E. **Comparability:** Enables users to identify and explain similarities and differences between two (or more) items of information. Includes *Consistency*: Conformity of information from period to period.

F. **Constraints:** Limits to help identify useful accounting information. Includes (1) *Benefits Greater Than Costs*: Benefits obtained by users of information must be greater than costs of providing information, and (2) *Materiality*: Monetary impact of the information must be large enough to make a difference in decision making (*quantitative constraint*).

V. ACCOUNTING ASSUMPTIONS AND PRINCIPLES

A. **Entity:** Information is recorded and reported about each separate economic entity (company).

B. **Continuity (Going Concern):** Company is assumed to continue future operations, unless substantial contrary evidence exists.

C. **Period of Time:** Information is reported in a company's financial statements at least on an annual basis.

D. **Monetary Unit:** National currency of company is used as stable unit of measure in preparing financial reports.

E. **Historical Cost:** Generally, exchange price is retained in the accounting records as the value of an item until it is consumed, sold, or liquidated and removed from records.

F. **Recognition:** Process of formally recording and reporting an item in a company's financial statements.

G. **Realization:** Process of converting noncash resources into cash or rights to cash.

H. **Accrual Accounting:** Process (matching) of relating financial effects of transactions, events, and circumstances having cash consequences to the period in which they occur rather than when the cash receipt or payment occurs.

I. **Prudence (Conservatism):** Process of ensuring, to extent possible, that uncertainties and risks related to a company are reflected in its accounting information.

VI. GENERALLY ACCEPTED ACCOUNTING PRINCIPLES (GAAP)

A. **Definition:** Guidelines, procedures, and practices that a company is required to use in recording and reporting the accounting information in its audited financial statements.

B. **Sources:** (in descending order of importance)
  1. **Category A:** FASB *Statements of Financial Accounting Standards* and *Interpretations*, FASB *Staff Positions*, FASB *Statement 133 Implementation Issues*, APB *Opinions*, and CAP (AICPA) *Accounting Research Bulletins* (as well as SEC releases such as *Regulation S-X*, *Financial Reporting Releases*, and *Staff Accounting Bulletins* for companies that file with the SEC).
  2. **Category B:** FASB *Technical Bulletins* and AICPA *Industry Audit and Accounting Guides*, and AICPA *Statements of Position*, (if cleared by the FASB).
  3. **Category C:** FASB Emerging Issues Task Force *Consensus Positions* and AICPA *Practice Bulletins* (if cleared by the FASB).
  4. **Category D:** FASB *Q's and A's* (Implementation Guides), AICPA *Accounting Interpretations*, and practices that are widely recognized and prevalent either generally or in the industry (e.g., AICPA *Accounting Trends and Techniques*).
  5. When none of the pronouncements in Categories A through D apply, then the company may consider other accounting literature such as FASB *Statements of Concepts*, AICPA *Issues Papers*, IASB *International Financial Reporting Standards*, AICPA *Technical Practice Aids*, and accounting textbooks, handbooks, and articles for GAAP guidance.

(Continued on inside back cover)

TENTH EDITION

INTERMEDIATE ACCOUNTING

LOREN A. NIKOLAI

**Ernst & Young Professor,
School of Accountancy,
University of Missouri-Columbia**

JOHN D. BAZLEY

**John J. Gilbert Professor,
School of Accountancy,
University of Denver**

Jefferson P. Jones

**Associate Professor,
School of Accountancy,
Auburn University**

THOMSON

SOUTH-WESTERN

Australia · Brazil · Canada · Mexico · Singapore · Spain · United Kingdom · United States

Intermediate Accounting, 10th Edition

Loren A. Nikolai, John D. Bazley, Jefferson P. Jones

VP/Editorial Director:
Jack W. Calhoun

Publisher:
Rob Dewey

Acquisitions Editor:
Keith Paul Chassé

Associate Developmental Editor:
Steven E. Joos

Marketing Manager:
Chris McNamee

Production Project Manager:
Robert Dreas

Manager of Technology, Editorial:
Vicky True

Sr. Technology Project Editor:
Sally Neiman

Web Coordinator:
Scott Cook

Manufacturing Coordinator:
Doug Wilke

Production House:
GEX Publishing Services

Printer:
QuebecorWorld
Versailles, Kentucky

Executive Art Director:
Ed Donald

Art Director:
Chris A. Miller

Internal Designer:
Lou Ann Thesing

Cover Designer:
Laura Brown

Cover Images:
Getty Images

Icon Illustrator:
Greg Grigorion

Photography Manager:
John Hill

Photo Researcher:
Darren Wright

COPYRIGHT © 2007
Thomson South-Western, a part of The Thomson Corporation. Thomson, the Star logo, and South-Western are trademarks used herein under license.

Printed in the United States of America
2 3 4 5 08 07 06

Student Edition: ISBN 0-324-30098-0

Instructor's Edition: ISBN 0-324-37579-4

Library of Congress Control Number:
2005932187

For more information about our products, contact us at:
Thomson Learning Academic Resource Center
1-800-423-0563

Thomson Higher Education
5191 Natorp Boulevard
Mason, OH 45040
USA

Loren A. Nikolai

Loren Nikolai is the Ernst & Young Professor and Director of the Masters Programs in the School of Accountancy at the University of Missouri—Columbia (MU). He received his B.A. and M.B.A. from St. Cloud State University and his Ph.D. from the University of Minnesota. Professor Nikolai has taught at the University of Wisconsin at Plattsville and at the University of North Carolina at Chapel Hill. Professor Nikolai has received numerous teaching awards. Most recently, he was the recipient of the MU Student-Athlete Advisory Council 2004 Most Inspiring Professor Award. Also, he has been awarded University of Missouri System 1999 Presidential Award for Outstanding Teaching, the MU Alumni Association 1996 Faculty Award, the MU College of Business 1994 Accounting Professor of the Year Award, the Missouri Society of CPAs 1993 Outstanding Accounting Educator of the Year Award, the MU 1992 Kemper Fellowship for Teaching Excellence, the St. Cloud State University 1990 Distinguished Alumni Award, and the Federation of Schools of Accountancy 1989 Faculty Award of Merit. He holds a CPA certificate in the state of Missouri and previously worked for the 3M Company. Professor Nikolai is the lead author of *Intermediate Accounting,* and has also been an author on four other accounting textbooks.

Professor Nikolai has published numerous articles in *The Accounting Review, Journal of Accounting Research, The Accounting Educator's Journal, Journal of Accounting Education, The CPA Journal, Management Accounting, Policy Analysis, Academy of Management Journal, Journal of Business Research,* and other professional journals. He was also lead author of a monograph published by the National Association of Accountants. Professor Nikolai has served as an ad hoc reviewer for *The Accounting Review* and *Issues in Accounting Education.* He has made numerous presentations around the country on curricular and pedagogical issues in accounting education, and was advisor for Beta Alpha Psi for twenty years.

Professor Nikolai is a member of the American Accounting Association, the American Institute of Certified Public Accountants (AICPA), and the Missouri Society of CPAs (MSCPA). He has chaired and served on numerous committees of the AICPA, the MSCPA, the Federation of Schools of Accountancy, and the AAA. Professor Nikolai is married and has two adult children and three grandsons. His family has two cats, and he is an avid basketball player, golfer, and weight lifter.

John D. Bazley

John Bazley is the John J. Gilbert Professor in the School of Accountancy of the Daniels College of Business at the University of Denver, where he has received numerous teaching awards, including the University's Distinguished Teaching Award. Professor Bazley earned a B.A. from the University of Bristol in England and an M.S. and Ph.D. from the University of Minnesota. He has taught at the University of North Carolina at Chapel Hill and holds a CPA certificate in the state of Colorado. He has taught national professional development classes for a major CPA firm and was consultant for another CPA firm. Professor Bazley is the coauthor of *Intermediate Accounting,* and has also been an author on three other accounting texts.

Professor Bazley has published articles in professional journals, including *The Accounting Review, Management Accounting, Accounting Horizons, Practical Accountant, Academy of Management Journal, The Journal of Managerial Issues,* and *The International Journal of Accounting,* and was a member of the Editorial Boards of *Issues in Accounting Education* and the *Journal of Managerial Issues.* He has served on numerous committees of The Federation of Schools of Accountancy (including chair of the Student Lyceum Committee), the American Accounting Association, and the Colorado Society of CPAs (including the Continuing Professional Education Board). He is also a coauthor of a monograph on environmental accounting published by the National Association of

Accountants. Professor Bazley is a member of the American Institute of Certified Public Accountants, the Colorado Society of CPAs, and the American Accounting Association. He has recently appeared as an expert witness for the Securities and Exchange Commission and as a consultant for a defendant in a securities fraud case. Professor Bazley is married and has two children, who especially enjoy their three cats, one dog, and eleven reptiles. He enjoys skiing, playing golf, car racing, and listening to jazz.

Jefferson P. Jones

Jeff Jones is an Associate Professor of Accounting in the School of Accountancy at Auburn University. He received his B.S. and Master of Accountancy from Auburn University and his Ph.D. from Florida State University. Professor Jones has received numerous teaching awards. He is the recipient of the 2004 Auburn University College of Business McCartney Teaching Award, the 2005, 2003, and 2001 Beta Alpha Psi Outstanding Teaching Award, and the 2000 Auburn University School of Accountancy Teaching Award. He has also been recognized in Who's Who Among America's Teachers (2002 and 2004). Professor Jones holds a CPA certificate in the state of Alabama and previously worked for Deloitte & Touche. Professor Jones is a coauthor of *Intermediate Accounting*.

Professor Jones has published articles in professional journals, including *Advances in Accounting, Review of Quantitative Finance and Accounting, Issues in Accounting Education, International Journal of Forecasting, The CPA Journal, Managerial Finance, Journal of Accounting and Finance Research*, and *The Journal of Corporate Accounting and Finance*. Professor Jones has made numerous presentations around the country on research and pedagogical issues. He is a member of the American Accounting Association, the American Institute of Certified Public Accountants (AICPA), and the Alabama Society of CPAs (ASCPA). Professor Jones is married, has two children, and enjoys playing golf.

Known for its balanced coverage of both concepts and procedures, *Intermediate Accounting* gives students an unparalleled look at financial accounting information and its increasingly varied uses in the world today. In addition to the thorough coverage of GAAP expected of a book of its caliber, the timely tenth edition illustrates the practices professional accountants execute daily, as well as the concepts behind those practices. Through this approach, this textbook equips students with the tools needed to critically assess evolving, accounting practices needed to meet the demands of a dynamic, professional world.

With three decades of experience, we continue to connect with the contemporary student with improved readability, while introducing them to the language of the profession. As before, compelling real world financial statements and research cases help students see the implication of the material at hand and learn to apply it in a real business context. Notably, Appendix A contains 2004 financial statements and supplemental data of The Coca-Cola Company for use throughout the book, but the tenth edition brings even more to the table.

With the new perspective brought by co-author Jeff Jones and the move to a lively, four-color design, *Intermediate Accounting* effectively imparts essential knowledge and skills through a student-friendly, easy to reference, and pedagogically sound presentation. Coupling that with the comprehensive coverage, professional language, and real world applications that have been the hallmarks of the text for many years, the tenth edition provides the perfect link between the academic and professional world. We believe this book simultaneously provides students with the vibrant pedagogy they need to understand the material and the technical complexity they need to succeed as professionals.

Intermediate Accounting, Tenth Edition consists of five parts containing 23 chapters, as follows:

Part 1 Financial Reporting: Concepts, Financial Statements, and Related Disclosures
(Chapters 1–6, and the Time Value of Money Module)
Part 2 Financial Reporting: Asset Measurement and Income Determination
(Chapters 7–12)
Part 3 Financial Reporting: Valuation of Liabilities and Investments
(Chapters 13–15)
Part 4 Financial Reporting: Stockholders' Equity
(Chapters 16–17)
Part 5 Financial Reporting: Special Topics
(Chapters 18–23)

TEACH THE LOGIC AND THE PRACTICE

CLEAR OBJECTIVES

Objectives at the beginning of each chapter prepare students for what they will be studying. We list each objective in the margin beside the topical coverage to reinforce students' learning.

4 Define the elements of a balance sheet.

CONCEPTUAL-ANALYTICAL-REAL REPORT FRAMEWORK (C-A-R)

Over the years, a major strength of *Intermediate Accounting* has been its comprehensive coverage of GAAP, but its unique hallmark is the authors' conceptual and analytical discussions related to those procedures. Through the C-A-R framework, the textbook draws out these important explanations and presents the underlying thought processes of financial analysis. Coupled with the interactive new and improved Real Reports, the C-A-R progression bolsters students' accounting savvy as they come to understand the logic and the practice of accounting.

Conceptual

Supported by the FASB conceptual framework introduced in Chapter 2, we relate the discussion of specific topics to the objectives of financial reporting, qualitative characteristics of accounting information, conceptual reporting guidelines, and to the concepts of liquidity, financial flexibility, risk, operating capability, and return on investment. With the conceptual discussions, students begin to understand the environment that gave rise to a specific procedure. Once that logic is place, they can begin the practice of accounting with a firm understanding of the environment in which they operate.

statements. Recall from Chapter 2 that **recognition is the process of formally recording and reporting an element in the financial statements.** It includes depiction of an element in both words and numbers, with the amount included in the totals. Generally, the most useful (i.e., the best combination of relevance and reliability) information about assets, liabilities, and equity should be recognized and reported in the main body of the balance sheet. There are four basic recognition criteria. To be recognized, an item (and information about it) must meet the definition of an element, and be measurable, relevant, and reliable.[5] Thus, to meet the objectives of a company's balance sheet—to provide

Analysis

To help bridge the gap between the conceptual and procedural, we indicate essential analytical coverage that illustrates the significance and application of certain key company characteristics and related ratio calculations to financial analysis. This material illuminates the critical thinking process, so that students can further understand how the logic of the conceptual framework translates to everyday accounting procedure and business practice. By effectively grounding this translation in specific business activities, this coverage further prepares students to intelligently apply this material on their own.

Offsetting Allowance for Doubtful Accounts against Accounts Receivable informs financial statement users of the net realizable value (the amount of cash expected to be collected) of the company's receivables.[12]

It is possible to base the estimate of bad debt expense on historical relationships

Reporting

In addition to a thorough understanding of business transactions and the environment of financial analysis, students need to be aware of issues that arise during financial reporting. Using concrete examples, we describe how items are reported in financial statements, which instills students with the knowledge and understanding they need to efficiently and effectively report their findings according to GAAP. A key aspect of the report coverage are the Real Reports. The unique Real Report feature gives students the opportunity to test their reporting mettle with real company data.

An audit report is *not* part of the financial statements because it is a report by the independent auditor. Nonetheless, it is considered an important item of information because external users place reliance on the report as to the fairness of the financial statements. The "standard" form of an auditor's report on *comparative* financial statements (often referred to as an *unqualified* report) is shown in Exhibit 6-1.[3] (The audit report of

Real Reports

When it's time to put it all together, this feature encourages students to test their understanding by providing excerpts from real company reports and challenging students to answer several questions about the information they see. As part of the Reporting material, students learn by doing, and stretch their understanding of each topic to its limit.

With the answers provided in the end of the chapter material, these self-contained features provide students a chance to test themselves as they read.

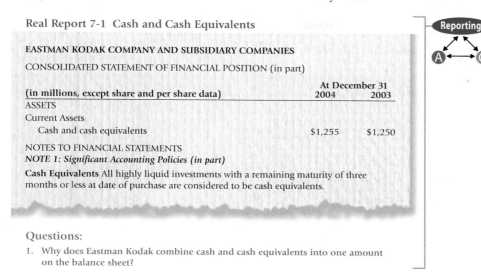

Real Report 7-1 Cash and Cash Equivalents

Reporting

EASTMAN KODAK COMPANY AND SUBSIDIARY COMPANIES

CONSOLIDATED STATEMENT OF FINANCIAL POSITION (in part)

(in millions, except share and per share data)	At December 31 2004	2003
ASSETS		
Current Assets		
Cash and cash equivalents	$1,255	$1,250

NOTES TO FINANCIAL STATEMENTS
NOTE 1: Significant Accounting Policies (in part)

Cash Equivalents All highly liquid investments with a remaining maturity of three months or less at date of purchase are considered to be cash equivalents.

Questions:
1. Why does Eastman Kodak combine cash and cash equivalents into one amount on the balance sheet?

Clarifying Computational Steps

Because complex computations can be hard for students to master, we reduce many computational procedures to a series of steps outlined in list format. For instance, Example 9-13 includes a series of steps for dollar-value LIFO calculations. Similar lists of steps for the gross profit inventory method, retail inventory method, and dollar-value LIFO retail method appear in Chapter 9. We include other computational steps where appropriate throughout the rest of the book.

Straightforward Design Distinguishes Important Material

- Key terms, definitions, and official statements are in boldface.
- Particularly important information is in italics.
- All real companies are in boldface.
- Exhibits of illustrations of journal entries, supporting schedules, and financial statements clarify concepts or procedures.
- All journal entries are now in blue.

Interest Expense	200	
Discount on Notes Payable		200
Notes Payable	10,000	
Cash		10,000

- Excerpts from real financial statements have a special background:

ConAgra Foods

NOTE 1: Summary of Significant Accounting Policies (in part):

Inventories   Grain, flour, and major feed ingredient inventories are hedged to the extent practicable and are principally stated at market, including adjustment to market of open contracts for purchases and sales.

NOTE 9: Senior Long-Term Debt, Subordinated Debt and Loan Agreements

Interest expense incurred to finance hedged inventories has been charged to cost of goods sold.

"I really like the design of these and do think they provide a valuable piece of the chapter coverage. Like I mentioned earlier, a move from the technical to the practical is very welcome and needed in the intermediate sequence."
Alee Phillips-University of Kansas

"Yes, I do like these examples and questions and particularly that the answers are in the end-of-chapter materials. This is a feature I would definitely like."
Vern Richardson-University of Arkansas

"I like these kind of problems because they use real-world companies and I strongly believe students pay more attention to examples dealing with the IBMs of the world versus the hypothetical ACMEs. Also, these kind of problems make the students critically think through the accounting and reporting issue as well as an application of the issue. They'll like the design of these kind of problems, and I think they are extremely valuable."
Rick Turpin-University of Tennesse-Chattanooga

"I really do think that these will be extremely helpful. The torn edge style of the box gives a real world feel to the information. I do like the examples that are used, the text is fine."
Rizvana Zameeruddin-University of Wisconsin-Parkside

Enhanced Design for Examples

In *Intermediate Accounting*, examples are clearly identified for easy reference. For in-text examples, the example text heading will be in red, and when the example ends, there will be a red bullet. Major, numbered examples, will also be in red, but will be in a box. This useful design ensures that students will know where they are in the material at all times.

EXAMPLE 7-3	Accounting for Short-Term Notes Receivable					
	Interest-Bearing			**Non-interest-Bearing**		
To record receipt of note on October 1, 2007	Notes Receivable Sales	5,000	5,000	Notes Receivable Interest Revenue Sales	5,100	100 5,000
To record receipt of maturity value on December 1, 2007	Cash Notes Receivable Interest Revenue*	5,100	5,000 100	Cash Notes Receivable	5,100	5,100

*$5,000 \times 0.12 \times 60/360$

UNDERSTAND THE LOGIC AND THE PRACTICE

Like no other book on the market, *Intermediate Accounting*, 10e moves beyond teaching just technical skills and makes even the most complex procedures accessible to students through an understanding of the conceptual framework.

Introduction of the FASB Conceptual Framework

Students are introduced to the "conceptual framework" in Chapter 2. This discussion involves an identification and explanation of the objectives of financial reporting (Exhibit 2-3) and the qualitative characteristics of useful accounting information (Exhibit 2-5). The chapter also includes an explanation of the interrelationship between financial reports, types of useful information, and external decision making (Exhibit 2-4), as well as a framework of financial accounting theory and practice (Exhibit 2-6).

Integrated Conceptual Discussion

Supported by the FASB conceptual framework introduced in Chapter 2, we relate the discussion of specific topics to the objectives of financial reporting, qualitative characteristics of accounting information, and conceptual reporting guidelines, and to the concepts of liquidity, financial flexibility, risk, operating capability, and return on investment. Where there are significant conceptual issues concerning an accounting principle, there is an objective discussion of the alternative views. Note that this coverage is indicated through the design.

 Information on cash management is important in financial accounting because one objective of financial reporting is to communicate how well the managers of a company have fulfilled their stewardship responsibility to stockholders for the use of the company assets. In this regard, cash management includes planning and control aspects. **Cash planning** systems

This integrated discussion of accounting theory is not at the expense of sound, procedural pedagogy, and we emphasize a balanced presentation of concepts and practice. For each topic, students will find a clear and concise discussion of the related generally accepted accounting principles. We enhance the discussion with a thorough explanation and illustration of the corresponding practices and procedures.

IASB Conceptual Framework

Because of the continuing globalization of companies, we briefly discuss the International Accounting Standards Board's Framework for the Preparation and Presentation of Financial Statements. This Framework provides the conceptual underpinning for the international accounting standards that we discuss in later chapters.

Conceptual Reference Guide

This guide provides a quick review of the concepts underlying financial accounting and is located inside the front and back covers of the book.

REINFORCE THE LOGIC AND THE PRACTICE

New and improved summary features help students identify key concepts and link them to a more complete understanding of the accounting process.

NEW! Secure Your Knowledge Summary

With all of the material presented to a student in an *Intermediate Accounting* text, these bulleted summaries help students identify key points, which helps them test their knowledge and review for tests.

SECURE YOUR KNOWLEDGE 5-2

- Income from continuing operations is a summary of the revenues, expenses (e.g., cost of goods sold, operating expenses, income tax expense), and other items that are expected to continue into the future.
- Income from continuing operations may be reported in a single-step format that classifies all items into either revenues or expenses, or it may be reported in a more useful multi-step format that contains additional classifications of the income statement elements.
- Discontinued operations (a component of a company's operations that has been, or will be, eliminated from ongoing operations) are reported net-of-tax directly after income from continuing operations.
- Extraordinary items, material gains or losses that are unusual in nature and infrequent in occurrence, are reported net-of-tax below the results of discontinued operations.
- Companies are required to report earnings per share amounts relating to income from continuing operations and net income on their income statements.
- The disclosure of additional information in the footnotes to the financial statements or in supplemental schedules is encouraged to overcome limitations of the income statement and provide external users with information useful for evaluating company performance.

Comprehensive Chapter Summaries

Each chapter ends with a summary of the key points for each major topic. Tied directly to the Objectives from the beginning of the chapter, these summaries provide students with a quick review of the important topical issues.

"I feel that this feature is extremely helpful and that students will use it to their advantage when reading the text the first time and then when reviewing for exams. What's nice about them is they are strategically located so students can test their knowledge before going on to the next topic, thus allowing them to take relatively small "bites" of knowledge as they progress through the chapter."
Herbert Hunt-
CSU Long Beach

"I think that the "Secure Your Knowledge" is excellent. They provide a valuable learning tool and should be used by just about all students."
Mary Loyland-
University of North Dakota

Helpful Summary Exhibits

Summary exhibits throughout the text help students pull together and understand what they have learned so far. For instance, Exhibit 5-3 summarizes corporate earnings and cash flow topics, Exhibit 21-2 summarizes the criteria and classifications for leases, and Exhibit 23-1 summarizes the impacts on financial statements of the methods used for accounting changes and errors.

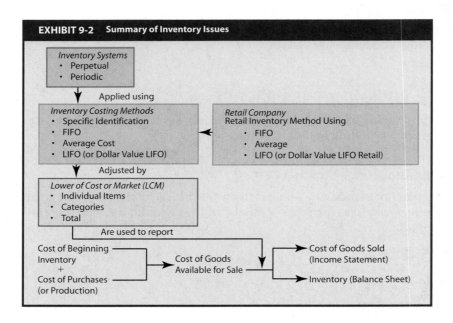

EXHIBIT 9-2   Summary of Inventory Issues

Apply the Logic and the Practice

Intermediate Accounting is the meeting point of many aspects of the discipline. Most notably, it is the link between Financial Principles and the professional world, but also, it links out to the other areas of the field such as ethical and global issues.

"I really like the way questions are embedded in the vignettes. This will help drive the student's discussion."
Abdul Qastin-
Lakeland College

NEW! Chapter Openers

These entertaining and informative vignettes briefly introduce concepts in the upcoming chapter through real aspects of the professional, accounting world. In addition, these openers include references to industry journals and newspapers for further reading. All of these sources are included in the Business and Company Resource Center (BCRC), which is automatically included with the new text.

For Further Investigation

For a discussion of ARC or Check 21, consult the Business & Company Resource Center (BCRC):

● Tear Out a Check, Then Watch it Vanish. Jeffrey Selingo, *The New York Times*, 0362-4331, October 9, 2003, pG6 col. 04.
● Why Check 21 Could Erase ARC's Gains. Will Wade, *American Banker*, 0002-7561, November 5, 2003, v168, i213, p1.

NEW! Link to Ethical Dilemmas

The ethical link between accounting practices and applications in the business world grows in importance daily. To help students develop their ethical compass, this feature puts the student in the role of the decision maker faced with an ethical dilemma. In addition, we provide a complete section on this topic in Chapter 1, as well as end-of-chapter cases sprinkled throughout the text.

LINK TO ETHICAL DILEMMA

As the controller for a struggling manufacturing company, you are in the process of closing the books for the year and notice that the company is going to be in technical violation of its debt covenants. Such a violation could result in bankruptcy, which would result in the loss of hundreds of jobs, including your own. You quickly analyze the financial statements and realize that by changing a few estimates involving accounts receivable, warranties, and pensions, the company will be able to avoid a violation of its debt covenants. While you don't believe the revised estimates would best represent the economic reality of your company's financial position, you also don't believe the estimates are unreasonably aggressive. Do you revise the estimates?

"The design is great! It definitely effectively separates the content and importantly draws attention to the issues. My feeling is that this is a good thing to do rather than simply burying the discussion points in the paragraphs with everything else. This is especially important in this course because there is so much material and it's often difficult for the students to think of every angle/consideration that might be important."
Herbert Hunt-
CSU Long Beach

Improved! Link to International Differences

Though *Intermediate Accounting* tackles the sizable topic of domestic GAAP, this feature enlightens students about the link between the FASB and International Accounting Standards Board (IASB), and encourages them to be mindful of possible global differences.

For the previous edition, we modified the discussion of international accounting standards in many chapters to expand the discussion and bring it up to date, and we continue that project in this edition.

LINK TO INTERNATIONAL DIFFERENCES

International accounting standards allow a company to record some internally generated intangibles as assets. Specifically, the company must classify activities leading to the generation of an intangible asset into a research and a development phase. Research costs are expensed but development costs may be capitalized if the company can demonstrate that the asset will generate probable future economic benefits. Also, the costs of items that are acquired for a particular research project and have no alternative future uses are expensed as the items are used in the project. In contrast, such costs are expensed when incurred under U.S. GAAP. Finally, international accounting standards allow intangibles to be revalued upwards. For example, in the United Kingdom, brand names such as Schweppes are accounted for in this manner.

NEW! Link to Ratio Analysis

After introducing ratios in an appendix to Chapter 6, this feature continues that discussion and introduces students to calculations accountants, investors, and creditors perform to link the numbers to specific types of real world analysis. Considering the usefulness of ratios as a tool for analyzing the health of a business, this feature should prove interesting and useful to students, while honing their critical thinking skills.

"I like the graphics and colors. This will allow instructors and students to identify and emphasize desired elements. It is a good way to include these challenging topics."
Mark Comstock-
Misouri Southern
State University

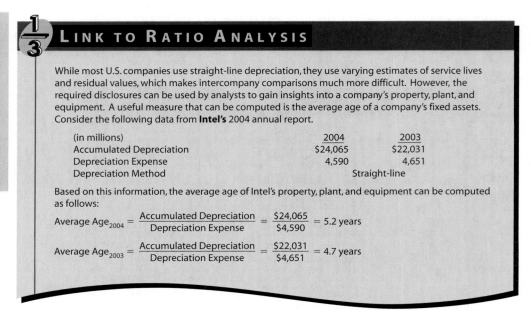

LINK TO RATIO ANALYSIS

While most U.S. companies use straight-line depreciation, they use varying estimates of service lives and residual values, which makes intercompany comparisons much more difficult. However, the required disclosures can be used by analysts to gain insights into a company's property, plant, and equipment. A useful measure that can be computed is the average age of a company's fixed assets. Consider the following data from **Intel's** 2004 annual report.

(in millions)	2004	2003
Accumulated Depreciation	$24,065	$22,031
Depreciation Expense	4,590	4,651
Depreciation Method	Straight-line	

Based on this information, the average age of Intel's property, plant, and equipment can be computed as follows:

$$\text{Average Age}_{2004} = \frac{\text{Accumulated Depreciation}}{\text{Depreciation Expense}} = \frac{\$24,065}{\$4,590} = 5.2 \text{ years}$$

$$\text{Average Age}_{2003} = \frac{\text{Accumulated Depreciation}}{\text{Depreciation Expense}} = \frac{\$22,031}{\$4,651} = 4.7 \text{ years}$$

End of Chapter

Extensive end-of-chapter materials allow students to test their understanding, and apply concepts to a variety of questions and problems.

Questions   primarily address key concepts and terms in the chapter. These questions allow students to solidify their understanding of the basics before moving on to specific applications.

Multiple-Choice Items   provide students with a variety of brief qualitative and quantitative tests of their knowledge. Starting with Chapter 2, each chapter contains ten multiple-choice activities based on past Uniform CPA Examination questions, providing sound preparation for the professional world.

Exercises   reinforce a chapter topic and provide students an opportunity to explore their answers more thoroughly.

Problems   consolidate a number of chapter topics or focus on a comprehensive analysis of a single topic. These multi-step items allow students to delve even further into the complex practice of accounting. Each problem is introduced by a subject reference in bold.

Cases   focus on the various conceptual and reporting issues within the chapter. In accordance with the Accounting Education Change Commission recommendations about improving certain skills of students, we present cases at the end of each chapter in three sections. Each case is introduced by a subject reference in bold.

> **Communication** cases are designed to help students improve their written communication skills. These cases prepare students for the future, when they will need to explain their findings to managers and other decision makers.

> **Creative and Critical Thinking** cases are designed to help students improve their thinking skills. Due to the increased emphasis on enhancing students' abilities to think creatively and critically in the accounting environment, we include a section on these topics in Chapter 1.

> **Ethics** cases deal with ethical and financial reporting issues in each chapter. Students should develop solutions from financial reporting and ethical perspectives, building on what they've learned through reading the discussion of ethical models in Chapter 1 and the Link to Ethical Dilemmas. Coverage of ethics is always denoted with this icon.

Research Simulations are found in most chapters, and simulate real scenarios in which research would be needed in the professional world. We designed these cases to be used with the *FARS* electronic database, pronouncements on the FASB web site, the FASB Current Text, or the FASB Original Pronouncements, which helps students develop the research skills needed as an accounting professional.

Other Features

Analysis of Coca-Cola's Financial Statements To give students insight into real-world financial reporting, several cases require students to review selected portions of The Coca-Cola Company's annual report (in Appendix A). These cases enhance critical-thinking skills as they require students to answer user-oriented and financial reporting questions related to the chapter topics.

AICPA Adapted In addition to being the only Intermediate Accounting textbook with AICPA adapted, multiple-choice questions, each chapter after Chapter 1 contains a variety of exercises, problems, and cases based on past Uniform CPA Examination questions.

User-Oriented Homework Selected exercises and problems require students to develop answers from a user-oriented perspective. These involve the computation of ratios as well as intracompany and intercompany analysis.

They provide many choices with different levels of difficulty. Creative and Critical Thinking Cases provide an opportunity to enhance writing and communication skills. The Research Simulation will enforce the need to use the technology and articulate findings to the stakeholders.
Abdul Qastin-
Lakeland College

Content Changes

We have included detailed coverage of the latest FASB statements as well as many other enhancements to the book's content. As new statements are issued, we will provide timely updates at our web site, *http://nikolai.swlearning.com*. A list of chapter key changes from the ninth to tenth editions follows:

Part 1 Financial Reporting: Concepts, Financial Statements, and Related Disclosures

Chapter 1
- Added FASB Staff Positions to GAAP
- Added discussion of objectives-oriented standard setting
- Added discussion of PCAOB

Chapter 2
- Modified Exhibit "Financial Reporting Environment" to add PCAOB

Chapter 3 (formerly Appendix C)
- Changed the entire example from a periodic to a perpetual inventory system
- Added a diagram to show information flow from source documents through to financial statements
- Added diagrams to show effect of each type of adjusting entry
- Added summary exhibit of adjusting entry framework
- Since switched to basic perpetual example, added a short section on periodic inventory, as well as returns, allowances, and discounts
- Moved worksheet ahead of reversing entries so it is in more proximity to the related financial statements
- Reduced the coverage of special journals to a basic discussion
- Moved cash-basis accounting to a chapter appendix

Chapter 4 (formerly Chapter 3)
- Added discussion of "fair value" based on new *FASB Statement.*

Chapter 5 (formerly Chapter 4)
- Added new section on purposes of the income statement
- Added discussion of FASB project on "financial performance reporting by business enterprises"

- Added discussion of FASB and IASB joint project on revenue recognition
- Added margin notes to income statement to highlight different sections
- Modified discussion to reflect perpetual inventory system for cost of goods sold
- Deleted exhibit dealing with cost of goods sold for manufacturing company
- Modified diagram of income from discontinued operations
- Deleted discussion of reporting "cumulative effects" on income statement
- Added discussion of reporting "change in accounting principle" in retained earnings statement
- Modified diagram of cash flows from operating, investing, and financing activities
- Added margin notes to a statement of cash flows to highlight different sections

Chapter 6 (formerly Chapter 5)

- Added diagram showing how "efficient market" works
- Added discussion of new audit "opinions" required for internal control and replaced old audit opinion with new audit opinions
- Added exhibit to illustrate segment reporting
- Added new brief section on XBRL supplemental information for SEC reporting
- In chapter Appendix, added new diagram for computing days in operating cycle from ratios
- Deleted redundant discussion of Management's Discussion and Analysis (MD&A) because it is covered in Chapter 4

Time Value of Money Module

- Created from Appendix D: Compound Interest and moved up for convenient, optional coverage

Part 2 Financial Reporting: Asset Measurement and Income Determination

Chapter 7 (formerly Chapter 6)

- Moved sections on Petty Cash and Bank Reconciliation to chapter appendix
- Added diagram showing pledging, assignment, and factoring conditions when financing with accounts receivable
- Clarified discounting notes receivable with recourse and without recourse
- Deleted appendix on four-column bank reconciliation
- Added an explanation of the effects of various accounts receivable and notes receivable transactions on the statement of cash flows

Chapter 8 (formerly Chapter 7)

- Updated for provisions of *FASB Statement No. 151*
- Deleted discussion of standard costs and variable costing
- Updated for provisions of *FASB Statement No. 154*
- Added an explanation of the effects of inventory transactions on the statement of cash flows

Chapter 9 (formerly Chapter 8)

- Clarified the discussion of the steps used for the gross profit method and retail inventory method of estimating inventory.

Chapter 10 (formerly Chapter 9)

- Added example of donation by nongovernmental entity
- Updated discussion of exchanges for *FASB Statement No. 153*, which eliminated similar asset exchanges. All nonmonetary asset exchanges are now recorded in the same way and all gains and losses are recognized in full
- Added an explanation of the effects of property, plant, and equipment transactions on the statement of cash flows

Chapter 11 (formerly Chapter 10)

- Moved discussion of activity-based depreciation methods
- Deleted discussion of retirement and replacement methods
- Updated discussion of Changes and Corrections of Depreciation for *FASB Statement No. 154*. A change in a depreciation method is now accounted for prospectively (instead of by a cumulative effect adjustment)

Chapter 12 (formerly Chapter 11)

- Deleted Appendix on Estimating the Value of Goodwill, but added a short discussion.

Part 3 Financial Reporting: Valuation of Liabilities and Investments

Chapter 13 (formerly Chapter 12)
- Shortened liquidity discussion
- Added a journal entry example for dividends
- Added a diagram to explain the differences in accounting for vacation time and sick pay
- Clarified the accounting for an unconditional purchase obligation

Chapter 14 (formerly Chapter 13)
- Added a diagram for the computation of the bond discount or premium amortization
- Added a diagram explaining the book value and market value methods for the conversion of bonds
- Added a diagram showing the payments for an impaired loan
- Added a discussion of accounting for guarantees under *FASB Interpretation No. 45*
- Added an explanation of the effects of long-term liability transactions on the statement of cash flows

Chapter 15 (formerly Chapter 14)
- Expanded the discussion of "other than temporary" losses
- Added an explanation of the effects of investment transactions on operating cash flows

Part 4 Financial Reporting: Stockholders' Equity

Chapter 16 (formerly Chapter 15)
- Adjusted discussion of stock subscriptions
- Added some discussion of political controversy about compensatory share (stock) option plans
- Revised discussion of compensatory share option plans
- Replaced discussion of intrinsic method for stock appreciation rights with discussion of newly required fair value method
- Eliminated discussion of intrinsic value method for compensatory share option plans
- Updated discussion of redeemable preferred stock for new GAAP
- Shortened discussion of par value method for treasury stock, eliminated numerical example, and moved to end of section.
- Added a section that explains the effects of capital stock transactions on the statement of cash flows

Chapter 17 (formerly Chapter 16)
- Added numerical example of computing simple basic earnings per share
- Clarified the discussion of effect of stock dividends and splits on EPS
- Shortened and clarified conceptual and procedural discussion of stock dividends
- Shortened discussion of restrictions of retained earnings
- Omitted chapter appendix on quasi-reorganizations because of their rarity

Part 5 Financial Reporting: Special Topics

Chapter 18 (formerly Chapter 17)
- Moved the discussion of Additional Revenue Recognition Issues to an Appendix

Chapter 19 (formerly Chapter 18)
- Changed "deductible temporary difference" to "future deductible amount" and changed "taxable temporary difference" to "future taxable amount"
- Shortened conceptual discussion of deferred assets, deferred liabilities, and measurement of deferred items and valuation allowance
- For each primary example, substituted series of steps explaining measuring and recording deferred taxes, instead of discussing in paragraph format
- Shortened conceptual discussion of operating carrybacks and forwards
- Adjusted intraperiod income tax allocation discussion for elimination of cumulative effect changes
- Eliminated discussion of investment tax credit
- Eliminated chapter appendix on additional conceptual issues regarding interperiod tax allocation
- Added a section that explains the effects of income tax transactions on the operating activities section of the statement of cash flows

Chapter 20 (formerly Chapter 19)

- Updated the discussion of disclosures for *FASB Statement No. 132R*
- Deleted the discussion of the transition requirements of *FASB Statement No. 87* and *No. 106*
- Added a section that explains the effects of pension transactions on the statement of cash flows

Chapter 21 (formerly Chapter 20)

- Increased clarity of account titles (e.g., Leased Equipment under Capital Lease is now Leased Equipment, and Obligation Under Capital Lease is now Capital Lease Obligation)
- Added a section that explains the effects of lease transactions on the statement of cash flows

Chapter 22 (formerly Chapter 21)

- Changed cash "inflows" to "receipts" and "outflows" to "payments" in many places to simplify
- Deleted Exhibit "Differences Between Revenues, Expenses, and Cash Flows from Operating Activities"
- Moved Exhibit "Calculation of Cash Flows from Operating Activities" and related revised discussion to chapter appendix because it relates more to direct method
- Added headings to discussion of worksheet method (indirect method) to make it easier for students to follow steps for completion
- Added "increase" or "decrease" to "Schedule to Compute Operating Cash Flows" to clarify changes in selected balance sheet accounts
- Added headings to discussion of worksheet method (direct method) in chapter appendix to make it easier for students to follow steps for completion

Chapter 23 (formerly Chapter 22)

- Completely revised the Chapter for *FASB Statement No. 154*. All changes in accounting principle are now accounted for by a retrospective application of the new accounting principle on the retained earnings statement instead of a cumulative effect adjustment on the income statement

RELATE, INNOVATE, AND MOTIVATE

Students master course concepts through cutting-edge, interactive supplements unparalleled in the market.

Your Course. Your Time. Your Way.

Introducing 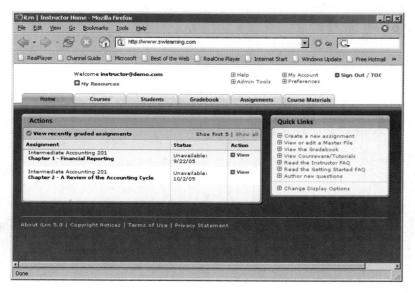 **NOW! for Nikolai/Bazley/Jones *Intermediate Accounting* 10e**
This powerful and fully integrated online teaching and learning system provides you with flexibility and control; saves valuable time and improves outcomes. Your students benefit by having choices in the way they learn through our unique personalized learning path. All this made possible by ThomsonNOW!

- Homework, including algorithms
- Integrated eBook
- Personalized Learning Paths
- Interactive Course Assignments
- Assessment Options with algorithms
- Test Delivery
- Course Management Tools, including Grade Book
- WebCT & Blackboard Integration

Understanding concepts, knowing GAAP rules, and learning exceptions is critical to a student's success in Intermediate Accounting. ThomsonNOW launches that success into the professional world by providing students with a Personalized Learning Path:

- Organized by topic, each student is directed to complete a diagnostic pre-assessment.
- The results of this pre-assessment generate an Individualized Learning Path that contains links to cases where students practice research, communication, tabulation, analysis and reporting.
- A post-assessment is also available, so that students can gauge their progress and comprehension of the concepts and skills necessary to successfully perform as an Accounting Professional.

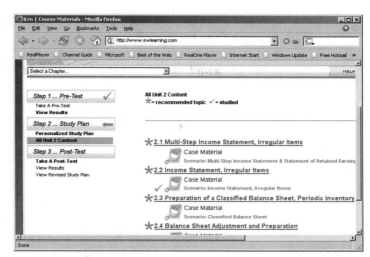

Intermediate Accounting Companion Web Site

http://nikolai.swlearning.com
This dramatically improved Internet site contains more resources for both students and instructors than ever before, and it's completely FREE!
For the STUDENT, it contains

- **BCRC Infomarks**: Direct links to the sources cited in the "For Further Research" boxes in each chapter opener, so there is no need to search for these articles.
- **Key Terms Quizzing**: This matching tool allows students to test themselves on key terms found in the text.

- **Crosswords**: Provides another way to familiarize students with the vocabulary of Intermediate Accounting through an entertaining game.
- **Interactive Quizzes**: Provide a test of basic knowledge of the chapter content and provide immediate feedback on the accuracy of the response. These quizzes contain multiple-choice, true/false, and brief exercise items that help students pinpoint areas in which they need more study.
- **Advanced Interactive Quizzes**: This next level of Interactive Quizzing is tied directly to the items recapped in the Secure Your Knowledge feature and Chapter Objectives. This test also consists of contain multiple-choice, true/false, and brief exercise items and provides immediate feedback.
- **Annotated Spreadsheets**: Similar to material found in the end of the chapter, these Excel® spreadsheet templates have annotated steps to help walk students through some of the most difficult problems types.
- **Internet Assignments**: Make full use of information that can be found on the Web with these research activities. These assignments require students to answer questions based on a company's most current financial statements. In many cases, students must analyze the disclosures from an external user's perspective.
- **Videos**: These brief videos provide overviews of the effects of certain characteristics of the business world. Such topics include the effect of fraud, goodwill, and SEC on everyday business.

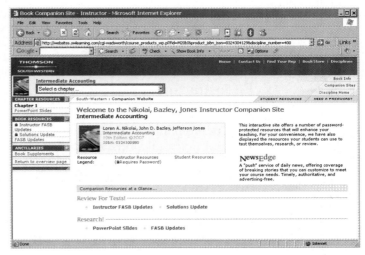

- Students can download many of the available supplements and see additional resources including,

Student PowerPoint® Presentation	Appendix: Accounting for Changes in Price
Enhanced Excel® Templates	Present Value Table
Links to accounting-related resources	Sample chapter for the Problem Solving Strategy Guide
Any FASB Updates	
Check Figures	

For INSTRUCTORS, this web site contains password protected downloads of the

Solutions Manual	Enhanced Excel® template solutions
Instructor's Manual	Links to accounting-related resources
Instructor's PowerPoint® Presentation	Any FASB Updates and related solutions
Test Bank files in Word	Appendix: Accounting for Changes in Price
Test Bank files in Examview	Present Value Tables
Check Figures	

There is a "Communicate with the Authors" link for sending e-mail. As mentioned, the authors will post updates to this site to keep adopters informed of the latest FASB pronouncements.

JoinIn on Turning Point is interactive PowerPoint®, simply the best classroom response system available today! JoinIn allows lectures to be transformed into powerful, two-way experiences. This lecture tool makes full use of the Instructor's PowerPoint® presentation, but moves it to the next level with interactive questions that provide immediate feedback on the students' understanding of the topic at hand. Visit *http://turningpoint. thomsonlearningconnections.com/index.html* to find out more!
ISBN: 0324378238

WebTutor® Toolbox on WebCT® or Blackboard®   Available on both platforms, this rich course management product is a specially designed extension of the classroom experience that enlivens the course by leveraging the power of the Internet with comprehensive educational content. Instructors or students can use these resources along with those on the Product Web Site to supplement the classroom experience. Use this effective resource as an integrated solution for your distance learning or web-enhanced course! Contact your local sales representative for details! *http://webtutor.swlearning.com*

SUPPLEMENTS

Intermediate Accounting's supplement package is comprised of a comprehensive set of teaching and learning tools that are as carefully developed as the book itself. From print-based supplements to electronic study aids, you're sure to find top-quality support in this thoroughly reviewed and verified set of supplements.

Instructors Resources

Solutions Manual   This two-volume manual includes: a suggested solution for each question, multiple-choice item, exercise, problem, case, and research simulation; all supporting calculations; and helpful notes to the instructor concerning any difficult areas within each problem. It also includes content and difficulty analysis of the exercises and problems in each chapter, as well as a sample syllabus and a list of assignments appropriate for group activities. This manual is personally prepared and verified by Loren Nikolai, John Bazley, and Jeff Jones.
Volume 1, Chapters 1–12 & Time Value of Money Module ISBN: 0324400594
Volume 2, Chapters 13–23 ISBN: 0324400640

Solution Transparencies   This two-volume set of acetates (set in large, bold type) for all problems and exercises adds an important visualization element to classroom presentations and discussions.

   Volume 1, Chapters 1–12 & Time Value of Money Module ISBN: 0324400586
   Volume 2, Chapters 13–23 ISBN: 0324400578

Instructor's Manual   For each chapter, this manual provides a list of objectives, synopsis, lecture outline, instructional notes, and content analysis of exercises and problems by topic. Illustrative teaching transparency masters consisting of selected exhibits from the text can be easily made into overheads for use in lecture presentations. Check figures of key answers to all text exercises and problems are also provided. Finally, there are suggested solutions for the Link to Ethics feature. Included with the Instructor's Manual files are the compound interest tables from the Time Value of Money Module. Prepared by Loren Nikolai, John Bazley, and Jeff Jones.

   Only available electronically on the IRCD and Companion web site

Test Bank   With examination materials covering each chapter, this updated two-volume bank includes approximately 2,100 multiple-choice, essay, and short-answer problems and solutions. In addition, it provides a grid that correlates each question to the individual chapter's objectives, as well as a ranking of difficulty based on a clearly described categorization. Through this helpful grid, making a test that is comprehensive and well-balanced is a snap!

   Volume 1, Chapters 1–12 & Time Value of Money Module ISBN: 0324406843
   Volume 2, Chapters 13–23 ISBN: 0324406835

ExamView®   This electronic testing software makes it easy to edit questions and customize exams. Containing the same questions as the printed Test Bank, the questions are correlated to the individual chapter's objectives and ranked by difficulty. This correlation is reflected in the general information for the question, so it's easy to sort by chapter objective or level of difficulty through ExamView®. This software requires PC compatibility.

   Only available electronically on the IRCD and Companion web site

Instructor's PowerPoint®   These colorful and detailed slides enhance lectures and class discussion, and include key exhibits from the text. MS-Windows® is required. Note that a separate outline version is available for students.

   Only available electronically on the IRCD and Companion web site

Instructor Excel® Templates   These templates provide the solutions for the problems and exercises that have Enhanced Excel® templates for students. Through these files, instructor's can see the solutions in the same format as the students.

   Only available electronically on the IRCD and Companion web site

Instructor's Resource CD-ROM   This CD-Rom contains electronic files for all the resources an instructor needs to teach from this text. It includes the computerized test bank in ExamView® format and the ExamView® testing software, as well as the Microsoft Word files for the Instructor's Manual, printed Test Bank, and Solutions Manual. Finally, this handy reference contains the Instructor PowerPoint Presentations and Excel® Templates.

   ISBN: 0324400527

Instructor's Edition for Nikolai/Bazley/Jones' Intermediate Accounting, 10th   This enhanced version of the core text comes equipped with a series of useful tabs that guide instructor's through the key features of the textbook and its accompanying supplements.

   ISBN: 0324375794

Thomson Custom Solutions   This service develops personalized solutions to meet your business education needs. Match your learning materials to your syllabus and create the perfect learning solution. Consider the following when looking at your customization options for Nikolai/Bazley/Jones, *Intermediate Accounting 10e*:

- Remove chapters you do not cover or rearrange their order, creating a streamlined and efficient text
- Customize our split volumes to meet the unique needs of your students or to match your two-semester sequence
- Add your own material to cover new topics or information, saving you time in planning and providing students a fully integrated course resource
- Adopt a loose-leaf version of the text allowing students to integrate your handouts; this money-saving option is also more portable than the full book

Students Resources

NEW! Problem Solving Strategy Guide Provides a variety of tutorial material to facilitate thorough understanding of the key points from each chapter. In addition, this guide provides a series of new exercises and problems, many of which are accompanied by worked out solutions and study tips. More than just a study guide, the PSSG includes detailed strategies for solving complex problems types similar to those from the textbook.
    Volume 1, Chapters 1–12 & Time Value of Money Module ISBN: 0324406819
    Volume 2, Chapters 13–23 ISBN: 0324374291

Student PowerPoint® These colorful and detailed slides provide an outline version of the presentation instructor's use in class lectures. Be prepared for each class meeting by viewing this helpful outline beforehand. MS-Windows® is required.
    Only available electronically on the IRCD and Companion web site

Enhanced Excel® Templates These templates are provided for selected long or complicated end-of-chapter exercises and problems, and provide assistance to the student as they set up and work the problem. Certain cells are coded to display a red asterisk when an incorrect answer is enter, which helps students stay on track. Selected problems that can be solved using these templates are designated by an icon.
    These helpful templates appear on both the Companion web site *http://nikolai.swlearning.com* and ThomsonNOW.

Intermediate Accounting Text, Volume 1, 10th This softbound volume of the core text provides a lighter and lower cost alternative to purchasing the complete, hardbound text. Perfect for students only taking one semester of *Intermediate Accounting*, Volume 1 contains material for Chapter 1–12 and the Time Value of Money Module.
    ISBN: 0324374275

Intermediate Accounting Text, Volume 2, 10th This softbound volume of the core text provides a lighter and lower cost alternative to purchasing the complete, hardbound text. Perfect for students only taking one semester of *Intermediate Accounting*, Volume 2 contains material for Chapter 13–23 and the Time Value of Money Module.
    ISBN: 0324374283

INTACCT: Internet Accounting Tutor Professors often find that the most basic rules and information that students learned in the introductory accounting course have long been forgotten when the students arrive in Intermediate Accounting. With the INTACCT Financial Accounting Tutorial, students easily review the basic introductory accounting concepts that they may have forgotten over the summer. It clearly explains the concept and then uses problem demonstrations to illustrate the concept and its applications.

    In addition to the Financial Tutorial, the INTACCT Intermediate Tutorial provides a variety of materials to help reinforce concepts that students learn in class and supplement the explanations given in the text. This Tutorial explains some of the difficult and basic Intermediate accounting concepts and then uses problem demonstrations to illustrate those concepts and their application. Review questions and interactive quizzing is available through this tool and the Financial Accounting Tutorial.

Check out the Companion web site for a link to purchase this useful tool!
http://rama.swlearning.com

Practice Cases

- Sharkey Incorporated—This case study allows the students to assume the role of a financial consultant for Sharkey, Inc. for a two-year term. The goal of the case study is for the student to maximize both earnings per share and return on assets.
- Foxcor Manufacturing Company—This comprehensive practice case pulls together the concepts learned in the first half of the intermediate accounting course. The case also draws on theory and concepts learned in foundation accounting courses. After completing this case, students will be able to read and interpret the financial statements and understand how individual journal entries support a set of financial statements and related footnote disclosures.

Check out the Companion web site for a link to purchase these useful tools!

Accounting and Auditing Research Tools and Strategies, Sixth Edition This step-by-step guide to professional research is integrated with ResearchLink, a new suite of online research tools, tutorials, demos, research cases, and links to accounting and business research sites and standard-setting organizations.

Completely revised and updated, the Sixth Edition now includes new guidance for research stemming from the Sarbanes-Oxley Act, principles- and rules-based standard setting, the PCAOB, the AICPA's SAS 99 fraud auditing standards, and the AICPA's anti-fraud program.

Written by Thomas R. Weirich, Central Michigan University; Thomas C. Pearson, University of Hawaii; and Alan Reinstein, Wayne State University.

Check out the Companion web site for a link to purchase this useful tool!

ACKNOWLEDGEMENTS

We are grateful to our respective Schools of Accountancy and to the American Institute of Certified Public Accountants, the Financial Accounting Standards Board, and the Institute of Certified Management Accountants of the Institute of Management Accountants for granting us permission to quote from their respective pronouncements and use their examination questions and unofficial answers. We are also grateful to our wives, children, and friends, who provided us with considerable moral support and understanding during the entire manuscript process. Finally, we'd like to acknowledge our publishing team, Keith Chasse, Chris McNamee, Steve Joos, and Bob Dreas for all of their assistance to ensure the textbook the best that it could be.

Most importantly, we would like to express our appreciation to those who served as reviewers and who provided insightful comments and valuable suggestions in the planning and writing of this textbook:

Advisory Board Members

Charlene Abendroth
California State University, East Bay

Matthew J. Anderson
Michigan State University

Gregory Brookins
Santa Monica College

Otto Chang
California State University, San Bernardino

S. Mark Comstock
Missouri Southern State University

Joanne Duke
San Francisco State University

Kathy L. Horton
College of DuPage

Herbert G. Hunt III
California State University, Long Beach

A. Rief Kanan
SUNY, New Paltz

Mary Loyland
University of North Dakota

Steven M. Mintz
Claremont McKenna College

Simon R. Pearlman
California State University, Long Beach

Alee S. Phillips
University of Kansas

Abe Qastin
Lakeland College

Vernon Richardson
University of Arkansas

William C. Schwartz, Jr.
University of Arizona

Vic Stanton
University of California, Berkeley

Rick Turpin
The University of Tennessee, Chattanooga

Nancy L. Wilburn
Northern Arizona University

Rizvana Zameeruddin
University of Wisconsin, Parkside

Chapter Reviewers

Florence Atiase
University of Texas at Austin

Sandra A. Augustine
Hilbert College

Thomas Badley
Baker College of Port Huron

Craig E. Bain
Northern Arizona University

Charles P. Baril
James Madison University

Allen Blay
University of California, Riverside

Helen Brubeck
San Jose State University

Eric Carlsen
Kean University

Otto Chang
California State University, San Bernardino

S. Mark Comstock
Missouri Southern State University

Araya Debessay
University of Delaware

Doug deVidal
University of Texas at Austin

Carolyn S. Dreher
Southern Methodist University

Tim V. Eaton
Marquette University

Karen M. Foust
Tulane University

Lucille S. Genduso
Nova Southeastern University

Donald F. Geren
Northeastern Illinois University

Kenneth R. Henry
Florida International University

Lori Holder-Webb
University of Wisconsin - Madison

Kevin L. Kemerer
Florida Memorial College

Saleha B. Khumawala
University of Houston

Dieter M. Kiefer
American River College

Mark Kohlbeck
University of Wisconsin – Madison

Patsy Lee
University of Texas at Arlington

Tim Lindquist
The University of Northern Iowa

Mary Loyland
University of North Dakota

Jim McDonald
Regis University

Steven M. Mintz
Claremont McKenna College

Barbara J. Muller
Arizona State University, West

Simon R. Pearlman
California State University, Long Beach

Donald J. Raux
Siena College

Randall Rentfro
Florida Atlantic University

Reginald Rezac
Texas Woman's University

Vernon Richardson
University of Arkansas

Angela H. Sandberg
Jacksonville State University

William C. Schwartz, Jr.
University of Arizona

Gim S. Seow
University of Connecticut

Leonard Stokes
Siena College

Sue Strickland
University of Texas at Arlington

Diane L. Tanner
University of North Florida

Robin M. Wagner
San Francisco State University

Tom Woods
Arizona State University, West

Rizvana Zameeruddin
University of Wisconsin, Parkside

Focus Group Participants

Gilda Agacer
Monmouth University

Joyce Allen
Xavier University

Bruce Bettinghause
Michigan State University

Jane Bozewicz
Babson University

Joan Monnin Callahan
University of Cincinnati

Gyan Chandra
Miami University

Lynn H. Clements
Florida Southern College

Clarence Coleman Jr.
Winthrop University

Richard H. Fern
Eastern Kentucky University

Linda Flaming
Monmouth University

Richard Fleischman
John Carroll University

Nashwa George
Montclair State University

Janet S. Greenlee
University of Dayton

Clayton H. Hock
Miami University

Afshad J. Irani
University of New Hampshire

Philip A. Lewis
Northern Kentucky University

Patricia Parker
Columbus State Community College

Bill Parrot
University of South Florida

Marc Percconi
Indiana University

Chuck Pier
Texas State University

Pat Poli
Fairfield University

Sally M. Schultz
SUNY New Paltz

John Surdick
Xavier University

Weimin Wong
Tulane University

Survey Participants

Joseph Adamo
Cazenovia College

Pierre Barakat
South University

Charles P. Baril
James Madison University

Debbie Beard
Southeast Missouri State University

Ronald. E. Blevins
Eastern New Mexico University

Jon Book
Tennessee Technological University

Martin A. Brady
Muskingum College

Angele Brill
Castleton State College

Star Brown
Western Piedmont Community College

Helen Brubeck
San Jose State University

Kurt H. Buerger
Angelo State University

Al B. Case
Southern Oregon University

B. Wayne Clark
Southwest Baptist University

Lynn H. Clements
Florida Southern College

S. Mark Comstock
Missouri Southern State University

Patricia Davis
Keystone College

Araya Debessay
University of Delaware

Joan H. Demko
Wor-Wic Community College

Julie L. Dilling
Fox Valley Technical College

Kathleen Fitzpatrick
University of Toledo

Frances Ann Ford
Spalding University

John Garlick
Fayetteville State University

Lucille S. Genduso
Nova Southeastern University

Saturnino (Nino) Gonzalez, Jr.
El Paso Community College

Teresa P. Gordon
University of Idaho

Janet S. Greenlee
University of Dayton

Lillian S. Grose
Delgado Community College

Steve Hall
University of Nebraska, Kearney

Penny Hanes
Mercyhurst College

Coby Harmon
University of California, Santa Barbara

Jean Hawkins
William Jewell College

Kenneth R. Henry
Florida International University

Joyce Lucas Hicks
Saint Mary's College

Clayton H. Hock
Miami University

Rich Houston
University of Alabama

Afshad J. Irani
University of New Hampshire

Philip Joos
University of Tilburg

A. Rief Kanan
SUNY, New Paltz

Kevin L. Kemerer
Florida Memorial College

Saleha B. Khumawala
University of Houston

Dieter M. Kiefer
American River College

Florence R. Kirk
SUNY, Oswego

Gordon Klein
UCLA Anderson School

David E. Laurel
South Texas College

David B. Law
Youngstown State University

Janice E. Lawrence
University of Nebraska, Lincoln

Chao-Shin Liu
University of Notre Dame

Marcia Lucas
Western Illinois University

Diane K. Marker
University of Toledo

Danny G. Matthews
Naval Postgraduate School

Cynthia McCall
Des Moines Area Community College

Jim McDonald
Regis University

Robert W. McGee
Barry University

Christine L. McKeag
University of Evansville

Dennis Moore
Worcester State College

Barbara J. Muller
Arizona State University

Susan Mundy
City University

Martha K. Nelson
Franklin and Marshall College

Leslie Oakes
University of New Mexico

Alfonso R. Oddo
Niagara University

Saundra Ohern
Evangel University

Pamela Ondeck
University of Pittsburgh at Greensburg

Stephen Owusu-Ansah
The University of Texas-Pan American

Janet C. Papiernik
Indiana University Purdue University Fort Wayne

Rob Parry
Indiana University, Bloomington

Deborah D. Pavelka
Roosevelt University

Simon R. Pearlman
California State University, Long Beach

Chuck Pier
Texas State University

Mary Ann M. Prater
Clemson University

Abe Qastin
Lakeland College

Vinita Ramaswamy
University of St. Thomas

Donald J. Raux
Siena College

Randall Rentfro
Florida Atlantic University

Vernon Richardson
University of Arkansas

Lyle M. Rupert
Hendrix College

Angela H. Sandberg
Jacksonville State University

James Schaefer
University of Evansville

Gim S. Seow
University of Connecticut

Robert J. Shore
Felician College

Gene Smith
Eastern New Mexico University

John L. Stancil
Florida Southern College

Leonard Stokes
Siena College

Norman Sunderman
Angelo State University

Mary Ann Swindlehurst
Carroll Community College

Lateef Syed
Robert Morris College

Diane L.Tanner
University of North Florida

James P. Trebby
Marquette University

John White
Elmhurst College

Donna Whitten
Purdue University North Central

Joni J. Young
University of New Mexico

Rizvana Zameeruddin
University of Wisconsin, Parkside

We wish to express appreciation to users of the earlier editions who provided meaningful comments and constructive criticism. We are grateful to Professors Larry Sallee, Winona State University; Scott Summers, Brigham Young University; Paul Miller, University of Colorado at Colorado Springs; Geri Wink, Colorado State University at Pueblo; James C. Buckley, Mesa State College; Norman A. Sunderman, Angelo State University; Peggy Dwyer, University of Central Florida; Robin Roberts, University of Central Florida; Kenneth R. Lambert, University of Memphis; Sandra D. Byrd, Missouri State University; Rita J. Hopewell; T.J. Atwood, Kansas State University; Ben Hsien Bao, Hong Kong Polytechnic University; John Sweeney, Washington State University; Sun Kim, SUNY-Buffalo; Brad Jordan, University of Kentucky; Ray Brooks, Oregon State University; Doug Cloud, Pepperdine University-Malibu; and Inder Khurana and Billie Cunningham, University of Missouri-Columbia for their reactions to selected topics. Special thanks go to Donald Green, Scott I. Jerris, San Francisco State University; Paula Kock; Walter Parker; Norma Powell, University of Massachusetts at Lowell; and Daryl G. Krause, CPA, for their contributions of homework. We also wish to thank our graduate and undergraduate students, including Jenny Reed, Beth Adair, JoAnne Leuders, Stephen Underhill, Devra Niemann, Teresa Hickam, Cherie Wadlin, Trish Nikolai, Lori Thompson, Lisa Klempert, Lori Hamilton, Terry Phillips, Theresa Spaedy, Kyle Newell, Carrie Hammond, Cassi Costner, Emily Kliethermes, Nathan Troup, Herman Eckerle, Kelli Strubinger, and Sarah Hooper. We are sincerely indebted to our typists, Anita Blanchar, Karen Staggs, and Mary Meyer, whose quality work and perseverance enabled us to complete the manuscript in a timely and orderly fashion.

Reviewers of the Ninth Edition

Richard C. Brooks
West Virginia University

Cheryl L. Fulkerson
University of Texas, San Antonio

David J. Harr
George Mason University

Penny Hanes, MBA, CPA
Mercyhurst College

Jeff Ritter
Associate Professor of Business Administration
St. Norbert College

Geri Wink
Colorado State University, Pueblo

Richard S. Sathe
University of St. Thomas

PART 1
Financial Reporting: Concepts, Financial Statements, and Related Disclosures

1	The Environment of Financial Reporting	2
2	Financial Reporting: Its Conceptual Framework	30
3	Review of a Company's Accounting System	64
4	The Balance Sheet and the Statement of Changes in Stockholders' Equity	116
5	The Income Statement and Statement of Cash Flows	168
6	Additional Aspects of Financial Reporting and Financial Analysis	242
Time Value of Money Module		M1

PART 2
Financial Reporting: Asset Valuation and Income Measurement

7	Cash and Receivables	304
8	Inventories: Cost Measurement and Flow Assumptions	358
9	Inventories: Special Valuation Issues	412
10	Property, Plant, and Equipment: Acquisition and Disposal	458
11	Depreciation and Depletion	502
12	Intangibles	548

PART 3
Financial Reporting: Valuation of Liabilities and Investments

13	Current Liabilities and Contingencies	586
14	Long-Term Liabilities and Receivables	638
15	Investments	704

PART 4
Financial Reporting: Stockholders' Equity

16	Contributed Capital	764
17	Earnings Per Share and Retained Earnings	824

PART 5
Financial Reporting: Special Topics

18	Income Recognition and Measurement of Net Assets	884
19	Accounting for Income Taxes	942
20	Accounting for Postemployment Benefits	994
21	Accounting for Leases	1064
22	The Statement of Cash Flows	1124
23	Accounting Changes and Errors	1198

APPENDIX A

The Coca-Cola Company 2004 Financial Statements and Supplementary Data — A1

APPENDIX B

List of the Official Pronouncements of the AICPA and FASB — B1

INDEX

INDEX — I1

Contents

PART 1
Financial Reporting: Concepts, Financial Statements, and Related Disclosures

1 The Environment of Financial Reporting 2
ACCOUNTING INFORMATION: USERS , USES, AND GAAP 4
External and Internal Users 5
Financial and Managerial Accounting Information Systems 6
Financial Reporting 7
Generally Accepted Accounting Principles 8
THE ESTABLISHMENT OF ACCOUNTING STANDARDS 9
Committee on Accounting Procedure (CAP) 10
Accounting Principles Board (APB) 10
Financial Accounting Standards Board (FASB) 11
Other Organizations Currently Influencing Generally Accepted Accounting Principles 16
ETHICS IN THE ACCOUNTING ENVIRONMENT 21
CREATIVE AND CRITICAL THINKING IN THE ACCOUNTING ENVIRONMENT 23

2 Financial Reporting: Its Conceptual Framework 30
FASB CONCEPTUAL FRAMEWORK 32
OBJECTIVES OF FINANCIAL REPORTING 34
Information Useful in Decision Making 35
Information Useful to External Users in Assessing Future Cash Receipts 35
Information Useful in Assessing Company Cash Flows 36
Information About Economic Resources and Claims to These Resources 36
Information About Comprehensive Income and Its Components 36
Information About Cash Flows 37
Other Issues 37
TYPES OF USEFUL INFORMATION 38
Return on Investment 38
Risk 38
Financial Flexibility 39
Liquidity 39
Operating Capability 39
QUALITATIVE CHARACTERISTICS OF USEFUL ACCOUNTING INFORMATION 40
Hierarchy of Qualitative Characteristics 40
Understandability 40
Decision Usefulness 41
Relevance 41
Reliability 42

Comparability and Consistency 43
Constraints to the Hierarchy 43
ACCOUNTING ASSUMPTIONS AND PRINCIPLES 45
Entity (Assumption) 45
Continuity (Assumption) 46
Period of Time (Assumption) 47
Monetary Unit (Assumption) 48
Historical Cost (Principle) 48
Recognition (Principle) 49
Matching and Accrual Accounting (Principles) 50
Conservatism (Principle) 51
GAAP AND FINANCIAL STATEMENTS 51
Balance Sheet 52
Income Statement 53
Statement of Cash Flows 53
Statement of Changes in Equity 54
Model of Business Reporting 54
IASB FRAMEWORK 56
OVERVIEW 56

3 Review of a Company's Accounting System 64
THE ACCOUNTING SYSTEM 66
Accounting Equation 66
Transactions, Events, and Supporting Documents 67
Accounts 67
Financial Statements 69
THE ACCOUNTING CYCLE 70
Recording in the General Journal (Step 1) 70
Posting to the Ledger (Step 2) 73
Preparation of Adjusting Entries (Step 3) 76
Preparation of the Financial Statements (Step 4) 81
Preparation of Closing Entries (Step 5) 84
Additional Issues 86
WORKSHEET (SPREADSHEET) 88
REVERSING ENTRIES 90
Example: Reversing Entry 91
SUBSIDIARY LEDGERS 92
SPECIAL JOURNALS 93
COMPUTER SOFTWARE 94
APPENDIX: CASH-BASIS ACCOUNTING 95

4 The Balance Sheet and the Statement of Changes in Stockholders' Equity 116
INTERRELATIONSHIP OF FINANCIAL STATEMENTS 118
PURPOSES OF THE BALANCE SHEET 119
Liquidity, Financial Flexibility, and Operating Capability 120
Capital and Capital Maintenance 120
RECOGNITION IN THE BALANCE SHEET 121
ELEMENTS OF THE BALANCE SHEET 121
Assets 122

Liabilities 122
Stockholders' Equity 123
MEASUREMENT OF THE ELEMENTS OF THE BALANCE SHEET 123
Historical Cost 123
Current Cost 123
Current Market Value 123
Net Realizable Value 124
Present Value 125
Valuations on Today's Balance Sheet 125
Limitations of the Balance Sheet 126
REPORTING CLASSIFICATIONS ON THE BALANCE SHEET 127
Current Assets 128
Current Liabilities 129
Working Capital 131
Long-Term Investments 132
Property, Plant, and Equipment 133
Intangible Assets 134
Other Assets 134
Long-Term Liabilities 134
Other Liabilities 136
Conceptual Guidelines for Reporting Assets and Liabilities 136
Stockholders' Equity 137
Contributed Capital 137
Capital Stock and Additional Paid-In Capital 138
Retained Earnings 139
Accumulated Other Comprehensive Income 139
Miscellaneous Items 140
STATEMENT OF CHANGES IN STOCKHOLDERS' EQUITY 140
OTHER DISCLOSURE ISSUES 141
Summary of Accounting Policies 141
Fair Value and Risk of Financial Instruments 142
Loss and Gain Contingencies 143
Subsequent Events 144
Related Party Transactions 144
Comparative Financial Statements 145
Auditor's Report 145
SEC Integrated Disclosures 145
Miscellaneous Disclosures 146
REPORTING TECHNIQUES 148
Statement Format (Balance Sheet) 148
Combined Amounts 148
Rounding 148
Notes, Supporting Schedules, and Parenthetical Notations 149
ILLUSTRATIVE STATEMENTS 149

5 The Income Statement and Statement of Cash Flows 168
CONCEPTS OF INCOME 170
Capital Maintenance Concept 170
Transactional Approach 171
PURPOSES OF THE INCOME STATEMENT 173

CONCEPTUAL REPORTING
GUIDELINES 173
  General Conceptual
  Guidelines 174
  Specific Conceptual
  Guidelines 174
  User Group Conceptual
  Guidelines 175
ELEMENTS OF THE INCOME
STATEMENT 176
  Revenues 176
  Expenses 178
  Gains and Losses 179
INCOME STATEMENT CONTENT 181
  All-Inclusive versus Current
  Operating 181
  Condensed Income Statements 183
INCOME STATEMENT: INCOME
FROM CONTINUING
OPERATIONS 183
  Sales Revenue (Net) 183
  Cost of Goods Sold 183
  Operating Expenses 184
  Other Items 185
  Income Tax Expense Related to
  Continuing Operations 186
  Single-Step and Multiple-Step
  Formats 187
  Alternative Income Captions 189
INCOME STATEMENT: RESULTS
FROM DISCONTINUED
OPERATIONS 189
  Operating Income (or Loss) 193
  Gain or Loss on Sale 193
  Disclosures 195
INCOME STATEMENT:
EXTRAORDINARY ITEMS 195
  Criteria 196
  Reporting Procedures 197
INCOME STATEMENT: EARNINGS
PER SHARE 199
INCOME STATEMENT: RELATED
ISSUES 200
  Change in Accounting Estimate 200
  Summary of Selected Financial
  Information 202
  Limitations of the Income
  Statement 202
STATEMENT OF RETAINED
EARNINGS 204
  Net Income and Dividends 204
  Adjustments of Beginning Retained
  Earnings 204
  Combined Statements 206
COMPREHENSIVE INCOME 206
  Reporting Alternatives 207
  Conceptual Evaluation 209
STATEMENT OF CASH FLOWS 209
  Overview and Uses of the
  Statement of Cash Flows 210
  Reporting Guidelines and
  Practices 210
  Operating Cash Flows: Direct
  Method 212
SUMMARY OF DISCLOSURES 214

6 Additional Aspects of Financial
   Reporting and Financial
   Analysis 242
   MARKET EFFICIENCY 244
   AUDITOR'S REPORT (OPINION) 246
   AUDIT COMMITTEE AND
   MANAGEMENT'S REPORT 249

SEGMENT REPORTING 251
  Reporting on Operating
  Segments 252
  Conceptual Evaluation 255
INTERIM FINANCIAL REPORTS 257
  Revenues 257
  Expenses 257
  Income Taxes 258
  Extraordinary Items and
  Discontinued Operations 259
  Earnings per Share 259
  Preparation and Disclosure of
  Summarized Interim Financial
  Data 260
SEC REPORTS 261
  Form 10-K 262
  Form 10-Q 262
  XBRL Supplemental
  Information 262
APPENDIX: FINANCIAL ANALYSIS
COMPARISONS 263
INTRACOMPANY
COMPARISONS 264
INTERCOMPANY
COMPARISONS 264
PERCENTAGE ANALYSES 264
  Horizontal Analysis 265
  Vertical Analysis 265
RATIO ANALYSIS 265
  Stockholder Profitability Ratios 268
  Company Profitability Ratios 269
  Liquidity Ratios 270
  Activity Ratios 272
  Stability Ratios 273
  Cash Flow Ratios 275

Time Value of Money Module   M1
SIMPLE INTEREST AND
COMPOUND INTEREST M2
FUTURE VALUE OF A SINGLE SUM
AT COMPOUND INTEREST M3
  The Idea M4
  Formula Approach M5
  Table Approach M5
  Summary and Illustration M6
PRESENT VALUE OF A SINGLE
SUM M7
  The Idea M7
  Shortcut Approaches M8
  Summary and Illustration M9
MEASUREMENTS INVOLVING AN
ANNUITY M10
FUTURE VALUE OF AN ORDINARY
ANNUITY M10
  Shortcut Approaches M11
  Summary and Illustration M12
FUTURE VALUE OF AN ANNUITY
DUE M13
  Solution Approach M14
PRESENT VALUE OF AN
ANNUITY M14
PRESENT VALUE OF AN ORDINARY
ANNUITY M14
  Solving by Determining the Present
  Value of a Series of Single
  Sums M15
  Shortcut Approaches M16
  Summary and Illustration M17
PRESENT VALUE OF AN ANNUITY
DUE M18
  Shortcut Approaches M19
  Another Application M21

PRESENT VALUE OF A DEFERRED
ORDINARY ANNUITY M21
  Another Application M23
SUMMARY OF PRESENT AND
FUTURE VALUE CALCULATIONS M24
CONCEPTUAL EVALUATION OF
PRESENT VALUE TECHNIQUES IN
FINANCIAL REPORTING M24

Part 2
Financial Reporting: Asset
Valuation and Income
Measurement

7 Cash and Receivables   304
   CASH 306
     Cash and Cash Equivalents 307
     Cash Management 307
     Electronic-Based Payments 309
     Compensating Balances 309
   RECEIVABLES 310
   REVENUE RECOGNITION AND
   VALUATION OF TRADE
   RECEIVABLES 310
     Normal Revenue Recognition 311
     Right of Return 311
     Valuation Issues 311
   ACCOUNTS RECEIVABLE 312
     Cash (Sales) Discounts 313
     Sales Returns and Allowances 314
   VALUATION OF ACCOUNTS
   RECEIVABLE FOR UNCOLLECTIBLE
   ACCOUNTS 315
     Allowance Method 316
     Percentage of Sales (or Net Credit
     Sales) 316
     Percentage of Outstanding
     Accounts Receivable 317
     Aging of Accounts Receivable 318
     Writing Off Uncollectible
     Accounts 320
     Collection of an Account Previously
     Written Off 321
     Direct Write-Off Method 322
   GENERATING IMMEDIATE CASH
   FROM ACCOUNTS RECEIVABLE 322
     Pledging of Accounts Receivable 324
     Assignment of Accounts
     Receivable 325
     Factoring (Sale) of Accounts
     Receivable 326
     Disclosure of Financing Agreements
     of Accounts Receivable 328
   NOTES RECEIVABLE 328
     Short-Term Interest-Bearing Notes
     Receivable 328
     Short-Term Non-Interest-Bearing
     Notes Receivable 329
     Notes Receivable Discounted 330
   FINANCIAL STATEMENT
   DISCLOSURES OF RECEIVABLES 331
   APPENDIX: INTERNAL CONTROLS
   FOR CASH 332
   PETTY CASH 333
   BANK RECONCILIATION 334
     Causes of the Difference 334
     Procedures for Preparing a Bank
     Reconciliation 335
     Example: Bank Reconcilation 336

8 **Inventories: Cost Measurement and Flow Assumptions 358**
 CLASSIFICATIONS OF INVENTORY 360
  Raw Materials Inventory 360
  Work in Process Inventory 360
  Finished Goods Inventory 361
  Reporting Inventory in a Company's Financial Statements 361
  Inventories of Service Companies 362
 ALTERNATIVE INVENTORY SYSTEMS 362
  Perpetual Inventory System 362
  Periodic Inventory System 362
 ITEMS TO BE INCLUDED IN INVENTORY QUANTITIES 363
 DETERMINATION OF INVENTORY COSTS 364
  Purchases Discounts 365
 COST FLOW ASSUMPTIONS 367
  Specific Identification 368
  First-In, First-Out (FIFO) 369
  Average Cost 370
  Last-In, First-Out (LIFO) 371
  Comparison of Inventory Cost Flow Assumptions 373
 CONCEPTUAL EVALUATION OF INVENTORY COST FLOW ASSUMPTIONS 374
  Income Measurement 374
  Income Tax Effects 375
  Liquidation of LIFO Layers 376
  Earnings (Income) Management 377
  Inventory Valuation 378
  Average Cost 378
  Management's Selection of an Inventory Cost Flow Assumption 379
 DOLLAR-VALUE LIFO 381
  Example: Dollar-Value LIFO 382
  Determination of Cost Index 383
  Inventory Pools 385
 ADDITIONAL LIFO CONSIDERATIONS 387
  LIFO Valuation Adjustment 387
  Interim Statements Using LIFO 387
  Change to or from LIFO 388
 DISCLOSURE OF INVENTORY VALUES AND METHODS 389
 APPENDIX: FOREIGN CURRENCY TRANSACTIONS INVOLVING INVENTORY 392
  Example: Exchange Gain 393
  Example: Exchange Loss 393

9 **Inventories: Special Valuation Issues 412**
 LOWER OF COST OR MARKET 414
  Application of Lower of Cost or Market Method 414
  Conceptual Evaluation of the Ceiling and Floor 416
  Approaches to Implementing Lower of Cost or Market Rule 418
  Recording the Reduction of Inventory to Market 419
  LCM: Direct Method (Periodic) 419

 LCM: Indirect Method (Periodic) 420
  LCM: Perpetual 420
  LCM: Reporting 420
  Lower of Cost or Market and Interim Financial Statements 421
 CONCEPTUAL EVALUATION OF LOWER OF COST OR MARKET 421
 PURCHASE OBLIGATIONS AND PRODUCT FINANCING ARRANGEMENTS 423
 VALUATION ABOVE COST 424
 GROSS PROFIT METHOD 426
  Example: Gross Profit Method 426
  Conceptual Evaluation of the Gross Profit Method 427
 RETAIL INVENTORY METHOD 428
  Example: Retail Inventory Method 428
  Retail Inventory Method Terminology 429
  Application of the Retail Inventory Method 429
  Additional Cost and Retail Adjustments 433
  Comparison of Methods 434
 CONCEPTUAL EVALUATION OF THE RETAIL INVENTORY METHOD 434
 DOLLAR-VALUE LIFO RETAIL METHOD 437
 EFFECTS OF INVENTORY ERRORS 439
 SUMMARY OF INVENTORY ISSUES 442

10 **Property, Plant, and Equipment: Acquisition and Disposal 458**
 CHARACTERISTICS OF PROPERTY, PLANT, AND EQUIPMENT 460
  Evaluation of Use of Historical Cost 460
 ACQUISITION OF PROPERTY, PLANT, AND EQUIPMENT 461
  Determination of Cost 461
  Lump-Sum Purchase 463
  Deferred Payments 464
  Issuance of Securities 464
  Assets Acquired by Donation 465
  Start-up Costs 466
 NONMONETARY ASSET EXCHANGES 466
  Example: Exchanges of Nonmonetary Assets 467
  Exceptions to the General Rule to Use Fair Value for Nonmonetary Exchanges 468
 SELF-CONSTRUCTION 469
  Interest During Construction 469
  Fixed Overhead Costs 474
  Income on Self-Construction 475
  Development Stage Companies 475
 COSTS AFTER ACQUISITION 476
  Additions 476
  Improvements and Replacements 476
  Rearrangement and Moving 477
  Repairs and Maintenance 477
 DISPOSAL OF PROPERTY, PLANT, AND EQUIPMENT 478
  Asset Retirement Obligations 479
 DISCLOSURE OF PROPERTY, PLANT, AND EQUIPMENT 481

 APPENDIX: OIL AND GAS PROPERTIES 483

11 **Depreciation and Depletion 502**
 FACTORS INVOLVED IN DEPRECIATION 504
  Asset Cost 504
  Service Life 504
  Residual Value 505
 METHODS OF COST ALLOCATION 505
  Time-Based Methods 506
  Activity Methods 509
 RECORDING DEPRECIATION 510
 CONCEPTUAL EVALUATION OF DEPRECIATION METHODS 511
 DISCLOSURE OF DEPRECIATION 513
 ADDITIONAL DEPRECIATION METHODS 515
  Group Depreciation 515
  Composite Depreciation 516
  Inventory Systems 518
 DEPRECIATION FOR PARTIAL PERIODS 518
  Compute Depreciation to the Nearest Whole Month 519
  Compute Depreciation to the Nearest Whole Year 520
  Compute One-Half Year's Depreciation on All Assets Purchased or Sold During the Year 520
 IMPAIRMENT OF PROPERTY, PLANT, AND EQUIPMENT 520
  Impairment Test 521
  Measurement of the Loss 521
  Recording and Reporting the Loss 521
  Disclosures 521
  Example: Impairment Loss 522
  Conceptual Evaluation of Asset Impairment 523
 DEPRECIATION AND INCOME TAXES 524
  MACRS Principles 525
  Example: MACRS 526
 CHANGES AND CORRECTIONS OF DEPRECIATION 528
 DEPLETION 528

12 **Intangibles 548**
 ACCOUNTING FOR INTANGIBLES 550
  Cost of Intangibles 550
  Amortization or Impairment of Intangible Assets 552
 RESEARCH AND DEVELOPMENT COSTS 554
  Conceptual Evaluation of Accounting for Research and Development Costs 556
 IDENTIFIABLE INTANGIBLE ASSETS 557
  Patents 557
  Copyrights 559
  Franchises 559
  Computer Software Costs 559
  Internal-Use Software 561
  Leases and Leasehold Improvements 562
  Trademarks and Tradenames 562

Deferred Charges 562
Organization Costs 562
UNIDENTIFIABLE INTANGIBLES 563
Internally Developed Goodwill 563
Purchased Goodwill 563
Impairment of Goodwill 564
Negative Goodwill 565
Estimating the Value of
Goodwill 566
DISCLOSURES FOR INTANGIBLE
ASSETS 567
CONCEPTUAL EVALUATION
OF ACCOUNTING FOR
INTANGIBLES 568

PART 3
**Financial Reporting: Valuation of
Liabilities and Investments**

13 **Current Liabilities and
Contingencies 586**
CONCEPTUAL OVERVIEW OF
LIABILITIES 588
NATURE AND DEFINITION OF
CURRENT LIABILITIES 589
Classification and the Operating
Cycle or Year 589
Liquidity, Financial Flexibility, and
Current Liabilities 589
Classification of Current
Liabilities 590
VALUATION OF CURRENT
LIABILITIES 591
CURRENT LIABILITIES HAVING A
CONTRACTUAL AMOUNT 591
Trade Accounts Payable 591
Notes Payable 592
Currently Maturing Portion of
Long-Term Debt 594
Dividends Payable 594
Advances and Refundable
Deposits 595
Accrued Liabilities 595
Unearned Items 598
CURRENT LIABILITIES WHOSE
AMOUNTS DEPEND ON
OPERATIONS 599
Sales and Use Taxes 599
Liabilities Related to Payrolls 600
Income Taxes Payable 602
Bonus Obligations 602
CURRENT LIABILITIES REQUIRING
AMOUNTS TO BE ESTIMATED 605
Property Taxes 605
Warranty Obligations 606
Premium and Coupon
Obligations 609
CONTINGENCIES 611
Accrual of Loss Contingencies 613
Disclosure of Loss Contingencies in
the Notes to the Financial
Statements 614
Disclosure of Gain Contingencies
in the Notes to the Financial
Statements 615
Executory Contracts 615
Illustrations of Contingency
Disclosures 615

OTHER LIABILITY CLASSIFICATION
ISSUES 617
Short-Term Debt Expected to Be
Refinanced 617
Classification of Obligations That
Are Callable by the Creditor 619
FINANCIAL STATEMENT
PRESENTATION OF CURRENT
LIABILITIES 620

14 **Long-Term Liabilities and
Receivables 638**
REASONS FOR ISSUANCE OF LONG-
TERM LIABILITIES 640
BONDS PAYABLE 640
Characteristics of Bonds 641
Bond Selling Prices 641
RECORDING THE ISSUANCE OF
BONDS 643
Bonds Issued Between Interest
Payment Dates 644
AMORTIZING DISCOUNTS AND
PREMIUMS 645
Straight-Line Method 645
Effective Interest Method 648
Bond Issue Costs 651
Accruing Bond Interest 652
Zero-Coupon Bonds 653
EXTINGUISHMENT OF
LIABILITIES 654
Bonds Retired at Maturity 654
Bonds Retired Prior to
Maturity 654
BONDS WITH EQUITY
CHARACTERISTICS 656
Bonds Issued with Detachable
Stock Warrants 656
Convertible Bonds 657
LONG-TERM NOTES PAYABLE 661
Notes Payable Issued for Cash 662
Notes Payable Exchanged for Cash
and Rights or Privileges 663
Notes Payable Exchanged for
Property, Goods, or Services 664
Disclosure of Long-Term
Liabilities 665
LONG-TERM NOTES
RECEIVABLE 667
Loan Fees 671
Impairment of a Loan 671
Guarantees 675
Future Developments 675
APPENDIX 1: TROUBLED DEBT
RESTRUCTURINGS 676
ACCOUNTING BY THE DEBTOR 676
Modification of Terms 677
Equity or Asset Exchange 679
Equity or Asset Exchange
Combined with a Modification of
Terms 679
Disclosure of Restructuring
Agreements 680
ACCOUNTING BY THE
CREDITOR 680
Equity or Asset Exchange 680
Modification of Terms 681
Equity or Asset Exchange
Combined with Modification of
Terms 682

CONCEPTUAL EVALUATION OF
ACCOUNTING FOR TROUBLED
DEBT RESTRUCTURINGS 683
APPENDIX 2: SERIAL BONDS 683
RECORDING THE ISSUANCE AND
INTEREST EXPENSE OF SERIAL
BONDS 683
Example: Serial Bonds 684
EARLY REDEMPTION OF SERIAL
BONDS 686

15 **Investments 704**
INVESTMENTS: CLASSIFICATION
AND VALUATION 706
INVESTMENTS IN DEBT AND
EQUITY TRADING SECURITIES 708
INVESTMENTS IN AVAILABLE-FOR-
SALE DEBT AND EQUITY
SECURITIES 708
Recording Initial Cost 709
Recording Interest and Dividend
Revenue 709
Recognition of Unrealized Holding
Gains and Losses 710
Realized Gains and Losses on Sales
of Available-for-Sale Securities 712
INVESTMENTS IN HELD-TO-
MATURITY DEBT SECURITIES 714
Recording Initial Cost 715
Recognition and Amortization of
Bond Premiums and Discounts 715
Amortization for Bonds Acquired
Between Interest Dates 718
Sale of Investment in Bonds Before
Maturity 719
TRANSFERS AND IMPAIRMENTS 720
Transfers of Investments Between
Categories 721
Impairments 722
DISCLOSURES 723
Financial Statement
Classification 726
FASB STATEMENT NO. 115: A
CONCEPTUAL EVALUATION 726
Fair Value Is Required for Certain
Investments 727
Fair Value Is Not Required for
Certain Liabilities 727
Reporting of Unrealized Gains and
Losses 728
Classification of Securities Is Based
on Management Intent 729
EQUITY METHOD 729
Accounting Procedures 730
Financial Statement
Disclosures 732
Special Issues 733
ADDITIONAL ISSUES FOR
INVESTMENTS 736
Nonmarketable Securities 736
Stock Dividends and Splits 736
Stock Warrants 737
Convertible Bonds 737
Cash Surrender Value of Life
Insurance 738
Investments in Funds 738
Investment Transactions and
Operating Cash Flows 739
APPENDIX: DERIVATIVES OF
FINANCIAL INSTRUMENTS 739

FAIR VALUE HEDGE 740
CASH FLOW HEDGE 745

PART 4
Financial Reporting: Stockholders' Equity

16 **Contributed Capital   764**
CORPORATE FORM OF
ORGANIZATION 766
    Types of Corporations 767
    Formation of a Corporation 767
CORPORATE CAPITAL
STRUCTURE 768
    Capital Stock and Stockholders'
    Rights 769
    Basic Terminology 769
    Legal Capital 770
    Additional Paid-in Capital 770
STOCKHOLDERS' EQUITY 771
ISSUANCE OF CAPITAL STOCK 772
    Authorization 772
    Issuance for Cash 772
    Stock Issuance Costs 773
    Stock Subscriptions 773
    Combined Sales of Stock 775
    Nonmonetary Issuance of
    Stock 776
    Stock Splits 777
    Stock Rights to Current
    Stockholders 779
NONCOMPENSATORY SHARE
PURCHASE PLANS 779
COMPENSATORY SHARE OPTION
PLANS 780
    Historical Perspective and
    Conceptual Overview 780
    Measurement of Fair Value 783
    Recognition of Compensation
    Expense 784
    Additional Disclosures 790
    Conceptual Evaluation 792
PREFERRED STOCK
CHARACTERISTICS 793
    Preference as to Dividends 793
    Cumulative Preferred Stock 793
    Participating Preferred Stock 794
    Convertible Preferred Stock 794
    Preferred Stock with Stock Warrants
    (Rights) 796
    Callable Preferred Stock 797
    Redeemable Preferred Stock 798
    Preference in Liquidation 798
    Voting Rights 799
CONTRIBUTED CAPITAL
SECTION 799
TREASURY STOCK (CAPITAL STOCK
REACQUISITION) 800
    Cost Method 801
    Balance Sheet Presentation 803
    Acquisition at Greater Than Market
    Value 803
    Donated Treasury Stock 804
    Retirement of Treasury Stock 804
    Par Value Method 804
CAPITAL STOCK TRANSACTIONS
AND THE STATEMENT OF CASH
FLOWS 805

17 **Earnings Per Share and Retained
Earnings 824**
EARNINGS AND EARNINGS PER
SHARE 826
OVERVIEW AND USES OF
EARNINGS PER SHARE
INFORMATION 826
BASIC EARNINGS PER SHARE 827
    Numerator Calculations 827
    Denominator Calculations 828
    Components of Earnings Per
    Share 829
    Example of Basic Earnings Per
    Share 830
DILUTED EARNINGS PER SHARE 831
    Share Options and Warrants 832
    Convertible Securities 834
    Computation of Tentative and Final
    Diluted Earnings Per Share 835
ADDITIONAL CONSIDERATIONS 837
    Conversion Ratios 837
    Contingent Issuances 837
    Additional Disclosures 837
EPS DISCLOSURE ILLUSTRATION 839
CONTENT OF RETAINED
EARNINGS 841
DIVIDENDS 841
    Cash Dividends 842
    Property Dividends 844
    Scrip Dividends 846
    Stock Dividends 846
    Liquidating Dividends 850
PRIOR PERIOD ADJUSTMENTS
(RESTATEMENTS) 852
RESTRICTIONS (APPROPRIATIONS)
OF RETAINED EARNINGS 853
STATEMENT OF RETAINED
EARNINGS 853
    Illustration of Retained Earnings
    Statement 854
    Accumulated Other Comprehensive
    Income 854
MISCELLANEOUS CHANGES IN
STOCKHOLDERS' EQUITY 855
STATEMENT OF CHANGES IN
STOCKHOLDERS' EQUITY 855

PART 5
**Financial Reporting: Special
Topics**

18 **Income Recognition and
Measurement of Net Assets 884**
OVERVIEW OF REVENUE
RECOGNITION ALTERNATIVES 886
EXAMPLES OF REVENUE
RECOGNITION ALTERNATIVES 887
    Example: Revenue Recognition at
    Time of Sale 887
    Example: Revenue Recognition
    During Production 887
    Example: Revenue Recognition at
    Time of Cash Receipt 889
    Summary of Revenue Recognition
    Alternatives 890
CONCEPTUAL ISSUES 891
ALTERNATIVE REVENUE
RECOGNITION METHODS 892

REVENUE RECOGNITION PRIOR TO
THE PERIOD OF SALE 894
    Long-Term Construction
    Contracts 894
    Percentage-of-Completion
    Method 895
    Completed-Contract Method 896
    Illustration of the Two Methods 897
    Losses on Long-Term Construction
    Contracts 901
    Additional Considerations in
    Accounting for Long-Term
    Construction Contracts 904
REPORTING AND DISCLOSING
LONG-TERM CONSTRUCTION
CONTRACTS 905
    Long-Term Service Contracts 906
    Proportional Performance
    Method 906
REVENUE RECOGNITION AFTER
THE PERIOD OF SALE 909
    Installment Method 909
    Example: Installment Method 910
    Additional Considerations for the
    Installment Method 912
    Cost Recovery Method 914
    Comparison of the Installment and
    Cost Recovery Methods 915
REVENUE RECOGNITION DELAYED
UNTIL A FUTURE EVENT
OCCURS 915
    Example: Deposit Method 915
ADDITIONAL ISSUES 916
    SAB No. 104 917
SUMMARY OF ALTERNATIVE
REVENUE RECOGNITION
METHODS 917
APPENDIX: ADDITIONAL REVENUE
RECOGNITION ISSUES 917
SOFTWARE REVENUE
RECOGNITION 917
FRANCHISES 919
    Option to Purchase 921
REAL ESTATE SALES 921
RETAIL LAND SALES 922
CONSIGNMENT SALES 923

19 **Accounting for Income Taxes 942**
OVERVIEW AND DEFINITIONS 944
    Causes of Differences 944
    Definitions 945
INTERPERIOD INCOME TAX
ALLOCATION: BASIC ISSUES 945
    Permanent Differences 946
    Temporary Differences 947
INTERPERIOD INCOME TAX
ALLOCATION: CONCEPTUAL
ISSUES 949
    Deferred Tax Liability 950
    Deferred Tax Asset 951
    Measurement 951
INTERPERIOD INCOME TAX
ALLOCATION: RECORDING AND
REPORTING OF CURRENT AND
DEFERRED TAXES 953
    Basic Entries 954
    Example: Deferred Tax Liability—
    Single Future Taxable Amount 954

Example: Deferred Tax Liability—
Single Future Taxable Amount and
Multiple Rates 956
Example: Deferred Tax Asset—Single
Future Deductible Amount 957
Example: Deferred Tax Asset and
Valuation Allowance 958
Example: Permanent and Temporary
Differences 959
OPERATING LOSS CARRYBACKS
AND CARRYFORWARDS 962
Conceptual Issues 963
Generally Accepted Accounting
Principles 964
Example: Operating Loss
Carryback 964
Example: Operating Loss
Carryforward and Valuation
Allowance 965
Example: Operating Loss
Carryforward and No Valuation
Allowance 966
COMPREHENSIVE
ILLUSTRATION 967
INTRAPERIOD INCOME TAX
ALLOCATION 970
Example: Intraperiod Income Tax
Allocation 971
FINANCIAL STATEMENT
PRESENTATION AND
DISCLOSURES 973
Balance Sheet Presentation 973
Statement of Cash Flows
Presentation 974
Financial Statement Disclosures 974
MISCELLANEOUS ISSUES 975
Change in Income Tax Laws or
Rates 975
Compensatory Share Option
Plans 975
Alternative Minimum Tax and Other
Tax Credits 976
ILLUSTRATIVE DISCLOSURES 978

**20 Accounting for Postemployment
Benefits 994**
CHARACTERISTICS OF PENSION
PLANS 996
HISTORICAL PERSPECTIVE OF
PENSION PLANS 997
ACCOUNTING PRINCIPLES FOR
DEFINED BENEFIT PENSION
PLANS 998
Key Terms Related to Pension
Plans 998
Pension Expense 999
Pension Liabilities and Assets 1003
Measurement Methods 1005
Disclosures 1005
EXAMPLES OF ACCOUNTING FOR
PENSIONS 1006
Example: Pension Expense Equal to
Pension Funding 1007
Example: Pension Expense Greater
Than Pension Funding 1008
Example: Pension Expense Less Than
Pension Funding, and Expected
Return on Plan Assets Different from
Both Actual Return and Discount
Rate 1009

Example: Pension Expense
Including Amortization of
Unrecognized Prior Service
Cost 1011
Example: Calculation of
Amortization of Unrecognized
Prior Service Cost 1012
Example: Pension Expense
Including Net Gain or Loss (to
Extent Recognized) 1014
Example: Recognition of Additional
Pension Liability 1016
Example: Disclosures 1018
Pension Worksheet 1019
Summary of Issues Related to
Pensions 1024
FASB Plans for Revision of
Postretirement Accounting 1026
CONCEPTUAL ISSUES RELATED TO
DEFINED BENEFIT PENSION
PLANS 1026
Pension Expense 1026
Pension Liabilities 1027
Balance Sheet Presentation of
Pension Plan Assets 1028
ADDITIONAL ASPECTS OF PENSION
ACCOUNTING 1029
Statement of Cash Flows
Disclosures 1029
Vested Benefits 1029
Accounting for Defined
Contribution Plans 1029
Disclosures by Funding
Agencies 1030
Employee Retirement Income
Security Act of 1974 1031
Pension Plan Settlements and
Curtailments 1031
Termination Benefits Paid to
Employees 1032
Multi-Employer Plans 1032
OTHER POSTEMPLOYMENT
BENEFITS 1033
Similarities to and Differences from
Pensions 1034
Accounting Principles 1035
OPEB Expense 1035
Components of OPEB Expense 1036
OPEB Liability or Asset 1037
Differences from Accounting for
Pensions 1037
EXAMPLE: ACCOUNTING FOR
OPEBS 1037
CONCEPTUAL EVALUATION OF
ACCOUNTING FOR OPEBS 1039
Relevance and Reliability 1039
Differences in Funding 1039
Attribution Period 1039
Interaction with Deferred Income
Taxes 1040
Minimum Liability 1041
Impacts of the Adoption of FASB
Statement No. 106 1041
APPENDIX: EXAMPLE OF PRESENT
VALUE CALCULATIONS FOR
DEFINED BENEFIT PENSION
PLANS 1042
SERVICE COST 1043
INTEREST ON PROJECTED BENEFIT
OBLIGATION 1044

EXPECTED RETURN ON PLAN
ASSETS 1046
AMORTIZATION OF
UNRECOGNIZED PRIOR SERVICE
COST 1046
Adjustments of Service Cost and
Projected Benefit Obligation 1047
PENSION EXPENSE AND
LIABILITY 1048

21 Accounting for Leases 1064
ADVANTAGES OF LEASING 1066
Advantages of Leasing from Lessee's
Viewpoint 1066
Advantages of Leasing from Lessor's
Viewpoint 1068
KEY TERMS RELATED TO
LEASING 1068
CLASSIFICATION OF PERSONAL
PROPERTY LEASES 1068
ACCOUNTING AND REPORTING BY
A LESSEE 1073
Example: Operating Lease
(Lessee) 1073
Capital Lease (Lessee) 1074
Examples of Lessee's Capital Lease
Method 1075
Other Lessee Capitalization
Issues 1080
Disclosure Requirements of the
Lessee 1082
ACCOUNTING AND REPORTING BY
A LESSOR 1083
Operating Lease (Lessor) 1084
Direct Financing Leases
(Lessor) 1086
Initial Direct Costs Involved in a
Direct Financing Lease 1092
Sales-Type Leases (Lessor) 1093
Initial Direct Costs Involved in a
Sales-Type Lease 1095
Unguaranteed and Guaranteed
Residual Values 1096
Disclosure Requirements for the
Lessor 1096
SUMMARY OF ACCOUNTING BY
LESSEE AND LESSOR 1096
ADDITIONAL LEASE ISSUES 1097
Statement of Cash Flows
Disclosures 1097
Conceptual Evaluation of
Accounting for Leases 1098
APPENDIX: SPECIALIZED LEASE
ISSUES AND CHANGES IN LEASE
PROVISIONS 1100
LEASE ISSUES RELATED TO REAL
ESTATE 1100
Lease of Land Only 1100
Lease of Both Land and Buildings
That Transfers Title or Contains a
Bargain Purchase Option 1100
Lease of Land and Buildings That
Does Not Transfer Title or Contain
a Bargain Purchase Option 1102
Lease Involving Equipment as Well as
Real Estate 1103
SALE-LEASEBACK ISSUES 1103
Lessor's Accounting Issues 1104
Lessee's Accounting Issues 1104
Leveraged Leases 1105

CHANGES IN LEASE
PROVISIONS 1106
  Review of Estimated Unguaranteed
  Residual Value 1107
  Impact of Renewal of Lease on
  Guarantee of Residual Value 1107
  Changes to Sales-Type or Direct
  Financing Lease Prior to Lease Term
  Expiration That Change the Lease
  to an Operating Lease 1107
  Renewal of Sales-Type or Direct
  Financing Lease Resulting in a New
  Lease That Qualifies as a Sales-Type
  Lease 1107

22 The Statement of Cash
Flows 1124
  CONCEPTUAL OVERVIEW AND
  REPORTING GUIDELINES 1126
    Reporting Guidelines and
    Practices 1127
    Example: Typical Statement of Cash
    Flows 1128
  CASH INFLOWS AND
  OUTFLOWS 1131
    Inflows of Cash 1131
    Outflows of Cash 1132
    Classifications of Cash Flows 1132
  NET CASH FLOW FROM OPERATING
  ACTIVITIES 1134
    Direct Method 1135
    Indirect Method 1136
  INFORMATION FOR PREPARATION
  OF STATEMENT 1138
  VISUAL INSPECTION METHOD OF
  ANALYSIS 1139
    Simple Example (Visual Inspection
    Method) 1140
  WORKSHEET (SPREADSHEET)
  METHOD OF ANALYSIS 1142
    Steps in Preparation (Worksheet
    Method) 1142
    Comprehensive Example
    (Worksheet Method) 1144
  SPECIAL TOPICS 1151
    Sale of Depreciable Asset 1151
    Interest Paid and Income Taxes
    Paid 1152

Flexibility in Reporting 1153
Partial Cash Investing and Financing
Activities 1154
Temporary and Long-Term
Investments 1154
Financial Institutions 1156
Cash Dividends Declared 1157
Cash Flows for Compensatory
Share Option Plans 1158
Effects of Exchange Rates 1159
Cash Flow Per Share 1159
Disclosure 1159
APPENDIX: DIRECT METHOD FOR
REPORTING OPERATING CASH
FLOWS 1162
OPERATING CASH FLOWS 1162
  Operating Cash Inflows 1162
  Operating Cash Outflows 1163
  Diagram of Operating Cash
  Flows 1163
PROCEDURES FOR STATEMENT
PREPARATION 1166
  Visual Inspection Method 1166
  Worksheet Method 1169
EXAMPLE: WORKSHEET
(SPREADSHEET) AND DIRECT
METHOD 1169
  Operating Cash Flows 1169
  Investing and Financing Cash Flows
  1169
  Completion of Worksheet and
  Statement 1171

23 Accounting Changes and
Errors 1198
  TYPES OF ACCOUNTING
  CHANGES 1200
  METHODS OF REPORTING AN
  ACCOUNTING CHANGE 1200
  ACCOUNTING FOR A CHANGE IN
  ACCOUNTING PRINCIPLE 1201
    Retrospective Adjustment
    Method 1201
  ACCOUNTING FOR A CHANGE IN AN
  ESTIMATE 1207
  ADDITIONAL ISSUES 1208
    Impracticability of Retrospective
    Adjustment 1208

A Change in Principle
Distinguished from a Change in an
Estimate 1209
Preferability of the New Accounting
Principle 1210
Direct and Indirect Effects 1210
Adoption of a New Accounting
Principle for Future Events 1211
Initial Public Sale of Common
Stock 1211
Transition Methods Required by the
FASB 1211
Accounting Changes in Interim
Financial Statements 1211
Litigation Settlement 1212
CONCEPTUAL EVALUATION OF
ACCOUNTING FOR A CHANGE IN
ACCOUNTING PRINCIPLE AND A
CHANGE IN ESTIMATE 1212
  Retrospective Application
  (Adjustment) 1212
  Prospective Adjustment 1213
ACCOUNTING FOR A CHANGE IN A
REPORTING ENTITY 1213
ACCOUNTING FOR A CORRECTION
OF AN ERROR 1214
  Error Analysis 1216
  Error Correction 1218
  Steps in Error Correction 1219
SUMMARY OF EFFECTS ON
FINANCIAL STATEMENTS 1224

APPENDIX A

The Coca-Cola Company 2004
Financial Statements and
Supplementary Data A1

APPENDIX B

List of the Official Pronouncements of
the AICPA and FASB B1

INDEX

Financial Reporting: Concepts, Financial Statements, and Related Disclosures

CHAPTER 1
The Environment of Financial Reporting

CHAPTER 2
Financial Reporting: Its Conceptual Framework

CHAPTER 3
Review of a Company's Accounting System

CHAPTER 4
The Balance Sheet and the Statement of
Changes in Stockholders' Equity

CHAPTER 5
The Income Statement and Statement of
Cash Flows

CHAPTER 6
Additional Aspects of Financial Reporting and
Financial Analysis

OBJECTIVES

After reading this chapter, you will be able to:

1 Understand capital markets and decision making.

2 Know what is included in financial reporting.

3 Explain generally accepted accounting principles (GAAP) and the sources of GAAP.

4 Identify the types of pronouncements issued by the FASB.

5 Understand how the Financial Accounting Standards Board (FASB) operates.

6 Describe the relationship between the Securities and Exchange Commission (SEC) and the FASB.

7 Use ethical models for decision making about ethical dilemmas.

8 Understand creative and critical thinking.

The Environment of Financial Reporting

The Future Is Bright!

With the accounting difficulties at **Enron**, **WorldCom**, **HealthSouth**, and others, the accounting profession has come under intense scrutiny from regulatory agencies and has become the subject of late-night talk show jokes. As a future accounting professional, a natural question is what the future holds for you upon graduation. Let's take a look at some recent evidence that may yield some answers.

As the regulatory environment has become more dynamic over the last several years, companies are faced with an increasing number of new accounting rules that pose a significant challenge for financial reporting. All indications are that future years will present even greater challenges. To deal with this changing environment, more and more companies are turning to accountants

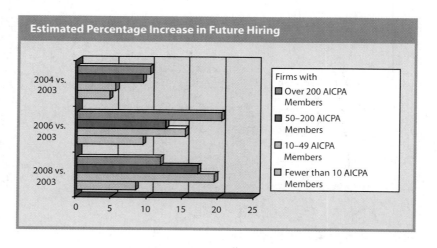

Estimated Percentage Increase in Future Hiring

Firms with
- Over 200 AICPA Members
- 50–200 AICPA Members
- 10–49 AICPA Members
- Fewer than 10 AICPA Members

Source: Adapted from "The Supply of Accounting Graduates and the Demand for Public Accounting Recruits – 2004."

Credit: Stockbyte

for assistance. Many companies have increased the importance of accounting skills in their executive training programs while other companies have emphasized the certified public accountant (CPA) credential in their executive searches. The trend toward increased hiring of individuals possessing accounting skills is not confined to industry. According to the 2004 American Institute of Certified Public Accountants (AICPA) survey, hiring of accounting graduates by public accounting firms increased approximately 10% in 2003. Future projections of hiring trends for accounting graduates (shown in the figure) are indicative of continued positive growth.

Finally, in a recent survey conducted by the National Association of Colleges and Employers, accounting was listed as the number one major on college campuses. By all indications, accounting skills appear in high demand, and your future professional career in accounting appears bright!

FOR FURTHER INVESTIGATION

For a discussion of the demand for accounting, consult the Business & Company Resource Center (BCRC) or the Internet for:

- CPA Ascendant. Kate O'Sullivan, *CFO, The Magazine for Senior Financial Executives*, 8756-7113, June 2004, v20, p102(2).
- American Institute of Certified Public Accountants. "The Supply of Accounting Graduates and the Demand for Public Accounting Recruits – 2004," http://www. aicpa.org/members/div/career/ edu/sagdpar.htm.

Accounting is the process of identifying, measuring, recording, and communicating economic information to enable users to make informed judgments and decisions. It is also called the "language of business." In the U.S. economy, most published accounting information is about different types of companies (primarily corporations). Companies engage in many transactions and generate large amounts of data. Since people can absorb only limited amounts of information, accounting systems are designed to report information in a concise, understandable format. In this sense, accounting is the link between a company's economic activities and decision makers.

In this chapter we review the uses of accounting information and who uses it, the development of principles for accumulating and communicating accounting information, and the ethical framework within which these accounting principles are applied.

ACCOUNTING INFORMATION: USERS , USES, AND GAAP

The U.S. economy is a free-market economy. In this type of economy, the decisions of many buyers and sellers influence the demand for and supply of products and services offered by companies. Individuals acting in this economy have limited resources to consume or to invest. But typically companies need large amounts of capital for their operations. Companies may obtain this capital from the issuance of capital stock (equity) and bonds (debt), from other borrowings, or from resources generated by their operations. The exchange of capital by investors for the stocks and bonds of companies occurs in **capital markets,** as we show in Exhibit 1-1. There are organized capital markets, such as the New York Stock Exchange (NYSE), the American Stock Exchange (AMEX), and the Nasdaq Stock Market, Inc. (NASDAQ). In these markets the capital stock and bonds of many corporations are purchased and sold daily. These corporations are called *publicly-held* (or *publicly-traded*) companies. These markets sometimes are referred to as *secondary markets* because the sales and purchases are among the investors themselves. That is, the corporation that initially issued the capital stock or bonds is not involved in the exchange.

There also are more loosely organized capital markets in which fewer exchanges occur. For instance, corporations may borrow from lending institutions or may issue new

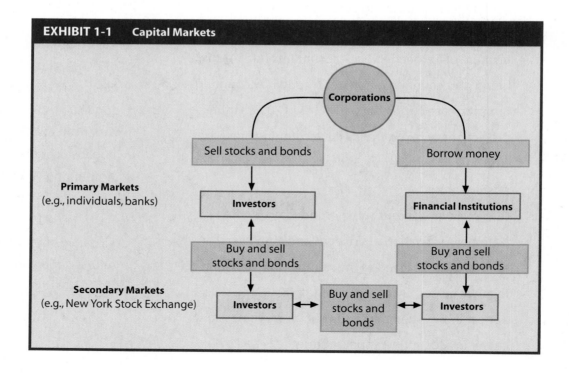

EXHIBIT 1-1   Capital Markets

capital stock or bonds, either through "public offerings" or through "private placements." Public offerings involve the sale to many investors (i.e., the general public). Private placements involve the sale to a few private institutions such as insurance companies and pension funds, or to employees. These markets sometimes are called *primary markets* because the exchange is directly between a corporation and the investors. Whether investors or lending institutions are involved in primary or secondary markets, they are interested in earning dividends and interest, and in a safe return of their resources. Investors in publicly traded securities participate in the increase (or decrease) in the market price of the capital stock and bonds. These investors are concerned with the efficient allocation of their scarce resources to achieve these objectives. Accounting information is useful in making decisions for this allocation process within these capital markets. It is also useful for other purposes.

External and Internal Users

Users of accounting information can be divided into two major categories, external users and internal users, as we show in Exhibit 1-2. These two user groups do not have the same information needs because of their different relationships to the company providing the economic information. **External users are actual or potential investors (stockholders and bondholders) and creditors (such as suppliers and lending institutions).** There are also other external users, such as employees, financial analysts, advisers, brokers, underwriters, stock exchanges, taxing and regulatory authorities, labor unions, and the general public. (Note that bondholders are "creditors" by contract and legal definition, but are considered "investors" as this term is commonly used.) Investors have a direct relationship with the company. Their capital market information needs revolve around three basic decisions:

1. *Buy.* A potential investor decides to purchase a particular security (e.g., a stock or bond) based on communicated accounting information.
2. *Hold.* An actual investor decides to retain a particular security based on communicated accounting information.
3. *Sell.* An actual investor decides to sell a particular security based on communicated accounting information.

1 Understand capital markets and decision making.

EXHIBIT 1-2   Accounting Information: Economic Activities and Decision Making

Impact

Company's Economic Activities → Accumulate → Accounting Information → Communicate → External User → External Decision Making

Communicate → Internal User → Internal Decision Making

Impact

Creditors, such as suppliers and lending institutions, also have a direct relationship with companies. Although creditors do not purchase securities, they make similar decisions that require accounting information. The decisions in this case are to extend credit, to maintain the credit relationship, or not to extend credit. Other users use accounting information in their decision making. For instance, stock exchanges use accounting information for listings, cancellations, and rule-making decisions. Labor unions use accounting information in negotiating wage agreements. Financial analysts use accounting information for making investment and credit recommendations.

Investment and credit decisions should be continuously reevaluated. Timely communication of information to external decision makers is very important. The publication of financial statements (e.g., in "hard copy" or on a company's web site) is a primary method by which relevant information is communicated. Studies have shown, however, that decision makers also use other reporting sources to satisfy their information needs.[1] We discuss this area of study, known as efficient capital markets research, in Chapter 6.

Internal users are the company managers who plan and control its operations on a day-by-day and a long-term basis. Internal users may request any information that the accounting system is capable of providing to help them make decisions on internal operations. For example, internal users may ask for information relating specifically to the purchase of new equipment or the addition of a new product.

Financial and Managerial Accounting Information Systems

Two branches of accounting are used to meet the needs of external and internal users. **Financial accounting is the information accumulation, processing, and communication system designed to provide investment and credit decision-making information for external users.** Financial accounting information is communicated (reported) through published financial statements and must follow the pronouncements of several policy-making groups. **Managerial accounting is the information accumulation, processing, and communication system designed to provide decision-making information for internal users.** Managerial accounting information is communicated via internal company reports and is not subject to the policy standards for externally communicated information. It is restricted by how useful the information is for a specific decision, and by the cost of providing that information. Financial and managerial accounting thus have somewhat different objectives because they provide information for different decisions. Exhibit 1-3 summarizes some of the more important differences.

The company's accountants prepare both the financial accounting and the managerial accounting reports, and the information comes from the same information system. The differences lie in selecting and presenting the communicated information. This book focuses on financial accounting and its usefulness in investors', creditors', and other users' decision making. We generally do not discuss managerial accounting information. On the other hand, the rules of a game influence how the game is played. The management of a company often is evaluated based on "performance criteria" (e.g., net income, rate of return) that are based on the accounting measures used in financial accounting reports. Thus, the financial accounting system may influence the managerial accounting system, or vice versa.

---

1. In addition to the use of published financial statements, accounting information may be communicated to external users by other methods, such as reports filed with the Securities and Exchange Commission (discussed later in the chapter), news releases, and management forecasts. Evidence from capital markets research studies tends to show that security prices fully reflect all *publicly* available information. For a more detailed discussion, see T. R. Dyckman and D. Morse, *Efficient Capital Markets and Accounting: A Critical Analysis*, 2nd ed. (Englewood Cliffs, N.J.: Prentice-Hall, 1986), R. L. Watts and J. R. Zimmerman, *Positive Accounting Theory* (Englewood Cliffs, N.J.: Prentice Hall, 1986), W. H. Beaver, *Financial Reporting: An Accounting Revolution*, 3rd ed. (Upper Saddle River, N.J.: Prentice Hall, 1998), or J. R. Macey, "Efficient Capital Markets, Corporate Disclosure, and Enron," *Cornell Law Review* (January 2004), p. 394–403.

EXHIBIT 1-3   Comparison of Financial and Managerial Accounting

	Financial Accounting	Managerial Accounting
1. Source of authority	Generally accepted accounting principles (GAAP)	Internal needs
2. Time frame of reported information	Primarily historical	Primarily present and future
3. Scope	Mainly total company	Individual departments, divisions, and total company
4. Type of information	Primarily quantitative	Qualitative as well as quantitative
5. Statement format	Prescribed by GAAP; oriented toward investment and credit decisions	Determined by company; focused on specific decisions being made
6. Decision focus	External	Internal

In other words, the amounts reported or methods used for financial accounting may influence management decisions. Or, the management of a company (perhaps in its own self-interest) may use the managerial accounting system to influence financial reporting. In this regard, the term *agency theory* describes the relationship between the manager (the "agent") and the stockholder (the "principal"). The theory suggests that agents do not always act in the best interests of the principals. For example, managers might make a decision that increases their compensation while reducing the wealth of the company and its stockholders. Research suggests that an effective way to align the interests of the agent and the principal is to base the manager's compensation on the performance of the company. Examples include the payment of bonuses that are a percentage of the company's income, and the awarding of stock options. We discuss bonuses and stock options in Chapters 13 and 16. In other chapters we discuss the effects on financial reporting from actual or potential agency theory relationships.

Financial Reporting

Financial reporting is the process of communicating financial accounting information about a company to external users. A company may report its financial accounting information in several ways. One important way is through its *annual report*. The financial reporting section of a company's annual report includes the company's financial statements and the notes to the financial statements. Companies present at least three major financial statements: (1) the *balance sheet* (or statement of financial position), which shows a company's financial position at a given date, (2) the *income statement*, which shows the results of a company's income-producing activities for a period of time, and (3) the *statement of cash flows*, which shows a company's cash inflows and cash outflows for a period of time. Many companies include the *statement of changes in stockholders' equity*, which shows the changes in each item of stockholders' equity for a period of time, as a fourth major financial statement.[2]

---

2. Some companies include a *statement of comprehensive income* as another major financial statement. We discuss this statement in Chapter 5.

2 Know what is included in financial reporting.

The *notes* to the financial statements include discussions that further explain items shown in the financial statements. Many of these notes also include supporting schedules of computations (some companies include the statement of changes in stockholders' equity here). The information in the notes is essential to understanding a company's activities. Most financial statements and accompanying notes presented to external users are *audited* by an independent certified public accountant (CPA). As we discuss in Chapters 4 and 6, after completion of the audit, the CPA expresses an opinion as to the fairness, in accordance with *generally accepted accounting principles,* of the financial statements and accompanying notes. These financial statements and notes (and supporting schedules) to the financial statements are the subject of this book.

SECURE YOUR KNOWLEDGE 1-1

- Accounting information aids in the efficient allocation of resources in capital markets.
- External users (investors, creditors, and others) use financial accounting information to make investment and credit decisions.
- Internal users (company management) use managerial accounting information to plan and control a company's operations.
- Financial reporting is the process of communicating financial information about a company to external users and includes the financial statements and the related notes to the financial statements.

Generally Accepted Accounting Principles

The information communicated to external users in financial reporting is based on standards that establish generally accepted accounting principles (GAAP). **Generally accepted accounting principles are the guidelines, procedures, and practices that a company is required to use in recording and reporting the accounting information in its audited financial statements.** GAAP define accepted accounting practices and provide a standard by which to report financial results. They are like laws and are the rules that must be followed in financial reporting.

3 Explain generally accepted accounting principles (GAAP) and the sources of GAAP.

The evolution of GAAP took place over many years. It involved several accounting policy-making bodies, including the Financial Accounting Standards Board (FASB), Accounting Principles Board (APB), American Institute of Certified Public Accountants (AICPA), and Securities and Exchange Commission (SEC). Unfortunately, there is no single document that includes all the accounting standards. [There are electronic databases such as the FASB *Financial Accounting Research System* (*FARS*) that include most accounting standards.] Nonetheless, an accountant must be able to determine the procedure for recording a transaction that is acceptable under GAAP. Accountants, therefore, must know the sources of generally accepted accounting principles. They must also know how to find authoritative sources to aid in recording and reporting a particular transaction. Throughout this book we discuss GAAP for various transactions, events, and circumstances. However, to aid in researching the sources of generally accepted accounting principles, Exhibit 1-4 provides a "hierarchy" of four categories of GAAP and the authoritative sources applicable to each category for companies.[3]

These categories are listed in descending order of importance, with Category A as the most important. Companies must follow the GAAP established by the pronouncements

---

3.   See "The Hierarchy of Generally Accepted Accounting Principles," *Proposed FASB Statement of Financial Accounting Standards* (April 28, 2005). This document will move the GAAP hierarchy contained in *AICPA Statement on Auditing Standards No. 69* into the FASB literature. The Proposed Statement is not controversial, but the timing of its release is dependent on the issuance of similar documents by the PCAOB and AICPA. Until its release, the hierarchy (which is essentially identical to that in the Proposed Statement) listed in the *AICPA Statement No. 69* applies.

EXHIBIT 1-4	Hierarchy of Sources of GAAP

Categories	Authoritative Sources (Pronouncements)
A	FASB *Statements of Financial Accounting Standards* and *Interpretations*, FASB *Staff Positions*, FASB *Statement 133 Implementation Issues*, APB *Opinions*, and CAP (AICPA) *Accounting Research Bulletins* (as well as SEC releases such as *Regulation S-X, Financial Reporting Releases*, and *Staff Accounting Bulletins* for companies that file with the SEC)
B	FASB *Technical Bulletins*, and, if cleared* by the FASB, AICPA *Industry Audit and Accounting Guides*, and AICPA *Statements of Position*
C	FASB Emerging Issues Task Force *Consensus Positions* and, if cleared* by the FASB, AICPA *Practice Bulletins*
D	FASB *Q's and A's* (Implementation Guides), AICPA *Accounting Interpretations*, AICPA *Industry and Audit Guides*, and AICPA *Statements of Position* not cleared by the FASB, and practices that are widely recognized and prevalent either generally or in the industry (e.g., AICPA *Accounting Trends and Techniques*)

*"Cleared" means that the FASB does not object to the pronouncement's issuance.

in this category unless, in unusual circumstances, they result in misleading financial statements. In situations where the accounting for a transaction or event is not specified by a pronouncement in Category A, then pronouncements in Categories B through D may be used in that order to identify GAAP. When none of the pronouncements in Categories A through D apply, then the company may consider other accounting literature such as FASB *Statements of Concepts*, AICPA *Issues Papers*, IASB *International Financial Reporting Standards*, AICPA *Technical Practice Aids*, and accounting textbooks, handbooks, and articles for GAAP guidance.

The FASB is currently working on a project that modifies the hierarchy so that it consists of only two levels—an "authoritative" level and a "nonauthoritative" level. The authoritative literature will be referred to as the "Codification." This Codification will be a compilation of existing U.S. GAAP, organized according to accounting topics, regardless of the authoritative pronouncement. This Codification project will be a multi-year effort.

THE ESTABLISHMENT OF ACCOUNTING STANDARDS

Accounting records dating back thousands of years have been discovered in various parts of the world. However, there was little organized effort to develop accounting standards in the United States prior to the 1930s. One of the most important initial attempts to develop standards began shortly after the onset of the Great Depression in 1929. In the early 1930s there were a series of meetings between representatives of the New York Stock Exchange and the American Institute of Accountants (later to become the American Institute of Certified Public Accountants). The goal was to discuss accounting and reporting issues involving the interests of investors, the New York Stock Exchange, and accountants.

The result of these meetings was a form of the auditor's opinion similar to the one used today. Specifically, the concepts of *fairness* and *consistency* in applying accounting principles were introduced into the auditor's opinion. Here, fairness means that the accounting methods and procedures adopted by a company comply with traditional practice and that they adequately portray the economic reality of the company. Since these meetings, several groups have been responsible for setting generally accepted accounting principles in the private sector of the United States. Exhibit 1-5 shows a "timeline" of the establishment of GAAP (Category A of Exhibit 1-4) in the private sector.

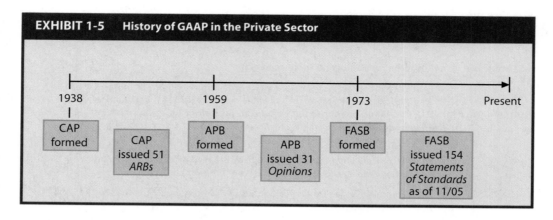

EXHIBIT 1-5 History of GAAP in the Private Sector

1938	1959	1973	Present

CAP formed

CAP issued 51 ARBs

APB formed

APB issued 31 Opinions

FASB formed

FASB issued 154 Statements of Standards as of 11/05

Committee on Accounting Procedure (CAP)

In 1938, the AICPA formed the **Committee on Accounting Procedure (CAP).** This group issued pronouncements to narrow the differences in accounting procedures and practice. Its conclusions were published as **Accounting Research Bulletins (ARBs).** However, because at that time the AICPA did not have the authority to require compliance, the CAP could not enforce its pronouncements and their application was optional. By 1953, the CAP had issued 42 *Accounting Research Bulletins.* It then reviewed these pronouncements and codified them into **Accounting Research Bulletin No. 43.** The CAP issued eight more *Accounting Research Bulletins,* ending with No. 51 before it was replaced by the Accounting Principles Board in 1959. All *Accounting Research Bulletins* are now sources of generally accepted accounting principles unless specifically superseded or amended.

Accounting Principles Board (APB)

After World War II the process of setting accounting principles was increasingly criticized and wider representation in rule making was sought. In 1959 the AICPA formed the **Accounting Principles Board (APB)** as an attempt to (1) alleviate this criticism and (2) create a policy-making body whose rules would be binding on companies rather than optional. The APB had between 17 and 21 members, selected primarily from the accounting profession. Representatives from industry, the government, and academia also served on the Board. The pronouncements of the APB were called **Opinions of the Accounting Principles Board,** and 31 of these Opinions were issued. *APB Opinions* are sources of generally accepted accounting principles unless specifically amended or rescinded. Some of these Opinions were based upon *Accounting Research Studies.* However, the conclusions in these studies were the opinion of the individuals commissioned by the APB to write them. In several cases the APB either did not act on the recommendations or came to different conclusions.

The members of the APB were volunteers whose employers allowed them time to serve on the Board. But by the late 1960s, many people again criticized the development of accounting principles. This criticism centered on three factors:

1. *Independence.* The members of the APB were part-time volunteers whose major responsibilities were to the business, governmental, or academic organizations employing them.
2. *Representation.* The public accounting firms and the AICPA were too closely associated with the development of accounting standards.
3. *Response time.* Emerging problems were not solved quickly enough by the part-time members of the APB.

The AICPA reacted to those criticisms by appointing a committee to evaluate the method of establishing accounting principles. This committee, called the Wheat Committee after its chairman Francis Wheat, recommended that the APB be abolished and that a new full-time body be created with even wider representation.

Financial Accounting Standards Board (FASB)

The AICPA adopted the recommendations of the Wheat Committee. The APB was phased out and replaced in 1973 by the **Financial Accounting Standards Board (FASB)**. Exhibit 1-6 shows the current structure of the FASB.

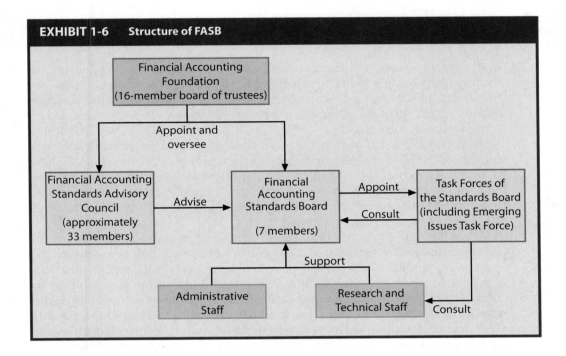

EXHIBIT 1-6   Structure of FASB

Organization

The Financial Accounting Foundation is the parent organization of the FASB. It is governed by a 16-member Board of Trustees appointed from the memberships of eight organizations interested in the establishment of accounting principles. These organizations are the AICPA, Financial Executives International, Institute of Management Accountants, CFA Institute, American Accounting Association, Securities Industry Association, Government Finance Officers Association, and National Association of State Auditors (Comptrollers and Treasurers).[4] The primary responsibilities of the Financial Accounting Foundation are to provide general oversight to its operations and to appoint the members of the Financial Accounting Standards Advisory Council (FASAC) and the FASB. The FASAC has about 33 influential members. It is responsible for advising the FASB about major policy issues, the priority of topics, the selection of task forces, the suitability of tentative decisions, and other matters.

There are seven members of the FASB. Appointees to the FASB are full-time, fully paid members with no other organizational ties. They are selected to represent a wide cross-section of interests. Each Board member is required to have a knowledge of accounting, finance, and business; high intelligence, integrity, and discipline; and a concern for the

---

4. The Financial Accounting Foundation also is the parent organization of the Governmental Accounting Standards Board (GASB), which establishes accounting principles for state and local governmental entities. We briefly discuss the GASB later in the chapter.

public interest regarding financial reporting. Currently, the FASB includes four members who are CPAs and who have been in public practice and three members from other areas related to accounting (e.g., academia and industry). The FASB is responsible for identifying financial accounting issues, conducting research to address these issues, and resolving them. The FASB is supported by a research and technical staff that researches issues, communicates with constituents, and drafts preliminary findings. The administrative staff assists the FASB by handling library, publications, personnel, and other activities.[5]

The FASB issues several types of pronouncements:

4 Identify the types of pronouncements issued by the FASB.

1. *Statements of Financial Accounting Standards.* These pronouncements establish generally accepted accounting principles. They indicate the methods and procedures required on specific accounting issues and are included in Category A of Exhibit 1-4.

2. *Interpretations.* These pronouncements provide clarification of conflicting or unclear issues relating to previously issued *FASB Statements of Financial Accounting Standards, APB Opinions,* or *Accounting Research Bulletins.* Interpretations also establish or clarify generally accepted accounting principles. They are included in Category A of Exhibit 1-4.

3. *Staff Positions.* The staff of the FASB issues these pronouncements to provide more timely and consistent application guidance in regard to FASB literature. In addition, at the direction of the FASB, the staff may issue *Staff Positions* to make narrow and limited revisions of *FASB Statements of Financial Accounting Standards* or *Interpretations* that previously would have been made through *Technical Bulletins.* They are included in Category A of Exhibit 1-4.

4. *Technical Bulletins.* The staff of the FASB issues these pronouncements to provide guidance on accounting and reporting problems related to *Statements of Financial Accounting Standards* or *Interpretations.* The guidance may clarify, explain, or elaborate upon an underlying standard. They are included in Category B of Exhibit 1-4.

5. *Statements of Financial Accounting Concepts.* These pronouncements establish a theoretical foundation on which to base financial accounting and reporting standards. They are the output of the FASB's "Conceptual Framework" project (which we discuss in Chapter 2).[6] They are not included in Exhibit 1-4 but are considered "other accounting literature" for GAAP guidance.

6. *Other Pronouncements.* On a major topic, the FASB staff also may issue a *Guide for Implementation,* which is in the form of questions and answers (referred to as *FASB Q's and A's*). These are included in Category D of Exhibit 1-4.

Many of these documents may be downloaded for free from the FASB web site (http://www.fasb.org) or may be purchased individually from the FASB. As a service to its constituency, the FASB also offers other publications. Two of these, published each year as part of the FASB's *Accounting Standards* series, are useful references for accountants. One three-volume set, titled *Original Pronouncements,* includes all of the first four types of pronouncements as of its date of publication. Another two-volume set, titled *Current Text* (*General Standards* and *Industry Standards*), is a topical integration of currently effective accounting and reporting standards as of its date of publication. These documents are also available on the *FARS* electronic database.

---

5.   For a more detailed look at the FASB's operations, see P. B. Miller, R. J. Redding, and P. R. Bahnson, *The FASB: The People, the Process, and the Politics,* 4th ed. (Boston: The McGraw-Hill Companies, Inc., 1998).

6.   The similarity in the titles *Statement of Financial Accounting Concepts* and *Statement of Financial Accounting Standards* makes an abbreviated reference to each potentially ambiguous. To avoid confusion, throughout this book a reference to **FASB Statement No. __** in the body of the text will always refer to a statement of *standards,* while a full reference will be presented for each statement of *concepts.*

Operating Procedures

Before issuing a statement of concepts or standards, the FASB generally completes a multi-stage process as outlined in Exhibit 1-7. Initially, a topic or project is identified and placed on the FASB's agenda. This topic may be the result of suggestions from the FASAC, the accounting profession, industry, or other interested parties. On major issues a Task Force may be appointed to advise and consult with the FASB's Research and Technical Staff. This may involve, for instance, the scope of the project and the nature and extent of additional research. The Staff conducts any research specifically related to the project.

5 Understand how the Financial Accounting Standards Board (FASB) operates.

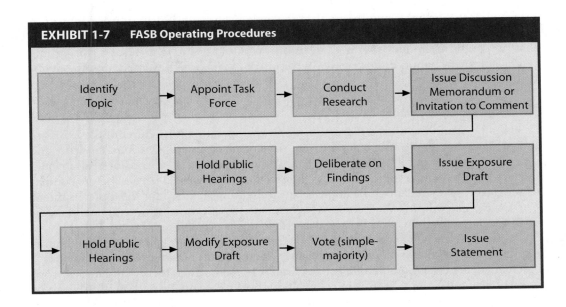

EXHIBIT 1-7   FASB Operating Procedures

Then the FASB usually publishes a Discussion Memorandum or Invitation to Comment (which outlines the research related to the issues) and sets a public comment period. During this period, the FASB may hold public hearings similar to those conducted by Congress. The intent is to receive information from and views of interested individuals and organizations on the issues. Many parties submit written comments ("position papers") or make oral presentations. These parties include representatives of CPA firms and interested corporations, security analysts, members of professional accounting associations, and academics. After deliberating on the views expressed and the information collected, the FASB issues an Exposure Draft of the proposed Statement. Interested parties generally have 30 to 90 days to provide written comments of reaction. On major issues, the FASB may hold more public hearings. Sometimes, the FASB conducts "field tests" of the proposed standards with selected companies to evaluate implementation issues. A modified draft is prepared, if necessary, and brought to the FASB for a final vote. After a *simple-majority* (i.e., 4 to 3) vote is attained, the *Statement* is issued.

The time involved to complete each of the steps varies depending on the complexity of the topic. For some complex topics it takes several years; for other, less complex topics only a few months are needed. For instance, the FASB deliberated on basic conceptual and practical issues involving the statement of cash flows for more than 10 years. The board issued a Discussion Memorandum in 1980, but then deferred consideration of cash flows reporting until it dealt with related theoretical issues in its Conceptual Framework project. In 1985 the FASB reactivated the topic. It held public hearings and received more than 450 comment letters in response to its Exposure Draft. *FASB Statement No. 95*, entitled "Statement of Cash Flows," was issued in November 1987, as shown in the following summary.

Step in Procedures	FASB Statement No. 95	FASB Statement No. 145
Issue *Discussion Memorandum*	Dec. 1980	None
Receive public comments	May 1981	None
Appoint Task Force	May 1985	None
Issue *Exposure Draft*	July 1986	Nov. 2001
Receive public comments	Through Mar. 1987	Through Jan. 14, 2002
Issue *Statement*	Nov. 1987	April 2002

On the other hand, *FASB Statement No. 145*, which rescinded *FASB Statement No. 4* in regard to reporting gains and losses from the extinguishment of debt, was issued within eight months after the related Exposure Draft was issued. In this case the FASB concluded that it could reach an informed decision without a public hearing. During the public comment period it did receive 30 comment letters, which were used in the deliberation process.

Sociopolitical Environment

As Exhibit 1-7 and the related discussion show, the operating procedures of the FASB are designed so that accounting standards are developed in an efficient manner, with due process, and in a public forum. The FASB is concerned that it considers all related research on a particular topic, as well as the views of all interested parties, before coming to a logical conclusion about the appropriate accounting standard for the topic. Its intent is to develop accounting standards that provide users with thorough, neutral, and credible information to help allocate capital as efficiently as possible.[7]

An inexperienced viewer of the FASB operating procedures might think that accounting standards are always "ideal" because they are the result of "rational policy making," where there are clearly defined objectives, an integrated body of theory, and known consequences of the actions. Yet this may not always be the case because accounting is part of a broader social system. Often, objectives are not clear, research results are conflicting, and only "best guesses" can be made of the future consequences of current standards.

Because the FASB has such a wide constituency and focuses on general purpose financial reporting, it often must establish accounting standards that are the result of *compromise*. To achieve "acceptable decisions" it is only natural for any affected parties to attempt to influence the FASB's decisions. Since the FASB holds public hearings and open meetings, it is relatively easy for various external user groups (e.g., investors and creditors) and other interested groups (e.g., affected corporations and CPA firms) to try to influence the FASB to develop new standards, continue existing standards, or change existing standards in their own best interests. These groups often hold conflicting views. For instance, in 1995 the FASB decided that a new accounting standard for "stock options" was desirable, but it could not get enough support from external user groups. Therefore, it issued a standard that allowed companies to use either the new standard or the existing standard. In this case, compromise led to a lack of "comparability" across companies as to the effect of stock option accounting on their financial statements. The serious financial reporting failures (e.g., Enron) that occurred in the early 2000s led to a review of this accounting. As a result, the FASB (despite opposition from some members of Congress) issued a new standard *requiring* the use of one method to account for stock options.

Compromise is inevitable as the FASB responds to the "globalization" of industry. In this regard, the FASB has been working with the International Accounting Standards Board (discussed later) and the accounting rule-making bodies of other countries to "harmonize" accounting standards among different countries. As Dennis Beresford (former Chair of the FASB) states: "Different countries have different domestic concerns that

---

7.   J. M. Foster, "The FASB and Capital Markets," *The FASB Report No. 245* (June 30, 2003). p. 3.

are reflected in the way they think about financial reporting. None of the viewpoints are more 'right' than one another, just different. Compromises are an inevitable part of harmonization."[8]

In regard to U.S. standards, for a given topic each FASB member will have certain issues of high priority and others of lower priority. In the FASB's deliberation process each Board member will attempt to persuade the other members to accept the important issues and to drop the less important ones. This negotiation is necessary to reach a consensus so that a majority vote may be attained on the topic.[9] Whenever a compromise is reached, some in the FASB's constituency may be unhappy because they perceive that the new GAAP is somehow "unfair" to them. In such a situation, many in the constituency have criticized the FASB for failing to listen to them, not considering the cost/benefit issues, creating logically inconsistent rules, and establishing complex standards that are too hard to implement. To help overcome these criticisms, the FASB now includes a discussion of its reasoning in each pronouncement it issues.

The Financial Accounting Foundation, in overseeing the FASB, has implemented procedures to overcome these criticisms. These procedures include use of an oversight committee to monitor the FASB's standard-setting process, periodic Financial Accounting Foundation and FASB discussions, stronger input by the FASAC on agenda determination and task force use, and additional publication and field testing of preliminary views. Furthermore, it is considering moving toward "objectives-oriented" rather than "rule-based" accounting standards, which we will discuss in Chapter 2.

Accounting standards are not unchangeable. The FASB fulfills its responsibility by (1) establishing standards that are the most acceptable, given the various affected constituencies, and (2) continually monitoring the consequences of its actions so that revised standards can be issued where appropriate. As Beresford points out, the FASB carries out its public responsibility in an environment characterized by subtlety, complexity, and an absence of clear-cut answers. The FASB works hard to develop accounting standards that can

---

8.   D. R. Beresford, "Notes from the Chairman," *FASB Status Report No. 282* (November 18, 1996), p. 2.
9.   For additional discussion of the FASB's political process, see Miller, Redding, and Bahnson, *op. cit.*, chap. 1.

be defended in terms of facts and circumstances, logic, and the fairness of the process that produces them. Reinforcing this fairness idea in testimony before Congress, Robert Herz (Chair of the FASB) stated that neutrality is a fundamental element of the FASB's standard-setting process. The Board strongly opposes any legislation that would impair its independent, objective, and open standard-setting process.[10]

Objectives-Oriented Standard Setting

As we noted in the preceding section, many constituents have said that they are concerned about the increasing level of detail ("rules-based" approach), lack of consistency, and complexity in the standards set by the FASB. As a result, the Board has begun a process whereby in the future, standards will be based on an internally consistent conceptual framework (we discuss the current conceptual framework in Chapter 2). Each "objectives-oriented" standard would: (1) clearly state the accounting objective of the standard, (2) provide enough (but not too much) detail so that the standard could be applied on a consistent basis, and (3) minimize exceptions to the standard. The intent is to allow preparers and auditors to exercise professional judgment in determining how to apply accounting standards to show the economic substance of transactions and events. It is likely that this process will take several years because, among other things, preparers and auditors have become less willing to exercise professional judgments due to increasing litigation risks.[11]

Other Organizations Currently Influencing Generally Accepted Accounting Principles

Several other organizations have had an impact on the development of generally accepted accounting principles during the past several decades.

Securities and Exchange Commission (SEC)

The SEC was created by Congress to administer the Securities Act of 1933 and the Securities Exchange Act of 1934. Under these Acts, **the SEC has the legal authority to prescribe accounting principles and reporting practices for all corporations issuing publicly traded securities.** About 17,000 (less than 1%) of the 4.9 million corporations in the United States are subject to the SEC's authority. Although this percentage is small, these corporations (e.g., Wal-Mart) are the major companies in our economy. While the SEC has seldom used this authority, from time to time the SEC has exerted pressure on the CAP, the APB, and the FASB. It has been especially interested in narrowing differences in accounting practice and in increasing disclosures.

The 1933 Act requires each company offering securities for sale to the public in the primary and secondary markets to file a registration statement. It also requires these "publicly-held" companies to provide each investor with a proxy statement prior to each stockholders' meeting. The 1934 Act established extensive reporting requirements to aid in full disclosure. Among the most commonly required reports are:

Form S-1. A registration statement.

Form 10-K. An annual report.

Form 10-Q. A quarterly report of operations.

Form 8-K. A report used to describe any significant events that may affect the company.

Proxy Statement. A report used when management requests the right to vote through proxies for shareholders at stockholders' meetings.

---

10. R. H. Herz, "FASB Chairman Appears before Congress on Stock Option Accounting," *The FASB Report No. 245* (June 30, 2003), p. 11.

11. For a more complete summary of the FASB's activities on objectives-oriented standards, see "On the Road to an Objectives-Oriented Accounting System," *The FASB Report No. 259* (August 31, 2004), pp. 1–7.

Companies are required to file these forms electronically with the SEC. These forms are located in the SEC's Electronic Data Gathering Analysis and Retrieval System (commonly known as EDGAR) on the Internet (http://www.sec.gov/edgar.shtml).

The SEC establishes accounting principles with respect to the information contained within the preceding reports. It issues reporting guidelines in its *Regulation S-X*, its *Financial Reporting Releases,* and its *Staff Accounting Bulletins* for companies that file with the SEC. In some instances the SEC has required the disclosure of information not typically found in published financial reports. We discuss these disclosures further in Chapters 4 and 6.

The impact of the SEC generally has been through its informal approval of *APB Opinions* and *FASB Statements* before their issuance. While the SEC has the authority to decide what constitutes "generally accepted accounting principles," in many cases it has exercised this authority through persuasion rather than edict. The SEC has endorsed the concept of "substantial authoritative support" by asserting that "principles, standards, and practices promulgated by the FASB in its *Statements* and *Interpretations* will be considered by the Commission as having substantial authoritative support, and those contrary to such FASB promulgations will be considered to have no such support."[12] The result of this position has been to *allow accounting principles to be formulated in the private sector* rather than by the government.

However, the SEC has been criticized for not exercising its responsibility, and there is no assurance that this position will remain in effect. In fact, during 1978 the SEC refused to support **FASB Statement No. 19** requiring the use of the successful-efforts method in the oil and gas industry, and the FASB reacted by suspending the effective date of this release. Then, in the late 1980s the House Energy and Commerce Committee's Oversight and Investigations Subcommittee was critical of the SEC for its alleged failure to monitor the detection of fraud and to establish an "early warning" system for identifying potential business failures. Although these hearings did not result in changes involving the establishment of generally accepted accounting principles, they did have an impact on *auditing* standards. Furthermore, the SEC pressured the FASB to adopt a standard requiring the use of market values by companies for reporting certain types of investments, and the Board issued **FASB Statement No. 115** in response to this pressure.

6 Describe the relationship between the SEC and the FASB.

American Institute of Certified Public Accountants (AICPA)

The AICPA dates back to 1887 and is the professional organization for all certified public accountants in the United States. To be a member of the AICPA, an individual must have passed the Uniform CPA Examination, hold a CPA certificate, agree to abide by its bylaws and Code of Professional Ethics, and have 150 hours of higher education. The primary purpose of the AICPA is to provide the necessary technical support to assure that CPAs serve the public interest in performing quality professional services.

To fulfill this purpose, the AICPA publishes numerous documents that, in certain circumstances, may be considered as sources of generally accepted accounting principles, as listed in Exhibit 1-4. *Industry Audit Guides* and *Industry Accounting Guides* (Category B of Exhibit 1-4) are publications designed to assist independent auditors in examining and reporting on financial statements of various types of entities in specialized industries (e.g., banking). *Statements of Position* (Category B of Exhibit 1-4) are publications intended to influence the development of financial accounting principles that best serve the public interest. *Practice Bulletins* (Category C of Exhibit 1-4) are publications that provide guidance on specific technical issues.

During the tenure of the Accounting Principles Board, the AICPA issued numerous *AICPA Accounting Interpretations* to provide timely guidance on accounting issues without

---

12. "Codification of Financial Reporting Policies," *SEC Accounting Rules* (Chicago: Commerce Clearing House, 2005), sec. 101. This Codification contains the accounting principles and reporting guidelines issued prior to 1982 in the SEC's *Accounting Series Releases.* In 1982, the name was changed to *Financial Reporting Releases* to better reflect the nature of the documents.

the formal procedures needed for an APB *Opinion*. These *Interpretations* (Category D of Exhibit 1-4) are still sources of generally accepted accounting principles unless specifically rescinded or amended. The AICPA also annually publishes *Accounting Trends and Techniques* (Category D of Exhibit 1-4), which provides a study of the latest accounting practices and trends identified from a survey of 600 published annual reports. This publication may be used to identify a consensus about generally accepted accounting principles for a particular issue or methods of disclosure. In this book we often cite disclosure information from *Accounting Trends and Techniques* that applies to a specific accounting practice. Finally, the AICPA develops *Issue Papers* to help the FASB identify accounting areas that need to be addressed and clarified.

FASB Emerging Issues Task Force (EITF)

The EITF was established in 1984 as a response by the FASB to criticisms that the Board did not always provide timely guidance on new accounting issues. Members of the EITF meet every six weeks; they include technical experts from all the major CPA firms and representatives from smaller CPA firms and from industry. These individuals are knowledgeable in accounting and financial reporting and are in positions to be aware of emerging problems. The Chief Accountant of the SEC also participates in EITF meetings. The primary objectives of the EITF are (1) to identify significant emerging accounting issues (i.e., unique transactions and accounting problems) that it feels the FASB should address and (2) to develop *consensus positions* on the implementation issues involving the application of standards. As shown in Category C of Exhibit 1-4, in some cases these consensus positions may be viewed as the "best available guidance" on generally accepted accounting principles, particularly as they relate to new accounting issues. The FASB publishes a summary of the proceedings of the EITF in a loose-leaf service and in an annual bound version titled *EITF Abstracts*. The summary is also available electronically on the FASB web site and the *FARS* database.

Cost Accounting Standards Board (CASB)

The CASB was established in 1970 as an agency of the U.S. Congress. In 1980, Congress did not vote funds for its continuance, but it was reinstated in 1988. The CASB is responsible only for negotiated federal contracts and subcontracts exceeding $500,000 and has issued several related *Cost Accounting Standards*. Since internal cost accounting procedures often affect externally reported financial information, these cost accounting standards occasionally influence external reporting. In the past, Congress considered replacing the FASB with a governmental board like the CASB. Although this change has not been made, the possibility of additional governmental involvement in setting accounting principles should not be discounted.

Internal Revenue Service (IRS)

The IRS administers the Internal Revenue Code enacted by Congress. Federal income tax laws have had a significant impact on financial reporting practices since they were first enacted in 1913. Although the Internal Revenue Code generally does not affect financial accounting practice directly, managers often prefer to lessen its impact on the accounting systems within their companies. The result in many cases has been that they have used accounting methods and procedures that result in the lowest taxable income, without considering the proper financial accounting theory and practice.

You should understand that accounting for income tax purposes and accounting for financial reporting purposes *are* and *should be* different. The goal of financial accounting is to provide information to financial statement users so that they may make decisions. The goal of income tax accounting is to legally minimize or postpone the payment of income taxes. Frequently, the goals of financial reporting and income tax reporting conflict. For this reason, in this book we are concerned with determining the proper *financial* accounting recording and reporting procedures. What is, or should be, proper under the

Internal Revenue Code is an entirely different question, which we only discuss when it has an impact on financial accounting and reporting. We discuss the impact of the Internal Revenue Code on financial accounting for income taxes in Chapter 19.

American Accounting Association (AAA)

The AAA is an organization primarily of academics and practicing accountants. The mission of the AAA is to foster worldwide excellence in the creation, dissemination, and application of accounting knowledge and skills. Its goals are to encourage excellence in accounting research and accounting instruction, and to contribute to excellence in accounting practice. These goals are primarily implemented through various meetings; the AAA's journals—*The Accounting Review, Issues in Accounting Education*, and *Accounting Horizons*; and the work of various committees such as the AAA Financial Accounting Standards Committee (FAS). The FAS responds to various documents of the FASB relating to proposed statements of concepts and standards. The AAA has no official stature in the development of financial accounting practice, so its impact is through education and persuasion. However, its members have served on the APB, FAF, and the FASB, and have appeared before the FASB in its hearings on particular issues.

International Accounting Standards Board (IASB)

Companies are becoming more international in their operations by producing, selling, and buying products and services in other countries. This globalization of business activity has led to increased information in a company's financial statements about its international operations. Investors and creditors in international markets, in turn, prefer that the information they use for decisions be internationally comparable from company to company across countries. The International Accounting Standards Committee (IASC) foundation is the parent organization of the International Accounting Standards Board (IASB). The objectives of the foundation are to: (1) develop high-quality, understandable, and enforceable global accounting standards that lead to useful, comparable financial reporting to help users in the world's capital markets make informed economic decisions, (2) promote the use and rigorous application of these standards, and (3) bring national accounting standards into agreement with international accounting standards.

The operating structure of the IASC Foundation consists of (1) a group of *Trustees* that is responsible for fund-raising, appointing IASB members, and overseeing the effectiveness of the IASB, (2) the *IASB*, which issues *International Financial Reporting Standards* and includes 12 full-time members (and 2 part-time members) from various countries, (3) an *International Financial Reporting Interpretations Committee* to interpret the application of the Standards, and (4) a *Standards Advisory Council* to give advice to the IASB on priorities and views of organizations on major standard setting projects. The operating procedure of the IASB is somewhat similar to that of the FASB and includes study of the topic, issuance of an Exposure Draft, evaluation of comments, and consideration of a revised draft. If approved by at least eight members of the IASB, the revised draft becomes an *International Financial Reporting Standard*. To date, the IASB (and its predecessor, the International Accounting Standards Committee) have issued 48 Standards.

There are, however, important differences between the environments in which the FASB and the IASB operate. The FASB operates as a private standard-setting organization, and focuses on setting accounting standards in the United States to improve the usefulness of accounting information to investors and creditors. On the other hand, in many other countries the emphasis in financial reporting is on meeting legal (e.g., tax) requirements, so that standard setting has evolved as a governmental rather than a private function. A role of the IASB, then, is to consolidate many countries' accounting regulations into international standards. In this regard, in response to an appeal from the International Organization of Securities Commissions, the IASB has developed a set of "core standards" of accounting principles for the financial statements of companies making "crossborder" offerings of their securities. As a result, the European Commission requires that listed European companies must use international accounting standards. Although there are areas of difference, financial statements prepared according to U.S. generally accepted accounting principles usually will comply with international accounting standards. Furthermore, as we noted earlier, the FASB and IASB are working together to harmonize accounting standards. However, financial statements prepared according to international accounting standards may *not* comply with U.S. GAAP. In later chapters, where U.S. accounting principles differ from international principles, we will discuss those differences briefly as they relate to the topics being covered.

Governmental Accounting Standards Board (GASB)

The GASB was established in 1984 and operates under the auspices of the Financial Accounting Foundation. The GASB operates in a manner similar to the FASB. It consists of a full-time chair and six other members, plus a supporting staff. The GASB's responsibility is to establish financial accounting standards for certain state and local governmental entities. Its impact on accounting principles for the private sector is minimal.

Public Company Accounting Oversight Board (PCAOB)

The PCAOB is a non-profit corporation that was created by Congress in the Sarbanes-Oxley Act of 2002. This was in response to fraudulent or misleading accounting practices by companies such as Enron and WorldCom. The PCAOB does not set generally accepted accounting principles. However, it indirectly influences public financial statements issued using GAAP. Its purpose is to protect the interests of investors by overseeing auditors of public companies in the preparation of informative, accurate, and independent audit reports for companies that sell securities to the public. The Board's responsibilities include registering public auditing firms; establishing auditing, quality control, and ethics standards; promoting high professional standards and improving the quality of audit services; and enforcing compliance with the securities laws as they relate to the preparation and issuance of audit reports. Any standards that the PCAOB proposes must be approved by the SEC.

Professional Associations

There are also several professional organizations that play an important role in the accounting standard-setting process. The **Financial Executives International (FEI)** consists primarily of high-level financial executives (such as financial vice presidents, treasurers, and controllers) of major corporations. The FEI publishes a monthly journal called the *Financial Executive* and has sponsored research projects dealing with financial reporting issues. Membership in the **Institute of Management Accountants (IMA)** is open to anyone, although its primary focus is on management accounting and financial management issues. The IMA publishes a monthly journal called *Strategic Finance*, which includes articles involving strategies in accounting, finance, and information management. Members of the **CFA Institute (CFAI)** are financial analysts who use accounting information in various investment management and security analysis decisions. The CFAI publishes the *Financial Analysts Journal*, and its members participate in FASB research studies that deal with the impact of proposed accounting standards on users of financial accounting information. As we noted earlier, each of these organizations is also a member of the Financial Accounting Foundation. They provide input to the FASB through position papers and oral presentations in the public hearings process.

Relationship of Organizations in Current Standard-Setting Environment

As we discussed earlier, accounting standards are set in a sociopolitical environment. Currently there are three major organizations in the private and public sector that develop GAAP for companies: the FASB, the AICPA, and the SEC. To a lesser extent, the other organizations we discussed in this section also are influential in the standard-setting process. We illustrate the relationship of the various participants in this process in Exhibit 1-8.

EXHIBIT 1-8   Participants in the Development of GAAP

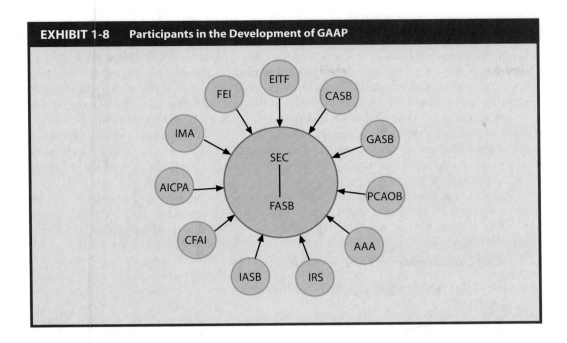

SECURE YOUR KNOWLEDGE 1-2

- The guidelines, procedures, and practices that a company is required to use in recording and reporting accounting information in its financial statements (GAAP) have evolved over many years and were set by several policy-making bodies.
- The major standard-setting bodies responsible for the establishment of GAAP include the Securities and Exchange Commission (SEC) and the Financial Accounting Standards Board (FASB).
- Before issuing a final standard, a proposed topic undergoes an extensive due process procedure that includes considerable research, numerous public hearings, and frequent deliberations.
- While final standards are intended to provide users with relevant and reliable information for their decision-making needs, social and political differences in FASB's constituency often result in final standards that are a result of compromise.
- Numerous other bodies (shown in Exhibit 1-8) have also impacted the development of GAAP.

ETHICS IN THE ACCOUNTING ENVIRONMENT

In recent years there have been an increasing number of news reports about unethical behavior on the part of companies or individuals acting in their own self-interest without regard to the impact on society. These unethical actions include, for instance, polluting lakes and streams, illegal shipments of weapons to foreign countries, savings and loan scandals, selling products that are hazardous to users' health, overcharging on government contracts, securities fraud, accounting fraud, false advertising, and "insider trading" activities. All of these unethical behaviors have a common theme: increased profits at the expense of some aspect of society. While these unethical actions often are sensational and capture the national headlines, there are also many situations of a smaller scale in which accountants face ethical dilemmas.

7 Use ethical models for decision making about ethical dilemmas.

Earlier we mentioned that accountants who record and report financial information must follow generally accepted accounting principles, and that auditors must express an opinion as to the fairness (in accordance with GAAP) of the financial statements. Among other things, the financial statements of a company communicate how well the employees of the company at the department, division, and corporate levels have performed in operating the company. The results reported in the audited financial statements are likely to have an effect on the company's ability to sell stock or borrow money, as well as on employees' compensation and promotion opportunities. Consequently, these employees have a vested interest in showing their performances in the best light and may pressure accountants to do so. For instance, executives at Enron and WorldCom were successful at defrauding the public.

We also mentioned that in the FASB's public hearings and open meetings various parties attempt to influence the Board in their own self-interest. These are just a few examples of situations in which accountants may be faced with *ethical dilemmas* (*ethical conflicts*), situations in which an accountant must make a decision about what is the "right" (ethical) action to take in a given set of circumstances. Because accounting is a service activity that plays an important role in society, professional accounting organizations have established "codes of ethics" for their members. One of these applies to members of the AICPA.[13]

Members of the AICPA recognize that they have an obligation of self-discipline above and beyond the requirements of laws and regulations. To help guide members in public practice, industry, government, and education in performing their responsibilities, the AICPA adopted the **Code of Professional Conduct (CPC)**. The CPC includes six *Principles* that express the basic tenets of ethical and professional conduct and call for an unswerving commitment to honorable behavior, even at the sacrifice of personal advantage. Exhibit 1-9 summarizes these Principles.[14]

EXHIBIT 1-9   Principles of the AICPA Code of Professional Conduct

I.   **Responsibilities:** In carrying out their responsibilities as professionals, members should exercise sensitive professional and moral judgments in all their activities.

II.   **The Public Interest:** Members should act in a way that will serve the public interest, honor the public trust, and demonstrate commitment to professionalism.

III.   **Integrity:** To maintain and broaden public confidence, members should perform all professional responsibilities with the highest sense of integrity.

IV.   **Objectivity and Independence:** A member should be objective and free from conflicts of interest in discharging professional responsibilities. A member in public practice should be independent in fact and appearance when providing auditing and other attestation services.

V.   **Due Care:** A member should observe the profession's technical and ethical standards, strive continually to improve competence and the quality of services, and discharge professional responsibility to the best of the member's ability.

VI.   **Scope and Nature of Services:** A member in public practice should observe the Principles of the CPC in determining the scope and nature of services to be provided.

While this code of ethics establishes guidelines for accountants in performing their responsibilities, it does not provide a structured approach for "moral reasoning" in ethical dilemmas. Ethical behavior may be different from legally acceptable behavior. What is

---

13. For the code of ethics of the IMA, another professional accounting organization, see *Ethics Center*, IMA: www.imanet.org.
14. *AICPA Code of Professional Conduct*, AICPA: www.aicpa.org.

legal may still be unethical in certain circumstances. Ethicists have developed alternative "models" to help individuals make sound moral judgments and guide their behavior when faced with ethical dilemmas involving various stakeholders. In the business environment of a company, the *stakeholders* may include past, current, and potential investors; creditors; employees; suppliers; competing companies; local, state, and federal governments; and citizens in the local, regional, national, and even international communities.

According to Manuel Velasquez, a noted ethicist, there are three basic approaches to moral reasoning. Each of these approaches uses a different set of moral standards in distinguishing between right and wrong. These approaches include (1) the *utilitarian* model, which evaluates actions based on the extent to which they result in the "greatest good for the greatest number," (2) the *rights* model, which embraces actions that protect individual moral rights, and (3) the *justice* model, which emphasizes a fair distribution of benefits and burdens. In determining if an action is ethical or which of several alternative behaviors is the most ethical, Velasquez says that no single set of moral standards is sufficient. Instead, he recommends a several-step process that combines all three types of moral standards. This process includes

1. gathering the facts (e.g., Who are the "stakeholders?" What are my responsibilities?);
2. asking whether the action is acceptable according to three ethical criteria:
   a. utility: Does the action optimize the satisfactions of all stakeholders?
   b. rights: Does the action respect the rights of all individuals? and
   c. justice: Is the action fair and just?;
3. considering whether there are any "overwhelming factors," such as conflicts between criteria that may justify disregarding one or more of the ethical criteria; and
4. deciding whether the action is ethical (or what ethical action to take) based on an evaluation of the applicable ethical criteria.[15]

Accountants are noted to have high ethical standards.[16] Acting ethically is not always easy; sometimes it is very difficult. However, because of the important role of accounting in society, every accountant must have high moral standards and strive to behave at the highest ethical level. Throughout this book, you will be exposed to ethical dilemmas that we urge you to consider using the framework we just discussed.

CREATIVE AND CRITICAL THINKING IN THE ACCOUNTING ENVIRONMENT

The business environment in which accountants work is constantly changing and becoming more complex. New products and services are continually introduced, and existing products are modified. Production techniques are changing, as are the channels of distribution and the approaches to promoting these products. There is an explosion of information technology as computers are networked, satellites allow global audiovisual communication, fax machines, the Internet, and e-mail enable nearly instantaneous information transmittal, and cell phones link customers and suppliers. More and more companies are becoming international in their operating activities by buying, producing, and selling products in foreign countries. Government regulations are increasing, as more concern is given to such issues as worker safety and environmental impacts.

In response to these changes, companies are becoming more innovative in the ways they manage their businesses, how they finance their activities, what they invest in to expand their operating capabilities, and what approaches they use in their credit and collection processes. They are restructuring their organizations and operations to increase

8 Understand creative and critical thinking.

---

15. M. Velasquez, *Business Ethics: Concepts and Cases*, 4th ed. (Englewood Cliffs, N.J.: Prentice Hall, 1998), ch. 2.
16. "The CPA Span of Influence Study," Research Study for AICPA by Peter W. Hart Research Associates (March 16, 2000).

efficiency, and are more sensitive to changing technology and product obsolescence. They are more creative in the ways they structure their executive and employee compensation packages. Accounting systems that are designed to accumulate, process, and communicate information for decision making in this changing environment must change to satisfy the needs of users. Accounting principles must evolve to reflect this changing environment. Accountants responsible for operating these systems, as well as for establishing and applying accounting principles, must be both *creative* thinkers and *critical* thinkers.

Research in psychology has found that each side of the brain deals with a different type of thinking. The right side focuses on creative thinking, involving visualizing and developing ideas. The left side focuses on critical thinking, involving analyzing and evaluating ideas. All individuals think creatively and critically, but they differ regarding the degree to which they use each side of the brain. However, through practice, it is possible for individuals to increase their ability to think creatively and critically.

Different aspects of creative thinking and critical thinking have been studied and discussed for many years and in numerous areas. Here, we discuss briefly what role these concepts play in financial accounting. There are many ways creative thinking and critical thinking are defined, in part because they are not mutually exclusive and the differences between the two types of thinking are not clear-cut. For our purposes, **creative thinking is the process of finding new relationships (ideas) among items of information that potentially can be used to solve a problem**. Creative thinking involves using imagination and insight to see issues in a different light. Terms that are used to describe a creative thinker include insightful, intuitive, imaginative, sensitive, flexible, original, adaptable, and tolerant of ambiguity.[17] In contrast, **critical thinking is the process of testing these new relationships (ideas) to determine how well they will work**. Critical thinking involves using inductive or deductive reasoning to analyze an issue logically. Terms that are used to describe a critical thinker include objective, independent, analytical, logical, rational, able to synthesize, consistent, and organized.[18]

In financial accounting, accountants tend to be "problem solvers." When an accounting issue or problem arises, the accountant is responsible for its resolution. Several steps have been identified in the **problem-solving process**, as we show in Exhibit 1-10. These steps include

1. recognizing a problem,
2. identifying alternative solutions,
3. evaluating the alternatives,
4. selecting a solution from among the alternatives, and
5. implementing the solution.

Creative thinking and critical thinking both play a role in each step of the problem-solving process. However, creative thinking is probably most critical in the *identification* of alternative solutions, while critical thinking is most critical in the *evaluation* of the alternative solutions.

The degree of complexity may differ from one problem to another. Problems can range from structured problems to unstructured problems. For *structured* problems, virtually complete information is known about the alternatives (in fact, there may be only one alternative) so that identifying, evaluating, selecting, and implementing an alternative is straightforward. At the other extreme are *unstructured* problems where even the basic issue may not be readily apparent, the alternative solutions are unclear once the problem is

---

17. For a more extensive discussion of creative thinking, see S. F. Isaksen, K. Dorval, and D. Treffinger, *Creative Approaches to Problem Solving,* 2nd ed. (Williamsville, NY: Creative Problem Solving Group-Buffalo, 2000).
18. For a more extensive discussion of critical thinking, see J. Chaffee, *Thinking Critically*, 6th ed. (New York: Houghton Mifflin Company, 2000).

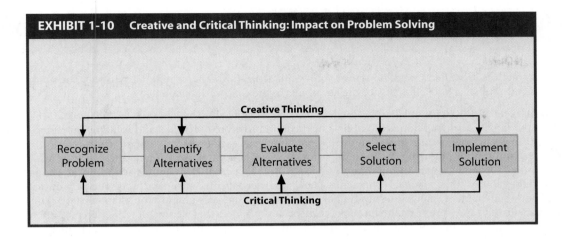

EXHIBIT 1-10   Creative and Critical Thinking: Impact on Problem Solving

identified, and there is a lack of information about the alternatives. Here the identification, evaluation, selection, and implementation process is much more complex. Between these extremes is the *partially structured* problem, where either the alternative solutions are unclear or there is a lack of information about the alternative solutions.

At the policy-making level, the FASB deals with complex unstructured problems. The Board members engage in higher-order creative thinking and critical thinking in their problem-solving processes involving the *establishment* of generally accepted accounting principles. In this book we discuss the major issues faced by the FASB in setting standards. However, our primary focus is on the *application* of generally accepted accounting principles in the recording and reporting of various topics. These topics may be general (e.g., income measurement) or specific (e.g., inventory). For each topic, we identify GAAP, discuss the related conceptual issues, and explain the recording and reporting procedures.

In the exercises and problems at the end of each chapter, we focus primarily on assignments intended to help you reinforce your understanding of the topical material. We do so by requiring you to prepare solutions to issues related to the chapter topics. These assignments generally involve structured problems for which there are only one or two correct solutions. Here the steps of identification, evaluation, and selection of alternatives in the problem-solving process are reduced or omitted. This approach does not mean that your creative thinking and critical thinking processes are not at work, however. In solving these assignments, you are practicing both creative and critical thinking, but at a lower level. It is important to master the understanding of basic recording and reporting issues in financial accounting. Then you can move on to more complex accounting issues that involve less structured problems and entail higher-level creative and critical thinking.

As a step in helping you develop your higher-level creative and critical thinking skills, there are also cases at the end of each chapter. These cases may require you to explain your understanding of interrelated concepts and practices. They may also require you to determine solutions to issues for which specific generally accepted accounting principles do not apply directly. These cases may deal with accounting issues that are emerging because of changes in the business environment we discussed earlier. They may focus on topics that are too "industry specific" to be included in the chapter material. In these latter situations, the cases ("research simulations") will require you to "research GAAP" in documents such as the FASB's *Current Text* or *Original Pronouncements* (or FARS) and, in so doing, stimulate your higher-level creative and critical thinking as you complete the problem-solving process. If your instructor does not assign these cases, you may still want to analyze them as a way of practicing creative and critical thinking. Your ability to think creatively and critically will be very important in your future accounting and business (as well as personal) activities.

SUMMARY

At the beginning of the chapter, we identified several objectives you would accomplish after reading the chapter. The objectives are listed below, each followed by a brief summary of the key points in the chapter discussion.

1. **Understand capital markets and decision making.** Capital markets are organized exchanges such as the NYSE, AMEX, and NASDAQ, where the capital stock and bonds of publicly held corporations are purchased and sold. Investors make buy-hold-sell decisions in regard to securities traded on these capital markets based on accounting information.
2. **Know what is included in financial reporting.** Financial reporting involves communicating financial accounting information about a company to external users. An important way to do so is in a company's annual report. In its annual report, a company includes at least three financial statements—a balance sheet, income statement, and statement of cash flows—and may include a statement of changes in stockholders' equity. It also includes notes to the financial statements.
3. **Explain GAAP and its sources.** GAAP are the guidelines, procedures, and practices that a company is required to use in recording and reporting the accounting information in its audited financial statements. The sources of GAAP included pronouncements by the FASB, APB, CAP, and SEC in four categories of descending order of importance.
4. **Identify the types of pronouncements issued by the FASB.** The FASB issues several types of pronouncements including *Statements of Financial Accounting Standards, Interpretations, Staff Positions, Technical Bulletins, Statements of Financial Accounting Concepts,* and other pronouncements, such as *Guides for Implementation* and *FASB Q's and A's.*
5. **Understand how the FASB operates.** The FASB is a seven-member board. Before issuing a statement of concepts or standards, the FASB goes through several steps which include conducting research and issuing a Discussion Memorandum or Invitation to Comment, holding public hearing and deliberating on findings before issuing an Exposure Draft, holding more public hearings, modifying its tentative conclusions, voting (simple-majority), and issuing the Statement.
6. **Describe the relationship between the SEC and the FASB.** The SEC has the legal authority to prescribe accounting principles and practices for all publicly traded companies. It, however, endorsed the workings of the FASB by stating that the standards set by the FASB will be considered by the SEC to have substantial authoritative support.
7. **Use ethical models for decision making about ethical dilemmas.** Models for ethical decision making include the *utilitarian* model, the *rights* model, and the *justice* model. In using these models, one several-step approach includes (1) gathering the facts; (2) asking whether the action is acceptable according to utility, rights, and justice ethical criteria; (3) considering any "overwhelming factors"; and (4) deciding whether the action is ethical.
8. **Understand creative and critical thinking.** Creative thinking is the process of finding new relationships (ideas) among items of information that potentially can be used to solve a problem. Critical thinking is the process of testing these new relationships (ideas) to determine how well they will work. In problem solving, creative thinking is most important in the *identification* of alternative solutions, while critical thinking is most important in the *evaluation* of the alternative solutions.

QUESTIONS

Q1-1 Distinguish between primary markets and secondary markets.

Q1-2 Distinguish between the categories of users of financial statements. Why might their decision-making needs be different?

Q1-3 Compare and contrast financial and managerial accounting.

Q1-4 What is financial reporting and what is an important way a company's financial information is reported?

Q1-5 What are the three major financial statements of a company and what do they show? What is the fourth major financial statement that many companies present, and what does it show?

Q1-6 What are generally accepted accounting principles? List the four accounting bodies that have established generally accepted accounting principles.

Q1-7 How many "categories" are in the hierarchy of generally accepted accounting principles? List the pronouncements that are included in Category A.

Q1-8 What are (were) the CAP, APB, and FASB? What documents that constitute generally accepted accounting principles have been issued by each of these organizations?

Q1-9 Briefly discuss the procedures followed by the FASB for issuing a statement of concepts or standards.

Q1-10 List and briefly discuss the types of pronouncements issued by the FASB.

Q1-11 List several organizations other than the FASB that have had an impact on the development of generally accepted accounting principles.

Q1-12 What is the IASB and how does it operate?

Q1-13 List several professional organizations that play an important role in the accounting standard-setting process.

Q1-14 What is the *Code of Professional Conduct* and what are the six areas covered in the Principles of this code?

Q1-15 List the steps a person should follow to determine whether an action is ethical.

Q1-16 What is creative thinking? How would you describe a creative thinker?

Q1-17 What is critical thinking? How would you describe a critical thinker?

CASES

COMMUNICATION

C1-1   Pronouncements
Several accounting groups have issued various pronouncements establishing or relating to generally accepted accounting principles. The following is a list of six pronouncements, as well as a list of statements describing each pronouncement.

    A. Statements of Financial Accounting Standards
    B. Opinions
    C. Technical Bulletins
    D. Statements of Financial Accounting Concepts
    E. Interpretations
    F. Staff Positions
    G. Accounting Research Bulletins

E   1. Pronouncements that provide clarification of conflicting or unclear issues relating to previously issued FASB *Statements of Standards*, APB *Opinions*, or *Accounting Research Bulletins*.

C   2. Issued by the FASB to provide guidance on accounting and reporting problems related to *Statements of Standards* or *Interpretations*.

G   3. Pronouncements of the APB that constitute generally accepted accounting principles unless specifically amended or rescinded, many of which were based on *Accounting Research Studies*.

D   4. Issued by the FASB as a series establishing a theoretical foundation upon which to base financial accounting and reporting standards.

B   5. Pronouncements of the Committee on Accounting Procedure (CAP) that constitute generally accepted accounting principles unless superseded or amended by other authoritative bodies.

A   6. Pronouncements issued by the FASB that establish generally accepted accounting principles and indicate the methods and procedures required on specific accounting issues.

F   7. Pronouncements issued to provide more timely and consistent application guidance in regard to FASB literature.

Required
Place the appropriate letter (A–G) identifying each pronouncement on the line in front of the statement describing the pronouncement.

C1-2   Organizations
Certain organizations have been influential in the establishment of accounting principles. The following is a list of abbreviations for several of these organizations, as well as a list of statements describing the organizations.

    A. IRS   G. CASB
    B. APB   H. FASB
    C. CAP   I. PCAOB
    D. IASB   J. GASB
    E. SEC   K. AICPA
    F. FASAC   L. EITF

____ 1. First organization in United States to be given authority to issue pronouncements on accounting procedures and practice. Issued *Accounting Research Bulletins*.

____ 2. Establishes cost accounting standards for U.S. government contracts.

____ 3. Administers the provisions of the Internal Revenue Code.

____ 4. Helps establish internationally comparable accounting principles.

____ 5. Establishes accounting standards for state and local governmental entities.

____ 6. Establishes generally accepted accounting principles in the private sector of the United States.

____ 7. Created by Congress in response to fraudulent accounting practices.

____ 8. Responsible for advising the FASB about technical areas, task forces, and other matters.

____ 9. Established 31 *Opinions*, many of which still constitute generally accepted accounting principles.

_____ 10. Has legal authority to prescribe accounting principles and reporting practices for all corporations issuing publicly traded securities.

_____ 11. Professional organization for all CPAs in the United States.

_____ 12. Develops consensus positions on the implementation issues involving the application of standards.

Required

Place the appropriate letter (A–L) for each organization in front of the statement describing the organization. In addition, write out the full name of the organization.

C1-3 Establishment of GAAP

Since the late 1930s, three organizations have been primarily responsible for the establishment of generally accepted accounting principles in the private sector of the United States.

Required

Write a brief report that identifies the three organizations and provides a brief chronological history of each, including the pronouncements issued that still constitute generally accepted accounting principles.

C1-4 Accounting Principles

AICPA Adapted At the completion of the Darby Department Store audit, the president asks about the meaning of the phrase "in conformity with generally accepted accounting principles" that appears in your audit report on the management's financial statements. He observes that the meaning of the phrase must include more than what he thinks of as "principles."

Required

1. Explain the meaning of the term "accounting principles" as used in the audit report. (Do not discuss in this part the significance of "generally accepted.")
2. The president wants to know how you determine whether or not an accounting principle is generally accepted. Discuss the sources of evidence for determining whether an accounting principle has substantial authoritative support. Do not merely list the titles of publications.

C1-5 Standard Setting

CMA Adapted When the Accounting Principles Board was founded in 1959, it planned to establish financial accounting standards using empirical research and logical reasoning only; the role of political action was little recognized at that time. Today, there is wide acceptance of the view that political action is as much an ingredient of the standard-setting process as is research evidence. Considerable political and social influence is wielded by user groups—those parties who are most interested in or affected by accounting standards.

Two basic premises of the Financial Accounting Standards Board (FASB) are (1) that it should be responsive to the needs and viewpoints of the entire economic community, and (2) that it should operate in full view of the public, affording interested parties ample opportunity to make their views known. The extensive procedural steps employed by the FASB in the standard-setting process support these premises.

Required

Write a brief report that describes why financial accounting standards inspire or encourage political action and social involvement during the standard-setting process.

C1-6 Organization of the FASB

The FASB is organized to establish generally accepted accounting principles. It is assisted by various groups and operates under a set of procedures.

Required

Prepare a short written report that summarizes the structure, types of pronouncements, and operating procedures of the FASB.

C1-7 GAAP and the AICPA

The American Institute of Certified Public Accountants (AICPA) has been in existence for many years to help CPAs provide high-quality professional services. Among other activities, in certain circumstances the AICPA establishes or provides guidance on generally accepted accounting principles (GAAP).

Required

Summarize the GAAP-related documents that the AICPA publishes.

C1-8 Code of Professional Conduct

In a few years, you may become a member of the AICPA and be subject to its Code of Professional Conduct (CPC).

Required

Identify and briefly discuss the first five principles of the CPC. Provide examples that illustrate each principle.

CREATIVE AND CRITICAL THINKING

C1-9 GAAP Hierarchy

A friend of yours says, "I understand there are 'rules' for financial reporting. But what are these rules, where can a person find them, and which ones are more important?"

Required

Prepare an answer for your friend.

C1-10 Lobbying the FASB

One of your friends remarks, "I understand that before voting on a Statement of Standards the FASB allows written comments and oral presentations in which interested parties can lobby for a particular ruling. Do you think this is a good idea?"

Required

Prepare a written response that discusses the advantages and disadvantages of the FASB's allowing interested parties to provide input to its deliberative process.

C1-11 Ethical Responsibilities

Each person in one of your accounting classes is required to write a report on an accounting topic. Included in the report must be a discussion from a specific library book. When you go to the library, you find that the only copy of the book is missing. While sitting at a study desk, you overhear one of your classmates say that he has "misfiled" the book in the library so he can use it again later without having to wait for other students to finish using it.

Required

Discuss the steps you would take to address this ethical dilemma. It is not necessary to state what ethical action you would take, but be prepared to discuss your reasoning for each step.

C1-12 Ethical Responsibilities

You and a friend are in the same accounting class. During the first test, you observe that your friend cheated by copying one of her answers from another student (who was unaware of the copying). When the exams are returned, your grade is a B, while your friend's grade is an A.

Required

Discuss the steps you would take to address this ethical dilemma. It is not necessary to state what ethical action you would take, but be prepared to discuss your reasoning for each step.

2

Financial Reporting: Its Conceptual Framework

If It's Broken ... Fix It!

U.S. GAAP is widely considered the most complete and well-developed set of accounting standards in the world. However, because of the recent accounting scandals, U.S. accounting standards have come under increasing criticism as being too rules-based. Some have also questioned the role of accounting standards in facilitating these financial reporting failures. The criticisms of U.S. accounting standards are that they had become too long and complex, contained too many percentage tests (bright lines), and allowed numerous exceptions to the principles underlying the standards. Together, the rules-based nature of the standard is seen to have fostered a "check-the-box mentality" that allowed financial "engineers" to comply with the letter of the standard while not always showing the underlying reality of the transaction. In its review of U.S. accounting standards, the **Securities and Exchange Commission (SEC)** noted that the lease accounting rules are made up of approximately 16 FASB Statements and Interpretations, 9 Technical Bulletins, and more than 30 EITF Abstracts. Also, there are more than 800 pages of accounting guidance relating to derivatives. One prominent controller described recently issued accounting guidance as a mistake that was so complicated that organizations are uncertain if they can even follow the rules. What is the solution?

The SEC has recommended that future accounting standards should not follow a rules-based, nor principles-only approach, but

should be "objectives-oriented." This principles-based standard setting approach should be built on an improved and consistently applied conceptual framework. This framework should clearly state the accounting objective of the standard, provide sufficient detail and structure so that the standard can be applied consistently, minimize exceptions to the standard, and avoid the use of bright-line tests. The development of objectives-oriented standards should improve the relevance, reliability, and comparability of financial information resulting in more meaningful and informative financial statements.

FOR FURTHER INVESTIGATION

For a discussion of principles-based accounting standards and the implications for accounting standard setting, consult the Business & Company Resource Center (BCRC) and the Internet:

- Defining Principles-Based Accounting Standards. Rebecca Toppe Shortridge, Mark Myring, *The CPA Journal*, 0732-8435, August 2004, v74 i8 p34(4).

- Study Pursuant to Section 108(d) of the Sarbanes-Oxley Act of 2002 on the Adoption by the United States Financial Reporting System of a Principles-Based Accounting System, Securities and Exchange Commission, http://www.sec.gov/news/studies/principlesbasedstand.htm.

As we saw in Chapter 1, accounting standards were developed in the United States by the Committee on Accounting Procedure (CAP) and the Accounting Principles Board (APB) before the inception of the Financial Accounting Standards Board (FASB). The CAP and the APB were not able to develop a broad, normative conceptual framework of accounting theory. The APB did issue **APB Statement No. 4**, "Basic Concepts and Accounting Principles Underlying Financial Statements of Business Enterprises." However, this document described current practice instead of what *should* be appropriate accounting. Although the CAP and APB considered some accounting concepts in setting of accounting standards, generally this was limited to the concepts related to the particular accounting issue at hand. This led, at times, to accounting principles that were inconsistently applied from one issue to another. These inconsistencies led to political pressure on the FASB to develop a general set of concepts and principles to guide its standard setting. In this chapter we discuss the FASB's conceptual framework of accounting theory. This framework includes:

- the objectives of financial reporting
- the types of useful accounting information
- the qualitative characteristics of accounting information
- accounting assumptions and principles

We also include a brief review of generally accepted accounting principles and financial statements.

FASB Conceptual Framework

The FASB has been given two charges. First, it is to develop a conceptual framework of accounting theory. Second, it is to establish standards (generally accepted accounting principles) for financial accounting practice. The intent is to develop **a theoretical foundation of interrelated objectives and concepts that leads to the establishment of consistent financial accounting standards.** In other words, the conceptual framework should provide a logical structure and direction to financial accounting and reporting. This conceptual framework is expected to:

1 Explain the FASB conceptual framework.

1. guide the FASB in establishing accounting standards
2. provide a frame of reference for resolving accounting questions in situations where a standard does not exist
3. determine the bounds for judgment in the preparation of financial statements
4. increase users' understanding of and confidence in financial reporting
5. enhance comparability

The FASB expects that the conceptual framework will encourage companies to provide financial (and related) information that is useful in efficiently allocating scarce economic resources in capital and other markets.[1]

Exhibit 2-1 shows the relationship among the objectives, concepts, and standards, their purposes, and the documents issued by the FASB. The outputs of the conceptual framework are *Statements of Financial Accounting Concepts*; to date, seven have been issued. The outputs of the standard-setting process are *Statements of Financial Accounting Standards*: to date 154 have been issued. The many "statements of standards" are required to identify the preferable accounting practice from the various alternatives that arise in response to the changing, dynamic business environment. As much as possible, the FASB considers its conceptual framework in establishing these standards.

---

1. This discussion is based on a background paper, "The Conceptual Framework Project," Financial Accounting Standards Board (Stamford, Conn., 1980).

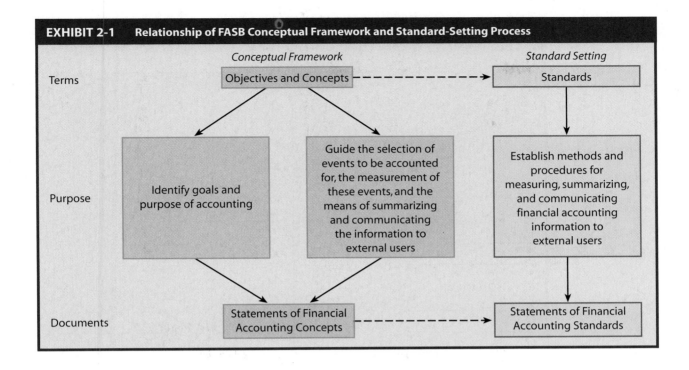

EXHIBIT 2-1   Relationship of FASB Conceptual Framework and Standard-Setting Process

Conceptual Framework   *Standard Setting*

Terms
Objectives and Concepts ----------> Standards

Purpose
Identify goals and purpose of accounting

Guide the selection of events to be accounted for, the measurement of these events, and the means of summarizing and communicating the information to external users

Establish methods and procedures for measuring, summarizing, and communicating financial accounting information to external users

Documents
Statements of Financial Accounting Concepts ----------> Statements of Financial Accounting Standards

Because of the large task, the FASB divided its conceptual framework activities into several projects. Exhibit 2-2 shows these projects. The first project dealt with identifying the objectives of financial reporting. This project resulted in **FASB Statement of Financial Accounting Concepts No. 1,** "Objectives of Financial Reporting by Business Enterprises." This document established the focus of the remaining projects, which are divided into two groups (accounting and reporting). The Qualitative Characteristics Project linked together the accounting and reporting projects, as illustrated by the dashed lines in Exhibit 2-2. It also resulted in **FASB Statement of Financial Accounting Concepts No. 2,** "Qualitative Characteristics of Accounting Information."

The accounting projects define the accounting elements (e.g., assets, liabilities, revenues, expenses) and identify which elements should be reported, when they should be reported (recognized), and how they should be measured.[2] The reporting projects deal with how the elements of financial reports are "displayed." Important issues include general questions such as what information should be provided, who should be required to provide the information, and where the information should be presented. Also included are more specific questions about income and its components, as well as cash flow and its components.

The FASB has issued several Statements of Concepts that deal with one or more of these accounting and reporting projects. **FASB Statement of Financial Accounting Concepts No. 3** was issued in 1980. However, this Statement of Concepts was replaced in 1986 by **FASB Statement of Financial Accounting Concepts No. 6,** "Elements of Financial Statements." **FASB Statement of Financial Accounting Concepts No. 5,** "Recognition and Measurement in Financial Statements of Business Enterprises," was issued in 1984.[3] **FASB Statement of Financial Accounting Concepts No. 7,** "Using Cash Flow Information and Present Value in Accounting Measurements," was issued in 2000. An Exposure Draft, *FASB Proposed Statement*

---

2. For a discussion of these and other issues, see L. T. Johnson and R. K. Storey, "Recognition in Financial Statements: Underlying Concepts and Practical Conventions," *Research Report* (Stamford, Conn.: FASB, 1982).

3. **FASB Statement of Financial Accounting Concepts No. 4,** titled "Objectives of Financial Reporting by Nonbusiness Organizations," has also been issued but is not discussed in this book.

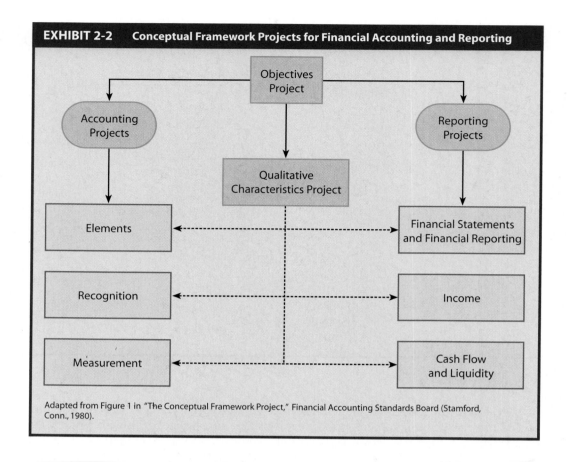

EXHIBIT 2-2   Conceptual Framework Projects for Financial Accounting and Reporting

Adapted from Figure 1 in "The Conceptual Framework Project," Financial Accounting Standards Board (Stamford, Conn., 1980).

of Financial Accounting Concepts, "Reporting Income, Cash Flows, and Financial Position of Business Enterprises," was issued regarding the reporting projects. In addition, several working documents dealing with both accounting and reporting issues were published that may eventually lead to the issuance of other statements of financial accounting concepts. We discuss the Statements of Concepts dealing with the elements, recognition and measurement, and reporting of income and cash flows in Chapters 4 and 5.

In this chapter we discuss the first two Statements of Concepts dealing with the objectives of financial reporting and the qualitative characteristics of accounting information. We also discuss parts of the Exposure Draft dealing with types of useful information.

OBJECTIVES OF FINANCIAL REPORTING

2 Understand the relationship among the objectives of financial reporting.

In its first concepts statement, the FASB stated that the objectives of financial reporting are those of *general-purpose* external reporting by companies. That is, the objectives relate to a *variety* of *external* users as opposed to specific internal users, such as management. These external users do not have the authority to prescribe the financial information they desire from a particular company. Therefore, they must use the information that the management of the company communicates to them.[4]

The FASB identified several objectives of financial reporting. These objectives proceed from the more general to the more specific. We show these objectives in Exhibit 2-3 and discuss them in the following sections.[5]

---

4.   "Objectives of Financial Reporting by Business Enterprises," *FASB Statement of Financial Accounting Concepts No. 1* (Stamford, Conn.: FASB, 1978), par. 28.

5.   The discussion in this section primarily is a summary of that presented by the FASB in its "Objectives of Financial Reporting by Business Enterprises."

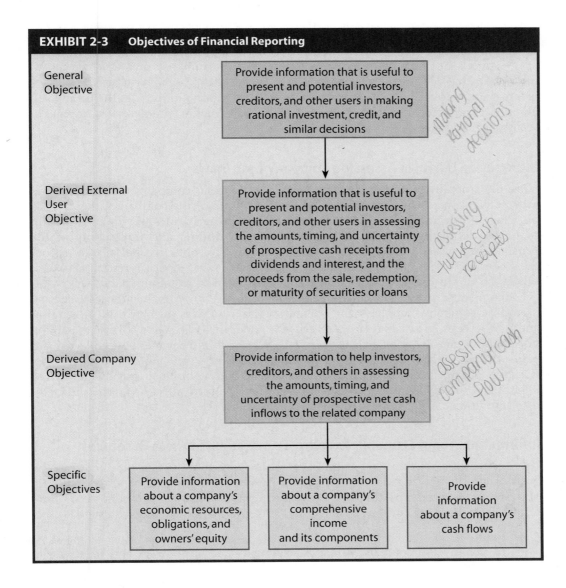

EXHIBIT 2-3   **Objectives of Financial Reporting**

General Objective: Provide information that is useful to present and potential investors, creditors, and other users in making rational investment, credit, and similar decisions

Derived External User Objective: Provide information that is useful to present and potential investors, creditors, and other users in assessing the amounts, timing, and uncertainty of prospective cash receipts from dividends and interest, and the proceeds from the sale, redemption, or maturity of securities or loans

Derived Company Objective: Provide information to help investors, creditors, and others in assessing the amounts, timing, and uncertainty of prospective net cash inflows to the related company

Specific Objectives:
- Provide information about a company's economic resources, obligations, and owners' equity
- Provide information about a company's comprehensive income and its components
- Provide information about a company's cash flows

Information Useful in Decision Making

The top of Exhibit 2-3 shows the most general objective. This objective states that **financial reporting should provide useful information for present and potential investors, creditors, and other external users in making their investment, credit, and similar decisions.** Investors include both equity security holders (stockholders) and debt security holders (bondholders). Creditors include suppliers, customers and employees with claims, individual lenders, and lending institutions. Other external users include brokers, lawyers, security analysts, and regulatory agencies. These external users are expected to have a reasonable understanding of business and economic activities. They are also expected to be willing to study carefully the information to comprehend it.

3 Identify the general objective of financial reporting.

Information Useful to External Users in Assessing Future Cash Receipts

The second objective shown in Exhibit 2-3 relates to external users' needs. It states that **financial reporting should provide information that is useful to external users in assessing the amounts, timing, and uncertainty of prospective cash receipts.** This objective is important because individuals and institutions make cash outflows for investing and lending activities primarily to increase their cash inflows. Whether or not they are successful depends on the extent to which they receive a return of cash, goods, or services greater than their investment or loan. That is, they must receive not only a return *of* investment, but also a return *on* investment relative to the risk involved. Investment and credit decisions involve choices between present and prospective future cash flows. External users need financial information to help set expectations about the timing and amount of prospective cash receipts (e.g., dividends, interest, proceeds from resale, or repayment) and assess the risk involved.

Information Useful in Assessing Company Cash Flows

Since investors invest in and creditors lend to a particular company, their current and prospective cash receipts are affected by the cash flows of the company. Thus, a third objective shown in Exhibit 2-3 is that **financial reporting should provide information to help external users in assessing the amounts, timing, and uncertainty of the prospective net cash inflows to the related company.** This objective logically flows from the second objective, because a company also invests cash in noncash resources to earn more cash and receive a return *on* its investment in addition to a return *of* its investment.

A company's investment activities are more complex, however, than those of external users. The company completes an "operating cycle" or cycles during which it acquires goods or services, increases their value, sells the goods or services, and collects the selling price. Within this operating cycle numerous cash receipts and payments are collected and paid, in no precise order. The company's ability to generate net cash inflows (i.e., cash inflows greater than cash outflows) affects both its ability to pay dividends and interest and the market prices of its securities. These, in turn, affect investors' and creditors' cash flows.

Information About Economic Resources and Claims to These Resources

4 Describe the three specific objectives of financial reporting.

The most specific objectives in Exhibit 2-3 are those in the bottom tier, which indicate the types of information that a company should provide in its financial reports. **A specific objective of financial reporting is to provide information about a company's economic resources, obligations, and owners' equity.** This information is useful to external users for four reasons:

- to identify the company's financial strengths and weaknesses and to assess its liquidity
- to provide a basis for evaluating information about the company's performance during a given period
- to provide direct indications of the cash flow potentials of some resources and the cash needed to satisfy obligations
- to indicate the potential cash flows that are the joint result of combining various resources in the company's operations

Information About Comprehensive Income and Its Components

Another specific objective of financial reporting is to provide information about a company's financial performance during a specified period to help external users form expectations about its future performance. **The** *primary* **focus of financial reporting about a company's performance is information concerning the company's** *comprehensive income* **and its components.** Information about comprehensive income is useful to external users in:

- evaluating management's performance
- estimating the company's "earning power," or other amounts that are representative of long-term income-producing ability
- predicting future income
- assessing the risk of investing in or lending to the company

We discuss comprehensive income in Chapter 5.

The measurement of comprehensive income should relate (i.e., match) the costs (sacrifices) of a company's operations to the benefits from its operations. The measurement should also include the benefits and costs of other nonoperating transactions, events, and circumstances. This is accomplished by using accrual accounting. Under **accrual accounting** the financial effects of a company's transactions, events, and circumstances having cash consequences are related to the period in which they occur instead of to when the cash receipt or cash payment takes place.[6]

Information About Cash Flows

Although information about comprehensive income is important to external users, **another specific objective of financial reporting is to provide information about a company's cash flows.** Cash flow information shows how a company obtains and spends cash for its operations, investments, borrowings, and capital transactions, including cash dividends and other distributions of company resources to owners. External users use cash (or cash and cash equivalents) flow information about a company to:

- help understand its operations
- evaluate its financing and investing activities
- assess its liquidity
- interpret the comprehensive income information provided

Other Issues

The FASB raised two other important issues in *FASB Statement of Concepts No. 1*. First, **financial reporting should provide information about how the management of a company has discharged its stewardship responsibility** to owners (stockholders) for using the company resources. The management is responsible to the owners for the custody and safekeeping of the resources, their efficient and profitable use, and their protection against unfavorable economic impacts, technological developments, and social changes.

Second, **a company's financial statements and other means of financial reporting should include explanations and interpretations by its management to help external users understand the financial information provided.** This is known as **full disclosure.** Since a company's management knows more about the company's activities than "outsiders," the usefulness of financial information can be enhanced by, for instance:

- explanations of certain transactions, events, and circumstances
- interpretations of the effects on the financial results of dividing continuous operations into accounting periods
- explanations of underlying assumptions or methods used and any related significant uncertainties

The FASB established the qualitative characteristics (e.g., relevance, reliability) that accounting information should possess to be included in financial reports in *FASB Statement of Concepts No. 2*. We include them in the next section of this chapter. The FASB includes definitions of the elements (e.g., assets, liabilities, revenues, and expenses) of financial statements in *FASB Statement of Concepts No. 6*. We include them later in this chapter. We discuss financial statement elements in Chapters 4 and 5.

The FASB's first step in developing its conceptual framework was to establish the objectives of financial reporting. The FASB intends that these objectives will be guidelines

---

6. *FASB Statement of Concepts No. 1* originally used the term "earnings" instead of "comprehensive income." This latter term was substituted in *FASB Statement of Concepts No. 5* because comprehensive income includes more components. We discuss this issue more fully in Chapter 4.

for providing financial information for investment and credit decisions. Thus, these guidelines will help in the efficient operation of the capital markets and in promoting the efficient allocation of scarce resources.

TYPES OF USEFUL INFORMATION

5 Discuss the types of useful information for investment and credit decision making.

The general objective of financial reporting is to provide information that is useful in investment and credit decision making. On a more specific level, a company's financial reports should provide information to help external users assess the amounts, timing, and uncertainty about its future net cash inflows. The FASB has identified five types of information as being useful in meeting this specific objective. Exhibit 2-4 shows the interrelationship of this useful information with financial reports and external decision making.

Return on Investment

Return on investment provides a measure of overall company performance. Shareholders (stockholders) invest capital for a share of the equity (stockholders' equity) of a company. These investors are concerned with a return *on* capital. Before a company can provide a return on capital, its capital must be maintained or recovered (i.e., first there must be a return *of* capital to the company). Once a company's capital is maintained, the return *on* capital (i.e., comprehensive income) may be distributed to investors or may be retained by the company for reinvestment.

Risk

Risk is the uncertainty or unpredictability of the future results of a company. The greater the range within which a company's future results are likely to fall, the greater the risk of an investment in or extension of credit to the company. Risk is caused by numerous factors including, for example, high rates of technological change, uncertainty about demand, exposure to the effects of price changes, and political changes in the United States and other countries. In general, the greater the risk of an investment in a particular company, the higher the rate of return expected by investors (or the higher the rate of interest charged by creditors).

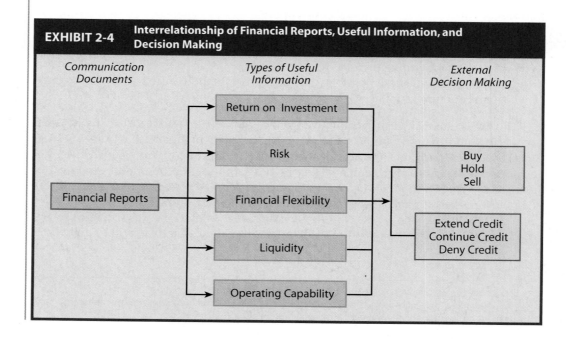

EXHIBIT 2-4   Interrelationship of Financial Reports, Useful Information, and Decision Making

Financial Flexibility

Financial flexibility is the ability of a company to use its financial resources to adapt to change. Financial flexibility is important because it enables a company to respond to unexpected needs and opportunities. Financial flexibility comes from a company's ability to:

- adapt operations to increase net operating cash inflows
- raise new capital through, for instance, the sale of debt or stock securities at short notice
- obtain cash by selling assets without disrupting ongoing operations

Financial flexibility affects risk as well as cash flows. It reduces the risk of failure in the event of a shortage in net cash flows from operations.

Liquidity

Liquidity refers to how quickly a company can convert its assets into cash to pay its bills. Liquidity reflects an asset's "nearness to cash." For operating assets, liquidity relates to the timing of cash flows in the normal course of business. For nonoperating assets, liquidity refers to marketability. The liquidity of a company is an indication of its ability to meet its obligations when they come due. Liquidity is positively related to financial flexibility but negatively related to both risk and return on investment. A more liquid company is likely to have a superior ability to adapt to unexpected needs and opportunities, as well as a lower risk of failure. On the other hand, liquid assets often offer lower rates of return than nonliquid assets.

Operating Capability

Operating capability refers to the ability of a company to maintain a given physical level of operations. This level of operations may be indicated by (1) the quantity of goods or services (e.g., inventory) of a specified quality produced in a given period or (2) the physical capacity of the fixed assets (e.g., property, plant, and equipment). Information about operating capability is helpful in understanding a company's past performance and in predicting future changes in its volume of activities. Operating capability may be affected by changes in methods of operations, changes in product lines, and the timing of the replacement of the service potential used up in operations.[7]

SECURE YOUR KNOWLEDGE 2-1

- The conceptual framework consists of a coherent system of interrelated objectives and concepts that prescribes the nature, function, and limitations of financial reporting.
- The conceptual framework serves as a conceptual underpinning that provides a unified and consistent structure and direction to financial accounting and reporting that allows the FASB to effectively fulfill its mission.
- The objective of financial reporting is to provide information that is useful for external users in making investment, credit, and similar decisions. More specifically, financial reporting should provide information about a company's:
  - economic resources, obligations, and owners' equity;
  - financial performance during a specified period of time; and
  - cash flows.

(continued)

---

7. "Reporting Income, Cash Flows, and Financial Position of Business Enterprises," *FASB Proposed Statement of Financial Accounting Concepts* (Stamford, Conn.: FASB, 1981), par. 7–33.

- Financial reporting should provide information about how the management of a company has discharged its stewardship responsibility and include explanations and interpretations that help external users understand the financial information provided (full disclosure).
- Information relating to return on investment, risk, financial flexibility, liquidity and operating capability is considered to be useful in assessing the amounts, timing, and uncertainty of a company's future net cash flows.

QUALITATIVE CHARACTERISTICS OF USEFUL ACCOUNTING INFORMATION

In the previous sections we discussed the types of information that are helpful in investment and credit decision making. But what are the characteristics of useful information? The purpose of *FASB Statement of Financial Accounting Concepts No. 2* is to specify the qualitative characteristics or "ingredients" that accounting information should have to be most useful.[8] These characteristics should be considered when choosing among accounting alternatives, because these qualities distinguish more useful from less useful information.

Each accounting alternative, however, may possess more of one quality and less of another. Although there is much agreement about the qualitative characteristics that "good" accounting information should possess, no "equation" can determine which information has the "best" combination of qualitative characteristics for decision-making purposes. Furthermore, the FASB strives to meet the needs of all users through *general-purpose* financial statements. However, the qualitative characteristics are still important for establishing common accounting standards. The qualitative criteria are helpful to the FASB in setting "minimum" and "maximum" limits of useful accounting information so that it can develop logical accounting standards consistent with these "limits."

Hierarchy of Qualitative Characteristics

6 Explain the qualities of useful accounting information.

Exhibit 2-5 shows a hierarchy of the qualitative characteristics of accounting information. This section presents an overview of the hierarchy, after which we define and discuss the components in detail. The hierarchy is bounded by *two constraints*: (1) **the benefits must be greater than the costs** (to justify providing the accounting information); and (2) **the dollar amount of the information must be material** (i.e., large enough to make a difference in decision making). The hierarchy is not designed to assign priorities among the qualitative characteristics in all situations. To be useful, **accounting information must have each of the qualitative characteristics to a minimum degree.** However, different situations may require tradeoffs, where the level of one quality is sacrificed for an increase in that of another quality.

Understandability

Accounting information should be **understandable to users who have a reasonable knowledge of business and economic activities and who are willing to study the information carefully.** *Understandability* serves as a "link" between the decision makers and the accounting information. Since the FASB establishes standards for general-purpose financial statements, it is concerned that *broad classes* of decision makers are able to understand the accounting information.

---

8. The discussion in this section primarily is a summary of that presented in "Qualitative Characteristics of Accounting Information," *FASB Statement of Financial Accounting Concepts No. 2* (Stamford, Conn.: FASB, 1980).

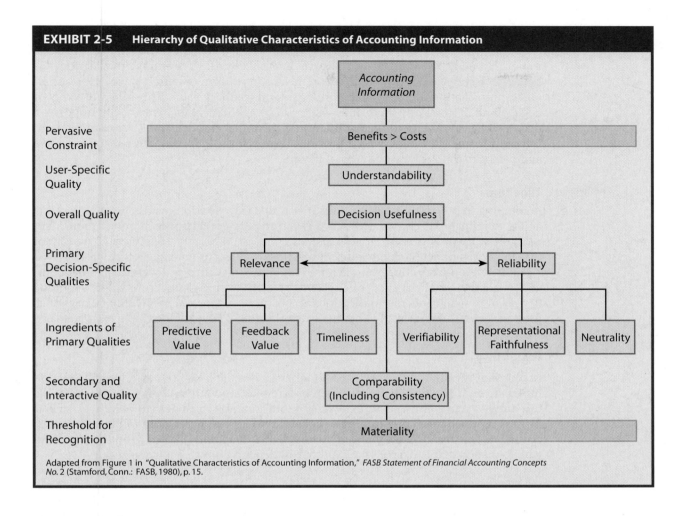

EXHIBIT 2-5   Hierarchy of Qualitative Characteristics of Accounting Information

Adapted from Figure 1 in "Qualitative Characteristics of Accounting Information," *FASB Statement of Financial Accounting Concepts No. 2* (Stamford, Conn.: FASB, 1980), p. 15.

Decision Usefulness

Decision usefulness is the *overall* qualitative characteristic to be used in judging the quality of accounting information. Whether or not information is useful depends on the decision to be made, the way in which it is made, the information already available, and the decision maker's ability to process the information. Since the FASB establishes standards for broad classes of users, however, it must consider the quality of decision usefulness in a broad context. This overall quality can be separated into the primary qualities of relevance and reliability.

Relevance

Accounting information is relevant if it can make a difference in a decision by helping users predict the outcomes of past, present, and future events or confirm or correct prior expectations. In this context, an "event" is a happening that is significant to a company (e.g., the purchase of a building). An "outcome" is the effect or result of an event or series of events (e.g., cash flows generated by use of the building). To be relevant, accounting information does not have to be expressed as a prediction. Information about a company's current resources or obligations or about its past performance commonly is used as a basis for expectations. To be relevant, accounting information should have either predictive or feedback value, or both. In addition, it should be timely.

Predictive Value and Feedback Value

Accounting information has **predictive value** when it helps decision makers forecast more accurately the outcome of past or present events. Accounting information has **feedback value** when it enables decision makers to confirm or correct prior expectations. Often, information has both predictive value and feedback value. This is because knowledge about a company's previous actions (i.e., feedback) generally will improve a decision maker's ability to predict the results of similar future actions. An example is an interim income statement, which provides feedback about a company's income to date and can be used to forecast its annual income.

Timeliness

Accounting information is **timely** when it is available to decision makers before it loses its ability to influence decisions. Timeliness is an ingredient of relevance. If information is not available when it is needed, it lacks relevance and is not useful. Timeliness alone cannot make information relevant, but a lack of timeliness reduces its potential relevance. However, a gain in relevance resulting from increased timeliness may involve a sacrifice of other desirable qualitative characteristics (e.g., reliability). The SEC has defined timeliness, requiring that each company under its jurisdiction file a Form 10-K annual report within 60 days of its fiscal year-end and a Form 10-Q quarterly report within 35 days of the end of each quarter.

Reliability

Accounting information is most useful when it is reliable as well as relevant. **Reliable information is reasonably free from error and bias, and faithfully represents what it is intended to represent.** That is, to be reliable, information must be verifiable, neutral, and possess representational faithfulness. Reliability does not necessarily imply certainty or precision. For instance, estimates may be reliable. Reliability has different degrees, and what is an acceptable degree of reliability will depend on the circumstances.

Verifiability

Accounting information is **verifiable** (sometimes called **objective**) when measurers (i.e., accountants) can agree that the selected method has been used without error or bias. That is, the measurement results can be duplicated. Verification is useful in reducing *measurer bias*, because by using the same method to repeat measurements, both unintentional and intentional errors are reduced.

Verification is a primary concern of auditing. The **Certified Public Accountant (CPA)** is an independent professional who reviews (audits) the published financial statements of a company. The performance of this duty is termed the **attest function.** It involves a review of a sample of a company's transactions during a reporting period to provide assurance that the recording and reporting of its financial information can be duplicated substantially by an independent measurer. As a result of the review, the CPA issues an auditor's report. (We discuss audit reports in Chapters 4 and 6.) Verification does not, however, ensure the appropriateness of the accounting methods used. That quality of accounting information is representational faithfulness.

Representational Faithfulness

Accounting information has **representational faithfulness** when there is a relationship between the reported accounting measurements or descriptions and the economic resources, obligations, and transactions and events causing changes in these items. Social scientists define this concept as "validity." For instance, a company may record an item leased on a long-term basis from another entity as an economic resource even though it does not own the item. This recording increases the representational faithfulness of the reported economic resources available to the company. Having a high degree of representational faithfulness is useful in reducing *measurement bias*. Having representational faithfulness in one decision-making context, however, does not mean that accounting information will be relevant for other decisions. For instance, the current value of an economic resource that a company expects to replace in the near future would be useful information, but it might not be useful if the company has no intention of replacing it.

Neutrality

Accounting information is **neutral** when it is not biased to attain a predetermined result or to influence behavior in a *particular* direction. Neutrality does not mean that accounting information has no purpose or does not influence human behavior. The purpose of providing accounting information is to serve different users with many interests. Furthermore, accounting information is intended to be useful in decision making, thereby influencing the decision makers' behavior, but not in a predetermined direction. Neutrality also implies *completeness* of information. An omission of information can lead to bias if it is intended to induce or inhibit a particular behavior. Sometimes, in conjunction with neutrality, you will hear that accounting information needs to be *transparent*. Transparent accounting information is clear and not distorted, which allows external users to clearly see the information they need to make decisions.

Comparability and Consistency

A secondary qualitative characteristic of accounting information is comparability (including consistency). Information about a company is more useful if it can be compared with similar information from other companies (this is referred to as *intercompany* comparison) or with similar information from past periods within the company (*intracompany* comparison). Comparability is not a primary quality of useful information, like relevance and reliability, because it must involve more than one item of information. It is an *interactive quality* of the relationship between two or more items of information. **Comparability of accounting information enables users to identify and explain similarities and differences between two or more sets of economic facts.**

Closely linked to comparability is consistency. **Consistency means conformity from period to period, with accounting policies and procedures remaining unchanged.** Consistency, like comparability, is a quality of the relationship between numbers rather than a quality of the numbers themselves. Consistency helps enhance comparability across periods. Without consistency, it would be difficult for a user to determine whether differences in results were caused by economic differences or simply by differences in accounting methods. On the other hand, a change in accounting method is sometimes desirable. Economic situations may change, or more preferable new accounting methods may evolve. A company must make some sacrifice in consistency at certain times to improve the usefulness of its accounting information.

Constraints to the Hierarchy

Two constraints to the hierarchy of qualitative characteristics help to identify further what accounting information should be disclosed in financial reports. The first is a benefit/cost constraint; the second is a threshold-for-recognition, or materiality, constraint.

Benefits Greater Than Costs

Accounting information is a commodity. Unless the benefits expected to be received from a commodity exceed its costs, the commodity will not be sought after. The preparer (the company) initially incurs the costs of providing financial information and then passes the costs on to consumers (external users). These costs include the cost of collecting, processing, auditing, and communicating the information. The costs also include those associated with losing a competitive advantage by disclosing the information. The benefits are enjoyed by a diverse group of investors and creditors, by customers (because they are assured a steady supply of goods and services), and by the preparer itself (for use in internal decision

the middle in question   *trustworthy*

making). To be reported, accounting information not only must be relevant and reliable but it also must satisfy the benefit/cost constraint. That is, the FASB must have reasonable assurance that the costs of implementing a standard will not exceed the benefits.

Materiality

The second constraint, that of materiality, is really a *quantitative "threshold"* constraint linked very closely to the qualitative characteristic of relevance. **Materiality refers to the magnitude of an omission or misstatement of accounting information that makes it likely the judgment of a reasonable person relying on the information would have been influenced by the omission or misstatement.** Materiality and relevance are both defined in terms of the influences that affect a decision maker, but there is a difference between the two terms. A company may make a decision to disclose certain information because users have a need for that information (it is relevant) *and* because the amount is large enough to make a difference (it is material). Alternatively, a decision not to disclose certain information may be made because the user has no need for the information (it is not relevant) *or* because the amount is too small to make a difference (it is not material).

The FASB did not set overall quantitative guidelines for materiality in the *Statements of Concepts*. It felt that materiality involves judgment, and that no general standards could be set that took into account all the elements of sound human judgment. Materiality judgments should be concerned with thresholds of recognition. Is an item large enough to pass over the threshold that separates material from immaterial items? To answer that question, the FASB suggested that a company give consideration to:

- the *nature* of the item (i.e., items considered too small to be significant when they result from routine transactions might be material if they arose from abnormal circumstances)
- the *relative size* rather than absolute size of an item (i.e., a $10,000 error in inventory of a large company may be insignificant while a similar $10,000 error by a small company may be material)

The FASB observed that quantitative guidelines have been and will continue to be set for specific accounting issues where appropriate.

In regard to the relative size of a misstatement, some companies establish an initial percentage threshold; for instance, 5% of net income for the income statement and 5% of total assets for the balance sheet. Thus, if the misstatement of an amount is less than 5% of net income it is not considered material for the income statement. External users feel that some companies are using a percentage threshold as an "absolute" cutoff without considering the qualitative factors of the information, such as the surrounding circumstances or the "total mix" of information. In response, several groups (the SEC, the AICPA, and the Big Five Audit Materiality Task Force) have provided guidance in assessing the materiality of a misstated item for a company. These include, for instance, whether the misstatement:

- has an effect on trends (particularly trends in profitability)
- masks a change in earnings (and earnings per share)
- is currently immaterial but may have a material impact in future periods because of a cumulative effect
- changes a loss into net income (or vice versa)
- misrepresents the company's compliance with loan agreements
- relates to a segment of the company that is of particular importance to the company's long-run profitability
- has the effect of increasing management's compensation.[9]

---

9. For a more extensive discussion, see "Materiality," *SEC Staff Accounting Bulletin No. 99* (Washington, D.C.: Securities and Exchange Commission, August 12, 1999) and "Audit Risk and Materiality in Conducting an Audit," *AICPA Professional Standards*, Volume 1 (New York: AICPA, 2004), sec. 312.

Thus, companies may use a quantitative threshold as an initial step in assessing materiality, but need to consider qualitative factors in making the final judgment on the materiality of an item.

SECURE YOUR KNOWLEDGE 2-2

- For accounting information to be useful for decision making, it must be understandable to users who possess a reasonable knowledge of business and economic activities and who are willing to study the information with reasonable diligence.
- The primary qualities that make accounting information useful for decision making are relevance and reliability.
  - Relevant information is available in a timely manner and assists users in predicting the outcome of past, present, or future events or confirming prior expectations.
  - Reliable information is reasonably free from error and bias, and faithfully represents what it is intended to represent.
- External decision makers need accounting information that is comparable across different companies and consistent within a company over time.
- Two constraints on the qualitative characteristics of accounting information are:
  - The costs of providing the information should not exceed the benefits received from the using the information; and
  - The information should be material (capable of influencing a decision).

ACCOUNTING ASSUMPTIONS AND PRINCIPLES

Certain accounting assumptions and principles have had an important impact on the development of GAAP. Exhibit 2-6 is useful in understanding the relationship among the objectives, types of useful information, qualitative characteristics, accounting assumptions and principles, generally accepted accounting principles, financial reports, and elements of financial statements. We discuss the accounting assumptions and principles listed in Exhibit 2-6 in this section. We will discuss others later in the book as they apply to specific accounting standards.

7 Understand the accounting assumptions and principles that influence GAAP.

Entity (Assumption)

Most of the economic activity in the United States can be directly or indirectly attributed to business enterprises, termed **economic entities.** These entities vary in size from small, one-owner companies such as hair salons or restaurants, to partnerships such as law or accounting firms, and to large multinational corporations such as **Wal-Mart.** Financial accounting is concerned with the economic activity of each of these entities, regardless of its size, and involves recording and reporting its transactions and events. A transaction involves the transfer of something of value between the entity and another party. In certain instances the financial records of related but separate legal entities may be *consolidated* (combined) to report more realistically the resources, obligations, and operating results of the overall economic entity.

Because the entity assumption distinguishes each organization from its owners, each separate entity prepares its own financial records and reports. The personal transactions of the owners are kept separate from those of the business enterprise. Throughout this book we refer to a business enterprise as a *company* (and when the discussion applies to a type of company, we use the specific type of entity, e.g., *corporation*).

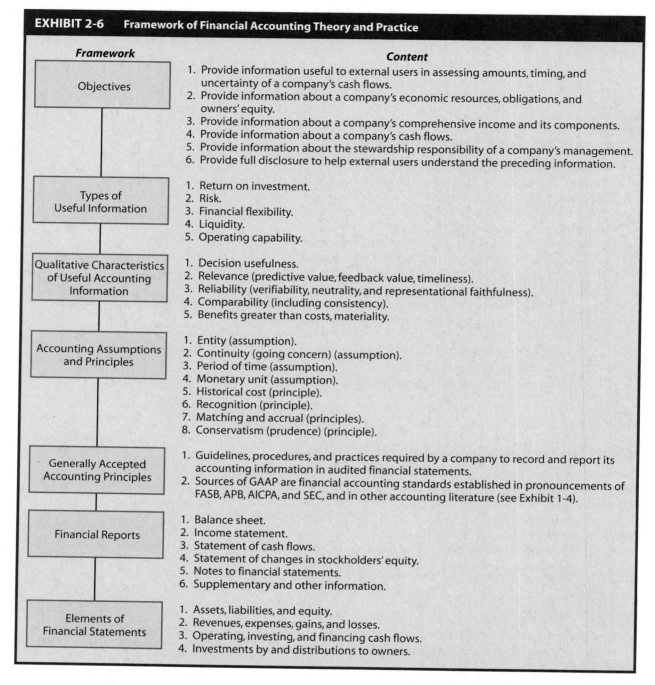

EXHIBIT 2-6   Framework of Financial Accounting Theory and Practice

Framework	Content
Objectives	1. Provide information useful to external users in assessing amounts, timing, and uncertainty of a company's cash flows. 2. Provide information about a company's economic resources, obligations, and owners' equity. 3. Provide information about a company's comprehensive income and its components. 4. Provide information about a company's cash flows. 5. Provide information about the stewardship responsibility of a company's management. 6. Provide full disclosure to help external users understand the preceding information.
Types of Useful Information	1. Return on investment. 2. Risk. 3. Financial flexibility. 4. Liquidity. 5. Operating capability.
Qualitative Characteristics of Useful Accounting Information	1. Decision usefulness. 2. Relevance (predictive value, feedback value, timeliness). 3. Reliability (verifiability, neutrality, and representational faithfulness). 4. Comparability (including consistency). 5. Benefits greater than costs, materiality.
Accounting Assumptions and Principles	1. Entity (assumption). 2. Continuity (going concern) (assumption). 3. Period of time (assumption). 4. Monetary unit (assumption). 5. Historical cost (principle). 6. Recognition (principle). 7. Matching and accrual (principles). 8. Conservatism (prudence) (principle).
Generally Accepted Accounting Principles	1. Guidelines, procedures, and practices required by a company to record and report its accounting information in audited financial statements. 2. Sources of GAAP are financial accounting standards established in pronouncements of FASB, APB, AICPA, and SEC, and in other accounting literature (see Exhibit 1-4).
Financial Reports	1. Balance sheet. 2. Income statement. 3. Statement of cash flows. 4. Statement of changes in stockholders' equity. 5. Notes to financial statements. 6. Supplementary and other information.
Elements of Financial Statements	1. Assets, liabilities, and equity. 2. Revenues, expenses, gains, and losses. 3. Operating, investing, and financing cash flows. 4. Investments by and distributions to owners.

Continuity (Assumption)

The **continuity assumption** is also known as the **going-concern assumption.** This assumption is that the company will continue to operate in the near future, unless substantial evidence to the contrary exists. Obviously, not all companies are successful, and failures do occur. However, the continuity assumption is valid in most cases and is necessary for many of the accounting procedures used. For example, if a company is not regarded as a going concern, the company should not depreciate its fixed assets over their expected useful lives, nor should the company record its inventory at its cost, because the receipt of future economic benefits from these items is uncertain.

The continuity assumption does not imply permanence. It simply indicates that the company will operate long enough to carry out its existing commitments. If a company appears to be going bankrupt, it must discard the continuity assumption. The company then reports its financial statements on a liquidation basis, with all assets and liabilities valued at the amounts estimated to be collected or paid when they are sold or liquidated.

Period of Time (Assumption)

The profit or loss earned by a company cannot be determined *accurately* until it stops operating. At that time the total lifetime profit or loss may be determined by comparing the cash on hand after liquidating the business (plus any cash payments to the owners during the period of operations) with the amount invested by the owners during the company's lifetime. Obviously, financial statement users need more current information to evaluate a company's profitability. Companies primarily use a year as the reporting period. In accordance with the **period-of-time assumption,** a company prepares financial statements at the end of each year and includes them in its annual report. Furthermore, the annual reporting period (called the **accounting period** or **fiscal year**) is used for reports issued to government regulators such as the Internal Revenue Service (IRS) and the Securities and Exchange Commission (SEC).

The period-of-time assumption is the basis for the adjusting entry process in accounting. If companies did not prepare financial statements on a yearly (or shorter time) basis, there would be no reason to determine the time frame affected by particular transactions. Historically, most companies adopted the calendar year as the accounting period. However, many companies now choose a fiscal year that more closely approximates their annual *business cycle*. (The yearly period from lowest sales through highest sales and back to lowest sales is known as a business cycle.) For example, consider Exhibit 2-7, which shows the annual sales pattern for Company G. Notice that peak sales occur each year in January, while the lowest sales volume occurs in June. A company that sells ski equipment might have such a sales pattern. If Company G were to report on a calendar-year basis, its financial reports would be prepared at about the time of peak yearly sales (i.e., the midpoint of the business cycle). Alternatively, a fiscal year that ended on June 30 would include a single complete annual business cycle. Many large retail chains have a fiscal year-end that follows the peak Christmas selling season. For example, **Wal-Mart's** year-end is January 31, which is after most of the returns and allowances related to those sales have occurred. Fiscal-year reports that include an annual business cycle contain information that is more easily comparable to past and future periods because annual sales patterns are not broken by the reporting period.

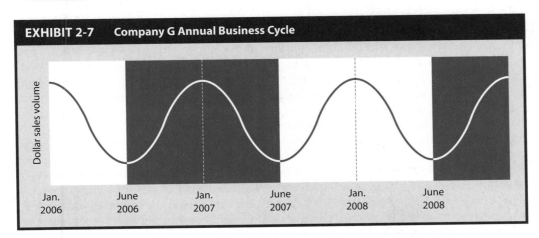

EXHIBIT 2-7   Company G Annual Business Cycle

In addition to annual reports, publicly traded companies issue financial statements for interim (quarterly) periods. These interim periods are integral parts of the annual period, and interim reports disclose summary information to provide investors with more timely information.

Monetary Unit (Assumption)

Since the time when gold and other precious metals were accepted in exchange for goods and services, there has been a unit of exchange. This unit of exchange is different for almost every nation. Accountants generally have adopted the national currency of the reporting company as the unit of measure in preparing financial statements.

In using the dollar or any other currency as the unit of measure, accountants traditionally have assumed that it is a stable measuring unit. Prior to the FASB, accounting policy-making bodies had felt that fluctuations in the value of the dollar were not a serious enough problem to affect the comparability of accounting information. Therefore, any adjustment in the monetary unit assumption was not needed.

In today's world the assumption that the dollar or any other national currency is a stable measure over time is not necessarily valid. Consider the building you are now in. If you were to measure its width in feet and inches today, next year, and five years from now, an accurate physical measurement would yield the same results each time. In contrast, consider the monetary value of the same building. Real estate prices have changed (increased or decreased) during the past several years and undoubtedly will continue to vary, resulting in changing monetary measures of value even though the physical capacity remains the same.

There are two primary reasons for changes in reported values over time:

1. The real value of the item in question may change in relation to the real value of all other goods and services in the economy.
2. The purchasing power of the measuring unit (in this case the dollar) may change.

Currently the dollar is considered to be a stable monetary unit for preparing a company's financial statements. As we mentioned earlier, however, to enhance comparability the FASB encourages companies to make supplemental disclosures relating to the impacts of changing prices.

Historical Cost (Principle)

The economic activities and resources of a company initially are measured using the exchange price at the time each transaction occurs. For many economic resources, usually the company retains the exchange price (the **historical cost**) in its accounting records as the value of the resource until the company consumes or sells it and removes it from the records. That is, a company usually delays recording gains and losses resulting from value changes of assets (or liabilities) until another exchange occurs. The reason for using historical cost (as opposed to other valuation methods such as current market value or appraisal value) is that it is reliable, and that source documents usually are available to confirm the recorded amount. Also, historical cost provides evidence that an independent buyer and seller were in agreement on the value of an exchanged good or service at the time of the transaction and thus has the qualities of representational faithfulness, neutrality, and verifiability.

One of the most frequently heard criticisms of accounting comes from those who prefer alternative valuation methods that they believe would report information more relevant for user decisions. Accountants understand that historical cost information may not always be completely *relevant* for all decisions, but it does have a significant degree of *reliability*. In certain cases accounting standards require the use of valuation methods other than historical cost to report the *fair value* of selected items in the financial statements. These methods are required when they provide more relevant information and possess an acceptable degree of reliability.[10] However, it is often felt that the measurement problems

---

10. See, for instance, "Fair Value Measurements," *FASB Proposed Statement of Financial Accounting Standards* (Norwalk, Conn.: FASB, 2004).

artifact

inherent in alternative valuation methods are greater than those of historical cost. That is, reliability often takes precedence over relevance. The FASB, however, understands the significance of this relevance/reliability tradeoff and encourages companies to disclose *supplemental* current value information in their annual reports. Also, you should understand that when a company changes the values of its assets and liabilities the company must include these value changes in its comprehensive income for the period. We discuss valuation methods in Chapter 4.

LINK TO ETHICAL DILEMMA

You have been hired as an accounting consultant to review the financial reporting policies of Parker Company as it enters merger negotiations with an interested buyer. Of particular interest is the way in which Parker Company accounts for its property, plant, and equipment. As rumors of possible mergers began several years ago, the company's management periodically began using independent valuation experts to determine fair market values for the company's net assets. As a result of these analyses, management was able to determine that its long-term productive assets had book values that were significantly less than their market values. Citing the increased reliability provided by the valuation experts, management decided to write the company's assets up to market value to provide investors and creditors with the most relevant information possible and to be consistent with the FASB's increasing use of fair value measurements. Do you agree with this decision?

Recognition (Principle)

Recognition means the process of formally recording and reporting an item in the financial statements of a company. A recognized item is shown in both words and numbers, with the amount included in the financial statement totals. The FASB has identified four fundamental recognition criteria. To be recognized, an item must:

- meet the definition of an element
- be measurable
- be relevant
- be reliable

In regard to revenues, two other factors provide guidance for revenue recognition. Revenues should be recognized when (1) realization has taken place, and (2) they have been earned. These factors provide acceptable assurance of the existence and amounts of revenues.

A company usually recognizes revenue at the time of sale because this is when realization occurs and its earning process is substantially complete. **Realization** means the process of converting noncash resources and rights into cash or rights to cash; that is, when the company receives cash or obtains a receivable. Actually, revenue is earned by a company throughout the earning process as it adds economic utility to goods. This **earning process** includes acquisition, production and/or distribution, sales, and the collection and payment of cash. A company could recognize revenue at one or more points in this process. In this regard, the FASB suggests that revenues are considered to be earned when a company has substantially completed what it must do to be entitled to the benefits (i.e., assets) generated by the revenues. Usually, this is the point of sale.[11]

Occasionally a company may advance (accrue) or delay (defer) the recognition of revenue in the earning process to increase the relevance of its income statement. Thus, a company may not recognize (record) revenue at the same time as realization. A company might recognize revenue (1) during production, (2) at the end of production, or (3) after the sale. In the case of certain long-term construction contracts extending over more than one accounting period, a company usually recognizes revenue during production to better depict economic reality by the use of the **percentage-of-completion** method. Similarly, revenue usually is recognized for certain long-term service contracts by use of the **proportional performance** method. These methods allocate the revenues of each contract to each period, based on an estimate of the percentage completed during the period. We discuss these revenue recognition methods in Chapters 5 and 8.

A company might recognize revenue at the completion of production if there is a fixed selling price and there is no limit on the amount that it can sell. This situation might be the case for certain valuable minerals or for farm products sold on the futures market. Finally, revenue may be recognized after the sale if the ultimate collectibility of the revenue is highly uncertain. This situation might arise, for instance, in the case of real estate land sales where a very small down payment is required and the payment terms extend over many years. In situations of high uncertainty about collections, a company uses either the installment or the cost-recovery method to recognize revenue. Under the **installment** method, a portion of each receipt is recognized as revenue. Under the **cost-recovery** method, no revenue is recognized until the cost of the product has been recovered.

Matching and Accrual Accounting (Principles)

Earlier, **accrual accounting** was defined as the process of relating the financial effects of transactions, events, and circumstances having cash consequences to the period in which they occur instead of to when the cash receipt or payment occurs. The **matching** principle is linked closely to accrual accounting and to revenue recognition. The matching principle states that to determine the income of a company for an accounting period, the company computes the total expenses involved in obtaining the revenues of the period and relates these total expenses to (matches them against) the total revenues recorded in the period. Thus, some expenses are advanced (accrued) or delayed (deferred) in a manner similar to revenues. The intent is to match the sacrifices against the benefits (i.e., the efforts against the accomplishments) in the appropriate accounting period.

A company recognizes and matches expenses against revenues on the basis of three principles:

- association of cause and effect
- systematic and rational allocation
- immediate recognition

Expenses recorded as a result of associating cause and effect include sales commissions and the **product costs** included in cost of goods sold. Expenses recorded on the basis of systematic and rational allocation include depreciation of property and equipment and amortization of intangibles. Immediate recognition is appropriate for **period costs—**those expenses related to a period of time, such as administrative salaries.[12]

Some smaller companies do not use accrual accounting and matching. Instead they use **cash basis** accounting for simplicity. In cash basis accounting, a company computes

---

11. "Recognition and Measurement in Financial Statements of Business Enterprises," *FASB Statement of Financial Accounting Concepts No. 5* (Stamford, Conn.: FASB, 1984), par. 63 and 83.
12. "Elements of Financial Statements," *FASB Statement of Financial Accounting Concepts No. 6* (Stamford, Conn.: FASB, 1985), par. 146–149.

its income for an accounting period by subtracting the cash payments from the cash receipts from operations. While this method may be convenient to use, it can lead to incorrect evaluations of a company's operating results. This may happen because the receipt and payment of cash may occur much earlier or later than the sale of goods or the providing of services to customers (benefits) and the related costs (sacrifices). Because cash basis accounting does not attempt to match expenses against revenues, it is not a generally accepted accounting principle.

Conservatism (Principle)

The principle of **conservatism** states that when alternative accounting valuations are equally possible, the accountant should select the one that is least likely to overstate the company's assets and income in the current period. Over the years conservatism gained prominence because of the optimism of management and the tendency, during the first three decades of the twentieth century, to overstate assets and net income on financial statements. Recently, conservatism has been criticized for being "anticonservative" in the years following the conservative act. That is, a deliberate understatement of an asset with a corresponding loss and understatement of income in one year will result in an over-statement of income in a later year when the asset is sold because of the greater difference between the selling price and lower recorded value of the asset. Furthermore, conservatism can conflict with qualitative characteristics such as neutrality. For instance, conservative financial statements may be unfair to present stockholders and biased in favor of future stockholders because the net valuation of the company does not include some future expectations. This factor may result in a relatively lower current market price of the company's common stock. These criticisms notwithstanding, conservatism has played an important role in the establishment of certain generally accepted accounting principles.

The FASB has attempted to modify the principle of conservatism so that it is more synonymous with **prudence.** That is, conservatism should be a prudent reaction to uncertainty so as to ensure, to the extent possible, that the uncertainties and risks inherent in business situations are adequately considered. These uncertainties and risks should be reflected in accounting information to improve its predictive value and neutrality. Prudent reporting based on a healthy skepticism promotes integrity and best serves the various users of financial reports.[13]

GAAP AND FINANCIAL STATEMENTS

As we noted in Chapter 1, generally accepted accounting principles (GAAP) are the guidelines, procedures, and practices that a company is required to use in recording and reporting its accounting information in its audited financial statements. In its *Conceptual Framework,* the FASB has identified various sources from which investors, creditors, and other users might obtain information useful in decision making. Exhibit 2-8 shows this model of financial reporting. We discuss components of this model in Chapters 4, 5, and 23.

Conceptually, the FASB identified the four specific financial statements listed in Exhibit 2-8. In practice, companies prepare at least three major financial statements: (1) the balance sheet (statement of financial position), (2) the income statement, and (3) the statement of cash flows. Many companies also prepare a statement of changes in equity as a major financial statement (or in a note to the financial statements).[14] In this section we discuss briefly these financial statements and the elements of the financial

8 Define the elements of financial statements.

---

13. *FASB Statement of Financial Accounting Concepts No. 2, op. cit.,* par. 95–97.
14. Each company also must report its comprehensive income and may choose to do so on its income statement, a statement of comprehensive income, or on its statement of changes in stockholders' equity. We will discuss these alternatives in Chapter 5.

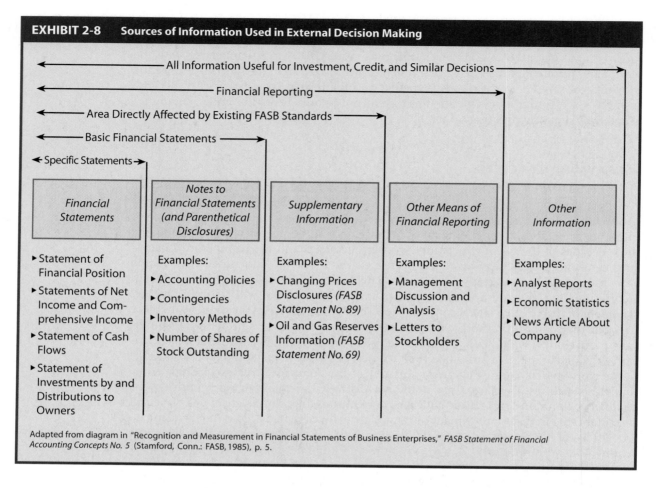

EXHIBIT 2-8   Sources of Information Used in External Decision Making

All Information Useful for Investment, Credit, and Similar Decisions

Financial Reporting

Area Directly Affected by Existing FASB Standards

Basic Financial Statements

Specific Statements

Financial Statements	*Notes to Financial Statements (and Parenthetical Disclosures)*	*Supplementary Information*	*Other Means of Financial Reporting*	*Other Information*
▸ Statement of Financial Position ▸ Statements of Net Income and Comprehensive Income ▸ Statement of Cash Flows ▸ Statement of Investments by and Distributions to Owners	Examples: ▸ Accounting Policies ▸ Contingencies ▸ Inventory Methods ▸ Number of Shares of Stock Outstanding	Examples: ▸ Changing Prices Disclosures *(FASB Statement No. 89)* ▸ Oil and Gas Reserves Information *(FASB Statement No. 69)*	Examples: ▸ Management Discussion and Analysis ▸ Letters to Stockholders	Examples: ▸ Analyst Reports ▸ Economic Statistics ▸ News Article About Company

Adapted from diagram in "Recognition and Measurement in Financial Statements of Business Enterprises," *FASB Statement of Financial Accounting Concepts No. 5* (Stamford, Conn.: FASB, 1985), p. 5.

statements. **The elements of each financial statement are the broad classes of items comprising it.** In other words, they are the "building blocks" with which each financial statement is prepared.[15] We discuss the financial statements and their elements in more depth in later chapters.

Balance Sheet

A **balance sheet** (or statement of financial position) is a financial statement that summarizes the financial position of a company on a particular date (usually the end of the accounting period). The financial position of a company includes its economic resources, economic obligations, and equity, and their relationships to each other. There are three elements of a balance sheet:

1. **Assets:** Assets are the probable future economic benefits obtained and controlled by a company as a result of past transactions or events.
2. **Liabilities:** Liabilities are the probable future sacrifices of economic benefits arising from present obligations of a company to transfer assets or provide services in the future as a result of past transactions or events.
3. **Equity:** Equity is the owners' residual interest in the assets of a company that remains after deducting its liabilities.

---

15. The discussion in this section primarily is a summary of that presented in "Elements of Financial Statements of Business Enterprises," *FASB Statement of Financial Accounting Concept No. 6* (Stamford, Conn.: FASB, 1985) and "Statement of Cash Flows," *FASB Statement of Financial Accounting Standards No. 95* (Stamford, Conn.: FASB, 1987).

In other words, the assets of a company are its economic resources, and the liabilities are its economic obligations. The equity of a corporation is referred to as stockholders' equity because the owners are the stockholders.

Income Statement

An **income statement** is a financial statement that summarizes the results of a company's operations (i.e., net income) for a period of time (generally a one-year or one-quarter accounting period). A company's operations (sometimes called the earning process) include its purchasing, producing, selling, delivering, servicing, and administrating activities. There are four elements of an income statement:

1. **Revenues:**   Revenues are inflows of assets of a company or settlement of its liabilities (or a combination of both) during a period from delivering or producing goods, rendering services, or other activities that are the company's ongoing major or central operations. Revenues increase the equity of a company.
2. **Expenses:**   Expenses are outflows of assets of a company or incurrences of liabilities (or a combination of both) during a period from delivering or producing goods, rendering services, or carrying out other activities that are the company's ongoing major or central operations. Expenses decrease the equity of a company.
3. **Gains:**   Gains are increases in the equity of a company from peripheral or incidental transactions, and from all other events and circumstances during a period, except those that result from revenues or investments by owners.
4. **Losses:**   Losses are decreases in the equity of a company from peripheral or incidental transactions, and from all other events and circumstances during a period, except those that result from expenses or distributions to owners.

Revenues may be thought of as measures of the accomplishments of a company during its accounting period, while expenses are measures of the efforts to achieve the revenues. Gains are similar to revenues and losses are similar to expenses, except that revenues and expenses relate to a company's primary operations, while gains and losses relate to its secondary activities.

Statement of Cash Flows

A **statement of cash flows** is a financial statement that summarizes the cash inflows and outflows of a company for a period of time (generally one year or one quarter). There are three elements of a statement of cash flows:

1. **Operating Cash Flows:**   Operating cash flows are the inflows and outflows of cash from acquiring, selling, and delivering goods for sale, as well as providing services.
2. **Investing Cash Flows:**   Investing cash flows are the inflows and outflows of cash from acquiring and selling investments, property, plant, and equipment, and intangibles, as well as from lending money and collecting on loans.
3. **Financing Cash Flows:**   Financing cash flows are the inflows and outflows of cash from obtaining resources from owners and paying them dividends, as well as obtaining and repaying resources from creditors on long-term credit.

In addition to these three elements, the statement of cash flows reconciles the amount of cash a company reports on its balance sheets at the beginning and end of the accounting period.

Statement of Changes in Equity

A **statement of changes in equity** summarizes the changes in a company's equity for a period of time (generally one year or one quarter). For a corporation, the statement is called the statement of changes in stockholders' equity. There are two elements in a statement of changes in equity:

1. **Investments by Owners:** Investments by owners are increases in the equity of a company resulting from transfers of something valuable (usually cash) to the company in order to obtain or increase ownership interests.

2. **Distributions to Owners:** Distributions to owners are decreases in the equity of a company caused by transferring assets, rendering services, or incurring liabilities.

In addition to these elements, the statement of changes in equity also reconciles the amounts of the equity items a company reports on its beginning and ending balance sheets for such items as net income and other comprehensive income.

Model of Business Reporting

The AICPA Special Committee on Financial Reporting issued a report that addressed concerns about the relevance and usefulness of reporting by companies. In this report the committee developed a comprehensive model of *business reporting*—the information that a company provides to help users with capital allocation decisions about the company. The model was designed to help focus attention on a broader, integrated range of information than that addressed in the FASB's conceptual framework. The goal was to provide the foundation for future improvement in business reporting. The model includes 10 items within five categories of information. These categories are designed to fit the decision processes of users to make projections, value companies, or assess the likelihood of loan repayments. The framework of the model is as follows:

1. *Financial and nonfinancial data* including (a) financial statements and related disclosures and (b) high-level operating data and performance measurements that a company's management uses to manage the business.

2. *Management's analysis of the financial and nonfinancial data,* including (a) reasons for changes in the financial, operating, and performance-related data and (b) the identity and past effect of key trends.

3. *Forward-looking information,* including (a) the assessment of opportunities and risks, including those resulting from key trends, (b) management's plans, including critical success factors, and (c) a comparison of actual business performance to previously disclosed opportunities, risk, and management's plans.

4. *Information about management and shareholders,* including (a) directors, management, compensation, and major shareholders and (b) transactions and relationships among related parties.

5. *Background about the company,* including (a) broad objectives and strategies, (b) scope and description of the company's business and properties, and (c) the impact of industry structure on the company.

The model is responsive to users' needs, but includes practical constraints to balance the costs and benefits of reporting. Since the AICPA committee is not a standard-setting body, the model is a recommendation to standard setters who have an interest in improving the cost-effective quality of business reporting.[16] We discuss components of this model in Chapters 4, 5, and 6.

---

16. "Improving Business Reporting—A Customer Focus," *AICPA Special Committee on Financial Reporting* (New York: AICPA, 1994), pp. 2–9.

SECURE YOUR KNOWLEDGE 2-3

- Four basic assumptions underlie GAAP. These are:
  - The entity assumption, which relates economic activities to a particular economic entity;
  - The continuity (going concern) assumption, which states that with no evidence to the contrary, a company will continue to operate in the near future;
  - The period of time assumption which allows the life of a company to be divided into artificial time periods and serves as the basis for the adjusting entry process; and
  - The monetary unit assumption, which requires financial statement elements to be expressed in terms of the dollar.
- Four broad principles have greatly influenced the development of GAAP. These are:
  - The historical cost principle, which provides highly reliable, although not always the most relevant, information by measuring economic activities at their historical exchange price;
  - The recognition principle, which determines when an item is to be reported in the financial statements (revenue recognition usually occurs when revenue is realized and the earnings process is complete);
  - The matching principle, which applies accrual accounting by stating that expenses should be recognized in the same period as the related revenues; and
  - The conservatism principle, which states that when given alternative accounting valuations, the accountant should select the one that is least likely to overstate current period assets and income.
- The FASB identified four basic financial statements (the balance sheet, the income statement, the statement of cash flows, and the statement of changes in stockholders' equity) as sources of useful information.

Credit: Michael Reynolds/EPA/Landov

IASB Framework

The International Accounting Standards Board (IASB) has issued a **Framework for the Preparation and Presentation of Financial Statements** that is similar, in many respects, to the FASB Conceptual Framework.

The IASB Framework states that the objective of financial statements is to provide information about the financial position, performance, and changes in financial position of a company that is useful to a wide range of users in making economic decisions. The Framework has two underlying assumptions; that a company is a going concern and uses accrual accounting. It identifies four qualitative characteristics of financial statements—understandability, relevance (including materiality), reliability (including faithful presentation, substance over form, neutrality, prudence, and completeness), and comparability. Three constraints on relevant and reliable information are identified; they include timeliness, balance between benefit and cost, and balance between the qualitative characteristics. The Framework calls for financial statements that present a true and fair view of the company and a fair presentation of the company's activities.

The IASB Framework identifies and defines the elements of a statement of financial position (i.e., assets, liabilities, and equity) and a statement of performance (i.e., income and expenses). It also discusses conceptual issues dealing with the recognition of the elements of financial statements, measurement of the elements, and concepts of capital and capital maintenance.

The IASB Framework is designed (1) to help the Board in developing future International Accounting Standards and reviewing existing Standards and (2) to promote the harmonization of regulations, accounting standards, and accounting procedures regarding the preparation of financial statements.[17]

In 2004, the FASB and the IASB added to their respective agendas a project to develop a common conceptual framework that is based on, and builds on, their existing frameworks. The Boards will focus on issues that are more likely to yield near term standard-setting benefits and cut across several current standard-setting projects. Issues relating to the definitions of assets and liabilities, historical cost versus fair value measurements, and relevance versus reliability will all be key concerns as the conceptual framework project progresses. In addition to promoting international harmonization of future accounting standards, the end result of this project should provide a more consistent and unified set of concepts that will result in accounting standards that are principles-based.

Overview

We discuss the financial statements and their elements, as they fit into the FASB's model of financial reporting and the AICPA's model of business reporting in depth in the later chapters of this book. In addition, we discuss supplementary schedules and notes to the financial statements, along with various recognition and measurement issues. As you read the discussions, it may be helpful for you to place them in the context of the *FASB Conceptual Framework* as we summarized in Exhibit 2-6, as well as the financial reporting environment as we summarize in Exhibit 2-9.

---

17. For further discussion, go to *International Accounting Reporting Standards* (London: IASCF, 2004).

EXHIBIT 2-9   Financial Reporting Environment (Major Activities)

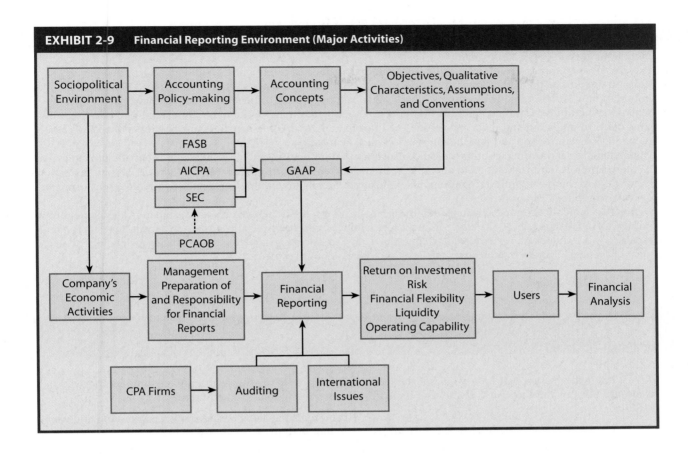

SUMMARY

At the beginning of the chapter, we identified several objectives you would accomplish after reading the chapter. The objectives are listed below, each followed by a brief summary of the key points in the chapter discussion.

1. **Explain the FASB conceptual framework.** The FASB conceptual framework is a theoretical foundation of interrelated objectives and concepts that leads to the establishment of consistent financial accounting standards. It provides a logical structure and direction to financial accounting and reporting.
2. **Understand the relationship among the objectives of financial reporting.** The FASB conceptual framework consists of four levels of objectives that proceed from the more general to the more specific. The top level is the general objective of financial reporting, the next level is the derived external user objective, the third level is the derived company objective, and the final level includes the specific objectives.
3. **Identify the general objective of financial reporting.** The general objective states that financial reporting should provide useful information for present and potential investors, creditors, and other external users in making their investment, credit, and similar decisions.
4. **Describe the three specific objectives of financial reporting.** The three specific objectives are to provide information about a company's: (1) economic resources, obligations, and owners' equity; (2) comprehensive income and its components; and (3) cash flows.

5. **Discuss the types of useful information for investment and credit decision making.** For investment and credit decision making, a company's financial reports should provide useful information about its return on investment, risk, financial flexibility, liquidity, and operating capability.

6. **Explain the qualities of useful accounting information.** Accounting information should be understandable and have decision usefulness. The two primary decision-specific qualities are relevance and reliability. To be relevant, accounting information must have predictive value, feedback value, and timeliness. To be reliable, it must have verifiability, representational faithfulness, and neutrality. In addition, accounting information should be comparable and consistent. Two constraints in preparing and reporting accounting information are that the benefits must be greater than the costs of preparing the information and that the information must be material.

7. **Understand the accounting assumptions and principles that influence GAAP.** Certain assumptions and principles play an important role in the development of GAAP. These include the entity, continuity (going-concern), accounting period, historical cost, monetary unit, recognition and realization, accrual accounting and matching, and conservatism (prudence) assumptions and principles.

8. **Define the elements of financial statements.** The elements of each financial statement are the broad classes of items comprising it. For a balance sheet, the elements are assets, liabilities, and equity. For an income statement, they are revenues, expenses, gains, and losses. For a statement of cash flows, they are operating, investing, and financing cash flows. For a statement of changes in equity, they are investments by and distributions to owners.

QUESTIONS

Q2-1 What is the "conceptual framework" of the FASB? What are the titles of the *Statements of Concepts* issued by the FASB?

Q2-2 What is the most general objective of financial reporting? Who are investors and creditors?

Q2-3 What is the "derived external user objective" and why is it important?

Q2-4 What is the "derived company objective" and what types of information about a company should be reported to satisfy this objective?

Q2-5 List the reasons why external users use information about a company's (a) economic resources and claims to these resources, (b) comprehensive income and its components, and (c) cash flows.

Q2-6 Define (a) return on investment, (b) risk, (c) financial flexibility, (d) liquidity, and (e) operating capability.

Q2-7 What is the overall qualitative characteristic of useful accounting information and what are its two primary qualities?

Q2-8 What is relevant accounting information? Identify and define the ingredients of relevant accounting information.

Q2-9 What is reliable accounting information? Identify and define the ingredients of reliable accounting information.

Q2-10 Identify the secondary quality of useful accounting information. Why is this important and how does it relate to consistency?

Q2-11 What is materiality and how does it relate to relevance?

Q2-12 What is the continuity assumption and why is it important in financial accounting?

Q2-13 What is the period-of-time assumption and why is it important in financial accounting?

Q2-14 Discuss the relationship between historical cost and reliability.

Q2-15 What is recognition? What is realization? What two factors provide guidance for revenue recognition? Why is revenue usually recognized at the time of sale?

Q2-16 What is accrual accounting and how does it relate to the matching principle?

Q2-17 List the three principles for matching expenses against revenues.

Q2-18 What is conservatism and how might it conflict with neutrality?

Q2-19 Define a balance sheet and list its three elements.

Q2-20 Define an income statement and list its four elements.

Q2-21 Define a statement of cash flows and list its three elements.

Q2-22 Define a statement of changes in equity and list its two elements.

Q2-23 For the IASB Framework, list the objective of financial statements and identify the underlying assumptions, qualitative characteristics, and constraints.

MULTIPLE CHOICE (AICPA Adapted)

Select the best answer for each of the following.

M2-1 Accruing net losses on non-cancelable purchase commitments for inventory is an example of the accounting concept of
a. Conservatism
b. Realization
c. Consistency
d. Materiality

M2-2 The information provided by financial reporting pertains to
a. Individual companies, rather than to industries or the economy as a whole or to members of society as consumers.
b. Individual companies and industries, rather than to the economy as a whole or to members of society as consumers.
c. Individual companies and the economy as a whole, rather than to industries or to members of society as consumers.
d. Individual companies, industries, and the economy as a whole, rather than to members of society as consumers.

M2-3 According to **Statement of Financial Accounting Concepts No. 2**, an interim earnings report is expected to have which of the following?

	Predictive value	Feedback value
a.	No	No
b.	Yes	Yes
c.	Yes	No
d.	No	Yes

M2-4 A patent, purchased in 2004 and being amortized over a 10-year life, was determined to be worthless in 2007. The write-off of the asset in 2007 is an example of which of the following principles?
a. Associating cause and effect
b. Immediate recognition
c. Systematic and rational allocation
d. Objectivity

M2-5 An accrued expense is an expense
a. Incurred but not paid
b. Incurred and paid
c. Paid but not incurred
d. Not reasonably estimable

M2-6 Which of the following accounting concepts states that an accounting transaction should be supported by sufficient evidence to allow two or more qualified individuals to arrive at essentially similar measures and conclusions?
a. Matching
b. Verifiability
c. Periodicity
d. Stable monetary unit

M2-7 Which of the following is considered a pervasive constraint by **Statement of Financial Accounting Concepts No. 2**?
a. Benefits/costs
b. Conservatism
c. Timeliness
d. Verifiability

M2-8 The valuation of a promise to receive cash in the future at present value on the financial statements of a company is valid because of the accounting concept of
a. Entity
b. Materiality
c. Going concern
d. Neutrality

M2-9 Under **Statements of Financial Accounting Concepts No. 2**, which of the following relates to both relevance and reliability?
a. Timeliness
b. Neutrality
c. Feedback value
d. Consistency

M2-10 Under **Statement of Financial Accounting Concepts No. 6**, which of the following, in the most precise sense, means the process of converting noncash resources and rights into cash or claims to cash?
a. Allocation
b. Recordation
c. Recognition
d. Realization

CASES

COMMUNICATION

C2-1 Qualitative Characteristics

In *FASB Statement of Concepts No. 2*, several qualitative characteristics of useful accounting information were identified. The following is a list of these qualities as well as a list of statements describing the qualities.

A. Comparability
B. Decision usefulness
C. Relevance
D. Reliability
E. Predictive value
F. Feedback value
G. Timeliness
H. Verifiability
I. Neutrality
J. Representational faithfulness
K. Consistency
L. Materiality

Verifiability 1. Ability of measurers to form a consensus that the selected accounting method has been used without error or bias.

Timeliness 2. Making information available to decision makers before it loses its capacity to influence decisions.

Relevance 3. Capacity to make a difference in a decision.

Decision 4. Overall qualitative characteristic.

neutral 5. Absence of bias intended to influence behavior in a particular direction.

Reliability 6. Reasonably free from error and bias.

Predictive value 7. Helps decision makers forecast correctly.

Rep. faithfulness 8. Validity.

Comparability 9. Interactive quality; helps explain similarities and differences between two sets of facts.

Materiality 10. Quantitative "threshold" constraint.

Consistent 11. Conformity from period to period.

Feedback 12. Helps decision makers confirm or correct prior expectations.

Required

Place the appropriate letter identifying each quality on the line in front of the statement describing the quality.

C2-2 Accounting Assumptions and Principles

Certain accounting assumptions and principles have had an important impact on the development of generally accepted accounting principles. The following is a list of these assumptions and principles as well as a list of statements describing certain accounting practices.

A. Entity   E. Monetary unit
B. Continuity   F. Realization
C. Period of time   G. Matching
D. Historical cost   H. Conservatism

A 1. The business, rather than its owners, is the reporting unit.

G 2. Depreciation costs are expensed in the periods of use rather than at the time the asset is acquired.

E 3. Accounting measurements are reported in dollars.

C 4. The year is the normal reporting unit.

B 5. In the absence of evidence to the contrary, the business will operate long enough to carry out its existing commitments.

F 6. Revenue is usually recognized at the time of sale.

D 7. Exchange price is retained in the accounting records.

H 8. An accounting alternative is selected that is least likely to overstate assets and income.

Required

Select the accounting assumption or principle that justifies each accounting practice and place the appropriate letter on the line preceding the statement.

C2-3   Objectives of Financial Reporting

The FASB has identified several objectives of financial reporting. These objectives proceed from the more general to the more specific and are intended to act as guidelines for providing accounting information in financial reports.

Required

Starting with the most general objective, prepare a written report that identifies and briefly explains the objectives of financial reporting.

C2-4   Qualities of Useful Accounting Information

A friend of yours, who is not an accounting major, is concerned about the "usefulness" of accounting information. The friend states: "I have watched you prepare many financial statements in completing your homework assignments. But how do you determine whether the information in these financial statements is useful? What are the characteristics or qualities of useful accounting information?"

Required

Prepare a written response for your friend that identifies and explains the qualitative characteristics of useful accounting information.

C2-5   Cost and Expense Recognition

AICPA Adapted An accountant must be familiar with the concepts involved in determining earnings of a company. The amount of earnings reported for a company is dependent on the proper recognition, in general, of revenue and expense for a given time period. In some situations costs are recognized as expenses at the time of product sale; in other situations guidelines have been developed for recognizing costs as expenses or losses by other criteria.

Required

1. Explain the rationale for recognizing costs as expenses at the time of product sale.
2. What is the rationale underlying the appropriateness of treating costs as expenses of a period instead of assigning the costs to an asset? Explain.
3. Some expenses are assigned to specific accounting periods on the basis of systematic and rational allocation of asset cost. Explain the underlying rationale for recognizing expenses on this basis.

C2-6   Characteristics of Useful Information

CMA Adapted Financial accounting and reporting provide information that is used in decision making regarding the allocation of resources. In **Statement of Financial Accounting Concepts No. 1,** "Objectives of Financial Reporting by Business Enterprises," the FASB defined the following basic objectives of financial reporting:

Financial reporting should provide understandable information to present and potential users:
- That is useful in making rational decisions.
- That facilitates assessing the amounts, timing, and uncertainty related to the company's cash flows.
- About the company's economic resources, its claims to those resources, and the changes in its resources and obligations occurring from earnings and other operating activities.

The qualitative characteristics of useful accounting information were identified in the FASB's **Statement of Financial Accounting Concepts No. 2,** "Qualitative Characteristics of Accounting Information." These characteristics distinguish better information (more useful) from inferior information (less useful).

Required

1. For the primary quality relevance,
   a. define relevance
   b. explain the meaning and importance of each of the three ingredients of relevance
2. For the primary quality reliability,
   a. define reliability
   b. explain the meaning and importance of each of the three ingredients of reliability
3. Explain the concepts of
   a. comparability
   b. consistency
   c. materiality

C2-7   Objectives, Users, and Stewardship

CMA Adapted   The owners of CSC Inc., a privately held company, are considering a public offering of the company's common stock as a means of acquiring additional funds. Prior to making a decision about a public offering, the owners had a lengthy conversation with John Duncan, CSC's chief financial officer. Duncan informed the owners of the reporting requirements of the Securities and Exchange Commission, including the necessity for audited financial statements. At the request of the owners, Duncan also discussed the objectives of financial reporting, the sophistication of users of financial information, and the stewardship responsibilities of management, all of which are addressed in **Statement of Financial Accounting Concepts No. 1,** "Objectives of Financial Reporting by Business Enterprises."

Required

1. Discuss the primary objectives of financial reporting.
2. Describe the level of sophistication that can be expected of the users of financial information.
3. Explain the stewardship responsibilities of management.

C2-8   Segment Reporting

The FASB requires that a company organized in different "operating segments" disclose the revenues, profits, and assets of each of its major operating segments.

Required

Prepare a short memo that briefly explains what types of useful information for investment decision making is provided by requiring these disclosures.

CREATIVE AND CRITICAL THINKING

C2-9   Relevance versus Reliability

You are listening to two accounting majors, both of whom are seniors. They are debating the merits of having relevant versus reliable accounting information for external decision making. One student states: "In my decision making, if given a choice between relevant and reliable accounting information, I would prefer to have relevant information." The other student replies: "Nonsense! If you cannot rely on the information, then of what use is it?"

Required

Based on your knowledge of the FASB's conceptual framework, define the qualitative characteristics of relevance and reliability. Include definitions of the ingredients of each. Which do you think is more important?

C2-10 Inconsistent Statements on Accounting Principles

AICPA Adapted   The following two statements have been taken directly or with some modification from the accounting literature. Each of them is either taken out of context, involves circular reasoning, and/or contains one or more fallacies, half-truths, erroneous comments, conclusions, or inconsistencies (internally or with generally accepted principles or practices).

Statement 1 Accounting is a service activity. Its function is to provide quantitative financial information that is intended to be useful in making economic decisions about and for economic entities. Thus the accounting function might be viewed primarily as being a tool or device for providing quantitative financial information to management to facilitate decision making.

Statement 2 Financial statements that were developed in accordance with generally accepted accounting principles, which apply the conservatism convention, can be free from bias (or can give a presentation that is fair with respect to continuing and prospective stockholders as well as to retiring stockholders).

Required

Evaluate each of the preceding numbered statements as follows:

1. List the fallacies, half-truths, circular reasoning, erroneous comments or conclusions, and/or inconsistencies.
2. Explain by what authority and/or on what basis each item listed in (1) can be considered to be fallacious, circular, inconsistent, a half-truth, or an erroneous comment or conclusion. If the statement or a portion of it is merely out of context, indicate the context(s) in which the statement would be correct.

C2-11 Accounting Entity

AICPA Adapted   The concept of the accounting entity often is considered to be the most fundamental of accounting concepts, one that pervades all of accounting.

Required

1. a. What is an accounting entity? Explain.
    b. Explain why the accounting entity concept is so fundamental that it pervades all of accounting.
2. For each of the following indicate whether the accounting concept of entity is applicable; discuss and give illustrations.
    a. A unit created by or under law
    b. The product-line operating segment of an enterprise
    c. A combination of legal units and/or product-line operating segments
    d. All of the activities of an owner or a group of owners
    e. An industry
    f. The economy of the United States

C2-12 Timing of Revenue Recognition

AICPA Adapted Revenue usually is recognized at the point of sale. Under special circumstances, however, bases other than the point of sale are used for the timing of revenue recognition.

Required

1. Why is the point of sale usually used as the basis for the timing of revenue recognition?
2. Disregarding the special circumstances when bases other than the point of sale are used, discuss the merits of each of the following objections to the sales basis of revenue recognition:
    a. It is too conservative because revenue is earned throughout the entire process of production.
    b. It is not conservative enough because accounts receivable do not represent disposable funds; sales returns and allowances may be made; and collection and bad debt expenses may be incurred in a later period.
3. Revenue may also be recognized (a) during production and (b) when cash is received. For each of these two bases of timing revenue recognition, give an example of the circumstances in which it is properly used and discuss the accounting merits of its use in lieu of the sales basis.

C2-13 Accruals and Deferrals

AICPA Adapted Generally accepted accounting principles require the use of accruals and deferrals in the determination of income.

Required

1. How does accrual accounting affect the determination of income? Include in your discussion what constitutes an accrual and a deferral, and give appropriate examples of each.
2. Contrast accrual accounting with cash accounting.

C2-14 Revenue Recognition

The following are brief descriptions of several companies in different lines of business.
A. Company A is a construction company. It has recently signed a contract to build a highway over a three-year period. A down payment was collected; the remaining collections will occur periodically over the construction period based upon the degree of completion.
B. Company B is a retailer. It makes sales on a daily basis for cash and on credit cards.
C. Company C is a health spa. It has recently signed contracts with numerous individuals to use its facilities over a two-year period. The contract price was collected in advance.
D. Company D is a land development company. It has recently begun developing a "retirement community" and has sold lots to senior citizens. The sales contract requires a small down payment and periodic payments until completion of the roads and a clubhouse, after which the remainder of the purchase price is due. Prior to this point, a purchaser may cancel the contract and receive a refund of all payments.

Required

Describe when revenue should be recognized by each company. If revenue should not be recognized at the time of sale, indicate what method should be used to recognize the revenue. Justify your decision.

C2-15 Violations of Assumptions and Principles

The following are accounting procedures and practices used by several companies.
A. As soon as it purchases inventory, Sokolich Company records the purchase price as cost of goods sold to simplify its accounting procedures.
B. At the end of each year Sloan Company records and reports its economic resources based on appraisal values.
C. Ebert Company prepares financial statements only every two years to reduce its costs of preparing the statements.
D. Guthrie Company sells on credit and records revenue at that time, even though it knows that collection is highly uncertain and very significant efforts have to be made to collect the accounts.
E. Because of inflation, Cross Company adjusts its financial statements each year to show the current purchasing power for all items.
F. David Thomas combines his personal transactions and business transactions when he prepares his company's financial statements so that he can tell how well he is doing on an "overall" basis.
G. At the end of each year Vann Company reports its economic resources on a liquidation basis even though it is likely to operate in the future.

Required

Identify what accounting assumption or principle each procedure or practice violates, and indicate what should be done to rectify the violation.

C2-16 Conceptual Framework

CMA Adapted The Financial Accounting Standards Board has developed a conceptual framework for financial accounting and reporting. The FASB has issued **7 Statements of Financial Accounting Concepts**. These statements set forth objectives and fundamentals that will be the basis for developing financial accounting and reporting standards. The objectives identify the goals and purposes of financial reporting. The fundamentals are the underlying concepts of financial accounting concepts that guide the selection of transactions, events, and circumstances to be accounted for; their recognition and measurement; and the means of summarizing and communicating them to interested parties.

The purpose of **Statement of Financial Accounting Concepts No. 2,** "Qualitative Characteristics of Accounting Information," is to examine the characteristics that make accounting information useful. The characteristics or qualities of information discussed in *Concepts No. 2* are the ingredients that make information useful and are the qualities to be sought when accounting choices are made.

Required

1. Identify and discuss the benefits which can be expected to be derived from the FASB's conceptual framework study.
2. What is the most important quality for accounting information as identified in **Statement of Financial Accounting Concepts No. 2**? Explain why it is the most important.
3. **Statement of Financial Accounting Concepts No. 2** describes a number of key characteristics or qualities for

accounting information. Briefly discuss the importance of understandability, relevance, and reliability for financial reporting purposes.

C2-17 Ethics and Income Reporting

You have been hired as an "accounting consultant" by Watson Company to evaluate its financial reporting policies. Watson is a small corporation with a few stockholders owning stock that is not publicly traded. In a discussion with you, Chris Watson, the company president, says "For the Watson Company's annual income statement, it is our policy to always record and report revenues when we collect the cash and to record and report expenses when we pay the cash. I like this approach and I think our stockholders and creditors do too. This policy results in income that is reliable and conservative, which is the way accounting should be. Besides, it is easy to keep track of our income. All I need are the receipts and payments recorded in the company's checkbook."

Required

From financial reporting and ethical perspectives, how would you reply to Chris?

Review of a Company's Accounting System

OBJECTIVES

After reading this chapter, you will be able to:

1 Understand the components of an accounting system.

2 Know the major steps in the accounting cycle.

3 Prepare journal entries in the general journal.

4 Post to the general ledger and prepare a trial balance.

5 Prepare adjusting entries.

6 Prepare financial statements.

7 Prepare closing entries.

8 Complete a worksheet (spreadsheet).

9 Prepare reversing entries.

10 Use subsidiary ledgers.

11 Understand special journals.

12 Convert cash-basis financial statements to accrual-basis (Appendix).

Houston, We Have a Problem!

Maintaining an accounting information system is essential to ensuring that economic transactions and financial information are properly entered into the accounting records and that financial reports are prepared in an accurate and timely fashion. The consequences of a dysfunctional accounting system can lead to widespread organizational problems. For example, at **NASA**, problems with the implementation of an enterprise-wide accounting system were blamed for more than $565 billion of inadequately documented year-end adjustments. A 2003 Government Accounting Office (GAO) report indicated that the existing accounting system impaired NASA's ability to collect, maintain, and report the full costs of its projects and programs. Further, the GAO noted that NASA's accounting system could not provide adequate cost data for planning purposes nor did it enable effective monitoring of work performed. Instances such as this illustrate the critical need of a well-functioning accounting system as an ingredient to any successful business endeavor.

In addition to organizational problems caused by sloppy bookkeeping, well-known cases such as **Enron**, **WorldCom**, and **HealthSouth** have shown how inadequate controls over accounting systems can result in massive financial frauds. To address these concerns, Section 404 of the **Sarbanes-Oxley Act** requires management to take responsibility for establishing and maintaining adequate internal controls over financial reporting

as well as providing an assessment of the effectiveness of the internal controls. The existence of effective internal controls over financial reporting, coupled with independent verification of these controls, should reduce the probability of accounting irregularities occurring while improving transparency of the financial reporting process. A 2004 survey by Financial Executives International (FEI) estimates that first-year compliance costs with Section 404 will average $4.6 million and 35,000 hours of internal manpower for each of the largest U.S. companies. While the costs and benefits of the internal control reporting responsibilities are controversial, one goal of these new regulations is to ensure that each company's accounting system produces relevant and reliable financial reports.

FOR FURTHER INVESTIGATION

For a discussion of the effects of Sarbanes-Oxley Act on the accounting profession, consult the Business & Company Resource Center (BCRC):

- Revenge of the Bean Counters: No longer frail in the face of fraud, accounting firms are thriving on new laws that give them real clout. Daren Fonda, *Time*, 0040-781X, March 29, 2004, v163, i13, p38.

A primary objective of financial reporting is to provide information that is useful to present and potential investors, and to creditors and other users in making rational investment, credit, and similar decisions.[1] A company provides this information in its financial statements and the accompanying notes. These statements are the result of the company's financial accounting process, which we discuss throughout this book. To understand financial accounting, you need to be familiar with the accounting system that a company uses to accumulate the information in its financial statements. This system is the topic of this chapter.

THE ACCOUNTING SYSTEM

A major purpose of a company's accounting system is to provide useful information to both external users and to the company's managers for making operating decisions. Many transactions result in important financial and managerial accounting information. **An accounting system is the means by which a company records and stores the financial and managerial information from its transactions so that it can retrieve and report the information in an accounting statement.** All companies have accounting systems, ranging from the very simple, such as a checkbook, to the very complex, involving the use of networked computers.

1 Understand the components of an accounting system.

In this chapter we present the basics of a *financial* accounting system that a company can use in either a manual or a computer accounting process. For convenience, our discussion is primarily in terms of a manual system. The components of an accounting system include (1) the framework for operation of the system, (2) the input source documents, (3) the records used to store accounting information, and (4) the output reports. We discuss each of these components in later sections.

Accounting Equation

The steps in a company's accounting system include:

- identifying the events occurring within its economic environment that are financial transactions,
- gathering the documents related to these transactions,
- analyzing the documents to determine the relevant financial information to be recorded,
- recording the financial information, and
- storing this information for future retrieval and use.

A basic accounting model provides a framework for the accounting system and is the basis for recording transactions. This model for a corporation, called the **residual equity theory** model, is usually expressed in an equation as follows:

Assets = Liabilities + Stockholders' Equity

where **assets** are the corporation's economic resources, **liabilities** are its obligations owed to creditors, and **stockholders' equity** is the owners' residual interest in its assets. This equation must remain in balance at all times because each side presents a different "picture" of the same information. That is, the left side summarizes the corporation's economic resources while the right side summarizes the sources of (or claims to) the economic resources. Other equations related to information wanted by external users evolve from this basic equation. We show these interrelated equations in Exhibit 3-1.

---

1. "Objectives of Financial Reporting by Business Enterprises," *FASB Statement of Financial Accounting Concepts No. 1* (Stamford, Conn.: FASB, 1978), par. 34.

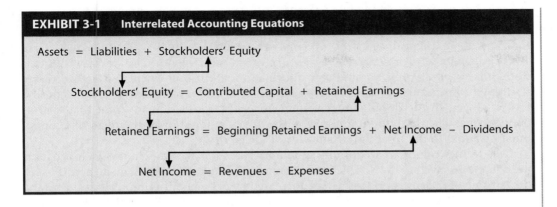

EXHIBIT 3-1   Interrelated Accounting Equations

Assets = Liabilities + Stockholders' Equity

Stockholders' Equity = Contributed Capital + Retained Earnings

Retained Earnings = Beginning Retained Earnings + Net Income – Dividends

Net Income = Revenues – Expenses

Contributed capital includes the amounts of stockholder investments resulting from the sale of shares of stock by the corporation, while **retained earnings** is the lifetime amount of net income reinvested in the corporation and not distributed to stockholders.[2] **Dividends** (which are *not* expenses) are the amounts distributed to stockholders as a return on their investment. **Revenues** are charges to customers for goods or services provided and **expenses** are the costs incurred by the corporation to provide the goods or services.[3]

Transactions, Events, and Supporting Documents

For financial accounting purposes, a change in a company's economic resources (assets), obligations (liabilities), or residual interest (stockholders' equity) may be caused by a transaction or an event. A **transaction** involves the transfer of something valuable between the company and another party. An **event** is a "happening" that affects the company. The event may be *internal*, such as using equipment in operations, or *external*, such as a decline in the value of an asset. The company records the transactions and events affecting its economic resources and obligations in its accounting system. The company uses business documents, or **source documents**, relating to these transactions and events as initial information for the recording process. These documents (such as sales invoices, checks, and freight bills) normally contain information about the monetary amount to be recorded, the parties involved, the terms of the transactions, and other relevant information. After the company records a transaction or event, it stores the supporting source documents to verify its accounting records.

Accounts

Within the accounting system, **a company uses accounts to store the recorded monetary information from its transactions and events.** It keeps a separate account for each asset, liability, revenue, expense, and other stockholders' equity item. Examples of these accounts include Cash, Accounts Receivable (amounts due from customers), Buildings, Accounts Payable (amounts owed to suppliers), Mortgage Payable, Sales Revenue, Cost of Goods Sold, Salaries Expense, Capital Stock, Retained Earnings, and Dividends Distributed. The company assigns each account a number in its **chart of accounts,** a numbering system designed to organize its accounts efficiently and to minimize errors in the recording process.

---

2. A company may also have accumulated other comprehensive income which we discuss in Chapters 4 and 5.
3. In this chapter, for simplicity, we include *gains* (those revenues from other than the sale of goods or services) in revenues and we include *losses* (those costs incurred that provide no revenues) in expenses. Throughout the book, we discuss and classify gains and losses separately from revenues and expenses.

An account can be in several physical forms. It might be a location on a computer disk or a standardized business form in a manual system. A single logical format is used for all accounts. The format for the accounts in a manual system is called a *T-account*. Each T-account has a left (or *debit*) and a right (or *credit*) side for storing monetary information. Since each account accumulates information about both increases and decreases resulting from various transactions or events, there is a "double-entry" rule for recording these changes. **In the double-entry system, for each transaction or event that a company records, the total dollar amount of the debits entered in all the related accounts must be equal to the total dollar amount of the credits.**

The framework of an accounting system includes the accounts in the basic accounting equation as well as the double-entry system. In an accounting system, all accounts on the left side of the equation (assets) are increased by debits (entries on the left side of the accounts) and decreased by credits, while accounts on the right side of the equation (liabilities and stockholders' equity) are increased by credits (entries on the right side of the accounts) and decreased by debits. The left side of Exhibit 3-2 shows this relationship.

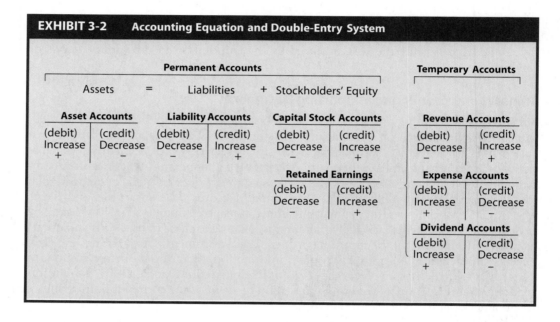

EXHIBIT 3-2   Accounting Equation and Double-Entry System

For example, suppose that stockholders invest $20,000 in a corporation by purchasing 2,000 shares of its no-par stock at $10 per share. The corporation records this transaction as a debit (increase) of $20,000 to an asset account, Cash, and as a $20,000 credit (increase) to a contributed capital account in stockholders' equity, Capital Stock. Note that the accounting equation remains in balance (both sides increase by $20,000) and that the total debits equal the total credits.

Assets	=	Liabilities	+	Stockholders' Equity
Cash				**Capital Stock**
(debit)				(credit)
+				+
20,000				20,000

Accounts are classified as permanent (or real) accounts and temporary (or nominal) accounts. The **permanent accounts** are the asset, liability, and stockholders' equity accounts whose balances at the *end* of the accounting period are carried forward into the next accounting period. The accounts on the far right of Exhibit 3-2, namely the revenue, expense, and dividend accounts, are **temporary accounts**. They are "temporarily" used to determine the changes in retained earnings that occur *during* an accounting period, and their account balances are *not* carried forward into the next period. Exhibit 3-2 also shows the rules for recording transactions in temporary accounts. Because an increase in revenues causes an increase in retained earnings, the rules for recording transactions in revenue accounts are the same as those for retained earnings. However, because an increase in temporary accounts such as expenses and dividends causes a decrease in retained earnings, the rules for recording transactions in these accounts are the *opposite* of those for retained earnings.[4] For instance, since the payment of dividends reduces retained earnings, an increase in a Dividend account is recorded as a debit.

Sometimes a company will use a **contra** (or negative) account to show a reduction in a related account. The rules for increasing or decreasing a contra account are also exactly the *opposite* of those for the related account. A contra account may be related to a permanent account or to a temporary account. For instance, a company uses an Accumulated Depreciation account to accumulate the depreciation recorded for Buildings. We illustrate contra accounts in a later section.

The balance of an account on a particular date is the difference between the total debits and credits recorded in that account. A company uses these balances in the preparation of its financial statements.

Financial Statements

A company's financial statements are summary reports from its accounting system. These statements are based on the interrelated equations presented earlier. As we introduced in Chapter 2, the major financial statements of a company include (1) the income statement, (2) the balance sheet (alternatively called the statement of financial position), and (3) the statement of cash flows.[5] A company prepares its financial statements at the end of each fiscal year, called the **accounting period.** The set of financial statements and accompanying supporting schedules and notes, along with other information distributed to the various external users, is called the company's **annual report**. A company often prepares financial statements for a shorter time period, such as three months. These are called **interim** (or quarterly) statements.

The income statement summarizes the results of a company's income-producing activities for the accounting period. In the income statement, the company's net income is determined by subtracting the total expenses from the total revenues. A supporting schedule (statement) is usually prepared to tie the income statement to the balance sheet. **The statement of retained earnings summarizes the amount of a company's net income retained in the business.** This procedure involves adding the net income for the period to the balance in the retained earnings account at the beginning of the period, and subtracting the dividends distributed to stockholders.

The balance sheet summarizes the amounts of a company's assets, liabilities, and stockholders' equity at the end of the accounting period. The stockholders' equity section includes the ending retained earnings balance from the statement of retained earnings. The balance sheet is so named because it is an expansion of the basic accounting equation, which always remains in balance. Because of the "linkage" between the income statement, statement of retained earnings, and balance sheet due to net income and retained earnings, these financial statements are said to be **articulated.** We illustrate these statements later in Examples 3-5, 3-6, and 3-7.

---

4. Since *gains* are similar to revenues and *losses* are similar to expenses, the rules for increasing these accounts are the same as those for revenues and expenses, respectively.

5. Some companies also have a fourth major financial statement for reporting their "comprehensive income." We discuss this topic in Chapters 4 and 5.

The third major statement, **the statement of cash flows, summarizes a company's cash receipts and cash payments during the accounting period.** We do not show it here but briefly discuss it in Chapter 4 and more fully in Chapter 22. The statement of cash flows articulates with the balance sheet because it reconciles the beginning cash balance with the ending cash balance. We also discuss other supporting schedules, such as the schedule of changes in stockholders' equity and the schedule of investing and financing activities not involving cash receipts or cash payments, in Chapters 4 and 22.

SECURE YOUR KNOWLEDGE 3-1

- The framework of the financial accounting system is based on an equality between the corporation's resources (assets) and the claims on those resources (liabilities and stockholders' equity).
- The inputs to this accounting system are source documents that contain information about transactions (internal or external) that affect a corporation's economic resources or obligations.
- The monetary information from transactions is recorded and stored in accounts so that each transaction has a dual effect on the accounting system (debits equal credits).
- The output of a financial accounting system is the financial statements: the income statement, the statement of retained earnings, the balance sheet, and the statement of cash flows.

THE ACCOUNTING CYCLE

2 Know the major steps in the accounting cycle.

A company completes a series of steps during each accounting period to record, store, and report the accounting information contained in its transactions. These steps are referred to as the **accounting cycle.** The *major* steps include:

1. Record the daily transactions in a journal
2. Post the journal entries to the accounts in the ledger
3. Prepare and post adjusting entries
4. Prepare the financial statements
5. Prepare and post closing entries for the revenue, expense, and dividend accounts

We explain each of the steps in the accounting cycle in the following sections. We explain the steps in terms of a manual accounting system, but most companies use a computer system based on accounting software. This software follows the same procedures as a manual system. We briefly discuss this software at the end of the chapter.

Before we discuss these steps, on the top of the next page we show a diagram so you can see how accounting information from one transaction "flows through" a company's accounting system. For simplicity, the diagram assumes the company purchases inventory of $100 on credit, but has not yet sold or paid for the inventory by the end of the accounting period. You can see that the accounting cycle starts with the company recording the transaction based on the information in a source document (in this case, an invoice). The information is then stored in the company's accounts until needed. Finally, the cycle ends with reporting the information on one of the company's financial statements (in this case, its balance sheet).

Recording in the General Journal (Step 1)

A company initially records its transactions (and events) in a journal. A company *could* record all its transactions in a single journal, called the **general journal**. We use a general

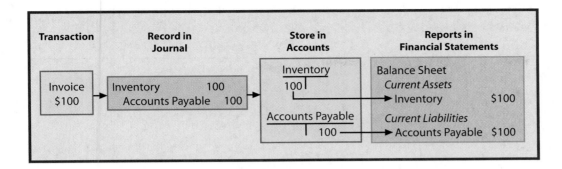

journal in this chapter. However, many companies have a number of different **special journals**, each designed to record a particular type of transaction. We briefly discuss special journals in a later section of this chapter.

The general journal consists of a date column, a column to list the accounts affected by each transaction, a column to list the account numbers (to save space, we do *not* use account numbers in the subsequent comprehensive illustration), a debit column, and a credit column to list the amounts recorded as a debit or credit to each account. Just below each journal entry is a written explanation of the transaction. **The process of recording the transaction in the journal is called journalizing. The resulting entry is referred to as a journal entry.** We show a general journal in Example 3-2 later in this chapter.

There are a number of advantages to using a general journal. First, it helps prevent errors. Because the accounts and debit and credit amounts for each transaction are initially recorded on a single journal page, rather than directly in the numerous accounts, it is easier to verify the equality of the debits and credits. Second, all the transactional information (including the explanation) is recorded in one place, thereby providing a complete "picture" of the transaction. This is especially useful during the auditing process, or if an error is discovered later in the accounting cycle, because the general journal can be reviewed to determine the nature of the transaction. Finally, since the transactions are recorded as they occur, the journal provides a chronological record of the company's financial transactions.

To show the entire accounting cycle, we present a comprehensive example throughout this section. Dapple Corporation incorporates on January 1, 2007 as a wholesaler. It purchases one product from suppliers and resells this inventory to commercial customers. It opens for business on April 1, 2007. The company uses a perpetual inventory system. Under a **perpetual inventory system**, the inventory account is updated each time the company makes a purchase or sale. When the company purchases inventory, it records the increase (debit) directly in its Inventory account. When it makes a sale, it makes *two* journal entries. The first entry records the sales revenue at the retail price. The second entry records an increase (debit) in the Cost of Goods Sold account (a major expense) and a decrease (credit) in the Inventory account for the cost of the inventory.[6] During 2007, the company engages in several transactions. Example 3-1 lists these transactions and an analysis of the accounts and amounts to be debited and credited. This analysis is based on a review of the related source documents. Some of these transactions are partially condensed and overly simplified so that we may show a variety of transactions.

Based on the transactional analysis listed in Example 3-1, the company prepares the general journal entries shown in Example 3-2. Traditionally, for each entry, the accounts to be debited are listed first. The accounts to be credited are listed next and indented. Finally, a brief explanation of the journal entry is made.

Analysis

3 Prepare journal entries in the general journal.

---

6. Some small companies use a periodic inventory system. We briefly discuss the periodic inventory system later in this chapter. We also discuss both the perpetual and periodic inventory systems more fully in Chapter 8.

EXAMPLE 3-1 **2007 Transactions and Analyses (Dapple Corporation)**

Date	Transaction	Analysis
01/01	Various stockholders invest in Dapple by purchasing 2,000 shares of no-par stock at $10 per share.	Asset account Cash increased (debited) by $20,000; stockholders' equity account Capital Stock increased (credited) by $20,000.
01/16	Dapple purchases 2 acres of land as a building site, paying $1,500 an acre.	Asset account Land increased (debited) by $3,000; asset account Cash decreased (credited) by $3,000.
03/30	A building is built and equipment purchased for $15,320 and $2,120, respectively. Dapple pays $10,840 and signs a 12% note (interest and principal to be paid after 2 years) for the $6,600 balance.	Asset accounts Building and Equipment increased (debited) by $15,320 and $2,120, respectively; asset account Cash decreased (credited) by $10,840; liability account Notes Payable increased (credited) by $6,600.
03/30	Dapple purchases a 1-year comprehensive insurance policy for $360.	Asset account Prepaid Insurance increased (debited) by $360; asset account Cash decreased (credited) by $360.
03/31	Dapple purchases $7,300 of inventory on credit from Bark Company.	Asset account Inventory increased (debited) by $7,300; liability account Accounts Payable increased (credited) by $7,300.
04/02	Dapple sells inventory at total cash selling price of $8,000. The cost of the inventory was $5,090.	Asset account Cash increased (debited) by $8,000; revenue account Sales Revenue increased (credited) by $8,000. Expense account Cost of Goods Sold increased (debited) by $5,090; Asset account Inventory decreased (credited) by $5,090.
04/08	Dapple pays $7,300 to Bark for inventory purchase on 03/31.	Liability account Accounts Payable decreased (debited) by $7,300; asset account Cash decreased (credited) by $7,300.
07/15	Dapple makes $3,300 cash purchase of inventory.	Asset account Inventory increased (debited) by $3,300; asset account Cash decreased (credited) by $3,300.
09/01	Dapple sells one acre of land (original cost $1,500) for $1,320. It accepts a 6-month, 15% note from buyer.	Asset account Notes Receivable increased (debited) by $1,320; loss account Loss on Sale of Land increased (debited) by $180; asset account Land decreased (credited) by $1,500.
10/01	Dapple pays the first 6 months' salaries (April through September) totaling $1,800 to employees.	Expense account Salaries Expense increased (debited) by $1,800; asset account Cash decreased (credited) by $1,800.
11/23	Dapple makes sales on credit of $5,000 to Frank Company and $4,000 to Knox Company. The cost of the inventory was $5,400.	Asset account Accounts Receivable increased (debited) by $9,000; revenue account Sales Revenue increased (credited) by $9,000. Expense account Cost of Goods Sold increased (debited) by $5,400; Asset account Inventory decreased (credited) by $5,400.
12/01	Dapple rents part of its building to Fritz Company, receiving 3 months' rent in advance at $150 per month.	Asset account Cash increased (debited) by $450; liability account Unearned Rent increased (credited) by $450.
12/02	Dapple collects $2,000 of accounts receivable from Frank Company.	Asset account Cash increased (debited) by $2,000; asset account Accounts Receivable decreased (credited) by $2,000.
12/27	Dapple purchases $1,900 of inventory on credit from Ajax Company.	Asset account Inventory increased (debited) by $1,900; liability account Accounts Payable increased (credited) by $1,900.
12/28	Dapple pays $428 of miscellaneous operating expenses.	Expense account Other Expenses increased (debited) by $428; asset account Cash decreased (credited) by $428.
12/29	Dapple distributes dividends of $500 ($0.25 per share for 2,000 shares) to stockholders.	Dividends Distributed account increased (debited) by $500; asset account Cash decreased (credited) by $500.

EXAMPLE 3-2   General Journal Entries (Dapple Corporation)

Date	Account Titles and Explanations	Debit	Credit
2007			
Jan. 1	Cash	20,000	
	Capital Stock		20,000
	Issued 2,000 shares of no-par stock at $10 per share.		
16	Land	3,000	
	Cash		3,000
	Purchased 2 acres of land at $1,500 per acre.		
Mar. 30	Building	15,320	
	Equipment	2,120	
	Cash		10,840
	Notes Payable		6,600
	Purchased a building and equipment. The note bears annual interest of 12% and the principal and interest are due on March 30, 2009.		
30	Prepaid Insurance	360	
	Cash		360
	Purchased a 1-year comprehensive insurance policy.		
31	Inventory	7,300	
	Accounts Payable		7,300
	Purchased inventory for resale on credit from Bark Company.		
Apr. 2	Cash	8,000	
	Sales Revenue		8,000
	To record cash sales.		
2	Cost of Goods Sold	5,090	
	Inventory		5,090
	To record cost of sales.		
8	Accounts Payable	7,300	
	Cash		7,300
	Paid Bark Company for purchases made on credit on March 31.		
July 15	Inventory	3,300	
	Cash		3,300
	Purchased inventory for resale.		
Sept. 1	Notes Receivable	1,320	
	Loss	180	
	Land		1,500
	Sold 1 acre of land at less than its cost, incurring a loss. Buyer issued a note due in 6 months and bearing 15% annual interest.		
Oct. 1	Salaries Expense	1,800	
	Cash		1,800
	Paid 6 months' of employees' salaries.		
Nov. 23	Accounts Receivable	9,000	
	Sales Revenue		9,000
	Made sales on credit to the Frank Company ($5,000) and Knox Company ($4,000).		
23	Cost of Goods Sold	5,400	
	Inventory		5,400
	To record cost of sales.		

(continued)

Posting to the Ledger (Step 2)

A general ledger is the entire group of accounts for a company. It might take several forms, such as a storage location on a computer disk, or in the case of our manual system, a loose-leaf binder with a page for each T-account. After a company journalizes its transactions and events in a general journal, it updates each account in the general ledger. This is done through the process of **posting.** Posting involves transferring the date and debit and credit amounts from the journal entries in the general journal to the debit and credit

4 Post to the general ledger and prepare a trial balance.

EXAMPLE 3-2 (Continued)

Date	Account Titles and Explanations	Debit	Credit
Dec. 1	Cash	450	
	Unearned Rent		450
	Received 3 months' rent in advance at $150 per month. Company owes use of portion of building to Fritz Company for the 3-month period.		
2	Cash	2000	
	Accounts Receivable		2000
	Frank Company paid a portion of its accounts receivable.		
27	Inventory	1,900	
	Accounts Payable		1,900
	Purchased inventory on credit from Ajax Company.		
28	Other Expenses	428	
	Cash		428
	Paid miscellaneous operating expenses.		
29	Dividends Distributed	500	
	Cash		500
	Distributed dividends of $0.25 per share to stockholders.		

sides of the accounts in the general ledger. Thus, **after posting, the general ledger accounts contain the same information as in the general journal, just in a different format.** Example 3-3 shows *all* the accounts in the general ledger of the Dapple Corporation. To conserve space, these accounts include the postings not only for the journal entries shown in Example 3-2, but also for the *adjusting* entries (*Adj* is shown in the account) and the *closing* entries (*Cl*) discussed later in Examples 3-4 and 3-9.[7]

Trial Balance

After a company prepares and posts its journal entries for the accounting period, it determines the balance in each account. Then a trial balance is often prepared. **A trial balance is a working paper that lists all the company's general ledger accounts and their account balances.** These account balances are listed in either the debit or the credit column. The trial balance is used to verify that the total of the debit balances is equal to the total of the credit balances. This working paper is not shown here but is included on the worksheet in Example 3-10.

If a trial balance does not balance, there is an error. To find the error, add the debit and credit columns of the trial balance again. If the column totals do not agree, check the amounts in the debit and credit columns to be sure that a debit or credit account balance was not mistakenly listed in the wrong column. If the error is still not found, compute the difference in the column totals and divide by 9. When the difference is evenly divisible by 9, there is a good chance that a *transposition* or a *slide* has occurred. A transposition occurs when two digits in a number are mistakenly reversed. For instance, if the $1,500 Land balance is listed as $5,100 on the trial balance in Example 3-10, the debit column would total $49,550 instead of $45,950. The difference, $3,600, is evenly divisible by 9. A slide occurs when the digits are listed in the correct order but are mistakenly moved one decimal place to the left or right. For instance, in Example 3-10 if the $1,900 Accounts Payable balance is listed as $190, the credit column would total $44,240 instead of $45,950. The $1,710 difference is evenly divisible by 9.

---

7. A company may also use subsidiary ledgers, such as an accounts receivable subsidiary ledger and an accounts payable subsidiary ledger. We discuss subsidiary ledgers later in this chapter.

EXAMPLE 3-3 General Ledger (Dapple Corporation)

Cash

01/01	20,000	01/16	3,000
04/02	8,000	03/30	10,840
12/01	450	03/30	360
12/02	2,000	04/08	7,300
		07/15	3,300
		10/01	1,800
		12/28	428
		12/29	500
Balance	2,922		

Accounts Receivable

11/23	9,000	12/02	2,000
Balance	7,000		

Allowance for Doubtful Accounts

	12/31 Adj	170

Notes Receivable

09/01	1,320

Interest Receivable

12/31 Adj	66

Inventory

03/31	7,300	04/02	5,090
07/15	3,300	11/23	5,400
12/27	1,900		
Balance	2,010		

Prepaid Insurance

03/30	360	12/31 Adj	270
Balance	90		

Land

01/16	3,000	09/01	1,500
Balance	1,500		

Building

03/30	15,320

Accumulated Depreciation: Building

	12/31 Adj	264

Equipment

03/30	2,120

Accumulated Depreciation: Equipment

	12/31 Adj	120

Accounts Payable

04/08	7,300	03/31	7,300
		12/27	1,900
		Balance	1,900

Notes Payable

	03/30	6,600

Salaries Payable

	12/31 Adj	900

Interest Payable

	12/31 Adj	594

Income Taxes Payable

	12/31 Adj	600

Unearned Rent

12/31 Adj	150	12/01	450
		Balance	300

Capital Stock

	01/01	20,000

Retained Earnings

12/31 Cl	500	12/31 Cl	1,400
		Balance	900

Dividends Distributed

12/29	500	12/31 Cl	500

Sales Revenue

12/31 Cl	17,000	04/02	8,000
		11/23	9,000

Interest Revenue

12/31 Cl	66	12/31 Adj	66

Rent Revenue

12/31 Cl	150	12/31 Adj	150

Cost of Goods Sold

04/02	5,090	12/31 Cl	10,490
10/23	5,400		

Salaries Expense

10/01	1,800	12/31 Cl	2,700
12/31 Adj	900		

Other Expenses

12/28	428	12/31 Cl	428

Loss on Sale of Land

09/01	180	12/31 Cl	180

Depreciation Expense: Building

12/31 Adj	264	12/31 Cl	264

Depreciation Expense: Equipment

12/31 Adj	120	12/31 Cl	120

Bad Debts Expense

12/31 Adj	170	12/31 Cl	170

Insurance Expense

12/31 Adj	270	12/31 Cl	270

Interest Expense

12/31 Adj	594	12/31 Cl	594

Income Tax Expense

12/31 Adj	600	12/31 Cl	600

Income Summary

12/31 Cl	15,816	12/31 Cl	17,216
12/31 Cl	1,400		

If a transposition or slide has occurred, the error may have occurred when the account balances were transferred from the accounts to the trial balance or when the account balances were computed initially. To find the error, first compare the account balances listed on the trial balance with the account balances listed in the ledger. Then recompute the ledger account balances, and if no error is found, double-check the postings. Finally, review the journal entries for accuracy.

If the trial balance is in balance, it is likely that (1) equal debit entries and credit entries were recorded for each transaction; (2) the debit and credit entries are posted to the accounts; and (3) the account balances are correctly computed. The equality of the debit and credit totals, however, does not necessarily mean that the information in the accounting system is error-free. A trial balance does not pick up several types of errors. First, an entire transaction may not have been journalized. Second, an entire transaction may not have been posted to the accounts. Third, equal debits and credits, but of the wrong amount, may have been recorded for a transaction. Fourth, a transaction may have been journalized to a wrong account. Finally, a journal entry may have been posted to the wrong account.

Preparation of Adjusting Entries (Step 3)

5 Prepare adjusting entries.

Most companies use generally accepted accounting principles which require the accrual method of accounting. Under *accrual accounting,* a company records revenues in the accounting period in which they are earned and realized (or realizable). The company also records (matches) expenses in the accounting period in which they are incurred, regardless of the inflow or outflow of cash. In many instances, not all accounts are up to date at the end of the accounting period. A company must *adjust* certain amounts so that all its revenues and expenses are recorded and its balance sheet accounts have correct ending balances. **Adjusting entries are journal entries made at the end of the accounting period so that a company's financial statements include the correct amounts for the current period.**

An adjusting entry ordinarily affects both a permanent (balance sheet) and a temporary (income statement) account. Adjusting entries may be classified into three categories. These categories and the types of balance sheet accounts involved in the adjusting entries are:

1. Apportionment of prepaid and deferred items
   a. Prepaid expenses
   b. Deferred revenues
2. Recording of accrued items
   a. Accrued expenses
   b. Accrued revenues
3. Recording estimated items

Prepaid Expenses

A prepaid expense (sometimes called a prepaid asset) is a good or service purchased by a company for its operations but not fully used up by the end of the accounting period. When the company initially purchases the good or service, it records the *cost* as an asset (prepaid expense). At the end of the accounting period, the company has used some of these goods or services to generate revenues. The costs are systematically *matched,* as expenses, against the current revenues, while the unused cost remains as an asset on the balance sheet. Examples of prepaid expenses include prepaid rent, office supplies, and prepaid insurance. Below we show the effect of a prepaid expense adjusting entry on a company's accounts. Then we explain Dapple Corporation's related adjusting entry.

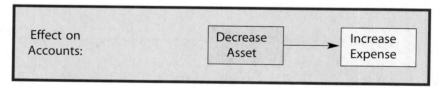

In the Dapple Corporation example, it purchased a one-year comprehensive insurance policy on March 30, 2007. It recorded an asset, Prepaid Insurance, for $360. At the end of the year, nine months of insurance coverage has expired while three months of coverage remains in force. The cost is apportioned as an expense on a straight-line basis (an equal amount each month). Insurance Expense is increased (debited) by $270 ($30 per month for nine months) and Prepaid Insurance decreased (credited) by $270. The result is a $270 increase in expenses and a $90 remaining balance in the asset Prepaid Insurance. Example 3-4 shows this adjusting entry which is posted to the ledger accounts shown in Example 3-3. Since the December 31 date of the adjusting entries is the same as

EXAMPLE 3-4 Adjusting Entries for 2007 (Dapple Corporation)

Date	Account Titles and Explanations	Debit	Credit
	Adjusting Entries		
Dec. 31	Insurance Expense	270	
	Prepaid Insurance		270
	To record expiration of 9 months of insurance coverage purchased on March 30.		
31	Unearned Rent	150	
	Rent Revenue		150
	To record earning of 1 month of rent revenue from receipt collected in advance on December 1.		
31	Salaries Expense	900	
	Salaries Payable		900
	To record 3 months' salaries earned by employees but not yet paid.		
31	Interest Expense	594	
	Interest Payable		594
	To record interest accumulated on the note payable issued on March 30 and due March 30, 2009.		
31	Interest Receivable	66	
	Interest Revenue		66
	To record interest accumulated on the note receivable accepted on September 1.		
31	Depreciation Expense: Building	264	
	Accumulated Depreciation: Building		264
	To record 9 months' depreciation on building acquired March 30.		
31	Depreciation Expense: Equipment	120	
	Accumulated Depreciation: Equipment		120
	To record 9 months' depreciation on equipment acquired March 30.		
31	Bad Debts Expense	170	
	Allowance for Doubtful Accounts		170
	To record estimated uncollectible accounts receivable.		
31	Income Tax Expense	600	
	Income Taxes Payable		600
	To record income taxes for the period.		

the December 31 date for the closing entries (which we discuss in Example 3-9), each adjusting entry date is followed by the abbreviation *Adj* to clarify the postings.

Deferred Revenues

Deferred (or unearned) revenue is payment received by a company in advance for the future sale of inventory or performance of services. Initially the company usually records a liability because it has an obligation to provide the goods or services. When the company has provided the goods or services to the customer, it eliminates the liability and records the revenue in an adjusting entry. Although the adjusting entry may be made at the time the goods or services are provided, it may also be made at the end of the accounting period. Below we show the effect of a deferred revenue adjusting entry on a company's accounts. Then we explain Dapple Corporation's related adjusting entry.

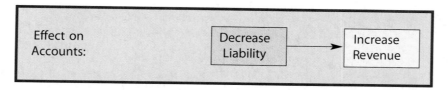

On December 1, Dapple Corporation received $450 for three months' rent in advance. It recorded the receipt as a liability, Unearned Rent. On December 31 it must make an adjusting entry because it has now earned one month of rent. The adjusting entry is a debit (decrease) of $150 to Unearned Rent and a credit (increase) of $150 to Rent Revenue. The result is a $150 increase in revenues and a $300 remaining balance in the liability Unearned Rent. Example 3-4 shows this adjusting entry.

A company might *initially* record the entire prepayment of a cost as an expense (instead of as an asset) or the entire receipt in advance as a revenue (instead of a liability). In this case the company must still make adjusting entries at the end of the accounting period, but they are different in form and amount. For example, Dapple Corporation *could* have recorded the March 30 payment as a $360 debit to Insurance Expense (instead of Prepaid Insurance) and it *could* have recorded the December 1 receipt of $450 as a credit to Rent Revenue (instead of Unearned Rent). In this case the adjusting entry procedure is to calculate the appropriate ending balances in the permanent accounts and adjust the accounts accordingly. For instance, Prepaid Insurance should have an ending balance of $90. The year-end adjusting entry must *reduce* the expense and *increase* the Prepaid Insurance account by this amount. The adjusting entry is a debit (increase) to Prepaid Insurance for $90 and a credit (decrease) to Insurance Expense for $90. Similarly, Unearned Rent should have an ending balance of $300. The year-end adjusting entry must *reduce* the revenue and *increase* the Unearned Rent account by this amount. The adjusting entry is a debit (decrease) to Rent Revenue for $300 and a credit (increase) to Unearned Rent for $300. The results of these adjusting entries are the *same* balances in the respective accounts as we show in the comprehensive illustration. Be careful to determine how advance payments and receipts were initially recorded before determining the adjusting entry.

Accrued Expenses

An accrued expense is an expense that a company has incurred during the accounting period but has neither paid nor recorded. To match expenses against revenues and to reflect the proper liabilities at the end of the period, a company must make an adjusting entry for each accrued expense. Below we show the effect of an accrued expense adjusting entry on a company's accounts. Then we explain Dapple Corporation's related adjusting entries.

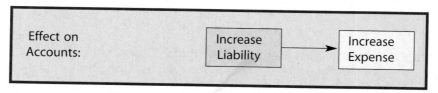

Dapple Corporation has three accrued expenses it has not yet recorded: employees' salaries, interest, and income taxes.

Accrued Salaries   For simplicity, assume the company pays employees' salaries every six months, making the last $1,800 payment on October 1. At the end of December, its employees have earned salaries for three months (October through December) although they have not been paid. The adjusting entry is a debit (increase) to Salaries Expense for $900 and a credit (increase) to Salaries Payable for $900. The result is a $900 increase in expenses and a $900 ending balance in the liability, Salaries Payable. Example 3-4 shows this adjusting entry.

Accrued Interest   On March 30, Dapple Corporation issued a $6,600, 12% note payable due at the end of two years. Although it will not *pay* the principal and interest until 2009,

nine months of interest expense has accumulated and is a liability at the end of 2007. The interest is computed using the equation: Interest = Principal × Rate × Time, where time is expressed as a fraction of a year. The adjusting entry involves a debit (increase) to Interest Expense for $594 ($6,600 × 0.12 × 9/12) and a credit (increase) to Interest Payable for $594, as we show in Example 3-4.

Accrued Income Taxes   Corporations are subject to a federal (and often state) income tax. Although a corporation may not pay its income taxes until the following period, they are an expense and year-end obligation of the period in which the corporation earned the income. The adjusting entry for income taxes is prepared *after* all the other adjusting entries because the amount is computed by multiplying the income tax rate times the current income before income taxes. Based on its current income before income taxes and on the current tax rate,[8] Dapple Corporation calculates that its 2007 income taxes are $600, with the entire amount payable in 2008. The adjusting entry is a debit (increase) to Income Tax Expense for $600 and a credit (increase) to Income Taxes Payable for $600, and is shown as the last item in Example 3-4.

Accrued Revenues   An accrued revenue is a revenue that a company has earned during the accounting period but has neither received nor recorded. The company must make an adjusting entry to increase its assets and revenues at the end of the period. Below we show the effect of an accrued revenue adjusting entry on a company's accounts. Then we explain Dapple Corporation's related adjusting entry.

On September 1, Dapple Corporation accepted a $1,320, 15% note as payment when it sold an acre of land. Although it will not collect the note and interest until 2008, the company has earned four months of interest in 2007. The company records the $66 of interest ($1,320 × 0.15 × 4/12) as a debit (increase) to Interest Receivable and a credit (increase) to Interest Revenue. The result is a $66 increase in revenues and a $66 increase in the asset Interest Receivable. Example 3-4 shows this adjusting entry.

---

8.   As we show in Example 3-6, the Dapple Corporation's income before income taxes is $2,000. Multiplying this amount by an assumed tax rate of 30% yields income taxes of $600.

Estimated Items

Certain other adjusting entries are based on estimated amounts because they relate, at least in part, to expected future events. Adjustments involving (1) the depreciation on assets such as buildings and equipment, and (2) the uncollectibility of some accounts receivable are both based upon estimates. Below we show the effect of an estimated item adjusting entry on a company's accounts. Then we explain Dapple Corporation's related adjusting entries.

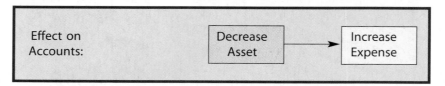

Depreciation Expense When a company acquires an asset such as a machine, sales fixture, or building to use in its operations, the company records the cost as an economic resource (asset). The company expects to use the asset for several periods after which it will dispose of the asset at a value much less than its original cost. The difference between the original cost and an estimate of this later value (alternatively called residual value, salvage value, scrap value, or trade-in value) is the asset's **depreciable cost.** This depreciable cost is allocated as an expense to each accounting period in which the asset is used. This cost allocation process is referred to as **depreciation.** One depreciation method is straight-line depreciation, which allocates a proportionate amount as an expense to each accounting period. Its computation is as follows:

$$\text{Annual Depreciation Expense} = \frac{\text{Cost} - \text{Estimated Residual Value}}{\text{Estimated Service Life}}$$

The company records depreciation at the end of the accounting period in an adjusting entry. The entry increases Depreciation Expense and decreases the remaining depreciable cost of the asset. However, the company does *not* record this decrease directly in the asset account. Instead it *increases* a contra (negative) asset account entitled Accumulated Depreciation. This contra account is subtracted from the asset account on the company's balance sheet. The resulting balance is referred to as the *book* value (or carrying value) of the asset.

Dapple Corporation has two depreciable assets, the building and equipment acquired on March 30, 2007. The company estimates that these assets will have lives of 35 years and 12 years, respectively. The company estimates that the residual value of the building will be $3,000 and the residual value of the equipment will be $200 at the end of these lives. Since it used the building and equipment for only nine months during 2007, the depreciation expense is $264 {[($15,320 − $3,000) ÷ 35] × 9/12} on the building and $120 {[($2,120 − $200) ÷ 12] × 9/12} on the equipment. The adjusting entry for the building is a debit (increase) to Depreciation Expense: Building for $264 and a credit (increase) to the contra-asset Accumulated Depreciation: Building for $264. The adjusting entry for the equipment is a debit to Depreciation Expense: Equipment for $120 and a credit to the contra-asset Accumulated Depreciation: Equipment for $120. The result is an increase in expenses and a *decrease* in the book value that the company reports on its balance sheet for the building and the equipment. Example 3-4 shows these adjusting entries.

Bad Debt Expense Many companies make a large amount of their sales on credit. Regardless of a company's collection efforts, it is likely to have a certain amount of bad debts—customer accounts that will not be collected. Although a company may not know which specific customers will not pay their accounts until a later accounting period, it must match bad debt expense against revenues in the *period of the sale*. Furthermore, the company must reduce its assets so that at the end of the period its accounting records show the amount of accounts receivable that it expects to collect. The adjusting entry to record the increase in expenses and the decrease in assets requires an estimate of future uncollectible accounts. However, since the company does not know in the period of sale which specific customers will default on their accounts, it does not directly reduce Accounts Receivable. Instead it *increases* a contra-asset account, Allowance for Doubtful Accounts. This account is deducted from Accounts Receivable on the company's balance sheet to report the estimated collectible amount.

For example, assume for simplicity that Dapple Corporation estimates its bad debts to be 1% of total sales. Since the balance in the Sales Revenue account totals $17,000, the adjusting entry is a debit (increase) to Bad Debts Expense for $170 and a credit (increase) to the contra-asset Allowance for Doubtful Accounts for $170. The result is an increase in expenses and a *decrease* in the collectible accounts receivable shown on the company's balance sheet. Example 3-4 shows this adjusting entry.

Summary   We show the basic framework for adjusting entries in Exhibit 3-3. This framework will be helpful to you in visualizing the appropriate debit and credit entry for each type of adjusting entry. However, you must be careful to identify the proper accounts to use in each adjusting entry. Note that for an estimated item, under the Accounts Credited column, we show the use of a contra-account because typically a company credits (increases) such an account (e.g., accumulated depreciation) to decrease the book value of the related asset.

EXHIBIT 3-3   Framework for Adjusting Entries

Type of Adjusting Entry	Accounts Debited	Accounts Credited
Prepaid Expense:	Debit (increase) Expense	Credit (decrease) Asset
Deferred Revenue:	Debit (decrease) Liability	Credit (increase) Revenue
Accrued Expense:	Debit (increase) Expense	Credit (increase) Liability
Accrued Revenue:	Debit (increase) Asset	Credit (increase) Revenue
Estimated Item:	Debit (increase) Expense	Credit (decrease) Asset
		[credit (increase) contra account]

LINK TO ETHICAL DILEMMA

As a newly hired accountant at a Fortune 500 company, you were excited when the controller showed confidence in your abilities by delegating to you the responsibility to make many of the routine adjusting entries related to the preparation of the year-end financial statements. The controller was pleased with the diligence with which you completed the task and assured you that he would not hesitate to increase your responsibilities in the financial reporting department. You were on the fast-track to a promotion. However, three months later, as you were preparing the adjusting entries for the next fiscal quarter, you realized that you had overlooked several adjustments that you should have recorded at year-end. While the overlooked adjustments would most likely not be considered material to last year's financial statements, you are certain that your boss would lose confidence in your abilities. Realizing that you can easily fix the mistake by incorporating the overlooked adjustments into the first quarter adjusting entries for this year, what course of action should you take?

Preparation of the Financial Statements (Step 4)

After a company prepares and posts the adjusting entries to the general ledger accounts, it prepares its financial statements. This procedure involves several steps. First, the balance

EXAMPLE 3-5 Adjusted Trial Balance (Dapple Corporation)

Adjusted Trial Balance
December 31, 2007

	Debit	Credit
Cash	$ 2,922	
Accounts receivable	7,000	
Allowance for doubtful accounts		$ 170
Notes receivable	1,320	
Interest receivable	66	
Inventory	2,010	
Prepaid insurance	90	
Land	1,500	
Building	15,320	
Accumulated depreciation: building		264
Equipment	2,120	
Accumulated depreciation: equipment		120
Accounts payable		1,900
Notes payable		6,600
Salaries payable		900
Interest payable		594
Income taxes payable		600
Unearned rent		300
Capital stock		20,000
Retained earnings		0
Dividends distributed	500	
Sales revenue		17,000
Interest revenue		66
Rent revenue		150
Cost of goods sold	10,490	
Salaries expense	2,700	
Other expenses	428	
Loss on sale of land	180	
Depreciation expense: building	264	
Depreciation expense: equipment	120	
Bad debts expense	170	
Insurance expense	270	
Interest expense	594	
Income tax expense	600	
Totals	$48,664	$48,664

of each account in the ledger is recomputed if necessary. Next, an adjusted trial balance is frequently prepared; it is similar to a trial balance. **An adjusted trial balance lists all the accounts and the account balances of a company *after* adjustments (but *before* closing) in either a debit or a credit column.** The adjusted trial balance is used to verify that the total of the debit balances is equal to the total of the credit balances. This working paper also helps in the preparation of the company's financial statements because all the accounts and amounts included in the financial statements are listed on the adjusted trial balance. Example 3-5 shows the Dapple Corporation's adjusted trial balance. Finally, the company prepares its income statement, statement of retained earnings, and balance sheet in sequential order directly from the information in the adjusted trial balance.

Income Statement

6 Prepare financial statements.

Example 3-6 shows Dapple Corporation's income statement for 2007. Sales revenue is listed first. Because the cost of goods sold is directly related to sales, it is shown next. Cost of Goods Sold is deducted to determine the Gross Profit. Operating Expenses (often classified into two groups, Selling Expenses and Administrative Expenses) are deducted next to determine the Income from Operations. The total of the Other Items section (for recurring items that are not directly related to ongoing operations) is deducted to determine the Income Before Income Taxes. Finally the Income Tax Expense is deducted to determine the Net Income of $1,400. The $0.70 Earnings Per Share is computed by dividing the $1,400 net income by the 2,000 shares owned by the stockholders.

Retained Earnings Statement

Example 3-7 shows the retained earnings statement of the Dapple Corporation for 2007. Because 2007 is its first year of operations, the company did not have a beginning retained earnings balance. It did, however, earn net income of $1,400 and distributed dividends of $500, resulting in ending retained earnings (the excess of total earnings over total dividends) of $900.

EXAMPLE 3-6   Income Statement

DAPPLE CORPORATION

Income Statement
For Year Ended December 31, 2007

Sales revenue		$17,000
Cost of goods sold		(10,490)
Gross profit		$ 6,510
Operating expenses		
Salaries expense	$ 2,700	
Other expenses	428	
Depreciation expense: building	264	
Depreciation expense: equipment	120	
Bad debts expense	170	
Insurance expense	270	
Total operating expenses		(3,952)
Income from operations		$ 2,558
Other items		
Loss on sale of land	$ (180)	
Interest revenue	66	
Rent revenue	150	
Interest expense	(594)	(558)
Income before income taxes		$ 2,000
Income tax expense		(600)
Net Income		$ 1,400
Earnings per share (2,000 shares)		$ 0.70

EXAMPLE 3-7   Retained Earnings Statement

DAPPLE CORPORATION

Statement of Retained Earnings
For Year Ended December 31, 2007

Retained earnings, January 1, 2007	$ 0
Add: Net income for 2007	1,400
	$1,400
Less: Dividends for 2007	(500)
Retained earnings, December 31, 2007	$ 900

Balance Sheet

Example 3-8 shows the Dapple Corporation's balance sheet at the end of 2007. It includes three sections: assets, liabilities, and stockholders' equity. The assets are divided into current assets and property and equipment. The *current assets* are cash and those assets that are expected to be converted into cash or consumed within one year or the operating cycle, whichever is longer. Current assets generally include cash, receivables, temporary investments in marketable securities, inventories, and prepaid items such as insurance and office supplies. *Property and equipment* contains the longer-lived operational assets of the company. This section includes both nondepreciable assets and depreciable assets listed at their book values. The liabilities are divided into current liabilities and long-term liabilities. *Current liabilities* are those obligations that will become due within one year or the operating cycle, whichever is longer, and are expected to be paid with current assets or the creation of other current liabilities. *Long-term liabilities* are obligations that do not meet the current liability criteria. Stockholders' equity includes contributed capital (capital stock) and retained earnings. Total assets amount to $31,794, and equal the total of liabilities plus stockholders' equity.

EXAMPLE 3-8   **Balance Sheet**

DAPPLE CORPORATION

Balance Sheet
December 31, 2007

Assets

Current Assets		
Cash		$ 2,922
Accounts receivable	$ 7,000	
Less: Allowance for doubtful accounts	(170)	6,830
Notes receivable (due March 1, 2008)		1,320
Interest receivable		66
Inventory		2,010
Prepaid insurance		90
Total current assets		$13,238
Property and equipment		
Land		$ 1,500
Building	$15,320	
Less: Accumulated depreciation	(264)	15,056
Equipment	$ 2,120	
Less: Accumulated depreciation	(120)	2,000
Total property and equipment		$18,556
Total Assets		$31,794

Liabilities

Current Liabilities	
Accounts payable	$ 1,900
Salaries payable	900
Income taxes payable	600
Unearned rent	300
Total current liabilities	$ 3,700
Long-Term Liablilities	
Notes payable (due March 30, 2009)	$ 6,600
Interest payable (due March 20, 2009)	594
Total long-term liabilities	$ 7,194
Total Liabilities	$10,894

Stockholders' Equity

Contributed Capital		
Capital stock, no par (2,000 shares)	$20,000	
Retained Earnings	900	
Total Stockholders' Equity		$20,900
Total Liabilities and Stockholders' Equity		$31,794

Preparation of Closing Entries (Step 5)

7 Prepare closing entries.

The next step in the accounting process involves preparing and posting closing entries. **Closing entries are journal entries that a company makes at the end of the accounting period (1) to reduce the balance in each temporary account to zero, and (2) to update the retained earnings account.**

A company uses the temporary accounts (namely, all the revenue, expense, and dividend accounts) during each accounting period to accumulate and summarize information for its net income and dividends *for that period.* After the period is over and the company's financial statements are prepared, the balances in these accounts are no longer needed. Furthermore, these accounts must begin the *next* accounting period with a zero balance to summarize the company's net income and dividend information for the next period. Also, the company's permanent stockholders' equity account, Retained Earnings, must be updated for the net income and dividend information contained in the temporary accounts.

The revenue and expense accounts are closed to a temporary closing account called Income Summary. The resulting balance in this account is the company's net income (or loss) for the period. This balance is then transferred to Retained Earnings.

The closing process is straightforward. Each temporary income statement account is debited or credited for the amount that will result in a zero balance in that account. The total of the credits to these accounts is recorded as a debit to the Income Summary account, and the total of the debits is recorded as a credit to Income Summary. A resulting *credit* balance in the Income Summary account is the net income for the period, and is the same amount as that shown on the company's income statement. This credit balance is closed to zero with a debit entry to Income Summary and a credit entry to Retained Earnings for the amount of the net income. If, on the other hand, there is a *debit* balance in the Income Summary account, this means there is a net loss for the period. This debit balance is closed to zero with a debit entry to Retained Earnings and a credit entry to Income Summary for the amount of the net loss. Finally, the Dividends Distributed account is credited for the amount necessary to reduce its balance to zero; the corresponding debit to Retained Earnings reduces it for the amount of the dividends.

Example 3-9 shows the closing entries for the Dapple Corporation which are posted to the ledger accounts shown in Example 3-3. The abbreviation *Cl* is used to identify each December 31 closing entry. The temporary income statement accounts that have a credit balance are closed first. These include all the revenue accounts. The total credit to Income Summary is $17,216.

The temporary income statement accounts that have a debit balance are closed next. These include all the expense accounts. The total debit to Income Summary is $15,816.

EXAMPLE 3-9   Closing Entries for 2007 (Dapple Corporation)

Date	Account Titles and Explanations	Debit	Credit
	Closing Entries		
Dec. 31	Sales Revenue	17,000	
	Interest Revenue	66	
	Rent Revenue	150	
	Income Summary		17,216
	To close the temporary accounts with credit balances.		
31	Income Summary	15,816	
	Cost of Goods Sold		10,490
	Salaries Expense		2,700
	Other Expenses		428
	Loss on Sale of Land		180
	Depreciation Expense: Building		264
	Depreciation Expense: Equipment		120
	Bad Debts Expense		170
	Insurance Expense		270
	Interest Expense		594
	Income Tax Expense		600
	To close the temporary accounts with debit balances.		
31	Income Summary	1,400	
	Retained Earnings		1,400
	To close the income summary balance (net income) to retained earnings.		
31	Retained Earnings	500	
	Dividends Distributed		500
	To close the dividends to retained earnings.		

The Income Summary account now has a credit balance of $1,400 ($17,216 credit less the $15,816 debit). This amount is the net income we computed on the income statement (Example 3-6). It is transferred to Retained Earnings by a debit to Income Summary for $1,400 (which creates a zero balance in this account) and a credit to Retained Earnings for $1,400 (which increases this account for the amount of the net income). Finally, the debit balance in the Dividends Distributed account is reduced to zero by a debit to Retained Earnings for $500 and a credit to Dividends Distributed for $500.

The result of the closing entries is that (1) all of the company's revenue, expense, and dividend accounts are closed (have zero balances) and are ready to accumulate the net income and dividend information for the next accounting period, (2) the ending balance in its Retained Earnings account is increased by $900 because of the excess of net income over dividends, and (3) only the permanent balance sheet accounts are open (have nonzero account balances).

After the closing entries are prepared and posted, many companies will prepare a post-closing trial balance. **A post-closing trial balance is prepared to verify that the total of the debit balances is equal to the total of the credit balances in all of the company's permanent accounts.** We do not show this working paper here. The accounting cycle is now complete and a new cycle for the next accounting period begins.

SECURE YOUR KNOWLEDGE 3-2

- An accounting cycle is composed of five key steps:
  - Recording in a journal
  - Posting to the ledger
  - Preparing and posting adjusting entries
  - Preparing financial statements
  - Preparing and posting closing entries
- Adjusting entries apply accrual accounting concepts to ensure that all revenues earned and all expenses incurred during a period are recorded, regardless of the inflow or outflow of cash.
- Deferred revenues and prepaid expenses result when the cash inflow or outflow occurs prior to the recognition of the revenue or the expense.
- Accrued revenues and expenses result when the recognition of the revenue or expense occurs prior to the cash inflow or outflow.
- Closing entries are required at the end of the accounting cycle to reduce the temporary accounts to zero and to update the retained earnings account for changes that have occurred during the period.

Additional Issues

For simplicity, we ignored several common items in the Dapple Corporation example. In this section we briefly discuss returns, allowances, and discounts, as well as the periodic inventory system.

Returns, Allowances, and Discounts

Most companies have sales returns and allowances, as well as purchases returns and allowances. Some also have sales discounts and purchases discounts. How a company records them depends on its accounting system.

When a customer returns merchandise and receives a refund, this is called a **sales return**. When a customer agrees to keep damaged merchandise and the company refunds a portion of the selling price, this is called a **sales allowance**. In either case, these are a reduction in the company's sales revenue. To record these transactions, some companies will create an account, Sales Returns and Allowances, which is a contra-account to the Sales Revenue account. Others will record these transactions directly as a reduction in the

Sales Revenue account. For instance, suppose that Dapple Corporation had previously made a $500 credit sale to a customer, but the customer returned the item because it was defective. We show both ways of recording this return below[9]:

Using Contra-Account			*Reducing Sales Revenue account*	
Sales Returns & Allowances	500		Sales	500
Accounts Receivable		500	Accounts Receivable	500

Note that by using a contra-account, Dapple can determine its total sales returns and allowances simply by looking at the account balance. However, this approach requires an additional account in the company's accounting system. If Dapple records the return directly as a reduction in the sales revenue account, it has one less account in its accounting system. However, it will have to examine the details of the sales revenue account to determine its sales returns and allowances. In a computerized accounting system it is not difficult, however, to design a program to do this.

Some companies offer a discount on credit sales for prompt payment within a discount period. If a customer pays within the discount period, the company receives an amount that is less than the original selling price. This difference is called a **sales (or cash) discount**. A sales discount is also a reduction in the company's sales revenue. We show how to record sales discounts in Chapter 7.

When a company has sales returns and allowances (and sales discounts), the company must report its net sales on its income statement. **Net sales** are a company's sales less its sales returns and allowances and sales discounts. For instance, we will slightly modify the amounts in the Dapple Corporation example. Still assume that Dapple Corporation had sales revenue of $17,000, but that it had sales returns and allowances of $250 and sales discounts of $40. In this case, its net sales would be $16,710 ($17,000 – $250 – $40) and it would report this amount on its 2007 income statement as follows:

Sales (net of $250 returns and $40 discounts) $16,710

A company usually also has purchases returns and allowances. When the company returns inventory to its supplier, this is called a **purchases return**. When the company agrees to keep damaged inventory and receives a refund from its supplier, this is called a **purchases allowance**. In either case, these are a reduction in the cost of the company's inventory. To record these transactions, some companies will create an account, Purchases Returns and Allowances, which is a contra-account to the Inventory account. Other companies will record these transactions directly as a reduction in the Inventory account. For instance, suppose that Dapple returned $300 of inventory that it had purchased on credit from its supplier. We show both ways of recording the return as follows:

Using Contra-Account			*Reducing Inventory Account*	
Accounts Payable	300		Accounts Payable	300
Purchases Returns & Allowances		300	Inventory	300

Some suppliers offer a discount on credit sales for prompt payment within the discount period. To the purchasing company, this is a **purchases discount**. A purchases discount is also a reduction in the company's inventory. We show how to record purchases discounts in Chapter 8.

Periodic Inventory System

As we noted earlier in the chapter, some small companies use a periodic inventory system. Under a **periodic inventory system**, a company records its purchases of inventory using a Purchases account, so that the Inventory account balance does not change during the

---

9. Since the inventory was returned by the customer, Dapple Corporation would also "reverse" its original Cost of Goods Sold entry by debiting Inventory and crediting Cost of Goods Sold for the cost of the returned inventory.

accounting period. Also, at the time of sale, the company does not make a second journal entry to record the increase in cost of goods sold and decrease in inventory. Instead, it takes a physical inventory at the end of the accounting period. The company then *derives* its cost of goods sold by first computing its cost of goods available for sale. The cost of goods available for sale is the beginning inventory plus the net purchases (purchases less returns and allowances and any purchases discounts). The company then deducts its ending inventory from the cost of goods available for sale to determine its cost of goods sold.

For instance, assume that Dapple Corporation uses a periodic inventory system instead of a perpetual inventory system, and that it also had purchases returns and allowances as well as purchases discounts. Using slightly different numbers than we did in the original example, assume that Dapple made purchases of $12,600, had purchases returns and allowances of $300, and had taken purchases discounts of $100. Also assume that Dapple takes a physical inventory at the end of 2007 to determine that its ending inventory is $2,140. On Dapple Corporation's income statement for 2007, it would show cost of goods sold of $10,060, computed as follows:

Inventory, 1/1/2007	$ 0
Purchases	12,600
Purchases returns and allowances	(300)
Purchases discounts	(100)
Cost of goods available for sale	$12,200
Less: Inventory, 12/31/2007	(2,140)
Cost of goods sold	$10,060

Even though a company uses a perpetual inventory system, in certain situations it may use a periodic inventory approach like we show above to estimate its inventory, as we discuss in Chapter 9.

We used a relatively simple accounting system to show a company's accounting cycle. Certain additional complexities are common in companies today. These include a worksheet (spreadsheet), reversing entries, subsidiary ledgers, special journals, and computer software. We discuss each of these topics in the sections that follow.

WORKSHEET (SPREADSHEET)

8 Complete a worksheet (spreadsheet).

At the end of an accounting period, a company prepares adjusting entries, closing entries, and its financial statements. **A company often first prepares a worksheet to minimize errors, simplify recording of adjusting and closing entries in the general journal, and make it easier to prepare the financial statements.** A worksheet is *not* a substitute for any accounting records or financial statements; it is merely a working paper designed for these purposes.

A worksheet may be a large sheet of multicolumn accounting paper. A common way of preparing an electronic worksheet is to use a software package such as Microsoft Excel®. Example 3-10 shows a worksheet for the Dapple Corporation. This worksheet is based on the same information as we presented earlier in the chapter. It has a column for listing all the ledger accounts, plus debit and credit columns for the trial balance, adjustments, adjusted trial balance, income statement, retained earnings statement, and balance sheet. There are five steps in completing a worksheet.

Step 1: The process of completing the worksheet begins with preparing the trial balance. All of the company's accounts and account balances (prior to adjustments) are listed and the debit and credit columns of the trial balance are totaled to verify the equality of the debits and credits. Note that since this is the first year of operations for the Dapple Corporation, the Inventory, Accumulated Depreciation: Building, Accumulated Depreciation: Equipment, and Retained Earnings accounts do not have balances (prior to adjustments). Normally these accounts *do* have balances so we include them in the illustrated trial balance.

EXAMPLE 3-10 Worksheet (Dapple Corporation)

Dapple Corporation
Worksheet
For Year Ended Dec. 31, 2007

Account Titles	Trial Balance Debit	Trial Balance Credit	Adjustments Debit	Adjustments Credit	Income Statement Debit	Income Statement Credit	Retained Earnings Statement Debit	Retained Earnings Statement Credit	Balance Sheet Debit	Balance Sheet Credit
Cash	2,922								2,922	
Accounts receivable	7,000								7,000	
Notes receivable	1,320								1,320	
Inventory	2,010								2,010	
Prepaid insurance	360			(a) 270					90	
Land	1,500								1,500	
Building	15,320								15,320	
Acc. depreciation : building		0		(f) 264						264
Equipment	2,120								2,120	
Acc. depreciation : equipment		0		(g) 120						120
Accounts payable		1,900								1,900
Notes payable		6,600								6,600
Unearned rent		450	(b) 150							300
Capital stock		20,000								20,000
Retained earnings (1/1/07)		0						0		
Dividends distributed	500						500			
Sales revenue		17,000				17,000				
Cost of goods sold	10,490				10,490					
Salaries expense	1,800		(c) 900		2,700					
Other expenses	428				428					
Loss on sale of land	180				180					
	45,950	45,950								
Insurance expense			(a) 270		270					
Rent revenue				(b) 150		150				
Salaries payable				(c) 900						900
Interest expense			(d) 594		594					
Interest payable				(d) 594						594
Interest receivable			(e) 66						66	
Interest revenue				(e) 66		66				
Depreciation expense: bldg			(f) 264		264					
Depreciation expense: equip			(g) 120		120					
Bad debts expense			(h) 170		170					
Allow. for doubtful accounts				(h) 170						170
			2,534	2,534	15,216	17,216				
Income tax expense			(i) 600		600					
Income taxes payable				(i) 600						600
					15,816	17,216				
Net income					1,400	→		1,400		
			3,134	3,134	17,216	17,216	500	1,400		
Retained earnings, 12/31/07							900	→		900
							1,400	1,400	32,348	32,348

(a) To record 9 months of insurance expense	
(b) To record 1 month of rent revenue	
(c) To record 3 months of accrued salaries expense	
(d) To record 9 months of accrued interest expense	
(e) To record 9 months of accrued interest revenue	
(f) To record 9 months depr expense on building	
(g) To record 9 months depr expense on equipment	
(h) To record estimated bad debts expense	
(i) To record income tax expense	

Step 2: The accounts are analyzed to determine the necessary adjustments, which are initially entered in the adjustments columns on the worksheet. If an adjustment involves an account that does not currently have a balance, the account title is entered on the first available line below the other account titles. Each of the adjusting journal entries we show in Example 3-4 is initially prepared as shown on the worksheet. Note that the adjusting entry for income taxes is not made until after the income before income taxes is computed. Note also that the accounts in each adjusting entry are *keyed* with the same letter of the alphabet to reduce the likelihood of error. Explanations keyed to these entries are entered at the bottom of the worksheet. They are similar to the adjusting entry explanations that we included in Example 3-4. The adjustments columns are subtotaled to prove the equality of the debits and credits. At this point, some companies prepare an adjusted trial balance in a next set of columns. For an adjusted trial balance, the adjustment amounts are combined with the trial balance amounts to determine the new account balances. This step may be omitted as we did in the Dapple Corporation worksheet. If we had included adjusted trial balance columns, they would look like Example 3-5.

Step 3: The trial balance amount of each account is combined with the adjustments to that account and carried over to the proper column of the financial statement in which the account is located. For instance, the $360 debit balance in Prepaid Insurance is combined with the $270 credit adjustment, and the new balance of $90 is carried over to the debit column of the balance sheet.

Step 4: The income statement debit and credit columns are subtotaled. Ordinarily the debit column total differs from the credit column total, the difference being the income (or loss) before income taxes. For the Dapple Corporation the $17,216 credit total exceeds the $15,216 debit total, indicating income before income taxes of $2,000. At this point, the applicable tax rate (30% in this case) is multiplied by the income before income taxes to determine the income taxes ($600). The adjusting entry for income taxes is recorded, and the amounts are carried to the proper columns of the financial statements.

Step 5: The financial statement debit and credit columns are totaled in sequential order. First the income statement columns are totaled. The difference between the debit and credit totals is the net income or loss for the period. For the Dapple Corporation the net income is $1,400. This amount is used to balance the income statement columns. It is also entered in the retained earnings statement credit column. We use the arrows in Example 3-10 for illustrative purposes; they ordinarily are not included on the worksheet. The beginning retained earnings balance ($0 in this case) is combined with the net income to determine the $1,400 credit total. The $500 debit total is the dividends distributed. The $900 difference is the ending retained earnings. It is used to balance the retained earnings statement columns and is also transferred to the balance sheet credit column. Finally, the balance sheet debit and credit columns are totaled. The $32,348 total of the debit and credit columns indicates that the system is in balance and the worksheet is complete.

The worksheet is prepared as a preliminary step, before recording the adjusting and closing entries in the general journal and preparing the financial statements. A brief review of the Dapple Corporation worksheet indicates how a worksheet helps in the accounting process. All the adjusting entries are developed and shown on the worksheet in their basic format. They now must be recorded in the general journal. The closing entries are also simplified. The $17,216 total of the income statement credit column is credited to Income Summary, while the individual accounts with credit balances are debited. Similarly, the $15,816 debit subtotal is debited to Income Summary, while the individual accounts with debit balances are credited. The remaining closing entries involve closing both net income and dividends to Retained Earnings. Finally, the worksheet helps in preparing the actual financial statements. The amounts from the worksheet columns for each financial statement are rearranged in the proper order on that financial statement. For instance, note how easy it would be to prepare the income statement, retained earnings statement, and balance sheet shown in Examples 3-6, 3-7, and 3-8 from the respective worksheet columns. The worksheet is very useful in preparing *interim* (such as quarterly) financial statements when a company does not actually adjust or close its accounts. The adjusting entries needed to update the financial statements may be made on the worksheet only, thereby enabling the company to keep its accounts on an annual basis.

REVERSING ENTRIES

9 Prepare reversing entries.

After a company adjusts and closes its accounts for the current period, it begins a new accounting cycle for the next accounting period. Prior to journalizing the daily transactions of the new accounting period in the general journal, most companies prepare reversing entries. **A reversing entry is the exact reverse (accounts and amounts) of an adjusting entry.** A company usually makes reversing entries at the same time as closing entries but dates them the first day of the *next* accounting period. A reversing entry is *optional* and has one purpose: to simplify the recording of a later transaction related to the adjusting entry. A reversing entry enables a company to routinely record the later transaction, without having to consider the possible impact of the prior adjusting entry.

As a general guideline, reversing entries *should* be made for any adjusting entry that creates a new balance sheet account as follows:

1. Adjusting entries that create accrued revenues or expenses to be collected or paid in the next accounting period
2. Adjusting entries related to prepayments of costs initially recorded as expenses or receipts-in-advance initially recorded as revenues

Reversing entries *should not* be made for:

1. Adjusting entries related to prepayments of costs initially recorded as assets or receipts-in-advance initially recorded as liabilities
2. Adjusting entries related to estimated items such as depreciation or bad debts

These guidelines are just that, *guidelines*. They are no substitute for good accounting judgment.

Example: Reversing Entry

The Dapple Corporation should consider reversing two of the adjusting entries recorded in Example 3-4. That is, the entries to record accrued interest revenue and accrued salaries expense. Each of these is related to a transaction that will occur in the *next* accounting period. The entry to record income taxes is generally not reversed because complex tax laws require careful analysis for each journal entry. Although the adjusting entry for interest expense created an accrued expense, Interest Payable, this entry is not reversed because the subsequent transaction will not occur until 2009. Example 3-11 illustrates reversing entries and how they simplify the recording of subsequent transactions for Interest Revenue and Salaries Expense.

For each of these accounts, in the left column we first assume a reversing entry is *not* made so you can see the complex subsequent journal entry and analysis that is needed. In the right column we assume a reversing entry is made so you can see the much simpler subsequent journal entry and analysis.

Whether or not it makes reversing entries, the Dapple Corporation will collect $1,419 on March 1, 2008 for the 15%, six-month note receivable accepted on September 1, 2007. The $1,419 includes the $1,320 note and $99 of interest ($1,320 × 0.15 × 6/12). If it does not make a reversing entry, when Dapple records this collection it must determine what portion of the interest relates to 2007 ($66 of Interest Receivable) and what portion is Interest Revenue for 2008 ($33 for two months). Often this analysis is complex and impractical. The use of a reversing entry eliminates this analysis. The entire amount of the $99 received in excess of the face value of the note is credited to Interest Revenue. Since the reversing entry created a $66 *debit* balance in Interest Revenue, the $99 credit results in a $33 *credit* balance, the two months of interest for 2008, in the Interest Revenue account.

Similarly, on April 1, 2008 the Dapple Corporation will pay its employees another 6 months of salaries, or $1,800. If Dapple does not make a reversing entry, when it pays the salaries it must determine what portion of the salary payment relates to 2007 ($900 of Salaries Payable) and what portion is Salaries Expense for 2008 ($900 for 3 months). The use of a reversing entry eliminates this analysis. The entire $1,800 payment is debited to Salaries Expense. When combined with the $900 *credit* balance in Salaries Expense established by the reversing entry, the result is a $900 *debit* balance, the amount representing three months of salaries expense for 2008. ♦

Alternative Procedures

As we indicated in the discussion of the adjusting entry for deferred revenues, some companies initially record the receipt of revenues in advance of being earned as a revenue instead of

---

EXAMPLE 3-11 Reversing Entries (Dapple Corporation)

Accrued Revenue

Adjusting Entry

| 12/31/07 | Interest Receivable | 66 | |
| | Interest Revenue | | 66 |

12/31/07 Revenues and expenses are CLOSED.

*If reversing entry is **not** made:*		*If reversing entry is made:*

Reversing Entry

| 1/1/08 | None | | | 1/1/08 | Interest Revenue | 66 | |
| | | | | | Interest Receivable | | 66 |

Subsequent Entry

3/1/08	Cash	1,419		3/1/08	Cash	1,419	
	Notes Receivable		1,320		Notes Receivable		1,320
	Interest Receivable		66		Interest Revenue		99
	Interest Revenue		33				

Analysis of Subsequent Entry

Interest of $99 is collected, but $66 was recorded in Interest Receivable at end of last period. Consequently, Interest Receivable must be credited for $66 and Interest Revenue credited for $33.

Interest of $99 is collected and credited to Interest Revenue. Because reversing entry was made for $66, the net result in Interest Revenue is a $33 credit balance.

Accrued Expense

Adjusting Entry

| 12/31/07 | Salaries Expense | 900 | |
| | Salaries Payable | | 900 |

12/31/07 Revenues and expenses are CLOSED.

*If reversing entry is **not** made:*		*If reversing entry is made:*

Reversing Entry

| 1/1/08 | None | | | 1/1/08 | Salaries Payable | 900 | |
| | | | | | Salaries Expense | | 900 |

Subsequent Entry

4/1/08	Salaries Expense	900		4/1/08	Salaries Expense	1,800	
	Salaries Payable	900			Cash		1,800
	Cash		1,800				

Analysis of Subsequent Entry

Salaries of $1,800 for 6 months are paid, but $900 was recorded in Salaries Payable at end of last period. Consequently, Salaries Payable must be debited for $900 and Salaries Expense debited for $900.

Salaries of $1,800 for 6 months are paid and debited to Salaries Expense. Because reversing entry was made for $900, the net result in Salaries Expense is a $900 debit balance.

---

a liability. We showed that Dapple Corporation *could* have recorded the December 1 receipt of three months' advance rent as a credit to Rent Revenue for $450. In this case the adjusting entry is a debit to Rent Revenue for $300 and a credit to Unearned Rent for $300. This adjusting entry creates a balance sheet account and should be reversed. On January 1, 2008 a reversing entry should be made debiting Unearned Rent for $300 and crediting Rent Revenue for $300. This entry eliminates the Unearned Rent account balance and creates a $300 balance in Rent Earned for the two months of 2008. No further adjusting entry is needed in 2008.

SUBSIDIARY LEDGERS

10 Use subsidiary ledgers.

Even in the relatively simple Dapple Corporation example, the general ledger contains many accounts. For a larger company that sells to many customers and purchases from many suppliers, the general ledger is much larger because the company incurs additional types of expenses and earns other types of revenues. The company also must keep adequate records of amounts owed by each customer and to each supplier.

To (1) reduce the size of the general ledger, (2) minimize errors, (3) divide the accounting task, and (4) keep up-to-date records of its credit customers and suppliers, a company creates subsidiary ledgers that are *not* part of the double-entry system. **A subsidiary ledger is a group of accounts, all of which relate to one specific company activity.** Most companies have separate subsidiary ledgers for accounts receivable and accounts payable. These ledgers enable a company to better focus on the collection and payment process for the receivables and payables. Many companies also use subsidiary ledgers for major categories of accounts, such as property and equipment, selling expenses, and administrative expenses. The *accounts receivable* subsidiary ledger contains the individual accounts of all the company's credit customers. Since the individual customer accounts have debit balances, this subsidiary ledger has a *total* debit balance (computed by preparing a *schedule* of the individual customer account balances).

When a company uses this subsidiary ledger, it still keeps an Accounts Receivable account in the general ledger. This account is referred to as a **control account** because its debit balance must be equal to that of the subsidiary ledger. In a computerized accounting system, each posting to the Account Receivable control account is also automatically posted to the applicable subsidiary ledger account. Similarly, the *accounts payable* subsidiary ledger contains the individual accounts of all the company's credit suppliers. Since these accounts have credit balances, the credit total of this subsidiary ledger must agree with the credit total of the Accounts Payable control account in the general ledger. If the Dapple Corporation used a subsidiary ledger for the accounts receivable, the ledger and control account balances at the end of 2007 would appear as we show in Example 3-12.

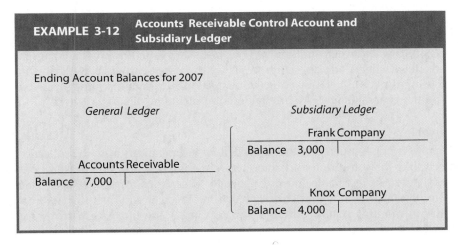

EXAMPLE 3-12   Accounts Receivable Control Account and Subsidiary Ledger

Ending Account Balances for 2007

General Ledger

Accounts Receivable
Balance   7,000

Subsidiary Ledger

Frank Company
Balance   3,000

Knox Company
Balance   4,000

SPECIAL JOURNALS

When a company increases in size and complexity, it needs to efficiently record and summarize many daily transactions. Special journals are used for this purpose. **A special journal is a journal used by a company to record its transactions with a similar characteristic.** A company uses these journals (1) to divide the accounting task, (2) to reduce the time needed to complete the various accounting activities, and (3) to provide for a chronological listing of similar transactions. There are four common types of transactions for which special journals are usually established: (1) sales of merchandise on credit, (2) purchases of merchandise on credit, (3) cash receipts, and (4) cash payments. A company still needs a general journal to record various other transactions or events not repetitive enough to require the use of special journals.

The major journals and their uses are:

1. *Sales Journal.* Used to record all (and only) sales of merchandise on credit.
2. *Purchases Journal.* Used to record all (and only) purchases of merchandise on credit.
3. *Cash Receipts Journal.* Used to record all cash receipts.
4. *Cash Payments Journal.* Used to record all cash payments.

11 Understand special journals.

5. *General Journal.* Used to record adjusting, closing, and reversing entries and other transactions not recorded in the special journals.

Because operating procedures and transactions vary across companies, each company organizes its special journals in a way best suited to its operations.

SECURE YOUR KNOWLEDGE 3-3

- A worksheet is a tool designed to minimize errors, simplify the recording of adjusting and closing entries in the general journal, and help in preparing financial statements.
- A reversing entry is the exact reverse of an adjusting entry and is used to simplify the recording of a later transaction related to the adjusting entry.
- A subsidiary ledger is a group of accounts for one specific company activity that sums to the total of the related control account in the general ledger.
- Special journals such as the sales journal, purchases journal, cash receipts journal and cash payments journal are tools used to record business transactions with similar characteristics that allow for increased efficiency and effectiveness in the accounting cycle.

COMPUTER SOFTWARE

In this chapter (and throughout the book) we use a manual accounting system for convenience. In the business world, however, most companies use computer software to process their accounting information. Software has been developed by software companies for the subsidiary ledgers and special journals we discussed earlier, as well as other financial accounting functions relating to accounts receivable, accounts payable, inventory, payroll, and the general ledger. We briefly describe each type of software next.

Accounts Receivable

Because a company generates much of the cash needed for its operations from the collection of accounts receivable, the software for accounts receivable is a very important aspect of a computer system. Accounts receivable software generally is designed to provide up-to-date balances in customers' accounts by immediately recording invoices and cash receipts from customers; print out monthly statements (bills) for customers; monitor sales returns and allowances as well as sales discounts taken by customers; generate a credit history of each customer to help avoid uncollectible accounts; and provide projections of future cash inflows.

Accounts Payable

Accounts payable software monitors and controls the cash a company pays to suppliers. In the case of a retailer or wholesaler, payments for purchases of inventory for resale is the primary activity. The software for accounts payable generally is designed to provide up-to-date balances in suppliers' accounts by immediately recording purchase orders and cash payments to suppliers; generate a list to verify the quantity and unit price of an order when it is received from a supplier; monitor purchases returns and allowances and purchases discounts taken; write checks; and provide projections of future cash outflows.

Inventory

Inventory is a very important asset for many companies. Most inventory software is linked to a company's accounts receivable and accounts payable software. Inventory software generally is designed to provide an up-to-date count of the number of units of each item of inventory by immediately recording all unit purchases and sales; highlight when a minimum or maximum stock level has been reached for each item of inventory; print price tags for newly acquired inventory; prepare reports on slow-moving or obsolete inventory items; and provide unit prices when a physical count of the inventory is taken.

Payroll

Software for a company's payroll was one of the first to be developed. Payroll software can be very complex because of the various federal, state, and local tax laws. Payroll software may be designed to compute the salaries earned by each employee based on pay rates and overtime; allocate the salaries across departments in the company; calculate federal, state, and local withholding taxes; compute other voluntary withholdings such as for investments in retirement plans; print payroll checks; generate comparisons of actual with projected salaries; and prepare various tax-withholding reports.

General Ledger

General ledger software is broader than the name implies and includes many aspects of a company's accounting system. General ledger software usually includes all special journals and the general journal for recording transactions, a chart of accounts, and the ledger accounts on disks for storing the recorded information. Usually, the software is capable of preparing a trial balance and financial statements at any point in time. Frequently, supporting schedules (e.g., depreciation) and budgets also may be generated. The general ledger software of a company usually is linked to its accounts receivable, accounts payable, inventory, and payroll software.

APPENDIX: CASH-BASIS ACCOUNTING

As we mentioned earlier in this chapter, most companies use accrual accounting. Under *accrual accounting*, a company records revenues in the accounting period in which they are earned and realized, and records expenses in the accounting period they are incurred. A few companies such as small retail stores and professionals such as dentists, doctors, and architects use cash-basis accounting. Under *cash-basis accounting*, a company records revenues when it collects cash from sales and records expenses when it pays cash for its operations. On its income statement, then, the company computes its net income as the difference between its cash receipts and cash payments. In other words, net income is the same as the net operating cash flow for the period. The company may choose not to prepare a balance sheet. However, it frequently will keep track of certain assets such as amounts owed by customers (accounts receivable), amounts paid in advance (prepaid expenses), and any property and equipment it owns. It also frequently will keep track of certain liabilities such as amounts owed to suppliers (accounts payable) and amounts owed to employees (accrued expenses). Cash-basis accounting, however, is not allowed under generally accepted accounting principles.

> **12** Convert cash-basis financial statements to accrual-basis.

Sometimes a company that is using cash-basis accounting must prepare its financial statements based on accrual accounting. This might happen, for instance, if it applies for a bank loan and the bank requires financial statements prepared using generally accepted accounting principles. In this case, the company must convert its cash-basis income statement to an accrual-basis income statement and must prepare a related balance sheet. This involves making adjustments to the cash receipts to convert them to sales revenues and making adjustments to the cash payments to convert them to cost of goods sold and operating expenses. It also involves combining the information it has about its assets and liabilities into a formal balance sheet.

Exhibit 3-4 shows the basic adjustments that a company must make to convert its cash receipts and cash payments into accrual-based revenues, cost of goods sold, and operating expenses. In addition, the company must include depreciation expense on its property and equipment in the operating expenses.

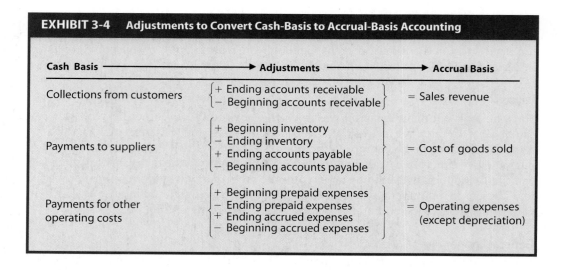

EXHIBIT 3-4   Adjustments to Convert Cash-Basis to Accrual-Basis Accounting

Cash Basis →	Adjustments →	Accrual Basis
Collections from customers	+ Ending accounts receivable − Beginning accounts receivable	= Sales revenue
Payments to suppliers	+ Beginning inventory − Ending inventory + Ending accounts payable − Beginning accounts payable	= Cost of goods sold
Payments for other operating costs	+ Beginning prepaid expenses − Ending prepaid expenses + Ending accrued expenses − Beginning accrued expenses	= Operating expenses (except depreciation)

Example: Cash-Basis Accounting

Assume that Gretta Gropples starts Gropples Company (a small retail store organized as a sole proprietorship) on January 1, 2007 by investing cash of $20,000. Gropples Company uses cash-basis accounting but wants to prepare its financial statements on an accrual basis. At the end of the year, the company's checkbook shows cash receipts from customers of $95,000, cash payments of $106,000, and an ending cash balance of $9,000. Based on a physical inventory, the company determined that its inventory at the end of 2007 is $7,200. It also determined that at the end of 2007, customers owed it $4,300, and that it owed suppliers $5,100 and employees $500. The company examined its checkbook and found that during 2007:

1. It paid suppliers $54,000 and paid other operating costs of $29,000. Included in the other operating costs was $6,000 that it paid on January 1 for two years of rent on store space.
2. It paid $8,000 for store equipment on January 1. It planned to use straight-line depreciation and expected to use the store equipment for five years, after which the store equipment would have a zero residual value.
3. Gretta withdrew $15,000 during the year.

Based on this information, using accrual accounting the company prepared its income statement for 2007 that we show in Example 3-13 and its balance sheet at the end of 2007 that we show in Example 3-14.

In Example 3-13, Gropples Company computed its $99,300 sales revenues by adding the $4,300 ending accounts receivable to the $95,000 it collected from customers. The company computed its $51,900 cost of goods sold by subtracting the $7,200 ending inventory and adding the $5,100 ending accounts payable to the $54,000 it paid to suppliers. It computed the $26,500 other operating expenses by subtracting the $3,000 prepaid rent (the cost of the remaining year of rent it had paid for in advance) and adding the $500 ending salaries payable to the $29,000 it paid for other operating costs. It computed the $1,600 depreciation expense by dividing the $8,000 cost of the store equipment by the five-year estimated life.

In Example 3-14, most of the amounts come from the initial information we presented for the company. The $1,600 accumulated depreciation is the depreciation to date (one year, in this example; in later years, this amount would increase each year by the amount of the annual depreciation expense). The company computed the $24,300 amount of the G. Gropples capital account by adding the $19,300 net income and subtracting the $15,000 withdrawals from the $20,000 initial investment.

In more complex situations, a company may have items such as deferred revenues and accrued revenues, sales returns and allowances, purchases returns and allowances,

---

EXAMPLE 3-13   Income Statement (Gropples Company)

GROPPLES COMPANY

Income Statement
For Year Ended December 31, 2007

Sales revenue		$99,300 [a]
Cost of goods sold		(51,900) [b]
Gross profit		$47,400
Operating expenses		
Depreciation expenses	$ 1,600 [d]	
Other operating expenses	26,500 [c]	
Total expenses		(28,100)
Net Income		$19,300

[a]$95,000 collections from customers + $4,300 ending accounts receivable.
[b]$54,000 payments to suppliers − $7,200 ending inventory + $5,100 ending accounts payable.
[c]$29,000 payments for other operating costs − $3,000 ending prepaid rent ($6,000 × 1/2) + $500 ending salaries payable.
[d]$8,000 store equipment ÷ 5 years.

---

and interest revenue and expense, as well as gains or losses on sales of equipment. In these cases the company may make additional adjustments to determine its revenues and expenses, and may provide more detail in the revenues, cost of goods sold, and operating expenses sections of its income statement. For convenience, the company may prepare a worksheet to help it determine these amounts. Regardless of how simple or complex the adjustments are, the intent is to report the company's financial statements on an accrual basis according to generally accepted accounting principles. ◆

EXAMPLE 3-14   Balance Sheet (Gropples Company)

GROPPLES COMPANY

Balance Sheet
December 31, 2007

Assets

Current Assets		
Cash	$ 9,000	
Accounts receivable	4,300	
Inventory	7,200	
Prepaid rent	3,000	
Total current assets		$23,500
Property and Equipment		
Store equipment	$ 8,000	
Less: Accumulated depreciation	(1,600)	
Total property and equipment		6,400
Total Assets		$29,900

Liabilities

Current Liabilities	
Accounts payable	$ 5,100
Salaries payable	500
Total liabilities	$ 5,600
Owner's Equity	
G. Gropples, capital	$24,300 [a]
Total Liabilities	$29,900

[a]$20,000 beginning investment + $19,300 net income (from Example 3-13) − $15,000 withdrawals.

SUMMARY

At the beginning of the chapter, we identified several objectives you would accomplish after reading the chapter. The objectives are listed below, each followed by a brief summary of the key points in the chapter discussion.

1. **Understand the components of an accounting system.** The components of an accounting system include: (1) the framework for operating the system, (2) the input source documents, (3) the records used to store accounting information, and (4) the output reports.

2. **Know the major steps in the accounting cycle.** The major steps in the accounting cycle include: (1) recording (journalizing) daily transactions in a journal, (2) posting the journal entries to the accounts in the general ledger, (3) preparing and posting adjusting entries, (4) preparing the financial statements, and (5) preparing and posting closing entries for the revenue, expense, and dividend accounts.

3. **Prepare journal entries in the general journal.** To make a journal entry to record a transaction, enter the date in the date column. Next, enter the title of the account and amount to be debited in the account titles column and debit column, respectively. Then, enter the title of the account and amount to be credited in the account titles column and credit column, respectively. Finally, write a short explanation of the transaction in the account titles column.

4. **Post to the general ledger and prepare a trial balance.** To post to the general ledger, for each journal entry, first transfer from the general journal the date and the amount debited to the account in the general ledger. Next, transfer the date and the amount credited to the account in the general ledger. To prepare a trial balance at the end of the accounting period, first compute the balance in each account. Then, list each account and list its balance in the debit or credit column of the working paper (trial balance). Finally, total the debit and credit columns to verify that the totals are equal.

5. **Prepare adjusting entries.** Adjusting entries are journal entries made at the end of the accounting period so that a company's financial statements include the correct amounts for the current period. Adjusting entries are made to: (1) apportion prepaid and deferred items, (2) record accrued items, and (3) record estimated items. Adjusting entries are made in the usual manner in the general journal.

6. **Prepare financial statements.** To prepare a company's financial statements, first prepare an adjusted trial balance to verify that the total of the debit balances is equal to the total of the credit balances in the company's accounts. Then, prepare the income statement, which includes the company's revenues, expenses, and net income. Next, prepare the retained earnings statement, which shows the change in retained earnings because of the company's net income and dividends. Finally, prepare the balance sheet, which includes the company's assets, liabilities, and stockholders' equity.

7. **Prepare closing entries.** Closing entries are journal entries of a company made at the end of the accounting period (1) to reduce the balance in each temporary account (revenue, expense, and dividend accounts) to zero, and (2) to update the retained earnings account. Closing entries are made in the usual manner in the general journal.

8. **Complete a worksheet (spreadsheet).** To complete a worksheet, first list each account and list its balance in the debit or credit column of the trial balance. Second, enter the adjusting entries as debits or credits in the adjustments columns. Third, combine the trial balance amount of each account with the adjustments to that account and carry over the resulting amount to the proper column of the financial statement in which the account is included. Fourth, subtotal the income statement debit and credit columns, make an adjusting entry for any income taxes on the difference between the columns (the pretax income), and carry the adjustment amounts to the appropriate financial statement columns. Finally, subtotal the income statement columns. List the difference as net income (or net loss), write the amount in the debit (credit) column and balance the income statement columns. Transfer the net income (net loss) amount to the retained earnings columns and balance these columns. Then transfer the retained earnings balance to the balance sheet credit column and balance these columns.

9. **Prepare reversing entries.** A reversing entry is the exact reverse (accounts and amounts) of an adjusting entry. Reversing entries are made at the end of an accounting period to simplify the recording of later transactions. A reversing entry enables a company to routinely record the later transaction without having to consider the possible impact of the prior adjusting entry.

10. **Use subsidiary ledgers.** A subsidiary ledger is a group of accounts, all of which pertain to one specific company activity. Most companies have subsidiary ledgers for accounts receivable and accounts payable to better focus on collections from customers and payments for payables. When a company uses a subsidiary ledger it still maintains a *control account* in its general ledger. The balance of the control account must be equal to the total of the balances of all the individual accounts in the subsidiary ledger.

11. **Understand special journals.** The major special journals are the: (1) sales journal (for sales on credit), (2) purchases journal (for purchases on credit), (3) cash receipts journal, (4) cash payments journal, and (5) general journal (for miscellaneous transactions).

12. **Convert cash-basis financial statements to accrual-basis (Appendix).** First, start with the income statement. Make adjustments to the collections from customers for any changes in accounts receivable. Make adjustments to the payments to suppliers for any changes in inventory and accounts payable. Make adjustments to the payments for other operating costs for any changes in prepaid expenses or accrued expenses, and for depreciation expense. Complete the accrual-basis income statement using the resulting amounts. Use the cash balance from the company's checkbook and the information from the preceding adjustments (e.g., accounts receivable, accounts payable, etc.) to prepare the ending balance sheet.

QUESTIONS

Q3-1 What is a primary objective of financial reporting?

Q3-2 What is an *accounting system*?

Q3-3 Discuss the relationship between the accounting equation and the double-entry system of recording transactions.

Q3-4 What is the difference between a *permanent* and a *temporary* account? Give examples of each.

Q3-5 What are the major financial statements of a company and what information does each summarize?

Q3-6 Define the following:
a. *Account*
b. *Contra account*
c. *Ledger*
d. *Journal*
e. *Posting*

Q3-7 Why is it advantageous to a company to initially record each of its transactions in a journal?

Q3-8 What is a perpetual accounting system? What journal entries are involved?

Q3-9 Give examples of transactions that:
a. Increase an asset and a liability.
b. Increase an asset and stockholders' equity.
c. Increase an asset and decrease an asset.
d. Decrease an asset and a liability.
e. Decrease an asset and stockholders' equity.

Q3-10 Give examples of transactions that:
a. Increase inventory account and a liability.
b. Decrease inventory account and a liability.
c. Increase inventory account and decrease an asset.
d. Decrease inventory account and increase an asset.

Q3-11 What are the steps that a company completes in the accounting cycle? Briefly discuss each step.

Q3-12 Why are adjusting entries necessary?

Q3-13 What are *prepaid expenses* and *deferred revenues*? Give an example of an adjusting entry to update each of these items at year-end.

Q3-14 What are *accrued expenses* and *accrued revenues*? Give an example of an adjusting entry to record each of these items.

Q3-15 Give two examples of adjusting entries to record estimated items. Include in one example a discussion of how depreciation is computed.

Q3-16 What is the difference between a *trial balance* and an *adjusted trial balance*? Why is the latter a useful accounting working paper?

Q3-17 What is the difference between a sales return and a sales discount? How does each affect net sales?

Q3-18 What is a periodic inventory system? How is cost of goods sold computed when a company uses a periodic inventory system?

Q3-19 What are the objectives of closing entries?

Q3-20 Show, without amounts, the form of the closing entries for a retail store using a perpetual inventory system.

Q3-21 What is a *worksheet*? How does the use of a worksheet facilitate the completion of the accounting cycle?

Q3-22 What are *reversing entries* and why are they used? Give an example of an adjusting entry and a reversing entry for salaries payable, and the later entry to pay the salaries.

Q3-23 What is a *subsidiary ledger* and a *control account*, and why are they used? Give an example of how they work.

Q3-24 What are *special journals* and what advantages are achieved by using them?

Q3-25 What are the major special journals? Give an example of transactions that would be recorded in each journal.

Q3-26 Identify the common software for the financial accounting functions.

Q3-27 What is cash-basis accounting? What must a company do to convert its cash-basis accounting records to an accrual-based income statement?

EXERCISES

E3-1   *Financial Statement Interrelationship* Draw a diagram that shows the interrelationship between the beginning balance sheet, income statement, retained earnings statement, and ending balance sheet.

E3-2   *Journal Entries* The Mead Company uses a perpetual inventory system and engaged in the following transactions during the month of May:

Date	Transaction
May 1	Made cash sales of $6,300; the cost of the inventory was $3,700.
5	Purchased $2,000 of inventory on credit.
9	Made credit sales of $3,300; the cost of the inventory sold was $1,900.
13	Paid sales salaries of $900 and office salaries of $600.
14	Paid for the May 5 purchases.
18	Purchased sales equipment costing $8,000; made a down payment of $2,000 and agreed to pay the balance in 60 days.
21	Purchased $600 of inventory for cash.
27	Sold land that had originally cost $1,900 for $2,600.

Required
Record the preceding transactions in a general journal.

E3-3   *Journal Entries* The following are selected accounts and account balances of the Sawyer Company on May 31:

	Debit (Credit)
Cash	$12,523
Accounts receivable	23,052
Inventory	16,300
Office equipment	35,860
Accumulated depreciation	(10,540)
Notes payable	(3,400)
Accounts payable	(3,500)
Sales revenue	(47,872)
Gain on sale of office equipment	(400)
Cost of goods sold	22,354
Utility expense	1,124

The Sawyer Company entered into the following transactions during June:

Date	Transaction
June 3	Sold for $700 office equipment that had cost $2,000 and has associated accumulated depreciation of $1,500.
7	Made sales of $2,000 on credit; the cost of the inventory sold was $1,200.
10	Purchased $1,000 of inventory for cash.
15	Purchased new office equipment costing $4,000, paying $1,500 and signing a 90-day note for the balance.
16	Received check for June 7 credit sale.
17	Made cash sales of $4,200; the cost of the inventory sold was $2,300.
20	Purchased $2,600 of inventory on credit.
24	Returned $200 of defective inventory from the June 20 purchase for a credit to its account.
29	Paid for the June 20 purchase less the return.
30	Paid the monthly utility bill, $210.

Required
1. Record the preceding transactions in a general journal.
2. Post to the accounts.

E3-4   *Basic Income Statement* The following are selected account balances of the Rule Corporation at the end of 2007:

	Debit	Credit
Operating expenses	$3,800	
Sales returns	600	
Sales revenue		$16,200
Cost of goods sold	8,300	
Interest expense	800	
Gain on sale of land		500

The company is subject to a 30% income tax rate and stockholders own 800 shares of its capital stock.

Required
Prepare a 2007 income statement for Rule Corporation.

E3-5   *Periodic Inventory System* Raynolde Company uses a periodic inventory system. At the end of 2007, the following information is available:

Purchases returns and allowances	$ 1,400
Inventory, 12/31/2007	11,900
Purchases	21,200
Inventory, 1/1/2007	10,800
Purchases discounts	600

Required
Prepare a schedule to compute Raynolde Company's cost of goods sold for 2007.

E3-6   *Financial Statements* The Turtle Company has prepared the following adjusted trial balance for the year ended December 31, 2007:

	Debit	Credit
Cash	$ 1,700	
Accounts receivable (net)	2,100	
Inventory	1,800	
Equipment	5,400	
Accumulated depreciation		$ 1,700
Accounts payable		2,300
Salaries payable		300
Income taxes payable		360
Capital stock (400 shares)		3,200
Retained earnings		2,500
Dividends distributed	200	
Sales revenue		7,900
Cost of goods sold	4,300	
Selling expenses	1,800	
Administrative expenses	600	
Income tax expense	360	
Totals	$18,260	$18,260

Required
Prepare for 2007 in proper form: (1) an income statement, (2) a retained earnings statement, (3) an ending balance sheet, and (4) closing entries.

E3-7   *Adjusting Entries* Your examination of the records of the Sullivan Company provides the following information for the December 31, 2007 year-end adjustments:
1. Bad debts are to be recorded at 2% of sales. Sales totaled $25,000 for the year.
2. Salaries at year-end that have accumulated but have not been paid total $1,400.
3. Annual straight-line depreciation for the company's equipment is based on a cost of $30,000, an estimated life of eight years, and an estimated residual value of $2,000.
4. Prepaid insurance in the amount of $800 has expired.
5. Interest that has been earned but not collected totals $500.
6. Unearned rent in the amount of $1,000 has become earned.

7. Interest on a note payable that has accumulated but has not been paid totals $600.
8. The income tax rate is 30% on current income and is payable in the first quarter of 2008. The pretax income before the preceding adjusting entries is $6,800.

Required
Prepare the adjusting entries to record the preceding information.

E3-8 *Adjusting Entries* The following are several transactions of the Pruitt Company that occurred during the current year and were recorded in *real* (that is, balance sheet) accounts unless indicated otherwise:

Date	Transaction
Apr. 1	Purchased a delivery van for $10,000, paying $1,000 down, and issuing a one-year, 12% note payable for the $9,000 balance. It is estimated that the van has a four-year life and an $800 residual value; the company uses straight-line depreciation. The interest on the note will be paid on the maturity date.
May 15	Purchased $830 of office supplies.
June 2	Purchased a two-year comprehensive insurance policy for $960.
Aug. 1	Received six months' rent in advance at $260 per month and recorded the $1,560 receipt as Rent Earned.
Sept.15	Advanced $600 to sales personnel to cover their future travel costs.
Nov. 1	Accepted a $6,000, six-month, 12% (annual rate) note receivable from a customer, the interest to be collected when the note is collected.

The following information also is available:
1. On January 1, the Office Supplies account had a $250 balance. On December 31, an inventory count showed $190 of office supplies on hand.
2. The weekly (five-day) payroll of Pruitt Company amounts to $2,000. All employees are paid at the close of business each Wednesday. A two-day accrual is required for the current year.
3. Sales personnel travel cost reports indicate that $490 of advances had been used to pay travel expenses.
4. The income tax rate is 30% on current income and is payable in the first quarter of next year. The pretax income before the adjusting entries is $8,655.

Required
On the basis of the above information, prepare journal entries to record whatever *adjustments* are necessary to bring the accounts up to date on December 31. Each journal entry explanation should show any related computations.

E3-9 *Adjusting Entries* The following partial list of accounts and account balances has been taken from the trial balance and the adjusted trial balance of the Barker Company:

	Trial Balance		Adjusted Trial Balance	
	Debit	Credit	Debit	Credit
Accumulated depreciation		$5,200		$6,600
Allowance for doubtful accounts		380		650
Income taxes payable		0		2,250
Interest payable		0		320
Prepaid insurance	$350		$90	
Salaries payable		0		720
Unearned rent		900		300

Required
Prepare the adjusting entry that caused the change in each account balance.

E3-10 *Closing Entries* The Collins Corporation shows the following inventory, dividends, revenue, and expense account balances before closing:

	Debit	Credit		Debit	Credit
Dividends distributed	$ 250		Gain on sale of land		$300
Sales revenue		$2,400	Salaries expense	$300	
Sales returns	200		Utilities expense	130	
Cost of goods sold	1,350		Miscellaneous expenses	120	
			Income tax expense	180	

Required
Prepare closing entries.

E3-11 *Worksheet for Service Company* The Grant Consulting Company has prepared a trial balance on the following partially completed worksheet for the year ended December 31, 2007:

	A	B	C	D	E	F	G	H	I	J	K
1									Retained		
2						Income		Earnings		Balance	
3		Trial Balance		Adjustments		Statement		Statement		Sheet	
4	Accounts	Debit	Credit	Debit	Credit	Debit	Credit	Debit	Credit	Debit	Credit
5	Cash	3,800									
6	Prepaid rent	2,400									
7	Office equipment	7,000									
8	Accumulated depreciation		1,400								
9	Notes payable (due 7/1/08)		2,000								
10	Capital stock (200 shares)		4,000								
11	Retained earnings (1/1/07)		3,200								
12	Dividends distributed	200									
13	Consulting revenues		6,100								
14	Salaries expense	2,500									
15	Miscellaneous expenses	800									
16	Totals	16,700	16,700								
17											

Additional information: (a) On January 1, 2007 the company had paid two years' rent in advance at $100 a month on its office space, (b) the office equipment is being depreciated on a straight-line basis over a 10-year life, and no residual value is expected, (c) interest of $150 has accrued on the note payable but has not been paid, and (d) the income tax rate is 30% on current income and will be paid in the first quarter of 2008.

Required
1. Complete the worksheet.
2. Prepare financial statements for 2007.

E3-12 *Worksheet, Including Inventory* The Murphy Company prepared a trial balance on the following partially completed worksheet for the year ended December 31, 2007:

	A	B	C	D	E	F	G	H	I	J	K
1									Retained		
2						Income		Earnings		Balance	
3		Trial Balance		Adjustments		Statement		Statement		Sheet	
4	Accounts	Debit	Credit	Debit	Credit	Debit	Credit	Debit	Credit	Debit	Credit
5	Cash	2,500									
6	Accounts receivable	4,000									
7	Allowance for doubtful accounts		300								
8	Inventory	8,200									
9	Prepaid rent	3,600									
10	Equipment	30,000									
11	Accumulated depreciation		12,000								
12	Accounts payable		3,700								
13	Notes payable (due 7/1/08)		5,000								
14	Capital stock (1,000 shares)		8,900								
15	Retained earnings (1/1/07)		10,200								
16	Dividends distributed	1,000									
17	Sales revenues		45,000								
18	Cost of goods sold	21,000									
19	Salaries expense	7,100									
20	Utilities expense	3,300									
21	Advertising expense	4,400									
22	Totals	85,100	85,100								
23											

Additional information: (a) The equipment is being depreciated on a straight-line basis over a 10-year life, with no residual value; (b) salaries accrued but not recorded total $500; (c) on January 1, 2007 the company had paid three years' rent in advance at $100 per month; (d) bad debts are expected to be 1% of total sales; (e) interest of $400 has accrued on the note payable; and (f) the income tax rate is 40% on current income and will be paid in the first quarter of 2008.

Required
1. Complete the worksheet.
2. Prepare financial statements for 2007.
3. Prepare closing entries in the general journal.

E3-13 *Reversing Entries* On December 31, 2007 Adams Company made the following adjusting entries for its annual accounting period:

Depreciation Expense	2,400	
Accumulated Depreciation		2,400

To record depreciation on buildings.

Interest Receivable	500	
Interest Revenue		500

To record interest on note receivable due January 28, 2008.

Rent Expense	400	
Prepaid Rent		400

To record expired prepaid rent.

Interest Expense	620	
Interest Payable		620

To record interest on note payable due March 16, 2008.

Required
Prepare whatever reversing entries are appropriate.

E3-14 *Special Journals* The following are several transactions of a company that uses special journals:

Transaction	Journal
1. Purchase of inventory for cash.	_____
2. Sale of inventory on credit.	_____
3. Payment of sales salaries.	_____
4. Purchase of inventory on credit.	_____
5. Sale of merchandise for cash.	_____
6. Purchase of land by issuing note payable.	_____
7. Collection of short-term note receivable and related interest.	_____
8. Return of defective inventory to supplier for credit to account.	_____
9. Preparation of adjusting entries.	_____
10. Purchase of equipment for cash.	_____

Required
In the space provided, indicate in which journal the transaction would be recorded using the codes: *G* for general journal, *S* for sales journal, *P* for purchases journal, *CR* for cash receipts journal, and *CP* for cash payments journal.

E3-15 *Cash-Basis Accounting (Appendix)* Ellis Company keeps its accounting records on a cash basis during the year. At year-end, it adjusts its books to the accrual basis for preparing its financial statements. At the end of 2006, Ellis Company reported the following balance sheet items:

	Debit	Credit
Cash	$ 2,700	
Accounts receivable	4,200	
Inventory	5,600	
Equipment	12,000	
Accumulated depreciation		$ 4,800
Accounts payable		6,100
M. Ellis, capital		13,600
Totals	$24,500	$24,500

It is now the end of 2007. The company's checkbook shows a balance of $4,700, which includes cash receipts from customers of $51,300 and cash payments of $49,300.

An examination of the cash payments show that: (1)$30,600 was paid to suppliers, (2) $12,700 was paid for other operating costs (including $7,200 paid on January 1 for two years' annual rent), and (3) $6,000 was withdrawn by M. Ellis.

On December 31, 2007, (1) customers owed Ellis Company $5,900, (2)Ellis Company owed suppliers and employees $7,000 and $900, respectively, and (3) the ending inventory was $6,300. Ellis is depreciating the equipment using straight-line depreciation over a 10-year life (no residual value).

Required
Using accrual-based accounting, prepare (1) a 2007 income statement and (2) a December 31, 2007 balance sheet (show supporting calculations).

PROBLEMS

P3-1 *Journal Entries, Posting, and Trial Balance* The account balances of the Antil Company on November 1, 2007 are as follows:

	Debit	Credit		Debit	Credit
Cash	$ 7,800		Patents	$25,000	
Accounts receivable	12,530		Accounts payable		$38,750
Allowance for doubtful accounts		$ 740	Notes payable		2,400
Notes receivable	6,000		Common stock, no par		165,000
Inventory	25,121		Retained earnings, January 1, 2007		24,958
Prepaid insurance	840		Sales revenue		38,400
Office supplies	465		Sales returns and allowances	1,567	
Land	74,350		Cost of goods sold	32,000	
Buildings	66,580		Sales salaries expense	6,200	
Accumulated depreciation:			Office salaries expense	4,300	
buildings		21,400	Advertising expense	1,250	
Equipment	37,620		Utility expense	1,845	
Accumulated depreciation:			Interest revenue		550
equipment		11,480	Interest expense	210	

During the month of November, the following transactions took place:

Date	Transaction
Nov. 2	Made cash sales of $3,400; the cost of the inventory sold was $2,040.
3	Purchased $900 of inventory for cash.
5	Sold an unused 1/2 acre of land for $4,000; the land had originally cost $3,650.
8	Purchased a two-year comprehensive insurance policy for $528.
12	Leased an unused portion of its building to Charles Company, collecting six months' rent in advance at $220 per month.
13	Made $2,300 of sales on credit to Smith Company; the cost of the inventory sold was $1,400.
16	Collected the $200 monthly payment plus $30 interest on a customer's note receivable.
17	Purchased $1,600 of inventory on credit from Mason Company.
19	Granted Smith Company a $200 allowance for defective inventory (from the November 13 transaction) and credited its account.
20	Purchased land for a future building site. Made a $2,000 down payment and signed a 12%, 90-day $6,000 note payable for the balance.
23	Collected the Smith Company account for the November 13 sale less the return.
26	Paid for the November 17 purchase of inventory.
27	Paid the city newspaper $420 for advertising that had appeared during November.
30	Paid $520 of sales salaries and $390 of office salaries.

Required
1. Prepare general journal entries to record the preceding transactions.
2. Post to the general ledger accounts.
3. Prepare a trial balance on November 30, 2007.

P3-2   *Financial Statements* The Stern Company uses a perpetual inventory system and has prepared the following *adjusted trial balance* on December 31, 2007:

	Debit	Credit
Cash	$ 2,000	
Accounts receivable	2,700	
Allowance for doubtful accounts		$ 250
Inventory	6,500	
Prepaid insurance	800	
Land	5,200	
Buildings and equipment	31,000	
Accumulated depreciation		15,000
Accounts payable		3,100
Salaries payable		420
Unearned rent		360
Income taxes payable		2,625
Note payable (due July 1, 2011)		5,000
Interest payable (due July 1, 2011)		750
Capital stock (1,500 shares)		9,000
Retained earnings, January 1, 2007		6,770
Dividends distributed	1,200	
Sales revenue		33,000
Sales returns	2,100	
Rent revenue		1,440
Cost of goods sold	15,040	
Selling expenses	4,800	
Administrative expenses	3,000	
Interest expense	750	
Income tax expense	2,625	
Totals	$77,715	$77,715

Required

Prepare in proper form for 2007 the company's: (1) income statement, (2) retained earnings statement, (3) ending balance sheet, and (4) closing entries in its general journal.

P3-3   *Financial Statements* The Nealy Company has prepared the following alphabetical adjusted trial balance on December 31, 2007:

	Debit	Credit
Accounts payable		$ 6,400
Accounts receivable	$ 5,700	
Accumulated depreciation: buildings		19,000
Accumulated depreciation: equipment		11,000
Additional paid-in capital		15,000
Administrative expenses	6,500	
Allowance for doubtful accounts		600
Buildings	42,000	
Capital stock, $1 par (4,000 shares)		4,000
Cash	5,000	
Cost of goods sold	27,400	
Current income taxes payable		4,035
Dividends distributed	2,400	
Equipment	22,000	

	Debit	Credit
Income tax expense	4,035	
Interest expense	650	
Interest payable (due July 1, 2008)		650
Inventory	10,800	
Land	6,800	
Notes payable (due July 1, 2011)		10,000
Rent revenue		2,800
Retained earnings, January 1, 2007		14,500
Sales returns	4,900	
Sales revenue		59,800
Selling expenses	9,700	
Unearned rent		700
Unexpired insurance	1,600	
Wages payable		1,000
	$149,485	$149,485

Required

Prepare the following 2007 items in proper form for the Nealy Company: (1) the income statement, (2) the retained earnings statement, (3) the ending balance sheet, and (4) the closing entries in the general journal. (*Hint*: For the ending balance sheet, the Capital Stock, Additional Paid-in Capital, and Retained Earnings accounts are summed to determine the total stockholders' equity.)

P3-4 *Adjusting Entries* The following 2007 information is available concerning the Drake Company, which adjusts and closes its accounts every December 31:

1. Salaries accrued but unpaid total $2,840 on December 31, 2007.
2. The $247 December utility bill arrived on December 31, 2007 and has not been paid or recorded.
3. Buildings with a cost of $78,000, 25-year life, and $9,000 residual value are to be depreciated; equipment with a cost of $44,000, eight-year life, and $2,000 residual value is also to be depreciated. The straight-line method is to be used.
4. A count of supplies indicates that the Store Supplies account should be reduced by $128 and the Office Supplies account reduced by $397 for supplies used during the year.
5. The company holds a $6,000, 12% (annual rate), six-month note receivable dated September 30, 2007 from a customer. The interest is to be collected on the maturity date.
6. Bad debts expense is estimated to be 1% of annual sales. 2007 sales total $65,000.
7. An analysis of the company insurance policies indicates that the Prepaid Insurance account is to be reduced for the $528 of expired insurance.
8. A review of travel expense reports indicates that $310 advanced to sales personnel (and recorded as Travel Expenses) has not yet been used by these personnel.
9. The income tax rate is 30% on current income and will be paid in the first quarter of 2008. The pretax income of the company before adjustments is $18,270.

Required

Journalize the necessary adjusting entries for the company at the end of 2007. Show supporting calculations in your journal entry explanations.

P3-5 *Adjusting Entries* The Franklin Retail Company entered into the following transactions during 2007. [The transactions were properly recorded in *real* (balance sheet) accounts unless otherwise indicated.]

Date	Transaction
Jan. 25	Purchased $480 of office supplies.
Feb. 1	Rented a warehouse from Tropple Company, paying one year's rent of $3,600 in advance. Recorded the $3,600 payment as rent expense.
Mar. 1	Borrowed $10,000 from the bank, signing a one-year note at an annual interest rate of 12%. The interest was collected in advance by the bank. The company recorded the transaction as a debit to Cash $8,800, debit to Interest Expense $1,200, and credit to Notes Payable $10,000.
May 1	Purchased office equipment for $15,000, paying $3,000 down and signing a two-year, 12% (annual rate) note payable for the balance. The office equipment is expected to have a useful life of 10 years and a residual value of $1,500. Straight-line depreciation is appropriate.

Date	Transaction
May 31	Purchased a three-year comprehensive insurance policy for $720.
Aug. 1	Sold land for $9,000. The purchaser made a $2,000 down payment and signed a one-year, 10% note for the balance. The interest and principal will be collected on the maturity date.
Oct. 1	Rented a portion of the retail floor space to a florist for $120 per month, collecting eight months' rent in advance. Recorded the $960 receipt as rent revenue.
Nov. 13	Issued checks to sales personnel totaling $900. The checks are advances for expected travel costs during the remainder of the year.

On December 31, 2007 the following additional information is available:

1. Property taxes for 2007 are due to be paid by April 1, 2008. The company has not paid or recorded its $2,300 property taxes for 2007.
2. The $302 December utility bill has not been recorded or paid.
3. Salaries accrued but not paid total $927.
4. Travel cost reports indicate that $787 of travel advances have been used to pay travel expenses.
5. The Office Supplies account had a balance of $129 on January 1, 2007. A physical count on December 31, 2007 showed $174 of office supplies on hand.
6. On January 1, 2007 the Buildings account and the Store Equipment account had balances of $100,000 and $65,000, respectively. The buildings are expected to have an $8,000 residual value, while the store equipment is expected to have a $2,000 residual value at the end of their respective lives. They are being depreciated using the straight-line method over 20- and 10-year lives, respectively.
7. The income tax rate is 30% on current income and is payable in the first quarter of 2008. The pretax income of the company before adjustments is $27,749.

Required

On the basis of the preceding information, prepare journal entries to adjust the company's books as of December 31, 2007. Each entry explanation should include supporting computations. (Round to the nearest dollar.)

P3-6   *Adjusting Entries* At the end of 2007 the Ritter Company prepared a trial balance, recorded and posted its adjusting entries, and then prepared an adjusted trial balance. Selected accounts and account balances from the trial balance and adjusted trial balance are as follows:

	Partial Trial Balance		Partial Adjusted Trial Balance	
	Debit	Credit	Debit	Credit
Depreciation expense	$ 0		$3,960	
Interest payable (due May 14, 2009)		$ 0		$ 810
Bad debts expense	0		410	
Utilities expense	1,480		1,682	
Rental revenue		1,650		2,635
Income tax expense	0		2,740	
Prepaid insurance	1,742		1,380	
Office salaries payable		0		540
Rent expense	0		800	
Accumulated depreciation		14,820		18,780
Interest receivable (due March 1, 2008)	0		320	
Prepaid rent	1,600		800	
Office salaries expense	5,600		6,140	
Income taxes payable		0		2,740
Insurance expense	300		662	
Allowance for doubtful accounts		130		540
Interest expense	0		810	
Unearned rent		600		0
Utilities payable		0		202
Interest revenue		620		940

	Partial Trial Balance		Partial Adjusted Trial Balance	
	Debit	Credit	Debit	Credit
Sales salaries expense	7,300		7,850	
Office supplies	1,150		700	
Rent receivable	0		385	
Advances to salespersons	770		220	
Office supplies expense	0		450	

Required
1. By comparing the partial trial balance to the partial adjusted trial balance, determine the adjusting entries that the company made on December 31, 2007. Prepare your answers in general journal form.
2. Assuming that the company uses reversing entries, indicate which adjusting entries should be reversed.

P3-7 *Adjusting Entries* The trial balance of the Trishia Company on December 31, 2007 (the end of its *annual* accounting period) included the following account balances *before* adjustments:

Notes receivable	$ 10,000 debit
Insurance expense	3,000 debit
Delivery equipment	14,000 debit
Building	60,000 debit
Unearned rent	4,320 credit
Notes payable	7,200 credit
Office supplies expense	1,000 debit

Reviewing the company's recorded transactions and accounting records for 2007, you find the following data pertaining to the December 31, 2007 adjustments:

1. On July 2, 2007 the company had accepted a $10,000, nine-month, 10% (annual rate) note receivable from a customer. The interest is to be collected when the note is collected.
2. On August 2, 2007 the company had paid $3,000 for a two-year insurance policy.
3. The building was acquired in 1995 and is being depreciated using the straight-line method over a 25-year life. It has an estimated residual value of $8,000.
4. The delivery equipment was purchased on April 2, 2007. It is to be depreciated using the straight-line method over a 10-year life, with an estimated residual value of $2,000.
5. On September 1, 2007 the company had received two years' rent in advance ($4,320) for a portion of a building it is renting to Oscar Company.
6. On December 1, 2007 the company had issued a $7,200, three-month, 12% (annual rate) note payable to a supplier. The interest is to be paid when the note is paid.
7. On January 2, 2007 the company purchased $1,000 of office supplies. A physical count on December 31, 2007 revealed that there are $400 of office supplies still on hand. No supplies were on hand at the beginning of the year.

Required
Prepare the adjusting entries that are necessary to bring the Trishia Company accounts up to date on December 31, 2007. Each journal entry explanation should summarize your calculations.

P3-8 *Income Statement Calculations* The Ferdon Company uses a periodic inventory system. The following is partial information from its income statements for 2007 and 2008:

	2007	2008
Beginning inventory	$ (2)	$ (4)
Sales	220,000	(6)
Purchases	118,000	140,000
Purchases returns	2,000	3,000
Ending inventory	48,000	74,000
Sales returns	1,000	3,000
Gross profit	(1)	77,000
Cost of goods sold	106,000	(5)
Expenses	65,000	62,000
Net income	(3)	15,000

Required

Fill in the blanks numbered 1 through 6. (*Hint*: It probably is easiest to work through the blanks according to the sequential numbers.)

P3-9 **Effects of Errors** During the current accounting period Page Company makes the following errors. The company uses a perpetual inventory system.

Error	Net Income	Total Assets	Total Liabilities	Total Stockholders' Equity
Example: Failed to record a cash sale.	U	U	N	U
1. The purchase of equipment for cash is recorded as a debit to Equipment and a credit to Accounts Payable.				
2. Failed to record the purchase of inventory on credit.				
3. Cash received from a customer in payment of its account is recorded as if the receipt were for a current period sale.				
4. Failed to record a credit sale.				
5. At the end of the year the receipt of money from a 60-day, 12% bank loan is recorded as a debit to Cash and a credit to Sales Revenue.				
6. Failed to record depreciation at the end of the current period.				

Required

Indicate the effect of the errors on the net income, total assets, total liabilities, and total stockholders' equity at the end of the accounting period by using the following code: O = overstated, U = understated, N = no effect. Disregard income taxes.

P3-10 **Errors in Financial Statements** At the end of the current year, the controller of the Jodi Corporation discovers the following items of information:

1. Salaries are paid every Friday for a five-day work week. The normal weekly payroll is $40,000. The year-end falls on a Tuesday this year.
2. The company has a $20,000, nine-month, 12% (annual rate) note payable outstanding at the end of the year. The note was issued on October 1; the interest is to be paid when the note is paid.
3. Examining the Rent Expense account, the controller finds that it includes a $4,800 advance payment for three months' rent. The payment was made on November 1.
4. There are $500 of office supplies left in the storeroom. At the beginning of the year there were no office supplies. During a year the company purchased $3,500 of office supplies, which were debited to the Office Supplies account.
5. The company received a large order in May with a $13,000 advance payment. The advance payment was credited to Unearned Revenue. In November, the last of the order was received by the customer.

Required

For each of the preceding items, indicate the effect on net income, assets, liabilities, and stockholders' equity in the financial statements of the company for the year if the controller fails to make an adjusting entry for the item (ignore income taxes). (*Contributed by Paula L. Koch*)

P3-11 **Worksheet** The Fiorillo Company has the following account balances on December 31, 2007 prior to any adjustments:

	Debit	Credit		Debit	Credit
Cash	$ 1,900		Accumulated depreciation:		
Accounts receivable	4,700		equipment		3,100
Allowance for doubtful accounts		$ 60	Accounts payable		4,300
Inventory	8,700		Notes payable (due March 1, 2008)		1,400
Prepaid insurance	600		Unearned rent		1,200
Land	4,100		Mortgage payable (due		
Buildings	38,000		January 1, 2012)		7,300
Accumulated depreciation:			Capital stock (2,000 shares)		10,000
buildings		11,500	Retained earnings (January 1, 2007)		18,075
Equipment	10,700		Dividends distributed	1,300	

(*continued*)

	Debit	Credit		Debit	Credit
Sales revenue		49,355	Utilities expense	2,000	
Cost of goods sold	27,185		Office supplies expense	770	
Salaries expense	4,080		Delivery expense	1,275	
			Other expenses	980	

Additional adjustment information: (a) depreciation on buildings, $1,100; on equipment, $600, (b) bad debts expense, $240, (c) interest accumulated but not paid: on note payable, $50; on mortgage payable, $530 (this interest is due during the next accounting period), (d) insurance expired, $175, (e) salaries accrued but not paid $370, (f) rent that was collected in advance and is now earned at year-end, $800, (g) office supplies on hand at year-end, $230 (expensed when originally purchased earlier in the year), and (h) the income tax rate is 30% on current income and is payable in the first quarter of 2008.

Required ▧
1. Transfer the account balances to a 10-column worksheet and prepare a trial balance.
2. Complete the worksheet.
3. Prepare the company's income statement, retained earnings statement, and balance sheet.
4. Prepare (a) adjusting, and (b) closing entries in the general journal.

P3-12 *Worksheet* The Langer Company has prepared the following partially completed worksheet for the year ended December 31, 2007:

	A	B	C	D	E	F	G	H	I	J	K
1								Retained			
2						Income		Earnings		Balance	
3		Trial Balance		Adjustments		Statement		Statement		Sheet	
4	Accounts	Debit	Credit	Debit	Credit	Debit	Credit	Debit	Credit	Debit	Credit
5	Cash	1,000									
6	Accounts receivable	2,700									
7	Allowance for doubtful accounts		30								
8	Note receivable (due 5/1/08)	1,200									
9	Inventory	9,200									
10	Land	4,500									
11	Buildings and equipment	20,600									
12	Accumulated depreciation		8,790								
13	Accounts payable		4,050								
14	Notes payable (due 4/1/2010)		4,000								
15	Capital stock (2,000 shares)		5,000								
16	Retained earnings (1/1/07)		6,120								
17	Dividends distributed	600									
18	Sales revenue		25,140								
19	Rent revenue		550								
20	Cost of goods sold	9,050									
21	Salaries expense	2,750									
22	Delivery expense	720									
23	Heat and light expense	820									
24	Other expenses	540									
25	Totals	53,680	53,680								
26											

The following additional information is available: (a) salaries accrued but unpaid total $250; (b) the $80 heat and light bill for December has not been recorded or paid; (c) depreciation expense totals $810 on the buildings and equipment; (d) interest accrued on the note payable totals $380 (this will be paid when the note is repaid); (e) the company leases a portion of its floor space to Brix Specialty Company for $50 per month, and Brix has not yet paid its December rent; (f) interest accrued on the note receivable totals $80; (g) bad debts expense is $70; and (h) the income tax rate is 30% on current income and is payable in the first quarter of 2008.

Required ▧
1. Complete the worksheet. (Round to the nearest dollar.)
2. Prepare the company's financial statements.
3. Prepare (a) adjusting, and (b) closing entries in the general journal.

P3-13 *Reversing Entries* During 2007, the Garson Company entered into two transactions involving promissory notes and properly recorded each transaction. These are listed next:

1. On November 1, 2007 it purchased land at a cost of $8,000. It made a $2,000 down payment and signed a note payable agreeing to pay the $6,000 balance in 6 months plus interest at an *annual* rate of 10%.

2. On December 1, 2007 it accepted a $4,200, three-month, 12% (*annual* interest rate) note receivable from a customer for the sale of merchandise. On December 31, 2007, the Garson Company made the following related adjustments:

Interest Expense	100	
Interest Payable		100

Interest Receivable	42	
Interest Revenue		42

Required

1. Assuming that the Garson Company uses reversing entries, prepare journal entries to record:
   a. The January 1, 2008 reversing entries
   b. The March 1, 2008 $4,326 collection of the note receivable
   c. The May 1, 2008 $6,300 payment of the note payable
2. Assuming instead that the Garson Company does *not* use reversing entries, prepare journal entries to record the collection of the note receivable and the payment of the note payable.

P3-14 *Reversing Entries* On December 31, 2007 Cochran Company made the following proper year-end adjusting entries:

Date	Account Titles	Debit	Credit
Dec. 31	Bad Debts Expense	530	
	Allowance for Doubtful Accounts		530
31	Salaries Expense	940	
	Salaries Payable		940
31	Unearned Rent	1,230	
	Rent Revenue		1,230
31	Interest Expense	220	
	Interest Payable (due July 1, 2008)		220
31	Rent Receivable	310	
	Rent Revenue		310
31	Depreciation Expense	5,100	
	Accumulated Depreciation		5,100
31	Insurance Expense	312	
	Prepaid Insurance		312
31	Interest Receivable (due February 1, 2009)	225	
	Interest Revenue		225
31	Office Supplies	100	
	Office Supplies Expense		100
31	Advances to Salespersons	300	
	Salaries Expense		300
31	Income Tax Expense	4,300	
	Income Taxes Payable		4,300

Required

1. Prepare journal entries to record whatever reversing entries you think are appropriate.
2. Explain your reasoning for each reversing entry.

P3-15 *Comprehensive* On November 30, 2007 the Zu Company had the following account balances:

	Debit	Credit		Debit	Credit
Cash	$ 3,090		Capital stock, no-par (2,000 shares)		$20,000
Accounts receivable	9,900		Retained earnings (1/1/2007)		42,400
Allowance for doubtful accounts		$ 100	Dividends distributed	$ 2,000	
Inventory	17,750		Sales revenue		76,000
Supplies	1,400		Sales returns	6,300	
Land	9,000		Cost of goods sold	36,860	
Buildings and equipment	42,000		Salaries expense	12,500	
Accumulated depreciation		4,200	Advertising expense	8,100	
Accounts payable		10,700	Other expenses	4,500	

During the month of December the Zu Company entered into the following transactions:

Date	Transaction
Dec. 4	Made cash sales of $3,000; the cost of the inventory sold was $1,800.
7	Purchased $2,400 of inventory on credit.
11	Customer returned $600 (retail price) of inventory for credit to its account; the cost of the inventory returned was $360.
14	Collected $900 of accounts receivable.
18	Sold land for $7,800; the land originally had cost $5,000.
20	Made credit sales of $4,000; the cost of the inventory sold was $2,400.
21	Returned $360 of defective inventory to supplier for credit to the Zu Company's account and reduced the inventory account.
27	Purchased $1,250 of inventory for cash.
28	Paid $1,100 of accounts payable.
31	Purchased land at a cost of $6,000; made a $1,000 down payment and signed a 12%, two-year note for the balance.

Required
1. Prepare general journal entries to record the preceding transactions.
2. Post to the general ledger accounts.
3. Prepare a year-end trial balance on a worksheet and complete the worksheet using the following information: (a) accrued salaries at year-end total $1,200; (b) for simplicity, the building and equipment are being depreciated using the straight-line method over an estimated life of 20 years with no residual value; (c) supplies on hand at the end of the year total $630; (d) bad debts expense for the year totals $830; and (e) the income tax rate is 30%; income taxes are payable in the first quarter of 2008.
4. Prepare the company's financial statements for 2007.
5. Prepare the 2007 (a) adjusting and (b) closing entries in the general journal.

P3-16 *Comprehensive (Appendix)* Tina Tunxis is the owner of Valley Sales, a distributor of horticulture supplies. The following is the balance sheet of the company as of December 31, 2006:

Cash	$ 2,300	Accounts payable	$ 6,400
Accounts receivable	10,400	Salaries payable	1,200
Inventory	12,500		
Equipment	8,000		
Less: Accumulated depreciation	(6,500)	T. Tunxis, Capital	$19,100
	$26,700		$26,700

Tina keeps very few records and has asked you to help her in the preparation of Valley Sales' 2007 financial statements. An analysis of the 2007 cash transactions recorded in the company's checkbook indicates deposits and checks as follows:

Total deposits: $173,200; all were collections from customers except for a long-term $10,000 bank loan.
Checks written: $169,800 summarized as follows:

Inventory	$123,100	Note payments (including interest of $650)	$ 2,650
Salaries	4,250	Office expense	3,400
Rent	4,800	Auto expense	4,100
Equipment	4,000	Withdrawals	23,500

Other information about the company is as follows:
1. Accounts receivable at December 31, 2007, $9,200.
2. Accounts payable at December 31:

2006: Inventory	$6,100	2007: Inventory	$8,500
Office expense	300	Auto expense	200
	$6,400		$8,700

3. Salaries payable at December 31, 2007, $1,800.
4. Equipment is depreciated by the straight-line method over a 10-year life. The equipment purchased in 2007 was acquired on July 1.
5. Interest payable at December 31, 2007, $140.
6. The company uses a periodic inventory system. Inventory at December 31, 2007, $17,400.

Required

1. Prepare a worksheet to summarize the transactions and adjustments of Valley Sales for 2007. (*Hint*: Include debit and credit columns for both transactions and adjustments.)
2. Prepare a 2007 income statement and a balance sheet as of December 31, 2007. (*Contributed by Walter A. Parker*)

P3-17 **AICPA Adapted** *Comprehensive (Appendix)* Presented next is information pertaining to Ward Specialty Foods, a calendar-year sole proprietorship, maintaining its books on the cash basis during the year. At year-end, however, Mary Ward's accountant adjusts the books to the accrual basis only for sales, purchases, and cost of sales, and records depreciation to more clearly reflect the business income.

Trial Balance
December 31, 2007

	Debit	Credit
Cash	$ 18,500	
Accounts receivable, 12/31/06	4,500	
Inventory, 12/31/06	20,000	
Equipment	35,000	
Accumulated depreciation, 12/31/06		$ 9,000
Accounts payable, 12/31/06		4,800
Payroll taxes withheld		850
Mary Ward, withdrawals	24,000	
Mary Ward, capital, 12/31/06		33,650
Sales		187,000
Purchases	82,700	
Salaries	29,500	
Payroll taxes	2,900	
Rent	8,400	
Miscellaneous expense	3,900	
Insurance	2,400	
Utilities	3,500	
	$235,300	$235,300

During 2007, Ward signed a new eight-year lease for the store premises and is in the process of negotiating a loan for remodeling purposes. The bank requires Ward to present financial statements for 2007 prepared on the accrual basis. To do so, Ward's accountant obtained the following additional information:

1. Amounts due from customers totaled $7,900 at December 31, 2007.
2. A review of the receivables at December 31, 2007 disclosed that an allowance for doubtful accounts of $1,100 should be provided. Ward had no bad debt losses from the inception of the business through December 31, 2007.
3. The inventory amounted to $23,000 at December 31, 2007 based on a physical count of goods priced at cost. No reduction to market was required.
4. On signing the new lease on October 1, 2007, Ward paid $8,400 representing one year's rent in advance for the lease year ending October 1, 2008. The $7,500 annual rental under the old lease was paid on October 1, 2006 for the lease year ended October 1, 2007.
5. On April 1, 2007, Ward paid $2,400 to renew the comprehensive insurance coverage for one year. The premium was $2,160 on the old policy, which expired on April 1, 2007.
6. Depreciation on the equipment was computed at $5,800 for 2007.
7. Unpaid vendors' invoices for food purchases totaled $8,800 at December 31, 2007.
8. Accrued expenses at December 31, 2006 and December 31, 2007 were as follows:

	12/31/06	12/31/07
Payroll taxes	$250	$400
Salaries	375	510
Utilities	275	450

After obtaining the preceding information, Ward's accountant prepared the following partially completed worksheet:

	A	B	C	D	E	F	G
1		Cash Basis		Adjustments		Accrual Basis	
2	Accounts	Debit	Credit	Debit	Credit	Debit	Credit
3	Cash	$18,500					
4	Accounts receivable	4,500					
5	Allowance for doubtful accounts						
6	Inventory	20,000					
7	Equipment	35,000					
8	Accumulated depreciation		$9,000				
9	Prepaid rent						
10	Prepaid insurance						
11	Accounts payable		4,800				
12	Accrued expenses						
13	Payroll taxes withheld		850				
14	Ward, withdrawals	24,000					
15	Ward, capital		33,650				
16							
17	Sales		187,000				
18	Purchases	82,700					
19	Income summary - inventory						
20	Salaries	29,500					
21	Payroll taxes	2,900					
22	Rent	8,400					
23	Miscellaneous expenses	3,900					
24	Insurance	2,400					
25	Utilities	3,500					
26	Depreciation						
27	Bad debts						
28	Totals	$235,300	$235,300				
29							

Required
1. Complete the preceding worksheet to convert the trial balance of Ward Specialty Foods to the accrual basis for the year ended December 31, 2007.
2. Prepare the statement of changes in Mary Ward, Capital, for the year ended December 31, 2007.

4

The Balance Sheet and the Statement of Changes in Stockholders' Equity

OBJECTIVES

After reading this chapter, you will be able to:

1 Understand the purposes of the balance sheet.

2 Define the elements of a balance sheet.

3 Explain how to measure the elements of a balance sheet.

4 Classify the assets of a balance sheet.

5 Classify the liabilities of a balance sheet.

6 Report the stockholders' equity of a balance sheet.

7 Prepare a statement of changes in stockholders' equity.

8 Understand the other disclosure issues for a balance sheet.

9 Describe the SEC integrated disclosures.

10 Explain the reporting techniques used in an annual report.

Do You Believe in Magic?

Walt Disney Company is well known for the magic that its "imagineers" have created in movie theaters and theme parks across the globe. To those not well versed in accounting, it appears that financial analysts may possess similar mystical qualities as they value a company's securities. Using several key financial variables (fundamentals) as their crystal ball, financial analysts will often make predictions of a company's future performance. For example, accounts receivable or inventory increases that are disproportionate to sales increases are often perceived as signals that a company is having trouble generating sales and that near-term economic prospects may be gloomy.

However, before you begin analyzing balance sheet information, you should be aware that the balance sheet has some significant limitations, or you could get the mistaken impression that a company's accountants possess as much financial magic as Disney's imagineers. For example, at the end of Disney's 2004 fiscal year, its market value of stockholders' equity (number of shares outstanding multiplied by stock price) was approximately $44 billion while the book value (reported amount) of this equity on its balance sheet was approximately $26 billion. What causes these differences between the market value of a company's stockholders' equity and its book value? Is it financial magic? Is it due to the mispricing in the stock market or in the way that accountants calculate book values? The explanations are varied and include the use of historical costs for valuing assets and liabilities, the use of estimates, and the existence of "off-balance sheet" assets and liabilities.

Credit: KIN CHEUNG/Reuters/Landov

Let's examine the sources of these differences in a little more detail. Disney's book value is based on past transactions measured at historical costs, yet its market value is based on market estimates of Disney's future prospects. For example, in the 1960s, Walt Disney was able to acquire about 43 acres (about twice the size of Manhattan Island) for a little over $5 million to build the Disney World Resort area. The market value of that land is certainly much more than that today, yet the increased value does not appear on Disney's balance sheet. Second, Disney makes many estimates of balance sheet items including accounts receivable, property, plant, and equipment, and contingent liabilities. These estimates are disclosed in the notes to the financial statements and should be considered in any financial analysis. Finally, many assets and liabilities are not recorded at all. The intellectual capital of Disney's imagineers is not shown as an asset on the balance sheet. Additionally, Disney reported contractual obligations of over $34 billion; however $20 billion of these obligations do not appear on the balance sheet.

With a clear understanding of the balance sheet and its limitations, we can see that the balance sheet isn't the result of magic but simply the result of current accounting rules and practices.

FOR FURTHER INVESTIGATION

For an article discussing a current balance sheet limitation of interest to accounting professionals (off-balance sheet structures), consult the Business & Company Resource Center (BCRC):

- All in the family: FIN 46 made companies admit paternity of special purpose entities. But it also resulted in some surprise adoptions. Tim Reason, *CFO, The Magazine for Senior Financial Executives*, 8756-7113, September 2004, v20, i11, p99(2).

FASB Statement of Concepts No. 5 recommends that a full set of financial statements for an accounting period should show a company's

- financial position at the end of the period,
- net income for the period,
- comprehensive income for the period,
- cash flows for the period, and
- investments by and distributions to owners for the period.[1]

Currently, companies include at least three major financial statements and several supporting schedules as the "full set" of financial statements in their **annual reports**. The three major financial statements are

1. the **balance sheet** or statement of financial position, which shows the company's financial position at the end of the accounting period,
2. the **income statement**, which shows the results of the company's income-producing activities for the accounting period, and
3. the **statement of cash flows**, which shows the cash inflows and cash outflows of the company for the accounting period.

Many companies include a statement of changes in stockholders' equity, which shows the changes in each item of stockholders' equity for the accounting period, as a fourth major financial statement.[2] A company also includes explanatory notes in its annual report to supplement these financial statements.

In this chapter, we focus primarily on the balance sheet, the statement of changes in stockholders' equity, and the accompanying notes. We discuss the balance sheet first because the FASB defines revenues and expenses in terms of changes in assets and liabilities. Thus, you need a clear understanding of the nature and measurement of assets and liabilities to understand net income and its components. Furthermore, the chapters of this book in general follow a balance sheet framework. Consequently, you need to know its purpose, content, format, and preparation to understand the more complex issues we discuss later. The statement of changes in stockholders' equity helps to explain the changes that occurred in each stockholders' equity item on a company's balance sheet from the beginning to the end of the accounting period. We also discuss this statement in this chapter as it relates to the balance sheet. The discussion focuses on the corporation, the major business entity in the United States. We discuss the income statement and statement of cash flows in Chapter 5.

INTERRELATIONSHIP OF FINANCIAL STATEMENTS

Exhibit 4-1 shows the interrelationship of the information in a company's major financial statements. The solid lines indicate the major flows of interrelated financial accounting information among the financial statements because of transactions and events during the period. For instance, the company may use assets from the beginning balance sheet (i.e., the ending balance sheet from the previous period) in an income-producing activity or it may sell them as a source of cash. The related financial accounting information will affect the company's income statement and statement of cash flows, respectively. Both the information about the income-producing activities reported in the income statement and the

---

1. "Recognition and Measurement in Financial Statements of Business Enterprises," *FASB Statement of Financial Accounting Concepts No. 5* (Stamford, Conn.: FASB, 1984), par. 13.
2. Some companies include a statement of comprehensive income as another major financial statement. We discuss this statement in Chapter 5.

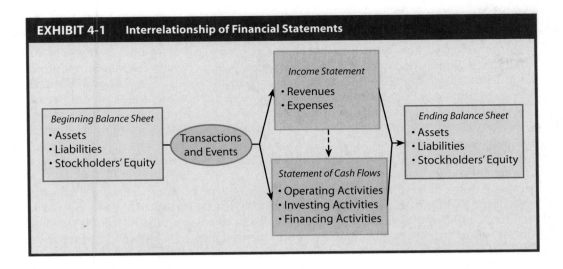

EXHIBIT 4-1   Interrelationship of Financial Statements

information about the cash inflows and cash outflows shown in the statement of cash flows will affect the accounting information reported in the ending balance sheet. The dashed line indicates a secondary flow of the interrelated information; that is, the income-producing activities that the company reports on its income statement also provide a net source of cash from operating activities. We further explain the relationships among the balance sheet, income statement, and statement of cash flows in the remaining sections of this chapter and in later chapters of this book.

PURPOSES OF THE BALANCE SHEET

One objective of financial reporting for a company is to help investors, creditors, and others assess the amounts, timing, and uncertainty of the prospective net cash inflows of the company. To meet this objective, the FASB suggested that a company should provide certain types of accounting information in its financial statements. A specific objective of a company's financial statements is to provide information about its economic resources, obligations, and owners' equity. This information is reported on a balance sheet. **A balance sheet shows the** *financial position* **of a company at a particular date.** A balance sheet also may be called a **statement of financial position.** The financial position of a company includes its economic resources (i.e., assets), economic obligations (i.e., liabilities), and equity, and their relationships to each other at a moment in time. A corporation's balance sheet, then, discloses its assets, liabilities, stockholders' equity, and related information on a specific date. The statement reports the corporation's *resource structure* (i.e., major classes and amounts of assets) and its *financial structure* (i.e., major classes and amounts of liabilities and equity). Its name evolved because the balance sheet is a detailed summary of the basic accounting equation (which must always remain in balance):

> **Assets = Liabilities + Stockholders' Equity**

The balance sheet does not attempt to show the total fair value of a company. Together with other financial statements and other information, however, it provides information that is useful to external users who want to make their own estimates of the company's fair value. More specifically, a company's balance sheet is intended to help external users (1) assess its liquidity, financial flexibility, and operating capability and (2) evaluate information about its income-producing performance during the period.

1 Understand the purposes of the balance sheet.

Liquidity, Financial Flexibility, and Operating Capability

Liquidity refers to how quickly a company can convert an asset into cash to pay its bills. That is, liquidity relates to the "nearness to cash" of a company's economic resources. Information about liquidity is important in evaluating the *timing* of cash flows in the near future. Information about short-term cash inflows is useful because these cash inflows are part of total cash inflows. Also, a company needs short-term cash inflows to take advantage of new investment opportunities as well as to pay its short-term obligations. Liquidity is also one aspect of a company's financial flexibility.

Financial flexibility refers to the ability of a company to use its financial resources to adapt to change. Adaptation may be thought of as being "offensive" or "defensive." A company uses offensive adaptation to take advantage of an unexpected new business opportunity, while it uses defensive adaptation to react to a negative business event. Financial flexibility may come from a quick access to the cash generated from more "liquid" economic resources. But liquidity is only part of financial flexibility. A company's financial flexibility comes from its ability to obtain enough net cash inflows from operations, from additional capital contributed by investors or long-term creditors, or from liquidating long-term economic resources without disrupting continuing operations. Information about a company's financial flexibility is important to external users in assessing the uncertainty of its future cash flows.

Operating capability refers to the ability of a company to maintain a given physical level of operations. This level may be indicated by the quantity of goods or services the company produced in a given period (i.e., inventory) or by the physical capacity of its operating assets (i.e., property, plant, and equipment) used to produce the goods or services. Information about a company's operating capability may be helpful to external users in understanding its performance and predicting future changes in its volume of activity and related cash flows.[3]

Capital and Capital Maintenance

A company's balance sheet provides a basis for evaluating its income-producing performance during a period. Therefore, a company's capital is important. **The capital (or *net assets*) of a company is its economic resources (assets) less its economic obligations (liabilities), or owners' equity.** For a corporation, the stockholders' equity is the capital. The management of the corporation uses this capital in fulfilling its responsibilities to the corporate stockholders. When a stockholder invests in a corporation, the stockholder is interested in a return *of* investment as well as a return *on* investment. To provide for a return of investment, the corporation's stockholders' equity (capital) must be maintained; this is referred to as **capital maintenance.** Once this capital is maintained, any income of the corporation is an increase in stockholders' equity. This increase is the basis for providing a return *on* investment to stockholders. Dividends are a return on investment, as is market price appreciation on the stock. Many investors prefer market price appreciation to dividends. Information about a corporation's capital is important in assessing its profitability and its ability to provide a return on investment. We discuss capital maintenance and income in Chapter 5.

Another way for you to look at Exhibit 4-1 is to think in terms of capital and capital maintenance. You can think of the beginning balance sheet as showing the corporation's capital at the beginning of the accounting period. The income statement and the statement of cash flows disclose the results of management's activities to use, maintain, and increase the capital during the accounting period. The ending balance sheet reports the capital at the end of the accounting period. But before it can be determined whether

3.   *Ibid.,* par. 24, 26, and 27 and "Reporting Income, Cash Flows, and Financial Position of Business Enterprises," *FASB Proposed Statement of Financial Accounting Concepts* (Stamford, Conn.: FASB, 1981), par. 25-32.

capital is maintained or a corporation has earned income, the initial (beginning) and subsequent (ending) capital must be determined.

Capital can be thought of in terms of (1) financial capital or (2) physical capital. **Financial capital is the monetary value of the net assets** from investments by stockholders as well as from earnings retained by the corporation. **Physical capital is a quantitative measure of the physical productive capacity** (e.g., square feet of factory space) of the corporation to provide goods or services. It is related to the concept of operating capability that we discussed in the previous section.[4] The difference between financial capital and physical capital is important in considering whether and when capital is maintained and income is earned (Chapter 5). The difference is not as important for reporting the capital at a point in time because accounting information primarily is expressed in dollars. Thus, a dollar value must be assigned to the physical capital before it is reported on a balance sheet. We discuss the alternative ways of measuring the net assets (capital) of a corporation later in the chapter.

RECOGNITION IN THE BALANCE SHEET

A company may disclose an item of information related to its financial position in its balance sheet, in a supporting schedule, or as part of the notes accompanying the financial statements. Recall from Chapter 2 that **recognition is the process of formally recording and reporting an element in the financial statements.** It includes depiction of an element in both words and numbers, with the amount included in the totals. Generally, the most useful (i.e., the best combination of relevance and reliability) information about assets, liabilities, and equity should be recognized and reported in the main body of the balance sheet. There are four basic recognition criteria. To be recognized, an item (and information about it) must meet the definition of an element, and be measurable, relevant, and reliable.[5] Thus, to meet the objectives of a company's balance sheet—to provide relevant and reliable information to assess its liquidity, financial flexibility, and operating capability and to evaluate its income-producing performance during the period—the company must determine what, how, and where to disclose the "elements" of the balance sheet. That is, the company must complete a three-stage process:

1. Identification of what items meet the definitions of the elements
2. Measurement (valuation) of the elements
3. Reporting (classification) of the elements

ELEMENTS OF THE BALANCE SHEET

For a company to report an item of information on its balance sheet, the item must meet the definition of an element. **The elements of the balance sheet are the broad classes of items comprising it.** They are the building blocks with which the balance sheet is prepared. The elements of financial statements are defined in **FASB Statement of Concepts No. 6.** We define and discuss each of the elements of a corporate balance sheet—assets, liabilities, and stockholders' equity—in the following sections.[6]

2 Define the elements of a balance sheet.

---

4. For a further discussion, see "Conceptual Framework for Financial Accounting and Reporting: Elements of Financial Statements and Their Measurement," *FASB Discussion Memorandum* (Stamford, Conn.: FASB, 1976), ch. 6.
5. "Recognition and Measurement in Financial Statements of Business Enterprises," *FASB Statement of Financial Accounting Concepts No. 5, op. cit.,* par. 58–64.
6. The discussion of the elements in the following sections is a summary of that presented in "Elements of Financial Statements of Business Enterprises," *FASB Statement of Financial Accounting Concepts No. 6* (Stamford, Conn.: FASB, 1985).

Assets

Assets are the probable future economic benefits obtained or controlled by a company as a result of past transactions or events.

Assets are the economic resources used to carry out a company's economic activities of consumption, production, and exchange. The primary attribute of all assets is *service potential*, the capacity to provide services or benefits to the company that uses them. To be considered an asset, an economic resource must have three characteristics:

1. The resource must be able to contribute directly or indirectly to the company's future net cash inflows. This service potential may exist because the asset is expected to be exchanged for something else of value to the company (e.g., accounts receivable), to be used in producing goods (e.g., factory) or services, to increase the value of other assets (e.g., patent), or to be used to settle its liabilities (e.g., cash).
2. The company must be able to obtain the future benefit and control others' access to it. Control means that the company can deny or regulate the ability of others to use the asset.
3. The transaction or event giving the company the right to or control over the benefit must have occurred. As a corollary, once an asset is acquired by a company, it continues to be an asset until it is exchanged or used up, or until some other event destroys the future benefit or removes the company's ability to obtain or control it.

Assets may be natural or man-made, tangible or intangible, and either exchangeable or useful only in the company's activities. Furthermore, they may be acquired by purchase, production, stockholder investments, discovery, or other nonreciprocal (one-way) transfers.

Liabilities

Liabilities are the probable future sacrifices of economic benefits arising from present obligations of a company to transfer assets or provide services in the future as a result of past transactions or events.

An obligation of a company must have three characteristics to be considered a liability:

1. It must involve a responsibility that will be settled by a sacrifice involving the transfer of assets, provision of services, or other use of assets at a specified or determinable date, on occurrence of a specified event, or on demand. The company does not need to know the specific identity of the "creditor" for a liability to exist, as long as a future transfer or use of assets to settle the liability is *probable*.
2. The responsibility must obligate the company so that it has little or no discretion to avoid the future sacrifice. Although most liabilities involve legal rights and duties, some are the result of equitable (ethical or moral) obligations or constructive (inferred from the facts) obligations. Thus, the company must be bound by a legal, equitable, or constructive responsibility to transfer assets or provide services.
3. The transaction or other event obligating the company must have occurred. Once a liability has been incurred, it continues to be a liability until the company settles it or another event removes it from the company's responsibility.

Liabilities arise primarily from purchasing goods or services on credit and from borrowing funds. Other liabilities result from collecting economic resources in advance of providing goods or services to customers. Liabilities also arise from selling products subject to warranties, from regulations imposed by governmental units, and from nonreciprocal transfers to owners or other entities.

Stockholders' Equity

Equity is the residual interest in the assets of a company that remains after deducting its liabilities.

The equity of a company is equal to its net assets (assets minus liabilities). Equity stems from ownership rights, and therefore it is the ownership interest. Since a company generally is not obligated to transfer assets to its owners, owners' equity ranks after liabilities as an interest in the assets and thus is a residual interest. For a corporation, stockholders' equity represents the interest of the stockholders, who bear the risks involved in the company's operations and activities and who obtain the resulting rewards. It is created by stockholders' investments of economic resources and later is modified by additional investments, net income, distributions to owners, and other changes in assets and liabilities. Stockholders' equity may not exist apart from the corporate assets and liabilities, since it is a residual interest.

MEASUREMENT OF THE ELEMENTS OF THE BALANCE SHEET

For a company to report an element on its balance sheet, the element must be reliably measured (valued) in monetary terms. The FASB has identified five alternatives for measuring elements. We show these alternative valuation methods in Exhibit 4-2 and discuss them in the following sections. Later in the chapter, when we discuss specific assets and liabilities, we identify the applicable valuation method. We do not include stockholders' equity in Exhibit 4-2 because it may not exist apart from assets or liabilities. That is, the measurement of assets and liabilities (i.e., net assets) will determine the dollar amount of stockholders' equity. To conserve space, we focus the discussion on the measurement of assets, but our comments generally also apply to liabilities.

3 Explain how to measure the elements of a balance sheet.

Historical Cost

The historical cost of an asset is the exchange price in the transaction in which the asset was acquired. The historical cost is measured by the cash paid for the asset or, in the case of a noncash exchange, by the estimated cash equivalent of the noncash asset or liability exchanged. After acquisition, the historical cost of an asset may be reduced due to the recognition of depreciation, amortization, impairment, or other adjustments.

Current Cost

The current cost of an asset is the amount of cash (or equivalent) that would be required on the date of the balance sheet to obtain the same asset. The "same asset" may be an identical asset or one with equivalent productive capacity. Alternative methods for obtaining the current cost include quoted market prices, the use of specific price indexes, and appraisals. Current cost is an *input value* and is sometimes referred to as *current replacement cost.*

Current Market Value

The current market value of an asset is the amount of cash (or equivalent) that could be obtained on the date of the balance sheet by selling the asset, in its present condition, in an orderly liquidation. An orderly liquidation means the asset is disposed of in a

EXHIBIT 4-2   Measurement (Valuation) of Assets and Liabilities

Alternative	Assets	Liabilities
1. Historical cost/historical proceeds	Initially, the amount of cash (or its equivalent) paid to acquire an asset (historical cost); subsequent to acquisition, the historical amount may be adjusted for depreciation, amortization, or other adjustments.	Initially, the amount of cash (or its equivalent) received when an obligation was incurred (historical proceeds); subsequent to incurrence, the historical amount may be adjusted for amortization.
2. Current cost/current proceeds	Amount of cash (or its equivalent) that would have to be paid if the same asset were acquired currently.	Amount of cash (or its equivalent) that would be obtained if the same obligation were incurred currently.
3. Current market value	Amount of cash (or its equivalent) that could be obtained currently by selling the asset in orderly liquidation.	Amount of cash (or its equivalent) that would be required currently to eliminate the liability.
4. Net realizable value	Amount of cash (or its equivalent) into which the asset is expected to be converted in due course of business less direct costs necessary to make that conversion.	Amount of cash (or its equivalent) expected to be paid to eliminate the liability in due course of business.
5. Present value	Present value of future cash inflows into which the asset is expected to be converted in due course of business less present value of future cash outflows necessary to obtain those inflows.	Present value of future cash outflows to eliminate the liability in due course of business.

Source: Adapted from "Conceptual Framework for Financial Accounting and Reporting: Elements of Financial Statements and Their Measurement," *FASB Discussion Memorandum* (Stamford, Conn.: FASB, 1976), p. 193 and "Recognition and Measurement in Financial Statements of Business Enterprises," *FASB Statement of Financial Accounting Concepts No. 5* (Stamford, Conn.: FASB, 1984), p. 23.

systematic and organized fashion. A current market value would be determined by obtaining a quoted market price for the sale of an asset of similar kind and condition. The term current market value is potentially confusing, because current cost and current market value are both "market values." Therefore, sometimes current market value is referred to as *current exit value*.

Net Realizable Value

The net realizable value of an asset is the amount of cash (or equivalent) into which the asset is expected to be converted in the ordinary operations of the company, less any expected conversion costs (e.g., completion, disposal, or collection costs). Net realizable value differs from current exit value by being based upon expected *future* sales proceeds of the asset (perhaps in a different form) rather than upon the *current* disposal value of an asset in its existing form. Net realizable value is sometimes referred to as *expected exit value*.

Present Value

The present value of an asset is the net amount of discounted future cash inflows less the discounted future cash outflows relating to the asset. Each future cash flow may be a single amount; in this case, the amount is referred to as an *estimated* cash flow. Or, each future cash flow may involve a range of possible amounts. In this case, a "weighted average" amount is determined and is referred to as an *expected* cash flow. When the estimated cash flows are used to determine present value, they are similar to those used to determine net realizable value; the difference between the two alternatives is that under the present value approach the time value of money (i.e., interest) is considered.[7] We discuss discounting and the computation of present value in the Time Value of Money module.

Valuations on Today's Balance Sheet

The valuation method primarily used in a company's balance sheet is historical cost. In general, each asset and liability of the company is recorded at the exchange price of the transaction in which the asset is obtained or the liability is incurred. Usually the company then reports this exchange price in its balance sheet until another exchange has taken place. Certain assets such as property, plant, and equipment are measured and reported at their exchange price (historical cost) adjusted for depreciation. Historical cost is used extensively as a valuation method because it is based on transactions and provides information that has a high degree of *reliability*. It has been criticized, however, because some users of financial statements argue that historical cost is not as *relevant* as the amounts reported under some alternative valuation methods. That is, historical cost may not represent the amount of future cash inflows (or outflows) that the company is likely to obtain (or pay) for the asset (or liability).

The FASB sometimes requires a company to report an asset or liability at its fair value. To clarify how to measure fair value, the FASB has issued a **Proposed FASB Statement of Standards**. This *Proposed Statement* defines **fair value** as the estimated price at which an asset (or liability) could be exchanged in a current transaction between knowledgeable, unrelated willing parties under normal business conditions. It indicates that the objective of determining a fair value is to estimate an exchange price for an asset (or liability) when an actual transaction has not occurred.

The *Proposed Statement* defines "market inputs" as the assumptions and data that would be used to estimate fair value. It groups these market inputs into a "hierarchy" of five broad categories (levels) for estimating fair value, as follows:

- *Level 1* market inputs are the best information for estimating fair value. These inputs are quoted prices in active markets for identical assets.
- *Level 2* market inputs are quoted market prices for similar assets, adjusted for differences between the assets.
- *Level 3* market inputs are direct market values other than quoted prices (e.g., current appraisals).
- *Level 4* market inputs are indirect market values (e.g., previous appraisals).
- *Level 5* measures are the lowest level of information and are "entity" inputs. These are based on the application of valuation techniques. Whenever possible (without undue cost and effort), multiple valuation techniques consistent with the market approach, income approach, and cost approach should be used. The *market*

---

7. *FASB Statement of Financial Accounting Concepts No. 5, op. cit.*, par. 67, and "Conceptual Framework for Financial Accounting and Reporting: Elements of Financial Statements and Their Measurement," *FASB Discussion Memorandum, op. cit.*, pp. 196–206, and "Using Cash Flow Information and Present Value in Accounting Measurements," *FASB Statement of Financial Accounting Concepts No. 7* (Norwalk, Conn.: FASB, 2000) p. 1.

approach requires observable prices based on actual transactions involving comparable assets. The *income approach* uses present value techniques to convert future amounts to a single present amount. The *cost approach* relates to the amount that would have to be paid to replace an asset's service capacity.

When measuring the fair value, a company must consider whether the asset will continue to be used in the business or will be sold. A company must also disclose certain information about its use of fair value to remeasure assets (and liabilities) reported on its balance sheet. This includes, for instance, how the fair value amount(s) were determined and the impact on the company's earnings for the period.[8]

Depending on the circumstances, to report the fair value of an asset or liability, a company might use current cost, current exit value, net realizable value, or present value. For instance, a company uses current cost for valuing certain "inventories," current exit value for "marketable securities," net realizable value for "receivables," and present value for "bonds payable." We identify the valuation method used for each type of asset and liability in the next section and we discuss these methods more fully in later chapters. As increased emphasis is placed on reporting information concerning a company's liquidity, financial flexibility, and operating capability, it is likely that the FASB will require more fair values to be reported on balance sheets (or related notes). The extent of the use of other valuation methods will depend, among other considerations, on the tradeoff between relevance and reliability. It is possible the FASB may develop GAAP in which "financial" assets and liabilities are valued at fair value while "non-financial" assets and liabilities are valued at historical cost.

LINK TO ETHICAL DILEMMA

As the controller for a struggling manufacturing company, you are in the process of closing the books for the year and notice that the company is going to be in technical violation of its debt covenants. Such a violation could result in bankruptcy, which would result in the loss of hundreds of jobs, including your own. You quickly analyze the financial statements and realize that by changing a few estimates involving accounts receivable, warranties, and pensions, the company will be able to avoid a violation of its debt covenants. While you don't believe the revised estimates would best represent the economic reality of your company's financial position, you also don't believe the estimates are unreasonably aggressive. Do you revise the estimates?

Limitations of the Balance Sheet

In addition to the criticism that the use of historical costs for valuing assets and liabilities does not help users assess the likely amounts of future cash flows relating to these items, there are other limitations of the balance sheet. First, a company's balance sheet does not include all of its economic resources and economic obligations. For instance, "human resources" or "intellectual capital" such as high-quality management or highly creative employees are not included as assets, primarily because of the difficulty of reliably measuring their values. Or, possible legal obligations for air or water pollution may not be reported as liabilities, again due to measurement problems. Second, many of the

---

8. "Fair Value Measurements," *FASB Proposed Statement of Financial Accounting Standards* (Norwalk, Conn.: FASB, 2004).

amounts that a company reports are based on estimates, which are subject to change. As we discuss in the next section, estimates are involved in determining the amounts for items such as uncollectible accounts and depreciation, as well as warranty and pension liabilities. Finally, in periods of inflation the amounts listed on a company's balance sheet do not show the "purchasing power" of its assets and liabilities. The FASB is aware of these limitations and in certain instances, as we discuss later in the chapter, requires companies to disclose additional information in the notes to the financial statements to help users in their decision making.

SECURE YOUR KNOWLEDGE 4-1

- By providing information about a company's resources and financial structure, the balance sheet should help users:
    - assess a company's liquidity, financial flexibility, and operating capability, and
    - evaluate a company's income-producing performance during a period.
- The elements of a balance sheet that should be recognized are assets, liabilities, and stockholders' equity.
- Various valuation methods can be used to measure elements on a balance sheet, with historical cost being the primary method employed; however, increasing use of fair value measurements is being required by FASB.
- The balance sheet does suffer from several limitations, including the use of historical cost, the exclusion of some economic resources and obligations, the use of estimates, and the lack of purchasing power adjustments.

REPORTING CLASSIFICATIONS ON THE BALANCE SHEET

A company's accounting system processes vast amounts of data. When the company prepares the financial statements, it simplifies, condenses, and classifies that data. The classifications are designed to help analysis by grouping items with similar characteristics. The intent is to improve the predictive value, and hence the usefulness, of the financial information for assessing the amounts, timing, and uncertainty of future cash flows.[9] **The arrangement of each company's balance sheet items and subtotals should be designed to be useful to its various external user groups.** But there are differences in companies, industries, and economic conditions. Therefore, there must be flexibility in classifications to ensure that a company's balance sheet is useful. Nonetheless, a general classification scheme may be presented that captures the majority of items reported by most companies.

A corporation usually divides its balance sheet into three sections, and groups the items reported within each section in some informative manner. A common classification would be:

1. *Assets*
    a. Current assets
    b. Long-term investments
    c. Property, plant, and equipment
    d. Intangible assets
    e. Other assets
2. *Liabilities*
    a. Current liabilities
    b. Long-term liabilities
    c. Other liabilities

4 Classify the assets of a balance sheet.

---

9.   *Ibid., FASB Statement of Financial Accounting Concepts No. 5,* par. 20–22.

3. *Stockholders' equity*
   a. Contributed capital
      (1) Capital stock
      (2) Additional paid-in capital
   b. Retained earnings
   c. Accumulated other comprehensive income

We discuss each of these groupings in the following sections. We show a comprehensive illustration of a balance sheet at December 31, 2007 for the Caron Manufacturing Company in Example 4-1 on pages 130 and 131. For selected items, we show illustrations of disclosures of actual companies in related exhibits. Appendix A includes **The Coca-Cola Company's** balance sheet at December 31, 2004.

Current Assets

Current assets are cash and other assets that a company expects to convert into cash, sell, or consume within one year or the normal operating cycle, whichever is longer. An *operating cycle* is the average time taken by a company to spend cash for inventory, process and sell the inventory, and collect the receivables, converting them back into cash. We show an example of a company's operating cycle in Exhibit 4-3. Note the relationship between current assets, current liabilities (discussed in the next section), and operating cash flows. Most companies have operating cycles of a year or less. A few, such as construction, lumber, distillery, and tobacco companies, have operating cycles that are longer than

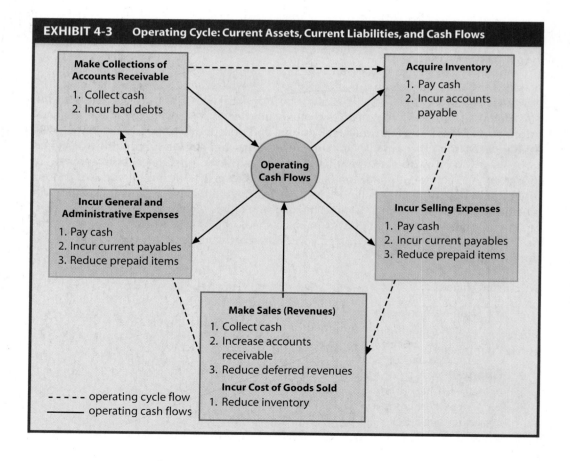

EXHIBIT 4-3   Operating Cycle: Current Assets, Current Liabilities, and Cash Flows

Make Collections of Accounts Receivable
1. Collect cash
2. Incur bad debts

Acquire Inventory
1. Pay cash
2. Incur accounts payable

Operating Cash Flows

Incur General and Administrative Expenses
1. Pay cash
2. Incur current payables
3. Reduce prepaid items

Incur Selling Expenses
1. Pay cash
2. Incur current payables
3. Reduce prepaid items

Make Sales (Revenues)
1. Collect cash
2. Increase accounts receivable
3. Reduce deferred revenues

Incur Cost of Goods Sold
1. Reduce inventory

- - - - - operating cycle flow
———— operating cash flows

one year. In that case, the longer time period should be used to determine the current assets.[10]

A company's current assets may include five items:

- cash (and cash equivalents),
- temporary investments in marketable securities,
- receivables,
- inventories, and
- prepaid items.

(Companies may use different titles than the ones we use here.) These items usually are presented in the current asset section in the order of their liquidity, as we show in Example 4-1 on pages 130 and 131.

Cash includes cash on hand and readily available in checking and savings accounts. Many companies also include "cash equivalents" with cash. *Cash equivalents* are risk-free securities, such as money market funds and treasury bills that will mature in three months or less from the date acquired by the holder. **Temporary investments in marketable securities** include debt and equity securities that are classified as "trading securities," "available-for-sale securities" that management intends to sell within one year or the normal operating cycle (whichever is longer), and "held-to-maturity" securities that will mature within a year. Also included are "derivative financial instruments," such as options to buy stock. Alternative titles include *short-term marketable securities* and *short-term investments*. They are listed at their fair value (current market value). **Receivables** include accounts receivable and notes receivable with short-term maturity dates. They are listed at their estimated collectible amounts (net realizable values).

Inventories include goods held for resale in the normal course of business plus, in the case of a manufacturing company, raw materials (items to be converted into finished goods) and work in process (partially completed goods) inventories. They are listed at their historical cost or market value (current cost), whichever is lower. The inventory costing method (LIFO, FIFO, average cost) is disclosed parenthetically or in the related notes. To reduce the detail on its balance sheet, a company might show a total inventory amount in current assets and include a schedule of the components in the notes to the financial statements. This procedure is used by **Johnson & Johnson,** as we show in Real Report 4-1 on page 132. **Prepaid items** such as insurance, rent, office supplies, and taxes will not be converted into cash but will be consumed. Conceptually, prepaid items should not be classified as current assets because they do not directly enter into the operating cycle. However, they are included as current assets because had they not been paid in advance, cash would have been paid out within the cycle. Also, even though a two-year prepayment of insurance would extend over more than an annual operating cycle, the payment is usually classified as a current asset because the amount is not material. Prepaid items are listed at the historical cost of the remaining amounts.

Current Liabilities

We discuss current liabilities next because of their close relation to current assets. **Current liabilities are obligations of a company that it expects to liquidate by using existing current assets, or creating other current liabilities within one year or the normal operating cycle, whichever is longer.** Several types of liabilities should be included as current liabilities:

1. Obligations for items (goods or services) that are in the operating cycle. These include, for instance, accounts payable and salaries payable.

---

10. "Restatement and Revision of Accounting Research Bulletins," *Accounting Research and Terminology Bulletins, Final Edition, No. 43* (New York: AICPA, 1961), ch. 3, sec. A, par. 4 and 5.

2. Advance collections for the future delivery of goods or performance of service—for instance, obligations under short-term derivative financial instruments (such as options to sell stock) as well as unearned rent and unearned ticket sales. These latter items sometimes are referred to as short-term deferred (unearned) revenues.

3. Other obligations that will be paid within one year or the operating cycle, such as short-term notes payable, interest payable, dividends payable, income taxes payable, the estimated liability for short-term product warranties, and the portions of long-term liabilities that mature during this period.[11]

These obligations are listed on the balance sheet at the amount owed (historical proceeds) or estimated to be owed. Example 4-1 shows the current liabilities section of the Caron Manufacturing Company.

EXAMPLE 4-1   Balance Sheet

CARON MANUFACTURING COMPANY

Balance Sheet
December 31, 2007

Assets

Current Assets			
Cash		$ 14,300	
Temporary investments in available for sale securities		19,700	
Accounts receivable	$ 68,200		
Less: Allowance for doubtful accounts	(3,200)	65,000	
Inventories			
Raw materials	$ 32,000		
Work in process	49,500		
Finished goods	66,100	147,600	
Prepaid items			
Insurance	$ 4,800		
Office supplies	2,200	7,000	
Total current assets			$253,600
Long-Term Investments			
Investment in held-to-maturity bonds		$ 17,000	
Fund to retire long-term bonds payable		17,400	
Total long-term investments			34,400
Property, Plant, and Equipment			

	Cost	Accumulated Depreciation	Book Value
Land	$ 36,000	—	$ 36,000
Buildings	428,000	$207,000	221,000
Equipment	192,000	63,700	128,300
Totals	$ 656,000	$270,700	$385,300

Total property, plant, and equipment			385,300
Intangible Assets			
Trademarks		$ 12,600	
Patents (net)		16,900	
Total intangible assets			29,500
Total Assets			$702,800

---

11. *Ibid.*, par. 7.

An obligation that is due within the next accounting period but which will be refinanced by issuing new long-term liabilities is not classified as a current liability. This obligation is not a current liability, because it will not require the use of current assets to satisfy the debt.

Working Capital

The working capital of a company is the financial resources it uses during its operating cycle. **Working capital is the excess of a company's current assets over its current liabilities.** Although a company seldom computes its working capital on the balance sheet, it is often used by creditors and others as an indicator of the short-run liquidity of the company. Often external users use a slightly different computation, the **current ratio** (current assets divided by current liabilities), for the same purpose. Users must be careful when using the current ratio because the liquidity *composition* of the current assets is very important. The FASB has suggested several general guidelines for more homogeneous classifications of assets to help external users assess the nature, amounts, and liquidity of available resources. One classification alternative might be to separate the current assets

---

EXAMPLE 4-1 (Continued)

Liabilities

Current Liabilities		
Accounts payable	$ 87,100	
Salaries payable	3,300	
Income taxes payable	27,400	
Advances from customers	19,600	
Current portion of mortgage payable	8,400	
Total current liabilities		$145,800
Long-Term Liabilities		
Bonds payable (10%, due 2020)	$ 90,000	
Less: Unamortized bond discount	(8,200)	$ 81,800
Mortgage payable (12%, due 2009–2012)		52,600
Accrued pension cost		34,700
Total long-term liabilities		169,100
Other Liabilities		
Deferred income taxes		14,300
Total Liabilities		$329,200

Stockholders' Equity

Contributed Capital (see Example 4-2)		
Common stock, $5 par (20,000 shares authorized,		
14,300 shares issued and outstanding)	$ 71,500	
Additional paid-in capital on common stock	173,900	
Total contributed capital		$245,400
Retained Earnings (see Example 4-2)		116,200
Accumulated Other Comprehensive Income		
Unrealized increase in value of available-for-		
sale securities (see Example 4-2)		12,000
Total Stockholders' Equity		$373,600
Total Liabilities and Stockholders' Equity		$702,800

into two groups. The first group would include the *liquid* assets of cash and temporary investments in marketable securities that are immediately convertible into cash. The second group would include *separable assets,* those assets that can be separated from the company and converted into cash but with some time lag and conversion costs. These would include items such as receivables and inventories.[12] Users can develop alternative groupings of current assets and current liabilities, as well as other ratios for assessing liquidity and financial flexibility.

Reporting

Real Report 4-1 Inventory Disclosures

JOHNSON & JOHNSON

At January 2, 2005 and December 28, 2003 (in millions)	2004	2003
Current assets (in part):		
Inventories (Notes 1 and 2)	$3,744	$3,588

NOTES TO CONSOLIDATED FINANCIAL STATEMENTS (in part):

2 Inventories

At the end of 2004 and 2003, inventories were comprised of:

(Dollars in Millions)	2004	2003
Raw materials and supplies	$ 964	$ 966
Goods in process	1,113	981
Finished goods	1,667	1,641
	$3,744	$3,588

Questions:

1. What is the percentage of each type of inventory for 2004 and 2003?
2. Why might you be concerned (or optimistic) in regard to the changes in the percentages?

Long-Term Investments

Companies make investments for several reasons. They may be interested in appreciation of the investment (the company expects the market value of the investment to increase), in income from interest or dividends, in exercising control over certain other companies, as in the case of a subsidiary or a major supplier, and in using the investment for specific future purposes such as the acquisition of property, plant, and equipment for expansion. Whether or not the investment is readily marketable, **if the company expects to hold the item for more than one year or the operating cycle, whichever is longer, it is classified as a long-term (noncurrent) investment.**

Long-term investments include holdings of available-for-sale debt and equity securities that the company does not intend to convert into cash within one year or the normal operating cycle (if longer than a year). Long-term investments also include investments in debt securities (e.g., bonds) expected to be held to maturity, noncurrent notes receivable from unaffiliated companies, long-term advances to unconsolidated affiliated companies, and financial instruments (such as options to buy stock) that are noncurrent. Investments in property and equipment being held for future operations, such as land being held for a future building site, also are included. Special funds established to retire

---

12. For a further discussion, see "Reporting Funds Flows, Liquidity, and Financial Flexibility," *FASB Discussion Memorandum* (Stamford, Conn.: FASB, 1980), ch. 8 and 9.

bonds payable or preferred stock (often called sinking funds) or to acquire future facilities are included as long-term investments. Finally, miscellaneous investments, including the cash surrender value of life insurance policies, should be listed in this section of the balance sheet. Investments are listed at their fair value, historical cost, book value, or present value, depending on the type of investment. The method of valuation for each long-term investment should be disclosed either parenthetically or in the notes to the financial statements. Example 4-1 illustrates the long-term investments section of Caron Manufacturing Company.

Property, Plant, and Equipment

The property, plant, and equipment section of a company's balance sheet includes the tangible assets used in its operations. Often these are called *fixed assets* because of their relative permanency in the company's operations. A merchandising company sometimes will title this section Property and Equipment because it does not have manufacturing (plant) facilities. Assets that have a physical existence, such as land, buildings, equipment, machinery, furniture, and natural resources are listed in this category. Except for land, all the fixed assets are depreciable or depletable (in the case of natural resources). Land is listed at its historical cost, while the remaining fixed assets are listed at their book values (historical cost less accumulated depreciation or depletion). A *contra-asset* account, such as accumulated depreciation, usually is used to reduce fixed assets to their book values while still disclosing the historical cost. The method of depreciating the fixed assets is disclosed in the notes to the financial statements. In the case where the earning power of a fixed asset has been impaired, it is reported at a reduced fair value. Example 4-1 illustrates the property, plant, and equipment section of Caron Manufacturing Company. Some companies show a total amount of property, plant, and equipment on their balance sheets and a breakdown in the related notes. This procedure is used by **Campbell Soup Company** for its plant assets, as we show in Real Report 4-2.

Contra asset (handwritten margin note)

Real Report 4-2 Plant Assets

CAMPBELL SOUP COMPANY

	August 1, 2004	August 3, 2003
(in millions)		
Assets (in part):		
Plant assets, net of depreciation (Note 14)	$1,901	$1,893

NOTES TO CONSOLIDATED FINANCIAL STATEMENTS (in part):

14 Plant Assets (in part):

	2004	2003
Land	$ 70	$ 66
Buildings	1,009	974
Machinery and equipment	2,977	2,827
Projects in progress	192	145
	4,248	4,012
Accumulated depreciation	(2,347)	(2,169)
	$1,901	$1,843

Questions:

1. What percentage of the total cost is "projects in progress" on August 3, 2003, and August 1, 2004?
2. What might this indicate?

Certain long-term lease contracts relating to leased property, plant, and equipment also are included in this section. Long-term leases of assets are a popular way for a lessee to acquire the rights to the use of the assets without a large cash down payment. In the case of a *capital lease*, one that has many of the characteristics of a purchase, both the assets and the liabilities sections of the lessee's balance sheet are affected. Since the lease allows the lessee company relatively unrestricted rights to the use of the asset for an extended period, the rights are economic resources to the company, even though the asset is not legally owned. The lessee initially records a capital lease as an asset, Leased Equipment, at the present value of the future lease payments. It is amortized in a manner similar to other legally owned assets of the company. The book value of the leased asset is reported in the property, plant, and equipment section. Similarly, since the capital lease payments are noncancelable over an extended number of years, these payments are a long-term liability of the lessee company. The obligation for a capital lease also is recorded initially at the present value of the future lease payments and then reduced by the amount of each lease payment (after adjustment for interest). As we discuss later in this chapter, the capital lease liability is reported in the long-term liabilities section of the balance sheet. We discuss the accounting for capital leases in Chapter 21.

Intangible Assets

Intangible assets are those noncurrent economic resources that a company uses in its operations but have no physical existence. They generally derive their value from the rights held by the company for their use. A company may have three categories of intangible assets: (1) intangible assets with finite useful lives, (2) intangible assets with indefinite lives, and (3) goodwill. Intangible assets with finite useful lives (such as patents, franchises, and computer software costs) are amortized over their useful lives and reported on the balance sheet at their book values (historical cost less accumulated amortization). The accumulated amortization of these intangibles is disclosed in the notes to the financial statements. Intangible assets with indefinite useful lives (such as trademarks) are not amortized, but are reviewed for impairment annually. Impairment arises when the earning power of an intangible asset has been reduced to the point where its fair value is less than its historical cost. These intangible assets are reported on the balance sheet at their historical cost or, if impaired, at their lower fair value. Goodwill, another type of intangible asset, is not amortized but is also reviewed for impairment annually. Goodwill is also reported on the balance sheet at its historical cost or, if impaired, at its lower fair value. Many companies have valuable "intangible assets," such as their human resources and intellectual capital (employees), but these resources are not reported on the balance sheet because of the difficulty in reliably measuring their value. Example 4-1 illustrates the intangibles section of Caron Manufacturing Company. We discuss the acounting for intangible assets in Chapter 12.

Other Assets

Finally an "Other Assets" section occasionally is used to report miscellaneous assets that may not "fit" in one of the previous sections. This section sometimes is referred to as *deferred charges*. Examples of items that have been classified in this section include long-term prepayments (such as for rent or insurance), deferred tax assets, prepaid pension costs, bond issue costs, assets of a component of the company that is being discontinued, advances to officers, idle fixed assets, cash from customers' security deposits on returnable containers, assets leased to others, and assets temporarily restricted by foreign countries. Classification within this section should be made judiciously. Many items that are listed in this section might be classified correctly in one of the previous sections.

Long-Term Liabilities

5 Classify the liabilities of a balance sheet.

Long-term liabilities are those obligations of a company that it does not expect to liquidate using current assets or creating current liabilities within one year or the normal operating cycle (whichever is longer). Long-term liabilities may be called **noncurrent liabilities.** Many of these obligations may be outstanding for several years. Items such as long-term notes payable, capital lease obligations, mortgages payable, obligations under noncurrent financial instruments (e.g., options to sell stock), estimated liabilities from long-term warranties, accrued pension cost (i.e., obligation for future pension payments), and bonds payable are included in this category.

To finance its activities, a corporation may issue long-term bonds (sometimes called debentures or notes). A bond is a written promise to repay a specific amount (its *face value*) at some future maturity date. Nearly all bonds also pay a specified interest rate (either semiannually or annually) that may vary from company to company. Many bonds sell in a bond market similar to that of a stock market. Frequently a corporation may issue a bond at more or less than its face value. This occurs when the bond pays a stated interest rate greater or less than the yield rate investors can earn elsewhere on a similar security, making it more or less valuable.

When a bond is issued for more than its face value, it is sold at a *premium*; when it is issued for less, it is sold at a *discount*. At the time of sale the Bonds Payable account is recorded at the face value of the bond, and an adjunct account called Premium on Bonds Payable (or a *contra* account called Discount on Bonds Payable) is used to record the amount by which the selling price is greater than (or less than) the face value. Then, each period this premium (or discount) is amortized as an adjustment to interest expense (generally by use of a present value approach), and at the maturity date only the face value of the bonds payable remains. Whenever a balance sheet is prepared, the remaining premium is added to (or the discount is subtracted from) the face value of the bonds payable to determine the book value. Most long-term liabilities are reported at their present value, but some are listed at cost. Any applicable interest rates, maturity values, and other provisions are disclosed parenthetically on the balance sheet or in the notes to the financial statements. Example 4-1 illustrates the long-term liabilities section of Caron Manufacturing Company. Some companies show a total amount of long-term liabilities on their balance sheets and a schedule of the individual amounts in the related notes. This procedure is used by **Kimberly-Clark** for its long-term debt, as we show in Real Report 4-3.

Real Report 4-3 Long-Term Debt

KIMBERLY-CLARK CORPORATION

Liabilities and Stockholders' Equity (in part):

	December 31	
	2004	2003
(in millions)		
Long-term Debt	$2,298.0	$2,733.7

NOTES TO CONSOLIDATED FINANCIAL STATEMENTS (in part):

Note 4. Debt (in part)

Long-term debt is composed of the following:

	Weighted-Average Interest Rate	Maturities	December 31	
			2004	2003
Notes and debentures	5.77%	2005–2038	$2,309.8	$2,342.9
Industrial development revenue bonds	2.58%	2006–2037	300.7	381.3
Bank loans and other financings in various currencies	7.22%	2005–2031	272.9	194.9
Total long-term debt			2,883.4	2,919.1
Less current portion			585.4	185.4
Long-term portion			$2,298.0	$2,733.7

Continued

Fair value of total long-term debt, based on quoted market prices for the same or similar debt issues, was approximately $3.0 billion and $3.1 billion at December 31, 2004 and 2003, respectively. Scheduled maturities of long-term debt for the next five years are $585.4 million in 2005, $64.8 million in 2006, $336.7 million in 2007, $19.7 million in 2008, and $5.1 million in 2009.

At December 31, 2004, the Corporation had $1.2 billion of revolving credit facilities. These facilities, unused at December 31, 2004, permit borrowing at competitive interest rates and are available for general corporate purposes, including backup for commercial paper borrowings. The Corporation pays commitment fees on the unused portion but may cancel the facilities without penalty at any time prior to their expiration. Of these facilities, $600 million expires in September 2005 and the balance expires in November 2009.

Debt payable within one year is as follows:

	December 31	
	2004	2003
	(Millions of dollars)	
Commercial paper	$ 526.3	$533.5
Current portion of long-term debt	585.4	185.4
Other short-term debt	103.0	145.4
Total	$1,214.7	$864.3

At December 31, 2004 and 2003, the weighted-average interest rate for commercial paper was 2.3 percent and 1.0 percent, respectively.

Questions:

1. What information regarding cash flows is available in the note but is not available in the balance sheet?
2. Compute the approximate interest expense on the notes and debentures for the year ended December 31, 2004.
3. Provide an estimate of what the interest expense on the notes and debentures will be for the year ended December 31, 2005. What assumptions must be made to provide this estimate?

Other Liabilities

A final section sometimes is used to report miscellaneous liabilities. This section might include items such as deferred tax liabilities, obligations of a component of the company that is being discontinued, and long-term advances from customers. As in the case of other assets, this category should be used judiciously.

Conceptual Guidelines for Reporting Assets and Liabilities

In the previous sections we discussed the typical classifications of assets and liabilities in a balance sheet. A company, however, should classify its assets and liabilities in the most informative manner for its external user groups. In addition to the "liquid" and "separable" subclassifications of current assets we discussed earlier, the FASB has suggested several guidelines for developing *homogeneous classes* of assets and liabilities. These guidelines include:

1. Reporting assets according to their type or expected function in the central operations or other activities of the company. For example, assets held for resale (inventory) should be reported separately from assets held for use in production (property, plant, and equipment).

2. Reporting as separate items assets and liabilities that affect the financial flexibility of the company differently; for example, assets used in operations, assets held for investment, and assets subject to restrictions (such as leased equipment).

3. Reporting assets and liabilities according to the fair value method used to value the items; for example, assets and liabilities measured at net realizable value versus those measured at current cost.

These general guidelines are intended to result in asset and liability classifications that help users assess the nature, amounts, and liquidity of available resources. This includes the intentions of management regarding their use, and the amounts and timing of obligations that require liquid resources for settlement.

The AICPA Special Committee on Financial Reporting extends these guidelines by suggesting that companies distinguish between "core" and "non-core" assets and liabilities. Core assets and liabilities result from a company's usual and recurring activities, transactions, and events. Conversely, non-core assets result from unusual or non-recurring activities, transactions, or events. For instance, non-core assets might include a receivable related to an unusually large sale of inventory that is not expected to recur in the future. Non-core liabilities might include those related to a discontinued component.[13]

Stockholders' Equity

Stockholders' equity is the residual interest of the stockholders in the assets of the corporation. A company may be organized in three different ways: as a sole proprietorship, a partnership, or a corporation.

A sole proprietorship is a single-owner company. This is usually a small company where the owner acts as manager and has direct access to the accounting records. Therefore, separate accounts typically are not used for the owner's investment and retained earnings. Normally, the total owner's equity is summarized in a single *capital* account.

A partnership involves two or more persons who have agreed to combine their capital and efforts in the operations of a company. The partnership generally has a *partnership agreement*, a legal document that includes the investment requirements, allocation of income, and withdrawal provisions for each partner. Separate capital accounts are used for each partner to summarize the partner's equity.

The corporation is the most complex business organization. Usually there is *absentee* ownership, where most of the stockholders are not involved in managing the corporation. To protect these absentee owners, state laws have been established, many of which relate to the accounting for stockholders' equity. Stockholders' equity consists of three components: (1) contributed capital, (2) retained earnings, and (3) accumulated other comprehensive income.

6 Report the stockholders' equity of a balance sheet.

Contributed Capital

The owners of a corporation hold shares of stock in that corporation. A stockholder may acquire shares directly from the corporation or by purchasing them on the stock market from another investor. The corporation's balance sheet is affected only in the first case. Most state laws protecting stockholders and creditors require a certain amount of legal capital. **Legal capital is the minimum amount of stockholders' equity that the corporation may not distribute as dividends;** it is one element of the total amount of contributed capital. Accounting for contributed capital follows these legal requirements. Contributed capital frequently is separated into two components, capital stock (relating to the legal capital) and additional paid-in capital.

---

13. "Reporting Income, Cash Flows, and Financial Position of Business Enterprises," *FASB Proposed Statement of Financial Accounting Concepts, op. cit.,* par. 50, 51, and 170, and "Improving Business Reporting—A Customer Focus," *AICPA Special Committee on Financial Reporting* (New York: AICPA, 1994), App. II, pp. 138–139.

Capital Stock and Additional Paid-In Capital

Corporations may issue two types of capital stock, preferred stock and comon stock. **Preferred stock** has different ownership features (which some investors consider more attractive) from common stock, including the first right to a specified dividend, if one is paid. **Common stock** carries the right to vote at the annual stockholders' meeting and to share in residual profits. The corporate charter includes the number of shares that a corporation is legally authorized to issue, as well as the types and characteristics of its capital stock. Common stock is the most prevalent type of capital stock. Each of these types of stock typically sells on a stock market, which establishes its *market value* per share.

Based upon state laws, a corporation may issue (1) par value, (2) stated value, or (3) no-par (no stated value) capital stock. Legally, capital stock may be required to carry a par value or a stated value. Par value or stated value refers to a specific dollar amount per share that is printed on the stock certificate.[14] Often this par value is a very small amount, say $1 or $5 per share, because states generally do not allow a corporation to issue stock at less than par. For instance, the par value of **Honeywell's** common stock is $1 per share. The par value of a share of stock has no direct relationship to the share's market value. Nonetheless, the legal (par) value must be accounted for separately.

When a corporation issues par value capital stock (common or preferred), it must allocate the amount it receives (market price) between a capital stock account for the par value and another contributed capital account for the difference between the par and the market value. This latter account has a title such as Additional Paid-in Capital, Paid-in Capital in Excess of Par, or Premium on Common (or Preferred) Stock. For instance, if a corporation sold 100 shares of its $5 par common stock for $30 per share, the journal entry to record the transaction is as follows (the number of shares issued in the transaction is also recorded):

Cash	3,000	
Common Stock, $5 par		500
Additional Paid-in Capital on Common Stock		2,500

Many states allow corporations to issue no-par capital stock. When a corporation issues no-par capital stock, the amount it receives from the sale usually is the legal capital, and the corporation records the entire amount in the capital stock account. Due to various other stock transactions, it is possible for a corporation issuing no-par stock to have certain additional paid-in capital accounts.

A corporation sometimes will repurchase its own capital stock. When it does, the number of shares outstanding is reduced. The corporation usually records the *cost* of the reacquisition in a contra stockholders' equity account entitled **Treasury Stock.** This account has a debit balance and the corporation deducts the amount from the total of

---

14. There are certain legal differences between par value and stated value. We discuss these in Chapter 16. Since the accounting for stated value stock generally is identical to that for par value stock, here we focus on par value stock.

contributed capital, retained earnings, and accumulated other comprehensive income to determine its total stockholders' equity.

Regardless of whether a corporation issues par or no-par stock, the corporation lists the balances in the Preferred Stock, Common Stock, and Additional Paid-in Capital accounts separately on its balance sheet and sums the amounts to determine the total amount of its contributed capital. The par value or stated value per share, as well as the number of shares authorized, issued, and outstanding, should be disclosed either parenthetically in the contributed capital section or in the notes to the financial statements. Example 4-1 illustrates the contributed capital section of Caron Manufacturing Company.

Retained Earnings

Retained earnings is the total amount of corporate net income that has not been distributed to stockholders as dividends. A corporation may retain the assets generated from this net income to use in its daily operations, to maintain its productive facilities, or for growth. In any event, a retained earnings balance has no relationship to the cash that is available for dividends. The resources generated by net income are invested in all assets. The Retained Earnings account balance is an addition in stockholders' equity. A negative (debit) retained earnings balance (due to cumulative net losses and dividends exceeding cumulative net income), called a *deficit*, is subtracted in stockholders' equity.

Sometimes a company *restricts* or *appropriates* a portion of retained earnings to indicate that it cannot be reduced by the distribution of dividends. This may occur as a result of a legal or contractual requirement. Usually, such a restriction is disclosed in the notes to the financial statements.

Accumulated Other Comprehensive Income

As we discuss in Chapter 5, a company is required to report its total comprehensive income for the accounting period. Comprehensive income includes both net income and "other comprehensive income." Other comprehensive income (loss) may include four items: (1) unrealized increases (gains) or decreases (losses) in the market (fair) value of investments in available-for-sale securities, (2) translation adjustments from converting the financial statements of a company's foreign operations into U.S. dollars, (3) certain gains and losses on "derivative" financial instruments, and (4) certain pension liability adjustments.

A corporation includes its total net income earned to date in its retained earnings amount reported in stockholders' equity. The corporation includes its other comprehensive income (or loss) accumulated to date in its **accumulated other comprehensive income (or loss)** amount reported in stockholders' equity. If a corporation has more than one item of other comprehensive income, it has a choice. It may report the amount of accumulated other comprehensive income for each item in stockholders' equity. Or, it may report the total amount of accumulated other comprehensive income for all the items in stockholders' equity. If the corporation uses this approach, it must disclose the amounts for each of the items in the notes to its financial statements.[15]

General Motors Corporation uses the first approach. In the stockholders' equity section of its December 31, 2004 balance sheet, General Motors reported an accumulated other comprehensive loss of $2,285 million, consisting of four items as follows:

Accumulated foreign currency translation adjustments	$(1,194)
Net unrealized gains on derivatives	589
Net unrealized gains on securities	751
Minimum pension liability adjustment	(3,031)
Accumulated other comprehensive loss	$(2,885)

---

15. "Reporting Comprehensive Income," *FASB Statement of Financial Accounting Standards No. 130* (Norwalk, Conn.: FASB, 1997), par. 17 and 26.

The Caron Manufacturing Company has one item of accumulated other comprehensive income, as we show in Example 4-1. Unless a corporation has miscellaneous items of equity (discussed next), it adds the totals for contributed capital, retained earnings, and accumulated other comprehensive income to determine the total stockholders' equity.

Miscellaneous Items

In rare instances a company may increase its assets without a corresponding outflow of assets, increase in liabilities, recognition of income, or issuance of capital stock. For instance, a company may receive donated assets from a governmental unit or it may discover previously unrecorded assets. In either case, when the company records the asset's fair value it also increases stockholders' equity. These items are listed separately in stockholders' equity.

SECURE YOUR KNOWLEDGE 4-2

- When presenting the elements of a balance sheet, a company will simplify, condense, and classify the financial information in order to improve the usefulness of the information for the external users.
- The classification of assets and liabilities as current and noncurrent is a key distinction made on a company's balance sheet that allows users to more easily assess its liquidity and financial flexibility.
- Assets that are expected to provide economic benefits for more than one year or the operating cycle, whichever is longer, are classified as noncurrent assets and include long-term investments, property, plant, and equipment, and intangible assets.
- Obligations that will not be satisfied within one year or the operating cycle, whichever is longer, are classified as noncurrent liabilities and include long-term notes payable, bonds, and capital lease contracts.
- Stockholders' equity, the residual interest in the assets of the corporation, consists of contributed capital, retained earnings, and accumulated other comprehensive income.

STATEMENT OF CHANGES IN STOCKHOLDERS' EQUITY

7 Prepare a statement of changes in stockholders' equity.

When a corporation issues financial statements, it must disclose the changes in its stockholders' equity accounts. This disclosure may be in a financial statement, a supporting schedule, or a note to the financial statements.[16] This reporting is consistent with the FASB's suggestion that a full set of financial statements should show, among other information, investments by and distributions to owners during the period. The intent is to help report on the changes in a company's financial structure to help users in assessing its financial flexibility.

FASB Statement of Concepts No. 6 defines investments by owners and distributions to owners, as follows:

> **Investments by owners are increases in the equity of a company resulting from transfers of something valuable to the company from other entities to obtain or increase ownership interests.**

> **Distributions to owners are decreases in the equity of a company caused by transferring assets, rendering services, or incurring liabilities to owners.**

Assets are the economic resources most commonly received by a company from investments by owners, but the items received may include services or the conversion of liabilities

---

16. "Omnibus Opinion—1967," *APB Opinion No. 12* (New York: AICPA, 1967), par. 10.

handwritten: investment used to begin or expand operation...
handwritten: Distribution decrease it net assets & decrease
handwritten: ownership interest

Other Disclosure Issues   **141**

of the company. Through investments by owners, a company obtains the resources it needs to begin or expand operations, to retire liabilities, or for other business purposes. Distributions by a company to its owners decrease its net assets and decrease or terminate ownership interests of those who receive them.[17]

To disclose investments by and distributions to owners, many companies will prepare a statement of changes in stockholders' equity, which combines the retained earnings changes and the changes in accumulated other comprehensive income with the other capital account changes. Example 4-2 illustrates this statement. Note that the totals of the columns in this example are the same as those shown in the stockholders' equity section of Example 4-1.

EXAMPLE 4-2   Statement of Changes in Stockholders' Equity

SCHEDULE A
CARON MANUFACTURING COMPANY

Statement of Changes in Stockholders' Equity
For Year Ended December 31, 2007

	Common Stock, $5 par	Additional Paid-in Capital	Retained Earnings	Accumulated Other Comprehensive Income	Total
Balance, January 1, 2007	$65,000	$143,400	$ 64,900	$10,000	$283,300
Unrealized increase in value of available-for-sale securities				2,000	2,000
Net income			62,500		62,500
Cash dividends paid			(11,200)		(11,200)
Common stock issued	6,500	30,500			37,000
Balance, December 31, 2007	$71,500	$173,900	$116,200	$12,000	$373,600

OTHER DISCLOSURE ISSUES

A company cannot report all the relevant financial information about its activities directly in the body of the financial statements because some items do not meet the recognition criteria we discussed earlier in the chapter. As indicated throughout the balance sheet discussion, a company may make many disclosures in the notes accompanying its financial statements. We discuss other significant disclosure issues here.

8 Understand the other disclosure issues for a balance sheet.

Summary of Accounting Policies

To understand a company's financial statements, an external user needs to know the company's accounting policies, practices, and methods. For this reason, generally accepted accounting principles require the disclosure of certain information in a company's annual report.

APB Opinion No. 22 requires that a company include a description of all its significant accounting policies. The disclosure should include principles relating to revenue recognition and asset allocation, particularly when these principles and methods involve (1) a selection from existing acceptable alternatives, (2) principles and methods peculiar to the industry in which the company operates, and (3) unusual or innovative applications of generally accepted accounting principles. Examples cited include, among others, those policies related to the basis for consolidation, depreciation methods, amortization of intangibles,

Analysis

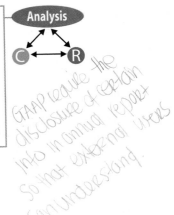

handwritten: GAAP require the disclosure of certain info in annual report so that external users can understand

---

17.   *FASB Statement of Financial Accounting Concepts No. 6, op. cit.,* par. 66–69.

inventory pricing, recognition of profits on long-term contracts, and revenue recognition from franchise and leasing operations. Although allowing for flexibility, the disclosure is particularly useful when made in a separate *Summary of Significant Accounting Policies* preceding the notes to the financial statements or as the initial note.[18] We show this summary (in part) for the **Black & Decker Corporation** in Real Report 4-4. We include a complete summary in the **Coca-Cola Company's** notes to its financial statements in Appendix A.

Reporting

Real Report 4-4   Summary of Accounting Policies

BLACK & DECKER CORPORATION

Notes to Consolidated Financial Statements (in part)

Note 1: Summary of Accounting Policies (in part):

Principles of Consolidation: The Consolidated Financial Statements include the accounts of the Corporation and its subsidiaries. Intercompany transactions have been eliminated.

Inventories: Inventories are stated at the lower of cost or market. The cost of United States inventories is based primarily on the last-in, first-out (LIFO) method; all other inventories are based on the first-in, first-out (FIFO) method.

Property and Depreciation: Property, plant, and equipment is stated at cost. Depreciation is computed generally on the straight-line method for financial reporting purposes.

Questions:

1. Why is it important to disclose the accounting method used to compute the cost of inventory and to compute depreciation?
2. If the company used accelerated deprecation for financial reporting purposes, how would the income statement and balance sheet be affected?

Fair Value and Risk of Financial Instruments

Some companies, many of which are banks and brokerage firms, deal in financial instruments. These *financial instruments* include items such as notes payable and receivable, contracts for loan commitments, collateralized mortgages, interest rate swaps, and put and call options on stocks. In recent years, both the types and uses of financial instruments have increased to the point where the FASB has addressed the reporting and disclosure of their fair values and risk. **FASB Statement No. 107** requires a company to disclose the fair value of all its financial instruments (both assets and liabilities), whether or not they are reported on its balance sheet. The *Statement* also requires a company to disclose all significant concentrations of credit risk due to its financial instruments. A company typically makes these disclosures in the notes to its financial statements.

FASB Statement No. 133 requires a company to report all *derivative financial instruments* as either assets or liabilities on its balance sheet, and to measure these items at their fair value. A derivative financial instrument is, for example, an option to buy stock where the value of the option depends on the price of the stock. The *Statement* also requires a company to disclose information such as the types of derivative instruments it holds, its objectives in holding the instruments, and its strategies for achieving these objectives. The description must indicate the company's risk management policy in regard to each type of instrument. The intent of these disclosures is to improve the reporting of a company's *risk, liquidity, and financial flexibility*.[19] We discuss disclosures about fair values and risks of financial instruments in Chapter 13 and the Appendix to Chapter 15.

---

18.   "Disclosure of Accounting Policies," *APB Opinion No. 22* (New York: AICPA, 1972), par. 8, 12, 13, and 15.
19.   "Disclosures About Fair Value of Financial Instruments," *FASB Statement of Financial Accounting Standards No. 107* (Norwalk, Conn.: FASB, 1991) and "Accounting for Derivative Instruments and Hedging Activities," *FASB Statement of Financial Accounting Standards No. 133* (Norwalk, Conn.: FASB, 1998).

possible gains or losses if occurs or fail to occur

Conditions met → report on fin. statement

Conditions Not met → disclose in notes.

Loss and Gain Contingencies

Certain situations may exist for a company on its balance sheet date that involve uncertainty as to possible losses or gains that the company may incur if some future event(s) occurs or fails to occur. These are known as **loss contingencies** or **gain contingencies** and may need to be included directly in the company's financial statements by recording a journal entry, or disclosed in a note accompanying the financial statements.[20]

A company accrues (reports a loss and a liability or a reduction of an asset) an estimated loss (or expense) from a loss contingency if (1) it is *probable* that a liability has been incurred (or an asset impaired) and (2) the amount of the loss can be *reasonably estimated*. Examples of this type of loss contingency include product warranties and uncollectible accounts receivable. If either of these conditions is *not* met—that is, if there is only a reasonable possibility that the loss may have been incurred or if the amount of the loss cannot be reasonably estimated—the company discloses the loss contingency in the notes to its financial statements.

The following diagram illustrates the alternative ways of accounting for loss contingencies:

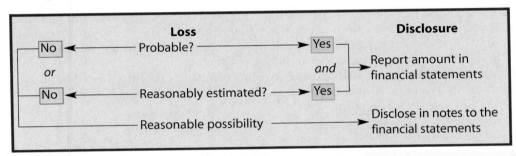

The disclosure of any loss contingencies of a company is important to provide external users with additional information for helping predict its use of its financial resources in the future. Examples of a loss contingency that are disclosed in the notes to the financial statements include guarantees of the debts of others and pending litigation against the company, where either the outcome of the litigation or the amount of possible loss is uncertain. An illustration of this type of contingency for **Pinnacle Entertainment Inc.** is shown in Real Report 4-5. Gain contingencies are not reported in a company's financial statements and, if disclosed in a note, should be carefully explained to avoid misleading implications as to the likelihood of future revenues or gains.[21] We discuss loss and gain contingencies in Chapter 13.

disclose in Notes

gains are not report!

Real Report 4-5 Contingency

PINNACLE ENTERTAINMENT INC.

Notes to Financial Statements (in part)

Note 11. Commitments and Contingencies

Legal

Columbia Sussex Litigation. On January 26, 2005, Columbia Sussex Corporation and three other plaintiffs filed a petition against the Missouri Gaming Commission and Casino One Corporation, a wholly owned subsidiary of the Company, in the Circuit Court of Cole County, Missouri. The plaintiffs seek to undo the Missouri Gaming Commission's approval of Casino One's docking site on the St. Louis riverfront under a claim for judicial review by

Continued

---

20. "Accounting for Contingencies," *FASB Statement of Financial Accounting Standards No. 5* (Stamford, Conn.: FASB, 1975), par. 1.

21. *Ibid.*, par. 8–17.

original writ, declaratory judgment, and writ of prohibition. The factual allegations for each claim are that the Commission could not grant approval to Casino One because the facility's planned gaming floor is allegedly not within 1,000 feet of the main channel of the Mississippi River, as required under the Missouri constitution. While the Company cannot predict the outcome of this litigation, management intends to defend it vigorously.

Question:

1. What possible impact might settlement of this litigation have on Pinnacle Entertainment's future financial position or results of operations?

Subsequent Events

A company usually does not issue its annual report for several weeks or months after the end of the accounting period because of the time needed for adjusting and closing the books and auditing the financial statements. During this time it is possible for significant business events and transactions to occur which, if not disclosed in the company's annual report, would cause this report to be misleading. Subsequent events are discussed more fully in an auditing book; we briefly summarize them here.

A subsequent event is one that occurs between a company's balance sheet date and the date when it issues its annual report, as we illustrate in the following time diagram:

End of Accounting Period	Annual Report Publication Date

Subsequent Events

If a subsequent event occurs that (1) provides additional evidence about conditions that *existed* on the balance sheet date and (2) significantly affects the estimate(s) used in preparing the company's financial statements, the company must make an adjustment to the financial statements. For instance, if a company obtains additional information indicating that a major customer's account receivable is unlikely to be collected, it makes an adjustment to the allowance for doubtful accounts and the bad debt expense.

When a subsequent event occurs that provides evidence concerning conditions that did *not* exist on the company's balance sheet date, but instead occurred after that date, the company does *not* adjust its financial statements. Instead, the information is disclosed in a note, pro forma ("as if") statement, or an explanatory paragraph in the audit report, depending upon the materiality of the financial impact. Examples of these events include a fire or flood loss, a litigation settlement, and the sale of a bond or stock issue after the balance sheet date.[22]

Related Party Transactions

Transactions between related parties frequently occur in the normal course of business. Related parties of a company include affiliated entities such as subsidiaries, trusts for the benefit of employees, its management, and its principal owners or immediate families. Relationships between related parties may enable one of the parties to influence the other so that it is given preferential treatment. To provide sufficient information for external users to understand a company's financial statements, **FASB Statement No. 57** requires certain disclosures by the company. For related party transactions these include (1) the

---

22. *AICPA Professional Standards,* Volume 1 (New York: AICPA, 2004), sec. 560.03–560.09.

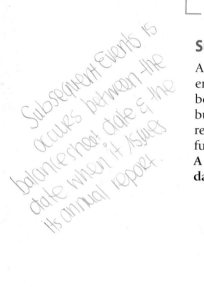

Handwritten margin notes: Subsequent Events is occurs between the balancesheet date & the date when it Issues its annual report

If evidence concerning conditions that did Not exist but Disclosed in a Note! No adjust its fin statement

Fire, flood loss

nature of the relationship involved, (2) a description of the transactions, (3) the dollar amounts of the transactions, and (4) any amounts due to or from the related parties on the balance sheet date.[23]

Comparative Financial Statements

Examples 4-1 and 4-2 show the ending balance sheet and the statement of changes in stockholders' equity of the Caron Manufacturing Company for one year. Many external users are interested in comparing the current financial statements with those of the previous year. Also, many times *trend* information about a company will reveal useful insights about its past performance and future success. For this reason, nearly all companies present **comparative financial statements** for the current and preceding accounting periods. Additionally, in a supplemental schedule, most companies will present a summary of key accounting information for, say, the past 5 to 10 years. For instance, some companies report their **debt ratio** (total liabilities ÷ total assets) to help external users (creditors and stockholders) assess the risk of their investment in the company. We show the **Coca-Cola Company's** comparative financial statements Debt Ratio in Appendix A.

Auditor's Report

Many major financial decisions by investors, bankers, other creditors, and other users are based on the financial information presented in a company's financial statements and related notes. These financial statements are the responsibility of the company's management. To help ensure a fair presentation of corporate financial resources, obligations, and activities, companies' financial statements and accompanying notes presented to external users are audited by an independent certified public accountant. In an audit, the certified public accountant is responsible for making an examination of a company's internal control, accounting system, records, and reports *in accordance with generally accepted auditing standards*. Based on this examination, the auditor expresses an *opinion* as to the *fairness in accordance with generally accepted accounting principles* of the company's financial statements and accompanying notes. Although this opinion is *not* itself part of the financial statements, it is an extremely important item of information, and one on which external users place much significance. We discuss the auditor's report in Chapter 6.

SEC Integrated Disclosures

As we noted in Chapter 1, the Securities and Exchange Commission has the legal authority to prescribe accounting principles and reporting practices for all regulated ("publicly-held") companies. Each year, within 60 days of its fiscal year-end, a regulated company must file a *Form 10-K* annual report with the SEC. This report must be filed electronically according to the EDGAR requirements. Each company's chief executive and chief financial officer both must "certify" that the company's annual report within the Form 10-K (or interim report within the company's Form 10-Q) is both complete and accurate. The SEC has also developed an "integrated" set of disclosure requirements that enable a company to satisfy certain Form 10-K disclosure requirements by referring to its stockholders' annual report, provided the latter report includes certain items. Since many regulated companies now include these items in their annual reports, we briefly summarize the items as follows. For a more detailed discussion, see *Regulation S-X* of the SEC.

9 Describe the SEC integrated disclosures.

---

23. "Related Party Transactions," *FASB Statement of Financial Accounting Standards No. 57* (Stamford, Conn.: FASB, 1982), par. 2.

Comparative Financial Statements

As we discussed in the previous section, most companies present comparative financial statements for at least two years. The SEC requires comparative balance sheets for *two* years and comparative income statements and statements of cash flows for *three* years.

Selected Financial Data

As we discussed in the previous section, most companies present a summary of important accounting information for several years. The SEC requires *specific* disclosures for a *five-year period*. These include net sales or operating revenues, income (loss) from continuing operations and related earnings per share, total assets, long-term obligations and redeemable stock, and cash dividends declared per share. The SEC encourages the inclusion of other information that will help users understand and highlight trends.

Management's Discussion and Analysis

A company's management must include a discussion and analysis (MD&A) of the company's financial condition, changes in financial condition, and results of operations. The intent is to give investors the opportunity to look at the company from management's perspective. Management is asked to discuss the dynamics of the company's business and to analyze the financial statements. The discussion is intended to provide "forward-looking" information that does not clearly appear in the financial statements but is useful in evaluating cash flows from operations and from outside sources. The major items covered should include, for instance, specific information about short-term and long-term liquidity and capital resources, a narrative discussion of the impact of inflation on sales and on income from continuing operations, a description of any significant unusual events and their effect on revenues and expenses, explanations of material changes in financial statement items between years, and known events and uncertainties expected to affect future operations. Other kinds of forward-looking information (e.g., trends) are required as well.

Common Stock Market Prices And Dividends

Several disclosures must be made. These include the principal trading markets for the company's common stock, the high and low market prices for each quarter in the last two years, the approximate number of stockholders, the dividends paid in the last two years, and any dividend restrictions.

Miscellaneous Disclosures

In addition to the disclosures discussed throughout this chapter, a company must make many other disclosures to provide adequate information concerning its activities. These include information about items such as the company's stock (share) option, pension, and insurance plans, long-term lease and purchase commitments, bond indenture provisions, notes receivable, and notes payable provisions. We discuss specific disclosure requirements as we address each topic in the remaining chapters.

SECURE YOUR KNOWLEDGE 4-3

- A statement of changes in stockholders' equity discloses investments by and distributions to owners, as well as changes in retained earnings and accumulated other comprehensive income.
- The notes accompanying the financial statements contain relevant information about a company's activities that cannot be reported in the body of the financial statements.

(continued)

- Examples of disclosures made in the notes include the accounting policies, practices, and methods used by a company, the fair values and risks of financial instruments, contingent losses and gains, the existence of subsequent events, and any related party transactions.

LINK TO INTERNATIONAL DIFFERENCES

One of the objectives of the IASB is to ensure, to the extent possible, that a company's published financial statements comply with international accounting standards. The financial statements required by the IASB are similar to those in the United States. They include a balance sheet, statement of changes in equity, income statement, and statement of cash flows, as well as related notes and other explanatory materials. However, International Accounting Standards do not *require* a particular format; the appropriate format depends on the type of company.

A company may classify its assets on the balance sheet into noncurrent assets and current assets, with noncurrent assets presented first. Noncurrent assets include property, plant, and equipment, as well as other items (investments, long-term receivables, intangibles). These classifications are similar to those in the United States. Current assets are also similar to those under U.S. GAAP.

The ordering of the liabilities and owners' equity sections is usually different than under U.S. GAAP, with "capital and reserves" listed first. The capital and reserves section includes issued capital, reserves, and accumulated profits (losses). The issued capital includes share capital and share premium. A company is required to disclose the par value, as well as the number of shares authorized, issued and fully paid, and issued but not fully paid. It must also disclose dividends that have been proposed but not formally approved for payment. Reserves may result from revaluations of properties and investments, as well as currency translation differences. A company must also provide a description of the nature and purpose of each reserve.

Noncurrent liabilities are usually listed next and include items such as interest-bearing borrowings, deferred income, deferred taxes, and retirement benefit obligations. Deferred income may include government grants, which are a form of financial assistance to a company for compliance with certain conditions. On the other hand, some government grants for the construction of assets are treated as a reduction in the book value of the asset. Current liabilities are listed last and are similar to those under U.S. GAAP. As with U.S. GAAP, a company is not required to separate its assets and liabilities into current and noncurrent classifications; it decides on the disclosures based on their usefulness.

A company's statement of changes in equity includes the changes in share capital and share premium, as well as any changes in the company's reserves due to, for instance, a surplus on the revaluation of properties or a deficit on the revaluation of investments. A company must also disclose any changes in accumulated profits (losses) due to changes in accounting policies, corrections of fundamental errors, net income, and dividends.

In the notes to its financial statements, a company is required to disclose items similar to those required under U.S. GAAP. These disclosures include its accounting policies, narrative descriptions of financial statement items, and contingencies. For revaluations, they also include the measurement basis used. Furthermore, companies in "hyperinflationary" economies (e.g., the cumulative inflation rate over three years exceeds 100 percent) are required to prepare general price-level-adjusted financial statements. In the following chapters, we briefly discuss the major differences between international and U.S. accounting standards as they apply to specific assets, liabilities, and income.[24]

---

24. For a more complete discussion, see Carrie Bloomer (editor), *The IASC—U.S. Comparison Project: A Report on the Similarities and Defferences between IASC Standards and U.S. GAAP*, 2nd ed. (Norwalk, Conn.: FASB, 1999).

REPORTING TECHNIQUES

Companies use several reporting techniques in the presentation of their annual reports. We discuss the major ones relating to the financial statement presentations next.

10 Explain the reporting techniques used in an annual report.

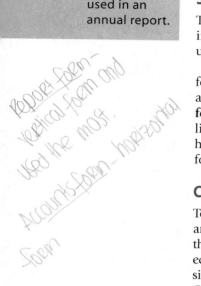

Statement Format (Balance Sheet)

The format that a company uses for its balance sheet depends upon its size, the industry in which it operates, certain regulatory requirements, and tradition. Two basic formats are used: the report form or the account form.

Most companies use the **report form.** Here the balance sheet is shown in a vertical format. The asset accounts are listed first, and the liability and stockholders' equity accounts are listed in sequential order directly below the assets. In contrast, the **account form** of the balance sheet is organized in a horizontal fashion, with the asset accounts listed on the left-hand side and liabilities and stockholders' equity accounts on the right-hand side. This is the format used in Example 4-1. Of 600 companies surveyed, the report form and account form are used by 506 and 94, respectively.[25]

Combined Amounts

To reduce the size of a company's financial statements, it may combine certain related amounts. For instance, a company may list a single amount for property and equipment on the face of its balance sheet and then itemize the amounts applicable to land, buildings, and equipment in a note to the financial statements. Frequently the amounts for inventories are similarly combined and itemized, as illustrated in Real Report 4-1 for **Johnson & Johnson.** Generally, it is *not* proper to offset asset and liability accounts. For instance, the amount in a special Bond Sinking Fund account to retire long-term bonds would not be offset against the Bonds Payable account balance. In a few circumstances, a *right of offset* exists whereby a debtor (Company A) has a legal right to discharge all or some of the liability owed to another party (Company B) by applying an amount that the other party (Company B) owes to the debtor (i.e., a receivable of Company A) against the liability.[26] For instance, when a bank loans money to a company in exchange for the company's accounts receivable that are assigned to the bank, the company would offset the assigned accounts receivable on its balance sheet against the liability owed to the bank. We discuss the right of offset in Chapter 7.

Rounding

In Examples 4-1 and 4-2 the amounts presented for each account, subtotal and total, were rounded to the nearest hundred dollars. Rounding is usually done to increase readability and to reduce the likelihood that readers will attach more precision to the numbers than is warranted. In fact, many major companies round to the nearest million dollars. In the **Coca-Cola Company** financial statements shown in Appendix A, the amounts are rounded as indicated.

---

25. *Accounting Trends and Techniques,* (New York: AICPA, 2004), p. 149.
26. For the criteria to be met for a right of offset to exist, see "Offsetting of Amounts Related to Certain Contracts," *FASB Interpretation No. 39* (Norwalk, Conn.: FASB, 1992), par. 5 and "Offsetting of Amounts Related to Certain Repurchase and Reverse Repurchase Agreements," *FASB Interpretation No. 41* (Norwalk, Conn.: FASB, 1994), par. 3.

Notes, Supporting Schedules, and Parenthetical Notations

Additional information not included in the accounts reported on a company's financial statements is disclosed in a note, supporting schedule, or parenthetical notation.

The **notes** (sometimes called *footnotes*) accompanying the financial statements are extremely useful ways of presenting additional information. Generally accepted accounting principles *require* that a company disclose certain information (for instance, contingent liabilities that are reasonably possible) in the notes to the financial statements, and it is good accounting practice to include additional note disclosures when they add to the completeness of the annual report. Notes usually contain narrative discussion, additional monetary amounts, and sometimes supplemental schedules.

We illustrated several notes of actual companies earlier in this chapter. We discuss required and suggested disclosures in notes throughout this book as they apply to specific topics. Because notes must communicate technical accounting information in a narrative format, there are several ways to improve their clarity and readability. When preparing and writing financial reporting notes, the accountant should (a) specify what data are to be disclosed, (b) outline the desired format of the note, (c) construct and use short sentences in the note, (d) use terminology understandable to the external user, and (e) be concise but complete.

Supporting schedules may be freestanding or part of the notes. A supporting schedule may complement an entire financial statement (such as the retained earnings statement) or may explain a summary amount on a specific financial statement (such as the categories of inventories, as we showed in Real Report 4-1). We discuss and illustrate supporting schedules throughout the book.

Parenthetical notations following specific accounts are used to explain items such as the method of valuation (e.g., cost, lower of cost or market) or of determining the ending inventory (e.g., average cost), or to cross-reference certain related asset and liability accounts (e.g., bond sinking fund and bonds payable).

ILLUSTRATIVE STATEMENTS

Appendix A shows the actual financial statements and accompanying notes of the **Coca-Cola Company** for the year ended December 31, 2004. Although you may not understand all of these items at this point, pay particular attention to each statement's format and content and, in particular, to the notes accompanying the reports. Your understanding will increase as you study this book.

SUMMARY

At the beginning of the chapter, we identified several objectives you would accomplish after reading the chapter. The objectives are listed below, each followed by a brief summary of the key points in the chapter discussion.

1. **Understand the purposes of the balance sheet.** A balance sheet summarizes the *financial position* of a corporation on a specific date by reporting on its assets, liabilities, and stockholders' equity. The balance sheet reports a corporation's *resource structure* and its *financial structure*.

2. **Define the elements of a balance sheet.** The elements of a balance sheet are the broad classes of items comprising it. The elements include assets, liabilities, and stockholders' equity. Briefly, assets are a corporation's economic resources, liabilities are its present obligations, and stockholders' equity is the residual interest in the assets.

3. **Explain how to measure the elements of a balance sheet.** There are five alternatives for measuring the elements (assets and liabilities) of a balance sheet. These include: (1) historical cost/historical proceeds (2) current cost/current proceeds, (3) current market value, (4) net realizable value, and (5) present value. Alternatives (2) through (4) are ways of measuring the fair value of an element. Each of these alternatives is used under specific circumstances for measuring certain assets and liabilities.

4. **Classify the assets of a balance sheet.** The assets of a balance sheet may be classified into five groups: (1) current assets, (2) long-term investments, (3) property, plant, and equipment, (4) intangible assets, and (5) other assets.

5. **Classify the liabilities of a balance sheet.** The liabilities of a balance sheet may be classified into three groups: (1) current liabilities, (2) long-term liabilities, and (3) other liabilities.

6. **Report the stockholders' equity of a balance sheet.** The stockholders' equity of a balance sheet consists of contributed capital (capital stock and additional paid-in capital), retained earnings, and accumulated other comprehensive income.

7. **Prepare a statement of changes in stockholders' equity.** A statement of changes in stockholders' equity starts with the beginning balances of capital stock, additional paid-in capital, retained earnings, and accumulated other comprehensive income. It then reconciles these beginning balances to the ending balances by showing the changes (and reasons for the changes) in each of these items.

8. **Understand the other disclosure issues for a balance sheet.** To help users understand the elements of its balance sheet (and other financial statements), a company also discloses useful information in the notes to the financial statements. This information includes a summary of the company's accounting policies, the fair value and risk of its financial instruments, any contingent liabilities and assets, any subsequent events, and any related party transactions. The company also includes comparative financial statements, all of which must be audited.

9. **Describe the SEC integrated disclosures.** A company can satisfy certain SEC 10-K disclosure requirements by including an "integrated" set of disclosures in its annual report. The company must include comparative financial statements, selected financial information for a five-year period, a management's discussion and analysis (MD&A), and common stock market prices and dividends.

10. **Explain the reporting techniques used in an annual report.** A company may use various reporting techniques in its annual report. It may use a *report form* or *account form* of balance sheet. It may combine amounts of certain elements, and may round the reported numbers. It may provide additional information in the notes to the financial statements, supporting schedules, or parenthetical notations.

ANSWERS TO REAL REPORT QUESTIONS

Real Report 4-1 Answers
1. Below are the percentages of each type of inventory (calculated by dividing the type of inventory by total inventory for each respective year)

	2004	2003
Raw materials and supplies	26%	27%
Goods in process	30%	27%
Finished goods	44%	46%

2. The reduction of finished goods inventory, coupled with the increase in the goods in process inventory, could be interpreted as a signal that Johnson & Johnson is expecting higher future demand and sales, and is increasing production to meet this forecast.

Real Report 4-2 Answers
1. Projects in progress represent 4.5% and 3.6% of the total cost of projects as of August 3, 2003, and August 1, 2004, respectively.
2. This indicates that Campbell's capital expenditures on new projects have remained fairly steady and represent a small portion of its fixed assets.

Real Report 4-3 Answers
1. Kimberly Clark has access to a significant source of cash through revolving credit facilities ($1.2 billion) which should be considered when evaluating the company's liquidity and financial flexibility. Additionally, the company, absent any refinancing of debt, will incur cash outflows of approximately $1.2 billion within the next year relating to the settlement of debt (both current maturities of long-term debt and other current debt). Finally, information on the scheduled maturities of long-term debt for the next five years is provided.
2. Interest expense (computed by multiplying the weighted average interest rate by the average debt outstanding) was approximately $134.2 million.
3. Assuming that the weighted average interest rate for 2005 remains the same as for 2004 and the average value of the notes and debentures for 2005 is equal to the value at December 31, 2004, interest expense relating to the notes and debentures is estimated to be $133.3 million ($2,309,800,000 × 5.77%). These assumptions can be modified to take into account predicted economic activity (e.g., rising interest rates).

Real Report 4-4 Answers

1. Users of financial statements need to understand the accounting methods used in the preparation of the financial statements to facilitate intercompany as well as intracompany comparisons. Because the use of different accounting methods can result in different valuations in the financial statements, the comparability and consistency of the information presented would be compromised if such disclosures were not made.

2. If the company had used accelerated depreciation instead of straight-line depreciation, the company would have recorded more depreciation expense than currently recorded. This additional expense would have resulted in lower income. Additionally, the book value of the company's assets (property, plant, and equipment) and equity (retained earnings) would be lower.

Real Report 4-5 Answer

1. If Pinnacle Entertainment were to lose this litigation, the company would lose approval for the docking site of its casino on the St. Louis riverfront. The loss of this docking site could result in (1) a write-down of assets that make up the docking site (since the assets' future benefits are certainly in doubt); (2) the relocation of the casino to another location at considerable cost; and (3) the loss of income due to the inability to operate the casino until an approved location is found.

QUESTIONS

Q4-1 What are the major financial statements of a company and what do they show?

Q4-2 What does a company's financial position include?

Q4-3 What are two purposes of a company's balance sheet?

Q4-4 Define liquidity, financial flexibility, and operating capability.

Q4-5 What is financial capital? Why is capital maintenance important?

Q4-6 What does "recognition" mean in accounting?

Q4-7 Define an asset. What are the three characteristics of an asset?

Q4-8 Define a liability. What are the three characteristics of a liability?

Q4-9 What is stockholders' equity?

Q4-10 Identify the five alternatives for measuring (valuing) assets. What is the fair value of an asset? Which valuation method is usually used in a company's balance sheet?

Q4-11 List the major sections (and the components of each section) of a company's balance sheet.

Q4-12 How are current assets defined and what are the major items that may be included in current assets? How are current liabilities defined? Give three examples of such liabilities.

Q4-13 Define a company's operating cycle. How does working capital relate to this cycle? How is working capital computed?

Q4-14 What items are classified as (a) long-term investments, (b) property, plant, and equipment, and (c) intangible assets?

Q4-15 What items are classified as (a) long-term liabilities and (b) other liabilities?

Q4-16 What is a bond? Give an illustration of how bonds payable would be disclosed on a company's balance sheet.

Q4-17 Define (a) capital stock, (b) additional paid-in capital in excess of par, (c) treasury stock, (d) retained earnings, (e) deficit, and (f) accumulated other comprehensive income.

Q4-18 What are investments by owners? Distributions to owners? In what statement do many companies report these items?

Q4-19 What accounting policies are disclosed in the notes accompanying a company's financial statements? Why is this disclosure important?

Q4-20 Give several examples of financial instruments and identify the required *disclosures* for a company's financial instruments.

Q4-21 What is a loss contingency? What criteria have to be met for a company to accrue a loss contingency? If these criteria are not met, how does a company disclose a loss contingency?

Q4-22 Why is it necessary for a company to disclose subsequent events? What kinds of subsequent events are disclosed by an adjustment to the company's financial statements and what kinds are disclosed in a note?

Q4-23 What must a company disclose for related party transactions?

Q4-24 Why are comparative financial statements important?

Q4-25 What is an audit and why is the auditor's report an important item of information?

Q4-26 Briefly describe the SEC "integrated" disclosures that most regulated companies include in their annual reports.

Q4-27 Briefly list the format of a company's balance sheet under international accounting standards.

Q4-28 What is the difference between the report form and the account form of the balance sheet?

Q4-29 What alternative methods are used to disclose additional information not included in the accounts reported on a company's financial statements? Give examples of the types of information disclosed by each method.

Q4-30 What factors should be considered when an accountant prepares and writes financial reporting notes?

MULTIPLE CHOICE (AICPA Adapted)

Select the best answer for each of the following.

M4-1 APB Opinion No. 22, "Disclosure of Accounting Policies"
a. Requires a description of every accounting policy followed by a reporting entity
b. Provides a specific listing of all types of accounting policies that must be disclosed
c. Requires disclosure of the format for the statement of cash flows
d. Requires a description of all significant accounting policies to be included as an integral part of the financial statements

M4-2 Which of the following contingencies should generally be accrued on the balance sheet when the occurrence of the contingent event is reasonably possible and its amount can be reasonably estimated?

	Gain Contingency	Loss Contingency
a.	Yes	Yes
b.	Yes	No
c.	No	Yes
d.	No	No

M4-3 A donated fixed asset (from a governmental unit) for which the fair value has been determined should be recorded as a debit to fixed assets and a credit to
a. Unrealized capital
b. Retained earnings
c. Deferred income
d. Other income

M4-4 On October 2, 2005, a company borrowed cash and signed a 3-year interest-bearing note on which both the principal and interest are payable on October 2, 2008. At December 31, 2007 the accrued interest should
a. Be reported on the balance sheet as a current liability
b. Be reported on the balance sheet as a noncurrent liability
c. Be reported on the balance sheet as part of long-term notes payable
d. Not be reported on the balance sheet as a liability

M4-5 Financial statements that are expressed assuming a stable monetary unit are
a. General-price-level financial statements
b. Historical-dollar financial statements
c. Current-value financial statements
d. Fair-value financial statements

M4-6 Rent revenue collected one month in advance should be accounted for as
a. Revenue in the month collected
b. A current liability
c. A separate item in stockholders' equity
d. An accrued liability

M4-7 Which of the following should be disclosed in the Summary of Significant Accounting Policies?
a. Rent expense amount
b. Maturity dates of long-term debt
c. Methods of amortizing intangibles
d. Composition of plant assets

M4-8 A company receives an advance payment for special-order goods to be manufactured and delivered within six months. The advance payment should be reported on the company's balance sheet as a
a. Deferred charge
b. Contra-asset account
c. Current liability
d. Noncurrent liability

M4-9 The FASB has identified five alternatives for measuring balance sheet elements. Which of the following alternatives may be used?

	Net Realizable Value	Present Value
a.	No	No
b.	No	Yes
c.	Yes	No
d.	Yes	Yes

M4-10 The balance sheet provides information about each of the following items, except
a. Operating capability of entity
b. Results of entity's operations
c. Entity's liquidity
d. Financial flexibility of entity

EXERCISES

E4-1 *Current Assets* Listed here are certain accounts of the Jenkins Company at the end of 2007:

Account	Debit (Credit)
Land	$12,000
Prepaid insurance	1,530
Cash on hand	1,120
Notes receivable (due 2010)	4,300
Cash in bank	5,400
Allowance for doubtful accounts	(1,100)
Marketable securities (short-term)	3,380
Accumulated depreciation	(8,700)
Accounts receivable	15,600
Office supplies	970
Buildings	27,200
Inventory	19,700

Required
Prepare the current asset section of Jenkins' balance sheet.

E4-2 *Plant and Equipment* Your analysis of the fixed asset accounts at the end of 2007 for the Moen Corporation reveals the following information:

1. The company owns two tracts of land. The first, which cost $18,000, is being held as a future building site. It has a current market value of $20,000. The second, which cost $19,000, was purchased 10 years ago. On this site were built the current office and factory buildings. The land has a current market value of $56,000.
2. The company owns two buildings. The office building and the factory building were both built 10 years ago at a cost of $50,000 and $120,000, respectively. At that time each was expected to have a life of 30 years, and a residual value of 10% of original cost. They are being depreciated on a straight-line basis.
3. The company owns factory machinery with a total cost of $51,000 and accumulated depreciation of $35,300. Included in factory machinery is one machine that cost $7,000 and has accumulated depreciation of $4,200. This machine is being held for resale and is not being used in operations.
4. The company owns office equipment that cost $14,500 and has a book value of $6,300. It owns office furniture that cost $17,900 and has a book value of $11,400.

Required
Prepare the property, plant, and equipment section of Moen's 2007 ending balance sheet.

E4-3 *Stockholders' Equity* The following are several accounts of the Graf Corporation at the end of 2007:

Account	Credit Balance
Common stock, $10 par	$ 47,100
Bonds payable (due 2014)	126,000
Premium on preferred stock	39,600
Retained earnings	209,000
Premium on bonds payable	12,300
Unearned rent	4,800
Preferred stock, $100 par	65,400
Premium on common stock	53,900
Unfunded accrued pension cost	18,400
Treasury stock (cost)	(7,600) debit
Accumulated other comprehensive income	8,200

Required
Prepare the stockholders' equity section of Graf's 2007 ending balance sheet.

E4-4 *Classifications on Balance Sheet* A balance sheet may contain the following major sections:

A. Current assets
B. Long-term investments
C. Property, plant, and equipment
D. Intangible assets

E. Other assets
F. Current liabilities
G. Long-term liabilities
H. Other liabilities

I. Contributed capital
J. Retained earnings
K. Accumulated other comprehensive income

Required

The following is a list of fifteen accounts. Using the letters A through K, indicate in which section of the balance sheet each account would most likely be classified. Place a check mark (√) beside each item that is a contra account. If an account cannot be classified in any of the preceding sections, indicate with an X and explain.

_E_ 1. Temporary investments in marketable securities
_G_ 2. Discount on bonds payable (bonds due in 5 years)
_I_ 3. Additional paid-in capital on common stock
_A_ 4. Accounts receivable
_G_ 5. Notes payable (due in 5 years)
_D_ 6. Patents (net)
_K_ 7. Unrealized decrease in value of available-for-sale securities

_I_ 8. Preferred stock
_F_ 9. Unearned rent (to be earned within next 6 months)
_E_ 10. Accrued pension cost
_D_ 11. Trademarks
_J_ 12. Deficit
_F_ 13. Salaries payable
_C_ 14. Land
____ 15. Investment in Ace Company preferred stock (to be held for 3 years)

E4-5 *Classifications on Balance Sheet* The balance sheet contains the following major sections:

A. Current assets
B. Long-term investments
C. Property, plant, and equipment
D. Intangible assets
E. Other assets
F. Current liabilities

G. Long-term liabilities
H. Other liabilities
I. Contributed capital
J. Retained earnings
K. Accumulated other comprehensive income

Required

The following is a list of several accounts. Using the letters A through K, indicate in which section of the balance sheet each of the accounts would be classified. Place a check mark (√) beside each item that is a contra account. If an account cannot be classified in any of the preceding sections, indicate with an X and explain.

____ 1. Cash
____ 2. Bonds payable (due in 8 years)
____ 3. Machinery
____ 4. Deficit
____ 5. Unexpired insurance
____ 6. Franchise (net)
____ 7. Fund to retire preferred stock
____ 8. Current portion of mortgage payable
____ 9. Accumulated depreciation
____ 10. Copyrights
____ 11. Investment in held-to-maturity bonds

____ 12. Allowance for doubtful accounts
____ 13. Notes receivable (due in 3 years)
____ 14. Property taxes payable
____ 15. Deferred taxes payable
____ 16. Premium on preferred stock
____ 17. Premium on bonds payable (due in 8 years)
____ 18. Work in process
____ 19. Common stock, $1 par
____ 20. Land
____ 21. Treasury stock (at cost)
____ 22. Unrealized increase in value of available-for-sale securities

E4-6 *Balance Sheet* The balance sheet accounts and amounts of the Baggett Company as of December 31, 2007 are shown in random order as follows:

Account	Debit (Credit)	Account	Debit (Credit)
Income taxes payable CL	$ (3,800)	Premium on preferred stock OE	$ (7,900)
Prepaid items CA	1,800	Allowance for doubtful accounts XCA	(1,600)
Premium on common stock OE	(9,300)	Bonds payable (due 2017) N CL	(23,000)
Land NCA	12,200	Buildings NCA	57,400
Notes payable (due 2010) NCL	(6,000)	Sinking fund to retire bonds payable NCL	5,000
Notes receivable (due 2009) NCA	16,400	Advances from customers (long-term) N CL	(2,600)
Accounts receivable CA	12,600	Cash CA	4,300
Premium on bonds payable CL	(1,400)	Accumulated depreciation: equipment XCA	(9,700)

Account	Debit (Credit)	Account	Debit (Credit)
Accounts payable	(13,100)	Retained earnings	(18,300)
Inventory	7,400	Preferred stock, $100 par	(18,600)
Accumulated depreciation: buildings	(21,000)	Wages payable	(1,400)
Patents (net)	4,600	Common stock, $10 par	(12,700)
Equipment	28,700		

Required
1. Prepare a December 31, 2007 balance sheet for the Baggett Company.
2. Compute the debt ratio.

E4-7 *Balance Sheet* The December 31, 2007 balance sheet accounts of the Hitt Company are shown here in alphabetical order:

Accounts payable	$ 22,400	Current taxes payable	$ 10,400
Accounts receivable	21,500	Discount on bonds payable	6,900
Accumulated depreciation: buildings	53,000	Equipment	72,400
Accumulated depreciation: equipment	35,100	Inventory	37,200
Additional paid-in capital on common stock	24,000	Land	30,000
		Marketable securities (short-term)	6,100
Additional paid-in capital on preferred stock	11,500	Patents (net)	9,800
		Preferred stock, $100 par	21,000
Allowance for doubtful accounts	800	Retained earnings	46,200
Bonds payable (due 2021)	77,000	Salaries payable	2,000
Buildings	144,000	Trademarks	3,700
Cash	2,900	Unrealized increase in value of	
Common stock, $10 par	30,000	marketable securities	1,100

Required
1. Prepare the December 31, 2007 balance sheet of the Hitt Company.
2. Compute the working capital and the current ratio.

E4-8 *Balance Sheet Calculations* The balance sheet information at the end of 2007 and 2008 for the Dawson Company is as follows:

	2007	2008
Current assets	$ (a)	$25,000
Long-term liabilities	(b)	34,900
Total contributed capital	(c)	(g)
Long-term investments	19,200	(h)
Retained earnings	50,000	60,000
Total liabilities	(d)	(i)
Intangible assets	10,400	9,200
Current liabilities	14,500	12,300
Capital stock, $5 par	(e)	20,000
Total assets	142,200	(j)
Additional paid-in capital	15,000	(k)
Property, plant, and equipment (net)	85,700	92,800
Accumulated other comprehensive income	6,900	7,000
Total stockholders' equity	(f)	(l)

Additional information: The company did not issue any common stock during 2008.

Required
Fill in the blanks labeled (a) through (l). All the necessary information is provided. (*Hint*: It is not necessary to calculate your answers in alphabetical order.)

E4-9 *Balance Sheet Calculations* The balance sheet information of the Fermer Company at the end of 2007 and 2008 is as follows:

	2007	2008
Total stockholders' equity	$ (1)	$100,700
Accumulated other comprehensive income	4,800	5,000
Current liabilities	(2)	9,800
Intangible assets	12,600	12,000
Property, plant, and equipment (net)	(3)	87,500
Current assets	19,100	(8)
Total contributed capital	51,000	(9)
Long-term liabilities	(4)	30,200
Retained earnings	40,900	(10)
Total assets	(5)	(11)
Common stock, $10 par	(6)	(12)
Working capital	9,900	10,200
Additional paid-in capital	(7)	36,000
Long-term investments	23,700	(13)
Total liabilities	38,100	(14)

Additional information: At the end of 2007, additional paid-in capital is twice the amount of capital stock. In 2008, the company issued (sold) 100 shares of common stock.

Required

Fill in the blanks numbered (1) through (14). All the necessary information is provided. (*Hint*: It is not necessary to calculate your answers in numerical order.)

E4-10 *Correction of Balance Sheet* On December 31, 2007, the Stevens Company bookkeeper prepared the following erroneously classified balance sheet:

STEVENS COMPANY
Balance Sheet
For Year Ended December 31, 2007

Current Assets		Current Liabilities	
Inventory	$ 6,000	Accounts payable	$ 9,900
Accounts receivable	5,900	Allowance for doubtful accounts	800
Cash	2,300	Salaries payable	1,500
Treasury stock (at cost)	3,300	Taxes payable	2,500
Long-Term Investments		Long-Term Liabilities	
Temporary investments in marketable		Bonds payable (due 2014)	11,000
securities	3,200	Unearned rent (for 3 months)	900
Investment in held-to-maturity bonds	10,000		
Plant and Equipment			
Land	8,100		
Office supplies	800	Owners' Equity	
Buildings and equipment	35,600	Retained earnings	24,200
Intangibles		Accumulated depreciation on buildings	
Patents (net)	5,000	and equipment	9,200
Prepaid insurance (for 6 months)	1,200	Premium on common stock	10,400
Discount on bonds payable	1,000	Common stock, $10 par	12,000
Total Assets	$82,400	Total Credits	$82,400

Required

You determine that the account balances listed on the balance sheet are correct but, in certain cases, incorrectly classified. Prepare a properly classified balance sheet for the Stevens Company as of December 31, 2007.

E4-11   *Changes in Stockholders' Equity* On January 1, 2007 the Powder Company listed the following stockholders' equity section of its balance sheet:

Contributed Capital
Preferred stock, $100 par	$ 92,800
Common stock, $5 par	37,400
Additional paid-in capital on preferred stock	21,500
Additional paid-in capital on common stock	58,700
Total contributed capital	$210,400
Retained Earnings	185,700
Total Stockholders' Equity	$396,100

During 2007, the following transactions and events occurred and were properly recorded:
1. The company issued 1,800 shares of common stock at $13 per share.
2. The company issued 340 shares of preferred stock at $130 per share.
3. The company earned net income of $38,950.
4. The company paid a $7 per share dividend on the preferred stock and a $1 per share dividend on the common stock outstanding at the end of 2007.

Required
Prepare a statement of changes in stockholders' equity of the Powder Company for 2007. (Include retained earnings.)

E4-12   *Changes in Stockholders' Equity* On January 1, 2007 the Osborne Company reported the following alphabetical list of stockholders' equity items:

Additional paid-in capital on common stock	$170,000
Additional paid-in capital on preferred stock	12,000
Common stock, $2 par	80,000
Preferred stock, $100 par	60,000
Retained earnings	209,000

During 2007, the company sold 3,000 shares of common stock for $10 per share and 500 shares of preferred stock for $125 per share. It also earned income of $99,000 and paid dividends of $8 per share on the preferred stock and $1.50 per share on the common stock outstanding at the end of 2007.

Required
Prepare a statement of changes in stockholders' equity of the Osborne Company for 2007. (Include retained earnings.)

PROBLEMS

P4-1   *Classifications on Balance Sheet* The current balance sheet of Day Company contains the following major sections:

A. Current assets
B. Long-term investments
C. Property, plant, and equipment
D. Intangible assets
E. Other assets
F. Current liabilities
G. Long-term liabilities
H. Other liabilities
I. Contributed capital
J. Retained earnings
K. Accumulated other comprehensive income

The following is a list of 37 accounts. Using the letters A through K, indicate in which section each account would most likely be classified. Place a check mark (√) beside each item that is a contra account. If an account cannot be classified in any of the preceding sections, indicate with an X and explain.

D 1. Patents (net)
F 2. Income taxes payable
A 3. Notes receivable (due in 5 months)
E 4. Unearned rent
G 5. Discount on bonds payable (long-term bonds)

C 6. Data processing center
C 7. Furniture
C 8. Land held for future expansion
C 9. Timberland (net)
I X 10. Treasury stock, at cost
C 11. Advances to sales personnel
___ 12. Idle machinery

_____ 13. Deferred taxes payable
_____ 14. Raw materials
_____ 15. Investment in held-to-maturity bonds
_____ 16. Pollution control facilities
_____ 17. Cash from security deposits
of customers on returnable
containers
_____ 18. Donated capital for industrial
park building site from
Toma City
_____ 19. Trademarks
_____ 20. Finished goods
_____ 21. Cash dividends payable
_____ 22. Bond sinking fund
_____ 23. Temporary investments
_____ 24. Retained earnings
_____ 25. Advances to affiliated company
(long-term)

_____ 26. Cash surrender value of life
insurance
_____ 27. Leased equipment under
capital lease
_____ 28. Additional paid-in capital
on preferred stock
_____ 29. Interest receivable (due in
5 months)
_____ 30. Office supplies
_____ 31. Accrued pension cost
_____ 32. Capital lease obligation
_____ 33. Investment in 8-year certificates
of deposit
_____ 34. Unearned ticket sales
_____ 35. Estimated warranty (6-months)
obligations
_____ 36. Unrealized decrease in value
of available-for-sale securities
_____ 37. Cash

P4-2   _Balance Sheet without Amounts_ The following is an alphabetical list of the accounts of the Oliver Manufacturing Company as of December 31, 2007:

Accounts payable
Accounts receivable
Accrued pension cost
Accumulated depreciation: buildings
Accumulated depreciation: equipment
Accumulated depreciation: machinery
Additional paid-in capital on common stock
Additional paid-in capital on preferred stock
Administrative expenses
Allowance for doubtful accounts
Bond sinking fund
Bonds payable (due 2019)
Buildings
Cash in bank
Cash on hand
Cash surrender value of life insurance
Common stock
Cost of goods sold
Deferred taxes payable
Dividends payable
Equipment
Estimated warranty (1-year) obligations
Finished goods
General expenses
Income tax expense
Income taxes payable
Interest expense

Interest payable
Interest receivable
Interest revenue
Investment in available-for-sale securities
Land
Land for future plant site
Loss on sale of equipment
Machinery
Mortgage payable (20 equal annual payments)
Notes payable (short-term)
Notes receivable (short-term)
Office supplies
Patents (net)
Preferred stock
Premium on bonds payable
Prepaid insurance
Raw materials
Retained earnings
Salaries payable
Sales
Sales discounts taken
Sales returns
Selling expenses
Temporary investments in marketable securities Trademarks
Treasury stock, at cost
Unearned rent
Unrealized increase in value of available-for-sale securitie
Work in process

Required

Prepare a balance sheet (without amounts) in proper format for the Oliver Manufacturing Company.

P4-3   _Balance Sheet_ The following is an alphabetical list of the December 31, 2007 balance sheet accounts and amounts for the Green Manufacturing Company:

Accounts payable	$20,900	Accumulated depreciation: machinery	
Accounts receivable	15,300	and equipment	30,000
Accrued pension cost	13,300	Allowance for doubtful accounts	1,000
Accumulated depreciation: buildings	32,400	Bond sinking fund	7,700

Bonds payable (due 2021)	29,000	Marketable securities (short-term)	8,400
Buildings	92,500	Notes payable (short-term)	5,000
Cash	7,200	Patents (net)	8,600
Common stock, $10 par	44,100	Preferred stock, $100 par	30,000
Deferred taxes payable	2,800	Premium on common stock	16,300
Discount on bonds payable	2,500	Premium on preferred stock	7,000
Dividends payable	5,600	Prepaid insurance	2,600
Finished goods	23,800	Raw materials	10,100
Income taxes payable	8,900	Retained earnings	28,100
Interest payable	500	Unearned rent	5,000
Investment in available-for-sale stock	16,400	Unrealized increase in value of available-	
Land	17,000	for-sale stock	2,000
Machinery and equipment	57,800	Wages payable	2,700
		Work in process	14,700

Required

Prepare a properly classified balance sheet for the Green Manufacturing Company on December 31, 2007. List the additional parenthetical or note disclosures (if any) that should be made for each item. Compute the working capital and the current ratio.

P4-4 *Balance Sheet* The following is a list (in random order) of the December 31, 2007 balance sheet accounts of the Midwest Company:

Additional paid-in capital on preferred stock	$ 1,600	Accounts payable	$16,500
Accounts receivable	13,800	Prepaid insurance	900
Dividends payable	1,800	Discount on bonds payable	2,000
Buildings	50,000	Common stock, $10 par	15,000
Bonds payable (due 2013)	29,000	Equipment	29,000
Retained earnings	25,800	Allowance for doubtful accounts	700
Office supplies	1,900	Preferred stock, $50 par	10,000
Current income taxes payable	4,200	Accumulated depreciation: buildings	12,400
Accumulated depreciation: equipment	8,300	Current interest payable	2,900
Patents (net)	2,400	Investment in held-to-maturity bonds	9,000
Notes payable (due January 1, 2010)	17,000	Cash	8,200
Inventory	24,400	Treasury stock (at cost)	1,500
Additional paid-in capital on common stock	7,700	Accrued wages	3,700
Sinking fund for bond retirement	4,000	Land	9,500

Required

Prepare a properly classified balance sheet for the Midwest Company on December 31, 2007.

P4-5 *Balance Sheet from Adjusted Trial Balance* The following is the alphabetical adjusted trial balance of the Meadows Company on December 31, 2007:

	Debits	Credits
Accounts payable		$ 9,800
Accounts receivable	$ 18,000	
Accrued payables		6,500
Accumulated depreciation		44,000
Additional paid-in capital		50,600
Cash	7,900	
Common stock, $5 par		29,600
Cost of goods sold	175,500	
Current portion of long-term debt		6,200
Deferred taxes payable		12,500
Dividends distributed	7,000	
General expenses	27,560	
Income tax expense	12,340	

	Debits	Credits
Income taxes payable		7,500
Interest expense	4,300	
Inventories	32,000	
Investment in held-to-maturity bonds	36,000	
Long-term debt		56,300
Long-term receivables	38,600	
Marketable securities (short-term)	10,100	
Patents (net)	13,000	
Prepaid insurance	5,000	
Property, plant, and equipment	148,000	
Retained earnings, 1/1/07		64,800
Sales		278,000
Sales returns	8,000	
Selling expenses	21,500	
Unrealized decrease in value of available-for-sale securities	1,000	
	$565,800	$565,800

Required

Prepare the December 31, 2007 balance sheet of the Meadows Company. Compute the debt ratio.

P4-6   *Balance Sheet and Notes*   Listed here in random order are the balance sheet accounts and related ending balances of the Eubanks Company as of December 31, 2007:

Income taxes payable	$ 24,700	Temporary investments	$19,100
Cash surrender value of life insurance	8,900	Bonds payable	80,000
Preferred stock	40,000	Additional paid-in capital on common stock	30,300
Premium on bonds payable	4,800	Inventories	98,500
Cash	11,600	Accounts receivable	32,300
Property, plant, and equipment (net)	229,300	Patents (net)	18,200
Accounts payable	58,000	Investment in bonds	25,000
Common stock	62,800	Additional paid-in capital on preferred stock	23,400
Retained earnings	123,400	Miscellaneous current payables	6,200
Land held for building site	19,500	Estimated liability for product warranties	7,300
Allowance for doubtful accounts	1,500		

Additional information:

1. The company uses control accounts for inventories and property, plant, and equipment and lists the latter at its book value.
2. The straight-line method is used to depreciate buildings, machinery, and equipment, based upon their cost and estimated residual values and lives. A breakdown of property, plant, and equipment shows the following: land at a cost of $32,000, buildings at a cost of $182,400 and a book value of $120,200, machinery at a cost of $63,900 and related accumulated depreciation of $18,600, and equipment (40% depreciated) at a cost of $53,000.
3. Patents are amortized on a straight-line basis directly to the patent account.
4. Inventories are listed at the lower of cost or market value using an average cost. The inventories include raw materials $22,200, work in process $34,700, and finished goods $41,600.
5. Common stock has a $10 par value per share, 12,000 shares are authorized, 6,280 shares have been issued.
6. Preferred stock has a $100 par value per share, 1,000 shares are authorized, 400 shares have been issued.
7. The investment in bonds is carried at the original cost, which is the face value, and is being held to maturity.
8. Temporary investments in marketable securities were purchased at year-end.
9. The bonds payable mature on December 31, 2012.
10. The company attaches a one-year warranty on all the products it sells.

Required

1. Prepare the December 31, 2007 balance sheet of the Eubanks Company (including appropriate parenthetical notations).
2. Prepare notes to accompany the balance sheet that itemize company accounting policies, inventories, and property, plant, and equipment.
3. Compute the current ratio. Which current assets would you classify as *liquid* and which as *separable* according to the FASB's conceptual guidelines? Why might these classifications be useful?

P4-7 *Comprehensive: Balance Sheet, Schedules, and Notes* The following is an alphabetical listing of the balance sheet accounts and account balances of the Blazer Company on December 31, 2007:

Accounts payable	$ 44,200	Income taxes payable	$ 19,700
Accounts receivable	37,100	Inventory	85,300
Accumulated depreciation	109,300	Investment in affiliate	30,000
Additional paid-in capital on common stock	20,000	Long-term liabilities (book value)	91,000
Additional paid-in capital on preferred stock	3,200	Miscellaneous current payables	6,800
Allowance for doubtful accounts	1,600	Notes receivable	17,000
Bond sinking fund	12,500	Preferred stock	32,000
Cash	13,800	Property and equipment	296,700
Common stock	80,000	Retained earnings	84,600

Additional information:
1. The company uses a control account for property and equipment, accumulated depreciation, and for long-term liabilities. The latter account is listed at its book value.
2. The straight-line method is used to depreciate property and equipment based upon cost, estimated residual value, and estimated life. The costs of the assets in this account are: land $29,500, buildings $164,600, store fixtures $72,600, and office equipment $30,000.
3. The accumulated depreciation breakdown is as follows: buildings $54,600, store fixtures $37,400, and office equipment $17,300.
4. The long-term debt includes 12%, $36,000 face value bonds that mature on December 31, 2012 and have an unamortized bond discount of $1,000; 11%, $48,000 face value bonds that mature on December 31, 2016, have a premium on bonds payable of $1,800, and whose retirement is being funded by a bond sinking fund; and a 13% note payable that has a face value of $6,200 and matures on January 1, 2010.
5. The noninterest-bearing note receivable matures on June 1, 2008.
6. Inventory is listed at lower of cost or market; cost is determined on the basis of average cost.
7. The investment in affiliate is carried at cost. The company has guaranteed the interest on 12%, $50,000, 15-year bonds issued by this affiliate, the Jay Company.
8. Common stock has a $10 par value per share, 10,000 shares are authorized, and 1,000 shares were issued during 2007 at a price of $13 per share, resulting in 8,000 shares issued at year-end.
9. Preferred stock has a $50 par value per share, 2,000 shares are authorized, and 140 shares were issued during 2007 at a price of $55 per share, resulting in 640 shares issued at year-end.
10. On January 15, 2008, before the December 31, 2007 balance sheet was issued, a building with a cost of $20,000 and a book value of $7,000 was totally destroyed. Insurance proceeds will amount to only $5,000.
11. Net income and dividends paid during the year were $50,500 and $21,000, respectively.

Required
1. Prepare the December 31, 2007 balance sheet (including appropriate parenthetical notations) of the Blazer Company.
2. Prepare a statement of changes in stockholders' equity for 2007. (*Hint*: Work back from the *ending* account balances.)
3. Prepare notes that itemize the balance sheet control accounts and those necessary to disclose any company accounting policies, contingent liabilities, and subsequent events.
4. Compute the debt ratio at the end of 2007. What is your evaluation of this ratio if it was 39% at the end of 2006?

P4-8 *Corrections to Balance Sheet* The Cable Company prepared the following balance sheet:

CABLE COMPANY
Balance Sheet For Year Ended December 31, 2007

Working capital	$ 22,800	Noncurrent liabilities	$ 62,000
Other assets	152,000	Stockholders' equity	112,800
Total	$174,800	Total	$174,800

Your analysis of these accounts reveals the following information:

1. Working capital consists of:

Land	$ 12,000
Accounts due from customers	18,000
Accounts due to suppliers	(22,700)
Inventories, including office supplies of $3,500	35,500
Income taxes owed	(16,400)
Wages owed	(3,600)
Note owed to bank (due December 31, 2009)	(17,000)
Securities held as a temporary investment	17,000
	$ 22,800

2. Other assets include:

Cash	$ 12,300
Prepaid insurance	2,400
Buildings and equipment	100,000
Discount on bonds payable	3,000
Investment in available-for-sale stock	29,000
Treasury stock (at cost)	5,300
	$152,000

3. Noncurrent liabilities consist of:

Bonds payable (due 2017)	$ 33,000
Allowance for doubtful accounts	1,400
Premium on preferred stock	2,600
Common stock, $5 par	25,000
	$ 62,000

4. Stockholders' equity includes:

Accumulated depreciation:	
buildings and equipment	$ 40,000
Preferred stock, $100 par	12,000
Premium on common stock	15,600
Retained earnings	40,000
Accrued pension cost	6,500
Unrealized decrease in value of	
available-for-sale securities	(1,300)
	$112,800

Required

Based on your analysis, prepare a properly classified December 31, 2007 balance sheet for the Cable Company.

P4-9 *Corrections to Balance Sheet* The Brandt Company presents the following December 31, 2007 balance sheet:

BRANDT COMPANY
Sheet of Balances
For Year Ended December 31, 2007

Current assets	$ 44,300	Current liabilities	$ 66,600
Long-term investments	13,600	Long-term liabilities	24,100
Property and equipment	123,500	Contributed capital	17,000
Intangible assets	7,700	Unrealized capital	22,500
Other assets	13,600	Retained earnings	72,500
Total assets	$202,700	Total equities	$202,700

The following information is also available:

1. Current assets include cash $3,800, accounts receivable $18,500, notes receivable (maturity date July 1, 2009) $10,000, and land $12,000.
2. Long-term investments include a $4,600 investment in available-for-sale securities that is expected to be sold in 2008 and a $9,000 investment in Dray Company bonds that are expected to be held until their December 31, 2016 maturity date.
3. Property and equipment include buildings costing $63,400, inventory costing $30,500, and equipment costing $29,600.
4. Intangible assets include patents that cost $8,200 and on which $2,300 amortization has accumulated, and treasury stock that cost $1,800.
5. Other assets include prepaid insurance (which expires on November 30, 2008) $2,900, sinking fund for bond retirement $7,000, and trademarks that cost $3,700 and are not impaired.
6. Current liabilities include accounts payable $19,400, bonds payable (maturity date December 31, 2018) $40,000, and accrued income taxes payable $7,200.
7. Long-term liabilities include accrued wages $4,100 and mortgage payable (which is due in five equal annual payments starting December 31, 2008) $20,000.
8. Contributed capital includes common stock ($5 par) $11,000 and preferred stock ($100 par) $6,000.
9. Unrealized capital includes premium on bonds payable $4,300, premium on preferred stock $2,400, premium on common stock $14,700, and unrealized increase in value of securities available for sale $1,100.
10. Retained earnings includes unrestricted retained earnings, $37,800, allowance for doubtful accounts $700, and accumulated depreciation on buildings and equipment of $21,000 and $13,000, respectively.

Required ✖

Based on the preceding information, prepare a properly classified December 31, 2007 balance sheet for the Brandt Company.

P4-10 *Balance Sheet Calculations* The balance sheet information of the John Company at the end of 2007 and 2008 is as follows:

	2007	2008
Long-term liabilities	$ (a)	$ 33,100
Accumulated other comprehensive income	8,000	8,900
Working capital	17,900	19,800
Intangible assets	19,100	18,600

	2007	2008
Common stock, $10 par	(b)	(i)
Total stockholders' equity	(c)	$179,000
Accumulated depreciation	$(37,500)	(48,600)
Total liabilities	51,900	(j)
Current assets	(d)	39,800
Retained earnings	83,300	(k)
Total contributed capital	66,700	(l)
Total assets	(e)	(m)
Additional paid-in capital	(f)	(n)
Long-term investments	40,100	(o)
Current liabilities	(g)	(p)
Property, plant, and equipment	(h)	180,000

Additional information: At the end of 2007, (a) the amount of long-term liabilities is twice the amount of current liabilities, and (b) there are 2,900 shares of common stock outstanding. During 2008, the company (a) issued 100 shares of common stock for $25 per share, (b) earned net income of $20,600, and (c) paid dividends of $1 per share on the common stock outstanding at year-end.

Required
Fill in the blanks lettered (a) through (p). All of the necessary information is provided. (*Hint:* It is not necessary to calculate your answers in alphabetical order.)

P4-11 *Erroneous Balance Sheet* The Cutler Corporation prepared the following balance sheet:

CUTLER CORPORATION
Balance Report For Year Ended December 31, 2007

Current Assets			Current Liabilities		
Cash		$ 6,300	Accounts payable		$13,000
Accounts receivable		15,900	Accumulated depreciation: buildings		17,100
Inventory, at higher of cost or market			Wages payable		3,000
(cost $27,200)		28,000	Additional paid-in capital		
Long-Term Investments			on common stock		23,200
Treasury stock (at cost)		1,400	Long-Term Liabilities		
Investment in D Company bonds			Bonds payable	$46,000	
(at book value)		7,300	Less: Sinking fund to retire		
Marketable securities,			bonds	(6,000)	40,000
short-term at market value		10,000	Preferred stock, $50 par		15,000
Property, Plant, and Equipment			Premium on preferred stock		5,100
Land		11,300	Accumulated depreciation: equipment		7,000
Patents	$8,000		Current taxes payable		9,600
Less: Accumulated amortization	(2,800)	5,200	Owners' Equity:		
Buildings		40,800	Common stock, $2 par		8,000
Equipment		19,000	Unrealized gain on write-up		
Intangibles			of marketable securities		
Trademarks		5,700	to market value		1,300
Other Assets			Unrealized gain on write-up		
Cash surrender value of life insurance		5,000	of inventory to market value		800
Discount on bonds payable		3,900	Retained earnings		16,000
Total Assets		$159,800	Allowance for doubtful accounts		700
			Total Equities		$159,800

Required
1. Identify the errors made in the Cutler balance sheet.
2. Prepare a corrected, properly classified balance sheet.

P4-12 **AICPA Adapted** *Complex Balance Sheet* Presented below is the unaudited balance sheet as of December 31, 2007, prepared by the bookkeeper of Zues Manufacturing Corporation.

ZUES MANUFACTURING CORPORATION
Balance Sheet For the Year Ended December 31, 2007

Assets		Liabilities & Stockholders' Equity	
Cash	$ 225,000	Accounts payable	$ 133,800
Accounts receivable (net)	345,700	Mortgage payable	900,000
Inventories	560,000	Notes payable	500,000
Prepaid income taxes	40,000	Lawsuit liability	80,000
Investments	57,700	Income taxes payable	61,200
Land	450,000	Deferred tax liability	28,000
Building	1,750,000	Accumulated depreciation	420,000
Machinery and equipment	1,964,000	Total Liabilities	$2,123,000
Goodwill	37,000	Common stock, $50 par; 40,000	
Total Assets	$5,429,400	shares issued	2,231,000
		Retained earnings	1,075,400
		Total Stockholders' Equity	$3,306,400
		Total Liabilities and	
		Stockholders' Equity	$5,429,400

Your firm has been engaged to perform an audit, during which the following data are found:

1. Checks totaling $14,000 in payment of accounts payable were mailed on December 31, 2007 but were not recorded until 2008. Late in December 2007, the bank returned a customer's $2,000 check, marked "NSF," but no entry was made. Cash includes $100,000 restricted for building purposes.
2. Included in accounts receivable is a $30,000 note due on December 31, 2010 from Zues' president.
3. During 2007, Zues purchased 500 shares of common stock of a major corporation that supplies Zues with raw materials. Total cost of this stock was $51,300, and market value on December 31, 2007 was $47,000. The decline in market value is considered temporary. Zues plans to hold these shares indefinitely.
4. Treasury stock was recorded at cost when Zues purchased 200 of its own shares for $32 per share in May 2007. This amount is included in investments.
5. On December 31, 2007, Zues borrowed $500,000 from a bank in exchange for a 10% note payable, maturing December 31, 2012. Equal principal payments are due December 31 of each year, beginning in 2008. This note is collateralized by a $250,000 tract of land acquired as a potential future building site, which is included in land.
6. The mortgage payable requires $50,000 principal payments, plus interest, at the end of each month. Payments were made on January 31 and February 28, 2008. The balance of this mortgage was due June 30, 2008. On March 1, 2008, prior to issuance of the audited financial statements, Zues consummated a noncancelable agreement with the lender to refinance this mortgage. The new terms require $100,000 annual principal payments, plus interest, on February 28 of each year, beginning in 2009. The final payment is due February 28, 2016.
7. The lawsuit liability will be paid in 2008.
8. Of the total deferred tax liability, $5,000 is considered a current liability.
9. The current income tax expense reported in Zues' 2007 income statement was $61,200.
10. The company was authorized to issue 100,000 shares of $50 par value common stock.

Required

Prepare a corrected classified balance sheet as of December 31, 2007. This financial statement should include a proper heading, format, and necessary descriptions.

P4-13 *Changes in Stockholders' Equity* On January 1, 2007 the Knox Company showed the following alphabetical list of stockholders' equity balances:

Additional paid-in capital on common stock	$130,000
Additional paid-in capital on preferred stock	6,000
Common stock, $10 par	100,000
Preferred stock, $100 par	50,000
Retained earnings	224,000

During 2007, the following events occurred and were properly recorded by the company:

1. The company purchased an investment in available-for-sale securities. At year-end the market value of the securities had increased by $9,000.
2. The company issued 2,000 shares of common stock for $25 per share.

3. The company issued 110 shares of preferred stock for $116 per share.
4. The company reacquired 400 shares of its common stock as treasury stock at a cost of $26 per share. (*Hint*: Record the reacquisition cost in a Treasury Stock account.)
5. The company earned net income of $57,000.
6. The company paid a $7 per share dividend on the preferred stock and a $1.25 per share dividend on the common stock outstanding at the end of 2007 (treasury stock is not entitled to dividends).

Required
Prepare a statement of changes in stockholders' equity for 2007. (Include retained earnings.)

P4-14 *Analyzing Coca-Cola's Balance Sheet Disclosures* Review the financial statements and related notes of the Coca-Cola Company in Appendix A.

Required
Answer the following questions. (*Note*: You do not need to make any calculations. All answers may be found in the financial report.) Indicate on what page of the annual report you located the answer.
1. What was the amount of the current assets on December 31, 2004?
2. What was the amount in the allowance for doubtful accounts on December 31, 2004?
3. What is the par value of the company's common stock? How many shares had been issued at the end of 2004?
4. What was the total amount of inventories on December 31, 2004? What were the principal categories of inventory on this date?
5. What was the long-term debt on December 31, 2004? Of this total, how much was for the 5¾%, U.S. dollar notes due 2011?
6. What was the allowance for depreciation on December 31, 2004? What method does the company use to depreciate its property, plant, and equipment?
7. What was the amount of accounts payable and accrued expenses on December 31, 2004? How much was for accrued marketing expenses?
8. What inventory costing method was used for most inventories in 2004?
9. What was the reinvested (retained) earnings on December 31, 2004?
10. What was the total property, plant, and equipment before and after allowance for depreciation on December 31, 2004?
11. What were the total assets on December 31, 2004?
12. What were the current liabilities on December 31, 2004?
13. What were the number of shares and cost of the treasury stock held by the company on December 31, 2004?
14. What was the amount of marketable securities on December 31, 2004? What was the unrealized gain (loss) on available for sale securities on December 31, 2004?
15. How much was the company contingently liable for guarantees of indebtedness owed by third parties on December 31, 2004?

CASES

COMMUNICATION

C4-1   Alternative Valuation Methods
A friend of yours who had a bookkeeping course in high school and who is currently a business major says, "I thought that assets were always reported at their historical cost on a company's balance sheet. Recently, however, I heard several accounting majors discussing 'alternative valuation methods' for measuring the value of assets. I know that historical cost is the exchange price paid for an asset, so I cannot understand how there can be any other 'value' for the asset."

Required
Write a short memo that identifies and briefly explains the valuation methods (other than historical cost) that a company could use to measure the value of an asset. For each valuation

method, include in your discussion examples of assets whose values are often reported based on the use of that method.

C4-2   Contingencies and Subsequent Events
The bookkeeper of a company you are auditing states, "Our balance sheet is dated December 31, the end of our accounting period. I don't understand loss contingencies and subsequent events. Also, I see no reason for disclosing these items on the company's balance sheet because they deal with events that might occur or have occurred *after* the balance sheet date."

Required
Write a short report to the bookkeeper that explains loss contingencies and subsequent events, as well as the importance of their disclosure on the company's balance sheet.

C4-3 Securities and Exchange Commission Disclosures

CMA Adapted The Securities and Exchange Commission (SEC) has encouraged managements of public companies to disclose more information in the shareholders' annual report. As a consequence, a significant amount of the information required in the SEC's Form 10-K now appears in published annual reports.

At the same time, the SEC has made the annual financial reporting process simpler and more efficient by approving an integrated disclosure system.

Required

1. Identify the major classes of information that must be included in both the annual report to shareholders and Form 10-K filed with the SEC.
2. The integrated disclosure system is intended to simplify the annual reporting process with the SEC by expanding the ability to incorporate by reference.
   a. Define what is meant by *incorporating by reference* and identify the documents that are involved when incorporating by reference.
   b. Explain how the integrated disclosure system reduces managements' efforts in filing annual reports with the SEC.
   c. Explain the SEC's principal reasons for making the changes in the annual reporting process.
   d. Identify and explain potential problems the integrated disclosure system could have on the annual reporting process from the aspect of users of financial information.

C4-4 Asset Valuation

It is the end of 2007 and you are an accountant for the Stone Company. During 2007, sales of the company's products slumped and the company's earnings are expected to be much less than those of 2006. The president comes to you with an idea. He says, "Our company's property, plant, and equipment cost $300,000, and that is the amount we usually report on our balance sheet. However, I just had these assets appraised by an independent appraiser, and she says they are worth $400,000. I think that the company should report the property, plant, and equipment at this amount on its December 31, 2007 balance sheet, and should report the $100,000 increase in value as a gain on the 2007 income statement. If we use this approach, it will show how much our company is really worth and increase our earnings. This will make our stockholders happy. What do you think?"

Required

Prepare a written response to the president.

CREATIVE AND CRITICAL THINKING

C4-5 Valuation of Assets and Stock

A friend has come to you for advice. He states that he owns several shares of stock in a corporation. He has examined the most recent balance sheet of the corporation and has found that the common stock issued and outstanding totals 40,000 shares, and the market price per share is $25 on the balance sheet date. He is sure that the balance sheet must be in error because, in his words, "the total assets are $1,100,000 and this current value should be the same as the $1,000,000 total value of the outstanding common stock."

Required

Explain to your friend how the "values" of the various assets of the corporation typically are measured and reported on its balance sheet, and how the "value" of the $1,100,000 total assets is determined. Continue the discussion by explaining to your friend why the "values" of the assets and the stock are not the same.

C4-6 Valuation of Assets

AICPA Adapted Valuation of assets is an important topic in accounting theory. Suggested valuation methods include the following:

Historical cost (past purchase price)
Historical cost adjusted to reflect general price-level changes
Discounted cash flow (future exchange price)
Market price (current selling price)
Replacement cost (current purchase price)

Required

1. Why is the valuation of assets a significant issue?
2. Explain the basic theory underlying each of the valuation methods cited, including the effect on earnings. Do not discuss advantages and disadvantages of each method.

C4-7 Analyzing Coca-Cola's Accounting Policies

A company must include a summary of its accounting policies in the notes to its financial statements. The Coca-Cola Company includes this summary as the first of its notes to the consolidated financial statements shown in Appendix A.

Required

1. Explain what is required to be disclosed about the accounting policies of a company.
2. Review the Coca-Cola Company's note on its accounting policies and answer the following questions:
   a. When does the company recognize revenue?
   b. What items are classified as cash equivalents?
   c. How are inventories valued, and generally what inventory costing method(s) is used?
   d. How are property, plant, and equipment stated, and what depreciation method is used?
   e. How are trademarks and other intangible assets amortized?
   f. How does the company account for production costs of print, radio, television, and other advertisements?

What was the amount of advertising and production costs included in prepaid expenses and other assets and noncurrent other assets as of December 31, 2004?

C4-8 Ethics and Accounts Receivable Adjustment

It is February 16, 2008 and you are auditing the Davenport Corporation's financial statements for 2007 (which will be issued in March, 2008). You read in the newspaper that Travis Corporation, a major customer of Davenport, is in financial difficulty. Included in Davenport's accounts receivable is $50,000 (a material amount) owed to it by Travis. You approach Jim Davenport, president, with this information and suggest that a reduction of accounts receivable and recognition of a loss for 2007 might be appropriate. Jim replies, "Why should we make an adjustment? Ted Travis, the president of Travis Corporation, is a friend of mine; he will find a way to pay us, one way or another. Furthermore, this occurred in 2008, so let's wait and see what happens; we can always make an adjustment later this year. Our 2007 income and year-end working capital are not that high; our creditors and stockholders wouldn't stand for lower amounts than they already are."

Required

From financial reporting and ethical perspectives, prepare a response to Jim Davenport regarding this issue.

C4-9 Ethics and Note Due from President

You are the accountant for Spaedy Company and are preparing the financial statements for 2007. Near the end of 2007, Spaedy Company loaned its president $100,000 (a material amount) because she was having financial difficulties. The note was properly recorded as a note receivable by Spaedy Company. You are unsure of how to classify this note on the 2007 ending balance sheet and ask the president when the note is due. She replies, "We never really set a due date; I might repay it in 2008 or maybe in a couple of years when I get more financially secure. It would be best to classify this note as a current asset in the usual manner because that will increase our working capital and current ratio, which will make our creditors and stockholders happy."

Required

From financial reporting and ethical perspectives, what do you think of the president's suggestion?

RESEARCH SIMULATION

R4-1 Researching GAAP

Situation

You are the assistant accountant for Tyler Corporation. It is mid-January, 2008 and you are helping to prepare the Tyler Corporation's balance sheet for December 31, 2007. Tyler will publish this balance sheet on March 1, 2008, after the auditors have completed their work. Tyler has a $100,000 note payable that was issued in 2006 and that is due March 6, 2008. On January 5, 2008, Tyler sold 2,000 shares of its $10 par common stock for $80,000. Its intent is to use these proceeds (plus $20,000 cash it already has on hand) to repay the note payable on March 6. The head accountant says "I'm not sure how to classify the $100,000 note payable on the December 31, 2007 balance sheet. Check this out for me."

Directions

Research the related generally accepted accounting principles and prepare a short memo to the head accountant that explains how Tyler Corporation should report the $100,000 note payable on its December 31, 2007 balance sheet.

5

The Income Statement and Statement of Cash Flows

OBJECTIVES

After reading this chapter, you will be able to:

1 Understand the concepts of income.

2 Explain the conceptual guidelines for reporting income.

3 Define the elements of an income statement.

4 Describe the major components of an income statement.

5 Compute income from continuing operations.

6 Report results from discontinued operations.

7 Identify extraordinary items.

8 Prepare a statement of retained earnings.

9 Report comprehensive income.

10 Explain the statement of cash flows.

11 Classify cash flows as operating, investing, or financing.

A New Standard for Income?

FASB Statement of Concepts No. 1 establishes the information on the income statement as the best indicator of company performance. However, many companies have increased their emphasis on non-GAAP performance measures. A recent earnings release by **Hewlett Packard** focuses on non-GAAP operating profit and earnings per share ahead of the GAAP operating profit and earnings per share. The graph below charts Hewlett Packard's non-GAAP and GAAP operating profit over the 2003 fiscal year.

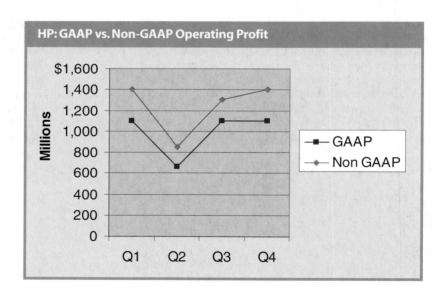

Using names such as pro-forma earnings, normalized earnings, and earnings before interest, taxes, depreciation, and amortization (EBITDA), many companies argue that these alternative performance measures increase users' understanding of a company's past performance and its prospects for the future. The

Credit: Associated Press/AP

implication is that GAAP income is an inadequate measure of performance. However, because pro-forma measures typically exclude significant negative components of GAAP income, resulting in much higher pro-forma results, many view the use of non-GAAP measures as an attempt to put a positive spin on operating results.

Because of concern over the proliferation of alternative and inconsistent financial performance measures, the **FASB** has begun a project that may help alleviate the problem. The current project, "Financial Performance Reporting by Business Enterprises," does not specifically address pro-forma reporting. Instead it focuses on redesigning the income statement by providing standards for the display of information. Such a standard may reduce flexibility in how a company reports financial information but the FASB hopes that improving the presentation of GAAP-based performance measures will result in more meaningful and useful disclosures of a company's operating results.

FOR FURTHER INVESTIGATION

For a discussion of pro-forma earnings and FASB's project to improve financial performance reporting, consult the Business & Company Resource Center (BCRC):

- "A Matter of Emphasis: Regulation G was Supposed to End the Abuses of Pro Forma Reporting. Has it Succeeded?" Alix Nyberg, *CFO, The Magazine for Senior Financial Executives*, 8756-7113, July 2004 v20 i9 p69(2).
- "Financial Performance Reporting: Striking a Balance Between Transparency and Simplicity." Colleen Sayther, *Financial Executive*, 0895-4186, Jan-Feb 2004 v20 i1 p6(1).

A company's **income statement** summarizes the results of its operations for the accounting period. This statement is alternatively referred to as a *statement of income, statement of earnings,* or *statement of operations.* The income statement and balance sheet are supported by a schedule entitled the *statement of retained earnings* (or simply the *retained earnings statement*), which serves as the link between the two statements. The operations of a company include routine ongoing activities, as well as activities that are infrequent or unusual. In addition, a company may divest itself of a major component of its operations, report extraordinary items, make changes in accounting principles, and make adjustments to prior periods' financial statements. We discuss how a company reports each of these items in this chapter as it relates to the company's income statement or its statement of retained earnings. We also discuss the alternative ways a company may report its comprehensive income in its financial statements. We also introduce the **statement of cash flows** in this chapter because of the relationship of operating, investing, and financing cash flows to different sections of the income statement and balance sheet. Before we do this, we first examine the concepts of income.

CONCEPTS OF INCOME

1 Understand the concepts of income.

Accountants and economists have long debated what "income" is and how it should be measured. One *concept* of income is that of capital maintenance; a useful way to *measure* income is by using the transactional approach.

Capital Maintenance Concept

The capital maintenance concept focuses upon the capital, or net assets (assets minus liabilities), of the corporation. Under this concept, a corporation's income for a period of time is the amount that it may pay to stockholders during that period and still be as well off at the end of the period as it was at the beginning.[1] In other words, **capital must be maintained before a corporation earns income on that capital.** Although capital may be thought of as financial capital or physical capital, the FASB uses a financial capital maintenance concept. To use this concept, the beginning and ending capital (that is, the net assets) must be compared after adjusting for any additional investments or disinvestments during the period. The resulting difference is the corporation's income. Given this definition, accountants and economists probably would agree on the total income that a corporation earned over its entire life. This lifetime income would be computed by comparing the total proceeds received from the liquidation of the net assets at the end of the life with the capital invested at the beginning of the life, adjusted for any additional investments or withdrawals. Here there is certainty regarding the value of the net assets at the two points in time.

However, **external (and internal) users need income information on a more timely basis** (for example, on an annual basis). Also, there is more uncertainty about the value of the net assets that have not been liquidated at the end of such a shorter time period. For a shorter time period the values of a company's assets and liabilities at the beginning and end of the period may be measured in several ways. For a particular corporation these might include use of (1) the historical cost, (2) the current cost, (3) the current market value, (4) the net realizable value, or (5) the present value of future cash flows. After measuring the values of the assets and liabilities at the two points in time using one of these methods, corporate income can be computed as the difference between the beginning and ending net assets (after any adjustments for additional investments or disinvestments). Many accountants and economists have advocated a particular valuation concept and

---

1. S. S. Alexander, "Income Measurement in a Dynamic Economy," *Five Monographs on Business Income* (New York: AICPA Study Group on Business Income, 1950), p. 15.

methodology.[2] (A thorough discussion of the conceptual merits of these alternatives is an appropriate topic for an accounting theory book.)

We provide a brief example of the capital maintenance approach to determining corporate income here, using the historical cost method of valuing net assets. Assume that a corporation has net assets of $50,000 at the beginning and $90,000 at the end of the year, and that no additional investments or withdrawals were made. Based upon a comparison of the ending and the beginning net assets, the corporation could pay out $40,000 to stockholders and still be as well off at year-end. This $40,000 is the corporation's income for the year, using the capital maintenance concept *based on historical costs*. To illustrate further, assume that a corporation has beginning net assets of $45,000 and ending net assets of $80,000. Also assume the stockholders made an additional capital investment of $10,000 during the year. The total income of the corporation for the year is $25,000 computed as follows:

Ending net assets	$80,000
Less: Additional investment	(10,000)
Ending net assets excluding additional investments	$70,000
Less: Beginning net assets	(45,000)
Total income for the year	$25,000

Unfortunately, in either of the two examples, **the corporation's total income is not very useful to various user groups.** The total income includes all amounts affecting net assets, whether they relate to usual or unusual, to extraordinary or ordinary events. But the total income is just that, a total. **The corporation's total income does not show a breakdown that identifies the causal relationships and operating activities** that may be helpful to a specific user group. This specific information is shown under the transactional approach to income measurement.

Transactional Approach

As we noted in Chapter 2, an objective of financial reporting is to provide information that is useful to investors, creditors, and other external user groups to evaluate the amounts, timing, and uncertainty of the future net cash inflows for a company. A derived specific objective is to **provide information about a company's comprehensive income and its components.** That is, user groups are interested in the resources obtained from and the resources given up for ongoing operations, discontinued operations, and unusual and/or infrequent activities. Accountants are also concerned with developing reliable (verifiable) evidence of the company's income-producing and other business activities reported in its financial statements.

As a result, a transactional approach to income measurement has evolved. Generally, **in the transactional approach, a company records its net assets at their historical cost, and it does not record changes in the assets and liabilities unless a transaction, event, or circumstance has occurred that provides reliable evidence of a change in value.** The transactional approach uses the accrual basis of accounting. **In accrual accounting, a company records the financial effects of transactions and other events and circumstances in the periods during which they occur rather than only in the periods in which it receives or pays cash.** In the transactional approach certain changes in values of the specific assets or liabilities are associated with the earning activities and are included in the company's income.

The transactional approach to income measurement is used in accounting today. It is consistent with the traditional capital maintenance concept because the income represents

2.   See, for instance, E. O. Edwards and P. W. Bell, *The Theory and Measurement of Business Income* (Berkeley: University of California Press, 1970).

Credit: ©Getty Images/PhotoDisc

the difference between the beginning and ending adjusted net assets on an historical cost basis. However, **the accrual-based transactional approach to income measurement** is more informative because **it relates (matches) the accomplishments and the efforts** so that the reported income measures the company's earnings activities.[3] The FASB has developed the concept of **comprehensive income** as follows:

> **Comprehensive income is the change in equity of a company during a period from transactions, other events, and circumstances relating to nonowner sources. It includes all changes in equity during a period except those resulting from investments by owners and distributions to owners.**[4]

The intent of the FASB is (1) to develop a concept of income broad enough to include changes in value not traditionally reported in net income under the transactional approach, and (2) to allow for flexibility as to where a company reports certain components of income in its financial statements. We discuss the reporting of a company's comprehensive income later in the chapter. First, we focus on its primary component, net income.

In the accrual-based transactional approach, a corporation's net income for an accounting period currently is measured as follows:

Net Income = Revenues − Expenses + Gains − Losses

The FASB has defined the various elements (revenues, expenses, gains, and losses) of net income. We discuss these definitions and their relationships later in the chapter and throughout the book as they relate to specific situations. The identification of what elements to include in net income, when these should be included (recognized), and how they should be measured depends on the definitions. Accounting rules and conventions (generally accepted accounting principles) also play a role in determining net income. Before we get into the details of determining net income, it is helpful to understand the purposes of the income statement.

---

3.   "Objectives of Financial Reporting by Business Enterprises," *FASB Statement of Financial Accounting Concepts No. 1* (Stamford, Conn.: FASB, 1978), par. 45.
4.   "Elements of Financial Statements," *FASB Statement of Financial Accounting Concepts No. 6* (Stamford, Conn.: FASB, 1985), par. 70.

PURPOSES OF THE INCOME STATEMENT

Because a company's income statement summarizes its income-generating activities, many external users consider the income statement to be the most important financial statement. The purposes of a company's income statement are:

1. **To help evaluate management's past performance**. Investors invest capital into a company. The management of the company has a responsibility to maintain and increase this capital. The income statement provides information that helps current and potential investors evaluate how well a company's management has performed in fulfilling this responsibility. It provides information about the company's accomplishments and efforts in earning net income.

2. **To help predict the company's future income and cash flows**. The past income of a company is useful for predicting the company's future income and cash flows. External users review the components of a company's net income to evaluate the "earnings quality" or ability to predict its future earnings. In turn, this information is useful in predicting the cash flows that the company will have to make current and future dividend payments to investors. It is also useful to help predict the future price of a company's stock.[5]

3. **To help assess the company's "creditworthiness."** The net income of a company is also useful for determining the risk associated with extending credit to the company. A study of the company's "earning power" as reported on its income statement helps lending institutions, suppliers, employees, and other external users evaluate the likelihood that the company will be able to convert its net income into cash to meet its obligations.

4. **To help in comparisons with other companies**. Investors are interested in evaluating the risk of investing in a company as compared to other companies in the same industry or other industries. They are also interested in comparing a company's return on investment and operating capability to those of other companies. These comparisons aid investors in evaluating a company's "attractiveness" as compared to other companies. A company's income statement helps in this comparative analysis.

With these factors in mind, we now turn to understanding the conceptual reporting guidelines for improving the measurement of net income under the transactional approach.

CONCEPTUAL REPORTING GUIDELINES

The FASB is concerned with how a company reports net income and its components to better achieve the purposes of the income statement. In particular, the FASB is interested in improving the reporting of income statement information relating to return on investment, risk, financial flexibility, and operating capability.

- **Return on investment is a measure of overall company performance**. Stockholders (investors) invest capital to obtain a return *on* capital. Before a company can provide a return on investment, its capital must be maintained.

- **Risk is the uncertainty or unpredictability of the future results of a company.** The greater the range and time frame within which future results are likely to fall, the greater the risk associated with an investment in or extension of credit to the company. Generally, the greater the risk, the higher the rate of return expected.

---

5. C. A. Finger, "The Ability of Earnings to Predict Future Earnings and Cash Flow," *Journal of Accounting Research* 32 (Autumn 1994), pp. 210–223; P. M. Dechow, S. P. Kothari, and R. L. Watts, "The Relation between Earnings and Cash Flows," *Journal of Accounting and Economics* 25(2) (May 1998), pp. 133–168.

- **Financial flexibility is the ability of a company to adapt to unexpected needs and opportunities.** Financial flexibility stems from, among other qualities, the ability to adjust operations to increase net operating cash flows and the ability to sell assets without disrupting operations.
- **Operating capability refers to a company's ability to maintain a given physical level of operations.** This level of operations may be measured by the quantity of goods or services (e.g., inventory) produced in a given period or by the physical capacity of the fixed assets (e.g., property, plant, and equipment).

The reporting of income statement information should also guard against "earnings management" by the managers of a company. **Earnings management** occurs when managers enter into transactions or select from alternative generally accepted accounting principles for the purpose of artificially influencing reported net income (by changing revenues/gains or expenses/losses).

2 Explain the conceptual guidelines for reporting income.

General Conceptual Guidelines

In regard to providing information about the preceding items, the FASB suggests that a company's income statement can be improved by:

1. Providing information about its operating performance separately from other aspects of its performance.
2. Presenting the results of significant activities or events that predict the amounts, timing, and uncertainty of its future income and cash flows.
3. Providing information useful for assessing the return on investment.
4. Providing feedback that enables users to assess their previous predictions of income and its components.
5. Providing information to help assess the cost of maintaining its operating capability.
6. Presenting information about how effectively management has discharged its stewardship responsibility regarding the company's resources.

To accomplish these goals, the FASB has established general concepts to guide decisions about reporting information on (or related to) the income statement. It suggests that **the components of net income may be more important than the total amount.** A company should report a component of net income separately if it is important for assessing some aspect of future income. This guide implies the separate reporting of income from ongoing central operations, discontinued operations, and one or more components relating to peripheral activities, unusual activities, and other events and circumstances affecting the company. The guide also indicates that it is desirable to report information about operating segments.

Specific Conceptual Guidelines

More specific guidelines may aid in decisions about how to report revenues, expenses, gains, and losses. We summarize these guidelines as follows:

1. Those items that are judged to be unusual in amount based on past experience should be reported separately.
2. Revenues, expenses, gains, and losses that are affected in different ways by changes in economic conditions should be distinguished from one another. For instance, changes in revenues are the joint result of changes in sales volume and selling prices. Information about both types of changes is helpful in assessing future operating results.
3. Sufficient detail should be given to help understand the primary relationships among revenues, expenses, gains, and losses. In particular, it is helpful to report separately (a) expenses that vary with volume of activity or with various components of

income, (b) expenses that are discretionary, and (c) expenses that are stable over time or depend upon other factors, such as the level of interest rates or the rate of taxation.

4. When the measurements of revenues, expenses, gains, or losses are subject to different levels of reliability, they should be reported separately.

5. Items whose amounts must be known for the calculation of summary indicators (e.g., rate of return) should be reported separately.[6]

These guidelines are intended to provide assistance for decisions about the grouping of items to show the components of net income and the elements that a company should report separately. The benefits of any additional information should, of course, be greater than the costs of providing the information.

User Group Conceptual Guidelines

The AICPA Special Committee on Financial Reporting suggests similar general and specific guidelines for the reporting of a company's income. Based on input from external user groups, the Committee developed a "model" for business reporting. In this model, the Committee recommends that a company report separately the effects on earnings from its "core" and "non-core" activities. Core activities are usual and recurring activities, transactions, or events, and continuing operations, excluding interest. Conversely, non-core activities, transactions, or events are unusual or nonrecurring.

Under this approach a company's income statement would present two categories of earnings:

1. core earnings, and

2. non-core earnings and financing costs

The *core earnings category* would include income (or loss) from core activities and recurring nonoperating gains and losses. The *non-core earnings and financing costs category* would include nonrecurring income (or loss) from such items as discontinued operations, unusually large nonrecurring transactions, the effects of a rare natural disaster, unique transactions, and interest income and expense. The Committee also recommends increasing the amount of detail on the income statement. This includes, for instance, dividing operating expenses into categories such as fixed and variable, controllable and noncontrollable, or discretionary and nondiscretionary, as well as providing more detail about the components and cost of goods sold.

In addition to the annual income statement disclosures, the Committee recommends improved interim reporting, as well as reporting disaggregated information on an operating segment basis. In regard to quarterly reporting, the Committee recommends that fourth-quarter results be shown separately within the annual report so that year-end adjustments can be reviewed for additional insight. Disaggregated information should be improved by aligning more closely what is reported in a company's annual report with what is reported internally to the company's management.[7]

These recommendations were made to enhance the predictive and feedback value of the information reported in a company's income statement and the related notes. The intent is to help external users to better identify the opportunities and risks of investments in or credit extensions to the company. Although the Committee is not a standard-setting body, the FASB has implemented some of its recommendations in regard to the reporting of operating segment information (which we discuss in Chapter 6).

---

6. "Reporting Income, Cash Flows, and Financial Position of Business Enterprises," *FASB Proposed Statement of Financial Accounting Concepts* (Stamford, Conn.: FASB, 1981), par. 34 and 46–48.

7. "Improving Business Reporting—A Customer Focus," *AICPA Special Committee on Financial Reporting* (New York: AICPA, 1994), Appendix II, pp. 137–140.

In addition, the FASB has added a project called "Financial Performance Reporting by Business Enterprises" to its agenda. The objective of this project is to set standards for presenting information in a company's financial statements that would help external users assess the financial performance of the company. It will take several years for these standards to be set, but the Board has reached some tentative conclusions. If implemented, these tentative standards would require a company to report all its revenues, expenses, gains, and losses in a single statement of comprehensive income. Then, within this statement:

- the comprehensive income would be separated into at least three categories: business activities, financing activities, and other gains and losses,
- extraordinary items (net of taxes) would be included in each of the categories to which they relate,
- income taxes would be presented as a separate classification after the categories,
- a subtotal called net income (loss) from continuing operations would be presented after the income taxes section,
- the effects of discontinued operations (net of taxes) would be presented as a separate category below the net income (loss) from continuing operations, and
- items of other comprehensive income (if any) would be included in a category below discontinued operations.

These tentative conclusions, however, will be revisited because the Board has agreed to work with the IASB to help in the international convergence of these standards. For more details on this long-range project, see the FASB website (*http://www.fasb.org*). We discuss how each of these items is currently reported in later sections of this chapter.

ELEMENTS OF THE INCOME STATEMENT

3 Define the elements of an income statement.

The elements of the income statement are the broad classes of items comprising the statement. They are the "building blocks" with which the income statement is prepared. Each of the four elements—revenues, expenses, gains, and losses—is defined in **FASB Statement of Concepts No. 6**.

Revenues

> **Revenues are inflows of (increases in) assets of a company or settlement of its liabilities during a period from delivering or producing goods, rendering services, or other activities that are the company's ongoing major or central operations.**

Revenues represent actual or expected cash inflows (or the equivalent) that occur as a result of the company's ongoing primary operating activities. Revenues are a measurement of the *accomplishments* of the operating activities during the accounting period. It is important to remember that revenues are a component of equity. The transactions that result in revenues are of various types, depending on the kinds of operations involved and the way revenues are recognized.[8]

Revenue Recognition

Recognition is the process of formally recording and reporting an item in a company's financial statements. To be recognized, an item must meet the definition of an element

---

8. The discussion in this section is a summary of that presented by the FASB in *FASB Statement of Financial Accounting Concepts No. 6, op. cit;* "Recognition and Measurement in Financial Statements of Business Enterprises," *FASB Statement of Financial Accounting Concepts No. 5* (Stamford, Conn.: FASB, 1984).

and be reliably measurable in monetary terms. Recognition involves the depiction of an item in both words and numbers, with the amount included in the totals of the financial statements. Most revenues are the joint result of many operating activities of a company and are "earned" gradually and continually as a result of this entire set of activities. These activities may be described as a company's earning process. **The earning process includes purchasing, producing, selling, delivering, administering, and collecting and paying cash.** Although revenues are defined in relation to this entire earnings (operating) process, **revenues generally are recognized when two criteria are met: (1) realization has taken place, and (2) they have been earned.** These criteria provide an acceptable level of assurance (i.e., reliability) of the existence and amounts of revenues. Sometimes one and sometimes the other criterion is more important, but both must be satisfied to a reasonable degree for revenue to be recognized.

In the first criterion, *realization* means the process of converting noncash resources into cash or rights to cash. Realization encompasses two terms: (1) realized and (2) realizable. *Realized* refers to the actual exchange of noncash resources into cash or near cash (e.g., receivables). *Realizable* refers to the situation where noncash resources are readily convertible into known amounts of cash or claims to cash. "Readily convertible" noncash resources (e.g., gold, wheat) have interchangeable units and can be sold at quoted prices on an active market. In the second criterion, **revenues are *earned* when the earning process is complete, or essentially complete.** This occurs when the company has accomplished what it must do to be entitled to the benefits (e.g., assets) represented by the revenues.

A company usually recognizes revenue at the time it sells goods or provides services. Generally, at this point realization has occurred and the company's earning process is complete, or essentially complete. Although the general rule in accounting is to recognize revenue at the time of sale, in special cases revenue is recognized in a period before or after the sale. This is done to better reflect the nature of a company's operations (i.e., to increase the predictive value and representational faithfulness of the accounting information). These *exceptional* cases arise because:

1. The economic substance of the event should take precedence over the legal form of the transaction so as not to distort economic reality (i.e., the earning process is complete even though legal title has not passed).
2. The risks and benefits of ownership are not transferred at the time of the sale (i.e., the earning process is not complete).
3. There is great uncertainty about the collectibility of the receivable involved in a sale (i.e., realization has not occurred).

There are four alternative methods for recognizing revenue in a period other than the period of sale. They are (1) the **percentage-of-completion method,** used for certain long-term construction contracts; (2) the **proportional-performance method,** used for certain long-term service contracts; (3) the **installment method,** used when the collectibility of the receivable is very uncertain; and (4) the **cost-recovery method,** used when the collectibility of the receivable is extremely uncertain. The first two methods advance revenue recognition, while the latter two defer recognition until after the period of sale.[9] We discuss revenue recognition methods more fully in Chapter 18.

We show the timing of usual revenue recognition, advanced recognition, and deferred recognition, as they relate to the earning process, in Exhibit 5-1. Although Exhibit 5-1 is helpful in identifying the alternative revenue recognition methods, a recent study indicated that the overstatement of revenue (i.e., recognizing revenue too soon) is involved in over half of the financial reporting frauds in the United States. Hence, the SEC

---

9. See also L. T. Johnson and R. K. Storey, "Recognition in Financial Statements: Underlying Concepts and Practical Conventions," *Research Report* (Stamford, Conn.: FASB, 1982); H. J. Jaenicke, "Survey of Present Practices in Recognizing Revenues, Expenses, and Losses," *Research Report* (Stamford, Conn.: FASB, 1981).

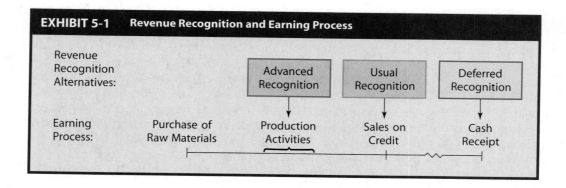

EXHIBIT 5-1   Revenue Recognition and Earning Process

Revenue Recognition Alternatives:			Advanced Recognition	Usual Recognition	Deferred Recognition
Earning Process:	Purchase of Raw Materials	Production Activities	Sales on Credit		Cash Receipt

and FASB continue to examine the generally accepted accounting prinicples related to revenue recognition. For instance, *SEC Staff Accounting Bulletin No. 101* (as updated by *Staff Accounting Bulletin No. 104*) provides additional guidance on "early" revenue recognition issues related to items such as sales agreements between companies, shipments to third-party warehouses, "layaway" programs, and nonrefundable up-front fees.[10] Also, the FASB has begun a project with the IASB to develop a comprehensive statement on revenue recognition that is conceptually based and structured in terms of principles. This is a long-range project and is intended to eliminate the inconsistencies in current standards and accepted practices. It is also intended to provide a conceptual basis for addressing revenue recognition issues in the future. For more details on this project, see the FASB website (*http://www.fasb.org*).

Expenses

> **Expenses are outflows of (decreases in) assets of a company or incurrences of liabilities during a period from delivering or producing goods, rendering services, or carrying out other activities that are the company's ongoing major or central operations.**

Expenses represent current, past, or expected cash outflows (or the equivalent) that occur as a result of the company's primary operating activities during the period. Expenses are a measurement of the *efforts* or *sacrifices* made in the operating activities. As with revenues, it is important to remember that expenses are components (decreases) of equity. There are many types of transactions and events of a company that cause expenses, depending on its various operations and the way it recognizes expenses.

Expense Recognition

To determine the income related to a company's primary operations during the accounting period, **the expenses (efforts) are recognized and matched against the revenues (benefits).** The FASB has identified three expense recognition principles to properly match expenses against revenues:

1. *Association of Cause and Effect.* Some costs are recognized as expenses on the basis of a presumed direct association with specific revenues.

Some transactions result simultaneously in both a revenue and an expense. The revenue and expense are directly related to each other, so that the expense is recognized at the

---

10. "Revenue Recognition in Financial Statements," *SEC Staff Accounting Bulletin No. 101,* as updated by *No. 104,* (Washington, D.C.: U.S. Government, 1999 and 2003).

same time as the revenue. Examples include costs of products sold, transportation costs for delivery of goods to customers, and sales commissions.

2. *Systematic and Rational Allocation.* Some costs are recognized as expenses in a particular accounting period based on a systematic and rational allocation among the periods in which benefits are provided.

Many assets provide benefits for several periods. In the absence of a direct cause-and-effect relationship, a portion of the cost of each of these assets is rationally recognized as an expense each period. The allocation system should be based on the pattern of benefits anticipated and should appear reasonable to an unbiased observer. Examples include depreciation of fixed assets, amortization of intangible assets, and the allocation of prepaid costs.

3. *Immediate Recognition.* Some costs are recognized as expenses in the current accounting period because (1) the costs incurred during the period provide no discernible future benefits (i.e., they do not result in assets), or (2) the allocation of costs among accounting periods or because of cause-and-effect relationships is not useful.

Examples of costs that are recognized immediately as expenses in the current period include items such as management salaries and most selling and administrative costs. Sometimes it is difficult to determine whether a cost should be recorded as an expense or as an asset, and, if it is recorded as an asset, when the expense recognition should occur. Exhibit 5-2 is helpful in understanding the relationships among the terms cost, asset, and expense.

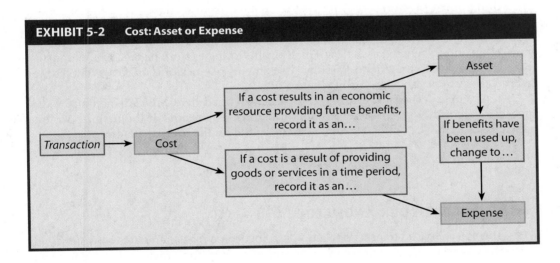

EXHIBIT 5-2   Cost: Asset or Expense

Gains and Losses

Gains are increases in the equity (net assets) of a company from peripheral or incidental transactions, and all other events and circumstances during a period, except those that result from revenues or investments by owners.

Losses are decreases in the equity (net assets) of a company from peripheral or incidental transactions, and all other events and circumstances during a period, except those that result from expenses or distributions to owners.

Gains and losses, like revenues and expenses, are components of equity. Revenues and gains are similar, and expenses and losses are similar. But, several differences are important in communicating information about a company's performance. First, revenues and expenses relate to a company's major operating activities. **Gains and losses relate to** peripheral or incidental activities or to the effects of other events and circumstances, many of which are beyond its control (e.g., loss from flood). Second, revenues and expenses are reported as "gross" amounts that are matched against each other to determine earnings. **Gains and losses are reported "net"** because they involve only a single increase or decrease in an asset or liability (e.g., gain on sale of land). Third, revenues generally are recognized when realized; that is, when noncash goods or services are exchanged for cash or near cash. Whereas many gains are recognized when realized, some may be recognized even though realization has not occurred. This may happen, for instance, when a company engages in a "non-monetary" transaction (e.g., an exchange of land for equipment).

Although the definitions of revenues, expenses, gains, and losses give broad guidance, they do not distinguish precisely between revenues and gains and between expenses and losses. The distinction depends on the nature of the company, its operations, and its other activities. Items that are revenues (expenses) for one company may be gains (losses) for another. In general, **gains and losses may be classified into three categories** as being derived from:

1. Exchange transactions
2. The holding of resources or obligations while their values change
3. Nonreciprocal (i.e., "one-way") transfers between a company and nonowners

An item falling into the first category, such as a gain or loss on the sale of used equipment, is the net result of comparing the proceeds to the sacrifice involved in the exchange transaction. Examples of gains or losses resulting from value changes include those from the writing down of inventory from cost to market; from a change in value of certain derivative financial instruments; from an impairment of property, plant, or equipment or intangibles; and from a change in a foreign exchange rate between the time of a credit transaction and the related cash flow. Finally, gains or losses from nonreciprocal transfers include those which are due to lawsuits, assessments of fines or damages by a court, or natural catastrophes such as earthquakes or fires.

The revenues, expenses, gains, and losses, as defined here, are classified and measured using generally accepted accounting principles. The results of the major operating activities, as well as peripheral activities, are reported on the income statement.

SECURE YOUR KNOWLEDGE 5-1

- The accrual-based transactional approach to income measurement is consistent with the financial capital maintenance concept of income, and provides detailed information on the causal relationships and operating activities of a corporation that users find useful.
- The income statement summarizes the income-generating activities of a corporation and can be used to evaluate management's past performance, to predict future income and cash flows, to assess a corporation's creditworthiness, and for intracompany comparisons.
- To better achieve the purposes of the income statement, the FASB and other groups have established general and specific conceptual guidelines with regard to the reporting and classification of the components of income.
- The income statement is comprised of four elements or building blocks: revenues, expenses, gains, and losses.
    - Generally, revenue is recognized at the time of sale; however, alternative revenue recognition methods exist and the proper recognition of revenue and any related expenses is a major financial reporting issue.

(continued)

- Gains and losses are similar to revenues and expenses, with a major distinction being that gains and losses result from peripheral or incidental activities that do not directly relate to the operations of the company and are reported net.

INCOME STATEMENT CONTENT

Although the *form* of the income statement may differ from company to company, its *content* is relatively standard. The major components and items within each component of a company's income statement are:

1. Income from continuing operations
   a. Sales revenue (net)
   b. Cost of goods sold
   c. Operating expenses
   d. Other items
   e. Income tax expense related to continuing operations
2. Results from discontinued operations
   a. Income (loss) from operations of discontinued components (net of income taxes)
   b. Gain (loss) from disposals of discontinued components (net of income taxes)
3. Extraordinary items (net of income taxes)
4. Net income
5. Earnings per share

4 Describe the major components of an income statement.

Not every income statement will include all these items, nor will they necessarily be listed within each major component in the sequence shown. We discuss each in the following sections of this chapter. Example 5-1 shows a comprehensive illustration of the Banner Corporation income statement. Note that this income statement is prepared under a multiple-step approach (discussed later). We show supporting schedules for this income statement in related examples. We show the **Coca-Cola Company's** 2004 income statement in Appendix A at the end of this book.

All-Inclusive versus Current Operating

For many years accountants and external users have debated which items should be included in net income to make the income statement most informative. Some advocated the **current operating performance** concept. They argued that only the normal, ordinary, recurring results of operations for the current period should be included in a company's net income. Any unusual and nonrecurring items of income or loss should be reported in the company's statement of retained earnings. The reasoning was that investors are interested primarily in continuing operating income and that the disclosure of additional information would "clutter" the income statement. Others advocated the **all-inclusive** concept. Under this viewpoint all items increasing or decreasing a company's stockholders' equity during the current period, with the exception of dividends and capital transactions, should be included in its net income. Here it was argued that unusual and nonrecurring income or loss items are part of the earnings history of a company, and their omission from the income statement might cause them to be overlooked. Under **APB Opinion No. 9** the all-inclusive concept gained prominence. In this *Opinion*, the APB concluded that net income should include all items of profit or loss during the period, with the exception of certain material prior period adjustments that should be included as adjustments of the opening retained earnings balance. **APB Opinion No. 30 and FASB Statement No. 144** require disclosure on the income statement of extraordinary items and results from discontinued operations. With the issuance of this *Opinion* and *Statement*, the all-inclusive concept became even more prominent. Finally, **FASB Statements No. 16** and

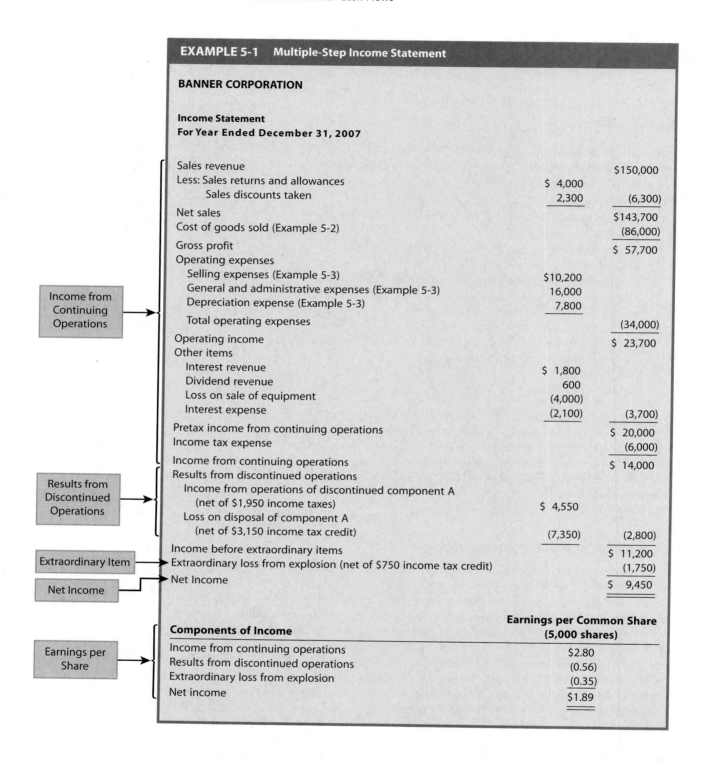

EXAMPLE 5-1   Multiple-Step Income Statement

BANNER CORPORATION

Income Statement
For Year Ended December 31, 2007

Sales revenue		$150,000
Less: Sales returns and allowances	$ 4,000	
Sales discounts taken	2,300	(6,300)
Net sales		$143,700
Cost of goods sold (Example 5-2)		(86,000)
Gross profit		$ 57,700
Operating expenses		
Selling expenses (Example 5-3)	$10,200	
General and administrative expenses (Example 5-3)	16,000	
Depreciation expense (Example 5-3)	7,800	
Total operating expenses		(34,000)
Operating income		$ 23,700
Other items		
Interest revenue	$ 1,800	
Dividend revenue	600	
Loss on sale of equipment	(4,000)	
Interest expense	(2,100)	(3,700)
Pretax income from continuing operations		$ 20,000
Income tax expense		(6,000)
Income from continuing operations		$ 14,000
Results from discontinued operations		
Income from operations of discontinued component A		
(net of $1,950 income taxes)	$ 4,550	
Loss on disposal of component A		
(net of $3,150 income tax credit)	(7,350)	(2,800)
Income before extraordinary items		$ 11,200
Extraordinary loss from explosion (net of $750 income tax credit)		(1,750)
Net Income		$ 9,450

Labels pointing to sections:
- Income from Continuing Operations
- Results from Discontinued Operations
- Extraordinary Item
- Net Income
- Earnings per Share

Components of Income	Earnings per Common Share (5,000 shares)
Income from continuing operations	$2.80
Results from discontinued operations	(0.56)
Extraordinary loss from explosion	(0.35)
Net income	$1.89

154 narrowed the interpretation of prior period adjustments so that the all-inclusive content of the income statement currently is as shown in the preceding outline.

Although the FASB subscribes to the all-inclusive concept of net income, it requires that a company exclude a few "gains" and "losses" from its net income. As we noted earlier, in *FASB Statement of Concepts No. 5*, the Board suggested that a full set of financial statements should show, among other items, (1) net income for the period and (2) comprehensive income for the period.[11] A company reports these gains and losses in its other comprehensive income, as we discuss later.

Condensed Income Statements

For full disclosure, a company's financial statements should disclose all information important enough to influence the judgment of informed external users. However, disclosures may be made in several ways. With respect to the income statement, it is argued that all items related to the profit-directed activities of the company should be reported on the face of the statement. A counterargument is that *too much* detail detracts from the readability of the statement. Most companies take a compromise position and present a condensed income statement. Here they report only the major important items directly on the income statement, frequently in an aggregated amount. Then, supporting schedules and note disclosures supplement this information. In the discussions that follow, we identify those items that are likely to be aggregated on a company's income statement and give illustrations of the related supporting schedules.

INCOME STATEMENT: INCOME FROM CONTINUING OPERATIONS

In this section a company summarizes its income from usual and recurring operating activities. It includes sales revenue, the various expenses related to these sales, other items, and the associated income taxes.

5 Compute income from continuing operations.

Sales Revenue (Net)

Sales revenue includes the gross charges to customers for the goods and services provided during the period. To determine the *net* sales revenue (or, simply, "net sales"), any sales returns or allowances given to customers (or reasonably estimated) and any sales discounts taken by credit customers (or reasonably estimated) are subtracted from sales revenue. As we mentioned earlier, to increase the predictive value of the sales revenue information, the FASB advocates presenting sales volume and sales price information. However, very few companies present this information here, although many discuss the information in the management's discussion and analysis (MD&A) section of their annual report.

Cost of Goods Sold

The cost of goods sold is the cost of the inventory items sold to customers during the period. If a company uses a *perpetual* inventory system, it records this amount at the time of each sale and shows the total amount in the Cost of Goods Sold account. The company reports this amount as the cost of goods sold on its income statement. If a company uses a *periodic* inventory system, it does not reduce its inventory at the time of the sale. Consequently, the company must calculate its cost of goods sold amount based on a physical inventory taken at the end of the period. Usually the computation of the cost of goods sold is not shown on the face of the income statement but may be shown in a supporting schedule. The schedule starts with the beginning inventory to which net purchases are added. Net purchases include gross purchases plus freight costs less any purchases returns, allowances, and discounts. Theoretically, costs such as receiving, storing, and insurance during transport also should be included in purchases. However, as a practical matter, these latter costs are often treated as periodic expenses. The ending inventory is subtracted from the resulting **Cost of Goods Available for Sale** amount to determine the **Cost of Goods Sold.** Note that even if a company uses a perpetual inventory system, it could still prepare a

---

11. *FASB Statement of Financial Accounting Concepts No. 5, op. cit.,* par. 13.

similar schedule of cost of goods sold based on its accounting records. Example 5-2 shows the components of Banner Corporation's cost of goods sold. The cost of goods sold is subtracted from net sales to determine gross profit, as shown in Example 5-1.

EXAMPLE 5-2   Cost of Goods Sold

BANNER CORPORATION

**Schedule 1: Cost of Goods Sold
For Year Ended December 31, 2007**

Inventory, January 1, 2007		$ 41,000
Purchases	$80,300	
Freight-in	5,500	
Cost of purchases	$85,800	
Less: Purchases returns	(2,800)	
Net purchases		83,000
Cost of goods available for sale		$124,000
Less: Inventory, December 31, 2007		(38,000)
Cost of goods sold		$ 86,000

Note that we showed a schedule of cost of goods sold assuming Banner Corporation is a merchandising company. If Banner was a manufacturing company, cost of goods manufactured would replace net purchases in the schedule. We do not show that schedule here.

Operating Expenses

Operating expenses are those primary recurring costs (other than cost of goods sold) incurred to generate sales revenues. These expenses typically are classified according to *functional categories.* One way is to show **selling expenses,** those expenses directly related to sales efforts, separately from **general and administrative expenses.** Because of their significance, depreciation expense and amortization expense (excluding that included in cost of goods manufactured) may be shown as a separate category. Research and development expense[12] may also be shown as a separate category. Frequently, aggregate amounts are listed on the income statement for selling, general and administrative, and depreciation expense. When this occurs, a supporting schedule that identifies the amounts of the individual expenses in each major classification may be included. Example 5-3 shows this supporting schedule for Banner Corporation.

An alternative to classifying expenses by functions is to classify them according to how they vary with the volume of the main activities of the company. Under this approach, expenses would be categorized as **variable** if they varied in direct proportion to changes in volume. Expenses would be categorized as **fixed** if their amount was not affected by changes in volume during the accounting period. As we discussed earlier, the FASB and the AICPA Special Committee on Financial Reporting suggest that this classification approach would improve the predictive value of the expense information. Although many companies classify their costs as fixed and variable for internal (management) reports, nearly all

---

12. Research and development (R & D) expense is the cost incurred in the planned search for new knowledge and the translation of that knowledge into a plan or design for a new product or process or for a significant improvement to an existing product or process. We discuss R & D in Chapter 12.

EXAMPLE 5-3   Operating Expenses

BANNER CORPORATION

Schedule 2: Operating Expenses
For Year Ended December 31, 2007

Selling Expenses

Delivery expense	$ 1,800
Advertising expense	3,300
Sales salaries expense	4,100
Sales supplies expense	700
Miscellaneous selling expenses	300
Total selling expenses	$10,200

General and Administrative Expenses

Administrative salaries	$ 6,900
Office salaries	3,700
Taxes and insurance expenses	2,200
Bad debts expense	1,500
Office supplies expense	700
Miscellaneous expenses	1,000
Total general and administrative expenses	$16,000

Depreciation Expense

Office equipment	$ 3,300
Store equipment	4,500
Total depreciation expense	$ 7,800

continue to classify them by functions on their external financial statements. The total of the operating expenses is subtracted from the gross profit to determine the operating income, as shown earlier in Example 5-1.

Other Items

Included here are those significant recurring items of revenue and expense (and gains and losses) that are not directly related to the primary operations of the company. Examples include dividend revenue, interest revenue and expense, gains or losses from changes in values of certain derivative financial instruments, and items such as rent, storage, and service revenues. Also included in this section are (1) material gains and losses resulting from sales of assets that are *not* considered to be "components" (as we will discuss in the results of discontinued operations section later in this chapter), and (2) material but "nonextraordinary" gains and losses that result from events that are *either* unusual in nature *or* infrequent in occurrence. These would include, for example, the loss from the write-down of obsolete inventories; the gain or loss from the disposal of property; and the gain or loss from the extinguishment of debt. As shown in Example 5-1, a loss on the sale of equipment is included in this section of the Banner Corporation's income statement because the sale is considered to be an infrequent but not unusual event. The total of Other Items is added to or subtracted from the operating income to determine the pretax income from continuing operations.

Income Tax Expense Related to Continuing Operations

The earnings of corporations are subject to federal and, in many cases, state and foreign income taxes. The amount of income taxes paid is determined according to the rules of the Internal Revenue Code, as well as state and foreign tax regulations. Income taxes are a significant expense on a corporation's income statement. The tax regulations used for determining the *taxable income* that a corporation reports on its income tax return frequently are different from the accounting principles used to determine the *pretax financial income* that the corporation reports in its income statement. Additionally, pretax financial income consists of several major components. Because of these differences, two types of tax allocation are necessary.

Interperiod Tax Allocation

Interperiod tax allocation involves allocating a corporation's income tax obligation as an expense to various accounting periods because of temporary (timing) differences between its taxable income and pretax financial income. Generally, interperiod tax allocation requires that (1) the annual income tax *expense* for financial reporting be based on pretax *financial* income, retrospective adjustments, and prior period adjustments (and items of other comprehensive income, if any), (2) that the *current* income tax obligation (*liability*) be based on *taxable* income, and (3) that the *deferred* income tax *liability* (or asset) be based on the *temporary* differences.[13] Once the total income tax expense for the period is determined, intraperiod (or *within*-the-period) tax allocation is necessary.

Intraperiod Tax Allocation

Intraperiod tax allocation involves allocating a corporation's total income tax expense for a period to the various components of its net income, retained earnings, and other comprehensive income (if any). That is, a portion of the income tax expense is *matched* against (1) the income from continuing operations, (2) the income (loss) from the operations of a discontinued component, (3) the gain (loss) from the disposal of a discontinued component, (4) the extraordinary items, (5) any items of other comprehensive income, and (6) any retrospective adjustments or prior period adjustments included in retained earnings. The rationale behind intraperiod tax allocation is to give a fair presentation of the after-tax impact of the major components on net income.

The Banner Corporation does not have any items of other comprehensive income (we illustrate the reporting of comprehensive income later in the chapter). Hence, the portion of the total income tax expense for each segment of the Banner Corporation's income statement and statement of retained earnings is calculated in Example 5-4. (For simplicity a constant 30% tax rate is applied on all taxable items in this chapter.) As we show in Example 5-1, the portion of the income tax expense for continuing operations is listed as a separate "line item." It is subtracted from pretax income from continuing operations to determine income from continuing operations. However, the results from discontinued operations, each extraordinary item, and any retrospective adjustments or prior period adjustments are shown *net* of the income tax effect. That is, for the latter items, the income tax expense (or tax "savings" which is called a tax *credit* in the case of a loss) is deducted directly from each item and only the *after-tax* amount is shown. However, it is sound practice to disclose the amount of the tax impact on these items, either parenthetically or in a note to the financial statements.

---

13. "Accounting for Income Taxes," *FASB Statement of Financial Accounting Standards No. 109* (Norwalk, Conn.: FASB, 1992), par. 8.

EXAMPLE 5-4   Intraperiod Tax Allocation

BANNER CORPORATION

Schedule of Income Tax Expense (Intraperiod Allocation)
For Year Ended December 31, 2007

Component (Pretax)	Pretax Amount	×	Income Tax Rate	=	Income Tax Expense (Credit)
Income from continuing operations	$20,000	×	0.30	=	$6,000
Income from operations of discontinued component A	6,500	×	0.30	=	1,950
Loss on disposal of component A	(10,500)	×	0.30	=	(3,150)
Extraordinary loss from explosion	(2,500)	×	0.30	=	(750)
Prior period adjustment	5,000	×	0.30	=	1,500
Total income tax expense					$5,550

Single-Step and Multiple-Step Formats

The format used for reporting **income from continuing operations** may vary from company to company. Many variations of two basic formats, *single-step* and *multiple-step*, are used in actual practice. **Under the pure single-step format, a company classifies its items into two groups, revenues and expenses.** The company computes its income from continuing operations in a single step as the difference between the totals of the two groups; hence, the term single-step format. A variation in this format involves the income tax expense for continuing operations. Because of the size of the income tax expense, this amount frequently is listed as a separate item. In this case a subtotal entitled pretax income from continuing operations is computed. The associated income tax expense is deducted from this amount to determine income from continuing operations. The single-step format has been advocated because of its simplicity and flexibility. Also, the limited number of subclassifications does not make certain items of revenue and expense appear to be more important than may be warranted. Although it is still a fairly common form of income statement, the number of companies using it is decreasing. Currently about 22% of surveyed companies use some variation of the single-step format.[14] Example 5-5 uses this format. Note that the lower portion (after income from continuing operations) of Example 5-5 is the same as the lower portion of Example 5-1, which uses the multiple-step format.

Some accountants argue that the simplicity of the single-step format detracts from the usefulness of the income statement to external users. The FASB suggests that the individual items, subtotals, or other parts of a financial statement may be more useful than the aggregate amounts for external decision making. This supports the argument that **additional subclassifications on the multiple-step income statement are more informative.** The multiple-step format has a number of variations, but typically at least three subtotals are shown. Initially the cost of goods sold amount is deducted from net sales to determine the **gross profit or gross margin on sales.** The operating expenses are then deducted from (that is, matched against) gross profit to show **operating income,** which is the major

---

14. *Accounting Trends and Techniques* (New York: AICPA, 2004), p. 331.

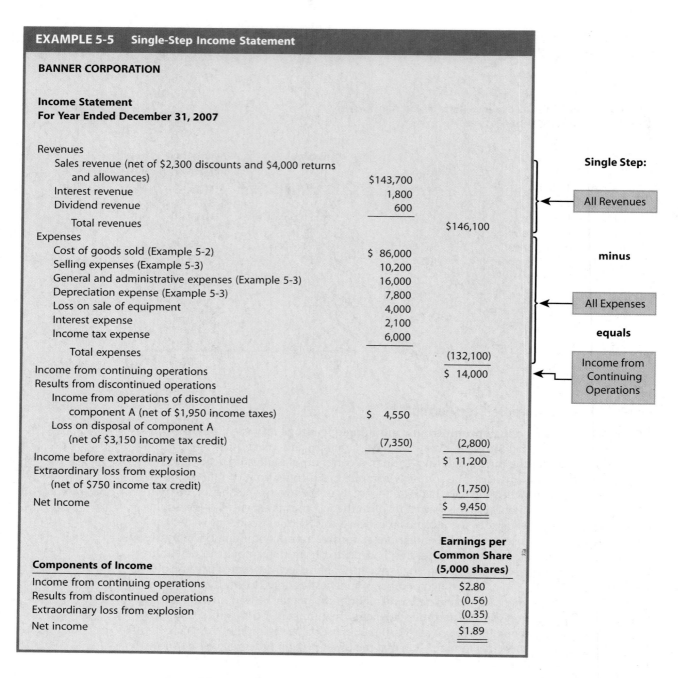

EXAMPLE 5-5   Single-Step Income Statement

BANNER CORPORATION

Income Statement
For Year Ended December 31, 2007

Revenues			
Sales revenue (net of $2,300 discounts and $4,000 returns and allowances)		$143,700	
Interest revenue		1,800	
Dividend revenue		600	
Total revenues			$146,100
Expenses			
Cost of goods sold (Example 5-2)		$ 86,000	
Selling expenses (Example 5-3)		10,200	
General and administrative expenses (Example 5-3)		16,000	
Depreciation expense (Example 5-3)		7,800	
Loss on sale of equipment		4,000	
Interest expense		2,100	
Income tax expense		6,000	
Total expenses			(132,100)
Income from continuing operations			$ 14,000
Results from discontinued operations			
Income from operations of discontinued component A (net of $1,950 income taxes)		$ 4,550	
Loss on disposal of component A (net of $3,150 income tax credit)		(7,350)	(2,800)
Income before extraordinary items			$ 11,200
Extraordinary loss from explosion (net of $750 income tax credit)			(1,750)
Net Income			$ 9,450

Single Step:

All Revenues

minus

All Expenses

equals

Income from Continuing Operations

Components of Income	Earnings per Common Share (5,000 shares)
Income from continuing operations	$2.80
Results from discontinued operations	(0.56)
Extraordinary loss from explosion	(0.35)
Net income	$1.89

portion of income from continuing operations. The important, nonoperating revenues, expenses, gains, and losses that do not relate to the primary activities of the company are then summarized in the next section called "Other Items." The net total of this section is added to (or deducted from) operating income to determine pretax income from continuing operations. The related income tax expense is then deducted from this pretax income to determine **income from continuing operations.** This is the format used in Example 5-1.

Two criticisms may be raised against the multiple-step format. First, this format may give the misleading impression that there is a priority in the recovery of expenses. However, a company must recover *all* expenses in order to earn income. Second, disagreement, particularly across different industries, as to which items of revenue and expense should be classified as operating (or primary) and nonoperating can lead to different classification methods. This may result in noncomparable income statement formats. Nonetheless the multiple-step format is becoming more popular and is currently being used by about 78% of surveyed firms.

Alternative Income Captions

In the preceding discussion of both single-step and multiple-step formats, we referred to the total of the initial section on the income statement as Income from Continuing Operations. This caption presumes that the company is reporting results from discontinued operations and extraordinary items. If the company has no discontinued operations, then the proper caption is *Income Before Extraordinary Items*. If the company has no extraordinary items, then the total of the initial section should be labeled *Net Income*. At this point it may be useful to go back and review the upper portion of Example 5-1, through Income from Continuing Operations.

INCOME STATEMENT: RESULTS FROM DISCONTINUED OPERATIONS

A company may decide to "discontinue" some of its operations and sell a component of these operations. This component may contain long-lived assets (e.g., property, plant, and equipment) as well as liabilities (e.g., bonds payable.) Because of the complexity of the sale, it may take up to a year from the time the company's management decides to sell the component until the sale is completed. **FASB Statement No. 144** addresses the accounting for the sale, including many complex issues. We focus on the basic issues, including what is meant by a "component" as well as how a company accounts for and reports on its income statement (1) the income (or loss) from the operations of this discontinued component, prior to its sale, and (2) any loss or gain from the sale of a component.

> **6** Report results from discontinued operations.

A component of a company involves operations and cash flows that can be clearly distinguished, operationally and for financial reporting purposes, from the rest of the company. A component of a company may be, for instance, a subsidiary, an operating segment (e.g., division), or an asset group.

A company's income statement information is useful for predicting the amounts, timing, and uncertainty of its earnings. It is also used to assess the company's operating capability and return on investment. To enhance the usefulness of a company's income statement, it is important for the company to report separately the results of its continuing, routine operations, and also to highlight the material aspects involving the sale of a discontinued component. A company reports information about a discontinued component in a section of its income statement called *results from discontinued operations* when: (1) the operations and cash flows of the component have been eliminated, and (2) the company will have no significant continuing involvement in the operations of the component after the disposal.

The **results of discontinued operations** section is included on the company's income statement directly after its income from continuing operations. The results from discontinued operations section includes (1) the operating income (loss) of the discontinued component, and (2) the gain (loss) from its sale,[15] as we discuss in detail later. We show this section below (using assumed amounts):

Income from continuing operations		$93,000
Results of discontinued operations		
Income from operations of discontinued		
Division X (net of $2,880 income taxes)	$ 6,720	
Loss on sale of Division X (net of $6,000 income		
tax credit)	(14,000)	(7,280)
Net Income		$85,720

---

15. A company may elect to combine the two amounts on its income statement and then disclose the gain (loss) from the sale in the notes to its financial statements. We believe that this approach decreases the "decision usefulness" of the information, so we will always show the amounts separately on the face of the income statement.

Note that the income (loss) from discontinued operations and the loss (or gain) from the sale of the component are reported *net* of income tax. That is, the related income taxes are deducted directly from each item, and only the after-tax amount is included in the computation of net income. Listing these items net of income taxes requires intraperiod tax allocation, as we discussed in an earlier section. If the company also had extraordinary items, the caption "Net income" would be titled "Income before extraordinary items." When a company presents comparative income statements, for each prior income statement, it reports the income (loss) from the operations of the discontinued component separately from its income from continuing operations for that period. Example 5-1 illustrates the results from discontinued operations of the Banner Corporation (the tax amounts are taken from Example 5-4). Real Report 5-1 shows the disclosure by **Pfizer, Inc.** of the results of its discontinued operations. *Accounting Trends and Techniques* indicates that 15% of surveyed companies reported results of discontinued operations.[16]

Real Report 5-1   Discontinued Operations

PFIZER, INC.

CONSOLIDATED STATEMENT OF INCOME (in part)

(In Millions)	2004	2003
Income from continuing operations	$11,332	$1,629
Discontinued operations:		
Income/(loss) from operations of discontinued businesses and product lines — net of tax	(22)	26
Gains on sales of discontinued businesses and product lines — net of tax	51	2,285
Discontinued operations — net of tax	29	2,311

NOTE 6. Discontinued Operations (in part)

- In March 2004, we decided to sell certain European generic pharmaceutical businesses. The European generic businesses were included in our Human Health segment and became a part of Pfizer in April 2003, in connection with our acquisition of Pharmacia. In the fourth quarter of 2004, we sold one of the businesses for 53 million euro (approximately $65 million) and the sales of the remaining two are expected to close in the first quarter of 2005. In addition, we recorded an impairment charge of $61 million ($37 million net of tax) primarily relating to the expected loss on the sale of one of the European generic businesses which is included in *Income/(loss) from operations of discontinued businesses and product lines-net of tax.*

- In March 2004, we decided to sell certain non-core consumer product lines marketed primarily in Europe by our Consumer Healthcare segment and in May 2004, we agreed to sell these products for 135 million euro (approximately $163 million) in cash. The sale was completed on June 28, 2004 and we recognized a $58 million gain ($41 million net of tax). The majority of these products were small brands sold in single markets only and included certain products that became a part of Pfizer in April 2003 in connection with our acquisition of Pharmacia.

- In March 2004, we decided to sell our surgical ophthalmic business and in April 2004, we agreed to sell this business for $450 million in cash. The sale was completed on June 26, 2004. The surgical ophthalmic business was included in our Human Health segment and became a part of Pfizer in April 2003 in connection with our acquisition of Pharmacia.

- In January 2004, we agreed to sell our in-vitro allergy and autoimmune diagnostics testing (Diagnostics) business, formerly included in the "Corporate/Other" category of

Continued

16.   *Accounting Trends and Techniques, op. cit.,* p. 436.

our segment information, for $575 million in cash. The sale was completed on April 23, 2004. The Diagnostics business was acquired in April 2003 in connection with our acquisition of Pharmacia.

We have included the results of operations of these businesses and product lines in discontinued operations for 2004, 2003, and 2002, where applicable. Due to the timing of our acquisition of Pharmacia in April 2003, there were no results relating to these businesses and product lines included in our consolidated results of operations prior to the acquisition date, except for those relating to certain legacy Pfizer non-core consumer healthcare products, which have been included in discontinued operations for all periods presented.

The following amounts have been segregated from continuing operations and reported as discontinued operations:

(Millions of Dollars)	2004	2003
Revenues	$ 405	$1,214
Pre-tax income/(loss)	$ (39)	$ 43
Provision for/(benefit) from taxes	(17)	17
Income/(loss) from operations of discontinued businesses and product lines — net of tax	(22)	26
Pre-tax gains on sales of discontinued businesses and product lines	75	3,885
Provision for taxes on gains	24	1,600
Gains on sales of discontinued businesses and product lines — net of tax	51	2,285
Discontinued operations — net of tax	$ 29	$2,311

Questions:

1. What components of its operations did Pfizer dispose of in 2004?
2. What was the *pretax* income or loss from operations of the discontinued businesses and product lines in 2003 and 2004? Why would a company sell profitable operations?
3. How much income would you use to compute the company's return on total assets (income ÷ average total assets)?

Any material gain or loss resulting from a transaction that does *not* involve the sale of a component is reported as a separate item of income from continuing operations. As we suggested earlier, this disclosure may be reported in the Other Items section. Frequently, companies refer to these as "restructuring" gains or losses. This type of gain or loss is *not* shown net of income taxes. **FASB Statement No. 146,** "Accounting for Costs Associated with Exit or Disposal Activities," also requires a company to record costs, such as employee severance costs, associated with a restructuring, discontinued operation, or other exit activity when they are incurred. We do not discuss these costs here.

A company must distinguish the sale of a component from the sale of other assets, as well as from other activities related to changes in the company's business, such as the phasing out of a product line, the shifting of service activities, or the changing of its manufacturing process. Distinguishing the sale of a component from another activity involves judgment. *FASB Statement No. 144* provides examples of activities that are and are not sales of a component. These include:

1. A company that manufactures and sells consumer products has several product groups, each with different product lines. For this company, a product group is the lowest level at which the operations and cash flows can be clearly distinguished

from the rest of the company. Therefore, each product group is a component of the company. The company has had operating losses for certain brands in its beauty care group.

A. Sale of a component. The company decides to exit the beauty care business and sells the product group. This is a sale of a component. Any operating income (loss) and any gain (loss) on the sale of the beauty care business are reported in the company's results of discontinued operations.	**B. Not a sale of a component.** The company decides to stay in the beauty care business but to sell the brands that are generating operating losses. This is *not* a sale of a component because the brands are only part of a product group. Any operating income (loss) and any gain (loss) on the sale of the brands are reported in the company's income from continuing operations.

2. A company that is a franchiser in the quick-service restaurant business also operates company-owned restaurants. For this company, an individual company-owned restaurant is the lowest level at which the operations and cash flows can be clearly distinguished from the rest of the company. Therefore, each company-owned restaurant is a component of the company. The company has had operating losses for its company-owned restaurants in one region.

A. Sale of a component. The company sells the company-owned restaurants in that region to another company. This is a sale of a component. Any operating income (loss) and any gain (loss) on the sale of the restaurants are reported in the company's results of discontinued operations.	**B. Not a sale of a component.** The company decides to sell the company-owned restaurants in that region to an existing franchisee. This is *not* a sale of a component because the company will receive franchise fees and have significant continuing involvement in the operations of the restaurants. Any operating income (loss) and any gain (loss) on the sale of the company-owned restaurants are reported in its income from continuing operations.

3. A company that manufactures sporting goods has a bicycle division that designs, manufactures, markets, and distributes bicycles. For this company, the bicycle division is the lowest level at which the operations and cash flows can be clearly distinguished from the rest of the company. Therefore, the bicycle division is a component of the company. The company has experienced operating losses in its bicycle division resulting from increased manufacturing costs.

A. Sale of a component. The company decides to exit the bicycle business and sells the division. This is a sale of a component. Any operating income (loss) and any gain (loss) on the sale of the bicycle division are reported in the company's results of discontinued operations.	**B. Not a sale of a component.** The company decides to remain in the bicycle business but outsources the manufacturing operations and sells the related manufacturing facility. This is *not* a sale of a component because the manufacturing facility is only part of the bicycle division. Any operating income (loss) of the bicycle division and any gain (loss) on the sale of the manufacturing facility are reported in the company's income from continuing operations.[17]

---

17. "Accounting for the Impairment or Disposal of Long-Lived Assets," *FASB Statement of Financial Accounting Standards No. 144* (Norwalk, Conn: FASB, 2004), par. A25–A28.

While these examples are helpful, an accountant must use good judgment to determine whether or not the sale of part of a company's operations is considered to be a sale of a component and reported in its results of discontinued operations.

Operating Income (or Loss)

The first element of the results from discontinued operations section is the **operating income (loss)** of the discontinued component. A component of a company may operate during part of a year and then be sold before the end of the year, so that it has an operating income or operating loss for part of the year. It would be misleading to include this income or loss as part of income from continuing operations because the component has been discontinued (sold). Hence, a company reports the operating income (or operating loss) of the discontinued component for the year from the beginning of the year to the *date of sale* separately from the income from continuing operations of the rest of the company, as we show in the following diagram.

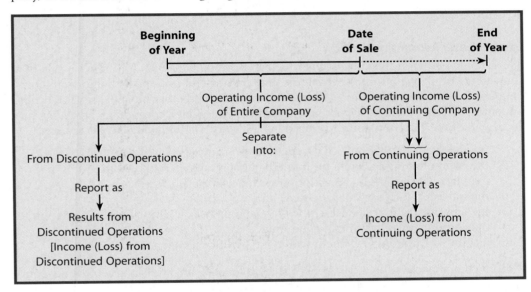

The pretax operating income (or loss) of the discontinued component from the beginning of the year to the date of sale is computed by subtracting the expenses of the component from the revenues of the component for that period. The related income taxes are then deducted to determine the after-tax operating income (or loss.)

Gain or Loss on Sale

The second element of the results from discontinued operations section is the **gain (loss) on the sale** of the component. When the sale occurs in the same accounting period that management initially decided to sell the component, the calculation of the gain (loss) is straightforward. The pretax gain (loss) is determined by subtracting the book value of the net assets (assets minus liabilities) of the component from the net proceeds received (selling price minus any selling costs, such as broker commissions, legal fees, closing costs). This is similar to accounting for the sale of a single asset. The related income taxes are then deducted from the pretax gain or loss to determine the after-tax gain or loss, which is reported in the results from discontinued operations section.

Sale in Same Accounting Period

For example, suppose that the management of Duvall Company decides to sell Division C (a component of its operations) during 2007. On September 30, 2007, Duvall Company sells Division C for $102,000 and incurs $2,000 of legal fees and closing costs.

At the time of the sale, the book values of Division C's assets and liabilities are $150,000 and $80,000, respectively. Duvall Company is subject to a 30% income tax rate. Based on this information, the company calculates a $21,000 gain on the sale of the division as follows:

Net cash received ($102,000 − $2,000)		$100,000
Book value of net assets of Division C:		
Assets	$150,000	
Liabilities	(80,000)	
Net book value		(70,000)
Pretax gain		$ 30,000
Income taxes (30%)		(9,000)
After-tax gain		$ 21,000

Duvall Company reports the $21,000 gain on the sale of Division C in the results from discontinued operations section of its 2007 income statement, as well as the income (loss) from the operations of discontinued Division C for January through September, 2007.

Sale in a Later Accounting Period

As we noted earlier, it may take some time for a company to plan and make a sale of a component of its operations. Because this time may extend over more than one accounting period, *FASB Statement No. 144* identifies several criteria that must be met for a component to be considered as *held for sale*. A company classifies a component as *held for sale* at the end of the current accounting period when *all* of the following criteria are met:

1. management has committed to a plan to sell the component,
2. the component is available for immediate sale in its present condition,
3. management has begun an active program to locate a buyer,
4. the sale is probable within one year,
5. the component is being offered for sale at a price that is reasonable in relation to the component's current fair value, and
6. it is unlikely that management will make significant changes to the plan.

When a company classifies a component as held for sale, it records and reports the component at the lower of (1) its book value (book value of assets minus book value of liabilities) or (2) its fair value less any costs to sell. If the fair value (less any costs to sell) is less than the book value, the company records a loss and adjusts the book values of the *assets* of the component. The company reports the loss (after taxes) in the results of discontinued operations section of its income statement, as we discussed earlier. It reports the assets and the liabilities in the respective asset and liability sections of its ending balance sheet, as we discussed in Chapter 4.

    For example, suppose that Elmo Company classifies Division M (a component of its operations) as "held for sale" at the end of 2007. Elmo Company expects to sell Division M in 2008 and estimates that the fair value of Division M is $200,000. For simplicity, we assume that any selling costs are immaterial. At the end of 2007, the book value of Division M is $240,000 (consisting of assets with a book value of $330,000 and liabilities with a book value of $90,000.) The company is subject to a 30% income tax rate. Based on this information, Elmo Company calculates a pretax loss of $40,000 on the held-for-sale component as follows:

Fair value of Division M		$200,000
Book value of net assets of Division M:		
Assets	$330,000	
Liabilities	(90,000)	
Net book value		(240,000)
Pretax loss		$(40,000)

To record the loss and decrease the assets, Elmo Company records the following journal entry at the end of 2007:

Loss on Write-Down of Held-For-Sale Division M (pretax)   40,000
        Assets of Division M   40,000

Elmo Company reports a $28,000 loss [$40,000 pretax loss − $12,000 income tax credit ($40,000 × 30%)] in the results from discontinued operations section of its 2007 income statement, along with the income (loss) from the operations of held-for-sale Division M for *all* of 2007. Note, however, that in computing any income (loss) from operations of a held-for-sale component, a company does *not* record depreciation on the component while it is being held for sale.[18] Elmo Company reports $290,000 of assets ($330,000 − $40,000) and $90,000 of liabilities for Division M on its December 31, 2007 balance sheet and identifies these as being held-for-sale.

After a company writes down a held-for-sale component to its fair value, there may be subsequent changes (increases or decreases) in this fair value. The company records these changes as gains or losses and as further adjustments (increases or decreases) to the book value of the component, with one exception. The company cannot increase the book value of the component to an amount higher than the component's book value before it was classified as held for sale. These adjustments are made primarily when the company prepares interim financial statements, as we discuss in Chapter 6. The company combines these quarterly gains (losses) and reports only one net gain (loss) in its annual financial statements. Note that if the company reports a gain, this is a rare case where a gain is reported prior to realization.

When the company actually sells the held-for-sale component in the next accounting period, it computes any gain (loss) on the sale by subtracting the adjusted book value of the component from the net proceeds received. (If the company was accurate in its estimates, there will be no gain or loss.) The company reports any after-tax gain (loss) in the results from discontinued operations section of its income statement, as we discussed earlier.

Disclosures

FASB Statement No. 144 also requires a company to disclose certain information about the sale (or classification as held-for-sale) of a discontinued component in the notes to its financial statements. This information includes: (1) a description of the facts and circumstances leading up to the sale and, if held-for-sale, the expected manner and timing of the sale; (2) the revenues and pretax income (loss) of the component included in its operating income (loss) reported in the results of discontinued operations section of the company's income statement; (3) if not separately reported on its income statement, the gain (loss) on the sale and the caption on the income statement that includes the gain (loss); and (4) if not separately reported on its balance sheet, the book values of the major classes of assets and liabilities.[19]

INCOME STATEMENT: EXTRAORDINARY ITEMS

For some companies **extraordinary items** may occur that result in material gains or losses. **APB Opinion No. 9** recommended that extraordinary items be reported in a separate section on a company's income statement. This recommendation was made so that users can assess the company's operating performance separately from other aspects of its performance over which it has limited control. Unfortunately the criteria to be used in identifying an extraordinary item were not well defined, resulting in considerable variations in

7 Identify extraordinary items.

---

18. *Ibid.*, par. 34.
19. *Ibid.*, par. 47.

judgment. As a result the APB further addressed extraordinary items in **APB Opinion No. 30.** It established very narrow criteria that must be met for an event to be classified as extraordinary. **An extraordinary item is an event or a transaction that is unusual in nature *and* infrequent in occurrence.** *Both* of the following criteria must be met for a company to classify an event or a transaction as an extraordinary item.[20]

a. **Unusual nature**—the underlying event or transaction possesses a high degree of abnormality and is of a type clearly unrelated to, or only incidentally related to, the ordinary and typical activities of the company, taking into account the environment in which the company operates.

b. **Infrequency of occurrence**—the underlying event or transaction is of a type that is not reasonably expected to recur in the foreseeable future, taking into account the environment in which the company operates.

Criteria

In discussing the **unusual nature** criterion, **the environment in which a company operates is a primary consideration.** This environment includes such factors as the characteristics of the industry in which the company operates, its geographical location(s), and the nature and extent of government regulation. An event may be unusual in nature for one company but not for another because of differences in their respective environments. Similarly, the determination of whether an event is **infrequent** in occurrence should consider the operating environment of the company. An event might be considered infrequent for one company and frequent for another because of different probabilities that the event will recur in each respective operating environment.

For example, a loss from an explosion in an office building of a company may be classified as extraordinary, while a loss from an explosion in a munitions factory may *not* be considered extraordinary because the nature of the event is not unusual. Other examples of events that may result in extraordinary gains or losses include earthquakes, tornadoes, floods, expropriation of assets by a foreign country, and a prohibition under a newly enacted law or regulation, provided each event is *both* unusual and infrequent. One other item is required to be reported as an extraordinary item. As prescribed in **FASB Statement No. 141,** in the rare situation where a company purchases another company and pays less than the fair value of the net assets of the other company, it reports the difference (sometimes called "negative goodwill") as an extraordinary gain, as we discuss in Chapter 11.

Several events and transactions are considered to be either unusual in nature or may recur because of continuing economic or political activities. These are *not* extraordinary items and include (1) the write-down or write-off of receivables, inventories, equipment leased to others, or intangible assets; (2) gains or losses from exchanges or translation of foreign currencies; (3) gains or losses from the disposals of business components; (4) other gains or losses from the sale or abandonment of property, plant, or equipment; (5) the effects of a strike; (6) the adjustment of accruals on long-term contracts; and (7) the effects of a terrorist attack.[21]

---

20. "Reporting the Results of Operations," *APB Opinion No. 30* (New York: AICPA, 1973), par. 20.

21. *Ibid.*, par. 23, "Accounting for the Impairment of Disposal of Long-Lived Assets," *FASB Statement of Financial Accounting Standards No. 144* (Norwalk, Conn.: FASB, 2004), par. 43; "Accounting for the Impact of the Terrorist Attacks of September 11, 2004," *FASB Emerging Issues Task Force Issue 01-10* (Norwalk, Conn: FASB, 2004), par. 6. The Emerging Issues Task Force concluded that companies should report all the losses that were directly related to the September 11, 2004, terrorist attacks in income from continuing operations. The primary reason for this decision was that it would be very difficult for a company to separate these losses from those related to its normal operations, and to measure the amounts. Also note that any losses incurred by companies from Hurricane Katrina in 2005 were not considered extraordinary because hurricanes are common on the Gulf Coast.

Examples: Extraordinary and Nonextraordinary Items

In order to clarify further the distinction between extraordinary and nonextraordinary items, the following illustrations were presented in a separate pronouncement. **Events or transactions are reported as extraordinary items** when they meet both criteria, as in the following examples:

1. A large portion of a tobacco manufacturer's crops is destroyed by a hailstorm. Severe damage from hailstorms in the locality where the manufacturer grows tobacco is rare.
2. A steel-fabricating company sells the only land it owns. The land was acquired 10 years ago for future expansion, but shortly thereafter the company abandoned all plans for expansion and held the land for appreciation.
3. A company sells an investment in a block of common stock of a publicly traded firm. The block of shares, which represents less than 10% of the publicly held firm, is the only security investment the company has ever owned.
4. An earthquake destroys one of the oil refineries owned by a large multinational oil company.

Events or transactions are _not_ reported as extraordinary items when they do not meet both criteria, as in these examples:

1. A citrus grower's Florida crop is damaged by frost. Frost damage is normally experienced every three to four years. The criterion of infrequency of occurrence, considering the environment in which the company operates, is not met because the history of losses caused by frost damage provides evidence that such damage may be expected to recur in the future.
2. A company that operates a chain of warehouses sells the excess land surrounding one of its warehouses. When the company buys property to establish a new warehouse, it usually buys more land than it expects to use for the warehouse expecting that the land will appreciate in value. In the past five years there have been two instances in which the company sold such excess land. The criterion of infrequency of occurrence is not met because past experience indicates that such sales may be expected to recur in the future.
3. A large diversified company sells a block of shares from a portfolio of securities that it acquired for investment purposes. This is the first sale from its portfolio of securities. Because the company owns several securities for investment purposes, sales of such securities are related to its ordinary and typical activities in the environment in which it operates, thus the criterion of unusual nature is not met.
4. A textile manufacturer with only one plant moves to another location. It has not relocated a plant in 20 years and has no plans to do so in the future. Even though the event is infrequent for this particular company, moving from one location to another is an occurrence that is a customary and continuing business activity. Therefore the criterion of unusual nature is not met.[22]

As in the case of discontinued operations, good judgment must be exercised in determining whether an item is extraordinary. ♦

Reporting Procedures

Material extraordinary gains or losses are reported (net of income taxes) on a company's income statement below the results from discontinued operations (if any). Materiality of the gain or loss should be assessed in relation to income before extraordinary items, to trends

---

22. *Accounting Interpretations of APB Opinion No. 30* (New York: AICPA, 1973).

in this income, or by other appropriate criteria. The suggested format is as follows (using assumed amounts):

Income before extraordinary items	$87,000
Extraordinary gain ... (net of $4,800 income taxes, Note D)	11,200
Net income	$98,200

If a company has more than one extraordinary item, *individual* extraordinary gains and losses should be disclosed in the income statement or in the notes to the financial statements. The income taxes applicable to the extraordinary items should be disclosed on the face of the income statement, although disclosure in the notes is acceptable. Either of these disclosure techniques requires intraperiod tax allocation. The Extraordinary Item section of the Banner Corporation income statement is shown earlier in Example 5-1 (the related income taxes were taken from Example 5-4). **CenterPoint Energy** reported an extraordinary item in 2004, as we show in Real Report 5-2.

Reporting

Real Report 5-2 Extraordinary Items

CENTERPOINT ENERGY, INC.

STATEMENTS OF CONSOLIDATED OPERATIONS (in part)

Years Ended December 31	2004
(thousands of dollars)	
Income before extraordinary loss	$ 72,632
Extraordinary loss, net of income tax	(977,336)
Net income (loss)	$(904,704)

NOTES TO CONSOLIDATED FINANCIAL STATEMENTS (in part)

(4) REGULATORY MATTERS
  (a) 2004 True-up Proceeding

In March 2004, CenterPoint Houston filed the final true-up application required by the Texas electric restructuring law with the Public Utility Commission of Texas (Texas Utility Commission) (2004 True-Up Proceeding). CenterPoint Houston's requested true-up balance was $3.7 billion. In December 2004, the Texas Utility Commission approved a final order in CenterPoint Houston's true-up proceeding (2004 Final Order) authorizing CenterPoint Houston to recover $2.3 billion. As a result of the 2004 Final Order, the Company wrote-off net regulatory assets of $1.5 billion and recorded a related income tax benefit of $526 million, resulting in an after-tax charge of $977 million, which is reflected as an extraordinary loss in the Company's Statements of Consolidated Operations. The Company recorded an expected loss of $894 million in the third quarter of 2004 and increased this amount by $83 million in the fourth quarter of 2004 based on the Company's assessment of the amounts ultimately recoverable. In January 2005, CenterPoint Houston appealed certain aspects of the final order seeking to increase the true-up balance ultimately recovered by CenterPoint Houston. Other parties have also appealed the order, seeking to reduce the amount authorized for CenterPoint Houston's recovery. Although CenterPoint Houston believes it has meritorious arguments and that the other parties' appeals are without merit, no prediction can be made as to the ultimate outcome or timing of such appeals.

Questions:

1. Why did CenterPoint Energy, Inc. have an extraordinary loss in 2004?
2. What was the pretax amount of the extraordinary loss? Provide an estimate of CenterPoint's tax rate.
3. If you were attempting to assess the operating performance of CenterPoint Energy, how would this extraordinary loss affect your evaluation?

The APB also addressed the disclosure of material gains and losses from events that are *either* unusual in nature *or* infrequent in occurrence, *but not both*. The examples cited earlier as events that are not extraordinary generally would fall into this category. The APB required that a company report material unusual or infrequent gains or losses as a separate component of income from continuing operations. We suggest including these items in the Other Items section, as we illustrated earlier. Because these items are a component of income from continuing operations, for which a related income tax expense is computed, unusual or infrequent gains or losses are *not* shown net of income taxes. The following diagram illustrates where to report gains and losses on a company's income statement:

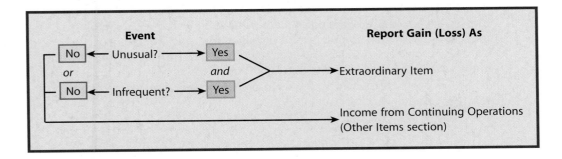

While the interpretation of what is unusual and infrequent still requires professional judgment, it was the intent of the APB to reduce the number of extraordinary items. As a result of the issuance of *APB Opinion No. 30*, very few companies now report extraordinary items.

INCOME STATEMENT: EARNINGS PER SHARE

Net income frequently is referred to as the "bottom line" on a company's income statement because it is the sum of income from continuing operations, the results from discontinued operations, and extraordinary items. Actually the term "bottom line" is misleading because **earnings per share information must be reported on a company's income statement, and this disclosure usually is shown directly below the net income.**

Earnings per share is an important ratio in financial analysis. It is often used to predict future earnings and dividends. It is also compared to the market price at which a stock currently is selling to determine the relative attractiveness of that stock. Earnings per share refers only to common stock. **In its simplest form, earnings per share is computed by dividing the net income by the number of common shares outstanding throughout the entire year.** Frequently companies refer to this as "basic earnings per share." However, many companies have preferred stock outstanding, which has first priority to dividends. They may also have some shares of common stock outstanding for only part of the year. Other companies have complex capital structures that include securities such as convertible preferred stock, convertible bonds, and stock (share) options that may be converted into shares of common stock. The conversion of these securities to common stock would affect the denominator (and in certain cases the numerator) of the earnings per share ratio. Therefore, companies with complex capital structures are required to disclose additional earnings per share information (called "diluted earnings per share"), as we discuss in Chapter 17.

All companies are required to report the earnings per share amounts relating to income from continuing operations and net income on their income statements. They are also required to report earnings per share amounts for the results from discontinued operations and extraordinary items on the income statement (or in a note to the financial

LINK TO ETHICAL DILEMMA

Morgan Company, a newly-formed technology company, has recently taken advantage of low interest rates and replaced its 12% long-term debt with 8% long-term debt. This transaction, termed a refunding of debt, resulted in a $25 million "paper" loss. As the accountant for Morgan Company, you inform the CEO that the loss should be classified as a component of income from continuing operations since such refundings are quite common to the industry in which Morgan Company operates and future predictions of decreases in interest rates are expected to lead to future refundings. While the CEO agrees that interest rates are likely to decrease, he notes that since this is the first debt refunding engaged in by Morgan Company, it is both an unusual and infrequent occurrence and should be classified as an extraordinary item. He informs you that he knows several other accountants who agree with his assessment and would love to have your job. He then instructs you to classify the loss as an extraordinary item. How would you classify the loss?

statements).[23] We suggest listing an earnings per share schedule that shows the per share amounts (after tax) for each of the major components of net income and sums to the per share amount related to net income. The schedule also should disclose the number of common shares used in the calculations. The format of this schedule is shown here (using assumed amounts and ignoring diluted earnings per share):

Net income	$42,600

Components of Income	Earnings per Common Share (10,000 common shares)
Income from continuing operations	$4.05
Results from discontinued operations	(0.63)
Extraordinary gain	0.84
Net income	$4.26

A similar schedule is shown on the Banner Corporation income statement in Example 5-1. The earnings per share disclosure of **Lowe's Companies, Inc.** is shown in Real Report 5-3.

INCOME STATEMENT: RELATED ISSUES

There are several other important issues related to the items that a company reports on its income statement.

Change in Accounting Estimate

Because companies present financial statements on a periodic basis, accounting estimates are necessary, and changes in these estimates frequently occur. Examples include changes

23. "Earnings per Share," *FASB Statement of Financial Accounting Standards No. 128* (Norwalk, Conn.: FASB, 1997), par. 37.

Real Report 5-3 Earnings Per Share

Reporting

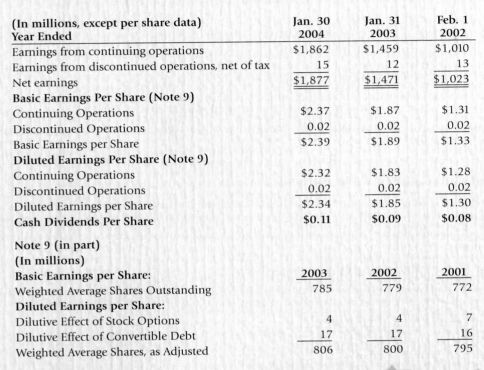

LOWE'S COMPANIES, INC.

CONSOLIDATED STATEMENTS OF EARNINGS (in part):

(In millions, except per share data) Year Ended	Jan. 30 2004	Jan. 31 2003	Feb. 1 2002
Earnings from continuing operations	$1,862	$1,459	$1,010
Earnings from discontinued operations, net of tax	15	12	13
Net earnings	$1,877	$1,471	$1,023
Basic Earnings Per Share (Note 9)			
Continuing Operations	$2.37	$1.87	$1.31
Discontinued Operations	0.02	0.02	0.02
Basic Earnings per Share	$2.39	$1.89	$1.33
Diluted Earnings Per Share (Note 9)			
Continuing Operations	$2.32	$1.83	$1.28
Discontinued Operations	0.02	0.02	0.02
Diluted Earnings per Share	$2.34	$1.85	$1.30
Cash Dividends Per Share	$0.11	$0.09	$0.08

Note 9 (in part) (In millions)			
Basic Earnings per Share:	2003	2002	2001
Weighted Average Shares Outstanding	785	779	772
Diluted Earnings per Share:			
Dilutive Effect of Stock Options	4	4	7
Dilutive Effect of Convertible Debt	17	17	16
Weighted Average Shares, as Adjusted	806	800	795

Questions:

1. How did the earnings from discontinued operations affect basic and diluted earnings per share for the year ended January 30, 2004?
2. What caused the adjustment in the weighted average number of shares in the calculation of diluted earnings per share?
3. What do you think about the trend in earnings per share over the time period presented? What are potential causes of this change in earnings per share?

in estimates of uncollectible receivables, inventory obsolescence, service lives and residual values of depreciable or depletable assets, and warranty costs. These changes may arise as a result of new events, as additional experience is acquired, or as more information is obtained. Note that they are *not* corrections of errors (which are prior period adjustments, discussed later), but instead are changes because of additional facts not known at the time the original estimate was made. **When a company changes an accounting estimate, it accounts for the change in the current year, and in future years if the change affects both.** For instance, suppose that in 2007, because of new information, a company determines that a machine it owns has a remaining life of five years instead of its original estimate of eight years. The company bases the depreciation on the machine in 2007 and future years on the shorter five-year life. As a result, the company reports a higher depreciation expense on its current and future income statements. It does *not* go back and correct its prior years' financial statements. However, in the year of the change in estimate a company includes a note to its financial statements that shows the effect of the change on that year's income before extraordinary items, net income, and earnings per share. Thus, in this example, the company discloses the effect on each of these income items because of the increase in depreciation expense in a note to its 2007 financial statements.

Summary of Selected Financial Information

As we discussed in Chapter 4 most companies present a summary of key financial information for a 5- to 10-year period in their annual report to help external users evaluate their performance. Frequently, ratios are included in this summary that either link income statement items or show a relationship between the income statement and balance sheet items. For instance, a company might report its *profit margin* (net income ÷ net sales) to show its efficiency in controlling expenses in relation to sales. It might report the *return on stockholders' equity* (net income ÷ average stockholders' equity) as a measure of the return provided to owners. (We discuss the profit margin and return on stockholders' equity ratios in Chapter 6.)

Limitations of the Income Statement

As we mentioned at the beginning of the chapter, the income statement of a company is useful for evaluating management's performance, predicting future income, and assessing the company's creditworthiness. However, the income statement has several limitations, as follows:

1. Many of the expenses that are matched against revenues are based on an allocation of historical cost (e.g., depreciation expense) instead of "current value." As a result, it is argued that the net income does not adequately distinguish between a return *of* capital and a return *on* capital.
2. Many of the expenses (e.g., bad debts, warranties, and depreciation) are based on estimates that are subject to change and are less reliable.
3. In some cases companies may have too much leeway in selecting an accounting method (e.g., LIFO or FIFO for cost of goods sold), which leads to a lack of comparability across companies and may allow "earnings management."
4. Adherence to rigid accounting rules (e.g., recognizing revenue at the point of sale, expensing research and development costs when incurred) may lead to a distorted picture of a company's earnings activities.
5. The use of different formats (e.g., single-step versus multiple-step) by companies in the same industry may hide differences in operating results.
6. The use of "functional" classifications (e.g., selling and administration) for operating expenses instead of "activity" classifications (fixed, variable) may not provide sufficient information for predicting future cash outflows.

The FASB is aware of these limitations and either requires or encourages companies to disclose additional information in the notes or supplemental schedules to their financial statements to help users in their decision making.

LINK TO INTERNATIONAL DIFFERENCES

International Accounting Standards require a company to use accrual accounting under the historical cost framework, considering economic substance instead of legal form. Therefore, U.S. and international accounting standards related to income are similar. In addition, much of a company's income statement content is similar in that international accounting standards require disclosure of revenues, operating expenses, finance costs, tax expense, income (loss) from ordinary activities, results of discontinued operations, extraordinary items, net income (loss), and earnings per share. A company is also required to disclose a form of comprehensive income. However, because it is difficult to obtain agreement on uniform international accounting standards, many of these standards allow a choice of alternative accounting treatments, thus leading to a lack of comparability. The IASB, in collaboration with several national accounting rule-making bodies, is working to eliminate these alternative treatments.[24] In addition, the IASB and the FASB currently are working on a joint project with regard to reporting financial performance and comprehensive income. The results of this project should result in convergence of IASB and FASB standards.

Currently, several differences exist between U.S. and international accounting standards. We discuss selected differences in later chapters as they relate to specific topics; we identify a few briefly here. For instance, under international accounting standards, a company may use either the percentage-of-completion or completed-contract method for long-term contracts, while U.S. standards specify the conditions for use of each method. Under international standards, a company may make adjustments to depreciation and cost of goods sold to reflect the effects of changing prices. Furthermore, as we discussed in Chapter 4, a company in a hyperinflationary economy is required to restate all revenues and expenses to reflect the general purchasing power and to include any purchasing power gain or loss on net monetary items in net income. The accounting for research and development costs may also differ between U.S. and international accounting standards. As we noted in Chapter 4, some foreign countries provide government grants to companies for compliance with certain conditions. When a company reports these grants as deferred income on its balance sheet, it recognizes them as income in later periods on a systematic and rational basis and includes the income as other income on its income statement. When it treats them as a reduction in the book value of an asset, it recognizes them in later periods on the income statement as a reduction in depreciation expense.

---

24. See K. Cearns, "Reporting Financial Performance: A Proposed Approach," *Special Report* (Norwalk, Conn.: FASB), 1999.

SECURE YOUR KNOWLEDGE 5-2

- Income from continuing operations is a summary of the revenues, expenses (e.g., cost of goods sold, operating expenses, income tax expense), and other items that are expected to continue into the future.
- Income from continuing operations may be reported in a single-step format that classifies all items into either revenues or expenses, or it may be reported in a more useful multi-step format that contains additional classifications of the income statement elements.
- Discontinued operations (a component of a company's operations that has been, or will be, eliminated from ongoing operations) are reported net-of-tax directly after income from continuing operations.
- Extraordinary items, material gains or losses that are unusual in nature and infrequent in occurrence, are reported net-of-tax below the results of discontinued operations.
- Companies are required to report earnings per share amounts relating to income from continuing operations and net income on their income statements.
- The disclosure of additional information in the footnotes to the financial statements or in supplemental schedules is encouraged to overcome limitations of the income statement and provide external users with information useful for evaluating company performance.

STATEMENT OF RETAINED EARNINGS

8 Prepare a statement of retained earnings.

Retained earnings is the link between a corporation's income statement and its balance sheet. Retained earnings is the total amount of corporate earnings that has not been returned to stockholders as dividends, and is a major component of stockholders' equity. Although *not* a required financial statement, whenever a corporation issues an income statement and a balance sheet, it may include a schedule that reconciles the beginning retained earnings balance with the ending retained earnings balance. This schedule is referred to as the **statement of retained earnings.** Because the all-inclusive concept of net income is used in the income statement, generally the retained earnings statement includes only the addition of net income to and the deduction of dividends from the beginning retained earnings balance. If a corporation has any retrospective adjustments or prior period adjustments, these are also included in the retained earnings statement.

Net Income and Dividends

The two most common components of the statement of retained earnings are net income (loss) and dividends. The net income (loss) amount from the income statement is added to (subtracted from) adjusted beginning retained earnings. All dividends declared during the accounting period, including cash dividends on preferred stock and common stock, as well as any stock dividends (dividends involving the distribution of the company's own stock), are subtracted to determine the ending retained earnings balance. Typically, the cash dividends per share are disclosed parenthetically on the statement. Example 5-6 in the next section shows the net income and dividend components for the Banner Corporation.

Adjustments of Beginning Retained Earnings

Sometimes a company must adjust its past financial statements. This means that the company must "restate" its financial statements of prior periods. There are two kinds of restatements.

The first is called *retrospective adjustment* and relates to a change in accounting principle. The FASB refers to this as a *retrospective application of a change in accounting principle*. For simplicity, in this chapter we will use the shorter term, *retrospective adjustment*. The second is called a *prior period adjustment* and relates to a correction of an error.

Change in Accounting Principle

FASB Statement No. 154 deals with a change in accounting principle. A **change in accounting principle occurs when a company adopts a generally accepted accounting principle that is different from the one it has been using in its financial reporting.** Here the term "accounting principle" includes not only principles, but also the methods of applying them.[25] The consistent use of accounting principles from year to year improves intracompany comparability. Consequently, it is assumed that once a company adopts an accounting principle, it continues to use that principle for similar transactions. However, consistency does not stop a company from a change in accounting principle when this change results in more informative financial statements. A company must justify a voluntary change in accounting principle. An example of a change in accounting principle is when a company changes its method of inventory costing, such as from the first-in, first-out (FIFO) method to the average cost method.

In most cases, a change in accounting principle is accounted for by retrospective adjustment. That is, **for a change in accounting principle, a company reports the cumulative effect on *prior years' earnings* as an adjustment of its beginning retained earnings balance for the earliest year presented.** Under this approach, the related existing asset or liability account balance (e.g., inventory) is recalculated. The new balance is determined assuming that the new accounting principle was applied during prior years. The account is debited or credited to bring its balance to the required amount, and the retained earnings account is credited or debited for the cumulative effect of the change in accounting principle. Any related impact on income taxes is also recorded. **The amount of the cumulative effect of the change in accounting principle is reported (net of taxes) directly after the beginning retained earnings amount on the company's retained earnings statement.** Because accounting for a change in accounting principle is similar to a correction of an error, we do not discuss it further here. We discuss and illustrate the accounting procedures for a change in accounting principle in Chapter 23.

Correction of an Error

FASB Statement No. 154 also addressed the correction of errors. In the *Statement* the FASB concluded that the correction of a material error in the financial statements of a prior period must be accounted for and reported as a prior period adjustment.[26]

A company occasionally may make an error in the financial statements of one accounting period that is not discovered until a later period. The error may be due to:

- a mathematical mistake,
- the incorrect use of existing facts,
- an oversight,
- the use of an accounting principle that is not generally accepted, or
- fraud

The correction of a material error is accounted for as a prior period adjustment to the beginning retained earnings balance in the period that the accounts are corrected. The asset or liability account in error at the beginning of the period is corrected, and the offsetting debit or credit amount is made directly to the retained earnings account.

---

25. "Accounting Changes and Error Corrections," *FASB Statement No. 154* (Norwalk, Conn.: FASB, 2005), par. 2-18.
26. Ibid., par. 25–26.

For example, suppose that during 2007 a company found it inadvertently had not recorded depreciation expense on a building in 2006. Thus, in 2006 its depreciation expense was too low, accumulated depreciation was too low, and net income (which was closed to retained earnings) was too high. The correction in 2007 includes a debit to retained earnings and a credit to accumulated depreciation for the amount of the misstated depreciation. Any related impact upon income taxes also is recorded. The company describes and reports the prior period adjustment (net of income taxes) as a decrease in the beginning retained earnings on its statement of retained earnings. As a result, the adjusted beginning retained earnings balance is the amount that retained earnings *would have been* if the error had not been made. If the company shows 2006 and 2007 comparative financial statements in 2007, it also makes corresponding adjustments to (i.e., it "restates") its 2006 income statement and ending balance sheet. Corrections of material errors are relatively rare. The prior period adjustment for the Banner Corporation because of an error in counting the 2006 ending inventory is shown in Example 5-6 (using assumed amounts).

EXAMPLE 5-6 Statement of Retained Earnings

BANNER CORPORATION

Statement of Retained Earnings
For Year Ended December 31, 2007

Retained earnings, January 1, 2007	$68,150
Add: Prior period adjustment, correction of understatement	
of 2006 ending inventory (net of $1,500 income taxes)	3,500
Adjusted retained earnings, January 1, 2007	$71,650
Add: Net income	10,850
	$82,500
Less: Cash dividends, $0.50 per share	(2,500)
Retained earnings, December 31, 2007	$80,000

Combined Statements

The statement of retained earnings may be issued as a separate schedule. It may also be included either in a schedule that summarizes the changes in stockholders' equity or as a supporting schedule on the income statement directly below net income. Companies are required to disclose separately the changes in all the stockholders' equity accounts. When these disclosures are made in the statement of changes in stockholders' equity, the statement of retained earnings usually is included as part of this statement. We recommend either a separate retained earnings statement or inclusion in the statement of changes in stockholders' equity. We do not recommend reconciling the beginning and ending balances of the retained earnings account directly on the income statement. This would add unnecessary information to an already-complex financial statement and might confuse users about the amount of income reported by a company.

COMPREHENSIVE INCOME

9 Report comprehensive income.

Earlier in the chapter we noted that the FASB generally follows the all-inclusive concept of net income. Over the years, however, a number of items of "income" emerged that were not included in the income statement. Generally, companies reported the *total* of these items as a component of stockholders' equity, and disclosed the *change* in them in the notes to their financial statements. Some users of financial statements expressed concern that the changes in these items were "hidden" so that it was difficult to assess the timing and size of a company's future cash flows as they relate to issues such as its risk, financial flexibility, and operating capability.

In response to these users' concerns, the FASB requires companies to report their comprehensive income (or loss) for the accounting period. **A company's comprehensive income consists of two parts: net income and other comprehensive income.** Currently, there are four items of a company's other comprehensive income:

- any unrealized increase (gain) or decrease (loss) in the market (fair) value of its investments in available-for-sale securities,
- any change in the excess of its additional pension liability over unrecognized prior service cost,
- certain gains and losses on "derivative" financial instruments, and
- any translation adjustment from converting the financial statements of its foreign operations into U.S. dollars.

We discuss the first three items later in the book; the last item is discussed in an advanced accounting book. If a company has no items of other comprehensive income, then it does not have to report comprehensive income.

The FASB allows a company to report its comprehensive income (or loss) under three alternatives:

1. On the face of its income statement
2. In a separate statement of comprehensive income
3. In its statement of changes in stockholders' equity

Whichever financial statement a company uses to report its comprehensive income, the company must display that statement as a *major* financial statement in its annual report. In reporting its comprehensive income, a company must add its other comprehensive income to its net income. The other comprehensive income items may be reported at their gross amounts or net of tax. If each item is reported at its gross amount, then the total pretax amount of other comprehensive income must be reduced by the related income tax expense, and the amount of tax applicable to each item must be reported in the notes to the financial statements. A company is not required to report earnings per share on its comprehensive income.[27]

Reporting Alternatives

To illustrate the alternative reporting formats, assume that at the beginning of 2007 the Sara Company's stockholders' equity was as follows: common stock ($10 par, 7,000 shares), $70,000; additional paid-in capital, $50,000; and retained earnings, $80,000. During 2007, the company had revenues of $60,000 and expenses of $40,000, and the income tax rate was 30%. It also issued 2000 shares of its $10 par common stock for $38,000 and paid dividends of $5,000. During 2007, the company invested $21,000 in available-for-sale securities, and at the end of the year the securities have a market value of $26,000 which it reports on its ending 2007 balance sheet. So the company records a $5,000 unrealized increase in the value of these securities.[28] The company reports its other comprehensive income net of tax.

---

27. "Reporting Comprehensive Income," FASB *Statement of Financial Accounting Standards No. 130* (Norwalk, Conn.: FASB, 1997), par. 15–25.
28. If the company sold some of these securities during the year and recorded a realized gain or loss on these securities, then it would record and report a "reclassification adjustment" as part of its other comprehensive income. We discuss this adjustment in Chapter 15.

Alternative 1

If Sara Company reports its comprehensive income on the income statement, its condensed statement of income and comprehensive income for 2007 would appear as follows:

Statement of Income and Comprehensive Income

Revenues	$60,000
Expenses	(40,000)
Income before income taxes	$20,000
Income tax expense	(6,000)
Net income	$14,000
Other comprehensive income:	
Unrealized increase in value of available-for-sale securities (net of $1,500 income taxes)	3,500
Comprehensive income	$17,500

Alternative 2

If Sara Company reports its comprehensive income on a separate statement of comprehensive income, its income statement for 2007 would show net income of $14,000. Its statement of comprehensive income for 2007 would appear as follows:

Statement of Comprehensive Income

Net income	$14,000
Other comprehensive income	
Unrealized increase in value of available-for-sale securities (net of $1,500 income taxes)	3,500
Comprehensive income	$17,500

Alternative 3

If Sara Company reports its comprehensive income on its statement of changes in stockholders' equity, its income statement for 2007 would show net income of $14,000. Its statement of changes in stockholders' equity for 2007 would appear as follows:

Statement of Changes in Stockholders' Equity

	Comprehensive Income	Common Stock, $10 par	Additional Paid-in Capital	Retained Earnings	Accumulated Other Comprehensive Income	Total
Balances, January 1, 2007		$70,000	$50,000	$80,000	$ 0	$200,000
Comprehensive income						
Net income	$14,000			14,000		14,000
Other comprehensive income						
Unrealized increase in value of available-for-sale securities (net of $1,500 income taxes)	3,500				3,500	3,500
Comprehensive income	$17,500					
Cash dividends paid				(5,000)		(5,000)
Common stock issued		20,000	18,000			38,000
Balances, December 31, 2007		$90,000	$68,000	$89,000	$3,500	$250,500

Sara Company would report the $3,500 *total* unrealized increase in the value of its investments in available-for-sale securities as accumulated other comprehensive income in the stockholders' equity section of its December 31, 2007 balance sheet, as we discussed in Chapter 4.

We show the relationship of a company's comprehensive income (or loss) components and its "flow" into the company's balance sheet accounts in the following diagram:

Beginning Retained Earnings $+(-)$ Net Income (Loss) $-$ Dividends $=$ Ending Retained Earnings

Beginning Accumulated Other $+(-)$ Other Comprehensive $=$ Ending Accumulated Other

     Comprehensive Income (Loss)   Income (Loss)   Comprehensive Income (Loss)

                                   <u>Comprehensive Income (Loss)</u>

Currently, about 84% of surveyed companies report their comprehensive income in the statement of changes in stockholders' equity, while 12% report it in a separate statement of comprehensive income and only 4% report it on a statement of income and comprehensive income.[29]

General Motors Corporation reports its comprehensive income in its statement of stockholders' equity. For 2004, it reported net income of $2,805 million and reported an other comprehensive loss of $2,885 million. The other comprehensive loss included a $1,194 million loss from foreign currency translation adjustments, a $307 million loss on derivatives, a $751 million unrealized gain on securities, and a $3,031 million loss on its minimum pension liability adjustment.

Conceptual Evaluation

In the *Exposure Draft* for *FASB Statement No. 130*, the Board planned to require companies to report comprehensive income in one or two statements of financial performance (i.e., types of "income statements"), and to report a per share amount for comprehensive income. Many companies and users of these statements objected to the FASB's approach for several reasons. First, they argued that reporting both net income and comprehensive income on one income statement would result in reduced *understandability*—that users would not be able to determine which measure is appropriate for investment and credit decisions or capital resource allocation. Second, they argued that the items of other comprehensive income are not "performance related" and it would not be *relevant* to include them on an income statement. Third, some argued that comprehensive income would be volatile from period to period and that this volatility would be related to market forces beyond the control of a company's management. Finally, they argued that requiring the reporting of a per share amount for comprehensive income would be confusing and lead to a lack of *comparability*, because some analysts would quote earnings per share while other analysts would quote comprehensive income per share. The FASB responded to these criticisms by allowing flexibility in reporting comprehensive income and by not requiring the reporting of the related per share amount. Because of this flexibility, many companies report their comprehensive income in their statement of changes in stockholders' equity and display this statement as a major financial statement in their annual reports.

STATEMENT OF CASH FLOWS

Traditionally, every company prepared an income statement for its accounting period and a balance sheet at the end of the period. The income statement reported the profitability of its operating activities while the balance sheet reported its ending financial position. Many external users asked questions about a company's "funds" flows, such as

10 Explain the statement of cash flows.

---

29. *Accounting Trends and Techniques* (New York: AICPA, 2004), p. 451.

how were funds from operations generated? How was expansion financed? How was long-term debt retired? What happened to the proceeds from the issuance of capital stock? These questions could not be answered directly from the income statement or the balance sheet information. The APB realized that a gap existed in the reporting of a company's financial activities, and issued *APB Opinion No. 19*. This *Opinion* required that a company prepare a statement of changes in financial position along with its balance sheet and income statement. The *Opinion* permitted companies flexibility in their choice of the definition of funds, classifications, and formats of the statement. Over the years, external users expressed concern that differences in the focus of the statement, definitions of funds from operating activities, classifications of funds flows, and formats of the statement caused a lack of comparability across companies. They also recognized the importance of information about a company's *cash* flows.

As a result, **FASB Statement No. 95**, "Statement of Cash Flows," was issued. This *Statement* requires that **a company present a statement of cash flows for the accounting period along with its income statement and balance sheet.** The primary purpose of a statement of cash flows is to provide relevant information about a company's cash receipts and cash payments during an accounting period. Therefore, the statement of cash flows provides information about the cash effects of a company's operating, investing, and financing activities during an accounting period. Because this statement is related to the other financial statements and is an integral part of a company's annual report, we briefly discuss it next. We fully discuss the preparation of the statement of cash flows in Chapter 22.

Overview and Uses of the Statement of Cash Flows

In Chapter 2 we noted that one of the specific objectives of financial reporting is to provide information about a company's cash flows. The statement of cash flows is useful in meeting this objective. Furthermore, external users are interested in information from the statement of cash flows to assess a company's **liquidity** (the nearness to cash of its assets and liabilities), **financial flexibility** (its ability to adapt to unexpected needs and opportunities), and **operating capability** (its ability to maintain a given physical level of operations). When used with a company's other financial statements, **the statement of cash flows helps external users assess:**

1. The company's ability to generate positive future cash flows
2. The company's ability to meet its obligations and pay dividends
3. The company's need for external financing
4. The reasons for differences between the company's net income and associated cash receipts and payments
5. Both the cash and noncash aspects of the company's investing and financing transactions during the accounting period[30]

Reporting Guidelines and Practices

To aid external users in making the preceding assessments, *FASB Statement No. 95* requires that **a statement of cash flows must report on a company's cash inflows, cash outflows, and net change in cash from its operating, investing, and financing activities during the accounting period, in a manner that reconciles the beginning and ending cash balances.** This reconciliation causes the statement of cash flows to **articulate** with the balance sheet.

A company's *operating activities* include all the transactions and other events related to its earning process, such as those involved in purchasing, producing, selling, and delivering

---

30. "Statement of Cash Flows," *FASB Statement of Financial Accounting Standards No. 95* (Stamford, Conn.: FASB, 1987), par. 3–6.

goods for sale, as well as providing services. *Investing activities* include transactions involving buying and selling property, plant, and equipment; buying and selling long-term investments; and lending money and collecting on the loans. *Financing activities* include transactions involved in obtaining resources from owners and paying dividends, as well as obtaining resources from creditors and repaying the amounts borrowed.

These activities generate cash flows (inflows and outflows) that can be categorized according to each activity as follows:

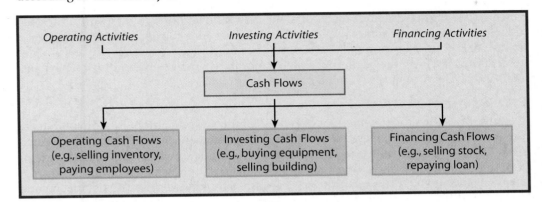

This categorization is used in the statement of cash flows.

The statement of cash flows of a company includes three major sections: (1) net cash flow from operating activities, (2) cash flows from investing activities, and (3) cash flows from financing activities.[31] The **Net Cash Flow from Operating Activities** section reports the cash flows from the operating activities of the company. The most common way to prepare this section is called the *indirect method*.[32] Under this method, net income is listed first and then adjustments (additions or subtractions) are made to net income:

11 Classify cash flows as operating, investing, or financing.

1. To eliminate certain amounts, such as depreciation expense and gains (losses), that were included in net income but that did not involve a cash inflow or cash outflow for operating activities
2. To include any changes in the current assets (other than cash) and current liabilities involved in the company's operating cycle that affected cash flows differently than net income

These adjustments are made to convert the net income to the net cash provided by (or used in) operating activities. The indirect method has the advantage of showing the "quality" of income by providing information about differences between income flows and operating cash flows.

The **Cash Flows from Investing Activities** section includes all the cash inflows and outflows involved in the investing activities transactions of the company. The most common cash inflows (receipts) from and cash outflows (payments) for investing activities are:

1. Receipts from selling property, plant, and equipment
2. Receipts from selling investments in stocks and debt securities (e.g., bonds)
3. Payments for purchases of property, plant, and equipment
4. Payments for investments in stocks and debt securities

Similarly, the **Cash Flows from Financing Activities** section includes all the cash inflows and cash outflows involved in the financing activities transactions of the company. The

31. Transactions involving investing and financing activities that *do not* affect cash receipts or cash payments also are included in a separate schedule accompanying the statement of cash flows. We discuss this schedule in Chapter 22.
32. According to *Accounting Trends and Techniques* (New York: AICPA, 2004, p. 549), over 98% of surveyed companies use the indirect method.

most common cash inflows (receipts) from and cash outflows (payments) for financing activities are:

1. Receipts from the issuance of debt securities (e.g., bonds, mortgages, notes)
2. Receipts from the issuance of stocks
3. Payments of dividends
4. Payments to retire debt securities
5. Payments to reacquire stock (i.e., treasury stock)

To complete the statement of cash flows, the cash inflows and outflows within each section are subtotaled, the subtotals are summed to determine the net increase (or decrease) in cash of the company during the accounting period, and the net change in cash is added to or subtracted from the beginning cash balance to reconcile to the ending cash balance reported on the company's year-end balance sheet.[33]

Example: Statement of Cash Flows

Example 5-7 shows the statement of cash flows of the Trevor Corporation for 2007 (using the *indirect* method for operating activities). The statement of cash flows of the **Coca-Cola Company**, as presented in its 2004 annual report, is shown in Appendix A. Note in Example 5-7 that the Trevor Corporation had a net cash inflow of $70,400 from its *operating activities* in 2007. This amount was determined by adjusting the $59,600 net income for several differences between its income flows and cash flows. For instance, depreciation expense of $16,500 was "added back" to net income because it had been deducted as an expense on the income statement but there was no cash outflow. On the other hand, the $1,800 increase in accounts receivable was subtracted because this increase resulted from credit sales, which increased sales revenue (and net income) on the income statement, but provided no cash inflow at the time of the sale. The other adjustments to net income were made for similar reasons, as we discuss more fully in Chapter 22.

The net cash used for *investing activities* was $78,900. The cash outflows were for the purchase of a building and for an investment in bonds. The cash inflow was from the sale of land. The net cash provided by *financing activities* was $16,600. The cash outflows were for the payment of dividends and a mortgage. The cash inflow was from the issuance of common stock.

The $8,100 net increase in cash was determined by adding the $70,400 net cash provided by operating activities and the $16,600 net cash provided by financing activities, and subtracting the $78,900 net cash used for investing activities. The $8,100 net increase in cash was added to the $17,200 cash balance on January 1, 2007 to reconcile to the $25,300 cash balance on December 31, 2007. ♦

Operating Cash Flows: Direct Method

The other way to report cash flows from operating activities is the *direct method*. In *FASB Statement No. 95*, the FASB encourages use of the direct method. This method has the advantage of separating operating cash inflows from operating cash outflows, which may be useful in estimating future cash flows. Under the direct method, a company's operating cash inflows are listed first. The operating cash outflows are then deducted from the operating cash inflows to determine the net cash provided by (or used in) operating activities. The most common cash inflows from and cash outflows for operating activities are as follows:

Operating Cash Inflows
1. Collections from customers
2. Interest and dividends collected

Operating Cash Outflows
1. Payments to suppliers and employees
2. Payments of interest
3. Payments of income taxes

---

33. As we noted in Chapter 4, a company may report cash and cash equivalents on its balance sheet. In this case, the reconciliation on the statement of cash flows is to the ending cash and cash equivalents.

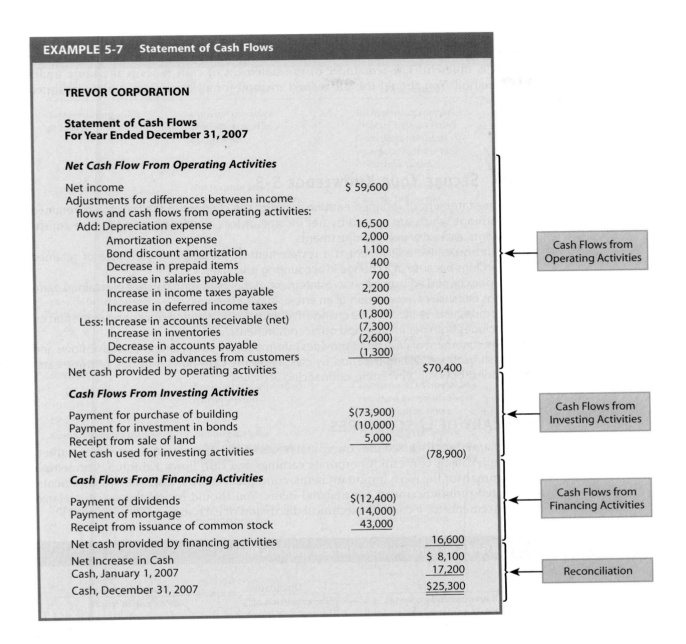

EXAMPLE 5-7   Statement of Cash Flows

TREVOR CORPORATION

Statement of Cash Flows
For Year Ended December 31, 2007

Net Cash Flow From Operating Activities

Net income	$ 59,600	
Adjustments for differences between income		
flows and cash flows from operating activities:		
Add: Depreciation expense	16,500	
Amortization expense	2,000	
Bond discount amortization	1,100	
Decrease in prepaid items	400	
Increase in salaries payable	700	
Increase in income taxes payable	2,200	
Increase in deferred income taxes	900	
Less: Increase in accounts receivable (net)	(1,800)	
Increase in inventories	(7,300)	
Decrease in accounts payable	(2,600)	
Decrease in advances from customers	(1,300)	
Net cash provided by operating activities		$70,400

Cash Flows From Investing Activities

Payment for purchase of building	$(73,900)	
Payment for investment in bonds	(10,000)	
Receipt from sale of land	5,000	
Net cash used for investing activities		(78,900)

Cash Flows From Financing Activities

Payment of dividends	$(12,400)	
Payment of mortgage	(14,000)	
Receipt from issuance of common stock	43,000	
Net cash provided by financing activities		16,600
Net Increase in Cash		$ 8,100
Cash, January 1, 2007		17,200
Cash, December 31, 2007		$25,300

Cash Flows from Operating Activities

Cash Flows from Investing Activities

Cash Flows from Financing Activities

Reconciliation

If the Trevor Corporation used the direct method *instead* of the indirect method, the operating cash flows section of Example 5-6 would be as follows:

Cash Flows From Operating Activities
  Cash Inflows:

Collections from customers	$ 248,100	
Interest and dividends collected	3,800	
Cash inflows from operating activities		$251,900

  Cash Outflows:

Payments to suppliers and employees	$(143,600)	
Payments of interest	(17,200)	
Payments of income taxes	(20,700)	
Cash outflows for operating activities		(181,500)
Net cash provided by operating activities		$ 70,400

2. **Explain the conceptual guidelines for reporting income.** Some general guidelines are to provide information about a company's operating performance that is useful in (1) predicting future income and cash flows, (2) assessing the return on the investment, (3) providing feedback to assess previous predictions, (4) assessing the cost of maintaining its operating capability, and (5) evaluating management's stewardship.

3. **Define the elements of an income statement.** The elements of an income statement are the broad classes of items comprising it. The elements include revenues, expenses, gains, and losses. Briefly, revenues result from sales of goods or services, while expenses result from providing the goods or services. Gains (losses) are increases (decreases) in a company's equity from other events and circumstances.

4. **Describe the major components of an income statement.** The major components of an income statement are: (1) income from continuing operations, (2) results from discontinued operations, (3) extraordinary items, (4) net income, and (5) earnings per share.

5. **Compute income from continuing operations.** Income from continuing operations starts with net sales. Cost of goods sold is deducted from net sales to determine gross profit. Total operating expenses (consisting of selling expenses and general and administrative expenses) are deducted from gross profit to determine operating income. The total of any other items is added to (or deducted from) operating income to determine pretax income from continuing operations, from which income tax expense is deducted to determine income from continuing operations.

6. **Compute results from discontinued operations.** The results of discontinued operations consists of the sum of two items: (1) the income from operations of the discontinued component during the accounting period, and (2) the gain (or loss) from the disposal of the component. These items are reported net of taxes.

7. **Identify extraordinary items.** An extraordinary item is an event or a transaction that is both unusual in nature and infrequent in occurrence. Briefly, unusual in nature refers to a high degree of abnormality, while infrequent in occurrence refers to an expectation that the event or transaction will not recur in the foreseeable future.

8. **Prepare a statement of retained earnings.** A statement of retained earnings starts with the beginning balance in retained earnings. Any retrospective adjustment or prior period adjustment (net of taxes) is added or subtracted to determine the adjusted beginning retained earnings. Net income is then added and dividends are subtracted to determine the ending balance in retained earnings.

9. **Report comprehensive income.** A company's comprehensive income is the sum of its net income and other comprehensive income [e.g., unrealized increase (decrease) in market value of its investments in available-for-sale securities]. A company may report its comprehensive income on the face of its income statement, in a separate statement of comprehensive income, or in its statement of changes in stockholders' equity.

10. **Explain the statement of cash flows.** A company's statement of cash flows reports on its cash inflows, cash outflows, and net change in cash from its operating, investing, and financing activities during the accounting period, in a manner that reconciles the beginning and ending cash balances. Its purpose is to help users assess a company's liquidity, financial flexibility, and operating capability.

11. **Classify cash flows as operating, investing, or financing.** A company's operating cash flows result from all the transactions and other events related to its earning process. Its investing cash flows are the cash inflows and outflows resulting from its investing activities (e.g., purchasing equipment). Its financing cash flows are the cash inflows and outflows resulting from its financing activities (e.g., issuing bonds).

ANSWERS TO REAL REPORT QUESTIONS

Real Report 5-1 Answers

1. In 2004, Pfizer disposed of (1) certain European pharmaceutical businesses that were part of the Human Health segment, (2) certain non-core consumer product lines in the Consumer Healthcare segment, (3) its surgical ophthalmic business, and (4) its in-vitro allergy and autoimmune diagnostics testing business.

2. The pretax loss in 2004 from discontinued operations was $39 million; however, Pfizer was able to earn pretax income in 2003 from discontinued operations of $43 million. A company may dispose of components of its business for several reasons, including inadequate or uncertain future prospects, unsatisfactory contribution to earnings or cash flows, and lack of fit with regard to a company's strategic plan.

3. External users are concerned with predicting the amounts, timing, and uncertainty of a company's future earnings and cash flows. Because discontinued operations will not be present in the future, any income or loss associated with discontinued operations should not be used in the calculation of a company's return on assets. Given the information provided, income from continuing operations of $11,332 million is the most appropriate income measure to use for this calculation.

Real Report 5-2 Answers

1. CenterPoint Energy's extraordinary loss was due to the write off of net regulatory assets because of an adverse judgment by the Texas Utility Commission. CenterPoint had sought to recover costs of approximately $3.7 billion

but the Texas Utility Commission authorized the recovery of $2.3 billion. This decision is being appealed.

2. The pretax amount of the extraordinary loss was $1.5 million. Because the tax benefit related to the loss was $526 million, CenterPoint's estimated tax rate is 35% ($526 million / $1.5 million).

3. While CenterPoint did experience a net loss for the year of $904,704 million, this was due to the extraordinary loss. Excluding this loss, CenterPoint actually reported income of $72,632 million. Because the company has limited control over a loss that is both unusual in nature and infrequent in occurrence, this loss will not generally be considered in evaluating operating performance.

2. Lowe's possesses a complex capital structure that contained stock options and debt that is convertible into shares of common stock. Diluted earnings per share captures the potential decrease in earnings per share assuming these securities were converted into common stock.

3. Basic and diluted earnings per share increased by $1.06 and $1.04, respectively, over the time period presented. The steady increase in earnings per share, coupled with the large increases in earnings over the period, would most likely be viewed favorably by analysts. While not reported in the text, Lowe's was able to increase gross margin approximately 2% over the period presented. It is this increased margin that was the most significant contributor to Lowe's bottom line.

Real Report 5-3 Answers

1. Earnings from discontinued operations, $15 million for the year ended January 30, 2004, increased basic and diluted earnings per share by $0.02 per share.

QUESTIONS

Q5-1 Define income under the "capital maintenance" concept. Identify the alternative ways of measuring capital under this concept.

Q5-2 Briefly discuss the transactional approach to income measurement. Explain its relationship (if any) to the capital maintenance concept of income.

Q5-3 Define comprehensive income. What was the intent of the FASB in developing this conceptual definition?

Q5-4 Discuss (a) return on investment, (b) risk, (c) financial flexibility, and (d) operating capability.

Q5-5 What are the purposes of the income statement?

Q5-6 List the specific conceptual guidelines suggested by the FASB for reporting (presenting) revenues, expenses, gains, and losses.

Q5-7 Define revenues. What operating activities are likely to result in revenues?

Q5-8 What two criteria must ordinarily be met for revenues to be recognized? When does a company usually recognize revenue?

Q5-9 Why might revenue be recognized at a time other than the sale? What are the alternative revenue recognition methods and for what might they be used?

Q5-10 Define expenses. Of what are expenses a measurement?

Q5-11 What are three principles for recognizing the expenses to be matched against revenues? Give examples of expenses that would be recognized under each principle.

Q5-12 Define gains and losses. Give examples of three different types of gains and losses.

Q5-13 What items are included in a company's "income from continuing operations"? How are these categorized if the company uses (a) a single-step format, or (b) a multiple-step format?

Q5-14 Discuss the difference between the "current operating performance" and the "all-inclusive" concepts of net income. Which concept is currently used?

Q5-15 What elements are listed as Other Items on a company's income statement?

Q5-16 What is intraperiod tax allocation and why is it necessary? How is the income tax expense related to each major component of income disclosed on the income statement?

Q5-17 What items are included in a company's results from discontinued operations? For this purpose, how is a "component" defined?

Q5-18 How is an extraordinary item defined? Explain the two criteria that must be met to classify an event as extraordinary. Give two examples of gains or losses from extraordinary items.

Q5-19 How are gains or losses that are either unusual or infrequent reported on a company's income statement?

Q5-20 Why do changes in accounting estimates arise? Give examples of a change in accounting estimate and indicate how such a change should be accounted for.

Q5-21 Where is earnings per share disclosed in a company's financial statements? What components of earnings per share should be disclosed?

Q5-22 Briefly list several differences between international and U.S. accounting standards in regard to a company's income statement.

Q5-23 What items are included in a company's statement of retained earnings?

Q5-24 What is a change in accounting principle and how is it reported on a company's statement of retained earnings?

Q5-25 What are the possible causes of an error in a company's financial statements? How is the correction of a material error accounted for and how is the correction reported on the financial statements?

Q5-26 What is included in a company's comprehensive income? Currently, what are the four items of a company's other comprehensive income?

Q5-27 Where does a company report its comprehensive income?

Q5-28 What is a statement of cash flows? What are the three major sections of the statement?

Q5-29 When used with a company's other financial statements, what does the statement of cash flows help external users assess?

Q5-30 What are the three types of activities that a statement of cash flows reports on for a company? Provide examples of transactions for each type of activity.

Q5-31 Under the indirect method, how is the net cash provided by operating activities determined in a company's statement of cash flows?

Q5-32 Under the direct method, what are the most common cash inflows from and the most common cash outflows for operating activities in a company's statement of cash flows?

MULTIPLE CHOICE (AICPA Adapted)

Select the best answer for each of the following.

M5-1 The following information is available for Cooke Company for the current year:

Net sales	$1,800,000
Freight-in	45,000
Purchases discounts	25,000
Ending inventory	120,000

The gross margin is 40% of net sales. What is the cost of goods available for sale?

a. $840,000   c. $1,200,000
b. $960,000   d. $1,220,000

M5-2 A transaction that is material in amount, unusual in nature, and infrequent in occurrence is presented in the income statement separately as a component of income
a. Net of applicable income taxes
b. As a prior period adjustment
c. From continuing operations
d. From discontinued operations

M5-3 Effective January 1, 2007, Younger Company adopted the accounting principle of expensing as incurred advertising and promotion costs. Previously, advertising and promotion costs applicable to future periods were recorded in prepaid expenses. Younger can justify the change, which was made for both financial statement and income tax reporting purposes. Younger's prepaid advertising and promotion costs totaled $500,000 at December 31, 2006. Assume that the income tax rate is 30% for 2006 and 2007. The adjustment for the effect of this change in accounting principle should result in a net adjustment in the 2007 retained earnings statement of
a. $0   c. $350,000
b. $150,000   d. $500,000

M5-4 A company changes from the first-in, first-out inventory method to the average cost method. The cumulative effect of the change on the amount of retained earnings at the beginning of the period in which the change is made is reported separately as a(n)
a. Extraordinary item
b. Component of income from discontinued operations
c. Component of income from continuing operations
d. Retrospective adjustment

M5-5 Palo Corporation incurred the following losses, net of applicable income taxes, for the year ended December 31, 2007:

Loss on disposal of a component of Palo's business	$400,000
Loss on translation of foreign currency because of devaluation	500,000

How much should Palo report as extraordinary losses on its 2007 income statement?
a. $0   c. $500,000
b. $400,000   d. $900,000

M5-6 Which of the following is expensed under the principle of systematic and rational allocation?
a. Salespeople's monthly salaries
b. Insurance premiums
c. Transportation to customers
d. Electricity to light office building

M5-7 The following information is available for Wagner Corporation for the current year:

Sales	$500,000
Beginning inventory	180,000
Ending inventory	95,000
Freight-out	45,000
Purchases	215,000

How much is the cost of goods sold?

a. $200,000   c. $345,000

b. $300,000   d. $440,000

M5-8   Dobbin Corporation, a manufacturer of household paints, is preparing annual financial statements at December 31, 2007. Because of a recently proven health hazard in one of its paints, the government has clearly indicated its intention of having Dobbin recall all cans of this paint sold in the last six months. The management of Dobbin estimates that this recall would cost $1,000,000. What accounting recognition, if any, should be accorded this situation?

a. No recognition

b. Footnote disclosure

c. Operating expense of $1,000,000

d. Extraordinary loss of $1,000,000

M5-9   A loss from the sale of a component of a business enterprise is reported separately as a component of income

a. After income from continuing operations and before extraordinary items

b. In income from continuing operations

c. After extraordinary items

d. Before income from continuing operations and extraordinary items

M5-10   In a statement of cash flows, receipts from sales of property, plant, and equipment generally are classified as

a. Investing activities

b. Selling activities

c. Operating activities

d. Financing activities

EXERCISES

E5-1   *Simple Income Statement* The following are selected accounts taken from the adjusted trial balance of the Dibb Company on December 31, 2007:

Loss on sale of land	$ 5,000	Sales (net)	$198,000
Cost of goods sold	130,000	Operating expenses	45,000
		Extraordinary gain (pretax)	6,000

Twelve thousand shares of common stock were outstanding the entire year.

Required

Assuming a 30% income tax rate on all items of income, prepare a 2007 income statement for Dibb Company using (1) a multiple-step format and (2) a single-step format.

E5-2   *Simple Income Statement* The following are selected account balances of the Albertson Company as of December 31, 2007:

Purchases (net)	$63,000	Sales (net)	$100,000
Merchandise inventory, January 1, 2007	20,000	Operating expenses	22,000
Gain on sale of equipment	5,000	Extraordinary loss (pretax)	8,000

The merchandise inventory on December 31, 2007 is $31,000. Ten thousand shares of common stock have been outstanding the entire year. The company uses a periodic inventory system.

Required

Assuming a 30% income tax rate on all items of income, prepare a 2007 income statement for Albertson Company using (1) a multiple-step format, and (2) a single-step format.

E5-3   *Classifications* Where would each of the following items most likely be reported in a company's financial statements? Assume the monetary amount of each item is material.

1. Bad debts expense

2. Sales discounts taken

3. Depreciation expense on sales equipment

4. Loss from operations of discontinued Division B

5. Earnings per share

6. Gain on sale of land

7. Administrative salaries

8. Cash dividends declared on common stock

9. Correction of an error made in a prior period

10. Gain from sale of discontinued Division B

11. Cumulative effect on prior years' income of change in accounting principle

12. Advertising expense

13. Merchandise inventory (ending)

14. Loss from write-off of obsolete inventory

15. Net income

16. Unrealized increase in market value of available-for-sale securities

E5-4 *Classifications* Where would each of the following items most likely be reported in a company's financial statements? Assume the monetary amount of each item is material and the company uses a periodic inventory system.

1. Loss on sale of equipment
2. Office supplies used
3. Correction of miscount of last year's ending finished goods inventory
4. Freight-in
5. Delivery expense
6. Dividend revenue
7. Gain from retirement of debt
8. Change in the estimated useful life of office equipment
9. Summary of accounting policies
10. Purchases returns and allowances
11. Income tax expense on continuing income
12. Stock dividend
13. Loss resulting from tornado damage
14. Merchandise inventory (ending)
15. Unrealized decrease in market value of available-for-sale securities

E5-5 *Multiple-Step and Single-Step Income Statements* Included in the December 31, 2007 adjusted trial balance of the Gold Company are the following accounts:

Cost of goods sold	$101,000	Selling expenses	$28,000
Sales	200,000	Sales returns and allowances	5,000
General and administrative expenses	20,000	Interest revenue	4,000
Loss from strike (pretax)	9,000	Extraordinary loss (pretax)	17,000

Additional data:
1. Seven thousand shares of common stock have been outstanding the entire year.
2. The income tax rate is 30% on all items of income.

Required
1. Prepare a 2007 multiple-step income statement.
2. Prepare a 2007 single-step income statement.

E5-6 *Multiple-Step and Single-Step Income Statements, and Statement of Comprehensive Income* On December 31, 2007 the Adandt Company listed the following items in its adjusted trial balance:

Extraordinary loss (pretax)	$ 8,000	Loss on sale of equipment (pretax)	$ 2,000
Interest revenue	2,500	General and administrative expenses	17,000
Sales returns and allowances	3,000	Sales	163,000
Selling expenses	14,000	Unrealized decrease in value of available-	
Cost of goods sold	95,000	for-sale securities	1,800

Additional data:
1. Seven thousand shares of common stock have been outstanding the entire year.
2. The income tax rate is 30% on all items of income.

Required
1. Prepare a 2007 multiple-step income statement.
2. Prepare a 2007 single-step income statement.
3. Prepare a 2007 statement of comprehensive income.

E5-7 *Cost of Goods Sold and Income Statement* The Fanta Company presents you with the following account balances taken from its December 31, 2007 adjusted trial balance:

Inventory, January 1, 2007	$ 43,000	Purchases returns	$3,500
Selling expenses	35,000	Interest expense	4,000
Extraordinary gain (pretax)	23,000	Sales discounts taken	2,000
Purchases	100,000	Gain on sale of property (pretax)	7,000
Sales	250,000	Freight-in	5,000
General and administrative expenses	22,000		

Additional data:
1. A physical count reveals an ending inventory of $22,500 on December 31, 2007.
2. Twenty-five thousand shares of common stock have been outstanding the entire year.
3. The income tax rate is 30% on all items of income.

Required
1. As a supporting document for Requirements 2 and 3, prepare a separate schedule for Fanta Company's cost of goods sold.
2. Prepare a 2007 multiple-step income statement.
3. Prepare a 2007 single-step income statement.

E5-8   *Cost of Goods Sold, Income Statement, and Statement of Comprehensive Income* The Engle Company lists the following accounts on its adjusted trial balance as of December 31, 2007.

Sales	$147,100	Interest revenue	$ 3,300
Purchases returns	5,200	Purchases discounts taken	2,700
Gain on sale of equipment (pretax)	3,800	Inventory, January 1, 2007	12,100
Freight-in	3,400	Sales returns	8,100
Selling expenses	15,600	Purchases	89,700
Unrealized increase in value of available-		Administrative expenses	24,200
for-sale securities	2,400	Extraordinary loss (pretax)	6,500

The following additional information is also available. The December 31, 2007, ending inventory is $14,700. During 2007, 4,200 shares of common stock were outstanding the entire year. The income tax rate is 30% on all items of income.

Required
1. As a supporting document for Requirements 2 and 3, prepare a separate schedule for Engle Company's cost of goods sold.
2. Prepare a 2007 single-step income statement.
3. Prepare a 2007 multiple-step income statement.
4. Prepare a 2007 statement of comprehensive income.

E5-9   *Income Statement and Retained Earnings* The Senger Company presents the following partial list of account balances taken from its December 31, 2007 adjusted trial balance:

Sales (net)	$124,000	Operating expenses	$30,400
Interest expense	3,700	Common stock, $5 par	22,000
Cost of goods sold	66,200	Retained earnings, 1/1/2007	45,800

The following information is also available for 2007 and is not reflected in the preceding accounts:
1. The common stock has been outstanding all year. A cash dividend of $1.28 per share was declared and paid.
2. Land was sold at a pretax gain of $6,300.
3. Division X (a component of the company) was sold at a pretax gain of $4,700. It had incurred a $9,500 pretax operating loss during 2007.
4. A tornado, which is an unusual and infrequent event in the area, caused a $5,400 pretax loss.
5. The income tax rate on all items of income is 30%.
6. The average stockholders' equity is $90,000.

Required
1. Prepare a 2007 multiple-step income statement for Senger Company.
2. Prepare a 2007 retained earnings statement.
3. Compute the 2007 return on stockholders' equity (net income ÷ average stockholders' equity).

E5-10 *Income Statement and Retained Earnings* The Cobler Company uses a periodic inventory system and presents the following partial list of account balances taken from its December 31, 2007 adjusted trial balance:

Operating expenses	$ 35,800	Common stock, $15 par	$45,000
Dividend revenue	1,000	Merchandise inventory, January 1, 2007	24,000
Retained earnings, January 1, 2007	68,700	Purchases (net)	79,200
Sales (net)	139,600		

The following information is also available for 2007 and is not reflected in the preceding accounts:
1. The common stock has been outstanding for the entire year. A cash dividend of $0.84 per share was declared and paid.
2. The income tax rate on all items of income is 30%.
3. The ending merchandise inventory is $27,300.
4. A pretax $4,000 loss was recognized on the sale of Division X (a component of the company). This division had earned a pretax operating income of $1,900 during 2007.
5. Damaged inventory was written off at a pretax loss of $6,600.
6. An earthquake, which is an unusual and infrequent event in the area, caused a $3,700 pretax loss.

Required
1. Prepare a cost of goods sold schedule for Cobler Company.
2. Prepare a 2007 single-step income statement.
3. Prepare a 2007 retained earnings statement.
4. Compute the 2007 profit margin (net income ÷ net sales).

E5-11   *Income Statement Calculations* The income statement information for 2007 and 2008 of the Caleb Company (a sole proprietorship) is as follows:

	2007	2008
Cost of goods sold	$ (a)	$59,300
Interest expense	600	0
Selling expenses	(b)	10,800
Operating income	21,800	(d)
Sales (net)	96,000	(e)
General expenses	7,900	(f)
Net income	(c)	21,600
Interest revenue	0	600
Gross profit	39,000	40,200

Required
Fill in the blanks labeled (a) through (f). All the necessary information is listed. (*Hint*: It is not necessary to calculate your answers in alphabetical order.)

E5-12   *Income Statement Calculations* The income statement information for 2007 and 2008 of the Connor Company (a sole proprietorship) is as follows:

	2007	2008
Beginning inventory	$ (a)	$ (d)
Sales	210,000	(e)
Purchases	130,000	140,000
Purchases returns and allowances	7,000	6,000
Ending inventory	62,000	(f)
Sales returns and allowances	4,000	9,000
Gross profit	(b)	100,000
Cost of goods sold	114,000	120,000
Selling expenses	35,000	36,000
Transportation-in	2,000	5,000
General and administrative expenses	20,000	(g)
Net income	(c)	43,000

Required
Fill in the blanks labeled (a) through (g). All the necessary information is listed. (*Hint*: It is not necessary to calculate your answers in alphabetical order.)

E5-13   *Results of Discontinued Operations* During December 2007, Smythe Company decides to sell Division F (a component of the company). On December 31, 2007, the company classifies Division F as held for sale. On that date, the book values of Division F's assets and liabilities are $950,000 and $600,000, respectively. Smythe expects to sell Division F in 2008 and estimates that the fair value of Division F is $250,000. During 2007, Division F earned revenues of $1,000,000 and incurred expenses of $1,300,000. Smythe Company is subject to a 30% income tax rate.

Required
Prepare the results from discontinued operations section of Smythe Company's income statement for 2007. Show supporting calculations.

E5-14   *Results of Discontinued Operations* On November 30, 2007, Feiner Company announced its plans to discontinue the operations of Division P (a component of the company) by selling the division. On December 31, 2007, Division P had not yet been sold and was classified as held for sale. On this date, Division P had assets with a book value of $920,000 and liabilities with a book value of $610,000. Feiner Company estimates that the fair value of Division P on this date is $190,000. During 2007, Division P earned revenues of $920,000 and incurred expenses of $980,000. Feiner Company is subject to a 30% income tax rate.

Required
Prepare the results from discontinued operations section of Feiner Company's income statement for 2007. Show supporting calculations.

E5-15 `AICPA Adapted`   *Income Statement Deficiencies* David Company's Statements of Income for the year ended December 31, 2008, and December 31, 2007, are presented here:

	Year Ended December 31,	
	2008	2007
Net sales	$900,000	$750,000
Costs and expenses:		
Cost of goods sold	$720,000	$600,000
Selling, general and administrative expenses	112,000	90,000
Other, net	11,000	9,000
Total costs and expenses	$843,000	$699,000
Income from continuing operations before income taxes	$ 57,000	$ 51,000
Income taxes	23,000	24,000
Income from continuing operations	$ 34,000	$ 27,000
Loss on sale of Dex Division, less applicable		
income taxes of $8,000	8,000	—
Cumulative effect on prior years of change		
in depreciation method, less applicable		
income taxes of $1,500	—	3,000
Net income	$ 26,000	$ 30,000
Earnings per share of common stock:		
Income before cumulative effect of change		
in inventory method	$ 2.60	$2.70
Cumulative effect on prior years of change		
in inventory method, less applicable		
income taxes	—	.30
Net income	$ 2.60	$ 3.00

Additional facts are as follows:
a. On January 1, 2007, David Company changed its inventory method from the average cost method to the first-in, first-out method, and justified the change.
b. The loss from operations of the discontinued Dex Division (a component of the company) from January 1, 2008 to September 30, 2008 (the portion of the year prior to the date of sale) and from January 1, 2007 to December 31, 2007 is included in David Company's Statements of Income for the year ended December 31, 2008 and December 31, 2007 respectively, in "other, net."
c. David Company has a simple capital structure with only common stock outstanding, and the net income per share of common stock was based on the weighted average number of common shares outstanding during each year.
d. David Company common stock is listed on the New York Stock Exchange and closed at $13 per share on December 31, 2008 and $15 per share on December 31, 2007.

Required
Determine from the additional facts listed whether the presentation of those facts in David Company's Statements of Income is appropriate. If the presentation is appropriate, discuss the rationale for the presentation. If the presentation is not appropriate, specify the appropriate presentation and discuss its rationale. Do *not* discuss disclosure requirements for the Notes to the Financial Statements.

E5-16 *Net Income and Comprehensive Income* On December 31, 2007 TNT Company lists the following accounts in its adjusted trial balance:

Sales (net)	$85,000
Unrealized increase in value of available-for-sale securities	4,000
Operating expenses	18,000
Cost of goods sold	47,000

The income tax rate is 30% on all items of income.

Required
1. Prepare a 2007 multiple-step income statement, which includes comprehensive income (disregard earnings per share).
2. Prepare (a) a 2007 multiple-step income statement (disregard earnings per share) and (b) a 2007 statement of comprehensive income.

E5-17 *Net Cash Flow From Operating Activities* The following are accounting items taken from the records of the Tyrone Company for 2007:

a. Net income, $22,900
b. Payment for purchase of land, $4,000
c. Payment for retirement of bonds, $6,000
d. Depreciation expense, $7,800
e. Receipt from issuance of common stock, $7,000

f. Patent amortization expense, $2,700
g. Bond discount amortization, $1,000
h. Increase in accounts receivable, $3,400
i. Payment of dividends, $5,000
j. Decrease in accounts payable, $2,600

Required
Prepare the net cash flow from operating activities section of the Tyrone Company's 2007 statement of cash flows.

E5-18 *Operating Cash Flows: Direct Method* The following are various cash flows and other information of the Lexie Company for 2007:

a. Payments of interest, $8,200
b. Receipt from sale of land, $7,900
c. Interest collected, $10,000
d. Payment of dividends, $12,100
e. Depreciation expense, $24,700

f. Collections from customers, $101,600
g. Payments of income taxes, $15,400
h. Receipt from issuance of stock, $18,900
i. Payments to suppliers and employees, $67,500
j. Increase in inventories, $4,600

Required
Using the direct method, prepare the cash flows from operating activities section of the Lexie Company's 2007 statement of cash flows.

E5-19 *Statement of Cash Flows* The following are several items involving the cash flow activities of the Rocky Company for 2007:

a. Net income, $41,000
b. Payment of dividends, $16,000
c. Ten-year, $28,000 bonds payable were issued at face value
d. Depreciation expense, $11,000
e. Building was acquired at a cost of $40,000

f. Accounts receivable decreased by $2,000
g. Accounts payable decreased by $4,000
h. Equipment was acquired at a cost of $8,000
i. Inventories increased by $7,000
j. Beginning cash balance, $13,000

Required
Prepare the statement of cash flows of the Rocky Company for 2007.

E5-20 *Statement of Cash Flows* The following are several items involving the cash flow activities of the Jones Company for 2007:

a. Net income, $60,400
b. Receipt from issuance of common stock, $32,000
c. Payment for purchase of equipment, $41,500
d. Payment for purchase of land, $19,600
e. Depreciation expense, $20,500

f. Patent amortization expense, $1,200
g. Payment of dividends, $21,000
h. Decrease in salaries payable, $2,600
i. Increase in accounts receivable, $10,300
j. Beginning cash balance, $30,700

Required
Prepare the statement of cash flows of the Jones Company for 2007.

PROBLEMS

P5-1 *Comprehensive Income Framework* The following is an alphabetical list of accounts for the Mack Company:

Accounts payable
Accounts receivable
Accumulated depreciation,
  buildings and office equipment
Accumulated depreciation,
  store and delivery equipment
Administrative salaries
Advertising expense

Allowance for doubtful accounts
Bad debts expense
Bonds payable
Buildings
Cash
Cash dividends declared
Common stock, $10 par
Correction of previous years' error

Delivery expense
Depreciation expense, buildings and
  office equipment
Depreciation expense, store and
  delivery equipment
Dividend revenue
Dividends payable
Freight on purchases
Fund to retire long-term bonds
Gain on sale of equipment
Gain on sale of Division T
Income tax expense
Insurance expense
Interest expense
Interest payable
Interest revenue
Investment in securities (long-term)
Loss from expropriation
Loss from operations of discontinued Division T
Loss on sale of office equipment
Merchandise inventory, January 1, 2007
Merchandise inventory, December 31, 2007
Miscellaneous office expenses
Miscellaneous sales expenses

Miscellaneous service revenues
Mortgage payable
Office salaries
Office supplies used
Paid-in capital on common stock
Prepaid office supplies
Property tax expense
Purchases
Purchases discounts taken
Purchases returns and allowances
Rent revenue
Retained earnings, January 1, 2007
Salaries payable
Sales
Sales commissions
Sales discounts taken
Sales returns and allowances
Sales salaries
Stock dividends declared
Unearned rent
Unexpired insurance
Unrealized increase in value of
  available-for-sale securities
Utilities expense

Required

Ignoring amounts, select the appropriate accounts of Mack Company and prepare for 2007:
1. A multiple-step income statement with proper subheadings
2. A statement of comprehensive income
3. A retained earnings statement

P5-2 *Account Classifications* Given the following code letters and components of financial statements, indicate where each item would most likely be reported in the financial statements by inserting the corresponding code letters. Assume the monetary amount of each item is material.

Code Letter	Component
A	Sales revenues (net)
B	Cost of goods sold
C	Selling expenses
D	General and administrative expenses
E	Other items
F	Results from discontinued operations
G	Extraordinary items
H	Prior period adjustments
I	Additions to retained earnings (other than H)
J	Deductions from retained earnings (other than H)
K	Notes to financial statements
L	Ending balance sheet

_____ 1. Purchases
_____ 2. Loss on sale of equipment
_____ 3. Utilities expense
_____ 4. Cash dividends declared on common stock
_____ 5. Bad debts expense
_____ 6. Sales salaries
_____ 7. Sales discounts taken
_____ 8. Transportation-in
_____ 9. Net income
_____ 10. Gain on retirement of long-term debt
_____ 11. Purchases returns and allowances
_____ 12. Premium on bonds payable
_____ 13. Gain on sale of land
_____ 14. Interest expense
_____ 15. Delivery expense
_____ 16. Expenses incurred as a result of a strike
_____ 17. Summary of accounting policies
_____ 18. Gain on disposal of Division J
_____ 19. Interest revenue
_____ 20. Additional paid-in capital on common stock

_____ 21. Loss from write-down of obsolete inventory
_____ 22. Administrative salaries
_____ 23. Stock dividends declared on common stock
_____ 24. Correction of erroneous understatement of last year's ending inventory
_____ 25. Operating loss related to discontinued Division J
_____ 26. Additional depreciation on office equipment resulting from decrease in estimated useful life

_____ 27. Gain on sale of factory
_____ 28. Loss from frost damage in southern Arizona
_____ 29. Sales returns
_____ 30. Depreciation expense for office equipment
_____ 31. Sales commissions
_____ 32. Promotion expense
_____ 33. Merchandise inventory (beginning)

P5-3   Income Statement, Lower Portion At the beginning of 2007, the retained earnings of the Cameron Company was $212,000. For 2007, the company has calculated its pretax income from continuing operations to be $120,000. During 2007, the following events also occurred:

1. During July the company sold Division M (a component of the company). It has determined that the pretax income from the operations of Division M during 2007 totals $39,000 and that a pretax loss of $40,500 was incurred on the sale of Division M.
2. The company had 21,000 shares of common stock outstanding during all of 2007. It declared and paid a $1 per share cash dividend on this stock.
3. The company experienced an extraordinary event. It recognized a material pretax gain of $26,000 on the event.
4. The company found and corrected a pretax $18,000 understatement of the 2006 ending inventory because of a mathematical error.

Required
Assuming that all the "pretax" items are subject to a 30% income tax rate:
1. Complete the lower portion of Cameron Company's 2007 income statement, beginning with "Pretax Income from Continuing Operations."
2. Prepare an accompanying retained earnings statement.

P5-4   Income Statement, Lower Portion Cunningham Company reports a retained earnings balance of $365,200 at the beginning of 2007. For the year ended December 31, 2007, the company reports pretax income from continuing operations of $150,500. The following information is also available pertaining to 2007:

1. The company declared and paid a $0.72 cash dividend per share on the 30,000 shares of common stock that were outstanding the entire year.
2. The company found and corrected a pretax $48,000 understatement of 2006 depreciation expense because of a mathematical error.
3. The company incurred a pretax $21,000 loss as a result of an earthquake, which is unusual and infrequent for the area.
4. The company sold Division P (a component of the company) in May. From January through May, Division P had incurred a pretax loss from operations of $33,000. A pretax gain of $15,000 was recognized on the sale of Division P.
5. Because of additional information, the company determined that the estimated useful life of certain depreciable assets had decreased. As a result, the current depreciation expense included in the 2007 pretax income from continuing operations is $7,000 higher than it would have been had the original estimated useful life been used in the calculations.

Required
Assuming that all the "pretax" items are subject to a 30% income tax rate:
1. Complete the lower portion of Cunningham Company's 2007 income statement beginning with "Pretax Income from Continuing Operations." Include any related note to the financial statements.
2. Prepare an accompanying retained earnings statement.

P5-5   Comprehensive: Income Statement and Retained Earnings The Houston Manufacturing Company presents the following partial list of account balances, after adjustments, as of December 31, 2007:

Sales salaries expense	$ 27,400	Sales personnel travel expenses	$ 8,300
Miscellaneous administrative expenses	3,000	Property taxes and insurance expense	9,000
Sales returns	5,000	Retained earnings, January 1, 2007	200,800
Sales	468,200	Depreciation expense: sales equipment	9,000
Interest revenue	3,200	Advertising expense	15,700
Office and administrative salaries	30,000	Miscellaneous rent revenue	5,900
Delivery expenses	11,700	Common stock, $10 par	200,000
Loss on sale of factory equipment (pretax)	4,100	Depreciation expense: buildings and	
Cost of goods sold	232,200	office equipment	14,400

The following information is also available but is not reflected in the preceding accounts:

1. The company sold Division E (a component of the company) on August 1, 2007. During 2007, Division E had incurred a pretax loss from operations of $16,000. However, because the acquiring company could vertically integrate Division E into its facilities, the Houston Manufacturing Company was able to recognize a $42,000 pretax gain on the sale.
2. On January 2, 2007, without warning, a foreign country expropriated a factory of Houston Manufacturing Company, which had been operating in that country. As a result of that expropriation, the company has incurred a pretax loss of $30,000.
3. In preparing its 2007 adjusting entries at year-end, the company discovered that it had not recorded $10,100 of depreciation on its office building during 2006. This error did not affect the 2007 depreciation expense.
4. The common stock was outstanding for the entire year. A cash dividend of $1.20 per share was declared and paid in 2007.
5. The 2007 income tax expense totals $28,020 and consists of the following:

Tax expense on income from continuing operations	$32,250
Tax credit on Division E operating loss	(4,800)
Tax expense on gain from sale of Division E	12,600
Tax credit on loss from expropriation	(9,000)
Tax credit on 2006 depreciation error	(3,030)
	$28,020

Required

1. As supporting documents for Requirement 2, prepare separate supporting schedules for selling expenses and for general and administrative expenses (include depreciation expense where applicable in these schedules).
2. Prepare a 2007 multiple-step income statement for the Houston Manufacturing Company.
3. Prepare a 2007 retained earnings statement.
4. What was Houston Manufacturing Company's return on stockholders' equity for 2007 if its average stockholders' equity during 2007 was $500,000? What is your evaluation of this return on stockholders' equity if its "target" for 2007 was 15%?

P5-6   *Comprehensive: Income Statement and Retained Earnings*   The following selected accounts are taken from the Crandle Corporation's December 31, 2007 adjusted trial balance:

Retained earnings, January 1, 2007	$428,900	Office supplies expense	$ 1,800
Interest expense	4,900	Transportation-out (deliveries)	6,000
Depreciation expense: sales fixtures	8,500	Cost of goods sold	191,200
Sales returns and allowances	11,300	Sales discounts taken	5,200
Advertising expense	14,100	Bad debt expense	1,900
Common stock, $10 par	110,000	Sales supplies expense	4,600
Administrative and office salaries expense	29,500	Sales salaries expense	16,500
Dividend revenue	900	Depreciation expense: buildings and	
Sales	378,000	office equipment	10,000
Property tax expense	7,700	Income tax expense	15,870
Gain on sale of sales fixtures (pretax)	5,000		

In addition to the preceding account balances, you have available the following information:

1. In the middle of December 2007 the company incurred a material $5,500 pretax loss as a result of a freak flood of a river that had never flooded before.
2. While making its December 31, 2007 adjusting entries, the company discovered the following:
    a. In recording its December 31, 2006 adjusting entries, it had inadvertently recorded depreciation expense twice for the same asset. The amount of the error was $4,000 pretax and is considered material. The error did not have any effect upon the depreciation recorded for 2007.
    b. Based on an analysis of the company's recent favorable experience with uncollectible accounts receivable, the company decided to reduce the percentage used in computing bad debt expense. The use of the new percentage resulted in the $1,900 bad debt expense being $500 less than the amount that would have been calculated using the old percentage.
3. On April 1, 2007 the company sold Division M (a component of the company), which had been unprofitable for several years. For the first 3 months of 2007, Division M had incurred a pretax operating loss of $8,800. Division M was sold at a pretax loss of $7,500.
4. The company paid cash dividends of $0.90 per share on its common stock. All the stock was outstanding for the entire year.
5. The company is subject to a 30% income tax rate. The $15,870 Income Tax Expense account balance consists of $21,210 tax on income from continuing operations and $1,200 tax on the depreciation correction, and tax credits of $2,640 on the operating loss of Division M, $2,250 on the loss from sale of Division M, and $1,650 on the loss because of the flood.

Required

1. As supporting documents for Requirement 2, prepare separate schedules for selling expenses and for general and administrative expenses (include each depreciation expense where applicable in these schedules).
2. Prepare a 2007 single-step income statement for the Crandle Corporation. Include any related note to the financial statements.
3. Prepare a 2007 retained earnings statement.
4. What was Crandle Corporation's profit margin for 2007? What is your evaluation of Crandle's 2007 profit margin if last year it was 8%?

P5-7 *Comprehensive: Income Statement and Supporting Schedules* The following is a partial list of the account balances, after adjustments, of the Silvoso Company on December 31, 2007:

Depreciation expense: buildings and office equipment	$ 14,500	Office supplies expense	$ 1,400
Sales commissions and salaries	18,200	Common stock, $10 par	80,000
Inventory, January 1, 2007	37,800	Loss on sale of office equipment (pretax)	5,000
Sales supplies used	5,600	Insurance and property tax expense	8,500
Retained earnings, January 1, 2007	83,700	Sales	340,700
Purchases returns and allowances	6,200	Rent revenue	6,900
Bad debts expense	2,700	Office and administrative salaries expense	32,000
Transportation-in	13,500	Promotion and advertising expense	17,000
Sales discounts taken	4,900	Sales returns and allowances	12,100
Purchases	173,000	Purchases discounts taken	4,100
Delivery expense	7,700	Depreciation expense: sales equipment	9,600
		Interest expense	3,700

The following information is also available:

1. The company declared and paid a $0.60 per share cash dividend on its common stock. The stock was outstanding the entire year.
2. A physical count determined that the December 31, 2007 ending inventory is $34,100.
3. A tornado destroyed a warehouse, resulting in a pretax loss of $12,000. The last tornado in this area had occurred 20 years earlier.
4. While making its December 31, 2007 adjusting entries, the company determined that:
    a. In 2006, it had inadvertently omitted $11,000 depreciation expense on its buildings and office equipment. The error did not have any effect upon the depreciation recorded in 2007.
    b. Because of recently increased obsolescence, its sales equipment should be depreciated over a shorter useful life. The resulting $2,500 of additional depreciation has been included in the 2007 depreciation expense.
5. On May 1, 2007, the company sold an unprofitable division (R). From January through April, Division R (a component of the company) had incurred a pretax operating loss of $8,700. Division R was sold at a pretax gain of $10,000.
6. The company is subject to a 30% income tax rate. Its income tax expense for 2007 totals $930. The breakdown is as follows:

Income Tax Expense (Credit) Related to	Amount
Continuing income	$ 7,440
Operating loss of Division R	(2,610)
Gain on sale of Division R	3,000
Loss from tornado	(3,600)
Error in recording 2006 depreciation expense	(3,300)
	$ 930

7. The company had average stockholders' equity of $150,000 during 2007.

Required

1. As supporting documents for Requirement 2, prepare separate supporting schedules for cost of goods sold, selling expenses, general and administrative expenses, and depreciation expense.
2. Prepare a 2007 multiple-step income statement for the Silvoso Company. Include any related note to the financial statements.
3. Prepare a 2007 retained earnings statement.
4. What was Silvoso Company's return on stockholders' equity for 2007? What is your evaluation of Silvoso Company's return on stockholders' equity if last year it was 10%?

P5-8   *Misclassifications* The Rox Corporation's multiple-step income statement and retained earnings statement for the year ended December 31, 2007, as developed by its bookkeeper, are shown here:

ROX CORPORATION
Revenue Statement
December 31, 2007

Sales (net)		$179,000
Plus: Income from operations of discontinued Division P (net of $960 income taxes)		2,240
Less: Dividends declared ($1.50 per common share)		(7,500)
Net revenues		$173,740
Less: Selling expenses		(19,000)
Gross profit		$154,740
Less: Operating expenses		
Interest expense	$ 4,100	
Loss on sale of Division P (net of $1,200 income tax credit)	2,800	
Cost of goods sold	110,700	
Income tax expense on income from continuing operations	5,370	
Total operating expenses		(122,970)
Operating income		$ 31,770
Miscellaneous items		
Dividend revenue	$ 1,800	
General and administrative expenses	(24,300)	(22,500)
Income before extraordinary items		$ 9,270
Extraordinary items		
Loss on sale of land	$ (4,800)	
Correction of error in last year's income (net of $1,500 income taxes)	3,500	(1,300)
Net income		$ 7,970

ROX CORPORATION
Retained Earnings Statement
December 31, 2007

Beginning retained earnings	$ 62,850
Add: Net income	7,970
Adjusted retained earnings	$ 70,820
Less: Loss from expropriation (net of $2,760 income tax credit)	(6,440)
Ending retained earnings	$ 64,380

You determine that the account *balances* listed in the statements are correct but are incorrectly classified in certain cases. No shares of common stock were issued or retired during 2007.

Required
1. Review both statements and indicate where each incorrectly classified item should be classified.
2. Prepare a correct multiple-step 2007 income statement.
3. Prepare a correct 2007 retained earnings statement.

P5-9   *Misclassifications* The bookkeeper for the Olson Company prepared the following income statement and retained earnings statement for the year ended December 31, 2007:

OLSON COMPANY
December 31, 2007
Expense and Profits Statement

Sales (net)	$196,000
Less: Selling expenses	(19,600)
Net sales	$176,400
Add: Interest revenue	2,300
Add: Gain on sale of equipment	3,200
Gross sales revenues	$181,900

Less: Costs of operations		
Cost of goods sold	$120,100	
Correction of overstatement in last year's income because of error		
(net of $1,650 income tax credit)	3,850	
Dividend costs ($0.50 per share for 8,000 common shares)	4,000	
Extraordinary loss because of earthquake (net of $1,800 income tax credit)	4,200	(132,150)
Taxable revenues		$ 49,750
Less: Income tax on income from continuing operations		(12,480)
Net income		$ 37,270
Miscellaneous deductions		
Loss from operations of discontinued Division L (net of $900 income tax credit)	$ 2,100	
Administrative expenses	16,800	(18,900)
Net revenues		$ 18,370

OLSON COMPANY
Retained Revenues Statement
For Year Ended December 31, 2007

Beginning retained earnings	$59,300
Add: Gain on sale of Division L (net of $1,350 income taxes)	3,150
Recalculated retained earnings	$62,450
Add: Net revenues	18,370
	$80,820
Less: Interest expense	(3,400)
Ending retained earnings	$77,420

The preceding account *balances* are correct but have been incorrectly classified in certain instances.

Required

Prepare a corrected 2007 multiple-step income statement and a 2007 retained earnings statement.

P5-10 *Classification of Unusual and/or Infrequent Items* The following are a number of unusual and/or infrequent gains or losses that might be disclosed on the income statement or retained earnings statement. All items are considered to be material in amount.

1. A loss from an earthquake that destroyed a chemical plant of a major chemical company. The region where the plant was destroyed had not had an earthquake in 15 years.
2. A gain resulting from the retirement of bonds payable. The bonds payable had been classified as current liabilities on last year's ending balance sheet because of their expected retirement during the current year.
3. A reduction in the current depletion expense as a result of the discovery of additional mineral deposits.
4. A gain from the sale of land. The land had been purchased for the construction of a new factory. The company has built several new factories over the past several years, and in each instance has acquired more land than necessary for the factory site. After completion of the factory, the excess land is sold at its appreciated value.
5. A loss incurred by a corporation on the sale of an investment in bonds of a publicly held company. The bonds constitute 5% of the net assets of the publicly held company. The corporation has been holding these bonds as an investment for several years. This is the only investment in securities the corporation has ever made.
6. A loss incurred as a result of an earthquake that destroyed a 2-year-old storage facility of a large retail chain. The storage facility is located in California. A major earthquake occurred in the same region 2 years ago, just prior to the construction of the facility.
7. A decrease in previous years' earnings as a result of a change from the first-in, first-out inventory method to the average cost inventory method at the beginning of the current year.
8. A loss incurred in the spring by a retail store in a shopping center as a result of a flood of a nearby stream. Although the stream has overflowed several times in the past six years, only 3 stores (out of 38) in the shopping center had previously incurred a significant flood loss.
9. A gain recognized as the result of the sale by a food processing company of a 15% interest in a professional baseball team.
10. A reduction in last year's income as a result of the discovery in the current year of a miscount (overstatement) of last year's ending inventory.
11. A loss incurred by a diversified citrus grower because of frost damage in southern California. No frost damage has occurred in the region for seven years, although last year the citrus grower had incurred a loss because of frost damage to its Florida operations.

Required
For each item, indicate in which section of the income statement or retained earnings statement it should be disclosed. Justify your disclosure.

P5-11 *Results of Discontinued Operations* On November 1, 2007, Woods Company announced its plans to sell Division J (a component of the company). By December 31, 2007, Woods Company had not sold Division J and so it classifies the division as held for sale.

During 2007, Woods Company recorded the following revenues and expenses for Division J and the remainder of the company.

	Division J	Remainder of Company
Sales revenues	$170,000	$950,000
Cost of goods sold	119,000	560,000
Operating expenses	42,000	190,000

The company is subject to a 30% income tax rate.

On December 31, 2007, the net book value of Division J is $500,000, consisting of assets of $910,000 and liabilities of $410,000. On this date, Woods Company estimates that the fair value of Division J is $420,000. The company had 50,000 shares of common stock outstanding during all of 2007.

Required
1. Prepare the journal entry on December 31, 2007 to record the pretax loss on held-for-sale Division J. Show supporting calculations.
2. Prepare a 2007 multiple-step income statement for Woods Company.
3. Show how Division J would be reported on Woods Company's December 31, 2007 balance sheet.

P5-12 *Analyzing Coca-Cola's Income Statement and Cash Flow Statement Disclosures* Review the financial statements and notes of the Coca-Cola Company in Appendix A.

Required (*Note:* You do not need to make any calculations).
1. Does the company use a multiple-step or a single-step format on its income statement? Explain.
2. What was the net income for 2004? What was the basic net income (earnings) per common share for 2004?
3. What was the gross profit for 2004? For 2003?
4. How much interest expense was incurred in 2004? In 2003?
5. What was the amount of the income taxes related to income before income taxes for 2004?
6. What was the amount of selling, general, and administrative expenses in 2004? Of this amount, what was the amount for stock-based compensation expense?
7. What amount of dividends on common stock were paid per share and in total in 2004?
8. What were the net operating revenues and gross profit, respectively, for the fourth quarter of 2004?
9. What method was used to determine the net cash provided by operating activities in 2004? What was the amount?
10. What was the net cash used in investing activities in 2004?
11. What was the cash provided by the issuances of debt in 2004?

P5-13 **AICPA Adapted** *Complex Income Statement* The following is the adjusted trial balance for the Woodbine Circle Corporation on December 31, 2007:

	Debit	Credit
Cash	$ 500,000	
Accounts receivable, net	1,500,000	
Inventory	2,500,000	
Property, plant, and equipment	15,100,000	
Accumulated depreciation		$ 4,900,000
Accounts payable		2,200,000
Income taxes payable		200,000
Notes payable		1,000,000
Common stock ($1 par value)		1,000,000
Additional paid-in capital		6,200,000
Retained earnings, Jan. 1, 2007		3,000,000
Sales—regular		10,100,000
Sales—AL Division		2,000,000
Cost of sales—regular	6,200,000	
Cost of sales—AL Division	900,000	

	Debit	Credit
Administrative expenses—regular	2,000,000	
Administrative expenses—AL Division	300,000	
Interest expense—regular	210,000	
Interest expense—AL Division	140,000	
Loss on sale of AL Division	250,000	
Gain from extraordinary event		300,000
Income tax expense	900,000	
	$30,500,000	$30,500,000

Other financial data for the year ended December 31, 2007:

Federal Income Taxes

Paid on Federal Tax Deposit Form	$700,000
Accrued	200,000
Total charged to income tax expense (estimated)	$900,000
Tax rate on all types of taxable income	40%

Discontinued Operations

On September 30, 2007 Woodbine sold its Auto Leasing (AL) Division for $4,000,000. The book value of this division was $4,250,000 at that date. For financial statement purposes, this sale was considered as discontinued operation of a component of the company.

Capital Structure

Common stock, par value $1 per share, traded on the New York Stock Exchange:

Number of shares outstanding during all of 2007	1,000,000

Required

Using the multiple-step format, prepare a formal income statement for Woodbine for the year ended December 31, 2007, together with the appropriate supporting schedules. All income taxes should be appropriately shown.

P5-14 **AICPA Adapted** *Comparative Income Statements* The Century Company, a diversified manufacturing company, had four separate operating divisions engaged in the manufacture of products in each of the following areas: food products, health aids, textiles, and office equipment. Financial data for the 2 years ended December 31, 2008 and 2007 are presented here:

Net Sales	2008	2007
Food products	$3,500,000	$3,000,000
Health aids	2,000,000	1,270,000
Textiles	1,580,000	1,400,000
Office equipment	920,000	1,330,000
	$8,000,000	$7,000,000

Cost of Sales	2008	2007
Food products	$2,400,000	$1,800,000
Health aids	1,100,000	700,000
Textiles	500,000	900,000
Office equipment	800,000	1,000,000
	$4,800,000	$4,400,000

Operating Expenses	2008	2007
Food products	$ 550,000	$ 275,000
Health aids	300,000	125,000
Textiles	200,000	150,000
Office equipment	650,000	750,000
	$1,700,000	$1,300,000

On January 1, 2008, Century adopted a plan to sell the assets and product line of the office equipment division and considered it a component of the company. On September 1, 2008, the division's assets and product line were sold for $2,100,000 cash, resulting in a gain of $640,000.

The company's textiles division had six manufacturing plants that produced a variety of textile products. In April 2008, the company sold one of these plants and realized a gain of $130,000. After the sale the operations at the plant that was sold were transferred to the remaining five textile plants, which the company continued to operate.

In August 2008, the main warehouse of the food products division, located on the banks of the Bayer River, was flooded when the river overflowed. The resulting damage of $420,000 is not included in the financial data given previously. Historical records indicate that the Bayer River normally overflows every 4 to 5 years, causing flood damage to adjacent property.

For the 2 years ended December 31, 2008 and 2007 the company had interest revenue earned on investments of $70,000 and $40,000, respectively.

The provision for income tax expense for each of the 2 years should be computed at a rate of 40%.

Required
Prepare in proper form a multiple-step comparative statement of income of the Century Company for the 2 years ended December 31, 2008 and December 31, 2007. Earnings per share information and footnotes are not required.

P5-15 **AICPA Adapted** *Financial Statement Deficiencies* The following is the complete set of financial statements prepared by Oberlin Corporation:

OBERLIN CORPORATION
Statement of Earnings and Retained Earnings
For the Fiscal Year Ended August 31, 2007

Sales		$3,500,000
Less returns and allowances		(35,000)
Net sales		$3,465,000
Less cost of goods sold		(1,039,000)
Gross margin		$2,426,000
Less:		
Selling expenses	$1,000,000	
General and administrative expenses (Note 1)	1,079,000	(2,079,000)
Operating earnings		$ 347,000
Add other revenues		
Purchase discounts	$ 10,000	
Gain on increased value of investments in real estate	100,000	
Gain on sale of treasury stock	200,000	
Correction of error in last year's statement	90,000	400,000
Ordinary earnings		$ 747,000
Add extraordinary item—gain on sale of fixed asset		53,000
Earnings before income tax		$ 800,000
Less income tax expense		(320,000)
Net earnings		$ 480,000
Add beginning retained earnings		2,690,000
		$3,170,000
Less:		
Dividends (12% stock dividend declared but not yet issued)		(120,000)
Contingent liability (Note 3)		(300,000)
Ending retained earnings		$2,750,000

Statement of Financial Position
August 31, 2007

Assets		
Current Assets		
Cash	$ 80,000	
Accounts receivable, net	110,000	
Inventory	130,000	
Total current assets		$320,000

Other Assets

Land and building, net	$4,000,000	
Investments in real estate (current value)	1,668,000	
Goodwill (Note 2)	250,000	
Discount on bonds payable	42,000	
Total other assets		5,960,000
Total assets		$6,280,000

Liabilities and Stockholders' Equity

Current Liabilities

Accounts payable	$ 160,000	
Income taxes payable	300,000	
Stock dividend payable	120,000	
Total current liabilities		$ 580,000

Other Liabilities

Due to Grant, Inc. (Note 3)	$ 300,000	
Accrued pension cost	450,000	
Bonds payable (including portion due within one year)	1,000,000	
Deferred taxes	58,000	
Total other liabilities		1,808,000
Total liabilities		$2,388,000

Stockholders' Equity

Common stock	$1,000,000	
Paid-in capital in excess of par	142,000	
Retained earnings	2,750,000	
Total stockholders' equity		3,892,000
Total liabilities and stockholders' equity		$6,280,000

Notes to Financial Statements

1. Goodwill is not being reviewed for impairment. The goodwill was "acquired" in 2007.
2. The amount, Due to Grant, Inc., is contingent upon the outcome of a lawsuit, which is currently pending. The amount of loss, if any, is not expected to exceed $300,000.

Required

Identify and explain the deficiencies in the presentation of Oberlin's financial statements. There are no arithmetic errors in the statements. Organize your answer as follows:

1. Deficiencies in the statement of earnings and retained earnings
2. Deficiencies in the statement of financial position
3. General comments

If an item appears on both statements, identify the deficiencies for each statement separately.

P5-16 **AICPA Adapted** *Financial Statement Violations of GAAP* The following are the financial statements issued by Allen Corporation for its fiscal year ended October 31, 2007:

ALLEN CORPORATION
Statement of Financial Position
October 31, 2007

Assets

Cash	$ 15,000
Accounts receivable, net	150,000
Inventory	120,000
Total current assets	$285,000
Patent (Note 3)	250,000
Land	125,000
Total assets	$660,000

Liabilities

Accounts payable	$ 80,000
Accrued expenses	20,000
Total current liabilities	$ 100,000
Deferred income tax payable (Note 4)	80,000
Total liabilities	$180,000

Stockholders' Equity

Common stock, par $1 (Note 5)	$100,000	
Additional paid-in capital	180,000	
Retained earnings	200,000	480,000
Total liabilities and stockholders' equity		$660,000

Earnings Statement
For the Fiscal Year Ended October 31, 2007

Sales		$1,000,000
Cost of goods sold		(750,000)
Gross margin		$ 250,000
Expenses		
Bad debt expense	$ 7,000	
Insurance	13,000	
Lease expenses (Note 1)	40,000	
Repairs and maintenance	30,000	
Pensions (Note 2)	12,000	
Salaries	60,000	(162,000)
Earnings before provision for income tax		$ 88,000
Provision for income tax		(28,740)
Net earnings		$ 59,260
Earnings per common share outstanding		$ 0.5926

Statement of Retained Earnings
For the Fiscal Year Ended October 31, 2007

Retained earnings, November 1, 2006	$150,000
Extraordinary gain, net of income tax	25,000
Net earnings for the fiscal year ended October 31, 2007	59,260
	$234,260
Dividends ($0.3426 per share)	(34,260)
Retained earnings, October 31, 2007	$200,000

Notes to Financial Statements:

1. *Long-Term Lease.* Under the terms of a 5-year noncancellable lease for buildings and equipment, the Company is obligated to make annual rental payments of $40,000 in each of the next four fiscal years. At the conclusion of the lease period, the Company has the option of purchasing the leased assets for $20,000 (a bargain purchase option) or entering into another 5-year lease of the same property at an annual rental of $5,000.

2. *Pension Plan.* Substantially all employees are covered by the Company's pension plan. Pension expense is equal to the total of pension benefits paid to retired employees during the year.

3. *Patent.* The patent had an estimated remaining life of 10 years at the time of purchase. The Company's patent was purchased from Apex Corporation on January 1, 2007, for $250,000.

4. *Deferred Income Tax Payable.* The entire balance in the deferred income tax payable account arose from tax-exempt municipal bonds that were held during the previous fiscal year, giving rise to a difference between taxable income and reported net earnings for the fiscal year ended October 31, 2007. The deferred liability amount was calculated on the basis of past tax rates.

5. *Warrants.* On January 1, 2006, one common stock warrant was issued to stockholders of record for each common share owned. An additional share of common stock is to be issued upon exercise of ten stock warrants and receipt of an amount equal to par value. For the six months ended October 31, 2007, the average market value for the Company's common stock was $5 per share and no warrants had yet been exercised.

6. *Contingent Liability.* On October 31, 2007, the Company was contingently liable for product warranties in an amount estimated to aggregate $75,000.

Required

Review the preceding financial statements and related notes. Identify any inclusions or exclusions from them that would be in violation of generally accepted accounting principles, and indicate corrective action to be taken. Do *not* comment as to format or style. Respond in the following order:

1. Statement of Financial Position
2. Notes
3. Earnings Statement
4. Statement of Retained Earnings
5. General

P5-17 *Comprehensive: Comparative Income Statements* The accountant for the Tiger Company prepared comparative income statements for 2007 and 2008 as follows:

TIGER COMPANY
Comparative Statements of Income
For Years Ended December 31

	2008	2007
Sales	$3,500,000	$4,600,000
Cost of goods sold	(1,600,000)	(2,600,000)
Gross profit	$1,900,000	$2,000,000
Operating expenses	(1,300,000)	(1,500,000)
Operating income	$ 600,000	$ 500,000
Other items	(200,000)	100,000
Income before income taxes	$ 400,000	$ 600,000
Income tax expense (30%)	(120,000)	(180,000)
Net income	$ 280,000	$ 420,000

The auditor of Tiger Company reviewed the accounting records and income statements and discovered the facts described in items 1 and 2 below. All amounts incurred during 2007 and 2008 are included in the preceding statements.
1. Included in the category "Other Items" (along with other smaller miscellaneous items) were the following:
   a. A casualty loss of $60,000 in 2007 that was considered to be both unusual and infrequent
   b. A $150,000 loss in 2008 from an unusually large write-down of inventory because of obsolescence
   c. A $250,000 gain in 2007 that was considered to be both unusual and infrequent
2. On July 1, 2008, Tiger has announced its intention to sell its backscratcher division. This division is considered a component of the company. Operating results for this division are included in the company's overall operating results for 2007 and 2008, as shown previously, and are as follows:

	2008 (7/1–12/31)	2008 (1/1–6/30)	2007
Sales	$200,000	$400,000	$700,000
Cost of goods sold	300,000	320,000	290,000
Operating expenses	100,000	180,000	110,000

The division had not been sold by the end of 2008, so the company classified it as held for sale. The division consisted of the following items with book values and fair values on December 31, 2008:

Item	Book Value	Fair Value
Assets	$720,000	$620,000
Liabilities	450,000	510,000

Required
Prepare corrected comparative statements of income for 2008 and 2007 for the Tiger Company. Ignore earnings per share.

P5-18 *Net Income and Comprehensive Income* At the beginning of 2007, JR Company's stockholders' equity was as follows:

Common stock, $5 par	$35,000
Additional paid-in capital	49,000
Retained earnings	63,000

During 2007, the following events and transactions occurred:
1. The company earned sales revenues of $108,000. It incurred cost of goods sold of $62,000 and operating expenses of $12,000.
2. The company issued 1,000 shares of its $5 par common stock for $14 per share.
3. The company invested $30,000 in available-for-sale securities. At the end of the year, the securities had a market value of $35,000.
4. The company paid dividends of $6,000.

The income tax rate on all items of income is 30%.

Required
1. Prepare a 2007 income statement for JR Company which includes comprehensive income (ignore earnings per share).
2. Instead, prepare (a) a 2007 income statement (ignore earnings per share), and (b) a 2007 statement of comprehensive income.

3. Instead, prepare (a) a 2007 income statement (ignore earnings per share), and (b) a 2007 statement of changes in stock-holders' equity that includes comprehensive income.

P5-19 *Statement of Cash Flows* A list of selected items involving the cash flow activities of the Topps Company for 2007 is presented here:

a. Patent amortization expense, $3,500
b. Machinery was purchased for $39,500
c. At year-end, bonds payable with a face value of $20,000 were issued for $17,000
d. Net income, $47,200
e. Dividends paid, $16,000
f. Depreciation expense, $12,900

g. Preferred stock was issued for $13,600
h. Investments were acquired for $21,000
i. Accounts receivable increased by $4,300
j. Land was sold at cost, $11,000
k. Inventories increased by $15,400
l. Accounts payable increased by $2,700
m. Beginning cash balance, $19,400

Required
Prepare the statement of cash flows of the Topps Company for 2007.

P5-20 *Statement of Cash Flows* The following are several items involving the cash flow activities of the Mueller Company for 2007:

a. Net income, $68,000
b. Increase in accounts receivable, $4,400
c. Receipt from sale of common stock, $12,300
d. Depreciation expense, $11,300
e. Dividends paid, $24,500
f. Payment for purchase of building, $65,000
g. Bond discount amortization, $2,700
h. Receipt from sale of long-term investments at cost, $10,600

i. Payment for purchase of equipment, $8,000
j. Receipt from sale of preferred stock, $20,000
k. Increase in income taxes payable, $3,500
l. Payment for purchase of land, $9,700
m. Decrease in accounts payable, $2,900
n. Increase in inventories, $10,300
o. Beginning cash balance, $18,000

Required
Prepare the statement of cash flows of the Mueller Company for 2007.

P5-21 *Statement of Cash Flows: Direct Method* The following are various cash flows and other information of the Trainer Company for 2007:

a. Payments of interest, $5,000
b. Depreciation expense, $22,700
c. Receipt from sale of land, $3,100
d. Payments of income taxes, $6,200
e. Beginning cash balance, $16,500
f. Decrease in receivables, $7,400
g. Interest and dividends collected, $6,300

h. Payments of dividends, $5,200
i. Decrease in accounts payable, $8,600
j. Payments to suppliers and employees, $50,300
k. Receipt from issuance of common stock, $11,000
l. Collections from customers, $61,700
m. Payment for purchase of investments, $17,800
n. Net income, $73,400

Required
Using the direct method for operating cash flows, prepare the Trainer Company's 2007 statement of cash flows.

P5-22 *Comprehensive: Balance Sheet from Statement of Cash Flows* Gibb Company prepared the following balance sheet at the *beginning* of 2007:

GIBB COMPANY
Balance Sheet
January 1, 2007

Assets		Liabilities and Stockholders' Equity	
Cash	$ 1,000	Accounts payable	$ 4,000
Accounts receivable (net)	3,900	Salaries payable	1,100
Inventory	4,700	Total Liabilities	$ 5,100
Land	9,800	Common stock, $10 par	13,500
Buildings and equipment	68,900	Additional paid-in capital	11,200
Less: Accumulated depreciation	(14,100)	Retained earnings	44,400
Total Assets	$74,200	Total Liabilities and Stockholders' Equity	$74,200

At the end of 2007 Gibb prepared the following statement of cash flows:

GIBB COMPANY
Statement of Cash Flows
For Year Ended December 31, 2007

Net Cash Flow From Operating Activities		
Net Income	$ 5,400	
Adjustments for differences between income		
flows and cash flows from operating activities:		
Add: Depreciation expense	1,900	
Decrease in inventory	500	
Increase in salaries payable	400	
Less: Increase in accounts receivable (net)	(1,100)	
Decrease in accounts payable	(1,000)	
Net cash provided by operating activities		$ 6,100
Cash Flows From Investing Activities		
Payment for purchase of building	$(13,900)	
Receipt from sale of land	3,000	
Net cash used for investing activities		(10,900)
Cash Flows From Financing Activities		
Payment of dividends	$ (3,100)	
Receipt from issuance of bonds	5,700	
Receipt from issuance of common stock	4,500	
Net cash provided by financing activities		7,100
Net Increase in Cash		$ 2,300
Cash, January 1, 2007		1,000
Cash, December 31, 2007		$ 3,300

Additional information related to the statement of cash flows:
1. The long-term bonds have a face value of $6,000 and were issued on December 31, 2007.
2. The building was purchased on December 30, 2007.
3. The land was sold at its original cost.
4. The common stock which was sold totaled 300 shares and had a par value of $10 per share.

Required
Prepare a classified balance sheet for the Gibb Company as of December 31, 2007. (*Hint*: Review the information on the statement of cash flows and the balances in the beginning balance sheet accounts to determine the impact on the ending balance sheet accounts.)

CASES

COMMUNICATION

C5-1   Revenue Recognition
A friend of yours who is not an accounting major states, "I always thought that a company recognizes revenues at the time of sale. Recently, however, I heard that there are specific criteria for revenue recognition and that included in the criteria is something about realization (whatever that means). Furthermore, I also heard that revenue may be recognized before or after the sale. Please explain revenue recognition to me."

Required
Prepare a written response for your friend. Include an explanation of the revenue recognition criteria and realization. Also include a discussion of the reasons for, and alternative methods of, recognizing revenue in a period other than the period of sale.

C5-2 Expense Recognition

The FASB states that expenses are recognized according to three principles to properly match expenses against revenues.

Required

Write a concise report that identifies the three principles, briefly explains each, and provide examples of expenses that would be recognized under each principle.

C5-3 Cost, Expense, and Loss

AICPA Adapted You were requested to personally deliver your auditor's report to the board of directors of Sebal Manufacturing Corporation and answer questions posed about the financial statements. While reading the statements, one director asked, "What are the precise meanings of the terms 'cost,' 'expense,' and 'loss'? These terms seem sometimes to identify similar items and other times dissimilar items."

Required

1. Explain the meanings of the terms (a) "cost," (b) "expense," and (c) "loss" as used for financial reporting in conformity with generally accepted accounting principles. In your explanation discuss the distinguishing characteristics of the terms and their similarities and interrelationships.
2. Classify each of the following items as a cost, expense, loss, or other category, and explain how the classification of each item may change:
   a. Cost of goods sold
   b. Bad debts expense
   c. Depreciation expense for plant machinery
   d. Spoiled goods
3. The terms "period cost" and "product cost" are sometimes used to describe certain items in financial statements. Define these terms and distinguish between them. To what types of items does each apply?

C5-4 Results of Discontinued Operations

FASB Statement No. 144 dealt with, among other issues, reporting the results of discontinued operations. In the *Statement*, a section of the income statement was created and several terms were defined, including "component."

Required

Identify the elements of a company's results of discontinued operations section of its income statement. Define the previously listed term and explain how the elements of the section are computed if the company sells a component in the same accounting period that its management decided to sell the component.

C5-5 Extraordinary Items

APB Opinion No. 30 establishes two narrow criteria that must be met in order for an event or transaction to be classified as an extraordinary item.

Required

1. Identify and explain each criterion.

2. Develop examples of events that might be extraordinary to one company but not extraordinary to another, such as:
   a. An earthquake
   b. A flood
   c. A tornado
   d. A severe frost
   Justify your reasoning.
3. Explain how the following are reported on a company's income statement:
   a. An extraordinary item
   b. An event or transaction that does not meet both criteria

C5-6 Extraordinary Items

AICPA Adapted Morgan Company grows various crops and then processes them for sale to retailers. In the latter part of this year, Morgan had a large portion of its crops destroyed by a hail storm. Morgan has incurred substantial costs in raising the crops destroyed by the hail storm. Severe damage from hail storms in the locality where the crops are grown is rare.

Required

1. Where should Morgan report the effects of the hail storm in its income statement? Why?
2. How does the classification in the income statement of an extraordinary item differ from that of an operating item? Why? Do not discuss earnings per share requirements.

C5-7 Nonrecurring Items

AICPA Adapted Lynn Company sells a component of its business in the middle of the year. On the date of sale, the net proceeds received were less than the aggregate book value of the component's net assets. The component was operating at a loss from the beginning of the year.

In addition, Lynn had one of its manufacturing plants destroyed by an earthquake during the year. The loss is properly reported as an extraordinary item.

Required

1. Explain how Lynn should report discontinued operations of a component of its business on its income statement for this year. Do not discuss earnings per share requirements.
2. What are the criteria for classification as an extraordinary item?
3. Explain how Lynn should report the extraordinary loss from the earthquake on its income statement for this year. Do not discuss earnings per share requirements.

C5-8 Statement of Cash Flows

The president of a company, which is being audited for the first time, is concerned about all the unnecessary financial information the company is being required to disclose, and says, "We have always prepared only a balance sheet and an income statement. Surely these are enough. The only information anyone is interested in is how much we earned and what we have left. Now I am told we must prepare a statement of cash flows. What is this statement, what information does it provide, what are the major sections of the statement, and what is included in each section (under the indirect method)?"

Prepare a written response that answers the president's questions.

CREATIVE AND CRITICAL THINKING

C5-9 Capital Maintenance

At the beginning of 1995, the Hill family organized the Hill Corporation and issued 8,000 shares of stock to family members for $20 per share. During 1998, it issued an additional 1,600 shares of stock for $25 per share to family members. The 9,600 shares were held by the family until the corporation was liquidated at the end of 2007. At that time the corporate assets were sold for $600,000 and the $50,000 of corporate liabilities were paid off. The remainder was returned to stockholders. During the 13 years of operation the corporation had a volatile operating life. It started out slowly but then increased its activities in later years. It had operated in several industry segments, being quite successful in some, not so successful in others. It had survived a major earthquake, but not without incurring significant losses. The corporation paid out dividends of $100,000 during its lifetime.

You are a member of the Hill family who has just inherited a sizable fortune from one of your relatives. Although you were quite young during the operating life of the Hill Corporation, you are considering establishing and investing in a new corporation that operates in some of the same lines of business, provided that the corporation would be profitable. You have just received your undergraduate accounting degree and upon investigation find that, with the exception of the preceding information, all the corporate accounting records were destroyed in a recent fire. You have been told that these records were sketchy at best, but that a capital maintenance approach to income measurement might yield some useful information.

Required

Compute the lifetime income of the Hill Corporation and comment upon what additional information you would desire before making your investment decision.

C5-10 Accrual Accounting

AICPA Adapted Generally accepted accounting principles require the use of accruals and deferrals in the determination of income.

Required

1. Explain how accrual accounting affects the determination of a company's income. Include in your discussion what constitutes an accrual and a deferral, and give appropriate examples of each.
2. Contrast accrual accounting with cash accounting.

C5-11 Ethics and Sale of Operating Component

It is the end of 2007, and, as an accountant for Newell Company, you are preparing its 2007 financial statements. On December 29, 2007, the management of Newell decided to sell one of its major divisions, subject to some legal work that is expected to be completed during the first week in April 2008 (after the 2007 financial statements have been issued). During 2007, the division earned a small operating income that is just enough for the company to report "record earnings" for the year. However, the estimated fair value of the division at the end of 2007 is less than its net book value, so that management anticipates the component will be sold at a loss.

The president of Newell stops by your office and says to you, "You have been doing a fine job. Keep up the good work, because you are heading for a promotion in early 2009. Once we report the record earnings for 2007, our stockholders and creditors will be happy. Then I think our earnings for 2008 will be high enough so that the loss we expect to report in 2008 on the sale of the division will not look so bad." After the president leaves your office, you continue preparing the 2007 financial statements.

Required

From financial reporting and ethical perspectives, what information, if any, will you include about the upcoming sale of the division in the 2007 financial statements?

RESEARCH SIMULATIONS

R5-1   Researching GAAP

Situation

During 2007, one of the customers of Klote Company declared bankruptcy. This customer had been a major purchaser of Klote's products and had owed $40,000 on account to Klote (a material portion of its receivables) at the time of bankruptcy. As a result of the bankruptcy, Klote had to write off the entire $40,000 account receivable of the customer as a loss. The president of Klote is concerned about how to report this loss on the company's 2007 income statement. The president says, "Since this company that went bankrupt was a major customer, surely that is an unusual and infrequent event, and the $40,000 should be reported as an extraordinary loss. What do you think?"

Directions

Research the related generally accepted accounting principles and prepare a short memo to the president that summarizes how to report the $40,000 loss on Klote's 2007 income statement. Cite your reference and applicable paragraph numbers.

R5-2   Researching GAAP

Situation

The Kelly Company, a small corporation, is preparing its 2007 financial statements. At the end of 2007, the company purchased a building for $100,000, paying $20,000 as a down payment and signing an $80,000 mortgage. The president of Kelly is concerned about how to report this transaction on the company's statement of cash flows and has asked you to "look into this issue for me."

Directions

Research the related generally accepted accounting principles and prepare a short memo to the president that summarizes how to report this transaction on the 2007 statement of cash flows. Cite your reference and applicable paragraph numbers.

6

Additional Aspects of Financial Reporting and Financial Analysis

OBJECTIVES

After reading this chapter, you will be able to:

1 Describe an auditor's report.

2 Understand the meaning of an operating segment.

3 Describe the disclosures in a segment report.

4 Explain interim reporting.

5 Prepare an interim report.

6 Understand intracompany and intercompany comparisons (Appendix).

7 Prepare horizontal and vertical percentage analyses (Appendix).

8 Perform ratio analysis (Appendix).

Can You Hear Me Now?

The rapid advancement of information technology, particularly the Internet and related technologies, has dramatically changed the way information flows between companies and users of financial information. It also presents unique opportunities and challenges for the financial reporting community. By leveraging technology, companies can provide investors with an expanded menu of relevant and timely information, such as audio and video clips of conference calls, downloadable spreadsheets that allow interactive analysis, and customer access to company databases. While the use of the Internet for financial reporting presents great opportunities, many challenges exist with regard to the quality, security, and reliability of electronic-based financial information.

Recognizing that the Internet has changed the way companies communicate with investors, creditors, and others, many have begun to embrace a technology known as **XBRL** (e**X**tensible **B**usiness **R**eporting **L**anguage) that may revolutionize financial reporting. XBRL is an Internet language for business reporting that will make it easier for users to extract and analyze information contained in annual reports, press releases, and other communications by directing that information into the many analytical tools they use. A recent forecast by a Big Four accounting firm has identified XBRL as one of the technologies that will most affect business in the coming years. With the

Credit: ©Getty Images/PhotoDisc

Securities and Exchange Commission's decision to allow voluntary filing of supplemental financial information using XBRL, its usage will almost certainly grow. The use of technologies such as XBRL should lead to improvements in communication between companies and investors and has the potential to contribute significantly to enhancing the transparency of financial reporting.

FOR FURTHER INVESTIGATION

For a discussion of the use of technology in financial reporting, consult the Business & Company Resource Center (BCRC):

- XBRL A Work in Progress: Accountants are taking a leadership role in making a breakthrough in financial reporting. Jeff Stimpson, *The Practical Accountant*, 0032-6321, June 2004, v37, i6, p39(4).
- Tap into XBRL's Power the Easy Way: the Microsoft Office Tool for XBRL benefits all financial reporting participants. Jeffrey W. Naumann, *Journal of Accountancy*, 0021-8448, May 2004, v197, i5, p32(8).

A company's financial statements summarize its various financial activities and operations. External users analyze the information in these statements and relate it to other information for many reasons. Current stockholders, for example, are concerned about their investment income, as well as about the company's future profitability and stability. Some potential investors are interested in "safe" companies, with stable earnings and dividends, and limited or moderate growth. Others prefer companies with a trend for financial flexibility, rapid growth, and diversification into different lines of business. Short-term creditors are interested in a company's short-run liquidity—its ability to pay current obligations as they mature. Long-term creditors are concerned about the long-term security of their interest income. These are just a few of the users and uses of financial statements.

This book is designed for *preparers* of **general purpose** financial statements—statements that serve the needs of many types of external users. The information in these statements should be understandable to users who are reasonably knowledgeable about business and economic activities and who are willing to carefully study the information.[1] These general purpose financial statements are published in a corporation's **annual report** to its stockholders. Besides the financial statements and accompanying notes, an annual report includes many items. These include the auditor's report, the report of management, and management's discussion and analysis. Companies also prepare *interim reports*. Many companies include their financial statements and additional financial information on their web sites on the Internet. However, users should be careful because companies sometimes only provide summary information. Accountants must be familiar with these additional aspects of financial reporting.

Accountants, in the role of *preparers of financial statements*, do not themselves use the statements for investment and credit decisions. However, a better understanding of how external users analyze the data contained in the financial statements can lead to insights on how to improve that information. In some cases, companies may be required or may choose to present certain reports and analyses in their annual reports as an aid to external users, and accountants must know how to prepare these documents. Finally, accountants often are asked by management, lending institutions, and other groups to provide additional analyses of the financial statements.

We include in this chapter a discussion of (1) market efficiency, (2) the auditor's report, (3) the report of management, (4) segment reports, (5) interim reports, and (6) SEC reports. We also discuss various aspects of financial analysis, including an Appendix that covers financial analysis comparisons as well as a horizontal analysis, vertical analysis, and ratio analysis.

MARKET EFFICIENCY

During the past 20 years, research studies have examined the **efficient markets** hypothesis. Evidence from this research tends to show that (1) the prices of securities traded in the capital markets fully reflect all *publicly* available information, and (2) these prices are adjusted almost *immediately* based on new information and in an *unbiased* manner. That is, as soon as new information becomes publicly available, it is interpreted, analyzed, and incorporated into the market prices. New information about companies may include, for instance, earnings amounts, cash flow and accrual components of earnings, and differences in accounting methods across companies. Information about companies becomes publicly available in a variety of ways, including news releases reported on the Internet and in newspapers such as *The Wall Street Journal*, and in published management forecasts, interim financial statements, and annual reports. The market prices adjust in an

---

1. "Objectives of Financial Reporting by Business Enterprises," FASB *Statement of Financial Accounting Concepts No. 1* (Stamford, Conn.: FASB, 1978), par. 34.

immediate and unbiased manner because of the market communication system and the sophistication of investors (professionals such as security analysts and stockbrokers) who continuously gather, interpret, analyze, and process information. We show this process in the following diagram.

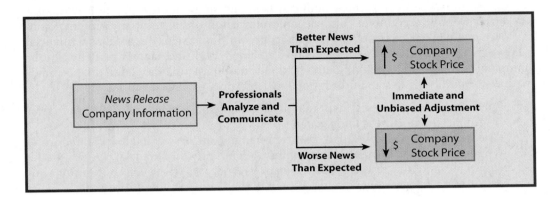

An efficient capital market means that an individual investor cannot use published information to earn an "abnormal" return on a security investment with a given amount of risk. That is, all securities with a similar amount of risk will yield approximately the same rate of return; only through the use of "insider information" can abnormal returns be obtained. On the other hand, some research appears to show that the market may not always be efficient. That is, the market may be mispricing the accrual component of earnings, thereby mispricing securities and enabling an astute investor to earn an abnormal return. If the efficient markets hypothesis is reasonably valid, how does the related research affect financial reporting and financial analysis, the topics of this chapter?

Since the market efficiently processes many types of public information, **full disclosure** of financial information is important for two reasons. First, full disclosure (so that the information becomes "public") helps to prevent the use of insider information by unscrupulous investors to earn abnormal returns. Second, full disclosure (at a reasonable cost) in the financial statements, the accompanying notes, or by other means helps the market operate efficiently and in a cost-effective fashion.

The efficiency of the capital markets does not detract from the use of various financial analysis techniques. In fact, one of the reasons why the markets tend to be efficient is because professional analysts interpret and analyze the information. Furthermore, financial analysis techniques are useful in situations where an investor is considering the investment potential of a company whose securities are *not* traded in an organized capital market, where a financial institution is considering a lending arrangement with a company, or where a company must be monitored to make sure that it is adhering to any financial restrictions set by various lending agreements. Finally, not all investors believe in the efficient market hypothesis; some continue to use financial analysis techniques to try to earn abnormal returns.[2]

---

2. For a further discussion of efficient capital markets research and its implications, see D. C. Nichols and J. M. Wahlen, "How Do Earnings Numbers Relate to Stock Returns? A Review of Classic Accounting Research with Updated Evidence," *Accounting Horizons* (December 2004), pp. 263–286; R. L. Watts and J. L. Zimmerman, "Positive Accounting Theory: A Ten Year Perspective," *The Accounting Review* (January 1990), pp. 131–156; T. R. Dyckman and D. Morse, *Efficient Capital Markets and Accounting: A Critical Analysis,* 2d ed. (Englewood Cliffs, N.J.: Prentice-Hall, 1986); and W. H. Beaven, *Financial Reporting: An Accounting Revolution,* 3rd ed. (Upper Saddle River, N.J.: Prentice Hall, 1998).

AUDITOR'S REPORT (OPINION)

Many investment and credit decisions are based on the information presented in a company's financial statements, which are prepared by and are the responsibility of its management. To provide an external perspective, most published financial statements are audited by an *independent* certified public accountant. In an **audit** of a public company, the certified public accountant conducts an examination of the company's internal control over its financial reporting, as well as its accounting system, records, and financial statements in accordance with generally accepted auditing standards. The Public Company Accounting Oversight Board sets these auditing standards. Based on this examination, the auditor issues an **audit report**, which expresses three opinions:

1 Describe an auditor's report.

1. That management's assessment that the company maintained internal control over its financial reporting is fairly stated
2. That the company maintained effective internal control over its financial reporting
3. That the company's financial statements present fairly the financial position of the company and the results of its operations and cash flows in conformity with accounting principles generally accepted in the United States of America.

The management of a company is responsible for maintaining internal control over the company's financial reporting. This means that the company

- has a reliable accounting system in which its transactions are appropriately recorded and stored,
- maintains records in reasonable detail that accurately reflect its transactions and events,
- has a process for providing reliable financial statements prepared according to GAAP, and
- has adequate procedures for preventing or detecting significant unauthorized acquisition, use, or disposal of its assets.

Before the company issues its financial statements, the company's management must evaluate the effectiveness of this internal control and must issue a report (we discuss this report in a later section) assessing this effectiveness.

As we noted earlier, the company's auditor then must express an opinion on whether the management's internal control assessment report is appropriate and whether the company did, in fact, maintain internal control over its financial reporting. To form a basis for issuing these opinions, the auditor must carefully examine (audit) the company's internal control system. The auditor must also audit (and issue an opinion on) the company's financial statements at the same time. This is necessary because the information obtained during the financial statement audit is relevant to the auditor's conclusion about the company's internal control over its financial reporting.

An audit report is *not* part of the financial statements because it is a report by the independent auditor. Nonetheless, it is considered an important item of information because external users place reliance on the report as to the fairness of the financial statements. The "standard" form of an auditor's report on *comparative* financial statements (often referred to as an *unqualified* report) is shown in Exhibit 6-1.[3] (The audit report of **The Coca-Cola Company** is shown in Appendix A at the end of this book.)

An audit report consists of five paragraphs. The first paragraph, known as the **introductory paragraph**, lists the financial statements that were audited, indicates that management's assessment of internal control was audited, declares that management is

---

3. Adapted from "An Audit of Internal Control Over Financial Reporting Performed in Conjunction with An Audit of Financial Statements," *Auditing Standard No. 2* (PCAOB, March 9, 2004), Example A-7.

Credit: ©Getty Images/PhotoDisc

responsible for the financial statements and related internal control, and asserts that the auditor is responsible for expressing three related opinions.

The second paragraph, known as the **scope paragraph**, describes what the auditor has done. Specifically, it states that the auditor has examined the financial statements and related internal control in accordance with generally accepted auditing standards, performed appropriate tests, and obtained an understanding of the company's internal control. The auditor does not examine all the information used to prepare the financial statements, but performs tests to evaluate the reasonableness of the information and related internal control. The auditor uses skills and judgment in deciding what evidence to examine, when to examine it, and how much to examine. As we see throughout this book, financial statements include many estimates made by management. An auditor also designs tests to evaluate the reasonableness of the assumptions and other factors used in the estimates. Because estimates are inherently imprecise, the auditor's involvement supports their reasonableness but does not guarantee their accuracy.

The third paragraph, known as the **definition paragraph**, defines internal control over financial reporting. It identifies the policies and procedures related to this internal control. The fourth paragraph, known as the **inherent limitations paragraph**, discusses the possibility that internal control over financial reporting may not prevent or detect misstatements of the financial statements. It also addresses the risk that current controls may become inadequate in the future.

The fifth paragraph, known as the **opinion paragraph**, gives the auditor's opinions. Like a doctor or lawyer, an auditor's opinion is based on professional judgment, not absolute certainty. When the financial statement opinion is unqualified, the auditor states that the financial statements present *fairly* in accordance with *generally accepted accounting principles* (GAAP). Thus the emphasis is not on presenting "fairly" in some general sense of the word but on presenting in accordance with GAAP. In other words, GAAP is defined as being fair. Therefore, the user of the financial statements must understand GAAP to be able to understand and interpret the statements. (In exceptional cases, the management of the company and the auditor may agree that a method other than GAAP provides more useful and "fairer" information about a transaction or event. In such a case, the non-GAAP method is fully disclosed.) The financial statement opinion also

---

EXHIBIT 6-1   Unqualified Audit Report

REPORT OF INDEPENDENT REGISTERED PUBLIC ACCOUNTING FIRM

We have audited the accompanying balance sheets of W Company as of December 31, 20X7 and 20X6, and the related statements of income, stockholders' equity and comprehensive income, and cash flows for each of the years in the three-year period ended December 31, 20X7. We also have audited management's assessment, included in the accompanying [title of management's report], that W Company maintained effective internal control over financial reporting as of December 31, 20X7, based on [Identify control criteria]. W Company's management is responsible for these financial statements, for maintaining effective internal control over financial reporting, and for its assessment of the effectiveness of internal control over financial reporting. Our responsibility is to express an opinion on these financial statements, an opinion on management's assessment, and an opinion on the effectiveness of the company's internal control over financial reporting based on our audits.

We conducted our audits in accordance with the standards of the Public Company Accounting Oversight Board (United States). Those standards require that we plan and perform the audits to obtain reasonable assurance about whether the financial statements are free of material misstatement and whether effective internal control over financial reporting was maintained in all material respects. Our audit of financial statements included examining, on a test basis, evidence supporting the amounts and disclosures in the financial statements, assessing the accounting principles used and significant estimates made by management, and evaluating the overall financial statement presentation. Our audit of internal control over financial reporting included obtaining an understanding of internal control over financial reporting, evaluating management's assessment, testing and evaluating the design and operating effectiveness of internal control, and performing such other procedures as we considered necessary in the circumstances. We believe that our audits provide a reasonable basis for our opinions.

A company's internal control over financial reporting is a process designed to provide reasonable assurance regarding the reliability of financial reporting and the preparation of financial statements for external purposes in accordance with generally accepted accounting principles. A company's internal control over financial reporting includes those policies and procedures that (1) pertain to the maintenance of records that, in reasonable detail, accurately and fairly reflect the transactions and dispositions of the assets of the company; (2) provide reasonable assurance that transactions are recorded as necessary to permit preparation of financial statements in accordance with generally accepted accounting principles, and that receipts and expenditures of the company are being made only in accordance with authorizations of management and directors of the company; and (3) provide reasonable assurance regarding prevention or timely detection of unauthorized acquisition, use, or disposition of the company's assets that could have a material effect on the financial statements.

(continued)

---

emphasizes that the statements comply with GAAP in all *material* respects; that is, the financial statements are free of material misstatements rather than precisely accurate. The paragraph concludes with the two opinions about management's assessment of the company's internal control over its financial reporting and whether this internal control was maintained by the company. An audit enhances the confidence of users because the auditor is an objective, independent expert who is knowledgeable about the company's business, internal control, and financial reporting requirements.

Note that there are three things that the audit report does *not* say. First, an unqualified opinion is not a "clean bill of health." The report does not, for example, endorse a company's policy decisions or its use of resources. Second, an unqualified opinion provides

---

EXHIBIT 6-1   (Continued)

Because of its inherent limitations, internal control over financial reporting may not prevent or detect misstatements. Also, projections of any evaluation of effectiveness to future periods are subject to the risk that controls may become inadequate because of changes in conditions, or that the degree of compliance with the policies or procedures may deteriorate.

In our opinion, the financial statements referred to above present fairly, in all material respects, the financial position of W Company as of December 31, 20X7 and 20X6, and the results of its operations and its cash flows for each of the years in the three-year period ended December 31, 20X7, in conformity with accounting principles generally accepted in the United States of America. Also in our opinion, management's assessment that W Company maintained effective internal control over financial reporting as of December 31, 20X6, is fairly stated, in all material respects, based on [Identify control criteria]. Furthermore, in our opinion, W Company maintained, in all material respects, effective internal control over financial reporting as of December 31, 20X7, based on [Identify control criteria].

[Signature]

[City and State or Country]

[Date]

---

no assurance of the future success of the company. Generally accepted auditing standards include procedures to be followed to examine the financial viability of the company. However, a company may suffer financial difficulty, or even failure, within a relatively short time of receiving an unqualified opinion, a situation that does not necessarily indicate that the audit was negligent. In other words, there is a difference between a business failure and an audit failure. Third, although an audit assesses a company's internal controls, an audit report does not provide an assurance that fraud has not been committed by a member(s) of the company unless such fraud is material. An audit is planned and performed with professional skepticism. The auditor assesses the risk of material misstatement and designs the audit to provide reasonable assurance of detection of significant errors or fraud. However, fraud that is concealed through forgery and collusion among the personnel of the company, especially management, may escape detection by the auditor. For large companies, such fraud would have to involve millions of dollars to be material.

In certain circumstances a qualified opinion, adverse opinion, or disclaimer of opinion may be expressed by the independent auditor in any of the three opinions. A *qualified* opinion states that except for the effects of the qualified item, the internal control was maintained or the financial statements present fairly the information in conformity with GAAP. An *adverse* opinion states that the internal control was not maintained or the financial statements do not present fairly the information in conformity with GAAP. A *disclaimer* of opinion states that the auditor does not express an opinion. These types of reports and opinions are discussed more fully in standard auditing books.

Audit Committee and Management's Report

Audit committees have existed for many years. The SEC requires all publicly-held companies to have an audit committee. An **audit committee is a group that has oversight over the financial reporting process of a company.** Since an auditor must closely communicate with a company's management, the possibility exists that the auditor will not maintain independence from this management. A lack of independence would reduce the reliability that external users place on the company's financial statements. Consequently, a primary responsibility of an audit committee is to help maintain auditor independence. Therefore, most audit committee members usually are "outside directors" (not officers or employees of the company). The audit committee acts as the liaison between the auditor and management. Although the duties of an audit committee vary among companies, generally an audit committee of a company: (1) oversees the internal control structure, (2) helps in the selection of accounting policies, (3) helps select the auditor, (4) approves all auditing services, (5) reviews the audit plan, (6) reviews suggestions by auditors concerning weaknesses in internal control, and (7) reviews the financial statements (both interim and annual) and audit report. Use of an audit committee enhances the credibility of a company's financial statements.

As we noted earlier, **the preparation and presentation of a company's financial statements are the responsibility of its management.** In the past, many external users have had the mistaken impression that because auditors reviewed the financial statements, the financial statements were the responsibility of the auditor. Then, if a company experienced financial difficulties that resulted in a "business failure," they erroneously thought this was an "audit failure." Consequently, officers of companies are encouraged to acknowledge their responsibilities regarding financial statements. Although not part of the financial statements, companies include a **"Management Report"** section in their annual report. In this report management acknowledges that it is responsible for preparing and presenting the financial statements. Furthermore, since sound internal control plays a vital role in these activities, the management of each public company is required to "certify" that

- the company's financial statements are not misleading and are fairly presented,
- it is responsible for designing and maintaining appropriate internal controls,
- it has evaluated the effectiveness of these internal controls and issued a report about the effectiveness of these controls, and
- it has communicated to the company's auditors and audit committee any significant deficiencies in these internal controls.

Finally, the report may identify the independent auditor's responsibilities. An example of the management report section of **Wachovia Corporation** is shown in Real Report 6-1. Note the references to management's responsibility, the auditor's role, internal control, and the reference to the auditor's reports.

Real Report 6-1 Management's Report

WACHOVIA CORPORATION AND SUBSIDIARIES

MANAGEMENT'S REPORT ON INTERNAL CONTROL OVER FINANCIAL REPORTING

Management of Wachovia Corporation and subsidiaries (the "Company") is responsible for establishing and maintaining effective internal control over financial reporting. Internal control over financial reporting is a process designed to provide reasonable assurance regarding the reliability of financial reporting and the preparation of financial statements for external purposes in accordance with U.S. generally accepted accounting principles.

Under the supervision and with the participation of management, including the principal executive officer and principal financial officer, the Company conducted an evaluation of the effectiveness of internal control over financial reporting based on the framework in Internal Control – Integrated Framework issued by the Committee of Sponsoring Organizations of the Treadway Commission. Based on this evaluation under the framework in Internal Control – Integrated Framework, management of the Company has

Continued

concluded the Company maintained effective internal control over financial reporting, as such term is defined in Securities Exchange Act of 1934 Rules 13a-15(f), as of December 31, 2004.

Internal control over financial reporting cannot provide absolute assurance of achieving financial reporting objectives because of its inherent limitations. Internal control over financial reporting is a process that involves human diligence and compliance and is subject to lapses in judgment and breakdowns resulting from human failures. Internal control over financial reporting can also be circumvented by collusion or improper management override. Because of such limitations, there is a risk that material misstatements may not be prevented or detected on a timely basis by internal control over financial reporting. However, these inherent limitations are known features of the financial reporting process. Therefore, it is possible to design into the process safeguards to reduce, though not eliminate, this risk.

Management is also responsible for the preparation and fair presentation of the consolidated financial statements and other financial information contained in this report. The accompanying consolidated financial statements were prepared in conformity with U.S. generally accepted accounting principles and include, as necessary, best estimates and judgments by management.

KPMG LLP, an independent, registered public accounting firm, has audited the Company's consolidated financial statements as of and for the year ended December 31, 2004, and the Company's assertion as to the effectiveness of internal control over financial reporting as of December 31, 2004, as stated in their reports, which are included herein.

Questions:

1. What does Wachovia Corporation say about its internal controls?
2. What do you think "reasonable assurance" means?

SECURE YOUR KNOWLEDGE 6-1

- Market efficiency, the relation between security prices and information, has implications for financial reporting, including the ability to earn abnormal returns based on reported financial information, as well as the form and content of financial statement disclosures.
- To provide assurance to external users about the quality of the financial information in the financial statements, auditors examine the effectiveness of a company's internal control over its financial reporting, as well as the company's accounting system, records, and financial statements.
- The audit report consists of an introductory paragraph, a scope paragraph, a definition paragraph, an inherent limitations paragraph, and an opinion paragraph.
- The "Management's Report" section of an annual report contains management's statement of responsibility for, and certification of, the company's financial statements and internal controls relating to the financial reporting process.

SEGMENT REPORTING

A company that has subsidiaries prepares its financial statements on a "consolidated" basis. That is, the accounting results of its various legal entities are *aggregated* into a set of financial statements for the entire economic entity (briefly discussed in Chapter 15).

Although investors and creditors know the importance of consolidated statements in evaluating overall company performance, the *disaggregation* of total financial data also can be important in their financial analysis.

The evaluations of risk and return are significant factors in investment and credit decisions. Risk may result from a number of factors including:

- the way that a company is organized and how its divisions are operated
- the nature of the economies in which the company operates
- the changing conditions in the geographic areas where the company operates
- the characteristics of its major customers

The profitability or return offered by a company also is affected by the same factors.

A company improves the financial analysis information on risk and return by presenting disaggregated financial information about its operating segments. The AICPA Special Committee on Financial Reporting considers operating segment reporting to be very important. It suggests that a company should provide disaggregated information on segments if they are critical "drivers" of the company's risks and opportunities. The information reported should be based on the way in which the company uses the information for internal reporting to operate its business.[4]

In light of the need for operating segment information, the FASB, in cooperation with its counterpart in Canada, issued **FASB Statement No. 131**, which requires that a company's financial statements include certain disaggregated information about its operations.[5] Exhibit 6-2 shows a diagram of the "breakdown" between a company's consolidated financial statements and its reportable operating segments. In the next sections we discuss how this breakdown (disaggregation) is done.

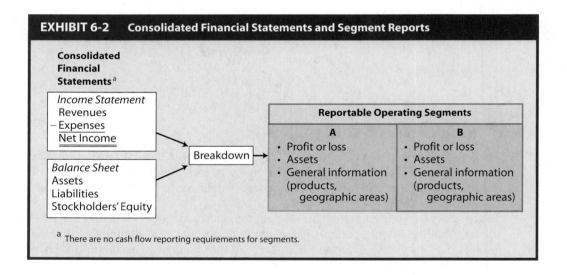

EXHIBIT 6-2   Consolidated Financial Statements and Segment Reports

Consolidated Financial Statements[a]

Income Statement
Revenues
− Expenses
Net Income

Breakdown

Balance Sheet
Assets
Liabilities
Stockholders' Equity

Reportable Operating Segments

A
- Profit or loss
- Assets
- General information (products, geographic areas)

B
- Profit or loss
- Assets
- General information (products, geographic areas)

[a] There are no cash flow reporting requirements for segments.

Reporting on Operating Segments

2 Understand the meaning of an operating segment.

A company's financial statements might be disaggregated in a number of ways, such as by products and services, geography, legal entity, or type of customer. The way a company identifies its operating segments for financial reporting is through the use of the

---

4.   "Improving Business Reporting—A Customer Focus," *AICPA Special Committee on Financial Reporting* (New York: AICPA, 1994), pp. 10 and 140.

5.   "Disclosures about Segments of an Enterprise and Related Information," *FASB Statement of Financial Accounting Standards No. 131* (Norwalk, Conn.: FASB, 1997), par. 1. Nonpublic companies, those whose securities are not traded publicly or that are not required to file financial statements with the SEC, are not required to report segment information.

"management approach." The management approach is based on the way a company's management organizes the company's segments for making operating decisions and for assessing performance. Thus, **an operating segment is a component of a company:**

1. **that engages in business activities to earn revenues and incur expenses,**
2. **whose operating results are regularly reviewed by the company's chief operating officer to make decisions about allocating resources to the segment and assessing its performance, and**
3. **for which financial information is available.**

Not all departments in a company are operating segments. For instance, a corporate headquarters normally does not earn revenues directly and is not an operating segment. Generally, an operating segment has a *segment manager* who is directly accountable for the segment's operating activities, and who maintains regular contact with the chief operating officer.

Reportable Segments

A company does not have to provide financial information about all its operating segments, however. Materiality determines whether or not a segment is a **reportable segment**—one whose operations are significant enough that its financial activities must be reported. **An operating segment is significant and is a reportable segment if it satisfies at least *one* of the three following tests:**

1. *Revenue Test.* Its reported revenues (including sales to external customers and intersegment sales) are 10% or more of the combined revenues of all the company's reported operating segments.
2. *Profit Test.* The absolute amount of its profit (loss) is 10% or more of the combined reported profits of all operating segments that did not report a loss.[6]
3. *Asset Test.* Its segment assets are 10% or more of the combined assets of all operating segments.

We discuss the terms "revenues," "profit (and loss)," and "segment assets" as applied in this *Statement* in the next section.

In addition to these tests, there is an overall materiality test. This test requires that the reportable segments must be a substantial portion of the company's total operations. That is, enough reportable segments must be disclosed so that their combined revenues are at least 75% of the entire company revenues. The remaining insignificant operating segments are combined and the segment information discussed in the next section is disclosed in an "all other" segment category. If a company has only one operating segment, it does not have disaggregated information to report, but it still must disclose the general information and company-wide information discussed in the next section.

Information Reported

The disclosure requirements of *FASB Statement No. 131* are quite detailed. We summarize them as follows:

3 Describe the disclosures in a segment report.

1. *General Information.* A company must (a) identify how it is organized (e.g., by product lines or geographic areas) and what factors were used to identify its operating segments, and (b) describe the types of products and services from which each reportable segment earns its revenues.
2. *Information about Profit (or Loss).* A company must report its profit (or loss) for each reportable segment. It must also disclose certain amounts used to compute each segment's profit (or loss). These amounts are the segment's (a) revenues (separated

---

6. If the combined losses of all operating segments that reported a loss exceed the combined profits as calculated earlier, the combined loss amount is used for this 10% test.

into sales to external customers and intersegment sales), (b) interest revenue and interest expense, and (c) depreciation, depletion, and amortization expense.[7]

3. *Information about Assets*. A company must report the total assets of each reportable segment. For these assets, a company also must disclose the total capital expenditures for long-lived assets of each reportable segment.

4. *Reconciliations*. A company must provide reconciliations of (a) the total of the reportable segments' revenues to the company's total revenues, (b) the total of the reportable segments' profit (or loss) to the company's pretax income from continuing operations, and (c) the total of the reportable segments' assets to the company's total assets. The revenues, profit (or loss), and segment assets of the "all other" segment category must be included in these reconciliations.

5. *Company-Wide Disclosures*. A company must disclose (a) its revenue from external customers for each product and service, and (b) information about geographic areas including (1) revenues from external customers in the United States and in individual foreign countries, and (2) total long-lived assets located in the United States and in all foreign countries. If a company's revenues from a single external customer are 10% or more of the company's total revenues, then the company must disclose this fact and identify the segment(s) reporting the revenues.[8]

A company is not required to follow a specific format in making the preceding disclosures. The FASB encourages a company to use a format that provides the information in the most understandable manner for its specific circumstances.

LINK TO ETHICAL DILEMMA

After preparing the segment disclosures required for your company (a large, multinational corporation), you have been confronted by the CEO about the classifications used. Her major concern is that the extremely profitable operations in the Middle East are reported separately from the significantly less profitable European operations. Given the political climate in the Middle East, the CEO is concerned that many investors may get the mistaken impression that the company is exploiting the political and economic situation that exists. Also, the CEO argues that, from a managerial viewpoint, since the Middle Eastern operations are headquartered and managed from London, the European and Middle Eastern operations should be considered one operating segment. She instructs you to combine the two segments and revise the disclosures. What is your response to this request?

Typically, a company will include its segment report and the related narrative discussion in the notes to the financial statements in its annual report. What a company includes in this segment report depends on the approach the company uses to evaluate

---

7. These are the amounts for the most common items included in a company's pretax income from continuing operations. If an operating segment is evaluated using a more complex "income" measure (or on an after-tax basis), then the company must also disclose any unusual items, equity method income, other significant noncash items, and extraordinary items (and income tax expense or benefit) for each reportable segment.

8. *FASB Statement No. 131, op. cit.,* par. 18–39.

its segment managers. For instance, a company may invest excess funds and borrow funds at the "corporate level" so that any interest revenue and interest expense are not attributable to segment activities. These items, frequently called "corporate interest revenue" and "corporate interest expense," are not assigned to each segment. Other types of corporate revenues, corporate expenses, and corporate assets related to the company's headquarters also are not assigned to each segment.

Thus, a company frequently prepares a worksheet (based on information from internal reports) that assigns its total sales revenues, cost of goods sold, operating expenses, and assets to each operating segment. Based on these assignments, the company performs the revenue, profit, and asset tests to determine the *reportable segments*. The required financial information of the reportable segments (and the "all other" segments) then is reported separately in the company's segment report. Because companies vary in their management approaches, it is not practical to illustrate all possible types of segment reports. We do, however, illustrate the way one hypothetical company (the Teal Company) discloses its disaggregated financial information in its annual report. The Coca-Cola Company has more extensive disclosures, which we show in Appendix A of this book.

For example, assume that on its 2007 income statement, the Teal Company reports sales of $3,800, cost of goods sold of $2,470, and operating expenses of $620, so that its pretax operating profit is $710 ($3,800 − $2,470 − $620). From this pretax operating profit, the company deducts interest expense of $80 to report pretax income from continuing operations of $630. The company also reports total assets of $19,000 on its December 31, 2007 balance sheet. The company's chief operating officer uses a segment's pretax operating profit to evaluate the segment manager; the company makes no intersegment sales, and interest expense is considered to be incurred at the corporate level. After preparing a worksheet to assign its segment revenues (sales), operating profits (sales minus cost of goods sold and operating expenses), and assets for segment reporting, Teal determines that it has three reportable segments (A, B, and C) and several insignificant operating segments. Teal also determines that it has $100 of general corporate expenses and $3,000 of general corporate assets.

Example 6-1 shows the schedule and narrative discussion that Teal Company includes in its annual report. Note that the revenues and profits of the segments are reconciled to the appropriate totals on the income statement. The segment revenues are reconciled to total sales. The segment profits are reconciled to the pretax income from continuing operations by deducting the general corporate expenses and corporate interest expense. Similarly, the segment assets are reconciled to the total corporate assets.

Conceptual Evaluation

FASB Statement No. 131 replaced *FASB Statement No. 14*, which was issued more than 30 years ago. *FASB Statement No. 14* focused on limited reporting of disaggregated information about a company's industry and geographic segments. During the 30-year period, external users found that they needed *more* and *better* disclosures. They argued that the disclosure of disaggregated information, along the lines that a company uses in its internal management decisions, is vital for investment and credit decision making. They felt that it is important for analysis and interpretation to be able to see the information "through the eyes of management." Furthermore, they argued that quarterly disaggregated information would be helpful in their decisions.

The FASB agreed and issued *FASB Statement No. 131*. It stated that the disaggregated reporting requirements are intended to provide information about the different types of company operations and the different economic environments in which it operates to help users (1) better understand the company's current and past performance, (2) better assess its prospects for future net cash flows, and (3) make more informed judgments about the company as a whole. It also requires the disclosure of certain segment information in a company's interim reports (discussed in the next section). In other words, the

EXAMPLE 6-1   **Segment Reporting**

TEAL COMPANY

Operating Segment Financial Results
For Year Ended December 31, 2007

	Reportable Operating Segments			All Other Segments	Total Results
	A	**B**	**C**		
Segment revenues (sales)	$ 300	$2,530	$ 370	$ 600	$ 3,800
Segment profit (pretax)	$ 70	$ 495	$ 105	$ 140	$ 810
General corporate expenses					(100)
Corporate interest expense					(80)
Pretax income from continuing operations					$ 630
Segment assets at December 31, 2007	$1,800	$9,400	$2,000	$2,800	$16,000
General corporate assets					3,000
Total assets at December 31, 2007					$19,000

NOTES: The company is organized into three major segments, A, B, and C (describe factors identifying segments). Operations in Segment A involve production and sales of (describe types of products and services). Operations in Segment B involve production and sales of (describe types of products and services). Operations in Segment C involve production and sales of (describe types of products and services). Total revenue by segment includes sales to external customers. The company makes no intersegment sales.

    Segment profit is total revenue less operating expenses. In computing segment profit, none of the following items have been deducted: general corporate expenses, corporate interest expense, or income taxes.

    Depreciation for Segments A, B, and C was $20, $300, and $40, respectively. Capital expenditures for the three segments were $100, $400, and $200, respectively. Segment assets are those assets that are used in the company's operations in each segment. General corporate assets are principally cash, temporary investments, and corporate headquarters.

    The company only makes sales in the U.S. Contracts with a U.S. government agency account for $600 of the sales to external customers of Segment B.

FASB expects that this disaggregation will provide more *relevant* information that will improve the *feedback value, predictive value,* and *timeliness* of a company's financial reports.

    The FASB adopted the "management approach" to disaggregated reporting to provide a viewpoint of the way a company manages its operations. Furthermore, it felt that since segment managers have a vested interest in the "quality" of the information used to evaluate them, the information is more likely to be accurate. In other words, the FASB expects the current disclosures to be more *reliable* by having more *representational faithfulness* and a higher degree of *verifiability.*

    There are at least three *comparability* issues, however. First, not all companies are organized in the same way. Therefore, one company's operating segment information may not be comparable to another's. Second, companies vary as to what price a segment is charged when it "purchases" goods from another segment (this is called "transfer pricing"). So one company's intersegment sales revenue may be based on market prices, while other companies may use "full costing" or "variable costing" transfer pricing methods. Finally, if a company allocates expenses in determining each segment's profit, this must be done on a "reasonable" basis. But what is reasonable to one company may not be reasonable to another. While these issues may result in reduced comparability across companies, there is increased *consistency* for each company. On balance, the FASB feels that the current requirements for disaggregated disclosures improve the financial reporting for external users by enhancing the *decision usefulness* of the information.

INTERIM FINANCIAL REPORTS

External users often want more frequent accounting information than that provided in the annual report. **Interim financial statements are reports for periods of less than a year.** Their purpose is to improve the *timeliness* of accounting information. These *interim reports* are issued by all publicly held companies on a quarterly basis (hence the term *quarterly financial statements*). One issue involving interim reports is the difficulty inherent in determining meaningful operating results for intervals of less than a year. Revenues of some businesses are seasonal and fluctuate widely across interim periods. Some companies incur heavy fixed costs in one interim period that benefit the operating activities in other periods. Other companies must estimate costs that will not be paid until later interim periods but that benefit the current one. Estimates also must be made of items such as inventories and income taxes if the interim reports are to be relevant and reliable.

In response to these concerns, the APB issued **APB Opinion No. 28.** This *Opinion* established the generally accepted accounting principles that apply to interim financial statements and specified the disclosures needed to present meaningful information for an interim period of less than a year. The Board was particularly concerned with reconciling two different views about interim periods. One view is that each interim period is a basic accounting period and the results of operations should be determined in the same way as if the interim period were an annual accounting period. The other view is that each interim period is an integral part of the annual accounting period. Thus, deferrals, accruals, and estimates made at the end of each interim period should consider the impact on the results of operations for the rest of the annual period. The Board concurred with the second view and concluded that **each interim period is viewed primarily as an integral part of an annual period.** Thus a company must continue to use the generally accepted accounting principles that it used in the preparation of its latest annual report. However, certain principles are modified for interim reporting purposes so that the results are more informative and articulate better with the annual report results. The FASB has issued one *Statement* (No. 131) and an *Interpretation* (No. 18) to expand and clarify various aspects of *APB Opinion No. 28.* The current generally accepted accounting principles focus primarily on the income statement items. We briefly summarize them in the following sections.

4 Explain interim reporting.

Revenues

A company must recognize revenues from products or services during an interim period in the same manner (when earned and realized) as during the annual accounting period. For example, when the percentage-of-completion method is used to recognize long-term construction contracts, revenues are recorded on the basis of the percent completed during that interim period. In cases where revenues are subject to seasonal variations, the company must disclose the seasonal nature of its activities and consider presenting supplemental information regarding revenues for previous periods.

Expenses

A company must match the expenses that are directly related to product sales or services against interim revenues in the period the revenues are recognized. These include items such as inventory costs, wages, and warranties. For inventories, a company generally must use the same inventory pricing methods (e.g., LIFO, FIFO, average) and make write-downs to market for interim reporting in the same way as it does for annual reporting, with the following exceptions:

1. A company that uses a periodic inventory system and estimated gross profit rates (or other estimation methods) to determine its cost of goods sold during interim periods must disclose the method used and any significant adjustments from reconciliation with the annual physical inventory.

2. If a company using the LIFO method has a temporary partial liquidation of its base-period inventory, but expects to replace that inventory by year-end, its cost of goods sold must include the expected cost to replace the liquidated inventory. Also, the inventory at the interim reporting date must *not* include the effect of the liquidation. Assuming rising prices, this requirement avoids the possibility of showing abnormally high interim period income due to LIFO "liquidation profits."

3. A company must recognize a permanent loss due to an inventory market decline by using the lower of cost or market procedures in the interim period during which the decline occurred. It must recognize any recovery of such a loss in a later interim period within the same year as a gain (not to exceed the previously recognized loss) in the later period. It does not have to recognize a temporary market decline in an interim period. (We discuss the recognition of losses using lower of cost or market procedures in Chapter 9.)

4. If a company uses a standard cost accounting system, it must follow routine annual procedures for all variances. The company must disclose any significant unplanned or unanticipated purchase price or volume variances in the interim period.

Expenses that are not directly associated with product sales (or services) are matched against revenues using a variety of methods. Expenses that affect the operating activities of more than one interim period are allocated among the interim periods based on an estimate of (1) time expired, (2) benefit received, or (3) activity associated with the periods. These allocations must be consistent with those used for annual reporting purposes. For example, accrued or deferred property taxes, advertising costs, depreciation charges, and uncollectible accounts (bad debts) expense are allocated among the interim periods. Expenses that relate only to the current interim period are allocated to that period. No arbitrary allocations are allowed. For example, office utilities, rent expense, and interest costs are expensed as incurred in the interim period. Gains and losses that occur in an interim period and that would not be deferred at year-end are recognized in that interim period. For example, a gain on the sale of land or a loss on the disposal of equipment is recognized in the interim period.[9]

Income Taxes

To present fairly the results of operations, at the end of *each* interim period a company must make its best estimate of the effective income tax rate expected to apply for the *entire* year. The effective rate includes the appropriate tax rate on *annual* income from continuing operations. In determining the rate, the company does not consider the income tax related to any items (such as extraordinary items) that are reported separately net of income taxes. Consequently, each quarter the company estimates its annual income from continuing operations and, based on this annual income, estimates its annual income taxes to derive an effective annual income tax rate. It then uses the effective rate to compute the income taxes related to income from continuing operations on a year-to-date basis. The amount of income taxes for the current interim period is the difference between the income tax computed on year-to-date income from continuing operations and the related income taxes reported on previous interim reports of the accounting period.[10] This procedure must be completed for each of the four interim periods; it follows the general principle of intraperiod tax allocation.

For example, assume Trull Corporation reported pretax income from continuing operations of $20,000 at the end of the first quarter and estimated its income tax on this income to be $5,220. (This estimate was made at the end of the first quarter, using the

---

9. "Interim Financial Statements," *APB Opinion No. 28* (New York: AICPA, 1973), par. 11–15.
10. "Accounting for Income Taxes in Interim Periods," *FASB Interpretation No. 18* (Stamford, Conn.: FASB, 1977), par. 9.

technique discussed previously.) The corporation now is preparing an interim income statement at the end of the second quarter for that quarter and the first six months. It determines that its pretax income from continuing operations for the second quarter is $26,000 and estimates it will earn $25,000 and $29,000 in each of the next two quarters, respectively. The corporate income tax rates are 15% on the first $20,000 of earnings and 30% on earnings in excess of $20,000. As we show in Example 6-2, based on an estimated effective income tax rate of 27%, Trull Corporation lists income tax expense of $12,420 for the first six months and $7,200 for the second quarter of operations.

EXAMPLE 6-2   Computation of Interim Income Taxes

1. Estimated Annual Income

First quarter	$ 20,000	actual income
Second quarter	26,000	actual income
Third quarter	25,000	estimated income
Fourth quarter	29,000	estimated income
	$100,000	estimated annual income

2. Estimated Effective Income Tax Rate

$$15\% \times \$20,000 = \$\ 3,000$$
$$30\% \times (\$100,000 - \$20,000) = \underline{\ 24,000}$$
$$\text{Estimated total tax} = \$27,000$$

$$27\% \text{ Effective income tax rate} = \frac{\$27,000 \text{ Estimated income tax}}{\$100,000 \text{ Estimated income}}$$

3. Estimated Income Tax for First Six Months

$$\$46,000 \times 27\% = \underline{\$12,420} \text{ estimated income tax on first six months' income}$$

4. Estimated Income Tax for Second Quarter

$12,420	estimated income tax on first six months of income
(5,220)	estimated income tax on first-quarter income
$ 7,200	estimated income tax on second-quarter income

Extraordinary Items and Discontinued Operations

Material extraordinary items and results of discontinued operations are reported (net of income taxes) in the usual manner in the interim period during which the events occurred. None of these items is prorated over the entire annual accounting period. Materiality, however, is determined on the basis of a relationship of the item to the estimated income for the entire *year* and not to the interim period results.

Earnings per Share

Earnings per share is computed for each interim period presented. In its simplest form, earnings per share is computed by dividing the net income by the average number of common shares outstanding for the accounting "period." The quarter (or year-to-date for longer periods) is considered the accounting period. The resulting earnings per share is reported on the face of the interim income statement. A breakdown of earnings per share related to income from continuing operations, results of discontinued operations, and extraordinary items is also disclosed.

Companies must be careful in disclosing comparative interim earnings per share because of differences arising from the short time periods. Shares issued in the second quarter result in a different number of outstanding shares than in the first quarter, making it difficult for a user to predict an annual earnings per share. Similarly, an extraordinary loss occurring in the fourth quarter affects earnings per share for that quarter and the year but does not affect the earnings per share listed in the first three quarters.

Preparation and Disclosure of Summarized Interim Financial Data

5 Prepare an interim report.

The accounting procedures a company uses to prepare its interim reports are similar to those for annual reports. Typically, a trial balance of the year-to-date account balances is prepared. The trial balance is entered on a worksheet, spreadsheet, or other working paper. Year-to-date adjusting entries are recorded on the working paper, after which the year-to-date financial statements are prepared. However, the interim accounting procedures differ in several respects from those completed at year-end.

First, for a company using a periodic inventory system, the ending inventory for the interim reports is usually based on an estimation technique rather than on a physical inventory. Thus, the gross profit method, retail inventory method, or some other estimation technique is used to estimate the ending interim inventory to be recorded on the working paper and reported in the financial statements. Second, the adjusting entries required at the end of the interim period to bring the accounts up to date usually are recorded only on the working paper and are not entered into the accounts. When this approach is used, only at the end of the year are the annual adjusting entries journalized and posted to the accounts.

Third, the accounts are not closed at the end of each interim period. Consequently, in an interim period subsequent to the first period, a company must be careful not to include amounts applicable to previous interim periods in the revenue and expense accounts. To avoid this problem, as we mentioned previously, a company typically prepares the interim income statement on a year-to-date basis and then eliminates the income statement results from any previous interim periods. For example, at the end of six months, a company would prepare a half-year income statement and then "back out" (subtract) the first-quarter income statement results to determine the second-quarter income statement. Finally, interim reports typically are not audited (except for SEC reports) because of the time and cost involved. However, auditing procedures have been developed for cases where an accountant is engaged to review a company's interim financial information.

While the APB recognized the advantages to users of more timely information in interim reports, it also felt that this advantage may be partially offset by the lesser amount of detail in the interim reports. Thus, it provided guidelines regarding *minimum* disclosure. When publicly held companies report interim summaries of financial information, the following data must be reported at a minimum: (1) sales or gross revenues, income taxes, extraordinary items (net of tax), and net income; (2) earnings per share for each period presented; (3) seasonal revenues, costs, and expenses; (4) significant changes in estimates of income taxes; (5) results of discontinued operations and material unusual or infrequent items; (6) contingent items; (7) changes in accounting principles[11] or estimates; and (8) significant changes in financial position (i.e., cash flows).

When a company presents the preceding information on a quarterly basis, it also provides current year-to-date information, along with comparable data from the previous year. Companies are encouraged to provide condensed balance sheet and cash flow data for the interim periods to assist external users in their analyses of *financial flexibility* and *liquidity*. When this information is not presented, a company must report any significant changes since the last reporting date in liquid assets, working capital, long-term liabilities,

---

11. *APB Opinion No. 28* established certain guidelines for reporting accounting changes in interim reports. These guidelines are not discussed in this chapter. As a result of difficulties in interpretation, *FASB Statement of Financial Accounting Standards No. 154*, "Accounting Changes and Error Corrections" (Norwalk, Conn.: FASB, 2005), clarified the reporting of such changes, and is discussed in Chapter 23.

and stockholders' equity. A company also must disclose selected information about each of its reportable operating segments. This information includes items such as segment revenues from external customers, intersegment revenues, segment profit or loss, and segment assets.[12] The SEC requires more extensive interim disclosures, as we discuss later in the chapter. Although interim financial statements are too lengthy to illustrate here, The Coca-Cola Company includes quarterly data at the end of the notes to it financial statements, as we show in Appendix A to this book.

SECURE YOUR KNOWLEDGE 6-2

- A company reports disaggregated financial information for any significant operating segments to help external users better understand the way in which it manages its operations.
- While no specific format is specified, extensive disclosures are required that include information on how a company is organized, the types of products and services of each reportable segment, the income and assets of each reportable segment, and how segment data reconciles to company-wide data.
- To provide more timely information, a company prepares interim financial reports that are viewed as an integral part of its annual reporting period.
- The preparation of interim financial reports requires the modification of certain generally accepted accounting principles to provide more meaningful reports that articulate with the annual report.

SEC REPORTS

The Securities and Exchange Commission (SEC) was created to administer various securities acts under powers provided by Congress in the Securities Act of 1933 and the Securities Exchange Act of 1934. The intent of Congress was to regulate the disclosure of all significant financial information provided by companies issuing publicly-traded securities (e.g., stocks and bonds). The SEC has the legal authority to prescribe accounting principles and reporting practices for these regulated (publicly-held) companies.

The SEC is a large organization with headquarters in Washington, D.C. Among the administrative offices, the **Office of the Chief Accountant** is important to accountants because it is responsible for providing the SEC with advice concerning accounting and auditing. The *Chief Accountant* helps to establish administrative policies regarding accounting matters. This office is directly responsible for *Regulation S-X* (which establishes the form and content of financial statements filed with the SEC), and is primarily responsible for the *Financial Reporting Releases* (which prescribe accounting principles for regulated companies). Among the divisions, the **Division of Corporation Finance** is also important to accountants. This division is responsible for assisting in the establishment of reporting standards (except those directly related to financial statements, which are the responsibility of the Chief Accountant) and the requirements for adherence to these standards by regulated companies. The division is also responsible for reviewing the financial reports submitted to the SEC by regulated companies. Since all these reports generally must be certified by a certified public accountant, an understanding of its activities is useful to accountants responsible for filing them.[13]

---

12. *FASB Statement No. 131, op. cit.*, par. 33.
13. For a more extensive discussion of the history and administrative responsibilities of the various segments of the SEC, see K. F. Skousen, S.M. Glover, and D.F. Prawitt, *An Introduction to Corporate Governance and the SEC* (Mason, Ohio: South-Western Publishing Company, 2005).

Numerous forms are required to be filed with the SEC by regulated companies. Two forms that are important to accountants are:

- *Form 10-K.* An annual report.
- *Form 10-Q.* A quarterly report of operations.

Form 10-K

Form 10-K is used to report a company's annual financial information to the SEC and is required to be filed within 60 days of a company's fiscal year-end. The SEC separates its required financial information in Form 10-K into two types: (1) information that must be reported *both* in annual reports filed with the SEC and annual reports issued to stockholders, and (2) information required to be filed only with the SEC.

Information of the first type includes items such as the financial statements, notes, management's discussion and analysis (MD&A), and market information on the company's common stock. This information can be included in Form 10-K by *reference* to the company's annual report issued to stockholders. Note, however, that all the information *must* be included in the annual report. Thus, for instance, many companies include an MD&A as well as three years of comparative financial statements in their stockholders' annual reports. Some regulated companies (e.g., The Coca-Cola Company) no longer publish a separate stockholders' annual report but only publish their Form 10-K. The second type of information (required to be filed only with the SEC) is considered to be important primarily to a limited and sophisticated group of users (e.g., security analysts). This type includes items such as directors and officers, executive compensation, legal proceedings, and voting matters.

Form 10-Q

Form 10-Q is used to report a company's quarterly financial information to the SEC and is required to be filed within 35 days of the end of each of the company's first three fiscal quarters. It contains similar disclosures to that of Form 10-K, but includes only quarterly and year-to-date information. The accounting principles established in *APB Opinion No. 28*, "Interim Financial Reporting," discussed earlier in the chapter, are used to prepare the Form 10-Q disclosures, so that this financial information is very similar to that provided in a company's quarterly report to stockholders. However, it may be more extensive because the SEC *requires* the presentation of comparative interim financial statements.

XBRL Supplemental Information

All companies are required to file Form 10-K and Form 10-Q electronically according to the EDGAR requirements. In addition, the SEC allows companies to voluntarily submit some or all of this electronically-transmitted financial information in XBRL (eXtensible Business Reporting Language). A financial report prepared using the XBRL format includes an identifying "tag" for each individual item (e.g., sales revenue, cost of goods sold) in the report. This allows computer software to recognize and extract items of information in the report in "real time" for various analytical purposes. For instance, the software can provide external users with virtually instantaneous comparisons of a company's operating results for the current year with its results from previous years or with the results of other companies. Although XBRL reporting is in its early stages, it is likely that more financial information will be transmitted to external users under this format. For more details on XBRL see http://www.xbrl.org.

LINK TO INTERNATIONAL DIFFERENCES

International accounting standards differ somewhat from U.S. accounting standards for both segment reporting and interim reporting. Segment reporting is required under international accounting standards, but reportable segments are identified differently than under U.S. standards. Under international standards, segments are reported as either business segments or geographic segments. A business segment is a component of a company that provides goods or services that are different from other business segments as to risks and returns. A geographic segment is a component of a company that provides goods or services within a particular economic environment that are different from other geographic segments as to risks and returns. International and U.S. standards require a company to make similar segment disclosures (e.g., segment profit or loss, revenues, assets), but there are some differences in measurement and reporting requirements. For instance, a company (1) measures its segment profit (or loss) under international standards in the same way as it reports its consolidated income (as opposed to the management approach in the United States) and (2) includes in segment revenues and segment assets any reasonably allocated items (as opposed to the management approach). International standards also require a company to disclose each segment's liabilities and encourages segment cash flow disclosures.

International accounting standards provide guidance for what to include in an interim report, but do not specify which companies must publish them or how frequently. Public companies, however, are encouraged to provide at least half-year reports. If a company issues an interim report, under international standards it is required to include a condensed balance sheet, income statement, cash flow statement, statement of changes in equity, and selected explanatory notes. However, international standards differ from U.S. standards in that they do not allow (1) the allocation of expenses between interim periods, (2) the deferral of manufacturing variances that are expected to be offset in a later interim period, or (3) the deferral of a temporary market decline in inventory that is expected to be recovered in a later interim period.

APPENDIX: FINANCIAL ANALYSIS COMPARISONS

This Appendix deals with various tools of financial analysis. The following diagram depicts financial analysis and its related tools that we discuss in later sections.

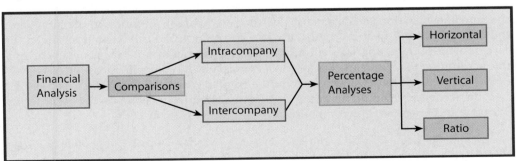

Before we discuss preparing these financial analyses, it is helpful to know how this information is used. The decision process of external users may be summarized as follows:

1. External users examine the current financial reports for information important to them.

2. They look for criteria that will assist them in analyzing the reports and making decisions; usually, although not exclusively, they make comparisons with a particular company's past results as well as with similar companies within the same or related industries.
3. They make their decision.
4. They evaluate their decision based on feedback.

INTRACOMPANY COMPARISONS

6 Understand intracompany and intercompany comparisons.

One method of evaluating a company's current financial performance and condition is to compare them with the company's past results. This is called **intracompany comparison.** An important issue in this type of comparison is the evidence of **trends**—indications that a company's performance is stable, improving, or deteriorating, not only in the short run but also in the longer run. Most companies now present at least 2 years of comparable data in their financial statements. Many also include 5-, 10-, or 15-year summaries of key financial data.

A critical point to remember when preparing financial analysis information for use in intracompany comparisons is the need for **consistency** over time. Whether a company prepares operating segment information, interim data, percentage analyses, ratios, or SEC reports, each year's information should be consistently presented so that valid and reliable comparisons may be made.

INTERCOMPANY COMPARISONS

A second method of evaluation is to compare a company's performance with that of competitors, with the industry as a whole, or with the results in related industries. This is known as **intercompany comparison** and may be made for a single period or for several past periods. A competitor's financial information may be obtained from its respective financial statements. Information on the performance of the industry as a whole or of related industries may be based on compilations of financial information by such financial analysis companies as Moody's Investors Service, Standard and Poor's, Dun and Bradstreet, and Robert Morris and Associates. These companies not only provide information from annual reports but also publish periodic updates and supplements. Other organizations and trade associations supply similar information on a more selective basis. Much of this information is available on the Internet.

A user preparing financial analysis information for an intercompany comparison is concerned not only with consistency over time, but also with comparability of data across companies. A preparer of a company's financial information cannot control the consistency of data across other companies. Nevertheless, the preparation of this data should take into consideration such factors as the use of comparable numbers in the numerator and denominator of financial ratios, the use of common industry classifications in the development of operating segment results, and the impact of different generally acceptable accounting practices (for example, LIFO versus FIFO for inventory costing or accelerated versus straight-line depreciation) on the results. When preparing financial analysis data, an accountant should be aware that this information may be used in both intracompany and intercompany comparisons.

PERCENTAGE ANALYSES

7 Prepare horizontal and vertical percentage analyses.

The comparison of a company's operating results and financial position across several periods or with other companies may be enhanced by converting the monetary amounts in the financial statements to percentage relationships. The three types of analyses that use percentage relationships are called horizontal analysis, vertical analysis, and ratio analysis. We discuss the first two in this section and discuss ratio analysis in the following section.

Horizontal Analysis

In horizontal analysis, a company shows the changes in its operating results and financial position *over time* in percentages as well as in dollars. This method is usually used with the income statement. Horizontal analysis sometimes is used for balance sheet comparisons. It is used less frequently in the analysis of the statement of cash flows because many items do not recur consistently on this statement.

When only two years of comparative data are disclosed in percentages, the earlier year is used as the base year and the amount of change in each item is shown as a percentage of that item's base-year amount. When data are shown for more than two years, two alternative approaches may be used. In the first approach, the preceding year is used as the base year for each later year, and the percentage change from year to year is shown. Column (1) of Example 6-3 shows this "year-to-year" approach for the Cooper Company. Although this approach identifies and highlights year-to-year changes, a user cannot easily analyze the relative changes over an extended period. Because different years are used as bases, it is not possible to add the changes from year to year to determine the total cumulative change. For this type of analysis, a second approach may be used. Here, the *initial* year is used as the base year, and the cumulative results from later years are compared with the initial year to determine the cumulative percentage changes. Column (2) of Example 6-3 shows this "base-year-to-date" approach for the Cooper Company. With this approach, if a weak initial year is selected, the cumulative percentage changes appear stronger than may be warranted.

Whenever horizontal analysis is used, a company must be be careful in computing and interpreting percentage changes. If a base figure is zero or negative, although an *amount* of change may be shown, *no percentage* change may be validly expressed. Also, in cases where changes are shown as percentages, no vertical addition or subtraction of the percentages (as we discuss in the next section) can be made because the percentage changes result from the use of different bases. Finally, for items with small base amounts, a relatively small dollar change may result in a very high percentage change, thus potentially making the item more significant than may be warranted.

Vertical Analysis

In vertical analysis, a company shows the monetary relationships between items on its financial statements for a particular *period* in percentages as well as in dollars. When vertical analysis is used for comparisons of financial statements from several periods, trends or changes in the relationships between items are more easily identified. Financial statements shown only in percentages are referred to as **common-size statements.**

Vertical analysis may be used with the income statement, retained earnings statement, balance sheet, or the statement of cash flows. In the case of the income statement, net sales usually are expressed as 100% and all other components are expressed accordingly. On the balance sheet, total assets represent 100%; on the retained earnings statement, beginning retained earnings is 100%; and for the statement of cash flows, the increase in cash is usually expressed as 100%. Examples 6-4 and 6-5 show vertical analyses for the Cooper Company.

Both vertical and horizontal analysis may be used with interim reports and reports of the results of operating segments. Vertical and horizontal analyses also are used with ratio analysis.

RATIO ANALYSIS

Another form of percentage analysis involves the use of ratios. Ratios involve the division of one or more items on the financial statements by another related item or items. They are frequently used to evaluate the financial aspects (i.e., return, risk, financial flexibility, liquidity, and operating capability) of a company. Many ratios have become standardized. They are

EXAMPLE 6-5 **Vertical Analysis (Balance Sheet)**

COOPER COMPANY

Comparative Condensed Balance Sheets
December 31, 2007 and 2008

	2008		2007	
	Amount	**Percent**	**Amount**	**Percent**
Cash	$ 3,900	3.0	$ 4,800	4.3
Receivables (net)	7,600	5.9	8,600	7.7
Inventories	8,900	6.9	10,100	9.0
Prepaid items	1,000	.8	1,200	1.1
Total current assets	$ 21,400	16.6	$ 24,700	22.1
Noncurrent assets (net)	107,800	83.4	87,300	77.9
Total Assets	$129,200	100.0	$112,000	100.0
Accounts payable	$ 5,000	3.9	$ 6,600	5.9
Other current liabilities	6,200	4.8	6,400	5.7
Total current liabilites	$ 11,200	8.7	$ 13,000	11.6
Long-term liabilities (12%)	25,000	19.3	20,000	17.9
Total liabilities	$ 36,200	28.0	$ 33,000	29.5
Preferred stock, 8%, $100 par*	$ 15,000	11.6	$ 15,000	13.4
Common stock, $5 par†	27,000	20.9	24,000	21.4
Additional paid-in capital	14,600	11.3	8,000	7.1
Retained earnings	36,400	28.2	32,000	28.6
Total stockholders' equity	$ 93,000	72.0	$ 79,000	70.5
Total Liabilities and Stockholders' Equity	$129,200	100.0	$112,000	100.0

*The 150 shares of preferred stock are noncumulative and have a liquidation value of $140 per share.
†December 31, 2008 market price is $14.25 per share.

Stockholder Profitability Ratios

Stockholder profitability ratios are used to evaluate how effective a company has been in meeting the profit (i.e., return) objectives of its owners. Example 6-6 shows several stockholder profitability ratios, along with the calculations for the Cooper Company. We discuss each ratio in the following sections.

Earnings Per Share

Earnings per share is probably the most frequently cited ratio in a financial analysis. It is considered important enough to be a required disclosure on the face of a company's income statement. As its name indicates, it shows the amount of earnings attributable to each share of common stock held by stockholders.

Price/Earnings

Although not precisely a stockholder profitability ratio, the price/earnings ratio is used by actual and potential stockholders to evaluate the attractiveness of an investment in the stock of a company. A higher price/earnings ratio compared to other similar companies may indicate that investors perceive expansion potential for the company. Be careful, however, that the comparison is made to other "similar" companies. The price/earnings ratios for companies in "growth" industries, such as the electronics industry, are likely to be higher than for, say, companies in the automobile or steel industries. Interpretation of the ratio also is affected by investors' perceptions of the company's quality and trend of earnings, relative risk, use of alternative accounting methods, and other factors. Earnings per share based on income from continuing operations usually is used as the denominator.

Dividend Yield

The market value of a company's stock represents the value a stockholder must forgo to continue holding the security. Stockholders are interested in their individual rates of return based on the actual dividends received as compared with the ending market price (or market price on another particular date) of the stock. The dividend yield provides this information. The dividend yield, combined with the percentage change in the market price of the stock held during the period, is the total annual return on the stockholders' investment.

EXAMPLE 6-6	Stockholder Profitablility Ratios	
Ratio	**Formula**	**Calculations (2008)**
1. Earnings per Share	$\dfrac{\text{Net Income} - \text{Preferred Dividends}}{\text{Average Common Shares Outstanding}}$	$\dfrac{\$11,000 - \$1,200}{5,400} = \$1.81$
2. Price/Earnings	$\dfrac{\text{Market Price per Common Share}}{\text{Earnings per Share}}$	$\dfrac{\$14.25}{\$1.81} = 7.9 \text{ times}$
3. Dividend Yield	$\dfrac{\text{Dividends per Common Share}}{\text{Market Price per Common Share}}$	$\dfrac{\$1.00}{\$14.25} = 7.0\%$

Company Profitability Ratios

Company profitability ratios are used to evaluate how effective a company has been in meeting its overall profit (return) objectives, particularly in relation to the resources invested. Example 6-7 shows several overall company profitability ratios, along with the calculations for the Cooper Company. We discuss each ratio in the following sections.

EXAMPLE 6-7	Company Profitability Ratios	
Ratio	**Formula**	**Calculations (2008)**
1. Profit Margin	$\dfrac{\text{Net Income}}{\text{Net Sales}}$	$\dfrac{\$11,000}{\$130,000} = 8.5\%$
2. Return on Total Assets	$\dfrac{\text{Net Income} + \text{Interest Expense (net of tax)}}{\text{Average Total Assets}}$	$\dfrac{\$11,000 + (\$3,000 \times 0.7)}{\dfrac{\$129,200 + \$112,000}{2}} = 10.9\%$
3. Return on Stockholders' Equity	$\dfrac{\text{Net Income}}{\text{Average Stockholders' Equity}}$	$\dfrac{\$11,000}{\dfrac{\$93,000 + \$79,000}{2}} = 12.8\%$

Profit Margin

The relationship of net income to net sales commonly is used to evaluate a company's efficiency in controlling costs and expenses in relation to sales. That is, the lower a company's expenses relative to sales, the higher the sales dollars remaining for other activities.

If a company has nonrecurring items of income, income from continuing operations typically is used as the numerator. The reporting of segment information permits a variation of this ratio to be computed for the major operating segments of a company. For each reportable segment, the profit margin *before* income taxes can be computed by dividing the segment's profit by its revenues. A weakness of the ratio is that it does not consider the investment (the total assets or stockholders' equity) necessary to generate the sales and income. A "return on investment" ratio (either total assets or stockholders' equity) overcomes this weakness.

Return on Total Assets

The amount of net income earned in relation to total assets indicates how efficiently a company uses its economic resources. When a comparison is made of the return on total assets of one company to the return of another company, the age of the assets of each company should be considered. That is, the return on a company's assets will get higher as the assets become older because the denominator will decrease each year due to the increase in accumulated depreciation. Also, since prices tend to increase due to inflation, a company that uses recently purchased assets will tend to show a relatively lower return on these assets. Typically, extraordinary items and results of discontinued operations are excluded from the numerator because they are the result of infrequent events not directly related to a company's ongoing operations. Interest expense (after income taxes)[14] is added back to net income because it is a financial cost paid to creditors to acquire the assets as opposed to a cost of generating sales. Since net income is earned over the entire period, the *average* total assets (beginning plus ending assets divided by two) for the period are used as the denominator. Reporting the results of segments permits the computation of a variation of this ratio for the major operating segments of a company. For each reportable segment, the *pretax* return on the segment's assets can be computed by dividing the segment's profit by its total assets.

Return on Stockholders' Equity

Net income may be divided by stockholders' equity to show the residual return on the owners' equity. When this return is higher than the return on total assets, the company has favorable financial leverage (that is, it is trading on the equity, which we discuss later). A weakness of the return on stockholders' equity ratio (as well as the return on total assets ratio), however, is that it does not consider the current value of the capital invested, since financial statements are based primarily on historical cost. Extraordinary items and other nonrecurring items usually are excluded from the numerator, and *average* stockholders' equity typically is used for the denominator. Some companies deduct preferred dividends from net income and use only common stockholders' equity in this ratio. They argue that preferred stock is more similar to long-term liabilities than it is to common stock.

Liquidity Ratios

Liquidity ratios are used to evaluate a company's ability to meet its currently maturing financial obligations. These ratios generally involve all or most of the components of a company's working capital, its current assets less its current liabilities. Current assets include cash, temporary investments, receivables, inventories, and prepaid items. Current liabilities include items such as accounts payable from the normal acquisition of goods

---

14. After-tax interest expense is usually computed by multiplying the pretax interest expense by 1 minus the effective income tax rate. In the case of the Cooper Company, the effective tax rate approximates 30% ($4,700 ÷ $15,700), so that the $3,000 pretax interest expense is multiplied by 70% (1 − 0.30) to determine the after-tax results.

or services; accruals for wages, taxes, and interest payable; short-term notes payable; advance collections of unearned revenues; and the currently maturing portion of long-term debt. Example 6-8 shows the common liquidity ratios, along with the calculations for the Cooper Company. We discuss each ratio in the following sections.

EXAMPLE 6-8	Liquidity Ratios	
Ratio	**Formula**	**Calculations (2008)**
1. Current Ratio	$\dfrac{\text{Current Assets}}{\text{Current Liabilities}}$	$\dfrac{\$21,400}{\$11,200}$ = 1.91 times
2. Acid-Test Ratio	$\dfrac{\text{Quick Assets}}{\text{Current Liabilities}}$	$\dfrac{\$11,500}{\$11,200}$ = 1.03 times

Current Ratio

The current ratio probably is the most commonly used ratio to evaluate a company's short-run liquidity. Sometimes it is referred to as the *working capital ratio*. It is considered to be a better indicator of a company's current debt-paying ability than simply working capital. This is because working capital shows only the absolute difference between a company's current assets and its current liabilities. By computing the current ratio, the *relative* relationship between the current assets and current liabilities is known, so that comparisons of different-sized companies can be made. In the past, as a "rule of thumb," a 2.0 current ratio was considered satisfactory. Today, however, more attention is given to (1) industry practices, (2) the length of a company's operating cycle, and (3) the mix of the current assets. Too *high* a current ratio relative to similar companies within the same industry may indicate inefficient management of current assets. The shorter a company's operating cycle, the less likely it is to need much working capital, or as high a current ratio, to operate efficiently. A company's operating cycle is evaluated through the use of activity ratios, which we discuss in the next section. The proportion of different items that make up the total current assets is referred to as the "mix" of the current assets. This mix has an effect on how quickly the current assets can be converted into cash. As an extreme, a high proportion of prepaid items in current assets may indicate a weak liquidity position, since prepaid assets are consumed within the operating cycle rather than converted back into cash. The mix of a company's current assets and the impact on its liquidity are considered in the acid-test ratio.

Acid-Test Ratio

The acid-test or *quick* ratio is a more severe test of a company's short-term debt-paying abilities. In this ratio, only the current assets that may be easily converted into cash are used in the calculation. These items, referred to as **quick assets**, generally consist of cash, temporary investments, accounts receivable, and short-term notes receivable. Inventories are excluded because their salability is uncertain and they frequently are sold on credit; thus they may not be quickly converted into cash. Prepaid items are excluded because they are not convertible into cash. The acid-test ratio highlights potential liquidity problems because of an inadequate mix of current assets. For instance, the use of this ratio usually reveals the lower liquidity of a company having a significant amount of inventories that would not be shown in the current ratio. However, be careful to consider which assets to include. Even though inventories usually are excluded from the acid-test ratio, sometimes these are, in fact, more liquid than certain receivables. A quick ratio of 1.0 used to be a general rule of thumb. Today, as with the current ratio, greater consideration is given to such factors as industry practices and the company's typical operations.

Activity Ratios

Activity ratios are used to evaluate the liquidity of certain current assets by estimating the length of various segments of a company's operating cycle. The ratios are indicators of the efficiency with which the company uses its short-term economic resources. Example 6-9 shows the three common activity ratios, along with the calculations for the Cooper Company. We discuss each ratio in the following sections.

EXAMPLE 6-9   **Activity Ratios**

Ratio	Formula	Calculations (2008)
1. Inventory Turnover	$\dfrac{\text{Cost of Goods Sold}}{\text{Average Inventory}}$	$\dfrac{\$74,100}{\dfrac{\$8,900 + \$10,100}{2}} = 7.8$ times or 47 days*
2. Receivables Turnover	$\dfrac{\text{Net Credit Sales}}{\text{Average Net Receivables}}$	$\dfrac{\$130,000 \times 0.70}{\dfrac{\$7,600 + \$8,600}{2}} = 11.2$ times or 33 days*
3. Payables Turnover	$\dfrac{\text{Cost of Goods Sold}}{\text{Average Accounts Payable}}$	$\dfrac{\$74,100}{\dfrac{\$5,000 + \$6,600}{2}} = 12.8$ times or 29 days*

*365-day business year.

Inventory Turnover

A company's operating cycle is the length of time it takes to invest in inventory, make credit sales, and convert the receivables into cash. Dividing a company's cost of goods sold for the accounting period by its average inventory indicates the number of times the inventory is "turned over" or sold during that period. As a general rule, the higher the inventory turnover, (1) the more effective the company is in its operations, (2) the lesser the amount that must be tied up in inventory, and (3) the shorter the operating cycle necessary to replenish cash. A company with a higher inventory turnover is usually more efficient and is also minimizing the chance of having obsolete inventory. A smaller investment in inventory means the company either needs less capital or can invest its capital in other earnings activities. However, *too* high an inventory turnover may indicate lost sales as a result of insufficient inventory on hand.

The inventory turnover often is divided into the number of operating days in a "business" year (365, 300, or 250, depending on the industry) so that the inventory segment of the operating cycle may be shown in days. Be careful in developing the average inventory; seasonal factors can affect this average substantially. Also, when a comparison is made of one company to another, both companies should be using similar inventory costing methods. In periods of rising prices, without an adjustment, no valid comparison of inventory turnovers can be made when one company is using FIFO and another company is using LIFO. This is because the company using LIFO will show a higher cost of goods sold and lower inventory than the FIFO company, even though their operations are similar. Therefore, the amounts for the company using LIFO must be adjusted to FIFO, as we discuss in Chapter 8.

Receivables Turnover

After a company has sold its inventory on credit, the company collects the receivables to complete its operating cycle. Dividing net credit sales by average net trade receivables indicates how many times receivables are "turned over" or collected each period. The receivables turnover is an indicator of how efficiently the company collects its receivables and converts them back into cash. As a general rule, the higher the turnover the better, because the company has less cash tied up in receivables, collects this cash at a faster pace, and usually has fewer uncollectible accounts. When net credit sales information is not available, net sales are used in the calculations. Be careful to consider seasonal factors and to exclude nontrade receivables in developing the average receivables.

The receivables turnover often is divided into the number of days in the business year to show the average collection period in days. A comparison of a company's average collection period to the days in its typical credit terms gives an indication of how aggressively the company's credit department collects overdue accounts.

Payables Turnover

The payables turnover ratio measures the number of times accounts payable turn over during the year. The higher the turnover, the shorter the time between the purchase of inventory and the cash payment. However, too high a turnover may indicate that the company is making payments too quickly and losing the "free" credit provided by accounts payable. Alternatively, if a company's payables turn over more slowly than the average for its industry, it may indicate that the company is having financial difficulty. It may be preferable to compute the ratio by using purchases as the numerator. In this case purchases can be computed by adding the ending inventory to the cost of goods sold and subtracting the beginning inventory. The payables turnover ratio also may be divided into the number of days in the business year to show the average payment period in days.

Days in Operating Cycle

The three turnover ratios may be analyzed together to estimate the total number of days in the company's operating cycle from the payment of cash to purchase inventory to the collection of cash from sales. This period is computed by adding the number of days in the inventory turnover to the number of days in the receivables turnover and subtracting the number of days in the payables turnover, as we show in the following diagram. For example, in Example 6-9, the Cooper Company's operating cycle is 51 (47 + 33 − 29) days.

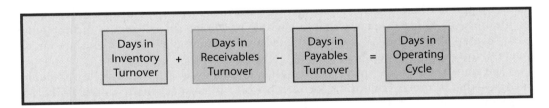

Stability Ratios

Stability ratios are used to evaluate the long-run solvency and stability of a company. They provide evidence of the safety (risk) of the investments in the company by long-term bondholders, preferred stockholders, and common stockholders. Example 6-10 shows several stability ratios, along with the calculations for the Cooper Company. We discuss each ratio in the following sections.

Debt Ratio

The debt ratio indicates the percentage of total assets contributed by creditors. Subtraction of this ratio from 100% shows the percentage of total assets (or *equity* ratio)

EXAMPLE 6-10   Stability Ratios

Ratio	Formula	Calculations (2008)	
1. Debt Ratio	$\dfrac{\text{Total Liabilities}}{\text{Total Assets}}$	$\dfrac{\$36{,}200}{\$129{,}200}$	= 28%
2. Interest Coverage	$\dfrac{\text{Pretax Operating Income}}{\text{Interest Expense}}$	$\dfrac{\$15{,}700 + \$3{,}000}{\$3{,}000}$	= 6.2 times
3. Book Value per Common Share	$\dfrac{\text{Common Stockholders' Equity}}{\text{Outstanding Common Shares}}$	$\dfrac{\$93{,}000 - (\$140 \times 150)}{5{,}400}$	= $13.33 per common share

contributed by stockholders.[15] Sometimes, when a company has issued a significant amount of preferred stock (which has some characteristics of both debt and common stock), the equity ratio is further divided into a preferred equity ratio and a common equity ratio. The appropriate relationship (or "mix") between the debt and equity ratios depends on the industry. In general, creditors prefer to see a lower debt ratio because, in the event of business decline, their interests are better protected and there is less risk. Up to a point, stockholders prefer a higher debt ratio, particularly when the company is favorably "trading on the equity," or applying favorable "financial leverage." This occurs when the company borrows money from creditors at an interest rate (net of income taxes) that is lower than the return the company can earn in its operations. However, an extremely high debt ratio is likely to be a disadvantage when a company wants to attract additional external capital. Investors in both long-term bonds and stocks usually consider a highly leveraged company to be a relatively unstable and more risky investment.

Interest Coverage

The interest coverage ratio (sometimes called the *times interest earned ratio*) is used to evaluate the ability of a company to cover its interest obligations through its annual earnings. It is a measure of the safety of creditors' (particularly long-term) investments in the company. As a general rule, the higher the interest coverage ratio the better able the company is to meet its interest obligations. While interest obligations are legal commitments, it is also true that continued interest payments are endangered by low earnings over an extended period of time. Because both earnings and interest expense are based on accrual accounting, the interest coverage ratio is slightly inaccurate, since it should include only cash payments for interest and cash receipts from earnings. Such refinements are rarely made to this ratio, however.

The numerator of the interest coverage ratio usually is a form of pretax *operating* income—that is, pretax continuing income to which interest expense is added back. If a company has preferred stock outstanding, a similar calculation may be made to evaluate the safety of preferred dividends. The *preferred dividends coverage ratio* is computed by dividing net income by the annual preferred dividends.

Book Value per Common Share

The book value per common share shows the net assets per share of stock. It is sometimes erroneously referred to as the liquidation value per share. Although the book value per common share frequently is computed, for several reasons it is not very useful as an indicator of a company's financial stability. First, most companies are going concerns and a related liquidation value is not important. Second, even if a liquidation value were important, the book value per share is based on assets recorded primarily in terms of

---

15. Sometimes total liabilities are divided by total stockholders' equity to determine the *debt/equity* ratio.

historical costs and thus has no relation to the liquidation value per share. Third, the market value per share of a company's common stock is important in evaluating its stability. Since book value is based on historical costs, it also has no direct relation to this market value. However, if the market price of a company's common stock falls below its book value per common share, some investors consider this to be unfavorable.

When the book value per share is computed and the company has both preferred and common stock outstanding, the equity relating to the common stock is determined first. To do so, stockholders' equity is separated into its preferred and common stock components on the basis of the legal claims of each class upon liquidation. Typically, preferred stock is allocated its par value unless the stock's characteristics include a liquidation value, in which case the latter value is used. When preferred dividends are cumulative and in arrears, an appropriate portion of retained earnings is also assigned as preferred stockholders' equity. The residual amount of stockholders' equity then is assigned as common stockholders' equity. The book value per common share is computed by dividing this residual stockholders' equity by the number of common shares outstanding. A book value per share of preferred stock also may be computed based on the preferred stockholders' equity and the number of preferred shares outstanding.

Cash Flow Ratios

Cash flow ratios assist a user in understanding relationships and trends among a company's cash flows. Example 6-11 summarizes four of these ratios. We do not compute these ratios for the Cooper Company, because they are not as generally accepted and the statement of cash flows is not provided.

EXAMPLE 6-11   Cash Flow Ratios

Ratio	Formula
1. Cash Flow From Operations to Sales	$\dfrac{\text{Cash Flow From Operations}}{\text{Sales}}$
2. Cash Flow From Operations to Net Income	$\dfrac{\text{Cash Flow From Operations}}{\text{Net Income}}$
3. Cash Flow From Operations Per Share	$\dfrac{\text{Cash Flow From Operations}}{\text{Average Shares of Common Stock Outstanding}}$
4. Cash Flow From Operations to Maturing Debt	$\dfrac{\text{Cash Flow From Operations}}{\text{Debt Maturing Next Year}}$

Cash Flow from Operations (CFO) to Sales

This ratio is used to evaluate the cash generated from sales, and the management of cash collections and payments. It enables users to understand the proportion of each sales dollar that is available for investing and financing activities. A comparison of the ratio with the profit margin may be useful. Generally, the CFO to sales ratio is higher than the profit margin, because noncash expenses such as depreciation are deducted in computing net income.

Cash Flow from Operations to Net Income

This ratio enables users to understand how the earning of net income relates to the receipt of CFO. While many users consider CFO as important as income, be careful because income is computed on the accrual basis, whereas CFO may vary depending on when cash flows occur. Management may find it easier to influence the timing of cash flows than the measurement of income.

Cash Flow from Operations per Share

Disclosure of CFO per share is expressly prohibited by GAAP for the reasons we discussed above. However, users may wish to compute it, using the weighted average number of shares that the company discloses for its computation of earnings per share.

Cash Flow from Operations to Maturing Debt

Since CFO is usually the primary source of cash, this ratio measures the ability of a company to make principal payments. It is an indicator of whether the company has the capacity to borrow additional debt.

Other cash flow ratios include CFO divided by cash operating expenses, total assets, or total liabilities, and CFO divided by the cash flows for investing activities that are needed to maintain the operating capacity of the company.

SUMMARY

At the beginning of the chapter, we identified several objectives you would accomplish after reading the chapter. The objectives are listed below, each followed by a brief summary of the key points in the chapter discussion.

1. **Describe an auditor's report.** In an audit report, the auditor expresses three opinions. The first relates to management's assessment of the company's internal control over its financial reporting. The second relates to whether this internal control was maintained by the company. The third relates to the fairness of the financial statements in accordance with generally accepted accounting principles.

2. **Understand the meaning of an operating segment.** An operating segment is a component of a company that engages in activities to earn revenues and incur expenses, whose operating results are regularly reviewed by the company's chief operating officer, and for which financial information is available.

3. **Describe the disclosures in a segment report.** In a segment report, a company provides general information (e.g., types of products); information about the profit (or loss) and total assets of each reportable segment; reconciliations to the company's total revenues, pretax income from continuing operations, and total assets; and various company-wide information.

4. **Explain interim reporting.** Interim financial statements are financial reports for periods of less than a year. Their purpose is to improve the timeliness of accounting information. In developing an interim report, each interim period is viewed primarily as an integral part of an annual period.

5. **Prepare an interim report.** To prepare an interim report, first a trial balance is prepared on a working paper. Next, year-to-date adjusting entries are recorded on the working paper. Then, the interim financial statements are prepared. In preparing the statements, inventory may have to be estimated, the adjusting entries are not entered into the accounts, and closing entries are not made.

6. **Understand intracompany and intercompany comparisons (Appendix).** Intracompany comparison involves comparing a company's current financial performance and condition to the company's past results. Intercompany comparison involves comparing a company's performance with that of competitors, with the industry as a whole, or with the results in related industries.

7. **Prepare horizontal and vertical percentage analyses (Appendix).** In horizontal analysis, changes in a company's operating results and financial position over time are shown in percentages as well as in dollars. In vertical analysis, the monetary relationships between items on a company's financial statements for a particular period are shown in percentages as well as in dollars.

8. **Perform ratio analysis (Appendix).** A ratio involves dividing one or more items on a company's financial statements by another related item or items. Ratio analysis involves computing ratios to evaluate a company's performance using intracompany and intercompany analysis. The six groups of ratios include (1) stockholder profitability, (2) company profitability, (3) liquidity, (4) activity, (5) stability, and (6) cash flow ratios.

ANSWERS TO REAL REPORT QUESTIONS

Real Report 6-1 Answers

1. Internal controls are in place to provide reasonable assurance as to the integrity and reliability of the financial statements. Wachovia also states that it has conducted an evaluation of its internal controls over financial reporting and concluded that the internal controls were effective. This conclusion (assertion) has been audited by Wachovia's auditors.

2. In this context, the concept of reasonable assurance takes into account that one cannot be absolutely sure that the financial statements are not materially misstated, that assets were improperly used or stolen, or that fraud has not occurred. Reasonable assurance takes into account that mistakes can still occur, differences in judgment may exist, and that controls in place can still be circumvented. Nevertheless, reasonable assurance is still a high level of assurance that most would interpret as a remote likelihood that the internal controls did not prevent or detect material misstatements on a timely basis.

QUESTIONS

Q6-1   What does *efficient markets hypothesis* research show and what does an "efficient capital market" mean?

Q6-2   In an audit report, what three opinions are expressed by the auditor?

Q6-3   What is an *audit committee*? Generally, what are its duties?

Q6-4   Why do investors and creditors desire financial information concerning the operating segments of a company?

Q6-5   Briefly describe the three alternative tests used to determine a "reportable segment."

Q6-6   Briefly describe the information that a company reports in regard to the profit (or loss) and assets of each reportable segment.

Q6-7   What company-wide disclosures must a company make related to its operating segments?

Q6-8   What are *interim financial statements* and why are they issued?

Q6-9   What specific principles must a company apply to the reporting of inventories in its interim financial reports?

Q6-10   What principles does a company apply to the accounting for expenses not directly associated with product sales during an interim period?

Q6-11   Briefly explain how the accounting procedures for preparing a company's interim reports are (a) similar and (b) dissimilar to those used in preparing annual reports.

Q6-12   List the minimum disclosures that must be made by a publicly held company in its interim financial report.

Q6-13   List the responsibilities of the Chief Accountant and the Division of Corporation Finance of the SEC.

Q6-14   What are the two SEC reports that are important to accountants?

Q6-15 (Appendix)   What two types of comparisons may external users make in their financial decision making? Why is knowledge of these comparisons important to accountants?

Q6-16 (Appendix)   What is *horizontal analysis* and how is it prepared?

Q6-17 (Appendix)   What is *vertical analysis* and how does it differ from horizontal analysis?

Q6-18 (Appendix)   What is *ratio analysis* and how is it used?

Q6-19 (Appendix)   Briefly describe how each of the stockholder profitability ratios is computed.

Q6-20 (Appendix)   Briefly describe how each of the company profitability ratios is computed.

Q6-21 (Appendix)   Which financial ratios may be used to evaluate the effectiveness and efficiency of a company's reportable operating segments?

Q6-22 (Appendix)   Briefly describe how each of the liquidity ratios is computed.

Q6-23 (Appendix)   Briefly describe how each of the activity ratios is computed.

Q6-24 (Appendix)   Briefly describe how each of the stability ratios is computed.

MULTIPLE CHOICE (AICPA Adapted)

Select the best answer for each of the following.

M6-1 The computation of a company's third-quarter provision for income taxes should be based on earnings
a. For the quarter at an expected annual effective income tax rate
b. For the quarter at the statutory rate
c. To date at an expected annual effective income tax rate less prior quarters' provisions
d. To date at the statutory rate less prior quarters' provisions

M6-2 Which of the following ratios measures short-term solvency?
a. Current ratio
b. Age of receivables
c. Creditors' equity to total assets
d. Return on investment

M6-3 Kaycee Corporation's revenues for the current year were as follows:

Consolidated revenue per income statement	$1,200,000
Intersegment sales	180,000
Intersegment transfers	60,000
Combined revenues of all operating segments	$1,440,000

Kaycee has a reportable segment if that operating segment's revenues exceed
a. $6,000
b. $24,000
c. $120,000
d. $144,000

M6-4 An inventory loss from a market decline occurred in the first quarter that was not expected to be restored in the fiscal year. For interim financial reporting purposes, how would the dollar amount of inventory in the balance sheet be affected in the first and fourth quarters?

	First Quarter	Fourth Quarter
a.	Decrease	No effect
b.	Decrease	Increase
c.	No effect	Decrease
d.	No effect	No effect

M6-5 Barr Corporation's capital stock at December 31, 2007 consisted of the following:

Common stock, $2 par value; 100,000 shares authorized, issued, and outstanding

10% noncumulative, nonconvertible preferred stock, $100 par value; 1,000 shares authorized, issued, and outstanding

Barr's common stock, which is listed on a major stock exchange, was quoted at $4 per share on December 31, 2007. Barr's net income for the year ended December 31, 2007 was $50,000. The 2007 preferred dividend was declared. No capital stock transactions occurred during 2007. What was the price/earnings ratio on Barr's common stock at December 31, 2007?
a. 8 to 1
b. 10 to 1
c. 16 to 1
d. 20 to 1

M6-6 In August 2007, Ella Company spent $150,000 on an advertising campaign for subscriptions to the magazine it sells on getting ready for the skiing season. There are only two issues: one in October and one in November. The magazine is only sold on a subscription basis and the subscriptions started in October 2007. Assuming Ella's fiscal year ends on March 31, 2008, what amount of expense should be included in Ella's quarterly income statement for the three months ended December 31, 2007 as a result of this expenditure?
a. $37,500
b. $50,000
c. $75,000
d. $150,000

M6-7 When a company reports the profit (or loss) for a reportable operating segment, it also must disclose the segment's
a. Revenues
b. Interest revenue and interest expense
c. Depreciation, depletion, and amortization expense
d. All of the above

M6-8 Utica Company's net accounts receivable were $250,000 at December 31, 2006 and $300,000 at December 31, 2007. Net cash sales for 2007 were $100,000. The accounts receivable turnover for 2007 was 5.0. What were Utica's total net sales for 2007?
a. $1,475,000
b. $1,500,000
c. $1,600,000
d. $2,750,000

M6-9 During 2007, Red, Incorporated purchased $2,000,000 of inventory. The cost of goods sold for 2007 was $2,200,000, and the ending inventory at December 31, 2007 was $400,000. What was the inventory turnover for 2007?
a. 4.0
b. 4.4
c. 5.5
d. 11.0

M6-10 The following data pertain to Cowl, Inc. for the year ended December 31, 2007:

Net sales	$ 600,000
Net income	150,000
Total assets, January 1, 2007	2,000,000
Total assets, December 31, 2007	3,000,000

What was Cowl's rate of return on assets for 2007?
a. 5%
b. 6%
c. 20%
d. 24%

EXERCISES

E6-1 *Segment Reporting* York Drug Company has two reportable operating segments, A and B. The 2007 condensed income statement for the entire company is as follows:

Sales	$90,000
Cost of goods sold	(50,000)
Gross profit	$40,000
Operating expenses	(18,000)
Income before income taxes	$22,000
Income tax expense	(8,800)
Net Income	$13,200

Additional Information:
1. Sales are made as follows: Segment A, $52,000; Segment B, $26,000; other segments, $12,000 of the total.
2. Cost of goods sold for each segment is as follows: Segment A, $30,000; Segment B, $12,500; other segments, $7,500.
3. Operating expenses are identified with the segments as follows: Segment A, $10,000; Segment B, $4,500; other segments, $3,500. There are no general corporate expenses.
4. The company has $110,000 total assets as of December 31, 2007. These assets are assigned to the segments as follows: Segment A, $49,500; Segment B, $38,500; other segments, $22,000. There are no general corporate assets.

Required
Prepare a schedule that reports on the 2007 revenues, profit, and assets of Segments A and B and the other segments of the York Drug Company.

E6-2 *Segment Reporting* The Wilson Diversified Company has total assets of $130,000 at the end of 2007 and the following condensed income statement for 2007:

Sales	$90,000
Operating expenses	(66,600)
Income before income taxes	$23,400
Income tax expense	(7,020)
Net income	$16,380

The company has two reportable operating segments and has developed the following related information:

		Segments		
	1	2	Other	Total
Sales	$51,700	$24,400	$13,900	$ 90,000
Operating expenses	36,780	15,400	10,420	66,600[a]
Segment assets	70,300	28,740	21,960	130,000[b]

a. Of the $66,600 total operating expenses, $4,000 are general corporate expenses.
b. Of the $130,000 total assets, $9,000 are general corporate assets.

Required
Prepare a schedule that reports on the revenues, profit, and assets of Segments 1 and 2 and the other operating segments of the Wilson Diversified Company for 2007. Be sure to include the appropriate reconciliations.

E6-3 *Segment Reporting* Parks Conglomerate Company does business in several different industries. The following is a 2007 condensed income statement for the entire company:

Sales		$300,000
Less:		
Cost of goods sold	$140,000	
Depreciation expense	30,000	
Other operating expenses	60,000	
Total expenses		(230,000)
Pretax income		$ 70,000
Income tax expense		(21,000)
Net income		$ 49,000
Earnings per share (20,000 shares)		$2.45

Parks has two major operating segments, A and B. No other operating segment contributes 10% or more of the company's activities. Segments A and B make no sales to each other or to the other segments of the company. An analysis reveals that $2,000 of the total depreciation expense and $6,000 of the total other operating expenses are related to general corporate activities. The *remaining* expenses and total revenues are directly allocable to segment activities according to the following percentages:

	Percent Identified with		
	Segment A	Segment B	Other Segments
Sales	40%	46%	14%
Cost of goods sold	35	50	15
Depreciation expense	40	45	15
Other operating expenses	42	40	18

Required

Prepare a schedule that reports on the revenues and profit of Segments A and B and the other operating segments of the Parks Conglomerate Company for 2007. Be sure to reconcile these amounts with the related totals on the preceding income statement. Include notes summarizing the depreciation related to each operating segment and the computation of segment profits.

E6-4 *Determination of Reportable Segments* Straub Diversified Company has five different operating segments. None of these segments makes sales to the other segments. The company has total assets of $155,000 at the end of 2007 and lists the following condensed income statement for 2007:

Sales	$100,000
Operating expenses	(72,000)
Pretax income	$ 28,000
Income taxes	(8,400)
Net income	$ 19,600

In preparing its segmental reporting schedule, the company determined that it has $7,000 of general corporate expenses and $10,000 of general corporate assets. It also developed the following information for each of its five segments:

	Segment				
	1	2	3	4	5
Sales	$ 9,200	$ 8,800	$ 9,000	$63,900	$ 9,100
Segment profit	3,300	3,200	3,400	21,500	3,600
Segment assets	15,100	13,900	14,300	87,900	13,800

Required

On the basis of the preceding information:

1. Determine which segments are reportable operating segments (justify your conclusions).
2. Prepare a schedule that reports on the revenues, profit, and assets of the reportable operating segments and the remaining segments of the Straub Diversified Company for 2007. Reconcile these amounts to the related totals on the income statement and to total assets. Notes to the schedule are not necessary.

E6-5 *Interim Reporting* Jersey Company is in the process of developing its first-quarter interim report. It has developed the following condensed trial balance as of March 31, 2007:

	Debit	Credit
Cash	$ 900	
Accounts receivable (net)	4,000	
Inventory	8,500	
Prepaid insurance	4,800	
Note receivable	6,000	
Land	3,000	
Buildings and equipment (net)	36,000	
Accounts payable		$ 9,100
Common stock, $1 par		6,000
Premium on common stock		12,400
Retained earnings (1/1/07)		23,080
Sales (net)		50,000

(continued)

	Debit	Credit
Cost of goods sold	26,500	
Selling expenses	6,500	
General and administrative expenses	4,380	
	$100,580	$100,580

Additional information:
1. The company makes formal adjusting entries at year-end and enters the amounts in the appropriate accounts at that time.
2. The company uses control accounts for selling expenses and for general and administrative expenses.
3. Uncollectible accounts typically average 1% of net sales.
4. On January 1, 2007, buildings and equipment (net) have an average remaining life of 10 years. One-third of the account balance consists of assets related to selling activities. The company uses straight-line depreciation with no residual value.
5. The note receivable is dated January 1, 2007, matures on January 1, 2009, and carries an annual interest rate of 12% (interest will not be collected until the maturity date).
6. On January 1, 2007, the company had purchased a 3-year insurance policy, debiting Prepaid Insurance for the $4,800 payment.
7. The company expects its annual effective income tax rate to be 30%. Income taxes for 2007 will be paid at the beginning of 2008.
8. No common stock has been issued or retired in 2007.

Required
On the basis of the preceding information, prepare the Jersey Company income statement for the first quarter of 2007 and a March 31, 2007 balance sheet. A worksheet is not required, but you should be prepared to document any adjustments you make to the preceding accounts.

E6-6 *Interim Reporting* The Howard Corporation presented the following trial balance for the quarter ended March 31, 2007:

	Debit	Credit
Cash	$ 9,800	
Accounts receivable	13,000	
Inventory (1/1/07)	10,000	
Prepaid insurance	9,600	
Land	16,000	
Buildings and equipment	108,000	
Accumulated depreciation		$ 36,000
Accounts payable		28,200
Common stock, $1 par		13,200
Additional paid-in capital		24,800
Retained earnings (1/1/07)		44,900
Sales (net)		100,000
Purchases (net)	59,000	
Selling expenses	12,000	
General and administrative expenses	9,700	
Totals	$247,100	$247,100

Additional information:
1. The company uses control accounts for selling expenses and for general and administrative expenses.
2. The company makes formal adjusting entries at year-end and enters the amounts in the appropriate accounts at that time.
3. The company uses a periodic inventory system. It uses the gross profit method to determine interim inventory. Historical gross profit has averaged 43% of net sales.
4. On January 1, 2007, the company purchased a 4-year insurance policy for $9,600.
5. No common stock has been issued or retired in 2007.
6. The buildings and equipment have an estimated life of 15 years with no residual value. The company uses straight-line depreciation; it records one-fourth of the depreciation as a selling expense and the remainder as a general and administrative expense.
7. The company expects its annual effective income tax rate to be 30%; income taxes will be paid at the beginning of the next year.

Required

On the basis of the preceding information, prepare the Howard Corporation income statement for the first quarter of 2007 and a March 31, 2007 balance sheet. A worksheet is not required, but you should be prepared to substantiate any adjustments you make to the preceding accounts.

E6-7   Interim Reporting The Hill Company prepares quarterly and year-to-date interim reports. The following is its interim income statement for the quarter ended March 31, 2007:

Sales (net)		$150,000
Cost of goods sold		(90,000)
Gross profit		$ 60,000
Operating expenses		
Selling expenses	$18,000	
General expenses	10,600	
Depreciation expense	8,000	(36,600)
Pretax operating income		$ 23,400
Other items		
Dividend revenue	$ 600	
Interest expense	(1,000)	(400)
Income before income taxes		$ 23,000
Income tax expense		(7,000)
Net income		$ 16,000
Earnings per share (20,000 shares)		$.80

On June 30, 2007, the company accountant completed a worksheet in preparation for developing the year-to-date interim income statement. The following are the accounts and amounts listed in the income statement debit and credit columns of this worksheet:

	Debit	Credit
Sales (net)		$340,000
Interest revenue		500
Dividend revenue		1,000
Cost of goods sold	$190,000	
Selling expenses	50,000	
General expenses	20,000	
Depreciation expense	16,000	
Interest expense	2,100	
Income tax expense	19,200	

Required

Based on the given information, and assuming 20,000 shares of common stock have been outstanding for the entire 6 months, for the Hill Company prepare:

1. A year-to-date interim income statement for the first 6 months of 2007.
2. An interim income statement for the second quarter of 2007.

E6-8   Interim Taxes Farris Company is subject to income taxes at a rate of 20% on its first $50,000 of income and 35% on any income in excess of $50,000. In the process of preparing its interim reports, each quarter Farris Company uses an estimated effective income tax rate based on its estimated annual income. The following is a schedule that shows the company's actual year-to-date pretax income and the estimate of the annual pretax income made at the end of each quarter. The company neither anticipates nor incurs any extraordinary items, and its pretax accounting income is the same as its taxable income.

	Pretax Income Amounts at End of			
	First Quarter	Second Quarter	Third Quarter	Fourth Quarter
Actual income (year-to-date)	$20,000	$42,000	$60,000	$82,000
Estimated remaining income	60,000	44,000	21,000	—
Estimated annual pretax income	$80,000	$86,000	$81,000	$82,000

Required 📝

Based on the preceding information, prepare a schedule for Farris Company to compute the income tax expense that would be listed on *each* quarterly income statement. (Carry your effective income tax rate computation to three decimal places.)

E6-9   Horizontal Analyses (Appendix) Slusher Company presents the following condensed comparative income statements for 2006, 2007, and 2008:

	For Years Ended December 31,		
	2008	**2007**	**2006**
Sales (net)	$120,000	$100,000	$85,000
Cost of goods sold	(72,000)	(55,000)	(45,000)
Gross profit	$ 48,000	$ 45,000	$40,000
Operating expenses	(22,000)	(20,000)	(18,000)
Operating income	$ 26,000	$ 25,000	$22,000
Other items			
Dividend revenue	400	500	200
Interest expense	(1,200)	(1,000)	(500)
Income before income taxes	$ 25,200	$ 24,500	$ 21,700
Income tax expense	(8,200)	(8,000)	(6,000)
Net income	$ 17,000	$ 16,500	$15,700
Number of common shares	6,000	6,000	5,000
Earnings per share	$2.83	$2.75	$3.14

Required

Based on the preceding information for Slusher Company, prepare horizontal analyses for the years 2006, 2007, and 2008 using (1) a year-to-year approach and (2) a base-year-to-date approach. Do your analyses reveal any favorable or unfavorable trends?

E6-10   Vertical Analyses (Appendix) The Samuels Company presents the following condensed income statement and balance sheet information for 2007 and 2008.

Income Statements

	For Years Ended December 31,	
	2008	**2007**
Sales (net)	$100,000	$90,000
Cost of goods sold	(60,000)	(51,000)
Gross profit	$ 40,000	$39,000
Operating expenses	(21,300)	(21,900)
Interest revenue	1,500	1,400
Interest expense	(3,700)	(2,500)
Income before income taxes	$ 16,500	$16,000
Income tax expense	(5,000)	(4,700)
Net income	$ 11,500	$ 11,300
Earnings per share	$1.92	$1.95

Balance Sheets

	December 31,	
	2008	**2007**
Cash	$ 3,000	$ 2,000
Receivables (net)	7,000	8,000
Inventories	11,000	12,000
Long-term investments (bonds)	20,000	15,000
Property and equipment (net)	79,000	63,000
Total Assets	$120,000	$100,000

	2008	2007
Current liabilities	$ 10,000	$ 11,400
Bonds payable, 10%	37,000	25,000
Common stock, $2 par	12,000	11,600
Premium on common stock	21,000	19,500
Retained earnings	40,000	32,500
Total Liabilities and Stockholders' Equity	$120,000	$100,000

Required

Based on the preceding information for Samuels Company, prepare vertical analyses of the income statements and balance sheets for 2008 and 2007. Do your analyses reveal any trends in the company's operations and financial position?

E6-11   *Ratios (Appendix)* The following are a condensed income statement for 2007 and a December 31, 2007 balance sheet for the Allen Company:

Income Statement

Sales (net)	$304,400
Cost of goods sold	(183,600)
Gross profit	$120,800
Operating expenses	(82,000)
Interest expense	(7,000)
Income before income taxes	$ 31,800
Income taxes	(10,000)
Net income	$ 21,800

Balance Sheet

Cash	$ 8,200	Accounts payable	$ 18,000
Receivables (net)	14,700	Other current liabilities	6,800
Inventory	19,300	Bonds payable, 10%	70,000
Property, plant, and equipment (net)	195,800	Common stock, $10 par	80,500
		Premium on common stock	24,000
		Retained earnings	38,700
Total Assets	$238,000	Total Liabilities and Stockholders' Equity	$238,000

Additional information: The corporate common stock was outstanding the entire year and is selling for $16 per share at year-end. On January 1, 2007, the inventory was $21,500, the total assets were $224,000, the accounts payable were $18,800, and the total stockholders' equity was $130,800. The company operates on a 300-day business year.

Required

For the Allen Company, compute the following ratios:

1. Price/earnings
2. Profit margin
3. Return on total assets
4. Return on stockholders' equity

5. Current
6. Inventory turnover (in days)
7. Payables turnover (in days)
8. Debt

Is the company favorably "trading on its equity"? Explain.

E6-12   *Ratios (Appendix)* The Byers Company presents the following condensed income statement for 2007 and condensed December 31, 2007 balance sheet:

Income Statement

Sales (net)		$267,000
Less:		
Cost of goods sold	$160,000	
Operating expenses	62,000	
Interest expense	11,000	
Income taxes	10,000	
Total expenses		(243,000)
Net income		$ 24,000

Balance Sheet

Cash	$ 10,000	Current liabilities	$ 40,000
Receivables (net)	22,000	Bonds payable, 10%	110,000
Inventory	56,000	Preferred stock, $100 par	50,000
Long-term investments	30,000	Common stock, $10 par	100,000
Property and equipment (net)	282,000	Additional paid-in capital	45,000
		Retained earnings	55,000
Total Assets	$400,000	Total Liabilities and Stockholders' Equity	$400,000

Additional information:
1. The company's common stock and preferred stock were outstanding the entire year.
2. Dividends of $1.50 per share on the common stock and $6 per share on the preferred stock were declared in 2007.
3. On December 31, 2007, the common stock is selling for $20 per share.
4. The preferred stock has a liquidation value of $110 per share.
5. On January 1, 2007, the accounts receivable (net) balance was $24,000 and the total stockholders' equity was $246,000.
6. Of the company's net sales, 78% are on credit.
7. The company operates on a 365-day business year.

Required
On the basis of the preceding information, compute the following ratios for the Byers Company:

1. Earnings per share
2. Dividend yield
3. Return on stockholders' equity
4. Current

5. Acid-test
6. Receivables turnover (in days)
7. Interest coverage
8. Book value per common share

On the basis of applicable "rules of thumb," what information is revealed by the acid-test ratio that is not disclosed by the current ratio?

E6-13 **AICPA Adapted** *Ratios (Appendix)* Daley, Inc. is consistently profitable. Daley's normal financial statement relationships are as follows:

I. Current ratio:	3 to 1
II. Inventory turnover:	4 times
III. Total debt/total assets ratio:	0.5 to 1

In 2007, Daley was involved in the following transactions and events:
1. Daley issued a stock dividend.
2. Daley declared, but did not pay, a cash dividend.
3. Customers returned invoiced goods for which they had not paid.
4. Accounts payable were paid on December 31, 2007.
5. Daley recorded both a receivable from its insurance company and a loss from fire damage to a factory building.
6. Early in 2007, Daley increased the selling price of one of its products that had a demand in excess of capacity. The number of units sold in 2006 and 2007 was the same.

Required
For items 1 through 6, determine whether each 2007 transaction or event increased (I), decreased (D), or had no effect (N) on each of the 2007 ratios.

PROBLEMS

P6-1 *Income Statement and Segment Reporting* Frahm Corporation presents the following account balances, after adjustments, on December 31, 2007:

Administrative and office salaries	$ 43,000	Sales salaries and commissions	$ 59,000
Interest expense	8,800	Property taxes	7,000
Bad debts expense	6,000	Depreciation expense: buildings,	
Sales (net)	600,000	sales equipment, and office equipment	31,000
Loss due to tornado (pretax)	12,000	Cost of goods sold	323,700
Advertising expense	40,000	Delivery expense	25,000
Miscellaneous office expenses	2,300	Interest revenue	3,000

The following information is also available:

1. The income tax rate on all items is 30%.
2. 10,000 shares of common stock have been outstanding the entire year.
3. Frahm Corporation operates several divisions, two of which, Divisions B and C, are considered reportable operating segments.
4. Sales (net) are made as follows: Division B, 60%; Division C, 25%; other divisions, 15% of the total. No intersegment sales are made.
5. The cost of goods sold as a *percentage of net sales* in each division is as follows: Division B, 55%; Division C, 52%; other divisions, 53%.
6. Operating expenses are traceable to divisions as follows:
   a. Sales salaries directly traceable to Division B total $27,000; Division C, $12,000; other divisions, $8,000.
   b. Sales commissions in each division are 2% of net sales.
   c. Bad debts average 1% of net sales in each division.
   d. Of the total delivery expense, 64% was spent in Division B, 20% was spent in Division C, and 16% was spent in the other divisions.
   e. Of the total advertising expense, $5,000 was spent on general advertising. Of the remainder, 52% was spent in Division B, 28% in Division C, and 20% in the other divisions.
   f. Administrative and office salaries are considered general corporate expenses, except for $17,000 allocated for the management of Division B, $12,000 for the management of Division C, and $10,000 for the management of the other divisions.
   g. Property taxes paid are $4,000 in Division B, $2,000 in Division C, and $1,000 in other divisions.
   h. Miscellaneous office expenses are not directly traced to divisions.
7. The depreciation expense is listed as a separate component on the corporate income statement. Of the total listed, $6,000 is due to depreciation on the corporate headquarters building and is not allocated. Of the remainder, $15,000 is traceable to Division B, $6,000 is traceable to Division C, and $4,000 is traceable to the other divisions.
8. Interest expense is for corporate bonds used to finance overall operating activities. Interest revenue is from corporate investments in marketable securities.
9. An infrequent and unusual tornado caused a warehouse used in Division B to be severely damaged, resulting in the material pretax loss shown earlier.
10. Of the $1,600,000 total company assets at year-end, $910,000 are assets of Division B, $420,000 are assets of Division C, $140,000 are assets of the remaining divisions, and $130,000 are assets related to corporate headquarters.
11. Capital expenditures of Divisions B and C amounted to $50,000 and $27,000, respectively, in 2007 and are included in the total company assets at year-end.

Required

1. Prepare a single-step 2007 income statement for the Frahm Corporation.
2. Prepare a separate schedule that shows the revenues, profit, and assets of Divisions B and C and the remaining operating divisions.
3. Prepare appropriate segment notes relating to depreciation, profits, and capital expenditures.
4. (*Appendix*) Compute the profit margin *before* income taxes for Divisions B and C, and for the other divisions. What do these ratios reveal?

P6-2 *Income Statement and Segment Reporting* The following accounts are taken from the December 31, 2007 adjusted trial balance of the Reed Company:

Cost of goods sold	$121,120	Loss due to flood (pretax)	$ 8,000
Interest expense	4,880	Sales (net)	200,000
Depreciation expense	7,000	Administrative expenses	16,000
Selling expenses	26,000	Interest revenue	1,000

Additional information:

1. The company had 5,000 shares of common stock outstanding the entire year.
2. The income tax rate is 30% on all items.
3. The Reed Company operates several divisions, two of which, Divisions 1 and 2, are reportable operating segments.
4. No intersegment sales are made by any division. Of the total sales (net), Division 1 made 49%; Division 2, 30%; and the remaining segments, 21%.
5. Cost of goods sold as a *percentage of net sales* in each division was: Division 1, 62%; Division 2, 60%; other segments, 58%.
6. Selling expenses consist of sales salaries, sales commissions, delivery costs, advertising, and miscellaneous expenses. These are traceable to the segments as follows:
   a. Sales salaries ($6,000): $3,000 to Division 1, $2,000 to Division 2, and $1,000 to the remaining segments.
   b. Sales commissions ($4,000): 2% of net sales in all segments.

c. Delivery costs ($5,000): 60% to Division 1, 30% to Division 2, and 10% to the remaining segments.

d. Advertising ($10,500): Of the total, $1,200 was spent on general advertising. The remainder was spent as follows: $4,600 in Division 1, $3,200 in Division 2, and $1,500 in the other segments.

e. The miscellaneous selling expenses of $500 are considered common costs and are not allocated to any segments.

7. Administrative expenses consist of bad debts, administrative salaries, property taxes, and miscellaneous expenses. These are allocable to the segments as follows:

a. Bad debts ($2,000): 1% of net sales in all segments.

b. Administrative salaries ($10,000): Of the total, $2,100 are considered general corporate salaries. The remainder is allocated $3,800 to Division 1, $2,500 to Division 2, and $1,600 to the other segments.

c. Property taxes ($3,000): Of the total, $1,600 are general corporate expenses. Of the remainder, 40% is allocable to Division 1, 35% to Division 2, and 25% to the remaining segments.

d. The miscellaneous administrative expenses of $1,000 are considered common costs and are not allocated to any segments.

8. Depreciation expense is listed as a separate item on the income statement. Of the total, $1,400 is a general corporate expense. Of the remainder, 40% is allocable to Division 1, 30% to Division 2, and 30% to the remaining segments.

9. Interest revenue is from corporate investments in marketable securities. Interest expense is related to corporate bonds used to finance general operating activities.

10. An unusual and infrequent flood causing the material pretax loss occurred in Division 1.

11. Of the $300,000 total assets on December 31, 2007, 45% are assets of Division 1, 29% are assets of Division 2, 18% are assets of the remaining segments, and 8% are assets related to corporate headquarters.

12. Capital expenditures amounted to $25,000 in Division 1 and $6,000 in Division 2 during 2007 and are included in the total assets on December 31, 2007.

Required

1. Prepare a 2007 multiple-step income statement for the Reed Company.

2. Prepare a separate schedule that discloses the revenues, profit, and assets of Divisions 1 and 2, and the remaining operating segments.

3. Prepare appropriate segment notes related to depreciation, profit, and capital expenditures.

4. (*Appendix*) Compute the *pretax* return on identifiable assets for Divisions 1 and 2, and for the other divisions. What do these ratios reveal?

P6-3 *Interim Reporting* The Schultz Company prepares interim financial statements at the end of each quarter. The income statement presented at the end of the first quarter of 2007 is as follows:

Sales (net)		$40,000
Cost of goods sold		(23,000)
Gross profit		$17,000
Operating expenses:		
Selling expenses	$8,800	
Administrative expenses	4,210	
Total operating expenses		(13,010)
Pretax operating income		$ 3,990
Other items:		
Interest revenue	$ 40	
Rent revenue	300	
Interest expense	(330)	10
Income before income taxes		$ 4,000
Income tax expense		(700)
Net income		$ 3,300
Earnings per share (8,000 shares)		$.41

Shown next is the Schultz Company trial balance as of June 30, 2007:

	Debit	Credit
Cash	$ 7,200	
Accounts receivable (net)	10,300	
Note receivable (due 9/1/07)	4,000	
Inventory	24,400	
Prepaid insurance	960	
Property and equipment	80,000	

	Debit	Credit
Accumulated depreciation		$ 20,000
Accounts payable		8,000
Dividends payable		3,200
Unearned rent		1,800
Bonds payable, 10% (due 1/1/2012)		12,000
Discount on bonds payable	600	
Common stock, $1 par		8,000
Premium on common stock		34,580
Retained earnings		26,400
Sales (net)		90,000
Cost of goods sold	48,600	
Selling expenses	19,750	
Administrative expenses	8,170	
	$203,980	$203,980

Additional information:

1. The company uses a perpetual inventory system.
2. The company uses control accounts for selling and administrative expenses.
3. The company journalizes and posts its adjusting entries to its accounts *only at year-end.*
4. Uncollectible accounts average 0.5% of net sales.
5. The $4,000 note receivable was received on March 1, 2007. The 6-month note carries an annual interest rate of 12%, the interest to be collected at the maturity date.
6. The balance in the Prepaid Insurance account represents payment made on January 1, 2007 for a one-year comprehensive insurance policy.
7. The Property and Equipment account consists of land, $5,000; buildings, $55,000; and equipment, $20,000. The buildings are being depreciated over a 25-year life; the equipment over an 8-year life. Straight-line depreciation is used; residual value is disregarded. No acquisitions have been made in 2007. The depreciation on the buildings is treated as an sadministrative expense; depreciation on the equipment as a selling expense.
8. On February 1, 2007, the company rented some floor space to another company, receiving one year's rent of $1,800 in advance.
9. The bonds pay interest semiannually on January 1 and July 1. Straight-line amortization of the discount is recorded at the end of each year.
10. The company estimates that its pretax income for the second half of 2007 will total $11,550. All items in income are subject to the same income tax rate schedule. The income tax rate schedule is 15% on the first $20,000 of taxable income and 30% on the excess. There is no difference between the company's pretax financial income and taxable income, and no tax credits are available. The company rounds its estimated effective income tax rate to the nearest tenth of a percent. Income taxes will be paid during the first quarter of 2008.
11. On June 29, 2007, the company had declared and recorded (directly in Retained Earnings) a semiannual dividend of 40¢ per share, payable on August 3, 2007.
12. The 8,000 shares of common stock have been outstanding the entire 6 months of 2007.

Required

1. Prepare a 10-column worksheet to develop the Schultz Company financial statements for the first 6 months of 2007 (refer to Chapter 3 for a worksheet illustration, if necessary).
2. Prepare the income statement for (a) the first 6 months of 2007 and (b) the second quarter of 2007.
3. Prepare a retained earnings statement for the first 6 months of 2007.
4. Prepare the June 30, 2007 balance sheet.

P6-4 **Interim Reporting** The Sikyta Company prepares quarterly and year-to-date financial statements at the end of each quarter. The income statement presented at the end of the first quarter of 2007 is:

Sales (net)	$62,000
Cost of goods sold	(37,200)
Gross profit	$24,800
Operating expenses	(14,074)
Pretax operating income	$10,726

Other items

Interest expense (bonds)	(726)
Income before income taxes	$10,000
Income tax expense	(2,000)
Net income	$ 8,000
Earnings per share (10,000 shares)	$.80

The following is the Sikyta Company trial balance as of June 30, 2007:

	Debit	Credit
Cash	$ 10,200	
Accounts receivable	14,700	
Allowance for doubtful accounts		$ 400
Note receivable (due April 2, 2008)	5,000	
Inventory	29,500	
Prepaid rent (warehouse)	2,400	
Land	12,000	
Buildings	80,000	
Equipment	18,000	
Accumulated depreciation: buildings and equipment		23,000
Accounts payable		9,100
Dividends payable		3,000
Note payable (due October 1, 2007)		6,000
Bonds payable, 12% (due January 1, 2017)		25,000
Premium on bonds payable		960
Common stock, $0.50 par		5,000
Additional paid-in capital		52,000
Retained earnings		22,968
Sales (net)		120,000
Cost of goods sold	71,420	
Operating expenses	24,208	
	$267,428	$267,428

Additional information:
1. The company uses a perpetual inventory system.
2. The company uses a control account for operating expenses.
3. Bad debts average 0.5% of net sales.
4. The company journalizes and posts adjusting entries only at the end of the year.
5. On March 1, 2007, the company rented a small warehouse, paying a year's rent of $2,400 in advance.
6. The note receivable was received from a customer on April 1, 2007. The customer will pay the note plus interest of 14% on April 1, 2008.
7. The buildings are being depreciated over a 25-year life, the equipment over a 10-year life. No acquisitions have been made in 2007. The company uses straight-line depreciation. Residual value is expected to be nominal and is not considered for depreciation.
8. The note payable was issued on April 1, 2007. It carries an annual interest rate of 13%; interest is payable on the maturity date.
9. The bonds pay interest semiannually on January 1 and July 1. Straight-line amortization of the premium is recorded at the end of each year.
10. At the end of the second quarter, it estimated that the pretax income for the remaining 6 months would total $20,000. The income tax rate schedule is 15% on the first $20,000 of taxable income and 30% on the excess. The company rounds its estimated effective income tax rate to the nearest tenth of a percent. There is no difference between the company's pretax financial income and taxable income. Income taxes will be paid during the first quarter of 2008.
11. The company declared and recorded (directly in Retained Earnings) a 30¢ per share semiannual dividend (on 10,000 shares) on June 30, 2007, payable on July 31, 2007.
12. The 10,000 shares of common stock have been outstanding the entire 6 months of 2007.

Required

1. Prepare a 10-column worksheet to develop the Sikyta Company financial statements for the first 6 months of 2007 (refer to Chapter 3 for a worksheet illustration, if necessary).
2. Prepare the income statement for (a) the first 6 months of 2007 and (b) the second quarter of 2007.
3. Prepare a retained earnings statement for the first 6 months of 2007.
4. Prepare the June 30, 2007 balance sheet.

P6-5 **AICPA Adapted** *Interim Reporting* The Anderson Manufacturing Company, a California corporation listed on the Pacific Coast Stock Exchange, budgeted activities for 2007 as follows:

	Amount	Units
Net sales	$6,000,000	1,000,000
Cost of goods sold	(3,600,000)	1,000,000
Gross margin	$2,400,000	
Selling, general, and administrative expenses	(1,400,000)	
Operating earnings	$1,000,000	
Nonoperating revenues and expenses	0	
Earnings before income taxes	$1,000,000	
Estimated income taxes (current and deferred)	(350,000)	
Net earnings	$ 650,000	
Earnings per share	$6.50	

Anderson has operated profitably for many years and has experienced a seasonal pattern of sales volume and production similar to the following forecasted for 2007. Sales volume is expected to follow a quarterly pattern of 10%, 20%, 35%, and 35%, respectively, because of the seasonality of the industry. Also, due to production and storage capacity limitations, it is expected that production will follow a pattern of 20%, 25%, 30%, and 25%, respectively.

At the conclusion of the first quarter of 2007, the controller of Anderson has prepared and issued the following interim report for public release:

	Amount	Units
Net sales	$ 600,000	100,000
Cost of goods sold	(360,000)	100,000
Gross margin	$ 240,000	
Selling, general, and administrative expenses	(275,000)	
Operating loss	$ (35,000)	
Loss from warehouse fire	(175,000)	
Loss before income taxes	$(210,000)	
Estimated income taxes	0	
Net loss	$(210,000)	
Loss per share of common stock	$(2.10)	

The following additional information is available for the first quarter just completed, but was not included in the public information released:

1. The company uses a standard cost system in which standards are set at currently attainable levels on an annual basis. At the end of the first quarter, there was underapplied fixed factory overhead (volume variance) of $50,000 that was treated as an asset at the end of the quarter. Production during the quarter was 200,000 units, of which 100,000 were sold.
2. The selling, general, and administrative expenses were budgeted on a basis of $900,000 fixed expenses for the year plus $0.50 variable expenses per unit of sales.
3. Assume that the warehouse fire loss met the conditions of an extraordinary loss. The warehouse had an undepreciated cost of $320,000; $145,000 was recovered from insurance on the warehouse. No other gains or losses are anticipated this year from similar events or transactions, nor has Anderson had any similar losses in preceding years; thus, the full loss will be deductible as an ordinary loss for income tax purposes.
4. The effective income tax rate, for federal and state taxes combined, is expected to average 35% of earnings before income taxes during 2007. There are no permanent differences between pretax financial income and taxable income.
5. Earnings per share were computed on the basis of 100,000 shares of capital stock outstanding. Anderson has only one class of stock issued, no long-term debt outstanding, and no stock option plan.

Required

1. Without reference to the specific situation described previously, what are the standards of disclosure for interim financial data (published interim financial reports) for publicly traded companies? Explain.

2. Identify the weaknesses in form and content of Anderson's interim report without reference to the additional information.

3. For each of the five items of additional information, indicate the preferable treatment for each item for interim reporting purposes and explain why that treatment is preferable.

P6-6 **AICPA Adapted** *Financial Statement Presentation and Ratios* The Horizon Company is listed on the New York Stock Exchange. The market value of its common stock was quoted at $18 per share at both December 31, 2007 and December 31, 2006. Horizon's balance sheets at December 31, 2007 and December 31, 2006, and statements of income and retained earnings for the years then ended are as follows:

Balance Sheets

	December 31,	
	2007	**2006**
Assets		
Current assets		
Cash	$ 3,500	$ 3,600
Marketable securities, at market	13,000	11,000
Accounts receivable, net of allowance for doubtful accounts	105,000	95,000
Inventories at lower of cost or market	126,000	154,000
Prepaid expenses	2,500	2,400
Total current assets	$250,000	$266,000
Property, plant and equipment, net of accumulated depreciation	311,000	308,000
Other assets	29,000	34,000
Total Assets	$590,000	$608,000
Liabilities		
Current liabilities		
Notes payable	$ 5,000	$ 15,000
Accounts payable and accrued expenses	62,500	74,500
Income taxes payable	1,000	1,000
Payments due within one year on long-term debt	6,500	7,500
Total current liabilities	$ 75,000	$ 98,000
Long-term debt	169,000	180,000
Deferred income taxes	74,000	67,000
Other liabilities	9,000	8,000
Stockholders' Equity		
Common stock, par value $1.00 per share; authorized 20,000 shares; issued and outstanding 10,000 shares	10,000	10,000
Additional paid-in capital	110,000	110,000
Retained earnings	142,000	134,000
Accumulated other comprehensive income		
Unrealized increase in value of marketable securities	1,000	1,000
Total stockholders' equity	263,000	255,000
Total Liabilities and Stockholders' Equity	$590,000	$608,000

Statement of Income and Retained Earnings

	Year Ended December 31,	
	2007	**2006**
Net sales	$600,000	$500,000
Costs and expenses		
Cost of goods sold	480,000	400,000
Selling, general and administrative expenses	74,200	68,000
Other, net	17,000	6,000
Total costs and expenses	571,200	474,000
Income before income taxes	$ 28,800	$ 26,000

	2007	2006
Income taxes	8,600	7,800
Net income	$ 20,200	$ 18,200
Retained earnings at beginning of period, as previously reported	141,000	132,000
Adjustment required for correction of an error	(7,000)	(6,000)
Retained earnings at beginning of period, as restated	$134,000	$126,000
Dividends on common stock	12,200	10,200
Retained earnings at end of period	$142,000	$134,000

Additional facts are as follows:
a. "Selling, general and administrative expenses" for 2007 included a usual but infrequently occurring charge of $9,000.
b. "Other, net" for 2007 included an extraordinary item (charge) of $10,000. If the extraordinary item (charge) had not occurred, income taxes for 2007 would have been $11,600, instead of $8,600.
c. "Adjustment required for correction of an error" was a result of a change from an accounting principle that is not generally accepted to one that is generally accepted.
d. Horizon Company has a simple capital structure and has disclosed earnings per common share for net income in the Notes to the Financial Statements.

Required
1. Determine from the preceding additional facts whether or not the presentation of those facts in the Horizon Company statements of income and retained earnings is appropriate. If the presentation is appropriate, discuss the theoretical rationale for the presentation. If the presentation is not appropriate, describe the appropriate presentation and discuss its theoretical rationale. Do not discuss disclosure requirements for the notes to the financial statements.
2. Describe the general significance of the following financial analysis tools: (a) quick (acid-test) ratio, (b) inventory turnover, and (c) return on stockholders' equity.
3. Based on the Horizon Company balance sheets, statements of income and retained earnings, and additional facts, describe how to determine each of the above financial analysis tools (for the year 2007 only).

P6-7 **AICPA Adapted** *Multiple-Step Income Statement* Before closing the books for the year ended December 31, 2007, Pitt Corp. prepared the following condensed trial balance:

	Debit	Credit
Total assets	$ 7,082,500	
Total liabilities		$ 1,700,000
Common stock		1,250,000
Additional paid-in capital		2,097,500
Donated capital		90,000
Retained earnings, 1/1/07		1,650,000
Net sales		6,250,000
Cost of sales	3,750,000	
Selling and administrative expenses	1,212,500	
Interest expense	122,500	
Gain on sale of long-term investments		130,000
Income tax expense	300,000	
Loss on disposition of plant assets	225,000	
Loss due to earthquake damage	475,000	
	$13,167,500	$13,167,500

Other financial data for the year ended December 31, 2007:
Federal income tax

Estimated tax payments	$200,000
Accrued	$100,000
Total charged to income tax expense (Does not properly reflect current or deferred income tax expense or interperiod income tax allocation for income statement purposes.)	$300,000

Pitt applied the provisions of FASB Statement No. 109, *Accounting for Income Taxes*, in its financial statements for the year ended December 31, 2007. The enacted tax rate on all types of taxable income for the current and future years is 30%. The alternative minimum tax is less than the regular income tax.

Temporary difference
> Excess of book basis over tax basis in depreciable assets (arising from equipment donated as a capital contribution on December 31, 2007, and expected to be depreciated over five years beginning in 2008). There were no temporary differences prior to 2007.

$90,000

Nondeductible expenditure
> Officers' life insurance expense

$70,000

Earthquake damage
> This damage is considered unusual and infrequent.

Capital structure
Common stock, par value $5 per share, traded on a national exchange:
Number of shares:

Outstanding at 1/1/07	200,000
Issued on 3/30/07 as a 10% stock dividend	20,000
Sold for $25 per share on 6/30/07	30,000
Outstanding at 12/31/07	250,000

Required
1. Using the multiple-step format, prepare a formal income statement for Pitt for the year ended December 31, 2007.
2. Prepare a schedule to reconcile net income to taxable income reportable on Pitt's tax return for 2007.

P6-8 *The Coca-Cola Company Disclosures* Review the financial statements and related notes of The Coca-Cola Company in Appendix A.

Required
1. What was the gross profit for 2004? The operating income?
2. What was the net income for 2004? What were the related earnings per share amounts?
3. What were the total assets on December 31, 2004? How much of this total were current assets?
4. What were the total liabilities on December 31, 2004?
5. What was the total shareowners' equity on December 31, 2004? How much was deducted from this shareowners' equity for treasury stock? What method does the company use to account for its treasury stock?
6. What was the net increase in cash and cash equivalents in 2004? How much of this was from net cash provided by operating activities?
7. Where does the company summarize its accounting policies? How are inventories valued and what costing methods are used? How are property, plant, and equipment depreciated?
8. What is the total of the lines of credit and other short-term credit facilities available, and how much was outstanding on December 31, 2004?
9. What was the net cash used in financing activities in 2004? What was the net cash used in investing activities in 2004?
10. How many stock options were outstanding at December 31, 2004? What was the weighted-average price per share for exercised stock options in 2004?
11. What was the net periodic pension cost of the company's pension plan in 2004? What was the fair value of the company's pension benefit plan assets on December 31, 2004?
12. For the third quarter of 2004, what were the (a) net operating revenues, (b) gross profit, and (c) net income? What were the related earnings per share for (c)?
13. What were the net operating revenues in Africa for 2004? What were the identifiable operating assets held in Latin America at December 31, 2004?
14. Who are the auditors of the company? On what date was the audit report issued?
15. What is the company's internal control over financial reporting designed to do, and how is it supported?

P6-9 *Horizontal Analysis and Ratios (Appendix)* The following are comparative financial statements of the Cohen Company for 2006, 2007, and 2008:

Comparative Income Statements

	For Years Ended December 31,		
	2008	**2007**	**2006**
Sales (net)	$ 102,200	$ 91,500	$ 81,700
Cost of goods sold	(61,100)	(52,800)	(47,150)
Gross profit	$ 41,100	$ 38,700	$ 34,550
Selling expenses	(11,400)	(10,000)	(8,900)
Administrative expenses	(8,700)	(7,843)	(6,950)
Interest expense	(3,000)	(4,000)	(4,000)
Total expenses	(23,100)	(21,843)	(19,850)
Income before income taxes	$ 18,000	$ 16,857	$ 14,700
Income tax expense	(5,400)	(5,057)	(4,410)
Net income	$ 12,600	$ 11,800	$ 10,290
Earnings per share	?	?	?

Comparative Retained Earnings Statements

	For Years Ended December 31,		
	2008	**2007**	**2006**
Beginning retained earnings	$ 28,800	$ 20,800	$ 14,310
Add: Net income	12,600	11,800	10,290
	$ 41,400	$ 32,600	$ 24,600
Less: Dividends distributed	(4,410)	(3,800)	(3,800)
Ending retained earnings	$ 36,990	$ 28,800	$ 20,800

Comparative Balance Sheets

	December 31,		
	2008	**2007**	**2006**
Cash	$ 4,200	$ 4,000	$ 4,100
Receivables (net)	7,600	7,000	6,200
Inventories	9,800	9,000	8,600
Noncurrent assets	119,390	112,000	107,100
Total Assets	$140,990	$132,000	$126,000
Current liabilities	$ 12,000	$ 10,000	$ 12,000
Bonds payable, 10%	30,000	40,000	40,000
Common stock, $2 par	8,400	7,600	7,600
Premium on common stock	53,600	45,600	45,600
Retained earnings	36,990	28,800	20,800
Total Liabilities and Stockholders' Equity	$140,990	$132,000	$126,000

Additional information: Credit sales were 65% of net sales in 2007 and 60% in 2008. At the beginning of 2008, 400 shares of common stock were issued, the first sale of stock in several years.

The Cohen Company is concerned. Although it increased the dividends paid per share by 5% in 2008 and its 2008 net income is higher than 2007 net income, the market price of its common stock dropped from $22 per share at the beginning of 2008 to $21 per share at year-end.

Required

1. For 2006, 2007, and 2008, prepare horizontal analyses for the Cohen Company using a year-to-year approach.
2. For 2007 and 2008, compute the following ratios:
   a. Current
   b. Acid-test
   c. Inventory turnover
   d. Receivables turnover

e. Earnings per share
f. Dividend yield
g. Return on total assets
h. Return on stockholders' equity
i. Debt
3. Based on your results, discuss the possible reasons for the decrease in the market price per share in 2008.

P6-10 *Vertical Analysis, Ratios (Appendix)* The Pierce Company operates a high-volume retail outlet. The following are comparative financial statements for the company:

Comparative Income Statements

	For Years Ended December 31,	
	2008	2007
Sales (net)	$180,000	$150,000
Cost of goods sold	(108,000)	(85,500)
Gross profit	$ 72,000	$ 64,500
Selling expenses	(21,600)	(15,000)
Administrative expenses	(23,770)	(23,410)
Interest expense	(3,200)	(2,800)
Income before taxes	$ 23,430	$ 23,290
Income tax expense	(7,030)	(6,990)
Net income	$ 16,400	$ 16,300
Earnings per share (6,000 shares)	$2.73	$2.72

Comparative Balance Sheets

	December 31,	
	2008	2007
Cash	$ 4,200	$ 3,000
Investments (short-term)	2,000	2,100
Receivables (net)	8,600	6,400
Inventory	11,300	9,700
Noncurrent assets (net)	129,900	118,800
Total Assets	$156,000	$140,000
Accounts payable	$ 12,000	$ 10,000
Other current liabilities	1,000	2,400
Bonds payable	40,000	35,000
Common stock, $3 par	18,000	18,000
Additional paid-in capital	30,000	30,000
Retained earnings	54,100	43,600
Accumulated other comprehensive income	900	1,000
Total Liabilities and Stockholders' Equity	$156,000	$140,000

Additional data: The company has not issued any common stock for several years and the price of its common stock has remained relatively constant over that time. At the beginning of 2007, it had outstanding accounts receivable (net) of $7,600, an inventory of $11,000, accounts payable of $7,400, total liabilities of $44,600, and stockholders' equity of $85,400. The company typically makes 50% of its sales on credit.

Pierce Company management has become concerned. Although it feels that progress has been made in "tightening up" the company's operating cycle, this has caused only a modest increase in profits and no increase in the company's stock market price. Management has asked for your assistance in identifying problem areas as well as strong points.

Required

1. Prepare a vertical analysis for the 2007 and 2008 financial statements of Pierce.
2. Compute the following ratios for 2007 and 2008:

   a. Current
   b. Acid-test
   c. Inventory turnover
   d. Receivables turnover
   e. Payables turnover

   f. Return on total assets
   g. Return on stockholders' equity
   h. Debt
   i. Interest coverage

3. Briefly discuss any findings that your analyses reveal.

P6-11 *Horizontal and Vertical Analyses (Appendix)* The following are comparative financial statements of the Perez Company for 2006, 2007, and 2008:

Comparative Income Statements

	For Years Ended December 31,		
	2008	**2007**	**2006**
Sales	$407,000	$361,500	$332,000
Sales returns	(7,000)	(11,500)	(12,000)
Net sales	$400,000	$350,000	$320,000
Cost of goods sold	(244,000)	(222,000)	(205,000)
Gross profit	$156,000	$128,000	$115,000
Selling expenses	(45,825)	(39,550)	(35,690)
Administrative expenses	(60,232)	(46,664)	(44,213)
Interest expense	(4,150)	(4,200)	(3,580)
Total expense	$(110,207)	$(90,414)	$(83,483)
Income before income taxes	$45,793	$37,586	$31,517
Income tax expense	(13,738)	(11,276)	(9,455)
Net income	$32,055	$26,310	$22,062
Number of common shares	10,000	9,000	8,000
Earnings per share	$3.21	$2.92	$2.76

Comparative Balance Sheets

	December 31,		
	2008	**2007**	**2006**
Cash	$15,500	$12,650	$9,300
Receivables (net)	11,000	9,350	6,600
Inventories	38,000	30,000	22,250
Noncurrent assets	286,500	250,000	220,350
Total Assets	$351,000	$302,000	$258,500
Accounts payable	$11,800	$9,500	$9,300
Notes payable	16,200	13,500	11,700
Bonds payable	38,000	39,000	36,500
Common stock, $5 par	50,000	45,000	40,000
Premium on common stock	90,000	72,000	56,000
Retained earnings	145,000	123,000	105,000
Total Liabilities and Stockholders' Equity	$351,000	$302,000	$258,500

Required 📧

On the basis of the given information:

1. Prepare horizontal analyses for Perez Company using a base-year-to-date approach for 2006 through 2007, and 2006 through 2008.
2. Prepare vertical analyses for the 2007 and 2008 financial statements.

P6-12 *Ratio Analysis (Appendix)* Comparative financial statements of the Boeckman Company for 2006 and 2007 are as follows:

Comparative Balance Sheets

	December 31,	
	2007	2006
Assets		
Current assets		
Cash	$ 7,940	$ 5,760
Temporary investments (at market)	10,060	4,240
Accounts receivable	18,000	19,500
Inventories	32,000	27,000
Prepaid insurance	15,000	14,000
Total current assets	$ 83,000	$ 70,500
Property and plant (net)	64,000	46,000
Investments	36,000	32,000
Long-term receivables	38,600	31,000
Patents, net	13,000	9,000
Other assets	30,000	27,500
Total Assets	$264,600	$216,000
Liabilities		
Current liabilities		
Accounts payable	$ 17,800	$ 16,500
Income taxes payable	7,500	6,800
Accrued payables	1,500	1,400
Current portion of long-term debt	3,200	3,200
Total current liabilities	$ 30,000	$ 27,900
Long-term debt	$ 56,300	$ 48,000
Deferred income taxes	12,500	11,800
Total other liabilities	7,200	8,300
Total liabilities	$106,000	$ 96,000
Stockholders' Equity		
Common stock, $5 par	$ 35,000	$ 30,000
Premium on common stock	36,000	24,600
Retained earnings	86,600	$ 64,800
Accumulated other		
comprehensive income	1,000	600
Total stockholders' equity	$158,600	$120,000
Total Liabilities and Stockholders' Equity	$264,600	$216,000

Comparative Income Statements

	For Years Ended December 31,	
	2007	2006
Sales	$278,000	$256,000
Sales returns	(8,000)	(6,000)
Net sales (68% on credit)	$270,000	$250,000
Cost of goods sold	(175,500)	(170,000)
Gross profit	$ 94,500	$ 80,000
Selling expenses	(21,500)	(18,200)
General expenses	(27,560)	(23,550)
Interest expense	(4,300)	(3,100)
Total expenses	$(53,360)	$ (44,850)

| | For Years Ended December 31, | |
	2007	2006
Income before income taxes	$ 41,140	$ 35,150
Income tax expense	(12,340)	(10,550)
Net income	$ 28,800	$ 24,600
Beginning retained earnings	64,800	43,200
Common stock dividends	(7,000)	(3,000)
Ending retained earnings	$ 86,600	$ 64,800

Additional information: The Boeckman Company is listed on the New York Stock Exchange. It issued 1,000 additional shares of common stock at the beginning of 2007. The market value of its common stock was quoted at $17 per share at December 31, 2007. The company uses a 365-day business year in its ratio analysis.

Required

1. Based on the preceding information, compute (for the year 2007 only) the following ratios for Boeckman:
   a. Dividend yield
   b. Price/earnings
   c. Profit margin
   d. Return on total assets
   e. Return on stockholders' equity
   f. Current
   g. Acid-test
   h. Inventory turnover (in days)
   i. Receivables turnover (in days)
   j. Payables turnover (in days)
   k. Average operating cycle (in days)
   l. Debt
   m. Interest coverage
   n. Book value per common share
2. Briefly discuss what a potential investor might do to evaluate the results of these ratios.

P6-13 **AICPA Adapted** *Ratio Analysis (Appendix)* The Printing Company is listed on the New York Stock Exchange. The market value of its common stock was quoted at $10 per share at December 31, 2007 and 2006. Printing's balance sheet at December 31, 2007 and 2006, and statement of income and retained earnings for the years then ended are as follows:

Balance Sheet

| | December 31, | |
	2007	2006
Assets		
Current Assets		
Cash	$ 3,500,000	$ 3,600,000
Marketable securities, at market	13,000,000	11,000,000
Accounts receivable (net)	105,000,000	95,000,000
Inventories, lower of cost or market	126,000,000	154,000,000
Prepaid expenses	2,500,000	2,400,000
Total current assets	$250,000,000	$266,000,000
Property and plant (net)	311,000,000	308,000,000
Investments, at equity	2,000,000	3,000,000
Long-term receivables	14,000,000	16,000,000
Goodwill and patents (net)	6,000,000	6,500,000
Other assets	6,000,000	7,600,000
Total Assets	$589,000,000	$607,100,000

	2007	2006
Liabilities		
Current Liabilities		
Notes payable	$ 5,000,000	$ 15,000,000
Accounts payable	38,000,000	48,000,000
Accrued expenses	24,500,000	27,000,000
Income taxes payable	1,000,000	1,000,000
Current portion of long-term debt	6,500,000	7,000,000
Total current liabilities	75,000,000	98,000,000
Long-term debt	169,000,000	180,000,000
Deferred income taxes	74,000,000	67,000,000
Other liabilities	9,000,000	8,000,000
Stockholders' Equity		
Common stock, $1 par value	10,000,000	10,000,000
5% cumulative preferred stock, $100 par value; $100 liquidating value	4,000,000	4,000,000
Additional paid-in capital	107,000,000	107,000,000
Retained earnings	142,000,000	134,000,000
Accumulated other comprehensive loss		
Unrealized decrease in value of marketable securities	(1,000,000)	(900,000)
Total stockholders' equity	262,000,000	254,100,000
Total Liabilities and Stockholders' Equity	$589,000,000	$ 607,100,000

Statement of Income and Retained Earnings

	Year Ended December 31,	
	2007	2006
Net sales	$600,000,000	$500,000,000
Costs and expenses		
Cost of goods sold	$490,000,000	$400,000,000
Selling and general expenses	71,900,000	66,000,000
Other, net	7,000,000	6,000,000
Total costs and expenses	568,900,000	472,000,000
Income before taxes	$ 31,100,000	$ 28,000,000
Income tax expense	10,900,000	9,800,000
Net income	$ 20,200,000	$ 18,200,000
Beginning retained earnings	134,000,000	126,000,000
Dividends on common stock	12,000,000	10,000,000
Dividends on preferred stock	200,000	200,000
Ending retained earnings	$142,000,000	$134,000,000

Required

Based on the preceding information, compute (for the year 2007 only) the following:

1. Current (working capital) ratio
2. Quick (acid-test) ratio
3. Number of days' sales in average receivables, assuming a business year consists of 300 days and all sales are on account
4. Inventory turnover
5. Book value per share of common stock
6. Earnings per share on common stock
7. Price/earnings ratio on common stock
8. Dividend yield ratio on common stock

CASES

COMMUNICATION

C6-1 Auditor's Report

Meyer Company is considering being audited for the first time. Mary Thomas, its president, has asked your advice. She says: "I understand that after an audit the certified public accountant issues a report that expresses some opinions, and that one type of report is 'unqualified.' What exactly is involved in an audit, what opinions does the auditor express, and what paragraphs are included in an unqualified audit report?"

Required

Prepare a written response to the president of Meyer Company.

C6-2 Management's Report

CMA Adapted The subject of management reports has been prominent the past few years. A *management report* is included in the annual report to shareholders. This report should not be confused with management's discussion and analysis of operations and financial condition that also is relatively new to the annual report.

The management report is included in the annual report to shareholders as a result of the urging of a number of groups and organizations. Consequently, the form and content of the annual report to shareholders continues to evolve as management attempts to present additional information that will be useful to the readers.

Required

1. Explain the general purposes of the management report.
2. Identify five subject areas or topics which have been recommended for inclusion in the management report.
3. Explain why the content of the management report influences the activities of the external auditor during the audit engagement?

C6-3 Securities and Exchange Commission

CMA Adapted The U.S. Securities and Exchange Commission (SEC) was created in 1934 and consists of five commissioners and a staff of approximately 1,900. The SEC professional staff is organized into four divisions and several principal offices. The primary objectives of the SEC are to support fair securities markets and to foster enlightened shareholder participation in major corporate decisions. The SEC has a significant presence in financial markets and corporation-shareholder relations and has the authority to exert significant influence on entities whose actions lie within the scope of its authority. The SEC chairman has identified enforcement cases and full disclosure filings as major activities of the SEC.

Required

1. The SEC must have some "license" to exercise power. Explain where the SEC receives its authority.
2. Explain, in general, the major ways in which the SEC:
    a. Supports fair securities markets.
    b. Fosters enlightened shareholder participation in major corporate decisions.
3. The major responsibilities of the SEC's Division of Corporation Finance include full disclosure filings. Describe the means by which the SEC attempts to assure the material accuracy and completeness of registrants' financial disclosure filings.

C6-4 Segment Reporting

To understand current generally accepted accounting principles with respect to accounting for and reporting on the operating segments of a company, as stated in *FASB Statement No. 131*, it is necessary to be familiar with certain terminology. Furthermore, central issues in reporting on operating segments of a company are the determination of which segments are reportable, and what is to be reported.

Required

1. Explain what is meant by an operating segment of a company.
2. What are the tests to determine whether or not an operating segment is reportable?
3. Briefly identify the information that a company must disclose in regard to its reportable operating segments.

C6-5 Interim Reporting

AICPA Adapted Interim financial reporting has become an important topic in accounting. There has been considerable discussion as to the proper method of reflecting results of operations at interim dates. Accordingly, the Accounting Principles Board issued an opinion clarifying some aspects of interim financial reporting.

Required

1. Explain generally how revenue should be recognized at interim dates and specifically how revenue should be recognized for industries subject to large seasonal fluctuations

in revenue and for long-term contracts using the percentage-of-completion method at annual reporting dates.

2. Explain generally how product and period costs should be recognized at interim dates. Also discuss how inventory and cost of goods sold may be afforded special accounting treatment at interim dates.

3. Explain how the provision for income taxes is computed and reflected in interim financial statements.

CREATIVE AND CRITICAL THINKING

C6-6   Segment Reporting

AICPA Adapted Many accountants and financial analysts contend that a company should report financial data for operating segments of the enterprise.

Required

1. Explain what financial reporting for the operating segments of a business enterprise involves.
2. Identify the reasons for requiring financial data to be reported by operating segments.
3. Identify the possible disadvantages of requiring financial data to be reported by operating segments.

C6-7   Interim Reporting

AICPA Adapted The unaudited quarterly statements of income issued by many corporations to their stockholders usually are prepared on the same basis as annual statements, the statement for each quarter reflecting the transactions of that quarter.

Required

1. Why do problems arise in using such quarterly statements to predict the income (before extraordinary items) for the year? Explain.
2. Discuss the ways in which quarterly income can be affected by the behavior of the costs recorded in a Repairs and Maintenance of Factory Machinery account.
3. Do such quarterly statements give management opportunities to manipulate the results of operations for a quarter? Explain your answer.

C6-8   Analyzing Coca-Cola's Segment and Interim Reporting

Refer to the financial statements and related notes of The Coca-Cola Company in Appendix A of this book.

Required

1. What are the company's operating segments?

2. What items are subtracted from an operating segment's net operating revenues to determine its profit or loss?
3. What does the North America operating segment include and what was its operating income for 2004?
4. What were the net operating revenues of the Latin America operating segment for 2004? What was the total amount of the net operating revenues of the various operating segments for 2004? How does this amount compare to the net operating revenues reported on the company's consolidated statement of income for 2004?
5. What was the depreciation and amortization of the Asia operating segment for 2004? What was the total amount of the depreciation and amortization of the various operating segments for 2004? How does this amount compare to the depreciation and amortization reported on the company's consolidated statement of cash flows for 2004?
6. What were the company's net operating revenues for the first quarter of 2004? How does this amount compare to the third quarter of 2004?
7. What was the company's gross profit for the second quarter of 2004? How does this amount compare to the second quarter of 2003?
8. What was the company's basic net income per share for the third quarter of 2004? What was the company's full-year net income per share for 2004? How does this amount compare to the basic net income per share reported on the company's consolidated statement of income for 2004?

 C6-9 Ethics and Quarterly Expenses

It is March 2008, and you have just been hired by the Tallas Company to be its accountant. Tallas is a small corporation that does a seasonal business of selling snow removal equipment, with most of its sales to retailers occurring in the last two quarters of the calendar year. Production is particularly heavy during the second quarter, in preparation for these sales. During the first quarter production is slowest, so this is when Tallas does the majority of its repairs and maintenance on its production equipment.

You are in the process of preparing Tallas Company's 2008 first quarter interim report. After preparing a preliminary income statement, which shows a modest $30,000 profit, you begin to prepare a preliminary balance sheet. In reviewing the asset accounts in the general ledger, you notice an account entitled Miscellaneous Factory Assets in the amount of $140,000. Since this is a large amount relative to the other assets and you are unclear how to classify this asset, you ask the controller for an explanation. The controller replies, "Oh that. Just include it under Property, Plant, and Equipment. That is the amount we spent on repairs and maintenance during the first quarter. If we expensed all of it now, we would show a loss for the first quarter. Instead, we record the amount as an asset, wait to see how the second quarter results are, and then expense some of it so we can show a reasonable profit. The remainder we expense during our busy season of the third and fourth quarters. We have been doing this for years. It makes all of our quarterly income statements look better. Besides, it makes no difference, since our total yearly income is the same regardless of when we report repairs and maintenance expense during the four quarters."

Required

From financial reporting and ethical perspectives, when do you think Tallas Company should report its quarterly repairs and maintenance expense?

Time Value of Money Module

OBJECTIVES

After reading this Module, you will be able to:

1. Understand simple interest and compound interest.

2. Compute and use the future value of a single sum.

3. Compute and use the present value of a single sum.

4. Compute and use the future value of an ordinary annuity.

5. Compute and use the future value of an annuity due.

6. Compute and use the present value of an ordinary annuity.

7. Compute and use the present value of an annuity due.

8. Compute and use the present value of a deferred ordinary annuity.

9. Explain the conceptual issues regarding the use of present value in financial reporting.

Suppose someone asked you, "Would you rather have $100 today or $100 next year?" Your answer should be, "I'd rather have $100 today." This reply involves considering the **time value of money**. The difference in worth between the two amounts, the time value of money, is interest. **Interest is the cost of the use of money over time.** It is an expense to the borrower and revenue to the lender. Therefore, it is a very important element in the decision making related to the acquisition and disposal of many of the resources of a company.

Interest concepts are involved in the development of many values that a company reports on its financial statements. Also, managers need to understand the concept of interest when making decisions where cash paid or received *now* must be compared with amounts that will be received or paid in the *future*.

The cash flows at various dates, say some at three years from now, some at two years from now, and some at one year from now, cannot be added together to produce a relevant value. Future cash flows, before they can be added, must be converted to a common denominator by being restated to their present values as of a specific moment in time (often referred to as *time period zero*). The dollars to be received or paid three years from now have a *smaller* present value than those to be received or paid two years or one year from now. **The conversion of these future value amounts to the present value common denominator is known as discounting** and involves the removal of the interest or discount—the time value of money—from those dollars that would be received or paid three years, two years, or one year from now.

Instead of restating some of the cash inflows and outflows to their present values at time period zero, a common denominator is also achieved by stating them at a future value by adding the time value of money (interest) to these inflows and outflows. The future value of any series of inflows or outflows is the sum of these periodic amounts plus the compound interest calculated on the amounts.

A company uses the present value or the future value in many situations, such as (1) for measurement and reporting of some of its assets and liabilities, since many accounting pronouncements require the use of present value concepts in a number of measurement and reporting issues; and (2) when it accumulates information for decision making involving, for example, property, plant, and equipment acquisitions. We discuss these concepts in this Module and we apply them in various chapters when we discuss how a company records and reports (1) long-term notes payable and notes receivable when the interest rate is not specified or differs from the market rate at the time of the transaction, (2) assets acquired by the issuance of long-term debt securities that carry either no stated rate of interest, or a rate of interest that is different from the market rate at the time of the transaction, (3) bonds payable and investments in bonds and the amortization of bond premiums and discounts in each case, (4) long-term leases, (5) various aspects of employees' post-employment benefits, and (6) impairment of noncurrent assets.

Various compound interest techniques are used in the measurement of the values (costs) of these and other types of transactions. Most compound interest applications can be calculated by a longhand arithmetic process. However, quicker approaches and shortcuts to the solutions of the problems are available. In this Module we illustrate the basic principles of compound interest in a way that leads to the development of tables used to resolve issues introduced throughout this book. Note that many of the calculations are rounded.

SIMPLE INTEREST AND COMPOUND INTEREST

Simple interest is interest on the original principal (amount originally received or paid) regardless of the number of time periods that have passed or the amount of interest that has been paid or accrued in the past. Interest rates are usually stated as an *annual* rate, which is adjusted for any other time period. Thus simple interest is calculated by the following equation:

Interest = Principal × Rate × Time

1 Understand simple interest and compound interest.

where time is either a fraction of a year or a multiple of years. If the term of a note is stated in days, say 90 days, the denominator of the time fraction in the preceding equation is usually stated in terms of a commercial year of 360 days rather than a full year of 365 days. In this practice the year is assumed to be a period of 12 months of 30 days each. For example, the simple interest on a $10,000, 90-day, 12% note given to a company by Allen Sanders is $300 ($10,000 × 0.12 × 90/360). However, if the term of this note is 15 months, the simple interest is $1,500 ($10,000 × 0.12 × 15/12). Observe that simple interest for more than one year is still calculated on only the principal amount (in this case $10,000).

Compound interest is the interest that accrues on both the principal and the past unpaid accrued interest. Simple interest of 12% for 15 months on the Allen Sanders note is $1,500. If, on the other hand, the 12% interest is *compounded quarterly* for 15 months (5 quarters), the total compound interest is $1,592.74, as we show in Example M-1. Note that in the compound interest computation, the future accumulated amount (value) at the end of each quarter becomes the principal sum used to compute the interest for the following period.

EXAMPLE M-1   Computation of Quarterly Compounded Interest

Period	Value at Beginning of Quarter*	× Rate ×	Time =	Compound Interest	Value at End of Quarter
1st quarter	$10,000.00	× 0.12 ×	1/4	$ 300.00	$10,300.00
2nd quarter	10,300.00	× 0.12 ×	1/4	309.00	10,609.00
3rd quarter	10,609.00	× 0.12 ×	1/4	318.27	10,927.27
4th quarter	10,927.27	× 0.12 ×	1/4	327.82	11,255.09
5th quarter	11,255.09	× 0.12 ×	1/4	337.65	11,592.74
Compound interest on $10,000 at 12% compounded quarterly for 5 quarters				$1,592.74	

* This value is the amount on which interest is calculated.

To help solve the many business issues stated in the introductory section of this Module, accountants need to know the various types of compound interest computations. Although there are many variations, there are only four basic types:

1. **Future value (amount) of a single sum** at compound interest
2. **Present value of a single sum** due in the future
3. **Future value (amount) of an annuity,** a series of receipts or payments
4. **Present value of an annuity,** a series of receipts or payments

FUTURE VALUE OF A SINGLE SUM AT COMPOUND INTEREST

As we stated previously, the main objective of this Module is to explain shortcut methods to determine and apply the compound interest techniques. We will use the following step-by-step procedure, introducing the entire topic *only* with the future value of a single sum at compound interest:

1. We diagram the idea or concept.
2. We make the computation using a longhand calculation.
3. We make the computation using formulas.
4. We discuss the method of constructing and using tables.
5. We illustrate the use of the tables to solve a compound interest problem.

The Idea

2 Compute and use the future value of a single sum.

The future value of a single sum at compound interest is the original sum plus the compound interest, stated as of a specific future date. It is also often referred to as the **future amount** of a single sum. For example, suppose you invest a single amount of $1,000 in a savings account on December 31, 2007. What will be the amount in the savings account on December 31, 2011 if interest at 6% is compounded annually each year? We show the issue graphically in Example M-2. Most compound interest calculations can be made by applying longhand arithmetic. We follow this procedure here only to clarify the various shortcut devices used.

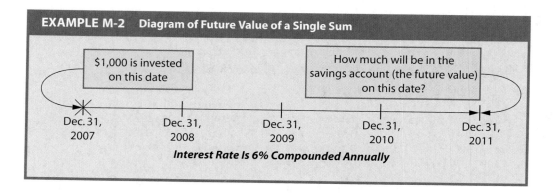

EXAMPLE M-2 **Diagram of Future Value of a Single Sum**

$1,000 is invested on this date

How much will be in the savings account (the future value) on this date?

Dec. 31, 2007   Dec. 31, 2008   Dec. 31, 2009   Dec. 31, 2010   Dec. 31, 2011

Interest Rate Is 6% Compounded Annually

The future value of $1,000 for four years at 6% a year can be calculated as we show in Example M-3. The single sum of $1,000 invested on December 31, 2007 has grown to $1,262.48 by December 31, 2011. This is the **future value.** The total interest of $262.48 for the four years is referred to as **compound interest.**

EXAMPLE M-3 **Calculation of Future Value of Single Sum at Compound Interest**

(1) Year	(2) Value at Beginning of Year	(3) Annual Compound Interest (Col. 2 × 0.06)	(4) Future Value at End of Year (Col. 2 + Col. 3)
2008	$1,000.00	$60.00	$1,060.00
2009	1,060.00	63.60	1,123.60
2010	1,123.60	67.42	1,191.02
2011	1,191.02	71.46	1,262.48

A slight variation of the longhand arithmetic approach is to determine what $1 invested on December 31, 2007 will amount to by December 31, 2011 if interest at 6% is compounded annually. Then this amount is multiplied by the principal sum to find the future value. In this case, $1 amounts to $1.26248 in four years. Knowing this fact, the value of 1,000 different $1 investments (or $1,000) at the end of four years can be calculated by multiplying the $1,000 by 1.26248 as follows: $1,000 × 1.26248 = $1,262.48. To avoid a significant rounding error in the final results, when solving this problem, the intermediate figures should *not* be rounded to the nearest cent.

Formula Approach

Each amount in column 4 of Example M-3 is 1.06 times the corresponding amount in column 2. The final future value is therefore $1,000 × 1.06 × 1.06 × 1.06 × 1.06 = $1,262.48. This means that 1.06 has been used as a multiplier four times; that is, 1.06 has been raised to the fourth power. The future value is therefore $1,000 multiplied by 1.06 to the fourth power:

$$\text{Future Value} = \$1,000(1.06)^4 = \$1,262.48$$

Thus the formula to compute the future value of a single sum at compound interest is:

$$f = p(1 + i)^n$$

where f = future value of a single sum at compound interest i for n periods
p = principal sum (present value)
i = interest rate for each of the stated time periods
n = number of time periods

It is important to understand that the interest rate i is the rate of interest applicable for the particular time period for which interest is compounded. For example, a stated annual rate of interest of 12% is

- 12% per year if interest is compounded annually
- 6% per one-half year if interest is compounded semiannually
- 3% per quarter if interest is compounded quarterly
- 1% per month if interest is compounded monthly

In general, **an interest rate per period (i) is the annual stated rate (sometimes called the nominal rate) divided by the number of compounding time periods in the year, and n is the number of time periods in the year multiplied by the number of years.**

The formula for the future value of 1 is:

$$f_{n,i} = (1 + i)^n$$

where $f_{n,i}$ is the future compound value of 1 ($1 or 1 of any other monetary unit) at interest rate i for n periods.

Using the preceding formula for the future value of 1, a short formula for the future compound value of any single amount at compound interest is:

$$f = p(f_{n,i})$$

The example of the future value of $1,000 invested at 6% with interest compounded annually can now be calculated in two steps:

Step 1 $f_{n = 4, \, i = 6\%} = (1.06)^4 = 1.2624796$

Step 2 $f = \$1,000(1.2624796) = \$1,262.48$

Recall that this is exactly the same as the *second* approach, which we used in the previous arithmetic method.

Table Approach

To develop additional shortcuts to the solution of the compound interest issue, tables for the future value of 1 have been constructed. These tables simply include calculations of the future values of 1 at different interest rates and for different time periods. They can be constructed by using the preceding formula with the desired interest rates and time periods. For example, suppose that you need tables of the future value of 1 at 2% and 14% for time periods 1 through 4 and for 40 years. The information for these can be calculated as follows:

$$f_{n=1, i=2\%} = (1.02)^1 = 1.020000 \qquad f_{n=1, i=14\%} = (1.14)^1 = 1.140000$$
$$f_{n=2, i=2\%} = (1.02)^2 = 1.040400 \qquad f_{n=2, i=14\%} = (1.14)^2 = 1.299600$$
$$f_{n=3, i=2\%} = (1.02)^3 = 1.061208 \qquad f_{n=3, i=14\%} = (1.14)^3 = 1.481544$$
$$f_{n=4, i=2\%} = (1.02)^4 = 1.082432 \qquad f_{n=4, i=14\%} = (1.14)^4 = 1.688960$$
$$f_{n=40, i=2\%} = (1.02)^{40} = 2.208040 \qquad f_{n=40, i=14\%} = (1.14)^{40} = 188.883514$$

This information can then be accumulated in a partial table as we show in Example M-4. In this kind of table the factors are shown without the use of the dollar sign. Each factor is an amount for a certain time period and rate. We provide more complete tables at the end of this Module.

EXAMPLE M-4   **Future Value of 1 Table** $(1 + i)^n$

Periods	2%	14%
1	1.020000	1.140000
2	1.040400	1.299600
3	1.061208	1.481544
4	1.082432	1.688960
.	.	.
.	.	.
.	.	.
40	2.208040	188.883514

Since the factors in Example M-4 and in Table 1 at the end of this Module are based on the formula $(1 + i)^n$, the table approach can be expressed as:

$$f = p(\text{Factor for } f_{n,i})$$

To calculate the future value that $1,000 will accumulate to in four years at 6% compounded annually, it is necessary to look up the table factor for $f_{n=4, i=6\%}$, namely, 1.262477; then, to arrive at the answer of $1,262.48, the calculation is: $f = \$1,000(1.262477) = \$1,262.48$.

Summary and Illustration

In addition to the straightforward situation of calculating the future value of a single sum at compound interest, you can solve other kinds of problems with the *future value of 1* table.

Example: Finding an Unstated Interest Rate

If $1,000 is invested on December 31, 2007 to earn compound interest and if the future value on December 31, 2014 is $2,998.70, what is the quarterly interest rate on the investment?

We show the facts in Example M-5. Using the table approach

$$f = p(\text{Factor for } f_{n,i})$$

and substituting in the formula the amounts shown in Example M-5, the factor is determined as follows:

$$\$2,998.70 = \$1,000(\text{Factor for } f_{n=28, i=?})$$

$$\text{Factor for } f_{n=28, i=?} = \frac{\$2,998.70}{\$1,000.00} = 2.99870$$

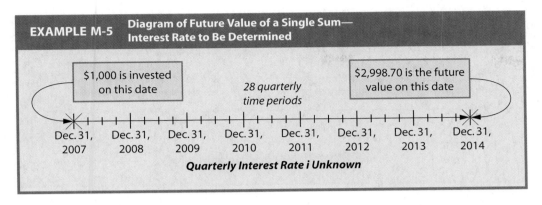

EXAMPLE M-5 | **Diagram of Future Value of a Single Sum—Interest Rate to Be Determined**

$1,000 is invested on this date

28 quarterly time periods

$2,998.70 is the future value on this date

Dec. 31, 2007   Dec. 31, 2008   Dec. 31, 2009   Dec. 31, 2010   Dec. 31, 2011   Dec. 31, 2012   Dec. 31, 2013   Dec. 31, 2014

Quarterly Interest Rate i Unknown

The factor of 2.99870 is the future value of 1 for 28 time periods at an unknown interest rate. Using the future value of 1 table (Table 1) at the end of this Module, you look down the periods (n) column until you get to 28. Then you move horizontally on the $n = 28$ line to the column factor closest to 2.99870. If the value appears in the table, you can determine the interest rate (shown at the top of the column) that produces this value. In this case, 2.99870 is equal to 2.998703 (rounded) located in the 4% column; thus the quarterly interest rate is 4%. This is often referred to as being a stated annual rate of 16%; you should understand, however, that a quarterly rate of 4% compounded four times yields an effective rate of more than 16%. If the factor of 2.99870 does not appear in the table, an interpolation procedure is required to approximate the quarterly interest rate.[1] Calculators and computer software that compute the interest rate are widely available. ◆

You can solve other problems by using the future amount of 1 tables. Keep in mind, however, that most tables are incomplete. At times it will be necessary to construct tables for odd interest rates and time periods, or to use a calculator or computer software.

PRESENT VALUE OF A SINGLE SUM

For the remaining compound interest techniques, we focus on the shortcut approach. After we discuss the idea, we state the formula and use factors derived from the formula.

The Idea

The present value is the principal that must be invested at time period zero to produce the known future value. Also, **discounting is the process of converting the future value to the present value.** For example, if $1,000 is worth $1,262.48 when it earns 6% compound interest per year for four years, then it follows that $1,262.48 to be received four years from now is worth $1,000 now at time period zero; that is, $1,000 is the present value of $1,262.48 discounted at 6% for four years. Example M-6 presents this information graphically.

---

1.   You can use the following six steps to determine an interest rate by linear interpolation: (1) Calculate the compound interest factor as shown in the preceding example. (2) Look up in compound interest tables the two interest rates that yield the next largest and the next smallest factors from the calculated factor determined in step 1. (3) Determine (a) the difference between the two factors in step 2, and (b) the difference between the calculated factor from step 1 and the factor of the smaller interest rate from step 2. (4) Find the difference between the two interest rates found in step 2. (5) Apportion the difference in the interest rates in step 4 by multiplying it by a fraction: The numerator is the difference determined in step 3b and the denominator is the difference determined in step 3a. (6) The interest rate is then the lower rate found in step 2 *plus* the apportioned difference from step 5.

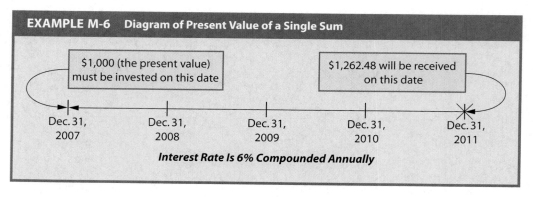

EXAMPLE M-6   **Diagram of Present Value of a Single Sum**

$1,000 (the present value) must be invested on this date

$1,262.48 will be received on this date

Dec. 31, 2007   Dec. 31, 2008   Dec. 31, 2009   Dec. 31, 2010   Dec. 31, 2011

Interest Rate Is 6% Compounded Annually

Shortcut Approaches

3   Compute and use the present value of a single sum.

While it is possible to calculate the present value of $1,262.48 to be received at the end of four years discounted at 6% by a longhand approach by reversing the process described in the calculation of the future value, we do not show this approach here. Instead we focus on the development of shortcut approaches to find the present value of a single sum. First we present the formula, then we explain how to create and use factors.

Formula Approach

Since the present value of a single future amount is the reciprocal value of the future value of a single sum, the formula for this calculation is:

$$p = f \frac{1}{(1 + i)^n}$$

where p = present value of any given future value due in the future
        f = future value
        i = interest rate for each of the stated time periods
        n = number of time periods

In this example the present value of $1,262.48 received at the end of 4 years discounted at 6% is $1,000, calculated as follows:

$$p = \$1,262.48 \frac{1}{(1.06)^4} = \$1,000$$

The formula for the present value of 1 is:

$$p_{n,i} = \frac{1}{(1 + i)^n}$$

where $p_{n,i}$ is the present value of 1 ($1 or 1 of any monetary unit) at interest rate i for n periods. It is now possible to express the formula for the present value of any given future amount as:

$$p = f(p_{n,i})$$

The example of the present value of $1,262.48 to be received four years from now with interest of 6% compounded annually can be calculated in two steps:

Step 1 $p_{n=4,\ i=6\%} = \dfrac{1}{(1.06)^4} = 0.792094$

Step 2 $p = \$1,262.48(0.792094) = \$1,000$

Table Approach

Using the formula for $p_{n,i}$ tables have been constructed for any interest rate and for any number of periods by simply substituting in the formula the selected various interest rates for the various time periods desired. Table 3 at the end of this Module shows the factors for the present value of 1 $(p_{n,i})$.

Since the factors in Table 3 are based on the formula $p_{n,i} = 1/(1 + i)^n$, the generalized table approach can be stated as:

$$p = f(\text{Factor for } p_{n,i})$$

To calculate the present value of $1,262.48 to be received at the end of four years, discounted at 6%, look up the factor for $p_{n = 4, i = 6\%}$ in Table 3; it is 0.792094. Then the future value of $1,262.48 is multiplied by this present value of 1 factor to obtain the present value amount of $1,000, as follows: $p = \$1,262.48(0.792094) = \$1,000$.

Summary and Illustration

In addition to calculating the present value of a single sum using compound interest, you can solve other kinds of problems with the present value of 1 table.

Example: Finding an Unstated Interest Rate

Assuming that the present value of $10,000 to be paid at the end of 10 years is $3,855.43, what interest rate compounded annually is used in the calculation of the present value?

Example M-7 shows the known facts. Since both the present value and the future amount are known, this problem can be solved in two different ways: (1) by using the method we described in the future value section, or (2) by using the present value approach we describe here. Since we discussed the future value approach earlier in this Module, we use only the present value approach here to solve the problem. Using the table approach

$$p = f(\text{Factor for } p_{n,i})$$

and substituting in the formula the known amounts shown in Example M-7, the factor is determined as follows:

$$\$3,855.43 = \$10,000.00 \, (\text{Factor for } p_{n = 10, i = ?})$$

$$\text{Factor for } p_{n = 10, i = ?} = \frac{\$3,855.43}{\$10,000.00} = 0.385543$$

The factor of 0.385543 is the present value of 1 for 10 periods at an unknown interest rate. Using the present value of 1 table (Table 3), you look down the periods (n) column until you get to 10. Then you move horizontally on the $n = 10$ line to the column factor closest to 0.385543. If the amount appears in the table, you can determine the interest rate (shown at the top of the column) that produces this amount. In this case, 0.385543 is in the 10% column. Thus the annual rate is 10%. If the factor of 0.385543 does not appear in the table, an interpolation procedure is required to approximate the annual interest rate (see footnote 1). ◆

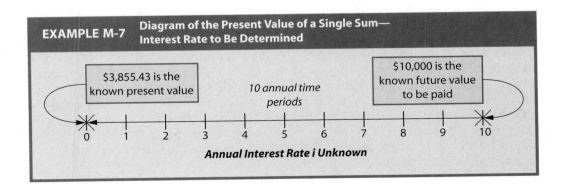

EXAMPLE M-7   **Diagram of the Present Value of a Single Sum— Interest Rate to Be Determined**

$3,855.43 is the known present value

10 annual time periods

$10,000 is the known future value to be paid

0 1 2 3 4 5 6 7 8 9 10

Annual Interest Rate i Unknown

MEASUREMENTS INVOLVING AN ANNUITY

An annuity is a series of equal cash flows (deposits, receipts, payments, or with-drawals), sometimes referred to as *rents*, **made at regular intervals with interest compounded at a certain rate.** The regular intervals between the cash flows may be any time period—for example, one year, a six-month period, one month, or even one day. In solving measurement problems involving the use of annuities, these four conditions must exist: (1) the periodic cash flows are equal in amount, (2) the time periods between the cash flows are the same length, (3) the interest rate is constant for each time period, and (4) the interest is compounded at the end of each time period.

FUTURE VALUE OF AN ORDINARY ANNUITY

The future value of an ordinary annuity is determined *immediately* **after the last cash flow in the series is made.** For the first example, assume that Debbi Whitten wants to calculate the future value of four cash flows of $1,000, each with interest compounded annually at 6%, where the first $1,000 cash flow occurs on December 31, 2007 and the last $1,000 occurs on December 31, 2010. Example M-8 presents this information graphically.

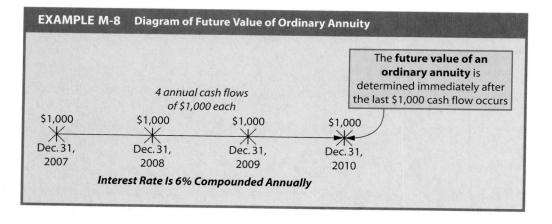

EXAMPLE M-8   Diagram of Future Value of Ordinary Annuity

The **future value of an ordinary annuity** is determined immediately after the last $1,000 cash flow occurs

4 annual cash flows of $1,000 each

$1,000 $1,000 $1,000 $1,000

Dec. 31,   Dec. 31,   Dec. 31,   Dec. 31,
2007   2008   2009   2010

Interest Rate Is 6% Compounded Annually

In drawing a **time line** such as that in Example M-8, some accountants prefer to add a beginning time segment to the left of the time when the first cash flow occurs. For example, they would draw the time line for the future amount of an ordinary annuity, as we show in Example M-9. This approach is acceptable if it is understood that the time from January 1, 2007 to December 31, 2007 (which is the period of time immediately *before* the first cash flow occurs) is not used to compute the future value of the ordinary annuity. It is similar to stating a decimal as .4 or 0.4. The zero in front of the decimal may help someone to understand the issue better, but does not change it. In the case of the future value of an ordinary annuity, however, placing the broken line segment to the left of the first cash flow may lead someone to think that the cash flows in an ordinary annuity *must occur* at the end of a given year. That statement is *not* true; the cash flows can occur, for example, on March 15 of each year, or November 5 of each year. For the calculation to be the future value of an *ordinary* annuity, the *future value* is determined *immediately after* the last cash flow in the series occurs. Because of the potential misinterpretation of the information, we prefer not to use the broken line segment to the left of the first cash flow in the time lines describing the future value of an ordinary annuity.

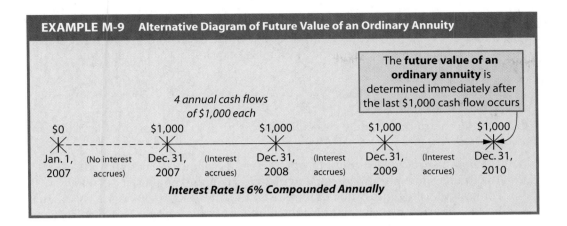

EXAMPLE M-9   Alternative Diagram of Future Value of an Ordinary Annuity

Shortcut Approaches

Formula Approach

The formula for the future value of an ordinary annuity of any amount is:

$$F_0 = C\left[\frac{(1+i)^n - 1}{i}\right]$$

where F_0 = future value of an ordinary annuity of a series of cash flows of any amount

C = amount of each cash flow

n = number of cash flows (not the number of time periods)

i = interest rate for each of the stated time periods

In the example, the future value of an ordinary annuity of four cash flows of $1,000 each at 14% compounded annually is as follows:

$$F_0 = \$1,000\left[\frac{(1.06)^4 - 1}{0.06}\right] = \$4,374.62$$

The formula for the future value of an ordinary annuity with cash flows of 1 each is as follows:

$$F_{0_{n,i}} = \left[\frac{(1+i)^n - 1}{i}\right]$$

where $F_{0_{n,i}}$ is the future value of an *ordinary* annuity of n cash flows of 1 each at interest rate i.

With the preceding formula for $F_{0_{n,i}}$ it is possible to express another formula for the future value of an ordinary annuity of cash flows of any size in this manner:

$$F_0 = C(F_{0_{n,i}})$$

In a two-step approach, the future value of an ordinary annuity of four cash flows of $1,000 each at 14% compounded annually is calculated as follows:

Step 1 $F_{0_{n=4,\ i=6\%}} = \dfrac{(1.06)^4 - 1}{0.06} = 4.37462$

Step 2 $F_0 = \$1,000(4.37462) = \$4,374.62$

This two-step approach is used to solve the problem when factors are not available.

4 Compute and use the future value of an ordinary annuity.

Table Approach

The formula for $F_{O_{n,i}}$ can be used to construct a table of the future value of any series of cash flows of 1 each for any interest rate. Here the number of cash flows of 1 and the interest rates are substituted into the formula

$$\frac{(1 + i)^n - 1}{i}$$

Table 2 at the end of this Module shows the factors for $F_{O_{n,i}}$. Turning to Table 2, observe the following:

1. The numbers in the first column (n) represent the number of cash flows.
2. The future values are always equal to or larger than the number of cash flows of 1. For example, the future value of four cash flows of 1 each at 6% is 4.374616. This figure comprises two elements: (a) the number of cash flows of 1 each *without* any interest, and (b) the compound interest on the cash flows, with the exception of the compound interest on the last cash flow in the series, which in the case of an ordinary annuity *does not* earn any interest.

Since Table 2 shows the calculation of $F_{O_{n,i}}$ or

$$\frac{(1 + i)^n - 1}{i}$$

values, the generalized table approach is as follows:

$$F_0 = C(\text{Factor for } F_{O_{n,i}})$$

To calculate the future value of an ordinary annuity of 4 cash flows of $1,000 each at 6%, you must look up the $F_{O_{n=4, \, i=6\%}}$ factor in the future value of an ordinary annuity of 1 table (Table 2); it is 4.374616. Then the amount of each cash flow, here $1,000, is multiplied by the Table 2 factor to obtain the future value of $4,374.62:

$$F_0 = \$1,000(4.374616) = \$4,374.62$$

Summary and Illustration

You can solve several kinds of problems using a future value of an ordinary annuity of 1 table, such as (1) calculating the future value when the cash flows and interest rate are known (the preceding problem); (2) calculating the value of each cash flow where the number of cash flows, interest rate, and future value are known; (3) calculating the number of cash flows when the amount of each cash flow, the interest rate, and the future value are known; and (4) calculating an unknown interest rate when the cash flows and the future value are known. To demonstrate the analysis used in the solution of all these problems, we show item (2) as follows.

Example: Determining the Amount of Each Cash Flow Needed to Accumulate a Fund to Retire Debt

At the beginning of 2007 the Rexson Company issued 10-year bonds with a face value of $1,000,000 due on December 31, 2016. The company will accumulate a fund to retire these bonds at maturity. It will make annual deposits to the fund beginning on December 31, 2007. How much must the company deposit each year, assuming that the fund will earn 12% interest compounded annually?

Example M-10 shows the facts of the problem. The future value and the compound interest rate are known. The amount of each of the 10 deposits (cash flows) is the unknown factor. Starting with the formula

$$F_0 = C(\text{Factor for } F_0)$$

and then shifting the elements and substituting the known amount and applicable factor (from Table 2), the amount of each annual deposit is \$56,984.16, calculated as follows:

$$C = \frac{F_0}{\text{Factor for } F_{0_{n,i}}}$$

$$= \frac{F_0}{\text{Factor for } F_{0_{n=10,\ i=12\%}}}$$

$$= \frac{\$1,000,000}{17.548735}$$

$$= \$56,984.16$$

The 10 annual deposits of \$56,984.16, plus the compound interest, will accumulate to \$1,000,000 by December 31, 2016. ◆

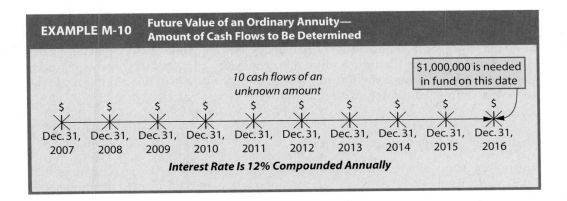

EXAMPLE M-10   **Future Value of an Ordinary Annuity— Amount of Cash Flows to Be Determined**

FUTURE VALUE OF AN ANNUITY DUE

The future value of an annuity due (F_d) is determined 1 period after the last cash flow in the series. For example, assume that Ronald Jacobson deposits in a fund four payments of \$1,000 each beginning December 31, 2007, with the last deposit being made on December 31, 2010. How much will be in the fund on December 31, 2010, 1 year after the final payment, if the fund earns interest at 6% compounded annually? Example M-11 shows the facts of this problem.

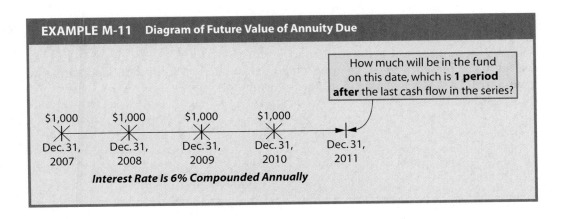

EXAMPLE M-11   **Diagram of Future Value of Annuity Due**

Solution Approach

5 Compute and use the future value of an annuity due.

By observing the information contained in Examples M-11 and M-8, you can determine a quick way to compute the future value of an annuity due.[2] When only the future value of an *ordinary* annuity table is available, you can use the factors by completing the following steps:

Step 1   In the *ordinary* annuity table (Table 2), look up the value of $n + 1$ cash flows at 6% or the value of 5 cash flows at 6%.   5.637093

Step 2   Subtract 1 without interest from the value obtained in step 1.   (1.000000)

This is the converted future value factor for $F_{d_{n=4,\ i=6\%}}$ 4.637093

Step 3   Multiply the amount of each cash flow, here $1,000, by the converted factor for $F_{d_{n=4,\ i=6\%}}$ determined in step 2:

$$F_d = \$1,000(4.637093) = \$4,637.09$$

Tables of the future value of an annuity due of cash flows of 1 each are available in some finance books, but not in this book. Therefore, these values must be calculated using the tables for the future value of an *ordinary* annuity. As we showed previously, **the general rule is to use the future value of an ordinary annuity factor for $n + 1$ cash flows and subtract 1 from the factor.** (Note that we do include in this Module a present value of an annuity due table, as we discuss later.)

PRESENT VALUE OF AN ANNUITY

The present value of an annuity is the present value of a series of equal cash flows that occur in the future. In other words, it is the amount that must be invested now and, if left to earn compound interest, will provide for a receipt or payment of a series of equal cash flows at regular intervals. Over time, the present value balance is *increased* periodically for interest and is *decreased* periodically for each receipt or payment. Thus, the last cash flow in the series exhausts the balance on deposit.

A company frequently uses the present value of an annuity concept to report many items in its financial statements, as we stated in the introduction to this Module. Because of the importance of the present value of an annuity, we will discuss the (1) present value of an ordinary annuity, (2) present value of an annuity due, and (3) present value of a deferred annuity.

PRESENT VALUE OF AN ORDINARY ANNUITY

6 Compute and use the present value of an ordinary annuity.

The present value of an ordinary annuity is determined 1 period before the first cash flow in the series is made. For example, assume that Kyle Vasby wants to calculate the present value on January 1, 2007 of four future withdrawals (cash flows) of $1,000, with the first withdrawal being made on December 31, 2007, 1 year after the determination of the present value. The applicable interest rate is 6% compounded annually. Example M-12 shows this information graphically.

---

2.   An alternative approach is to multiply the future value of an ordinary annuity factor by 1 plus the interest rate. Thus, the future value in this example would be computed as $1,000 × (4.374616 × 1.06) = $4,637.09.

EXAMPLE M-12   Diagram of Present Value of an Ordinary Annuity

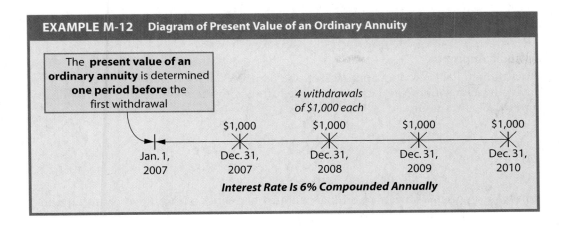

Solving by Determining the Present Value of a Series of Single Sums

The solution to this problem can be determined by using the present value of a single sum. For instance, the answer can be calculated in the following two steps: (1) determine the present value of four individual cash flows of 1 each for one, two, three, and four years, as we show in Example M-13; and (2) multiply the final results of the summation by $1,000.

Step 1   The present value of four cash flows of 1 for one, two, three, and four years discounted at 6% is determined in Example M-13.

Step 2   Now it is possible to determine the present value of the four cash flows of $1,000 each by multiplying the $1,000 by 3.465105:

$1,000 × 3.465105 = $3,465.11

The present value on January 1, 2007 is $3,465.11; or we can say that $3,465.11 must be invested on January 1, 2007 to provide for four withdrawals of $1,000 each starting on December 31, 2007, given an interest rate of 6%.

EXAMPLE M-13   Present Value of Four Cash Flows of 1 for One, Two, Three, and Four Years at 6%

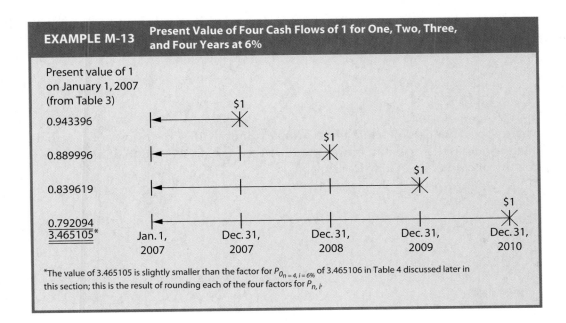

*The value of 3.465105 is slightly smaller than the factor for $P_{0_{n=4,\,i=6\%}}$ of 3.465106 in Table 4 discussed later in this section; this is the result of rounding each of the four factors for $P_{n,\,i}$.

Shortcut Approaches

Formula Approach

Even though the preceding approach can be used, it is time-consuming for calculations involving a large number of cash flows. The formula for the present value of an ordinary annuity of any amount is:

$$P_0 = C \left[\frac{1 - \frac{1}{(1+i)^n}}{i} \right]$$

where P_0 = present value of an ordinary annuity of a series of cash flows of any amount
C = amount of each cash flow
n = number of cash flows (not the number of time periods)
i = interest rate for each of the stated time periods

In the example, the present value of an ordinary annuity of four cash flows of $1,000 each at 6% compounded annually can be calculated as follows:

$$P_0 = \$1,000 \left[\frac{1 - \frac{1}{(1.06)^4}}{0.06} \right] = \$3,465.11$$

Based on these calculations and formula observe that:

1. The results are the same as those produced in the first approach, $3,465.11.
2. The formula is developed from the formulas for both the future value of $1(f)$ and the present value of $1(p)$:

$$(1 + i)^n = f$$

$$\frac{1}{(1 + i)^n} = p$$

3. Thus the formula can be restated as follows:

$$P_0 = C \left(\frac{1-p}{i} \right)$$

The formula for the present value of an ordinary annuity can be converted to that for a series of cash flows of 1 each as follows:

$$P_{0_{n,i}} = \left[\frac{1 - \frac{1}{(1+i)^n}}{i} \right]$$

where $P_{0_{n,i}}$ is the present value of an ordinary annuity of n cash flows of 1 each at interest rate i. This formula can be expressed for the present value of an ordinary annuity of cash flows of *any size* as:

$$P_0 = C(P_{0_{n,i}})$$

In a two-step approach the present value of four future withdrawals (cash flows) of $1,000 each discounted at 6% is recalculated as follows:

Step 1 $\quad P_{0_{n=4, i=6\%}} = \left[\dfrac{1 - \dfrac{1}{(1.06)^4}}{0.06}\right] = 3.46511$

Step 2 $\quad P_0 = \$1,000(3.46511) = \$3,465.11$

This calculation is exactly the same as that of the first formula, except that the process is divided into two steps. The two-step approach is the one used when tables of the present value of an ordinary annuity of 1 are available.

Table Approach

The formula for $P_{0_{n,i}}$ can be used to construct a table of the present value of any series of cash flows of 1 each for any interest rate. All that is necessary is to substitute in the formula the desired number of cash flows for the various required interest rates. Table 4 at the end of the Module shows the factors for $P_{0_{n,i}}$. Turning to Table 4, observe the following:

1. The numbers in the first column (n) represent the number of cash flows of 1 each. In this calculation the number of cash flows and time periods are equal.
2. The present value amounts are always smaller than the number of cash flows of 1. For example, the present value of three cash flows of 1 at 2% is 2.883883.

Since Table 4 shows the precalculation of $P_{0_{n,i}}$ or

$$\dfrac{1 - \dfrac{1}{(1+i)^n}}{i}$$

the generalized table approach is as follows:

$$P_0 = C(\text{Factor for } P_{0_{n,i}})$$

Thus, to calculate the present value on January 1, 2007 of four future withdrawals (cash flows) of $1,000 discounted at 6%, with the first cash flow being withdrawn on December 31, 2007, it is necessary to look up the $P_{0_{n=4,\ i=6\%}}$ value in the present value of an ordinary annuity of 1 table (Table 4); it is 3.465106. This factor is then multiplied by $1,000 to determine the present value figure of $3,465.11:

$$P_0 = \$1,000(3.465106) = \$3,465.11$$

Over the 4 periods, the annuity yields interest each period as follows:

Period	Beginning Balance	Interest	Cash Flow	Ending Balance
1	$3,465.11	$207.91	$(1,000)	$2,673.02
2	2,673.02	160.38	(1,000)	1,833.40
3	1,833.40	110.00	(1,000)	943.40
4	943.40	56.60	(1,000)	0

Summary and Illustration

You can solve several kinds of problems by using the present value of an ordinary annuity of 1 table. We present one additional example: a problem involving the calculation of the periodic cash flows when the present value and interest rate are known.

Example: Determining the Value of Periodic Cash Flows When the Present Value Is Known

Suppose that on January 1, 2007 Rex Company borrows $100,000 to finance a plant expansion project. It plans to pay this amount back with interest at 12% in equal annual payments over a 10-year period, with the first payment due on December 31, 2007. What is the amount of each payment?

Example M-14 shows the facts of the problem. The present value and the compound interest rate are known. The amount of each of the 10 cash flows is the unknown item and is $17,698.42, calculated as follows:

$$C = \frac{P_0}{\text{Factor for } P_{0_{n,i}}}$$

$$= \frac{P_0}{\text{Factor for } P_{0_{n=10,\ i=12\%}}}$$

$$= \frac{\$100,000}{5.605223}$$

$$= \$17,698.42$$

Remember that each of these payments of $17,698.42 includes (1) a payment of annual interest, and (2) a retirement of debt principal. For example, the interest for 2007 is $12,000 (12% × $100,000). Thus the amount of the payment on principal is $5,698.42 ($17,698.42 − $12,000). For the year 2008 the interest is $11,316.19 [12% × ($100,000 − $5,698.42)], and the retirement of principal is $6,382.23 ($17,698.42 − $11,316.19). The *last* payment of $17,698.42 on December 31, 2016, will be sufficient to retire the remaining principal and to pay the interest for the tenth year. ♦

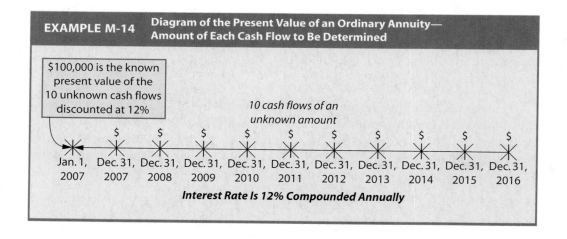

EXAMPLE M-14 — **Diagram of the Present Value of an Ordinary Annuity— Amount of Each Cash Flow to Be Determined**

$100,000 is the known present value of the 10 unknown cash flows discounted at 12%

10 cash flows of an unknown amount

Jan. 1, 2007   Dec. 31, 2007   Dec. 31, 2008   Dec. 31, 2009   Dec. 31, 2010   Dec. 31, 2011   Dec. 31, 2012   Dec. 31, 2013   Dec. 31, 2014   Dec. 31, 2015   Dec. 31, 2016

Interest Rate Is 12% Compounded Annually

PRESENT VALUE OF AN ANNUITY DUE

7 Compute and use the present value of an annuity due.

The present value of an annuity due (P_d) is determined on the date of the first cash flow in the series. For example, assume that Barbara Livingston wants to calculate the present value of an annuity on December 31, 2007, which will permit four annual future receipts of $1,000 each, the first to be received on December 31, 2007. The interest rate is 6% compounded annually. Example M-15 shows the facts of this problem.

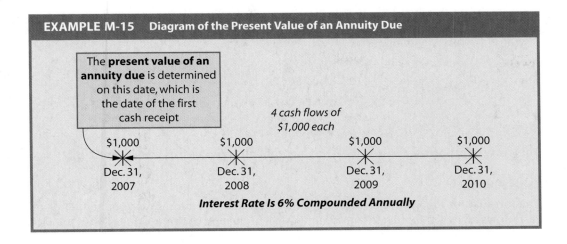

EXAMPLE M-15   Diagram of the Present Value of an Annuity Due

The **present value of an annuity due** is determined on this date, which is the date of the first cash receipt

4 cash flows of $1,000 each

$1,000 $1,000 $1,000 $1,000

Dec. 31,   Dec. 31,   Dec. 31,   Dec. 31,
2007   2008   2009   2010

Interest Rate Is 6% Compounded Annually

Shortcut Approaches

Formula Approach

The formula for the present value of an annuity due of any amount is:

$$P_d = C\left[\frac{1 - \dfrac{1}{(1+i)^{n-1}}}{i} + 1\right]$$

where P_d = present value of an ordinary annuity of a series of cash flows of any amount
C = amount of each cash flow
n = number of cash flows (not the number of time periods)
i = interest rate for each of the stated time periods

In the example, the present value of an annuity due of four cash flows of $1,000 each at 6% compounded annually is calculated as follows:

$$P_d = \$1,000\left[\frac{1 - \dfrac{1}{1.06^3}}{0.06} + 1\right] = \$3,673.01$$

The formula for the present value of an annuity due with cash flows of 1 each is:

$$P_{d_{n,i}} = C\left[\frac{1 - \dfrac{1}{(1+i)^{n-1}}}{i} + 1\right]$$

where $P_{d_{n,i}}$ is the present value of an annuity *due* of n cash flows of 1 each at interest rate i.

With the preceding formula for $P_{d_{n,i}}$ it is possible to express another formula for the future value of an ordinary annuity of cash flows of any size as:

$$P_d = C(P_{d_{n,i}})$$

In a two-step approach the present value of an annuity due of four cash flows of $1,000 each at 6% compounded annually is calculated as follows:

$$\text{Step 1} \quad P_{d_{n=4, i=6\%}} = \left[\frac{1 - \dfrac{1}{1.06^3}}{0.06} + 1 \right] = 3.673012$$

$$\text{Step 2} \quad P_d = \$1,000(3.673012) = \$3,673.01$$

This two-step approach is used to solve the problem when factors are not available.

Table Approach

The formula for $P_{d_{n,i}}$ can be used to construct a table of the future value of any series of cash flows of 1 each for any interest rate. Table 5 at the end of this Module shows the factors for $P_{d_{n,i}}$. Since the factors in Table 5 are based on the formula for $P_{d_{n,i}}$ or

$$\frac{1 - \dfrac{1}{(1+i)^{n-1}}}{i} + 1$$

values, the generalized table approach is as follows:

$$P_d = C(\text{Factor for } P_{d_{n,i}})$$

To calculate the present value of an annuity due of four cash flows of $1,000 each at 6%, the $P_{d_{n=4,\ i=6\%}}$ factor is found in the present value of an annuity due table (Table 5); it is 3.673012. Then the amount of each cash flow, here $1,000, is multiplied by the Table 5 factor to obtain the present value of $3,673.01:

$$P_d = \$1,000(3.673012) = \$3,673.01$$

Alternative Table Approach

By observing the information contained in Examples M-15 and M-12, you can determine another way to compute the present value of an annuity due.[3] When only the present value of an *ordinary* annuity table is available, you can use the factors to determine the present value of an annuity due by completing the following steps:

Step 1	In the ordinary annuity table (Table 4), look up the present value of $n - 1$ cash flows at 6%, or the value of three cash flows at 6%.	2.673012
Step 2	Add 1 without interest to the value obtained in step 1.	<u>1.000000</u>
	This is the converted present value factor for $P_{d_{n=4,\ i=6\%}}$.	<u>3.673012</u>
Step 3	Multiply the amount of each cash flow, here $1,000, by the converted factor for $P_{d_{n=4,\ i=6\%}}$ determined in step 2:	

$$P_d = \$1,000(3.673012) = \$3,673.01$$

---

3. An alternative approach is to multiply the present value of an ordinary annuity factor by 1 plus the interest rate, which is consistent with the formula:

$$\frac{1 - \dfrac{1}{(1+i)^n}}{i} \times (1+i)$$

Thus, the present value in this example would be computed as $1,000 × (3.465106 × 1.06) = $3,673.01.

Thus, if the present value of an annuity due is calculated using tables for the present value of an *ordinary* annuity, **the general rule is to use present value of an ordinary annuity factor for $n - 1$ cash flows and add 1 to the factor.**

Another Application

Besides determining the present value of an annuity due where the amount of each cash flow is known, you can solve other types of problems by using the preceding approaches. Suppose, for example, that Katherine Spruill purchases on January 1, 2007 an item that costs $10,000. She agrees to pay for this item in 10 equal annual installments, with the first installment on January 1, 2007 as a down payment. The equal installments include interest at 8% on the unpaid balance at the beginning of each year. After the interest is deducted, the balance of each payment reduces the principal of the debt. This problem involves the present value of an annuity due. It requires the determination of the amount of each of 10 cash flows that have a present value of $10,000 when discounted at an annual rate of 8%. Example M-16 shows these facts graphically.

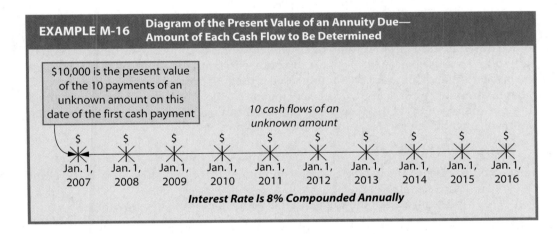

EXAMPLE M-16 — Diagram of the Present Value of an Annuity Due—Amount of Each Cash Flow to Be Determined

$10,000 is the present value of the 10 payments of an unknown amount on this date of the first cash payment

10 cash flows of an unknown amount

Jan. 1, 2007 — Jan. 1, 2008 — Jan. 1, 2009 — Jan. 1, 2010 — Jan. 1, 2011 — Jan. 1, 2012 — Jan. 1, 2013 — Jan. 1, 2014 — Jan. 1, 2015 — Jan. 1, 2016

Interest Rate Is 8% Compounded Annually

The solution to this problem requires the rearrangement of the present value of an annuity due formula:

$$C = \frac{P_0}{\text{Factor for } P_{d_{n,i}}}$$

$$= \frac{\$10,000}{7.246888} = \$1,379.90$$

The down payment of $1,379.90 plus nine more payments of this same amount will retire the principal in nine years, plus pay interest at 8% on the balance of the principal outstanding at the beginning of each year.

PRESENT VALUE OF A DEFERRED ORDINARY ANNUITY

The present value of a deferred ordinary annuity ($P_{deferred}$) is determined on a date two or more periods before the first cash flow in the series. Suppose, for example, that Helen Swain buys an annuity on January 1, 2007 that yields her four annual receipts of $1,000 each, with the first receipt on January 1, 2011. The interest rate is 6% compounded annually. What is the cost of the annuity—that is, what is the present value on January 1, 2007 of the four cash flows of $1,000 each to be received on January 1, 2011, 2012, 2013, and 2014—discounted at 6%? Example M-17 shows the facts of this problem diagrammatically.

8 Compute and use the present value of a deferred ordinary annuity.

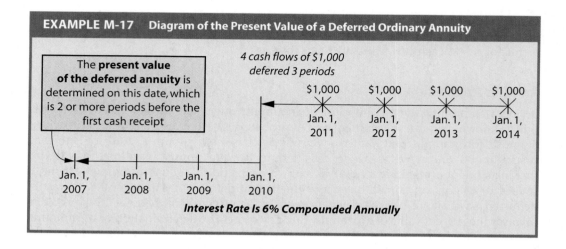

EXAMPLE M-17 **Diagram of the Present Value of a Deferred Ordinary Annuity**

The **present value of the deferred annuity** is determined on this date, which is 2 or more periods before the first cash receipt

4 cash flows of $1,000 deferred 3 periods

$1,000 — Jan. 1, 2011
$1,000 — Jan. 1, 2012
$1,000 — Jan. 1, 2013
$1,000 — Jan. 1, 2014

Jan. 1, 2007
Jan. 1, 2008
Jan. 1, 2009
Jan. 1, 2010

Interest Rate Is 6% Compounded Annually

There are two ways to compute the present value of a deferred annuity. The first method involves a combination of the present value of an ordinary annuity (P_0) and the present value of a single sum due in the future (p). For the stated problem it is necessary to determine first the present value of an *ordinary* annuity of four cash flows of $1,000 each to find a single present value figure discounted to January 1, 2010. Note that because the present value of an ordinary annuity table is used, the present value of the four cash flows is computed on January 1, 2010, *not* January 1, 2011. That single sum is discounted for three more periods at 6% to arrive at the present value on January 1, 2007. Using the factors of $1 each, the present value is stated as follows:

$$P_{deferred} = C[(P_{0_{n,i}})(p_{k,i})]$$

where $P_{0_{n,i}}$ = present value of the ordinary annuity of the n cash flows of 1 at the given interest rate i

$p_{k,i}$ = present value of the single sum of 1 for k periods of deferment

Substituting appropriate factors from Tables 4 and 3, respectively, in this formula, the following solution is obtained:

$$P_{deferred} = C[(P_{0_{n=4, i=6\%}})(p_{k=3, i=6\%})]$$
$$= \$1,000[(3.465106)(0.839619)]$$
$$= \$2,909.37$$

An alternative approach involves a combination of two ordinary annuities. For example, it is possible to calculate the present value of an ordinary annuity of $n + k$ cash flows of 1. From this amount is subtracted the present value of the k (the period of deferment, which is 3 in this example) cash flows of 1. This procedure removes the cash flows that were not available to be received; yet the discount factor for the three periods of deferments on the four cash flows that are to be received remains in the calculated factor. This difference is multiplied by the value of each cash flow to determine the final present value of the deferred annuity. Example M-18 illustrates this approach.

In effect, the present value of an ordinary annuity of $n + k$ cash flows, minus the present value of an ordinary annuity of the k cash flows, becomes a converted factor for the present value of a deferred annuity, as follows:

$$P_{deferred} = C(\text{Converted Factor for Present Value of Deferred Annuity of 1})$$

Using the factors from Table 4, the converted factor for the deferred ordinary annuity stated in the preceding problem is determined as follows:

$$P_{0_{n+k=7, i=6\%}}(5.582381) - P_{0_{k=3, i=6\%}}(2.673012) = 2.909369$$

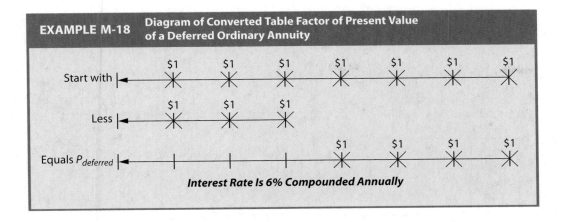

EXAMPLE M-18 | Diagram of Converted Table Factor of Present Value of a Deferred Ordinary Annuity

The present value of the four cash flows of $1,000 each, deferred three periods, is $2,909.37, calculated as follows:

$$P_{deferred} = \$1,000(2.909369) = \$2,909.37$$

Note that the two methods produce the same present value figure. Also, note that the period of deferment is *only* three periods and *not* four because the present value of an ordinary annuity table is used (see Example M-18 in the second approach). This assumption *is* required if the problem is to be solved by the use of *ordinary* annuity factors rather than annuity due factors.

Another Application

Besides determining the present value of a deferred annuity, other types of problems can be solved by using the previous approaches. For example, suppose that David Jones wants to invest $50,000 on January 1, 2007 so that he may withdraw 10 annual cash flows of equal amounts beginning January 1, 2013. If the fund earns 12% annual interest over its life, what will be the amount of each of the 10 withdrawals?

Example M-19 shows the facts of this problem. A simpler method that can be used to solve this problem is a variation of the second suggested solution. Here, the value of C can be determined from the following expression of the present value of a deferred annuity formula:

$$C = \frac{P_{deferred}}{\text{Converted Factor for Present Value of Deferred Annuity of 1}}$$

Using Table 4, the converted factor for 10 cash flows of 1 each, deferred 5 periods at 12%, is as follows:

$$\text{Converted Factor} = P_{0_{n+k=15,\ i=12\%}}(6.810864) - P_{0_{k=5,\ i=12\%}}(3.604776)$$
$$= 3.206088$$

Then the amount of each cash flow is

$$C = \frac{\$50,000}{3.206088} = \$15,595.33$$

The accuracy of the answer produced by the second approach can be tested using the amount of each cash flow and the solution from the first approach. The present value of 10 cash flows of $15,595.33 deferred 5 periods and discounted at 12% must be $50,000 if the first solution is correct. The proof can be calculated as follows:

$$P_{deferred} = \$15,595.33[(5.650223)(0.567427)]$$
$$= \$50,000$$

A slight rounding-error difference may occur with this method because the solution requires the multiplication of two factors, $P_{0_{n,i}}$ and $p_{k,i}$, which are rounded.

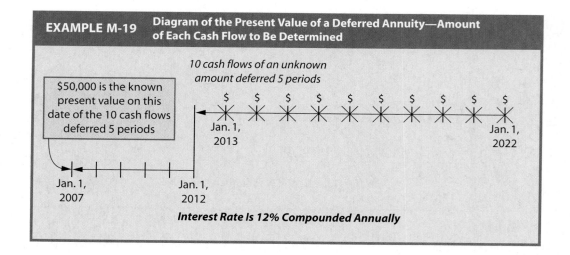

EXAMPLE M-19   Diagram of the Present Value of a Deferred Annuity—Amount of Each Cash Flow to Be Determined

SUMMARY OF PRESENT AND FUTURE VALUE CALCULATIONS

The present and future value calculations discussed in this Module may be summarized by the following diagrams:

	Present Value	**Future Value**
of a single sum for 3 periods		
of a 3-payment ordinary annuity		
of a 3-payment annuity due		

CONCEPTUAL EVALUATION OF PRESENT VALUE TECHNIQUES IN FINANCIAL REPORTING

9 Explain the conceptual issues regarding the use of present value in financial reporting.

Accounting principles have evolved without a unifying objective or rationale for determining when present value techniques should and should not be used. Among the issues are the use of present value for the initial valuation of assets and liabilities, the amortization of those assets and liabilities, and any subsequent revaluation when interest rates change.

Present values are used in generally accepted accounting principles for certain monetary items. A monetary item is money or a claim to money that is not affected by changes in the prices of specific goods or services. For example, a note payable is a monetary item, whereas a warranty payable is a nonmonetary item. Monetary items for which present values are used in generally accepted accounting principles include bonds payable and bond investments, long-term notes payable and receivable, leases, and postretirement benefits (e.g., pensions). Present value is not used for items such as deferred income taxes. Some accountants argue that present value should be used for nonmonetary items such as property, plant, and equipment. However, accounting principles have not been extended to the use of present value for these nonmonetary items, except for the impairment of noncurrent assets. Therefore, present values are not used for warranties, unearned revenue, compensated absences, or for nonmonetary assets. We discuss each of these topics in this book.

Most accountants would argue that the use of present value creates a *relevant* accounting measurement. For example, in the situations we discussed earlier, present value amounts are more relevant than, say, the total of the undiscounted cash flows because they represent the equivalent current cash amount. However, the use of present value may create measurements that are less *reliable* (especially if used for nonmonetary items) because the computation requires:

1. The estimation of the future cash flows, including the timing, amount, and risk of those cash flows.
2. The estimation of the interest rate. Interest rates that could be used include the historical rate, the current rate, the average expected rate, the weighted average cost of capital, or the incremental borrowing rate.[4]
3. The degree to which the cash flows from the individual assets may be added (and the liabilities subtracted) to give a measure of the value of the company.

In 2000, the FASB issued **FASB Statement of Concepts No. 7,** "Using Cash Flow Information and Present Value in Accounting Measurements."[5] The *Statement* provides a framework for using future cash flows as the basis for an accounting measurement of both assets and liabilities. It provides general principles governing the use of present value, as well as the objectives of present value accounting measurements. The *Statement* does not address recognition issues, and therefore does not address when fair value should be based on present value, or when assets or liabilities should be remeasured using present value. It describes five elements that together may be used to determine the value of various assets and liabilities:

1. An estimate of the future cash flow(s) and the timing of those cash flows
2. Estimates about variations in the amount or timing of those cash flows
3. The risk-free interest rate
4. An increase in the interest for any expected risk
5. Other factors, including a lack of liquidity and market imperfections

The methodology introduced in the *Statement* permits development of a fair value using cash flow information even if uncertainties exist about the timing and/or amount of the cash flows. Present value calculations have typically been based on a single set of cash flows and a single discount rate. The *Statement* introduces the concept of "expected cash flows" when using present value techniques for accounting measurements.

Expected cash flows are a probability-weighted average of the range of possible estimated cash flow amounts and/or estimated timing of cash flows. For example, in regard to differing expected amounts, a company may estimate that there is a 20% probability that the cash flow in a given year will be $1,000, a 50% probability that it will be $1,200, and a 30% probability that it will be $1,400. The company would use the expected cash flow of $1,220 [($1,000 × 0.20) + ($1,200 × 0.50) + ($1,400 × 0.30)] in its present value calculations. Or in regard to the timing of its cash flows, a company might determine that it has a 30% probability of receiving $1,000 in one year but a 70% probability of receiving $1,000 in two years. The present value would be calculated as [(30% × the present value of $1,000 in one year) + (70% × the present value of $1,000 in two years)].

The *Statement* also discusses the use of present value to estimate the fair value for a transaction between willing parties or to develop entity-specific measurements. The entity-specific value (or value in use) is the value of an asset or liability to a particular entity. In other words, the measurement substitutes the entity's assumptions for those of the market place. The FASB concluded that an entity-specific measurement might be appropriate in some situations. As with all *FASB Statements of Concepts,* the conclusions do not create specific GAAP, but will provide guidance for the development of future *FASB Statements of Financial Accounting Standards.* The FASB has also issued an *Exposure Draft* on fair value measurements that would clarify the use of present value techniques to estimate fair value.[6]

---

4. R. Aggarwal and C. H. Gibson, *Discounting in Financial Accounting and Reporting* (Morristown, N.J.: Financial Executives Research Foundation, 1989), p. 45.
5. "Using Cash Flow Information and Present Value in Accounting Measurements," *FASB Statement of Financial Accounting Concepts No. 7* (Norwalk, Conn.: FASB, 2000).
6. "Fair Value Measurements," *FASB Proposed Statement of Financial Accounting Standards* (Norwalk, Conn.: FASB, 2004).

SUMMARY

At the beginning of the Module, we identified several objectives you would accomplish after reading the Module. The objectives are listed below, each followed by a brief summary of the key points in the Module discussion.

1. **Understand simple interest and compound interest.** Simple interest is interest on the original principal regardless of the number of time periods that have passed or the amount of interest that has been paid or accrued in the past. Compound interest is the interest that accrues on both the principal and the past unpaid accrued interest.

2. **Compute and use the future value of a single sum.** The future value of a single sum is the original sum plus the compound interest, stated as of a specific future date. The future value may be computed using a formula approach or a table approach (Table 1 at the end of this Module).

3. **Compute and use the present value of a single sum.** The present value is the principal that must be invested at time period zero to produce the known future value. Discounting is the process of converting the future value to the present value. The present value may be computed using a formula approach or a table approach (Table 3).

4. **Compute and use the future value of an ordinary annuity.** An annuity is a series of equal cash flows made at regular intervals with interest compounded at a certain rate. The future value of an ordinary annuity is determined immediately after the last cash flow in the series is made. The future value may be computed using a formula approach or a table approach (Table 2).

5. **Compute and use the future value of annuity due.** The future value of an annuity due is determined one period after the last cash flow in the series. The general rule for determining the future value of an annuity due factor is to take the future value of an ordinary annuity factor (Table 2) for $n + 1$ cash flows and subtract 1 from the factor.

6. **Compute and use the present value of an ordinary annuity.** The present value of an ordinary annuity is determined one period before the first cash flow in the series is made. The present value may be computed using a formula approach or a table approach (Table 4).

7. **Compute and use the present value of annuity due.** The present value of an annuity due is determined on the date of the first cash flow in the series. The present value may be computed using a formula approach or a table approach (Table 5). The general rule for determining the present value of an annuity due factor is to take the present value of an ordinary annuity factor (Table 4) for $n - 1$ cash flows and add 1 to the factor.

8. **Compute and use the present value of a deferred ordinary annuity.** The present value of a deferred ordinary annuity is determined on a date two or more periods before the first cash flow in the series. The general rule for determining the present value of a deferred ordinary annuity factor is to take the factor for the present value of an ordinary annuity of $n + k$ cash flows and subtract the factor for the present value of an ordinary annuity of the k cash flows.

9. **Explain the conceptual issues regarding the use of present value in financial statements.** The conceptual issues include the lack of a unifying objective or rationale for determining when present value techniques should and should not be used. These include the use of present value for the initial valuation of assets and liabilities, the amortization of those assets and liabilities, and any subsequent revaluation when interest rates change. Another issue is that present value may create measurements that are less reliable. In 2000, the FASB issued *FASB Statement of Concepts No. 7*, "Using Cash Flow Information and Present Value in Accounting Measurements." The *Statement* identifies five elements that together may be used to determine the value of various assets and liabilities: (1) an estimate of the future cash flow(s) and the timing of those cash flows, (2) estimates about variations in the amount or timing of those cash flows, (3) the risk-free interest rate, (4) an increase in the interest for any expected risk, and (5) other factors, including a lack of liquidity and market imperfections. The FASB has issued an *Exposure Draft* that would clarify the use of present value to estimate fair value.

QUESTIONS

QM-1   Define *interest*. Explain how the cost of interest is similar to the price of any merchandise item.

QM-2   Discuss the following concepts of interest: *simple interest, compound interest, time value of money, discount.*

QM-3   Distinguish between the *future value of 1* and the *future value of an ordinary annuity of 1.*

QM-4   What is the interest rate per period and the frequency of compounding per year in each of the following?
a. 18% compounded semiannually
b. 16% compounded quarterly
c. 15% compounded monthly

QM-5   Distinguish between the *future value of 1* and the *present value of 1* and between the *present value of 1* and the *present value of an ordinary annuity of 1.*

QM-6   Distinguish between the *future value of an ordinary annuity* and the *future value of an annuity due.* Draw a time line of each.

QM-7   Distinguish between the *present value of an annuity due* and the *present value of a deferred annuity.* Draw a time line of each.

QM-8   Explain how to solve each of the following without tables (in each case use the quickest approach possible):
a. The present value of $10,000 for four years at 10% compounded annually
b. The present value of $5,000 for five years at 10% [start with information developed in (a)]
c. The future value of five cash flows of an ordinary annuity of $3,000 each at 10% compound interest

QM-9   Potter wishes to deposit a sum that at 12% interest, compounded semiannually, will permit two withdrawals: $40,000 at the end of 4 years and $50,000 at the end of 10 years. Analyze the problem to determine the required deposit, stating the procedure to follow and the tables to use in developing the solution.

QM-10 The following factors are taken from the compound interest tables for the same number of time periods and/or cash flows for the same interest rate:
a. 8.137249
b. 50.980352
c. 6.265060
d. 7.142168
e. 0.122892

Identify each of the five compound interest table factors without reference to the tables. Discuss briefly.

QM-11 Explain how to determine the converted table factor for any deferred annuity by using the present value of an ordinary annuity table.

QM-12 Samuel Ames owes $20,000 to a friend. He wants to know how much he would have to pay if he paid the debt in three annual installments at the end of each year, which would include interest at 14%. Draw a time line for the problem. Indicate what table to use. Look up the table value and place in a brief formula, but do not solve.

QM-13 Starting with the given value for $(1.16)^{10} = 4.411435$, describe the fastest way to solve each of the following:
a. $P_{n=10, i=16\%}$
b. $f_{n=20, i=16\%}$
c. $F_{0_{n=10, i=16\%}}$
d. $P_{0_{n=10, i=16\%}}$
e. $F_{0_{n=20, i=16\%}}$

Select the best answer for each of the following.
Items 1 through 4 require use of present value tables. The following are the present value factors of $1 discounted at 8% for one to five periods. Each item is based on 8% interest compounded annually from day of deposit to day of withdrawal.

Periods	Present Value of $1 Discounted at 8% per Period
1	0.926
2	0.857
3	0.794
4	0.735
5	0.681

MM-1   What amount should be deposited in a bank today to grow to $1,000 three years from today?
a. $\dfrac{\$1,000}{0.794}$
b. $1,000 × 0.926 × 3
c. ($1,000 × 0.926) + ($1,000 × 0.857) + ($1,000 × 0.794)
d. $1,000 × 0.794

MM-2   What amount should an individual have in his bank account today, before withdrawal, if he needs $2,000 each year for four years, with the first withdrawal to be made today and each subsequent withdrawal at one-year intervals? (He is to have exactly a zero balance in his bank account after the fourth withdrawal.)
a. $2,000 + ($2,000 × 0.926) + ($2,000 × 0.857) + ($2,000 × 0.794)
b. $\dfrac{\$2,000}{0.735} × 4$

c. ($2,000 × 0.926) + ($2,000 × 0.857) + ($2,000 × 0.794) + ($2,000 × 0.735)
d. $\dfrac{\$2,000}{0.926} × 4$

MM-3   If an individual put $3,000 in a savings account today, what amount of cash will be available two years from today?
a. $3,000 × 0.857
b. $3,000 × 0.857 × 2
c. $\dfrac{\$3,000}{0.857}$
d. $\dfrac{\$3,000}{0.926} × 2$

MM-4   What is the present value today of $4,000 to be received six years from today?
a. $4,000 × 0.926 × 6
b. $4,000 × 0.794 × 2
c. $4,000 × 0.681 × 0.926
d. Cannot be determined from the information given

MM-5   On January 1, 2007 Kern Company sold a machine to Burns Company. Burns signed a non-interest-bearing note requiring payment of $30,000 annually for seven years. The first payment was made on January 1, 2007. The prevailing rate of interest for this type of note at the date of issuance was 10%. Information on present value factors is as follows:

Periods	Present Value of 1 at 10%	Present Value of Ordinary Annuity of 1 at 10%
6	0.56	4.36
7	0.51	4.87

Kern should record the sale in January 2007 at

a. $107,100

b. $130,800

c. $146,100

d. $160,800

MM-6 On May 1, 2007, a company purchased a new machine that it does not have to pay for until May 1, 2009. The total payment on May 1, 2009 will include both principal and interest. Assuming interest at a 10% rate, the cost of the machine would be the total payment multiplied by what time value of money concept?

a. Future value of annuity of 1

b. Future value of 1

c. Present value of annuity of 1

d. Present value of 1

MM-7 An office equipment representative has a machine for sale or lease. If you buy the machine, the cost is $7,596. If you lease the machine, you will have to sign a noncancellable lease and make five payments of $2,000 each. The first payment will be paid on the first day of the lease. At the time of the last payment you will receive title to the machine. The present value of an ordinary annuity of $1 is as follows:

Present Value

Number of Periods	10%	12%	16%
1	0.909	0.893	0.862
2	1.736	1.690	1.605
3	2.487	2.402	2.246
4	3.170	3.037	2.798
5	3.791	3.605	3.274

The interest rate implicit in this lease is approximately

a. 10%

b. 12%

c. Between 10% and 12%

d. 16%

MM-8 An accountant wishes to find the present value of an annuity of $1 payable at the beginning of each period at 10% for eight periods. He has only one present value table, which shows the present value of an annuity of $1 payable at the end of each period. To compute the present value factor

he needs, the accountant would use the present value factor in the 10% column for

a. Seven periods

b. Seven periods and add 1

c. Eight periods

d. Nine periods and subtract 1

MM-9 On July 1, 2007, James Rago signed an agreement to operate as a franchisee of Fast Foods, Inc., for an initial franchise fee of $60,000. Of this amount, $20,000 was paid when the agreement was signed and the balance is payable in four equal annual payments of $10,000 beginning July 1, 2008. The agreement provides that the down payment is not refundable and no future services are required of the franchisor. Rago's credit rating indicates that he can borrow money at 14% for a loan of this type. Information on present and future value factors is as follows:

Present value of $1 at 14% for four periods	0.59
Future value of $1 at 14% for four periods	1.69
Present value of an ordinary annuity of $1 at 14% for four periods	2.91

Rago should record the acquisition cost of the franchise on July 1, 2007 at

a. $43,600

b. $49,100

c. $60,000

d. $67,600

MM-10 For which of the following transactions would the use of the present value of an annuity due concept be appropriate in calculating the present value of the asset obtained or liability owed at the date of incurrence?

a. A capital lease is entered into with the initial lease payment due one month subsequent to the signing of the lease agreement.

b. A capital lease is entered into with the initial lease payment due upon the signing of the lease agreement.

c. A 10-year, 8% bond is issued on January 2, with interest payable semiannually on July 1 and January 1 yielding 7%.

d. A 10-year, 8% bond is issued on January 2, with interest payable semiannually on July 1 and January 1 yielding 9%.

EXERCISES

EM-1 *Future Value of an Investment and Compound Interest* Using the future value tables, solve the following:

Required

1. What is the value on January 1, 2014 of $40,000 deposited on January 1, 2007 which accumulates interest at 12% compounded annually?

2. What is the value on January 1, 2013 of $10,000 deposited on July 1, 2007 which accumulates interest at 16% compounded quarterly?

3. What is the compound interest on an investment of $6,000 left on deposit for five years at 10% compounded annually?

EM-2 *Future Value of an Investment* Hugh Colson deposited $20,000 in a special savings account that provides for interest at the annual rate of 12% compounded semiannually if the deposit is maintained for four years.

Required

Calculate the balance of the savings account at the end of the four-year period.

EM-3   *Present Value of a Sum and Compound Discount* Using the present value tables, solve the following problems:

Required
1. What is the present value on January 1, 2007 of $30,000 due on January 1, 2012 and discounted at 12% compounded annually?
2. What is the present value on July 1, 2007 of $8,000 due January 1, 2012 and discounted at 16% compounded quarterly?
3. What is the compound discount on $8,000 due at the end of five years at 10% compounded annually?

EM-4   *Future Value of Annuity* Using appropriate tables, solve the following future value of annuity problems:

Required
1. What is the future value on December 31, 2013 of seven cash flows of $10,000, with the first cash payment being made on December 31, 2007 and interest at 12% being compounded annually?
2. What is the future value on December 31, 2014 of seven cash flows of $10,000, with the first cash payment made on December 31, 2007 and interest at 12% being compounded annually?

EM-5   *Present Value of an Annuity* Samuel David wants to make five equal annual withdrawals of $8,000 from a fund that will earn interest at 10% compounded annually.

Required
How much would David have to invest on:
1. January 1, 2007 if the first withdrawal is made on January 1, 2008?
2. January 1, 2007 if the first withdrawal is made on January 1, 2007?

EM-6   *Amount of Each Cash Flow* Six equal annual contributions are made to a fund, with the first deposit on December 31, 2007.

Required
Using the future value tables, determine the equal contributions that, if invested at 10% compounded annually, will produce a fund of $30,000, assuming that this sum is desired on December 31, 2012.

EM-7   *Amount of an Annuity* Beginning December 31, 2011, five equal annual withdrawals are to be made.

Required
Using the appropriate tables, determine the equal annual withdrawals if $25,000 is invested at an interest of 12% compounded annually on
1. December 31, 2010
2. December 31, 2011
3. December 31, 2007

EM-8   *Amount of Each Cash Flow* R. Lee Rouse borrows $10,000 that is to be repaid in 24 equal monthly installments payable at the end of each subsequent month with interest at the rate of 1½% a month.

Required
Using the appropriate table, calculate the equal installments.

EM-9   *Amount of Each Cash Flow* On January 1, 2007 Charles Jamison borrows $40,000 from his father to open a business. The son is the beneficiary of a trust created by his favorite aunt from which he will receive $25,000 on January 1, 2017. He signs an agreement to make this amount payable to his father and, further, to pay his father equal annual amounts from January 1, 2008 to January 1, 2016, inclusive, in retirement of the debt. Interest is 12%.

Required
What are the annual payments?

EM-10   *Amount of an Annuity* Beginning with January 1, 2007, five equal deposits are to be made in a fund.

Required
Using the appropriate tables, determine the equal deposits if interest at 10% is compounded annually and if $200,000 must be in the fund on
1. January 1, 2012
2. January 1, 2013

EM-11   *Series of Compound Interest Techniques* The following are several situations involving compound interest.

Required
Using the appropriate table, solve each of the following:
1. Hope Dearborn invests $40,000 on January 1, 2007 in a savings account that earns interest of 8% compounded semiannually. What will be the amount in the fund on December 31, 2012?

2. Ben Johnson receives a bonus of $5,000 each year on December 31. He starts depositing his bonus on December 31, 2007 in a savings account that earns interest of 12% compounded annually. What will be the amount in the fund on December 31, 2011 after he deposits his bonus received on that date?

3. Ron Sewert owes $30,000 on a non-interest-bearing note due January 1, 2017. He offers to pay the amount on January 1, 2007 provided that it is discounted at 10% on a compound annual discount basis. What would he have to pay on January 1, 2007 under this assumption?

4. June Stickney purchased an annuity on January 1, 2007 which, at a 12% annual rate, would yield $6,000 each June 30 and December 31 for the next six years. What was the cost of the annuity to Stickney?

5. Five equal annual contributions are to be made to a fund, the first deposit on December 31, 2007. Determine the equal contributions that, if invested at 10% compounded annually, will produce a fund of $30,000 on December 31, 2012.

6. Beginning on December 31, 2008, six equal annual withdrawals are to be made. Determine the equal annual withdrawals if $11,000 is invested at 10% interest compounded annually on December 31, 2007.

EM-12 *Amount of an Annuity* John Goodheart wishes to provide for six annual withdrawals of $3,000 each beginning January 1, 2017. He wishes to make 10 annual deposits beginning January 1, 2007, with the last deposit to be made on January 1, 2016.

Required

If the fund earns interest compounded annually at 10%, how much is each of the 10 deposits?

EM-13 *Present Value of Leased Asset* On January 1, 2007 Ashly Farms leased a hay baler from Agrico Tractor Company. Ashly was having cash flow problems, so Agrico drew up the lease to allow Ashly to reestablish itself. The lease requires Ashly to make $3,000 payments on January 1 of each year for five years beginning in 2007. The interest rate is 12%.

Required

Calculate the present value of the cost of the lease payments to Ashly on January 1, 2007.

EM-14 *Number of Cash Flows* On July 1, 2007 Boston Company purchased a machine at a cost of $80,000. It paid $56,046.06 in cash and signed a 10% note for the difference. This note is to be paid off in annual installments of $5,000 each, payable each July 1, beginning immediately. The $5,000 includes a payment of interest on the balance of the principal at the beginning of each period and a payment on the principal.

Required

Calculate the number of annual payments to be made by Boston Company.

PROBLEMS

PM-1 *Future Value of an Investment* Using the future value tables, solve the following:

Required

1. What is the future value on December 31, 2011 of a deposit of $35,000 made on December 31, 2007 assuming interest of 10% compounded annually?

2. What is the future value on December 31, 2011 of a deposit of $10,000 made on December 31, 2007 assuming interest of 16% compounded quarterly?

3. What is the future value on December 31, 2011 of a deposit of $25,000 made on December 31, 2007 assuming interest of 12% compounded semiannually?

PM-2 *Present Value Issues* Using the present value tables, solve the following:

Required

1. What is the present value on January 1, 2007 of $30,000 due on January 1, 2011 and discounted at 10% compounded annually?

2. What is the present value on January 1, 2007 of $40,000 due on January 1, 2011 and discounted at 11% compounded semiannually?

3. What is the present value on January 1, 2007 of $50,000 due on January 1, 2011 and discounted at 16% compounded quarterly?

PM-3 *Future Value Issues* Using the future values tables, solve the following:

Required

1. What is the future value on December 31, 2016 of 10 cash flows of $20,000 with the first cash payment made on December 31, 2007 and interest at 10% being compounded annually?

2. What is the future value on June 30, 2017 of 20 cash flows of $15,000 with the first cash payment made on December 31, 2007 and the annual interest rate of 10% being compounded semiannually?

3. What is the future value on December 31, 2017 of 20 cash flows of $15,000 with the first cash payment made on December 31, 2007 and the annual interest rate of 10% being compounded semiannually?

PM-4   *Amount of Each Cash Flow* On December 31, 2014 Michael McDowell desires to have $60,000. He plans to make six deposits in a fund to provide this amount. Interest is compounded annually at 12%.

Required
Compute the equal annual amounts that McDowell must deposit assuming that he makes the first deposit on
1.   December 31, 2009
2.   December 31, 2008

PM-5   *Value of an Annuity* John Joshua wants to make five equal annual withdrawals of $20,000 from a fund that will earn interest at 12% compounded annually.

Required
How much would Joshua have to invest on January 1, 2007 if he makes the first withdrawal on
1.   January 1, 2008?
2.   January 1, 2007?
3.   January 1, 2012?

PM-6   *Value of an Annuity* Ralph Benke wants to make eight equal semiannual withdrawals of $8,000 from a fund that will earn interest at 11% compounded semiannually.

Required
How much would Benke have to invest on:
1.   January 1, 2007 if the first withdrawal is made on July 1, 2007?
2.   July 1, 2007 if the first withdrawal is made on July 1, 2007?
3.   January 1, 2007 if the first withdrawal is made on January 1, 2010?

PM-7   *Various Compound Interest Issues* You are given the following situations:

1.   Thomas Petry owes a debt of $7,000 from the purchase of a boat. The debt bears interest of 12% payable annually. Petry will pay the debt and interest in five annual installments beginning in one year. Calculate the equal annual installments that will pay off the debt and interest at 12% on the unpaid balance.

2.   On January 1, 2007 John Cothran offers to buy Ruth House's used tractor and equipment for $4,000 payable in 12 equal semiannual installments, which are to include payment of 10% interest on the unpaid balance and payment of a portion of the principal, with the first installment to be made on January 1, 2007. Calculate the amount of each of these installments.

3.   Nadine Love invests in a $60,000 annuity at 12% compounded annually on March 1, 2007. The first of 15 receipts from the annuity is payable to Love on March 1, 2017, 10 years after the annuity is purchased and on the date Love expects to retire. Calculate the amount of each of the 15 equal annual receipts.

Required
Using the appropriate tables, solve each of the preceding situations.

PM-8   *Value of an Annuity* Using the appropriate tables, solve each of the following:

Required
1.   Beginning December 31, 2008, five equal withdrawals are to be made. Determine the equal annual withdrawals if $30,000 is invested at 10% interest compounded annually on December 31, 2007.

2.   Ten payments of $3,000 are due at annual intervals beginning June 30, 2008. What amount will be accepted in cancellation of this series of payments on June 30, 2007 assuming a discount rate of 14% compounded annually?

3.   Ten payments of $2,000 are due at annual intervals beginning December 31, 2007. What amount will be accepted in cancellation of this series of payments on January 1, 2007 assuming a discount rate of 12% compounded annually?

PM-9   *Amount of Each Cash Flow* On January 1, 2007 Philip Holding invests $40,000 in an annuity to provide eight equal semiannual payments. Interest is 10%, compounded semiannually.

Required
Compute the equal semiannual amounts that Holding will receive, assuming that the first withdrawal is to be received on
1.   July 1, 2007
2.   January 1, 2007
3.   July 1, 2010
4.   January 1, 2012

PM-10   *Number of Cash Flows*   The following are two independent situations.

1. Houser wishes to accumulate a fund of $40,000 for the purchase of a house and lot. He plans to deposit $4,000 semiannually at the end of each six months. Assuming interest at 14% a year compounded semiannually, how many deposits of $4,000 each will be required and what is the amount of the last deposit?

2. On January 1, 2007 Joan Campbell borrows $20,000 from Susan Rone and agrees to repay this amount in payments of $4,000 a year until the debt is paid in full. Payments are to be of an equal amount and are to include interest at 12% on the unpaid balance of principal at the beginning of each period. Assuming that the first payment is to be made on January 1, 2008, determine the number of payments of $4,000 each to be made and the amount of the final payment.

Required

Using the appropriate tables, solve each of the preceding situations.

PM-11   *Serial Installments; Amounts Applicable to Interest and Principal*   Ronald McDuffie purchases a new car at a cost of $14,400. He pays $3,000 down and issues an installment note payable by which he promises to pay the balance in 18 equal monthly installments, which include interest at an annual rate of 18% on the remaining unpaid balance at the beginning of each month, starting with the first month after the purchase.

Required

1. Compute the equal installment payments.
2. Compute the interest that will be paid for each of the first two periods. Indicate the amount of each payment that will be a reduction of principal.

PM-12   *Determining Loan Repayments*   Rockness needs $40,000 to pay off a loan due on December 31, 2016. His plans included the making of 10 annual deposits beginning on December 31, 2007 in accumulating a fund to pay off the loan. Without making a precise calculation, Rockness made three annual deposits of $4,000 each on December 31, 2007, 2008, and 2009, which have been earning interest at 10% compounded annually.

Required

What is the equal amount of each of the next seven deposits for the period December 31, 2010 to December 31, 2016 to reach the fund objective, assuming that the fund will continue to earn interest at 10% compounded annually?

PM-13   *Purchase of Asset*   William Thomas intends to purchase a tractor on credit. Two local implement dealers have offered him the following payment plans for identical tractors:

1. Redd Truck & Tractor's plan calls for five annual payments of $10,350, with the first payment now and the remaining payments at the beginning of each of the next four years.
2. Greene Farm Implements requires semiannual payments of $5,750 at the end of each of the next 10 semiannual periods, with the first payment to be in six months.

Required

Determine which of the preceding plans offers Thomas the lower present value. The applicable annual interest rate is 10% for both alternatives.

PM-14   *Fund to Retire Bonds*   At the beginning of 2007 Shanklin Company issued 10-year bonds with a face value of $1,000,000 due on December 31, 2016. The company wants to accumulate a fund to retire these bonds at maturity by making annual deposits beginning on December 31, 2007.

Required

How much must the company deposit each year, assuming that the fund will earn 12% interest a year compounded annually?

PM-15   *Asset Purchase Price*   BWP, Inc., is considering the purchase of an asset. BWP's required rate of return on new assets is 12%. The expected net cash inflows generated by the new asset are as follows:

Years	Amount	Nature of the Cash Inflows
1–4	$3,000	Net operating revenues
5–9	2,500	Net operating revenues
10	2,000	Net operating revenues
10	1,000	Sale of asset

Required

Given that the net cash inflows can be realized, what is the maximum amount BWP should be willing to pay for the new asset? Assume that each cash inflow occurs at the end of the year. (*Contributed by Norma C. Powell*)

PM-16   *Acquisition of Asset*   SuMar Company purchased a new piece of machinery by paying $2,000 down and agreeing to pay $1,000 at the end of each year for five years. The appropriate interest rate is 8%.

Required

1. What is the cost of the machinery?

2. Prepare the journal entry to record the purchase of the machinery.
3. Prepare a table that shows the interest and ending balance of the liability each year. (*Contributed by Norma C. Powell*)

PM-17 *Present Value Issues* Nello Construction Company has just purchased several major pieces of road-building equipment. Since the purchase price is so large, the equipment company is giving Nello an option of choosing one of four different payment plans:

1. $600,000 immediately in cash.
2. $200,000 down payment now; $65,000 per year for 12 years, beginning at the end of the current year.
3. $200,000 down payment now; $25,000 per year for 3 years beginning at the end of the current year; $75,000 per year for 11 years beginning at the end of the fourth year after the purchase.
4. $80,000 now and at the beginning of each of the next 13 years.

Required
You have been asked by the Nello Construction Company to decide which payment plan will provide the smallest present value. The expected effective interest rate during the future periods stated above is 12%.

PM-18 **AICPA Adapted** *Comprehensive*

Part a. Reproduced in the following table are the first three lines from the 2% columns of each of several tables of mathematical values. For each of the following items, you are to select from among these fragmentary tables the one from which the amount required can be obtained *most directly* (assuming that the complete table was available in each instance):

Periods	Table A	Table B	Table C	Table D	Table E	Table F
0	1.0000		1.0000			
1	0.9804	1.0200	1.0200	1.0000	0.9804	1.0200
2	0.9612	2.0604	1.0404	0.4950	1.9416	0.5150
3		3.1216		0.3268	2.8839	0.3468

1. The amount to which a single sum would accumulate at compound interest by the end of a specified period (interest compounded annually).
2. The amount that must be appropriated at the end of each of a specific number of years to provide for the accumulation, at annually compounded interest, of a certain sum.
3. The amount that must be deposited in a fund that will earn interest at a specified rate, compounded annually, in order to make possible the withdrawal of certain equal sums annually over a specified period starting one year from date of deposit.
4. The amount of interest that will accumulate on a single deposit by the end of a specified period (interest compounded semiannually).
5. The amount, net of compound discount, that if paid now would settle a debt of larger amount due at a specified future date.

Part b. The following tables of values at 10% interest may be used as needed to answer the questions in this part of the problem.

Periods	Future Value of 1 at Compound Interest	Present Value of 1 at Compound Interest	Future Value of Annuity of 1 at End of Each Period	Present Value of Annuity of 1 at End of Each Period
1	1.100	0.9091	1.0000	0.9091
.	.	.	.	.
.	.	.	.	.
.	.	.	.	.
6	1.7716	0.5645	7.7156	4.3553
7	1.9487	0.5132	9.4872	4.8684
8	2.1436	0.4665	11.4359	5.3349
9	2.3579	0.4241	13.5795	5.7590
10	2.5937	0.3855	15.9374	6.1446
11	2.8531	0.3505	18.5312	6.4951
12	3.1384	0.3186	21.3843	6.8137
13	3.4523	0.2897	24.5227	7.1034
14	3.7975	0.2633	27.9750	7.3667
15	4.1772	0.2394	31.7725	7.6061
16	4.5950	0.2176	35.9497	7.8237

1. Your client has made annual payments of $2,500 into a fund at the close of each year for the past three years. The fund balance immediately after the third payment totaled $8,275. He has asked you how many more $2,500 annual payments

will be required to bring the fund to $22,500, assuming that the fund continues to earn interest at 10% compounded annually. Compute the number of full payments required and the amount of the final payment if it does not require the entire $2,500. Carefully label all computations supporting your answer.

2. Your client wishes to provide for the payment of an obligation of $200,000 due on July 1, 2014. He plans to deposit $20,000 in a special fund each July 1 for 7 years, starting July 1, 2008. He wishes to make an initial deposit on July 1, 2007 of an amount that, with its accumulated interest, will bring the fund up to $200,000 at the maturity of the obligation. He expects that the fund will earn interest at the rate of 10% compounded annually. Compute the amount to be deposited July 1, 2007. Carefully label all computations supporting your answer.

PM-19   *Comprehensive*   The following are three independent situations:

1. M. Herman has decided to set up a scholarship fund for students. She is willing to deposit $5,000 in a trust fund at the end of each year for 10 years. She wants the trust fund to then pay annual scholarships at the end of each year for 30 years.
2. Charles Jordy is planning to save for his retirement. He has decided that he can save $3,000 at the end of each year for the next 10 years, $5,000 at the end of each year for years 11 through 20, and $10,000 at the end of each year for years 21 through 30.
3. Patricia Karpas has $200,000 in savings on the day she retires. She intends to spend $2,000 per month traveling around the world for the next two years, during which time her savings will earn 18%, compounded monthly. For the next five years, she intends to spend $6,000 every six months, during which time her savings will earn 12%, compounded semiannually. For the rest of her life expectancy of 15 years, she wants an annuity to cover her living costs. During this period her savings will earn 10% compounded annually. Assume that all payments occur at the end of each period.

Required

1. In Situation 1, how much will the annual scholarships be if the fund can earn 6%? 10%?
2. In Situation 2,
   (a) How much will Jordy have at the end of 30 years if his savings can earn 10%? 6%?
   (b) If Jordy expects to live for 20 years in retirement, how much can he spend each year if his savings earn 10%? 6%?
   (c) How much would Jordy need to invest today to have the same amount available at the time he retires as calculated in 2(a) at 10%? 6%?
3. In Situation 3, how much will Karpas's annuity be?

CASES

CM-1   Cost of Insurance Plans

The Johnson Company is considering three different time periods for an insurance policy on its main office building. The premiums on a fire insurance policy covering the building for the amount of $2,000,000 on a one-year, three-year, and five-year basis are as follows:

One year	$ 4,480
Three years	11,200
Five years	17,920

In each case the entire premium for the full term of the policy is payable at the beginning of the year in which the policy is purchased.

Required

Evaluate the annual cost of each insurance plan for the insured, assuming that money is worth 12% compounded annually. Which plan do you recommend? State the savings for the company.

CM-2   Acquisition of Equipment

The manager of the Taylor Company has consulted you, the controller, as to which of the following plans you would recommend in acquiring the use of a piece of heavy equipment:

1. Purchase the equipment and pay immediately a cash price of $36,800. The service life of the heavy equipment

is estimated to be five years, with a resale value at the end of that time of $5,500.
2. Lease the equipment at the rate of $9,100 per year for five years, payable at the beginning of each year.

Required

Assuming that the time value of money is 12%, evaluate the two alternatives and indicate which plan you would recommend to the manager, stating the value of savings to the company.

CM-3   Effective Interest in Various Situations

On March 1, 2007 the White Company purchased $400,000 worth of inventory on credit with terms of 1/20, n/60. In the past, White has always followed the policy of making payment one month (30 days) after the goods are purchased.

A new member of White's staff has indicated that the company he previously worked for never passed up its cash discounts, and he wonders if this is not a sound policy. It was pointed out, however, that if White were to pay the bill on March 20 rather than on March 30, it would have to borrow the necessary funds for the 10 extra days. White's borrowing terms with a local bank were estimated to be at 14% (annual rate), with a 15% compensating balance (a requirement by the bank that White maintain an amount in its account equal to 15% of the loan) for the term of the loan. Most members of White's staff felt that it made little sense to take out a 14% loan with a compensating balance of 15% in order to save 1% on $400,000 by paying the account 10 days earlier than planned.

Required

1. In terms of simple effective annual interest cost, explain whether it would be to White's advantage to borrow the amount necessary to take the 1% discount by paying the bill 10 days early.
2. It has also been pointed out to White that if it does not take advantage of the cash discount, it should wait the entire 60-day period to pay the full bill rather than pay within 30 days. Explain how your answer to Requirement 1 would change if White undertook this policy.
3. Your answer to Requirement 2 indicates that, in relation to Requirement 1, it has become either more desirable or less desirable to borrow in order to take advantage of the 1% cash discount.
   a. If you said *more desirable,* explain why.
   b. If you said *less desirable,* make a similar explanation.

CM-4 Future Value of Single Investment and Annuity

Jane Dough was a teller in a large northeastern bank. She was single and approaching age 30, and she considered herself an honest and upright citizen. After considering what she might do to build a retirement plan for the future, she decided to embezzle $1,500,000. Subsequently she gave herself up to the authorities but did not return the $1,500,000. She was tried, convicted, and sentenced to 20 years in prison. After completing her 20-year term, she returned the $1,500,000 that she had stolen. She then decided to take a world cruise. On the ship someone asked her how she had accumulated enough money to afford the trip. She replied, "Do you know how much *interest* $1,500,000 will earn in 20 years if invested at an annual rate of 16% compounded quarterly?"

Required

1. Determine the answer to Jane Dough's question. The table factor for $f_{n=40,\ i=4\%}$ is 4.801021.
2. Evaluate Jane's retirement decision, assuming that she could have earned $21,000 each year for each of the 20 years she was in prison. Assume that $11,000 is

required each year to cover living expenses and that she could have invested the remaining $10,000 at the end of each year to earn interest at 16% compounded annually.

CM-5 Value of a Note

You have just been promoted to manager at a national CPA firm. On your first job a new accountant approaches you with the following situation: He has discovered that the president of the client company has a brother who is both the major stockholder and the president of a local bank. Your client has a $300,000, five-year note payable to the bank at 4% interest compounded annually. Since the going interest rate is 16%, the accountant suggests that the note be recorded at its present value using this going rate. The president says that the effective liability is $300,000 and should be reported on the balance sheet at this figure. The note was issued on January 1, 2007 and is due on January 1, 2012.

Required

1. Explain who is correct.
2. At what amount should the company have valued the note on January 1, 2007, assuming that the accountant's assessment is correct?

CM-6 Future Value and Present Value Issues

Jean Perry has a $25,000 whole-life insurance policy that she began many years ago. She is presently 55 years old. One of the benefits of the policy is that Perry can borrow up to a given amount at 12% interest (2% below the current rate), with the principal due two years after the loan is made. The policy states that should Perry default on the principal payment, it will simply be deducted from the amount given her beneficiary when she dies. However, the interest will continue to accrue as long as the note is not paid. Perry has just borrowed $5,000 on this policy to take a vacation in Hawaii.

Required

Assuming that a woman of Perry's health is expected to live to be 72, explain whether it would be financially advantageous for Perry to repay the principal on the loan in two years. (Calculations are not required.)

COMPOUND INTEREST TABLES

Table 1: Future Value of 1: $f_{n,i} = (1 + i)^n$

Table 2: Future Value of an Ordinary Annuity of 1: $F_{0_{n,i}} = \dfrac{(1+i)^n - 1}{i}$

Table 3: Present Value of 1: $p_{n,i} = \dfrac{1}{(1 + i)^n}$

Table 4: Present Value of an Ordinary Annuity of 1: $P_{0_{n,i}} = \dfrac{1 - \dfrac{1}{(1+i)^n}}{i}$

Table 5: Present Value of Annuity Due: $P_{d_{n,i}} = \dfrac{1 - \dfrac{1}{(1+i)^{n-1}}}{i} + 1$

Table 1 FUTURE VALUE OF 1: $f_{n,i} = (1 + i)^n$

n	1.5%	4.0%	4.5%	5.0%	5.5%	6.0%	7.0%
1	1.015000	1.040000	1.045000	1.050000	1.055000	1.060000	1.070000
2	1.030225	1.081600	1.092025	1.102500	1.113025	1.123600	1.144900
3	1.045678	1.124864	1.141166	1.157625	1.174241	1.191016	1.225043
4	1.061364	1.169859	1.192519	1.215506	1.238825	1.262477	1.310796
5	1.077284	1.216653	1.246182	1.276282	1.306960	1.338226	1.402552
6	1.093443	1.265319	1.302260	1.340096	1.378843	1.418519	1.500730
7	1.109845	1.315932	1.360862	1.407100	1.454679	1.503630	1.605781
8	1.126493	1.368569	1.422101	1.477455	1.534687	1.593848	1.718186
9	1.143390	1.423312	1.486095	1.551328	1.619094	1.689479	1.838459
10	1.160541	1.480244	1.552969	1.628895	1.708144	1.790848	1.967151
11	1.177949	1.539454	1.622853	1.710339	1.802092	1.898299	2.104852
12	1.195618	1.601032	1.695881	1.795856	1.901207	2.012196	2.252192
13	1.213552	1.665074	1.772196	1.885649	2.005774	2.132928	2.409845
14	1.231756	1.731676	1.851945	1.979932	2.116091	2.260904	2.578534
15	1.250232	1.800944	1.935282	2.078928	2.232476	2.396558	2.759032
16	1.268986	1.872981	2.022370	2.182875	2.355263	2.540352	2.952164
17	1.288020	1.947900	2.113377	2.292018	2.484802	2.692773	3.158815
18	1.307341	2.025817	2.208479	2.406619	2.621466	2.854339	3.379932
19	1.326951	2.106849	2.307860	2.526950	2.765647	3.025600	3.616528
20	1.346855	2.191123	2.411714	2.653298	2.917757	3.207135	3.869684
21	1.367058	2.278768	2.520241	2.785963	3.078234	3.399564	4.140562
22	1.387564	2.369919	2.633652	2.925261	3.247537	3.603537	4.430402
23	1.408377	2.464716	2.752166	3.071524	3.426152	3.819750	4.740530
24	1.429503	2.563304	2.876014	3.225100	3.614590	4.048935	5.072367
25	1.450945	2.665836	3.005434	3.386355	3.813392	4.291871	5.427433
26	1.472710	2.772470	3.140679	3.555673	4.023129	4.549383	5.807353
27	1.494800	2.883369	3.282010	3.733456	4.244401	4.822346	6.213868
28	1.517222	2.998703	3.429700	3.920129	4.477843	5.111687	6.648838
29	1.539981	3.118651	3.584036	4.116136	4.724124	5.418388	7.114257
30	1.563080	3.243398	3.745318	4.321942	4.983951	5.743491	7.612255

n	8.0%	9.0%	10.0%	12.0%	14.0%	16.0%	18.0%
1	1.080000	1.090000	1.100000	1.120000	1.140000	1.160000	1.180000
2	1.166400	1.188100	1.210000	1.254400	1.299600	1.345600	1.392400
3	1.259712	1.295029	1.331000	1.404928	1.481544	1.560896	1.643032
4	1.360489	1.411582	1.464100	1.573519	1.688960	1.810639	1.938778
5	1.469328	1.538624	1.610510	1.762342	1.925415	2.100342	2.287758
6	1.586874	1.677100	1.771561	1.973823	2.194973	2.436396	2.699554
7	1.713824	1.828039	1.948717	2.210681	2.502269	2.826220	3.185474
8	1.850930	1.992563	2.143589	2.475963	2.852586	3.278415	3.758859
9	1.999005	2.171893	2.357948	2.773079	3.251949	3.802961	4.435454
10	2.158925	2.367364	2.593742	3.105848	3.707221	4.411435	5.233836
11	2.331639	2.580426	2.853117	3.478550	4.226232	5.117265	6.175926
12	2.518170	2.812665	3.138428	3.895976	4.817905	5.936027	7.287593
13	2.719624	3.065805	3.452271	4.363493	5.492411	6.885791	8.599359
14	2.937194	3.341727	3.797498	4.887112	6.261349	7.987518	10.147244
15	3.172169	3.642482	4.177248	5.473566	7.137938	9.265521	11.973748
16	3.425943	3.970306	4.594973	6.130394	8.137249	10.748004	14.129023
17	3.700018	4.327633	5.054470	6.866041	9.276464	12.467685	16.672247
18	3.996019	4.717120	5.559917	7.689966	10.575169	14.462514	19.673251
19	4.315701	5.141661	6.115909	8.612762	12.055693	16.776517	23.214436
20	4.660957	5.604411	6.727500	9.646293	13.743490	19.460759	27.393035
21	5.033834	6.108808	7.400250	10.803848	15.667578	22.574481	32.323781
22	5.436540	6.658600	8.140275	12.100310	17.861039	26.186398	38.142061
23	5.871464	7.257874	8.954302	13.552347	20.361585	30.376222	45.007632
24	6.341181	7.911083	9.849733	15.178629	23.212207	35.236417	53.109006
25	6.848475	8.623081	10.834706	17.000064	26.461916	40.874244	62.668627
26	7.396353	9.399158	11.918177	19.040072	30.166584	47.414123	73.948980
27	7.988061	10.245082	13.109994	21.324881	34.389906	55.000382	87.259797
28	8.627106	11.167140	14.420994	23.883866	39.204493	63.800444	102.966560
29	9.317275	12.172182	15.863093	26.749930	44.693122	74.008515	121.500541
30	10.062657	13.267678	17.449402	29.959922	50.950159	85.849877	143.370638

Table 2 FUTURE VALUE OF AN ORDINARY ANNUITY OF 1: $F_{0_{n,i}} = \dfrac{(1+i)^n - 1}{i}$

n	1.5%	4.0%	4.5%	5.0%	5.5%	6.0%	7.0%
1	1.000000	1.000000	1.000000	1.000000	1.000000	1.000000	1.000000
2	2.015000	2.040000	2.045000	2.050000	2.055000	2.060000	2.070000
3	3.045225	3.121600	3.137025	3.152500	3.168025	3.183600	3.214900
4	4.090903	4.246464	4.278191	4.310125	4.342266	4.374616	4.439943
5	5.152267	5.416323	5.470710	5.525631	5.581091	5.637093	5.750739
6	6.229551	6.632975	6.716892	6.801913	6.888051	6.975319	7.153291
7	7.322994	7.898294	8.019152	8.142008	8.266894	8.393838	8.654021
8	8.432839	9.214226	9.380014	9.549109	9.721573	9.897468	10.259803
9	9.559332	10.582795	10.802114	11.026564	11.256260	11.491316	11.977989
10	10.702722	12.006107	12.288209	12.577893	12.875354	13.180795	13.816448
11	11.863262	13.486351	13.841179	14.206787	14.583498	14.971643	15.783599
12	13.041211	15.025805	15.464032	15.917127	16.385591	16.869941	17.888451
13	14.236830	16.626838	17.159913	17.712983	18.286798	18.882138	20.140643
14	15.450382	18.291911	18.932109	19.598632	20.292572	21.015066	22.550488
15	16.682138	20.023588	20.784054	21.578564	22.408663	23.275970	25.129022
16	17.932370	21.824531	22.719337	23.657492	24.641140	25.672528	27.888054
17	19.201355	23.697512	24.741707	25.840366	26.996403	28.212880	30.840217
18	20.489376	25.645413	26.855084	28.132385	29.481205	30.905653	33.999033
19	21.796716	27.671229	29.063562	30.539004	32.102671	33.759992	37.378965
20	23.123667	29.778079	31.371423	33.065954	34.868318	36.785591	40.995492
21	24.470522	31.969202	33.783137	35.719252	37.786076	39.992727	44.865177
22	25.837580	34.247970	36.303378	38.505214	40.864310	43.392290	49.005739
23	27.225144	36.617889	38.937030	41.430475	44.111847	46.995828	53.436141
24	28.633521	39.082604	41.689196	44.501999	47.537998	50.815577	58.176671
25	30.063024	41.645908	44.565210	47.727099	51.152588	54.864512	63.249038
26	31.513969	44.311745	47.570645	51.113454	54.965981	59.156383	68.676470
27	32.986678	47.084214	50.711324	54.669126	58.989109	63.705766	74.483823
28	34.481479	49.967583	53.993333	58.402583	63.233510	68.528112	80.697691
29	35.998701	52.966286	57.423033	62.322712	67.711354	73.639798	87.346529
30	37.538681	56.084938	61.007070	66.438848	72.435478	79.058186	94.460786

n	8.0%	9.0%	10.0%	12.0%	14.0%	16.0%	18.0%
1	1.000000	1.000000	1.000000	1.000000	1.000000	1.000000	1.000000
2	2.080000	2.090000	2.100000	2.120000	2.140000	2.160000	2.180000
3	3.246400	3.278100	3.310000	3.374400	3.439600	3.505600	3.572400
4	4.506112	4.573129	4.641000	4.779328	4.921144	5.066496	5.215432
5	5.866601	5.984711	6.105100	6.352847	6.610104	6.877135	7.154210
6	7.335929	7.523335	7.715610	8.115189	8.535519	8.977477	9.441968
7	8.922803	9.200435	9.487171	10.089012	10.730491	11.413873	12.141522
8	10.636628	11.028474	11.435888	12.299693	13.232760	14.240093	15.326996
9	12.487558	13.021036	13.579477	14.775656	16.085347	17.518508	19.085855
10	14.486562	15.192930	15.937425	17.548735	19.337295	21.321469	23.521309
11	16.645487	17.560293	18.531167	20.654583	23.044516	25.732904	28.755144
12	18.977126	20.140720	21.384284	24.133133	27.270749	30.850169	34.931070
13	21.495297	22.953385	24.522712	28.029109	32.088654	36.786196	42.218663
14	24.214920	26.019189	27.974983	32.392602	37.581065	43.671987	50.818022
15	27.152114	29.360916	31.772482	37.279715	43.842414	51.659505	60.965266
16	30.324283	33.003399	35.949730	42.753280	50.980352	60.925026	72.939014
17	33.750226	36.973705	40.544703	48.883674	59.117601	71.673030	87.068036
18	37.450244	41.301338	45.599173	55.749715	68.394066	84.140715	103.740283
19	41.446263	46.018458	51.159090	63.439681	78.969235	98.603230	123.413534
20	45.761964	51.160120	57.274999	72.052442	91.024928	115.379747	146.627970
21	50.422921	56.764530	64.002499	81.698736	104.768418	134.840506	174.021005
22	55.456755	62.873338	71.402749	92.502584	120.435996	157.414987	206.344785
23	60.893296	69.531939	79.543024	104.602894	138.297035	183.601385	244.486847
24	66.764759	76.789813	88.497327	118.155241	158.658620	213.977607	289.494479
25	73.105940	84.700896	98.347059	133.333870	181.870827	249.214024	342.603486
26	79.954415	93.323977	109.181765	150.333934	208.332743	290.088267	405.272113
27	87.350768	102.723135	121.099942	169.374007	238.499327	337.502390	479.221093
28	95.338830	112.968217	134.209936	190.698887	272.889233	392.502773	566.480890
29	103.965936	124.135356	148.630930	214.582754	312.093725	456.303216	669.447450
30	113.283211	136.307539	164.494023	241.332684	356.786847	530.311731	790.947991

Table 3 PRESENT VALUE OF 1: $p_{n,i} = \dfrac{1}{(1+i)^n}$

n	1.5%	4.0%	4.5%	5.0%	5.5%	6.0%	7.0%
1	0.985222	0.961538	0.956938	0.952381	0.947867	0.943396	0.934579
2	0.970662	0.924556	0.915730	0.907029	0.898452	0.889996	0.873439
3	0.956317	0.888996	0.876297	0.863838	0.851614	0.839619	0.816298
4	0.942184	0.854804	0.838561	0.822702	0.807217	0.792094	0.762895
5	0.928260	0.821927	0.802451	0.783526	0.765134	0.747258	0.712986
6	0.914542	0.790315	0.767896	0.746215	0.725246	0.704961	0.666342
7	0.901027	0.759918	0.734828	0.710681	0.687437	0.665057	0.622750
8	0.887711	0.730690	0.703185	0.676839	0.651599	0.627412	0.582009
9	0.874592	0.702587	0.672904	0.644609	0.617629	0.591898	0.543934
10	0.861667	0.675564	0.643928	0.613913	0.585431	0.558395	0.508349
11	0.848933	0.649581	0.616199	0.584679	0.554911	0.526788	0.475093
12	0.836387	0.624597	0.589664	0.556837	0.525982	0.496969	0.444012
13	0.824027	0.600574	0.564272	0.530321	0.498561	0.468839	0.414964
14	0.811849	0.577475	0.539973	0.505068	0.472569	0.442301	0.387817
15	0.799852	0.555265	0.516720	0.481017	0.447933	0.417265	0.362446
16	0.788031	0.533908	0.494469	0.458112	0.424581	0.393646	0.338735
17	0.776385	0.513373	0.473176	0.436297	0.402447	0.371364	0.316574
18	0.764912	0.493628	0.452800	0.415521	0.381466	0.350344	0.295864
19	0.753607	0.474642	0.433302	0.395734	0.361579	0.330513	0.276508
20	0.742470	0.456387	0.414643	0.376889	0.342729	0.311805	0.258419
21	0.731498	0.438834	0.396787	0.358942	0.324862	0.294155	0.241513
22	0.720688	0.421955	0.379701	0.341850	0.307926	0.277505	0.225713
23	0.710037	0.405726	0.363350	0.325571	0.291873	0.261797	0.210947
24	0.699544	0.390121	0.347703	0.310068	0.276657	0.246979	0.197147
25	0.689206	0.375117	0.332731	0.295303	0.262234	0.232999	0.184249
26	0.679021	0.360689	0.318402	0.281241	0.248563	0.219810	0.172195
27	0.668986	0.346817	0.304691	0.267848	0.235605	0.207368	0.160930
28	0.659099	0.333477	0.291571	0.255094	0.223322	0.195630	0.150402
29	0.649359	0.320651	0.279015	0.242946	0.211679	0.184557	0.140563
30	0.639762	0.308319	0.267000	0.231377	0.200644	0.174110	0.131367

n	8.0%	9.0%	10.0%	12.0%	14.0%	16.0%	18.0%
1	0.925926	0.917431	0.909091	0.892857	0.877193	0.862069	0.847458
2	0.857339	0.841680	0.826446	0.797194	0.769468	0.743163	0.718184
3	0.793832	0.772183	0.751315	0.711780	0.674972	0.640658	0.608631
4	0.735030	0.708425	0.683013	0.635518	0.592080	0.552291	0.515789
5	0.680583	0.649931	0.620921	0.567427	0.519369	0.476113	0.437109
6	0.630170	0.596267	0.564474	0.506631	0.455587	0.410442	0.370432
7	0.583490	0.547034	0.513158	0.452349	0.399637	0.353830	0.313925
8	0.540269	0.501866	0.466507	0.403883	0.350559	0.305025	0.266038
9	0.500249	0.460428	0.424098	0.360610	0.307508	0.262953	0.225456
10	0.463193	0.422411	0.385543	0.321973	0.269744	0.226684	0.191064
11	0.428883	0.387533	0.350494	0.287476	0.236617	0.195417	0.161919
12	0.397114	0.355535	0.318631	0.256675	0.207559	0.168463	0.137220
13	0.367698	0.326179	0.289664	0.229174	0.182069	0.145227	0.116288
14	0.340461	0.299246	0.263331	0.204620	0.159710	0.125195	0.098549
15	0.315242	0.274538	0.239392	0.182696	0.140096	0.107927	0.083516
16	0.291890	0.251870	0.217629	0.163122	0.122892	0.093041	0.070776
17	0.270269	0.231073	0.197845	0.145644	0.107800	0.080207	0.059980
18	0.250249	0.211994	0.179859	0.130040	0.094561	0.069144	0.050830
19	0.231712	0.194490	0.163508	0.116107	0.082948	0.059607	0.043077
20	0.214548	0.178431	0.148644	0.103667	0.072762	0.051385	0.036506
21	0.198656	0.163698	0.135131	0.092560	0.063826	0.044298	0.030937
22	0.183941	0.150182	0.122846	0.082643	0.055988	0.038188	0.026218
23	0.170315	0.137781	0.111678	0.073788	0.049112	0.032920	0.022218
24	0.157699	0.126405	0.101526	0.065882	0.043081	0.028380	0.018829
25	0.146018	0.115968	0.092296	0.058823	0.037790	0.024465	0.015957
26	0.135202	0.106393	0.083905	0.052521	0.033149	0.021091	0.013523
27	0.125187	0.097608	0.076278	0.046894	0.029078	0.018182	0.011460
28	0.115914	0.089548	0.069343	0.041869	0.025507	0.015674	0.009712
29	0.107328	0.082155	0.063039	0.037383	0.022375	0.013512	0.008230
30	0.099377	0.075371	0.057309	0.033378	0.019627	0.011648	0.006975

Table 4 **PRESENT VALUE OF AN ORDINARY ANNUITY OF 1:** $P_{0_{n,i}} = \dfrac{1 - \dfrac{1}{(1+i)^n}}{i}$

n	1.5%	4.0%	4.5%	5.0%	5.5%	6.0%	7.0%
1	0.985222	0.961538	0.956938	0.952381	0.947867	0.943396	0.934579
2	1.955883	1.886095	1.872668	1.859410	1.846320	1.833393	1.808018
3	2.912200	2.775091	2.748964	2.723248	2.697933	2.673012	2.624316
4	3.854385	3.629895	3.587526	3.545951	3.505150	3.465106	3.387211
5	4.782645	4.451822	4.389977	4.329477	4.270284	4.212364	4.100197
6	5.697187	5.242137	5.157872	5.075692	4.995530	4.917324	4.766540
7	6.598214	6.002055	5.892701	5.786373	5.682967	5.582381	5.389289
8	7.485925	6.732745	6.595886	6.463213	6.334566	6.209794	5.971299
9	8.360517	7.435332	7.268790	7.107822	6.952195	6.801692	6.515232
10	9.222185	8.110896	7.912718	7.721735	7.537626	7.360087	7.023582
11	10.071118	8.760477	8.528917	8.306414	8.092536	7.886875	7.498674
12	10.907505	9.385074	9.118581	8.863252	8.618518	8.383844	7.942686
13	11.731532	9.985648	9.682852	9.393573	9.117079	8.852683	8.357651
14	12.543382	10.563123	10.222825	9.898641	9.589648	9.294984	8.745468
15	13.343233	11.118387	10.739546	10.379658	10.037581	9.712249	9.107914
16	14.131264	11.652296	11.234015	10.837770	10.462162	10.105895	9.446649
17	14.907649	12.165669	11.707191	11.274066	10.864609	10.477260	9.763223
18	15.672561	12.659297	12.159992	11.689587	11.246074	10.827603	10.059087
19	16.426168	13.133939	12.593294	12.085321	11.607654	11.158116	10.335595
20	17.168639	13.590326	13.007936	12.462210	11.950382	11.469921	10.594014
21	17.900137	14.029160	13.404724	12.821153	12.275244	11.764077	10.835527
22	18.620824	14.451115	13.784425	13.163003	12.583170	12.041582	11.061240
23	19.330861	14.856842	14.147775	13.488574	12.875042	12.303379	11.272187
24	20.030405	15.246963	14.495478	13.798642	13.151699	12.550358	11.469334
25	20.719611	15.622080	14.828209	14.093945	13.413933	12.783356	11.653583
26	21.398632	15.982769	15.146611	14.375185	13.662495	13.003166	11.825779
27	22.067617	16.329586	15.451303	14.643034	13.898100	13.210534	11.986709
28	22.726717	16.663063	15.742874	14.898127	14.121422	13.406164	12.137111
29	23.376076	16.983715	16.021889	15.141074	14.333101	13.590721	12.277674
30	24.015838	17.292033	16.288889	15.372451	14.533745	13.764831	12.409041

n	8.0%	9.0%	10.0%	12.0%	14.0%	16.0%	18.0%
1	0.925926	0.917431	0.909091	0.892857	0.877193	0.862069	0.847458
2	1.783265	1.759111	1.735537	1.690051	1.646661	1.605232	1.565642
3	2.577097	2.531295	2.486852	2.401831	2.321632	2.245890	2.174273
4	3.312127	3.239720	3.169865	3.037349	2.913712	2.798181	2.690062
5	3.992710	3.889651	3.790787	3.604776	3.433081	3.274294	3.127171
6	4.622880	4.485919	4.355261	4.111407	3.888668	3.684736	3.497603
7	5.206370	5.032953	4.868419	4.563757	4.288305	4.038565	3.811528
8	5.746639	5.534819	5.334926	4.967640	4.638864	4.343591	4.077566
9	6.246888	5.995247	5.759024	5.328250	4.946372	4.606544	4.303022
10	6.710081	6.417658	6.144567	5.650223	5.216116	4.833227	4.494086
11	7.138964	6.805191	6.495061	5.937699	5.452733	5.028644	4.656005
12	7.536078	7.160725	6.813692	6.194374	5.660292	5.197107	4.793225
13	7.903776	7.486904	7.103356	6.423548	5.842362	5.342334	4.909513
14	8.244237	7.786150	7.366687	6.628168	6.002072	5.467529	5.008062
15	8.559479	8.060688	7.606080	6.810864	6.142168	5.575456	5.091578
16	8.851369	8.312558	7.823709	6.973986	6.265060	5.668497	5.162354
17	9.121638	8.543631	8.021553	7.119630	6.372859	5.748704	5.222334
18	9.371887	8.755625	8.201412	7.249670	6.467420	5.817848	5.273164
19	9.603599	8.950115	8.364920	7.365777	6.550369	5.877455	5.316241
20	9.818147	9.128546	8.513564	7.469444	6.623131	5.928841	5.352746
21	10.016803	9.292244	8.648694	7.562003	6.686957	5.973139	5.383683
22	10.200744	9.442425	8.771540	7.644646	6.742944	6.011326	5.409901
23	10.371059	9.580207	8.883218	7.718434	6.792056	6.044247	5.432120
24	10.528758	9.706612	8.984744	7.784316	6.835137	6.072627	5.450949
25	10.674776	9.822580	9.077040	7.843139	6.872927	6.097092	5.466906
26	10.809978	9.928972	9.160945	7.895660	6.906077	6.118183	5.480429
27	10.935165	10.026580	9.237223	7.942554	6.935155	6.136364	5.491889
28	11.051078	10.116128	9.306567	7.984423	6.960662	6.152038	5.501601
29	11.158406	10.198283	9.369606	8.021806	6.983037	6.165550	5.509831
30	11.257783	10.273654	9.426914	8.055184	7.002664	6.177198	5.516806

Table 5 PRESENT VALUE OF ANNUITY DUE: $P_{d_{n,i}} = \dfrac{1 - \dfrac{1}{(1+i)^{n-1}}}{i} + 1$

n	1.5%	4.0%	4.5%	5.0%	5.5%	6.0%	7.0%
1	1.000000	1.000000	1.000000	1.000000	1.000000	1.000000	1.000000
2	1.985222	1.961538	1.956938	1.952381	1.947867	1.943396	1.934579
3	2.955883	2.886095	2.872668	2.859410	2.846320	2.833393	2.808018
4	3.912200	3.775091	3.748964	3.723248	3.697933	3.673012	3.624316
5	4.854385	4.629895	4.587526	4.545951	4.505150	4.465106	4.387211
6	5.782645	5.451822	5.389977	5.329477	5.270284	5.212364	5.100197
7	6.697187	6.242137	6.157872	6.075692	5.995530	5.917324	5.766540
8	7.598214	7.002055	6.892701	6.786373	6.682967	6.582381	6.389289
9	8.485925	7.732745	7.595886	7.463213	7.334566	7.209794	6.971299
10	9.360517	8.435332	8.268790	8.107822	7.952195	7.801692	7.515232
11	10.222185	9.110896	8.912718	8.721735	8.537626	8.360087	8.023582
12	11.071118	9.760477	9.528917	9.306414	9.092536	8.886875	8.498674
13	11.907505	10.385074	10.118581	9.863252	9.618518	9.383844	8.942686
14	12.731532	10.985648	10.682852	10.393573	10.117079	9.852683	9.357651
15	13.543382	11.563123	11.222825	10.898641	10.589648	10.294984	9.745468
16	14.343233	12.118387	11.739546	11.379658	11.037581	10.712249	10.107914
17	15.131264	12.652296	12.234015	11.837770	11.462162	11.105895	10.446649
18	15.907649	13.165669	12.707191	12.274066	11.864609	11.477260	10.763223
19	16.672561	13.659297	13.159992	12.689587	12.246074	11.827603	11.059087
20	17.426168	14.133939	13.593294	13.085321	12.607654	12.158116	11.335595
21	18.168639	14.590326	14.007936	13.462210	12.950382	12.469921	11.594014
22	18.900137	15.029160	14.404724	13.821153	13.275244	12.764077	11.835527
23	19.620824	15.451115	14.784425	14.163003	13.583170	13.041582	12.061240
24	20.330861	15.856842	15.147775	14.488574	13.875042	13.303379	12.272187
25	21.030405	16.246963	15.495478	14.798642	14.151699	13.550358	12.469334
26	21.719611	16.622080	15.828209	15.093945	14.413933	13.783356	12.653583
27	22.398632	16.982769	16.146611	15.375185	14.662495	14.003166	12.825779
28	23.067617	17.329586	16.451303	15.643034	14.898100	14.210534	12.986709
29	23.726717	17.663063	16.742874	15.898127	15.121422	14.406164	13.137111
30	24.376076	17.983715	17.021889	16.141074	15.333101	14.590721	13.277674

n	8.0%	9.0%	10.0%	12.0%	14.0%	16.0%	18.0%
1	1.000000	1.000000	1.000000	1.000000	1.000000	1.000000	1.000000
2	1.925926	1.917431	1.909091	1.892857	1.877193	1.862069	1.847458
3	2.783265	2.759111	2.735537	2.690051	2.646661	2.605232	2.565642
4	3.577097	3.531295	3.486852	3.401831	3.321632	3.245890	3.174273
5	4.312127	4.239720	4.169865	4.037349	3.913712	3.798181	3.690062
6	4.992710	4.889651	4.790787	4.604776	4.433081	4.274294	4.127171
7	5.622880	5.485919	5.355261	5.111407	4.888668	4.684736	4.497603
8	6.206370	6.032953	5.868419	5.563757	5.288305	5.038565	4.811528
9	6.746639	6.534819	6.334926	5.967640	5.638864	5.343591	5.077566
10	7.246888	6.995247	6.759024	6.328250	5.946372	5.606544	5.303022
11	7.710081	7.417658	7.144567	6.650223	6.216116	5.833227	5.494086
12	8.138964	7.805191	7.495061	6.937699	6.452733	6.028644	5.656005
13	8.536078	8.160725	7.813692	7.194374	6.660292	6.197107	5.793225
14	8.903776	8.486904	8.103356	7.423548	6.842362	6.342334	5.909513
15	9.244237	8.786150	8.366687	7.628168	7.002072	6.467529	6.008062
16	9.559479	9.060688	-8.606080	7.810864	7.142168	6.575456	6.091578
17	9.851369	9.312558	8.823709	7.973986	7.265060	6.668497	6.162354
18	10.121638	9.543631	9.021553	8.119630	7.372859	6.748704	6.222334
19	10.371887	9.755625	9.201412	8.249670	7.467420	6.817848	6.273164
20	10.603599	9.950115	9.364920	8.365777	7.550369	6.877455	6.316241
21	10.818147	10.128546	9.513564	8.469444	7.623131	6.928841	6.352746
22	11.016803	10.292244	9.648694	8.562003	7.686957	6.973139	6.383683
23	11.200744	10.442425	9.771540	8.644646	7.742944	7.011326	6.409901
24	11.371059	10.580207	9.883218	8.718434	7.792056	7.044247	6.432120
25	11.528758	10.706612	9.984744	8.784316	7.835137	7.072627	6.450949
26	11.674776	10.822580	10.077040	8.843139	7.872927	7.097092	6.466906
27	11.809978	10.928972	10.160945	8.895660	7.906077	7.118183	6.480429
28	11.935165	11.026580	10.237223	8.942554	7.935155	7.136364	6.491889
29	12.051078	11.116128	10.306567	8.984423	7.960662	7.152038	6.501601
30	12.158406	11.198283	10.369606	9.021806	7.983037	7.165550	6.509831

Financial Reporting: Asset Valuation and Income Measurement

CHAPTER 7
Cash and Receivables

CHAPTER 8
Inventories: Cost Measurement and Flow
Assumptions

CHAPTER 9
Inventories: Special Valuation Issues

CHAPTER 10
Property, Plant, and Equipment: Acquisition
and Disposal

CHAPTER 11
Depreciation and Depletion

CHAPTER 12
Intangibles

OBJECTIVES

After reading this chapter, you will be able to:

1 Identify items of cash (and cash equivalents).

2 Understand the importance of cash management.

3 Discuss revenue recognition when the right of return exists.

4 Understand the credit policies and internal control related to accounts receivable.

5 Explain the gross and net methods to account for cash discounts.

6 Estimate and record bad debts using a percentage of sales.

7 Estimate and record bad debts using an aging analysis.

8 Explain pledging, assignment, and factoring of accounts receivable.

9 Account for short-term notes receivable.

10 Understand a petty cash fund (Appendix).

11 Prepare a bank reconciliation (Appendix).

Cash and Receivables

Show Me the Money!

Cash is the lifeblood for companies and infusions are coming more frequently from nontraditional sources. According to the 2004 Federal Reserve Payments Study, Americans are for the first time using electronic "money" such as debit and credit cards more frequently than checks to pay their bills.

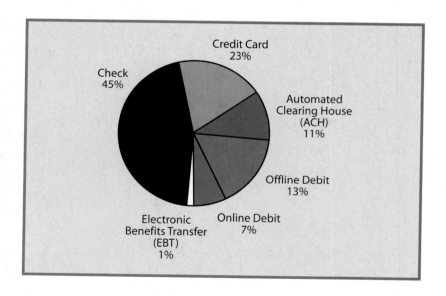

Hastening the decline in the use of checks is a process known as accounts receivable conversion (ARC). In ARC, when paper checks arrive at a bank lockbox, they are converted into automated clearing house debits and the check itself is then

destroyed. For banks, the savings are obvious—ARC payments are about one-third cheaper than handling checks and float time (the time it takes for a check to clear the bank) is cut in half. Additionally, the Check Clearing for the 21st Century Act is a recently enacted law that gives legal status to substitute checks. Termed Check 21, this act allows merchants to scan checks and transmit the digital images to the bank instead of sending the actual check. Whether it is ARC or Check 21, one thing is clear—making payments will never be the same again.

FOR FURTHER INVESTIGATION

For a discussion of ARC or Check 21, consult the Business & Company Resource Center (BCRC):

- Tear Out a Check, Then Watch it Vanish. Jeffrey Selingo, *The New York Times*, 0362-4331, October 9, 2003, pG6 col. 04.
- Why Check 21 Could Erase ARC's Gains. Will Wade, *American Banker*, 0002-7561, November 5, 2003, v168, i213, p1.

Analysis

Financial statement users focus on a variety of information in making credit and investment decisions. Investors, long-term creditors, and short-term creditors are interested in a company's **financial flexibility**, the ability to use its financial resources to adapt to change. One part of a company's financial flexibility that external users are concerned about is liquidity. **Liquidity** is the availability of a company's liquid assets (cash or assets that may be quickly converted into cash) to pay its bills. The most common liquid assets are cash, temporary investments, accounts receivable, and notes receivable. In this chapter we discuss the measurement and valuation procedures for cash, accounts receivable, and notes receivable. Because the accounting principles for temporary investments are similar to those for most long-term investments, we do not discuss temporary investments until Chapter 15.

CASH

Cash is the resource on hand to meet planned payments and emergency situations. **The amount a company reports as cash in the current assets section on its balance sheet must be available to pay current obligations.** There must not be any contractual restrictions that prevent the company from using this money to pay its current debts. For example, some companies create sinking funds into which they deposit cash over an extended period. At the end of the period, the cash (plus accumulated interest) is to be used for a specific purpose (e.g., to retire long-term bonds). Amounts in sinking funds are not classified as cash on the balance sheet; a company normally reports these amounts in the long-term investments category.

1 Identify items of cash (and cash equivalents).

Cash classified as a current asset includes coins, currency, unrestricted funds on deposit with a bank (either checking accounts or savings accounts[1]), **negotiable checks,** and **bank drafts.** On the other hand, some items may be confused with cash but normally are listed under other balance sheet captions. Among these items are certificates of deposit, bank overdrafts, postdated checks, travel advances, and postage stamps. *Certificates of deposit (CDs)* are short-term investments issued by banks that allow a company to invest idle cash for short periods of time. CDs normally are classified as temporary investments. *Bank overdrafts* are overdrawn checking accounts. They are reported as current liabilities and should *not* be offset against positive balances in other bank accounts. *Postdated checks* from customers are checks dated in the future so they become payable on a date later than the issue date. Postdated checks are included as receivables until the date they become negotiable. *Travel advances* are funds or checks given to company employees to cover out-of-pocket expenses while traveling on company business. Since travel advances are satisfied when the employee submits receipts for business expenses, they are classified as prepaid items. *Postage stamps* on hand are classified as prepaid items because they will be used rather than exchanged for cash. Below is a diagram that summarizes what is, and what is not, included in cash.

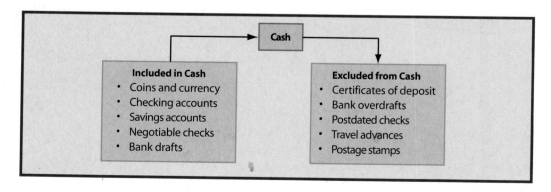

---

1. Although some banks place restrictions on the withdrawal of funds from savings accounts, they generally are included as a component of cash.

In summary, to be classified under the current asset—Cash—caption on a company's balance sheet, amounts must be available immediately to pay its bills and may not be bound by any contractual or legal restrictions. Items that do not meet these criteria are reported elsewhere within the assets (or liabilities) section on the balance sheet.

Cash and Cash Equivalents

Some companies use the title Cash on their balance sheets. An increasing number (approximately 88%)[2], however, use a title such as *Cash and Cash Equivalents*. In addition to cash, these companies include in this category items that are considered to be "cash equivalents" because of their liquidity and low risk. **Cash equivalents** are short-term, highly liquid investments that are readily convertible into known amounts of cash and so near their maturity that there is little risk of changes in value because of changes in interest rates. Generally, only investments with maturity dates of three months or less from the date acquired by the holder are cash equivalents.[3] Securities such as commercial paper, treasury bills, and money market funds are examples of cash equivalents. For instance, in its December 31, 2004 balance sheet, **Eastman Kodak Company** reported cash and cash equivalents as a current asset. Then it included a note describing its cash equivalents in the notes to its financial statements, as we show in Real Report 7-1.

Real Report 7-1 Cash and Cash Equivalents

EASTMAN KODAK COMPANY AND SUBSIDIARY COMPANIES

CONSOLIDATED STATEMENT OF FINANCIAL POSITION (in part)

(in millions, except share and per share data)	At December 31 2004	2003
ASSETS		
Current Assets		
Cash and cash equivalents	$1,255	$1,250

NOTES TO FINANCIAL STATEMENTS
NOTE 1: Significant Accounting Policies (in part)

Cash Equivalents All highly liquid investments with a remaining maturity of three months or less at date of purchase are considered to be cash equivalents.

Questions:

1. Why does Eastman Kodak combine cash and cash equivalents into one amount on the balance sheet?

A clear understanding of what items a company includes in Cash and Cash Equivalents is important because when preparing its statement of cash flows, it must reconcile its cash inflows and outflows to the change in cash and cash equivalents. In this chapter for simplicity we focus our discussion on Cash.

Cash Management

2 Understand the importance of cash management.

Efficient cash management is very important to every company. Each company must ensure that it has enough cash to pay its current obligations. However, it must recognize the fact that idle cash is a nonproductive resource.

---

2. *Accounting Trends and Techniques* (New York: AICPA, 2004), p. 150.
3. "Statements of Cash Flows," *FASB Statement of Financial Accounting Standards No. 95* (Stamford, Conn.: FASB, 1987), par. 8.

Although a company may wish to protect itself against business failure by amassing a large amount of cash to keep itself liquid, it can improve its performance by investing these funds and earning interest. Proper cash management requires that a company invest its idle cash and estimate the timing of its cash inflows and outflows to ensure that it has enough cash to meet its needs. Having too much cash, however, may make a company the target of a takeover attempt.

Information on cash management is important in financial accounting because one objective of financial reporting is to communicate how well the managers of a company have fulfilled their stewardship responsibility to stockholders for the use of the company assets. In this regard, cash management includes planning and control aspects. **Cash planning** systems are those methods and procedures that a company uses to ensure that it has adequate cash available to meet maturing obligations and that it invests any unused or excess cash. **Cash control** systems are the methods and procedures a company uses to safeguard its funds.

A company's cash budget is the major component of its cash planning system. **The cash budget is a plan of cash activity that forecasts cash receipts and payments, and identifies when the company might have too much or too little cash.** The cash budget is primarily a managerial accounting technique and is outside the scope of this book.

Cash control systems require adequate internal control measures. **Internal control** is the process (policies and procedures) a company uses so that its financial reports are reliable, its operations (including safeguarding its assets) are effective and efficient, and that it complies with applicable laws and regulations.[4] This control is so important that a federal law requires all publicly traded companies to maintain adequate internal control systems. Since cash cannot be traced easily, internal control over cash is enhanced by routine reviews of the accuracy of recorded cash transactions and by the separation of employee duties. These procedures help to prevent theft unless there is collusion among employees. However, whenever a company adopts internal control measures, the cost of using these measures should not exceed the value of the benefits. Any measure that costs more than its benefits ultimately will result in lower profits for the company.

Cash control systems can be subdivided into two main functions: (1) control over receipts and (2) control over payments. The control procedures a company adopts for its cash receipts should be designed to safeguard all cash inflows from the time they arrive at the company until they are deposited in its bank account. The key elements in a cash receipts internal control system are

- immediate counting of receipts by the person opening the mail or the salesperson using the cash register,
- daily recording of all cash receipts in the accounting records, and
- daily deposit of all receipts in the company's bank account.

The control procedures for payments should ensure that only authorized payments are made for actual company expenditures. The key elements in a cash payments internal control system include

- making all payments by check so there is a record for every company expenditure,
- authorizing and signing checks only after an expenditure is approved, and
- periodically reconciling the cash balance in the bank statement with the company's accounting records.

Two important elements of the internal control over cash are a petty cash system and a bank reconciliation. We discuss each of these elements in more detail in the Appendix at the end of this chapter.

---

4. For auditing purposes, a company's internal control structure consists of its control environment, risk assessment procedures, control activities, information and communication system, and monitoring process. For more detail, see *AICPA Professional Standards* vol. 1 (New York: AICPA, 2004), sec. 319.

Electronic-Based Payments

Many companies prepare and process hundreds or even thousands of checks each month to pay their suppliers and employees. Furthermore, they receive and process an equally large number of checks from their customers. Whether for payments or receipts, processing the paperwork for checks is expensive. With the increased use of computer networks, banks offer **electronic funds transfers (EFT)** to their customers. Under EFT, funds are transferred between companies electronically without the need of a check. EFT systems are becoming more compatible, and their networking capabilities are increasing. In addition to EFT systems, banks are also using accounts receivable conversion (ARC) and Check 21 (as we discussed at the opening of the chapter) for faster processing of "checks." As more and more companies and banks use EFT, ARC, and Check 21 systems, fewer physical documents (e.g., checks) are processed. Therefore, greater emphasis is being placed on internal control systems as they apply to computer technology because fewer physical source documents are available to verify cash inflows and outflows.

Compensating Balances

It is common for banks to require a portion of any amount loaned to a company to remain on deposit in the bank (usually earning a low interest rate) for the loan period. These required deposits are called **compensating balances** because they "compensate" the bank for granting the loan. For example, a bank loaning a company $100,000 may require that the company maintain a $10,000 deposit with the bank until the company repays the loan. Such arrangements have two main effects. First, they reduce the amount of cash available to the borrower, and second, they increase the effective interest rate the borrower pays for the use of the funds. For example, if the stated interest rate for the $100,000 loan is 12%, the effective rate for the actual funds used for a year is 13.33% ($12,000 ÷ $90,000), assuming the $10,000 compensating balance does not earn any interest.

The SEC studied funds subject to these withdrawal or usage restrictions. This study was partially in response to *liquidity* problems that were reported by companies with apparently adequate cash balances. The SEC found many cases in which a portion of the reported cash balance was legally restricted. Therefore, it requires that a public company with a compensating balance against its short-term borrowings separately report the amount in the current assets section of its balance sheet. Compensating balances for long-term borrowings are separately reported as noncurrent assets (as either investments or other assets). Compensating balance agreements that do not legally restrict the amount of funds shown on the balance sheet are disclosed in the notes to the financial statements.

SECURE YOUR KNOWLEDGE 7-1

- To be reported as cash, the resource must be readily available to pay current obligations and may not be bound by any contractual or legal restrictions.
- Cash equivalents are short-term, highly liquid investments with a maturity date of three months or less from the date of purchase; they are often combined with cash for financial reporting purposes.
- A well-functioning cash management system ensures that a company has enough cash to fulfill its needs, invests any idle cash, and safeguards its cash receipts and cash payments.
- Compensating balances required in connection with loans serve to increase the effective interest rate on the loan and must be adequately disclosed.

RECEIVABLES

Receivables are amounts owed to the company by customers and other parties arising from the company's operations. Most receivables are canceled through the receipt of cash, although others may be canceled through the receipt of other assets or services. A company reports receivables on its balance sheet as either **current** or **noncurrent** items. Those receivables expected to be collected within one year or the current operating cycle, whichever is longer, are classified as current assets; the remainder are classified as noncurrent. Also, a company may group receivables within its classified balance sheet as trade receivables and nontrade receivables.

Trade receivables arise from the sale of the company's products or services to customers. For instance, manufacturers may sell on credit to retailers (or other manufacturers), and retailers may sell on credit to consumers. Trade receivables generally are the majority of a company's total receivables balance. Trade receivables may be subclassified into **accounts receivable** (nonwritten promises by customers to pay for goods or services) and **notes receivable** (unconditional written agreements to receive a certain sum of money on a specific date). We discuss these subclassifications later in the chapter.

Nontrade receivables arise from transactions that are not directly related to the sale of the company's goods and services. Nontrade receivables are recorded in separate accounts. They are reported on the balance sheet in individual groups as current or noncurrent assets, depending upon the length of their collection period. Examples of nontrade receivables include deposits with utilities, advances to subsidiary companies, loans made by nonfinancial companies, deposits made to guarantee performance, and declared dividends and accrued interest on investments.

Utility companies often require a company to make a deposit to guarantee utility expense payments. This deposit normally is classified by the depositor as a noncurrent receivable because the timing of repayment by the utility company is indeterminate. An advance to a subsidiary typically is classified as long-term because repayment may be postponed indefinitely. A deposit made to guarantee contract performance is classified as either current or noncurrent, depending on the expected completion date of the project guaranteed. Declared dividends to be received and accrued interest on investments are disclosed as current assets. In this chapter we focus upon the valuation issues associated with current trade receivables. We discuss nontrade receivables and noncurrent receivables in other chapters in this book.

Accounting for trade receivables involves a number of issues. We include the following diagram to provide you with an overview of our related discussion.

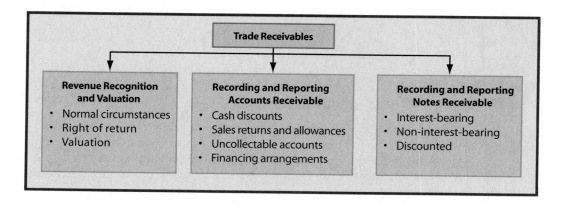

REVENUE RECOGNITION AND VALUATION OF TRADE RECEIVABLES

First, we look at several issues related to revenue recognition and receivables valuation.

Normal Revenue Recognition

A company usually makes sales of goods and services on "open accounts" that result in short-term extensions of credit. **A company records revenue from credit sales based on the revenue recognition criteria.** Revenue is recognized when **realization has occurred** (i.e., a noncash resource is exchanged for cash or a near cash resource) and the **revenue is earned** (i.e., the earning process is complete or virtually complete). Typically, the sale of goods and services on credit results in an asset called a trade receivable (account receivable or note receivable) and the recognition of revenue at the time of sale. This approach is used because the company expects to collect the asset (receivable), and very few activities remain in the earning process. However, in some cases a company may defer revenue recognition because it is not sure it will collect the receivable (which we will discuss in Chapter 18). In other cases, a company may defer revenue because a right of return exists.

Conceptual

Right of Return

In most industries sales returns and allowances are not material, so that companies typically record them at the time of the return or allowance even if they occur in a period later than the period of sale. In some industries, such as book publishing, the right of return is common and the amounts may be material. In these cases, credit "sales" in one period may be followed by substantial returns in another. These factors create a revenue recognition issue for the selling company because sometimes (1) it cannot make reliable estimates of the collectibility of the receivable and (2) the risks and benefits of ownership are not transferred (the earning process is not complete) to the buyer. As a result, **FASB Statement No. 48** identifies criteria for recording sales revenue when the right of return exists. **For a seller to recognize revenue at the time of sale, each of the following criteria must be satisfied when the right of return exists.** If they are not, then the seller must defer revenue recognition.

3 Discuss revenue recognition when the right of return exists.

1. The sales price is known at the date of sale.
2. The buyer has paid or will pay the seller, and the obligation is not contingent upon resale of the product.
3. The buyer's obligation to the seller would not be changed by theft or damage to the product.
4. The buyer has an economic substance apart from the seller.
5. The seller does not have significant obligations to help the buyer sell the product.
6. The seller can reasonably estimate the amount of future returns.[5]

If a company defers recognizing sales revenue and cost of goods sold because one or more of these conditions are not met, it records the sales revenue and cost of goods sold either when the return privilege expires or when the conditions are met, whichever occurs first.

Conceptual

Valuation Issues

When the conditions in the previous section are met so that the company records a receivable and revenue at the time of sale, there still is an issue of valuing the trade receivable. As we discussed in Chapter 4, one purpose of reporting current assets is to disclose the **liquidity** of a company; that is, the "nearness to cash" of its economic resources. In this regard, the accounting issues related to the valuation of current trade receivables are (1) the initial recording of the receivables based on the total future cash flows, and (2) the estimation of the probability of collection. Since there is a time value of money,

---

5. "Revenue Recognition When Right of Return Exists," *FASB Statement of Financial Accounting Standards No. 48* (Stamford, Conn.: FASB, 1981), par. 6.

there is a difference between the maturity value of a receivable and its present value. The longer the time until maturity, the greater the difference. **APB Opinion No. 21** (discussed in Chapter 15) provides specific guidelines for recording and reporting receivables at their present values. However, the provisions do not apply to "receivables . . . arising from transactions with customers . . . in the normal course of business which are due in customary trade terms not exceeding approximately one year."[6] Consequently **most trade receivables are recorded initially at their maturity values** and not at their present values. Also, since the collection period for most trade receivables is 60 days or less, the difference between their present value and maturity value is usually not material.

The uncertainty of collection also affects the value of trade receivables. Whenever a company extends credit, it may not collect a few receivables. The company should consider this issue in valuing its receivables on its balance sheet to report on their liquidity. We discuss the accounting procedures used to deal with the uncertainty of collecting receivables later in this chapter.

ACCOUNTS RECEIVABLE

As we discussed earlier, trade accounts receivable result from credit sales. A company sells on credit in order to increase sales. But credit sales create the need for a credit department to investigate credit ratings, approve the extension of credit, and attempt to collect delinquent accounts. Credit sales result in a certain amount of bad debts due to nonpayment by customers. When a company considers whether or not to sell on credit, it must evaluate the trade-off between the additional gross profit received from the expected credit sales and the additional expenses incurred due to these credit sales. In this regard, most companies establish a credit policy.

A credit policy reflects the degree of risk a company is willing to accept to increase sales. Credit policies are closely associated with customers' credit ratings. High credit ratings indicate low risk, whereas low credit ratings indicate high risk. A company should adopt a credit policy that results in the maximum increased profit consistent with maintaining customer satisfaction. That is, it should determine the combination of increased sales revenue and bad debt losses that results in the highest incremental profit and cash inflows. However, it should also consider other factors, such as the cost of additional sales and credit personnel to handle these increased sales. A few companies have decided that this trade-off is negative. These companies believe that they can lower costs and increase profits by selling exclusively for cash. Note that retail "credit card" sales involving bank credit cards are treated as cash sales, as we discuss later in the chapter.

If a company decides to sell on credit and establishes a credit department, it must install an effective internal control system for processing credit sales and cash collections. We discussed the internal control procedures used for cash collections earlier in the chapter, but a company must also establish internal control procedures for processing its accounts receivable. These control features include (1) prenumbered sales invoices so that all invoices are accounted for, and (2) the separation of the sales function from the cash collection responsibilities so that theft should not occur unless there is collusion between employees.

Once a company feels that a reasonable trade-off exists between the incremental revenues and expenses of credit sales, and has established an adequate system of internal control for credit sales, other issues may arise in recording accounts receivable. These issues include cash discounts and sales returns and allowances. We discuss uncollectible accounts (bad debts) in a later section.

4 Understand the credit policies and internal control related to accounts receivable.

---

6. "Interest on Receivables and Payables," *APB Opinion No. 21* (New York: AICPA, 1971), par. 3.

Cash (Sales) Discounts

Companies may offer a discount to induce prompt payment. This discount is called a **cash discount** (or **sales discount**) and frequently is expressed as 2/10, n/30 or perhaps 2/10, n/EOM (end of month). In both cases **the first component refers to the discount rate and period, and the second to the invoice due date.** These terms are read in the first case as: A 2% discount may be subtracted from the invoice price[7] if payment is made by the purchaser within 10 days, and the total invoice price is due within 30 days. In the second example full payment is due by the end of the month. For example, assume that Company S sells $5,000 of merchandise to Company B with terms of 2/10, n/30. If Company B pays for the merchandise within 10 days, it only has to pay $4,900. This $100 cash discount is a strong inducement to pay within the discount period because it is a relatively high effective annual interest rate for Company B. By paying within the discount period, Company B is giving up the use of funds for 20 days (that is, the invoice is due 20 days after the discount period expires) to earn a discount of 2%. This is approximately equal to an annual effective interest rate of 36% ($0.023 \times 60/20$).

Cash discounts are important in the financial management of companies. Both sellers and purchasers should carefully analyze the potential effects of cash discounts. As we noted, the theory behind cash discounts is that they will induce prompt payment. A purchasing company should take advantage of any cash discounts that have a higher effective annual interest rate than the rate it must pay to borrow money. For a selling company, a cash discount has two main positive effects: (1) it stimulates faster collection of cash for use in current operations, and (2) it tends to reduce the losses resulting from uncollectible accounts. However, the seller should not overlook the negative effect of its reduced total cash inflow because of the discount. Sellers should attempt to set the cash discount rate at a level so that its positive effects exceed any negative effects.

If a selling company extends cash discounts to its customers, it may use one of two methods (a "gross" method or a "net" method) to account for the discounts:[8]

5 Explain the gross and net methods to account for cash discounts.

1. *Accounts Receivable and Sales Recorded at Gross Price.* When the selling company uses the gross price method, it records the total invoice price in both the Accounts Receivable and Sales accounts at the time of sale as if no cash discount were involved. When the customer pays and takes the allowable cash discount, the company records the difference between the cash received and the original amount of Accounts Receivable as a debit to Sales Discounts Taken. If the customer does not take the cash discount, it pays an amount that is equal to the original balance in the company's Accounts Receivable account, and no further adjustment is needed. Sales discounts taken are deducted from sales on the income statement to determine net sales.

2. *Accounts Receivable and Sales Recorded at Net Price.* When the selling company uses the net price method, it records the net invoice price (after deducting the allowable cash discount) in both the Accounts Receivable and Sales accounts at the time of sale. When the customer pays and takes the allowable cash discount, no adjustment is needed because the amount of cash received is equal to the recorded amount of the receivable. However, if the customer does *not* take the cash discount, it pays an amount that is greater than the amount in the company's Accounts Receivable

---

7. Another type of discount is the **trade** (or *quantity*) discount, which is offered for purchases in excess of a certain quantity. For example, if a company offers a 10% trade discount and a customer purchases 100 units of an item with a list price of $80 per unit subject to the trade discount, the customer is billed $7,200 [$8,000−(0.10 × $8,000)] as the invoice price. This $7,200 invoice price then is subject to the cash discount.

8. In a third method, accounts receivable are recorded at the gross price, sales are recorded at the net price, and the difference is recorded in an allowance account (a contra account to accounts receivable). The allowance account then is reduced by the difference between the cash collected from the customer and the accounts receivable balance. It also is adjusted for sales discounts not taken.

account. The company credits this excess to an account entitled Sales Discounts Not Taken, which is interest revenue and is reported in the Other Items section of the income statement.[9]

To illustrate these methods, assume that the Howe Corporation sold $8,000 of merchandise to various customers on December 4, 2007, with terms of 2/10, n/EOM. On December 13 Howe received payment on goods originally billed at $5,500. Howe received payment on goods billed at $1,500 on December 30. The remaining $1,000 was not collected by the end of the year. Example 7-1 shows the journal entries to record these transactions and the year-end adjustments.

EXAMPLE 7-1   Alternative Methods of Accounting for Sales Discounts

	Gross Price Method			Net Price Method		
To record sale on December 4, 2007	Accounts Receivable Sales	8,000	8,000	Accounts Receivable [$8,000 − (0.02 × $8,000)] Sales	7,840	7,840
To record payment received on December 13, 2007	Cash [$5,500 − ($5,500 × 0.02)] Sales Discounts Taken Accounts Receivable	5,390 110	5,500	Cash Accounts Receivable	5,390	5,390
To record payment received on December 30, 2007	Cash Accounts Receivable	1,500	1,500	Cash Accounts Receivable [$1,500 − ($1,500 × 0.02)] Sales Discounts Not Taken	1,500	1,470 30
To adjust the accounts at the end of the period	No entry required			Accounts Receivable Sales Discounts Not Taken	20	20

Conceptual Evaluation

Theoretically the use of the net price method is sound because it values the accounts receivable at the net realizable value and also separates the amount of sales revenue from interest revenue. The gross price method has the advantage over the net price method of reporting receivable accounts at gross amounts, which simplifies communications with customers (because discussions are based on the gross amount). The gross price method also has the advantage of enabling sales returns and allowances (discussed later) to be recorded at gross instead of net amounts. But since a company expects most customers to take advantage of the cash discount, the gross price method overstates its current sales and accounts receivable at the end of the period. However, because the gross price method requires less record keeping, most companies use this method. Furthermore, when the timing of collections does not vary much from period to period, there is no material difference from using either method.

Sales Returns and Allowances

When a company sells merchandise, a few defective items may be returned by customers. In other cases contractual agreements also may allow products that are *not* defective to be returned. **When goods are sold that are found to be defective, the customer may retain**

---

9.   At the end of the accounting period, an adjusting entry may be made for any cash discounts no longer available on the outstanding accounts receivable. This entry involves a debit to Accounts Receivable and a credit to Sales Discounts Not Taken. A reversing entry is usually made so that when these sales are collected, the collections may be recorded in the usual manner for when no discount is taken.

the goods and be allowed a reduction in the purchase price. **This reduction is called a** *sales allowance.* **When the customer returns goods to the seller, the exchange is called a** *sales return.* Often a sales return or allowance occurs in an accounting period after the sale. From a theoretical standpoint, if a company can make reliable estimates, it should **record the estimated amount of future returns and allowances in the period of sale so as to correctly report net sales revenue and value ending accounts receivable.**

To illustrate the accounting for sales returns and allowances, assume that the Barclay Corporation sells $500,000 of goods during 2007 and the company estimates that returns and allowances will be 2% of sales. To anticipate the returns and allowances, the company records the following adjusting entry at the end of the period of sale (assuming it uses the gross price method of recording sales):

Sales Returns and Allowances ($500,000 × 0.02)	10,000	
Allowance for Sales Returns and Allowances		10,000

Consequently, when sales returns and allowances of $8,000 actually occur for goods sold on credit, the company records this transaction as follows:

Allowance for Sales Returns and Allowances	8,000	
Accounts Receivable		8,000

If the company used the net price method to record sales, it would base the preceding entries on the net price after deducting the cash discounts.

When a company estimates its sales returns and allowances in the period of sale, it includes any balance in the Allowance for Sales Returns and Allowances account on the balance sheet as a valuation account offset against Accounts Receivable. In cases where returns and allowances are not material, most companies do not estimate these items. Instead they record the returns and allowances on credit when they actually occur by debiting Sales Returns and Allowances and crediting Accounts Receivable (at the gross price or net price depending on which method they are using). Whether estimated or actual, a company reports sales returns and allowances on its income statement as a deduction from sales revenue.

VALUATION OF ACCOUNTS RECEIVABLE FOR UNCOLLECTIBLE ACCOUNTS

The preceding discussion focused on the issues involved in initially recording trade accounts receivable. Not all accounts receivable will be collected, however. Some will become bad debts. A company might record uncollectible accounts (bad debts) by either of two procedures:

1. In the year of sale, based upon an estimate of the amount of uncollectible accounts, or
2. When it determines that a specific customer account is uncollectible.

FASB Statement No. 5 requires that companies estimate their losses from loss contingencies and deduct the amounts from income and assets when both of the following conditions are met:

1. Information available prior to the issuance of the financial statements indicates that it is probable that an asset has been impaired at the date of the financial statements.
2. The amount of the loss can be reasonably estimated.[10]

---

10. "Accounting for Contingencies," *FASB Statement of Financial Accounting Standards No. 5* (Stamford, Conn.: FASB, 1975), par. 8.

Since both conditions normally are met in regard to uncollectible accounts, most companies estimate bad debts. For instance, over 93% of surveyed companies reported estimates of bad debts on their financial statements.[11] This approach enables these companies to **properly value their receivables and match expenses against revenues in the current period.**

Allowance Method

Under the **allowance method** a company studies the historical data about the actual bad debts it has incurred. It compares this information to its current sales or accounts receivable to determine relationships to use to estimate its current uncollectible accounts. **These relationships provide the information the company needs to prepare the adjusting entry to record the estimated bad debt expense for the period.**

When the company records the estimate of bad debts, the journal entry is a debit to Bad Debt Expense and a credit to Allowance for Doubtful Accounts (or, alternatively, Allowance for Bad Debts or Allowance for Uncollectible Accounts). A company normally reports bad debt expense on its income statement as an operating expense. However, some companies offset the account against gross sales, or report it as a financial expense in the Other Items section. The authors suggest reporting bad debt expense as an operating expense because it is similar to other operating expenses. Also, financial statement users normally expect companies to report bad debt expense in this manner.

Allowance for Doubtful Accounts is a valuation (contra) account that is offset against Accounts Receivable in the current assets section of the company's balance sheet. Although current credit sales create a likelihood of losses from bad debts, the company does not know at the time of sale which actual customer accounts will not be collected (if they were known, the company would not have extended credit to these customers). Offsetting Allowance for Doubtful Accounts against Accounts Receivable informs financial statement users of the net realizable value (the amount of cash expected to be collected) of the company's receivables.[12]

It is possible to base the estimate of bad debt expense on historical relationships between the actual bad debts incurred and (1) sales or (2) accounts receivable. These relationships may be classified as we show in the following diagram:

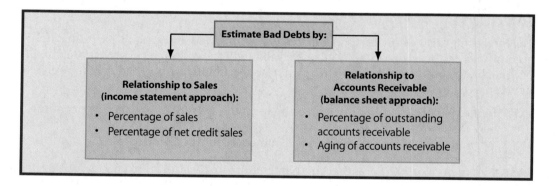

Percentage of Sales (or Net Credit Sales)

Estimating bad debts based on the historical relationship to sales matches current expenses against current revenues. This method is income statement oriented because it

6 Estimate and record bad debts using a percentage of sales.

---

11. *Accounting Trends and Techniques* (New York: AICPA, 2004), p. 177.
12. If a company has other accounts, such as Allowance for Sales Returns and Allowances, Allowance for Sales Discounts, and Deferred Gross Profit, it also deducts these accounts from Accounts Receivable to determine the net realizable value.

is based on the matching principle. It results in recording bad debt expense in the period during which credit sales occur. A percentage of total sales may be used for the estimate when there is a stable relationship between cash and credit sales. However, if the proportion of credit sales to total sales varies from period to period, it is not appropriate to use a percentage of total sales in any given period. For this reason most accountants favor estimating bad debts based on the historical relationship between bad debts and net *credit* sales. For example, if Lema Company's net credit sales during the year were $525,000 and bad debts have historically amounted to 2% of net credit sales, the company makes the following year-end adjusting entry:

Bad Debt Expense ($525,000 × 0.02)	10,500	
Allowance for Doubtful Accounts		10,500

Since this method focuses on an expense account, any existing balance in the allowance account is ignored when determining the amount of the adjusting entry. Also, if a company sells many products in different locations, it may choose to estimate bad debts based on the historical credit sales of particular products or in specific locations. Although basing bad debt expense on sales is a relatively straightforward income statement approach and adheres to the matching concept, it may not provide the best estimate of the net realizable value of accounts receivable. This is because the balance in the allowance account is ignored when making the adjusting entry. Also, if the company materially over (or under) estimates the net realizable value of the accounts receivable, a change in the accounting estimate may be necessary. Furthermore, it provides only limited information for the credit department to use in its collection activities. Because of these disadvantages a company may use a balance sheet approach.

LINK TO ETHICAL DILEMMA

As the accountant for SaveMart, the nation's largest retail company, you have performed an extensive analysis and estimated bad debts to be 3% of credit sales. While this estimate is slightly higher than last year's estimate of 2%, you feel the increase is warranted since the company, in an effort to stimulate sales, significantly relaxed its credit policy in the current fiscal year. However, if the 3% estimate is used, SaveMart's earnings will fall slightly below analysts' estimates. If the bad debt estimate is lowered to 2.5%, SaveMart will meet earnings expectations, and you will receive a large bonus. Because bad debt estimates have historically been between 2% and 3%, you are quite certain that the auditors will accept any estimate in this range. What are your responsibilities?

Percentage of Outstanding Accounts Receivable

Bad debts may be estimated based on the historical relationship between actual amounts not collected and accounts receivable. This approach is balance sheet oriented because the resulting accounts receivable is reported on the balance sheet at its estimated net realizable value. A relatively simple balance sheet approach is to base the estimated expense on the historical relationship between the actual bad debts and the outstanding accounts receivable balance at the end of the year.

In using this method, the goal is to determine the ending balance in Allowance for Doubtful Accounts. To determine the amount of its adjusting entry, a company must consider the existing balance (prior to adjustment) in the allowance account. The company records Bad Debt Expense at the amount necessary to adjust the existing allowance account balance to the required ending balance. For example, assume that Weir Company has determined that historically there has been a 4% relationship between actual bad debts and the year-end accounts receivable balance. The company's accounts at the end of the year (prior to adjustment) are as follows:

Accounts Receivable	475,000
Allowance for Doubtful Accounts	4,500 (credit balance)

The expected net realizable value of Accounts Receivable is $456,000 [$475,000−($475,000 × 0.04)], and the required balance in Allowance for Doubtful Accounts is therefore $19,000 ($475,000−$456,000, or simply $475,000 × 0.04). However, since the current credit balance in the allowance account is $4,500, only the amount necessary to increase the allowance account to its required ending balance is recorded as Bad Debt Expense. In this example the amount is $14,500 ($19,000−$4,500), as we show in the following T-account:

Allowance for Doubtful Accounts

	4,500 (current balance)
	14,500 (required adjustment)
	19,000 (required ending balance)

Based on the preceding information, Weir Company records the following year-end adjusting entry:

Bad Debt Expense	14,500	
Allowance for Doubtful Accounts		14,500

A potential weakness of basing bad debts on a percentage of total outstanding accounts receivable is that it does not consider the due date of the many individual accounts comprising the total balance. This weakness is overcome by "aging" the accounts receivable.

Aging of Accounts Receivable

7 Estimate and record bad debts using an aging analysis.

The length of time an account is outstanding is important in estimating the probability of its future collection. A company is much more likely to collect an account that is 20 days old than one that is 360 days old. For this reason a more sophisticated method of estimating bad debts as a percentage of accounts receivable is used. **A company that "ages" its accounts receivable first classifies the individual accounts based on the length of time they have been outstanding, and then applies an historically developed bad debts percentage to each age category.** This information is available from the company's accounts receivable subsidiary ledger. The information in Example 7-2 is taken from the accounts receivable subsidiary ledger of the Rhorke Corporation and illustrates how bad debts are estimated with the use of an *aging schedule* (or aging analysis).[13]

In developing the aging schedule, the company reviewed the unpaid invoices in each customer's account, classified the invoice amounts according to the length of time the invoice has been outstanding, and totaled the amounts in each group. It then multiplied the total amount in each age group by the applicable estimated uncollectible percentage to determine the estimated amount uncollectible for that age group. It determines the

---

13. A company with few accounts receivable would probably not find an aging analysis to be a useful procedure, because each customer could be evaluated individually. Aging is appropriate when there are large numbers of customers who cannot reasonably be evaluated individually at the end of the period. In this example, for simplicity, only a few customers are used.

EXAMPLE 7-2   Aging Analysis

Rhorke Corporation
December 31, 2007

(a) Aging Schedule of Accounts Receivable

		Length of Time Outstanding				
Customer	Balance 12/31/07	Under 60 Days	60–120 Days	121–240 Days	241–360 Days	Over 1 Year
Goodwin Co.	$ 33,100	$21,000	$12,100			
Hobson Inc.	14,500					$14,500
Lomas Manufacturing	20,600	15,000	5,600			
McClendon Co.	15,700				$15,700	
Schauer Corporation	37,900	17,500	16,800	$3,600		
	$121,800	$53,500	$34,500	$3,600	$15,700	$14,500

(b) Estimated Uncollectibles

Age	Amount	×	Estimated Percentage Uncollectible	=	Estimated Amounts Uncollectible
Under 60 days	$ 53,500		2%		$ 1,070
60–120 days	34,500		8		2,760
121–240 days	3,600		15		540
241–360 days	15,700		30		4,710
Over 1 year	14,500		50		7,250
	$121,800				$16,330

total estimated uncollectible amount by adding the estimated uncollectible amounts related to each age group.

This analysis indicates that the ending balance of Allowance for Doubtful Accounts should be $16,330 on December 31, 2007. **Since the objective in an aging analysis is to determine the ending allowance account balance, a company also considers the previous balance of the allowance account in recording the amount of bad debt expense at the end of the period.** If Rhorke has a current $1,350 *debit* balance in its allowance account, the amount of recorded expense necessary to bring the allowance account up to its required balance is $17,680 ($16,330+$1,350). Note that in this case the current *debit* balance in its allowance account is added. (We discuss the events that might cause the allowance account to have a debit balance in the next section.) A credit balance would be *subtracted* to determine the necessary adjustment amount. Based upon the preceding calculations, Rhorke makes the following year-end adjusting entry:

Bad Debt Expense   17,680
   Allowance for Doubtful Accounts   17,680

Use of the aging method, particularly when the company prepares interim (monthly) financial reports, is very helpful to its credit department. As it prepares each new aging schedule, this method focuses attention on any accounts that have not been collected and that have shifted to an older age category. Frequently, a company will compute its "receivables turnover" (net credit sales÷average net accounts receivable) along with its aging schedule, to determine how efficient it is in collecting its accounts receivable. The aging method has the advantage of properly reporting the net realizable value of accounts receivable on the balance sheet and of providing useful information to the credit department. However, it may not precisely match bad debt expense against revenue in the year of sale.

Conceptual Evaluation

In summary, a company should estimate and record bad debt expense in the period of sale rather than record bad debts as accounts are written off. There are two main approaches to estimating bad debts. **The income statement approach, in which a percentage of sales (or net credit sales) is used, results in a matching of expenses with sales in the current period.** However, this approach may not report accounts receivable at their net realizable value, because it does not consider the age of the individual accounts. **The balance sheet approach, which uses a percentage of outstanding accounts receivable or an aging analysis for estimating bad debts, results in reporting accounts receivable at their expected net realizable value on the balance sheet.** Also, the aging analysis provides useful credit information. With the FASB's concern for reporting on a company's *liquidity* and *future expected cash flows*, the balance sheet method may be more appropriate. Currently, both methods are used in practice, and both are allowed under generally accepted accounting principles.

LINK TO RATIO ANALYSIS

Cash is the lifeblood for any company and often results from billing and collecting credit sales. Therefore, many managers and investors carefully monitor accounts receivable to gain insight into future profitability and cash flow. The receivables turnover ratio (net credit sales ÷ average net receivables) is one measure often used as an indicator of the efficiency with which a company collects its receivables and converts them back to cash. Using data obtained from the **Walt Disney Company's** annual report, the receivables turnover computation is shown in the following table:

(amounts in millions)	2004	2003	2002
Receivables (net)	$ 4,558	$ 4,238	$4,049
Net Revenues	$30,752	$27,061	

$$2004: \text{Receivables Turnover} = \frac{\$30,752}{\left(\dfrac{\$4,558 + \$4,238}{2}\right)} = 6.99$$

$$2003: \text{Receivables Turnover} = \frac{\$27,061}{\left(\dfrac{\$4,238 + \$4,049}{2}\right)} = 6.53$$

Disney turned its receivables over 6.99 and 6.53 times per year for fiscal years 2004 and 2003, respectively. Dividing the turnover ratio into 365 days, it appears that it took Disney, on average, 52.2 days and 55.9 days to collect its accounts receivables in 2004 and 2003, respectively. Overall, it appears that over the two-year period examined, Disney was successful at speeding up the collections of receivables and, as a result, had fewer resources tied up in receivables.

Writing Off Uncollectible Accounts

If a company records bad debt expense based on an estimate, it writes off an individual account when it determines that the account is uncollectible. The journal entry is a debit to Allowance for Doubtful Accounts and a credit to Accounts Receivable. This write-off is simply an adjustment required because the company has confirmed a previously estimated expense. The write off does not affect the carrying value of the accounts receivable on the balance sheet. Consider the following information for Shy Company:

Accounts Receivable	$175,000
Allowance for Doubtful Accounts	8,750 (credit balance)
Customer account determined to be uncollectible	1,000

At the time of the write-off, the company makes the following journal entry:

Allowance for Doubtful Accounts	1,000	
Accounts Receivable		1,000

This write-off has *no effect* on the net realizable value of the accounts receivable because the allowance account and the accounts receivable balance are reduced by the same amount. As shown in the following schedule, before the write-off the net realizable accounts receivable was $166,250 ($175,000 − $8,750). After the write-off the net carrying value of the accounts receivable is still $166,250, but it now consists of a $174,000 accounts receivable balance and a $7,750 allowance account balance. Similarly, there is no affect on the income statement as a result of this write-off because it did not involve a revenue or expense account.

	Before Write-off	Write-off	After Write-off
Accounts receivable	$175,000	$(1,000)	$174,000
Less: Allowance for doubtful accounts	(8,750)	1,000	(7,750)
Net realizable value	$166,250		$166,250

A company records its write-offs of accounts receivable when it determines the individual accounts that are uncollectible. Occasionally write-offs occur during the period of sale *prior to* recording the estimated bad debts at the end of the period. In these cases the journal entry for the write-off is the same as shown previously: a debit to Allowance for Doubtful Accounts and a credit to Accounts Receivable. This entry may cause a *debit* balance in Allowance for Doubtful Accounts prior to the year-end adjustment. When the company is using a balance sheet approach, the debit balance is considered in determining the amount of the adjusting entry. When the income statement approach is used, a debit (or credit) balance is ignored (unless it becomes significant). Additionally, estimates always involve future uncertainties, and the actual losses incurred from bad debts may be greater than the amount of estimated expense. As new information becomes available, a company may need to change its estimated percentage of bad debts. If the company uses the balance sheet approach, it modifies the balance of the allowance account each year based on the most current information. When a company changes the estimated percentage of bad debts, it treats this change as an adjustment of bad debt expense in current and future periods. This change is considered to be a change in estimate as defined by *FASB Statement No. 154*. We discuss changes in estimates in Chapter 23.

Collection of an Account Previously Written Off

Occasionally a company will receive payment from a customer whose account it has already written off. Most accountants favor reestablishing the customer's account receivable in the subsidiary ledger and then recording the payment. This procedure has the advantage of providing a complete credit history for each customer account and also eliminates the previous write-off entry. For example, if Uphoff Company receives a $300 payment from a customer whose account it had previously written off, the company makes the following journal entries:

Accounts Receivable	300	
Allowance for Doubtful Accounts		300
Cash	300	
Accounts Receivable		300

Note that the first entry "reverses" the initial write-off and the second entry records the cash collection in the usual manner. Also note that both entries to accounts receivable are also recorded in the customer's account in the subsidiary ledger.

Direct Write-Off Method

The second method of recording uncollectible accounts is called the direct write-off method. This method has the advantages of simplicity and of reporting actual bad debts expense rather than an estimate. **When a company uses the direct write-off method, it records bad debt expense when it determines that a specific customer account is uncollectible.** At that time it writes off the account by debiting Bad Debt Expense and crediting Accounts Receivable. However, this determination and write-off may not occur until a later period than the period of sale. The use of the direct write-off method has the disadvantage of matching the bad debt expenses associated with previous sales against revenues of the current period. It also overstates accounts receivable associated with previous sales. Furthermore, it allows the manipulation of income because management selects the period of write-off (and expense). For these reasons the direct write-off method is not allowed under generally accepted accounting principles. However, some companies use it for financial reporting because they are required to use it for income tax purposes and the results do not differ materially from those obtained under the estimated methods we discussed earlier.

SECURE YOUR KNOWLEDGE 7-2

- Revenue from credit sales is normally recognized at the time of sale; however, if collectibility of the receivable is not reasonably assured or if a right of return exists, revenue recognition may be deferred until a later period.
- Accounts receivable are normally reported at the amount the company expects to receive (net realizable value).
- Cash discounts taken are recorded as a reduction of net sales; however, cash discounts *not* taken are left in sales (gross method) or recorded as interest revenue (net method).
- If sales returns and allowances can be reliably estimated, they should be recorded as a reduction in net sales and net receivables in the period of the sale.
- Because bad debt expense is a cost of granting credit, the matching principle requires that this expense be estimated and recorded in the period of the credit sale.
- Bad debt expense may be estimated as a percentage of sales (an income statement approach) or through an analysis of accounts receivable (a balance sheet approach).
- The write off of an uncollectible account under the allowance bad debt method does not affect the carrying value of net accounts receivable.

GENERATING IMMEDIATE CASH FROM ACCOUNTS RECEIVABLE

The net realizable value of the accounts receivable reported on a company's balance sheet is usually the amount of cash the company expects to collect in its normal operating cycle. However, in some circumstances a company may find that it needs to accelerate the cash inflows from its accounts receivable.

In today's business environment there are many companies that specialize in "financing" other companies' accounts receivable. These finance companies include, for instance, **General Motors Acceptance Corporation (GMAC)**, **Ford Motor Credit Company (Ford Credit)**, and **General Electric Capital Services (GECS)**, as well as credit card companies such as VISA, MasterCard, American Express, and Diner's Club. There are many variations in financing arrangements, including which receivables are involved, which company collects the receivables, who has title, and who incurs bad debts.

In this section we discuss the accounting issues faced by a company that "transfers" its accounts receivable to a financing company in exchange for cash. For financial reporting, these issues involve revenue recognition and asset valuation. For **revenue recognition,** the issue relates to whether the risks of ownership of the receivables have been transferred (so revenue should be recognized). For **asset valuation,** the issue relates to who has control over the future benefits from the receivables (to determine who "owns" the asset). In addition, reporting on these types of arrangements provides important information about a company's **liquidity,** the nearness to cash of its receivables; and **financial flexibility,** its ability to use its receivables to adapt to changing financial conditions.

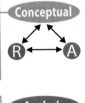

There are three basic forms of financing agreements to obtain cash from accounts receivable: (1) **pledging,** (2) **assigning,** and (3) **factoring (sale).** There may be variations in the conditions of each agreement so that the distinctions are not always clear-cut.[14] These agreements are evaluated on a "continuum," based on the transfer of risks of ownership and control over the benefits of the receivables, as we show in Exhibit 7-1.

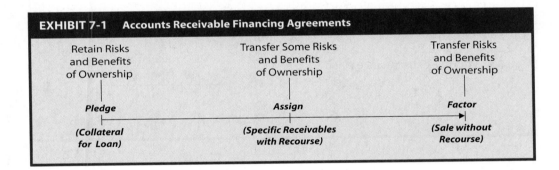

EXHIBIT 7-1   Accounts Receivable Financing Agreements

Retain Risks and Benefits of Ownership	Transfer Some Risks and Benefits of Ownership	Transfer Risks and Benefits of Ownership
Pledge	*Assign*	*Factor*
(Collateral for Loan)	*(Specific Receivables with Recourse)*	*(Sale without Recourse)*

The FASB addressed these issues in **FASB Statement No. 140** related to financing agreements. It concluded that a company (transferor) records the transfer of financial assets (e.g., accounts receivable) in which it surrenders control over the financial assets to another company (the transferee) as a sale when *all* the following conditions are met:

1. The transferred assets have been isolated from the transferor (i.e., put beyond the reach of the transferor).
2. The transferee obtains the right to exchange (e.g., sell) the transferred assets.
3. The transferor does not maintain effective control over the transferred assets through an agreement in which it can repurchase the transferred assets before their maturity.

If financial assets are transferred, the transferor continues to report on its balance sheet any retained interest in the transferred assets. If the transfer meets the conditions for a sale, the transferor records the proceeds, eliminates the financial assets, and records a

---

14. For a broad discussion, see "Asset Securitization: Economic Effects and Accounting Issues," *Accounting Horizons* (March 1992), pp. 5–16.

gain or loss. If the conditions for a sale are *not* met, the transferor records the proceeds from the transfer of financial assets as a secured borrowing.[15]

Of 600 surveyed companies nearly 26% reported pledging, assigning, or factoring their accounts receivable.[16] Exhibit 7-2 briefly shows how to determine whether to account for an accounts receivable financing agreement as a pledge, assignment, or factor (sale). We discuss the specific accounting for these three arrangements in the following sections.

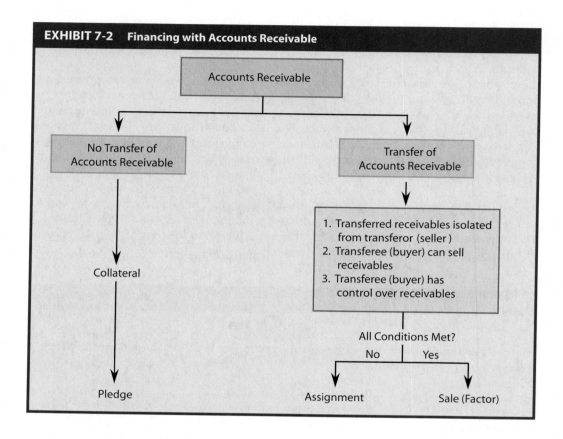

EXHIBIT 7-2 Financing with Accounts Receivable

Pledging of Accounts Receivable

8 Explain pledging, assignment, and factoring of accounts receivable.

When a company *pledges* its accounts receivable, it is using these accounts only as collateral for a loan, and the servicing activities remain its responsibility. (*Servicing activities* are the routine collection and administration functions.) The company records the loan as a liability in the usual manner. Then when it collects the receivable, it uses the cash to repay the loan plus any interest charges. Upon full payment of the loan the pledge is canceled. If the company defaults, the lender has the legal right to take title to the pledged receivables and sell them to recover the amount of the loan. Pledge agreements usually are not formally entered in a company's accounting records because there is no transfer of risk, and the company retains control over the receivables. A company generally discloses these agreements parenthetically or in the notes to its financial statements to indicate that a portion of the accounts receivable balance may not be available to general creditors.

---

15. "Accounting for Transfers and Servicing of Financial Assets and Extinguishment of Liabilities," *FASB Statement of Financial Accounting Standards No. 140* (Norwalk, Conn.: FASB, 2000), par. 9–12.
16. *Accounting Trends and Techniques* (New York: AICPA, 2004), p. 173.

Assignment of Accounts Receivable

When a company *assigns* its accounts receivable to a financial institution, it enters into a lending agreement with the institution to receive cash on specific customer accounts. Frequently, these are long-term agreements. Assignment agreements can be very complex and involve issues such as interest rate swaps, call options, and unique servicing charges, as addressed in *FASB Statement No. 140*. Here, we discuss basic assignment agreements. Under a basic assignment agreement, the borrowing company (assignor) usually retains ownership of the assigned accounts, incurs any bad debts, collects the amounts due from customers, and uses these funds to repay the loan. Occasionally, the financial institution (assignee) will require the assigned accounts to make their payments directly to it (this procedure is called *notification*). The assignee may impose collection guidelines on the assigned accounts or may agree to share in the risks of nonpayment. In these cases some of the risks and control of ownership are transferred to the assignee. This is the major difference between assigning and pledging accounts receivable. Since the assignor (borrowing company) usually retains the risks of ownership, accounts are assigned *with recourse*. This means that if the cash collected from the accounts is not enough to repay the amount owed by the assignor, the assignee still can demand payment from (has recourse against) the assignor. This is the major difference between assignment agreements and factoring agreements, where the receivables are sold without recourse and the buyer assumes all the risks of ownership.

In assignment agreements the assignor company's relationship with the purchasers of its goods and services is not disrupted because the purchaser usually makes payments directly to the company (*non-notification*) and is unaware of the financing arrangement. Usually, the amount of receivables assigned is greater than the amount of the advance; the excess amount protects the assignee from sales returns and allowances. Under assignment arrangements the assignor pays a service charge and interest on the loan, and makes periodic payments (including interest) to the assignee based on collections of assigned accounts receivable. The assignor is also required to absorb any reductions due to sales returns and allowances or losses from uncollectible accounts. On the assignor company's balance sheet, it reports assigned accounts receivable separately from unassigned accounts receivable because it must use cash receipts from these assigned receivables for a specific purpose. That is, some of the benefits of ownership of the asset are transferred to the assignee. The assignor company reports the note payable as a current or noncurrent liability, depending on the due date.

Example: Assignment

Assume that on December 1, 2007, the Trussel Company assigns $60,000 of its accounts receivable to a finance company. The finance company advances 80% of the accounts receivable assigned less a service charge of $500. It also charges an annual interest rate of 12% on any outstanding loan balance. The journal entries that Trussel makes to record this assignment are:

Cash [($60,000 × 0.80) − $500]	47,500	
Assignment Service Charge Expense	500	
Note Payable ($60,000 × 0.80)		48,000
Accounts Receivable Assigned	60,000	
Accounts Receivable		60,000

The first journal entry records the receipt of cash. The Assignment Service Charge Expense account is a cost of borrowed funds and most companies usually record it as an expense at the time of the advance. The second journal entry reclassifies the receivables as assigned accounts receivable.

On December 31, 2007, Trussel collects $10,000 on assigned accounts. It pays this amount along with the 12% interest for 1 month to the finance company. Trussel records these transactions as follows:

Cash	10,000	
Accounts Receivable Assigned		10,000
Note Payable	10,000	
Interest Expense ($48,000 × 0.12 × 1/12)	480	
Cash		10,480

The interest expense on any future payments is based upon the balance *remaining* in the Note Payable account (for example, the interest expense for the next payment in our example is based on the $38,000 note payable balance). During the period the note is outstanding, Trussel credits any bad debt losses and sales returns and allowances related to the assigned accounts receivable against the Accounts Receivable Assigned account. After Trussel pays the note, it reclassifies any remaining balance in Accounts Receivable Assigned as Accounts Receivable.

On the December 31, 2007 balance sheet of the Trussel Company, it reports the assigned accounts and the remaining liability (assuming it is short-term) as follows:

Current Assets		*Current Liabilities*	
Accounts receivable assigned	$50,000	Note payable	$38,000

Trussel includes a description of the financing agreement in the notes to its financial statements. ♦

Factoring (Sale) of Accounts Receivable

When a company factors its accounts receivable, it sells individual accounts to a financial institution (called a factor). Since the company *sells* the receivables, it transfers title to the factor who assumes all the risks of ownership. That is, the company sells the accounts receivable *without recourse*, which means that if any receivables are not collected the factor cannot demand payment from it. Consequently, factoring agreements focus on control of the receivables and usually require (1) notification of the credit customers to remit the amounts owed directly to the factor, and (2) assumption by the factor of all collection activities, setting of credit policies, and losses from uncollectible accounts.

At the time of sale the factor (finance company) charges the selling company a commission. The commission usually is based on the amount of receivables transferred and is relatively high, although it varies depending on the risk of noncollection. The way in which the selling company records the commission depends on its normal operating activities. A selling company records the commission as an *expense* if it normally factors its accounts receivable, or as a *loss* if it usually does not sell its accounts receivable. In addition to charging a commission, the factor usually will pay only 80% to 90% of the value of the accounts receivable transferred, as a protection against sales returns and allowances. The selling company records the amount withheld (i.e., the 20% to 10%) in a separate Receivable from Factor account to indicate the amount that may be returned by the factor. Since title is transferred, the selling company reduces (credits) Accounts Receivable for the amount of the receivables sold.

Example: Factoring

Assume that the Farber Corporation sells $80,000 of accounts receivable to a factor, receives 90% of the value of the factored accounts, and is charged a 15% commission based on the gross amount of factored accounts receivable. Farber records the following journal entry (assuming that it normally factors its accounts receivable):

Cash [($80,000 × 0.90) − $12,000]	60,000	
Receivable from Factor ($80,000 × 0.10)	8,000	
Factoring Expense ($80,000 × 0.15)	12,000	
Accounts Receivable		80,000

If sales returns or allowances occur on factored accounts, the selling company debits Sales Returns and Allowances and credits Receivable from Factor. At the conclusion of the factoring agreement for a particular group of receivables, the selling company collects any balance remaining in the Receivable from Factor account from the factor and debits Cash and credits Receivable from Factor. When a factoring agreement exists, the selling company discloses the agreement in a note to its financial statements. Factoring agreements are common in the furniture and textile industries; another common example is the sale of home mortgages from one financial institution to another. However, many companies are reluctant to use factoring agreements because of the cost of notifying their customers, and because their customers may dislike being required to make payments to a bank or finance company rather than to the seller. ◆

Credit Card Sales

Many retail companies make agreements with national credit card companies, which operate either independently or in affiliation with banks. Among the most popular are VISA, MasterCard, American Express, and Diner's Club. Under these arrangements, card holders establish a **line of credit** (with the credit card company) which may be used for retail purchases of goods and services. After customers make credit purchases, the retailer deposits the credit card receipts in its bank account (or receives an electronic transfer of cash from the credit card company). The customers then repay the bank or credit card company. These types of agreements are *factoring* agreements.

The retailer accepting these credit cards charges its customers the selling price for goods and services, but is assessed a service charge on credit card sales by the bank or credit card company. This charge is usually a percentage of each sale, and the fee is for the use of a credit and collection department. Thus, the retailer usually records the fee as an operating expense. The individual retailer assumes little or no risk in accepting national credit cards, because most risk is borne by the bank or credit card company (except where there is fraud or negligence by the retailer) since the bank or credit card company originally granted the line of credit. The service charge assessed on credit card sales usually varies between 1 and 5% and is partially determined by the annual amount of sales or by exclusive arrangements. In an **exclusive arrangement** a retailer will accept only one national credit card, and in return the credit card company charges the retailer a lower service charge. For example, **Sam's Club** accepts only Discover cards in its stores.

For example, assume that Kerns Shoes sold $1,500 of merchandise on credit which was billed to a national credit card company. If the collection fee charged by the credit card company is 5%, Kerns makes the following journal entry when it deposits the credit card sales receipts (assuming it is using the gross price method of recording sales):

Cash	1,425	
Credit Card Expense ($1,500 × 0.05)	75	
Sales		1,500

Some large retailers (e.g., Sears, JCPenney) have their own credit cards. When a customer makes a credit purchase using a retail company's credit card, the company records accounts receivable in the usual manner.

Disclosure of Financing Agreements of Accounts Receivable

As we noted in the previous discussion, a company should disclose the existence of pledge, assignment, or factor (sale) agreements parenthetically or in the notes to its financial statements. An example of this type of disclosure for a factoring agreement is shown in the first note of **UNIFI, Inc.**, 2004 financial statements in Real Report 7-2.

Real Report 7-2   Disclosure of Factoring Agreement

UNIFI, INC.

NOTES TO CONSOLIDATED FINANCIAL STATEMENTS (IN PART)
1. Accounting Policies and Financial Statement Information (in part)

Receivables: . . . Prior to March 28, 2004, certain customer accounts receivable were factored without recourse. Effective March 26, 2004, the Company ended its factoring relationships due to the cost savings derived from in-house collections. The remaining factored receivables at June 27, 2004 were $0.8 million compared to $20.1 million at June 29, 2003. An allowance for losses is provided for known and potential losses arising from yarn quality claims and for amounts owed by customers that are not factored. . . . The reserve for such losses was $10.7 million at June 27, 2004 and $12.3 million at June 29, 2003.

Questions:

1. Why didn't UNIFI provide an allowance for losses on the accounts receivable that it factored?
2. Why did UNIFI end its factoring relationships?

NOTES RECEIVABLE

A note receivable is an unconditional written agreement to collect a certain sum of money on a specific date. Notes receivable generally have two attributes that accounts receivable do not have:

1. They are negotiable instruments, which means that they are legally transferable among parties and may be used to satisfy debts by the holders of these instruments.
2. They usually involve interest, requiring the separation of the receivable into its principal and interest components.

Companies frequently require their customers to issue notes receivable when the customers wish to extend the repayment period on an account receivable. Sometimes a company may require notes receivable when it extends credit to new customers, and in some cases it may require them for all credit sales. Notes receivable also may result from long-term contracts.

A company may receive two types of short-term notes: (1) those bearing interest on the face amount of the note and (2) non-interest-bearing notes. We discuss these short-term notes in the following sections. We discuss recording long-term notes at their fair (present) value in Chapter 14.

Short-Term Interest-Bearing Notes Receivable

9 Account for short-term notes receivable.

When an interest-bearing note is issued, the amount borrowed (the principal) is listed as the face value, and the interest charged is stated as a specific rate applied to this face value. When a company receives a note, it debits the Note Receivable account for the face value. After issuance, it records interest revenue on the note in the usual fashion, including any year-end adjustments for interest receivable. To illustrate, assume that on October 1, 2007, Trent Company made a $5,000 credit sale to Jaynik Company and required the company to sign a $5,000, 60-day, 12% note. The middle column of Example 7-3 shows the journal

EXAMPLE 7-3   Accounting for Short-Term Notes Receivable

	Interest-Bearing				Non-interest-Bearing		

To record receipt of note on October 1, 2007	Notes Receivable
	  Sales
		5,000		5,000	Notes Receivable
					  Interest Revenue
					  Sales
						5,100	100
							5,000

To record receipt of maturity value on December 1, 2007	Cash
	  Notes Receivable
	  Interest Revenue*
		5,100		5,000
				100
					Cash
					  Notes Receivable
						5,100	5,100

*$5,000 \times 0.12 \times 60/360$

entries on October 1, 2007 for the Trent Company to record the receipt of the interest-bearing note, and on December 1, 2007 to record the receipt of the principal and interest (assuming, for simplicity, a 360-day business year). If the note had extended past the end of the year, Trent Company would have made a year-end adjusting entry to record the interest receivable and recognize the interest revenue.

Bad debt losses may occur on transactions involving short-term notes receivable, particularly when it is common practice to require customers to sign notes for all credit sales. In these cases the company should assess the likelihood of these losses and establish an Allowance for Doubtful Notes. This procedure is the same as we discussed earlier for accounts receivable and results in an increase in its expenses and a decrease in the net realizable value of its notes receivable.

Short-Term Non-Interest-Bearing Notes Receivable

In the case of a non-interest-bearing note, the maturity value (the amount to be collected, which includes both principal and implicit interest) is listed as the face value. Actually the term non-interest-bearing is a misnomer because all notes implicitly include interest. It is simply a case of the interest being included in the face value rather than being stated as a separate rate. A better term would be a note with no *stated interest rate*. APB Opinion No. 21 does not *require* current trade receivables to be recorded at their present values because the difference between the present value and the maturity value is not likely to be significant. Consequently, many companies record short-term non-interest-bearing trade notes receivable at their maturity values. This approach, however, overstates sales revenue and understates interest revenue.

A conceptually better approach is to record the note receivable at its present value and to recognize interest revenue as it is earned. To illustrate, assume the same facts as in the earlier example except that Jaynik Company signs a $5,100 non-interest-bearing note, due on December 1, 2007. The top of the right column of Example 7-3 shows the journal entry on October 1, 2007 for the Trent Company to record the receipt of the non-interest-bearing note. Observe in this entry that interest revenue is credited[17] for $100. Although technically the company has not yet earned the interest, it will do so before the end of the accounting period. This procedure simplifies the accounting process. The journal entry on December 1, 2007 to record the receipt of the face value is shown at the bottom of the right column of Example 7-3. If the note had extended past the end of the year, Trent Company would have made a year-end adjusting entry to *reduce* (debit) the interest revenue for the interest not yet earned and to adjust (credit) an account entitled Discount on Notes Receivable. This Discount account is a contra account and is deducted from the Notes Receivable account to report the net realizable value on the balance sheet.

---

17. Alternatively, Discount on Notes Receivable could be credited (instead of Interest Revenue) at the time of issuance. Then, when the face value is collected (or at year-end if an adjustment is required), a journal entry must be made to reduce the discount account and increase interest revenue for the amount of interest earned.

Notes Receivable Discounted

Occasionally a company may find that it needs additional cash on a short-term basis, but the company does not wish to borrow money or sell or assign its accounts receivable. In these cases the company may discount a customer's note receivable at a bank in return for cash. **When a company discounts a customer's note receivable at the bank, it transfers the note to the bank.** This financing arrangement is subject to the conditions of *FASB Statement No. 140* summarized in Exhibit 7-2. If all the conditions are met, the company records the transfer as a sale (without recourse). If the conditions are not met, the company records the transfer as an assignment (with recourse). Typically, the customer is notified to pay the bank directly on the maturity date. If the agreement is an assignment with recourse, there is a contingent liability during the period between the discount date and the maturity date. During this period, the company must disclose the assignment in the notes to its financial statements, even if the possibility of default by the customer is remote.[18]

When a customer's note receivable is discounted, the proceeds (cash received) are determined by multiplying the discount rate times the maturity value of the note (face value of the note plus total interest) for the discount period, and deducting the resulting discount from the maturity value. The *discount rate* is the interest rate charged by the bank. It has no relationship to the interest rate charged the customer on the note receivable. The *discount period* is the length of time from the date of discount to the maturity date. Any gain or loss from the discounting is computed by comparing the current book value of the note receivable (including accrued interest revenue) to the proceeds received. The company discounting the note makes journal entries on the date of the discount to record any accrued interest revenue, the proceeds received, and any gain or loss on the discounting of the note. It eliminates the discounted note on the maturity date.

Example: Note Assignment

Assume that on August 31, 2007, the Kasper Corporation discounts (with recourse) a customer's note at its bank at a 14% discount rate. The note was received from the customer on August 1, is for 90 days, has a face value of $5,000, and carries an interest rate of 12%. The customer pays the note on the October 30, 2007 maturity date. The calculations on August 31 for the discounted note are as follows (assuming a 360-day business year for simplicity):

1.	Face value of note	$5,000.00
2.	Interest to maturity ($5,000 × 0.12 × 90/360)	150.00
3.	Maturity value of note	$5,150.00
4.	Discount ($5,150 × 0.14 × 60/360)	(120.17)
5.	Proceeds received	$5,029.83
6.	Accrued interest revenue: $50 ($5,000 × 0.12 × 30/360)	
7.	Book value of note ($5,000 + $50)	(5,050.00)
8.	Loss from discounting of note	$ (20.17)

Kasper Corporation makes the following journal entry to record the discounted note on August 31:

Cash	5,029.83	
Loss from Discounting of Note	20.17	
Notes Receivable		5,000.00
Interest Revenue		50.00

When a note is discounted, the difference between the book value of the note and its proceeds is recorded as a gain or loss (as we did in this example) if a company usually does

---

18. *FASB Statement No. 5, op. cit.,* par. 12.

not discount its notes. Alternatively, if a company normally discounts its notes, the difference is reported as interest revenue or interest expense.

If the Kasper Corporation prepares an interim balance sheet on September 30, 2007, it discloses the contingent liability in the notes to its financial statements. This note might read as follows: "The company is contingently liable for a discounted note receivable of $5,000. The company does not anticipate that this note will be defaulted on its maturity date."

In this illustration the contingent liability was eliminated on the maturity date when the customer paid the note. If the customer does not pay this note at maturity, the bank would require Kasper to pay the maturity value of the note plus a service charge on the dishonored note. Kasper's only recourse is to attempt to collect these amounts from the customer. Consequently, upon default Kasper establishes a Notes Receivable Dishonored account. For example, assume instead that on November 2, 2007, the bank notified Kasper that the note had not been paid and also charged Kasper a $10 fee. At that time Kasper would record the following journal entry:

Notes Receivable Dishonored	5,160	
Cash [$5,000 + ($5,000 × 0.12 × 90/360) + $10]		5,160

If Kasper does not collect the dishonored note in the future, it recognizes a loss on the default. ◆

SECURE YOUR KNOWLEDGE 7-3

- Three basic forms of financing arrangements that allow a company to accelerate the cash flow from its accounts receivable are pledging, assigning, and factoring (sale).
- If a company surrenders control over its receivables, the transaction is recorded as a sale; otherwise, the transaction is considered a secured borrowing (either an assignment with recourse or a pledge as collateral).
- Short-term, interest-bearing notes are recorded at the face value of the note receivable, and interest is recognized by applying a specific interest rate to this face value.
- Non-interest–bearing notes receivable are recorded at their maturity value (which includes both principal and implicit interest), and interest is recognized over the term of the note.
- Similar to accounts receivable, a note receivable may be discounted or transferred to a bank in exchange for cash.

FINANCIAL STATEMENT DISCLOSURES OF RECEIVABLES

Companies are required to disclose any accounting policies related to their receivables that might be helpful to external users. Furthermore, **FASB Statement No. 133** requires a company to *recognize* as assets any derivative financial instruments that involve rights of the company (e.g., a "hedge" of the exposure to changes in the fair value of receivables), based on their fair value. The *Statement* also requires a company to disclose information such as the types of derivative instruments it holds, its objectives in holding the instruments, and its strategies for achieving these objectives. The description must indicate the company's risk management policy in regard to each type of instrument. **FASB Statement No. 107** requires a company to *disclose* the fair value of all its financial instruments, whether recognized or not on the balance sheet. The *Statement* also requires a company to disclose all significant concentrations of credit risk due to its financial instruments. A company typically makes these disclosures in the notes to its financial statements. The intent of these disclosures is to improve the reporting of a company's *risk, liquidity, and*

financial flexibility.[19] Real Report 7-3 shows an excerpt from **Apple Computer's** 2004 year-end balance sheet and related Note 2 illustrating the presentation of receivables.

Reporting

Real Report 7-3   Disclosure of Accounts Receivable

APPLE COMPUTER, INC.

CONSOLIDATED BALANCE SHEETS

September 25, 2004 and September 27, 2003

	2004	2003
(in millions)		
Current Assets: (in part)		
Accounts receivable, less allowances		
of $47 and $49, respectively	$774	$776

Notes to Consolidated Financial Statements (in part)

NOTE 2

Trade Receivables

The following table summarizes the activity in the allowance for doubtful accounts (in millions):

	2004	2003
Beginning allowance balance	$49	$51
Charged to costs and expenses	3	4
Deductions (a)	(5)	(6)
Ending allowance balance	$47	$49

(a) Represents amounts written off against the allowance, net of recoveries.

Questions:

1. For 2004 recreate the summary journal entries that Apple Computer must have made for its Allowance account.
2. Based on the information presented, comment on the effect of Apple Computer's estimate of bad debt expense on the financial statements for the period presented.

A company includes collections of its accounts receivable and notes receivable from sales in the operating activities section of its statement of cash flows. If a company normally factors its accounts receivable, it generally reports the cash proceeds from the sale in the operation activities section. However, if a company assigns its accounts receivable, the cash proceeds from the loan are reported in the financing section of its statement of cash flows. Collections of interest on notes receivable are included in operating cash flows. However, the receipt by a company of the principal on a note receivable issued for a loan is treated as a cash inflow from an investing activity. When a company discounts a note receivable, the cash received is treated as a cash inflow from a financing activity on its statement of cash flows.

APPENDIX: INTERNAL CONTROLS FOR CASH

Two important elements of internal control over cash are a petty cash fund and a bank reconciliation. We discuss each of these elements in the following sections.

---

19. "Accounting for Derivative Instruments and Hedging Activities," *FASB Statement of Financial Accounting Standards No. 133* (Norwalk, Conn.: FASB, 1998), par. 17 and 44; and "Disclosures about Fair Value of Financial Instruments," *FASB Statement of Financial Accounting Standards No. 107* (Norwalk, Conn.: FASB, 1991), par. 7 and 15A.

PETTY CASH

A petty cash system involves a cash fund under the control of an employee that enables a company to pay for small amounts that might be impractical or impossible to pay by check. For example, a company requiring employees to work overtime may have a policy of sending late-working employees home by taxi. Since taxi drivers do not usually accept checks, the company may give these employees cash to pay the taxi fare. Small amounts of cash may also be needed to pay for postage, deliveries, the purchase of small amounts of office supplies, and other items. A company may use a petty cash system for these purposes. The design and operation of a petty cash system includes the following steps:

10 Understand a petty cash fund.

1. An employee is appointed petty cash custodian. The petty cash fund is established at an amount estimated to be enough to cover expenditures over a short period of time, and the fund is turned over to the employee. The journal entry to record the establishment of the fund is a debit to Petty Cash and a credit to Cash for $500 (amount assumed).

2. Petty cash vouchers are printed, prenumbered, and given to the custodian of the fund. The vouchers are used as evidence of expenditures. Therefore at all times the total of the cash in the fund plus the amounts of expenditure vouchers should be equal to the original amount of the fund, in this case $500. The custodian completes a petty cash voucher each time a payment from the fund is made, but journal entries are *not* recorded at this time.

3. When the amount of cash in the petty cash fund becomes low and/or at the end of an accounting period, the vouchers are sorted into expense categories and the remaining cash is counted. The expenses are then recorded and the fund is replenished. At this time, a Cash Short and Over account is used to record any "shortage" or "overage" between the original petty cash fund balance and the remaining cash in the fund plus the amounts of the petty cash vouchers. The account helps to highlight errors and improve internal control. For example, assume that a count at the end of the month shows $67.54 remaining in the petty cash fund, and the sorting of vouchers indicates the following costs were incurred during the month:

Office supplies	$ 34.16
Postage	178.00
Transportation	132.14
Miscellaneous	83.76
Total expenses	$428.06

Since these expenses total $428.06 and the amount needed to replenish the fund is $432.46 ($500 − $67.54), the fund is "short" by $4.40. The company records (debits) the actual expenses (along with Cash Short and Over), rather than petty cash, as follows when it replenishes the fund:

Office Supplies Expense	34.16	
Postage Expense	178.00	
Transportation Expense	132.14	
Miscellaneous Expense	83.76	
Cash Short and Over	4.40	
Cash		432.46

The $432.46 is given to the fund custodian, and the actual amount of cash in the petty cash fund is now equal to the original fund balance of $500. The company reports the expenses on its income statement. It reports a debit balance in the Cash Short and Over account at the end of the accounting period as a miscellaneous expense; it reports a credit balance as a miscellaneous revenue. The company includes the balance of the petty cash fund as part of the Cash amount reported on its balance sheet when it issues financial statements.

BANK RECONCILIATION

The information in a company's Cash account is also kept by an external independent party, the company's bank. Therefore it is a good internal control procedure to use one to verify the other. **A bank reconciliation is a schedule that a company prepares to analyze the difference between the ending cash balance in its accounting records and the ending cash balance reported by its bank in a bank statement to determine the correct ending cash balance.**

Banks send a monthly statement to each depositor summarizing the activities that have taken place in the depositor's account. These activities include deposits, checks cleared, miscellaneous items, and the ending balance in the checking account. Also included with the bank statement may be photos of the depositor's canceled checks. Every company has a checking account and keeps its own accounting records of its deposits and checks. The bank statement and the company's accounting records usually will not be in complete agreement. When the company receives the bank statement each month, it prepares a bank reconciliation to compare the bank statement balance and its cash balance to reconcile these records.

Credits: Getty Images/PhotoDisc (both images)

Causes of the Difference

The causes of the difference between the cash balance listed on a company's bank statement and the balance shown in the company's cash account include the following items:

1. *Outstanding Checks.* **An outstanding check is a check written by the company and deducted from its cash balance that the bank has not yet deducted from the balance reported on the bank statement.** On the date a company issues a check, it reduces its Cash account. A period of time is necessary for the check to be received by the payee (the recipient of the check), deposited in the payee's bank, and subtracted from the company's bank balance. Therefore a company has a certain number of outstanding checks at the end of each month that causes its Cash account balance to be less than the balance on the bank statement.

2. *Deposits in Transit.* **A deposit in transit is a cash receipt added to the company's cash balance but not yet added to the balance reported on the bank statement.** When a company receives a check, it increases its Cash account. A period of time may pass before the check is deposited by the company and recorded by the bank. At the end of each month the company may have deposits in transit (either cash or checks) that cause its Cash account balance to be greater than the balance on the bank statement.

3. *Charges Made Directly by the Bank.* A bank frequently imposes a service charge for a depositor's checking account and deducts this charge directly from the account.

Banks also charge for the cost of printing checks and for stopping payment on checks. The bank reports these charges on the bank statement.

When the company receives a customer's check, it deposits the check in its bank as a cash receipt even though the customer's bank has not yet transferred the cash from the customer's bank account to the company's bank account. Occasionally, the company's bank is unable to collect the amount of the customer's check. That is, the customer's check has "bounced." **NSF (not sufficient funds) is the term used for a customer's check that a company has deposited in its bank account but has not been paid by the customer's bank because there is not enough cash in the customer's account.** Because the bank has not received payment from the customer, it deducts this amount from the company's bank account. Consequently, there may be some NSF checks included in the bank statement that the company has not recorded.

At the end of the month the bank lists all of these charges as deductions from the company's cash balance on the bank statement even though the company may not have deducted them from its cash balance in its accounting records. Therefore the bank statement balance is less than the balance in the company's Cash account.

4. *Deposits Made Directly by the Bank.* A bank often acts as a collection agency for its customers on items such as notes receivable. In addition, most checking accounts earn interest. When the bank collects a note, it records the amount (principal and interest) as an increase in the company's bank account. Consequently, the bank statement may include notes received by the bank that the company has not yet recorded in its accounting records. The company may not know the amount of interest it has earned on its checking account until it receives the bank statement. In both these situations the bank statement balance is greater than the balance in the company's Cash account.

5. *Errors.* Despite the internal control procedures established by the bank and the company, the company may discover errors in either the bank's records or its records when it prepares the bank reconciliation. For example, a bank may include a deposit or a check from another customer's account or make an error in recording an amount. A company may similarly make an error in recording an amount. For example, a common error is to transpose two numbers, so that the correct amount of $426 is recorded as $462.

Procedures for Preparing a Bank Reconciliation

Given the items that might cause a difference between the ending balance in a company's Cash account and the ending cash balance from the bank statement, the company should follow a list of procedures in preparing its bank reconciliation:

11 Prepare a bank reconciliation.

1. **Compare the deposits listed in the company's records with the deposits shown on the bank statement.** Determine that the deposits in transit included in the *last* month's bank reconciliation are listed in this month's bank statement. These deposits do not need any adjustment in the bank reconciliation. If they are *not* shown on the bank statement, immediately investigate to determine if an error or theft has occurred. Identify any deposits for the current month that are not listed on the bank statement. Add the amounts of all the deposits in transit to the ending cash balance of the bank statement in the reconciliation.

2. **Compare the checks listed in the company's records with the checks shown on the bank statement.** Determine that the outstanding checks included in last month's bank reconciliation are listed in this month's bank statement. These checks do not need any adjustment in the bank reconciliation. If they are *not* shown on the bank statement, investigate to determine if the checks were received by the creditors so that the company's "credit rating" is not affected. Identify any checks for the current month not deducted in the bank statement. Subtract the amounts of all the outstanding checks from the ending cash balance of the bank statement in the reconciliation.

3. **Identify any deposits or charges made directly by the bank that are not included in the company's records.** These items include collections of notes receivable, interest earned on the checking account, service charges, NSF checks, and so on, which are listed on the bank statement. Add the collections to or subtract the charges from the company's ending cash balance in the bank reconciliation.

4. **Determine the effect of any errors.** If an error is found, the nature of the error determines whether to add the error to or subtract the error from the company's ending cash balance or from the ending cash balance of the bank statement.

5. **Complete the bank reconciliation.** Use the format we discuss below.

A company is required to report on its balance sheet the amount of cash over which it has control at the end of an accounting period. Our discussion focuses on the form of reconciliation that arrives at an *adjusted*, or *corrected*, cash balance, indicating the amount of cash that a company reports on its balance sheet. We illustrate this form of bank reconciliation as follows (using assumed amounts):

Cash balance from bank statement		$7,218
Add:	Receipts recorded on the company's records but not reported on the bank statement. *Examples*: deposits in transit and cash received and recorded but not yet deposited	629
		$7,847
Deduct:	Payments recorded on the company's records but not reported on the bank statement. *Example*: outstanding checks	(516)
Adjusted Cash Balance		$7,331
Cash balance from company records		$6,925
Add:	Receipts reported on the bank statement but not recorded on the company's records. *Examples*: notes receivable and interest collected by the bank or interest earned on the funds on deposit	715
		$7,640
Deduct:	Payments reported on the bank statement but not recorded on the company's records. *Examples*: bank service charge and customers' checks returned for lack of funds (NSF checks)	(309)
Adjusted Cash Balance		$7,331

After the company completes the bank reconciliation, it makes journal entries to bring its accounts up to date. The company only makes journal entries for the adjustments it made to *its* records on the bank reconciliation. It does *not* make journal entries for the adjustments it made to the bank statement balance on the reconciliation; the bank will record these adjustments in its accounts at the appropriate time.

Example: Bank Reconcilation

The following example shows the preparation of a bank reconciliation and the required adjusting entries for the Craig Corporation for the month ended June 30, 2007. The unadjusted cash balances are as follows:

Cash balance from bank statement, June 30	$12,461.15
Cash balance from company records, June 30	12,437.94

The bank statement disclosed the following information:

1. A customer note for $1,200 plus $12 interest was collected on June 29.
2. A customer check for $138.14 was returned because of insufficient funds (NSF check).
3. The monthly service charge was $15.

A review of the company records disclosed the following:

1. A deposit for $1,142.87 at the end of the day on June 30 did not appear on the bank statement.
2. Customer checks totaling $327.40 were on hand at the end of June awaiting deposit.
3. The following company checks were outstanding at the end of June:
   #862 $ 96.19
   #864   147.18
   #865   263.25
4. Check #843, written for $91.20 in payment of an account payable and included with the canceled checks in the bank statement, was erroneously recorded as $19.20 in the company's records.

The upper part of Example 7-4 shows the preparation of a bank reconciliation based on this information. After completing the reconciliation, the Craig Corporation prepares adjusting entries to record those items not previously included in its accounts. We show these entries in the bottom part of Example 7-4 (with arrows to indicate which items are adjusted). These adjusting entries adjust the Cash account to $13,424.80, the amount that Craig Corporation reports as its cash balance (along with any petty cash) on its June 30, 2007 balance sheet. ♦

EXAMPLE 7-4   **Bank Reconciliation and Adjusting Entries**

Craig Corporation
Bank Reconciliation
June 30, 2007

Cash balance from bank statement			$12,461.15
Add: Deposit in transit	$1,142.87		
Checks on hand	327.40		1,470.27
			$13,931.42
Deduct: Outstanding checks:			
#862	$ 96.19		
#864	147.18		
#865	263.25		(506.62)
Adjusted Cash Balance			$13,424.80
Cash balance from company records			$12,437.94
Add: Note collected by bank	$1,200.00		
Interest on note	12.00		1,212.00 ←
			$13,649.94
Deduct: Bank service chanrge	$ 15.00		
NSF check returned	138.14		
Error in recording check #843	72.00		(225.14) ←
Adjusted Cash Balance			$13,424.80

Adjusting Entries

June 30 Cash		1,212.00 ←	
Notes Receivable (note collected)			1,200.00
Interest Revenue (interest collected)			12.00
30 Miscellaneous Expense			
(bank service charge)		15.00	
Accounts Receivable (NSF check)		138.14	
Accounts Payable (error)		72.00	
Cash			225.14 ←

SUMMARY

At the beginning of the chapter, we identified several objectives you would accomplish after reading the chapter. The objectives are listed below, each followed by a brief summary of the key points in the chapter discussion.

1. **Identify items of cash (and cash equivalents).** Cash consists of coins and currency, unrestricted funds on deposit with a bank (checking and savings accounts), negotiable checks, and bank drafts. Cash equivalents are short-term, highly liquid investments (having maturity dates of three months or less from the date acquired) that are readily convertible into known amounts of cash.

2. **Understand the importance of cash management.** Cash management is important so that a company has enough cash available to pay its bills, but does not have idle cash as a nonproductive resource. To do so, a company must have sound cash planning systems (cash budget) and sound cash control systems (internal control).

3. **Discuss revenue recognition when the right of return exists.** When the right of return exists, a company recognizes revenue at the time of the sale only when six conditions are met. Briefly, these are: (1) the sales price is known, (2) the buyer has paid or will pay, (3) the buyer's obligation is not affected by theft or damage, (4) the buyer is a separate entity from the seller, (5) the seller does not have to help resell the product, and (6) the seller can estimate the future returns.

4. **Understand the credit policies and internal control related to accounts receivable.** A company sells on credit to increase sales. Credit policies should be closely associated with customers' credit ratings. A company should adopt a credit policy that combines increased customer satisfaction with increased sales revenue, credit department costs, and bad debt losses in a way that results in the highest incremental profit and cash flows. A company should use prenumbered invoices and separate the sales function from the collection function to help maintain internal control over accounts receivable.

5. **Explain the gross and net methods to account for cash discounts.** Under the gross method, a company records accounts receivable and sales at the gross price. If the customer takes the cash discount, the company debits Sales Discounts Taken for the amount of the discount. Under the net method, a company records accounts receivable and sales at the net price. If the customer does not take the cash discount, the company credits Sales Discount Not Taken for the amount of the lost discount.

6. **Estimate and record bad debts using a percentage of sales.** Under the percentage of sales method, a company debits the bad debts expense account and credits the allowance account for an amount based on an estimate of the percentage of the current sales that will not be collected.

7. **Estimate and record bad debts using an aging analysis.** Under the aging method, a company first classifies its accounts receivable into categories based on their age. Then it multiplies the amount in each category by the percentage estimated to be uncollectible, and sums the expected uncollectible amounts. Finally, it deducts this sum from the balance in the allowance account to determine the amount to record as a debit to bad debts expense and a credit to the allowance account.

8. **Explain pledging, assignment, and factoring of accounts receivable.** When a company *pledges* accounts receivable, it uses these accounts as collateral for a loan. When a company *assigns* accounts receivable, it enters into a lending agreement with a financial institution to receive cash on specific customer accounts. When a company *factors* accounts receivable, it sells individual accounts to a financial institution.

9. **Account for short-term notes receivable.** When a company receives an interest-bearing note receivable, it records the note at its face value. It then records interest revenue when it collects the note. When a company receives a non-interest-bearing note, it records the note at its maturity value and, for simplicity, also records interest revenue at this time.

10. **Understanding a petty cash fund (Appendix).** A petty cash system involves assigning a cash fund to an employee who has control over the fund, and who pays for small amounts (e.g., postage) that might be impractical or impossible to pay by check. At all times the amount of the cash in the fund plus the amount of expenditure vouchers should be equal to the original amount in the fund.

11. **Prepare a bank reconciliation (Appendix).** To prepare a bank reconciliation, add the amounts of any deposits in transit to, and subtract the amounts of any outstanding checks from, the ending bank statement balance. Next, add any collections or subtract any charges made directly by the bank to or from the company's ending cash balance. Then adjust the ending bank statement balance or company's ending cash balance for any errors, and complete the bank reconciliation.

ANSWERS TO REAL REPORT QUESTIONS

Real Report 7-1 Answers

1. Cash and cash equivalents are reported as one combined amount because the investment is readily convertible into cash (three months or less at the date of purchase), and the risk that that the short-term investment's value will change significantly due to a change in interest rates is minimal.

Real Report 7-2 Answers

1. In a factoring arrangement, the receivables are sold, without recourse, to the factor. Because the factor assumes all risks of ownership and cannot demand payment from UNIFI for any uncollectible accounts, no allowance for uncollectible accounts is needed. The factor is assuming all losses from uncollectible accounts.

2. The factors will charge UNIFI a commission which is usually based on the amount of the receivables transferred. Additionally, UNIFI will incur costs related to notifying its customers that their receivables have been factored. Apparently, UNIFI believes it will be cheaper to collect the receivables itself rather than incur the costs associated with the factoring arrangement.

Real Report 7-3 Answers

1. The appropriate jounal entries (dollars in millions) would be:

Bad Debt Expense	3	
Allowance for Doubtful Accounts		3
Allowance for Doubtful Accounts	5	
Accounts Receivable		5

2. Assuming that delinquent accounts receivable are written off relatively quickly (e.g., when they are six months overdue), Apple appears to be underestimating bad debt expense since write-offs exceed the expense by approximately $2 million. This underestimate of expense would have the effect of increasing Apple Computer's reported income.

QUESTIONS

Q7-1 What are the components of cash? What items may be confused with cash, but normally are categorized under other balance sheet captions? What are "cash equivalents"?

Q7-2 What is internal control?

Q7-3 What are the two revenue recognition criteria and how do they relate to receivables in some industries?

Q7-4 Briefly discuss the two methods of recording accounts receivable when cash discounts are involved.

Q7-5 What is a sales return? A sales allowance? Conceptually, when should sales returns and allowances be recorded?

Q7-6 Discuss the differences between the estimation (allowance) methods of recording bad debts and the direct write-off method.

Q7-7 Explain how a company estimates bad debts using (a) the sales or income statement approach, and (b) the accounts receivable or balance sheet approach.

Q7-8 Define the *net realizable value* of a company's accounts receivable. How is the net realizable value of accounts receivable reported on the company's balance sheet?

Q7-9 What method of bad debt estimation categorizes individual accounts receivable based on the length of time outstanding? Why is this length of time an important factor?

Q7-10 Why does the write-off of uncollectible accounts have no effect on the net realizable accounts receivable on the balance sheet if bad debts are estimated? What is the effect of this write-off on the income statement?

Q7-11 Define pledging, assigning, and factoring of accounts receivable.

Q7-12 When does a company record the transfer of accounts receivable as a sale? As a liability?

Q7-13 What is a note receivable? How do notes receivable differ from accounts receivable?

Q7-14 What is a non-interest-bearing note? How does accounting for a short-term non-interest-bearing note differ from a short-term interest-bearing note?

Q7-15 What are notes receivable discounted? How are discounted notes disclosed on the financial statements during the period between the discount date and maturity date?

Q7-16 How are the cash proceeds determined when a note receivable is discounted?

Q7-17 (Appendix) What is the purpose of a petty cash system?

Q7-18 (Appendix) Why are actual expenses, rather than the petty cash account, debited when the fund is replenished?

Q7-19 (Appendix) What is a bank reconciliation? List the causes of the difference between the cash balance listed on a company's bank statement and the balance shown in the company's cash account.

Q7-20 (Appendix) Why are adjusting entries made after the bank reconciliation is completed? Give an example of an item on a bank reconciliation which requires an adjusting entry.

MULTIPLE CHOICE (AICPA Adapted)

Select the best answer for each of the following.

M7-1 Which of the following items should be classified under the heading of cash on the balance sheet?

	Postdated checks	Certificates of deposit
a.	Yes	Yes
b.	Yes	No
c.	No	No
d.	No	Yes

M7-2 Greenfield Company had the following cash balances at December 31, 2007:

Cash in banks	$1,500,000
Petty cash funds (all funds were reimbursed on December 31, 2007)	20,000
Cash legally restricted for additions to plant (expected to be disbursed in 2009)	2,000,000

Cash in banks includes $500,000 of compensating balances against short-term borrowing arrangements at December 31, 2007. The compensating balances are not legally restricted as to withdrawal by Greenfield. In the current assets section of Greenfield's December 31, 2007 balance sheet, what total amount should be reported as cash?

a. $1,020,000   c. $3,020,000
b. $1,520,000   d. $3,520,000

M7-3 On January 1, 2007, King Company's Allowance for Doubtful Accounts had a credit balance of $15,000. During 2007 King, (1) charged $32,000 to bad debt expense, (2) wrote off $23,000 of uncollectible accounts receivable, and (3) unexpectedly recovered $6,000 of bad debts written off in the prior year. The Allowance for Doubtful Accounts balance at December 31, 2007 should be:

a. $47,000   c. $30,000
b. $32,000   d. $24,000.

M7-4 A company is in its first year of operations and has never written off any accounts receivable as uncollectible. When the allowance method of recognizing bad debt expense is used, the entry to recognize that expense
a. Increases net income
b. Decreases current assets
c. Has no effect on current assets
d. Has no effect on net income

M7-5 Tallent Company received a $30,000, 6-month, 10% interest-bearing note from a customer. After holding the note for two months, Tallent was in need of cash and discounted the note at the United National Bank at a 12% discount rate. The amount of cash received by Tallent from the bank was

a. $31,260   c. $30,300
b. $30,870   d. $30,240

M7-6 When the accounts receivable of a company are sold outright to a company that normally buys accounts receivable of other companies without recourse, the accounts receivable have been
a. Factored   c. Pledged
b. Assigned   d. Collateralized

M7-7 A method of estimating bad debts that focuses on the income statement rather than the balance sheet is the allowance method based on
a. Direct write-off
b. Aging the trade receivable accounts
c. Credit sales
d. The balance in the trade receivable accounts

M7-8 Prior to adjustments, Barrett Company's account balances at December 31, 2007 for Accounts Receivable and the related Allowance for Doubtful Accounts were $1,200,000 and $60,000, respectively. An aging of accounts receivable indicated that $106,000 of the December 31, 2007 receivables may be uncollectible. The net realizable value of accounts receivable was

a. $1,034,000   c. $1,140,000
b. $1,094,000   d. $1,154,000

M7-9 Marmol Corporation uses the allowance method for bad debts. During 2007 Marmol charged $30,000 to bad debt expense and wrote off $25,200 of uncollectible accounts receivable. These transactions resulted in a decrease in working capital of

a. $0   c. $25,200
b. $4,800   d. $30,000

M7-10 The following bank reconciliation is presented for the Kingston Company for the month of November 2007:

Balance per bank statement, 11/30/07		$18,040
Add: Deposit in transit		4,150
		$22,190
Less: Outstanding checks	$ 6,300	
Bank credit recorded in error	20	(6,320)
Balance per books, 11/30/07		$15,870

Data for the month of December 2007 follow:

Per bank	
December deposits	$26,100
December disbursements	22,420
Balance, 12/31/07	21,720

All items that were outstanding as of November 30 cleared through the bank in December, including the bank credit. In addition, $2,500 in checks were outstanding as of December 31, 2007. What is the balance of cash per books at December 31, 2007?

a. $19,220   c. $21,720
b. $19,240   d. $24,220

EXERCISES

E7-1 *Computing the Cash Balance* Indicate whether or not each of the following ten items should be included in the cash balance presented on the balance sheet. Also indicate the normal balance sheet treatment for those items not included as cash.

Item	Include in Cash Balance	Classification of Items Excluded
1. NSF checks		
2. Savings account		
3. Postage stamps		
4. Postdated checks		
5. IOUs		
6. Cash on hand		
7. Cash in sinking fund		
8. Travel advance		
9. Bank draft		
10. Traveler's checks		

E7-2 *Reporting Cash on the Balance Sheet* Your audit of the Watt Corporation discovers the following information:

1.	Reconciled balance in First National Bank checking account	$ 2,360.75
2.	Reconciled balance in City National Bank checking account	(40.20)
3.	Balance in First Federal savings account	28,750.00
4.	Certificate of deposit	30,000.00
5.	Postage stamps	100.00
6.	Employee's IOU	125.00
7.	Employees' travel advances	1,640.00
8.	Cash on hand (undeposited sales receipts)	3,609.40
9.	Traveler's checks	600.00
10.	Customer's postdated check	290.40

Required
1. What amount should be reported as cash on Watt's balance sheet?
2. Describe the balance sheet treatment of the items not included in the cash balance.

E7-3 *Journal Entry to Separate Receivables* An examination of the accounting records for the Hutton Corporation indicates that all receivables are being recorded in a single account entitled Receivables. An analysis of the account reveals the following:

Accounts receivable (trade)	$15,500
Accounts receivable (officers)	3,600
Common stock subscriptions receivable (current)	12,000
Advances to employees	1,800
Notes receivable (trade), due in 3 years	6,000
Deposit to guarantee contract performance	5,000
Utility deposit	500
Total	$44,400

Required
1. Prepare a journal entry to separate the preceding items into their proper accounts.
2. How would each of the preceding items normally be reflected on Hutton's balance sheet?

E7-4 *Accounting for Sales Discounts* On December 8, 2007, Lynch Incorporated sold $9,000 of merchandise with terms 2/10, n/EOM. On December 18, 2007, collections were made on sales originally billed for $5,000, and on December 31, 2007, additional collections on sales originally billed for $3,000 were received.

Required
Prepare the journal entries to record the sale, collections, and any required year-end adjustments under (1) the gross price method, and (2) the net price method.

E7-5 *Comparison of Discount Methods* The Eastman Corporation sells merchandise with a list price of $13,000 on February 1, 2007, with terms of 1/10, n/30. On February 10, 2007, payment was received on merchandise originally billed for $7,500, and the balance due was received on February 28, 2007.

Required
Prepare journal entries to record the preceding information using (1) the gross price method, and (2) the net price method.

E7-6 *Returns and Allowances* Towbin Products sells merchandise on credit for $7,000 on December 1, 2007. The company estimates that returns and allowances will amount to 4% of sales. On December 22, 2007, a customer returns for credit merchandise originally sold on December 1 for $200.

Required
1. Prepare journal entries to record the preceding sale and the return of merchandise if returns are recorded as they occur.
2. Prepare journal entries to record the preceding sale, the estimation of returns and allowances, and the actual return of goods, if returns and allowances are estimated at the end of the period of sale.
3. How would the preceding information be reflected on Towbin's December 31, 2007 financial statements if (a) returns are recorded as they occur, and (b) returns are estimated in the period of sale?

E7-7 *Estimation vs. Direct Write-Off of Bad Debts* The Blunt Company makes credit sales of $21,000 during the month of February 2007. During 2007 collections are received on February sales of $20,400, accounts representing $600 of these sales are written off as uncollectible, and a $100 account previously written off is collected.

Required
Prepare the journal entries necessary to record the preceding information if (1) bad debts are estimated as 3% of sales at the time of sale, and (2) the bad debts are recorded as they actually occur.

E7-8 *Estimating Bad Debts from Receivables Balances* The following information is extracted from the accounting records of the Shelton Corporation at the beginning of 2007:

Accounts Receivable	$63,000
Allowance for Doubtful Accounts	1,400 (credit)

During 2007, sales on credit amounted to $575,000, $557,400 was collected on outstanding receivables, and $2,600 of receivables were written off as uncollectible. On December 31, 2007, Shelton estimates its bad debts to be 4% of the outstanding gross accounts receivable balance.

Required
1. Prepare the journal entry necessary to record Shelton's estimate of bad debt expense for 2007.
2. Prepare the Accounts Receivable section of Shelton's December 31, 2007 balance sheet.
3. Compute Shelton's receivables turnover.

E7-9 *Aging Analysis of Accounts Receivable* Cowen's, a large department store located in a metropolitan area, has been experiencing difficulty in estimating its bad debts. The company has decided to prepare an aging schedule for its outstanding accounts receivable and estimate bad debts by the due dates of its receivables. This analysis discloses the following information:

Balance	Age of Receivable	Estimated Percentage Uncollectible
$193,000	Under 30 days	0.8%
114,000	30–60 days	2.0%
73,000	61–120 days	5.0%
41,000	121–240 days	20.0%
25,000	241–360 days	35.0%
19,000	Over 360 days	60.0%
$465,000		

Required
1. Use the preceding analysis to compute the estimated amount of uncollectible receivables.
2. Prepare the journal entry to record Cowen's estimated uncollectibles, assuming the balance in the Allowance for Doubtful Accounts prior to adjustment is:
   a. 0
   b. $3,000 (debit)
   c. $2,800 (credit)

E7-10   *Comparison of Bad Debt Estimation Methods*   The following information (prior to adjustment) is available from the accounting records of the Bradford Company on December 31, 2007:

Cash sales	$ 93,100	
Net credit sales	262,900	
Total sales (net)		$356,000
Accounts receivable		126,300
Allowance for doubtful accounts		2,150 (credit)

Required
Prepare journal entries to record the estimate of Bradford's bad debt expense for 2007 assuming:
1. Bad debts are estimated to be 1.5% of total sales (net).
2. Bad debts are estimated to be 2% of net credit sales.
3. Bad debts are estimated to be 5% of gross accounts receivable.

E7-11   `AICPA Adapted`   *Receivables—Bad Debts*   At January 1, 2007 the credit balance in the Allowance for Doubtful Accounts of the Master Company was $400,000. For 2007 the provision for doubtful accounts is based on a percentage of net sales. Net sales for 2007 were $50,000,000. Based on the latest available facts, the 2007 provision for doubtful accounts is estimated to be 0.7% of net sales. During 2007 uncollectible receivables amounting to $410,000 were written off against the allowance for doubtful accounts.

Required
Prepare a schedule computing the balance in Master's Allowance for Doubtful Accounts at December 31, 2007. Show supporting computations in good form.

E7-12   *Assigning Accounts Receivable*   White Corporation has entered into a long-term assignment agreement with a finance company. Under the terms of this agreement, White receives 80% of the value of all accounts assigned and is charged a 1% service charge which is based upon the actual dollar amount of cash received. Additionally, the finance company charges White 12% annual interest on the outstanding loan. The following selected transactions relate to this agreement:

December 1, 2007	Accounts receivable of $160,000 are assigned.
December 11, 2007	A sales return of $1,000 on an assigned account is allowed by White.
December 31, 2007	Collections are made on $86,000 of assigned accounts. This amount and 1 month's interest on the outstanding loan are remitted to the finance company. (For simplicity, compute interest to the nearest month.)
January 29, 2008	$50,000 of assigned accounts are collected and the remainder of the loan is repaid.

Required
1. Prepare journal entries on White's books to record the preceding transactions.
2. How would this assignment agreement be reported on White's December 31, 2007 balance sheet (assume the note payable is short-term)?

E7-13   *Factoring Accounts Receivable*   The Inder Corporation is experiencing a temporary cash shortage and decides to factor a group of its accounts receivable. The factor accepts $80,000 of Inder's accounts receivable, remits 90% of the accounts receivable factored, and charges a 16% commission on the gross amount of the factored receivables. During the period, sales returns and allowances on factored accounts amounted to $1,500.

Required
Prepare all the journal entries necessary by Inder to record the preceding information.

E7-14   `AICPA Adapted`   *Generating Cash from Receivables*   The Guide Company requires additional cash for its business. Guide has decided to use its accounts receivable to raise the additional cash as follows:
1. On June 30, 2007, Guide assigned $200,000 of accounts receivable to the Cell Finance Company. Guide received an advance from Cell of 85% of the assigned accounts receivable, less a commission on the advance of 3%. Prior to December 31, 2007, Guide collected $150,000 on the assigned accounts receivable and remitted $160,000 to Cell, $10,000 of which represented interest on the advance from Cell.
2. On December 1, 2007, Guide sold $300,000 of net accounts receivable to the Factoring Company for $260,000. The receivables were sold outright on a nonrecourse basis.
3. On December 29, 2007, Guide received an advance of $100,000 from the Domestic Bank by pledging $120,000 of Guide's accounts receivable. Guide's first payment to Domestic is due on January 29, 2008.

Required

Prepare a schedule showing the income statement effect for the year ended December 31, 2007, as a result of the preceding facts. Show supporting computations in good form.

E7-15 *Interest-Bearing and Non-Interest-Bearing Notes* On December 11, 2007, the Hooper Bank loans a customer $12,000 on a 60-day, 12% note.

Required

Prepare the journal entries necessary to record the receipt of the note by Hooper, the accrual of interest on December 31, 2007, and the customer's repayment on February 9, 2008, assuming:
1. Interest was assessed in addition to the face value of the note.
2. The note was issued as a $12,000 non-interest-bearing note.

E7-16 *Computing the Proceeds from Discounted Notes* Below are several customer notes.
1. An $8,000, 60-day, non-interest-bearing note discounted after 15 days at 12%.
2. A $9,000, 12%, 60-day note discounted after 30 days at 14%.
3. A $6,000, 10%, 90-day note discounted after 30 days at 12%.
4. A $10,000, 12%, 120-day note discounted after 45 days at 15%.

Required

Determine the proceeds from each of the preceding discounted customer notes.

E7-17 *Recording Notes Receivable Discounted* The following are events of the Singer Corporation for the current year:

June 30	Barney Manufacturing gives Singer a $5,000, 11%, 90-day note for merchandise purchased.
July 15	Dillon Construction Co. gives Singer a $6,000, 10%, 60-day note for merchandise originally purchased on April 20 of the current year.
July 30	The Barney and Dillon notes are discounted with recourse by Singer at its bank at 12%.
Sept. 15	The bank notifies Singer that the Dillon note was paid.
Sept. 30	The bank notifies Singer that Barney defaulted on the note and charges the amount of principal, interest, and a fee of $10 against Singer's bank account.

Required

Prepare journal entries to record the preceding information on Singer's accounting records. (Assume that the company does not normally discount its notes.)

E7-18 *Petty Cash Transactions (Appendix)* The Crown Company established a petty cash fund of $600 for incidental expenditures on January 2, 2007. At the end of the month the count of cash on hand indicated that $57.35 remained in the fund. A sorting of petty cash vouchers disclosed that the following expenses had been incurred during the month, and the fund was replenished.

Postage expense	$250.40
Office supplies expense	165.90
Miscellaneous expense	119.05

Required

Prepare the journal entries necessary to record the Crown Company's petty cash transactions during the month of January 2007.

E7-19 *Adjusting an Unknown Cash Balance (Appendix)* The information that follows is available from the general ledger and the bank statement of the Gentry Corporation for the month of August 2007:

1. Bank statement balance, August 31	$1,342.50
2. Note collected by the bank not previously recorded by Gentry	600.00
3. Interest on the preceding note (not previously recorded)	25.00
4. NSF check returned with the bank statement (not previously recorded)	212.60
5. Outstanding checks at the end of August	684.70
6. Bank service charge for August	12.85
7. Deposit in transit, August 31	329.42

Required

1. Starting with the bank statement balance, prepare a schedule to determine Gentry's cash balance on August 31, 2007, prior to any required adjustments.
2. Prepare a bank reconciliation to determine Gentry's adjusted cash balance on August 31, 2007.
3. Prepare the journal entries necessary to bring Gentry's cash account balance up to date.

E7-20 *Bank Reconciliation (Appendix)* The following information is extracted from the bank statement and the accounting records of the Sun Corporation for the month of July 2007:

1. Cash balance from books, July 31	$1,967.35
2. Cash balance from bank, July 31	1,980.20
3. NSF check returned by bank with bank statement	81.00
4. Note collected by bank on July 31	190.00
5. Interest on preceding note	5.50
6. Bank service charge for July	4.40
7. Outstanding checks at end of July	150.00
8. Deposit in transit at end of July	247.25

Required
1. Prepare a bank reconciliation for the Sun Corporation for July 31, 2007.
2. Prepare the journal entries necessary to adjust Sun's books on July 31, 2007.

E7-21 *Bank Reconciliation and Adjusting Entries (Appendix)* The Odum Corporation's cash account showed a balance of $17,198 on March 31, 2007. The bank statement balance for the same date indicated a balance of $17,924.55. The following additional information is available concerning Odum's cash balance on March 31, 2007.
1. Undeposited cash on hand on March 31 amounted to $724.50.
2. A customer's NSF check for $173.80 was returned with the bank statement.
3. A note for $2,000 plus interest of $25 was collected for Odum by the bank during March. The bank notified Odum of this collection on the bank statement.
4. The bank service charge for March was $15.
5. A deposit of $951.75 mailed to the bank on March 31 did not appear on the bank statement.
6. The following checks mailed to creditors had not been processed by the bank on March 31:

#429	$ 57.40	#433	$214.80
#432	$147.50	#434	$191.90

7. A customer check for $149.50 in payment of his account and listed correctly for that amount on the bank statement had been incorrectly recorded on the accounting records as $194.50.

Required
1. Prepare a bank reconciliation for the Odum Corporation for March 31, 2007.
2. Prepare any adjusting journal entries necessary to record the information from Requirement 1.

E7-22 *Computing the Bank Statement Balance (Appendix)* Your cashier I. Amakrook has notified you that he has misplaced all the bank statements for the past year. You decide to review selected accounting records during the year and discover that the following journal entry was made to reconcile the June 30, 2007 bank statement and the accounting records:

Accounts Receivable	1,520.24	
Miscellaneous Expense	12.50	
Notes Receivable		200.00
Interest Revenue		10.00
Cash		1,322.74

Required
1. What events might have caused each of the preceding reconciling items to occur?
2. Compute the amount that would have appeared as the balance per bank statement on a bank reconciliation if the preadjustment cash balance in the accounting records was $7,683.70, outstanding checks were $207.50, and no other adjustments were required.
3. Assume that you contact the bank and are informed that a balance of $5,542.90 had been reported on the June 30, 2007 bank statement. What does this discrepancy indicate and how would you begin investigating it?

PROBLEMS

P7-1 *Cash and Other Items* The following information has been extracted from the accounting records of the Atwood Corporation:

1. Cash on hand (undeposited sales receipts)	$ 1,020

2. Certificates of deposit	25,000
3. Customer's note receivable	1,000
4. Reconciled balance in University National Bank checking account	(350)
5. Reconciled balance in Second National Bank checking account	9,350
6. Balance in City Federal savings account	8,560
7. Customer's postdated check	1,350
8. Employee travel advances	1,600
9. Cash in bond sinking fund	1,200
10. Bond sinking fund investments	8,090
11. Postage stamps	430

Required

Determine the balance in Atwood's Cash account, and discuss the balance sheet treatment of any items not included as cash.

P7-2 *Analyzing Bad Debt Expense* In 2008, 3 years after it began operations, the Pearce Corporation decided to change from the direct write-off method of recording bad debts to estimating bad debts. The following information is available to you:

	Year			
	2005	**2006**	**2007**	**2008**
Sales	$125,000	$180,000	$250,000	$280,000
Credit sales	90,000	158,000	210,000	235,000
Collections on accounts receivable				
2005 sales	78,000	8,500	200	
2006 sales		137,000	15,000	300
2007 sales			178,800	19,500
2008 sales				200,000
Accounts receivable written off				
2005 accounts	2,500	500	300	0
2006 accounts		4,600	700	400
2007 accounts			6,200	1,000
2008 accounts				6,800

Required

1. Prepare an analysis to determine Pearce's estimated bad debt expense percentage based upon the average relationship of actual bad debts to credit sales.
2. Prepare an analysis to determine Pearce's estimated percentage of allowance for doubtful accounts based on year-end accounts receivable.
3. What amount should Pearce record as bad debts expense for 2008 if:
   a. Bad debts are estimated as a percentage of credit sales?
   b. Allowance for doubtful accounts is estimated as a percentage of outstanding year-end accounts receivable?

P7-3 *Analyzing Accounts Receivable* The June 30, 2006 balance sheet of the Upham Company included the following information:

Accounts receivable	$224,000	
Less: Allowance for doubtful accounts	(14,100)	$209,900
Notes receivable*		21,800
Total receivables		$231,700

*The company is contingently liable for discounted notes receivable of $38,000.

During the company's fiscal year ending June 30, 2007 the following transactions occurred:

1. Sales on credit	$874,600
2. Collections of accounts receivable	841,000
3. Accounts receivable written off as uncollectible	13,800
4. Notes receivable collected	29,000
5. Customer notes received in payment of accounts receivable	72,000
6. Notes receivable discounted that were paid at maturity	36,000
7. Notes receivable discounted that were defaulted, including interest of $20 and a $5 fee. This amount is expected to be collected during the 2008 fiscal year	2,025
8. Proceeds from customer notes discounted with recourse (face value $45,000, accrued interest revenue $200)	45,075
9. Collections on accounts previously written off	500

10. Sales returns and allowances (on credit sales)   2,000
11. Bad debts were estimated to be 1.5% of credit sales

Required
1. Prepare journal entries necessary for Upham to record the preceding transactions.
2. Prepare an analysis and schedule that shows the amounts of the accounts receivable, allowance for doubtful accounts, notes receivable, and notes receivable dishonored accounts that will be disclosed on Upham's June 30, 2007 balance sheet.

P7-4 *Recording Note Transactions* The following information is extracted from the accounting records of the Tara Corporation:

May 1	Received a $6,000, 12%, 90-day note from V. Leigh, a customer.
May 6	Received a $9,000, 10%, 120-day note from C. Gable, a customer.
May 11	Discounted the Leigh and Gable notes with recourse at the bank at 13%. In addition, borrowed $10,000 from the bank for 90 days at 12%. The bank remits the face value less the interest.
July 31	The July bank statement indicated that the Leigh note had been paid.
Sept. 4	Received notice that Gable had defaulted on the May 6 note. The bank charged a fee of $10. Paid the amount due on the Gable note to the bank. Informed Gable to pay Tara the entire amount due plus 11% interest on the total of the face amount of the note, the accrued interest, and the fee from the maturity date until Gable remits the amount owed.
Sept. 23	Received the amount due from Gable.

Required
Prepare journal entries to record the preceding information, assuming that Tara usually does not discount its notes.

P7-5 *Reconstructing Accounts Receivable and Expense Journal Entries* The 2008 audit of the accounting records of the Lane Company discloses the following information:

	2007	2008
Accounts receivable (ending)	$186,000	$187,100
Allowance for doubtful accounts (ending)	7,400	7,000
Allowance for sales returns and allowances (ending)	4,700	3,916
Gross sales returns and allowances (estimated for the year)	4,900	5,200
Accounts receivable written off during the year	6,800	7,900
Estimated bad debts for the year	7,200	7,500
Actual gross sales returns and allowances for the year	4,700	6,000
Sales discounts not taken at end of year	0	400
Credit sales during the year (terms, 2/10, n/60)	375,000	380,000
Cash collected on accounts receivable during the year (net of discounts taken)	352,000	367,500

Required
1. Reconstruct the journal entries that were made by Lane during 2008 to record changes in the following accounts, assuming sales returns and allowances are estimated in the period of sale and the net price method is used to account for sales discounts.
   a. Allowance for doubtful accounts
   b. Allowance for sales returns and allowances
   c. Accounts receivable
2. What is the 2008 ending balance in each of the accounts in Requirement 1 and how will it be reported on Lane's 2008 financial statements?

P7-6 *Cash Discounts* The Lambert Corporation sells merchandise at a list price of $70,000 with accompanying terms of 2/10, n/30 on December 8, 2007. By December 18, 2007, Lambert had collected from customers for merchandise originally billed at $46,000. By December 31, 2007, additional collections had been received on sales originally billed for $18,000, and sales returns and allowances of $1,500 had been granted by Lambert. By January 15, 2008, all the remaining balances due had been collected.

Required
1. Prepare the journal entries using (a) the gross price method and (b) the net price method to record each of the following items:
   a. The sale of the merchandise
   b. Collections received by December 18, 2007
   c. Collections received by December 31, 2007
   d. Sales returns and allowances (*not* estimated in the period of sale)
   e. Any required year-end adjustments

f. Any January 1, 2008 reversing entries

g. The collections received by January 15, 2008

2. Calculate the accounts receivable balance that would be reported under (a) the gross price method and (b) the net price method on the Lambert Corporation's December 31, 2007, balance sheet.

P7-7   *Aging Accounts Receivable* On September 30, 2007 (the end of its fiscal year), the Lufkin Corporation reported accounts receivable of $331,750 and an allowance for doubtful accounts of $16,700. During fiscal 2008 the following transactions occurred:

Credit sales (terms, n/EOM)	$2,017,800
Collections on accounts receivable	1,956,000
Accounts receivable written off	16,200

On September 30, 2008 an aging of the accounts receivable balance indicated the following:

Age	Amount	Estimated Percentage Uncollectible
Under 30 days	$169,250	0.8%
30–90 days	100,000	1.6
91–180 days	55,900	5.0
181–360 days	38,200	15.0
Over 360 days	14,000	40.0
	$377,350	

Required

1. Prepare the journal entries necessary to record the credit sales, collections on account, write-off of accounts receivable, and the bad debts expense for Lufkin for fiscal 2008.

2. What are Lufkin's September 30, 2008 balances in Accounts Receivable and in its Allowance for Doubtful Accounts and how will they be disclosed on the September 30, 2008 balance sheet?

3. Compute Lufkin's receivables turnover in days, assuming a 360-day business year (as discussed earlier in the chapter and in the Appendix to Chapter 6). What is your evaluation of its collection policies?

P7-8   *Estimating Bad Debts* An examination of the accounting records of the Keegan Corporation disclosed the following information for 2007:

Cash sales	$680,000
Net credit sales	527,000
Accounts receivable (12/31/07)	190,000
Allowance for doubtful accounts (12/31/07, prior to adjustment)	1,500 (debit)

Keegan wishes to examine the effect of various alternative bad debt estimation policies.

Required

1. Prepare the adjusting entry that would be required under each of the following methods:
   a. Bad debts are estimated at 1.4% of total sales (net).
   b. Bad debts are estimated at 3% of net credit sales.
   c. Bad debts are estimated at 7.5% of gross accounts receivable.
   d. An aging of accounts receivable indicates that half of the outstanding accounts will incur a 3% loss, a quarter will incur a 6% loss, the remaining quarter will incur a 20% loss.

2. Discuss the difference between the income statement and balance sheet approaches to estimating bad debts.

P7-9   *Notes Receivable and Notes Receivable Discounted* The following notes receivable transactions occurred for the Harris Company during the last three months of the current year. (Assume all notes are dated the day the transaction occurred.)

Oct.	9	Received a $5,000, 12%, 60-day note from K. Weedon, a customer.
Oct.	12	Received a $6,000, 10%, 90-day note from M. Black, a customer.
Oct.	15	Discounted the Weedon note with recourse at the bank at 14%.
Nov.	11	Discounted the Black note with recourse at the bank at 15%.
Nov.	16	Received an $8,000, 12%, 60-day note from B. Butcher, a customer.
Nov.	20	Received a $6,000, 11%, 120-day note from D. Goldman, a customer.
Dec.	1	Received a $9,000, 13%, 60-day note from S. Lambert, a customer.
Dec.	8	Received notice that the Weedon note was paid at maturity.
Dec.	10	Discounted the Goldman note with recourse at the bank at 13%.

Required

1. Prepare journal entries to record the preceding note transactions and the necessary adjusting entries on December 31. (Assume that Harris does not normally discount its notes.)
2. Show how Harris Company's notes receivable would be disclosed on the December 31 balance sheet. (Assume these are the only note transactions encountered by Harris during the year.)

P7-10 *Assigning Accounts Receivable* The Furman Corporation entered into an assignment agreement with a finance company whereby Furman would be advanced 80% of all accounts assigned, less a $2,000 service charge. During the year, $300,000 of accounts receivable were assigned, $220,000 collections were made on outstanding assigned accounts, and $210,000 was remitted to the finance company. This remittance included interest charges of $2,100. Sales returns and allowances on assigned accounts amounted to $5,000.

Required

1. Prepare the journal entries necessary to record the preceding information.
2. Show how the preceding information would be reported on Furman's year-end balance sheet (assume the note payable is short-term).

P7-11 *Factoring Accounts Receivable* Faeber Textile Company frequently factors its accounts receivable. During 2007, Faeber made credit sales of $100,000 to customers, under terms of 2/10, n/30. Faeber records its credit sales using the gross price method. From past experience, sales returns and allowances are expected to be minimal. In 2007, Faeber sold $70,000 of these receivables to a factor. The factor remitted 90% of the accounts receivable factored and charged a 12% commission on the gross amount of the factored receivables. The factoring agreement also requires Faeber to be responsible for any cash discounts taken by customers upon payment of the factored receivables. Faeber is charged for these cash discounts upon reimbursement by the factor. During 2007, sales returns and allowances were $3,000 on the factored accounts receivable and $1,300 on the unfactored accounts receivable. The factor collected the remaining amount of the factored receivables, less the 2% discount on 94% of the collected receivables, and returned the balance owed to Faeber. Faeber collected the remaining amount of the unfactored accounts receivable, less the 2% discount on 96% of the collected receivables.

Required

Prepare all the journal entries necessary for Faeber to record the preceding information.

P7-12 *Factoring and Assignment of Accounts Receivable* The Lazard Corporation has experienced cash flow problems and decides to improve its current cash position by factoring 30% of its receivables and assigning the remainder with the same finance company. The agreement with the finance company stipulates that a 10% commission will be assessed on factored accounts and 15% annual interest will be charged on the outstanding note payable balance related to the assigned accounts. Additionally, the finance company will advance only 80% of the factored and assigned accounts, and Lazard must continue the collection responsibilities on the assigned accounts. At the beginning of the last month of the company's fiscal year, the accounts receivable transferred to the finance company amounted to $187,000. During the month, collections on factored accounts were $46,000, and collections on assigned accounts amounted to $84,000. All collections on assigned accounts plus accrued interest were remitted to the finance company at the end of the month. The remaining amounts owed will be remitted within these months.

Required

1. Prepare all journal entries to record the preceding information on Lazard's books.
2. How would the accounts related to Lazard's factoring and assignment agreements be reported on Lazard's year-end financial statements?

P7-13 **AICPA Adapted** *Examination of Accounts Receivable* You are engaged in the annual examination of Faulane Company, a wholesale office supply business, for the year ended June 30, 2007. You have been assigned to examine the accounts receivable. The following information is available at June 30, 2007.

1. Your review of accounts receivable and discussions with the client disclose that the following items are included in the accounts receivable (of both the control and the subsidiary ledgers):
   a. Accounts with credit balances total $1,746
   b. Receivables from officers total $8,500
   c. Advances to employees total $1,411
   d. Accounts that are definitely uncollectible total $1,187
2. Uncollectible accounts are estimated to be 0.50% of the year's net credit sales of $16,750,000.

Required

Prepare any journal entry (entries) required:

1. to reclassify items that are not trade accounts receivable,
2. to write off uncollectible accounts, and
3. to adjust the allowance for doubtful accounts.

P7-14 `AICPA Adapted` *Allowance for Bad Accounts* The Installment Jewelry Company has been in business for 5 years but has never had an audit made of its financial statements. Engaged to make an audit for 2007, you find that the company's balance sheet carries no allowance for bad accounts, bad accounts having been expensed as written off and recoveries credited to income as collected. The company's policy is to write off at December 31 of each year those accounts on which no collections have been received for 3 months. The installment contracts generally are for 2 years.

On your recommendation the company agrees to revise its accounts for 2007 to give effect to bad account treatment on the allowance basis. The allowance is to be based on a percentage of sales that is derived from the experience of prior years. Statistics for the past 5 years are shown in the following table:

	Charge Sales	Accounts Written Off and Year of Sale			Recoveries and Year of Sale
2003	$100,000	(2003) $ 550			
2004	250,000	(2003) 1,500	(2004) $1,000		(2003) $100
2005	300,000	(2003) 500	(2004) 4,000	(2005) $1,300	(2004) 400
2006	325,000	(2004) 1,200	(2005) 4,500	(2006) 1,500	(2005) 500
2007	275,000	(2005) 2,700	(2006) 5,000	(2007) 1,400	(2006) 600

Accounts receivable at December 31, 2007 were as follows:

2006 Sales	$ 15,000
2007 Sales	135,000
	$150,000

Required

Prepare the adjusting journal entry or entries with appropriate explanations to set up the Allowance for Bad Accounts. (Support each item with organized computations; income tax implications should be ignored.)

P7-15 `AICPA Adapted` *Allowance for Doubtful Accounts* From inception of operations to December 31, 2006, Harris Corporation provided for uncollectible accounts receivable under the allowance method: Provisions were made monthly at 2% of credit sales; bad debts written off were charged to the allowance account; recoveries of bad debts previously written off were credited to the allowance account; and no year-end adjustments to the allowance account were made. Harris's usual credit terms are net 30 days.

The balance in the Allowance for Doubtful Accounts was $130,000 at January 1, 2007. During 2007, credit sales totaled $9,000,000, interim provisions for doubtful accounts were made at 2% of credit sales, $90,000 of bad debts were written off, and recoveries of accounts previously written off amounted to $15,000. Harris upgraded its computer facility in November 2007 and an aging of accounts receivable was prepared for the first time as of December 31, 2007. A summary of the aging is as follows:

Classification by Month of Sale	Balance in Each Category	Estimated % Uncollectible
Nov.–Dec. 2007	$1,140,000	2%
July–Oct.	600,000	10
Jan.–June	400,000	25
Prior to 1/1/07	130,000	75
	$2,270,000	

Based on the review of collectibility of the account balances in the "prior to 1/1/07" aging category, additional receivables totaling $60,000 were written off as of December 31, 2007. Effective with the year ended December 31, 2007, Harris adopted a new accounting method for estimating the allowance for doubtful accounts at the amount indicated by the year-end aging analysis of accounts receivable.

Required

1. Prepare a schedule analyzing the changes in the allowance for doubtful accounts for the year ended December 31, 2007. Show supporting computations in good form.
2. Prepare the journal entry for the year-end adjustment to the Allowance for Doubtful Accounts balance as of December 31, 2007.

P7-16 **AICPA Adapted** *Correction of Allowance Account* From inception of operations in 2004 Summit carried no allowance for doubtful accounts. Uncollectible receivables were expensed as written off, and recoveries were credited to income as collected. On March 1, 2008 (after the 2007 financial statements were issued), management recognized that Summit's accounting policy with respect to doubtful accounts was not correct, and determined that an allowance for doubtful accounts was necessary. A policy was established to maintain an allowance for doubtful accounts based on Summit's historical bad debt loss percentage applied to year-end accounts receivable. The historical bad debt loss percentage is to be recomputed each year based on the relationship of net write-offs to credit sales for all available past years up to a maximum of five years.

Information from Summit's records for five years is as follows:

Year	Credit Sales	Accounts Written Off	Recoveries
2004	$1,500,000	$15,000	$ 0
2005	2,250,000	38,000	2,700
2006	2,950,000	52,000	2,500
2007	3,300,000	65,000	4,800
2008	4,000,000	83,000	5,000

Accounts receivable balances were $1,250,000 and $1,460,000 at December 31, 2007 and December 31, 2008 respectively.

Required

1. Prepare the journal entry, with appropriate explanation, to set up the Allowance for Doubtful Accounts as of January 1, 2008. Disregard income taxes. Show supporting computations in good form.
2. Prepare a schedule analyzing the changes in the Allowance for Doubtful Accounts account for the year ended December 31, 2008. Show supporting computations in good form.

P7-17 *Comprehensive Receivables Problem* The December 31, 2006 balance sheet of the Blackmon Corporation disclosed the following information relating to its receivables:

Accounts receivable	$245,000	
Less: Allowance for doubtful accounts	(15,000)	
		$230,000
Notes receivable*		50,000
Total receivables		$280,000

*The company is contingently liable for a discounted note receivable of $10,000.

During 2007, credit sales (terms, n/EOM) totaled $2,200,000 and collections on accounts receivable (unassigned) amounted to $1,900,000. Uncollectible accounts totaling $18,000 from several customers were written off, and a $1,350 accounts receivable previously written off was collected. Additionally, the following transactions relating to Blackmon's receivables occurred during the year:

Mar. 6   Received payment of $12,460 on a note from the Renko Company. The payment included interest revenue of $460.

Mar. 31   The March bank statement indicated that the discounted note had been paid at maturity.

May 1   Accepted a 120-day, 13% note from the Licata Company in exchange for its account receivable of $4,800.

May 18   Received a $6,900, 90-day, 12% note from the Eagle Manufacturing Corporation for a credit sale.

June 2   Discounted both the Licata and Eagle notes with recourse at the bank at 14% (assume that Blackmon normally does not discount its notes).

July 1   Assigned $140,000 of accounts receivable to a finance company. Under the terms of the agreement, Blackmon receives 85% of the value of the accounts assigned, less a service charge of $5,000, and is charged 1.5% per month on the outstanding loan balance.

July 6   A sales allowance of $2,500 on an assigned account is allowed by Blackmon.

July 13   A sales return of $800 on an assigned account is granted by Blackmon.

July 31   Collections of $50,000 are made on assigned accounts. This amount and 1 month's interest are remitted to the finance company.

Aug. 31   Assigned accounts of $60,000 are collected, and the remainder of the loan is repaid, including interest.

Aug. 31   The August bank statement indicated the Eagle note had been paid.

Sept. 1   The bank notifies Blackmon that Licata defaulted on its note and charges a fee of $25.

Sept. 4   Collected the amount due from the Licata Company.

Dec. 31   Collected interest of $5,000 on the outstanding notes receivable.

On December 31, 2007 an aging of the accounts receivable balance indicated the following:

Age	Amount	Estimated Percentage Uncollectible
Under 30 days	$240,487	0.5%
31–60 days	113,421	1.5
61–90 days	30,933	8.0
91–240 days	17,185	35.0
Over 240 days	6,874	70.0
	$408,900	

Required

1. Prepare the journal entries to record the preceding receivable transactions during 2007 and the necessary adjusting entry on December 31, 2007.
2. Prepare the receivables portion of Blackmon's December 31, 2007 balance sheet.
3. Compute Blackmon's accounts receivable turnover in days, assuming a 365-day business year (as discussed earlier in the chapter and in the Appendix to Chapter 6). What is your evaluation of its collection policies?

P7-18 *Reconciliation of Bank and Company Cash Amounts (Appendix)* The December 31, 2007 bank statement for Miller Corporation showed a $2,049.25 balance. On this date the company's Cash account reflected a $325.60 overdraft. In reconciling these amounts, the following information is discovered:

1. Cash on hand for undeposited sales receipts, December 31, 2007, $130.25.
2. Customer NSF check returned with bank statement, $420.40.
3. Cash sales of $640.25 for the week ended December 18, 2007 were recorded on the books. The cashier reports this amount missing, and it was not deposited in the bank.
4. Note receivable of $2,500 and interest of $25 collected by the bank and not recorded on the books.
5. Deposit in transit December 31, 2007, $350.00.
6. A customer check for $290.40 in payment of its account was recorded on the books at $940.20.
7. Outstanding checks, $2,040.55. Includes a duplicate check of $70.85 to C. Brown, who notified Miller that the original was lost. Miller stopped payment on the original check and has already adjusted the cash account in the accounting records for this amount.

Required

1. Prepare a December 31, 2007 bank reconciliation for Miller.
2. Prepare any journal entries necessary by Miller to record the information from Requirement 1.

P7-19 *Unknown Book Balance (Appendix)* The following information pertains to the Cash account of the Nakamoto Corporation for the month of July 2007:

Bank statement

Balance July 31	$22,639.54
Service charge for July	15.00
NSF check returned with July bank statement	184.50
Note receivable collected by bank (not previously recorded on the books)	2,000.00
Interest on note collected by bank (not previously recorded on the books)	60.00

Books

Balance July 31	?
Cash on hand awaiting deposit	1,824.42
Outstanding checks:	
#257 $42.17	
#271 $120.19	
#272 $80.82	
Deposit in transit	2,420.98

Required 🖎
1. Prepare a bank reconciliation to determine Nakamoto's adjusted cash balance on July 31, 2007.
2. Determine Nakamoto's unadjusted cash balance (per books) on July 31, 2007.
3. Prepare the adjusting entries necessary to bring Nakamoto's cash account balance up to date on July 31, 2007.

P7-20 *Bank Reconciliation (Appendix)* The Daisy Company received a bank statement for February 2007, as follows:

From: Central Bank, Denver, Co. 80222
To: Daisy Company, 1313 Williams St., Denver, Co. 80218

Date		Checks	Deposits	Balance
Feb.	1			$4,524.80
	7	$2,700.33	$8,642.61	
	9	3,484.81		
	14	6.00 SC	460.00 CM	
	16	274.09		
	21	4,133.60	3,385.49	
	23	69.69 NSF		
	28			$6,344.38

SC 5 Service Charge   NSF 5 Check Returned
CM 5 Credit Memo   DM 5 Debit Memo

The receipt of $460 on February 14 was for a $445 note collected by the bank, plus $20 current interest, less a $5 service charge. The company's accounting records contained the following information:

Cash balance on February 28 from the books: $2,610.42

Cash Disbursements			Cash Receipts		
Check No.	155	$2,700.33	Feb.	7	$8,624.61
	156	3,484.81		21	3,385.49
	157	274.09	All receipts are verified and correct		
	158	589.02			
	159	4,133.60			
	160	2,742.63			

Required
1. Prepare a bank reconciliation on February 28, 2007 for the Daisy Company.
2. Prepare the journal entries that the Daisy Company should record as a result of the reconciliation.

P7-21 **AICPA Adapted** *Comprehensive Reconciliation (Appendix)* In auditing the Train Company, you obtain directly from the bank Train's bank statement, canceled checks, and other memoranda which relate to the company's bank account for December 2007. In reconciling the bank balance on December 31, 2007 with that shown on the company's books, you observe the following facts:

1. Balance per bank statement	$91,174.63
2. Balance per books	59,088.46
3. Outstanding checks, 12/31/07	33,378.82
4. Receipts of 12/31/07 deposited on 1/1/08	5,317.20
5. Service charge for December	22.50
6. Proceeds of bank loan, 12/15/07 omitted from company records (discounted for 3 months at 12% per year)	11,640.00
7. Deposit of 12/20/07 omitted from the bank statement	2,892.41
8. Check of Rome Products Co. charged back on 12/22/07 for lack of countersignature. Redeposited 1/5/08. No entry was made for the chargeback or the redeposit.	873.74
9. Error on bank statement in entering deposit of 12/18/07:	
Correct amount	$3,182.40
Entered in statement	3,181.40 1.00
10. Check No. 3917 of Trait Manufacturing Co. charged in error to company's account	2,690.00

11. Proceeds of note of J. Somers & Co. collected by bank 12/11/07 not entered on books:

Principal	$2,000.00	
Interest	40.00	
	$2,040.00	
Less: collection charge	5.00	2,035.00

12. Erroneous debit memo of 12/22/07 to charge company's account with settlement of bank loan, which was paid by check No. 8714 on same date 5,000.00

13. Error on bank statement in entering deposit of 12/4/07

Entered as	$4,817.10	
Correct amount	4,807.10	10.00

14. Deposit of Trait Manufacturing Co. of 12/8/07 credited in error to the company 1,819.20

Required

1. Prepare a reconciliation of the Train Company's bank account.
2. Prepare journal entries to adjust the Train Company's books to reflect the correct bank balance on December 31, 2007.

CASES

COMMUNICATION

C7-1   Cash Management

The president of Poor Corporation, who likes to have large balances of cash on hand, has recently been reading articles in highly respected financial magazines about very successful businesses. The president noticed that each company stressed the importance of cash management and internal control in making it a success. The president of Poor Corporation comes to you, the accountant, and asks you to explain the concept of cash management.

Required

Explain the concept of cash management, including the two major subdivisions and their components.

C7-2   Bad Debt Expense

AICPA Adapted   When a company has a policy of making sales for which credit is extended, it is reasonable to expect a portion of those sales to be uncollectible. As a result of this, a company must recognize bad debt expense. There are basically two methods of recognizing bad debt expense: (1) direct write-off method, and (2) allowance method.

Required

1. Describe fully both the direct write-off method and the allowance method of recognizing bad debt expense.
2. Explain the reasons why one of these methods is preferable to the other and the reasons why the other method is not usually in accordance with generally accepted accounting principles.

C7-3   Accounts Receivable

The Moore Company is undergoing a period of financial stress due to the depressed economy. The company is in desperate need of cash. The only liquid asset that the company holds is $500,000 of accounts receivable.

Required

1. Explain the various types of arrangements that may be used to obtain cash from outstanding accounts receivable.
2. Indicate how each method should be disclosed in the financial statements.
3. If Moore Company decides to sell its accounts receivable, should it account for the transfer as a pledge or a factoring agreement? Why?

C7-4   Receivables Issues

AICPA Adapted   Magrath Company has an operating cycle of less than one year and provides credit terms for all of its customers. On April 3, 2007, the company factored, without recourse, some of its accounts receivable.

On August 1, 2007, Magrath sold special order merchandise and received an interest-bearing note due April 30, 2008.

Magrath uses the allowance method to account for uncollectible accounts. During 2007, some accounts were written off as uncollectible, and other accounts previously written off as uncollectible were collected.

Required

1. Explain how Magrath should account for and report the accounts receivable factored on April 3, 2007. Why is this accounting treatment appropriate?
2. Explain how Magrath should report the effects of the interest-bearing note on its income statement for the year ended December 31, 2007 and its December 31, 2007 balance sheet.

3. Explain how Magrath should account for the collection of the accounts previously written off as uncollectible.
4. What are the two basic approaches to estimating uncollectible accounts under the allowance method? What is the rationale for each approach?

C7-5   Bank Reconciliations (Appendix)

A discrepancy usually will exist between a company's bank statement balance and its cash records due to the time lag associated with the use of a checking account. The time lag results in many transactions being recorded on the company's records prior to their appearance on the bank statement. The bank statement balance and the cash records must be brought into agreement to determine their accuracy. This result can be achieved by using a bank reconciliation.

Required
Prepare a written report that explains a bank reconciliation.

C7-6   Lockbox Account Bank Reconciliation (Appendix)

DGK Company maintains a lockbox account to facilitate the collection of its accounts receivable. All of the company's cash receipts from credit sales are sent directly to a post office box held in the company's name, which is accessed directly by bank personnel. Each day the bank processes the receipts, credits DGK's account, and provides the company with a hard copy package, which includes a detail and summary listing of all checks deposited, copies of actual checks, invoices, enclosures, and envelopes. The company usually receives its hard copy packages a day after the bank has processed the receipts.

In addition, DGK Company has authorized the bank to apply "collected balances" (balances for which the holding period allowed for collection and return of deposited items has elapsed) directly against the company's outstanding line of credit with the bank, unless instructed otherwise by the company. The company receives hard copy notices of amounts applied, generally within two business days.

The accounting records for DGK Company contain the following details for December 2007:

1. Balance per bank for the lockbox account, 12/31/07	$55,000
2. Balance per books, 12/31/07	50,050
3. Deposit in transit from cash sales	5,000
4. Lockbox receipts, 12/31/07	30,000
5. Collected balances applied to line of credit on 12/31/07	20,000
6. Bank service charge for December	50
7. No checks are drawn on the lockbox account	

Required
1. Explain how a lockbox account might benefit a company.
2. Prepare a December 31, 2007 bank reconciliation of DGK Company's lockbox bank account.
3. Prepare any journal entries necessary to adjust DGK Company's books to reflect the results of the reconciliation performed in Requirement 2. (*Contributed by Daryl G. Krause.*)

CREATIVE AND CRITICAL THINKING

C7-7   Components of Cash

AICPA Adapted   Cash is an important asset of a company.
1. What are the normal components of cash?
2. Under what circumstances, if any, do valuation problems arise in connection with cash?

C7-8   Estimated Bad Debts

AICPA Adapted   On December 31, 2007, Carme Company had significant amounts of accounts receivable as a result of credit sales to its customers. Carme Company uses the allowance method based on credit sales to estimate bad debts. Based on past experience, 1% of credit sales normally will not be collected. This pattern is expected to continue.

Required
1. Explain the rationale of using the allowance method based on credit sales to estimate bad debts. Contrast this method with the allowance method based on the balance in the trade receivables accounts.
2. Explain how Carme Company should report the allowance for bad debts account on its balance sheet at December 31, 2007. Also, describe the alternatives, if any, for presentation of bad debt expense in Carme Company's 2007 income statement.

C7-9   Cash Discounts

In order to induce prompt payment, the Swope Company offers a cash discount of 2% to customers who make payment on their account within 10 days of the invoice date. The company's bookkeeper is not sure how these discounts should be recorded.

Required
1. Explain the methods of recording accounts receivable with cash discounts.
2. Discuss the theoretical soundness of each method.

C7-10   Assignment and Factoring

AICPA Adapted   Marie Company has significant amounts of trade accounts receivable as a result of credit sales to its customers. On October 2, 2007, some trade accounts receivable were assigned to Daniel Finance Company on a with-recourse, nonnotification basis for an advance of 75% of their amount at an interest charge of 20% on the balance outstanding.

On November 3, 2007, other trade accounts receivable were factored on a without-recourse basis. The factor withheld 5% of the trade accounts receivable factored as protection against sales returns and allowances and charged a finance charge of 3%.

Required

1. How should Marie account for subsequent collections on the trade accounts receivable assigned on October 2, 2007, and the payments to Daniel Finance? Why?

2. How should Marie account for the trade accounts receivable factored on November 3, 2007? Why?

C7-11 Receivables Issues

AICPA Adapted Hogan Company uses the net method of accounting for sales discounts. Hogan also offers trade discounts to various groups of buyers. On August 1, 2007, Hogan factored some accounts receivable on a without-recourse basis. Hogan incurred a finance charge.

Hogan also has some notes receivable bearing an appropriate rate of interest. The principal and total interest are due at maturity. The notes were received on October 2, 2007, and mature on October 1, 2008. Hogan's operating cycle is less than one year.

Required

1. Using the net method, how should Hogan account for the sales discounts at the date of sale? What is the rationale for the amount recorded as sales under the net method?

2. a. Using the net method, what is the effect on Hogan's sales revenues and net income when customers do not take the sales discounts?

   b. What is the effect of trade discounts on sales revenues and accounts receivable? Why?

   c. How should Hogan account for the accounts receivable factored on August 1, 2007? Why?

   d. How should Hogan report the effects of the interest-bearing notes receivable on its December 31, 2007 balance sheet and on its income statement for the year ended December 31, 2007? Why?

C7-12 Assignment and Discounting

AICPA Adapted Tidal Company has significant amounts of trade accounts receivable. In March of this year, Tidal assigned specific trade accounts receivable to Herb Finance Company on a with-recourse, nonnotification basis as collateral for a loan. Tidal signed a note and received 70% of the amount assigned. Tidal was charged a 5% finance fee and agreed to pay interest at 12% on the unpaid balance. Some specific accounts of the assigned receivables were written off as uncollectible. The remainder of the trade accounts receivable assigned were collected by Tidal in March and April of this year. Tidal paid Herb Finance in full at the end of April of this year.

Tidal also sold some special order merchandise and received a 90-day, 10%, interest-bearing note receivable on July 1 of this year. After 30 days, the note receivable was discounted with recourse at 14% at a bank.

Required

1. Explain how Tidal should account for the transactions described here for the assignment of trade accounts receivable.

2. a. Explain how Tidal should determine the amount of the discount for the note receivable.

   b. Explain how the discounting transaction should be accounted for.

C7-13 Analyzing Coca-Cola's Cash and Receivables Disclosures

Refer to the financial statements and related notes of the Coca-Cola Company in Appendix A of this book.

Required

1. What were the cash and cash equivalents at the end of 2004? What does the company classify as cash equivalents?

2. What were the trade accounts receivable (net) at the end of 2004? At the end of 2003?

3. Assuming that all net operating revenues were net credit sales and that the trade accounts receivable (net) at the end of 2002 were $2,097 million, compute the receivables turnover for 2004 and 2003. What is your evaluation of the difference?

 C7-14 Ethics and Sales Returns

At the end of 2007, the accounting firm for which you work is auditing the books of Debitus Publishing Inc. for the first time. Debitus, a calendar year company, publishes textbooks that are used in colleges and universities across the country. These textbooks are purchased by students through their campus bookstores. Debitus normally makes its biggest sales at the beginning of the fall semester. In the past, Debitus has always recorded sales returns in the spring semester when the campus bookstores return any unsold textbooks. This has been satisfactory because the returns have been immaterial in amount.

In 2006, as a promotional strategy to stimulate sales, Debitus began offering bookstores a reduced price if they ordered more textbooks. There is no penalty for returns of these textbooks if the bookstores cannot sell them to customers. This strategy worked; sales increased by 10% during 2006. In early 2007, however, a substantial amount of unsold textbooks were returned by bookstores to Debitus. Continuing the promotional strategy, sales increased by 15% during 2007.

While reviewing the sales returns account for 2007, you notice that the only entry was for the textbooks returned earlier in the year. You note that these returns amounted to about 5% of the sales for the fall semester of 2006. Since this pattern of returns seems to you to be a trend that will continue, you raise the issue with the company controller as to whether all of the "sales" for the fall semester of 2007 are actually revenue. The controller responds, "Of course they are revenue; we sold the textbooks. Just because there will be some returns doesn't mean we haven't made sales. Besides, we don't know what percentage the returns will be; they might be as much as 5 percent, but definitely not more. Furthermore, we have already recorded all those returns at the beginning of 2007 that really applied to 2006. So we already have recorded our fair share of returns for 2007. As long as we record returns consistently, it will all work out. We don't want a drop in earnings for 2007 because of a change in customer returns; our shareholders wouldn't like that. Let's just leave this issue alone."

Required

From financial reporting and ethical perspectives, what do you think about Debitus Publishing Inc.'s policy in regard to sales returns?

RESEARCH SIMULATION

R7-1   Researching GAAP

Situation

Hamilton Company operates in an industry with numerous competitors. It is experiencing a shortage of cash and decides to obtain money from a large bank by using some of its receivables as collateral. Hamilton pledges $100,000 of its receivables, is charged a 12% fee on this amount, and notifies these credit customers to make their payments directly to the bank. Hamilton transfers the receivables to the bank and the bank assumes the servicing activities, but Hamilton is responsible for all bad debts, which it reasonably estimates to be 2% of the receivables amount. When the balance of the receivables pledged is reduced to $3,000, Hamilton is required to "repurchase" the receivables, notify the remaining credit customers to make payments to it, and reassume the servicing activities. The bank has the right to sell the receivables, except to Hamilton's major competitor. Hamilton's president has asked you how to account for (and record) this transaction.

Directions

Research the related generally accepted accounting principles and prepare a short memo to the president that answers his question. Cite your reference and applicable paragraph numbers.

Inventories: Cost Measurement and Flow Assumptions

Objectives

After reading this chapter, you will be able to:

1 Describe how inventory accounts are classified.

2 Explain the uses of the perpetual and periodic inventory systems.

3 Identify how inventory quantities are determined.

4 Determine the cost of inventory.

5 Compute ending inventory and cost of goods sold under specific identification, FIFO, average cost, and LIFO.

6 Explain the conceptual issues regarding alternative inventory cost flow assumptions.

7 Understand dollar-value LIFO.

8 Explain additional LIFO issues.

9 Understand inventory disclosures.

10 Record foreign currency transactions involving inventory (Appendix).

Keep Your Eye on the Ball

Effective management and control of inventory is critical to the profitability and overall performance of many companies. For example, **Wal-Mart** executives closely monitor the $26.612 billion of inventory reported in its 2004 annual report. With approximately 25% of its total assets represented by inventory, the level of inventory has widespread effects on its financial performance. Management of inventory involves widespread tasks such as making sure that a company has sufficient quantities of the right items, controlling shrinkage (the reduction of inventory because of theft or loss), and evaluating the impact of interest costs related to the debt financing of inventory. Company executives realize that effective inventory management may be the difference between operating success and failure. To enhance inventory management, Wal-Mart has begun implementing radio frequency identification (RFID), a scanning technology similar to bar codes that allows inventory to be tracked from the supplier to the final customer, and promises dramatic reductions in inventory losses.

In addition to merchandising companies such as Wal-Mart, manufacturing companies, such as **General Mills**, also face special challenges in management of its inventory. Proper inventory management can allow managers to achieve significant operational efficiencies and economies of scale. A well-functioning inventory system allows managers to take advantage of quantity

Credit: RICHARD SHEINWALD/Bloomberg News/Landov

discounts in the purchase of inventory, increase productivity, and lower manufacturing costs through the scheduling of longer production runs. However, given the demand and supply uncertainties that exist in business, inventory also serves as a buffer to ensure that adequate goods exist that allow management to maintain desired service levels. Inventory decisions are not made in isolation. Because General Mills sells large amounts of inventory to Wal-Mart, the two companies are "partners" that have inevitable conflicts. For example, General Mills would like to deliver its products as soon as they are manufactured; however, Wal-Mart would prefer to receive the items when they are ready to put them on store shelves. The resolution of these intercompany conflicts is also a consideration in effective inventory management. Whether your company is a manufacturer or a merchandiser, inventory is something that will be watched closely.

FOR FURTHER INVESTIGATION

For a discussion of recent innovations in inventory management, consult the Business & Company Resource Center (BCRC):

- "Radio Frequency Identification: The Wave of the Future," Harold E. Davis and Michael S. Luehlfing, *Journal of Accountancy*, 0021-8448, November 2004, v198, i5, p43–49.
- "NCR Corp.'s Retail-Checkout Technology Likely to Shape Future of Shopping," *Knight Ridder/Tribune Business News*, September 20, 2004.

Inventories are assets of a company that are (1) held for sale in the ordinary course of business, (2) in the process of production for sale, or (3) held for use in the production of goods or services to be made available for sale. Inventory specifically *excludes* any assets that a company does not sell in the normal course of business, such as marketable securities, or property, plant, and equipment that the company intends to sell.

Accounting for inventories is important because the purchase, manufacture, and sale of products are critical to the profitability of many companies. The cost (carrying value) of the inventory usually has a material effect on a company's balance sheet. Since the ending inventory of one period is the beginning inventory of the next period, the cost of the inventory on a company's balance sheet will have an effect on its cost of goods sold and net income of the next period. In addition, various accounting practices, such as alternative cost flow assumptions and valuation principles, are widely used and may have a significant effect on asset valuation and income determination. In this chapter we discuss the classifications of inventory, the perpetual and periodic inventory systems, the determination of inventory quantities and costs, and alternative inventory cost flow assumptions.

CLASSIFICATIONS OF INVENTORY

1 Describe how inventory accounts are classified.

A company may use several different accounts to classify inventory, depending on its business. A merchandising company, whether wholesale or retail, purchases goods for resale and *does not* alter their physical form. Consequently, it needs only one type of inventory account, usually called **(merchandise) inventory.** A manufacturing company *does* change the physical form of the goods and typically uses three inventory accounts, usually called **raw materials inventory, work in process inventory,** and **finished goods inventory.** We show the flow of inventory costs for these two types of companies in Exhibit 8-1. We discuss the three categories of inventory accounts used by a manufacturing company in the following sections. Both types of companies may use more accounts internally, and may combine account balances in their financial statements.

Raw Materials Inventory

Raw materials inventory includes the tangible goods acquired for direct use in the production process. This inventory includes materials that a company acquired from natural sources, such as the iron ore used by a steel mill. Raw materials also may include products purchased from other companies, such as the steel or subassemblies used in the manufacture of appliances. Raw materials are different from **parts inventory,** which is the term often used for the inventory of replacement parts.

Sometimes, a company includes in raw materials inventory those materials that are not directly a part of its manufacturing process but are needed for its successful operation. However, the company often includes them in an account called **factory supplies, manufacturing supplies,** or **indirect materials.** Examples of materials in this category include lubricating oil and cleaning supplies.

Work in Process Inventory

Work (or goods) in process inventory includes the products that are started in the manufacturing process but are not yet complete. This partially completed inventory includes three cost components: (1) raw materials, (2) direct labor, which is the cost of the labor used directly in the manufacture of the product, and (3) manufacturing (or factory) overhead, which includes the costs other than raw materials and direct labor that are part of the manufacturing process. These latter costs include **variable manufacturing overhead,** such as supplies and some indirect labor, and **fixed manufacturing overhead,** such as insurance, utilities, and depreciation on the assets used in the production activities.

EXHIBIT 8-1   Flow of Inventory Costs

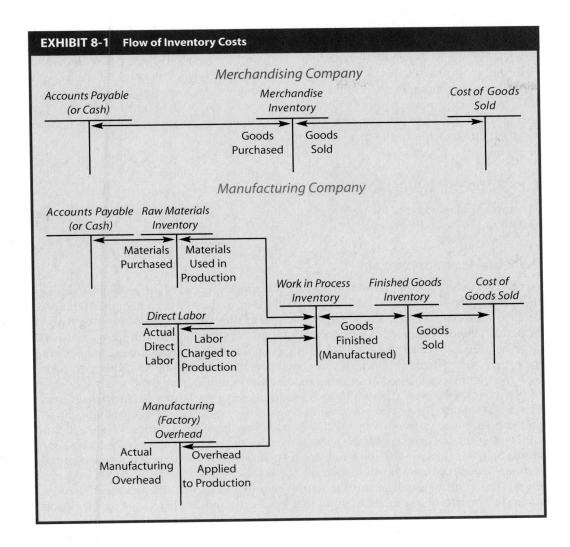

Finished Goods Inventory

Finished goods inventory includes the completed manufactured products awaiting sale. The inventory includes the same three cost components as the work in process inventory, but all the costs are combined into a single cost per unit for all the completed units.

Reporting Inventory in a Company's Financial Statements

A company reports the cost of the inventory that it sold as cost of goods sold on its income statement, and deducts the amount from net sales to determine its gross profit. A company reports the cash it paid to purchase or produce its inventory in the operating activities section of its statement of cash flows. The inventory cost that a company reports on its balance sheet is the final amount that results from a series of steps. First the company must decide what items to include in the inventory and count the physical inventory quantities. Then it must determine the costs of the units it purchased or produced during the accounting period, taking into consideration the costs for freight-in and the reductions for purchases discounts, returns, and allowances. The company uses a cost flow assumption to allocate the costs of the beginning inventory plus the units purchased or produced during the year between the ending inventory and the cost of goods sold. We discuss each of these steps in the following sections.

Inventories of Service Companies

A service company generally doesn't have a physical inventory. However, it often has an "inventory" of services that it has provided but not yet billed. For example, a company that provides computer consulting services will pay its employees each period but may only bill its services when certain "contract milestones" are reached. The company has an inventory of "unbilled services provided" that it reports as an asset, and then recognizes as an expense when it recognizes the revenue.

ALTERNATIVE INVENTORY SYSTEMS

2 Explain the uses of the perpetual and periodic inventory systems.

A company may account for inventory quantities and costs using either the **perpetual system** or the **periodic system**.

Perpetual Inventory System

A company using a perpetual system keeps a continuous record of the physical quantities in its inventory. It records the purchase, or production, and use of each item of inventory in detailed subsidiary records, although it often only records units without including costs. A perpetual physical system allows management to plan and control the inventory and avoid stock-outs. To help inventory control and the preparation of periodic financial statements, many perpetual systems also include costs. Such systems are becoming much more common with today's computer-based accounting systems. For example, most retail stores use "point of sale" cash register systems in which each product has a unique code, such as the UPC code, that is entered into the system as each unit is sold. Some companies are adopting radio frequency identification technology (RFID) to track inventory by attaching RFID tags. Both UPC codes and RFID tags enable the retailer to immediately update its Inventory and Cost of Goods Sold accounts as each sale is made. A company maintains these accounts as summary accounts, which makes it possible to know the inventory and the cost of goods sold at all times. The company usually records purchases returns and allowances, purchases discounts taken, and freight-in in separate accounts that it uses to compute the income for the period.

When a company uses a perpetual system, it should take a physical count at least once a year to confirm the balance in the inventory account. Any difference between the physical count and the inventory account balance results from errors in recording, shrinkage, waste, breakage, theft, and other causes. The company adjusts its inventory account and also increases cost of goods sold (or recognizes a loss) for the cost of the difference in the two quantities so that the perpetual records are in agreement with the physical count. The size of the difference provides useful information for inventory control purposes and is another advantage of the perpetual system.

Periodic Inventory System

A company using a periodic system does *not* maintain a continuous record of the physical quantities (or costs) of inventory on hand. It takes physical counts periodically, which should be at least once a year and generally at the end of the year. This is the only time(s) when it knows the physical quantities on hand, and therefore the quantities used or sold during the period. The company determines the cost of the ending inventory by assigning costs to the physical quantities on hand based on the cost flow assumption it is using. Then it calculates the cost of goods sold by subtracting the ending inventory from the cost of goods available for sale. The cost of goods available for sale is the sum of the beginning inventory and either the net purchases for a merchandising company or the costs of the units produced for the period for a manufacturing company. This system is adequate for relatively low cost inventory items, particularly when the costs of a perpetual inventory system are likely to be greater than its benefits.

In the periodic system, a company typically does not record (debit) the costs of the purchases of inventory in an inventory account. This would lead to an overstatement of the permanent Inventory account, because the company does not reduce (credit) the account during the period for the cost of the inventory sold. Therefore, in a periodic system the company usually records (debits) costs of purchases of inventory in a temporary account, Purchases, while the beginning inventory cost remains in the Inventory account.

In both the perpetual and periodic systems, the company usually records purchases returns and allowances, purchases discounts taken, and freight-in in separate accounts. It uses each of these amounts in the computation of net purchases as follows:

$$\text{Net Purchases} = \text{Purchases} + \text{Freight-in} - \begin{array}{c}\text{Purchases Returns} \\ \text{and Allowances}\end{array} - \begin{array}{c}\text{Purchases} \\ \text{Discounts} \\ \text{Taken}\end{array}$$

In summary, the difference between a perpetual and a periodic inventory system may be illustrated by the following equations:

Perpetual Inventory System

Beginning Inventory + Purchases (net) − Goods Sold = Ending Inventory

Periodic Inventory System

Beginning Inventory + Purchases (net) − Ending Inventory = Goods Sold

Note that you can think of each equation in terms of *units* or *costs*.

ITEMS TO BE INCLUDED IN INVENTORY QUANTITIES

The basic criterion for including items in inventory is *economic control* rather than physical possession or legal ownership. In simple situations, all three occur at the same time. However, because there may be differences in more complex situations, the *economic substance* of the transaction should always take precedence over its *legal form* to determine whether the buyer or the seller has economic control. While control is often easy to determine, it may be affected by the following issues.

3 Identify how inventory quantities are determined.

Goods are often shipped under one of two alternatives: **FOB** (free-on-board) **shipping point** or **FOB destination**. When goods are in transit at the end of the accounting period, the terms of shipment determine whether the seller or the buyer includes them in its inventory. **If the goods are shipped FOB shipping point, control of (and legal title to) the goods is transferred at the shipping point when the seller delivers them to the buyer,** or to a transportation company that is acting as an agent for the buyer. The buyer has economic control and includes those goods in its inventory, and the seller excludes them. **If goods are shipped FOB destination, control of (and legal title to) the goods is not transferred until the goods are delivered to the buyer's destination.** The seller has economic control and includes those goods in its inventory, and the buyer excludes them. We show these situations in Exhibit 8-2.

Conceptual

Economic control may also transfer before or after physical possession (and legal ownership) transfer. For example, suppose the buyer requests that the seller holds the goods to be delivered later, and the goods are segregated from the seller's other inventory so that the risk of ownership has passed to the buyer. In this case, control has passed and the seller should exclude the goods from inventory and the buyer should include them. This is known as a "bill and hold" sale. Also, goods may be transferred on **consignment.** As we discuss in Chapter 18, the company delivering the goods, the **consignor,** retains economic control (and ownership), while the company receiving the goods, the **consignee,** attempts to sell them. The consignor includes the goods in its inventory until they are sold by the consignee. Transfer of control may also be affected by product financing arrangements (discussed in Chapter 9), and by sales made when there is a right of return (discussed in Chapter 6).

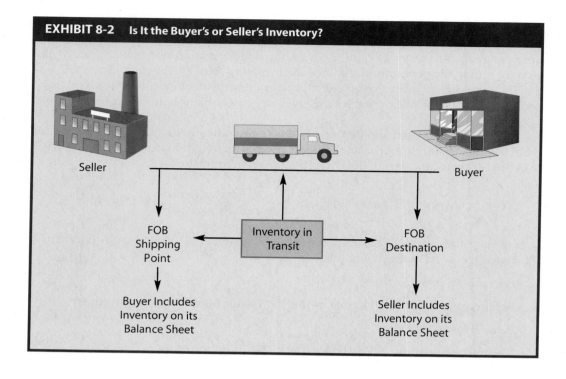

EXHIBIT 8-2   Is It the Buyer's or Seller's Inventory?

Physical transfer of goods usually determines when the seller records the sale and the buyer records the inventory, respectively, in their accounting systems. However, both companies should adjust the recorded amounts in situations where physical possession is not consistent with economic control on the balance sheet date. However, companies may ignore these adjustments if the effects are not material.

As we discuss in Chapter 18, what a company includes in inventory depends on its revenue recognition decisions. A company first decides when it is appropriate to recognize revenue and then matches the cost of goods sold against that revenue. As it recognizes the cost of goods sold, it reduces its inventory.

DETERMINATION OF INVENTORY COSTS

4 Determine the cost of inventory.

There are two issues in determining inventory costs. We discuss the costs attached to each unit *available for sale* in this section. We discuss the costs attached to the *ending inventory* and *cost of goods sold* (the inventory cost flow assumption) later in this chapter.

The cost of inventory is the price paid or consideration given to acquire it.[1] Thus, **inventory cost includes costs directly or indirectly incurred in bringing an item to its existing condition and location.** For each item of inventory, purchased or manufactured, a company must make a decision as to whether or not each cost meets this definition. If it does, the company includes it in the cost of the inventory. If it does not, the company immediately recognizes it as an expense. The cost of purchased inventory should include the purchase price (net of purchases discounts, as we discuss later) plus payments directly related to the inventory, such as freight-in, receiving, unpacking, inspecting, storage, insurance, personal property taxes, sales and other applicable taxes, and similar costs. When a company purchases more than one type of inventory for a

---

1.   "Restatement and Revision of Accounting Research Bulletins," *Accounting Research and Terminology Bulletins, Final Edition, No. 43* (New York: AICPA, 1961), ch. 4, par. 4; and "Inventory Costs—An Amendment of ARB No. 43, Chapter 4," *FASB Statement of Financial Accounting Standards No. 151* (Norwalk, Conn.: FASB, 2004).

single sum and it cannot identify the costs of each type, it should use the relative fair value method to apportion the cost, as we discuss in Chapter 10.

Some costs that should be attached to inventor normally are excluded because of the cost/benefit relationship. For example, the costs of operating a purchasing department are necessary to bring the item to its existing condition and location, but the practical difficulties involved in allocating these costs to the separate inventories often exceed the benefits that result from not

Credit: JASON M. CARRIER/Bloomberg News/Landov

making an allocation. Also, **FASB Statement No. 151** requires that abnormal amounts of idle facility costs, freight and handling costs, and spoilage are expensed in the period and are *not* included in the cost of inventory.

Another cost that *may* be included in the cost of inventory is the interest cost for amounts a company borrowed to finance the purchase of the inventory. It can be argued that this interest cost is incurred indirectly in order to bring an item to its existing condition and location and, therefore, should be added to the inventory cost. Alternatively, it can be argued that borrowing costs are period costs associated with the general activities of the company, and none is related specifically to the acquisition of a particular inventory item. According to *FASB Statement No. 34*, interest costs are *not* included in the cost of inventory that is *routinely manufactured* (discussed in Chapter 10). However, interest cost is included in the cost of inventory that is manufactured over an extended period of time (as we discuss in Chapter 18).

When a company manufactures inventory, it adds the **product costs** that are directly and indirectly incurred in the production activity to the cost of inventory. The costs that it includes are acquisition and production costs (including manufacturing overhead). The company expenses **period costs**, such as general and administrative costs, except for the portion of such costs that are clearly related to production and thus are included in inventory costs. Selling costs are not associated with bringing the item to its existing condition and location. Instead, they are an expense of the period and not an inventory cost because they apply to the units sold during the period and not to the units held in inventory.

Purchases Discounts

Many sellers offer discounts to buyers to encourage prompt payment. These discounts, called purchases discounts, may be accounted for by the gross price method or the net price method. These methods raise questions about whether purchases discounts should directly affect a company's income or its inventory cost. They also can be used to show how efficient managment is.

Under the gross price method, a company records the purchase at the gross price and records the amount of the discount in the accounting system only if the discount is *taken*. This discount should be deducted from the purchase price of the inventory. **Under the net price method, a company records the purchase at its net price and records the amount of the discount in the accounting system only if the discount is**

not taken. This discount lost should be treated as a period expense.[2] We illustrate these two alternatives in Example 8-1 for a company that purchases $1,000 of goods under terms of 1/10, n/30 (a 1% discount is allowed if payment is made within 10 days; otherwise, full payment is due within 30 days).

EXAMPLE 8-1	Alternative Methods of Accounting for Purchases Discounts					
	Gross Price Method			**Net Price Method**		
To record the purchase	Inventory (or Purchases)	1,000		Inventory (or Purchases)	990	
	Accounts Payable		1,000	Accounts Payable		990
To record payment within the discount period	Accounts Payable	1,000		Accounts Payable	990	
	Purchases Discounts Taken		10	Cash		990
	Cash		990			
To record payment outside the discount period	Accounts Payable	1,000		Accounts Payable	990	
	Cash		1,000	Purchases Discounts Lost	10	
				Cash		1,000
Adjusting entry at end of period if discount has expired and invoice is unpaid	No entry required			Purchases Discounts Lost	10	
				Accounts Payable		10

Conceptual Evaluation of the Two Methods

The correct inventory cost is the invoice price less all available discounts. Therefore, a company should treat the purchases discounts lost under the net price method as a financing expense for the period and should not include it in inventory cost, because **losing the discount does not increase the economic benefit to be derived from the inventory.** To be consistent, a company should treat the purchases discounts taken under the gross price method as a reduction in inventory cost. However, if some discounts were not taken, the inventory cost would include those discounts lost, even though they do not increase the economic benefits of the inventory. **Therefore, the correct inventory cost is always recorded under the net price method, but under the gross price method only if all discounts are taken** (or if the company makes an adjustment to remove the discounts lost from the cost of the inventory and records the cost as a financing expense).

Sometimes it is argued that the discounts taken under the gross method should be treated as an increase in income. This is not correct because the matching principle would be violated, since the discounts may relate to goods that have not yet been sold. Furthermore, a company does not earn income by buying goods and paying bills. **The revenue recognition principle requires that a sale of goods (or services) occur before a company recognizes income.** However, for practical reasons, a company may include purchases discounts in income; this is acceptable provided that the amount is not material. Retailing companies often follow this procedure.

Another advantage of the net price method is that it isolates the purchases discounts lost, thereby highlighting inefficiencies, which assists the management control process. For example, if a company purchases goods on terms of 2/10, n/30 and does not take the discount, it is paying 2% to delay payment by 20 days (the 30-day maximum less the 10 days allowed to take the discount), which is an approximate annual rate of 36% (2% × 360/20).

---

2. In a third method, the allowance method, the purchase is recorded at the net price, the accounts payable at the gross price, and the difference is debited to an allowance account. The allowance account is reduced by the difference between the cash paid to the supplier and the accounts payable balance. It is also adjusted for purchases discounts not taken.

The net price method can be criticized, though, because Accounts Payable does not represent the maximum amount of the liability that the company may be required to pay, although it does reflect the most likely amount if the company generally takes the discounts. However, the adjusting entry illustrated in Example 8-1 for expired discounts will ensure that the correct liability (the gross price) appears on the company's balance sheet. Despite the advantages of the net price method, the gross price method is more common because it is simpler to use and the results produced usually are not materially different from the net price method.

Purchases discounts are different from trade discounts. As we discussed in Chapter 7, **trade discounts are discounts deducted prior to arriving at the invoice price** and do not enter into the accounting system.

SECURE YOUR KNOWLEDGE 8-1

- Common inventory classifications used by companies range from a single (merchandise) inventory account for merchandisers to raw materials inventory, work in process inventory, and finished goods inventory for manufacturers.
- Two alternative inventory systems may be used to account for inventory:
  - A perpetual inventory system, which makes inventory management and control easier, and keeps a continuous record of inventory quantities and cost of goods sold.
  - A periodic inventory system relies on physical counts of inventory to determine inventory quantities and cost of goods sold.
- Economic control is the key factor that a company should consider in determining whether an item is a part of inventory (substance over form).
- Inventory costs should include all costs (e.g., purchase price, freight-in, insurance, taxes) that are directly or indirectly incurred to obtain the inventory.

COST FLOW ASSUMPTIONS

A company typically starts an accounting period with some units in the beginning inventory and then purchases or produces additional units during the period. Together these are the *goods available for sale*, which the company then either sells or retains in its ending inventory.

For financial statement purposes, a company must attach *costs* to these units. The cost of the beginning inventory (the cost of the ending inventory of the preceding period) is the beginning balance in the Inventory account. The beginning balance in Inventory plus the cost of purchases or production (discussed earlier) is the *cost of the goods available for sale*. This total cost is allocated between the cost of goods sold and ending inventory using a *cost flow assumption*. The major cost flow assumptions are specific identification; first-in, first-out (FIFO); average cost; and last-in, first-out (LIFO). We show both the unit relationship and the cost flow relationship in Exhibit 8-3.

Cost flow assumptions are important for two reasons. First, a company has inventories at each year-end. If there were none, all the cost of goods available for sale would be transferred to cost of goods sold. Second, the costs of purchases and production change during the year. If these costs did not change, all units would have the same cost. Therefore, alternative cost flow assumptions would not affect the cost of goods sold or the ending inventory. Note that we are discussing *cost* flow assumptions here. There is no requirement that they be related to the *physical* flow (except for the specific identification method).

We discuss each cost flow assumption in the following sections and apply it to both the perpetual and the periodic inventory systems using the information for the Dalton

5 Compute ending inventory and cost of goods sold under specific identification, FIFO, average cost, and LIFO.

Reporting

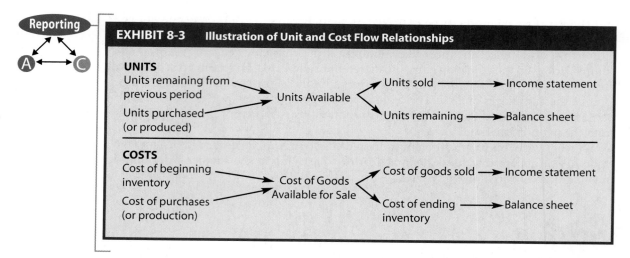

EXHIBIT 8-3 Illustration of Unit and Cost Flow Relationships

UNITS

Units remaining from previous period → Units Available → Units sold → Income statement

Units purchased (or produced) → Units Available → Units remaining → Balance sheet

COSTS

Cost of beginning inventory → Cost of Goods Available for Sale → Cost of goods sold → Income statement

Cost of purchases (or production) → Cost of Goods Available for Sale → Cost of ending inventory → Balance sheet

Company shown in Example 8-2. Recall that under the periodic system, the ending inventory is computed before the cost of goods sold, whereas under the perpetual system, the cost of goods sold is calculated first. To make the example less complicated, we use a merchandising company, although a manufacturing company uses the same principles.

EXAMPLE 8-2 Inventory Inflows and Outflows for Dalton Company

Inventory, April 1	100	units @ $10 per unit	$1,000
Purchases, April 10	80	units @ $11 per unit	880
Purchases, April 20	70	units @ $12 per unit	840
Goods Available for Sale	250	units	$2,720
Sales, April 18	(90)	units ⎫ 140 units	
Sales, April 27	(50)	units ⎭	
Inventory, April 30	110	units	

Notes: (1) The beginning inventory is valued at $10 per unit for all the flow assumptions. However, if costs are changing, this value would be different for different flow assumptionsbecause the beginning inventory for the current period is the ending inventory of the preceding period.
(2) The company uses a monthly accounting period.

Specific Identification

Under the specific identification inventory cost flow assumption, a company identifies each unit sold and each unit remaining in the ending inventory and includes the actual costs of those units in cost of goods sold and ending inventory, respectively. For example, the company must specifically identify each unit sold on April 27. If all the units are from beginning inventory, the company's cost of goods sold is $10 for each unit. However, if they are from the units purchased on April 10 or April 20, its cost of goods sold would be either $11 or $12 for each unit, respectively. Similarly, the company must identify each unit in the ending inventory and attach the appropriate cost of $10, $11, or $12 to it.

The specific identification method can be applied in either a perpetual or a periodic inventory system. However, it is more reasonable to use it with a perpetual system in which each unit is identified as it is sold and the appropriate cost attached. While the specific identification method seems simple and matches costs as expenses against revenues, there are significant objections to its use. It may be practical in a few situations in which units are costly and can be easily distinguished (for example, a car dealership). But, in many complex manufacturing and retailing situations it is not practical to apply the specific identification method because the cost of each individual unit is not identifiable (e.g., a single can of soup), and it is not known which specific units are sold. In addition, as volume increases, so does the cost of record keeping, and the method may become too expensive to use.

Another argument against the method is that the amount of profit varies even though the units of inventory are identical. Continuing the preceding example, if the units were sold on April 27 for $30, then using a $10 unit or a $12 unit for sale would make the gross profit either $20 per unit or $18 per unit, respectively. In summary, the specific identification method can produce ending inventory and cost of goods sold amounts at the two extremes of FIFO and LIFO, or at values in between. This ability of a company's management to select, or "manipulate," its profits is not desirable. However, the method is appropriate if each item is unique. We do not show any summary amounts in this section because they are so dependent on the assumptions regarding the particular units selected for sale.

First-In, First-Out (FIFO)

Under the FIFO cost flow assumption, a company includes the earliest costs incurred in the cost of goods sold, and includes the most recent costs in the ending inventory. We show these relationships as follows:

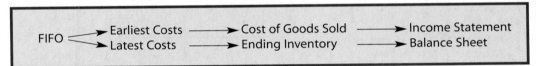

In other words, the first costs incurred are the first transferred to cost of goods sold. Consequently, the ending inventory consists of the most recent costs incurred. Therefore, in periods of rising costs, FIFO produces a lower cost of goods sold amount based on older and lower costs. However, the ending inventory is based on the most recent and higher costs, as we discuss in the evaluation section later in this chapter.

If the Dalton Company uses the periodic method, it computes the ending inventory of $1,280 first, as we show in Example 8-3. The ending inventory of 110 units is based on the most recent costs incurred. It includes 40 units purchased on April 10 for $11 each and 70 units purchased on April 20 for $12 each. The company calculates the cost of goods sold of $1,440 by subtracting the ending inventory from the cost of goods available for sale as we show in Example 8-3. Therefore, it is based on the earliest costs incurred and includes the beginning inventory of 100 units at $10 each and 40 units from the April 10 purchase at $11 each.

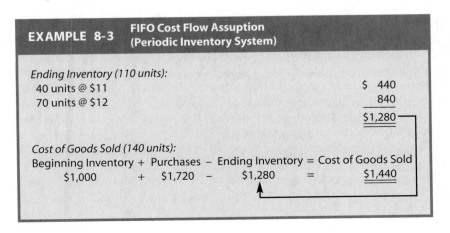

EXAMPLE 8-3   **FIFO Cost Flow Assuption (Periodic Inventory System)**

Ending Inventory (110 units):

40 units @ $11	$ 440
70 units @ $12	840
	$1,280

Cost of Goods Sold (140 units):

Beginning Inventory	+	Purchases	–	Ending Inventory	=	Cost of Goods Sold
$1,000	+	$1,720	–	$1,280	=	$1,440

If the Dalton Company uses the perpetual inventory system (for costs as well as physical quantities), it calculates the cost of goods sold of $1,440 and the ending inventory of $1,280 as we show in Example 8-4. The $1,440 cost of goods sold for 140 units is based on the earliest costs incurred. For the April 18 sale, the 90 units have a cost of $10 per unit (from the beginning inventory). For the April 27 sale of 50 units, 10 units have a cost of $10 per unit from the beginning inventory and 40 units have a cost of $11 per unit (from the April 10 purchase). The company determines the $1,280 ending inventory by deducting the $1,440 cost of goods sold from the $2,720 cost of goods available for sale. The ending inventory is 110 units and includes the most recent costs: the cost of the remaining 40 units from the first purchase on April 10 and the 70 units purchased on April 20.

EXAMPLE 8-4   **FIFO Cost Flow Assuption (Perpetual Inventory System)**

Cost of Goods Sold (140 units):

April 18	90 units @ $10	$ 900
April 27	50 units: 10 units @ $10	100
	40 units @ $11	440
Total		$1,440

Ending Inventory (110 units):

Beginning Inventory + Purchases − Cost of Goods Sold = Ending Inventory
$1,000   + $1,720   − $1,440   = $1,280*

*40 units @ $11 = $ 440
70 units @ $12 =   840
                   $1,280

Note that the ending inventory and the cost of goods sold under both the perpetual and the periodic systems are identical; this always is true for the FIFO cost flow assumption because the most recent costs incurred always are included in the ending inventory.

Average Cost

Under the average cost flow assumption, a company considers all the costs and units to be combined so that no individual units or costs are identified. When a company uses the periodic inventory system, the average cost method is known as the **weighted average** method. The company calculates the cost of the units for the period based on the cost of the beginning inventory and the average cost of the units purchased or manufactured, weighted according to the number of units at each cost. In other words, **under the weighted average method, the average cost per unit for the period is the cost of goods available for sale divided by the number of units available for sale.** The company uses this average cost for both its ending inventory and the cost of goods sold.

The weighted average unit cost for the Dalton Company in April is $10.88 (the cost of goods available for sale of $2,720 ÷ the number of units available for sale of 250), as we show in Example 8-5. It records the ending inventory at this $10.88 cost per unit, resulting in a total cost of $1,197. The company computes the $1,523 cost of goods sold by deducting the ending inventory from the cost of goods available for sale of $2,720. It is also equal to the 140 units sold multiplied by the $10.88 weighted average cost.

When a company uses the average cost method under a perpetual inventory system (for costs as well as physical quantities), the same principles are applied. But it is known as

EXAMPLE 8-5	Weighted Average Cost Flow Assumption (Periodic Inventory System)	
Cost of goods available for sale ($1,000 + $1,720)		$2,720
Units available for sale		250
Average cost (Cost ÷ Number of units)		$10.88
Ending inventory (110 units @ $10.88)		$1,197

Beginning Inventory + Purchases − Ending Inventory = Cost of Goods Sold
    $1,000   + $1,720   − $1,197   = $1,523

a **moving average** method because a new weighted average cost must be calculated after *each* purchase, as we show in Example 8-6. The new weighted average is computed in the same way as in the weighted average method. That is, **under the moving average method, the average cost per unit is the cost of the units available for sale after the purchase divided by the number of units available for sale at that time.** This average cost is used to determine the cost of each sale made until the next purchase, when a new average cost is calculated. The average cost after the April 10 purchase is $10.44 (cost of goods available for sale of $1,880 ÷ the number of units available for sale of 180). Therefore, the sales on April 18 have a cost of $10.44 per unit for a total cost of goods sold of $940. The purchase on April 20 increases the average cost to $11.125 per unit, and therefore the 50 units sold on April 27 have a total cost of $556. The total cost of goods sold for April is $1,496 ($940 + $556). The company records the ending inventory at the final average cost for the period, which it calculates after the last purchase. The cost of $11.125 per unit for the 110 units results in a total ending inventory of $1,224 (see Example 8-6).

EXAMPLE 8-6	Moving Average Cost Flow Assumption (Perpetual Inventory System)		
April 1, Beginning Inventory	100	units @ $10	$ 1,000
April 10, Purchases	80	units @ $11	880
April 10, Balance	180	units @ $10.44	$ 1,880
April 18, Sales	(90)	units @ $10.44	(940)
April 18, Balance	90	units @ $10.44	$ 940
April 20, Purchases	70	units @ $12	840
April 20, Balance	160	units @ $11.125	$ 1,780
April 27, Sales	(50)	units @ $11.125	(556)
April 30, Balance	110	units @ $11.125	$ 1,224
Cost of Goods Sold (140 units)	$940 + $556		$ 1,496
Ending Inventory (110 units @ $11.125)			$ 1,224

Last-In, First-Out (LIFO)

Under the LIFO cost flow assumption, a company includes the most recent costs incurred in the cost of goods sold, and includes the earliest costs (part or all of which

are costs incurred in previous periods) in the ending inventory. We show these relationships as follows:

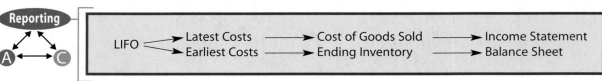

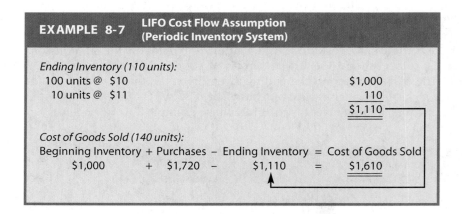

Therefore, in periods of rising costs, LIFO produces a higher cost of goods sold figure based on the most recent costs. However, the ending inventory is based on the oldest and lowest costs. We discuss the logic behind this procedure later in this chapter.

If the Dalton Company uses the periodic inventory system, it gives no consideration to the timing of the individual sales. It calculates the ending inventory of $1,110 and the cost of goods sold of $1,610 as we show in Example 8-7. The ending inventory includes the earliest costs, which are the cost of the beginning inventory and the cost of the 10 units from the first purchase on April 10. The company computes the cost of goods sold by subtracting the ending inventory from the cost of goods available for sale. This implicitly includes the cost of the 70 units purchased on April 20 ($840) and the cost of 70 units purchased on April 10 ($770).

EXAMPLE 8-7   **LIFO Cost Flow Assumption (Periodic Inventory System)**

Ending Inventory (110 units):

100 units @ $10	$1,000
10 units @ $11	110
	$1,110

Cost of Goods Sold (140 units):

Beginning Inventory	+	Purchases	−	Ending Inventory	=	Cost of Goods Sold
$1,000	+	$1,720	−	$1,110	=	$1,610

If the Dalton Company uses the perpetual inventory system (for costs as well as physical quantities), it calculates the cost of goods sold for each sale at the cost(s) of the most recent purchase(s). The $1,580 cost of goods sold for 140 units includes the sale of 90 units on April 18, and 50 units on April 27, as we show in Example 8-8. For the April 18 sale, 80 of the 90 units have a cost of $11 each from the April 10 purchase and 10 units have a cost of $10 each from the beginning inventory. The 50 units on April 27 have a cost of $12 from the April 20 purchase. The company computes the $1,140 ending inventory by deducting the $1,580 cost of goods sold from the $2,720 cost of goods available for sale. It consists of 110 units and includes the earliest costs: the cost of the 90 units left from the beginning inventory and the remaining 20 units from the April 20 purchase.

Note that the cost of goods sold and the ending inventory are *not* the same for the LIFO perpetual method and the LIFO periodic method because of different assumptions about the timing of the sales. Under the periodic method, the whole accounting period (a month in this example) is treated as a single time period, and all the sales are assumed to take place after all the units have been purchased during the period. Therefore, the cost of goods sold includes the costs of the *most recent purchases of the period*. Under the perpetual method, each event is recorded as it occurs. Therefore, the cost of goods sold is calculated when each sale is made and includes the costs of the *most recent purchase(s) at that time*.

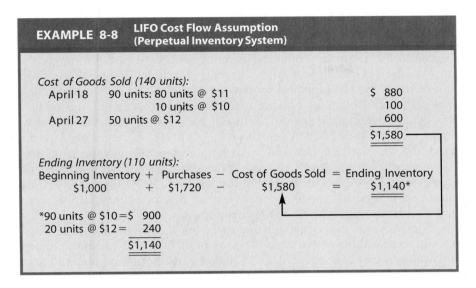

EXAMPLE 8-8   **LIFO Cost Flow Assumption (Perpetual Inventory System)**

Cost of Goods Sold (140 units):

April 18	90 units: 80 units @ $11	$ 880
	10 units @ $10	100
April 27	50 units @ $12	600
		$1,580

Ending Inventory (110 units):

Beginning Inventory + Purchases − Cost of Goods Sold = Ending Inventory

$1,000   + $1,720   − $1,580   = $1,140*

*90 units @ $10 = $ 900
20 units @ $12 =   240
                $1,140

In the Dalton Company example, unit sales are less than unit purchases for the period. Therefore, under the *periodic* inventory system, the company does *not* include costs from the beginning inventory in cost of goods sold. However, the first sale in the month is larger than the first purchase. Therefore, under the *perpetual* inventory system, the company includes the costs of 10 units of its beginning inventory in cost of goods sold. Furthermore, under the perpetual system, the second sale of 50 units has a cost of $12 per unit from the second purchase, leaving 20 units of that purchase in inventory. However, under the periodic system, the company includes the entire purchase of units at $12 each in its cost of goods sold, leaving none in inventory. These factors explain the difference of $30 in the cost of goods sold and the ending inventory between the two methods.

In each case the LIFO ending inventory of the Dalton Company consists of two layers. Each period in which the number of units in inventory *increases*, the company adds a layer of costs to its LIFO inventory. When the number of units in inventory *decreases*, the company removes costs from its beginning inventory of the period in the reverse order in which it added them—that is, it removes the most recent layers first and includes them in cost of goods sold.

Comparison of Inventory Cost Flow Assumptions

We summarize the cost of goods sold and the inventory amounts for the Dalton Company calculated in the preceding examples in Example 8-9. However, we exclude the specific identification method because, as we discussed previously, the results are dependent on the assumptions regarding the particular units selected for sale.

EXAMPLE 8-9   **Effects of Inventory Cost Flow Assumptions**

Cost Flow Assumption and Method	Cost of Goods Available for Sale	Cost of Goods Sold	Ending Inventory
FIFO, periodic	$2,720	$1,440	$1,280
FIFO, perpetual	2,720	1,440	1,280
Weighted average, periodic	2,720	1,523	1,197
Moving average, perpetual	2,720	1,496	1,224
LIFO, periodic	2,720	1,610	1,110
LIFO, perpetual	2,720	1,580	1,140

Analysis

In this example, costs rose throughout the period. As a result, the FIFO method produces the lowest cost of goods sold because it includes the oldest and lowest costs. Since the cost of goods sold is lowest, the gross profit (and income) is highest. Correspondingly, the ending inventory using FIFO has the highest cost because it includes the most recent and highest costs. In contrast, the LIFO method produces the highest cost of goods sold and the lowest gross profit (and income) because it includes the most recent and highest costs. The LIFO ending inventory is lowest because it includes the earliest and lowest costs. The average cost amounts are between the FIFO and LIFO extremes because the ending inventory and the cost of goods sold include an average of both the lower and higher costs of the period. Note that this example is simplified because we assumed that the beginning inventory was $10 per unit for FIFO, average, and LIFO. When an inventory cost flow assumption is used in consecutive periods, the beginning inventory in each period is different under the alternative cost flow assumptions.

The Dalton Company was experiencing rising costs, but if costs were falling consistently, the opposite relationships would occur. The use of LIFO would produce a higher ending inventory, a lower cost of goods sold, and a higher gross profit (and income) than FIFO. When costs fluctuate, no general relationships can be described. The differences between the amounts under the periodic and the perpetual inventory systems for each cost flow assumption result from the different calculations and not from any differences in the logic underlying the cost flow assumptions.

CONCEPTUAL EVALUATION OF INVENTORY COST FLOW ASSUMPTIONS

6 Explain the conceptual issues regarding alternative inventory cost flow assumptions.

Many arguments are made in favor of each of the alternative cost flow assumptions. These arguments focus on a comparison of LIFO and FIFO, although the average cost method may be considered as similar to FIFO for this discussion. Sometimes, the FIFO and average cost methods are referred to as nonLIFO methods. Initially, our discussion assumes that inventory costs are rising. The advantages of LIFO are that it provides a better measure of income in times of rising costs, and it results in the payment of less income taxes. The disadvantages of LIFO are the impact of the liquidation of LIFO layers, the possibility of income manipulation, the inventory valuation on the balance sheet, and the lack of comparability among companies using LIFO. There also are several issues involved in selecting a method. We discuss and evaluate each of these issues in the following sections. In addition, we discuss specific arguments that relate solely to the average cost method. We discussed the arguments for and against the specific identification method earlier in the chapter.

Income Measurement

For financial reporting, the basic criterion a company uses to select a cost flow assumption is to achieve a "proper determination of income through the process of matching appropriate costs and revenues."[3] **There is no requirement that the assumed flow of costs be related to the actual physical flow of goods.** Most companies use a FIFO method for the physical management of inventory to reduce the likelihood of obsolescence. Such companies may use any of the alternative cost flow assumptions in their financial statements.

Conceptual

But what are "appropriate" costs? Unfortunately, there is no simple answer as to whether income is better measured under LIFO or FIFO. Both methods match historical costs with revenues, but **the major argument in favor of LIFO is that it matches the most recent costs with revenue.** The most recent costs are closer to replacement costs. Therefore, LIFO excludes from a company's income some (but not all) of the holding gains, so that the income reflects the earnings after capital has been maintained and is a

---

3. *Accounting Research and Terminology Bulletins, Final Edition, op. cit.*

better measure of the increase in wealth of the company. **A holding gain (or inventory profit) is the difference between the historical cost and the replacement cost of units sold.** In contrast, FIFO matches the earliest costs with revenue and *includes* all the holding gains in income.

In the Dalton Company example, when the company sells a unit on April 27 for $30, if the unit cost of the goods sold is $10 (FIFO) and the most recent acquisition cost was $12 per unit, the gross profit of $20 per unit (the selling price of $30 minus the cost of $10) includes a holding gain of $2 per unit (the most recent cost to replace the inventory of $12 less the cost of $10). The LIFO method records in cost of goods sold the cost of $12 per unit, resulting in a gross profit of $18 per unit, thereby *excluding* the holding gain of $2 from income. We show these two alternatives in Example 8-10. To continue this example, suppose that the company started with $10 cash, which it used to purchase a unit of inventory. When the company sells that unit for $30, it recognizes $20 of income under FIFO. If the company distributes the $20 income as a dividend, it is left with $10 cash, which is not enough to purchase a unit of inventory at its higher price of $12. Thus the income of $20 includes a holding gain of $2, which is not real income since the company cannot distribute it to the owners without leaving it worse off in terms of its ability to maintain the same level of inventory.

EXAMPLE 8-10	Alternative Cost Flow Assumptions and Holding Gains (per Unit)		
	FIFO	**LIFO ($12)**	**LIFO ($11)**
Revenue	$30	$30	$30
Cost of goods sold	(10)	(12)	(11)
Gross profit	$20	$18	$19
Holding gains (excluded from income)		2	1
		$20	$20

In this example, the LIFO method excluded all the holding gains. However, in other situations, it may not exclude them all. Under LIFO the Dalton Company included units at $11 per unit in the cost of goods sold (for the periodic method), whereas the most recent purchase price was $12 per unit. Therefore, the income included holding gains of $1 on each of these units. We also show this alternative in Example 8-10.

Also note that if the replacement cost of the inventory was $13 at the end of the month, the Dalton Company has not achieved the matching of current costs with revenue, even on the $12 units, and would include even more holding gains in income. In summary, it can be seen that "matching appropriate costs and revenues" is interpreted very widely. FIFO, LIFO, average cost, and specific identification all match historical cost with revenue, and are generally accepted accounting principles.

Income Tax Effects

As we have seen, LIFO produces the highest cost of goods sold and the lowest income under conditions of rising costs. Although it might be thought that a company would consider it undesirable to report low *accounting* income, it must be remembered that lower *taxable* income results in payment of lower income taxes. For example, three long-time LIFO users—**Exxon, General Motors,** and **General Electric**—have together saved more than $2 billion in taxes compared to what they would have paid using FIFO.

The use of LIFO for the computation of federal income taxes presents a special situation. The Internal Revenue Code permits a company to use LIFO for income tax purposes only if it also uses LIFO in its financial statements. This requirement is known as the **LIFO conformity rule.** A company might prefer to report a higher income for accounting purposes when costs are rising by using FIFO even though, as discussed before, its income is overstated because it includes holding gains. The LIFO conformity rule prevents a company from having "the best of both worlds" by using FIFO for financial reporting and LIFO for income taxes. This is in contrast to many situations in which a company can use different methods (e.g., when it uses straight-line depreciation for financial reporting and accelerated depreciation for income tax reporting). A company must decide whether it is willing to report a lower accounting income in order to achieve the advantages of the real economic benefits of reduced cash payments for income taxes.

Because of rulings by the Internal Revenue Service that allow a company using LIFO more latitude in the supplementary reporting of cost of goods sold and income on a FIFO basis, the Securities and Exchange Commission issued a ruling indicating how such disclosures should be made.[4] Also, since there was a lack of authoritative literature on the specifics of applying LIFO in complex situations, the tendency was to follow the income tax rules, which were much more specific. Since this did not always lead to appropriate financial reporting, the AICPA published an *Issues Paper* that was endorsed by the SEC, thereby giving it authoritative status.[5] The specific topics included in these two publications are beyond the scope of this book.

The Tax Reform Act of 1986 established "uniform capitalization rules" that require a company to include in inventory certain costs that previously it expensed as incurred for tax purposes. These costs include such items as purchasing, warehousing, and distribution costs, including related officer salaries and administrative costs. Because a cost must be capitalized for income tax purposes does not mean that capitalizing it for financial reporting is preferable, or even appropriate. Each situation must be analyzed based on the particular circumstances. The likely result in many situations is that inventory cost is different between financial reporting and income tax reporting.

Liquidation of LIFO Layers

A company using the LIFO method may liquidate inventory during a period. This occurs when the number of units in ending inventory is less than the number in beginning inventory because unit sales are more than the units acquired during the period. Therefore, some of the beginning inventory costs are included in cost of goods sold. In other words, the layers of LIFO inventory costs added in previous periods are removed in reverse order; the last costs added are the first expensed. Assuming rising costs, these units have lower costs attached to them; thus cost of goods sold is lower and gross profit (and income) is higher than if the liquidation did not occur. This increased amount of income is often referred to as a **LIFO liquidation profit.**

Many companies adopted LIFO in 1939 when the method was first allowed to be used by all companies for income tax purposes, and also in the higher inflation period between 1975 and 1985. Therefore, a company's LIFO liquidation profit may be significant because it includes some very old costs in cost of goods sold. An extreme example of LIFO liquidation profits occurs when a company liquidates its inventory down to the base (the beginning inventory in the year it adopted LIFO). In summary, liquidations bring units with a cost from previous years into cost of goods sold and produce an unrealistically high income.

---

4.   "Codification of Financial Reporting Policies," *SEC Accounting Rules* (Chicago: Commerce Clearing House, August 2005), sec. 205.

5.   "Identification and Discussion of Certain Financial Accounting and Reporting Issues Concerning LIFO Inventories," *Issues Paper* (New York: AICPA, 1984), and "LIFO Inventory Accounting Practices for Financial Statement Purposes," *Staff Accounting Bulletin 58* (Washington, D.C.: SEC, 1985).

Example: LIFO Liquidation Profit To illustrate the concept of a LIFO liquidation profit, assume that a company was formed in 2003. Its 2007 beginning inventory of $644,000 is made up of four layers as follows:

2003:	10,000 units at $20 per unit =	$200,000
2004:	6,000 units at $22 per unit =	132,000
2005:	8,000 units at $24 per unit =	192,000
2006:	4,000 units at $30 per unit =	120,000
Inventory, January 1, 2007		$644,000

In 2007 the company purchases (or manufactures) 50,000 units at $35 per unit but sells 60,000 units. The company has an inventory liquidation of 10,000 units. It includes these 10,000 units in cost of goods sold at the most recent beginning inventory costs; that is, the most recently added layers. Therefore, the company's cost of goods sold for 2007 includes costs from 2007, 2006, and 2005, as follows:

50,000 units at $35 per unit =	$1,750,000	(2007 costs)
4,000 units at $30 per unit =	120,000	(2006 costs)
6,000 units at $24 per unit =	144,000	(2005 costs)
60,000	$2,014,000	

If, instead, the company had purchased (or produced) 60,000 units at $35 each (thus avoiding the LIFO liquidation), the company would have had a cost of goods sold in 2007 of $2,100,000 (60,000 units × $35 per unit) consisting entirely of 2007 costs. The difference of $86,000 ($2,100,000 − $2,014,000) is the LIFO liquidation profit (before income taxes). If we assume an income tax rate of 30%, the effect of the LIFO liquidation is to increase gross profit by $86,000, income tax expense by $25,800 ($86,000 × 30%), and net income by $60,200 ($86,000 × 70%). Note that the company's income is higher (because cost of goods sold includes older and lower costs) even though there is **no economic substance to the higher income, and the company pays the additional income taxes** (because of the higher taxable income reported under the LIFO conformity rule). A company that reports to the SEC is required to disclose the amount of its LIFO liquidation profit so that users of the financial statements may obtain a better understanding of the profit earned by the company. For example, **Eastman Kodak Company** reported LIFO liquidation profits of $69 million and $45 million in 2004 and 2003, respectively. ♦

Earnings (Income) Management

As we have seen, a company's liquidation of inventory under LIFO, whether intentional or not, results in higher income (assuming rising costs). Such a liquidation may be caused by economic factors beyond the control of the company, such as a strike or a scarcity of raw materials, or as a result of a management decision such as the adoption of a "just-in-time" inventory system, which results in a permanent reduction in the size of the inventory. Also a liquidation may be deliberately created by delaying purchases. Intentional liquidation to artificially increase income is a significant concern. If a company is facing a period of lower income, management can increase income intentionally by liquidating inventory. This can be achieved by delaying purchases until after the end of the fiscal year.

Also, a company may influence (manage) its income by increasing its purchases. To illustrate, refer back to the Dalton Company periodic LIFO example and assume that the company purchased an additional 40 units on April 29 at $12 per unit. Total purchases then would be $2,200 ($1,720 + $480). The ending inventory would then consist of 150 units (110 + 40) and have a cost of $1,550 (100 units at $10 each from the beginning inventory + 50 units at $11 each from the April 10 purchase). The cost of goods sold would be computed as follows:

$$\text{Beginning Inventory} + \text{Purchases} - \text{Ending Inventory} = \text{Cost of Goods Sold}$$
$$\$1,000 \qquad + \quad \$2,200 \quad - \qquad \$1,550 \qquad = \qquad \underline{\underline{\$1,650}}$$

Thus purchasing additional units has increased cost of goods sold by $40 ($1,650 − $1,610) even though unit sales remain unchanged. **It is inconsistent with the revenue recognition principle for income to be affected by the purchasing activities of a company,** but it is an inevitable result of the LIFO method. The FIFO and average cost methods do not produce unusual results when inventory liquidation occurs, nor are they as susceptible to earnings management.

Management should make decisions about purchasing or manufacturing inventory on the basis of economic and operating factors. The use of LIFO, however, allows management to influence the company's income through the acceleration of, or delay in, acquiring inventory.

Inventory Valuation

The LIFO method produces a lower ending (and beginning) inventory value on a company's balance sheet (again assuming rising costs) because the oldest costs remain in this inventory. The recorded amount of this inventory often has little or no relationship to the costs of the current period or to the costs that will be incurred to replace the inventory, and therefore is *not relevant*. This low valuation affects the computation and evaluation of current assets, working capital, total assets, and any financial ratios that include inventory, thereby *reducing comparability* between companies using LIFO and those using FIFO. Furthermore, comparability between two or more companies using LIFO is impaired, because each company's inventory valuation depends on the year in which it adopted LIFO. For example, if companies in the same industry adopted LIFO in different years, each company's LIFO base will include costs of different years. (The year of adoption is *not* a required disclosure.) In addition, if the companies increase their inventories by different amounts in later years, the additional LIFO layers were added at different costs.

Therefore, a user evaluating a company that uses LIFO should always convert the inventory to nonLIFO (FIFO or average) amounts. As we show later, a company that uses LIFO and files with the SEC must disclose the nonLIFO value of its inventory.

The FIFO method produces a higher ending inventory value on the balance sheet (assuming rising costs) because it includes the most recent costs. This value approximates the costs that will be incurred to replace the inventory, but how closely depends on when the purchases included in the ending inventory were made and how fast costs are rising. Therefore, the FIFO inventory value is more *relevant*.

Average Cost

The average cost method is based on the assumption that during the period a company combines all the costs so that the unit costs included in cost of goods sold are the same as those remaining in inventory. Thus the method produces the same cost in a particular period for identical units that have the same utility. The weighted average method treats the accounting period as a single time period and produces the same unit cost for cost of goods sold and ending inventory. The general principle underlying the moving average method is the same, except that the period used is the time between the respective purchases. The same unit cost is used for the sales made in that time period and for the inventory at the end of that period. However, over the total accounting period, the unit costs used for the cost of goods sold vary as each purchase is made, and the unit cost for the ending inventory is the average cost calculated after the last purchase of the period.

The disadvantage of the average cost method is that the average is affected by the costs incurred in previous periods. Although the influence from these past periods becomes minimal as time passes, it still means that the average cost does not reflect the actual costs paid, either for the units sold or for those held in inventory in the current period.

LINK TO ETHICAL DILEMMA

As the CFO of a large manufacturing company, you realize that, although the company performed well over the past fiscal year, reported earnings will fall short of analysts' expectations. Knowing that failure to meet these expectations will likely result in a fall in the company's stock price and possibly the loss of your job, you assemble your most trusted financial experts to provide advice as to how to increase earnings. A plan is developed that would:

- Delay all inventory purchases until the next fiscal year (because you are using LIFO, this delay would result in the liquidation of inventory and a corresponding increase in income)
- Implement a sales program that would allow customers who accepted delivery of merchandise in the current year to defer payment for six months (normal practice requires payment within 30 days)

The financial experts all agree that these two actions are acceptable under GAAP and would allow the company to meet its earnings target. Discuss the ethical implications of these actions.

Management's Selection of an Inventory Cost Flow Assumption

The previous discussion shows that there are many financial accounting and tax issues involved in selecting an inventory cost flow assumption. In most cases, however, the decision should focus on the expected future cost changes.

If a company expects that costs will *rise* for several years, it should select LIFO because, as we discussed earlier, LIFO is a better measure of income. Also the LIFO conformity rule will allow the use of LIFO for income tax reporting and the company will save income taxes. Therefore, the financial reporting rules and the income tax rules are consistent. However, most companies probably consider the tax savings to be more important than the financial reporting issues!

The additional cash that results from the tax savings is reduced because the LIFO method is more costly to use than the FIFO method. These costs result from the additional costs of record keeping and financial statement preparation, such as keeping track of the LIFO layers for each type of inventory and the requirements imposed by the Internal Revenue Service. For a small company, these additional costs may be greater than the income tax savings that would result from the adoption of LIFO. For larger companies, however, the income tax savings are likely to exceed the additional costs (assuming rising prices), as is evidenced by the number of companies that use LIFO (see Exhibit 8-5).

Alternatively, if costs are expected to *fall* for several years, the decision is not as simple. For financial reporting purposes it can be argued that LIFO is still preferable because the most recent (and lowest) costs should be included in cost of goods sold because the inventory can be replaced at those lower costs. However, for income tax purposes, the use of FIFO is preferable because the company pays less income taxes. Although a company could use LIFO internally and FIFO for income taxes, it is unlikely to do so because of the additional record keeping costs it would incur. Therefore, if a company expects falling costs, it will use FIFO. Unfortunately, this means that income tax considerations are determining the accounting principle used for financial reporting.

Arguments are made that a company should not adopt LIFO even when its costs are expected to rise. This is because of the lower income that will result and a possible perception that the company is less successful and that its stock price will be lower. However, efficient capital markets research, discussed in Chapter 1, has indicated that stock market prices are *not* affected by the selection of an inventory cost flow assumption. That is, the stock market compensates for the lower reported income under LIFO.

In most situations the FIFO and weighted average *cost* flow assumptions approximate the *physical* flow of the items in inventory, whereas LIFO does not. For example, a retail store will try to impose a FIFO physical flow on its customers by selling the oldest items first. But, the customers may impose more of an average flow on the store by the way they select items from the shelves. However, accounting principles do *not* require that the selected cost flow method approximate the physical flow of goods but only that the method be systematic, based on cost, and match costs and revenues appropriately, as we discussed earlier. Therefore, a company's selection of a cost flow assumption should *not* depend on the perceived physical flow of goods.

Management also may be reluctant to adopt LIFO if the company pays them bonuses on the basis of accounting income. This tends to discourage management from using LIFO in periods of rising costs, since the lower reported income produces lower bonuses. In addition, a higher income results in higher earnings per share and a higher rate of return. These factors are considered important by many users of financial statements. Remember, however, that using a method other than LIFO in periods of rising costs causes the company to pay additional taxes.

There are several additional miscellaneous disadvantages of LIFO that a company should consider before adopting LIFO. First, adopting LIFO could increase its income taxes initially because the income tax rules require that the opening inventory in the year that LIFO is adopted must be stated at cost. Therefore, if the inventory previously had been written down to a market value lower than cost for income tax purposes (as we discuss in Chapter 9), it would be necessary to write the inventory back up and pay additional taxes on that amount. Second, the use of LIFO might also cause a company to be limited in its *financial flexibility*, because of covenants included in its bond indentures or other borrowing agreements. For example, the company might be required to maintain a certain current ratio or debt-to-equity ratio. Finally, the use of LIFO might cause a company to be less concerned about controlling the level of its inventories because of the company's lower *apparent* investment in those inventories.

Many manufacturing companies that expect falling costs use the average cost flow assumption in their financial statements. A company uses this method because (1) it operates a standard cost system (discussed in a cost accounting book) for its budgeting and control, and (2) it is unlikely to result in significantly more income taxes than FIFO.

Secure Your Knowledge 8-2

- Because a company carries inventory and the cost of the inventory changes during a period, it uses a cost flow assumption to assign costs to the physical units in ending inventory and cost of goods sold.
- The specific identification cost flow assumption (under which the company identifies the actual cost of each unit in ending inventory and cost of goods) is appropriate for perpetual inventory systems in which each item is unique.

(continued)

- The FIFO cost flow assumption (under which the company includes the earliest costs in costs of goods sold and the most recent costs in ending inventory) is generally viewed as providing a more relevant inventory valuation and a better approximation of the physical flow of inventory compared to LIFO.
- The LIFO cost flow assumption (under which the company includes the most recent costs in costs of goods sold and the earliest costs in ending inventory) is generally viewed as providing both a more relevant measure of income when costs are rising, as well as tax benefits. However, it is more susceptible to income distortions because of inventory liquidations or management of inventory quantities.
- The average cost flow assumption (under which the company combines all costs and units and applies a weighted average cost to both ending inventory and cost of goods sold) produces income measures and inventory valuations that fall between the FIFO and LIFO values and is often used by manufacturers.

DOLLAR-VALUE LIFO

The dollar-value LIFO method follows the same cost flow assumption as the LIFO method, but it overcomes three difficulties involved in applying the simple LIFO approach.

7 Understand dollar-value LIFO.

First, the LIFO method requires a company to keep numerous detailed records. As with other methods, the company must record the physical quantities of each item in its inventory from either a physical count or the perpetual inventory records. Then, it must apply unit costs from the years since it adopted LIFO, in the LIFO order. Finally, it must correctly account for the liquidations in LIFO inventory that occurred over the years.

Second, fluctuations in the physical quantities of similar inventory items may occur. For example, the quantity of one inventory item may significantly decline during a period causing a partial liquidation of its LIFO layers, whereas the quantity of a very similar inventory item may increase. As these fluctuations occur over time, the LIFO layers for each individual item would be reduced, thereby removing many of the advantages of LIFO.

Third, as technological changes take place, inventory made with one material is replaced by inventory made with substitute materials, or an outdated design is replaced by a newer design. Strict application of the LIFO method would require a company to start a new LIFO base for the new inventory item, and as the old item is phased out to reduce its inventory to zero. This would eliminate the advantages of LIFO built up in previous periods. With the rate of technological change in many industries, the advantages of LIFO would be lost.

Dollar-value LIFO overcomes part of the first problem by the use of *current costs* and *cost indexes*, and the second and third problems by the use of *inventory pools*. Under the dollar-value LIFO method, a company may group the inventory into pools that are similar as to types of material or use. Some companies may consider their entire inventory as one pool, but usually several pools are used. We discuss cost indexes and inventory pools in more detail later in the chapter.

The general principle of the dollar-value LIFO method is that a company initially values its ending inventory at current cost and "rolls back" this cost to the cost at the beginning of the base year (the year in which it adopted LIFO) to *eliminate the change in costs* from the physical quantity of the ending inventory. A comparison of the year's beginning and ending inventory at base-year costs indicates whether there has been a real increase (or decrease) in the physical quantity of the inventory. The company "rolls forward" the increase (or decrease) to the appropriate current cost level, and adds this layer of current cost (or subtracts it from) the beginning inventory to determine its ending inventory. The application of the dollar-value LIFO method requires the four steps we show in Exhibit 8-4.

It is necessary to convert the inventory to base-year costs in order to isolate the *quantity* increase from the *cost* increase. To show that a comparison of base-year *costs* reflects changes in *quantity*, consider the following two simplified examples. First, assume a company has a beginning inventory of 100 units at $20 each, or $2,000, when it adopts

---

EXHIBIT 8-4   Dollar-Value LIFO Calculation Steps

Step 1.   Value the total ending inventory at current-year costs.

Step 2.   Convert (roll back) the ending inventory cost to base-year costs by applying the base-year conversion index:

$$\text{Ending Inventory at Base-Year Costs} = \text{Ending Inventory at Current-Year Costs} \times \frac{\text{Base-Year Cost Index}}{\text{Current Cost Index}}$$

Step 3.   Compute the change in the inventory level (physical quantity) for the year at base-year costs by comparing the ending inventory at base-year costs with the beginning inventory at base-year costs.

Step 4.   a.   If there is an increase in the inventory level at base-year costs, there has been a real *increase* in the physical quantity of the inventory over the year. Convert (roll forward) this increase to current-year costs by applying the current-year conversion index:

$$\text{Layer Increase at Current-Year Costs} = \text{Increase at Base-Year Costs} \times \frac{\text{Current Cost Index}}{\text{Base-Year Cost Index}}$$

The ending inventory cost is the dollar-value LIFO inventory cost at the beginning of the year *plus* the layer increase at current-year costs.

b.   If there is a decrease in the inventory level at base-year costs, there has been a real decrease in the physical quantity of the inventory over the period. This decrease reduces the inventory on a LIFO layer basis, and therefore it must be converted to the costs of the most recently added layer or layers:

$$\frac{\text{Decrease at Costs of}}{\text{Most Recently Added Layer(s)}} = \text{Decrease at Base-Year Costs} \times \frac{\text{Cost Index of Most Recently Added Layer(s)}}{\text{Base-Year Cost Index}}$$

The ending inventory cost is the dollar-value LIFO cost at the beginning of the year *minus* the decrease at the costs of the most recently added layer(s). Note that the decrease may eliminate more than one layer of LIFO inventory, and therefore the decrease at base-year costs has to be converted to the costs of as many layers as is necessary to eliminate the total decrease.

---

dollar-value LIFO. At the end of the year, it has an ending inventory of 100 units at a current cost of $21 each, or $2,100. It might appear from a simple comparison of the two costs ($2,100 versus $2,000) that the *physical quantity* of the inventory has increased. However, this is not the case. The quantity has remained unchanged, and the cost change (from $20 to $21 per unit, or an increase of 5%) has accounted for the entire change in the cost of the inventory. Reducing the inventory of $2,100 to the base-year costs gives an amount of $2,000 [$2,100 × (100 ÷ 105) = $2,000]. Since the beginning and ending inventory amounts are $2,000 when they are both measured in terms of the same costs (base year), there has been no increase in quantity. The increase from $2,000 to $2,100 resulted solely from the increase in costs.

In the second example, we can isolate the quantity increase from the cost increase without knowing the number and costs of the units. To illustrate, assume a company has a beginning inventory of $1,000 and a cost index (discussed later) of 100 when it adopted dollar-value LIFO. Assume further that the ending inventory at current cost is $1,430 and costs have increased 10%. That is, the cost index is 110 (100 × 1.10 = 110). The quantity increase in the inventory is not 43% ($1,430 ÷ $1,000 = 1.43). Rather, the ending inventory at base-year costs is $1,300 [$1,430 × (100 ÷ 110) = $1,300], and therefore inventory has increased in quantity by 30% ($1,300 ÷ $1,000 = 1.30). The total increase of 43% in the cost of the inventory is made up of an increase in the quantity of 30% and a cost increase of 10% (1.30 × 1.10 = 1.43). To complete the example, the increase in inventory of $300 at base-year costs is converted to ending costs of $330 [$300 × (110 ÷ 100)], and therefore the LIFO ending inventory is valued at $1,330 ($1,000 + $330).

Example: Dollar-Value LIFO

We show how to apply the four steps discussed in Exhibit 8-4 for the Wagner Company using the basic data in Example 8-11. The Wagner Company adopted LIFO at the beginning of 2006 and has taken an ending inventory at the *current costs* for each year as indicated. In addition, the company has experienced yearly changes in the level of its costs as indicated by its cost index for each year. (We discuss the determination of a cost index later.)

EXAMPLE 8-11   Data for Wagner Company

Date	Ending Inventory at Current Costs	Cost Index
January 1, 2006	$10,000	100
December 31, 2006	12,100	110
December 31, 2007	13,125	125
December 31, 2008	16,800	140
December 31, 2009	12,360	120

We show the calculation of the dollar-value LIFO ending inventory in Example 8-12. The base year is 2006, so the beginning inventory needs no adjustment. The 2006 ending inventory at the current cost of $12,100 is reduced to $11,000 at base-year costs. Therefore, the real (quantity) increase in inventory is $1,000 ($11,000 − $10,000 at base-year costs), which is $1,100 [$1,000 × (110 ÷ 100)] in 2006 costs. The ending LIFO inventory cost for 2006 is $11,100, which is made up of two layers, the base layer of $10,000 plus the layer added in 2006 of $1,100.

In 2007, the company reduces its ending inventory of $13,125 at the current cost to $10,500 at base-year costs. This indicates a real (quantity) *decrease* in inventory of $500 (the $10,500 2007 ending inventory less the $11,000 2006 ending inventory, *both* at base-year costs). The company subtracts the decrease from the most recently added layer, which is the layer added in 2006. Therefore it converts the decrease of $500 in base-year costs to 2006 costs and *not* to 2007 costs. Consequently it applies the 110 cost index to the $500 decrease, resulting in a decrease of $550 in terms of 2006 costs and an ending inventory of $10,550.

In 2008, the company has an increase in inventory at base-year costs, and therefore adds another layer, so that its ending LIFO inventory of $12,650 consists of three layers.

In 2009, the company has a decrease in its cost index. It calculates the ending inventory at base-year costs in exactly the same manner as we discussed previously. In this case the $10,300 ending inventory at base-year costs is $1,700 lower than the $12,000 beginning inventory at base-year costs. This completely eliminates the layer of $1,500 (at base-year costs) added in 2008, and so the company must go back into the 2006 layer to account for the remaining decrease of $200 at base-year costs (no layer was added in 2007). The ending LIFO inventory of $10,330 consists of the base inventory plus the remainder of the layer added in 2006. ◆

Determination of Cost Index

The preceding discussion refers to the use of a cost index rather than a price index. A **cost index** refers to an internally generated index that is specific to a company's particular inventory, whereas a **price index** is a more general index prepared by an external organization, such as a government or trade association. Although the concepts underlying the two are identical, we use the term *cost index* because IRS regulations require that in most situations a company use an internally developed index specific to the company's particular operations. However, the IRS has simplified the LIFO method by allowing the use of published price indexes in certain situations.

EXAMPLE 8-12 Dollar-Value LIFO Inventory Calculations

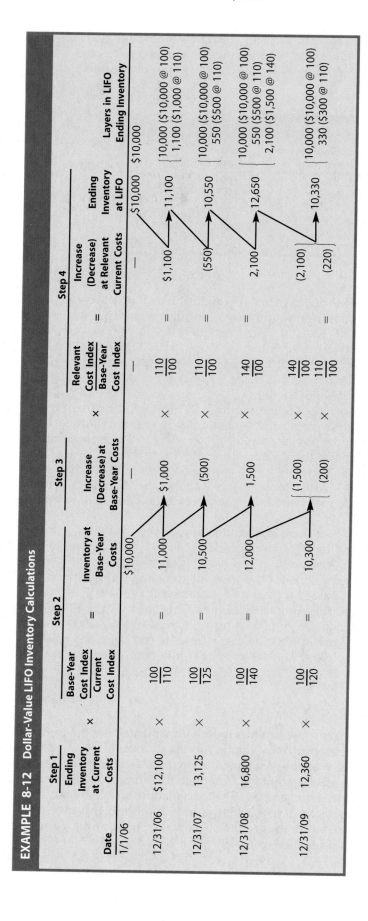

If a company uses an internally developed cost index, it must compute an index based on the particular cost per unit it has experienced in the current year as compared to the base year. Typically, the company prepares the index using a sample of its total inventory. Two methods to compute the cost index are used in practice: the double-extension method and the link-chain method.

Under the **double-extension** method, a sample of the ending inventory is priced at current-year costs and at base-year costs, and the cost index is computed as follows:

$$\text{Cost Index} = \frac{\text{Sample of Ending Inventory at Current-Year Costs}}{\text{Sample of Ending Inventory at Base-Year Costs}} \times 100$$

This is known as the double-extension method because the ending inventory is priced and "extended" twice—once at current costs and once at base-year costs. The double-extension method is appropriate for companies that have little change in the characteristics of their inventory items. When changes are frequent, determination of base-year costs for new items is difficult. For example, if a company adopted LIFO in 1990 and develops a new product in 2007, the double-extension method would require the computation of the cost in 1990 of the new product. Since the product, perhaps including the technology, did not exist in 1990, the difficulties of such a calculation are obvious. In such situations the link-chain method should be used.

Under the **link-chain** method, a company prices a sample of the ending inventory at current costs for the current year and for the previous year, and therefore the method avoids the problems of the double-extension method we just discussed. The ratio of the current-year current cost to the previous-year current cost is used to compute a cost index for the *year*. This index is multiplied by the cost index carried forward from the previous year to determine the current year cumulative index as follows:

$$\text{Cost Index} = \frac{\text{Sample of Ending Inventory at Current-Year Costs}}{\text{Sample of Ending Inventory at Previous-Year Costs}} \times \begin{array}{c} \text{Previous-Year} \\ \text{Cost Index} \end{array}$$

Inventory Pools

As we discussed earlier in the chapter, a company may use inventory pools in conjunction with dollar-value LIFO. The purpose of the pools is to maintain the benefits from using LIFO when fluctuations in the physical quantities of similar inventory items occur and when technological change takes place.

To illustrate the concept of an inventory pool, consider the Herrmann Soup Company, which adopts dollar-value LIFO on January 1, 2007 using a single pool. The pool includes three types of soup that the company manufactures, and we show the calculation of the total cost of the beginning inventory in Example 8-13. The company assigns a cost index of 100 to the beginning inventory and uses it as the base for calculating the cost index in later years.

EXAMPLE 8-13	Herrmann Soup Company Inventory, January 1, 2007		
Type	**Quantity**	**Cost per Unit**	**Total Cost**
Mushroom	10,000	$0.25	$2,500
Vegetable	8,000	0.20	1,600
Tomato	22,000	0.16	3,520
	40,000		$7,620

During 2007, the transactions we show in Example 8-14 occurred. The company purchased 150,000 cans of soup and sold 139,000 cans, leaving 51,000 cans in ending inventory, including the quantities of each type as shown. Using the double-extension method, the company calculates a cost index of 107 for the ending inventory by dividing the ending inventory at current-year costs by the ending inventory at base-year costs. Completing the remaining steps in the dollar-value LIFO calculations results in an ending inventory at LIFO cost of $10,167, as we show in Example 8-14.

EXAMPLE 8-14   Inventory Pools

Purchases and Sales During 2007

Type	Beginning Quantity	Quantity Purchased	Cost per Unit	Quantity Sold	Inventory Quantity December 31, 2007
Mushroom	10,000	60,000	$0.30	54,000	16,000
Vegetable	8,000	40,000	0.24	38,000	10,000
Tomato	22,000	50,000	0.14	47,000	25,000
	40,000	150,000		139,000	51,000

$$\text{Cost Index} = \frac{\text{Ending Inventory at Current-Year Costs}}{\text{Ending Inventory at Base-Year Costs}} \times 100$$

$$= \frac{(16,000 \times \$0.30) + (10,000 \times \$0.24) + (25,000 \times \$0.14)}{(16,000 \times \$0.25) + (10,000 \times \$0.20) + (25,000 \times \$0.16)} \times 100$$

$$= \frac{\$10,700}{\$10,000} \times 100$$

$$= 107$$

LIFO Cost of Ending Inventory

$$\text{Ending Inventory at Base-Year Costs} = \frac{\text{Ending Inventory}}{\text{at Current-Year Costs}} \times \frac{\text{Base-Year Cost Index}}{\text{Current Cost Index}}$$

$$= \$10,700 \times \frac{100}{107}$$

$$= \$10,000$$

$$\text{Increase in Inventory at Base-Year Costs} = \frac{\text{Ending Inventory at}}{\text{Base-Year Costs}} - \frac{\text{Beginning Inventory}}{\text{at Base-Year Costs}}$$

$$= \$10,000 - \$7,620$$

$$= \$2,380$$

$$\text{Layer Increase at Current-Year Costs} = \frac{\text{Increase at}}{\text{Base-Year Costs}} \times \frac{\text{Current Cost Index}}{\text{Base-Year Cost Index}}$$

$$= \$2,380 \times \frac{107}{100}$$

$$= \$2,547 \text{ (rounded)}$$

$$\text{Total LIFO Ending Inventory Cost} = \$7,620 + \$2,547$$

$$= \$10,167$$

The preceding discussion assumed that the entire ending inventory cost was a single inventory "pool." When a company uses the dollar-value LIFO method, however, it may include the inventory in one or several "inventory pools." IRS regulations do not specify what types of items are to be included in the same pool, other than to say they should be "substantially similar." If a company uses more than one pool, it must compute a separate cost index for each (or a representative sample of the pool). In general, the fewer the pools and the more items included in each pool, the more likely it is that increases in some items will offset decreases in other items in the pool, thereby avoiding the liquidation of LIFO layers and the loss of the tax benefits of LIFO. In other words, a company would typically prefer to have the fewest number of pools allowed. In a surprising decision several years ago, **Stauffer Chemical Company** increased its LIFO pools from 8 to 280, which increased its income by $16.5 million (and resulted in additional taxes being paid).

Note also that the current cost used in the dollar-value LIFO calculations can be the cost of the first purchases in a year, the last purchases in a year, or the average cost of all purchases during the year as assumed in the preceding example. Once a choice is made, however, it must be applied consistently.

ADDITIONAL LIFO CONSIDERATIONS

Several other items concerning LIFO are important, including the LIFO valuation adjustment, interim statements using LIFO, a change to or from LIFO, and international accounting differences. We discuss these topics in the following sections.

8 Explain additional LIFO issues.

LIFO Valuation Adjustment

Frequently, a company uses LIFO for external financial reporting and income tax purposes but uses another method for internal management. In this case, the company makes a valuation adjustment to convert its internally reported ending inventory to LIFO for external reporting. This adjustment increases (decreases) cost of goods sold for the period and decreases (increases) the ending inventory by the amount of the *change* in the difference between the beginning and ending inventories under the two methods. However, the company usually does not adjust the inventory account directly. Instead, it uses a valuation adjustment. This adjustment has a variety of names including *Valuation Allowance* or (inappropriately) *LIFO Reserve*. Typically, this adjustment is not part of the company's formal accounting system, but the company does report the amount in its balance sheet or its notes because the SEC requires the disclosure. When this occurs, the company subtracts the *cumulative* balance of the adjustment to report the ending inventory at LIFO. We illustrate this situation with the disclosures of **General Mills** and **Marathon Oil** in Real Report 8-1 later in the chapter.

You should also note that the *change* in the adjustment for the year is the difference between the LIFO cost of goods sold and what the cost of goods sold would have been under the method used internally (FIFO or average). A user can use this change to adjust the cost of goods sold of a company using LIFO to the other method, which improves the comparability of the two companies. The *total* amount of the adjustment is the cumulative difference between the two cost of goods sold amounts since LIFO was adopted. Multiplying this amount by the income tax rate gives the cumulative savings in income tax expense, while multiplying the amount by the after-tax rate gives the cumulative effect on income.

Interim Statements Using LIFO

If a company uses LIFO for annual reporting purposes, it must use LIFO for interim (i.e., quarterly) reporting purposes (discussed in Chapter 5). **APB Opinion No. 28** states that if a company using LIFO has an inventory liquidation at an interim date that it expects to replace by the end of the annual period, it does not include the LIFO liquidation in its inventory, and its cost of sales includes the expected cost of replacement of the liquidated LIFO inventory.[6]

Consequently, when a company has an inventory liquidation at the end of a quarter, it must forecast its year-end physical quantities. If the forecast indicates that the company will not liquidate any inventory at the end of the year, it removes the effect of the LIFO liquidation from the interim financial statements. The company decreases the inventory value and increases the cost of goods sold by the difference between the replacement cost and the LIFO cost for the number of units that it has liquidated. If the forecast indicates that the liquidation will still exist at the end of the year, the company includes the effect of the LIFO liquidation in its interim financial statements.

---

6. "Interim Financial Reporting," *APB Opinion No. 28* (New York: AICPA, 1973), par. 14(b).

LINK TO RATIO ANALYSIS

Analysts often use financial ratios such as inventory turnover and average days in inventory to evaluate the effectiveness of a company's inventory management and control activities. It is important to note that the accounting choice between FIFO and LIFO can have a significant impact on this evaluation since each method will produce different income statement and balance sheet amounts. Therefore, it would not be useful to compare companies that make different accounting choices without first adjusting for these differences. Fortunately, the disclosure of the "LIFO reserve" allows the following adjustments to be made:

FIFO Inventory = LIFO Inventory + LIFO Reserve

FIFO Cost of Goods Sold = LIFO Cost of Goods Sold − Increase (or + Decrease) in LIFO Reserve

Using amounts obtained from General Mills' annual report, we show this conversion below:

	2004	2003
Inventory (as reported, LIFO)	$ 1,063	$1,082
Add: LIFO Reserve	+ 41	+ 27
Inventory (FIFO)	$ 1,104	$1,109
Cost of Sales (as reported)	$ 6,584	
Less: Increase in LIFO Reserve	− 14	
Cost of Sales (FIFO)	$ 6,570	

With these adjustments, you can now perform an appropriate analysis.

Change to or from LIFO

Although the adoption of an inventory cost flow assumption is a long-term decision, a company may occasionally change its method. When the company changes *to* LIFO from another method, usually the effect on the results of prior periods is not determinable. Then *FASB Statement No. 154* requires that the company apply the change prospectively, as of the earliest date practicable. A company that changes to another method *from* LIFO retroactively restates the results of prior periods and treats the change as a retrospective adjustment.[7] We discuss these changes in Chapter 23.

LINK TO INTERNATIONAL DIFFERENCES

International accounting standards for inventories also require a company to base its inventory values on cost. However, the IASB does not allow the use of LIFO because it is clearly inconsistent with any presumed physical flow of the inventory, an issue that has not been considered relevant for U.S. accounting principles. Also, LIFO is not permitted to be used for income tax purposes in most countries and, therefore, there has been no incentive to allow its use for financial reporting.

---

7.   "Accounting Changes and Error Corrections," *FASB Statement No. 154* (Norwalk, Conn.: 2005), par. 7–9.

SECURE YOUR KNOWLEDGE 8-3

- Dollar-value LIFO was developed to overcome practical difficulties with the application of LIFO.
- The calculation of a cost index is necessary to convert the inventory to base-year costs so that *quantity* increases (decreases) may be isolated from *cost* increases (decreases).
- Inventory is often included in one or more inventory pools to keep the advantages of LIFO when there are fluctuations in the physical quantities of similar products and/or technological change.
- For a company that uses LIFO for financial reporting purposes but an alternative cost flow assumption for internal management, a LIFO valuation adjustment is necessary to convert the internally reported ending inventory to a LIFO basis.
- If a company has a LIFO liquidation in an interim reporting period but expects to replace the inventory by year-end, the impact of the liquidation is removed from its interim financial statements.

DISCLOSURE OF INVENTORY VALUES AND METHODS

Exhibit 8-5 shows the relative use of alternative inventory methods by 600 surveyed companies and the proportion of the inventory cost determined by LIFO. The trend to the use of LIFO between 1973 and 1982 is clearly indicated, although the trend has reversed somewhat with the lower inflation since then. There were more than 600 responses to the methods used, since many companies use more than one method, as indicated by the categories listed in the second section.

9 Understand inventory disclosures.

EXHIBIT 8-5 Inventory Cost Determination

	Number of Companies										
	2003	2000	1997	1994	1991	1988	1985	1982	1979	1976	1973
Methods											
First-in, first-out (FIFO)	384	386	415	417	421	396	381	373	390	389	394
Last-in, first-out (LIFO)	251	283	326	351	361	379	402	407	374	331	150
Average cost	167	180	188	192	200	213	223	238	241	232	235
Other	31	38	32	42	50	50	48	53	56	50	57
	833	887	961	1,002	1,032	1,038	1,054	1,071	1,061	1,002	836
Use of LIFO											
All inventories	26	23	17	17	23	20	26	28	20	9	8
50% or more inventories	120	148	170	186	186	207	231	206	194	167	49
Less than 50% of inventories	77	82	99	98	95	90	83	88	94	84	78
Not determinable	28	30	40	50	57	62	62	85	66	71	25

Source: Accounting Trends and Techniques (New York: AICPA, 1974, 1977, 1980, 1983, 1986, 1989, 1992, 1995, 1998, 2001, and 2004).

Real Report 8-1 shows examples of the way in which three companies disclose the methods used for inventory. Companies are required to disclose the inventory method, or methods, used. **Marathon Oil** reports a single inventory amount in the balance sheet and shows the breakdown in the notes to the financial statements. It categorizes its inventory by functional groups, while **General Mills** categorizes its inventory by type and product.

Hewlett-Packard uses FIFO, while General Mills uses LIFO in the United States and FIFO elsewhere. Marathon Oil discloses the difference between LIFO costs and current costs.

Real Report 8-1 Examples of Disclosure of Inventory Values and Methods

HEWLETT-PACKARD COMPANY

(millions)

Balance Sheet

Assets (in part)	October 31, 2004	October 31, 2003
Inventory	$7,071	$6,065

Notes to Consolidated Financial Statements (in part)

Note 1 Summary of Significant Accounting Policies (in part)

Inventory—Inventory is valued at the lower of cost or market, with cost computed on a first-in, first-out basis.

GENERAL MILLS, INC.

Notes to Consolidated Financial Statements (in part)

Note 1 Summary of Significant Accounting Policies (in part)

C. Inventories. Inventories are valued at the lower of cost or market. We generally use the LIFO method of valuing inventory because we believe that it is a better match with current revenues. However, FIFO is used for most foreign operations, where LIFO is not recognized for statutory purposes.

Note 6 Inventories
The components of inventories are as follows:

In Millions	May 30, 2004	May 25, 2003
Raw materials, work in process and supplies	$ 234	$ 221
Finished goods	793	818
Grain	77	70
Reserve for LIFO valuation method	(41)	(29)
Total inventories	$1,063	$1,082

At May 30, 2004 and May 25, 2003, respectively, inventories of $765 million and $767 million were valued at LIFO. LIFO accounting decreased fiscal 2004 earnings by $0.02 per share and had a negligible impact on fiscal 2003 and 2002 earnings. Results of operations were not materially affected by a liquidation of LIFO inventory. The difference between replacement cost and the stated LIFO inventory value is not materially different from the reserve for LIFO valuation method.

MARATHON OIL

Notes to Financial Statements (in part)

Note 12. Inventories

(In millions) December 31	2004	2003
Liquid hydrocarbons and natural gas	$ 676	$ 674
Refined products and merchandise	1,192	1,151
Supplies and sundry items	129	130
Total	1,995	1,955

The LIFO method accounted for 92 percent and 91 percent of total inventory value at December 31, 2004 and 2003. Current acquisition costs were estimated to exceed the LIFO inventory values at December 31, 2004 and 2003, by approximately $1,294 million and $655 million. Cost of revenues was reduced and income from operations was

Continued

increased by $4 million in 2004 and $11 million in 2003 and less than $1 million in 2002 as a result of liquidations of LIFO inventories.

Questions

1. Why do you think Hewlett-Packard uses FIFO while General Mills uses LIFO?
2. Why does General Mills use LIFO in the United States and FIFO elsewhere?
3. If the inventory costs of General Mills are rising throughout the world, what is the effect on the financial statements of its use of FIFO?
4. How would you explain the meaning of General Mills' disclosure about the impact of LIFO accounting to a shareholder?
5. For Marathon Oil, how would you explain the statement that the LIFO liquidation increased income from operations?

LINK TO RATIO ANALYSIS

Effective inventory management and control is a critical ingredient to a company's success. While management wants to keep an adequate supply of inventory on hand to meet customer demands and maintain desired service levels, there is a cost associated with carrying high levels of inventory (e.g., storage costs, risk of obsolescence, damage, theft, insurance, and taxes). Unfortunately, reducing costs by reducing inventory levels can also have adverse consequences such as lost sales, stockouts, and dissatisfied customers. Companies use a variety of tools, such as computerized inventory tracking systems, to manage and control their inventories. The effectiveness of an inventory management program can be evaluated using financial ratios such as inventory turnover and average days in inventory.

Using data obtained from the company's annual report, the computation of inventory turnover ratios for **General Mills** and **ConAgra** are shown below:

(amounts in millions)	General Mills		ConAgra	
	2004	2003	2004	2003
Cost of Goods Sold (assuming FIFO)	$6,570		$11,326.1	
Inventories (on FIFO basis)	$1,104	$1,109	$2,625.6	$2,455.6

General Mills: Inventory Turnover $= \dfrac{\$6,750}{\left(\dfrac{\$1,104 + \$1,109}{2}\right)} = 5.94$

ConAgra: Inventory Turnover $= \dfrac{\$11,326.1}{\left(\dfrac{\$2,625.6 + \$2,455.6}{2}\right)} = 4.46$

Dividing the turnover ratio into 365 days shows that General Mills and ConAgra hold inventory an average of 61.45 and 81.84 days, respectively. The industry average, obtained from **Thomson Analytics** is approximately 61 days. Because higher inventory turnover ratios generally signal more effective inventory management and control, General Mills appears to manage and control its inventory better than ConAgra; however, there is still room for improvement since General Mills' inventory turnover is approximately average for the industry.

APPENDIX: FOREIGN CURRENCY TRANSACTIONS INVOLVING INVENTORY

10 Record foreign currency transactions involving inventory.

Many U.S. companies conduct inventory transactions with customers and suppliers in foreign countries. Sometimes the transaction is expressed in U.S. dollars. For example, most purchases and sales of crude oil are expressed in terms of the U.S. dollar. In these situations there is no accounting issue. For example, if a U.S. oil company purchases 10,000 barrels of crude oil from Saudi Arabia, the price is quoted in dollars and not in the equivalent amount of riyals. If the price is $50 per barrel, the company records a purchase of inventory and the related payment of $500,000 ($50 × 10,000).

In many situations, however, the transaction is expressed in terms of the foreign currency. In these cases the company must record the transaction in U.S. dollars. Therefore, it converts the foreign currency amount into dollars at the exchange rate on the day of the transaction. Exhibit 8-6 shows selected foreign exchange rates. For example, suppose a U.S. company purchases inventory of electronic components from a Japanese company for 50 million yen (¥) when the exchange rate is $0.008 (1 yen = $0.008). If the U.S. company pays cash of $400,000 (¥50,000,000 × $0.008) on the same day to purchase yen to settle the transaction, the U.S. company records the transaction as follows:

Inventory (or Purchases)	400,000	
Cash		400,000

EXHIBIT 8-6   Selected Foreign Exchange Rates

Currency (Country)	Price in U.S. dollars*
Pound (Britain)	$1.81
Dollar (Canada)	0.83
Euro	1.25
Shekel (Israel)	0.22
Yen (Japan)	0.0091
Peso (Mexico)	0.09
Riyal (Saudi Arabia)	0.27
Franc (Switzerland)	0.80

*Note that the exchange rates are stated in terms of $ per unit of foreign currency. Exchange rates are often stated in terms of units of foreign currency per $.

Source: *The Wall Street Journal* (August 12, 2005).

More often, transactions between companies in different countries involve credit terms. This allows time for processing the order and payment across international borders. In addition, currency exchange rates change continuously. As a result, the exchange rate is likely to have changed between the date the U.S. company records a purchase transaction and the date it makes the payment. On the date of the payment, the company records an exchange gain or loss to account for the difference between the purchase price of the inventory and the amount of the payment. **An exchange gain or loss is caused by a change in the exchange rate between the date of a purchase or sale on credit and the date of the payment or receipt.** More specifically, when exchange rates are stated in terms of $ per unit of foreign currency, exchange gains and losses occur for purchases or sales on credit as follows:

1. An exchange *gain* occurs when the exchange rate *declines* between the date a company records a *payable* from a purchase of inventory and the date of the cash *payment*.

2. An exchange *gain* occurs when the exchange rate *increases* between the date a company records a *receivable* from a sale of inventory and the date of the cash *receipt*.
3. An exchange *loss* occurs when the exchange rate *increases* between the date a company records a *payable* from a purchase of inventory and the date of the cash *payment*.
4. An exchange *loss* occurs when the exchange rate *declines* between the date a company records a *receivable* from a sale of inventory and the date of the cash *receipt*.

Example: Exchange Gain

We first illustrate an exchange gain that occurs when the exchange rate declines between the date a company records a credit purchase of inventory and the date of the cash payment. Suppose that in the preceding example the U.S. company made the purchase of the electronic components on credit. Because the company purchased the inventory when the exchange rate was $0.008, it records the acquisition as follows:

Inventory	400,000	
Accounts Payable		400,000

The Japanese company has a right to receive 50 million yen, and the U.S. company is obligated to pay sufficient dollars that will convert to 50 million yen on the date that the payment is made. Now assume that the exchange rate on the date of payment is $0.0078 (1 yen = $0.0078). In this case, since only $0.0078 now is needed to buy 1 yen, the U.S. company will have to pay fewer dollars to buy 50 million yen. That is, the yen has become less expensive. More specifically, the U.S. company has to pay only $390,000 (¥50,000,000 × $0.0078). Therefore, the company has incurred an exchange *gain* of $10,000 ($400,000 − $390,000), which it records at the time of payment for the inventory as follows:

Accounts Payable	400,000	
Cash		390,000
Exchange Gain		10,000

The exchange gain occurs because the U.S. company has to pay only $390,000 to settle its credit purchase originally recorded at $400,000. The gain can also be computed by multiplying the amount owed by the change in the exchange rate [¥50,000,000 × ($0.008 − $0.0078) = $10,000]. Remember that the Japanese company still receives 50 million yen; it is the U.S. company that has the exchange gain. ♦

Example: Exchange Loss

We now illustrate an exchange loss that occurs when the exchange rate declines between the date a company records a credit sale and the date of the cash receipt. Suppose that a U.S. company sells computer equipment to a German company on credit and agrees to a price of 300,000 euros rather than a price in dollars. On the date of the sale, the exchange rate is $1.20 (1 euro = $1.20), and therefore the U.S. company records the sale of $360,000 (300,000 euros × $1.20) as follows (assuming the inventory has a cost of $200,000):

Accounts Receivable	360,000	
Sales Revenue		360,000
Cost of Goods Sold	200,000	
Inventory		200,000

The German company has an obligation to pay 300,000 euros regardless of the exchange rate on the date of payment. If the exchange rate is $1.18 when it pays the amount owed, the U.S. company can convert those euros into only $354,000 (300,000 euros × $1.18). As a result, it has incurred an exchange *loss* of $6,000 ($354,000 − $360,000), which it records at the time of the cash collection as follows:

Cash	354,000	
Exchange Loss	6,000	
Accounts Receivable		360,000

The exchange loss can also be computed by multiplying the amount receivable by the change in the exchange rate [300,000 euros × ($1.20 − $1.18) = $6,000]. For financial reporting purposes, the company usually reports the net amount of Exchange Gains and Losses in the Other Items section of its income statement. This amount is included in the income statement because the exchange gains and losses were caused by fluctuations in the exchange rates that resulted in increased or decreased dollar cash flows during the accounting period.

Note that the U.S. company experienced exchange gains and losses in the preceding situations because it agreed to transactions expressed in terms of foreign currencies. Therefore, the U.S. company accepts the risks associated with exchange rate changes. When the transactions are expressed in U.S. dollars, the foreign company accepts, and the U.S. company avoids, the risks associated with exchange rate changes. ♦

SUMMARY

At the beginning of the chapter, we identified several objectives you would accomplish after reading the chapter. The objectives are listed below, each followed by a brief summary of the key points in the chapter discussion.

1. **Describe how inventory accounts are classified.** A retailer needs only one type of inventory account, usually called (merchandise) inventory. A manufacturer typically uses three inventory accounts, usually called raw materials inventory, work in process inventory, and finished goods inventory.
2. **Explain the uses of the perpetual and periodic inventory systems.** A company using a perpetual system keeps a continuous record of the physical quantities in its inventory. A company using a periodic system does not keep a continuous record of the physical quantities (or costs) of inventory on hand.
3. **Identify how inventory quantities are determined.** The basic criterion for including items in inventory is economic control rather than physical possession. Issues include goods shipped FOB shipping point and FOB destination, and goods transferred on consignment.
4. **Determine the cost of inventory.** Inventory cost includes costs directly or indirectly incurred in bringing an item to its existing condition and location. Purchases discounts may be recorded under the gross or net method.
5. **Compute ending inventory and cost of goods sold under specific identification, FIFO, average cost, and LIFO.** Under the specific identification cost flow assumption, a company identifies each unit sold and each unit remaining in the ending inventory, and includes the actual costs of those units in cost of goods sold and ending inventory. Under the FIFO cost flow assumption, a company includes the earliest costs incurred in the cost of goods sold and includes the most recent costs in the ending inventory. Under the average cost flow assumption, a company considers all the costs and units to be combined so that no individual units or costs can be identified. Under the weighted average method, a company computes an average cost for the period. Under the moving average method, a company computes an average cost after each acquisition of inventory. Under the LIFO cost flow assumption, a company includes the most recent costs incurred in the cost of goods sold and includes the earliest costs (including costs incurred in previous periods) in the ending inventory.
6. **Explain the conceptual issues regarding alternative inventory cost flow assumptions.** Conceptual issues include income measurement, income tax effects, liquidation of LIFO layers, earnings (income) management, inventory valuation, average cost, and management's selection of an inventory cost flow assumption.

7. **Understand dollar-value LIFO.** Exhibit 8-4 summarizes the four dollar-value calculation steps.
8. **Explain additional LIFO issues.** Additional LIFO issues include the LIFO valuation adjustment, interim statements using LIFO, a change to or from LIFO, and international accounting differences.
9. **Understand inventory disclosures.** Exhibit 8-5 illustrates the proportion of companies using various methods. Companies must disclose the inventory method, or methods, used. A company using LIFO must disclose the difference between the LIFO and the nonLIFO inventory value.
10. **Record foreign currency transactions involving inventory (Appendix).** A U.S. company records a credit purchase from (or sale to) a company in a foreign country in the usual way. An exchange gain or loss is caused by a change in the exchange rate between the date of the credit purchase (sale) and the date of the payment (receipt). It is recorded as the difference between the accounts payable (receivable) and cash payment (receipt).

ANSWERS TO REAL REPORT QUESTIONS

Real Report 8-1 Answers

1. General Mills' choice to use LIFO is appropriate for a company with rising inventory costs and appears to be driven primarily by tax considerations since LIFO will produce lower income amounts in periods of rising prices. Hewlett-Packard, which possesses a much larger inventory balance, uses FIFO, which is consistent with costs that fall over time (or increase very slowly) and results in relevant balance sheet amounts.
2. LIFO is generally not allowed for tax purposes in foreign countries. With this tax advantage eliminated and the fact that LIFO is typically more complex and costly to implement, the benefits of FIFO (higher income and balance sheet amounts in periods of rising prices) most likely outweigh any remaining benefits of using LIFO.
3. Given rising inventory costs, General Mills' decision to use LIFO will result in lower inventory values, earnings, and taxes (assuming the use of LIFO for income tax purposes) relative to FIFO.

4. The use of the LIFO cost flow assumption resulted in increased cash flow for General Mills. While reported earnings decreased $0.02 per share in the current fiscal year, the company was able to use LIFO for tax purposes, resulting in lower taxable income and increased cash flow. Additionally, if the company was still able to meet analyst expectations of earnings while using LIFO, the use of the LIFO assumption could be interpreted as a positive signal regarding the company's ability to generate future earnings.
5. The majority of Marathon Oil's inventory (92% and 91% at December 31, 2004 and 2003, respectively) is accounted for under the LIFO method which, during periods of rising prices, results in inventory layers with that have lower (noncurrent) costs attached to them. Even though total inventory increased from 2003 to 2004, Marathon Oil sold more inventory than it purchased at some point during the year causing the lower costs in inventory to be expensed. This liquidation of inventory valued at noncurrent costs led to lower cost of revenues (cost of goods sold) and higher income from operations.

QUESTIONS

Q8-1 Distinguish among the types of inventory accounts used for merchandising and manufacturing companies.

Q8-2 What are the cost components of each of the three inventory accounts of a manufacturing company?

Q8-3 Explain the differences between the perpetual and periodic inventory systems in terms of inventory quantity and cost. Does the use of a perpetual system eliminate the need for taking a physical inventory count?

Q8-4 What is the general rule used to determine if a company includes an item in inventory? Apply the concept to the accounting for goods in transit and goods on consignment.

Q8-5 Which of the following items does a manufacturing company include in its inventory account? (a) Goods in transit

purchased FOB shipping point, invoice received, (b) Raw materials, (c) Goods out on consignment, (d) Goods in transit sold to Breyer, Inc., shipped FOB destination, (e) Manufacturing supplies.

Q8-6 Which of these costs does a company include in its inventory cost? (a) Sales commissions, (b) Supervisor's salary, (c) Freight charges, (d) Indirect factory production labor, (e) Storage costs, (f) Corporate executive salaries.

Q8-7 Discuss the advantages and disadvantages of the two methods of accounting for purchases discounts taken in regard to management's needs, inventory cost, and the valuation of accounts payable.

Q8-8 What criteria should a company use to decide between alternative inventory cost flow assumptions?

Evaluate the relevance of the LIFO cost flow assumption. Why is LIFO not allowed under international accounting standards?

Q8-9 During a period of rising costs, indicate whether the LIFO cost flow assumption results in a larger or a smaller net income as compared to the FIFO cost flow assumption and explain why. Explain how a company's net income would compare during a period of falling costs.

Q8-10 Discuss the cost flow assumptions of the LIFO inventory method. Under what conditions would a company's ending inventory differ under a perpetual and a periodic LIFO system?

Q8-11 Explain the issue of inventory liquidation when a company uses the LIFO cost flow assumption. Why is this an issue exclusive to LIFO?

Q8-12 Discuss the LIFO and FIFO cost flow assumptions relative to the issue of holding gains (inventory profits).

Q8-13 Explain the dollar-value LIFO method of inventory valuation. What are the advantages of dollar-value LIFO as compared to simple LIFO?

Q8-14 Describe the double-extension and link-chain methods used in dollar-value LIFO and when each should be used.

Q8-15 When a company changes from FIFO to LIFO, what effect does the change have on its net income and working capital of the current period?

Q8-16 What is the impact of LIFO inventory liquidation on a company's interim financial statements?

Q8-17 **(Appendix)** Explain what causes an exchange gain or loss and when each occurs.

MULTIPLE CHOICE (AICPA Adapted)

Select the best answer for each of the following.

M8-1 The moving average inventory cost flow method is applicable to which of the following inventory systems?

	Periodic	Perpetual
a.	Yes	Yes
b.	Yes	No
c.	No	No
d.	No	Yes

Questions M8-2 and M8-3 are based on the following data: City Stationers, Inc., had 200 calculators on hand on January 1, 2007, costing $18 each. Purchases and sales of calculators during the month of January were as follows:

Date	Purchases	Sales
Jan. 12		150 @ $28
15	100 @ $20	
27	100 @ $22	
30		100 @ $32

City does not maintain perpetual inventory records. According to a physical count, 150 calculators were on hand at January 31, 2007.

M8-2 The cost of the inventory on January 31, 2007 under the FIFO method is
a. $400
b. $2,700
c. $3,100
d. $3,200

M8-3 The cost of the inventory on January 31, 2007 under the LIFO method is
a. $400
b. $2,700
c. $3,100
d. $3,200

M8-4 Goods on consignment should be included in the inventory of
a. The consignor but not the consignee
b. Both the consignor and the consignee
c. The consignee but not the consignor
d. Neither the consignor nor the consignee

M8-5 On December 31, 2006 Kern Company adopted the dollar-value LIFO inventory method. All of Kern's inventories constitute a single pool. The inventory on December 31, 2006 using the dollar-value LIFO inventory method, was $600,000. Inventory data for 2007 are as follows:

Dec. 31, 2007 inventory at year-end prices	$780,000
Relevant price index at year-end (base year 2006)	120

Under the dollar-value LIFO inventory method, Kern's inventory method, Kern's inventory on December 31, 2007 would be
a. $650,000
b. $655,000
c. $660,000
d. $720,000

M8-6 Assuming no beginning inventory, what can be said about the trend of inventory prices if cost of goods sold computed when inventory is valued using the FIFO method exceeds cost of goods sold when inventory is valued using the LIFO method?
a. Prices decreased.
b. Prices remained unchanged.
c. Prices increased.
d. Price trend *cannot* be determined from information given.

M8-7 Dixon Menswear Shop regularly buys shirts from Colt Company and is allowed trade discounts of 20% and

10% from the list price. Dixon purchased shirts from Colt on May 28, 2007, and received an invoice with a list price amount of $5,000, and payment terms of 2/10, n/30. Dixon uses the net method to record purchases. Dixon should record the purchase at
a. $3,600
b. $3,528
c. $3,500
d. $3,430

M8-8 The following items were included in Venicio Corporation's inventory account on December 31, 2007:

Merchandise out on consignment, at sales price,
  including 40% markup on selling price $14,000
Goods purchased, in transit, shipped F.O.B.
  shipping point   12,000
Goods held on consignment by Venicio   9,000

Venicio's inventory account at December 31, 2007 should be reduced by
a. $14,600
b. $17,400
c. $23,000
d. $35,000

M8-9 When the double-extension approach to the dollar-value LIFO inventory cost flow method is used, the inventory layer added in the current year is multiplied by an index number. How would the following be used in the calculation of this index number?

	Ending inventory at current-year cost	Ending inventory at base-year cost
a.	Numerator	Denominator
b.	Numerator	Not Used
c.	Denominator	Numerator
d.	Not Used	Denominator

M8-10 The LIFO inventory cost flow method may be applied to which of the following inventory systems?

	Periodic	Perpetual
a.	No	No
b.	No	Yes
c.	Yes	Yes
d.	Yes	No

EXERCISES

E8-1 *Inventory Accounts for a Manufacturing Company* The Fujita Company produces a single product. Costs accumulated at the end of the period are as follows:

Raw material purchases	$54,000	Production supervisor's salary	$ 20,000
Depreciation on manufacturing equipment	3,000	Shipping costs on units sold	43,500
Sales commissions	20,000	Materials used in production	81,400
Factory labor	36,000	Goods completed	115,000
Property tax on manufacturing equipment	3,500	Costs of units sold	150,000

Assume the beginning raw material inventory to be $67,400, the beginning finished goods inventory to be $123,500, and no beginning work in process inventory.

Required
Compute the closing account balances of each of the three inventory accounts: Raw Materials, Work in Process, and Finished Goods.

E8-2 *Goods in Transit* The Gravais Company made two purchases on December 29, 2007. One purchase for $3,000 was shipped FOB destination, and the second for $4,000 was shipped FOB shipping point. Neither purchase had been received on December 31, 2007.

Required
Which of these purchases, if either, does the Gravais Company include in inventory on December 31, 2007? What is the cost?

E8-3 *Items Included in Inventory* The following are several items that the controller of the Golosow Company has questioned regarding their inclusion in Inventory:

1. An invoice has been received for goods ordered. The goods were shipped FOB destination but have not been received.
2. Purchases have been ordered and received, but no invoice has arrived.
3. Product was shipped to a customer today, FOB destination, and the invoice mailed.
4. Purchases are in the receiving department but they are damaged and will be returned.
5. Product is in the shipping department and the invoice has not been mailed to the customer.
6. Product is in the receiving department. It was returned by a customer without notification.

Required
For each of the preceding items indicate whether Golosow should include them in Inventory.

E8-4   *Inventory Valuation* A retailer of washing machines receives a rebate of $25 per machine purchased if total purchases exceed 1,000 units. On reviewing the inventory records in December, it discovers that it has purchased 1,100 units during the year. The company claims the rebate immediately but it is not received until January.

Required

Prepare journal entries to record the claiming of the rebate and its receipt. What effect do these events have on the inventory valuation on December 31?

E8-5   *Discounts* The Hirsch Company buys inventory for $20,000 on terms of 2/10, n/30. It pays within the discount period.

Required

Prepare the journal entries to record the purchase and the payment under both the (1) gross price and (2) net price methods.

E8-6   *Discounts* The Nelson Company bought inventory for $50,000 on terms of 2/15, n/60. It pays for the first $37,500 of inventory purchased within the discount period and pays for the remaining $12,500 two months later.

Required

Prepare the journal entries to record the purchase and the payment under both the (1) gross price and (2) net price methods.

E8-7   *Alternative Inventory Methods* The Nevens Company uses a periodic inventory system. During November the following transactions occurred:

Date		Transaction	Units	Cost/Unit
November	1	Balance	500	$3.50
	8	Sale	350	
	13	Purchase	300	4.00
	21	Purchase	200	5.00
	28	Sale	150	

Required

Compute the cost of goods sold for November and the inventory at the end of November for each of the following cost flow assumptions:

1. FIFO
2. LIFO
3. Average cost

E8-8   *Alternative Inventory Methods* The perpetual inventory records of the Park Company indicate the following transactions in the month of June:

	Units	Cost/Unit
Inventory, June 1	200	$3.20
Purchases		
June 3	200	3.50
June 17	250	3.60
June 24	300	3.65
Sales		
June 6	300	
June 21	200	
June 27	150	

Required ⬚

Compute the cost of goods sold for June and the inventory at the end of June, using each of the following cost flow assumptions:

1. FIFO
2. LIFO
3. Average cost (round unit costs to 2 decimal places)

E8-9 | AICPA Adapted | *Alternative Inventory Methods* The Frate Company was formed on December 1, 2006. The following information is available from Frate's inventory records for Product Ply:

	Units	Unit Cost
January 1, 2007		
(beginning inventory)	800	$ 9.00
Purchases:		
January 6, 2007	1,500	10.00
January 24, 2007	1,200	10.50
February 17, 2007	600	11.00
March 27, 2007	900	11.50

A physical inventory on March 31, 2007 shows 1,600 units on hand.

Required
Prepare schedules to compute the ending inventory at March 31, 2007 under each of the following inventory methods:

1. FIFO
2. LIFO
3. Weighted average

Show supporting computations in good form.

E8-10 *LIFO, Perpetual and Periodic* The inventory records of the Riedel Company showed the following transactions for the fiscal period ended June 30:

	Units	Cost/Unit
June 1 Inventory	700	$6.20
June 3 Purchases	400	6.40
June 15 Sales @ $12.00	300	
June 22 Sales @ $12.50	600	
June 30 Purchases	600	6.70

Required
Compute the ending inventory and the cost of goods sold under the LIFO cost flow assumption, assuming both a perpetual and a periodic inventory system. Explain any difference in the final inventory valuations.

E8-11 *Dollar-Value LIFO* A company adopted the LIFO method when its inventory was $1,800. One year later its ending inventory was $2,100 and costs had increased 5% during the year.

Required
What is the ending inventory using dollar-value LIFO?

E8-12 *Dollar-Value LIFO* On January 1, 2006 the Sato Company adopted the dollar-value LIFO method of inventory costing. The company's ending inventory records appear as follows:

Year	Current Cost	Index
2006	$40,000	100
2007	56,100	120
2008	58,500	130
2009	70,000	140

Required 🖎
Compute the ending inventory for the years 2006, 2007, 2008, and 2009, using the dollar-value LIFO method (round to the nearest dollar).

E8-13 **AICPA Adapted** *Dollar-Value LIFO* The Belstock Company manufactures one product. On December 31, 2006 Belstock adopted the dollar-value LIFO inventory method. The inventory on that date, using the dollar-value LIFO inventory method, was $200,000. Inventory data for succeeding years are as follows:

Year	Inventory at Respective Year-End Prices	Price Index (Base Year 2006)
2007	$231,000	1.05
2008	299,000	1.15
2009	300,000	1.20

Required
Compute the inventory for the following dates using the dollar-value LIFO method for each year:

1. December 31, 2007,
2. December 31, 2008, and
3. December 31, 2009.

E8-14 **AICPA Adapted** *Dollar-Value LIFO* The Acute Company manufactures a single product. On December 31, 2006 Acute adopted the dollar-value LIFO inventory method. It computes the inventory on that date using the dollar-value LIFO inventory method as $300,000. Inventory data for succeeding years are as follows:

Year Ended December 31,	Inventory at Respective Year-End Prices	Relevant Price Index (Base Year 2003)
2007	$363,000	1.10
2008	420,000	1.20
2009	430,000	1.25

Required
Compute the inventory amounts at December 31, 2007, 2008, and 2009, using the dollar-value LIFO inventory method for each year.

E8-15 *Inventory Pools* The Stone Shoe Company adopted dollar-value LIFO on January 1, 2007. The company produces four products and uses a single inventory pool. The company's beginning inventory consists of the following:

Type	Quantity	Cost per Unit	Total Cost
Running	80,000	$16	$1,280,000
Tennis	30,000	15	450,000
Basketball	60,000	14	840,000
Soccer	40,000	17	680,000
	210,000		$3,250,000

During 2007, the company has the following purchases and sales:

Type	Quantity Purchased	Cost per Unit	Quantity Sold	Selling Price per Unit
Running	150,000	$19	140,000	$40
Tennis	130,000	16	100,000	38
Basketball	100,000	14	90,000	37
Soccer	120,000	18	140,000	42
	500,000		470,000	

Required
1. Compute the LIFO cost of the ending inventory. (Round the cost index to 4 decimal places.)
2. By how much would the company's gross profit be different if it had used four pools instead of a single pool?

E8-16 *FIFO Used Internally, LIFO Used Externally* The Grimstad Company uses FIFO for internal reporting purposes and LIFO for financial reporting and income tax purposes. At the end of 2007 the following information was obtained from the inventory records:

	2006	2007
Ending inventory, FIFO	$100,000	$140,000
Ending inventory, LIFO	80,000	115,000

Required

1. Prepare the necessary adjusting journal entry, assuming that the company converts the accounts to LIFO at the end of 2007.
2. Indicate how the company would disclose the inventory value on its comparative balance sheets prepared at the end of 2007.
3. By how much would the company's cost of goods sold be different in 2007 if it used FIFO for external reporting?

E8-17 *LIFO and Interim Financial Reports* The following values were obtained from the inventory records of the Harris Company, which has a fiscal year ending on December 31:

Inventory, January 1, 2007, LIFO	$80,000
Inventory, March 31, 2007, LIFO	70,000

Required

1. Under what conditions is the company's inventory liquidation not reflected in its first-quarter interim financial statements?
2. Assuming that the liquidation is not to be reflected, what adjusting worksheet entry would the company make and how would you determine the amount?

E8-18 *Exchange Gains and Losses (Appendix)* On January 15, 2007, the Searle Company, a U.S. company, acquired machinery on credit from a British company for £12,000. The company paid for the machine on January 30, 2007. The exchange rates on January 15 and 30 were $1.85 and $1.80, respectively.

Required

Record the journal entries for the acquisition and payment by the Searle Company.

E8-19 *Exchange Gains and Losses (Appendix)* On June 21, 2007, the Livingston Company, a U.S. company, sold merchandise on credit to a Swiss company for 25,000 francs. The company received payment for the merchandise on July 10, 2007. The exchange rates on June 21 and July 10 were $0.69 and $0.68, respectively.

Required

Record the journal entries for the sale and collection by the Livingston Company.

PROBLEMS

P8-1 *Items to Be Included in Inventory* As the auditor of the Hayes Company for the year ended December 31, 2007, you found the following transactions occurred near its closing date:

1. Merchandise received on January 8, 2008, and costing $800, was recorded on January 6, 2008. An invoice on hand showed the shipment was made FOB supplier's warehouse on December 31, 2007. Since the merchandise was not on hand at December 31, 2007, it was not included in the inventory.
2. A product costing $600 was in Hayes' shipping room when the physical inventory was taken. It was not included in the inventory because it was marked "Hold for customer's shipping instructions." Investigation revealed that the customer's order was dated December 18, 2007, but that the case was shipped and the customer billed on January 10, 2008.
3. A machine, made to order for a customer, was finished on December 31, 2007. The customer had inspected it and was satisfied with it. The customer was billed in full for $2,000 on that date. The machine was excluded from inventory although it was shipped on January 2, 2008.
4. Merchandise costing $800 was received on December 26, 2007, but a purchase was not recorded. The goods were "on consignment from Milliken Company."
5. Merchandise costing $4,000 was received on January 2, 2008, and the related purchase invoice recorded January 5. The invoice showed that the shipment was made on December 29, 2007, FOB destination.

Required

For each situation, state whether the Hayes Company should include the merchandise in its inventory. Give your reason for the decision on each item.

P8-2 *Valuation of Inventory* The inventory on hand at the end of 2007 for the Reddall Company is valued at a cost of $87,450. The following items were not included in this inventory:

1. Purchased goods in transit, under terms FOB shipping point, invoice price $3,700, freight costs $170.
2. Goods out on consignment to Marlman Company, sales price $2,800, shipping costs of $210.
3. Goods sold to Grina Co. under terms FOB destination, invoiced for $1,700, which included $251 freight charges to deliver the goods. Goods are in transit.

4. Goods held on consignment by the Reddall Company at a sales price of $2,700, which included sales commission of 20% of sales price.
5. Purchased goods in transit, shipped FOB destination, invoice price $2,100 which included freight charges of $190.

Required
Determine the cost of the ending inventory that Reddall should report on its December 31, 2007 balance sheet, assuming that its selling price is 140% of the cost of the inventory.

P8-3 *Cost of Sales* As an accountant for the Lee Company, your supervisor gave you the following calculations of the gross profit for the first quarter:

Alternative	Sales ($50 per unit)	Cost of Goods Sold	Gross Profit
A	$500,000	$200,000	$300,000
B	500,000	228,000	272,000
C	500,000	213,333	286,667

The three alternative cost flow assumptions are FIFO, Average, and LIFO (the alternatives are not necessarily presented in this sequence). The company uses the periodic inventory system. The computation of the cost of goods sold under each alternative is based on the following data:

	Units	Cost/Unit
Inventory, January 1	12,000	$20
Purchase, January 10	4,000	21
Purchase, February 15	6,000	22
Purchase, March 10	8,000	23

Required
Prepare schedules computing the ending inventory (in units and dollars) and proving the cost of goods sold shown here under each of the three alternatives.

P8-4 *Discounts* On April 11, Edwards Construction Company purchased inventory for $20,000 on terms of 2/10, n/30. It pays the account balance on April 21.

Required
1. Prepare the journal entries to record the purchase and payment using each of the following methods: (a) gross price, (b) net price.
2. If the company sold half the inventory during April for $12,000, how much income would it recognize under each method?
3. Assume that the invoice was misfiled and, as a result, the company did not pay until April 30. Prepare the journal entries to record the purchase and payment under each of the methods. If the company sold half the inventory during April for $12,000, how much income would it recognize under each method?

P8-5 *Alternative Inventory Methods* The Garrett Company has the following transactions during the months of April and May:

Date		Transaction	Units	Cost/Unit
April	1	Balance	400	
	17	Purchase	200	$5.50
	25	Sale	150	
	28	Purchase	100	5.75
May	5	Purchase	250	5.50
	18	Sale	300	
	22	Sale	50	

The cost of the inventory on April 1 is $5, $4, and $2 per unit, respectively, under the FIFO, average, and LIFO cost flow assumptions.

Required

1. Compute the costs of goods sold for each month and the inventories at the end of each month for the following alternatives:
   a. FIFO periodic
   b. FIFO perpetual
   c. LIFO periodic
   d. LIFO perpetual
   e. Weighted average (round unit costs to 2 decimal places)
   f. Moving average (round unit costs to 2 decimal places)
2. Reconcile the difference between the LIFO periodic and the LIFO perpetual results.

P8-6   *Alternative Inventory Methods* The Totman Company has the following transactions during the months of January and February:

Date		Transaction	Units	Cost/Unit
January	1	Balance	200	
	10	Purchase	50	$25
	22	Sale	40	
	28	Purchase	60	$27
February	4	Purchase	40	$28
	14	Sale	50	
	23	Sale	20	

The cost of the inventory at January 1 is $24, $23, and $15 per unit, respectively, under the FIFO, average, and LIFO cost flow assumptions.

Required

1. Compute the cost of goods sold for each month and the inventories at the end of each month for the following alternatives:
   a. FIFO periodic
   b. FIFO perpetual
   c. LIFO periodic
   d. LIFO perpetual
   e. Weighted average (round unit costs to 2 decimal places)
   f. Moving average (round unit costs to 2 decimal places)
2. Reconcile the difference between the LIFO periodic and the LIFO perpetual results.
3. If the company had purchased an additional 25 units for $30 each on February 27, compute the cost of goods sold for February under FIFO periodic and LIFO periodic.
4. For February, compute the company's inventory turnover under the FIFO and LIFO periodic methods. Use ending inventory instead of average inventory for convenience. Which measure would you use in your evaluation of the company? How would you convert a monthly inventory turnover into an annual measure to use for comparison with other companies? What assumptions are involved?

P8-7   *Alternative Inventory Methods* The Habicht Company was formed in 2006 to produce a single product. The production and sales for the next four years were as follows:

	Production		Sales		Units in Ending Inventory
	Units	Total Costs	Units	Sales Revenue	
2006	100,000	$200,000	80,000	$400,000	20,000
2007	120,000	234,000	110,000	550,000	30,000
2008	130,000	247,000	150,000	750,000	10,000
2009	130,000	240,500	120,000	600,000	20,000

Required
1. Determine the gross profit for each year under each of the following periodic inventory methods:
   a. FIFO
   b. LIFO
   c. Average cost (round unit costs to 3 decimal places)
2. Explain whether the company's return on assets (net income divided by average total assets, as we discussed in Chapter 6) would be higher under FIFO or LIFO.

P8-8   AICPA Adapted   *LIFO and Inventory Pools*   On January 1, 2004 Grover Company changed its inventory cost flow method to the LIFO cost method from the FIFO cost method for its raw materials inventory. It made the change for both financial statement and income tax reporting purposes. Grover uses the multiple-pools approach, under which it groups substantially identical raw materials into LIFO inventory pools; it uses weighted average costs in valuing annual incremental layers. The composition of the December 31, 2006 inventory for the Class F inventory pool is as follows:

	Units	Weighted Average Unit Cost	Total Cost
Base year inventory—2004	9,000	$10.00	$ 90,000
Incremental layer—2005	3,000	11.00	33,000
Incremental layer—2006	2,000	12.50	25,000
Inventory, December 31, 2006	14,000		$148,000

Inventory transactions for the Class F inventory pool during 2007 were as follows:
- On March 2, 2007, 4,800 units were purchased at a unit cost of $13.50 for $64,800.
- On September 1, 2007, 7,200 units were purchased at a unit cost of $14.00 for $100,800.
- A total of 15,000 units were used for production during 2007.

The following transactions for the Class F inventory pool took place during 2008:
- On January 11, 2008, 7,500 units were purchased at a unit cost of $14.50 for $108,750.
- On May 14, 2008, 5,500 units were purchased at a unit cost of $15.50 for $85,250.
- On December 29, 2008, 7,000 units were purchased at a unit cost of $16.00 for $112,000.
- A total of 16,000 units were used for production during 2008.

Required
1. Prepare a schedule to compute the inventory (units and dollar amounts) of the Class F inventory pool at December 31, 2007. Show supporting computations in good form.
2. Prepare a schedule to compute the cost of Class F raw materials used in production for the year ended December 31, 2007.
3. Prepare a schedule to compute the inventory (units and dollar amounts) of the Class F inventory pool at December 31, 2008. Show supporting computations in good form.

P8-9   *Dollar-Value LIFO*   The Olson Company adopted the dollar-value LIFO method for inventory valuation at the beginning of 2006. The following information about the inventory at the end of each year is available from the company records:

Year	Current Costs	Index
2005	$50,000	100
2006	60,000	108
2007	70,000	115
2008	73,000	125
2009	78,000	135

Required
1. Calculate the dollar-value LIFO inventory at the end of each year.
2. Prepare the appropriate disclosures for the year 2009 annual report if the company uses current cost internally and LIFO for financial reporting. Why would the company use current cost internally?

P8-10 *Dollar-Value LIFO* The Kwestel Company adopted the dollar-value LIFO method for inventory valuation at the beginning of 2006. The following information about the inventory at the end of each year is available from the company records:

Year	Current Cost	Index
2005	$ 8,000	100
2006	10,800	120
2007	11,500	130
2008	14,000	145
2009	10,500	125

Required

Calculate the dollar-value LIFO inventory at the end of each year.

P8-11 *Dollar-Value LIFO and Inventory Pools* The Webster Company adopted dollar-value LIFO on January 1, 2007. The company produces three products: X, Y, and Z. The company's beginning inventory consisted of the following:

Type	Quantity	Cost per Unit	Total Cost
X	30,000	$4.25	$127,500
Y	10,000	3.50	35,000
Z	25,000	2.00	50,000
	65,000		$212,500

During 2007, the company had the following purchases and sales:

Type	Quantity Purchased	Cost per Unit	Quantity Sold	Selling Price per Unit
X	110,000	$4.75	90,000	$10.00
Y	100,000	3.75	85,000	7.50
Z	75,000	2.10	70,000	5.00
	285,000		245,000	

Required

1. Compute the LIFO cost of the ending inventory assuming Webster Company uses a single inventory pool. (Round cost index to 4 decimal places.)
2. Compute the LIFO cost of the ending inventory assuming Webster Company uses three inventory pools. (Round cost indexes to 4 decimal places.)

P8-12 *Comprehensive* The Kelly Company adopted dollar-value LIFO on January 1, 2006 using two inventory pools, each of which includes two types of inventory items. The following information about the inventory at the end of each year is available:

	Pool 1			Pool 2		
Year	Number of Units	Type	Average Cost per Unit	Number of Units	Type	Average Cost per Unit
2006	20,000	A	$10	40,000	C	$5
	10,000	B	20	20,000	D	8
2007	30,000	A	11	50,000	C	7
	12,000	B	24	22,000	D	9
2008	40,000	A	12	46,000	C	6
	14,000	B	22	20,000	D	8
2009	45,000	A	12	60,000	C	7
	13,000	B	25	25,000	D	8

Required

1. Compute the cost index for each year for each pool using a base of 100 for each index. (Round each cost index to 4 decimal places.)
2. Compute the dollar-value LIFO inventory at the end of each year.

P8-13 **AICPA Adapted** *Double-Extension: Dollar-Value LIFO* On January 1, 2007 Lucas Distributors, Inc., adopted the dollar-value LIFO inventory method for income tax and external financial reporting. However, Lucas continued to use the FIFO inventory method for internal accounting and management purposes. In applying the LIFO method, Lucas uses internal conversion cost indexes and the multiple-pools approach under which substantially identical inventory items are grouped into LIFO inventory pools. The following data were available for Inventory Pool No. 1, which is comprised of products A and B, for the 2 years following the adoption of LIFO:

	FIFO Basis per Records		
	Units	Unit Cost	Total Cost
Inventory, 1/1/07			
Product A	12,000	$30	$360,000
Product B	8,000	25	200,000
			$560,000
Inventory, 12/31/07			
Product A	17,000	$35	$595,000
Product B	9,000	28	252,000
			$847,000
Inventory, 12/31/08			
Product A	13,000	$40	$520,000
Product B	10,000	32	320,000
			$840,000

Required

1. Prepare a schedule to compute the internal conversion cost indexes for 2007 and 2008. Round indexes to two decimal places.
2. Prepare a schedule to compute the inventory amounts at December 31, 2007 and 2008, using the dollar-value LIFO inventory method.

P8-14 *LIFO Liquidation Profit* The Hammond Company adopted LIFO when it was formed on January 1, 2005. Since then, the company has had the following purchases and sales of its single inventory item:

Year	Units Purchased	Cost per Unit	Units Sold	Price per Unit
2005	10,000	$5	8,000	$12
2006	12,000	6	9,000	13
2007	15,000	8	14,000	16

In December 2008, the controller realized that because of an unexpected increase in demand, the company had sold 22,000 units but had purchased only 19,000 units during the year. In 2008, each unit had been sold for $19, and each unit purchased had cost $10. The income tax rate is 30%.

Required

1. If the company makes no additional purchases in 2008, how much LIFO liquidation profit will it report?
2. Prepare the appropriate annual report disclosures for 2008.
3. If the company purchases an additional 7,000 units in December 2008, how much income tax will the company save?
4. If the company purchases the additional 7,000 units, how much income tax has the company saved over the four-year period by using LIFO instead of the FIFO cost flow assumption?

P8-15 *Comprehensive* The following information for 2007 is available for the Marino Company:

1. The beginning inventory is $100,000.
2. Purchases of $300,000 were made on terms of 2/10, n/30. Eighty percent of the discounts were taken.
3. Purchases returns of $4,000 were made.
4. At December 31, purchases of $20,000 were in transit, FOB destination, on terms of 2/10, n/30.
5. The company made sales of $640,000. The gross selling price per unit is twice the net cost of each unit sold.
6. Sales allowances of $6,000 were made.
7. The company uses the LIFO periodic method and the gross method for purchases discounts.

Required
1. Compute the cost of the ending inventory before the physical inventory is taken.
2. Compute the amount of the cost of goods sold that came from the purchases of the period and the amount that came from the beginning inventory.

P8-16 **AICPA Adapted** *Inventory Valuation* You are engaged in an audit of the Roche Mfg. Company for the year ended December 31, 2007. To reduce the workload at year-end, the company took its annual physical inventory under your observation on November 30, 2007. The company's inventory account, which includes raw materials and work in process, is on a perpetual basis and it uses the first-in, first-out method of pricing. It has no finished goods inventory. The company's physical inventory revealed that the book inventory of $60,570 was understated by $3,000. To avoid distorting the interim financial statements, the company decided not to adjust the book inventory until year-end except for obsolete inventory items. Your audit revealed this information about the November 30 inventory:
a. Pricing tests showed that the physical inventory was overpriced by $2,200.
b. Footing and extension errors resulted in a $150 understatement of the physical inventory.
c. Direct labor included in the physical inventory amounted to $10,000. Overhead was included at the rate of 200% of direct labor. You determined that the amount of direct labor was correct and the overhead rate was proper.
d. The physical inventory included obsolete materials recorded at $250. During December, these materials were removed from the inventory account by a charge to cost of sales. Your audit also disclosed the following information about the December 31, 2007 inventory.
e. Total debits to certain accounts during December are:

	December
Purchases	$24,700
Direct labor	12,100
Manufacturing overhead expense	25,200
Cost of sales	68,600

f. The cost of sales of $68,600 included direct labor of $13,800.
g. Normal scrap loss on established product lines is negligible. However, a special order started and completed during December had excessive scrap loss of $800, which was charged to Manufacturing Overhead Expense.

Required
1. Compute the correct amount of the physical inventory at November 30, 2007.
2. Without prejudice to your solution to Requirement 1, assume that the correct amount of the inventory at November 30, 2007 was $57,700. Compute the amount of the inventory at December 31, 2007.

P8-17 **AICPA Adapted** *Comprehensive* The Allen Company is a wholesale distributor of automotive replacement parts. Initial amounts taken from Allen's accounting records are as follows:

Inventory at December 31, 2007 (based on physical	
count of goods in Allen's warehouse on December 31, 2007)	$1,250,000

| Sales in 2007 | $9,000,000 |

Accounts payable at December 31, 2007:

Vendor	Terms	Amount
Baker Company	2% 10 days, net 30	$ 265,000
Charlie Company	Net 30	210,000
Dolly Company	Net 30	300,000
Eager Company	Net 30	225,000
Full Company	Net 30	—
Greg Company	Net 30	—
		$1,000,000

Additional information is as follows:
1. Parts held on consignment from Charlie to Allen, the consignee, amounting to $155,000, were included in the physical count of goods in Allen's warehouse on December 31, 2007 and in accounts payable at December 31, 2007.
2. $22,000 of parts, which were purchased from Full and paid for in December 2007 were sold in the last week of 2007 and appropriately recorded as sales of $28,000. The parts were included in the physical count of goods in Allen's warehouse on December 31, 2007 because the parts were on the loading dock waiting to be picked up by customers.

3. Parts in transit on December 31, 2007 to customers, shipped FOB shipping point on December 28, 2007, amounted to $34,000. The customers received the parts on January 7, 2008. Sales of $40,000 to the customers for the parts were recorded by Allen on January 3, 2008.

4. Retailers were holding $210,000 at cost ($250,000 at retail) of goods on consignment from Allen, the consignor, at their stores on December 31, 2007.

5. Goods were in transit from Greg to Allen on December 31, 2007. The cost of the goods was $25,000, and they were shipped FOB shipping point on December 29, 2007.

6. A quarterly freight bill in the amount of $2,000 specifically relating to merchandise purchases in December 2007, all of which was still in the inventory at December 31, 2007, was received on January 4, 2008. The freight bill was not included in either the inventory or in accounts payable at December 31, 2007.

7. All of the purchases from Baker occurred during the last seven days of the year. These items have been recorded in accounts payable and accounted for in the physical inventory at cost before discount. Allen's policy is to pay invoices in time to take advantage of all cash discounts, adjust inventory accordingly, and record accounts payable, net of cash discounts.

Required 🖎

Prepare a schedule of adjustments to the initial amounts of inventory, accounts payable, and sales. Show the effect, if any, of each of the transactions separately and indicate if the transactions would have no effect on the amount.

CASES

COMMUNICATION

C8-1   Dollar-Value LIFO

AICPA Adapted In January Broome, Inc., requested and secured permission from the Commissioner of Internal Revenue to compute inventories under the last-in, first-out (LIFO) method and elected to determine inventory cost under the dollar-value method. Broome, Inc., satisfied the Commissioner that cost could be accurately determined by use of an index number computed from a representative sample selected from the Company's single inventory pool.

Required

1. Why should a company include inventories in (a) its statement of financial position and (b) the computation of its net income?

2. The Internal Revenue Code allows some accountable events to be considered differently for income tax reporting purposes and financial accounting purposes, while other accountable events must be reported the same for both purposes. Discuss why it might be desirable to report some accountable events differently for financial accounting purposes than for income tax reporting purposes.

3. Discuss the ways and conditions under which the FIFO and LIFO inventory costing methods produce different inventory valuations. Do not discuss procedures for computing inventory cost.

4. Discuss the specific advantages and disadvantages of using the dollar-value LIFO application as compared to traditional LIFO methods. Ignore income tax considerations.

C8-2   FIFO and LIFO

AICPA Adapted *Part a.* A company may compute inventory under one of various cost flow assumptions. Among these assumptions are first-in, first-out (FIFO) and last-in, first-out (LIFO). In the past, some companies have changed from FIFO to LIFO for computing portions or all of their inventory.

Required

1. Ignoring income tax, explain what effects a change from FIFO to LIFO has on a company's net earnings and working capital.

2. Explain the difference between the FIFO assumption of earnings and operating cycle and the LIFO assumption of earnings and operating cycle.

Part b. A company using LIFO inventory may establish a "Reserve for the Replacement of LIFO Inventory" account.

Required

Explain why and how a company establishes this "reserve" account and where it should show the account on its statement of financial position.

C8-3 Cash Discounts, FIFO, and LIFO

AICPA Adapted Taylor Company, a household appliances dealer, purchases its inventories from various suppliers. Taylor has consistently stated its inventories at the lower of cost (FIFO) or market.

Required

1. Taylor is considering alternate methods of accounting for the cash discounts it takes when paying its suppliers promptly. From a theoretical standpoint, discuss the acceptability of each of the following methods:
   a. Financial income when payments are made.
   b. Reduction of cost of goods sold for period when payments are made.
   c. Direct reduction of purchase cost.
2. Identify the effects on both the balance sheet and the income statement of a company using the LIFO inventory method instead of the FIFO method over a substantial time period when purchase prices of household appliances are rising. State why these effects take place.

C8-4 Specific Identification

AICPA Adapted Happlia Co. imports expensive household appliances. Each model has many variations and each unit has an identification number. Happlia pays all costs for getting the goods from the port to its central warehouse in Des Moines. After repackaging, the goods are consigned to retailers. A retailer makes a sale, simultaneously buys the appliance from Happlia, and pays the balance due within one week.

To alleviate the overstocking of refrigerators at a Minneapolis retailer, some were reshipped to a Kansas City retailer where they were still held in inventory at December 31, 2007. Happlia paid the costs of this reshipment.

Happlia uses the specific identification inventory costing method.

Required

1. In regard to the specific identification inventory costing method
   a. Describe its key elements.
   b. Discuss why it is appropriate for Happlia to use this method.
2. a. What general criteria should Happlia use to determine inventory carrying amounts at December 31, 2007? Ignore lower of cost or market considerations.
   b. Give four examples of costs included in these inventory carrying amounts.
3. What costs should be reported in Happlia's 2007 income statement? Ignore lower of cost or market considerations.

CREATIVE AND CRITICAL THINKING

C8-5 Cash Discounts

AICPA Adapted The Atgar Corporation records all purchases and the corresponding liabilities net of cash discounts. Whenever it pays after the discount period, it credits cash for the full amount of the invoice, and debits accounts payable for the net amount and an expense account for the discount lost.

Required

Explain the arguments for and against this treatment of cash discounts.

C8-6 Purchases Discounts

The Auge Company annually purchases 1,000 tons of raw material at a cost of $100,000 with terms of 2/10, n/30. Freight costs amount to $10,000 and storage and handling costs to $7,500.

Required

1. What is the correct inventory cost?
2. Explain whether your answer to Requirement 1 would change if the discount were not taken.
3. Would your answer to Requirement 1 change if the storage and handling costs were fixed costs and therefore not dependent on the volume of material stored?

C8-7 Cost Flow Assumptions

AICPA Adapted A company should determine cost for inventory purposes by the inventory cost flow method most clearly reflecting its periodic income.

Required

1. Explain the fundamental cost flow assumptions of the average cost, FIFO, and LIFO inventory cost flow methods.
2. Discuss the reasons a company uses LIFO in an inflationary economy.
3. Where there is evidence that the utility of goods, in their disposal in the ordinary course of business, will be less than cost, explain the proper accounting treatment and under what concept that treatment is justified.

C8-8 LIFO

The 1970s were a period of historically high inflation. The 1976 financial statements of the Ford Motor Company included the following note:

Note 1 (in part): Inventory valuation. Inventories are stated at the lower of cost or market. In 1976 the company changed its method of accounting from first-in, first-out (FIFO) to last-in, first-out (LIFO) for most of its U.S. inventories.

The change to LIFO reduced net income in 1976 by $81 million or $0.86 a share. There is no effect on prior years' earnings resulting from the change to LIFO in 1976 and, accordingly, prior years' earnings have not been restated. If the FIFO method of inventory accounting had been used by the company, inventories on December 31, 1976, would have been $166 million higher than reported.

Required
1. Explain the arguments that must have been used in favor of LIFO for the management of Ford to accept a reduction in net income of $81 million.
2. Explain the disadvantages that are likely to result from the adoption of LIFO.
3. Explain why the effect on earnings is $81 million when the effect on the inventory valuation is $166 million.
4. Explain whether your answers to Requirements 1 and 2 would change if you were discussing a change to LIFO for a Ford dealer.

C8-9 Selection of an Inventory Method and Ethical Issues

The Kelly Company uses FIFO. It has experienced rising costs for the last 5 years and expects that trend to continue. The King Company increased the number of LIFO pools it uses to account for its inventory.

Required
1. Explain why you think each company follows its policy.
2. Does either practice create ethical issues?

C8-10 Interpretation of GAAP and Ethical Issues

Robin Smith is considering buying shares in the Mah Company. The company has reported an increase in net income this year. On careful reading of the notes to the financial statements, Robin learns that the company had a LIFO liquidation this year. Robin understands what caused the liquidation but has asked you for advice about how to interpret it.

Required
1. Prepare a short memo to Robin to answer the question.
2. Could a LIFO liquidation profit create ethical issues?

C8-11 Exchange Rates (Appendix)

The Gasper Company has transactions with companies in many countries. It purchases components from companies in Korea and several European countries and sells its products throughout the world. The CEO is concerned that the stock market does not like companies to have volatile earnings. However, she is more willing to accept volatility if earnings are higher than they otherwise would be.

Required
Select a type of business with which you are familiar and that would be appropriate for Gasper Company's international activities. Write a memo to the CEO outlining how to eliminate her concerns.

C8-12 Analyzing Coca-Cola's Inventory Disclosures

Refer to the financial statements and related notes of the Coca-Cola Company in Appendix A of this book.

Required
1. Which inventory method(s) does the company use? Explain why you think the company selected this method(s).
2. Compute the inventory turnover ratio for 2004 and 2003 using the ending inventory instead of the average inventory. What is your evaluation of the difference?
3. Recreate summary journal entries to record the transactions that affected inventory during 2004.

C8-13 Ethics and Free Textbooks

Textbook publishers provide a copy of a particular book to each professor who is making a decision about adopting a book for the class. These books may be solicited by the professor or may be unsolicited. Some of the books are stamped "For Faculty Use Only." "Used book" companies send out reps who are reimbursed for their travel expenses and are paid a commission to buy these books from the professors at a low price. A lot of these books are purchased at the end of spring, held as inventory over the summer, and sold to university bookstores before the beginning of fall classes. The bookstores sell them to students or return them. Depending on the condition of the book, it is sold to students as either "new" or "used."

Required
From financial reporting and ethical perspectives, discuss the issues raised by the above situation.

RESEARCH SIMULATIONS

R8-1 Researching GAAP

Situation
To pump up sales of all brands, **Philip Morris** is moving aggressively to ship extra cases of cigarettes into distributors' warehouses and record them as sales, a practice generally known as "trade loading." (Adapted from *Fortune*, April 6, 1992). Philip Morris' president has asked you whether these shipments may be recognized as revenue.

Directions
Research the related generally accepted accounting principles and prepare a short memo to the president. Cite your references and applicable paragraph numbers.

R8-2 Researching GAAP

Situation

The Fenimore Manufacturing Company uses the average cost method. It has followed a policy of expensing all its manufacturing cost variances. It is considering a change in its policy that will involve allocating them between cost of goods sold and inventory. Fenimore's president has asked you which of these alternative policies is consistent with GAAP.

Directions

Research the related generally accepted accounting principles and prepare a short memo to the president. Cite your references and applicable paragraph numbers.

9

Inventories: Special Valuation Issues

Relationships That Matter

Inventory is a major asset of many companies, and the measurement of inventory involves management decisions that have a major impact on both the balance sheet and the income statement. Accordingly, financial statement users will pay close attention to inventory changes as they assess the financial health of companies. Typically, increases in raw materials and work-in-process inventories signal increases in production to meet higher anticipated future demand. Increases in finished goods inventory, on the other hand, typically indicate lower demand.

Perceptive users need to understand some special valuation issues related to inventory so that they can more clearly understand inventory's impact on the financial statements. For example, assuming that costs and selling prices move together, a decrease in the cost of inventory may signal a future decline in selling price and usefulness of inventory. Following the principle of conservatism, companies employ a lower of cost or market rule so that they will report inventory losses as soon as they discover them. Other companies, with large amounts of inventory, may

OBJECTIVES

After reading this chapter, you will be able to:

1. Understand the lower of cost or market method.

2. Explain the conceptual issues regarding the lower of cost or market method.

3. Understand purchase obligations and product financing arrangements.

4. Explain the valuation of inventory above cost.

5. Use the gross profit method.

6. Understand the retail inventory method.

7. Explain the conceptual issues regarding the retail inventory method.

8. Understand the dollar-value LIFO retail method.

9. Understand the effects of inventory errors on the financial statements.

Credit: Comstock Images

find it either impractical to conduct physical inventory counts to prepare interim reports or inefficient to maintain records of individual inventory purchases. Recognizing the relationship between the costs of inventory purchases and selling prices, a company may be able to more efficiently manage its inventory using estimation techniques such as the retail inventory method. In any event, an understanding of key relationships between inventory and other financial and economic phenomena is essential for effective inventory management and control.

FOR FURTHER INVESTIGATION

For a discussion of the relationship between inventory and the business cycle, consult the Business & Company Resource Center (BCRC):

- Inventories and the Business Cycle: An Overview. Terry J. Fitzgerald, *Economic Review (Cleveland)*, 0013-0281, Summer 1997, v33, n3, p11.

In Chapter 8 we described the various methods to determine the historical cost of inventory. In certain situations a company does not report its inventory at the historical cost. The alternatives to historical cost are valuation at the lower of cost or market, valuation above cost, and estimation of cost by the gross profit or retail inventory methods, including the dollar-value LIFO retail inventory method. We discuss each of these topics in this chapter, as well as purchase obligations, product financing arrangements, and the effects of errors in inventory on a company's financial statements.

LOWER OF COST OR MARKET

1 Understand the lower of cost or market method.

Valuation of inventory at historical cost, based on the cost flow assumption used, is modified when the market value of a company's inventory has declined below its historical cost. This might occur for reasons such as declining costs, obsolescence, or physical deterioration. In these situations the lower of cost or market rule is applied. **The lower of cost or market rule requires that a company write down its inventory to its market value when the inventory's utility has declined.** The write-down of the inventory is appropriate because the utility of the asset has declined. Also, to leave the inventory at its historical cost would overstate both its value and the expected future cash inflows. The lower of cost or market rule is consistent with the conservatism principle. Since the company writes down the asset, it reports a loss (or expense) in its income statement because the decline is an economic event of the period.[1]

Since utility is difficult to measure except through a changed market value, the measurement of the decline in utility is, in practice, always made by valuing the inventory at the lower of cost or market (LCM). **Market value is the current replacement cost** (either by purchase or manufacture) and *not* the selling price.

Application of Lower of Cost or Market Method

When a company applies the lower of cost or market method, it compares the cost to the market value. It does not always use the current replacement cost as the market value, however. An upper (*ceiling*) and a lower (*floor*) constraint on the market value are imposed as follows:

1. **The upper constraint is that the market value should not exceed the net realizable value** (the estimated selling price in the ordinary course of business, less reasonably predictable costs of completion and disposal).
2. **The lower constraint is that the market value should not be below the net realizable value, reduced by an allowance for a normal profit margin** (normal markup).

These two constraints are used to determine which "market value" (current replacement cost, ceiling, or floor) is to be compared to cost. Note that the appropriate market value is determined before the comparison with the cost is made. **The purpose of the ceiling is to ensure that the write-down of the inventory is enough to cover all expected losses and therefore prevent the recognition of further losses in the future.** In contrast, **the purpose of the floor is to prevent an excessive loss from being recognized and therefore prevent the recognition of excessive profits in the future** (as we discuss later in this section).

---

1. "Restatement and Revision of Accounting Research Bulletins," *Accounting Research Bulletins, Final Edition, No. 43* (New York: AICPA, 1961), ch. 4, par. 7.

Thus, to apply the lower of cost or market (LCM) method a company completes three steps: it (1) selects the market value, (2) compares the market value to cost, and (3) reports the results in its financial statements, as we show in the following diagram:

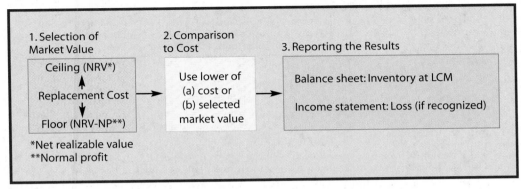

In the first step, the company calculates the current replacement cost, ceiling, and floor. It selects the middle value of the three. Then, it chooses the lower of the selected market value or the historical cost. Finally, the company reports the lower value on its balance sheet and, if it recognizes a loss, it reports the amount on the income statement, perhaps including it in cost of goods sold.

To illustrate the first step in the application of the lower of cost or market method, suppose that a company's unit of inventory has the following characteristics:

Selling price	$165
Packaging cost	10
Transportation cost	15
Profit margin	40

The company computes the ceiling and floor as follows:

Selling price	$165
Less: Costs of completion (i.e., packaging)	(10)
Costs of disposal (i.e., transportation)	(15)
Ceiling (net realizable value)	$140
Less: Normal profit margin	(40)
Floor (net realizable value less normal profit)	$100

If the current replacement cost is between $100 and $140, it would be used as the market value. If the replacement cost is above $140, the ceiling would be used; if the replacement cost is below $100, the floor would be used.

We show all three steps in applying the lower of cost or market method in Example 9-1 for a single unit of inventory. We use Cases 5 and 6 to explain the logic behind the ceiling and floor. If in Case 5 the ceiling constraint was ignored and the current replacement cost was used as market, the inventory would be written down only to $105 and a loss of $5 would be recognized. However, in a later period when the unit is sold for $90 (net), there would be an additional loss of $15. Therefore, the inventory would not have been written down to its expected utility, and the total loss due to the decline in utility would not have been recognized in the period in which it occurred. Imposing an upper limit of net realizable value ensures that the full decline in utility is recognized in the period in which it occurred. At first it might be considered unusual that the net realizable value is below the replacement cost (of a new asset), but this can happen when there is physical deterioration to the inventory. If the volume of such items becomes significant, they should be transferred to a separate account.

If the floor constraint was ignored in Case 6 and the current replacement cost was used as market, the inventory would be written down to $80 and a loss of $30 would be recognized. However, in a later period when the unit is sold for $140 (net), there would

EXAMPLE 9-1   **Application of the Lower of Cost or Market Rule**

Case	Current Replacement Cost	Net Realizable Value (Ceiling)	Net Realizable Value Less a Normal Markup (Floor)	Market (Constrained by Ceiling and Floor)	Cost	Lower of Cost or Market Inventory Value*	Loss
1	$120	$140	$100	$120	$110	$110	$ 0
2	150	140	100	140	110	110	0
3	75	140	120	120	110	110	0
4	105	140	100	105	110	105	5
5	105	90	80	90	110	90	20
6	80	140	100	100	110	100	10

*Cases 1, 2 and 3: Cost is used because it is lower than market.
Case 4: Replacement cost is used because it is between floor and ceiling and is less than cost.
Case 5: Net realizable value (ceiling) is used because replacement cost is higher than ceiling and net realizable value is less than cost.
Case 6: Net realizable value less a normal markup (floor) is used because replacement cost is less than floor and net realizable value less a normal markup is less than cost.

be a profit of $60, which is higher than the normal profit of $40. Therefore, the inventory would have been written down below its expected utility, and an excessive loss followed by an excessive profit would have been recognized. Imposing a lower limit of net realizable value less normal profit prevents a write-down below the expected utility of the inventory and the arbitrary transfer of profit from one accounting period to another.

Conceptual Evaluation of the Ceiling and Floor

The implicit assumption for the lower of cost or market method is that selling (exit) prices move in parallel to replacement costs (entry prices) within the constraints of the ceiling and floor. While the two prices are likely to move together, there will be exceptions. Also, the lower of cost or market method may be criticized because it uses three different concepts for the loss recognized in the period. This loss recognition also affects the amount of profit a company will recognize in future periods. These differences create conceptual inconsistencies both within the lower of cost or market method and between that method and other conservative methods.

To illustrate these issues, assume the following facts for 1 unit of inventory of the Sahara Company, a retailer:

Cost: $19
Ceiling: 14   (Net realizable value)
Floor: 10   (Net realizable value − Normal profit)

Situation 1

If we also assume that the replacement cost is $15, the ceiling of $14 is used as the market value. Why would the Sahara Company sell an item for $14 when the replacement cost is $15? One explanation would be that the supplier of the inventory has set a lower price on a new product so that the inventory held by the Sahara Company has become obsolete.

The loss in the period of the *write-down* is equal to the net realizable value (ceiling) less the historical cost. The expected profit in the period of *sale* is equal to the net realizable value less the ceiling (the new carrying value of the inventory). The loss and expected profit are:

$$\textbf{Loss in period of write-down} = \$14 - \$19$$
$$= \underline{\underline{\$(5)}}$$

$$\textbf{Expected profit in period of sale} = \$14 - \$14$$
$$= \underline{\underline{\$\ 0}}$$

The loss of $5 is a measure of the expected loss that *would* have been recognized at the time of sale if the lower of cost or market rule had *not* been used. The loss is recognized in the current period instead of in a future period and, therefore, the expected profit at the time of the sale is zero. This loss concept is the same as that applied in other areas where the conservatism principle is used (such as contingencies and construction contracts, which we discuss in Chapters 13 and 18, respectively) because no provision is made for the recognition of a profit when the sale occurs in a future period.

Situation 2

Assume now that the replacement cost is $12. In this situation the replacement cost is used as the market value. Why would the Sahara Company sell an item for $14 when the replacement cost is $12 and its normal profit (the difference between the ceiling and floor) is $4? One explanation would be that the supplier has reduced its price on the product, so that the Sahara Company has to reduce its selling price to remain competitive with other retailers who have reduced their prices.

The loss in the period of the *write-down* is equal to the replacement cost less the historical cost. The expected profit in the period of *sale* is the net realizable value less the replacement cost (the new carrying value of the inventory). The loss and expected profit are:

$$\textbf{Loss in period of write-down} = \$12 - \$19$$
$$= \underline{\underline{\$(7)}}$$

$$\textbf{Expected profit in period of sale} = \$14 - \$12$$
$$= \underline{\underline{\$\ 2}}$$

The loss of $7 is the cost saving that was missed because the inventory was purchased before the price decline. This alternative allows the company to recognize a profit of $2 at the time of sale, although it is less than the normal profit of $4.

Situation 3

Assume now that the replacement cost is $9. In this situation the floor of $10 is used as the market value. Why would the Sahara Company be able to sell an item for $14 when the replacement cost is $9 and its normal profit is $4? One explanation would be that the supplier has reduced the price on the product and has so stimulated demand that the retail price has not fallen as much.

The loss in the period of the *write-down* is equal to the floor (net receivable value minus the normal profit) less the historical cost. The expected profit in the period of *sale* is equal to the net realizable value less the floor (the new carrying value of the inventory). The loss and expected profit are:

$$\textbf{Loss in period of write-down} = \$10 - \$19$$
$$= \underline{\underline{\$(9)}}$$

$$\textbf{Expected profit in period of sale} = \$14 - \$10$$
$$= \underline{\underline{\$\ 4}}$$

The loss of $9 is the amount needed to provide a normal profit in the future. The expected profit at the time of sale is the normal profit of $4.

The loss concept in Situations 2 and 3 is *not* consistent with the conservatism principle applied in other situations because it allows a company to recognize profits in future periods when the sale is made. Note also that the total loss in all three situations is $5 [$(5) + $0; $(7) + $2; $(9) + $4]. The issue is the inconsistent application of accounting principles, which results in different amounts of loss and profit that a company may recognize in the period of write-down and the period of sale.[2]

---

2. For additional discussion of these issues, see S.E. Warner and F.D. Whitehurst, "An Illustration of Inventory Loss Measurements Under the LCM Rule," *The Accounting Educators' Journal* (Fall 1988), pp. 32–7.

Approaches to Implementing Lower of Cost or Market Rule

A company may apply the lower of cost or market rule to each item or to the total of the inventory (or, in some cases, to the total of the components of each major category). The method used should clearly reflect periodic income.[3]

Applying the rule to each individual item in inventory results in an inventory value less than (or equal to) the values obtained by the other two alternatives. Under these other two alternatives the price declines of some of the units in inventory are offset by price rises in other items. You can see this in Example 9-2, which illustrates the three alternative methods of implementing the lower of cost or market rule for a company in the first year of its operations. To simplify the example, we assume that there was no beginning inventory. Similar results would be obtained if the cost of the beginning inventory was less than or equal to the market value. If the company applies the lower of cost or market rule to individual items, the inventory value is $6,100 and it recognizes a loss of $600 ($6,100 market − $6,700 cost). This method is the most conservative alternative. If the company applies the rule to each category, the inventory value is $6,500 and it recognizes a loss of $200. If the company applies the rule to the total inventory, the value is $6,600 and it recognizes a loss of $100.

EXAMPLE 9-2   Approaches to Implementing Lower of Cost or Market

| | | | LCM applied to: | | |
Inventory	Cost	Market	Individual Items	Inventory Categories	Total Inventory
Category A:					
Item 1	$1,000	$ 700	$ 700		
Item 2	1,200	1,300	1,200		
	$2,200	$2,000		$2,000	
Category B:					
Item 3	$2,000	$2,400	2,000		
Item 4	2,500	2,200	2,200		
	$4,500	$4,600		4,500	
Total	$6,700	$6,600			$6,600
Inventory valuation			$6,100	$6,500	$6,600
Loss recognition			$ 600	$ 200	$ 100

The use of three alternative methods to account for the *same economic events* is inappropriate, since the qualitative characteristic of *comparability* among companies is enhanced when only one method is allowed. However, in many situations there will be no material differences from the use of the alternative methods. The most common practice is to apply the lower of cost or market rule to each individual item since it is required for income tax purposes and is the most conservative alternative. Of course, the method chosen should be applied consistently each period.

Once the inventory is reduced to market, it is *not* written back up to cost even if the market value subsequently rises above cost. Effectively, the written-down value becomes the new "cost" for subsequent valuation purposes. If the company is using the FIFO or average cost flow assumptions this affects the cost of goods sold in the next period. Therefore, the company may *implicitly* recognize recoveries of losses, as we show in the next section.

---

3. *Accounting Research Bulletin No. 43, op. cit.,* par. 10.

Recording the Reduction of Inventory to Market

It is acceptable for a company to record the write-down of inventory cost to market value directly in its inventory and cost of goods sold accounts (*direct* method). However, it is more desirable to use a separate inventory valuation account and a loss account (*allowance* method) so that the effects of the write-down can be clearly identified. We illustrate the journal entries for both methods in Example 9-3 for a company using FIFO and the periodic inventory system that has the following inventory values:

	Cost	Market
December 31, 2006	$20,000	$20,000
December 31, 2007	25,000	22,000
December 31, 2008	30,000	28,000

EXAMPLE 9-3   Recording the Reduction of Inventory to Market

	Periodic Inventory System			
	Direct Method		Allowance Method	
December 31, 2007				
1. To close beginning inventory:				
Income Summary	20,000		20,000	
Inventory		20,000		20,000
2. To record ending inventory:				
Inventory	22,000		25,000	
Income Summary		22,000		25,000
3. To record inventory at market:				
Loss Due to Market Valuation	Not required		3,000	
Allowance to Reduce Inventory to Market				3,000
December 31, 2008				
1. To close beginning inventory:				
Income Summary	22,000		25,000	
Inventory		22,000		25,000
2. To record ending inventory:				
Inventory	28,000		30,000	
Income Summary		28,000		30,000
3. To record inventory at market:				
Allowance to Reduce Inventory to Market	Not required		1,000	
Loss Recovery Due to Market Valuation				1,000

LCM: Direct Method (Periodic)

In the *direct* method, the company includes the $3,000 decline in the value of the inventory at the end of 2007 in the year-end closing entry by recording the ending inventory at its lower *market* value of $22,000. Consequently, the Inventory account balance is $3,000 *lower* and Cost of Goods Sold is $3,000 *higher* than they otherwise would be. This lower inventory value of $22,000 is the beginning inventory for 2008. At the end of 2008 the market value is $2,000 below the cost of $30,000, and so the market value of $28,000 is included in the closing entry. The effect of the value of the beginning and ending inventory on cost of goods sold in 2008 should be considered carefully. The market value of the beginning inventory is $3,000 below cost, and this causes the cost of goods sold to be $3,000 *lower* than it otherwise would be. The market value of the ending inventory is $2,000 below cost, and this causes the cost of goods sold to be $2,000 *higher* than it otherwise would be. Therefore, the net effect is that the cost of goods sold is $1,000 lower and gross profit (and income) is $1,000 higher in 2008, because the lower of cost or market value method is used.

LCM: Indirect Method (Periodic)

The same net results are obtained when the *allowance* method is used. However, the method reveals more information about the effect of the lower of cost or market method on a company's cost of goods sold. In the allowance method, a company records the amount by which the market value is below cost in an Allowance account, and shows the effect on the cost of goods sold explicitly in a Loss (or Loss Recovery) account. In the closing entry at the end of 2007, the company records the inventory at its cost of $25,000, and records the decline in value of $3,000 separately in the Loss account and the Allowance account. At the end of 2008 the company records the inventory in the closing entry at its cost of $30,000. As we discuss later, the net effect of recording the beginning inventory at a book value of $3,000 below cost and the ending inventory at a book value of $2,000 below cost is to make cost of goods sold $1,000 lower than it otherwise would be. Therefore, the company reduces the Allowance account by $1,000 and recognizes a Loss Recovery of $1,000. These losses and recoveries are shown as adjustments to cost of goods sold (as in the example in Example 9-4) and therefore disclose more information than the direct method. However, many companies may combine the two amounts in their published financial statements by reporting just the net amount of the inventory and a single amount for the cost of goods sold.

LCM: Perpetual

If the company was using a perpetual inventory system instead of a periodic system, the net results would again be the same. The journal entries to record the reductions to market would be as follows:

| | Direct Method | | Allowance Method | |
	2007	2008	2007	2008
Cost of Goods Sold	3,000	2,000		
Inventory	3,000	2,000		
Loss (Loss Recovery) due to Market Valuation			3,000	1,000
Allowance to Reduce Inventory to Market			3,000 1,000	

If the company was using the *direct* method, it would recognize the reduction of $3,000 in the 2007 ending inventory by increasing cost of goods sold and reducing inventory. In 2008 it recognizes the reduction of $2,000 in the ending inventory in exactly the same way. Again note that the net effect of the reduction of the beginning and ending inventory ($3,000 and $2,000, respectively) on cost of goods sold in 2008 is that it is $1,000 lower than it would otherwise be. If the company was using the *allowance* method, the amount it records in the Allowance and in the Loss (or Loss Recovery) accounts is the same as for the periodic method.

LCM: Reporting

We show the financial statement reporting of the direct and allowance methods for the periodic inventory method in Example 9-4, assuming purchases in each year are $100,000. The advantage of the allowance method is that it clearly discloses the loss and loss recovery in the company's income statements (but not as extraordinary items) and the valuation adjustment in its respective balance sheets. Although this method is recommended and is used for many companies' internal financial reporting, published financial statements generally do not disclose the size of the loss and the valuation allowance (unless one, or both, is material) but merely disclose that the company is using the lower of cost or market method.

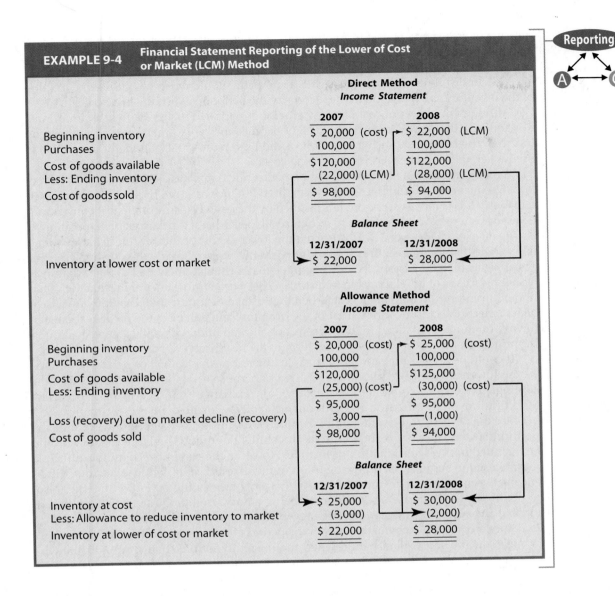

Reporting
A   C

EXAMPLE 9-4 Financial Statement Reporting of the Lower of Cost or Market (LCM) Method

Direct Method
Income Statement

	2007	2008
Beginning inventory	$ 20,000 (cost)	$ 22,000 (LCM)
Purchases	100,000	100,000
Cost of goods available	$120,000	$122,000
Less: Ending inventory	(22,000) (LCM)	(28,000) (LCM)
Cost of goods sold	$ 98,000	$ 94,000

Balance Sheet

	12/31/2007	12/31/2008
Inventory at lower cost or market	$ 22,000	$ 28,000

Allowance Method
Income Statement

	2007	2008
Beginning inventory	$ 20,000 (cost)	$ 25,000 (cost)
Purchases	100,000	100,000
Cost of goods available	$120,000	$125,000
Less: Ending inventory	(25,000) (cost)	(30,000) (cost)
	$ 95,000	$ 95,000
Loss (recovery) due to market decline (recovery)	3,000	(1,000)
Cost of goods sold	$ 98,000	$ 94,000

Balance Sheet

	12/31/2007	12/31/2008
Inventory at cost	$ 25,000	$ 30,000
Less: Allowance to reduce inventory to market	(3,000)	(2,000)
Inventory at lower of cost or market	$ 22,000	$ 28,000

Lower of Cost or Market and Interim Financial Statements

APB Opinion No. 28 specifies that if a company experiences a temporary market decline in an interim period the company should ignore the decline in its interim financial statements. If the company is unlikely to recover the decline, it should recognize the amount. If the company recognizes a decline and then reverses it in a later *interim* period, it should recognize a loss recovery and increase the inventory value by the amount of the recovery, but only up to the original cost.[4]

CONCEPTUAL EVALUATION OF LOWER OF COST OR MARKET

Conceptual
R   A

The reduction of the value of the inventory to market and the recognition of a loss are appropriate for both a company's balance sheet and income statement. As we discussed in Chapter 4, *FASB Statement of Concepts No. 6* defines *assets* as "probable future economic benefits." When the cost of the inventory exceeds the expected benefits, the lower market value is a better

---

4.   "Interim Financial Reporting," *APB Opinion No. 28* (New York: AICPA, 1973), par. 14(c).

2 Explain the conceptual issues regarding the lower of cost or market method.

measure of the expected benefits. In other words, an unrecoverable cost is not an asset. As we discussed in Chapter 5, the *Statement* also defines *losses* as "decreases in net assets from peripheral or incidental transactions . . . and other events . . . except those that result from expenses or distributions to owners." Thus a company should recognize the decline in value of the inventory as a reduction in the income of the period in which the loss occurs.

Although the lower of cost or market method is applied to all cost flow assumptions, it is unlikely that it will be used with LIFO because the replacement cost should not be less than the LIFO cost. Such a situation would be very unusual, especially since LIFO is used when there is an expectation of rising costs.

A major criticism of the lower of cost or market rule is that it is applied only in one direction. Declines and (holding) losses are recognized but increases and (holding) gains are not. Obviously this is inconsistent, but it is justified by the conservatism (prudence) convention. Conservatism requires a company to recognize all losses that it can reasonably expect and to anticipate no possible gains, which is what the lower of cost or market rule achieves. Some users argue that the market value of inventory should be recognized when the replacement cost is *higher* than the historical cost. They argue that the replacement cost of the inventory is *reliable* regardless of its relationship to historical cost. Furthermore, they argue that the valuation of inventory at replacement cost (when higher than historical cost) is *relevant* because it better reflects the **cash flow potential** of the inventory and enhances the predictive value of the information. This valuation, however, is not allowed under generally accepted accounting principles, because it would be a violation of the historical cost principle.

It could be argued that another principle, the *revenue recognition* principle, is violated by the lower of cost or market method. This is because a loss is recognized before the earning process is complete and before an exchange transaction has occurred. Modification of the revenue recognition principle is justified in these circumstances because the decline in the value of the company's inventory is an **economic event of the period** that has caused a reduction in its stockholders' equity. Therefore the loss should be included in the determination of income. However, the revenue recognition principle may be used to support the nonrecognition of increases in value, because the total difference between selling price and cost is usually recognized in the period of the sale. Also, recognition of an increase in the value of the inventory would require the recognition of income and would be a violation of the revenue recognition principle.

Since a company recognizes a loss in the period of the market decline, its income will be *higher* in the subsequent period when the inventory is sold than it would otherwise have been. In other words, the loss is transferred from the future period of the sale to the current period of the decline in market value. Total income over the two periods will be the same whether or not the lower of cost or market rule is used. This is shown by the earlier

Credit: ©Getty Images/PhotoDisc

example in which recording the inventory at the lower of cost or market caused income to be lower by $3,000 in 2007 and higher by $1,000 in 2008. If the company recorded the inventory at cost in a subsequent year(s), its income will be higher by the $2,000 remaining in the Allowance account in that year(s). Therefore the company's total income over the years in which it recorded inventory at lower of cost or market will be the same as if it had recorded the inventory at cost for those years. This occurs because the beginning and ending inventory for the several years are both at cost.

LINK TO ETHICAL DILEMMA

Your company, Acquirer Inc., has recently acquired a related business, TargetCo, to take advantage of possible synergies. You have been appointed CFO of TargetCo and hope to restore it to profitability. You realize that this will not be an easy task and that this opportunity will make or break your career. One of your first priorities is for your staff to conduct an extensive review of the value of TargetCo's inventory. The resulting review determines that approximately 10% of the inventory should be written down under the lower of cost or market rule. However, to be conservative, you authorize a 25% reduction in the inventory valuation that you term a restructuring charge. Discuss the ethical implications.

LINK TO INTERNATIONAL DIFFERENCES

International accounting standards also require the use of the lower of cost or market method. However, market is defined as net realizable value and should typically be applied to individual items. International accounting standards also allow a reversal of a write-down and require disclosures about inventory that is written down, as well as any reversals.

PURCHASE OBLIGATIONS AND PRODUCT FINANCING ARRANGEMENTS

Accounting principles generally require that a company not record a purchase obligation in its accounts (except in governmental accounting), because neither an asset nor a liability is created by placing an order. **If a company has incurred an unconditional purchase obligation at a definite price, the company discloses this commitment in a note to its financial statements.**[5] This disclosure is required because the commitment is important for the prediction of the cash outflows that the company will make in the future.

If a company has an unconditional (noncancelable) purchase obligation to acquire inventory and the current market price (i.e., replacement cost) is less than the fixed purchase price, the company must recognize the loss in the period in which the decline occurs. This procedure is consistent with the conservatism principle and also

3 Understand purchase obligations and product financing arrangements.

5. "Disclosure of Long-Term Obligations," *FASB Statement of Financial Accounting Standards No. 47* (Stamford, Conn.: FASB, 1981), par. 7.

provides the users of the financial statements with information about the decision-making ability of the management. For example, if a company entered into a noncancelable commitment to purchase inventory at a fixed price of $500,000 and the market price (replacement cost) at the end of the year is $450,000, it would make the following year-end adjusting entry:

Loss on Purchase Commitments	50,000	
Accrued Loss on Purchase Commitments		50,000

The company reports the accrued loss as a liability on its year-end balance sheet.

The company writes it off the accrued loss when it purchases the goods as follows:

Inventory (or Purchases)	450,000	
Accrued Loss on Purchase Commitments	50,000	
Accounts Payable		500,000

If the market price rises by the time the company makes the purchase, it reduces the accrued loss and recognizes a loss recovery. It then records the purchases at the market price (cost) on the date of acquisition.

The company accrues the loss only when there is a loss on a *noncancelable* purchase commitment. Such a loss is a contingent loss and is recognized because it is probable and can be reasonably estimated, as we discussed in Chapter 4. Losses on *cancelable* purchase commitments are not accrued because it is assumed that the purchase commitment can be canceled and the loss avoided.

Some companies have engaged in product financing arrangements as a way of financing the cost of inventory before the sale to the ultimate purchaser occurs. **In a product financing arrangement the company "sells" the inventory to another company. Then, in a related transaction, it agrees to purchase the inventory (or a substantially identical item) back from the other company at specified prices over specified periods.** Typically the inventory is not delivered to the "buyer" and is repurchased at a higher price, the difference being an interest charge. When the "sale" under the product financing arrangement occurs, the transaction is similar to borrowing cash with the inventory being used as collateral, sometimes referred to as a "parking" transaction. Thus, according to **FASB Statement No. 49,** the company does *not* record sales revenue but instead records the proceeds received as a liability.[6] This procedure avoids the overstatement of revenues and stockholders' equity and the understatement of liabilities. As a result of not recording a sale, the inventory also remains in the accounts at cost. Note, however, that this *Statement* does *not* apply to agreements to repurchase at prices that are not specified.

VALUATION ABOVE COST

4 Explain the valuation of inventory above cost.

We stated earlier in this chapter that the lower of cost or market method does not result in a valuation of inventory above cost. However, generally accepted accounting principles do allow a company to value its inventory above cost in certain circumstances. **Accounting Research Bulletin No. 43** states that in exceptional cases inventories may be reported above cost. For example, precious metals having a fixed monetary value with no major cost of marketing may be reported above cost. Any other exceptions must be justified by an inability to determine appropriate costs, immediate marketability at a quoted market price, and unit interchangeability. When goods are reported above cost, this fact should be fully disclosed. Inventories of agricultural, mineral, and other products, where

---

6. "Accounting for Product Financing Arrangements," *FASB Statement of Financial Accounting Standards No. 49* (Stamford, Conn.: FASB, 1981).

units are interchangeable and are immediately marketable at quoted prices, and for which appropriate costs may be difficult to obtain may also be reported above cost.[7]

Real Report 9-1 shows an example of valuation at market prices for **ConAgra Foods**. Justification for this method exists when it is highly certain that the inventory can be sold at the market price. Such a situation indicates that the income is earned by production rather than by sale. Therefore, valuation at market, above cost, is appropriate. However, this practice violates the conservatism principle and the usual application of the revenue recognition principle, and is acceptable only in selected industries.

Real Report 9-1 Inventory Valuation Above Cost

ConAgra Foods

NOTE 1: Summary of Significant Accounting Policies (in part):

Inventories   Grain, flour, and major feed ingredient inventories are hedged to the extent practicable and are principally stated at market, including adjustment to market of open contracts for purchases and sales.

NOTE 9: Senior Long-Term Debt, Subordinated Debt and Loan Agreements

Interest expense incurred to finance hedged inventories has been charged to cost of goods sold.

Question:

1. What allows ConAgra to value its inventory at market price instead of cost?

SECURE YOUR KNOWLEDGE 9-1

- The lower of cost or market (LCM) rule is an application of the conservatism principle that requires a company to write down its inventory to market value when the market value of the inventory has declined below its historical cost.
- In applying the LCM method, market value is defined as the current replacement cost; it is constrained by the net realizable value (ceiling) and the net realizable value less a normal profit margin (floor).
- LCM may be applied to individual inventory items (the most conservative approach), to major categories of inventory items, or to the entire inventory.
- The write-down of inventory cost under the LCM method can be accomplished by recording the write-down using either the:
  - direct method (recorded directly in the inventory and cost of goods sold accounts) or
  - indirect method (recorded in an inventory valuation/allowance account and a loss account).
- Unconditional purchase obligations should generally be disclosed in a note to the financial statements; however, if the market price is less than the fixed purchase price, a loss should be recognized in the period of the decline.
- Product financing arrangements are similar to borrowing cash with inventory as collateral; therefore, a liability is recorded for the proceeds of the transaction.

---

7. *Accounting Research Bulletin No. 43, op. cit.,* ch. 4, par. 15 and 16.

GROSS PROFIT METHOD

5 Use the gross profit method.

Two commonly used methods of estimating inventory costs are (1) the gross profit method and (2) the retail inventory method (which we discuss in the next section).

A company uses the gross profit method to estimate the cost of the inventory by applying a gross profit rate from previous period(s) to the net sales of the current period. It may be used in the following situations:

1. To determine the cost of the inventory at the end of an interim period without taking a physical count. Because of the cost of taking a physical inventory, a company using a periodic inventory system may use the gross profit method for its internal financial statements. It is also an acceptable method for interim financial statements, provided that the company "disclose the method used at the interim date and any significant adjustments that result from reconciliations with the annual physical inventory."[8]
2. For the internal or external auditor to check the reasonableness of an inventory cost developed from a physical inventory or perpetual inventory system. Also, the auditor can take a physical inventory count before the end of the year and then estimate the cost of the ending inventory.
3. To estimate the cost of inventory that is destroyed by a casualty, such as a fire.
4. To estimate the cost of the inventory from incomplete records. For example, if a company's inventory records are destroyed, the inventory can be estimated if the cost of goods available for sale and the sales are known or can be reconstructed.
5. To develop a budget of cost of goods sold and ending inventory from a sales budget.

The gross profit method assumes that a company's gross profit rate (the rate of gross profit on net sales from the company's income statement) in the current period is not materially different from that of the previous period(s). If there are any identifiable differences, adjustments should be made, as we discuss later. The steps that a company completes when using the gross profit method include the following:

1. Calculate the historical gross profit rate by dividing the gross profit of the prior period(s) by the net sales of the prior period(s).
2. Estimate the gross profit for the current period by multiplying the historical gross profit rate by the actual net sales for the period.
3. Subtract the estimated gross profit from the actual net sales to determine the estimated cost of goods sold for the period.
4. Subtract the estimated cost of goods sold from the actual cost of goods available for sale (the beginning inventory plus the net purchases) for the period to determine the estimated cost of the ending inventory.

Example: Gross Profit Method

We show how a company applies the gross profit method in Example 9-5 and list each of the preceding steps in parentheses. The company uses the historical gross profit rate of 40% because it believes this rate is the best estimate of conditions in the current year; that is, no material changes in conditions from previous years have occurred.[9]

---

8. *APB Opinion No. 28, op. cit.,* par. 14(a).
9. Sometimes a company will express gross profit as a percent of cost of goods sold instead of as a percent of net sales. In this case it must convert the gross profit percent to a percent of net sales before it can apply the gross profit method, as follows:

$$\text{Gross Profit to Net Sales Ratio} = \frac{\text{Gross Profit to Cost of Goods Sold Ratio}}{1 + \text{Gross Profit to Cost of Goods Sold Ratio}}$$

Alternatively, if the gross profit to net sales ratio is known, and calculation of the gross profit to cost of goods sold ratio (often called the markup percentage) is required, the following formula can be used:

$$\text{Gross Profit to Cost of Goods Sold Ratio} = \frac{\text{Gross Profit to Net Sales Ratio}}{1 - \text{Gross Profit to Net Sales Ratio}}$$

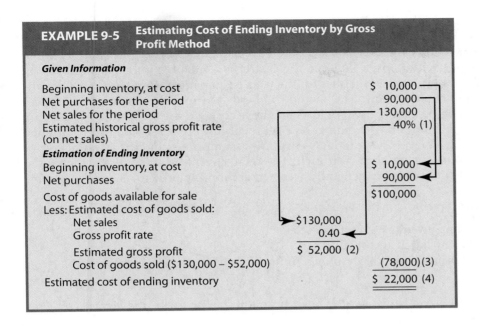

EXAMPLE 9-5 — Estimating Cost of Ending Inventory by Gross Profit Method

Given Information

Beginning inventory, at cost	$ 10,000
Net purchases for the period	90,000
Net sales for the period	130,000
Estimated historical gross profit rate (on net sales)	40% (1)

Estimation of Ending Inventory

Beginning inventory, at cost		$ 10,000
Net purchases		90,000
Cost of goods available for sale		$100,000
Less: Estimated cost of goods sold:		
Net sales	$130,000	
Gross profit rate	0.40	
Estimated gross profit	$ 52,000 (2)	
Cost of goods sold ($130,000 − $52,000)		(78,000) (3)
Estimated cost of ending inventory		$ 22,000 (4)

One step may be removed from the calculation shown in Example 9-5. Since the gross profit is 40% of net sales, the cost of goods sold is 60% of net sales. Therefore, the cost of goods sold could be calculated directly as $78,000 (60% × $130,000). ♦

Conceptual Evaluation of the Gross Profit Method

The gross profit method is useful in the situations outlined at the beginning of this section, but the relevance of the results depends on the accuracy of the gross profit percentage. Three modifications may enhance its accuracy.

First, a company should adjust the gross profit rate for known changes in the relationship between its gross profit and net sales. For example, if the company's costs of purchases have increased, but it has not passed on the increases to customers through increased sales prices, it should reduce the gross profit percentage accordingly. The company may also need to adjust the gross profit rate if its productivity or sales (and purchases) returns and allowances have changed.

Second, a company may use a separate gross profit rate for each department or type of inventory that has a different markup percentage. It would then apply separate rates to each department's net sales, and add the resulting amounts to compute the total inventory. Use of a single, overall gross profit rate assumes that all types of inventory are sold or held in inventory in equal proportions at all times. Since this is unlikely, use of separate gross profit rates enhances the accuracy of the cost of the ending inventory and the cost of goods sold.

Third, a company may use an average gross profit rate based on several past periods to average out period-to-period fluctuations. However, use of an average rate assumes that no significant changes occurred over the periods selected for calculating the average rate and that the company made no adjustments to account for such changes. The use of an average rate is particularly appropriate when there are relatively stable costs, selling prices, and operating methods.

The ending inventory estimated by the gross profit method is consistent with the cost flow assumption previously (and currently) used by the company. This occurs because the gross profit rate is based on past results developed from using the particular cost flow assumption. However, if there has been a special situation in the past, such as the reduction of the inventory to market, or a liquidation of LIFO inventory, the gross profit rate must be adjusted.

RETAIL INVENTORY METHOD

6 Understand the retail inventory method.

The retail inventory method is used widely to estimate the cost of inventory when there is a consistent pattern between the cost of a company's purchases and selling prices. This pattern may exist either for the whole company or for identifiable departments within the company. The method is best used by retail stores where prices often are set based on a consistent markup above cost and the accounting systems are based on retail values rather than costs. The retail inventory method can be applied based on the average, FIFO, and LIFO cost flow assumptions, and the lower of cost or market method can be used with each. The retail inventory method is widely used because it is allowed under generally accepted accounting principles and for income tax purposes.

The retail inventory method requires a company to use the following information:

1. Beginning inventory at cost and retail
2. Goods purchased at cost and retail
3. Changes in selling price resulting from additional markups and markdowns
4. Sales

Assuming that a company uses the retail inventory method with the *average* cost flow assumption, the following steps are necessary:

1. Compute the total goods available for sale (beginning inventory plus purchases) at both cost and retail value (selling price).
2. Compute a cost-to-retail ratio by dividing the cost of the goods available for sale by the retail value of the goods available for sale.
3. Compute the ending inventory at retail by subtracting the sales for the period from the retail value of the goods available for sale.
4. Compute the ending inventory at cost by multiplying the ending inventory at retail by the cost-to-retail ratio.

Example: Retail Inventory Method

We show how a company applies the retail inventory method using the following simplified data:

	Cost	Retail
Beginning inventory	$10,000	$17,000
Purchases	50,000	83,000
Sales		80,000

The ending inventory at cost is computed as follows (and we list each of the preceding steps in parentheses):

	Cost	Retail	
Beginning inventory	$ 10,000	$ 17,000	
Purchases	50,000	83,000	
Goods available for sale	$60,000	$ 100,000	(1)

Cost-to-retail ratio: $\dfrac{\$\,60{,}000}{\$100{,}000} = 0.60$ (2)

Less: Sales		(80,000)	
Ending inventory at retail		$ 20,000	(3)

Ending inventory at cost (0.60 x $20,000) $12,000   (4) ◆

Retail Inventory Method Terminology

In the preceding example we assumed that the retail value of the goods available for sale is the original sales price, and that the company made no subsequent changes in retail prices. However, the typical retail store makes many changes in selling prices after setting the original price. (For the average retail food store there are likely to be hundreds of changes each week.) The following seven terms describe these changes:

1. *Markup.* The original markup from cost to the first selling price (also known as *mark-on*).
2. *Additional Markup.* An increase above the original sales price.
3. *Markup Cancellation.* A reduction in the selling price after there has been an additional markup. The markup cancellation cannot be greater than the additional markup.
4. *Net Markup.* The total additional markups less the total markup cancellations.
5. *Markdown.* A decrease below the original sales price.
6. *Markdown Cancellation.* An increase in the selling price after there has been a markdown. The markdown cancellation cannot be greater than the markdown.
7. *Net Markdown.* The total markdowns less the total markdown cancellations.

To illustrate the meaning of these terms, suppose that a company purchased an item for $6 and initially priced the item to sell for $10. The markup is $4. If the company subsequently increases the selling price to $12, there is an additional markup of $2. If it then lowers the selling price to $7, there is a markup cancellation of $2 and a markdown of $3. If the company then raises the selling price to $8, there is a markdown cancellation of $1. The net markup is zero ($2−$2), and the net markdown is $2 ($3−$1).

Application of the Retail Inventory Method

In the simplified example shown earlier, we used the average cost flow assumption. However, companies may use the retail inventory method to develop inventory valuations under four alternatives (we do not illustrate the lower of cost or market used with FIFO and LIFO):

1. *FIFO.* Exclude the cost and the retail value of the beginning inventory from the computation of the cost-to-retail ratio for the period. The ratio includes both net markups and net markdowns.
2. *Average Cost.* Include the cost and the retail value of the beginning inventory and net markups and markdowns in the cost-to-retail ratio.
3. *LIFO.* Compute separate ratios for each layer in the beginning inventory and for the purchases of the current period; include both net markups and net markdowns in the cost-to-retail ratio for the current period.
4. *Lower of Average Cost or Market.* Include the cost and retail value of the beginning inventory and net markups in the cost-to-retail ratio. Thus, the net markdowns are excluded from the computation of the cost-to-retail ratio. This method is also known as the *conventional retail* method.

We summarize the calculation of the cost-to-retail ratio of the current period for each of the alternative methods as follows:

	FIFO	Average Cost	LIFO*	Lower of Average Cost or Market
Beginning inventory	Exclude	Include	Exclude	Include
Purchases	Include	Include	Include	Include
Markups (net)	Include	Include	Include	Include
Markdowns (net)	Include	Include	Include	Exclude

*A separate cost-to-retail ratio is also computed for each layer in the beginning inventory.

Note that these alternative methods differ in the calculation of the cost-to-retail ratio. However, the net markups and markdowns *always* are added and subtracted in order to compute the retail value of the ending inventory. Also note that markups and markdowns are recorded only at *retail*. We show each of these methods in the following sections, using the data for the Thompson Company given in Example 9-6.

EXAMPLE 9-6   Thompson Company Inventory Cost and Retail Value

	Cost	Retail
Beginning inventory	$20	$ 35
Purchases	40	80
Net markups	—	5
Net markdowns	—	(10)
Goods available for sale	$60	$110
Sales		(66)
Ending inventory at retail		$ 44

Note: It is assumed that the beginning inventory is valued at a cost of $20 for all flow assumptions, although this value would be different for different cost flow assumptions because the beginning inventory for the current period is the ending inventory of the previous period.

FIFO

Under the FIFO cost flow assumption the beginning inventory is excluded from the computation of the cost-to-retail ratio for the period. The Thompson Company would compute the cost of its ending inventory as $23.45, as we show in Example 9-7.

EXAMPLE 9-7   Retail Inventory Method — FIFO

	Cost	Retail
Purchases	$40	$ 80
Net markups		5
Net markdowns		(10)
	$40	$ 75

Cost-to-retail ratio: $\dfrac{\$40}{\$75} = 0.533$
(for purchases)

	Cost	Retail
Beginning inventory	20	35
Goods available for sale	$60	$110
Less: Sales		(66)
Ending inventory at retail		$ 44
Ending inventory at FIFO cost (0.533 × $44)	$23.45	

Excluding the beginning inventory from the computation of the cost-to-retail ratio produces the layering effect of FIFO for cost of goods sold. Since the ending inventory cost is based only on the activities of the current period, the entire beginning inventory is included in the cost of goods sold. Therefore the *cost of goods sold* is made up of two layers as follows:

	Cost	Retail
Beginning inventory	$20.00	$35
Purchases at retail		31
Purchases at cost ($31 × 0.533)	16.52	
	$36.52	$66

Thus the cost of goods available for sale of $60 is allocated (amounts rounded) between cost of goods sold ($36.52) and ending inventory ($23.45).[10]

Average Cost

Under the average cost flow assumption the beginning inventory and the net markups and markdowns are included in the cost-to-retail ratio. The Thompson Company would estimate the cost of its ending inventory as $24, as we show in Example 9-8.

EXAMPLE 9-8   Retail Inventory Method — Average Cost

	Cost	Retail
Beginning inventory	$20	$ 35
Purchases	40	80
Net markups		5
Net markdowns		(10)
Goods available for sale	$60	$110

Cost-to-retail ratio: $\dfrac{\$60}{\$110} = 0.545$

Less: Sales		(66)
Ending inventory at retail		$ 44
Ending inventory at average cost (0.545 × $44)	$24	

There are similarities between applying this average cost flow assumption and the more general average cost method we discussed in the preceding chapter. The beginning inventory and the purchases are combined. Since the company sold at retail 60% ($66 ÷ $110) of the goods available for sale, 40% of the goods are left in ending inventory. The cost of the inventory is $24, which is 40% of the cost of the goods available for sale (40% × $60 = $24).

LIFO

Separate cost-to-retail ratios for the beginning inventory and the purchases must be calculated when the LIFO cost flow assumption is applied to the retail inventory method.

---

10. Note that in this example we assumed that the units sold during the period exceed the units in the beginning inventory; therefore, under FIFO the company includes the cost of the entire beginning inventory in cost of goods sold during the current period. If some of the beginning inventory still remained at the end of the period, the ending inventory would include two layers, each with its own cost-to-retail ratio.

The ratio for the purchases includes both markups and markdowns if the cost basis is used. (Remember that a company may use LIFO for income tax purposes only if it also uses LIFO for financial reporting.) The layers of inventory are accounted for by using the same principles as those discussed in Chapter 8. The Thompson Company would compute the cost of its ending inventory as $24.80, as we show in Example 9-9.

EXAMPLE 9-9   Retail Inventory Method — LIFO

	Cost	Retail
Beginning inventory	$20	$ 35
Cost-to-retail ratio: $\frac{\$20}{\$35} = 0.57$ (for beginning inventory)		
Purchases	40	80
Net markups		5
Net markdowns		(10)
		$ 75
Cost-to-retail ratio: $\frac{\$40}{\$75} = 0.533$ (for purchases)		
Goods available for sale	$60	$110
Less: Sales		(66)
Ending inventory at retail		$ 44
Ending inventory at LIFO cost:		
$35 × 0.57 (beginning inventory layer)	$20.00	
$ 9 × 0.533 (added layer)	4.80	
	$24.80	

The company had sales of $66, which left an inventory at retail of $44. This inventory consists of two layers, one of which is the base inventory at retail of $35, and the other an addition at retail of $9. Each layer is converted to cost at its own cost-to-retail ratio. Another way of looking at this example is to see that the Thompson Company sold 88% ($66 ÷ $75) of the goods purchased during the period. Therefore at cost the company sold $35.20 (88% × $40) of the purchases, leaving $4.80 ($40 − $35.20) as an added layer in inventory.

Note that in the Thompson Company example, the LIFO method does not produce the lowest ending inventory cost (in comparison to FIFO or average). The reason is that the cost-to-retail ratio for the purchases is less than the cost-to-retail ratio for the beginning inventory. This situation was caused by the large markdowns during the period, indicating the existence of falling costs. These may be caused by a decline in the prices charged by the supplier or by obsolescence due to a change in tastes or the season of the year. When costs are rising, the retail method using LIFO will produce a lower inventory cost.

If there was a decrease in inventory over the period, the ending inventory would include only of a portion of the beginning inventory, and there would be no need to compute a cost-to-retail ratio for the purchases of the current period. In more complex situations the beginning inventory would include LIFO layers, each with its own cost-to-retail ratio, and the decrease would be removed according to the general LIFO principles discussed in the preceding chapter.

Lower of Average Cost or Market

The retail inventory method can be used with lower of cost or market under either the average, FIFO, or LIFO cost flow assumptions. In all three cases, net markdowns are excluded from the cost-to-retail ratio for the period to achieve the effects of the lower of cost or market method. Because the lower of average cost or market is commonly used, we will illustrate this alternative. The calculations follow the average cost example earlier, except that the net markdowns are *excluded* from the computation of the cost-to-retail ratio. The Thompson Company would compute the value of its ending inventory as $22, as we show in Example 9-10.

EXAMPLE 9-10	Retail Inventory Method — Lower of Average Cost or Market	
	Cost	**Retail**
Beginning inventory	$20	$ 35
Purchases	40	80
Net markups		5
	$60	$120
Cost-to-retail ratio: $\frac{\$60}{\$120} = 0.50$		
Net markdowns		(10)
Goods available for sale	$60	$110
Less: Sales		(66)
Ending inventory at retail		$ 44
Ending inventory at lower of cost or market (0.50 × $44)	$22	

Since the net markdowns are excluded from the computation of the cost-to-retail ratio, the denominator of the ratio is higher ($120 in Example 9-10 as compared to $110 in Example 9-8). Therefore, the ratio is lower (0.50 versus 0.545) and the cost of the ending inventory is lower ($22 versus $24). We discuss the assumptions for this calculation later in the chapter.

Additional Cost and Retail Adjustments

A company has to consider how to treat other costs and activities when it applies the retail inventory method. The cost of purchases includes the costs directly or indirectly incurred in bringing the items to their existing condition and location (as we discussed in Chapter 8). Two items that affect net purchases are (1) freight charges, which are added to the cost of purchases, and (2) purchases discounts taken under the gross price method, which are subtracted from the cost of purchases. These two items affect only the *cost* of purchases and not the retail amount of purchases, because it is assumed that the original markup applied to the invoice cost by the company covers such incidental items. A third item that affects net purchases is purchases returns and allowances. Once the purchases are recorded by a company at retail, any subsequent purchases returns and allowances are subtracted from *both the cost and the retail value* of the purchases so as not to distort the computation of the cost-to-retail ratio.

Several items also affect the estimate of the ending inventory at retail. Sales returns and allowances are subtracted from sales at retail to determine net sales. Net sales are then subtracted from goods available for sale at retail to compute ending inventory at retail. Sales discounts taken are *not* deducted to determine the ending inventory at retail, because they are considered to be financing items and not part of the original markup. Inventory shrinkage due to breakage and theft is a common problem in retail stores. Therefore, whenever the retail inventory method is used for interim financial statements, an estimate should be made of normal shrinkage (such as 1% of sales) based on past experience. This estimate is then subtracted, in addition to the usual items, to determine the ending inventory at retail. An estimate is not necessary at year-end because a physical inventory is taken. Employee discounts—discounts from the normal sales price that are made available to employees— also are subtracted to compute ending inventory at retail (in the same way as sales). Both inventory shrinkage and employee discounts are subtracted because they are normal costs incurred by the company and therefore were reflected in the retail selling price determined by the original markup. Abnormal inventory spoilage would be subtracted at both cost and retail to determine the goods available for sale so as not to distort the cost-to-retail ratio.

Comparison of Methods

The retail inventory method is similar to the gross profit method because it estimates inventory based on a profit percentage. It differs, however, and is more sensitive to price changes because it uses a current-period estimate of the profit percentage, whereas the gross profit method uses an estimate based on past periods. This similarity is summarized as follows:

Gross Profit Method	Retail Inventory Method
Beginning inventory at cost	Beginning inventory at retail
+ Purchases at cost	+ Purchases at retail
= Cost of goods available	= Retail value of goods available
− Cost of goods sold	− Retail value of goods sold (sales)
[sales × (1 − estimated gross profit rate)]	= Ending inventory at retail
	× actual cost-to-retail ratio
= Ending inventory at cost	= Ending inventory at cost

The major advantages of the retail inventory method are:

1. It allows a company to prepare interim reports without taking a physical inventory; but as with any inventory system, the company should take a physical count at least annually.
2. It simplifies a company's record-keeping procedures because the company does not need to keep track of the costs of *individual* purchases and does not have to relate them to the particular units in inventory. In addition, retail stores typically price and display merchandise immediately, and base their record keeping on retail prices.
3. It speeds up verifying a company's ending inventory by physical count because the company records the inventory in the retail store at retail values and can therefore compare it directly with the accounting records, which are also based on retail prices. Thus, the company does not need to refer to the individual purchase invoices to determine the cost of each item.

CONCEPTUAL EVALUATION OF THE RETAIL INVENTORY METHOD

7 Explain the conceptual issues regarding the retail inventory method.

Two general assumptions underlie the retail inventory method. The first is that the items in a company's inventory are sufficiently homogeneous so that all have the same markup. Or, if they have different markups, that the proportion of the different items in the ending inventory is the same as that in the goods available for sale. The company can reduce the limitations of this assumption by using a separate cost-to-retail ratio for each category of inventory or for each department. The second general assumption is that the cost-to-retail ratio remains constant over the accounting period or that changes in the retail prices parallel the changes in the costs of purchases. The limitations of this assumption can also be reduced by weighting the different cost-to-retail ratios by the volume of activity for inventory items under each ratio.

Since the lower of average cost or market method is the most used version of the retail inventory method, it is important to consider whether this method actually does result in an inventory at lower of cost or market, or just a value that is lower than cost. We evaluate this in the three examples of Example 9-11, which use the same basic information for the Thompson Company.

EXAMPLE 9-11	Assumptions Underlying the Use of the Retail Inventory Method: Lower of Average Cost or Market					
	Example 1 (no markdowns)		Example 2 (no markups)		Example 3 (all markdowns sold)	
	Cost	Retail	Cost	Retail	Cost	Retail
Beginning inventory	$20	$ 35	$20	$ 35	$20	$ 35
Purchases	40	80	40	80	40	80
Net markups		5		—		5
	$60	$120	$60	$115	$60	$120
Cost-to-retail ratio:		0.50[1]		0.52[2]		0.50[3]
Net markdowns		—		(10)		(10)
Goods available for sale	$60	$120	$60	$105	$60	$110
Less: Sales		(72)[4]		(63)[5]		(62)[6]
Ending inventory at retail		$ 48		$ 42		$ 48
Ending inventory at lower of cost or market	$24[7]		$21.91[8]		$24[9]	

[1] $\frac{\$60}{\$120} = 0.50$ [2] $\frac{\$60}{\$115} = 0.52$ [3] $\frac{\$60}{\$120} = 0.50$ [4] ($120 × 60%)   [5] ($105 × 60%)

[6] ($120 × 60% − $10)   [7] $\frac{\$60}{\$120} × \$48$ [8] $\frac{\$60}{\$115} × \$42$ [9] $\frac{\$60}{\$120} × \$48$

In all three examples we assume that the company sells 60% of the goods available for sale, but we use different assumptions regarding the markups and markdowns in each example. In the first example we assume that there are only markups and no markdowns. Thus, the cost-to-retail ratio is $60 ÷ $120 and the ending inventory is $24. This cost is the same as the average cost figure computed in Example 9-8. Since there were no markdowns, it can be assumed that the market value has not declined below cost, and therefore the inventory value is the lower of cost or market.

In the second example we assume that there are no markups but that there are markdowns. This results in a cost-to-retail ratio of $60 ÷ $115 and an ending inventory of $21.91. Since there are markdowns of $10, it can be assumed that prices have declined by a factor of 10 ÷ 115. To reflect this change, the ending inventory is valued at the lower of cost or market, which is $21.91 [$24 − ($24 × 10 ÷ 115)]. Therefore, in this situation the method again has resulted in an inventory amount equal to the lower of cost or market.

Now refer back to the original computation of the lower of cost or market in Example 9-10. Since $22 is greater than $21.91, the $22 value is *not* the true lower of cost or market of the inventory, but simply a value that is lower than cost. This indicates that the lower of cost or market method is accurate only if the goods in the inventory are perfectly homogeneous. In other words, markups and markdowns for separate items within inventory cannot exist at the same time.

In the third example, again there are both markups and markdowns. The cost-to-retail ratio is $60 ÷ $120. But now we assume that all the goods that are marked down are sold. Since we also assumed that 60% of the goods available for sale are sold, sales would be equal to 60% of the goods available for sale, less the $10 markdowns [(60% × $120) − $10 = $62]. The ending inventory is $24, which is again the lower of cost or market, because we assumed that all goods marked down have been sold and thus the ending inventory contains items that have a retail value that is higher than their cost. Therefore, for the lower of cost or market method to be accurate, the goods in inventory do not have to be perfectly homogeneous if it can be assumed that all the units that have been marked down have been sold.

To summarize, **the lower of average cost or market method is accurate only if either markups and markdowns do not exist at the same time or if all the marked-down items have been sold.** Under other conditions the method produces an inventory value that is less than cost but only approximates the lower of cost or market. We show **Wal-Mart's** disclosure of its use of the retail method in Real Report 9-2.

Real Report 9-2 Example of Inventory Disclosure

WAL-MART STORES

Balance Sheets
(in millions)

| | January 31, | |
	2004	2003
Assets (in part)		
Current Assets:		
Cash and cash equivalents	$ 5,199	$ 2,736
Receivables	1,254	1,569
Inventories	26,612	24,401
Prepaid expenses and other	1,356	837
Current assets of discontinued operation	—	1,179
Total Current Assets	$34,421	$30,722

NOTES TO FINANCIAL STATEMENTS (IN PART)

Inventories

The Company values inventories at the lower of cost or market as determined primarily by the retail method of accounting, using the last-in, first-out ("LIFO") method for substantially all domestic merchandise inventories, except SAM'S CLUB merchandise, which is based on average cost using the LIFO method. Inventories of foreign operations are primarily valued by the retail method of accounting, using the first-in, first-out ("FIFO") method. Our inventories at FIFO did not exceed inventories of LIFO by a significant amount.

Questions:

1. What method does Wal-Mart use to value its inventory? Describe how this method is applied.
2. Why do you think Wal-Mart uses the inventory method you identified in the previous question to value its inventory?
3. Why does Wal-Mart use the retail LIFO inventory method for domestic operations but the retail FIFO inventory method for international operations?

DOLLAR-VALUE LIFO RETAIL METHOD

We discussed the advantages of the dollar-value LIFO method in Chapter 8, and we discussed the advantages of the retail method earlier in this chapter. Many retail companies take advantage of both these methods by using the dollar-value LIFO retail method, which combines the principles of the retail LIFO method with the dollar-value LIFO method. Although no new principles are involved, we provide an illustration of the dollar-value retail LIFO inventory method for the Weston Company because of the complexity involved. We show the basic information in Example 9-12, and we show the calculation of the cost of the ending inventory in Example 9-13.

8 Understand the dollar-value LIFO retail method.

EXAMPLE 9-12   **Weston Company Cost and Retail Values and Price Indexes**

	2007 Cost	2007 Retail	2008 Cost	2008 Retail	2009 Cost	2009 Retail
Jan. 1, inventory	$ 8,000	$12,000				
Purchases	20,400	32,000	$25,600	$41,000	$26,040	$45,000
Net markups		3,000		2,000		1,000
Net markdowns		(1,000)		(3,000)		(4,000)
Sales		(29,800)		(32,240)		(42,990)

Price Index:
Jan. 1, 2007	100
Dec. 31, 2007	108
Dec. 31, 2008	115
Dec. 31, 2009	120

Note: It is assumed that LIFO is adopted on January 1, 2007.

In Example 9-13, the cost-to-retail ratio is computed in the same manner as we described earlier for the LIFO retail method. That is, the ratio includes both net markups and net markdowns but excludes the beginning inventory. The dollar-value LIFO concepts are applied to the retail values as follows (the numbers in parentheses are from Example 9-13 for 2007):

1. The ending inventory at retail ($16,200) is computed by adding the beginning inventory, purchases, and the markups, and subtracting the markdowns and sales. Alternatively, it is computed at year-end by taking a physical inventory in which the number of units in ending inventory is multiplied by the current-year retail prices.
2. The ending inventory at retail ($16,200) is converted to base-year retail prices ($15,000) by applying the base-year conversion index:

$$\frac{\text{Ending Inventory at}}{\text{Base-Year Retail Prices}} = \frac{\text{Ending Inventory}}{\text{at Retail}} \times \frac{\text{Base-Year Retail Price Index}}{\text{Current-Year Price Index}}$$

Note that the conversion index used here is based on a *price* index, while the conversion index used in Chapter 8 was based on a *cost* index. A price index is computed in the same way as a cost index, except that retail prices are used.
3. The increase (decrease) in the inventory at retail in base-year prices is computed by comparing the ending inventory with the beginning inventory when both are measured at retail in base-year prices (an increase of $3,000).

EXAMPLE 9-13 Dollar-Value LIFO Retail Inventory Method

	2007 Cost	2007 Retail	2008 Cost	2008 Retail	2009 Cost	2009 Retail
Beginning inventory*	$ 8,000	$12,000	$ 9,944	$16,200	$14,238	$23,960
Purchases	20,400	$32,000	25,600	$41,000	26,040	$45,000
Net markups		3,000		2,000		1,000
Net markdowns		(1,000)		(3,000)		(4,000)
		34,000		40,000		42,000
Goods available for sale	$28,400	$46,000	$35,544	$56,200	$40,278	$65,960
Sales		(29,800)		(32,240)		(42,990)
Ending inventory at retail		$16,200 (1)		$23,960		$22,970
Ending inventory at retail at base-year prices:						
$16,200 × (100 ÷ 108)		$15,000 (2)				
$23,960 × (100 ÷ 115)				$20,835		
$22,970 × (100 ÷ 120)						$19,142
Inventory change at retail base-year prices:						
$15,000 − $12,000		$ 3,000 (3)				
$20,835 − $15,000				$ 5,835		
$19,142 − $20,835						$ (1,693)
Change at retail at relevant current prices:						
$3,000 × (108 ÷ 100)		$ 3,240 (4)				
$5,835 × (115 ÷ 100)				$ 6,710		
($1,693) × (115 ÷ 100)						$ (1,947)
Change at relevant current costs:*						
$3,240 × 0.60	$ 1,944 (5)					
$6,710 × 0.64			$ 4,294			
($1,947) × 0.64					$ (1,246)	
Year-end LIFO inventory:						
Base-year layer	$ 8,000		$ 8,000		$ 8,000	
Layer added in 2007	1,944		1,944		1,944	
Layer added in 2008			4,294		4,294	
Layer subtracted in 2009 at 2008 costs					(1,246)	
Ending inventory	$ 9,944 (6)		$14,238		$12,992	

*2007 cost-to-retail ratio for beginning inventory: $8,000 ÷ $12,000 = 0.667; 2007 cost-to-retail ratio for purchases: $20,400 ÷ $34,000 = 0.60; 2008 cost-to-retail ratio for purchases: $25,600 ÷ $40,000 = 0.64.

4. The increase (decrease) in the inventory at retail in base-year prices ($3,000) is converted to current-year retail prices ($3,240) by multiplying by the appropriate conversion index. If there is an *increase*, the current year conversion index is used as follows:

$$\text{Layer Increase at Current-Year Retail Prices} = \text{Increase at Base-Year Retail Prices} \times \frac{\text{Current-Year Price Index}}{\text{Base-Year Price Index}}$$

Alternatively, if there is a *decrease*, the conversion index for the appropriate LIFO layer is used as follows:

$$\text{Decrease at Retail Prices of Most Recently Added Layer} = \text{Decrease at Base-Year Retail Prices} \times \frac{\text{Price Index of Most Recently Added Layer}}{\text{Base-Year Price Index}}$$

Note that for large decreases that affect more than one layer of inventory, the price index applicable to each layer must be used in the conversion index.

5. The increase (decrease) at current-year retail prices is converted to cost ($1,944) by multiplying by the cost-to-retail ratio for the appropriate year. If there is an increase, the cost-to-retail ratio for the current year is used (0.60). If there is a decrease, the cost-to-retail ratio(s) for the LIFO layer(s) being removed is used.

6. The ending inventory at cost ($9,944) is computed by adding (subtracting) the increase (decrease) at cost to the beginning inventory at cost ($1,944 + $8,000).

Continuing the example, in 2008 the ending inventory at retail of $23,960 is converted to base-year retail prices of $20,835 by multiplying by the base-year conversion index (100 ÷ 115). Comparing the $20,835 to the ending inventory at retail base-year prices in 2007 of $15,000 results in an increase in inventory at base-year retail prices of $5,835. This increase is multiplied by the current-year conversion index of 115 ÷ 100 to compute the increase at current retail prices of $6,710. The $6,710 is multiplied by the cost-to-retail ratio of 0.64 to compute the $4,294 increase at current-year costs, which is added to the $9,944 ending inventory cost from 2007 to determine the $14,238 cost of the ending inventory for 2008.

In 2009 there is a *decrease* in the inventory of $1,693 at base-year retail prices. This is converted into a $1,947 decrease by applying the conversion index for 2008, since part of the layer added in 2008 is being removed. This decrease of $1,947 at retail is converted to cost by applying the cost-to-retail ratio for 2008 of 0.64, resulting in a decrease at cost of $1,246. Note that the conversion index of 115 ÷ 100 and the cost ratio of 0.64 would be used only for a reduction in inventory at base-year retail prices of $5,835, because this is the amount of the increase from 2008. The next $3,000 reduction at base-year retail prices would be at the conversion index of 108 ÷ 100 and the cost ratio of 0.60 (for the layer added in 2007) and the remaining $12,000 at a conversion index of 100 ÷ 100 and the cost ratio of 0.667 (for the beginning inventory from 2007).

EFFECTS OF INVENTORY ERRORS

In addition to the special methods we described earlier in the chapter, errors made by a company may affect its ending inventory valuation. Errors in the valuation of inventory and the recording of purchases can result in inaccurate values on the company's balance

9 Understand the effects of inventory errors on the financial statements.

sheet and income statement. We summarize the effects of some common errors in Exhibit 9-1 (assuming a periodic inventory system and ignoring income taxes):

EXHIBIT 9-1   Effects of Inventory Errors

I.   A purchase on credit is omitted from both the Purchases account and ending inventory and is *not* recorded in the succeeding year.
  A. **Current year**
    1. *Income Statement*. Income is correct because the errors in the purchases and ending inventory offset each other.
    2. *Balance Sheet*. Ending inventory and accounts payable are understated.
  B. **Succeeding year**
    1. *Income Statement*. Income is overstated because beginning inventory is understated and therefore cost of goods sold is understated.
    2. *Balance Sheet*. Accounts payable is understated and retained earnings is overstated. Note that if the purchase omitted from the current year was included in the succeeding year, the income would be correct in the second year because the errors would again offset each other. Accounts payable and retained earnings would also be correct.

II. A purchase on credit is omitted from the Purchases account but ending inventory is correct.
  A. **Current year**
    1. *Income Statement*. Income is overstated because purchases are understated and therefore cost of goods sold is understated.
    2. *Balance Sheet*. Accounts payable is understated because a purchase has been omitted. Retained earnings is overstated because income is overstated.
  B. **Succeeding year**
    1. *Income Statement*. No effect because the beginning inventory, purchases, and ending inventory are correct.
    2. *Balance Sheet*. Accounts payable is understated and retained earnings is overstated, due to the error in the previous period.

III. Ending inventory is over(under)stated due to quantity and/or costing errors, but purchases are correct.
  A. **Current year**
    1. *Income Statement*. Income is over(under)stated because cost of goods sold is under(over)stated.
    2. *Balance Sheet*. Ending inventory and retained earnings are over(under)stated.
  B. **Succeeding year**
    1. *Income Statement*. Income is under(over)stated because beginning inventory is over(under)stated, and therefore cost of goods sold is over(under)stated.
    2. *Balance Sheet*. Correct because the errors in inventory and retained earnings in the previous year were counterbalanced in this year.

Note that in the third situation in Exhibit 9-1 the total income for the two years combined is correct, as is the ending inventory for the succeeding year. For example, assume that a company's periodic inventory at December 31, 2007 is overstated by $5,000 but purchases are correct. The following errors occur (ignoring income taxes) in the company's financial statements:

2007: *Income Statement*. Cost of goods sold is understated by $5,000 and income is overstated by $5,000.

Balance Sheet. Ending inventory and retained earnings are overstated by $5,000.

2008: *Income Statement*. Cost of goods sold is overstated by $5,000 and income is understated by $5,000.

Balance Sheet. Ending inventory and retained earnings are correct because the errors have counterbalanced each other.

These errors are illustrated by the following equations:

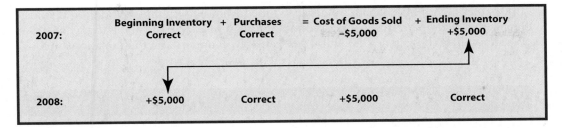

	Beginning Inventory + Purchases		= Cost of Goods Sold	+ Ending Inventory
2007:	Correct	Correct	−$5,000	+$5,000
2008:	+$5,000	Correct	+$5,000	Correct

Note that if income taxes are considered, the effect of the error on income is reduced. For example, if the company has an income tax rate of 30%, the inventory is still overstated by $5,000, but net income in 2007 is overstated by only $3,500 [$5,000 × (1 − 0.30)] and income taxes payable is increased by $1,500 ($5,000 × 0.30). Thus the errors affect more items on the company's balance sheet, but the balance sheet still balances because assets are overstated by $5,000, liabilities by $1,500, and stockholders' equity by $3,500.

Many companies use a perpetual inventory system. Under this system, they still take a physical inventory and may make similar errors. The discovery of inventory errors requires careful analysis and adjusting entries to correct the company's accounts. If a company discovers a material error after it has closed the books, it treats the correction as a prior period adjustment. In this case it corrects the permanent (real) accounts. The company makes the corrections it would have made to temporary (nominal) accounts to Retained Earnings instead, as we discuss in Chapter 23.

SECURE YOUR KNOWLEDGE 9-2

- When it is impractical, infeasible, or impossible to perform a physical count of inventory, inventory estimation techniques such as the gross profit method or the retail inventory method may be used.
- The gross profit method estimates the cost of inventory by
  - Calculating a historical gross profit rate,
  - Applying this gross profit rate to the net sales of the current period to get an estimate of gross profit,
  - Subtracting the estimated gross profit from net sales to get estimated cost of goods sold, and
  - Subtracting the estimated cost of goods sold from actual cost of goods available for sale.
- The retail method is a commonly used estimation technique that can produce inventory valuations under FIFO, average cost, LIFO, or lower of average cost or market cost flow assumptions by modifying the calculation of the cost-to-retail ratio. Ending inventory is estimated by:
  - Calculating cost of goods available for sale at both cost and retail,
  - Subtracting sales from the retail value of cost of goods available for sale to obtain ending inventory at retail,
  - Computing a cost-to-retail ratio that will allow inventory valuations under FIFO, average cost, LIFO, or lower of average cost or market cost flow assumptions, and
  - Applying the appropriate cost-to-retail ratio to ending inventory at retail.
- The dollar-value LIFO retail method combines the principles of the retail LIFO method with the dollar-value LIFO method
- Errors in the valuation of inventory can result in inaccurate balance sheet and income measurements that affect multiple years. Careful analysis is required to determine the effects of such errors.

SUMMARY OF INVENTORY ISSUES

In Chapter 8 and this chapter, we discussed the inventory systems, methods, and adjustments that a company may use to account for its cost of goods sold and ending inventory. We summarize these issues in Exhibit 9-2 to help you understand their relationships.

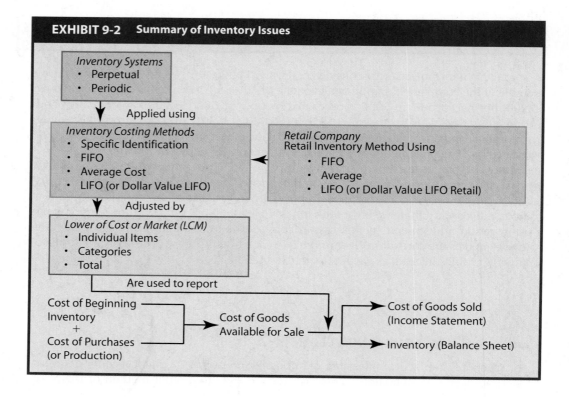

EXHIBIT 9-2   Summary of Inventory Issues

Inventory Systems
• Perpetual
• Periodic

Applied using

Inventory Costing Methods
• Specific Identification
• FIFO
• Average Cost
• LIFO (or Dollar Value LIFO)

Retail Company
Retail Inventory Method Using
• FIFO
• Average
• LIFO (or Dollar Value LIFO Retail)

Adjusted by

Lower of Cost or Market (LCM)
• Individual Items
• Categories
• Total

Are used to report

Cost of Beginning Inventory
+
Cost of Purchases (or Production)

Cost of Goods Available for Sale

Cost of Goods Sold (Income Statement)

Inventory (Balance Sheet)

SUMMARY

At the beginning of the chapter, we identified several objectives you would accomplish after reading the chapter. The objectives are listed below, each followed by a brief summary of the key points in the chapter discussion.

1. **Understand the lower of cost or market method.** The lower of cost or market rule requires that a company write down its inventory to market value (replacement cost) when its utility has declined. The upper constraint on the market value is that the market value should not exceed the net realizable value. The lower constraint is that the market value should not be below the net realizable value reduced by an allowance for a normal profit margin. A company may apply the method to each item in inventory, to major categories, or to the inventory as a whole.

2. **Explain the conceptual issues regarding the lower of cost or market method.** The conceptual issues include the appropriateness of recognizing a loss and a reduction in the value of the inventory before a transaction occurs. Another issue is that a company only recognizes declines in value. The method also affects the amount of income a company recognizes in future periods.

3. **Understand purchase obligations and product financing arrangements.** If a company has incurred an unconditional purchase obligation at a definite price, the company discloses this commitment in a note to its financial statements. In a product financing arrangement, the company does not recognize the transfer of the inventory as a sale, but records the proceeds received as a liability.

4. **Explain the valuation of inventory above cost.** Inventory may be valued above cost only in rare circumstances, such as for precious metals and certain agricultural and mineral products.

5. **Use the gross profit method.** A company uses the gross profit method to estimate the cost of the inventory by applying a gross profit rate based on its income statements of previous periods to the net sales of the current period. It deducts the estimated gross profit from the actual net sales to determine the estimated cost of goods sold and deducts the latter amount from the cost of goods available for sale to determine the estimated ending inventory.

6. **Understand the retail inventory method.** Retail companies often use the retail inventory method in which they compute the ending inventory at cost by multiplying the ending inventory at retail by a cost-to-retail ratio. The computation of the cost-to-retail ratio varies depending on which cost flow assumption the company is using, and whether it is using the lower of cost or market method.

7. **Explain the conceptual issues regarding the retail inventory method.** The retail inventory method involves two assumptions. First, the items in inventory are assumed to be relatively homogeneous so that they have the same markup. Second, the cost-to-retail ratio is assumed to remain constant over the period. Furthermore, the lower of average cost or market retail method (the most widely used method) is accurate only if either markups and markdowns do not exist at the same time or if all the marked-down items have been sold.

8. **Understand the dollar-value LIFO retail method.** Under the dollar-value LIFO retail method, a company determines its ending inventory at retail and then converts this amount to the ending inventory at base-year retail prices by applying a base-year conversion index. It then determines the increase (decrease) in inventory at base-year retail prices and converts this amount to current-year retail prices using the appropriate conversion index. It converts the increase (decrease) to cost using the cost-to-retail ratio for the current year and then adds (subtracts) this amount to the beginning inventory at cost to determine the ending inventory at cost. The dollar-value LIFO retail method combines the advantages of the dollar-value LIFO method with those of the retail method.

9. **Understand the effects of inventory errors on the financial statements.** Errors in the valuation of inventory and the recording of purchases can result in inaccurate values on a company's balance sheet and income statement. The company must carefully examine each error to determine the appropriate correction.

ANSWERS TO REAL REPORT QUESTIONS

Real Report 9-1 Answer

1. While inventory is normally valued using the lower of cost or market method, ConAgra is able to value its inventory of grain, flour, and feed ingredients at market value because of their immediate marketability at quoted prices. This represents an exception to the general rule of inventory valuation and should only be used in exceptional cases.

Real Report 9-2 Answers

1. Wal-Mart values its inventory at the lower of cost or market using the retail method. The retail inventory method requires records of beginning inventory and goods purchased to be kept at cost (Wal-Mart uses a LIFO assumption) and retail. The retail inventory method then estimates the cost of inventory by applying a cost-to-retail ratio to the ending inventory valued at retail. To achieve a lower of cost or market valuation of the ending inventory, the cost and retail value of the beginning inventory and net markups are included in the computation of the cost-to-retail ratio (net markdowns are excluded). This method is known as the conventional retail method.

2. With inventory over $26 billion, a physical count of inventory is a major undertaking. Wal-Mart most likely uses the retail method because this permits it to compute cost of goods sold and income without having to take a physical count of inventory.

3. Given rising inventory costs, Wal-Mart's use of the LIFO cost flow assumption will result in lower inventory values, earnings, and taxes (assuming the use of LIFO for tax purposes). However, LIFO is not generally allowed for tax purposes in foreign countries and with these benefits removed, the advantages of a FIFO cost flow assumption (higher income and balance sheet amounts) likely outweigh any remaining benefits of using LIFO.

QUESTIONS

Q9-1 Define the terms *cost* and *market* as used in the lower of cost or market inventory valuation rule.

Q9-2 Define the *upper* and *lower* constraints used in the lower of cost or market rule. What is the purpose of each constraint?

Q9-3 How may a company apply the lower of cost or market method to its inventory?

Q9-4 What arguments may be used against the lower of cost or market rule?

Q9-5 Under what conditions does a company anticipate price declines?

Q9-6 How, and under what conditions, does a company recognize a purchase obligation or a product financing arrangement in its financial statements?

Q9-7 What are the exceptions to historical cost valuation of inventory allowed under generally accepted accounting principles? Under what conditions is each allowed?

Q9-8 Describe four situations in which the gross profit method of estimating inventory would be useful.

Q9-9 What is the basic assumption underlying the gross profit method? How may the gross profit percentage for the prior year be modified to provide a better estimate of the inventory value?

Q9-10 What are the necessary conditions for the retail inventory method to provide valid results?

Q9-11 Explain the meaning of the following terms: *markup, additional markup, markup cancellation, net markup, markdown, markdown cancellation, net markdown.*

Q9-12 Describe how a company computes the cost-to-retail ratio for the following cost flow assumptions: FIFO, average cost, LIFO, lower of average cost or market. Why do the different methods approximate each cost flow assumption?

Q9-13 What assumptions are necessary for the lower of cost or market retail inventory method to actually produce an inventory value equal to the lower of average cost or market?

Q9-14 The retail inventory method indicated an inventory value of $80,000. A physical inventory indicated a value of $70,000. Suggest possible causes of this discrepancy.

Q9-15 Indicate the effect of each of the following errors on a company's balance sheet and income statement of the current and succeeding years:
a. The ending inventory is overstated.
b. Merchandise received was not recorded in the Purchases account until the succeeding year although the item was included in inventory of the current year.
c. Merchandise purchases shipped FOB shipping point were not recorded in either the Purchases account or the ending inventory.
d. The ending inventory was understated as a result of the exclusion of goods sent out on consignment.

MULTIPLE CHOICE (AICPA Adapted)

Select the best answer for each of the following.

M9-1 Moore Company carries product A in inventory on December 31, 2007 at its unit cost of $7.50. Because of a sharp decline in demand for the product, the selling price was reduced to $8.00 per unit. Moore's normal profit margin on product A is $1.60, disposal costs are $1.00 per unit, and the replacement cost is $5.30. Under the rule of cost or market, whichever is lower, Moore's December 31, 2007 inventory of product A should be valued at a unit cost of
a. $5.30
b. $5.40
c. $7.00
d. $7.50

M9-2 Under the retail inventory method, freight-in would be included in the calculation of the goods available for sale for which of the following?

	Cost	Retail
a.	No	No
b.	No	Yes
c.	Yes	No
d.	Yes	Yes

M9-3 The following information is available for the Silver Company for the three months ended March 31, 2007:

Merchandise inventory, January 1, 2007	$ 900,000
Purchases	3,400,000
Freight-in	200,000
Sales	4,800,000

The gross margin recorded was 25% of sales. What should be the merchandise inventory at March 31, 2007?

a. $700,000
b. $900,000
c. $1,125,000
d. $1,200,000

M9-4 The retail inventory method would include which of the following in the calculation of the goods available for sale at both cost and retail?

a. Freight-in
b. Purchases returns
c. Markups
d. Markdowns

M9-5 During 2007 R Corp., a manufacturer of chocolate candies, contracted to purchase 100,000 pounds of cocoa beans at $1.00 per pound, delivery to be made in the spring of 2008. Because a record harvest is predicted for 2008, the price per pound for cocoa beans had fallen to $.80 by December 31, 2007.

Of the following journal entries, the one that would properly reflect in 2007 the effect of the commitment of R Corp. to purchase the 100,000 pounds of cocoa is

		Debit	Credit
a.	Cocoa Inventory	100,000	
	Accounts Payable		100,000
b.	Cocoa Inventory	80,000	
	Loss on Purchase Commit-ments (an expense account)	20,000	
	Accounts Payable		100,000
c.	Loss on Purchase Commit-ments (an expense account)	20,000	
	Accrued Loss on Purchase Commitments (a liability account)		20,000

d. No entry would be necessary in 2007.

M9-6 The replacement cost of an inventory item is below the net realizable value and above the net realizable value less the normal profit margin. The original cost of the inventory item is above the replacement cost and below the net realizable value. As a result, under the lower of cost or market method, the inventory item should be valued at the

a. Net realizable value
b. Original cost
c. Replacement cost
d. Net realizable value less the normal profit margin

M9-7 At December 31, 2007 the following information was available from Crisford Company's books:

	Cost	Retail
Inventory, 1/1/07	$14,700	$ 20,300
Purchases	83,300	115,500
Additional markups	—	4,200
Available for sale	$98,000	$140,000

Sales for the year totaled $110,600; markdowns amounted to $1,400. Under the approximate lower of average cost or market retail method, Crisford's inventory at December 31, 2007 was

a. $30,800
b. $28,000
c. $21,560
d. $19,600

M9-8 Hestor Company's records indicate the following information:

Merchandise inventory, January 1, 2007	$ 550,000
Purchases, January 1 through December 31, 2007	2,250,000
Sales, January 1 through December 31, 2007	3,000,000

On December 31, 2007 a physical inventory determined that ending inventory of $600,000 was in the warehouse. Hestors gross profit on sales has remained constant at 30%. Hestor suspects some of the inventory may have been taken by some new employees. At December 31, 2007 what is the estimated cost of missing inventory?

a. $100,000
b. $200,000
c. $300,000
d. $700,000

M9-9 Estimates of price-level changes for specific inventories are required for which of the following inventory methods?

a. Conventional retail
b. Weighted average cost
c. FIFO
d. Dollar-value retail LIFO

M9-10 A company forgets to record a purchase on credit in the Purchases account, but ending inventory is correct. The effect of this mistake in the current year is:

	Income	Cost of goods sold	Accounts payable	Retained earnings
a.	Overstated	Understated	Understated	Overstated
b.	Understated	Overstated	Overstated	Understated
c.	Overstated	Understated	Overstated	Understated
d.	Understated	Overstated	Understated	Overstated

EXERCISES

E9-1 *Lower of Cost or Market* The Stiles Corporation uses the lower of cost or market method for each of two products in its ending inventory. A profit margin of 30% on the selling price is considered normal for each product. Specific data for each product are as follows:

	Product A	Product B
Historical cost	$ 68	$ 91
Replacement cost	60	93
Estimated cost of disposal	32	52
Estimated selling price	140	200

Required
What is the correct inventory value for each product?

E9-2 *Lower of Cost or Market* The following information for the Tuell Company is available:

	Case				
	1	2	3	4	5
Cost	$5.00	$5.00	$5.00	$5.00	$5.00
Net realizable value	5.10	5.50	4.80	4.20	4.70
Net realizable value less normal profit	4.80	5.30	4.70	4.00	4.60
Replacement cost	5.30	5.20	4.60	4.10	4.80

Required
What is the correct inventory value in each of the preceding situations?

E9-3 *Lower of Cost or Market* The following information is taken from the records of the Aden Company:

Product	Group	Units	Cost/Unit	Market/Unit
A	1	600	$ 1.00	$ 0.80
B	1	250	1.50	1.55
C	2	150	5.00	5.25
D	2	100	6.50	6.40
E	3	80	25.00	24.60

Required
What is the correct inventory value if the company applies the lower of cost or market to each of the following?

1. Individual items
2. Groups of items
3. The inventory as a whole

E9-4 *Lower of Cost or Market* The inventories of the Berry Company for the years 2007 and 2008 are as follows:

	Cost	Market
January 1, 2007	$10,000	$10,000
December 31, 2007	13,000	11,500
December 31, 2008	15,000	14,000

Required
Prepare the necessary journal entries at the end of each year to record the correct inventory valuation. Use the allowance method and assume that a periodic inventory system is used.

E9-5 *Loss on Purchase Commitment* During 2007 the Boge Corporation signed a noncancelable contract to purchase 10,000 bushels of soybeans at $5 per bushel with delivery to be made in 2008. On December 31, 2007, the price of soybeans had fallen to $4.50 per bushel. On May 1, 2008, the Boge Corporation takes delivery of the soybeans when the price is $4.75 per bushel.

Required
Prepare the journal entries required on December 31, 2007 and May 1, 2008.

E9-6   *Estimation of Fire Loss*   On September 28, 2007 a fire destroyed the entire merchandise inventory of the Carroll Corporation. The following information is available:

Sales, January 1—September 28, 2007	$540,000
Inventory, January 1, 2007	$150,000
Merchandise purchases, January 1—September 28, 2007 (including $60,000 of goods in transit on September 28, 2007, shipped FOB shipping point)	$465,000
Markup percentage on cost	20%

Required
What is the estimated inventory on September 28, 2007 immediately prior to the fire?

E9-7   **AICPA Adapted**   *Gross Profit Method*   On November 21, 2007 a fire at Hodge Company's warehouse caused severe damage to its entire inventory of Product Tex. Hodge estimates that all usable damaged goods can be sold for $10,000. The following information was available from Hodge's accounting records for Product Tex:

Inventory at November 1, 2007	$100,000
Purchases from November 1, 2007 to date of fire	140,000
Net sales from November 1, 2007 to date of fire	220,000

Based on recent history, Hodge had a gross margin (profit) on Product Tex of 30% of net sales.

Required
Prepare a schedule to calculate the estimated loss on the inventory in the fire, using the gross margin (profit) method. Show supporting computations in good form.

E9-8   *Gross Profit*   The following gross profit data are taken from the financial records of the Eckhardt Company:

	2007	2008
Sales	$300,000	$296,000
Cost of goods sold	(200,000)	(203,300)
Gross profit	$100,000	$ 92,700

Required
1. If it is known that volume declined 5% from 2007 to 2008, by how much did selling prices change?
2. If it is known that volume declined 5% from 2007 to 2008, by how much did costs change?
3. If selling prices increased 4% from 2007 to 2008, what effect would this factor alone have on gross profit?
4. If costs increased by 7% from 2007 to 2008, what effect would this factor have on gross profit?

E9-9   *Gross Profit Percentage*   An accountant sometimes must convert gross profit percentages.

Required
1. Convert the following gross profit percentages based on net sales to gross profit as a percentage of the cost of goods sold: 20%, 25%, and 40%.
2. Convert the following gross profit percentages based on the cost of goods sold to gross profit as a percentage of net sales: 20%, 25%, and 40%.

E9-10   *Retail Inventory Method*   The Harmes Company is a clothing store that uses the retail inventory method. The following information relates to its operations during 2007:

	Cost	Retail
Inventory, January 1	$28,400	$ 40,200
Purchases	65,200	100,000
Markups (net)	—	1,900
Markdowns (net)	—	400
Sales	—	80,000

Required 🖾
Compute the ending inventory by the retail inventory method for the following cost flow assumptions:

1. FIFO
2. Average cost

3. LIFO
4. Lower of cost or market (based on average cost)

E9-11 AICPA Adapted *Retail Inventory Method* The following data were available from the records of the Hegge Department Store for the year ended December 31, 2007:

	At Cost	At Retail
Merchandise inventory, January 1, 2007:	$ 90,000	$130,000
Purchases	330,000	460,000
Markups	—	10,000
Markdowns	—	40,000
Sales	—	480,000

Required
Using the retail method, what is the estimate of the merchandise inventory at December 31, 2007 valued at the lower of cost or market?

E9-12 *Retail Inventory Method* The following information relates to the retail inventory method used by the Jeffress Company:

	Cost	Retail
Beginning inventory	$11,160	$18,000
Purchases	54,600	92,400
Freight-in	840	—
Net markups	—	600
Net markdowns	—	1,144
Sales	—	94,056

Required
Compute the ending inventory by the retail inventory method, using the following cost flow assumptions:
1. FIFO
2. Average cost
3. LIFO
4. Lower of cost or market (based on average cost)

E9-13 *Dollar-Value LIFO Retail* The Johns Company adopts the dollar-value LIFO retail inventory method on January 1, 2007. The following information for 2007 is obtained from the company's records:

	Cost	Retail
Inventory, January 1, 2007	$20,000	$29,000
Purchases	60,000	92,000
Net markups	—	1,000
Net markdowns	—	3,000
Sales	—	75,000

The price index on January 1, 2007 was 100 and on December 31, 2007 it was 110.

Required
Compute the cost of the inventory on December 31, 2007.

E9-14 *Dollar-Value LIFO Retail* The Wyatt Company adopts the dollar-value LIFO retail inventory method on January 1, 2007. The company's records reveal that the inventory on January 1, 2007 had a cost of $75,000 and a retail value of $120,000. During 2007 the cost of purchases made was $110,000, and the retail value was $165,000. In addition, net markdowns were $6,000, net markups were $8,000, and sales were $147,000. The price index on January 1, 2007 was 100 and the index for 2004 was 110.

Required
Compute the cost of inventory on December 31, 2007. (Round the cost-to-retail index to 3 decimal places.)

E9-15 AICPA Adapted *Dollar-Value LIFO Retail* On December 31, 2006 Davison Company adopted the dollar-value LIFO retail inventory method. Inventory data for 2007 are as follows:

	LIFO Cost	Retail
Inventory, 12/31/06	$360,000	$500,000
Inventory, 12/31/07	?	660,000
Increase in price level for 2007		10%
Cost-to-retail ratio for 2007		70%

Required
Compute the cost of Davison Company's inventory at December 31, 2007.

E9-16 *Errors* A company that uses the periodic inventory system makes the following errors:

1. It omits a purchase on credit from the Purchases account and the ending inventory.
2. It omits a purchase on credit from the Purchases account, but the ending inventory is correct.
3. It overstates the ending inventory, but purchases are correct.

Required
Indicate the effect of the preceding errors on the income statement and the balance sheet of the current and succeeding years.

E9-17 **AICPA Adapted** *Errors* During the course of your examination of the financial statements of Burnett Co., a new client, for the year ended December 31, 2007, you discover the following:

Inventory at January 1, 2007 was understated by $6,000.
Inventory at December 31, 2007 was overstated by $5,000.

During 2007 the company received a $1,000 cash advance from a customer for merchandise to be manufactured and shipped during 2008. It had credited the $1,000 to sales revenue. The company's gross profit on sales is 50%. Net income reported on the 2007 income statement (before reflecting any adjustments for the above items) is $20,000.

Required
What is the correct net income for 2007?

PROBLEMS

P9-1 *Lower of Cost or Market* The Palmquist Company has five different inventory items that it values by the lower of cost or market method. The normal markup on all items is 20% of cost. The following information is obtained from the company's records:

Item	Units	Cost	Replacement Cost	Net Realizable Value
1	500	$10.00	$ 9.10	$ 9.20
2	400	8.00	8.10	7.80
3	300	15.00	13.50	14.00
4	200	18.00	12.00	17.00
5	100	25.00	25.50	25.30

Required
1. Compute the lower of cost or market value for each item.
2. Compute the total inventory value if the lower of cost or market is applied to (a) each individual item and (b) the inventory as a whole. Explain the reason for the difference between the two values.

P9-2 *Lower of Cost or Market* The following are the inventories for the years 2007, 2008, and 2009 for the Parry Company:

	Cost	Market
January 1, 2007	$50,000	$50,000
December 31, 2007	64,000	60,000
December 31, 2008	71,000	70,000
December 31, 2009	75,000	78,000

Required
Prepare journal entries to record the lower of cost or market for each of the following alternatives:

1. Allowance method, periodic inventory system
2. Allowance method, perpetual inventory system
3. Direct method, periodic inventory system
4. Direct method, perpetual inventory system

P9-3 *Lower of Cost or Market and Interim Financial Statements* The following values were obtained from the inventory records of the Robb Company, which has a fiscal year ending on December 31:

	Cost	Market
Inventory, January 1, 2007	$10,000	$10,500
Inventory, March 31, 2007	12,000	11,500

Required
1. Under what conditions does the company ignore the decline in inventory value below cost in its interim financial statements?
2. Assuming that the company records the market value, what is the journal entry to record the decline if the company uses the perpetual inventory system and the allowance method?

P9-4 *Lower of Cost or Market* The inventory records of the Frost Company for the years 2007 and 2008 reveal the cost and market of the January 1, 2007 inventory to be $125,000. On December 31, 2007 the cost of inventory was $130,000, while the market value was only $128,000. The December 31, 2008 market value of inventory was $140,000, and the cost was only $135,000. The Frost Company uses a periodic inventory system. Purchases for 2007 were $100,000 and for 2008 were $110,000.

Required
1. Prepare the journal entries at the end of 2007 and 2008 to record the lower of cost or market under the (a) allowance method, and (b) direct method.
2. Prepare the cost of goods sold section of the income statement and show how the company would record the inventory on its balance sheet for 2007 and 2008 under the (a) allowance method, and (b) direct method.

P9-5 *Gross Profit* The following information relates to the activities of the Skeen Corporation for 2007:

Work in process, January 1	$25,000	Finished goods, December 31	$ 30,000
Work in process, December 31	40,000	Cost of production	70,000
Finished goods, January 1	37,000	Sales (net)	100,000

Required
What is the gross profit as a percentage of net sales?

P9-6 *Estimation of Theft Loss* You are requested by a client on September 28 to prepare an insurance claim for a theft loss which occurred on that day. You immediately take an inventory and obtain the following data:

Inventory, September 1	$38,000	Sales, September 1–September 28	$52,000
Purchases received, September 1–September 28	19,000	Sales returns	1,000

The inventory on September 28 indicates that an inventory of $15,000 remains after the theft. During the past year net sales were made at 50% above the cost of goods sold.

Required
Compute the inventory lost during the theft.

P9-7 *Estimation of Fire Loss* On January 20, 2008 the records of the Stewart Company revealed the following information:

Inventory, July 1, 2007	$ 53,600	Purchases discounts taken	$5,800
Purchases, July 1, 2007–January 20, 2008	368,000	Freight-in	3,800
Sales, July 1, 2007–January 20, 2008	583,000	Sales returns	6,600
Purchases returns	11,200		

A fire destroyed the entire inventory on January 20, 2008 except for purchases in transit, FOB shipping point, of $6,000 and goods having a selling price of $4,700 that were salvaged from the fire. The salvaged goods had an estimated salvage value of $2,900. The average gross profit on net sales in previous periods was 40%.

Required
1. Compute the cost of the inventory lost in the fire.
2. If a company discloses that it uses a periodic inventory system, what concerns might you have about its interim financial statements?

P9-8 *Estimation of Loss* On February 17, 2007 a flood destroyed the work in process inventory and half the raw materials inventory of the LRT Company. There was no damage to the finished goods inventory. A physical inventory taken after the flood indicated the following values:

Raw materials	$35,000	Finished goods	$79,000

A review of the accounting records indicated the following:

Inventories, December 31, 2006

Raw materials	$70,000	Raw materials purchases	$20,000
Work in process	80,000	Direct labor cost	30,000
Finished goods	72,000	Manufacturing overhead cost	15,000
Sales (to February 17)	50,000	Gross profit rate (on sales)	40%

Required
Compute the value of the inventory destroyed by the flood.

P9-9 **AICPA Adapted** *Estimation of Flood Loss* On June 30, 2007 a flash flood damaged the warehouse and factory of Padway Corporation, completely destroying the work-in-process inventory. There was no damage to either the raw materials or finished goods inventories. A physical inventory taken after the flood revealed the following valuations:

Raw materials	$ 62,000
Work in process	-0-
Finished goods	119,000

The inventory on January 1, 2007 consisted of the following:

Raw materials	$ 30,000
Work in process	100,000
Finished goods	140,000
	$270,000

A review of the books and records disclosed that the gross profit margin historically approximated 25% of sales. The sales for the first six months of 2007 were $340,000. Raw material purchases were $115,000. Direct labor costs for this period were $80,000, and manufacturing overhead was historically applied at 50% of direct labor.

Required
Compute the value of the work-in-process inventory lost at June 30, 2007. Show supporting computations in good form.

P9-10 *Retail Inventory Method* The Turner Corporation uses the retail inventory method. The following information relates to 2007:

	Cost	Retail		Cost	Retail
Inventory, January 1	$ 29,000	$ 45,000	Additional markups	—	$ 50,000
Purchases (gross price)	140,000	190,000	Markup cancellations	—	10,000
Purchases discounts taken	3,000	—	Markdowns	—	15,000
Purchases returns	5,000	8,000	Markdown cancellations	—	3,000
Freight-in	20,000	—	Sales	—	190,000
Employee discounts	—	3,000			

Required
Compute the cost of the ending inventory under each of the following cost flow assumptions:

1. FIFO
2. Average cost
3. LIFO
4. Lower of cost or market (based on average cost)

P9-11 *Comprehensive* The EKC Company uses the retail inventory method. The following information for 2007 is available:

	Cost	Retail		Cost	Retail
Inventory, January 1	$100,000	$180,000	Markdowns	—	$ 15,000
Purchases (gross price)	320,000	600,000	Markdown cancellations	—	4,000
Purchases discounts taken	6,000	—	Sales	—	610,000
Freight-in	16,000	—	Sales returns	—	30,000
Additional markups	—	60,000	Sales discounts	—	10,000
Markup cancellations	—	12,000			

Required

Compute the cost of the ending inventory under each of the following cost flow assumptions:

1. FIFO
2. Average cost
3. LIFO
4. Lower of cost or market (based on average cost)

P9-12 ▐ AICPA Adapted ▐   *Retail Inventory Method*   The Red Department Store uses the retail inventory method. Information relating to the computation of the inventory at December 31, 2007 is as follows:

	Cost	Retail		Cost	Retail
Inventory at January 1, 2007	$ 32,000	$ 80,000	Markups	—	$60,000
Sales	—	600,000	Markup cancellations	—	10,000
Purchases	270,000	590,000	Markdowns	—	25,000
Freight-in	7,600	—	Markdown cancellations	—	5,000

Estimated normal shrinkage is 2% of sales.

Required

Prepare a schedule to calculate the estimated ending inventory at the lower of average cost or market at December 31, 2007, using the retail inventory method. Show supporting computations in good form.

P9-13   *Retail Inventory Method*   The Weber Corporation uses the retail inventory method to estimate its inventory balances. The following information is available on June 30:

	Cost	Retail		Cost	Retail
Inventory, January 1	$25,000	$ 60,000	Markdowns	—	$7,000
Purchases	75,000	180,000	Additional markups	—	3,000
Sales	—	210,000	Markdown cancellations	—	2,000
Purchases returns	2,000	5,000	Markup cancellations	—	1,000
Sales returns	—	5,000			

Required

1. Compute the inventory on June 30 using the "normal" retail inventory method (lower of average cost or market).
2. Independent of Requirement 1, assume that the June 30 inventory was $80,000 at retail and that the cost-to-retail ratio is 50%. If the price level of the inventory has risen by 5% during the period, compute the cost of the June 30 inventory under the dollar-value retail LIFO method, assuming that the company adopted the method at the beginning of the year.

P9-14   *Dollar-Value LIFO Retail*   The following information is obtained from the records of the Burger Company, which uses the dollar-value LIFO retail method:

	2007		2008		2009	
	Cost	Retail	Cost	Retail	Cost	Retail
Purchases	$200,000	$420,000	$250,000	$550,000	$240,000	$500,000
Net markups	—	20,000	—	30,000	—	10,000
Net markdowns	—	10,000	—	40,000	—	20,000
Sales	—	400,000	—	600,000	—	450,000

The company adopted LIFO on January 1, 2007, when the cost and retail values of the inventory were $50,000 and $100,000, respectively. The following price indexes were experienced by the Burger Company:

January 1, 2007	100	December 31, 2008	115
December 31, 2007	108	December 31, 2009	120

Required

Compute the cost of the ending inventory for 2007, 2008, and 2009.

P9-15   *Dollar-Value LIFO Retail*   Intella, Inc. adopted the dollar-value retail LIFO method on January 1, 2006. The following data apply to the 4 subsequent years:

		Cost	Retail			Cost	Retail
2006	Inventory, January 1	$40,000	$ 80,000	2008	Purchases	$117,600	$280,000
	Purchases	85,500	190,000		Sales	—	260,000
	Sales	—	200,000	2009	Purchases	147,200	320,000
2007	Purchases	92,000	230,000		Sales	—	300,000
	Sales	—	210,000				

In addition the following price indexes are available:

January 1, 2006	100	December 31, 2008	120
December 31, 2006	105	December 31, 2009	125
December 31, 2007	110		

Required ◩
Compute the inventory at the end of each of the 4 years.

P9-16 *Dollar-Value LIFO Retail and Fire Loss* The Golden Company adopted the dollar-value retail LIFO method on January 1, 2007. The following information relates to the following 2 years:

	2007			2008 (through September 7)	
	Cost	Retail		Cost	Retail
Inventory, January 1	$ 40,000	$ 90,000	Purchases	$160,000	$350,000
Purchases	100,000	210,000	Sales	—	280,000
Sales	—	200,000	Net markups	—	40,000
Net markups	—	20,000	Net markdowns	—	70,000
Net markdowns	—	40,000			

In addition the following price indexes are available:

January 2007	100
December 2007	106
September 2008	110

On September 8, 2008 a fire destroyed the inventory except for goods in transit (properly recorded), FOB shipping point, at a cost of $8,000, and undamaged goods salvaged from the fire, which had a retail value of $10,000.

Required
Compute the cost of the inventory destroyed in the fire.

P9-17 *Errors* As controller of the Lerner Company, which uses a periodic inventory system, you discover the following errors in the current year:
1. Merchandise with a cost of $17,500 was properly included in the final inventory, but the purchase was not recorded until the following year.
2. Merchandise purchases are in transit under terms of FOB shipping point. They have been excluded from the inventory, but the purchase was recorded in the current year on the receipt of the invoice of $4,300.
3. Goods out on consignment have been excluded from inventory.
4. Merchandise purchases under terms FOB shipping point have been omitted from the Purchases account and the ending inventory. The purchases were recorded in the following year.
5. Goods held on consignment from Talbert Supply Co. were included in the inventory.

Required
For each error indicate the effect on the ending inventory and the net income for the current year and on the net income for the following year.

P9-18 **AICPA Adapted** *Comprehensive* Layne Corporation, a manufacturer of small tools, provided the following information from its accounting records for the year ended December 31, 2007:

Inventory at December 31, 2007 (based on physical count of goods in Layne's plant at cost on December 31, 2007)	$1,750,000
Accounts payable at December 31, 2007	1,200,000
Net sales (sales less sales returns)	8,500,000

Additional information is as follows:
1. Included in the physical count were tools billed to a customer FOB shipping point on December 31, 2007. These tools had a cost of $28,000 and had been billed at $35,000. The shipment was on Layne's loading dock waiting to be picked up by the common carrier.
2. Goods were in transit from a vendor to Layne on December 31, 2007. The invoice cost was $50,000, and the goods were shipped FOB shipping point on December 29, 2007.
3. Work-in-process inventory costing $20,000 was sent to an outside processor for plating on December 30, 2007.
4. Tools returned by customers and held pending inspection in the returned goods area on December 31, 2007 were not included in the physical count. On January 8, 2008 the tools costing $26,000 were inspected and returned to inventory. Credit memos totaling $40,000 were issued to the customers on the same date.

5. Tools shipped to a customer FOB destination on December 24, 2007 were in transit at December 31, 2007 and had a cost of $25,000. Upon notification of receipt by the customer on January 2, 2008, Layne issued a sales invoice for $42,000.

6. Goods, with an invoice cost of $30,000, received from a vendor at 5:00 p.m. on December 31, 2007, were recorded on a receiving report dated January 2, 2008. The goods were not included in the physical count, but the invoice was included in accounts payable at December 31, 2007.

7. Goods received from a vendor on December 24, 2007 were included in the physical count. However, the related $60,000 vendor invoice was not included in accounts payable at December 31, 2007 because the accounts payable copy of the receiving report was lost.

8. On January 4, 2008, a monthly freight bill in the amount of $4,000 was received. The bill specifically related to merchandise purchased in December 2007, one-half of which was still in the inventory at December 31, 2007. The freight charges were not included in either the inventory or in accounts payable at December 31, 2007.

Required

Prepare a schedule of adjustments as of December 31, 2007 to the initial amounts in inventory, accounts payable, and sales. Show separately the effect, if any, of each of the eight transactions on the December 31, 2007 amounts. Indicate if the transactions would have no effect on the initial amount shown.

CASES

COMMUNICATION

C9-1   Retail Inventory Method

AICPA Adapted The Sandberg Paint Company, your client, manufactures paint. The company's president, Ms. Sandberg, has decided to open a retail store to sell Sandberg paint as well as wallpaper and other supplies that it would purchase from other suppliers. She has asked you for information about the retail method of pricing inventories at the retail store.

Required

Prepare a report to the president explaining the retail method of pricing inventories. Your report should include these four points:

1. Description and accounting features of the method.
2. The conditions that may distort the results under the method.
3. A comparison of the advantages of using the retail method with those of using cost methods of inventory pricing.
4. The accounting theory underlying the treatment of net markdowns and net markups under the method.

C9-2   Gross Profit

AICPA Adapted The Shelly Corporation is an importer and wholesaler. Its merchandise is purchased from several suppliers and is warehoused by Shelly Corporation until sold to consumers.

In conducting her audit for the year ended June 30, 2007 the corporation's CPA determined that the system of internal control was good. Accordingly, she observed the physical inventory at an interim date, May 31, 2007, instead of at year-end.

The CPA obtained the following information from the general ledger:

Inventory, July 1, 2006	$ 87,500
Physical inventory, May 31, 2007	95,000
Sales for 11 months ended May 31, 2007	840,000
Sales for year ended June 30, 2007	960,000
Purchases for 11 months ended May 31, 2007 (before audit adjustments)	675,000
Purchases for year ended June 30, 2007 (before audit adjustments)	800,000

The CPA's audit disclosed the following information:

Shipments received in May and included in the physical inventory but recorded as June purchases	$7,500
Shipments received in unsalable condition and excluded from physical inventory; credit memos had not been received nor had chargebacks to vendors been recorded:	
Total at May 31, 2007	$1,000
Total at June 30, 2007 (including the May unrecorded chargebacks)	$1,500
Deposit made with vendor and charged to purchases in April 2007. Product was shipped in July 2007.	$2,000
Deposit made with vendor and charged to purchases in May 2007. Product was shipped, FOB destination, on May 28, 2007, and was included in May 31, 2007 physical inventory as goods in transit.	$5,500

Through the carelessness of the receiving department, a June shipment was damaged by rain. This shipment was later sold in June at its cost of $10,000.

Required

In audit engagements in which interim physical inventories are observed, a frequently used auditing procedure is to test the reasonableness of the year-end inventory by the application of gross profit ratios. Prepare in good form the following schedules:

1. Computation of the gross profit ratio for 11 months ended May 31, 2007.
2. Computation by the gross profit ratio method of cost of goods sold during June 2007.
3. Computation by the gross profit ratio method of June 30, 2007 inventory.

CREATIVE AND CRITICAL THINKING

C9-3 Lower of Cost or Market Method

AICPA Adapted Blaedon Co. makes ongoing design refinements to lawnmowers that are produced for it by contractors. Blaedon stores the lawnmowers in its own warehouse and sells them at list price, directly to retailers. Blaedon uses the FIFO inventory method. Approximately two-thirds of new lawnmower sales involve trade-ins. For each used lawnmower traded in and returned to Blaedon, retailers receive a $40 allowance regardless of whether the trade-in was associated with a sale of a 2007 or 2008 model. Blaedon's net realizable value on a used lawnmower averages $25.

At December 31, 2007, Blaedon's inventory of new lawnmowers includes both 2007 and 2008 models. When the 2008 model was introduced in September 2007, the list price of the remaining 2007 model lawnmowers was reduced below cost. Blaedon is experiencing rising costs.

Required

1. At December 31, 2007, how should Blaedon determine the carrying amounts assigned to its lawnmower inventory of
   a. 2008 models?
   b. 2007 models?
2. Considering only the 2008 model lawnmower, explain the impact of the FIFO cost flow assumptions on Blaedon's 2007
   a. Income statement amounts.
   b. Balance sheet amounts.

C9-4 Retail Inventory Method

AICPA Adapted Retail, Inc., sells normal brand-name household products both from its own store and on consignment through The Mall Space Company.

Required

1. Explain whether Retail, Inc., should include in its inventory normal brand-name goods purchased from its suppliers but not yet received if the terms of purchase are FOB shipping point (manufacturer's plant).

2. Explain whether Retail, Inc., should include freight-in expenditures as an inventoriable cost.
3. Retail, Inc., purchased cooking utensils for sale in the ordinary course of business three times during the current year, each time at a higher price than the previous purchase. Explain the effect on ending inventory and cost of goods sold if Retail, Inc., used the weighted-average cost method instead of the FIFO method.
4. Explain how and why Retail, Inc., will treat net markdowns when it calculates the estimated cost of ending inventory using the conventional (lower of cost or market) retail inventory method.
5. Explain what products on consignment are and how they are presented on the balance sheets of Retail, Inc., and The Mall Space Company.

C9-5 Various Inventory Issues

AICPA Adapted Diane Company, a retailer and wholesaler of national brand-name household lighting fixtures, purchases its inventories from various suppliers.

Required

1. a. What criteria are used to determine which of Diane's costs are inventoriable?
   b. Are Diane's administrative costs inventoriable? Defend your answer.
2. a. Diane uses the lower of cost or market rule for its wholesale inventories. Explain the theoretical arguments for that rule.
   b. The replacement cost of the inventories is below the net realizable value less a normal profit margin, which, in turn, is below the original cost. Explain the amount that is used to value the inventories.
3. Diane calculates the estimated cost of its ending inventories held for sale at retail using the conventional (lower of average cost or market) retail inventory method. Explain how Diane would treat the beginning inventories and net markdowns in calculating the cost ratio used to determine its ending inventories.

C9-6   LCM, Dollar-Value LIFO, and Consignments

AICPA Adapted   Caddell Company, a wholesaler, purchases its inventories from various suppliers FOB destination; it incurs substantial warehousing costs. Caddell uses the dollar-value LIFO inventory cost flow method. Caddell also consigns some of its inventories to Reed Company.

Reed also has items for sale that it purchases from other wholesalers. Reed uses the lower of FIFO cost or market inventory method.

Required

1. When are the purchases from various suppliers generally included in Caddell's inventory? Why?
2. Theoretically, how should Caddell account for the warehousing costs? Why?
3. a. Explain the advantages of using the dollar-value LIFO inventory cost flow method as opposed to the conventional quantity of goods LIFO method.
   b. How does the calculation of dollar-value LIFO differ from the conventional quantity of goods method?
4. Explain how Caddell should account for the inventories consigned to Reed Company.
5. When Reed applies the lower of cost or market method, what are the ceiling and floor limits?

C9-7   Inventory Valuation Issues

AICPA Adapted   Hanlon Company purchased a significant amount of raw materials inventory for a new product that it is manufacturing. Hanlon purchased insurance on these raw materials while they were in transit from the supplier.

Hanlon uses the lower of cost or market rule for these raw materials. The replacement cost of the raw materials is above the net realizable value and both are below the original cost.

Hanlon uses the average cost inventory method for these raw materials. In the last two years, each purchase has been at a lower price than the previous purchase, and the ending inventory quantity for each period has been higher than the beginning inventory quantity for that period.

Required

1. Explain the theoretically appropriate method that Hanlon should use to account for the insurance costs on the raw materials while they were in transit from the supplier.
2. a. Explain the amount at which Hanlon should report the raw materials inventory on its balance sheet.
   b. In general, explain why the lower of cost or market rule is used to report inventory.
3. Explain what would have been the effect on ending inventory and cost of goods sold had Hanlon used the LIFO inventory method instead of the average cost inventory method for the raw materials.

C9-8   Various Inventory Issues

AICPA Adapted   Hudson Company, which is both a wholesaler and a retailer, purchases its inventories from various suppliers. Additional facts for Hudson's wholesale operations are as follows:

- Hudson incurs substantial warehousing costs.
- Hudson uses the lower of cost or market method.
- The replacement cost of the inventories is below the net realizable value and above the net realizable value less the normal profit margin. The original cost of the inventories is above the replacement cost and below the net realizable value.

Additional facts for Hudson's retail operations are as follows:

- Hudson determines the estimated cost of its ending inventories held for sale at retail using the conventional retail inventory method, which approximates lower of average cost or market.
- Hudson incurs substantial freight-in costs.
- Hudson has net markups and net markdowns.

Required

1. Theoretically, how should Hudson account for the warehousing costs related to its wholesale inventories? Why?
2. a. In general, explain why the lower of cost or market method is used to report inventory.
   b. At which amount should Hudson report the wholesale inventories on its balance sheet? Explain the application of the lower of cost or market method in this situation.
3. In the calculation of the cost-to-retail percentage used to determine the estimated cost of its ending retail inventories, how should Hudson treat
   a. Freight-in costs?
   b. Net markups?
   c. Net markdowns?
4. Explain why Hudson's retail inventory method approximates lower of average cost or market.

C9-9   Ethics and Retail Inventory

You are the accountant for the South-Western Division of HiValue Grocery Stores. Late in December, Kelly Cholak, the CEO of the Division stops by your office and says "I have a couple of questions. I recently received a report from the head office on the first 11 months of the year. We are not doing as well as we budgeted and they are not happy with the gross profit we have earned. But the good news is that I just got off the phone with a big supplier who has excess inventory and could sell us enough of their products to last us three months. They have offered us a great price—lower than we have paid in a couple of years. Then I remembered that you use that funny LIFO retail inventory method where you play with such confusing numbers. Will the purchase reduce our retail ratio, or whatever you call it, so that our inventory is lower and cost of goods sold higher, because that would only make us look worse? Alternatively, I thought that we could delay this purchase until after January 1 and we might be able to have one of those LIFO liquid profits and make ourselves look good for the year's results. Give these issues some thought and let's have a drink after work today to discuss them."

Required

From financial reporting and ethical perspectives, how would you reply to Kelly?

Property, Plant, and Equipment: Acquisition and Disposal

OBJECTIVES

After reading this chapter, you will be able to:

1 Identify the characteristics of property, plant, and equipment.

2 Record the acquisition of property, plant, and equipment.

3 Determine the cost of a nonmonetary asset acquired by the exchange of another nonmonetary asset.

4 Compute the cost of a self-constructed asset, including interest capitalization.

5 Record costs after acquisition.

6 Record the disposal of property, plant, and equipment.

7 Understand the disclosures of property, plant, and equipment.

8 Explain the accounting for oil and gas properties (Appendix).

To Capitalize or Not to Capitalize, That is the Question

The issue of capitalizing (recording as an asset) versus expensing expenditures for property, plant, and equipment has historically been controversial and one that can have dramatic consequences for the balance sheet, income statement, and statement of cash flows. It was precisely this issue that triggered one of the largest financial restatements in U.S. history by **WorldCom**. According to U.S. accounting standards, line costs, the various fees paid to telecommunications companies to use their communication networks, are considered expenses. By improperly capitalizing approximately $3.8 billion in line costs, WorldCom was able to conceal large losses and falsely portray itself as a profitable business. In addition, the expenditures for line costs were treated as investing cash flows instead of operating cash flows, which resulted in WorldCom reporting higher net operating cash flows than if the costs were expensed. While the practices used by WorldCom were clear violations of GAAP, in many situations (e.g., oil and gas exploration) managers have choices and must use their judgment as to whether certain expenditures are capitalized or expensed.

Credit: Adam Rountree/Bloomberg News/Landov

What are the financial impacts of these choices? First, companies that choose to capitalize rather than expense costs will report higher asset and equity balances, which tend to make them appear more solvent (lower debt ratios). Second, capitalizing costs will raise current-year income by the amount capitalized; however, future income will be lowered by the amount of the depreciation expense. While the income effect on any single year depends on the actual size of the expenditures, the pattern of reported income will tend to be smoother for firms that capitalize costs because of the systematic allocation of costs through the recording of depreciation. When faced with the question of capitalizing or expensing certain costs, it is crucial to understand the financial statement impacts of your decision.

FOR FURTHER INVESTIGATION

For a discussion of capitalizing expenditures, consult the Business & Company Resource Center (BCRC):

- Accounting Practice On Trial with WorldCom: Should Cable Companies be Able to Capitalize Expenses? *Investment Dealers' Digest*, 0021-0080, Oct 13, 2003.

Property, plant, and equipment are very important components of a company's assets. They include assets that a company needs to conduct its business, such as land, office buildings, factories, machinery, equipment, warehouses, retail stores, and delivery vehicles. They usually are a major portion of a company's total assets. In this chapter we include a discussion of the costs of acquisition, costs subsequent to acquisition, and disposal of property, plant, and equipment. We include additional issues related to oil and gas properties in an Appendix at the end of this chapter.

CHARACTERISTICS OF PROPERTY, PLANT, AND EQUIPMENT

1 Identify the characteristics of property, plant, and equipment.

Property, plant, and equipment are the tangible noncurrent assets that a company uses in the normal operations of its business. Alternative terms are **plant assets, fixed assets, and operational assets.** To be included in this category, an asset must have three characteristics:

1. *The asset must be held for use and not for investment.* Only assets used in the normal course of business should be included. However, the asset does not have to be used continuously. Therefore, a company includes machinery it owns for standby purposes in case of breakdowns. However, it does not include idle land or buildings; these should be reported as investments. A particular type of asset may be classified as property, plant, and equipment by one company and as inventory by another. For example, trucks owned by a trucking company are included in its property, plant, and equipment. However, trucks owned by a dealer are categorized as inventory.

2. *The asset must have an expected life of more than one year.* The asset represents a bundle of future services that the company will receive over the life of the asset. To be included in property, plant, and equipment, the benefits must extend for more than one year or the normal operating cycle, whichever is longer. Therefore, a company distinguishes the asset from other assets, such as supplies, that it expects to consume within the current year. However, assets remain in the property, plant, and equipment category, even if the company intends to sell them in the next year.

3. *The asset must be tangible in nature.* There must be a physical substance that can be seen and touched. In contrast, intangible assets such as goodwill or patents do not have a physical substance. Unlike raw materials, generally property, plant, and equipment do not change their physical characteristics and are not added into the product. Wasting assets are natural resources, such as minerals, oil and gas, and timber, that are used up by extraction. A company usually includes them under the category of property, plant, and equipment, even though it may add them in a product. For example, an iron mine owned by a steel company produces iron ore, which changes its characteristics as it is used in the manufacture of steel.

A company initially records an asset included in its property, plant, and equipment category at its acquisition cost. The asset provides benefits to the company over a period of more than one year. Therefore, the matching principle requires that the company allocate the cost of the asset as an expense to each period in which it consumes the asset and receives benefits. We discuss this process of depreciation in the next chapter.

Evaluation of Use of Historical Cost

The use of acquisition (historical) cost as the basis for reporting property, plant, and equipment is consistent with the reporting of most other assets, liabilities, and stockholders' equity items. The advantages are that

1. the cost is equal to the fair value at the date of acquisition,
2. the cost is a *reliable* valuation, and
3. gains and losses from holding the asset are recognized only when realized through a sale transaction.

However, the use of historical cost for reporting property, plant, and equipment on a company's financial statements raises more issues than for other assets because the time since acquisition is usually greater. For example, many users question the continued use of historical cost for reporting an asset such as land. How *relevant* is the cost of land purchased in the past, perhaps as much as 50 years ago? Similar issues arise with depreciable assets such as office buildings. Although depreciation is a process of cost allocation rather than of valuation, the book value of the assets (cost less accumulated depreciation) may become less relevant as it becomes much less than the asset's current value. In addition, as we discuss in the next chapter, a company writes down property, plant, and equipment to its fair value when its value is impaired.

Another factor to be considered is the manner in which a company uses the asset. The process of allocating the historical cost may be more relevant if the company uses the asset in its productive operations, because there is an appropriate matching of the cost of the asset against the revenues it produces. Alternatively, the current value may be more relevant if the company intends to sell the asset, or the entire company is for sale.

Since generally accepted accounting principles require that a company report its property, plant, and equipment at historical cost, their current cost generally is not available to users of financial statements. However, companies are encouraged to provide supplementary disclosures of the current cost of their property, plant, and equipment.

ACQUISITION OF PROPERTY, PLANT, AND EQUIPMENT

The major types of assets that a company includes in the category of property, plant, and equipment are land, buildings, equipment, machinery, furniture and fixtures, leasehold improvements, and wasting assets. The acquisition of an item of property, plant, and equipment raises many issues. These include the determination of the cost of an asset acquired singly or by a lump-sum purchase, with deferred payments, through the issuance of securities, or by donation. Also, in more complex situations, assets may be acquired in exchange for other assets or by self-construction. We discuss each of these issues in the following sections.

> **2** Record the acquisition of property, plant, and equipment.

Determination of Cost

The cost of property, plant, and equipment is the cash outlay (not the "list" price) or its equivalent that is necessary to acquire the asset and put it in operating condition. In other words, **the acquisition costs that are necessary to obtain the benefits to be derived from the asset are capitalized** (recorded as an asset). These costs include the contract price, less discounts available, plus freight, assembly, installation, and testing costs. As for inventory, discounts *available* should be subtracted from the cost of the asset rather than recorded as discounts *taken*, because the benefits to be received from the asset are not increased by a discount not taken.

Example: Recording the Acquisition

Assume that the Devon Company purchases a machine with a contract price of $100,000 on terms of 2/10, n/30. The company does not take the cash discount of $2,000, and incurs transportation costs of $2,500, as well as installation and testing costs of $3,000. Sales tax is 7% of the invoice price, or $7,000. During the installation of the machine, uninsured damages of $500 are incurred and paid by the company. The company makes the following summary journal entry to record these costs:

Machine		
($100,000 − $2,000 + $2,500 + $3,000 + $7,000)	110,500	
Repair Expense	500	
Discounts Lost	2,000	
Cash		113,000

The company does not include the $500 of damages in the cost of the asset because it was not a "necessary" cost. We discuss the issues related to the cost of various types of property, plant, and equipment in the following sections. ♦

Land

The recorded cost of land includes the:

- contract price
- costs of closing the transaction and obtaining title, including commissions, options, legal fees, title search, insurance, and past due taxes
- costs of surveys
- costs of preparing the land for its particular use, such as clearing, grading, and razing old buildings (net of any proceeds from salvage) when such improvements have an indefinite life

A company should record the costs of improvements with a limited economic life, such as landscaping, streets, sidewalks, and sewers, in a Land Improvements account and depreciate these costs over their economic lives. Alternatively, if the local government authority is responsible for the continued upkeep of the improvements, then effectively the improvements have an indefinite economic life to the company. In this case, the company should add the costs of the improvements to the cost of the land. Since land is considered *not* to have a limited economic life and its residual value is unlikely to be less than its acquisition cost, land generally is not depreciated.

Land purchased for future use or as an investment should not be considered part of property, plant, and equipment. Issues arise about accounting for interest and property taxes on such land. **FASB Statement No. 34** (discussed later in the chapter) requires that a company capitalize interest only when an asset is undergoing the activities needed to get it ready for its intended use. Therefore, if the company is involved in any planning activity, such as architectural design or the obtaining of permits, it capitalizes interest. The *Statement* does not address the issue of property taxes (or other costs such as insurance).

FASB Statement No. 67 applies to real estate held for sale or rental. It requires a company to capitalize the costs incurred for property taxes and insurance only during periods in which activities needed to get the property ready for its intended use are in progress. Costs incurred for these items after the property is substantially complete and ready for its intended use are expensed as incurred.[1] Thus the rules for interest, property taxes, and insurance are the same for real estate projects developed for sale or lease to others. However, the *Statement* does not apply to real estate developed by a company for use in its own operations. Therefore, the company could capitalize or expense the property taxes and insurance during the development period.

Arguments in favor of capitalizing property taxes are (1) the matching principle does not require expensing the costs since the asset is not being used in a revenue-producing activity, and (2) if the advance purchase of the land had been made at a lower price, capitalizing the costs would result in a cost nearer to that which the company would have paid later. Arguments in favor of expensing the property taxes are (1) property taxes are a maintenance cost that do not add value to the property, and (2) it is consistent with the conservatism convention. Once the land is used in the operating activities, both interest and property taxes must be expensed.

Buildings

The recorded cost of buildings includes:

- the contract price
- the costs of remodeling and reconditioning

---

1.   "Accounting for Costs and Initial Rental Operations of Real Estate Projects," *FASB Statement of Financial Accounting Standards No. 67* (Stamford, Conn.: FASB, 1982), par. 6.

- the costs of excavation for the specific building
- architectural costs and the costs of building permits
- capitalized interest costs in the particular circumstances discussed later in the chapter
- unanticipated costs resulting from the condition of the land (such as blasting rock or channeling an underground stream)

A company should expense unanticipated costs, such as a strike or a fire, associated with the construction of the building. The different treatment is justified because the avoidable costs of the unanticipated events were not necessary to obtain the economic benefits of the building. The costs of property taxes and insurance during construction may be capitalized or expensed, as we discussed for land.

Leasehold Improvements

Improvements made by the lessee to leased property, unless specifically exempted in the lease agreement, revert to the lessor at the end of the lease. Therefore, **a lessee capitalizes the cost of a leasehold improvement,** such as the interior design of a retail store, **and amortizes the cost over its economic life or the life of the lease, whichever is shorter.**

The preceding discussion indicates the general rules to be followed but does not provide solutions for all possible situations. A company's decision to expense a cost immediately, to capitalize it as an asset, such as a building that will be depreciated, or to capitalize the cost as a nondepreciable asset, such as land, has an impact on both the company's income statement and balance sheet. **The general procedure is to determine whether incurring the cost will provide economic benefits for the company beyond the current period, and which asset is associated with the increase in benefits.** For example, when a company purchases land, the cost of demolishing an old building on the land is properly capitalized to the land because the benefits to be derived from the land are increased as a result of the old building no longer being there. Also, if the seller had demolished the old building, the selling price presumably would have been higher. When a company demolishes an old building on land already owned so that a new building can be erected, the cost is associated with the benefits previously realized from the old building. Therefore, the cost is included in the calculation of the gain or loss on disposal. The new building does not have greater benefits because the old building is obsolete. Similarly if a company purchases an old building with the expectation of incurring some costs of renovation, but the actual costs exceed the planned costs because of unforeseen difficulties, the added cost should not be capitalized. This is because it resulted from an error of judgment and did not increase the economic benefits of the building above those benefits originally expected. However, given the difficulties of accurate budgeting, the total costs often are capitalized whether or not those total costs exceed the budgeted amount.

Lump-Sum Purchase

A company may acquire several dissimilar assets for a single lump-sum purchase price. The purchase price is allocated to the individual assets purchased. This allocation is necessary because some of the assets may be depreciable and some not, and the depreciable assets may have different economic lives and be depreciated by different methods. **A company allocates the acquisition price in a lump-sum purchase based on the relative fair values of the individual assets.**

Example: Lump Sum Purchase

Suppose Sample Company pays $120,000 for land and a building. If there is no evidence in the contract of separate prices agreed upon for the land and the building, the company allocates the $120,000 between the two assets based on their relative fair values. The company can obtain evidence of such values from several sources, such as an appraisal or the assessed values for property taxes, if it considers those values to be reasonably accurate indications of relative market values. Suppose that an appraisal of the land and building indicates values of $50,000 and $75,000, respectively. Sample Company computes the cost of each as follows:

	Appraisal Value	Relative Fair Value	× Total Cost	= Allocated Cost
Land	$ 50,000	$50,000/$125,000	× $120,000 =	$ 48,000
Building	75,000	$75,000/$125,000	× $120,000 =	72,000
Total	$125,000			$120,000

Sample Company records the land at a cost of $48,000 and the building at a cost of $72,000. If the cost of obtaining an appraisal is material, the company should add it to the purchase price so it is allocated to the respective assets. In some situations, it may be possible to determine only one of the market values. Then the remaining portion of the total cost is assigned to the other asset. ♦

Deferred Payments

When a company acquires property, plant, and equipment on a deferred payment basis, such as by issuing notes or bonds or assuming a mortgage, **it records the asset at its fair value or the fair value of the liability on the date of the transaction, whichever is more *reliable*.** If neither is determinable, the company records the asset at the present value of the deferred payments at the stated interest rate, unless the stated rate is materially different from the market rate, in which case it uses the market rate.[2]

Example: Deferred Payments

Suppose that Antush company purchases equipment by issuing a $10,000 non-interest-bearing five-year note, when the market rate for obligations of this type is 12%. The note will be paid off at the rate of $2,000 at the end of each year. Neither the fair value of the equipment nor the note is determinable directly. In this case the company values both the equipment and the note at the present value of the payments, which is $7,210 ($2,000 × 3.604776, the factor from Table 4 of the Time Value of Money Module for five years and a 12% rate). Antush Company records the acquisition of the equipment as follows:

Equipment	7,210	
Discount on Notes Payable	2,790	
Notes Payable		10,000

If the company purchased the equipment by issuing a $7,500 5-year note with a stated interest rate of 12%, the present value of the note is $7,500 (assuming that 12% is a fair rate). In this case, Antush Company would record the acquisition as follows:

Equipment	7,500	
Notes Payable		7,500

Property, plant, and equipment may be purchased by issuing bonds, as we discuss in Chapter 14. The same principles are followed, and the asset is recorded at the present value of the future payments. ♦

Issuance of Securities

When a company acquires assets by issuing securities such as common stock or preferred stock, the company must determine the fair value of the transaction. In many cases two measures of fair value are available: the fair value of the asset acquired and the fair value of the securities issued. **The general rule is to record the exchange at the fair value of**

---

2. "Interest on Receivables and Payables," *APB Opinion No. 21* (New York: AICPA, 1971), par. 11.

the asset acquired or of the stock issued, whichever is more *reliable*. Normally the two values would be very similar, but if they are materially different, it is necessary to select one. In some situations, one of the values may be considered more reliable because it is quoted in an active market. For example, if the security is actively traded on a stock exchange and the asset being acquired is very specialized, the security value would be the preferred choice. Alternatively, if the security is not actively traded but the asset is one that is commonly traded, the asset value would be the better choice. But what if neither of the two values can be readily determined?

For example, suppose that a company whose stock is not traded publicly issues stock to acquire a mining claim. Conceptually, the value of the asset is preferred to the value of the stock, because the value of the acquired asset is independent of the value of the stock. However, the value of the stock is *not* independent of the asset being acquired, because the more valuable the asset is, the more valuable is the stock. In the absence of any other valuation approach, the directors of the company assign a value on the transaction. State laws generally allow this procedure, provided the value is established in good faith.

Assets Acquired by Donation

When a company acquires property, plant, and equipment through donation (usually by a governmental unit or an individual), a strict interpretation of the cost concept would require that the asset be valued at zero. However, these transactions are defined by **APB Opinion No. 29** as nonreciprocal transfers of nonmonetary assets. A **nonreciprocal transfer** is a transfer of assets or services in one direction. A company receiving an asset in such an exchange must record it at its fair value. The justification is that when an asset is donated, cost provides an inadequate method of accounting for the asset and for income measurement. Therefore, the cost principle is modified to produce more relevant asset and income values.

Generally accepted accounting principles require different treatment for recording an asset donated by a governmental unit and an asset donated by a nongovernmental unit (such as an individual stockholder). In both situations, the company records (debits) the asset at its fair value. In the case of a donation by a governmental unit, the credit is recorded in a donated capital account. The argument for this treatment is that the company should not increase earnings as a result of a donation by a governmental unit.

Example: Donation by Governmental Unit

Suppose the city of Julesberg (a governmental unit) donates land worth $20,000 to the Klemme Company because the company relocates its production facilities to Julesberg. The Klemme Company records this event as follows:

Land	20,000	
Donated Capital		20,000

Donations of this type often are accompanied by conditions. For example, the Klemme Company might be required to employ 100 people for 10 years. The company reports the condition in the notes to the financial statements, if material, but does not record it as a liability. Klemme Company includes the Donated Capital account in the Stockholders' Equity section of its balance sheet. ♦

Example: Donation by Nongovernmental Agency

In the case of a donation by a nongovernmental unit, the company records a gain.[3] The argument for this treatment is that receiving something of value from a nongovernmental unit (e.g., a stockholder) represents earnings to the company. For example, suppose

---

3.   "Accounting for Contributions Received and Contributions Made," *FASB Statement of Financial Accounting Standards No. 116* (Norwalk, Conn.: FASB, 1993), par. 8.

the CEO of Hrouda Company donates a building worth $50,000 to the company. The company records this event as follows:

Building	50,000	
Gain on Receipt of Donated Building		50,000

The company reports the gain in the other items section of its income statement. ♦

Start-up Costs

Many companies incur start-up costs as they expand their activities. For example, a retail company that opens a new store would incur start-up costs for hiring and training new employees and pre-opening advertising. Other examples are costs of opening new restaurants, new plants, new hotels, new casinos, and new golf courses.

AICPA Statement of Position No. 98-5 requires that a company expense the costs of start-up activities as incurred.[4] The *SOP* defines start-up costs as those costs related to one-time activities for opening a new facility, introducing a new product or service, conducting business in a new territory, conducting business with a new class of customer, initiating a new process in an existing facility, or starting some new operation. Costs associated with organizing a new entity, often referred to as organization costs, (e.g., costs of preparing a charter, bylaws, minutes of organizational meetings, and original stock certifications) are also included as start-up costs. Start-up activities do *not* include activities that are related to routine, ongoing efforts to refine or otherwise improve the qualities of an existing product, service, process or facility.

LINK TO INTERNATIONAL DIFFERENCES

The primary difference between U.S. and international accounting standards is that international standards allow a company to write the value of its property, plant, and equipment assets up to fair value if fair value can be reliably measured. Any increase is credited to stockholders' equity as a revaluation surplus. Such write-ups create significant differences that reduce international comparability among companies. There are some other minor differences between U.S. and international accounting standards that are beyond the scope of the book.

NONMONETARY ASSET EXCHANGES

3 Determine the cost of a nonmonetary asset acquired by the exchange of another nonmonetary asset.

Accounting for assets acquired by the exchange of other assets (e.g., trade-in, swap) is covered by **APB Opinion No. 29 and FASB Statement No. 153.**[5] A **nonmonetary exchange** is a reciprocal transfer between a company and another entity, in which the company acquires nonmonetary assets or services by surrendering other nonmonetary assets or services. (A nonmonetary transaction may also include paying or incurring liabilities.) **The general principle is that the cost of a nonmonetary asset acquired in exchange for another nonmonetary asset is the fair value of the asset surrendered.** The company acquiring the asset recognizes a gain or loss on the exchange as the difference between the fair value of the asset surrendered and its book value. When a small

---

4. "Reporting on the Costs of Start-up Activities," *AICPA Statement of Position No 98-5* (New York: AICPA, 1998).
5. "Accounting for Nonmonetary Transactions," *APB Opinion No. 29* (New York: AICPA, 1973), and "Exchanges of Nonmonetary Assets, an amendment of APB Opinion No. 29," *FASB Statement No. 153* (Norwalk, Conn.: FASB, 2004).

amount of cash is also given or received, the cost of the asset acquired and the gain or loss on the nonmonetary asset surrendered is determined by these equations:

$$\text{Cost of Asset Acquired} = \frac{\text{Fair Value of}}{\text{Asset Surrendered}} + \text{Cash Paid or} - \text{Cash Received}$$

and

$$\text{Gain (Loss)} = \frac{\text{Fair Value of}}{\text{Asset Surrendered}} - \text{Book Value of Asset Surrendered}$$

If the fair value of the asset received is more reliable than the fair value of the asset surrendered, it is used to measure the cost of the asset acquired. Of course, the recorded cost of the asset acquired cannot be greater than its fair value.

Example: Exchanges of Nonmonetary Assets

We show an exchange of nonmonetary assets between Arnold Company and Carbon Company, both with and without cash included in the exchange, in Example 10-1. Arnold Company exchanges a building for Carbon Company's equipment. Before studying the example, it is helpful to refer back to the equations for nonmonetary asset exchanges.

EXAMPLE 10-1   Exchange of Nonmonetary Assets

(a) No Cash Included in Exchange

	Arnold Company (Building)	Carbon Company (Equipment)
Cost of asset surrendered	$100,000	$60,000
Accumulated depreciation	54,000	32,000
Fair value of asset surrendered	40,000	40,000

Arnold Company		Carbon Company	
Equipment	40,000	Building	40,000
Accumulated Depreciation	54,000	Accumulated Depreciation	32,000
Loss [$40,000 –		Equipment	60,000
($100,000 – $54,000)]	6,000	Gain [$40,000 –	
Building	100,000	($60,000 – $32,000)]	12,000

(b) Cash Included in Exchange

	Arnold Company (Building)	Carbon Company (Equipment)
Cost of asset surrendered	$100,000	$60,000
Accumulated depreciation	54,000	32,000
Fair value of asset surrendered	40,000	35,000
Cash received (paid)	5,000	(5,000)

Arnold Company		Carbon Company	
Equipment		Building	
($40,000 – $5,000)	35,000	($35,000 + $5,000)	40,000
Accumulated Depreciation	54,000	Accumulated Depreciation	32,000
Cash	5,000	Equipment	60,000
Loss [$40,000 –		Cash	5,000
($100,000 – $54,000)]	6,000	Gain [$35,000 –	
Building	100,000	($60,000 – $32,000)]	7,000

In example (a), there is no cash exchanged. Each company gives up and receives an asset with a fair value of $40,000, which is, therefore, the fair value of the transaction. Since Arnold Company gives up a building with a fair value of $40,000 and a book value of $46,000 (the cost of $100,000 less the accumulated depreciation of $54,000), it recognizes a loss of $6,000 ($40,000 − $46,000). It also records the cost of the acquired equipment at the fair value of $40,000. Carbon Company gives up equipment with a fair value of $40,000 and a book value of $28,000 ($60,000 − $32,000). Therefore, it recognizes a gain of $12,000 ($40,000 − $28,000) and records the cost of the building acquired at the fair value of $40,000.

In example (b), Arnold Company receives cash of $5,000. Since Arnold Company gives up a building with a fair value of $40,000 and a book value of $46,000, it recognizes a loss of $6,000. It records the acquired equipment at a cost of $35,000 (the $40,000 fair value of the building surrendered minus the $5,000 cash received). Carbon Company gives up equipment with a fair value of $35,000 and a book value of $28,000. Therefore, it records a gain of $7,000 and the acquired building at a cost of $40,000 (the $35,000 fair value of the equipment surrendered plus the $5,000 cash paid). ◆

Exceptions to the General Rule to Use Fair Value for Nonmonetary Exchanges

FASB Statement No. 153 was issued to make U.S. GAAP more similar to international GAAP. Therefore, it made three exceptions to the general rule to use fair value that we discussed earlier. A company would record the nonmonetary exchange transaction at book value and would not recognize a gain or loss when:

1. Neither the fair value of the asset received or given up is reasonably determinable.
2. The transaction is an exchange of inventory to facilitate sales to a third party. For example, when a company exchanges its inventory with another company in order to sell the newly acquired inventory to a third company.
3. The transaction lacks "commercial substance." A nonmonetary exchange does *not* have commercial substance if the company's future cash flows are *not* expected to change significantly.

For example, assume that the Messenger Company owned a truck with a cost $50,000 and accumulated depreciation of $20,000. The company exchanged the truck for a used truck from Leninger Company and paid $2,000. Since the trucks were so similar, the Messenger Company's cash flows are not expected to change significantly as a result of this exchange. Messenger would record the truck it received at $32,000, which is the book value of the truck it gave up of $30,000 ($50,000 − $30,000) plus the $2,000 cash it paid. Messenger would record the exchange as follows:

Truck	32,000	
Accumulated Depreciation	30,000	
Truck		50,000
Cash		2,000

SECURE YOUR KNOWLEDGE 10-1

- Property, plant, and equipment is reported in the financial statements at historical cost, and includes tangible assets with expected lives of greater than one year that a company uses in the normal course of business to generate revenue.
- The initial cost of the various types of property, plant, and equipment includes all the costs necessary to acquire the asset, bring it to its desired location, and get it ready for its intended use.

(continued)

- The initial valuation of property, plant, and equipment is often complicated by the manner in which the asset is acquired. In these situations, the acquisition cost is generally based on fair value, as noted below:
  - When more than one asset is acquired for a single lump-sum purchase price, the purchase price is allocated to the individual assets based on their relative fair values.
  - Assets acquired on a deferred payment basis (long-term credit contract) are recorded at the fair value of the asset or the fair value of the liability, whichever can be more clearly determined.
  - Assets acquired through the exchange of stock are recorded at the fair value of the asset or the fair value of the stock, whichever can be more clearly determined.
  - Donated assets are recorded at fair value with a corresponding increase in either an equity account (if the donation was made by a governmental entity) or a gain (if the donation was made by a nongovernmental entity).
  - In general, exchanges of nonmonetary assets should be recorded at fair value, with any gains or losses recognized in income.

LINK TO ETHICAL DILEMMA

As the accountant for Magna Corporation, you have been carefully analyzing a nonmonetary exchange of assets that occurred in the current fiscal year. Toward the end of the third quarter, Magna obtained 10 used Ford delivery trucks by exchanging 10 of its own General Motors delivery trucks. Because the fair value of Magna's trucks exceeded their book value, Magna was able to recognize a gain on the transaction. The Ford trucks obtained in the exchange had the same cargo capacity as the General Motors trucks and approximately the same amount of miles on the odometer. In fact, as far as you can tell, other than the manufacturer's names, the trucks were virtually identical! In discussions with management, you determine that, prior to the exchange, third-quarter earnings were slightly lower than analyst expectations, and the exchange appears to be prompted by a desire to record a gain that would increase earnings to meet the earnings forecast. As support for the decision to enter into the exchange, management offers a brief memo stating that the new trucks are expected to generate significantly more cash flow than the trucks given up. Therefore, the exchange has commercial substance and GAAP requires the exchange to be recorded at fair value. What is your response?

SELF-CONSTRUCTION

Sometimes a company constructs an item of property, plant, and equipment that it intends to use in its production process. The costs directly related to the construction are added to the cost of the asset, including materials, labor, engineering, and variable manufacturing overhead. Three other components of the asset cost need additional consideration: (1) interest costs, (2) fixed manufacturing overhead costs, and (3) profit on the construction. We discuss each of these in the following sections.

4 Compute the cost of a self-constructed asset, including interest capitalization.

Interest During Construction

There has been a great deal of controversy as to whether a company should capitalize the interest on the funds borrowed to finance construction of an asset as part of the acquisition cost, or expense the interest. Also, if the company uses internally generated funds to finance the acquisition, should it add imputed interest to the cost of the asset? Regulating authorities for public utilities usually allow a company to include both actual and imputed interest in the cost of the asset because the impact of the interest on the utility rates is deferred until the new plant is in operation. Therefore, the company assigns the cost of the plant (through depreciation expense) to the periods of use and to the customers who use the product. **FASB Statement No. 34** requires the capitalization of interest in certain instances as we discuss later in this section.[6]

Conceptual Alternatives

The *Statement* discussed three alternatives that the FASB considered to account for interest during construction.

(a) *No interest is capitalized during construction.* Under this alternative a company would treat interest as a cost of borrowing funds, and would record the interest as an expense during the period incurred. This approach would be consistent with all other interest costs, such as interest on cash borrowed to purchase inventory, or to purchase property, plant, and equipment. The principal argument in favor of this alternative is that interest is the price paid for borrowing funds for a period of time, and the benefit received is the availability of the funds. Therefore, the matching principle requires that the cost be expensed against the company's revenues in the period in which the funds are made available. Another argument is that expensing interest as incurred results in income amounts that are more similar to cash flows.

(b) *Capitalize an amount of interest for all funds used for construction.* Under this alternative a company would assign an interest cost to all funds used in construction, whether borrowed or not. Therefore, the company would have to impute and capitalize an interest cost for the equity funds (common stock) used in construction in addition to the cost of borrowed funds. While it often is argued that this alternative provides the fairest economic cost of the asset, two major problems have prevented its adoption. First, there might be disagreement about the rate to be used for the imputed cost of the equity funds, and this amount would lack *reliability*. Second, since the computed interest cost of the equity funds would be debited to the asset, it would be necessary to record a credit. The credit could be to a revenue account, but that would violate the revenue recognition principle, since revenue should not be recognized as a result of acquiring assets. Another alternative would be to credit stockholders' equity directly, but there has been no contribution of capital by the owners, and the net worth of the company has not increased.

(c) *Capitalize the interest on funds borrowed for the construction.* Under this alternative a company would treat the cost of borrowed funds as part of the cost of acquiring an asset and therefore as equivalent to the other costs of construction, such as materials and labor. The advantages are (1) the cost of the borrowed funds is necessary to obtain the benefits from the asset, and (2) since the asset is not yet generating revenue, the matching principle requires that the cost of interest (and depreciation) not be expensed during construction. The disadvantage is that the cost of the asset will differ depending on the type of financing (debt or equity) used for construction. There are two ways of interpreting this third alternative. The cost to be capitalized could be either the cost of funds *specifically* borrowed to finance the project or the *average* cost of all borrowed funds. Elements of both approaches are required by *FASB Statement No. 34.*

---

6. "Capitalization of Interest Cost," FASB *Statement of Financial Accounting Standards No. 34* (Stamford, Conn.: FASB, 1979).

GAAP for Interest Capitalization

FASB Statement No. 34 requires a company to complete three steps for its interest capitalization:

- Determine whether an asset qualifies for interest capitalization
- Calculate the amount of interest to capitalize
- Identify the period over which to capitalize interest

We discuss each step in the following sections.

Assets Qualifying for Interest Capitalization **A company is required to capitalize interest on assets that are either constructed for its own use or constructed as discrete projects for sale or lease to others** (for example, long-term construction projects such as ships or real estate developments, as we discuss in Chapter 18). Interest *cannot* be capitalized for the following types of assets:

1. Inventories that are routinely manufactured. Inventories are not qualifying assets because, in the view of the FASB, "the informational benefit does not justify the cost"[7] of capitalization.
2. Assets that are in use or ready for their intended use.
3. Assets that are not being used in the earning activities of the company and are not undergoing the activities necessary to get them ready for use.

Amount of Interest to Be Capitalized The amount of interest capitalized for a qualifying asset is based on the actual amounts borrowed and the cost of those borrowings. The amount is "intended to be that portion of the interest cost incurred during the asset's acquisition periods that theoretically could have been avoided."[8] **A company determines the amount of interest to capitalize by applying an interest rate to the average cumulative invested costs (expenditures) for the qualifying asset during the capitalization period.**

If a company incurs a specific borrowing for a qualifying asset, it applies the interest rate on that borrowing to the expenditures for the asset. If the expenditures on the asset exceed the cost of the specific borrowing or if no specific borrowing is made, the company applies the weighted average interest rate on all other borrowings. Because no imputed interest is allowed to be capitalized, **the total amount of interest cost that a company capitalizes each period may not exceed the interest cost incurred during the period.**

The expenditures to which a company applies this rate are the cumulative capitalized expenditures (which include any capitalized interest on the qualifying asset from previous periods). The company may assume for simplicity that the expenditures are incurred evenly throughout the period. Therefore, the average cumulative capitalized expenditures for a period are computed as follows: [(beginning cumulative costs + ending cumulative costs) ÷ 2]. If a company does not incur expenditures evenly throughout the period, a weighted average calculation would be used. If the company receives any progress payments from the eventual purchaser of the asset, it deducts these amounts from its expenditures, so that it capitalizes interest on its net expenditures.

Period of Interest Capitalization The capitalization period begins when **(a) expenditures for the asset have been made, (b) activities that are necessary to get the asset ready for its intended use are in progress, and (c) interest cost is being incurred.** Interest capitalization continues as long as the three conditions are present. *Activities* include all the steps necessary to prepare the asset for its intended use. For example, they include administrative and technical activities during the preconstruction stage and activities undertaken to overcome technical difficulties after construction has begun, such as labor disputes or litigation. If a company suspends

---

7. *Ibid.*, par. 10.
8. *Ibid.*, par. 12.

substantially *all* the activities related to the construction of the asset, however, it suspends interest capitalization until the activities are resumed.

The capitalization period ends when the asset is (a) substantially complete and (b) ready for its intended use. If the asset is completed in parts and each part can be used independently, interest capitalization stops for each part when that part meets the two criteria. In this case the interest capitalized is based on the average cost for that part. If the asset must be completed in its entirety before any part of the asset may be used, however, interest capitalization continues until the entire asset meets the two criteria.

Example : Interest Capitalization

To illustrate these provisions of *FASB Statement No. 34*, consider the Cia Company, which started a building project on January 1, 2007 and completed it on December 31, 2008. Example 10-2 shows the relevant facts.

The company incurred the costs (expenditures) evenly during each year. It computes the average cumulative capitalized costs in the project to date for each year using the equations discussed earlier as we show in Example 10-2.

EXAMPLE 10-2   Capitalization of Interest Costs

Capitalization period: January 1, 2007 through December 31, 2008

Annual expenditures on the project (excluding capitalized interest):
  2007 $1 million
  2008 $2.9 million

Amounts borrowed and outstanding:

  $1.5 million at 10% borrowed specifically for the project
  $4 million at 12%
  $6 million at 13%

Average cumulative costs: 2007, $500,000 [($0 + $1,000,000) ÷ 2]

Capitalized interest, 2007 = Average cumulative cost × Interest rate

$$= \$500,000 \times 10\%$$
$$= \underline{\$50,000}$$

Average cumulative costs: 2008, $2,500,000
  [($1,000,000 + $50,000[a]) +($1,050,000 + $2,900,000)] ÷ 2

Capitalized interest, 2008 = Average cumulative cost × Interest rate

$$= (\$1,500,000^{b} \times 10\%) + (\$1,000,000^{c} \times 12.6\%^{d})$$
$$= \$150,000 + \$126,000$$
$$= \underline{\$276,000}$$

[a]$50,000 capitalized interest for 2007
[b]$1.5 million specific borrowing
[c]$2,500,000 average cumulative cost for 2008 – $1,500,000 specific borrowing

[d]Weighted average interest rate $= \left(12\% \times \dfrac{\$4,000,000}{\$10,000,000}\right) + \left(13\% \times \dfrac{\$6,000,000}{\$10,000,000}\right)$

$$= 4.8\% + 7.8\%$$
$$= 12.6\%$$

Since the company borrowed $1.5 million specifically for the project, it uses the 10% interest rate on this borrowing for each of the two years on the first $1.5 million of costs. It computes interest each year on costs greater than $1.5 million based on the weighted average of its remaining borrowings. It calculates the amount of interest to be capitalized in each of the two years as we show in Example 10-2.

Cia Company calculates the $50,000 interest capitalized in 2007 by multiplying the $500,000 average cumulative cost by the 10% interest rate on the specific borrowing for the project. The interest capitalized in 2008 requires two calculations, because the $2,500,000 average cumulative cost exceeds the $1,500,000 specifically borrowed for the project. First, the company calculates the $150,000 ($1,500,000 × 10%) annual interest on the specific borrowing. Next, it multiples the $1,000,000 excess of average cost over specific borrowing ($2,500,000 − $1,500,000) by the 12.6% weighted average interest rate to determine the $126,000 additional interest to be capitalized. Thus it capitalizes a total of $276,000 ($150,000 + $126,000) interest in 2008.

As we mentioned earlier, the total amount of interest that is capitalized each period may not exceed the interest cost incurred during the period. Each year the company incurs interest costs of $1.41 million [($1.5 million × 10%) + ($4 million × 12%) + ($6 million × 13%)]. This amount is clearly more than the capitalized interest in either year. If it were less, however, it would be the maximum amount that the company could capitalize in any given year. Assuming Cia Company has recorded interest expense for the $1.41 million interest cost each year, it would record the capitalized interest at the end of 2007 and 2008, respectively, as follows:

End of 2007

Building	50,000	
Interest Expense		50,000

End of 2008

Building	276,000	
Interest Expense		276,000

Note that these journal entries *reduce* the net interest expense for each year and *increase* the cost of the building because of the capitalized interest. The company reports the remaining net interest expense amounts of $1,360,000 ($1,410,000 − $50,000) and $1,134,000 ($1,410,000 − $276,000), respectively, on its 2007 and 2008 income statements. Therefore, its pretax income is increased by $50,000 in 2007 and $276,000 in 2008. In addition, the company discloses the capitalized interest amounts of $50,000 and $276,000 in the notes to its financial statements. (Note that it also discloses the total interest paid each year, as we discuss in Chapter 22.)

The company reports a cost of $1,050,000 ($1 million construction cost + $50,000 interest cost) for the construction-in-process on its December 31, 2007 balance sheet, and a cost of $4,226,000 ($3.9 million total construction costs + $326,000 total interest cost) for the building on its December 31, 2008 balance sheet. The total interest capitalized over the two years is $326,000 ($50,000 + $276,000). Therefore, the cost of the asset is increased by this amount. This will reduce the gross profit on the sale if the asset is sold when completed, or increase the depreciation expense each year if the asset is held by the company. ♦

In some cases, a company may borrow a larger amount than it requires for its immediate construction needs. A question arises as to whether the company should offset the interest revenue earned by investing the excess funds against the interest cost to determine the amount of interest to be capitalized. Since *FASB Statement No. 34* states that the amount of interest to be capitalized is the portion of the interest that theoretically could have been avoided, the interest revenue should *not* be offset against the interest cost. The decision of a company to borrow greater amounts than needed and to invest the excess does not affect the avoidable interest and therefore does not affect the amount of interest to be capitalized.[9] Therefore, the interest earned is recognized and reported as interest revenue in the normal way.

---

9. "Offsetting Interest Cost to Be Capitalized with Interest Income," *FASB Technical Bulletin No. 81–5* (Stamford, Conn.: FASB, 1981).

LINK TO INTERNATIONAL DIFFERENCES

International accounting standards for the capitalization of interest may be different from U.S. standards. International standards state that the "benchmark" method is to expense all interest costs. However, the capitalization of interest during the acquisition, construction, or production of a qualifying asset is an allowable alternative. This allowed alternative approach is similar to the capitalization rules under U.S. GAAP. So the flexibility allowed under international standards may create a lack of comparability with companies following U.S. standards. (There are also some differences in the two sets of capitalization rules that are beyond the scope of this book.)

Fixed Overhead Costs

There are three alternatives for a company to include fixed overhead costs in the cost of a self-constructed asset. They are (1) to allocate a portion of the total fixed overhead, (2) to include only the incremental fixed overhead, and (3) not to include any fixed overhead in the cost of the asset. Each alternative should be considered for two production situations. First, the company may be operating at full capacity, so that the construction activity reduces normal production activity. Second, the company may be operating at below-normal capacity, so that the construction activity does not affect normal production activity.

1. *Allocate a portion of potal fixed overhead to the self-constructed asset.* Under this alternative, the company allocates the fixed overhead to the construction in the same manner as to units of inventory produced. This is a "full costing" concept, because the total overhead costs of the period are allocated to the production of inventory and the construction of the asset. Arguments in favor of this alternative are (1) the construction should be accounted for in the same way as regular products, even though this means that the regular products will be allocated less of the overhead, and (2) the cost of the constructed asset will tend to approximate more closely the cost of an equivalent purchased asset, since the seller normally would include fixed overhead in its selling price. The first argument is especially relevant if the company is operating at full capacity prior to the construction, so that the construction causes less regular production to take place. Then the lower total overhead allocated to production coupled with lower productive output results in more consistent unit costs. When the company is operating at below-normal capacity prior to construction, allocation of some fixed overhead to self-constructed assets reduces the costs allocated to regular production and therefore increases the income reported for these products when they are sold. Thus there is a transfer of overhead costs from regular production to the self-constructed asset.

2. *Include only incremental fixed overhead in the cost of the self-constructed asset.* Under this alternative, the company includes only the fixed overhead that increases as a result of the construction (but no allocated overhead) in the cost of the self-constructed asset. Arguments in favor of this alternative are (1) the cost of an asset is the additional cost incurred to produce it, (2) the normal operations should not receive different treatment by reducing the cost of the regular product and increasing income because of the construction, (3) the overhead would be incurred whether or not the construction takes place, and (4) the decision to construct the asset should be based on the total incremental cost and not include allocated fixed overhead. This method is particularly appropriate when the company has excess capacity available so that regular production and income are not affected by the construction. If this method is used in a full-capacity situation, the unit cost of the regular production is increased because the same total fixed overhead is allocated to the reduced production.

3. *Include no fixed overhead in the cost of the self-constructed asset.* The primary argument in favor of this alternative is that the company's fixed overhead does not change as a result of the construction. Therefore, if the company included some overhead, this would result in less overhead being expensed in the current period (or included in the cost of inventory) and an increase in income. Of course, this alternative is reasonable only if the fixed overhead does not increase as a result of the construction.

In summary,

- the allocation of fixed overhead to a self-constructed asset is most appropriate when the company is operating at full capacity,
- the inclusion of only incremental fixed overhead is most appropriate in excess-capacity situations, and
- no allocation is appropriate if the overhead does not change.

Otherwise, the self-construction activity affects income, an effect that many people consider undesirable. Income should be a measure of the success of selling goods and services, and it should not depend on the amount of construction undertaken.

However, the first alternative of allocating a portion of the total fixed overhead to the self-constructed asset is supported for both situations by the Cost Accounting Standards Board as follows:

> **Tangible capital assets constructed for a contractor's own use must be capitalized at amounts that include general and administrative [costs] when such [costs] are identifiable with the constructed asset and are material in amount. When the constructed assets are identical with or similar to the contractor's regular product, such assets must be capitalized at amounts that include a full share of indirect costs.**[10]

This method is the most commonly used and tends to produce an asset cost that is closer to the cost of a purchased asset, because an independent contractor would include an allowance to cover its overhead and income. However, it also tends to result in increased income during construction.

Income on Self-Construction

If a company constructs an asset for less than it would cost to purchase, should it recognize income for the difference between the two costs? An argument can be made in favor of recognizing income, since it would tend to produce an asset cost similar to the purchase price of the asset. However, generally accepted accounting principles do not allow recognition of income in this case. To do so would violate the revenue recognition principle that requires a company to recognize income through asset use and disposal and not through acquisition. In addition, accounting is based on actions taken, not on what might have been. The company will realize the saving from self-construction with reduced depreciation charges in the future. However, the conservatism convention requires that, if the construction cost materially exceeds the fair value of the asset, the company must write down the capitalized construction costs of the asset to fair value and recognize a loss.

Development Stage Companies

Development stage companies devote substantially all their efforts to establishing a new business, and their planned principal operations have not yet started or no significant revenue has been generated. Some people argue that a new company should capitalize the costs of interest, taxes, and general overhead during its development stage—that is, before it makes

---

10. "Capitalization of Tangible Assets," *CASB Standard 404* (Washington, D.C.: CASB, 1973).

significant sales. They argue that the costs incurred in the development stage will benefit future periods. Therefore, the company should not report losses before it makes sales. In **FASB Statement No. 7** this argument was rejected. Instead normal capitalization criteria are applied to development stage companies. Therefore, a company expenses such costs as interest (except for the provisions of *FASB Statement No. 34*), taxes, and general overhead in the period incurred. *FASB Statement No. 7* does impose some special disclosure requirements on development stage companies, but these are beyond the scope of this book.

COSTS AFTER ACQUISITION

5 Record costs after acquisition.

A company incurs costs over the life of its property, plant, and equipment for purposes ranging from routine repairs to major overhauls and improvements. The related accounting decision is whether these costs should be added (capitalized) to an asset account (a **capital expenditure**) or expensed (an **operating** or **revenue expenditure**). **A cost that increases the future economic benefits of the asset above those that originally were expected is a capital expenditure.** The future economic benefits can be increased by (1) extending the life of the asset, (2) improving productivity, (3) producing the same product at lower cost, or (4) increasing the quality of the product. **A cost that does not increase the economic benefits but is incurred to maintain the existing benefits is an operating expenditure.** We discuss additions, improvements and replacements, rearrangement and moving, and repairs and maintenance in the following sections.

Additions

The cost of an **addition** represents a new asset and therefore is capitalized. Adding a new wing to a building and installing a pollution-control device are examples of additions. When the addition involves removing an old asset, an issue arises as to how to account for the cost of the removal. For example, when a company adds a new wing to a building, it frequently makes alterations to the old building. If these alterations increase the economic benefits originally anticipated for the old building, then the cost of alteration is capitalized. If the alterations do not increase the original benefits of the old building, then the cost is expensed. In addition, the cost of any part of the asset that is demolished (for example, a connecting wall) should be removed from the accounts as the disposal of an asset, although this is rarely done because of immateriality or the difficulty of measurement.

Improvements and Replacements

Improvements (sometimes called **betterments**) and **replacements** (sometimes called **renewals**) involve the substitution of new parts for old ones, and increase the economic benefits to be obtained from the asset. An improvement is the substitution of a better asset for the one currently used, such as the installation of a solar heating system in a building. A replacement is the substitution of an equivalent asset, such as a new engine in a truck. The related costs of improvements and replacements are capitalized. There are three alternative ways for a company to account for such capitalized expenditures, and the choice depends on the particular circumstances.

1. Example: Substitution Method

When the book value of the old asset is known, it is removed from the accounts and the new asset recorded. For example, suppose that Pippa Company decides to replace its oil furnace with a gas furnace. The oil furnace is carried on the books at a cost of $50,000 with accumulated depreciation of $30,000. The scrap value of the old furnace is $5,000, and the new furnace costs $70,000. Pippa Company records this transaction as follows:

Furnace	70,000	
Accumulated Depreciation: Furnace	30,000	
Loss on Disposal of Furnace		
($20,000 − $5,000)	15,000	
Furnace		50,000
Cash ($70,000 − $5,000)		65,000 ◆

Although this is the ideal method, it often is not practical because the company does not know the book value of the asset being replaced. For example, when the company replaces the engine on a truck, it may not know the book value of the engine. In these situations, it should use one of the following two alternative methods.

2. Example: Reduce Accumulated Depreciation

The costs of improvements and replacements are often debited to Accumulated Depreciation because some of the service potential that previously was written off has been restored. Therefore, it is appropriate to use this method for replacements when the service life of the asset has been extended. For example, suppose that Ellen Company incurs a capital expenditure of $60,000 to replace a roof on its factory. Ellen Company had not planned to replace the roof, but it has extended the life of the factory. Ellen Company records the cost as follows:

Accumulated Depreciation	60,000	
Cash		60,000 ◆

3. Example: Increase the Asset Account

The costs of improvements and replacements may be capitalized directly to the asset account because an addition to the service potential of the asset has been made. This method is particularly appropriate for improvements when the benefits are increased above those originally expected. For example, Matt Company records a capital expenditure of $80,000 to enlarge a factory that increases its usefulness as follows:

Factory	80,000	
Cash		80,000 ◆

Note that examples 2 and 3 have exactly the same effect on the book value of the asset, although the gross amounts in the two accounts would be different. In both cases, a new depreciation rate would be computed, as we discuss in the next chapter.

Rearrangement and Moving

The costs of rearranging the facilities within a building or moving them to a new location are capitalized and expensed over the period expected to benefit. (This period is shorter than the economic life of the assets being moved if the company expects that it will move the assets again before the end of their service lives.) However, many companies expense such costs immediately, which is an acceptable procedure if the difference is immaterial.

Repairs and Maintenance

When a company incurs routine repair and maintenance costs to maintain an asset in its operating condition, it expenses the costs in the period incurred. However, the classification of an expenditure as a repair may depend on how the company accounts for its assets. For example, if the company includes landscaping costs in a Land Improvements account, it would account for the replacement of some trees as repairs and maintenance. If the company included the landscaping costs in a separate account, then it would most likely account for the replacement of these trees as an improvement or replacement.

Since a company may incur repair and maintenance costs unevenly during the year (e.g., it may schedule repairs for slack production periods), its interim financial statements (such as quarterly reports) will include different amounts of repair costs that, in turn, may give a misleading picture of the company's income. The amount of repair costs that a company records as an expense in each interim period may be averaged by using an allowance account.

Example: Repairs and Maintenance

Suppose Sanner Company anticipates spending $60,000 on repair and maintenance during the year, but $45,000 will be spent in the third quarter, with the remainder spread equally over the remaining three quarters. Sanner Company records these events as follows:

First Quarter

Repair Expense ($60,000 ÷ 4)	15,000	
Allowance for Repairs		10,000
Cash, Accounts Payable, Inventory, etc.		5,000

Second Quarter

Repair Expense	15,000	
Allowance for Repairs		10,000
Cash, Accounts Payable, Inventory, etc.		5,000

Third Quarter

Repair Expense	15,000	
Allowance for Repairs		30,000
Cash, Accounts Payable, Inventory, etc.		45,000

Fourth Quarter

Repair Expense	15,000	
Allowance for Repairs		10,000
Cash, Accounts Payable, Inventory, etc.		5,000

The repair expense for each quarter is $15,000 (one-fourth of the annual cost of $60,000), and Allowance for Repairs has a zero balance at the end of the year. This procedure is acceptable for *interim* reporting because it allows a company to record equal expenses in each interim period. Sanner Company reports the balance in Allowance for Repairs as an addition to or offset from its property, plant, and equipment and not as a liability because nothing is owed. However, a balance in Allowance for Repairs is not carried over from one *annual* fiscal period to another, because such smoothing of income is not allowed under generally accepted accounting principles. If a balance does remain in the Allowance for Repairs account at the end of the year, it is closed to the Repair Expense account. ♦

DISPOSAL OF PROPERTY, PLANT, AND EQUIPMENT

6 Record the disposal of property, plant, and equipment.

A company may dispose of property, plant, and equipment by sale, involuntary conversion, abandonment, or exchange (which we discussed earlier in the chapter). Ideally, the depreciation, which is accumulated up to the time of disposal, will have reduced the book value down to the disposal value. Usually, however, this does not occur, and the company must recognize a gain or a loss on the disposal. The gain or loss may be considered a correction of the income that has been recorded in the years the asset has been owned, since it is an indication that the depreciation was not correct. However, GAAP requires that a company record a gain or loss on disposal in the period of the disposal. The company usually includes the gain or loss in ordinary income, but it could also be reported as an extraordinary item or a disposal of a component of a business if it meets the appropriate criteria established in **FASB Statement No. 144,** as we discussed in Chapter 4.

To account for the disposal of property, plant, and equipment, the company first records the depreciation up to the date of the disposal (as we discuss in the next chapter). It then removes the cost of the asset and the related amount of accumulated depreciation from the respective accounts.

Example: Disposal of Machine

Assume that Bean Company has a machine that originally cost $10,000, has accumulated depreciation of $8,000 at the beginning of the current year, and is being depreciated at $1,000 per year. If the company sells the machine for $600 on December 30, it must first bring the depreciation up to date as follows:

Depreciation Expense	1,000	
Accumulated Depreciation		1,000

Once the book value is up to date, the company compares it to the proceeds to determine the gain or loss. Comparing the $1,000 [$10,000 − ($8,000 + $1,000)] book value of the asset on December 30 to the $600 proceeds yields a loss of $400, which Bean Company records as follows:

Cash	600	
Accumulated Depreciation	9,000	
Loss on Disposal	400	
Machine		10,000

An involuntary disposal, such as condemnation of land by a governmental unit, is accounted for in the same way.[11] An abandonment is handled in a similar way, except that there is no receipt of cash, so the loss is equal to the remaining book value. ♦

Asset Retirement Obligations

The acquisition of some assets automatically creates a legal obligation related to the retirement of the asset. For example, companies owning power plants, mines, and industrial manufacturing sites frequently are legally required to incur significant costs related to their closure. **FASB Statement No. 143** requires a company to record a legal liability for the obligation at its fair value when the obligation is incurred, which is usually when the asset is acquired. The most common method of measuring the fair value is likely to be the present value of the future cash flows that will be paid by the company. When the company acquires the asset (and records the liability) the present value is less than the future cash flows, and therefore, it must increase the liability over time. So the company recognizes interest expense (called accretion expense) each year it uses the asset. It calculates the expense by multiplying the book value of the liability by the discount rate it used to compute the original present value. On the date the company retires the asset and pays the retirement costs, it debits the obligation and credits cash. The company recognizes any difference between the estimated retirement costs (i.e., the liability) and the actual costs as a gain or loss.

When the company records (credits) the initial liability, it also records (debits) the same amount as an increase in the carrying value of the related asset. The company expenses (depreciates) this cost in the usual way by means of a systematic and rational allocation method over its useful life.[12]

---

11. "Accounting for Involuntary Conversions of Nonmonetary Assets to Monetary Assets," *FASB Interpretation No. 30* (Stamford, Conn.: FASB, 1979), requires that a gain or loss be recognized when a nonmonetary asset is involuntarily converted to monetary assets even though a company reinvests or is obligated to reinvest the monetary assets in replacement nonmonetary assets.
12. "Accounting for Asset Retirement Obligations," *FASB Statement of Financial Accounting Standards No. 143* (Norwalk, Conn.: FASB, 2001), par. 3, 11, and 14.

SECURE YOUR KNOWLEDGE 10-2

- The initial cost of self-constructed assets includes direct material, direct labor, and a portion of the company's overhead costs.
  - If the asset qualifies for interest capitalization, avoidable interest (computed by applying an appropriate interest rate to the average cumulative cost) is capitalized as long as it does not exceed the actual interest cost incurred during the period.
  - Management may choose to allocate a portion of fixed overhead, include incremental fixed overhead, or exclude fixed overhead from the cost of a self-constructed asset.
  - Income recognition is not allowed if a company constructs an asset for less than it would have cost to purchase it.
- Expenditures that increase the future economic benefits of an asset (e.g., extend the useful life of the asset, improve productivity, decrease operating costs, or increase the quality of the product) are capital expenditures and are added to the cost of the asset.
- Expenditures that simply maintain the existing level of benefits are operating (or revenue) expenditures and are expensed in the current period.
- When a company disposes of property, plant, and equipment by sale, involuntary conversion, or abandonment, any resulting gain or loss is included in current period income.
- An asset retirement obligation (any liability related to the retirement or disposition of property, plant, and equipment) is required to be capitalized at fair value on the date the obligation is incurred. After acquisition, a company increases the liability over time by recognizing interest expense (accretion expense), and depreciates the asset using a systematic and rational method.

Credit: ©Getty Images/PhotoDisc

DISCLOSURE OF PROPERTY, PLANT, AND EQUIPMENT

APB Opinion No. 12 requires a company to disclose the balances of its major classes of depreciable assets by nature or function.[13] We show an example of each of these methods in Real Report 10-1. **Johnson & Johnson** discloses by the nature of the assets, such as land, buildings, and machinery. **Norfolk Southern** discloses by function, such as road and equipment.

7 Understand the disclosures of property, plant, and equipment.

Real Report 10-1   Disclosures of Depreciable Assets

JOHNSON & JOHNSON AND SUBSIDIARIES
Notes to Consolidated Financial Statements (in part)

1. Summary of Accounting Principles (in part):
Property, Plant, and Equipment and Depreciation
Property, plant, and equipment are stated at cost. The Company utilizes the straight-line method of depreciation over the estimated useful lives of the assets:

Building and building equipment	20–40 years
Land and leasehold improvements	10–20 years
Machinery and equipment	2–13 years

3 Property, Plant and Equipment
At the end of 2004 and 2003, property, plant and equipment at cost and accumulated depreciation were:

(Dollars in Millions)	2004	2003
Land and land improvements	$ 515	$ 491
Buildings and building equipment	5,907	5,242
Machinery and equipment	10,455	9,638
Construction in progress	1,787	1,681
	18,664	17,052
Less accumulated depreciation	8,228	7,206
	$ 10,436	$ 9,846

The Company capitalizes interest expense as part of the cost of construction of facilities and equipment. Interest expense capitalized in 2004, 2003 and 2002 was $136 million, $108 million and $98 million, respectively.

Upon retirement or other disposal of fixed assets, the cost and related amount of accumulated depreciation or amortization are eliminated from the asset and accumulated depreciation accounts, respectively. The difference, if any, between the net asset value and the proceeds is adjusted to earnings.

NORFOLK SOUTHERN CORPORATION AND SUBSIDIARIES
Notes to Consolidated Financial Statements (in part)

1. Summary of Significant Accounting Policies (in part):
Properties: "Properties" are stated principally at cost and are depreciated using group depreciation. Rail is depreciated primarily on the basis of use measured by gross ton

Continued

13. "Omnibus Opinion—1967," *APB Opinion No. 12* (New York: AICPA, 1967), par. 5.

miles. Other properties are depreciated generally using the straight-line method over the lesser of estimated service or lease lives. NS capitalizes interest on major capital projects during the period of their construction. Expenditures, including those on leased assets, that extend an asset's useful life or increase its utility, are capitalized. Maintenance expense is recognized when repairs are performed. When properties other than land and non-rail assets are sold or retired in the ordinary course of business, the cost of the assets, net of sale proceeds or salvage, is charged to accumulated depreciation, and no gain or loss is recognized through income. Gains and losses on disposal of land and non-rail assets are included in "Other income-net."

NS reviews the carrying amount of properties whenever events or changes in circumstances indicate that such carrying amount may not be recoverable based on future undiscounted cash flows. Assets that are deemed impaired as a result of such review are recorded at the lower of carrying amount or fair value.

6. Properties

($ in millions)	December 31, 2004	December 31, 2003	Depreciation Rate for 2004
Railway property:			
Road	$19,530	$11,243	3.0%
Equipment	6,661	5,779	4.2%
Other property	574	569	2.9%
	26,765	17,591	
Less: Accumulated depreciation	6,239	5,812	
Net properties	$20,526	$11,779	

Railway property includes $618 million at Dec. 31, 2004 and $477 million at Dec. 31, 2003, of assets recorded pursuant to capital leases. Other property includes the costs of obtaining rights to natural resources of $341 million at Dec. 31, 2004 and 2003.

Total interest cost incurred on debt in 2004, 2003 and 2002 was $499 million, $509 million and $529 million respectively, of which $10 million, $12 million and $11 million was capitalized.

Questions:

1. If Johnson & Johnson had not capitalized interest in 2004, how would its financial statements be different?
2. What are the effects on the financial statements of the method used by Norfolk Southern for the sale of its properties? Is it different from the method used by Johnson & Johnson?
3. Why does Norfolk Southern account for the sale of land differently than the sale of other properties?

LINK TO RATIO ANALYSIS

The analysis of property, plant, and equipment is often concerned with a company's ability to use its investment in assets to generate income. An examination of a company's return on assets, a profitability ratio, provides an indication of how efficiently a company uses its economic resources. Consider the following information from **Microsoft's** 2004 annual report:

(in millions)

Net Sales	$36,835
Net Income	5,355
Total Assets, beginning of year	81,732
Total Assets, end of year	92,389

Microsoft's return on assets[14] is shown in the following equation:

$$\text{Return on Assets} = \frac{\text{Net Income}}{\text{Average Total Assets}} = \frac{\$5,355}{\left(\dfrac{\$81,732 + \$92,389}{2}\right)} = 6.1\%$$

A company's return on assets is driven by two factors: how effective a company is at controlling its costs and expenses in relation to sales (profit margin) and how well a company manages its assets to generate sales (asset turnover). Additional insights into Microsoft's profitability can be obtained by separating its return on assets into these two ratios as shown in the following equation:

$$\text{Return on Assets} = \text{Profit Margin} \times \text{Asset Turnover} = \frac{\text{Net Income}}{\text{Net Sales}} \times \frac{\text{Net Sales}}{\text{Average Total Assets}}$$

$$= \frac{\$5,355}{\$36,835} \times \frac{\$36,835}{\left(\dfrac{\$81,732 + \$92,389}{2}\right)} = 14.5\% \times 42.3\% = 6.1\%$$

Based on this equation, Microsoft's profit margin indicates that every dollar of sales generated approximately $0.145 of income and that Microsoft was able to generate $0.423 of sales per dollar invested in assets.

APPENDIX: OIL AND GAS PROPERTIES

A company faces special issues when accounting for oil and gas properties that are included in its property, plant, and equipment. Two alternative methods of accounting for the cost of oil and gas properties are widely used. The principal difference between the two methods concerns the cost of dry wells—those that do not result in the production of oil or gas. Under the **successful-efforts** method, those costs are expensed; under the **full-cost** method, they are capitalized as part of the cost of oil and gas reserves, and then amortized.

Proponents of the *successful-efforts method* argue that a direct relationship between costs incurred and specific reserves discovered is required before costs are recorded as assets. Costs of acquisition and development activities that are known not to have resulted in the discovery of reserves are expensed. In contrast, the *full-cost method* regards the costs of unsuccessful

8 Explain the accounting for oil and gas properties.

---

14. Return on assets is often computed by adding interest expense (net of tax) back to net income because interest is a financial cost to pay creditors, not a cost of generating sales. However, because Microsoft has such a small percentage of long-term debt, we ignore interest cost for this calculation.

acquisition and exploration activities as necessary for the discovery of reserves. Thus, all costs incurred in oil and gas drilling are regarded as integral to the development of whatever reserves ultimately result from the efforts as a whole, and are thus associated with the company's reserves. Establishing a direct cause-and-effect relationship between drilling costs incurred and specific reserves discovered is not relevant to full costing.

The basic difference between the two methods focuses on the nature of an asset. If the asset is viewed as an individual well, it is appropriate for a company to expense the costs incurred if no oil or gas is found, because no future cash flows will result. Alternatively, if the asset is viewed as the oil or gas that lies underground, it is appropriate for a company to capitalize the costs of drilling even if no oil or gas is found from a particular well, because the activity was necessary in searching for oil or gas. It is the oil or gas that is discovered that will contribute to the future cash flows rather than the costs incurred to drill any particular well. A company that uses the full-cost method is required (by the SEC, as discussed later) to use a country as a cost center. Thus if costs are incurred in a new country and no oil or gas results, the costs are expensed.

Because both methods are widely used, difficulties are created for users of financial statements when making comparisons between companies that are each using different methods. Large oil and gas companies generally use the successful-efforts method, whereas small independent producers prefer the full-cost method because it enables them to defer more costs, thereby reducing current expenses and increasing current income.

In 1977 **FASB Statement No. 19** was issued, which required the use of the successful-efforts method. The FASB cited two primary reasons to justify the adoption of the successful-efforts method. First, an asset is an economic resource that is expected to provide future benefits, so costs that are known not to have resulted in identifiable future benefits should be expensed. Second, financial statements should reflect risk and unsuccessful results. The successful-efforts method highlights the cost of failures and the risks involved in the search for oil and gas reserves. In a politically motivated decision, the SEC decided not to support the FASB's position. Many of the owners and managers of oil and gas companies that were using full-cost accounting objected to its elimination and lobbied Congress. They argued that the use of successful efforts would cause reported income and assets to be lower, and would impair the ability of their companies to raise capital and search for oil and gas. This argument is inconsistent with efficient markets research, which indicates that users of financial statements would not be "fooled" by the different reporting of the same underlying economic facts. However, Congress accepted the argument and directed that the SEC must accept the use of the full-cost method in reports filed with it, thereby allowing both methods to continue to be used. Consequently, the FASB suspended *FASB Statement No. 19.*

It can be argued that neither method satisfies the needs of users of financial statements because they do not reflect the economic substance of oil and gas exploration. That is, neither one includes the current values of a company's oil and gas reserves in its financial statements. Thus, the SEC established a completely new method of accounting called Reserve Recognition Accounting (RRA). RRA allowed a company to report the current values of reserves on its balance sheet and changes in the values of those reserves to be included on its income statement. Effective in 1979, companies were required to present a supplementary income statement, based on RRA, while continuing to use successful-efforts or full-cost accounting. Later, the SEC rescinded the requirement to use RRA, and therefore oil companies now use either the full-cost or the successful-efforts method. Once a company has selected one of the two alternative methods, it must follow specific SEC accounting rules.[15] If the successful-efforts method is chosen, the SEC requires that the rules of *FASB Statement No. 19* must be followed. In addition, *FASB Statement No. 69* requires that oil companies disclose the physical and dollar amounts of reserves at year-end and changes in these amounts. Since these accounting problems relate to a specific industry, we do not discuss them further.

---

15. "Codification of Financial Reporting Policies," *SEC Accounting Rules* (Chicago: Commerce Clearing House, 2005), sec. 406.

SUMMARY

At the beginning of the chapter, we identified several objectives you would accomplish after reading the chapter. The objectives are listed below, each followed by a brief summary of the key points in the chapter discussion.

1. **Identify the characteristics of property, plant, and equipment.** Property, plant, and equipment is the title used to classify tangible noncurrent assets a company uses in the normal operations of its business. The asset must be held for use and not for investment, must have an expected life of more than one year, and must be tangible in nature.

2. **Record the acquisition of property, plant, and equipment.** Property, plant, and equipment is recorded at the total cost necessary to acquire the asset and put it in operating condition; that is, the costs that are necessary to obtain the benefits to be derived from the asset.

3. **Determine the cost of a nonmonetary asset acquired by the exchange of another nonmonetary asset.** The cost of the nonmonetary asset acquired is the fair value of the nonmonetary asset surrendered plus any cash paid or minus any cash received.

4. **Compute the cost of a self-constructed asset, including interest capitalization.** When a company constructs an item of property, plant, and equipment, the costs included in the asset cost are materials, labor, engineering, variable manufacturing overhead, interest, and perhaps allocated fixed manufacturing overhead. A company is required to capitalize interest on assets that are either constructed for its own use or constructed as discrete projects for sale or lease to others. The company determines the amount of interest to capitalize by applying an interest rate to the average cumulative invested costs for the qualifying asset during the capitalization period.

5. **Record costs after acquisition.** A subsequent cost that increases the future economic benefits of the asset above those that originally were expected is a capital expenditure. A subsequent cost that does not increase the economic benefits but is incurred to maintain existing benefits is an operating expenditure and is expensed.

6. **Record the disposal of property, plant, and equipment.** A company may dispose of property, plant, and equipment by sale, involuntary conversion, or abandonment. The company records depreciation up to the date of the sale and records a gain or loss for the difference between the book value of the asset and the proceeds received.

7. **Understand the disclosures of property, plant, and equipment.** A company is required to disclose the balances of its major classes of depreciable assets by nature or function.

8. **Explain the accounting for oil and gas properties** (Appendix). A company may account for oil and gas properties using either the full cost method, in which the cost of dry holes is capitalized, or the successful efforts method, in which the cost of dry holes is expensed.

ANSWERS TO REAL REPORT QUESTIONS

Real Report 10-1 Answers

1. The capitalization of interest in 2004 by Johnson & Johnson resulted in a $136 million decrease in interest expense reported on the income statement, and a $136 million increase in income, assets (property, plant, and equipment), and stockholders' equity.

2. Norfolk Southern uses the group depreciation method for "properties" (group depreciation is discussed in Chapter 11). Under this method, the sale of properties other than land and non-rail assets is recorded by a debit to cash for any sale proceeds and a credit to the asset account. Any gain or loss on the sale (the difference between the cost of the asset and the sale proceeds) is recorded as an adjustment to accumulated depreciation. For land and non-rail assets, Norfolk Southern includes any gain or loss in income. Johnson & Johnson records retirements or disposals in a manner consistent with the latter method.

3. Norfolk Southern uses group depreciation for its railway property because the assets are homogeneous (similar) and this method simplifies the company's record-keeping. However, the unique nature of land necessitates a different accounting method relative to the similar, relatively lower cost railway properties.

QUESTIONS

Q10-1   What characteristics are necessary for a company to include an asset in the category of property, plant, and equipment?

Q10-2   What is the general criterion a company uses to decide whether to include an expenditure in the cost of property, plant, and equipment rather than expensing it?

Q10-3   How does a company categorize land held for investment on its balance sheet?

Q10-4   What is the book value of an asset?

Q10-5   What is the relationship between the book value and the market value of an asset during the life of the asset?

Q10-6   When a company purchases several assets for a single lump sum, what principle does it use for cost apportionment? Why is it necessary to apportion the cost?

Q10-7   How does a company determine the acquisition cost of an asset when it acquires the asset in exchange for securities?

Q10-8   At what amount does a company record the cost of a nonmonetary asset acquired in exchange for another non-monetary asset?

Q10-9   How much does a company recognize as a gain or loss when it exchanges nonmonetary assets?

Q10-10   Under what conditions does a company capitalize the interest incurred during self-construction of an asset? Contrast your answer with accounting for interest on a note payable that is not associated with the construction of an asset.

Q10-11   Explain how a company determines the amount of interest to capitalize when it constructs an asset.

Q10-12   A company borrows some money which it uses to acquire a parcel of land for a real estate development project. Before construction begins, a period of time passes while the company obtains the necessary planning permission. May the company capitalize interest during this period? If so, should it capitalize the interest to the land or the building account?

Q10-13   What are the three common alternative treatments of overhead costs during self-construction of an asset? What are the arguments in favor of each?

Q10-14   May a company recognize profit during self-construction of an asset under generally accepted accounting principles? May it recognize a loss?

Q10-15   What is the distinction between a capital and an operating expenditure? Give two examples of each.

Q10-16   Distinguish between additions and improvements/replacements. How should a company account for each?

Q10-17   Distinguish between ordinary repairs and maintenance, and extraordinary repairs. How should a company account for each?

Q10-18   What are leasehold improvements? How should a company account for them?

Q10-19   Under what conditions would you expect to see Allowance for Repairs in a company's balance sheet?

Q10-20   How does a company account for the disposal of an asset? How does it report gains and losses on its financial statements?

Q10-21 (Appendix)   Distinguish between successful efforts and full cost accounting for oil and gas properties.

MULTIPLE CHOICE (AICPA Adapted)

Select the best answer for each of the following.

M10-1   The Hickory Company made a lump-sum purchase of three pieces of machinery for $115,000 from an unaffiliated company. At the time of acquisition Hickory paid $5,000 to determine the appraised value of the machinery. The appraisal disclosed the following values:

Machine A $70,000   Machine B $42,000
Machine C $28,000

What cost should be assigned to machines A, B, and C, respectively?

	A	B	C
a.	$40,000	$40,000	$40,000
b.	$57,500	$34,500	$23,000
c.	$60,000	$36,000	$24,000
d.	$70,000	$42,000	$28,000

M10-2   A donated plant asset for which the fair value has been determined, and for which incidental costs were incurred in acceptance of the asset, should be recorded at an amount equal to its

a. Incidental costs incurred
b. Fair value and incidental costs incurred
c. Book value on books of donor and incidental costs incurred
d. Book value on books of donor

M10-3 The following expenditures were among those incurred by Jensen Corporation during the year ended December 31, 2007:

Replacement of tiles on portion of roof that had been leaking	$4,000
Overhaul of machinery that is expected to extend its useful life for another two years	6,000

How much should be charged to repairs and maintenance in 2007?

a. $0
b. $4,000
c. $6,000
d. $10,000

M10-4 The sale of a depreciable asset resulting in a loss indicates that the proceeds from the sale were

a. Less than current market value
b. Greater than cost
c. Greater than book value
d. Less than book value

M10-5 Electro Corporation bought a new machine and agreed to pay for it in equal annual installments of $5,000 at the end of each of the next five years. Assume a prevailing interest rate of 15%. The present value of an ordinary annuity of $1 at 15% for five periods is 3.35. The future amount of an ordinary annuity of $1 at 15% for five periods is 6.74. The present value of $1 at 15% for five periods is 0.5. How much should Electro record as the cost of the machine?

a. $12,500
b. $16,750
c. $25,000
d. $33,700

M10-6 When a company purchases land with a building on it and immediately tears down the building so that the land can be used for the construction of a plant, the costs incurred to tear down the building should be

a. Expensed as incurred
b. Added to the cost of the plant
c. Added to the cost of the land
d. Amortized over the estimated time period between the tearing down of the building and the completion of the plant

M10-7 When a company replaces an old asphalt roof on its plant with a new fiberglass insulated roof, which of the following types of expenditure occurs?

a. Ordinary repair and maintenance
b. Addition
c. Rearrangement
d. Betterment

M10-8 On January 2, 2007 Yuki Yogurt Company decided to replace its obsolete refrigeration system with a more efficient one. The old system had a book value of $9,000 and a fair value of $1,000. Yuki's new refrigeration system has a fair value of $190,000, for which Yuki paid $189,000 after permitting the contractor to keep the old refrigeration equipment. How much should Yuki capitalize as the cost of the new refrigeration system?

a. $189,000
b. $190,000
c. $197,000
d. $198,000

M10-9 During 2007, Belardo Corporation constructed and manufactured certain assets, and incurred the following interest costs in connection with those activities:

	Interest Costs Incurred
Warehouse constructed for Belardo's own use	$20,000
Special-order machine for sale to unrelated customer, produced according to customer's specifications	9,000
Inventories routinely manufactured, produced on a repetitive basis	7,000

All of these assets required an extended period of time for completion. Assuming that the effect of interest capitalization is material, what is the total amount of interest costs to be capitalized?

a. $0
b. $20,000
c. $29,000
d. $36,000

M10-10 Lyle, Inc., purchased certain plant assets under a deferred payment contract on December 31, 2007. The agreement was to pay $20,000 at the time of purchase and $20,000 at the end of each of the next five years. The plant assets should be valued at

a. The present value of a $20,000 ordinary annuity for five years
b. $120,000
c. $120,000 less imputed interest
d. $120,000 plus imputed interest

EXERCISES

E10-1 *Determination of Cost* Which of the following 22 items does a company include in the cost of property, plant, and equipment?

1. Contract price
2. List price
3. Freight costs

4. Discounts taken
5. Discounts not taken
6. Installation costs
7. Testing costs
8. Cost of overhaul before initial use
9. Costs of grading land prior to construction
10. Tax assessment for street improvements
11. Delinquent property taxes on acquired property
12. Cost of tearing down an old building (already owned) in preparation for new construction
13. Cost of insurance during construction
14. Excess of costs over revenues during the development stage of the company
15. Interest costs during construction
16. Landscaping costs
17. Severance pay for employees dismissed because of the acquisition of a new machine
18. Cost of tearing down a building on newly acquired land
19. Replacement of an electric motor in a machine
20. Expansion of the heating/cooling system to accommodate an expansion of a building and certain expected future needs
21. Service contract for two years on the acquired asset
22. Cost of training new employees

E10-2 *Inclusion in Property, Plant, and Equipment* Which of the following does a company include in property, plant, and equipment on the balance sheet?
1. Idle equipment awaiting sale
2. Land held for future use as a plant site
3. Land held for investment
4. Deposits on machinery not yet received
5. Progress payments on building being constructed by a contractor
6. Fully depreciated assets still being used
7. Leasehold improvements
8. Assets leased to others

E10-3 *Acquisition Costs* The Voiture Company manufactures compact, energy efficient cars. On April 1, it purchased a machine for its assembly line at a contract price of $200,000 with terms of 2/10, n/30. The company paid the contract price on April 8 and also incurred installation and transportation costs of $5,000, sales tax of $10,000, and testing costs of $2,000. During testing the machine was accidentally damaged, so the company had to pay $1,000 to repair it.

Required
Prepare the journal entry to record the acquisition of the machine.

E10-4 *Determination of Acquisition Cost* In January 2007 Cordova Company entered into a contract to acquire a new machine for its factory. The machine, which has a cash price of $215,000, was paid for as follows:

Down payment	$ 55,000
Note payable in four equal annual payments starting in January 2008	120,000
600 shares of Cordova preferred stock with a mutually agreed value of $100 per share (par value $100)	60,000
Fair rate of interest on the non-interest-bearing note	10%

Required
1. Prepare the journal entry to record the acquisition of the machine.
2. How would your answer change, if at all, if the $215,000 cash price were not available?

E10-5 **AICPA Adapted** *Determination of Acquisition Cost* On August 1, 2007 Darmow Corporation purchased a new machine on a deferred payment basis. It made a down payment of $1,000 and will make four monthly installments of $2,500 each beginning on September 1, 2007. The cash equivalent price of the machine was $9,500. Darmow incurred and paid installation cost amounting to $300.

Required
Prepare the journal entry to record the acquisition of the machine.

E10-6 **AICPA Adapted** *Acquisition of Land and Building* On February 1, 2007 Edwards Corporation purchased a parcel of land as a factory site for $50,000. It demolished an old building on the property, and began construction on a new building that was completed on October 2, 2007. Costs incurred during this period are:

Demolition of old building	$ 4,000
Architect's fees	20,000
Legal fees for title investigation and purchase contract	2,000
Construction costs	500,000

The company sold salvaged materials resulting from the demolition for $3,000.

Required
At what amount should Edwards record the cost of the land and the new building, respectively?

E10-7 *Lump-Sum Purchase* The Garrett Corporation paid $200,000 to acquire land, buildings, and equipment. At the time of acquisition, the company paid $20,000 for an appraisal, which revealed the following values: land, $100,000; buildings, $125,000; and equipment, $25,000.

Required
What cost does the company assign to the land, buildings, and equipment, respectively?

E10-8 *Exchange of Assets* Two independent companies, Denver and Bristol, each own a warehouse, and they agree to an exchange in which no cash changes hands. The following information for the two warehouses is available:

	Denver	Bristol
Cost	$90,000	$45,000
Accumulated depreciation	55,000	25,000
Fair value	30,000	30,000

Required
Prepare journal entries for the Denver Company and the Bristol Company to record the exchange.

E10-9 *Exchange of Assets* Use the same information as in E10-8, except that the warehouse owned by Denver Company has a fair value of $28,000, and therefore Denver agrees to pay Bristol $2,000 to complete the exchange.

Required
Prepare journal entries for the Denver Company and the Bristol Company to record the exchange.

E10-10 *Exchange of Assets* Use the same information as in E10-8, except that the warehouse owned by Denver Company has a fair value of $33,000, and therefore the Bristol Company agrees to pay the Denver Company $3,000 to complete the exchange.

Required
Prepare journal entries for the Denver Company and the Bristol Company to record the exchange.

E10-11 *Exchange of Assets* The Goodman Company acquired a truck from the Harmes Company in exchange for a machine. The machine cost $30,000, has a book value of $6,000, and has a market value of $9,000. The truck has a cost of $12,000 and a book value of $8,000 on Harmes' books.

Required
Prepare journal entries for the Goodman Company and the Harmes Company to record the exchange.

E10-12 *Exchange of Assets* Use the same information as in E10-11, except that the machine has a market value of $8,500, and therefore the Goodman Company agrees to pay $500 to complete the exchange.

Required
Prepare journal entries for the Goodman Company and the Harmes Company to record the exchange.

E10-13 **AICPA Adapted** *Exchange of Assets* Minor Baseball Company had a player contract with Doe that was recorded in its accounting records at $145,000. Better Baseball Company had a player contract with Smith that was recorded in its accounting records at $140,000. Minor traded Doe to Better for Smith by exchanging each player's contract. The fair value of each contract was $150,000.

Required
What amounts should each company show in its accounting records for the exchange of player contracts?

E10-14 *Self-Construction* The Harshman Company constructed a building for its own use. The company incurred costs of $20,000 for materials and supplies, $48,000 for direct labor, and $4,000 for a supervisor's overtime that was caused by the construction. The company uses a factory overhead rate of 50% of direct labor cost. Before construction, the company had received a bid of $100,000 from an outside contractor.

Required
1. At what value should the company capitalize the building? Justify your answer.
2. Would your answer change if the bid from the outside contractor had been $80,000? $60,000?

E10-15 *Asset Acquired by Donation* The city of Littleton donated a building and land to the Hetting Co. without charge. The agreement provided that the company employ 350 people for 10 years. The land was appraised at $65,000 and the building at $44,000.

Required
1. Prepare the journal entry to record the acquisition of the land and building.
2. How should the 10-year agreement be reported in the financial statements?
3. If the title were not to pass until after 10 years, would your answer change?

E10-16 *Interest During Construction* The Snowbird Company is constructing a building that qualifies for interest capitalization. It is built between January 1 and December 31, 2007. Expenditures, which occur evenly throughout the year, totaled $800,000. The company borrowed $500,000 at 12% to help finance the project. In addition, the Snowbird Company had outstanding borrowings of $2 million at 8%.

Required
1. Compute the amount of interest capitalized on the building.
2. What effect does the interest capitalization have on the company's financial statements after it completes the building?

E10-17 *Calculating Capitalized Interest* The Kit Company borrows $5 million at 12% on January 1, 2007 specifically for the purpose of financing a construction project. The company invests the total amount at 11% until it makes payments for the construction project. During the first year of construction, the company incurs construction costs of $4 million evenly over the year.

Required
Compute the amount of interest that the company would capitalize and the amount of interest revenue it would recognize.

E10-18 *Capital and Operating Expenditures* Which of the following 10 items does a company record as a capital expenditure and which as an operating expenditure?
1. Cost of installing machinery
2. Cost of moving machinery
3. Repairs as a result of an accident
4. Cost of major overhaul
5. Installation of safety device as a result of an OSHA inspection
6. Property taxes on land and buildings
7. Property taxes on land and buildings held for investment
8. Cost of rearranging offices
9. Cost of repainting offices
10. Ordinary repairs

E10-19 *Oil and Gas Accounting (Appendix)* The Lawrence Company spends $4 million in 2007 drilling oil wells. Sixty percent of the drilling is successful and results in commercial quantities of oil being found.

Required
1. How much drilling expense does the company recognize under
   a. The successful-efforts method?
   b. The full-cost method?
2. At what value does the company report the asset, Oil and Gas Properties, in its balance sheet under
   a. The successful-efforts method?
   b. The full-cost method?

PROBLEMS

P10-1 *Acquisition Costs* The Mawn Company bought land and built a warehouse during 2007. It debited the following related costs to an account titled Land and Buildings:

Land purchase	$22,000
Demolition of old building	3,000

Legal fees for land acquisition	1,500
Interest on loan for construction (based on average costs incurred)	2,900
Building construction	53,000
Assessment by city for sewer connection	1,200
Landscaping	3,500
Equipment purchased for excavation	18,800
Fixed overhead charged to building	15,000
Insurance on building during construction	1,000
Profit on construction	12,000
Compensation for injury to construction worker	3,000
Modifications to building ordered by building inspectors	7,500
Property taxes on land paid in 2007	2,500

The following credits were made to the account:	
Salvage from demolished old building	$ 700
Sale of excavation equipment	14,000

In addition, you discover that compensation for the worker's injury was necessary because it was not covered by the particular insurance policy purchased by the company. Accident insurance that would have covered the injury would have cost an additional $350. The modifications ordered by the building inspectors resulted from poor planning by the company.

Required
Prepare adjusting entries on December 31, 2007 to properly reclassify the preceding items.

P10-2 *Costs Subsequent to Acquisition* As the first auditor of the Newberg Company you discover that the following entries have been made in the property, plant, and equipment account:

Property, Plant, and Equipment				
2006			**2006**	
Plant purchased	60,000		Depreciation	6,310
Legal fees	700			
Insurance	2,400			
2007			**2007**	
Repairs	2,000		Depreciation	6,879
Addition to building	10,000			
2008			**2008**	
Repairs	3,000		Machine sold	500
Insurance	2,800		Depreciation	7,421
Machine purchased	7,000			

You discover the following additional information:

1. The purchase of the plant included a building and machinery. When the plant was purchased, an appraisal showed that the building was valued at $39,000 and the machinery at $26,000.
2. Depreciation has been recorded each year at 10% of the balance in the account. The 10% was chosen because the property is being depreciated over 10 years for tax purposes. Subsequent investigation indicates that the expected lives at the time of acquisition were: building, 20 years; machinery, 8 years.
3. Each insurance payment was made on January 1 and was for a two-year policy.
4. The machine that was sold in 2008 had an original cost of $800.
5. All purchases and sales of property, plant, and equipment items occurred at the beginning of the year indicated.

Required
Prepare adjusting entries at December 31, 2008 to correct the books assuming they have not been closed for the year.

P10-3 *Classification of Costs Associated with Assets* The following account balances were included in the balance sheet of the Bromley Company on December 31, 2006:

Land	$100,000
Land improvements	20,000
Buildings	300,000
Machinery and equipment	500,000

During 2007 the following transactions occurred:

1. Land was acquired for $70,000 for a future building site. Commissions of $4,000 were paid to a real estate agent.
2. A factory and land were acquired from the Kent Development Company by issuing 20,000 shares of $3 par common stock. At that time the stock was selling for $10 per share on the New York Stock Exchange. The independently appraised values of the land and the factory were $60,000 and $180,000, respectively.
3. Machinery and equipment was acquired at a cost of $120,000. In addition, sales tax, freight costs, and installation costs were $7,000, $10,000, and $16,000, respectively. During installation, the machinery was damaged and $2,000 was spent in repairs.
4. A new parking lot was installed at a cost of $30,000.
5. A machine that had cost $20,000 on January 1, 2003 and had a book value on December 31, 2007 of $4,000 was sold on that date for $6,000.
6. Half the land purchased in item 1 was prepared as a building site. Costs of $26,000 were incurred to clear the land, and the timber recovered was sold for $3,000. A new building was built for $60,000 plus architect's fees and imputed interest on equity funds used during construction of $18,000 and $15,000, respectively. No debt is outstanding.
7. Costs of $20,000 were incurred to improve some leased office space. The lease will terminate in 2009 and is not expected to be renewed.
8. A group of new machines was purchased under a royalty agreement that provides for payment of annual royalties based on units produced. The invoice price of the machines was $30,000, freight costs were $2,000, and royalty payments for 2007 were $12,000.

Required

Prepare journal entries to record all the preceding events. Unless otherwise indicated, assume the company makes all payments in cash.

P10-4 **CMA Adapted** *Self-Construction*   The Olson Machine Company manufactures small and large milling machines. Selling prices of these machines range from $35,000 to $200,000. During the five-month period from August 1, 2007 through December 31, 2007, the company manufactured a milling machine for its own use. This machine was built as part of the regular production activities. The project required a large amount of time from planning and supervisory personnel, as well as that of some of the company's officers, because it was a more sophisticated type of machine than the regular production models.

Throughout the five-month period, the company charged all costs directly associated with the construction of the machine to a special account entitled "Asset Construction Account." An analysis of the charges to this account as of December 31, 2007 follows:

ASSET CONSTRUCTION ACCOUNT

Item Description	Cost	
Raw Materials		
Iron castings:		
Main housing, 3 sections	$37,480	
Movable heads, 2 heads @ $3,900	7,800	
Machine bed	4,760	
Table, 2 sections @ $5,500	11,000	$ 61,040
Other raw materials:		
Electrical components and wiring	$28,000	
Worm screws and housing	8,600	
Cutter housings	2,700	
Conveyor system	8,400	
Other parts	2,500	50,200
Direct Labor Costs		
Layout 90 hr. @ $5.00	$ 450	
Electricians 380 hr. @ 9.00	3,420	
Machining 1,100 hr. @ 8.00	8,800	
Heat treatment 100 hr. @ 7.50	750	
Assembly 450 hr. @ 7.00	3,150	
Testing 180 hr. @ 8.00	1,440	18,010
Other Direct Charges		
Repairs and maintenance during testing period	$ 1,340	
Interest expense from 8/1/07 to 12/31/07 on funds borrowed for construction purposes	4,260	
Additional labor to assist during machine testing period, 180 hr. @ $5.00	900	6,500
Balance, December 31, 2007		$135,750

The company allocates factory overhead to normal production as a percent of direct labor dollars as follows:

Departments	Factory Overhead Rates (applied as a percent of direct labor dollars)		
	Variable	Fixed	Total
Layout and electricians	50%	20%	70%
Machining,* heat treatment, and assembly	50%	50%	100%

*All testing is conducted by employees in the machining department.

The company uses a flat rate of 40% of direct labor dollars to allocate general and administrative overhead.

During the machine testing period, a cutter head malfunctioned and did extensive damage to the machine table and one cutter housing. This damage was not anticipated and was the result of an error in the assembly operation. Although no additional raw materials were needed to make the machine operational after the accident, the following labor for rework was required:

	Direct Labor Hours
Electric	80
Machining	200
Assembly	100
Testing (conducted by machining department)	20

The company has included all these labor charges in the Asset Construction account. In addition, it included in the account the repairs and maintenance charges of $1,340 that it incurred as a result of the malfunction.

Required

1. Compute, in accordance with generally accepted accounting principles, the amount that Olson Machine Company should capitalize for the milling machine as of December 31, 2007 when it declares the machine operational.
2. Identify the costs you included in Requirement 1 for which there are acceptable alternative procedures. Describe the alternative procedure(s) in each case.

P10-5 *Acquisition Cost* The following transactions of the Weber Company occurred during 2007:

1. The company acquired a tract of land in exchange for 1,000 shares of $10 par value common stock. The stock was traded on the New York Stock Exchange at $24 on the date of exchange. The land had a book value on the selling company's records of $5,000, and it was believed to be worth "anything up to $30,000."
2. An engine on a truck was replaced. The truck originally cost $10,000 three years ago and was being depreciated at $2,000 per year. The engine cost $1,000 to replace.
3. The company acquired a tract of land that was believed to have mineral deposits by issuing 500 shares of preferred stock of $50 par value. The preferred stock was rarely traded. The last transaction was two months earlier, when 50 shares were sold at $75 per share. The owner of the land was willing to accept cash of $55,000, and an appraisal had shown a value of $60,000.
4. The company purchased a machine with a list price of $8,500 by issuing a two-year $10,000 non-interest-bearing note when the market rate of interest was 10%.

Required
Prepare journal entries to record the preceding events.

P10-6 **AICPA Adapted** *Comprehensive* At December 31, 2006 certain accounts included in the property, plant, and equipment section of the Townsand Company's balance sheet had the following balances:

Land	$100,000	Leasehold improvements	$500,000
Buildings	800,000	Machinery and equipment	700,000

During 2007, the following transactions occurred:

1. Land site number 621 was acquired for $1,000,000. Additionally, to acquire the land Townsand paid a $60,000 commission to a real estate agent. Costs of $15,000 were incurred to clear the land. During the course of clearing the land, timber and gravel were recovered and sold for $5,000.
2. A second tract of land (site number 622) with a building was acquired for $300,000. The closing statement indicated that the land value was $200,000 and the building value was $100,000. Shortly after acquisition, the building was demolished at a cost of $30,000. A new building was constructed for $150,000 plus the following costs:

Excavation fees	$11,000
Architectural design fees	8,000
Building permit fee	1,000

The building was completed and occupied on September 29, 2007.

3. A third tract of land (site number 623) was acquired for $600,000 and was put on the market for resale.

4. Extensive work was done to a building occupied by Townsand under a lease agreement that expires on December 31, 2016. The total cost of the work was $125,000, which consisted of the following:

Painting of ceilings	$ 10,000 (estimated useful life is one year)
Electrical work	35,000 (estimated useful life is ten years)
Construction of extension to current working area	80,000 (estimated useful life is thirty years)
	$125,000

The lessor paid one-half of the costs incurred in connection with the extension to the current working area.

5. During December 2007 costs of $65,000 were incurred to improve leased office space. The related lease will terminate on December 31, 2009, and is not expected to be renewed.

6. A group of new machines was purchased under a royalty agreement which provides for payment of royalties based on units of production for the machines. The invoice price of the machines was $75,000, freight costs were $2,000, unloading charges were $1,500, and royalty payments for 2007 were $13,000.

Required

1. Prepare a detailed analysis of the changes in each of the following balance sheet accounts for 2007:

Land	Leasehold improvements
Buildings	Machinery and equipment

Disregard the related accumulated depreciation accounts.

2. List the items in the fact situation which were not used to determine the answer to Requirement 1, and indicate where, or if, these items should be included in Townsand's financial statements.

P10-7   Assets Acquired by Exchange The Bremer Company made the following exchanges of assets during 2007:

1. Acquired a more advanced machine worth $10,000 by paying $2,000 cash and giving a machine that had originally cost $40,000 and has a book value of $12,000.
2. Acquired a building worth $55,000 by paying $5,000 cash and giving a piece of land that had originally cost $35,000.
3. Acquired a more advanced machine worth $20,000 by paying $5,000 cash and giving a machine that had originally cost $13,000 and has a book value of $11,000.
4. Acquired a car by giving a truck that had originally cost $20,000, has a book value of $15,000, and has a "blue book" value of $16,800. In addition the company received $1,000 cash.

Required ▨

Prepare the journal entry of the Bremer Company for each exchange.

P10-8   Assets Acquired by Exchange The Bussell Company exchanged the following assets during 2007:

1. Acquired a newer machine by paying $4,000 cash and giving a machine that originally cost $40,000, has a book value of $25,000, and is worth $30,000.
2. Same facts as in item 1, except that the asset being surrendered has a book value of $33,000.
3. Acquired a newer machine by giving a machine that originally cost $45,000, has a book value of $20,000, and is worth $32,000. In addition $5,000 cash was received.
4. Same facts as in item 3, except that the asset being surrendered has a book value of $36,000.
5. Acquired a newer machine worth $90,000 by giving up a machine of equal value. The machine surrendered had originally cost $150,000 and has a book value of $80,000.
6. Same facts as in item 5, except that the asset being surrendered has a book value of $94,000.
7. Acquired a building in exchange for land that had originally cost $130,000 and is now worth $200,000.
8. Same facts as in item 7, except that $30,000 was paid.
9. Same facts as in item 7, except that $20,000 was received.

Required

Prepare the journal entry to record each acquisition of the Bussell Company.

P10-9   Interest During Construction The Alta Company is constructing a production complex which qualifies for interest capitalization. The following information is available:

Capitalization period: January 1, 2007 to June 30, 2009

Expenditures on project (incurred evenly during each period and excluding capitalized interest from previous years):

2007	$2,000,000
2008	$3,760,000
2009	$4,324,000

Amounts borrowed and outstanding:

$3 million borrowed at 12%, specifically for the project
$6 million borrowed on July 1, 2003, at 14%
$14 million borrowed on January 1, 1999, at 8%

Required
1. Compute the amount of interest costs capitalized each year.
2. If it is assumed that the production complex has an estimated life of 20 years and a residual value of zero, compute the straight-line depreciation in 2010.
3. Explain the effects of the interest capitalization on the financial statements for all three years. Ignore income taxes.

P10-10 *Comprehensive* The Foothills Power Company begins a two-year construction project on a power plant on January 1, 2007. The following information is available:

1. The company borrows $10 million on January 1, 2007 at 12%, specifically for use on the project.
2. The company's other borrowings are:

   $20 million at 10%
   $60 million at 8%

3. The expenditures for the project, incurred evenly each year (excluding capitalized interest from previous years), are as follows:

   $6,000,000 in 2007
   $11,460,000 in 2008
   $1,800,000 in 2009

4. The project is completed on March 31, 2009. It took longer than originally planned because the company suspended construction for the last three months of 2007 because of a concern about the salability of the electricity produced by the plant.
5. Because of reduced demand for electricity, the plant does not begin operations until October 1, 2009.
6. The company invests at 11% the unused amounts of the $10 million borrowed in item 1.
7. Assume all transactions are in cash unless otherwise indicated.

Required
1. Prepare all the necessary journal entries for each of the three years. Record all construction costs in a Construction in Progress inventory account.
2. How would your answer to Requirement 1 change if the three-month suspension in the construction activity was due to an environmental dispute with the federal government?

P10-11 *Events Subsequent to Acquisition* The following selected events occurred during 2007:

Jan. 10 A motor breaks on a machine and is replaced for $800. This replacement was expected when the machine was purchased.
Jan. 24 A machine that was purchased for $10,000 and has a book value of $1,000 is sold for $600.
Feb. 3 A fully depreciated building that originally cost $25,000 is demolished so that a new building may be constructed. The demolition cost $2,200 and resulted in $700 of salvageable materials.
Feb. 14 A machine breaks down unexpectedly and requires repairs of $700.
Mar. 10 An accident damages some equipment. Repairs cost $2,000.
Mar. 19 A motor breaks on a machine and is replaced for $900. The new motor is of an improved design that increases the capacity of the machine.
Mar. 27 Office layout is rearranged at a cost of $700. At the same time, the walls are repainted for $500.

Required
Prepare journal entries for the preceding transactions.

P10-12 `AICPA Adapted` *Comprehensive* You are engaged in the examination of financial statements of the Dewoskin Company and are auditing the Machinery and Equipment account and the related depreciation accounts for the year ended December 31, 2007. Your permanent file contains the following schedules:

	Balance 12/31/05	2006 Retirements	2006 Addition	Balance 12/31/06
	Machinery and Equipment			
1996	$ 8,000	$2,100	—	$ 5,900
1997	400	—	—	400
1998	—	—	—	—
1999	—	—	—	—
2000	3,900	—	—	3,900
2001	—	—	—	—
2002	5,300	—	—	5,300
2003	—	—	—	—
2004	4,200	—	—	4,200
2005	—	—	—	—
2006	—	—	$5,700	5,700
	$21,800	$2,100	$5,700	$25,400

	Balance 12/31/05	2006 Retirements	2006 Addition	Balance 12/31/06
	Accumulated Depreciation			
1996	$ 7,840	$2,100	$ 160	$ 5,900
1997	340	—	40	380
1998	—	—	—	—
1999	—	—	—	—
2000	2,145	—	390	2,535
2001	—	—	—	—
2002	1,855	—	530	2,385
2003	—	—	—	—
2004	630	—	420	1,050
2005	—	—	—	—
2006	—	—	285	285
	$12,810	$2,100	$1,825	$12,535

Here is a transcript of the Machinery and Equipment account for 2007:

2007	Machinery and Equipment	Ref.	Debit	Credit
Jan. 1	Balance forward		$25,400	
Mar. 1	Burnham grinder	VR	1,200	
May 1	Air compressor	VR	4,500	
June 1	Power lawnmower	VR	600	
June 1	Lift-truck battery	VR	320	
Aug. 1	Rockwood saw	CR		$ 150
Nov. 1	Electric spot welder	VR	4,500	
Nov. 1	Baking oven	VR	2,800	
Dec. 1	Baking oven	VR	236	
			$39,556	150
Dec. 31	Balance			$39,406
			$39,556	$39,556

Your examination reveals the following eight items:

1. The company uses a 10-year life for all machinery and equipment for depreciation purposes. Depreciation is computed by the straight-line method. Six months' depreciation is recorded in the year of acquisition or retirement. For 2007 the company recorded depreciation of $2,800 on machinery and equipment.

2. The Burnham grinder was purchased for cash from a firm in financial distress. The chief engineer and a used machinery dealer agreed that the machine, which was practically new, was worth $2,100 in the open market.

3. For production reasons, the new air compressor was installed in a small building that was erected in 2007 to house the machine. The building will also be used for general storage. The cost of the building, which has a 25-year life, was $2,000 and is included in the $4,500 voucher for the air compressor.

4. The power lawnmower was delivered to the home of the company president for personal use.

5. On June 1, the battery in a battery-powered lift truck was accidentally damaged beyond repair. The damaged battery was included at a price of $600 in the $4,200 cost of the lift truck purchased on July 1, 2004. The company decided to rent a replacement battery instead of buying a new battery. The $320 expenditure is the annual rental for the battery paid in advance, net of a $40 allowance for the scrap value of the damaged battery that was returned to the battery company.

6. The Rockwood saw sold on August 1 had been purchased on August 1, 1994, for $1,500. The saw was in use until it was sold.

7. On September 1, the company determined that a production casting machine was no longer needed and advertised it for sale for $1,800 after having determined from a used machinery dealer that this was its market value. The casting machine had been purchased for $5,000 on September 1, 2002.

8. On November 1 a baking oven was purchased for $10,000. A $2,800 down payment was made, and the balance will be paid in monthly installments over a three-year period. The December 1 payment includes interest charges of $36. Legal title to the oven will not pass to the company until the payments are completed.

Required

1. Prepare the auditor's adjusting journal entries required on December 31, 2007, for machinery and equipment and the related depreciation.

2. Prepare schedules for detailing the effect of additions and retirements on the assets and related accumulated depreciation balances.

P10-13 AICPA Adapted *Adjusting Entries* In your examination of the financial statements of Ericson Corporation at December 31, 2007 you observe the contents of certain accounts and other pertinent information as follows:

Building

Date	Explanation	Post REF	Debit	Credit	Balance
12/31/06	Balance	X	$100,000	—	$100,000
7/1/07	New boiler	CD	16,480	$1,480	115,000
9/1/08	Insurance recovery	CR	—	2,000	113,000

Accumulated Depreciation—Building

Date	Explanation	LF	Debit	Credit	Balance
12/31/06	Balance: 15 years @ 4% of $100,000 (no salvage value)	X		$60,000	$60,000
12/31/07	Annual depreciation	GJ		4,440	64,440

You learn that on June 15 the company's old high-pressure boiler exploded and was partially damaged. Damage to the building was insignificant, but the boiler was replaced by a more efficient oil-burning boiler. The company received $2,000 as an insurance adjustment under terms of its policy for damage to the boiler. The disbursement voucher charged to the Building account on July 1, 2007 is reproduced here:

To: Leetsdale Heating Company

Fair value—new oil-burning boiler (including fuel oil tank and 1,000 gallons fuel oil)	$16,000
Sales tax—3% of $16,000	480
Total	$16,480
Less: Allowance (fair value) for old coal-burning boiler in building—to be removed at the expense of the Leetsdale Heating Company	1,480
Total price	$15,000

In vouching the expenditure, you determine that the terms included a 2% cash discount that was properly computed and taken. Neither the sales tax nor the trade-in allowance on the old boiler is subject to discount. Your audit discloses that a voucher for $1,000 was paid to Monaco Company on July 3, 2007 and charged to the Repair Expense account. The voucher is adequately supported and is marked "installation costs for new oil-burning boiler."

The company's fuel oil supplier advises that fuel oil had a market price of 80 cents per gallon on July 1 and 85 cents per gallon on December 31. The fuel oil inventory at December 31 was 100 gallons.

A review of subsidiary property records discloses that the replaced coal-burning boiler was installed when the building was constructed and was recorded at a cost of $10,000. According to its manufacturers, the new boiler should be serviceable for the estimated useful life of the building.

In computing depreciation for retirements, Ericson Corporation consistently treats a fraction of a month as a full month.

Required

Prepare the adjusting journal entries that you would suggest for entry on the books of the Ericson Corporation. The books have not been closed. Support your entries with computations in good form. Assume that the building has no salvage value.

P10-14 *Oil and Gas Accounting Methods (Appendix)* The Iwata Oil Company incurred costs of $6 million during 2007 drilling for oil. Half the costs resulted in oil being found and half resulted in dry wells. The company expects the oil wells to produce 10% of their capacity each year from 2008 to 2017.

Required

1. What amounts appear in the financial statements for 2008 under
   a. The successful-efforts method?
   b. The full-cost method?
2. Why do small oil companies generally prefer the full-cost method?

CASES

COMMUNICATION

C10-1 Acquisition and Retirement

AICPA Adapted Among the principal topics related to the accounting for property, plant, and equipment of a company are acquisition and retirement.

Required

1. Explain the expenditures that a company capitalizes when it acquires equipment for cash.
2. Assume that a company cannot determine the market value of equipment acquired by reference to a similar purchase for cash. Explain how the company determines the capitalizable cost of equipment purchased by exchanging it for each of the following three items:
   a. Bonds having an established market price.
   b. Common stock not having an established market price.
   c. Similar equipment having a determinable market value.
3. Explain the factors that a company uses to determine whether it capitalizes expenditures relating to property, plant, and equipment already in use.
4. Explain how a company accounts for the gain or loss on the sale of property, plant, and equipment for cash.

C10-2 Capitalization Issues

AICPA Adapted George Company purchased land for use as its corporate headquarters. A small factory that was on the land when it was purchased was torn down before construction of the office building began. Furthermore, a substantial amount of rock blasting and removal had to be done to the site before construction of the building foundation began. Because the office building was set back on the land, far from the public road, George Company had the contractor construct a paved road that led from the public road to the parking lot of the office building.

Three years after it occupied the office building, George Company added four stories to the office building. The four stories had an estimated useful life of five years more than the remaining estimated useful life of the original office building.

Ten years later George Company sold the land and building at an amount more than their book value and had a new office building constructed in another state for use as its new corporate headquarters.

Required

1. Which of the preceding expenditures does the company capitalize? How does it depreciate or amortize each? Explain the rationale for your answers.
2. How does a company account for the sale of the land and building? Include in your answer how to determine the book value at the date of sale. Explain the rationale for your answer.

C10-3 Cost Issues

AICPA Adapted Deskin Company purchased a new machine to be used in its operations. The new machine was delivered by the supplier, installed by Deskin, and placed into operation. It was purchased under a long-term payment plan for which the interest charges approximated the prevailing market rates. The estimated useful life of the new machine is 10 years, and its estimated residual (salvage) value is significant. Normal maintenance was performed to keep the new machine in usable condition.

Deskin also added a wing to the manufacturing building that it owns. The addition is an integral part of the building. Furthermore, Deskin made significant leasehold improvements to office space used as corporate headquarters.

Required

1. What costs should Deskin capitalize for the new machine?
2. Explain how Deskin should account for the normal maintenance performed on the new machine.
3. Explain how Deskin should account for the wing added to the manufacturing building. Where should the added wing be reported on Deskin's financial statements?
4. Explain how Deskin should account for the leasehold improvements made to its office space. Where should the leasehold improvements be reported on Deskin's financial statements?

C10-4 Acquisition Costs

AICPA Adapted A company may acquire plant assets (among other ways) for cash, on a deferred-payment plan, by exchanging other assets, or by a combination of these ways.

Required
1. Identify six costs that a company should capitalize as the cost of land. For your answer, assume that a company acquires land with an existing building for cash and that it removes the existing building immediately in order that it can construct a new building on that site.
2. At what amount should a company record a plant asset acquired on a deferred-payment plan?
3. In general, at what amount should a company record plant assets received in exchange for other nonmonetary assets? Specifically, at what amount should a company record a new machine acquired by exchanging an older, similar machine and paying cash? What amount should it recognize as a gain or loss?

C10-5 Capital and Revenue Expenditures

AICPA Adapted Bristol Company purchased land as a site for construction of a factory. Outside contractors were engaged to:

1. Construct the factory
2. Grade and pave a parking lot adjacent to the factory for the exclusive use of the factory workers.

Operations at the new location began during the year and normal factory maintenance costs were incurred after production began.

Required
1. Distinguish between capital and revenue (operating) expenditures.
2. Indicate how the company should account for and report expenditures for each of the following at the time incurred and in subsequent accounting periods.
   a. Purchase of land
   b. Construction of factory
   c. Grading and paving parking lot
   d. Payment of normal factory maintenance costs

Do not discuss capitalization of interest during construction in your response.

CREATIVE AND CRITICAL THINKING

C10-6 Lump-Sum Acquisition

In 1975 a trial was held to settle a tax dispute between the owners of the **Atlanta Falcons,** a National Football League franchise, and the Internal Revenue Service. In 1966, the owners had paid $8.5 million to purchase the franchise. They considered $50,000 to be the cost of the franchise (which is not depreciable for income tax reporting), $727,000 was deferred interest, and the remaining $7.7 million was claimed to be the cost of the players' contracts and options. The dispute centered on several variables:

1. How much of the purchase price was assignable to television rights?
2. Is the value assignable to television rights depreciable? If so, what is the expected life?
3. How much of the purchase price was assignable to player contracts and options?
4. Over what life should the value assigned to the players be depreciated?
5. What is the value of the franchise?

Required
1. As an independent accountant, explain the approach you would take and the information you would need to provide advice to the court for the resolution of the points in dispute.
2. Do these valuation issues also create ethical issues?

C10-7 Interest Capitalization

The Gold Creek Company has borrowed large amounts of money to purchase 5,000 acres of land, which it will develop as a new ski area over the next 10 years. Development is currently under way on the first 2,000 acres, with trails being cut and ski lifts being built. When the company completes this initial development after four years, it will develop the remaining acreage at the rate of approximately 500 acres per year. The company also used some of the money it borrowed to purchase adjacent land, which it will use to expand the ski area if it is successful.

Since this is the first year of the company's existence, it has not developed a policy about interest capitalization. Specifically, it is uncertain about whether it is entitled to capitalize interest on the amounts borrowed to acquire the first 2,000 acres, the total 5,000 acres, the 5,000 acres plus the adjacent land, or the land and the development.

Required
1. Explain the interest capitalization that is appropriate under these circumstances.
2. How might the decision be influenced if the company were interested in earnings management?

C10-8 Purchase Options

The Morgan Company was planning to expand its production facilities. Therefore it acquired one-year options to purchase two alternative sites. Each option cost $5,000 and could not be applied against the contract. One of the sites was bought for $100,000. The company was unsure whether to capitalize the land at $100,000, $105,000, or $110,000.

Required
Write a short report that presents arguments in favor of each alternative.

C10-9 Donated Asset and Its Modification

The Birkby Company acquires a building as a donation from the City of Avalon. The controller argues that since there was no payment by the company, it is not necessary to record the asset and therefore no depreciation should be recorded.

The company has to spend $15,000 altering the building to suit its unique needs. The controller argues that the $15,000 should be expensed because if the building is sold or returned to the city, it cannot recover the $15,000. In addition, expensing the $15,000 results in a closer approximation of the apparent market value of the asset and reduces income taxes immediately.

Required

Write a short memo to the controller that evaluates each of the arguments made by the controller.

C10-10 Natural Resource Assets

AICPA Adapted You have been engaged to examine the financial statements of Brahe Corporation for the year ending December 31, 2007. Brahe Corporation was organized in January 2007 by Messrs. Moses and Price, original owners of options to acquire oil leases on 5,000 acres of land for $350,000. They expected that first the oil leases would be acquired by the corporation and subsequently 180,000 shares of the corporation's common stock would be sold to the public at $6 per share. In February 2007 they exchanged their options, $150,000 cash, and $50,000 of other assets for 75,000 shares of common stock of the corporation. The corporation's board of directors appraised the leases at $600,000, basing its appraisal on the price of other acreage recently leased in the same area. The options were therefore recorded at $250,000 ($600,000 − $350,000 option price).

The options were exercised by the corporation in March 2007 prior to the sale of common stock to the public in April 2007. Leases on approximately 500 acres of land were abandoned as worthless during the year.

Required

1. Explain why the valuation of assets acquired by a corporation in exchange for its own common stock is sometimes difficult.
2. a. Explain the reasoning Brahe Corporation might use to support valuing the leases at $600,000, the amount of the appraisal by the board of directors.
   b. Assuming the board's appraisal was sincere, what steps might Brahe Corporation have taken to strengthen its position to use the $600,000 value and to provide additional information if questions were raised about possible overvaluation of the leases?
3. Discuss the propriety of charging one-tenth of the recorded value of the leases against income at December 31, 2007 because leases on 500 acres of land were abandoned during the year.

C10-11 Ethics and Construction Costs

You are the accountant for a division of a company that is constructing a building for its own use. It is January 2008, and you are working on closing the books for 2007. The CEO of the division stops by your office and says, "I have some questions about our building. Although we started construction at the beginning of June this year, we started planning it at the beginning of the previous year. I believe that we can capitalize interest since then. Check to see if we did capitalize some in 2006. If not, we can take it out of this year's expense and get a double dose. Also, I want you to add lots of overhead to the cost of the building so we can increase our profit for this year. For example, you spent quite a bit of time on the project. So perhaps we could add 1/12 of your salary to the cost of the building. You get the idea?" When the CEO leaves, you check the files and find a letter to an architect dated January 2, 2006. There are numerous subsequent letters to and from the architect.

Required

From financial reporting and ethical perspectives, how would you reply to the CEO?

RESEARCH SIMULATIONS

R10-1 Researching GAAP

Situation

The Tenth National Bank had taken possession of a shopping mall in foreclosure of a mortgage. When the mall was inspected prior to being sold by the bank to a real estate company, it was discovered that it had extensive asbestos problems. An estimate indicated that it would cost $1 million to remove the asbestos. The bank has also purchased an office building for its headquarters. The building was inspected before the purchase and a similar asbestos problem was discovered. An estimate indicated that it would cost $2 million to remove the asbestos, and the bank completed the purchase. The bank's president has asked you how to account for these transactions.

Directions

1. Research the related generally accepted accounting principles and prepare a short memo to the president that answers her question. Cite your references and applicable paragraph numbers.
2. Does this situation create ethical issues?

R10-2 Researching GAAP

Situation

The Perry Park Company (a privately-held company) was searching for a way to expand its operating capacity even though it was short of cash. The president of the company was playing golf and mentioned his concern to his playing partner, who owned some land and a building, and was interested in disposing of them. After some negotiation, the two agreed to swap the land and building for shares in the company. The president of the company has asked you how to account for this transaction, including whether the transaction qualifies as an exception to the general rule to use fair value and the value to place on the transaction and its components.

Directions

1. Research the related generally accepted accounting principles and prepare a short memo to the president. Cite your references and applicable paragraph numbers.

2. Does this situation create ethical issues?

11

Depreciation and Depletion

OBJECTIVES

After reading this chapter, you will be able to:

1 Identify the factors involved in depreciation.

2 Explain the alternative methods of cost allocation, including time-based and activity-based methods.

3 Record depreciation.

4 Explain the conceptual issues regarding depreciation methods.

5 Understand the disclosure of depreciation.

6 Understand additional depreciation methods, including group and composite methods.

7 Compute depreciation for partial periods.

8 Explain the impairment of property, plant, and equipment.

9 Understand depreciation for income tax purposes.

10 Explain changes and corrections of depreciation.

11 Understand and record depletion.

The Financial Effect of Impairments

Accounting for property, plant, and equipment involves many choices that affect the balance sheet and the income statement, but perhaps no choice involving property, plant, and equipment has generated as much regulatory scrutiny as the decision to record asset impairments. Under U.S. accounting standards, companies are required to evaluate their property, plant, and equipment when events or circumstances indicate that an asset may be impaired. For example, in November 2004, **DirecTV** announced that it was taking a $1.47 billion write-down because of the company's decision to use several new satellites for high-definition TV broadcasting rather than their intended use to deliver Internet service. In DirecTV's third-quarter press release, this write-down was listed as a contributing factor to the company's quarterly loss of $1.01 billion.

Because impairments produce conservative financial results (income is reduced and asset values lowered), why would asset impairment accounting be a focus of the Securities and Exchange Commission? One concern is that companies often take large

write-downs to help their future earnings. When an asset impairment charge is taken, there is often very little of the asset's book value left to depreciate in future periods. For example, the book value of the DirecTV satellites was approximately $1.9 billion prior to the impairment. After the impairment loss, the remaining book value to be depreciated was $430 million, approximately 23% of the assets' original book value. Given a useful life of 12 to 16 years for satellites, as disclosed in DirecTV's annual report, the asset impairment taken by DirecTV will reduce depreciation expense by approximately $90 million to $120 million per year. With financial statement effects of this size, the SEC and investors will certainly take notice.

FOR FURTHER INVESTIGATION

For a discussion of asset impairments, consult the Business & Company Resource Center (BCRC):

- The Perils of Impairment. Daniel Berninger, *Telephony*, 0040-2656, Jan 31, 2005, v245, i2.

In Chapter 10, we described property, plant, and equipment as a group of assets held by a company for use for a period of more than one year. That is, the company acquired the assets for their long-term revenue-generating ability. Since the company uses these assets to earn revenue, the matching principle requires that the company match the expenses of the assets' use against the revenue. Over the life of the asset, the expense is the difference between the purchase price of the asset and its residual value (that is, future selling price). **Depreciation is the process of allocating in a systematic and rational manner this total expense to each period benefited by the asset.** Land is not depreciated because it generally does not have a limited life and its residual value usually is higher than its cost. Thus, there is no expense to be recognized over the life of the asset and, therefore, no periodic cost allocation.

Terms used to describe this allocation process depend on the type of asset:

1. **Depreciation** is the allocation of the cost of *tangible assets*, such as property, plant, and equipment.
2. **Depletion** is the allocation of the cost of *natural resource assets*, such as oil, gas, minerals, and timber.
3. **Amortization** is the allocation of the cost of *intangible assets*, such as patents and copyrights. It may be used as a general term to describe the periodic allocation of costs; in that case, it is synonymous with depreciation and depletion.

These three terms all describe the same principle of a company allocating costs to match its expenses with revenue. However, they differ in their application to different types of assets. It is important to note that a company does **not** record depreciation, depletion, and amortization in an attempt to report the fair value of the asset. We discuss depreciation and depletion in this chapter, and the amortization of intangible assets in the next chapter.

FACTORS INVOLVED IN DEPRECIATION

1 Identify the factors involved in depreciation.

A company considers four factors in the computation of depreciation for a period:

- Asset cost
- Service life
- Residual value
- Method of cost allocation[1]

Asset Cost

The cost of an asset includes all the acquisition costs a company incurs to obtain the benefits from the asset. These costs include the contract price plus freight, assembly, installation, and testing costs, as we discussed in Chapter 10.

Service Life

The service life of an asset is the measure of the service units a company expects from the asset before its disposal. Service life may be measured in *units of time*, such as years and months, or *units of activity or output*, such as hours of operation of a machine, tons produced for a steel mill, or miles driven for a truck.

---

1. The service life, residual value, and method of cost allocation are different for income tax purposes under the Modified Accelerated Cost Recovery System (MACRS), as we discuss later in the chapter.

The factors that limit the service life of an asset can be divided into two general categories:

- Physical causes include wear and tear because of operational *use*, deterioration and decay that is independent of use but is a function of *time* (such as rust), and damage and destruction.
- Functional causes limit the service life of the asset through obsolescence and inadequacy, *even though the physical life is not exhausted.*

Obsolescence is common in a technologically advanced economy when an asset becomes obsolete because of new technology. *Inadequacy* refers to the situation in which an asset is no longer suitable for the size of the company's operations. For example, a warehouse may be physically sound and useful, but too small for the company's operations.

When a company estimates the service life, it should consider all these factors because in many situations the service life is affected by a combination of factors. For example, the service life of a truck is likely to be affected by the passage of time (deterioration, decay, and possibly obsolescence) as well as by the amount of use. In addition, the company may be able to increase or decrease the service life by the amount it spends on repairs and maintenance as well as on improvements and replacements. You will have to rely on others, such as engineers, for advice about such estimates, but will still have to make your own judgment.

Residual Value

The residual (salvage) value is the net amount that a company expects to obtain from disposing of an asset at the end of its service life. It is the expected value of the asset at the end of its service life minus the costs of disposal, such as dismantling, removing, and selling the asset. The service life and the residual value are determined by company policy. A company may plan to hold an asset until it is physically exhausted or functionally obsolete and not useful to anyone else. Then, the expected residual value is the expected scrap value, which is probably very low. Alternatively, a company may plan to dispose of the asset when it still has considerable economic usefulness to others (the service life to the company is less than the physical life). Then, the expected residual value is the estimated net market value of the asset (the selling price less the disposal costs) at the time of the disposal, which may be relatively high. For example, many airlines sell their planes long before the end of their physical lives to replace them with technologically more advanced planes and to avoid passenger resistance to flying in old planes. In some situations, such as a nuclear power plant, the acquisition of an asset automatically creates an obligation related to the retirement of the asset. As we discussed in Chapter 10, a company computes the present value of the obligation and adds the same amount to the cost of the asset.

In practice, because the residual value is difficult to estimate, it often is ignored in computing the depreciation amount, or else a standard rate, such as 10% of original cost, is used. This practice is acceptable if it does not have a material effect on the measurement of income and the book value of the asset.

METHODS OF COST ALLOCATION

Accounting principles require that a company use a method of cost allocation that is "systematic and rational."[2] *Systematic* means that the calculation should follow a formula and not be determined in an arbitrary manner. *Rational* means that the amount of the depreciation should relate to the benefits that the asset produces in each period.

2 Explain the alternative methods of cost allocation, including time-based and activity-based methods.

2. *Accounting Terminology Bulletin No. 1* (New York: AICPA, 1953), par. 56.

Although these criteria may appear to be very general and to allow numerous methods, only the following methods are used frequently in practice:

1. Time-based methods
   a. Straight line
   b. Accelerated (declining charge)
      (1) Sum of the years' digits
      (2) Declining balance
2. Activity (or use) methods

We discuss each of these methods in the following sections, using the data for the Troup Company shown in Example 11-1. **The depreciation base (depreciable cost) of the asset is the cost less the estimated residual value,** or $100,000. The different depreciation methods all allocate the total of $100,000 over the expected service life of the asset. However, they differ in the pattern in which the cost is allocated to each year or each unit produced. We discuss additional special depreciation methods later in the chapter.

EXAMPLE 11-1	Asset Information of the Troup Company
Asset cost	$120,000
Date of purchase	January 1, 2006
Estimated residual value	$20,000
Estimated service life	5 years; 10,000 hours; 20,000 units

Time-Based Methods

A company should use a time-based method when the service life of the asset is affected primarily by the passage of time and not by the use of the asset. This situation includes the physical causes of deterioration and decay and the functional causes of obsolescence and inadequacy. Two general categories of time-based methods are the straight-line method and the accelerated methods. **The straight-line method is appropriate when a company estimates that the benefits it will derive from the asset will be approximately constant each period of its life.** Since straight-line depreciation is the same each period, the matching principle is satisfied because the company matches, as an expense, an equal cost each period against benefits that are approximately the same each period. The straight-line method is appropriate if maintenance costs are expected to be the same each period. Then the total costs of depreciation and maintenance each period are equal and matched against benefits that are approximately the same each period.

    The accelerated (or declining-charge) methods are appropriate when a company estimates that the benefits it will derive from the asset will decline each period. Thus, the accelerated methods match a depreciation cost that declines each period against revenues that also are declining each period. The benefits to be derived from the asset may be measured in physical terms or in dollars of revenue, as we discuss later. The choice of a particular accelerated method is basically arbitrary. This is because, in most situations, the particular declining depreciation amount of each method cannot be matched against the expected pattern of declining revenue. The estimates required cannot be that accurate. Instead, the general principle is that if declining benefits are expected, then an accelerated (declining-charge) method is selected.

Straight Line

The straight-line method allocates an equal cost to each period. For the Troup Company, we show the calculation in Example 11-2. The depreciation base of $100,000 is allocated equally to the estimated life of five years at the rate of $20,000 per year. The straight-line depreciation sometimes is expressed as a percentage of original cost

($20,000 ÷ $120,000 = 16.67%) or of depreciable cost ($20,000 ÷ $100,000 = 20%). Although widely adopted, the use of the straight-line method may be criticized because it often is used for convenience when an activity method would be more appropriate.

EXAMPLE 11-2   Straight-Line Depreciation

Year	Book Value of Asset at Beginning of Year	Depreciation	Book Value of Asset at End of Year[b]
2006	$120,000	$20,000[a]	$100,000
2007	100,000	20,000	80,000
2008	80,000	20,000	60,000
2009	60,000	20,000	40,000
2010	40,000	20,000	20,000

$$^a Depreciation = \frac{Cost - Residual\ Value}{Service\ Life}$$

$$= \frac{\$120,000 - \$20,000}{5}$$

$$= \$20,000\ per\ year$$

[b] Cost minus depreciation; in 2006, $120,000 − $20,000

Sum of the Years' Digits

The sum-of-the-years'-digits method produces declining depreciation each period by applying a declining fraction each year to the depreciation base. The denominator of the fraction is the sum of the years' digits. So, for an asset with a five-year life, the sum is $5 + 4 + 3 + 2 + 1 = 15$.[3] The numerator of the fraction is the years' digits taken in reverse order—that is, 5 the first year, 4 the second year, etc. An alternative way of looking at the numerator is that it is the number of years remaining in the asset's life as of the *beginning* of the year. The fractions for the five years of the asset's life are 5/15, 4/15, 3/15, 2/15, and 1/15. We show the calculation of the depreciation for the Troup Company in Example 11-3. Each year, the depreciation declines, and at the end of the fifth year, the book value of the asset is equal to the estimated residual value of $20,000. Note that in this method, the depreciation base remains constant, while the fraction decreases each year.

EXAMPLE 11-3   Sum-of-the-Years'-Digits Depreciation

Year	Depreciation Base	Fraction	Depreciation	Book Value of Asset at End of Year*
2006	$100,000	5/15	$ 33,333	$86,667
2007	100,000	4/15	26,667	60,000
2008	100,000	3/15	20,000	40,000
2009	100,000	2/15	13,333	26,667
2010	100,000	1/15	6,667	20,000
			$100,000	

*Cost minus accumulated depreciation; in 2006, $120,000 − $33,333

---

3.   The general formula to compute the sum of the years' digits is $n(n + 1)/2$. So, for an asset with a 50-year life, the sum is $50(50 + 1)/2 = 1,275$.

Declining Balance

The declining-balance methods produce a declining depreciation amount each period by applying a *constant* rate to the book value of the asset at the beginning of the period. Note that the periodic depreciation declines because the book value is used and *not* the depreciation base. Also, the residual value is ignored in the calculation of the depreciation each period. However, the asset is not depreciated below the estimated residual value. The constant rate is a function of the straight-line rate. The highest rate that can be used is double the straight-line rate. This rate was established as the highest rate by the income tax regulations and was also adopted as the highest rate for financial reporting. An asset that has a five-year life is depreciated on a straight-line basis at the rate of 20% per year, so the double-declining rate is 40%. However, an alternative rate could be chosen, such as a 150% declining rate, which is 1½ times the straight-line rate or, in this example, 30% per year. We show both alternatives for the Troup Company in Example 11-4.

EXAMPLE 11-4   Declining-Balance Depreciation Methods

(a) Double-Declining-Balance

Year	Book Value of Asset at Beginning of Year	Rate	Depreciation	Book Value of Asset at End of Year
2006	$120,000	40%	$ 48,000	$72,000
2007	72,000	40%	28,800	43,200
2008	43,200	40%	17,280	25,920
2009	25,920	—	5,920	20,000
2010	20,000	—	—	20,000
			$100,000	

(b) 150%-Declining-Balance

Year	Book Value of Asset at Beginning of Year	Rate	Depreciation	Book Value of Asset at End of Year
2006	$120,000	30%	$ 36,000	$84,000
2007	84,000	30%	25,200	58,800
2008	58,800	30%	17,640	41,160
2009	41,160	30%	12,348	28,812
2010	28,812	—	8,812	20,000
			$100,000	

Note the special situations that arise toward the end of the asset's life. Under the double-declining-balance method, the book value at the beginning of 2009 is $25,920. A strict application of the 40% rate would result in depreciation of $10,368 ($25,920 × 40%). However, this would reduce the book value below the estimated residual value. Therefore, the 2009 depreciation is only $5,920, which reduces the $25,920 book value to the $20,000 residual value, and there is no depreciation in 2010. A similar issue arises under the 150%-declining-balance method. Applying the 30% rate in 2010 would result in depreciation of $8,643.60 ($28,812 × 30%), which would not reduce the book value to the residual value. Consequently, the depreciation in 2010 is $8,812, which reduces the book value to the $20,000 residual value.

Many companies avoid these problems by switching from the declining-balance method to the straight-line method during the life of the asset. The change in the depreciation method might be made at the midpoint of the life of the asset, or when the depreciation under the straight-line method exceeds the declining-balance depreciation. Either method is systematic and rational if the company decides on the policy at the time of purchase and applies it to all assets. In addition, this practice avoids the possible distortion in the depreciation in the last years of the asset's life. The depreciation under this procedure probably will not be materially different from the continued application of the accelerated method.[4]

Activity Methods

A company should use an activity method when the service life of the asset is affected primarily by the amount the asset is used and not by the passage of time. The activity usually is measured in terms of the number of hours worked or the output produced (such as miles driven or tons produced). In the case of the Troup Company, one measure of the life of the asset is estimated to be 10,000 hours of activity. We show the calculation of the depreciation per hour in Example 11-5.

EXAMPLE 11-5   Depreciation Based on Activity

$$\text{Depreciation Rate} = \frac{\text{Cost} - \text{Residual Value}}{\text{Total Lifetime Activity Level}}$$

$$= \frac{\$120,000 - \$20,000}{10,000 \text{ hours}}$$

$$= \$10 \text{ per hour}$$

The depreciation base of $100,000 is divided by the life of 10,000 hours to derive a depreciation rate of $10 per hour. The total depreciation for the period is determined by multiplying the depreciation rate by the number of hours the asset is used in the period. For example, if the Troup Company uses the asset for 2,100 hours during 2006, the depreciation for the year is $21,000 ($10 × 2,100).

It is important to note that this application of the activity method has produced a constant depreciation rate per *hour*, but one that varies per *unit* of production as the output per hour changes. For example, if the company produces 2 units per hour, the depreciation cost per unit is $5. If productivity increases so that the company produces 2.5 units per hour, the depreciation cost per unit is $4, although the depreciation per hour remains at $10. In contrast, if the activity method is based on the number of *units* expected to be produced over the life of the asset, then a depreciation rate is developed that is constant per *unit* produced but would vary per *hour* as productivity changes. For example, if the depreciation is based on the expected lifetime production of 20,000 units, the depreciation rate is $5 per unit produced ($100,000 ÷ 20,000). If productivity

---

4.   Another depreciation method also solves the issue of computing the correct amount of depreciation in the last year of an asset's life. It is the **fixed-percentage-of-declining-balance method,** in which a percentage depreciation rate is calculated that is multiplied by the book value to reduce it to the residual value at the end of the service life. The depreciation rate is calculated as follows:

$$\text{Depreciation Rate} = 1 - n\sqrt{\frac{\text{Residual Value}}{\text{Cost}}}$$

where *n* is the life of the asset. (The residual value cannot be zero because that makes the fraction zero and the depreciation rate 100%.) The Troup Company would compute the rate as follows:

$$\text{Depreciation Rate} = 1 - 5\sqrt{\frac{\$20,000}{\$120,000}} = 0.3012$$

This method is rarely used in practice because of its complexity.

increases so that the company produces 2.5 units per hour, the depreciation cost per unit remains at $5, but the depreciation per hour increases to $12.50.

Although an activity method is appropriate for many assets because their lives are limited by physical causes, it often is not used because of the difficulty of estimating the lifetime units of activity. Also it would be a costly method to implement because of the need to measure and record the activity level of each asset each period. However, it is the method used for depletion, as we discuss later in the chapter.

LINK TO RATIO ANALYSIS

While most U.S. companies use straight-line depreciation, they use varying estimates of service lives and residual values, which makes intercompany comparisons much more difficult. However, the required disclosures can be used by analysts to gain insights into a company's property, plant, and equipment. A useful measure that can be computed is the average age of a company's fixed assets. Consider the following data from **Intel's** 2004 annual report.

(in millions)	2004	2003
Accumulated Depreciation	$24,065	$22,031
Depreciation Expense	4,590	4,651
Depreciation Method	Straight-line	

Based on this information, the average age of Intel's property, plant, and equipment can be computed as follows:

$$\text{Average Age}_{2004} = \frac{\text{Accumulated Depreciation}}{\text{Depreciation Expense}} = \frac{\$24,065}{\$4,590} = 5.2 \text{ years}$$

$$\text{Average Age}_{2003} = \frac{\text{Accumulated Depreciation}}{\text{Depreciation Expense}} = \frac{\$22,031}{\$4,651} = 4.7 \text{ years}$$

Based on the above analysis, it appears that the average age of Intel's assets has increased slightly during 2004. Analysts may monitor this trend for three reasons. First, the age of a company's assets affects its competitive position since old assets tend to be less efficient than newer assets. Second, the age of assets provides an indication of a company's capital replacement policy and assists analysts in estimating future capital expenditures. Third, all things being equal, a company's return on assets will increase as the company's assets get older, which may affect the company's perceived profitability.

RECORDING DEPRECIATION

3 Record depreciation.

It is important to note that a company may not expense all its depreciation cost in the period. **A company includes depreciation on manufacturing assets as a cost of the inventory produced and records the depreciation as an increase (debit) to the Work in Process Inventory account.** In other words, the company capitalizes the depreciation to inventory rather than expensing it directly. Costs incurred during the period either remain in the inventory accounts, Work in Process and Finished Goods Inventory, or they are included in Cost of Goods Sold. Only the portion of the total depreciation included in the units sold appears in the company's income statement as part of the cost of goods sold (and not separately as depreciation expense). Consequently, depreciation included in the cost of the units produced but not sold is part of the two inventory accounts on the company's balance sheet. Therefore, when a company sells in the current period units produced in previous periods, its cost of goods sold includes some depreciation cost from previous periods.

A manufacturing company records depreciation on assets used for its selling, general, and administrative functions as an expense in the period, and includes the total Depreciation Expense each period on its income statement. Similarly, a merchandising company records depreciation on all its assets as an expense each period. Note, however, that many companies choose to disclose their expenses under functional classifications, such as selling, general, and administrative expenses. Therefore, they would not separately report depreciation expense on their income statements. However, the total depreciation expense for the period is a required disclosure.

The credit entry to record depreciation is to a contra-asset account usually called Accumulated Depreciation, or Allowance for Depreciation. A company maintains a separate contra-asset account for each class of assets and should deduct this amount on its balance sheet directly from the cost of that asset class. Alternatively, the company may report the book value on the balance sheet and disclose the cost and accumulated depreciation in the notes to its financial statements. However, many companies combine all the accumulated depreciation amounts and report only the total since this limited disclosure is allowed by GAAP.

CONCEPTUAL EVALUATION OF DEPRECIATION METHODS

A company may use any of the previously discussed depreciation methods, provided the method relates the allocation of the depreciable cost of the asset to the expected pattern of benefits to be derived from the asset. The choice of a particular method can have a significant impact on a company's income and assets, as you can see by comparing the various depreciation amounts and the book value of the asset computed for the Troup Company. We show these differences in Example 11-6. Use of an inappropriate method has an adverse impact on the measurement of a company's income each year. However, the company's total income over the life of the asset is unaffected because it expenses the same total depreciable cost. For example, if an asset produces equal (or increasing) benefits each year but a company uses an accelerated depreciation method, its income will increase each year of the asset's life (if other factors remain the same each period). This will occur even though there has been no change in the activity each period. The rising income may be misleading to users of the financial statements.

4 Explain the conceptual issues regarding depreciation methods.

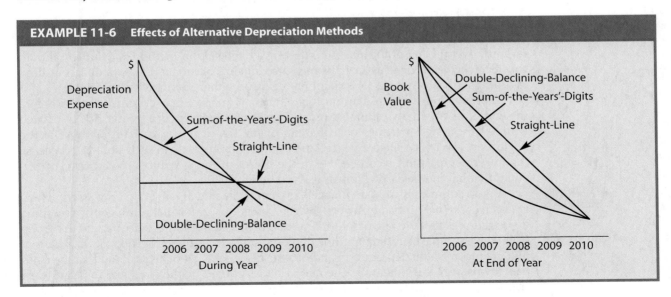

EXAMPLE 11-6   Effects of Alternative Depreciation Methods

Three additional factors that should be considered when a company selects a depreciation method are repair and maintenance costs, changing prices, and the risk associated with the cash flows from the asset. However, none have been addressed by generally accepted accounting principles. A company should consider the selection of the depreciation method together with the expected repair and maintenance costs, so that it evaluates the matching of the *total* costs associated with the asset and the benefits derived from the asset. For example, if a company expects that repair and maintenance costs and the total economic benefits of the asset all will remain similar each period, a similar total cost each period can be achieved through straight-line depreciation and the similar repair and maintenance costs. Alternatively, if a company expects increasing repair and maintenance costs, accelerated (declining-charge) depreciation and the increasing repair and maintenance costs each period may produce similar total costs each period. However, repair and maintenance costs would have to increase significantly to offset the decreasing depreciation amounts. We show these two situations in Exhibit 11-1. Alternatively, a company may expect that benefits will decline each year for the life of the asset, and that repair and maintenance costs are constant each period or are not rising as fast as the depreciation is declining. Then, a declining total cost will be achieved by using accelerated (declining-charge) depreciation along with the expected repair and maintenance costs.

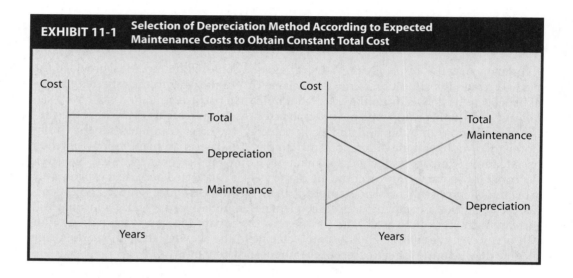

EXHIBIT 11-1 Selection of Depreciation Method According to Expected Maintenance Costs to Obtain Constant Total Cost

Inflation is likely to have a significant effect on the measurement of the benefits, or revenue, over the life of the asset. In selecting a depreciation method, a company should consider whether its benefits are to be measured in terms of current dollars or dollars realized in future periods. Since GAAP is silent on this issue, either alternative is acceptable.

In these periods of rapid technological change, an asset may become obsolete before the end of its originally estimated useful life. Therefore, there is a greater risk associated with the estimated revenues near the end of the life of the asset than for those at the beginning. Use of accelerated depreciation may be appropriate in such situations because the lower depreciation recorded late in the life of the asset reduces the amount of revenues that have to be earned for the asset to be profitable.

A ratio commonly used in financial analysis is the rate of return on total assets, which is defined as (net) income divided by the assets. An unfortunate impact of recording depreciation is that the rate of return on assets increases over time. Refer back to the Troup Company example using straight-line depreciation in Example 11-2. Suppose, in addition, that net income after depreciation and income taxes is $12,000 per year and that the company owns only this one asset. The rate of return earned by the company increases each year as we show in Example 11-7. (The calculation of the rate of return could also be based on the average of the beginning and ending book values of the asset.) The increase in the rate of return over the life of the asset would be even more dramatic if an accelerated depreciation method were used. As a result of this relationship, a user should always be careful when calculating the rate of return during financial statement analysis. Comparison between two companies can be distorted if one company has a newer asset base and hence a lower rate of return. Alternatively, if one company is analyzed over time, its rate of return will increase as its asset base gets older, other things being equal.

		EXAMPLE 11-7 **Effect of Depreciation on Rate of Return**		

Year	Net Income	Book Value of Asset at Beginning of Year	Rate of Return
2006	$12,000	$120,000	10%
2007	12,000	100,000	12
2008	12,000	80,000	15
2009	12,000	60,000	20
2010	12,000	40,000	30

Depreciation is intended only to allocate the cost in a systematic and rational manner. It is *not* an attempt to measure the *fair value* of the asset. The only times that a company should expect to report the fair (market) value of a property, plant, and equipment asset is on the date of acquisition and the date of disposal. Therefore, accounting principles match the cost of the asset against the benefits it produces, rather than an alternative approach of valuing the asset at its fair value. Many users consider the fair value only to be relevant for assets that are held for sale rather than held for use.

Depreciation is *not* recorded in an attempt to provide funds for the replacement of the asset. Over the life of the asset, the total depreciation expense is equal to the depreciable cost. Since depreciation is a tax-deductible expense, there is an income tax savings over the life of the asset. However, the savings is equal only to the tax rate multiplied by the total amount of tax depreciation. Therefore, there will not be sufficient cash saved over the life of the asset to replace it. Also, the purchase of an asset requires that cash be available at the time of the purchase, or that the company be able to obtain the necessary funds by borrowing or selling stock. However, the cash saved in income taxes may have been used to help finance the company's operations and may not be available for asset acquisitions. Also, in times of rising prices, the cost of replacing the asset will be higher than the original cost, so that additional funds will be required for the replacement.

DISCLOSURE OF DEPRECIATION

APB Opinion No. 12 requires the following disclosure requirements for depreciation:

5 Understand the disclosure of depreciation.

a. Depreciation expense for the period
b. Balances of major classes of depreciable assets, by nature or function, at the balance sheet date
c. Accumulated depreciation, either by major classes of depreciable assets or in total, at the balance sheet date
d. A general description of the method or methods used in computing depreciation with respect to major classes of depreciable assets[5]

---

5. "Omnibus Opinion—1967," *APB Opinion No. 12* (New York: AICPA, 1971), par. 5.

We show the disclosure of these items for **Anheuser-Busch** in Real Report 11-1. The depreciation (and amortization) expense of $932.7 million in 2004 was disclosed (after adjusting for the amortization expense) in the company's statement of cash flows under the indirect method.

Reporting

Real Report 11-1   Consolidated Balance Sheet

ANHEUSER-BUSCH COMPANIES, INC. AND SUBSIDIARIES

NOTES TO CONSOLIDATED FINANCIAL STATEMENTS (in part)

Note 1. Summary of Significant Accounting Principles and Policies (in part):

FIXED ASSETS

Fixed assets are carried at original cost less accumulated depreciation, and include expenditures for new facilities as well as those that increase the useful lives of existing facilities. The cost of routine maintenance, repairs and minor renewals is expensed as incurred. Depreciation expense is recognized using the straight-line method based on the following weighted average useful lives: buildings, 25 years; production machinery and equipment, 15 years; furniture and fixtures, 10 years; computer equipment, 3 years. When fixed assets are retired or sold, the book value is eliminated, and any gain or loss on disposition is recognized in cost of sales.

The components of plant and equipment as of December 31 are summarized below (in millions):

	December 31	
	2004	**2003**
Land	$ 278.9	$ 278.8
Buildings	4,750.6	4,546.1
Machinery and equipment	11,907.4	11,208.0
Construction in progress	475.6	488.3
Plant and equipment, at cost	17,412.5	16,521.2
Accumulated depreciation	(8,565.1)	(8,022.3)
Net plant and equipment	$ 8,847.4	$ 8,498.9

Questions:

1. Why do you think the company selected its depreciation method?
2. What is the estimated average age of Anheuser-Busch's property, plant, and equipment at the end of 2004?

Analysis

We show the relative use of alternative depreciation methods by 600 surveyed companies in Exhibit 11-2. Note that the straight-line method is used by most companies. There are more than 600 responses because many companies use more than one method of depreciation. Even with the current disclosure requirements, the reader of a company's

EXHIBIT 11-2   Use of Alternative Depreciation Methods

	Number of Companies							
	2003	**2000**	**1997**	**1994**	**1990**	**1986**	**1982**	**1978**
Straight-line	580	576	578	573	560	561	562	560
Declining-balance	22	22	26	27	38	49	57	67
Sum-of-the-years'-digits	5	7	10	9	11	14	20	35
Accelerated method, not specified	41	53	50	49	69	77	69	67
Units-of-production	30	34	39	49	50	48	62	44

Source: Accounting Trends and Techniques (New York: AICPA, 2004, 2001, 1998, 1995, 1991, 1987, 1983 and 1979).

financial statements is not able to evaluate whether the chosen depreciation method(s) is appropriate for the particular assets, but must accept that management and the company's auditors consider the method(s) to be systematic and rational. Nor is the reader able to estimate accurately the effect on income and assets of the use of an alternative depreciation method, which might be useful when comparing the financial activities of two companies using different depreciation methods.

LINK TO INTERNATIONAL DIFFERENCES

International accounting standards for depreciation are essentially the same as those in the United States. However, they only require that depreciation be "systematic," rather than "systematic and rational." International standards also require that the estimated useful lives and residual values of the assets, and the depreciation method, be reviewed at least once a year. They also require that companies disclose the accumulated depreciation for each class of asset, not just the total amount as allowed by U.S. standards. Also note that international standards allow a company to write up the value of its property, plant, and equipment assets to fair value, as we discussed in Chapter 10. Such a write-up would affect the amount of depreciation that the company records each period.[6]

ADDITIONAL DEPRECIATION METHODS

Some additional depreciation methods are **group-rate** and **composite-rate** methods, which are used frequently with the straight-line or accelerated methods, and **inventory systems.**[7]

Group and composite depreciation are conceptually similar methods of applying depreciation to more than one asset. Group depreciation is applied to *homogeneous* assets that are expected to have similar service lives and residual values. Composite depreciation is applied to *heterogeneous* assets having some similar characteristics, but are expected to have varying service lives and residual values. Thus, group depreciation would be used for homogeneous assets such as laptops, whereas composite depreciation would be applied to heterogeneous assets such as office machines.

6 Understand additional depreciation methods, including group and composite methods.

Group Depreciation

A company uses group depreciation when it owns a group of homogeneous (similar) assets. Under this method, the company uses the following procedures:

- It capitalizes the assets in one asset account.
- It treats the group as one "asset" for purposes of depreciation.
- It bases the group depreciation rate on the average life of the assets in the group.
- It accumulates the depreciation in a single contra-asset account.
- It calculates the depreciation each period by multiplying this rate by the balance in the asset account.
- When an item in the group is retired, the company does not recognize a gain or loss on that item because the entire "asset" is not retired.

---

6. For additional discussion see Carrie Bloomer (editor), *The IASC–U.S. Comparison Project: A Report on the Similarities and Differences between IASC Standards and U.S. GAAP*, 2nd ed. (Norwalk, Conn: FASB, 1999).

7. Two other methods, the **compound-interest** and **sinking-fund** methods, are based on present value concepts. They result in an *increasing* depreciation amount and a constant rate of return on the asset each period. They are very rarely used because increasing depreciation each period generally is not considered to satisfy the matching principle.

- It records the retirement of an item in the group by a credit to the asset account for the original cost, and a debit to the accumulated depreciation account for the difference between the cost and the proceeds received.
- It recognizes a total net gain or loss on the group as a whole when the final unit in the group is retired.

Example: Group Depreciation

Suppose that a company purchases 10 cars for $20,000 each, and the average expected service life is three years with a residual value of $5,000 each. Of those cars, three are sold after two years for $8,000 each, five after three years for $6,000 each, and two after four years for $4,800 each. The company computes the depreciation rate as follows:

$$\text{Depreciation} = \frac{\text{Cost} - \text{Residual Value}}{\text{Life}}$$

$$= \frac{\$200,000 - \$50,000}{3}$$

$$= \$50,000 \text{ (or 25\% of the cost of the assets)}$$

We show the journal entries used to record these events in Example 11-8. Depreciation expense is based on the original estimates, and the rate is not changed by the early retirement of three cars after the second year. No gain or loss is recognized on the retirement at the end of the second and third years. The journal entries in the fourth year (the year of the final retirement) need further explanation. First, the usual procedure in group depreciation is to multiply the asset cost by the group depreciation rate to determine the annual depreciation expense. However, it is a general rule that assets are not depreciated below their residual value. Since the book value of the group asset is $11,000 ($40,000 Cars − $29,000 Accumulated Depreciation) at the beginning of the year and the residual value of the two remaining cars is $10,000 (2 × $5,000), the depreciation expense must be $1,000 in this year. Second, the $400 loss on the *entire* group is determined by comparing the $9,600 (2 × $4,800) proceeds to the $10,000 book value at the end of the fourth year. ♦

Suppose the company purchases a new asset (i.e., more cars) before the group is retired. In this case, it computes a new depreciation rate by dividing the new depreciation base (book value at the beginning of the period plus the additional cost less the estimated residual value of the group) by the new weighted average of the remaining lives of the assets in the group.

Composite Depreciation

A company may apply composite depreciation to heterogeneous (dissimilar) assets that have somewhat similar characteristics or purposes. It uses similar prodecures to group depreciation, as follows:

- The company combines the assets in one asset account and depreciates them accordingly.
- The company uses one accumulated depreciation account.
- The company does not recognize a gain or loss on each item retired.
- The company recognizes a net gain or loss when it retires the final asset.

Example: Composite Depreciation

Suppose that a company purchases three assets with the following characteristics:

Asset	Cost	Residual Value	Life	Annual Depreciation
A	$25,000	$5,000	10 years	$2,000
B	13,000	1,000	6	2,000
C	12,000	—	4	3,000
	$50,000	$6,000		$7,000

EXAMPLE 11-8   Journal Entries for Group Depreciation

1. To record the purchase:

Cars	200,000	
Cash		200,000

2. To record the first year's depreciation expense:

Depreciation Expense	50,000	
Accumulated Depreciation		50,000

3. To record the second year's depreciation expense:

Depreciation Expense	50,000	
Accumulated Depreciation		50,000

4. To record the disposal of three cars at the end
of the second year for $8,000 each:

Cash	24,000	
Accumulated Depreciation	36,000	
Cars		60,000

5. To record the third year's depreciation expense:

Depreciation Expense [25% $\times$ ($200,000 – $60,000)]	35,000	
Accumulated Depreciation		35,000

6. To record the disposal of five cars at the end of
the third year for $6,000 each:

Cash	30,000	
Accumulated Depreciation	70,000	
Cars		100,000

7. To record the depreciation expense for the fourth
year, the disposal of two cars at the end of the
fourth year for $4,800 each, and the *net* gain or
loss of the *entire* group:

Depreciation Expense	1,000[a]	
Accumulated Depreciation		1,000
Cash	9,600	
Accumulated Depreciation	30,000	
Loss on Disposal	400[b]	
Cars		40,000

[a] The depreciation expense is the amount needed to reduce the $11,000 book value ($40,000 remaining cost minus $29,000 remaining accumulated depreciation) of the group to the estimated residual value (2 $\times$ $5,000).
[b] The loss is equal to the proceeds of $9,600 (2 $\times$ $4,800) minus the remaining book value of $10,000 ($40,000 – $30,000).

Assuming that the company uses straight-line depreciation, it computes the composite depreciation rate as follows:

$$\text{Depreciation Rate} = \frac{\$7,000}{\$50,000} = 14\%$$

The company computes the depreciation by multiplying 14% by the cost of the assets remaining in service until the book value equals the estimated residual value of $6,000. If the company purchases another asset, it may include the asset in the group by adding the cost to the asset account. Then it calculates a new composite depreciation rate.

The advantage of both the group and the composite methods is that they simplify a company's record keeping, especially when it acquires a large number of low-cost items. The methods also recognize that depreciation estimates are based on averages and that gains or losses on disposals of single assets are often immaterial. The major disadvantage of the two methods is that faulty estimates might be concealed for long periods. Also, gains and losses may be deferred beyond the period in which they actually occurred. This is particularly true when heterogeneous assets are combined for the composite depreciation method, and the average life is the result of combining varying individual lives. ◆

Inventory Systems

The inventory (or appraisal) system typically is used in situations where there are large numbers of similar low-cost items, such as tools for a manufacturing company or dishes for a restaurant. The method is similar to a periodic inventory system, in that a cost is assigned to an expense by a physical count at the end of the year. That is, the cost that a company assigns to depreciation is determined by multiplying the physical number of units at the end of the year by the replacement cost. Then, it subtracts that amount from the "inventory" cost at the beginning of the year to determine the depreciation expense. The ending inventory usually is computed as the value (not the cost) of the assets, so that the depreciation becomes a measure of the change in the value of the assets. The method is criticized because it does not result in a systematic and rational allocation of cost, but rather is a measure of the value of the assets. Also, the value assigned to the inventory tends to be less reliable than cost.

SECURE YOUR KNOWLEDGE 11-1

- Depreciation, depletion, and amortization are allocation processes that attempt to match the cost of an asset against the revenue that the asset helps to generate.
- The four factors that must be considered in computing depreciation are:
  - Asset cost—acquisition cost, as discussed in Chapter 10.
  - Service life—the amount of use that the company expects from the asset prior to disposal, measured in units of time or in units of activity.
  - Residual value—the amount that a company expects to receive for an asset at the end of its useful life.
  - Method of cost allocation—must be systematic and rational.
- Time-based depreciation methods result in a depreciation amount that is related to the passage of time.
  - The straight-line method allocates an equal amount of the asset's depreciable cost to each year of the service life.
  - Accelerated methods (sum-of-the-years'-digits and declining balance) result in periodic depreciation amounts that decline over the asset's service life.
- Activity-based depreciation methods result in a depreciation rate that is based on estimated usage (e.g., number of hours worked or output produced), and this rate is then multiplied by actual usage to compute the depreciation amount.
- Depreciation on assets used for selling, general, and administrative functions is recorded as a current period expense on the income statement; however, depreciation on manufacturing assets is recorded as part of the cost of inventory.
- While a company selects from acceptable depreciation methods that are systematic and rational, this choice can have a significant impact on a company's income and assets.
- A company may choose to combine multiple assets into one asset account and use group depreciation (for homogeneous assets) or composite depreciation (for heterogeneous assets) to simplify record keeping.

DEPRECIATION FOR PARTIAL PERIODS

7 Compute depreciation for partial periods.

Our discussion so far has assumed that assets are purchased on the first day of the fiscal year and disposed of on the last day. Of course, transactions occur throughout the fiscal year. Also, depreciation could be computed to the nearest day, but such precision is unnecessary, since the calculation of depreciation uses estimates. There are three common alternative policies that companies use to compute depreciation for partial periods.

Compute Depreciation to the Nearest Whole Month

Under this method, assets purchased on or before the 15th of the month are considered owned for the whole month; assets purchased after the 15th are considered *not* to be owned during the month. Similarly, assets sold on or before the 15th are considered not to be owned for the month; assets sold after the 15th are considered owned for the whole month. Depreciation is based on the fraction of the year the asset is used. When a company uses straight-line depreciation and calculates depreciation for months instead of years, it usually states the denominator of the depreciation calculation as the total months in the estimated service life. This results in a monthly depreciation amount. We show the more complex issues when a company uses accelerated depreciation methods.

Example: Depreciation for Partial Periods

Suppose Vann Company purchases a $6,000 asset with a three-year life and no residual value on August 18. Thus four months remain in the year. It uses the *sum-of-the-years'-digits depreciation* method over four fiscal years and computes the amounts as follows:

Fiscal Year	Annual Depreciation by Sum-of-the-Years'-Digits Method	Months	Computation	Annual Depreciation
1	$3,000	4	4/12 × $3,000	$1,000
2	2,000	12	8/12 × $3,000 + 4/12 × $2,000	2,667
3	1,000	12	8/12 × $2,000 + 4/12 × $1,000	1,667
4	—	8	8/12 × $1,000	666*
	$6,000			$6,000

*Adjusted for $1 rounding error

If Vann Company use *double-declining depreciation* for partial periods, two alternatives are available. In the first alternative, it can use the double-declining-balance method in the same way as we just described for the sum-of-the-years'-digits method. That is, the depreciation on an annual basis is allocated to each fiscal year on the basis of the number of months. In the second alternative, after computing the depreciation for the first year as described for the first alternative, it can apply the double-declining-balance method by multiplying the book value by the appropriate percentage (66.7%). Using the same example of a $6,000 asset with a three-year life and no residual value, Vann Company computes the depreciation under the two alternatives as follows:

Fiscal Year	Annual Depreciation by the Double-Declining-Balance	Months	Computation	Reported Annual Depreciation
Alternative 1				
1	$4,000	4	4/12 × $4,000	$1,333
2	1,333	12	8/12 × $4,000 + 4/12 × $1,333	3,111
3	667	12	8/12 × $1,333 + 4/12 × $667	1,111
4	—	8	8/12 × $667	445
	$6,000			$6,000
Alternative 2				
Depreciation Year 1			4/12 × $4,000	$1,333
Depreciation Year 2			0.667* × ($6,000 − $1,333)	3,113
Depreciation Year 3			0.667 × ($4,667 − $3,113)	1,037
Depreciation Year 4			Remaining balance	517
				$6,000 ◆

*Two times straight-line rate = 2 × 1/3

Compute Depreciation to the Nearest Whole Year

For this partial depreciation method, exactly the same procedure is used as for the monthly situation, except that six months is used as the cutoff instead of the 15th of the month. That is, assets purchased during the first six months of the year are considered to be owned for the entire year, and assets purchased during the second six months are not depreciated for that year. Using the same example, with straight-line deprecation there is no depreciation in the first fiscal year, since the asset was purchased in the second half of the year. However, a full year's depreciation is recorded in the last year. Under the sum-of-the-years'-digits method, depreciation in the four fiscal years is $0, $3,000, $2,000, and $1,000, respectively.

Compute One-Half Year's Depreciation on All Assets Purchased or Sold During the Year

Under this method, all assets purchased or sold during the fiscal year are considered to have been purchased or sold at the midpoint of the year. Therefore, one-half year's depreciation is recorded in all such situations. Using the same example, the depreciation for each fiscal year is computed as follows:

Fiscal Year	Annual Depreciation by Sum-of-the-Years'-Digits Method	Computation	Reported Annual Depreciation
1	$3,000	1/2 × $3,000	$1,500
2	2,000	1/2 × $3,000 + 1/2 × $2,000	2,500
3	1,000	1/2 × $2,000 + 1/2 × $1,000	1,500
4	—	1/2 × $1,000	500
	$6,000		$6,000

IMPAIRMENT OF PROPERTY, PLANT, AND EQUIPMENT

8 Explain the impairment of property, plant, and equipment.

Conceptual

Users have been concerned for a long time about the values that a company assigns to its property, plant, and equipment. If the fair value of these noncurrent assets is less than their book value, then the company's past earnings may be overstated (because it did not record sufficient depreciation in prior years). Conservatism would suggest that the company write down these assets and recognize a loss. Also, if a company writes down an asset by too much, then future profits will be overstated (because it would record too little depreciation in future years). **FASB Statement No. 144**[8] requires that a company review its property, plant, and equipment for impairment whenever events or changes in circumstances indicate that the book value of the property, plant, and equipment may not be recoverable. Examples of such events or changes in circumstances include:

- a significant decrease in the fair value of the asset,
- a significant change in the way the asset is used,
- a significant change in the business or regulatory environment,
- costs of constructing the asset that exceed the planned amount,
- a current period operating loss,
- a negative cash flow from operating activities,
- or an expectation that the asset will more-likely-than-not (i.e., more than 50% chance) be sold or otherwise disposed of before the end of its useful life.

8. "Accounting for the Impairment or Disposal of Long-Lived Assets," *FASB Statement of Financial Accounting Standards No. 144* (Norwalk, Conn.: FASB 2001). Certain assets are excluded from the scope of the *Statement,* including specialized assets in the record, music, broadcasting, and software industries. The *Statement* replaced, but made only minor changes to, *FASB Statement of Financial Accounting Standards No. 121* which was issued in 1995.

After the company identifies that an asset may be impaired, two steps are taken: (1) an impairment test, and (2) measurement of the loss.

Impairment Test

To test for impairment, the company estimates the future net cash flows expected to result from the use of the asset and its eventual sale. If the total expected cash flows (undiscounted) are less than the book value of the asset, the company must recognize an impairment loss. One of the major issues faced by the FASB was asset grouping. That is, does the company test individual assets or large groups of assets? The FASB resolved this issue by requiring that assets be grouped at the lowest level at which identifiable cash flows are largely independent of the cash flows of other groups of assets. (We will use the singular term "asset" to describe the group of assets identified by a company.) If the future cash flows exceed the book value, an impairment loss is *not* recognized, but a review of the company's depreciation policies may be appropriate.

Measurement of the Loss

The impairment loss for an asset that the company intends to hold and use is the difference between the asset's book value and its lower fair value.[9] The fair value is the amount at which the asset could be bought or sold in a current transaction between willing parties. However, quoted market prices will often not be available for the assets covered by *FASB Statement No. 144*. Therefore, fair value may be measured by using the present value method to determine the discounted cash flows (as we discuss in the Time Value of Money Module). The discount rate is the rate of return that the company would require for a similar investment with similar risks. For example, this could be the rate used to evaluate capital budgeting projects.

Recording and Reporting the Loss

When a company recognizes an impairment loss (debit), it writes down the asset (credit) to reduce its book value to the lower fair value (as we show in the example that follows). The company reports the impairment loss on its income statement as part of income from continuing operations and reports the new (reduced) book value on its ending balance sheet. The reduced book value (i.e., fair value) becomes the new "cost" of the asset and is used to compute the depreciation over the remaining life of the asset. Once an asset has been written down, if the fair value later increases, the asset may *not* be written back up.

Disclosures

A company must include in its disclosures in the year of the write-down and the next two years (1) a description of the impaired asset and the circumstances leading to the impairment, (2) the amount of the loss, how the asset's fair value was determined, (3) the income statement caption which includes the loss, and (4) the operating segment affected (if applicable).

---

9. The *Statement* also discusses the measurement of an impairment loss for an asset that the company *intends to sell*. The asset is reported at the lower of the (1) book value or (2) fair value less the costs to sell. The impairment loss is calculated in the same way as for an asset held for use, except that the estimated selling price less the costs to sell is used instead of the present value of the cash flows (or other measure of fair value). Thus, the GAAP related to an asset the company expects to sell is similar to that we discussed in Chapter 5 for the disposal of a component of a company and we do not discuss it further.

In summary, an impairment loss involves the following steps:

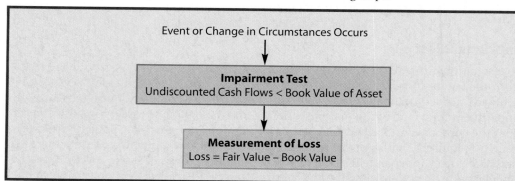

Example: Impairment Loss

Suppose that on January 1, 2004, the Hall Company purchased a factory for $1 million and machinery for $3 million. The asset(s) is held for use and not for sale. The company is depreciating the factory over 20 years and the machinery over 10 years, both by the straight-line method, to zero residual values. Late in 2007, because of technological changes in the industry and reduced selling prices for its products, the company believes that its asset(s) may be impaired and will have a remaining useful life of five years. The company combines the factory and machinery as a group because the cash flows from each are not separable and are independent of the company's other activities. To test for impairment, the company estimates that the asset will produce cash inflows of $700,000 and will incur cash outflows of $300,000 each year for the next five years. The company tests for impairment and measures the loss as follows:

Impairment Test

December 31, 2007

Factory cost	$1,000,000	
Less: Accumulated depreciation (4 years × $50,000)	(200,000)	
Book value		$ 800,000
Machinery cost	$3,000,000	
Less: Accumulated depreciation (4 years × $300,000)	(1,200,000)	
Book value		1,800,000
Total Book Value		$2,600,000

$$\text{Undiscounted expected net cash flows} = 5 \text{ years} \times (\$700,000 \text{ cash inflows} -$$
$$\$300,000 \text{ cash outflows})$$
$$= 5 \times \$400,000$$
$$= \$2,000,000$$

Because $2,000,000 is less than $2,600,000, the company must recognize an impairment loss.

Since the company is not able to determine the fair value based on the selling price of the factory and machinery, it uses the present value method instead. To apply this method, the company uses a discount rate of 16% (which is the rate of return it uses to evaluate capital budgeting projects). It calculates the impairment loss of $1,290,282 as follows:

Measurement of the Loss

Present value of the expected net cash flows (fair value) = $400,000 × 3.274294
($n = 5$, $i = 0.16$ from
Table 4 in the Time Value
of Money Module)
= $1,309,718 (rounded)

Impairment loss = $1,309,718 fair value − $2,600,000 book value
= $(1,290,282)

Although the *Statement* does not specify how to record the write-down, it does indicate that the reduced book value of the asset is to be accounted for as the new cost. Therefore, we will treat the write-down as a "sale" with an acquisition at the new "cost." We also assume that the new cost is allocated among the individual assets based on their relative fair values at their original acquisition date. Then the Hall Company records the loss as follows:

Loss from Impairment	1,290,282	
Accumulated Depreciation: Factory	200,000	
Accumulated Depreciation: Machinery	1,200,000	
Factory (new cost)	327,429[a]	
Machinery (new cost)	982,289[b]	
Factory (old cost)		1,000,000
Machinery (old cost)		3,000,000

[a]$1,309,718 × [$1,000,000 ÷ ($3,000,000 + $1,000,000)]
[b]$1,309,718 × [$3,000,000 ÷ ($3,000,000 + $1,000,000)]

The company will depreciate the factory and machinery over their remaining useful life of five years. It reports the $1,290,282 loss in income from continuing operations on its 2007 income statement, and the property, plant, and equipment at a total of $1,309,718 on its 2007 ending balance sheet. ♦

LINK TO ETHICAL DILEMMA

The fortunes of NetWorth, Inc. are in serious jeopardy. Several years ago, NetWorth was the high-technology darling of Wall Street with the business press constantly heaping praises on NetWorth's innovative business model and solid management team. However, the recession during the last two years and increasing competition has certainly dampened its future prospects. During the last 18 months, NetWorth has reported only one quarterly profit and the Board of Directors is calling for a quick return to profitability. With current quarterly results looking disappointing, the CFO has called on you to perform an extensive analysis of all property, plant, and equipment items in an effort to identify the nonproductive assets and improve operational efficiency. After informing the CFO that preliminary results indicated an impairment loss of almost $700 million needed to be recognized, you are instructed to increase the impairment amount by $300 million and record a $1 billion impairment loss. When you question the increase in the impairment amount, you are told that upper management thought your estimates of the usefulness of the assets were overly optimistic and that they changed several of your estimates, including the discount rate used in measuring the impairment loss. Since the changes resulted in more conservative financial statements, the CFO was sure you would not object. What is your reaction?

Conceptual Evaluation of Asset Impairment

FASB Statement No. 121 first established the impairment rules we just discussed. Although it has been replaced by *FASB Statement No. 144*, the principles it established have only changed slightly. *FASB Statement No. 121* was issued to enhance the usefulness of a company's financial statements by recognizing the loss when incurred and reporting the fair value of productive assets. This should provide better financial reporting because the asset value reflects the value of the company's investment. Thus, the information is expected to be more relevant and help users assess the return on investment, operating capability, and risk of the company. The information should also improve comparability across companies.

Although the *Statement* narrows GAAP, it still allows for significant management flexibility. For example, it does not require that assets be tested for impairment on a regular basis, because the FASB concluded that would be too costly. Management will also have some flexibility in deciding which assets to include in, and exclude from, each grouping. Also, estimating future cash flows is very subjective. For example, the company could use current or expected cost and volume information. Furthermore, the discount rate used to value the cash flows is a management choice.

The *Statement* was adopted by a 5-to-2 vote. The dissenters believed that the use of fair value is not appropriate if the asset will continue to be used, because there has not been an exchange transaction. They argued that such use of fair value is a precedent-setting departure from the transaction-based historical cost model (other than for certain investments in marketable securities, as we discuss in Chapter 15). Therefore, the dissenters argued that the asset should be recorded at recoverable cost, either measured on a present value or undiscounted basis. One dissenter also argued that fair value is not relevant and reliable information for property, plant, and equipment that is held and used in the normal course of business. Therefore, the fair value of an impaired asset is also not relevant and reliable. Also the write-down will "guarantee" future profits because of the lower depreciation expense in the future.

Two other concerns were also expressed. First, the cash flows expected by a company from using a specific asset are not necessarily the same as those used to determine the market value of the asset, since the company may use the asset differently from other companies. Therefore, the specific cash flows may not result in a measure of fair value. Second, the test for an impairment may differ for identical assets simply because of the depreciation method (or life) selected by the company. An asset depreciated by an accelerated method will have a lower book value than one depreciated by the straight-line method, and therefore be less likely to meet the impairment test. Even with these concerns, it is hoped that the *Statement* has improved financial reporting. For example, in 2004, **Corning** reported that it would record noncash charges of $2.8 billion to $2.9 billion as it reduced the value of the assets in its telecommunication business.

LINK TO INTERNATIONAL DIFFERENCES

Although international accounting standards for the impairment of assets are similar to those of the United States, there are some differences. International standards use the higher of the asset's net selling price or value in use to determine if an asset is impaired compared to the undiscounted cash flows used in U.S. principles. Typically, this should mean that international companies will recognize impairment losses earlier than U.S. companies. Under international standards, the impairment loss is the difference between the book value and the "trigger" value defined above. Therefore, it is likely that the impairment losses measured under the two sets of principles would be different. Also, international standards allow impairment losses to be reversed, which is not allowed under U.S. standards.

DEPRECIATION AND INCOME TAXES

9 Understand depreciation for income tax purposes.

Companies follow different depreciation rules for computing taxable income than for computing income for financial reporting purposes. The use of different methods is appropriate because the purpose of the depreciation methods required by the income tax laws is to stimulate capital investment through the rapid recovery of capital costs. However, the purpose of accounting income is to present fairly the activities of the company over a particular period. Therefore, companies that are *not* required to follow GAAP may use the tax method in their financial statements.

For assets acquired before 1981, depreciation for income tax purposes is based on use of the straight-line, sum-of-the-years'-digits, and declining-balance methods we discussed earlier. The asset may not be depreciated below the estimated residual value, and the IRS publishes tables that give a range of the estimated lives to use. For assets purchased in the years 1981 through 1986, the Accelerated Cost Recovery System (ACRS) is used. For assets purchased in 1987 and later, ACRS was modified and is known as MACRS.[10] The following discussion is based on these latest rules.

MACRS Principles

For an asset purchased in 1987 or later, a company's computations of depreciation for federal income tax purposes and financial reporting purposes differ in three major respects:

1. A mandated tax life, which is usually shorter than the economic life
2. Acceleration of the cost recovery (except for a building)
3. Elimination of the residual value

Each of these differences tends to cause depreciation early in the life of an asset to be higher for income tax purposes than for financial statement reporting. This results in lowering income taxes payable in those years. Over the life of an asset, the sum of the total depreciation and the gain or loss on disposal for both income tax reporting and financial reporting usually will be the same for both methods. Therefore, a company's taxable income over the asset's life usually will be equal to its income before income taxes reported in its financial statements. However, the transfer of income tax payments from early in the life of the asset to later in the life is desirable when present value concepts are considered. Since MACRS depreciation is so different from the depreciation used in a company's financial statements, we briefly discuss it. You should also note that for income tax reporting a company may use the straight-line method over the mandated tax life instead of MACRS. Refer to the Internal Revenue Code, or an income tax book, for a more detailed and technical discussion.

Shorter Life

The MACRS establishes lives (recovery periods) of 3, 5, 7, 10, 15, 20, 27½ (residential rental buildings), and 39 (commercial buildings) years. Each asset is defined to be in one of the categories, and a company uses that life no matter what economic life it uses for financial reporting purposes.

Acceleration of Cost Recovery

The depreciation is computed based on the *cost* of the asset. The method used depends on the life of the asset mandated by MACRS, as follows:

Method	MACRS Life (in years)
Double-declining-balance	3, 5, 7, 10
150%-declining-balance	15, 20
Straight-line	27½, 39

All the depreciation calculations for income tax purposes are based on the half-year convention. That is, a company records depreciation for half a year in the year of acquisition and in the last year of the MACRS life. Therefore, the depreciation for tax purposes is spread over one more tax year than the number of calendar years listed previously. Also, when one of the accelerated methods is used, a change is made to the straight-line

---

10. Following the terrorist attacks of 9/11/01, Congress enacted a temporary change in the MACRS rules. For assets (other than buildings) placed in service between 9/10/01 and 9/11/04, a company receives a tax deduction of 30% of the cost of the asset and then applies MACRS procedures to the remaining 70%. To assist in the economic recovery, Congress enacted a temporary change in the MACRS rules. For new assets (other than buildings) placed in service between 5/6/03 and 12/31/04, a company receives a tax deduction of 50% of the cost of the asset and then applies MACRS procedures to the remaining 50%. We do not include the effects of these temporary rules in the examples and homework throughout the book.

method in the period in which the straight-line depreciation exceeds the amount calculated under the accelerated method. The IRS has published tables to simplify the application of these methods, as we show in Exhibit 11-3.

EXHIBIT 11-3   MACRS Depreciation as a Percentage of the Cost of the Asset

Year of Life	Tax Life of Asset in Years					
	3	5	7	10	15	20
1	33.33%	20.00%	14.29%	10.00%	5.00%	3.750%
2	44.45	32.00	24.49	18.00	9.50	7.219
3	14.81	19.20	17.49	14.40	8.55	6.677
4	7.41	11.52	12.49	11.52	7.70	6.177
5		11.52	8.93	9.22	6.93	5.713
6		5.76	8.92	7.37	6.23	5.285
7			8.93	6.55	5.90	4.888
8			4.46	6.55	5.90	4.522
9				6.56	5.91	4.462
10				6.55	5.90	4.461
11				3.28	5.91	4.462
12					5.90	4.461
13					5.91	4.462
14					5.90	4.461
15					5.91	4.462
16					2.95	4.461
17						4.462
18						4.461
19						4.462
20						4.461
21						2.231

Residual Value

The residual value is *not* considered when the MACRS system is used, and so the asset is depreciated to a zero value at the end of its MACRS life. However, the entire proceeds from the disposal of the asset will be taxable since the entire value received will be a gain.

Example: MACRS

To show the use of the MACRS system and the differences from the calculation of depreciation for financial reporting, consider the following facts for an asset purchased by the Melville Company on January 1, 2006:

Cost	$200,000
Estimated economic life	8 years
Estimated residual value	$20,000
Depreciation method for financial statements	Straight-line
MACRS life	5 years
MACRS method	200% declining balance
Disposal	$15,000 on January 3, 2014

The company computes the MACRS depreciation using the rates from Exhibit 11-3 as follows:

2006:	$200,000 × 20%	= $ 40,000
2007:	$200,000 × 32%	= $ 64,000
2008:	$200,000 × 19.20%	= $ 38,400
2009:	$200,000 × 11.52%	= $ 23,040
2010:	$200,000 × 11.52%	= $ 23,040
2011:	$200,000 × 5.76%	= $ 11,520
		$200,000

Note that the total depreciation deductions on the company's income tax returns for 2006 through 2011 are $200,000. Thus, the MACRS depreciation recovers the total cost of the asset on an accelerated basis and ignores any residual value. Also note that the MACRS depreciation is spread over six tax years, even though the tax life is five years. This is because of the half-year MACRS convention. Therefore, the MACRS depreciation is zero in 2012 and 2013. The taxable gain in 2014 when the asset is sold is $15,000, since the company has depreciated the asset to a zero residual value. Therefore, the total effect on its taxable income for the years 2006 through 2013 is $185,000 ($200,000 − $15,000).

The depreciation for financial reporting purposes is $22,500 [($200,000 − $20,000) ÷ 8] for each of the eight years of the asset's economic life from 2006 through 2013. The loss on disposal in 2014 is $5,000 ($20,000 book value − $15,000 proceeds). The total effect on the company's income before income taxes for the years 2006 through 2013 in its income statement is $185,000 ($180,000 + $5,000), which is the same as the total effect on taxable income. The different amounts of depreciation for income tax reporting and financial reporting in each year result in temporary differences, which require interperiod tax allocation, as we discuss in Chapter 19. ♦

Credit: ©Getty Images/PhotoDisc

CHANGES AND CORRECTIONS OF DEPRECIATION

10 Explain changes and corrections of depreciation.

FASB statement No. 154, which we discuss more fully in Chapter 23, describes how a company may make each of the various changes in and corrections of depreciation for the following situations:

Reporting

1. A change in an estimate of the residual value or the service life of a currently owned asset is accounted for prospectively. The company allocates the undepreciated cost of the asset at the beginning of the year of the change over the new remaining life, considering the new residual value. We include an example (using depletion) in the next section of the chapter.

2. A change in the depreciation method for currently owned assets is also accounted for prospectively. A company may change its depreciation method because of a change in the estimated future benefits expected from the asset. In this case, the company allocates the undepreciated cost of the asset at the beginning of the year over the remaining life (considering the residual value) using the new depreciation method. This change is called a change in accounting estimate that is effected by a change in accounting principle.[11]

3. A correction of an error in depreciation is accounted for as a prior period restatement. The effect on the current period's financial statements involves a correction to the amount in the accumulated depreciation account and an adjustment to retained earnings (net of income taxes) for the amount of the error in previously reported net income. The company's previous financial statements are also corrected (restated). We show this reporting in Chapters 5 and 17, and more fully in Chapter 23, and it is consistent with the requirements of **FASB Statement No. 154.**

DEPLETION

11 Understand and record depletion.

Depletion is the allocation of the depletable cost for the use of a natural resource (wasting asset) to the periods in which benefits are received. It is the same concept as depreciation, but the different term is used for natural resources. Examples of such resources are oil, gas, minerals, timber, and gravel.

A company determines the recorded cost of natural resources by the same principles used for property, plant, and equipment. It is possible that there will be extensive reclamation costs. In this case the company would report a liability and add the same amount to the cost of the asset, as we discussed in Chapter 10.

A company usually records depletion using an activity method. The activity measure is the number of units of the resource that the company expects to extract over the life of the asset. A unit depletion rate is calculated as follows:

$$\text{Unit Depletion Rate} = \frac{\text{Cost} - \text{Residual Value}}{\text{Units}}$$

To determine the actual depletion for a period, the unit depletion rate is multiplied by the actual production for that period.

Example: Coal Mine Depletion

Suppose that the Reggio Company purchases land for $3,000,000 from which it expects to extract 1,000,000 tons of coal, the estimated residual value is $200,000, and it mines

---

11. If a company has a policy of switching depreciation methods at a specific point in the service life of an asset, this is *not* considered to be a change in accounting estimate that is effected by a change in accounting principle.

80,000 tons of coal in the first year. It calculates the depletion for that year as follows:

$$\text{Unit Depletion Rate} = \frac{\$3,000,000 - \$200,000}{1,000,000 \text{ tons}}$$
$$= \underline{\underline{\$2.80 \text{ per ton}}}$$

$$\text{Depletion for Year} = \$2.80 \times 80,000 \text{ tons}$$
$$= \underline{\underline{\$224,000}}$$

Reggio Company typically makes the journal entry to record the depletion directly to an inventory account. The reason for this is so that the cost is included in Cost of Goods Sold for the units that are sold and in ending inventory for the units on hand at the end of the period. The credit is made either to Accumulated Depletion or directly to the asset account because disclosure of the accumulated depletion amount is not required by GAAP. However, this disclosure is required by the SEC.

The nature of natural resources is such that additional capital expenditures may be made in future periods. In addition, the estimation of the remaining number of units is often uncertain and therefore subject to revision based on new geological information. When additional capital expenditures are incurred or estimates are revised, a new depletion rate is calculated. The new depletion rate is based on the current book value of the asset (including the additional capital expenditures), the new estimate of the residual value, and the new estimate of the remaining units as of the beginning of the year. ♦

Example: Revised Estimate   Continuing the preceding example, suppose that at the beginning of the second year of operation of the coal mine, a new estimate indicates that the mine has a capacity to produce another 1,600,000 tons (for a lifetime production of 1,680,000 tons). The Reggio Company computes a new unit depletion rate as follows:

$$\text{Unit Depletion Rate} = \frac{\text{Book Value} - \text{Residual Value}}{\text{Remaining Units}}$$
$$= \frac{(\$3,000,000 - \$224,000) - \$200,000}{1,600,000}$$
$$= \underline{\underline{\$1.61 \text{ per ton}}}$$

The company uses the new unit depletion rate to compute each year's depletion until it makes new estimates and calculates another depletion rate. ♦

The cost of a natural resource asset may include certain tangible assets, such as buildings and roads on the site of a mine. Since the useful life of the tangible assets is limited by the life of the mine, a company depreciates their cost on the basis of the same activity method as it uses for the mine. Of course, if other improvements have a life shorter than the expected life of the mine, the company depreciates them over their expected economic lives.

Depletion for income tax purposes involves a different concept than for financial reporting. A company can deduct as depletion expense either the **cost depletion** just shown (based on the units sold) or **percentage depletion.** Under percentage (or **statutory**) depletion, the company deducts a stated percentage of gross income as depletion expense. This percentage varies, depending on the type of natural resource, from a minimum of 5% to a maximum of 22%. Also, the total depletion over the life of the asset for income tax purposes may exceed the cost of the asset less the expected residual value. Therefore, most companies use percentage depletion for income tax purposes and cost depletion for financial reporting. The percentage depletion in excess of cost depletion results in a permanent tax difference, as we discuss in Chapter 19.

SECURE YOUR KNOWLEDGE 11-2

- When assets are not purchased or disposed of on the first or last day of the fiscal year, depreciation may be allocated to the partial periods by:
  - Computing depreciation to the nearest whole month,
  - Computing depreciation to the nearest whole year, or
  - Computing one-half year's depreciation on all assets purchased or sold during the year.
- When the book value of property, plant, and equipment may not be recoverable, a company should:
  - Determine if an impairment exists by comparing the undiscounted cash flows to the book value of the asset, and
  - If an impairment has occurred, measure and record the impairment loss as the difference between the book value of the asset and the fair value of the asset.
- For income tax reporting, a company uses the Modified Accelerated Cost Recovery System (MACRS), an accelerated depreciation method in which assets are placed in defined recovery periods (useful lives) and depreciation is determined by applying predetermined depreciation rates to the cost of the asset. Alternatively, it may use the straight-line depreciation method.
- A change in depreciation method (e.g., straight-line to accelerated method) or any change in the estimates used to compute depreciation (e.g., residual value, service life) are accounted for prospectively.
- A correction of an error in depreciation is accounted for as a prior period restatement.
- Depletion of the cost of a natural resource is recorded using the activity method with the journal entry typically made directly to an inventory account.

SUMMARY

At the beginning of the chapter, we identified several objectives you would accomplish after reading the chapter. The objectives are listed below, each followed by a brief summary of the key points in the chapter discussion.

1. **Identify the factors involved in depreciation.** To record depreciation, a company considers the asset cost, its service life, its residual value, and the method of cost allocation.
2. **Explain the alternative methods of cost allocation, including time-based and activity-based methods.** Accounting principles require that the method of cost allocation be systematic and rational. The available methods include time-based methods, including straight-line, sum of the years' digits, and declining balance, and activity (or use) methods.
3. **Record depreciation.** A company includes depreciation on manufacturing assets as a cost of the inventory produced and records the depreciation as an increase to the Work in Process Inventory account. Depreciation on the remaining assets is expensed in the period.
4. **Explain the conceptual issues regarding depreciation methods.** The choice of a depreciation method has an impact on a company's income measurement and asset valuation. The method should be chosen so that it matches the cost of the asset against the benefits the asset produces. Additional factors that should be considered are repair and maintenance costs, changing prices, and the risk associated with the cash flows from the asset. Also, the rate of return on the asset increases as it ages.
5. **Understand the disclosure of depreciation.** A company is required to disclose depreciation expense for the period, balances of major classes depreciable assets by nature or function, accumulated depreciation either by major classes or in total, and a general description of the method or methods used in computing depreciation.
6. **Understand additional depreciation methods, including group and composite depreciation.** Group depreciation is used for homogeneous assets, whereas composite depreciation is used for heterogeneous assets. In both cases the individual assets are capitalized in one asset account and this asset is treated as a single asset for depreciation. A gain or loss on disposal is only recognized when the final individual asset is disposed of.

7. **Compute depreciation for partial periods.** Depreciation may be computed to the nearest whole month or to the nearest whole year. Alternatively, one-half year's depreciation may be computed on all assets purchased or sold during the year.
8. **Explain the impairment of property, plant, and equipment.** A company must review its property, plant, and equipment for impairment whenever events or changes in circumstances indicate the book value of the asset may not be recoverable. If the total expected cash flows (undiscounted) are less than the book value of the asset, an impairment loss is recognized. The impairment loss is the difference between the asset's book value and its lower fair value.
9. **Understand depreciation for income tax purposes.** Depreciation for income tax purposes uses the Modified Accelerated Cost Recovery System (MACRS). MACRS usually involves a shorter life, an accelerated method (except for buildings), and does not recognize a residual value.
10. **Explain changes and corrections of depreciation.** A change in an estimate of the residual value or the service life of a currently owned asset is accounted for prospectively. A change in the depreciation method for currently owned assets is accounted for prospectively. Adoption of a new depreciation method for newly acquired assets must be disclosed in the notes to the financial statements. A correction of an error in depreciation is treated as a prior period restatement.
11. **Understand and record depletion.** Depletion is the allocation of the depletable cost for the consumption of a natural resource asset to the periods in which the benefits are received. A company normally records depletion using an activity method.

ANSWERS TO REAL REPORT QUESTIONS

Real Report 11-1 Answers

1. Straight-line depreciation is the most widely used and easily understood of all the depreciation methods. The straight-line method tends to produce higher income and stockholders' equity amounts compared with the accelerated methods. Furthermore, many of Anheuser-Busch's fixed assets (land, buildings, machinery, and equipment) may provide benefits evenly over time, which is consistent with the results of the straight-line method. Additionally, any benefit derived from using an alternative depreciation method may not exceed the increased costs associated with that method. Finally, while Anheuser-Busch may use the straight-line method for financial reporting purposes, it is still free to use the IRS's modified accelerated cost recovery system (an accelerated method that would produce a higher amount of depreciation expense and lower taxable income relative to the straight-line method) for tax purposes.

2. The average age of Anheuser-Busch's property, plant, and equipment can be estimated by dividing accumulated depreciation by the annual depreciation expense. For Anheuser-Busch, the average age of its property, plant, and equipment at the end of 2004 is 9.2 years ($8,565.1 ÷ $932.7).

QUESTIONS

Q11-1 Distinguish among the use of the terms *depreciation*, *depletion*, and *amortization*.

Q11-2 Briefly explain the meaning of the four factors that are involved in the computation of a company's periodic charge for depreciation.

Q11-3 What is the *depreciation base*?

Q11-4 What is the objective of accounting for depreciation?

Q11-5 Explain how recording depreciation affects a company's (a) income statement, (b) balance sheet, and (c) statement of cash flows.

Q11-6 Does recording depreciation generate funds for the replacement of the asset? Explain.

Q11-7 Under what circumstances is depreciation a fixed cost or a variable cost?

Q11-8 What are the primary causes of depreciation? For each cause, indicate which depreciation method may be most appropriate. Would it be desirable to require all companies to use the same method?

Q11-9 Under what circumstances are accelerated methods of depreciation most appropriate?

Q11-10 Compare the group and composite methods of depreciation.

Q11-11 Under what circumstances is an asset's depreciation amount not included in total in a company's current income statement?

Q11-12 In a year in which the cost of replacing an asset rises, should a company record depreciation for that asset? Why?

Q11-13 A company should use an accelerated depreciation method because of the large decline in the value of an asset early in its life. Evaluate this statement.

Q11-14 The manager of a utility stated that since its transmission lines are kept in good condition by regular repairs and maintenance and their efficiency remains constant, the lines do not depreciate. Do you agree with this statement?

Q11-15 What disclosures of depreciation are required in a company's financial statements and the accompanying notes?

Q11-16 Why might depreciation on a company's financial statements be different from depreciation the company computed for income tax purposes?

Q11-17 How does a company's depletion for income tax purposes vary from its depletion for financial reporting purposes?

MULTIPLE CHOICE (AICPA Adapted)

Select the best answer for each of the following.

M11-1 A method that excludes residual value from the base for the depreciation calculation is
a. Straight-line
b. Sum-of-the-years'-digits
c. Double-declining-balance
d. Productive-output

Items 2 through 4 are based on the following information:

Vorst Corporation's schedule of depreciable assets at December 31, 2007 was as follows:

Asset	Cost	Accumulated Depreciation	Acquisition Date	Residual Value
A	$100,000	$ 64,000	2006	$20,000
B	55,000	36,000	2005	10,000
C	70,000	33,600	2005	14,000
	$225,000	$133,600		$44,000

Vorst takes a full year's depreciation expense in the year of an asset's acquisition, and no depreciation expense in the year of an asset's disposition. The estimated useful life of each depreciable asset is five years.

M11-2 Vorst depreciates asset A on the double-declining-balance method. How much depreciation expense should Vorst record in 2008 for asset A?
a. $32,000
b. $25,600
c. $14,400
d. $6,400

M11-3 Using the same depreciation method as used in 2005, 2006, and 2007, how much depreciation expense should Vorst record in 2008 for asset B?
a. $6,000
b. $9,000
c. $11,000
d. $12,000

M11-4 Vorst depreciates asset C by the straight-line method. On June 30, 2008, Vorst sold asset C for $28,000 cash. How much gain (loss) should Vorst record in 2008 on the disposal of asset C?
a. $2,800
b. ($2,800)
c. ($5,600)
d. ($8,400)

M11-5 The composite depreciation method
a. Is applied to a group of homogeneous assets
b. Is an accelerated method of depreciation
c. Does not recognize gain or loss on the retirement of single assets in the group
d. Excludes residual value from the base of the depreciation calculation

M11-6 On July 1, 2006, Mundo Corporation purchased factory equipment for $50,000. Residual value was estimated at $2,000. The equipment will be depreciated over 10 years using the double-declining-balance method. Counting the year of acquisition as one-half year, Mundo should record 2007 depreciation expense of
a. $7,680
b. $9,000
c. $9,600
d. $10,000

M11-7 A fixed asset with a five-year estimated useful life is sold during the second year. How would the use of the straight-line method of depreciation instead of the double-declining-balance method of depreciation affect the amount of gain or loss on the sale of the fixed asset?

	Gain	Loss
a.	No effect	No effect
b.	No effect	Increase
c.	Decrease	Increase
d.	Increase	Decrease

M11-8 Crowder Company acquired a tract of land containing an extractable natural resource. Crowder is required by the purchase contract to restore the land to a condition suitable for recreational use after it has extracted the natural resource. Geological surveys estimate that the recoverable reserves will be 5,000,000 tons and that the land will have a value of $1,000,000 after restoration. Relevant cost information follows:

Land	$9,000,000
Estimated restoration costs	1,500,000

If Crowder maintains no inventories of extracted material, what should be the depletion expense per ton of extracted material?

a. $2.10   c. $1.80
b. $1.90   d. $1.60

M11-9 A machine with a four-year estimated useful life and an estimated 15% residual value was acquired on January 1. Would depreciation expense using the sum-of-the-years'-digits method be higher or lower than depreciation expense using the double-declining-balance method in the first and second years?

	First year	Second year
a.	Higher	Higher
b.	Higher	Lower
c.	Lower	Higher
d.	Lower	Lower

M11-10 At the end of the expected useful life of a depreciable asset with an estimated 15% residual value, the accumulated depreciation would equal the original cost of the asset under which of the following depreciation methods?

	Straight-line	Sum-of-the-years'-digits
a.	Yes	Yes
b.	No	No
c.	Yes	No
d.	No	Yes

EXERCISES

E11-1 *Depreciation Methods* The Gruman Company purchased a machine for $220,000 on January 2, 2004. It made the following estimates:

Service life	5 years or 10,000 hours
Production	200,000 units
Residual value	$20,000

In 2007, the company uses the machine for 1,800 hours and produces 44,000 units.

Required
Compute the depreciation for 2007 under each of the following methods:
1. Straight-line
2. Hours worked
3. Units of output

E11-2 *Depreciation Methods* The Sorter Company purchased equipment for $200,000 on January 2, 2007. The equipment has an estimated service life of eight years and an estimated residual value of $20,000.

Required
Compute the depreciation for 2007 under each of the following methods:
1. Straight-line
2. Sum-of-the-years'-digits
3. Double-declining-balance
4. Compute the company's return on assets (net income divided by average total assets, as we discussed in Chapter 6) for each method in 2007 if the income before depreciation is $100,000. For simplicity, use ending assets, and ignore interest, income taxes, and other assets.

E11-3 *Acquisition Cost and Depreciation* Reveille, Inc. purchased Machine #204 on April 1, 2007 and placed the machine into production on April 3, 2007. The following information is relevant to Machine #204:

Price	$60,000
Freight-in costs	2,500
Preparation and installation costs	3,900
Labor costs during regular production operation	10,200
Credit terms	2/10, n/30
Total productive output	138,500 units

The company expects that the machine could be used for 10 years, after which the salvage value would be zero. However, Reveille, Inc. intends to use the machine only eight years, after which it expects to be able to sell it for $9,800. The invoice for Machine #204 was paid April 10, 2007. The number of units produced in 2007 and 2008 were 23,200 and 29,000, respectively. Reveille computes depreciation to the nearest whole month.

Required

Compute the depreciation for the years indicated, using the following methods (round your answer to the nearest dollar):
1. 2007: Units of production
2. 2008: Sum-of-the-years'-digits method (*Contributed by Norma C. Powell*)

E11-4 *Depreciation Methods* The Nickle Company purchased an asset for $17,000 on January 2, 2007. The asset has an expected residual value of $1,000. The depreciation expense for 2007 and 2008 is shown next for three alternative depreciation methods:

Year	Method A	Method B	Method C
2007	$4,000	$6,400	$6,375
2008	4,000	4,800	3,984

Required
1. Which depreciation method is the company using in each example?
2. Compute the depreciation expense for 2009 and 2010 under each method.

E11-5 *Depreciation and Rate of Return* The Burrell Company purchased a machine for $20,000 on January 2, 2007. The machine has an estimated service life of five years and a zero estimated residual value. The asset earns income before depreciation and income taxes of $10,000 each year. The tax rate is 30%.

Required 🖎

Compute the rate of return earned (on the average net asset value) by the company each year of the asset's life under the straight-line and the double-declining-balance depreciation methods. Assume that the machine is the company's only asset.

E11-6 *Determination of Acquisition Cost* On January 1, 2006, the Emming Corporation purchased some machinery. The machinery has an estimated life of 10 years and an estimated residual value of $5,000. The depreciation on this machinery was $20,000 in 2008.

Required

Compute the acquisition cost of the equipment under the following depreciation methods:
1. Straight-line
2. Sum-of-the-years'-digits
3. Double-declining-balance

E11-7 *Group Depreciation* The Loban Company purchased four cars for $9,000 each, and expects that they would be sold in three years for $1,500 each. The company uses group depreciation on a straight-line basis.

Required
1. Prepare journal entries to record the acquisition and the first year's depreciation.
2. If one of the cars is sold at the beginning of the second year for $7,000, what journal entry is required?

E11-8 *Composite Depreciation* The Wilcox Company acquires four machines that have the following characteristics:

Machine	Cost	Estimated Residual Value	Estimated Service Life
A	$26,000	$2,000	6 years
B	19,000	1,000	9
C	30,000	5,000	5
D	28,000	—	7

Required
1. Prepare journal entries to record the acquisition and the first year's depreciation, assuming that the composite method is used on a straight-line basis.
2. If the company sells machine B after four years for $10,000, prepare the journal entry.
3. What arguments may be used to support the composite depreciation method?

E11-9 **AICPA Adapted** *Depreciation* On January 2, 2007, Lapar Corporation purchased a machine for $50,000. Lapar paid shipping expenses of $500, as well as installation costs of $1,200. The company estimated that the machine would have a useful life of 10 years and a salvage value of $3,000. In January 2008, the company made additions costing $3,600 to the machine in order to comply with pollution-control ordinances. These additions neither prolonged the life of the machine nor increased the salvage value.

Required 🖎

If Lapar records depreciation under the straight-line method, how much is the depreciation expense for 2008?

E11-10 *Partial Periods* On May 10, 2007, the Horan Company purchased equipment for $25,000. The equipment has an estimated service life of five years and zero residual value. Assume that straight-line depreciation is used.

Required

Compute the depreciation for 2007 for each of the following four alternatives:
1. The company computes depreciation to the nearest day. (Use 12 months of 30 days each.)
2. The company computes depreciation to the nearest month. Assets purchased in the first half of the month are considered owned for the whole month.
3. The company computes depreciation to the nearest whole year. Assets purchased in the first half of the year are considered owned for the whole year.
4. The company records one-half year's depreciation on all assets purchased during the year.

E11-11 *Asset Impairment* On January 1, 2003, the Vallahara Company purchased machinery for $650,000 which it installed in a rented factory. It is depreciating the machinery over 12 years by the straight-line method to a residual value of $50,000. Late in 2007, because of increasing competition in the industry, the company believes that its asset may be impaired and will have a remaining useful life of five years, over which it estimates the asset will produce total cash inflows of $1,000,000 and will incur total cash outflows of $825,000. The cash flows are independent of the company's other activities and will occur evenly each year. The company is not able to determine the fair value based on a current selling price of the machinery. The company's discount rate is 10%.

Required

1. Prepare schedules to determine whether, at the end of 2007, the machinery is impaired and, if so, the impairment loss to be recognized.
2. If the machinery is impaired, prepare the journal entry to record the impairment.

E11-12 *Depreciation for Financial Statements and Income Tax Purposes* The Dinkle Company purchased equipment for $50,000. The equipment has an estimated residual value of $5,000 and an expected useful life of 10 years. The company uses straight-line depreciation for its financial statements.

Required

What is the difference between the company's income before taxes reported on its financial statements and the taxable income reported on its tax return in each of the first two years of the asset's life if the asset was purchased on January 2, 2007 and its MACRS life is five years?

E11-13 *Changes and Corrections of Depreciation* The Bailand Company purchased a building for $210,000 that had an estimated residual value of $10,000 and an estimated service life of 10 years. The company purchased the building four years ago, and has used straight-line depreciation. At the beginning of the fifth year (before it records depreciation for the year), the following *independent* situations occur:
1. The company estimates that the asset has 8 years' life remaining (for a total of 12 years).
2. The company changes to the sum-of-the-years'-digits method
3. The company discovers that the estimated residual value has been ignored in the computation of the depreciation.

Required

For each of the independent situations, prepare all the journal entries relating to the building for the fifth year. Ignore income taxes.

E11-14 *Depletion* The Feller Company purchased a site for a limestone quarry for $100,000 on January 2, 2007. It estimates that the quarry will yield 400,000 tons of limestone. It estimates that its retirement obligation has a fair value of $20,000, after which the land could be sold for $10,000. In 2007, 80,000 tons were quarried and 60,000 tons sold. Costs of production (excluding depletion) are $4 per ton.

Required

1. Compute the depletion cost per ton.
2. Compute the total cost of the inventory at December 31, 2007.
3. Compute the total cost of goods sold for 2007.

E11-15 **AICPA Adapted** *Depletion* The Lorton Company acquired land containing coal. Lorton will restore the land to a condition suitable for recreational use after it has extracted the coal. Geological surveys estimate that the recoverable reserves will be 4,000,000 tons and that the land will have a value of $1 million after restoration. Relevant cost information follows:

Land	$12,000,000
Estimated fair value of retirement obligation	1,200,000

Required

If Lorton maintains no inventories of coal, what is the depletion expense per ton of coal?

PROBLEMS

P11-1 *Depreciation Methods* The Winsey Company purchased equipment on January 2, 2007 for $700,000. The equipment has the following characteristics:

Estimated service life	20 years	Estimated residual value	$50,000
	100,000 hours		
	950,000 units of output		

During 2007 and 2008, the company used the machine for 4,500 and 5,500 hours, respectively, and produced 40,000 and 60,000 units, respectively.

Required

Compute the depreciation for 2007 and 2008 under each of the following methods:
1. Straight-line
2. Hours worked
3. Units of output
4. Sum-of-the-years'-digits
5. Double-declining-balance
6. 150%-declining-balance
7. Compute the company's return on assets (net income divided by average total assets, as discussed in Chapter 6) for each method for 2007 and 2008, assuming that income before depreciation is $100,000. For simplicity, use ending assets, and ignore interest, income taxes, and other assets.

P11-2 *Depreciation Methods* The Lord Company purchased a machine on January 2, 2007 for $70,000. The machine had an expected residual value of $10,000, an expected life of eight years or 24,000 hours, and a capacity to produce 100,000 units. During 2007, the company produced 12,000 units in 2,500 hours. In 2008, the company produced 15,000 units in 3,000 hours.

Required

Prepare a schedule showing the depreciation for 2007 and 2008 and the book value of the asset at the end of 2007 and 2008 for each of the following methods:
1. Straight-line
2. Hours worked
3. Units of output

P11-3 *Depreciation Methods* The Sayers Company purchased a building for $250,000 on January 2, 2007. The building has an expected residual value of $20,000 at the end of its expected life of 20 years.

Required

Prepare a schedule showing the depreciation for 2007 and 2008 and the book value on December 31, 2007 and December 31, 2008 for each of the following methods:
1. Straight-line
2. Sum-of-the-years'-digits
3. Double-declining-balance

4. 150%-declining-balance
5. Compute the company's return on assets (net income divided by average total assets, as discussed in Chapter 6) for each method in 2007 and 2008 assuming that income before depreciation is $50,000. For simplicity, use ending assets, and ignore interest, income taxes, and other assets. Why does the rate of return increase each year?

P11-4 Fixed Percentage of Declining Balance The Tubbs Company purchased a machine for $8,000 that has an estimated residual value of $1,000 and a life of three years.

Required
1. Compute the depreciation rate under the fixed-percentage-of-the-declining-balance method.
2. Compute the depreciation for each year of the asset's life.

P11-5 Changing Depreciation The Kam Company purchased a machine on January 2, 2007 for $20,000. The machine had an expected life of eight years and a residual value of $300. The double-declining-balance method of depreciation is used.

Required
1. Compute the depreciation for each year of the asset's life.
2. Assuming that the company has a policy of always changing to the straight-line method at the midpoint of the asset's life, compute the depreciation for each year of the asset's life.
3. Assuming that the company always changes to the straight-line method at the beginning of the year when the annual straight-line amount exceeds the double-declining-balance amount, compute the depreciation for each year of the asset's life.

P11-6 Cost of Asset and Depreciation Method The Heist Company purchased a machine on January 2, 2007 and uses the 150%-declining-balance depreciation method. The machine has an expected life of 10 years and an expected residual value of $5,000. The following costs relate to the acquisition and use of the machine during the first year of its operations:

Invoice price	$50,000	Testing	$1,100
Discounts available and taken	1,000	Normal spoilage of materials during	
Freight	700	the year	750
Installation	900	Abnormal spoilage of materials	
		during the year	250
		Wages of machine operator	15,000

Required
Compute the depreciation expense for 2007 and 2008.

P11-7 Depreciation and Partial Periods The following assets are owned by the Dinnell Company:

	Asset		
	A	B	C
Year purchased	2005	2006	2007
Cost	$20,000	$40,000	$100,000
Expected life	5 years	8 years	10 years
Residual value	$2,000	—	$10,000
Depreciation method	Straight-line	Sum-of-the-years'-digits	Double-declining-balance

In the year of acquisition and retirement of an asset, the company records depreciation for one-half year. During 2008, asset A was sold for $7,000.

Required
Prepare the journal entries to record depreciation on each asset for 2005 through 2008 and the sale of asset A.

P11-8 Group and Composite Depreciation The Cheadle Company purchased a fleet of 20 delivery trucks for $8,000 each on January 2, 2007. It decided to use composite depreciation on a straight-line basis, and calculated the depreciation from the following schedule:

Year	Number of Trucks to Be Retired at Year-End	Estimated Residual Value per Truck
2008	2	$4,000
2009	6	4,000
2010	8	2,000
2011	4	—

The company actually retired the trucks according to the following schedule (assume each truck was retired at the beginning of the year):

Year	Number of Trucks Retired	Total Proceeds from Retirements
2008	1	$ 4,000
2009	3	11,000
2010	6	19,000
2011	5	6,000
2012	3	4,000
2013	2	1,000

Required
1. Prepare the journal entries necessary to record the preceding events.
2. Assume that the company expected all the trucks to last four years and be retired for $1,600 each. Using group depreciation, prepare journal entries for all six years, assuming the company retired the trucks as shown by the latter schedule.

P11-9 *Composite Depreciation* The Borrell Company purchased four delivery trucks on January 2, 2007 for $22,000 each. The company expected two of the trucks to last five years and have a residual value of $3,500 each. The other two trucks had an expected life of eight years and no residual value. The company uses straight-line depreciation on a composite basis.

Required
Prepare journal entries to record the following events:
1. January 1, 2009. One of the two trucks expected to last five years is destroyed in an accident. The truck was not insured and the scrap value is $400.
2. January 5, 2009. A new truck is acquired for $26,000. It has an expected life of four years and a residual value of $3,920.
3. Depreciation expense for 2009.

P11-10 *Asset Impairment* On January 1, 2002, the Borstad Company purchased a factory for $180,000 and machinery for $1 million. It is depreciating the factory over 30 years and the machinery over 20 years, both by the straight-line method to zero residual values. Late in 2007, because of technological changes in the industry and reduced selling prices for its products, the company believes that its asset(s) may be impaired and will have a remaining useful life of eight years. The cash flows from the factory and machinery are not separable, and are independent of the company's other activities. The company estimates that the asset will produce cash inflows of $400,000 and will incur cash outflows of $295,000 each year for the next 8 years. It is not able to determine the fair value of the asset based on a current selling price of the factory and machinery. The company's discount rate is 12%.

Required
1. Prepare schedules to determine whether, at the end of 2007, the machinery is impaired and, if so, the impairment loss to be recognized.
2. Prepare the journal entry to record the impairment.
3. How would your answer to Requirement 1 change if the discount rate was 16% and the cash flows were expected to continue for 6 years?
4. How would your answer change if management planned to implement efficiencies that would save $10,000 each year?

P11-11 *Depreciation for Financial Statements and Income Tax Purposes* The Hunter Company purchased a light truck on January 2, 2007 for $18,000. The truck, which will be used for deliveries, has the following characteristics:

Estimated life: 5 years
Estimated residual value: $3,000
Depreciation for financial statements: straight-line
Depreciation for income tax purposes: MACRS (three-year-life)

From 2007 through 2011, each year, the company had sales of $100,000, cost of goods sold of $60,000, and operating expenses (excluding depreciation) of $15,000. The truck was disposed of on December 31, 2011 for $2,000.

Required
1. Prepare an income statement for financial reporting through pretax accounting income for each of the five years, 2007 through 2011.
2. Prepare, instead, an income statement for income tax purposes through taxable income for each of the five years, 2007 through 2011.
3. Compare the total income for all five years under Requirement 1 and Requirement 2.

P11-12 *Depletion* On January 2, 2007, the Whistler Company purchased land for $450,000, from which it is estimated that 400,000 tons of ore could be extracted. It estimates that it will cost $80,000 to restore the land, after which it could be sold for $30,000.

During 2007, the company mined 80,000 tons and sold 50,000 tons. During 2008, the company mined 100,000 tons and sold 120,000 tons. At the beginning of 2009, the company spent an additional $100,000, which increased the reserves by 60,000 tons. In 2009, the company mined 140,000 tons and sold 130,000 tons. The company uses a FIFO cost flow assumption.

Required
1. Calculate the depletion included in the income statement and ending inventory for 2007, 2008, and 2009.
2. Prepare the natural resources section of the balance sheet on December 31, 2007, 2008, and 2009, assuming that an accumulated depletion account is used.

P11-13 *Depletion* On July 1, 2007, the Amplex Company purchased a coal mine for $2 million. The estimated capacity of the mine was 800,000 tons. During 2007, the company mines 10,000 tons of coal per month and sells 9,000 tons per month. The selling price is $30 per ton and production costs (excluding depletion and depreciation) are $8 per ton. At the end of the mine's life, it is expected that it will cost $300,000 to restore the land, after which it can be sold for $100,000. The company also purchased some temporary housing for the miners at a cost of $170,000. The housing has an expected life of 10 years but is expected to be sold for $10,000 at the end of the mine's life. The company uses the FIFO cost flow assumption.

Required
1. Compute the company's expenses included on the 2007 income statement.
2. Compute the cost of the company's inventory at December 31, 2007.
3. In January 2008 a new estimate indicated that the capacity of the mine was only 500,000 tons at that time. Compute the company's expenses included on the 2008 income statement if the company mines and sells 10,000 tons per month.

P11-14 *Changes and Corrections of Depreciation* During 2007, the controller of the Ryel Company asked you to prepare correcting journal entries for the following three situations:

1. Machine A was purchased for $50,000 on January 1, 2002. Straight-line depreciation has been recorded for five years, and the Accumulated Depreciation account has a balance of $25,000. The estimated residual value remains at $5,000, but the service life is now estimated to be one year longer than estimated originally.
2. Machine B was purchased for $40,000 on January 1, 2005. It had an estimated residual value of $5,000 and an estimated service life of 10 years. It has been depreciated under the double-declining-balance method for two years. Now, at the beginning of the third year, Ryel has decided to change to the straight-line method.
3. Machine C was purchased for $20,000 on January 1, 2006. Double-declining-balance depreciation has been recorded for one year. The estimated residual value of the machine is $2,000 and the estimated service life is five years. The computation of the depreciation erroneously included the estimated residual value.

Required
Prepare any necessary correcting journal entries for each situation. Also prepare the journal entry necessary for each situation to record the depreciation for 2007. (Assume that the debit is to Depreciation Expense.)

P11-15 **AICPA Adapted** *Adjusting Entries* You are engaged in the examination of the financial statements of the Madle Corporation for the year ended December 31, 2007. The schedules for the property, plant, and equipment and the related accumulated depreciation accounts that follow have been prepared by the client. You have checked the opening balances to your prior year's audit workpapers. Your examination reveals the following information:

1. All equipment is depreciated on the straight-line basis (no salvage value taken into consideration) using the following estimated lives: buildings 25 years, all other items 10 years. The company's policy is to take one-half year's depreciation on all asset acquisitions and disposals during the year.
2. The company completed the construction of a wing on the plant building on June 30. The useful life of the building was not extended by this addition. The lowest construction bid received was $17,500, the amount recorded in the Buildings account. Company personnel were used to construct the addition at a cost of $16,000 (materials $7,500, labor $5,500, and overhead $3,000).
3. On August 18, $5,000 was paid for paving and fencing a portion of land owned by the company and used as a parking lot for employees. The expenditure was capitalized to the Land account.
4. The amount shown in the Machinery and Equipment asset retirement column represents cash received on September 4 upon disposal of a machine purchased four years ago in July for $48,000. The bookkeeper recorded depreciation expense of $3,500 on this machine in 2007.
5. Sydney City donated land and building appraised at $10,000 and $40,000, respectively, to the Madle Corporation for a plant. On September 1, the company began operating the plant. Because no costs were involved, the bookkeeper made no entry to record the transaction.

MADLE CORP.
Analysis of Property, Plant, and Equipment, and of
Related Accumulated Depreciation Accounts
Year Ended December 31, 2007

Description	Final 12/31/06	Additions	Retirements	Per Books 12/31/07
Assets:				
Land	$ 22,500	$ 5,000	—	$ 27,500
Buildings	120,000	17,500	—	137,500
Machinery and Equipment	385,000	40,400	$26,000	399,400
	$527,500	$62,900	$26,000	$564,400
Accumulated Depreciation:				
Buildings	$ 60,000	$ 5,150*		$ 65,150
Machinery and Equipment	173,250	39,220*		212,470
	$233,250	$44,370		$277,620

*Depreciation expenses for the year

Required

Prepare the formal journal entries that you would suggest at December 31, 2007 to adjust the accounts for the transactions noted previously. Disregard income tax implications. The books have not been closed. Computations should be rounded off to the nearest dollar.

P11-16 *Comprehensive* On December 31, 2007, the Vail Company owned the following assets:

Asset	Date of Purchase	Cost	Accumulated Depreciation	Life in Years	Residual Value
Building	1/1/2005	$50,000	$ 3,750[a]	40	$ 0
Office machinery	1/1/2005	20,000	9,760[b]	10	2,000
Office fixtures	1/1/2005	30,000	20,000[c]	5	5,000

a. Straight-line depreciation
b. Double-declining-balance depreciation
c. Sum-of-the-years'-digits depreciation

The company computes depreciation and amortization expense to the nearest whole year. During 2008, the company engaged in the following transactions:

Jan. 3   Extended the building at a cost of $30,000. The extension provided an addition to the service potential of the building.

Mar. 7   Sold a piece of office machinery that had originally cost $4,000 and that had accumulated depreciation of $1,952 on December 31, 2007. The machine was sold for $3,000.

Apr. 28 Obtained a patent on an invention by paying $7,000. The company expected that the patent would provide protection against competition for 10 years.

May 16   Purchased office fixtures and office machinery for $9,200. The supplier reduced the price because of the joint purchase. If purchased separately, the office fixtures would have cost $6,000 and the office machinery $4,000. Delivery costs paid by Vail were $200. The machinery was accidentally damaged during installation and cost $230 to repair. The office fixtures have an estimated life of five years and a residual value of $250. The office machinery has an estimated life of 10 years and a residual value of $500.

Aug. 10 Exchanged the president's desk (classified as office fixtures) for a larger desk belonging to a friend of the president. The desk had cost $600 and had accumulated depreciation on December 31, 2007 of $400 and an estimated residual value of $100. The new desk had a value of $900 and $700 cash was paid.

Oct. 20 Serviced and adjusted the office machinery at a cost of $125.

Required

1. Check the accuracy of the accumulated depreciation balances at December 31, 2007. (Round to the nearest whole dollar in all requirements.)
2. Prepare journal entries to record the preceding events in 2008, as well as the year-end recording of depreciation expense.
3. Prepare an Accumulated Depreciation account for each category of assets, enter the beginning balance, post the journal entries from Requirement 2, and compute the ending balance.

P11-17 AICPA Adapted   *Comprehensive* On January 2, 2007, Brock Corporation purchased a tract of land (site number 101) with a building for $600,000. Additionally, Brock paid a real estate broker's commission of $36,000, legal fees of $6,000, and title guarantee insurance of $18,000. The closing statement indicated that the land value was $500,000 and the building value was $100,000. Shortly after acquisition, the building was razed at a cost of $75,000.

Brock entered into a $3,000,000 fixed-price contract with Barnett Builders, Inc. on March 2, 2007 for the construction of an office building on land site number 101. The building was completed and occupied on September 30, 2008. Additional construction costs were incurred as follows:

Plans, specifications, and blueprints	$12,000
Architects' fees for design and supervision	95,000

The company estimates that the building will have a 40-year life from date of completion and decides to use the 150%-declining-balance depreciation method.

To finance the construction cost, Brock borrowed $3,000,000 on March 2, 2007. The loan is payable in 10 annual installments of $300,000 plus interest at the rate of 14%. Brock's average amounts of accumulated building construction expenditures were as follows:

For the period March 2 to December 31, 2007	$ 900,000
For the period January 1 to September 30, 2008	2,300,000

Required
1. Prepare a schedule that discloses the individual costs making up the balance in the Land account with respect to land site number 101 as of September 30, 2008.
2. Prepare a schedule that discloses the individual costs that the company should capitalize in the Office Building account as of September 30, 2008. Show supporting computations in good form.
3. Prepare a schedule showing the depreciation expense computation of the office building for the year ended December 31, 2008.

P11-18 AICPA Adapted *Comprehensive* Logan Corporation, a manufacturer of steel products, began operations on October 1, 2006. The accounting department of Logan has started the fixed asset and depreciation schedule shown as follows:

Assets	Acquisition Date	Cost	Salvage	Depreciation Method	Estimated Life in Years	Depreciation Expense Year Ended September 30 2007	2008
Land A	October 1, 2006	(1) ___	N/A*	N/A	N/A	N/A	N/A
Building A	October 1, 2006	(2) ___	$47,500	Straight line	(3) ___	$14,000	(4) ___
Land B	October 3, 2006	(5) ___	N/A	N/A	N/A	N/A	N/A
Building B	Under construction	$210,000 to date	—	Straight line	30	—	(6) ___
Donated equipment	October 3, 2006	(7) ___	2,000	150% declining balance	10	(8) ___	(9) ___
Machinery A	October 3, 2006	(10) ___	5,500	Sum of the years' digits	10	(11) ___	(12) ___
Machinery B	October 1, 2007	(13) ___	—	Straight line	15	—	(14) ___

* "N/A" means "not applicable"

You have been asked to assist in completing this schedule. In addition to ascertaining that the data already on the schedule are correct, you have obtained the following information from the company's records and personnel:

1. Depreciation is computed from the first of the month of acquisition to the first of the month of disposition.
2. Land A and building A were acquired from a predecessor corporation. Logan paid $812,500 for the land and building together. At the time of acquisition, the land had an appraised value of $72,000 and the building had an appraised value of $828,000.
3. Land B was acquired on October 3, 2006 in exchange for 3,000 newly issued shares of Logan's common stock. At the date of acquisition, the stock had a par value of $5 per share and a fair value of $25 per share. During October 2006, Logan paid $10,400 to demolish an existing building on this land so that it could construct a new building.
4. Construction of building B on the newly acquired land began on October 2, 2007. By September 30, 2008 Logan had paid $210,000 of the estimated total construction costs of $300,000. Estimated completion and occupancy are July 2009.
5. Certain equipment was donated to the corporation by a local university. An independent appraisal of the equipment when donated placed the fair value at $16,000 and the salvage at $2,000.

6. Machinery A's total cost of $110,000 includes installation expense of $550 and normal repairs and maintenance of $11,000. Salvage value is estimated at $5,500. Machinery A was sold on February 1, 2008.
7. On October 1, 2007, machinery B was acquired with a down payment of $4,000 and the remaining payments to be made in ten annual installments of $4,000 each beginning October 1, 2008. The prevailing interest rate was 10%. The data that follow were abstracted from present value tables:

Present Value of $1.00 at 10%		Present Value of Annuity of $1.00 in Arrears at 10%	
10 years	0.386	10 years	6.145
11 years	0.350	11 years	6.495
15 years	0.239	15 years	7.606

Required
For each numbered item in the schedule, supply the correct amount next to the corresponding number. Round each answer to the nearest dollar. Show supporting computations in good form.

P11-19 *Errors* Soon after December 31, 2007 the auditor requested a depreciation schedule for trucks of the Jarrett Trucking Company, showing the additions, retirements, depreciation, and other data affecting the income of the company in the four-year period 2004 to 2007, inclusive. The following data were in the truck account as of January 1, 2004:

Truck no. 1	Purchased January 1, 2001	$12,000
Truck no. 2	Purchased July 1, 2001	10,400
Truck no. 3	Purchased January 1, 2003	12,800
Truck no. 4	Purchased July 1, 2003	15,000
Balance January 1, 2004		$50,200

The Accumulated Depreciation—Trucks account, previously adjusted to January 1, 2004 and duly entered in the ledger, had a balance on that date of $16,460. This amount represented the straight-line depreciation on the four trucks from the respective dates of purchase, based on a five-year life and no residual value. No debits had been made to this account prior to January 1, 2004.

Transactions between January 1, 2004 and December 31, 2007 and their record in the ledger were as follows:

1. July 1, 2004: Truck no. 1 was sold for $1,000 cash. The entry was a debit to Cash and a credit to Trucks, $1,000.
2. January 1, 2005: Truck no. 3 was traded for a larger one (no. 5) with a five-year life. The agreed purchase price was $12,000. The Jarrett Company paid the other company $1,780 cash on the transaction. The entry was a debit to Trucks, $1,780, and a credit to Cash, $1,780.
3. July 1, 2006: Truck no. 4 was damaged in a wreck to such an extent that it was sold as junk for $50 cash. Jarrett Company received $950 from the insurance company. The entry made by the bookkeeper was a debit to Cash, $1,000, and credits to Miscellaneous Revenue, $50, and Trucks, $950.
4. July 1, 2006: A new truck (no. 6) was acquired for $20,000 cash and debited at that amount to the Trucks account. The truck has a five-year life.

Entries for depreciation had been made at the close of each year as follows: 2004, $8,840; 2005, $5,436; 2006, $4,896; 2007, $4,356.

Required
1. For each of the four years, calculate separately the increase or decrease in earnings arising from the company's errors in determining or entering depreciation or in recording transactions affecting trucks.
2. Prove your work by one compound journal entry as of December 31, 2007; the adjustment of the Trucks account is to reflect the correct balances, assuming that the books have not been closed for 2007.

P11-20 **AICPA Adapted** *Comprehensive* Information for Blake Corporation's property, plant, and equipment for 2007 is:

Account Balances at January 1, 2007

	Debit	Credit
Land	$ 150,000	
Building	1,200,000	
Accumulated depreciation		$263,100
Machinery and equipment	900,000	
Accumulated depreciation		250,000
Automotive equipment	115,000	
Accumulated depreciation		84,600

<u>Depreciation Method and Useful Life</u>

Building: 150%-declining-balance; 25 years.

Machinery and equipment: Straight-line; 10 years.

Automotive equipment: Sum-of-the-years'-digits; 4 years.

Leasehold improvements: Straight-line.

The residual value of the depreciable assets is immaterial.

Depreciation is computed to the nearest month.

Transactions during 2007 and other information were as follows:

1. On January 2, 2007, Blake purchased a new car for $10,000 cash and a trade-in of a two-year-old car with a cost of $9,000 and a book value of $2,700. The new car has a cash price of $12,000; the market value of the trade-in is not known.
2. On April 1, 2007, a machine purchased for $23,000 on April 1, 2002 was destroyed by fire. Blake recovered $15,500 from its insurance company.
3. On May 1, 2007, costs of $168,000 were incurred to improve leased office premises. The leasehold improvements have a useful life of eight years. The related lease, which terminates on December 31, 2013, is renewable for an additional six-year term. The decision to renew will be made in 2013 based on office space needs at that time.
4. On July 1, 2007, machinery and equipment were purchased at a total invoice cost of $280,000; additional costs of $5,000 for freight and $25,000 for installation were incurred.
5. Blake determined that the automotive equipment comprising the $115,000 balance at January 1, 2007 would have been depreciated at a total amount of $18,000 for the year ended December 31, 2007.

Required

1. For each asset classification, prepare schedules showing depreciation and amortization expense, and accumulated depreciation and amortization that would appear on Blake's income statement for the year ended December 31, 2007 and on the balance sheet at December 31, 2007, respectively.
2. Prepare a schedule showing the gain or loss from disposal of assets that would appear in Blake's income statement for the year ended December 31, 2007.
3. Prepare the property, plant, and equipment section of Blake's December 31, 2007 balance sheet.

P11-21 AICPA Adapted *Comprehensive* The Plant Asset and Accumulated Depreciation accounts of Pell Corporation had the following balances at December 31, 2006:

	Plant Asset	Accumulated Depreciation
Land	$ 350,000	$ —
Land improvements	180,000	45,000
Building	1,500,000	350,000
Machinery and equipment	1,158,000	405,000
Automobiles	150,000	112,000

Depreciation method and useful lives:

- Land improvements: Straight-line; 15 years.
- Building: 150%-declining-balance; 20 years.
- Machinery and equipment: Straight-line; 10 years.
- Automobiles: 150%-declining-balance; 3 years.
- Depreciation is computed to the nearest month. No salvage values are recognized.

Transactions during 2007:

1. On January 2, 2007, machinery and equipment were purchased at a total invoice cost of $260,000, which included a $5,500 charge for freight. Installation costs of $27,000 were incurred.
2. On March 31, 2007, a machine purchased for $58,000 on January 3, 2003 was sold for $36,500.
3. On May 1, 2007, expenditures of $50,000 were made to repave parking lots at Pell's plant location. The work was necessitated by damage caused by severe winter weather.
4. On November 2, 2007, Pell acquired a tract of land with an existing building in exchange for 10,000 shares of Pell's $20 par common stock, which had a market price of $38 a share on this date. Pell paid legal fees and title insurance totaling $23,000. The last property tax bill indicated assessed values of $240,000 for land and $60,000 for building. Shortly after acquisition, the building was razed at a cost of $35,000 in anticipation of new building construction in 2008.
5. On December 31, 2007, Pell purchased a new automobile for $15,250 cash and trade-in of an automobile purchased for $18,000 on January 1, 2006. The new automobile has a cash value of $19,000.

Required

1. Prepare a schedule analyzing the changes in each of the plant assets during 2007, with detailed supporting computations. Disregard the related accumulated depreciation accounts.
2. For each asset classification, prepare a schedule showing depreciation expense for the year ended December 31, 2007.
3. Prepare a schedule showing the gain or loss from each asset disposal that Pell would recognize in its income statement for the year ended December 31, 2007.

P11-22 *Comprehensive* The Lurch Company's December 31, 2006 balance sheet follows:

Assets		
Cash		$ 540,000
Inventory		450,000
Prepaid rent		60,000
Machine	$500,000	
Less: Accumulated depreciation	(135,000)	365,000
		$1,415,000

Liabilities and Equities		
Accounts payable		$ 400,000
Common stock, $10 par		300,000
Additional paid-in capital		515,000
Retained earnings		200,000
		$1,415,000

During 2007, the following transactions occurred:

1. To avoid paying monthly rent of $5,000 on existing plant facilities, the company decided to buy a tract of land and construct a building of its own on it. On January 2, 2007, Lurch exchanged 6,000 shares of its common stock to acquire the land; the stock was selling for $25 per share. Construction of the building also began on January 2, 2007. At the time, Lurch borrowed funds by issuing a one-year, $500,000 note at 12% to help finance the project. The principal and interest on the note are due January 3, 2008. Construction costs (paid in cash) that occurred evenly throughout the year totaled $700,000. The building was completed on December 30, 2007 and the move-in to the new building was to occur during the next week.
2. On January 2, 2007 Lurch exchanged its one existing machine plus $50,000 for a newer machine with a fair value of $430,000. The new machine is to be depreciated using straight-line depreciation based on an economic life of five years and a residual value of $55,000.
3. Lurch uses a FIFO perpetual inventory system. Lurch sold $350,000 of its inventory for $700,000 cash, paid for its beginning accounts payable, and purchased $480,000 of inventory on account during the year.
4. On July 31, 2007, Lurch declared and paid a $2.50 per share cash dividend to its shareholders.
5. Lurch is subject to a 30% income tax rate, and income taxes are accrued at year-end.

Required

Prepare Lurch's income statement and statement of retained earnings for the fiscal year ended December 31, 2007 and a balance sheet as of December 31, 2007. Show all supporting journal entries and computations made during 2007. (*Contributed by Scott I. Jerris*)

CASES

COMMUNICATION

C11-1 Depreciation

AICPA Adapted The certified public accountant is frequently called upon by management for advice regarding methods of computing depreciation. Although the question arises less frequently, of comparable importance is whether the depreciation method should be based on the consideration of the assets as units, as a group, or as having a composite life.

Required

1. Briefly describe the depreciation methods based on treating assets as:
   a. Units
   b. A group or as having a composite life
2. Explain the arguments for and against the use of each of the two methods.
3. Explain how retirements are recorded under each of the two methods.

C11-2 Capitalization and Depreciation

AICPA Adapted Gehl Company purchased significant amounts of new equipment this year to be used in its operations. The equipment was delivered by the suppliers, installed by Gehl, and placed into operation. Gehl purchased some for cash with discounts available for prompt payments. It purchased some under long-term payment plans, for which the interest charges approximate prevailing rates. As a result, Gehl is studying its capitalization and depreciation policies.

Required

1. What costs should Gehl capitalize for the new equipment purchased this year?
2. What factors cause the equipment to lose its future economic benefit?
3. What factors should be considered in computing the equipment's depreciation expense?
4. What theoretical justifications are there for the use of accelerated depreciation methods?

C11-3 Capitalization and Depreciation

AICPA Adapted At the beginning of the year, Patrick Company acquired a computer to be used in its operations. The computer was delivered by the supplier, installed by Patrick, and placed into operation. The estimated useful life of the computer is five years, and its estimated residual (salvage) value is significant.

During the year, Patrick received cash in exchange for an automobile that was purchased in a prior year.

Required

1. a. What costs should Patrick capitalize for the computer?
   b. Explain the objective of depreciation accounting. (Do not discuss specific methods of depreciation.)
2. Explain the rationale for using accelerated depreciation methods.
3. How should Patrick account for and report the disposal of the automobile?

C11-4 Straight-Line and Composite Depreciation

AICPA Adapted Portland Co. uses the straight-line depreciation method for depreciable assets. All assets are depreciated individually, except manufacturing machinery, which is depreciated by the composite method.

During the year, Portland exchanged a delivery truck with Maine Co. for a larger delivery truck. It paid cash equal to 10% of the larger truck's value.

Required

1. Explain the factors that should influence Portland's selection of the straight-line depreciation method.
2. Explain how Portland should account for and report the truck exchange transaction.
3. a. What benefits should Portland derive from using the composite method rather than the individual basis for manufacturing machinery?
   b. How should Portland calculate the manufacturing machinery's annual depreciation expense in its first year of operation?

C11-5 Operating and Capital Expenditures

AICPA Adapted Property, plant, and equipment (plant assets) generally represent a material portion of the total assets of most companies. Accounting for the acquisition and usage of such assets is, therefore, an important part of the financial reporting process.

Required

1. Distinguish between operating (revenue) and capital expenditures and explain why this distinction is important.
2. Briefly define depreciation as used in accounting.
3. Identify the factors that are relevant in determining the annual depreciation and explain whether these factors are determined objectively or whether they are based on judgment.
4. Explain why depreciation is usually shown in the net cash flow from operating activities section of the statement of cash flows.

CREATIVE AND CRITICAL THINKING

C11-6 Depreciation Concepts

AICPA Adapted Depreciation continues to be one of the most controversial, difficult, and important problem areas in accounting.

Required

1. a. Explain the conventional accounting concept of depreciation accounting, and
   b. Discuss its conceptual merit with respect to (1) the value of the asset, (2) the amount(s) expensed, and (3) the discretion of management in selecting the method.
2. a. Explain the factors that should be considered when applying the conventional concept of depreciation to the determination of how the value of a newly acquired computer system should be assigned to

expense for financial reporting purposes. (Ignore income tax considerations for this case.)
   b. What depreciation methods might be used for the computer system?

C11-7 Depreciation Concepts

Prepare a short report that evaluates each of the following statements separately:

1. "Since our plant was shut down for part of the year, we will not depreciate it. Depreciating it for the full year would increase our costs and overstate the inventory."
2. "I think we should have increasing depreciation each period because it will increase the funds recovered near the end of the asset's life when maintenance costs are high and we will need to replace the asset. Also, I think tax rates will be higher toward the end of

the asset's life, so we will be better off to have larger depreciation then."

C11-8 Depreciation

AICPA Adapted May Manufacturing Company was organized January 2, 2007. During 2007, it has used in its reports to management the straight-line method of depreciating its plant assets.

On November 9, you are having a conference with May's officers to discuss the depreciation method to be used for income tax and stockholder reporting. The president of May has suggested the use of a new method, which he feels is more suitable than the straight-line method for the needs of the company during the period of rapid expansion of production and capacity that he foresees. The following is a schedule in which the proposed method is applied to a fixed asset with an original cost of $32,000, an estimated useful life of five years, and a scrap value of approximately $2,000.

Year	Years of Life Used	Fraction Rate	Depreciation Expense	Accumulated Depreciation, Year-End	Book Value at Year-End
1	1	1/15	$ 2,000	$ 2,000	$30,000
2	2	2/15	4,000	6,000	26,000
3	3	3/15	6,000	12,000	20,000
4	4	4/15	8,000	20,000	12,000
5	5	5/15	10,000	30,000	2,000

The president favors the new method because he has heard that:

1. It will increase the funds recovered during the years near the end of the asset's useful life when maintenance and replacement disbursements are high.
2. It will result in increased write-offs in later years, thereby reducing taxes.

Required

1. Explain the purpose and, hence, the nature of accounting for depreciation.
2. Is the president's proposal within the scope of generally accepted accounting principles? In making your decision, explain the circumstances, if any, under which the method would be reasonable and those, if any, under which it would not be reasonable.
3. The president wants your advice.
   a. Explain whether depreciation recovers or creates funds.
   b. Assume that the Internal Revenue Service accepts the proposed depreciation method in this particular case. If the proposed method were used for stockholder and tax reporting purposes, explain how it would affect the availability of funds generated by operations.

C11-9 Asset Writedowns

NBC paid $401 million for the rights to televise the 1992 Summer Olympic Games, and it was widely reported that it had a loss of more than $60 million. CBS purchased the rights to the 1992 and 1994 Winter Olympic Games for a combined $543 million. CBS reported a $322 million pretax loss on its baseball and football contracts in 1991.

Required

1. Under what conditions, if any, should NBC and CBS have written-down the value of their assets?
2. Does this situation allow opportunities for earnings management?

C11-10 Analyzing Coca-Cola's Property, Plant, and Equipment Disclosures

Refer to the financial statements and related notes of the Coca-Cola Company in Appendix A of this book.

Required

1. Which depreciation method does the company use? Why do you think the company selected this method?
2. Compute the estimated average age of the property, plant, and equipment.
3. Assuming the company estimates a residual value of 10% of the cost, compute the estimated average life of the property, plant, and equipment.
4. Recreate summary journal entries to record the transactions and events that affected property, plant, and equipment during 2004.

C11-11 Ethics and Depreciation Issues

You are auditing the financial records of a company and are reviewing the depreciation computations. Included in the assets are two buildings and numerous machines in each building. One of the buildings is used to manufacture components of toys and the other for assembly and packing, using the manufactured components as well as others purchased from suppliers. You see that the company uses straight-line depreciation over 40 years for the buildings and 20 years for the machinery. You decide to ask the CFO about these calculations, and he replies, "We use 40 years for the buildings because it is close to the 39 we use for tax. And our best guess is that we will replace the machines twice while we use the building. And the method is easy to use and most companies use it, don't they? Or have things changed that much since I was in college?" You feel as if you have annoyed the CFO with your questions, so you decide to leave. As you walk back to your office, you recall from earlier in the audit that the company uses FIFO and LIFO for different segments of its inventory and that all top-level managers receive bonuses based on reported income.

Required

From financial reporting and ethical perspectives, what depreciation methods and lives would you recommend?

RESEARCH SIMULATIONS

R11-1 Researching GAAP

Situation

The Magic Movie Company has been formed to produce films for showing in movie theaters. The president knows that there are some unusual accounting issues regarding asset valuation and income recognition and has asked for your advice.

Directions

1. Research the related generally accepted accounting principles and prepare a short memo to the president. Cite your references and applicable paragraph numbers.
2. Does this situation allow opportunities for earnings management?

R11-2 Researching GAAP

Situation

Scientific Software sells software to the oil industry. Its policy is to recognize revenue when it signs a licensing agreement for the software. It uses a 13-year amortization period for the software products it capitalizes. The president has asked you to evaluate these revenue recognition and amortization policies.

Directions

1. Research the related generally accepted accounting principles and prepare a short memo to the president. Cite your references and applicable paragraph numbers.
2. Why do you think the company might have selected a 13-year amortization period? (*Adapted from* The Wall Street Journal, *11/6/90*)

Intangibles

OBJECTIVES

After reading this chapter, you will be able to:

1 Explain the accounting alternatives for intangibles.

2 Understand the amortization or impairment of intangibles.

3 Identify research and development costs.

4 Explain the conceptual issues for research and development costs.

5 Account for identifiable intangible assets including patents, copyrights, franchises, computer software costs, and trademarks and tradenames.

6 Account for unidentifiable intangibles including internally developed and purchased goodwill.

7 Understand the disclosure of intangibles.

8 Explain the conceptual issues regarding intangibles.

Managing Intangibles Can Lead to Large Profits

With the move to a more knowledge-based economy over the last three decades, intangible assets are replacing tangible assets as the key value driver for the economy. A recent study by Accenture estimates that, on average, 60% of a company's value is tied to intangible assets. Of the executives surveyed, 49% indicated that their company primarily relies on intangible assets to create shareholder wealth; however, only 5% of executives indicated that their company had an effective system for measuring the performance of intangible assets.

Given the high degree of uncertainty in valuing the future benefits from intangibles, it is easy to see why management may often become frustrated with tracking intangible assets. Consider the recent events affecting **Merck & Co**. In September 2004, Merck withdrew its arthritis medicine, Vioxx, from the market because of a link between the medicine and increased risk of heart problems. As a result, its stock plunged more than 26%. In January 2005, Merck's stock fell 10% after a federal appeals court effectively nullified a patent and granted a competitor the right to market a version of Merck's second-biggest selling drug. Finally, Merck will soon lose patent protection on its top-selling product, the cholesterol-lowering drug Zocor.

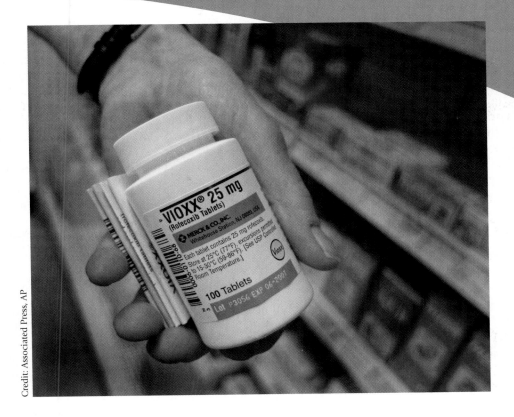

While companies like Merck may have experienced negative financial effects related to intangible assets, other companies have effectively defended the value of their intangible assets. For example, **Intergraph Corp.** reported that it has received approximately $860 million in 2003 and 2004 relating to the protection and enforcement of its intellectual property. Trying to measure, track, and analyze intangible assets is a difficult task. However, if companies can effectively manage their intangibles, they should be able to enhance company performance and increase shareholder value.

FOR FURTHER INVESTIGATION

For a discussion of intangible assets, consult the Business & Company Resource Center (BCRC):

- Developing an Effective Strategy for Managing Intellectual Assets. John Tao, Joseph Daniele, Edward Hummel, David Goldheim, Gene Slowinski, *Research-Technology Management*, 0895-6308, Jan–Feb 2005, v48, i1, p50–58.
- The High Price of Popularity. David Kelly, Monica Riva Talley, *Managing Intellectual Property*, 0960-5002, Feb. 2004, i136 p57–61.

As we discussed in Chapter 10, tangible noncurrent assets have a physical substance that can be seen and touched. In contrast, **intangible assets, which generally result from legal or contractual rights, do not have a physical substance.** Intangible and tangible noncurrent assets do have characteristics in common, as both (1) are held for use and not for investment (although they are "used" in very different ways), (2) have an expected life of more than one year, (3) derive their value from their ability to generate revenue for their owners, and (4) are expensed by a company in the periods in which it receives their benefits, if the assets have finite lives.

Intangible assets have four additional characteristics that distinguish them from tangible assets:

1. There is generally a higher degree of uncertainty regarding the future benefits that may be derived.
2. Their value is subject to wider fluctuations because it may depend, to a considerable extent, on competitive conditions.
3. They may have value only to a particular company.
4. Goodwill and intangible assets with indefinite lives are not expensed.

Accounting terminology includes only noncurrent assets in intangible assets. However, legal terminology includes as intangibles all assets without physical substance and therefore includes such current assets as accounts and notes receivable, and investments in securities. Accounting practice restricts the use of the term *intangible* to such items as patents, licenses, copyrights, franchises, computer software costs, trademarks and tradenames, and goodwill. We discuss each of these items later in the chapter.

ACCOUNTING FOR INTANGIBLES

1 Explain the accounting alternatives for intangibles.

Accounting for intangible assets follows some of the general principles used for tangible assets. They are both initially recorded at cost. As we discuss later, some intangibles are amortized and others are not amortized, but instead are reviewed for impairment. Those that are amortized are reported on a company's balance sheet at their book value, which is the cost less the accumulated amortization. The accumulated amortization results from a periodic allocation of the cost as amortization expense on the company's income statement. As we discussed in Chapter 11, amortization follows the same principle as depreciation, but is the term used specifically for intangible assets. We discuss the specific issues related to whether or not a company amortizes an intangible asset and the measurement of any amortization expense on its income statement in the following sections. The other accounting principles that we discussed in the previous two chapters also apply to intangible assets. Thus, the principles used for determining the acquisition cost, capital and operating expenditures, impairment, and disposal apply to both tangible and intangible assets. However, the measurement of any impairment may be different, as we discuss later.

Cost of Intangibles

Intangibles may be classified by a company according to whether they are *purchased* from others (externally acquired) or *internally developed*. In addition they may be classified according to whether they are *identifiable* or *unidentifiable*. **Identifiable intangible assets** include items such as patents, franchises, and trademarks, whereas the primary **unidentifiable intangible asset** is goodwill. These classifications lead to the four alternatives, and the proper method of accounting for each, which we show in Exhibit 12-1.

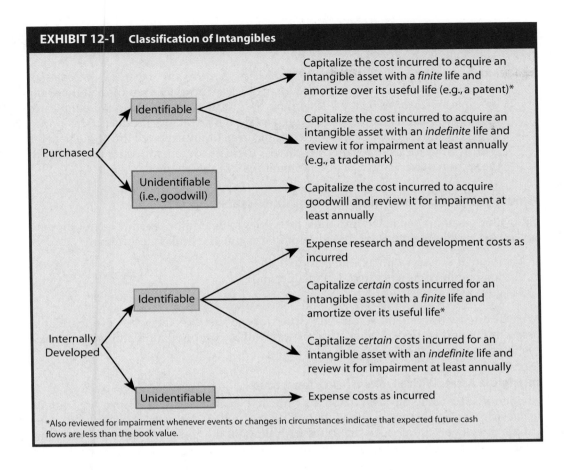

EXHIBIT 12-1   Classification of Intangibles

Purchased
- Identifiable
  - Capitalize the cost incurred to acquire an intangible asset with a *finite* life and amortize over its useful life (e.g., a patent)*
  - Capitalize the cost incurred to acquire an intangible asset with an *indefinite* life and review it for impairment at least annually (e.g., a trademark)
- Unidentifiable (i.e., goodwill)
  - Capitalize the cost incurred to acquire goodwill and review it for impairment at least annually

Internally Developed
- Identifiable
  - Expense research and development costs as incurred
  - Capitalize *certain* costs incurred for an intangible asset with a *finite* life and amortize over its useful life*
  - Capitalize *certain* costs incurred for an intangible asset with an *indefinite* life and review it for impairment at least annually
- Unidentifiable
  - Expense costs as incurred

*Also reviewed for impairment whenever events or changes in circumstances indicate that expected future cash flows are less than the book value.

Accounting for the cost of intangibles is discussed in **FASB Statement No. 142** as follows:[1]

1. *Purchased Identifiable Intangibles.* A company may purchase an intangible asset, such as a patent, from another company. The acquisition of a purchased intangible involves no special issues. It is accounted for in the same way as we discussed in Chapter 10 for the acquisition of a single asset, in a group of assets, or in an exchange of assets.

2. *Purchased Unidentifiable Intangibles.* A company capitalizes the cost of a purchased unidentifiable intangible asset. Goodwill is the major unidentifiable intangible. Goodwill can be acquired only through the purchase of another company or segment of a company. We discuss the nature of and accounting for goodwill in more detail later in this chapter.

3. *Internally Developed Identifiable Intangibles.* When a company internally develops an intangible asset, such as a patent, it can capitalize only certain costs. The costs of a patent include the legal and related costs of establishing the rights associated with a patent but *not* the costs of developing the product or process that is being patented. A company includes those latter costs in research and development costs and must expense them as incurred according to **FASB Statement No. 2.** Thus, the

---

1.   "Goodwill and Other Intangible Assets," *FASB Statement of Financial Accounting Standards No. 142* (Norwalk, Conn.: FASB, 2001).

expensing of research and development costs is an exception to the general rule of capitalization of internally developed identifiable intangibles. (We discuss this topic later in the chapter.)

4. *Internally Developed Unidentifiable Intangibles.* A company expenses the costs of internally developed unidentifiable intangibles as incurred, even though they may be expected to have benefits extending beyond the current period. Examples of these costs include employee training and design of quality products. This procedure is justified because either the costs incurred or the expected life of the benefits is difficult to measure reliably. We discuss these measurement issues more fully in the section on research and development costs in this chapter.

Amortization or Impairment of Intangible Assets

2 Understand the amortization or impairment of intangibles.

Intangible assets are separated into three categories to determine whether or not they are amortized, and how they are reviewed for impairment. The three categories are:

1. intangible assets with a finite (limited) life,
2. intangible assets with an indefinite life, and
3. goodwill.

We will discuss the general accounting issues for the first two categories of identifiable assets in the next sections. We will discuss goodwill as part of the unidentifiable intangibles section later in the chapter.

Intangible Assets With a Finite Life Are Amortized

An identifiable intangible asset that has a finite life (such as a patent) is *amortized over its useful life*. That is, the useful life is the period over which the asset is expected to contribute directly or indirectly to the future cash flows of the company. Factors that a company should consider in estimating the useful life of an intangible asset include: (1) the expected life of the asset; (2) the expected useful life of another asset that is related to the life of the intangible asset, such as the mineral rights that relate to a depleting asset; (3) any legal or contractual provisions that enable renewal or extension of the asset's legal or contractual life without substantial economic cost; (4) the effects of obsolescence, demand, competition, and other economic factors; and (5) the level of maintenance costs required to obtain the expected future cash flows from the asset.[2]

The calculation of the amortization of intangible assets follows the same principles as the depreciation of tangible assets. The amount of an intangible asset to be amortized is the cost less the residual value, if any. As with depreciation, a company selects the amortization method based on the expected pattern of benefits the intangible asset will produce. If the company cannot reliably determine the pattern, then it must use the straight-line method. As for tangible assets, the amortization (debit entry) may be either a production cost and included in Work in Process (such as a patent on a manufacturing process) or an operating expense (such as a copyright). The credit entry is made to a contra account, Accumulated Amortization: Intangibles.

Example: Amortization Suppose that Schultz Company purchases a patent for $85,000 and amortizes it using the straight-line method over 10 years (the estimated economic life) with no expected residual value. The journal entries to record the acquisition and the amortization for the first year are as follows:

Patent	85,000	
Cash		85,000
Amortization Expense (or Factory Overhead)	8,500	
Accumulated Amortization: Patent		8,500

---

2. *Ibid.,* par. 11.

The company reports the $76,500 book value ($85,000 cost − $8,500 accumulated amortization) of the patent in the intangible assets section of its balance sheet.

FASB Statement No. 142 requires a company to evaluate the estimated economic life every year to determine whether a revised estimate is warranted.[3] Such a change in estimate is accounted for by computing a new periodic amortization amount based on the current book value and the new estimated remaining economic life, as we discussed in Chapter 11.

If an intangible asset is impaired because its expected future net cash flows are less than its book value, a company must write down the asset to its fair value using the procedures of **FASB Statement No. 144**, as we discussed in Chapter 11. ♦

Intangible Assets With an Indefinite Life Are Reviewed for Impairment

Some identifiable intangible assets, such as trademarks and tradenames, have a potentially indefinite life. An intangible asset with an indefinite life is *not* amortized (until its life is no longer considered to be indefinite), but is *reviewed for impairment*.[4] A company must review these intangible assets for impairment annually, *or* more frequently when events or circumstances occur that indicate the intangible may be impaired.

A company tests an intangible asset for impairment by first estimating the fair value of the asset. The fair value of an intangible asset is the amount at which the asset could be bought or sold in a current transaction between willing parties. The quoted market price in an active market is the best measure of fair value. However, because a quoted market price is often unavailable for an intangible asset, a company may estimate the value by using the value of similar assets, or by using present value techniques.

An intangible asset is impaired when its fair value is less than its carrying value. The impairment loss is the amount by which the fair value of the intangible asset is less than its carrying value (i.e., the original cost, unless the asset was impaired in a previous period). The loss is recorded by debiting an impairment loss account and crediting the intangible asset account.

Example: Impairment Suppose the Norton Company purchased a trademark two years ago for $60,000. The company considered the trademark to have an indefinite life and it still has a carrying value of $60,000. At the end of the current year, the company determines that the fair value of the trademark is $20,000. Norton Company records the $40,000 loss ($20,000 fair value − $60,000 cost) as follows:

Impairment Loss on Trademark	40,000	
Trademark		40,000

Norton Company reports the loss as a component of income from continuing operations on its income statement. The company reports the $20,000 fair value of the trademark in the intangible asset section of its balance sheet. Every year the company must compare the fair value with the $20,000 carrying value to determine if the trademark is again impaired.

In the remaining sections of this chapter we discuss specific intangibles, starting with research and development costs. Although research and development costs are not capitalized, we discuss them first because of the impact they have on the capitalization of many other intangibles. ♦

---

3.   *Ibid.*, par. 14.
4.   *Ibid.*, par. 16. Before *FASB Statement No. 142*, all intangible assets were amortized over their economic lives, not to exceed 40 years (except those acquired before November 1, 1970, and for which there is no evidence of a decline in value or a limited economic life).

RESEARCH AND DEVELOPMENT COSTS

Many companies spend large sums each year on research and development (R&D). *FASB Statement No. 2* requires that **a company must expense all its research and development costs as incurred.**[5] Even though R&D costs often benefit future periods, the decision to require expensing in all circumstances was made primarily in the belief that uniformity would enhance *comparability* and would eliminate the possibility of income manipulation. It also avoids the *reliability* problems of how much to capitalize and over what period to amortize the capitalized costs. We evaluate the FASB's decision to require expensing of R&D costs at the end of this section.

Two issues in the expensing of R&D are the activities and costs that a company includes in each category. Research and development activities are defined by the FASB as follows:

3 Identify research and development costs.

(a) **Research** is the planned search or critical investigation aimed at discovering new knowledge with the hope that the knowledge will be useful in developing a new product or service ("product") or a new process or technique ("process") or in significantly improving an existing product or process.

(b) **Development** is the translation of research findings into a plan or design for a new product or process or for significantly improving an existing product or process, whether intended for sale or use. It includes the conceptual formulation, design, and testing of product alternatives, construction of prototypes, and operation of pilot plants. It does not include routine or periodic alterations to existing products, production lines, manufacturing processes, and other ongoing operations, even though those alterations may be improvements; it does not include market research or market testing activities.[6]

To help you understand these general definitions, we show examples of activities that are included as R&D and those that are excluded in Exhibit 12-2.

Costs of activities *excluded* from R&D are either expensed or capitalized according to the normal capitalization criteria, as we discussed in Chapter 10. When an activity is included in R&D, a company must identify the costs so that it may record the correct amount of R&D expense. The costs for the following elements of R&D activities are *included* in R&D costs, and thus are expensed as incurred:

1. Materials, equipment, and facilities
2. Personnel
3. Intangibles purchased from others
4. Contract services—the costs of services performed by others in connection with the R&D activities of an enterprise
5. Indirect costs—R&D includes a reasonable allocation of indirect costs; however, general and administrative costs that are not clearly related to R&D activities are not included as R&D costs[7]

The inclusion in R&D expense of the cost of materials, equipment, facilities, and intangibles purchased from others requires further explanation. If the items have **alternative future uses**, then a company follows normal accrual procedures. For example, a company includes the costs of R&D personnel in R&D expense as payments are made and accrued at year-end. It also records the costs of materials in inventory and then includes them as R&D expense when it uses the materials. Also, a company capitalizes the cost of a machine that has alternative future uses (even if only in other R&D projects) and *depreciates* the cost over the asset's estimated useful life. The company includes the depreciation in R&D expense.

---

5. "Accounting for Research and Development Costs," *FASB Statement of Financial Accounting Standards No. 2* (Stamford, Conn.: FASB, 1974), par. 8.

6. *Ibid.*

7. *Ibid.*, par. 9–10.

EXHIBIT 12-2   Examples of Activities Included in and Excluded from R&D

Included in R&D

(a) Laboratory research aimed at discovery of new knowledge.
(b) Searching for applications of new research findings or of other knowledge.
(c) Conceptual formulation and design of possible product or process alternatives.
(d) Testing in search for or evaluation of product or process alternatives.
(e) Modification of the formulation or design of a product or process.
(f) Design, construction, and testing of preproduction prototypes and models.
(g) Design of tools, jigs, molds, and dies involving new technology.
(h) Design, construction, and operation of a pilot plant that is not of a scale economically feasible to the company for commercial production.
(i) Engineering activity required to advance the design of a product to the point that it meets specific functional and economic requirements and is ready for manufacture.

Excluded from R&D

(a) Engineering follow-through in an early phase of commercial production.
(b) Quality control during commercial production, including routine testing of products.
(c) Troubleshooting in connection with breakdowns during commercial production.
(d) Routine, ongoing efforts to refine, enrich, or otherwise improve upon the qualities of an existing product.
(e) Adaptation of an existing capability to a particular requirement or customer's need as part of a continuing commercial activity.
(f) Seasonal or other periodic design changes to existing products.
(g) Routine design of tools, jigs, molds, and dies.
(h) Activity, including design and construction engineering, related to the construction, relocation, rearrangement, or start-up of facilities or equipment other than (1) pilot plants and (2) facilities or equipment whose sole use is for a particular research and development project.
(i) Legal work in connection with patent applications or litigation, and the sale or licensing of patents.

Source: FASB Statement No. 2, par. 9 and 10.

However, the company includes in R&D expense the costs of any materials, equipment, facilities, and intangibles purchased from others that have **no alternative future uses** in research and development or other activities. For example, if a company can use inventory or a machine only for one R&D project and so has no alternative future uses for it, the company includes the total acquisition costs in R&D expense in the period it incurs the cost.

Example: R&D Costs Assume that the Kent Company incurred the following costs for R&D activities:

Material used from inventory	$50,000
Wages and salaries	90,000
Allocation of general and administrative costs	20,000
Depreciation on building housing R&D activities	25,000
Machine purchased for R&D project that has no alternative future uses	30,000

The company includes all these costs in R&D expense and records them as follows:

Research and Development Expense	215,000	
Cash, Payables, etc.		140,000
Inventory		50,000
Accumulated Depreciation: Building		25,000

FASB Statement No. 2 does not cover the costs of R&D activities conducted for others (including the government) under a contractual arrangement. A company capitalizes these costs as incurred and expenses them when it recognizes the revenue from the contract. ♦

Conceptual Evaluation of Accounting for Research and Development Costs

The FASB considered four methods for companies to account for R&D costs when *FASB Statement No. 2* was being prepared:

1. Expense all costs when incurred
2. Capitalize all costs when incurred and amortize them over the periods expected to benefit
3. Capitalize costs when incurred if specified conditions are fulfilled and record all other costs as expenses
4. Accumulate all costs in a special category until the existence of future benefits can be determined

4 Explain the conceptual issues for research and development costs.

The first alternative is supported and the second alternative countered by the argument that there is a high degree of uncertainty about the future benefits of a company's individual R&D projects. Most projects do not result in any identifiable future benefits. Therefore, it is desirable to expense all costs in the periods incurred. In addition, it is difficult to show a direct relationship between R&D costs and specific future revenue generated. Therefore, it is not possible to *reliably* estimate the expected life and the pattern of the benefits received, and thereby determine the appropriate amortization. If R&D costs are about the same each period, the amount of the expense each period will be similar, whether the cost was capitalized and then expensed by the straight-line method or simply expensed immediately. However, immediate expensing means that the company does not record an asset on its balance sheet. This omission may lead to a very significant understatement of assets for some companies, if the costs incurred on their R&D projects often will generate future benefits.

The second alternative, capitalizing all costs as incurred, would be supported by the argument that a company undertakes R&D projects only to develop future benefits. Therefore, an asset should be recognized by capitalizing the entire costs of R&D without regard to the certainty of future benefits from individual projects. However, this approach would be inconsistent with other areas of accounting where the cost of each asset is recorded and expensed over its individual life. In addition, capitalization of the entire costs of R&D would make it difficult to develop a meaningful amortization period.

The third alternative, selective capitalization, would have desirable conceptual features. A company would accumulate the costs of each individual project. It would then capitalize and expense the costs over the life of the benefits to be received. If no such benefits were expected, the costs would be expensed immediately. Thus, R&D costs would be capitalized and expensed on the same basis as other costs. However, this alternative would be difficult to implement. What criteria for capitalization would be used? The FASB considered a number of criteria, such as definition of the product or process, technological feasibility, marketability and usefulness, economic feasibility, management action, and distortion of net income comparisons. Any criteria would have been very difficult to define and implement reliably, and would probably have led to a lack of comparability. In addition, it might be several periods after the costs have been incurred before the company could reasonably evaluate the likelihood of benefits being received.

The fourth alternative would be to classify the costs in a special category on the company's balance sheet. The two alternative categories suggested were below the assets or as a reduction of stockholders' equity. This procedure would not be desirable because it would violate the basic concepts underlying the fundamental accounting equation. It was suggested as an alternative to draw attention to the basic uncertainty surrounding the nature of R&D costs, and to delay the decision regarding capitalizing or expensing until sufficient information for a reliable decision would become available.

The FASB's choice basically was between an alternative that has desirable conceptual features but significant implementation difficulties (capitalization), and an alternative that is less desirable conceptually but is much easier to implement and is likely to lead to greater *comparability* between companies (immediate expensing). As in so many situations, the choice was between *relevance* and *reliability*. It is not surprising that the FASB decided on the latter alternative. In addition, income tax regulations allow a company to immediately expense its R&D costs, so a major difference between financial income and taxable income was eliminated.

SECURE YOUR KNOWLEDGE 12-1

- The accounting for intangible assets follows many of the same general principles as the accounting for tangible assets; however, intangible assets have unique characteristics (e.g., uncertainty regarding future benefits, wide fluctuations in value, possibility of indefinite lives) that lead to different accounting treatments.
- Purchased (externally acquired) intangible assets are recorded at their historical cost, while only *certain* costs of internally developed assets may be capitalized.
- Intangible assets with finite lives are amortized over their useful lives. Intangible assets with indefinite lives are not amortized but instead are reviewed for impairment (fair value less than carrying value) at least annually.
- Research and development (R&D) costs, which include expenditures for materials, equipment, facilities, personnel, purchased intangible assets, contract services, and other indirect costs, are required to be expensed as incurred.
- Capitalizing R&D costs has conceptual merit because these costs should lead to future benefits; however, the implementation difficulties with capitalization (it is not possible to reliably estimate the pattern of future benefits) led the FASB to decide on the more reliable, but perhaps less relevant, alternative of expensing R&D costs.

IDENTIFIABLE INTANGIBLE ASSETS

Identifiable intangible assets are those intangibles that can be purchased or sold separately from the other assets of the company. A company capitalizes the costs of identifiable intangibles (except for R&D costs). Because a company expenses R&D and operating costs, it capitalizes only certain costs of *internally developed* identifiable intangibles—not the total costs that might be related to the item. For example, it capitalizes only the direct legal costs of applying for and registering a tradename, and it expenses all indirect costs as incurred, such as advertising to promote the tradename. If a company *purchases* an identifiable intangible asset, it capitalizes the cost on the same basis as for a tangible asset by including all necessary costs. Exhibit 12-3 shows the differences between the amortization and impairment of intangible assets and the expensing of R&D costs in the period incurred. We discuss each of these identifiable intangible assets in the following sections.

> **5** Account for identifiable intangible assets including patents, copyrights, franchises, computer software costs, and trademarks and tradenames.

Patents

A patent is an exclusive right granted by the federal government giving the owner control of the manufacture, sale, or other use of an invention for 20 years from the date of filing. Patents cannot be renewed, but their effective life may be extended by obtaining new patents on modifications and improvements to the original invention.

A patent has value if it enables the company to obtain higher income by selling products at a higher price, producing products at a lower cost, or producing a product for which there is less competition. In many situations, the value of a patent is eliminated

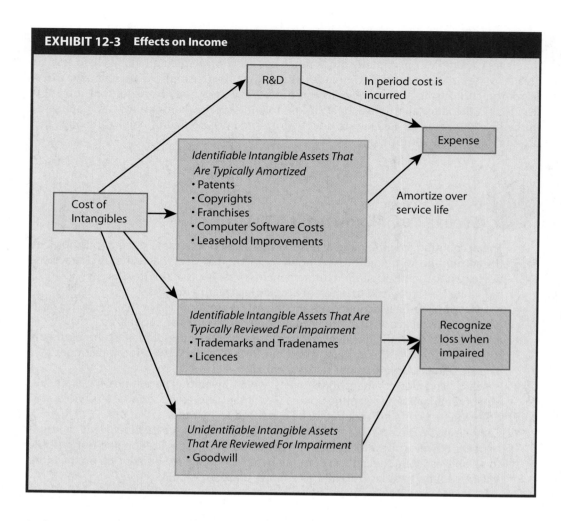

EXHIBIT 12-3   Effects on Income

R&D → In period cost is incurred

Cost of Intangibles

Identifiable Intangible Assets That Are Typically Amortized
• Patents
• Copyrights
• Franchises
• Computer Software Costs
• Leasehold Improvements

Expense

Amortize over service life

Identifiable Intangible Assets That Are Typically Reviewed For Impairment
• Trademarks and Tradenames
• Licences

Recognize loss when impaired

Unidentifiable Intangible Assets That Are Reviewed For Impairment
• Goodwill

before the end of its legal life by the actions of other companies that produce a competing product without violating the patent, or through technological change or a change in demand for the product. Therefore, a patent has a finite life. A company amortizes the cost of a patent over its expected *useful* life if that life is shorter than 20 years.[8]

Licenses often are granted to others to use the invention covered by a patent. A company accounts for amounts received under such agreements under the normal revenue recognition criteria by including them in income when earned and realizable rather than when received. A company should disclose license agreements in the notes to its financial statements if their effect on its income is material.

It may be necessary for the owner of a patent to defend it against infringement by others. A company capitalizes the costs of successfully defending the legal validity of a patent because the benefits of the patent are maintained for its remaining economic life. However, given the length of time it may take to resolve a patent infringement suit, some companies may expense the legal costs when incurred because of the uncertainty about winning the suit. If the company loses the suit, it immediately expenses all legal costs not previously expensed. It also writes off the remaining book value of the patent because there is no remaining economic value. However, if a company expenses the legal costs and then wins the suit, it does *not* make a prior period adjustment.

---

8.   Prior to 1994, the legal life of a patent was 17 years from the date of grant.

Copyrights

A copyright is a grant by the federal government covering the right to publish, sell, or otherwise control literary or artistic products for the life of the author plus 70 years.[9] Copyrights cover items such as books, music, and films. Accounting for copyrights follows the same principles as those used for patents. A copyright has a finite life. The cost is amortized over the useful life either on a straight-line basis, or on an activity basis if that is a better measure of the pattern of benefits.

It is possible that a fully amortized copyright may develop a significant value, such as in the case of some old films or music. Under current generally accepted accounting principles, which require that assets are recorded at cost, such an increase in value is not recognized in the financial statements.

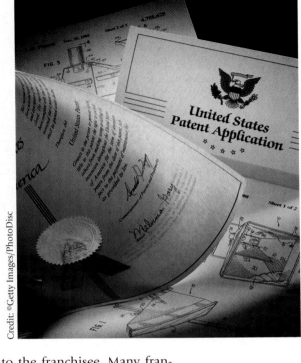

Credit: ©Getty Images/PhotoDisc

Franchises

Franchises are agreements entered into by two parties in which, for a fee, one party (the franchisor) gives the other party (the franchisee) rights to perform certain functions or sell certain products or services. In addition the franchisor may agree to provide certain services to the franchisee. Many franchises exist between governments and companies, such as a franchise to provide a monopoly service (e.g., utilities) or to use public property to provide a service (e.g., a ferry). A common example of a franchise between two companies is in the restaurant business, where many units of national chains such as **McDonald's** are locally owned and operated under the terms of a franchise agreement. Another example is the selling of name-brand items in the automotive parts market, such as **Midas Muffler.** A franchisee capitalizes the initial cost it pays to acquire the franchise, whereas it expenses the continuing franchise fees that it pays for services provided by the franchisor in subsequent years according to the normal matching criteria. If a franchise is granted in perpetuity, it would be considered to have an indefinite life and would be tested for impairment at least annually, as we discussed earlier. However, most franchises have a finite legal life that is specified in the franchise agreement. For these franchises, the franchisee amortizes the related initial franchise cost over its useful life. We discuss accounting for franchises by the franchisor in Chapter 18.

Computer Software Costs

FASB Statement No. 86 specifies the accounting for the costs of computer software to be sold or leased. There are three categories of costs associated with software that is to be sold, leased, or otherwise marketed directly or indirectly as part of a product, process, or service.[10] The first category of costs relates to the development stage. **Software production costs** are the costs of designing, coding, testing, and preparing documentation and training

---

9. Prior to 1999, the legal life of a copyright was the life of the author plus 50 years.

10. "Accounting for the Costs of Computer Software to Be Sold, Leased, or Otherwise Marketed," *FASB Statement of Financial Accounting Standards No. 86* (Stamford, Conn.: FASB, 1985). For additional discussion, see N. Erikson and D. Herskovits, "Accounting for Software Costs: Cracking the Code," *Journal of Accountancy,* November 1985, pp. 81–96.

materials. A company includes these costs in research and development expense until technological feasibility of the product is established. Because companies use different development methods, **technological feasibility is established either on the date the company completes a detailed program design or, in its absence, when it completes a working model of the product.** After this date, a company capitalizes all software production costs until the product is available for general release to customers. No software production costs may be capitalized after the product is ready for general release; they are expensed as incurred. The accounting for software production costs may be summarized as follows:

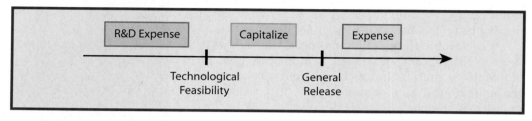

The company amortizes the capitalized software production costs incurred during the period between technological feasibility and general release over the expected life of the product, which typically will be a relatively short period, such as five years. The amortization expense is the greater of the amount calculated from either the

1. ratio of current gross revenues from the software to the total amount of current and anticipated future gross revenues from the software multiplied by the cost of the asset, or
2. straight-line method.

If the net realizable value of the software product is lower than the asset's book value, a company writes down the asset to this value and recognizes a loss. The lower value is then the new "cost" and the write-down may not be recovered. Note that two new concepts are involved. First, a new concept of amortization based on estimated revenues is introduced. Second, the lower of cost or market method is applied to this one intangible asset.

The second category of costs is the **unit cost of producing the software.** This would include amounts for the cost of the disks and duplication of the software, packaging, documentation, and training materials. A company records these unit costs as inventory and expenses them as cost of goods sold when it recognizes the related revenue. The third category of costs is the **maintenance and customer support costs** incurred after the software is released. These costs are expensed as incurred.

Conceptual Evaluation

FASB Statement No. 86 resulted in most computer software costs being expensed because, for many companies, the detailed program design occurs after the detailed logic of the program is complete and after coding has already begun. For many companies, software may be a significant, or perhaps the only, revenue-generating asset. As the U.S. economy moves toward intangible outputs and creative processes, accounting could accommodate this transition by allowing the results of a company's creative processes to be recorded as an asset when they are likely to result in probable future cash flows. Another issue is that many costs incurred before the completion of the detailed program design are not part of research and development but are incurred to perform an activity, just like other production processes. Therefore, *FASB Statement No. 86* expands the definitions of research and development established in *FASB Statement No. 2*. Finally, the amount of cost that a company may capitalize depends on how it organizes its programming process and, in particular, the date on which it establishes technological feasibility. Because the capitalization criterion is based on a point in time rather than a function, the costs capitalized may vary significantly from company to company depending on whether the coding and testing parallels, or follows, the detailed program design.

LINK TO ETHICAL DILEMMA

Quality Technology Systems (QTS) is a high-technology company that focuses on developing software that controls and manages industrial machinery used in automated manufacturing processes. As an accountant for QTS, one of your responsibilities is to determine which expenditures can be capitalized as software development costs. Because you are not an expert in software design, you rely extensively on status reports provided by the company's engineering department and have, over the years, developed a friendship with one of the engineers. Based on the latest status report, you have decided that a new wireless operating system had reached technological feasibility, which resulted in the capitalization of approximately $1,000,000 during the current quarter.

During lunch today, you mention to the engineer that you were impressed at the progress they had made on the wireless operating system. After making you promise that you would not repeat anything he says, the engineer responded that the project has really been time-consuming, and he wasn't sure if it would ever result in a functioning technology. In fact, recent setbacks had resulted in much of the previous work being scrapped and the project effectively having to start over from scratch. He further confided in you that he overheard a conversation between the CEO and the chief engineer in which the CEO instructed the engineer to achieve technological feasibility by the end of the quarter "by any means necessary." What are your responsibilities upon learning of these events?

Internal-Use Software

AICPA Statement of Position No. 98-1 specifies the accounting for the costs of internal-use computer software.[11] Costs that are incurred in the preliminary stage of development are expensed as incurred. Capitalization of costs begins when

1. the preliminary stage is completed, and
2. management agrees to fund a computer software project and
   (a) it is probable that the project will be completed, and
   (b) the software will be used to perform the function intended.

Once a company has met these capitalization criteria, it capitalizes the cost of

1. external direct costs of materials and services used in developing the internal-use software,
2. payroll costs for employees who are directly associated with the project, and
3. interest costs incurred when developing the software.

The company then amortizes the capitalized cost using the straight-line method over the estimated useful life of the software unless another method provides better matching.

---

11. "Accounting for the Costs of Computer Software Developed or Planned for Internal Use," *AICPA Statement of Position No. 98-1* (New York: AICPA, 1998).

Training costs for using the software are expensed as incurred. Costs incurred for upgrades and enhancements of the software are capitalized if they meet the capitalization criteria of the *SOP*. However, costs incurred for maintaining the software are expensed as incurred. Impairment is measured and recognized according to *FASB Statement No. 144*.

Leases and Leasehold Improvements

Leases (or leaseholds) are intangible assets because a right to use the property is held by the lessee, but the property itself is still owned by the lessor. However, capital leases are normally included on the lessee's balance sheet within its property, plant, and equipment rather than under intangible assets, as we discuss in Chapter 21. Leasehold improvements are also intangible assets of the lessee but normally are included as a separate item in its property, plant, and equipment, as we discussed in Chapter 10.

Trademarks and Tradenames

Registration of a trademark or tradename with the U.S. Patent Office establishes a right to exclusive use of a name, symbol, or other device used for product identification (e.g., **Coke**™ or **Scotch**™ **Tape**). The right lasts for 20 years and is renewable indefinitely as long as the trademark or tradename is used continuously. Therefore, it typically is considered to have an indefinite life and is not amortized (unless the company decides its useful life is no longer indefinite). The company must review the asset for impairment at least annually, as we discussed earlier.

Deferred Charges

Deferred charges (or other "noncurrent assets") is a category often used on a company's balance sheet as a catchall category in which it accumulates several individually immaterial items. Examples of items included are intangibles from any of the categories previously discussed if the company does not include intangibles as a separate category in the balance sheet. In addition, long-term prepayments such as for insurance, rent, taxes, or moving and plant rearrangement costs may be included in deferred charges. All deferred charges are amortized over their expected economic lives. As we discussed in Chapter 4, most of these deferred charges can, and should, be included in other asset categories on the company's balance sheet.

Organization Costs

When a corporation is formed, it incurs organization costs such as legal fees, stock certificate costs, underwriting fees, accounting fees, and promotional fees. Because these costs are essential to forming a corporation and the life of the company is indefinite, it can be argued that these organization costs are an intangible asset with an indefinite life.

However, **AICPA Statement of Position No. 98-5** (which we discussed in Chapter 10) requires that the costs of start-up activities (including organization costs) be expensed as incurred.[12] An argument in favor of expensing the organization costs is that once the costs have been incurred and the company is formed, all the benefits associated with the costs have been realized. However, it can be argued that the matching principle is violated because the cost of forming the company is not matched against the revenue generated by the newly formed company. Also, income tax regulations allow organization costs to be amortized and deducted from taxable income over 60 months.

---

12. "Reporting on the Costs of Start-Up Activities," *AICPA Statement of Position No. 98-5* (New York: AICPA, 1998).

LINK TO INTERNATIONAL DIFFERENCES

International accounting standards allow a company to record some internally generated intangibles as assets. Specifically, the company must classify activities leading to the generation of an intangible asset into a research and a development phase. Research costs are expensed but development costs may be capitalized if the company can demonstrate that the asset will generate probable future economic benefits. Also, the costs of items that are acquired for a particular research project and have no alternative future uses are expensed as the items are used in the project. In contrast, such costs are expensed when incurred under U.S. GAAP. Finally, international accounting standards allow intangibles to be revalued upwards. For example, in the United Kingdom, brand names such as Schweppes are accounted for in this manner.

UNIDENTIFIABLE INTANGIBLES

We discussed identifiable intangible assets in previous sections of this chapter. However, many additional intangibles of a company also contribute to its earning power. These unidentifiable intangibles are often called "goodwill." Accounting for such goodwill depends on whether it is internally developed or purchased through a transaction.

6 Account for unidentifiable tangibles, including internally developed and purchased goodwill.

Internally Developed Goodwill

All companies develop unidentifiable intangibles. For example, employees at all levels are an integral part of a company. They are a key component in using the assets and that produce the company's products and services. Superior employees may produce the products with a higher quality and enable a company to earn a higher income. Also, service companies and companies that produce computer software rely almost entirely on their employees to generate revenue, yet record no asset related to their skills and talents. This unrecorded "asset" is often referred to as "intellectual capital." Another example of an unidentifiable intangible is a company that has an advantageous geographical location. Perhaps it is closer to its raw materials or suppliers or to its major customers. Such a geographical advantage may enable the company to earn a higher income. Yet a company's balance sheet does not include assets relating to such internally developed intangibles as quality, reputation, human resources, or geographical location.[13]

Two characteristics distinguish intangibles of this type. First, they are considered to be unidentifiable because they are not separable from the identified and recorded assets. For example, the employees of the company cannot be sold to another company, and the geographical location cannot be sold without selling the other assets of the company. Second, measuring the value of these unidentifiable intangibles would be very difficult and less *reliable* than measuring the value of identifiable intangibles. Because of these two characteristics, the costs associated with such *internally developed* intangibles (internally developed goodwill) are expensed as incurred.

Purchased Goodwill

Goodwill arises when a company is purchased. It is the difference between the purchase price of the acquired company and the fair value of the reported identifiable

---

13.   A few attempts have been made to value human resources and record them on the balance sheet. See, for instance, E. H. Caplan and S. Landkich, *Human Resource Accounting* (New York: National Association of Accountants, 1974).

net assets. Goodwill is recorded only when a transaction occurs—that is, when a company (or a significant part of a company) is purchased by another company. The purchased goodwill is the price paid by the acquiring company for the unidentifiable intangibles that were internally developed by the acquired company. It is recorded as an asset by the acquiring company because a transaction has occurred that establishes a *reliable* valuation. From this perspective, goodwill is a residual valuation account for the additional value of the unidentifiable intangible assets. In other words, it is the amount paid in excess of the cost of the identifiable net assets (assets less liabilities) acquired. The capitalization of purchased goodwill is required by **FASB Statement No. 141**, which defines goodwill as the excess of the cost of an acquired entity over the net of the amounts assigned to assets acquired and liabilities assumed.[14]

Example: Recording the Purchase

The purchase of a company can be a very complex matter. To show a simple alternative, suppose that after negotiation the Sara Company purchases all the assets of the Trevor Company for $790,000 cash and the Trevor Company is dissolved. If the Trevor Company has identifiable assets with a fair value of $920,000 and liabilities with a fair value of $530,000, Sara Company would record the purchase as follows:

Identifiable Assets	920,000	
Goodwill	400,000	
Liabilities		530,000
Cash		790,000

To record an actual purchase, instead of debiting Identifiable Assets and crediting Liabilities as shown, the company would debit or credit each of the individual asset and liability accounts based on their current fair values. Also, if the Trevor Company had any "in-process" R&D, the Sara Company would expense that amount of the purchase price. Alternatively, if the Trevor Company is not dissolved, the Sara Company would record the entire purchase cost in an Investments account. Then, it would use the equity method (discussed in Chapter 15) and consolidated financial statements (discussed in advanced accounting books) to account for and report on the investment. ♦

Impairment of Goodwill

A company must review its goodwill for impairment at least annually at the reporting unit level. (Goodwill is not amortized.[15]) The reporting unit is the same as the operating segment that we discussed in Chapter 6 for segment reporting. A company must also review its goodwill for impairment whenever events or changes in circumstances occur that would more-likely-than-not reduce the fair value of the goodwill below its carrying value. Examples include: a significant adverse change in the business climate or market, a legal issue, an action by regulators, unanticipated competition, a loss of key personnel, and an expectation that a reporting unit may be sold.

A company reviews its purchased goodwill for impairment using two steps. First, it compares the fair value of the reporting unit with its book value (including goodwill).[16] The fair value of a reporting unit is the amount at which the unit could be bought or sold in a current transaction between willing parties. Sometimes this information is not available. In this case, the company might determine the reporting unit's fair value by multiplying the market price of its common stock by the number of shares outstanding (known as the *market cap*). However, the reporting unit may not have shares that trade in

---

14. "Business Combinations," *FASB Statement of Financial Accounting Standards No. 141* (Norwalk, Conn.: FASB, 2001), Appendix F.

15. Before *FASB Statement No. 142*, goodwill was amortized over its useful life, not to exceed 40 years.

16. Impairment tests must be performed on other assets of the reporting unit first, so that the resulting fair value of the reporting unit that is less than the book value must be from goodwill impairment.

an active market. In this case, estimates of the fair value may be based on valuation techniques, such as multiples of earnings or revenues, or measured as the present value of the estimated future cash flows of the reporting unit. Those cash flow estimates must be based on reasonable assumptions and should consider all available evidence.

If the fair value of the reporting unit is greater than the book value, goodwill is not impaired, and the second step is not necessary. If the fair value of the reporting unit is *less than* its book value, the second step of the impairment test must be performed to measure the *amount* of the impairment loss, if any. The second step is the recognition of an impairment loss for the amount by which the implied fair value of the goodwill is less than its carrying value.

To determine the implied fair value of the goodwill, the company first allocates the fair value of the reporting unit to all the identifiable assets and liabilities of the unit as if the unit had been acquired and the fair value was the purchase price. Then the implied fair value of the goodwill is the excess "purchase price" over the amounts assigned to the identifiable assets and liabilities. The impairment loss is the difference between the carrying value of the goodwill and the lower implied fair value of the goodwill. When the company records the impairment loss, it reduces the carrying value of the goodwill to the lower fair value.

Example: Goodwill Impairment

Suppose that the Kent Company purchased the Devon Company as a subsidiary several years ago. The Devon Company has a book value (assets minus liabilities) of $3.6 million, including goodwill of $400,000. To test for the impairment of its goodwill, the Kent Company first estimates that the fair value of the Devon Company is $3 million. Because this $3 million fair value is less than its $3.6 million book value, the Kent Company must perform the second step. If Kent allocates $2.7 million of the fair value to Devon Company's identifiable assets and liabilities, this means that $300,000 ($3 million − $2.7 million) is the implied fair value of the goodwill. Because the $300,000 implied fair value of the goodwill is $100,000 less than the $400,000 carrying value, Kent Company records the $100,000 impairment loss as follows:

Impairment Loss on Goodwill	100,000	
Goodwill		100,000

Kent Company reports the impairment loss as a separate line item on its income statement as part of income from continuing operations. It reports the new (reduced) $300,000 carrying value on its ending balance sheet. Every year, Kent Company must compare the fair value with the $300,000 carrying value to determine if the goodwill is again impaired.

Note also that the book value of the Devon Company's identifiable net assets is $3,200,000 ($3,600,000 − $400,000 goodwill). Because the fair value of the identifiable net assets is $2,700,000, the Kent Company should recognize additional impairment losses of $500,000 ($2,700,000 − $3,200,000) on the relevant assets. It is likely that other intangible assets recorded at the time of the purchase of the Devon Company are impaired. Other assets that may also be impaired include accounts receivable, inventory, property, plant and equipment, and investments (which we discuss in Chapter 15). ♦

Negative Goodwill

The discussion and examples in this chapter have assumed that purchased goodwill is positive. That is, the price paid for the company is greater than the fair value of the net assets acquired. However, it is possible that the cash paid is less than the fair value of the net assets acquired. In this case goodwill is a negative amount. This situation tends to raise questions about the rational behavior of the parties involved. The best course of action for the current owners of the company would be to liquidate it rather than to sell it. An exception is when the acquisition is made by buying common stock that is trading at less than the value of the net assets.

If such a purchase transaction does occur, *FASB Statement No. 141* requires that negative goodwill *not* be recorded. Instead, the acquiring company allocates the negative amount proportionately to reduce the amounts assigned to the noncurrent assets acquired. The exceptions to this allocation are financial assets other than those accounted for by the equity method, assets to be sold, deferred tax assets (discussed in Chapter 19), prepaid assets relating to pension and other postretirement benefits (discussed in Chapter 20), and any other current assets. Any excess that remains after reducing those assets to zero is reported as an extraordinary gain (as we discussed in Chapter 5).

Estimating the Value of Goodwill

When one company is negotiating to buy another company, the price offered is typically much greater than the book value of the net assets to be acquired. Three factors can account for the difference between the value of the company as a whole and the book value of the net assets (assets less liabilities). First, **identifiable net assets are generally listed on the balance sheet at their historical costs.** While some assets and liabilities are listed at amounts that approximate their fair values, others (such as land and buildings) may have current fair values that are very different from the recorded historical costs. Second, **identifiable intangible assets may be unrecorded** (or undervalued). As we discussed earlier in the chapter, R&D costs and operating costs are expensed as incurred. Therefore, internally developed intangibles either are not recorded or are recorded at only the costs directly associated with the intangible after all R&D costs and operating costs have been expensed. Third, **unidentifiable intangibles may exist that are categorized as goodwill.**

There are several methods that might be used to estimate the value of the goodwill for a purchased company. The most conceptually correct way is to compute the present value of a purchased company's estimated "excess" earnings. This involves four steps: (1) estimate the company's future annual earnings, (2) calculate an appropriate annual future return on the fair value of the company's identifiable net assets, (3) subtract the amount in step 2 from the amounts in step 1 to determine the estimated excess average annual earnings, and (4) compute the present value of the amounts in step 3 using an appropriate discount rate. The amount calculated in step 4 is the estimated value of the purchased company's goodwill. However, remember that this method provides only an estimate of goodwill. The purchase price of a company must be agreed upon by both the purchaser and the seller. Therefore, the amount paid for goodwill in any purchase transaction is determined solely by the parties involved and is not defined by generally accepted accounting principles.

Secure Your Knowledge 12-2

- Identifiable intangible assets may be purchased or sold separately from the other assets of a company and include patents, copyrights, franchises, computer software costs, and trademarks or tradenames.
- Only certain costs of internally developed identifiable intangible assets (e.g., costs of a successful legal defense of a patent, filing costs of a copyright) are capitalized; all other costs are expensed as incurred.
- Computer software costs are capitalized after technological feasibility of the product is established; these costs are amortized over the expected life of the product.
- The right to use a trademark or tradename that can be renewed indefinitely is considered to be an intangible asset with an indefinite life.
- Organization costs are expensed in the period incurred.

(continued)

- The primary unidentifiable intangible asset is goodwill and is measured as the difference between the purchase price of the acquired company and the fair value of its identifiable net assets.
- A two-step approach is used to test for an impairment of goodwill:
  - Step 1: Compare the fair value of the reporting unit with its book value to determine if goodwill may be impaired.
  - Step 2: Measure the impairment loss as the difference between the lower implied fair value of goodwill and the carrying value of goodwill.

DISCLOSURES FOR INTANGIBLE ASSETS

FASB Statement No. 142 requires a company to disclose certain information about its intangible assets, including:

7 Understand the disclosure of intangibles.

1. In the period it acquires intangible assets:
   a. The cost of any intangible assets acquired, separated into assets that are, and are not, amortized, and goodwill
   b. For assets that are amortized, the residual value and the weighted-average amortization period
   c. The cost of any research and development acquired and written off, and where it is included in the income statement
2. In each period for which it presents a balance sheet:
   a. For intangible assets that are amortized, the total cost, the accumulated amortization, the amortization expense, and the estimated amortization expense for the next five years
   b. For intangible assets that are not amortized, the total cost and the cost of each major intangible asset class
   c. For goodwill, the amount of goodwill acquired and the amount of any impairment losses recognized
   d. For any intangible asset impairment, the facts leading to the impairment, the amount of the impairment loss, and the method of determining the fair value

In addition, a company must report, as a minimum, the total of all identifiable intangible assets as a separate line item (asset) on the balance sheet. A company must include amortization expense and impairment losses in its income from continuing operations. It must report goodwill impairment losses as a separate line item in income from continuing operations (unless the impairment is related to a discontinued operation).

Real Report 12-1 shows the disclosures of intangible assets by **Johnson & Johnson**.

Real Report 12-1 Disclosure of Intangible Assets

JOHNSON & JOHNSON AND SUBSIDIARIES

Notes to Financial Statements (in part)

1 SUMMARY OF SIGNIFICANT ACCOUNTING POLICIES (in part)

GOODWILL AND INTANGIBLE ASSETS

SFAS No. 142 requires that goodwill and non-amortizable intangible assets be assessed annually for impairment. The Company completed the annual impairment test in the fourth quarter and no impairment was determined. Future impairment tests will be performed in the fiscal fourth quarter, annually.

Intangible assets that have finite useful lives continue to be amortized over their useful lives, and are reviewed for impairment when warranted by economic conditions.

Continued

7 INTANGIBLE ASSETS

At the end of 2004 and 2003, the gross and net amounts of intangible assets were:

(Dollars in Millions)	2004	2003
Goodwill—gross	$ 6,597	$ 6,085
Less accumulated amortization	734	695
Goodwill—net	$ 5,863	$ 5,390
Tradmarks (non-amortizable)—gross	$ 1,232	$ 1,098
Less accumulated amortization	142	136
Tradmarks (non-amortizable)—net	$ 1,090	$ 962
Patents and trademarks—gross	$ 3,974	$ 3,798
Less accumulated amortization	1,125	818
Patents and trademarks—net	$ 2,849	$ 2,980
Other intangibles—gross	$ 3,302	$ 3,187
Less accumulated amortization	1,262	980
Other intangibles—net	$ 2,040	$ 2,207
Total intangible assets—gross	$15,105	$14,168
Less accumulated amortization	3,263	2,629
Total intangible asssets—net	$11,842	$ 11,539

Goodwill as of January 2, 2005, as allocated by segments of business is as follows:

(Dollars in Millions)	Consumer	Pharm	Med Dev and Diag	Total
Goodwill, net of accumulated amortization at December 28, 2003	$ 882	$781	$3,727	$5,390
Acquisitions	232	32	138	402
Translation & other	46	19	6	71
Goodwill at January 2, 2005	$1,160	$832	$3,871	$5,863

The weighted average amortization periods for patents and trademarks and other intangible assets are 15 years and 17 years, respectively. The amortization expense of amortizable intangible assets for the fiscal year ended January 2, 2005, was $603 million before tax. Certain patents and intangibles were written down to fair value during 2004 with the resulting charge included in amortization expense. The estimated amortization expense for the five succeeding years approximates $550 million before tax, per year. Substantially all of the amortization expense is included in cost of products sold.

Questions:

1. Why does Johnson & Johnson classify "Trademarks" as non-amortizable?
2. As of the end of 2004, how many more years does Johnson & Johnson expect "Patents and Trademarks" to provide value to the company?
3. What is important about allocating goodwill to various segments of the business?

CONCEPTUAL EVALUATION OF ACCOUNTING FOR INTANGIBLES

8 Explain the conceptual issues regarding intangibles.

Generally accepted accounting principles for internally developed and purchased intangibles are complex and have some inconsistencies. For example, earlier in the chapter we discussed the arguments for and against expensing the R&D costs incurred by a company. Also, when one company acquires another company, it may acquire the R&D that is in-process in that other company. The acquiring company expenses, at the date of purchase, the cost of that in-process R&D. This is consistent with the principle of expensing R&D costs incurred by a company but is inconsistent with the general rule that items purchased are assets. It is possible that the purchasing company may have an incentive to reduce or increase the amount of the purchase price it allocates to the acquired in-process R&D. A reduction would increase the amount the company assigns to goodwill and reduce the total expenses it will recognize (unless the goodwill becomes impaired). An increase would reduce the assets reported on its balance sheet and increase its rate of return in future periods.

Another inconsistency may occur because only purchased goodwill is recorded as an asset, while internally developed goodwill is expensed. Suppose Conner Company internally develops goodwill, while Schuster Company has purchased a company identical to Conner and records goodwill as an asset. Both companies expense the continuing costs of developing internal goodwill, but only Schuster Company reports a goodwill asset. However, there are two different elements. One is the recognition of goodwill that was developed in the *past* and was purchased; the other is the expensing of the costs of internally generated goodwill in the *current period*.

There are three major arguments in favor of expensing internally generated goodwill. First, it would be very difficult to measure the cost of internally generated goodwill to reliably record the cost as an asset. Second, to capitalize internally developed goodwill would raise issues similar to those for R&D, such as which costs should be capitalized and which should be expensed. For example, do some or all of a company's marketing costs provide benefits for just the current period, or do they also provide benefits for future periods? Third, capitalization would require amortization of those assets with a finite life. However, it would be very difficult to identify the revenues generated and therefore to decide over which periods, and by which method, to match the amortization expense against the benefits.

The FASB argued that not amortizing certain intangible assets is appropriate because they have indefinite future lives, and amortizing those assets would not meet the criterion of being *representationally faithful*. To classify an asset as having an indefinite life requires the asset to generate cash flows indefinitely. Examples of such intangible assets may include airport route authorities, certain trademarks, and taxicab medallions. There is little disagreement that these few intangible assets that have an indefinite life should not be amortized until there is evidence that they have a finite life.

An argument in favor of capitalizing purchased goodwill is that the cost of purchased goodwill is *reliable* because it is based on an exchange price (the cost of purchasing the company). The decision not to require amortization of purchased goodwill was more controversial. The FASB argued that the life of goodwill cannot be predicted with a satisfactory level of *reliability*, nor can the pattern of benefits it generates. Therefore, the amount that would be amortized would be only a rough estimate of the decrease in goodwill for the period. The FASB also argued that many financial analysts ignore goodwill amortization in their evaluation of a company's income.

In contrast, many people argue that purchased goodwill is an asset with benefits that expire over time and therefore it should be amortized over a maximum life of, for example, 20 years. Supporters of this view argue that the goodwill recorded as a result of a transaction is an asset that is consumed over time and is replaced by internally generated goodwill. Many of these people would also argue that internally generated goodwill should also be capitalized and amortized over its useful life.

Another alternative considered by the FASB was to require the immediate write off of purchased goodwill. The Board rejected this alternative because the goodwill that is acquired and paid for meets the definition of an asset. It is also difficult to argue that the amount paid for goodwill suddenly has no value. However, this alternative was supported by **Accounting Research Study No. 10**.[17] Several major arguments can be made in

---

17. G. R. Catlett and N. O. Olson, "Accounting for Goodwill," *Accounting Research Study No. 10* (New York: AICPA, 1968).

favor of this position. First, purchased goodwill is different in nature than a company's other assets and cannot be sold or used independently of the other assets. Therefore, it is inappropriate to include it with the other assets on the company's balance sheet. Second, because internally developed goodwill is expensed immediately, this alternative creates a degree of consistency between internally developed and purchased goodwill. Third, as it is so difficult to estimate the life of the benefits, any choice of periods over which to amortize the goodwill is arbitrary, thus immediate write-off is justifiable.

Intangible assets are amortized over 15 years for computing taxable income. Therefore, there is a temporary difference between financial income and taxable income for intangible assets (unless those with a finite life are amortized for over 15 years for computing financial income). This temporary difference results in deferred income taxes. Some users would argue that for a growing company (which is increasing its tangible assets), there is no temporary difference because the company will never pay the deferred taxes. Some users would also argue that reporting deferred taxes for goodwill is not appropriate because there is no temporary difference since the goodwill is not being systematically amortized.

Once the FASB concluded that goodwill (and intangible assets with indefinite lives) would not be amortized, it had to develop an impairment test, as we discussed earlier in this chapter. Because the impairment test has to be applied annually, it may add a significant cost to companies. Many users are also concerned that the impairment loss will not be *reliable* because of the numerous estimates that a company has to make.

SUMMARY

At the beginning of the chapter, we identified several objectives you would accomplish after reading the chapter. The objectives are listed below, each followed by a brief summary of the key points in the chapter discussion.

1. **Explain the accounting alternatives for intangibles.** The cost of a purchased identifiable intangible with a finite life is recorded as an asset and is amortized. The cost of a purchased identifiable intangible with an indefinite life and an unidentifiable intangible (goodwill) is recorded as an asset and is reviewed for impairment annually (but not amortized). The cost of an internally developed identifiable intangible is recorded as an asset and is amortized, except for research and development costs, which are expensed as incurred. The cost of an internally developed unidentifiable intangible is expensed as incurred.

2. **Understand the amortization or impairment of intangibles.** An intangible asset with a finite life must be amortized over its economic life. A company selects the amortization method based on the expected pattern of benefits that the intangible asset will produce, but if the company cannot reliably determine the pattern it uses the straight-line method. An intangible asset with an indefinite life is not amortized but is reviewed for impairment at least annually. A company tests an intangible asset for impairment by first estimating the fair value of the asset. An intangible asset is impaired when its fair value is less than its carrying value. The impairment loss is the amount by which the fair value is less than the carrying value.

3. **Identify research and development costs.** Research is the planned search or critical investigation aimed at discovery of new knowledge with the hope that such knowledge will be useful in developing a new product or service, or a new process or technique, or in bringing about a significant improvement to an existing product or process. Development is the translation of research findings or other knowledge into a plan or design for a new product or process, or for a significant improvement to an existing product or process, whether intended for sale or use. Research and development costs include materials, equipment, and facilities, personnel, intangibles purchased from others, contract services, and indirect costs. Research and development costs are expensed, including the costs of materials, equipment, facilities, and intangibles purchased from others that have no alternative future uses.

4. **Explain the conceptual issues for research and development costs.** The conceptual alternatives for research and development costs are to expense all costs as incurred, to capitalize all costs as incurred and amortize them over the periods expected to benefit, to capitalize costs when incurred if specified conditions are fulfilled and record all other costs as expenses, and to accumulate all costs in a special category until the existence of future benefits can be determined.

5. **Account for identifiable intangible assets including patents, copyrights, franchises, computer software costs, and trademarks and tradenames.** Each of these identifiable intangible assets is recorded at cost and amortized over its economic life, unless it has an indefinite life, such as trademarks and tradenames, in which case it is reviewed for impairment annually.

6. **Account for unidentifiable intangibles including internally developed and purchased goodwill.** The costs of internally developed goodwill are expensed as incurred. Purchased goodwill arises when a company is acquired and is the difference between the purchase price of the company and the fair value of the identifiable net assets. Purchased goodwill is recorded as an asset and is reviewed for impairment annually at the reporting unit level. A company uses a two-step approach. First, the company compares the fair value of the reporting unit with its book value. If the fair value is less than the book value, the second step must be performed. The company first allocates the fair value of the reporting unit to all the identifiable assets and liabilities of the unit as if the unit had been acquired. The implied fair value of the goodwill is the excess "purchase price" over the amount assigned to the identifiable assets and liabilities. The impairment loss is the difference between the carrying value of the goodwill and the lower implied fair value.

7. **Understand the disclosure of intangibles.** A company must disclose its total research and development expense. Intangible assets and goodwill are distinguished from tangible assets in the financial statements. A company must also disclose amortization expense, impairment losses, the method and period of amortization, as well as other disclosures.

8. **Explain the conceptual issues regarding intangibles.** The major conceptual issues are whether some internally developed intangibles, such as research and development, should be capitalized, and whether some intangible assets, such as purchased goodwill, should be amortized instead of being reviewed for impairment.

ANSWERS TO REAL REPORT QUESTIONS

Real Report 12-1 Answers

1. Intangible assets with indefinite lives are not amortized but reviewed for impairment. For Johnson & Johnson, a portion of the trademarks are considered intangible assets with indefinite lives and are tested for impairment annually in the fourth quarter of each fiscal year.

2. The average life of Johnson & Johnson's patents and trademarks can be calculated by dividing accumulated amortization of the patents and trademarks ($1,125) by the gross amount of the patents and trademarks ($3,974), which gives a percentage of the intangible assets that have been amortized (28.3%). Therefore, approximately 71.7% (100% – 28.3%) of the patents and trademarks value remains to be amortized.

Multiplying this by an expected useful life of 15 years (for patents) and 17 years (for trademarks), it appears that Johnson & Johnson expects to receive benefits related to its patents and trademarks for another 11 to 12 years, respectively.

3. A company is required to review its goodwill for impairment at least annually, and this impairment test is to be performed at the reporting unit level. The reporting unit level is generally the same as the operating segment. Therefore, this provides the financial statement user with insights into the operations of the company. For example, goodwill increased by $402 million in the current year because of acquisitions. Of this amount, over half ($232 million) related to the consumer segment.

QUESTIONS

Q12-1 How are intangible assets distinguished from tangible assets? What do they have in common?

Q12-2 How are identifiable intangibles distinguished from unidentifiable intangibles?

Q12-3 Explain how a company accounts for the cost of identifiable and unidentifiable intangibles.

Q12-4 Are all intangible assets amortized? If not, which ones are not? Why?

Q12-5 Which amortization method is required for intangibles? Are there any exceptions?

Q12-6 What factors should a company consider in estimating the useful life of an intangible?

Q12-7 What is meant by the terms *research* and *development*?

Q12-8 What activities are included in R&D? Which are excluded?

Q12-9 What expenditures for R&D does a company include in R&D costs?

Q12-10 What alternative methods of accounting for R&D were considered in *FASB Statement No. 2*? List an argument in favor and one against each alternative.

Q12-11 Over how many years are patents amortized? Trademarks? Goodwill?

Q12-12 How does a company record a patent worth $100,000 if: (a) It has just purchased it for $90,000? (b) The company has developed it?

Q12-13 List four possible causes of goodwill.

Q12-14 What is the definition of *goodwill* from an asset valuation perspective? From an income perspective?

Q12-15 What are the three factors that may account for the difference between the value of the company as a whole and the book value of the net assets?

Q12-16 Under what conditions is goodwill capitalized at acquisition? Expensed at acquisition? Explain the arguments used to justify this accounting.

Q12-17 Distinguish between internal and external goodwill. In which situations is each capitalized or expensed?

Q12-18 Under what conditions is purchased goodwill amortized? Explain how a company determines its goodwill impairment, if any.

Q12-19 It has been proposed that purchased goodwill should be written off immediately to stockholders' equity. Evaluate the arguments in favor of and against this proposal.

Q12-20 What is meant by the term *negative goodwill*? How is it recorded?

MULTIPLE CHOICE (AICPA Adapted)

Select the best answer for each of the following.

M12-1 The Plaza Company originated late in 2006 and began operations on January 2, 2007. Plaza is engaged in conducting market research studies on behalf of manufacturers. Prior to the start of operations, the following costs were incurred:

Attorney's fees in connection with organization of Plaza	$ 4,000
Improvements to leased offices prior to occupancy	7,000
Meetings of incorporators, state filing fees and other organization expenses	5,000
	$16,000

What is the amount of expense recognized for 2007?
a. $16,000
b. $9,000
c. $7,000
d. $4,000

M12-2 A purchased patent has a remaining legal life of 15 years. It should be
a. Expensed in the year of acquisition
b. Amortized over 15 years regardless of its useful life
c. Amortized over its useful life if less than 15 years
d. Not amortized

M12-3 Frye Company incurred research and development costs in 2007 as follows:

Equipment acquired for use in research and development projects	$1,000,000
Depreciation on the equipment	150,000
Materials used	200,000
Compensation costs of personnel	500,000
Outside consulting fees	100,000
Indirect costs appropriately allocated	250,000

The total research and development costs charged in Frye's 2007 income statement should be
a. $650,000
b. $900,000
c. $1,200,000
d. $1,800,000

M12-4 Which of the following assets typically are amortized?

	Patents	Trademarks
a.	No	No
b.	Yes	Yes
c.	No	Yes
d.	Yes	No

M12-5 What is the proper time or time period over which to match the cost of an intangible asset with revenues if it is likely that the benefit of the asset will last for an indefinite period?
a. 40 years
b. 50 years
c. Immediately
d. At such time as a reduction in value can be quantitatively determined

M12-6 The general ledger of the Flint Corporation as of December 31, 2007 includes the following accounts:

Organization costs	$ 5,000
Deposits with advertising agency (will be used to promote goodwill)	8,000
Discounts on bonds payable	15,000
Excess of cost over book value of net assets of acquired subsidiary	70,000
Trademarks	12,000

In the preparation of Flint's balance sheet as of December 31, 2007, what should be reported as total intangible assets?
a. $82,000
b. $87,000
c. $95,000
d. $110,000

M12-7 Goodwill represents the excess of the cost of an acquired company over the
a. Sum of the fair values assigned to tangible assets acquired less liabilities assumed
b. Sum of the fair values assigned to identifiable assets acquired less liabilities assumed
c. Sum of the fair values assigned to intangible assets acquired less liabilities assumed
d. Book value of an acquired company

M12-8 During 2003, Traco Machine Company spent $176,000 on research and development costs for an invention. This invention was patented on January 2, 2004 at a nominal cost that was expensed in 2004. The patent had a legal life of 20 years and an estimated useful life of eight years. In January 2008 Traco paid $16,000 for legal fees in a successful defense of the patent. Amortization for 2008 should be
a. $0
b. $1,000
c. $4,000
d. $26,000

M12-9 Which of the following amounts incurred in connection with a trademark should be capitalized?

	Cost of a Successful Defense	Registration Fees
a.	Yes	No
b.	Yes	Yes
c.	No	Yes
d.	No	No

M12-10 Sherwood Corporation incurred $68,000 of research and development costs in its laboratory to develop a patent that was granted on January 2, 2007. Legal fees and other costs associated with registration of the patent totaled $13,600. Sherwood estimates that the economic life of the patent will be eight years. What amount should Sherwood charge to patent amortization expense for the year ended December 31, 2007?
a. $0
b. $800
c. $1,700
d. $10,200

EXERCISES

E12-1 *Cost of a Patent* The Befort Company filed for a patent on a new type of machine. The application costs totaled $12,000. R&D costs incurred to create the machine were $75,000. In the year in which the company filed for and received the patent, it spent $20,000 in the successful defense of a patent infringement suit.

Required
1. At what amount should the company capitalize the patent?
2. How would you determine the economic life of the patent?

E12-2 *Cost of a Patent* On January 3, 2007 the Franc Company purchased for $27,000 a patent that had been filed eight years earlier. The patent covers a manufacturing process that the company plans to use for 15 years. On January 2, 2008 the company paid its lawyers $10,000 for successfully defending the patent in a lawsuit.

Required
Prepare all the journal entries associated with the patent in 2007 and 2008.

E12-3 *Cost of a Tradename* On January 10, 2007 the Hughes Company applied for a tradename. Legal costs associated with the application were $20,000. In January 2008 the company incurred $8,000 of legal fees in a successful defense of its tradename. The tradename was not impaired in 2007 and 2008.

Required
Compute the ending carrying value of the tradename for 2007 and 2008. Should the company amortize the tradename?

E12-4 *Start-Up Costs* Kling Company was organized in late 2007 and began operations on January 2, 2008. Prior to the start of operations, it incurred the following costs:

Costs of hiring new employees	$ 3,000
Attorney's fees in connection with the organization of the company	12,000
Improvements to leased offices prior to occupancy (10-year lease)	6,000
Costs of pre-opening advertising	5,000

Required
What amount should the company expense in 2007? In 2008?

E12-5 *Research and Development Costs* The KLK Clothing Company manufactures professional clothing for women. In order to keep costs low while still producing quality clothes, KLK conducts many research and development projects. On a current project, KLK researchers used $35,000 of cotton and $27,000 of wool from its inventory. KLK paid its researchers $30,000 in wages and purchased a special weaving machine for $60,000 cash. The machine was not suitable for use in production activities and was not expected to be used in other research projects. In addition, depreciation of the project's research lab amounted to $20,000.

Required

Prepare the journal entry to record KLK's research and development costs.

E12-6 **AICPA Adapted** *Research and Development Costs* In 2007, Lalli Corporation incurred R&D costs as follows:

Materials and equipment	$100,000
Personnel	100,000
Indirect costs	50,000
	$250,000

These costs relate to a product that will be marketed in 2008. The company estimates that these costs will be recouped by December 31, 2011.

Required

What is the amount of R&D costs expensed in 2007?

E12-7 *Research and Development Activities* Which of the following activities are considered R&D? Justify your reasons for each answer.
1. Building an oil shale plant to test the feasibility of large-scale exploitation
2. Testing a new type of machine to evaluate its potential usefulness in production
3. Modifying a machine to make it suitable for filling a customer's order
4. Designing a new plant to produce the same products more efficiently
5. Testing in an attempt to find a more efficient production method

E12-8 *Research and Development Costs* Which of the following are included in R&D costs of the current period? Justify each answer.
1. Current-period depreciation on the building housing the R&D activities
2. Cost of a market research study
3. Current-period depreciation on a machine used in R&D activities
4. Salary of the director of R&D
5. Salary of the vice president who spends one-third of her time overseeing the R&D activities
6. Pension costs for the salaries in items 4 and 5

E12-9 *Intangibles* The Barnum Company acquired several small companies at the end of 2006 and, based on the acquisitions, reported the following intangibles in its December 31, 2006 balance sheet:

Patent	$20,000
Tradename	35,000
Computer software	10,000
Goodwill	90,000

The company's accountant determines the patent has an expected life of 10 years and no expected residual value, and that it will generate approximately equal benefits each year. The company expects to use the tradename for the foreseeable future. The accountant knows that the computer software is used in the company's 120 sales offices. The company has replaced the software in 60 offices in 2007, and expects to replace the software in 40 more offices in 2008 and the remainder in 2009.

Required

How much amortization expense should the company recognize on each intangible asset in 2007?

E12-10 *Tradename* Probst Company acquired a tradename several years ago at a cost of $60,000. The company has never considered the tradename to be impaired. However, at the end of 2007, the company has determined that the tradename is impaired because of a change in market conditions. It estimates that the tradename has a fair value of $40,000 at the end of 2007.

Required

Prepare the journal entry (if any) for Probst Company to record the impairment of its trademark at the end of 2007.

E12-11 *Goodwill* Several years ago, Blaha Company purchased Husker Company as a subsidiary. At that time, Blaha Company recorded goodwill of $100,000 related to the purchase. Since that time, the company has not considered the goodwill to be impaired. However, at the end of 2007, Blaha Company decides to evaluate the goodwill for impairment because of technological changes in the industry. The subsidiary has a book value (including the goodwill) of $900,000. Blaha Company estimates that the fair value of the subsidiary is $720,000, of which it allocates $660,000 to the subsidiary's identifiable assets and liabilities.

Required

Prepare the journal entry (if any) for Blaha Company to record the impairment of its goodwill at the end of 2007.

E12-12 *Goodwill* The Marino Company had the following balance sheet on January 1, 2007:

Current assets	$ 50,000	Current liabilities	$ 30,000
Property, plant, and equipment	200,000	Noncurrent liabilities	100,000
Intangible assets	20,000	Stockholders' equity	140,000
	$270,000		$270,000

On January 2, 2007 the Paul Company purchased the Marino Company by acquiring all its outstanding shares for $300,000 cash. On that date the fair value of the current assets was $40,000, and the fair value of the property, plant, and equipment was $240,000. In addition, the fair value of a previously unrecorded intangible asset was $25,000.

Required
Compute the goodwill associated with the purchase of the Marino Company.

PROBLEMS

P12-1 *Cost of Intangibles* The Brush Company engaged in the following transactions at the beginning of 2007:

1. Purchased a patent for $70,000 that had originally been filed in January 2001. The purchase was made to protect another patent that the company had filed for in January 2003 and subsequently received.
2. Purchased the rights to a novel by a best-selling novelist in exchange for 10,000 shares of $10 par value common stock selling for $60 per share. The book sells one million copies in 2007 and is expected to sell a total of 500,000 copies in future years.
3. Purchased the franchise to operate a ferry service from the state government for $10,000. A bridge has been planned to replace the ferry, and it is expected that it will be completed in five years. Brush hopes that the ferry will continue as a tourist attraction, but profits are expected to be only 20% of those earned before the bridge is opened.
4. Paid $28,000 of legal costs to successfully defend the patent acquired in transaction 1.
5. Paid a race car driver $50,000 to have the Brush Company name prominently displayed on his car for two years.

Required
Prepare journal entries to record the preceding transactions, including the first year's amortization of intangible assets where appropriate. Amortize over the legal life unless a better alternative is indicated.

P12-2 *Cost of Intangibles* The Byrd Corporation engaged in the following transactions at the beginning of 2007:

1. Purchased a Hogburger franchise for a five-year, $60,000, 10%-interest-bearing note. The franchise has an indefinite life providing the terms of the franchise are not violated.
2. Sold a tradename for $50,000. The tradename had a carrying value of $5,000.
3. Paid an advertising agency $60,000 to develop a two-year advertising campaign to promote a new tradename.
4. Incurred legal fees of $5,000 to register a new tradename.
5. Purchased the copyright to a new movie for $500,000. The movie is made during 2007 at a cost of $15 million. It will begin showing in 2008 and is expected to gross $10 million during 2008, $20 million during 2009, and $10 million during 2010.

Required
Prepare journal entries to record the preceding transactions, including any appropriate adjusting entries for 2007.

P12-3 *Correct Classification of Intangibles* During the current year, the accountant for the Cartwright Corporation recorded numerous transactions in an account labeled Intangibles as follows:

Jan.	2	Incorporation fees	$17,500
Jan.	10	Legal fees for the organization of the company	7,500
Jan.	25	Paid for large-scale advertising campaign for the year	15,000
Apr.	1	Acquired land for $15,000 and a building for $20,000 to house the R&D activities. The building has a 20-year life.	35,000
May	15	Purchased materials exclusively for use in R&D activities. Of these materials, 20% are left at the end of the year and will be used in the same project next year. (They have no alternative use.)	15,000
June	30	Filed for a patent	10,000
July	1	Operating loss for first six months of the year	12,000
Dec.	11	Purchased an experimental machine from an inventor. The machine is expected to be used for a particular R&D activity for two years, after which it will have no residual value.	12,000
Dec.	31	Paid employees involved in R&D	30,000

Required

Prepare adjusting journal entries to eliminate the Intangibles account and correctly record all the items. The company amortizes patents over 10 years.

P12-4 *Correcting Entries for Patents* During the year-end audit of the Cressman Corporation's financial statements for 2007, you discover the following items:

1. The company had capitalized $57,000 to the Patent account at the beginning of 2006 for the cost of a patent. This amount included $50,000 of R&D costs. The patent was amortized over a 20-year life in 2006 and 2007.
2. At the beginning of 2006, the company had paid its lawyers $8,000 to successfully defend a patent infringement suit regarding the patent in item 1. The company debited this cost to legal fees expense.
3. At the beginning of 2007, the company purchased a patent for $30,000 from the Baylor Company to prevent potential competition. It recorded the cost in the Patent account and amortized this cost over the remaining legal life of the patent obtained in item 1. However, the company agreed to a suggestion by the auditors that the life of the company patent obtained in item 1 was protected for only seven more years as of the beginning of 2007.

Required

Prepare adjusting journal entries on December 31, 2007.

P12-5 *Cost of Patents* The Davis Research Company engaged in the following six transactions during 2007:

1. Purchased a patent for $35,000. Legal costs of $5,000 were also incurred.
2. Costs of improving patent:

Engineering costs	$20,000
Assembling and testing prototypes	10,000
Other R&D costs	25,000

3. Sold a prototype machine for $7,000. The research and development were performed in previous years.
4. Licensed a manufacturing process to another company and received $80,000 as an advance payment.
5. Successfully defended a patent infringement suit at a cost of $12,000.
6. Earned $5,000 of the advance payment on the licensed manufacturing process in Item 4.

Required

Prepare journal entries to record the preceding transactions.

P12-6 AICPA Adapted **Research and Development Costs** Cressman Company incurred research and development costs in 2007 as follows:

Materials used in research and development projects	$ 400,000
Equipment acquired that will have alternate future uses in future research and development projects for four years	2,000,000
Personnel costs of employees involved in research and development projects	1,000,000
Consulting fees paid to outsiders for research and development projects	100,000
Indirect costs reasonably allocable to research and development projects	200,000

Required

What is the amount of research and development costs charged to Cressman's 2007 income?

P12-7 *Intangibles* The Jolis Company has provided information on the following items:

1. A patent was purchased from the Totley Company for $500,000 on January 1, 2006. At that time, Jolis estimated the remaining useful life to be 10 years. The patent was carried on Totley's books at $20,000 when it sold the patent.
2. On March 2, 2007 a franchise was purchased from the Unal Company for $240,000. In addition, 8% of the revenue from the franchise must be paid to Unal. Revenue earned during 2007 was $620,000. Jolis believes that the life of the franchise is indefinite and that the franchise is not impaired at the end of 2007.
3. Research and development costs were incurred as follows: (a) materials and equipment: $50,000; (b) personnel: $80,000; and (c) indirect costs: $40,000. The costs were incurred to develop a product that will go on sale in 2008 and will have an expected life of five years.
4. A tradename had been purchased for a sugar substitute at the beginning of 2003 for $80,000. In January 2007 it was suspected that the product caused cancer and so the tradename was abandoned.
5. The company purchased the net assets of Lansing Company on September 1, 2004 for $950,000, and the Lansing Company was liquidated. The Lansing Company had the following book (fair) values: current assets, $200,000 ($210,000); property, plant, equipment, $750,000 ($900,000), liabilities, $250,000 ($250,000). Any goodwill is not impaired at the end of 2007.

Required

Prepare journal entries for the Jolis Company for 2007. The company uses the straight-line method of amortization computed to the nearest month over the maximum allowable life. Assume that the company pays all costs in cash, unless otherwise indicated.

P12-8 *Cost of a Copyright* The Gansac Publishing Company signed a contract with an author to publish her book. The signing took place on January 1, 2007 and a payment of $20,000 was made. The agreement was that the author would receive 10% of the selling price of $10 per book. The company expects sales of the book to be 100,000 copies in 2007, 80,000 in 2008, and 20,000 in 2009. It incurred production costs of $800,000 for 200,000 copies during 2007.

Required
1. Prepare journal entries to record the preceding events during 2007 and 2008, assuming that sales were as projected.
2. How would your answer change if the projected sales were considered to be "probable"?

P12-9 *R&D Costs* The controller of the Halpern Company prepared the following income statement and balance sheet at the end of the first year of the company's existence:

Income Statement

Sales revenue	$40,000
Cost of sales	(20,000)
Operating expenses	(8,000)
Net income	$12,000

Balance Sheet

Cash	$ 33,000	Accounts payable	$ 5,000
Inventory	24,000	Notes payable	40,000
R&D costs	30,000	Common stock	50,000
Property, plant, and equipment (net)	20,000	Retained earnings	12,000
	$107,000		$107,000

Investigation shows that R&D costs include, among others, half the year's operating costs because "the company is not yet operating at capacity." In addition R&D costs include $5,000 of materials that were wasted during early production because "our employees made some unnecessary mistakes."

Required
1. Prepare the financial statements according to generally accepted accounting principles.
2. Compute the company's return on assets (net income divided by average total assets, as we discussed in Chapter 6.) under both the original and revised financial statements.

P12-10 *Intangibles* The Bailey Company was formed in January 2005 and is preparing its financial statements under GAAP for the first time at the end of 2007. Its general ledger at December 31, 2007 includes the following assets:

Patent	$120,000
Copyright	140,000
Tradename	150,000
Computer software	90,000
Organization costs	30,000
Research and development	250,000
Intellectual capital	150,000
Goodwill	90,000

As the recently hired accountant for the company, you have been asked to make sure that the company's accounting for intangibles follows GAAP. You know that, because the company has never issued financial statements according to GAAP, any adjustments that are made to correct violations of GAAP are recorded as an adjustment to its retained earnings. You determine that the patent has an expected life of 15 years at the end of 2007 and no residual value, and that it will generate approximately equal benefits each year. You also determine that the company will use the copyright and tradename for the foreseeable future. The computer software is used in the company's 20 offices around the country; it was replaced in 40% of the offices in 2007 and will be replaced in the remaining offices next year. On further examination, you find that the company had previously capitalized the expected value of its "human resources" as intellectual capital, with a corresponding increase in additional paid-in capital.

You also determine that the tradename and goodwill arose from an acquisition of a subsidiary company at the end of 2006. Because of a significant adverse change in the market, you decide that both assets are impaired. You estimate that the fair value of the tradename is $50,000. The subsidiary company has a book value of $500,000, including the goodwill of $90,000. You estimate that the subsidiary's fair value is $300,000, of which $250,000 is allocated to its identifiable assets and liabilities.

Required
Prepare journal entries to provide the correct information under GAAP at the end of 2007.

P12-11 *Impairment* Wember Company acquired a subsidiary company on December 31, 2003, and recorded the cost of the intangible assets it acquired as follows:

Patent	$100,000
Tradename	80,000
Goodwill	150,000

The patent is being amortized by the straight-line method over an expected life of 10 years with no residual value. The trade-name was considered to have an indefinite life.

Because of continued success of the subsidiary, Wember has not considered any of the intangibles to be impaired. However, because of a recession and technological changes in the subsidiary's industry, Wember decides to review all its intangibles for impairment and record any adjustments at December 31, 2007.

Wember estimates that the fair value of the patent and copyright are $42,000 and $25,000, respectively. The company estimates the fair value of the tradename to be $90,000 but decides that it now has a limited life of five years. The subsidiary company has a book value of $700,000, including the goodwill of $150,000. Wember estimates that the fair value of the subsidiary company is $400,000, of which it allocates 80% to the identifiable assets and liabilities.

Required
1. Prepare journal entries for Wember Company to record the impairment of its intangible assets at December 31, 2007.
2. Prepare journal entries for Wember Company to record the amortization expense for its intangibles at December 31, 2008.

P12-12 *Goodwill* The Hamilton Company balance sheet on January 1, 2007 was as follows:

Cash	$ 30,000	Current liabilities	$ 20,000
Accounts receivable	80,000	Bonds payable	120,000
Marketable securities (short-term)	40,000	Pension liability	50,000
Inventory	100,000	Common stock	200,000
Property, plant, and equipment (net)	200,000	Retained earnings	60,000
	$450,000		$450,000

The Korbel Company is considering purchasing the Hamilton Company (a privately held company) and discovers the following about the Hamilton Company:
1. No allowance for uncollectibles has been established. A $10,000 allowance is considered appropriate.
2. Marketable securities are valued at cost. The current market value is $60,000.
3. The LIFO inventory method is used. The FIFO inventory of $140,000 would be used if the company is acquired.
4. Land, included in property, plant, and equipment, which is recorded at its cost of $50,000, is worth $120,000. The remaining property, plant, and equipment is worth 10% more than its depreciated cost.
5. The company has an unrecorded trademark that is worth $70,000.
6. The company's bonds are currently trading for $130,000 and the common stock for $300,000.
7. The pension liability is understated by $40,000.

Required 📈
1. Compute the value of the implied goodwill if the Korbel Company agrees to pay $500,000 cash for the Hamilton Company.
2. Prepare the journal entry to record the acquisition on the books of the Korbel Company, assuming the Hamilton Company is liquidated.
3. If the Korbel Company agrees to pay only $400,000 cash, how much is the implied goodwill?
4. If the Korbel Company pays only $400,000 cash, prepare the journal entry to record the acquisition on its books assuming the Hamilton Company is liquidated.

P12-13 AICPA Adapted *Intangibles: Expense and Disclosure* Munn, Inc., had the following intangible account balances at December 31, 2006:

Patent	$192,000
Accumulated amortization	(24,000)

Transactions during 2007 and other information relating to Munn's intangible assets were as follows:
1. The patent was purchased from Grey Company for $192,000 on January 1, 2005, at which date the remaining legal life was 16 years. On January 1, 2007, Munn determined that the useful life of the patent was only eight years from the date of acquisition.
2. On January 2, 2007, in connection with the purchase of a trademark from Cody Corporation, the parties entered into a noncompetition agreement and a consulting contract. Munn paid Cody $800,000, of which three-quarters was for the trademark and one-quarter was for Cody's agreement not to compete for a five-year period in the line of business covered by the trademark. Munn considers the life of the trademark to be indefinite. Under the consulting contract, Munn agreed to pay Cody $50,000 annually on January 2 for five years. The first payment was made on January 2, 2007. The trademark is not impaired at the end of 2007.

Required 📈
1. Prepare a schedule of the expenses for 2007 relating to Munn's intangible asset balances at December 31, 2006 and transactions during 2007.
2. Prepare the intangible assets section of Munn's balance sheet at December 31, 2007.

P12-14 AICPA Adapted *Intangibles: Assets and Expenses* The Barb Company has provided information on intangible assets as follows:

1. A patent was purchased from the Lou Company for $1,500,000 on January 1, 2006. Barb estimated the remaining useful life of the patent to be 10 years. The patent was carried in Lou's accounting records at a net book value of $1,250,000 when Lou sold it to Barb.
2. During 2007, a franchise was purchased from the Rink Company for $500,000. In addition, 5% of revenue from the franchise must be paid to Rink. Revenue from the franchise for 2007 was $2,000,000. Barb estimates the useful life of the franchise to be 10 years and takes a full year's amortization in the year of purchase.
3. Barb incurred research and development costs in 2007 as follows:

Materials and equipment	$120,000
Personnel	140,000
Indirect costs	60,000
	$320,000

Barb estimates that these costs will be recouped by December 31, 2008.

4. On January 1, 2007 Barb, based on new events that have occurred in the field, estimates that the remaining life of the patent purchased on January 1, 2006 is only five years from January 1, 2007.

Required
1. Prepare a schedule showing the intangibles section of Barb's balance sheet at December 31, 2007. Show supporting computations in good form.
2. Prepare a schedule showing the income statement effect for the year ended December 31, 2007 as a result of the previously mentioned facts. Show supporting computations in good form.

P12-15 AICPA Adapted *Comprehensive* Lee Manufacturing Corporation was incorporated on January 3, 2006. The corporation's financial statements for its first year's operations were not examined by a CPA. You have been engaged to examine the financial statements for the year ended December 31, 2007, and your examination is substantially completed. The corporation's trial balance at December 31, 2007 appears as follows:

	Debit	Credit
Cash	$ 61,000	
Accounts receivable	92,500	
Allowance for doubtful accounts		$ 500
Inventories	38,500	
Machinery	75,000	
Equipment	29,000	
Accumulated depreciation		10,000
Patents	85,000	
Leasehold improvements	26,000	
Prepaid expenses	10,500	
Organization costs	29,000	
Goodwill	24,000	
Licensing agreement No. 1	50,000	
Licensing agreement No. 2	49,000	
Accounts payable		147,500
Unearned revenue		12,500
Capital stock		300,000
Retained earnings, January 1, 2007	27,000	
Sales		768,500
Cost of goods sold	454,000	
Selling and general expenses	173,000	
Interest expense	3,500	
Extraordinary losses	12,000	
Total	$1,239,000	$1,239,000

The following information relates to accounts that may yet require adjustment:

1. Patents for Lee's manufacturing process were acquired January 2, 2007 at a cost of $68,000. An additional $17,000 was spent in December 2007 to improve machinery covered by the patents and charged to the Patents account. Depreciation on fixed assets has been properly recorded for 2007 in accordance with Lee's practice, which provides a full year's depreciation

for property on hand June 30 and no depreciation otherwise. Lee uses the straight-line method for all depreciation and amortization and amortizes its patents over their legal life.

2. On January 3, 2006 Lee purchased Licensing Agreement No. 1, which was believed to have an indefinite useful life. The balance in the Licensing Agreement No. 1 account includes its purchase price of $48,000 and costs of $2,000 related to the acquisition. On January 1, 2007 Lee purchased Licensing Agreement No. 2, which has a life expectancy of 10 years. The balance in the Licensing Agreement No. 2 account includes its $48,000 purchase price and $2,000 in acquisition costs, but it has been reduced by a credit of $1,000 for the advance collection of 2008 revenue from the agreement. In late December 2006 an explosion caused a permanent 60% reduction in the expected revenue-producing value of Licensing Agreement No. 1, and in January 2008 a flood caused additional damage that rendered the agreement worthless.

3. The balance in the Goodwill account includes (a) $8,000 paid December 30, 2006 for newspaper advertising for the next four years following the payment, and (b) legal costs of $16,000 incurred for Lee's incorporation on January 3, 2006.

4. The Leasehold Improvements account includes (a) the $15,000 cost of improvements with a total estimated useful life of 12 years, which Lee, as tenant, made to leased premises in January 2006, (b) movable assembly line equipment costing $8,500 that was installed in the leased premises in December 2007, and (c) real estate taxes of $2,500 paid by Lee in 2007, which under the terms of the lease should have been paid by the landlord. Lee paid its rent in full during 2007. A 10-year nonrenewable lease was signed January 3, 2006 for the leased building that Lee used in manufacturing operations.

5. The balance in the Organization Costs account includes costs incurred during the organizational period.

Required

Prepare a worksheet (spreadsheet) to adjust accounts that require adjustment and prepare financial statements. A separate account should be used for the accumulation of each type of amortization and for each prior period adjustment. Formal adjusting journal entries and financial statements are not required. No intangibles are impaired at the end of 2007. Ignore income taxes.

P12-16 **AICPA Adapted** *Comprehensive* Information concerning Tully Corporation's intangible assets is as follows:

a. On January 1, 2007 Tully signed an agreement to operate as a franchisee of Rapid Copy Service, Inc., for an initial franchise fee of $85,000. Of this amount, $25,000 was paid when the agreement was signed, and the balance is payable in four annual payments of $15,000 each beginning January 1, 2008. The agreement provides that the down payment is not refundable and no future services are required of the franchisor. The present value at January 2, 2007 of the four annual payments discounted at 14% (the implicit rate for a loan of this type) is $43,700. The agreement also provides that 5% of the revenue from the franchise must be paid to the franchisor annually. Tully's revenue from the franchise for 2007 was $900,000. Tully estimates the useful life of the franchise to be 10 years.

b. Tully incurred $78,000 of experimental and development costs in its laboratory to develop a patent, which was granted on January 2, 2007. Legal fees and other costs associated with registration of the patent totaled $16,400. Tully estimates that the useful life of the patent will be eight years.

c. A trademark was purchased from Walton Company for $40,000 on July 1, 2004. Expenditures for successful litigation in defense of the trademark totaling $10,000 were paid on July 1, 2007. Tully estimates that the useful life of the trademark will be 20 years from the date of acquisition.

Required

1. Prepare a schedule showing the intangibles section of Tully's balance sheet at December 31, 2007. Show supporting computations in good form.

2. Prepare a schedule showing all expenses resulting from the transactions that would appear on Tully's income statement for the year ended December 31, 2007. Show supporting computations in good form.

P12-17 **AICPA Adapted** *Comprehensive* Bryant Corporation was incorporated on December 1, 2006 and began operations one week later. Before closing the books for the fiscal year ended November 30, 2007, Bryant's controller prepared the following financial statements:

Balance Sheet
November 30, 2007

Assets		Liabilities and Stockholders' Equity	
Current assets		Current liabilities	
Cash	$ 180,000	Accounts payable and accrued expenses	$ 592,000
Accounts receivable	480,000	Income taxes payable	168,000
Less: Allowance for doubtful accounts	(59,000)	Total current liabilities	$ 760,000
Inventories	430,000	Stockholders' equity	
Prepaid insurance	15,000	Common stock, $10 par value	$ 400,000
Total current assets	$1,046,000	Retained earnings	392,000
Property, plant, and equipment	426,000	Total stockholders' equity	$ 792,000
Less: Accumulated depreciation	(40,000)	Total Liabilities and Stockholders' Equity	$1,552,000
Research and development costs	120,000		
Total Assets	$1,552,000		

Statement of Income
For Year Ended November 30, 2007

Net sales	$2,950,000
Operating expenses	
Cost of sales	$1,670,000
Selling and administrative	650,000
Depreciation	40,000
Research and development	30,000
Total expenses	$2,390,000
Income before income taxes	$ 560,000
Income tax expense	168,000
Net Income	$ 392,000

Bryant Corporation is in the process of negotiating a loan for expansion purposes, and the bank has requested audited financial statements. During the course of the audit, the following additional information was obtained:

1. Included in selling and administrative expenses were $5,000 of costs incurred on software being developed for sale to others. The technological feasibility of the software has been established.
2. Based on an aging of the accounts receivable as of November 30, 2007, it was estimated that $36,000 of the receivables will be uncollectible.
3. Inventories at November 30, 2007 did not include work-in-process inventory costing $12,000 sent to an outside processor on November 26, 2007.
4. A $3,000 insurance premium paid on November 30, 2007 on a policy expiring one year later was charged to insurance expense.
5. Bryant adopted a pension plan on June 1, 2007 for eligible employees to be administered by a trustee. Based upon actuarial computations, the first 12 month's accrued pension plan expense was estimated at $45,000.
6. On June 1, 2007 a production machine purchased for $24,000 was charged to repairs and maintenance. Bryant depreciates machines of this type on the straight-line method over a five-year life, with no salvage value, for financial and tax purposes.
7. Research and development costs of $150,000 were incurred in the development of a patent that Bryant expects to be granted during the fiscal year ending November 30, 2008. Bryant initiated a five-year amortization of the $150,000 total cost during the fiscal year ended November 30, 2007.
8. During December 2007 a competitor company filed suit against Bryant for patent infringement claiming $200,000 in damages. Bryant's legal counsel believes that an unfavorable outcome is probable. A reasonable accrual based on an estimate of the court's award to the plaintiff is $50,000.
9. The 30% effective tax rate was determined to be appropriate for calculating the provision for income taxes for the fiscal year ended November 30, 2007. Ignore computation of deferred portion of income taxes.

Required
1. Prepare the necessary correcting entries.
2. Prepare a corrected balance sheet of Bryant Corporation as of November 30, 2007 and a corrected statement of income for the year ended November 30, 2007.

P12-18 Goodwill The Elm Company is considering purchasing the EKC Company. The balance sheet of the EKC Company at December 31, 2007 is as follows:

Cash	$ 50,000	Current liabilities	$ 60,000
Accounts receivable	70,000	Bonds payable	200,000
Inventory	120,000	Common stock	300,000
Property, plant, and equipment (net)	600,000	Retained earnings	280,000
	$840,000		$840,000

At December 31, 2007 the Elm Company discovered the following about the EKC Company:
1. No allowance for uncollectible accounts has been established. An allowance of $5,000 is considered appropriate.
2. The LIFO inventory method has been used. The FIFO inventory method would be used if EKC were purchased by Elm. The FIFO inventory valuation of the December 31, 2007 ending inventory would be $180,000.
3. The fair value of the property, plant, and equipment (net) is $730,000.
4. The company has an unrecorded patent that is worth $120,000.
5. The book values of the current liabilities and bonds payable are the same as their market values.

Required
Compute the value of the goodwill if the Elm Company pays $1,350,000 for EKC.

CASES

COMMUNICATION

C12-1 Patents

AICPA Adapted In examining the books of Samson Manufacturing Company, you find on the December 31, 2007 balance sheet the item, "Costs of patents, $308,440." Referring to the ledger accounts, you note the following items regarding one patent acquired in 2004:

2004	Legal costs incurred in defending the validity of the patent	$3,500
2006	Legal costs in prosecuting an infringement suit	7,900
2006	Legal costs (additional expenses) in the infringement suit	1,500
2006	Cost of improvements (unpatented) on the patented device	4,800

There are no credits in the account, and the company has not recorded any amortization for any of the patents. There are three other patents issued in 2001, 2003, and 2004; all were developed by the staff of the client. The patented articles are presently very marketable, but are estimated to be in demand only for the next few years.

Required

Discuss the items included in the Patent account from an accounting standpoint.

C12-2 Patent and R&D

AICPA Adapted Clonal, Inc., a biotechnology company, developed and patented a diagnostic product called Trouver. Clonal purchased some research equipment to be used exclusively for Trouver and other research equipment to be used on Trouver and subsequent research projects. Clonal defeated a legal challenge to its Trouver patent and began production and marketing operations for the product.

Clonal allocated its corporate headquarters' costs to its research division as a percentage of the division's salaries.

Required

1. Explain how Clonal should report the equipment purchased for Trouver in its income statements and balance sheets.
2. a. Describe the matching principle.
   b. Describe the accounting treatment of research and development costs and consider whether this is consistent with the matching principle. What is the justification for the accounting treatment of research and development costs?
3. Explain how Clonal should classify its corporate headquarters' costs allocated to the research division in its income statement.
4. Explain how Clonal should report the legal costs incurred in defending Trouver's patent in its statement of cash flows.

C12-3 Research and Development Costs

AICPA Adapted The Gratwick Company is in the process of developing a revolutionary new product. A new division of the company was formed to develop, manufacture, and market this new product. As of year-end (December 31, 2006), the new product has not been manufactured for resale; however, a prototype unit was built and is in operation.

Throughout 2007 the new division incurred certain costs. These costs include design and engineering studies, prototype manufacturing costs, administrative expenses (including salaries of administrative personnel), and market research costs. In addition, the company purchased approximately $500,000 in equipment (estimated useful life, 10 years) for use in developing and manufacturing the new product. The company built approximately $200,000 of this equipment specifically for the design and development of the new product; it used the remaining $300,000 of equipment to manufacture the preproduction prototype and will use it to manufacture the new product once it is in commercial production.

Required

1. What is the definition of *research* and of *development* as defined in *FASB Statement No. 2*?
2. Briefly indicate the practical and conceptual reasons for the conclusion reached by the FASB on accounting practices for research and development costs.
3. In accordance with *FASB Statement No. 2*, how should Gratwick record the various costs in the financial statements for the year ended December 31, 2007?

C12-4 Goodwill

AICPA Adapted After extended negotiations, Rothman Corporation bought from Felzar Company most of the latter's assets on June 30, 2007. At the time of the sale, Felzar's accounts (adjusted to June 30, 2007) reflected the following descriptions and amounts for the assets transferred:

	Cost	Contra (Valuation) Account	Book Value
Receivables	$ 83,600	$ 3,000	$ 80,600
Inventory	107,000	5,200	101,800
Land	20,000	—	20,000
Buildings	207,500	73,000	134,500
Fixtures and equipment	205,000	41,700	163,300
Goodwill	50,000	—	50,000
	$673,100	$122,900	$550,200

You ascertain that the contra (valuation) accounts were allowance for doubtful accounts, allowance to reduce inventory to market, and accumulated depreciation. During the extended negotiations, Felzar held out for a consideration of approximately $600,000 (depending on the level of the receivables and inventory). As of June 30, 2007, however, Felzar agreed to accept Rothman's offer of $450,000 cash plus 1% of the net sales (as defined in the contract) of the next five years, with payments at the end of each year. Felzar expects that Rothman's total net sales during this period will exceed $15 million.

Required

1. Explain how Rothman Corporation should record this transaction.
2. Discuss the propriety of recording goodwill in the accounts of Rothman Corporation for this transaction.

C12-5 Goodwill

AICPA Adapted   Elson Corporation, a retail fuel oil distributor, has increased its annual sales volume to a level three times greater than the annual sales of a dealer it purchased in 2003 in order to begin operations.

The board of directors recently received an offer to negotiate the sale of Elson Corporation to a large competitor. As a result, the majority of the board wants to increase the stated value of goodwill on the balance sheet to reflect the larger sales volume developed through intensive promotion and the current market price of sales gallonage. A few of the board members, however, would prefer to eliminate goodwill altogether from the balance sheet in order to prevent "possible misinterpretations." Goodwill was recorded properly in 2003.

Required

1. Explain the meaning of the term *goodwill*.
2. Explain why the book and fair values of the goodwill of Elson Corporation are different.
3. Discuss the propriety of (a) increasing the stated value of goodwill prior to the negotiations and (b) eliminating goodwill completely from the balance sheet prior to negotiations.

CREATIVE AND CRITICAL THINKING

C12-6 Intangibles

Some intangibles that companies may report on their balance sheets include patents, copyrights, tradenames, computer software, and goodwill.

Required

1. Which of these intangibles would typically be amortized? How would they be amortized? Which of these intangibles would typically not be amortized? Why would they not be amortized? Which of these intangibles would never be amortized?
2. Which of these intangibles must be reviewed for impairment annually?

C12-7 Nature of Intangibles

AICPA Adapted   The Johnson Company operates several plants at which it processes limestone into quicklime and hydrated lime. The Bland Plant, where most of the equipment was installed many years ago, continually deposits a dusty white substance over the surrounding countryside. Citing the unsanitary condition of the neighboring community of Adeltown, the pollution of the Adel River, and the high incidence of lung disease among workers at Bland, the state's Pollution Control Agency has ordered the installation of air pollution control equipment. Also, the Agency has assessed a substantial penalty, which will be used to clean up Adeltown. After considering the costs involved (which could not have been reasonably estimated prior to the Agency's action), Johnson decides to comply with the Agency's orders, the alternative being to cease operations at Bland at the end of the current fiscal year. The officers of Johnson agree that the air pollution control equipment should be capitalized and depreciated over its useful life, but they disagree over the period(s) to which the penalty should be expensed.

Required

Explain the conceptual merits and reporting requirements of accounting for the penalty as a
1. Charge to the current period
2. Correction of prior periods
3. Capitalizable item to be amortized over future periods

C12-8 Patents

AICPA Adapted   On June 30, 2007 your client, Sprauge Corporation, was granted two patents covering plastic cartons that it has been producing and marketing profitably for the past three years. One patent covers the manufacturing process and the other covers the related products.

Sprauge executives tell you that these patents represent the most significant breakthrough in the industry in the past 30 years. The products have been marketed under the registered trademarks Safetainer, Duratainer, and Sealrite. Your client has already granted licenses under the patents to other manufacturers in the United States and abroad and they are producing substantial royalties.

On July 1 Sprauge commenced patent infringement actions against several companies whose names you recognize as those of substantial and prominent competitors. Sprauge management is optimistic that these suits will result in a permanent injunction against the manufacture and sale of the infringing products and collection of damages for loss of profits caused by the alleged infringement. The financial vice-president has suggested that the patents be recorded at the discounted value of expected net royalty receipts.

Required

1. Explain the meaning of *discounted value of expected* net receipts.
2. How would such a value be calculated for net royalty receipts?

3. Explain the basis of valuation of Sprauge's patents that would be generally accepted in accounting.
4. Assuming no practical problems of implementation and ignoring generally accepted accounting principles, explain the preferable basis of valuation for patents.
5. Explain what would be the preferable theoretical basis of amortization.
6. Explain what recognition, if any, the company should make of the infringement litigation in the financial statements for the year ending September 30, 2007.

C12-9 Cost of Intangibles

AICPA Adapted   After securing lease commitments from several major stores, Silver Springs Shopping Center, Inc., was organized and built a shopping center in a growing suburb. The shopping center would have opened on schedule on January 2, 2008 if it had not been struck by a severe tornado in December; it opened for business on October 2, 2008. All the additional construction costs incurred as a result of the tornado were covered by insurance.

In July 2007 in anticipation of the scheduled January opening, a permanent staff was hired to promote the shopping center, obtain tenants for the uncommitted space, and manage the property. A summary of some of the costs incurred in 2007 and the first nine months of 2008 follows:

	2007	Jan. 1, to Sept. 30, 2008
Interest on mortgage bonds	$60,000	$90,000
Cost of obtaining tenants	28,000	58,000
Promotional advertising	34,000	34,000

The promotional advertising campaign was designed to familiarize shoppers with the center. Had the company known in time that the center would not open until October 2008, it would not have made the 2007 expenditure for promotional advertising. The company had to repeat the advertising in 2008.

All the tenants who had leased space in the shopping center at the time of the tornado accepted the October occupancy date on condition that the monthly rental charges for the first nine months of 2008 be canceled.

Required

Explain how the company should treat each of the costs for 2007 and the first nine months of 2008. Give the reasons for each treatment.

C12-10 Analyzing Coca-Cola's Intangibles Disclosures

Refer to the financial statements and related notes of the Coca-Cola Company in Appendix A of this book.

Required

1. What was the total amount of intangible assets that the company reported at the end of 2004, and what was the amount of each component?
2. Do you think that the company has additional "intangibles" that are not recorded on the balance sheet? Why? How would this issue affect your understanding of the company's financial performance?
3. Re-create summary journal entries to record the transactions and events that affected the "amortized intangible assets" in 2004, assuming there were no sales.
4. Compute the estimated average life of the "amortized intangible assets."
5. Why does the company amortize some of its intangible assets but not others?

C12-11 Ethics and Intangibles

You are auditing the financial records of a company and you are aware that it has grown quickly in the last few years by acquiring other companies. You look up the disclosure in last year's annual report, which states, "The company amortizes its intangibles over periods ranging from 3 to 15 years." As you review the company's records, you find that the company made an acquisition of a "high-tech" company three years ago and has not recognized any impairment on the related goodwill. In the last six years, the company has made five other acquisitions and has not recognized any impairment related to them. Included in the acquisitions are several patents that are amortized over nine years and some intangibles with indefinite lives.

Required

From financial reporting and ethical perspectives, discuss the issues raised by this situation.

Financial Reporting: Valuation of Liabilities and Investments

CHAPTER 13
Current Liabilities and Contingencies

CHAPTER 14
Long-Term Liabilities and Receivables

CHAPTER 15
Investments

13

Current Liabilities and Contingencies

OBJECTIVES

After reading this chapter, you will be able to:

1 Explain the characteristics of a liability.

2 Define current liabilities.

3 Account for compensated absences.

4 Understand and record payroll taxes and deductions.

5 Record property taxes.

6 Account for warranty costs.

7 Explain the terms "probable," "reasonably possible," and "remote" related to contingencies.

8 Record and report a loss contingency.

9 Disclose a gain contingency.

All I Want for Christmas

What do you get the person who has everything? For more and more consumers, the answer to this question is a gift card. According to a survey conducted by the National Retail Federation, consumers spent approximately $17.34 billion on gift cards during the 2004 holiday season. What does this mean for retailers? Many view the gift card as having significant benefits for the bottom line. Research shows that when gift cards are redeemed, as many as 60% of consumers will spend considerably more than the card's face value. In addition, gift card advocates claim benefits in the form of reduced returns, lower processing and administrative costs relative to paper gift certificates, and increased value due to unredeemed gift cards (termed breakage revenue, the average consumer is estimated to leave as much as 15% of a gift card's value unredeemed).

However, gift cards also present a hidden danger. While companies receive cash when the gift card is sold, the company must record a current liability, and delay the recognition of revenue,

until the card is redeemed. Therefore, "holiday" sales may not actually appear until months later. As reported in a January 11, 2005 press release, **Williams-Sonoma Inc.** noted that the disappointing sales for the eight-week period ending December 26, 2004 were due, in part, to significant increases in gift card sales, which caused retail sales to be shifted into a later reporting period. Furthermore, if gift card redemptions coincide with markdowns (e.g., after-Christmas sales), retailers may also see reductions in their gross margins.

FOR FURTHER INVESTIGATION

For a discussion of gift cards, consult the Business & Company Resource Center (BCRC):

- Gift Card Sales Help Boost Final Retail Numbers for Holiday Season, *Knight Ridder/Tribune Business News* Jan 5, 2005.
- Turn in Unwanted Gift Card for Another, Betsy Taylor, *The Seattle Times (Seattle, WA)*, 0745-9696, Jan 1, 2005, pC3.

This is the first of two chapters on liabilities. In Chapter 13 we focus on current liabilities (including contingencies). In Chapter 14 we discuss long-term (noncurrent) liabilities. The topics in both chapters depend on an understanding of the term *liabilities*. Our initial discussion expands on the concept and definition of a liability we presented in the review of the balance sheet in Chapter 4. We discuss the nature, definition, and valuation of current liabilities, and explain the items in three major groups of current liabilities. Then we examine the important issue of contingencies, after which we discuss short-term debt expected to be refinanced and obligations that are callable by the creditor. Last, we discuss specific methods of reporting current liabilities on the balance sheet and in the notes to the financial statements.

CONCEPTUAL OVERVIEW OF LIABILITIES

1 Explain the characteristics of a liability.

In its *Conceptual Framework*, the FASB defines liabilities as follows:

> **Liabilities are the probable future sacrifices of economic benefits arising from present obligations of a company to transfer assets or provide services in the future as a result of past transactions or events.**[1]

The FASB also explained two of the terms. The word *probable* **refers to what can be expected or believed based on available evidence or logic.** The word *obligations* **refers to duties imposed legally or socially which one is bound to do by contract, promise, or moral responsibility.** In other words, liabilities include both legal and nonlegal (but not illegal) obligations. **Legal liabilities are incurred in transactions that are contractual—based on written or oral agreements to pay cash or to provide goods or services to other entities in the future.** Legal liabilities include such items as accounts payable, notes payable, and sales tax payable. **The nonlegal group (also called accounting liabilities) includes those obligations where there is *no legal requirement* for assets to be transferred, but a transfer of assets typically occurs as a part of the normal operations of a business.**[2] Nonlegal liabilities include equitable and constructive obligations, such as the liability to employees for vacation pay or year-end bonuses. These are obligations that a company accepts by paying them every year even though it is not contractually required and has not announced a policy to do so. We discuss the accounting for both types of liabilities later in this chapter.

As we introduced in Chapter 3, there are **three characteristics of a liability** for a company:

1. A liability involves a responsibility that will be settled by the probable *future transfer* or *use of assets* at a specified or determinable date, on occurrence of a specific event, or on demand.
2. The responsibility obligates the company *so that it has little or no discretion to avoid the future sacrifice.*
3. The transaction or other event obligating the company *has already happened.*

The main features of these three characteristics are highlighted by italics: the requirement that a company transfer or use assets, that the obligation cannot be avoided, and that the liability transaction has already occurred.

There are two additional factors involving a liability. First, the company does not need to know the identity of the recipient before the time of settlement. Second, a legally enforceable claim is not a prerequisite for an obligation to qualify as a liability.[3] Note,

---

1. "Elements of Financial Reporting of Business Enterprises," *FASB Statement of Financial Accounting Concepts No. 6* (Stamford, Conn.: FASB, December 1985), par. 28.
2. *Ibid.*, fn. 21 and 22 and par. 38.
3. *Ibid.*, par. 36.

however, that some liabilities are "liquidated" by conversion into common or preferred stock or by refinancing into other liabilities, as we discuss in Chapter 14.

The financial accounting issues related to liabilities are important in both balance sheet valuation and income statement measurement. The primary issues discussed in the remainder of this chapter are:

- *Identification* of liabilities—the detection of a company's obligations
- *Valuation* of the liabilities and measurement of the related expense—the determination of an amount to record for each obligation and to match as an expense against revenues
- *Reporting* on the financial statements—the specific disclosures in both the company's financial statements and the related notes

Liabilities generally are classified as either current or long-term. We discuss the preceding issues in this chapter as they relate to current liabilities.

NATURE AND DEFINITION OF CURRENT LIABILITIES

The specific meaning, nature, and classification of current liabilities are important to users of financial statements.

Classification and the Operating Cycle or Year

Recall that **current liabilities are obligations of a company that it expects to liquidate by using existing current assets or creating other current liabilities within one year or the normal operating cycle, whichever is longer.** The usual criterion is one year. For certain companies, however, where the **operating cycle—from cash to inventory to receivables and back to cash—**is longer than a year, the length of the operating cycle determines the classification of the liability. Many current liabilities, such as accounts payable, wages payable, warranty obligations, and notes payable, are incurred (and paid) during the operating cycle. For example, a current liability—Accounts Payable—is created when an inventory item is acquired. Also, a current liability, Salaries Payable, arises as a result of accrued salaries for sales, as well as general and administrative, personnel.

Some users question using different time periods for classifying liabilities as current. They prefer to use the length of the operating cycle as the period for classifying liabilities, regardless of whether it is longer or shorter than a year. Since this issue deals primarily with the question of liquidity, we discuss liquidity and the related issue of financial flexibility next.

2 Define current liabilities.

Liquidity, Financial Flexibility, and Current Liabilities

One attribute of a liability (and also an asset) is its liquidity. **Liquidity refers to how quickly a company can convert its assets to cash to pay its liabilities.** One aspect of a company's liquidity is how soon its bills (liabilities) must be paid. The FASB is concerned about reporting the liquidity of liabilities and assets because users evaluate future cash flows in their decision-making processes. In part, these *future cash flows are predicted based on the nearness to cash of liabilities and assets.* Therefore, knowledge of the liquidity of liabilities and assets is important in these decision-making processes. The Board studied ways of relating liabilities and assets to each other and to other financial statement data to obtain information about a company's liquidity. It listed five "liquidity" ratios as providing information to lending institutions, creditors, and other external users of financial information: (1) cash flows to total debt, (2) net income to total assets (return on total assets ratio), (3) total debt to total assets (debt ratio), (4) current assets to current liabilities (current ratio), and (5) cash to current liabilities.[4] Four of the five require information about a company's liabilities; two require information about its current liabilities. Since we discussed ratio analysis in detail in Chapter 6, we do not discuss these ratios here.

The AICPA Special Committee on Financial Reporting reinforced the Board's view by stating that in a company's MD&A, its management should identify and describe internal and external sources of liquidity, and significant unused sources of liquid assets. It also believes that a company should disclose the impact of "illiquidity" on financial flexibility.[5] **Financial flexibility refers to a company's ability to use its financial resources to adapt to change.** This ability primarily involves the management of cash and other resources to achieve certain financial advantages from both an offensive and defensive point of view. In part, it also involves the potential to create new current and long-term liabilities, to restructure existing debt, and to manage debt in other ways. We discuss these features relating to financial flexibility later in this chapter and in other chapters.

LINK TO RATIO ANALYSIS

Companies experience liquidity problems when their cash inflows are not sufficient to meet their cash outflows. Because companies that violate debt covenants could be forced into bankruptcy, managers should closely monitor a company's liquidity. As we discussed in Chapter 6, two useful ratios for assessing a company's liquidity are the current ratio and the acid-test (quick) ratio. Selected financial information for **Circuit City** and **Best Buy** for fiscal year 2004 is shown below.

Selected Financial Information (in millions)	Circuit City	Best Buy
Current Assets	$2,919	$5,724
Quick Assets	1,363	2,943
Current Liabilities	1,177	4,501

Circuit City and Best Buy have current ratios (current assets ÷ current liabilities) of 2.48 and 1.27, respectively. While this ratio should be examined with respect to industry practices and any circumstances specific to the company, it appears that Circuit City is in a much more favorable position relative to Best Buy. Examining the acid-test (quick) ratio (quick assets ÷ current liabilities), a much more severe test of a company's liquidity, Circuit City is again in a much more favorable position than Best Buy (acid-test ratios of 1.16 and 0.65, respectively).

Classification of Current Liabilities

A company reports its current liabilities in the first section of its liabilities on its balance sheet. Many current liabilities are easily identifiable and have a "contractual" amount. Some current liabilities, though identifiable, have amounts that depend on operations. Others require that amounts be estimated. We classify the primary types of current liabilities in three groups, as we show in Exhibit 13-1, although some types might fit in more than one category. We organize our discussion according to these three types.

---

4. "Reporting Income, Cash Flows, and Financial Flexibility of Business Enterprises," *FASB Proposed Statement of Financial Accounting Concepts* (Stamford, Conn.: FASB, November 16, 1981), par. 28.
5. "Improving Business Reporting—A Customer Focus," *Report of the AICPA Committee on Financial Reporting* (New York: AICPA, 1994), Appendix II, p. 145.

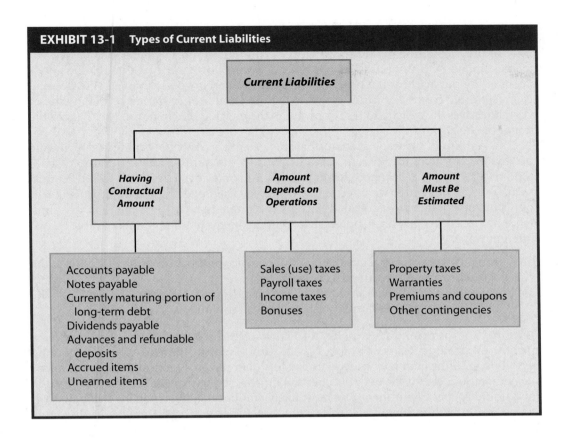

EXHIBIT 13-1   Types of Current Liabilities

Current Liabilities

- **Having Contractual Amount**
  - Accounts payable
  - Notes payable
  - Currently maturing portion of long-term debt
  - Dividends payable
  - Advances and refundable deposits
  - Accrued items
  - Unearned items

- **Amount Depends on Operations**
  - Sales (use) taxes
  - Payroll taxes
  - Income taxes
  - Bonuses

- **Amount Must Be Estimated**
  - Property taxes
  - Warranties
  - Premiums and coupons
  - Other contingencies

VALUATION OF CURRENT LIABILITIES

Conceptually, a company should record (and report on its balance sheet) all its liabilities at the present value of the future payments they will require. In practice, however, most current liabilities are measured, recorded, and reported at their maturity or face amount. The difference between the maturity amount and the present value of the maturity amount is usually not material because of the short time period involved (usually one year or less). Although a slight overstatement of liabilities results from reporting current liabilities at their maturity amount, this overstatement is justified on the basis of cost/benefit and materiality constraints.

CURRENT LIABILITIES HAVING A CONTRACTUAL AMOUNT

The short-term liabilities in this group result from the terms of contracts or from the existence of laws. In these cases the debt and its maturity are known with reasonable certainty. The accounting issues we discuss in this section for each current liability are (1) identifying the item, (2) measuring it, and (3) recording it in the accounts.

Trade Accounts Payable

A company's trade accounts payable arise from the purchase of inventory, supplies, or services on credit. The credit period generally varies from 30 to 120 days without any interest being charged. A company usually records the amount of the liability in its accounting system when it receives the invoice from the supplier.

Issues often arise when a company purchases inventory near the end of its accounting period. Goods may be shipped by the supplier and still be in transit at year-end, as we discussed in Chapter 8. The purchaser should record both the purchase and the liability in the accounting period in which the economic control of the goods passes. For goods shipped FOB shipping point, economic control of (and legal title to) the goods passes to the purchaser at the supplier's shipping point. For goods shipped FOB destination, economic control of (and legal title to) the goods is transferred to the purchaser when it receives the merchandise. The owner of the merchandise in transit usually pays the cost of the freight.

The amount of the trade accounts payable usually is easily determined by reviewing the invoice. An accounting issue arises when cash discount terms (for example, 2/10, n/30; or 3/10 EOM) are offered. A company should take advantage of all cash discounts because of the high effective interest rate involved. Theoretically, it should show inventory (purchases) and the associated liability (accounts payable) less the cash discount. As we discussed in Chapter 8, however, a company may record accounts payable in two different ways:

1. using the *gross price method*, that is, at the invoice price—the liability is stated at the maximum amount required to be paid, or
2. using the *net price method*, that is, at the invoice price less the cash discount—the liability is stated at its current cash equivalent amount.

Assuming the company has a policy of taking cash discounts, use of the gross price method overstates accounts payable (a valuation issue) at the end of the accounting period because the company expects to pay less than the gross amount. We recommend the net method. Use of the net price method more accurately measures accounts payable (and liquidity) because it shows the most likely amount that the company will pay. Also, the net price method highlights management inefficiency because purchases discounts lost are recorded when an invoice is paid after the cash discount period has expired. The gross price method is more widely used, however, because of its simplicity and the lack of materiality of the differences between the two methods. For an illustration of the two methods, refer to Chapter 8.

Notes Payable

A note payable is an unconditional written agreement to pay a sum of money to the bearer on a specific date. Notes payable may be either short term (discussed here) or long term (discussed in Chapter 14). Notes arise either out of a trade situation—the purchase of goods or services on credit—or the borrowing of money. The promissory note is the source document a company uses to determine and record the initial amount of the liability. However, interest is important in determining the value of the liability at a later date. The interest for a note payable may be stated or implied in different ways. One note may be *interest-bearing*, with the principal listed as the face value and the interest rate stated on the note, and with interest payable at maturity. Another note may be *non-interest-bearing* in which the note is stated at its maturity value that includes both the principal and interest to maturity. For a non-interest-bearing note, the note is discounted and the borrower receives less than the face value. The interest on this type of note is the amount of the discount.

Issuance of an Interest-Bearing Trade Note for Merchandise

For an interest-bearing note, the principal amount (face value) is the present value of the liability and is used to record the current liability. Interest expense then is recorded over the life of the note by applying the stated interest rate to the face value. For example, assume that Trishan Corporation uses a perpetual inventory system and purchases merchandise for $7,000 on September 1, 2007 by issuing a $7,000, 12%, 30-day note to the supplier. The company records the issuance of the note and the payment of the principal and interest (assuming, for simplicity, a 360-day business year) on September 1, 2007 and October 1, 2007, respectively, as follows:

September 1, 2007

Inventory	7,000	
Notes Payable		7,000

October 1, 2007

Interest Expense ($7,000 × 0.12 × 30/360)	70	
Notes Payable	7,000	
Cash		7,070

If the note spans two fiscal periods, the company makes an adjusting entry at the end of the first fiscal period to accrue the interest expense and to report the amount as a current liability, Interest Payable.

Issue of Non-Interest-Bearing Note to Borrow Money

For a non-interest-bearing note, the face value (which includes the interest to maturity) and the discount (the interest to maturity) of the note are used to record the current liability. Interest expense is then recorded over the life of the note as an adjustment of this discounted amount. For example, assume that on December 1, 2007, the Trollingwood Corporation (which has a fiscal year ending December 31) borrows money at First National Bank by issuing a $10,000, 90-day, non-interest-bearing note that is discounted on a 12% basis. Trollingwood receives only $9,700 [$10,000 − ($10,000 × 0.12 × 3/12)]. It makes four journal entries to record the events related to this note. First, it records the proceeds of the note on December 1, 2007 as follows:

Cash	9,700	
Discount on Notes Payable	300	
Notes Payable		10,000

Observe that $10,000 is the maturity (face) value of the note, but the company records the liability at its present value. The company debits the $300 discount (the interest expense applicable to the entire term of the note) to Discount on Notes Payable, and shows this account on its balance sheet as a contra account to Notes Payable to report the net amount of the current liquidation value.[6] Since the life of this note extends into 2008, the company makes a second journal entry on December 31, 2007 to record a portion of the discount (1/3 × $300) as interest expense[7] for 2007 as follows:

Interest Expense	100	
Discount on Notes Payable		100

---

6. Alternatively, the company could record the Notes Payable at the current value ($9,700), in which case it would show the maturity value parenthetically on the balance sheet. Then the company would make the Interest Expense adjusting entry credit directly to Notes Payable to increase it to the maturity value.
7. In this situation, for simplicity we use the "straight-line" method to allocate the interest expense. In Chapter 14, we use the more conceptually correct "effective interest" method to calculate interest expense for long-term notes.

Observe that the reduction in the Discount on Notes Payable account increases the current liability amount shown on the company's balance sheet.[8] The company records the last two journal entries at maturity on March 1, 2008 as follows:

Interest Expense	200	
Discount on Notes Payable		200
Notes Payable	10,000	
Cash		10,000

After the company makes the journal entry adjusting Interest Expense, Discount on Notes Payable has a zero balance so that the carrying value of the current liability equals the maturity value of the note. The second journal entry records the payment of the maturity value, which includes the $9,700 borrowed, plus the $300 total interest recognized (i.e., the amount of the discount).

In borrowing money, a manager must be aware of the effective interest rate, referred to as the annual percentage rate (or APR), for each source of credit. In the preceding case, the approximate effective annual interest on the cash actually borrowed is higher than the discount rate of 12%. It is 12.37% [($300 ÷ $9,700) × 4 quarters]. Federal laws require lenders to disclose the APR to borrowers.

Currently Maturing Portion of Long-Term Debt

As a general rule, a company classifies the currently maturing portion of long-term debt as a current liability to show the effect on its liquidity. Two different situations are involved here. First, any long-term debt requiring the use of current assets for its retirement will become a current liability on the balance sheet prepared immediately before the year of retirement. If a company has issued 20-year bonds and these are due on July 1, 2008, the company reports their total amount as a current liability on the balance sheet prepared as of December 31, 2007. The second situation involves the issuance of serial bonds—that is, bonds that are retired in periodic installments. (We discuss serial bonds in an Appendix to Chapter 14). For example, assume that on July 1, 2006, Rexlow Corporation issues 9% serial bonds with a face value of $1 million. These bonds are to be retired in installments of $100,000, beginning on July 1, 2008 and for each year thereafter until all bonds are retired.

The company's balance sheet prepared as of December 31, 2007 would show the currently maturing installment of $100,000 as a current liability and the $900,000 (the installments due after December 31, 2008) as a long-term liability item. The current portion of other long-term debt (such as the current amount of lease obligations and certain deferred taxes) is treated in the same manner. These items, however, are not included in current liabilities if they will be refinanced on a long-term basis, as we discuss later in this chapter.

Dividends Payable

A company may declare (on the dividend declaration date by the board of directors) a cash dividend, a property dividend (a dividend payable in property other than cash), or a scrip dividend (a dividend that creates a promissory note). When a company declares a dividend, it reduces retained earnings and recognizes a current liability if it expects to distribute the dividend in the coming year or operating cycle. These dividends are recorded and reported at the amount to be paid. The liability is titled Dividends Payable, Property Dividends Payable, or Dividends Payable in Scrip. For

---

8. An alternative approach involves debiting the original discount amount first to Interest Expense. Then, at the end of the period, an adjusting entry would be necessary to transfer the *unexpired* portion of the expense to the Discount on Notes Payable account. The Discount on Notes Payable account would be shown on the balance sheet as a contra account to Notes Payable, as we discussed earlier.

instance, if Brown Corporation declared a $50,000 cash dividend, on the date of declaration it would record the dividend as follows:

Retained Earnings	50,000	
Dividends Payable		50,000

Note that accounting for the declaration of a dividend results in a shift of a stockholders' equity element—retained earnings—to a current liability element. The company eliminates the liability on the date of payment. We discuss dividends in Chapter 17.

There are two exceptions to the recording of current liabilities for dividends. First, a company does *not* report a stock dividend to be issued as a current liability. Since a corporation distributes a stock dividend by issuing its own stock, it reports a stock dividend declared as an element of stockholders' equity. Second, a company does *not* report undeclared dividends in arrears on cumulative preferred stock (which we discuss in Chapter 16) as liabilities until they are formally declared by the corporation's board of directors. However, it discloses them in the notes to the financial statements because they potentially affect its future liquidity.

Advances and Refundable Deposits

Many utility and other companies require customers and employees to make deposits. These deposits may be required as guarantees to cover equipment used by the customer, to cover payments that may arise in the future, or to guarantee performance of a contract or service. Since these deposits either are refundable or are later offset against a trade receivable, they are a special type of liability. Accounting for these deposits involves an increase in a liability describing the nature of the refundable deposit. For example, the liability for a refundable deposit received by a utility company may be called Refundable Deposits Received from Customers. The law frequently requires that interest be paid on these deposits. Therefore, most utility companies refund the deposit as soon as a customer has established a good credit standing. The utility company must accrue any related interest expense and report the amount as a current liability, Interest Payable.

Accrued Liabilities

Accrued liabilities are obligations that *accumulate* in a systematic way over time. For convenience, a company usually waits until the end of the accounting period to make adjusting entries to record these liabilities and the related expenses. Most accrued liabilities are current liabilities. Some are definite in amount, while the amounts of others are based on operations or estimates.

Accrued Liability for Compensated Absences

FASB Statement No. 43 defines the accounting for compensated absences. **Compensated absences include vacation, holiday, illness, or other personal activities for which a company pays its employees.** They do not include items such as severance pay, stock options, or long-term fringe benefits. A company recognizes an expense and accrues a liability for employees' compensation for future absences if *all* the following conditions are met:

1. The company's obligation relating to the employee's rights to receive compensation for future absences is based on the employee's services already rendered;
2. The obligation relates to rights that vest or accumulate;
3. Payment of the compensation is probable; and
4. The amount can be reasonably estimated.[9]

3 Account for compensated absences.

Reporting

---

9. "Accounting for Compensated Absences," *FASB Statement of Financial Accounting Standards No. 43* (Stamford, Conn.: FASB, November, 1980), par. 6. These criteria also apply to postemployment benefits under *FASB Statement of Financial Accounting Standards No. 112.*

If the company meets the first three conditions but does not accrue a liability because the last condition is not met, it discloses the known facts about these compensated absences in the notes to its financial statements.

Two terms need more explanation. A **vested right** exists when an employer has an obligation to make payment to an employee that is not contingent on the employee's future services. An **accumulated right** is one that can be carried forward by the employee to future periods if the employee does not take them in the period in which they are earned. The most common type is *vacation time* that is allowed to accumulate and for which payment is probable. Even if these rights do not vest, they accumulate and the employer must recognize an expense and accrue a current liability. In doing so, it allows for those rights it does not expect employees to exercise.

The second most frequent compensated absence is *sick pay*, which is treated by *FASB Statement No. 43* differently from vacation pay. If sick pay benefits *vest* and are not used by the end of the period, then the employer must recognize an expense and accrue a current liability. If sick pay benefits *accumulate* but do *not* vest, recognition and accrual is optional. The reason for this exception to the general recognition rule is that employers administer sick pay in at least two different ways. Some companies permit employees to accumulate unused sick pay and take compensated time off from work even though they are not ill. A company must accrue a current liability for this type of sick pay because it is probable that it will be paid in the future, regardless of whether or not the employees are ill. Other companies require that employees receive accumulated sick pay only if they are absent from work because of illness. In this case, accrual is optional because payment is less likely and measurement of the amount is less reliable.

There is a **conceptual difference** between vacation pay and sick pay. *Vacation pay is earned as a result of past employment* (the services rendered by the employee), whereas *sick pay is earned only when the future event* (sickness) *occurs*. In the latter case, the criteria for a liability have *not* been met during employment because the event obligating the company has not yet occurred.

When an accrual is made, the company records an expense and related current liability in the period in which the sick pay benefits are earned by the employees. In measuring the amount of the accrual, the rate of pay the company uses to record the liability is either: (1) the rate for the current period, or (2) the rate for the estimated future time of absence. Since the current period's rate is more reliable than the future period's rate, and the difference is unlikely to be material, most companies use the current period's rate for the accrual. If the amount paid in the future for the compensated absence is larger than the amount of the previous accrual (because of a pay raise or promotion), the company records the difference as an adjustment to the expense recorded in the period of the payment. In other words, the difference is treated as a change in estimate, as we discuss in Chapter 23.

We show the differences in accounting for vacation time and sick pay in the following diagram.

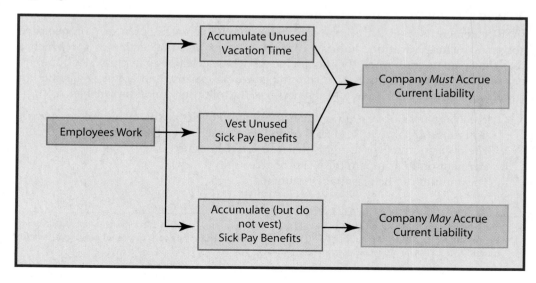

Example: Compensated Absence

To show a compensated absence for vacations, assume that the Milton Company has 100 employees who are each paid an average of $200 per day. The company has a policy (which meets the *FASB Statement No. 43* conditions) of allowing each employee 12 days of paid vacation per year. The total annual cost of the paid vacations—a form of compensated absence—is $240,000 (100 × 12 × $200). The company records the related current liability on a quarterly basis for interim reporting purposes. Employees are paid monthly; half the employees are in the sales force and the remaining half are in the office staff. Assuming no vacation days were taken in the first quarter of 2008, the company records the expense and accrued liability on March 31, 2008 as follows:

Sales Salaries Expense: Compensated Absences	30,000	
Office Salaries Expense: Compensated Absences	30,000	
Liability for Employees' Compensation for		
Future Absences (3/12 × $240,000)		60,000

Some companies prefer to record the debit entry as Vacation Pay Expense. Generally, no payroll taxes are recorded at this time because companies wait until payment of the payroll to do so. Note that as a result of this journal entry **the salaries expense is recognized in the period during which the employees work and earn the vacation time and *not* during the vacation period,** thus adhering to the matching principle. The company's first-quarter interim financial statements include the expense and current liability for compensated absences.

The liability for compensated absences will be satisfied when the employees take their vacations. The company will record the elimination of the current liability, however, when it pays the regular payroll after the employees take their vacations. For example, assume that the $400,000 April 30, 2008 payroll, including paid vacation time taken by the sales and office staff, is as follows:

	Payroll for	
	Time Worked	**Vacation Taken**
Sales staff	$194,000	$6,000
Office staff	193,000	7,000

The company records the payment of this payroll (ignoring payroll taxes) on April 30, 2008 as follows:

Sales Salaries Expense	194,000	
Office Salaries Expense	193,000	
Liability for Employees' Compensation		
for Future Absences	13,000	
Cash		400,000

As we discussed earlier, if the $13,000 payroll for vacation time was larger than the respective amount accrued earlier (because of a pay raise or promotion), the company would reduce the liability by the accrued amount, and would add the difference to the two expense accounts. In addition, payroll taxes would normally be recorded at this time. For simplicity however, since we discuss payroll taxes later in the chapter, we do not illustrate them here. If payroll taxes had been recorded, the withheld payroll taxes of the employees would apply to the entire $400,000 as of April 30, 2008 (the date of payment of the salaries and the vacation time) because the taxes are legally assessable. Also, the payroll taxes applicable to the employer would be recorded at this time.

Similar journal entries are made to record the expense for compensated absences and accrue (and eliminate) the liability during the remaining quarters for interim reporting purposes. At year-end, the Milton Company reports any remaining balance in the liability account as a current liability on its ending balance sheet.[10] ♦

Liabilities from Noncancelable Obligations

FASB Statement No. 47 deals with liability issues relating to *off-balance-sheet financing*. We discussed this topic in Chapter 9 as it relates to inventories; we also discuss it in Chapter 21 as it applies to leasing arrangements. Here we discuss it briefly as it relates to current liabilities. This *Statement* focuses on accounting for an unconditional purchase obligation. An **unconditional purchase obligation** is one requiring payment in the future for fixed amounts of goods or services at set prices. If a company has an unconditional (noncancelable) obligation to purchase an asset (e.g., inventory) at a specified price and the market price goes below this price, the company must accrue a loss and record a liability.[11] If any part of the future payment falls within a year (or operating cycle, if longer), the company reports this amount as a current liability. This helps users evaluate the company's liquidity and financial flexibility.

Liabilities from Product Financing Arrangements

FASB Statement No. 49 deals with off-balance-sheet financing transactions in which a company "sells" inventory and agrees to repurchase it (perhaps additionally processed) at a specified price. As we discussed in Chapter 9, the company does not record the transaction as a sale or remove the inventory from its balance sheet. Instead, the company records a liability for the proceeds received. *FASB Statement No. 49* also addresses transactions where a company has another entity purchase a product on its behalf. In this case the company records the asset (often an inventory item) and related liability when the product is purchased by the other entity.[12] The company reports the amount as a current liability on its balance sheet if it expects to pay it in the next year (or operating cycle, if longer).

Unearned Items

A company's unearned items (sometimes called deferred revenues) include amounts that it has collected in advance for future sales but has not yet earned and has not recorded as revenues. These unearned items are liabilities because it has not yet provided the product or service.

Examples of unearned items are amounts collected in advance, such as interest, rent, magazine subscriptions, royalties, tickets, tokens, gift certificates, and service contracts. Most of these items are current liabilities. If more than one year (or one operating cycle, if longer) is required in the earning process, then the unearned item is classified as a long-term liability.

The accounting by a company for these unearned items involves the recognition of a liability when it recieves the cash. The company makes an adjusting entry at the end of the accounting period to correctly state the amount of revenue earned that it reports on its income statement, and the ending current or long-term liability that it reports on its balance sheet.

---

10. *FASB Statement No. 43* does not specifically address the allocation of the costs of compensated absences to interim periods. If a company did not make quarterly accruals for compensated absences because they were not material, it would need to determine its remaining liability for compensated absences at year-end and make the related accrual journal entry at that time.

11. "Disclosure of Long-Term Obligations," *FASB Statement of Financial Accounting Standards No. 47* (Stamford, Conn.: FASB, June, 1981), par. 10.

12. "Accounting for Product Financing Arrangements," *FASB Statement of Financial Accounting Standards No. 49* (Stamford, Conn.: FASB, June, 1981), par. 8.

SECURE YOUR KNOWLEDGE 13-1

- Liabilities are unavoidable obligations, which may or may not be legally enforceable, that arise from past transactions, and are settled at a future date through the transfer or use of assets.
- Current liabilities provide insights into a company's liquidity and financial flexibility, and are useful in assessing a company's future cash flows.
- Most current liabilities are measured, recorded, and reported at their maturity amount.
- Accounts payable, current maturities of long-term debt, dividends payable, advances and refundable deposits, accrued liabilities, and unearned items are examples of liabilities that are contractual in nature.
- A company's obligation for compensated absences that vest or accumulate and result from employee's services already rendered must be accrued in the current period, if the payment of the obligation is probable and can be reasonably estimated.

CURRENT LIABILITIES WHOSE AMOUNTS DEPEND ON OPERATIONS

Several kinds of current liabilities relate to operations, and their amounts depend on these operations. Included are liabilities related to sales and use taxes, payrolls, a corporation's income taxes, and bonus agreements.

Sales and Use Taxes

A sales tax is a tax levied on the transfer of tangible personal property and on certain services. A seller must collect sales tax from the customer and pay the amount—usually on a monthly basis—to the proper governmental authority. **A use tax is a tax levied by a state or local governmental unit on goods bought from a nonsales-tax area or sector.** It is levied on the buyer of merchandise purchased for the buyer's own use or consumption. For example, suppose that a company goes out of state to buy trucks because of a better price. When the company registers the trucks in its own state, it has to file a use tax return and pay the tax. A sales tax and a use tax are essentially the same, except for collection and payment. In the following discussion, we only discuss the sales tax in two situations.

Sales Tax Separate from Sales

The first situation is a typical sale when the sales tax is added to the invoice price. For example, assume that Selleroy Company sells merchandise for cash with a retail sales price of $50,000 on which a sales tax of 6% is levied. The company collects $53,000 from its customers and records the collection as follows:

Cash	53,000	
Sales		50,000
Sales Taxes Payable		3,000

The Selleroy Company owes the $3,000 sales taxes it collected to the state or local government levying the tax. Therefore, the amount is *not* part of revenues (sales). Instead the company records it as a current liability, Sales Taxes Payable. Later, when Selleroy files the sales tax return and pays the tax to the governmental agency, it eliminates the current liability.

Sales Tax Included in Sales

The second situation arises when a company includes the amount of the sales taxes directly in the price it charges for merchandise. In this case, at the time of sale it credits the Sales account for the sum of the sales taxes payable and the sales amount. When a company uses this procedure, since sales taxes generally must be paid monthly, it must make an adjusting entry at the end of each month to reduce the Sales account and to create the current liability, Sales Taxes Payable. For example, suppose that the Smally Company collects sales taxes but records the combined amount of both the sales and the sales taxes in the Sales account. To calculate the sales for the month, the amount in the Sales account must be divided by 1 plus the tax rate. The sales taxes owed are determined by subtracting the calculated sales from the amount in the Sales account. For instance, suppose that at the end of January, the Sales account shows a credit balance of $169,600. Assuming a 6% sales tax on all goods, the company makes an adjusting entry for $9,600 [$169,600 − ($169,600 ÷ 1.06)] at the end of January as follows:

Sales	9,600	
Sales Taxes Payable		9,600

In some cases the sales taxes payable computed by the company may differ slightly from the amount calculated by the governmental authority (e.g., because of the use of graduated sales tax tables). In these cases the company makes an adjustment to Sales Taxes Payable and to Sales. This is a change in accounting estimate.

Liabilities Related to Payrolls

4 Understand and record payroll taxes and deductions.

Companies are required by law to withhold from the pay of each employee a legal amount for the anticipated federal and state (and sometimes local government) taxes payable by employees. They also may voluntarily withhold amounts for union dues, group insurance, retirement savings, and various other amounts payable by the employees to third parties. In addition to these withheld items, federal and state (and sometimes local) laws levy on employers other taxes that are based on the payroll amount. These include social security taxes and unemployment insurance taxes. Since a company must pay these taxes and voluntary withholdings within a few months, it classifies them as current liabilities.

Exhibit 13-2 shows an overview of the withheld groups of items and related voluntary payroll deductions. We discuss each item briefly in the following sections.

Payroll Tax Group

The federal income tax law, most state income tax laws, and some local government laws require employers to withhold from the pay of each employee an amount of the anticipated income taxes payable by the employee to the respective governmental units. (Since only a few local governments levy taxes based on the payroll, we ignore these taxes in the following discussion.) The amount withheld depends on the number of exemptions claimed and the amount of income earned by the employee. Employers determine the amount to be withheld from each employee's pay by using applicable legal rates or by referring to withholding tax tables. The employer must pay withheld amounts to the respective governmental unit at specified times and through specified channels. For example, the withheld federal income taxes must be paid to the Internal Revenue Service either electronically or through local depositories (e.g., banks).

Social security legislation requires that employers withhold Federal Insurance Contribution Act taxes (F.I.C.A.) from the wages of each employee under certain conditions. Also, employers must match the taxes of the employee and pay the sum of both taxes to the Internal Revenue Service along with the income taxes withheld. F.I.C.A. taxes have a dual purpose. The first is to pay federal old-age, survivor, and disability insurance (O.A.S.D.I.) benefits. The second is to pay federal hospital insurance (Medicare) benefits. Together, these taxes are referred to as *social security taxes*. As shown in Exhibit 13-2, the 2005 F.I.C.A. taxes are 15.30% (6.20% + 1.45% + 6.20% + 1.45%) on the first $90,000 earned by each employee. One half of this amount—7.65% (6.20% + 1.45%)—is paid by the employee; the other half is paid by the employer. On income between $90,000 and the total income earned by the employee, additional F.I.C.A. taxes of 1.45% are paid by both the employee and employer.

EXHIBIT 13-2   **Payroll Taxes and Voluntary Deductions**

Payroll Tax Group	2005 Rate on		2005 Annual Salary per Employee Subject to Tax
	Employee	Employer	
Federal income tax	Graduated rates	—	100%
State income tax	Graduated rates	—	100%
F.I.C.A. taxes			
O.A.S.D.I.	6.20%	6.20%	$90,000
Medicare	1.45%	1.45%	100%
Federal unemployment tax	—	0.8%	$ 7,000
State unemployment tax	—	5.4%	$ 7,000

Voluntary Payroll Deductions Group

Union dues
Government bonds
Group insurance } Amount withheld is stated in contract
Retirement savings
Others

The actual tax rates and wage base for future years will be determined by Congress. Because Congress changes (generally increases) these items frequently, for simplicity in the following examples and homework, we will use an assumed rate of 16%—8% on the employee and 8% on the employer—and a taxable wage base of $90,000 on *both* F.I.C.A taxes.

The fifth and sixth taxes shown in Exhibit 13-2 are unemployment insurance taxes, another type of social security tax. These taxes are used by governmental units to make payments for a limited time to individuals who become unemployed. The Federal Unemployment Tax Act (F.U.T.A.) requires a tax with a maximum rate of 6.2% to be levied wholly on employers of one or more persons, but the rate applies to only the first $7,000 paid to each employee. The law provides, however, that 5.4% of the 6.2% is payable to the state, assuming that the state levies an approved unemployment insurance tax. Thus, in these cases, the net effective federal unemployment tax rate is 0.8%. Most state laws allow for a reduction of the 5.4% tax through merit-rating plans for those employers who maintain steady employment, because that reduces the amount paid from the fund.

Voluntary Payroll Deduction Group

Through a contractual arrangement between individual employees and their employer, many kinds of payroll deductions can be authorized. Typical examples of these voluntary contractual deductions are for payment of group hospital insurance, accident insurance, life insurance, union dues, government bonds, and tax-sheltered retirement savings. These payroll deductions are made for the convenience of the employees of a company.

Accounting for Payroll Taxes and Deductions

To show the accounting for payroll taxes and voluntary payroll deductions, assume that the Wager Corporation summarizes the following weekly payroll from its payroll records during early February 2008:

Type of Salary	Gross Pay	Withheld Amounts				Net Pay
		F.I.C.A. Tax*	Federal Income Tax	State Income Tax	Union Dues	
Sales staff	$20,000	$1,600	$1,460	$ 600	$200	$16,140
Office staff	8,000	640	520	400	160	6,280
	$28,000	$2,240	$1,980	$1,000	$360	$22,420

*Assumed 8% rate.

Further assume that the effective federal and state unemployment tax rates are 0.8% and 5.4%, respectively, and *that all wages are subject to all payroll taxes*. The company makes the following two journal entries to record the payment of the payroll and the payroll taxes imposed on the employer:

1. To record salaries and employee withholding items:

Sales Salaries Expense	20,000	
Office Salaries Expense	8,000	
F.I.C.A. Taxes Payable		2,240
Employee Federal Income Taxes		
Withholding Payable		1,980
Employee State Income Taxes		
Withholding Payable		1,000
Employee Union Dues Withholding Payable		360
Cash		22,420

2. To record employer payroll taxes:

Payroll Taxes Expense	3,976	
F.I.C.A. Taxes Payable (8% × $28,000)		2,240
Federal Unemployment Taxes Payable		
(0.8% × $28,000)		224
State Unemployment Taxes Payable		
(5.4% × $28,000)		1,512

The company reports the various "payable" accounts as current liabilities. Instead of recording Payroll Taxes Expense in the second entry, the company may increase the respective Salaries Expense accounts for the appropriate amounts that are the additional cost of employing the sales and office staff. Regardless of approach, when Wager Corporation pays the payroll deductions, it eliminates the related current liability accounts.

Income Taxes Payable

The income of corporations is subject to a federal income tax separate from that of individuals. In addition, corporations may be subject to state and foreign income taxes. The federal corporate income tax imposes a rate schedule for 2006 that is a four-step progressive structure, which ranges from a low of 15% on taxable income of less than $50,000 to 35% on taxable income over $10,000,000. Because Congress may change the income tax rates and because actual income tax computations are complex, for simplicity we generally assume an effective income tax rate (e.g., 30%) in our discussions and homework.

A corporation must file its Form 1120, Corporate Income Tax Return, two and one half months after the end of the taxable fiscal year. Most corporations must pay estimated taxes throughout the fiscal year. The Internal Revenue Service provides guidelines for the calculation of both estimated and actual income taxes. Since these guidelines are subject to change, we do not discuss them in this book.

When a corporation accrues its estimated income taxes for either interim or end-of-period financial statement purposes, it records a debit to Income Tax Expense and a credit to a current liability, Income Taxes Payable. Later, when the corporation pays its actual income taxes, it records a debit to Income Taxes Payable (to eliminate the current liability) and a credit to Cash. If the estimated amount differs from the actual amount, the corporation makes an adjustment to the Income Tax Expense account. This is a change in accounting estimate.

Bonus Obligations

As incentives to certain employees—particularly officers and managers—to increase company earnings, many companies establish an earnings-based bonus agreement. The

LINK TO ETHICAL DILEMMA

You are on the management team of Crystal Clear Electronics (CCE) Inc., a company that specializes in high-quality home theater systems. In addition to selling home theater systems, your company provides custom installation on all purchases and is known for the professionalism of its installation staff. This reputation is due to the rigorous policies its home installation staff must follow. All employees are required to attend bimonthly training sessions, wear CCE Inc. uniforms, observe the installation dates and times agreed on by CCE and the customer, and follow any instructions given by CCE as to how to perform the installation.

Faced with shrinking margins and cash flow problems, CCE is looking to cut costs and increase cash flows. You realize that by reclassifying the installation staff as independent contractors, CCE will be able to accomplish both objectives. Because the installation staff would be independent contractors, the company would not have to pay payroll taxes, social security, and medicare expenses. The reduction in these costs and the corresponding increase in cash flow would certainly help the company's liquidity. Furthermore, such a change would not affect the quality of the service provided and would be virtually invisible to customers. Is this reclassification an acceptable interpretation of GAAP?

bonus is usually payable shortly after the end of the year. The bonus, which is additional salary, is an operating expense of the company. The company records the bonus as an expense and as a current liability when it has been earned by the employees. Also, the company deducts the bonus payments when computing its taxable income. Legal documents for bonus agreements may be written in several different ways. Two typical plans provide for the calculation of the bonus as follows:[13]

1. The bonus is based on the corporation's income after deducting income taxes, but before deducting the bonus.
2. The bonus is based on the corporation's net income after deducting both the bonus and the income taxes.

In either of these two approaches, the corporation cannot determine its income tax until it calculates the bonus. Thus, the computation requires solving two simple simultaneous equations. Example 13-1 shows the computation of the bonus and income tax for each of these approaches.

The Bonex Corporation records the bonus and income taxes in Part 2 of Example 13-1 as follows:

1. To record the bonus:

Salaries Expense (Officer's Bonus)	17,009	
Officer's Bonus Payable		17,009

---

13. Two other approaches are: (1) the bonus could be based on the corporation's income before income taxes and before the bonus, or (2) the bonus could be based on the corporation's income before income taxes and after the bonus is deducted. The computations involved in these two approaches are similar to (but simpler than) the methods we discuss and we do not present them here.

EXAMPLE 13-1 Computation of Bonus and Income Tax

Basic Information

The two examples involve these assumptions: the Bonex Corporation reported income for the current year of $260,000 before deducting income taxes and before a bonus to the chief executive officer; the effective tax rate is 30%, and the bonus rate is 10%. In the two examples, let: B = bonus and T = income tax.

Part 1

Bonus computed on income after deducting income taxes but before deducting the bonus.
The two equations for calculating the bonus are:

$B = 0.10$ ($260,000 – T)   (1)
$T = 0.30$ ($260,000 – B)   (2)

To solve the simultaneous equations, the value of T is substituted in Equation (2) for the element T in Equation (1) as follows:

$B = 0.10$ [$260,000 – 0.30 ($260,000 – B)]   (3)

Now Equation (3) has only one unknown and is solved as follows:

B = 0.10 [$260,000 – $78,000 + 0.30$B$]
B = $26,000 – $7,800 + 0.03$B$
B – 0.03B = $18,200
0.97B = $18,200
B = $18,200 ÷ 0.97
B = <u>$18,763</u> (rounded to nearest dollar)

To calculate the amount of the income tax, the amount of the bonus is substituted into Equation (2) as follows:

T = 0.30 ($260,000 – $18,763)
T = <u>$72,371</u> (rounded to nearest dollar)

Part 2

Bonus computed on net income after deducting both income taxes and the bonus.
The two equations for calculating the bonus are:

$B = 0.10$ ($260,000 – B – T)   (4)
$T = 0.30$ ($260,000 – B)   (5)

To solve the simultaneous equations, the value of T in Equation (5) is substituted for the element T in Equation (4) as follows:

$B = 0.10$ [$260,000 – B – 0.30 ($260,000 – B)]   (6)
B = 0.10 [$260,000 – B – $78,000 + 0.30$B$]
B = $26,000 – 0.10$B$ – $7,800 + 0.03$B$
B + 0.10B – 0.03B = $18,200
1.07B = $18,200
B = $18,200 ÷ 1.07
B = <u>$17,009</u> (rounded to nearest dollar)

To calculate the amount of the income tax, the amount of the bonus is substituted into Equation (5) as follows:

T = 0.30 ($260,000 – $17,009)
T = <u>$72,897</u> (rounded to nearest dollar)

2. To record the income tax expense:

Income Tax Expense	72,897	
Income Taxes Payable		72,897

The Bonex Corporation reports both the Officer's Bonus Payable and Income Taxes Payable as current liabilities on its balance sheet. Note that bonuses *may* have an undesirable effect on management's decisions regarding accounting principles. That is, management might choose an accounting principle, method, or procedure only because it increases the company's income, thereby increasing management's bonuses. This action is consistent with "agency theory" that we discussed in Chapter 1.

CURRENT LIABILITIES REQUIRING AMOUNTS TO BE ESTIMATED

A number of liabilities have amounts that a company must estimate as of the balance sheet date. We discuss the obligations that typically are current liabilities in this section. These include property taxes, warranties, and premium obligations. These items are specific types of "contingent liabilities." We discuss contingencies in the following section.

Property Taxes

Property taxes are assessed by municipal, county, and some state governments on the value of certain property as of a given date. They become a lien against the property at a date specified by law. Legally, a liability arises on this lien date. The lien date may precede the billing date by several months. For example, in Columbia, Missouri, the property tax is assessed on the value of the property as of January 1 of each year. The date that the tax becomes a lien against the property is July 1. The fiscal year of the city is July 1 to June 30. Property tax statements are mailed to property owners during November. Thus if a company records its property taxes before it receives the tax statement, it must estimate the amount. Also, the accounting year of the company may be different from the fiscal year of the municipality. In this case, the issue arises as to when the company should record the property tax liability and in which accounting period the property taxes should be expensed.

A company should accrue property taxes in equal monthly amounts during the fiscal periods of the taxing authority for which the taxes are levied. The accounting records then will show, at any closing date, the appropriate current liability or prepaid asset.[14] This method is preferred because the company recognizes the property tax expense in the same period it receives services from the governmental unit(s).

It is not difficult to estimate the amount of property taxes applicable to the fiscal year of the taxing authority. By law, the tax rate generally cannot vary too much from past rates. Also, the value of the property being taxed is generally determined by the municipality with a notification to the owner. Thus, the company can determine the total valuation subject to the tax. The company calculates the estimated property tax by applying the estimated rate to the assessed valuation amount. If a variation between the actual property taxes and the estimated property taxes occurs, the company accounts for it as a change in accounting estimate.

Example: Recording Property Taxes   Assume that the Ezzell Company's fiscal year-end is December 31. The fiscal year-end for the town and county in which the Ezzell Company is located is June 30 of the next year. The tax becomes a lien against the property on July 1 of each year. The estimated property taxes for the period July 1, 2007 to June 30, 2008 are $7,200. The tax bill is mailed in October with a requirement that the tax be paid before December 31, 2007. The tax bill for the Ezzell Company reported an actual tax of $7,290, and the company pays this amount on October 31, 2007. The company records monthly property tax adjustments for interim statements required by its management.

5 Record property taxes.

---

14. "Restatement and Revision of Accounting Research Bulletins," *Accounting Research Bulletin No. 43* (New York: AICPA, 1961), par. 14.

Assuming that the Ezzell Company did not recognize any property tax liability at the lien date and it records the property tax on a monthly accrual basis, it records the following series of journal entries:

Three Monthly Entries: July 31–September 30, 2007

Property Tax Expense ($7,200 ÷ 12)	600	
Property Taxes Payable		600

October 31, 2007: Payment of Property Taxes

Property Taxes Payable	1,800	
Prepaid Property Taxes	5,490	
Cash		7,290

Three Monthly Entries: October 31–December 31, 2007

Property Tax Expense	610	
Prepaid Property Taxes		610

The company reports an $1,800 ($600 × 3) current liability for property taxes on its September 30, 2007 interim balance sheet. Note that the $610 amount in the last journal entry is the result of allocating the $90 difference ($7,290 − $7,200) between the actual and estimated property taxes to the remaining 9-month period ending June 30, 2008. That is, the $610 is computed by subtracting the previously estimated property tax expense to date ($600 × 3) from the total actual property tax ($7,290) and dividing the difference ($5,490) by the remaining months (9) in the year.

Assuming that Ezzell had recorded $598 each month from January 31 to June 30, 2007 (the portion of the tax authority's *previous* fiscal year occurring during the company's *current* accounting year), its property tax expense for 2007 is $7,218 [($598 × 6) + ($600 × 3) + ($610 × 3)]. ♦

Warranty Obligations

Product warranty agreements require the seller, over a specified time after the sale, to correct any defect in the quality of the merchandise sold, to replace the item, or to refund the selling price. These promises are made by manufacturers and retailers to promote sales.

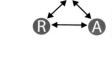

The period of the warranty may span two or more accounting periods. **The matching principle requires that a company recognize the warranty expense in the period during which it makes the sale,** because the flaws in the merchandise are assumed to be present at the time of the sale. The actual use of resources to correct the defects in the merchandise, however, may occur partly in the period of sale and partly in a later period. Consequently, recognition of the warranty expense in the period of sale and the resulting current liability requires a company to estimate the costs it will incur after the sale to correct any defects. There are three methods of accounting for warranty costs:

6 Account for warranty costs.

- expense warranty accrual method,
- sales warranty accrual method, and
- modified cash basis method.

We discuss each method in the following sections.

Expense Warranty Accrual Method

Under the expense warranty accrual method, a company recognizes the estimated warranty expense and a liability for future performance in the period of sale. This method assumes that the company makes the warranty offer to increase sales; hence, the estimated warranty expense is matched against these sales. The company classifies the estimated portion of the warranty liability for the next accounting period (or operating cycle, if longer) as a current liability; it classifies the remainder as a long-term liability. During the period when it uses resources to fulfill the warranty agreement, it debits the liability and credits the respective assets.

Example: Expense Warranty Accrual Method Assume that Anglee Machinery Corporation begins production on a new machine in April 2007 and sells 200 of these machines at $6,000 each by December 31, 2007. Each machine carries a warranty for one year. Experience from the sale of similar machinery in the past has shown that the warranty costs will average $150 per unit, or a total of $30,000 (200 × $150). The corporation spent $5,000 in 2007 and $25,150 in 2008 to fulfill the warranty agreements for the 200 machines sold in 2007. The company records this information under the expense warranty accrual method for the year 2007 in a series of journal entries as follows:

> **Sale of 200 Machines during April–December, 2007**
>
> | | | |
> |---|---|---|
> | Cash or Accounts Receivable ($6,000 × 200) | 1,200,000 | |
> | Sales | | 1,200,000 |
>
> **Recognition of Warranty Expense for Period, April–December, 2007**
>
> | | | |
> |---|---|---|
> | Warranty Expense ($150 × 200) | 30,000 | |
> | Estimated Liability under Warranties | | 30,000 |
>
> **Payment or Incurrence of Warranty Costs for Period, April–December, 2007**
>
> | | | |
> |---|---|---|
> | Estimated Liability under Warranties | 5,000 | |
> | Cash (or other assets) | | 5,000 |

The company reports the Warranty Expense as an operating expense on its 2007 income statement. It reports the remaining $25,000 ($30,000 accrued − $5,000 paid) unpaid Estimated Liability under Warranties as a current liability on its December 31, 2007 balance sheet since the warranty period is a year in length.

The company records the transactions in 2008 relating to the 200 machines sold in 2007 as follows:

> **Payment or Incurrence of Warranty Costs during 2008**
>
> | | | |
> |---|---|---|
> | Estimated Liability under Warranties | 25,000 | |
> | Warranty Expense | 150 | |
> | Cash (or other assets) | | 25,150 |

In the preceding journal entry, the actual warranty costs are $150 more than were estimated. The company debited this amount to Warranty Expense for 2008 because it resulted from a change in accounting estimate. ✦

Sales Warranty Accrual Method

Many companies encourage customers to buy a "service contract" when they buy merchandise. Service contracts require customers to make fixed payments for future services. In other cases, there is no explicit separate service contract but the sales price of each product includes the sale of two items: the product and an implied warranty contract. Use of the **sales warranty accrual method** separates the accounting for these two items *even when no separate service contract is involved*. Under this method, a company assumes that its revenue from the implied warranty contract is equal to the estimated warranty costs, and it defers and recognizes revenue in an amount equal to the warranty costs it incurred. This is a *cost recovery approach to warranty revenue recognition*. (We discuss the cost recovery method of revenue recognition in Chapter 18.)

Example: Sales Warranty Accrual Method In the case of the Anglee Machinery Corporation, assume that the $6,000 selling price of each machine includes both an implied service contract (sale of the warranty) of $150 and a sale of a machine with a selling price of $5,850 ($6,000 − $150). Under the sales warranty accrual method, the company records the transactions for 2007 as follows:

Sale of 200 Machines during April–December, 2007

Cash or Accounts Receivable ($6,000 × 200)	1,200,000	
Sales ($5,850 × 200)		1,170,000
Unearned Warranty Revenue ($150 × 200)		30,000

Recognition of Warranty Expense for Period, April–December, 2007

Warranty Expense	5,000	
Cash (or other assets)		5,000

Recognition of Warranty Revenue for Period, April–December, 2007

Unearned Warranty Revenue	5,000	
Warranty Revenue		5,000

The company reports the $25,000 balance ($30,000 – $5,000) in Unearned Warranty Revenue as a current liability on its December 31, 2007 balance sheet. Note that on the company's 2007 income statement the Sales amount is $30,000 smaller than under the expense warranty accrual method. The 2007 income statement lists Warranty Revenue of $5,000 and also Warranty Expense of $5,000 (as compared to $30,000 under the expense warranty accrual approach). Thus, while the company's net income for 2007 is the same under each method, the amounts of revenue and expense and the classifications of revenues are different, reflecting the different nature of revenue earned.

The company records the transactions for 2008 related to the 200 machines sold in 2007 as follows:

Recognition of Warranty Expense during 2008

Warranty Expense	25,150	
Cash (or other assets)		25,150

Recognition of Warranty Revenue during 2008

Unearned Warranty Revenue	25,000	
Warranty Revenue		25,000

Generally, it is assumed that a company realizes no profit from the sale of an implied warranty contract. As a matter of fact, in the Anglee Machinery Corporation example, there is a loss of $150. This loss results from the actual warranty costs exceeding the estimated costs by that amount. Thus, this method assumed the most conservative possible recognition of that part of the revenue related to the warranty. ◆

Modified Cash Basis Method

Under the modified cash basis, a company records the warranty costs as an expense during the period in which it makes the repairs to merchandise under warranty. Thus, it recognizes the expense in the period of the *repair*, and this period may be later than the period of the sale. The modified cash basis is the only method accepted for federal income tax purposes. For this reason companies often use it for financial reporting if the results are not materially different than those from either of the two previous methods. Since the company does not estimate and recognize the warranty costs during the period of sale, it does not record a liability for these future warranty costs. The company records a current liability only if it incurs an obligation for the repair that it does not pay at the time of the repair. This method is *not* appropriate for financial reporting because it violates the matching principle. In general, since the company expects to use resources in the future, a liability *does* in fact exist from the date of sale to the end of the warranty period. Therefore, the modified cash basis is conceptually unsound. It is justified for accounting under two conditions: (1) from a cost/benefit standpoint, when the warranty period is relatively short, (2) when it is not possible for the company to make a reliable estimate of the warranty obligation amount at the time of sale, or (3) when its results are not materially different from the expense warranty accrual method or the sales warranty accrual method.

Premium and Coupon Obligations

Many companies offer premiums such as toys, dishes, CDs, and small appliances in exchange for labels, coupons, box tops, and wrappers from their products. Other companies offer coupons printed in newspapers and magazines that can be used to reduce the purchase price of their products. Still others offer a cash rebate when customers return a cash register receipt for the purchase of their products. Many of these offers expire after a specified time, but some do not have an expiration date. All of these offers are intended to increase a company's sales. Accordingly, **a company matches the related costs as expenses against revenues in the period of sale.** Also, at the end of the accounting period, the company reports any outstanding offers that it expects to be redeemed or claimed within the next year (or operating cycle, if longer) as a current liability.

Example: Premium Obligation Assume that on October 1, 2007, the American Spaghetti Corporation began offering to customers a CD in return for 30 spaghetti can labels. This offer expires on April 1, 2008. The cost of each premium CD is $2. Based on past experience, the company estimates that only 60% of the labels will be redeemed. During 2007, the company purchased 6,000 CDs. In 2007, it sold 300,000 cans of spaghetti at $1.80 per can. From these sales 105,000 labels were returned for redemption in 2007. The company records the following series of journal entries in 2007 to match expenses against revenues and to record its current liabilities:

Purchase of 6,000 CDs

Inventory of Premium CDs	12,000	
Cash (or Accounts Payable)		12,000

Sale of 300,000 Cans of Spaghetti

Cash (or Accounts Receivable)	540,000	
Sales		540,000

Redemption of 105,000 Labels

Premium Expense [(105,000 ÷ 30) × $2]	7,000	
Inventory of Premium CDs		7,000

End-of-Year Recording of Estimated Liability for Outstanding Premium Offers

Premium Expense	5,000	
Estimated Premium Claims Outstanding		5,000

The company computes the year-end adjustment to premium expense as follows:

Total spaghetti cans (with labels) sold in 2007	300,000
Total labels estimated for redemption (60% × 300,000)	180,000
Deduct labels redeemed during 2007	(105,000)
Estimated number of labels for future redemption	75,000
Premium expense for estimated future redemptions [(75,000 ÷ 30) × $2]	$ 5,000

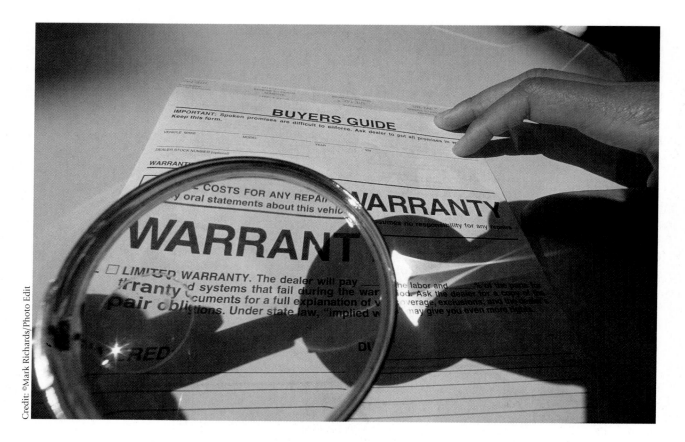

Credit: ©Mark Richards/Photo Edit

The company reports the Premium Expense as a selling expense on its 2007 income statement. The company reports the Inventory of Premium CDs as a current asset and the Estimated Premium Claims Outstanding as a current liability on its December 31, 2007 balance sheet since the offer expires in less than a year.

The future redemptions of these labels in 2008 will require a debit to the Estimated Premium Claims Outstanding liability account and a credit to Inventory of Premium CDs. If customers redeem fewer labels than the company estimated, it disposes of the remaining CDs. It debits Premium Expense and credits Inventory of Premium CDs for the remaining cost because it resulted from a change in accounting estimate.

Some companies prefer to record an estimate of the premium expense and current liability at the time of sale and reduce the liability each time a premium is claimed. Others prefer to record an estimate of the entire current liability at the end of the accounting period, but reduce the liability as premiums are claimed during the period. In either case, the effects on the financial statements are the same as those we showed. ♦

Advertising Costs

Companies are required to expense their advertising costs as incurred or at the first time the advertising takes place because it is difficult to measure the future economic benefits. This advertising can be very expensive. For instance, a 30-second advertisement during the 2005 Super Bowl cost $2.4 million dollars. A company running such an ad would expense the cost of preparing it as well as the $2.4 million fee at the time the ad was first run (i.e., at the time of the Super Bowl).

In the case of "direct-response" advertising, however, the AICPA issued a *Statement of Position* that requires companies to record certain costs initially as assets. **Direct-response advertising** is advertising that is expected to result in a customer's decision to buy the company's product based on a specific response to the advertising. The specific response must be documented through, for instance, a coded coupon turned in by the customer or a coded order form included with an advertisement. In this case, the company capitalizes specific costs if it has evidence (e.g., historical patterns) that they will result in future revenues in excess of future costs. If this evidence is not available, the company expenses the direct advertising costs as incurred. In a "cease-and-desist order," several years ago **America Online (AOL)** was required to pay a $3.5 million fine because it violated GAAP with regard to its direct advertising costs. AOL had been recording as assets the costs of sending its disks to potential customers. The SEC found that the Internet marketplace was too unstable for AOL to have evidence that its future revenues from these potential customers would exceed the amount of its capitalized costs.

The costs of direct-response advertising that a company capitalizes include (1) incremental direct costs incurred in transactions with independent third parties (e.g., costs of artwork, magazine space, mailing), and (2) payroll costs for activities (e.g., idea development, writing advertising copy) of employees directly related to the advertising. As we discussed in the previous section, also included as assets are premiums, contest prizes, gifts, and similar promotions directly related to the direct-response advertising activities. Costs for administration and occupancy (e.g., depreciation) are *not* included as assets. The costs of direct-response advertising that are reported as assets are amortized as advertising expense over the period during which the future benefits are expected to be received (e.g., up to the date a coupon expires).[15] A company generally reports any unpaid direct advertising costs as current liabilities because they will be paid in the near future.

SECURE YOUR KNOWLEDGE 13-2

- Sales and use taxes, payroll and payroll taxes, corporate income taxes, and bonus agreements are examples of current liabilities whose amounts depend on operations.
- In addition to the amounts withheld from employees' pay, a company also has a current liability for payroll taxes (e.g., social security, Medicare) until these amounts are sent to the appropriate governmental agencies.
- Property taxes are usually estimated and accrued in equal monthly amounts during the fiscal year of the taxing authority.
- When a warranty offer is made to stimulate sales, warranty obligations are estimated and recognized in the period of the sale even though the actual use of resources to satisfy the warranty agreement may not occur until a future period.
- If the warranty is considered a separate element from the sale itself (e.g., an implied service contract), revenue equal to the warranty costs must be deferred (creating a current liability) until service is actually performed or the warranty period expires.
- The accounting for obligations relating to premiums and coupons is similar to that of warranties—any obligation is estimated and recorded in the period of the sale.

CONTINGENCIES

External users are interested in information that helps them assess the amounts, timing, and uncertainty of the net cash inflows of a company. They need accounting information that has predictive value to help them forecast the future outcome of past or present events. The financial information that a company reports in its financial statements is based primarily on transactions that have affected it. However, there may be some information available at

---

15. "Reporting on Advertising Costs," *AICPA Statement of Position 93-7* (New York: AICPA, 1993), par. 25–47.

year-end about the company that is not yet recorded in its accounting system but may be useful in predicting what might happen to the company. These items commonly are referred to as "contingencies."

Specifically, **FASB Statement No. 5** defines a **contingency** for a company as:

an existing condition, situation, or set of circumstances involving uncertainty as to a possible gain (a *"gain contingency"*) or loss (a *"loss contingency"*) that will be resolved when a future event occurs or fails to occur.[16]

We discuss gain contingencies later in this section. Examples of loss contingencies are product warranties and premium offers that we discussed in earlier sections. We will discuss other loss contingencies later.

When a loss contingency exists for a company, the likelihood that the future event will confirm the loss can vary over a wide range. *FASB Statement No. 5* uses the terms *probable, reasonably possible,* and *remote* to identify three areas within this range. These terms are defined as follows:

1. **Probable.** The future event is *likely* to occur.
2. **Reasonably possible.** The chance of the future event occurring is *more* than remote but *less* than likely.
3. **Remote.** The chance of the future event occurring is *slight*.[17]

7 Explain the terms "probable," "reasonably possible," and "remote" related to contingencies.

A company's **accounting for a loss contingency** depends on the likelihood that the future event will occur. Two separate methods of accounting are defined by *FASB Statement No. 5*.

1. *Recognition in Financial Statements.* A company accrues an estimated loss from a loss contingency and reports a loss (or expense) and a liability (or as a reduction in an asset) in its financial statements if *both* of the following conditions are met:
   a. The company has information prior to issuing its financial statements that indicates it is *probable* that a liability has been incurred (or an asset impaired) at the date of the financial statements.
   b. The company can *reasonably estimate* the amount of the loss. In certain situations a company's reasonable estimate of the loss may be a range of amounts. When some amount within the range is a better estimate than any other amount in the range, *the better estimate is accrued.* When no amount within the range is a better estimate, *the minimum amount in the range is accrued* because it is not likely that the loss will be less than this minimum.[18]

2. *Disclosure in Notes to Financial Statements.* If either of the preceding conditions are not met but there is at least a reasonable possibility that a loss may have been incurred, then the company discloses the loss contingency in the notes to its financial statements. (Some remote loss contingencies are also disclosed in the notes, as we discuss later.)

To summarize, **a company recognizes a loss contingency in its financial statements if the future event is *probable* and if its amount can be *reasonably estimated*.** If a liability is recorded in this process, it is *not* necessary to know the payee or the date that it is to be paid. A company discloses a loss contingency in the notes to its financial statements if one of

---

16. "Accounting for Contingencies," *FASB Statement of Financial Accounting Standards No. 5* (Stamford, Conn.: FASB, 1975), par. 1. (Emphasis added.)
17. *Ibid.*, par. 3. (Emphasis added.)
18. "Reasonable Estimation of the Amount of a Loss," *FASB Interpretation No. 14* (Stamford, Conn.: FASB, 1976), par. 3.

these criteria is not met and if there is a reasonable possibility that the company may have incurred a loss.

The following diagram is helpful in determining how to report a loss contingency.

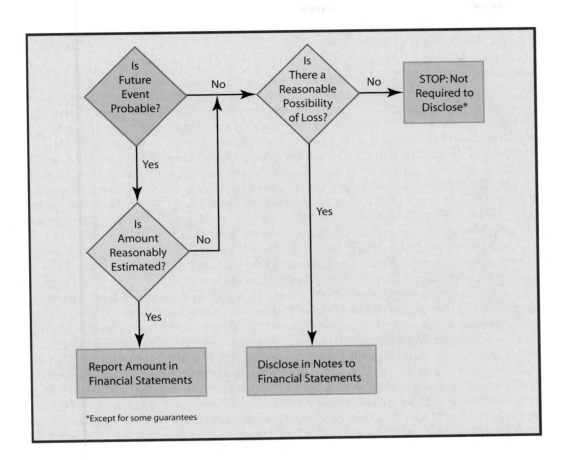

We discuss accounting for the accrual of loss contingencies, disclosure of loss contingencies in the notes to the financial statements, and disclosure of gain contingencies in the notes to the financial statements.

Accrual of Loss Contingencies

Companies usually accrue certain loss contingencies because they are probable and can be reasonably estimated. They include the noncollectibility of receivables (bad debts), sales returns and allowances (which we discussed in Chapter 7), and the obligations related to property taxes, product warranties, and premium offers that we discussed earlier in this chapter. Several other loss contingencies *may be* accrued provided they meet the two stated conditions. These include the threat of expropriation of assets, pending litigation, actual claims and assessments, guarantees of indebtedness of others, and agreements to repurchase receivables (or the related property) that were sold. On the other hand, at least three contingencies are *usually not* accrued. These include the uninsured risk of damage to company property by fire, explosion, or other hazards, general or unspecified business risks, and risk of loss from catastrophes assumed by property and casualty insurance companies. For this latter group of items, a company's mere exposure to risk does not mean that an asset is impaired or that a liability has been incurred.

8 Record and report a loss contingency.

When a company recognizes a loss contingency, it records a debit to an *expense* (or *loss*) account and a credit to a *liability* account, *asset* account, or *contra-asset* account. For example, assume Roberts Company estimates that its bad debt expense is $12,000 for 2007. The company records this loss contingency at the end of the year as follows:

Bad Debt Expense	12,000	
Allowance for Doubtful Accounts		12,000

Lawsuits

Accounting for lawsuits is a very difficult issue. A defendant company must analyze these lawsuits as loss contingencies. The company should consider the opinion of its legal counsel, the nature of the litigation, its previous experience in similar cases, and management reaction to the lawsuit. If the cause of the litigation has occurred before the date of its financial statements, if the loss of the lawsuit is *probable*, and if the loss amount can be *reasonably estimated*, the company must accrue the loss and related liability. Management may decide only to disclose the pending lawsuit in the notes to the financial statements because the loss is not probable or because it is not possible to reasonably estimate the loss. However, this decision may be influenced by management's desire to maintain higher reported earnings and to minimize the amount of reported liabilities.

In regard to potential unfiled lawsuits and other possible assessments and unasserted claims, a company must determine the likelihood that the suit may be filed or the claim or assessment asserted, and the probability of an unfavorable outcome. For example, if Patterson Corporation is being investigated for a possible patent infringement suit, it must determine the probability that the suit will be filed and that the suit will be lost. If these future events are probable, if the loss is reasonably estimable, and if the cause for action has occurred before the date of the issuance of the financial statements, it must accrue the loss and related liability.

In practice, companies usually do *not* accrue the costs of actual or pending litigation. In the case where a company is being sued for a specific situation by a single complainant, it is unlikely that the company will have sufficient evidence to conclude that the likelihood of loss is probable. Or in a situation where there is a lack of precedence relating to the particular circumstances of a lawsuit, even if a company admits guilt it is unlikely to conclude that it can reasonably estimate the amount of the loss. However, a company may be sued by many complainants over the same, or similar, issue (a "class action" suit) in which case the thresholds of probable and reasonably estimable may be reached. In this situation, the company typically will accrue the costs of the litigation. For instance, **Union Carbide Corporation** (a wholly owned subsidiary of **Dow Chemical Company**) has accrued losses of $1.6 billion in regard to its potential liability for a class action lawsuit involving its manufacture of asbestos.

Disclosure of Loss Contingencies in the Notes to the Financial Statements

If a company does not accrue a loss for a loss contingency, it must disclose the contingency when there is at least a reasonable possibility that it has incurred a loss. Recall that a loss contingency is reasonably possible when the chance of the future event occurring is more than remote but less than likely. Most of the examples of loss contingencies listed earlier could fall into this category, particularly the threat of expropriation of assets, pending or threatened litigation, and actual or possible claims and assessments. For this type of loss contingency, a company makes this disclosure in the notes to its financial statements. The disclosure must indicate the nature of the contingency and give an estimate of the possible loss or range of loss or state that such an estimate cannot be made.

Certain loss contingencies, where the possibility of loss is only remote, are also disclosed in the notes to a company's financial statements. Examples of these loss contingencies include direct and indirect guarantees of indebtedness of others, obligations of commercial banks under "standby letters of credit," and guarantees to repurchase receivables that have been sold or otherwise assigned. **An indirect guarantee involves an agreement requiring** one company to transfer funds to another entity if specified events occur whereby (1) the funds are legally available to creditors of the other entity, and (2) those creditors may enforce that entity's claims against the company under the agreement.[19] A common characteristic of these remote contingencies is a guarantee, normally with a right to proceed against an outside party in the event that the guarantor has to satisfy the guarantee.[20] The disclosure of this group of guarantees must include the nature and amount of the guarantee and, if estimable, the value of any recovery that could be expected to result. This latter requirement would result from the guarantor's right to proceed against an outside party.

Disclosure of Gain Contingencies in the Notes to the Financial Statements

If a company has a gain contingency, there is a potential increase in its assets or a potential decrease in its liabilities. Adhering to the convention of conservatism and to the revenue recognition criteria, *FASB Statement No. 5* requires that these gains usually are *not* accrued, but are disclosed in the notes to the company's financial statements. It states:

9 Disclose a gain contingency.

> (a) **Contingencies that might result in gains usually are not reflected in [a company's] accounts since to do so might be to recognize revenue prior to its realization.**
>
> (b) **Adequate disclosure shall be made of contingencies that might result in gains, but care shall be exercised to avoid misleading implications as to the likelihood of realization.[21]**

Therefore, gain contingencies are generally recognized when realized. An example of a gain contingency is where a company is suing another company for patent infringement, and the probability of winning the suit is excellent. A second example is a probable expropriation of a company's property by a government where probable reimbursement will exceed the book value of the property expected to be taken over by the government.

Executory Contracts

An **executory contract** is a contract in which two parties agree to a future exchange of resources or services, but neither party has performed any of its responsibilities. Examples of executory contracts include an unused line of credit, a purchase commitment, an agreement to pay future compensation, and a contract for having a factory built. For instance, **Mariah Carey** and **Universal** agreed to a $20 million contract for future albums. Since in an executory contract (sometimes called an *unexecuted* contract) no exchange of resources or services has occurred, no liability (or asset reduction) or contingent liability exists. However, when an executory contract has a likely material impact on the future cash flows of a company, the company discloses this information in the notes to its financial statements to enhance the predictive value of the information.

Illustrations of Contingency Disclosures

Real Report 13-1 illustrates the loss contingency disclosures in the notes to the 2004 financial statements of several companies. These disclosures involve the potential violation of environmental regulations by **Baker Hughes**, a value-added tax dispute of **Englehard**, and financial guarantees of customers' lines of credit by **Whirlpool**.

---

19. "Disclosure of Indirect Guarantees of Indebtedness of Others," *FASB Interpretation No. 34* (Stamford, Conn.: FASB, 1981), par. 2.

20. *FASB Statement No. 5, op. cit.*, par. 10 and 12.

21. *Ibid.*, par. 17.

Real Report 13-1 Disclosure of Contingencies

BAKER HUGHES INCORPORATED

NOTES TO CONSOLIDATED FINANCIAL STATEMENTS (in part):
NOTE 16. Commitments and Contingencies (in part)

[The Company has] been identified as a potentially responsible party ("PRP") in remedial activities related to various Superfund sites. We participate in the process set out in the Joint Participation and Defense Agreement to negotiate with government agencies, identify other PRPs, determine each PRP's allocation and estimate remediation costs. We have accrued what we believe to be our pro-rata share of the total estimated cost of remediation and associated management of these Superfund sites. This share is based upon the ratio that the estimated volume of waste we contributed to the site bears to the total estimated volume of waste disposed at the site. Applicable United States federal law imposes joint and several liability on each PRP for the cleanup of these sites leaving us with the uncertainty that we may be responsible for the remediation cost attributable to other PRPs who are unable to pay their share. No accrual has been made under the joint and several liability concept for those Superfund sites where our participation is minor since we believe that the probability that we will have to pay material costs above our volumetric share is remote. We believe there are other PRPs who have greater involvement on a volumetric calculation basis, who have substantial assets and who may be reasonably expected to pay their share of the cost of remediation. For those Superfund sites where we are a major PRP, remediation costs are estimated to include recalcitrant parties. In some cases we have insurance coverage or contractual indemnities from third parties to cover the ultimate liability.

Our total accrual for environmental remediation is $13.6 million and $15.6 million, which includes accruals of $3.6 million and $4.3 million for the various Superfund sites, at December 31, 2004 and 2003, respectively. The determination of the required accruals is subject to uncertainty, including the evolving nature of environmental regulations and the difficulty in estimating the extent and type of remediation activity that will be utilized. We believe that the likelihood of material losses in excess of the recorded accruals is remote.

ENGELHARD CORPORATION

NOTES TO CONSOLIDATED FINANCIAL STATEMENTS (in part):
NOTE 22. Litigation and Contingencies (in part)

The Company is involved in a value-added tax dispute in Peru. Management believes the Company was targeted by corrupt officials within a former Peruvian government... In late October 2000, a criminal proceeding alleging tax fraud and forgery related to this value-added tax dispute was initiated against two Lima-based officials of Engelhard Peru, S.A. Although Engelhard Peru, S.A. is not a defendant, it may be civilly liable in Peru if its representatives are found responsible for criminal conduct. In its own investigation, and in detailed review of the materials presented in Peru, management has not seen any tax fraud by these officials. Accordingly, Engelhard Peru, S.A. is assisting in the vigorous defense of this proceeding. Management believes the maximum economic exposure is limited to the aggregate value of all assets of Engelhard Peru, S.A. That amount, which is approximately $30 million, including unpaid refunds, has been fully provided for in the accounts of the Company.

WHIRLPOOL CORPORATION

NOTES TO CONSOLIDATED FINANCIAL STATEMENTS (in part):
NOTE (9) Guarantees, Commitments and Contingencies (in part)

The Company has guarantee arrangements in place in a Brazilian subsidiary. As a standard business practice in Brazil, the subsidiary guarantees customer lines of credit at commercial banks, supporting purchases from the Company, following its normal credit policies. In the event that a customer were to default on its line of credit with the bank, the subsidiary would be required to satisfy the obligation with the bank, and the receivable would revert back to the subsidiary. As of December 31, 2004 and December 31, 2003, these amounts totaled $184 million and $109 million, respectively. The only

Continued

recourse the Company has related to these agreements would be legal or administrative collection efforts directed against the customer.

Questions:

1. Describe the journal entries made by Baker Hughes in 2004 related to its remediation costs?
2. Does Baker Hughes accrue the remediation costs attributable to other PRPs who were unable to pay their share? Why or why not?
3. What is likelihood that Engelhard will incur a loss relating to the tax fraud, and what amount does Engelhard expect to pay?
4. Does the disclosure of the guarantee arrangements indicate that Whirlpool thinks it is probable that a loss will be incurred relating to these arrangements?

LINK TO INTERNATIONAL DIFFERENCES

International accounting standards and U.S. accounting standards are similar in regard to contingencies, but there are some critical differences. International standards deal with loss contingencies but refer to them as provisions. A company is required to recognize a provision when it has a present obligation as a result of a past event, when it is probable that the company will have a future outflow of resources to settle the obligation, and when it can make a reliable estimate of the amount. These provisions are similar to U.S. GAAP but international standards use probable to mean that the outcome is more likely than not to occur, while U.S. standards use probable to mean the outcome is likely to occur (a more stringent test). Furthermore, in a situation where a company cannot determine whether the obligating event has occurred, international standards require recognition of a liability if it is probable that the event has occurred. International standards also require a company to measure the provision at the settlement price on the balance sheet date using present value techniques whenever the effect on the measurement of the liability is material. A company is not allowed to recognize gain contingencies until realized, but discloses a gain contingency in the notes to its financial statements if an inflow of economic benefits is probable.

OTHER LIABILITY CLASSIFICATION ISSUES

We discuss two additional liability classification issues in this section: (1) short-term debt expected to be refinanced, and (2) classification of obligations that are callable by the creditor.

Short-Term Debt Expected to Be Refinanced

Generally, a company classifies debt that is maturing within one year (or the operating cycle, if longer) as a current liability. This classification affects the company's liquidity ratios such as its current ratio and acid-test ratio. In some situations, short-term debt that is expected to be refinanced on a long-term basis is *not* classified as a current liability. A company may refinance its short-term debt on a long-term basis by either:

- replacing the short-term debt with long-term debt (such as bonds payable) or with ownership securities (such as common stock); or
- extending, renewing, or replacing the short-term debt with other short-term obligations.

FASB Statement No. 6 states that short-term obligations are *excluded* from a company's current liabilities if two conditions are met: (1) it intends to refinance the obligation on a *long-term basis*, and (2) it has an ability to refinance. The **intent to refinance** on a long-term basis means that the company intends to refinance the short-term obligations so that it will not have to use working capital during the next year (or operating cycle, if longer). The **ability to refinance** on a long-term basis means that the company (1) has issued long-term obligations or equity securities after the date of its balance sheet but before it issues its balance sheet, or (2) has entered into a bona fide long-term financing agreement before it issues its balance sheet that clearly permits the company to refinance the short-term obligations on a long-term basis.

If a company actually has refinanced short-term debt after the year-end but before it issues its financial statements, it excludes an amount from the current liabilities shown on its year-end balance sheet. The amount excluded is *only* that portion of the short-term obligation that is equal to the proceeds from the new long-term obligations or equity securities issued to retire the short-term obligation. For example, assume that Rayvon Corporation, with $2,000,000 of short-term debt on December 31, 2007, issued 75,000 shares of common stock for $20 per share on January 9, 2008. The proceeds of $1,500,000 were scheduled to be used to retire the short-term obligation when it matured. On the December 31, 2007 balance sheet (issued on February 25, 2008), the company reports the short-term debt of $1,500,000 expected to be refinanced as a noncurrent liability. Note that the company reports the refinanced portion as a liability and *not* as stockholders' equity since, as of year-end, the item was debt and not equity. It reports the other $500,000 as a current liability.

When a company relies on a **financing agreement** to show its the ability to refinance, the amount of the short-term debt that it excludes from current liabilities is reduced to an amount that is the *lesser* of

1. The amount available for refinancing under the agreement, or
2. The amount obtainable under the agreement after considering the restrictions included in other agreements, or
3. A reasonable estimate of the minimum amount expected to be available for future refinancing if the amount that could be obtained fluctuates (for example, in relation to the company's needs, in proportion to the value of the collateral, or according to other terms of the agreement).[22]

If the company cannot make a reasonable estimate, it must include the entire outstanding short-term obligation as a current liability.

When a company excludes a short-term obligation to be refinanced from its current liabilities, the notes to its financial statements must include a description of the financing agreement and the terms of any new debt, or equity securities issued or expected to be issued as a result of the refinancing. These obligations also may be shown in captions distinct from both the current liabilities and long-term debt, such as "Interim Debt" or "Short-Term Debt Expected to Be Refinanced."

Repayment and Replacement

After the issuance of *FASB Statement No. 6*, an issue arose as to whether a company should exclude a short-term debt from its current liabilities if it repays the debt after the balance sheet date and then later issues long-term debt (or common stock) before the balance sheet actually is published. **FASB Interpretation No. 8** concluded that a company must *not* exclude such short-term debt from its current liabilities at the balance sheet date.[23] Thus, since the repayment of a short-term debt required the use of an existing actual current asset (even though it is later replaced), the company reports the short-term debt on its preceding year-end balance sheet as a current liability.

---

22. "Classification of Short-Term Obligations Expected to Be Refinanced," *FASB Statement of Financial Accounting Standards No. 6* (Stamford, Conn.: FASB, 1975), par. 9–12.
23. "Classification of a Short-Term Obligation Repaid Prior to Being Replaced by a Long-Term Security," *FASB Interpretation No. 8* (Stamford, Conn.: FASB, 1976), par. 3.

Classification of Obligations That Are Callable by the Creditor

As we noted earlier in the chapter, a company generally reports the *currently maturing portion* of its long-term debt as a current liability. Also, **FASB Statement No. 78** concluded that a company must report the *entire amount* of a long-term obligation as a current liability if the company is in violation of a long-term debt agreement (a requirement in the debt contract) at the balance sheet date, and the violation makes the liability callable by the creditor within one year (or operating cycle, if longer) from the balance sheet date.

An exception to this requirement is a callable obligation that meets the following conditions: (1) the creditor has waived the right to request repayment for more than one year (or operating cycle, if longer) from the balance sheet date, or (2) it is probable that the company will resolve the violation of a debt agreement for a long-term obligation within a specified grace period, thus preventing it from becoming callable. In this case, the company reports the obligation as long-term debt. It also discloses the circumstances involving an obligation under item (2) in the notes to its financial statements.[24]

The preceding GAAP indicate that the FASB concluded that a company's current liability classification is intended to include obligations that are (or will be) due on demand within one year (or the operating cycle, if longer) from the balance sheet date, *even though liquidation may not be expected within that period.* As indicated by the italicized phrase, this concept does not conform to the requirement that a current liability is one that "a company expects to liquidate by using current assets..." Instead, it substitutes a rule that obligations are classified as current when they are legally callable within one year, whether or not they are likely to be called. In dissenting to *FASB Statement No. 78*, three Board members stated that:

> **It is asserted that this amendment will improve comparability. It will, in fact, cause situations to appear the same even when underlying facts and circumstances are sufficiently different to justify different reasonable expectations. This is not comparability; it is substituting an arbitrary rule for judgment.**[25]

SECURE YOUR KNOWLEDGE 13-3

- A contingency is an existing uncertainty as to possible gains or losses, where the uncertainty can only be resolved when a future event occurs or fails to occur.
- A loss contingency is accrued when it is probable that the future confirming event will occur and the amount of the loss can be reasonably estimated.
- If the future confirming event is not probable or cannot be reasonably estimated and there is a reasonable possibility of a loss, the loss contingency is disclosed in the notes to the financial statements.
- Certain loss contingencies that involve a guarantee (e.g., standby letters of credit, guarantees of indebtedness of others) are disclosed in the notes to the financial statements even though the possibility of a loss is remote.
- Gain contingencies are usually not accrued but are disclosed in the notes to the financial statements. Gain contingencies are generally recognized when realized.
- If a company has both the intent and ability to refinance short-term debt on a long-term basis, the debt is excluded from the company's current liabilities.

---

24. "Classification of Obligations That Are Callable by the Creditor," *FASB Statement of Financial Accounting Standards No. 78* (Stamford, Conn.: FASB, 1983), par. 5.

25. *Ibid.*, page 4.

FINANCIAL STATEMENT PRESENTATION OF CURRENT LIABILITIES

Conceptually, a company should report its three main balance sheet elements—assets, liabilities, and equity—in homogeneous classes. This disclosure is helpful to users in assessing the nature, amount, timing, and liquidity of its resources and obligations. A company can report liabilities and assets as items in its balance sheet in various ways. The FASB has suggested broad guidelines as follows:

1. Assets and liabilities with different implications for the *financial flexibility* of the company should be reported as separate items.
2. Assets and liabilities with different general *liquidity* characteristics should be reported as separate items.
3. Assets and liabilities that differ regarding the attribute that is measured should be reported in separate categories.[26]

These guidelines suggest that a company should arrange its current liabilities in a way that will **highlight their liquidity characteristics and their effect on its financial flexibility.**

Most companies report current liabilities at the top of the Liabilities classification. Items within the current liability section typically may be listed (1) in the order of their average length of maturity, (2) according to amount (largest to smallest), or (3) in the order of liquidation preference—that is, in the order of their legal claims against assets. A popular way of presenting these items is as follows:

- Accounts payable
- Notes payable
- Accrued liability items
- Unearned revenue items
- Other current liabilities

A company includes any major issue affecting its current liabilities in a note to its financial statements. This presentation is made so that the notes and other supplemental information about current liabilities meet the requirement of full disclosure. For example, secured liabilities are clearly identified, along with the related assets pledged as collateral. If the due date of any liability can be extended, that fact and any related details are disclosed. Current liabilities are *not* offset against the assets that the company plans to use for their liquidation, and currently maturing long-term debt is classified as a current liability (unless refinanced).

Real Report 13-2 is an excerpt of the **General Mills** balance sheets showing how it reports its current liabilities, along with the related note to the financial statements. This disclosure is representative of the reporting techniques used by most large companies.

Real Report 13-2 Disclosure of Current Liabilities

GENERAL MILLS		
	May 30, 2004	**May 25, 2003**
(millions of dollars)		
Liabilities (in part)		
Current Liabilities:		
Accounts payable	$1,145	$1,303
Current portion of long-term debt	233	105
Notes payable	583	1,236
Other current liabilities	796	800
Total Current Liabilities	$2,757	$3,444

Continued

---

26. "Reporting Income, Cash Flows, and Financial Flexibility of Business Enterprises," *FASB Proposed Statement of Financial Accounting Concepts, op. cit.,* par. 50 and 51. (Emphasis added.)

NOTES TO CONSOLIDATED FINANCIAL STATEMENTS (in part):

5. BALANCE SHEET INFORMATION (in part)

The components of certain balance sheet accounts are as follows:

In Millions	May 30, 2004	May 25, 2003
Other Current Liabilities:		
Accrued payroll	$ 230	$ 243
Accrued interest	186	178
Accrued taxes	249	129
Miscellaneous	131	250
Total other current liabilities	$ 796	$ 800

8. DEBT (in part)

NOTES PAYABLE – The components of notes payable and their repective weighted average interest rates at the end of the periods were as follows:

In Millions	May 30, 2004		May 25, 2003	
	Notes Payable	Weighted Average Interest Rate	Notes Payable	Weighted Average Interest Rate
U.S. commercial paper	$ 441	1.2%	$ 1,415	1.4%
Canadian commercial paper	159	2.1	28	3.3
Euro commercial paper	499	2.1	527	1.5
Financial institutions	234	6.7	366	1.4
Amounts reclassified to long-term debt	(750)	–	(1,100)	–
Total Notes Payable	$ 583		$ 1,236	

See Note Seven for a description of related interest-rate derivative instruments.

To ensure availability of funds, we maintain bank credit lines sufficient to cover our outstanding short-term borrowings. As of May 30, 2004, we had $1.85 billion in committed lines and $264 million in uncommitted lines.

In the third quarter of fiscal 2004, we entered into an agreement for a new $750 million credit facility, expiring in January 2009. That facility replaced a $1.1 billion, 364-day facility, which expired January 22, 2004. The new credit facility, along with our existing $1.1 billion multi-year facility that expires January 2006, brings our total committed back-up credit amount to $1.85 billion. These revolving credit agreements provide us with the ability to refinance short-term borrowings on a long-term basis; accordingly, a portion of our notes payable has been reclassified to long-term debt.

Questions:

1. What must the revolving credit agreement include so that General Mills can reclassify a portion of its notes payable as long-term debt?
2. If current assets were $3,215 million on May 30, 2004, compute the current ratio.
3. If cost of goods sold was $6,584 million on May 30, 2004, compute the payables turnover.

SUMMARY

At the beginning of the chapter, we identified several objectives you would accomplish after reading the chapter. The objectives are listed below, each followed by a brief summary of the key points in the chapter discussion.

1. **Explain the characteristics of a liability.** The characteristics of a liability are: (1) a present responsibility for the probable future transfer or use of assets, (2) the obligation cannot be avoided, and (3) the liability transaction has already occurred.
2. **Define current liabilities.** Current liabilities are obligations that are expected to require the use of current assets or the creation of current liabilities within one year or the normal operating cycle, whichever is longer.
3. **Account for compensated absences.** Compensated absences include vacation, holiday, illness, or other personal activities for which an employee is paid. A company records an expense and a liability for an employee's compensation for future absences when: (1) its obligation relates to employee's services already rendered, (2) the obligation relates to rights that vest or accumulate, (3) payment is probable, and (4) it can estimate the amount.
4. **Understand and record payroll taxes and deductions.** Payroll taxes include social security taxes (F.I.C.A. taxes, including O.A.S.D.I and Medicare) levied on both the employee and employer, as well as unemployment taxes (F.U.T.A. and state) levied only on the employer. Payroll deductions include income tax withholdings and items such as union dues. A company records these items as liabilities at the time it records salaries expense and payroll tax expense.
5. **Record property taxes.** A company records property taxes in equal monthly amounts during the fiscal period of the taxing authority for which the taxes are levied. By doing so, at the end of the company's accounting period it reports the appropriate accrual or prepayment.
6. **Account for warranty costs.** Under the expense warranty accrual method, a company recognizes in the period of sale the estimated warranty expense and a liability for future performance. Under the sales warranty accrual method, a company separates the accounting for the product sale from the accounting for the (implied) warranty contract. Under the modified cash basis method, a company records the warranty cost as an expense during the period that repairs are made.
7. **Explain the terms "probable," "reasonably possible," and "remote" related to contingencies.** "Probable" means the future event is likely to occur. "Reasonably possible" means that the chance of the future event occurring is more than remote but less than likely. "Remote" means that the chance of the future event occurring is slight.
8. **Record and report a loss contingency.** A loss contingency is recognized if the future event is probable and if its amount can be reasonably estimated. If these two criteria are met, a company records a loss contingency by debiting an expense (or loss) and crediting a liability (or contra asset). Otherwise, it discloses a loss contingency in the notes to its financial statements.
9. **Disclose a gain contingency.** A gain contingency is usually not accrued; a company discloses a gain contingency in the notes to its financial statements. A company generally recognizes a gain contingency when it is realized.

ANSWERS TO REAL REPORT QUESTIONS

Real Report 13-1 Answers

1. Baker Hughes makes a journal entry that debits an expense account and credits a liability account for its share of expected environmental remediation costs. As the remediation costs are paid, Baker Hughes reduces the liability account. For 2004, the liability account decreased by $700,000 ($4.3 million less $3.6 million), indicating that the net remediation costs paid in 2004 exceeded the accruals for 2004.
2. Under the concept of joint and several liability, Baker Hughes may be liable for remediation costs attributable to other PRPs. However, where its involvement is minor, Baker Hughes believes there is a remote chance that it would be held responsible for costs in excess of its share, and no liability is accrued for these excess costs. Where it is considered a major PRP, Baker Hughes accrues its share of remediation costs as well as the estimate of the remediation costs of other PRPs that are not expected to be able to pay their share.

3. Although Engelhard's note disclosure states that no evidence of tax fraud by company officials has been found, the fact that Engelhard accrued this liability indicates that the company thinks it is probable it will have a loss of $30 million, its reasonable estimate of the liability. While Engelhard discloses the $30 million as the *maximum* amount it expects to pay, the disclosure suggests a range of possible outcomes. It should be noted that, if a range of outcomes is likely, GAAP requires a company to accrue the most likely estimate within the range. If all amounts in the range are equally likely, GAAP requires the *minimum* amount within the range to be accrued. Therefore, the user of the financial statement should not interpret this disclosure as stating that Engelhard expects to settle the amount for less than the $30 million that is accrued.
4. Whirlpool's disclosure does not indicate that a future loss is probable. Certain loss contingencies, such as guarantees of indebtedness of others, are disclosed in the notes to the financial statements even when the possibility of loss is remote.

Real Report 13-2 Answers

1. In order to reclassify a portion of its notes payable as long-term debt, the revolving credit agreement must clearly permit the company to refinance the portion of the notes payable reclassified after considering any restrictions.

2. The current ratio for General Mills at May 30, 2004 is 1.17 ($3,215 million ÷ $2,757 million).

3. The payables turnover ratio for General Mills at May 30, 2004 is 5.38 [$6,584 million ÷ {($1,145 million ÷ $1,303 million) ÷ 2}].

QUESTIONS

Q13-1 Define *liabilities*. Explain the meanings of *probable* and *obligations* in the context of a liability.

Q13-2 Distinguish between a legal and a nonlegal (accounting) liability. Give an example of each.

Q13-3 List the three characteristics of a liability. Discuss briefly.

Q13-4 Before a liability can be reported, a company must know the identity of the recipient. True or false? Justify your answer.

Q13-5 What are the primary issues in accounting for current liabilities?

Q13-6 Define a company's operating cycle.

Q13-7 Why is the liquidity of liabilities important in the accounting for liabilities?

Q13-8 How does the constraint of materiality affect the accounting for current liabilities?

Q13-9 Define a non-interest-bearing note that is discounted at a bank at a specific rate. How are the proceeds computed for a non-interest-bearing note?

Q13-10 What are compensated absences? How does a company account for them?

Q13-11 *FASB Statement No. 49* requires that a company selling inventory and agreeing to repurchase it later neither record the transaction as a sale nor remove the inventory from the balance sheet. If so, does a new current liability arise? How is its amount measured?

Q13-12 Identify how to account for warranty costs under the expense warranty accrual method, sales warranty accrual method, and modified cash basis.

Q13-13 Define *contingency*. What exactly is the company uncertain about—whether a future event will take place and result in a liability, or whether a future event will take place that will confirm that a liability exists from an event that has already taken place?

Q13-14 How do the matching principle and the conservatism convention enter into the accounting for contingencies?

Q13-15 What two criteria must be met before a loss contingency is reported in a company's financial statements?

Q13-16 With regard to a loss contingency, by what date must the event that results in a probable loss have occurred before accrual is required? By what date must information be available for a company to assess the probability that a loss has been incurred?

Q13-17 What conditions would have to be met for a company to accrue the loss from an unfiled lawsuit?

Q13-18 Define *gain contingency*. Describe the accounting requirements for a gain contingency.

Q13-19 What two criteria must be met before a company can classify short-term debt that is expected to be refinanced as a noncurrent liability?

Q13-20 How does a company demonstrate the ability to refinance currently maturing short-term debt?

Q13-21 *FASB Statement No. 78* requires that a company report certain obligations due on demand within one year (or operating cycle, if longer) as current liabilities. Do you agree with this statement? Explain.

MULTIPLE CHOICE (AICPA Adapted)

Select the best answer for each of the following.

M13-1 Which of the following is classified as an accrued payroll liability?

	Federal Income Tax Withheld	Employee's Share of F.I.C.A. Taxes
a.	No	Yes
b.	No	No
c.	Yes	No
d.	Yes	Yes

M13-2 During 2007 Lawton Company introduced a new line of machines that carry a three-year warranty against manufacturer's defects. Based on industry experience, warranty costs are estimated at 2% of sales in the year of sale, 4% in the year after sale, and 6% in the second year after sale. Sales and actual warranty expenditures for the first three-year period were as follows:

	Sales	Actual Warranty Expenditures
2007	$ 200,000	$ 3,000
2008	500,000	15,000
2009	700,000	45,000
	$1,400,000	$63,000

What amount should Lawton report as a liability at December 31, 2009?

a. $0

b. $5,000

c. $68,000

d. $105,000

M13-3 How should a loss contingency that is reasonably possible and for which the amount can be reasonably estimated be reported?

	Accrued	Disclosed
a.	Yes	No
b.	No	Yes
c.	Yes	Yes
d.	No	No

M13-4 All of Rolf Co.'s employees are entitled to two weeks of paid vacation for each full year in Rolf's employ. Unused vacation time can be accumulated and carried forward to succeeding years and will be compensated at the salary in effect when the vacation is taken. Mary Beal started her employment with Rolf on January 1, 2001. As of December 31, 2007, when Beal's salary was $500 per week, Beal had used 10 weeks of her accumulated vacation time. In December 2007 Beal notified Rolf of her intention to use her accumulated vacation weeks in June 2008. Rolf regularly scheduled salary adjustments in July of each year. Rolf properly did not deduct compensation for unused vacations in Rolf's 2007 income tax return. How much should Rolf report as a liability at December 31, 2007 for Beal's accumulated vacation time?

a. $0

b. $500

c. $1,000

d. $2,000

M13-5 Bronson Apparel, Inc., operates a retail store and must determine the proper December 31, 2007 year-end accrual for the following expenses:

The store lease calls for fixed rent of $1,000 per month, payable at the beginning of the month, and additional rent equal to 6% of net sales over $200,000 per calendar year, payable on January 31 of the following year. Net sales for 2007 are $800,000.

Bronson has personal property subject to a city property tax. The city's fiscal year runs from July 1 to June 30 and the tax, assessed at 3% of personal property on hand at April 30, is payable on June 30. Bronson estimates that its personal property tax will amount to $6,000 for the city's fiscal year ending June 30, 2008.

In its December 31, 2007 balance sheet, Bronson should report accrued expenses of

a. $39,000

b. $39,600

c. $51,000

d. $51,600

M13-6 When a company receives a deposit from a customer to protect itself against nonpayment for future services, the deposit should be classified by the company as

a. Revenue

b. A liability

c. Part of the allowance for doubtful accounts

d. A deferred credit deducted from accounts receivable

M13-7 The balance in Ashwood Company's Accounts Payable account at December 31, 2007 was $900,000 before any necessary year-end adjustment relating to the following:

Goods were in transit from a vendor to Ashwood on December 31, 2007. The invoice cost was $50,000, and the goods were shipped FOB shipping point on December 29, 2007. The goods were received on January 2, 2008.

Goods shipped FOB shipping point on December 19, 2007 from a vendor to Ashwood were lost in transit. The invoice cost was $25,000. On January 5, 2008 Ashwood filed a $25,000 claim against the common carrier.

Goods shipped FOB destination on December 22, 2007 from a vendor to Ashwood were received on January 6, 2008. The invoice cost was $15,000.

What amount should Ashwood report as accounts payable on its December 31, 2007 balance sheet?

a. $925,000

b. $940,000

c. $950,000

d. $975,000

M13-8 On September 1, 2007 a company borrowed cash and signed a one-year, interest-bearing note on which both the principal and interest are payable on September 1, 2008. How will the note payable and the related interest be classified in the December 31, 2007 balance sheet?

	Note Payable	Accrued Interest
a.	Current liability	Noncurrent liability
b.	Noncurrent liability	Current liability
c.	Current liability	Current liability
d.	Noncurrent liability	No entry

M13-9 Morgan Company determined that (1) it has a material obligation relating to employees' rights to receive compensation for future absences attributable to employees' services already rendered, (2) the obligation relates to rights that vest, and (3) payment of the compensation is probable. The amount of Morgan's obligation as of December 31, 2007 is reasonably estimated for the following employee benefits:

Vacation pay	$100,000
Holiday pay	25,000

What total amount should Morgan report as its liability for compensated absences in its December 31, 2007 balance sheet?

a. $0

b. $25,000

c. $100,000

d. $125,000

M13-10 Gain contingencies are usually recognized in the income statement when
a. Realized
b. Occurrence is reasonably possible and the amount can be reasonably estimated
c. Occurrence is probable and the amount can be reasonably estimated
d. The amount can be reasonably estimated

EXERCISES

E13-1 *Accounts Payable and Cash Discounts* On January 4, 2007 Dunbar Company purchased, on credit, 2,000 television sets at $500 each. Terms of the purchase were 2/10, n/30. Dunbar paid for one-fifth of these sets within 10 days and the remaining four-fifths by January 31.

Required
Prepare the journal entries on Dunbar Company's books, assuming that it uses the net price method to record its merchandise. (Dunbar uses a perpetual inventory system.)

E13-2 *Notes Payable* On December 1, 2007 Insto Photo Company purchased merchandise, invoice price $25,000, and issued a 12%, 120-day note to Ringo Chemicals Company. Insto uses the calendar year as its fiscal year and uses the perpetual inventory system.

Required
Prepare journal entries on Insto Photo's books to record the preceding information, including the adjusting entry at the end of the year and payment of the note at maturity.

E13-3 *Non-interest-bearing Notes Payable* On November 16, 2007 the Clear Glass Company borrowed $20,000 from First American Bank by issuing a 90-day, non-interest-bearing note. The bank discounted this note at 12% and remitted to Clear Glass Company the difference.

Required
1. Prepare the journal entries of Clear Glass to record the preceding information, the related calendar year-end adjusting entry, and payment of the note at maturity.
2. Show how the preceding items would be reported on the December 31, 2007 balance sheet.
3. What is Clear Glass Company's effective interest rate?

E13-4 *Discounting of Notes Payable* On October 30, 2007 the Sanchez Company acquired a piece of machinery and signed a 12-month note for $24,000. The face value of the note includes the price of the machinery and interest. The note is to be paid in four $6,000 quarterly installments. The value of the machinery is the present value of the four quarterly payments discounted at an annual interest rate of 16%.

Required
1. Prepare all the journal entries required to record the preceding information including the year-end adjusting entry and the installment payments. Present value techniques should be used.
2. Show how the preceding items would be reported on the December 31, 2007 balance sheet.

E13-5 *Compensated Absences* The Bettinghaus Corporation began business on January 2, 2007 with five employees. It created a sick leave and vacation policy stated as follows: Each employee is allowed eight days of paid sick leave each year and one day of paid vacation leave for each month worked. The accrued vacation leave cannot be taken until the employee has been with the company one year. The sick leave, if not used, accumulates to an 18-day maximum. The vacation leave accumulates for five years, but at any time the employee may request additional compensation in lieu of taking paid vacation leave. The company considers that the requirements of *FASB Statement No. 43* have been met and desires to record the liability for both compensated absences on a quarterly basis. The daily gross wages for each employee are $160.

Required
1. Prepare journal entries to record the liability for compensated absences for the first quarter of 2007. Assume no sick leave had been taken by the employees.
2. Prepare a partial interim balance sheet showing how the liability created in Requirement 1 would be reported on March 31, 2007.

E13-6 *Sales Taxes* During August the Hill Sales Company had these summary transactions:
1. Cash sales of $210,000, subject to sales taxes of 6%
2. Sales on account of $260,000, subject to sales taxes of 6%
3. Paid the sales taxes to the state

Required
Prepare journal entries to record the preceding transactions.

E13-7 *Payroll and Payroll Taxes* The payroll of the Rand Company on December 31 of the current year is as follows:
1. Total payroll, $500,000
2. Payroll in excess of $90,000 to each employee, $350,000
3. Payroll in excess of $7,000 to each employee, $400,000
4. Income taxes withheld, $85,000
5. Union dues withheld, $10,000
6. Tax rates: State unemployment tax, 5.4%; F.I.C.A. tax, 8% for both employees and employers; federal unemployment tax, 0.8%; 1% merit-rating reduction of state unemployment tax from normal rate of 5.4%

Required
Prepare the journal entries for Rand's payroll and payroll taxes.

E13-8 *Bonus Obligation* Raymond Moss, vice president of Moss Auto Parts, gets an annual bonus of 15% of net income after bonus and income taxes. Income before bonus and income taxes is $250,000. The effective income tax rate is 30%.

Required
1. Compute the amount of Raymond Moss's bonus.
2. Compute the income tax expense.

E13-9 *Property Taxes* Family Practice Associates has an estimated property tax liability of $7,200 assessed as of January 1, 2007 for the year May 1, 2007 to April 30, 2008. The property tax is paid on September 1, 2007. The property tax becomes a lien against the property on May 1.

Required
Prepare the necessary monthly journal entries to record the preceding information for the period from May 1 to September 30, 2007 (assuming actual taxes are the same as estimated). What would be the amount of the liability on December 31, 2007?

E13-10 *Property Taxes* The Ames Company is located in a city and county that issue property tax statements in May of each year. The fiscal year for the two local governmental units is May 1 to April 30. Property taxes of $48,000 are assessed against the Ames Company property held on January 1, 2007. The taxes become a lien against Ames Company property on May 1, 2007. The actual amount of the property taxes of $48,000 is determinable on May 1, 2007; therefore, no estimate of taxes is required. The tax bills are payable in two equal installments on July 10 and September 10.

Required
Assuming that monthly accruals are recorded, prepare all property tax journal entries for the period May 1 to September 30, 2007.

E13-11 *Expense Warranty Accrual Method* On September 1, 2007 Carolina Electronics Company has ready for sale 1,000 CD players. On October 1, 2007, 900 are sold at $50 each with a one-year warranty. Carolina estimates that the warranty cost on each CD player sold will probably average $2 per unit. During the final three months of 2007, Carolina incurred warranty costs of $800, and in 2008 warranty costs were $1,000.

Required
1. Prepare the journal entries for the preceding transactions, using the expense warranty accrual method.
2. Show how the preceding items would be reported on the December 31, 2007 balance sheet.

E13-12 *Sales Warranty Accrual Method* On August 1, 2007 Pereira Corporation has ready for sale 2,000 Wiglow instruments. During the next 5 months, 1,600 Wiglows are sold at $460 each with a one-year warranty. Pereira estimates that the warranty cost on each Wiglow will probably average $10 per unit. In this period, Pereira incurred warranty costs of $9,200. Costs for 2008 were $7,000.

Required
1. Prepare the journal entries for the preceding transactions, using the sales warranty accrual method.
2. Show how the items would be reported on the December 31, 2007 balance sheet.

E13-13 *Premium Obligation* The Sweet Dates Company offers to its customers a premium—a glass bowl (cost to Sweet Dates, $0.90) upon return of 40 coupons. Two coupons are placed in each box of dates sold. The company estimates, on the basis of past experience, that only 70% of the coupons will ever be redeemed. During 2007, 10 million boxes of dates are sold at $0.30 each. Eight million coupons are redeemed during 2007. Sweet Dates purchased 360,000 glass bowls for the plan in 2007.

Required
1. Prepare the journal entries related to the sales of dates and the premium plan in 2007.
2. Show how the preceding items would be reported on the December 31, 2007 balance sheet.

E13-14 *Premium Obligation* On the back of its cereal boxes, the Tiger Cereal Company offers a premium to its customers. The premium, a toy truck, may be claimed by sending in $1 plus 10 coupons; one coupon is included in each box of cereal sold. The company estimates, based on past experience, that 60% of the coupons will be redeemed. During 2007, the company purchased 240,000 toy trucks at $1.25 each for the premium promotion and sold 5,000,000 boxes of cereal at $1.80 per box. In 2007, 2,200,000 coupons were redeemed.

Required
1. Prepare the journal entries related to the previous promotion (including sales) for 2007.
2. Show how the items related to the premium plan would be reported on the December 31, 2007 balance sheet.

E13-15 *Gift Certificates* On December 5, 2007 Super Circuit Store sold gift certificates totaling $4,000. By December 31, 2007 all but $750 worth of these certificates had been redeemed for merchandise. Outstanding certificates were then redeemed by January 15, 2008.

Required
1. Prepare journal entries on Super Circuit Store's books to reflect the preceding transactions.
2. How would the gift certificates be reported on Super Circuit's balance sheet on December 31, 2007?

E13-16 *Loss Contingency* On December 4, 2007 Dan Johnson, delivery truck driver for Farmers Products, Inc., ran a stop sign and collided with another vehicle. On January 8, 2008 the driver of the other vehicle filed suit against Farmers Products for damages to the vehicle. Estimated damages to this vehicle were $6,500. The dairy issued its 2007 financial statements on March 3, 2008.

Required
Prepare the disclosures and/or journal entries Farmers Products should make in preparing its December 31, 2007 financial statements.

E13-17 *Gain Contingency* On December 31, 2007 Braino Tech., Inc. learned that its competitor had introduced a product making use of an accessory over which Braino Tech. has exclusive patent rights. Braino Tech. planned to file suit and in all likelihood, its attorneys felt, Braino should recover at least $500,000. Braino Tech.'s December 31, 2007 year-end financial statements were issued March 2, 2008. At that date Braino Tech. still planned to file suit, even though it had not yet done so.

Required
Discuss the accounting treatment in regard to the 2007 financial statements of Braino Tech. called for by *FASB Statement No. 5* concerning the described circumstances.

E13-18 *Disclosure of Serial Bonds Payable* On May 1, 2007 the Ramden Company issues 13% serial bonds with a face value of $2 million. The bond contract calls for retirement of the bonds in periodic installments of $200,000, starting on May 1, 2008 and continuing on each May 1 thereafter until all bonds are retired.

Required
How would the preceding information appear in the Ramden Company's balance sheets on December 31, 2007 and 2008?

E13-19 *Short-Term Debt Expected to Be Refinanced* On December 31, 2007 Excello Electric Company had $1 million of short-term notes payable due February 7, 2008. Excello expected to refinance these notes on a long-term basis. On January 15, 2008 the company issued bonds with a face value of $900,000 at 98; brokerage fees and other costs of issuance were $3,450. On January 22, 2008 the proceeds from the bond issue plus additional cash held by the company on December 31, 2007 were used to liquidate the $1 million of short-term notes. The December 31, 2007 balance sheet is issued on February 12, 2008.

Required
Prepare a partial balance sheet as of December 31, 2007 showing how the $1 million of short-term notes payable should be disclosed. Include an appropriate footnote for proper disclosure.

E13-20 *Short-Term Debt Expected to Be Refinanced* On December 31, 2007 Carrboro Textile Company had short-term debt in the form of notes payable totaling $600,000. These notes were due on June 1, 2008. Carrboro expected to refinance these notes on a long-term basis. On February 1, 2008 Carrboro entered into an agreement with Worldwide Life Insurance Company whereby Worldwide will lend Carrboro $450,000, payable in five years at 12%. The money will be available to Carrboro on May 20, 2008. Carrboro issues its December 31, 2007 year-end financial statements on March 2, 2008.

Required
Show how the $600,000 notes payable will be classified on Carrboro Textile Company's balance sheet on December 31, 2007.

PROBLEMS

P13-1 Accounts Payable and Cash Discounts The Byrd Company had the following transactions during 2007 and 2008:
1. On December 24, 2007 a computer was purchased on account from Computers International for $60,000. Terms of the sale were 2/10, n/30.
2. Byrd calculated that to forgo the discount for the computer would be the equivalent of paying 36% interest annually on the $58,800 for the extra 20 days. Therefore, Byrd went to First Local Bank and signed a $60,000, 30-day note at 12% in order to take advantage of the discount terms. This transaction took place on December 29, 2007. (The account payable was paid on January 2, 2008 and the note was paid at maturity.)
3. On December 30, 2007, Byrd declared a $2.00 cash dividend to the common stockholders. Ten thousand shares were outstanding on this date. The dividend is to be paid on January 5, 2008.

Required
1. Prepare the journal entries for the Byrd Company for both 2007 and 2008. Assume that the net price method is used to account for the credit terms.
2. Show how the preceding items would be reported in the current liabilities section of Byrd's December 31, 2007 balance sheet.
3. Assuming Byrd's current assets were $1,200,000 and its current ratio was 2.4 at the end of 2006, compute the current ratio at the end of 2007 (based solely on the effects of the preceding transactions).

P13-2 Notes Payable and Effective Interest On November 1, 2007 Edwin, Inc., borrowed cash and signed a $60,000, one-year note payable.

Required
1. Compute the following items assuming (i) an interest-bearing note at 12%, (ii) a non-interest-bearing note discounted at 12%:
    a. Cash received
    b. Effective interest rate
    c. Interest expense for 2007
2. Prepare the journal entries for Edwin, Inc. under each case for 2007 and 2008.

P13-3 Trade Note Transactions The Adjusto Corporation (which is on a December 31 fiscal year-end) engaged in the following transactions during 2007 and 2008:

2007
Nov. 1 Issued a 120-day, 12% note, face value of $15,000, to Johnson Company to settle an open account of that amount
Dec. 1 Issued a 90-day, 12% note, face value of $22,000, to Winslow Corporation for the purchase of merchandise (the perpetual inventory method is used)

2008
Mar. 1 Paid the principal and interest on both the Johnson and the Winslow notes

Required
Prepare journal entries to record the preceding transactions on Adjusto's books, including the adjusting entries at the end of 2007.

P13-4 Compensated Absences The Rexallo Company begins business on January 2, 2007 with 15 employees. Its company policy is to permit each employee to take six days of paid sick leave each year and one and one half days of paid vacation leave for each month worked. The accrued vacation leave cannot be taken until the employee has been with the company nine months. The sick leave, if not used, accumulates to a 24-day maximum. The vacation leave accumulates for two years, but at any time after a one-year period the employee may request additional compensation in lieu of taking paid vacation leave. The company desires to record the liability for compensated absences on a quarterly basis. Assume that the gross wages for each employee are $100 per day.
   The following selected events take place during the first two quarters of 2007:

1. On March 31, 2007 the quarterly liability for compensated absences is to be recorded.
2. On April 30, 2007 the following $45,000 monthly payroll, including paid vacation and sick leave, is summarized from the records of Rexallo:

	Payroll for		
	Time Worked	Vacation Taken	Sick Leave Taken
Salaries	$42,000	$1,800	$1,200

3. On June 30, 2007 the quarterly liability for compensated absences is to be recorded.

Required

1. Prepare journal entries to record the preceding events, ignoring payroll taxes and assuming that both sick leave and vacation time meet the requirements of *FASB Statement No. 43* for accrual.
2. Prepare a partial interim balance sheet as of March 31, 2007 to disclose the liability created in Requirement 1.

P13-5 *Sales Taxes* The Mauldin Company makes sales on which a 5% sales tax is assessed. The following summary transactions were made during 2007:

1. Sales for cash of $1,665,400, excluding sales taxes
2. Sales on credit of $2,820,500, excluding sales taxes
3. Sales taxes of $168,220 were paid to the state government during 2007

Required

1. Prepare journal entries to record the preceding transactions.
2. Show how the unpaid sales taxes would be reported on the December 31, 2007 balance sheet of Mauldin.

P13-6 *Payroll and Payroll Taxes* Bailey Dry Cleaners has six employees who were paid the following wages during 2007:

Frank Johnson	$ 27,000
Bill Long	18,000
Duff Morse	95,000
Laura Stewart	28,000
Cindy Sharpe	26,000
Melissa Ledbetter	20,000
Total	$214,000

The state allows the company a 1% unemployment compensation merit-rating reduction from the normal rate of 5.4%. The federal unemployment rate is 0.8%. The maximum unemployment wages per employee are $7,000 for both the state and the federal government. Income tax withholdings of 20% are applied to all employees. An 8% F.I.C.A. tax for both employees and employers is applied to the first $90,000 of each employee's wages.

Required

1. Calculate the amount of payroll taxes to be paid by Bailey.
2. Prepare the journal entries to record the payment of payroll and the payroll tax expense.

P13-7 *Bonus Obligation and Income Tax Expense* James Kimberley, president of National Motors, receives a bonus of 10% of National's profits after his bonus and the corporation's income taxes are deducted. National's effective income tax rate is 30%. Profits before income taxes and his bonus are $5,000,000 for 2007.

Required

1. Compute the amount of Kimberley's bonus for 2007.
2. Compute National Motors' income tax expense for 2007.
3. Prepare journal entries at the end of 2007 to record the bonus and income taxes.
4. Show how the bonus and income taxes would be reported on National Motors' December 31, 2007 balance sheet.

P13-8 *Property Taxes* The Rosen Corporation was formed on December 12, 2006. It plans to close its books annually each December 31. The corporation is located in Lanmark City and Apple County. The fiscal period of these two governmental units runs from July 1 to June 30. The property tax that they assess on property held on January 1 of each year becomes a lien against the property on July 1. The estimated property taxes for Rosen Corporation for the period July 1, 2007 to June 30, 2008 are $15,300. The tax bill is mailed in October with a requirement that the tax be paid before December 31. The tax bill received on October 30, 2007 for the Rosen Corporation revealed an actual tax of $15,680, and the corporation paid this amount on November 30, 2007. The corporation elects to record monthly property tax adjustments for interim statements required by management.

Required

1. Prepare all property-tax related entries for Rosen for the period July 1, 2007 to June 30, 2008.
2. Show how the preceding information would be reported on the December 31, 2007 balance sheet of Rosen Corporation.

P13-9 *Expense Warranty Accrual Method* Clean-All, Inc., sells washing machines with a three-year warranty. In the past Clean-All has found that in the year after sale, warranty costs have been 3% of sales; in the second year after sale, 5% of sales; and in the third year after sale, 7% of sales. The following data are also available:

Year	Sales	Warranty Expenditures
2007	$500,000	$62,000
2008	650,000	82,000
2009	700,000	85,000

Required

1. Prepare the journal entries for the preceding transactions for 2007–2009, using the expense warranty accrual method. Closing entries are not required.
2. What amount would Clean-All report as a liability on its December 31, 2009 balance sheet, assuming the liability had a balance of $88,200 on December 31, 2006?

P13-10 *Sales Warranty Accrual Method* Wright Machinery Corporation manufactures automobile engines for major automobile producers. These engines have a warranty against any defects for a period of five years. Even though Wright Machinery does not have a separate warranty contract, it assumes that the $993 selling price of each engine includes an implied service contract of $73 per engine. During 2007 Wright Machinery sold 8,000 engines to National Motors. During 2007 Wright Machinery repaired defective motors at a cost of $94,400.

Required

Prepare the journal entries for the preceding transactions, assuming that Wright Machinery uses the sales warranty accrual method to account for warranties.

P13-11 *Premium Obligation* Yummy Cereal Company is offering one toy shovel set for 15 box tops of its cereal. Year-to-date sales have been off, and it is hoped that this offer will stimulate demand. Each shovel set costs the company $3. The following data are available for the last three months of 2007:

Month	Boxes of Cereal Sold	Shovel Sets Purchased by the Company	Box Tops Redeemed by Customers
October	21,000	880	12,000
November	24,000	1,083	16,005
December	33,000	1,697	20,745

It is estimated that only 70% of the box tops will be redeemed. The cereal sells for $2.80 per box.

Required

1. Prepare journal entries for each month to record sales, shovel set purchases, redemptions, and closing entries, assuming that the books are closed at the end of each month.
2. Assuming Yummy prepares monthly financial statements, indicate how the premiums and the estimated liability would be disclosed on Yummy's ending balance sheets for October, November, and December.

P13-12 *Contingencies* Fallon Company, a toy manufacturer that also operates several retail outlets, is preparing its December 31, 2007 financial statements. It has identified the following legal situations that may qualify as contingencies:

1. A customer is suing the company for $800,000 in damages because her child was injured in November 2007 while riding an escalator that stopped suddenly in one of its stores. The child was hurt when he tripped and fell while walking "down" an escalator that was going "up." Legal counsel feels that the child is partially at fault, but that it is probable that the lawsuit will be settled for between $50,000 and $100,000, with $80,000 being the most likely amount.
2. The company has discovered that a skateboard it began manufacturing and selling in 2007 has defective bearings, sometimes causing a wheel to fall off. The company has issued a "recall" notice in newspapers and magazines in which it offers to replace the bearings. It estimates a cost of $200,000 for these repairs. No lawsuits have been filed for injury claims, although the company feels that there is a reasonable possibility that claims may total as high as $2 million.
3. The company has an incinerator behind one of its retail outlets which is used to burn cardboard boxes received in shipments of inventory from suppliers. The state environmental protection agency filed suit against the company in August 2007 for air pollution. The company expects to stop using the incinerator and begin recycling. However, its lawyers believe that it is probable that a fine of between $40,000 and $60,000 will be levied against the company, although they cannot predict the exact amount.
4. In early 2007 the company signed a contract with a computer vendor to install "state of the art" cash registers in all of its retail outlets. Because of the vendor's inability to acquire sufficient cash registers, the vendor canceled the contract. The company has filed a breach of contract suit against the vendor, claiming $300,000 in damages. The company's lawyers expect that it will settle the suit "out of court" for $150,000.

Required

For each situation, prepare the journal entry (if any) on December 31, 2007 to record the information for Fallon Company, and explain your reasoning. If no journal entry is recorded, explain how the information would be disclosed in Fallon Company's 2007 annual report.

P13-13 ⬛ AICPA Adapted *Contingencies* Greenlaw, Inc., a publishing company, is preparing its December 31, 2007 financial statements and must determine the proper accounting treatment for each of the following situations:

1. Greenlaw sells subscriptions to several magazines for a one-year, two-year, or three-year period. Cash receipts from subscribers are credited to magazine subscriptions collected in advance, and this account had a balance of $2,500,000 at December 31, 2007. Outstanding subscriptions at December 31, 2007 expire as follows:

     During 2008 — $600,000
     During 2009 — 900,000
     During 2010 — 400,000

2. On January 3, 2007 Greenlaw discontinued collision, fire, and theft coverage on its delivery vehicles and became self-insured for these risks. Actual losses of $45,000 during 2007 were charged to delivery expense. The 2006 premium for the discontinued coverage amounted to $100,000, and the controller wants to set up a reserve for self-insurance by a debit to delivery expense of $55,000 and a credit to the reserve for self-insurance of $55,000.

3. A suit for breach of contract seeking damages of $1,000,000 was filed by an author against Greenlaw on July 3, 2007. The company's legal counsel believes that an unfavorable outcome is probable. A reasonable estimate of the court's award to the plaintiff is in the range between $100,000 and $500,000. No amount within this range is a better estimate of potential damages than any other amount.

4. During December 2007 a competitor company filed suit against Greenlaw for industrial espionage claiming $2,000,000 in damages. In the opinion of management and company counsel, it is reasonably possible that damages will be awarded to the plaintiff. However, the amount of potential damages awarded to the plaintiff cannot be reasonably estimated.

Required
For each of the preceding situations, prepare the journal entry that should be recorded as of December 31, 2007, or explain why an entry should not be recorded. Show supporting computations in good form.

P13-14 *Short-Term Debt Expected to Be Refinanced* Several times during 2007, Palmer Company issued short-term commercial paper totaling $7 million. On December 31, 2007, the company's year-end, Palmer intends to refinance the commercial paper by issuing long-term debt. However, because of the temporary existence of excess cash, $3 million of the liability is liquidated in February 2008, as the commercial paper matures. On March 1, 2008 Palmer issues $9 million of long-term bonds, with $3 million of the proceeds going to replenish the working capital used to liquidate the $3 million of commercial paper, $4 million to pay the remaining balance of the commercial paper due after April, and the remaining $2 million to finance an equipment modernization program at Palmer's plant. Palmer's December 31, 2007 year-end financial statements are issued on March 13, 2008.

Required
1. How will the $3 million of commercial paper liquidated prior to the refinancing be classified on Palmer's December 31, 2007 balance sheet? Explain your reasoning.
2. How will the remaining $4 million of commercial paper be classified on Palmer's December 31, 2007 balance sheet? Explain your reasoning.

P13-15 *Short-Term Debt Expected to Be Refinanced* On December 31, 2007 Atwood Table Company has $8 million of short-term notes payable owed to City National Bank. On February 1, 2008 Atwood negotiates a revolving credit agreement providing for unrestricted borrowings up to $6 million. Borrowings will bear interest at 1% over the prevailing prime rate, will have stated maturities of 120 days, and will be continuously renewable for 120-day periods for four years. Atwood plans to refinance as much as possible of the notes outstanding with the proceeds available from this agreement. Assume that Atwood's December 31, 2007 year-end financial statements are issued on March 30, 2008.

Required
Prepare a partial December 31, 2007 balance sheet for Atwood Table Company showing how the $8 million short-term debt should be reported.

P13-16 *Non-interest-bearing Note Payable: Present Value* On January 1, 2007 Northern Manufacturing Company bought a piece of equipment by signing a non-interest-bearing $80,000, one-year note. The face value of the note includes the price of the equipment and the interest. The effective interest rate is an annual rate of 16%, and the note is to be paid in four $20,000 quarterly installments. The price of the equipment is the present value of the four payments discounted at the effective interest rate.

Required 🖎
1. Prepare all journal entries to record the preceding information. Present value techniques should be used.
2. If Northern's financial statements were issued on June 30, 2007, what amount would the company report as notes payable?

P13-17 *Comprehensive* Selected transactions of the Lizard Lick Corporation during 2007 are as follows:

Jan. 5   Purchased merchandise from Boston Company for $30,000; terms, 2/10, n/30. Purchases and accounts payable are recorded by Lizard Lick using the net price method.

Jan. 26   Paid the January 5 invoice.

Mar. 31   Purchased a van for $19,950 from the Hill Sales Company, paying $9,950 in cash and issuing a 12%, one-year note for the balance of the purchase price.

May 1   Borrowed money from the Mebane National Bank by discounting its own one-year, non-interest-bearing note made out for the maturity value of $50,000 at an interest rate of 12%.

Nov. 2   Received $500 from the Carr Mill Playhouse as a deposit to be refunded after certain rental furniture to be used in a play is returned on January 7, 2008.

Nov. 5   Made sales on credit to Jones Company for $15,000. Sales taxes of 6½% were added to the $15,000 price. (Ignore cost of goods sold.)

Nov. 6   Purchased another van at a cost of $18,000 from a company located in a state that does not levy a sales tax. The entire purchase price was paid in cash. Lizard Lick is located in a state that assesses a use tax of 6½% on non-salable equipment bought outside its sales tax authority. The van and the liability for the use tax are to be recorded.

Dec. 1   Estimated property taxes for the year December 1, 2007 to November 30, 2008 are $36,000 (ignore previous property taxes). The corporation follows the practice of recording its property tax by a monthly accrual starting one month following the lien date. The tax becomes a lien on December 1 and is payable in two installments on May 1 and October 1.

Dec. 31   Estimated quarterly income taxes for the last quarter of the year are $150,000.

Required
Prepare journal entries to record the preceding transactions for 2007. Include year-end interest accruals.

P13-18 *Comprehensive* Selected transactions of the Shadrach Computer Corporation during November and December of 2007 are as follows:

Nov. 1   Borrowed money from the bank by issuing a non-interest-bearing, $40,000, 90-day note. The note is discounted on a 12% basis.

     9   Sold 100 computers with a one-year warranty for $5,000 each on credit (ignore cost of goods sold). Past experience indicates that warranty costs average $125 per computer. The corporation uses the expense warranty accrual method for record keeping.

    12   Sold 100 software packages at $300 each on credit (ignore cost of goods sold). With each software package the corporation offered a premium in the form of a package of disks for the return of one proof of purchase. The offer expires June 30, 2008. The cost of each package of disks is $5, and the company estimates that 80% of the premiums will be redeemed; therefore, 80 packages of disks were purchased on credit.

    20   Paid $2,900 in fulfillment of the warranty agreement on several of the computers sold on November 9.

    30   Accrued monthly vacation pay. Shadrach Computer Corporation has 90 employees, who are each paid an average of $160 per day. The corporation has a policy of allowing each employee 12 days' paid vacation per year; the related liability is recorded on a monthly basis. Employees are paid monthly; two-thirds of the employees work in the sales force and one-third work in the office.

    30   Paid monthly payroll. Gross salaries for the sales force were $288,000 and for the office staff were $144,000. No vacations were taken during November. Income tax withholdings of 20% are applicable to the salaries of all employees. An 8% F.I.C.A. tax for both employees and employers is also applicable. These rates apply to all salaries because no employee's salary has exceeded the maximum wage limit. The state allows the corporation a 1% unemployment compensation merit-rating reduction from the normal rate of 5.4%. The federal unemployment rate is 0.8%. Prior to October, each individual employee had accumulated a gross salary in excess of $7,000 for 2007.

Dec. 14   Twenty proofs of purchase were returned from the November 12 sale.

    29   An individual filed suit against Shadrach Computer Corporation for damages caused in a November 5 accident that resulted when a member of the sales force hit the individual's car while on personal business. The amount of the suit filed was $1,500. Because the employee was on personal business, the company's insurance company will not pay the claim. In the opinion of the company's attorney, the amount of the suit is reasonable; furthermore, the company believes it is likely to lose the suit.

    31   Accrued monthly vacation pay.

    31   Paid monthly payroll. Gross salaries for the sales force were $290,000 and for the office staff were $145,000. The salaries included $6,800 of vacation pay in the sales force and $3,200 of vacation pay in the office staff. The F.I.C.A. tax rate still applies to all wages, because no employee's salary exceeded the maximum wage limit.

31 Recorded president's bonus. The president receives a 10% bonus computed on income after deducting income taxes but before deducting the bonus. The corporation's effective income tax rate is 30%, and income before income taxes and bonus for 2007 was $560,000. The bonus will be paid in January 2008.

Required
Prepare journal entries to record the preceding transactions of the Shadrach Computer Corporation for 2007. Include year-end accruals. Round all calculations to the nearest dollar.

CASES

COMMUNICATION

C13-1 Short-Term Debt Expected to Be Refinanced

The following is the current liability section of Hollo Hardware Company on December 31, 2007:

Accounts payable, trade	$ 50,000
Notes payable, 12%, due February 19, 2008	70,000
Unearned interest and revenue	12,000
Total current liabilities	$132,000

On January 15, 2008 Hollo enters into an agreement with the local bank to receive a line of credit for $60,000, available for the next two years with payment due 2 years after the date of the loan. Interest at 1% above the prime rate will be charged quarterly. On February 15, 2008 Hollo borrows the money to refinance the short-term note due in three days.

Required
1. Does the preceding agreement allow Hollo to exclude any of the short-term note from current liabilities on the December 31, 2007 balance sheet? If so, how much? Explain.
2. Would the result be the same if Hollo borrowed the money on February 26, 2008?

C13-2 Short-Term Debt Expected to Be Refinanced

While auditing the 2007 financial statements of Warder Corporation, you found evidence that the following were not included in its current liabilities on the December 31, 2007 balance sheet:

1. Convertible bonds maturing in 60 days that were never converted.
2. Note payable due two months after the balance sheet date, with refinancing agreement entered into four weeks after the balance sheet date.
3. Notes payable of Warder's completely owned subsidiary due its stockholders and payable upon demand.
4. Deposits from customers on equipment ordered by them from Warder.

Required
Discuss the assumptions needed for Warder to correctly exclude the previously mentioned items from the December 31, 2007 current liabilities. The balance sheet was issued on March 3, 2008.

C13-3 Loss Contingencies

AICPA Adapted *Part a.* The two basic requirements for the accrual of a loss contingency are supported by several basic concepts of accounting. Three of these concepts are: periodicity (time periods), measurement, and objectivity.

Required
Discuss how the two basic requirements for the accrual of a loss contingency relate to the three concepts listed previously.

Part b. The following three **independent** sets of facts relate to (1) the possible accrual or (2) the possible disclosure by other means of a loss contingency.

Situation I
A company offers a one-year warranty for the product that it manufactures. A history of warranty claims has been compiled and the probable amount of claims related to sales for a given period can be determined.

Situation II
Subsequent to the date of a set of financial statements, but prior to the issuance of the financial statements, a company enters into a contract that will probably result in a significant loss to the company. The amount of the loss can be reasonably estimated.

Situation III
A company has adopted a policy of recording self-insurance for any possible losses resulting from injury to others by the company's vehicles. The premium for an insurance policy for the same risk from an independent insurance company would have an annual cost of $2,000. During the period covered by the financial statements, there were no accidents involving the company's vehicles that resulted in injury to others.

Required

Explain the accrual and/or type of disclosure necessary (if any) and the reason(s) why such disclosure is appropriate for each of the three independent sets of facts in the situations described here. Complete your response to each situation before proceeding to the next situation.

C13-4 Contingency Conditions and Disclosure

AICPA Adapted Loss contingencies may exist for companies. Write a short memo that answers the following questions.

Required

1. What conditions should be met for an estimated loss from a loss contingency to be accrued by a charge to income?
2. When is disclosure required, and what disclosure should be made for an estimated loss from a loss contingency that need not be accrued by a charge to income?

C13-5 Contingency and Commitment

AICPA Adapted Supey Chemical Co. encountered the following two situations in 2007:

1. Supey must pay an indeterminate amount for toxic waste cleanup on its land. An adjoining land owner, Gap

Toothpaste, sold its property because of possible toxic contamination by Supey of the water supply and resulting potential adverse public reaction towards its product. Gap sued Supey for damages. There is a reasonable possibility that Gap will prevail in the suit.

2. At December 31, 2007, Supey had a noncancellable purchase contract for 10,000 pounds of Chemical XZ, for delivery in June 2008. Supey does not hedge its contracts. Supey uses this chemical to make Product 2-Y. In December 2007, the U.S. Food and Drug Administration banned the sale of Product 2-Y in concentrated form. Supey will be allowed to sell Product 2-Y in a diluted form; however, it will take at least five years to use the 10,000 pounds of Chemical XZ. Supey believes the sales price of the diluted product will not be sufficient to recover the contract price of Chemical XZ.

Required

1. (a) In its 2007 financial statements, how should Supey report the toxic waste cleanup? Why is this reporting appropriate?
   (b) In its 2007 financial statements, how should Supey report Gap's claim against it? Why is this reporting appropriate?
2. In its 2007 financial statements, how should Supey report the effects of the contract to purchase Chemical XZ? Why is this reporting appropriate?

CREATIVE AND CRITICAL THINKING

C13-6 Various Liability Issues

AICPA Adapted Angela Company is a manufacturer of toys. During the year, the following situations arose:

1. A safety hazard related to one of its toy products was discovered. It is considered probable that liabilities have been incurred. Based on past experience, a reasonable estimate of the amount of loss can be made.
2. One of its small warehouses is located on the bank of a river and could no longer be insured against flood losses. No flood losses have occurred after the date that the insurance became unavailable.
3. This year, Angela began promoting a new toy by including a coupon, redeemable for a movie ticket, in each toy's carton. The movie ticket, which costs Angela $2, is purchased in advance and then mailed to the customer when the coupon is received by Angela. Angela estimated, based on past experience, that 60% of the coupons would be redeemed. Forty percent of the coupons were actually redeemed this year, and the remaining 20% of the coupons are expected to be redeemed next year.

Required

1. How should Angela report the safety hazard? Explain why. Do not discuss deferred income tax implications.
2. How should Angela report the noninsurable flood risk? Explain why.

3. How should Angela account for the toy promotion campaign in this year?

C13-7 Pending Damage Suit Disclosure

On January 15, 2008 a truck driver for Cork Transfer Company negligently rounded a curve that was also a bridge covering several local merchant shops. The truck jumped the guardrail and fell 30 feet onto one of the shops, causing highly flammable chemicals in the truck to explode. Although by February 22, 2008 (the date on which Cork's financial statements for 2007 are issued), no claims had been filed against Cork, it fully expected that some will be filed in the future.

Required

Explain the accounting treatment, if any, Cork should give the contingent loss occurring from the wreck in the December 31, 2007 financial statements.

C13-8 Estimate Liability Arising from Loss Contingency

Worldwide Motors has produced "Stallions" for 10 years as of December 31, 2007. In a civil judgment against it on July 20, 2007, it was found that for the period of January 1, 2004 until the present, Worldwide was negligent in the design of the cars because the gasoline tank was positioned in the rear in such a way that it would explode upon impact with another car. On December 31, 2007 Worldwide estimated that its ultimate liability on the Stallions would total $9 million.

Required

Explain fully the accounting treatment World-wide should give to the contingency on its financial statements as of December 31, 2007.

C13-9 Various Contingency Issues

AICPA Adapted Skinner Company has the following contingencies:

1. Potential costs due to the discovery of a possible defect related to one of its products. These costs are probable and can be reasonably estimated.
2. A potential claim for damages to be received from a lawsuit filed this year against another company. It is probable that proceeds from the claim will be received by Skinner next year.
3. Potential costs due to a promotion campaign whereby a cash refund is sent to customers when coupons are redeemed. Skinner estimated, based on past experience, that 70 percent of the coupons would be redeemed. Forty percent of the coupons were actually redeemed and the cash refunds sent this year. The remaining 30 percent of the coupons are expected to be redeemed next year.

Required

1. How should Skinner report the potential costs due to the discovery of a possible product defect? Explain why.
2. How should Skinner report this year the potential claim for damages that may be received next year? Explain why.
3. This year, how should Skinner account for the potential costs and obligations due to the promotion campaign?

C13-10 Various Contingency Issues

AICPA Adapted At December 31, 2007, Niki Company reviewed the following situations to consider their impact on its 2007 financial statements:

1. In December 2007, Niki became aware of a safety hazard related to one of its products. Estimates of the probable costs resulting from the hazard include highest, most likely, and lowest amounts.
2. During 2007, Niki received a note for goods sold to a customer. The note was sold, with recourse, to a bank. The customer filed for bankruptcy in December 2007, before the note's 2008 due date.
3. In 2003, Niki moved and assigned the remaining 10 years of its old lease to Pro Company, an unrelated third party. Pro agreed to make all payments due on the assigned lease, but Niki has prime responsibility for the lease to the lessor. At December 31, 2007, it is reasonably possible that Pro will be unable to make all payments due on the assigned lease.

Required

For each of the preceding situations, state how Niki should report the impact, if any, on its 2007 financial statements, and explain why the reporting is appropriate.

C13-11 Product and Lawsuit Contingencies

AICPA Adapted Reese Company sells two types of merchandise, Type A and Type B. Each carries a one-year warranty.

Type A merchandise: Product warranty costs, based on past experience, will normally be 1% of sales.

Type B merchandise: Product warranty costs cannot be reasonably estimated because this is a new product line. However, the chief engineer believes that product warranty costs are likely to be incurred.

Reese Company is also being sued for $2,000,000 for an injury caused to a child as a result of alleged negligence while the child was visiting the Reese Company plant in March 2007. The suit was filed in July 2007. Reese's lawyer states that it is probable that Reese will lose the suit and be found liable for a judgment costing anywhere from $200,000 to $900,000. However, the lawyer states that the most probable judgment is $400,000.

Required

1. How should Reese report the estimated product warranty costs for each of the two types of merchandise mentioned earlier? Explain the rationale for your answer. Do not discuss deferred income tax implications, or disclosures that should be made in Reese's 2007 financial statements or notes.
2. How should Reese report the suit in its 2007 financial statements? Explain the rationale for your answer. Include in your answer disclosures, if any, that should be made in Reese's financial statements or notes.

C13-12 Analyzing Coca-Cola's Current Liabilities and Contingencies Disclosures

Refer to the financial statements and related notes of the Coca-Cola Company in Appendix A of this book.

Required

1. What were the total current liabilities at the end of 2004? What was the largest current liability?
2. What did accounts payable and accrued expenses consist of at the end of 2004?
3. What was the total loans and notes payable and what did they consist of at the end of 2004? What was the total of the lines of credit (and other short-term credit facilities) that were available to the company at the end of 2004? How much is outstanding? Why do you think the company disclosed the lines-of-credit information?
4. How much was the company contingently liable for in regard to the guarantees of indebtedness owed by third parties at the end of 2004? What does this mean? How likely is it that the company will have to satisfy these guarantees?

C13-13 Ethics and Environmental Damage

Hart Corporation is a chemical company that produces cleaning fluids of different types; it is the main employer in a small town. Stan Hart has been the company president for 15 years and is paid a salary plus a 10% bonus based on pretax income; he is also the major stockholder. After treatment to remove pollutants, Hart Company has been draining the waste water from its production process into a nearby river for many years. Over the past year (2007) there have been several "fish kills" in the river and at the end of 2007 the Environmental Protection Agency (EPA) filed a $1 million lawsuit against Hart for violation of pollution control laws.

You are an accountant for the firm that is auditing Hart's 2007 financial statements. Preliminary calculations show that Hart earned a pretax income of $600,000 for 2007, before considering the effects of the lawsuit. In a discussion with Stan Hart and Bob Brandt, the company's attorney, you raise the issue of whether or not to report the lawsuit in the company's 2007 financial statements. Stan says, "I've been president of this company for long enough to know that we didn't cause the fish kills; it must be something else. Furthermore, I don't want anything included in the income statement that would jeopardize the company's well being; the town depends on us. If we shut down, the town will die." Bob replies "I generally agree with you. But you need to be realistic. I don't expect the outcome of the lawsuit to be determined for a couple of years. However, there is a pretty good chance the company will lose. If that happens, then there is a 60 percent chance the loss will be $400,000 and a 40 percent chance the loss will be $1 million." Stan replies "Okay, then lets put it in a note to the financial statements."

Required

From a financial reporting and ethical standpoint, prepare a written report that recommends how to account for the lawsuit.

RESEARCH SIMULATIONS

R13-1 Researching GAAP

Situation

Bogan Company is in need of cash to finance its operations. The company creates a new company, Hall Company, which is wholly owned by Bogan. On November 1, 2007 Bogan sells inventory on credit to Hall Company for $50,000, which in turn immediately uses the inventory for a $40,000, 12% loan (guaranteed by Bogan) from 8th National Bank. Hall then uses the proceeds from the loan to repay $40,000 of the $50,000 owed to Bogan. Bogan agrees to continue to extend credit for nine months to Hall for the remaining $10,000. The inventory is Hall's only asset and is stored in a public warehouse. Bogan agrees to pay Hall the $200 monthly storage fee and $400 per month for a financing fee at the end of each month. Bogan also agrees to repurchase the inventory from Hall for $50,000 at the end of July 2008. Bogan uses a perpetual inventory system; the cost of the inventory sold to Hall is $42,000. The president of Bogan has asked you how to account for this series of transactions in 2007.

Directions

Research the related generally accepted accounting principles and prepare a short memo to the president that explains how Bogan Company should record the sale of the inventory on November 1, 2007 and the payment of the fees at the end of November and December. Also explain how Bogan should report the recorded items in its 2007 financial statements. Cite your reference and applicable paragraph numbers.

R13-2 Researching GAAP

Situation

Gilmatt Company developed a new product that it planned to sell directly to customers and to promote heavily because of "stiff" competition in the market place. Its marketing department did extensive market surveys and developed a marketing plan for this product. The plan called for a series of television commercials and magazine advertisements. The television commercials aired for two months (September and October) in 2007 to (a) advertise the product and (b) indicate to viewers that "$5 off" coupons would be appearing in forthcoming magazine advertisements. The magazine advertisements appeared evenly over a three-month period from November 2007 through January 2008 and further promoted the product, as well as included the coded $5-off coupons (which expired at the end of February 2008.) Gilmatt expected 20,000 coupons to be redeemed. During November and December 2007, Gilmatt sold 2,000 units of the new product at the $50 regular price and 8,000 units at the $45 coded-coupon price. In January 2008, the company sold another 3,000 units at $50 each and 7,000 units at $45 each. It expects customers to redeem another 5,000 coupons before the coupons expire. It is now late January 2008 and the company is preparing its 2007 annual report.

The marketing department has prepared the following schedule of its 2007 costs related to the advertising and promotion of the new product: supervisor's salary, $10,000; payroll of employees working on magazine advertising copy, $40,000; depreciation, $7,500; cost of television commercials (independently produced), $180,000; cost of magazine space for advertisements, $100,000; cost of television airtime, $300,000.

Direction

Research the related generally accepted accounting principles and indicate how Gilmatt Company should report the costs of marketing the new product and the related sales revenues on its 2007 financial statements. Cite your reference and applicable paragraph numbers.

14

Long-Term Liabilities and Receivables

OBJECTIVES

After reading this chapter, you will be able to:

1 Explain the reasons for issuing long-term liabilities.

2 Understand the characteristics of bonds payable.

3 Record the issuance of bonds.

4 Amortize discounts and premiums under the straight-line method.

5 Compute the selling price of bonds.

6 Amortize discounts and premiums under the effective interest method.

7 Explain extinguishment of liabilities.

8 Understand bonds with equity characteristics.

9 Account for long-term notes payable.

10 Understand the disclosure of long-term liabilities.

11 Account for long-term notes receivable, including impairment of a loan.

12 Understand troubled debt restructurings. (Appendix)

13 Account for serial bonds. (Appendix)

A Double-Edged Sword

A company's capital structure refers to the mix of debt and equity it uses to finance its operations. Because debt requires fixed interest and principal payments at specified times, debt financing is considered more risky than equity financing. Despite this increased risk, most companies consider the use of some debt to be beneficial. In fact, debt can be used to increase earnings, a concept known as financial leverage. If a company invests borrowed money in assets earning an amount greater than the after-tax cost of the debt, the excess return will increase the return on equity for the company's shareholders. For example, assume three companies each have income before taxes of $120, a return on assets of 12%, and an effective tax rate of 40%, but differ in terms of financial leverage, as follows:

	Company A	Company B	Company C
Average Assets	$1,000	$1,000	$1,000
Debt (10%)	0	500	800
Average Equity	1,000	500	200
Interest Expense (Debt × 10%)	0	50	80
Net Income	120	90*	72*
Return on Equity	12%	18%	36%

* Computed as net income less interest expense, net of taxes. For Company B = [$120 − .6($50)]; For Company C = [$120 − .6($80)].

Because Company A is not leveraged, its return on equity (net income divided by average equity) will be the same as its return

Credit: Daniel Acker/Bloomberg News/Landov

on assets. However, Companies B and C are using financial leverage to generate greater returns on equity. Results are not always so positive. Financial leverage also makes a company more risky. If times are bad and the company's return on assets is less than the after-tax cost of debt, shareholders' earnings are reduced and return on equity will deteriorate rapidly.

Companies such as **Maytag** and **General Motors** are considered highly leveraged while **Microsoft** is an extreme example of a company with virtually no debt. Because financial leverage magnifies the financial effects of both good and bad years, an understanding of the benefits and risks of financial leverage are critical to analyzing a company's return and risk.

FOR FURTHER INVESTIGATION

For a discussion of capital structure and financial leverage, consult the Business & Company Resource Center (BCRC):

- The Determination of Capital Structure: Is National Culture a Missing Piece to the Puzzle? Andy C.W. Chui, Alison E. Lloyd, Chuck C.Y. Kwok, *Journal of International Business Studies*, 0047-2506, Spring 2002, v33, i1, p99(29).
- Framework for Financial Statement Analysis Part 2: Financial Leverage and Return on Equity. George W. Gallinger, *Business Credit*, 0897-0181, March 2000, v102, i3, p33.

A company classifies an item as a long-term liability if it is *not* expected to be repaid within one year or the current operating cycle, whichever is longer. The most common examples of long-term liabilities are bonds payable, long-term notes payable, lease obligations, pension obligations, deferred income taxes and other long-term deferrals, and, occasionally, contingent liabilities. In this chapter we examine the recording and reporting requirements for bonds payable and long-term notes payable. We also discuss long-term notes receivable in this chapter, including accounting for an impairment in such notes. We discuss the other types of long-term liabilities listed above elsewhere in this book.

REASONS FOR ISSUANCE OF LONG-TERM LIABILITIES

1 Explain the reasons for issuing long-term liabilities.

Borrowing, which results in a long-term liability, is one of the choices available to companies seeking to obtain financial resources. There are five basic reasons why a company might issue long-term debt rather than offer other types of securities.

1. *Debt financing may be the only available source of funds.* Many small- and medium-sized companies may appear too risky to investors to attract equity (i.e., capital stock) investments. Debt securities issued by a company may be a less risky investment because by law interest is required to be paid on each interest payment date. Also, some types of debt are secured by a lien against specific company assets.
2. *Debt financing may have a lower cost.* Historically, since debt has a lesser investment risk than stock, it usually has offered a relatively lower rate of return. In general, investors in equity securities have earned a higher return. However, because market conditions change, the cost of debt financing varies, so this advantage depends on the particular market conditions.
3. *Debt financing offers an income tax advantage.* Interest payments to debt holders are deductible by a corporation as interest expense for income tax purposes, whereas dividend payments on equity securities are not.
4. *The voting privilege is not shared.* Corporate stockholders may not wish to share ownership. Thus, by issuing debt, which does not provide voting rights, ownership interests are not diluted.
5. *Debt financing offers the opportunity for leverage.* The term **leverage** (or **trading on the equity**) refers to a company's use of borrowed funds. By investing these funds, the company expects to **earn a return greater than the interest it will pay for their use** and thereby benefit the stockholders. Earnings in excess of interest charges (net of the applicable income tax reduction) increase earnings per share. However, if the return falls below the effective interest rate, earnings per share will decline. Expectations of current and future earnings, inflation, and the debt/equity relationship influence the rate of interest needed to issue debt.

BONDS PAYABLE

2 Understand the characteristics of bonds payable.

One common method for a company to incur long-term liabilities is by issuing bonds. There are several key terms you should know about bonds, as follows:

- **Bond:** A bond is a type of note in which a company agrees to pay the holder the face value at the maturity date and usually to pay interest periodically at a specified rate on the face value. Thus the company that issues the bonds (the *issuer*) is borrowing money from the holder of the bonds (the *lender*).
- **Face Value:** The face (or par) value is the amount of money that the issuer agrees to pay at maturity. It is the same concept as the principal of a note.
- **Maturity Date:** The maturity date is the date on which the issuer of the bond agrees to pay the face value to the holder. The issuer also agrees to pay interest.

- **Contract Rate:** The contract rate is the rate at which the issuer of the bond agrees to pay interest each period until maturity. The contract rate is also called the *stated, face,* or *nominal* rate. This information is printed on a bond certificate, which is the document that indicates ownership of the bond.
- **Bond Certificate:** A bond certificate is a legal document that specifies the face value, the annual interest rate, the maturity date, and other characteristics of the bond issue. Each bond usually has a bond indenture.
- **Bond Indenture:** A bond indenture is a document (contract) that defines the rights of the bondholders.

Since bonds usually are issued to borrow large amounts of money, corporations (and government entities) are the most common issuers of bonds. Corporate bonds usually are issued so that each bond has a face value of $1,000. The entire bond issue may be sold to one purchaser or to numerous individual purchasers. Thus a $1 million bond issue includes 1,000 bonds, each with a $1,000 face value. In addition, interest usually is paid twice each year (semiannually) on dates stated on the bond certificate. Therefore, the stated annual interest rate must be halved to obtain the interest rate per semiannual period. For example, a 10%, $1,000 bond will pay the annual interest of $100 (10% × $1,000) in two semiannual installments of $50 (10% × 1/2 × $1,000).

Characteristics of Bonds

Companies issue bonds that may have different characteristics, as we summarize in Exhibit 14-1. While some of these characteristics are mutually exclusive, several can be combined for a bond issue. The characteristics of a particular bond issue are listed on the bond certificates for that issue and spelled out in detail in the bond indenture. A company may also include in the bond indenture certain restrictions on its financial operations to protect the bondholders and improve the marketability of a bond issue. These restrictions may include limitations on dividends, adherence to certain minimum working capital amounts, or the maintenance of a certain debt/equity relationship. In this chapter, we focus primarily on the accounting for debenture bonds. We also discuss the accounting principles that apply when a bond issue includes a callable, convertible, or serial (Appendix 2) feature.

Bond Selling Prices

When a company issues bonds, it may offer them to the public or privately to an institution, such as an insurance company or a pension fund. When the bonds are offered to the public, the company usually deals with an underwriter (a stockbrokerage firm or an investment banker). The underwriter agrees on a price for the bonds, pays the company for them and then sells the bonds to its clients. Because the issuing company avoids having to find the purchasers and being involved in cash transactions with each purchaser, it pays the underwriter a fee for this service.

There are certain steps a company must follow when it issues bonds. The company must:

1. Receive approval from regulatory authorities such as the Securities and Exchange Commission
2. Set the terms of the bond issue, such as the contract rate and the maturity date
3. Make a public announcement of its intent to sell the bonds on a particular date and print the bond certificates

At the time of the sale, the underwriter negotiates with the company to determine an appropriate selling price. The selling price is based on the terms of the bond issue and factors such as the general bond market conditions, the relative risk of the bonds, and the expected state of the economy. The underwriter determines the rate (yield) that it believes

---

EXHIBIT 14-1   Characteristics of Bonds

1. *Debenture Bonds.* Debenture bonds are bonds that are not secured by specific property. Their marketability is based on the general credit rating of the company. Generally, a company must have a long period of earnings and continued favorable predictions of future earnings and liquidity to sell debenture bonds. Debenture bondholders are considered to be general creditors, with the same rights as other creditors if the issuer fails to pay the interest or principal and declares bankruptcy.
2. *Mortgage Bonds.* Mortgage bonds are bonds that are secured by a lien against specific property of the company. If the company becomes bankrupt and is liquidated, the holders of these bonds have first claim against the proceeds of the sale of the assets that secured their debt. If the proceeds from the sale of pledged assets are not sufficient to repay the debt, mortgage bondholders become general creditors for the balance of the unpaid debt.
3. *Registered Bonds.* Registered bonds are bonds whose ownership is registered with the company. That is, the company maintains a record of the holder of each bond. Therefore, on each interest payment date, interest is paid to the individuals listed on the corporate records as owners of the bonds. When an owner sells registered bonds, the issuer or transfer agent must be notified so that interest will be paid to the proper person.
4. *Coupon Bonds.* Coupon bonds are unregistered bonds on which interest is claimed by the holder presenting a coupon to the company. These bonds can be transferred between individuals without the company or its agent being notified. Currently, coupon bonds are rarely issued because bonds issued after December 31, 1982 must be registered for the related interest expense to be deductible for income tax purposes.
5. *Zero-Coupon Bonds.* Zero-coupon bonds (also called *deep-discount bonds*) are bonds on which the interest is not paid until the maturity date. That is, the bonds are sold at a price considerably below their face value, interest accrues until maturity, and then the bondholders are paid the interest along with the principal at maturity.
6. *Callable Bonds.* Callable bonds are bonds that are callable by the company at a predetermined price for a specified period. That is, the company has the right to require the bondholders to return the bonds before the maturity date, with the company paying the predetermined price and interest to date.
7. *Convertible Bonds.* Convertible bonds are bonds that are convertible into a predetermined number of shares. That is, the owner of each bond has the right to exchange it for a predetermined number of shares of the company. Thus, upon conversion, the bondholder becomes a stockholder of the company.
8. *Serial Bonds.* Serial bonds are bonds issued at one time, but portions of the total face value mature in periodic installments at different future dates. For example, a serial bond issued in 2007 may have a face value of $50,000, and bonds with a face value of $10,000 mature each year for five years from 2013 through 2017.

---

best reflects the current market conditions for the particular bond issue. **The yield (effective rate) is the market rate at which the bonds are actually sold.**[1] The yield on the bonds may be different from the contract (stated) rate set by the company and printed on the bond certificates. This difference may result from a difference of opinion between the underwriter and the company about the correct yield. It may also result from a change of economic conditions between the date the company set the terms of the bond issue and the date it was issued.

Once the company has set the terms of the bond issue, the selling price, and therefore the effective yield of the bonds, is determined. We show the calculation later in the chapter. Three alternatives are possible for a company selling bonds.

---

1.   After a company has issued bonds, their yield will fluctuate in the bond market as changes occur in the risk premium and expected inflation rate. It is the yield at the time of *issuance*, however, that is relevant to the company in accounting for the bonds.

1. **If the yield is *equal* to the contract rate, the purchasers of the bonds pay the face value of the bonds—the bonds are sold at *par*.**
2. **If the yield is *more* than the contract rate, the purchasers of the bonds pay *less* than the face value of the bonds—the bonds are sold at a *discount*.**
3. **If the yield is *less* than the contract rate, the purchasers of the bonds pay *more* than the face value of the bonds—the bonds are sold at a *premium*.**

The issuance price of bonds sold at a premium or discount is often quoted as a percentage of the face value. For example, bonds with a face value of $100,000 that are quoted at 103 (meaning 103% of the face value) are sold for $103,000—that is, at a premium of $3,000. Alternatively, bonds with a $200,000 face value quoted at 98 are sold for $196,000 ($200,000 × 0.98), a $4,000 discount.

It is important to understand why bonds sell at a price different from the face value when the yield is different from the contract rate. The difference between the price paid and the face value enables the purchaser to earn a return on the bonds equal to the yield at the time the bonds are purchased. For instance, bonds are sold at a discount when the yield is higher than the contract rate. The "savings" (i.e., the discount) between the lower purchase price and the face value at maturity, along with the contract interest received by the purchaser each interest period, result in a return equal to the higher yield. Alternatively, bonds are sold at a premium when the yield is lower than the contract rate. The "excess" (i.e., the premium) between the higher selling price and the face value, along with the contract interest received by the purchaser each interest period, results in a return equal to the lower yield. These relationships may be summarized as follows:

Bonds Sold at	Yield Compared to Contract Rate	Interest Over the Life of the Bonds
Premium	Yield < Contract Rate	Interest Expense < Interest Paid
Par	Yield = Contract Rate	Interest Expense = Interest Paid
Discount	Yield > Contract Rate	Interest Expense > Interest Paid

When the bonds yield a rate either lower (for bonds sold at a premium) or higher (for bonds sold at a discount) than the contract rate, the interest *expense* recorded by the issuing company each period is different from the interest *paid*. When bonds are sold at a *premium*, the interest expense is *less* than the interest paid. When bonds are sold at a *discount*, the interest expense is *more* than the interest paid. The difference between the interest expense and the interest payment is the amount of the premium or discount amortized by the issuing company in the period (which we discuss later).

RECORDING THE ISSUANCE OF BONDS

At the time of sale, the issuing company records the face value of bonds in a Bonds Payable account, and it records any premium or discount in a separate account titled Premium on Bonds Payable or Discount on Bonds Payable. For example, assume the company sells bonds with a face value of $400,000 on the authorization date at 102. It records the sale as follows:

3 Record the issuance of bonds.

Cash ($400,000 × 1.02)	408,000	
Bonds Payable		400,000
Premium on Bonds Payable		8,000

A Premium account is an *adjunct* account and is added to the Bonds Payable account in the long-term liability section of the balance sheet. A Discount account is a *contra* account and is subtracted from the Bonds Payable account. **The book value (carrying value) of the bond issue at any time is the face value plus any unamortized premium or minus any unamortized discount.** In the preceding example, the book value on the issue date is $408,000.

Bonds Issued Between Interest Payment Dates

Recall that the interest on bonds usually is paid semiannually on the dates indicated on the bond certificates. Bonds often are sold after their authorization date and between interest payment dates. In such cases, the issuing company must pay interest only for the period of time the bonds are outstanding—that is, from the sale date to the next interest payment date. When a company sells bonds between interest dates, the company normally will collect from the investors both the selling price and the interest accrued on the bonds from the interest payment date prior to the date of sale. This procedure reduces the record keeping for the first interest payment. This interest amount collected typically is *credited* to Interest Expense and is computed by multiplying the face value by the stated interest rate for the fraction of the year from the interest payment date prior to the sale date. On the next interest payment date, the company pays each bondholder six months of interest and records Interest Expense as usual. The following diagram illustrates this situation:

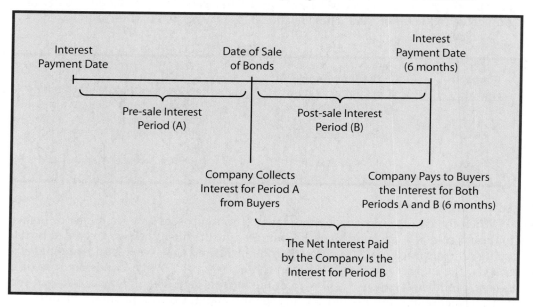

For example, assume that on March 1, 2007, Grimes Corporation issues $800,000 of 10-year bonds dated January 1, 2007 at par. The bonds have a contract (stated) interest rate of 12% and pay interest semiannually on January 1 and July 1. On March 1, because two months have elapsed since the interest payment date prior to the sale, Grimes collects $16,000 ($800,000 × 0.12 × 2/12) accrued interest in addition to the face value. Grimes records the issue of the bonds on March 1, 2007 as follows:

Cash	816,000	
Interest Expense		16,000
Bonds Payable		800,000

On July 1, 2007, Grimes records the semiannual interest payment as follows:

Interest Expense ($800,000 × 0.12 × 6/12)	48,000	
Cash		48,000

As a result of the preceding journal entries, on July 1, 2007 the Interest Expense account has a debit balance of $32,000 ($48,000 − $16,000) representing the interest cost ($800,000 × 0.12 × 4/12) since the bonds were issued.

Alternatively, it is possible to record the previous transaction by using a liability account because part of the proceeds (i.e., the accrued interest) will be repaid in the future. Using this approach, Grimes would record the original transaction as follows:

Cash	816,000	
Interest Payable		16,000
Bonds Payable		800,000

On July 1, 2007, Grimes would record the first interest payment as follows:

Interest Expense ($800,000 × 0.12 × 4/12)	32,000	
Interest Payable	16,000	
Cash		48,000

Companies generally use the first method because it has less potential for errors in later transactions. Also, this method enables a company to develop a single routine in its computerized accounting system for recording and distributing all interest payments.

AMORTIZING DISCOUNTS AND PREMIUMS

Recall that when a company sells bonds at a discount or premium, it is incurring an effective interest (yield) rate that is more, or less, than the stated rate of interest. When a company pays the interest on the bonds, this *payment* is an amount based on the *stated* rate. However, to properly report the interest cost on the bonds, the Interest *Expense* on the company's income statement must show an amount based on the *effective* interest rate and the book value of the bonds. **The effective interest expense amount is computed by multiplying the effective interest rate (yield) times the book value of the bonds at the beginning of the period.** Consequently, a portion of the bond discount or premium is amortized, and **this amortization is the difference between the amount of interest expense and the cash payment.** This process is known as the *effective interest method* (sometimes called the *interest method*) of amortization. Another approach is the **straight-line method** of amortization. APB Opinion No. 21 requires the use of the effective interest method unless the results produced by the straight-line method are *not materially different* from those obtained by using the effective interest method.[2] However, we discuss the straight-line method first because it is often used if the amounts are not materially different from the preferred effective interest method amounts.

4 Amortize discounts and premiums under the straight-line method.

Straight-Line Method

When using the straight-line method, the discount or premium is amortized to interest expense in *equal amounts* each period during the life of the bonds. Therefore, the straight-line method amortizes the bond discount or premium so that the interest expense is an average cost for the period. We will show an example of each.

Example: Bond Discount (Straight Line) Assume that the Jet Company sells bonds for $92,976.39 on January 1, 2007. The bonds have a face value of $100,000 and a 12% stated annual interest rate. Interest is paid semiannually on June 30 and December 31, and the

2. "Interest on Receivables and Payables," *APB Opinion No. 21* (New York: AICPA, 1971), par. 15.

bonds mature on December 31, 2011. Thus, the bonds have a five-year life, with 10 semi-annual interest periods. Jet records the sale on January 1, 2007 as follows:

Cash	92,976.39	
Discount on Bonds Payable	7,023.61	
Bonds Payable		100,000.00

On the first interest payment date, Jet records both the cash payment and discount amortization. It computes the discount amortization of $702.36 per semiannual period by dividing the total discount ($7,023.61) by the number of semiannual periods (10) *until maturity*[3] (it may also use monthly or yearly amortization periods, whichever is more convenient). The interest expense is the sum of the cash payment and the discount amortization. Jet records the first interest payment on June 30, 2007 as follows:

Interest Expense ($6,000 + $702.36)	6,702.36	
Discount on Bonds Payable ($7,023.61 ÷ 10)		702.36
Cash ($100,000 × 0.12 × 1/2)		6,000.00

In this case, the interest expense is higher than the cash paid, indicating that the effective rate is higher than the stated rate. Jet makes a similar journal entry to record the second interest payment on December 31, 2007 and every six months after that. After this second entry, the long-term liabilities section of Jet's December 31, 2007 balance sheet includes the following:

Bonds Payable	$100,000.00
Less: Discount on Bonds Payable	(5,618.89)
	$ 94,381.11

Note that the $5,618.89 ($7,023.61 − $702.36 − $702.36) unamortized discount is subtracted from the $100,000 face value of the bonds to determine the $94,381.11 book value. ♦

Example: Bond Premium (Straight Line) The straight-line amortization of a bond premium follows the same principles. Suppose the Jet Company sold the bonds on January 1, 2007 for $107,721.71. In this case, the premium amortization per semiannual period is $772.17 ($7,721.71 ÷ 10) and the interest expense is the cash payment less the premium amortization. Jet records the sale and first interest payment as follows:

January 1, 2007

Cash	107,721.71	
Bonds Payable		100,000.00
Premium on Bonds Payable		7,721.71

June 30, 2007

Interest Expense ($6,000 − $772.17)	5,227.83	
Premium on Bonds Payable ($7,721.71 ÷ 10)	772.17	
Cash ($100,000 × 0.12 × 1/2)		6,000.00

Here the interest expense is lower than the cash paid, indicating an effective rate lower than the stated rate. After a similar journal entry to record the second interest payment, Jet's December 31, 2007 balance sheet includes the following:

Bonds Payable	$100,000.00
Add: Premium on Bonds Payable	6,177.37
	$106,177.37

Note that the $6,177.37 ($7,721.71 − $772.17 − $772.17) unamortized premium is added to the $100,000 face value of the bonds to determine the $106,177.37 book value.

---

3.   Note that the maturity date of bonds is established on the date they are authorized. When bonds are issued later than the authorization date, any discount or premium is amortized over the *remaining* life until the maturity date.

In both situations, the total discount or premium will be amortized by the maturity date, and the book value will equal the maturity value. ◆

Summary For both premiums and discounts, **the straight-line method results in a constant amount of interest expense each semiannual period** even though the book value of the liability changes each period. A schedule may be developed that summarizes the interest expense, discount or premium amortization, and book value of the bonds each period. Example 14-1 shows a partial schedule for the Jet Company bonds sold at a discount. Example 14-2 presents a partial schedule for the same bonds sold at a premium. Again, remember that the straight-line method is acceptable only when it results in amounts of interest expense and book value that are not materially different from those computed by using the effective interest method.

EXAMPLE 14-1	**Bond Interest Expense and *Discount* Amortization Schedule: *Straight-Line Method***			
Date	**Cash Credit[a]**	**Unamortized Discount Credit[b]**	**Interest Expense Debit[c]**	**Book Value of Bonds[d]**
1/01/07				$ 92,976.39
6/30/07	$6,000.00	$702.36	$6,702.36	93,678.75
12/31/07	6,000.00	702.36	6,702.36	94,381.11
6/30/08	6,000.00	702.36	6,702.36	95,083.47
⋮	⋮	⋮	⋮	⋮
12/31/10	6,000.00	702.36	6,702.36	98,595.27
6/30/11	6,000.00	702.36	6,702.36	99,297.63
12/31/11	6,000.00	702.37[e]	6,702.37	100,000.00

a. $100,000 (face value) × 0.12 (stated annual interest rate) × 1/2 (year).
b. [$100,000 – $92,976.39 (issue price)] ÷ 10 (semiannual periods until maturity).
c. $6,000.00 + $702.36.
d. Previous book value + amount from footnote *b*.
e. Difference due to $0.01 rounding error.

EXAMPLE 14-2	**Bond Interest Expense and *Premium* Amortization Schedule: *Straight-Line Method***			
Date	**Cash Credit[a]**	**Unamortized Premium Debit[b]**	**Interest Expense Debit[c]**	**Book Value of Bonds[d]**
1/01/07				$107,721.71
6/30/07	$6,000.00	$772.17	$5,227.83	106,949.54
12/31/07	6,000.00	772.17	5,227.83	106,177.37
6/30/08	6,000.00	772.17	5,227.83	105,405.20
⋮	⋮	⋮	⋮	⋮
12/31/10	6,000.00	772.17	5,227.83	101,544.35
6/30/11	6,000.00	772.17	5,227.83	100,772.18
12/31/11	6,000.00	772.18[e]	5,227.82	100,000.00

a. $100,000 (face value) × 0.12 (stated annual interest rate) × 1/2 (year).
b. [$107,721.71 (issue price) – $100,000] ÷ 10 (semiannual periods until maturity).
c. $6,000.00 – $772.17.
d. Previous book value – amount from footnote *b*.
e. Difference due to $0.01 rounding error.

Effective Interest Method

5 Compute the selling price of bonds.

Conceptual

The basic assumption underlying the straight-line method that interest *expense* is the same every year is not realistic when a premium or discount is involved. Instead, the use of a stable interest *rate* per year (the *yield*) is appropriate. The yield is used to calculate the proceeds received when bonds are issued. The selling price of a bond issue is calculated by summing the present value of the principal and interest payments discounted at the effective interest (yield) rate. Recall the Jet Company discount example of $100,000 of five-year bonds paying semiannual interest with a stated rate of 12%. Jet Company sold these bonds for $92,976.39, a price that yields an effective interest rate of 14%. **To determine this selling price and the related discount, the effective rate is applied to both the future principal and periodic interest payments,** as we show in the following computations. As we point out in the Time Value of Money Module, in present value analyses when interest is paid semiannually, the effective rate (14%) is divided by the interest periods per year (two) to determine the effective rate (7%) per semiannual period. Similarly, the time to maturity is expressed in semiannual periods (10). The discount of $7,023.61 is computed[4] as follows:

Present value of principal: $100,000 × 0.508349[a]	$ 50,834.90
Present value of interest: $6,000[b] × 7.023582[c]	42,141.49
Selling price	$ 92,976.39
Face value	$100,000.00
Selling price	(92,976.39)
Discount	$ 7,023.61

a. From Present Value of 1 Table in Time Value of Money Module ($n=10$; $i=0.07$).
b. $100,000 × 0.12 × 1/2.
c. From Present Value of an Ordinary Annuity of 1 Table in Time Value of Money Module ($n=10$; $i=0.07$).

Similarly, in the second example, in which the Jet Company sold the bonds at a premium, they yielded 10%. The premium of $7,721.71 is computed as follows:

Present value of principal: $100,000 × 0.613913[a]	$ 61,391.30
Present value of interest: $6,000 × 7.721735[b]	46,330.41
Selling price	$107,721.71
Selling price	$107,721.71
Face value	(100,000.00)
Premium	$ 7,721.71

a. From Present Value of 1 Table in Time Value of Money Module ($n=10$; $i=0.05$).
b. From Present Value of an Ordinary Annuity of 1 Table in Time Value of Money Module ($n=10$; $i=0.05$).

---

4. The discount (or premium) and the selling price to yield a given interest rate can also be calculated by another method. The amount of the discount is the present value of the *deficiency* produced by the difference between the yield multiplied by the face value of the bonds and the stated rate multiplied by the face value of the bonds, discounted at the yield. The calculations of the discount and selling price for the Jet Company bonds are:

Face value		$100,000.00
Less: Discount on bonds payable		
Yield amount: 7% × $100,000	$7,000	
Stated amount: 6% × $100,000	(6,000)	
Deficiency	$1,000	
Discount [$1,000 × 7.023582 (Present Value		
of an Ordinary Annuity Table in Time Value of Money Module)]		(7,023.58)*
Selling Price		$ 92,976.42

* The difference between the $7,023.61 calculated in the text and the $7,023.58 calculated by this alternative method is due to a rounding error.

Again, to compute the present value, the effective rate is expressed on a semiannual basis, and the time to maturity is expressed in semiannual periods.

As we noted earlier, the book (carrying) value of the bond issue at any time is its face value plus any unamortized premium or minus any unamortized discount. Thus, this book value changes with each successive premium or discount amortization and is equal to **the present value of the remaining cash payments.** (Under the straight-line method, the book value is *not* equal to the present value of the remaining cash payments.) Since the bonds were issued to yield a particular interest rate, interest expense over the life of the bond issue should be based on this interest rate (yield). Also, as we noted earlier, *APB Opinion No. 21* requires the use of the effective interest method, unless another method produces results that are *not materially* different. The effective interest method applies the semiannual yield to the book value of the bonds at the beginning of each successive semiannual period to determine the interest expense for that period. In this procedure, **the discount or premium amortization is the difference between the interest expense computed under the effective interest method and the cash payment.** This method is based on the compound interest techniques discussed in the Time Value of Money Module.

6 Amortize discounts and premiums under the effective interest method.

We show the relationship among the interest paid, interest expense, and the amortization in Exhibit 14-2.

EXHIBIT 14-2   Interest and Amortization

Contractual Amount		Market Determined Amount		Difference
Bond Interest Paid	—	Bond Interest Expense	=	Amortization Amount
Face Value of Bonds × Contract Rate		Book Value of Bonds at Beginning of Period × Yield		

Example: Bond Discount (Effective Interest)   To illustrate, after the Jet Company sold bonds for $92,976.39 (yielding an effective annual interest rate of 14%), it records the first two interest payments under the effective interest method as follows:

June 30, 2007

Interest Expense ($92,976.39 × 0.14 × 1/2)	6,508.35	
Discount on Bonds Payable ($6,508.35 − $6,000.00)		508.35
Cash ($100,000 × 0.12 × 1/2)		6,000.00

December 31, 2007

Interest Expense [($92,976.39 + $508.35) × 0.14 × 1/2]	6,543.93	
Discount on Bonds Payable ($6,543.93 − $6,000.00)		543.93
Cash		6,000.00 ♦

Example: Bond Premium (Effective Interest) Alternatively, if the Jet Company sold the bonds for $107,721.71 (equivalent to an annual yield rate of 10%), it records the first two interest payments under the effective interest method as follows:

June 30, 2007

Interest Expense ($107,721.71 × 0.10 × 1/2)	5,386.09	
Premium on Bonds Payable		
($6,000.00 − $5,386.09)	613.91	
Cash ($100,000 × 0.12 × 1/2)		6,000.00

December 31, 2007

Interest Expense		
[($107,721.71 − $613.91) × 0.10 × 1/2]	5,355.39	
Premium on Bonds Payable		
($6,000.00 − $5,355.39)	644.61	
Cash		6,000.00 ♦

Summary Schedules may be developed to show the interest expense, amortization of discounts and premiums, and book values using the effective interest method. Example 14-3 illustrates a schedule for the Jet Company bonds issued at a discount. Example 14-4 illustrates a schedule for these bonds issued at a premium. Note that **the amount of interest expense using the effective interest method is based on a constant** *rate* **applied to the remaining book value of the bonds.** (In contrast, in Examples 14-1 and 14-2 for the straight-line method, the *amount* of interest expense was constant.) The following diagram shows how the book values of bonds are different between the straight-line and effective interest methods for both a premium and a discount:

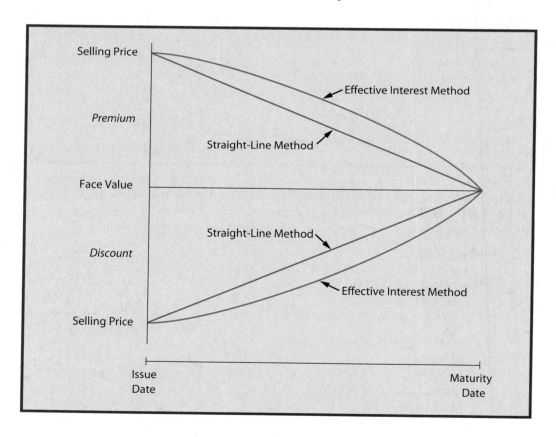

EXAMPLE 14-3	**Bond Interest Expense and *Discount* Amortization Schedule: *Effective Interest Method***

12% Bonds Sold to Yield 14%

Date	Cash Credit[a]	Interest Expense Debit[b]	Unamortized Discount Credit[c]	Book Value of Bonds[d]
1/01/07				$ 92,976.39
6/30/07	$6,000.00	$6,508.35	$508.35	93,484.74
12/31/07	6,000.00	6,543.93	543.93	94,028.67
6/30/08	6,000.00	6,582.01	582.01	94,610.68
12/31/08	6,000.00	6,622.75	622.75	95,233.43
6/30/09	6,000.00	6,666.34	666.34	95,899.77
12/31/09	6,000.00	6,712.98	712.98	96,612.75
6/30/10	6,000.00	6,762.89	762.89	97,375.64
12/31/10	6,000.00	6,816.29	816.29	98,191.93
6/30/11	6,000.00	6,873.44	873.44	99,065.37
12/31/11	6,000.00	6,934.63[e]	934.63	100,000.00

a. $100,000 (face value) × 0.12 (stated annual interest rate) × 1/2 (year).
b. Previous book value × 0.14 (effective interest rate) × 1/2 (year).
c. Amount from footnote *b* − $6,000.00.
d. Previous book value + amount from footnote *c*.
e. Difference due to $0.05 rounding error.

EXAMPLE 14-4	**Bond Interest Expense and *Premium* Amortization Schedule: *Effective Interest Method***

12% Bonds Sold to Yield 10%

Date	Cash Credit[a]	Interest Expense Debit[b]	Unamortized Premium Debit[c]	Book Value of Bonds[d]
1/01/07				$107,721.71
6/30/07	$6,000.00	$5,386.09	$613.91	107,107.80
12/31/07	6,000.00	5,355.39	644.61	106,463.19
6/30/08	6,000.00	5,323.16	676.84	105,786.35
12/31/08	6,000.00	5,289.32	710.68	105,075.67
6/30/09	6,000.00	5,253.78	746.22	104,329.45
12/31/09	6,000.00	5,216.47	783.53	103,545.92
6/30/10	6,000.00	5,177.30	822.70	102,723.22
12/31/10	6,000.00	5,136.16	863.84	101,859.38
6/30/11	6,000.00	5,092.97	907.03	100,952.35
12/31/11	6,000.00	5,047.65[e]	952.35	100,000.00

a. $100,000 (face value) × 0.12 (stated annual interest rate) × 1/2 (year).
b. Previous book value × 0.10 (effective interest rate) × 1/2 (year).
c. $6,000.00 − amount from footnote *b*.
d. Previous book value − amount from footnote *c*.
e. Difference due to $0.03 rounding error.

Bond Issue Costs

APB Opinion No. 21 requires that a company defer any costs connected with a bond issue (such as legal and accounting fees, printing costs, or registration fees). Conceptually a company with deferred bond issue costs should compute a new yield. However, because of a lack of materiality, these deferred bond issue costs are often amortized over the life of the bond issue by the *straight-line* method. For example, assume that on January 1, 2007 Bergen Company issues 10-year bonds with a face value of $500,000 at 104, or $520,000. Costs connected with the issue totaled $8,000. Bergen records this issue as follows:

Cash ($520,000 − $8,000)	512,000	
Deferred Bond Issue Costs	8,000	
Premium on Bonds Payable (0.04 × $500,000)		20,000
Bonds Payable		500,000

Bergen amortizes deferred bond issue costs of $800 to bond interest expense (i.e., debit Bond Interest Expense and credit Deferred Bond Issue Costs) each year over the 10-year life of the bonds. The unamortized deferred bond issue costs typically are reported as other assets or deferred charges on the balance sheet. The FASB is considering changing GAAP so that all debt issue costs, including those for bonds, will be expensed as incurred.

Accruing Bond Interest

In the previous examples, the semiannual interest payments coincided with the company's fiscal year. However, frequently companies issue bonds with interest payment dates that differ from the fiscal year. In such cases, the matching principle requires that the company record an accrual of interest and a partial premium or discount amortization at the end of the fiscal year. For example, assume that McAdams Company issues $200,000 of 10%, five-year bonds on October 1, 2007 for $185,279.87. Interest on these bonds is payable each October 1 and April 1. McAdams records this issue as follows:

Cash	185,279.87	
Discount on Bonds Payable	14,720.13	
Bonds Payable		200,000.00

At the end of the fiscal year, December 31, 2007, the company must accrue interest and amortize the discount for the months of October, November, and December. Thus, it must compute and record the amount of interest expense in 2007 for these three months. It records this adjusting entry (assuming straight-line amortization) as follows:

Interest Expense	5,736.01	
Discount on Bonds Payable		
[($14,720.13 ÷ 5) × 3/12]		736.01
Interest Payable ($200,000 × 0.10 × 3/12)		5,000.00

Typically, the company will record a reversing entry on January 1, 2008 so that it can make the April 1, 2008 entry to record interest expense as usual. If the company does not make a reversing entry, when it records interest expense it eliminates the Interest Payable account and records the three months of interest expense incurred in 2008.

If a company uses the effective interest method to amortize a premium or discount, it determines the amount of interest expense it accrues on December 31, 2007 by computing the semiannual effective interest cost for the next interest and amortization period, and using the straight-line approach to allocate this amount over the number of months of interest accrual. For example, the effective annual interest rate on the McAdams bonds is 12%. Therefore, the amount of semiannual interest for the six-month period ending April 1, 2008 is $11,116.79 ($185,279.87 × 0.12 × 1/2). There are six months in the interest period and the elapsed time since the date of issue (October 1) is three months; therefore, the company expenses $5,558.40, or 3/6 of the $11,116.79 semiannual interest charge. It computes the amount of discount amortization as the difference between the effective interest expense, $5,558.40, and the $5,000.00 ($200,000 × 0.10 × 3/12) amount of interest owed, or $558.40. Using the effective interest method of discount amortization, McAdams records the accrued interest on December 31, 2007, as follows:

Interest Expense	5,558.40	
Discount on Bonds Payable		558.40
Interest Payable		5,000.00

Zero-Coupon Bonds

Zero-coupon bonds are bonds sold at a "deep" discount. As the name implies, zero-coupon bonds *pay* no interest each period. The only cash outflow for the bonds is the payment of the face value on the maturity date. The calculation of the selling price follows the principles we discussed earlier; that is, it is the present value (based on the yield) of the face value. A company records the issuance of zero-coupon bonds in the usual way; that is, it debits the discount account for the difference between the selling price and the face value.

Even though the bonds *pay* no interest each period, the company must still recognize interest *expense* because it has incurred a cost each period on the amount borrowed. It computes the interest expense, as we discussed earlier, by multiplying the yield times the book value of the bonds at the beginning of the period. (Alternatively, the company may use the straight-line method.) Since the company makes no cash payment for interest each period, it recognizes the interest expense each period as a decrease (credit) in the discount account (and therefore increases the book value of the bonds). On page 662, we illustrate the accounting for a non-interest-bearing note. Accounting for a zero-coupon bond follows the same procedures.

SECURE YOUR KNOWLEDGE 14-1

- Bonds are notes that obligate a company to repay a stated amount (the face value) plus interest by a specified maturity date.
- The selling price of a bond is based on the relationship between the yield (effective rate) and the contract rate of interest.
  - If the yield is equal to the contract rate, the bonds sell at par and the periodic interest expense is equal to the interest paid.
  - If the yield is lower than the contract rate, the bonds sell at a premium and the periodic interest expense is less than the interest paid.
  - If the yield is greater than the contract rate, the bonds sell at a discount and the periodic interest expense is greater than the interest paid.
- The book value of a bond issue is the face value plus any unamortized premium or minus any unamortized discount.
- When a bond is sold between interest payment dates, the issuing company will normally collect the selling price plus any accrued interest since the last interest payment date.
- Because a company pays interest based on the contract rate but records interest expense based on the effective interest rate (yield), any premium or discount is amortized to account for this difference.
- Under the straight-line method, the premium or discount is amortized to interest expense in equal amounts, resulting in a constant amount of interest expense being recognized each period.
- Under the effective interest method, periodic interest expense is computed by multiplying the effective interest rate by the book value of the bonds and reflects a constant rate based on the book value of the bonds.

LINK TO INTERNATIONAL DIFFERENCES

International accounting standards for long-term liabilities are generally similar to U.S. principles. One exception is that any financial liability (or asset) *may* be measured at fair value, with the change in value included in net income.

EXTINGUISHMENT OF LIABILITIES

7 Explain extinguishment of liabilities.

The agreement between the bondholders and the issuing company always includes a specified maturity date. On this date the company agrees to repay the face value of the bonds to the bondholders. At this time any premium or discount will be completely amortized so that the book value of the bonds is equal to the face value. Occasionally, under certain circumstances, bonds may be retired (extinguished) prior to their scheduled maturity date.

Over the past three decades, both the APB and the FASB have considered the various circumstances under which liabilities should be considered to be extinguished and what, if any, gain or loss should be recognized on that extinguishment. Under **FASB Statement No. 140,** a liability is derecognized (extinguished) for financial reporting purposes if either of the following occurs:[5]

1. The debtor pays the creditor and is relieved of its obligation for the liability.
2. The debtor is released legally from being the primary obligor under the liability.

Bonds may be extinguished by retirement at maturity or prior to maturity. We discuss the accounting issues related to these retirements in the following sections.

Bonds Retired at Maturity

On the balance sheet issued immediately prior to the maturity date, a company reclassifies the face value (and any related premium or discount) of the bonds to be retired from a noncurrent (long-term) to a current liability if it will use current assets to repay the obligation. On the maturity date, after the last interest payment is recorded, any premium or discount on bonds payable is fully amortized. Therefore, the book value of the bonds is equal to the maturity value. The company records the retirement of bonds on the maturity date by a debit to Bonds Payable to eliminate the liability and a credit to Cash.

Bonds Retired Prior to Maturity

To reduce their level of debt, eliminate any restrictions on operations included in the bond contract, or protect themselves from the inability to take advantage of future favorable changes in market conditions, many companies will include a **call provision** on long-term debt. **This provision allows the company to recall the debt issue at a prestated percentage of the face value prior to the maturity date.** Since the call price generally is above the issue price (if not, it is unlikely that the company would be able to sell the debt issue), a loss or, in unusual circumstances, a gain occurs when the company recalls the debt. An alternative method of retiring bonds prior to their maturity is for the company to purchase them on the open market. Then a gain or loss arises depending on the relationship between the book value and the market value of the bonds. The extinguishment of debt may take two forms: (1) the borrowed funds may no longer be needed, and the debt is not replaced (**debt retirement**), or (2) the existing debt may be replaced with another debt issue (**debt refunding**).

---

5. "Accounting for Transfers and Servicing of Financial Assets and Extinguishments of Liabilities," *FASB Statement of Financial Accounting Standards No. 140* (Norwalk, Conn.: FASB, 2000), par 16.

Conceptually, a company could recognize a gain or loss from a refunding:

- over the remaining life of the old issue,
- over the life of the new bond issue, or
- in the current period.

Recognizing the gain or loss over the remaining life of the old issue is favored by some because they view this as the period affected by the refunding. That is, a different interest cost would have been incurred if the old issue had been for a shorter period. Those who favor recognizing the gain or loss over the life of the new issue base their arguments on the matching principle. That is, the different interest cost obtained for the life of the new issue should be adjusted to reflect any refunding gain or loss. Finally, those who favor an immediate write-off argue that this method is the most logical because the value of the debt has changed in prior periods and paying the call (or purchase) price recognizes this change in value through a transaction of the current period.

When **APB Opinion No. 26** was issued, the Board took the position that all extinguishments of debt securities prior to maturity were basically alike (whether retirements or refundings) and should be accounted for in the same way. Since a company reports gains or losses on retirements of liabilities in the period of recall, *APB Opinion No. 26* concluded that current income should reflect any gains or losses from refunding.[6] Thus, the gain or loss reported in a refunding transaction is computed in exactly the same way as a retirement and is included as a component of income from continuing operations.[7] A company would only report the gain or loss as extraordinary if it is considered to be unusual and infrequent according to the criteria in *APB Opinion No. 30*.

In summary, whether a company recalls, retires, or refunds bonds prior to maturity, **it reports any difference between the book value of the bonds (plus any unamortized bond issue costs) and the call price (or market price) as a gain or loss in income from continuing operations in the year the cancellation occurs.**

Example: Retirement Prior to Maturity Assume that Channing Corporation originally issued $100,000 of 12% bonds at 97 on January 1, 2002. The bonds have a 10-year life, pay interest on January 1 and July 1, and are callable at 105 plus accrued interest. Assume, for simplicity, that the company amortizes the discount by the straight-line method. On June 30, 2007 the company recalls the bonds. First, Channing records the current interest expense and liability, including the amortization of the discount that expired since the last interest payment, as follows:

Interest Expense	6,150	
Discount on Bonds Payable [($3,000 ÷ 10) × 1/2]		150
Interest Payable ($100,000 × 0.12 × 1/2)		6,000

Channing then records the reacquisition of the bonds as follows:

Bonds Payable	100,000	
Interest Payable	6,000	
Loss on Bond Redemption	6,350[b]	
Discount on Bonds Payable		1,350[a]
Cash [($100,000 × 1.05) + $6,000]		111,000

a. Original discount $ 3,000

   Amortization on straight-line basis for 5 1/2 years = 5.5 × $300   (1,650)

   Unamortized discount 6/30/07 $ 1,350

b. Call price (excluding interest) $105,000

   Less: Face value $100,000

       Unamortized discount   (1,350)   (98,650)

   Loss on bond redemption $ 6,350

---

6. "Early Extinguishment of Debt," *APB Opinion No. 26* (New York: AICPA, 1972).
7. "Rescission of FASB Statements No. 4, 44, and 64, Amendment of FASB Statement No. 13, and Technical Corrections," *FASB Statement of Financial Accounting Standards No. 145* (Norwalk, Conn.: FASB, 2002), par. 6.

Channing reports the loss of $6,350 in income from continuing operations on its 2007 income statement. ◆

Earlier we noted that the FASB has concluded that, in addition to retirement at maturity or prior to maturity, a liability can be extinguished if the debtor is legally released from being the primary obligor of the liability. This is sometimes referred to as *defeasance*. It might arise when an affiliated company agrees to become the primary obligor for the liability. The parent company removes the liability (e.g., bonds payable) from its balance sheet and reports a gain (or perhaps a reduction in an investment in affiliate account). The parent company may still be required to disclose a contingent liability. This situation would arise if the parent has been released from being the primary obligor because a third party has assumed the debt, but the creditor requires the parent to be a guarantor of the third party's debt.

BONDS WITH EQUITY CHARACTERISTICS

8 Understand bonds with equity characteristics.

A company may issue bonds that allow creditors to ultimately become stockholders either by attaching **stock warrants** to the bonds or including a **conversion feature** in the bond indenture. In either case, the investor has acquired a dual set of rights:

- The right to receive interest on the bonds
- The right to acquire common stock and to participate in the potential appreciation of the market value of the company's common stock

Conceptual

Conceptually, it can be argued that the economic substance of issuing bonds with either detachable warrants or a conversion feature is similar. For consistency, therefore, a portion of the proceeds of a bond issue carrying either of these features could be assigned to stockholders' equity. However, GAAP differ in their treatment of these securities.

Bonds Issued with Detachable Stock Warrants

When a company issues bonds with detachable stock warrants, these **warrants represent rights that enable the security holder to acquire a specified number of common shares at a given price within a certain time period.** Stock warrants are attached to bonds to increase their marketability. They generally result in either a relatively lower interest rate or greater proceeds when compared with other bond issues with similar risk but without such rights. (The terms stock *warrants* and stock *rights* often are used interchangeably.) Because these warrants are detachable, they usually trade separately from the bonds on the open market.

APB Opinion No. 14 requires that a portion of the proceeds of bonds issued with detachable warrants is allocated to the stock warrants and accounted for as additional paid-in capital. This allocation is based on the relative fair values of the bonds and warrants as soon as both elements trade separately on the open market. The allocation is made as follows:

$$\text{Amount Assigned to Bonds} = \frac{\text{Market Value of Bonds Without Warrants}}{\text{Market Value of Bonds Without Warrants} + \text{Market Value of Warrants}} \times \text{Issuance Price}$$

$$\text{Amount Assigned to Warrants} = \frac{\text{Market Value of Warrants}}{\text{Market Value of Bonds Without Warrants} + \text{Market Value of Warrants}} \times \text{Issuance Price}$$

Example: Bonds Issued with Warrants Assume Paul Company sold $800,000 of 12% bonds at 101, or $808,000. Each $1,000 bond carried 10 warrants, and each warrant allows the holder to acquire one share of $5 par common stock for $25 per share. After issuance, the bonds are quoted at 99 *ex rights* (without the rights attached), and the warrants (rights) are quoted at $3 each. The company calculates the values assigned to each security as follows:

$$\text{Value Assigned to Bonds} = \frac{\$990 \times 800}{(\$990 \times 800) + (\$3 \times 800 \times 10)} \times \$808,000$$

$$= \frac{\$792,000}{\$792,000 + \$24,000} \times \$808,000 = \underline{\underline{\$784,235.29}}$$

$$\text{Value Assigned to Warrants} = \frac{\$3 \times 800 \times 10}{(\$990 \times 800) + (\$3 \times 800 \times 10)} \times \$808,000$$

$$= \frac{\$24,000}{\$792,000 + \$24,000} \times \$808,000 = \underline{\underline{\$\ 23,764.71}}$$

In the denominator of each equation, note that the $792,000 fair value of the bonds without warrants is computed by multiplying the $990 (99 ex rights) quoted price times the 800 bonds. The fair value of the warrants is determined by multiplying the $3 quoted price times the 8,000 warrants (800 × 10). Paul records the transaction as follows:

Cash	808,000.00	
Discount on Bonds Payable		
($800,000 − $784,235.29)	15,764.71	
Bonds Payable		800,000.00
Common Stock Warrants		23,764.71

Each warrant is assigned a value of $2.971 ($23,764.71 ÷ 8,000). If 500 of the warrants were later exercised at the $25 per share exercise price, Paul records the following journal entry:

Cash ($25 × 500)	12,500.00	
Common Stock Warrants ($2.971 × 500)	1,485.50	
Common Stock ($5 × 500)		2,500.00
Additional Paid-in Capital on Common Stock		11,485.50

If the remaining warrants expire, Paul would record the following journal entry:

Common Stock Warrants		
($23,764.71 − $1,485.50)	22,279.21	
Additional Paid-in Capital from Expired		
Warrants		22,279.21

This journal entry transfers the value assigned to the warrants to the existing stockholders. ◆

Convertible Bonds

A company may also issue bonds that are convertible into common stock. **At conversion, the bondholder (creditor) exchanges the bonds for a specified number of common shares (and becomes a stockholder).** Debt securities that are convertible into common stock often have played a role in corporate financing, and this role appears to be growing. The use of these financial instruments raises two questions. Why do companies issue such securities? Are the securities really bonds or are they a form of common stock?

Most financial analysts agree that a company sells convertible bonds for one of two primary reasons. One, the company wants to increase its equity capital at a later date and decides that the issuance of convertible bonds is the best way to do so. Two, it wants to increase its debt and finds the conversion feature necessary to make the security sufficiently marketable at a reasonable interest rate.

Several other factors have motivated companies to issue convertible bonds rather than common stock. For example, a company may wish to:

- Avoid the downward price pressures on its stock that placing a large new issue of common stock on the market would cause
- Avoid the direct sale of common stock when it believes its stock currently is undervalued in the market
- Penetrate that segment of the capital market that is unwilling or unable to participate in a direct common stock issue
- Minimize the costs associated with selling securities

For similar reasons, companies may issue convertible preferred stock (which we discuss in Chapter 17). In this chapter, we focus only on accounting for convertible bonds.

Recording the Issuance

When a company issues convertible debt, it must determine the value of these securities and their balance sheet presentation. Conceptually, there are two methods for recording the issuance of convertible debt. The company could either:

- attribute part of the proceeds from the sale of the security to the conversion privilege and allocate this to additional paid-in capital as part of stockholders' equity, or
- treat the issue solely as debt.

Both the conversion feature and the right to receive interest on the debt are valuable to an investor. Additionally, advocates of the first position argue that a lower interest rate or a higher selling price (or both) than might otherwise have been available usually accompanies the conversion feature. This indicates that investors are paying for the right to acquire common stock. Thus, an amount equal to the difference between the price at which the bonds might have been sold without the conversion privilege and the actual issue price should be allocated to additional paid-in capital. This position was taken in *APB Opinion No. 10* but soon was suspended in *APB Opinion No. 12*.[8] Companies had opposed the convertible debt provisions of the earlier *Opinion*, and this viewpoint may have influenced the APB's suspension decision.

The decision was reversed in **APB Opinion No. 14**[9] and **companies are required to treat the proceeds from the issuance of convertible debt solely as debt**. The APB argued that the debt and the conversion option are not separable, and that the values were not reliable. That is, the difficulty in assigning a *reliable* value to the conversion feature outweighed the arguments cited for the first method. Thus, treating the issue solely as debt is now the only generally accepted accounting principle. Thus, a company records the issuance of convertible debt in the same manner as the issuance of nonconvertible debt, without separately recording a value for the conversion feature. However, the FASB is considering a proposal to require that the equity component be separately valued, as we discuss later in the chapter.

Recording the Conversion

When bonds are converted into common stock, a company must determine the amount to record as stockholders' equity. If the conversion takes place between interest dates, the company first must record interest expense and any discount or premium amortization to bring the book value of the bonds up to date. There are two generally accepted methods for a company to record the conversion, as we show in the following diagram and summary.

---

8. "Omnibus Opinion—1966," *APB Opinion No. 10* (New York: AICPA, 1966), par. 8 and "Omnibus Opinion 1967," *APB Opinion No. 12* (New York: AICPA, 1967), par. 11.

9. "Accounting for Convertible Debt and Debt Issued with Stock Purchase Warrants," *APB Opinion No. 14* (New York: AICPA, 1969), par. 12.

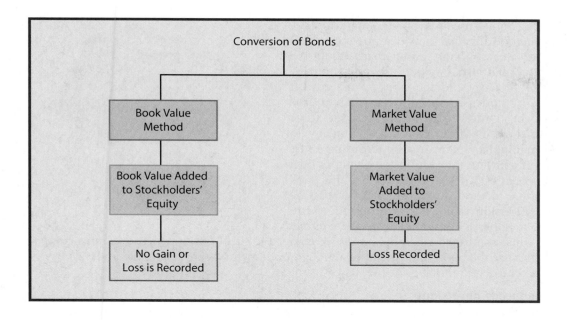

1. *Book Value Method.* The stockholders' equity (common stock and additional paid-in capital) is recorded at the book value of the convertible bonds on the date of conversion, and no gain or loss is recorded upon conversion. (If the par value of the common stock is greater than the book value of the bonds, the difference is recorded as a reduction of retained earnings.)
2. *Market Value Method.* The stockholders' equity (common stock and additional paid-in capital) is recorded at the market value of the shares issued on the date of conversion, and a loss is recorded. The loss is computed by comparing the market value of the shares with the book value of the bonds at the time of conversion. (For a gain to be recognized, the market value of the shares would have to be less than the book value of the bonds—an unlikely event.) This loss is reported in income from continuing operations on the company's income statement.

Example: Conversion of Bonds Assume that Shannon Corporation has outstanding convertible bonds with a face value of $10,000, it has just paid interest on these bonds, and the bonds have a book value of $10,500. Each $1,000 bond is convertible into 40 shares of common stock (par value $20 per share). If all the bonds are converted into common stock when the market value of Shannon's common stock is $26.50 per share, it may record the following alternative journal entries:

Book Value Method

Bonds Payable	10,000	
Premium on Bonds Payable	500	
Common Stock (40 × 10 × $20)		8,000
Additional Paid-in Capital from Bond Conversion		
($10,500 − $8,000)		2,500

Market Value Method

Bonds Payable	10,000	
Premium on Bonds Payable	500	
Loss on Conversion ($10,600 − $10,500)	100	
Common Stock (40 × 10 × $20)		8,000
Additional Paid-in Capital from Bond Conversion		
(40 × 10 × $6.50)		2,600

Credit: Comstock Images

Some users favor the market value method because they view the conversion as an economic event that should be recorded at fair value. Also, the company could have sold the stock at the market price and used the proceeds to retire the debt. Others criticize the market value method because it allows a company to manipulate its income by recording a loss (or gain) on transactions involving its own securities. They also argue that the book value method should be used because the conversion is not a new economic event, but rather a continuation of the contract terms established when the bonds were issued initially. For these reasons, most companies use the book value method, although both methods are acceptable under generally accepted accounting principles. ♦

Induced Conversions

A company that has issued convertible bonds may want to induce conversion of these bonds to common stock to reduce interest costs, improve its debt/equity ratio, or for other reasons. To induce conversion, the company may add a "sweetener" to the convertible bond issue so that the conversion privileges are changed or additional consideration is paid to the bondholder.

FASB Statement No. 84 applies in situations where the conversion privileges are changed after the initial issuance, are effective for a limited period of time, involve additional consideration, and are made to induce conversion. The changed terms (privileges) may involve a reduction of the original conversion price resulting in the issuance of additional shares of common stock, the issuance of warrants or other securities not included in the original conversion terms, or the payment of cash to bondholders who convert during the specified time period.

When convertible bonds are converted to common stock in such a situation, the debtor company recognizes an expense equal to the excess of the fair value of the common stock (and any other consideration) transferred in the transaction over the fair value of the common stock issuable under the original conversion terms. The fair values are measured on the date the inducement offer is accepted by the convertible bondholders.[10]

For example, assume that the Harmon Company previously had issued convertible bonds with a face value of $10,000 at par. At the time of issuance, the conversion terms allowed each $1,000 bond to be converted into 40 shares of no-par common stock. To induce conversion, the company later changed the conversion terms so that each bond is convertible into 50 shares of no-par common stock if conversion is made in 60 days. All the bonds are converted within the time limit when the market price of the common stock is $30 per share. The bond conversion expense is $3,000 because the $15,000 (10 × 50 × $30) fair value of the no-par common stock issued in the transaction is in excess of the $12,000 (10 × 40 × $30) fair value of the shares that would have been issued under the original terms. Under the *book value method*, Harmon records the bond conversion expense at $3,000, eliminates the $10,000 par value of the bonds payable, and records the no-par common stock at $13,000 as follows:

Bonds Payable	10,000	
Bond Conversion Expense	3,000	
Common Stock, no par		13,000

Harmon reports the bond conversion expense in its income from continuing operations.

10. "Induced Conversions of Convertible Debt," *FASB Statement of Financial Accounting Standards No. 84* (Stamford, Conn.: FASB, 1985), par. 3 and 4.

SECURE YOUR KNOWLEDGE 14-2

- If bonds are extinguished prior to their maturity date, any difference between the book value of the bonds and the amount paid to retire the bonds is recognized as either a gain or loss in income from continuing operations.
- If bonds are issued with detachable stock warrants that give the bondholder the option to acquire shares of stock, the issue price is allocated between the bonds and the warrants based on their relative fair values.
- When convertible bonds contain both debt and equity components, current standards require that the issuance of such bonds is accounted for solely as debt due to the inseparability of the debt and conversion options and the lack of sufficiently reliable market valuations.
- Companies may record the conversion of bonds into stock using either the book value method (the equity is recorded at the book value of the debt) or the market value method (the equity is recorded at market value, which generally results in a loss).

LINK TO INTERNATIONAL DIFFERENCES

International accounting standards require a company that issues a compound financial instrument containing both liability and equity components to report each component separately on its balance sheet. While this is similar to U.S. GAAP with respect to bonds with detachable stock warrants, international standards require that companies with convertible debt value and report the debt instrument and the conversion option (an equity instrument) separately.

LONG-TERM NOTES PAYABLE

A long-term note is similar to a debenture bond because it represents a future obligation of the borrower to repay debt in more than a year. Also, in many cases no collateral backs the note. Similarly, a long-term note generally includes a provision for interest on the borrowed funds, and the rate of interest charged will depend on such factors as the credit standing of the borrower, the amount of current debt, and other issues.

9 Account for long-term notes payable.

The APB reviewed procedures used by various companies to account for notes receivable and payable and found that some note transactions did not have an interest charge (i.e., these transactions involved *non-interest-bearing notes*). These transactions apparently were used to maintain favorable customer or supplier relations or to ensure future services. *APB Opinion No. 21* was issued to provide guidelines for cases in which a note does not stipulate a rate of interest or the stated interest rate is clearly not appropriate. The basic principle is that, regardless of how a note is structured legally, **the note is recorded at its present value and the effective interest method is used to record the interest.**[11] In essence, accounting for a note is based on its economic substance and not its legal form. The variety of transactions discussed in the *Opinion* did not allow the use of the same interest rate in all situations. In some situations, the borrower knows the present value so that it calculates the interest rate implicit in the transaction and uses this rate to apply the effective interest method. In other situations, where the present value is not known, the

---

11. The straight-line method may be used if the results obtained are not materially different from the effective interest method.

borrower uses its incremental interest rate to determine the present value and to apply the effective interest method. **The incremental interest rate is the rate that the borrower would be required to pay to obtain similar financing in the credit market at the time the note is issued.** Three major categories of notes were addressed:

- Notes exchanged for cash
- Notes exchanged for cash and rights or privileges
- Notes exchanged for property, goods, or services

Although *APB Opinion No. 21* addressed the accounting for most notes receivable and payable, it specifically exempted normal trade transactions not exceeding one year, as we discussed in Chapter 7.[12]

Notes Payable Issued for Cash

When a company borrows cash and issues a long-term note payable bearing a stated (and fair) interest rate, it records the note initially at its face value (because it is equal to the present value). Subsequently, it records interest payments and accruals as debits to Interest Expense and credits to Cash or Interest Payable. Upon payment at maturity, it eliminates the Notes Payable account.

A more complex situation involves receiving cash in exchange for a long-term non-interest-bearing note (or a zero-coupon bond, as discussed earlier). **When a long-term non-interest-bearing note is exchanged solely for cash, the note is assumed to have a present value equal to the cash proceeds. The difference between the cash proceeds and the face value of the note is recorded as a discount and amortized over the life of the note by the effective interest method.** To apply the effective interest method, a company must determine the implicit (effective) interest rate of the note. Since the cash received is the present value of the note and the face value is the future value of the note at maturity, **the effective (implicit) interest rate is the rate that equates the future value on the maturity date to the present value.**

Example: Note Payable Issued for Cash Assume that on January 1 of the current year Johnson Company issues a three-year, non-interest-bearing note with a face value of $8,000 and receives $5,694.24 in exchange. Johnson records the issuance of the note as follows:

Cash	5,694.24	
Discount on Notes Payable	2,305.76	
Notes Payable		8,000.00

The discount account is a contra account and is subtracted from the Notes Payable account on the company's balance sheet to report the carrying (book) value of the note.[13] From the Present Value of 1 Table (Time Value of Money Module), we find that the effective (implicit) interest rate that equates the present value of $5,694.24 to $8,000 at the end of three years is 12%.[14] The company computes the interest expense each year by multiplying the 12% effective interest rate by the carrying value at the beginning of the year. This

---

12. *APB Opinion No. 21, op. cit.,* par. 1, 3, and 15.
13. An alternative method is to record the Notes Payable account at its present value without the use of a Discount account. In this case, the adjusting entries for interest involve a debit to Interest Expense and a credit directly to the Notes Payable account. When a company uses this method, it discloses the difference between the maturity value and the carrying value parenthetically on its balance sheet as the amount of the discount.
14. Present Value = Future Value × Factor
    $5,694.24 = $8,000 × Factor
    $Factor_{n=3, i=?} = \$5,694.24 \div \$8,000 = 0.711780$
        $i = 12\%$

amount also increases the carrying value of the note by reducing the discount. The company computes the interest each year as follows:

	Year 1	Year 2	Year 3
Note payable	$ 8,000.00	$ 8,000.00	$8,000.00
Less: Unamortized discount	(2,305.76)	(1,622.45)[a]	(857.14)[b]
Carrying value at beginning of year	$ 5,694.24	$ 6,377.55	$7,142.86
× Effective interest rate	0.12	0.12	0.12
Interest expense and discount amortization	$ 683.31	$ 765.31	$ 857.14

a. $2,305.76 − $683.31
b. $1,622.45 − $765.31

Johnson records the $683.31 interest expense for the first year as follows:

Interest Expense ($5,694.24 × 0.12)	683.31	
Discount on Notes Payable		683.31

The company records interest expense for the next two years in the same way so that the Discount account has a zero balance at the end of the third year. Therefore, the carrying value at the end of the third year is $8,000 (the face value of the note), and the repayment involves a debit to Notes Payable and credit to Cash for the $8,000 face value of the note. ♦

Notes Payable Exchanged for Cash and Rights or Privileges

Long-term notes exchanged for cash may include special rights or privileges. A company must consider these rights or privileges when accounting for such long-term notes. For instance, a company might sign a contract with a customer in which the company borrows cash from the customer on a non-interest-bearing basis, with the understanding that the customer has the right to purchase certain goods from the company at less than prevailing prices over the period of the contract. In this situation the consideration received from the customer for the note is, in essence, a prepayment for future purchases. In such a case, for the company issuing the note:

1. **The note is recorded at its present value at the time of issuance by discounting the maturity value using the incremental interest rate of the borrower.**
2. **Interest expense is recorded each period over the life of the note using the effective interest method.**
3. **The difference between the cash proceeds and the present value of the note is recorded as unearned revenue, and revenue is recognized over the life of the contract using appropriate revenue recognition criteria.**

For instance, revenue might be recognized on a per-unit basis as goods are sold, or evenly throughout the contract on a straight-line basis.

Example: Exchange for Cash and Rights or Privileges Assume that the Verna Company borrows $100,000 by issuing a three-year, non-interest-bearing note to a customer. In addition, Verna Company agrees to sell inventory to the customer at reduced prices over a five-year period. Verna's incremental borrowing rate is 12%, so the present value of $100,000 to be repaid at the end of three years is $71,178 ($100,000 × 0.711780, from the Present Value of 1 Table in the TVM Module). The customer agrees to purchase an equal amount of inventory each year over the five-year period so that a straight-line method of revenue recognition is appropriate. In this situation, Verna Company records the following journal entries during the first two years:

Issuing the Note

Cash	100,000.00	
Discount on Notes Payable		
($100,000 − $71,178)	28,822.00	
Notes Payable		100,000.00
Unearned Revenue		28,822.00

End of First Year

Interest Expense ($71,178 × 0.12)	8,541.36	
Discount on Notes Payable		8,541.36
Unearned Revenue ($28,822 ÷ 5 years)	5,764.40	
Sales Revenue		5,764.40

End of Second Year

Interest Expense [($71,178 + $8,541.36) × 0.12]	9,566.32	
Discount on Notes Payable		9,566.32
Unearned Revenue	5,764.40	
Sales Revenue		5,764.40

Recording the transactions according to these procedures results in the proper recognition of both the revenue and expense components. The company recognizes revenue as it earns it and recognizes the expense over the life of the loan. ♦

Notes Payable Exchanged for Property, Goods, or Services

When a note is exchanged solely for property, goods, or services in an external transaction, *APB Opinion No. 21* states that the stated rate of interest should be presumed fair. This presumption can be overcome only if:

- No interest is stated, or
- The stated rate of interest is clearly unreasonable, or
- The face value of the note is materially different from the cash sales price of the property, goods, or services, or the fair value of the note at the date of the transaction.[15]

In any of these cases, **the note is recorded at the fair value of the property, goods, or services, or the fair value of the note, whichever is more reliable.** The interest rate implicit in the transaction then is calculated and used to calculate the interest expense each period using the effective interest method. **If neither of these fair values is determinable, the note is recorded at its present value by discounting the future cash flow(s) using the incremental interest rate of the borrower.** The incremental interest rate then is used to apply the effective interest method to determine the interest expense.

In either situation, the carrying value of the note and the cost of the assets or services acquired are recorded at an amount that is less than the face value of the note. If the liability and asset had been erroneously recorded at the face value of the note, both would be overstated in the current period. Additionally, this would result in an overstatement of depreciation expense (or cost of goods sold) and an understatement of interest expense over the life of the asset and note, respectively. Recording the note at its fair (present) value results in correct asset and liability valuations and in the proper timing of expense recognition.

Example: Exchange for Property Assume that on January 1, 2007 the Marsden Company purchases used equipment from the Joyce Company, issuing a non-interest-bearing $10,000, five-year note in exchange. Neither the fair value of the equipment nor that of the note is determinable, so Marsden uses its incremental interest rate to compute

---

15. *APB Opinion No. 21, op. cit.,* par. 12.

the present value. If Marsden's incremental borrowing rate is 12%, the present value of $10,000 to be repaid at the end of five years at 12% is $5,674.27 ($10,000 × 0.567427, from Present Value of 1 Table in the TVM Module). Assume the remaining asset life is 10 years (no residual value). Marsden records the issuance of the note, the first two interest payments, and annual straight-line depreciation as follows:

January 1, 2007

Equipment	5,674.27	
Discount on Notes Payable	4,325.73	
Notes Payable		10,000.00

December 31, 2007

Interest Expense [($10,000 − $4,325.73) × 0.12]	680.91	
Discount on Notes Payable		680.91
Depreciation Expense	567.43	
Accumulated Depreciation ($5,674.27 ÷ 10)		567.43

December 31, 2008

Interest Expense		
{[$10,000 − ($4,325.73 − $680.91)] × 0.12}	762.62	
Discount on Notes Payable		762.62
Depreciation Expense	567.43	
Accumulated Depreciation		567.43

This example assumes that a 12% interest rate is appropriate for the transaction, but a borrower should attempt to determine the fair values of the property and of the note before applying its incremental interest rate. If either the fair value of the property or of the note is used, the note payable is recorded at the fair value, and the company must find the implicit interest rate that equates the recorded (fair) value to the face value over the term of the loan. For example, assume in the previous example that Marsden determines that the fair value of the equipment is $6,209.21. From the Present Value of 1 Table (TVM Module), we find that the rate that equates $6,209.21 to $10,000 at the end of five years is 10%.[16] Marsden would record the note payable initially at $6,209.21, and then would record the interest expense of 10% on the carrying value of the note each year over the life of the note.

This example also assumes the issuance of a non-interest-bearing note. As discussed earlier, the same principles apply in the case where a note carries a stated interest rate that is unreasonable. For example, assume that on January 1, 2007 Fox Company issues a $30,000, three-year note bearing interest of 2% for equipment when its incremental borrowing rate is 10%. If the fair value of the equipment or the note is not determinable, Fox records the transaction using the present value of the future cash flows with the 10% rate for the three-year life. In this case, it records the equipment and note at $27,015.78 [($30,000 face value × 0.751315) + ($1,800 annual interest × 2.486852)]. It then applies the effective interest method using the 10% rate at the end of each year to determine the interest expense. For instance, at the end of 2007, it debits Interest Expense for $2,701.58 ($27,015.78 × 0.10), credits Cash for $1,800 ($30,000 × 0.06), and increases the book value of the note by $901.58. ♦

Disclosure of Long-Term Liabilities

We discussed how a company reports its long-term liabilities on its balance sheet in various sections earlier in the chapter. We also discussed how a company reports any gains or losses on the retirement of its long-term liabilities on its income statement. A company generally reports its long-term liability transactions involving cash in the financing section of its statement of cash flows. It reports the cash received from the issuance of notes

10 Understand the disclosure of long-term liabilities.

---

16. $6,209.21 ÷ $10,000 = 0.620921. In the $n = 5$ row, we find 0.620921 in the 10% column.

payable or bonds payable—whether issued at face value, at a premium, or at a discount—as a cash inflow from financing activities. It reports the cash paid to retire bonds payable or notes payable as a cash outflow for financing activities. It includes the cash paid for interest, however, in the operating activities section. Even though the interest paid is related to a financing activity, GAAP requires it to be included in operating activities because the related interest expense is included in the company's income statement. If a company has amortized a discount (premium) on bonds payable, under the indirect method, the company adds (subtracts) the discount (premium) to net income in the operating activities section of its statement of cash flows. It also includes any gains or losses on the retirement of its long-term liabilities as adjustments to net income in the operating activities section of its statement of cash flows. If a company converts bonds into common stock, it discloses this transaction as a non-cash financing activity.

A company also must disclose the various characteristics of its long-term debt. It normally does so in the notes to its financial statements. We show the disclosure by **IBM Corporation** of its long-term (and short-term) debt in Real Report 14-1 on page 668. Also included are disclosures about scheduled repayments of long-term debt, interest payments, capitalized interest, and lines of credit.

LINK TO RATIO ANALYSIS

Investors, creditors, and others are interested in a company's long-run solvency and stability. As companies acquire more debt, risk typically increases for equity owners. This risk arises from two sources. First, debt usually requires periodic interest payments, and failure to make these payments can lead to default and possibly bankruptcy. Second, in the event of bankruptcy, the creditors' claims are satisfied first. Two ratios that provide evidence of this risk that can affect a company's long-run solvency and stability are the debt ratio and the times interest earned ratio. Below are excerpts from the 2004 annual report of **Deere and Company**.

(in millions)	2004	2003
Total Assets	$28,754.0	$26,258.0
Total Liabilities	22,361.2	22,255.9
Interest Expense	592.1	628.5
Income before Income Taxes	2,113.7	971.3

Deere's debt ratio is:

2004: $\dfrac{\text{Total Liabilities}}{\text{Total Assets}} = \dfrac{\$\,22{,}361.2}{\$\,28{,}754.0} = 0.78$ 2003: $\dfrac{\text{Total Liabilities}}{\text{Total Assets}} = \dfrac{\$\,22{,}255.9}{\$\,26{,}258.0} = 0.85$

Subtracting this ratio from 100%, stockholders have contributed just 22% and 15% of the total assets for 2004 and 2003, respectively. The interest coverage ratio, a measure of the safety of creditors' investments in the company is:

2004: $\dfrac{\text{Pretax Operating Income}}{\text{Interest Expense}} = \dfrac{\$\,2{,}113.7 + \$\,592.1}{\$\,592.1} = 4.57$

2003: $\dfrac{\text{Pretax Operating Income}}{\text{Interest Expense}} = \dfrac{\$\,971.3 + \$\,628.5}{\$\,628.5} = 2.55$

These results show that Deere is a highly leveraged company, which is usually viewed as a more risky investment.

LINK TO ETHICAL DILEMMA

TLM, Inc., a struggling software development company, has been experiencing cash flow problems. To address working capital deficiencies, TLM entered into an agreement with one of its customers, MoneyTree, Inc. and issued a two-year, non-interest-bearing note with a face value of $5,000,000 and received $4,853,310 in exchange. This equates to an effective (implicit) interest rate of 1.5%. As the accountant for TLM, such a low interest rate (TLM's normal borrowing rate is 10%) has led you to question how this favorable rate was obtained. In your investigation, you discover that the CEO of TLM has an oral agreement with MoneyTree to provide free software support (e.g., installation, troubleshooting) over the next five years and it was the existence of this side agreement that resulted in the unreasonably low interest rate. You conclude that the note and future interest charges should be recorded at the market interest of 10%, resulting in larger yearly interest charges. Furthermore, the value of the software support should be recorded as unearned revenue and recognized over the next five years. Upper management disagrees with your conclusion and tells you that the interest expense that would be required under your assessment would turn the company's small positive net income into a net loss, as well as cause the company to be in technical violation of existing debt covenants. Furthermore, the CEO states that the verbal agreement is nonbinding and to record revenue in such a situation would be earnings management. The CEO instructs you to record the transaction as if the side agreement did not exist. What are your responsibilities?

LONG-TERM NOTES RECEIVABLE

Although this is a chapter on long-term liabilities, we discuss accounting for long-term notes receivable here because the generally accepted accounting principles that apply to notes receivable are very similar to those for notes payable. Companies may acquire long-term notes receivable as a result of lending cash to another entity or in return for the extension of certain rights or privileges. However, except for financial institutions, long-term notes receivable are acquired primarily as a result of an exchange for property, goods, or services. We focus on this type of exchange in this section.

11 Account for long-term notes receivable, including impairment of a loan.

As we discussed in the previous section, when a company receives a note in exchange for property, goods, or services, it should presume that the stipulated interest rate is fair unless:

- No interest rate is stated
- The stated interest rate is clearly unreasonable
- The face value of the note is materially different from the cash sales price of the property, goods, or services, or from the fair value of the note on the transaction date

In any of these situations, **the note receivable is recorded at the fair value of the property, goods, or services or the fair value of the note, whichever is more reliable. If neither of these values is reliable, the note is recorded at its present value by using the** *borrower's* **incremental interest rate.** The effective interest method is used to record the periodic interest revenue. Recording the note at its fair value (present value) and using the effective interest method results in the correct asset valuation and in the proper timing of revenue recognition.

Reporting

Real Report 14-1 Disclosure of Long-Term Liabilities

INTERNATIONAL BUSINESS MACHINES CORPORATION

k. Borrowings

SHORT-TERM DEBT

(Dollars in millions)

AT DECEMBER 31:	2004	2003
Commercial paper	$3,151	$2,349
Short-term loans	1,340	1,124
Long-term debt—current maturities	3,608	3,173
Total	$8,099	$6,646

The weighted-average interest rates for commercial paper at December 31, 2004 and 2003, were 2.2 percent and 1.0 percent, respectively. The weighted-average interest rates for short-term loans were 1.5 percent and 2.5 percent at December 31, 2004 and 2003, respectively.

LONG-TERM DEBT

Pre-Swap Activity

(Dollars in millions)	Maturities	2004	2003
U.S. Dollars:			
Debentures:			
5.875%	2032	$ 600	$ 600
6.22%	2027	469	500
6.5%	2028	313	319
7.0%	2025	600	600
7.0%	2045	150	150
7.125%	2096	850	850
7.5%	2013	532	550
8.375%	2019	750	750
3.43% convertible notes*	2007	278	309
Notes: 5.9% average	2006–2013	2,724	3,034
Medium-term note program: 4.5% average	2005–2018	3,627	4,690
Other: 3.0% average**	2005–2010	1,555	508
		12,448	12,860
Other currencies (average interest rate at December 31, 2004, in parentheses):			
Euros (5.0%)	2005–2009	1,095	1,174
Japanese yen (1.2%)	2005–2015	3,435	4,363
Canadian dollars (7.8%)	2005–2011	9	201
Swiss francs (1.5%)	2008	220	—
Other (5.5%)	2005–2014	513	770
		17,720	19,368
Less: Net unamortized discount		49	15
Add: SFAS No. 133 fair value adjustment+		765	806
		18.436	20,159
Less: Current maturities		3,608	3,173
Total		$14,828	$16,986

*On October 1, 2002, as part of the purchase price consideration for the PwCC acquisition, ... the company issued convertible notes bearing interest at a stated rate of 3.43 percent with a face value of approximately $328 million to certain of the acquired PwCC partners. The notes are convertible into 4,764,543 shares of IBM common stock at the option of the holders at any time after the first anniversary of their issuance based on a fixed conversion price of

Continued

$68.81 per share of the company's common stock. As of December 31, 2004, a total of 720,034 shares had been issued under this provision.

**Includes $249 million and $153 million of debt collateralized by financing receivables at December 31, 2004 and 2003, respectively.

+In accordance with the requirements of SFAS No. 133, the portion of the company's fixed rate debt obligations that is hedged is reflected in the Consolidated Statement of Financial Position as an amount equal to the sum of the debt's carrying value plus an SFAS No.133 fair value adjustment representing changes recorded in the fair value of the hedged debt obligations attributable to movements in market interest rates and applicable foreign currency exchange rates.

Annual contractual maturities on long-term debt outstanding, including capital lease obligations, at December 31, 2004, are as follows:

(Dollars in millions)

2005	$ 3,221
2006	3,104
2007	1,300
2008	499
2009	2,116
2010 and beyond	7,480

INTEREST ON DEBT

(Dollars in millions)

FOR THE YEAR ENDED DECEMBER 31:	2004	2003	2002
Cost of Global Financing	$428	$503	$633
Interest expense	139	145	145
Interest expense—discontinued operations	—	—	2
Interest capitalized	4	15	35
Total interest paid and accrued	$571	$663	$815

LINES OF CREDIT

On May 27, 2004, the company completed the renegotiation of a new $10 billion 5-year Credit Agreement with JP Morgan Chase Bank, as Administrative Agent, and Citibank, N.A., as Syndication Agent, replacing credit agreements of $8 billion (5 year) and $2 billion (364 day). The total expense recorded by the company related to these facilities was $8.9 million, $7.8 million and $9.1 million for the years ended December 31, 2004, 2003, and 2002, respectively. The new facility is irrevocable unless the company is in breach of covenants, including interest coverage ratios, or if it commits an event of default, such as failing to pay any amount due under this agreement. The company believes that circumstances that might give rise to a breach of these covenants or an event of default, as specified in these agreements, are remote. The company's other lines of credit, most of which are uncommitted, totaled $9,041 million and $8,202 million at December 31, 2004 and 2003, respectively. Interest rates and other terms of borrowing under these lines of credit vary from country to country, depending on local market conditions.

(Dollars in millions)

AT DECEMBER 31:	2004	2003
Unused lines:		
From the committed global credit facility	$ 9,804	$ 9,907
From other committed and uncommitted lines	6,477	5,976
Total unused lines of credit	$16,281	$15,883

Questions:

1. What is the remaining life of the debt with the longest maturity?
2. Why would financial statement users be concerned with the amount of long-term debt maturing in the next five years?
3. Did total interest paid and accrued increase or decrease in 2004?
4. Does IBM have financial flexibility?

Example: Exchange for Equipment To illustrate, consider the previous example in which the Joyce Company accepted a $10,000, non-interest-bearing, five-year note on January 1, 2007 in exchange for used equipment it sold to Marsden Company. Since a reliable fair value for the equipment or the note was not available, Joyce uses *Marsden's* 12% incremental borrowing rate to determine a present value of $5,674.27 for the note. Assume further that the equipment had originally cost the Joyce Company $8,000 and had a book value of $5,000 on the date of sale. The Joyce Company records the following journal entries for the exchange and the first two interest receipts:

January 1, 2007

Notes Receivable	10,000.00	
Accumulated Depreciation	3,000.00	
Discount on Notes Receivable		
($10,000 − $5,674.27)		4,325.73
Equipment		8,000.00
Gain on Sale of Equipment		674.27

December 31, 2007

Discount on Notes Receivable	680.91	
Interest Revenue		
[($10,000 − $4,325.73) × 0.12]		680.91

December 31, 2008

Discount on Notes Receivable	762.62	
Interest Revenue		
{[$10,000 − ($4,325.7 − $680.91)] × 0.12}		762.62

At the date of exchange, Joyce records the difference between the present value and face value of the note in a Discount on Notes Receivable account.[17] This account is a contra account and is subtracted from the Notes Receivable account to report the carrying (book) value of the note on the company's balance sheet. Joyce computes the $674.27 gain by comparing the book value ($5,000) of the equipment with the present value ($5,674.27) of the note. If the exchange takes place in the middle of the year, the company must make a depreciation adjusting entry to bring the book value of the equipment up to date. If the company receives cash in addition to the note, it computes the gain by comparing the book value of the equipment with the sum of the cash received plus present value of the note.

At the end of each year the company records interest revenue using the effective interest method. By the maturity date, it will have amortized the entire discount to interest revenue, and the carrying value will equal the face value of the note. If a reliable value for the equipment or the note is available, the company records the note at this fair value and computes the implicit interest rate as we discussed in the previous section. The company then uses this interest rate to recognize periodic interest revenue under the effective interest method. ♦

---

17. An alternative method is to record the Notes Receivable account at its present value without the use of a Discount account. The Notes Receivable account is then increased by each subsequent entry to record interest revenue and is equal to the maturity value on the due date.

Loan Fees

The proper matching of revenues and expenses for the lending activities of financial services companies is defined by **FASB Statement No. 91.** Lending activities precede the payment of funds and generally include efforts to identify and attract potential borrowers and to originate a loan or loan commitment. The nonrefundable fees charged to borrowers for these activities are called *loan origination fees* and *commitment fees.* Generally, any loan origination fees or commitment fees are deferred and recognized over the life of the loan as an increase in the interest revenue related to the note receivable. Likewise, the direct loan origination costs are deferred and recognized over the life of the loan as a decrease in the interest revenue. In either case, a new, effective interest rate (yield) is computed. In other words, the revenues and expenses for these lending activities are matched over the life of the loan rather than recognized in the period in which the loan is originated.[18]

Impairment of a Loan

Since loans typically are made by financial institutions such as banks, it is helpful to understand how they estimate bad debts as compared to retailers or manufacturers which make sales on credit. The retailer or manufacturer estimates bad debts in the period of the sales because it is probable that a portion of the asset (accounts receivable) has been impaired and the amount of the loss can be reasonably estimated based on historical information (as we discussed in Chapter 7). Thus, the bad debt expense is matched against revenues in the period of sale, and the receivables are reported at their net realizable value at the end of the period. In a later period, a specific account receivable is written off when it is determined that the amount is not collectible.

There are several differences between the receivables of a financial institution and those of a retailer or manufacturer. In the case of the financial institution:

- The notes receivable result primarily from loans made to customers.
- The loans are made to more heterogeneous customers.
- The repayment periods for the loans are frequently longer (i.e., several years).
- There are fewer receivables because fewer loans are made.
- More thorough credit analyses are made before extending loans.

These differences affect when and how bad debt expense is recognized by a financial institution.

A financial institution is likely to make a more thorough credit analysis before granting a loan and to analyze the noncollectibility of each individual loan. Therefore, it is likely to recognize bad debts in a later period than a retailer or manufacturer. In a later period, however, a financial institution will recognize bad debt expense when, for instance, there is evidence that a loan may not be collectible (e.g., when the customer misses a payment on a loan). Then, in an even later period, a specific note receivable is written off when it is determined that the amount is not collectible, perhaps after taking possession of, and selling, the collateral provided by the borrower. We illustrate the difference between bad debt recognition for a retailer or manufacturer and a financial institution in the diagram on the next page of events occurring during several (perhaps nonconsecutive) accounting periods.

Note that because there is a delay in the recognition of bad debts by a financial institution, it does not recognize bad debt expense in the period in which the loan originates (and the financial institution does not recognize revenue from the loan origination), and it does not report its receivables at their net realizable value at the end of that period. However, *relevant* expense recognition and receivables valuation does occur when *reliable* information becomes available that a loan is impaired.

18.˙ "Accounting for Nonrefundable Fees and Costs Associated with Originating or Acquiring Loans and Initial Direct Costs of Leases," *FASB Statement of Financial Accounting Standards No. 91* (Stamford, Conn.: FASB, 1986), par. 5–9.

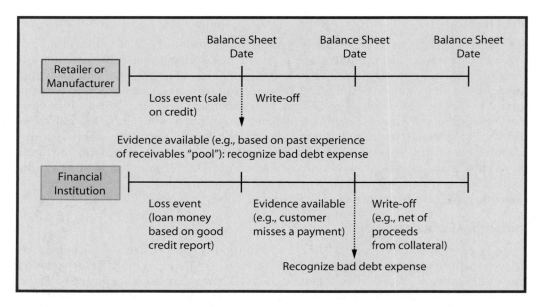

A loan (note receivable) is impaired if it is *probable* that the creditor will be unable to collect all amounts due according to the contractual terms of the loan agreement.[19] Impairment occurs when there is a delay or reduction in the payment of the principal or interest. The creditor company, often a financial institution, applies its normal loan review procedures in making this determination. A loan is *not* impaired even if there is a delay in making interest or principal payments provided the creditor expects to collect all amounts due, including interest accrued during the period of delay. When a loan is found to be impaired, **the creditor company computes the present value of the expected future cash flows of the impaired loan using the effective interest rate on the loan. The effective interest rate is the original (contractual) interest rate on the loan** (adjusted for any loan fees, discount, or premium). The creditor recognizes the amount by which the present value is less than the recorded investment in the loan as Bad Debt Expense and Allowance for Doubtful Notes. Alternatively, the creditor may measure the impairment based on the loan's market price, or the fair value of the collateral if it expects repayment of the loan to be provided solely by the underlying collateral (net of the costs of selling the loan or the collateral).

Once the creditor has written down the loan, it computes the interest revenue each period by multiplying the carrying value of the loan by the effective interest rate. It recognizes the interest revenue as a reduction of the allowance account.[20] If there are additional changes in the amount or timing of an impaired loan's expected cash flows, or if actual cash flows are different than expected cash flows, the creditor recalculates the amount of the impairment. It recognizes the difference, whether an increase or decrease, as an adjustment to Bad Debt Expense and the Allowance account.

---

19. "Accounting by Creditors for Impairment of a Loan," *FASB Statement No. 114* (Norwalk, Conn.: FASB, 1993). This *Statement* also applies to the impairment of accounts receivable of more than one year (which we do not discuss here). It does *not* apply to investments in debt securities, as defined in *FASB Statement No. 115* (which we discuss in Chapter 15).

20. This method is the conceptually preferred method for recognizing income. Alternatively, *FASB Statement No. 114* allows for the entire change in the present value (the bad debt expense *and* the interest revenue) to be recognized as a single amount and reported as an increase or decrease in bad debt expense. However, because the two alternatives were inconsistent with the accounting for impaired loans required by bank and thrift regulators, **FASB Statement No. 118** was issued in 1994. This amendment allows the use of any method of income recognition, such as cash basis or cost recovery, even though the current value of the impaired loan may be less than the present value of the expected cash flows discounted at the loan's effective interest rate. Thus, the Board decided to allow for a reduction of *comparability* in order to reduce implementation *costs* for companies. It also increased disclosure by requiring that companies must report their policy for recognizing interest income. Since illustrations of all the methods are beyond the scope of the book, we use the conceptually preferred effective interest method.

Example: Impairment of Loan To illustrate the impairment of a loan using present value calculations, assume that the Snook Company has a $100,000 note receivable from the Ullman Company that it is carrying at face value. The original loan agreement specifies that interest of 8% is payable each December 31 and the principal is to be paid on December 31, 2012. The Ullman Company paid the interest due on December 31, 2007, but informed the Snook Company at that time that it probably would miss the next two year's interest payments because of its financial difficulties.[21] After that, it expects to resume the $8,000 annual interest payments, but the principal payment would be made one year late with interest paid for that additional year. We show these different cash flows in the following diagram:

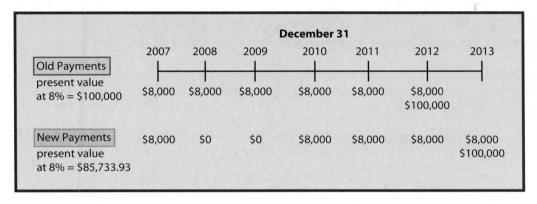

On December 31, 2007 the Snook Company computes the present value of the impaired loan as we show below. Note that the company discounts the principal for six years, the period from December 31, 2007 to December 31, 2013, but only discounts the interest for four years, deferred two years, because Ullman will not pay interest for two years.

Present value of principal = **$100,000 × present value of a single sum for 6 years at 8% (from Time Value of Money Module)**
= **$100,000 × 0.630170**
= **$63,017.00**

Present value of interest = **$8,000 × present value of an annuity for 4 years at 8% deferred 2 years (from Time Value of Money Module)**
= **$8,000 × 3.312127 × 0.857339**
= **$22,716.93**

Value of the impaired loan = **$63,017.00 + $22,716.93**
= **$85,733.93**

At December 31, 2007, the Snook Company recognizes the impairment of $14,266.07 ($100,000 carrying value − $85,733.93 present value) as follows:

Bad Debt Expense	14,266.07	
Allowance for Doubtful Notes		14,266.07

At December 31, 2008, the Snook Company recognizes interest revenue of $6,858.71 [8% × $85,733.93 ($100,000 − $14,266.07)] as follows:

Allowance for Doubtful Notes	6,858.71	
Interest Revenue		6,858.71

At December 31, 2009 the Snook Company recognizes interest revenue of $7,407.36 [8% × $92,592.64 ($100,000 − $7,407.36), adjusted for $0.04 rounding error]. This eliminates

---

21. In a more complex situation, knowledge of the loan impairment would occur when a payment is missed. If the company has accrued interest revenue for the period, the bad debt expense would be the difference between the carrying value (including the accrued interest) and the present value of the expected cash flows (including any late interest payments).

the balance in the Allowance for Doubtful Notes account, and the carrying value of the receivable is now $100,000. Snook will recognize interest revenue of $8,000 each year for 2010 through 2013 as the cash payment is received. Snook will eliminate the $100,000 carrying value on December 31, 2013 when it receives the principal payment. If Snook's expectations of future cash flows decrease (increase) before December 31, 2009, it would debit (credit) Bad Debt Expense and credit (debit) the Allowance account for the decrease (increase) in the present value. In either situation, the company would recognize interest revenue each year, as we discussed earlier. ♦

LINK TO INTERNATIONAL DIFFERENCES

When a loan (note receivable) is impaired, international accounting standards, similar to U.S. standards, require a company to compute the loss as the difference between the carrying value of the receivable and the present value of the future cash flows. However, international standards allow the company to record the loss by reducing the receivable directly or through the use of an allowance account. Also, if in a later period the impairment loss decreases, international standards allow the company to reverse the impairment loss with the reversal included in income.

Conceptual Evaluation

FASB Statement No. 114 was issued because companies were using a variety of practices when a loan was impaired. Some would make no adjustment to the value of the loan, some would value the loan based on undiscounted cash flows, and some would use discounted cash flows. Thus, one objective of issuing the *Statement* was to establish a consistent method for valuing impaired loans. Another objective was to require companies to measure the economic losses on impaired loans and to include them in their income.

Perhaps the only controversial issue in the required principles is the use of the original (contractual) interest rate rather than a current market rate that would reflect the risk involved in the loan (which is now higher than at the origination of the loan). The FASB concluded that the loan impairment measurement should reflect only the deterioration in the borrower's credit quality (which is evidenced by the reduced future cash inflows), and should not reflect changes in interest rates.

The *Statement* was adopted by a 5-to-2 vote, however, with the two dissenters arguing that the *fair value* of the loan should be recognized. Such a fair value would be the market value of the loan or the present value of the expected cash flows discounted at the *market* rate of interest. The market rate reflects current economic events and conditions, and is consistent with the risk involved. The dissenters argued that the fair value provides the most *relevant* information about the amount and riskiness of the expected future cash flows. The historical effective interest rate reflects the risk characteristics of the loan at the time it was originated or acquired, but not at the time it was impaired. Also they note that bad debt expense would be *overstated* if the historical rate is *higher* than the current market rate.

Initially, it may seem surprising that interest revenue (based on the new carrying value) is recognized even though a loan is impaired. For example, the Snook Company recognizes interest revenue in 2008 when it receives no cash. However, remember that in 2007, it recognizes the economic loss of $14,266.07 associated with the receivable and values the loan at the present value of the future cash flows. It then recognizes interest revenue on that reduced value. As always, one of the major issues of income recognition is the period in which income (and losses) should be recognized. These principles for the impairment of a loan recognize the true economic situation appropriately because a loss is recognized in the period of impairment and interest revenue is recognized in later periods.

Guarantees

Sometimes a company may guarantee another company's debt. For example, suppose the Probst Company sells a product to the Metcalf Company for $10 million. Since Metcalf does not have sufficient cash, it decides to take out a bank loan to finance the purchase. However, its financial status is such that the bank will not provide an unsecured loan. So the Probst Company agrees to guarantee Metcalf's loan from the bank so that it can make the sale. **FASB Interpretation No. 45** requires the Probst Company to determine the fair value of the guarantee and recognize it as a liability.[22] The company has a liability because it has an obligation to "stand ready" to perform over the life of the guarantee if the specific triggering events or conditions occur. For the Probst Company, it would have to repay the bank loan if the Metcalf Company defaulted. In addition to recognizing a liability, Probst would reduce the profit it recognizes on the sale.

The *Interpretation* does not explicitly state how the guarantee is to be accounted for in future periods. However, it is presumed that the company would determine the fair value each period, and recognize the change in value in its income for the period. In most situations, the fair value would decrease each period and a gain would be recognized.

The *Interpretation* also requires the company to make certain disclosures including the nature of the guarantee, its approximate term, how it arose, and the events or circumstances that would require the company to perform under the guarantee. Other disclosures include the maximum potential future undiscounted payments that the company could be required to make and the current carrying value of the liability. The *Interpretation* does not apply to some guarantees, such as insurance and warranty contracts.

SECURE YOUR KNOWLEDGE 14-3

- Long-term notes are recorded at their present value with periodic interest determined using the effective interest method.
- When a note is exchanged for cash and special rights or privileges, these rights and privileges represent unearned revenue (measured as the difference between the cash proceeds and the present value of the note) which is recognized over the life of the contract.
- A note issued in exchange for property, goods, or services is recorded at the fair value of the property, goods, or services or the fair value of the note, whichever is more reliable.
- The accounting for long-term notes receivable is similar to that of long-term notes payable, with any loan fees being deferred and recognized over the life of the loan.
- If a loan (note receivable) becomes impaired, a company must write down the loan to the present value of the expected future cash flows by setting up an allowance account; it then records future interest revenue as a reduction to the allowance account.

Future Developments

At the time of writing this book, the FASB has issued an *Exposure Draft* that, if implemented, will have significant effects on how some companies account for liabilities. *Exposure Draft No. 213-B*, "Accounting for Financial Instruments with Characteristics of Liabilities, Equity, or Both," will, if adopted, change the accounting for what the FASB has identified as **multiple-component instruments**. These financial instruments have characteristics of both liabilities and equity. This *Exposure Draft* would require a company that issues a multiple component instrument to separately classify the liability component and the equity component. In measuring the amount to classify as each component, it must allocate the proceeds received to its liabilities and its stockholders' equity using the relative-fair-value-method.

---

22. "Guarantor's Accounting and Disclosure Requirements for Guarantees, Including Indirect Guarantees of Indebtedness of Others," *FASB Interpretation No. 45* (FASB: Norwalk, Conn.: 2002).

This new GAAP would affect how a company accounts for the issuance of convertible bonds. When a company issues convertible bonds, it would allocate a portion of the proceeds to the conversion feature and account for this amount as additional paid-in capital. This allocation is based on the relative independent fair values of the liability (bonds) component and the equity (conversion rights) component.

When convertible bondholders exercise their rights to convert the bonds to common stock, the company must determine any gain or loss, as well as the amount to record as stockholders' equity. To determine these amounts, the company would complete a series of steps. It would:

1. Determine the total fair value of the convertible bonds on the conversion date
2. Determine the independent fair values of the liability (bonds) component and the stockholders' equity (conversion rights) component
3. Allocate the total fair value from step (1) to the liability component and the stockholders' equity component based on the relative independent fair values of each of these components
4. Subtract the fair value of the bonds component from the book value of the bonds to determine the gain or loss after conversion before
5. Assign the fair value of the bond component to the separate elements (i.e., common stock and additional paid-in capital) of the equity component

The company would then prepare a journal entry to eliminate the book value of the bonds, record the gain or loss on the conversion, and record the common stockholders' equity at the fair value of the bonds.

APPENDIX 1: TROUBLED DEBT RESTRUCTURINGS

12 Understand troubled debt restructurings.

Some companies that experience difficulty in repaying long-term debt obligations enter into financial arrangements with their creditors to allow them to avoid bankruptcy. **FASB Statement No. 15** states that **a troubled debt restructuring occurs when a creditor for economic or legal reasons related to a debtor's financial difficulties grants a concession to the debtor that it would not otherwise consider.** A troubled debt restructuring may include, but is not limited to, one or any combination of the following:

1. **Modification of terms** of a debt, such as one or a combination of:
   a. Reduction of the stated interest rate for the remaining original life of the debt.
   b. Extension of the maturity date at a stated interest rate lower than the current market rate for new debt with similar risk.
   c. Reduction of the face amount or maturity amount of the debt.
   d. Reduction of accrued interest.
2. **Issuance or other granting of an equity interest** to the creditor by the debtor to satisfy a debt unless the equity interest is granted under existing terms for converting the debt into an equity interest.
3. **Transfer of receivables, real estate, or other assets** from the debtor to the creditor to satisfy a debt.[23]

ACCOUNTING BY THE DEBTOR

We first discuss the debtor's accounting for a troubled debt restructuring. Later we discuss the creditor's accounting.

---

23. "Accounting by Debtors and Creditors for Troubled Debt Restructurings," *FASB Statement of Financial Accounting Standards No. 15* (Stamford, Conn.: FASB, 1977), par. 2 and 5.

Modification of Terms

When a restructuring agreement involves only a modification of terms, the carrying value of the *liability* (face value of the debt plus any unpaid accrued interest) is compared to the *undiscounted* future cash payments (principal plus interest) specified by the new terms. Then, two different situations may arise:

1. If the undiscounted total future cash payments are *greater* than (or equal to) the carrying value of the liability, the debtor does *not* recognize a gain, the carrying value of the liability is *not* reduced, and interest expense is recognized in future periods using an imputed interest rate.
2. If the future cash payments are *less* than the carrying value of the liability, the debtor recognizes a gain, the carrying value of the liability is reduced, and interest expense is *not* recognized in future periods.

Example: No Gain Recognized by the Debtor

When there is a modification of terms and the total cash to be repaid over the remaining life of the loan is greater than (or equal to) the carrying value of the liability, the debtor makes no adjustment to the carrying value. The debtor recognizes annual interest expense using the effective interest method. **The imputed interest rate used is the rate that equates the total amount of cash to be paid with the current carrying value of the debt.** In this situation, the debtor records a portion of each cash payment as interest expense and records the remainder as a reduction in the carrying value of the liability.

For example, assume that on December 31, 2007 Chapin Company restructures a $1,178,073 debt with its bank (a note payable of $1,100,000 plus accrued interest of $78,073). The bank (1) forgives the $78,073 of accrued interest and $100,000 of principal, (2) extends the maturity date from December 31, 2007 to December 31, 2012, and (3) reduces the interest rate from 10% to 8%. The total future cash payments under the new terms are $1,400,000 (principal of $1,000,000 at the end of five years and interest of $80,000 at the end of each year for five years). Since the *undiscounted* amount of the principal and interest to be paid ($1,400,000) exceeds the carrying value of the liability ($1,178,073), Chapin does not record a gain and therefore does not reduce the carrying value of the liability. It records the difference of $221,927 as interest expense over the next five years by using the effective interest method. It determines the interest expense each period by multiplying the effective interest rate times the carrying value at the beginning of the period.

The effective interest rate is that rate which discounts the principal of $1,000,000 and the interest payments of $80,000 to the $1,178,073 carrying value of the note. This discounting procedure involves two present value calculations, as we summarize in the following diagram:

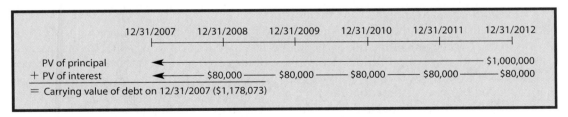

This rate is found to be 4%, as proven below:

Present value of interest payments:
(Present Value of an Ordinary Annuity Table in
   Time Value of Money Module, $n=5, i=0.04$) $80,000 × 4.451822 = \$ 356,146

Present Value of Principal:
(Present Value of 1 Table in Time Value
   of Money Module, $n=5, i=0.04$) $1,000,000 × 0.821927 =   821,927
Carrying Value of the Debt on 12/31/2007 $1,178,073

On December 31, 2007 Chapin transfers the accrued Interest Payable balance to the Notes Payable account as follows:

Interest Payable	78,073	
Notes Payable		78,073

The Notes Payable account now contains the entire $1,178,073 carrying value of the note. Chapin computes the interest expense to be recorded in each period by applying the effective interest rate of 4% to the carrying value of the note each year. Example 14-5 illustrates the computation of the interest expense and principal reduction for each year of the Chapin Company's restructuring agreement.

EXAMPLE 14-5 — Debt Restructuring Agreement: Schedule to Compute Interest Expense

Date	Cash Credit[a]	Interest Expense Debit[b]	Notes Payable Debit[c]	Carrying Value of Note[d]
12/31/07				$1,178,073.00
12/31/08	$ 80,000	$47,122.92	$ 32,877.08	1,145,195.92
12/31/09	80,000	45,807.84	34,192.16	1,111,003.76
12/31/10	80,000	44,440.15	35,559.85	1,075,443.91
12/31/11	80,000	43,017.76	36,982.24	1,038,461.67
12/31/12	1,080,000	41,538.33[e]	1,038,461.67	-0-

a. From terms of restructuring agreement.
b. Previous carrying value × 0.04.
c. Amount from footnote a − amount from footnote b.
d. Previous carrying value − amount from footnote c.
e. Difference due to $0.14 rounding error.

In reviewing Example 14-5, note that each cash payment is separated into its principal and interest components by multiplying the carrying value of the note in each year by the imputed interest rate in the agreement (4% in this case). Chapin Company records the difference between the interest expense and each cash payment as a reduction in the carrying value of the note payable. For example, Chapin Company records the following journal entry on December 31, 2008:

Interest Expense	47,122.92	
Notes Payable	32,877.08	
Cash		80,000.00 ◆

Example: Gain Recognized by the Debtor

An adjustment to the carrying value of the liability is required if the total cash to be repaid over the remaining life of the loan is less than that carrying value. In this case, the debtor recognizes a gain equal to the excess of the carrying value (face value plus accrued interest) over the sum of the future payments.

For example, assume that the Chapin Company was allowed the terms stated previously (reduction of principal by $100,000, forgiving of $78,073 of accrued interest, and extension of repayment period by five years), except that the stated interest rate was reduced to 3%. The aggregate future cash payments in this case total $1,150,000 ($1,000,000 principal and $30,000 interest per year for five years). This amount is $28,073 less than the carrying value of $1,178,073 ($1,100,000 face value + $78,073 accrued interest). Chapin Company reports this amount as a gain in its income from continuing operations for 2007, eliminates the accrued interest, and credits the difference between the gain and the accrued interest to the Notes Payable account so that the balance is now $1,150,000. Chapin records the restructuring on December 31, 2007 is as follows:

Interest Payable	78,073	
Notes Payable		50,000
Gain on Debt Restructure		28,073

Each future cash payment reduces the carrying value of the payable and Chapin does *not* recognize interest expense, since the effective interest rate is 0%. That is, since the amount to be repaid is less than the original carrying value of the liability, the creditor is, in effect, accepting repayment without an accompanying interest charge. Chapin records the first cash payment on December 31, 2008 as follows:

Notes Payable	30,000	
Cash		30,000

The reduction of the Notes Payable account by $30,000 each year for five years will reduce this account to $1,000,000. This amount will then be eliminated at the time of the lump-sum principal payment at the end of the fifth year. ♦

Equity or Asset Exchange

When a debtor satisfies a liability by exchanging an equity interest or an asset of lesser value, it records the transfer on the basis of the fair value of the equity interest or asset transferred and recognizes a gain on the debt restructuring. Also, when an *asset* is exchanged, if the fair value is greater or less than its carrying value, the debtor also records a gain or loss on the disposal of the asset.

Example: Equity Exchange

To illustrate an equity exchange, assume that on December 31, 2007 the Chapin Company repays the note payable and the accrued interest totaling $1,178,073 by issuing 35,000 shares of its own common stock to the bank. The shares have a par value of $10 per share and are selling currently for $25 per share on the open market. Chapin records the stock at the fair value of $875,000 (35,000 × $25), reduces the liability by $1,178,073, and recognizes a gain of $303,073. Chapin Company records the debt restructuring as follows:

Notes Payable	1,100,000	
Interest Payable	78,073	
Common Stock (35,000 × $10)		350,000
Additional Paid-in Capital on Common Stock		525,000
Gain on Debt Restructure		303,073 ♦

Example: Asset Exchange

To illustrate an asset exchange, assume the same information as the equity exchange except that the Chapin Company repays the liability by transferring land it owns to the bank. The land has a fair value of $800,000 and had cost the Chapin Company $600,000 five years ago. The Chapin Company recognizes a gain of $378,073 ($1,178,073 − $800,000) on the restructuring and a gain of $200,000 ($800,000 − $600,000) on the disposal of the land. Chapin Company records the debt restructuring as follows:

Notes Payable	1,100,000	
Interest Payable	78,073	
Gain on Debt Restructure		378,073
Gain on Disposal of Land		200,000
Land		600,000 ♦

Equity or Asset Exchange Combined with a Modification of Terms

In some situations, a troubled debt restructuring includes an equity or asset exchange as well as a modification of terms. In this case, the debtor records the equity or asset transfer first at the fair value as we discussed previously. It then compares the *remaining* carrying value of the liability, after deducting the fair value of the equity or assets transferred, to the total undiscounted future cash payments specified under the new terms. If the remaining carrying value is less than the total payments, the debtor does *not* recognize a gain, does *not* reduce the carrying value of the liability, and recognizes interest expense in future periods using an imputed interest rate. If the remaining carrying value is greater than the total payments, it recognizes a gain and reduces the carrying value of the liability, but does *not* record interest expense in future periods. The accounting procedures to be followed in these two situations are the same as those we discussed earlier.

Disclosure of Restructuring Agreements

The following disclosures are required for debtors who have entered into restructuring agreements: (1) A description of the principal changes in terms and/or the major features of settlement for each restructuring agreement; (2) the aggregate gain on debt restructures and the related income tax effect; (3) the per share amount of the aggregate gain on restructuring, net of the related income tax effect; (4) the aggregate gain or loss recognized during the period on transfers of assets; and (5) information on any contingent payments.[24]

The following is an example of the disclosure required for the Chapin Company's exchange of equity securities we discussed previously (ignoring income taxes):

> **During the year Chapin Company gave common stock with a fair value of $875,000 to the bank in exchange for full settlement of a 10% note in the amount of $1,100,000 and accrued interest of $78,073. As a result of this exchange, the company recognized a gain of $303,073 and increased earnings per share by $0.11.**

ACCOUNTING BY THE CREDITOR

The accounting principles for the creditor are defined by *FASB Statement No. 15* and *FASB Statement No. 114*. Some of the principles are "mirror images" of those for the debtor, while others are not.

Equity or Asset Exchange

The accounting by the creditor (e.g., the bank) for a troubled debt restructuring that involves an equity or asset exchange is a "mirror image" of the accounting by the debtor. These principles are defined by *FASB Statement No. 15*. Thus, when a creditor receives an equity interest or asset to satisfy the receivable, **the creditor records the equity or asset investment at fair value, eliminates the carrying value of the receivable, and recognizes a loss.**

Example 14-6 shows the journal entries used by Tenth National Bank to record the equity and asset exchanges for the troubled debt restructuring of the Chapin Company we discussed earlier. It is helpful to observe the mirror image by contrasting the bank's journal entries with those of the Chapin Company shown earlier.

EXAMPLE 14-6	Creditor Journal Entries for Troubled Debt Restructuring		
Equity Exchange			
12/31/07	Investment in Chapin	875,000	
	Loss on Restructured Loan	303,073	
	Notes Receivable		1,100,000
	Interest Receivable		78,073
Asset Exchange			
12/31/07	Land	800,000	
	Loss on Restructured Loan	378,073	
	Notes Receivable		1,100,000
	Interest Receivable		78,073

---

24. *Ibid.*, par. 25 and 26.

Modification of Terms

The accounting principles for a modification of terms are *not* a mirror image because the creditor must recognize a new value for the loan. **The investment in the restructured loan is valued by discounting the total future cash flows specified by the new contractual terms to their present value.** A loss is recognized as the difference between the present value of the future cash flows and the carrying value of the receivable. **The effective interest rate used in the present value calculation is the original (contractual) interest rate on the loan** (i.e., the same interest rate used for a loan impairment), and *not* the rate specified in the restructuring agreement.[25]

A loan whose terms are modified in a troubled debt restructuring usually will have been identified as impaired in a previous period. We discussed the accounting principles for an impaired loan earlier in the chapter.

Example: Modification of Terms To illustrate the accounting for a modification of terms in a troubled debt restructuring, consider the first Chapin Company example that we discussed earlier. Assume that the loan was from the Tenth National Bank and that the bank has *not* recognized a previous impairment. The bank's note receivable is $1,100,000 and the accrued interest is $78,073. On December 31, 2007, the bank restructures the note so that the new principal is $1,000,000, payable in five years, with an interest rate of 8% (i.e., the annual interest payment is $80,000). Since 10% is the original interest rate on the loan to the Chapin Company, the loan is valued as follows:

$$\begin{aligned}
\text{Present value of principal} &= \$1,000,000 \times \text{present value of a single sum for} \\
&\quad \text{5 years at 10\% (from Time Value of Money} \\
&\quad \text{Module)} \\
&= \$1,000,000 \times 0.620921 \\
&= \$620,921.00
\end{aligned}$$

$$\begin{aligned}
\text{Present value of interest} &= \$80,000 \times \text{present value of an annuity for} \\
&\quad \text{5 years at 10\% (from Time Value of Money} \\
&\quad \text{Module)} \\
&= \$80,000 \times 3.790787 \\
&= \$303,262.96
\end{aligned}$$

$$\begin{aligned}
\text{Value of the restructured loan} &= \$620,921.00 + \$303,262.96 \\
&= \$924,183.96
\end{aligned}$$

On December 31, 2007, the bank records a loss of $253,889.04 ($1,178,073 − $924,183.96) on the restructuring as follows:

Loss on Restructured Loan	253,889.04	
Interest Receivable		78,073.00
Notes Receivable		175,816.04

The carrying value of the Notes Receivable is now $924,183.96 ($1,100,000 − $175,816.04).

In later periods, the bank earns interest at the original rate of 10% applied to the current carrying value. The bank recognizes interest revenue for 2008 of $92,418.40 (10% × $924,183.96) on December 31, 2008 as follows:

Cash	80,000.00	
Notes Receivable	12,418.40	
Interest Revenue		92,418.40

After five years of recording interest under the effective interest method, the Notes Receivable will grow to the principal amount of $1,000,000.

For another illustration, consider the second Chapin Company example, where the stated interest rate is reduced to 3% (i.e., the annual interest payment is $30,000) by the

---

25. "Accounting by Creditors for Impairment of a Loan," *FASB Statement No. 114, op. cit.*

Tenth National Bank. Since the original interest rate for the loan is 10%, the bank computes the value of the loan as follows:

$$
\begin{aligned}
\textbf{Present value of principal} &= \$1,000,000 \times \textbf{present value of a single sum for} \\
&\quad \textbf{5 years at 10\% (from Time Value of Money Module)} \\
&= \$1,000,000 \times 0.620921 \\
&= \$620,921.00
\end{aligned}
$$

$$
\begin{aligned}
\textbf{Present value of interest} &= \$30,000 \times \textbf{present value of an annuity for} \\
&\quad \textbf{5 years at 10\% (from Time Value of Money Module)} \\
&= \$30,000 \times 3.790787 \\
&= \$113,723.61
\end{aligned}
$$

$$
\begin{aligned}
\textbf{Value of the restructured loan} &= \$620,921.00 + \$113,723.61 \\
&= \$734,644.61
\end{aligned}
$$

On December 31, 2007, the bank records a loss of $443,428.39 ($1,178,073 − $734,644.61) on the restructuring as follows:

Loss on Restructured Loan	443,428.39	
Interest Receivable		78,073.00
Notes Receivable		365,355.39

The carrying value of the Notes Receivable is now $734,644.61 ($1,100,000 − $365,355.39).

Since the bank earns interest at the original rate of 10%, it recognizes interest revenue for 2008 of $73,464.46 (10% × $734,644.61) on December 31, 2008 as follows:

Cash	30,000.00	
Notes Receivable	43,464.46	
Interest Revenue		73,464.46

After five years of recording interest under the effective interest method, Notes Receivable will grow to the principal amount of $1,000,000. ♦

It is important to note the difference between the accounting by the debtor and creditor for a modification of terms. As we discussed earlier, the debtor does *not* record the liability at a present value and, therefore, either recognizes no interest expense at all or recognizes an interest expense that is based on a below-market rate that was never part of the contractual agreement. In contrast, the creditor records the receivable at a present value and, therefore, recognizes interest revenue at the original contractual rate. The FASB may eventually require that the debtor also use a present value.

Equity or Asset Exchange Combined with Modification of Terms

When an equity interest or asset is received and a modification of terms is made, the creditor records the equity or asset first at its fair value. It then discounts the future cash receipts to their present value at the effective (contractual) rate of interest. It records a loss as the difference between the carrying value of the receivable and the sum of the fair value of the equity interest or asset plus the present value of the future cash flows.

Following is a summary of the accounting principles we have discussed:

Modification of Terms		Equity or Asset Exchange	
Debtor	**Creditor**	**Debtor**	**Creditor**
(a) If undiscounted cash flows > carring value, no gain and impute new interest rate	Compute present value using the original (contractual) interest rate	Record at fair value, recognize gain	Record at fair value, recognize loss
(b) If undiscounted cash flows < carring value, recognize gain (no interest recognized)			

CONCEPTUAL EVALUATION OF ACCOUNTING FOR TROUBLED DEBT RESTRUCTURINGS

When *FASB Statement No. 15* was issued, many accountants and financial statement users criticized the accounting principles for the modification of terms for a troubled debt restructuring. With the issuance of *FASB Statement No. 114*, these criticisms apply only to the accounting by the debtor because there is no longer a mirror image between the debtor and creditor, as we discussed earlier. The critics argue that the procedures for the debtor (i.e., a limited or no gain) lead to inconsistencies in recording events that have similar economic substance (i.e., a modification of terms and an asset or equity exchange). They view a modification of terms as an economic event that should be recorded at a present value. In other words, they argue that the debtor should follow the procedures that are now required for the creditor. However, as we discussed earlier in the chapter for loan impairment, the *Statement* was adopted by a 5-to-2 vote with the two dissenters arguing that the fair value of the loan should be recognized.

At the time that *FASB Statement No. 15* was issued, it was widely believed that the rules to be followed by the creditor in a modification of terms were the result of lobbying by financial institutions. These institutions argued that the recognition of large losses under the fair value approach would undermine the public's confidence in the banking system and have an adverse effect on the economy. A counterargument was that the nonrecognition of losses enabled banks to continue in business longer than they should have, resulting in larger payments by taxpayers to "bail out" failing banks.

Since these original rules for the creditor have now been superseded, it seems logical that the rules for the debtor should also be modified. However, some supporters of the original rules point out that the FASB was just being conservative in its approach so as to minimize the gain recognized by a financially distressed debtor in a restructuring. Therefore, the choice of the accounting principle for debtors is based on whether a person believes that conservatism or the recognition of fair value is more important to external decision makers.

APPENDIX 2: SERIAL BONDS

In the main part of this chapter, we focused on accounting for bonds in which the entire face value was due on one maturity date. Bonds also may contain provisions that require the issuer to **repay the face value in periodic installments over a number of years;** these bonds are termed **serial bonds.** Serial bonds may be especially attractive in cases where the bond issue is used to finance a particular project, because the issuer can use the yearly cash flow from that project to retire the bond issue.

RECORDING THE ISSUANCE AND INTEREST EXPENSE OF SERIAL BONDS

Serial bonds may sell at a premium or discount because of differences between the prevailing market rate and the stated rate of interest. Since the bonds mature over a number of periods and interest rates depend partly on the terms of the issue, some accountants have questioned the use of a single interest rate to record the initial issue of serial bonds. There are, however, no generally accepted principles for determining the different interest rates to assign to each individual installment. So it is assumed that they all yield the same rate of interest. Thus, a company records the initial issuance of serial bonds in the same manner as other bonds. That is, it records the entire face value in a Bonds Payable account and any discount or premium in a separate contra or adjunct account. After issuance, it computes interest expense and any premium or discount amortization on serial bonds by the **effective interest method.** Alternatively, it may use a method similar to the straight-line method, known as the **bonds outstanding method.** This method results in recording an amount of discount or premium amortization proportionate to the face value of the bonds outstanding. Under this method, if $400,000 of 13% serial bonds are to be repaid

13 Account for serial bonds.

in four $100,000 installments, a proportionate (fractional) share of any premium or discount is amortized over the number of periods each installment is outstanding. The denominator of this fraction is derived by summing the face values of the bonds outstanding at the *beginning* of each period over the life of the entire issue. The numerator of this fraction is the face value of bonds outstanding at the *beginning* of each period.

Example: Serial Bonds

To illustrate these two methods, assume that the Wallace Corporation issues $400,000 of serial bonds with a 13% stated rate of interest for $410,460.92 on January 1, 2005. The company is to repay the bonds in four semiannual $100,000 installments beginning June 30, 2007 and to pay interest semiannually. The $410,460.92 selling price of this serial bond issue reflects a yield of 12%, as we show in the following calculations using factors from the Time Value of Money Module:

Present Value of Principal		
Installment due 6/30/07		
Present value of $100,000 ($n = 5$, $i = 0.06$) × 0.747258	$74,725.80	
Installment due 12/31/07		
Present value of $100,000 ($n = 6$, $i = 0.06$) × 0.704961	70,496.10	
Installment due 6/30/08		
Present value of $100,000 ($n = 7$, $i = 0.06$) × 0.665057	66,505.70	
Installment due 12/31/08		
Present value of $100,000 ($n = 8$, $i = 0.06$) × 0.627412	62,741.20	
Present Value of Principal		$274,468.80
Present Value of Interest Payments		
Installment due 6/30/07		
Present Value of an annuity of $6,500 ($n = 5$, $i = 0.06$) × 4.212364	$27,380.37	
Installment due 12/31/07		
Present value of an annuity of $6,500 ($n = 6$, $i = 0.06$) × 4.917324	31,962.61	
Installment due 6/30/08		
Present value of an annuity of $6,500 ($n = 7$, $i = 0.06$) × 5.582381	36,285.48	
Installment due 12/31/08		
Present value of an annuity of $6,500 ($n = 8$, $i = 0.06$) × 6.209794	40,363.66	
Present value of Interest		135,992.12
Selling Price of Serial Bonds		$410,460.92

The company records the issuance as follows:

Cash	410,460.92	
Bonds Payable		400,000.00
Premium on Bonds Payable		10,460.92

Example 14-7 shows the use of the bonds outstanding (straight-line) method of amortization for these serial bonds. Example 14-8 shows the use of the effective interest method for the same bonds.

In both Examples 14-7 and 14-8, the interest expense debit column shows the interest that Wallace records for each period. The interest expense for the semiannual periods in 2007 and 2008 decreases because the company makes partial repayments during these periods. The cash credit column during these periods also reflects these repayments. For example, on December 31, 2007, the company records the interest expense and partial retirement of the bonds (using straight-line amortization) as follows:

Bonds Payable	100,000.00	
Premium on Bonds Payable	1,207.03	
Interest Expense	18,292.97	
Cash		119,500.00 ♦

EXAMPLE 14-7　Interest Expense and Premium Amortization Schedule for Serial Bonds: *Straight-Line (Bonds Outstanding) Method*

Date	Fraction of Premium Amortized[a]	Cash Credit[b]	Premium Amortization Debit[c]	Interest Expense Debit[d]	Unamortized Premium[e]	Bonds Payable Debit[f]	Bonds Outstanding[g]	Book Value of Bonds[h]
1/01/05					$10,460.92		$ 400,000	$410,460.92
6/30/05	4/26	$ 26,000	$1,609.37	$24,390.63	8,851.55		400,000	408,851.55
12/31/05	4/26	26,000	1,609.37	24,390.63	7,242.18		400,000	407,242.18
6/30/06	4/26	26,000	1,609.37	24,390.63	5,632.81		400,000	405,632.81
12/31/06	4/26	26,000	1,609.37	24,390.63	4,023.44		400,000	404,023.44
6/30/07	4/26	126,000	1,609.37	24,390.63	2,414.07	$100,000	300,000	302,414.07
12/31/07	3/26	119,500	1,207.03	18,292.97	1,207.04	100,000	200,000	201,207.04
6/30/08	2/26	113,000	804.69	12,195.31	402.35	100,000	100,000	100,402.35
12/31/08	1/26	106,500	402.35[i]	6,097.65	-0-	100,000	-0-	-0-
	26/26					$2,600,000		

a. Bonds outstanding at beginning of each period ÷ sum of bonds outstanding, or $400,000 ÷ $2,600,000 in the first period.
b. Bonds outstanding ($400,000 in first period) × interest rate (0.13) × 6/12 + installment payment (amount from footnote f).
c. $10,460.92 × fraction from footnote a.
d. Amount from footnote b − amount from footnote c − installment payment.
e. Previous balance − amount from footnote c.
f. Installment payment.
g. Face value − amount from footnote f.
h. Amount from footnote e + amount from footnote g.
i. Difference due to $0.01 rounding error.

| EXAMPLE 14-8 | Interest Expense and Premium Amortization Schedule for Serial Bonds: Effective Interest Method: 13% Bonds Sold to Yield 12% | | | | | |

Date	Cash Credit[a]	Interest Expense Debit[b]	Premium Amortization Debit[c]	Unamortized Premium[d]	Bonds Payable Debit[e]	Book Value of Bonds[f]
1/01/05				$10,460.92		$410,460.92
6/30/05	$ 26,000	$24,627.66	$1,372.34	9,088.58		409,088.58
12/31/05	26,000	24,545.31	1,454.69	7,633.89		407,633.89
6/30/06	26,000	24,458.03	1,541.97	6,091.92		406,091.92
12/31/06	26,000	24,365.52	1,634.48	4,457.44		404,457.44
6/30/07	126,000	24,267.45	1,732.55	2,724.89	$100,000	302,724.89
12/31/07	119,500	18,163.49	1,336.51	1,388.38	100,000	201,388.38
6/30/08	113,000	12,083.30	916.70	471.68	100,000	100,471.68
12/31/08	106,500	6,028.32[g]	471.68	-0-	100,000	-0-

a. Bonds outstanding ($400,000 in first period) × interest rate (0.13) × 6/12 + installment payment (amount from footnote e).
b. Previous balance of footnote f × 0.12 × 6/12.
c. Amount from footnote a − amount from footnote b − installment payment.
d. Previous balance − amount from footnote c.
e. Installment payment.
f. Previous balance − amount from footnote c − amount from footnote e.
g. Difference due to $0.02 rounding error.

EARLY REDEMPTION OF SERIAL BONDS

If a company redeems bonds from any individual series prior to their maturity date, it eliminates the amount of unamortized discount or premium for these bonds. When the bonds outstanding method is used, this amount can be determined from the amortization table by applying the following formula:

$$\frac{\text{Number of Periods Before Maturity of Issue} \times \text{Par Value of Bonds Redeemed}}{\text{Total of Bonds Outstanding Column}} \times \text{Total Premium or Discount}$$

For example, assume that on January 1, 2007 the $100,000 of the Wallace Corporation bonds due December 31, 2008 are redeemed. The unamortized premium associated with this redemption is calculated as:

$$\frac{4 \text{ periods} \times \$100,000}{\$2,600,000} \times \$10,460.92 = \$1,609.37$$

When the company records the redemption, it debits the Unamortized Premium account for $1,609.37, and calculates a gain or loss on the transaction by comparing the book value of the bonds redeemed with the redemption price. In addition, it reduces the amount of premium amortization shown in Example 14-7 by $402.34 ($1,609.37 ÷ 4) for each semiannual period in 2007 and 2008.

When a company uses the effective interest method, the book value of the bonds being retired is the present value of the future cash payments required (principal and interest) on the bonds being retired at that time. The company calculates the book value by discounting the future principal and interest payments to the retirement date, using the effective interest rate. It computes and reports the gain or loss as we discussed in the preceding paragraph, and eliminates the book value of the retired bonds.

SUMMARY

At the beginning of the chapter, we identified several objectives you would accomplish after reading the chapter. The objectives are listed below, each followed by a brief summary of the key points in the chapter discussion.

1. **Explain the reasons for issuing long-term liabilities.** The five basic reasons why a company might issue long-term debt rather than offer other types of securities are as follows: (1) debt may be the only available source of funds, (2) debt financing may have a lower cost, (3) debt financing offers an income tax advantage, (4) the voting privilege is not shared, and (5) debt financing offers the opportunity for leverage.

2. **Understand the characteristics of bonds payable.** A bond is a type of note in which a company agrees to pay the holder the face value at the maturity date and usually to pay interest periodically at a specified rate on the face value. The face (or par) value is the amount of money that the issuer agrees to pay at maturity. The maturity date is the date on which the issuer of the bond agrees to pay the face value to the holder. The contract rate is the rate at which the issuer of the bonds agrees to pay interest each period until maturity.

3. **Record the issuance of bonds.** At the time of sale, the company records the face value of the bonds in a Bonds Payable account and it records any premium or discount in a separate account entitled Premium on Bonds Payable or Discount on Bonds Payable. A premium account is an adjunct account and a discount account is a contra account.

4. **Amortize discounts and premiums under the straight-line method.** Any discount or premium is amortized to interest expense in equal amounts each period during the life of the bonds. The interest expense is the sum of the cash payment plus the discount amortization or minus the premium amortization.

5. **Compute the selling price of bonds.** The selling price of a bond issue is calculated by summing the present value of the principal and interest payments discounted at the effective interest (yield) rate.

6. **Amortize discounts and premiums under the effective interest method.** The effective interest method applies the semiannual yield to the book value of the bonds at the beginning of each successive semiannual period to determine the interest expense for that period. The discount or premium amortization is the difference between the interest expense and the cash payment.

7. **Explain extinguishment of liabilities.** A liability is extinguished for financial reporting purposes when either (1) the debtor pays the creditor and is relieved of its obligation for the liability, or (2) the debtor is released legally from being the primary obligor under the liability.

8. **Understand bonds with equity characteristics.** A company may issue bonds that allow creditors to ultimately become stockholders by attaching stock warrants to the bonds or including a conversion feature. In either case, the investor has acquired the right to receive interest on the bonds and the right to acquire common stock and to participate in the potential appreciation of the market value of the company's common stock.

9. **Account for long-term notes payable.** A note payable is recorded at its present value, and the effective interest method is used to record the subsequent interest. A note exchanged for property, goods, or services is recorded at the fair value of the property, goods, or services, or the fair value of the note, whichever is more reliable. If neither of these fair values is determinable, the note is recorded at its present value by discounting the future cash flow(s) using the incremental interest rate of the borrower.

10. **Understand the disclosure of long-term liabilities.** A company must disclose many characteristics of its long-term debt, including the book value, interest rates, maturity dates, scheduled repayments for each of the next five years, interest expense, interest paid, and capitalized interest. It normally makes these disclosures in the notes to its financial statements.

11. **Account for long-term notes receivable including impairment of a loan.** A note receivable is recorded at the fair value of the property, goods, or services or the fair value of the note, whichever is more reliable. If neither of these values is reliable, the note is recorded at its present value by using the borrower's incremental interest rate. A loan is impaired if it is probable that the creditor will be unable to collect all amounts due according to the contractual terms of the loan agreement. When a loan is impaired, the creditor company computes the present value of the expected future cash flows of the impaired loan using the effective interest rate, which is the original (contractual) interest rate on the loan. It records an expense for the difference between the carrying value and the present value, and recognizes future interest revenue based on the contractual rate applied to the new carrying (present) value.

12. **Understand troubled debt restructurings (Appendix).** A troubled debt restructuring occurs when a creditor for economic or legal reasons related to a debtor's financial difficulties grants a concession to the debtor that it would not otherwise consider. A troubled debt restructuring may include a modification of terms, the issuance or other granting of an equity interest, and the transfer of an asset.

13. **Account for serial bonds (Appendix).** Serial bonds require the issuer to repay the face value in periodic installments over a number of years. The initial issuance of the bonds is recorded in the same manner as other bonds. Subsequently, the company computes the interest expense and any premium or discount amortization by the effective interest method. Alternatively, it may use a method similar to the straight-line method known as the bonds outstanding method.

ANSWERS TO REAL REPORT QUESTIONS

Real Report 14-1 Answers
1. IBM has 7.125% debentures that mature in 2096. As of 2004, the remaining maturity is 92 years.
2. The scheduled maturities allow a financial statement user to assess the company's obligation to repay the principal amount of debt over the next five years. Coupled with interest payments, this schedule will allow the financial statement user insight as to the future cash flow needed to service the company's debt.
3. Total interest paid and accrued decreased by $92 million ($663 million less $571 million) in 2004.
4. Financial flexibility allows a company to change the amounts and timing of its cash flows in response to unexpected needs and opportunities. With more than $16 billion in unused lines of credit as of December 31, 2004, IBM would be considered to have financial flexibility.

QUESTIONS

Q14-1 Why may a company that requires additional funds choose to issue long-term liabilities rather than equity securities?

Q14-2 What is a *bond*? Define *face value, maturity date, contract rate, bond certificate,* and *bond indenture*.

Q14-3 Distinguish between mortgage and debenture bonds.

Q14-4 Distinguish between registered and coupon bonds.

Q14-5 What are callable bonds? Convertible bonds?

Q14-6 Why does the stated (contract) rate and the effective rate (yield) of interest on bonds frequently differ?

Q14-7 Why do bond discounts and bond premiums arise at the time of sale?

Q14-8 Distinguish between bond premiums or discounts and bond issue costs.

Q14-9 Why does the recorded amount of interest expense for the first interest payment differ from the expense recorded for other interest payments when bonds are issued between interest payment dates?

Q14-10 What two methods may a company use to allocate a premium or discount over the life of a bond issue? Briefly describe each method.

Q14-11 How is the amount of interest expense a company records each period affected by the amortization of a bond discount using the straight-line method?

Q14-12 How is the amount of interest expense a company records each period affected by the amortization of a bond premium using the straight-line method?

Q14-13 How is the amount of proceeds from a bond issue determined once the market (yield) rate of interest is specified?

Q14-14 What is a call provision? Why do companies often include call provisions on bond issues?

Q14-15 Distinguish between bond retirements and bond refundings.

Q14-16 What are the three alternatives that could be used to account for gains or losses on bond refundings? What reasons support each of these methods? Which method did the APB finally favor? Why?

Q14-17 Why does a company issue a bond with detachable warrants (rights)? At what value is each of these securities recorded at the time of the bond issuance?

Q14-18 What are convertible bonds? Why would a company issue convertible debt?

Q14-19 What two alternative methods are available to account for the issuance of convertible debt? What method did the APB finally require? Why?

Q14-20 When a company exchanges a long-term non-interest-bearing note for cash and no interest rate is stated, how does it determine the effective interest?

Q14-21 Describe the steps necessary for a company to determine the value at which to record a non-interest-bearing note payable exchanged for property, goods, or services.

Q14-22 What is the incremental interest rate of a borrower? When and for what calculations is this rate used if a company exchanges a note for property, goods, or services?

Q14-23 (Appendix 1) When does a troubled debt restructuring occur? What are three conditions a troubled debt restructuring may involve?

MULTIPLE CHOICE (AICPA Adapted)

Select the best answer for each of the following.

M14-1 Should the following bond issue costs be expensed as incurred?

	Legal Fees	Underwriting Costs
a.	No	No
b.	No	Yes
c.	Yes	No
d.	Yes	Yes

M14-2 On December 31, 2006 Dumont Corporation had outstanding 8%, $2,000,000 face value convertible bonds maturing on December 31, 2010. Interest is payable annually on December 31. Each $1,000 bond is convertible into 60 shares of Dumont's $10 par value common stock. The unamortized balance on December 31, 2007 in the Premium on Bonds Payable account was $45,000. On December 31, 2007 an individual holding 200 of the bonds exercised the conversion privilege when the market value of Dumont's common stock was $18 per share. Using the book value method, Dumont's entry to record the conversion should include a credit to additional paid-in capital of

a. $80,000
b. $84,500
c. $96,000
d. $125,000

M14-3 On January 1, 2007 when the market rate for bond interest was 14%, Luba Corporation issued bonds in the face amount of $500,000, with interest at 12% payable semiannually. The bonds mature on December 31, 2017, and were issued at a discount of $53,180. How much of the discount should be amortized by the effective interest method at July 1, 2007?

a. $1,277
b. $2,659
c. $3,191
d. $3,723

M14-4 When the cash proceeds from a bond issued with detachable stock purchase warrants exceed the sum of the par value of the bonds and the fair value of the warrants, the excess should be credited to

a. Additional paid-in capital
b. Retained earnings
c. Premium on bonds payable
d. Detachable stock warrants outstanding

M14-5 When the issuer of bonds exercises the call provision to retire the bonds, the excess of the cash paid over the carrying amount of the bonds should be recognized separately as a(n)

a. Extraordinary loss
b. Extraordinary gain
c. Loss from continuing operations
d. Loss from discontinued operations

M14-6 Peterson Company has a $500,000, 15%, three-year note dated January 1, 2006, payable to Forest National Bank. On December 31, 2007 the bank agreed to settle the note and unpaid interest of $75,000 for 2007 for $50,000 cash and marketable securities having a current market value of $375,000. Peterson's acquisition cost of the securities is $385,000. Ignoring income taxes, what amount should Peterson report as a gain from the debt restructuring in its 2007 income statement?

a. $65,000
b. $75,000
c. $140,000
d. $150,000

M14-7 When the interest payment dates of a bond are May 1 and November 1, and a bond issue is sold on June 1, the amount of cash received by the issuer will be

a. Increased by accrued interest from June 1 to November 1
b. Increased by accrued interest from May 1 to June 1
c. Decreased by accrued interest from June 1 to November 1
d. Decreased by accrued interest from May 1 to June 1

M14-8 On January 1, 2007 Parke Company borrowed $360,000 from a major customer evidenced by a non-interest-bearing note due in three years. Parke agreed to supply the customer's inventory needs for the loan period at lower than market price. At the 12% imputed interest rate for this type of loan, the present value of the note is $255,000 at January 1, 2007. What amount of interest expense should be included in Parke's 2007 income statement?

a. $43,200
b. $35,000
c. $30,600
d. $0

M14-9 For the issuer of a 10-year term bond, the amount of amortization using the effective interest method would increase each year if the bond was sold at a

	Discount	Premium
a.	No	No
b.	Yes	Yes
c.	No	Yes
d.	Yes	No

M14-10 On April 1, 2007 Girard Corporation issued at 98 plus accrued interest, 200 of its 10%, $1,000 bonds. The bonds are dated January 1, 2007, and mature on January 1, 2017. Interest is payable semiannually on January 1 and July 1. From the bond issuance Girard would realize net cash receipts of

a. $191,000
b. $196,000
c. $198,500
d. $201,000

EXERCISES

E14-1   *Recording Bond Issue and Interest Payments*   The Kurten Corporation is authorized to issue $500,000 of 8% bonds. Interest on the bonds is payable semiannually; the bonds are dated January 1, 2007 and are due December 31, 2012.

Required
Prepare the journal entries to record the following:

April 1, 2007   Sold the bonds at par plus accrued interest
June 30, 2007   First interest payment
Dec. 31, 2007   Second interest payment

E14-2   *Straight-Line Premium Amortization*   On April 30, 2007 Hackman Corporation issued $1 million face value 12% bonds dated January 1, 2007, for $1,023,000 plus accrued interest. The bonds pay interest semiannually on June 30 and December 31 and are due December 31, 2014. The company uses the straight-line amortization method.

Required
Record the issuance of the bonds and the first two interest payments.

E14-3   *Straight-Line Discount Amortization*   The Bryan Company issued $500,000 of 10% face value bonds on January 1, 2007 for $486,000. The bonds are due December 31, 2009, and pay interest semiannually on June 30 and December 31. The company uses the straight-line amortization method.

Required
Prepare the journal entries to record the issuance of the bonds and the first two interest payments.

E14-4   *Effective Interest Discount Amortization*   The Cotton Corporation issued $100,000 of 10% bonds dated January 1, 2007 for $97,158.54 on July 1, 2007. The bonds are due December 31, 2010, were issued to yield 11%, and pay interest semi-annually on June 30 and December 31. The company uses the effective interest method of amortization.

Required
Record (1) the issuance of the bonds, and (2) the payment of interest and the discount amortization on December 31, 2007, June 30, 2008, and December 31, 2008.

E14-5   *Effective Interest Premium Amortization*   Addison Incorporated issued $200,000 of 13% bonds on July 1, 2007 for $206,801.60. The bonds were dated January 1, 2007, pay interest on each June 30 and December 31, are due December 31, 2011, and were issued to yield 12%. The company uses the effective interest method of amortization.

Required
Prepare the journal entries to record the issue of the bonds on July 1, 2007, and the interest payments on December 31, 2007 and June 30, 2008.

E14-6   *Determining the Proceeds from Bond Issues*   The Madison Corporation is authorized to issue $800,000 of five-year bonds dated June 30, 2007, with a face rate of interest of 11%. Interest on the bonds is payable semiannually and the bonds are sold on June 30, 2007.

Required
Determine the proceeds that the company will receive if it sells (1) the bonds to yield 12%, and (2) the bonds to yield 10%.

E14-7   *Effective Interest Amortization of Premium or Discount*   The Taylor Company issued $100,000 of 13% bonds on January 1, 2007. The bonds pay interest semiannually on June 30 and December 31 and are due December 31, 2009.

Required
1. Assume the company sells the bonds for $102,458.71 to yield 12%. Prepare the journal entries to record:
    a. The sale of the bonds.
    b. Each 2007 semiannual interest payment and premium amortization, using the effective interest method.
2. Assume the company sells the bonds for $97,616.71 to yield 14%. Prepare the journal entries to record:
    a. The sale of the bonds.
    b. Each 2007 semiannual interest payment and discount amortization, using the effective interest method.

E14-8   *Bond Amortization Tables*   On January 1, 2007 the Calvert Company issues 12%, $100,000 face value bonds for $103,545.91, a price to yield 10%. The bonds mature on January 1, 2009. Interest is paid semiannually on June 30 and December 31.

Required ⬛
1. Prepare a bond interest expense and premium amortization schedule using the straight-line method.
2. Prepare a bond interest expense and premium amortization schedule using the effective interest method.
3. Prepare the journal entries to record the interest payments on June 30, 2007 and December 31, 2007, using both methods.

E14-9 *Premium Amortization and Partial Retirement* Rockwood Company issued $100,000 of 10% bonds on November 1, 2007 at 103. Interest on the bonds is payable on November 1 and May 1 of each year, and the maturity date is November 1, 2017. Rockwood Company retired bonds with a face value of $20,000 on February 1, 2009, at 98 plus accrued interest. The company uses straight-line amortization and reverses any calendar year-end adjusting entries.

Required
1. Prepare the journal entry to record the issuance of the bonds on November 1, 2007.
2. Prepare all the journal entries to record the interest expense during 2008.
3. Prepare the journal entries to record the retirement of $20,000 of the bonds on February 1, 2009.

E14-10 *Effective Interest vs. Straight-Line Discount Amortization* Burr Motor Company, a manufacturer of small- to medium-sized electric motors, needs additional funds to market a revolutionary new motor. Burr has arranged for private placement of a $50,000, five-year, 11% bond issue. Interest on these bonds is paid annually each year on August 31. The issue was dated and sold on September 1, 2006, for proceeds of $48,197.62 to yield 12%. The company reverses any year-end adjusting entries.

Required
1. Prepare a bond interest expense and discount amortization schedule showing interest expense for each year, using the effective interest method.
2. Prepare journal entries to record the issuance of the bonds and the interest payments for 2007 and 2008, using (a) the effective interest method, and (b) the straight-line method.

E14-11 *Redemption of Bonds Prior to Maturity* The Hill Corporation issued $1,500,000 of 11% bonds at 98 on January 2, 2005. Interest is paid semiannually on June 30 and December 31. The bonds had a 10-year life from the date of issue, and the company uses the straight-line method of amortization. On March 31, 2008 the company recalls the bonds at the call price of 107 plus accrued interest.

Required
Prepare the journal entries to record the reacquisition (recall) of the Hill Corporation bonds.

E14-12 **AICPA Adapted** *Extinguishment of Bonds Prior to Maturity* On December 1, 2005 the Cone Company issued its 10%, $2 million face value bonds for $2.3 million, plus accrued interest. Interest is payable on November 1 and May 1. On December 31, 2007 the book value of the bonds, inclusive of the unamortized premium, was $2.1 million. On July 1, 2008 Cone reacquired the bonds at 98, plus accrued interest. Cone appropriately uses the straight-line method for the amortization because the results do not materially differ from those of the interest method.

Required
Prepare a schedule to compute the gain or loss on this extinguishment of debt. Show supporting computations in good form.

E14-13 *Convertible Bond Entries* On July 2, 2006 the McGraw Corporation issued $500,000 of convertible bonds. Each $1,000 bond could be converted into 20 shares of the company's $5 par value stock. On July 3, 2008, when the bonds had an unamortized discount of $7,400, and the market value of the McGraw shares was $52 per share, all the bonds were converted into common stock.

Required
1. Prepare the journal entry to record the conversion of the bonds under (a) the book value method, and (b) the market value method.
2. Compute the company's debt-to-equity ratio (total liabilities divided by total stockholders' equity, as mentioned in Chapter 6) under each alternative. Assume the company's other liabilities are $2 million and stockholders' equity before the conversion is $3 million.

E14-14 **AICPA Adapted** *Convertible Bonds* On January 1, 2006, when its $30 par value common stock was selling for $80 per share, a corporation issued $10 million of 10% convertible debentures due in 10 years. The conversion option allowed the holder of each $1,000 bond to convert it into six shares of the corporation's $30 par value common stock. The debentures were issued for $11 million. At the time of issuance the present value of the bond payments was $8.5 million, and the corporation believes the difference between the present value and the amount paid is attributable to the conversion feature. On January 1, 2007 the corporation's $30 par value common stock was split 3 for 1. On January 1, 2008, when the corporation's $10 par value common stock was selling for $90 per share, holders of 40% of the convertible debentures exercised their conversion options. The corporation uses the straight-line method for amortizing any bond discounts or premiums.

Required
1. Prepare the journal entry to record the original issuance of the convertible debentures.
2. Prepare the journal entry to record the exercise of the conversion option, using the book value method. Show supporting computations in good form.

E14-15 *Induced Conversion* On July 1, 2008 the Tuttle Company had bonds payable outstanding with a face value of $200,000 and a book value of $194,000. The interest on these bonds was paid on June 30. When these bonds were issued, each $1,000 bond was convertible into 20 shares of $10 par common stock. To induce conversion, on June 15, 2008 the terms were changed so that each bond was convertible into 22 shares of common stock if the conversion was made within 30 days. All the bonds were converted on July 1, 2008 when the market price of the common stock was $50 per share.

Required
Using the book value method, record the conversion of the bonds on July 1, 2008.

E14-16 *Detachable Stock Warrants* Conroe Corporation sold $500,000 of 13% bonds at 107. Each $1,000 bond carried 20 warrants, and each warrant allowed the holder to acquire one share of $10 par value common stock for $20 per share. Subsequent to the issuance of the securities, the bonds were quoted at 102 ex rights, and the warrants were quoted at $4 each.

Required
1. Determine the value to be assigned to the bonds and the warrants, and prepare the journal entry to record the issuance of the convertible bonds.
2. Assume that 4,000 warrants are subsequently exercised. Prepare the journal entry for the issuance of the common stock.

E14-17 **AICPA Adapted** *Bonds with Detachable Warrants* On July 1, 2007 Salem Corporation issued $3 million of 12% bonds payable in 10 years. The bonds pay interest semiannually. The bonds include detachable warrants giving the bondholder the right to purchase for $30, one share of $1 par value common stock at any time during the next 10 years. The company sold the bonds for $3 million. The value of the warrants at the time of issuance was $200,000.

Required
Prepare in general journal format the entry to record the issuance of the bonds.

E14-18 *Long-Term Notes Payable* On January 1, 2007 the Johnson Corporation issued a two-year note due December 31, 2008, with a face value of $10,000, receiving $7,694.68 in exchange.

Required
Prepare the journal entries to account for the note:
1. On the date the note is issued
2. At the end of 2007
3. At the end of 2008

E14-19 *Note Payable Exchanged for Cash and Rights* The Spath Company borrows $75,000 by issuing a four-year, non-interest-bearing note to a customer on January 1, 2007. In addition, Spath Company agrees to sell inventory to the customer at reduced prices over a five-year period. Spath's incremental borrowing rate is 12%. The customer agrees to purchase an equal amount of inventory each year over the five-year period so that a straight-line method of revenue recognition is appropriate.

Required
Prepare the journal entries on Spath Company's books for 2007 and 2008. (Round answers to two decimal places.)

E14-20 *Exchange of a Note Payable for an Asset* The Webb Corporation purchased an asset from the Shaw Corporation on January 1, 2007. Shaw accepted a three-year, non-interest-bearing note of $18,000 due December 31, 2009 in exchange for the asset. Neither the fair value of the asset nor that of the note is available. Webb's incremental borrowing rate is 12%.

Required
Prepare the journal entries to record the issuance of the note, retirement, and any interest expense on the books of Webb on each of the following dates:
1. January 1, 2007
2. December 31, 2007
3. December 31, 2008
4. December 31, 2009

E14-21 *Note Payable Issued in Exchange for an Asset* On January 1, 2007 the Sanders Corporation purchased equipment having a fair value of $68,301.30 by issuing a non-interest-bearing, $100,000, four-year note due December 31, 2010.

Required
Prepare the journal entries to record (1) the purchase of the equipment, (2) the annual interest charges over the life of the note, and (3) the repayment of the note.

E14-22 *Note Payable in Installments* On January 1, 2007 the Billips Corporation purchased equipment having a fair value of $72,054.94 by issuing a $90,000 note, payable in three $30,000 annual installments beginning December 31, 2007.

Required
Prepare (1) the journal entry to record the purchase of the equipment, (2) a schedule to compute the annual interest expense, and (3) the journal entries to record yearly interest expense and note repayments over the life of the note.

E14-23 *Notes Receivable* On January 1, 2007 Crouser Company sold land to Chad Company, accepting a two-year, $150,000 non-interest-bearing note due January 1, 2009. The fair value of the land was $123,966.90 on the date of sale. The company purchased the land for $120,000 on January 1, 2001.

Required
Prepare all the journal entries on Crouser Company's books for January 1, 2007 through January 1, 2009 in regard to the Chad Company note.

E14-24 *Notes Receivable* On January 1, 2007 Worthylake Company sold used machinery to Brown Company, accepting a $25,000 non-interest-bearing note maturing on January 1, 2009. Worthylake Company carried the machinery on its books at a cost of $22,000 and a current book value of $15,000. Neither the fair value of the machinery nor the note was determinable at the time of sale; however, Brown's incremental borrowing rate was 12%.

Required
Prepare the journal entries on Worthylake Company's books to record:
1. The sale of the machinery
2. The related adjusting entries on December 31, 2007 and 2008
3. The payment of the note by Brown Company on January 1, 2009

E14-25 *Note Receivable in Installments* On January 1, 2007 Tabor Company sold land with a book value of $50,000 to Wilson Company, accepting a $60,000 note, payable in three $20,000 annual installments beginning December 31, 2007. The note carried no stated interest rate and the fair values of the land and the note were not determinable. An appropriate interest rate for this note is 12%.

Required
Prepare the journal entries on Tabor Company's books to record:
1. The sale
2. The annual interest revenue and receipt of each $20,000 installment

E14-26 *Notes Receivable Discounted* On January 1, 2007 Boiler Company received two notes for merchandise sold:

Note 1: A $10,000, 10%, 60-day note from Wildcat, Inc.
Note 2: A $20,000, 8%, three-year interest-bearing note from Gopher, Inc.

On January 1, 2007 the fair rate of interest was 10%. Needing cash to meet the upcoming payroll, Boiler Company discounted the Wildcat, Inc. note at the local bank at 14% on January 12, 2007. On March 2, 2007 Wildcat, Inc. remitted the full amount owed to the bank.

Required
Prepare journal entries on the books of Boiler Company to record the receipt of the two notes on January 1, 2007, the discounting of the Wildcat note on January 12, 2007, the payment by Wildcat to the bank on March 2, 2007, and the interest on the Gopher note on December 31, 2007. Round all calculations to the nearest dollar and use a 360-day year. (*Contributed by Scott I. Jerris*)

E14-27 **AICPA Adapted** *Notes Receivable and Income* On January 1, 2007 the Pitt Company sold a patent to Chatham, Inc., which had a carrying value on Pitt's books of $10,000. Chatham gave Pitt a $60,000 non-interest-bearing note payable in five equal annual installments of $12,000, with the first payment due and paid on January 1, 2008. There was no established price for the patent, and the note has no ready market value. The prevailing rate of interest for a note of this type at January 1, 2007 is 12%. Information on present value and future amount factors is as follows:

	\multicolumn{5}{c}{Period}				
	1	2	3	4	5
Present value of $1 at 12%	0.89	0.80	0.71	0.64	0.57
Present value of an annuity of $1 at 12%	0.89	1.69	2.40	3.04	3.60
Future amount of $1 at 12%	1.12	1.25	1.40	1.57	1.76
Future amount of an annuity of $1 at 12%	1.00	2.12	3.37	4.78	6.35

Required

Prepare a schedule showing the income or loss before income taxes (rounded to the nearest dollar) that Pitt should record for the years ended December 31, 2007 and 2008 as a result of the preceding facts. Show supporting computations in good form.

E14-28 *Loan Impairment* The Perry National Bank has a note receivable of $200,000 from the Mogren Company that it is carrying at face value and is due on December 31, 2011. Interest on the note is payable at 9% each December 31. The Mogren Company paid the interest due on December 31, 2007, but informed the bank that it would probably miss the next two years' interest payments because of its financial difficulties. After that, it expected to resume its annual interest payments, but it would make the principal payment one year late, with interest paid for that additional year at the time of the principal payment.

Required

1. Compute the value of the impaired loan on December 31, 2007.
2. Prepare the journal entries from 2007 to 2012 for the bank to record the above events.

E14-29 *Loan Impairment* The Oaks National Bank has a note receivable of $500,000 from the Haldane Company that it is carrying at face value and is due on December 31, 2013. Interest on the note is payable at 6% each December 31. The Haldane Company paid the interest due on December 31, 2007, but informed the bank that it would probably miss the next three years' interest payments because of its financial difficulties. After that, it expected to resume its annual interest payments, but it would make the principal payment two years late, with interest paid for the additional years. On January 1, 2010 the bank received new information and now expected the Haldane Company to pay the interest for 2010 through 2015 on December 31 of each year.

Required

1. Compute the value of the impaired loan on December 31, 2007.
2. Prepare the journal entries from 2007 to 2015 for the bank to record the above loan impairment events.

E14-30 *Troubled Debt Restructuring (Debtor)—Modification of Terms (Appendix 1)* On January 1, 2007 Northfield Corporation becomes delinquent on a $100,000, 14% note to the First National Bank, on which $16,651 of interest has accrued. On January 2, 2007 the bank agrees to restructure the note. It forgives the accrued interest, extends the repayment date to December 31, 2009, and reduces the interest rate to 10%.

Required

Prepare a schedule for Northfield Corporation to compute the annual interest expense in regard to the preceding note for each year of the restructuring agreement.

E14-31 *Troubled Debt Restructuring (Debtor)—Equity and Asset Exchange (Appendix 1)* On January 1, 2007 the Boonville Corporation is delinquent on a $300,000 note to the Great National Bank on which $66,000 of interest has accrued. On January 2, 2007 Boonville enters into a debt restructuring agreement with the bank.

Required

Prepare the journal entries for Boonville to record the restructuring agreement assuming:
1. The bank accepts 10,000 shares of Boonville's $10 par common stock that is currently selling for $35 per share in full settlement of the debt.
2. The bank accepts land with a fair value of $342,000 in full settlement of the debt. The land is being carried on Boonville's books at a cost of $324,000.

E14-32 *Troubled Debt Restructuring (Creditor)—Modification of Terms (Appendix 1)* On December 31, 2007 Central Bank agrees to a restructuring of a 12% note with a $200,000 face value and $60,000 of accrued interest owed to the bank by Carter Company. The bank agrees to forgive the accrued interest, extend the maturity date to December 31, 2010, and reduce the annual interest rate to 6%. Carter Company paid the interest due on December 31, 2008.

Required

1. Prepare the journal entry for Central Bank to record the restructuring of the note on December 31, 2007.
2. Prepare the journal entry for Central Bank to record the receipt of the interest on December 31, 2008.

E14-33 *Troubled Debt Restructuring (Creditor)—Equity and Asset Exchange (Appendix 1)* Refer to the debt restructuring information in E14-31.

Required

Prepare the journal entries for Great National Bank to record the restructuring agreement assuming:
1. The bank accepts the 10,000 shares of Boonville's stock.
2. The bank accepts the land.

E14-34 *Serial Bonds Entries (Appendix 2)* On July 1, 2006 the Nicholsen Corporation issued $300,000 of bonds, with a 13% face rate of interest, for $318,000. The bonds pay interest semiannually on each January 1 and July 1 and are to be repaid in three equal semiannual installments beginning July 1, 2008. Assume the company's fiscal year ends May 31 and it makes reversing entries for year-end accruals.

Required

Prepare the journal entries to account for this serial bond issue on each of the following dates, using the bonds outstanding method of amortization:

1. July 1, 2006
2. January 1, 2007
3. July 1, 2007
4. January 1, 2008
5. July 1, 2008
6. January 1, 2009
7. July 1, 2009

E14-35 *Serial Bond Issue Using the Effective Interest Method (Appendix 2)* The Lewis Company sells $200,000 of 13% bonds dated January 1, 2006, on that date, for $204,650.74 to yield 12%. The bonds pay interest *annually* on December 31, and bonds of $40,000 mature on each December 31 for the next 5 years. The company uses the effective interest method of amortization.

Required

1. Prepare a serial bond premium amortization schedule for these bonds.
2. Prepare the journal entries necessary to record the yearly interest payments, premium amortization, and serial bond redemption.

E14-36 **AICPA Adapted**   *Serial Bonds (Appendix 2):* On January 1, 2006 Mykoo Corporation issued $1 million in five-year, 10% serial bonds to be repaid in the amount of $200,000 on January 1, 2007, 2008, 2009, 2010, and 2011. Interest is payable at the end of each year. The bonds were sold to yield a rate of 12%. Information on present value and future amount factors is as follows:

	Present Value of an Ordinary Annuity of $1 for 5 Years		Future Amount of an Ordinary Annuity of $1 for 5 Years	
	10%	12%	10%	12%
	3.7908	3.6048	6.1051	6.3528

Number of Years	Present Value of $1		Future Amount of $1	
	10%	12%	10%	12%
1	.9091	.8929	1.1000	1.1200
2	.8264	.7972	1.2100	1.2544
3	.7513	.7118	1.3310	1.4049
4	.6830	.6355	1.4641	1.5735
5	.6209	.5674	1.6105	1.7623

Required

1. Prepare a schedule showing the computation of the total amount received from the issuance of the serial bonds. Show supporting computations in good form.
2. Assume the company originally sold the bonds at a discount of $46,498. Prepare a schedule of amortization of the bond discount for the first two years after issuance, using the interest (effective rate) method. Show supporting computations in good form.

PROBLEMS

P14-1 *Amortizing Bond Issue Costs and Bond Premiums* On January 1, 2006 the Baker Corporation issued $100,000 of five-year bonds due December 31, 2010 for $103,604.79 less bond issue costs of $3,000. The bonds carry a face rate of interest of 13% payable annually on December 31 and were issued to yield 12%. The company uses the effective interest method of amortization.

Required

Prepare the journal entries to record the issuance of the bonds, all the interest payments, premium amortizations, bond issue cost amortizations, and the repayment of the bonds.

P14-2 *Computation of Effective Interest Rate* On June 30, 2007 the Watson Corporation sold $800,000 of 11% face value bonds for $761,150.96. On December 31, 2007 the Watson Corporation sold $700,000 of this same bond issue for $734,645.28. The bonds were dated January 1, 2007, pay interest semiannually on each December 31 and June 30, and are due December 31, 2014.

Required

Compute the effective yield rate on each issuance of the Watson Corporation 11% bonds.

P14-3 *Premium Amortization Schedule with Retirement Before Maturity* The Dorsett Corporation issued $600,000 of 13% bonds on January 1, 2006 for $614,752.24. The bonds are due December 31, 2008, were issued to yield 12%, and pay interest semiannually on June 30 and December 31. The company uses the effective interest method.

Required ▨

1. Prepare a bond interest expense and premium amortization schedule.
2. Assume the company retired the bonds on September 30, 2008 for $630,000, which includes accrued interest. Prepare the journal entry to record the bond retirement.

P14-4 *Comprehensive* The Batson Corporation issued $800,000 of 12% face value bonds for $851,705.70. The bonds were dated and issued on April 1, 2007, are due March 31, 2011, and pay interest semiannually on September 30 and March 31. The company sold the bonds to yield 10%.

Required

1. Prepare a bond interest expense and premium amortization schedule using the straight-line method.
2. Prepare a bond interest expense and premium amortization schedule using the effective interest method.
3. Prepare any adjusting entries for the end of the fiscal year, December 31, 2007, using:
   a. The straight-line method of amortization
   b. The effective interest method of amortization
4. Assume the company retires the bonds on June 30, 2008, at 103 plus accrued interest. Prepare the journal entries to record the bond retirement using:
   a. The straight-line method of amortization
   b. The effective interest method of amortization

P14-5 *Discount Amortization Schedule and Retirement Before Maturity* Donaldson Incorporated sold $500,000 of 12% bonds on January 1, 2006 for $470,143.47, a price that yields a 14% interest rate. The bonds pay interest semiannually on June 30 and December 31 and are due December 31, 2009. The company uses the effective interest method.

Required

1. Prepare an interest expense and discount amortization schedule.
2. Assume the company reacquired the bonds on July 1, 2008 at 104. Prepare journal entries to record the bond retirement.

P14-6 *Comprehensive* The Wilkerson Corporation issued $1 million of 13.5% bonds for $985,071.68. The bonds are dated and issued October 1, 2007, are due September 30, 2011, and pay interest semiannually on March 31 and September 30. Assume an effective yield rate of 14%.

Required

1. Prepare a bond interest expense and discount amortization schedule using the straight-line method.
2. Prepare a bond interest expense and discount amortization schedule using the effective interest method.
3. Prepare adjusting entries for the end of the fiscal year December 31, 2007 using:
   a. The straight-line method of amortization
   b. The effective interest method of amortization
4. If income before interest and income taxes of 30% in 2008 is $500,000, compute net income under each alternative.
5. Assume the company retired the bonds on June 30, 2008 at 98 plus accrued interest. Prepare the journal entries to record the bond retirement using:
   a. The straight-line method of amortization
   b. The effective interest method of amortization
6. Compute the company's times interest earned (pretax operating income divided by interest expense) under each alternative.

P14-7 *Bond Refunding* The Baxter Corporation issued $400,000 of 11% bonds for $385,279.91 on January 1, 2006. The bonds pay interest semiannually on June 30 and December 31, were issued to yield 12%, and are due on December 31, 2010. Interest is amortized using the effective interest method, and the bonds are callable at 105. In 2008 Baxter wishes to take advantage of more favorable market interest rate conditions and issues $450,000 of 11%, 10-year bonds at 102 on June 1. Interest on these bonds is payable each May 31 and November 30. Sufficient proceeds from this issue are used to recall the original issue on July 1, 2008.

Required

1. Prepare the journal entries to record (a) the original issue, (b) the new issue, and (c) the recall of the old issue.
2. If the company were required to reflect the current yield each year, explain how it would account for the bonds. For simplicity, assume that the yield changes from 12% to 11% on January 1, 2008. No calculations are required.

P14-8 *Convertible Bonds* The Shank Corporation issued $1,500,000 of 10% convertible bonds for $1,620,000 on March 1, 2006. The bonds are dated March 1, 2006, pay interest semiannually on August 31 and February 28, and the premium is amortized using the straight-line method. The bonds are due on February 28, 2016, and each $1,000 bond is convertible into 25 shares of Shank Corporation $10 par common stock. On March 1, 2008, when the shares were selling for $28 per share, $300,000 of bonds were converted. On September 1, 2010, when the shares were selling for $30 per share, the remainder of the bonds were converted.

Required

1. Prepare the journal entries to record each bond conversion using (a) the book value method, and (b) the market value method.
2. If the company were required under GAAP to assign a value to the conversion feature, explain how the valuation would be determined (no calculations are required).
3. Compute the company's debt-to-equity ratio (total liabilities divided by total stockholders' equity, as mentioned in Chapter 6) under each alternative. Assume the company's other liabilities are $3 million, and that stockholders' equity before conversion is $3.5 million.

P14-9 *Bonds with Detachable Warrants* On January 1, 2007 the London Corporation issued $500,000 of 11.5% bonds due January 1, 2017 at 102. The bonds pay interest semiannually on June 30 and December 31. Each $1,000 bond carried 20 warrants, and the exchange of two warrants allowed the holder to acquire one share of $10 par common stock for $50. Shortly after the time of issue, the bonds were quoted at 98 ex rights and each individual warrant was quoted at $5. Subsequently, on March 31, 2007, 8,000 rights were exercised.

Required

1. Prepare the journal entry to record the bond issue.
2. Prepare the journal entries on March 31, 2007 to record the exchange of the warrants for common shares.

P14-10 *Notes Payable* The Houston Corporation acquires machinery from the South Company in exchange for a $20,000 non-interest-bearing, five-year note on June 30, 2006. The note is due on June 30, 2011. The machinery has a fair value of $11,348.54, is subject to straight-line depreciation, and has an estimated life of 10 years (no residual value). Houston's fiscal year ends June 30.

Required

Prepare the journal entries on each of the following dates to record the preceding information for Houston Corporation:

1. June 30, 2006
2. June 30, 2007
3. June 30, 2008
4. June 30, 2009
5. June 30, 2010
6. June 30, 2011

P14-11 *Notes Payable in Installments* Hamlet Corporation purchases computer equipment at a price of $100,000 on January 1, 2007, paying $40,000 down and agreeing to pay the balance in three $20,000 annual installments beginning December 31, 2007. It is not possible to value either the equipment or the $60,000 note directly; however, Hamlet's incremental borrowing rate is 12%.

Required

1. Prepare a schedule to compute the interest expense and discount amortization on the note.
2. Prepare all the journal entries for Hamlet to record the issuance of the note, each annual interest expense, and the three annual installment payments.

P14-12 *Notes Receivable* On January 1, 2007 the Somerville Corporation sold a used truck to the Cornelius Company and accepted a $28,000 non-interest-bearing note due January 1, 2010. Somerville carried the truck on its books at a cost of $30,000 and a current book value of $23,000. Neither the fair value of the truck nor the note was available at the time of the sale; however, Cornelius's incremental borrowing rate was 12%.

Required

1. Prepare the journal entries on Somerville's books to record:
   a. The sale of the truck
   b. The related adjusting entries on December 31, 2007, 2008, and 2009
   c. The collection of the note on January 1, 2010
2. Prepare the notes receivable portion of Somerville's December 31, 2007, 2008, and 2009 balance sheets.

P14-13 *Notes Receivable* On January 1, 2007 Lisa Company sold machinery with a book value of $118,000 to Mark Company. Mark Company signed a $180,000 non-interest-bearing note, payable in three $60,000 annual installments on December 31, 2007, 2008, and 2009. The fair value of the machinery was $149,211.12 on the date of sale. The machinery had been purchased by Lisa Company at a cost of $160,000.

Required
1. Prepare all the journal entries on Lisa Company's books for January 1, 2007 through December 31, 2009.
2. Prepare the notes receivable portion of the Lisa Company's balance sheet on December 31, 2007 and 2008.

P14-14 *Comprehensive* On January 1, 2007 Seaver Company sold land with a book value of $23,000 to Bench Company. Bench Company paid $15,000 down and signed a $15,000 non-interest-bearing note, payable in two $7,500 annual installments on December 31, 2007 and 2008. Neither the fair value of the land nor of the note is determinable. Bench Company's incremental borrowing rate is 12%. Later in the year, on July 1, 2007, Seaver Company sold a building to Hane Company, accepting a two-year, $100,000 non-interest-bearing note due July 1, 2009. The fair value of the building was $82,644.60 on the date of the sale. The building had been purchased at a cost of $90,000 on January 1, 2002, and had a book value of $67,500 on December 31, 2006. It was being depreciated on a straight-line basis (no residual value) over a 20-year life.

Required
1. Prepare all the journal entries on Seaver Company's books for January 1, 2007 through December 31, 2008 in regard to the Bench Company note.
2. Prepare all the journal entries on Seaver Company's books for July 1, 2007 through July 1, 2009 in regard to the Hane Company note.
3. Prepare the notes receivable portion of the Seaver Company's balance sheet on December 31, 2007 and 2008.

P14-15 **AICPA Adapted** *Comprehensive* Linden, Inc., had the following long-term receivable account balances at December 31, 2006:

Note receivable from sale of division	$1,500,000
Note receivable from officer	400,000

Transactions during 2007 and other information relating to Linden's long-term receivables were as follows:

1. The $1,500,000 note receivable is dated May 1, 2006, bears interest at 9%, and represents the balance of the consideration received from the sale of Linden's electronics division to Pitt Company. Principal payments of $500,000 plus appropriate interest are due on May 1, 2007, 2008, and 2009. The first principal and interest payment was made on May 1, 2007. Collection of the note installments is reasonably assured.
2. The $400,000 note receivable is dated December 31, 2004, bears interest at 8%, and is due on December 31, 2009. The note is due from Robert Finley, president of Linden, Inc., and is collateralized by 10,000 shares of Linden's common stock. Interest is payable annually on December 31, and all interest payments were paid on their due dates through December 31, 2007. The quoted market price of Linden's common stock was $45 per share on December 31, 2007.
3. On April 1, 2007 Linden sold a patent to Bell Company in exchange for a $100,000 non-interest-bearing note due on April 1, 2009. There was no established exchange price for the patent, and the note had no ready market. The prevailing rate of interest for a note of this type at April 1, 2007 was 15%. The present value of $1 for two periods at 15% is 0.756. The patent had a carrying value of $40,000 at January 1, 2007, and the amortization for the year ended December 31, 2007 would have been $8,000. The collection of the note receivable from Bell is reasonably assured.
4. On July 1, 2007 Linden sold a parcel of land to Carr Company for $200,000 under an installment sale contract. Carr made a $60,000 cash down payment on July 1, 2007 and signed a four-year, 16% note for the $140,000 balance. The equal annual payments of principal and interest on the note will be $50,000, payable on July 1, 2008 through July 1, 2011. The land could have been sold at an established cash price of $200,000. The cost of the land to Linden was $150,000. Circumstances are such that the collection of the installments on the note is reasonably assured.

Required
1. Prepare the long-term receivables section of Linden's balance sheet at December 31, 2007.
2. Prepare a schedule showing the current portion of the long-term receivables and accrued interest receivable that would appear in Linden's balance sheet at December 31, 2007.
3. Prepare a schedule showing interest income from the long-term receivables and gains recognized on sale of assets that would appear on Linden's income statement for the year ended December 31, 2007.

P14-16 *Comprehensive* An examination of the accounting records of the Durham Corporation on January 1, 2008 (after reversing entries had been made for all accrued interest at the end of 2007) disclosed the following information regarding the company's long-term debt:

12.5% bonds, dated January 1, 2004, paying interest semiannually on June 30 and December 31, and due December 31, 2010.	$1,300,000
11% convertible bonds, dated April 1, 2006, paying interest semiannually on March 31 and September 30, and due March 31, 2011.	$ 500,000
Discount on convertible bonds payable	(17,500)
	$ 482,500
9% bonds, dated March 1, 2007, paying interest annually on February 28, and due February 28, 2012.	$ 100,000
Discount on bonds payable	(3,960)
	$ 96,040
4-year, non-interest-bearing note issued January 1, 2007. (Durham's incremental borrowing rate on the date the note was issued was 10%.)	$ 80,000
Discount on note payable	(19,895)
	$ 60,105

Additional information disclosed in the notes to Durham Corporation's 2007 financial statements:

1. The conversion option allows the holder of each $1,000 bond to exchange it for 30 shares of $10 par common stock. Durham uses the book value method to record conversions of bonds to common stock.
2. Each $1,000 bond of the 9% bonds dated March 1, 2007 carries 15 detachable warrants. The company had recorded the 1,500 warrants on the bonds at $4,800 in a Common Stock Warrants account. The exchange of three warrants allows the holder to acquire one share of $10 par common stock for $27.
3. The discount on the convertible bonds and the discount on the 9% bonds with detachable warrants are being amortized using the straight-line method.
4. The discount on the note payable is being amortized annually using the effective interest method.

During 2008, the Durham Corporation engaged in the following long-term debt transactions:

Jan.	1	Issued 11%, $800,000 face value bonds for $820,302, a price to yield 10%. Interest on these bonds is payable semiannually on June 30 and December 31, and they are due December 31, 2010. The effective interest method is to be used to amortize the premium. The bonds are callable at 107.
May	1	Six hundred warrants from the 9% bonds were exercised when the common stock was selling for $42 per share.
Sept.	29	Convertible bonds of $100,000 were exchanged when the common stock was selling for $45 per share.
Nov.	1	Retired $200,000 of the bonds issued on January 1, 2008, at the call price plus accrued interest.

Required
1. Prepare the journal entries for Durham Corporation to record all the transactions that occurred during 2008 relating to the preceding information.
2. Prepare the long-term debt section of the Durham Corporation's balance sheet on December 31, 2008.

P14-17 *Troubled Debt Restructuring (Debtor) (Appendix 1)* The Oakwood Corporation is delinquent on a $2,400,000, 10% note to the Second National Bank that was due January 1, 2007. At that time Oakwood owed the principal amount plus $34,031.82 of accrued interest. Oakwood enters into a debt restructuring agreement with the bank on January 2, 2007.

Required
Prepare the journal entries for Oakwood to record the debt restructuring agreement and all subsequent interest payments assuming the following independent alternatives:
1. The bank extends the repayment date to December 31, 2010, forgives the accrued interest owed, reduces the principal by $200,000, and reduces the interest rate to 8%.
2. The bank extends the repayment date to December 31, 2010, forgives the accrued interest owed, reduces the principal by $200,000, and reduces the interest rate to 1%.
3. The bank accepts 160,000 shares of Oakwood's $5 par value common stock, which is currently selling for $14.50 per share, in full settlement of the debt.
4. The bank accepts land with a fair value of $2,300,000 in full settlement of the debt. The land is being carried on Oakwood's books at a cost of $2,200,000.

P14-18 *Troubled Debt Restructuring (Creditor) (Appendix 1)* Refer to the debt restructuring information listed in P14-17.

Required

For each of the independent alternatives listed in Requirements 1 through 4 of P14-17, prepare the journal entries for Second National Bank to record the debt restructuring agreement and all subsequent interest receipts.

P14-19 *Comprehensive—Loan Impairment and Troubled Debt Restructuring* The 10th National Bank has a $200,000, 12% note receivable from the Priday Company that is due on December 31, 2010. On December 31, 2007 the company misses the interest payment due on that date. The bank expects that the company will also miss the next payment, but will pay the principal on the maturity date. On December 31, 2008 the company misses the interest payment due on that date. On December 31, 2009 the company pays half the interest payment due on that date and is not expected to pay the other half.

In early January 2010 the bank and the company agree to a loan restructuring because of the financial condition of the company. The bank forgives the unpaid interest, extends the loan to December 31, 2012, and reduces the interest rate to 6%. The market rate for the loan is estimated to be 10% at this time.

Required

1. Compute the value of the impaired loan on December 31, 2007.
2. Prepare the journal entries from 2007 to 2012 for the bank to record the above events.

P14-20 *Serial Bond Amortization and Repayment Schedule (Appendix 2)* On July 1, 2007 the Hubbard Corporation issued $600,000 of bonds with an 8% face rate of interest. The bonds were issued for $589,381.93, pay interest semiannually on June 30 and December 31, carry an effective yield rate of 9%, and are payable in three annual installments of $200,000 each, beginning June 30, 2008.

Required

1. Prepare a serial bond discount amortization schedule using the bonds outstanding method.
2. Prepare a serial bond discount amortization schedule using the effective interest method.
3. Prepare the journal entries necessary to record the payment of interest and the bond retirements on June 30, 2008, June 30, 2009, and June 30, 2010 using (a) the bonds outstanding method, and (b) the effective interest method.

P14-21 *Call Provision of Serial Bonds (Appendix 2)* The Case Corporation issued $600,000 of 13% bonds on January 1, 2006 for $636,000. The bonds are payable in three annual $200,000 installments beginning December 31, 2007, pay interest semiannually on June 30 and December 31, and are callable at 107. On January 1, 2008 the bonds due December 31, 2009 are recalled at the call price. The corporation uses the bonds outstanding method of amortization.

Required

Prepare a serial bond premium amortization schedule and the journal entries to record the bond issue, payment of interest, and bond retirement on each of the following dates:
1. January 1, 2006
2. December 31, 2006
3. December 31, 2007
4. January 1, 2008
5. December 31, 2008

CASES

COMMUNICATION

C14-1 Amortization of Bond Premium or Discount

AICPA Adapted The appropriate method of amortizing a premium or discount on issuance of bonds is the effective interest method.

Required

1. What is the effective interest method of amortization and how is it different from and similar to the straight-line method of amortization?

2. Explain how a company computes amortization using the effective interest method, and why and how do amounts obtained using the effective interest method differ from amounts computed under the straight-line method.

C14-2 Various Bond Characteristics

AICPA Adapted One way for a corporation to accomplish long-term financing is through the issuance of long-term debt instruments in the form of bonds.

Required

1. Explain how to account for the proceeds from bonds issued with detachable stock purchase warrants.
2. Contrast a serial bond with a term (straight) bond.
3. For a five-year term bond issued at a premium, why is the amortization in the first year of the life of the bond different using the interest method of amortization instead of the straight-line method? Include in your discussion whether the amount of amortization in the first year of the life of the bond is higher or lower using the interest method instead of the straight-line method.
4. When a company sells a bond issue between interest dates at a discount, what journal entry does it make and how is the subsequent amortization of bond discount affected? Include in your discussion an explanation of how the amounts of each debit and credit are determined.
5. Explain how to account for and classify the gain or loss from the reacquisition of a long-term bond prior to its maturity.

C14-3 Convertible and Nonconvertible Bonds

AICPA Adapted On February 1, 2004 Aubrey Company sold its five-year, $1,000 par value, 9% bonds, which were convertible at the option of the investor into Aubrey Company common stock at a ratio of 10 shares of common stock for each bond. Aubrey Company sold the convertible bonds at a discount. Interest is payable annually each February 1. On February 1, 2007 Mel Company, an investor in the Aubrey Company convertible bonds, tendered 1,000 bonds for conversion into 10,000 shares of Aubrey Company common stock, which had a market value of $110 per share at the date of the conversion.

On May 1, 2007 Aubrey Company sold its 10-year, $1,000 par value, 10% nonconvertible term bonds dated April 1, 2007. Interest is payable semiannually, and the first interest payment date is October 1, 2007. Due to market conditions, the company sold the bonds at an effective interest rate (yield) of 12%.

Required

1. Explain how Aubrey Company accounts for the conversion of the convertible bonds into common stock under both the book value and market value methods. Discuss the rationale for each method.

2. Were the nonconvertible term bonds sold at par, at a discount, or at a premium? Discuss the rationale for your answer.
3. Identify and discuss the effects on Aubrey Company's 2007 income statement associated with the nonconvertible term bonds.

C14-4 Bond Refunding

AICPA Adapted A company's gains or losses from the early extinguishment of debt theoretically can be accounted for in three ways:

a. Amortized over remaining life of old debt
b. Amortized over the life of the new debt issue
c. Recognized in the period of extinguishment

Required

1. Discuss the supporting arguments for each of the three theoretical methods of accounting for gains and losses from the early extinguishment of debt.
2. Which of the preceding methods is generally accepted?

C14-5 Serial Bonds (Appendix 2)

AICPA Adapted On November 1, 2007 Janine Company sold directly to underwriters at a lump-sum price, $1,000 face value, 9% serial bonds dated November 1, 2007 at an effective annual interest rate (yield) of 11%. A total of 25% of these serial bonds are due on November 1, 2009, a total of 35% on November 1, 2010, and a total of 40% on November 1, 2011. Interest is payable semiannually and the first interest payment date is May 1, 2008. Janine uses the interest method of amortization and incurred bond issue costs in preparing and selling the bond issue.

Required

1. How does the company determine the market price of the serial bonds?
2. How does the company present all items related to the serial bonds, except for bond issue costs, in a balance sheet prepared immediately after it sold the serial bond issue?
3. How does the company determine the amount of interest expense for the serial bonds for 2007?

CREATIVE AND CRITICAL THINKING

C14-6 Recording Convertible Debt

AICPA Adapted Zakin Co. recently issued $1,000,000 face value, 10%, 30-year subordinated debentures at 97. The debentures are redeemable at 103 upon demand by the issuer at any date upon 30 days notice 10 years after the issue. The debentures are convertible into $10 par value common stock of the Company at the conversion price of $12.50 per share for each $500 or multiple thereof of the principal amount of the debentures.

Required

1. Explain how the conversion feature of convertible debt has a value to the:
   a. Issuer
   b. Purchaser
2. Management of Zakin Co. has suggested that in recording the issuance of the debentures, it should assign a portion of the proceeds to the conversion feature.
   a. What are the arguments for according separate accounting recognition to the conversion feature of the debentures?

b. What are the arguments supporting accounting for the convertible debentures as a single element?

3. Assume that the company assigns no value to the conversion feature upon issue of the debentures. Assume further that five years after issue, debentures with a face value of $100,000 and book value of $97,500 are tendered for conversion on an interest payment date when the market price of the debentures is 104 and the common stock is selling at $14 per share and that the Company records the conversion as follows:

Bonds Payable	100,000	
Bond Discount		2,500
Common Stock		80,000
Premium on		
Common Stock		17,500

Discuss the propriety of the preceding accounting treatment.

C14-7 Debt with Detachable Stock Warrants

AICPA Adapted Incurring long-term debt with an arrangement whereby lenders receive an option to buy common stock during all or a portion of the time the debt is outstanding is a frequently used corporate financing practice. In some situations, the result is achieved through the issuance of convertible bonds; in others, the debt instruments and the warrants to buy stock are separate.

Required

1. a. Explain the differences that exist in current accounting for original proceeds of the issuance of convertible bonds, and of debt instruments with separate warrants to purchase common stock.
   b. Explain the underlying rationale for the differences described in Requirement 1a.
   c. Summarize the arguments that have been presented for the alternative accounting treatment.
2. At the start of the year, AB Company issued $6 million of 7% notes along with warrants to buy 400,000 shares of its $10 par value common stock at $18 per share. The notes mature over the next 10 years, starting one year from date of issuance, with annual maturities of $600,000. At the time, AB had 3,200,000 shares of common stock outstanding and the market price was $23 per share. The company received $6,680,000 for the notes and the warrants. For AB Company, 7% was a relatively low borrowing rate. If offered alone, at this time, the notes would have been issued at a 20 to 24% discount. Prepare journal entries for the issuance of the notes and warrants for the cash consideration received.

C14-8 Long-Term Notes Payable

AICPA Adapted Business transactions often involve the exchange of property, goods, or services for notes or similar instruments that may stipulate no interest rate or an interest rate that varies from prevailing rates.

Required

1. When a company exchanges a note for property, goods, or services, what value does it place on the note:
   a. If it bears interest at a reasonable rate and is issued in a bargained transaction entered into at arm's length? Explain.
   b. If it bears no interest and/or is not issued in a bargained transaction entered into at arm's length? Explain.
2. If the recorded value of a note differs from the face value:
   a. Explain how the company should account for the difference.
   b. Explain how the company should present this difference in the financial statements.

C14-9 Bonds: Sale, Interest, and Recall

AICPA Adapted On March 2, 2007 Wesley Company sold its five-year, $1,000 face value, 8% bonds dated March 2, 2007 at an effective annual interest rate (yield) of 10%. Interest is payable semiannually and the first interest payment date is September 2, 2007. Wesley uses the interest method of amortization and incurred bond issue costs in preparing and selling the bond issue. Wesley can call the bonds at 101 at any time on or after March 2, 2008.

Required

1. a. How does the company determine the selling price of the bonds?
   b. Specify how the company presents all items related to the bonds in a balance sheet prepared immediately after the bond issue is sold.
2. What items related to the bond issue does Wesley include in its 2007 income statement, and how does it determine each?
3. Will the amount of bond discount amortization using the interest method of amortization be lower in the second or third year of the life of the bond issue? Why?
4. Assuming that the bonds are called in and retired on March 2, 2008, how does Wesley report the retirement of the bonds on the 2008 income statement?

C14-10 Bonds: Issuance, Expense, and Conversion

AICPA Adapted On January 1, 2006 Brewster Company issued 2,000 of its five-year, $1,000 face value, 11% bonds dated January 1 at an effective annual interest rate (yield) of 9%. Brewster uses the effective interest method of amortization. On December 31, 2007 Brewster extinguished the 2,000 bonds early through acquisition in the open market for $1,980,000.

On July 1, 2006 Brewster issued 5,000 of its six-year, $1,000 face value, 10% convertible bonds dated July 1 at an effective annual interest rate (yield) of 12%. The bonds are convertible at the option of the investor into Brewster's common stock at a ratio of 10 shares of common stock for each bond. Brewster uses the effective interest method of amortization. On July 1, 2007 an investor in Brewster's convertible bonds tendered 1,500 bonds for conversion into 15,000 shares of Brewster's common stock, which had a market value of $105 per share at the date of the conversion.

Required

1. a. Were the 11% bonds issued at par, at a discount, or at a premium? Why?
    b. Is the amount of interest expense for the 11% bonds using the effective interest method of amortization higher in the first or second year of the life of the bond issue? Why?
2. a. How is a gain or loss on early extinguishment of debt determined? Does the early extinguishment of the 11% bonds result in a gain or loss? Why?
    b. How does Brewster report the early extinguishment of the 11% bonds on the 2007 income statement?
3. a. Does recording the conversion of the 10% convertible bonds into common stock under the book value method affect net income? What is the rationale for the book value method?
    b. Does recording the conversion of the 10% convertible bonds into common stock under the market value method affect net income? What is the rationale for the market value method?

C14-11 Analyzing Coca-Cola's Long-Term Debt Disclosures

Refer to the financial statements and related notes of the Coca-Cola Company in Appendix A of this book.

Required

1. What was the difference between the interest expense and interest paid in 2004?
2. How much long-term debt will mature in 2005?
3. Assuming no long-term debt was issued or retired during 2004, which U.S. dollar notes were issued at par? At a premium? At a discount?
4. Was the current yield at December 31, 2004 on the company's long-term debt the same as, greater, or less than the average yield at issuance? At December 31, 2003?

 ## C14-12 Ethics and Long-Term Liabilities

You are an accountant for the Virden Company, which has two items of long-term convertible debt on its balance sheet. The president of the company calls you into his office and says, "We are too leveraged. So, you remember that convertible debt we issued at the beginning of the year? Let's figure out the value of the conversion feature and assign that to equity so that we can reduce the amount we report as debt. And I have also been thinking about that convertible debt we issued at par five years ago. If you remember, each $1,000 bond is convertible into 25 shares. Now that our shares are trading at $70, obviously that is no longer debt. So let's classify that debt as equity now."

Required

From financial reporting and ethical perspectives, discuss the issues raised by this situation.

RESEARCH SIMULATIONS

R14-1 Researching GAAP

Situation

You are auditing the York Company when you come across a note receivable signed by the president of a company that is a major supplier. The note has a face value of $100,000, is payable to the York Company, is dated January 1, 2007, and is payable January 1, 2008. The interest rate on the note is 1%. You ask the president of the York Company about the note and she responds "That is fine. We lent him some money to help him through a difficult divorce. We wanted him to pay interest, but he couldn't afford the going rate of 8%. So how do you think we should account for the note?"

Directions

1. Research the related generally accepted accounting principles and prepare a short memo to the president that answers her question. Cite your references and applicable paragraph numbers.
2. How would your answer change if the interest rate on the note was 16%?
3. Do these valuation issues also create ethical issues?

R14-2 Researching GAAP

Situation

The Wales Company has a $90,000, non-interest-bearing four-year note receivable from the Spenser Company that was received on July 1, 2007 when Wales sold a used machine. The machine was custom made five years ago, cost the Wales Company $100,000, and was being depreciated over a 10-year life by the straight-line method to a zero residual value. As the accountant for the Wales Company you know that *APB Opinion No. 21* requires that the note be discounted using the borrower's interest rate. You phone the accountant for the Spenser Company and ask her what that company's incremental borrowing rate is. She responds cheerfully, "Sorry, I have no idea. We never borrow money because the owner provides all the capital we need." The president asks you to resolve this issue.

Directions

Research the related generally accepted accounting principles and prepare a short memo to the president that answers her question. Cite your references and applicable paragraph numbers.

Investments

OBJECTIVES

After reading this chapter you will be able to:

1 Explain the classification and valuation of investments.

2 Account for investments in debt and equity trading securities.

3 Account for investments in available-for-sale debt and equity securities.

4 Account for investments in held-to-maturity debt securities, including amortization of bond premiums and discounts.

5 Understand transfers and impairments.

6 Understand disclosures of investments.

7 Explain the conceptual issues regarding investments in marketable securities.

8 Account for investments using the equity method.

9 Describe additional issues for investments.

10 Account for derivatives of financial instruments. (Appendix)

Gains Trading—Good Business or Earnings Management?

A company invests in securities of other companies for reasons ranging from obtaining additional income to improving its competitive position. For some companies, such as financial institutions and insurers, these investments are a major part of the financial position of the company. For example, the health and accident insurance provider, **Aflac**, reported more than $48 billion of investments on its 2004 balance sheet. As the following chart shows, investments in other companies represent the majority of Aflac's total assets.

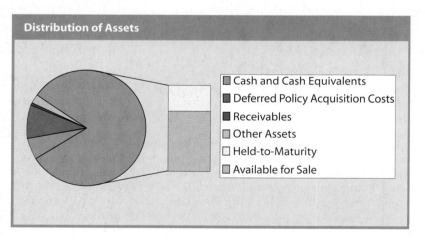

Distribution of Assets

- Cash and Cash Equivalents
- Deferred Policy Acquisition Costs
- Receivables
- Other Assets
- Held-to-Maturity
- Available for Sale

Furthermore, of the almost $48 billion of investments, nearly 70% are classified as available-for-sale, with the remainder classified as held-to-maturity. Finally, more than $2 billion in unrealized gains on the available-for-sale securities appear as accumulated

other comprehensive income on its balance sheet and have never been recognized on the income statement.

An historical criticism of accounting for investments is the ability of a company to selectively sell assets that have risen in value so that it can include the gains in income, while not selling securities that have declined in value and thereby avoid recognizing the losses. This practice has often been referred to as "gains trading." By allowing unrealized gains or losses on available-for-sale securities to bypass the income statement and be reported directly in stockholders' equity on a company's balance sheet, current accounting standards provide the company with the ability to manage its income through its decisions as to which securities to sell. Because the financial effects can be quite significant for companies with large investments like Aflac, it is critical to analyze the extensive disclosures in the notes to the financial statements to gain a clear picture of the financial condition and operating performance of a company.

FOR FURTHER INVESTIGATION

For a discussion of investments, consult the Business & Company Resource Center (BCRC):

- FAS 115: The Effect of Gains Trading. Lynn Suberly. *Bank Accounting and Finance*. 0894-3958, February 2004, v17, i2, p17(7).

A corporation buys securities of other corporations for many reasons. One reason is to obtain additional income. In Chapter 7 we emphasized that proper cash management requires the temporary investment of excess cash. Many companies have excess cash because the period of highest cash inflows does not coincide with the period of highest cash needs. Seasonal fluctuations in sales patterns frequently result in the period of greatest cash needs preceding the peak production or purchasing period when inventories are increasing. On the other hand, peak cash inflows follow the highest levels of sales activity. For efficient cash management, a company must invest excess cash from the time of peak inflows until the next period of cash outflows. For example, a department store must purchase large amounts of inventory for its peak Christmas selling season. Cash inflows from credit sales do not occur until the receivables are collected. The company may have excess cash until purchases are made for the next Christmas season. Companies may also have excess cash available to invest for longer periods of time.

As we discussed in Chapter 7, companies may invest excess cash in financial instruments called cash equivalents. Alternatively, to earn a higher return, companies may invest in other financial instruments, such as common stock, preferred stock, or bonds of other corporations, as well as municipal, state, or federal bonds. All these securities are classified as investments, and the entire group of securities is often referred to as a **portfolio of marketable securities**. Another reason why securities of other corporations are purchased is to establish long-term relationships with suppliers or to obtain significant influence or control over related companies. It is also common practice to include the cash surrender value of life insurance policies and sinking funds under the Investments category on the balance sheet. We discuss the recording and reporting issues for these types of investments in this chapter.

INVESTMENTS: CLASSIFICATION AND VALUATION

1 Explain the classification and valuation of investments.

FASB Statement No. 115 establishes generally accepted accounting principles for investments in debt securities and those equity securities that have readily determinable fair values.[1] A fair value is readily determinable if a sales price is currently available on a securities exchange registered with the SEC (e.g., the New York Stock Exchange) or in an over-the-counter market for which prices are publicly reported. A foreign market must be comparable to one of the U.S. markets. At acquisition, a company classifies each investment in debt and equity "marketable" securities into one of three categories. The three categories are:

1. *Trading Securities*. Investments in debt and equity securities that are purchased and held principally to sell in the near term are classified as trading securities. Trading generally involves active and frequent buying and selling, and the securities are held to make a profit on short-term differences in price. For example, a stock-brokerage firm that holds an "inventory" of securities for sale to its customers classifies them as trading securities. A bank that holds securities for active and frequent buying and selling to make a profit on short-term differences in price also classifies them as trading securities.
2. *Available-for-Sale Securities*. Investments in available-for-sale securities are (a) debt securities that are not classified as being held to maturity (see next category), and (b) debt and equity securities that are not classified as trading securities.

---

1. "Accounting for Certain Investments in Debt and Equity Securities," *FASB Statement of Financial Accounting Standards No. 115* (Norwalk, Conn.: FASB, 1993), par. 3–13. This *Statement* applies, in the case of equity securities, to investments in equity securities when the investor does *not* have "significant influence." *Significant influence* generally occurs when the ownership percentage is more than 20%, as we discuss later in the chapter.

3. *Held-to-Maturity Debt Securities*. Investments in held-to-maturity debt securities are debt securities for which the company has the "positive intent and ability to hold those securities to maturity."[2] Any sales of these securities prior to their maturity should be rare. A company does not classify a security as being held to maturity if it intends to hold the security only for an indefinite period. So the classification is *not* appropriate if the security will be sold for reasons such as a change in market interest rates or a need for liquid funds.[3] The sale of a debt security is *not* inconsistent with the original classification if there is a change of circumstances, or other events that are isolated, nonrecurring, and unusual for the company.

A company uses the "fair value" method to account for trading and available-for-sale securities, but not for held-to-maturity debt securities. The fair value method results in "unrealized holding gains and losses." Before we discuss the accounting for these securities, you need to know some additional definitions.

Conceptual

R ← → A

1. **An equity security involves an ownership interest in another company.** Thus, *investments* in equity securities include common stocks, preferred stocks, preferred stocks that are redeemable at the option of the company that issued the stock, stock warrants, stock rights, and put and call options. Investments in convertible debt or preferred stock with a mandatory redemption feature or that is redeemable at the option of the holder are *not* investments in equity securities.

2. **A debt security involves a creditor relationship with another entity.** Thus, *investments* in debt securities include U.S. treasury securities, municipal securities, corporate bonds, convertible debt, and commercial paper. Also included are investments in preferred stock that have a mandatory redemption feature or are redeemable at the option of the holder (discussed in Chapter 16). Trade accounts receivable are *not* investments in debt securities.

3. **Fair value is the amount at which a security could be exchanged in a current transaction between willing parties.** Thus, the fair value is the number of units of the security times the quoted market price on a stock exchange. Note that there is no adjustment for any estimated change in the market price that might result from the attempted sale of a large number of a particular security.

fair value = # of units x quoted market price.

There are two additional methods for reporting investments. However, these methods are *not* alternatives, but are applied depending on the level of ownership that the investor has in the investee. The **equity method** is used for investments in equity securities when the investor has *significant influence* over the investee. Significant influence generally occurs when the investor owns between 20% and 50% of the voting common stock of the investee, as we discuss later in the chapter. **Consolidation** occurs when the investor *controls* the investee through an investment in equity securities. Control generally occurs when the investor owns more than 50% of the voting common stock of the investee. The FASB is considering a change so that consolidation will occur whenever a company controls another entity (unless control is temporary). Control will be defined as the power to use the individual assets of the other entity in essentially the same way as the company can use its own assets. This effective control can occur at a lower ownership level than legal control. The investor issues consolidated financial statements, which are the combined financial statements of both companies. The preparation of consolidated financial statements is discussed in an advanced accounting book and is beyond the scope of this chapter, although we briefly discuss the underlying concepts of consolidation accounting in a later section.

---

2. *Ibid.*, par. 7.
3. Sales of held-to-maturity debt securities are considered to be at maturity if (1) the security is sold near enough to its maturity (or its call date, if exercise of the call is probable) that interest rate risk is substantially eliminated (e.g., within three months of maturity or the call date), or (2) the sale occurs after the company has collected a substantial portion (e.g., 85%) of the principal.

We provide an overview of the various categories and methods for recording and reporting investments in securities in Exhibit 15-1. We explain the related accounting principles in the following sections.

EXHIBIT 15-1 Accounting for Investments

	Method	Reporting of Unrealized Holding Gains and Losses
Investments in Equity Securities		
1. No significant influence (less than 20% ownership)		
a. Trading	Fair value	Net income
b. Available for sale	Fair value	Other comprehensive income
2. Significant influence (20% to 50% ownership)	Equity method	Not recognized
3. Control (more than 50% ownership)	Consolidation	Not recognized
Investments in Debt Securities		
1. Trading	Fair value	Net income
2. Available for sale	Fair value	Other comprehensive income
3. Held to maturity	Amortized cost	Not recognized

INVESTMENTS IN DEBT AND EQUITY TRADING SECURITIES

2 Account for investments in debt and equity trading securities.

The generally accepted accounting principles for investments in debt and equity securities classified as trading securities are:

- the investment is initially recorded at cost,
- it is then reported at fair value on the ending balance sheet(s),
- unrealized holding gains and losses from changes in the fair value are included in net income of the current period, and
- interest and dividend revenue, as well as realized gains and losses on sales, are included in net income of the current period.

As we noted earlier, investments in debt and equity trading securities are held primarily by such institutions as banks and stockbrokers. Since the accounting principles for trading securities tend to apply to a relatively few companies, we do not illustrate them here. However, they are the same as those we discuss in the next section on available-for-sale securities, *except* that for investments in trading securities (1) unrealized holding gains and losses on changes in value are included in net income for the current period, and (2) any realized gains or losses on sales are computed by comparing the selling price to the *fair value* recorded on the most recent balance sheet date.

INVESTMENTS IN AVAILABLE-FOR-SALE DEBT AND EQUITY SECURITIES

3 Account for investments in available-for-sale debt and equity securities.

The accounting principles for investments classified as available-for-sale debt and equity securities are:

- the investment is initially recorded at cost,
- it is then reported at fair value on the ending balance sheet(s),
- unrealized holding gains and losses from changes in the fair value are reported as a component of other comprehensive income,

- the cumulative unrealized holding gains and losses are reported in the accumulated other comprehensive income section of stockholders' equity, and
- interest and dividend revenue, as well as realized gains and losses on sales, are included in net income for the current period.

To illustrate each of these issues, assume that the Kent Company purchases the following securities on May 1, 2006 as an investment in available-for-sale securities:

A Company common stock	100 shares at $50 per share
B Company common stock	300 shares at $80 per share
C Company preferred stock	200 shares at $120 per share
D Company 10% bonds	Face value of $15,000, acquired at par plus accrued interest. Interest is paid on May 31 and November 30 each year.

Recording Initial Cost

A company records all investments in securities initially at the acquisition price of the securities plus any other costs necessary for the transaction. Thus, the cost of equity securities is simply the quoted market price at the time of the transaction plus any brokerage fees and taxes. A special issue arises with debt securities because any accrued interest must be separated from the purchase price. Recall from Chapter 14 that bondholders receive six months' interest on each interest payment date. Since interest accrues over time, whenever bonds are purchased between interest payment dates, the purchaser pays the previous bondholder for the interest earned to date.

The accrued interest on the D Company bonds purchased by the Kent Company is the interest from November 30, 2005 to May 1, 2006, or five months, and is $625 ($15,000 × 0.10 × 5/12). Therefore, the payment for the bonds includes the $15,000 cost of the bonds plus the $625 accrued interest. Thus, the total cost of the securities purchased by the Kent Company is $68,000 [(100 × $50) + (300 × $80) + (200 × $120) + $15,000].[4] The total payment is $68,625 ($68,000 cost + $625 accrued interest) and the company records the purchase as follows:

Investment in Available-for-Sale Securities	68,000	
Interest Revenue	625	
Cash		68,625

Note that Kent debited Interest Revenue for the accrued interest. This procedure reduces the possibility of error in recording the next interest revenue transaction.[5]

Recording Interest and Dividend Revenue

A company records interest revenue as it is earned during the period. On May 31, 2006 the Kent Company receives the semiannual interest on the D Company bonds and records it as follows:

Cash	750	
Interest Revenue ($15,000 × 0.10 × 6/12)		750

---

4. Any costs necessary for the acquisition, such as brokerage fees and taxes, are included in the cost of the securities. However, those amounts then would be allocated among each security purchased to determine its cost. We do not discuss this procedure because the amounts would not be material.

5. Alternatively, Kent Company could have debited Interest Receivable for $625, in which case it would eliminate the Interest Receivable account when it receives the interest on May 31, 2006.

Because the Kent Company initially debited interest revenue for five months of accrued interest on the date of acquisition, it credits interest revenue for the full six months of interest received. Therefore, by May 31 it has earned one month's interest and has that amount recorded in its accounting system. If the company purchased the D Company bonds at a premium or discount, it computes the interest revenue using the effective interest (or straight-line) method and amortizes a portion of the premium or discount, as we discuss later in the chapter.

On November 30, 2006 Kent Company receives the next interest payment and records it with the same journal entry. On December 31, 2006, it accrues one month's interest as follows:

Interest Receivable	125	
Interest Revenue ($15,000 × 0.10 × 1/12)		125

For the year, the Kent Company has earned interest revenue for eight months, or $1,000 ($750 − $625 + $750 + $125, or $15,000 × 0.10 × 8/12).

Dividend revenue is recorded as it is received. So if the Kent Company receives dividends during 2006 of $3,000 on its investments in the stock of A, B, and C Companies, it records the following:

Cash	3,000	
Dividend Revenue		3,000

It is conceptually more correct to record the Dividend Revenue when the dividends are declared by the investee company because that is the date on which the investor has the right to receive them. However, the date of receipt of the dividends is usually used for convenience. If the investee company has declared dividends at year-end but the investor company has not received them, it should record Dividends Receivable and Dividend Revenue to recognize the appropriate asset values and income, and also because the dividends receivable affect the calculation of any unrealized holding gain or loss, as we discuss later.

Note the different recognition of interest revenue and dividend revenue. Interest revenue accrues continuously over time, whereas dividend revenue is recognized only when dividends are received (or declared).

Recognition of Unrealized Holding Gains and Losses

On its ending balance sheet, a company reports any investments in available-for-sale securities at fair value. The fair values are determined by the year-end market prices on a securities exchange. *FASB Statement No. 115* uses the phrase "unrealized holding gains and losses" to describe the change in the value of investment securities. Note that a company reports its *realized* gains and losses for the year from sales of securities in its net income on its income statement, but reports its *unrealized* gains and losses for the year in its other comprehensive income. Also, a company reports its *cumulative* net unrealized gains and losses on investments in available-for-sale securities in its accumulated other comprehensive income section of stockholders' equity on its balance sheet. We use the terms "unrealized holding gains and losses" in the text but prefer a more appropriate title for the account, Unrealized Increase/Decrease in Value of Available-for-Sale Securities, in recording journal entries and reporting in the financial statements. Note that this account is a permanent account whose value carries over to the next period.[6] A *credit balance* in the account represents the *cumulative* net unrealized holding *gains* and is reported as a positive element in the accumulated other comprehensive income section of stockholders' equity. A *debit balance* in the account represents the *cumulative* net unrealized holding *losses* and is reported as a negative element in

---

6. The term "unrealized holding gains and losses" for investments in trading securities is appropriate because the amounts are included in net income for the current period. Also the account is a temporary one that is closed to Income Summary each year.

the accumulated other comprehensive income section of stockholders' equity. Also note that a credit (debit) *change* in this account represents the net unrealized holding gains (losses) on the securities for the *year* and is included as a positive (negative) component of other comprehensive income for the year, as we discussed in Chapter 5.

To illustrate, assume that the total fair value of the available-for-sale securities held by the Kent Company is $71,000 on December 31, 2006 as follows:

Security	Cost	12/31/06 Fair Value	Cumulative Change in Fair Value
100 shares of A Company common stock	$ 5,000	$ 6,000	$1,000
300 shares of B Company common stock	24,000	23,500	(500)
200 shares of C Company preferred stock	24,000	26,000	2,000
$15,000 face value of D Company 10% bonds	15,000	15,500	500
Totals	$68,000	$71,000	$3,000

The Kent Company determined the fair value of the securities based on the December 31, 2006 ending quoted market prices, with one adjustment. The quoted market price of the 10% D Company bonds was $15,625, but this included the $125 of accrued interest that Kent Company previously recorded. To avoid double-counting, Kent eliminates this interest to determine the $15,500 ($15,625 − $125) fair value of the bonds. (If dividends had been declared but not paid on the equity securities, a similar adjustment would be made.) Furthermore, if the company had purchased bonds at a premium or discount, it would use the amortized cost (i.e., carrying value) in the "cost" column.

The Kent Company records the $3,000 increase (unrealized holding gain) in the value of the securities at the end of 2006 as follows:

Allowance for Change in Value of Investment	3,000	
Unrealized Increase/Decrease in Value of Available-for-Sale Securities		3,000

The Allowance account is an adjunct/contra account to the Investment in Available-for-Sale Securities account. On its December 31, 2006 balance sheet, Kent Company reports the investment as an asset at the $71,000 fair value of the securities ($68,000 cost *plus* the $3,000 increase in fair value recorded in the Allowance account). If some investments are current and some noncurrent, the asset account is separated between the current and noncurrent components, as we show in a later section of the chapter. We are assuming that the Kent Company uses an Allowance account to record the changes in the fair values of the securities so that information about the original cost of each security is retained in its accounts and can be used to compute the realized gain or loss on the sale of a security, as we discuss later.[7] Also, note that the fair value method is not allowed for federal income tax purposes so a company has to retain cost information to compute its taxable income.[8]

---

7. Alternatively, a company may choose to record any changes in fair value directly in the Investment account. For example, companies investing in *trading securities* generally may *not* use an Allowance account because these securities "turn over" quickly. When this "direct" method is used for investments in available-for-sale securities, however, it is more difficult for a company to determine information needed for transactions in subsequent periods; therefore, we do not use this method for these securities.

8. A company includes the unrealized holding gains and losses on investments in *trading securities* in its net income for the current period. If it does not include them in its taxable income, the difference is a temporary difference on which the company recognizes deferred income taxes, as we discuss in Chapter 19. A company also recognizes deferred income taxes on a change in the unrealized increase/decrease in the value of investments in available-for-sale securities because the amount included in other comprehensive income is not included in taxable income.

Reporting

The Unrealized Increase/Decrease account is an adjunct/contra stockholders' equity account. Kent Company reports the $3,000 *change* (increase) in the Unrealized Increase/Decrease account as an unrealized holding gain in its other comprehensive income for 2006 (as we discussed in Chapter 5). It also reports the $3,000 credit *balance* in the Unrealized Increase/Decrease account as an addition to stockholders' equity on its balance sheet in the accumulated other comprehensive income section.[9] We show this disclosure in a later section in the chapter. In other words, the change in this account is included in other comprehensive income for the year, and its total is included in accumulated other comprehensive income. In this first year that Kent owns securities, the two amounts are the same.

To illustrate subsequent increases or decreases in fair value, suppose that on December 31, 2007, the fair value of the available-for-sale securities held by Kent Company is $66,000 as follows:

Security	Cost	12/31/07 Fair Value	Cumulative Change in Fair Value
100 shares of A Company common stock	$ 5,000	$ 6,100	$ 1,100
300 shares of B Company common stock	24,000	22,700	(1,300)
200 shares of C Company preferred stock	24,000	23,200	(800)
$15,000 face value of D Company 10% bonds	15,000	14,000	(1,000)
Totals	$68,000	$66,000	$(2,000)

Once a company has established an Allowance account, it determines the amount of the year-end adjustment in a subsequent period by comparing the required amount of the Allowance account with the previous balance in the account. At December 31, 2007 the required amount of the Kent Company's Allowance account is a $2,000 *credit* balance, but the previous balance at December 31, 2006 was a $3,000 *debit* balance. Therefore, the Kent Company credits the Allowance account for $5,000 at the end of 2007 to record the decline in value (unrealized holding loss) as follows:

Unrealized Increase/Decrease in Value of Available-for-Sale Securities	5,000	
Allowance for Change in Value of Investment		5,000

Reporting

On its December 31, 2007 balance sheet, the Kent Company reports the investment as an asset at the $66,000 fair value of the securities ($68,000 cost − $2,000 allowance) as we showed earlier.[10] It reports the $5,000 *change* (decrease) in the Unrealized Increase/Decrease account as an unrealized holding loss in its other comprehensive income for 2007. It also reports the $2,000 *debit balance* in the Unrealized Increase/Decrease account as a subtraction from stockholders' equity in the accumulated other comprehensive income section.

Realized Gains and Losses on Sales of Available-for-Sale Securities

A company reports realized gains and losses on sales of investments in available-for-sale securities in net income. They are measured as the difference between the selling price and the *cost* (of an equity security) or the *amortized cost* (of a debt security). Furthermore, since the security is no longer in the portfolio of available-for-sale securities, the portion of the

---

9. The amounts included in other comprehensive income for the year and accumulated other comprehensive income are reported net of tax. We do not include the tax effects in this discussion.

10. A company preparing interim (quarterly) financial statements would use the same accounting procedures, applied each quarter.

balances in the Allowance and Unrealized Increase/Decrease accounts reported at the previous balance sheet date for the security sold must be "reversed" out of the accounts.

For example, suppose that on March 1, 2008 the Kent Company sold the 100 shares of A Company common stock for $6,000. The cost of the securities was $5,000 and the fair value at the previous balance sheet was $6,100, as follows:

Security	Cost	12/31/07 Fair Value	Cumulative Change in Fair Value
100 shares of A Company common stock	$5,000	$6,100	$1,100

The company recognizes a gain of $1,000 ($6,000 selling price − $5,000 cost) and eliminates the $1,100 cumulative unrealized gain (and allowance) on the A Company stock. The company records the sale and the "reversal" on March 1, 2008 in two journal entries as follows:

Cash	6,000	
Investment in Available-for-Sale Securities		5,000
Gain on Sale of Available-for-Sale Securities		1,000
Unrealized Increase/Decrease in Value of		
Available-for-Sale Securities	1,100	
Allowance for Change in Value of Investment		1,100

The first journal entry records the sale and the $1,000 realized gain in 2008. The second journal entry reverses (eliminates) the $1,100 cumulative unrealized gain that had accumulated from May 1, 2006 (the date the company purchased the securities) until December 31, 2007 (the most recent balance sheet date). This is called a "reclassification adjustment," which we discuss in the next section. A sale of an investment in securities at a loss would be recorded in the same way. The company would record the sale and realized loss in the first journal entry and would reverse (eliminate) any cumulative unrealized loss (or gain) and allowance on that security.

At the end of 2008, Kent Company must adjust the Allowance and Unrealized Increase/Decrease accounts to report the fair values of the securities it still owns. To illustrate, assume that the total fair value of the remaining securities is $62,300 on December 31, 2008 as follows:

Security	Cost	12/31/08 Fair Value	Cumulative Change in Fair Value
300 shares of B Company common stock	$24,000	$23,500	$(500)
200 shares of C Company preferred stock	24,000	24,100	100
$15,000 face value of D Company 10% bonds	15,000	14,700	(300)
Totals	$63,000	$62,300	$(700)

Before the 2008 year-end adjusting entry, the Allowance account has a credit balance of $3,100 ($2,000 12/31/07 credit balance + $1,100 from 3/1/08 reversal) and the Unrealized Increase/Decrease account has a $3,100 debit balance.[11] At December 31, 2008 the required amount of the Allowance account is a $700 credit balance, so the Kent

---

11. The $3,100 debit balance (cumulative unrealized holding loss) in the Unrealized Increase/Decrease account is the difference between the $63,000 cost ($24,000 + $24,000 + $15,000) of the remaining securities held (in Company B, C, and D securities) and the 12/31/07 fair value of $59,900 ($22,700 + $23,200 + $14,000).

Company debits the Allowance account for $2,400 ($3,100 − $700) to record the increase in value (unrealized holding gain) as follows:

Allowance for Change in Value of Investment	2,400	
Unrealized Increase/Decrease in Value of		
Available-for-Sale Securities		2,400

Reporting

The Kent Company reports the $1,000 gain on the sale of its investment in the A Company common stock in its 2008 net income because this amount is realized. The company reports the $2,400 unrealized holding gain (on the Company B, C, and D securities) in its 2008 other comprehensive income.

Reclassification Adjustment

As we discussed in Chapter 5, a company's comprehensive income consists of two parts: net income and other comprehensive income. A reclassification adjustment is made to avoid "double-counting" in the company's comprehensive income. Recall that the Kent Company reports the $1,000 gain on the sale of the Company A common stock in its income statement for 2008. So the company includes the $1,000 in the net income that it reports as the first part of its comprehensive income. Also recall that it computed the $1,000 gain by comparing the $6,000 selling price to the $5,000 *cost*. But the company had already reported a $1,100 cumulative unrealized gain ($6,100 fair value − $5,000 cost) on these securities in its other comprehensive income for 2006 and 2007. So to avoid double-counting, the Kent Company *reduced* its other comprehensive income for 2008 by the $1,100 adjustment of the Unrealized Increase/Decrease account that it made on March 1, 2006 (when it sold the Company A common stock). This offsets the $1,100 cumulative unrealized holding gain that it reported in the prior years. It reports the $1,100 reclassification adjustment as a *negative* component of other comprehensive income.

INVESTMENTS IN HELD-TO-MATURITY DEBT SECURITIES

4 Account for investments in held-to-maturity debt securities, including amortization of bond premiums and discounts.

The generally accepted accounting principles for investments in held-to-maturity debt securities are:

- the investment is initially recorded at cost,
- it is then reported at amortized cost on the ending balance sheet(s)[12],
- unrealized holding gains and losses are *not* recorded, and
- interest revenue and realized gains and losses on sales (if any) are all included in net income.

In Chapter 14 we pointed out that bonds carrying a stated interest rate above the prevailing yield for securities with a similar amount of risk sell at a premium. This premium lowers the stated interest rate to the market (yield) rate. Bonds carrying a stated interest rate below the prevailing market rate for securities with a similar amount of risk sell at a discount. The discount effectively increases the stated interest rate to the market rate. Therefore, accounting for investments in bonds is essentially a "mirror image" of accounting for bonds payable. However, in contrast to accounting for premiums and discounts by debtor companies, investor companies generally do *not* use a separate valuation account for the premiums and discounts on investments in bonds. Instead, the purchase price is recorded in the investment account, which is directly adjusted for any premium and discount amortization, even though *APB Opinion No. 21* recommended separate disclosure. The effect of not separately

---

12. "Amortized cost" is the remaining amount (i.e., carrying value) of the cost (face value plus any premium or less any discount at acquisition) after any premium or discount has been amortized each period as interest revenue is recognized.

disclosing premiums or discounts is to report the Investment in Held-to-Maturity Bonds account directly at its carrying value (amortized cost) on each balance sheet date.

Recording Initial Cost

Investments in debt securities held to maturity are recorded in the same way as we discussed earlier. For example, assume that a company purchases 9% bonds with a face value of $100,000 on August 1, 2006 at 99 plus accrued interest. Interest on these bonds is payable semiannually on May 31 and November 30. The company records this purchase on August 1, 2006 as follows:

Investment in Held-to-Maturity Debt Securities ($100,000 × 0.99)	99,000	
Interest Revenue ($100,000 × 0.09 × 2/12)	1,500	
Cash		100,500

Note that the company debits the Investment account for $99,000. Therefore, it includes the $1,000 discount directly in the Investment account and amortizes it as an adjustment to interest revenue, as we discuss later. Note also that, as we showed for investments in available-for-sale securities, the company debits the Interest Revenue account for the two months of accrued interest ($1,500). It will credit the Interest Revenue account for $4,500 when it receives the November 30, 2006 semiannual interest, resulting in the recognition of $3,000 interest earned for the period August 1 through November 30, 2006.

Recognition and Amortization of Bond Premiums and Discounts

Investments in held-to-maturity debt securities that are purchased at a premium or discount result in an effective interest rate that is different than the stated rate, as we discussed in Chapter 14. Consequently, for these investments in bonds, **the amount of interest revenue recognized each accounting period is based on the effective interest rate (yield) at the time of acquisition.** Therefore, **any premium or discount is amortized over the remaining life of the bonds to record the proper amount of interest revenue for each accounting period.** The effective interest method and straight-line method are the alternative procedures that are used to record interest revenue and account for premiums and discounts. However, *APB Opinion No. 21* requires use of the effective interest method, unless the use of the straight-line method does not result in a material difference in the amount of interest revenue recognized in any year. Premium amortizations result in an effective interest rate lower than the stated rate, whereas discount amortizations result in an effective interest rate higher than the stated rate.

Accounting for Premiums

Assume that the Colburn Company invests in bonds that will be held to maturity, with a face value of $100,000, paying $102,458.71 on January 1, 2006. These bonds carry a stated interest rate of 13% payable semiannually on June 30 and December 31; they mature on December 31, 2008, and yield an effective interest rate of 12%. The Colburn Company records the acquisition on January 1, 2006 as follows:

Investment in Held-to-Maturity Debt Securities	102,458.71	
Cash		102,458.71

Examples 15-1 and 15-2 show the schedules for computing interest revenue, the premium amortization, and the carrying value under the straight-line and effective interest methods for these bonds. We explained the preparation of similar schedules for bonds payable in Chapter 14, so our discussion here is limited. The Colburn Company records the first interest receipt on June 30, 2006 using the *effective interest method* (see Example 15-2) for the bonds purchased at a premium, as follows:

Cash	6,500.00	
Investment in Held-to-Maturity Debt Securities		352.48
Interest Revenue		6,147.52

Note that the company credits the premium amortization directly to the Investment account. If it uses the straight-line method, it makes a similar entry using the amounts from Example 15-1.

EXAMPLE 15-1   **Bond Investment Interest Revenue and Premium Amortization Schedule: *Straight-Line Method***

Date	Cash Debit[a]	Investment in Debt Securities Credit[b]	Interest Revenue Credit[c]	Carrying Value of Investment in Debt Securities[d]
1/1/06				$102,458.71
6/30/06	$6,500.00	$409.79	$6,090.21	102,048.92
12/31/06	6,500.00	409.79	6,090.21	101,639.13
6/30/07	6,500.00	409.79	6,090.21	101,229.34
12/31/07	6,500.00	409.79	6,090.21	100,819.55
6/30/08	6,500.00	409.79	6,090.21	100,409.76
12/31/08	6,500.00	409.76[e]	6,090.24	100,000.00

a. $100,000 (face value) × 0.13 (stated rate of interest) × 1/2 (year).
b. ($102,458.71 − $100,000) = $2,458.71 ÷ 6 (remaining semiannual periods of bond life).
c. $6,500 − $409.79.
d. Previous investment carrying value − amount from footnote *b*.
e. Difference due to $0.03 rounding error.

EXAMPLE 15-2   **Bond Investment Interest Revenue and Premium Amortization Schedule: *Effective Interest Method***

Date	Cash Debit[a]	Interest Revenue Credit[b]	Investment in Debt Securities Credit[c]	Carrying Value of Investment in Debt Securities[d]
1/1/06				$102,458.71
6/30/06	$6,500.00	$6,147.52	$352.48	102,106.23
12/31/06	6,500.00	6,126.37	373.63	101,732.60
6/30/07	6,500.00	6,103.96	396.04	101,336.56
12/31/07	6,500.00	6,080.19	419.81	100,916.75
6/30/08	6,500.00	6,055.01	444.99	100,471.76
12/31/08	6,500.00	6,028.24[e]	471.76	100,000.00

a. $100,000 (face value) × 0.13 (stated rate of interest) × 1/2 (year).
b. Previous investment carrying value × 0.12 (effective interest rate) × 1/2 (year).
c. Amount from footnote *a* − amount from footnote *b*.
d. Previous investment carrying value − amount from footnote *c*.
e. Difference due to $0.07 rounding error.

Accounting for Discounts

Now assume that Colburn acquired the bonds at a discount for $97,616.71. This discount indicates that the rate of interest desired by investors is greater than the stated rate of 13%. These bonds yield an effective interest rate of 14%. Examples 15-3 and 15-4 illustrate the schedules for computing interest revenue, the discount amortization, and the carrying value under the straight-line and effective interest methods for these bonds. On January 1, 2006 Colburn records the acquisition as follows:

Investment in Held-to-Maturity Debt Securities	97,616.71	
Cash		97,616.71

Colburn records the first interest receipt on June 30, 2006, using the *effective interest method* (see Example 15-4) for the bonds purchased at a discount, as follows:

Cash	6,500.00	
Investment in Held-to-Maturity Debt Securities	333.17	
Interest Revenue		6,833.17

Note that the company debits the discount amortization directly to the Investment account. If it uses the straight-line method, it makes a similar entry using the amounts from Example 15-3.

EXAMPLE 15-3 **Bond Investment Interest Revenue and Discount Amortization Schedule: *Straight-Line Method***

Date	Cash Debit[a]	Investment in Debt Securities Debit[b]	Interest Revenue Credit[c]	Carrying Value of Investment in Debt Securities[d]
1/1/06				$ 97,616.71
6/30/06	$6,500.00	$397.22	$6,897.22	98,013.93
12/31/06	6,500.00	397.22	6,897.22	98,411.15
6/30/07	6,500.00	397.22	6,897.22	98,808.37
12/31/07	6,500.00	397.22	6,897.22	99,205.59
6/30/08	6,500.00	397.22	6,897.22	99,602.81
12/31/08	6,500.00	397.19[e]	6,897.19	100,000.00

a. $100,000 (face value) × 0.13 (stated rate of interest) × 1/2 (year).
b. ($100,000 − $97,616.71) = $2,383.29 ÷ 6 (remaining semiannual periods of bond life).
c. $6,500 + $397.22.
d. Previous investment carrying value + amount from footnote *b*.
e. Difference due to $0.03 rounding error.

EXAMPLE 15-4 **Bond Investment Interest Revenue and Discount Amortization Schedule: *Effective Interest Method***

Date	Cash Debit[a]	Interest Revenue Credit[b]	Investment in Debt Securities Debit[c]	Carrying Value of Investment in Debt Securities[d]
1/1/06				$ 97,616.71
6/30/06	$6,500.00	$6,833.17	$333.17	97,949.88
12/31/06	6,500.00	6,856.49	356.49	98,306.37
6/30/07	6,500.00	6,881.45	381.45	98,687.82
12/31/07	6,500.00	6,908.15	408.15	99,095.97
6/30/08	6,500.00	6,936.72	436.72	99,532.69
12/31/08	6,500.00	6,967.31[e]	467.31	100,000.00

a. $100,000 (face value) × 0.13 (stated rate of interest) × 1/2 (year).
b. Previous investment carrying value × 0.14 (effective interest rate) × 1/2 (year).
c. Amount from footnote *b* − amount from footnote *a*.
d. Previous investment carrying value + amount from footnote *c*.
e. Difference due to $0.02 rounding error.

Amortization for Bonds Acquired Between Interest Dates

As we showed earlier, held-to-maturity bonds may be acquired between interest dates. When these bonds are purchased at a premium or discount, the premium or discount is amortized over the remaining life of the bonds. For example, assume that the Tallen Company purchased 13% bonds with a face value of $200,000 for $204,575.07 on April 3, 2006. Interest on these bonds is payable June 30 and December 31, and the bonds mature December 31, 2008 (33 months after the date of purchase). Tallen records the acquisition on April 3, 2006 as follows:

Investment in Held-to-Maturity		
Debt Securities	204,575.07	
Interest Revenue ($200,000 × 0.13 × 3/12)	6,500.00	
Cash		211,075.07

The company amortizes the $4,575.07 premium ($204,575.07 − $200,000) over the remaining 33-month life of the bond issue. If it uses straight-line amortization, it amortizes $138.64 ($4,575.07 ÷ 33) of the premium to reduce interest revenue for each month it holds the bonds.

When the effective interest method is used, the actual yield[13] is computed and then used to amortize the premium over the length of time the investment is to be held. The purchase of a $200,000 investment due in 33 months with a stated 13% interest rate, payable semiannually, for $204,575.07 results in an effective interest rate of 12%. Using the effective interest method of amortization, the company would record the first two interest receipts as follows:

June 30, 2006

Cash	13,000.00	
Interest Revenue		
[($204,575.07 × 0.12 × 1/4) + $6,500*]		12,637.25
Investment in Held-to-Maturity		
Debt Securities ($13,000 − $12,637.25)		362.75

* Amount debited to interest revenue on the date the bonds were acquired.

December 31, 2006

Cash	13,000.00	
Interest Revenue		
[($204,575.07 − $362.75) × 0.12 × 1/2]		12,252.74
Investment in Held-to-Maturity		
Debt Securities ($13,000 − $12,252.74)		747.26

In calculating the premium amortization for the first interest payment, note that the actual amount of interest revenue is only $6,137.25 ($204,575.07 × 0.12 × 3/12)[14] even though Tallen credited the interest revenue account for $12,637.25. The additional $6,500 credit reflects the interest payment to the former owner. Subsequently, Tallen computes the amount of interest revenue by multiplying the carrying value of the investment (acquisition price less amortized premium) by the 6% semiannual yield (0.12 × 6/12). It records the difference between the amount of cash received and the amount of interest revenue as premium amortization in each successive period.

---

13. See Chapter 14 for an illustration of the calculation of yields.
14. This calculation assumes that the purchase price yields 12% interest for 33 months. Normally, it is necessary to find the present value of the bonds at the last interest payment date (December 31, 2005 in this case), subtract the present value of the bonds on the next interest payment date (June 30, 2006), and apply the straight-line method to amortize the premium for the interim period. See Chapter 14 (pp. 652–653) for an illustration of this procedure.

Sale of Investment in Bonds Before Maturity

Selling an investment in held-to-maturity bonds before the maturity date should be rare because the sale may violate the reason for their classification. Alternatively, as we discussed earlier in the chapter, certain changes in circumstances are *not* inconsistent with the classification. When such a sale occurs, a company must record any gain or loss from the transaction. Also, the company eliminates its Investment account, and collects any interest earned since the last interest date from the purchaser.

Before computing the gain or loss on the sale of an investment, the company amortizes any premium or discount on the bonds from the last interest date to the sale date. This procedure is necessary to record the correct amount of interest revenue, and to determine the carrying value of the investment on the date of the sale. The carrying value of the bonds is then compared with the sales price (*excluding* any accrued interest) to determine the gain or loss. To illustrate, assume that the $100,000 of 13% bonds purchased by the Colburn Company for $97,616.71 that we discussed earlier were sold on March 31, 2007 for $102,000 plus accrued interest. Colburn records the following journal entries on March 31, 2007 (assuming it amortizes the bond discount by the straight-line method illustrated in Example 15-3):

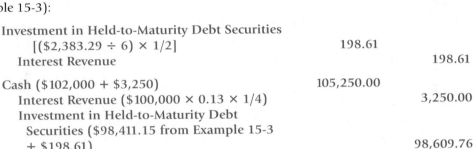

Investment in Held-to-Maturity Debt Securities		
[($2,383.29 ÷ 6) × 1/2]	198.61	
Interest Revenue		198.61
Cash ($102,000 + $3,250)	105,250.00	
Interest Revenue ($100,000 × 0.13 × 1/4)		3,250.00
Investment in Held-to-Maturity Debt		
Securities ($98,411.15 from Example 15-3		
+ $198.61)		98,609.76
Gain on Sale of Debt Securities		3,390.24

The first journal entry brings the investment carrying value up to date. In the second journal entry, the debit to Cash records the sales price plus the $3,250 interest earned in the three months since the last interest payment date. The credit to the Investment account eliminates the current carrying value of the investment on the sale date. The Colburn Company computes the gain by comparing the $98,609.76 current carrying value of the Investment account on the sale date with the $102,000 selling price of the investment. Colburn reports this gain as ordinary income, unless considered unusual and infrequent, in which case it reports the gain as an extraordinary item.

The diagram at the bottom of this page and top of the next page summarizes the accounting issues we have discussed for the three categories of investments in securities.

Event	Classify According to Management Intent as:	Initially Record at:	Classify Cash Flow as:	Report on the Ending Balance Sheet at:
	Trading	Cost	Operating	Fair Value
Company Purchases Securities	Available-for-Sale	Cost	Investing	Fair Value
	Held-to-Maturity	Cost	Investing	Amortized Cost

(continued)

Classify According to Management Intent as:	Recognize Unrealized Holding Gains and Losses in:	Recognize Interest and Dividend Revenue in:	Recognize Realized Gain or Loss in:	Compute Realized Gain or Loss as:
Trading	Net Income	Net Income	Net Income	Selling Price minus Fair Value at Most Recent Balance Sheet Date
Available-for-Sale	Other Comprehensive Income	Net Income	Net Income	Selling Price minus (Amortized) Cost
Held-to-Maturity	—	Net Income	Net Income*	Selling Price* minus (Amortized) Cost

*Sales of held-to-maturity securities should be rare.

SECURE YOUR KNOWLEDGE 15-1

- Investments in the financial instruments (debt and equity securities) of other companies in which the investor does not have significant influence or control are classified as either trading securities, available-for-sale securities, or held-to-maturity securities.
- While all investment securities are initially recorded at cost with dividend revenue, interest revenue, and realized gains and losses recorded on the income statement, the subsequent valuation of these securities depends on their classification.
- Investments in debt and equity trading securities are subsequently reported at fair value on each balance sheet date with any unrealized holding gains and losses included in current period income.
- Investments in debt and equity securities classified as available-for-sale are subsequently reported at fair value on each balance sheet date with any unrealized holding gains and losses included in comprehensive income for the year and as a component of accumulated other comprehensive income in stockholders' equity on the balance sheet.
    - Unrealized holding gains and losses result from increases or decreases in the fair value of the securities.
    - If a company has a realized gain or loss on available-for-sale securities (measured as the difference between the selling price and the cost of the security), it recognizes this gain in income and "reverses" any previously recognized unrealized gain or loss.
- Investments in held-to-maturity debt securities are subsequently reported at amortized cost on each balance sheet date with no recognition of any unrealized holding gains and losses.
    - Any premium or discount resulting from the purchase of a held-to-maturity debt security is amortized over the remaining life of the security.
    - If the held-to-maturity securities are acquired between interest payment dates, any accrued interest since the last interest payment date is recorded as a debit to interest revenue.

TRANSFERS AND IMPAIRMENTS

5 Understand transfers and impairments.

Two additional issues arise in accounting for investments. The first involves transfers between investment categories. The second involves impairments of investments.

Transfers of Investments Between Categories

The transfer of a security between investment categories is accounted for at the fair value at the time of the transfer. However, transfers into or out of the trading category should be rare, as should transfers *from* the held-to-maturity category. In the journal entry to record the transfer, the fair value is used as the "new" investment carrying value, and the "old" investment carrying value is eliminated. However, the accounting for any related unrealized gain or loss varies, depending on the type of transfer.

1. A transfer *from the trading* category. No accounting for the unrealized holding gain or loss is needed because it has already been recognized in net income.
2. A transfer *into the trading* category. The previous unrealized holding gain or loss is eliminated and a gain or loss is included in net income.
3. A transfer *into the available for sale* category *from the held-to-maturity* category. An unrealized holding gain or loss is established and included in other comprehensive income.
4. A transfer of a debt security *into the held-to-maturity* category *from the available-for-sale* category. The unrealized holding gain or loss on the available-for-sale security is eliminated and an unrealized holding gain or loss on the held-to-maturity security is recorded for the same amount and included in other comprehensive income. The amount is amortized over the remaining life of the security as an adjustment of interest revenue by computing a new yield to maturity for that security.

We will use three examples to illustrate transfers (we do not discuss a transfer *from* the trading category).

Example: Transfer *into* Trading Category *from* Available-for-Sale Category

Assume the same facts as earlier for the Kent Company at December 31, 2007. Assume also that in 2008 Kent transfers the Company A securities into the trading category when their fair value is $6,300. Because Kent does not use an Allowance account for its investments in trading securities, it debits the asset account directly for the fair value of the securities. Since the available-for-sale securities had a cost of $5,000, it records a $1,300 realized holding gain. Also, it debits the Unrealized Increase/Decrease account and credits the Allowance account related to the available-for-sale securities for $1,100, respectively, to eliminate the December 31, 2007 adjustment ($6,100 fair value − $5,000 cost) recorded on that date. It records the transfer as follows:

Investment in Trading Securities	6,300	
Investment in Available-for-Sale Securities		5,000
Gain on Transfer of Securities		1,300
Unrealized Increase/Decrease in Value of		
Available-for-Sale Securities	1,100	
Allowance for Change in Value of Investment		1,100

Kent includes the gain in its net income for 2008, and as we discussed earlier, includes the $1,100 as a reduction in its other comprehensive income for 2008. ♦

Example: Transfer *into* Available-for-Sale Category *from* Held-to-Maturity Category

Assume that the Devon Company has bonds included in the category of investments held to maturity. The bonds have a face value of $10,000 and the company purchased them at par. When the fair value of the bonds is $9,500, the company transfers the bonds into the available-for-sale category. Since an Investment in Available-for-Sale Securities is recorded at cost and an Allowance account is used to adjust the carrying value to fair value (with a corresponding adjustment to the Unrealized Increase/Decrease account), the company records the transfer as follows:

Investment in Available-for-Sale Securities	10,000	
Investment in Held-to-Maturity Debt Securities		10,000
Unrealized Increase/Decrease in Value of		
Available-for-Sale Securities	500	
Allowance for Change in Value of Investment		500

If the company purchased bonds being held to maturity at a premium or discount, it would record the investment in available-for-sale securities at the amortized cost, and it would compute the adjustment to the Allowance and Unrealized Increase/Decrease accounts by comparing the fair value to the amortized cost. ♦

Example: Transfer *into* Held-to-Maturity Category *from* Available-for-Sale Category

Assume the same facts for the Devon Company except that it currently classifies the bonds as available for sale and transfers them into the held-to-maturity category. Assume further that the available-for-sale bonds had a fair value of $9,700 on the previous balance sheet date. In this case, the company records the investment in debt securities at the current fair value of $9,500, and eliminates the previous $300 ($9,700 − $10,000) amounts in the Allowance and Unrealized Increase/Decrease accounts. It creates a new stockholders' equity account, Unrealized Increase/Decrease in Value of Held-to-Maturity Debt Securities for the $500 difference between the current fair value and the original cost. It records the transfer as follows:

Investment in Held-to-Maturity Debt Securities	9,500	
Unrealized Increase/Decrease from Transfer		
of Securities	500	
Investment in Available-for-Sale Securities		10,000
Allowance for Change in Value of Investment	300	
Unrealized Increase/Decrease in Value of		
Available-for-Sale Securities		300

In later periods the company amortizes the $500 discount in the Investment account ($10,000 face value − $9,500 carrying value) using the effective interest method over the remaining life of the bonds. This requires the computation of a new effective interest rate. The new rate is computed by equating, on a present value basis, the future cash flows and the new "carrying value."[15] Interest revenue is then computed by multiplying the carrying value each period by the effective interest rate. We discussed this procedure in Chapter 14 in the section on troubled debt restructuring. The $500 unrealized amount is also amortized as an adjustment to interest revenue, using the effective interest method over the remaining life of the debt security (bonds), and this amount offsets the amortization of the discount. ♦

Impairments

There may be an "other than temporary" decline below the amortized cost of an investment in a debt security classified as available for sale or held to maturity. A company uses factors such as the reason for the decline, the length of the decline, the future potential of the investee, and the current state of the economy to determine whether a particular decrease in the value of a security is other than temporary. Impairment occurs when it is probable that the company will be unable to collect all the amounts due. The company writes down the amortized cost of the security to the fair value and includes the amount of the write-down in net income as a realized loss. The fair value becomes the new "cost" and is not changed for

---

15. This procedure is used for investments in marketable debt securities. We discussed accounting for the impairment of a loan (which does not have a fair value available on a stock exchange) in Chapter 14.

Credit: RAMIN TALAIE/Bloomberg News/Landov

subsequent recoveries in fair value. However, increases and decreases in the fair value of available-for-sale securities are included in stockholders' equity as we discussed earlier.

To illustrate this situation, suppose that the Tracy Company has a bond investment categorized as held to maturity, which has a carrying value (amortized cost) of $21,500 and a fair value of $6,500. If it considers the decline in value to be other than temporary, the company records the decline of $15,000 ($21,500 − $6,500) as follows:

Realized Loss on Decline in Value	15,000	
Investment in Held-to-Maturity Debt Securities		15,000

The $6,500 becomes the new "cost" of the security. The company computes interest revenue using the effective interest method based on the new effective interest rate computed. We discussed this approach earlier for bonds transferred into the held-to-maturity category.

A similar procedure is followed for an investment in a security classified as available for sale which has a decline in value that is considered to be other than temporary. Since a company is already reporting the security at fair value by using an allowance account, it establishes a new cost basis at the fair value. It eliminates the allowance and unrealized increase/decrease accounts, and records the loss from the write-down as a realized loss. It includes any subsequent changes in value (that are considered to be temporary) as unrealized holding gains and losses in other comprehensive income. The realized gain or loss on the eventual sale of the security is the difference between the selling price and the new "cost."

The SEC has also been involved in the issue of how the "other than temporary" criterion is to be applied by publicly-traded companies. It suggests that companies should consider the length of time a security has been impaired, the severity of the impairment, and the financial condition of the issuer of the security. While it has not issued a specific rule, it has indicated that a loss should be recognized if recovery of the loss is not probable within a year.

Also, at the time of writing this book, interest rates were rising. These increases reduce the present (market) value of investments in debt securities. Therefore, companies must decide whether these decreases in value should be considered "other than temporary" and recognize losses in their income statements. For this, and other reasons, the FASB is re-evaluating the whole issue of other-than-temporary impairments for investments in debt and equity securities.

DISCLOSURES

A company is required to make the following major disclosures for investments in securities by *FASB Statement No. 115*:

6 Understand disclosures of investments.

1. *Trading Securities.* Disclose the change in the net unrealized holding gain or loss that is included in each income statement.

2. *Available-for-Sale Securities.* For each balance sheet date, disclose the aggregate fair value, gross unrealized holding gains and gross unrealized holding losses, and (amortized) cost by major security types. For each income statement period, disclose (1) the proceeds from sales and the gross realized gains and gross realized losses on those sales, (2) the basis on which cost was determined (e.g., the average cost method), (3) the gross gains and gross losses included in net income from transfers of securities from this category into the trading category, and (4) the change in the net unrealized holding gain or loss included as a separate component of other comprehensive income.

3. *Held-to-Maturity Debt Securities.* For each balance sheet date, disclose the aggregate fair value, gross unrealized holding gains, gross unrealized holding losses, and amortized cost by major security types. For any sales or transfers from this category, the disclosures must include the amortized cost, the related realized or unrealized gain or loss, and the circumstances leading to the decision to sell or transfer the security.

Real Report 15-1 shows the disclosures of **Intel Corporation** in its 2004 annual report. Financial institutions must make additional disclosures, which we do not discuss here.

Real Report 15-1 Disclosure of Marketable Securities

INTEL CORPORATION

NOTES TO CONSOLIDATED FINANCIAL STATEMENTS (in part):

Note 2: Accounting Policies (in part)

Investments

Trading Assets. Trading assets are stated at fair value, with gains or losses resulting from changes in fair value recognized currently in earnings.

Available-for-Sale Investments. Investments designated as available-for-sale include marketable debt and equity securities. Investments that are designated as available-for-sale are reported at fair value, with unrealized gains and losses, net of tax, recorded in stockholders' equity. The cost of securities sold is based on the specific identification method. Realized gains and losses on the sale of debt securities are recorded in interest and other, net. Realized gains or losses on the sale or exchange of equity securities and declines in value judged to be other than temporary are recorded in gains (losses) on equity securities, net. Marketable equity securities are presumed to be impaired if the fair value is less than the cost basis continuously for at least six months, absent evidence to the contrary.

NOTE 6: Investments (in part)

Trading Assets

Trading assets outstanding at fiscal year-ends were as follows:

(In Millions)	2004		2003	
	Net Unrealized Gains	Estimated Fair Value	Net Unrealized Gains	Estimated Fair Value
Debt instruments	$187	$2,772	$174	$2,321
Equity securities offsetting deferred compensation	81	339	60	304
Total trading assets	$268	$3,111	$234	$2,625

Continued

Net holding gains on fixed income debt instruments classified as trading assets were $80 million in 2004, $208 million in 2003 and $79 million in 2002. Net holding losses on the related derivatives were $(77) million in 2004, $(192) million in 2003 and $(75) million in 2002. These amounts were included in interest and other, net in the consolidated statements of income.

Available-for-Sale Investments

Available-for-sale investments at December 25, 2004 were as follows:

(In Millions)	Adjusted Cost	Gross Unrealized Gains	Gross Unrealized Losses	Estimated Fair Value
Commercial paper	$9,024	$—	$ (4)	$ 9,020
Floating rate notes	3,419	—	(1)	3,418
Bank time deposits	1,936	—	—	1,936
Corporate bonds	794	—	—	794
Marketable strategic equity securities	589	118	(51)	656
Preferred stock and other equity	200	—	—	200
Other debt securities	234	—	—	234
Total available-for-sale investments	**$16,196**	**$118**	**$(56)**	**$16,258**

Available-for-sale investments at December 27, 2003 were as follows:

(In Millions)	Adjusted Cost	Gross Unrealized Gains	Gross Unrealized Losses	Estimated Fair Value
Commercial paper	$ 9,948	$	$(1)	$ 9,947
Bank time deposits	1,900	—	—	1,900
Floating rate notes	1,078	—	—	1,078
Corporate bonds	703	—	—	703
Marketable strategic equity securities	467	47	—	514
Preferred stock and other equity	224	9	—	233
Other debt securities	352	—	—	352
Total available-for-sale investments	**$14,672**	**$56**	**$(1)**	**$14,727**

The duration of the unrealized losses on available-for-sale investments at December 25, 2004 did not exceed 12 months. The company's unrealized losses of $51 million on investments in marketable strategic equity securities at December 25, 2004 related primarily to a $450 million investment in Micron Technology, Inc. The unrealized losses were due to market-price movements. Management does not believe that any of the unrealized losses represented an other-than-temporary impairment based on its evaluation of available evidence as of December 25, 2004.

The company sold available-for-sale securities, primarily equity securities, with a fair value at the date of sale of $85 million in 2004, $39 million in 2003, and $114 million in 2002. The gross realized gains on these sales totaled $52 million in 2004, $16 million in 2003, and $15 million in 2002. The company recognized impairment losses on available-for-sale and non-marketable investments of $117 million in 2004, $319 million in 2003, and $524 million in 2002.

Questions:

1. What was the pretax amount of the unrealized gain or loss on available-for-sale securities that Intel included in other comprehensive income for 2004, excluding the reclassification amounts from sales?
2. How much did Intel include in accumulated other comprehensive income (pretax) at December 31, 2004 for available-for-sale securities?
3. How much gain or loss did Intel include in its income statement for 2004 related to marketable securities?

Financial Statement Classification

Investments in trading securities are always classified as current assets (if the company presents a classified balance sheet). Investments in available-for-sale securities are classified as current or noncurrent assets depending on whether or not they will be sold within one year or the operating cycle, whichever is longer.[16] For example, if the Kent Company investments in A and B are current and in C and D are noncurrent at December 31, 2006, it reports the $71,000 fair value (from our earlier example on page 711) as follows:

Assets	
Current Assets	
Temporary investment in available-for-sale securities (at cost)	$29,000
Plus: Allowance for change in value of investment	500
Temporary investment in available-for-sale securities (at fair value)	$29,500
Noncurrent Assets	
Investment in available-for-sale securities (at cost)	$39,000
Plus: Allowance for change in value of investment	2,500
Investment in available-for-sale securities (at fair value)	$41,500

Investments in held-to-maturity debt securities are classified as noncurrent assets unless they mature within the next year.

Kent Company would show the $3,000 ($500 + $2,500) related total balance of the Unrealized Increase in Value of Available-for-Sale Securities in stockholders' equity as follows:

Stockholders' Equity	
Accumulated other comprehensive income:	
Unrealized increase in value of available-for-sale securities	$3,000

Cash flows from purchases, sales, and maturities of available-for-sale securities and held-to-maturity securities are classified as cash flows from investing activities. The gross amounts of inflows and outflows are reported for each category. Cash flows from purchases, sales, and maturities of trading securities are classified as cash flows from operating activities.

FASB STATEMENT NO. 115: A CONCEPTUAL EVALUATION

7 Explain the conceptual issues regarding investments in marketable securities.

Before *FASB Statement No. 115*, investments in marketable equity securities were accounted for by the lower of cost or market (LCM) method. There were no specific general principles for investments in debt securities. Most companies used the cost method, but financial institutions followed regulatory accounting principles, which require that some securities be accounted for by the fair value method.

The LCM method was widely criticized for two primary reasons. First, it was argued that it was not a *relevant* value because it did not show the *liquidity* of the securities when the fair value exceeded the cost. In that situation, more funds could be obtained through a sale in the current market than was indicated by the balance sheet. Secondly, the method allowed companies to engage in what was often referred to as "gains trading." Gains trading meant that companies would sell those securities that had a fair value above cost so that the realized gain on the sale would be included in income.

The major controversies involved in the new principles focus on four issues: (1) fair value is required in the balance sheet for trading securities and available-for-sale securities, but amortized cost is required for held-to-maturity securities, (2) fair value is *not* required for certain liabilities, (3) unrealized holding gains and losses are reported in net

---

16. *FASB Statement No. 115, op. cit.,* par. 17.

income for trading securities but in other comprehensive income for available-for-sale securities, and (4) the classification of securities is based on management intent. The *Statement* was adopted by a 5-to-2 majority. The dissenters argued that a company should report all three categories at fair value, and include all unrealized holding gains and losses in net income.

Fair Value Is Required for Certain Investments

It may be argued that the fair value of trading securities and available-for-sale securities is more *relevant* than the LCM value. In particular, reporting the fair value may assist users in evaluating the performance of a company's investment strategies and increase the *comparability* of balance sheets. Fair value is the market's estimate of the present value of the net future cash flows of those securities, discounted to reflect both the current interest rate and the market's estimate of the *risk* associated with those cash flows.

The fair value of investments also may provide a better indication of the *financial flexibility*, or *solvency*, of companies, particularly for financial institutions that have a large portion of their assets in such securities. In a *liquidity* shortage, the fair value of investments is the amount available to cover a company's obligations.

It also may be argued that the fair value of held-to-maturity debt securities is *not* relevant. Amortized cost may provide relevant information because it focuses on the decision to acquire the asset, the earnings effects of that decision that will be realized over time, and the future recoverable value of the asset. Fair value ignores those concepts and focuses instead on the effects of transactions and events that do not directly involve the company. If a debt security is held to maturity, the maturity value will be realized and any interim unrealized holding gains and losses will reverse. If a company has no intent to sell a security and has no need to, then the fair value may *not* be relevant because that cash flow will not occur.

The FASB made the held-to-maturity category restrictive, so that the use of the amortized cost method must be justified for each investment in a debt security. At each acquisition, the company must establish the positive intent and ability to hold the security to maturity, which is *not* the same as the absence of an intent to sell. Thus the amortized cost method is appropriate if the security is actually held to maturity, but is not appropriate if the company merely has no intent to sell it. Of course, the classification does involve judgment and that judgment may prove to be incorrect. Also, the judgment may be changed by unforeseen circumstances such as changes in tax laws or in the security's credit risk.

Note that the arguments in favor of reporting fair value for some securities do not necessarily apply to the reporting of other assets, such as inventories. Therefore, the arguments do not invalidate the use of the LCM method for inventories.

Fair Value Is Not Required for Certain Liabilities

The FASB also considered requiring certain liabilities to be reported at fair value because they are "mirror images" of the assets. This was supported by financial institutions, which manage their interest rate risk by coordinating their holdings of financial assets and liabilities. Therefore, they argued that financial statements would provide a more *relevant* view of a company's exposure to *risk* if some liabilities were also reported at fair value. In other words, they felt that recognizing fair value on only one side of their portfolios introduced bias into their financial statements.

The FASB rejected the fair value reporting of liabilities because of the difficulty of (1) determining which liabilities should be reported at fair value, and (2) obtaining a *reliable* value because many of the liabilities do not trade in an established market. Also nonfinancial companies do not manage risk in the same way and use the proceeds from borrowing to invest in physical and intangible assets that are not reported at fair value. Since liabilities are not reported at fair value, the FASB concluded that it would not require all investments (i.e., those held to maturity) to be valued at fair value. The FASB admitted that this conclusion represents a compromise, and one of the dissenters voted against adoption partly for this reason. However, the FASB has since announced an *intent* to change GAAP so that liabilities would be reported at fair value.

Reporting of Unrealized Gains and Losses

Since trading securities are actively managed, the FASB concluded that income measurement for those securities is more relevant if it includes the results of changes in fair value—the unrealized holding gains and losses. Therefore, a company's net income includes the results of economic events that occur in the period and provides a better measure of the company's *return on investment.*

Partly in response to the issue of not reporting liabilities at fair value, the FASB concluded that including unrealized holding gains and losses in income for available-for-sale securities would create unnecessary volatility in a company's reported net income. Such volatility does not represent the way that the company manages its business and the impact of economic events of the period. In addition, when the intent is to hold securities for a long period, it is more likely that any unrealized holding gains and losses will offset before the sale occurs. Therefore, including those gains and losses in net income would also create unnecessary volatility in income. For these reasons, the FASB concluded that unrealized holding gains and losses on available-for-sale securities should not be included in net income, but instead should be reported as a component of other comprehensive income.

This reporting of unrealized holding gains and losses, however, does not eliminate the possibility of "gains trading," because the realized gain on a sale is the difference between the selling price and the cost of the security, and is included in net income. Note also that a company may tend to avoid selling a security classified as available for sale when its fair value is less than its cost. The sale would result in the recognition of a realized loss in net income. However, if the company continues to hold the security, the decline in value is included in other comprehensive income. Therefore the decision not to sell avoids the recognition of the decline in value in net income. Thus, companies are able to "manage" the amount of net income they report by selecting which securities to sell.

LINK TO ETHICAL DILEMMA

As you complete the audit of Blanket Insurance Company, an interesting item has come to your attention. One of the staff accountants on the job noted that at the end of each quarter, the company has sold a portion of its investments classified as available-for-sale. With each sale, the company was able to recognize a gain and increase income so that it would be able to just meet analyst forecasts. As the audit manager, you began to look into this finding and an interesting pattern has emerged. For the last five years, if the company's income appeared to fall short of the analysts' expectations, the company would sell available-for-sale investments that had increased in value and recognize a gain that would allow the company to meet the analysts' forecasts. Because the company has a significant investment portfolio, you had overlooked these sales in previous years. In discussions with the company's management, the CEO noted that this practice was part of the company's financial reporting strategy. Also, the CEO argued that the recognition of these gains and losses was entirely within GAAP. What is your reaction to the CEO's comments?

Classification of Securities Is Based on Management Intent

Classifying securities into three categories using management intent as a criterion to distinguish among the categories may result in an inconsistent application of the principles. Companies with three identical securities could account for those securities using three different accounting methods. Both issues may create a lack of *comparability*.

In addition, transfers between categories, which are also based partly on management intent and judgment, allow for the management of earnings because the gain (or loss) is included in net income. Combined with the opportunities for gains trading, the new principles may not produce sufficient *relevance*.

LINK TO INTERNATIONAL DIFFERENCES

International accounting standards also use the trading, available-for-sale, and held-to-maturity categories but apply them to all financial assets, not just investments in securities. The valuation methods are the same for each category as U.S. principles, but companies are allowed to make a one-time election to choose whether to record the changes in value of any financial asset or liability in net income or equity (which would be similar to other comprehensive income) if it meets certain restrictions. Additionally, international accounting standards allow for the reversal of impairment losses related to held-to-maturity securities and available-for-sale *equity* securities.

EQUITY METHOD

When an investor corporation owns a sufficiently large percentage of common stock, it is able to exert significant influence over the operating and financial policies of the investee corporation. In particular, the investor may be able to influence the investee's dividend policy. The dividends paid may be affected by the investor's cash needs, desire to raise its income, or by tax considerations. The fair value methods, which recognize income when dividends are received (declared), are not appropriate when significant influence exists because the investor could influence its income. Also, the fair value of the stock does not represent the cash that would be received if such a large number of shares were sold. The equity method of accounting is used to account for these investments.

8 Account for investments using the equity method.

The equity method is based on the existence of a material economic relationship between the investor and the investee. **APB Opinion No. 18 requires that an investor use the equity method when it is able to exercise significant influence over the operating and financial policies of an investee.** "Significant influence" is determined by factors such as:

- Representation on the board of directors
- Participation in policy-making processes
- Material intercompany transactions
- Interchange of managerial personnel
- Technological dependency.

In the absence of evidence to the contrary, however, **an investment of *20% or more* in the outstanding common stock of the investee leads to the *presumption* of significant influence and the use of the equity method.**[17] An investor also uses the equity method when significant influence exists even though the investor holds less than a 20% investment in the common stock of the investee.

On the other hand, there are situations in which an investor holds 20% or more of the outstanding common stock of an investee and does not have the ability to exercise

---

17. "The Equity Method of Accounting for Investments in Common Stock," *APB Opinion No. 18* (New York: AICPA, 1971), par. 17.

significant influence over the investee. In these cases, the investor does not use the equity method to account for the investment. For example, an investor holding an investment of 20% or more in the investee should *not* use the equity method when; (1) the investee challenges the investor's ability to excercise significant influence through litigation or complaints to governmental regulatory authorities; (2) the investor and investee sign an agreement that the investor surrenders significant rights as a shareholder; (3) a small group of shareholders hold majority ownership and operate the investee and ignore the views of the investor; (4) the investor needs more financial information to apply the equity method than is available to the investee's other shareholders, and cannot obtain that information (the application of the equity method requires information not typically included in published financial statements); or (5) the investor cannot obtain representation on the investee's board of directors.[18]

Accounting Procedures

When an investor company uses the equity method, it uses the following procedures:

- The investor initially records an investment in common stock at its acquisition cost. However, in contrast to the fair value method, the investor records income when it is *reported* by the investee.
- The investor records income and an increase in the carrying value of the investment account at an amount that is based on the investor's percentage of ownership in the investee.
- The investor records dividends received (or receivable) as reductions in the carrying value of the investment account when they are paid (or declared) by the investee.

Also, (1) since a material relationship is presumed, the investor removes from its investment account the effects of all intercompany items of revenue and expense to avoid "double-counting," and (2) if the acquisition cost is greater than the proportionate book value of the investee, the investor may recognize additional depreciation. Therefore, the investor must make certain adjustments to its investment income. The most frequent are to:

1. Eliminate intercompany transactions in the determination of investor income (e.g., a sale from the investor to the investee that results in revenue to the investor and an expense to the investee).
2. Depreciate the proportionate share of any difference between the fair values and book values of investee depreciable assets implied by the acquisition price of the investee shares. [In the event the investor cannot determine the fair value of the specific investee assets, the entire excess of cost (i.e., acquisition price) over the proportionate book value is treated as goodwill and is *not* amortized.]
3. Treat the proportionate share of investee extraordinary items as investor extraordinary items. The proportionate share of investee results of discontinued operations are treated similarly.[19]

In summary, the investor accounts for the investment and income under the equity method as follows:

$$\text{Investment} = \text{Acquisition Cost} + \frac{\text{Investor's Share of}}{\text{Investee Income}} - \text{Dividends Received}$$

---

18. "Criteria for Applying the Equity Method of Accounting for Investments in Common Stock," *FASB Interpretation No. 35* (Stamford, Conn.: FASB, 1981), par. 4.
19. In addition, the investor recognizes deferred income taxes for any difference between income reported under the equity method for financial reporting purposes and dividend income reported for income tax purposes. We do not consider deferred income taxes further in this chapter; we discuss them in Chapter 19.

where

$$\text{Investor's Share of Investee Income} = (\text{Investee's Net Income} \times \text{Ownership \%}) - \text{Adjustments}$$

and

$$\text{Dividends Received} = \text{Total Dividends Paid by Investee} \times \text{Ownership \%}$$

The use of the equity method more closely fits the requirements of accrual accounting because the investor's share in investee income is reported by the investor during the period in which it is earned rather than as cash is received. The equity method, therefore, supplies more relevant information for decision makers who rely on financial statements.

Example: Equity Method   Assume Cliborn Company purchases 4,200 shares of the S Company's outstanding common stock on January 1, 2007. (On that date, S Company had 16,800 shares outstanding, so Cliborn's investment is 25% and significant influence is presumed to exist.) Cliborn paid $125,000 for the shares, and on the date of acquisition obtains the following information concerning S Company:

	Balance Sheet Book Value	Fair Value
Depreciable assets (remaining life, 10 years)	$400,000	$450,000
Other nondepreciable assets (e.g., land)	190,000	246,000
Total	$590,000	$696,000
Liabilities	$200,000	$220,000
Common stock	250,000	
Retained earnings	140,000	
Total	$590,000	

There were no intercompany transactions during the year. S Company paid a $20,000 dividend on August 27, 2007, and reported net income for 2007 of $81,000, consisting of ordinary income of $73,000 and an extraordinary gain of $8,000. Cliborn Company records these events as follows:

1. To record the original investment on January 1, 2007:

Investment in Stock: S Company	125,000	
Cash		125,000

2. To record the receipt of dividends on August 27, 2007:

Cash	5,000	
Investment in Stock: S Company		5,000
(0.25 × $20,000)		

The effect of this transaction is simply to exchange one asset (Investment in Stock: S Company) for another (Cash).

3. To record Cliborn Company's 25% share in the year's net income on December 31, 2007:

Investment in Stock: S Company		
(0.25 × $81,000)	20,250	
Investment Income: Ordinary		
(0.25 × $73,000)		18,250
Investment Income: Extraordinary		
(0.25 × $8,000)		2,000

Note that Cliborn increases the investment account by its share of the total net income, and separates the investment income into its share of the ordinary and extraordinary income.

4. To depreciate the increase in the recorded value of depreciable assets acquired:

Investment Income: Ordinary	1,250	
Investment in Stock: S Company		
($12,500 ÷ 10)		1,250

The depreciable assets acquired have a fair value that exceeds book value by $50,000 ($450,000 − $400,000) and the remaining useful life of the assets is 10 years. Cliborn acquired 25% of this increase in asset value, so it depreciates $12,500 (0.25 × $50,000) of the additional depreciable asset value over the remaining useful life of the assets according to the matching principle. This $12,500 divided by the 10-year life results in $1,250 additional depreciation, which Cliborn records directly as a deduction from the ordinary investment income and the investment on December 31, 2007. ♦

The investment must also be reviewed for impairment.[20] *APB Opinion No. 18* requires a company to recognize an impairment loss and reduce the investment to its fair value if there is an "other than temporary" decline in value, as we discuss later in the chapter. ♦

Financial Statement Disclosures

Cliborn computes the carrying value of its Investment in Stock: S Company account by adding the reported income for the year and deducting the dividends, depreciation, and goodwill amortization. It reports the Investment in Stock: S Company account in the long-term investment section of its December 31, 2007 balance sheet. This account has a carrying value of $139,000, computed as follows:

Investment in S Company

Acquisition price January 1, 2007		$125,000
Add: Share of 2007 reported ordinary income	$18,250	
Share of 2007 reported extraordinary income	2,000	20,250
		$145,250
Less: Dividends received August 27, 2007	$ 5,000	
Depreciation on excess fair value of		
acquired assets		
($12,500 ÷ 10; see earlier computation)	1,250	(6,250)
Carrying value		$139,000

The total amount of investee income that Cliborn reports on its income statement for 2007 is $19,000. This amount consists of $17,000 that it reports as income from continuing operations and $2,000 that it reports as an extraordinary item. The accompanying notes to the financial statements include a supporting schedule reconciling these amounts. This schedule appears as follows:

Income from Investment

Share of 2007 ordinary income	$18,250
Less: Depreciation on excess fair value of acquired assets	(1,250)
Ordinary investment income	$17,000
Plus: Share of investee extraordinary income	2,000
Net investment income	$19,000

---

20. "Goodwill and Other Intangible Assets," *FASB Statement of Financial Accounting Standards No. 142* (Norwalk, Conn.: FASB, 2001), par. 40 states that any implied goodwill at the purchase of the equity investment is *not* reviewed for impairment.

Special Issues

Sometimes an investor acquires enough additional common shares during a year to justify a change from the fair value method to the equity method, or an investor may dispose of a portion of its investment so that a change from the equity method to the fair value method is necessary. Additionally, an investment carried under the equity method may be acquired for a cost that is less than the fair value of the assets. Or investments carried under the equity method may have impairments and/or declines in value that are not temporary. Finally, a company may acquire enough of an investee's outstanding common stock to issue consolidated financial statements.

Change to Equity Method

When an investor currently using the fair value method acquires enough additional common shares during a year to exercise significant influence over the investee, the investor is required to adopt the equity method of accounting. It is most likely (and assumed in this discussion) that the shares were accounted for as available-for-sale securities. When the equity method is adopted, the investor restates its investment in the investee by debiting the Investment account and crediting Retained Earnings for its *previous* percentage of investee income (less dividends) for the period from the original date of acquisition to the date that significant influence was obtained. This is a retrospective restatement (adjustment). The company also eliminates any amounts included in the allowance and unrealized increase/decrease accounts that it used to record these shares at fair value. Thereafter, the equity method is applied in the usual manner based on the *current* percentage ownership.

For example, assume that on January 2, 2006, Short Company purchased as its only investment 15% of the outstanding common stock of J Corporation for $150,000 (when the book value of net assets was $1,000,000). At the end of 2006, the J Corporation reported net income of $300,000 and paid dividends of $60,000; at this time, the market value of the shares was $186,000 so the company wrote up the carrying value of the investment (using an allowance account) to fair value. On January 2, 2007, to exert significant influence on J Corporation, Short Company purchased an additional 25% of the outstanding common stock of the J Corporation for $310,000.

We show the journal entries that Short Company recorded in 2006 and 2007 related to this information in the upper portion of Example 15-5. In 2006, Short Company used the fair value method to account for its investment. It recorded the dividends received as dividend revenue and made an adjustment to the Allowance and Increase/Decrease accounts to record the increase in the investment's carrying value to fair value. In 2007, the Short Company recorded the $310,000 additional investment that increased its ownership to 40%. The company also made two journal entries to account for its *previous* 15% ownership under the equity method. First, it recognized $45,000 ($300,000 × 0.15) of the 2006 net income of J Corporation as an increase in its Investment account and in Retained Earnings. Second, it reduced its Investment account and Retained Earnings by $9,000, its share of the 2006 dividends of J Corporation. (Note that Retained Earnings was adjusted directly for the share of net income and dividends because these are from the *prior* year.) Thus, the company recognized an increase in value of $36,000 ($45,000 − $9,000) in the Investment and Retained Earnings accounts. The company also "reversed" its December 31, 2006 adjustment to increase the carrying value of the investment. Because the purchase price (fair value) of the shares was equal to their underlying book value, no additional depreciation was recorded. Had this adjustment been necessary, it would have been recorded (based on the 15% ownership) as a reduction in the Investment and Retained Earnings accounts.

The lower portion of Example 15-5 explains the rationale behind the adjustments. Note that the book value of the net assets of J Corporation was $1,240,000 on January 2, 2007. By increasing the $150,000 initial investment for the $45,000 share of 2006 net income and decreasing it for the $9,000 share of the 2006 dividends, the book value of

---

EXAMPLE 15-5 **Journal Entries to Illustrate a Change to the Equity Method**

Fair Value Method

1/2/06	Investment in J	150,000	
	Cash		150,000
12/31/06	Cash	9,000[a]	
	Dividend Revenue[b]		9,000
12/31/06	Allowance for Change in Value of Investment	36,000	
	Unrealized Increase/ Decrease in Value of Available-for-Sale Securities		36,000

Change to Equity Method

1/2/07	Investment in J	310,000	
	Cash		310,000
1/2/07	Investment in J	45,000[c]	
	Retained Earnings		45,000
1/2/07	Retained Earnings	9,000	
	Investment in J		9,000
1/2/07	Unrealized Increase/Decrease in Value of Available-for-Sale Securities	36,000	
	Allowance for Change in Value of Investment		36,000

Comparison of Book Values

	J Corporation Net Assets	Investment in J
Book value, 1/2/06	$1,000,000	$150,000
+ Net Income for 2006	300,000	45,000
− Dividends for 2006	(60,000)	(9,000)
Book value, 1/2/07	$1,240,000	$186,000 (15%[d])
Additional investment (25%)		310,000 (25%)
Book value, 1/2/07 (40%)		$496,000

a. $60,000 × 0.15
b. Closed to Retained Earnings
c. $300,000 × 0.15
d. $186,000 ÷ $1,240,000

---

the Investment account is $186,000 (prior to the additional investment), or 15% of the $1,240,000 net assets of J Corporation on January 2, 2007. Increasing the $186,000 for the $310,000 (25%) additional investment results in an Investment account balance of $496,000, or 40% of the net assets. From this point on, Short Company will apply the equity method using the 40% ownership interest.

Change from Equity Method

Sometimes an investor using the equity method sells a portion of the investment so that its portion of ownership falls below 20%, or the investor may lose significant influence over the investee. Under these conditions, the use of the equity method is no longer appropriate and the investor no longer accrues its share of investee income. However, previously recorded income remains as a part of the book value of the Investment account. The company then accounts for the investment under the fair value method. The investor company deducts from the book value of its Investment account any dividends received in later periods that exceed its share of income for those periods.

Acquisition at Less Than Fair Value

When the purchase price of an investment in common stock accounted for by the equity method is less than the proportionate fair value of the net assets acquired, the investment initially is recorded at cost. However, the difference between the cost and proportionate fair value of the net assets acquired (i.e., "negative goodwill") is allocated to reduce the value assigned to noncurrent assets, as we discussed in Chapter 12.

Impairment: Declines Other Than Temporary

The investor must recognize "other than temporary" declines in the value of investments accounted for under the equity method. Evidence of these declines may be provided by the bankruptcy of the investee, by lengthy declines in the market value of the stock, or by a number of years of operating losses. These events bring into question the ability of the investee to sustain income sufficient to justify the carrying value of the investment. When a decline that is considered to be other than temporary occurs, the investor debits a Loss account and credits the Investment account for the difference between the carrying value of the investment and the fair value. If the market value of the investment later increases, the investor does not recognize the recovery in value.

Consolidated Financial Statements

When an investor using the equity method acquires *control* over the investee's operations, the entity concept is enhanced by preparing financial statements for the combined set of companies. However, the two (or more) companies continue to maintain separate accounting records. During the year, the investor accounts for its investment in the investee by the equity method, as we previously discussed. At the end of the year, the accounting results of the investor and investee are combined (and the Investment account is eliminated) and reported in consolidated financial statements.

The logic of consolidation accounting is to present financial statements for a single economic entity, even though there are separate legal entities. The two guiding principles for the preparation of consolidated financial statements are:

1. The entity cannot make a profit by selling to itself. That is, intercompany sales and profits must be eliminated from the consolidated financial statements.
2. The entity cannot own or owe itself. That is, intercompany receivables and payables are not reported in consolidated financial statements.

Discussion of the preparation of consolidated financial statements is included in an advanced accounting book.

LINK TO INTERNATIONAL DIFFERENCES

The application of the equity method is generally the same under both international and U.S. accounting standards. However, the U.S. standards require more detailed disclosures.

SECURE YOUR KNOWLEDGE 15-2

- The transfer of a security between investment categories is accounted for at the fair value at the time of the transfer, with the accounting for any unrealized gain or loss dependent on the type of transfer.
- If a held-to-maturity or available-for-sale security experiences a decline in fair value that is judged to be "other than temporary," an impairment is recognized in income as a realized loss with the fair value becoming the new "cost" of the security.
- If the investor company is able to exert significant influence over the investee company, the fair value methods are inappropriate and the investor is required to use the equity method.

(continued)

Under the equity method:

- Significant influence is presumed if the investor owns between 20% and 50% of the investee's outstanding common stock.
- The initial investment is recorded at cost, is increased by the investor's proportionate share of the investee's reported income, and is reduced by the investor's proportionate share of any dividends declared.
- The investor depreciates its proportionate share of any difference between the fair value and the book value of the investee's depreciable assets by reducing the investment account.
- If a company changes its accounting for investments to the equity method, a retrospective restatement (adjustment) is made to adjust the accounts to the balance they would have shown if the equity method had always been used.
- If the equity method is no longer appropriate (e.g., the investor's ownership percentage falls below 20%), the company will then account for the investment under the fair value method.

ADDITIONAL ISSUES FOR INVESTMENTS

9 Describe additional issues for investments.

Additional issues for investments include accounting for investments in nonmarketable securities, stock dividends and stock splits, stock warrants, convertible bonds, the cash surrender value of life insurance, and investments in funds. We discuss each of these in the following sections.

Nonmarketable Securities

Nonmarketable securities are those that are not traded in a "qualifying" market (e.g., New York Stock Exchange), as we discussed earlier in the chapter. For example, shares or bonds issued by a privately held company are considered nonmarketable (even though they may be traded between individual investors). Investments in nonmarketable securities are outside the scope of *FASB Statement No. 115*. Therefore, there is no requirement to report them at fair value. Companies typically report them at their historical cost and, therefore, ignore any unrealized holding gains and losses.

Stock Dividends and Splits

Corporations occasionally distribute additional shares of stock to current shareholders (as we discuss in Chapters 16 and 17). In such cases the investor retains the same relative percentage of ownership in the investee because it does not acquire an additional percentage of outstanding shares. Consequently, the investor records no income from the distribution when it receives the new shares. The fair value of each share typically falls. The fair value at year-end, however, is simply the new number of shares multiplied by the year-end fair value.

The investor does not make a formal journal entry to record the receipt of shares of stock from either a stock dividend or a stock split. However, its cost is now spread over a larger number of shares, thereby lowering its average unit cost of the shares. It records a memorandum entry to assign the average unit cost to the old and new shares. It then uses this average cost when there is a sale transaction involving the shares.

For example, assume that the Smith Corporation purchased 2,000 shares of Kell Company common stock for $30 per share, or a total of $60,000. Two months later Kell issued a 50% stock dividend and Smith Corporation received another 1,000 shares. Smith records a memo entry for the receipt of the stock dividend as follows:

> **Memo: Received 1,000 shares of Kell Company common stock as a stock dividend. The cost of the shares is now $20 per share, computed as follows: $60,000 ÷ 3,000 (2,000 + 1,000) shares.**

Later, Smith sold 500 of the shares for $25 per share, and the fair value at the most recent balance sheet date was $23 per share. Smith records the *sale* of the 500 shares as follows:

Cash (500 × $25)	12,500	
Investment in Available-for-Sale Securities		
(500 × $20)		10,000
Gain on Sale of Investment [500 × ($25 − $20)]		2,500
Unrealized Increase/Decrease in Value of Available-		
for-Sale Securities [500 × ($23 − $20)]	1,500	
Allowance for Change in Value of Investment		1,500

Note that the reduction of the Investment account and calculation of the Gain are based on the $20 per share cost and not the $30 original purchase price. Smith still owns a total of 2,500 (2,000 + 1,000 − 500) shares and will report them on its balance sheet at fair value.

Stock Warrants

As we discussed in Chapter 14, stock warrants are certificates that enable their holders to purchase a specified number of shares of common stock at a predetermined price. They generally are issued to current stockholders as evidence of preemptive rights (discussed in Chapter 16), or for other reasons. Each stockholder usually receives a warrant for each share owned, although it may take more than one warrant to purchase a share. Warrants are defined as equity securities under *FASB Statement No. 115*.

    Stock warrants have value because they usually allow the holder the right to purchase additional shares at a fixed price, usually slightly less than their current market price. Thus, the warrants for these rights will trade on the stock market soon after they are issued. Eventually, the right to purchase additional shares expires, so the stockholder (the investor corporation) who receives these warrants has three alternatives:

Analysis

1. Purchase additional shares by exercising the warrants.
2. Sell the warrants.
3. Do nothing and allow the warrants to expire.

Option 3 obviously is not a good choice in most circumstances because by selling the warrants, the shareholder can convert them into cash and still retain the original number of shares held. The shareholder thus should choose either alternative 1 or 2, although either the exercise or the sale of the warrants creates a valuation issue. To determine the cost of the new investment shares, or the gain or loss on the sale of the warrants, a cost must be assigned to the warrants. Since no additional cost is incurred when the warrants are received by the investor corporation, it must assign a portion of the cost of the stock to the warrants upon their receipt. This amount is determined by using a weighted average based on the market value of the stock *ex rights* (without the rights attached) and the market value of the warrants (rights) as we discussed in Chapter 14.[21] The accounting for the purchase of additional shares by exercising the warrants (or the sale of the warrants) would use the amount assigned to the warrants.

Convertible Bonds

As we discussed in Chapter 14, some bonds (and preferred stock) carry a conversion privilege that allows investors to exchange them for common stock. Investments in convertible bonds are *not* included in the held-to-maturity category because the intent is that conversion will occur before the bonds mature. These investments in convertible bonds are included in the available-for-sale (or trading) category and valued at fair value.

---

21. If the market value is not available when the warrants are received, this process must be delayed until the market value becomes known.

Therefore, conversion requires only a memorandum entry, which specifies the number of shares that are now owned instead of the bonds. Also, the cost per share is calculated to help account for future transactions, such as the sale of the shares.

Cash Surrender Value of Life Insurance

Since a company is dependent on the skill and expertise of its officers, frequently it will purchase insurance policies on their lives. The reason for this is that the company will be at least partly compensated for the loss of executive skill in the event of an unexpected death.

Many insurance policies allow a portion of accumulated premiums to build up as a savings plan; if the policy is canceled, this savings plan or **cash surrender value** of the policy is returned to the company buying the life insurance policy. When a company is guaranteed a return equal to the amount of the cash surrender value of the policy, part of each annual premium represents an investment. The company records the portion of the yearly premium that does not increase the cash surrender value of the policy as insurance expense. It includes the amount of the cash surrender value of life insurance policies as a long-term investment on the balance sheet. The investment increases from year to year and is stated in the policy. Typically, the company records the yearly increase in this investment at the end of the year. Additionally, some life insurance policies pay dividends. The company holding such a policy treats any dividends received as a reduction of insurance expense.

For example, suppose that at the beginning of the year the Mele Corporation pays an annual insurance premium of $5,500 to cover the lives of its officers. It records the payment as follows:

Prepaid Insurance	5,500	
Cash		5,500

According to the terms of the insurance contract, the cash surrender value of the policies increases from $7,200 to $8,300 during that year. The adjusting entry at the end of the year to record the Insurance Expense and the increase in the Cash Surrender Value of Life Insurance is as follows:

Insurance Expense	4,400	
Cash Surrender Value of Life Insurance		
($8,300 − $7,200)	1,100	
Prepaid Insurance		5,500

Upon the death of any of the insured officers, Mele would collect the face amount of the insurance policy and credit the cash surrender value account to close out the balance in the account related to this policy. The difference between the proceeds and the cash surrender value is reported as an ordinary gain, because the insuring of officers' lives is a usual operating procedure. For income tax purposes the premiums are not tax deductible and the gain is not taxable.

Investments in Funds

Companies may place assets in special funds for specific purposes, and some of these assets then become unavailable for normal operations because of indenture or other contractual arrangements. Special funds may be current, such as petty cash funds, or they may be long term. The most common long-term funds are as follows:

- Funds used to accumulate cash to retire long-term liabilities (**sinking funds**)
- Funds used to retire preferred stock (**stock redemption funds**)
- Funds used to purchase long-term assets (**plant expansion funds**)

A company reports its long-term funds as investments on its balance sheet. It is important to understand the distinction between a fund and an appropriation (restriction) of retained earnings. A fund actually sets aside cash and other assets to accomplish specific objectives. In contrast, an appropriation of retained earnings discloses legal or contractual restrictions (as we discuss in Chapter 17). An appropriation does not provide any cash.

Accounting for long-term funds requires separate accounts. In essence, the fund is accounted for as an individual set of books. For example, the accounts that a company might use in connection with a bond sinking fund are Sinking Fund Cash, Sinking Fund Securities, Sinking Fund Revenues, Sinking Fund Expenses, Allowance for Change in Value of Sinking Fund Securities, Unrealized Increase/Decrease in Value of Sinking Fund Securities, Gain on Sale of Sinking Fund Securities, and Loss on Sale of Sinking Fund Securities. This company makes journal entries to these accounts to record its (1) initial and/or periodic cash contributions to the sinking fund, (2) investments in various securities to earn dividends and interest, (3) expenses to administer the fund, (4) unrealized increases and decreases in value, and (5) sale of the securities to acquire cash to retire the bonds. The company reports any revenues, expenses, gains, and losses in the usual manner on its income statement.

Investment Transactions and Operating Cash Flows

We discussed how a company reports its investments on its balance sheet and statement of cash flows in various sections earlier in the chapter. We also discussed how a company reports any gains or losses related to its investments on its income statement. We did not discuss how a company reports certain investment-related transactions in the operating activities section of its statement of cash flows. A company includes the cash received for interest in the operating activities section. Even though the interest received is related to an investing activity, GAAP requires it to be included in operating activities because the related interest revenue is included in the company's income statement. If a company has amortized a discount (premium) on an investment in bonds, under the indirect method the company subtracts (adds) the discount (premium) to net income in the operating activities section of its statement of cash flows. Similarly, if a company is accounting for an investment under the equity method, it subtracts (adds) any increase (decrease) in the equity investment to net income in the operating activities section.

APPENDIX: DERIVATIVES OF FINANCIAL INSTRUMENTS

Companies have always held or issued financial instruments. However, derivatives of those financial instruments are relatively new and are becoming increasingly common. Companies often use derivatives to reduce the risk of adverse changes in interest rates, commodity prices, and foreign currency exchange rates. It is important for financial statements to show the effects of that risk management. In this Appendix, we discuss recording and reporting issues as they relate to selected derivative transactions.

A **financial instrument** is cash, evidence of an ownership interest in an entity, or a contract that both (1) imposes on one entity a contractual obligation (a) to deliver cash or another financial instrument to a second entity or (b) to exchange other financial instruments on potentially unfavorable terms with the second entity, and (2) conveys to that second entity a contractual right (a) to receive cash or another financial instrument from the first entity or (b) to exchange other financial instruments on potentially favorable terms with the first entity.[22] Thus, financial instruments include cash, accounts and notes receivable, accounts and notes payable, and investments in debt and equity securities, as well as bonds payable and common stock. We discuss accounting for these financial instruments throughout the book.

10 Account for derivatives of financial instruments. (Appendix)

---

22. "Accounting for Derivative Instruments and Hedging Activities," *FASB Statement of Financial Accounting Standards No. 133* (Norwalk, Conn.: FASB 1998), Appendix F and "Accounting for Certain Derivative Instruments and Certain Hedging Activities," *FASB Statement of Financial Accounting Standards No. 138* (Norwalk, Conn.: FASB 2000).

A **derivative financial instrument** (or simply **derivative**) derives its value from an underlying asset or index. Thus, derivatives include futures, forward, swap, and option contracts. Derivative contracts can be very complex, and they involve the following concepts:[23]

1. A derivative's cash flows or fair value must fluctuate and vary based on the changes in one or more underlying variables.
2. The contract must be based on one or more notional (defined later) amounts or payment provisions or both, even though title to that amount never changes. The underlying and notional amounts determine the amount of the settlement.
3. Many contracts require no initial net investment.
4. The contract can be readily settled by a net cash payment.

A recent study indicated that more than $41 trillion of derivative contracts are outstanding worldwide. Derivatives contracts have been in the news in recent years and include situations in which **Procter & Gamble** sustained significant losses, **Bankers Trust** has been sued by numerous clients, **Barings Bank** in London was bankrupted, **Orange County, California**, lost millions of dollars, and **Fannie Mae** restated its results by $9 billion.

A **hedge** is a means of protecting against a financial loss. For a derivative to be considered a hedge, it must be "highly effective" in offsetting risk exposure because of changes in fair values or cash flows of the hedged item. The three types of hedges are:

- Fair value hedges
- Cash flow hedges
- Hedges of foreign currency exposures of net investments in foreign operations

FASB Statement No. 133 requires a different accounting treatment for each type of hedge. Accounting for derivatives can be very complex. To explain the basic issues, we show the accounting for a fair value hedge using an interest-rate swap, and briefly discuss the accounting issues for a cash flow hedge (the third type is beyond the scope of this book). In our examples we use simplifying assumptions (such as a flat yield curve) and facts so that you can understand the basic accounting issues and avoid many real-world complexities regarding valuation.

An **interest-rate swap** is an agreement in which two companies agree to exchange the interest payments on debt over a specified period. The interest payments are based on a principal amount that often is referred to as a **notional** (i.e., imaginary) amount because the swap does not involve an actual exchange of principal at either inception or maturity. An example of a *fair value hedge* is an interest rate swap in which a company *receives* a fixed rate of interest and *pays* a variable rate. An example of a *cash flow hedge* is an interest rate swap in which a company *receives* a variable rate of interest and *pays* a fixed rate.

Although we discuss investments in this chapter, we focus on accounting for a derivative of a financial instrument that is a liability, because they are more common for nonfinancial companies. However, a derivative can result in either an "investment" asset or a liability being recognized by either party, as market conditions change. The other company involved in the original transaction, a bank in our example, has a financial instrument that is an asset.

FAIR VALUE HEDGE

A fair value hedge protects against the risk from changes in value caused by *fixed* terms, rates, or prices. For example, a company with debt that has a fixed interest rate that enters into an interest rate swap to receive a fixed rate of interest and pay a variable rate protects itself against paying a higher than market rate of interest if interest rates decline. Of

---

23. *FASB Statement of Financial Accounting Standards No. 133, ibid.,* par 6–9.

course, it will pay a higher rate than the fixed rate if interest rates rise. Another example would be a company that purchases a commodity, such as oil, and agrees to a fixed price contract. It can enter into a futures contract so that if, for example, the purchase price of oil decreases, it pays an above market price for the oil that is offset by the value of the futures contract. In each case, the company has converted a fixed-rate contract (for interest or oil) into a variable-rate contract.

For a fair value hedge, *FASB Statement No. 133* requires a company to recognize in its current *net income* (1) any gain or loss from a change in the fair value of the derivative (fair value hedge), and (2) any gain or loss from the change in the fair value of the financial instrument being hedged, along with any interest revenue or expense. As a result the company reports both the derivative and the financial instrument on its balance sheet at their respective fair values. Note that the FASB is requiring the use of the *fair value method* in the valuation of derivatives *and* the related financial instruments.

To illustrate the accounting for an interest rate swap that is a fair value hedge, suppose that Laki Company has had a $1 million, 6% bank loan (the financial instrument) from MidAmerica Bank outstanding for several years. On January 1, 2007, when the $1 million loan (debt) has five years remaining, Laki contracts with Jordan Investment Bank (a swaps dealer) for a five-year interest-rate swap (the derivative) with a $1 million notional amount. The company agrees to *receive* from Jordan a fixed interest rate of 6% and to *pay* Jordan an interest rate each year that is variable. The variable rate is the LIBOR (London Interbank Offer Rate) interest rate at the beginning of each year. In other words, Laki has converted ("swapped") its fixed interest rate debt into the variable LIBOR interest rate debt. If the LIBOR interest rate debt is 5.3% at January 1, 2007, the company has converted 6% debt into 5.3% debt for that year. This type is called a "matched" swap because the notional amount is the same as the actual loan amount and the fixed interest rate on the derivative is equal to the fixed interest rate paid on the loan. Therefore, the derivative is an effective hedge of the risk of interest rate changes. We summarize the facts for the loan and swap involving Laki Company, MidAmerica Bank, and Jordan Investment Bank in Example 15-6.

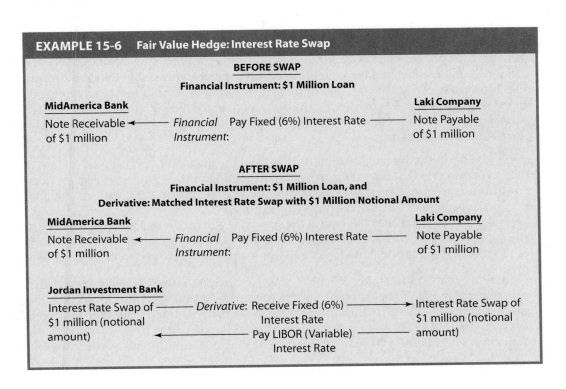

EXAMPLE 15-6   Fair Value Hedge: Interest Rate Swap

The Laki Company recorded the following journal entry for the financial instrument (the original loan):

Original Bank Loan

Cash	1,000,000	
Notes Payable		1,000,000

Laki accounts for the derivative (the fair value hedge) in 2007 and 2008, as follows:

Interest Payment on Loan: December 31, 2007

Laki pays MidAmerica the fixed rate of 6% on the $1 million loan and records this as interest expense, as follows:

Interest Expense	60,000	
Cash		60,000

Interest Rate Swap Payment: December 31, 2007

Since the LIBOR rate that was set at January 1, 2007 is 5.3%, there is a net payment (settlement) between Laki Company and Jordan Investment Bank. Since Laki owes to Jordan the LIBOR 5.3% rate and receives from Jordan the fixed 6% rate, it receives from Jordan the *net* 0.7% on the notional amount of $1 million, or $7,000. Laki records the cash received as a *decrease* to interest expense, as follows:

Cash	7,000	
Interest Expense		7,000

Thus, Laki records a total interest expense of $53,000 ($60,000 − $7,000) in 2007, which is the equivalent of the variable rate of 5.3% on the $1 million loan.

Fair Values and Gains and Losses: December 31, 2006

The fair value method uses market values to recognize the value of derivatives if they are available, such as for futures contracts traded on exchanges. However, many derivatives are forward contracts that are custom-designed for the two entities, and market values are not available for such distinctive contracts, as in this example. In these cases, discounted cash flows are used to value the derivative.

Laki determines the gain or loss for 2007 on the derivative (fair value hedge) by computing the net present value of the future cash flows over the remaining life of the derivative. It is based on the difference between the fixed interest rate contracted in the derivative and the current market fixed interest rate applied to the notional amount for the remaining life of the swap. Note that this rate is typically different than the LIBOR rate that is a short-term variable rate and has no inherent fair value because it can be obtained at any time. Thus, there are three interest rates:

1. The fixed interest rate (6%) on the loan and the derivative.
2. The variable LIBOR interest rate at the beginning of the year that is used to determine the swap payment at the end of the year (5.3% for 2007, and we assume it changes to 6.8% for 2008).
3. The fixed market rate of interest at the end of the year for the remaining life of the loan or derivative (7% for a four-year loan or derivative at December 31, 2007, and we assume it changes to 5.5% for a three-year loan or derivative at December 31, 2008).

We assume that, at December 31, 2007, the fixed market rate of interest for the four-year remaining life of the derivative is 7% (compared to the LIBOR rate of 6.8% that is set at January 1, 2008). Thus, the difference in the fixed interest rates at the end of 2007 is 1% (6% fixed rate − 7% four-year market rate). The $33,872 value of the derivative is $10,000 per year (the difference of 1% multiplied by the notional amount of $1,000,000) discounted at the current fixed market rate of 7% for the remaining four years, as follows:

$$\text{Present value of derivative} = \$10,000 \times 3.387211 \; (n = 4, \; i = 0.07)$$
$$= \$33,872$$

A swap derivative *liability* and *loss* exist because the 7% current market rate is higher than the 6% fixed interest rate that Laki receives on the derivative. Laki records the liability and loss as follows:

Loss in Value of Derivative	33,872	
Liability from Interest Rate Swap		33,872

Since interest rates have changed, the value of the Laki's debt (financial instrument) has also changed. The increase in interest rates decreases the value of the debt. The current value of the debt is computed based on the 7% market rate as follows:

$$\text{Present value of principal} = \$1,000,000 \times 0.762895 \; (n = 4, \; i = 0.07)$$
$$= \$762,895$$

$$\text{Present value of interest} = \$60,000 \times 3.387211 \; (n = 4, \; i = 0.07)$$
$$= \$203,233$$

$$\text{Total present value of debt} = \$762,895 + \$203,233$$
$$= \$966,128$$

Laki recognizes the $33,872 ($1,000,000 − $966,128) decrease in the value of the debt and the related *gain* as follows:

Notes Payable	33,872	
Gain in Value of Debt		33,872

The Laki Company reports both the $33,872 gain in the value of the debt and the $33,872 loss in value of the derivative in the other items section of its 2007 income statement. There is no net effect because it is an effective hedge. Laki reports the $33,872 derivative liability and the $966,128 ($1,000,000 − $33,872) value of the note payable on its December 31, 2007 balance sheet. Therefore, its total liability in regard to this debt is $1,000,000.

Interest Payment on Loan: December 31, 2008

Laki pays MidAmerica the fixed rate of 6% on the $1 million loan and records this as interest expense, as follows:

Interest Expense	60,000	
Cash		60,000

Interest Rate Swap Payment: December 31, 2008

We assume that at the beginning of 2008, the LIBOR interest rate is 6.8%. Since Laki pays Jordan the LIBOR 6.8% rate and receives from Jordan the fixed 6% rate, it pays to Jordan the *net* 0.8% on the notional amount of $1 million, or $8,000. Laki records the payment as an *increase* in interest expense, as follows:

Interest Expense	8,000	
Cash		8,000

Thus, Laki records a total interest expense of $68,000 ($60,000 + $8,000) in 2008, which is the equivalent of the variable rate of 6.8% on the $1 million loan.

Fair Values and Gains and Losses: December 31, 2008

Laki again determines the gain or loss for 2008 on the derivative (fair value hedge) by computing the net present value of the future cash flows over the remaining life of the derivative. It is again based on the difference between the fixed interest rate contracted in the derivative and the current market fixed interest rate, applied to the notional amount for the remaining life of the swap. We assume that at December 31, 2008 the three-year fixed interest rate is 5.5%. Thus, the difference in fixed interest rates at the end of 2008 is 0.5% (6% fixed rate − 5.5% three-year market rate). The $13,490 value of the derivative is $5,000 per year (the difference of 0.5% multiplied by the notional amount of $1,000,000) discounted at the current market rate of 5.5% for the remaining three years, computed as follows:

$$\text{Present value of derivative} = \$5,000 \times 2.697933 \ (n = 3, i = 0.055)$$
$$= \$13,490$$

A swap derivative *asset* and *gain* exist because the current 5.5% market rate is lower than the 6% fixed interest rate that Laki receives on the derivative. So Laki has moved from a $33,872 liability at the end of 2007 to a $13,490 asset position at the end of 2008, and has a $47,362 ($33,872 + $13,490) gain which it records as follows:

Liability from Interest Rate Swap	33,872	
Asset from Interest Rate Swap	13,490	
Gain in Value of Derivative		47,362

Again, since interest rates have changed, the value of Laki's debt (financial instrument) has also changed. The decrease in interest rates increases the value of the debt. The current value of the debt is computed based on the 5.5% current market rate as follows:

$$\text{Present value of principal} = \$1,000,000 \times 0.851614 \ (n = 3, i = 0.055)$$
$$= \$851,614$$

$$\text{Present value of interest} = \$60,000 \times 2.697933 \ (n = 3, i = 0.055)$$
$$= \$161,876$$

$$\text{Total present value of debt} = \$851,614 + \$161,876$$
$$= \$1,013,490$$

Laki recognizes the $47,362 ($1,013,490 current value − $966,128 previous value) increase and the related loss as follows:

Loss in Value of Debt	47,362	
Notes Payable		47,362

Reporting

The Laki Company reports the $47,362 gain in value of the derivative and the $47,362 loss in value of the debt in the other items section of its 2008 income statement. There is no net effect for this effective hedge. It reports the $13,490 derivative asset as a long-term investment and the $1,013,490 ($966,128 + $47,362) value of the note payable on its December 31, 2008 balance sheet. Note that Laki's *net* liability in regard to the debt is still $1,000,000. Laki would account for the loan and the derivative (fair value hedge) in a similar manner for the years 2009 through 2012.

In summary, the Laki Company has converted a fixed interest rate bank loan into a variable interest rate loan with this interest rate swap. Laki pays a variable net interest rate on this loan and reports the amount each year as interest expense on its income statement. Laki reports the derivative asset or liability and the related financial instrument (note payable) on its balance sheet at their respective fair values. There is no effect from the change in the fair value of this derivative on the income statement because the change in the fair value of the derivative is offset by the change in the fair value of the financial instrument (i.e., an effective hedge of the fixed rate debt). Note that when a hedge is not perfect or is ineffective (e.g., the notional amount is not equal to the actual principal amount), then a net amount is reported on the income statement. The financial reporting reflects Laki's interest rate risk management strategy. Laki discloses the characteristics of its financial instrument and derivative in the notes to its financial statements.

CASH FLOW HEDGE

A cash flow hedge protects against the risk caused by *variable* prices, costs, rates, or terms that cause future cash flows to be uncertain. A cash flow hedge is a hedge of an expected transaction that will probably occur in the future, but the amount of the transaction has not been fixed. This contrasts with a fair value hedge that protects against the risk from changes in value caused by *fixed* terms, rates, or prices.

For example, a company with a variable rate debt that enters into an interest rate swap to receive a variable rate of interest and pay a fixed rate protects itself against paying a higher rate of interest if interest rates increase. Of course, it will pay a higher rate than the variable rate if interest rates fall. The company has converted a variable rate contract into a fixed rate contract.

For a cash flow hedge, *FASB Statement No. 133* requires a company to recognize in its current *other comprehensive income* any gain or loss from a change in the fair value of the derivative (cash flow hedge). The company reports the derivative at its fair value and the related accumulated other comprehensive income in its stockholders' equity on its ending balance sheet. The company does *not* recognize in its financial statements any change in value of the financial instrument being hedged. When the hedged expected transaction occurs, the company transfers the accumulated other comprehensive income to its current net income.

To illustrate an interest rate swap that is a cash flow hedge, assume the same facts as for the fair value hedge, except that Laki has a 5.3% (for 2007) variable rate $1 million loan (debt) with MidAmerica Bank that is based on the LIBOR rate. It enters into an interest rate swap with Jordan Investment Bank in which it will receive a variable (5.3% for 2007) interest rate and pay a 6% fixed rate. Since this hedge protects against the risk caused by variable interest rates, it is a cash flow hedge. We summarize the facts for the loan and swap involving Laki Company, MidAmerica Bank, and Jordan Investment Bank in Example 15-7.

EXAMPLE 15-7   Cash Flow Hedge: Interest Rate Swap

BEFORE SWAP

Financial Instrument: $1 Million Loan

MidAmerica Bank		**Laki Company**
Note Receivable ◄— *Financial* Pay LIBOR (Variable) Interest ——	Note Payable
of $1 million *Instrument*: Rate, Reset Annually	of $1 million

AFTER SWAP

Financial Instrument: $1 Million Loan, and
Derivative: Matched Interest Rate Swap with $1 Million Notional Amount

MidAmerica Bank   **Laki Company**

Note Receivable ◄——— *Financial*   Pay LIBOR (Variable) ——— Note Payable
of $1 million   *Instrument*: Interest Rate   of $1 million

Jordan Investment Bank

Interest Rate Swap of ——— *Derivative*: Receive LIBOR ———► Interest Rate Swap of
$1 million (notional   (Variable) Interest Rate $1 million (notional
amount)   ◄——— Pay Fixed (6%) ———   amount)
                        Interest Rate

Laki reports this swap at its fair (present) value on the balance sheet and reports any change in the fair value for the period in other comprehensive income. It reports the total change in fair value as accumulated other comprehensive income in the stockholders' equity section of its balance sheet. This type of interest rate swap does not hedge the liability. Instead, it hedges the interest payments. Thus, as Laki makes each interest payment, a hedged expected transaction occurs and Laki must transfer an amount from the accumulated other comprehensive income to its net income, based on the change in the present value. In this case, Laki must compute the present value of each interest payment separately. Because each payment occurs at a different point on the yield curve, Laki would use a different interest rate to determine its present value. These procedures are beyond the scope of this book.

SUMMARY

At the beginning of the chapter, we identified several objectives you would accomplish after reading the chapter. The objectives are listed below, each followed by a brief summary of the key points in the chapter discussion.

1. **Explain the classification and valuation of investments.** Trading securities are the investments in debt and equity securities that are purchased and held principally for the purpose of selling them in the near term. Trading securities are valued at their fair values on the balance sheet date. Available-for-sale securities are investments in (a) debt securities that are not classified as held-to-maturity, and (b) debt and equity securities that are not classified as trading securities. Available-for-sale securities are valued at their fair values on the balance sheet date. Held-to-maturity debt securities are investments in debt securities for which the company has the positive intent and ability to hold to maturity. Held-to-maturity securities are valued at their amortized cost on the balance sheet date.

2. **Account for investments in debt and equity trading securities.** Investments in debt and equity trading securities are initially recorded at cost and then recorded at fair value. Unrealized holding gains and losses are included in net income of the period, and interest and dividend revenue, as well as realized gains and losses on sales, are included in net income of the current period.

3. **Account for investments in available-for-sale debt and equity securities.** Investments in available-for-sale debt and equity securities are initially recorded at cost and then recorded at fair value. Unrealized holding gains and losses are reported as a component of other comprehensive income of the period, and interest and dividend revenue, as well as realized gains and losses on sales, are included in net income of the current period. The cumulative net unrealized holding gains or losses are reported in the accumulated other comprehensive income section of stockholders' equity.

4. **Account for investments in held-to-maturity debt securities, including amortization of bond premiums and discounts.** Investments in held-to-maturity debt securities are initially recorded at cost and then recorded at amortized cost. Unrealized holding gains and losses are not recorded, and interest and dividend revenue, as well as realized gains and losses on sales (if any), are included in net income of the current period.

5. **Understand transfers and impairments.** The transfer of a security between categories is accounted for at the fair value at the time of the transfer. Depending on the classification of the security transferred, the unrealized gain or loss is either eliminated or established. An impairment occurs when there is an other than temporary decline below the amortized cost of a debt security classified as available for sale or held to maturity. The company writes down the amortized cost of the security to the fair value and includes the amount of the write-down in net income as a realized loss.

6. **Understand disclosures of investments.** For trading securities, a company must disclose the change in the net unrealized holding gain or loss that is included in each income statement. For available-for-sale securities, a company must disclose for each balance sheet date the aggregate fair value, gross unrealized holding gains and gross unrealized holding losses, and amortized cost by major security types. For each income statement period, the company must disclose (1) the proceeds from the sales and the gross realized gains and losses on those sales as well as the basis on which cost was determined, (2) the gross gains and gross losses included in net income from transfers of securities from this category into the trading category, and (3) the change in the net unrealized holding gain or loss included as a separate component of other comprehensive income. For held-to-maturity securities a company must disclose for each balance sheet date the aggregate fair value, gross unrealized holding gains, gross unrealized holding losses, and amortized cost by major security types. For any sales or transfers from this category, the disclosures must include the amortized cost, the related realized or unrealized gain or loss, and the circumstances leading to the decision to sell or transfer security.

7. **Explain the conceptual issues regarding investments in marketable securities.** The use of fair value creates a relevant value because it reflects the liquidity of the securities. The value is also reliable because the fair value is available on a securities exchange. The following points reflect the major controversies: (1) the fair value is required for trading and available-for-sale securities whereas amortized cost is required for held-to-maturity securities; (2) fair value is not required for certain liabilities; (3) unrealized holding gains and losses are reported in net income for trading securities but in other comprehensive income for available-for-sale securities; and (4) the classification of securities is based on management intent.

8. **Account for investments using the equity method.** An investor company uses the equity method when it is able to exercise significant influence over the operating and financial policies of an investee. The company initially records its investment at cost and records income and an increase in the carrying value of the asset at an amount based on its percentage ownership in the investee. The investor company records dividends received as reductions in the carrying value of the investment account. The investor must also eliminate any intercompany transactions and recognize any additional depreciation expense.

9. **Describe additional issues for investments.** Additional issues for investments include accounting for investments in nonmarketable securities, stock dividends and stock splits, stock warrants, convertible bonds, the cash surrender value of life insurance, and investments in funds.

10. **Account for derivatives of financial instruments (Appendix).** A derivative derives its value from an underlying financial instrument. A hedge is a means of protecting against a financial loss. The two types of hedges discussed in the Appendix are fair value hedges and cash flow hedges. A *fair value hedge* protects against the risk from changes in value caused by fixed terms, rates, or prices. A company recognizes in its current net income (1) any gain or loss from a change in the fair value of the derivative (fair value hedge), and (2) any gain or loss from the change in the fair value of the financial instrument being hedged, along with any interest revenue or expense. As a result the company reports both the derivative and the financial instrument on its balance sheet at their respective fair values.

A *cash flow hedge* protects against the risk caused by variable prices, costs, rates, or terms that cause future cash flows to be uncertain. A cash flow hedge is a hedge of an expected transaction that will probably occur in the future, but the amount of the transaction has not been fixed. A company recognizes in its current other comprehensive income any gain or loss from a change in the fair value of the derivative (cash flow hedge). The company reports the derivative at its fair value and the related accumulated other comprehensive income in its stockholders' equity on its ending balance sheet.

ANSWERS TO REAL REPORT QUESTIONS

Real Report 15-1 Answers

1. Other comprehensive income for 2004 included any change in the unrealized gains and losses from securities that are classified as available-for-sale. The total pretax unrealized gains and losses for Intel for 2003 and 2004 are shown below:

(in millions)	2004	2003	Net Change
Gross Unrealized Gain	$118	$56	$ 62
Gross Unrealized Loss	(56)	(1)	(55)
Net Unrealized Gain			$ 7

Intel's other comprehensive income for 2004 would include the pretax net unrealized gain of $7 million.

2. Accumulated other comprehensive income would include the cumulative unrealized gains and losses for the available for sale securities. At December 25, 2004, Intel has a cumulative pretax gross unrealized gain of $62 million ($118 million gross unrealized gain less $56 million gross unrealized loss).

3. On its income statement for 2004, Intel reported a net gain of $52 million from the sale of marketable securities classified as available-for-sale. A $268 million unrealized gain was reported on the 2004 income statement related to trading securities. An impairment loss of $117 million (which included losses on non-marketable securities) was also reported on the 2004 income statement.

QUESTIONS

Q15-1 Why do companies purchase securities of other corporations?

Q15-2 What are the three categories of investments in debt and equity securities when there is no significant influence?

Q15-3 Provide brief definitions for the following terms: (a) *debt security*, (b) *equity security*, and (c) *fair value*.

Q15-4 Identify the accounting methods a company uses for investments of 20% or more in the voting common stock of the investee.

Q15-5 Briefly summarize the accounting for an investment in trading securities.

Q15-6 Briefly summarize the accounting for an investment in available-for-sale securities.

Q15-7 Briefly summarize the accounting for an investment in debt securities held to maturity.

Q15-8 Briefly describe how to determine and record any subsequent increases or decreases in the fair value of an investment in available-for-sale securities.

Q15-9 Briefly describe how to determine and record the gain or loss on the sale of an investment in available-for-sale securities.

Q15-10 When are investments in bonds held to maturity purchased at a premium? How does the amortization of a premium under the effective interest method affect interest revenue?

Q15-11 When are investments in bonds held to maturity purchased at a discount? How does the amortization of a discount under the effective interest method affect interest revenue?

Q15-12 Briefly describe the two methods available to determine interest revenue and account for premiums and discounts on investments in bonds held to maturity.

Q15-13   Briefly describe how to record the transfer of an investment in a debt security (a) from the held-to-maturity category to the available-for-sale category, and (b) from the available-for-sale category to the held-to-maturity category.

Q15-14   Show the balance sheet disclosures of an investment in available-for-sale securities that a company classifies as current and has a fair value in excess of cost.

Q15-15   Discuss the rationale behind the use of the equity method for an investment in common stock.

Q15-16   Briefly describe the accounting for an investment in common stock under the equity method.

Q15-17   Identify the facts and circumstances that would preclude an investor from using the equity method, even if it owns more than a 20% investment in an investee.

Q15-18   Discuss the appropriate accounting treatment to use when (a) an investor acquires enough additional common stock during a year to change from using the fair value method to using the equity method, and (b) an investor using the equity method sells enough common stock so that its portion of ownership falls below 20%.

Q15-19   Why is the cash surrender value of a life insurance policy on which the company is the beneficiary carried as an investment? How does the company determine the increase in this amount and the amount of insurance expense determined each year?

Q15-20   What is a fund? Distinguish between a fund and an appropriation of retained earnings.

MULTIPLE CHOICE   (AICPA Adapted)

Select the best answer for each of the following.

M15-1   On its December 31, 2006 balance sheet, Fay Company appropriately reported a $2,000 credit balance in its Allowance for Change in Value of Investment. There was no change during 2007 in the composition of Fay's portfolio of marketable equity securities held as available for sale. Pertinent data are as follows:

Security	Cost	Market Value at 12/31/07
A	$ 60,000	$ 63,000
B	45,000	40,000
C	80,000	78,500
Totals	$185,000	$181,500

What amount of loss on these securities should be included in Fay's income statement for the year ended December 31, 2007?
a. $0
b. $1,500
c. $3,500
d. $5,500

M15-2   A security in a portfolio of available-for-sale securities is transferred to the trading category. The security should be transferred between the corresponding portfolios at
a. The book value at date of transfer if higher than the fair value at date of transfer
b. The fair value at date of transfer, regardless of its cost
c. Its cost, regardless of the fair value at date of transfer
d. The lower of its cost or fair value at date of transfer

M15-3   On April 1, 2007, Aldrich Company purchased as an available-for-sale security $200,000 face value, 9% U.S. Treasury notes for $198,500, which included accrued interest of $4,500. The notes mature July 1, 2008, and pay interest semiannually on January 1 and July 1. The notes were sold on December 1, 2007 for $206,500, which included accrued interest of $7,500. Aldrich uses straight-line amortization. In its income statement for the year ended December 31, 2007, what amount should Aldrich report as a gain on the sale of the available-for-sale security?
a. $1,800
b. $5,000
c. $6,500
d. $8,000

M15-4   When the market value of a company's portfolio of available-for-sale securities is lower than its cost, the difference should be
a. Accounted for as a liability
b. Disclosed and described in a note to the financial statements but not accounted for
c. Accounted for as a valuation allowance deducted from the asset to which it relates
d. Accounted for as an addition in the shareholders' equity section of the balance sheet

M15-5   On January 2, 2007, Portela, Inc. bought 30% of the outstanding common stock of Bracero Corporation for $258,000 cash. Portela accounts for this investment by the equity method. At the date of acquisition of the stock, Bracero's property, plant, and equipment had a fair value in excess of its book value of $150,000. Bracero's property, plant, and equipment has a remaining life of 10 years. Bracero's net income for the year ended December 31, 2007 was $180,000. During 2007, Bracero declared and paid cash dividends of $20,000. On December 31, 2007, Portela should have carried its investment in Bracero in the amount of
a. $258,000
b. $301,500
c. $306,000
d. $312,000

M15-6   Cash dividends declared out of current earnings were distributed to an investor. How will the investor's investment account be affected by those dividends under each of the following accounting methods?

	Fair Value Method	Equity Method
a.	Decrease	No effect
b.	No effect	Decrease
c.	Decrease	Decrease
d.	No effect	No effect

M15-7 During 2007, Anthony Company purchased securities as a long-term investment and classified them as available for sale. Pertinent data are as follows:

Security	Cost	Market Value at 12/31/07
A	$ 20,000	$ 18,000
B	40,000	30,000
C	90,000	93,000
Totals	$150,000	$141,000

The amount of the holding gain or loss included in Anthony's year-end balance sheet should be
a. $0
b. $3,000
c. $9,000
d. $12,000

M15-8 For an available-for-sale securities portfolio included in noncurrent assets, which of the following should be included in net income of the period?
a. Realized gains during the period
b. Unrealized losses during the period
c. Accumulated changes in the valuation allowance
d. Increases in the valuation allowance during the period

M15-9 In 2006, Cromwell Corporation bought 30,000 shares of Fleming Corporation's listed stock for $300,000 and classified the investment as available for sale. In 2007, the market value declined to $200,000. In 2008, the market value of the Fleming stock rose to $230,000 and the stock was sold. How much should Cromwell record as a realized gain or loss in its determination of net income for 2008?
a. $0
b. $30,000 gain
c. $70,000 loss
d. $100,000 loss

M15-10 On January 1, 2007, Weaver Company purchased as held-to-maturity debt securities $500,000 face value of Park Corporation's 8% bonds for $456,200. The bonds were purchased to yield 10% interest and pay interest annually. The bonds mature on January 1, 2012. Weaver uses the effective interest method of amortization. What amount should Weaver report on its December 31, 2007 balance sheet as an investment in held-to-maturity debt securities?
a. $450,580
b. $456,200
c. $461,820
d. $466,200

EXERCISES

E15-1 *Trading Securities* Midwest Bank invests in trading securities. At the beginning of December 2007, the bank held no trading securities. During December of 2007, it entered into the following trading securities transactions:

Dec. 10   Purchased 500 shares of C Company common stock for $76 per share
Dec. 21   Purchased 800 shares of D Company common stock for $34 per share

At the end of December, the C Company common stock had a quoted market price of $79 per share and the D Company common stock had a quoted market price of $33 per share.

Required
1. Prepare journal entries to record the preceding information.
2. What is the unrealized holding gain or loss and where is it reported in the 2007 financial statements?
3. Show how the bank reports the trading securities on its December 31, 2007 balance sheet.

E15-2 *Trading Securities* Southeast Bank invests in trading securities and prepares quarterly financial statements. At the beginning of the fourth quarter of 2007, the bank held as trading securities 200 shares of Company E common stock that had originally cost $5,500. At that time, these securities had a fair value of $5,200. During the fourth quarter, the bank engaged in the following trading securities transactions:

Oct. 26   Purchased 300 shares of Company F common stock for $35 per share
Nov. 26   Sold 200 shares of Company E common stock for $25 per share
Dec. 10   Purchased 400 shares of Company G common stock for $41 per share

On December 31, 2007 the quoted market prices of the shares were as follows: E, $52 per share; F, $38 per share; and G, $40 per share.

Required

1. Prepare journal entries to record the preceding information for the fourth quarter.
2. Show what the bank reports on its fourth quarter 2007 income statement for these trading securities.
3. Show how the bank reports these trading securities on its balance sheet at the end of the fourth quarter of 2007.

E15-3 *Long-Term Investments* On December 31, 2006 Marsh Company held 1,000 shares of X Company common stock in its portfolio of long-term investments in available-for-sale securities. The stock had cost $15 per share and has a current market value of $13 per share. The December 31, 2006 balance sheet showed the following:

Assets

Long-term investment in available-for-sale securities	$15,000
Less: Allowance for change in value of investment	(2,000)
	$13,000

Stockholders' Equity

Unrealized decrease in value of available-for-sale securities	$ (2,000)

During 2007 the company acquired as long-term investments 900 shares of Y Company common stock for $18 per share and 800 shares of Z Company common stock for $22 per share. At the end of 2007 the respective market values per share were: X—$14, Y—$17, and Z—$20.

Required

Record the purchase of the investments in 2007 and the adjusting entry on December 31, 2007, and show the respective December 31, 2007 balance sheet accounts.

E15-4 *Available-for-Sale Securities* At the beginning of 2007 Ace Company had the following portfolio of investments in available-for-sale securities (common stock):

Security	Cost	12/31/06 Fair Value
A	$20,000	$25,000
B	30,000	29,000
Totals	$50,000	$54,000

During 2007 the following transactions occurred:

May	3	Purchased C securities (common stock) for $13,500
July	16	Sold all of the A securities for $25,000
Dec.	31	Received dividends of $800 on the B and C securities, for which the following information was available:

Security	12/31/07 Fair Value
B	$32,000
C	15,500

Required ▨

1. Prepare journal entries to record the preceding information.
2. What is the balance in the Unrealized Increase/Decrease account on December 31, 2007?

E15-5 *Available-for-Sale Securities* At the end of 2006 Terry Company prepared the following schedule of investments in available-for-sale securities (common stock):

Security	Cost	12/31/06 Fair Value	Cumulative Change in Fair Value
M	$37,000	$34,200	$(2,800)
N	42,000	43,100	1,100
Totals	$79,000	$77,300	$(1,700)

During 2007, the following transactions occurred:

June	8	Purchased O securities (common stock) for $50,000
Oct.	11	Sold all of the M securities for $35,400
Dec.	31	Received dividends of $900 on the N and O securities, and the following year-end total market values were available: N common stock, $43,900; O common stock, $49,600

Required
1. Prepare journal entries to record the preceding information.
2. Show how the preceding items are reported on the December 31, 2007 balance sheet of the Terry Company. Assume all investments are noncurrent.

E15-6 *Purchase of Bonds Between Interest Dates* On March 31, 2007 the Brodie Corporation acquired bonds with a par value of $400,000 for $425,800. The bonds are due December 31, 2012, carry a 12% annual interest rate, pay interest on June 30 and December 31, and are being held to maturity. The accrued interest is included in the acquisition price of the bonds. The company uses straight-line amortization.

Required
1. Prepare journal entries for Brodie to record the purchase of the bonds and the first two interest receipts.
2. If the company failed to separately record the interest at acquisition, explain the errors that would occur in the company's financial statements (no calculations are required).

E15-7 *Amortizing a Discount on a Bond Investment* On January 1, 2007 the Kelly Corporation acquired bonds with a face value of $500,000 for $483,841.79, a price that yields a 10% effective annual interest rate. The bonds carry a 9% stated rate of interest, pay interest semiannually on June 30 and December 31, are due December 31, 2010 and are being held to maturity.

Required
Prepare journal entries to record the purchase of the bonds and the first two interest receipts using:
1. The straight-line method of amortization.
2. The effective interest method of amortization.

E15-8 *Purchase, Discount Amortization, and Sale of Bond Investment* On November 1, 2006 the Reid Corporation acquired bonds with a face value of $700,000 for $673,618.61. The bonds carry a stated rate of interest of 10%, were purchased to yield 11%, pay interest semiannually on April 30 and October 31, were purchased to be held to maturity, and are due October 31, 2011. On November 1, 2007, in contemplation of a major acquisition, the bonds were sold for $700,000. Reid Corporation is on a fiscal year accounting period ending October 31. The company uses the effective interest method.

Required
Prepare journal entries to record the purchase of the bonds, the interest receipts on April 30, 2007 and October 31, 2007, and the sale of the bonds.

E15-9 *Investment Discount Amortization Schedule* On January 1, 2007 Rodgers Company purchased $200,000 face value, 10%, three-year bonds for $190,165.35, a price that yields a 12% effective annual interest rate. The bonds pay interest semiannually on June 30 and December 31.

Required
1. Record the purchase of the bonds.
2. Prepare an investment interest revenue and discount amortization schedule, using the effective interest method.
3. Record the receipts of interest on June 30, 2007 and June 30, 2009.

E15-10 *Investment Premium Amortization Schedule* On January 1, 2007 Lynch Company acquired 13% bonds with a face value of $50,000. The bonds pay interest on June 30 and December 31 and mature on December 31, 2009. Lynch Company paid $51,229.35, a price that yields a 12% effective annual interest rate.

Required
1. Record the purchase of the bonds.
2. Prepare an investment interest revenue and premium amortization schedule using the effective interest method.
3. Record the receipts of interest on June 30, 2007 and December 31, 2009.

E15-11 *Purchase, Premium Amortization, and Sale of Bond Investment* The Glover Corporation purchased bonds with a face value of $300,000 for $307,493.34 on January 1, 2007. The bonds carry a face rate of interest of 12%, pay interest semiannually on June 30 and December 31, were purchased to be held to maturity, are due December 31, 2009, and were purchased to yield 11%. On January 1, 2008, in contemplation of a major acquisition, the bonds were sold for $300,000. The company uses the effective interest method.

Required
Prepare journal entries to record the purchase of the bonds, the first two interest receipts, and the sale of the bonds.

E15-12 *Transfer Between Categories* On December 31, 2006 the Leslie Company held an investment in bonds of Kaufmann Company which it categorized as being held to maturity. At that time, the 8%, $100,000 face value bonds had a carrying value of $107,023.56 and were being amortized using the effective interest method based on a yield of 7%. Interest on these bonds is paid annually each December 31.

On December 31, 2007, after recording the interest earned, the Leslie Company decided to reclassify the Kaufmann bonds to its available-for-sale category in anticipation of a major restructuring. At that time, the ending quoted market price for the bonds was 105.

Required

Prepare the journal entries on December 31, 2007 to record the interest earned and the reclassification.

E15-13 *Equity Method* The Miller Corporation acquired 30% of the outstanding common stock of the Crowell Corporation for $160,000 on January 1, 2007 and obtained significant influence. The purchase price of the shares was equal to their book value. During 2007, the following information is available for Crowell:

Mar.	31	Declared and paid a cash dividend of $50,000 × 30%
June	30	Reported semiannual earnings of $120,000 for the first half of 2007
Sept.	30	Declared and paid a cash dividend of $50,000
Dec.	31	Reported semiannual earnings of $140,000 for the second half of 2007

Required

1. Prepare journal entries for Miller to reflect the preceding information.
2. What is the balance in Miller's investment account on December 31, 2007? (Show your computations.)

E15-14 *Equity Method* On January 1, 2007 the Field Company acquired 40% of the North Company by purchasing 8,000 shares for $144,000 and obtained significant influence. On the date of acquisition, Field calculated that its share of the excess of the fair value over the book value of North's depreciable assets was $15,000, and that the purchased goodwill was $12,000. At the end of 2007, North reported net income of $45,000 and paid dividends of $0.70 per share. Field Company depreciates its depreciable assets over a 12-year remaining life.

Required

Prepare all the journal entries of Field Company to record the preceding information for 2007.

E15-15 *Equity Method* On January 1, 2007 Jones acquires a 30% interest in Fink Company by purchasing 3,000 of its 10,000 common shares for $16 per share and obtains significant influence. On the date of acquisition, the net assets of Fink Company were as shown here:

	Book Value	Fair Value
Nondepreciable assets (for example, land)	$ 15,000	$ 25,000
Depreciable assets (10-year remaining life)	90,000	115,000
	$105,000	$140,000
Liabilities	$ 10,000	$ 15,000

During 2007 Fink Company earned income of $22,000 and paid dividends of $6,000.

Required

Prepare all journal entries on Jones Company's books to record the acquisition, dividends, and income from the investment in Fink Company. Show supporting calculations.

E15-16 *Convertible Bonds* On January 1, 2006 the Taylor Corporation purchased $20,000 of the Kalanda Corporation's 12% convertible bonds for $19,760. The bonds pay interest semiannually each December 31 and June 30 and are due December 31, 2010. Each $1,000 bond is convertible into 15 shares of the Kalanda Corporation's $10 par common stock. Taylor uses the straight-line method of discount amortization. At the end of 2006 and 2007, the quoted market price of the bonds was not materially different from the amortized cost. On July 1, 2008 Taylor exchanged all of the bonds for Kalanda common stock. At that time the market value of the common stock was $72 per share.

Required

Prepare whatever entries are necessary to record the acquisition and conversion of the Kalanda bonds.

E15-17 *Receipt of Stock Dividends* On March 2, 2007 the Dawson Corporation acquired 5,000 common shares, representing a 1% interest in the Foreman Corporation, for $60,000. On May 1, 2007 Foreman issued a 20% stock dividend, and on December 31, 2007 the market value was $10 per share. On February 1, 2008 Dawson sold 1,500 shares for $12 per share.

Required

Prepare journal entries for Dawson to record the acquisition, stock dividend, and sale of the shares.

E15-18 *Cash Surrender Value of Life Insurance* The Westford Corporation purchases life insurance policies on its officers, and these policies all carry a cash surrender value clause. At the beginning of 2007, Westford paid $13,300 in life insurance premiums for one year. During 2007 the cash surrender value of the policies increased from $98,450 to $103,900. At the beginning of 2008 the corporation's vice president lost his life in an automobile accident. The policy carried on this officer paid $50,000, and the cash surrender value of the policy was $6,480.

Required

Prepare journal entries to record the preceding information on the Westford Corporation's books.

E15-19 *Sinking Funds Entries* The following information is available concerning the Nunan Corporation's sinking fund:

Jan.	1, 2007	Established a sinking fund to retire an outstanding bond issue by contributing $425,000
Feb.	3, 2007	Purchased securities for $400,000
July	30, 2007	Sold securities originally costing $48,000 for $45,000
Dec.	31, 2007	Collected dividends and interest on the remaining securities in the amount of $49,000; the securities had a market value of $355,000 at this time
Dec.	31, 2008	Collected dividends and interest on the remaining securities in the amount of $40,000
Dec.	31, 2008	Paid sinking fund expenses of $4,500
Dec.	31, 2008	Sold the remaining securities in the fund for $360,000
Dec.	31, 2008	Retired an outstanding bond issue of $500,000 with the cash from the fund and transferred the remaining fund balance back to the cash account

Required

Prepare journal entries to record the preceding transactions for the Nunan Corporation.

E15-20 *Derivatives (Appendix)* Anglar Company has a $3 million 7% bank loan from Castle Rock Bank. On January 1, 2007, when the $3 million loan has three years remaining, Anglar contracts with Susan Investment Bank to enter into a three-year interest-rate swap with a $3 million notional amount. Anglar agrees to receive from Susan a fixed interest rate of 7% and to pay Susan an interest amount each year that is variable based on the LIBOR interest rate at the beginning of the year. The interest payments are made at year-end. The applicable interest rate on the swap is reset each year after the annual interest payment is made. The LIBOR interest rate is 6.6% at the beginning of 2007. The three-year fixed interest rate is 8% at December 31, 2007.

Required

1. Prepare the journal entries of Anglar for the bank loan and derivative for 2007.
2. Prepare the appropriate disclosures in Anglar's financial statements for 2007.

PROBLEMS

P15-1 *Trading Securities* The investment manager of 4th National Bank invests some of the bank's financial resources in trading securities. During the last quarter of 2007 the following transactions occurred in regard to these trading securities:

Nov.	5	Purchased 200 shares of M Company common stock at $86 per share
Nov.	19	Purchased 300 shares of P Company preferred stock at $63 per share
Nov.	29	Sold 100 shares of M Company common stock at $89 per share
Dec.	15	Purchased 400 shares of T Company common stock at $37 per share
Dec.	17	Sold 100 shares of P Company preferred stock at $62 per share

On December 31, 2007 the market values of the shares were as follows: M, $87 per share; P, $61 per share; and T, $37.25 per share. The bank held no trading securities at the beginning of the last quarter of 2007.

Required

1. Prepare journal entries to record the preceding information.
2. Show what the bank reports on its fourth quarter 2007 income statement for these trading securities.
3. Show how the bank reports these trading securities on its December 31, 2007 balance sheet.

P15-2 *Trading Securities* The 8th State Bank prepares interim financial statements and follows an investment strategy of investing in trading securities. At the beginning of the third quarter of 2007, the bank held the following portfolio of trading securities:

		June 30, 2007
Security	Cost	Fair Value
100 shares of G Company common stock	$ 2,900	$ 2,800
600 shares of O Company common stock	12,000	12,600
Totals	$14,900	$15,400

During the third quarter of 2007, the bank entered into the following trading securities transactions:

July	2	Received dividends of $1.50 per share on the G Company common stock
July	14	Sold 600 shares of O Company common stock for $20 per share

Aug.	9	Purchased 300 shares of P Company common stock for $36 per share
Aug.	24	Sold 100 shares of G Company common stock for $30 per share
Sept.	17	Purchased 500 shares of U Company common stock for $22 per share

On September 30, 2007 the P Company common stock had a quoted market price of $36.50 per share and the U Company common stock had a quoted market price of $21 per share.

Required
1. Prepare journal entries to record the preceding information.
2. Show what the bank reports on its third-quarter 2007 income statement for these trading securities.
3. Show how the bank reports these trading securities on its September 30, 2007 balance sheet.

P15-3 *Available-for-Sale Securities* Holly Company invests its excess cash in marketable securities. At the beginning of 2007 it had the following portfolio of investments in available-for-sale securities:

Security	Cost	12/31/06 Fair Value
400 shares of I Company common stock	$ 8,400	$ 9,400
700 shares of O Company common stock	23,100	21,700
Totals	$31,500	$31,100

During 2007, the following transactions occurred:

Mar.	31	Purchased U Company 8% bonds with a face value of $10,000 for $10,000 plus accrued interest; interest is payable on the bonds each June 30 and December 31
May	17	Sold 200 shares of O Company common stock for $30 per share
June	30	Received the semiannual interest on the U Company bonds
Oct.	12	Sold 100 shares of I Company common stock for $24 per share
Dec.	31	Received the semiannual interest on the U Company bonds and dividends of $1 per share and $1.50 per share on the I and O Company common stock, respectively

The December 31 closing market prices were as follows: I Company common stock, $25 per share; O Company common stock, $31 per share; U Company 8% bonds, 101.

Required
1. Prepare journal entries to record the preceding information.
2. Show what is reported on the Holly Company's 2007 income statement.
3. Assuming the investment in I Company stock is considered to be a current asset and the remaining investments are noncurrent, show how all the items are reported on the December 31, 2007 balance sheet of the Holly Company.
4. If GAAP required that unrealized holding gains and losses on available-for-sale securities be included in income, how much would Holly recognize in 2007?

P15-4 *Investments in Equity Securities* The Noonan Corporation prepares quarterly financial statements and invests its excess funds in marketable securities. At the end of 2006 Noonan's portfolio of investments available for sale consisted of the following equity securities:

Security	Number of Shares	Cost Per Share	Fair Value Per Share
Keene Company	500	$60	$60
Sachs, Inc.	800	43	44
Bacon Company	400	70	72

During the first half of 2007, Noonan engaged in the following investment transactions:

Jan.	6	Sold one-half of the Sachs shares for $45 per share
Feb.	3	Purchased 700 shares of Jackson Corporation common stock for $45 per share
Mar.	31	Dividends of $2,500 were received on the investments, and the following information is available on market prices:

Security	Fair Value Per Share
Keene Company	$59
Sachs, Inc.	45
Bacon Company	70
Jackson Corporation	43

Apr.	14	Purchased 300 shares of Quinn Company preferred stock for $52 per share
May	11	Sold the remainder of the Sachs shares for $42 per share
June	30	Dividends of $2,800 were received on investments, and the following information is available:

Security	Fair Value Per Share
Keene Company	$62
Bacon Company	69
Jackson Corporation	46
Quinn Company	50

Required

1. Record Noonan's investment transactions for January 6 through June 30, 2007.
2. Show the items of income or loss from investment transactions that Noonan reports for each of the first and second quarters of 2007.
3. Show how the preceding items are reported on the first and second quarter 2007 ending balance sheets, assuming that management expects to dispose of the Keene and Sachs securities within the next year.

P15-5 *Temporary Available-for-Sale Investments* Manson Incorporated reported the following current asset on its December 31, 2006 balance sheet:

Temporary investment in available-for-sale securities (at cost)	$63,475
Less: Allowance for change in value of investment	(2,980)
Temporary investment in available-for-sale securities (at fair value)	$60,495

An analysis of Manson's temporary investments on December 31, 2006 reveals the following:

Equity Security	Cost	Fair Value
400 shares of Turben Company, common	$14,275	$13,590
500 shares of Cook Corp., common	12,650	13,175
700 shares of Hill Corp., common	17,450	18,180
200 shares of Web Engines, preferred	19,100	15,550
Totals	$63,475	$60,495

During 2007 the following transactions related to Manson's temporary investments occurred:

Jan.	6	Received a $265 dividend on the Turben Company common
Mar.	31	Received the semiannual dividend of $500 on the Web Engines preferred

On March 31, 2007 the following information is available concerning Manson's temporary investments:

Equity Security	Fair Value
Turben Company	$13,470
Cook Corp.	13,765
Hill Corp.	18,940
Web Engines	15,500

June	30	Received a $375 dividend on the Cook Corp. common and a $700 dividend on the Hill Corp. common

On June 30, 2007 the following information is available concerning Manson's temporary investments:

Equity Security	Fair Value
Turben Company	$13,300
Cook Corp.	14,125
Hill Corp.	19,300
Web Engines	15,400

July	6	Sold the Turben Company common for $13,750
Sept.	29	Received the semiannual dividend of $500 on the Web Engines preferred

On September 30, 2007 the following information is available concerning Manson's temporary investments:

Equity Security	Fair Value
Cook Corp.	$14,230
Hill Corp.	19,500
Web Engines	15,900

Nov.   2   Sold the Hill Corp. common for $19,780
Dec.   30   Received a $375 dividend on the Cook Corp. common

On December 31, 2007, the following information is available:

Equity Security	Fair Value
Cook Investment Corp.	$14,280
Web Engines	16,400

Required
1. Assuming Manson prepares quarterly financial statements, prepare journal entries to record the preceding information.
2. Show the items of income or loss from temporary investment transactions that Manson reports for each quarter of 2007?
3. Show how Manson's temporary investments are reported on the balance sheet on March 31, 2007; June 30, 2007; September 30, 2007; and December 31, 2007.

P15-6 *Investment in Available-for-Sale Bonds* The following information relates to the Starr Company's Investment in Available-for-Sale Bonds account for 2007:

Jan.   1   Purchased $30,000 face value of Bradford Company 8% bonds at 97 to yield 10%; interest on the bonds
                       is payable each June 30 and December 31
Jan.   1   Purchased $40,000 face value of Morris Company 10% bonds at 101 to yield 9.8%; interest on the
                       bonds is payable each June 30 and December 31

On June 30, collected the interest and the following information is available:

Security	Fair Value
Bradford Company 8%	97.2
Morris Company 10%	102.0

July   1   Purchased $25,000 face value of Whipple Corporation 11% bonds at 92 to yield 12%; interest on the
                       bonds is payable each June 30 and December 31
Nov.   30   Sold the Whipple bonds at 91 plus accrued interest

On December 31, collected the interest, sold the Morris bonds at 102, and the following information is also available:

Security	Fair Value
Bradford Company 8%	96

Required
1. Prepare journal entries to record the previous information for 2007. Use the effective interest method and round all amounts to the nearest *dollar*. Assume that Starr prepares semiannual financial statements.
2. Show the items of income or loss from investment transactions that Starr reports for each 2007 semiannual income statement.
3. Show how the investment items are reported on each of the 2007 semiannual balance sheets, assuming that management expects to dispose of all investments within one year of purchase.

P15-7 *Temporary Investments in Available-for-Sale Bonds and Equity Securities* During 2007 the Dana Company decided to begin investing its idle cash in marketable securities. The information contained below relates to Dana's 2007 marketable security transactions:

Feb.   3   Purchased 3,000 shares of Blair Company common stock for $12 per share
Apr.   1   Purchased $20,000 face value of Solomon Inc. 12% bonds at par plus accrued interest; interest on the
                       bonds is payable each June 30 and December 31
June   30   Received the semiannual interest on the Solomon bonds and a $0.25 per share dividend on the Blair
                       common
Sept.   1   Purchased 4,000 shares of Woodman Corporation common for $22 per share
Nov.   1   Purchased $30,000 face value of Edwards Company 11% bonds at par plus accrued interest; interest on
                       the bonds is payable each June 1 and December 1
Dec.   1   Received the interest on the Edwards bonds and sold the bonds at 101
Dec.   30   Received a $0.25 dividend per share on the Blair common and sold all the shares for $35,300
Dec.   31   Received the interest on the Solomon bonds

On December 31, the following information is available concerning the year-end market prices:

Security	Quoted Market
Solomon 12% bonds	101
Woodman common	$23

Required

1. Record Dana's transactions in temporary investments for 2007.
2. Show the items of income or loss on temporary investments Dana reports on its 2007 income statement.
3. Show the carrying value of Dana's Temporary Investment account on its December 31, 2007 balance sheet.

P15-8   *Investments, Petty Cash, Bank Reconciliation*   During the first quarter of 2007 the Payne Corporation entered into the following transactions:

Jan.	1	Acquired 150 shares of Block Corporation common stock for $20 per share, 200 shares of Bridle Corporation common stock for $30 per share, and 100 shares of Alpha Corporation common stock for $25 per share. These are the only shares the company owns and all are classified as securities available for sale.
Feb.	1	Purchased 12% A Company bonds with a face value of $20,000 at par, plus accrued interest. Interest on the bonds is payable February 28 and August 31 each year, and the bonds are due August 31, 2010. Also purchased 10% B Company bonds with a face value of $12,000 at par, plus accrued interest. Interest on the bonds is payable March 31 and September 30, and the bonds are due September 30, 2013. These are the only bonds the company owns and all are classified as securities available for sale.
Feb.	1	Established a petty cash fund for incidental expenditures at $500.
Feb.	28	Received the semiannual interest on the A Company bonds.
Feb.	28	A count of cash on hand indicated that $125.50 remained in the petty cash fund. A sorting of petty cash vouchers disclosed that $110.00 was spent for postage, $170.65 was spent for office supplies, $45.00 was spent for transportation, and $43.50 was spent for miscellaneous items. The fund was replenished.
Mar.	31	Received first quarter dividends of $1,500 and the semiannual interest on the B Company bonds. On this date, the aggregate fair value of Payne's securities available for sale is $42,600.
Mar.	31	A count of cash on hand indicated that $230.50 remained in the petty cash fund. A sorting of petty cash vouchers disclosed that $140.00 was spent for postage, $75.30 was spent for office supplies, and $54.20 was spent for miscellaneous items. The fund was replenished.

The bank statement and the accounting records of the Payne Corporation for the month of March 2007 indicated that the cash collected from the dividends and the B Company bond interest was deposited on March 31 but did not appear on the March bank statement. There were no other deposits in transit. The bank statement showed a balance on March 31 of $13,459.75, which included collection of a $1,500 note and $100 of interest by the bank for the Payne Corporation. Also listed was a $20 bank service charge and a $75.60 NSF check returned by the bank. The cash balance per the accounting records on March 31 was $11,689.95, which included checks totaling $2,365.40 that had not yet cleared the bank.

Required

1. Prepare journal entries to record the preceding transactions of the Payne Corporation for the first quarter of 2007.
2. Prepare a bank reconciliation for Payne for March 31, 2007.
3. Prepare any journal entries necessary to adjust Payne's books on March 31, 2007.

P15-9   *Premium Amortization on Bond Investment and Partial Sale of the Investment Using the Effective Interest Method*   On January 1, 2007 the Hyde Corporation purchased bonds with a face value of $300,000 for $308,373.53. The bonds are due June 30, 2010, carry a 13% stated interest rate, and were purchased to yield 12%. Interest is payable semiannually on June 30 and December 31. On March 31, 2008, in contemplation of a major acquisition, the company sold one-half the bonds for $159,500 including accrued interest; the remainder were held until maturity.

Required

Prepare the journal entries to record the purchase of the bonds, each interest payment, the partial sale of the investment on March 31, 2008, and the retirement of the bond issue on June 30, 2010.

P15-10   *Bond Investment Discount Amortization Schedule*   The Tudor Company acquired $500,000 of Carr Corporation bonds for $487,706.69 on January 1, 2007. The bonds carry an 11% stated interest rate, pay interest semiannually on January 1 and July 1, were issued to yield 12%, and are due January 1, 2010.

Required

1. Prepare an investment interest revenue and discount amortization schedule using:
   a. The straight-line method
   b. The effective interest method
2. Prepare the July 1, 2009 journal entries to record the interest revenue under both methods.

P15-11   *Discount Amortization on Bonds Purchased Between Interest Dates*   On October 1, 2006 the Jenkins Corporation bought bonds with a face value of $200,000 for $199,175, which included accrued interest. The bonds are due December 31, 2008 and carry a face rate of interest of 10.5%. Interest on the bonds is payable semiannually on June 30 and December 31. The company uses the straight-line method to amortize the discount.

Required

1. Prepare journal entries to record the purchase of the bonds, each interest receipt, and the retirement of the issue on December 31, 2008.
2. If the company failed to separately record the interest at acquisition, explain the errors that would occur in the company's financial statements (no calculations are required).

P15-12 *Bond Investment Premium Amortization Schedule*   The Mercer Corporation acquired $400,000 of the Park Company's bonds on June 30, 2006 for $409,991.12. The bonds carry a 12% stated interest rate, pay interest semiannually on June 30 and December 31, were issued to yield 11%, and are due June 30, 2009.

Required

1. Prepare an investment interest revenue and premium amortization schedule, using:
   a. The straight-line method
   b. The effective interest method
2. Prepare journal entries to record the December 31, 2006 and December 31, 2008 interest receipts using both methods.

P15-13 *Discount Amortization on Bond Investment and Partial Sale of Investment Using Effective Interest Method*   On January 1, 2007 the Mark Corporation purchased bonds with a face value of $500,000 for $475,413.60. The bonds are due December 31, 2009, carry a 10% stated rate, and were purchased to yield 12%. Interest is payable semiannually on June 30 and December 31. On January 1, 2009, in contemplation of a major acquisition, one-fourth of the bonds were sold for $127,000. The remainder were held until maturity.

Required ☒

Prepare journal entries to record the purchase of the bonds, each interest payment, the partial sale of the investment on December 31, 2008, and the retirement of the bond issue on December 31, 2009.

P15-14 *Comparison of Fair Value and Equity Methods*   On January 1, 2006 Snow Corporation purchased 20% of the 200,000 outstanding shares of common stock of Garvey Company for $4.00 per share as a long-term investment. The purchase price of the shares was equal to their book value. The following information is available about Garvey Company for 2006 and 2007:

End of 2006	Reported net income	$80,000
	Cash dividends declared and paid	$30,000
	Market value of shares	$3.80 per share
End of 2007	Reported net income	$90,000
	Cash dividends declared and paid	$35,000
	Market value of shares	$4.25 per share

Required

1. Prepare journal entries to record this information, assuming:
   a. The fair value method is used by Snow
   b. The equity method is used by Snow
2. Assume 10,000 of the Garvey shares are sold on January 4, 2008 by Snow for $4.25 per share. Prepare the journal entry for this sale, assuming:
   a. Snow is using the fair value method
   b. Snow is using the equity method

P15-15 *Application of Equity Method*   On January 1, 2007 Doe Company purchased 3,000 of the 10,000 common shares outstanding of the Ray Company for $15 per share and obtained significant influence. Doe amortizes its patents over 10 years. The December 31, 2006 condensed balance sheet of the Ray Company is shown here:

Current assets	$ 10,000	Liabilities	$ 50,000
Fixed assets (net)	100,000	Common stock, no par	30,000
Patents (net)	40,000	Retained earnings	70,000
	$150,000		$150,000

Doe Company was unable to determine the fair value of the Ray Company identifiable net assets shown on the preceding balance sheet. It did, however, determine that Ray Company uses the straight-line method (no residual value) to depreciate its fixed assets and to amortize its patents over 20 years and 10 years, respectively. At the end of 2007 Ray Company disclosed the following condensed income statement and retained earnings statement for 2007:

Revenues	$ 100,000	Beginning retained earnings	$ 70,000
Expenses	(60,000)	Add: Net income	32,000
Operating income	$ 40,000		$ 102,000
Extraordinary loss	(8,000)	Less: Cash dividends	(20,000)
Net income	$ 32,000	Ending retained earnings	$ 82,000

Required
Prepare all the 2007 journal entries that Doe should make related to this investment. Show and label all supporting calculations.

P15-16 *Recording Investments Under the Equity Method* The Harper Corporation acquired 80,000 of the 200,000 outstanding shares of the Moore Corporation on April 1, 2007 for $400,000 and obtained significant influence. The following information concerning the Moore Corporation is available on the date of acquisition:

	Book Value	Fair Value
Depreciable assets (remaining life, 15 years)	$ 600,000	$ 700,000
Other assets	500,000	450,000
Total	$1,100,000	$1,150,000
Liabilities	$ 300,000	$ 320,000
Common stock	250,000	
Retained earnings	550,000	
Total	$1,100,000	

Subsequently, Moore Corporation paid a cash dividend of $40,000 on August 31, 2007 and reported annual income from operations of $125,000 and extraordinary income (earned in the third quarter) of $30,000 on December 31, 2007.

Required
1. Prepare journal entries for Harper to record the preceding information.
2. What is the balance in Harper's investment account on December 31, 2007? (Show all computations.)
3. Prepare Harper's net cash flow from operating activities section of its 2007 statement of cash flows under the indirect method, assuming the equity investment income is the only income Harper reports. Ignore income taxes.

P15-17 *Equity Method and Subsequent Sale* On January 1, 2007 the Easton Corporation acquired 30% of the outstanding common shares of Feeley Corporation for $140,000, and 25% of the outstanding common shares of Holmes Company for $82,500 and obtained significant influence in both situations. On this date the financial statements of Feeley and Holmes disclosed the following information:

	Feeley	Holmes
Current assets	$190,000	$140,000
Long-term assets	370,000	180,000
	$560,000	$320,000
Liabilities	$120,000	$ 90,000
Common stock (no par)	200,000	150,000
Retained earnings	240,000	80,000
	$560,000	$320,000

During 2007 Feeley reported a loss of $70,000 and paid dividends of $40,000; Holmes reported income of $45,000 and paid dividends of $28,000. On January 1, 2008 Feeley sold all the Holmes shares for $90,000. Assume the company records both investments under the equity method and considers that any difference between each purchase price and the respective book value of the net assets acquired is goodwill.

Required
Prepare journal entries to record (1) the purchase of the Feeley and Holmes shares, (2) the recognition of investment income, (3) the receipt of investee dividends, and (4) the sale of the Holmes shares.

P15-18 *Change to Equity Method* On January 1, 2007 Lion Company paid $600,000 for 10,000 shares of Wolf Company's voting common stock, which was a 10% interest in Wolf. Lion does not have the ability to exercise significant influence over the operating and financial policies of Wolf. Lion received dividends of $1.00 per share from Wolf on October 2, 2007. Wolf reported net income of $400,000 for the year ended December 31, 2007 and the ending market price of its shares was $63.

On July 2, 2008 Lion paid $1,950,000 for 30,000 additional shares of Wolf Company's voting common stock, which represents a 30% investment in Wolf. The fair values of all of Wolf's assets, net of liabilities, were equal to their book values of $6,500,000. As a result of this transaction, Lion has the ability to exercise significant influence over the operating and financial policies of Wolf. Lion received dividends of $1.00 per share from Wolf on April 2, 2008 and $1.35 per share on October 1, 2008. Wolf reported net income of $500,000 for the year ended December 31, 2008, and $200,000 for the 6 months ended December 31, 2008.

Required
1. For the Lion Company show the dividend revenue for 2007, as well as the December 31, 2007 unrealized increase in value of available-for-sale securities and carrying value of the investment account.
2. Assuming that Lion Company issues comparative financial statements for 2007 and 2008, show the investment income for 2007 and 2008, as well as the December 31, 2007 and 2008 carrying value of the Investment account.

P15-19 *Cash Surrender Value of Life Insurance* On January 1, 2006 Kehoe Corporation insured the lives of its president, vice president, controller, and treasurer for $100,000 each. The annual premium on each policy is $4,200, payable on January 1 of each year, and the cash surrender values for the policies increase by 4% of the annual premiums paid. Premium payments were made on the scheduled date by the Kehoe Corporation through 2008, and the following dividends were received at the end of the year on each policy: 2006, $450; 2007, $575; 2008, $550. On February 1, 2009 the treasurer died and Kehoe Corporation collected the face value of his policy plus 11 months' premium.

Required
Prepare journal entries to record the preceding information for the years 2006 through 2009. (Round calculation to the nearest dollar.)

P15-20 *Derivatives (Appendix)* Danburg Company has a $5 million 9% bank loan outstanding with its local bank. On January 1, 2007, when the loan has four years remaining, Danburg contracts with Bradford Investment Bank to enter into a four-year interest-rate swap with a $5 million notional amount. Danburg agrees to receive from Bradford a fixed interest rate of 9% and to pay Bradford an interest amount each year that is variable based on the LIBOR interest rate at the beginning of the year. The interest payments are made at year-end. The applicable interest rate on the swap is reset each year after the annual interest payment is made. The LIBOR interest rate is 8.6% and 9.5% at the beginning of 2007 and 2008, respectively. The three-year fixed interest rate is 10% at December 31, 2007, and the two-year rate is 8% at December 31, 2008.

Required
1. Prepare the journal entries of Danburg for the bank loan and derivative for 2007 and 2008.
2. Prepare the appropriate disclosures in Danburg's financial statements for 2007 and 2008.

CASES

COMMUNICATION

C15-1 Realized and Unrealized Losses: Temporary Investments

FASB Statement No. 115 changed accounting principles with respect to certain marketable securities. An important part of this *Statement* is the distinction between investments categorized as trading, available for sale, or held to maturity.

Required
1. What types of securities are covered by this *Statement?*
2. Explain how the distinction between the three categories is made.
3. Discuss the distinction between realized and holding gains and losses on investments in debt and equity securities.
4. Explain how a company discloses realized and holding gains and losses on investments in equity securities on its financial statements.

C15-2 Investments in Securities

Cane Company has two portfolios of investments in marketable equity securities. It classifies one as trading securities and the other as available-for-sale securities. Cane does not have the ability to exercise significant influence over any of the companies in either portfolio. It sold some securities from each portfolio during the year. The company reclassified one of the securities in the available-for-sale category to the trading category when its fair value was less than cost. At the beginning and end of the year, the aggregate cost of each portfolio exceeded its aggregate market value by different amounts.

Required
1. Explain how Cane measures and reports the income statement effects of the securities sold during the year from each portfolio.
2. Explain how Cane accounts for the security which it reclassified.
3. Explain how Cane reports the effects of investments in each portfolio on its balance sheet as of the end of the year and on its income statement for the year. Do not discuss the securities sold.
4. Explain gains trading. Can Cane use gains trading on either portfolio? Does gains trading raise ethical issues?

C15-3 Investments in Securities

FASB Statement No. 115 was issued to change accounting methods and procedures with respect to investments in debt and equity securities. An important part of the *Statement* concerns the distinction between trading securities, available-for-sale securities, and held-to-maturity securities.

Required
1. Explain why a company invests in debt and equity securities.
2. Explain what factors a company should consider in determining which investments it should classify in each of the three categories, and how these factors affect the accounting treatment for unrealized gains and losses.

C15-4 Equity Method

AICPA Adapted The most common method of accounting for unconsolidated subsidiaries is the equity method.

Required

Answer the following questions with respect to the *equity* method.

1. Under what circumstances does a company apply the equity method?
2. At what amount does a company record the initial investment and what events subsequent to the initial investment (if any) change this amount?
3. How does a company recognize investment earnings under the equity method, and how does it determine the amount?

C15-5 Investments in Equity Securities

AICPA Adapted Walker Company has an investment portfolio of equity securities available for sale. Walker does not own more than 5% of the outstanding voting stock for any of the securities in the portfolio. At the beginning of the year, the aggregate market value of the portfolio exceeded its cost. It received cash dividends on these securities during the year. It sold none of the securities in the portfolio during the year. At the end of the year, the aggregate cost of the portfolio exceeded its market value. The decline in the market price of the securities in the portfolio is attributable to general market decline.

During this year, Walker purchased for cash 35% of the outstanding voting stock of Sipe Company. It received cash dividends on this investment from Sipe during the year, and Sipe reported its earnings after the acquisition date to Walker.

Required

1. Explain how Walker reports on its balance sheet and income statement the effects of its investment in the securities available for sale portfolio for the year.

2. Explain how Walker reports on its balance sheet and income statement the effects of its investment in Sipe for the year.

C15-6 Various Investments

AICPA Adapted Houston Company has a portfolio of investments in available-for-sale securities that it classifies as a noncurrent asset. Houston owns less than 5% of the outstanding voting stock of each company's securities in the portfolio. At the beginning of the year, the aggregate market value of the portfolio exceeded its aggregate cost. Houston received cash dividends on these securities during the year. All cash dividends received represent distribution of earnings subsequent to Houston's acquisition of these securities. Houston sold some of the securities in the portfolio during the year. At the end of the year, the aggregate cost of the portfolio exceeded its aggregate market value.

Houston also owns 40% of the outstanding voting stock of Joy Company. The remainder of Joy's outstanding voting stock is widely dispersed among unrelated investors.

Required

1. a. Explain how Houston reports the income statement effects of the cash dividends received during the year on the securities in the available-for-sale portfolio.
   b. Explain how Houston reports the income statement effects of the securities sold during the year.
2. Explain how Houston reports the effect of ownership of the portfolio of securities available for sale in its balance sheet as of the end of the year and on its income statement for the year. Do *not* discuss the cash dividends or the securities sold.
3. Identify the method of accounting that Houston uses for its 40% investment in the outstanding voting stock of Joy. Why is this method appropriate?

CREATIVE AND CRITICAL THINKING

C15-7 Available-for-Sale Securities

AICPA Adapted The following are four *unrelated* situations involving investments in available-for-sale securities:

Situation I

A portfolio of available-for-sale securities with an aggregate fair value in excess of cost includes one particular security whose fair value has declined to less than one-half of the original cost. The decline in value is considered to be other than temporary.

Situation II

The statement of financial position of a company does not classify assets and liabilities as current and noncurrent. The portfolio of available-for-sale securities includes securities normally considered current that have a net cost in excess of fair value of $2,000. The remainder of the portfolio has a net fair value in excess of cost of $5,000.

Situation III

An available-for-sale security, whose fair value is currently less than cost, is reclassified as a trading security.

Situation IV

A company's portfolio of available-for-sale securities consists of the common stock of one company. At the end of the prior year, the fair value of the security was 50% of original cost, and the effect was properly reflected in an allowance account. However, at the end of the current year, the fair value of the security had appreciated to twice the original cost.

Required

Explain the effect on classification, carrying value, and earnings for each of the preceding situations.

C15-8 Change in Percent Ownership

AICPA Adapted For the past five years, Herbert has maintained an investment (properly accounted for and reported upon) in Broome amounting to a 10% interest in the voting common stock of Broome. The purchase price was $700,000 and the underlying net equity in Broome at the date of purchase was $620,000. On January 2 of the current year, Herbert purchased an additional 15% of the voting common stock of Broome for $1,200,000; the underlying net equity of additional investment at January 2 was $1,000,000. Broome has been profitable and has paid dividends annually since Herbert's initial acquisition.

Required

Discuss how this increase in ownership affects the accounting for and reporting upon the investment in Broome. Include in your discussion adjustments, if any, to the amount shown prior to the increase in investment to bring the amount into conformity with generally accepted accounting principles. Also include how the company would report in current and subsequent periods.

C15-9 Investments in Stocks and Bonds

AICPA Adapted Victoria Company has investments in equity securities classified as trading and available for sale. At the beginning of the year, the aggregate market value of each portfolio exceeded its cost. During the year, Victoria sold some securities from each portfolio. At the end of the year, the aggregate cost of each portfolio exceeded its market value.

Victoria also has investments in bonds classified as held to maturity, all of which were purchased for face value. During the year, some of these bonds held by Victoria were called prior to their maturity by the bond issuer. Three months before the end of the year, additional similar bonds were purchased for face value plus two months' accrued interest.

Required

1. a. Explain how Victoria accounts for the sale of securities from each portfolio.
    b. Explain how Victoria accounts for each equity securities portfolio at year-end.
2. Explain how Victoria accounts for the disposition prior to their maturity of the long-term bonds called by their issuer.
3. Explain how Victoria reports the purchase of the additional similar bonds at the date of the acquisition.

C15-10 Analyzing Coca-Cola's Investments Disclosures

Refer to the financial statements and related notes of The Coca-Cola Company in Appendix A of this book.

Required

1. Was the fair value of the company's available-for-sale securities higher or lower than the cost at the end of 2004? By how much?
2. Is the fair value of the company's held-to-maturity securities different from their cost at December 31, 2004? At December 31, 2003?
3. Explain why the company has cost method investments.
4. If the company included the assets and liabilities of its equity investments in its December 31, 2004 balance sheet instead of using the equity method, determine whether the effects on the assets, liabilities, and debt ratio would be material.

C15-11 Ethics and Investments

You are an accountant for the Davanzo Company. The president of the company calls you into her office and says, "I want to ask you about two issues. First, we need to sell one of our investments to raise $1 million because I think I have found a better investment. We could sell the shares of Company X, which are currently worth $1 million even though they originally cost us $400,000. But I don't want to sell them, because the company seems to be getting better all the time. Or we could sell the shares in that dog, Company Z. These shares are also worth $1 million, but they cost us $1.5 million and I hate to admit we made such a big mistake. And then there's that loss. I don't want to report that. I am going to use the $1 million to buy about 20% of the shares of Company M, but I seem to remember that there is some accounting rule that might affect how much we buy. I was also wondering about buying some of Company M's convertible preferred stock so we can convert that into a large ownership position in the future. Let me know what you think." You are aware that Company M is a new company that is not yet listed on the stock market, has been making losses, and is expected to continue making losses for a few more years.

Required

From financial reporting and ethical perspectives, discuss the issues raised by this situation.

Financial Reporting: Stockholders' Equity

CHAPTER 16
Contributed Capital

CHAPTER 17
Earnings Per Share and Retained Earnings

Contributed Capital

OBJECTIVES

After reading this chapter, you will be able to:

1 Explain the corporate form of organization.

2 Know the rights and terms that apply to capital stock.

3 Account for the issuance of capital stock.

4 Describe a compensatory share option plan.

5 Recognize compensation expense for a compensatory share option plan.

6 Account for a fixed compensatory share option plan.

7 Account for a performance-based compensatory share option plan.

8 Account for share appreciation rights.

9 Describe the characteristics of preferred stock.

10 Know the components of contributed capital.

11 Understand the accounting for treasury stock.

What is the Future of Executive Compensation?

Over the last two decades, stock ownership has increased dramatically. According to the Federal Reserve Board's Survey of Consumer Finances, more than 50% of U.S. households own stock, directly or indirectly—the highest percentage recorded by the Federal Reserve since it started regularly tracking stock ownership in 1983. Many factors have contributed to this growth in stock ownership, including the increasing use of mutual funds that have allowed small investors to diversify their portfolios at a low cost. According to the Investment Company Institute's 2004 Mutual Fund Fact Book, approximately 91 million individuals owned mutual funds in 2003.

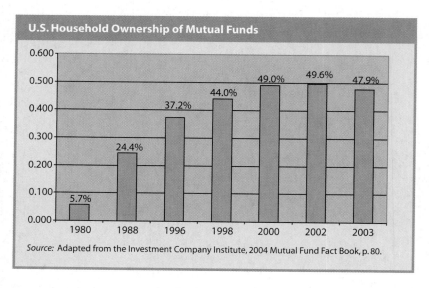

U.S. Household Ownership of Mutual Funds

Source: Adapted from the Investment Company Institute, 2004 Mutual Fund Fact Book, p. 80.

This growth in stock ownership has been enhanced by the increasing use of employee share (stock) option plans designed to reward employees for their long-term contributions and provide incentives for them to remain with the company. Historically,

Credit: Greg Pease/The Image Bank

companies usually did not record the "cost" of share options as an expense. For companies that make extensive use of share options, this form of compensation can be quite significant. For example, **Cisco** disclosed in its 2004 annual report that if it had been required to expense the fair value of share options, the additional expense would have decreased income by $1.215 billion (net of tax). However, after a long and controversial battle, new accounting standards require companies to record the fair value of these options as an expense. One impact of these new standards has already been observed. Because the cost of options are recorded as an expense over the vesting period, many companies have begun to accelerate the vesting of options to avoid having to record an expense once the new rules come into effect. As reported by the *Wall Street Journal*, this practice has already saved **HCA, Inc.** from having to record approximately $83 million in future compensation expense. Other companies, such as **Dow Jones & Co.**, have employed similar strategies to avoid the recognition of expenses related to share options. Because options must now be recorded as an expense, it is likely that boards of directors will soon be turning to other forms of pay for top executives. Only time will tell what lies ahead for executive compensation.

FOR FURTHER INVESTIGATION

For a discussion of stock options, consult the Business & Company Resource Center (BCRC):
- FASB Adopts Stock-Option Rule. *The Daily Deal* Dec 17, 2004.
- FASB Final Stock Option Ruling Lacks Real World Application; Future of Young, Emerging Growth Companies, IPO Market at Stake. *PR Newswire* Dec 16, 2004.

This chapter is the first of two on stockholders' equity. **FASB Statement of Concepts No. 6** defines **equity** as **the residual interest in the assets of a company that remains after deducting its liabilities.**[1] That is, the equity in a company is the ownership interest. Equity, which arises because of ownership rights, is created originally by owners' investments in the company. It may change because of several transactions or events, including cash dividends or other distributions of assets. Exhibit 16-1 summarizes these items.[2]

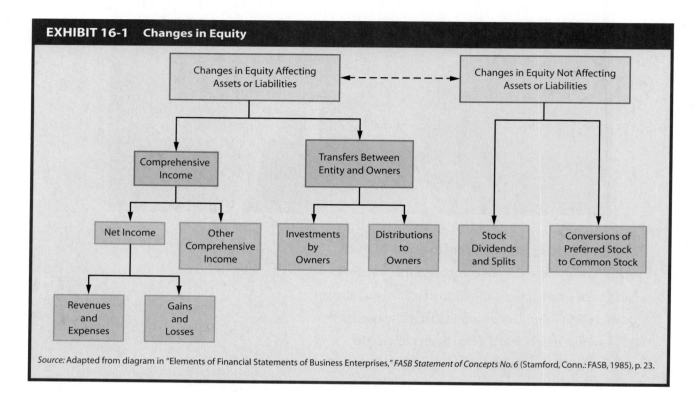

EXHIBIT 16-1   Changes in Equity

Source: Adapted from diagram in "Elements of Financial Statements of Business Enterprises," *FASB Statement of Concepts No. 6* (Stamford, Conn.: FASB, 1985), p. 23.

In the previous chapters we focused primarily on changes in assets and liabilities and their impact on net income (and equity). The main focus of Chapters 16 and 17, however, is on investments by owners, distributions to owners, and changes in equity not affecting assets or liabilities, as they apply to corporations.

In Chapter 16 we primarily discuss topics involving contributed capital. These issues include the formation of a corporation, the terminology relating to capital stock, the issuance of capital stock, compensatory share (stock) option plans, the contributed capital section of stockholders' equity, and the reacquisition of capital (treasury) stock. In Chapter 17 we primarily discuss issues involving retained earnings.

CORPORATE FORM OF ORGANIZATION

The corporation is the dominant form of company in the U.S. economy today. The number of sole proprietorships and partnerships is much greater than the number of corporations. However, corporations produce and sell many more goods and services. For example, according to recent government statistics, only 20% of companies in the United States are corporations, but they provide more than 86% of the total revenues of all companies.

---

1. "Elements of Financial Statements of Business Enterprises," *FASB Statement of Concepts No. 6* (Stamford, Conn.: FASB, 1985), par. 49.
2. *Ibid.*, par. 60–63.

Types of Corporations

Corporations may be classified in several ways. These classifications include private versus public, open versus closed, and domestic versus foreign. We summarize each of these classifications as follows:

1. **Private** corporations are privately owned. They include *nonstock* companies that do not issue stock and do not operate for profit (e.g., universities, hospitals, and churches). They also include *stock* companies that issue shares of stock to stockholders and operate for profit. Stock companies include open and closed corporations.
    a. **Open** corporations are those whose stock can be purchased by the public on a stock exchange or over-the-counter, and so are widely held. Open corporations often are called *publicly-traded* corporations.
    b. **Closed** corporations do not allow the sale of stock to the general public. This stock usually is held by a few stockholders. Closed corporations often are called *privately-held* corporations.
2. **Public** corporations are owned or operated by governmental units, such as the Federal Deposit Insurance Corporation.
3. **Domestic** corporations, as viewed by a particular state, are companies that are incorporated in that state.
4. **Foreign** corporations, as viewed by a particular state, are companies that are operating in the state but are incorporated in another state.

The federal government applies a more global definition to domestic and foreign corporations. To the federal government a domestic corporation is one incorporated in the United States; a foreign corporation is one incorporated in another country.

In this book, we are concerned primarily with private corporations that issue shares of stock.

Formation of a Corporation

Although a corporation actually is a collection of individual owners, legally it is treated as an artificial entity, separate from and independent of these individuals. Thus, ownership is readily transferable. Owners (**stockholders**) have limited liability. That is, they ordinarily have no personal liability for the corporation's debts and risk only their capital investment. Also, owners frequently are not active in its management. As a result, the success of the corporation generally depends on its ability to attract large amounts of capital (from a diverse set of stockholders, each with limited liability), which is controlled by a professional management group for an indefinite period.

> **1** Explain the corporate form of organization.

In the United States a corporation is a legal entity of a particular state. Each state has its own laws of incorporation. Many are uniform throughout the country, others are not. Normally, one or more individuals may apply for approval to form a corporation. The application includes:

- the names of the individual incorporators;
- the corporate name, address, and nature of business;
- the types, par value (if any), and number of shares of capital stock to be issued; and
- any other information required by the state's law.

The application may also include the names and addresses of the initial subscribers to the capital stock, the number of subscribed shares, the subscription price, and the down payment (if any). If approved, the application is referred to as the **articles of incorporation** (or corporate *charter*). A stockholders' meeting then may be held. At this meeting the initial issuance of capital stock is made to the incorporators, a board of directors is elected, a set of rules (bylaws) regulating the corporate operations is established, and the board appoints the executive officers ("top management") of the corporation.

For a corporation to perform its functions, the state gives it various rights and powers. These include the right to enter into contracts, to hold, buy, and sell property, to sue and be sued, and to continue in perpetuity. A corporation also has a number of responsibilities. A corporation may engage only in the activities for which it was established, it must adhere to state laws concerning the distribution of income, and it must pay state and federal taxes. Because a corporation's management has the responsibility to abide by state and federal laws and to safeguard and ensure the proper use of capital contributed by a diverse set of owners, accounting for corporate capital is important.

In this chapter we focus on capital stock transactions and their impact on the corporate capital structure. Any statements we make about the characteristics of corporations, capital stock, and a corporation's capital structure are general statements. In any particular state, or for any particular corporation, these statements may not hold.

CORPORATE CAPITAL STRUCTURE

Ownership in a corporation is evidenced by a **stock certificate**, a serially numbered document that indicates the number of shares owned and the par value (if any). Exhibit 16-2 shows a stock certificate for **The Coca-Cola Company.** Because stock certificates are easily transferred from one individual to another, state laws require that each corporation keep appropriate records of its stockholders. The **stockholders' ledger** contains an account for each stockholder that shows the number of shares held. Whenever new shares are issued or shares are exchanged between stockholders, the ledger must be updated. Exchanges of stock are recorded initially in a **stock transfer journal.** This journal contains the names and addresses of the new and former stockholders involved in each stock transfer, the date of exchange, the stock certificate numbers, and the number of shares exchanged.

EXHIBIT 16-2   Illustration of Stock Certificate

"Coca-Cola" is a registered trademark of the Coca-Cola Company

Many corporations employ an independent **transfer agent** (such as a bank) to handle the issuance of stock certificates, as well as a **registrar** to maintain the stockholder records.

Capital Stock and Stockholders' Rights

Capital stock refers to the shares of stock issued by the corporation and owned by its stockholders. Each stockholder has various rights. Generally, these rights include:

- the right to share in the profits when a dividend is declared,
- the right to elect directors and to establish corporate policies,
- the right (called a **preemptive right**) to maintain a proportionate interest in the ownership of the corporation by purchasing a proportionate (pro rata) share of additional capital stock, if more stock is issued, and
- the right to share in the distribution of the assets of the corporation if it is liquidated.

2 Know the rights and terms that apply to capital stock.

These rights may be modified or waived for some types of capital stock or in specific circumstances. For instance, stockholders who own a certain class of stock may be entitled to vote only on particular issues. Another example involves waiving the preemptive right to allow a corporation to raise significant capital or acquire another company by issuing a large number of additional shares of stock.

A corporation may issue capital stock for cash, through installment sales, for nonmonetary assets, for compensatory share option plans, and for other types of transactions. It may issue two basic classes of stock, generally designated as common stock and preferred stock. **Common stock** is capital stock that carries all of the preceding rights. Some corporations, however, issue more than one type of common stock such as Class A and Class B common stock. In this situation, usually one type of common stock has greater voting rights than the other to maintain control over the corporate activities. In exchange for certain other privileges, **preferred stock** usually is not granted all of the common stock's rights. We discuss the various stock transactions, as well as the characteristics and privileges of preferred stock, later in this chapter.

Basic Terminology

Several terms are often used in the discussion of capital stock and related transactions:

- **Authorized capital stock.** The number of shares of capital stock (both preferred and common) that a corporation may issue as stated in its corporate charter.
- **Issued capital stock.** The number of shares of capital stock that a corporation has issued to its stockholders as of a specific date.
- **Outstanding capital stock.** The number of shares of capital stock that a corporation has issued to stockholders and that are still being held by them as of a specific date.
- **Treasury stock.** The number of shares of capital stock that a corporation has issued to stockholders and has reacquired but not retired. The number of treasury shares is the difference between the number of issued shares and the number of outstanding shares.
- **Subscribed capital stock.** The number of shares of capital stock that a corporation will issue upon the completion of an installment purchase contract with an investor.

These terms relate to each other as follows:

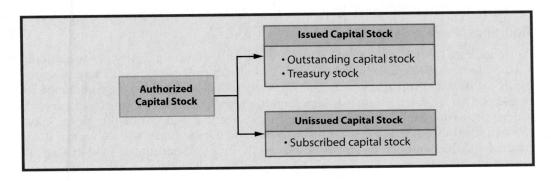

Legal Capital

As we indicated earlier, stockholders have *limited liability*. Generally they cannot be held legally responsible for the debts of the corporation unless the corporation has been operated for the personal benefit of particular stockholders. To protect the corporation's creditors, state laws have established the concept of **legal capital** as the **amount of stockholders' equity that the corporation cannot distribute to stockholders.** A corporation may not pay dividends or reacquire capital stock if such a transaction would impair its legal capital. The definition of legal capital varies among states. An investor must refer to the corporate laws of each state to determine the corporate legal capital in that state. However, in most states the par value or stated value of the issued capital stock is some or all of the legal capital.

Par Value Stock

Historically, the primary way a corporation establishes its legal capital is by issuing par value stock. **The par value of a corporation's capital stock (either common or preferred) is a designated dollar amount per share that is established in the articles of incorporation and is printed on each stock certificate.** When a corporation issues par value stock, most states designate that the par value of all its issued stock is the legal capital. The legal capital of the corporation is the par value per share multiplied by the number of shares issued. The par value of a share often is set very low—perhaps $5, $1, or even less per share. Note that the par value of the common stock listed on the stock certificate of The Coca-Cola Company in Exhibit 16-2 is $0.25 per share.

Since capital stock normally will sell at a price much higher than the par value (e.g., Coke's common stock was recently selling for $43.50 per share), the legal capital is usually only a small portion of the total proceeds received. Stock rarely sells initially for less than its par value, because it is illegal to do so in most states. If such a sale occurs, the stock is said to have been sold at a *discount*, in which case the stockholder is contingently responsible to contribute sufficient additional capital to meet the corporation's legal capital requirements. In any event, par value has no direct relationship to the **market value,** the price at which the stock is issued. Generally, state regulations require only that a corporation separately account for its legal capital.

No-Par Stock

To avoid the contingent liability that would arise if stock were issued at less than par value, many states allow corporations to issue no-par capital stock. As the term implies, this stock does not carry a par value. When a corporation issues no-par stock, some states require that the corporation designate the entire proceeds received as legal capital. Many states, however, allow the corporate board of directors to establish a **stated value** per share of no-par stock. This stated value, when multiplied by the number of shares issued, generally determines the amount of the corporation's legal capital. The accounting for stated value, no-par stock parallels that of the accounting for par value stock.

The concept of legal capital has had a significant effect on corporate reporting practices, particularly as they apply to the accounting for stockholders' equity. A corporation creates capital stock accounts (for either common stock or preferred stock) to accumulate at least part of the legal capital. It uses Additional Paid-in Capital accounts for the remainder of the capital contributed by stockholders (part of which also may be legal capital).

Additional Paid-in Capital

As we indicated earlier, a corporation may issue capital stock in a variety of transactions. Each of these transactions is likely to involve an exchange price (i.e., market value) significantly higher than the par or stated value of the stock. State law requires the corporation to record the par or stated value. Sound accounting practice (as well as state law in certain states) also requires the corporation to identify, measure, and record the excess value received (the difference between the market value and the par value) in each type of stock transaction. The corporation records this excess in a specific **Additional Paid-in Capital** account. This account alternatively is titled *Paid-in Capital in Excess of Par* (or *Stated*) *Value, Premium on Capital Stock,* or *Contributed Capital in Excess of Par* (or *Stated*) *Value,* or by an outdated term, *Capital Surplus.* Because this additional paid-in capital is likely to arise from a variety of transactions, a corporation may create a single Additional Paid-in Capital *control* account and then have a subsidiary ledger containing separate additional paid-in capital accounts for each different source. When this occurs, it reports only the control account balance on its balance sheet. In this chapter we assume a control account is *not* used.

STOCKHOLDERS' EQUITY

As we discussed earlier, total stockholders' equity is the residual interest of the owners in the net assets of the corporation—the equity or *capital* of the owners is the corporation's assets less its liabilities. In Chapter 4 we noted that the value of the assets and liabilities could be measured by several methods. The way in which a corporation measures its assets and liabilities will determine its measurement of total stockholders' equity, since the accounting equation: Assets = Liabilities + Stockholders' Equity must remain in balance. Total stockholders' equity, however, may be made up of several components.

A corporation reports the various components of its capital structure in the stockholders' equity section of its balance sheet. We noted earlier that a corporation records the results of all its stock transactions in capital stock accounts and additional paid-in capital accounts. To report the total amount invested by stockholders, a corporation lists and adds together these accounts in the **Contributed Capital** (or **Paid-in Capital**) section of its stockholders' equity.

In addition to disclosing total investments by stockholders, state laws and sound accounting practice require a corporation to disclose any net income that has been reinvested in the corporation and not paid out to stockholders as dividends. A corporation reports this element of its corporate capital structure in the **Retained Earnings** section of stockholders' equity. Also, stockholders' equity may increase or decrease as a result of other comprehensive income. A corporation reports this element of its capital structure in an **Accumulated Other Comprehensive Income** section of stockholders' equity. We discuss retained earnings and accumulated other comprehensive income in Chapter 17.

The basic framework of a corporation's stockholders' equity is as follows:

Stockholders' Equity

Contributed Capital	
Capital stock	$ XX
Additional paid-in capital	XX
Retained earnings	XX
Accumulated other comprehensive income	XX
Total stockholders' equity	$XXXX

SECURE YOUR KNOWLEDGE 16-1

- A corporation, the dominant form of a company in terms of revenues generated, is a legal entity that is separate from and independent of its owners.
- As a legal entity of a particular state, a corporation must follow the laws of the particular state in which it was incorporated.
- Capital stock represents the basic ownership interest in a corporation and possesses various rights including:
  - The right to share in the corporation's profits when a dividend is declared
  - The right to elect directors and establish corporate policies (voting right)

(continued)

- ■ The right to maintain a proportionate share in the ownership of the corporation when new stock is issued (preemptive right)
- ■ The right to share in the distribution of the assets if the corporation is liquidated
- ● Legal capital, the amount of stockholders' equity that cannot be distributed to stockholders, is often based on the par value or stated value of the capital stock.
- ● While par and stated values have no direct relationship to market value, these values are needed in many states to properly separate a corporation's legal capital from its other capital accounts.
- ● Additional Paid-in Capital represents any capital contributed by stockholders in excess of the par or stated value.
- ● Stockholders' equity, the residual interest of the owners in the assets of the corporation, is generally separated into three primary components: Contributed Capital, Retained Earnings, and Accumulated Other Comprehensive Income.

ISSUANCE OF CAPITAL STOCK

3 Account for the issuance of capital stock.

When a corporation issues only one class of capital stock, it is referred to as common stock. Common stockholders are the claimants to the residual interest in the corporation. Unless waived or modified, common stockholders generally have all the rights we discussed earlier in the chapter. As we pointed out previously, corporations may engage in a variety of transactions related to the issuance of capital stock. We describe the proper accounting for each of these transactions next. Because most capital stock is common stock, our examples are in terms of common stock. However, the journal entries we show apply equally to preferred stock.

Authorization

The corporate charter contains the authorization to issue capital stock. A corporation usually records this authorization in a memorandum journal entry. The entry identifies the number of authorized shares, the par or stated value per share, and, in the case of preferred stock, any preference provisions. Generally, the corporation creates a separate account for each class of capital stock, and makes a similar memorandum entry in each account.

Issuance for Cash

A corporation may issue capital stock with a par value, as no-par stock with a stated value, or as true no-par stock. In the case of par value stock issued for cash, it records the difference between the proceeds and the total par value in an Additional Paid-in Capital account. For example, assume Tyler Corporation issues 500 shares of its $10 par common stock for $18 per share. The corporation records the transaction as follows:

Cash ($18 × 500)	9,000	
Common Stock, $10 par ($10 × 500)		5,000
Additional Paid-in Capital on Common Stock		4,000

If, instead, the stock were no-par stock with a stated value of $10 per share, it would record the preceding transaction as follows:

Cash	9,000	
Common Stock, $10 stated value		5,000
Additional Paid-in Capital on Common Stock		4,000

Note that, with the exception of the terminology change, accounting for the issuance of no-par stock with a stated value is identical to that of par value stock.

Alternatively, Tyler Corporation may be authorized to issue no-par stock without a stated value. In this case, unless otherwise stipulated, the entire amount of the proceeds is the legal capital and is recorded in the capital stock account. If the preceding transaction involved no-par, no-stated-value stock, the corporation would record it as follows:

Cash	9,000	
Common Stock, no-par (500 shares)		9,000

Note that in this journal entry the number of *shares* issued is included. This is necessary because the number of shares issued in this transaction cannot be determined by dividing the total increase in the Common Stock account by the par value per share. In the remaining examples of stock issuances we assume a par value for the stock.

As we discussed earlier, most states prohibit a corporation from issuing capital stock at a price below its par or stated value (at a discount). If such a transaction occurs, the original stockholder may be required to pay into the corporation the amount of the discount if the corporation is unable to meet its financial obligations. The corporation *debits* the difference between the proceeds and the par value to an account titled Discount on Common Stock. It reports this account as a contra (negative) account in the Contributed Capital section of its stockholders' equity.

Stock Issuance Costs

A corporation may incur miscellaneous costs that are related directly to issuing its capital stock. They include items such as legal fees, accounting fees, stock certificate costs, underwriter's fees, promotional costs, and postage. When related to the initial issuance of stock at incorporation, the corporation records these costs as an expense. On the other hand, the costs related to later issuances of stock are considered to be normal financing expenditures and reduce the proceeds from the issuances. When a corporation incurs these costs, it reduces additional paid-in capital for the amount of the costs. The FASB is considering changing GAAP so that all stock issuance costs will be expensed as incurred.

Stock Subscriptions

Investors sometimes agree to purchase capital stock from a corporation on an "installment" basis. This means the corporation and the future stockholder enter into a legally-binding subscription contract. This contract requires the subscriber (investor) to buy a certain number of shares at an agreed-upon price, with payment spread over a specified time period. The contract often requires a down payment and may require the subscribers to issue a promissory note. It may also contain provisions for the handling of any defaults (nonpayments) by the subscriber. Usually, the corporation does not issue shares of capital stock to a subscriber until the subscriber has completed full payment of the subscription price.

Example: Subscription Contract Assume that Pellogrini Corporation enters into a subscription contract with several subscribers. The contract requires the subscribers to purchase 1,000 shares of $6 par common stock at a price of $13 per share. The contract further requires a down payment of $3 per share, with the remaining $10 per share collectible at the end of one month. The stock will be issued to each subscriber upon full payment. The corporation records the subscription as follows:

Cash ($3 × 1,000)	3,000	
Subscriptions Receivable:		
Common Stock ($10 × 1,000)	10,000	
Common Stock Subscribed ($6 × 1,000)		6,000
Additional Paid-in Capital on Common Stock		7,000

Note that the balance to be received is recorded in a Subscriptions Receivable account. There is disagreement as to how a corporation should report the subscriptions receivable on its balance sheet. Some argue that because the subscription contract is legally binding, the receivable will be collected. Hence, Subscriptions Receivable should be reported as an asset on the corporation's balance sheet. Others contend that Subscriptions Receivable should be listed as a contra-stockholders' equity account because collection is uncertain and the corporation is not assured of obtaining a future benefit. They claim that the receivable does not meet the definition of an asset established in *FASB Statement of Concepts No. 6.* They also claim that receivables from subscriptions are different from normal trade receivables in that no goods or services were provided. The Securities and Exchange Commission supports this view by requiring a corporation to report its subscriptions receivable as a contra-stockholders' equity account in financial statements filed with it. The SEC also felt that a subscription contract could be a "sham" transaction used to inflate the corporation's assets and stockholders' equity. In fact, this is what happened with **Enron Corporation**. Enron created "special purpose entities" and agreed to issue its stock to these entities as part of its investment in these entities. It reported more than $1 billion of notes (subscription) receivable as assets and an equal amount as stockholders' equity. This overstated Enron's assets and stockholders' equity, which helped lead to its collapse. Most companies report Subscriptions Receivable as a contra-stockholders' equity account.

Note in the Pellogrini example that a Common Stock Subscribed account is credited for the par value of the shares subscribed. This account is used because the shares have not yet been issued. Since the corporation expects the contract to be completed, the Common Stock Subscribed account is reported in the Contributed Capital section of its stockholders' equity. It indicates that the corporation has contracted to issue additional stock. Additional Paid-in Capital is credited for the entire difference between the subscription price (the proceeds) and the par value of the subscribed stock under the assumption that the contract will be completed and the stock fully paid for.

When the corporation receives payment, it debits Cash and credits the Subscriptions Receivable account. At the final payment by a subscriber, it makes a journal entry to transfer the balance in the Common Stock Subscribed account to the Common Stock account, and issues stock certificates for the number of subscribed shares fully paid for by that subscriber. For example, assume that Pellogrini received the $10 per share final payment from subscribers to 950 shares at the end of the month. The corporation makes the following journal entries to record the final payment and the issuance of the 950 shares of stock:

Cash (950 × $10)	9,500	
Subscriptions Receivable: Common Stock		9,500
Common Stock Subscribed (950 × $6)	5,700	
Common Stock, $6 par		5,700 ♦

Example: Default Occasionally, a subscriber will not pay the entire amount as required by the subscription contract. When a default occurs, the accounting is based on the contract provisions, such as: (1) return to the subscriber the entire amount paid in, (2) return to the subscriber the amount paid in, less any costs incurred by the corporation to reissue the stock, (3) issue to the subscriber a lesser number of shares based on the total amount paid in, or (4) require the forfeiture of all amounts paid in.

For example, assume the subscriber to the 50 remaining shares of Pellogrini defaults on the contract. If the contract requires forfeiture of the entire amount paid in, the corporation makes the following journal entry:

Common Stock Subscribed (50 × $6)	300	
Additional Paid-in Capital on		
Common Stock (50 × $7)	350	
Subscriptions Receivable:		
Common Stock (50 × $10)		500
Additional Paid-in Capital from Subscription		
Default (50 × $3)		150

If the subscription contract does not address defaults, a default is handled according to the laws of the state in which the corporation is incorporated. ♦

LINK TO ETHICAL DILEMMA

Muddy Water, Inc. catches and supplies fresh seafood to a variety of restaurants across the country. While the company remains profitable, increased competition from South American seafood suppliers has lowered the company's return on equity (net income divided by average stockholders' equity) to a level that the Board of Directors finds unacceptable. In response to these competitive pressures, the company decided to modernize its processing plants in hopes that the resulting increase in efficiency would lead to lower costs and higher profit margins. You were in charge of assembling a team to develop financing options. After carefully analyzing the various options, your team recommended that the modernization be financed by issuing stock. The CEO agreed with your recommendation that equity financing was in the best long-term interest of the company and instructed you to proceed with the stock issuance. However, after returning from a business trip, the CEO informs you that she has changed her mind and the modernization will be financed by debt instead of equity. The CEO confessed that she had discussed the matter with another business professional who informed her that issuing stock would only serve to increase stockholders' equity, which would lower the company's return on equity. Debt financing, on the other hand, might actually help the company reach its return on equity targets. While you confirm that this may be true, you inform the CEO that the debt option is much riskier and the required interest payments would put the company in a shaky cash position. The CEO stated that she understood the risk, but that she really needed to reach the return on equity target to achieve bonuses for her executive team, and any cash flow concerns would not surface until after she retired in two years. Do you have any ethical responsibilities to report the CEO's decision to the Board of Directors?

Combined Sales of Stock

Instead of issuing different classes of securities separately, a corporation may combine two or more classes and issue them in a single "package" transaction. To make the package attractive to investors, the corporation will set the selling price of the package at less than the amount it would receive if it sold each class of securities separately. These transactions may include combinations of common stock, preferred stock, and long-term bonds. When a corporation issues different classes of securities in a combined sale, it allocates the proceeds between the two (or more) securities. This allocation is based on the **relative fair values of the separate securities**. If a fair (e.g., market) value is not known, the securities with the known fair values are assigned a portion of the proceeds equal to their fair values. The remaining proceeds are assigned to the security with the unknown fair value.

Suppose, for example, that Brandt Corporation issues 100 "packages" of securities for $82.80 per package, or a total of $8,280. Each package includes two shares of $10 par common stock and one share of $50 par preferred stock. If the separate market values are

$16 per share for the common stock and $60 per share for the preferred stock, the corporation makes the following journal entry and supporting computations*:

Cash	8,280	
Common Stock, $10 par (200 shares)		2,000
Additional Paid-in Capital on Common Stock		880
Preferred Stock, $50 par (100 shares)		5,000
Additional Paid-in Capital on Preferred Stock		400

*Computations:

Aggregate Fair Value

Common Stock: $16 × 2 Shares × 100 Packages = $3,200
Preferred Stock: $60 × 1 Share × 100 Packages = <u>6,000</u>
$9,200

Allocation

Common Stock: $\dfrac{\$3,200}{\$9,200} \times \$8,280 = \$2,880$

Preferred Stock: $\dfrac{\$6,000}{\$9,200} \times \$8,280 = \underline{\;5,400\;}$
$8,280

Note that the corporation separates the fair value assigned to each class of stock into the par value and additional paid-in capital in the journal entry.

If only the separate market value of $16 per share for the common stock is known, Brandt Corporation assigns $3,200 ($16 × 2 shares × 100 packages) of the proceeds to the common stock, and allocates the remainder of $5,080 to the preferred stock, as follows:

Cash	8,280	
Common Stock, $10 par		2,000
Additional Paid-in Capital on Common Stock		1,200
Preferred Stock, $50 par		5,000
Additional Paid-in Capital on Preferred Stock		80

In the rare case when none of the securities has a market value, a corporation must estimate the fair values. A reasonable allocation must be made to the various elements of equity. If a fair value is established for one (or all) of the securities in the near future that makes this allocation unreasonable, it makes an adjustment of the allocation. If, in the preceding examples, the stock was issued in combination with bonds, then the corporation would record the bonds at a premium or discount based on their relative fair value.

Nonmonetary Issuance of Stock

In some cases a corporation may issue capital stock for assets other than cash, or for services performed. This type of transaction is called a *nonmonetary exchange*. The corporation must assign an appropriate value to the transaction so it can record the exchange properly. This valuation is a particularly troublesome issue when it involves intangible assets such as patents, copyrights, or organization costs. The general rule is to **record the exchange at the fair value of the stock issued or the asset received, whichever is more** *reliable.* For instance, at the time of the exchange the stock may be selling on the stock market at a specified price but a verifiable value of the asset may be difficult to determine. In this case, the stock market price is used as the fair value at which to record the exchange transaction.

Example: Fair Value of Stock Known   Suppose Cody Corporation issues 200 shares of $10 par common stock for a patent. The stock currently is selling for $22 per share on the open market, and no significant impact on the market price by the issuance of the additional shares is expected. The corporation assigns a value of $4,400 to the exchange, and records the transaction as follows:

Patent ($22 × 200)	4,400	
Common Stock, $10 par		2,000
Additional Paid-in Capital on Common Stock		2,400

If a large number of additional shares are issued, this may significantly reduce the market price. In this case, the corporation does not record the transaction until the reduced market price is known, and records the asset at that price. ♦

Example: Fair Value of Asset Unknown   Alternatively, the stock may be closely held and not actively traded. Here, using the fair value of the assets received may be more reliable for recording the transaction. This value may be based on recent transactions involving similar assets or on an appraisal by an independent appraiser. For example, assume that Elk Corporation issues 500 shares of $8 par common stock that is not widely traded for an acre of land. An independent appraiser indicates the land has a value of $20,000. The corporation uses the appraisal value of the land as the fair value and records the transaction as follows:

Land	20,000	
Common Stock, $8 par		4,000
Additional Paid-in Capital on Common Stock		16,000 ♦

When a corporation issues two or more securities for an asset, it uses the combination of the most reliable fair values to determine the total value at which to record the transaction. If reliable fair values for both the stock and the asset are not available, the corporate board of directors must assign the value used to record the exchange. Such an assignment should be based on available supporting evidence. Incorrect valuation of the exchange would lead either to an overstatement of the corporation's assets and its stockholders' equity (referred to as **watered stock**), or to an understatement of its assets and stockholders' equity (referred to as **secret reserves**). Also, errors would arise in later financial statements if the asset is depreciated or amortized against future revenues, or sold.

Stock Splits

The market price of a corporation's common stock may increase to the point where it discourages investments by some investors. Many corporations believe that wide distribution of ownership improves their public image, increases the demand for their stock, and may increase product sales to these stockholders. To reduce the market price so that it falls within the "trading range" of most investors, a corporation's board of directors—upon meeting state legal requirements—may authorize a stock split. **A stock split (or stock split-up) decreases the par value per share of stock and proportionally increases the number of shares issued.** Generally, a stock split also results in a proportional increase in the number of shares authorized.

Example: Proportionate Stock Split   Assume that Ollar Corporation has 250,000 authorized shares and has issued 60,000 shares of $10 par common stock. The corporation declares a two-for-one stock split with a reduction to a $5 par value. After the split 500,000 shares are authorized and a total of 120,000 shares of $5 common stock are issued. Generally, the additional shares participating in the same amount of earnings will cause a corresponding decrease in the market price per share.

When a corporation has a stock split, it generally does not recall the existing shares. Instead, each stockholder is informed of the new par value per share and is issued an additional number of shares to compensate for the split. From an accounting standpoint, a stock split has no dollar effect on any element of the corporation's stockholders' equity. Consequently, a stock split has no effect on total stockholders' equity. In the previous example, the total par value of the issued common stock is $600,000 prior to and after the stock split.

A corporation ordinarily records a stock split by a memorandum entry that indicates the new par value, the total number of shares issued, and the impact (if any) on the number of authorized shares. For instance, the memorandum entry of Ollar Corporation might read as follows:

> **The board of directors split the common stock two for one, increasing the issued stock from 60,000 to 120,000 shares. The par value of the stock has been reduced from $10 per share to $5 per share and the authorized shares have been increased to 500,000 shares.** ◆

Example: Disproportionate Stock Split Occasionally, a corporation will issue a **disproportionate stock split in which the reduction in par value is not proportionate to the increase in the number of shares.** In this case the corporation must make a journal entry to adjust the legal capital and additional paid-in capital. In the previous example, assume instead that Ollar Corporation reduced the par value to $4 per share. The corporation would record the disproportionate stock split as follows:

Common Stock, $10 par (60,000 × $10)	600,000	
Common Stock, $4 par (60,000 × 2 × $4)		480,000
Additional Paid-in Capital from Stock Split		120,000

Although a disproportionate stock split does not affect total stockholders' equity, it does affect the components of Contributed Capital. Occasionally, a corporation may declare a reverse stock split to increase the market value of its stock. **A reverse stock split decreases the number of shares and increases the par value per share,** and is recorded in a manner opposite to that of a stock split. ◆

Some corporations issue *stock dividends* instead of, or with, cash dividends. Certain large stock dividends are similar to stock splits. We discuss stock dividends in Chapter 17.

SECURE YOUR KNOWLEDGE 16-2

- When common stock is issued for cash, the total par value (number of shares multiplied by the par value per share) is recorded in the Common Stock account, with any excess recorded as Additional Paid-in Capital.
  - For stock with no par or stated value, the total amount received from the sale is recorded as Common Stock.
- Stock issuance costs are recorded either as an expense (if the costs relate to the initial issuance of stock at incorporation) or as a reduction of additional paid-in capital (if the costs relate to subsequent issuances of stock).
- Stock is sometimes issued on a subscription or "installment" basis:
  - The initial entry results in a debit to Cash for the subscription price received; a debit to Subscriptions Receivable (a contra-equity account) for any cash not yet received; a credit to Common Stock Subscribed (a contributed capital account) for the par value of the subscribed shares that have not yet been issued; and a credit to Additional Paid-in Capital for any excess of the subscription price.
  - Final receipt of the amount owed by investors results in the corporation issuing the shares by transferring the balance in Common Stock Subscribed to Common Stock.
- If more than one class of security (common stock, preferred stock, bonds) is issued for a single price, the proceeds are allocated to the different securities based on their relative fair values.
- Capital stock issued for services or assets other than cash should be recorded at the fair value of the stock issued or noncash consideration received, whichever is more reliable.
- A stock split increases the number of shares issued and proportionately decreases the par value per share, resulting in no dollar impact to any element of stockholders' equity. A reverse split works in the opposite manner.

Stock Rights to Current Stockholders

The preemptive right gives current stockholders the opportunity to maintain their proportionate share in the ownership of the corporation if it issues additional shares of the same class of stock. If a corporation's board of directors authorizes the issuance of additional shares, it must extend the preemptive right to the present stockholders, unless they have waived that right. The corporation fulfills the **right** by issuing stock **warrants** to each present stockholder who may then exchange them for additional shares of stock. One stock warrant (right) usually attaches to each share outstanding. However, a stockholder usually must exchange more than one warrant to acquire each additional share. A corporation may also issue stock rights to stockholders for a new issue of stock to encourage rapid sale of the stock. In either case, the rights usually allow stockholders to purchase the additional shares at a price slightly less than the current market price. The rights thus acquire a value themselves. Because the warrants are certificates that are readily transferable, they trade on the stock market in a manner similar to stocks. These stock warrants (rights) generally expire within a short period of time, usually a few weeks.

At the time a corporation issues the warrants, it makes a memorandum entry listing the number of additional shares that may be acquired through the exercise of the stock rights. This entry also provides information for disclosing the outstanding warrants in the notes to its financial statements. If the rights are exercised, the corporation makes the usual journal entry to record the issuance of the stock. If the rights expire, it makes another memorandum entry noting the expiration.

Many corporations also have **share purchase plans** or **share option plans** that enable employees to buy shares of stock, often at a price less than the current market price. These programs involve the issuance of warrants (rights) to the employees. The degree of allowed participation in these plans varies. At one extreme, all employees are eligible to participate. At the other extreme, a plan is available only to one, or a few, key employees within the company. Also, the purchase price may be at a small discount from the current market price, or a price established when the options were granted. These plans are established for various reasons: (1) the need to attract more equity capital, (2) the belief that employee ownership will lead to a greater commitment to corporate activities, and (3) the desire to provide further compensation for certain employees. **FASB Statement No. 123R** addresses the accounting for the warrants involved in employee share purchase and option plans. It is a complex *Statement*; we summarize only the primary elements here. The *Statement* differentiates between noncompensatory share purchase plans and compensatory share option plans.

NONCOMPENSATORY SHARE PURCHASE PLANS

A noncompensatory employee plan (share purchase plan) is designed by a corporation to raise capital or to obtain more widespread employee ownership of the corporate stock. Three criteria must be met for a share option plan to be noncompensatory:

1. Substantially all employees who meet limited employment qualifications may participate in the plan on an equitable basis.
2. The discount from the market price does not exceed the per-share amount of stock issuance costs avoided by not issuing the stock to the public. A purchase discount of up to 5% automatically complies with this criterion.
3. The plan has no option features other than the following: (a) employees are allowed a short time (no longer than 31 days) from the date the purchase price is set to decide whether to enroll in the plan, and (b) the purchase price is based solely on the market price of the stock on the purchase date, and employees are permitted to cancel their participation before the purchase date and obtain a refund of any amounts previously paid.[3]

---

3. "Share-Based Payment," *FASB Statement of Financial Accounting Standards No. 123* (revised 2004) (Norwalk, Conn.: FASB, 2004), par. 12. In the text, we will refer to this as *FASB Statement No.123R*.

If **all** these criteria are met, the plan is a **noncompensatory plan** because no compensation is considered to be paid to employees. The corporation makes a memorandum entry when it issues the stock warrants, indicating the number of additional shares that may be acquired. If the warrants are exercised, the corporation makes the usual journal entry to record the stock issuance. If not exercised, it makes a memorandum entry noting the expiration.

In some cases, employees of a corporation (with its assistance) will set up an employee share ownership plan (called an ESOP) for investment purposes. ESOPs vary from corporation to corporation. In one type of ESOP, a trustee borrows money from a financial institution and uses the funds to purchase shares in the corporation for the employees. Usually, the corporation guarantees the liability of the ESOP (using the shares as collateral). It also may agree to make contributions to the ESOP to pay the interest on the liability and to help the ESOP acquire more of the corporation's stock. If the corporation only assists in the initial financing of the ESOP, at the time of borrowing the corporation records an increase in cash (for the amount received from the trustee for the stock) and a liability. It also records the issuance of the stock and a contra-equity account for the unearned ESOP shares that are used as collateral on the loan. It reduces the liability and contra-equity accounts (and increases stockholders' equity) as the ESOP makes payments on the debt that it guaranteed. If the corporation also makes contributions to the ESOP, it treats these contributions as interest expense and "deferred compensation" (a "negative" component of stockholders' equity), which it allocates to compensation expense.[4]

COMPENSATORY SHARE OPTION PLANS

4 Describe a compensatory share option plan.

In addition to cash salaries, many corporations have share-based compensation plans. A **share-based compensation plan** (often called a **stock option plan**) is a compensation arrangement (award) established by a corporation. Under this plan, its employees, in exchange for their services, receive shares of stock, share options, or other equity instruments (or the corporation incurs liabilities to employees in amounts based on the price of its stock). In this chapter we focus primarily on share options (stock options), because they are the most common type of plan.

A share option plan that does *not* possess *all* three criteria we listed in the previous section is a compensatory plan. **A compensatory share option plan is intended to provide additional compensation to selected employees within the corporation.** The terms of a compensatory share option plan are often complex and relate to items such as the number of shares to which each employee is entitled and the option price (both of which may depend on some future event), whether cash may be received instead of shares, the period of service the employee must complete before becoming eligible, the date the option can first be exercised, and the date of expiration (if any).

Historical Perspective and Conceptual Overview

Before we discuss the current generally accepted accounting principles for compensatory share option plans, it is useful to review how these plans work, how corporations accounted for them in the past, and related conceptual issues. Under a common type of plan, a corporation grants selected employees (e.g., top managers) the rights to purchase shares of stock at a set price (called the **exercise price** or **option price**; these terms are used interchangeably) some time in the future (usually several years) in exchange for their services. The corporation generally issues nontransferable warrants to the employees as evidence of the rights. Each warrant generally allows the employee to acquire one share of common stock. So, for instance, a corporation may grant an employee the right to purchase 1,000 shares of common stock at the end of three years at an exercise (option) price of $20 per share. If the market price increases to

---

4. For a more detailed discussion, see "Employer's Accounting for Employee Stock Ownership Plans," *AICPA Statement of Position 93-6* (AICPA: November 23, 1993).

$35 per share at the end of three years, the employee can exercise the option and acquire shares with a value of $35,000 ($35 × 1,000) by paying only $20,000 ($20 × 1,000). Clearly, this is a valuable share option for the employee.

Intrinsic Value

APB Opinion No. 25 initially governed the accounting for compensatory share option plans. It required the use of the "intrinsic value method." **Under the intrinsic value method,** a corporation measured the total compensation cost for each employee as the excess of the market price of the stock over the exercise price for the specified number of shares on the date the corporation grants the option. The corporation recognized this total compensation cost as an expense on a "straight-line" basis over the years from the date of grant to the date the shares could first be purchased.

In cases where the exercise price was *equal to or higher than* the market price on the grant date, the corporation incurred *no* compensation cost and therefore recognized *no* compensation expense. This situation frequently occurred because compensatory share option plans usually are written to take advantage of Internal Revenue Service rules regarding the income taxes of the employees participating in the plans. These plans are called *qualified (incentive) stock option plans*. That is, according to the tax rules, if the exercise price is set at (or greater than) the market price of the stock on the grant date, then the plan qualifies for special tax treatment. The options are not considered to be taxable compensation of the employee on that date. Instead, the income taxes generally are deferred until the employee exercises the stock option (or in some cases even later when the stock is sold). At that time any gain is taxed at a lower, long-term capital gains rate.

Fair Value

From a conceptual standpoint, many external users were critical of the intrinsic value measurement method. They noted that the fair value of a share option may be a significant portion of the total compensation of each employee. For instance, a study showed that share option grants averaged 81% of the total cash compensation of the top executives of the nation's 100 largest financial institutions. In addition, the dollar value of compensatory share option plans can be quite large. For example, **Wal-Mart's** compensation expense for its plan was $102 million in 2004. External users felt that measuring a corporation's compensation cost as the difference between the market price of the stock and the exercise price on the grant date understated—in many cases, significantly—the fair value of the share option and the corresponding compensation expense (and overstates the corporation's net income). They argued that while this measurement approach was *reliable*, it was *not relevant*. They were concerned that this approach overstated a corporation's *return on investment* (because of overstated net income) and misstated the *risk* associated with an investment (because of potential earnings dilution if the options were exercised) in the corporation. They were also concerned about the lack of *comparability* across corporations because of the inability to identify similarities and differences among different compensatory share option plans.

There are many views about what should be the proper value (and compensation expense) of a compensatory share option plan. We summarize these views under two alternatives. One alternative is that a corporation should measure the compensation based on the fair value of the *benefits received* (that is, the value of the employee's services) by the corporation at the time of grant. This might involve estimating the cash salary forgone in lieu of the share option, perhaps adjusted to a present value basis, as a measurement of the share option value. The second alternative is that the fair value of the option should be based on the *costs sacrificed* (the value of the shares given up) by the corporation. This might involve estimating the fair value of the option using an "option pricing model." With these conceptual issues as well as practical concerns in mind, amid considerable controversy the FASB studied compensatory share option plans for several years before issuing the initial version of *FASB Statement No. 123*.

Political Controversy Prior to issuing *FASB Statement No. 123*, the FASB issued an *Exposure Draft* as part of its due process. This Exposure Draft, if enacted, would have required a company to use a fair value method to account for the compensation cost resulting from its compensatory share option plan. The Exposure Draft was extremely controversial. Various constituencies were strongly opposed to the fair value method. They lobbied the FASB (the Board received nearly 1,800 comment letters, mostly negative) to persuade it not to require use of the fair value method. They even had bills introduced in Congress to outlaw it use. These efforts threatened the very existence of the FASB. As a result, when *FASB Statement No. 123* was initially issued, the FASB allowed a company the option of using the fair value method or the intrinsic method to account for its compensatory share option plan. Not surprisingly, most companies continued to use the intrinsic value method (and generally did not recognize any compensation expense related to their plans).

The serious financial reporting failures that occurred in the early 2000s led external users, accountants, and even Congress to revisit this issue. Many people felt that because compensation expense was not recognized under the intrinsic method, many companies' income statements were misleading. In response to the need for high-quality "transparent" financial reporting, more and more companies began to use the fair value method. However, these companies were using different methods to measure fair value, which led to noncomparability across companies. Also, about the same time, the International Accounting Standards Board issued an Exposure Draft that proposed a single fair value method to account for all share-based compensation plans. To help increase comparability and to harmonize U.S. and international accounting standards, in December 2004, the FASB issued *FASB Statement No. 123R*.

Conceptual Overview *FASB Statement No. 123R* requires the use of the fair value method. Since accounting for a compensatory share option plan under the fair value method affects both a corporation's income statement and balance sheet, *FASB Statement No. 123R* addresses several related issues. These issues include (1) how to measure the fair value of stock options issued for employees' services, (2) how to recognize and report the related compensation expense, and (3) what additional disclosures should be made for the plan.[5]

The following conceptual diagram of the recommended method of accounting will help you see the "big picture" before we discuss the detailed accounting issues.

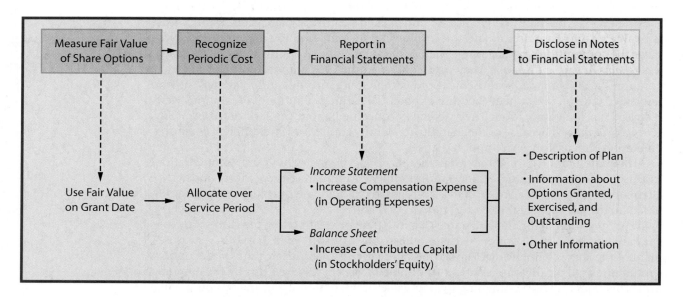

---

5.   The discussion in the following three sections primarily is a summary of the generally accepted accounting principles established in *FASB Statement No. 123* (revised 2004), par. 5–64. The *Statement* also addresses share-based payment transactions with nonemployees and for which it is not possible to estimate fair value. We do not discuss these topics.

Measurement of Fair Value

A corporation must use a fair value method to account for its compensatory share option plan. This approach is consistent with the general principle we discussed earlier in the chapter that a nonmonetary exchange is recorded at the fair value of the stock issued or the asset received, whichever is more reliable. For a compensatory share option plan, it is the fair value of the share options or the services received. Usually it is very difficult for a corporation to determine the fair value of the services it received (in part, because the employees will provide these services in the future and also will receive a cash salary), so the focus is on determining the fair value of the share options.

The fair value of a share option in a compensatory plan is measured based on the market price of an option with the same or similar terms and conditions. Most of the time, similar options don't exist so that the fair value must be estimated. A corporation estimates the fair value of a share option on the grant date using an option pricing model (e.g., the Black-Scholes-Merton model or a lattice model). The **grant date** is the date on which the corporation and an employee have an agreement concerning the terms of the share-based compensation award. On this date, the corporation becomes contingently obligated to issue common stock to the employee who fulfills the service requirements of the plan (e.g., working for the corporation for a certain number of years). Once the fair value is measured on the grant date, it is *not* remeasured for later changes in the underlying variables of the option pricing model (which we discuss below).

Option Pricing Model

The option pricing model that a corporation uses must take into account, as of the grant date, the following variables: (1) exercise price, (2) expected life of the option, (3) current market price of the underlying common stock, (4) expected volatility of the stock, (5) expected dividends on the stock, and (6) risk-free interest rate for the expected term of the option. We do not illustrate complex option pricing models in this chapter because they involve the use of standard deviations and natural logarithms. Also, computer programs of these models have been designed so that the fair value of a share option can be estimated by including the preceding variables. However, it is helpful to understand that a complex option pricing model is an expansion of the basic option pricing model. The basic model (for a share option where it is known with certainty that the share price at maturity will exceed the exercise price) is as follows:

Option value (fair value) = Current stock price − Present value[6] of exercise price

or

$$O = M - \frac{E}{(1 + i)^n}$$

where: O = option value on grant date
         M = market price of stock on grant date
         E = exercise price
         i = risk-free interest rate
         n = number of years until option expires

Based on this basic equation, we can make the following observations:

- the higher the market price of the stock (M) on the grant date, the more the option is worth;
- the higher the exercise price (E), the less the option is worth;
- the higher the risk-free interest rate (i), the more the option is worth; and
- the longer the years (n) until the option expires, the more the option is worth.

---

6.   See the TVM Module for a discussion of present value.

For instance, a higher market price of the stock on the grant date means that there is a greater difference between this price and the set exercise price; hence, the option is more valuable. The more complex option pricing models expand on this equation by including expected dividends and volatility variables in the equation.[7] For simplicity, in the examples that follow and the end-of-chapter exercises and problems we always assume a fair value (option value) for each option on the grant date.

Recognition of Compensation Expense

5 Recognize compensation expense for a compensatory share option plan.

The total compensation cost is the total fair value of the share options that actually become vested. Share options become **vested** on the date the employee's right to exercise the share options is no longer contingent on the employee performing services in exchange for the options. A corporation does not recognize the total compensation cost in its financial statements on the grant date. Instead, **it recognizes the total compensation cost as compensation expense over the requisite service period using the straight-line method.** The **requisite service period (or simply service period)** is the years during which the employee must perform service (e.g., work for the company) in exchange for the share options. Generally, the service period is the same as the vesting period.[8]

If the corporation expects that a significant number of employees will forfeit their nonvested stock options (because they will not fulfill the service requirements for vesting), then it records the compensation expense each year based on an estimate. The estimated total compensation cost is determined at the grant date by multiplying the fair value per option times the estimate of the number of share options expected to vest. If additional information becomes available after the grant date and estimated forfeitures change, the change is included in compensation expense in the year of the change (we will illustrate this in a later example).

The corporation records the compensation expense[9] each year as follows:

Compensation Expense	XXX	
Common Stock Option Warrants		XXX

The corporation includes the compensation expense[10] as an operating expense on its income statement. It includes the Common Stock Option Warrants[11] account balance in the contributed capital section of stockholders' equity on its ending balance sheet.

FASB Statement No. 123R deals with many different types of share-based compensation plans. Appendix A of the *Statement* illustrates the accounting for share option plans that are fixed (with cliff vesting and graded vesting) or performance-based

---

7. For an explanation of option pricing, see, for instance, J. Marlow, *Option Pricing: Black-Scales Made Easy: A Visual Way to Understand Stock Options, Option Prices, and Stock-Market Volatility* (New York: Wiley, 2001).

8. Typically, share options that are vested are also immediately exercisable. However, if the exercise date (or exercise price) is affected by the service the employee must complete, the service period used to allocate the compensation expense must be consistent with the assumptions used to estimate the fair value of the share options.

9. In many cases the amount of compensation expense a corporation recognizes for financial reporting purposes in a given year will be more (less) than the amount of compensation expense the corporation reports on its income tax return. This temporary difference is a future deductible amount and results in an increase (decrease) in a deferred tax asset. Thus, a corporation would make an additional journal entry to record the change in the deferred tax asset and the adjustment of income tax expense. Since we do not discuss deferred taxes until Chapter 19, we do not deal with deferred tax journal entries in this chapter.

10. For simplicity, we record and report the entire amount as compensation expense. Some companies might capitalize a portion of the amount as part of inventory or another asset.

11. For simplicity, the *FASB Statement No. 123R* examples initially record the credit entry directly to Additional Paid-in Capital. We use a Common Stock Option Warrants account for two reasons. First, reporting this account on a corporation's balance sheet alerts users that warrants are outstanding which, if exercised, may decrease earnings per share. Second, use of a Common Stock Option Warrants account makes it easier to see how the fair value assigned to the warrants flows through the different elements of a corporation's contributed capital as some (or all) of the options are exercised (or expire).

(where the number of options to be earned or the exercise price varies); share option plans with indexed exercise prices, with an exercise price that increases by a fixed amount, or with share appreciation rights; and share option plans for which the terms are modified. We show examples of the measurement and recognition procedures for three of these plans.[12]

Fixed Share Option Plan (with Cliff Vesting)

Assume that on January 1, 2007 Fox Corporation adopts a compensatory share option plan and grants 9,000 stock options (to acquire 9,000 shares of common stock) with a maximum life of 10 years to 30 selected employees. The $50 exercise price is equal to the market price of the stock on this grant date. All the options vest at the end of three years (this is known as **cliff vesting**), so the service period is three years. This plan is called a **fixed plan** because all the terms (e.g., exercise price, number of shares) are set ("fixed") on the grant date.

6 Account for a fixed compensatory share option plan.

Fox has had historical employee turnover rates of about 3% per year and it expects this rate to continue. Therefore, at the beginning of 2007 it uses a 3% annual forfeiture rate in its compensation cost (and expense) calculations. At the end of 2008, because of increased employee turnover rates in 2007 and 2008, Fox changes its estimated forfeiture rate to 6% per year for the entire service period. At the end of 2009, a total of 7,500 stock options for 25 employees actually vest and the other 1,500 are forfeited.

Using an option pricing model in accordance with *FASB Statement No. 123R*, Fox determines that the fair value of each option is $17.15 on the grant date. To determine the total estimated compensation cost on the grant date, Fox multiplies the fair value per option times the estimated options that will become vested. This amounts to $140,871 [$17.15 × (9,000 × 0.97 × 0.97 × 0.97), rounded]. On January 1, 2007 (the grant date), Fox makes a memorandum entry to summarize the terms of the compensatory share option plan as follows:

> *Memorandum entry*: **On January 1, 2007 the company granted compensatory share options to 30 employees. The plan allows each employee to exercise 300 options to acquire the same number of shares of the company's common stock at an exercise price of $50 per share. The options vest at the end of 3 years and expire at the end of 10 years. The estimated fair value of the options expected to be exercised is $140,871.**

Example 16-1 shows the compensation computations for Fox Corporation's fixed compensatory share option plan over the three-year service period. The 2007 compensation expense is $46,957, computed by multiplying the $140,871 total estimated

---

EXAMPLE 16-1   Fixed Compensatory Share Option Plan

	2007	2008	2009
Estimated (actual) total compensation cost	$140,871[a]	$128,201[b]	$128,625[c]
Fraction of service period expired	× 1/3	× 2/3	× 3/3
Estimated compensation expense to date	$ 46,957	$ 85,467	$128,625
Previously recognized compensation expense	(0)	(46,957)	(85,467)[d]
Current compensation expense	$ 46,957	$ 38,510	$ 43,158

a. $17.15 fair value per option × (9,000 options × 0.97 × 0.97 × 0.97 retention rate), rounded
b. $17.15 × (9,000 × 0.94 × 0.94 × 0.94), rounded
c. $17.15 × 7,500 vested; actual total compensation cost
d. $46,957 (2004) + $38,510 (2005)

---

12. The three examples are adapted from Appendix A of *FASB Statement No. 123* (revised 2004), par. A87–A96, A105–A108, and A127–A133. For simplicity, in each of these examples we show the adoption of a share option plan in a single year. In reality, a company usually grants new share options *every* year so that the impact on the company's net income is much greater than that shown.

compensation cost (fair value) times the fraction of the service period expired (1/3). On December 31, 2007, Fox records the compensation expense as follows:

Compensation Expense	46,957	
Common Stock Option Warrants		46,957

The computation of the 2008 compensation expense involves adjusting for the change in the estimated forfeitures. Based on the new estimate, at the end of 2008 the revised total compensation cost is $128,201 [$17.15 × (9,000 × 0.94 × 0.94 × 0.94), rounded]. Since two-thirds of the service period has expired, $85,467 ($128,201 × 2/3) of the cost is the compensation expense to date. Because Fox recorded $46,957 compensation expense in 2007, it recognizes $38,510 ($85,467 − $46,957) as compensation expense in 2008. By using this approach, it makes a "catch-up" correction for the change in the previous measurement regarding the estimated forfeitures. On December 31, 2008, Fox records the compensation expense as follows:

Compensation Expense	38,510	
Common Stock Option Warrants		38,510

The last year of the service period is 2009. Because the actual forfeitures were different from the estimated forfeitures, Fox includes another "catch up" correction in the computation of the compensation expense. The 2009 compensation expense is $43,158, computed as we show in Example 16-1. The December 31, 2009 journal entry is the same as those shown earlier (except for the amount) so we do not repeat it here. After this journal entry, Fox has recorded the entire $128,625 actual compensation cost (fair value) as an expense over the three-year service period. Also, the Common Stock Option Warrants account has a balance of $128,625 because each of the 7,500 vested stock options was recorded at its fair value of $17.15.[13]

When an employee exercises share options, the employee pays the exercise price per share and turns in the option warrants to the corporation in exchange for the stock. The corporation records the issue of the common stock in the usual manner at **a price that is the sum of the cash received plus the previously recorded value of the warrants received.** For instance, suppose that on January 5, 2010 one employee exercises options to purchase 300 shares of Fox Corporation's $10 par common stock. On this date the stock is selling for $70 per share on the stock market. Fox records this transaction as follows:

Cash (300 × $50)	15,000	
Common Stock Option Warrants (300 × $17.15)	5,145	
Common Stock, $10 par		3,000
Additional Paid-in Capital on Common Stock		17,145

The common stock is recorded at a price of $67.15 ($50 exercise price + $17.15 option price). The current market price of $70 is *not* used because these shares were committed to the employee based on the terms (and values) set in the compensation agreement on the grant date. If an employee does not exercise share options before they expire, the amount recorded in the Common Stock Option Warrants account for these options is transferred to Additional Paid-in Capital.

Performance-Based Share Option Plan

Now suppose that instead of the fixed stock option plan, the Fox Corporation adopts a performance-based compensatory share option plan. A **performance-based plan** has one

7 Account for a performance-based compensatory share option plan.

---

13. In *graded vesting,* a certain percentage of the share options vest each year (rather than in cliff vesting where all the options vest at the end of the service period). In the case of graded vesting, in addition to adjusting each year's computations for the estimated retention rate, the computations must also be adjusted for the percentage of options that vest in that year. See *FASB Statement No. 123* (revised 2004) (par. A97–A104) for an illustration.

or more terms that are *not* fixed at the grant date. These plans are set up so that the terms will vary depending on how well the selected employees perform during the service period (sometimes these plans are called *variable-term* plans). In other words, the better the employees manage the corporation, the better the terms in the share option plan are for the employees. Performance may be based, for instance, on measures such as earnings or market share for the corporation's products. As earnings or market share increases, the terms of the plan may involve a decrease in the exercise price or an increase in the number of options awarded to the employees.

Assume that the terms of Fox Corporation's performance-based plan adopted on January 1, 2007 are the same as in the previous example (three-year vesting and service period, $50 exercise price, $17.15 fair value per option), except that Fox grants each of the 30 selected employees a *maximum* of 300 share options. The options vest in differing numbers depending on the increase in market share of Fox's products over the three-year service period. The terms are as follows: By December 31, 2009:

1. If the market share has increased by at least 5%, at least 100 share options will vest for each employee on that date.
2. If the market share has increased by at least 10%, another 100 share options will vest for each employee, for a total of 200.
3. If the market share has increased by more than 20%, all 300 share options will vest for each employee.

In a performance-based plan, the estimated total fair value depends on the number of options that are expected to be earned during the vesting period. For Fox Corporation's plan, on the grant date it bases the estimated total compensation cost on the estimate of market growth over the three-year vesting period. This cost then is adjusted in later years for any changes in the expected or actual market share growth. On the grant date Fox Corporation estimates that its market share will increase between 10 and 20%, so it assumes 200 share options will vest for each employee. However, at the end of 2009, Fox determines that its market share has increased over the three-year period by more than 20% (so that 300 stock options actually vest for each employee). Furthermore, on the grant date Fox estimates the forfeiture rate on the stock options to be 3% per year, but changes it to 6% at the end of 2008. At the end of 2009, 25 employees vest in 7,500 stock options.

Example 16-2 shows the compensation computations for Fox Corporation's performance-based compensatory share option plan over the three-year service period. In 2007 the $93,914 estimated total compensation cost is based on the 200 share options expected to vest and an expected annual forfeiture rate of 3%. At the end of 2008 the $85,467 estimated total compensation cost is based on the same expected share options, but on an expected 6% annual forfeiture rate. At the end of 2009 the $128,625 actual total compensation cost is based on the 300 actual share options that vest and the actual 25 employees who vest in the plan. Fox Corporation allocates the compensation cost to

---

EXAMPLE 16-2   Performance-Based Compensatory Share Option Plan

	2007	2008	2009
Estimated (actual) total compensation cost	$93,914[a]	$85,467[b]	$128,625[c]
Fraction of service period expired	× 1/3	× 2/3	× 3/3
Estimated compensation expense to date	$31,305	$56,978	$128,625
Previously recognized compensation expense	(0)	(31,305)	(56,978)
Current compensation expense	$31,305	$25,673	$ 71,647

a.   200 options × (30 employees × 0.97 × 0.97 × 0.97 retention rate) × $17.15 fair value per option, rounded.
b.   200 × (30 × 0.94 × 0.94 × 0.94) × $17.15, rounded
c.   300 × 25 × $17.15; actual total compensation cost

compensation expense each year using the same procedure as we showed in the previous example. Because the memorandum entry and journal entries to recognize the yearly compensation expense are the same as in the previous example (except, of course, for the amounts), we do not repeat them here.

Share Appreciation Rights

8 Account for share appreciation rights.

Analysis

Although compensatory share option plans provide selected employees with the opportunity to buy shares of stock with a market value in excess of the option price, these plans have some disadvantages. At the time of exercise, the employee must have enough cash to pay the option price and any income taxes. For some employees, this is a significant cash flow problem. To remedy at least part of this problem, corporations have developed compensatory share option plans involving share appreciation rights. **Share appreciation rights (SARs)** are rights granted to selected employees that enable them to receive cash, stock, or a combination of both equal to the *excess* of the market value over a stated price of the corporation's stock on the date of *exercise*. SARs are an advantage to an employee because the employee can receive the market appreciation of the corporation's stock in cash on the date of exercise, without paying cash to actually acquire the stock.

FASB Statement No. 123R treats SARs the same way as other compensatory share option plans, with several exceptions. A company accounts for a SARs plan using the fair value method. So, it estimates the fair value of the SARs on the date of grant (and makes a memorandum entry summarizing the grants). For fixed share option plans, the estimated fair value of the total compensation cost is set on the grant date because this is the date when the variables used to determine the fair value are known. However, for SARs, the fair value can only be determined on the *date the rights are exercised* because the cash payment is a function of the stock price on that date.[14] Therefore, for a SARs plan, a company (1) estimates the total compensation cost at the end of *each* year based on the fair value of the SARs *at that time*, (2) records compensation expense over the service period based on these estimates (and any corrections of previous estimation errors), and (3) makes additional adjustments to compensation expense at the end of each year *after* the service period has expired, up to the date of exercise, as we show in the following diagram:

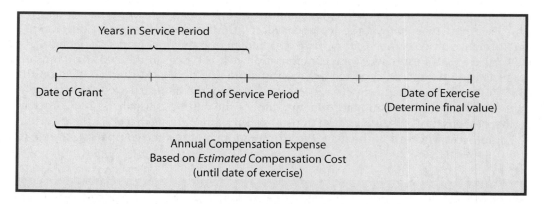

Accounting for a SAR plan also differs from the accounting for a compensatory share option plan in two ways. First, the adjustments (increases or decreases) that are made at the end of each year to compensation expense *after* the service period has expired (until the date of exercise) are based on the difference between 100% of the estimated total compensation cost and the accrued compensation expense recognized to date. Second, the credit entry to recognize the accrued compensation is made to a *liability* account if the company can be required to pay cash to the employee on the date of exercise.[15]

---

14. *FASB Statement No. 123* (revised 2004), par. 36.
15. *Ibid.*, par. 32.

For example, assume that on January 1, 2006, when the market price is $60 per share, Wolf Corporation grants share appreciation rights to a selected employee. (For simplicity, in this example we show the calculations for one executive who is expected to remain employed by the company. If more employees were involved, estimates of turnover would be included in the calculations, as we showed in the previous two examples.) Under the SAR plan, the executive will receive cash for the difference between the quoted market price and $60 for 1,000 shares of the company's common stock on the date of exercise. The service period is four years and the rights must be exercised within 10 years from the grant date.

On the grant date, using an option pricing model, the corporation estimates that the fair value of each SAR is $19. Therefore, the corporation makes a memorandum entry on January 1, 2006 indicating that the estimated fair value of this SAR award is $19,000 ($19 × 1,000). At the end of each year until the date of exercise, the corporation estimates the fair value of each SAR on that date. We show the year-end fair value per SAR in Example 16-3. The executive exercises the rights on December 31, 2010 when the quoted market price of the company's common stock was $94 per share. The calculations of the annual compensation expense are shown in Example 16-3. At the end of each year, the corporation records the SAR compensation by debiting Compensation Expense and crediting SAR Compensation Payable for the amount calculated in the last column of Example 16-3. For instance, on December 31, 2007, Wolf Corporation makes the following journal entry:

Compensation Expense	10,000	
SAR Compensation Payable		10,000

EXAMPLE 16-3   SAR Annual Compensation Expense

Date	Fair Value per SAR	Estimated Total Compensation Cost[a]	Percent Accrued[b]	Total Compensation Expense to Date[c]	Accrued Compensation Expense to Date[d]	Yearly Compensation Expense[e]
12/31/06	$20	$20,000	25%	$ 5,000	—	$ 5,000
12/31/07	30	30,000	50	15,000	$ 5,000	10,000
12/31/08	18	18,000	75	13,500	15,000	(1,500)
12/31/09[f]	26	26,000	100	26,000	13,500	12,500
12/31/10[g]	34	34,000	100	34,000	26,000	8,000
						$ 34,000

a. Fair value per SAR × 1,000 shares; at end of 2006, $20 × 1,000 shares
b. Service years to date ÷ Total service period; at end of 2006, 1 ÷ 4 = 25%
c. Amount from footnote *a* × Percent from footnote *b*; at end of 2006, $20,000 × 0.25
d. Amount for previous year from footnote *c*
e. Amount from footnote *c* − Amount from footnote *d*
f. End of service period
g. Date of exercise

An exception to this procedure occurs in 2008. Because the fair value at the end of 2008 decreased below that of 2006, the corporation makes an adjusting entry *debiting* SAR Compensation Payable and *crediting* Compensation Expense for $1,500 to reduce the total accrued liability. Of course, the SAR Compensation Payable account can never have a debit *balance* because the cumulative compensation expense can never be negative. On December 31, 2010 the corporation makes the following journal entry to recognize the SAR compensation expense for 2010 and to record the exercise of the rights:

Compensation Expense	8,000	
SAR Compensation Payable	26,000	
Cash[($94 market price − $60 option price)		
× 1,000]		34,000

Note that by the end of 2010, the corporation has recognized total compensation expense of $34,000 for this SAR plan, the amount paid to the employee on the date of exercise.

Additional Disclosures

A corporation must disclose several items of information about its compensatory share option plan. This information includes:

1. A description of the plan, including the general terms, such as the service period, number of shares authorized for grants of options, and maximum term of options granted.
2. The number and weighted-average exercise prices for options granted, exercised, outstanding, forfeited, and expired during the year.
3. The weighted-average grant-date fair values of options granted during the year.
4. A description of the method and assumptions (e.g., risk-free interest rate, expected life, and volatility) used during the year to estimate the fair values of options.
5. The total compensation cost for the year related to its plan.

Illustration of Disclosure

Real Report 16-1 shows Note 15 of the 2004 annual report of the **Target Corporation** relating to its share option plans.

Real Report 16-1 Disclosure of Share Option Plan

TARGET CORP.

SUMMARY OF SIGNIFICANT ACCOUNTING POLICIES (in part)

Stock-based Compensation In December 2004, the Financial Accounting Standards Board finalized Statement of Financial Accounting Standards No. 123R, "Share-Based Payment" (SFAS No. 123R). SFAS No. 123R eliminates accounting for share-based compensation transactions using the intrinsic value method prescribed in APB Opinion No. 25, "Accounting for Stock Issued to Employees," and requires instead that such transactions be accounted for using a fair-value-based method.

STOCK-BASED COMPENSATION (in part)

We maintain a long-term incentive plan for key employees and non-employee members of our Board of Directors. Our long-term incentive plan allows for the grant of equity-based compensation awards, including stock options, performance share awards, restricted stock awards, or a combination of awards. A majority of the awards are non-qualified stock options that vest annually in equal amounts over a four-year period. Therefore, in accordance with SFAS No. 123R, we recognize compensation expense for these awards on a straight-line basis over the four-year vesting period. These options generally expire no later than ten years after the date of the grant. Options granted to the non-employee members of our Board of Directors vest after one year and have a ten-year term. Performance share awards represent shares issuable in the future based upon attainment of specified levels of future financial performance. We use a three- or four-year performance measurement period for performance share awards. The number of unissued common shares reserved for future grants under the stock-based compensation plans was 51,560,249 at January 29, 2005 and 19,279,658 at January 31, 2004.

OPTIONS AND PERFORMANCE SHARE AWARDS OUTSTANDING

	Options						
	Total Outstanding			Currently Exercisable			Performance Shares Potentially Issuable
(options and shares in thousands)	Number of Options	Average Price*	Average Life**	Number of Options	Average Price*	Average Life**	
February 2, 2002	31,315	$24.07	5.7	17,629	$17.04	5.7	—
Granted	6,096	30.60					552
Canceled	(561)	35.55					
Exercised	(2,063)	12.22					

Continued

(options and shares in thousands)	Options						Performance Shares Potentially Issuable
	Total Outstanding			Currently Exercisable			
	Number of Options	Average Price*	Average Life**	Number of Options	Average Price*	Average Life**	
February 1, 2003	34,787	$25.73	5.5	21,931	$20.89	5.4	552
Granted	4,638	38.34					573
Canceled	(407)	34.77					
Exercised	(2,859)	12.58					
January 31, 2004	36,159	$28.28	6.2	23,689	$24.48	5.2	1,125
Granted	4,072	49.12					629
Canceled/forfeited	(513)	35.32					(73)
Exercised/earned	(7,727)	20.95					(73)
January 29, 2005	31,991	$32.59	5.8	22,102	$28.79	5.3	1,608

* Weighted average exercise price.

** Weighted average contractual life remaining in years.

Total compensation expense related to stock-based compensation, which is the total fair value of shares vested was $60 million, $57 million, and $49 million, during 2004, 2003, and 2002, respectively. The weighted-average grant date fair value of options granted during 2004, 2003, and 2002 was $13.10, $11.04, and $10.07, respectively. The total intrinsic value of options (the amount by which the stock price exceeded the strike price of the option on the date of exercise) that were exercised during 2004, 2003, and 2002 was $201 million, $72 million, and $66 million, respectively.

NONVESTED OPTIONS AND PERFORMANCE SHARE AWARDS

(options and shares in thousands)	Stock Options	Weighted Average Fair Value at Grant Date	Performance Shares	Weighted Average Fair Value at Grant Date
Nonvested at February 1, 2004	12,470	$11.07	1,125	$34.33
Granted	4,072	13.10	419	49.43
Vested/earned	(6,237)	11.25	(73)	34.44
Forfeited/cancelled	(416)	11.00	(73)	34.44
Nonvested at January 29, 2005	9,889	$11.83	1,398	$38.84

As of January 29, 2005, there was $104 million of total unrecognized compensation expense related to nonvested share-based compensation arrangements granted under our plans. That cost is expected to be recognized over a weighted-average period of 1.5 years.

The Black-Scholes model was used to estimate the fair value of the options at the grant date based on the following assumptions:

	2004	2003	2002
Dividend yield	.7%	.8%	.8%
Volatility	22%	29%	35%
Risk-free interest rate	3.8%	3.0%	3.0%
Expected life in years	5.5	5.0	5.0

Questions:

1. The market price of Target shares at the end of fiscal 2004 was $49.41 per share. Assuming that all share (stock) options were exercised at fiscal year-end, what was the "profit" or "loss" made by employees who exercised their options in 2004?

2. How many options are currently exercisable at the end of fiscal 2004? How many shares does Target have reserved for future grants under its share option plan?

3. How much compensation expense was unrecognized at the end of fiscal 2004? When is this expense expected to be recognized?

Conceptual Evaluation

From a conceptual standpoint, by requiring corporations to use a fair value method of accounting for their compensatory share option plans, *FASB Statement No. 123R* goes a long way toward remedying the criticisms raised about the intrinsic method. Use of the fair value method increases the *relevance* of the accounting information because it shows the fair value of the share options. Although some people argue that the *reliability* of the accounting information is decreased because of the use of estimates, this is similar to using estimates for items such as depreciation and bad debts. Whereas the estimates involve complex issues, the issues are no more complex than those involving postemployment benefits (which we discuss in Chapter 20). Other people argue that the reliability is increased because the result is more *representationally faithful* in that the accounting information better depicts the economic obligation. Use of the fair value method provides a more relevant measure of a corporation's *return on investment* and *earnings per share* because compensation expense (based on fair value) is included in the corporation's net income. Similarly, a better assessment of *risk* is possible because external users are able to better evaluate the likelihood of the exercise of the share options. Finally, *comparability* is improved because external users can better contrast the terms of different plans with the information provided in the notes to the financial statements.

On the other hand, there are several criticisms of the way the fair value method is applied in *FASB Statement No. 123R*. First, the fair value of the share options is measured only on the grant date using an option pricing model. This fair value is not further adjusted for changes in the variables of the model, even though some of these variables (e.g., volatility and risk-free interest rate) change with changes in the underlying economy. Not allowing adjustment of the fair value may distort reporting of the real value of the share options. However, not adjusting is consistent with generally accepted accounting principles that are based on transactions. Second, under the fair value method, a corporation will have an expense even if its employees never exercise their share options because the market price is less than the option price. Finally, many people argue that an "opportunity cost" method should be used because under this method a corporation would recognize compensation expense based on actual market values and not estimates.

SECURE YOUR KNOWLEDGE 16-3

- Noncompensatory employee share purchase plans are not intended to compensate employees for services performed but are instead designed to raise capital or obtain more widespread employee ownership of the company's stock.
- The accounting objective of compensatory share option plans, designed to provide additional compensation to selected employees, is to recognize compensation expense over the periods in which the employees perform a service and earn the options.
- Compensatory share option plans are accounted for under the fair value method, which:
    - Measures total compensation cost using the fair value of the options on the date the options are granted (estimated using an option-pricing model),
    - Adjusts total compensation cost for estimated forfeitures of the nonvested share options, and
    - Recognizes total compensation cost as compensation expense over the service period using the straight-line method.
- In a fixed share option plan, all terms (e.g., exercise price, number of shares) are set at the grant date which allows a company to measure total compensation cost at the grant date. Any subsequent adjustments to compensation cost involve only changes in estimated forfeitures.
- In a performance-based share option plan, one or more of the terms (e.g., exercise

(continued)

price, number of shares) vary with managerial performance which requires total compensation cost to be adjusted during the vesting period in response to changes in the terms of the share option plan.

- Stock appreciation rights (SARs) allow employees to receive cash, stock, or a combination of both equal to the increase of the stock price over a stated value on the date of exercise.
  - SARs are accounted for using the fair value method, with compensation expense recorded over the service period.
  - The value of the SAR plan is estimated based on the fair value of the SARs on the date of grant and is later adjusted each year until the SARs are *exercised*.
  - Any adjustments to compensation expense that occur after the service period has expired are accounted for in the period the estimate is revised.

PREFERRED STOCK CHARACTERISTICS

Some investors consider certain stockholder rights to be more important than others. Therefore, they are willing to give up some rights in exchange for preferences for other rights. To attract these investors, a corporation may issue a class of capital stock called **preferred stock**. The preferred stock contract identifies the stockholders' rights as well as the rights of the corporation. Various preferred stock characteristics may be specified in the contract, including:

9 Describe the characteristics of preferred stock.

- preference as to dividends,
- accumulation of dividends,
- participation in excess dividends,
- convertibility into common stock,
- attachment of stock warrants (rights),
- callability by the corporation,
- mandatory redemption at a future maturity date,
- preference as to assets upon liquidation of the corporation, and
- lack of voting rights.

We discuss each characteristic in the following sections.

Preference as to Dividends

Holders of preferred stock have a preference as to dividends because a corporation must pay any applicable dividends to preferred stockholders before a dividend may be paid to common stockholders. Since most preferred stock is issued with a par value, the preferred dividend may be expressed as a percentage of this par value. If no-par stock is issued, the preferred dividend is expressed as a dollar amount per share.

For example, assume that Trask Corporation has outstanding 2,000 shares of 8%, $100 par preferred stock. In this case:

- Each stockholder is entitled to an $8 ($100 × 0.08) annual dividend per share.
- The corporation must pay $16,000 of dividends (8% × $100 × 2,000 shares) to preferred stockholders before it may pay any dividends to common stockholders.

A preference as to dividends does not guarantee, however, that a corporation will pay a preferred dividend in any given year. This is because dividend payments are at the discretion of the board of directors. To protect preferred stockholders further, a corporation may issue cumulative preferred stock.

Cumulative Preferred Stock

A corporation's stockholders are not legally entitled to share in dividends unless these dividends have been declared by its board of directors. If dividends are "passed" (that is, *not* declared) in a particular year, a holder of **noncumulative** preferred stock will never be paid that dividend. For this reason, corporations seldom issue noncumulative preferred stock because investors think this feature is a distinct disadvantage.

Most preferred stock is **cumulative.** If a corporation fails to declare a dividend on cumulative preferred stock at the stated rate on the usual dividend date, the amount of passed dividends becomes **dividends in arrears.** Dividends in arrears accumulate from period to period. A corporation cannot pay common stockholders any dividends until it has paid the preferred dividends in arrears. The dividends in arrears are *not* a liability to the corporation, because no liability exists until the dividend declaration. Nonetheless, this information is very important to investors and other interested parties in predicting future cash flows, and so a corporation discloses dividends in arrears in a note to its financial statements.

For example, assume that Richland Corporation has outstanding 1,000 shares of 10%, $100 par cumulative preferred stock. Each share of stock is entitled to a $10 annual dividend (computed by multiplying the 10% times the $100 par value). If the corporation does not pay dividends in 2007 and 2008, preferred stockholders would be entitled to dividends in arrears of:

- $10,000 at the end of 2007 and
- $20,000 at the end of 2008.

At the end of 2009, Richland Corporation would have to pay $30,000 (for three years) to preferred stockholders before it could pay any dividends to common stockholders.

Participating Preferred Stock

When preferred stock is **participating,** preferred stockholders share with the common stockholders in any "extra" dividends. Extra dividends are paid only after preferred stockholders have been paid their stated dividend *amount* and common stockholders have been paid at a *rate* equal to that paid on the preferred stock.

For example, if Pierce Corporation has 9%, $100 par participating preferred stock and $10 par common stock outstanding, it must pay preferred stockholders $9 per share (9% of the $100 par) and common stockholders 90 cents per share (9% of the $10 par). Then, if the total dividends paid are greater than the amount needed to meet these dividend requirements, an extra dividend arises.

Participating preferred stock may be either fully or partially participating. **Fully participating preferred stockholders share equally with the common stockholders in any extra dividends.** When a corporation pays extra dividends, they are distributed to the fully participating preferred stockholders and common stockholders proportionately based on the respective total par values of each class of stock. **Partially participating preferred stockholders share in extra dividends, but this participation is limited to a fixed rate or amount per share.**

In the preceding example, if the 9% preferred stockholders participated up to a maximum of 12% of the preferred stock par value, their share in any extra dividends would be limited to 3% of this par value. We show an example of participating preferred stock dividends in Chapter 17 in the section dealing with cash dividends. Participating preferred stock, whether fully or partially participating, is rare. Corporations generally agree that preferred stockholders receive too much preference when they are given first preferences as to dividends and also are allowed to share in all dividends.

Convertible Preferred Stock

Convertible preferred stock allows stockholders, at their option and under specified conditions, to convert the shares of preferred stock into another security of the corporation. Usually this security is common stock, and the conversion provisions stipulate the conditions and a specific exchange ratio. This exchange ratio is modified, however, if there is a stock split. Since most preferred stock is not participating, the conversion feature

Credit: Comstock Images

allows the holder to exchange the dividend preferences attached to preferred stock for the unlimited rights to corporate income held by common stockholders. This feature is attractive to investors because the exchange ratio tends to tie the market price of the preferred stock to the market price of the common stock when that price is rising. This increases the value of the preferred stock. Conversely, the preferred stock dividend rate tends to stabilize the market price of the preferred stock when common stock prices are falling.

Theoretically, both the preferred features and the potential for common stock equity are valuable to (and paid for by) an investor in convertible preferred stock. Conceptually, then, a corporation could separate the proceeds received when it issues the stock into preferred and common stockholders' equity. However, **APB Opinion No. 14** requires that when convertible preferred stock is issued, no value is assigned to the conversion provision. Any difference between par and market value is recorded as additional paid-in capital on preferred stock.[16] Thus, a corporation accounts for the *issuance* of convertible preferred stock in the same way as for the issuance of nonconvertible stock. This method of accounting is required because of the inseparability of the stock and conversion option, and the difficulty of reliably determining the fair value to attach to the conversion provision. Unfortunately, use of this method places more importance on the legal form of the security than the economic substance of the transaction. The FASB is currently considering whether the conversion feature should be valued separately. However, at the time of writing this book no decision has been made and the accounting for convertible preferred stock continues to follow the generally accepted accounting principles in *APB Opinion No. 14*.

Accounting for the *conversion* of preferred to common stock is very straightforward because the *book value method* is used. (We discussed the book value method in Chapter 14.) The book value method is used (and the market value method is *not* allowed) because it does not result in a corporation recording a gain or loss on a transaction involving its own capital stock, which would violate the concept of income. Under the book value method, the corporation eliminates the contributed capital (that is, the par value and additional paid-in capital) associated with the preferred stock and replaces it with the par (or stated) value of the common stock. If the total contributed capital eliminated for the preferred stock is more than the common stock par value, the corporation records the excess as an increase in additional paid-in capital related to the conversion. If less, the corporation reduces retained earnings because it is considered to be a dividend distribution to the preferred stockholders.

Example: Conversion of Preferred Stock Assume that Ness Corporation originally issued 500 shares of $100 par convertible preferred stock at $120 per share. If each preferred

16. "Accounting for Convertible Debt and Debt Issued with Stock Purchase Warrants," *APB Opinion No. 14* (New York: AICPA, 1969), par. 12.

share may be converted into four shares of $20 par common stock and all the shares are converted, Ness makes the following journal entry at conversion:

Preferred Stock, $100 par	50,000	
Additional Paid-in Capital on Preferred Stock	10,000	
Common Stock, $20 par (4 × 500 × $20)		40,000
Additional Paid-in Capital from Preferred Stock		
Conversion ($60,000 − $40,000)		20,000

Alternatively, if each preferred share may be converted into seven shares of common stock, upon conversion Ness makes the following entry:

Preferred Stock, $100 par	50,000	
Additional Paid-in Capital on Preferred Stock	10,000	
Retained Earnings ($70,000 − $60,000)	10,000	
Common Stock, $20 par (7 × 500 × $20)		70,000

The conversion of preferred to common stock changes the components of, but does not affect the corporation's total, stockholders' equity. ♦

Preferred Stock with Stock Warrants (Rights)

A corporation may also attach warrants to preferred stock to enhance their attractiveness. As we discussed earlier in the chapter and in Chapter 14 for bonds payable, these **warrants** represent **rights** that allow the holder to purchase additional shares of common stock at a specified price over some future period. This period frequently involves a number of years, and in some cases no time limit is set. The longer the time period, the greater the attractiveness of such warrants, since stock prices over the long run have tended to increase. Because these warrants are separable (*detachable*) from the preferred stock, they usually begin trading on the stock market at some market price. This happens whether the specified purchase price of the common stock is greater than, less than, or the same as the current market price.

Theoretically, an investor in preferred stock with attached (detachable) warrants is investing in "dual" rights, each of which has a value. These rights include:

1. the right to dividends that will be paid on the preferred stock, and
2. the right to the market value appreciation of the common stock that may be purchased as a result of the warrants.

Accounting theory suggests that, in recording the issuance of these securities, the economic substance of the event should take precedence over the legal form of the security. Following this theory, *APB Opinion No. 14* states that **the proceeds from the issuance of preferred stock with attached warrants is allocated to preferred stockholders' equity and to common stockholders' equity, based on the relative independent fair values of the two securities at the time of issuance.**[17]

Example: Issuance of Preferred Stock and Exercise of Warrants Assume Ponce Corporation issues 1,000 shares of $100 par value preferred stock at a price of $121 per share. It attaches a warrant to each share of stock that allows the holder to purchase one share of $10 par common stock at $40 per share. Immediately after the issuance, the preferred stock begins selling ex rights (without rights attached) on the market for $119 per share. The warrants begin selling for $6 each. Based on the $119,000 ($119 × 1,000) and $6,000 ($6 × 1,000) relative market values of the preferred stock (ex rights) and the

---

17. *Ibid.*, par. 16.

warrants, respectively, Ponce Corporation makes the following journal entry to allocate the $121,000 ($121 × 1,000) issuance price:*

Cash ($121 × 1,000)	121,000	
Preferred Stock, $100 par		100,000
Additional Paid-in Capital on Preferred Stock		15,192
Common Stock Warrants		5,808

Computations

Preferred Stock: $\dfrac{\$119,000}{\$119,000 + \$6,000} \times \$121,000 = \$115,192$

Common Stock Warrants: $\dfrac{\$6,000}{\$119,000 + \$6,000} \times \$121,000 = \underline{5,808}$

$\underline{\underline{\$121,000}}$

If the warrants did not begin trading, the corporation must make the allocation based on an estimate of the value paid for the warrants.

The corporation lists the Common Stock Warrants account as an element of contributed capital in its stockholders' equity. Assuming all warrants are exercised, Ponce Corporation makes the following journal entry to record the issuance of the 1,000 shares of common stock in exchange for the warrants and $40 per share:

Cash ($40 × 1,000)	40,000	
Common Stock Warrants	5,808	
Common Stock, $10 par		10,000
Additional Paid-in Capital on Common Stock		35,808

If any warrants are not exercised, the corporation makes a journal entry debiting Common Stock Warrants and crediting Additional Paid-in Capital from Expired Warrants to transfer the value assigned to the warrants to the existing common stockholders. ◆

Callable Preferred Stock

Preferred stock frequently has a *call* provision. **Callable preferred stock may be retired (recalled) under specified conditions by a corporation at *its* option.** The corporation includes the specified conditions and call price in the stock contract. The call price is usually several points (dollars) higher than the issuance price and usually establishes a ceiling on the market value of the stock. Typically, the stock contract requires the payment of dividends in arrears before the call is made. Occasionally, callable preferred stock also will be convertible. In this case, the call price may be lower than the issuance price but usually will be higher than the par value. When a corporation recalls convertible preferred stock, the corporation will ordinarily allow the stockholder the choice of conversion or recall.

When a corporation *issues* callable preferred stock, no special accounting is required. The corporation credits the difference between the issuance price and par value to Additional Paid-in Capital. Upon *recall*, the corporation does *not* treat the difference between the call price and the original issuance price as a gain or loss. This prevents a corporation from influencing its earnings by recognizing a gain (or incurring a loss) in transactions involving its own equity securities, in violation of the concept of income. Instead, the corporation eliminates the original contributed capital. That is, it eliminates the par value in the preferred stock account and the additional paid-in capital associated with the recalled preferred stock. If the call price exceeds the total of these amounts, the corporation debits the difference to retained earnings because it is treated as a dividend distribution. In the case in which the call price is less than the total of these amounts, the corporation records the difference as a credit to Additional Paid-in Capital because it is considered to be an additional contribution by the stockholder.

Example: Recall of Preferred Stock Assume that Li Corporation has outstanding 1,000 shares of $100 par callable preferred stock that were issued at $110 per share and that no dividends are in arrears. If the call price is $112 per share, Li Corporation makes the following journal entry to record the recall of these shares:

Preferred Stock, $100 par	100,000	
Additional Paid-in Capital on Preferred Stock	10,000	
Retained Earnings ($112,000 − $110,000)	2,000	
Cash ($112 × 1,000)		112,000

Although unlikely, if the call price had been $105 per share, the corporation makes the following journal entry:

Preferred Stock, $100 par	100,000	
Additional Paid-in Capital on Preferred Stock	10,000	
Cash ($105 × 1,000)		105,000
Additional Paid-in Capital from Recall of		
Preferred Stock ($110,000 − $105,000)		5,000

The recall and retirement of preferred stock causes a permanent reduction in the corporation's stockholders' equity. (This is not to be confused with *treasury stock*, which is reacquired but not retired, as we discuss later in the chapter.) ♦

Redeemable Preferred Stock

In contrast to convertible preferred stock and callable preferred stock, some preferred stock is redeemable. **Redeemable preferred stock either may be subject to mandatory redemption at a specified future maturity date for a specified price, or redeemable at the option of the holder** (instead of being callable at the option of the issuer). Redeemable preferred stock has a key characteristic of a liability because of the likelihood of a cash outflow in the future that the company has no ability to prevent. Therefore, a corporation with mandatorily redeemable preferred stock is required to report the preferred stock as a *liability*. If both the maturity date and redemption price are fixed, at the end of each year the corporation reports the liability at the present value of the amount to be paid at settlement. To determine the present value, the corporation uses the implicit interest rate when it issued the redeemable preferred stock. It records interest expense for the change in the present value during the year. If either the maturity date or the redemption price is not known, at the end of each year the corporation reports the liability at its current market value. It records interest expense for the change in market value during the year.[18] The corporation is also required to disclose the redemption features, shares issued and redeemed, and other related issues in the notes to its financial statements.[19] Preferred stock that is redeemable at the option of the holder is *not* reported as a liability. It is reported in stockholders' equity.

Preference in Liquidation

If a corporation is liquidated, the preferred stock contract usually allows the preferred stockholders **preference** over the common stockholders (but secondary to the creditors) with respect to the corporate assets. The preference is typically expressed as a percentage of (or equal to) the par value. It also frequently requires the payment of dividends in arrears. This liquidation preference is important to external users. A corporation discloses this information either parenthetically in its stockholders' equity section or in the notes accompanying its financial statements.[20]

---

18. "Accounting for Certain Financial Instruments with Characteristics of both Liabilities and Equity," *FASB Statement of Financial Accounting Standards No. 150* (Norwalk, Conn.: FASB, 2003) par. 18 and 22.

19. "Disclosure of Information about Capital Structure," *FASB Statement of Financial Accounting Standards No. 129* (Norwalk, Conn.: FASB, 1997) par. 4, 5, and 8.

20. *Ibid.*, par. 6.

Voting Rights

In exchange for the previously discussed provisions, the preferred stock contract often states that the holder has **no voting rights**. Otherwise, the preferred stockholder has full voting rights.

CONTRIBUTED CAPITAL SECTION

A corporation includes the results of the various transactions involving its issuance of capital stock in the Contributed Capital (frequently called Paid-in Capital) section of stockholders' equity on its balance sheet. Contributed capital is usually separated into the par (or stated) value of the outstanding capital stock (or, in the case of no-par stock, the total proceeds received from the stock issue) and the additional paid-in capital arising from the different transactions. A corporation's contributed capital section may include:

10 Know the components of contributed capital.

1. Capital stock
   a. Par value of preferred stock
   b. Par value of common stock
   c. Common (or preferred) stock subscribed
   d. Stock warrants
   e. Stock dividends to be distributed (discussed in Chapter 17)
2. Additional paid-in capital
   a. On preferred stock
   b. On common stock
   c. From other sources (e.g., stock splits, preferred stock conversions, treasury stock)

In addition to reporting the specific amounts for the Capital Stock and Additional Paid-in Capital accounts, a corporation is required to disclose certain other information. For each class of stock this disclosure includes the par value and the number of shares authorized, issued, and outstanding. The FASB also requires certain disclosures.[21] These include the preferred stock dividend rate, preferred stock characteristics, any dividends in arrears, and any relevant details relating to the common stock. A corporation may present this information parenthetically adjacent to each capital stock account or in a note to its financial statements. As we discuss in the next chapter, a schedule summarizing the changes in these various components of contributed capital is also an integral part of a corporation's financial statements.

To illustrate the preceding contributed capital framework, Example 16-4 presents the Contributed Capital section of a hypothetical company, Newsom Corporation.

EXAMPLE 16-4   Newsom Corporation

Contributed Capital
December 31, 2007

Stockholders' Equity
Contributed Capital

Preferred stock, $100 par (9%, cumulative, convertible, 10,000 shares authorized, 4,300 shares issued and outstanding)	$ 430,000
Common stock, $5 par (80,000 shares authorized, 32,800 shares issued and outstanding)	164,000
Common stock subscribed, $5 par (3,600 shares at a subscription price of $34 per share)	18,000
Common stock option warrants	23,000
Additional paid-in capital on preferred stock	107,500
Additional paid-in capital on common stock	590,400
Additional paid-in capital from conversion of preferred stock into common stock	10,100
Total Contributed Capital	$1,343,000

Real Report 16-2 shows the contributed capital of **Alcoa, Inc.** on its comparative balance sheets dated December 31, 2004 and 2003, and the accompanying Note M (in part), which describes the capital stock.

---

21. *Ibid.*, par. 4–7.

Real Report 16-2 Contributed Capital

ALCOA AND SUBSIDIARIES

CONSOLIDATED BALANCE SHEET (in part):

Shareholders' Equity (in part):

	December 31	
(in millions)	2004	2003
Preferred stock (R)	$ 55	$ 55
Common stock (R)	925	925
Additional capital	5,775	5,831

NOTES TO CONSOLIDATED FINANCIAL STATEMENTS (in part):

R. PREFERRED AND COMMON STOCK

Preferred Stock. Alcoa has two classes of preferred stock. Serial preferred stock has 546,024 shares authorized and outstanding, with a par value of $100 per share and an annual $3.75 cumulative dividend preference per share. Class B serial preferred stock has 10 million shares authorized (none issued) and a par value of $1 per share.

Common Stock. There are 1.8 billion shares authorized at a par value of $1 per share. As of December 31, 2004, 136.6 million shares of common stock were reserved for issuance under the long-term stock incentive plans.

Questions:

1. How many classes of preferred stock does Alcoa have? What is the par value per share of each class and how many shares of each class are outstanding?
2. What is the par value per share of the common stock?
3. How many shares of common stock were reserved on December 31, 2004, and for what purpose?

This concludes the discussion of the major items affecting contributed capital. We now turn to a discussion of accounting for the reacquisition of capital (treasury) stock, which may or may not affect contributed capital.

TREASURY STOCK (CAPITAL STOCK REACQUISITION)

11 Understand the accounting for treasury stock.

In most states a corporation may reacquire its own previously issued capital stock, after which it may formally retire (cancel) the stock or hold the stock in its corporate treasury. **Treasury stock is a corporation's own capital stock that (1) has been fully paid for by stockholders, (2) has been legally issued, (3) is reacquired by the corporation, and (4) is being held by the corporation for future reissuance.** A corporation typically pays cash to reacquire its capital stock, but it may exchange other assets. Treasury stock may also be donated to the corporation by its stockholders.

A corporation may acquire treasury stock for various reasons:

- to use for share option, bonus, and employee purchase plans;
- to use in the conversion of convertible preferred stock or bonds;
- to use excess cash;
- to use in acquiring other companies;
- to reduce the number of shares outstanding and thereby increase the earnings per share and help maintain or increase the market price of its stock;
- to reduce the number of shares held by hostile shareholders and thereby reduce the likelihood of being acquired by another company; and
- to use for the issuance of a stock dividend.

Treasury stock is clearly *not* an asset of a corporation; the corporation cannot own itself. A corporation cannot recognize a gain or loss when reacquiring its own stock. This restricts a corporation from influencing its net income by buying and selling its own stock. Consequently, a corporation treats treasury stock as a reduction of its stockholders' equity as we will discuss later.

To ensure that treasury stock is handled in the best interests of the stockholders, states have passed laws regulating corporate activities as follows:

- A corporation must acquire treasury stock for some legitimate corporate purpose.
- Treasury stock does not vote, has no preemptive rights, ordinarily cannot participate in any type of dividends, and has no rights at liquidation.
- Treasury stock does participate in stock splits, because the par value must be reduced.
- The acquisition of treasury stock does not formally reduce a corporation's legal capital.
- The amount that a corporation may pay to acquire treasury stock is usually limited to the balance in its retained earnings (and perhaps additional paid-in capital) so that its legal capital is not impaired.
- Treasury stock transactions may reduce retained earnings but may never increase retained earnings.
- A corporation ordinarily must restrict the amount of retained earnings available for dividends by the cost of the treasury stock held so that the payment of dividends does not reduce contributed capital.

The original issuance of capital stock causes an increase in a corporation's stockholders' equity and the number of shares outstanding. Its reacquisition has an opposite effect. The corporation's stockholders' equity (and the number of shares outstanding) is reduced. Reacquired capital stock may be formally retired. The shares then revert to authorized but unissued shares, and the corporation's legal capital is appropriately reduced. If the shares are *not* retired, the corporation may reissue the treasury stock at a price above or below the acquisition price, or the par value. Ordinarily, the board of directors does not need to consider the par value when treasury stock is reissued because it met the legal capital requirements when it originally issued the stock. Upon reissuance, the corporation again increases its stockholders' equity and the number of shares outstanding.

A corporation may account for treasury stock transactions by either (1) the cost method or (2) the par (or stated) value method. Both are generally accepted accounting principles, although they affect the various components of stockholders' equity differently. Because the cost method is used by 96% of companies that hold treasury stock[22] we discuss and illustrate this method in the following section. We briefly discuss the par value method in a later section.

Cost Method

When a corporation uses the cost method, it treats the treasury stock "event" as though it consists of two parts: (1) the purchase (reacquisition) of the treasury stock that starts the event, and (2) the reissuance that completes the event. Under this method, when the corporation reacquires its capital stock, it assumes it will reissue rather than retire the stock. Therefore, it debits a temporary account entitled Treasury Stock (and credits Cash, or other appropriate asset account) for the *cost* of the shares. A separate Treasury Stock account should be established for each class of stock (common and preferred). During the period between reacquisition and reissuance, the corporation treats the Treasury Stock account as a contra-stockholders' equity account. This account represents a temporary reduction in its stockholders' equity, as we show later in the chapter.

When the corporation reissues the treasury shares, it reduces (credits) the Treasury Stock account for the *cost* of the shares reissued and records the difference between the cash received and this cost as an adjustment of stockholders' equity. If the cash exceeds

---

22. *Accounting Trends and Techniques* (New York: AICPA, 2004, p. 322) reports that of the companies disclosing treasury stock holdings in common stock, 96% used the cost method and only 4% used the par or stated value method.

the cost of the reissued treasury stock, it records the excess as an increase in additional paid-in capital from the treasury stock transaction. If the cash is less than the cost, it records the "deficit" as a reduction of additional paid-in capital related to previous issuances or retirements of treasury stock. If this additional paid-in capital is insufficient to absorb the deficit, the corporation records the remainder as a reduction in retained earnings.[23] Since a corporation may reacquire treasury stock at different dates and at different costs, it may use the specific identification, FIFO, or average cost methods to record the reduction in the Treasury Stock account when the stock is reissued.

Example: Treasury Stock Assume that Ball Corporation is authorized to issue 20,000 shares of $10 par common stock and enters into several treasury stock transactions. These transactions (1 through 5) are listed in Example 16-5, followed by the journal entries Ball makes to record the transactions. In journal entry 4, note that the treasury stock was reissued at less than par. However, this is not relevant because the legal capital requirements were met in journal entry 1. Only the *cost* of the treasury stock is used to determine the impact on additional paid-in capital.[24]

EXAMPLE 16-5   Journal Entries for Treasury Stock: Cost Method

1. *Issuance of 6,000 shares of $10 par common stock for $12 per share:*

Cash	72,000	
Common Stock, $10 par		60,000
Additional Paid-in Capital on Common Stock		12,000

2. *Reacquisition of 1,000 shares of common stock at $13 per share:*

Treasury Stock	13,000	
Cash		13,000

3. *Reissuance of 600 shares of treasury stock at $15 per share:*

Cash	9,000	
Treasury Stock (600 shares at $13 per share)		7,800
Additional Paid-in Capital from Treasury Stock		1,200

4. *Reissuance of another 200 shares of treasury stock at $8 per share:*

Cash	1,600	
Additional Paid-in Capital from Treasury Stock	1,000	
Treasury Stock (200 shares at $13 per share)		2,600

5. *Reissuance of another 100 shares of treasury stock at $10 per share:*

Cash	1,000	
Additional Paid-in Capital from Treasury Stock	200	
Retained Earnings	100	
Treasury Stock (100 shares at $13 per share)		1,300

---

23. "Status of Accounting Research Bulletins", *APB Opinion No. 6* (New York: AICPA, 1965), par. 12.

24. Some corporations prepare a slightly different journal entry from that shown in transaction 4 when they reissue treasury stock at substantially less than cost. This involves reducing the additional paid-in capital from all the *original* issuances of the same class of stock by an average pro rata amount per share. Any deficit below the average original issuance price is then debited to retained earnings. For example, recall from transaction 1 that the original issuance price of $12 per share resulted in a $2 per share increase in additional paid-in capital (because this is the only issuance, the $2 excess per share is also the *average* excess per share). Since the reissuance price for $8 per share in transaction 4 is $5 below the per share cost of the treasury stock, a corporation might record transaction 4 as follows:

Cash	1,600	
Additional Paid-in Capital on Common Stock ($2 per share)	400	
Retained Earnings ($3 per share)	600	
Treasury Stock (200 shares at $13)		2,600

After journal entry 4 the additional paid-in capital related to common treasury stock transactions is $200 ($1,200 − $1,000). In transaction 5, Ball Corporation reissues 100 shares of treasury stock at $10 per share. When Ball records this transaction, it reduces the Additional Paid-in Capital from Treasury Stock account to zero and records the remaining deficit as a reduction of Retained Earnings (as a kind of dividend). The accounting for no-par treasury stock follows the same procedures. ♦

Balance Sheet Presentation

If a corporation holds treasury stock on the balance sheet date, it deducts the Treasury Stock account from the total of contributed capital, retained earnings, and accumulated other comprehensive income (if any). For example, assume that the Ball Corporation prepares its stockholders' equity section immediately after recording transactions 1–5 of the preceding example (assume further that retained earnings is $40,000 *prior to* recording any treasury stock transactions). We show this stockholders' equity in Example 16-6. Note that state laws generally require retained earnings to be restricted by the amount of the cost of the treasury stock, as we show in Example 16-6. We discuss restrictions of retained earnings in Chapter 17.

EXAMPLE 16-6   Treasury Stock and Stockholders' Equity

Stockholders' Equity	
Contributed Capital	
Common stock, $10 par (20,000 shares authorized, 6,000 shares issued, of which 100 are being held as treasury stock)	$ 60,000
Additional paid-in capital on common stock	12,000
Total contributed capital	$ 72,000
Retained earnings (see note)	39,900
Accumulated other comprehensive income	10,000
Total contributed capital, retained earnings, and accumulated other comprehensive income	$ 121,900
Less: Treasury stock (100 shares at cost)	(1,300)
Total Stockholders' Equity	$ 120,600

Note: Retained earnings are restricted regarding dividends in the amount of $1,300, the cost of the treasury stock.

Acquisition at Greater Than Market Value

Over the years, there have been numerous "takeover" attempts by hostile stockholders. Their goal is to acquire a sufficient number of shares of a company's common stock to exercise control over its activities. To thwart these attempts, some companies have reacquired their common stock from these stockholders at prices in excess of the fair value of the stock. This excess is often referred to as "greenmail." In return for this greenmail, the selling stockholders may agree to abandon certain acquisition plans, to restrict purchases of additional shares, or to other limitations. When this occurs, a question arises as to how to account for the acquisition of this treasury stock and the related greenmail.

In a situation where a corporation pays more than the fair value to acquire treasury stock, *FASB Technical Bulletin 85-6* requires that the corporation record the treasury stock at its fair value. The difference between the price paid to acquire the treasury stock and the fair value is recorded as an expense. The corporation does *not* report this expense as an extraordinary item on its income statement.[25] The corporation records any later reissuances in the usual manner.

---

25. *FASB Technical Bulletin No. 85-6* (Stamford, Conn.: FASB, 1985), par. 3–7.

Donated Treasury Stock

Stockholders sometimes may donate treasury stock to a corporation, which the corporation then reissues. This usually occurs when the corporation needs more cash without increasing the number of outstanding shares. According to *FASB Statement No. 116*, a corporation records a donation from a nongovernmental unit (e.g., stockholders) as a gain in the period received, based on the fair value of the exchange.[26] On the date of the donation the corporation debits the Treasury Stock account and credits a gain for the fair value of the stock. It reports the gain in the Other Items section of its income statement. When the stock is reissued, it records the transaction in the usual manner.

A corporation must adhere to state laws regarding donated treasury stock. Many of these laws were established to discourage what is referred to as *treasury stock subterfuge*, an activity that occurred in times of high par values and resulted in *watered stock* (discussed earlier). A corporation would issue an excess number of shares of par value stock in exchange for a nonmonetary asset. A limited number of shares then would be donated back to the corporation and reissued at a price less than par, thereby avoiding the contingent liability on the part of the stockholder. However, such subterfuges are unlikely in today's financial world with its legal restrictions.

Retirement of Treasury Stock

Occasionally, a corporation's board of directors may decide to retire treasury stock. As a result, the corporation's legal capital is reduced. In the journal entry a corporation makes to record the retirement, it offsets the cost of the retired shares in the Treasury Stock account against both the par value in the Capital Stock account and a pro rata share from the Additional Paid-in Capital (on common or preferred) account. Any difference between these latter amounts and the cost of the treasury stock either is debited to Retained Earnings or credited to an Additional Paid-in Capital from Treasury Stock account. For example, assume the Ball Corporation retires the remaining 100 shares of treasury stock from the previous example. The journal entry to record the retirement is:

Common Stock, $10 par	1,000	
Additional Paid-in Capital on Common Stock	200*	
Retained Earnings	100	
Treasury Stock (100 shares at $13 per share)		1,300

$^{*}\dfrac{\$12,000}{6,000} \times 100 \text{ shares} = \$200$

Note that the pro rata reduction per share in additional paid-in capital on common stock was computed based on the current balance in Additional Paid-in Capital on Common Stock ($12,000) divided by the number of shares *issued* (6,000). After retirement, it accounts for the shares as authorized but unissued stock. Also note that when a corporation retires treasury stock, retained earnings is no longer restricted so the corporation eliminates the related note describing the restriction.

Par Value Method

If a corporation uses the par value method to account for treasury stock, it treats the *reacquisition* of capital stock as an event entirely separate from the stock's *reissuance*. When the corporation reacquires its capital stock, it debits the Treasury Stock (either common or preferred) account for the *par* value of the stock and debits the original Additional Paid-in Capital (on common or preferred) account for an amount based on the average price received from all the *original* issuances of the stock. If the reacquisition

---

26. "Accounting for Contributions Received and Contributions Made," *FASB Statement of Financial Accounting Standards No. 116* (Norwalk, Conn.: FASB, 1993), par. 8.

price is less than the original average issuance price, it credits the excess to a new Additional Paid-in Capital from Treasury Stock account. If the reacquisition price is more than the original average issuance price, it first records the deficit as a reduction of Additional Paid-in Capital from Treasury Stock (if any) and then as a reduction of Retained Earnings (as a kind of dividend paid upon reacquisition).

During the period between reacquisition and reissuance, the corporation treats the Treasury Stock account as a contra-capital stock account. Since fewer shares are outstanding, it deducts the Treasury Stock account from the Capital Stock (common or preferred) account to reduce the total par value.

When the corporation reissues the treasury stock, it increases its contributed capital (and the number of outstanding shares) by crediting the Treasury Stock account at *par* and crediting the existing Additional Paid-in Capital (on common or preferred) account for the excess of the proceeds over the par value. If the cash received is less than par, it reduces the Additional Paid-in Capital account. If no additional paid-in capital exists related to this class of stock, it debits Retained Earnings. A Discount on Capital Stock account is *not* debited because no contingent liability exists on the part of the new stockholders.

If the corporation retires treasury stock, it debits the capital stock account and credits the treasury stock account for the par value of the retired stock. Because the par value method is not widely used, we do not show an example.

CAPITAL STOCK TRANSACTIONS AND THE STATEMENT OF CASH FLOWS

A company reports the proceeds it receives from the issuance of common stock or preferred stock (or the reissuance of treasury stock) as a cash inflow in the financing activities section of its statement of cash flows. A company reports the cash its pays to purchase treasury stock or recall preferred stock as cash outflow in the financing activities section of its statement of cash flows. If a company has recorded compensation expense in regard to a compensatory share option plan, the amount is a non-cash expense. Therefore, the company adds this amount as an adjustment of net income under the indirect method in the operating activities section on its statement of cash flows. If a company converts preferred stock in common stock, it discloses this transaction as a non-cash financing activity.

SECURE YOUR KNOWLEDGE 16-4

- Preferred stock has several features including (1) preference as to dividends, (2) accumulation of dividends (dividends in arrears), (3) participation in excess dividends, (4) convertibility into common stock (using the book value or market value method), (5) attachment of stock warrants (requiring the allocation of proceeds between the stock and the warrants based on fair value), (6) callability by the corporation, (7) mandatory redemption at a future date (requires classification of the preferred stock as a liability), (8) preference in the company's net assets in the event of a liquidation, and (9) lack of voting rights.
- Treasury stock, resulting from a company reacquiring its own shares, can be accounted for using either the cost method or the par value method.
  - Under the cost method:
    - The reacquired shares (reported as a reduction of stockholders' equity) are recorded at cost, with any later reissuance accounted for as either:
      - a credit to Additional Paid-in Capital from Treasury Stock (if the proceeds from the reissuance exceed the cost of the treasury stock) or

(continued)

- • a debit to Additional Paid-in Capital from Treasury Stock (if the cost exceeds the proceeds from the reissuance of the treasury stock), with any excess deficit recorded as a reduction of Retained Earnings.
  - ♦ The retirement of treasury stock involves a reduction in the legal capital of the company.
    - ■ Under the par value method, the treasury stock account (reported as a contra-capital account) is recorded at par value with any reissuance of treasury stock accounted for in a manner similar to that of an original issuance of stock.

LINK TO RATIO ANALYSIS

One key ratio that is used to evaluate a company's profitability is the return on stockholders' equity (ROE). This ratio shows how many dollars of net income were earned for every dollar invested by the owners. While the overall ROE ratio can be useful, many financial statement users prefer a more detailed examination of the components of this ratio. This analysis is commonly known as the DuPont model and enables the analyst to "decompose" the ROE ratio into three major components as shown below:

$$ROE = \text{Profitability} \times \text{Activity} \times \text{Stability} = \frac{\text{Net Income}}{\text{Net Sales}} \times \frac{\text{Net Sales}}{\text{Average Assets}} \times \frac{\text{Average Assets}}{\text{Average Stockholder's Equity}}$$

The formula above provides the financial statement analyst insights into whether a change in ROE is caused by a change in profitability (income/sales), a change in activity or turnover (sales/average assets), or a change in stability or financial leverage (average assets/average equity).

Below is information obtained from the 2004 annual report of **Starbucks Corporation**:

(in millions)	2004	2003
Average Assets	$3,084,541	$2,514,448
Average Stockholders' Equity	2,272,664	1,892,247
Net Sales	5,294,247	4,075,522
Net Income	390,559	266,848

Using the formula above, Starbucks' ROE for 2004 and 2003 can be computed as:

2004: $ROE = \dfrac{\$390,559}{\$5,294,247} \times \dfrac{\$5,294,247}{\$3,084,541} \times \dfrac{\$3,084,541}{\$2,272,664} = 0.074 \times 1.716 \times 1.357 = 0.17$

2003: $ROE = \dfrac{\$266,848}{\$4,075,522} \times \dfrac{\$4,075,522}{\$2,514,448} \times \dfrac{\$2,514,448}{\$1,892,247} = 0.065 \times 1.621 \times 1.329 = 0.14$

The above analysis indicates that while Starbucks' ROE has increased by approximately 3%, Starbucks' financial leverage (the degree to which assets are internally financed) has remained relatively steady (1.357 vs. 1.329). Therefore, any increase in ROE is due primarily to the fact that Starbucks was more successful in controlling cost and expenses relative to sales (profitability measure increased from 0.065 to 0.074) and was more efficient in using its assets to generate sales (asset turnover increased from 1.621 to 1.716).

SUMMARY

At the beginning of the chapter, we identified several objectives you would accomplish after reading the chapter. The objectives are listed below, each followed by a brief summary of the key points in the chapter discussion.

1. **Explain the corporate form of organization.** A corporation is a legal entity of a particular state. A corporation's articles of incorporation states the types, par value, and number of shares of capital stock to be issued. A corporation's owners (stockholders) have limited liability. A corporation may enter into contracts, hold property, sue and be sued, and continue in perpetuity.
2. **Know the rights and terms that apply to capital stock.** Each stockholder of a corporation generally has the right to: (1) share in the corporation's profits by receiving dividends, (2) elect directors and establish corporate policies, (3) maintain a proportionate interest in the ownership if additional shares are issued (preemptive right), and (4) share in the distribution of assets if the corporation is liquidated. The terms that apply to capital stock include authorized, issued, and outstanding capital stock, par (or stated) value, and additional paid-in capital.
3. **Account for the issuance of capital stock.** When a corporation issues capital stock for cash, it debits cash for the amount received, credits capital stock for the par value, and credits additional paid-in capital for the difference. It modifies this entry accordingly for the issuance of stock subscriptions, for combined sales of stock, and for nonmonetary issuances of stock.
4. **Describe a compensatory share option plan.** A compensatory stock option plan is intended to provide additional compensation to selected employees within the corporation. The employees receive shares of stock, share options, or other equity instruments in exchange for their services.
5. **Recognize compensation expense for a compensatory share option plan.** Under the fair value method, the total compensation cost is the total fair value of the share options that actually become vested. Under this method, a corporation recognizes the total compensation cost as compensation expense over the service period using the straight-line method, making adjustments each year for any changes in circumstances or changes in estimates.
6. **Account for a fixed compensatory share option plan.** Under a fixed plan, a corporation estimates the total compensation cost by multiplying the fair value per option times the number of options granted times the estimated retention rate. It allocates the total compensation cost over the service period, adjusting for changes in the estimated turnover rate and for the number of options that actually vest.
7. **Account for a performance-based compensatory share option plan.** Under a performance-based plan, a corporation estimates the total compensation cost by multiplying the fair value per option times the number of options expected to be granted times the estimated retention rate. It allocates the total compensation cost over the service period, adjusting for changes in estimates and for the number of options that actually vest.
8. **Account for share appreciation rights.** Under a SAR plan, a corporation estimates the total compensation cost at *the end of each year* by multiplying the fair value per SAR times the number of SARs expected to be exercised. It allocates the total compensation cost over the service period, adjusting for changes in estimates. It then continues to make adjustments to compensation expense each year until the SARs are exercised.
9. **Describe the characteristics of preferred stock.** Preferred stock may have (1) a preference as to dividends, (2) accumulation of dividends, (3) participation in excess dividends, (4) convertibility into common stock, (5) attachment of stock warrants (rights), (6) callability by the corporation, (7) redemption at a future maturity date, (8) preference as to assets if the corporation is liquidated, and (9) lack of voting rights.
10. **Know the components of contributed capital.** Contributed capital usually includes capital stock (par value of preferred and common stock) and additional paid-in capital (on preferred and common stock).
11. **Understand the accounting for treasury stock.** Treasury stock is a corporation's own capital stock that it has reacquired. Treasury stock is not an asset; a corporation cannot recognize a gain or loss when reacquiring (or reissuing) its own stock. Under the cost method (the most common method), when a corporation acquires treasury stock, it debits the treasury stock account for the amount paid. When it reissues treasury stock, it debits cash for the proceeds received, credits the treasury stock account for the cost, and credits (or debits) additional paid-in capital from treasury stock for the difference.

ANSWERS TO REAL REPORT QUESTIONS

Real Report 16-1 Answers

1. During 2004, 7,727,000 options were exercised at a weighted average exercise price of $20.95. If these options were exercised when the share price was $49.41, these employees made a "profit" of $28.46 per share ($49.41 − $20.95) or $219,910,000 (7,727,000 shares × $28.46 profit per share).

2. At the end of fiscal 2004, 22,102,000 options were currently exercisable at an average price of $28.79, and Target has unissued common shares of 51,560,249 reserved for future grants under its share option plan.

3. Under the fair value method, Target recognizes total compensation expense on a straight-line basis over a four-year vesting period. At the end of fiscal 2004, Target reported $104 million of unrecognized compensation expense which represents the portion of total compensation expense that has not yet vested. This compensation cost is expected to be recognized over the subsequent 1.5 years.

Real Report 16-2 Answers

1. Alcoa has two classes of preferred stock. The first class of preferred stock has 546,024 shares authorized and outstanding with a par value of $100 per share. The second class of preferred stock (Class B) has 10 million shares authorized but no shares are issued. Its par value is $1 per share.

2. The common stock has a par value of $1 per share.

3. On December 31, 2004, 136.6 million shares of common stock were reserved for issuance. This stock is reserved to meet Alcoa's commitment to its long-term stock incentive plans.

QUESTIONS

Q16-1 What information is contained in a corporation's articles of incorporation?

Q16-2 What is the difference between (a) a public and private corporation, (b) an open and closed corporation, and (c) a domestic and foreign corporation (as viewed by a particular state)?

Q16-3 What is (a) a *stock certificate*, (b) a *stockholders' ledger*, (c) a *stock transfer journal*, and (d) a *transfer agent*?

Q16-4 List the various rights of a stockholder. Which do you consider to be the most important?

Q16-5 What is the meaning of the following terms: (a) *authorized capital stock*, (b) *issued capital stock*, (c) *outstanding capital stock*, and (d) *treasury stock*? What is the difference between the number of issued and outstanding capital shares?

Q16-6 What is a corporation's *legal capital* and why is it important?

Q16-7 How is a corporation's legal capital determined, assuming its capital stock has a par value, a stated value, or no par value?

Q16-8 What are the three components and the basic framework of stockholders' equity?

Q16-9 How does preferred stock differ from common stock?

Q16-10 What amount of the proceeds from the issuance of no-par, no-stated-value stock is recorded in the Capital Stock account?

Q16-11 What is a *stock subscription?* How does a corporation report the accounts Subscriptions Receivable and Preferred Stock Subscribed on its balance sheet? Why?

Q16-12 What alternatives are possible if a subscriber defaults on a stock subscription? How would you determine which alternative to use?

Q16-13 How would you record the proceeds received from the combined issuance by a corporation of shares of common stock with shares of preferred stock?

Q16-14 If a corporation issues capital stock for an asset other than cash, what amount would you use to record the transaction?

Q16-15 When do (a) watered stock or (b) secret reserves result from the recording of a nonmonetary issuance of stock? What impact does each have on a corporation's balance sheet?

Q16-16 What is a *stock split* and a *disproportionate stock split?* How do they affect each element of a corporation's stockholders' equity?

Q16-17 (a) What are the criteria for a noncompensatory share option plan? (b) How does a compensatory share option plan differ from a noncompensatory plan? (c) What is the intent of a noncompensatory plan? Of a compensatory plan?

Q16-18 Under the fair value method, how does a corporation determine the total compensation cost for a compensatory share option plan? How does it recognize this amount as compensation expense?

Q16-19 What are share appreciation rights? Why are they advantageous to an employee?

Q16-20 Define the following terms regarding preferred stock: (a) *dividend preference*, (b) *cumulative*, (c) *participating*, (d) *convertible*, (e) *warrants*, (f) *callable*, and (g) *redeemable*.

Q16-21 Why is a preferred stock similar to a long-term bond? Why is it similar to common stock?

Q16-22 What are the two segments of a corporation's contributed capital and what might be included in each segment?

Q16-23 (a) What is *treasury stock?* (b) Why might a corporation acquire treasury stock?

Q16-24 If a corporation uses the cost method to account for treasury stock, the treasury stock "event" is treated as though it consists of two elements; if it uses the par value method, the reacquisition and reissuance transactions are viewed as separate events. Explain the accounting differences resulting from these concepts.

Q16-25 How does a corporation report the Treasury Stock account under the cost method of accounting for treasury stock? Under the par value method?

Q16-26 What accounting procedures are involved under the cost method when a corporation retires treasury stock?

MULTIPLE CHOICE (AICPA Adapted)

Select the best answer for each of the following.

M16-1 On July 14, JX Corporation exchanged 1,000 shares of its $8 par value common stock for a plot of land. JX's common stock is listed on the NYSE and traded at an average price of $21 per share on July 14. The land was appraised by independent real estate appraisers on July 14 at $23,000. As a result of this exchange, JX's additional paid-in capital will increase by

a. $0
b. $8,000
c. $13,000
d. $15,000

M16-2 When treasury stock is purchased for cash at more than its par value, what is the effect on total stockholders' equity under each of the following methods?

	Cost Method	Par Value Method
a.	Increase	Increase
b.	Decrease	Decrease
c.	No effect	Decrease
d.	No effect	No effect

M16-3 On July 9, 2007 Metaro Corporation purchased for $108,000, 2,000 shares of Jean Corporation's newly issued 6% cumulative $20 par value preferred stock. Each share also had one stock warrant attached, which entitled the holder to acquire, at $19, one share of Jean $10 par value common stock for each two warrants held. On July 10, 2007 the market price of the preferred stock (without warrants) was $50 per share and the market price of the stock warrants was $10 per warrant. On September 3, 2007 Metaro sold all the stock warrants for $19,800. What should be the gain on the sale of the stock warrants?

a. $0
b. $800
c. $1,800
d. $9,800

M16-4 What is the most likely effect of a stock split on the par value per share and the number of shares outstanding?

	Par Value Per Share	Number of Shares Outstanding
a.	Decrease	Increase
b.	Decrease	No effect
c.	Increase	Increase
d.	No effect	No effect

M16-5 Landy Corporation was organized on January 2, 2007 with authorized capital of 100,000 shares of $10 par value common stock. During 2007 Landy had the following transactions:

Jan. 12 Issued 20,000 shares at $12 per share
Apr. 23 Issued 1,000 shares for legal services when the market price was $14 per share

What should be the amount of additional paid-in capital at December 31, 2007?

a. $4,000
b. $14,000
c. $40,000
d. $44,000

M16-6 During 2007 Bradley Corporation issued for $110 per share, 5,000 shares of $100 par value convertible preferred stock. One share of preferred stock can be converted into three shares of Bradley's $25 par value common stock at the option of the preferred shareholder. On December 31, 2008 all of the preferred stock was converted into common stock. The market value of the common stock at the conversion date was $40 per share. What amount should be credited to the common stock account on December 31, 2008?

a. $375,000
b. $500,000
c. $550,000
d. $600,000

M16-7 The Amlin Corporation was incorporated on January 1, 2007, with the following authorized capitalization:

- 20,000 shares of common stock, no par value, stated value $40 per share
- 5,000 shares of 5% cumulative preferred stock, par value $10 per share

During 2007 Amlin issued 12,000 shares of common stock for a total of $600,000 and 3,000 shares of preferred stock at $16 per share. In addition, on December 21, 2007 subscriptions for 1,000 shares of preferred stock were taken at a purchase price of $17. These subscribed shares were paid for on January 4, 2008. What should Amlin report as total contributed capital on its December 31, 2007 balance sheet issued on February 1, 2008?

a. $520,000
b. $648,000
c. $665,000
d. $850,000

M16-8 On January 1, 2007 Stoner Corporation granted compensatory share options to key employees for the purchase of shares of the company's common stock at $25 per share. The options are intended to compensate employees for the next two years. The options are exercisable within a four-year period beginning January 1, 2009 by grantees still in the employ of the company. The fair value of each option was $7 on the date of grant. Stoner expects to distribute 10,000 shares of treasury stock when options are exercised. The treasury stock was acquired by Stoner during 2006 at a cost of $28 per share and was recorded under the cost method. How much should Stoner charge to compensation expense for the year ended December 31, 2007?

a. $70,000
b. $35,000
c. $30,000
d. $15,000

M16-9 When treasury stock accounted for by the cost method is subsequently sold for more than its purchase price, the excess of the cash proceeds over the carrying value of the treasury stock should be recognized as an
a. Extraordinary gain
b. Increase in additional paid-in capital
c. Income from continuing operations
d. Increase in retained earnings

M16-10 Preferred stock that may be retired by the corporation at its option is known as
a. Convertible
b. Redeemable
c. Cumulative
d. Callable

EXERCISES

E16-1 *Par Value and No-Par Stock Issuance* Cutler Corporation is authorized to issue 10,000 shares of common stock. It sells 6,000 shares at $19 per share.

Required
Record the sale of the common stock, given the following independent assumptions:
1. The stock has a par value of $10 per share.
2. The stock is no-par stock, but the board of directors has assigned a stated value of $8 per share.
3. The stock has no par and no stated value.

E16-2 *Combined Sale of Stock* Estes Company issues 300 shares of $50 par preferred stock and 1,000 shares of $10 par common stock in a "package" sale. Total proceeds received amount to $39,000.

Required
Record the transaction for each independent assumption shown:
1. The common stock has a current market value of $19 per share; the current market value of preferred stock is not known.
2. The common stock and the preferred stock have a current market value per share of $22 and $60 respectively.

E16-3 *Sale of Stock with Bonds* Kelly Company issues 12% bonds with a face value of $10,000 and 600 shares of $10 par common stock in a combined sale, receiving total proceeds of $23,000.

Required
Record the transaction for each independent assumption shown:
1. The common stock has a current market value of $21 per share; the market value of the bonds is not known.
2. The common stock has a current market value of $24.50 per share; the bonds are selling at 98.

E16-4 *Issuance of Stock for Land* The Putt Company issues 500 shares of $100 preferred stock for land. This land was carried on the seller's books for $40,000.

Required
1. Prepare the journal entry to record the acquisition of the land for each of the following independent situations:
   a. The preferred stock is currently selling for $120 per share. No appraisal is available on the land.
   b. The land is appraised at $65,000. There have been no recent sales of the preferred stock.
   c. The preferred stock is currently selling for $125 per share. The land is appraised at $64,000.
2. For Requirement 1(c), discuss why you chose the value used in the journal entry.

E16-5 *Stock Subscription* On February 3 the Teel Corporation enters into a subscription contract with several subscribers for 5,000 shares of $10 par common stock at a price of $16 per share. The contract requires a down payment of 25%, with the remaining balance to be paid on May 3. The stock will be issued to each subscriber upon full payment.

Required
Prepare journal entries to record the following:
1. The February 3 receipt of the down payment and signing of the contract.
2. The May 3 receipt of the remaining balance from subscribers to 4,000 shares. The market price is currently $17 per share.
3. The default of a subscriber to 1,000 shares. These shares are sold on the open market for $17 per share on May 4, and the down payment is returned to the subscriber.

E16-6 *Stock Split* Holton Company currently has 9,000 shares of $12 par common stock outstanding that had been issued at an average price of $60 per share. It declares a three-for-one stock split.

Required
Prepare whatever entry is necessary to record the stock split, assuming the following independent alternatives:
1. The par value is reduced to $4 per share.
2. The par value is reduced to $6 per share.
3. The par value is reduced to $3 per share.

E16-7 *Fixed Compensatory Share Option Plan* McEnroe Company has 20 executives to whom it grants compensatory share options on January 1, 2007. At that time it grants each executive the right to purchase 100 shares of its $5 par common stock at $40 per share after a three-year service period. The value of each option is estimated to be $10.25 on the grant date. Based on its average employee turnover rate each year, McEnroe expects that two executives will not vest in the plan. At the end of 2009 McEnroe confirms that the actual turnover was the same as expected. On January 5, 2010, three executives exercise their options.

Required
Prepare the journal entries of McEnroe Company for 2007 through 2010 in regard to its compensatory share option plan (round all calculations to the nearest whole number).

E16-8 *Fixed Compensatory Share Option Plan* On January 1, 2007 Sampress Company adopts a compensatory share option plan for its 50 executives. The plan allows each executive to purchase 200 shares of its $2 par common stock for $30 per share after completing a three-year service period. Sampress estimates the value of each option to be $14.00 on the grant date. It has had a 4% employee turnover rate each year and uses this rate in its compensation cost calculations in 2007. Because of higher turnover, at the end of 2008 Sampress changes it estimated turnover rate to 5% per year for the entire service period. At the end of 2009, Sampress determined that the actual turnover was seven executives for the entire service period. On January 6, 2010, eight executives exercise their options.

Required
1. Prepare a schedule of the Sampress Company's compensation computations for its compensatory share option plan for 2007 through 2009 (round all computations to the nearest dollar).
2. Prepare the journal entries of Sampress Company for 2007 through 2010 in regard to this plan.

E16-9 *Performance-Based Share Option Plan* On January 1, 2007 Seles Company adopts a performance-based share option plan for its 80 key executives. Each executive is granted a maximum of 70 share options, but the number of options that vest depends on the percentage increase in Seles Company's sales over a three-year service period. If by December 31, 2009, sales have increased by at least 10%, 50 options will vest for each executive; if sales have increased by at least 15%, all 70 options will vest. On the grant date, Seles estimates that its sales will increase by 12% over the service period, and that its annual employee turnover rate will be 2%. It also determines that the fair value of an option expected to vest is $13.40. At the end of 2009, actual sales had increased by 16% for the service period and the actual turnover was six key executives for the service period.

Required
1. Prepare a schedule of the Seles Company's computations for its compensatory share option plan for 2007 through 2009 (round all computations to the nearest dollar).
2. Prepare the compensation expense journal entry for 2007.

E16-10 *Share Appreciation Rights* On January 1, 2006, as a form of executive compensation, Wadlin Corporation grants share appreciation rights to Robert Brandt. These rights entitle Brandt to receive cash equal to the excess of the quoted market price over a $20 option price for 4,000 shares of the company's common stock on the exercise date. The service period is three years (which Brandt is expected to complete) and the rights must be exercised within five years. Brandt exercises his rights on December 31, 2009. The fair value per SAR was as follows: 12/31/06, $3.00; 12/31/07, $4.20; 12/31/08, $4.00; and 12/31/09, $5.00. The quoted market price per share of common stock was $25 on December 31, 2009.

Required
1. Prepare a schedule to compute the compensation expense related to this SAR plan for 2006 through 2009.
2. Prepare the December 31, 2009 journal entry related to this SAR plan.

E16-11 *Convertible Preferred Stock* On January 2, 2007 the Bray Corporation issues 900 shares of $100 par convertible preferred stock for $117 per share. On January 7, 2008, all the preferred stockholders convert their shares to common stock.

Required
1. Prepare the January 2, 2007 journal entry to record the issuance of the preferred stock.
2. Prepare the January 7, 2008 journal entry to record the conversion, assuming the preferred stock contract states that
   a. Each share of preferred stock is convertible into seven shares of $10 par common stock.
   b. Each share of preferred stock is convertible into twelve shares of $10 par common stock.

E16-12 *Callable Preferred Stock* On March 4, 2007 the Hein Corporation issues 1,000 shares of $100 par preferred stock for $125 per share. The stock is not callable by the corporation until three years have expired. On April 7, 2010, all the stock is called by the corporation.

Required
1. Prepare the journal entry to record the issuance of the stock.
2. Prepare the journal entry to record the recall
   a. At a price of $130 per share.
   b. At a price of $114 per share.

E16-13 *Stock Rights with Preferred Stock* The Nelson Corporation issues 6,000 shares of $100 par preferred stock at a price of $112 per share. A stock warrant is attached to each share of preferred stock that enables the holder to purchase one share of $10 par common stock for $25. Immediately after issuance, the preferred stock begins selling ex rights for $110 per share. The warrants (which expire in 30 days) also begin trading for $4 per warrant.

Required
1. Prepare the journal entry to record the sale of the preferred stock.
2. Prepare the journal entry to record the issuance of 5,000 shares of common stock in exchange for 5,000 warrants and $25 per share.
3. Prepare the journal entry to record the expiration of 1,000 warrants.

E16-14 *Various Journal Entries* Sapp Company is authorized to issue 20,000 shares of no-par, $5 stated-value common stock and 5,000 shares of 9%, $100 par preferred stock. It enters into the following transactions:
1. Accepts a subscription contract to 7,000 shares of common stock at $42 per share and receives a 30% down payment.
2. Collects the remaining balance of the subscription contract and issues the common stock.
3. Acquires a building by paying $23,000 cash and issuing 2,000 shares of common stock and 600 shares of preferred stock. Common stock is currently selling at $46 per share; preferred stock has no current market value. The building is appraised at $180,000.
4. Sells 1,000 shares of common stock at $45 per share.
5. Sells 900 shares of preferred stock at $112 per share.
6. Declares a two-for-one stock split on the common stock, reducing the stated value to $2.50 per share.

Required
Prepare journal entries to record the preceding transactions.

E16-15 *Contributed Capital* The following is a list of selected accounts and ending account balances taken from the books of the Adams Company on December 31, 2007:

Account Title	Amount
Premium on preferred stock	$ 17,000
Common stock	75,000
Premium on bonds payable	4,000
Preferred stock	80,000
Bonds payable	100,000
Preferred stock subscribed	20,000
Retained earnings	121,000
Premium on common stock	84,000

Additional information:
1. Common stock has a $5 par value, 50,000 shares are authorized, 15,000 shares have been issued and are outstanding.
2. Preferred stock has a $100 par value, 3,000 shares are authorized, 800 shares have been issued and are outstanding. Two hundred shares have been subscribed at $120 per share. The stock pays an 8% dividend, is cumulative and callable at $130 per share.
3. Bonds payable mature on January 1, 2011. They carry a 12% annual interest rate, payable semiannually.

Required
Prepare the contributed capital section of the December 31, 2007 balance sheet for the Adams Company. Include appropriate parenthetical notes.

E16-16 *Treasury Stock, Cost Method* On January 1 the Sanders Corporation had 1,000 shares of $10 par common stock authorized and outstanding. These shares were originally issued at a price of $26 per share. In addition, 500 shares of $50 par preferred stock were outstanding. These were issued at a price of $75 per share. During the year the following stock transactions occurred:
1. March 3: Sanders Corporation reacquired 100 shares of its own common stock at a cost of $24 per share.
2. April 27: It sold 25 shares of the stock acquired on March 3 for $30 per share.
3. July 10: It sold 25 shares of the stock acquired on March 3 for $22 per share.
4. October 12: It retired the remaining shares acquired on March 3.

Required

Prepare journal entries to record the treasury stock transactions of Sanders Corporation assuming it uses the cost method.

E16-17 *Treasury Stock, Cost Method* The records of TMP Incorporated provide the following information on January 1, 2007:

Preferred stock, $50 par (5,000 shares authorized, issued, and outstanding)	$250,000
Common stock, $10 par (20,000 shares authorized, 10,000 shares issued and outstanding)	100,000
Additional paid-in capital on preferred stock	50,000
Additional paid-in capital on common stock	80,000
Retained earnings	95,000

During 2007 the following transactions were recorded by TMP:

1. Reacquired 250 shares of preferred stock for $53 per share.
2. Reacquired 500 shares of common stock for $20 per share.
3. Sold 200 shares of the common stock acquired in (2) for $27 per share.
4. Sold 250 shares of preferred stock acquired in (1) for $59 per share.
5. Sold 100 shares of the common stock acquired in (2) for $18 per share.

Required

1. Prepare journal entries to record the stock transactions of TMP Incorporated, assuming it uses the cost method of accounting for treasury stock.
2. Prepare the stockholders' equity section of the TMP balance sheet at December 31, 2007 (assume 2007 net income was $30,000 and dividends distributed were $10,000).

E16-18 *Treasury Stock, Cost and Par Value Methods* On January 1 the West Company had outstanding 10,000 shares of $10 par common stock, which had been originally issued at an average price of $35 per share. During the year the company engaged in the following treasury stock transactions:
1. Reacquired 1,000 shares of its common stock for $33 per share.
2. Reissued 600 shares of the treasury stock for $35 per share.
3. Reissued 300 shares of the treasury stock for $32 per share.
4. Retired the remaining 100 shares of treasury stock.

Required

Prepare journal entries to record the preceding treasury stock transactions for West Company assuming it uses (1) the cost method and (2) the par value method.

E16-19 *Treasury Stock, No Par* The following information is taken from the accounting records of the Propst-Steele Production Corporation:

1. Issued 5,000 shares of no-par common stock at $15 per share.
2. Issued an additional 5,000 shares of no-par common stock at $17 per share.
3. Reacquired 500 shares of its no-par common stock at a cost of $12.50 per share.
4. Reissued 200 of its treasury shares at $14 per share.
5. Reissued the remaining treasury shares at $11 per share.

Required

Prepare journal entries to account for the preceding stock transactions of the Propst-Steele Production Corporation assuming it uses the cost method for treasury stock.

PROBLEMS

P16-1 *Issuances of Stock* The Cada Corporation is authorized to issue 10,000 shares of $100 par, convertible, callable preferred stock and 80,000 shares of no-par, no-stated-value common stock. There are currently 7,000 shares of preferred and 30,000 shares of common stock outstanding. The following are several *alternative* transactions:

1. Purchased land by issuing 640 shares of preferred stock and 1,000 shares of common stock. Preferred and common are currently selling at $113 and $36 per share, respectively. No reliable appraisal of the land is available.
2. Same as transaction 1, except that land is appraised at $104,000 and the preferred stock has no current market value.

3. Issued, for $99,000 cash, a combination of 400 shares of preferred stock and bonds payable with a face value of $50,000. Currently, the preferred stock is selling for $120 per share and the bonds at 104.
4. Same as transaction 3, except that the bonds do not have a current market value.
5. Same as transaction 3, except that the preferred stock does not have a current market value.
6. Preferred stockholders (who had originally paid the corporation $110 per share for their stock) convert 6,500 preferred shares into 19,500 shares of common stock. The current market prices of the preferred stock and the common stock are $120 and $41 per share, respectively.
7. The corporation calls the 7,000 shares of preferred stock (originally issued at $110 per share) at $123 per share. Common stock is currently selling for $42 per share. Stockholders elect *not* to convert into common stock.
8. Same as transaction 7, except that stockholders owning 2,000 shares of preferred stock elect to convert each share into three shares of common stock. The remaining 5,000 preferred shares are retired.

Required
Prepare the journal entry necessary to record each transaction. Below each entry, explain your reason for the values used.

P16-2   *Issuances of Stock* The Epple Corporation is authorized to issue 20,000 shares of $100 par, convertible, callable preferred stock and 100,000 shares of $10 stated value common stock. Currently, the company has outstanding 6,000 shares of preferred stock and 40,000 shares of common stock. The following are several *alternative* transactions:
1. Acquired a patent by issuing 2,500 shares of common stock and bonds with the face value of $100,000. The stock is currently selling for $27 per share and the bonds are selling at 98.
2. Sold, for $96,000 cash, a "package" consisting of 500 shares of preferred stock and 2,000 shares of common stock. Currently, the preferred and common stock are independently selling for $112 and $22 per share, respectively.
3. Purchased land by issuing 300 shares of preferred stock and 1,000 shares of common stock. The common stock is selling for $25 per share, but the preferred stock is not being actively traded. The value of the land is appraised at $57,000.
4. The corporation calls the 6,000 shares of preferred stock (originally issued at $108 per share) at a call price of $112 per share. Common stock is currently selling for $23 per share. The stockholders elect *not* to convert into common stock.
5. Same as transaction 4, except that stockholders owning 4,000 shares of preferred stock elect to convert each share into five shares of common stock. The remaining 2,000 shares of preferred stock are retired.
6. Upon approval by the state, the board of directors decides to split the common stock two for one, reducing the stated value to $5 per share and increasing the authorization to 200,000 shares. (Remember, only 40,000 shares are issued and outstanding.)
7. Same as transaction 6, except that the stated value is reduced to $4 per share.

Required
Prepare the journal entry necessary to record each transaction. Below each entry, explain your reason for the values used.

P16-3   *Subscriptions* On August 3, 2007, the date of incorporation, the Quinn Company accepts separate subscriptions for 1,000 shares of $100 par preferred stock at $104 per share and 9,000 shares of no-par, no-stated-value common stock for $22 per share. The subscription contracts require a 10% down payment, with the balance due by November 1, 2007. Shares are issued to each subscriber upon full payment. Any defaulted shares will be sold on November 2, 2007, and the down payment returned to the defaulting subscribers.

On November 1 the company received the remaining balances for 920 shares of preferred stock and 8,900 shares of common stock. The defaulted preferred shares and common shares were sold for $105 and $22.50 per share, respectively, on November 2 and the down payment was returned to the defaulting subscribers.

Required
Prepare journal entries to record all the transactions related to
1. The preferred stock
2. The common stock

P16-4   *Subscriptions* On July 3 the Wallace Company enters into a subscription contract with various investors. Terms of the contract are as follows:
1. Number of shares: 10,000 shares of no-par, $6 stated-value common stock.
2. Price and payment schedule: Subscription price is $13 per share. A $3 per share down payment is required, with a $5 per share payment due on both August 3 and October 3. Shares are issued to each subscriber upon full payment.
3. Default provisions: Defaulted shares are to be sold on October 4 at the then-current market price. If the proceeds from this sale are less than the total subscription price of the defaulted shares, an amount necessary to bring the proceeds up to the total subscription price is to be withheld from defaulted subscribers. Any remaining payments received from defaulted subscribers are to be returned to them.

Required
Record the July 3, August 3, and the October 3 and 4 journal entries, assuming that a subscriber to 500 shares of stock defaulted after making the down payment. The 500 shares were sold on October 4 for $11 per share.

P16-5   *Stock Rights to Stockholders* The Nichols Electronics Corporation has been experiencing a steadily growing demand for its products. In order to meet this demand, a major expansion of production facilities is necessary. The company plans to raise the money for this proposed expansion by issuing 10,000 shares of $50 par preferred stock and 50,000 shares of $10 par common stock. These shares were previously authorized but have not yet been issued.

There are presently 200,000 shares of $10 par common stock issued and outstanding. In order that the preemptive right of the current stockholders be maintained, the board of directors authorizes the issuance of stock rights to the current common stockholders on March 2, 2007. The current market price of the common stock at this date is $24 per share. Each common stockholder is to receive one stock warrant for each share of common stock owned. One additional share of common stock may be purchased at any time prior to April 7, 2007 for $23 and four of the stock warrants.

There are presently 20,000 shares of the $50 par preferred stock issued and outstanding. They were selling for $78 per share on March 5, 2007. No preemptive right applies to the preferred stock. In order to assure the sale of the additional 10,000 shares of the preferred stock, the board of directors also authorizes one stock warrant to be attached to each share of preferred stock in the new issue. One of these stock warrants allows the preferred stockholder to purchase one share of $10 par common stock for $18 per share at any time prior to April 7, 2007. The preferred shares with warrants attached are issued on March 6, 2007 at a price of $83 per share. The warrants begin trading in the market at $6 each.

Required
1. Prepare the entry to record the issuance of the common stock warrants on March 2, 2007.
2. Prepare journal entries to record the following transactions:
   a. The sale of the 10,000 shares of $50 par preferred stock with detachable warrants on March 6, 2007.
   b. The exercise on March 19, 2007 of 6,000 of the stock warrants that had been attached to the preferred stock (the common stock price is currently $24 per share and the preferred stock is selling ex rights for $79 per share).
   c. The exercise on April 2, 2007 of 120,000 stock warrants issued in conjunction with the preemptive right (the common stock is currently selling at $23.50 per share).
   d. 4,000 stock warrants related to the preferred stock and 80,000 stock warrants related to the preemptive right expire on April 6, 2007.

P16-6   *Fixed Compensatory Share Option Plan* On January 1, 2007 Roswall Corporation's common stock is selling for $55 per share. On this date, Roswall creates a compensatory share option plan for its 60 key employees. The plan document states that each employee may purchase 500 shares of its $10 par common stock for $55 per share after working for the company for three years. On this date, based on an option pricing model, Roswall estimates that each option has a value of $18. Historically, Roswall has experienced an employee turnover rate of 5% per year and, on the grant date, it expects this rate to continue over the next three years. Because of lower turnover, at the end of 2008 Roswall changes its estimated turnover rate to 4% for the entire service period. At the end of 2009, the options vest for 54 employees. On January 13, 2010, ten executives exercise their options when the stock is selling for $75 per share.

Required
1. Prepare a schedule of the Roswall Corporation's compensation computations for its compensatory share option plan for 2007 through 2009 (round all computations to the nearest dollar).
2. Prepare the journal entries of Roswall Corporation for 2007 through 2010 in regard to this plan.
3. Show how the account(s) related to the plan is (are) reported in the stockholders' equity section of Roswall Corporation's balance sheet on December 31, 2008.

P16-7   *Performance-Based Compensatory Share Option Plan* Connors Company has 70 executives to whom it grants compensatory share options on January 1, 2007. The plan grants each executive options to acquire a maximum of 100 shares of the company's $5 par common stock at $50 per share after completing three years of continuous service. However, the number of options that vest depends on the increase in the company's market share over the three-year period. The following schedule shows the number of options granted to each executive based on the increase in market share by the end of the service period:

Increase in Market Share	Number of Share Options Granted
0 to 4%	40
5 to 8%	60
More than 8%	100

Based on past trends, on the grant date Connors predicts that its market share will increase about 3% by the end of 2009. At the end of 2008, due to improved market position over the previous two years, Connors revises this estimate to 7%. At the end of 2009, Connors determines that its market share has increased 9% over the three-year period.

On the grant date, Connors Company estimates that (1) the fair value of each option is $16.25, and (2) its employee turnover rate will be 3% per year over the service period. At the end of 2008; because of increased resignations, Connors changes its estimated turnover rate to 5% for each year in the service period. At the end of 2009, 59 executives vest in the plan. On January 17, 2010, 30 executives exercise their options when the stock is selling for $68 per share.

Required

1. Prepare a schedule of the Connors Company's compensation computations for its compensatory share option plan for 2007 through 2009 (round all computations to the nearest dollar).
2. Prepare the journal entries of Connors Company for 2007 through 2010 in regard to this plan.
3. Show how the account(s) related to the plan is (are) reported in the stockholders' equity section of Connors Company's balance sheet on December 31, 2008.
4. Do you see a problem with your answer to Requirement 3 and the eventual value of the vested stock options? How might this problem be avoided?

P16-8 *Performance-Based Compensatory Share Option Plan* On January 1, 2007 Pierce Company establishes a performance-based share option plan for its 80 top executives. The terms of the plan are that each executive is granted a maximum of 200 options after completing a three-year service period. The exact number of options granted, however, depends on the percentage increase in sales over the three-year period. The terms are: (1) if sales increase between 0 and 3%, each executive is granted 90 options; (2) if, instead, sales increase between 4 and 6%, each executive is granted 140 options; and (3) if, instead, sales increase at least 7%, each executive is granted the maximum number of options. Each option entitles the executive to acquire one share of the company's $10 par common stock at a price of $45. The options expire at the end of six years.

On the grant date Pierce Company uses an option pricing model to estimate that the fair value of each share option is $15.50. Pierce's employee turnover rate has averaged 6% per year and, on the grant date, it expects this rate to continue over the service period. At the end of 2008, because of lower turnover, Pierce revises its estimated annual turnover rate to 4% for the service period. At the end of 2009, options vest for 68 executives. On February 3, 2010, 50 executives exercise their options when the market price of the company's common stock is $62 per share. During the remainder of the year, the market price declines so that at the end of 2010 the other 18 executives allow their options to expire.

Based on a projection of past trends, on the grant date Pierce Company estimates that its sales will increase about 5% by the end of 2009. This estimate appears accurate through 2008. However, in the last half of 2009, sales increase so much that at the end of 2009 Pierce determines that its total sales have increased by 7% over the three-year service period. All inventory is shipped by Pierce to its customers under FOB destination terms.

Required

1. Prepare a schedule of the Pierce Company's compensation computations for its compensatory share option plan for 2007 through 2009 (round all computations to the nearest dollar).
2. Prepare the journal entries of Pierce Company for 2007 through 2010 in regard to this plan.
3. Show how the account(s) related to the plan is (are) reported in the stockholders' equity section of Pierce Company's December 31, 2008 balance sheet.
4. Do you see any problems with the way the terms of Pierce Company's compensatory share option plan are structured? Explain.

P16-9 *Share Appreciation Rights* Smythe Company has a share appreciation rights plan for its key executives. This SAR plan gives each qualifying executive the right to receive cash, stock, or a combination of both equal to the excess of the quoted market price over the option price of the company's $10 par common stock on the date of exercise. The key characteristics and requirements of this SAR plan are as follows:

Option price: Market price on date of grant
Service period: 4 years
Exercise limit: Within 6 years after the service period has expired

On January 1, 2006 Sarah Mendelson was granted SARs to 10,000 shares of the company's common stock under the requirements of the SAR plan. She is expected to complete the service period and receive cash on the date of exercise. On December 31, 2010 Mendelson exercised her rights to receive $27,000 cash and the remainder in common stock. The fair value per SAR was as follows: 12/31/06, $4.00; 12/31/07, $4.10; 12/31/08, $3.80; 12/31/09, $5.50; and 12/31/10, $6.00. The quoted market price per share of common stock was $16 on January 1, 2006 and $22 on December 31, 2010.

Required 🖎

1. Prepare a schedule to compute the compensation expense related to this SAR plan for 2006 through 2010.
2. Prepare the journal entries related to the SAR plan on December 31, 2006 through December 31, 2010.

P16-10 *Comprehensive* The Young Corporation has been operating successfully for several years. It is authorized to issue 24,000 shares of no-par common stock and 6,000 shares of 8%, $100 par preferred stock. The Contributed Capital section of its January 1, 2007 balance sheet is as follows:

8% preferred stock, $100 par	$190,000
Common stock, no par	184,000
Premium on preferred stock	15,200
	$389,200

Part a. A stockholder has raised the following questions:

1. What is the legal capital of the corporation?
2. At what average price per share has the preferred stock been issued?
3. How many shares of common stock have been issued (the common stock has been issued at an average price of $23 per share)?

Part b. The company engaged in the following transactions in 2007:

Mar. 2 Received a subscription to 400 shares of the 8% preferred stock. The total subscription price is $122 per share and the contract requires a $10 per share down payment. The remaining balance must be paid within 60 days or the stock subscription is defaulted. In the case of default, 20% of the down payment on the defaulted shares is forfeited, and the remainder is returned to the defaulting subscribers.
Apr. 5 Sold 900 shares of common stock for $34 per share.
Apr. 13 Issued 400 shares of common stock in exchange for land. The stock is currently selling at $33 per share.
Apr. 30 Received remaining subscription balance (from March 2) owed on 350 shares of preferred stock and issued the stock.
May 4 Returned 80% of their down payment to defaulting subscribers and canceled the related account balances.
June 1 Reacquired 500 shares of common stock at $36 per share. The company uses the cost method to account for treasury stock.
Oct. 19 Issued for $27,000 a combination of 500 shares of common stock and 100 shares of preferred stock. The common and preferred stock are currently selling for $35 and $125 per share, respectively.
Nov. 16 Reissued the 500 shares of treasury stock at $38 per share.
Dec. 31 Distributed an $8 per share dividend on all preferred stock outstanding and a $2 per share dividend on all common stock outstanding on this date (debit Retained Earnings and credit Cash for each dividend).

Required
1. Answer the questions in part *a*.
2. Prepare journal entries to record the transactions in part *b*.
3. Prepare the contributed capital section of Young's December 31, 2007 balance sheet.

P16-11 *Comprehensive* The Byrd Company's Contributed Capital section of its January 1, 2007 balance sheet is as follows:

Preferred stock (6%, $50 par, 8,000 shares authorized, 3,400 shares issued and outstanding)	$170,000
Common stock ($10 stated value, 30,000 shares authorized, 12,000 shares issued and outstanding)	120,000
Preferred stock subscribed (800 shares subscribed at $54 per share)	40,000
Additional paid-in capital on preferred stock	12,800
Additional paid-in capital on common stock	72,000
Total contributed capital	$414,800

During 2007 the company entered into the following transactions:

Jan. 3 Established a compensatory share option plan for its key executives. The options vest after a three-year service period. The estimated fair value of the options expected to be exercised is $81,000.
Mar. 6 Received the remaining $40 per share on the subscribed preferred stock and issued the shares.
Apr. 24 Sold 300 shares of preferred stock at $55 per share.
May 4 Received a subscription down payment of $6 per share on 1,000 shares of common stock. The remaining $11 per share balance is due in 60 days.
June 7 Sold 600 shares of common stock at $17 per share.
July 3 Received the remaining balance on subscribed common stock and issued the shares.
Sept. 21 Purchased building by paying $9,000 cash and issuing 800 shares of common stock and 450 shares of preferred stock. Common and preferred stock are currently selling for $19 and $57 per share, respectively.
Oct. 12 Reacquired 900 shares of common stock at $19.50 per share. The company uses the cost method to account for treasury stock.
Nov. 15 Issued for $32,000 a combination of 700 shares of common stock and 12% bonds with a face value of $20,000. The common stock is currently selling for $18 per share. No market value exists for the bonds.
Dec. 14 Reissued the 900 shares of treasury stock at $20.50 per share.
Dec. 28 Distributed a $3.00 per share dividend to all outstanding preferred stock and a $1.50 per share dividend to all common stock outstanding on this date (debit Retained Earnings and credit Cash for each dividend).
Dec. 31 Declared a two-for-one stock split on the common stock, reducing the stated value to $4 per share and increasing the authorized shares to 60,000.

Required
1. Prepare journal entries to record the preceding transactions.
2. Prepare the contributed capital section of Byrd's December 31, 2007 balance sheet.

P16-12   *Contributed Capital* A partial list of the accounts and ending account balances taken from the post-closing trial balance of the Jordan Corporation on December 31, 2007 is shown as follows:

Account Title	Amount
Retained earnings	$410,000
Bonds payable	220,000
Common stock subscribed	60,000
Long-term investments in stock	210,000
Additional paid-in capital on common stock	460,000
Premium on bonds payable	30,000
Common stock	500,000
Preferred stock subscribed	35,000
Additional paid-in capital on preferred stock	112,000
Preferred stock	300,000
Additional paid-in capital from treasury stock	4,000
Unrealized increase in value of securities available for sale	3,000
Common stock option warrants	20,000

Additional information:
1. Common stock is no-par, with a stated value of $10 per share, 90,000 shares are authorized, 50,000 shares are issued and outstanding, 6,000 shares have been subscribed at a price of $28 per share.
2. Preferred stock has a $50 par value, 8,000 shares are authorized, 6,000 shares are issued and outstanding, 700 shares have been subscribed at a price of $70 per share. Each share is cumulative, convertible into five shares of common stock, and pays a 7% annual dividend. Dividends are not in arrears.
3. Bonds payable mature on July 1, 2019. They carry a 12% annual interest rate, payable semiannually. The premium is being amortized using the straight-line method.

Required
Prepare the contributed capital section of the December 31, 2007 balance sheet for the Jordan Corporation. Include appropriate parenthetical notes for the common and preferred stock.

P16-13   *Contributed Capital* The following is a partial list of the accounts and ending account balances taken from the post-closing trial balance of the Clett Corporation on December 31, 2007:

Common stock subscribed	$ 10,000	Long-term investments in	
Premium on bonds payable	50,000	preferred stock	$ 90,000
Preferred stock	400,000	Preferred stock subscribed	100,000
Temporary investments in common stock	110,000	Retained earnings	610,000
Bonds payable	500,000	Premium on common stock	542,000
Common stock	150,000	Unrealized decrease in value of	
Premium on preferred stock	76,000	securities available for sale	6,000

Additional information:
1. Bonds payable mature on December 31, 2022. They carry a 12% interest rate, payable semiannually. The premium is being amortized using the straight-line method.
2. The 7.5% preferred stock is cumulative and convertible into three shares of common stock. It has a par value of $100 per share, 20,000 shares are authorized, 4,000 shares are issued and outstanding, 1,000 shares have been subscribed at $125 per share.
3. Common stock has a par value of $5 per share, 100,000 shares are authorized, 30,000 shares are issued and outstanding, 2,000 shares have been subscribed at $41 per share.

Required
Prepare the contributed capital section of the December 31, 2007 balance sheet for the Clett Corporation. Include appropriate parenthetical notes for the common and preferred stock.

P16-14 *Reconstruct Journal Entries* At the end of its first year of operations, the Leo Company lists the following accounts and ending account balances related to stock transactions and dividends:

Account	Balance Debit	Balance Credit
Cash (from stock and for dividends paid)	$250,000	
Subscriptions receivable: common stock	14,000	
Subscriptions receivable: preferred stock	33,600	
Equipment	69,000	
Preferred stock subscribed (for 300 shares)		$ 30,000
8% preferred stock, $100 par (2,300 shares)		230,000
Additional paid-in capital on preferred stock		33,000
Common stock subscribed (2,000 shares)		10,000
Common stock, $5 stated value (9,000 shares)		45,000
Additional paid-in capital on common stock		46,000
Retained earnings		2,600

During the first year the following events occurred:

1. Subscription contracts were entered into for common stock at $9 per share and preferred stock at $112 per share. Common stock subscriptions required a $2 per share down payment. Preferred stock subscriptions required no down payment. Shares (either common or preferred) were issued to subscribers upon full payment.
2. One thousand shares of common stock were sold for $11 per share, and the stock was issued to stockholders.
3. Equipment with an appraised value of $69,000 was acquired by issuing 600 shares of preferred stock. The appraised value of the equipment was used to record the transaction.
4. Net income of $30,000 was closed to Retained Earnings from Income Summary at the end of the year.
5. Dividends of $8 per share on all the preferred stock outstanding and $1 per share on all the common stock outstanding were distributed at the end of the year (the company debited Retained Earnings and credited Cash for each dividend).

Required
On the basis of the preceding information, reconstruct all the journal entries that the company made to record the stock transactions, net income, and dividends.

P16-15 *Treasury Stock, Cost Method* Bush-Caine Company reported the following data on its December 31, 2006 balance sheet:

Preferred stock, $50 par	$50,000	Common stock, $10 par	$100,000
Additional paid-in capital on		Additional paid-in capital on common stock	80,000
preferred stock	4,000	Retained earnings	95,000

The following transactions were reported by the company during 2007:

1. Reacquired 200 shares of its preferred stock at $57 per share.
2. Reacquired 500 shares of its common stock at $16 per share.
3. Sold 100 shares of preferred treasury stock at $58 per share.
4. Sold 200 shares of common treasury stock at $17 per share.
5. Sold 100 shares of common treasury stock at $9 per share.
6. Retired the shares of common stock remaining in the treasury.

The company maintains separate treasury stock accounts and related additional paid-in capital accounts for each class of stock.

Required
1. Prepare the journal entries required to record the treasury stock transactions using the cost method.
2. Assuming the company earned a net income in 2007 of $30,000 and declared and paid dividends of $10,000, prepare the stockholders' equity section of its balance sheet at December 31, 2007.

P16-16 *Treasury Stock Analysis* The Ray Holt Corporation has retained you as a consultant on accounting policies and procedures. During 2007 the company engaged in a number of treasury stock transactions, having foreseen an opportunity to report its treasury stock as an asset, and to recognize a profit in trading its own stock. The transactions were as follows:

1. Reacquired 100 shares of its $10 par common stock at $20 per share. The shares had originally been issued at $23 per share.
2. Reacquired 150 shares of its $10 par common stock at $24 per share. The shares had originally been issued at $23 per share.
3. Reacquired 50 shares of its $100 par preferred stock at $140 per share. The shares had originally been issued at $170 per share.
4. Sold all common treasury shares held at $25 per share.
5. Reacquired 150 shares of its $100 par preferred stock at $130 per share. The shares had originally been issued at $170 per share.
6. Retired all preferred shares held in the treasury.

Required

1. Is the corporation correct in assuming that its treasury stock is an asset and that it can recognize a profit or gain from its treasury stock transactions? Explain.
2. Prepare an analysis of treasury stock accounting for Mr. Robert Richter, the controller. This analysis should contain proper journal entries for each of the treasury stock transactions occurring during 2007, prepared using the cost method discussed in the chapter.
3. Conclude the analysis by discussing how "gains" on treasury stock are reported and how treasury stock is reported on a corporation's balance sheet.

P16-17 AICPA Adapted *Comprehensive* Udall Corporation's post-closing trial balance at December 31, 2007 was as follows:

	Debit	Credit
Accounts payable		$ 290,000
Accounts receivable	$ 550,000	
Accumulated depreciation—building and equipment		200,000
Additional paid-in capital—common		
In excess of par value		1,560,000
From sale of treasury stock		250,000
Allowance for doubtful accounts		30,000
Bonds payable		400,000
Building and equipment	1,100,000	
Cash	220,000	
Common stock ($1 par value)		150,000
Dividends payable on preferred stock—cash		4,000
Inventories	620,000	
Land	380,000	
Long-term equity securities (at market)	285,000	
Marketable equity securities (at market)	215,000	
Preferred stock ($50 par value)		500,000
Prepaid expenses	40,000	
Retained earnings		231,000
Treasury stock—common (at cost)	180,000	
Unrealized decrease in value of available-for-sale securities	25,000	
Totals	$3,615,000	$3,615,000

At December 31, 2007 Udall had the following number of common and preferred shares:

	Common	Preferred
Authorized	500,000	50,000
Issued	150,000	10,000
Outstanding	140,000	10,000

The dividends on preferred stock are $4 cumulative. In addition, the preferred stock has a preference in liquidation of $50 per share.

Required

Prepare the stockholders' equity section of Udall's balance sheet at December 31, 2007.

CASES

COMMUNICATION

C16-1 Stockholder Rights and Preferences

A stockholder has several rights as an "owner" of a corporation. Furthermore, the rights of preferred stockholders are sometimes modified upon the issuance of preferred stock.

Required
1. List and briefly explain stockholders' rights as they pertain to common stockholders. Indicate the relative importance of each.
2. List and briefly explain what characteristics might be attached to preferred stock. Indicate the set of characteristics that makes preferred stock more like a long-term bond than a common stock.

C16-2 Exchange of Stock for Asset

As a general rule, when a corporation issues capital stock for assets other than cash, it is said that the exchange should be valued at the fair value of the stock or the asset, whichever is more reliable.

Required
Write a short report that explains the reasoning behind this rule, including the concepts of *watered stock* and *secret reserves*. Give an example of a situation where the fair value of (1) the stock or, alternatively, (2) the asset is used to record an exchange.

C16-3 Issuance of Security Packages

Occasionally, a corporation will combine securities into a "package" (for example, common stocks, preferred stocks, bonds) and issue these securities as a single unit.

Required
Assuming that two securities (common stock and preferred stock) are issued as a unit, explain the alternative ways of valuing the separate stocks of the unit in an exchange for (1) cash, or (2) an asset(s) other than cash.

C16-4 Subscriptions

A corporation may enter into subscription contracts for the purchase of its stock.

Required
What is a subscription contract and how does it work? What provisions are usually included in the contract? What are the arguments for reporting the Subscriptions Receivable account as a contra-stockholders' equity item and for reporting it as a current asset? Why is the Capital Stock account not credited at the time of the subscription instead of the Capital Stock Subscribed account? How is this latter account reported on the corporation's balance sheet?

What are the alternative methods of handling subscription defaults?

C16-5 Share Options

AICPA Adapted A corporation has a noncompensatory share purchase plan for all its employees and a compensatory share option plan for some of its corporate officers.

Required
1. Compare and contrast the accounting at the date the stock is issued for the noncompensatory share purchase plan with that for the compensatory share option plan.
2. What entry should be made for the compensatory share option plan at the date of the grant?

C16-6 Capital Stock

AICPA Adapted Capital stock is an important area of a corporation's equity section. Generally the term "capital stock" embraces common and preferred stock issued by a corporation.

Required
1. What are the basic rights inherent in ownership of common stock, and how are they exercised?
2. What is preferred stock? Discuss the various preferences afforded preferred stock.

C16-7 Treasury Stock

A corporation sometimes engages in treasury stock transactions.

Required
1. Define *treasury stock*.
2. Why would a corporation acquire treasury stock?
3. Briefly explain the cost method of accounting for the reacquisition and reissuance of treasury stock. Assume the treasury stock is common stock and has a par value.
4. Briefly explain the balance sheet presentation of treasury stock under this method.

C16-8 Definitions

AICPA Adapted In dealing with the various equity securities of a corporate entity, it is important to understand certain related terminology.

Required
Define the following terms: (1) treasury stock, (2) legal capital, (3) stock right, and (4) stock warrant.

CREATIVE AND CRITICAL THINKING

C16-9 Compensatory Share Options

AICPA Adapted On November 6, 2006, Gunpowder Corp.'s board of directors approved a share option plan for key executives. On January 2, 2007, a specific number of share options were granted. These options were exercisable between January 2, 2009 and December 31, 2011 at 90% of the quoted market price on January 2, 2007. The service period is for 2007 and 2008. Some options were forfeited when an executive resigned in 2008. All other options were exercised during 2009.

Required
1. How should Gunpowder determine the compensation expense, if any, for the share option plan in 2007?
2. What is the effect of forfeiture of the share options on Gunpowder's financial statements for 2008?
3. What is the effect of the share option plan on the balance sheet at December 31, 2009? Be specific as to the changes in balance sheet accounts between November 6, 2006 and December 31, 2009.

C16-10 Share Appreciation Rights

Instead of a fixed compensatory share option plan, Wright Company is considering providing its key executives with a plan that involves share appreciation rights (SAR).

Required
1. Explain what is meant by an SAR plan.
2. Identify the key differences between accounting for an SAR plan and a fixed compensatory share option plan.
3. Briefly summarize the steps in accounting for an SAR plan (assume that the executive is expected to receive cash on the date of exercise).

C16-11 Compensatory Share Option Plan

Tom Twitlet, president of Twitlet Corporation, is considering establishing a compensatory share option plan for the company's 20 top executives. Tom desires to set the terms of the plan so that the number of options the executives can exercise increases based on a specified increase in the company's future earnings. Tom is concerned about how to specify and account for the terms of the plan, and has asked for your advice.

Required
Prepare a memo to Tom that briefly explains the issues involved in specifying and accounting for the terms of this type of compensatory share option plan.

C16-12 Convertible Preferred Stock and Warrants

The stockholders' equity of a corporation may include both preferred stock and common stock. Preferred stock may (1) be convertible into common stock, or (2) be issued with warrants attached enabling the acquisition of common stock.

Required
Discuss the following three items:
1. The similarities and differences between these types of preferred stock.
2. Theoretically, the appropriate accounting treatment for the proceeds from the issuance of both types of preferred stock.
3. Which accounting treatment is generally acceptable for each type and why?

C16-13 Treasury Stock

AICPA Adapted For numerous reasons a corporation may reacquire shares of its own capital stock. When a corporation purchases treasury stock, it has two options as to how to account for the shares: (1) cost method, and (2) par value method.

Required
Write a short report that compares and contrasts the cost method with the par value method for each of the following:
1. Purchase of shares at a price less than par value.
2. Purchase of shares at a price greater than par value.
3. Subsequent resale of treasury shares at a price less than purchase price, but more than par value.
4. Subsequent resale of treasury shares at a price greater than both purchase price and par value.
5. Effect on net income.

C16-14 Changes in Equity

FASB Statement of Concepts No. 6 defines a company's equity and discusses the various changes in equity.

Required
Define and discuss the term equity. Identify the various changes in a company's equity in regard to their impact on assets and liabilities.

C16-15 Analyzing Coca-Cola's Contributed Capital

Refer to the financial statements and related notes of The Coca-Cola Company in Appendix A of this book.

Required
1. How many shares of preferred stock were authorized and issued at the end of 2004?
2. How many shares of common stock were authorized and issued at the end of 2004? What is the par value per share?
3. What does the company call its additional paid-in capital? What was the amount at the end of 2004?
4. How many shares of treasury stock did the company hold at the end of 2004? What was the average cost per share?
5. How many shares of treasury stock did the company reacquire during 2004? What was the average cost per share?
6. Briefly describe the company's 2002 Stock Option Plan. What was the weighted-average fair value of the stock options the company granted in 2004? How much was

the company's total stock-based compensation expense for 2004 and where was it reported? How many stock options were granted and exercised during 2004, and how many were outstanding at the end of 2004? At what weighted-average price per share were the options exercised in 2004? Assuming the stock options were exercised in 2004 at the weighted-average price per share and that the average market price per share was $46, by how much did the officers "gain" from exercising the options?

C16-16 Ethics and Share Options

Smaller Corporation has been in operation for several years. Each year, at Christmas time, the company has given a cash bonus to each of its employees, and properly recorded the bonuses as compensation expense. Smaller has reached the point at which it is now making a reasonable return on its stockholders' equity. At the end of the current year, the president of the company is considering establishing a compensatory share option plan for Smaller's key executives, instead of paying cash bonuses to any of its employees. At this time the market price and the planned option (exercise) price of the company's common stock are the same. The plan would allocate a specified number of options to each executive based on the executive's level within the company and meeting the company's targeted income goals. The service period would be three years and the options would have to be exercised within 10 years.

You are the controller for Smaller and one of the key executives who would participate in the plan. You also already own a substantial number of shares of Smaller common stock. The company president comes to you for advice about this plan and says, "If Smaller Corporation establishes this plan, it will work out for all of us. It looks like the plan is pretty valuable, since an option pricing model shows a high fair value for each option. The corporation will be saving cash because it won't have to pay bonuses to either the executives or the other employees. But executives will manage better because their share options will depend on meeting the company's targeted income. Since the market price and the option price are the same, there won't be any compensation cost or expense related to this plan. Furthermore, since no bonuses would be paid to any employees, the corporation will decrease its compensation expense. This will increase its net income and earnings per share compared to last year, as well as its return on stockholders' equity. So the stock value will go up. This seems like a win-win situation for everyone. Am I right on this? Do you think the company should adopt this compensatory share option plan?"

Required
From financial reporting and ethical perspectives, how would you reply to the president?

RESEARCH SIMULATIONS

R16-1 Researching GAAP

Situation
Russell International, a publicly traded company, reacquired 500,000 shares of its common stock during July 2008 at a cost of $25 per share. The current market price of the stock was $20 per share when the 500,000 shares were reacquired.

The shares that were reacquired had been owned by a group of minority shareholders who had been dissatisfied with Russell International's earnings trend, stock price, and dividends paid. In fact, these minority shareholders had been so disgruntled that they had filed a suit against Russell's directors during 2007. The minority shareholders' suit claimed damages of $3 million because of the board's failure to fulfill its fiduciary responsibility to maximize shareholders' value.

In August 2008 the minority shareholders' suit was dropped, with neither Russell International nor its directors having to offer or pay a settlement. Russell International accounts for its treasury stock transactions using the cost method.

Directions
Research the related generally accepted accounting principles and explain how Russell International should account for the treasury stock transaction. Cite your reference and applicable paragraph numbers. (*Contributed by Daryl G. Krause*)

R16-2 Researching GAAP

Situation
Bowsher Company had 10% bonds payable outstanding with a total face value of $185,000. Each bond had an individual face value of $1,000 and paid interest semiannually on June 30 and December 31. On July 1 of the current year the 10% bonds had a total book value of $210,000. At that time, because of a financial restructuring, the company executed an "exchange agreement" in which all of these 10% bonds were extinguished. In exchange for their 10% bonds, the bondholders were given cash of $125 per 10% bond, six shares of 7%, $100 preferred stock per 10% bond, and 50 warrants per 10% bond allowing the holder to acquire 50 shares of $5 par common stock for $25 per share. On July 1 the 7% preferred stock was selling at $106 per share and the warrants were selling at $5 each on the open market. You are the assistant accountant for Bowsher Company and have been asked by the head accountant to recommend how to record this transaction.

Directions
Research the related generally accepted accounting principles and prepare a short memo that explains and justifies your recommended journal entry to record the transaction. Cite your reference and applicable paragraph numbers.

17

OBJECTIVES

After reading this chapter you will be able to:

1 Compute basic earnings per share (EPS).

2 Understand how to compute the weighted average common shares for EPS.

3 Identify the potential common shares included in diluted EPS.

4 Apply the treasury stock method for including share options and warrants in diluted EPS.

5 Calculate the impact of a convertible security on diluted EPS.

6 Compute diluted EPS.

7 Record the declaration and payment of cash dividends.

8 Account for a property dividend.

9 Explain the difference in accounting for small and large stock dividends.

10 Understand how to report accumulated other comprehensive income.

11 Prepare a statement of changes in stockholders' equity.

Earnings Per Share and Retained Earnings

Are Dividends Making a Comeback?

While earnings per share (EPS) is one of the most-watched numbers in corporate America, the ability of a company to earn a profit does not always translate to the ability to pay a large dividend. For example, **Microsoft** chose not to pay a dividend from its inception. Instead it reinvested its earnings to fuel future growth. Eventually, Microsoft grew to a point where it could no longer grow at the rate it had maintained for so long. With analysts estimating that Microsoft was generating roughly $1 billion in extra cash each month, management was forced to act. In early 2003, Microsoft declared its first dividend ever on common stock. This was followed in mid-2004 with a special one-time dividend of $3 per share, a payout worth approximately $32 billion. And Microsoft is not alone. According to a *New York Times* article, the number of companies that decided to increase dividends in 2004 increased for the third consecutive year.

Why the sudden popularity of dividends?[1] While investors seemed to avoid dividend-paying stocks in the 1990s as companies focused on growth, U.S. companies paid a record $213.6 billion in dividends in 2004. Two reasons have been cited for this increase. First, faced with lackluster stock performance and burned by accounting scandals that made profits disappear, shareholders have increasingly put pressure on companies to pay

---

1. Adapted from "Tax Cut, Shareholder Pressure Stoke Surge in Stock Dividends," *Wall Street Journal*, Jan. 18, 2005.

dividends. Second, in 2003, new tax legislation was enacted that slashed the tax rate on dividends to 15%, a move viewed by many as effectively ending the practice of double taxation of dividends. With S&P 500 companies only distributing 34% of their earnings as dividends (the historical average is 56%), many analysts believe that this comeback for dividends is likely to continue.

FOR FURTHER INVESTIGATION

For a discussion of dividends, consult the Business & Company Resource Center (BCRC):

- The Market's Differential Reactions to Forward-Looking and Backward-Looking Dividend Changes. Bong-Soo Lee, Nairong Allen Yan, *Journal of Financial Research*, 0270-2592, Winter 2003, v26, i4, p449-468.

- Get Thy Yield: President Bush Wants to Hand Down a Repeal of the Stock-Dividend Tax. (Panel Discussion) Daniel Kadlec, *Time*, 0040-781X, Feb 10, 2003, v161, i6, pA11+.

In the previous chapter we introduced the topic of stockholders' equity by discussing the contributed capital that arises when a corporation issues capital stock. We also discussed the impact of the reacquisition of a corporation's capital stock (treasury stock) on its stockholders' equity. In this chapter we continue discussing stockholders' equity by focusing primarily on retained earnings. The chapter begins with a discussion of earnings per share (EPS) because its computation involves items of contributed capital (common stock) and retained earnings (net income). The chapter then moves to a discussion of items affecting retained earnings, such as dividends, prior period and retrospective adjustments, and restrictions (appropriations). We conclude the chapter by discussing the statement of retained earnings, other changes in stockholders' equity, and the statement of changes in stockholders' equity.

EARNINGS AND EARNINGS PER SHARE

Net income (loss) is the amount of earnings from a corporation's income-producing activities during its accounting period. A corporation summarizes the components of its net income on its income statement. As we discussed in Chapter 5, the primary components are: (1) **income (loss) from continuing operations,** which includes operating revenues and operating expenses; (2) **results from discontinued operations,** which includes the income (loss) from the operations of a discontinued component as well as the gain (loss) from the disposal of the discontinued component; and (3) **extraordinary gains or losses,** the results of unusual *and* infrequent events. A corporation also reports its earnings per share on its income statement.

Corporations are required to disclose earnings per share information. **FASB Statement No. 128** contains the generally accepted accounting principles for earnings per share. We discuss the major issues involved in computing and reporting earnings per share in the following sections.

OVERVIEW AND USES OF EARNINGS PER SHARE INFORMATION

Earnings per share often is considered to be the best measure summarizing the performance of a corporation, particularly for common shareholders. Earnings per share information is *relevant* to these users in evaluating the *return on investment* and *risk* of a corporation.

The amount of earnings per share, the change in earnings per share from the previous period, and the trend in earnings per share are all important indicators of a corporation's success. Many investors also are interested in the corporation's cash flow per share. Although corporations are prohibited from reporting cash flow per share, earnings per share may be a long-run indicator of cash flow per share.

One ratio used to evaluate return and risk is the price/earnings ratio, which investors often use in intercompany comparisons. To compute the price/earnings ratio, earnings per share is divided into the market price per share (of the common stock). For example, at the time of writing this book, two department stores, **Kohl's Corporation** and **J.C Penney Company**, had price/earnings ratios of 21 and 17, respectively. Kohl's price/earnings ratio indicates that the stock is selling for a price of 21 times the most recent year's earnings per share. The difference in the ratios indicates that compared to Penney's price/earnings ratio, investors are more optimistic about the future of Kohl's and expect that it will have a higher growth in earnings per share.

Investors often are interested in predicting earnings per share for future periods. One required earnings per share computation is intended to indicate the effects of possible future events. When a corporation has issued common share options (discussed in Chapter 16), convertible debt (discussed in Chapter 14), or convertible preferred stock (discussed in Chapter 14), it will issue additional common shares if the options are exercised or the securities converted, thereby affecting earnings per share. Diluted earnings per share (which we define and discuss later) includes the potential effects of such conversions. Also, earnings per share may be computed on past reported earnings, or on future earnings as estimated by financial analysts. When using earnings per share information (e.g., price/earnings ratios) for intercompany comparisons, a user must be sure that the calculations are *comparable*.

BASIC EARNINGS PER SHARE

For computing earnings per share, there are two types of corporate capital structures—simple and complex. We begin by discussing earnings per share for a corporation with a simple capital structure. **A simple capital structure is one that consists only of common stock outstanding.** A corporation with a simple capital structure is required to report basic earnings per share (sometimes called earnings per common share).[2] **Basic earnings per share** is computed as follows:

1 Compute basic earnings per share (EPS).

$$\text{Basic Earnings Per Share} = \frac{\text{Net Income} - \text{Preferred Dividends}}{\text{Weighted Average Number of Common Shares Outstanding}}$$

Example: Basic Earnings per Share

Assume that during 2007, Lapan Corporation reports net income of $48,000, and declares and pays dividends of $8,000 on its preferred stock. It also declares and pays dividends of $12,000 on its 16,000 shares of common stock that have been outstanding for the entire year. Lapan Corporation computes its $2.50 basic earnings per share for 2007 as follows:

$$\underline{\$2.50} = \frac{\$48,000 - \$8,000}{16,000}$$

Note that Lapan Corporation deducts the dividends on its preferred dividends but not the dividends on its common stock in computing its basic earnings per share. This is because the numerator of the basic earnings per share calculation is the earnings available to common stockholders, and preferred dividends must be paid before common dividends may be distributed.

Lapan Corporation reports its $2.50 basic earnings per share on its 2007 income statement, directly below net income. If it had a net loss, it would have reported the basic loss per share. It also reports basic earnings per share (or basic loss per share) for each comparative income statement presented. ♦

There are several complexities that affect the numerator and denominator of the earnings per share equation. Although we discuss these issues for basic earnings per share, they also apply to corporations that report diluted earnings per share (which we discuss in a later section).

Numerator Calculations

Only the amount of *earnings available to common stockholders* is used in the numerator of the earnings per share computation. If a corporation has outstanding *noncumulative* preferred stock, it deducts the dividends declared during the current period from the net income to determine the earnings available to common stockholders (as we did in the

---

2. "Earnings per Share," *FASB Statement of Financial Accounting Standards No. 128* (Norwalk, Conn.: FASB, 1997), par 36. A corporation also has a simple capital structure if it has nonconvertible preferred stock outstanding, in addition to its common stock.

previous example). If the corporation has *cumulative* preferred stock outstanding, it deducts the dividends for the *current* period, *whether declared or not*. It discloses the amount of the dividends deduction in the notes to its financial statements, as we show in Example 17-3.

Denominator Calculations

There are two types of denominator calculations: weighted average shares and stock dividends and splits.

Weighted Average Shares

2 Understand how to compute the weighted average common shares for EPS.

Since a corporation earns its net income over the entire year, the earnings relate to the common shares outstanding during the year. If a corporation has not issued or reacquired any shares during the year, it uses the number of common shares outstanding at the end of the accounting period as the denominator. If a corporation has issued or reacquired common shares during the period, the denominator is the weighted average number of common shares outstanding during the period.

A corporation calculates the weighted average by starting with the actual number of common shares outstanding at the beginning of the period. It then multiplies this "layer" of shares by the fraction of the year it is outstanding until more common stock is issued (or shares are reacquired). These new shares are added to (or subtracted from) the actual beginning number of outstanding shares, and the new layer is multiplied by the fraction of the year it is outstanding. This process is continued for all the issuances of common stock during the year. The resulting "equivalent whole units" of stock for all the layers are added to determine the weighted average number of common shares.

Example: Weighted Average Shares

Assume McTeal Corporation had 12,000 shares of common stock outstanding at the beginning of the year. On March 2, it issued 2,700 shares; on July 3, it issued another 3,300 shares; and on December 1, it reacquired 480 shares as treasury stock. The weighted average number of common shares the corporation uses in computing its earnings per share is 15,860 shares, as we show in Example 17-1. McTeal Corporation discloses this number in the notes to its financial statements. Note that for simplicity, the nearest whole month is used to determine the fraction of the year each layer of shares was outstanding. ♦

EXAMPLE 17-1   Weighted Average Shares

Months Shares Are Outstanding	Shares Outstanding	×	Fraction of Year Outstanding	=	Equivalent Whole Units
January–February	12,000	×	2/12	=	2,000
March–June	14,700	×	4/12	=	4,900
July–November	18,000	×	5/12	=	7,500
December	17,520	×	1/12	=	1,460
		Total weighted average common shares			15,860

Stock Dividends or Splits

A corporation's common shares outstanding may increase because of a stock dividend or stock split. In these cases, it must give *retroactive* recognition to these events for all comparative income statements that it presents.[3] This retroactive adjustment results in comparable earnings per share amounts for all periods, based on the most recent capital structure. The

---

3.   A corporation must also give retroactive recognition if the stock dividend or split occurs after the end of the accounting period but before it issues its financial statements.

simplest way of giving retroactive recognition is to first assume (for earnings per share computations) that the stock dividend or split occurred at the *beginning* of the earliest comparative period. Then assume that all stock transactions between this beginning date and the *actual* date of the stock dividend or split included the additional shares resulting from the assumed dividend or split.

Example: Stock Dividend and Split

Assume that Wallers Corporation begins operations in January 2007, and issues 5,000 shares of common stock that are outstanding during all of 2007. On December 31, 2007, it issues a two-for-one stock split. At the end of 2007, the weighted average number of shares that it uses in the earnings per share computation for 2007 is 10,000 ($5,000 \times 200\% \times 12/12$) because the two-for-one stock split is *assumed* to have occurred on January 1, 2007.

On May 28, 2008, the corporation issues 5,000 shares of common stock; on August 3, 2008, it issues a 20% stock dividend; and on October 5, 2008, it issues 2,000 shares of stock. At the end of 2008, when it reports comparative earnings per share for 2007 and 2008, the weighted average numbers of shares it uses in the computation are 12,000 shares for 2007 and 16,000 shares for 2008, as we show in Example 17-2.

EXAMPLE 17-2   Comparative Weighted Average Shares

Retroactive Recognition of Stock Split and Stock Dividend: At end of 2008, for 2007 and 2008

Months Shares Are Outstanding	Actual Shares Outstanding	Assumed Shares Outstanding	×	Fraction of Year Outstanding	=	Equivalent Whole Units
2007						
January–December	5,000	$5,000 \times 200\% \times 120\% = 12,000$	×	12/12	=	12,000
2008						
January–May	10,000	$10,000 \times 120\% = 12,000$	×	5/12	=	5,000
June–July	15,000	$15,000 \times 120\% = 18,000$	×	2/12	=	3,000
August–September	18,000	$15,000 \times 120\% = 18,000$	×	2/12	=	3,000
October–December	20,000	$15,000 \times 120\% + 2,000 = 20,000$	×	3/12	=	5,000
						16,000

In Example 17-2, for comparative purposes at the end of 2008, the two-for-one stock split actually issued on December 31 *and* the 20% stock dividend actually issued on August 3, 2008 are both *assumed* to have been issued on January 1, 2007. Under this assumption, 12,000 shares of stock would have been outstanding during all of 2007. Similarly, during 2008, 12,000 shares initially would have been outstanding. The 5,000 shares issued on May 29 would have increased by 20% to 6,000 shares, resulting in 18,000 shares outstanding until October 5, 2008. The 2,000 shares issued on October 5, 2008 would not have increased because this issuance occurred *after* the actual stock dividend. The resulting weighted average number of shares is 16,000 at the end of 2008. Although these assumptions do not reflect the actual timing of the transactions, they are necessary to compute comparable earnings per share amounts for each year. ◆

Components of Earnings Per Share

Net income is the final earnings amount on a corporation's income statement. If the net income includes any results from discontinued operations or extraordinary items, the corporation must report separate earnings per share amounts for *both* income from continuing operations and net income on its income statement. It is also required to disclose the earnings per share related to the results from discontinued operations and extraordinary items. The corporation may report these component amounts on its income statement or in the notes to its financial statements.[4] Each of these earnings per share component amounts is based on the same weighted average number of shares. When reported on the income statement, the components are summed to report the total earnings per share. The intent is to show the contribution of each income statement component to the total earnings per share. When a corporation has deducted preferred dividends in the computation of total earnings per share, it also deducts these dividends from the income related to continuing operations to reconcile the earnings per share amounts.

Example of Basic Earnings Per Share

Example 17-3 shows the computation of basic earnings per share for Stanton Corporation.

EXAMPLE 17-3   **Computation and Reporting of Basic Earnings Per Share**

1. Income statement information for Stanton Corporation:
   a. Net income for 2007 is $14,000.
   b. An extraordinary gain (net of income taxes) of $3,600 is included in net income.
2. Stockholders' equity information (end of 2007):
   a. 8% Preferred stock, $100 par $30,000
   b. Common stock, $10 par $60,000
3. Additional information:
   a. No preferred stock was issued or reacquired during 2007.
   b. Preferred dividends were declared during 2007 at the stated rate.
   c. A review of the common stock account shows that on January 1, 2007, 2,000 shares of common stock were outstanding. On April 2, 500 shares of common stock were issued for cash. On June 1, a two-for-one stock split occurred, resulting in 5,000 total common shares. On November 2, 1,000 shares of common stock were issued for cash.
4. Basic earnings per share computations for 2007:

Explanation	Earnings (Adjustments)	÷	Shares (Adjustments)	=	Earnings Per Share
Net income	$14,000				
Preferred dividends[a]	(2,400)				
Common shares[b]			4,917		
Earnings and shares	$11,600	÷	4,917	=	$2.36

   a. Preferred dividends: $30,000 × 0.08 = $2,400
   b. Weighted average shares:

4,000 (2,000 × 200% stock split) × 3/12 =	1,000	
5,000 (2,500 × 200%) × 7/12 =	2,917	
6,000 (2,500 × 200% + 1,000) × 2/12 =	1,000	
Weighted average common shares	4,917	

5. Condensed income statement presentation of Stanton Corporation for 2007:

Income before extraordinary items	$10,400
Extraordinary gain (net of income taxes)	3,600
Net income	$14,000
Basic earnings per share (see Note A):	
Income before extraordinary items	$1.63
Extraordinary gain	0.73
Net income	$2.36

6. Note A to financial statements: Preferred dividends of $2,400 are deducted from income before extraordinary items and net income to determine earnings available to common stock. The resulting amounts of $8,000 and $11,600 divided by the 4,917 weighted average number of common shares yield $1.63 and $2.36 basic earnings per share, respectively. A total of 6,000 common shares were outstanding at the end of 2007.

---

4.   *FASB Statement of Financial Accounting Standards No. 128, op. cit.,* par. 37. These disclosures are also required for diluted earnings per share, as we discuss later.

DILUTED EARNINGS PER SHARE

Many corporations have a more complex capital structure. Their capital structure includes securities such as share options and warrants, convertible preferred stock and convertible bonds, participating securities and two-class stocks, and contingent shares. These securities are referred to as **potential common shares** because they can be used by the holder to acquire common stock. Since conversion of these securities into common stock would affect the earnings available to each common stockholder, they are considered in computing a corporation's earnings per share.

3 Identify the potential common shares included in diluted EPS.

Instead of a single earnings per share disclosure, **a corporation with a complex capital structure is required to report two earnings per share amounts on the face of its income statement.** The two amounts are basic earnings per share and diluted earnings per share. Basic earnings per share is computed, as we discussed earlier, for corporations with a simple capital structure. **Diluted earnings per share shows the earnings per share after including** *all* **potential common shares that would reduce earnings per share.** If a corporation has a *loss* from continuing operations, then it does **not** include potential common shares in diluted earnings per share (even if it reports a positive net income). In this case, the corporation's basic and diluted earnings per share are the same.[5]

When a corporation with a complex capital structure computes diluted earnings per share, it must consider the impact of potential common shares. It considers these in addition to the weighted average common shares calculation, stock dividends and stock split assumptions, and earnings presentations we discussed earlier. We discuss only the more common types of potential common shares—share options (sometimes called stock options) and warrants, and convertible preferred stock and bonds—in this section.

To be included in the diluted earnings per share calculation, any potential common share must have a *dilutive* **effect on (that is, decrease) earnings per share.** Thus, a corporation may include a potential common share in the diluted earnings per share computation in one accounting period and not in another. Consequently, you must be familiar with the types of potential common shares, the tests to determine the dilution of each security, and the diluted earnings per share computations.

To evaluate the dilutive effect of each security, a corporation must include potential common shares in the diluted earnings per share (DEPS) calculations in a certain order. Therefore, **the steps for computing DEPS are as follows**:

Step 1. Compute the basic earnings per share.
Step 2. Include dilutive share options and warrants and compute a tentative DEPS.
Step 3. Develop a ranking of the impact of each convertible preferred stock and convertible bond on DEPS.
Step 4. Include each dilutive convertible security in DEPS in a sequential order based on the ranking and compute a new tentative DEPS.
Step 5. Select as the diluted earnings per share the lowest computed tentative DEPS.

Since we already have discussed how to compute basic earnings per share, the following discussion explains steps 2 through 5 for computing diluted earnings per share. Exhibit 17-1 shows a flowchart summarizing these steps.

---

5. *Ibid.*, par. 11 and 16.

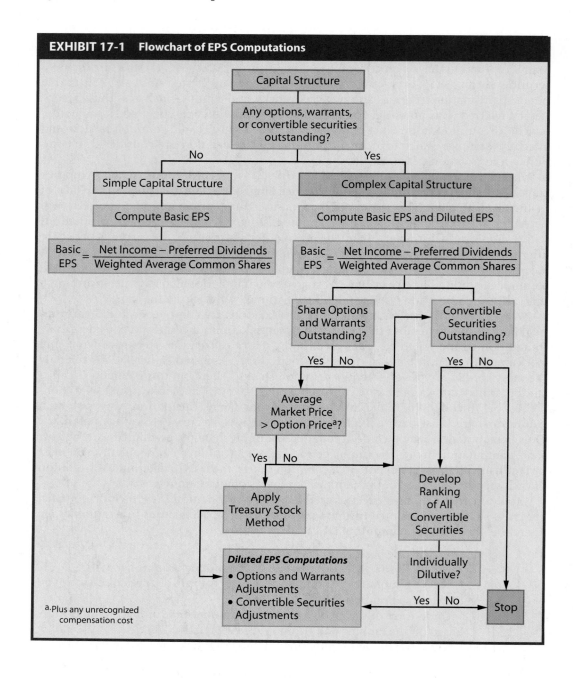

EXHIBIT 17-1   Flowchart of EPS Computations

a. Plus any unrecognized compensation cost

Share Options and Warrants

A corporation always first considers share options, warrants, and similar arrangements in its diluted earnings per share calculations. However, they are included in diluted earnings per share only if they are *dilutive*. Since the exercise of share options or warrants does not affect the corporation's net income, the focus is on the earnings per share denominator. **The treasury stock method is used to determine the change in the number of shares.** In this method, the impact on common shares is computed under the assumption (for earnings per share computations) that the options were exercised at the beginning of the period (or at the time the options were issued, if later). Then, it is assumed that the proceeds obtained from the exercise were used by the corporation to reacquire common stock at the *average* market price during the period.

Under the treasury stock method, the number of shares added to the earnings per share denominator is the difference between the assumed shares issued and the assumed shares reacquired. We show this relationship in the following diagram (we will discuss how to compute the proceeds shortly):

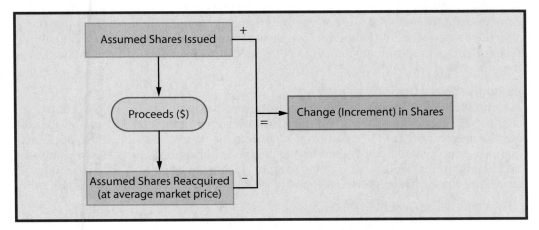

Whenever the shares issued exceed the shares reacquired, the effect is a dilution of earnings per share. **Dilution occurs whenever the average market price is greater than the option (exercise) price.**[6] In this case, it is assumed that fewer shares are reacquired than are issued. If the average market price is less than the option price, the assumed exercise would be antidilutive (i.e., would *increase* earnings per share). Therefore, the options are *excluded* from the diluted earnings per share computation (and the employees would not exercise their options under these circumstances). **The steps for the treasury stock method are as follows:**

Step 1. Determine the average market price of common shares during the period (if less than the option price, stop; the assumed exercise of the options and warrants would be antidilutive).[7]

Step 2. Compute the shares issued from the assumed exercise of all options and warrants.

Step 3. Compute the proceeds received from the assumed exercise by multiplying the shares issued by the option price [plus any unrecognized compensation cost (net of tax) per share].

Step 4. Compute the assumed shares reacquired by dividing the proceeds (step 3) by the average market price (step 1).

Step 5. Compute the incremental common shares (the results of step 2 minus step 4).

Step 3 needs further explanation. Recall from Chapter 16 that a corporation uses the fair value method to account for its compensatory share option plan. It determines its total compensation cost on the grant date (based on the estimated fair value of the stock) and recognizes a portion of this cost as an expense over the service period. For its earnings per share, the portion of the compensation cost (net of tax) that the corporation has *not* yet recognized as compensation expense is included in the proceeds received from the assumed exercise of compensatory share options.[8] This approach is used to estimate the fair value per share that the corporation would receive from the share options for the common stock assumed issued before the service period has expired. That is, if an

4 Apply the treasury stock method for including share options and warrants in diluted EPS.

---

6.   The option price is adjusted for any unrecognized compensation cost, as we discuss below.

7.   The FASB has issued a *Proposed Statement of Financial Accounting Standards* that explains how to compute the average market price of common shares for computing quarterly and year-to-date periods. These can be complex calculations. For simplicity, we always provide the average market price.

8.   *FASB Statement of Financial Accounting Standards No. 128, op. cit.*, par. 21.

employee exercised a share option before the service period had expired, the corporation would require the employee to pay both the option price and a "premium" for the early exercise. The unrecognized compensation cost per share is an estimate of this premium. By adding this amount to the exercise price, the computation includes an estimate of the fair value per share of common stock that the corporation would receive at the point of early exercise. The computation of the unrecognized compensation cost is complex; for simplicity, in the text and homework we always state the amount per share of any unrecognized compensation cost (net of tax) that should be included in the computation of the proceeds.

Example: Share Options

Assume Plummer Corporation has compensatory share options for employees to purchase 1,000 common shares at $18 per share outstanding the entire year, and that the average market price for the common stock during the year was $25 per share. The unrecognized compensation cost (net of tax) related to the share options is $2 per share. The net increase in the denominator is 200 shares, which has a dilutive effect on earnings per share. The share calculation is as follows:

Shares issued from assumed exercise: 1,000

Shares assumed reacquired:

$$\frac{\text{Proceeds}}{\text{Average Market Price Per Share}} = \frac{1,000 \times (\$18 + \$2)}{\$25} = \frac{\$20,000}{\$25} = \underline{(800)}$$

Assumed increment in common shares for computing diluted earnings per share $\underline{200}$

After Plummer Corporation has computed the number of incremental shares resulting from the assumed exercise of the options or warrants, it adds the increase to the denominator of the basic earnings per share. Then it divides the original numerator by the new denominator to determine the tentative diluted earnings per share. If no convertible securities are outstanding, this tentative figure is the final diluted earnings per share. We show this procedure later in part 4 of Example 17-5. ♦

Convertible Securities

Convertible bonds and convertible preferred stock are considered for inclusion in diluted earnings per share after stock options and warrants. A corporation includes convertible securities in its diluted earnings per share only if they are *dilutive*. It must be careful to include the individual convertible securities, one at a time, in the proper sequence. If it does not, it may make a mistake by including an antidilutive security in diluted earnings per share. That is, **a convertible security that may appear to be individually dilutive may, in fact, be antidilutive in combination with other convertible securities.**

To determine the sequence in which to include convertible securities in diluted earnings per share, the securities are ranked. This ranking is determined by comparing the individual impacts on diluted earnings per share resulting from the assumed conversion of each convertible security into common shares. To compute this impact, the *if-converted* method is used. Under this method, **each convertible stock or bond is *assumed* (for computing diluted earnings per share) to have been converted into common stock at the beginning of the earliest period reported** (or at the date of issuance of the security, if later).

This assumed conversion causes two changes in the earnings per share calculation: an increase in the denominator and an increase in the numerator. The denominator increases by the number of common shares issued in the assumed conversion. If bonds are assumed to be converted into common stock, the numerator increases because net income would be larger since the interest expense (net of income taxes) for the converted bonds would not exist.[9] If preferred stock is assumed to be converted into common stock, the numerator increases because the preferred dividends would not exist.

The numerical value impact on the corporation's diluted earnings per share for each convertible security is computed by dividing the increase in the numerator by the increase in the denominator,[10] as we show in the following equation:

$$\text{Impact on DEPS} = \frac{\text{Increase in Earnings Per Share Numerator}}{\text{Increase in Earnings Per Share Denominator}}$$

5 Calculate the impact of a convertible security on diluted EPS.

After the corporation has computed the impact on its diluted earnings per share for each convertible security, it ranks the securities. The convertible security having the *lowest* impact on diluted earnings per share is listed at the *top* of the ranking, and the other convertible securities are ranked in sequential order so that the security with the *highest* impact is listed at the *bottom* of the ranking. Beginning with the convertible security listed at the top of the ranking, the corporation sequentially enters the dilutive securities into its diluted earnings per share computations.

It is important to understand that the convertible security with the lowest numerical value impact on diluted earnings per share causes the least increase in the numerator relative to the increase in the denominator from the assumed conversion. Consequently, **that security, which has the *lowest impact* and which *causes the greatest decrease* in diluted earnings per share, is the most dilutive convertible security and is the first (after options and warrants) to be considered for inclusion in diluted earnings per share.** The ranking enables the corporation to sequentially include dilutive convertible securities in its diluted earnings per share in the descending order of their individual dilutive effect on earnings per share.

Example 17-4 shows the calculation of the impact of each convertible security on diluted earnings per share and the development of the ranking for a corporation that has four convertible securities outstanding the entire year. As you can see, security C has the lowest impact on diluted earnings per share and is the most dilutive. It is the first convertible security (after options and warrants) to be included in diluted earnings per share (assuming it is dilutive).

Computation of Tentative and Final Diluted Earnings Per Share

As we indicated earlier, a corporation begins the computation of its diluted earnings per share by calculating its basic earnings per share. Then, it computes the increment in shares from the assumed exercise of share options and warrants. It adds this increment to the denominator from basic earnings per share, and calculates an initial tentative diluted earnings per share. Next, it includes the dilutive convertible securities in diluted earnings per share in sequential order according to the ranking we discussed earlier. The convertible security listed at the top of the ranking is considered first. If its impact is *less* than the initial tentative diluted earnings per share, it is dilutive and is included in diluted earnings per share. This involves computing a new numerator and denominator by adding the increase in the numerator and the increase in the denominator resulting from the assumed conversion to the amounts used to compute the initial tentative diluted earnings per share.[11] A second (and lower) tentative diluted earnings per share is computed based on the revised numerator and denominator.

6 Compute diluted EPS.

---

9. The pretax savings in interest expense includes the interest paid or accrued, plus any bond discount amortization or less any bond premium amortization. The net-of-tax interest-expense savings is computed by multiplying the pretax interest-expense savings times one minus the effective income tax rate.

10. This and the later discussion dealing with the computation of tentative diluted earnings per share is adapted from the presentation by S. Davidson and R. Weil in "A Shortcut in Computing Earnings Per Share," *Journal of Accountancy* (December, 1975), pp. 45–47.

11. If no share options or warrants are outstanding, the corporation adds the increases in the numerator and denominator resulting from the assumed conversion of the top-ranked convertible security to the numerator and denominator it used to compute its basic earnings per share.

EXAMPLE 17-4	Computation of Impact of Convertible Securities on Diluted Earnings Per Share

A. Summary of Convertible Securities

Security	Description
A	9% convertible preferred stock. Dividends of $5,400 were declared during the year. The preferred shares are convertible into 3,000 shares of common stock.
B	10% convertible bonds. Interest expense (net of income taxes) of $4,800 was recorded during the year. The bonds are convertible into 1,920 shares of common stock.
C	8% convertible preferred stock. Dividends of $8,000 were declared during the year. The preferred shares are convertible into 5,000 shares of common stock.
D	7% convertible bonds. Interest expense (net of income taxes) of $6,300 was recorded during the year. The bonds are convertible into 3,150 shares of common stock.

B. Computations and Rankings

Security	Impact	Order in Ranking
A	$\dfrac{\$5,400}{3,000} = \$1.80$	2
B	$\dfrac{\$4,800}{1,920} = \$2.50$	4
C	$\dfrac{\$8,000}{5,000} = \$1.60$	1
D	$\dfrac{\$6,300}{3,150} = \$2.00$	3

We show this procedure in the following diagram.

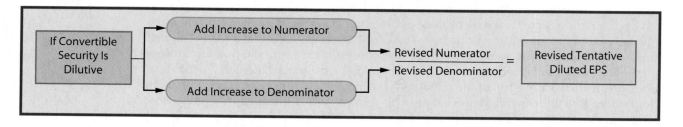

The second convertible security in the ranking is considered next. If its impact is *less* than the previously computed tentative diluted earnings per share, it is dilutive. The increase in the numerator and denominator from this convertible security is added to the revised numerator and denominator and a third (and still lower) tentative earnings per share is computed. This procedure is repeated for each security in the ranking until the impact of the next convertible security is *more* than the previously computed tentative diluted earnings per share (or until the ranking is exhausted). The remaining securities in the ranking are antidilutive and are excluded from diluted earnings per share. The final diluted earnings per share is the last tentative figure. It contains all the dilutive convertible securities included in the tentative diluted earnings per share computations.

If a corporation reports extraordinary gains and losses or results of discontinued operations in its net income, then the comparison of the impact of a convertible security on earnings per share to test for dilution is different. Instead of comparing the impact to the initial tentative *total* diluted earnings per share, it is compared to the initial tentative diluted earnings per share related to *income from continuing operations* to test for dilution.[12]

Example 17-5 shows the computation of diluted earnings per share for Rush Corporation, assuming (1) share options are outstanding, (2) both convertible bonds and convertible preferred stock are outstanding, and (3) the convertible bonds are dilutive but the convertible preferred stock is antidilutive. The computations result in diluted earnings per share of $1.94. Note that Rush Corporation reports *both* basic and diluted earnings per share on its income statement. Note, also, that if no ranking had been prepared, and if both the convertible preferred stock and bonds had been included in diluted earnings per share, the corporation would have reported an erroneous $1.96 [($2,000 + $800 + $224) ÷ (985 + 400 + 160)] diluted earnings per share.

ADDITIONAL CONSIDERATIONS

The previous sections focused on the main issues related to computing earnings per share. Several other issues are relevant to basic and diluted earnings per share. These issues involve conversion ratios, contingent issuances, and disclosures in the notes to the financial statements.

Conversion Ratios

After issuing convertible securities or share options, a corporation may declare a stock dividend or stock split. Typically, the "conversion ratio" for convertible securities and stock options is proportionally adjusted for the stock dividend or split. For instance, assume a share of preferred stock is convertible into four shares of common stock before a two-for-one stock split on the common stock. *After* the stock split, the preferred stock is convertible into eight shares of common stock. The corporation uses the *current* conversion ratio for convertible securities and share options in its diluted earnings per share computations.

Contingent Issuances

A corporation may be obligated to issue common shares in the future. This stock is referred to as contingently issuable common stock. Its issuance may depend on satisfying certain conditions, such as attaining or maintaining a certain level of earnings. When no further conditions must be met before issuance, the corporation considers these shares to be outstanding for basic and diluted earnings per share purposes. If the conditions have not been met, if dilutive, the corporation includes the shares in diluted earnings per share. They are included based on the number of shares that would be issuable if the end of the accounting period were the end of the contingency period.

Additional Disclosures

When a corporation reports its basic and diluted earnings per share on its income statement, it also is required to make additional disclosures in the notes to its financial statements. These include a schedule or note identifying and reconciling the numerators and denominators on which it calculated both basic and diluted earnings per share. For

---

12. Unless we indicate otherwise, for simplicity we assume in the text and homework that the corporation does not report any of these items in its net income.

EXAMPLE 17-5   Computation and Reporting of Diluted Earnings Per Share

1. Income statement information for Rush Corporation:
   a. Net income for 2007 is $2,800.
   b. The income tax rate is 30%.
2. Balance sheet information:
   a. 900 shares of common stock were outstanding the entire year.
   b. Options were outstanding the entire year. The assumed exercise of these options results in an increment of 85 shares of common stock.
   c. 100 shares of 8%, $100 par (and issuance price) convertible preferred stock were outstanding the entire year. $800 dividends were declared on this stock in 2007. Each share of preferred stock is convertible into 4 shares of common stock.
   d. 6% convertible bonds, $5,000 face value were outstanding the entire year. These bonds were issued to yield 6.5%. Bond interest expense of $320 was recorded in 2007; the total discount is being amortized at the rate of $20 per year. Each $1,000 bond is convertible into 32 shares of common stock.
3. Impact on diluted earnings per share and resulting ranking:

Security	Impact	Ranking
Preferred	$\dfrac{\$800}{100 \times 4} = \dfrac{\$800}{400} = \$2.00$	2
Bonds	$\dfrac{[(\$5,000 \times 0.06) + \$20] \times (1 - 0.3)}{5 \times 32} = \dfrac{\$224}{160} = \$1.40$	1

4. Diluted earnings per share computations for 2007:

Explanation	Earnings (Adjustments)	÷	Shares (Adjustments)	=	Earnings Per Share
Basic earnings per share	$2,000[a]	÷	900	=	$2.22 Basic
Increment in shares (options)			85		
DEPS$_1$ earnings and shares	$2,000	÷	985	=	$2.03 DEPS$_1$[b]
Savings in interest expense (bonds)	224[c]				
Increment in shares (bonds)			160[d]		
Diluted earnings and shares	$2,224	÷	1,145	=	$1.94 Diluted[e]

   a. $2,000 = $2,800 net income − $800 preferred dividends
   b. $1.40 is less than $2.03; therefore, the convertible bonds are individually dilutive and are included in diluted earnings per share.
   c. $224 = [($5,000 × 0.06) + $20] × (1 − 0.3)
   d. 160 = 5 bonds × 32 common shares
   e. The $2.00 impact on diluted earnings per share of the convertible preferred stock is more than $1.94; therefore, inclusion of the preferred stock in diluted earnings per share would be antidilutive.

5. Condensed income statement presentation of Rush Corporation for 2007:

Net income	$2,800
Earnings per share (see Note A):	
Basic earnings per share	$2.22
Diluted earnings per share	$1.94

6. Note A to financial statements: Basic earnings per share is based on 900 average common shares outstanding. Preferred dividends of $800 are deducted from income before extraordinary items and net income to determine earnings available to common stockholders. Diluted earnings per share is based on 900 average common shares outstanding plus 245 incremental shares from giving effect to the assumed exercise of share options and the conversion of 6% convertible bonds. Earnings available to common stockholders are adjusted for the $224 savings in interest expense (net of taxes). The 8% convertible preferred stock is antidilutive and is not included in diluted earnings per share. A total of 900 common shares were outstanding at the end of 2007.

example, Rush Corporation could disclose the information included in the schedule in part 4 of Example 17-5. The schedule or note also includes information that:

1. Identifies the amount of preferred dividends deducted to determine the income available to common stockholders.
2. Describes the potential common shares that were *not* included in the diluted earnings per share computation because they were antidilutive.
3. Describes any material impact on the common shares outstanding of transactions after the close of the accounting period but before the issuance of the financial report.[13]

For example, Rush Corporation would disclose the information in part 6 of Example 17-5.

EPS DISCLOSURE ILLUSTRATION

An illustration of the earnings per share disclosures of **International Business Machines (IBM)** in its 2004 annual report is shown in Real Report 17-1.

Real Report 17-1 Earnings Per Share Disclosures

Reporting
A ◄──► C

INTERNATIONAL BUSINESS MACHINES CORPORATION

CONSOLIDATED STATEMENT OF EARNINGS (in part)

In millions, except per share data

FOR THE YEAR ENDED DECEMBER 31:	**2004**	**2003**
Income from Continuing Operations	$8,448	$7,613
Discontinued Operations:		
Loss from discontinued operations	18	30
Net Income	$8,430	$7,583
Earnings/(Loss) per share of Common Stock:		
Assuming Dilution:		
Continuing Operations	$ 4.94	$ 4.34
Discontinued Operations	(0.01)	(0.02)
Total	$ 4.93	$ 4.32
Basic:		
Continuing Operations	$ 5.04	$ 4.42
Discontinued Operations	(0.01)	(0.02)
Total	$ 5.03	$ 4.40
Weighted Average Number of Common Shares Outstanding		
Assuming Dilution	1,708,872,279	1,756,090,689
Basic	1,674,959,086	1,721,588,628

Questions:

1. What effect did discontinued operations have on earnings per share in 2004? Is this important? Why or why not?
2. Why would the average number of common shares used in the diluted earnings per share computation be more than the weighted average number of common shares used in the basic earnings per share computation?

13. *FASB Statement of Financial Accounting Standards No. 128*, par. 40 and 41.

LINK TO INTERNATIONAL DIFFERENCES

International accounting standards and U.S. standards are similar with regard to computing and reporting basic and diluted earnings per share. However, one difference occurs in the application of the treasury stock method for potentially dilutive share options. International standards do not require a company to include any unrecognized compensation cost in the assumed proceeds from issuing the stock. The exclusion of unrecognized compensation cost would result in lower earnings per share amounts under international standards.

SECURE YOUR KNOWLEDGE 17-1

- A company that has a simple capital structure (only common stock is outstanding) is required to report separate basic earnings per share amounts for income from continuing operations and net income on its income statement, with any per share amounts related to discontinued operations or extraordinary items disclosed either on the income statement or in the notes to the financial statements.
- Basic earnings per share is computed by dividing a company's earnings available to common stockholders by the weighted average number of common shares outstanding.
  - Preferred dividends reduce earnings available to common shareholders unless the preferred stock is noncumulative and no dividends were declared during the year.
  - In the event of a stock dividend or stock split, the number of common shares outstanding at the date of the split are retroactively adjusted as if the stock dividend or split occurred at the beginning of the earliest period presented.
- When securities that have the potential to dilute earnings per share exist (e.g., share options and warrants, convertible preferred stock, convertible bonds), the company has a complex capital structure and, in addition to basic earnings per share, is required to report diluted earnings per share.
- The treasury stock method, used to calculate the dilutive effect of share options and warrants, assumes that the options or warrants were exercised at the beginning of the earliest period presented, and any proceeds obtained from this exercise were used to reacquire common stock at the average market price. The difference between the shares assumed to be issued and the shares assumed to be repurchased is the dilutive effect of the share options or warrants.
- The if-converted method is used to determine the dilutive effect for all other potentially dilutive securities (e.g., convertible preferred stock or convertible bonds). Under this method:
  - The individual impact of each potentially dilutive security is computed (both numerator and denominator effects) as if the security were converted into common stock at the beginning of the earliest period presented; and
  - The securities are ranked in order of their impact on earnings per share, with the most dilutive security being considered first for inclusion in diluted earnings per share.

CONTENT OF RETAINED EARNINGS

Now that we have discussed earnings per share, we turn to retained earnings. Retained earnings is the primary link between a corporation's income statement and balance sheet. The corporation's assets are financed by liabilities and stockholders' equity. The stockholders' share of assets results primarily from their investments and from net income (earnings) not distributed as dividends. A corporation uses its Retained Earnings account to summarize this latter component of its stockholders' equity.

Most corporations (78%) prefer the account title **Retained Earnings**, with the terms *Earnings* or *Income* (with additional words) used by about 5%. A number of corporations (about 17%) have *negative* retained earnings and use the terms *Retained Earnings (Deficit)* or *Accumulated Deficit* (a **deficit**, or a negative retained earnings balance, is the result of a corporation's accumulated prior net losses or dividends in excess of its earnings).[14]

In addition to net income (or net loss), the primary factors that affect Retained Earnings include (1) dividends, (2) retrospective and prior period adjustments, and (3) appropriations.

DIVIDENDS

Whereas a corporation's net income increases its assets (and capital) and the corporation records this increase in its retained earnings, the distribution of dividends has the opposite effect. The distribution of cash or property dividends decreases the assets (and capital) and is recorded as a reduction in retained earnings. Thus, the phrase "retained earnings paid out in dividends," or some similar phrase, often found in summaries of corporate financial activities is somewhat misleading. A corporation pays cash (or property dividends) out of *cash* (or some other asset), and reduces its retained earnings (and capital) because the payment is a return *of* capital to the stockholders.

To pay cash or property dividends, a corporation must meet legal requirements and have assets available for distribution. The board of directors is responsible for establishing a dividend policy and determines the amount, timing, and type of dividends to be declared. It must consider the articles of incorporation, applicable state regulations for dividends, the impact on legal capital (established to protect corporate creditors), and compliance with contractual agreements, as well as the financial well-being of the corporation.

Legal requirements for dividends vary from state to state, but most states require a corporation to have a positive (credit) retained earnings balance before it may declare dividends. Also, the amount of dividends it declares generally cannot exceed this retained earnings balance. Usually a corporation must restrict the amount of retained earnings available for dividends by the cost of treasury shares held. However, a few states allow a corporation to declare a dividend equal to the amount of current income even though it may have a prior deficit. In certain instances, some states allow dividends that reduce contributed capital, as long as legal capital is not impaired. Other states may allow a dividend from donated capital but not from other unrealized items in stockholders' equity. Also, contractual agreements (such as long-term bond provisions) may restrict a corporation from declaring dividends. Corporate legal counsel is responsible for reviewing applicable state laws and corporate contracts to determine the legality of dividends. Nonetheless, accountants also should be aware of state regulations and contractual obligations, particularly as they affect restrictions of dividends.

Besides meeting legal requirements, the board of directors must evaluate the financial desirability of a particular dividend. In this case, the board may consult with the corporate accountants. Consideration should be given to the corporation's *financial flexibility* and *operating capability*. Factors such as the impact of a dividend on its current

---

14. *Accounting Trends and Techniques* (New York: AICPA, 2004), p. 314.

assets and working capital, the ability to finance capital expansion projects, the effect on the stock market price per share, and the ability to maintain a liquidity "cushion" against possible future deteriorating economic conditions should be evaluated. The declaration of a dividend must be in the financial long- and short-term interests of the stockholders.

A corporation's board of directors may consider several types of dividends, including cash, property, scrip, stock, and liquidating dividends. The impact of each type of dividend upon a corporation's capital structure is as follows:

1. *cash, property, and scrip dividends:* decrease retained earnings (and stockholders' equity);
2. *stock dividends:* decrease retained earnings and increase contributed capital by the same amount (so there is no change in total stockholders' equity);
3. *liquidating dividends:* decrease contributed capital (and stockholders' equity); and
4. *stock splits:* do not affect the balance of any element of stockholders' equity.

Cash Dividends

The most common type of dividend is the cash dividend—the distribution of cash by the corporation to its common (and any preferred) stockholders. When used without a qualifying adjective, the term *dividends* refers to cash dividends.

Four dates are important for a cash dividend (or any type of dividend):

1. the date of declaration,
2. the ex-dividend date,
3. the date of record, and
4. the date of payment.

For instance, on March 17, 2005, **Dollar General** declared a $0.04 per-share quarterly dividend, payable on April 14, 2005 to stockholders of record on March 31, 2005.

On the date of declaration, the board of directors formally declares that a dividend will be paid to *stockholders of record* **on a specific future date,** typically four to six weeks later. At this declaration date, the corporation becomes legally liable to pay the dividend. Before this date, stockholders ordinarily have no power to require that a dividend be paid; dividend policy has been legally entrusted to the board of directors. Since the corporation incurs a liability on the date of declaration, it makes a journal entry to reduce retained earnings and record the current liability. It usually reduces (debits) Retained Earnings directly. However, some corporations prefer to use a contra-retained earnings account titled Dividends Declared for the dividends related to each class of stock. It either increases (credits) a current liability, Dividends Payable, or else increases separate liability accounts for the amounts owed to each class of stockholder.

After the date of declaration, the outstanding stock of the corporation trading in the open market normally sells "with dividends attached" (that is, at a higher market price that includes the amount of the future dividend payment). The ex-dividend date occurs several days before the date of record to enable the corporation to update its *stockholders' ledger* by the date of record. The ex-dividend date is important to investors because **on the ex-dividend date the stock stops selling with dividends attached.** Any purchaser of the stock on or after this date will not receive the current dividend. No accounting entry is required on the ex-dividend date.

Normally, it takes a corporation some time to process the dividend checks. Thus, a "cut-off" date is needed—the date of record. **Only investors listed in the stockholders' ledger on the date of record can receive the dividend.** The date of record usually occurs several weeks after the declaration date and several weeks before the payment date, as specified in the dividend provisions. On the date of record, the corporation makes a memorandum entry indicating that the date of record has been reached and showing the future dividend payment date.

On the date of payment, the corporation distributes the dividend checks, and makes a journal entry to eliminate the liability and reduce the cash. After the date of payment, the corporation has completed the dividend process. It reports the payment of dividends as a cash outflow in the financing section of its statement of cash flows.

The following diagram summarizes the accounting procedures for a cash dividend.

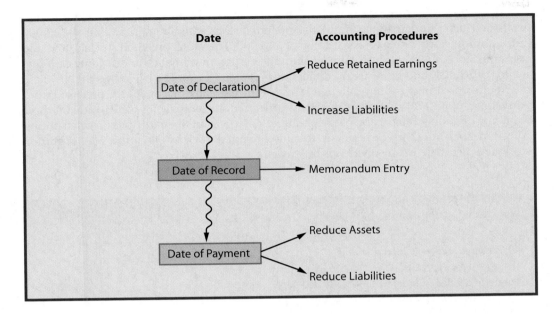

Example: Declaration and Payment of Dividends Assume that on November 2, 2007, the board of directors of Bay Corporation declares preferred dividends totaling $10,000 and common dividends totaling $20,000. These dividends are payable on December 14, 2007 to stockholders of record on November 23, 2007. The corporation makes the following journal entries to record the dividend:

7 Record the declaration and payment of cash dividends.

November 2, 2007

Retained Earnings	30,000	
Dividends Payable: Preferred Stock		10,000
Dividends Payable: Common Stock		20,000

November 23, 2007

Memorandum entry: The company will pay dividends on December 14, 2007, to preferred and common stockholders of record as of today, the date of record.

December 14, 2007

Dividends Payable: Preferred Stock	10,000	
Dividends Payable: Common Stock	20,000	
Cash		30,000

If its accounting period ends before the dividend payment, Bay Corporation reports the Dividends Payable account(s) as a current liability on its balance sheet. If it uses the contra account, Dividends Declared, it closes this account directly to Retained Earnings as part of the year-end closing process. ♦

Reporting
A ↔ C

Participating Preferred Stock

Usually the amounts of dividends payable to each class of stock can be easily determined. In certain cases, however, preferred stock may be either fully or partially participating. In these cases, a corporation must compute the dividends payable to preferred and common stockholders. Recall from Chapter 16 that *fully participating* preferred stock shares equally with the common stock in any extra dividends. These extra dividends are distributed proportionally, based on the respective *total* par values of each class of stock. *Partially participating* preferred stock is limited in its participation to a fixed rate (based on the respective par value) or amount per share.

Example: Participating Preferred Stock Dividends   Assume that Everett Corporation has issued 10%, participating, cumulative preferred stock with a total par value of $20,000 and common stock with a total par value of $30,000. Therefore, preferred stock is 40% and common stock is 60% of the total par value. The corporation intends to distribute cash dividends of $9,000, and there are no dividends in arrears. Example 17-6 shows the dividend distribution assuming (a) the preferred stock is fully participating, or (b) the preferred stock participates up to 12% of its par value. If any preferred stock dividends were in arrears, these would be distributed *before* any participation calculations. In the participation calculations, common stock initially receives a rate equal to preferred stock *for the current year*. Common stock does *not* share in any dividends in arrears. ♦

EXAMPLE 17-6   **Dividend Distribution**

		Preferred	Common
(a) Preferred Stock Is Fully Participating			
10% dividend to Preferred (on $20,000 par)		$2,000	
Common dividend (equal to 10% of $30,000 par)			$3,000
Extra dividend proportionate to par values:			
Total to allocate	$9,000		
Allocated ($2,000 + $3,000)	(5,000)		
Remainder (40% to preferred, 60% to common)	$4,000	1,600	2,400
Dividends to each class of stock		$3,600	$5,400
(b) Preferred Stock Participates up to 12%			
10% dividend to Preferred		$2,000	
Common dividend (equal to 10% of par)			$3,000
2% dividend on par of Preferred (2% × $20,000)		400	
2% dividend on par of Common (2% × $30,000)			600
Remainder to common ($9,000 − $6,000 allocated)			3,000
Dividends to each class of stock		$2,400	$6,600

Property Dividends

Occasionally, a corporation will declare a **property dividend that is payable in assets other than cash.** The corporation typically uses marketable securities of other companies that it owns for the property dividend because they can be distributed more easily to the stockholders. However, it may pay the dividend with any assets designated by its board of directors.

A property dividend is classified as a *nonreciprocal, nonmonetary transfer to owners.* That is, the corporation enters into an exchange in which it gives up something of value (the asset) but for which it receives no asset or service in return. Also, because no cash is involved, the exchange is a nonmonetary transfer. According to **APB Opinion No. 29,** a corporation records a property dividend at the fair value of the asset transferred, and recognizes a gain or a loss.[15]

---

15.   "Accounting for Nonmonetary Transactions," *APB Opinion No. 29* (New York: AICPA, 1973), par. 18.

The logic behind using fair value for a property dividend is that the corporation could have sold the assets distributed in the dividend for cash and used the proceeds (fair value) to pay a cash dividend. The fair value is determined *on the date of declaration* (because this is the date the dividend becomes a legal liability) by referring to existing stock or bond market prices, recent cash exchanges of similar assets, or objective independent appraisals.

Example: Bonds Distributed as Project Dividend Assume the board of directors of Asel Corporation declares a property dividend, payable in bonds of Bard Company being "held to maturity" (in accordance with paragraph 8 of *FASB Statement No. 115*). The bonds are carried on Asel Corporation's books at a book value of $40,000 but their current fair value is $48,000. On the date of declaration, the corporation revalues the investment account to its fair value and records the dividend obligation at this value so that the amounts of both the gain and the dividend liability are properly reported. Asel Corporation makes the following journal entries to record this property dividend:

8 Account for a property dividend.

Date of Declaration

Investment in Bard Company Bonds		
($48,000 − $40,000)	8,000	
Gain on Disposal of Investments		8,000
Retained Earnings	48,000	
Property Dividends Payable		48,000

Date of Payment

Property Dividends Payable	48,000	
Investment in Bard Company Bonds		48,000

On the date of payment, Asel Corporation does not adjust the gain or loss, even though the fair value may have changed since the date of declaration. It reports the gain or loss in the Other Items section of its income statement. If the corporation will not pay the dividend until next year, it reports the dividend liability as a current liability on its balance sheet. ♦

In the case where a corporation distributes "available-for-sale" debt or equity securities (as defined in *FASB Statement No. 115*) as a property dividend, the computation of the gain or loss is more complex because the corporation must consider any previously recorded unrealized increase or decrease in value. The corporation is carrying its investment in available-for-sale securities (whether current or noncurrent) at the fair value (by use of an Allowance account) of the securities *on the last balance sheet date.* It is also reporting an "unrealized increase (or decrease) in value" amount (whose balance is the difference between the cost and the fair value) in its accumulated other comprehensive income section of its stockholders' equity as we discussed in Chapter 15. However, the realized gain or loss on this type of property dividend is computed as the difference between the fair value of the securities *on the date of declaration* and the original *cost* of the securities. The journal entry that the corporation makes on the date of declaration to revalue the investment (by adjusting the Allowance account) and to record the realized gain or loss also must eliminate the unrealized increase (decrease) in value for these securities.

Example: Stock Distributed as Property Dividend Assume Cleek Corporation declares a property dividend on March 14, 2008, payable in Dunn Company stock. The Dunn Company stock was purchased early in 2007 for $24,000 and was reported as an asset at a fair value of $29,000 (i.e., at a cost of $24,000 plus an allowance for an increase in value of $5,000, along with an unrealized increase in value of $5,000 reported in its accumulated other comprehensive income) on the December 31, 2007 balance sheet. If the market value is $31,000 on March 15, 2008, the gain is $7,000, computed by comparing the current fair value ($31,000) to the original cost ($24,000).

Cleek Corporation makes the following journal entries on the date of declaration to record this property dividend:

Allowance for Change in Value of Investment in Available-for-Sale Securities	2,000	
Unrealized Increase in Value of Available-for-Sale Securities	5,000	
Gain on Disposal of Investments		7,000
Retained Earnings	31,000	
Property Dividends Payable		31,000

Cleek Corporation makes the following journal entry on the date of payment to record the distribution of the securities to stockholders:

Property Dividends Payable	31,000	
Investment in Available-for-Sale Securities		24,000
Allowance for Change in Value of Investment in Available-for-Sale Securities		7,000 ♦

Scrip Dividends

As we discussed earlier, in establishing dividend policy, the board of directors must consider both the legal requirements and the corporation's financial status. A corporation may have adequate retained earnings to meet the legal dividend requirements but insufficient cash to justify a current cash dividend. In this case, it may declare a **scrip dividend.** Here, the corporation issues promissory notes (called "scrip") requiring it to pay dividends at some future date. It makes the usual journal entries on the date of declaration (although some companies may credit Notes Payable instead of Dividends Payable) and date of payment, except when the notes carry an interest rate. In this case, it also records interest expense on the date of payment. If the corporation will not make the scrip payment until next year, it must make a year-end adjusting entry to record accrued interest expense. It must review the maturity date to determine the proper classification of the dividend liability on the balance sheet. Scrip dividends are rare, however. If a corporation is having liquidity problems, it is usually unwise for the board of directors to commit it to cash outflows, even if these would be made in the future.

Stock Dividends

Another type of dividend that a corporation may declare and distribute is a stock dividend. **A stock dividend is a proportional (pro rata) distribution of additional shares of a corporation's own stock to its stockholders.** For instance, on March 17, 2005, **Sun Bancorp** of New Jersey declared a 5% stock dividend, distributable on April 20, 2005 to stockholders of record on April 6, 2005.

A stock dividend usually consists of the same class of shares; that is, a common stock dividend is declared on common stock outstanding. This type of distribution is called an *ordinary* stock dividend. The distribution of a different class of stock (common on preferred or preferred on common) sometimes is called a *special* stock dividend. A corporation usually issues a stock dividend out of authorized but unissued shares, although it may use shares of treasury stock. Unlike other dividends, a corporation may legally rescind the declaration of a stock dividend. A stock dividend also differs from other dividends in that *no corporate assets are distributed.* Each stockholder maintains the same percentage ownership in the corporation as was held prior to the distribution.

Stockholders often view stock dividends favorably even though (1) they receive no corporate assets, (2) their percentage ownership does not change, (3) theoretically the total market value of their investment will remain the same because the decrease in the stock market price per share will be offset by the increased number of shares each stockholder owns, and (4) future cash dividends may be limited because retained earnings is decreased by the amount of the stock dividend and most states set legal dividend restrictions based on positive retained earnings. However, the following factors may enhance the perceived attractiveness of a stock dividend:

1. The stockholders may see the stock dividend as evidence of corporate growth.
2. The stockholders may see the stock dividend as evidence of sound financial policy.
3. Other investors may see the stock dividend in a similar light, and increased trading in the stock may cause the market price *not* to decrease proportionally.
4. The corporation may state that it will pay the same fixed cash dividend per share, in which case individual stockholders will receive higher total future cash dividends.
5. The stockholders may see the market price decreasing to a lower trading range, making the stock more attractive to additional investors so that the market price may eventually rise.

LINK TO ETHICAL DILEMMA

The CEO of Advanced Micro Technologies (AMT) is extremely upset and has just called an emergency meeting of her management team. She has just learned that, for the third time in four months, a key executive has left the company to pursue a better-paying opportunity with a competitor. The CEO is concerned that without a proper incentive compensation plan, the company will lose several other key executives and the company's future could be in jeopardy. The CEO has determined that the modest returns predicted for the stock market over the next several years have led many of the departed executives to conclude that the company's share option plan will not produce the large gains that were historically observed. Based on analysis of a highly respected compensation consulting firm, the CEO has proposed eliminating the share option plan and replacing it with a restricted stock plan. Under the CEO's plan, company executives would be given shares of restricted stock that could not be sold unless the executive remained with AMT for 10 years. If the employee were to leave prior to the 10-year period, the shares would be forfeited. It is the CEO's belief that such a plan would increase retention. Furthermore, the restricted stock plan has three other features that make it attractive. First, because restricted stock consists of actual shares rather than the option to buy future shares, the company will grant fewer shares than it would under the share option plan, resulting in lower compensation expense and higher income. Second, executives would also receive dividend payments on the restricted stock, even if the stock has not vested. Therefore, by increasing the dividend, the company could actually pay the executives a "cash bonus" without having to recognize compensation expense. Finally, employees will have something of value, even if the stock price doesn't increase. As the accountant for AMT, what is your reaction to the CEO's proposal?

Conceptual Issues for Stock Dividends

The **economic substance** of a stock dividend is that it is not really a "dividend" but instead is similar to a stock split. In both cases, even though the number of shares increases, a corporation does not distribute any assets to the stockholders and each stockholder's percentage ownership stays the same. So, the corporation's total assets and stockholders' equity remain unchanged. To show the similar economic substance, in theory a corporation should record a stock dividend like a stock split.

From an accounting standpoint, however, a corporation does *not* account for a stock dividend like a stock split, but instead records it like other dividends. When a stock dividend is recorded, total stockholders' equity is not changed. Retained earnings is decreased by the amount of the "dividend," and contributed capital is increased by the same amount because of the additional shares issued. This treatment is based on an "**opportunity cost**" argument. That is, the corporation should record the "dividend" at the fair value of the stock because this is the value it forgoes to issue the stock dividend.

Under this method, the fair value may be determined by assuming the stock is sold for cash at the current market price and the proceeds used to pay a cash dividend. The appropriate fair value at which to record the stock dividend is the market price *after* the declaration of the dividend. If a very small number of shares were issued in a stock dividend, this would cause only a small decrease in the market price. Larger stock dividends would cause greater decreases in the market price. To use this fair value approach, a method for estimating the decrease in fair value would need to be developed. However, no such method has been implemented. Instead, a distinction is made between "small" and "large" stock dividends, and different generally accepted accounting principles apply to each.

GAAP for Stock Dividends

In the case of a **small stock dividend** (presumably having no apparent effect on the market price per share), the Committee on Accounting Procedure accepted the view that a stock dividend is like a simultaneous sale of stock and payment of a dividend. **Therefore, a corporation accounts for a *small* stock dividend by transferring from retained earnings to contributed capital an amount equal to the fair value of the additional shares issued.** In distinguishing between a small and a large stock dividend, the Committee said that **fair value is ordinarily the appropriate value to use whenever the stock dividend (that is, small dividend) is less than 20 or 25% of the previously outstanding shares.**

9 Explain the difference in accounting for small and large stock dividends.

State legal requirements govern the *minimum* amount that a corporation must capitalize (transfer from retained earnings to contributed capital as part of legal capital) for a stock dividend. Generally, this amount is the par or stated value of the additional shares distributed. The accounting for a large stock dividend relates to this legal capital. **Therefore, a corporation accounts for a *large* stock dividend by transferring from retained earnings to contributed capital an amount equal to the par value of the additional shares issued.** In this case, the Committee suggested that the use of the term *dividend* be avoided or, when this is not possible because of legal restrictions, the transaction should be described in terminology such as *a stock split effected in the form of a dividend.*[16]

Given the Committee's acceptance of the argument that a stock dividend should be based on fair value, use of par value to record a large stock dividend seems inappropriate. Par value has no direct relationship to fair value. Also, use of par value for large stock dividends and fair value for small stock dividends can lead to illogical accounting results. For example, assume a corporation with 2,000 shares of $10 par common stock outstanding issued a 15% (300 shares) small stock dividend when the market price per share is $40. In this case it would reduce retained earnings and increase contributed capital by $12,000. If it issued a 50% (1,000 shares) large stock dividend, the corporation would reduce retained earnings and increase contributed capital by only $10,000. In this example, a small stock dividend has a greater effect on the components of the corporation's stockholders' equity than a large stock dividend! Nonetheless, use of fair value to record a small stock dividend and use of par value to record a large dividend are generally accepted accounting principles. The following diagram shows the effects on the various elements of stockholders' equity of a small and large stock dividend, respectively.

16. "Restatement and Revision of Accounting Research Bulletins," *Accounting Research Bulletin No. 43* (New York: AICPA, 1961), ch. 7, sec. B, par. 10 and 11.

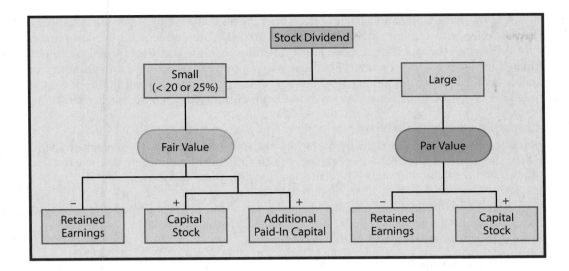

To show the accounting for the two sizes of stock dividend, assume Ringdahl Corporation has the following stockholders' equity prior to the stock dividend:

Common stock, $10 par (20,000 shares issued and outstanding)	$200,000
Additional paid-in capital	180,000
Retained earnings	320,000
Total Stockholders' Equity	$700,000

Note that in this example there are 20,000 shares issued and outstanding; therefore, there is no treasury stock. Treasury stock normally does not participate in a small stock dividend because the dividend is based on the outstanding shares of stock. However, treasury stock may participate in a large stock dividend because the dividend is considered to be similar to a stock split.

Example: Small Stock Dividend

Assume that Ringdahl Corporation declares and issues a 10% stock dividend. On the date of declaration, the stock is selling for $23 per share. The corporation records the 2,000-share stock dividend at the fair value of $46,000, as we show in the following journal entries:

Date of Declaration

Retained Earnings	46,000	
Common Stock To Be Distributed		20,000
Additional Paid-in Capital From Stock Dividend		26,000

Date of Issuance

Common Stock To Be Distributed	20,000	
Common Stock, $10 par		20,000

Ringdahl's resulting stockholders' equity is as follows:

Common stock, $10 par (22,000 shares issued and outstanding)	$220,000
Additional paid-in capital	206,000
Retained earnings	274,000
Total Stockholders' Equity	$700,000

Note that the amounts of the components of Ringdahl Corporation's stockholders' equity have changed, but its total stockholders' equity ($700,000) remains the same as before the small stock dividend.

If a corporation prepares a balance sheet after the declaration but before the issuance of the stock dividend, it reports the Common Stock To Be Distributed account as a component of Contributed Capital. The account is *not* a liability like the dividend payable accounts related to other types of dividends because it will not be satisfied by the distribution of assets. Instead, it is a temporary stockholders' equity item representing the legal capital related to the stock to be issued. As we showed, it is eliminated when the stock is issued. ♦

Example: Large Stock Dividend

Assume, *instead*, that Ringdahl Corporation declares and issues a 40% stock dividend when the stock is selling for $23 per share. In this case, the corporation uses the par value of $80,000 for the 8,000 shares to record the stock dividend as follows:

Date of Declaration

Retained Earnings	80,000	
Common Stock To Be Distributed		80,000

Date of Issuance

Common Stock To Be Distributed	80,000	
Common Stock, $10 par		80,000

The resulting stockholders' equity is as follows:

Common stock, $10 par (28,000 shares issued and outstanding)	$280,000
Additional paid-in capital	180,000
Retained earnings	240,000
Total Stockholders' Equity	$700,000

Note again that Ringdahl's total stockholders' equity ($700,000) remains the same as before the large stock dividend. ♦

Fractional Shares

In the case of a stock dividend, the number of shares that many stockholders own will not entitle them to receive additional whole shares from the dividend. For example, if a corporation declared a 10% stock dividend, a stockholder owning 43 shares would be entitled to 4.3 additional shares. Some corporations have a policy of not issuing fractional shares. These corporations usually offer stockholders two alternatives: (1) to receive cash equal to the market price of the fractional share, or (2) to pay in sufficient cash to receive a full share. In the first case, the corporation accounts for the cash it pays as a cash dividend and issues fewer shares. In the second case, it records the stock dividend in the usual manner and adjusts contributed capital for the cash it receives.

Liquidating Dividends

Liquidating dividends represent a return of contributed capital rather than a distribution of retained earnings. A corporation usually declares these dividends when it is ceasing or reducing operations. A liquidating dividend also may arise when a natural resources corporation pays a dividend based on earnings before depletion. That portion of the dividends equal to the amount of depletion is considered the liquidating dividend.

When a corporation pays a dividend that is in part (or in total) a liquidating dividend, it must adhere to state legal requirements in recording the dividend. It records the *normal* portion of the dividend as a reduction of retained earnings and the *liquidating* portion as a reduction of contributed capital. The latter may be recorded as a debit either to an additional paid-in capital account or to a special contra-contributed capital account entitled, for instance, Contributed Capital Distributed as a Liquidating Dividend. The corporation should disclose the liquidating dividend in a note to its financial statements to notify stockholders that a portion of contributed capital is being returned.

SECURE YOUR KNOWLEDGE 17-2

- Four important dates for any type of dividend are the:
  - Date of declaration—the date the board of directors formally declares that a dividend will be paid and the dividend becomes a liability of the company;
  - Ex-dividend date—the date the stock stops selling with the right to receive dividends (usually several days before the date of record);
  - Date of record—only registered owners of stock on this date will receive a dividend; and
  - Date of payment—the date the dividend is distributed and the liability is eliminated.
- A property dividend (a dividend payable in assets other than cash) is recorded at fair value, which involves revaluing the property to be distributed to fair value and recognizing a gain or loss for the difference between the fair value and the carrying value.
- A company without enough cash to justify paying a cash dividend may declare a scrip dividend, which obligates the company to pay the dividend plus interest at a future date.
- A stock dividend, the distribution of additional shares of stock to a company's shareholders, does not change total stockholders' equity and is accounted for based on the size of the dividend:
  - A small stock dividend (less than 20 or 25% of the outstanding shares) transfers the fair value of the shares issued from retained earnings to contributed capital.
  - A large stock dividend (more than 20 or 25% of the outstanding shares) transfers the par value of the shares issued from retained earnings to contributed capital.
- Liquidating dividends are a return of contributed capital rather than a distribution of retained earnings.

LINK TO RATIO ANALYSIS

Investors, creditors, and others use various measures to assess how effective a company has been at meeting its profit objective. While one such measure (earnings per share) has been discussed earlier in the chapter, two other measures are often used—price/earnings ratio and dividend yield. The price/earnings ratio measures the market's assessment of future earnings potential of the company. While price/earnings ratios should be evaluated in the context of the industry in which the company operates, higher price/earnings ratios relative to other similar companies are generally interpreted as a positive signal regarding a company's future prospects. Using information obtained from the 2004 annual report, **McDonald's Corporation's** price/earnings ratio at December 31, 2004 can be computed as:

$$\text{Price/Earnings Ratio} = \frac{\text{Market Price per Common Share}}{\text{Earnings Per Share}} = \frac{\$32.06}{\$1.81} = \$17.71$$

Another useful measure of stockholder profitability is dividend yield. This ratio provides investors with information pertaining to the rate of return that was received in cash dividends. For McDonald's, the dividend yield for the fiscal year ending December 31, 2004 was:

$$\text{Dividend Yield} = \frac{\text{Dividends per Common Share}}{\text{Market Price per Common Share}} = \frac{\$0.55}{\$32.06} = \$0.017$$

The dividend yield, together with the percentage change in the market price of the stock held during the period, is the total return on the stockholders' investment.

Credit: ©Michael Ventura/PhotoEdit

PRIOR PERIOD ADJUSTMENTS (RESTATEMENTS)

Corporations are required to report a few events as either retrospective adjustments or prior period adjustments (restatements) of retained earnings. These include changes in accounting principles, a change in accounting entity, and corrections of errors of prior periods.[17] We discuss the specific accounting treatment of these items in Chapter 23. The following discussion illustrates prior period adjustments by focusing on corrections of errors and their impact on retained earnings.

A corporation may make an error in the financial statements of one accounting period that it does not discover until a later period. These errors may be due to oversights, the incorrect use of existing facts, mathematical mistakes, or errors in applying accounting principles. Usually these errors affect an asset or liability and a revenue or expense of a prior year. A corporation is required to treat corrections of all material errors as prior period adjustments (restatements) of retained earnings. That is, in the year of correction, the asset or liability account balance is corrected (debited or credited). The offsetting credit or debit (which involved a revenue or expense previously closed to retained earnings) is made directly to the Retained Earnings account (or to an account such as Correction of Prior Years' Income Due to Material Error in . . .). If the latter account is used, it is closed directly to Retained Earnings in the year-end closing entries. Any related impact on income taxes is similarly recorded.

Example: Prior Period Adjustment Assume that in 2008 Fox Corporation discovers that it inadvertently did not accrue $10,000 of interest expense for 2007. This material error overstated 2007 income before income taxes by a similar amount. Assuming a related income tax effect of $3,000, Fox makes the following correcting entries in 2008:

Retained Earnings (or Correction of Prior . . .)	10,000	
Interest Payable		10,000
Income Tax Refund Receivable	3,000	
Retained Earnings (or Correction of Prior . . .)		3,000

When a corporation makes a prior period adjustment, it reports the item (net of the applicable income taxes) as an adjustment of the beginning balance of retained earnings on its statement of retained earnings. If the January 1, 2008 retained earnings balance of the Fox Corporation was $102,400, it reports the correction on its December 31, 2008 statement of retained earnings as a prior period adjustment as follows:

Retained earnings, as previously reported January 1, 2008	$102,400
Less: Correction of overstatement in 2007 net income due to	
interest expense understatement (net of $3,000 income taxes)	(7,000)
Adjusted retained earnings, January 1, 2008	$ 95,400

Fox then completes the remaining portion of the statement as we show in Example 17-7 later in the chapter. It discloses the effect of the error on the prior year's net income and earnings per share in the period in which the correction is made. With these disclosures, users can see the impact of the error on the company's financial statements. If Fox presents comparative financial statements, it makes corresponding adjustments to its net income, retained earnings, asset, or liability account balances for all the periods reported.[18] ◆

---

17. "Accounting Changes and Error Corrections," *FASB Statement of Financial Accounting Standards No. 154* (Norwalk, Conn.: FASB, 2005), par. 4–26.

18. *Ibid.*, par. 25 and 26 and "Reporting the Results of Operations," *APB Opinion No. 9* (New York: AICPA, 1966), par. 18 and 26.

RESTRICTIONS (APPROPRIATIONS) OF RETAINED EARNINGS

A corporation's board of directors is responsible for establishing dividend policy, while following legal requirements and sound financial practice. Stockholders sometimes consider only the legal requirements. As the corporation's Retained Earnings account balance increases, they may expect to be paid higher dividends. However, the corporation must use the *assets* represented by retained earnings for many activities, including financing on-going operations and long-term expansion projects, paying the principal and interest on debt securities, and paying dividends.

To indicate that a certain portion of retained earnings is not available for dividends, a corporation may restrict (appropriate) retained earnings. A **restriction (appropriation)** of retained earnings means that the board of directors establishes a formal policy that a portion of retained earnings is unavailable for dividends. It is important to understand that such a policy does *not* directly restrict the use of any assets. It merely requires that the corporation not distribute any assets that would reduce this restricted retained earnings. A board of directors may restrict retained earnings (1) to meet *legal* requirements, or (2) to meet *contractual* restrictions.

Corporations must follow the laws of the state in which they are incorporated. Certain states require restrictions of retained earnings when a corporation reacquires its own stock as treasury stock. Usually, the restriction is in an amount equal to the cost of the treasury shares. The argument for this restriction is that acquiring treasury stock reduces the amount of invested (permanent) capital. By restricting retained earnings for an equal amount, the corporation's permanent capital is not impaired.

A corporation also may restrict retained earnings because of a contractual agreement. This type of agreement may be made when a corporation issues long-term bonds. To provide some assurance that sufficient assets will be kept in the corporation to satisfy bondholders' claims, the bond provisions (sometimes called "debt covenants") may require the restriction of a certain amount of retained earnings.

Corporations disclose restrictions of retained earnings in a note (or sometimes by parenthetical notations) to the financial statements. In the note, a clear description of the legal or contractual provisions and the amount of the restriction is required. For example, assume Johnstone Corporation has a $300,000 retained earnings balance when it acquires treasury stock at a cost of $20,000. It would report the $300,000 retained earnings balance and disclose the restriction of retained earnings as follows:

Retained earnings (see *Note A*) $300,000

Notes to the Financial Statements

Note A: Retained earnings are restricted in the amount of $20,000, the cost of the treasury stock.

When a corporation cancels a restriction (because, for instance, it no longer has treasury stock), it does not include the note in its financial statements.

STATEMENT OF RETAINED EARNINGS

Although not a required separate financial statement, many corporations include a statement of retained earnings in their financial statements. To disclose the earnings, dividends, prior period adjustments, and other reductions, we suggest the format shown in Example 17-7.

A corporation may include the retained earnings statement as a separate statement within the financial statements, as a supporting schedule directly beneath the income statement, or, as is common, in the statement of changes in stockholders' equity which we discuss later in the chapter. Although the format in Example 17-7 includes all items affecting retained earnings, prior period adjustments, reductions because of conversions, or reductions because of the retirement of capital stock are relatively rare. A retained earnings statement usually includes only adjustments to retained earnings for net income and

---

EXAMPLE 17-7   Statement of Retained Earnings for 2007

Retained earnings, as previously reported, January 1, 2007
   Plus (minus): Prior period and retrospective adjustments (net of income tax effect)
Adjusted retained earnings, January 1, 2007
   Plus (minus): Net income (loss)
   Minus: Dividends (specifically identified, including per share amounts)
            Reductions because of retirement or reacquisition of capital stock
            Reductions because of conversion of bonds or preferred stock
Retained earnings, December 31, 2007

---

dividends. Any restrictions of retained earnings are disclosed in a note to the financial statements.

Illustration of Retained Earnings Statement

We show the 2004 and 2003 consolidated statements of retained earnings for **Merck & Co., Inc.** in Real Report 17-2.

Reporting
A ↔ C

Real Report 17-2 Retained Earnings Statement

MERCK & CO., INC. AND SUBSIDIARIES

CONSOLIDATED STATEMENT OF RETAINED EARNINGS

| ($ in millions) | Years Ended December 31 | |
	2004	2003
Balance, January 1	$34,142.0	$35,434.9
Net Income	5,813.4	6,830.9
Common Stock Dividends Declared	(3,329.1)	(3,264.7)
Spin-off of MedCo Health	—	(4,859.1)
Balance, December 31	$36,626.3	$34,142.0

Questions:

1. Why does the company use the term "Common Stock Dividends Declared" in this statement?
2. What is the common stock dividend as a percentage of net income for 2004 and 2003? What does this indicate?
3. Why does the spin-off of MedCo Health affect retained earnings?

Accumulated Other Comprehensive Income

10 Understand how to report accumulated other comprehensive income.

As we discussed in Chapters 4 and 5, a corporation is required to report its total comprehensive income for the accounting period. Comprehensive income includes both net income and "other comprehensive income." Other comprehensive income (loss) might include four items:

- unrealized increases (gains) or decreases (losses) in the market (fair) value of investments in available-for-sale securities,
- translation adjustments from converting the financial statements of a company's foreign operations into U.S. dollars,
- certain gains and losses on "derivative" financial instruments, and
- certain pension liability adjustments.

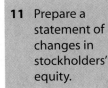

A corporation may report its comprehensive income (net of income taxes) on the face of its income statement, in a separate statement of comprehensive income, or in its statement of changes in stockholders' equity. We showed these alternatives in Chapter 5.

A corporation includes its total net income *earned to date* in its retained earnings amount which it reports in its stockholders' equity. The corporation includes its other comprehensive income (or loss) *accumulated to date* in its **accumulated other comprehensive income** (or **loss**) amount[19] which it also reports in its stockholders' equity. If a corporation has more than one type of comprehensive income, it has a choice. It may report the amount of accumulated other comprehensive income for *each item* in its stockholders' equity. Or, it may report the *total amount* of accumulated other comprehensive income for *all the items* in its stockholders' equity. If the corporation uses this approach, it must disclose the amounts for each of the items in the notes to its financial statements.[20] Unless a corporation has miscellaneous items of stockholders' equity (which we discuss next), it adds the totals for contributed capital, retained earnings, and accumulated other comprehensive income (and subtracts the cost of any treasury stock) to determine its total stockholders' equity.

MISCELLANEOUS CHANGES IN STOCKHOLDERS' EQUITY

In rare instances, a corporation may increase stockholders' equity for events not related to the issuance of stock or to retained earnings. For example, as we discussed in Chapter 10, it is possible for a corporation to receive donated assets (e.g., a plant site) from a governmental unit to induce it to locate in a particular community. Since this is a nonreciprocal, nonmonetary transfer, the corporation records the asset at its fair value. It records the resulting credit in a Donated Capital account. The *discovery value* of natural resources is another example. Here, a corporation might record an increase in assets and stockholders' equity as a result of the discovery of previously unknown valuable natural resources. A corporation lists these items separately in its stockholders' equity.

STATEMENT OF CHANGES IN STOCKHOLDERS' EQUITY

A corporation may engage in various transactions that affect some component of its stockholders' equity. **FASB Statement of Concepts No. 5** suggests that a full set of financial statements should show investments by and distributions to owners during the period. To inform external users of a corporation's financial statements about its capital activities, **APB Opinion No. 12** states:

> . . . **disclosure of changes in the separate accounts comprising stockholders' equity (in addition to retained earnings) and of the changes in the number of shares of equity securities during at least the most recent annual fiscal period . . . is required to make the financial statements sufficiently informative.**[21]

11 Prepare a statement of changes in stockholders' equity.

Thus, a corporation must disclose the changes in the different classes of common stock, additional paid-in capital, retained earnings, accumulated other comprehensive income, and treasury stock in its annual report. The intent is to help report on the changes in the corporation's financial structure to help users assess its *financial flexibility, profitability*, and *risk*. Most corporations prepare a statement of changes in stockholders' equity that includes an analysis of the changes in these items. The ending amounts in this statement then tie to the stockholders' equity section of the year-end balance sheet. Also, if a corporation chooses to report its comprehensive income on its statement of changes in stockholders' equity, it must include this statement as a *major* financial statement.

---

19. This amount may create deferred taxes and is reported net of taxes. However, since we do not discuss deferred taxes until Chapter 19, for simplicity we ignore the tax effect in this chapter.
20. "Reporting Comprehensive Income," *FASB Statement of Financial Accounting Standards No. 130* (Norwalk, Conn.: FASB, 1997), par. 17 and 26.
21. "Omnibus Opinion—1967," *APB Opinion No. 12* (New York: AICPA, 1967), par. 10.

Examples 17-8 and 17-9 show a statement of changes in stockholders' equity and the ending stockholders' equity for the hypothetical Bardwell Corporation.[22] Notice the interrelated amounts in both examples. We show **Colgate-Palmolive Company's** ending 2004 and 2003 consolidated shareholders' equity and statements of retained earnings, comprehensive income, and changes in capital accounts in Real Report 17-3.

EXAMPLE 17-8   Bardwell Corporation

Statement of Changes in Stockholders' Equity for 2007

Explanation	Common Stock		Additional Paid-in Capital		Common Stock Option Warrants	Retained Earnings	Accumulated Other Comprehensive Income	Treasury Stock (Cost)
	Shares Issued	Par Value	Common Stock	Treasury Stock				
Balances, 1/1/2007	10,000	$50,000	$170,000	$2,300	$11,200	$322,000	$15,200	$(7,500)
Issued for cash	1,100	5,500	22,000					
Reissued treasury stock				2,700				4,500
Issued for exercise of share options	300	1,500	5,400		(900)			
Compensation expense for share options					3,300			
Unrealized increase in value of available-for-sale securities							4,800	
Net income						97,000		
Cash dividends						(32,800)		
Balances, 12/31/2007	11,400	$57,000	$197,400	$5,000	$13,600	$386,200	$20,000	$(3,000)

EXAMPLE 17-9   Bardwell Corporation

Stockholders' Equity
December 31, 2007

Contributed capital	
Common stock, $5 par (30,000 shares authorized, 11,400 shares issued, of which 100 shares are being held as treasury stock)	$ 57,000
Additional paid-in capital on common stock	197,400
Additional paid-in capital from treasury stock	5,000
Common stock option warrants	13,600
Total contributed capital	$273,000
Retained earnings (see Note A)	386,200
Accumulated other comprehensive income	
Unrealized increase in value of available-for-sale securities	20,000
Total contributed capital, retained earnings, and accumulated other comprehensive income	$679,200
Less: Treasury stock (at cost)	(3,000)
Total Stockholders' Equity	$676,200

Notes to the Financial Statements
Note A: Retained earnings are restricted regarding dividends in the amount of $3,000, the cost of the treasury stock.

---

22.   Bardwell Corporation reports its comprehensive income in a separate financial statement.

LINK TO INTERNATIONAL DIFFERENCES

Under international accounting standards, a corporation's shareholders' interests (the term used for stockholders' equity) consists of two sections: (a) share capital, and (b) other equity. Many of the disclosures required under share capital are the same as those required under U.S. GAAP; for example, the number of shares authorized, issued, and outstanding, par value, reacquired shares, and rights, preferences, and restriction regarding dividends. The differences from those required by U.S. GAAP include disclosure of any capital not yet paid in, any restrictions on the repayment of capital, and the shares reserved for future issuance under sales contracts.

Share premium (additional paid-in capital) is disclosed in the *other equity* section, along with revaluation surplus, reserves, and retained earnings. Revaluation surplus and reserves are equity items that are different from those allowed under U.S. GAAP. Although International Accounting Standards are based on historical cost, some countries allow companies to revalue (upward and downward) their property, plant, and equipment (and intangibles) based on professionally qualified appraisals. When a company increases its asset values because of a revaluation, it also credits a revaluation surplus account. (A decrease because of revaluation would reduce this revaluation account, or if no balance exists in revaluation surplus, would be recognized in income.) In some respects, reserves under international accounting standards are similar to restrictions (appropriations) of retained earnings under U.S. GAAP. They may differ, however, in that reserves may be required by foreign statutes or tax laws, whereas there are no such requirements in the United States.

A company must disclose the "movement" in share capital accounts and in other equity for the period. In effect, these international disclosure requirements result in reporting the changes in shareholders' interests and are similar to the requirements of U.S. GAAP regarding the statement of changes in stockholders' equity, although the format of the disclosures may be different.

Real Report 17-3 Shareholders' Equity and Related Changes

COLGATE-PALMOLIVE COMPANY

Consolidated Balance Sheets (in part)

	December 31	
(In millions)	2004	2003
Shareholders' Equity		
Preference stock	$ 274.0	$ 292.9
Common stock, $1 par value (1,000,000,000 shares authorized, 732,853,180 shares issued)	732.9	732.9
Additional paid-in capital	1,093.8	1,126.2
Retained earnings	8,223.9	7,433.0
Accumulated other comprehensive income	(1,806.2)	(1,866.8)
	$ 8,518.4	$ 7,718.2
Unearned compensation	(307.6)	(331.2)
Treasury stock, at cost	(6,965.4)	(6,499.9)
Total shareholders' equity	$ 1,245.4	$ 887.1

Continued

COLGATE-PALMOLIVE COMPANY

Consolidated Statements of Retained Earnings, Comprehensive Income and Changes in Capital Accounts (in part)

(Dollars in millions except per share amounts)	Common Shares Shares	Amount	Additional Paid-in Capital	Treasury Shares Shares	Amount	Retained Earnings	Accumulated Other Comprehensive Income	Comprehensive Income
Balance, December 31, 2002	536,001,784	$732.9	$1,133.9	196,873,236	$6,152.3	$6,518.5	$(1,865.6)	
Net income						1,421.3		$1,421.3
Other comprehensive income:								
Cumulative translation adjustment							4.0	4.0
Other							(5.2)	(5.2)
Total comprehensive income								$1,420.1
Dividends declared:								
Series B Convertible Preference Stock, net of income taxes						(25.5)		
Preferred stock						(.2)		
Common stock						(481.1)		
Shares issued for stock options	4,928,861		(20.9)	(4,928,861)	(96.9)			
Treasury stock acquired	(10,146,986)			10,250,146	554.9			
Other	2,913,518		13.2	(3,038,518)	(110.4)			
Balance, December 31, 2003	533,697,177	$732.9	$1,126.2	199,156,003	$6,499.9	$7,433.0	$(1,866.8)	
Net income						1,327.1		$1,327.1
Other comprehensive income:								
Cumulative translation adjustment							75.4	75.4
Other							(14.8)	(14.8)
Total comprehensive income								$1,387.7
Dividends declared:								
Series B Convertible Preference Stock, net of income taxes						(25.9)		
Common stock						(510.3)		
Shares issued for stock options	2,142,895		2.1	(2,142,895)	(60.5)			
Treasury stock acquired	(12,383,273)			12,383,273	637.9			
Other	3,168,259		(34.5)	(3,168,259)	(111.9)			
Balance, December 31, 2004	526,625,058	$732.9	$1,093.8	206,228,122	$6,965.4	$8,223.9	$(1,806.2)	

Questions:

1. How many shares of treasury stock were issued for stock options in 2004? At what average price were they issued?
2. How many shares of treasury stock were acquired in 2004? At what average price per share were they acquired?
3. What were the total dividends declared during 2004?
4. What was the average dividend per common share outstanding during 2004?

SECURE YOUR KNOWLEDGE 17-3

- Prior period adjustments (restatements) are reported as adjustments of the beginning balance of retained earnings, net of taxes, on the statement of retained earnings.
- A restriction of retained earnings, to meet legal requirements or contractual restrictions, indicates that a portion of retained earnings is unavailable for dividends.
- A statement of retained earnings is often used to disclose the items affecting retained earnings—net income (loss), dividends, prior period (and retrospective) adjustments, and other reductions.
- Accumulated other comprehensive income may be reported on the face of the income statement, in a separate statement of comprehensive income, or in the statement of changes in stockholders' equity.
- A statement of changes in stockholders' equity is used to disclose the changes in different classes of common stock, additional paid-in capital, retained earnings, accumulated other comprehensive income, and treasury stock.

SUMMARY

At the beginning of the chapter, we identified several objectives you would accomplish after reading the chapter. The objectives are listed below, each followed by a brief summary of the key points in the chapter discussion.

1. **Compute basic earnings per share.** The numerator for computing basic earnings per share is net income minus preferred dividends. The denominator is the weighted average number of common shares outstanding.
2. **Understand how to compute the weighted average common shares for EPS.** The weighted average is computed by summing the "equivalent whole units" of shares for all the "layers" of stock. The equivalent whole units are computed by multiplying the number of shares for that layer times the fraction of the year the layer is outstanding.
3. **Identify the potential common shares included in diluted EPS.** The most common "potential common shares" that may be included in computing diluted EPS are share options and warrants, as well as convertible preferred stock and convertible bonds. These securities are included in diluted EPS only if they decrease EPS.
4. **Apply the treasury stock method for including share options and warrants in diluted EPS.** To apply the treasury stock method, compute the assumed shares issued and the proceeds received from the assumed exercise. Then compute the assumed shares reacquired by dividing the proceeds by the average market price. Finally, deduct the assumed shares reacquired from the assumed shares issued to determine the incremental shares.
5. **Calculate the impact of a convertible security on diluted EPS.** The impact is computed by dividing the increase in the EPS numerator by the increase in the EPS denominator, assuming the convertible security is converted into common stock. For a convertible bond, the numerator increases by the savings in interest expense (net of taxes). For a convertible bond, the numerator increases by the savings in preferred dividends.
6. **Compute diluted EPS.** Begin with the calculation of basic EPS. Then, increase the denominator for the increased shares from the assumed exercise of share options and warrants. Then include the impact on the numerator and denominator of the assumed conversion of each dilutive convertible security in sequential order until the impact of the next security is antidilutive.
7. **Record the declaration and payment of cash dividends.** A corporation records the declaration by debiting retained earnings and crediting dividends payable. It records the payment by debiting dividends payable and crediting cash.

8. **Account for a property dividend.** A corporation accounts for a property dividend at the fair value of the asset transferred, and records a gain (or loss) on the date of declaration.

9. **Explain the difference in accounting for small and large stock dividends.** A corporation accounts for a small stock dividend by transferring from retained earnings to contributed capital an amount equal to the fair value of the additional shares issued. It accounts for a large stock dividend by transferring an amount equal to the par value.

10. **Understand how to report accumulated other comprehensive income.** A corporation reports its accumulated other comprehensive income in the stockholders' equity section of its balance sheet. It may report the amount of accumulated other comprehensive income for each item or it may report the total. If it reports the total, it must disclose the amounts for each of the items in the notes to its financial statements.

11. **Prepare a statement of changes in stockholders' equity.** Start with the beginning balance of each stockholders' equity account. Then add (or deduct) the change in each account resulting from the related transactions during the accounting period. Report the ending amounts on the stockholders' equity section of the balance sheet.

ANSWERS TO REAL REPORT QUESTIONS

Real Report 17-1 Answers

1. Discontinued operations caused both basic and diluted earnings per share for net income to be $0.01 per share lower than the basic and diluted earnings per share for income from continuing operations. While some may consider a $0.01 per share effect significant, the fact that this was caused by discontinued operations should be considered. Because these operations will not persist into the future, analysts may disregard this component of earnings per share and instead focus on the continuing operations of the company as they assess the timing, amount, and uncertainty of the company's future cash flows.

2. International Business Machines (IBM) has a complex capital structure that includes securities that are potentially convertible into common shares. The diluted earnings per share computation uses a weighted average number of common shares that considers all potential common shares that would reduce earnings per share.

Real Report 17-2 Answers

1. The declaration of common stock dividends reduces the assets of the company (e.g., cash) and is considered a return of capital that reduces retained earnings.

2. The common stock dividend as a percentage of net income (dividends declared ÷ net income) is 57.3% and 47.8% for 2004 and 2003, respectively. Generally, companies that pay a higher percentage of their income

to stockholders in the form of dividends are considered "mature" companies. Because Merck is paying out such a large percentage of its income in the form of dividends (and conversely retaining a smaller portion of its earnings for reinvestment in the business), Merck may be reaching a mature stage in which it does not expect to experience rapid future growth opportunities.

3. The spin-off of MedCo Health is an unusual transaction that is similar to a dividend. As Merck disposed of the net assets of MedCo Health, existing stockholders received a pro-rata dividend of MedCo Health shares. Similar to any other dividend, this is treated as a reduction of retained earnings.

Real Report 17-3 Answers

1. During 2004, Colgate-Palmolive issued 2,142,895 shares of treasury stock for stock options at an average price per share of $29.21 [increase in equity of $62.6 million ($60.5 million + $2.1 million) ÷ 2,142,895 shares].

2. During 2004, Colgate-Palmolive acquired 12,383,273 shares of treasury stock at an average price of $51.51 per share ($637.9 million ÷ 12,383,273 shares).

3. Total dividends declared were $536.2 million, which consisted of $25.9 million of dividends declared on preference stock and $510.3 million of dividends declared on common stock.

4. The average dividend per common share for 2004 was $0.70 per share ($510.3 million ÷ 732,853,180 shares).

QUESTIONS

Q17-1 What is a *simple capital structure*?

Q17-2 How is "basic earnings per share" computed for a corporation with a simple capital structure?

Q17-3 What is the "weighted average" number of shares for computing earnings per share and how is it calculated?

Q17-4 On what date are stock dividends and splits considered to be issued for computing earnings per share?

Q17-5 Identify several securities that might be found in the complex capital structure of a corporation.

Q17-6 What two earnings per share figures generally are reported by a corporation with a complex capital structure? Besides common shares outstanding, what additional securities are included in the second earnings per share calculation?

Q17-7 What is the *treasury stock method*? How is the increase in the diluted earnings per share denominator determined under the treasury stock method?

Q17-8 Discuss how to develop a ranking for determining in which order to include convertible securities in a corporation's diluted earnings per share calculations.

Q17-9 What additional disclosures does a corporation make concerning the basic and diluted earnings per share it reports on its income statement?

Q17-10 What are the four important dates in regard to a cash dividend? What journal entry does the corporation make on each date?

Q17-11 What is fully participating preferred stock? Partially participating preferred stock?

Q17-12 Discuss how a corporation records the declaration of a property dividend.

Q17-13 Distinguish between an ordinary and special stock dividend.

Q17-14 Distinguish between a small and large stock dividend. What amounts does a corporation use to record the declaration of each dividend?

Q17-15 How does the accounting for a liquidating dividend differ from that for a normal cash dividend?

Q17-16 How does a corporation record and report a correction of a material error made in a previous year in its current year's financial statements?

Q17-17 For what reasons would a corporation restrict its retained earnings? How does it report a restriction?

Q17-18 What is the suggested format for the statement of retained earnings? What are the two most common elements in this statement?

Q17-19 What items might a corporation include in the accumulated other comprehensive income section of its stockholders' equity?

Q17-20 What changes does a corporation include in its statement of changes in stockholders' equity?

MULTIPLE CHOICE (AICPA Adapted)

Select the best answer for each of the following.

M17-1 For purposes of computing the weighted average number of shares outstanding during the year, a midyear event that must be treated as occurring at the beginning of the year is the
a. Issuance of stock warrants
b. Purchase of treasury stock
c. Sale of additional common stock
d. Declaration and payment of stock dividend

M17-2 In determining basic earnings per share, dividends on nonconvertible cumulative preferred stock should be
a. Deducted from net income only if declared
b. Deducted from net income whether declared or not
c. Added back to net income whether declared or not
d. Disregarded

M17-3 Redford Corporation's capital structure at December 31, 2006 was as follows:

	Shares Issued and Outstanding
Common stock	100,000
Nonconvertible preferred stock	20,000

On July 2, 2007, Redford issued a 10% stock dividend on its common stock, and paid a cash dividend of $2.00 per share on its preferred stock. Net income for the year ended December 31, 2007 was $780,000. What should be Redford's 2007 basic earnings per share?
a. $7.80   c. $7.05
b. $7.09   d. $6.73

M17-4 Faucet Company has 2,500,000 shares of common stock outstanding on December 31, 2006. An additional 500,000 shares of common stock were issued on April 2, 2007, and 250,000 more on July 2, 2007. On October 1, 2007, Faucet issued 5,000, $1,000 face value, 7% convertible bonds. Each bond is dilutive and convertible into 40 shares of common stock. No bonds were converted into common stock in 2007. What is the number of shares to be used in computing basic earnings per share and diluted earnings per share, respectively, for the year ended December 31, 2007?
a. 2,875,000 and 2,925,000
b. 2,875,000 and 3,075,000
c. 3,000,000 and 3,050,000
d. 3,000,000 and 3,200,000

M17-5 At December 31, 2007, Gravin Corporation had 90,000 shares of common stock and 20,000 shares of convertible preferred stock outstanding, in addition to 9% convertible bonds payable in the face amount of $2,000,000. During 2007, Gravin paid dividends of $2.50 per share on the preferred stock. The preferred stock is convertible into

20,000 shares of common stock. The 9% convertible bonds are convertible into 30,000 shares of common stock. Net income for 2007 was $970,000. Assume an income tax rate of 30%. How much is the diluted earnings per share for the year ended December 31, 2007?

a. $7.83
b. $8.82
c. $9.35
d. $10.22

M17-6 A prior period adjustment should be reflected, net of applicable income taxes, in the financial statements of a business entity in the

a. Retained earnings statement after net income but before dividends
b. Retained earnings statement as an adjustment of the opening balance
c. Income statement after income from continuing operations
d. Income statement as part of income from continuing operations

M17-7 Cash dividends on the $10 par value common stock of Ray Company were as follows:

1st quarter of 2007	$ 800,000
2nd quarter of 2007	900,000
3rd quarter of 2007	1,000,000
4th quarter of 2007	1,100,000

The 4th-quarter cash dividend was declared on December 21, 2007 to stockholders of record on December 31, 2007. Payment of the 4th-quarter cash dividend was made on January 18, 2008.

In addition, Ray declared a 5% stock dividend on its $10 par value common stock on December 3, 2007 when there were 300,000 shares issued and outstanding and the market value of the common stock was $20 per share. The shares were issued on December 24, 2007.

What was the effect on the stockholders' equity accounts of Ray Company as a result of the preceding transactions?

	Common Stock	Additional Paid-in Capital	Retained Earnings
a.	$ 0	$ 0	$3,800,000 dr
b.	$150,000 cr	$ 0	$3,950,000 dr
c.	$150,000 cr	$150,000 cr	$4,100,000 dr
d.	$300,000 cr	$300,000 dr	$3,800,000 dr

M17-8 The following information was abstracted from the accounts of the Oar Corporation at December 31, 2007:

Total income since incorporation	$840,000
Total cash dividends paid	260,000
Proceeds from sale of donated stock	90,000
Total value of stock dividends distributed	60,000
Excess of proceeds over cost of treasury stock sold	140,000

What should be the current balance of retained earnings?

a. $520,000   c. $610,000
b. $580,000   d. $670,000

M17-9 Effective April 27, 2007 the stockholders of Bennett Corporation approved a two-for-one split of the company's common stock, and an increase in authorized common shares from 100,000 shares (par value $20 per share) to 200,000 shares (par value $10 per share). Bennett's stockholders' equity accounts immediately before issuance of the stock split shares were as follows:

Common stock, par value $20; 100,000 shares authorized; 50,000 shares outstanding	$1,000,000
Additional paid-in capital (premium of $3 per share on issuance of common stock)	150,000
Retained earnings	1,350,000

What should be the balances in Bennett's additional paid-in capital and retained earnings accounts immediately after the stock split is effected?

	Additional Paid-in Capital	Retained Earnings
a.	$ 0	$ 500,000
b.	$ 150,000	$ 350,000
c.	$ 150,000	$1,350,000
d.	$1,150,000	$ 350,000

M17-10 Newton Corporation was organized on January 1, 2005. On that date it issued 200,000 shares of $10 par value common stock at $15 per share (400,000 shares were authorized). During the period January 1, 2005 through December 31, 2007, Newton reported net income of $750,000 and paid cash dividends of $380,000. On January 5, 2007, Newton purchased 12,000 shares of its common stock at $12 per share. On December 28, 2007, 8,000 treasury shares were sold at $8 per share. Newton used the cost method of accounting for treasury shares. What is the total stockholders' equity of Newton as of December 31, 2007?

a. $3,290,000
b. $3,306,000
c. $3,338,000
d. $3,370,000

EXERCISES

E17-1 *Weighted Average Shares* At the beginning of the current year, Heath Company had 20,000 shares of $10 par common stock outstanding. During the year, it engaged in the following transactions related to its common stock, so that at year-end it had 63,800 shares outstanding:

Apr.	2	Issued 5,000 shares of stock
June	4	Issued 4,000 shares of stock
July	1	Issued a 10% stock dividend
Sept.	28	Issued a two-for-one stock split, reducing the par value to $5 per share
Oct.	3	Reacquired 1,000 shares as treasury stock
Nov.	27	Reissued the 1,000 shares of treasury stock

Required
Determine the weighted average number of shares outstanding for computing the current earnings per share.

E17-2 *Comparative Earnings Per Share* Ryan Company reports net income of $5,125 for the year ended December 31, 2007, its first year of operations. On January 3, 2007, the company issued 9,000 shares of common stock. On August 1, 2007 it issued an additional 3,000 shares of stock, resulting in 12,000 shares outstanding at year-end.

During 2008 Ryan Company earned net income of $16,400. It issued 2,000 additional shares of stock on March 3, 2008 and declared and issued a two-for-one stock split on November 3, 2008, resulting in 28,000 shares outstanding at year-end.

During 2009 Ryan Company earned net income of $23,520. The only common stock transaction during 2009 was a 20% stock dividend issued on July 2, 2009.

Required
1. Compute the basic earnings per share that would be disclosed in the 2007 annual report.
2. Compute the 2007 and 2008 comparative basic earnings per share that would be disclosed in the 2008 annual report.
3. Compute the 2007, 2008, and 2009 comparative basic earnings per share that would be disclosed in the 2009 annual report.

E17-3 *Basic Earnings Per Share* Sardel Company reported net income of $29,975 for 2007. During all of 2007 the company had 1,000 shares of 10%, $100 par, nonconvertible preferred stock outstanding, on which the year's dividends had been paid. At the beginning of 2007 the company had 7,000 shares of common stock outstanding. On April 2, 2007 the company issued another 2,000 shares of common stock, so that 9,000 common shares were outstanding at the end of 2007. Common dividends of $17,000 had been paid during 2007. At the end of 2007 the market price per share of common stock was $17.50.

Required
1. Compute the basic earnings per share of Sardel Company for 2007.
2. Compute the price/earnings ratio for 2007.

E17-4 *Basic Earnings Per Share* Burke Company shows the following condensed income statement information for the year ended December 31, 2007:

Income before extraordinary items	$29,936
Less: Extraordinary loss (net of income tax credit)	(2,176)
Net income	$27,760

The company declared dividends of $6,000 on preferred stock and $17,280 on common stock. At the beginning of 2007, 10,000 shares of common stock were outstanding. On May 4, 2007 the company issued 2,000 additional common shares, and on October 19, 2007 it issued a 20% stock dividend on its common stock. The preferred stock is not convertible.

Required
1. Compute the 2007 basic earnings per share.
2. Show the 2007 income statement disclosure of basic earnings per share.
3. Draft a related note to accompany the 2007 financial statements.

E17-5 *Impact on EPS and Rankings* Matthews Company had five convertible securities outstanding during all of 2007. It paid the appropriate interest (and amortized any related premium or discount using the straight-line method) and dividends on each security during 2007. Each convertible security is described in the following table. The corporate income tax rate is 30%.

Security	Description
9.5% preferred stock	$200,000 par value. Issued at 112. Each $100 par preferred stock is convertible into 4.2 shares of common stock.
11.0% bonds	$220,000 face value. Issued at par. Each $1,000 bond is convertible into 44 shares of common stock.
8.0% preferred stock	$150,000 par value. Issued at par. Each $100 par preferred stock is convertible into 3.8 shares of common stock.
10.0% bonds	$100,000 face value. Issued at 94. Discount being amortized over 20-year life. Each $1,000 bond is convertible into 55 shares of common stock.
9.0% bonds	$200,000 face value. Issued at 108. Premium being amortized over 25-year life. Each $1,000 bond is convertible into 48 shares of common stock.

Required
1. Prepare a schedule that lists the impact of the assumed conversion of each convertible security on diluted earnings per share.
2. Prepare a ranking of the order in which the securities would be included in the diluted earnings per share computations.

E17-6 *Share Options, EPS* Butler Company has 30,000 shares of common stock outstanding during all of 2007. This common stock has been selling at an average market price of $45 per share. The company also has outstanding for the entire year compensatory share options to purchase 4,000 shares of common stock at $32 per share. The unrecognized compensation cost (net of tax) relating to these share options is $3 per share. During 2007 Butler Company earned income of $36,000 after income taxes of 30%.

Required
Compute the 2007 diluted earnings per share.

E17-7 *Convertible Preferred Stock and EPS* Jamieson Company earned net income of $43,800 during 2007. At the beginning of 2007 it had 10,000 shares of common stock outstanding; an additional 4,000 shares were issued on July 2. During 2007, 600 shares of 8%, $100 par, convertible preferred stock were outstanding the entire year. Dividends on this preferred stock were paid in 2007. Each share is convertible into 5 shares of common stock. The corporate income tax rate is 30%.

Required
Compute the 2007 diluted earnings per share.

E17-8 *Convertible Bonds and EPS* Clark Company's capital structure consists of common stock and convertible bonds. At the beginning of 2007 the company had 15,000 shares of common stock outstanding; an additional 4,500 shares were issued on May 4. The 7% convertible bonds have a face value of $80,000 and were issued in 2004 at par. Each $1,000 bond is convertible into 25 shares of common stock; to date, none of the bonds has been converted. During 2007, the company earned net income of $79,200 and was subject to an income tax rate of 30%.

Required
Compute the 2007 diluted earnings per share.

E17-9 *Convertible Securities and Earnings Per Share* Walker Company has 15,000 shares of common stock outstanding during all of 2007. It also has two convertible securities outstanding at the end of 2007. These are:
1. Convertible preferred stock: 1,000 shares of 9%, $100 par, preferred stock were issued in 2006 for $140 per share. Each share of preferred stock is convertible into 3.5 shares of common stock. The current dividends have been paid. To date, no preferred stock has been converted.
2. Convertible bonds: Bonds with a face value of $100,000 and an interest rate of 10% were issued at par on July 6, 2007. Each $1,000 bond is convertible into 35 shares of common stock. To date, no bonds have been converted.

The company earned net income of $54,000 during 2007. Its income tax rate is 30%.

Required
Compute the 2007 diluted earnings per share. What earnings per share amount(s) would Walker report on its 2007 income statement?

E17-10 *Convertible Securities and Earnings Per Share* Caldwell Company has 20,000 shares of common stock outstanding during all of 2007. It also has two convertible securities outstanding at the end of 2007. These are:
1. Convertible preferred stock: 2,000 shares of 9.5%, $50 par, preferred stock were issued on January 2, 2007 for $60 per share. Each share of preferred stock is convertible into 3 shares of common stock. Current dividends have been declared. To date, no preferred stock has been converted.

2. Convertible bonds: Bonds with a face value of $200,000 and an interest rate of 5.7% were issued at par in 2006. Each $1,000 bond is convertible into 22 shares of common stock. To date, no bonds have been converted.

The company earned net income of $61,500 during 2007. Its income tax rate is 30%.

Required
Compute the 2007 diluted earnings per share. What earnings per share amount(s) would Caldwell report on its 2007 income statement?

E17-11 *Dividends* Uphoff Company has $80,000 available to pay dividends. It has 2,000 shares of 10%, $100 par, preferred stock and 30,000 shares of $10 par common stock outstanding. The preferred stock is selling for $125 per share and the common stock is selling for $20 per share.

Required
1. Determine the amount of dividends to be paid to each class of stockholder for each of the following independent assumptions:
   a. Preferred stock is nonparticipating and noncumulative.
   b. Preferred stock is nonparticipating and cumulative. Preferred dividends are two years in arrears at the beginning of the year.
   c. Preferred stock is fully participating and cumulative. Preferred dividends are one year in arrears at the beginning of the year.
   d. Preferred stock is participating up to a maximum of 15% of its par value and is noncumulative.
2. For 1(a), compute the dividend yield on the preferred stock and the common stock.

E17-12 *Various Dividends* The Goodson Company listed the following account balances on December 31, 2006:

Investment in Xurk Company bonds	$ 25,000	Common stock, $10 par	$400,000
Dividends payable: preferred	4,000	Additional paid-in capital on preferred stock	20,000
Dividends payable: common	40,000	Additional paid-in capital on common stock	210,000
Preferred stock, 8%, $100 par	100,000	Retained earnings	270,000

During 2007, the following transactions occurred:

Feb.	2	Paid the semiannual dividends declared on December 15, 2006.
Mar.	5	Declared a property dividend, payable to common stockholders on April 5 in Xurk Company bonds being held to maturity. The bonds (which have a book value of $25,000) have a current market value of $31,000.
Apr.	5	Paid the property dividend.
July	6	Declared a $4 per share semiannual cash dividend on preferred stock and a $1.10 per share semiannual dividend on common stock, to be paid on August 17.
Aug.	17	Paid the cash dividends.
Oct.	15	Declared a 2% stock dividend on common stock to be issued on December 3. The current market price is $22 per share.
Dec.	3	Issued the stock dividend.
Dec.	28	Declared a $4 and $1.20 per share semiannual cash dividend on preferred and common stock, respectively, to be paid on February 15, 2008.

Required
Prepare journal entries to record the preceding transactions.

E17-13 *Various Dividends* Mills Company lists the following condensed balance sheet as of the beginning of 2007:

Current assets	$ 60,000	Current liabilities	$ 30,000
Investment in M bonds	9,000	Common stock, no par	150,000
Fixed assets (net)	200,000	Retained earnings	89,000
	$269,000		$269,000

Mills is considering the impact of various types of dividends on this balance sheet. Each dividend would be declared and paid in 2007. These include:
1. Cash dividend of $1.00 per share on the 10,000 shares outstanding.
2. Stock dividend of 5% on the 10,000 shares outstanding when the market price is $17 per share.
3. Property dividend consisting of the $9,000 (book value) investment in M bonds being held to maturity. This investment has a current market value of $13,000. (For Requirement 2, assume any gain or loss is to be reflected in retained earnings. Disregard income taxes.)
4. Scrip dividend of $0.80 per share on the 10,000 shares outstanding. The scrip earns interest at a 12% annual rate and is to be declared on January 30 and paid on December 30, 2007. (For Requirement 2, assume any interest expense is to be reflected in retained earnings. Disregard income taxes.)
5. Cash dividend consisting of a $0.70 per share normal dividend and a $0.30 per share liquidating dividend.

Required

For each preceding *independent* dividend:
1. Prepare the appropriate journal entries for the declaration and payment of the dividend.
2. Prepare a condensed balance sheet after the dividend has been *paid*.

E17-14 *Stock Dividend* The stockholders' equity of the Sadler Company is as shown:

Common stock, $10 par	$250,000
Additional paid-in capital on common stock	150,000
Retained earnings	200,000
	$600,000

The company is considering the declaration and issuance of a stock dividend at a time when the market price is $30 per share.

Required

1. Assuming the board of directors recommends a 6% stock dividend, prepare:
   a. the journal entry at the date of declaration
   b. the journal entry at the date of issuance
   c. the stockholders' equity after the issuance
2. Assuming, instead, that a 40% stock dividend is recommended, repeat (a), (b), and (c) of Requirement 1.

E17-15 *Stock Dividend Comparison* Although Weaver Company has enough retained earnings legally to declare a dividend, its working capital is low. The board of directors is considering a stock dividend instead of a cash dividend. The common stock is currently selling at $34 per share. The following is Weaver's current stockholders' equity:

Common stock, $10 par	$ 400,000
Premium on common stock	800,000
Total contributed capital	$1,200,000
Retained earnings	1,300,000
Total stockholders' equity	$2,500,000

Required

1. Assuming a 15% stock dividend is declared and issued, prepare the stockholders' equity section immediately after the date of issuance.
2. Assuming, instead, that a 30% stock dividend is declared and issued, prepare the stockholders' equity section immediately after the date of issuance.
3. What unusual result do you notice when you compare your answers from (1) with (2)? From a theoretical standpoint, how might this have been avoided?

E17-16 *Prior Period Adjustments* Miles Company began 2007 with a retained earnings balance of $142,400. During an examination of its accounting records on December 31, 2007, the company found it had made the following material errors, for both financial reporting and income tax reporting, during 2006.

1. Depreciation expense of $15,000 inadvertently had been recorded twice for the same machine.
2. No accrual had been made at year-end for interest; therefore, interest expense had been understated by $4,000.

The Miles Company's net income during 2007 was $60,000. The company has been subject to a 30% income tax rate for the past several years. It declared and paid dividends of $13,000 during 2007.

Required

1. Prepare whatever journal entries in 2007 are necessary to correct the Miles Company books for its previous errors. Make your corrections directly to the retained earnings account.
2. Prepare the statement of retained earnings for 2007.

E17-17 *Restrictions* Perry Company has a retained earnings balance of $400,000 at the end of 2007. During 2007 it had issued $100,000 of five-year, 12%, long-term bonds. The bond provisions require that each year over the five-year period an additional $20,000 of retained earnings be unavailable for dividends. This restriction is in addition to any other retained earnings restrictions that the company might make. At the end of 2007, Perry Company held treasury stock costing $15,000.

Required

Show how Perry Company would report its retained earnings in its 2007 financial statements. Include a note to the financial statements fully describing the restrictions.

E17-18 *Retained Earnings Statement*   Hernandez Company began 2007 with a $120,000 balance in retained earnings. During the year, the following events occurred:

1. The company earned net income of $80,000.
2. A material error in net income from a previous period was corrected. This error correction increased retained earnings by $9,800 after related income taxes of $4,200.
3. Cash dividends totaling $13,000 and stock dividends totaling $17,000 were declared.
4. One thousand shares of callable preferred stock that originally had been issued at $110 per share were recalled and retired at the beginning of 2007 for the call price of $120 per share.
5. Treasury stock (common) was acquired at a cost of $20,000. State law requires a restriction of retained earnings in an equal amount. The company reports its retained earnings restrictions in a note to the financial statements.

Required
1. Prepare a statement of retained earnings for the year ended December 31, 2007.
2. Prepare the note to disclose the restriction of retained earnings.

E17-19 *Retained Earnings Statement*   On January 1, 2007 Franklin Company had a retained earnings balance of $206,000. During 2007 the following events occurred:

1. Treasury stock (common) was acquired at a cost of $14,000. State law requires a restriction of retained earnings in an equal amount. The company reports its retained earnings restrictions in a note to the financial statements.
2. Cash dividends totaling $9,000 and stock dividends totaling $6,000 were declared and distributed.
3. Net income was $58,000.
4. Two thousand shares of callable preferred stock were recalled and retired at a price of $150 per share. This stock had originally been issued at $130 per share.
5. A material error in net income for a previous period was corrected. This error correction decreased retained earnings by $12,600 after a related income tax credit of $5,400.

Required
1. Prepare a statement of retained earnings for the year ended December 31, 2007.
2. Prepare a note to disclose the restriction of retained earnings.

E17-20 *Stockholders' Equity*   Wilk Manufacturing Corporation completed the following transactions during its first year of operation, 2007:

1. The state authorized the issuance of 30,000 shares of $5 par common stock; 15,000 shares were issued at $22 per share.
2. The state authorized the issuance of 6,000 shares of $50 par preferred stock. All 6,000 shares were issued at $70 per share.
3. Wilk reacquired 1,000 shares of its outstanding common stock at $18 per share. The cost method is used to account for treasury stock.
4. Wilk invested $50,000 of excess cash, not needed to finance operations, in long-term available-for-sale equity securities. At year-end, the market value of these securities was $47,500.
5. Wilk sold 500 shares of treasury stock for $23 per share.
6. Net income for the first year of operations was $16,000. No dividends were declared.

Required
Prepare the stockholders' equity section (and any related notes to the financial statements) of the Wilk Manufacturing Corporation balance sheet as of December 31, 2007.

E17-21 *Changes in Stockholders' Equity*   The stockholders' equity section of Winslow Design Company's December 31, 2006 balance sheet appeared as follows:

Contributed capital	
Preferred stock, $100 par (10,000 shares authorized, 1,250 shares issued)	$125,000
Additional paid-in capital on preferred stock	55,000
Common stock, $10 par (60,000 shares authorized, 15,000 shares issued)	150,000
Additional paid-in capital on common stock	105,000
Total contributed capital	$435,000
Retained earnings	78,000
Contributed capital and retained earnings	$513,000
Less: Treasury stock (300 shares of common at $14 per share)	(4,200)
Total Stockholders' Equity	$508,800

During 2007 the company entered into the following transactions affecting stockholders' equity:

1. Issued 250 shares of preferred stock at $164 per share.
2. Issued 3,000 shares of common stock at $17 per share.
3. Reacquired 200 of its own common shares as treasury stock for $15 per share.
4. Reissued 250 shares of treasury stock at $17 per share (FIFO basis).
5. Net income for 2007 was $46,500. Dividends of $25,000 were distributed.

Required

1. Prepare a statement of changes in stockholders' equity for the year ended December 31, 2007.
2. Compute the return on stockholders' equity for 2007.

PROBLEMS

P17-1   *Income Statement and Basic EPS* Manty Company listed the following selected pretax items in its December 31, 2007 adjusted trial balance:

	Debit	Credit
Nonconvertible, 8% preferred stock, $100 par		$ 60,000
Common stock, $5 par		90,000
Sales		206,000
Cost of goods sold	$131,000	
Gain on disposal of discontinued Division B		8,000
Extraordinary gain from bond retirement		15,000
Operating expenses	19,250	
Loss from operations of discontinued Division B	20,000	

Additional information:

The preferred shares had been outstanding the entire year; annual dividends were declared and paid in 2007. During 2007, 2,000 common shares were issued on July 2, and 6,000 common shares were issued on November 3. Common dividends of $12,500 were declared and paid in 2007. The company is subject to a 30% income tax rate.

Required

Prepare the Manty Company's 2007 income statement (multiple-step) and the related note.

P17-2   *Comparative Income Statements and Basic EPS* Agocha Company reported the following selected items in the stockholders' equity section of its balance sheet on December 31, 2007 and 2008:

	December 31,	
	2007	2008
7% preferred stock (nonconvertible), $100 par	$50,000	$50,000
Common stock, $10 par	70,000	84,000

In addition, it listed the following selected pretax items in its December 31, 2007 and 2008 adjusted trial balances:

	December 31, 2007		December 31, 2008	
	Debit	Credit	Debit	Credit
Sales		$124,300		$140,000
Extraordinary gain		6,000		—
Cost of goods sold	$75,000		$80,000	
Operating expenses	18,000		20,000	
Extraordinary loss	—		9,000	

The preferred shares were outstanding during all of 2007 and 2008; annual dividends were declared and paid in each year. During 2007, 2,000 common shares were sold for cash on October 3. During 2008, a 20% stock dividend was declared and issued in early May. At the end of 2007 and 2008, the common stock was selling for $25.75 and $32.20, respectively. The company is subject to a 30% income tax rate.

Required
1. Prepare the comparative 2007 and 2008 income statements (multiple-step), and the related note that would appear in the Agocha Company's 2008 annual report.
2. Compute the price/earnings ratio for 2008. How does this compare to 2007? Why is it different?

P17-3 *Earnings Per Share* Wheeler Company began 2007 with 10,000 shares of $10 par common stock and 2,000 shares of 9.4%, $100 par, convertible preferred stock outstanding. On April 2 and June 1, respectively, the company issued 2,000 and 6,000 additional shares of common stock. On November 16 the company declared a two-for-one stock split. Compensatory share options that currently allow the purchase of 2,000 shares of common stock at $16 per share were outstanding during 2007. To date, none of these options have been exercised. The unrecognized compensation cost (net of tax) related to these options is $2 per share. The preferred stock was issued in 2006. Each share of preferred stock is currently convertible into 4 shares of common stock. To date, no preferred stock has been converted. Current dividends have been paid on both preferred and common stock. Net income for 2007 totaled $109,800. The company is subject to a 30% income tax rate. The common stock sold at an average market price of $24 per share during 2007.

Required
1. Prepare supporting calculations and compute:
   a. Basic earnings per share
   b. Diluted earnings per share
2. Show how Wheeler Company would report the earnings per share on its 2007 income statement. Include an accompanying note to the financial statements.

P17-4 *Impact on EPS, Rankings, and Computations* Madsen Company had five convertible securities outstanding during all of 2007. It paid the appropriate interest (and amortized any related premium or discount using the straight-line method) and dividends on each security during 2007. Each of the convertible securities is described in the following table:

Security	Description
10.2% bonds	$200,000 face value. Issued at par. Each $1,000 bond is convertible into 28 shares of common stock.
12.0% bonds	$160,000 face value. Issued at 110. Premium being amortized over 20-year life. Each $1,000 bond is convertible into 47 shares of common stock.
9.0% bonds	$200,000 face value. Issued at 95. Discount being amortized over 10-year life. Each $1,000 bond is convertible into 44 shares of common stock.
8.3% preferred stock	$120,000 par value. Issued at 108. Each $100 par preferred stock is convertible into 3.9 shares of common stock.
7.5% preferred stock	$180,000 par value. Issued at par. Each $100 par preferred stock is convertible into 6 shares of common stock.

Additional data:
Net income for 2007 totaled $119,460. The weighted average number of common shares outstanding during 2007 was 40,000 shares. No share options or warrants are outstanding. The effective corporate income tax rate is 30%.

Required
1. Prepare a schedule that lists the impact of the assumed conversion of each convertible security on diluted earnings per share.
2. Prepare a ranking of the order in which each of the convertible securities should be included in diluted earnings per share.
3. Compute basic earnings per share.
4. Compute diluted earnings per share.
5. Indicate the amount(s) of the earnings per share that Madsen Company would report on its 2007 income statement.

P17-5 *Comprehensive: EPS* Newton Company is preparing its annual earnings per share amounts to be disclosed on its 2007 income statement. It has collected the following information at the end of 2007:

1. Net income: $120,400. Included in the net income is income from continuing operations of $130,400 and an extraordinary loss (net of income taxes) of $10,000. Corporate income tax rate, 30%.
2. Common stock outstanding on January 1, 2007: 20,000 shares.
3. Common stock issuances during 2007: July 6, 4,000 shares; August 24, 3,000 shares.
4. Stock dividend: On October 19, 2007 the company declared a 10% stock dividend that resulted in 2,700 additional outstanding shares of common stock.
5. Common stock prices: 2007 average market price, $30 per share; 2007 ending market price, $27 per share.

6. 7% preferred stock outstanding on January 1, 2007: 1,000 shares. Terms: $100 par, nonconvertible. Current dividends have been paid. No preferred stock issued during 2007.
7. 8% convertible preferred stock outstanding on January 1, 2007: 800 shares. The stock was issued in 2006 at $130 per share. Each $100 par preferred stock is currently convertible into 1.7 shares of common stock. Current dividends have been paid. To date, no preferred stock has been converted.
8. Bonds payable outstanding on January 1, 2007: $100,000 face value. These bonds were issued several years ago at 97 and pay annual interest of 9.6%. The discount is being amortized in the amount of $300 per year. Each $1,000 bond is currently convertible into 22 shares of common stock. To date, no bonds have been converted.
9. Compensatory share options outstanding: Key executives may currently acquire 3,000 shares of common stock at $20 per share. The options were granted in 2006. To date, none have been exercised. The unrecognized compensation cost (net of tax) related to the options is $4 per share.

Required

1. Compute the basic earnings per share. Show supporting calculations.
2. Compute the diluted earnings per share. Show supporting calculations.
3. Show how Newton Company would report these earnings per share figures on its 2007 income statement. Include an explanatory note to the financial statements.

P17-6 *Comprehensive: EPS* The Frost Company has accumulated the following information relevant to its 2007 earnings per share.

1. Net income for 2007, $150,500.
2. Bonds payable: On January 1, 2007 the company had issued 10%, $200,000 bonds at 110. The premium is being amortized in the amount of $1,000 per year. Each $1,000 bond is currently convertible into 22 shares of common stock. To date, no bonds have been converted.
3. Bonds payable: On December 31, 2005, the company had issued $540,000 of 5.8% bonds at par. Each $1,000 bond is currently convertible into 11.6 shares of common stock. To date, no bonds have been converted.
4. Preferred stock: On July 3, 2006 the company had issued 3,800 shares of 7.5%, $100 par, preferred stock at $108 per share. Each share of preferred stock is currently convertible into 2.45 shares of common stock. To date, no preferred stock has been converted and no additional shares of preferred stock have been issued. The current dividends have been paid.
5. Common stock: At the beginning of 2007, 25,000 shares were outstanding. On August 3, 7,000 additional shares were issued. During September, a 20% stock dividend was declared and issued. On November 30, 2,000 shares were reacquired as treasury stock.
6. Compensatory share options: Options to acquire common stock at a price of $33 per share were outstanding during all of 2007. Currently, 4,000 shares may be acquired. To date, no options have been exercised. The unrecognized compensation cost (net of tax) related to these options is $5 per share.
7. Miscellaneous: Stock market prices on common stock averaged $41 per share during 2007, and the 2007 ending stock market price was $40 per share. The corporate income tax rate is 30%.

Required

1. Compute the basic earnings per share. Show supporting calculations.
2. Compute the diluted earnings per share. Show supporting calculations.
3. Indicate which earnings per share figure(s) Frost Company would report on its 2007 income statement.

P17-7 **AICPA Adapted** *Earnings Per Share* The controller of Lafayette Corporation has requested assistance in determining income, basic earnings per share, and diluted earnings per share for presentation in the company's income statement for the year ended September 30, 2008. As currently calculated, the company's net income is $540,000 for fiscal year 2007–2008.

Your working papers disclose the following opening balances and transactions in the company's capital stock accounts during the year:

1. Common stock (at October 1, 2007, stated value $10, authorized 300,000 shares; effective December 1, 2007, stated value $5, authorized 600,000 shares):
    Balance, October 1, 2007—issued and outstanding 60,000 shares
    December 1, 2007—60,000 shares issued in a two-for-one stock split
    December 1, 2007—280,000 shares (stated value $5) issued at $39 per share
2. Treasury stock—common:
    March 3, 2008—purchased 40,000 shares at $38 per share
    April 1, 2008—sold 40,000 shares at $40 per share
3. Noncompensatory stock purchase warrants, Series A (initially, each warrant was exchangeable with $60 for one common share; effective December 1, 2007, each warrant became exchangeable for two common shares at $30 per share):
    October 1, 2007—25,000 warrants issued at $6 each

4. Noncompensatory stock purchase warrants, Series B (each warrant is exchangeable with $40 for one common share):
   April 1, 2008—20,000 warrants authorized and issued at $10 each.
5. First mortgage bonds, 5 1/2%, due 2020 (nonconvertible; priced to yield 5% when issued):
   Balance October 1, 2007—authorized, issued, and outstanding—the face value of $1,400,000
6. Convertible debentures, 7%, due 2027 (initially, each $1,000 bond was convertible at any time until maturity into 20 common shares; effective December 1, 2007, the conversion rate became 40 shares for each bond):
   October 1, 2007—authorized and issued at their face value (no premium or discount) of $2,400,000.

The following table shows the average market prices for the company's securities during 2007–2008 :

	Average for Year Ended September 30, 2008
Common stock	$37\frac{1}{2}$*
First mortgage bonds	87
Convertible debentures	115
Series A Warrants	15
Series B Warrants	$9\frac{1}{2}$

*Adjusted for stock split.

Required
Prepare a schedule computing:
1. The basic earnings per share.
2. The diluted earnings per share that should be presented in the Company's income statement for the year ended September 30, 2008.

A supporting schedule computing the numbers of shares to be used in these computations should also be prepared. Assume an income tax rate of 30%.

P17-8 AICPA Adapted *Earnings Per Share* Mason Corporation's capital structure is as follows:

	December 31	
	2007	2006
Outstanding shares of:		
Common stock	336,000	300,000
Nonconvertible preferred stock	10,000	10,000
8% convertible bonds	$1,000,000	$1,000,000

The following additional information is available:

1. On September 1, 2007, Mason sold 36,000 additional shares of common stock.
2. Net income for the year ended December 31, 2007 was $750,000.
3. During 2007 Mason paid dividends of $3 per share on its nonconvertible preferred stock.
4. The 8% convertible bonds are convertible into 40 shares of common stock for each $1,000 bond.
5. Unexercised compensatory share options to purchase 30,000 shares of common stock at $20.50 per share were outstanding at the beginning and end of 2007. The average market price of Mason's common stock was $36 per share during 2007. The market price was $33 per share at December 31, 2007. The unrecognized compensation cost (net of tax) related to the options is $2 per share.
6. Warrants to purchase 20,000 shares of common stock at $38 per share were attached to the preferred stock at the time of issuance. The warrants, which expire on December 31, 2012, were outstanding at December 31, 2007.
7. Mason's effective income tax rate was 30% for 2006 and 2007.

Required
(Show supporting computations in good form, and round earnings per share to the nearest penny.)
1. Compute the number of shares that should be used for the computation of basic earnings per share for the year ended December 31, 2007.
2. Compute the basic earnings per share for the year ended December 31, 2007.
3. Compute the number of shares that should be used for the computation of diluted earnings per share for the year ended December 31, 2007.
4. Compute the diluted earnings per share for the year ended December 31, 2007.

P17-9 *Dividends* The Keener Company has had 1,000 shares of 7%, $100 par-value preferred stock and 40,000 shares of $5 stated-value common stock outstanding for the last three years. During that period, dividends paid totaled $6,000, $28,000, and $30,000 for each year, respectively.

Required

Compute the amount of dividends that Keener must have paid to preferred stockholders and common stockholders in each of the three years, given the following four independent assumptions:
1. Preferred stock is nonparticipating and noncumulative
2. Preferred stock is nonparticipating and cumulative
3. Preferred stock is fully participating and cumulative
4. Preferred stock participates up to a maximum of 9% of its par value and is cumulative

P17-10 **AICPA Adapted** *Dividends* Tomasco, Inc., began operations in January 2003 and had the following reported net income or loss for each of its five years of operations:

2003	$ 150,000 loss
2004	130,000 loss
2005	120,000 loss
2006	250,000 income
2007	1,000,000 income

At December 31, 2007, the Tomasco capital accounts were as follows:

Common stock, par value $10 per share; authorized	
100,000 shares; issued and outstanding 50,000 shares	$ 500,000
4% nonparticipating noncumulative preferred stock, par value	
$100 per share; authorized, issued, and outstanding 1,000 shares	100,000
8% fully participating cumulative preferred stock, par value	
$100 per share; authorized, issued, and outstanding 10,000 shares	1,000,000

Tomasco has never paid a cash or stock dividend. There has been no change in the capital accounts since Tomasco began operations. The appropriate state law permits dividends only from retained earnings.

Required

Prepare a work sheet showing the maximum amount available for cash dividends on December 31, 2007 and how it would be distributable to the holders of the common shares and each of the preferred shares. Show supporting computations in good form.

P17-11 *Comprehensive* The Gray Company lists the following stockholders' equity items on its December 31, 2006 balance sheet:

Preferred stock, 8%, $100 par	$120,000
Common stock, $10 par	180,000
Additional paid-in capital on preferred stock	21,600
Additional paid-in capital on common stock	90,000
Total contributed capital	$411,600
Retained earnings	230,000
Accumulated other comprehensive income	
Unrealized increase in value of available-for-sale securities	6,000
Contributed capital, retained earnings, and accumulated other comprehensive income	$647,600
Less: Treasury stock (2,000 shares of common at $21 per share, acquired on March 3, 2006)	(42,000)
Total Stockholders' Equity	$605,600

The following stock transactions occurred during 2007:

Jan.	2	Issued 3,000 shares of common stock at $25 per share.
Jan.	30	Paid the annual 2006 per share dividend on preferred stock and the $2 per share dividend on common stock. These dividends had been declared on December 31, 2006.
Mar.	2	Issued 400 shares of preferred stock at $125 per share.
May	7	Reissued 600 shares of treasury stock at $24 per share.
June	15	Split the common stock two for one, reducing the par value to $6 per share.
July	2	Declared a 5% stock dividend on the outstanding common stock, to be issued on August 3. The stock is selling for $14 per share.
Aug.	3	Issued the stock dividend.
Oct.	1	Declared a property dividend payable to common stockholders on November 1. The dividend consists of 2,000 shares of an investment in Lamb Company available-for-sale common stock, which had been acquired at a cost of $12 per share and which have a carrying value of $15 per share. The stock is currently selling for $16 per share.

Nov. 1   Issued the property dividend to common stockholders.

Dec. 31   Declared the annual per share dividend on the outstanding preferred stock and a $1 per share dividend on the outstanding common stock, to be paid on January 30, 2008.

Required
1. Prepare journal entries to record the preceding transactions.
2. Prepare the December 31, 2007 stockholders' equity section (assume that 2007 net income was $225,000).

P17-12 *Comprehensive* Included in the December 31, 2006 Jacobi Company balance sheet was the following stockholders' equity section:

Preferred stock, 6%, $100 par	$200,000	
Premium on preferred stock	12,000	$ 212,000
Common stock, $5 par	$150,000	
Premium on common stock	240,000	390,000
Total contributed capital		$ 602,000
Retained earnings		627,000
Accumulated other comprehensive income (loss)		
Unrealized decrease in value of available-for-sale securities		(41,000)
Contributed capital, retained earnings, and accumulated other comprehensive income		$1,188,000
Less: Treasury stock (1,000 shares of common stock at cost, acquired on 2/3/2006)		(20,000)
Total Stockholders' Equity		$1,168,000

The company engaged in the following stock transactions during 2007:

Jan. 2   Paid the semiannual dividend on the outstanding preferred stock and a $1.60 per share annual dividend on the outstanding common stock. These dividends had been declared on December 1 of 2006.

Jan. 5   Issued 500 shares of preferred stock at $110 per share.

Jan. 23   Issued 4,000 shares of common stock at $23 per share.

Apr. 2   Reissued 700 shares of treasury stock at $24 per share.

May 14   Declared a 10% stock dividend on the outstanding common stock, payable on June 29. The common stock is currently selling for $25 per share.

June 5   Declared the semiannual cash dividend on the outstanding preferred stock, payable on July 5.

June 29   Issued the stock dividend declared on May 15.

July 5   Paid the cash dividend declared on June 5.

July 20   Split the common stock two for one and reduced the par value to $2.50 per share.

Aug. 3   Declared a property dividend, payable to common stockholders on September 14. The dividend consists of an investment in 5,000 shares of available-for-sale Drot Company common stock. The stock had been acquired at $9 per share, but has a carrying value of $6 per share. The stock is currently selling for $4 per share.

Sept. 14   Paid the property dividend declared on August 3.

Dec. 3   Declared the semiannual cash dividend on the outstanding preferred stock and a $0.90 per share annual dividend on the outstanding common stock.

Required
1. Prepare journal entries to record the preceding transactions.
2. Prepare the December 31, 2007 stockholders' equity section (assume that 2007 net income was $270,000).

P17-13 *Stock Dividends, Splits* The stockholders' equity of the Nance Company prior to any of the following events is as follows:

Preferred stock, 8%, $100 par	$100,000
Common stock, $10 par	150,000
Premium on preferred stock	16,000
Premium on common stock	220,000
Retained earnings	264,000
	$750,000

The company is considering the following *alternative* items:

1. An 8% stock dividend on the common stock when it is selling for $30 per share.
2. A 30% stock dividend on the common stock when it is selling for $32 per share.
3. A *special* stock dividend to common stockholders consisting of one share of preferred stock for every 100 shares of common stock. The preferred stock and common stock are selling for $123 and $31 per share, respectively.

4. A two-for-one stock split on the common stock, reducing the par value to $4 per share (assume the same date for declaration and issuance). The market price is $30 per share on the common stock.
5. A property dividend to common stockholders consisting of 1,000 shares of West Company common stock. This stock is being carried on the Nance Company books at a cost of $48 per share; it has a current value of $54 per share.
6. A cash dividend, consisting of a normal dividend and a liquidating dividend, on both the preferred and the common stock. The 10% preferred dividend includes a 2% liquidating dividend, and the $2.30 per share common dividend includes a $0.30 per share liquidating dividend (separate liquidating dividend contra accounts should be used).

Required
For each of the preceding *alternative* items:
1. Record (a) the journal entry at the date of declaration, and (b) the journal entry at the date of issuance.
2. Compute the balances in the stockholders' equity accounts immediately after the issuance (any gains or losses are to be reflected in the retained earnings balance; ignore income taxes).

P17-14 *Retained Earnings Statement* The Tate Company began 2007 with a Retained Earnings account balance of $180,000. During 2007 the following eight events occurred and were properly recorded by the company:

1. Bonds payable with a face value of $100,000 were issued on January 1 at 98. The bonds mature in 10 years. The bond provisions require the restriction of retained earnings (by means of a note to the financial statements) equal to one-half the face value of the bonds during the period the bonds are outstanding.
2. On April 13 the company reissued 2,400 shares of treasury stock for $25 per share. The company had reacquired these shares in 2005 at a cost of $20 per share. At that time, it had restricted retained earnings (by means of a note to the financial statements) in an amount equal to the cost of the treasury shares.
3. On January 5 the company recalled and retired 800 shares of $100 par preferred stock at the call price of $120 per share. The stock had originally been issued for $108 per share.
4. During June the company declared and issued a two-for-one stock split on its common stock, reducing the par value from $10 to $5 per share. Immediately prior to the split, 10,000 shares of common stock were outstanding. The stock market price on the date of the split was $25 per share.
5. In August the company declared and issued a 15% stock dividend when the common stock was selling at $13 per share.
6. During December the company declared and paid its annual $1.30 per share cash dividend on the outstanding common stock.
7. Net income amounted to $72,000.
8. During the year-end audit, it was found that in 2006 the company had recorded depreciation on a particular machine twice. The error resulted in a $13,000 overstatement of depreciation during 2006. It was also found that, due to an oversight, a $10,000 loss on the sale of land was omitted from the 2006 income statement. Both items are material. The company has been subject to a 30% income tax rate for several years.

Required
Prepare Tate Company's statement of retained earnings and any related notes to its financial statements for the year ended December 31, 2007.

P17-15 *Corrections, Dividends, Retained Earnings Statement* On January 1, 2007 the Fastor Company had a retained earnings balance of $218,600. It is subject to a 30% corporate income tax rate. During 2007 the company earned net income of $67,000, and the following events occurred:

1. Cash dividends of $3 per share on 4,000 shares of common stock were declared and paid.
2. A small stock dividend was declared and issued. The dividend consisted of 600 shares of $10 par common stock. On the date of declaration the market price of the company's common stock was $36 per share.
3. The company recalled and retired 500 shares of $100 par preferred stock. The call price was $125 per share; the stock had originally been issued for $110 per share.
4. The company discovered that it had erroneously recorded depreciation expense of $45,000 in 2006 for both financial reporting and income tax reporting. The correct depreciation for 2006 should have been $20,000. This is considered a material error.

Required
1. Prepare journal entries to record items 1 through 4.
2. Prepare Fastor Company's statement of retained earnings for the year ended December 31, 2007.

P17-16 *Comprehensive* The stockholders' equity of the Cory Company on January 1, 2007 is as follows:

Preferred stock, 8%, $100 par, callable at $116	$100,000
Preferred stock, 7%, $100 par	150,000
Common stock, $10 par	220,000
Premium on capital stock	160,000
Retained earnings	182,200
	$812,200

In January 2007 the company recalled and retired the 8% preferred stock. This stock originally had been issued for $105 per share. In April it declared and issued a 10% stock dividend on the common stock; the stock was then selling for $16 per share. This was the only issuance of common or preferred stock during the year. During November the company reacquired as treasury stock 1,000 shares of its common stock at $18 per share (it uses the cost method for treasury stock). State law requires a restriction of retained earnings equal to the cost of all treasury shares held. The company discloses this restriction by means of a note to the financial statements. In December the annual cash dividends on the outstanding preferred stock and a $1 per share cash dividend on the outstanding common stock were declared and paid. At the end of December net income of $87,000 was closed from Income Summary to Retained Earnings. During the year-end audit it was found that two errors had been made during 2006 for both financial reporting and income tax reporting. First, depreciation on certain machinery in the amount of $10,000 was inadvertently omitted. Second, a mathematical mistake was made in the calculation of the accumulated depreciation related to the sale of equipment. Consequently, the reduction in accumulated depreciation and the amount of the gain recognized were both understated by $8,000. Both errors are considered material. The company has been subject to a 30% income tax rate for the past several years.

Required
1. Prepare journal entries to record the preceding transactions.
2. Prepare Cory Company's statement of retained earnings and any related notes to its financial statements for the year ended December 31, 2007.

P17-17 *Corrections* You are engaged to perform the first audit of the Marble Company for the year ended December 31, 2007. You find the following account balances related to stockholders' equity:

Preferred stock, $100 par	$ 30,000
Common stock, $10 par	65,000
Capital surplus	(16,400)
Retained earnings	150,000

Because of the antiquated terminology and negative balance, you examine the Capital Surplus account first and find in it the following entries:

	Credit (Debit)
Premium on common stock	$ 27,100
Capital from donated land	16,000
Treasury stock (500 common shares at cost)	(7,500)
Premium on preferred stock	3,000
Stock dividend (50%)	(20,000)
Prior period adjustment (net of income taxes)	(12,000)
Loss from fire (uninsured), 2006	(18,000)
Property dividend declared	(6,000)
Cash dividends declared	(24,000)
Balance	$(41,400)

Your examination of the Preferred Stock and Common Stock accounts reveals that the amounts shown correctly state the total par value of the issued capital stock. The Retained Earnings account contains the accumulated earnings of the company, with the exception of any items of retained earnings that were inappropriately debited or credited to the Capital Surplus account.

Required

1. Prepare whatever journal entries are necessary to eliminate the Capital Surplus account and to correct the Marble Company's stockholders' equity accounts.
2. Prepare a corrected stockholders' equity section of Marble Company's December 31, 2007 balance sheet. Include any related notes to its financial statements.

P17-18 AICPA Adapted *Comprehensive* Ashwood, Inc. is a public enterprise whose shares are traded in the over-the-counter market. At December 31, 2006 Ashwood had 6,000,000 authorized shares of $10 par value common stock, of which 2,000,000 shares were issued and outstanding. The stockholders' equity accounts at December 31, 2006 had the following balances:

Common stock	$20,000,000
Additional paid-in capital	7,500,000
Retained earnings	6,470,000

Transactions during 2007 and other information relating to the stockholders' equity accounts were as follows:

1. On January 5, 2007, Ashwood issued at $54 per share, 100,000 shares of $50 par value, 9%, cumulative convertible preferred stock. Each share of preferred stock is convertible, at the option of the holder, into two shares of common stock. Ashwood had 600,000 authorized shares of preferred stock.
2. On February 2, 2007, Ashwood reacquired 20,000 shares of its common stock for $16 per share. Ashwood uses the cost method to account for treasury stock.
3. On April 27, 2007, Ashwood sold 500,000 shares (previously unissued) of $10 par value common stock to the public at $17 per share.
4. On June 18, 2007, Ashwood declared a cash dividend of $1 per share of common stock, payable on July 13, 2007 to stockholders of record on July 2, 2007.
5. On November 9, 2007, Ashwood sold 10,000 shares of treasury stock for $21 per share.
6. On December 14, 2007, Ashwood declared the yearly cash dividend on preferred stock, payable on January 14, 2008 to stockholders of record on December 31, 2007.
7. On January 18, 2008, before the books were closed for 2007, Ashwood became aware that the ending inventories at December 31, 2006 were understated by $300,000 (the after-tax effect on 2006 net income was $210,000). The appropriate correcting entry was recorded the same day.
8. After correcting the beginning inventory, net income for 2007 was $4,500,000.

Required

1. Prepare a statement of retained earnings for Ashwood for the year ended December 31, 2007. Assume that only single-period financial statements for 2007 are presented.
2. Prepare the stockholders' equity section of Ashwood's balance sheet at December 31, 2007.

P17-19 AICPA Adapted *Comprehensive* Carr Corporation had the following stockholders' equity account balances at December 31, 2006:

Preferred stock	$1,800,000
Additional paid-in capital from preferred stock	90,000
Common stock	5,150,000
Additional paid-in capital from common stock	3,500,000
Retained earnings	4,000,000
Unrealized decrease in value of marketable equity securities	245,000
Treasury common stock	270,000

Transactions during 2007 and other information relating to the stockholders' equity accounts were as follows:

1. Carr's preferred and common shares are traded on the over-the-counter market. At December 31, 2006, Carr had 100,000 authorized shares of $100 par, 10%, cumulative preferred stock; and 3,000,000 authorized shares of no-par common stock with a stated value of $5 per share.
2. On January 9, 2007, Carr formally retired all 30,000 shares of its treasury common stock and had them revert to an unissued basis. The treasury stock had been acquired on January 20, 2006. The shares were originally issued at $10 per share.
3. Carr owned 10,000 shares of Bush, Inc. common stock purchased in 2004 for $750,000. The Bush stock was included in Carr's short-term marketable securities portfolio at the end of 2006 at a value of $650,000. On February 13, 2007, Carr declared a dividend-in-kind of one share of Bush for every hundred shares of Carr common stock held by stockholders of record on February 27, 2007. The market price of Bush common stock was $63 per share on February 13, 2007. The dividend-in-kind was distributed on March 12, 2007.

4. On April 2, 2007, 250,000 stock rights were issued to the common stockholders permitting the purchase of one new share of common stock in exchange for one right and $11 cash. On April 23, 2007, 210,000 stock rights were exercised when the market price of Carr's common stock was $13 per share. Carr issued new shares to settle the transaction. The remaining 40,000 rights were not exercised and expired.

5. On December 10, 2007, Carr declared the yearly cash dividend on preferred stock, payable on January 14, 2008 to stockholders of record on December 31, 2007.

6. After the year-end adjustment, the Unrealized Decrease in Value of Marketable Equity Securities account had a debit balance of $135,000 at December 31, 2007.

7. On January 14, 2008, before the accounting records were closed for 2007, Carr became aware that rent income for the year ended December 31, 2006 was overstated by $500,000. The after-tax effect on 2006 net income was $275,000. The appropriate correcting entry was recorded the same day.

8. After correcting the rent income, net income for 2007 was $2,600,000.

Required

1. Prepare Carr's statement of retained earnings for the year ended December 31, 2007. Assume that only single-period financial statements for 2007 are presented.
2. Prepare the stockholders' equity section of Carr's balance sheet at December 31, 2007.

P17-20 *Comprehensive* Dana Company reported the following amounts in the stockholders' equity section of its December 31, 2006 balance sheet:

Preferred stock, 9%, $100 par (10,000 shares authorized, 1,000 shares issued)	$100,000
Common stock, $10 par (20,000 shares authorized, 9,000 shares issued)	90,000
Additional paid-in capital on preferred stock	20,000
Additional paid-in capital on common stock	99,000
Retained earnings	330,000

During 2007, the company's net income was $83,000 and its dividends on preferred and common stock were $9,900 and $17,600, respectively. In addition, the following transactions affected its stockholders' equity:

1. Purchased 750 shares of its outstanding common stock as treasury stock for $22 per share.
2. Sold 500 shares of treasury stock at $27 per share. The company uses the cost method to account for treasury stock.
3. Retired 200 of the common shares held in the treasury.
4. Issued 100 shares of preferred stock for $125 per share.
5. The aggregate market value of the company's long-term investments in available-for-sale equity securities dropped below the carrying value of these securities at year-end. The difference between the carrying value and the year-end market value totals $10,000 (net of taxes).

Required

1. Prepare Dana Company's statement of changes in stockholders' equity for 2007. (*Hint:* This statement will include more than 10 numerical columns.) Assume Dana Company reports its comprehensive income in this statement.
2. Prepare the stockholders' equity section of Dana Company's balance sheet as of December 31, 2007. Include any related notes to its financial statements.

P17-21 *Comprehensive* The stockholders' equity section of Gaines Industries' balance sheet appeared as follows at December 31, 2006:

Contributed capital	
Preferred stock, 8%, $100 par (5,000 shares authorized, 3,000 shares issued)	$ 300,000
Common stock, $10 par (25,000 shares authorized, 20,000 shares issued of	
which 500 shares are being held as treasury stock)	200,000
Premium on preferred stock	120,000
Premium on common stock	280,000
Common stock option warrants	32,000
Total contributed capital	$ 932,000
Retained earnings	260,000
Total contributed capital and retained earnings	$1,192,000
Less: Treasury stock (500 common shares at $31)	(15,500)
Total Stockholders' Equity	$1,176,500

During 2007, the following chronological transactions were recorded:

1. The company issued 1,000 shares of common stock for $40 per share.
2. The company has a share option plan for key executives. In accordance with the plan, the shares under option and the option price per share for each executive are known on the grant date. During 2007 no new options were granted, and compensation expense of $3,000 was recorded in regard to the existing options.
3. Share options to 500 common shares were exercised in 2007 at an option price of $30 per share. The share option value originally recorded in the Common Stock Option Warrants account in regard to these shares amounted to $3 per share.
4. The company reissued 200 shares of its treasury stock for $41 per share.
5. The company accepted land in an industrial park for a factory building site from the Columbus Development Association. The fair value of the land is estimated by an independent appraiser to be $50,000.
6. The law firm of Crook, Rezich, and Romero agreed to accept 100 shares of preferred stock in lieu of legal fees. At the time the preferred stock was selling for $142 per share.
7. Net income for 2007 of $182,000 was transferred from Income Summary to Retained Earnings. Dividends on preferred and common were $24,800 and $43,000, respectively (debit Retained Earnings and credit Cash).

Required

1. Prepare journal entries to record the preceding 2007 transactions for Gaines Industries.
2. Prepare the statement of changes in stockholders' equity for 2007. (*Hint:* This statement will require 10 numerical columns.)
3. Prepare the stockholders' equity section of the December 31, 2007 balance sheet. Include appropriate notes to the financial statements.
4. Compute the return on stockholders' equity for 2007.

P17-22 **AICPA Adapted** *Stockholders' Equity* Raun Company had the following account titles on its December 31, 2007 trial balance:

9% cumulative convertible preferred stock, $100 par value
Premium on preferred stock
Common stock, $1 stated value
Premium on common stock
Retained earnings

The following additional information about the Raun Company was available for the year ended December 31, 2007:

1. There were 2 million shares of preferred stock authorized, of which 1 million were outstanding. All 1 million shares outstanding were issued on January 2, 2004 for $120 a share. The preferred stock is convertible into common stock on a one-for-one basis until December 31, 2013; thereafter, the preferred stock ceases to be convertible and is callable at par value by the company. No preferred stock has been converted into common stock, and there were no dividends in arrears at December 31, 2007.
2. The common stock has been issued at amounts above stated value per share since incorporation in 1989. Of the 5 million shares authorized, 3,580,000 were outstanding at January 1, 2007. The market price of the outstanding common stock has increased slowly but consistently for the last 5 years.
3. The company has an employee share option plan where certain key employees and officers may purchase shares of common stock at 100% of the market price at the date of the option grant. All options are exercisable in installments of one-third each year, commencing one year after the date of the grant, and expire if not exercised within four years of the grant date. On January 1, 2007, options for 70,000 shares were outstanding at prices ranging from $47 to $83 a share. Options for 20,000 shares were exercised at $47 to $79 a share during 2007. During 2007, no options expired and additional options for 15,000 shares were granted at $86 a share. The 65,000 options outstanding at December 31, 2007 were exercisable at $54 to $86 a share; of these, 30,000 were exercisable at that date at prices ranging from $54 to $79 a share.
4. The company also has an employee share purchase plan whereby the company pays one-half and the employee pays one-half of the market price of the stock at the date of the subscription. During 2007, employees subscribed to 60,000 shares at an average price of $87 a share. All 60,000 shares were paid for and issued late in September 2007.
5. On December 31, 2007, there was a total of 355,000 shares of common stock set aside for the granting of future share options and for future purchases under the employee share purchase plan. The only changes in the stockholders' equity for 2007 were those described previously, 2007 net income, and cash dividends paid.

Required

Prepare the stockholders' equity section of the balance sheet of Raun Company at December 31, 2007. Substitute, where appropriate, X's for unknown dollar amounts. Use good form and provide full disclosure. Write appropriate notes as they should appear in the published financial statements.

P17-23 **AICPA Adapted**   *Comprehensive* Fay, Inc. finances its capital needs approximately one-third from long-term debt and two-thirds from equity. At December 31, 2006, Fay had the following liability and equity account balances:

11% debenture bonds payable, face amount	$5,000,000	Additional paid-in capital	$2,295,000
Premium on bonds payable	352,400	Retained earnings	2,465,000
Common stock	8,000,000	Treasury stock, at cost	325,000

Transactions during 2007 and other information relating to Fay's liabilities and equity accounts were as follows:

1. The debenture bonds were issued on December 31, 2004 for $5,378,000 to yield 10%. The bonds mature on December 31, 2019. Interest is payable annually on December 31. Fay uses the interest method to amortize bond premium.
2. Fay's common stock shares are traded on the over-the-counter market. At December 31, 2006, Fay had 2,000,000 authorized shares of $10 par common stock.
3. On January 16, 2007, Fay reissued 15,000 of its 25,000 shares of treasury stock for $225,000. The treasury stock had been acquired on February 24, 2006.
4. On March 2, 2007, Fay issued a 5% stock dividend on all issued shares. The market price of Fay's common stock at the time of issuance was $14 per share.
5. On November 2, 2007, Fay borrowed $4,000,000 at 9%, evidenced by an unsecured note payable to United Bank. The note is payable in five equal annual principal installments of $800,000. The first principal and interest payment is due on November 2, 2008.
6. On December 31, 2007, Fay owned 10,000 shares of Ryan Corp.'s common stock, which represented a 1% ownership interest. Fay treats this marketable equity investment as a long-term investment in available-for-sale securities. The stock was purchased on November 2, 2007 at $20 per share. The market price was $18 per share on December 31, 2007.
7. Fay's net income for 2007 was $2,860,000.

Required
1. Prepare the long-term liabilities section of Fay's December 31, 2007 balance sheet, including all disclosures applicable to each obligation.
2. Prepare the stockholders' equity section of Fay's December 31, 2007 balance sheet.
3. Prepare a schedule showing interest expense for the year ended December 31, 2007.

P17-24 **AICPA Adapted**   *Comprehensive* Min Co. is a publicly held company whose shares are traded in the over-the-counter market. The stockholders' equity accounts at December 31, 2006 had the following balances:

Preferred stock, $100 par value, 6% cumulative; 5,000 shares authorized; 2,000 issued and outstanding	$ 200,000
Common stock, $1 par value, 150,000 shares authorized; 100,000 issued and outstanding	100,000
Additional paid-in capital	800,000
Retained earnings	1,586,000
Total Stockholders' Equity	$2,686,000

Transactions during 2007 and other information relating to the stockholders' equity accounts were as follows:

*   February 2, 2007—Issued 13,000 shares of common stock to Ram Co. in exchange for land. On the date issued, the stock had a market price of $11 per share. The land had a carrying value on Ram's books of $135,000, and an assessed value for property taxes of $90,000.
*   March 2, 2007—Purchased 5,000 shares of its own common stock to be held as treasury stock for $14 per share. Min uses the cost method to account for treasury stock. Transactions in treasury stock are legal in Min's state of incorporation.
*   May 11, 2007—Declared a property dividend of marketable securities held by Min to common shareholders. The securities had a carrying value of $600,000; fair value on relevant dates were:

Date of declaration (May 11, 2007)	$720,000
Date of record (May 28, 2007)	758,000
Date of distribution (June 4, 2007)	736,000

*   October 1, 2007—Reissued 2,000 shares of treasury stock for $16 per share.
*   November 2, 2007—Declared a cash dividend of $1.50 per share to all common shareholders of record November 16, 2007. The dividend was paid on November 26, 2007.
*   December 21, 2007—Declared the required annual cash dividend on preferred stock for 2007. The dividend was paid on January 4, 2008.

- January 14, 2008—Before closing the accounting records for 2007, Min became aware that no amortization had been recorded for 2006 for a patent purchased on July 1, 2006. The patent was properly capitalized at $320,000 and had an estimated useful life of eight years when purchased. Min's income tax rate is 30%. The appropriate correcting entry was recorded on the same day.
- Adjusted net income for 2007 was $838,000.

Required
Determine the amounts of each of the following items. Show supporting calculations.
1. Prior period adjustment
2. Preferred dividends
3. Common dividends—cash
4. Common dividends—property
5. Number of common shares issued at December 31, 2007
6. Total legal capital of common stock issued
7. Additional paid-in capital, including treasury stock transactions
8. Total dollar amount of treasury stock
9. Numerator used in calculation of 2007 earnings per share for the year

CASES

COMMUNICATION

C17-1 Earnings Per Share

AICPA Adapted "Earnings per share" (EPS) is the most featured single financial statistic about modern corporations. Daily published quotations of stock prices also include a "times earnings" figure for many securities that is based on EPS. Often, the focus of analysts' discussions will be on the EPS of the corporations receiving their attention.

Required
1. Explain how dividends or dividend requirements on any class of preferred stock that may be outstanding affect the computation of basic EPS.
2. One of the technical procedures applicable in diluted EPS computations is the "treasury stock method." Briefly describe the circumstances under which it might be appropriate to apply the treasury stock method.
3. In the case of convertible bonds that are assumed to be converted and are dilutive, explain how they are handled for purposes of diluted EPS computations.

C17-2 Complex Capital Structure

AICPA Adapted The earnings per share data required of a company depend on the nature of its capital structure. A corporation may have a simple capital structure and compute only "basic earnings per share" or it may have a complex capital structure and have to compute basic earnings per share and "diluted earnings per share."

Required
Define the term *complex capital structure* and discuss the disclosures (both financial and explanatory) necessary for earnings per share when a corporation has a complex capital structure.

C17-3 Categories of Capital

AICPA Adapted A corporation's capital (stockholders' equity) is a very important part of its statement of financial position.

Required
Identify and explain the general categories of capital (stockholders' equity) for a corporation. Be sure to enumerate specific sources included in each general category.

C17-4 Dividends and Journal Entries

AICPA Adapted Problems may be encountered in accounting for transactions involving the stockholders' equity section of the balance sheet.

Required
1. Explain the significance of the three dates that are important in accounting for cash dividends to stockholders. State the journal entry, if any, needed at each date.
2. Assume retained earnings can be used for stock dividends distributable in shares. What is the effect of an ordinary 10% common stock dividend on retained earnings and total stockholders' equity?

C17-5 Stock Dividends and Splits

AICPA Adapted   Stock splits and stock dividends may be used by a corporation to change the number of shares of its stock outstanding.

Required

1. Explain what is meant by a stock split effected in the form of a dividend.

2. From an accounting viewpoint, explain how a stock split effected in the form of a dividend differs from an ordinary stock dividend.

3. How should a stock dividend that has been declared but not yet issued be classified in a statement of financial position? Why?

CREATIVE AND CRITICAL THINKING

C17-6 Convertible Securities

AICPA Adapted   Public enterprises are required to present earnings per share data on the face of the income statement.

Required

In regard to the computation of diluted earnings per share, discuss:

1. The effect of dilutive convertible securities.
2. The effect of antidilutive convertible securities.

C17-7 Share Options and EPS

AICPA Adapted   Jones Company has adopted a traditional share option plan for its officers and other employees. This plan is properly considered a compensatory plan.

Required

Explain how this plan will affect diluted earnings per share.

C17-8 Dividends and Treasury Stock

AICPA Adapted   Brady Company has 30,000 shares of $10 par value common stock authorized and 20,000 shares issued and outstanding. On August 13, 2007 Brady purchased 1,000 shares of treasury stock for $12 per share. Brady uses the cost method to account for treasury stock. On September 14, 2007 Brady sold 500 shares of the treasury stock for $14 per share.

In October 2007 Brady declared and distributed 2,000 shares as a stock dividend from unissued shares when the market value of the common stock was $16 per share.

On December 21, 2007 Brady declared a $1 per share cash dividend, payable on January 11, 2008 to shareholders of record on December 31, 2007.

Required

1. How should Brady account for the cash dividend, and how would it affect Brady's balance sheet at December 31, 2007? Explain why.

2. How should Brady account for the stock dividend, and how would it affect Brady's stockholders' equity at December 31, 2007? Explain why.

3. How should Brady account for the purchase and sale of the treasury stock, and how should the treasury stock be presented in Brady's balance sheet at December 31, 2007?

C17-9 Analyzing Coca-Cola's Retained Earnings and EPS

Refer to the financial statements and related notes of The Coca-Cola Company in Appendix A to this book.

1. What does the company call its retained earnings? What was the amount at the end of 2004?

2. What was the balance of accumulated other comprehensive income on December 31, 2004? What caused it to change during 2004 and by what amounts?

3. What was the company's basic net income per share for 2004? How much preferred dividends were subtracted in the computation of this income per share? What was the average number of common shares outstanding used in the computation of this income per share? What was the company's diluted net income per share for 2004? How does this amount compare to 2003? What potential common shares were included why?

4. What were the dividends per share and in total for 2004?

5. Compute the return on shareowners' equity for 2004. How does this compare to 2003 (the shareowners' equity was $11,800 million at the end of 2002)?

C17-10 Ethics and EPS Adjustment

Ryan Company has as a goal that its earnings per share should increase by at least 3% each year; this goal has been attained every year over the past decade. As a result, the market price per share of Ryan's common stock also has increased each year. Last year (2006) Ryan's earnings per share was $3. This year, however, is a different story. Because of decreasing sales, preliminary computations at the end of 2007 show that earnings per share will be only $2.99 per share.

You are the accountant for Ryan Company. Ryan's controller, Jim Nastic, has come to you with some suggestions. He says, "I've noticed that the decrease in revenues has been primarily related to credit sales. Since we have fewer credit sales, I believe we are justified in reducing our bad debts expense from 4 to 2% of net sales. I also think that because of the decreased sales, we won't use our factory equipment as much, so we can extend its estimated remaining life from 10 to 15 years for computing our straight-line depreciation expense. Based on my calculations, if we make these changes, Ryan Company's 2007 earnings per share will be

$3.06. This will sure make our stockholders happy, not to mention our CEO. You may even get a promotion. What do you think?"

Required

From financial reporting and ethical perspectives, prepare a response to Jim Nastic regarding his suggestions.

RESEARCH SIMULATION

R17-1 Researching GAAP

Situation

In 2007, its first year of operations, Tara Corporation appropriately reported basic earnings per share of $1.05 on its income statement. During 2008 the company instituted a share option plan and is required to report both basic and diluted earnings per share of $1.12 and $0.98, respectively, on its 2008 income statement. In its 2008 annual report, Tara Company presents comparative income statements for 2007 and 2008.

Directions

Research the related generally accepted accounting principles and prepare a short memo to Tara Corporation's president that explains how to report the 2007 and 2008 comparative earnings per share in its 2008 annual report. Cite your reference and applicable paragraph numbers.

PART

5

Financial Reporting: Special Topics

CHAPTER 18
Income Recognition and Measurement of Net Assets

CHAPTER 19
Accounting for Income Taxes

CHAPTER 20
Accounting for Postemployment Benefits

CHAPTER 21
Accounting for Leases

CHAPTER 22
The Statement of Cash Flows

CHAPTER 23
Accounting Changes and Errors

18

Income Recognition and Measurement of Net Assets

OBJECTIVES

After reading this chapter, you will be able to:

1 Understand the revenue recognition alternatives.

2 Explain revenue recognition at the time of sale, during production, and at the time of cash receipt.

3 Explain the conceptual issues regarding revenue recognition alternatives.

4 Describe the alternative revenue recognition methods.

5 Account for revenue recognition prior to the period of sale, including the percentage-of-completion and completed-contract methods.

6 Account for revenue recognition after the period of sale, including the installment and cost recovery methods.

7 Account for revenue recognition delayed until a future event occurs.

8 Understand software revenue recognition, franchises, real estate sales, retail land sales, and consignment sales (Appendix).

Cooking the Books?

Over the last several years, Securities and Exchange Commission (SEC) investigations have uncovered numerous earnings management practices that have ranged from aggressive accounting practices to outright fraud. Recently, **Bristol-Myers Squibb** has agreed to pay $150 million to settle SEC accusations of improperly inflating its sales and income by approximately $1.5 billion through a practice known as "channel stuffing"—pressuring wholesalers to accept shipments of products well ahead of anticipated demand, particularly toward the end of a quarter, to help meet revenue targets. **Nortel Networks Corp.** is investigating improper revenue recognition practices that led to the recording of approximately $3 billion in revenue over a three-year period. In particular, Nortel mentioned instances of revenue being recorded prior to title being transferred to customers and recording revenue prior to delivery of the product—a practice known as "bill and hold." As stated by Walter Schuetze, former chief accountant of the SEC, improper revenue recognition appears to be the "recipe of choice for cooking the books."

Revenue recognition is a key element in reporting financial performance. However, there currently exists no comprehensive standard on revenue recognition. While conceptual and general guidance can be found in *FASB Statement of Financial*

Robert H. Herz
Chairman
Financial Accounting Standards Board

Accounting Concepts No. 5 and the SEC's *Staff Accounting Bulletins No. 101* and *No. 104*, much of the authoritative literature concerning revenue recognition contains departures from this guidance and allows revenue to be recognized at various points in the earnings process in order to increase the usefulness of a company's financial statements. This guidance typically is concerned with specific types of revenue transactions or industry-specific revenue recognition issues. However, help is on the way. The FASB is currently working on a revenue recognition project that may dramatically change the manner in which revenue is recognized. While this project will likely not be effective for several years, the Financial Executive's Institute has already identified this project as a major reporting challenge that should be closely followed by all executives.

FOR FURTHER INVESTIGATION

For a discussion of revenue recognition and earnings management, consult the Business & Company Resource Center (BCRC):

- Abusive Earnings Management and Early Warning Signs. Lorraine Magrath, Leonard G. Weld, *The CPA Journal*, 0732-8435, August 2002, v72, i8, p50-54.
- Revenue Recognition: A Project to Watch. Colleen Cunningham, *Financial Executive*, 0895-4186, December 2004, v20, i9, p.6.

Revenues and expenses are defined in terms of changes in assets and liabilities. A company typically *recognizes* revenues in the period of sale even though they are earned gradually and continuously during the company's earning process. This recognition of revenue occurs if, at the time of sale, (1) realization has taken place, and (2) the revenues have been earned. There is a difference between recognition and realization. **Recognition** is the process of formally recording and reporting an item in the financial statements, whereas **realization** means the process of converting noncash resources into cash or rights to cash.

As we discussed in Chapter 5 revenue is recognized when *earned* and *realizable*. Generally, this recognition occurs at the time of sale. At this time, the company matches its expenses against its revenues. However, a company may advance and recognize revenues (and expenses) prior to the period of sale. In other situations, a company may defer and recognize revenues (and expenses) after the period of the sale. The purpose of advancing or deferring recognition is to increase the *usefulness* of a company's financial statements. This is achieved by a more *relevant* portrayal of the nature of its operations without a significant decrease in the *reliability* of the information. Note that in this discussion, we are referring to the "sale" as the transaction in which the product is transferred or the service is performed. It is also usually, but not necessarily, the point at which legal title is transferred. It is helpful to understand that the "sale," the transfer of legal title, and the recognition of revenue are three separate but related events. In this chapter we discuss the conceptual and practical issues of revenue recognition, the matching of expenses against the revenue, and the related issue of the measurement of the net assets (assets minus liabilities).

OVERVIEW OF REVENUE RECOGNITION ALTERNATIVES

1 Understand the revenue recognition alternatives.

We show the alternatives for recognizing revenue at various points in the earning process in Exhibit 18-1. In this simple example, a manufacturer purchases raw materials, converts them to finished goods in the production process, sells the finished goods on credit, and later collects the cash. The usual point of revenue recognition at the time of sale is shown in the middle, preceded by the alternative of advancing revenue recognition by recording revenue during production, and followed by the alternative of deferring revenue recognition until the receipt of cash. (Note also that the cash receipt may be spread out over several time periods.)

As we evaluate alternative revenue recognition methods, you must consider the related asset and liability recognition. The period in which a company recognizes revenue and expenses is also the period in which it recognizes an increase in the value of its net assets. We show this relationship in the next section.

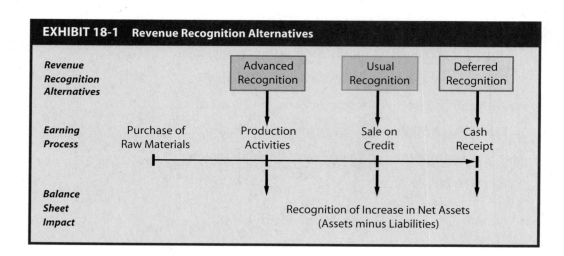

EXHIBIT 18-1   Revenue Recognition Alternatives

EXAMPLES OF REVENUE RECOGNITION ALTERNATIVES

The discussion of revenue recognition alternatives tends to focus on a company's income statement through the recognition of revenue and the matching of expenses. However, it is very important to understand the relationship between income (revenue and expense) recognition on a company's income statement and the measurement of the net assets (assets minus liabilities) on its balance sheet. In this section we show the effects on the financial statements of the three basic revenue recognition alternatives using the following facts for the Ringwood Company. This company is a small manufacturer of special order items in its first year of operations, and uses the perpetual inventory system:

1. The company begins the year with cash and contributed capital of $100.
2. The company contracts to produce and sell an item of inventory to a customer for $150. It costs $100 cash to manufacture the item.
3. The company sells the item on credit.
4. The company collects $60 cash from the customer in partial payment.

Example: Revenue Recognition at Time of Sale

Assume the company recognizes the revenue, expense, and increase in net assets at the time of sale. In this case, it records the preceding events as follows:

1. The company manufactures the inventory:

Inventory	100	
Cash		100

2. The company sells the inventory, recognizes revenue of $150, the related expense of $100, and the increase in net assets of $50 ($150 − $100):

Accounts Receivable	150	
Revenue		150
Cost of Goods Sold	100	
Inventory		100

3. The company collects cash of $60:

Cash	60	
Accounts Receivable		60

Following these events, the company prepares the financial statements shown in the first section of Example 18-1. The income statement reports the revenue of $150, the cost of goods sold of $100, and the resulting gross profit of $50. The balance sheet reports the accounts receivable at $90, which is the billing of $150 less the partial payment of $60. The contributed capital is unchanged at $100, and the retained earnings is the gross profit for the period of $50. Note that the (net) assets have increased by $50 ($150 − $100) which is the amount of profit recognized. ♦

Example: Revenue Recognition During Production

Now assume the same facts for the Ringwood Company, except that the company has not yet delivered the item to its customer, but advances the recognition of revenue to the period of production. During production the company recognizes a gross profit of $50 (revenue of $150 minus the related expense of $100) and bills the customer for a partial billing of $130. The company now records the preceding events as follows:

1. The company manufactures the inventory:

Inventory	100	
Cash		100

2 Explain revenue recognition at the time of sale, during production, and at the time of cash receipt.

EXAMPLE 18-1   Ringwood Company: Revenue Recognition Alternatives

Revenue Recognition at Time of Sale

Income Statement

Revenue	$150
Cost of goods sold	(100)
Gross profit	$ 50

Balance Sheet

Assets		Stockholders' Equity	
Cash	$ 60	Contributed capital	$100
Accounts receivable	90	Retained earnings	50
Total Assets	$150	Total Stockholders' Equity	$150

Revenue Recognition During Production

Income Statement

Revenue	$150
Production expense	(100)
Gross profit	$ 50

Balance Sheet

Assets			Stockholders' Equity	
Cash		$ 60	Contributed capital	$100
Accounts receivable		70	Retained earnings	50
Inventory	$150			
Less: Partial billings	(130)	20		
Total Assets		$150	Total Stockholders' Equity	$150

Revenue Recognition at Time of Cash Receipt

Income Statement

Revenue	$60
Cost of goods sold	(40)
Gross profit	$20

Balance Sheet

Assets			Stockholders' Equity	
Cash		$ 60	Contributed capital	$100
Accounts receivable	$90		Retained earnings	20
Less: Deferred gross profit	(30)	60		
Total Assets		$120	Total Stockholders' Equity	$120

---

2. The company recognizes revenue of $150, the related expense of $100, and the increase of $50 in the value of the inventory during production:

Production Expense	100	
Inventory	50	
Revenue		150

In this situation the company recognizes revenue of $150 and an expense of $100 during production even though it has not transferred the inventory to the customer. Since the company does not yet have a receivable (prior to the billing of $130), the value of the inventory is increased from its cost of $100 to its selling price of $150. In other words, since the company has recognized a gross profit, it must also increase the value of its net assets (inventory).

3. The company bills the customer for a partial billing of $130:

Accounts Receivable	130	
Partial Billings		130

When the company bills the customer, it credits Partial Billings, which is a contra account to the inventory. Thus, the net value of the inventory is reduced to the selling price less the amount billed, or $20 ($150 − $130). In other words, the $20 is the net investment of the Ringwood Company in the inventory.

4. The company collects cash of $60:

Cash	60	
Accounts Receivable		60

Following these events, the company prepares the financial statements in the second section of Example 18-1. The income statement reports the revenue of $150, the production expense of $100, and the resulting gross profit of $50. The balance sheet reports the accounts receivable at $70 ($130 − $60), and the inventory at its net value of $20. Again, note that the (net) assets have increased by $50, which is the amount of profit recognized.

After the company bills the remaining $20 to its customer, the inventory and partial billings accounts have equal balances (of $150). So the company would credit and debit them respectively, to eliminate their balances. Since the company recognized all the gross profit (revenue and expense) during production, it does not recognize any more income. ◆

Example: Revenue Recognition at Time of Cash Receipt

Now assume the original facts for the Ringwood Company, except that the company defers the recognition of revenue to the period when the cash is received. The company now records the preceding events as follows:

1. The company manufactures the inventory:

Inventory	100	
Cash		100

2. The company "sells" (i.e., delivers) the inventory and defers the recognition of revenue:

Accounts Receivable	150	
Inventory		100
Deferred Gross Profit		50

Since the company has transferred the item, it records the receivable of $150, removes the inventory of $100, and records the difference as Deferred Gross Profit, which is a contra account to accounts receivable. Thus, the net value of its accounts receivable is the *cost* of the item of $100 ($150 − $50).

3. The company collects cash of $60:

Cash	60	
Accounts Receivable		60

4.   The company recognizes revenue based on the cash received:

Cost of Goods Sold	40	
Deferred Gross Profit	20	
Revenue		60

Since the company collects $60, it recognizes revenue of $60. This collection is 40% ($60 ÷ $150) of the total sale price of $150. Therefore, it recognizes 40% of the cost of the item as cost of goods sold of $40 (40% × $100). It reduces the deferred gross profit by $20 ($60 − $40), thereby increasing the value of the net receivable.

Following these events, the company prepares the financial statements shown in the third section of Example 18-1. The income statement reports the revenue of $60, the cost of goods sold of $40, and the resulting gross profit of $20. The balance sheet reports the accounts receivable at a net value of $60, which is the remaining $90 ($150 − $60) balance of the receivable, less the remaining $30 ($50 − $20) balance of the deferred gross profit. In other words, the $60 is the *cost* of the receivable (60% of the cost of $100) to the Ringwood Company since it has not yet recognized revenue on that portion. Note that the (net) assets have increased by $20 ($120 − $100), which is the amount of profit recognized.

As the company collects the remaining $90 (60% of the total sale price of $150), it recognizes 60% of the total revenue (60% × $150 = $90) and cost of goods sold (60% × $100 = $60). This recognition eliminates the balance of $30 in the deferred gross profit account, thereby increasing the value of its net assets. ♦

Summary of Revenue Recognition Alternatives

As we discuss in later sections of the chapter, a company advances or defers revenue recognition in certain situations because realization and the completion of the earning process occur in periods other than the period of sale (delivery). These alternative methods increase the relevance of the financial statements. For all three examples discussed earlier, note that when the company recognizes revenue, it also recognizes expenses, and increases its net assets from cost to selling price. In the first example, the company recognizes revenue and expense at the time of sale, and records accounts receivable at the selling price and reduces inventory cost. At this point, realization has occurred, revenue and expense are recognized, and net assets are increased by the amount of the gross profit.

In the second example, the company recognizes revenue and expense during production, and increases the inventory from cost to selling price. Therefore, it records the increase in net assets when it recognizes revenue and expense. Even though the "sale" has not occurred, realization has occurred and the earning process is complete. We discuss this situation later in the chapter for the percentage-of-completion method.

Alternatively, if revenue is not recognized at the time of "sale," the net assets remain at cost. In the third example the company recognizes revenue at the time of cash receipt. Even though it records an account receivable at the selling price at the time of "sale," it reduces the receivable to cost through the subtraction of deferred gross profit. The increase to selling price only occurs as cash is received, revenue and expense are recognized, and deferred gross profit is reduced. In this situation realization occurs only as cash is received, as we discuss later in the chapter for the installment method.

Note also that the company starts the period with assets of $100. In the first and second examples, it recognizes a gross profit of $50 and the net assets increase to $150. In the third example, it recognizes a gross profit of $20 and the net assets increase to $120.

In the last two examples, the expenses are matched against the revenues so that they are either advanced or deferred in a consistent manner. Note that this matching occurs only for certain expenses, usually those for which there is a direct "association of cause and effect" (as we discussed in Chapter 5). Other expenses are recognized on the basis of "systematic and rational allocation" or "immediate recognition." They are usually recognized in the normal manner, unless they can be directly associated with the product. For example, depreciation on a machine used by a company to make a product is included in its inventory cost, and the company advances or defers recognition of the expense consistent with its revenue recognition. A company expenses depreciation on an office building used by selling and administrative personnel in the normal manner. Therefore, the recognition of that expense is *not* related to the revenue recognition alternative the company uses.

The selection of a revenue recognition alternative depends on the particular circumstances faced by each company. We discuss the conceptual issues that influence the decision in the next section.

CONCEPTUAL ISSUES

The decision as to when to recognize revenue focuses on three factors:

3 Explain the conceptual issues regarding revenue recognition alternatives.

1. **The economic substance of the event takes precedence over the legal form of the transaction.** Usually an exchange (sale) is considered to occur at the time of the legal transaction at which title to the property is transferred. However, if economic "reality" is substantially different from the legalities of a transaction, the recognition of revenue may be advanced to a period prior to the sale or deferred to a period after the sale. That is, revenue is recognized in the period in which the revenue is *earned* and *realizable*. For example, as we discuss in Chapter 21, a lessor recognizes the gross profit on a sales-type lease even though it retains legal title. As we discuss later in this chapter, a company may recognize the gross profit on a long-term construction contract each year during the contract, instead of when the construction is completed. In each of these situations, the revenue is earned before title is transferred. Also, as we discussed in Chapter 9, a company does not recognize revenue on a product financing arrangement even though title has passed, because the exchange is, in an economic sense, a loan (borrowing) and not a sale.

2. **The risks and benefits of ownership have been transferred to the buyer.** For revenue to be *earned* (and recognized) by the seller, the risks and benefits of ownership must be substantially transferred from the seller to the buyer. The benefits are the expected net cash flows, while the risks are the likelihood of larger or smaller net cash flows actually being received. For example, as we discussed in Chapter 7, when the buyer has certain rights to return items it has purchased, several criteria must be met for the seller to recognize revenue. Also, a company may recognize revenue during a long-term construction contract because the risks and benefits are transferred to the buyer, as we discuss later in this chapter. Alternatively, if the seller of a franchise has not substantially completed its obligations related to the exchange, then it has not transferred the benefits of ownership to the buyer, and its earning process is not complete. In this case, it defers revenue recognition, as we discuss later in this chapter. Also, if the seller of receivables can reacquire the benefits under a recourse provision, the exchange of benefits may not have occurred and the seller does not recognize revenue, as we discussed in Chapter 7. If the seller of real estate has substantial exposure to risk after the sale, a "full exchange" has not taken place and it defers revenue recognition, as we discuss later in this chapter. Finally, the lessor recognizes revenue on sales-type leases because the transfer of the risks and benefits of ownership has occurred, even though a legal sale has not taken place, as we discuss in Chapter 21.

3. **The collectibility of the receivable from the sale is reasonably assured.** If the collectibility is "*not* reasonably assured,"[1] then *realization* has not taken place and the earning process is not complete. In this case, the company defers the recognition of

---

1. "Omnibus Opinion—1966," *APB Opinion No. 10* (New York: AICPA, 1966), par. 12. In "Recognition and Measurement in Financial Statements of Business Enterprises," *FASB Statement of Concepts No. 5* (Stamford, Conn.: FASB, 1984), par. 84(g), the term "doubtful" is used. It is assumed that these two terms have the same meaning.

revenue. This occurs when it is difficult to predict whether customers will pay their accounts or when significant collection efforts may be required, as for certain real estate situations and franchises discussed later in this chapter. Deferral of revenue recognition may also be appropriate when future refunds or returns cannot be reasonably estimated, as we discussed in Chapter 7.

In this chapter we discuss several revenue recognition methods. In some specialized situations the FASB has not issued *Statements of Standards*. In these situations generally accepted accounting principles are defined by alternative sources, such as *Statements of Position*, *Industry Accounting Guides*, and *Industry Audit Guides*, which cover particular industries and are issued by the AICPA, as we discussed in Chapter 1.

ALTERNATIVE REVENUE RECOGNITION METHODS

4 Describe the alternative revenue recognition methods.

Once a company has decided when to recognize revenue (during, before, or after the period of sale), then it selects a particular accounting method. We briefly summarize the revenue recognition alternatives and the methods used as follows:

1. *Revenue Recognition in the Period of Sale.* This method is generally used because realization has occurred and revenue is earned at the time of sale. The *accrual method* of accounting is used, in which revenue (accomplishment) is recognized at the time of the sales transaction and expenses (sacrifices) are matched against the revenue in the period of sale. The inventory is recorded at cost and the resulting accounts receivable are recorded at net realizable value. The completed-contract method is used for some long-term contracts and recognizes revenue and expenses in the period of sale.

2. *Revenue Recognition Prior to the Period of Sale.* This method is used to reflect economic substance instead of legal form, so that economic reality is not distorted. The *percentage-of-completion method* is used for most long-term construction contracts (or some real estate sales). The *proportional performance method* is used for long-term service contracts to advance revenue recognition. These methods recognize revenue (and certain expenses) based on the percentage completed during the period. The inventory for a long-term construction project, for example, is recorded at cost until revenue is recognized, at which time it is raised to net realizable value.

3. *Revenue Recognition at the Completion of Production.* This method has been advocated for certain precious metals and farm products with immediate marketability at quoted prices, unit interchangeability, and an inability of the producer to determine unit acquisition costs. This method has become less appropriate over time as markets with fixed prices become less common. Also, since mining and agricultural companies generally recognize revenue in the period of the sale, we do not discuss this method in this chapter.[2] The inventory is recorded at replacement cost or net realizable value, and we presented a brief example in Chapter 9.

4. *Revenue Recognition After the Period of Sale.* This method is appropriate when the collectibility of the receivable is not reasonably assured or there is no reliable basis for estimating the collectibility. In this case, revenue recognition is deferred. In the *installment method* a portion of the total gross profit on the sale is recognized in proportion to the cash received. In the *cost recovery method* no gross profit is recognized until the cost of the product is recovered. After the cost recovery, gross profit is recognized as an amount equal to the subsequent cash receipts. The account receivable, less the deferred gross profit, is recorded at cost until the revenue is recognized.

---

2. H. J. Jaenicke, "Survey of Present Practices in Recognizing Revenues, Expenses, Gains, and Losses," *Research Report* (Stamford, Conn.: FASB, 1981), p. 75.

5. *Revenue Recognition Delayed Until a Future Event Occurs*. This method is appropriate when there has been an insignificant transfer of the risks and benefits of ownership. In this case, revenue is not recognized either at the time of the sale or as cash is received. The *deposit method* is used and all cash receipts are recorded as deposits until an event occurs that transfers sufficient risks and benefits to the buyer. Then revenue is recognized. Related assets are recorded at their cost or book value until the revenue recognition occurs.

The following diagram summarizes many of the revenue recognition issues we have discussed:

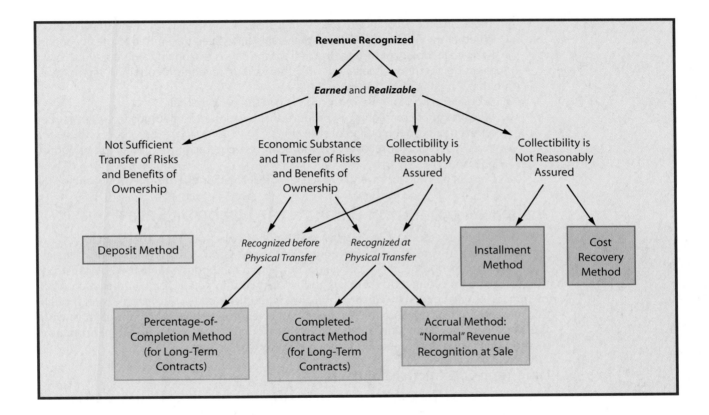

We discuss the accounting issues involved in the recognition of revenue (and expenses) in the period of sale in several places throughout this book and we will not discuss them further in this chapter. In the next section, we discuss revenue recognition prior to sale as it applies to construction contracts and service contracts. Following this section, we discuss revenue recognition after the period of sale.

SECURE YOUR KNOWLEDGE 18-1

- Revenues are recognized when earned and realized (or realizable). Generally, this involves recording revenue, the related expense, and the increase in net assets (for the amount of gross profit recognized) at the time of sale.

(continued)

- When the completion of the earning process and realization occur in periods other than the period of sale, companies may accelerate (advance) or delay (defer) the recognition of revenue to increase the usefulness of its financial statements:
  - If a company recognizes revenue and expense during production, it recognizes gross profit (revenues less expenses) during production and it increases inventory (net assets) from its cost to its selling price.
  - If a company is uncertain as to the ultimate collection of cash, it may defer the recognition of revenue until cash is received by crediting a contra-account to accounts receivable (Deferred Gross Profit). When cash is ultimately received, the deferred gross profit account is reduced (net assets increase), and revenues and expenses are recognized.
- In deciding when to recognize revenue, a company should consider:
  - The economic substance of the event instead of the legal form of the transaction,
  - Whether the risks and benefits of ownership have been transferred to the buyer, and
  - If the collectibility of the receivable from the sale is reasonably assured.
- Accounting methods associated with the various revenue recognition alternatives are the:
  - Accrual method for revenue recognized in the period of sale;
  - Percentage of completion or proportional performance methods for revenue recognized prior to the period of sale;
  - Installment or cost recovery methods for revenue recognized after the period of sale; and
  - Deposit method for revenue which will be delayed until a future event occurs.

REVENUE RECOGNITION PRIOR TO THE PERIOD OF SALE

5 Account for revenue recognition prior to the period of sale, including the percentage-of-completion and completed-contract methods.

We discuss three methods of revenue recognition in this section. Each applies to long-term contracts where the production of a product or the provision of a service extends over several accounting periods. The percentage-of-completion method is widely used by construction companies for long-term contracts and we discuss it in detail. The completed-contract method also may be used by construction companies for long-term contracts. Even though this method does *not* advance the recognition of revenue, we show it here for contrast with the percentage-of-completion method. We also discuss the proportional performance method that is used by companies for long-term service contracts.

Long-Term Construction Contracts

Some companies engage in long-term construction contracts in which they agree to construct an asset for another entity (e.g., company or governmental agency) over an extended period. Long-term construction contracts involve projects such as buildings, ships, roads, bridges, and dams, which can take several years to complete. Such a contract may involve advance payments by the buyer to help the seller finance the construction and to show the buyer's ownership interest in the asset under construction. The contract also may include specific responsibilities of the seller, such as the use of certain materials and the completion of production on a specific timetable. At completion, the buyer typically inspects and approves the finished asset before the legal "sale" takes place.

Because the construction process usually extends over more than one period, the question arises as to how the construction company should recognize revenue. The **percentage-of-completion method** is generally used. Under this method the company recognizes profit each period during the life of the contract in proportion to the amount of the contract completed during the period. As it recognizes the profit, it also increases the value of the inventory, so that it values the inventory at the costs incurred plus the profit recognized to date (less any partial billings). In certain situations, the **completed-contract method** is used. Under this method the company does *not* recognize profit during the life of the contract, but recognizes it only when the contract is completed. During the life of the contract, therefore, it records the inventory at cost (less any partial billings).

Most long-term contracts are accounted for by the percentage-of-completion method, because it produces a *more relevant* measure of periodic income. When a company uses this method, **economic substance takes precedence over legal form.** That is, the legal sale occurs at the completion of the contract, but revenue recognition is advanced to better depict economic reality.

The earning process is virtually complete because a "continuous sale" takes place. The arguments to support a continuous sale are that (1) the buyer and the seller obtain enforceable rights, including the right of the buyer to enforce specific performance, (2) the buyer usually makes progress payments to support its ownership investment and therefore realization is actually occurring, and (3) the buyer has the right to take over the work in progress.[3]

Thus, in accordance with the continuous sale concept, revenue is recognized continuously using the percentage-of-completion method. The method also has the following advantages:

- It achieves the goal of accrual accounting to report the effects of transactions and other events in the periods in which they occur.
- It is consistent with the argument that revenue is earned continuously over the entire earning process.
- It results in a more relevant measure of periodic income because income includes the results of the activities that occurred during the period.

Generally accepted accounting principles support the use of the percentage-of-completion method. **Accounting Research Bulletin No. 45** recommended its use when the total gross profit on the contract could be estimated with reasonable accuracy and ultimate realization is reasonably assured.[4] However *ARB No. 45* allowed the use of both the percentage-of-completion and completed-contract methods in all circumstances and did not specify the situations under which each method would be preferable. To clarify the use of the two methods, **AICPA Statement of Position No. 81-1** requires that a construction company use the percentage-of-completion method for long-term contracts when *all* the following conditions are met:

1. The company can make reasonably dependable estimates of the extent of progress toward the completion, contract revenues, and contract costs.
2. The contract clearly specifies the enforceable rights regarding goods or services to be provided and received by both the company and the buyer, the consideration to be exchanged, and the manner and terms of settlement.
3. The buyer can be expected to satisfy its obligations under the contract.
4. The company expects to perform its contractual obligations.[5]

The *Statement* also requires that a company use the completed-contract method only when at least one of the preceding conditions is *not* met or for short-term contracts. *SOP No. 81-1* narrowed the generally accepted accounting principles for long-term contracts. Instead of the two methods being allowed in all circumstances, each is acceptable only under specific and separate circumstances.

Percentage-of-Completion Method

When a company uses the percentage-of-completion method, it may determine the percentage completed by using either "input" or "output" measures.

---

3. "Accounting for Performance of Construction-Type and Certain Production-Type Contracts," *AICPA Statement of Position No. 81–1* (New York: AICPA, 1981), par. 22.
4. "Long-Term Construction-Type Contracts," *Accounting Research Bulletin No. 45* (New York: AICPA, 1955), par. 4.
5. "Accounting for Performance of Construction-Type and Certain Production-Type Contracts," *op. cit.*, par. 23.

% x Total revenue =
-total revenue recognize.

Input Measures

An input to the production activity may be used to measure the percentage of completion if a relationship exists between the input and the production activity. Two input measures are the cost-to-cost method and the efforts-expended method. In the **cost-to-cost** method, the company measures the percentage of completion by comparing the costs incurred to date with the expected total costs for the contract. This percentage is multiplied by the total revenue on the contract to compute the total revenue recognized to date. This revenue to date, minus the revenue recognized in previous years, is the revenue recognized in the current year. The expense recognized is the costs incurred in the current year (except when the company incurs a loss, as we discuss later).

In the **efforts-expended** method, the company measures the percentage of completion by the work performed to date, such as labor hours, labor dollars, machine hours, or material quantities compared to the expected total work to be performed in the contract. The revenue recognized in the current year is computed by following the same procedures as for the cost-to-cost method. The expense recognized is computed using the same procedures as for the revenue.

Output Measures

Output measures use the results achieved to date compared to the total expected results of the contract to measure the percentage of completion. Theoretically, output measures are preferable to input measures, since they measure the results achieved (that is, the actual production completed). However, output measures often cannot be reliably measured. For example, it is difficult to measure output for a contract that involves research, engineering, and physical construction. Examples of output measures are units produced, units delivered, contract milestones, value added, or units of work completed (such as cubic yards of pavement laid on a highway contract). Once a company has determined the output percentage of completion, the revenue and expense recognized each period are computed in the same way as for the efforts-expended method.

Accounting Procedures

In accounting for a long-term contract under the percentage-of-completion method, a company uses an inventory account, Construction in Progress, to record all costs incurred on the project. In addition, it adds the gross profit that it recognizes on the project to the account, so that at the end of the period the account is valued at cost plus gross profit recognized (i.e., net realizable value). Most long-term projects are financed by receipts from partial billings paid by the buyer, which are usually less than the amount of revenue recognized. When these partial billings are made, the company debits a receivable account and credits a Partial Billings account. The company reports the balance in the Partial Billings account on its balance sheet as an offset (contra account) to the Construction in Progress account. Therefore the net balance sheet amount is an asset if Construction in Progress (which includes incurred costs plus gross profit recognized) exceeds Partial Billings, or a liability if Partial Billings exceeds Construction in Progress.

If the project's total estimated cost exceeds the contract price, then the company expects a loss on the project. The conservatism convention requires that the company recognize the total expected loss in the current year and reduce the carrying value of the inventory. We discuss the recognition of losses later in this chapter.

Completed-Contract Method

Under the completed-contract method, no revenue is recognized until the project is completed or substantially so (although anticipated losses are recognized immediately). In effect, this method is just like the production and sale of any unit of inventory. The recording and reporting of inventory costs and partial billings are handled in the same way as for the percentage-of-completion method. The principal advantage of the completed-contract method is that the revenue recognized is *more reliable* because it is based on final results rather than on estimates. The principal disadvantage is that it is *less relevant* because a company's net income does not reflect its current performance, but rather is a function of the date the contract is completed. Indeed, a company's net income may be negative if it completes no contracts in a period and expenses its selling and administrative costs.

Illustration of the Two Methods

To illustrate the two methods, assume that the Calder Company contracted to construct a dam that takes three years to complete. We show the contract price, costs incurred, estimated costs to complete, partial billings, and collections in Example 18-2. The company estimates the percentage completed by the cost-to-cost method.

EXAMPLE 18-2   Calder Company: Dam Construction Contract Amounts

	2007	2008	2009
Construction costs incurred during the year	$100,000	$186,000	$314,000
Estimated costs to complete the contract	400,000	264,000	—
Partial billings to customer	80,000	350,000	270,000
Collections from customer	50,000	330,000	320,000
Total contract price: $700,000			

Example: Computations for the Percentage-of-Completion Method

We show the gross profit recognized each year under the percentage-of-completion method in Example 18-3.

EXAMPLE 18-3   Gross Profit Recognition: Percentage-of-Completion Method

	2007	2008	2009
Construction costs incurred to date	$100,000	$286,000	$600,000
Estimated costs to complete	400,000	264,000	—
Total estimated costs	$500,000	$550,000	$600,000
Percent complete (construction cost incurred to date ÷ total estimated costs)	20%	52%	100%
Revenue to date (% complete × $700,000 contract price)	$140,000	$364,000	$700,000
Revenue recognized for the year (revenue to date − revenue previously recognized)	$140,000	$224,000	$336,000
Construction cost (expense) incurred for the year	(100,000)	(186,000)	(314,000)
Gross profit recognized	$ 40,000	$ 38,000	$ 22,000

2007: In 2007 the Calder Company incurred $100,000 of construction costs and estimates that it will incur another $400,000 to complete the contract. Therefore, the company expects that the total cost of the contract will be $500,000. Since the contract price is $700,000, the company projects a gross profit of $200,000. The contract is 20% complete ($100,000 ÷ $500,000), and therefore the company recognizes 20% of the total revenue on the contract. This amounts to $140,000 (20% × $700,000). Since total estimated construction costs are $500,000, the construction expense recognized for 2007 is

$100,000 (20% $\times$ $500,000)[6] and the gross profit is $40,000. Note that the contract is 20% complete, and the company recognizes 20% of the $200,000 projected gross profit.

2008: In 2008 the company follows the same procedure. The total costs incurred *to date* are $286,000 (the sum of the costs incurred in 2007 and 2008). Since estimated costs to complete the project are $264,000, the contract is 52% complete. Therefore, the company's total revenue *to date* is $364,000 (52% $\times$ $700,000), and the revenue it recognizes for *the year* is $224,000 (the revenue to date of $364,000 less the revenue previously recognized of $140,000). Since total estimated construction costs are $550,000, the construction expense recognized for 2008 is $186,000 [(52% $\times$ $550,000)$-$ $100,000], and there is a gross profit of $38,000. Note that the contract is 52% complete, the total profit expected on the contract is now $150,000 ($700,000 $-$ $550,000). Therefore, the total profit recognized to date is $78,000 (52% $\times$ $150,000). This amount is consistent with the $40,000 and $38,000 gross profit recognized in the two years.

2009: In 2009 the company completes the contract at a total cost of $600,000. The revenue for *the year* is $336,000, which is the total revenue of $700,000 less the revenue *to date* of $364,000. Since construction costs for *the year* are $314,000, the gross profit for the year is $22,000. Note that the total gross profit for the three years is $100,000 ($40,000 + $38,000 + $22,000), which is consistent with the total revenue less the total actual costs ($700,000 $-$ $600,000). ◆

Example: Computations for the Completed-Contract Method

Under the completed-contract method, the company does not recognize a gross profit until the contract is complete. The Calder Company recognizes the entire gross profit on the contract at the end of 2009. The total construction costs incurred over the three years (and recorded in Construction in Progress) are $600,000 ($100,000 + $186,000 + $314,000). The revenue recognized is the total contract price of $700,000, and therefore the company recognizes a gross profit of $100,000 ($700,000 $-$ $600,000) in 2009. ◆

Journal Entries for the Two Methods

Example 18-4 show the journal entries to record the activities of the Calder Company for both the percentage-of-completion and the completed-contract methods. Under both methods, in 2007 through 2009 the company debits the construction costs (from Example 18-2) to the inventory account Construction in Progress. The accompanying credits are to various accounts such as Accounts Payable, Raw Materials Inventory, Cash, Prepaid Expenses, Accumulated Depreciation, etc. It debits the billings to the customer to Accounts Receivable and credits the Partial Billings, which is a contra account to Construction in Progress. It records the collection of cash from the customer in the normal manner. Under the percentage-of-completion method, the company recognizes the gross profit (calculated in Example 18-3) each year by a journal entry to a revenue and an expense account. It debits the difference between these two amounts, the gross profit, to Construction in Progress. This raises the asset value from cost to net realizable value and eventually to the contract selling price. The increase in stockholders' equity (the gross profit) is accompanied by a corresponding increase in an asset value. Under the completed-contract method the company does not recognize a profit in 2007 or 2008, so no journal entry is required.

In 2009, when the contract is completed, closing entries for the contract are required. Under the percentage-of-completion method, the company closes Partial Billings against Construction in Progress. Note that both accounts include the selling price. Under the completed-contract method, the company recognizes the total gross profit on the contract

---

6. Under the cost-to-cost method, construction expenses recognized for the year are equal to the construction costs incurred during the year (unless a loss is expected on the contract, as we discuss later). Therefore, the construction expense computations are simplified, as we show in Example 18-3. If this method is not used, construction expenses recognized in a given year may differ from the actual yearly construction costs incurred.

at the completion date. It does this by closing Partial Billings against Construction Revenue because both accounts include the selling price. It also closes Construction in

---

EXAMPLE 18-4   Journal Entries to Record Dam Construction

	Percentage-of-Completion Method		Completed-Contract Method	
2007				
1. *To record construction costs:*				
Construction in Progress	100,000		100,000	
Accounts Payable, Raw Materials Inventory, Cash, etc.		100,000		100,000
2. *To record partial billings:*				
Accounts Receivable	80,000		80,000	
Partial Billings		80,000		80,000
3. *To record collections:*				
Cash	50,000		50,000	
Accounts Receivable		50,000		50,000
4. *To record gross profit:*			No Entry	
Construction Expense	100,000			
Construction in Progress	40,000			
Construction Revenue		140,000		
2008				
1. *To record construction costs:*				
Construction in Progress	186,000		186,000	
Accounts Payable, Raw Materials Inventory, Cash, etc.		186,000		186,000
2. *To record partial billings:*				
Accounts Receivable	350,000		350,000	
Partial Billings		350,000		350,000
3. *To record collections:*				
Cash	330,000		330,000	
Accounts Receivable		330,000		330,000
4. *To record gross profit:*			No Entry	
Construction Expense	186,000			
Construction in Progress	38,000			
Construction Revenue		224,000		
2009				
1. *To record construction costs:*				
Construction in Progress	314,000		314,000	
Accounts Payable, Raw Materials Inventory, Cash, etc.		314,000		314,000
2. *To record partial billings:*				
Accounts Receivable	270,000		270,000	
Partial Billings		270,000		270,000
3. *To record collections:*				
Cash	320,000		320,000	
Accounts Receivable		320,000		320,000
4. *To record gross profit and to close out Construction in Progress and Partial Billings:*			No Entry	
Construction Expense	314,000			
Construction in Progress	22,000			
Construction Revenue		336,000		
Partial Billings	700,000		No Entry	
Construction in Progress		700,000		
Partial Billings	No Entry		700,000	
Construction Revenue				700,000
Construction Expense	No Entry		600,000	
Construction in Progress				600,000

Progress against Construction Expense because both accounts include the cost. At the end of the period, it closes the revenue and expense accounts to Income Summary.

We show how the Calder Company reports its activities for this contract under each method in Example 18-5. To complete the income statement under each method, the company deducts its operating expenses from the gross profit to determine its income. On the balance sheet under each method, it offsets Partial Billings against Construction in Progress. At the end of 2007, Construction in Progress exceeds Partial Billings, so the company reports the net amount as inventory in the current asset section of its balance

---

EXAMPLE 18-5   Financial Statement Reporting

1. Percentage-of-Completion Method

	2007	2008	2009
Income Statement (partial):			
Construction revenue	$140,000	$224,000	$336,000
Construction expense	(100,000)	(186,000)	(314,000)
Gross profit	$ 40,000	$ 38,000	$ 22,000
Balance Sheet (partial; end of year):			
Current Assets			
Accounts receivable	$ 30,000	$ 50,000	
Inventories			
Construction in progress	140,000		
Less: Partial billings	(80,000)		
Costs and recognized profit not yet billed	$ 60,000		
Current Liabilities			
Partial billings		$430,000	
Less: Construction in progress		(364,000)	
Billings in excess of costs and recognized profit		$ 66,000	

Notes to Financial Statements: Summary of Significant Accounting Policies (in part): The company reports profits from long-term construction contracts in progress using the percentage-of-completion method of accounting. Profits are accrued based on the ratio of cost incurred to total estimated costs. Costs include direct material, direct labor, and job-related overhead. General and administrative expenses are charged to operations as incurred and are not allocated to contract costs.

2. Completed-Contract Method

	2007	2008	2009
Income Statement (partial):			
Construction revenue	—	—	$700,000
Construction expense	—	—	(600,000)
Gross profit			$100,000
Balance Sheet (partial; end of year):			
Current Assets			
Accounts receivable	$ 30,000	$ 50,000	
Inventories			
Construction in progress	100,000		
Less: Partial billings	(80,000)		
Excess of costs over related billings	$ 20,000		
Current Liabilities			
Partial billings		$430,000	
Less: Construction in progress		(286,000)	
Excess of billings over related costs		$144,000	

Notes to Financial Statements: Summary of Significant Accounting Policies (in part): The company reports profit from long-term construction contracts using the completed-contract method of accounting. Under this method, billings and costs are accumulated during the period of construction, but no profits are recorded before the contract is either completed or substantially completed. A contract is considered substantially completed if the costs to complete are not significant in amount. Costs include direct labor, direct materials, and job-related overhead. General and administrative expenses are charged to operations as incurred and are not allocated to contract costs.

sheet. At the end of 2008, Partial Billings exceeds Construction in Progress, so the company reports the net amount as a current liability in its balance sheet. Note that the difference in the book values under the two methods is equal to the gross profit to date on the contract. Thus, at December 31, 2007, the book value under the percentage-of-completion method is $60,000 and under the completed-contract method it is $20,000. The difference of $40,000 is the gross profit for 2007 (which the company recognizes under the percentage-of-completion but not under the completed-contract method).

LINK TO ETHICAL DILEMMA

Titanic Inc. is a construction company that specializes in the construction of commercial cruise ships. Because the construction period for a ship may last as long as three years, Titanic recognizes revenue from its construction contracts based on the percentage-of-completion method where the percentage of completion is determined by the cost-to-cost method. (Sales and gross profit are recognized as work is performed based on the ratio of actual costs incurred to the estimated total costs of the contract.) As the accountant for Titanic, you recently informed the CEO that labor difficulties, which caused the company to halt construction earlier in the year, would cause Titanic to fall short of its revenue projections. The CEO calmly replied that he still had "a few tricks up his sleeve," and the company would meet these projections.

Later in the month, as you were completing your quarterly physical inspection of the various construction projects, you noticed large amounts of material on hand and waiting to be used in the various projects. Several of the workers commented that most of this material had been delivered over the last two weeks, and if any more were to arrive, they wouldn't have any place to store it. In fact, most of this material was not even going to be needed in the construction process for several more weeks! Returning to the corporate offices, you discovered that the CEO had personally placed the order for this material. The CEO explained to you that he had managed to negotiate a fantastic deal with some of the suppliers if Titanic would take possession of the materials immediately. (A later review of the invoices revealed that the purchase price for this material was equal to the average market price during the month.) Furthermore, the CEO noted that he really wanted the company to complete the projects ahead of schedule to take advantage of the large cash incentives being offered for early completion of the contract, and he didn't want the projects to be delayed because of lack of the necessary materials. Remembering the CEO's earlier comment about meeting earnings projections, you wonder if this purchase of materials was one of the tricks the CEO had up his sleeve. What are the potential effects of this purchase of materials on the company's financial statements, and is this action ethical?

Losses on Long-Term Construction Contracts

A loss on a construction contract can be of two types. First, the estimate of future costs may indicate that there is a **loss in the current period**, but that there will still be a profit on the total contract. Second, the estimate may indicate that an **overall loss on the contract** is expected. In this case, *SOP 81-1* requires that a company recognize the total estimated loss on the entire contract under both the percentage-of-completion and the completed-contract methods. This procedure is consistent with the *conservatism* convention of anticipating all foreseeable losses.

Example: Loss in Current Period

To show the computation of a loss for a period under the percentage-of-completion method, suppose that in 2008 the Calder Company estimates that the costs to complete are $364,000 *instead of* $264,000. Assuming that the data for 2007 are the same as in Example 18-2, it recognizes an $18,000 loss in 2008, which it calculates as follows:

	2008
Construction costs incurred to date	$ 286,000
Estimated costs to complete	364,000
Total estimated costs	$ 650,000
Percent complete ($286,000 ÷ $650,000)	44%
Revenue to date (44% × $700,000)	$ 308,000
Revenue recognized for year ($308,000 − $140,000)	$ 168,000
Construction costs incurred for year	(186,000)
Loss recognized	$ (18,000)

If the costs in 2009 are $364,000 as expected, the Calder Company recognizes the remaining 56% of the revenue, or $392,000. Therefore, the company reports a gross profit of $28,000 in 2009, with a total profit over the three years of the contract of $50,000 ($40,000 − $18,000 + $28,000). This is equal to the total revenue of $700,000 less the total cost of $650,000. Under the completed-contract method, no adjustment is needed in 2008 because the company expects an overall profit on the contract. ♦

Example: Overall Loss on Contract

A more complicated situation arises if the estimated total costs exceed the contract price, so that an overall loss on the contract is anticipated.

Percentage-of-Completion Method Assume that at the end of 2008 the Calder Company estimates that its costs to complete are $429,000. Therefore, it expects that its total costs will be $715,000 ($286,000 + $429,000), indicating an overall loss of $15,000 by the end of the contract. Therefore, it has to remove the gross profit to date and recognize the loss of $15,000 in 2008. It recognizes the revenue for 2008 in the normal way, as we show in Example 18-6. Because the project is 40% complete ($286,000 ÷ $715,000), the revenue to date is $280,000 (40% × $700,000). The revenue recognized in 2008 is $140,000 ($280,000 − $140,000). The total expense recognized includes two components: (1) the amount needed to create a cumulative profit of zero, and (2) the amount of the overall loss recognized.

Since the revenue to date is $280,000 and the expense recognized in 2007 was $100,000, the company recognizes an expense of $180,000 in 2008 to make the cumulative profit equal to zero.[7] In addition, it recognizes the overall loss of $15,000, so the total expense for 2008 is $195,000. The company records the revenue and expense as follows:

Construction Expense	195,000	
Construction in Progress		40,000
Construction Revenue		140,000
Provision for Loss on Contract		15,000

The credit to the Construction in Progress account removes the increase in value resulting from the gross profit recognized in 2007. Therefore, the account includes only the project costs incurred to date. The Provision for Loss on Contract is reported as a contra account to Construction in Progress (less Partial Billings), or it may be reported as a liability. Note that the negative gross profit of $55,000 ($140,000 − $195,000) is equal to the gross profit of $40,000 in 2007 that is reversed plus the anticipated loss of $15,000.

---

7. "Accounting for Performance of Construction-Type and Certain Production-Type Contracts," *op. cit.*, par. 88, requires that the amount of the loss is added to the contract cost. However, if the amount is material, unusual, or infrequent, the amount is reported separately.

If costs in 2009 are $429,000 as projected, the company recognizes a zero gross profit in 2009. The revenue recognized is the remaining amount of $420,000 ($700,000 − $140,000 − $140,000) left to be recognized on the contract. The expense is also $420,000. Thus the company recognizes the total loss incurred on the contract in the year in which it was first estimated (2008).

The company debits the costs incurred on the contract in 2009 to the Construction in Progress account in the normal way up to a total of $700,000 ($414,000 in 2009). The balance in the account should not exceed the contract price, since the asset value cannot be greater than the total proceeds to be received on the contract. The company debits any additional costs incurred over $700,000 to the Provision for Loss on Contract account. Since the total costs incurred are $715,000, the excess of $15,000 eliminates the balance established in the account at the end of 2008.

Example 18-6 summarizes the calculations we just discussed. The company records the construction costs and the revenue and expense in 2009 as follows:

Construction in Progress	414,000	
Provision for Loss on Contract	15,000	
Cash, Accounts Payable, etc.		429,000
Construction Expense	420,000	
Construction Revenue		420,000

Note that the amounts ($429,000 and $420,000) in these two journal entries are not equal. This difference occurs because each year the percent completed is computed based on the different expected total costs. In 2007 the percent completed of 20% is based on the expected total costs of $500,000. In 2008 the 40% completion is based on the expected total cost of $715,000.

EXAMPLE 18-6 **Calculation of Revenues and Expenses When a Loss Is Expected on the Contract**

	Current Year	Total to Date
2007		
Construction revenue	$140,000[a]	$140,000
Construction expense	(100,000)[b]	(100,000)
Gross profit	$ 40,000	$ 40,000
2008		
Construction revenue	$140,000	$280,000
Construction expense	(195,000)[d]	(295,000)[c]
Gross profit	$ (55,000)	$ (15,000)
2009		
Construction revenue	$420,000	$700,000
Construction expense	(420,000)	(715,000)
Gross profit	$ 0	$ (15,000)

a. (20% × $700,000)
b. (20% × $500,000)
c.

Contract price	$700,000
Percent complete	40%
Cost of earned revenue before loss provision	$280,000
Estimated total loss	15,000
Construction expense to date	$295,000

d.

Cumulative construction expense	$295,000
Less: Construction expense in previous year	(100,000)
Current construction expense	$195,000

Completed-Contract Method   Under this method, the company recognizes the loss in 2008 because there is an overall loss on the contract. It records this loss as follows:

Construction Expense	15,000	
Provision for Loss on Contract		15,000

The company debits an expense account to recognize the "loss" because the construction activity is *not* an incidental or peripheral activity. Note that there is no credit to the Construction in Progress account because under the completed-contract method the company did not add the gross profit to the account in previous years.

The company would recognize a gross profit or loss if the actual costs incurred in 2009 were less, or greater, than its estimated amount. This procedure is consistent with accounting for a change in estimate under *FASB Statement No. 154*, as we discuss in Chapter 23. ♦

Additional Considerations in Accounting for Long-Term Construction Contracts

We discuss several additional factors that affect the accounting for long-term construction contracts in this section.

Overhead Costs

Contract costs include all direct costs, such as materials and direct labor, and indirect costs (overhead) identifiable with or allocable to the contract. This is consistent with generally accepted accounting principles for inventory and production costs. Therefore a company usually expenses general and administrative costs as incurred when it uses the percentage-of-completion method. However, it may account for these costs as contract costs under the completed-contract method. Accounting for these costs theoretically provides a better matching of costs as expenses against revenues than would result from treating such costs as period expenses. This is particularly true in years when no contracts are completed, and it is less likely to be misleading to users of financial statements.

Operating Cycle

Accounting Research Bulletin No. 45 requires that the net amounts of Construction in Progress and Partial Billings be included as current assets or current liabilities. The operating-cycle concept is used to justify this classification.

Offsetting Amounts

It is a basic principle of accounting that the offsetting, or netting, of assets and liabilities is not acceptable, except when a right of offset exists. However, *Accounting Research Bulletin No. 45* does allow offsetting when contracts are closely related—for example, when separate contracts are parts of the same project. Therefore, in these circumstances a contract that has a net liability (Partial Billings exceeds Construction in Progress) may be offset against one that has a net asset balance. A company should base its decision as to whether offsetting is appropriate in any situation on economic substance rather than legal form. For example, if separate legal contracts are economically one contract, then the right to offset exists in spite of the legal form of the separate contracts.

Capitalized Interest

When a company constructs an asset, it includes in the cost of the asset the interest cost associated with the funds used in the construction, as we discussed in Chapter 10. Thus, if it incurs interest costs that are related to a long-term construction contract, it includes these costs in the Construction in Progress account rather than as interest expense.

Disclosure

Example 18-5 shows how a company discloses the method it used to account for long-term construction contracts. Note that simply disclosing the use of an "accrual basis" is not sufficient, because both the percentage-of-completion and the completed contract methods are accrual methods. The SEC requires additional long-term contract disclosures for financial statements filed with it. The overall effect is to require more detailed disclosure of accounts receivable and inventory components, as well as the accounting policies and assumptions on which the amounts are based.

REPORTING AND DISCLOSING LONG-TERM CONSTRUCTION CONTRACTS

Real Report 18-1 shows how **Johnson Controls** reports and discloses its long-term construction contracts under the percentage-of-completion method.

Real Report 18-1 Percentage-of-Completion Method

JOHNSON CONTROLS

(in millions)

Consolidated Statement of Financial Position (in part)

Assets	2004	2003
Costs and earnings in excess of billings on uncompleted contracts	$328.6	$323.0
Liabilities		
Billings in excess of costs and earnings on uncompleted contracts	197.2	186.2

Notes to Consolidated Financial Statements (in part)

SUMMARY OF SIGNIFICANT ACCOUNTING POLICIES

Revenue Recognition. The Company recognizes revenue from long-term systems installation contracts of the Controls Group over the contractual period under the percentage-of-completion method of accounting (see "Long-Term Contracts"). In all other cases, the Company recognizes revenue at the time products are shipped and title passes to the customer or as services are performed.

Long-Term Contracts. Under the percentage-of-completion method of accounting used for long-term contracts, sales and gross profit are recognized as work is performed based on the relationship between actual costs incurred and total estimated costs at completion. Sales and gross profit are adjusted prospectively for revisions in estimated total contract costs and contract values. Estimated losses are recorded when identified. Claims against customers are recognized as revenue upon settlement. The amount of accounts receivable due after one year is not significant.

Questions:

1. What method does Johnson Controls use to estimate the percentage of the project that has been completed?
2. How much does Johnson Controls report as an asset from construction activities? As a liability? Is the asset or liability larger?
3. Why does the company not net the asset and liability in its balance sheet?
4. How does Johnson Controls' treatment of claims against customers affect the gross profit recognized on the projects?

Long-Term Service Contracts

A company uses the percentage-of-completion method when it has a long-term contract for the construction and sale of a *product*. Other companies are in the business of providing a *service* instead of a product. **APB Statement No. 4** indicated that a company should recognize revenues from services rendered when these services have been performed and are billable.[8] Many service transactions involve a single service "act." In these cases a company recognizes revenues (and expenses) under the accrual method of accounting in the period when it performs the service. Some companies, however, have long-term contracts in which they agree to provide a service over an extended period. Generally, at the inception of the agreement, a service contract is signed at an agreed-on price and the seller agrees to perform certain service "acts" at a later date. The service contract may require performance of:

- a specified number of similar acts,
- a specified number of defined but not similar acts, or
- an unspecified number of similar acts.

In these cases revenue should be based on performance, but when has the "performance" been completed and how should revenue be recognized? This is a difficult question to answer because long-term service contracts can be complex. Sometimes service contracts are sold in conjunction with products, and the performance activities can vary depending on the industry involved.

There are many companies in service industries such as advertising agencies, cable television companies, computer service firms, and companies engaged in research and development for the government. The accounting principles in some of these industries are underdeveloped; in others they are very specialized. The FASB issued an *Invitation to Comment* titled "Accounting for Certain Service Transactions" as a prelude to its deliberations on setting general accounting standards of revenue (and expense) recognition for service transactions. The FASB deferred these deliberations because it decided to focus first on more conceptual revenue and expense recognition issues. However, the content of this *Invitation to Comment* does provide a good overview of revenue and expense recognition for long-term service contracts and forms the basis for the following general discussion.[9]

Proportional Performance Method

A company recognizes revenue for service transactions based on performance because performance determines the extent to which its earnings process is complete. **When a long-term service contract requires services to be performed in more than one act, revenue is recognized by the proportional performance method—that is, based on the proportionate performance of each act.** A company recognizes revenue depending on the type and number of service acts as follows:

1. *Specified Number of Similar Acts.* Recognize an equal amount of revenue for each act.
2. *Specified Number of Defined but Not Similar Acts.* Recognize revenue for each act based on the ratio of the direct costs (defined next) incurred to perform each act to the total estimated direct costs for the long-term contract.
3. *Unspecified Number of Similar Acts.* Recognize revenue on a straight-line method over the performance period.

---

8. "Basic Concepts and Accounting Principles Underlying Financial Statements of Business Enterprises," *APB Statement No. 4* (New York: AICPA, 1970), par. 151.
9. The following discussion summarizes par. 10–19 of "Accounting for Certain Service Transactions," *FASB Invitation to Comment* (Stamford, Conn.: FASB, 1978), par. 5.

Several types of service costs are involved in a long-term service contract. These include:

- **Initial direct costs**—those costs that are directly associated with negotiating and signing a service contract (e.g., legal fees)
- **Direct costs**—those costs that have a clear causal relationship to the services performed (e.g., labor costs)
- **Indirect costs**—those costs other than initial direct costs and direct costs (e.g., advertising and depreciation)

Under the proportional performance method, a company recognizes these costs as expenses as follows:

1. *Initial Direct Costs.* Defer and allocate over the performance period in proportion to the recognition of service revenues, because initial direct costs are expensed when revenue is recognized.
2. *Direct Costs.* Expense as incurred, because there is a close relationship between the direct costs incurred and the extent of performance achieved.
3. *Indirect Costs.* Expense as incurred, because indirect costs provide no discernible future benefits.

Example: Proportional Performance Method   To illustrate revenue recognition under the proportional performance method, assume the Health Spa Company sells memberships to use its facilities. For $500 in advance, a person signs a two-year contract that allows use of area X (exercise room) 50 times and area Y (whirlpool and sauna) 100 times during the two-year period. At the beginning of 2007, 120 people sign the service contract and the company collects $60,000 (120 × $500). Thus, the company is obligated to perform a total of 6,000 (120 × 50) and 12,000 (120 × 100) service acts in 2007 and 2008 involving areas X and Y, respectively. This service contract involves a specified number of defined but not similar acts, so the company recognizes revenue based on a ratio of direct costs per act to total estimated direct costs.

During 2007 members used area X 3,600 times and area Y 4,800 times. In 2008 members used area X 2,400 times and area Y 7,200 times.[10] The following is a summary of the relevant cost information regarding the 120 membership contracts:

Initial direct costs	$ 1,000
Annual indirect costs	2,000
Estimated (and actual) total direct costs (for two-year period)	24,000
Direct cost per service act:	
Area X	$1.00
Area Y	1.50

Example 18-7 shows the condensed income statements of the Health Spa Company for 2007 and 2008. The direct costs incurred in 2007 and 2008 are $10,800 and $13,200, or 45% and 55% of the total estimated (and actual) direct costs. Thus, the company recognizes revenues of $27,000 (45% × $60,000) and $33,000 (55% × $60,000) in each year. It allocates $450 of the $1,000 initial direct costs to 2007 and $550 to 2008 based on the 45% and 55% recognition of revenues. Use of the proportional performance method is appropriate in this case because the company recognizes revenues neither too early (at the time of the signing), before the earning process is complete, nor too late (at the completion of the contract). Therefore, the method helps to ensure that economic reality is not distorted. ♦

---

10.   In this example all members used the health spa facilities their entire permissible number of times. In reality this usage would probably not occur. In such a situation the company would have to make estimates of the expected usage, and make adjustments for the differences between actual and estimated usage. This topic is beyond the scope of this chapter. Also, in this example we assumed for simplicity that the company sold no new memberships in 2008.

EXAMPLE 18-7	Condensed Income Statements (Proportional Performance Method)			

	For Year Ended December 31			
	2007		**2008**	
Revenues		$27,000[b]		$33,000[e]
Expenses:				
Initial direct costs	$ 450[c]		$ 550[f]	
Direct costs	10,800[a]		13,200[d]	
Indirect costs	2,000		2,000	
Total expenses		(13,250)		(15,750)
Net Income		$13,750		$17,250

a. ($1 × 3,600) + ($1.50 × 4,800) = $10,800

b. $\frac{($1 \times 3,600) + ($1.50 \times 4,800)}{$24,000 \text{ total direct costs}}$ = 45%; $60,000 receipts × 45% = $27,000

c. 45% × $1,000 = $450

d. ($1 × 2,400) + ($1.50 × 7,200) = $13,200

e. $\frac{($1 \times 2,400) + ($1.50 \times 7,200)}{$24,000}$ = 55%; $60,000 receipts × 55% = $33,000

f. 55% × $1,000 = $550

SECURE YOUR KNOWLEDGE 18-2

- The two methods of accounting for long-term construction contracts are the:
  - Percentage-of-completion method—revenues and expenses are allocated to, and inventory is increased, each period during the life of the contract based on the progress made toward completion, and
  - Completed contract method—no profit is recognized until the project is completed.
- For the percentage-of-completion method, a company can determine the percentage of the project completed by using either:
  - Input measures that use the percentage of the costs incurred to date divided by the total estimated costs for the contract (cost-to-cost method) or the percentage of work performed to date (e.g., measured as labor hours, machine hours) divided by the estimated total work to be performed (efforts-expended method), or
  - Output measures that use the results achieved to date (e.g., units delivered, tons produced) divided by the total estimated results of the contract.
- Under the percentage-of-completion method:
  - The total revenue recognized to date is computed by multiplying the percentage of the project completed by the estimated total revenue.
  - The total revenue to be recognized in the current period is computed by subtracting the total revenue recognized to date from the total revenue recognized in prior periods.
  - The Construction in Progress account is increased by the amount of gross profit (revenues less expenses).
  - Any partial billings are recorded in a contra-account to Construction in Progress. If the net amount is a debit, it is reported as an asset, and if the net amount is a credit, it is reported as a liability.
- A loss on long-term construction contracts may be either a(n):
  - Loss in the current period, which is recorded in the current period as an adjustment to the Construction in Progress account under the percentage-of-completion method (no adjustment is necessary under the completed contract method); or

(continued)

- Overall loss on the contract—under both the percentage-of-completion and completed-contract methods, the total estimated loss is recognized in the current period.
- Revenue from long-term service contracts is recognized based on the proportionate performance of each act (proportionate performance method).

REVENUE RECOGNITION AFTER THE PERIOD OF SALE

As we discussed earlier in the chapter, the installment and cost recovery methods are the two principal ways of recognizing revenue after the sale. We discuss each method in this section.

Installment Method

Installment *sales* involve a financing agreement whereby the customer signs a contract, makes a small down payment, and agrees to make periodic payments over an extended period, often several years. The customer accepts possession of the item when the contract is signed (thereby enjoying its use during the payment period), while the seller retains legal title until the payments are complete. Companies may use installment sales contracts for merchandise because of a customer's lower credit rating, and in certain real estate transactions. **APB Opinion No. 10** found the installment *method* of recognizing revenue for installment *sales* generally to be unacceptable. The Board, however, did agree that there are *exceptional* cases where receivables are collected over an extended period and the probability of collection is not reasonably assured. In these exceptional cases, the installment method is used.[11] In addition, the installment method is still acceptable for income tax purposes under certain circumstances.

It is important to distinguish between an "installment sale" as a legal contract involving a buyer and a seller, and the "installment method" of revenue recognition. For example, for an installment *sale*, a company may recognize revenue in full at the time of the sale if collectibility is reasonably assured. In such a case the company must estimate the costs to be incurred in the future, such as costs of collection and bad debts, so that appropriate matching occurs. Alternatively, a company may use the installment *method* of revenue recognition for a sales transaction that is *not* an installment *sale*. In summary, a company selects the installment method of revenue recognition because the collectibility of the receivable from the sale is not reasonably assured. This decision is independent of the legal form of the contract. Therefore, we discuss the installment method of revenue recognition in this chapter irrespective of the legal form of the contract.

A company completes the following steps when it uses the installment method:

1. It records total sales, cost of goods sold, and collections in the normal manner during the year.
2. At the end of the year, it identifies sales for which the installment method is used. It reverses the revenue and the related cost of goods sold that were recorded during the year, and it recognizes the deferred gross profit.
3. At the end of the year, it computes the gross profit rate on the sales recognized under the installment method for that year. It calculates the rate by dividing the deferred gross profit recognized in step 2 by the related installment sales for the year.
4. It recognizes a portion of the deferred gross profit as gross profit for the year by multiplying the cash collected on the sales recognized under the installment method during the year times the gross profit rate calculated in step 3.
5. In future years it reduces the remaining deferred gross profit and recognizes the gross profit. It calculates the amount of gross profit to recognize by mulitplying the cash collected each year from the previous sales recognized under the installment method times the gross profit rate for the year in which those sales were made.

---

11. "Omnibus Opinion—1966," *op. cit.*, par. 12 and fn. 8.

Example: Installment Method

To illustrate the installment method, consider the following information for the Lee Company in the first two years of its operations:

	2007	2008
Total credit sales	$500,000	$600,000
Total cost of goods sold	390,000	430,000
Installment method sales*	100,000	150,000
Installment method cost of goods sold*	75,000	105,000
Gross profit rate on installment method sales	25%	30%
Cash receipts on installment method sales		
2007 sales	20,000	30,000
2008 sales		40,000
Cash receipts on other credit sales	300,000	480,000

* Included in total credit sales and total cost of goods sold, respectively.

Assume that the company uses the perpetual inventory method and that, for simplicity, interest on the installment receivables is ignored. The Lee Company records the preceding events as follows:

During 2007

Accounts Receivable	500,000	
Sales		500,000
Cost of Goods Sold	390,000	
Inventory		390,000

The company records the total sales and cost of goods sold for the year in the normal manner. It does not separate the sales recognized under the installment method.

During 2007

Cash	320,000	
Accounts Receivable		320,000

The company recognizes cash collections in the normal manner. Of these collections, $20,000 is for installment sales and $300,000 for other credit sales.

December 31, 2007

Sales	100,000	
Cost of Goods Sold		75,000
Deferred Gross Profit, 2007 ($100,000 × 25%)		25,000

The company identifies the sales recognized under the installment method and the related cost of goods sold from the accounting records and "reverses" them. It also recognizes the deferred gross profit. It computes a 25% gross profit rate for 2007 (deferred gross profit of $25,000 divided by the sales of $100,000).

December 31, 2007

Deferred Gross Profit, 2007	5,000	
Gross Profit Realized on Installment Method Sales		5,000

The company uses the gross profit rate of 25% to recognize the gross profit on the cash collected. Since the company collected $20,000 on these sales for 2007, it reduces the deferred gross profit and recognizes a gross profit of $5,000 ($20,000 × 25%). It closes the gross profit account to Income Summary along with the other sales, cost of goods sold, and expense accounts (not illustrated). The company reports the preceding events in its financial statements as we show in Example 18-8.

EXAMPLE 18-8   Lee Company: Partial Financial Statements

Partial Income Statement
For Year Ended December 31, 2007

Sales	$ 400,000[a]
Cost of goods sold	(315,000)[b]
Gross profit	$ 85,000
Gross profit realized on installment method sales	5,000
Total gross profit	$ 90,000

Partial Balance Sheet
December 31, 2007

Current Assets

Accounts receivable		$100,000[c]
Installment accounts receivable	$ 80,000[d]	
Less: Deferred gross profit	(20,000)[e]	60,000

a. $500,000 — $100,000
b. $390,000 — $75,000
c. $500,000 — $320,000 — $80,000 (from footnote *d*)
d. $100,000 — $20,000
e. $25,000 — $5,000

You should understand three aspects of the financial statements. First, in the income statement a company should report the gross profit on the sales recognized under the installment method separately from the gross profit on the other sales. In Example 18-8, Lee Company reported the $5,000 of gross profit on its installment sales separately from the $85,000 of gross profit on its "regular" sales. Some companies, however, might combine the two amounts and disclose the gross profit on these sales in the notes to the financial statements. Second, a company usually includes installment accounts receivable in current assets on the balance sheet under the operating cycle concept. Finally, a company usually deducts the deferred gross profit from the installment accounts receivable on the balance sheet, as we show in the lower part of Example 18-8. Some companies, however, include the deferred gross profit as a current liability rather than as a contra asset. Such reporting is inconsistent with the concept of a liability, because no future cash outflow will occur. We support reporting the deferred gross profit as a contra asset because, as we discussed earlier in the chapter, accounts receivable is reduced from selling price to cost.

In 2008 the Lee Company records the following:

During 2008

Accounts Receivable	600,000	
Sales		600,000
Cost of Goods Sold	430,000	
Inventory		430,000
Cash	550,000	
Accounts Receivable		550,000

Of these $550,000 collections, $70,000 is for installment sales and $480,000 for other credit sales. Note that the cash collections on the installment sales in 2008 include amounts from sales made in 2007 ($30,000) and 2008 ($40,000).

December 31, 2008

Sales	150,000	
Cost of Goods Sold		105,000
Deferred Gross Profit, 2008 ($150,000 × 30%)		45,000

The company "reverses" the sales recognized under the installment method and the related cost of goods sold for 2008, and recognizes the deferred gross profit for 2008. The gross profit rate in 2008 is 30% ($45,000 ÷ $150,000).

December 31, 2008

Deferred Gross Profit, 2007	7,500	
Deferred Gross Profit, 2008	12,000	
Gross Profit Realized on Installment Method Sales		19,500

During 2008 the company collected $30,000 on its 2007 installment method sales, for which its gross profit is 25%. As we show, the company reduces the deferred gross profit from 2007 and recognizes a gross profit of $7,500 ($30,000 × 25%). The company also collected $40,000 on its 2008 installment method sales, for which its gross profit is 30%. In the entry the company reduces the deferred gross profit for 2008 and recognizes a gross profit of $12,000 ($40,000 × 30%) on those collections. The combined gross profit for 2008 is $19,500, which the company closes to Income Summary.

The Lee Company includes the realized gross profit of $19,500 in its 2008 income statement, in addition to the sales and the cost of goods sold from those sales on which it recognized revenue at the time of sale. The company includes the installment accounts receivable of $160,000 ($100,000 − $20,000 + $150,000 − $30,000 − $40,000) and a deferred gross profit of $45,500 ($25,000 − $5,000 + $45,000 − $7,500 − $12,000) on its December 31, 2008 balance sheet. Note that the balance in the deferred gross profit account is the balance of the installment receivables multiplied by the gross profit percentage. ♦

Additional Considerations for the Installment Method

We discuss several additional factors that affect the accounting under the installment method in this section.

Alternative Accounting and Reporting

In the preceding example we assumed that it is acceptable to report only the gross profit amount in the income statement because the installment sales revenue is not material. If a company considered the installment sales to be material, then it should report separately both the installment sales and the cost of goods sold (a procedure that we used in the discussion of long-term construction contracts earlier in the chapter). In this situation the Lee Company would record an alternative journal entry as follows (using the amounts for 2007):

Deferred Gross Profit, 2007	5,000	
Installment Cost of Goods Sold	15,000	
Installment Sales		20,000

Under this alternative, when the company receives cash, it reduces the deferred gross profit as before. However, it records sales revenue at an amount equal to the cash collected. It also recognizes an appropriate amount of cost of goods sold; in this case, 75% of the sales amount. Then the company would report the installment sales of $20,000 and deduct the installment cost of goods sold of $15,000 to show its gross profit of $5,000 for 2007.

Operating Expenses

As we have seen, a company matches the cost of goods sold against the installment sales in the same period as the sales. It does *not* defer operating expenses. Instead, it recognizes them in the normal way on an accrual basis. That is, the company recognizes them either in the period incurred, such as general and administrative salaries, or by systematic and rational allocation, such as depreciation on an office building.

Interest Charges

A company making an installment sale typically charges the buyer interest because of the extended collection period. The company usually includes the interest charge as a component of the periodic payment specified in the sales contract. The normal practice is to make the installment payment an equal amount each period, so that each succeeding payment includes a smaller interest component and a larger principal payment. In other words, the interest is treated in the same way as a loan.

When a company includes interest in an installment sale, it accounts for the interest revenue separately. It separates each installment payment received into two components, interest revenue and a reduction in the installment accounts receivable. It records the interest revenue on an accrual basis in the normal manner (in the period earned), and recognizes the gross profit as it receives cash, as we discussed earlier.

Uncollectible Accounts

Installment sales contracts usually allow a company to repossess the item if the buyer defaults. If the experience of the company indicates that the price at which the repossessed item can be sold will be greater than the remaining payments on the original installment sale, then a provision for bad debts is not necessary. However, if past experience indicates that the expected resale price will be less than the payments, the company should recognize bad debt expense and an allowance for doubtful installment accounts receivable.

and vice versa

Defaults and Repossessions

When a company repossesses an item, it records the inventory and writes off the related receivable and deferred gross profit. For example, assume that the Lee Company repossesses an item it sold in 2007 with a gross profit of 25%, and that the fair value of the repossessed item is $600. If $1,000 remained unpaid, it records the repossession as follows:

Repossessed Inventory	600	
Deferred Gross Profit	250	
Allowance for Doubtful Installment Accounts		
Receivable	150	
Accounts Receivable		1,000

The company eliminates the deferred gross profit ($1,000 × 25%) related to the remaining cash payments and debits the $150 "lost" on the recovery to Allowance for Doubtful Installment Accounts Receivable, which it established when it recognized the bad debt expense.

Incidental Sales

As we mentioned earlier, a company is most likely to use the installment method in special situations. In these cases, it is likely that the company recognizes a gain rather than a revenue and expense, because the transaction is incidental or peripheral to its normal operations. For example, suppose a company sold for $100,000 land that had originally cost $40,000. The company uses the installment method and collects $30,000 the first year. It make the following journal entries:

To Record the Sale

Accounts Receivable	100,000	
Land		40,000
Deferred Gain		60,000

To Record the Cash Collection and the Gain for the Year

Cash	30,000	
Accounts Receivable		30,000
Deferred Gain	18,000	
Gain on Sale of Land		18,000*

*$30,000 × ($60,000 ÷ $100,000)

In later years, the company eliminates a proportion of the deferred gain and recognizes a gain when it collects each remaining cash receipt.

Cost Recovery Method

If a company makes a sale in which there is a very high degree of uncertainty about the collectibility of the sales price, it defers recognition of any profit until the company has recovered the cost of the entire sale. As with the installment method, **APB Opinion No. 10** found the **cost recovery method** of recognizing revenue generally to be unacceptable. The Board, however, did agree that there are exceptional cases where receivables are collected over an extended period and where the terms of the transaction provide no reasonable basis for estimating the degree of collectibility. In these exceptional situations, the cost recovery method may be used. For example, a company may sell an unprofitable division, thereby transferring the risks and benefits of ownership, but agree that the purchaser will pay with the net operating cash inflows generated by the division.

Under the cost recovery method a company records sales, cost of goods sold, and collections during the year in the usual manner (as with the installment method). In contrast to the installment method, however, it does *not* recognize a gross profit under the cost recovery method until it has recovered *all* the cost of the item sold. Once it has recovered the cost, it records gross profit at an amount equal to the cash it receives in the period.

Example: Cost Recovery Method   Consider the following information for the Patken Company:

Sale of property under cost recovery method	$20,000
Cost of property sold (net)	12,000
Cash collections	
2007	5,000
2008	9,000
2009	6,000

The company records the preceding events using the cost recovery method as follows:

During 2007

Accounts Receivable	20,000	
Deferred Gross Profit		8,000
Property (net)		12,000
Cash	5,000	
Accounts Receivable		5,000

The company records the transaction and defers the profit. It does not recognize a gross profit when it collects the cash because it has not yet recovered the $12,000 cost of the property sold.

During 2008

Cash	9,000	
Accounts Receivable		9,000

December 31, 2008

Deferred Gross Profit	2,000	
Gross Profit Realized on Cost Recovery Transactions		2,000

In 2007, the company recovered $5,000 of the $12,000 cost of the property sold. Therefore, of the $9000 cash collected in 2008, the first $7,000 collected completes the recovery of the cost, and the remaining $2,000 collected results in the recognition of a gross profit of $2,000.

During 2009

Cash	6,000	
Accounts Receivable		6,000

December 31, 2009

Deferred Gross Profit	6,000	
Gross Profit Realized on Cost Recovery Transactions		6,000

Since the company recovered the total cost in 2008, the $6,000 cash collected in 2009 results in the recognition of an equal amount of gross profit. The Patken Company includes the gross profit in its income statement each year, and includes the Accounts Receivable, less the balance in the Deferred Gross Profit account, on its ending balance sheet. ♦

Comparison of the Installment and Cost Recovery Methods

As we discussed earlier, *APB Opinion No. 10* allows the use of either the installment or cost recovery methods in certain exceptional circumstances and makes no distinction between the situations in which each should be applied. If collectibility is not reasonably assured, revenue should *not* be recognized at the time of sale. Instead, the installment method should be used. (Also, income tax rules allow the installment method to be used in certain situations for computing taxable income.) Since the cost recovery method is a more conservative revenue recognition method, it should be used only when such conservatism is appropriate. For example, **if the collectibility is *extremely* uncertain or there is *no* reliable basis for estimating the collectibility, then the cost recovery method is appropriate.** The method may also be used if there is significant uncertainty about the profitability of a new venture or product and for certain real estate transactions, as we discuss later in the chapter.

REVENUE RECOGNITION DELAYED UNTIL A FUTURE EVENT OCCURS

In certain situations **there may not be a sufficient transfer of the risks and benefits of ownership for a company to recognize revenue.** For example, a company may "sell" a subsidiary and accept a long-term interest-bearing note receivable. However, it may still be involved in the subsidiary's management through representation on the board of directors, perhaps because the buyer made a very small down payment. In such situations, the company should not recognize either the receivable or the deferred gross profit. Instead, the company uses the deposit method.

7 Account for revenue recognition delayed until a future event occurs.

Example: Deposit Method

Assume that the Oscar Company sells a subsidiary to the Pet Company and accepts a $500,000 down payment and a 10% note for the balance of the sale price of $7 million. The net assets (i.e., book value) of the subsidiary are $5 million and the Pet Company uses the deposit method because it has the right to cancel the agreement for the next year. **The deposit method postpones the recognition of revenue until a company can determine whether it has made a sale for accounting purposes.** Until Oscar Company recognizes revenue (by any of the revenue recognition methods), it does not record a note receivable, and continues to report the property and any related debt (even if assumed by the Pet Company) on its balance sheet. However, it separately classifies the assets and liabilities under such headings as "assets of business transferred under contract" and "liabilities of business transferred." Also, for depreciable assets the Oscar Company continues to record depreciation expense on the property. It records the down payment and all payments of principal and interest received from Pet Company as a deposit. It reports them as a liability on its balance sheet if the interest will be returned because the terms of the contract are not fulfilled. For example, the Oscar Company records the receipt of the down payment as follows:

Cash	500,000	
Deposit from Purchaser		500,000

When the company eliminates the liability for the deposit because the circumstances have changed, it recognizes the revenue. For example, suppose that the Oscar Company recognizes revenue (gain) one year after the original transaction. It records the note receivable and a gain, eliminates the net assets of the subsidiary and the deposit, and recognizes the interest revenue as follows:

Interest Receivable (10% × $6,500,000)	650,000	
Note Receivable	6,500,000	
Deposit from Purchaser	500,000	
Interest Revenue		650,000
Gain ($7,000,000 − $5,000,000)		2,000,000
Net Assets of Subsidiary		5,000,000

Alternatively, the company recognizes any interest that is *not* subject to refund as earned in the normal manner, and records only the principal portion of any payments as a deposit. If, instead, the contract is canceled without a refund, Oscar recognizes the deposits forfeited by Pet Company as income.

SECURE YOUR KNOWLEDGE 18-3

- In extreme cases where the ultimate collection of cash is uncertain, a company may delay the recognition of revenue using either the installment method or the cost recovery method.
  - Under the installment method, the company defers any gross profit (revenues less cost of goods sold) on installment sales in the period of the sale. It then recognizes gross profit each period by multiplying the gross profit percentage (deferred gross profit for the year divided by installment sales for the year) by the cash actually collected.
  - Under the cost recovery method, the company defers any gross profit on the sale in the period of the sale. Once the cost of the item sold has been recovered, the company will recognize gross profit at an amount equal to the cash it receives each period.
- If there was not a sufficient transfer of the risks and benefits of ownership, a company may use the deposit method and defer revenue recognition until a future event occurs.
  - Under the deposit method, any cash received is recorded as a deposit (a liability). Once circumstances change so that there has been a sufficient transfer of the risks and benefits of ownership, revenue is recognized.

ADDITIONAL ISSUES

We dicuss the special revenue recognition guidance of the SEC and international issues in this section.

SAB No. 104

In 1999, the Securities and Exchange Commission issued *Staff Accounting Bulletin No. 101*. The SEC updated it with *SAB No. 104* in 2004. These *Bulletins* provided guidance on revenue recognition issues. Although they did not change accounting principles, they did have some significant effects on the practice of revenue recognition, with many companies changing their policies. The *Bulletins* also give many examples of applying revenue recognition to specific factual situations. They also require that all companies disclose their revenue recognition policies.

LINK TO INTERNATIONAL DIFFERENCES

The basic international accounting standards for revenue recognition are generally very similar to those of the United States. However, there are some terminology differences. For example, international standards say that revenue is recognized when it is probable that future economic benefits will flow to the company and these benefits can be measured reliably. Some of the specific criteria are that the significant risks and rewards of ownership are transferred, the company retains neither continuing managerial involvement nor effective control, and can measure the costs reliably.

For construction contracts, international accounting standards also require the use of the percentage-of-completion method if the outcome can be estimated reliably, although they do not give as much guidance as U.S. principles on how to measure the estimated cost to complete. Otherwise, international standards require the use of the zero-profit method, which is a cost recovery method, in contrast to the completed contract method required by U.S. principles.

SUMMARY OF ALTERNATIVE REVENUE RECOGNITION METHODS

Exhibit 18-2 summarizes the various alternative revenue recognition methods. It includes the reasons for the use of each method and the primary impacts on the financial statements.

APPENDIX: ADDITIONAL REVENUE RECOGNITION ISSUES

The specific accounting principles used for software revenue recognition, sales of franchises, real estate sales, and retail land sales are important. These are significant industries and their rules should help you understand revenue recognition. In certain industries, consignment sales also are used frequently and the recognition of revenue on such sales is an important issue.

8 Understand software revenue recognition, franchises, real estate sales, retail land sales, and consignment sales.

SOFTWARE REVENUE RECOGNITION

The recognition of revenue by a company selling software can be complicated. *AICPA Statement of Position No. 97-2* provides the following guidance[12]:

1. If a company has an agreement to deliver software that requires significant production, modification, or customization of software, it uses contract accounting (e.g., percentage of completion) for the agreement.
2. If a company has an agreement to deliver software that does *not* require significant production, modification, or customization of software, it recognizes revenue

---

12. "Software Revenue Recognition," *AICPA Statement of Position No. 97-2* (New York: AICPA, 1997).

EXHIBIT 18-2   **Summary of Alternative Revenue Recognition Methods**

Method	Reasons for Use	Impact on Financial Statements
Accrual	Revenue is earned and realized or realizable in the period of sale.	Revenue and expenses are recognized in the period of sale, and net assets are increased.
Percentage-of-completion	Revenue is recognized during production because all four criteria are met (see p. 895).	Revenue and expenses are recognized in the period of production and inventory (net assets) is increased.
Completed-contract	Revenue is recognized at the completion of the contract because at least one of the four criteria is not met.	Revenue and expenses are recognized at the completion of production (sale) and net assets are increased.
Proportional performance	Same principles as percentage-of-completion, but applied to service contracts.	
Completion-of-production	Revenue is recognized at the completion of production because it is earned and the selling price is realizable due to the immediate marketability at quoted prices and unit interchangeability.	Revenue and expenses are recognized at the completion of production and inventory (net assets) is increased.
Installment	Revenue is recognized as cash is received because it is earned in the period of sale but is not realizable until the period of collection.	Gross profit is deferred in the period of sale and recognized as cash is received, at which time net assets are increased (deferred gross profit is reduced).
Cost recovery	Revenue is recognized after the cost has been recovered because it is earned in the period of sale but is not realizable due to the extreme uncertainty of collection.	Gross profit is deferred in the period of sale and recognized after the cost has been recovered, at which time net assets are increased (deferred gross profit is reduced).
Deposit	Revenue is not recognized until a future event occurs since it has not been earned because the risks and benefits of ownership have not been transferred.	All cash receipts are recorded as liabilities until a future event occurs, at which time revenue is recognized using one of the alternative methods.

    when (a) evidence of an agreement exists, (b) delivery has occurred, (c) its fee is fixed or determinable, and (d) collectibility is probable.

3. A company separately accounts for a service element if (a) the services are not essential to any other element of the transaction, and (b) the services are stated separately in the contract so that the total price would vary as the result of including the services.

4. Software arrangements may include multiple elements such as additional software products, upgrades and/or enhancements, rights to exchange or return software, and customer support. If contract accounting does not apply, a company must allocate its fee to the various elements based on fair values. Fair value is determined by either the price charged when the element is sold separately, or by a price set by management for each element when the element is not sold separately. If fair values do not exist, the company defers all revenue until it can determine the fair value, or until it has delivered all the elements.

5. A company must allocate any discounts proportionately to all the elements, except that none can be allocated to upgrade rights.

FRANCHISES

A **franchise agreement** involves the granting of business rights by the **franchisor** to a **franchisee** who will operate the franchised business. Franchises are common in several industries, such as fast foods (**McDonald's**), motels (**Holiday Inn**), and auto rentals (**Hertz**). Franchise agreements vary but usually involve an initial payment (called an **initial franchise fee**) by the franchisee and ongoing payments of **continuing franchise fees.** For the initial franchise fee, the franchisor may provide assistance in site selection and construction, equipment acquisitions, projections of franchisee's revenues and expenses, and other matters. For the continuing franchise fees, the franchisor may provide advertising, quality control, training of personnel, and budgeting and other accounting services.

Sometimes the franchisor collects the initial franchise fee far in advance of performing its services. At other times collection of part of the initial franchise fee is deferred until the franchise is operating successfully. Occasionally, the continuing franchise fee is not large enough to cover the franchisor's cost of the ongoing services provided. However, the initial franchise fee is unusually large (so, in effect, it involves a prepayment by the franchisee for the continuing services). Or the franchise agreement may involve the potential refund of the initial franchise fee if certain conditions or obligations are not met by the franchisor.

All these revenue recognition issues of the franchisor are addressed by **FASB Statement No. 45.**[13] The franchisor recognizes the initial franchise fee as revenue when it has substantially performed all material services. **Substantial performance** means that (1) the franchisor has no obligation to refund any cash received or forgive any unpaid notes receivable, and (2) the franchisor has performed substantially all the initial services required by the franchise agreement. The start of operations by the franchisee is the earliest point at which substantial performance has occurred, unless the franchisor can demonstrate earlier performance. At this point it recognizes revenue under the accrual method. A franchisor uses installment or cost recovery methods for revenue recognition only in those exceptional cases when revenue is collectible over an extended period and no reasonable basis exists for estimating collectibility.

The franchisor recognizes continuing franchise fees as revenue as it earns the fees and they are receivable from the franchisee. The continuing fee may not cover the cost of continuing services provided by the franchisor because there is a large initial fee that is, in effect, a prepayment for continuing services. In such cases, the franchisor records a portion of the initial fee as a liability and amortizes the amount to franchise revenue over the life of the franchise.

Example: Accounting for Initial Franchise Fees

Assume that the Castle Company sells a franchise that requires an initial franchise fee of $70,000. A down payment of $20,000 cash is required, with the balance covered by the issuance of a $50,000, 10% note, payable by the franchisee in five equal annual installments. The following are alternatives to account for this fee by the Castle Company (the franchisor):

1. Castle has substantially performed all material services, the refund period has expired, and the collectibility of the note is reasonably assured. Castle recognizes revenue as follows:

Cash	20,000	
Notes Receivable	50,000	
Franchise Revenue		70,000

---

13. "Accounting for Franchise Fee Revenue," *FASB Statement of Financial Accounting Standards No. 45* (Stamford, Conn.: FASB, 1981), par. 3–7.

2. The refund period has expired and the collectibility of the note is reasonably assured, but Castle has not substantially performed all material services. Castle does not recognize revenue, but instead recognizes a liability as follows:

Cash	20,000	
Notes Receivable	50,000	
Unearned Franchise Fees		70,000

Castle will recognize the unearned franchise fees as revenue when it has performed all material services.

3. Castle has substantially performed all services and the collectibility of the note is reasonably assured, but the refund period has not expired. Castle does not recognize revenue, but instead recognizes a liability as follows:

Cash	20,000	
Notes Receivable	50,000	
Unearned Franchise Fees		70,000

Castle will recognize the unearned franchise fees as revenue when the refund period expires.

4. Castle has substantially performed all services and the refund period has expired, but the collectibility of the note is not reasonably assured. Castle recognizes revenue by the installment or cost recovery method. If we assume that Castle uses the installment method, it recognizes revenue of $20,000 as follows:

Cash	20,000	
Notes Receivable	50,000	
Unearned Franchise Fees		50,000
Franchise Revenue		20,000

Since Castle is using the installment method, it recognizes the unearned franchise fees as revenue in the amount of $10,000 each year as it receives cash.

5. The refund period has expired, but Castle has not substantially performed all services and there is no basis for estimating the collectibility of the note. Castle does *not* recognize the note as an asset. Instead, it uses a form of the deposit method. For example, suppose Castle has developed an entirely new product whose success is uncertain and the franchisee will pay the note from the cash flows from the sale of the product, if any. Castle records the initial transaction as follows:

Cash	20,000	
Unearned Franchise Fees		20,000

Castle may recognize the unearned franchise fees as revenue under the accrual method in the normal manner at the completion of the services to be performed (if collectibility is reasonably assured). Alternatively, it may recognize revenue under the installment method if it has no basis for estimating the collectibility of the note. Alternatively, if Castle has earned the franchise fees through the substantial performance of all services, it would recognize franchise revenue of $20,000 instead of the liability.

6. Now assume that Castle has earned only $30,000 from providing initial services, with the balance being a down payment for continuing services. If the refund period has expired and the collectibility of the note is reasonably assured, Castle recognizes revenue of $30,000 as follows:

Cash	20,000	
Notes Receivable	50,000	
Franchise Revenue		30,000
Unearned Franchise Fees		40,000

Castle recognizes the unearned franchise fees of $40,000 as revenue when it performs the continuing services.

In all these cases except the fifth, Castle accounts for the collection of interest and principal on the note receivable in the usual manner. In the fifth situation, it does not recognize the note and revenue until a future event occurs. In addition, Castle accounts for its costs in the same way as its revenue recognition. That is, if it defers revenue, then it defers the related cost of goods sold. Then, when it recognizes revenue, it matches the cost of goods sold against the revenues. The *franchisee* accounts for its payments as an intangible asset. ♦

Example: Accounting for Continuing Franchise Fees

Assume that the Castle Company also charges the franchisee a continuing franchise fee of $9,000 per year. The following are alternatives to account for this fee by the Castle Company (the franchisor):

1. The fee is earned for providing continuing services:

Cash	9,000	
Continuing Franchise Fee Revenue		9,000

2. $1,000 of the fee is for national advertising:

Cash	9,000	
Continuing Franchise Fee Revenue		8,000
Unearned Franchise Fees		1,000

Castle recognizes the unearned franchise fees as revenue when it performs the advertising services and also records the costs as expenses.

In addition to providing services as part of the continuing franchise fee, a franchisor often sells supplies to the franchisee. These sales occur because the franchisor may be able to obtain quantity discounts from manufacturers or wholesalers, or to ensure the quality of the supplies. The franchisor records these sales and related expenses in the normal manner. ♦

Option to Purchase

In some franchise situations, the franchise agreement will include a provision allowing the franchisor an option to purchase the franchisee's business. If, at the time the franchise agreement is signed and the option is granted, an understanding exists that the option will be exercised (or it is probable that the franchisor ultimately will acquire the franchise), the franchisor does not recognize the initial franchise fee as revenue. Instead it records the initial franchise fee as a liability. When the franchisor exercises its option and acquires the franchise, it records the liability as a reduction in its investment.

REAL ESTATE SALES

In real estate sales, a company may sell land or a building or both. The land may be developed or undeveloped and the seller may be responsible for making improvements. The building may be completed or in the process of construction and may be for commercial use, such as a factory or office building, or residential use, such as a house or apartment building. Accounting for real estate sales is defined by **FASB Statement No. 66.** We discuss only the basic rules here because of their relevance to an understanding of revenue recognition alternatives.[14]

---

14. "Accounting for Sales of Real Estate," *FASB Statement of Financial Accounting Standards No. 66* (Stamford, Conn.: FASB, 1982), par. 5–43.

For real estate sales, **a selling company recognizes revenue and related expenses on the accrual basis in the normal manner in the period of the sale if** *all* **of the following conditions are met:**

1. A sale occurs.
2. The buyer's initial and continuing investments show a commitment to pay for the property.
3. The seller's receivable is not subject to having its liquidation rights reduced.
4. The seller has transferred to the buyer the usual risks and rewards of ownership, and does not have a continuing involvement with the property.

It is important to understand that these criteria address the conceptual issues we discussed earlier in the chapter, namely the economic substance of the transaction, the transfer of the risks and benefits of ownership, and the collectibility (realizability) of the receivable. **When any of the criteria are** *not* **met, the selling company recognizes revenue under an alternative method as follows:**

Credit: Digital Vision

- If the sale does not occur, the *deposit method* is used.
- If the buyer's initial and continuing investment is not adequate, the *installment method* is used if the recovery of the cost of the property is reasonably assured. The *cost recovery method* is used if recovery of the cost is not reasonably assured.
- If the seller's receivable is subject to having its liquidation rights reduced, the *cost recovery method* is used.
- If the seller has continuing involvement with the property and does not transfer substantially all the risks and benefits of ownership, generally revenue and related expenses are recognized at the time of sale with an adjustment to recognize its maximum possible loss.

Thus, various revenue recognition methods are appropriate depending on the circumstances. When a company has earned revenue and the related receivable is realized or realizable, the company recognizes revenue in full using the accrual method. When the earning process is not complete or realization has not occurred, the company uses an alternative method.

RETAIL LAND SALES

In retail land sales, a company may acquire a large tract of unimproved land that it divides into lots. It then "sells" these lots to widely dispersed retail customers (individuals) through intensive marketing programs. Generally, part of the marketing program involves an agreement by the company to improve the lots by installing roads, utilities, and related amenities such as golf courses, lakes, and recreational centers. These improvements will require large future capital outlays by the company. The company may agree to be continually involved in the operations of the recreational centers and to provide ongoing maintenance. The "sales contract" often has a low down payment, no (or limited) credit investigation of the buyer, periodic payments by the buyer that extend over several years, and the ability of the buyer to cancel the contract and obtain a refund within a specified period.

Several factors involved in retail land sales may affect the timing of revenue recognition by the company. These include the collectibility of the receivables, the financial ability of the company to fulfill its obligations, the length of the refund period, the accumulation of collections, and the ongoing completion of the project. For retail land sales, **the selling company recognizes revenue and the related expenses in the period of the sale on the accrual basis if *all* of the following conditions are met:**

1. The buyer has made the down payment and each required subsequent payment until the period of cancellation with refund has expired.
2. The cumulative payments of principal and interest equal or exceed 10% of the contract sales price.
3. Collection experience for the project indicates that at least 90% of the contracts will be collected in full (a down payment of 20% is an acceptable indication of collectibility).
4. The receivable from the sale is not subject to subordination to new loans on the property.
5. The seller is not obligated to complete improvements of lots sold or to construct amenities or other facilities applicable to lots sold.

As with real estate sales, the intent of these rules is to be consistent with the conceptual issues related to revenue recognition. **When at least one of the preceding criteria is *not* met, the selling company recognizes revenue under an alternative method as follows:**

- The *percentage-of-completion method* is used if the first four criteria are met, there has been progress on the improvements, the work is likely to be completed according to plan, significant delays are not likely, and development is practical.
- The *installment method* of accounting is used if only the first two criteria are met and the seller is financially capable of meeting its obligations.
- The *deposit method* is used if the first two criteria are not met.

Again, the selling company recognizes revenue in full using the accrual method if it is earned and the receivable is realized or realizable. It uses an alternative method if either criterion is not met.[15]

CONSIGNMENT SALES

A manufacturer or wholesaler may transfer goods to a dealer to sell but retain the risks and benefits of ownership (as well as legal title). In these situations the dealer is acting as an *agent* for the manufacturer or wholesaler in the sale of the goods to a third party. The transfer of goods is a **consignment,** the manufacturer or wholesaler is the **consignor,** and the dealer is the **consignee.** The consignor is usually responsible for all costs associated with the goods and the consignee must exercise due care in storing and selling the goods. When the sale to the third party takes place, legal title passes directly to the third party from the consignor.

Accounting for consignments may be summarized as follows:

1. Since title remains with the consignor, when the goods are transferred from the consignor to the consignee, the consignor does *not* record the sale of inventory, and the consignee does *not* record the acquisition of inventory. → obtain, toget
2. The consignor recognizes revenue only when the sale to the third party occurs, because that is when it earns the revenue. The consignee must notify the consignor of the sale and must maintain detailed records of items held on consignment and various costs incurred.
3. The consignee uses a **Consignment-in** account. It credits the account for the proceeds received from the sale of the consigned goods and debits the same account

---

15. *Ibid.*, par. 45–49.

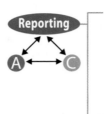

for costs that will be reimbursed by the consignor and for commissions it earns. At the end of the period, if the account has a debit balance, the consignor has an obligation for that amount to the consignee. That is, it represents a receivable of the consignee. Alternatively, if the account has a credit balance, the consignee has an obligation to the consignor. That is, it represents a liability of the consignee. The consignee reports the Commissions Earned account as operating revenue on its income statement.

4. The consignor uses a **Consignment-out** account, which is a special inventory account. When it ships goods on consignment, it debits the account for the cost of the inventory shipped (and credits the normal inventory account). In addition, the consignor debits any consignment costs (e.g., transportation charges) it incurs to the account. When notified by the consignee, the consignor credits the account for the costs incurred for the sale of consigned goods and debits these costs to the respective expense accounts. The consignor reports any balance in the Consignment-out account as consignment inventory on its ending balance sheet.

SUMMARY

At the beginning of the chapter, we identified several objectives you would accomplish after reading the chapter. The objectives are listed below, each followed by a brief summary of the key points in the chapter discussion.

1. **Understand the revenue recognition alternatives.** The usual point of revenue recognition is the time of sale (delivery). Revenue recognition may also be advanced by recording revenue during production, or deferred until cash receipt.
2. **Explain revenue recognition at the time of sale, during production, and at the time of cash receipt.** If a company recognizes revenue at the time of sale, it recognizes revenue, the related expense, and the increase in net assets at the same time. If a company recognizes revenue during production, it recognizes the gross profit (revenue less the related expense) during production even though the inventory has not been transferred to the customer. It increases the value of the inventory from its cost to its selling price, and the increase in the value of the net assets occurs at the same time. If a company recognizes revenue as it receives cash, it records the receivable, removes the inventory, and records the deferred gross profit as a contra account to Accounts Receivable. It recognizes the gross profit (revenue less the related expense) as it collects the cash.
3. **Explain the conceptual issues regarding revenue recognition.** The decision to recognize revenue focuses on three factors: (1) the economic substance of the event takes precedence over the legal form of the transaction; (2) the risks and benefits of ownership have been transferred to the buyer; and (3) the collectibility of the receivable from the sale is reasonably assured.
4. **Describe the alternative revenue recognition methods.** Revenue generally is recognized in the period of the sale. Revenue may also be recognized prior to the period of the sale under the percentage-of-completion method or the proportional performance method. Revenue may also be recognized at the completion of production. Revenue may also be recognized after the period of the sale under the installment method or the cost recovery method. Finally, revenue recognition may be delayed until a future event occurs, in which case the deposit method is used.
5. **Account for revenue recognition prior to the period of sale, including the percentage-of-completion and completed contract methods.** Under the percentage-of-completion method, the company recognizes profit each period during the life of the contract in proportion to the amount of the contract completed during the period. As it recognizes the profit, it also increases the value of the inventory, so that it values the inventory at the costs incurred plus the profit recognized to date, less any partial billings. Under the completed contract method, the company does not recognize profit during the life of the contract, but it recognizes the profit only when the contract is completed. During the life of the contract, the company records the inventory at cost, less any partial billings.
6. **Account for revenue recognition after the period of sale, including the installment and cost recovery methods.** Under the installment method, a company recognizes gross profit each period by multiplying the amount of cash it receives by the gross profit rate. Under the cost recovery method, a company does not recognize gross profit until it has recovered the cost of the item sold. Then it recognizes gross profit in an amount equal to the additional cash received during the period.
7. **Account for revenue recognition delayed until a future event occurs.** In certain situations, there may not be a sufficient transfer of the risks and benefits of ownership for a company to recognize revenue. In these situations, the company uses the deposit method and records all cash receipts as a liability, until it may recognize revenue.

8. **Understand software revenue recognition, franchises, real estate sales, retail land sales, and consignment sales.** (Appendix) If a company selling software has an agreement to deliver software that requires significant production, modifications, or customization, it uses "contract accounting". If contract accounting does not apply, a company must allocate its fee to the various elements based on fair values. If sufficiently objective evidence of fair values does not exist, the company defers all revenue until it has sufficient evidence, or until it has delivered all the elements.

A franchisor recognizes the initial franchise fee as revenue when it has substantially performed all material services. It recognizes continuing franchise fees as revenue as it earns the fees. For real estate sales, a company recognizes revenue in the period of sale if all of four conditions are met. For retail land sales, a company recognizes revenue in the period of sale if all of five conditions are met. In a consignment, the consignor transfers goods to the consignee for sale to a third party. The consignor recognizes revenue when the goods are transferred to the third party. The specific accounting rules for these industries are explained in the Appendix.

ANSWERS TO REAL REPORT QUESTIONS

Real Report 18-1 Answers

1. Johnson Controls uses the cost-to-cost method to determine the percentage complete. Under this method, the percentage of completion is measured by the ratio of actual costs incurred to date to expected total costs of the contract. This ratio is then multiplied by the total revenue on the contract to compute total revenue recognized to date. The expense recognized is the costs incurred during the current year.

2. In 2004, Johnson Controls reports an asset for the excess of construction in progress over partial billings of $328.6 million and a liability for partial billing in excess of construction in progress of $197.2 million. Combining these figures, Johnson Controls reports construction-in-progress in excess of partial billings (an asset) of $131.4 million.

3. By reporting a separate asset and liability on its balance sheet (as required by GAAP), Johnson Controls provides a more informative disclosure relating to its construction contracts than would be provided by netting these two amounts. Such a method provides more information to help financial statement users assess the risk of contract losses and the possibility of inaccurate estimates of the completion percentage.

4. By delaying the recognition of revenue until settlement, Johnson Controls is taking a conservative approach to revenue recognition. A more aggressive approach (allowable under generally accepted accounting principles) would be to estimate the amount of claims against customers in which collection is considered probable and include this estimated settlement amount in calculating profit on the contract. By including these probable settlements, the amount of gross profit recognized would be larger than if these claims were not included until the claim is settled.

QUESTIONS

Q18-1 Why is revenue sometimes recognized at a time other than the sale?

Q18-2 Distinguish between the terms *recognition* and *realization*.

Q18-3 Describe the effects on a company's financial statements of recognizing revenue at the time of sale, during production, and at the time of cash receipt.

Q18-4 What three factors affect the decision as to when to recognize revenue?

Q18-5 What are the five revenue recognition alternatives?

Q18-6 Under what circumstances does a company recognize revenue prior to the period of sale? What two methods may it use?

Q18-7 What are the differences between the two methods of accounting for long-term construction contracts?

Q18-8 Under what circumstances does a company use the percentage-of-completion method for long-term contracts?

Q18-9 How may the departure from the principle of recognizing revenue only at the time of the sale be justified when a company uses the percentage-of-completion method?

Q18-10 Describe input and output measures used in the percentage-of-completion method. Give an example of each.

Q18-11 How does a company account for losses under the two methods of accounting for long-term construction contracts?

Q18-12 How does a company classify the following accounts in its financial statements: Construction in Progress, Partial Billings, Construction Revenue, and Construction Expense?

Q18-13 How does a company recognize initial direct costs, direct costs, and indirect costs as expenses under the proportional performance method? Explain the reason for each method.

Q18-14 Under what circumstances does a company recognize revenue after the period of the sale? What two methods are used?

Q18-15 Describe the steps involved in the installment method.

Q18-16 Describe the differences between the cost recovery method and the installment method.

Q18-17 Describe the basic characteristics of the deposit method.

Q18-18 **(Appendix)** Distinguish between the initial franchise fee and continuing franchise fee. When is each recognized as revenue?

Q18-19 **(Appendix)** How is revenue recognized for real estate sales?

Q18-20 **(Appendix)** How is revenue recognized for retail land sales?

Q18-21 **(Appendix)** In a consignment, does the consignee or consignor retain title to the property? When is revenue recognized by the consignor? The consignee?

MULTIPLE CHOICE (AICPA Adapted)

Select the best answer for each of the following.

M18-1 Real estate sales are recognized by the accrual method if all of the conditions defined by *FASB Statement No. 66* are met. Which of the following is *not* one of the conditions defined by the *Statement?*
a. The seller has transferred to the buyer the usual risks and rewards of ownership in a transaction that is in substance a sale and does not have a continuing involvement with property.
b. A sale is consummated.
c. The buyer's initial and continuing investments are adequate to demonstrate a commitment to pay for the property.
d. The seller's receivable is subject to future subordination.

M18-2 Green Company, which began operations on January 1, 2007, appropriately uses the installment method of accounting. The following information is available for 2007:

Gross profit on sales	40%
Deferred gross profit at 12/31/07	$240,000
Cash collected on installment sales	450,000

What is the total amount of Green's installment sales for 2007?
a. $600,000   c. $850,000
b. $690,000   d. $1,050,000

M18-3 When should an indicated loss on a long-term contract be recognized under the completed-contract method and the percentage-of-completion method, respectively?

	Completed-Contract	Percentage-of-Completion
a.	Immediately	Over life of project
b.	Immediately	Immediately
c.	Contract complete	Over life of project
d.	Contract complete	Immediately

M18-4 In accounting for a long-term construction contract for which there is a projected profit, the balance in the construction-in-progress asset account at the end of the first year of work using the completed-contract method would be
a. Zero
b. The same as the percentage-of-completion method
c. Lower than the percentage-of-completion method
d. Higher than the percentage-of-completion method

M18-5 Warren Construction Company has consistently used the percentage-of-completion method of recognizing income. In 2007 Warren started work on a $6,000,000 construction contract, which was completed in 2008. The accounting records disclosed the following data:

	2007	2008
Progress billings	$2,200,000	$3,800,000
Costs incurred	1,800,000	3,600,000
Collections	1,400,000	4,600,000
Estimated cost to complete	3,600,000	—

How much income should Warren have recognized in 2007?
a. $200,000   c. $300,000
b. $220,000   d. $400,000

M18-6 Kramer Manufacturing Company ships goods to Sikes Company on consignment. When the consigned goods are delivered to Sikes, Kramer should record

	Sale of Inventory	Revenue
a.	No	Yes
b.	No	No
c.	Yes	No
d.	Yes	Yes

M18-7 During 2007 Morgan Company recognized $30,000 of sales under the cost recovery method. This is the first time the Morgan Company has used the cost recovery method in recognizing sales. The cost of goods sold related to these sales was $21,000. Cash collections in 2007 were $15,000, in 2008 were $10,000, and in 2009 were $5,000. What amount of gross profit should be recognized in 2007, 2008, and 2009?

	2007	2008	2009
a.	$9,000	$ 0	$ 0
b.	$4,500	$3,000	$1,500
c.	$ 0	$ 0	$9,000
d.	$ 0	$4,000	$5,000

M18-8 On January 1, 2006, Bartell Company sold its idle plant facility to Cooper, Inc., for $1,050,000. On this date, the plant had a depreciated cost of $735,000. Cooper paid $150,000 cash on January 1, 2006, and signed a $900,000 note bearing interest at 10%. The note was payable in three annual installments of $300,000 beginning January 1, 2007. Bartell appropriately accounted for the sale under the installment method. Cooper made a timely payment of the first installment on January 1, 2007 of $390,000, which included interest of $90,000 to date of payment. At December 31, 2007, Bartell has deferred gross profit of

a. $153,000   c. $225,000
b. $180,000   d. $270,000

M18-9 The Schmidt Company sells a franchise that requires an initial franchise fee of $50,000. A $10,000 down payment is required, with the balance covered by the issuance of a 12% note, payable in four equal installments. All material services have been substantially performed by the Schmidt Company, the refund period has expired, and the collectibility of the note is reasonably assured. The journal entry recorded by Schmidt Company should be

a.	Cash	10,000	
	Notes Receivable	40,000	
	Franchise Revenue		10,000
	Unearned Franchise Fees		40,000
b.	Cash	10,000	
	Notes Receivable	40,000	
	Franchise Revenue		50,000
c.	Cash	10,000	
	Notes Receivable	40,000	
	Unearned Franchise Fees		50,000
d.	Cash	10,000	
	Franchise Revenue		10,000

M18-10 On April 1, 2006, Pine Construction Company entered into a fixed-price contract to construct an apartment building for $6,000,000. Pine appropriately accounts for this contract under the percentage-of-completion method. Information relating to the contract is as follows:

	At December 31, 2006	At December 31, 2007
Percentage of completion	20%	60%
Estimated costs at completion	$4,500,000	$4,800,000
Income recognized (cumulative)	$ 300,000	$ 720,000

What is the amount of contract costs incurred during the year ended December 31, 2007?

a. $1,200,000   c. $1,980,000
b. $1,920,000   d. $2,880,000

EXERCISES

E18-1 *Revenue Recognition Alternatives* The Smith Construction Company received a contract on September 30, 2007 to build a warehouse over a period of 18 months. The contract price was $600,000 and the estimated cost to build was $400,000. The actual (and estimated) costs incurred and the payments made by the purchaser are as follows:

	Costs	Payments
September 30–December 31, 2007	$120,000	$ 90,000
January 1–December 31, 2008	240,000	210,000
January 1–March 31, 2009	40,000	300,000

Required
1. Compute the amount of revenue, expense, and gross profit each year for each of the following methods:
   a. Revenue recognition at the time of sale (completion)
   b. Revenue recognition during production
   c. Revenue recognition at the time of cash receipt
   d. Cost recovery (compute only the gross profit)
2. Which method provides the most useful information to users? Under what circumstances would the other methods provide more useful information?

E18-2 *Percentage-of-Completion Method* In 2007 Tarlo Company agrees to construct a highway for Brice County over a three-year period (2007 through 2009). The contract price is $1,200,000 and the construction costs (both actual and estimated) total $705,000 for the three years. The percentage completed at the end of each year is as follows: 2007, 20%; 2008, 75%; 2009, 100%.

Required

1. Prepare a schedule showing the amount of gross profit that Tarlo Company recognizes each year using the percentage-of-completion method.
2. Prepare a schedule showing the amount of gross profit that Tarlo Company recognizes each year using the completed-contract method.

E18-3 *Percentage of Completion* The King Construction Company began work on a contract in 2007. The contract price is $4,000,000, and the company uses the percentage-of-completion method. Other information relating to the contract is as follows:

	2007
Costs incurred during the year	$ 800,000
Estimated costs to complete, December 31	2,400,000
Billings during the year	600,000
Collections during the year	400,000

Required

1. How much gross profit or loss does King recognize in 2007?
2. Prepare the appropriate sections of the 2007 income statement and ending balance sheet.

E18-4 *Percentage of Completion* The Koolman Construction Company began work on a contract in 2007. The contract price is $3,000,000, and the company uses the percentage-of-completion method. Other information relating to the contract is as follows:

	2007	2008
Costs incurred during the year	$ 600,000	$ 700,000
Estimated costs to complete, December 31	1,400,000	1,200,000
Billings during the year	500,000	850,000
Collections during the year	400,000	800,000

Required

1. Compute the gross profit or loss recognized in 2007 and 2008.
2. Prepare the appropriate sections of the income statement and ending balance sheet for each year.

E18-5 **AICPA Adapted** *Percentage of Completion* Newberg Construction Corporation contracted to construct a building for $400,000. Construction began in 2007 and was completed in 2008. Data relating to the contract are as follows:

	Year Ended December 31,	
	2007	2008
Costs incurred	$200,000	$110,000
Estimated costs to complete	100,000	—

Required

Newberg uses the percentage-of-completion method as the basis for income recognition. For the years ended December 31, 2007 and 2008, respectively, how much income should Newberg report?

E18-6 **AICPA Adapted** *Long-Term Construction Contract* The Osborn Construction Company began operations January 2, 2007. During the year, Osborn entered into a contract with Redbeard Razor Corporation to construct a manufacturing facility. At that time, Osborn estimated that it would take five years to complete the facility at a total cost of $4,800,000. The total contract price for construction of the facility is $6,000,000. During the year, Osborn incurred $1,250,000 in construction costs related to the construction project. The estimated cost to complete the contract is $3,750,000. Redbeard was billed and paid 30% of the contract price.

Required

Prepare schedules to compute the amount of gross profit to be recognized for the year ended December 31, 2007 and the amount to be shown as "cost of uncompleted contract in excess of related billings" or "billings on uncompleted contract in excess of related costs" on December 31, 2007, under each of the following methods:

1. Completed-contract method
2. Percentage-of-completion method

Show supporting computations in good form.

E18-7 *Proportional Performance Method* The New Recreational Company sells two-year memberships to its recreational facilities. For $2,200 in advance, each member receives the right to 30 nights at the company's campgrounds, 20 rounds on its golf courses, and 50 hours on its bowling lanes. In 2007 the company sold 400 memberships. Members used the campgrounds for 4,100 nights, played 3,000 rounds of golf, and bowled for 10,000 hours. The relevant cost information for the 400 contracts is as follows:

Initial direct costs	$ 40,000
Annual indirect costs	100,000
Estimated (and actual) total direct costs for two-year period	340,000
Direct cost per	
Night at campground	10
Round of golf	15
Hour of bowling	5

Required
Prepare the income statement for 2007.

E18-8 *Revenue Recognition at Completion of Production* In 2007 the Sterling Farm Company produced 100,000 bushels of wheat at a cost of $2.00 per bushel. The company has a contract to deliver 80,000 bushels at $2.15 per bushel in 2008. Delivery costs are estimated to be $0.02 per bushel. For guaranteed price contracts, the company recognizes revenue at the completion of production; otherwise, it recognizes revenue at the time of delivery.

Required
1. Prepare summary journal entries for 2007 and 2008.
2. At what value is the inventory of the company carried after the delivery of the 80,000 bushels? Why?

E18-9 *Sales Under the Installment Method* Anibonita Company began operations in 2007. It sells goods on installment sales contracts; these transactions are considered to be exceptional, so it uses the installment method to recognize gross profit. The following is a summary of the installment sales, costs of installment sales, operating expenses, and collections for 2007 and 2008:

	2007	2008
Installment method sales	$80,000	$90,000
Costs of installment method sales	52,000	59,400
Operating expenses	13,000	15,000
Cash collections from		
2007 installment method sales	42,000	21,000
2008 installment method sales		41,000

Required
Using the installment method to recognize gross profits, prepare 2007 and 2008 condensed income statements for the Anibonita Company.

E18-10 *Sales Under the Installment Method* The following information is available for the Butler Company in 2007, its first year of operations:

Total credit sales (including installment method sales)	$205,000
Total cost of goods sold (including installment method cost of goods sold)	130,000
Installment method sales	65,000
Installment method cost of goods sold	39,000
Cash receipts on credit sales (including installment method sales of $20,000)	120,000

Required
1. Prepare the journal entries for 2007.
2. If the company collected $45,000 in 2008 on its 2007 installment method sales, prepare the appropriate journal entries in 2008.

E18-11 *Sales Under the Installment Method* The following information is available for the Butler Company, which began operations in 2007:

	2007	2008
Total credit sales (including installment method sales)	$100,000	$160,000
Total cost of goods sold (including installment method cost of goods sold)	72,000	105,000
Installment method sales	60,000	80,000
Installment method cost of goods sold	42,000	52,000
Cash receipts on installment method sales		
2007 sales	25,000	26,000
2008 sales		30,000
Cash receipts on other credit sales	28,000	85,000

Required
1. Prepare the journal entries for 2007 and 2008.
2. Prepare a partial income statement and a partial balance sheet for 2007.

E18-12 *Analysis of Installment Sales* The following partial information is available for the Cupp Company:

Installment method sales	$120,000	(3)
Installment method cost of goods sold	(1)	$63,000
Gross profit percentage	(2)	30%
Cash receipts on installment method sales		
2007 sales	25,000	(4)
2008 sales		(5)
Realized gross profit on installment method sales		
2007 sales	5,000	7,000
2008 sales		9,000

Required
Compute the unknown amounts. (Note: It is not necessary to compute the amounts in the numerical sequence.)

E18-13 *Adjusting Entries for Installment Sales* The Smookler Company uses the installment method for certain sales and experiences a constant gross profit rate of 20%. The following are the account balances at December 31, 2007 and 2008:

	Installment Receivables	Deferred Gross Profit	Installment Method Sales
2007	$50,000	$10,000	$100,000
2008	80,000	16,000	130,000

Required
Prepare the journal entries for 2008.

E18-14 *Cost Recovery* In 2007 the Huxley Company, a real estate company, purchased some raw land for $60,000 and resold it on credit for $90,000. Because of the speculative nature of the usefulness of the land, the company used the cost recovery method for the sale of the land. The cash collections in 2007, 2008, and 2009 were $25,000, $45,000, and $20,000, respectively.

Required
Prepare the journal entries for each year.

E18-15 *Deposit Method* On January 1, 2007, the Fritz Company sold a building in a depressed area for $200,000. The building had originally cost $500,000 and had a book value of $100,000. The sale agreement required the purchaser to pay $5,000 down and sign an 8% note for the balance. Interest on the note is payable at the end of each year; the interest is refundable if the following contingency is not met. The sale agreement is contingent on the commitment by the city government to support redevelopment of the area in which the building is located. Therefore, the company used the deposit method to record the sale.

Required
1. Prepare the journal entries for 2007.
2. On January 1, 2008 the city government made the necessary commitments. Prepare the appropriate journal entry.

E18-16 *Franchise (Appendix)* The Chocomalt Company sells franchises. For each franchise, the company charges an initial franchise fee of $28,000. The franchise agreement requires a down payment of $8,000, with the balance covered by the issuance of a $20,000, 12% note, payable by the franchisee in two equal annual installments.

Required
Prepare the journal entry required by the Chocomalt Company to record each initial franchise fee under each of the following independent situations:
1. All material services have been substantially performed, the refund period has expired, and the collectibility of the note is reasonably assured.
2. All material services have been substantially performed, the refund period has expired, and the collectibility of the note is not reasonably assured.
3. All material services have been substantially performed, the refund period has not expired, and the collectibility of the note is reasonably assured.

4. All material services have not been substantially performed, the refund period has expired, and there is no basis for esti-mating the collectibility of the note.
5. The refund period has expired and the collectibility of the note is reasonably assured, but all material services have not been substantially performed.

E18-17 *Consignee (Appendix)* On April 16, 2007 the Winger Company shipped 10 tractors to the Yuma Farm Supply Company on consignment. Each tractor cost $30,000 and the Winger Company incurred cash shipment costs of $100 per tractor. The consignment agreement required payment to Winger at year-end. On December 31, 2007 the consignee reported that it had sold six tractors for $36,000 each. The consignee paid the Winger Company the amount required under the agree-ment, after deducting the commission of 5% and advertising costs of $2,000 incurred by the consignee.

Required
Prepare the 2007 journal entries for the Yuma Farm Supply Company.

E18-18 *Consignor (Appendix)* Refer to the information in E18-17.

Required
1. Prepare the 2007 journal entries for the Winger Company.
2. What amount related to the consignment activities, and in what category, would the company report on its balance sheet on December 31, 2007?

PROBLEMS

P18-1 *Revenue Recognition Alternatives* Each of the following independent situations relates to the recognition of revenue:
a. Interest on loans made by a bank
b. Interest on loans made by a bank when the loans are in default
c. Collection of fares by an airline when the passengers make the reservations
d. Shipment of freight and mail by an airline before it receives payment
e. Imposition of a penalty (service charge) by a retailer on overdue accounts
f. Building a submarine for a foreign government
g. Growing and harvesting soybeans
h. Selling lots for vacation homes on long-term contracts with small down payments
i. Building houses in a subdivision
j. Growing timber over a 10-year period
k. Payments received by a producer for films that are licensed to movie theaters for two years, after which the rights are licensed to television networks for one year, and finally the rights revert to the producer
l. Rental of a building to another company for five years, with no payment of rent in the first year
m. "One cent" sale in which the first item is sold at full price and the second identical item is sold for $0.01
n. Sale of a season pass by a ski resort

Required
For each situation indicate when a company should recognize revenue.

P18-2 *Revenue Recognition Alternatives* The Slattery Company was formed on January 1, 2007 to build a single product. The company issued no-par common stock on that date for $300,000 cash. The product costs $20 to make, all of which is paid in cash at the time of production. The company sells each unit of the product for $35 on credit and incurs sales com-missions per unit of $5 cash. In 2007 the company produced 10,000 units, shipped 9,000 units, and received payment for 8,000 units.

Required
1. Prepare the 2007 income statement and ending balance sheet under each of the following methods:
   a. Revenue recognition at the time of sale (shipment)
   b. Revenue recognition during production
   c. Revenue recognition at the time of cash receipt

2. Which method provides the most useful information to users? Under what circumstances would the other methods provide more useful information?

3. In 2008 the company produced 15,000 units, shipped 16,000 units, and received payment for 17,000 units. What conclusion can you make about the balance in Retained Earnings on December 31, 2008 for each method of revenue recognition?

P18-3 **AICPA Adapted** *Percentage of Completion* In 2007 Dreyer Corporation began construction work under a three-year contract. The contract price is $800,000. Dreyer uses the percentage-of-completion method. The financial statement presentations relating to this contract on December 31, 2007 follow:

Balance Sheet

Accounts receivable		$15,000
Construction in progress	$50,000	
Less contract billings	(47,000)	
Cost of uncompleted contract in excess of billings		3,000

Income Statement

Gross profit (before tax) on the contract	$10,000

Required

1. How much cash did Dreyer collect during 2007?
2. What was the initial estimated total income before tax on this contract?

P18-4 *Long-Term Construction Contracts* The Fender Construction Company receives a contract to build a building over a period of three years for a price of $700,000. Information relating to the performance of the contract is summarized as follows:

	2007	2008	2009
Construction costs incurred during the year	$150,000	$242,000	$168,000
Estimated costs to complete	350,000	168,000	—
Billings during the year	120,000	250,000	330,000
Collections during the year	100,000	260,000	340,000

Required

Prepare journal entries for all three years under (1) the percentage-of-completion method, and (2) the completed-contract method.

P18-5 *Long-Term Construction Contracts* The Forman Company has contracted to build a dam over a period of four years for $3,000,000. Information relating to the performance of the contract is summarized as follows:

	2007	2008	2009	2010
Construction costs incurred during the year	$ 300,000	$1,100,000	$ 863,000	$837,000
Estimated costs to complete	2,200,000	1,400,000	837,000	—
Billings during the year	280,000	870,000	1,030,000	820,000
Collections during the year	270,000	875,000	1,010,000	845,000

Required

1. Compute the profit or loss for each year of the contract under (a) the percentage-of-completion method, and (b) the completed-contract method.
2. Prepare the relevant sections of the income statement and ending balance sheet for each year under (a) the percentage-of-completion method, and (b) the completed-contract method.

P18-6 *Long-Term Construction Contracts* The Rice Company signed a contract to build a dam over a period of three years for a price of $10,000,000. Information relating to the performance of the contract is summarized as follows:

	2007	2008	2009
Construction costs incurred during the year	$2,000,000	$4,000,000	$6,000,000
Estimated costs to complete	6,000,000	6,000,000	—
Billings during the year	1,500,000	3,500,000	5,000,000
Collections during the year	1,300,000	3,600,000	5,100,000

Required

Prepare journal entries for all three years under (1) the percentage-of-completion method, and (2) the completed-contract method.

P18-7   *Proportional Performance Method* The Hilt Company, a public relations company, signs two-year contracts with its clients. For $80,000 in advance, the company agrees to ensure that the client's name is mentioned five times on a network national news program, 10 times in a national news magazine, and 15 times on a local news program. In 2007 the company signed eight contracts; no additional contracts were signed in 2008.

In 2007 the company's clients were mentioned 10 times on network national news programs, 40 times in national news magazines, and 22 times on local news programs. In 2008 the company's clients were mentioned 30 times on national news programs, 40 times in national news magazines, and 98 times on local news programs. The relevant cost information for the eight contracts is as follows:

Initial direct costs	$ 20,000
Annual indirect costs	80,000
Estimated (and actual) total direct costs for two-year period	260,000
Direct cost per	
National news program	2,000
National news magazine	1,500
Local news program	500

Required
1. Prepare the income statements for 2007 and 2008.
2. From a theoretical viewpoint, how should the company compute the depreciation of its office building and office equipment that would be included in the preceding costs? Why?

P18-8   *Sales Under the Installment Method* The following information is available for the Dassler Company, which began its operations in 2007:

1. Installment method sales
2007	$520,000
2008	600,000

2. Gross profit percentage
2007	20%
2008	24%

3. Cash collections on installment method sales
2007	25% of 2007 sales
2008	55% of 2007 sales
	30% of 2008 sales

4. Bad debt policy
   The company estimates its bad debts to be 2% of installment method sales.

5. Defaults and repossessions
2007	$10,000 of 2007 installment method sales, of which $1,000 had been collected
2008	$20,000 of 2007 installment method sales, of which $4,000 had been collected
	$15,000 of 2008 installment method sales, of which $2,000 had been collected

The policy of the company is to value repossessed items at 40% of their original selling price.

Required
Prepare the journal entries for 2007 and 2008.

P18-9   *Sales Under the Installment Method* The Dyson Company sells computer games to teenagers. Selected accounts included in the trial balance at December 31, 2007 and 2008 are as follows:

	2006	2007
Installment accounts receivable, 2006	$80,000	$ 20,000
Installment accounts receivable, 2007		112,500
Allowance for doubtful installment accounts receivable, 2006	(5,000)	(3,700)
Allowance for doubtful installment accounts receivable, 2007		(7,000)
Deferred gross profit, 2006	(16,000)	(3,500)
Deferred gross profit, 2007		(22,500)

During 2007 installment method sales and cost of goods sold were $200,000 and $160,000, respectively. In 2007 the company repossessed games that had been sold in 2006 for $6,000 and on which $2,500 had been collected. The games were believed to be worth $1,000. No repossessions occurred on 2007 sales.

Required

Prepare summary journal entries for 2007.

P18-10 **AICPA Adapted** *Cost Recovery Method* After a two-year search for a buyer, Hobson, Inc. sold its idle plant facility to Jackson Company for $700,000 on January 1, 2005. On this date the plant had a depreciated cost on Hobson's books of $500,000. Under the agreement Jackson paid $100,000 cash on January 1, 2005, and signed a $600,000 note bearing interest at 10%. The note was payable in installments of $100,000, $200,000, and $300,000 on January 1, 2006, 2007, and 2008, respectively. The note was secured by a mortgage on the property sold. Hobson appropriately accounted for the sale under the cost recovery method since there was no reasonable basis for estimating the degree of collectibility of the note receivable. Jackson repaid the note with three late installment payments, which were accepted by Hobson, as follows:

Date of Payment	Principal	Interest
July 1, 2006	$100,000	$90,000
December 31, 2007	200,000	75,000
February 1, 2009	300,000	32,500

Required

Prepare a schedule (using the following format) to record the initial transaction for the sale of the idle plant facility, the application of subsequent cash collections on the note, and the necessary journal entry on the date the transaction is complete.

Date	Cash Received Debit	Note Receivable Dr. (Cr.)	Idle Plant (Net) (Credit)	Deferred Income Dr. (Cr.)	Income Recognized (Credit)
Jan. 1, 2005	$100,000				
July 1, 2006	190,000				
Dec. 31, 2007	275,000				
Feb. 1, 2009	332,500				
Feb. 1, 2009					

P18-11 *Revenue Recognition Alternatives* The following are the operating activities of three different companies:

Company A: Engages in long-term construction contracts. Uses the percentage-of-completion method to recognize gross profits. Started contract X in 2006, contract Y in 2007, and contract Z in 2008. The total gross profit (estimated and actual) and the percentage completed for each contract during 2007 through 2009 are:

	Contract X	Contract Y	Contract Z
Gross profit	$600,000	$400,000	$500,000
% completed during			
2007	60%	40%	—
2008	25%	35%	30%
2009	—	25%	50%

Company B: Engages in long-term service contracts involving a specific number of defined but not similar service acts. Uses proportional performance method to recognize revenues. Sells two-year service contracts for $400 in advance. Each service contract requires Company B to perform service act 1 a total of 50 times and service act 2 a total of 20 times during the two-year period. At the beginning of 2007, 100 service contracts were sold. The following is a summary of the related cost information for the 100 service contracts:

Initial direct costs	$ 3,500
Annual indirect costs	4,500
Estimated (and actual) total direct costs (for two-year period)	10,000
Direct cost per service act	
Service act 1	$ 1.20
Service act 2	2.00

During 2007, service act 1 was performed 2,700 times and service act 2 was performed 800 times. During 2008, service acts 1 and 2 were performed 2,300 and 1,200 times, respectively.

Company C: Sells goods on the installment basis. Uses the installment method (because these are exceptional cases) to recognize gross profits. The following is a summary of the installment sales, costs of installment sales, operating expenses, and collections for 2007 and 2008:

	2007	2008
Installment method sales	$80,000	$100,000
Costs of installment method sales	48,000	62,000
Operating expenses	17,000	20,000
Cash collections from		
2006 installment method sales (2006 gross profit is 39%)	58,000	—
2007 installment method sales	56,000	24,000
2008 installment method sales	—	68,000

Required
1. Prepare a schedule that shows Company A's gross profit for 2007, 2008, and 2009.
2. Prepare 2007 and 2008 condensed income statements for Company B.
3. Prepare 2007 and 2008 condensed income statements for Company C.

P18-12 *Revenue Recognition Alternatives* The following are the operating activities of three different companies.

Company X: Engages in long-term service contracts involving a specific number of defined but not similar service acts. Uses proportional performance method to recognize revenues. Sells two-year service contracts for $600 in advance. Each service contract requires Company X to perform service act 1 a total of 30 times and service act 2 a total of 50 times during the two-year period. At the beginning of 2007, 200 service contracts were sold. The following is a summary of the related cost information for the 200 service contracts:

Initial direct costs	$ 8,500
Annual indirect costs	9,300
Estimated (and actual) total direct costs (for two-year period)	20,000
Direct cost per service act	
Service act 1	$ 1.60
Service act 2	1.04

During 2007, service act 1 was performed 5,000 times and service act 2 was performed 4,000 times. During 2008, service acts 1 and 2 were performed 1,000 and 6,000 times, respectively.

Company Y: Sells goods on the installment basis. Uses the installment method (because these are exceptional cases) to recognize gross profits. The following is a summary of the installment sales, gross profit, operating expenses, and collections for 2007 and 2008:

	2007	2008
Installment method sales	$90,000	$110,000
Gross profit	35,100	45,100
Operating expenses	18,000	21,000
Cash collections from:		
2006 installment method sales (2006 gross profit is 40%)	35,000	—
2007 installment method sales	67,000	23,000
2008 installment method sales	—	80,000

Company Z: Engages in long-term construction contracts. Uses the percentage-of-completion method to recognize gross profits. Started contract 1 in 2006, contract 2 in 2007, and contract 3 in 2008. The total gross profit (estimated and actual) and the percentage complete for each contract at the end of 2007 through 2009 are:

	Contract 1*	Contract 2	Contract 3
Gross profit	$800,000	$350,000	$600,000
% complete at the end of			
2007	75%	40%	—
2008	100%	70%	35%
2009	—	100%	80%

*30% was complete at the end of 2006.

Required
1. Prepare 2007 and 2008 condensed income statements for Company X.
2. Prepare 2007 and 2008 condensed income statements for Company Y.
3. Prepare a schedule that shows Company Z's gross profit for 2007, 2008, and 2009.

P18-13 *Franchise (Appendix)* Year-Round Golf sells franchises for indoor golf driving ranges and putting greens. For each franchise, the company charges a nonrefundable initial franchise fee of $45,000. The franchise agreement requires a down payment of $10,000, with the balance covered by the issuance of a $35,000, 10% note, payable by the franchisee at the end of five years. Interest does not begin to accrue until the franchise opens, and the first interest payment is required 12 months after the franchise opens. The company sells only to qualified buyers so the collectibility of the note is always reasonably assured. The services required for the initial franchise fee are completed six months after the agreement is signed.

The franchisee is also required to pay a continuing fee of $6,000 per year, plus 10% of its gross sales. Half the $6,000 is applied against purchases of supplies from the franchisor, which are paid for in cash at the time of purchase. The franchisor charges a sales price of 50% above its cost on these supplies.

In the first six months of 2007, the company sold four franchises which began operating at the end of December. These franchisees had sales of $160,000 in 2008, and purchased the allowable amount of supplies. In the second six months of 2007, the company sold one franchise which began operating on April 1, 2008. The franchisee had sales of $25,000 in 2008 and purchased $1,500 of supplies.

Required

Prepare the journal entries required by Year-Round Golf in 2007 and 2008 to record the preceding events.

P18-14 *Real Estate (Appendix)* On January 1, 2007 the Hogback Company sold the Red Rocks Ranch, which constituted 20,000 acres of undeveloped land, to a limited partnership for $50 million. The land had originally cost Hogback $5 million. The terms of the sale included a cash payment of $9 million and a 10% note for $41 million to be paid in equal annual installments for 30 years. The note is secured by the land. Hogback paid a commission to a real estate company of 5% on the selling price.

Required

1. Should Hogback record the transaction as a sale? If so, prepare all the journal entries for 2007.
2. Assume, instead, that the company uses the installment method. Prepare all the journal entries for 2007.
3. Assume, instead, that the payments made to the Hogback Company were returnable at the option of the purchaser until June 30, 2008. Prepare all the journal entries for 2007. Ignore the sales commission.
4. Assume, instead, that the Hogback Company is obligated to make improvements costing $4 million over the next three years. In 2007 it made improvements costing $1 million. Prepare all the journal entries for 2007.
5. If the Hogback Company were the general partner of the limited partnership, would your answer to Requirement 1 change? If it were a limited partner?

P18-15 *Consignments (Appendix)* On January 1, 2007 the Hadad Company entered into a consignment agreement with the Trinidad Company. The agreement specifies that the consignee (Trinidad) is to sell the merchandise at a price of 30% above cost. Trinidad is required to pay Hadad the net sales price within 15 days of each sale to a third party. The net sales price is defined as the sales price, less any advertising costs incurred by Trinidad, and less a commission of 10% deducted from the sales price less the advertising costs. Hadad pays any costs incurred in shipping the merchandise to Trinidad.

In 2007 Hadad shipped merchandise costing $300,000 to Trinidad and incurred delivery costs of $8,000. During the year (through December 15), Trinidad made sales of $195,000 and incurred advertising costs of $15,000, and paid the required amount to Hadad. On December 31, 2007, Hadad phoned Trinidad and was told that since December 15 additional sales of $39,000 had been made and advertising costs of $3,000 incurred. (Record this information in separate journal entries.)

Required

1. Prepare the journal entries for the Hadad Company.
2. What amount, and in what category, would Hadad Company report on its balance sheet on December 31, 2007?
3. Prepare the journal entries for the Trinidad Company.
4. What amount related to the consignment activities, and in what category, would the Trinidad Company report on its balance sheet on December 31, 2007?

CASES

COMMUNICATION

C18-1 Criteria for Revenue Recognition

AICPA Adapted The earning of revenue by a company is recognized for accounting purposes when the transaction is recorded. In some situations, revenue is recognized approximately as it is earned in the economic sense; in others, accountants have developed guidelines for recognizing revenue by other criteria, for example, at the point of sale.

Required (*ignore income taxes*)

1. Explain and justify why revenue is often recognized as earned at the time of sale.
2. Explain in what situations it would be appropriate to recognize revenue as the productive activity takes place.
3. Explain at what times it may be appropriate to recognize revenue other than those included in items (1) and (2).

C18-2   Revenue Recognition Methods

In special cases, revenue is recognized by the use of several methods, including (a) percentage-of-completion method, (b) proportional performance method, and (c) installment method.

Required

Briefly explain each of the methods and indicate the situations in which each is used.

C18-3   Construction Contracts

AICPA Adapted   Village Company is accounting for a long-term construction contract using the percentage-of-completion method. It is a three-year, fixed-fee contract that is presently in its first year. The latest reasonable estimates of total contract costs indicate that the contract will be completed at a profit. Village will submit progress billings to the customer and has reasonable assurance that collections on these billings will be received in each year of the contract.

Required

1. a. What is the justification for the percentage-of-completion method for long-term construction contracts?
   b. What facts in the preceding situation indicate that Village should account for this long-term construction contract using the percentage-of-completion method?
2. How would the income recognized in each year of this long-term construction contract be determined using the cost-to-cost method of determining percentage of completion?
3. What is the effect on income, if any, of the progress billings and the collections on these billings?

C18-4   Long-Term Contracts

AICPA Adapted   In accounting for long-term contracts (those taking longer than one year to complete), the two methods commonly followed are the percentage-of-completion method and the completed-contract method.

Required

1. Explain how earnings on long-term contracts are recognized and computed under these two methods.
2. Under what circumstances is it preferable to use one method over the other?
3. Why is earnings recognition as measured by interim billings not generally accepted for long-term contracts?
4. How are job costs and interim billings reflected on the balance sheet under the percentage-of-completion method and the completed-contract method?

C18-5   Installment Method Sales

AICPA Adapted   Installment sales usually are accounted for by one of the following methods: (1) the profit may be recognized as earned in the period of sale; (2) the profit may be recognized on a proportionate basis in the periods of collection (commonly called the "installment method").

Required

1. Discuss the propriety of the two methods, including in your discussion a list of the circumstances under which recognition of profit in the period of sale would be preferable to recognition of profit on the installment method.
2. The collection period of an installment sale contract is frequently 24 months or longer. Discuss, in terms of both methods, the presentation of the installment contracts receivable on the balance sheet.
3. Deferred gross profit arising from installment sales has been reported on the balance sheet variously as a contra or valuation account to installments receivable, an estimated liability, a part of stockholders' equity, or a deferred credit. Discuss the nature and, hence, the appropriate balance sheet classification(s) of "deferred gross profit" for an accrual-basis business that uses the installment sales method for financial reporting and income tax purposes.

CREATIVE AND CRITICAL THINKING

C18-6   Revenue Recognition Methods

The following situations are independent.

1. Carlson Company is an international consulting firm that has received a two-year engagement from a client for a fee of $2 million. The company will assign differing numbers of personnel to the project depending on the needs of the project and the availability of personnel. The company requires a down payment of 10% and makes periodic billings based on the hours worked by the personnel, plus 20% profit. At the end of the engagement, the company and the client will negotiate whether an adjustment to the fee is appropriate.

2. The Fast Loss Health Club has three types of memberships: 1-year, 3-year, and 10-year. Each type of membership requires an initial fee as well as monthly fees. To encourage memberships, the company offers numerous incentives, such as free dues for the first two months and drawings for free vacation trips. In addition, the company advertises heavily at certain times of the year, such as during the Christmas period. The company also offers special programs to its members for a fee and allows nonmembers to participate for a higher fee.

3. The New Encyclopedia Company ships five complete sets of its 12-volume encyclopedia to each of its new

distributors. Each distributor has six months to sell all the encyclopedias and pay the company the selling price, less a 40% commission, within five days of each sale. During this period, the distributor may return the encyclopedias without obligation and at the company's expense. At the end of six months, the distributor must pay the selling price of the unsold encyclopedias, less a 60% commission.

Required

Discuss the revenue recognition issues that exist in each independent situation. Discuss any issues that exist in matching the expenses against the revenues.

C18-7 Revenue Recognition

AICPA Adapted Bonanza Trading Stamps, Inc. was formed early this year to sell trading stamps throughout the Southwest to retailers who distribute them free to their customers. Books for accumulating the stamps and catalogs illustrating the merchandise for which the stamps may be exchanged are given free to retailers for distribution to stamp recipients. Centers with inventories of merchandise premiums have been established for redemption of the stamps. Retailers may not return unused stamps to Bonanza.

The following schedule expresses Bonanza's expectations of the percentages of a normal month's activity that will be attained. For this purpose, a normal month's activity is defined as the level of operations expected when expansion of activities ceases or tapers off to a stable rate. The company expects that this level will be attained in the third year, and that sales of stamps will average $2,000,000 per month throughout the third year.

Month	Actual Stamp Sales Percentage	Merchandise Premium Purchases Percentage	Stamp Redemptions Percentage
6	30%	40%	10%
12	60	60	45
18	80	80	70
24	90	90	80
30	100	100	95

Required

1. Explain the factors to be considered in determining when revenue should be recognized in measuring the income of a business enterprise.
2. Explain the accounting alternatives that Bonanza Trading Stamps, Inc. should consider for the recognition of its revenues and related expenses.
3. For each accounting alternative discussed in (2), give balance sheet accounts that Bonanza should use and indicate how it should classify each.

C18-8 Exchanges and Revenue Recognition Issues

Certain business "exchanges" are very complex and may qualify as exceptional cases in which the related revenues

and expenses are advanced or deferred. The following are four such cases:

1. Franchisor grants a franchise to a franchisee; it collects part of the initial franchise fee and agrees to perform related initial services over an extended period.
2. Land development company acquires land for future development into a "sports retirement community," subdivides the land into lots, and sells the lots on "credit" with payment to be made on a long-term basis.
3. Lessor leases equipment to a lessee on a long-term noncancelable lease; the fair value of the leased item is greater than the cost, and the ownership of the leased item is transferred to the lessee by the end of the lease life.
4. A construction company builds bridges; it enters into a contract to construct a bridge for Rice County over a two-year period.

Required

For each of the preceding exchanges, (a) explain the revenue recognition issues involved, and (b) discuss when the revenue is recognized and by what method.

C18-9 Construction Contracts

AICPA Adapted At December 31, 2007, Roko Co. has two fixed price construction contracts in progress. Both contracts have monthly billings supported by certified surveys of work completed. The contracts are:

a. The Ski Park contract, begun in 2006, is 80% complete, is progressing according to bid estimates, and is expected to be profitable.
b. The Nassu Village contract, a project to construct 100 condominium units, was begun in 2007. Thirty-five units have been completed. Work on the remaining units is delayed by conflicting recommendations on how to overcome unexpected subsoil problems. While the total cost of the project is uncertain, a loss is not anticipated.

Required

1. Identify the alternatives available to account for long-term construction contracts, and specify the criteria used to determine which method is applicable to a given contract.
2. Identify the appropriate accounting method for each of Roko's two contracts, and describe each contract's effect on net income for 2007.
3. Indicate how the accounts related to the Ski Park contract should be reported on the balance sheet at December 31, 2007.

C18-10 Franchise and Revenue Recognition

AICPA Adapted Southern Fried Shrimp sells franchises to independent operators throughout the southeastern part of the United States. The contract with the franchisee includes the following provisions:

1. The franchisee is charged an initial fee of $25,000. Of this amount, $5,000 is payable when the agreement is signed and a $4,000 non-interest-bearing note is payable at the end of each of the five subsequent years.

2. All of the initial franchise fee collected by Southern Fried Shrimp is to be refunded and the remaining obligation canceled if, for any reason, the franchisee fails to open the franchise.

3. In return for the initial franchise fee, Southern Fried Shrimp agrees to (1) assist the franchisee in selecting the location for the business, (2) negotiate the lease for the land, (3) obtain financing and assist with building design, (4) supervise construction, (5) establish accounting and tax records, and (6) provide expert advice over a five-year period relating to such matters as employee and management training, quality control, and promotion.

4. In addition to the initial franchise fee, the franchisee is required to pay to Southern Fried Shrimp a monthly fee of 2% of sales for menu planning, recipe innovations, and the privilege of purchasing ingredients from Southern Fried Shrimp at or below prevailing market prices.

Management of Southern Fried Shrimp estimates that the value of the services rendered to the franchisee at the time the contract is signed amounts to at least $5,000. All franchisees to date have opened their locations at the scheduled time and none has defaulted on any of the notes receivable.

The credit ratings of all franchisees would entitle them to borrow at the current interest rate of 10%. The present value of an ordinary annuity of five annual receipts of $4,000 each, discounted at 10%, is $15,163.

Required

1. Explain the alternatives that Southern Fried Shrimp might use to account for the initial franchise fee, evaluate each by applying generally accepted accounting principles to this situation, and give illustrative entries for each alternative.

2. Given the nature of Southern Fried Shrimp's agreement with its franchisees, when should it recognize revenue? Discuss the question of revenue recognition for both the initial franchise fee and the additional monthly fee of 2% of sales and give illustrative entries for both types of revenue.

3. Assume that (a) Southern Fried Shrimp sells some franchises for $35,000 (which includes a charge of $10,000 for the rental of equipment for its useful life of 10 years); (b) $15,000 of the fee is payable immediately and the balance on non-interest-bearing notes at $4,000 per year; (c) no portion of the $10,000 rental payment is refundable in case the franchisee goes out of business; and (d) title to the equipment remains with the franchisor. What would be the preferable method of accounting for the rental portion of the initial franchise fee? Explain.

C18-11 Publishing and Revenue Recognition

AICPA Adapted After the presentation of your report on the examination of the financial statements to the board of directors of the Savage Publishing Company, one of the new directors says he is surprised the income statement assumes that an equal proportion of the revenue is earned with the publication of every issue of the company's magazine. He feels that the "crucial event" in the process of earning revenue in the magazine business is the cash sale of the subscription. He says that he does not understand why—other than for the smoothing of income—most of the revenue cannot be "recognized" in the period of the sale.

Required

Explain the propriety of timing the recognition of revenue in the Savage Publishing Company's accounts with

1. The cash sale of the magazine subscription.
2. The publication of the magazine every month.
3. Both events, by recognizing a portion of the revenue with the cash sale of the magazine subscription and a portion of the revenue with the publication of the magazine every month.

C18-12 Recognition of Revenues and Expenses

AICPA Adapted On May 6, 2006, Sterling Corporation signed a contract with Stony Associates under which Stony agreed (1) to construct an office building on land owned by Sterling, (2) to accept responsibility for procuring financing for the project and finding tenants, and (3) to manage the property for 50 years. The annual profit from the project, after debt service, is to be divided equally between Sterling Corporation and Stony Associates. Stony is to accept its share of future profits as full payment for its services in construction, obtaining finances and tenants, and management of the project.

By April 30, 2007, the project was nearly completed and tenants had signed leases to occupy 90% of the available space at annual rentals aggregating $2,600,000. It is estimated that, after operating expenses and debt service, the annual profit will amount to $850,000. The management of Stony Associates believed that the economic benefit derived from the contract with Sterling should be reflected on its financial statements for the fiscal year ended April 30, 2007 and directed that revenue be accrued in an amount equal to the commercial value of the services Stony had rendered during the year, that this amount be carried in contracts receivable, and that all related expenditures be charged against the revenue.

Required

Is the belief of Stony's management in accord with generally accepted accounting principles for the measurement of revenue and expense for the year ended April 30, 2007? Support your opinion by discussing the application to this case of the factors to be considered for asset measurement and revenue and expense recognition.

C18-13 Recognition of Expenses

AICPA Adapted Kwik-Bild Corporation sells and erects shell houses. These are frame structures that are completely finished on the outside but are unfinished on the inside except for flooring, partition studding and ceiling joists. Shell houses are sold chiefly to customers who are handy with tools and who have time to do the interior wiring, plumbing, wall completion and finishing, and other work necessary to make the shell houses livable dwellings.

Kwik-Bild buys shell houses from a manufacturer in unassembled packages consisting of all lumber, roofing, doors, windows and similar materials necessary to complete a shell house. Upon commencing operations in a new area, Kwik-Bild buys or leases land as a site for its local warehouse, field office and display houses. Sample display houses are erected at a total cost of from $10,000 to $30,000, including the cost of the unassembled packages. The chief element of cost of the display houses is the unassembled packages, since erection is a short, low-cost operation. Old sample models are torn down or altered into new models every three to seven years. Sample display houses have little salvage value because dismantling and moving costs amount to nearly as much as the cost of an unassembled package.

Required

1. A choice must be made between (a) expensing the costs of sample display houses in the period in which the expenditure is made, and (b) spreading the costs over more than one period. Discuss the advantages of each method.
2. Is it preferable to amortize the cost of display houses on the basis of (a) the passage of time, or (b) the number of shell houses sold? Explain.

C18-14 Installment Method Sales

AICPA Adapted On October 2, 2007 the Television Company sold a set costing $400 to Jones for $600. Jones made a down payment of $150 and agreed to pay $25 the first of each month for 18 months thereafter.

Jones paid the first two installments due on November 1 and December 1, 2007. In 2008 Jones made five payments, but then defaulted on the balance of the payments. The set was repossessed on November 1, 2008. The company closes its books as of December 31.

Required

1. Give three different amounts that might be shown as realized income for 2007 and indicate the circumstances under which each of these amounts would be acceptable.
2. Assuming that the repossessed television set has a wholesale value of $50 and a retail value of $75, prepare a journal entry to record the repossession under the "installment method" of accounting. Explain fully the reasoning applicable to your entry.

C18-15 Analyzing Coca-Cola's Revenue Recognition and Advertising Costs Disclosures

Refer to the financial statements and related notes of The Coca-Cola Company in Appendix A of this book.

Required

1. What does the company disclose about its revenue recognition policies? Why?
2. When does the company expense the production cost of its advertisements? Does this result in appropriate matching?

C18-16 Ethics and Revenue and Expense Recognition

You are employed by a local CPA firm, and one of your clients is Tiger Manufacturing Company. Tiger has been very successful in recent years, averaging approximately 10% increase in earnings each year. The company is planning a public stock offering early next year, which would bring significant fees to your firm. It would also allow the company to finance a much needed expansion that would allow the company to hire additional employees.

The audit is nearing completion, and it appears that the company will again report a significant increase in earnings. However, two issues have arisen. First, the company has a large order from a purchaser to be shipped FOB shipping point in early January. The inventory was completed and warehoused late in December, but it was not segregated. Management has included the selling price (less the related expense) in the current year's net income. Second, the company has added capitalized interest to the cost of two large special orders that are nearing completion. If both these issues are resolved in a way that decreases net income, the company's net income will be lower than the amount reported last year.

Required

From financial reporting and ethical perspectives, discuss the issues raised by this situation.

RESEARCH SIMULATIONS

R18-1 Researching GAAP

Situation

When asked about a $518 million "prepaid expense and deferred charge" on its balance sheet for 1990, Sears says that about $100 million of the figure—mainly for the catalog—consists of advertising costs whose impact on profit has been deferred. "These costs are paid but aren't charged against profits" yet, says a spokesman.

Procter and Gamble generally allocates advertising costs based on the number of cases of products it ships.

A spokesman for McDonald's says that a "small portion" of the $108 million in prepaid expenses and other current assets on its balance sheet for 1990 is deferred production costs for certain commercials and creative development.

Nike says that it deducts all advertising costs immediately, and calls advertising-cost deferral "a bogus exercise."

Philip Morris accrued $1.4 billion in marketing costs on the liability side of its balance sheet for 1990. This means that Philip Morris is deducting advertising costs it has not yet paid to help smooth out profits from year to year. An analyst says, "I call such amounts 'hidden earnings' for future years when financial results aren't as good as Philip Morris would like. Then, it could lower its advertising-cost deductions with this accrual." (*Adapted from* The Wall Street Journal, 1/8/92).

Directions

1. Research the generally accepted accounting principles and prepare a short memo that summarizes how to report advertising costs. Cite your reference(s) and applicable paragraph numbers.
2. Are each of the companies complying with the policy? Assume that all the companies recognize revenue at the time of sale.

R18-2 Researching GAAP

Situation

Amre Inc. capitalized its marketing costs, such as the cost of purchasing mailing lists, instead of treating the costs as expenses.

Inspeech capitalized estimated selling, general, and administrative costs of various acquired companies' accounting and billing activities for a period of three months following the acquisition. Similarly, the company capitalized search costs to hire new management employees, salaries of individuals involved with the integration of newly acquired companies, and fees for studies by outside consultants. Management justified capitalizing these expenses because they were required to implement the company's expansion strategy and would benefit future periods.

Among the costs Chambers deferred were portions of executives' salaries for time spent on developing projects such as new landfills. In addition, the company delayed recognizing some public relations and legal costs, as well as executive travel expenses.

Directions

Research the generally accepted accounting principles and prepare a short memo that summarizes how to report advertising costs. Cite your reference(s) and applicable paragraph numbers.

19

Accounting for Income Taxes

OBJECTIVES

After reading this chapter, you will be able to:

1 Understand permanent and temporary differences.

2 Explain the conceptual issues regarding interperiod tax allocation.

3 Record and report deferred tax liabilities.

4 Record and report deferred tax assets.

5 Explain an operating loss carryback and carryforward.

6 Account for an operating loss carryback.

7 Account for an operating loss carryforward.

8 Apply intraperiod tax allocation.

9 Classify deferred tax liabilities and assets.

Tax-Advantaged Transactions

The complexity of the Internal Revenue Code is well known. With thousands of new pronouncements being issued annually by the Internal Revenue Service (IRS) and the court system, there are many developing areas of tax law that present significant challenges to company management. When faced with having to make difficult choices as to the tax treatment of transactions that have no clear-cut answers, many managers will choose to take aggressive positions to minimize the company's tax liability. These managers know that an aggressive tax position will likely draw challenges from the IRS, with some positions ultimately being accepted and others being rejected. Many companies will record the tax benefits from these transactions in the financial statements on an "as-filed" basis. That is, they record a tax liability consistent with their tax return, even though it is probable that, after an IRS review, some of their tax positions will be reversed and additional taxes will be owed. In such a case, companies will report a tax contingency reserve on their financial statements based on the risk of being challenged by the IRS and a reasonable estimate of the amount of adjustment that will be required. The amount in such reserves can be significant. For example, **Hershey Foods Corp.** reported a reduction of income tax expense in the second quarter of 2004, of $61.1 million related to the settlement of federal tax audits as well as a number of state tax audit issues.

Believing that some companies may try to manage earnings through their estimate of tax contingencies, the financial reporting

implications of such tax-advantaged transactions have drawn the attention of the Securities and Exchange Commission (SEC). In several speeches by SEC staff, the SEC has reiterated its view that it would be inappropriate to recognize any benefit (e.g., reduced income tax expense) resulting from a tax-advantaged transaction unless it was probable that the tax position will be accepted. However, because the FASB is currently developing guidance on the treatment of such transactions, the "as-filed" basis will be allowed as long as it is consistently applied. In addition the SEC has repeatedly stressed the need for adequate disclosures of any tax contingencies. Companies, however, are afraid that detailed financial statement disclosures or information contained in the auditor's tax accrual work papers will provide a roadmap for the IRS to follow in identifying transactions to be examined. While such concerns are valid, the SEC view is that companies voluntarily accepted the disclosure requirements when they chose to access public markets, and the presentation of information useful to investors should be the overriding concern.

FOR FURTHER INVESTIGATION

For a discussion of accounting issues related to income taxes, consult the Business & Company Resource Center (BCRC):

- Learning to Think Like Warren Buffett. David Henry, *Business Week*, 0007-7135, Feb 14, 2005 i3920 p29.
- Do firms use the deferred tax asset valuation allowance to manage earnings? Christine C. Bauman, Mark P. Bauman, Robert F. Halsey, *Journal of the American Taxation Association*, 0198-9073, Spring 2002, v24, i1, pS27(25).

The objectives of financial reporting and the Internal Revenue Code are different. The objective of generally accepted accounting principles for financial reporting is to provide useful information to decision makers about companies. This information enables external users to make the investment and credit decisions we discussed in Chapter 1. The overall objective of the Internal Revenue Code, on the other hand, is to obtain funds, in an equitable manner, to operate the federal government. Additionally, tax laws frequently have been used to stimulate and regulate the economy. For example, the percentage depletion deduction attempts to stimulate new investment in natural resource assets.

As a result of their differing objectives, financial reporting is governed by generally accepted accounting principles (GAAP) and income tax reporting is governed by the Internal Revenue Code (IRC).[1] If a corporation reports different revenues and/or expenses for financial reporting than it does for income tax reporting, it must determine (1) the current and noncurrent deferred income tax liabilities and/or assets to report on its balance sheet, and (2) the income tax expense to match against its pretax financial income[2] on its income statement. We discuss the procedures used to determine and report these items in the following sections.

OVERVIEW AND DEFINITIONS

Consider the condensed income statements and income tax returns for the Freese Corporation for 2007 and 2008 that we show in Exhibit 19-1.

EXHIBIT 19-1   Freese Corporation

**Income Statement and Income Tax Return
Years Ended December 31, 2007 and 2008**

	Income Statement		Income Tax Return	
	2007	**2008**	**2007**	**2008**
Revenues	$180,000	$200,000	$170,000	$210,000
Cost of goods sold	(75,000)	(85,000)	(70,000)	(90,000)
Gross profit	$105,000	$115,000	$100,000	$120,000
Other expenses	(60,000)	(50,000)	(60,000)	(60,000)
Pretax income from continuing operations	$ 45,000	$ 65,000	$ 40,000	$ 60,000
Income taxes	(11,000)	(16,000)	(9,200)	(15,300)
Income from continuing operations	$ 34,000	$ 49,000	$ 30,800	$ 44,700
Extraordinary item (net of income tax effect)	—	(10,000)	—	—
Net income	$ 34,000	$ 39,000	$ 30,800	$ 44,700

Causes of Differences

There are several differences between the Freese Corporation's income statements and income tax returns in Exhibit 19-1: (1) the amounts of revenues recognized in 2007 and 2008 are different, (2) the cost of goods sold subtracted from revenues differ in 2007 and 2008, (3) other expenses differ in 2008, and (4) an extraordinary item is separately reported on the income statement in 2008 but does not appear on the income tax

---

1. Corporations may be subject to federal, state, and foreign income taxes. In this chapter we limit the discussion to the impact of federal income taxes on financial reporting.
2. The terms *financial income, financial accounting income, book income,* and *accounting income* are synonymous and may be used interchangeably. Because the FASB uses the term *financial income* in its discussion of accounting for income taxes, we use that term throughout this chapter.

return for that year. The causes of differences between a corporation's pretax financial income and taxable income (and potentially between its income tax expense and its income tax obligation) can be categorized into five groups:

1. *Permanent Differences.* Some items of revenue and expense that a corporation reports for financial accounting purposes are never reported for income tax purposes under the IRC. Other items classified as allowable deductions for income tax reporting do not qualify as expenses under GAAP. These items cause permanent differences between the corporation's pretax financial income and taxable income.

2. *Temporary Differences.* A corporation reports some items of revenue and expense in one period for financial accounting purposes, but in an earlier or later period for income tax purposes. These items cause temporary differences between the corporation's pretax financial income and taxable income.

3. *Operating Loss Carrybacks and Carryforwards.* When a corporation reports an operating loss in a given year, the IRC allows the corporation to carry back or carry forward the loss to offset previous or future reported taxable income on its income tax return. The corporation reports its pretax financial income or loss in the current year on its income statement.

4. *Tax Credits.* To stimulate certain investments, or to provide tax relief in special circumstances, the IRC provides specific tax credits that a corporation may deduct from its income taxes owed to determine its current income taxes payable. Although use of a tax credit does not cause a difference between the corporation's pretax financial income and taxable income, it may cause a difference between the corporation's income tax expense and income tax obligation.

5. *Intraperiod Tax Allocation.* A corporation allocates its income tax for financial accounting purposes to (a) income from continuing operations, (b) results from discontinued operations, (c) extraordinary items, (d) retrospective and prior period adjustments, and (e) other comprehensive income. No similar allocation is made on its income tax return.

Definitions

The FASB studied the impact of using different accounting procedures for financial reporting and income tax reporting. Based on its findings, the Board issued **FASB Statement No. 109**, which currently defines GAAP for income taxes. The following sections discuss the provisions of the *Statement* as they apply to the differences between income reported for financial reporting purposes and income reported for taxation purposes. The discussion includes a number of definitions[3] related to a corporation's income taxes, which we list in Exhibit 19-2.

INTERPERIOD INCOME TAX ALLOCATION: BASIC ISSUES

Interperiod income tax allocation is the allocation of a corporation's income tax obligation as an expense to various accounting periods. Differences between a corporation's pretax financial income and taxable income arise from both temporary and permanent differences. Temporary differences ultimately reverse and require interperiod tax allocation. Permanent differences are *not* subject to interperiod tax allocation. We discuss them first in this section because you must be able to classify differences as permanent or temporary for interperiod tax allocation purposes.

1 Understand permanent and temporary differences.

---

3. These definitions are adapted from "Accounting for Income Taxes," *FASB Statement of Financial Accounting Standards No. 109* (Stamford, Conn.: FASB, 1992), par. 289.

EXHIBIT 19-2   Key Terms Related to a Corporation's Income Taxes

Deferred tax asset. The deferred tax consequences of future deductible amounts and operating loss carryforwards. A deferred tax asset is measured using the enacted tax rate for the period of recovery or settlement and provisions of the tax law. A deferred tax asset is reduced by a valuation allowance if, based on the available evidence, it is more likely than not that some portion or all of a deferred tax asset will not be realized.

Deferred tax consequences. The future effects on income taxes, as measured by the enacted tax rate and provisions of the tax law, resulting from temporary differences and operating loss carryforwards at the end of the current year.

Deferred tax expense (or benefit). The change during the year in deferred tax liabilities and assets.

Deferred tax liability. The deferred tax consequences of future taxable amounts. A deferred tax liability is measured using the enacted tax rate for the period of recovery or settlement and provisions of the tax law.

Future deductible amount. Temporary difference that will result in deductible amounts in future years when the related asset or liability is recovered or settled, respectively (also called a *deductible temporary difference*).

Future taxable amount. Temporary difference that will result in taxable amounts in future years when the related asset or liability is recovered or settled, respectively (also called *taxable temporary difference*).

Income tax expense (or benefit). The sum of income tax obligation and deferred tax expense (or benefit).

Income tax obligation (or refund). The amount of income taxes paid or payable (or refundable) for a year, as determined by applying the enacted tax law to the taxable income or operating loss for that year. Sometimes called *current tax expense* (or *benefit*).

Operating loss carryback. An excess of tax-deductible expenses over taxable revenues in a year that may be carried back to reduce taxable income in a prior year.

Operating loss carryforward. An excess of tax-deductible expenses over taxable revenues in a year that may be carried forward to reduce taxable income in a future year.

Permanent difference. A difference between pretax financial income and taxable income in an accounting period, which will never reverse in a later accounting period.

Taxable income. The excess of taxable revenues over tax deductible expenses and exemptions for the year.

Temporary difference. A difference between the tax basis of an asset or liability and its reported amount in the financial statements that will result in taxable or deductible amounts in future years when the reported amount of the asset is recovered or the liability is settled.

Valuation allowance. The portion of a deferred tax asset for which it is more likely than not that a tax benefit will not be realized.

Permanent Differences

A **permanent difference** is a difference between a corporation's pretax financial income and taxable income in an accounting period that will *never* reverse in a later accounting period. These differences arise because the U.S. Congress sets economic policy or partially offsets a provision of the tax code that may impose too heavy a tax burden on a particular segment of the economy. There are three types of permanent differences between a corporation's pretax financial income and taxable income. We show a diagram of these permanent differences in the upper part of Exhibit 19-3. We explain the examples in the lower part.

Permanent differences affect *either* a corporation's reported pretax financial income *or* its taxable income, *but not both*. In other words, permanent differences do *not* have deferred tax consequences. They do not require interperiod income tax allocation because GAAP and the IRC differ on what revenues and expenses a corporation recognizes. A corporation that has nontaxable revenue or additional deductions for income tax reporting purposes will report a lower taxable income (compared to its pretax financial income) than it would have if these items did not occur. A corporation with expenses that are not tax deductible will report a higher taxable income.

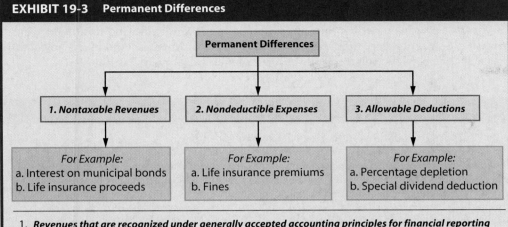

EXHIBIT 19-3   Permanent Differences

1. **Revenues that are recognized under generally accepted accounting principles for financial reporting purposes but are never taxable.** For example:
   a. Interest on municipal bonds. For income tax purposes the interest received by a corporation on an investment in municipal bonds generally is never taxable. The provision enables municipalities to offer bonds that pay a relatively lower rate of interest than corporate bonds of a similar quality. This reduces the cost of borrowing for these municipalities.
   b. Life insurance proceeds payable to a corporation upon the death of an insured employee. For income tax purposes the proceeds received are not taxable to the corporation. Instead, they are treated as partial compensation for the loss of the employee.
2. **Expenses that are recognized under generally accepted accounting principles for financial reporting purposes but are never deductible for income tax purposes.** For example:
   a. Life insurance premiums on officers. For income tax purposes the periodic premiums for life insurance policies on officers are not deductible as expenses. This procedure is consistent with the treatment of the insurance proceeds discussed in 1(b).
   b. Fines. For income tax purposes, fines or other expenses related to the violation of a law are not deductible.
3. **Deductions that are allowed for income tax purposes but do not qualify as expenses under generally accepted accounting principles.** For example:
   a. Percentage depletion in excess of cost depletion. Certain corporations that own wasting assets are allowed to deduct a percentage depletion in excess of the cost depletion on a wasting asset from their revenues for income tax purposes. This provision of the tax code was designed to encourage exploration for natural resources.
   b. Special dividend deduction. For income tax purposes corporations are allowed a special deduction (usually 70% or 80%) for certain dividends from investments in equity securities.

Temporary Differences

A **temporary difference** is a difference between the tax basis (i.e., book value) of a corporation's asset or liability for income tax purposes and the reported amount (i.e., book value) of the asset or liability in its financial statements that will result in taxable or deductible amounts in future years when the corporation recovers the reported amount of the asset (or settles the liability).[4] In other words, a temporary difference causes a difference between a corporation's pretax financial income and taxable

4.   Temporary differences also include items that a corporation cannot identify with a particular asset or liability for financial reporting but which (a) result from events that it has recognized in the financial statements, and (b) will result in taxable or deductible amounts in future years based on provisions in the tax law.

income that "originates" in one or more years and "reverses" in later years. A corporation's temporary differences sometimes are called *timing* differences because of the different time periods in which they affect pretax financial income and taxable income. A corporation's temporary differences generally relate to its individual assets and liabilities and may be classified into four groups[5], which we show in Exhibit 19-4.

EXHIBIT 19-4   Temporary Differences

Future Taxable Income Will Be More Than Future Pretax Financial Income

1. *Revenues or gains are included in pretax financial income prior to the time they are included in taxable income.* For example, gross profit on installment sales normally is recognized at the point of sale for financial reporting purposes. However, for income tax purposes, in certain situations it is recognized as cash is collected. Or, gross profit on long-term construction contracts may be recognized for financial reporting purposes under the percentage-of-completion method. But for income tax purposes it may be recognized by certain corporations under the completed-contract method. Also, investment income may be recognized under the equity method for financial reporting purposes. But for income tax purposes it is recognized in later periods as dividends are received.

2. *Expenses or losses are deducted to compute taxable income prior to the time they are subtracted to compute pretax financial income.* For example, a depreciable asset purchased after 1986 may be depreciated by the Modified Accelerated Cost Recovery System (MACRS) over the prescribed tax life (discussed in Chapter 11) for income tax purposes.[a] For financial reporting purposes, however, it may be depreciated by a financial accounting method (often straight-line) over a different period. Also, interest and taxes on certain self-construction projects may be deducted as incurred in arriving at taxable income. However, these costs may be capitalized in certain instances as a part of the cost of the self-constructed assets for financial reporting.

Future Taxable Income Will Be Less Than Future Pretax Financial Income

3. *Revenues or gains are included in taxable income prior to the time they are included in pretax financial income.* For example, items such as rent, interest, and royalties received in advance are taxable when received. However, they are not reported for financial reporting purposes until the service actually has been provided. Additionally, gains on "sales and leasebacks" are taxed at the date of sale, but are reported over the life of the lease contract for financial reporting purposes.

4. *Expenses or losses are subtracted to compute pretax financial income prior to the time they are deducted to compute taxable income.* For example, product warranty costs, bad debts, compensation expense for share option plans, and losses on inventories in a later year may be estimated and recorded as expenses in the current year for financial reporting purposes. However, they may be deducted as actually incurred to determine taxable income. Or, indirect costs of producing inventory may be recorded as expenses in the current year for financial reporting purposes. However, these costs may be capitalized in the cost of inventory and therefore deducted as part of cost of goods sold in a later year to determine taxable income. Also, a contingent liability may be expensed for financial reporting purposes if a loss is probable and is measurable, but deducted in arriving at taxable income when it is actually paid.

[a] A depreciable asset purchased before 1981 may be depreciated by an accelerated method for income tax purposes and the straight-line method for financial accounting purposes. Or, a depreciable asset purchased between 1981 and 1986 may be depreciated by the Accelerated Cost Recovery System (ACRS).

Temporary differences between pretax financial income and taxable income raise several conceptual issues about measuring and reporting the income tax liability (asset) and the income tax expense (benefit) in the affected accounting periods.

---

5. *FASB Statement No. 109* identifies four other temporary differences: (1) a reduction in the tax basis of depreciable assets because of an investment tax credit accounted for by the deferred method, (2) a reduction in the tax basis of depreciable assets because of other tax credits, (3) an increase in the tax basis of assets because of indexing whenever the local currency is the functional currency, and (4) business combinations accounted for by the purchase method. We do not discuss these temporary differences in this chapter.

INTERPERIOD INCOME TAX ALLOCATION: CONCEPTUAL ISSUES

The accounting principles for income taxes initially were defined in *APB Opinion No. 11*, issued in 1967. This *Opinion* required a corporation to use comprehensive income tax allocation applied under the deferred method. Under this approach a corporation's annual income tax expense was based on all transactions and events included in pretax income on its income statement (i.e., comprehensive allocation), and the deferred tax amount reported on its ending balance sheet was based on the existing income tax rates when the temporary differences originated (i.e., deferred method). *APB Opinion No. 11* was very controversial because of disagreements about its conclusions. Also, the *FASB Statements of Concepts* issued after the *Opinion* contradicted these conclusions.

> **2** Explain the conceptual issues regarding interperiod tax allocation.

   FASB Statement No. 96 was issued in 1987. It required a corporation to use comprehensive income tax allocation applied under the asset/liability method. Under this approach a corporation's deferred tax asset or liability reported on its ending balance sheet was based on the enacted *future* income tax rates when the temporary differences were scheduled to reverse. The conclusions of the FASB in this *Statement* also were controversial because of scheduling complexities (sometimes involving schedules for 20 to 30 years in the future) and restrictions imposed for recognizing deferred tax assets. It was superseded in 1992 by *FASB Statement No. 109*. In its deliberations, the FASB reexamined several conceptual questions (identified in Exhibit 19-5):

1. Should corporations be required to make interperiod income tax allocations for temporary differences, or should there be no interperiod tax allocation?
2. If interperiod tax allocation is required, should it be based on a comprehensive approach for all temporary differences or on a partial approach for only the temporary differences that it expects to reverse in the future?
3. Should interperiod tax allocation be applied using the asset/liability method (based on enacted future tax rates), the deferred method (based on originating tax rates), or the net-of-tax method (where deferred taxes are allocated as adjustments of the accounts to which they relate)?

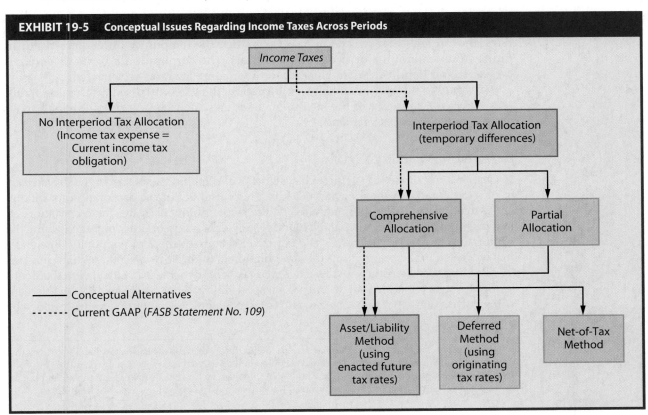

EXHIBIT 19-5   Conceptual Issues Regarding Income Taxes Across Periods

In *FASB Statement No. 109*, the Board identified two objectives of accounting for income taxes. First, a corporation should recognize the amount of its income tax obligation or refund for the current year. Second, a corporation should recognize deferred tax liabilities and assets for the future tax consequences of all events that it has reported in its financial statements or income tax returns. Based on these objectives, the FASB concluded that GAAP requires:

1. Interperiod income tax allocation of temporary differences
2. The comprehensive allocation approach
3. The asset/liability method of income tax allocation

To support its conclusions, the FASB argued that interperiod tax allocation is appropriate because income taxes are an expense of doing business for a corporation and should be accrued and deferred just like other expenses. It argued that comprehensive allocation is applicable because income tax expense should be based on *all* temporary differences, regardless of how significant and how often they reoccur. Finally, it argued that deferred tax items should be based on the enacted tax rates that will be in existence when the temporary differences reverse because that is when the cash flows will occur. Thus, nonallocation, partial allocation, and the deferred and net-of-tax methods listed in Exhibit 19-5 were rejected and are *not* GAAP.

To implement the objectives, the FASB listed four principles that a corporation is to apply to account for its income taxes. A corporation must:

1. Recognize a current tax liability or asset for the estimated income tax obligation or refund on its income tax return for the current year.[6]
2. Recognize a deferred tax liability or asset for the estimated future tax effects of each temporary difference.
3. Measure its deferred tax liabilities and assets based on the provisions of the enacted tax law; the effects of future changes in tax laws or rates are not anticipated.
4. Reduce the amount of deferred tax assets, if necessary, by the amount of any tax benefits that, based on available evidence, are not expected to be realized.[7]

Thus, according to *FASB Statement No. 109*, **a corporation uses interperiod income tax allocation to determine its deferred tax assets and liabilities for all temporary differences. These deferred items are measured based on the currently enacted income tax rates and on laws that will be in existence when the temporary differences result in future taxable amounts or deductible amounts. The corporation adjusts its deferred tax assets and liabilities when changes in the income tax rates are enacted.**

In regard to interperiod income tax allocation, the FASB discussed deferred tax liabilities, deferred tax assets, and the measurement of these items by a corporation in the context of the *FASB Conceptual Framework*.

Deferred Tax Liability

In Chapter 4, we discussed the three characteristics of a liability established in *FASB Statement of Concepts No. 6*. Briefly, they are: (1) it is a responsibility of the corporation to another entity that will be settled in the future, (2) the responsibility obligates the corporation, so that it cannot avoid the future sacrifice, and (3) the transaction or other event obligating the corporation has already occurred. The deferred tax consequences of temporary differences that will result in taxable amounts for a corporation in future years meet these characteristics.

The first characteristic is met by a deferred tax liability because (a) the deferred tax consequences stem from the tax law and are a responsibility to the government, (b) settlement will involve a future payment of taxes, and (c) settlement will result from events specified by

---

6. Since a corporation may make estimated tax payments during the year, the current tax liability or asset that it reports on its ending balance sheet may be different than its total tax obligation or refund.
7. *FASB Statement No. 109, op. cit.,* par. 6 and 8. *FASB Statement No. 109* also addressed the accounting for operating loss carrybacks and carryforwards. For simplicity, we discuss these items in a later section.

the tax law. The second characteristic is met because income taxes will be payable when the temporary differences result in taxable amounts in future years. The third characteristic is met because the past events that result in the deferred tax liability have already occurred.

Deferred Tax Asset

Briefly, the three characteristics of an asset are: (1) it will contribute to the corporation's future net cash inflows, (2) the corporation must be able to obtain the benefit and control other entities' access to it, and (3) the transaction or other event resulting in the corporation's right to or control of the benefit has already occurred.[8] The deferred tax consequences of temporary differences of a corporation that will result in deductible amounts in future years meet these characteristics.

The first characteristic is met because the deductible amounts in future years will result in reduced taxable income, and contribute to the corporation's future net cash inflows through reduced taxes paid. The second characteristic is met because the corporation will have an exclusive right to the reduced taxes paid. Finally, the third characteristic is met because the past events that result in the deferred tax asset have already occurred.

Measurement

After a corporation has identified a future taxable or deductible amount, it "measures" the temporary difference to record the amount of the deferred tax liability or deferred tax asset to report in its financial statements. The FASB addressed two issues regarding the measurement of deferred tax liabilities and assets: (1) the applicable income tax rates, and (2) whether a valuation allowance should be created for deferred tax assets.

Income Tax Rate

The U.S. federal corporate income tax is assessed based on a "several step" rate schedule. However, if a corporation's taxable income exceeds a specified amount, its entire taxable income essentially is taxed at a "single flat rate." For deferred taxes, the question arose as to what rate to use in measuring deferred tax liabilities and assets. For simplicity, the FASB decided to require a corporation to use the enacted income tax rate expected to apply to its *last* dollar of taxable income (i.e., its *marginal tax rate*) in the periods when it expects the deferred tax liability or asset to be settled or realized. In other words, most corporations are required to use the single flat rate in their deferred tax calculations.[9]

Valuation Allowance

The second issue—the possible use of a valuation allowance for deferred tax assets—was more controversial. A corporation will realize the tax benefits from a deferred tax asset only if it will have enough future taxable income from which to subtract the future deductible amount. If there is sufficient uncertainty about a corporation's future taxable income, the FASB decided that it must establish a valuation allowance to reduce its deferred tax asset(s) to the realizable amount. (This approach is similar to reporting accounts receivable at a gross amount and then reducing the amount by an allowance for doubtful accounts.)

But how much uncertainty is "sufficient" and how does a corporation make a judgment about the realizable amount? In regard to sufficiency, the FASB applied a "more likely than not" (a likelihood of more than 50%) criterion to measure uncertainty. In other words, a corporation needs a valuation allowance if, based on available evidence, it is *more likely than not* that the deferred asset will *not* be realized.

To make a judgment about the realizable amount, a corporation should consider all available evidence, both positive and negative, in determining whether it needs a valuation

---

8.   "Elements of Financial Statements of Business Enterprises," *FASB Statement of Financial Accounting Concepts No. 6* (Stamford, Conn.: FASB, 1985), par. 26 and 36.

9.   Corporations for which graduated rates are a significant factor must use an "average graduated tax rate" approach for measuring their deferred tax liabilities and assets. We do not discuss this approach in this book.

allowance. Positive evidence that a corporation will realize the tax benefits from a deferred tax asset includes, for instance, future reversals of existing taxable temporary differences and prudent and feasible tax-planning strategies.[10] These may be sufficient for a corporation to conclude that it does not need a valuation allowance.

The Board stated that it would be difficult for a corporation to conclude that a valuation allowance is *not* needed when there is negative evidence, such as cumulative losses in recent years. It also provided other examples of negative evidence, such as (1) a history of unused operating loss carryforwards, (2) losses expected in the near future years, and (3) unsettled circumstances that are potentially unfavorable. The Board noted, however, that other positive evidence (e.g., a strong earnings history and expected future profitability) may overcome negative evidence, making a valuation allowance unnecessary. A corporation must use good judgment in weighing the verifiable positive and negative evidence to determine if it needs a valuation allowance for some or all of a deferred tax asset.

If a corporation does establish a valuation allowance, a future change in circumstances may cause a change in judgment about the realizability of the related deferred tax asset. There also may be a change in tax laws or rates that would affect the amount of previously recorded deferred tax assets and liabilities. Therefore, the corporation must evaluate its valuation allowance on each balance sheet date. In each of the preceding cases, the corporation includes the effect of the change as an adjustment to the income tax expense related to its income from continuing operations in the year of the change.[11]

SECURE YOUR KNOWLEDGE 19-1

- Because the objectives of financial reporting differ from the objectives of the Internal Revenue Code, a company's pretax financial income and income tax expense (computed under GAAP) will differ from its taxable income and income tax obligation.
- Differences between a company's pretax financial income and its taxable income arise from both permanent and temporary differences.
- Permanent differences arise from revenues or expenses that are recognized for financial reporting purposes but never affect taxable income, or deductions that reduce taxable income but do not qualify as expenses for financial reporting. Permanent differences do not have deferred tax consequences.
- Temporary (timing) differences arise when a company reports a revenue or expense in one period for financial accounting purposes but in an earlier or later period for income tax purposes. This causes a difference between a company's tax basis of its assets or liabilities and the book value of the asset or liability in the financial statements, which creates a:
  - future taxable amount, which increases taxable income in the future; or
  - future deductible amount, which decreases taxable income in the future.
- In accounting for income taxes, a company should:
  - Recognize the amount of its income tax obligation or refund for the current year; and
  - Recognize deferred tax liabilities or assets for the future tax consequences of events that have been reported in the financial statements or income tax returns.
- A deferred tax liability is the increase in future taxes payable due to currently existing temporary differences (future taxable amounts). A deferred tax asset is the reduction in future taxes payable due to currently existing temporary differences (future deductible amounts).
- Deferred tax liabilities and assets are measured using the enacted tax rate that will be in existence when the temporary differences result in future taxable or deductible amounts.

(continued)

---

10. A tax planning strategy is an action a corporation ordinarily would not take except to ensure that it can realize a deductible temporary difference (e.g., acceleration of taxable income).
11. *FASB Statement No. 109, op. cit.,* par. 18–27.

- A deferred tax asset should be reduced by a valuation allowance if it is more likely than not that the deferred tax asset will not be realized (e.g., the future deductible amount will not be used because of insufficient future taxable income).

INTERPERIOD INCOME TAX ALLOCATION: RECORDING AND REPORTING OF CURRENT AND DEFERRED TAXES

To measure and record the amount of its current and deferred income taxes, a corporation completes the following steps:

Step 1. Measure the income tax obligation for the year by applying the applicable tax rate to the current taxable income.

Step 2. Identify the temporary differences and classify each as either a future taxable amount or a future deductible amount.

Step 3. Measure the year-end deferred tax liability for each future taxable amount using the applicable tax rate.

Step 4. Measure the year-end deferred tax asset for each future deductible amount using the applicable tax rate.

Step 5. Reduce deferred tax assets by a valuation allowance if, based on available evidence, it is *more likely than not* that some or all of the year-end deferred tax assets will not be realized.

Step 6. Record the income tax expense (including the deferred tax expense or benefit), income tax obligation, change in deferred tax liabilities and/or deferred tax assets, and change in valuation allowance (if any).

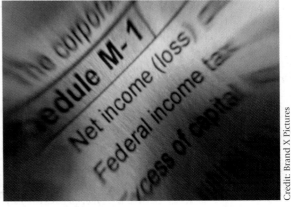

Credit: Brand X Pictures

A corporation reports its federal taxable income on *Form 1120,* "U.S. Corporation Income Tax Return." Included in this form is Schedule M-1 (or Schedule M-3 for large corporations), which identifies the differences between the corporation's pretax financial income and its taxable income. Because of its length, we do not include Form 1120 here. However, information about the taxable income and temporary differences we discussed in the previous steps is obtained from this form.

We show the previous steps in the following diagram, after which we explain the related journal entries.

Item		Balance Sheet Impact		Change in Balance Sheet Accounts		Income Statement Impact
Taxable Income	→	Current Tax Liability[a]	→	Income Taxes Payable		
				+ or −		
Future Taxable Amount	→	Deferred Tax Liability[b]	→	Change in Deferred Tax Liability		
				+ or −		(=) Income Tax Expense[e]
Future Deductible Amount	→	Deferred Tax Asset[c]	→	Change in Deferred Tax Asset		
				+ or −		
Realization Concern	→	Valuation Allowance[d]	→	Change in Valuation Allowance		
Permanent Difference				No tax consequences		

[a]Taxable income for year × Tax rate
[b]Year-end future taxable amount × Tax rate
[c]Year-end future deductible amount × Tax rate
[d]Unrealizable amount of year-end deferred tax asset × Tax rate
[e]May affect other financial statements (as we discuss later)

Basic Entries

A corporation's deferred tax expense or benefit is the change in its deferred tax liabilities or assets during the year. The amount of this change is combined with the amount of its income tax obligation (or refund) to determine the amount of its income tax expense (or benefit) for the year. Thus, if a corporation has one deferred tax liability at the beginning of the year, earns pretax income for the year, and has an increase in the liability (the deferred tax expense), it makes the following journal entry (amounts assumed):

Income Tax Expense	11,600	
Income Taxes Payable		10,000
Deferred Tax Liability		1,600

For a similar situation involving one deferred tax asset (and *no* valuation allowance) instead of a deferred tax liability, the corporation makes the following journal entry (amounts assumed):

Income Tax Expense	12,800	
Deferred Tax Asset	1,300	
Income Taxes Payable		14,100

The corporation allocates the amount of income tax expense to the various components of its comprehensive income, as we discuss in a later section. It determines the amount of the income tax obligation by multiplying the taxable income for the year by the current tax rate(s). For simplicity, we assume here (and in the later examples and homework) that the corporation does *not* make estimated income tax payments during the year. Therefore, it records the entire obligation for the year as income taxes payable.

The corporation calculates the amount of the adjustment to the deferred tax liability (asset) in the journal entry by determining the amount of the year-end deferred tax liability (asset) and comparing this ending amount to the beginning amount of the deferred tax liability (asset). The corporation reports the amount of the year-end deferred tax liability (asset) on its ending balance sheet, classified as "current" or "noncurrent," as we discuss in a later section.

If, in the last example, the corporation previously had no valuation allowance but determined that one was necessary, it would make the following additional journal entry (amounts assumed):

Income Tax Expense	400	
Allowance to Reduced Deferred Tax Asset to Realizable Value		400

The corporation combines the $400 debit to income tax expense with the $12,800 amount of Income Tax Expense from the journal entry in the last example to determine its $13,200 *total* Income Tax Expense. If the amount of the Allowance is equal to the adjustment to the Deferred Tax Asset, then the Income Tax Expense is equal to the Income Taxes Payable. The corporation subtracts the Allowance account from the Deferred Tax Asset account on its ending balance sheet to report the expected net realizable value of the deferred tax asset.

When a corporation has more than one future taxable amount or future deductible amount, permanent differences, and changes in enacted future tax rates, completion of the steps listed earlier becomes more complex. We provide several examples in the following sections.

Example: Deferred Tax Liability—Single Future Taxable Amount

Assume that in 2007, Track Company purchased an asset at a cost of $6,000. For financial reporting purposes, the asset has a four-year life, no residual value, and is depreciated by the units-of-output method over 6,000 units (2007: 1,600 units; 2008: 2,800 units;

2009: 1,100 units; 2010: 500 units). For income tax purposes the asset is depreciated under MACRS using the 200% declining balance method over a three-year life (no residual value), as we discussed in Chapter 11. Prior to 2007, Track Company had no deferred tax liability or asset. The difference between the company's depreciation for financial reporting purposes and income tax purposes is the only temporary difference between its pretax financial income and taxable income.[12] In 2007 the company has taxable income of $7,500 (after deducting the MACRS depreciation). The income tax rate for 2007 is 30% and no change in the tax rate has been enacted for future years.

Based on the preceding information:

- The depreciation expense for 2007 is $1,600 [1,600 × ($6,000 ÷ 6,000)] for financial reporting purposes and $2,000 [$6,000 × 33.33% (from Exhibit 11-3)] for income tax purposes.
- At the end of 2007 the asset has a book value of $4,400 for financial reporting purposes and a book value of $4,000 for income tax purposes, as we show in the top part of Example 19-1.

The $400 difference in book values is the result of a temporary difference in depreciation that originated in 2007 (and that caused taxable income to be lower than pretax financial income in that year). This difference will reverse in future years because tax depreciation will be *lower* than financial depreciation by $400 (to depreciate each book value to zero). Thus, the $400 is the ending *future taxable amount* for 2007 because future taxable income will be *higher* than future pretax financial income.

EXAMPLE 19-1 Asset Book Value and Deferred Tax Liability

	Financial Reporting (12/31/07)	Income Tax Reporting (12/31/07)
Cost of asset	$6,000	$6,000
Accumulation depreciation	(1,600)	(2,000)
Book value of asset	$4,400	$4,000
Ending future taxable amount	$400	
Enacted future tax rate	0.30	
Ending deferred tax liability	$120	
Beginning deferred tax liability	(0)	
Change (increase) in deferred tax liability	$120	(Deferred tax expense)

Track Company applies the following steps that we listed earlier on page 953 to determine its current and deferred income taxes:

Step 1: It calculates (measures) its $2,250 ($7,500 taxable income × 0.30 current tax rate) current income tax obligation for 2007.

Step 2: It identifies the depreciation difference as the only future taxable amount for 2007, as we show in Example 19-1.

---

12. In reality, a corporation would have several depreciable assets of different ages and with varying lives, perhaps resulting in both originating (and deductible) and reversing (and taxable) depreciation differences in a given year. For simplicity, when dealing with depreciable assets in the text and homework, we generally focus on a single depreciable asset, with depreciation that results in a reversing (and taxable) difference in the future.

Step 3: It calculates (measures) the $120 total deferred tax liability at the end of 2007 by multiplying the $400 total future taxable amount times the 30% enacted future tax rate, as we show in the middle of Exhibit 19-1.

Step 4: It skips this step because it has no future deductible amount.

Step 5: It skips this step because it has no deferred tax asset.

Step 6: It records its income taxes for 2007. It credits income taxes payable for its $2,250 current income tax obligation. Since the company has no deferred tax liability at the beginning of 2007, it credits the deferred tax liability for $120, the amount we show at the bottom of Example 19-1. [If a deferred liability had existed at the beginning of 2007, the change needed to bring the balance up (or down) to the ending deferred tax liability would be recorded in the journal entry.] It determines the debit for its $2,370 income tax expense by adding the $120 deferred tax liability to the $2,250 income taxes payable. Track Company makes the following journal entry at the end of 2007:

Income Tax Expense ($2,250 + $120)	2,370	
Income Taxes Payable		2,250
Deferred Tax Liability		120

Track Company reports the $2,370 income tax expense on its 2007 income statement, subject to intraperiod tax allocation (which we discuss in a later section of the chapter). The company reports the income taxes payable as a current liability on its 2007 ending balance sheet. As we discuss in a later section, the company reports the deferred tax liability on its ending balance sheet. ♦

Example: Deferred Tax Liability—Single Future Taxable Amount and Multiple Rates

Now assume the same information as in the previous example, except that the income tax rate for 2007 is 40%, but Congress has enacted tax rates of 35% for 2008, 33% for 2009, and 30% for 2010 and beyond. In the previous example, the calculation of the deferred tax liability is straightforward. This is because a 30% tax rate is applicable to all the future years in which the depreciation temporary difference reverses and results in higher taxable income. However, when different enacted tax rates apply to taxable income in different future years, the calculation of the amount of the ending deferred tax liability is more complicated. The calculation requires a corporation to:

- Prepare a schedule to determine the reversing difference (i.e., taxable amount) for each future year,
- Multiply each yearly taxable amount by the applicable tax rate to determine the additional income tax obligation (deferred taxes) for that year, and
- Sum the yearly deferred taxes to determine the total deferred tax liability.

In this example, before the Track Company can prepare a deferred tax liability schedule, it must first prepare a schedule to compute the 2008 through 2010 depreciation expense for financial reporting and income tax purposes. We show this schedule in the upper portion of Example 19-2. Based on the differences in depreciation for financial reporting and income tax purposes, the company prepares a schedule to calculate its deferred tax liability. We show this schedule in the lower portion of Example 19-2.

In Example 19-2, for each year Track Company deducts the income tax depreciation from the financial reporting depreciation to determine the taxable amount. Given the enacted tax rates for the respective years, the income taxes payable on the taxable amounts are $47 in 2008, $70 in 2009, and $17 in 2010. Thus, the total deferred tax liability is $134 at the end of 2007. Since the taxable income for 2007 is $7,500, the income

EXAMPLE 19-2 **Depreciation and Deferred Tax Schedules**

Depreciation Expense

Year	Financial Depreciation	Income Tax Depreciation
2008	$2,800[a]	$2,667[b]
2009	1,100	889[c]
2010	500	444[d]

Deferred Tax Liability

	2008	2009	2010	
Financial depreciation	$2,800	$1,100	$500	
Income tax depreciation	(2,667)	(889)	(444)	
Taxable amount[e]	$ 133	$ 211	$ 56	= $400
Income tax rate	0.35	0.33	0.30	
Deferred tax liability[f]	$ 47 +	$ 70 +	$ 17	= $134

a. Units produced × $1/unit.
b. $6,000 × 44.45% from Exhibit 11-3.
c. $6,000 × 14.81% from Exhibit 11-3.
d. $6,000 × 7.41% from Exhibit 11-3; $1 rounding error.
e. Lower income tax depreciation results in higher taxable income.
f. Amounts rounded to nearest dollar.

tax obligation is $3,000 ($7,500 × 0.40) based on the 40% tax rate for 2007. Track Company makes the following journal entry at the end of 2007:

Income Tax Expense ($3,000 + $134)	3,134	
Income Taxes Payable		3,000
Deferred Tax Liability		134

The company reports the expense and liabilities in its financial statements as we discussed in the first example. ♦

Example: Deferred Tax Asset—Single Future Deductible Amount

Assume that Klemper Company has been operating profitably for several years selling a product on which it provides a three-year warranty. It expects to be profitable in the future. For financial reporting purposes, the company estimates its future warranty costs and records a warranty expense and liability at year-end. For income tax purposes the company deducts its warranty costs when paid. This difference in reporting warranty costs is the only temporary difference between the company's pretax financial income and taxable income. It is a *future deductible amount* (resulting in a deferred tax asset) because in future years the warranty costs that the company deducts for income tax purposes will exceed the warranty expense it deducts for financial reporting purposes. This will cause its future taxable income to be *lower* than its future pretax financial income. At the beginning of 2007, the company had a deferred tax asset of $330 related to the warranty liability on its balance sheet. At the end of 2007 the company estimates that its ending warranty liability is $1,400, as we show in Example 19-3. In 2007 the company has taxable income of $5,000. The income tax rate for 2007 is 30% and no change in the tax rate has been enacted for future years.

4 Record and report deferred tax assets.

EXAMPLE 19-3   Liability Book Value and Deferred Tax Asset

	Financial Reporting (12/31/07)	Income Tax Reporting (12/31/07)
Book value of warranty liability	$1,400	$0
Ending future deductible amount	$1,400	
Enacted future tax rate	0.30	
Ending deferred tax asset	$ 420	
Beginning deferred tax asset	(330)	
Change (increase) in deferred tax asset	$ 90	(Deferred tax benefit)

Klemper Company applies the following steps that we listed earlier on page 953 to determine its current and deferred income taxes:

Step 1: It calculates (measures) its $1,500 ($5,000 × 0.30) current income tax obligation for 2007.

Step 2: It identifies the warranty liability difference as the only future deductible amount for 2007, as we show in Example 19-3.

Step 3: It skips this step because it has no future taxable amount.

Step 4: It calculates (measures) the $420 total deferred tax asset at the end of 2007 by multiplying the $1,400 total future deductible amount times the 30% enacted future tax rate, as we show in the middle of Example 19-3.

Step 5: It skips this step because it does not need a valuation allowance since it has a successful earnings history and expects to be profitable in the future.

Step 6: It records its income taxes for 2007. It credits income taxes payable for its $1,500 current income tax obligation. It calculates the $90 change (increase) in the deferred tax asset by deducting the $330 beginning deferred tax asset from the required $420 ending deferred tax asset, as we show in the bottom part of Example 19-3. This $90 is the amount of the debit to the deferred tax asset. It is subtracted from the $1,500 income taxes payable to determine the $1,410 debit to income tax expense for 2007. The Klemper Company makes the following journal entry at the end of 2007:

Income Tax Expense ($1,500 − $90)	1,410	
Deferred Tax Asset	90	
Income Taxes Payable		1,500

Klemper Company reports the deferred tax asset on its balance sheet, as we discuss in a later section. ♦

Example: Deferred Tax Asset and Valuation Allowance

Now assume the same information as in the previous example, except that during the past few years the Klemper Company's sales and profits have been declining. At the end of 2007, because of uncertain future economic conditions, the company decides that it is "more likely than not" that $600 of the ending $1,400 future deductible amount will not be realized. Therefore, in addition to the income tax entry made in the previous example, Track Company also records a valuation allowance of $180 ($600 × 0.30) at the end of 2007 as follows:

Income Tax Expense	180	
Allowance to Reduce Deferred		
Tax Asset to Realizable Value		180

The company subtracts the $180 ending balance in the allowance account from the $420 deferred tax asset ending balance to report the realizable value of $240 on its ending balance sheet as follows:

Deferred tax asset	$420
Less: Allowance to reduce deferred tax asset to realizable value	(180)
	$240

In 2008 and future years, the company must review the available evidence to determine whether it needs to make an adjustment (increase or decrease) in the valuation allowance. ♦

LINK TO ETHICAL DILEMMA

Classical Notes Inc. manufactures and sells various types of classical sheet music. Over the last several years, there has been a decrease in the interest in classical music and, as a result, Classical Notes has reported annual losses over this period. However, recent scientific evidence that classical music stimulates brain development has sparked renewed interest in classical music, resulting in the company reporting its first operating profit ($80,000) in five years. At the end of the current fiscal year, Classical Notes has recognized $4,000,000 of deferred tax assets, net of a $1,000,000 valuation allowance, which primarily consists of operating loss carryforwards that will expire evenly over the next 10 years.

As the recently hired accountant for Classical Notes, you are in charge of preparing the income tax accrual for the current year. You are particularly concerned with the amount of the valuation allowance (which was decreased from $1.2 million to $1 million in the current year) and have requested a meeting with the CEO concerning this matter. During the meeting, you inform the CEO that you think the valuation allowance is too small and should be increased by at least $500,000. You have based your conclusions on the fact that the company has reported historical operating losses in four of the last five years. Furthermore, the current operating profit was due largely to a one-time surge in the demand for classical music and all economic analyses expect this demand to level off within the next year. Therefore, you do not think the company will have sufficient future taxable income to use the operating loss carryforwards. The CEO is extremely upset at your recommendation. She informs you that the company's fortunes have finally turned around and the demand for classical music will continue to grow despite what the experts say. Furthermore, if the valuation allowance is increased, this would cause the company to report a net loss for the year and send the wrong signal to the market. After a heated exchange, the CEO tells you that the amount of the valuation allowance is a judgment call, and as the experienced leader of the company, it is her judgment that the valuation allowance is appropriate. She then instructs you to drop the matter and leave the major decisions to her. What is your response?

Example: Permanent and Temporary Differences

Assume that the Sand Company has been in operation for several years and has earned income in each of those years. For *financial reporting purposes*, at the end of 2007, the company reports pretax income of $75,500. Included in the calculation of this income are the following items: (1) interest revenue of $1,500 on investments in municipal bonds, (2) gross profit of $10,000 on installment sales recognized under the accrual method, and (3) rent revenue of $3,000 for the first year of a three-year, $9,000 rental contract collected in advance.

For *income tax purposes*, the company reports gross profit on installment sales under the installment sales method as cash is collected. It also reports rent revenue for tax purposes as cash is collected. During 2007 the company reports gross profit of $2,000 on installment sales. The company had a deferred tax liability of $300 related to an installment sales temporary difference of $1,000 at the beginning of 2007. The income tax rate is 30% for 2007 and no change in the tax rate has been enacted for future years.

To determine the Sand Company's current and deferred income taxes, the company must first compute its 2007 taxable income. This amount is $72,000, as we show in Example 19-4. This schedule is similar to the schedule required to reconcile a corporation's pretax financial income to its taxable income on Form 1120, the federal corporate income tax return. In preparing the schedule in Example 19-4, there is one permanent difference and two temporary differences. The permanent difference ($1,500 tax-exempt interest revenue) is deducted from pretax financial income to determine taxable income. Although the interest revenue is included in pretax financial income, it is not taxable. Thus, it is ignored for deferred tax calculations because it will *never* reverse and never be taxable.

EXAMPLE 19-4   Computation of 2007 Taxable Income

Pretax financial income	$75,500
Less: Tax-exempt interest revenue on municipal bonds (permanent difference)	(1,500)
Excess of gross profit on installment sales over gross profit for taxes (temporary difference)	(8,000)a
Add: Excess of rent collected in advance over rent revenue (temporary difference)	6,000b
Taxable Income	$72,000

a. $10,000 gross profit on installment sales recognized under accrual method for financial reporting minus $2,000 gross profit recognized under installment sales method for income taxes.
b. $9,000 collected in advance and reported for income taxes minus $3,000 rent revenue recognized for financial reporting.

The $8,000 *excess* of the gross profit on installment sales included in pretax financial income ($10,000) over the gross profit reported for taxes ($2,000) is subtracted to determine taxable income, because less cash is collected (and taxed). This difference is a *future taxable amount* because it will be included in future taxable income when the cash is collected. On the other hand, the $6,000 *excess* of rent collected in advance is added to pretax financial income to determine taxable income, because more cash ($9,000) is collected (and taxed) than reported as rent revenue ($3,000) in pretax financial income. This difference is a *future deductible amount* because future taxable income will be less than future pretax financial income when the rent is recognized as rent revenue for financial reporting purposes.

Sand Company applies the following steps that we listed earlier on page 953 to determine its current and deferred income taxes:

Step 1: It calculates (measures) its $21,600 ($72,000 taxable income from Example 19-4 × 0.30) current income tax obligation for 2007.
Step 2: It identifies the installment sales difference of $9,000 ($1,000 beginning + $8,000 increase during 2007) as the total *future taxable amount* for 2007. This amount is the difference between the book value of the installment accounts receivable that it reported under the accrual method for financial reporting purposes and the book value of the receivable that it reported under the

installment sales method for income tax purposes. It identifies the rent difference of $6,000 ($6,000 book value of unearned rent reported for financial reporting purposes − $0 book value reported for income tax purposes) as the total *future deductible amount* for 2007.

Step 3: It calculates (measures) the $2,700 total deferred tax liability at the end of 2007 by multiplying the $9,000 total future taxable amount times the 30% enacted future tax rate. Since the company had a $300 beginning deferred tax liability, it must increase this liability by $2,400 ($2,700 − $300).

Step 4: It calculates (measures) the $1,800 total deferred tax asset at the end of 2007 by multiplying the $6,000 total future deductible amount times the 30% enacted future tax rate.

Step 5: It skips this step because its $9,000 total future taxable amount is greater than its $6,000 total future deductible amount so that it does not need a valuation allowance for the deferred tax asset.

Step 6: It records its income taxes for 2007. It credits income taxes payable for its $21,600 current income tax obligation. It credits (increases) the deferred tax liability for $2,400. It debits (increases) the deferred tax asset for $1,800. It determines the $22,200 debit to income tax expense by adding the $2,400 to and subtracting the $1,800 from the $21,600 income taxes payable. Sand Company makes the following journal entry at the end of 2007:

Income Tax Expense ($21,600 + $2,400 − $1,800)	22,200	
Deferred Tax Asset	1,800	
Income Taxes Payable		21,600
Deferred Tax Liability		2,400 ♦

SECURE YOUR KNOWLEDGE 19-2

- The following steps are necessary to measure and record a company's current and deferred income taxes:
  - Step 1: Calculate the current income tax obligation by multiplying the current taxable income by the applicable tax rate.
  - Step 2: Identify any temporary differences and classify them as future taxable amounts or future deductible amounts.
  - Step 3: Calculate the deferred tax liability for each future taxable amount using the applicable tax rate.
  - Step 4: Calculate the deferred tax asset for each future deductible amount using the applicable tax rate.
  - Step 5: Reduce any deferred tax assets by a valuation allowance if necessary.
  - Step 6: Prepare journal entries to record income tax expense, the income tax obligation, the change in deferred liabilities and/or deferred tax assets, and the change in the valuation allowance (if any).
- Two basic journal entries are required to account for income taxes:
  - The first journal entry is based on the fact that income tax expense is made up of an amount payable in the current period (income taxes payable) and an amount deferred until a later period (deferred expense or benefit). Note that a company's deferred tax expense or benefit is the change in its deferred tax liability or asset during the year.
  - The second journal entry adjusts the valuation allowance (if necessary) with a matching adjustment to income tax expense. The valuation allowance is reported as a contra-account to the deferred tax asset.

(continued)

- When there are multiple enacted tax rates, the company prepares a schedule to determine the reversing temporary difference each year and uses the applicable enacted tax rate for each year to compute the deferred tax liability or asset.
- Permanent differences are ignored for deferred tax calculations because they will never reverse and will never be taxable.

OPERATING LOSS CARRYBACKS AND CARRYFORWARDS

The previous section and examples dealt with the recognition of a deferred tax liability or asset when a corporation had taxable *income* in the current year. This section deals with the situation where a corporation has a *loss* for income tax purposes (and a pretax financial loss) in the current year, resulting in an operating loss carryback or carryforward for income tax purposes.

The IRC allows a corporation reporting an operating loss for income tax purposes in the current year to carry this loss back or carry it forward to offset previous or future taxable income. The corporation may first carry a reported operating loss back two years (in sequential order, starting with the *earliest* of the two years). This procedure is called an **operating loss carryback**. In this case, the corporation files amended income tax returns showing lower taxable income for those years and receives a refund of income taxes previously paid. Operating loss carrybacks can provide significant refunds for companies. For instance, in 2004, **Lucent Technologies** was able to obtain an $816 million tax refund for carrying back its 2001 operating loss to 1996. (It was able to carry back for more than the usual two years because of a provision in the Job Creation and Worker Assistance Act of 2002, which allowed a longer carryback period to help companies hurt by the economic downturn at that time.)

If a corporation's taxable income for the past two years is not enough to offset the amount of the currently reported operating loss, it then sequentially carries forward the loss for 20 years and offsets the loss against future taxable income, if there is any.[13] This procedure is called an **operating loss carryforward**. The corporation then pays lower income taxes in the future based on lower future taxable income. Exhibit 19-6 shows a diagram of the operating loss carryback and carryforward sequence. A corporation also may elect to forgo the carryback and, instead, only carry forward an operating loss. Unless higher future income tax rates have been enacted, most corporations do not make this election because an operating loss carryback will result in a definite and immediate income tax refund. However, a carryforward will reduce income taxes payable in future years only to the extent that taxable income is earned.

5 Explain an operating loss carryback and carryforward.

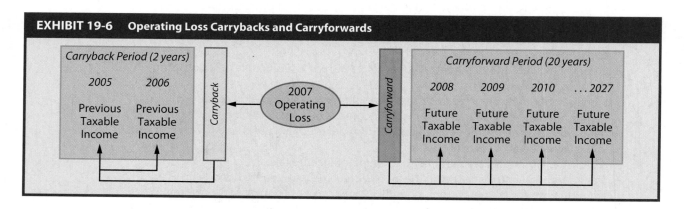

EXHIBIT 19-6 Operating Loss Carrybacks and Carryforwards

---

13. Prior to 1998, a corporation could carry back an operating loss 3 years, but it was limited to a 15-year carryforward period.

Conceptual Issues

When a corporation reports an operating loss for financial reporting purposes in a given year, there are several important accounting questions about valuing assets, recognizing income tax expense, and reporting net income. These issues primarily involve operating loss carryforwards, but also relate to operating loss carrybacks.

Operating Loss Carrybacks

The FASB considered two conceptual issues related to an operating loss carryback in *FASB Statement No. 109*.

1. Should a corporation recognize the tax benefit of an operating loss carryback as a retrospective adjustment or in the current period?

For an operating loss carryback, the corporation obtains a tax benefit in the year of the operating loss. This benefit is a refund of income taxes paid in prior periods (which the corporation reported as income tax expense in those periods). An argument in favor of the corporation reporting the tax benefit of a carryback as a retrospective adjustment is that its prior income is what makes possible the realization of the benefit. The counterargument is that the corporation's prior income that enables use of the carryback only gives value to the carryback. It is the corporation's current operating loss that creates the tax benefit.

2. Should the corporation incurring the operating loss recognize a current receivable for the tax benefit of the carryback?

The recognition of a receivable by a corporation for the tax benefit of an operating loss carryback is conceptually sound. The corporation will realize the tax benefit as an income tax refund when the refund is issued by the federal government. Thus, it is an economic benefit (asset).

Operating Loss Carryforwards

The FASB considered two conceptual issues related to an operating loss carryforward that arises because a corporation either has no prior taxable income or its prior taxable income is not enough to absorb the entire operating loss carryback.

1. Should a corporation recognize the tax effect of an operating loss carryforward in the current period or in the future when it is realized?

For an operating loss carryforward, the tax effect is the result of the corporation's operating loss in the *current* year that it will realize in a *future* year(s) if it earns enough future taxable income. One alternative accounting treatment for the corporation is to recognize the tax effect (i.e., future tax savings) as an asset in the year of its operating loss. This approach is consistent with the concepts of interperiod tax allocation and matching. Arguments for this alternative are: (1) the tax effects are an economic resource of the corporation because it has a right to and control over the future tax benefit, (2) there is better matching because the corporation offsets the tax benefit against the operating loss in the year the loss generated the benefit, (3) it enables better comparisons, because a corporation with an available operating loss carryforward is better off than one without it, and (4) it is consistent with the going-concern assumption.

Another alternative is for the corporation to defer recognition of an operating loss carryforward until it is realized. If this approach were taken, the corporation would not recognize an asset in the loss year. If realization occurs, it would recognize the tax benefit as a reduction in its income taxes payable for that future period. Arguments for this alternative are: (1) an operating loss carryforward is not a current economic resource of the corporation because it will provide a future tax benefit only if the corporation has sufficient future taxable income, (2) this approach is consistent with the consensus that realization should take precedence over matching (that is, when collectibility is not reasonably assured, recognition should be deferred), and (3) the corporation's operating loss is the past event that created a right to the future benefit; however, it is the future event of earning taxable income that gives value to the carryforward.

2. How should the corporation report the tax effect of an operating loss carryforward on its financial statements?

If the corporation recognizes an operating loss carryforward in the year of the loss, it is generally agreed that the corporation should deduct the tax benefit from its operating loss. If the corporation recognizes the tax effect in the year of realization, it could (1) deduct the tax effect from that year's income tax expense, or (2) report the tax effect as a retrospective adjustment of the year in which the operating loss occurred. An argument for the first approach is that the earning of taxable income in that year enables the corporation to reduce its income taxes, so it should decrease its income tax expense accordingly. An argument for reporting the tax benefit as a prior period adjustment is that the tax benefit arose in the year of the operating loss; it was just a matter of confirming the amount at the time of realization.[14]

Generally Accepted Accounting Principles

In *FASB Statement No. 109*, the FASB accepted parts of both alternatives. It concluded that the GAAP for the financial reporting of operating loss carrybacks and carryforwards are as follows:

1. A corporation must recognize the tax benefit of an operating loss carryback in the period of the loss as an asset (current receivable) on its balance sheet and as a reduction of the operating loss on its income statement.
2. A corporation must recognize the tax benefit of an operating loss carryforward in the period of the loss as a deferred tax asset. However, it must reduce the deferred tax asset by a valuation allowance if, based on the available evidence, it is *more likely than not* that the corporation will *not* realize some or all of the deferred tax asset.[15]

In other words, a corporation handles operating loss carryforwards in the same manner as the future deductible amounts we discussed earlier in the chapter. That is, at year-end:

- The corporation measures a deferred tax asset for an operating loss carryforward using the enacted future tax rate.
- If necessary, it measures a valuation allowance and deducts the amount from the deferred tax asset to determine its net realizable value.
- In the year-end journal entry to record its current and deferred taxes, the corporation treats any increase (decrease) in the deferred tax asset and valuation allowance as an adjustment of its income tax expense (benefit).

It is more likely that a corporation will need a valuation allowance for a deferred tax asset related to an operating loss carryforward, because the operating loss itself provides negative evidence as to the likelihood of having sufficient future taxable income to realize the tax benefits. We show several examples in the following sections.

Example: Operating Loss Carryback

6 Account for an operating loss carryback.

Assume that Monk Company reports a pretax operating loss of $90,000 in 2007 for both financial reporting and income tax purposes. Also assume that reported pretax financial

---

14. For a further discussion, see "Accounting for Income Taxes," *FASB Discussion Memorandum* (Stamford, Conn.: 1983), and D. Beresford, L. Best, P. Craig, and J. Weber, "Accounting for Income Taxes: A Review of Alternatives," *FASB Research Report* (Stamford, Conn.: FASB, 1983), par. 150–164 and pp. 95–106.
15. *FASB Statement No. 109, op. cit.*, par. 17.

income and taxable income for the previous two years had been: 2005 — $40,000 (tax rate 25%); and 2006 — $70,000 (tax rate 30%). Thus, the $110,000 total pretax income in the previous two years is more than enough to offset the $90,000 pretax operating loss. When the company carries back its 2007 operating loss, it is entitled to a tax refund of $25,000, calculated as we show in Example 19-5.

EXAMPLE 19-5	Refund from Operating Loss Carryback		
Year	Pretax Financial Income and Taxable Income Offset by Carryback	Income Tax Rate	Income Tax Refund
2005	$40,000	0.25	$10,000
2006	50,000	0.30	15,000
	$90,000		$25,000

Note in Example 19-5 that all of the 2005 income of $40,000 is offset by the $90,000 operating loss carryback, but only $50,000 of the $70,000 income in 2006 is offset because the carryback is first applied to the earlier year. (Therefore, the remaining $20,000 of the 2006 income is available to offset any operating losses that might occur in 2008.) At the end of 2007, Monk Company makes the following journal entry:

Income Tax Refund Receivable	25,000	
Income Tax Benefit from		
Operating Loss Carryback		25,000

Monk Company reports the receivable on its balance sheet as a current asset until it collects the receivable. The company reports the operating loss carryback tax benefit in the lower portion of its 2007 income statement as follows:

Pretax operating loss	$(90,000)
Less: Income tax benefit from operating loss carryback	25,000
Net loss	$(65,000) ♦

Example: Operating Loss Carryforward and Valuation Allowance

Assume that Lake Company reports a pretax operating loss of $60,000 in 2007 (its first year of operation) for both financial reporting and income tax purposes. The income tax rate is 30% and no change in the tax rate has been enacted for future years. Because the company had no income prior to 2007, it cannot carry back the operating loss. Since it carries forward the operating loss, the company reports a deferred tax asset at the end of 2007 for the deferred tax consequences (future tax benefit) of the carryforward. It calculates the deferred tax asset to be $18,000 ($60,000 × 0.30). Lake Company makes the following journal entry at the end of 2007:

7 Account for an operating loss carryforward.

Deferred Tax Asset	18,000	
Income Tax Benefit from		
Operating Loss Carryforward		18,000

Because Lake Company has no history of taxable income and has insufficient positive evidence of future taxable income, it must also reduce the deferred tax asset by a valuation allowance. If we assume the company establishes a valuation allowance for the entire amount of the deferred tax asset, it also makes the following journal entry at the end of 2007:

Income Tax Benefit from Operating Loss Carryforward	18,000	
Allowance to Reduce Deferred Tax Asset to Realizable Value		18,000

Lake Company reports the $60,000 operating loss as a net loss on its 2007 income statement because it did not realize any tax benefit from the operating loss carryforward in 2007. The deferred tax asset, offset by the valuation allowance, normally is reported on a company's balance sheet, but the net amount is zero in this example. (Lake Company discloses both the deferred tax asset and the valuation allowance amounts in the notes to its 2007 financial statements, however.) Lake Company also discloses the operating loss carryforward as follows in a note to its 2007 financial statements: "The company has a $60,000 operating loss carryforward that can be used within 20 years to offset future taxable income and reduce income taxes."

Now assume that in 2008, Lake Company operates successfully and earns pretax operating income of $100,000 for both financial reporting and income tax purposes. The company realizes the tax benefit of the operating loss carryforward in 2008 as a reduction of its income tax obligation. It offsets the $60,000 carryforward from 2007 against the $100,000 pretax income in 2008, resulting in taxable income of $40,000. Based on the 30% income tax rate, its income taxes payable (and income tax expense) are $12,000 ($40,000 × 0.30). Since the company has used up the tax benefit of the operating loss carryforward, it eliminates the deferred asset and related valuation allowance. Lake Company makes the following journal entry the end of 2008:

Income Tax Expense	12,000	
Allowance to Reduce Deferred Tax Asset to Realizable Value	18,000	
Income Taxes Payable		12,000
Deferred Tax Asset		18,000

The lower portion of Lake Company's 2008 income statement is as follows:

Pretax operating income	$100,000
Less: Income tax expense	(12,000)
Net income	$ 88,000

The effect of the operating loss carryforward is to reduce the company's income tax expense for 2008 from $30,000 ($100,000 × 0.30)—the amount without the tax benefit of the carryforward—to $12,000, so that its 2008 net income (after tax) is increased by $18,000. ♦

Example: Operating Loss Carryforward and No Valuation Allowance

Now assume the same information as in the previous example, except that the Lake Company has signed a substantial number of contracts for the sales of its products in 2008. Based on this verifiable positive evidence, the company decides that the tax benefit of its operating loss carryforward will be realized in 2008 and that it does not need a valuation allowance at the end of 2007.

In this case, Lake Company makes the same journal entry to record the $18,000 deferred tax asset as it did in the previous example. However, since it does not record a valuation allowance, the lower portion of Lake Company's 2007 income statement is as follows:

Pretax operating loss	$(60,000)
Less: Income tax benefit from operating loss carryforward	18,000
Net loss	$(42,000)

The realizable tax benefit reduces the company's $60,000 pretax operating loss to a $42,000 net loss. This is in contrast to the previous example, where the company reported a $60,000 net loss on its 2007 income statement.

Continuing with the same assumptions as in the previous example, Lake Company earns pretax operating income of $100,000 in 2008. The $60,000 operating loss carryforward reduces the company's taxable income to $40,000, so that its income tax obligation is $12,000 as in the previous example. The company eliminates the deferred tax asset but since it does not have a valuation allowance, the 2008 income tax expense is $30,000. Lake Company makes the following 2008 year-end journal entry:

Income Tax Expense	30,000	
Income Taxes Payable		12,000
Deferred Tax Asset		18,000

The lower portion of Lake Company's 2008 income statement is as follows:

Pretax operating income	$100,000
Income tax expense	(30,000)
Net income	$ 70,000

Note that Lake Company's total net income for 2007 and 2008 is $28,000 in both the previous and this example. Its income recognition is accelerated in this example, however (through a lower net loss in 2007), because the company had sufficient positive verifiable evidence in 2007 that it would realize the tax benefit from its operating loss carryforward in 2008.

In some cases a corporation's pretax operating income of a given year is not enough to offset the entire amount of an operating loss carryforward. In this situation, it offsets a portion of the operating loss against the income and continues to carry forward the remainder as a deferred tax asset (and discloses the amount in a note). For instance, if in the last example, Lake Company had earned only $50,000 pretax operating (and taxable) income in 2008, then it would offset $50,000 of the $60,000 operating loss carryforward against this income and would pay no income taxes for 2008. The company would report income tax expense of $15,000 ($50,000 × 0.30) and would reduce its deferred tax asset by $15,000. It would eliminate the $3,000 ($18,000 − $15,000) deferred tax asset (30% of the $10,000 remaining operating loss carryforward) in a future year(s) when it realized the tax benefit. ◆

COMPREHENSIVE ILLUSTRATION

The examples in the previous sections showed the accounting for temporary differences separately from operating losses. In this comprehensive example, we show a temporary difference and also an operating loss carryback and an operating loss carryforward. Assume that Branson Company begins operations in 2004 and is profitable through 2006. In 2007 the company reports a pretax financial loss of $8,000 and a taxable loss of $8,800. In 2008 and 2009, the company is again profitable, although at the end of 2007 the company felt that future profits were not likely. The income tax rate is 30%. Example 19-6 shows the company's pretax financial income (loss) and taxable income (loss) for the years 2004 through 2009, as well as its income taxes payable (receivable). It is assumed that the only difference between pretax financial income (loss) and taxable income (loss) in any year results from additional (MACRS) depreciation reported for income tax purposes.

As we show in Example 19-6, Branson Company pays $360 of income taxes in 2004 and $840 in 2005 and 2006. In 2007, $2,800 of the $8,800 operating loss is carried back to offset the 2005 and 2006 taxable income, resulting in a tax refund of $840. Note that the 2007 operating loss is *not* carried back to 2004 because of the two-year carryback limitation. In 2008 and 2009, the $6,000 remaining operating loss is carried forward and (1) offsets the $1,500 taxable income in 2008 so that no income taxes are paid, and (2) offsets $4,500 of the $6,400 taxable income in 2009 so that $570 of income taxes are paid.

EXAMPLE 19-6   Income Taxes Payable or Receivable

Year	Pretax Financial Income (Loss)	Depreciation Difference	Taxable Income (Loss)	Income Taxes Payable (Receivable)
2004	$2,000	$ 800	$ 1,200	$ 360[a]
2005–2006	5,000	2,200	2,800	840[a]
2007	(8,000)	800	(8,800)	(840)[b]
2008	2,200	700	1,500	0[c]
2009	7,000	600	6,400	570[d]

a. Taxable income × 0.30 income tax rate.
b. $2,800 carryback to years 2005 and 2006, resulting in tax refund of $840; remaining carryforward of $6,000 ($8,800 − $2,800).
c. $1,500 taxable income offset by carryforward, therefore no income taxes owed; remaining carryforward of $4,500 ($6,000 − $1,500).
d. $6,400 taxable income offset by $4,500 carryforward; $1,900 × 0.30.

For financial reporting purposes, Branson Company must determine its deferred tax liability (or asset) and income tax expense (or refund) for each year. Both the depreciation taxable temporary difference and the operating loss carryforward for each year affect the company's deferred taxes; Example 19-7 shows these calculations. Note in Example 19-7 that the depreciation taxable temporary difference increases each year by the difference in depreciation for financial reporting purposes and income tax purposes shown in Example 19-6.

EXAMPLE 19-7   Deferred Tax Information

Year	Depreciation Temporary Difference Beginning	Addition	Ending[a]	Operating Loss Carryforward
2004	$ 0	$ 800	$ 800	—
2005–2006	800	2,200	3,000	—
2007	3,000	800	3,800	(6,000)[b]
2008	3,800	700	4,500	(4,500)[c]
2009	4,500	600	5,100	—

a. Beginning depreciation temporary difference + additional difference for current year.
b. $8,800 taxable loss − $2,800 operating loss carryback (see Example 19-6).
c. $6,000 operating loss carryforward from 2007 − $1,500 taxable income in 2008 (see Example 19-6).

The operating loss carryforward of $6,000 at the end of 2007 is the $8,800 operating loss in 2007 less the $2,800 operating loss carryback, as we discussed earlier. The operating loss carryforward at the end of 2008 is only $4,500, because $1,500 was used to offset the taxable income in 2008. The following "timeline" diagram further explains the relationships between the taxable incomes and the operating loss carrybacks and carryforwards for the various years:

	2004	2005 2006	2007	2008	2009
Taxable income before adjustments	$1,200	$2,800	$(8,800)	$1,500	$6,400
Loss carrybacks		(2,800) ◄———	2,800		
			$(6,000)		
Loss carryforward (to 2008)				1,500 ►(1,500)	
Loss carryforward (to 2009)				4,500 ————————►	(4,500)
Taxable income			$ 0	$ 0	$1,900

Example 19-8 shows the computations of Branson Company's deferred tax liability and asset (and valuation allowance) for each year, based on the information in Example 19-7. As we show in Example 19-7, the company has $800 additional depreciation for tax purposes at the end of 2004, which will result in taxable income of the same amount in future years. As we show in Example 19-8, applying the 30% tax rate to the future taxable amount results in a deferred tax liability of $240 at the end of 2004. Since there was a $0 deferred tax liability at the beginning of 2004, the company makes a $240 adjustment (credit) to the deferred tax liability. The company makes similar computations for 2005 through 2009.

EXAMPLE 19-8   Annual Deferred Taxes

Year	Deferred Tax Liability			Deferred Tax Asset			Valuation Allowance		
	Beginning	Ending[a]	Adjustment	Beginning	Ending	Adjustment	Beginning	Ending	Adjustment
2004	$ 0	$ 240	$240	—	—	—	—	—	—
2005–06	240	900	660	—	—	—	—	—	—
2007	900	1,140	240	—	$1,800[b]	$1,800	—	$660[c]	$660
2008	1,140	1,350	210	$1,800	1,350[d]	(450)	$660	0[e]	(660)
2009	1,350	1,530	180	1,350	0	(1,350)	—	—	—

a. Ending depreciation taxable temporary difference (from Example 19-7) × 0.30.
b. $6,000 operating loss carryforward (from Example 19-7) × 0.30.
c. [$6,000 carryforward − $3,800 ending depreciation temporary difference (from Example 19-7)] × 0.30.
d. $4,500 operating loss carryforward × 0.30.
e. ($4,500 carryforward − $4,500 ending depreciation temporary difference) × 0.30.

At the end of 2007, the $6,000 operating loss carryforward results in an ending deferred tax asset of $1,800 ($6,000 × 0.30). Since there was a $0 deferred tax asset at the beginning of 2007, the company makes an $1,800 adjustment (debit) to the deferred tax asset. A valuation allowance is required at the end of 2007 because the company does not expect to be profitable in future years. However, the valuation allowance does not have to be for the full amount of the deferred tax asset resulting from the operating loss carryforward. This is because the company has an existing depreciation temporary difference that will result in additional future taxable income against which to offset the operating loss carryforward. Since the operating loss carryforward is $6,000, but the total ending depreciation taxable temporary difference is $3,800 at the end of 2007 (see Example 19-7), a valuation allowance of only $660 [($6,000 − $3,800) × 0.30] is required and the company makes an adjustment (credit) for that amount.

At the end of 2008 Branson Company has a $1,350 deferred tax asset ($4,500 operating loss carryforward × 0.30), which requires a $450 adjustment (credit) to that account. Since the $4,500 total ending depreciation taxable temporary difference is the same as the $4,500 remaining operating loss carryforward, it does not need a valuation allowance. This requires an adjustment (debit) of $660 to the valuation allowance account. In 2009 the company uses the $4,500 remaining operating loss carryforward to offset an equal amount of taxable income, so it eliminates (credits) the $1,350 related deferred tax asset.

At the end of each year, the company prepares a journal entry to record its income taxes, based on the information in Examples 19-6 and 19-8. For instance, at the end of 2007, Branson Company makes the following journal entry:

Income Tax Refund Receivable	840	
Deferred Tax Asset	1,800	
Deferred Tax Liability		240
Allowance to Reduce Deferred Tax Asset to Realizable Value		660
Income Tax Benefit from Operating Loss Carryback		840
Income Tax Benefit from Operating Loss Carryforward		900

The $840 income tax benefit from the operating loss carryback relates to the income tax refund receivable. The $900 income tax benefit from the operating loss carryforward is the net amount that the company will realize in future years and that is related to the deferred tax asset, valuation allowance, and deferred tax liability.

Branson Company reports operating loss carryback and carryforward tax benefits on its 2007 income statement as follows:

Pretax operating loss		$(8,000)
Less: Income tax benefit from operating loss carryback	$840	
Income tax benefit from operating loss carryforward	900	1,740
Net loss		$(6,260)

The company discloses the remaining operating loss carryforwards in 2007 and 2008 in a note accompanying the respective year's financial statements.

INTRAPERIOD INCOME TAX ALLOCATION

8 Apply intra-period tax allocation.

Intraperiod income tax allocation is the allocation of a corporation's total income tax expense for a period to the various components of its income statement (and occasionally the statement of retained earnings, statement of comprehensive income, or statement of changes in stockholders' equity). Income tax allocation within a period is required under GAAP. *APB Opinion No. 9* and *FASB Statement No. 154* require an allocation of the income tax effects to extraordinary items, retrospective adjustments, and prior period adjustments, and *APB Opinion No. 30* requires an allocation of the income tax effects to a disposal of a segment of a business. *FASB Statement No. 109* and *FASB Statement No. 130* extend the disclosures to the income tax effects of gains and losses included in other comprehensive income.[16] When a corporation has these types of income, it allocates income taxes between them and income from continuing operations. The rationale behind intraperiod tax allocation is based on the matching concept. A corporation *matches* its income tax expense against the major components of its pretax income to give a fair presentation of the after-tax impact of each of these items on net income.

For intraperiod income tax allocation purposes, on its income statement a corporation reports the income tax expense applicable to its pretax income from continuing operations separately. The disclosure of the tax effect on its income from continuing operations is important because external users are very interested in the corporation's business activities that are expected to continue. The amount is based on the normal income tax rates applied to this income. However, the corporation reports any extraordinary items, the income or loss from the operations of a discontinued component, the gain or loss from the disposal of a discontinued component, retrospective adjustments and prior period adjustments (reported on the statement of retained earnings), and any other comprehensive income items *net* of the related income tax effects. That is, for these items the corporation deducts the income tax expense (or tax "savings" which is called a tax *credit* in the case of a loss) directly from each item and reports only the *after-tax* amount. (It discloses the amount of the income tax expense or tax credit for each of these items either parenthetically or in a note to its financial statements.) Because these items are "incremental," the corporation determines the amount of the income tax expense or tax credit for each item by applying the marginal (incremental) tax rate to each item.

---

16. Currently, there are four items of other comprehensive income, as we discussed in Chapter 5. For instance, when a company records a change in the unrealized increase (decrease) stockholders' equity account for investments in available-for-sale securities, this causes a change in the deferred tax liability (or asset). In the journal entry to record the change in the deferred tax liability (or asset), the offsetting entry is a reduction of the unrealized increase (decrease) account.

Example: Intraperiod Income Tax Allocation

Assume the Kalloway Company reports the following items of *pretax* financial (and taxable) "income" for 2007:

Income from continuing operations	
(revenues of $270,000 less expenses of $190,000)	$80,000
Gain on disposal of discontinued Division X	18,000
Loss from operations of discontinued Division X	(5,000)
Extraordinary loss from tornado	(10,000)
Prior period adjustment	
(error in calculating bad debt expense for 2006)	(8,000)
Amount subject to income taxes	$75,000

The company is subject to income tax rates of 20% on the first $50,000 of income and 30% on all income in excess of $50,000. Example 19-9 shows the schedule to allocate the total income tax expense, and Example 19-10 shows Kalloway Company's 2007 income statement[17] and statement of retained earnings as a result of applying intraperiod income tax allocation.

EXAMPLE 19-9   Schedule of Income Tax Expense for 2007

Component (Pretax)	Pretax Amount	×	Income Tax Rate	=	Income Tax Expense (Credit)
Income from continuing operations	$50,000	×	0.20	=	$10,000
	30,000	×	0.30	=	9,000
Gain on disposal of discontinued Division X	18,000	×	0.30	=	5,400
Loss from operations of discontinued Division X	(5,000)	×	0.30	=	(1,500)
Extraordinary loss from tornado	(10,000)	×	0.30	=	(3,000)
Prior period adjustment	(8,000)	×	0.30	=	(2,400)
Total income tax expense					$17,500

As we show in Example 19-9, the total income taxes for the Kalloway Company on the $90,000 subject to income taxes in 2007 are $17,500. The company computes the $19,000 [(0.20 × $50,000) + (0.30 × $30,000)] income tax expense applicable to its pretax income from continuing operations by multiplying this $80,000 income by the normal income tax rates. This provision for income tax does *not* consider the tax consequences of any items not included in pretax income from continuing operations. The company reports the $19,000 income tax expense applicable to pretax income from continuing operations on its income statement in Example 19-10 on a separate line directly below pretax income from continuing operations, and subtracts this amount to determine its income from continuing operations. The company reports the gain on the disposal of the discontinued Division X, the loss from the operations of the discontinued Division X, and the extraordinary loss *net of income tax* on its income statement in Example 19-10, and discloses each related income tax effect in parentheses. It reports the prior period adjustment net of its income tax effect on the statement of retained earnings in Example 19-10. The company computed each of the related income tax effects in

---

17. For simplicity, in Example 19-10 and related homework we do not include earnings per share information.

Example 19-9 by multiplying the marginal tax rate (30%) by the pretax gain or loss.[18] Kalloway Company makes the following journal entry to record its 2007 intraperiod income tax allocation:

Income Tax Expense	19,000	
Gain on Disposal of Division X	5,400	
Loss from Operations of Discontinued Division X		1,500
Extraordinary Loss from Tornado		3,000
Retained Earnings (prior period adjustment)		2,400
Income Taxes Payable		17,500

EXAMPLE 19-10   Kalloway Company

Income Statement
For Year Ended December 31, 2007

Revenues (listed separately)		$270,000
Expenses (listed separately)		(190,000)
Pretax income from continuing operation		$ 80,000
Income tax expense		(19,000)
Income from continuing operations		$ 61,000
Results of discontinued operations:		
Gain on disposal of discontinued Division X		
(net of $5,400 income taxes)	$12,600	
Loss from operations of discontinued Division X		
(net of $1,500 income tax credit)	(3,500)	9,100
Income before extraordinary loss		$ 70,100
Extraordinary loss from tornado (net of $3,000 income tax credit)		(7,000)
Net Income		$ 63,100

Statement of Retained Earnings
For Year Ended December 31, 2007

Retained earnings, January 1, 2007	$435,000
Less: Prior period adjustment, understatement of 2006 bad debt expense	
(net of $2,400 income tax credit)	(5,600)
Adjusted retained earnings, January 1, 2007	$429,400
Add: Net income	63,100
	$492,500
Less: Cash dividends	(23,500)
Retained Earnings, December 31, 2007	$469,000

Note that the debit to Income Tax Expense of $19,000 relates *only* to the income taxes applicable to income from continuing operations. Since the company reports its results of discontinued operations, extraordinary items, and prior period adjustments on the financial statements *net* of their respective income tax effects, it debits or credits the income tax expense or credit related to each of these items directly to the related account

---

18. In our example only two tax rates were in effect, and the income from continuing operations was large enough so that the gain and losses were taxed at a single marginal rate. It is possible for several tax rates to be in effect at the same time, and for the total income to be increased or decreased by other gains and losses, so that more than one marginal tax rate may be applicable. In these cases, a corporation uses a weighted averaging process to determine the appropriate tax effects on the gains and losses. This process is beyond the scope of this book.

(as we show in the journal entry) to reduce the account balance to its after-tax amount, as it reports in Example 19-10. Note also, in this example, we assume that taxable income and pretax financial income are the same. If a corporation's taxable income is not the same as its pretax financial income because of temporary differences, the total income tax expense is the sum of the income tax obligation and the adjustments to the deferred tax liabilities and assets. In this case, the corporation must determine the impact of the adjustments on each component of pretax financial income before it can properly allocate the income tax expense. For adjustments of (1) a valuation allowance because of changes in circumstances, and (2) deferred tax liabilities and assets because of changes in tax rates or laws, the corporation includes the amounts of the adjustments in its income tax expense related to continuing operations.[19] ♦

FINANCIAL STATEMENT PRESENTATION AND DISCLOSURES

FASB Statement No. 109 specifies what is required for (1) reporting deferred tax liabilities and assets on a corporation's balance sheet, and (2) disclosures in the notes to the corporation's financial statements. *FASB Statement No. 95* specifies the related statement of cash flows disclosures.

Balance Sheet Presentation

A corporation must report its deferred tax liabilities and assets in two classifications:

- A *net* current amount
- A *net* noncurrent amount

It bases these classifications on the classifications of the related assets or liabilities for financial reporting. For instance, a corporation reports a deferred tax liability related to the excess of tax depreciation over financial depreciation as a noncurrent liability because the depreciable assets are noncurrent assets. It classifies a deferred tax liability or asset not directly related to an asset or liability (e.g., related to an operating loss carryforward) according to the expected reversal date of the temporary difference. A valuation allowance is allocated between current and noncurrent deferred assets on a proportional basis.[20]

In other words, a corporation must:

1. separate its deferred tax liabilities into current and noncurrent groups,
2. separate its deferred tax assets into current and noncurrent groups,
3. combine (*net*) the amounts in the current groups, and
4. combine (*net*) the amounts in the noncurrent groups.[21]

If the net amount of the current groups is a debit balance, the corporation reports the amount as a current asset, whereas it reports a net credit amount as a current liability. The corporation reports a net debit balance for the noncurrent groups as a noncurrent asset, and reports a net credit balance as a noncurrent liability. This procedure is one of the few situations in which "offsetting" of assets and liabilities is allowed in financial reporting. The FASB requires this approach because of the close relationship between deferred tax assets and liabilities, and to avoid the detailed analyses necessary for more refined classification methods.

9 Classify deferred tax liabilities and assets.

---

19. *FASB Statement No. 109, op. cit.,* par. 35.
20. *Ibid.,* par. 41.
21. This "offsetting" applies to each tax jurisdiction. Furthermore, a corporation may have some assets and liabilities (e.g., warranty liability) for which it classifies the portion due to be collected or paid in the next year as current and classifies the remainder as noncurrent. In such a case, it must also proportionally classify the related deferred tax liability or asset into current and noncurrent amounts.

Example: Balance Sheet Presentation

Assume that the Anicar Company has the four deferred tax items we show in Example 19-11. In this situation, the company combines the $6,000 credit balance of the current deferred tax liability (Item 1) with the $3,400 debit balance of the current deferred tax asset (Item 3), and reports a $2,600 net deferred tax liability as a *current liability* on its year-end balance sheet. Likewise, the company combines the $12,000 credit balance of the noncurrent deferred tax liability (Item 2) with the $2,500 debit balance of the noncurrent deferred tax asset (Item 4), and reports a $9,500 net deferred tax liability as a *noncurrent liability* on its year-end balance sheet. ◆

EXAMPLE 19-11	Schedule of Deferred Assets and Liabilities		
Deferred Tax Accounts	**Account Balance**	**Related Balance Sheet Account**	**Deferred Income Tax Reporting Classification**
Deferred Tax Liabilities			
1. Installment sales	$ 6,000 credit	Accounts receivable	Current
2. Depreciation	12,000 credit	Property, plant, and equipment	Noncurrent
Deferred Tax Assets			
3. Warranty costs	3,400 debit	Warranty liability	Current
4. Rent revenue (long-term)	2,500 debit	Unearned rent	Noncurrent

Statement of Cash Flows Presentation

If a corporation uses the indirect method to report its operating cash flows, it adds any increase in its income taxes payable, any increase in its deferred tax liability, or any decrease in its deferred tax asset to net income in the operating activities section of its statement cash flows. It subtracts from net income any decrease in its income taxes payable, any decrease in its deferred tax liability, or any increase in its deferred tax asset. Because of the significance of income taxes, a corporation using the indirect method of reporting its operating cash flows is also required to disclose its income taxes paid. This disclosure may be made in a separate schedule, narrative description, or in the notes to its financial statements.

Financial Statement Disclosures

To help users evaluate a corporation's income taxes, *FASB Statement No. 109* also requires extensive income tax disclosures in the notes to the corporation's financial statements (or directly on the statements themselves). We briefly summarize the major disclosures. For the net deferred tax liability or asset, it discloses the causes of the deferred tax assets and liabilities, the total deferred tax liabilities, the total deferred tax assets, and the total valuation allowance. For the income tax expense, it discloses the amount of income tax expense or benefit allocated to continuing operations, discontinued operations, extraordinary items, retrospective adjustments, prior period adjustments, and gains and losses included in other comprehensive income. It also discloses the significant components of income tax expense related to continuing operations for each year. These include, for instance, (1) current tax expense or benefit (i.e., income tax obligation or refund), (2) deferred tax expense or benefit, (3) tax credits, (4) benefits of operating loss carryforwards, and (5) adjustments of the valuation allowance for changes in circumstances.[22]

The intraperiod allocation of income taxes on the face of a corporation's income statement (and statement of retained earnings, statement of changes in stockholders' equity, or statement comprehensive income), as we previously illustrated, partially

---

22. *Ibid.*, par. 43–48.

satisfies the preceding disclosure requirements. A corporation typically discloses the remaining information in a note to its financial statements. We show these disclosures in Real Report 19-1 later in the chapter for **Emerson Radio Corp**.

MISCELLANEOUS ISSUES

The previous discussion and examples focused on the major issues involved in accounting for income taxes. For simplicity, we omitted several topics.

Change in Income Tax Laws or Rates

As we discussed earlier, a corporation determines the balances of its deferred tax liabilities (or assets) at the end of a given year by applying the currently enacted income tax rate(s) and laws to its taxable (or deductible) temporary differences. Occasionally, Congress may change the income tax laws or rates so that they differ from the laws or rates a corporation previously used to calculate its deferred tax liabilities (or assets). A corporation must disclose the financial impact of this congressional action because it is an event that has economic consequences to the corporation. That is, a corporation's financial condition improves if it owes a smaller amount of future taxes (or would receive a larger refund) and its condition weakens if it owes more future taxes (or would receive a smaller refund).

When a change in the income tax laws or rates occurs, a corporation adjusts the deferred tax liabilities (and assets) for the effect of the change. It makes the adjustment to the balance of each deferred tax liability (and asset) as of the beginning of the year in which the change is made, and includes the resulting tax effect in the income tax expense related to its income from continuing operations.[23] The amount of the adjustment is the difference between the deferred tax liability (or asset) balance at the beginning of the year, based on the newly enacted laws or rates, and the balance that was computed under the old law or rates.

For instance, refer back to the example (page 954) for a deferred tax liability. If, in May 2008, Congress increases the income tax rate from 30% to 35%, then Track Company's deferred tax liability at the end of 2007 should be $140 ($400 × 0.35) instead of $120, as we previously computed. Therefore, the company increases the deferred tax liability and recognizes a tax effect in the amount of $20 ($140 − $120). In May 2008, Track Company records the increase and recognizes the expense as follows:

Income Tax Expense	20	
Deferred Tax Liability		20

The company increases the income tax expense related to income from continuing operations by $20 on its 2008 income statement, and reports the deferred tax liability at a credit balance of $140. At the end of 2008 the company computes its deferred taxes in the usual manner, except that it uses the newly enacted 35% income tax rate. A change in the balance of a valuation allowance—because of changes in circumstances concerning the future realization of a deferred tax asset—is recorded and reported in a similar way.

Compensatory Share Option Plans

In Chapter 16, we discussed compensatory share option plans. Since we had not yet discussed deferred taxes, we did not deal with the related deferred tax journal entries. We provide you with a brief overview here.

Recall that a corporation determines the compensation cost of its compensatory share option plan using the fair value method based on an option pricing model. Under this method, it computes the total compensation cost by multiplying the estimated fair value per share option times the estimated number of share options that are expected to

---

23. *Ibid.*, par. 27.

become vested. This compensation cost is then expensed each year over the service period. This expense reduces the corporation's pretax income for financial reporting purposes and, hence, its income tax expense. However, for income tax purposes the corporation is not allowed to deduct any compensation expense related to the share option plan until the employees exercise the share options. Therefore, during the service period, the corporation's pretax financial accounting income is lower than its taxable income, resulting in a future deductible difference and the need to record a journal entry to increase the related deferred tax asset (and decrease income tax expense).

When the employees exercise the share options, income tax rules allow the corporation to take a tax deduction (compensation expense) for the difference between the market price of the shares on the exercise date and the exercise price. Since the exercise date will be *after* the service period, the corporation will have *no* compensation expense for financial reporting purposes at this time because it already deducted the compensation expense during the service period. Hence, the corporation's pretax accounting income will be higher than the corporation's taxable income. In other words, the previous future deductible difference has "reversed" and is now deducted for income tax purposes. This requires a journal entry to eliminate the deferred tax asset (and increase income tax expense).

If the actual market price at the time of exercise is different from the market price estimated under the option pricing model (which is likely because of the use of estimates), the deferred tax issues become more complicated. The difference is a "permanent" difference that decreases income tax expense and income taxes payable. The net tax savings is treated as an increase in additional paid-in capital in the deferred tax journal entry.

Alternative Minimum Tax and Other Tax Credits

The Tax Reform Act of 1986 imposed an *alternative minimum tax* (AMT) on corporations, designed to help ensure equity in income tax payments. A corporation pays the higher of its AMT (as computed according to the income tax laws) or its regular income tax liability. Thus, the AMT may affect the corporation's income tax obligation in a given year. The AMT also may affect the corporation's deferred tax liability or asset because calculation of the AMT depends, in part, on "adjusted current earnings (ACE)" adjustments related to certain temporary differences. Also, if a corporation pays the AMT, generally it can credit the amount paid against its future income taxes. The corporation uses this credit in a given future year when the regular tax liability exceeds the AMT. It may not carry back the minimum tax credit, but may carry it forward indefinitely.

The federal tax law also allows certain other "tax credits" that a corporation may deduct from its computed income taxes to determine the income taxes it owes. Among the tax credits that are, or have been, in the tax law are credits for certain research and experimental activities, for foreign taxes paid, for hiring certain employees, and for using certain fuels. To illustrate a foreign tax credit, assume the following situation for a corporation (amounts in millions):

	U.S.	Foreign
Taxable income	$100	$ 20
Tax rate (assumed)	0.35	0.40
Income taxes payable	$ 35	$ 8

On its U.S. income tax return, the corporation reports a total taxable income of $120 ($100 + $20), receiving a foreign tax credit based on the foreign taxes paid. However, the amount of the foreign tax credit cannot exceed an amount equal to the U.S. income tax imposed on the foreign-source income. Therefore, its foreign tax credit is the lesser of $8, the foreign tax imposed, or $7 ($20 × 35%), the U.S. tax imposed on foreign income. The corporation pays $35 [($120 × 35%) − $7] to the U.S. government. However, it pays total income tax of $43 ($35 + $8), which is also its income tax expense (assuming there are no temporary differences). In the notes to its financial statements, the corporation discloses that there is a difference between the statutory tax rate in the United States of 35% and its effective tax rate of 36% ($43 ÷ $120).

As we showed, specific restrictions apply to tax credits, and sometimes a corporation cannot use all of its tax credits in a given year. In some circumstances, the corporation may carry forward these tax credits and apply them against future taxes owed in a manner similar to operating loss carryforwards. When this arises, the steps we outlined earlier in the chapter for computing a corporation's deferred taxes must be modified to include measurement of a deferred tax asset for each type of tax credit. Because the AMT and tax credits are complex and vary across corporations, we do not discuss them further.

LINK TO INTERNATIONAL DIFFERENCES

The international accounting principles for deferred income taxes differ in certain respects from those in the United States. Recall that *FASB Statement No. 109* requires comprehensive income tax allocation of temporary differences using the asset/liability method. International accounting standards require a company to use comprehensive allocation (in most cases) of temporary differences using the "balance sheet liability method" (which is very similar to the asset/liability method). However, there are differences between U.S. and International GAAP. For instance, for deferred tax assets, international accounting standards allow a company to recognize a deferred tax asset only when it is *probable* that it will have sufficient future taxable income against which to utilize the deferred tax asset. For deferred tax liabilities, a company recognizes a deferred tax liability if it revalues its assets. The measurement of a company's deferred tax assets and liabilities is based on future tax rates as well as how the tax laws of the country in which it is located allow it to recover or settle the deferred tax asset or liability.

International accounting standards require a company to report the income tax expense related to its pretax income from ordinary activities as a separate line item on its income statement and to show extraordinary items net of tax. It reports the tax effects of any equity adjustments (e.g., asset revaluations) directly in equity. A company is required to report its deferred tax balances as separate items on its balance sheet. However, in some instances it may offset any debit and credit balances representing deferred tax items. It may *not* report deferred tax assets or liabilities as current items.

SECURE YOUR KNOWLEDGE 19-3

- If a company has an operating loss for income tax purposes (tax deductible expenses exceed taxable revenue), it can choose to:
  - Carry the operating loss back two years (in sequential order starting with the earliest year) to offset previous taxable income and create a refund of income taxes previously paid; any remaining loss can then be carried forward sequentially for 20 years to offset future taxable income, or
  - Forgo the operating loss carryback and choose to carry forward sequentially the operating loss for 20 years to offset future taxable income.
- The income tax benefit of an operating loss carryback is recognized in the year the operating loss occurs as a current receivable on the balance sheet and as a reduction of the operating loss on the income statement.

(continued)

- The income tax benefit of an operating loss carryforward is recognized in the year the operating loss occurs as a deferred tax asset (reduced by a valuation allowance, if necessary) on the balance sheet and as a reduction of the operating loss on the income statement.
- Intraperiod income tax allocation is the allocation of a corporation's total income tax expense for a period to the various components of its income statement (and occasionally the statement of retained earnings, statement of comprehensive income, or statement of changes in stockholders' equity).
  - Intraperiod tax allocation is based on the concept of matching income tax expense against the major components of pretax income to provide more useful information to external users.
  - Extraordinary items, the income or loss from a discontinued component, retrospective adjustments, prior period adjustments, and any other comprehensive income item are reported net of the related income tax effects where the income tax effect is based on the company's marginal tax rate.
- A company reports deferred tax liabilities and assets as a net current amount and a net noncurrent amount based on the classifications of the related assets or liabilities for financial reporting. Extensive disclosure in the notes to the financial statements is also required.
- A change in income tax laws or rates requires an adjustment of the deferred tax liabilities (and assets) as of the beginning of the year in which the change is made with the resulting tax effect included in income tax expense relating to income from continuing operations.
- The recording of compensation expense relating to compensatory share options (no tax deduction is allowed until the options are exercised) results in a decrease in income tax expense and an increase in the related deferred tax asset. Upon exercise of the share options, the deferred tax asset is eliminated and income tax expense is increased.
- In computing its income tax obligation, a corporation may be allowed tax credits (i.e., credits for alternative minimum tax paid in previous years, research and experimental activities) that reduce the amount of income taxes owed and create a deferred tax asset for each type of tax credit.

ILLUSTRATIVE DISCLOSURES

Real Report 19-1 shows the 2004 income tax disclosures (in part) of **Emerson Radio Corp.** These disclosures are representative of the type necessary under the generally accepted accounting principles of *FASB Statement No. 109*.

Reporting

Real Report 19-1 Income Tax Disclosures

EMERSON RADIO CORP.

(in thousands)

Income Statement (in part):

| | Years Ended March 31 | |
	2004	2003
Income (loss) before income taxes	$(1,585)	$16,924
Provision (benefit) for income taxes	2,150	(9,282)
Income (loss) from continuing operations	$(3,735)	$26,206

Balance Sheet (in part):

| | March 31 | |
	2004	2003
Assets		
Current Assets (in part):		
Deferred tax assets	$ 5,887	$ 6,761

Continued

	March 31	
	2004	2003
Noncurrent Assets (in part):		
Deferred tax assets	15,263	17,595
Current Liabilities (in part):		
Income taxes payable	509	752

Notes to Consolidated Financial Statements (in part):

NOTE 7—INCOME TAXES (in part)

	2004	2003	2002
		(In thousands)	
Current:			
Federal	$ —	$ —	$ (160)
Foreign, state and other	667	2,018	468
Deferred:			
Federal	1,843	(11,300)	(7,899)
Foreign, state and other	(360)	—	—
	$2,150	$ (9,282)	$(7,591)

The difference between the effective rate reflected in the provision for income taxes and the amounts determined by applying the statutory U.S. rate of 34% to income before income taxes from continuing operations for the years ended March 31, 2004, 2003, and 2002 are analyzed below:

	2004	2003	2002
		(In thousands)	
Statutory provision (recovery)	$ (539)	$ 5,389	$ 4,089
Increase (decrease) in valuation allowance	1,981	(13,069)	(12,057)
Foreign income taxes	434	(1,192)	254
State taxes	662	559	372
Minority interest	(268)	(706)	(606)
Other, net	(120)	(263)	357
Total income tax (benefit)	$2,150	$ (9,282)	$ (7,591)

As of March 31, 2004 and 2003, the significant components of the Company's deferred tax assets and liabilities are as follows:

	2004	2003
	(In thousands)	
Deferred tax assets:		
Accounts receivable reserves	$ 3,405	$ 4,707
Inventory reserves	1,710	1,963
Net operating loss carryforwards	24,791	25,005
Other	1,248	637
Total deferred tax assets	31,154	32,312
Valuation allowance	(7,543)	(5,562)
Net deferred tax assets	23,611	26,750
Deferred tax liabilities:		
Intangible assets	(578)	(415)
Investment in affiliate	(1,883)	(1,883)
Other	—	(96)
Net deferred taxes	$21,150	$24,356

Total deferred tax assets for the consumer electronics segment at March 31, 2004 and 2003 include the tax benefit of net operating loss carry forwards subject to annual limitations

Continued

(as discussed below) and future deductible temporary differences to the extent management believes it is more likely than not that such benefits will be realized.

Total deferred tax assets for the sporting goods segment at March 31, 2004 and 2003 include the tax benefit of net operating loss carryforwards, which expire in the years 2011 through 2023. Such assets are recorded net of a valuation allowance of $7,543,000 to reflect the extent to which management believes it is more likely than not that such tax benefits will be realized.

Income (loss) of foreign subsidiaries before taxes was $(2,872,000), $6,198,000, and $2,808,000 for the years ended March 31, 2004, 2003, and 2002, respectively.

As of March 31, 2004, Emerson and its consolidated subsidiaries had a federal net operating loss carryfoward of approximately $98,000,000, which will expire in the years 2006 through 2019. The utilization of these net operating losses are subject to limitations under IRC section 382. In addition, SSG has federal net operating loss carryforwards of approximately $25,500,000, which will expire in the years 2011 though 2022.

Questions:

1. What does Emerson call its income tax expense?
2. How much of the income tax expense shown on the 2004 income statement is currently payable and how much is deferred?
3. Does the company have an operating loss carryback or carryforward?
4. Explain why Emerson reports a provision for taxes in a year in which it has a loss before taxes and reports a benefit from income taxes in a year that it has income before taxes?
5. Does the schedule of deferred tax assets (liabilities) shown in Note 7 reconcile to the deferred tax items shown on the balance sheet?

SUMMARY

At the beginning of the chapter, we identified several objectives you would accomplish after reading the chapter. The objectives are listed below, each followed by a brief summary of the key points in the chapter discussion.

1. **Understand permanent and temporary differences.** A *permanent* difference is a difference between pretax financial income and taxable income in an accounting period, that will never reverse in a later accounting period. A *temporary* difference is a difference between the tax basis of an asset (or liability) and the financial statement reported amount of the asset (or liability) that will result in taxable or deductible amounts in future years when the reported amount of the asset is recovered (or the liability is settled).

2. **Explain the conceptual issues regarding interperiod tax allocation.** Conceptually, there are two objectives of income tax reporting. The first is that a corporation should recognize the amount of its income tax obligation (or refund) for the current year. The second is that the corporation should recognize deferred tax liabilities and assets for the future tax consequences of all events that it has recognized in its financial statements or income tax returns.

3. **Record and report deferred tax liabilities.** Measure the ending deferred tax liability for each future taxable amount using the applicable tax rate. Record the increase (or decrease) in the deferred tax liability. Report the ending deferred tax liability as a current or noncurrent liability on the ending balance sheet.

4. **Record and report deferred tax assets.** Measure the ending deferred tax asset for each future deductible amount using the applicable tax rate. Record the increase (or decrease) in the deferred tax asset. Report the ending deferred tax asset as a current or noncurrent asset on the ending balance sheet. Reduce the deferred tax asset by a valuation allowance when appropriate.

5. **Explain an operating loss carryback and carryforward.** An operating loss *carryback* occurs when a corporation carries back a current year operating loss to offset any taxable income in the previous two years. An operating loss *carryforward* occurs when a corporation's taxable income for the previous two years is not enough to offset the amount of the current year operating loss, so that it carries forward the loss to offset any future taxable income over the next 20 years.

6. **Account for an operating loss carryback.** Determine the amount of pretax financial (and taxable) income, as well as the income taxes paid in the previous two years. Carry back the pretax operating loss of the current year to the previous years and offset the previous pretax financial (and taxable) income. Report the resulting income tax refund of the income taxes

previously paid as a receivable on the balance sheet and subtract the income tax benefit due to the carryback from the pretax operating loss on the income statement.

7. **Account for an operating loss carryforward.** Recognize the tax benefit of an operating loss carryforward in the current year as a deferred tax asset. Determine the amount by multiplying the current income tax rate times the pretax operating loss. Establish a valuation allowance for the amount of the deferred tax asset that the corporation is not likely to realize.

8. **Apply intraperiod tax allocation.** Report the income tax expense applicable to pretax income from continuing operations separately on the income statement, basing the expense on the normal income tax rates. Report any results of discontinued operations, extraordinary items, retrospective adjustments, and prior period adjustments net of the income tax effects (with each related income tax effect reported in parentheses).

9. **Classify deferred tax liabilities and assets.** A corporation reports its deferred tax liabilities and assets in two classifications, a *net* current amount and a *net* noncurrent amount. To do so, it separates its deferred tax liabilities and deferred tax assets into current and noncurrent groups, and then combines (nets) the amounts in the current groups and the noncurrent groups.

ANSWERS TO REAL REPORT QUESTIONS

Real Report 19-1 Answers

1. Emerson calls its income tax expense "provision (benefit) for income taxes." The provision represents income tax expense while the benefit represents income tax savings.

2. At the end of 2004, Emerson has current income tax payable of $509,000 and deferred tax assets of $21,150,000 ($5,887,000 current asset + $15,263,000 noncurrent asset).

3. The company has a operating loss carryforward of approximately $98,000,000.

4. In 2003, when Emerson reported income before income taxes of $16,924,000 it recorded an income tax provision of $5,389,000 (disclosed in Note 7). However, the company also changed its estimate of the amount of the operating loss carryforward that was expected to be applied against future taxable income. Expecting future taxable income, the valuation allowance related to the deferred tax asset was decreased by $13,069,000 with a corresponding decrease in the provision for income taxes. This was the primary contributing factor to Emerson recognizing an income tax benefit in 2003 although it had future taxable income. In 2004, Emerson's loss before income taxes ($1,585,000) resulted in a tax benefit of $539,000. However, the company again revised its estimate of the amount of the deferred tax asset to be realized and increased the valuation allowance, with a corresponding increase in the provision for income taxes, by $1,981,000. This action, along with taxable income in foreign countries and various states contributed to Emerson reporting income tax expense in a year in which it reported a loss on the income statement.

5. The schedule of deferred tax assets shows a net deferred tax asset of $21,150,000 and $24,356,000 for 2004 and 2003, respectively. This reconciles to the total of the current and noncurrent deferred tax asset shown on the balance sheet for the respective years.

QUESTIONS

Q19-1 Distinguish between the objectives of financial reporting and the Internal Revenue Code.

Q19-2 Identify the five groups of possible differences between pretax financial income and taxable income (or between income tax expense and income taxes payable).

Q19-3 What is a permanent difference? Give two examples.

Q19-4 What is a temporary difference? Give two examples.

Q19-5 What did the FASB conclude in *FASB Statement No. 109* regarding interperiod income tax allocation?

Q19-6 What are the two objectives of accounting for income taxes identified in *FASB Statement No. 109*?

Q19-7 How does a corporation determine its deferred taxes under generally accepted accounting principles?

Q19-8 What are the three characteristics of a liability and why does a deferred tax liability of a corporation meet these characteristics?

Q19-9 What are the three characteristics of an asset and why does a deferred tax asset of a corporation meet these characteristics?

Q19-10 When does a corporation establish a valuation allowance? Give an example of positive evidence that might be used to justify that a valuation allowance is not needed.

Q19-11 List the steps necessary to measure and record a corporation's current and deferred income taxes.

Q19-12 Describe an operating loss carryback. List the two conceptual questions concerning accounting for a carryback.

Q19-13 Describe an operating loss carryforward. List the two conceptual questions concerning accounting for a carryforward.

Q19-14 Briefly summarize the generally accepted accounting principles for the financial reporting of operating loss carrybacks and carryforwards.

Q19-15 What is intraperiod income tax allocation? How is income tax expense reported on a corporation's income statement and retained earnings statement?

Q19-16 How are deferred tax liabilities and assets reported on a corporation's balance sheet?

Q19-17 Briefly describe the adjustment of a deferred tax liability (or asset) and the related income statement disclosure for a change in the income tax rate.

MULTIPLE CHOICE

Select the best answer for each of the following.

M19-1 A permanent difference is a difference between pretax financial income and taxable income in an accounting period that will never reverse in a later period. Which of the following is *not* an example of a permanent difference?
a. Fine for air pollution
b. Percentage depletion in excess of cost depletion on a wasting asset
c. Interest on municipal bonds
d. Rent received in advance

M19-2 Prior to and during 2007, the Shadrach Company reported tax depreciation at an amount higher than the amount of financial depreciation, resulting in a book value of the depreciable assets of $24,500 for financial reporting purposes and of $20,000 for tax purposes at the end of 2007. In addition, the company recognized a $3,500 estimated liability for legal expenses in the financial statements during 2007; it expects to pay this liability (and deduct it for tax purposes) in 2011. The current tax rate is 30%, no change in the tax rate has been enacted, and the company expects to be profitable in future years. What is the amount of the net noncurrent deferred tax liability at the end of 2007?
a. $300
b. $450
c. $1,050
d. $1,350

M19-3 Which of the following is an argument in favor of the asset/liability method of interperiod income tax allocation?
a. Deferred taxes are the result of historical transactions and should be reported in a similar manner.
b. Tax effects should be recorded in the same manner as all other revenue and expense transactions that involve changes in specific asset and liability accounts.
c. The predictive value of future cash flows, liquidity, and financial flexibility are increased when deferred taxes are reported based on enacted tax rates that will be in effect when the temporary differences reverse.
d. Historical tax rates are more verifiable and, therefore, the deferred tax amount is more reliable.

M19-4 At the beginning of 2007, Conley Company purchased an asset at a cost of $10,000. For financial reporting purposes, the asset has a four-year life with no residual value, and is depreciated by the straight-line method beginning in 2007. For tax purposes, the asset is depreciated under MACRS using a five-year recovery period. Prior to 2007, the company had no deferred tax liability or

asset. The difference between depreciation for financial reporting purposes and income tax purposes is the only temporary difference between pretax financial income and taxable income. The current income tax rate is 30% and no change in the tax rate has been enacted for future years. In 2007 and 2008, taxable income will be higher or lower than financial income by what amount?

	2007	2008
a.	Higher by $150	Lower by $210
b.	Higher by $500	Lower by $700
c.	Lower by $500	Higher by $700
d.	Lower by $1,500	Higher by $100

M19-5 Brooks Company reported a prior period adjustment of $12,000 in pretax financial "income" and taxable income for 2008. The prior period adjustment was the result of an error in calculating bad debt expense for 2007. The current tax rate is 30% and no change in the tax rate has been enacted for future years. When the company applies intraperiod income tax allocation, the prior period adjustment will be
a. Shown on the income statement at $12,000
b. Shown on the income statement at $8,400 (net of $3,600 income taxes)
c. Shown on the retained earnings statement at $12,000
d. Shown on the retained earnings statement at $8,400 (net of $3,600 income taxes)

M19-6 In 2007 Swope Company reports a pretax operating loss of $70,000 for both financial reporting and income tax purposes. Pretax financial income and taxable income for the previous three years had been: 2004—$15,000 (tax rate 20%); 2005—$24,000 (tax rate 25%); and 2006—$49,000 (tax rate 30%). The current tax rate is 30% and no change in the tax rate has been enacted for future years. At the end of 2007 the journal entry recorded would contain an income tax benefit from an operating loss carryback of
a. $0
b. $18,300
c. $19,800
d. $19,950

M19-7 *FASB Statement No. 109* came to which of the following conclusions regarding interperiod income tax allocation?
a. The partial allocation approach should be applied.
b. The net-of-tax method of income tax allocation should be used.
c. Nonallocation of income tax expense is appropriate.
d. The asset/liability method of income tax allocation should be used.

M19-8 Which of the following is *not* a cause of a difference between pretax financial income and taxable income in a given period?
a. Operating loss carrybacks and carryforwards
b. Permanent differences
c. Applicable tax rates
d. Temporary differences

M19-9 Which component of current income is not disclosed on the income statement net of tax effects?
a. Extraordinary loss from flood
b. Gain on disposal of milling machine
c. Gain from sale of discontinued segment
d. Loss from operations of discontinued component

M19-10 The Oliver Company earned taxable income of $7,500 during 2007, its first year of operations. A reconciliation of pretax financial income and taxable income indicated that an additional $2,500 of accelerated depreciation was deducted for tax purposes and that an estimated expense of $5,800 was deducted for financial reporting purposes. The estimated expense is not expected to be deductible for tax purposes until 2010, when the liability is paid. The current tax rate is 30% and no change in the tax rate has been enacted for future years. The resulting journal entry for 2007 would be:

a.
Income Tax Expense	1,260	
Deferred Tax Asset	1,740	
Deferred Tax Liability		750
Income Taxes Payable		2,250

b.
Income Tax Expense	1,260	
Deferred Tax Asset	990	
Income Taxes Payable		2,250

c.
Income Tax Expense	3,240	
Deferred Tax Liability		990
Income Taxes Payable		2,250

d.
Income Tax Expense	3,000	
Deferred Tax Liability		750
Income Taxes Payable		2,250

EXERCISES

E19-1 Future Taxable Amount The Durn Company began operations at the beginning of 2007. At the end of 2007 the company reported taxable income of $9,800 and pretax financial income of $11,200, because of a single temporary difference. The income tax rate for the current year is 30%, but Congress has enacted a 40% tax rate for 2008 and beyond.

Required
Prepare the income tax journal entry of the Durn Company at the end of 2007.

E19-2 Temporary Difference At the end of 2007, its first year of operations, the Slater Company reported a book value for its depreciable assets of $40,000 for financial reporting purposes and $33,000 for income tax purposes. The company earned taxable income of $97,000 during 2007. The company is subject to a 30% income tax rate and no change has been enacted for future years. The depreciation was the only temporary difference between taxable income and pretax financial income.

Required
1. Prepare the income tax journal entry of the Slater Company at the end of 2007.
2. Show how the deferred taxes would be reported on the Slater Company's December 31, 2007 balance sheet.

E19-3 Single Temporary Difference: Multiple Rates At the end of 2007, Fulhage Company reported taxable income of $9,000 and pretax financial income of $10,600. The difference is due to depreciation for tax purposes in excess of depreciation for financial reporting purposes. The income tax rate for the current year is 40%, but Congress has enacted tax rates of 35% for 2008 and 30% for 2009 and beyond.
    Fulhage Company has calculated the excess of its financial depreciation over its tax depreciation for future years as follows: 2008, $600; 2009, $700; and 2010, $300. Prior to 2007, the company had no deferred tax liability or asset.

Required
Prepare the income tax journal entry of the Fulhage Company at the end of 2007.

E19-4 Future Deductible Amount Pito Company has been in operation for several years. During those years the company has been profitable, and it expects to continue to be profitable in the foreseeable future. At the beginning of 2007, the company has a deferred tax asset of $360 pertaining to one future deductible amount. During 2007, the company earned taxable income of $51,000, which was taxed at a rate of 30% (no change in the tax rate has been enacted for future years). At the end of 2007, the book value of the current liability to which the deferred tax asset relates for financial reporting purposes exceeded the book value for income tax purposes by $6,000.

Required
1. Prepare the income tax journal entry of the Pito Company at the end of 2007.
2. Show how the deferred tax asset is reported on the Pito Company's December 31, 2007 balance sheet.

E19-5   *Valuation Account*   At the end of 2007, its first year of operations, the Beattie Company reported taxable income of $38,000 and pretax financial income of $34,400. The difference is due to the way the company handles its warranty costs. For tax purposes, the company deducts the warranty costs as they are paid. For financial reporting purposes, the company provides for a year-end estimated warranty liability based on future expected costs. The company is subject to a 30% tax rate for 2007 and no change in the tax rate has been enacted for future years. Based on verifiable evidence, the company decides it should establish a valuation allowance of 60% of its ending deferred tax asset.

Required
1. Prepare the income tax journal entry of the Beattie Company at the end of 2007.
2. Prepare the lower portion of the Beattie Company's 2007 income statement.

E19-6   *Income Taxes*   Thun Company has been in operation for several years. It has both a deductible and a taxable temporary difference. At the beginning of 2007, its deferred tax asset was $690 and its deferred tax liability was $750. The company expects its future deductible amount to be "deductible" in 2008 and its future taxable amount to be "taxable" in 2009. In 2006 Congress enacted income tax rates for future years as follows: 2007, 30%; 2008, 34%; and 2009, 35%. At the end of 2007, the company reported income taxes payable of $12,600, an increase in its deferred tax liability of $300, and an ending balance in its deferred tax asset of $860. The company has prepared the following schedule of items related to its income taxes for 2007.

Item	Amount
Taxable income for 2007	_____
Future taxable amount, 12/31/07	_____
Increase in future deductible amount during 2007	_____
Income tax expense for 2007	_____

Required
Fill in the blanks in the preceding schedule. Show your calculations.

E19-7   *Originating and Reversing Difference*   The Tanner Corporation begins operations in 2006 and reports the following amounts of pretax financial income and taxable income for the years 2006 through 2010. The company has only one temporary difference, and only one originating or reversing difference occurs in any single year. The company is subject to a tax rate of 30% for all the years.

Year	Pretax Financial Income	Taxable Income
2006	$70,000	$ 50,000
2007	85,000	75,000
2008	90,000	90,000
2009	82,000	92,000
2010	93,000	113,000

Required
1. Prepare the income tax journal entry for each year.
2. What do you notice about the balance in the deferred taxes over the five years?

E19-8   *Multiple Temporary Differences*   Vickers Company reports taxable income of $4,500 for 2007. The company has two temporary differences between pretax financial income and taxable income at the end of 2007. The first difference is expected to result in taxable amounts totaling $2,470 in future years. The second difference is expected to result in deductible amounts totaling $1,360 in future years. The company has a deferred tax asset of $372 and a deferred tax liability of $690 at the beginning of 2007. The current tax rate is 30% and no change in the tax rate has been enacted for future years. The company has positive, verifiable evidence of future taxable income.

Required
Prepare the income tax journal entry of the Vickers Company at the end of 2007.

E19-9   *Operating Loss*   At the end of 2007, Keil Company reports a pretax operating loss of $80,000 for both financial reporting and income tax purposes. Prior to 2007 the company had been successful and had reported and paid taxes on the following pretax financial income and taxable income: 2004, $37,000; 2005, $50,000; and 2006, $54,000. The company had been subject to tax rates of 20% in 2004, 25% in 2005, and 30% in 2006.

Required ▧
1. Prepare the income tax journal entry of the Keil Company at the end of 2007.
2. Prepare the lower portion of Keil's 2007 income statement.

E19-10 *Operating Loss* At the end of 2007, its first year of operations, the Swelland Company reported a pretax operating loss of $32,000 for both financial reporting and income tax purposes. At that time the company had no positive verifiable evidence that it would earn future taxable income. However, due to successful management, the company reported pretax operating income (and taxable income) of $70,000 in 2008. During both years, the income tax rate was 30% and no change had been enacted for future years.

Required
1. Prepare the income tax journal entries of the Swelland Company at the end of 2007.
2. Prepare the income tax journal entry of the Swelland Company at the end of 2008.
3. Prepare the lower portion of Swelland's 2008 income statement.

E19-11 *Operating Loss* Baxter Company began operations in 2003 and was profitable through 2006, during which time the tax rate was 30%. At the end of 2007, the company reported a pretax operating loss of $135,000 for both financial reporting and income taxes. Because the tax rate was increased to 40% in 2007, the company elects to forgo any carryback of the operating loss. In 2008 the company reported pretax operating income of $150,000.

Required
1. Prepare the income tax journal entry of the Baxter Company at the end of 2007.
2. Prepare the lower portion of Baxter's 2007 income statement.
3. Explain why Baxter Company elected to forgo any carryback in 2007.
4. Prepare the income tax journal entry of the Baxter Company at the end of 2008.
5. Prepare the lower portion of Baxter's 2008 income statement.

E19-12 *Intraperiod Tax Allocation* The Wright Company reports the following information for the year ended December 31, 2007:

Pretax income from continuing operations	$160,000[a]
Pretax gain from sale of investment (extraordinary item)	30,000
Pretax income from operations of discontinued Division M	27,000
Pretax loss on disposal of Division M	(45,000)
Pretax correction of error in understating depreciation in 2006	(8,000)
Retained earnings, January 1, 2007	410,000
Cash dividends during 2007	48,000
Total income tax	36,000[b]

a. Of this amount, revenues are $400,000 and expenses are $240,000.
b. Of this amount $7,500 relates to the extraordinary item; $6,750 relates to the pretax income from the operations of discontinued Division M; the pretax loss on the disposal of Division M resulted in an income tax savings of $11,250; and the pretax correction of the depreciation error resulted in an income tax savings of $2,000.

Required
1. Prepare the year-end journal entry necessary to record the 2007 intraperiod income tax allocation in regard to the preceding information.
2. Prepare Wright's 2007 income statement and statement of retained earnings.

E19-13 *Calculating Intraperiod Income Taxes* The Stam Corporation reports the following *pretax* accounting (and taxable) income items during 2007:

Income from continuing operations	$90,000[a]
Loss from operations of a discontinued division	(10,000)
Gain from the disposal of the discontinued division	25,000
Extraordinary gain	20,000

a. Of this amount, revenues are $320,000 and expenses are $230,000.

Required ✉
1. Prepare the journal entry necessary to record the 2007 intraperiod income tax allocation in regard to the preceding information. Assume a tax rate of 15% on the first $40,000 of income and a rate of 30% on income in excess of $40,000.
2. Prepare Stam's 2007 income statement.

E19-14 *Disclosure of Intraperiod Tax Allocation* The Lester Corporation reports $119,000 of both *pretax* accounting "income" and taxable income in 2007. In addition to income from continuing operations (of which revenues are

$500,000), included in this "income" is a $25,000 extraordinary loss from a fire, a $17,000 loss from operations of discontinued Division W, a $15,000 gain on the disposal of Division W, and a $14,000 correction of an error due to the understatement of bad debt expense in 2006. The company is subject to a 20% tax rate on the first $50,000 of income and a rate of 25% on income in excess of $50,000.

Required
1. Show how this information is disclosed on Lester's 2007 income statement.
2. Prepare Lester's 2007 statement of retained earnings. (Assume a beginning retained earnings balance of $191,000 and cash dividends during 2007 amounting to $65,000.)

E19-15 *Balance Sheet Presentation* The Thiel Company reports the following deferred tax items at the end of 2007:

Deferred Tax Item #	Account Balance	Related Asset or Liability
1	$ 7,200 credit	Current asset
2	6,700 debit	Current liability
3	15,500 credit	Noncurrent asset
4	10,600 debit	Noncurrent liability

Required
Show how the preceding deferred tax items are reported on the Thiel Company's December 31, 2007 balance sheet.

E19-16 *Change in Tax Rates* At the end of 2007, Rowet Company reported a deferred tax liability of $6,120 based on an income tax rate of 30%. On June 1, 2008 Congress changed the income tax rate to 35%.

Required
1. Calculate the amount of the adjustment to Rowet Company's 2007 year-end deferred tax liability.
2. Prepare the journal entry to correct Rowet Company's deferred tax liability.

PROBLEMS

P19-1 *Temporary and Permanent Differences* In the current year you are calculating a diversified company's deferred taxes. Based on an analysis of the company's current taxable income and pretax financial income, you have identified the following items that create differences between the two amounts and that may result in differences between the company's future taxable income and its future pretax financial income:

_____ 1. Percentage depletion deducted for taxes in excess of cost depletion for financial reporting
_____ 2. Warranty costs to be deducted for taxes that were deducted as warranty expense for financial reporting
_____ 3. Gross profit to be recognized for taxes under the completed-contract method that was recognized for financial reporting under the percentage-of-completion method
_____ 4. Officers' life insurance premium expense deducted for financial reporting
_____ 5. Rent revenue to be recognized for financial reporting that was reported for taxes when collected in advance
_____ 6. Loss from writedown of inventory that was recognized for financial reporting but that will be deducted for taxes when the inventory is sold
_____ 7. Interest revenue on municipal bonds recognized for financial reporting
_____ 8. Loss due to contingent liability that was deducted for financial reporting that will be deducted for taxes when the liability is actually paid
_____ 9. Gross profit to be recognized under installment method for tax purposes that was recognized on accrual basis for financial reporting
_____ 10. Depreciation to be recognized for financial reporting in excess of MACRS depreciation to be deducted for tax purposes
_____ 11. Investment income that has been recognized under the equity method for financial reporting that will be recognized as fully taxable for tax purposes when dividends are collected

Required
For each difference, indicate whether it is a temporary difference (*T*) or a permanent difference (*P*) by placing the appropriate letter on the line provided. If the difference is a temporary difference, also indicate for the current year whether it will result in a future taxable amount (*T*) or a future deductible amount (*D*).

P19-2 *Definitions* The FASB has defined several terms in regard to accounting for income taxes. Below are various code letters (for terms) followed by definitions.

Code Letter	Term	Code Letter	Term
A	Future deductible amount	H	Deferred tax consequences
B	Income tax obligation (or refund)	I	Future taxable amount
C	Operating loss carryback	J	Deferred tax liability
D	Valuation allowance	K	Temporary difference
E	Deferred tax asset	L	Income tax expense (or benefit)
F	Operating loss carryforward	M	Deferred tax expense (or benefit)
G	Taxable income		

_____ 1. The deferred tax consequences of future deductibles amounts and operating loss carryforwards

_____ 2. A difference between the tax basis of an asset or liability and its reported amount in the financial statements that will result in taxable or deductible amounts in future years when the reported amount of the asset or liability is recovered or settled, respectively

_____ 3. Temporary difference that results in taxable amounts in future years when the related asset or liability is recovered or settled, respectively

_____ 4. The future effects on income taxes, as measured by the applicable enacted tax rate and provisions of the enacted tax law, resulting from temporary differences and operating loss carryforwards at the end of the current year

_____ 5. The change during the year in a corporation's deferred tax liabilities and assets

_____ 6. The deferred tax consequences of future taxable amounts

_____ 7. The portion of a deferred tax asset for which it is more likely than not that a tax benefit will not be realized

_____ 8. Temporary difference that results in deductible amounts in future years when the related asset or liability is recovered or settled, respectively

_____ 9. The sum of income tax obligation and deferred tax expense (or benefit)

_____ 10. The amount of income taxes paid or payable (or refundable) for the current year

_____ 11. An excess of tax deductible expenses over taxable revenues in a year that may be carried forward to reduce taxable income in a future year

_____ 12. The excess of taxable revenues over tax deductible expenses and exemptions for the year

_____ 13. An excess of tax deductible expenses over taxable revenues in a year that may be carried back to reduce taxable income in a prior year

Required

Indicate which terms belongs with each definition by inserting the corresponding code letter on the line preceding the definition.

P19-3 *Multiple Temporary Differences* Wilcox Company has prepared the following reconciliation of its pretax financial income with its taxable income for 2007:

Pretax financial income	$3,000
Add: Estimated expense on one-year warranties recognized for financial reporting in excess of actual warranty costs deducted for income taxes	100
Less: MACRS depreciation deducted for income taxes in excess of depreciation recognized for financial reporting	(150)
Taxable income	$2,950

At the beginning of 2007, Wilcox Company had a deferred tax liability of $495. The current tax rate is 30% and no change in the tax rate has been enacted for future years. At the end of 2007, the company anticipates that actual warranty costs will exceed estimated warranty expense by $100 next year and that financial depreciation will exceed tax depreciation by $1,800 in future years. The company has earned income in all past years and expects to earn income in the future.

Required

1. Prepare the income tax journal entry of the Wilcox Company at the end of 2007.
2. Prepare the lower portion of Wilcox's 2007 income statement.
3. Show how the income tax items are reported on Wilcox's December 31, 2007 balance sheet.

P19-4 *Interperiod Tax Allocation* Klerk Company had four temporary differences between its pretax financial income and its taxable income during 2007, as follows:

Number	Temporary Difference
1	Gross profit on certain installment sales is recognized under the accrual method for financial reporting and under the installment method for income taxes
2	MACRS depreciation is used for income taxes; a different depreciation method is used for financial reporting
3	Rent receipts are included in taxable income when collected in advance; rent revenue is recognized under the accrual method for financial reporting
4	Warranty expense is estimated for financial reporting; warranty costs are deducted as incurred for income taxes

At the beginning of 2007, the company had a deferred tax liability of $84,300 related to temporary difference #2 and a deferred tax asset of $21,090 related to temporary difference #4. Based on its tax records, the company earned taxable income of $270,000 for 2007. The company's accountant has prepared the following schedule showing the total future taxable and deductible amounts at the end of 2007 for its four temporary differences:

Future Taxable Amounts		Future Deductible Amounts	
#1	#2	#3	#4
$77,900	$241,000	$20,000	$55,300

The company has a history of earning income and expects to be profitable in the future. The income tax rate for 2007 is 40%, but in 2006 Congress enacted a 30% tax rate for 2008 and future years.

During 2007, for financial accounting purposes, the company reported revenues of $750,000 and expenses of $447,100. The deferred tax related to temporary differences #1, #2, and #4 are considered to be noncurrent by the company; the deferred tax related to temporary difference #3 is considered to be current.

Required
1. Prepare the income tax journal entry of the Klerk Company for 2007.
2. Prepare a condensed 2007 income statement for the Klerk Company.
3. Show how the income tax items are reported on Klerk Company's December 31, 2007 balance sheet.

P19-5 *Interperiod Tax Allocation* Peterson Company has computed its pretax financial income to be $66,000 in 2007 *after* including the effects of the appropriate items from the following information:

1. Depreciation taken for tax purposes	$40,000
2. Officers' life insurance premium expense recorded on accounting records	15,000
3. Interest revenue on investment in municipal bonds recorded on accounting records	25,000
4. Percentage depletion taken for tax purposes in excess of cost depletion taken for financial reporting purposes	10,000
5. Depreciation taken for financial reporting purposes	48,000
6. Actual product warranty costs deducted for tax purposes	20,000
7. Gross profit on installment sales recognized for tax purposes	80,000
8. Estimated product warranty expense recorded on accounting records	27,000
9. Gross profit on installment sales recognized for financial reporting purposes	91,000

The company's accountant has prepared the following schedule showing the future taxable and deductible amounts at the end of 2007 for its three temporary differences:

	Totals
Future Taxable Amounts	
Depreciation difference	$33,800
Installment sales: gross profit difference	26,700
Future Deductible Amounts	
Warranty difference	56,500

At the beginning of 2007 the company had a deferred tax liability of $12,540 related to the depreciation difference and $4,710 related to the installment sales difference. In addition, it had a deferred tax asset of $14,850 related to the warranty difference. The current tax rate is 30% and no change in the tax rate has been enacted for future years.

Required
1. Compute the Peterson Company's taxable income for 2007.
2. Prepare the income tax journal entry of the Peterson Company for 2007 (assume no valuation allowance is necessary).
3. Identify the permanent differences in Items 1–9 and explain why you did or did not account for them as deferred tax items in Requirement 2.

P19-6 *Interperiod Tax Allocation* Quick Company reports the following revenues and expenses in its pretax financial income for the year ended December 31, 2007:

Revenues	$229,600
Expenses	(160,100)
Pretax financial income	$ 69,500

The revenues included in pretax financial income are the same amount as the revenues included in the company's taxable income. A reconciliation of the expenses reported for pretax financial income to the expenses reported for taxable income, however, reveals four differences:

1. Depreciation deducted for financial reporting exceeded depreciation deducted for income taxes by $11,000
2. Percentage depletion deducted for income taxes exceeded cost depletion deducted for financial reporting by $15,600

3. Warranty costs deducted for income taxes exceeded warranty expenses deducted for financial reporting by $8,900
4. Legal expense of $9,800 was deducted for financial reporting; it will be deducted for income taxes when paid in a future year

The company expects its percentage depletion to exceed its cost depletion in each of the next five years by the same amount as in 2007. At the end of 2007 the other three expenses are expected to result in total future taxable or deductible amounts as follows:

	Totals
Future Taxable Amounts	
Depreciation expense difference	$63,000
Future Deductible Amounts	
Warranty expense difference	48,400
Legal expense difference	9,800

At the beginning of 2007 the company had a deferred tax liability of $22,200 related to the depreciation difference and a deferred tax asset of $17,190 related to the warranty difference. The income tax rate for 2007 is 35%, but in 2006 Congress enacted a 30% rate for 2008 and future years.

Required

1. Compute the Quick Company's taxable income for 2007.
2. Prepare the income tax journal entry of the Quick Company for 2007. Assume no valuation allowance is necessary.
3. Prepare a condensed 2007 income statement for the Quick Company.

P19-7 *Deferred Tax Liability: Depreciation* At the beginning of 2007, its first year of operations, Cooke Company purchased an asset for $100,000. This asset has an eight-year economic life with no residual value, and it is being depreciated by the straight-line method for financial reporting purposes. For tax purposes, however, the asset is being depreciated using the MACRS (200%, 5-year life) method.

During 2007, the company reported pretax financial income of $51,500 and taxable income of $44,000. The depreciation temporary difference caused the difference between the two income amounts. The tax rate in 2007 was 30% and no change in the tax rate had been enacted for future years.

Required

1. Prepare a schedule that shows for each year, 2007 through 2014, (a) MACRS depreciation, (b) straight-line depreciation, (c) the annual depreciation temporary difference, and (d) the accumulated temporary difference at the end of each year.
2. Prepare a schedule that computes for each year, 2007 through 2014, (a) the ending deferred tax liability, and (b) the change in the deferred tax liability.
3. Prepare the income tax journal entry at the end of 2007.
4. Explain what happens to the balance of the deferred tax liability at the end of 2007 through 2014.

P19-8 *Deferred Tax Liability: Depreciation* Gire Company began operations at the beginning of 2007, at which time it purchased a depreciable asset for $60,000. For 2007 through 2010, the asset was depreciated on the straight-line basis over a four-year life (no residual value) for financial reporting. For income tax purposes the asset was depreciated using MACRS (200%, three-year life).

For 2007 through 2010, the company reported pretax financial income and taxable income of the following amounts (the differences are due solely to the depreciation temporary differences):

Year	Pretax Financial Income	Taxable Income
2007	$24,998	$20,000
2008	38,670	27,000
2009	27,886	34,000
2010	29,446	40,000

Over the entire four-year period, the company was subject to an income tax of 30% and no change in the tax rate had been enacted for future years.

Required

1. Prepare a schedule that shows for each year, 2007 through 2010, the (a) MACRS depreciation, (b) straight-line depreciation, (c) annual depreciation temporary difference, and (d) accumulated temporary difference at the end of each year.
2. Prepare the income tax journal entry at the end of (a) 2007, (b) 2008, (c) 2009, and (d) 2010. (Round to the nearest dollar.)
3. Prepare the lower portion of the income statement for (a) 2007, (b) 2008, (c) 2009 and (d) 2010.

P19-9 *Deferred Taxes: Multiple Rates* Wicks Corporation began operations on January 1, 2007. At the end of 2007 the company reported pretax financial income of $60,000 and taxable income of $57,700, due to two temporary differences. The income tax rate is 30% for 2007, but Congress has enacted a tax rate of 35% for 2007 and beyond. To determine its deferred taxes, the company prepared the following schedule of expected future taxable and deductible amounts for the two temporary differences:

	2008	2009	2010	2011
Future taxable amounts	$4,900	$4,200	$ 4,600	$4,100
Future deductible amount			(15,500)	

Required

1. Prepare the income tax journal entry of the Wicks Corporation at the end of 2007. Assume a valuation allowance is not required.
2. Prepare the lower portion of the 2007 income statement for the Wicks Corporation.

P19-10   *Operating Loss* Ross Company has been in business for several years, during which time it has been profitable. For each of those years, the company reported (and paid taxes on) taxable income in the same amount as pretax financial income based on the following revenues and expenses:

	Revenues	Expenses
2003	$182,000	$150,000
2004	220,000	170,000
2005	253,000	180,000
2006	241,000	196,000

The company was subject to the following income tax rates during this period: 2003, 20%; 2004, 25%; 2005, 30%; and 2006, 25%. During 2007 the company experienced a severe decrease in the demand for its products. The company tried to offset this decrease with an expensive marketing campaign, but was unsuccessful. Consequently, at the end of 2007 the company determined that its revenues were $60,000 and its expenses were $193,000 during 2007 for both income taxes and financial reporting.

The company decided to carry back its 2007 operating loss because it was not confident it could earn taxable income in the future carryforward period. The income tax rate was 30% in 2007 and no change in the tax rate had been enacted for future years.

In 2008 the company developed and introduced a new product that proved to be in high demand. On June 1, 2008 the company received a refund check from the government based on the tax information it filed at the end of 2007. For 2008 the company reported revenues of $181,000 and expenses of $155,000 for both income taxes and financial reporting. The applicable income tax rate was 30%.

Required

1. Prepare the income tax journal entries of the Ross Company at the end of 2007.
2. Prepare the Ross Company's 2007 income statement. Include a note for any operating loss carryforward.
3. Prepare the journal entry to record the receipt of the refund check on June 1, 2008.
4. Prepare the income tax journal entry at the end of 2008.
5. Prepare the Ross Company's 2008 income statement.

P19-11   *Operating Loss* Refer to the information in Problem 19-10 and modify it as follows: The company decided to carry back its 2007 operating loss. Furthermore, since the company had already begun to develop the new product at the end of 2007 and had contracts for its sale in 2008, the company was confident at the end of 2007 that it would earn sufficient taxable income in the future carryforward period.

Required

1. Prepare the income tax journal entries of the Ross Company at the end of 2007.
2. Prepare the Ross Company's 2007 income statement. Include a note for any operating loss carryforward recognition.
3. Prepare the journal entry to record the receipt of the refund check on June 1, 2008.
4. Prepare the income tax journal entry at the end of 2008.
5. Prepare the Ross Company's 2008 income statement.

P19-12   *Balance Sheet Reporting and Tax Rate Change* At the end of 2006, Dolf Company prepared the following schedule of its deferred tax items (based on the currently enacted tax rate of 30%):

Deferred Tax Item #	Account Balance	Related Asset or Liability
1	$ 8,400 debit	Current asset
2	10,200 debit	Noncurrent asset
3	5,700 credit	Current liability
4	17,700 credit	Noncurrent liability

On April 30, 2007 Congress changed the income tax rate to 40% for 2007 and future years. At the end of 2007 the company reported taxable income of $62,500 for 2007. At that time, the company determined that its deferred tax items should have balances as follows at the end of 2007 (based on the 40% tax rate): #1, $10,700 debit; #2, $15,000 debit; #3, $7,000 credit; #4, $25,900 credit.

Required
1. Show how the deferred tax items are reported on the Dolf Company's December 31, 2006 balance sheet.
2. Prepare the April 30, 2007 journal entry to correct Dolf Company's deferred tax items.
3. Prepare the income tax journal entry of the Dolf Company at the end of 2007.
4. Show how the current and deferred tax items are reported on the Dolf Company's December 31, 2007 balance sheet.
5. Calculate the total income tax expense for 2007.

P19-13 *Comprehensive* Colt Company reports *pretax* financial "income" of $143,000 in 2007. In addition to pretax income from continuing operations (of which revenues are $295,000), the following items are included in this pretax "income":

Extraordinary gain	$30,000
Loss from disposal of Division B	(10,000)
Income from operations of discontinued Division B	16,000
Prior period adjustment	(8,000)

The taxable income of the company totals $123,000 in 2007. The difference between the pretax financial income and the taxable income is due to the excess of tax depreciation over financial depreciation on assets used in continuing operations.

At the beginning of 2007 the company had a retained earnings balance of $310,000 and a deferred tax liability of $8,100. During 2007 the company declared and paid dividends of $48,000. It is subject to tax rates of 15% on the first $50,000 of income and 30% on income in excess of $50,000. Based on proper interperiod tax allocation procedures, the company has determined that its 2007 ending deferred tax liability is $14,100.

Required
1. Prepare a schedule for the Colt Company to allocate the total 2007 income tax expense to the various components of pretax income.
2. Prepare the income tax journal entry of the Colt Company at the end of 2007.
3. Prepare Colt Company's 2007 income statement.
4. Prepare Colt Company's 2007 statement of retained earnings.
5. Show the related income tax disclosures on the Colt Company's December 31, 2007 balance sheet.

P19-14 *Comprehensive* At the beginning of 2007 Norris Company had a deferred tax liability of $6,400, because of the use of MACRS depreciation for income tax purposes and units-of-production depreciation for financial reporting. The income tax rate is 30% for 2006 and 2007, but in 2006 Congress enacted a 40% tax rate for 2008 and future years.

The accounting records of the Norris Company show the following *pretax* items of financial income for 2007: income from continuing operations, $120,000 (revenues of $352,000 and expenses of $232,000); gain on disposal of Division F, $23,000; extraordinary loss, $18,000; loss from operations of discontinued Division F, $10,000; and prior period adjustment, $15,000, due to an error that understated revenue in 2006. All of these items are taxable; however, financial depreciation for 2007 on assets related to continuing operations exceeds tax depreciation by $5,000. The company had a retained earnings balance of $161,000 on January 1, 2007 and declared and paid cash dividends of $32,000 during 2007.

Required
1. Prepare the income tax journal entry of the Norris Company at the end of 2007.
2. Prepare Norris Company's 2007 income statement.
3. Prepare Norris Company's 2007 statement of retained earnings.
4. Show the related income tax disclosures on the Norris Company's December 31, 2007 balance sheet.

P19-15 *Comprehensive* Jayryan Company sells products in a volatile market. The company began operating in 2005 and reported (and paid taxes on) taxable income in 2005 and 2006. It has one taxable temporary difference (future taxable amount), and reconciled its taxable income to its pretax financial income for 2005 and 2006 as follows:

	2005	2006
Taxable income	$25,000	$53,000
Temporary difference	2,500	4,800
Pretax financial income	$27,500	$57,800

In 2007, because of a downturn in the market, the company reported a taxable loss of $90,000 and it was uncertain as to future profits. A temporary difference of $2,700 resulted in an $87,300 pretax operating loss for financial reporting. In 2008 and 2009 the company was again profitable and reported the following items:

	2008	2009
Taxable income	$7,000	$19,000
Temporary difference	2,300	2,800
Pretax financial income	$9,300	$21,800

The income tax rate has been 30% since 2003 and no change in the tax rate has been enacted for future years.

Required
1. Prepare a schedule that shows the Jayryan Company's income taxes payable (or receivable) for each year, 2005 through 2009.
2. Prepare a schedule that shows the deferred tax information (change in temporary difference and operating loss carryforward) for each year, 2005 through 2009.
3. Prepare a schedule that shows the deferred taxes for each year, 2005 through 2009.
4. Based on the schedule prepared in Requirement 3, prepare the income tax journal entry at the end of 2007.
5. Prepare a partial income statement for 2007. Include a note for any operating loss carryforward.

CASES

COMMUNICATION

C19-1 Asset/Liability Method and Temporary Differences

Interperiod tax allocation is necessary because there are differences in the timing of revenues and expenses between a corporation's financial statements and its federal income tax returns.

Required
1. Identify the two goals and four basic principles of accounting for income taxes.
2. Briefly explain interperiod income tax allocation under generally accepted accounting principles.
3. List the four groups of items that result in temporary differences and give examples for each group.

C19-2 Interperiod Tax Allocation

A friend in a business policy class says, "I always thought the income taxes reported on a corporation's income statement were the same as the income taxes paid during that period. Now I am not so sure because some other students mentioned interperiod income tax allocation. Furthermore, I have heard about comprehensive and partial allocation. I am confused. Please explain this to me."

Required
Prepare a written response for your friend. In your discussion be sure to discuss permanent and temporary differences, and to compare comprehensive allocation with partial allocation. Include the reasons for interperiod allocation and comprehensive allocation.

C19-3 Methods of Interperiod Tax Allocation

Three methods of interperiod income tax allocation have been advocated. These include (1) the asset/liability method, (2) the deferred method, and (3) the net-of-tax method.

Required
Define *interperiod income tax allocation* and briefly explain the three methods that have been advocated. Conclude by summarizing the generally accepted accounting principles for interperiod income tax allocation.

C19-4 Operating Losses

The Internal Revenue Code allows a corporation to carry back or carry forward an "operating loss" for a given year.

Required
1. Describe an operating loss carryback and a carryforward.
2. For a carryback, identify and briefly explain the two important conceptual questions.
3. For a carryforward, identify and briefly explain the two important conceptual questions.
4. Briefly summarize the generally accepted accounting principles for the financial reporting of (a) an operating loss carryback and (b) an operating loss carryforward.

C19-5 Intraperiod Tax Allocation

Income tax allocation is an integral part of generally accepted accounting principles. Income tax allocation consists of both intraperiod and interperiod tax allocation.

Required
1. Explain the difference between interperiod and intraperiod income tax allocation.
2. Explain how a corporation discloses its income tax expense (or credit) for the year under intraperiod allocation.
3. Provide an example of intraperiod tax allocation on a corporation's income statement that includes income from continuing operations, a loss from the sale of a discontinued component, a gain from the operations of the discontinued component, and an extraordinary gain. Assume a 30% tax rate.

CREATIVE AND CRITICAL THINKING

C19-6 Permanent and Temporary Differences

To implement interperiod income tax allocation, an accountant must be able to distinguish between permanent and temporary differences. The following is a list of three differences between a corporation's pretax financial income and taxable income:

a. Estimated warranty costs (covering a three-year warranty) are expensed for financial reporting purposes at the time of sale but are deducted for tax purposes when incurred.
b. MACRS depreciation for income tax purposes exceeds straight-line depreciation for financial reporting purposes.
c. Percentage depletion for tax purposes exceeds cost depletion for financial reporting purposes.

Required
1. Define (a) *permanent difference* and (b) *temporary difference*.
2. Define *interperiod income tax allocation* and briefly describe its application under generally accepted accounting principles.
3. Indicate and explain whether each of the three differences listed in this case should be treated as a temporary or permanent difference.

C19-7 Deferred Tax Assets and Liabilities

A friend says to you, "I don't understand how taxable temporary differences can be 'liabilities' and how deductible temporary differences can be 'assets.' It seems to me that these temporary differences relate only to the future, and that accounting is based on 'historical cost.' Furthermore, the government frequently changes the tax laws, so no one knows what the future tax laws will be."

Required
Prepare a written response for your friend that explains why deferred tax assets and deferred tax liabilities are recognized and reported on a corporation's balance sheet. Include a discussion of a valuation allowance.

C19-8 Interperiod Tax Allocation

AICPA Adapted Chris Green, CPA, is auditing Rayne Co.'s 2007 financial statements. For the year ended December 31, 2007, Rayne is applying *Statement of Financial Accounting Standards No. 109*, "Accounting for Income Taxes." Rayne's controller, Dunn, has prepared a schedule of all differences between financial statement and income tax return income. Dunn believes that as a result of pending legislation, the enacted tax rate at December 31, 2007 will be increased for 2008. Dunn is uncertain which differences to include and which rates to apply in computing deferred taxes under *FASB 109*. Dunn has requested an overview of *FASB 109* from Green.

Required
Prepare a brief memo to Dunn from Green that identifies the objectives of accounting for income taxes, defines temporary differences, explains how to measure deferred tax assets and liabilities, and explains how to measure deferred income tax expense or benefit.

C19-9 Analyzing Coca-Cola's Income Tax Disclosures

Refer to the financial statements and related notes of The Coca-Cola Company in Appendix A of this book.

Required
1. What was the total income tax expense relating to income before income taxes for 2004? How much of this was current? How much was deferred?
2. What were the total deferred tax assets at the end of 2004? Total deferred tax liabilities? Net deferred tax liability?
3. How much was the noncurrent deferred tax liability at the end of 2004 and where was it reported?
4. How much were the operating loss carryforwards at the end of 2004? Over what time periods must these be utilized?

 ## C19-10 Ethics and Deferred Taxes

It is the end of 2008, and the auditing firm for which you work is auditing the Weiss Company for the first time. Prior to 2008, Weiss was audited by another firm. A substantial amount of Weiss Company's revenues for 2007 came from installment sales. Weiss has considerable property, plant, and equipment. It also has a large amount of debt outstanding, and one of the debt covenants is that the company maintain a 2.00 current ratio.

You have been reviewing the deferred taxes of Weiss at the end of 2008. On its preliminary ending balance sheet for 2008, Weiss has included a noncurrent deferred tax liability of $45,000. On its ending 2007 balance sheet, Weiss had also reported a noncurrent deferred tax liability. Upon examining the calculations supporting the $45,000, you find that one-third relates to the receivables from the installment sales and two-thirds relates to the depreciation on the property, plant, and equipment. Nearly all of the 2007 deferred tax liability related to the latter.

Based on your analysis, you raise the issue with Weiss Company's controller about the possibility of reclassifying $15,000 of the deferred taxes as a current liability. The controller responds, "We have always listed our deferred taxes as a noncurrent liability. This was okay with our previous auditor. It just isn't worth the hassle of splitting the amount into current and noncurrent portions. It is clearly not material, since our total equity is over $400,000. Besides, if we did that it would bring our current ratio down to 1.95 and we would have our creditors on our backs. Everyone knows that deferred taxes are never really paid, so that is a good reason for not including the amount in our current liabilities."

Required
From financial reporting and ethical perspectives, prepare a response to Weiss Company's controller.

Accounting for Postemployment Benefits

OBJECTIVES

After reading this chapter, you will be able to:

1 Understand the characteristics of pension plans.

2 Explain the historical perspective of accounting for pension plans.

3 Explain the accounting principles for defined benefit plans, including computing pension expense and recognizing pension liabilities and assets.

4 Account for pensions.

5 Understand disclosures of pensions.

6 Explain the conceptual issues regarding pensions.

7 Understand several additional issues related to pensions.

8 Explain other postemployment benefits (OPEBs).

9 Account for OPEBs.

10 Explain the conceptual issues regarding OPEBs.

11 Understand present value calculations for pensions. (Appendix).

It's Never too Early to Plan for Retirement

If you've picked up a newspaper lately, it is likely that you've read about the problems facing the pension plans of many companies. For fiscal year 2004, the **Pension Benefit Guaranty Corporation** (PBGC), the government agency that insures the basic pension benefits of 44.4 million workers, reported that it had a record deficit of more than $23 billion. What has caused this problem? First, falling stock prices and the economic recession have contributed to a drop in the value of pension plan assets. Second, record low interest rates experienced at the beginning of this decade have significantly contributed to the increase in companies' pension liabilities. Falling asset values and increasing liabilities have left many pension plans insolvent.

The airline industry was responsible for much of the PBCG's record loss of $12.1 billion. The takeover of **U.S. Airways'** pension plan relating to flight attendants, machinists, and other employees is estimated to have cost the PBGC $2.3 billion. Combined with the $726 million claim related to U.S. Airways pilots' pension plans, the combined $3 billion claim is the second largest in the history of the pension insurance program. In addition, **UAL Corp.** has announced that it will terminate United Airlines' four pension plans in an effort to emerge from bankruptcy—the largest default in U.S. corporate history. The PBGC is estimated to assume costs of $6.6 billion when it takes over United's pension plans while United would avoid more than $3 billion of minimum-funding contributions over the next five years. This period of record-breaking claims has already led to one proposal to raise the insurance premiums that companies pay to the PBGC by an estimated $15 billion over the next five years. In addition, legislation is being proposed that would toughen the disclosure rules in hopes that

increased transparency with regard to pension plan assets and liabilities will create pressure on companies to keep their promises to employees.

In spite of the many problems facing pension plans, many companies are contributing large amounts of cash to their pension plans and recognizing sizeable financial benefits.[1] Of the many benefits of putting excess cash into pension plans are an increase in future earnings, reduced taxes, and freeing up future cash. For example, **Boeing Co.** contributed $3.6 billion into its pension plan during 2004, which was much more than the $100 million that it was required to contribute. Because companies use an expected rate of return on pension plan assets rather than the actual return on the assets (Boeing is currently using 8.75%) in pension calculations, this large contribution ensures Boeing an increase in income of $315 million in 2005. Because the contribution is tax-deductible, Boeing is expected to receive a tax benefit of more than $1 billion. Finally, the sizable contribution in 2004 will most likely mean that Boeing has pre-funded its plan for years to come, freeing up cash flow in future years to use for other business purposes. Clearly, the accounting for pensions has far-reaching impacts—socially and financially.

FOR FURTHER INVESTIGATION

For a discussion of pensions, consult the Business & Company Resource Center (BCRC):

- Make Your Pension Count: Use These Three Tips to Evaluate Your Benefits Plan and Safeguard Your Retirement. Janice Revell, *Fortune*, 0015-8259, Feb 21, 2005, v151, i4, p.134.

- Pumped-Up Pension Plays? Regulators are Investigating How Some Companies Tinker with Retiree Accounting. *Business Week*, 0007-7135, Oct 25, 2004 i3905 p92.

---

1. Adapted from "How Companies Make the Most of Pensions" by Karen Richardson, *Wall Street Journal*, January 24, 2005.

The average life expectancy of a male and female born in the United States in 1990 has increased to over 72 and 79 years, respectively. Consequently, most people are living long enough to retire and to become dependent on other sources of income. Both the government and companies are concerned about providing income to these individuals. In response, Congress passed the *Federal Insurance Contribution Act* (commonly called Social Security) in 1935. This Act requires most employers and employees to contribute to a federal retirement program. To supplement Social Security, many companies also have adopted private retirement plans. More than $12 trillion is invested in company pension funds.[2] Because these pension plans are important, Congress passed legislation affecting their operation. This legislation, the *Employee Retirement Income Security Act of 1974* (ERISA), often is referred to as the *Pension Reform Act of 1974*.

We discussed the accounting for the cost of social security taxes in Chapter 13. In this chapter we focus on the recording, reporting, and disclosure procedures for company pension plans under generally accepted accounting principles and the *Pension Reform Act of 1974*. In addition to pensions, many employers provide other postemployment benefits to their employees. We discuss the accounting for these benefits later in the chapter.

CHARACTERISTICS OF PENSION PLANS

1 Understand the characteristics of pension plans.

A pension plan requires that a company provide income to its retired employees for the services they provided during their employment. This retirement income, normally paid monthly, usually is determined on the basis of the employee's earnings and length of service with the company. For instance, under the retirement plan of one major company, employees who retire at age 65 receive annual retirement income according to the following formula:

Average of last five years' salary × number of years of service × 0.0257.

Thus, an individual who worked for this company for 30 years and had an average salary of $100,000 for the last five years of service receives annual pension benefits of $77,100 ($100,000 × 30 × 0.0257).

A pension plan of this type is a **defined benefit plan** because the plan specifically states either the *benefits* to be received by employees after retirement or the method of determining such benefits. In contrast, a pension plan is a **defined contribution plan** when the employer's *contribution* is based on a formula, so that future benefits are limited to an amount that can be provided by the contributions and the returns earned on the investment of those contributions.

These two types of plans involve different risks to the company and the employees. With a defined benefit plan, most of the risks lie with the company because the payments to the retired employees are defined and the company has the responsibility of ensuring that those amounts are paid. In contrast, with a defined contribution plan, most of the risks lie with the employees because the company's responsibilities essentially end once the required contribution for the period has been made by the company. There are many accounting issues related to defined benefit plans. These issues are the primary focus of this chapter. We briefly discuss defined contribution plans later in the chapter.

Companies' pension plans are **funded.** Under a funded plan, the company makes periodic payments to a *funding agency*. The funding agency assumes the responsibility for both safeguarding and investing the pension assets to earn a return on the investments for the pension plan. The funding agency also makes payments to the retirees. An **unfunded** plan, on the other hand, is one in which no periodic payments are made to an external agency; instead, the pension payments to retired employees are made from current resources. (Although the *Pension Reform Act of 1974* has eliminated *un*funded plans for companies, some plans are *under*funded. Also, many governmental plans are unfunded.)

---

2. Estimated for 2005. This amount does not include government pension funds.

The amounts needed to fund a pension plan are estimated by actuaries. **Actuaries** are individuals trained in actuarial science who use compound interest techniques, projections of future events, and *actuarial funding methods* to calculate required current contributions by the company.

Companies' pension plans are usually **noncontributory.** With noncontributory plans, the entire pension cost is borne by the employer (company). Under a **contributory** plan, employees bear part of the cost of the plan and make contributions from their salaries into the pension fund. We discuss noncontributory plans in this chapter.

In addition, most companies design their pension plans to meet the Internal Revenue Code rules:

1. The maximum amount of employer contributions that are deductible for income tax purposes
2. Pension fund earnings are exempt from income taxes
3. Employer contributions to the pension fund are not taxable to the employees until they receive their pension benefits

Exhibit 20-1 summarizes the relationships among the employees, the company, and the funding agency for a noncontributory defined benefit pension plan.

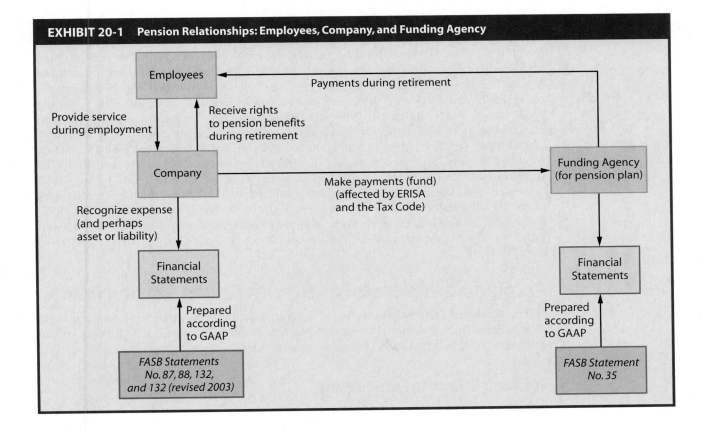

EXHIBIT 20-1   Pension Relationships: Employees, Company, and Funding Agency

HISTORICAL PERSPECTIVE OF PENSION PLANS

Accounting for the cost of pension plans has been analyzed for many years. The first authoritative statement was **Accounting Research Bulletin No. 47**, which recommended recognizing pension cost on the accrual basis instead of the cash basis. That is, it recommended that pension expense be recorded by an employer during the periods of employment as benefits are earned by employees, and *not* delayed until the periods when retirement

2 Explain the historical perspective of accounting for pension plans.

benefits are actually paid. The pension expense is based on the present value of the future benefits earned by employees during the current accounting period. We use present value techniques (which we explain in the Time Value of Money Module) in this chapter for computing the amounts related to pension plans.

Since the pronouncements of the Committee on Accounting Procedure were not mandatory, most companies continued to use the cash basis of accounting for pension plans after the issuance of *ARB No. 47*. The use of the cash basis, however, violated the accrual concept and resulted in a lack of comparability among companies in reporting pension expense. This sometimes caused wide year-to-year fluctuations in the pension expense for a single company. In an effort to solve this problem, **APB Opinion No. 8,** "Accounting for the Cost of Pension Plans" was issued. This *Opinion* required the use of the accrual method for the recognition of the pension expense. However, it allowed a choice of actuarial methods in determining the amount of the pension expense, which caused a lack of comparability. Also companies with plans for which the obligation to pay benefits greatly exceeded the plan assets available did not record a liability. As a result, in 1974 the FASB added pension accounting to its agenda, and over a long period developed and refined the accounting for pensions. The FASB first issued a Discussion Memorandum in 1975 and then issued several Exposure Drafts in subsequent years. Then, in 1980 **FASB Statement No. 35,** "Accounting and Reporting by Defined Benefit Pension Plans," was issued. This *Statement* defined the principles to be used and the disclosures required by the funding agency for a company's pension plan. This information, which we briefly discuss later in the chapter, is primarily for the benefit of the participants in the plan. However, it is also used by the employer company for its pension plan accounting calculations and disclosures. In 1985, the FASB issued **FASB Statement No. 87,** "Employers' Accounting for Pensions," which established the measurement, recognition, and disclosure principles for employers' pension plans. Also, in 1985, the FASB issued **FASB Statement No. 88,** "Employers' Accounting for Settlements and Curtailments of Defined Benefit Plans and for Termination Benefits," which we briefly discuss later in this chapter. In 1998, the FASB issued **FASB Statement No. 132,** which modified the disclosure requirements of *FASB Statement No. 87,* but did not change its measurement and recognition principles. Finally, in 2003, the FASB issued **FASB Statement No. 132 (revised 2003),** which modified the disclosures that companies must make. We refer to this as *FASB Statement No. 132R* in the rest of the chapter. In this chapter, we discuss the recording and reporting requirements of *FASB Statement No. 87* and the disclosure requirements of *FASB Statements No. 132 and 132R.*

ACCOUNTING PRINCIPLES FOR DEFINED BENEFIT PENSION PLANS

The principles of *FASB Statement No. 87* are very complex and we include only the basic elements in the following discussion. Note that the minimum amount funded by the employer is defined by ERISA (which we discuss later).

Key Terms Related to Pension Plans

Before we discuss the accounting principles for pension plans, you should understand the terms in Exhibit 20-2.[3] You should study these terms now and carefully review them as we introduce each in the chapter. In addition, we introduce several other terms later in the chapter as they relate to specific issues. Note that actuaries often use the term *accrue* to refer to amounts associated with the pension plan, in contrast to the more specific meaning used by accountants.

---

3.   "Employers' Accounting for Pensions," *FASB Statement of Financial Accounting Standards No. 87* (Stamford, Conn.: FASB, 1985), Appendix D and par. 44.

EXHIBIT 20-2   Key Terms Related to Pension Plans

Accumulated Benefit Obligation. The actuarial present value of all the benefits attributed by the pension benefit formula to employee service rendered before a specified date. The amount is based on current and past compensation levels of employees and, therefore, includes no assumptions about future pay increases.

Actual Return on Plan Assets. The difference between the fair value of the plan assets at the end of the period and the fair value at the beginning of the period, adjusted for contributions and payments of benefits during the period.

Actuarial Funding Method. Any technique that actuaries use in determining the amounts and timing of employer contributions to provide for pension benefits.

Actuarial Present Value. The value, on a specified date, of an amount or series of amounts payable or receivable in the future. The present value is determined by discounting the future amount or amounts at a predetermined discount rate. The future amounts are adjusted for the probability of payment (affected by factors such as death, disability, or withdrawal from the plan).

Assumptions. Estimates of the occurrence of future events affecting pension costs, such as mortality, withdrawal, disablement and retirement, changes in compensation, and discount rates. Sometimes called *actuarial* assumptions.

Expected Return on Plan Assets. An amount calculated by applying the expected long-term rate of return on plan assets to the fair market value of the plan assets at the beginning of the period.

Discount Rate. The rate at which the pension benefits can be effectively settled (e.g., the rate implicit in current prices of annuity contracts that could be used to settle the pension obligation). The discount rate is used in computing the service cost, the projected benefit obligation, and the accumulated benefit obligation.

Gain or Loss. A change in the value of either the projected benefit obligation (or the plan assets) resulting from experience different from that assumed, or from a change in an actuarial assumption. Sometimes called *actuarial* or *experience* gain or loss.

Pension Benefit Formula. The basis for determining payments to which employees will be entitled during retirement.

Prior Service Cost. The cost of retroactive benefits granted in a plan amendment or at the initial adoption of the plan. The cost is the present value of the additional benefits attributed by the pension benefit formula.

Projected Benefit Obligation. The actuarial present value, at a specified date, of all the benefits attributed by the pension benefit formula to employee service rendered prior to that date. The amount includes future increases in compensation that the company projects it will pay to employees during the remainder of their employment, provided the pension benefit formula is based on those future compensation levels. The projected benefit obligation differs from the accumulated benefit obligation because it includes anticipated future pay increases.

Service Cost. The actuarial present value of benefits attributed by the pension benefit formula to services of employees during the current period. If the pension benefit formula is based on future compensation levels (e.g., average of last five years' salary), the service cost is based on those future compensation levels.

Vested Benefit Obligation. The actuarial present value of the vested benefits, which are those benefits that the employees have the right to receive if the employee no longer works for the employer.

3 Explain the accounting principles for defined benefit plans, including computing pension expense and recognizing pension liabilities and assets.

Pension Expense

In defining the annual pension cost, *FASB Statement No. 87* uses the term *net periodic pension cost* because a company may capitalize some of its annual pension cost as part of the cost of an asset, such as inventory. For simplicity, we will use the term *pension expense* and assume that none of the pension costs are capitalized. The pension expense that a company recognizes includes five components: service cost, interest cost, expected return on plan assets, amortization of unrecognized prior service cost, and gain or loss.[4]

1. *Service Cost.* **The service cost is the actuarial present value of the benefits attributed by the pension benefit formula to services of the employees during the current period.** This amount is the present value of the deferred compensation to be paid to employees during their retirement in return for their current services. The service cost is computed using the *discount* rate selected by the company. The discount rate will vary as economic conditions change. If the rate increases (decreases), the present value decreases (increases). We show the nature of the service cost in the following diagram:

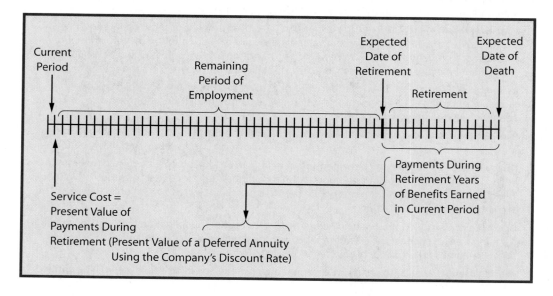

2. *Interest Cost.* **The interest cost is the increase in the projected benefit obligation due to the passage of time.** The projected benefit obligation is the present value of the deferred compensation earned by the employees to date (based on their expected future compensation levels). The interest cost is the projected benefit obligation at the beginning of the period multiplied by the *discount* rate used by the company. Since the pension plan is a deferred compensation agreement in which future payments are discounted to their present values, interest accrues because of the passage of time. The interest cost is added in the computation of pension expense.

3. *Expected Return on Plan Assets.* **The expected return on plan assets is the expected increase in the plan assets due to investing activities.**[5] Plan assets are held by the funding agency and consist of investments in securities such as stocks and bonds, as well as other investments. The expected return is calculated by multiplying the fair value of the plan assets at the beginning of the period by the expected long-term rate of return on plan assets. The rate of return reflects the average rate of earnings expected on the assets invested to provide for the benefits included in the projected benefit obligation. The expected return on plan assets is subtracted because the

---

4. A sixth component is the amortization of any unrecognized liability or asset that existed at the initial application of *FASB Statement No. 87*. This item is a result of the transition from the requirements of *APB Opinion No. 8* and we do not discuss it. There is a similar transition adjustment for other postretirement benefits.

5. Note that *FASB Statement No. 87* specifies that the third component of the pension expense is the actual return on plan assets. It then includes the difference between the actual and expected return in the computation of the fifth component (the gain or loss). Under the disclosure requirements of *FASB Statement No. 132R*, a company is only required to disclose the expected return in the computation of its pension expense. Therefore, in our discussion we combine the two amounts from *FASB Statement No. 87* into the expected return.

earnings "compensate" for the interest cost on the projected benefit obligation, as we show in the following diagram:

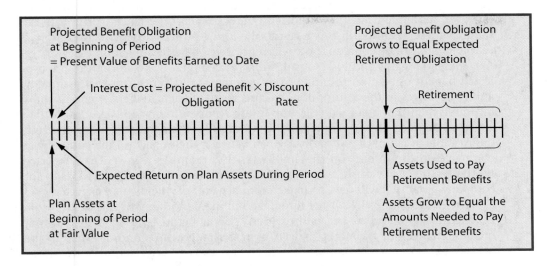

4. *Amortization of Unrecognized Prior Service Cost.* Amendments to a pension plan may include provisions that grant increased retroactive benefits to employees based on their employment in prior periods, thereby increasing the projected benefit obligation. Similar retroactive benefits may also be granted at the initial adoption of a plan. The cost of these retroactive benefits is the **prior service cost.** The prior service cost is "unrecognized" because it is *not* recognized in the financial statements (i.e., is not recorded in the accounts) in total in the period granted. Instead, it is "recognized" by the actuaries as a relevant cost and the amortization is included in the computation of pension expense.

The unrecognized prior service cost is amortized by assigning an equal amount to each future service period of each active employee who, at the date of the amendment, is expected to receive future benefits under the plan. Alternatively, straight-line amortization over the average remaining service life of active employees may be used for simplicity. Employees hired after the date of the amendment or the plan adoption are not included in either calculation. The plan amendment usually increases the projected benefit obligation. Therefore, the amortization is added in the computation of pension expense. However, there have been several instances in recent years where companies in financial difficulty or under pressure from competitors have amended their pension plans to reduce the projected benefit obligation. In this case, the amortization is subtracted in the computation. We show the unrecognized prior service cost and its amortization in the following diagram:

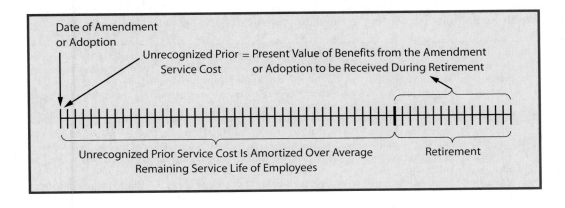

5. *Gain or Loss.* The gain or loss arises because actuaries make assumptions about many of the items included in the computation of pension costs and benefits. These include future compensation levels, the interest (discount) rate, employee turnover, retirement rates, and mortality rates. Actual experience will not be the same as these assumptions. As a result, the *actual* projected benefit obligation at year-end will not be equal to the *expected* projected benefit obligation.

Therefore, gains and losses result from (a) changes in the amount of the projected benefit obligation resulting from experience different from that assumed[6], and (b) changes in the assumptions.[7] Gains result when actual experience is more favorable than that assumed (e.g., the future compensation levels are lower than expected because of lower inflation). Losses result when the actual experience is unfavorable. It is important to distinguish between the impact on the company as compared to the impact on the employees. For example, a lower-than-expected mortality rate is obviously favorable to the employees, but it creates a loss to the company because it will have to make more pension payments than expected.

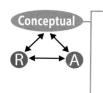

The entire gain or loss is *not* recognized in the period in which it occurs (so it is called an *unrecognized* net gain or loss). This is because the gain or loss may include changes in estimates as well as real changes in economic values, and because gains in one period may be offset by losses in another period. Also, immediate recognition in full might create significant fluctuations in the pension expense. Therefore, the amount of any unrecognized net gain or loss is amortized over *future* periods. **Amortization of any unrecognized net gain or loss is included in the pension expense of a given year if, at the beginning of the year, the cumulative unrecognized net gain or loss from previous periods exceeds a "corridor." The corridor is defined as 10% of the greater of the actual projected benefit obligation or the fair value of the plan assets.**[8] If amortization is required, the minimum amortization is computed as follows:

$$\frac{\text{Net gain or loss} - \text{Corridor at beginning of year}}{\substack{\text{Average remaining service period of the active employees} \\ \text{expected to receive benefits under the plan}}}$$

The amortization of an unrecognized net gain (loss) is subtracted (added) in the computation of pension expense.[9]

To summarize, the gain or loss component of pension expense generally consists of one of the following two items:
(1) Amortization of any unrecognized net loss from previous periods (added to compute pension expense), or
(2) Amortization of any unrecognized net gain from previous periods (deducted to compute pension expense).

Gains and losses that arise from a single occurrence not directly related to the pension plan are recognized in the period in which they occur. For example, a gain or loss that is directly related to the disposal of a component is included in the "gain or loss on disposal" and reported according to the requirements of *FASB Statement No. 144*.

---

6. In addition, gains and losses can occur because of the use of the market-related value of the plan assets, as we explain in footnote 8. These gains and losses are handled in a manner similar to those for changes in the projected benefit obligation, so for simplicity we do not discuss them further.

7. Although these gains and losses frequently are referred to as *experience* gains and losses or *actuarial* gains and losses, the FASB avoided using these terms.

8. In *FASB Statement No. 87*, the term **market-related value** is used. The market-related value of plan assets is either the fair value or a calculated value that recognizes changes in fair value in a systematic and rational manner over not more than five years. The use of the market-related value is allowed in order to reduce the volatility of the pension expense amount. For simplicity, we always use the fair value of the plan assets as the market-related value.

9. Alternatively, any systematic method of amortization may be used instead of the minimum just described, as long as it results in greater amortization. We use the minimum amount each period.

Components of Pension Expense

In summary, the pension expense a company reports on its income statement generally includes the following components:

Service cost (Present value of benefits earned during the year using the discount rate)

+ Interest cost (Projected benefit obligation at beginning of the year × Discount rate)

− Expected return on plan assets (Fair value of plan assets at the beginning of the year × Expected long-term rate of return on plan assets)

+ Amortization of prior service cost (Present value of additional benefits granted at adoption or modification of the plan amortized over the remaining service lives of active employees)

∓ Gain or loss (Amortization of the cumulative unrecognized net gain or loss from previous periods in excess of the corridor)

= Pension Expense

Note that the amortization of a reduction in unrecognized prior service cost is deducted in the pension expense calculation.

Pension Liabilities and Assets

The amount of a company's pension expense usually is different from the amount contributed by the company to the pension plan (the amount funded) because they are defined by different sets of rules. The expense is defined by *FASB Statement No. 87*, whereas the funding must be consistent with the rules of ERISA, as we discuss later. Therefore, the company records a liability if its pension expense is greater than the amount it funded. Alternatively, the company records an asset if its pension expense is less than the amount it funded. This asset or liability is similar to the assets and liabilities that arise from using the accrual basis of accounting and it increases or decreases every year. Since either an asset or a liability can occur (but not both at the same time), we use a single title for the account, **prepaid/accrued pension cost.** If the account has a debit balance at the end of the year, the company reports the amount as an asset (prepaid pension cost) on its balance sheet. If the account has a credit balance at the end of the year, the company reports it as a liability (accrued pension cost). Typically, the amount is classified as noncurrent.

Credit: ©Getty Images/PhotoDisc

The minimum total pension liability that a company must recognize is the **unfunded accumulated benefit obligation.** This is the excess of the *accumulated* benefit obligation over the fair value of the plan assets at the end of the period. Therefore, a company may have to report an additional pension liability on its balance sheet. The accumulated benefit obligation is the present value of the deferred compensation earned by employees to date, based on *current* compensation levels. (Thus, the difference between the projected and accumulated benefit obligation is the inclusion of expected salary increases in the projected amount.)

Therefore, the unfunded accumulated benefit obligation is a measure of the obligation of the company based on the legal concept of a liability. That is, it is based on historical events such as the actual service of the employees and their current pay levels.

Therefore, the unfunded accumulated benefit obligation provides information about the liability a company would have if its pension plan were discontinued. Alternatively, if the plan is continued, the unfunded accumulated benefit obligation provides a minimum measure of the additional funds that a company will have to contribute in future periods.

If a company has to report an Additional Pension Liability on its balance sheet, it calculates the amount as follows:

$$
\begin{array}{rl}
& \textbf{Accumulated benefit obligation} \\
- & \textbf{Fair value of plan assets} \\
\hline
= & \textbf{Unfunded Accumulated Benefit Obligation} \\
- & \textbf{Prepaid/accrued pension cost (credit balance)} \\
\text{or } + & \textbf{Prepaid/accrued pension cost (debit balance)} \\
\hline
= & \textbf{Additional Pension Liability}
\end{array}
$$

So the additional pension liability "adjusts" the company's existing pension liability or asset to the amount of the unfunded accumulated benefit obligation.

Generally, a company must recognize an additional liability in two situations. First, a company may have an unrecognized prior service cost. In this case, the company also recognizes an intangible asset, **deferred pension cost**, of the same amount. The reason for recognizing an intangible asset is that the prior service cost has created an expectation of enhanced future performance by employees. That is, the employer would take on an increased obligation only if future benefits of at least an equal amount were expected.

The second cause of an additional liability is that the company has funded minimal amounts and/or earned low or negative returns on its plan assets. In this case, the company also recognizes a negative component of other comprehensive income.

Note that a company might have both a prior service cost and poor returns on its plan assets. In this case, the amount of the intangible asset must not exceed the amount of any unrecognized prior service cost (plus any unrecognized transition liability or asset, as we noted in footnote 4). If the additional liability exceeds the unrecognized prior service cost, the company recognizes the intangible asset, and reports the excess (debit) as other comprehensive income.

The asset and accumulated other comprehensive income accounts related to the recognition of the additional pension liability are *not* amortized. Instead, the company recomputes the amount of the additional liability at each balance sheet date and adjusts or eliminates the related intangible asset or accumulated other comprehensive income as necessary.

In summary, a company may report the following pension asset, liability, and accumulated other comprehensive income items, depending on the circumstances, on its balance sheet:

Assets	Liabilities
1. Prepaid/accrued pension cost (debit balance)	1. Prepaid/accrued pension cost (credit balance)
2. Deferred pension cost (intangible asset)	2. Additional pension liability

Stockholders' Equity

1. Accumulated other comprehensive income: Excess of additional pension liability over unrecognized prior service cost (negative element)

Measurement Methods

The pension benefit formula usually is based on future compensation levels and defines benefits similarly for all years of service. Then, in computing the service cost, a constant amount of the total estimated pension benefit, based on an estimate of final salary, usually is **attributed** to each period (this method is known as the **benefit/years-of-service approach**). Using the pension benefit formula we showed at the beginning of the chapter, the service cost would be based on the employee earning a benefit of $1/30 \times$ $77,100 each year for 30 years.

The company uses a **discount rate that reflects the rates at which the pension benefits could be effectively settled** when it computes the service cost, the projected benefit obligation, and the accumulated benefit obligation. For example, if the company could settle its obligation by purchasing an annuity from an insurance company for each employee, it would use the rate on that annuity as the appropriate discount rate. The rate of return on high-quality fixed-income investments currently available and expected to be available in the future could also be used. Companies are required by the SEC to evaluate the rate each year.

On the other hand, the expected (assumed) long-term rate of return on plan assets used to compute the expected return on assets is based on the average rate of earnings expected on the funds invested (or to be invested). Actual experience is considered along with the rates of return expected to be available in the future.

Disclosures

The disclosure requirements for defined benefit pension plans of employers are established in **FASB Statement No. 132** and **FASB Statement No. 132R.**[10] They are very detailed and are intended to provide users with relevant information. We summarize the major required disclosures below:

1. A narrative description of investment policies and strategies, including target allocations for each major category of plan assets and other factors that are pertinent to an understanding of the investment goals, risk management strategies, and permitted and prohibited investments.
2. A narrative description of the basis used to determine the expected rate of return on plan assets.
3. Other information that would be useful in understanding the risk associated with each asset category and the rate of the return on plan assets.
4. The benefits expected to be paid in each of the next five years, and the total for the next five years.
5. The contributions to be made by the company to the plan in the next year.
6. A reconciliation of the beginning and ending balances of the projected benefit obligation, including the amounts of the service cost, interest cost, actuarial gains and losses, benefits paid, and plan amendments.
7. A reconciliation of the beginning and ending balances of the fair value of the plan assets, including the actual return on plan assets, contributions by the company, and benefits paid.
8. The funded status of the plan, the amounts not recognized on the balance sheet, and the amounts recognized on the balance sheet.
9. The amount of pension expense, including the service cost, the interest cost, the expected return on plan assets, the amortization of any unrecognized prior service cost, the amortization of any net gains or losses, and the amortization of any unrecognized transition obligation or asset.

---

10. "Employers' Disclosures about Pensions and Other Postemployment Benefits," *FASB Statement No. 132* and *132R* (Norwalk, Conn.:FASB, 1998 and 2003). There are additional disclosures beyond those we have listed.

10. The discount rate, the rate of compensation increase, and the expected long-term rate of return on the plan assets.
11. The amounts and types of securities included in the plan assets.

SECURE YOUR KNOWLEDGE 20-1

- A pension plan requires a company to provide income to its retired employees in return for services they provided during their employment and classify as a:
  - Defined benefit plan that promises fixed retirement benefits determined by a formula that is usually based on the employee's earnings and length of service, or a
  - Defined contribution plan in which the employer's annual contribution is based on a formula but no commitment is made as to the future benefits to be paid to employees.
- Pension expense consists of five components:
  - Service cost—the actuarial present value of the benefits earned by employees during the year (the discount rate used is a settlement rate reflecting the rate at which the pension benefits could be effectively settled),
  - Interest cost—the increase in the projected benefit obligation (the present value of the benefits earned by employees based on their expected future compensation levels) due to the passage of time,
  - Expected return on plan assets—the expected increase in plan assets that are invested,
  - Amortization of unrecognized prior service cost—the amortization of the cost of retroactive benefits granted to employees; and
  - Amortization of gain or loss—the amortization of the change in the projected benefit obligation resulting from actual experience being different from that which is assumed.
- Because pension expense (determined by generally accepted accounting principles) usually differs from the amount funded, the difference is recorded as an:
  - Asset—prepaid pension cost—if pension expense is less than the amount funded, or a
  - Liability—accrued pension cost—if pension expense is greater than the amount funded.
- A company must record a minimum liability equal to the unfunded accumulated benefit obligation (the excess of the accumulated benefit obligation over the fair value of the plan assets at the end of the period).
- If the balance in the accrued pension cost account is not sufficient to satisfy the minimum pension liability requirement, an additional pension liability must be recognized.
- If the cause of this additional pension liability is unrecognized prior service cost, the company will recognize an intangible asset equal to the unrecognized prior service cost (deferred pension cost). If the cause is minimal funding and/or poor returns on its plan assets, the company will recognize a negative component of stockholders' equity (excess of the additional pension liability over unrecognized prior service cost).

EXAMPLES OF ACCOUNTING FOR PENSIONS

4 Account for pensions.

We show various situations related to accounting for defined benefit pension plans in this section using *assumed* amounts. In the Appendix to the chapter, we show the present value calculations for pension plans. In that example, we calculate the amounts of the service cost, the projected benefit obligation, the prior service cost, and the pension expense from basic information about a company's pension plan.

Example: Pension Expense Equal to Pension Funding

Assume the following facts for the Carlisle Company:

1. The company adopts a pension plan on January 1, 2007. No retroactive benefits were granted to employees.
2. The service cost each year is: 2007, $400,000; 2008, $420,000; and 2009, $432,000.
3. The projected benefit obligation at the beginning of each year is: 2008, $400,000; and 2009, $840,000.
4. The discount rate is 10%.
5. The expected long-term rate of return on plan assets is 10%, which is also equal to the actual rate of return.
6. The company adopts a policy of funding an amount equal to the pension expense and makes the payment to the funding agency at the end of each year.[11]
7. Plan assets are based on the amounts contributed each year, plus a return of 10% per year, less an assumed payment of $20,000 at the end of each year to retired employees (beginning in 2008).

2007 Based on the preceding information, the service cost of $400,000 is the only component of the pension expense in 2007. This situation occurs because the company has (1) no interest cost because it has no projected benefit obligation at the beginning of the year since no employees had pension coverage before that time, (2) no expected return on plan assets because its expense recognition and funding were made at the end of the first year, (3) no prior service cost, and (4) no gain or loss. Since the company funds an amount equal to the pension expense, it records the following journal entry on December 31, 2007:

Pension Expense	400,000	
Cash		400,000

2008 The calculation of the pension expense for 2008 is more complex because it now has three components: service cost, interest cost, and expected return on plan assets. The service cost is $420,000. Since the projected benefit obligation at January 1, 2008 is $400,000 (the service cost for 2007), the interest cost is $40,000 (the projected benefit obligation of $400,000 multiplied by the discount rate of 10%). The $40,000 expected return on the plan assets is the $400,000 invested by the funding agency for the pension fund at the end of 2007 multiplied by the 10% expected rate of return. Therefore, the company computes its pension expense for 2008 as follows:

Service cost (assumed)	$420,000
Interest cost ($400,000 × 10%)	40,000
Expected return on plan assets ($400,000 × 10%)	(40,000)
Pension expense	$420,000

Since the company funds an amount equal to the expense, it records the following journal entry on December 31, 2008:

Pension Expense	420,000	
Cash		420,000

---

11. Companies are required by law to make payments to funding agencies on a quarterly basis. For simplicity, in all examples and homework we assume a single annual payment is made at the end of each year.

2009 For 2009 the service cost is $432,000. The projected benefit obligation at the beginning of 2009 is $840,000 ($400,000 beginning amount for 2008 + $420,000 service cost for 2008 + $40,000 interest cost − $20,000 payment to retired employees at end of 2008). The assets at the beginning of 2009 are $840,000 ($400,000 invested at the end of 2007 + $40,000 expected return in 2008 − $20,000 payment to retired employees at the end of 2008 + $420,000 invested at the end of 2008). Therefore, the company computes its pension expense for 2009 as follows:

Service cost (assumed)	$432,000
Interest cost ($840,000 × 10%)	84,000
Expected return on plan assets ($840,000 × 10%)	(84,000)
Pension expense	$432,000

Since the company funds an amount equal to the expense, it records the following journal entry on December 31, 2009:

Pension Expense	432,000	
Cash		432,000

Note that the interest cost and the expected return on the plan assets offset each other in this example. This situation occurs because the discount rate and the expected long-term rate of return on plan assets are both 10%, and because the company funds an amount equal to the expense. ◆

Example: Pension Expense Greater Than Pension Funding

Assume the same facts for the Carlisle Company as in the first example, except that instead of funding an amount equal to the pension expense, the company funds $385,000 in 2007, $400,000 in 2008, and $415,000 in 2009.[12] Since the company provides *fewer* assets to the pension fund, the expected return on those assets each year is less and, therefore, the pension expense must be larger to compensate for the lower expected return.

2007 The company's pension expense in 2007 is the $400,000 service cost, so the journal entry on December 31, 2007 is:

Pension Expense	400,000	
Cash		385,000
Prepaid/Accrued Pension Cost		15,000

Since the company funds only $385,000 in 2007 when the expense is $400,000, it recognizes a liability, Prepaid/Accrued Pension Cost, of $15,000.

2008 In 2008 the only difference from the previous example in the computation of the pension expense is the reduced expected return on the plan assets. Since the company

---

12. For illustrative purposes, the amount funded is less than the service cost. In some circumstances this procedure might be a violation of the minimum funding requirements of ERISA. However, the amount funded may be less than the *total* pension expense.

contributed only $385,000 on December 31, 2007, an expected return of only $38,500 was earned in 2008. The company computes its pension expense for 2008 as follows:

Service cost	$420,000
Interest cost ($400,000 × 10%)	40,000
Expected return on plan assets ($385,000 × 10%)	(38,500)
Pension expense	$421,500

Since the company funds $400,000 in 2008, it records the following journal entry on December 31, 2008:

Pension Expense	421,500	
Cash		400,000
Prepaid/Accrued Pension Cost		21,500

The balance in the liability account at the end of 2008 is $36,500 ($15,000 + $21,500).

2009 In 2009 the computation of the pension expense is again affected by the reduced expected return on the plan assets. Since the company contributed only $400,000, the assets of the pension fund on January 1, 2009 are $803,500 ($385,000 invested at the end of 2007 + $38,500 actual return in 2008 − $20,000 payment to retired employees at the end of 2008 + $400,000 invested at the end of 2008), and an expected return of $80,350 on those assets was earned during 2009. Therefore, the company computes its pension expense for 2009 as follows:

Service cost	$432,000
Interest cost ($840,000 × 10%)	84,000
Expected return on plan assets ($803,500 × 10%)	(80,350)
Pension expense	$435,650

Since the company funds $415,000 in 2009, it records the following journal entry on December 31, 2009:

Pension Expense	435,650	
Cash		415,000
Prepaid/Accrued Pension Cost		20,650

The balance in the liability account at the end of 2009 is $57,150 ($36,500 + $20,650). ◆

Example: Pension Expense Less Than Pension Funding, and Expected Return on Plan Assets Different from Both Actual Return and Discount Rate

Assume the same facts for the Carlisle Company as in the first example, except that (a) instead of funding an amount equal to the pension expense, the company funds $415,000 in 2007, $425,000 in 2008, and $440,000 in 2009, and (b) the expected return is 11% in each year, whereas the actual return is 12% in 2008. Since the company provides *more* assets to the pension fund and expects to earn a higher return on those assets, the pension expense is less to compensate for the higher return.

2007 The company's pension expense in 2007 is the $400,000 service cost and the journal entry on December 31, 2007 is:

Pension Expense	400,000	
Prepaid/Accrued Pension Cost	15,000	
Cash		415,000

Since the company funds $415,000 in 2007 when the expense is $400,000, it recognizes an asset, Prepaid/Accrued Pension Cost, of $15,000.

2008 In 2008 the only difference in the computation of the pension expense from the first example is the increased expected return on the plan assets. Since the company contributed $415,000 on December 31, 2007, its expected return on the plan assets is $45,650 in 2008. The company computes the pension expense for 2008 as follows:

Service cost	$420,000
Interest cost ($400,000 × 10%)	40,000
Expected return on plan assets ($415,000 × 11%)	(45,650)
Pension expense	$414,350

Since the company funds $425,000 in 2008, it records the following journal entry on December 31, 2008:

Pension Expense	414,350	
Prepaid/Accrued Pension Cost	10,650	
Cash		425,000

The balance in the Prepaid asset account at the end of 2008 is $25,650 ($15,000 + $10,650).

2009 In 2009, the computation of the pension expense is slightly more complicated. This is because the company earned a higher actual return (12%) than its expected return (11%) on its plan assets in 2008, so it has more total plan assets. Its plan assets at the beginning of 2009 are $869,800 [$415,000 invested at the end of 2007 + $49,800 ($415,000 × 0.12) actual return on plan assets − $20,000 payment to retired employees + $425,000 invested at the end of 2008]. Assuming the company continues to expect to earn 11% on its plan assets, its expected return for 2009 is $95,678. Therefore, the company computes its pension expense for 2009 as follows:

Service cost	$432,000
Interest cost ($840,000 × 10%)	84,000
Expected return on plan assets ($869,800 × 11%)	(95,678)
Pension expense	$420,322

Since the company funds $440,000 in 2009, it records the following journal entry on December 31, 2009:

Pension Expense	420,322	
Prepaid/Accrued Pension Cost	19,678	
Cash		440,000

The balance in the Prepaid asset account at the end of 2009 is $45,328 ($25,650 + $19,678). ♦

It is important that you understand the impact of the *expected* and *actual* rates of return on plan assets. As we have discussed, a company uses the expected return to compute its pension expense for the year. However, the actual return for the year increases the value of the plan assets at the end of the year. In the next year, the company multiplies those actual plan assets by the expected return to compute the amount that it subtracts to compute its the pension expense for that next year. In its pension plan disclosures, the company includes the actual return on its plan assets in the reconciliation of the beginning and ending balances of the fair value of its plan assets, as we show in a later example on page 1019.

Example: Pension Expense Including Amortization of Unrecognized Prior Service Cost

The previous three examples showed relatively simple computations of pension expense and the related pension liability or asset. The remaining examples deal with additional issues. Recall that a company may grant increased retroactive benefits based on services performed by employees in prior periods. The cost of providing these benefits is called a prior service cost. A prior service cost also may arise when a company adopts a pension plan. A prior service cost causes an increase in the projected benefit obligation. However, the company does not recognize the prior service cost (so it is called "unrecognized") in the balance sheet, but amortizes it as a component of pension expense.

To show this amortization, assume the same facts for the Carlisle Company as in the last example, except that the company awarded retroactive benefits to the employees when it adopted the pension plan on January 1, 2007. The company's actuary computed the unrecognized prior service cost to be $2 million. This amount is added to the projected benefit obligation on January 1, 2007. To fund this projected benefit obligation, the company decided to increase its contribution by $260,000 per year. For simplicity, we also assume that the company amortizes the unrecognized prior service cost by the straight-line method over the remaining 20-year service life of its active employees. Thus, its amortization is $100,000 ($2,000,000 ÷ 20) per year.

2007 The company's pension expense in 2007 now has three components. In addition to the service cost of $400,000, the company recognizes both the interest cost on the $2 million projected benefit obligation and the $100,000 amortization of the unrecognized prior service cost. Therefore, it computes the pension expense for 2007 as follows:

Service cost	$400,000
Interest cost ($2,000,000 × 10%)	200,000
Amortization of unrecognized prior service cost	100,000
Pension expense	$700,000

Since the company funds $675,000 ($415,000 + $260,000) in 2007, it records the following journal entry on December 31, 2007:

Pension Expense	700,000	
Cash		675,000
Prepaid/Accrued Pension Cost		25,000

Note that the company does *not* include the unrecognized prior service cost of $1.9 million ($2 million − $100,000 amortized) in its balance sheet, but includes it in the disclosures we discussed earlier.[13]

---

13. It is possible that the company might include an additional pension liability in its year-end balance sheet. We discuss this topic in a later example on page 1016.

2008 On January 1, 2008 the projected benefit obligation is $2,600,000 ($2 million beginning amount + $400,000 service cost + $200,000 interest cost). Therefore, the company computes the pension expense for 2008 as follows:

Service cost	$420,000
Interest cost ($2,600,000 × 10%)	260,000
Expected return on plan assets ($675,000 × 11%)	(74,250)
Amortization of unrecognized prior service cost	100,000
Pension expense	$705,750

Since the company funds $685,000 ($425,000 + $260,000) in 2008, it records the following journal entry on December 31, 2008:

Pension Expense	705,750	
Cash		685,000
Prepaid/Accrued Pension Cost		20,750

2009 On January 1, 2009 the projected benefit obligation is $3,260,000 ($2,600,000 beginning amount + $420,000 service cost + $260,000 interest cost − $20,000 paid to retired employees), the plan assets are $1,421,000 ($675,000 invested at the end of 2007 + $81,000 ($675,000 × 12%) actual return on plan assets + $685,000 invested at the end of 2008 − $20,000 paid to retired employees), and the company computes the pension expense for 2009 as follows:

Service cost	$432,000
Interest cost ($3,260,000 × 10%)	326,000
Expected return on plan assets ($1,421,000 × 11%)	(156,310)
Amortization of unrecognized prior service cost	100,000
Pension expense	$701,690

Since the company funds $700,000 ($440,000 + $260,000) in 2009, it records the following journal entry on December 31, 2009:

Pension Expense	701,690	
Cash		700,000
Prepaid/Accrued Pension Cost		1,690

Note that the plan assets at the end of 2009 are $2,271,520 [$1,421,000 + $170,520 ($1,421,000 × 12%) + $700,000 − $20,000]. ♦

Example: Calculation of Amortization of Unrecognized Prior Service Cost

In the last example the pension expense included the amortization of unrecognized prior service cost. In that example, we used an "average life" of 20 years to determine the amount of the amortization. We explain two methods of calculating the amount of the amortization in this example. The preferred method assigns an equal amount to each future service period for each active participating employee who is expected to receive future benefits under the plan. Since the FASB did not give this method a title, we will refer to it as the "years-of-future-service" method. Alternatively, a company may use straight-line amortization over the average remaining service life of employees for simplicity.

Examples 20-1 and 20-2 show the preferred years-of-future-service method of amortization. We assume that at the beginning of 2007 the Watts Company has nine employees participating in its pension plan who are expected to receive benefits. One employee (A) is expected to retire after three years, one (B) after four, two (C and D) after five, two (E and F) after six, and three (G, H, and I) after seven years. Example 20-1 shows the computation of the amortization fraction. First, the company computes the number of service years rendered by the nine employees in each calendar year. Thus, in 2007 there are nine service years rendered, while in 2011 there are only seven service years rendered because employees A and B have retired. The total number of these service years is 50. Then, the company computes the amortization fraction for each year by dividing the total service years in each calendar year by the total of 50. Thus, in 2007, 9/50 is the amortization fraction, whereas in 2011, 7/50 is the fraction.

EXAMPLE 20-1 Computation of Amortization Fraction

Employees	Expected Years of Future Service	Number of Service Years Rendered in Each Year						
		2007	2008	2009	2010	2011	2012	2013
A	3	1	1	1				
B	4	1	1	1	1			
C, D	5	2	2	2	2	2		
E, F	6	2	2	2	2	2	2	
G, H, I	7	3	3	3	3	3	3	3
Total		9	9	9	8	7	5	3 = 50
Amortization Fraction		9/50	9/50	9/50	8/50	7/50	5/50	3/50

If we assume that the company's actuary computed the total unrecognized prior service cost at the beginning of 2007 to be $400,000, the company calculates the amount of the amortization each year as we show in Example 20-2. For instance, the company amortizes $72,000 ($400,000 × 9/50) in 2007, while it amortizes $56,000 ($400,000 × 7/50) in 2011.[14] The company includes this amount in the total pension expense on its income statement for each year. The remaining unrecognized prior service cost is the balance at the end of the previous year less the amount amortized for the year. Remember that the company does not include this amount in its balance sheet, but does include it in the required pension plan disclosures, as we discussed earlier.

To compute the alternative straight-line amortization, the company calculates the average remaining service life of the participating employees. We show this method using the same employee group as we assumed earlier. The company computes the total number of service years rendered (50) by adding the expected years of service for all employees [i.e., 3(A) + 4(B) + 5(C) + 5(D) + 6(E) + 6(F) + 7(G) + 7(H) + 7(I)] and dividing by the number of employees (9) to give an average service life of 5.56 years. Example 20-3 shows the computation of the straight-line amortization. Under this method, the company amortizes $71,942 each year from 2007 through 2011 to increase the pension expense. In 2012 the amortization is only $40,290, the amount needed to reduce the remaining unrecognized prior service cost to zero. This straight-line method is also used for amortizing the

---

14. In *FASB Statement No. 87* (par. 85 and 86), a similar schedule and an amortization table are shown, but an assumption that an equal number of employees retire each year is made. This assumption provides a "pure" sum-of-the-years'-digits set of fractions that yield a constantly decreasing amortization amount each period. Since this is not a realistic assumption, we assume a varying number of employees retiring each period, which results in a modified sum-of-the-years'-digits set of fractions.

	EXAMPLE 20-2	**Amortization of Unrecognized Prior Service Cost: Years-of-Future-Service Method**		
Year	**Total Unrecognized Prior Service Cost**[a]	**Amortization Fraction**[b]	**Amortization to Increase Pension Expense**[c]	**Remaining Unrecognized Prior Service Cost**[d]
2007	$400,000	9/50	$72,000	$328,000
2008	400,000	9/50	72,000	256,000
2009	400,000	9/50	72,000	184,000
2010	400,000	8/50	64,000	120,000
2011	400,000	7/50	56,000	64,000
2012	400,000	5/50	40,000	24,000
2013	400,000	3/50	24,000	—

a. Computed by actuary
b. From Example 20-1
c. $400,000 × amortization fraction
d. Balance from end of previous year (or initial balance) − amortization for the current year

unrecognized net gain or loss we discuss in the next example. Note that if an amendment caused a decrease in future benefits, the resulting "negative" prior service cost is amortized in the same manner to decrease pension expense each period. ♦

	EXAMPLE 20-3	**Amortization of Unrecognized Prior Service Cost: Straight-Line Method**		
Year	**Total Unrecognized Prior Service Cost**[a]		**Amortization to Increase Pension Expense**[b]	**Remaining Unrecognized Prior Service Cost**[c]
2007	$400,000		$71,942	$328,058
2008	400,000		71,942	256,116
2009	400,000		71,942	184,174
2010	400,000		71,942	112,232
2011	400,000		71,942	40,290
2012	400,000		40,290[d]	—

a. Computed by actuary
b. $400,000 total unrecognized prior service cost ÷ 5.56 (50 total service years ÷ 9 employees) average remaining service life
c. Balance from end of previous year (or initial balance) − amortization for the year
d. To reduce the remaining unrecognized prior service cost to zero

Example: Pension Expense Including Net Gain or Loss (to Extent Recognized)

An unrecognized gain or loss from previous periods arises from (a) changes in the amount of the projected benefit obligation from experience different from that assumed, and (b) changes in actuarial assumptions. The excess of this unrecognized gain or loss over a "corridor" amount (discussed later) is amortized over the remaining service life of active employees expected to receive benefits under the plan. A company *adds* amortization of an unrecognized net loss to pension expense. It *subtracts* any amortization of an unrecognized net gain from pension expense as part of the net gain or loss.

Example 20-4 shows the computation of the net gain or loss included in pension expense for the years 2007 through 2010. This example is for the Bliss Company, which has had a defined benefit pension plan for its employees for several years. The amounts

EXAMPLE 20-4   Computation of Net Gain or Loss

Year	Cumulative Unrecognized Net Loss (Gain)[a]	Projected Benefit Obligation: Actual[a]	Fair Value of Plan Assets[a]	Corridor[b]	Excess Unrecognized Net Loss (Gain)[c]	Recognized Net Loss (Gain)[d]
2007	$13,000	$110,000	$100,000	$11,000	$2,000	$200
2008	(2,300)	135,000	130,000	13,500	—e	—
2009	18,700	168,000	170,000	17,000	1,700	170
2010	27,500	230,000	215,000	23,000	4,500	450

a. At the beginning of the year
b. 10% of the greater of the actual projected benefit obligation or the fair value of the plan assets at the beginning of the year
c. Absolute value of the cumulative unrecognized net loss (gain) − corridor
d. Excess unrecognized net loss (gain) ÷ average remaining service life (10 years)
e. Since the absolute value of the cumulative unrecognized net loss (gain) is less than the corridor, there is no excess unrecognized net loss (gain)

of the cumulative unrecognized net loss (gain), the projected benefit obligation (actual), and the fair value of the plan assets are based on information provided by the company's actuary and funding agency.

To compute the amortization, the first step is to determine the cumulative unrecognized net gain or loss at the beginning of the year. The company's actuary calculates the amounts in the Cumulative Unrecognized Net Loss (Gain) column of Example 20-4 at the beginning of the year, based on previous periods. Thus, for instance, the $13,000 amount of cumulative unrecognized net loss at the beginning of 2007 is a result of experience different from that assumed and changes in actuarial assumptions in periods prior to 2007. Note in this example that we have assumed a high volatility to better explain the calculations. Also note that we show a cumulative unrecognized net *loss* without parentheses because the related amortization is *added* to pension expense, whereas we show a *gain* in parentheses because the amortization is *deducted*.

The company's actuary also calculates the amounts in the Projected Benefit Obligation and the Fair Value of Plan Assets columns at the beginning of the year. For instance, the company has a $110,000 projected benefit obligation and a $100,000 fair value of the plan at the beginning of 2007. These amounts are used to determine the **corridor** amount. **The corridor is 10% of the greater of the actual projected benefit obligation or the fair value of the plan assets at the beginning of the period.** As we discussed earlier, the corridor reduces the volatility of the pension expense.

A company amortizes any cumulative unrecognized net gain or loss in a given year only if, at the beginning of the year, the (absolute value of the) cumulative unrecognized net gain or loss exceeds the corridor. This 10% threshold (the corridor) is intended to reduce fluctuations in pension expense. In many cases the corridor will not be exceeded, so no amortization is recorded. Also, if a company had a large cumulative unrecognized net gain (loss) at the beginning of a given year, it would reduce (increase) its pension expense only by the amortization of the cumulative unrecognized net gain (loss) in excess of the corridor amount. It is unlikely that the company would have a cumulative unrecognized net loss (gain) at the beginning of the next year in excess of the corridor amount. Even in such an extreme situation, the pension expense would be increased (decreased) only by the amount of the amortization of the cumulative unrecognized net loss (gain) in excess of the corridor amount.

In Example 20-4 the amount in the Corridor column for a given year is 10% of the higher of the actual projected benefit obligation or the fair value of the plan assets at the beginning of that year. Thus, in 2007 the company computes the $11,000 corridor as 10% of the $110,000 actual projected benefit obligation because it is the higher of the two amounts. In 2009, however, it computes the $17,000 corridor as 10% of the $170,000 fair value of the plan assets.

The amount in the Excess Unrecognized Net Loss (Gain) column for a given year is the excess of the (absolute value of the) cumulative unrecognized net loss (gain) over the corridor at the beginning of that year. Thus, in 2007 the $2,000 excess unrecognized net loss is the difference between the $13,000 cumulative unrecognized net loss and the $11,000 corridor. In 2008, however, the corridor exceeds the cumulative unrecognized net gain, so there is no excess.

The amount in the Recognized Net Loss (Gain) column for a given year is the adjustment to pension expense. The company computes each amortization amount by dividing the excess unrecognized net loss (gain) for that year by the average remaining service life of the active employees expected to receive benefits under the plan. In this example, we assume a 10-year average service life for all years. In reality, the company may have to recompute the average service life each year for changes in its employee work force. For instance, in 2007 the $200 amortization that the company *adds* to pension expense as the recognized net loss is determined by dividing the $2,000 excess unrecognized net loss by the 10-year average service life. ♦

Example: Recognition of Additional Pension Liability

The previous examples focused on computing a company's pension expense and the related pension liability or asset. This example deals with recognizing an additional pension liability when the company's accumulated benefit obligation is greater than the fair value of the plan assets. For example, the recognition of the additional liability, assume the following facts for the Devon Company at the end of 2007:

Projected benefit obligation	$2,000,000
Accumulated benefit obligation	1,200,000
Plan assets	1,000,000 fair value
Prepaid/accrued pension cost	50,000 liability
Unrecognized prior service cost	300,000

Remember that the difference between the two benefit obligations is that the *projected* benefit obligation includes assumed future pay increases, whereas the *accumulated* benefit obligation is based on current pay levels (see the definitions in Exhibit 20-2). The company computes the unfunded *accumulated* benefit obligation as the difference between the accumulated benefit obligation and the fair value of the plan assets as follows:

Accumulated benefit obligation	$1,200,000
Plan assets (fair value)	(1,000,000)
Unfunded accumulated benefit obligation	$ 200,000

This unfunded accumulated benefit obligation of $200,000 is the minimum liability that the company must recognize. Since the company already has recorded a liability (prepaid/accrued pension cost) of $50,000, it calculates the *additional* liability of $150,000 that it needs to recognize at the end of 2007 as follows:

Unfunded accumulated benefit obligation	$200,000
Prepaid/accrued pension cost (liability)	(50,000)
Additional pension liability	$150,000

Besides recognizing the additional liability, the company also recognizes an intangible asset of an equal amount because the intangible asset is less than the unrecognized prior service cost of $300,000. Since the FASB did not suggest a title, we call it Deferred Pension Cost. Thus, the journal entry on December 31, 2007 to record the intangible asset and to increase the pension liability from $50,000 to $200,000 is as follows:

Deferred Pension Cost	150,000	
Additional Pension Liability		150,000

The Devon Company reports the Deferred Pension Cost account balance of $150,000 as an intangible asset on its 2007 year-end balance sheet. It combines the balances of the Additional Pension Liability and Prepaid/Accrued Pension Cost accounts to report a total pension liability of $200,000 on the balance sheet. The company also includes the additional liability ($150,000) in its pension plan disclosures.

The company makes a different journal entry if the preceding facts remained the same, except that the company had a prepaid/accrued pension cost *asset* of $40,000 instead of the liability of $50,000. In this case, the minimum liability must still be $200,000, but a $40,000 asset exists. Consequently, the company must record a liability and an intangible asset of $240,000 (the unfunded accumulated benefit obligation of $200,000 + the prepaid/accrued pension cost asset of $40,000). The journal entry is as follows:

Deferred Pension Cost	240,000	
Additional Pension Liability		240,000

The company combines (nets) the balances of the Additional Pension Liability and Prepaid/Accrued Pension Cost accounts to report a net pension liability of $200,000 on its balance sheet. The company also includes the additional liability in its pension plan disclosures.

In the previous situations we assumed that the intangible asset does not exceed the unrecognized prior service cost. In other words, the need to recognize the additional liability arose because of amendments to the plan that created prior service costs and increased the accumulated benefit obligation, but have not yet been funded by the company.

Another issue in the recognition of the additional liability occurs if there is no unrecognized prior service cost, or if it exceeds the unrecognized prior service cost. Typically, this situation arises because there have been negative returns on the plan assets. Since it would be inappropriate for a company to record such declines in value of the plan assets as an intangible asset of the company, it includes the amount as a negative component of the year's other comprehensive income, which reduces the balance in accumulated other comprehensive income. To illustrate this situation, we use the same facts as originally given for the Devon Company, but, in addition, the company has an unrecognized prior service cost of $120,000 instead of $300,000. The company recognizes the same additional liability of $150,000, but the intangible asset cannot exceed the unrecognized prior service cost of $120,000. Therefore, the company records the $30,000 difference as a negative component of other comprehensive income. The journal entry by the Devon Company is as follows:

Deferred Pension Cost	120,000	
Excess of Additional Pension Liability Over		
Unrecognized Prior Service Cost	30,000	
Additional Pension Liability		150,000

In this case, the Devon Company reports the $120,000 balance in Deferred Pension Cost as an intangible asset on its 2007 year-end balance sheet. It combines the Prepaid/Accrued

Pension Cost liability of $50,000 and the Additional Pension Liability of $150,000 in a single amount, and reports the $30,000 excess as a negative component of the accumulated other comprehensive income component of its stockholders' equity section as follows (other amounts assumed):

Stockholders' Equity

Common stock	$600,000
Additional paid-in capital	230,000
Retained earnings	170,000
Accumulated other comprehensive income (loss)	
Excess of additional pension liability over unrecognized prior	
service cost	(30,000)
Total stockholders' equity	$970,000

Note that the additional liability, the intangible asset, and the amount included in accumulated other comprehensive income (loss) are *not* amortized. The company computes the appropriate amounts each year and includes them in its balance sheet for that year. For example, refer back to the original facts for the Devon Company. In that situation, it recorded the additional liability of $150,000 at the end of 2007. Now suppose that at the end of 2008, the following information is available:

Accumulated benefit obligation	$1,300,000
Plan assets	1,220,000 fair value
Prepaid/accrued pension cost	60,000 liability
Unrecognized prior service cost	110,000

The unfunded accumulated benefit obligation is $80,000 ($1,300,000 − $1,220,000) and the required additional liability at the end of 2008 is $20,000 ($80,000 − $60,000). Since the additional liability is less than the unrecognized prior service cost of $110,000, the company does not include any reduction in its accumulated other comprehensive income for the year. The journal entry on December 31, 2008 to adjust the additional liability is as follows:

Additional Pension Liability	130,000	
Deferred Pension Cost		130,000

This entry reduces the existing account balances of $150,000 by $130,000 to $20,000. Note that the changes in the account balances have no effect on the income statement. Also note that when a company has recognized accumulated other comprehensive income at the end of one year, it must adjust that amount each year based on the new calculations. It reports the change in the accumulated other comprehensive income as a "reclassification adjustment" in its other comprehensive income for the year, as we discussed in Chapter 15. ♦

Example: Disclosures

5 Understand disclosures of pensions.

To improve the usefulness of a company's disclosures about its defined benefit pension plan, as we discussed earlier, the company must report certain information in the notes to its financial statements, in addition to the amounts contained in its financial statements. *FASB Statement No. 132R* requires disclosure of, among other items, a reconciliation of the beginning and ending amounts of the projected benefit obligation, a reconciliation of the beginning and ending fair value of the plan assets, the components of the pension expense, and the discount rate used and the expected long-term rate of return on plan assets. We show these disclosures in Example 20-5 for the Carlisle Company for 2009 using the facts from the third example that we illustrated earlier in the chapter on pages 1009 and 1010.

EXAMPLE 20-5   Disclosure of Defined Benefit Pension Plan Information

Reconciliation of the beginning and ending amounts of the projected benefit obligation

Beginning projected benefit obligation	$ 840,000
Service cost	432,000
Interest cost	84,000
Actuarial gains and losses	0
Benefits paid	(20,000)
Plan amendments	0
Ending projected benefit obligation	$1,336,000

Reconciliation of the beginning and ending fair value of the plan assets

Beginning fair value of plan assets	$ 869,800
Actual return on plan assets	95,678
Contributions	440,000
Benefits paid	(20,000)
Ending fair value of plan assets	$1,385,478

Components of the pension expense

Service cost	$ 432,000
Interest cost	84,000
Expected return on plan assets	(95,678)
Amortization of prior service cost	0
Amortization of gains and losses	0
Amortization of any transition amount	0
Total pension expense	$ 420,332

Assumptions

Discount rate: 10%
Expected long-term rate of return on plan assets: 11%

Note that in the reconciliation of the beginning and ending fair value of the plan assets, a company discloses the *actual* return on its pension plan assets. In the schedule listing the components of the pension expense, however, the company discloses the *expected* return on the pension plan assets. This aspect of the pension plan disclosures is important because it enables external users to compare the difference between the expected and actual returns to evaluate how well the pension funds are being managed. ♦

Real Report 20-1 on page 1021 shows these 2004 disclosures for **Yum! Brands** (owner of Pizza Hut, Taco Bell, and KFC). (These disclosures include information about postretirement benefit plans that we discuss later in the chapter.) Note that Yum! Brands includes the information we have shown for the Carlisle Company, as well as the additional required disclosures.

Pension Worksheet

In Example 20-6 we show a worksheet that you can use to help understand the first four examples that we explained earlier in the chapter. We have completed the worksheet using the amounts in the fourth example on pages 1011 and 1012. It will be helpful for you to go back to this example and see how the amounts are included in the worksheet. Also, you should note three important aspects of this worksheet. First, the amounts at the bottom of the "Pension Expense" columns provide the information that Carlisle Company uses to determine the debit (dr) to the Pension Expense account, and the credits (cr) to the Cash and the Prepaid/Accrued Pension Cost accounts. Second, the ending projected benefit obligation and plan assets amounts for one year are the beginning amounts for the next year. Third, the calculations for the projected benefit obligation and the plan assets provide much of the information that Carlisle would report in its notes to its financial statements that we illustrated in the last example. Also, the worksheet is simplified because it does not include certain complexities, such as when the corridor needs to be used to determine the net gain or loss to be included in the pension expense, or the calculation of the minimum pension liability.

EXAMPLE 20-6 **Pension Plan Worksheet (using amounts in example on page 1011)**

Item	2007 Amount	2007 Pension Expense	2008 Amount	2008 Pension Expense	2009 Amount	2009 Pension Expense
Beginning projected benefit obligation	$2,000,000[a]		$2,600,000		$3,260,000	
× Discount rate	× 0.10		× 0.10		× 0.10	
= Interest cost	$ 200,000 ──▶	$200,000	$ 260,000 ──▶	$260,000	$ 326,000 ──▶	$326,000
Beginning projected benefit obligation	2,000,000		2,600,000		3,260,000	
+ Service cost	400,000 ──▶	400,000	420,000 ──▶	420,000	432,000 ──▶	432,000
− Benefits paid	(0)		(20,000)		(20,000)	
= Ending projected benefit obligation	$2,600,000		$3,260,000		$3,998,000	
Beginning plan assets	$ 0		$ 675,000		$1,421,000	
× Expected rate of return	× 0.11		× 0.11		× 0.11	
= Expected return	$ 0 ──▶	(0)	$ 74,250 ──▶	(74,250)	$ 156,310 ──▶	(156,310)
Beginning plan assets	$ 0		$ 675,000		$1,421,000	
+ Actual return[b]	0		81,000		170,520	
+ Contributions	675,000		685,000		700,000	
− Benefits paid	(0)		(20,000)		(20,000)	
= Ending plan assets	$ 675,000		$1,421,000		$2,271,520	
Unrecognized prior service cost	$ 2,000,000		$ 2,000,000		$ 2,000,000	
÷ Average service life (years)[c]	÷ 20		÷ 20		÷ 20	
= Amortization of unrecognized prior service cost	$ 100,000 ──▶	100,000	$ 100,000 ──▶	100,000	$ 100,000 ──▶	100,000
Net gain or loss[d]	$ 0 ──▶	0	$ 0 ──▶	0	$ 0 ──▶	0
Total Pension Expense		$700,000 dr		$705,750 dr		$701,690 dr
Contribution (Cash)		675,000 cr		685,000 cr		700,000 cr
Adjustment to Prepaid/Accrued Pension Cost		$ 25,000 cr		$ 20,750 cr		$ 1,690 cr

a   Unrecognized prior service cost at adoption of plan
b   The actual return is assumed to be 12% each year × Beginning plan assets
c   Or times amortization fraction
d   Calculated using the corridor approach; see Example 20-4

Real Report 20-1 Illustration of Pension Disclosures

YUM! BRANDS

NOTE 15 PENSION AND POSTRETIREMENT MEDICAL BENEFITS

Pension Benefits We sponsor noncontributory defined benefit pension plans covering substantially all full-time U.S. salaried employees, certain U.S hourly employees and certain international employees. The most significant of these plans, the YUM Retirement Plan (the "Plan"), is funded while benefits from the other plans are paid by the Company as incurred. During 2001, the plans covering our U.S. salaried employees were amended such that any salaried employee hired or rehired by YUM after September 30, 2001 is not eligible to participate in those plans. Benefits are based on years of service and earnings or stated amounts for each year of service.

Postretirement Medical Benefits Our postretirement plan provides health care benefits, principally to U.S. salaried retirees and their dependents. This plan includes retiree cost sharing provisions. During 2001, the plan was amended such that any salaried employee hired or rehired by YUM after September 30, 2001 is not eligible to participate in this plan. Employees hired prior to September 30, 2001 are eligible for benefits if they meet age and service requirements and qualify for retirement benefits.

We use a measurement date of September 30 for our pension and postretirement medical plans described above.

Obligation and Funded Status at September 30:

	Pension Benefits		Postretirement Medical Benefits	
	2004	2003	2004	2003
Change in benefit obligation				
Benefit obligation at beginning of year	$ 629	$ 501	$ 81	$ 68
Service cost	32	26	2	2
Interest cost	39	34	5	5
Plan amendments	1	—	—	—
Curtailment gain	(2)	(1)	—	—
Benefits and expenses paid	(26)	(21)	(4)	(4)
Actuarial (gain) loss	27	90	(3)	10
Benefit obligation at end of year	$ 700	$ 629	$ 81	$ 81
Change in plan assets				
Fair value of plan assets at beginning of year	$ 438	$ 251		
Actual return on plan assets	53	52		
Employer contributions	54	157		
Benefits paid	(26)	(21)		
Administrative expenses	(1)	(1)		
Fair value of plan assets at end of year	$ 518	$ 438		
Funded status	$(182)	$(191)	$(81)	$(81)
Employer contributions[a]	1	—	—	—
Unrecognized actuarial loss	225	230	23	28
Unrecognized prior service cost	9	12	—	—
Net amount recognized at year-end	$ 53	$ 51	$(58)	$(53)

(a) Reflects contributions made between the September 30, 2004 measurement date and December 25, 2004.

Continued

	Pension Benefits		Postretirement Medical Benefits	
	2004	2003	**2004**	2003
Amounts recognized in the statement of financial position consist of:				
Accrued benefit liability	**$(111)**	$(125)	**$(58)**	$(53)
Intangible asset	**11**	14	—	—
Accumulated other comprehensive loss	**153**	162	—	—
	$ 53	$ 51	**$(58)**	$(53)
Additional information				
Other comprehensive (income) loss attributable to change in additional minimum liability recognition	**$ (9)**	$ 48		
Additional year-end information for pension plans with accumulated benefit obligations in excess of plan assets				
Projected benefit obligation	**$ 700**	$ 629		
Accumulated benefit obligation	**629**	563		
Fair value of plan assets	**518**	438		

While we are not required to make contributions to the Plan in 2005, we may make discretionary contributions during the year based on our estimate of the Plan's expected September 30, 2005 funded status.

Components of Net Periodic Benefit Cost

	Pension Benefits		
	2004	2003	2002
Service cost	**$32**	$ 26	$ 22
Interest cost	**39**	34	31
Amortization of prior service cost	**3**	4	1
Expected return on plan assets	**(40)**	(30)	(28)
Recognized actuarial loss	**19**	6	1
Net periodic benefit cost	**$53**	$ 40	$ 27

Additional loss recognized due to:			
Curtailment	**$—**	$ —	$ 1

	Postretirement Medical Benefits		
	2004	2003	2002
Service cost	**$2**	$2	$2
Interest cost	**5**	5	4
Amortization of prior service cost	—	—	—
Recognized actuarial loss	**1**	1	1
Net periodic benefit cost	**$8**	$8	$7

Prior service costs are amortized on a straight-line basis over the average remaining service period of employees expected to receive benefits. Curtailment gains and losses have been recognized in facility actions as they have resulted primarily from refranchising and closure activities.

Weighted-Average Assumptions Used to Determine Benefit Obligations at September 30:

	Pension Benefits		Postretirement Medical Benefits	
	2004	2003	**2004**	2003
Discount rate	**6.15%**	6.25%	**6.15%**	6.25%
Rate of compensation increase	**3.75%**	3.75%	**3.75%**	3.75%

Continued

Weight-Average Assumptions Used to Determine the Net Periodic Benefit Cost for Fiscal Years:

	Pension Benefits			Postretirement Medical Benefits		
	2004	2003	2002	**2004**	2003	2002
Discount rate	**6.25%**	6.85%	7.60%	**6.25%**	6.85%	7.58%
Long-term rate of return on plan assets	**8.50%**	8.50%	10.00%	—	—	—
Rate of compensation increase	**3.75%**	3.85%	4.60%	**3.75%**	3.85%	4.60%

Our estimated long-term rate of return on plan assets represents the weighted average of expected future returns on the asset categories included in our target investment allocation based primarily on the historical returns for each asset category, adjusted for an assessment of current market conditions.

Assumed Health Care Cost Trend Rates at September 30:

	Postretirement Medical Benefits	
	2004	2003
Health care cost trend rate assumed for next year	**11%**	12%
Rate to which the cost trend rate is assumed to decline (the ultimate trend rate)	**5.5%**	5.5%
Year that the rate reaches the ultimate trend rate	**2012**	2012

There is a cap on our medical liability for certain retirees. The cap for Medicare eligible retirees was reached in 2000 and the cap for non-Medicare eligible retirees is expected to be reached between the years 2007–2008; once the cap is reached, our annual cost per retiree will not increase.

Assumed health care cost trend rates have a significant effect on the amounts reported for our postretirement health care plans. A one-percentage-point change in assumed health care cost trend rates would have the following effects:

	1-Percentage-Point Increase	1-Percentage-Point Decrease
Effect on total of service and interest cost	$ —	$ —
Effect on postretirement benefit obligation	$ 2	$ (2)

Plan Assets Our pension plan weighted-average asset allocations at September 30, by asset category are set forth below:

Asset Category	2004	2003
Equity securities	70%	65%
Debt securities	28%	30%
Cash	2%	5%
Total	100%	100%

Our primary objectives regarding the pension assets are to optimize return on assets subject to acceptable risk and to maintain liquidity, meet minimum funding requirements and minimize plan expenses. To achieve these objectives, we have adopted a passive investment strategy in which the asset performance is driven primarily by the investment allocation. Our target investment allocation is 70% equity securities and 30% debt securities, consisting primarily of low cost index mutual funds that track several sub-categories of equity and debt security performance. The investment strategy is primarily driven by our Plan's participants' ages and reflects a long-term investment horizon favoring a higher equity component in the investment allocation.

Continued

A mutual fund held as an investment by the Plan includes YUM stock in the amount of $0.2 million at both September 30, 2004 and 2003 (less than 1% of total plan assets in each instance).

Benefit Payments The benefits expected to be paid in each of the next five years and in the aggregate for the five years thereafter are set forth below:

Year ended:	Pension Benefits	Postretirement Medical Benefits
2005	$ 17	$ 5
2006	22	5
2007	25	6
2008	28	6
2009	32	6
2010–2014	242	35

Expected benefits are estimated based on the same assumptions used to measure our benefit obligation on our measurement date of September 30, 2004 and include benefits attributable to estimated further employee service.

Questions:

1. What types of pension plans does YUM! Brands have? How are they funded?
2. How much was the company's pension expense (cost) for 2004?
3. Was the company's actual return on plan assets in 2004 greater or less than the expected return?
4. How much are the accumulated and projected benefit obligations at the end of 2004? Why are the amounts different?
5. Is the company in a net asset or a net liability position for its pension plans at the end of 2004?
6. If YUM! Brands had used a lower discount rate during 2004, what would be the effect on the amounts disclosed by the company for 2004?
7. Describe the investment strategy employed by the company.

Summary of Issues Related to Pensions

In Example 20-7, we summarize the major issues related to accounting for the defined benefit pension plan of a company in T-account form for 2007. While each "entry" balances, note that four of the "accounts" (plan assets, projected benefit obligation, unrecognized loss or gain, and unrecognized prior service cost) are *not* included in the company's financial statements. The other three accounts [pension expense, cash, and prepaid (accrued) pension cost] are included in the financial statements. In this summary, the balance in the Prepaid (Accrued)Pension Cost is equal to the net balance of the Plan Assets, Projected Benefit Obligation, Unrealized Loss/Gain, and Unrecognized Prior Service Cost accounts. Thus, at the beginning of the year, $10,000 = $100,000 − $90,000. All amounts are assumed. We discuss each entry in the following sections.

We assume that the company started the plan in 2006, it had no prior service costs, and no employees retired during the year. Based on the actuarial computation of the service cost (the only component of pension expense for 2006), the company makes its first journal entry for the plan on December 31, 2006 as follows:

Pension Expense	90,000	
Prepaid (Accrued) Pension Cost	10,000	
Cash		100,000

EXAMPLE 20-7	Summary of Issues Related to Defined Benefit Pension Plan for 2007

Not included in the company's financial statements:

Plan Assets

Beginning balance	100*	(f) Payments to retirees	14
(c) Actual return on plan assets	9		
(g) Funding	98		
Ending balance	193		

Projected Benefit Obligation (Liability)

(f) Payments to retirees	14	Beginning balance	90
		(a) Service cost	95
		(b) Interest	7
		(d) Prior service cost	40
		Ending balance	218

Unrecognized Prior Service Cost

(d) Prior service cost	40	(e) Amortization	3
Ending balance	37		

Included in the company's financial statements:

Pension Expense

(a) Service cost	95	(c) Expected return on plan assets	9
(b) Interest	7		
(e) Amortization of prior service cost	3		
(g) Total expense	96		

Cash

		(g) Funding	98

Prepaid (Accrued) Pension Cost

Beginning balance	10		
(g) Funding exceeds expense	2		
Ending balance	12		

*All amounts in thousands of dollars.

Therefore, at the beginning of 2007 the plan assets are $100,000, the projected benefit obligation is $90,000, and the prepaid (accrued) pension cost is $10,000. The following information is for 2007.

(a) **Service Cost.** The service cost for 2007 of $95,000 is a component of the pension expense and increases the projected benefit obligation.

(b) **Interest Cost.** The interest cost for 2007 of $7,000 is a component of the pension expense and increases the projected benefit obligation.

(c) **Expected and Actual Return on Plan Assets.** The actual and expected return on plan assets for 2007 of $9,000 increases the plan assets and reduces the pension expense. Any difference between the actual and expected return on plan assets would be a component of the net gain or loss.

(d) **Unrecognized Prior Service Cost.** During 2007 the company provides retroactive benefits with a present value of $40,000. This creates an unrecognized prior service cost and increases the projected benefit obligation.

(e) **Amortization of the Unrecognized Prior Service Cost.** During 2007 the company amortizes the unrecognized prior service cost by $3,000. This increases the pension expense and decreases the unrecognized prior service cost.

(f) **Payments to Retired Employees.** Payments of $14,000 by the funding agency to retired employees in 2007 decrease the plan assets and the projected benefit obligation.

(g) Pension Expense and Funding by the Company. The $96,000 pension expense consists of the $95,000 service cost (a), plus the $7,000 interest cost (b), minus the $9,000 expected return on plan assets (c), plus the $3,000 amortization of the prior service cost (e). The payment of $98,000 by the company to the funding agency increases the plan assets. The prepaid (accrued) pension cost is also increased because the journal entry to record the payment of $98,000 involves a debit to pension expense for $96,000 and a debit to prepaid (accrued) pension cost for $2,000.

At the end of 2007, note that the balance in the Prepaid (Accrued) Pension cost account of $12,000 is equal to the balance in the Plan Assets of $193,000, minus the balance in the Projected Benefit Obligation of $218,000, plus the balance in the Unrecognized Prior Service Cost account of $37,000. In its disclosures the company reconciles the plan's funded status (the difference between the fair value of the assets and the projected benefit obligation) to the prepaid (accrued) pension cost as follows:

Fair value of plan assets	$ 193
Projected benefit obligation	(218)
Funded status	$ (25)
Unrecognized prior service cost	37
Prepaid (accrued) pension cost	$ 12

FASB Plans for Revision of Postretirement Accounting

The FASB has announced plans to review all the accounting principles for postretirement benefits. The Board has decided to split the project into two parts. The first revisions are expected by the end of 2006. Among those revisions are expected to be a requirement that a company include a *net* asset or liability (with an offsetting increase or decrease in accumulated other comprehensive income in stockholders' equity) on its balance sheet to reflect the amount by which its pension and other postretirement benefits plans are overfunded or underfunded. In other words, the amount that a company now includes in the disclosures in the notes to its financial statements would be reported on its balance sheet. Changes in the value of the net asset or liability would *not* be included in net income, but would be reported as a component of other comprehensive income. In the second phase, the Board would reconsider most, if not all, aspects of the existing standards for accounting for postretirement benefits. It will coordinate these changes with the IASB.

CONCEPTUAL ISSUES RELATED TO DEFINED BENEFIT PENSION PLANS

6 Explain the conceptual issues regarding pensions.

In their analyses of pension accounting, the APB and the FASB have considered several conceptual issues related to pension expense, prior service cost, pension liabilities, and pension assets. We briefly discuss these conceptual issues in the following sections.[15]

Pension Expense

The first conceptual issue in accounting for pension plans involves the proper amount of pension cost that the employer-company should recognize and when it should report that amount as pension expense on its income statement. *Expenses* are outflows of assets or incurrences of liabilities (during a period) from delivering or producing goods, rendering services, or carrying out other activities that are the company's ongoing major or central operations. Recall also that once a company has assigned revenues to an accounting period, it matches expenses against the revenues by association of cause and effect, systematic and rational allocation, or immediate recognition.

---

15. This discussion is a brief summary of that presented in "Employers' Accounting for Pensions and Other Postemployment Benefits," *FASB Discussion Memorandum* (Stamford, Conn.: FASB, 1981).

Pension cost may include several components. The primary component of pension cost is the deferred compensation (*service cost*) the employer will pay to employees in the future for their current services. However, since employees' compensation is deferred until retirement, the employees are, in effect, providing a "loan" to the employer. The *interest* on that loan may be a component of pension cost. In addition, an employer generally invests its pension contributions a pension fund with the intent of earning a return on these assets. A possible *negative* component of pension cost is the *return* earned on the pension fund assets. An employer that begins a pension plan or makes modifications in its existing plan may provide additional benefits to employees for *services they performed in previous years*. Part or all of the cost of these previously earned benefits may be a component of pension cost. Finally, unforeseen events related to a pension plan may result in (a) deviations in the current period between actual experience and the assumptions used, and (b) changes in the assumptions about the future. The resulting *gains* and *losses* may be a component of pension cost. Pension expense computed under *FASB Statement No. 87* includes all these components, although some are in a modified form.

Prior Service Cost

Four alternative methods have been suggested for an employer to account for its prior service cost. The first is to account for it prospectively, which is the approach adopted by *FASB Statement No. 87*. This method requires that the cost is expensed in the current and future periods, and that no liability is recorded when the cost arises. It is often argued that this method violates the matching concept because all the services performed by the employees were completed in previous periods. Also, the lack of recognition of a pension obligation is a violation of the concept of a liability.

The second alternative would be for an employer to recognize the total amount as an expense in the period in which it arises (i.e., the current period) and to record a liability. This procedure would also violate the matching concept because the services were performed by the employees in previous periods and not in the current period. It might also tend to dissuade companies from adopting, or changing, pension plans because of the related effect (i.e., decrease) on net income of the current period.

The third alternative would be for an employer to debit retained earnings (as a retrospective period adjustment) and to record a liability. This procedure would violate the all-inclusive income concept because the total amounts would never be included in the income statement. Also, many companies would resist the recording of a liability because of the effect it would have on their debt-to-equity ratios and on similar measures of financial performance.

The fourth alternative would be for an employer to record an intangible asset and liability of equal amounts. Although it is difficult to see how an asset is created by recognizing pension benefits earned by employees in previous periods, the argument is that the employer's decision to improve a pension plan is forward-looking and rational. That is, the employer would accept an increased obligation only if it expected future benefits of at least an equal amount. In this sense, the future economic benefits (intangible asset) should be recognized along with the liability and should be expensed over some future period. Similarly, gains and losses could be accounted for prospectively, currently, as a retrospective adjustment, or as a deferred item.

Pension Liabilities

A second conceptual issue regarding accounting for pension plans involves identifying and recording pension plan liabilities. *Liabilities* are probable future sacrifices of economic benefits arising from present obligations of a company to transfer assets or provide services in the future as a result of past transactions or events. Also, once a liability is identified, it must be measurable to be reported on a company's balance sheet.

Generally, it is agreed that a pension is a form of deferred compensation. An employer's pension obligation may be viewed as an obligation to make contributions to the plan, or as an obligation to employees for pensions promised. A company cannot know the exact amount of the pension obligation for each employee until the employee (or related beneficiary) dies. Therefore, actuaries can only estimate the amount of the obligation using assumptions about employee turnover, life expectancy, and other variables.

We briefly summarize the five alternatives for meeting the recognition-measurement criteria of a liability that have been identified, as follows:

1. *Contributions Based on an Actuarial Funding Method.* Under this alternative, it is argued that the employer has an obligation to make contributions to the plan rather than directly to employees. In this situation, the employer's liability is based on the actuarial funding method used for funding the plan, in which case the only recorded pension liability would be for contributions due but not yet paid. This is the approach adopted by *FASB Statement No. 87.*

2. *Amount Attributed to Employee Service to Date.* This alternative would be based on the concept that the employer's pension obligation arises as the employees work and that the transaction resulting in the obligation is the employees' service. The pension transaction would be an exchange whereby employees render service for pension benefits (deferred compensation) in addition to current compensation. The resulting obligation for deferred compensation (the projected benefit obligation) would be recorded in a manner similar to current compensation.

3. *Termination Liability.* This alternative would be based on the argument that the employer's obligation should be limited to the amount that it must pay when the plan is terminated. Those disagreeing believe that a company is a going concern and that an assumption of plan termination would be inappropriate unless there is clear evidence to the contrary.

4. *Amount of Vested Benefits.* Under this alternative the employer's obligation would be based on the vested benefits earned by the employees. Nonvested benefits are contingent on and result from future services and, therefore, create a liability only as they become vested in future periods. Those disagreeing believe that vesting is a legal transaction, and that a portion of the nonvested benefits will become vested and, therefore, meet the definition of a liability.

5. *Amount Payable to Retirees.* This alternative is a form of "pay-as-you-go" accounting whereby the employer's liability arises only during the period in which pension benefits will be paid to employees. Under this alternative, the liability would be readily measurable. Those disagreeing believe that this approach is a violation of the accrual concept of accounting.

If one of these alternatives meets the definition of a liability, the amount of the liability must be measurable for the employer to record and report the amount on its balance sheet. Most of the amounts are estimates. If uncertainty is so great that a reasonable estimate cannot be made because of the long-term nature of pension plans, then a liability would not be recorded (although disclosure may be required).

Balance Sheet Presentation of Pension Plan Assets

A third conceptual issue involves the disclosure of assets used in the pension plan. *Assets* are probable future economic benefits obtained or controlled by a company as a result of past transactions or events. As indicated earlier, a company having a pension plan typically makes periodic payments to a funding agency. This agency, then, assumes the responsibility for safeguarding and investing the pension assets (to earn a return on the assets), and for making benefit payments to retired employees. There are two alternative views for accounting by the employer-company for these pension assets.

1. **Funding is a discharge of the pension liability.** This alternative says that the assets of the pension plan held by the funding agency are *not* assets of the employer. The principal reasons are that: (1) the funding agency is a separate legal entity (e.g., a trust)

with legal title to the plan assets; (2) the assets can be used only for the benefit of the employees and retirees, and ordinarily cannot be returned to the employer; (3) the employer's obligation is to make contributions to the funding agency, and the agency pays the actual pension benefits; and (4) the employer's obligation may be limited by termination of the plan. This is the approach adopted by *FASB Statement No. 87.*

2. **The pension liability is not discharged until the retiree receives the pension payment.** This alternative says that the pension plan assets are assets of the employer. The employer remains obligated to provide benefits defined by the plan, and the trust is a legal device controlled by the employer for funding the pension obligation. Although the funding agency holds legal title to the assets, the employer is at risk with regard to the assets and ultimately reaps the rewards of economic ownership of them. If the assets grow, the employer's future contributions will be reduced. If the assets do not grow, or if losses are sustained, future contributions will be increased. If this alternative was adopted it would still need to be decided whether the employer should show the plan assets separately on the asset side of the balance sheet or deduct them from the pension liability.

Additional Aspects of Pension Accounting

Several other issues have an impact on some aspects of pension accounting. These include statement of cash flows disclosures, vested benefits, accounting for defined contribution plans, disclosures by funding agencies, the Employee Retirement Income Security Act of 1974, pension settlements and curtailments, termination benefits paid to employees, and multi-employer plans. We briefly discuss each of these topics, along with international accounting differences, in the following sections.

7 Understand several additional issues related to pensions.

Statement of Cash Flows Disclosures

A company reports the cash it paid to fund its pension plan as a cash outflow in the operating activities section of its statement of cash flows. If a company uses the indirect method to report its operating cash flows, it adds any increase in its accrued pension cost (liability), or any decrease in its prepaid pension cost (asset) to net income in the operating activities section of its statement of cash flows. It subtracts from net income any decrease in its accrued pension cost (liability), or any increase in its prepaid pension cost (asset).

Vested Benefits

Vested benefits are pension benefits earned by employees that are not contingent on future service with the company. That is, the employees will receive retirement benefits based on service to date, even if they terminate employment. ERISA specifies the minimum vesting requirements that companies must follow. A company must disclose the vested portion of the accumulated benefit obligation. Also, the vesting provisions affect calculations made by the company's actuary because it is necessary to estimate the number of employees who will leave before vesting of their pension benefits occurs.

Accounting for Defined Contribution Plans

As we explained earlier, some pension plans are defined contribution plans because the employer-company determines its contribution based on a formula. Therefore, any future benefits paid to retired employees are limited to those that can be provided by the contributions and the earnings on those contributions. A common example is a 401(k) plan. Accounting for defined contribution plans is very straightforward and is specified in *FASB Statement No. 87.*

A company records its pension expense at an amount equal to the contribution that it is required to make in that period. Thus, its journal entry is a debit to Pension Expense and a credit to Cash for the annual contribution. A company recognizes a liability only if the contribution for a given year has not been paid in full.

The company also is required to disclose the following two items:

Reporting

1. A description of the plan, including employee groups covered, the basis for determining contributions, and the nature and effect of significant matters affecting the comparability of the information for all periods presented.
2. The amount of the pension expense recognized during the period.[16]

LINK TO ETHICAL DILEMMA

Cloud Nine Airlines provides airline service to most major cities in the continental United States. Due mainly to high fuel costs and the reduced demand for air travel, Cloud Nine has been unable to generate enough cash flow to pay many of its short-term operating costs. Seeking to remedy the situation and keep the airline solvent, the CEO of Cloud Nine has been aggressively pursuing short-term loans from various creditors. However, the airline has nearly exhausted its borrowing capacity, and the CEO is finding it increasingly difficult to find a lender willing to provide the company with the needed cash. In a move to keep the airline solvent, the CEO approached the trustee of the company's defined benefit pension plan, who happened to be an old college friend, and convinced him to loan the company $10,000,000 in cash at the market rate of interest, with the loan secured by Cloud Nine common stock. While this amount represented only 10% of the assets of the pension plan, it was enough cash to keep the airline solvent for the next 12 months.

As the accountant for Cloud Nine, you are in charge of preparing the financial statements and related note disclosures for the current year. Upon reviewing the note disclosure that you prepared related to the pension plan, the CEO is furious. Specifically, he demands that you remove the detailed explanation of the lending arrangement between the airline and the pension plan. The CEO states that the dollar amount of the loan is already reflected in the financial statements as a component of long-term debt, and any further disclosure in the notes is irrelevant to the financial statements. How would you respond to the CEO?

Disclosures by Funding Agencies

A company typically makes its periodic pension plan payments to a funding agency that administers the plan. A funding agency may be a specific corporate trustee or an insurance company. These agencies issue financial statements that summarize the financial aspects of a company's pension plan, aimed primarily toward providing financial information about the pension plan's ability to pay benefits when due. **FASB Statement No. 35** requires that the annual financial statements issued by a funding agency for a company's pension plan include: (1) a financial statement (on an accrual accounting basis) presenting information about the net assets (at fair value) available for benefits at the end of the plan year, (2) a financial statement presenting information about the

Reporting

---

16. *FASB Statement No. 87, op. cit.,* par. 65.

changes during the year in the net assets available for benefits, (3) information regarding the actuarial present value of accumulated plan benefits as of either the beginning or the end of the plan year, and (4) information regarding the significant effects of factors affecting the year-to-year change in the actuarial present value of accumulated plan benefits.[17] Although these funding agency financial statements are beyond the scope of this book, the *company* sponsoring the pension plan discloses some of this information in the notes to its financial statements, as we discussed earlier.

Employee Retirement Income Security Act of 1974

The primary purpose of the Employee Retirement Income Security Act of 1974 (ERISA), alternatively known as the *Pension Reform Act of 1974* is to create standards for the operation and maintenance of pension funds. This Act was passed to prevent abuses in the handling of these funds. Also, it attempts to increase the protection given to employees covered by such plans. For example, at the congressional hearings, it was revealed that some companies routinely followed a policy of terminating employees at ages 60 to 62, even though service until age 65 was a requirement for pension eligibility. This practice greatly minimized the company's pension liabilities and deprived these employees of pension income on their retirement.

The *Pension Reform Act of 1974* provides guidelines for employee participation in pension plans, vesting provisions, minimum funding requirements, financial statement disclosure, and the administration of the plan. In addition, the administrators of pension plans are required to file annual reports with the Department of Labor that include a description of the plan and copies of the relevant financial statements.

The Act also created the Pension Benefit Guaranty Corporation (PBGC), an organization that provides benefits to employees covered by plans that have been terminated (usually because of the bankruptcy of the sponsoring company). The PBGC receives an annual fee for every employee covered by a pension plan that is subject to the PBGC. The PBGC can also impose a lien against 30% of the net assets of the company. This lien has the status of a tax lien and, therefore, ranks above the claims of most other creditors. Since the company may be bankrupt, however, this lien may not result in the PBGC receiving many assets.

Pension Plan Settlements and Curtailments

In recent years many companies have either settled (terminated) or reduced (curtailed) their defined benefit pension plans. Some have settled their defined benefit pension plans and substituted defined contribution plans. Others have reduced the benefits to be paid to employees, while continuing the defined benefit pension plans. For example, a company may decide to terminate its pension plan and buy from an insurance company an annuity for each of its employees that provides the same expected benefits during retirement.

FASB Statement No. 88 requires that a company include the net gain or loss from a settlement or curtailment in its net income of the period. When a plan is *settled*, the net gain or loss is the unrecognized net gain or loss that has not been recognized as part of pension expense, as we discussed earlier. When a plan is *curtailed*, the portion of the unrecognized prior service cost associated with the estimated reduced future benefits is a loss. The company combines this amount with any gain or loss from a change in the projected benefit obligation due to the curtailment in order to determine the net gain or loss.[18]

---

17. "Accounting and Reporting by Defined Benefit Pension Plans," *FASB Statement of Financial Accounting Standards No. 35* (Stamford, Conn.: FASB, 1980), par. 5 and 6.

18. "Employers' Accounting for Settlements and Curtailments of Defined Benefit Pension Plans and for Termination Benefits," *FASB Statement of Financial Accounting Standards No. 88* (Stamford, Conn.: FASB, 1985), par. 9–14.

Termination Benefits Paid to Employees

When a company wishes to reduce the size of its work force without firing employees, it may provide special benefits for a period of time to encourage some employees to terminate voluntarily. These benefits may include lump-sum cash payments, payments over future periods, or similar inducements. *FASB Statement No. 88* requires that a company record a loss and a liability for these *termination benefits* when the following two conditions are met:

1. The employee accepts the offer, and
2. The amount can be reasonably estimated.[19]

The amount of the loss includes the amount of any lump-sum payments and the present value of any expected future benefits.

Multi-Employer Plans

In the previous discussion we assumed that the pension plan is a single-employer plan. That is, the plan is maintained by one company for its employees. In contrast, **a multi-employer plan involves two or more unrelated companies in which assets contributed by each company are available to pay benefits to the employees of all the involved companies.** Generally, these plans result from collective-bargaining agreements with unions. Each company recognizes as pension expense the required contribution for the period. In other words, cash basis accounting is used for these plans. This difference in accounting principles results from the difference in the nature of the obligation of the company and the difficulty of obtaining *reliable* information for each separate company.

LINK TO INTERNATIONAL DIFFERENCES

The basic principles of accounting for defined benefit plans under international accounting standards are the same as U.S. principles. However, there are some differences. One is the requirement under international standards to expense prior service costs immediately. A second is that there is no requirement to recognize a minimum liability. It is also important to understand that it is common for foreign governments to provide significantly higher state-funded benefits to retirees. Therefore, pension benefits provided by foreign companies are less likely to have a material effect on their financial statements. In addition, international accounting standards allows defined benefit accounting for multi-employer plans, whereas U.S. standards require such plans to be accounted for on a defined contribution basis.

SECURE YOUR KNOWLEDGE 20-2

- Service cost and interest cost (computed as the discount rate multiplied by the projected benefit obligation at the beginning of the period) increase pension expense.
- The expected return (computed as the fair value of the plan assets at the beginning of the period multiplied by the expected long-term rate of return) is a reduction in pension expense. The actual return increases the plan assets.

(continued)

---

19. *Ibid.*, par. 15.

- The difference between pension expense and the amount funded is recorded in an asset/liability account (prepaid/accrued pension cost).
- If a company grants retroactive benefits to its employees, the prior service cost is amortized into pension expense using either the straight-line method over the average remaining service life of the employees or the years-of-future-service method.
- The excess of an unrecognized gain or loss over a corridor amount (determined as 10% of the greater of the projected benefit obligation or the fair value of the plan assets at the beginning of the period) is amortized into pension expense on a straight-line basis over the average remaining service life of the employees.
- If an additional pension liability is required to be recorded, an intangible asset (deferred pension cost) is recorded to the extent of unrecognized prior service cost, with any excess of the additional pension liability over the unrecognized prior service cost recorded as a negative component of other comprehensive income. This additional pension liability is not amortized but is recomputed and adjusted each year.
- Several conceptual issues arise in accounting for pensions:
  - Any prior service cost is expensed in the current and future periods with no liability being recorded when the cost arises (arguably a violation of the matching concept and the definition of a liability).
  - The employer's pension liability is based on the actuarial funding method used, resulting in the only recorded liability being for contributions due but not yet paid (i.e., the projected benefit obligation is not recorded as a liability) and any additional pension liability.
  - Pension plan assets are not considered assets of the employer.
- Other issues that impact pension accounting include transition requirements, vested benefits, accounting for defined contribution plans, disclosures by funding agencies, the Employee Retirement Income Security Act, pension settlements and curtailments, termination benefits paid to employees, and multi-employer plans.

OTHER POSTEMPLOYMENT BENEFITS

In addition to providing pensions to their employees, many companies also offer two types of additional benefits. *Postemployment* benefits are provided to former employees after employment but *before* retirement. Under **FASB Statement No. 112**,[20] a company must accrue the cost of these benefits during employment and recognize the amount as an expense and a liability if the four criteria for the recognition of compensated absences defined in *FASB Statement No. 43* are met, as we discussed in Chapter 13. If any one of the criteria is not met, the company records the expense and liability when the liability is probable and the amount can be reasonably estimated, in accordance with the provisions of *FASB Statement No. 5*.

8 Explain other postemployment benefits (OPEBs).

In the rest of this section we discuss *postretirement* benefits, which include all forms of benefits provided to former employees *after* their retirement, other than pensions. For convenience, we use the widely-used acronym, OPEB, for these benefits. Healthcare benefits typically are the most significant of these OPEBs, but some companies also provide dental benefits, eye care, tuition assistance, life insurance, legal services, and financial advisory services. Our discussion focuses on accounting for healthcare benefits because they usually are the largest dollar amount, present the greatest measurement difficulties, and are the most controversial.

When Medicare was first created in the 1960s, many companies decided to offer an additional benefit by agreeing to pay for the medical costs of retirees who were not covered by the federal plan. At that time healthcare costs and the retiree population were relatively small, so management believed that it was providing a valuable benefit to

---

20. "Employers' Accounting for Postemployment Benefits," *FASB Statement No. 112* (Norwalk, Conn.: FASB, 1992).

employees at a low cost. Companies accounted for OPEBs by recording the costs as they were paid. This cash basis accounting was accepted because the liability was thought to be immaterial and because the benefits were considered to be revocable. However, the costs of the plans have increased significantly in recent years because (1) inflation in healthcare costs has significantly exceeded general inflation, (2) Medicare reimbursements have been decreasing, leaving a larger portion to be covered by companies, (3) the number of retired employees has increased both absolutely and relative to the number of current employees as companies have matured (and down-sized) and life expectancies have increased, and (4) many companies have encouraged early retirement and their healthcare programs cover the entire healthcare costs of the retired employees until age 65, when Medicare is available.

In reaction to these changes, the FASB issued **FASB Statement No. 106.**[21] The *Statement* requires that a company accrue the cost of OPEBs during the periods in which its employees earn the benefits. This accounting has had a dramatic impact on the financial statements of many companies, as we discuss later.

Many companies provided OPEBs without computing the long-term costs involved. It is interesting, for example, that companies generally have refused to index *pension* benefits because of the inflation risk involved. However, *healthcare* benefits essentially are indexed because companies have committed to benefits in terms of *services* rather than in terms of a specific dollar amount of those services. Also, healthcare benefits are more egalitarian, because they usually are *not* based on length of service or salary, but rather on some minimum length of service, after which the same benefits are provided equally to every employee. Since pensions and OPEBs are both postemployment benefits, it is helpful to understand their similarities and differences in considering GAAP for OPEBs.

Similarities to and Differences from Pensions

The basic argument that accounting for OPEBs should be similar to the principles used for pensions involves the concept of a liability. Recall that a liability of a company is a probable future sacrifice of economic benefits arising from present obligations of the company to transfer assets or provide services to other entities in the future as a result of past transactions or events. The term "obligations" includes not only legal duties defined in a contract, but also equitable and constructive obligations based on promises or moral responsibility.

Some argue that a company offering OPEBs is essentially providing deferred compensation to employees because the benefits received during retirement were earned during the period of employment. Therefore, the company incurs an obligation as its employees provide services. *FASB Statement No. 106* follows this viewpoint.

Others argue that many OPEBs do not have the same explicit legal contract as a pension agreement, and the obligation of the company to continue to provide benefits is not as clear. In other words, they argue that there is no liability because the company has the right to withdraw the benefits. That is, a company has no obligation for OPEBs until its employees retire, since they must retire to obtain the benefit. However, recent court decisions have not allowed companies to withdraw rights from retired employees, and there are indications that it may be difficult to withdraw rights already earned by current employees. Therefore, the concept of a liability appears to have been satisfied.

Also, if a liability does exist prior to the employees' retirement, it can be argued that it arises only when employees become eligible for the benefits. OPEB plans typically specify a minimum number of years of active service before the employees are eligible for the benefits. Vesting for these plans is "cliff" vesting, because vesting occurs when the requirements are met. A liability would be recorded then and not gradually over a period of years.

---

21. "Employers' Accounting for Postretirement Benefits Other Than Pensions," *FASB Statement of Financial Accounting Standards No. 106* (Norwalk, Conn.: FASB, 1990).

We summarize the major differences between healthcare OPEBs and pensions in Exhibit 20-3. While the beneficiary of a pension plan is generally the retired employee, a company usually provides OPEBs to the retired employee, spouse, and dependents up to, say, age 21. The pension benefit is defined as a fixed dollar amount that is paid monthly. The OPEB, however, usually is not limited in amount because benefits are paid no matter how long or serious the illness, benefits are paid as used, and the amount of benefits varies geographically. Also, the amount is difficult to predict because of the incidence of new illnesses, such as SARS, and the use of new treatments. Finally, companies fund pension plans because of ERISA requirements, and the contributions are tax-deductible. On the other hand, companies generally do not fund OPEBs because there are no legal requirements and the contributions are *not* tax-deductible.

EXHIBIT 20-3	Major Differences Between Postretirement Healthcare Benefits and Pensions	
Item	**Pensions**	**Healthcare**
Beneficiary	Retired employee (some residual benefit to surviving spouse)	Retired employee, spouse, and dependents
Benefit	Defined, fixed dollar amount, paid monthly	Not limited, paid as used, varies geographically
Funding	Funding legally required and tax-deductible	Usually not funded because not legally required and not tax-deductible

Accounting Principles

FASB Statement No. 106 requires that companies follow accounting principles for OPEBs that closely parallel those for pensions. (Because we assume that you have studied the discussion of accounting for pensions, this section is simplified. However, it may be helpful to review those principles as we discuss the OPEB principles.)

Two concepts also need to be understood. The **expected postretirement benefit obligation** (*EPBO*) is the actuarial present value on a specific date of the benefits a company expects to pay under the terms of the postretirement benefit plan. The amount is measured based on the benefits that employees will receive after their expected retirement dates. In contrast, the **accumulated postretirement benefit obligation** (*APBO*) is the actuarial present value of the benefits attributed to employee service rendered to a specific date. Prior to an employee's full eligibility date, the APBO is the portion of the EPBO attributed to that employee's service rendered to that date. On or after the full eligibility date, the APBO and EPBO for an employee are the same. Thus, the difference between the EPBO and APBO is that the accumulated amount is based on benefits earned to date. However, the expected amount is based on all benefits expected to be paid to employees. (In comparison, the difference between the projected and accumulated benefit obligation for pensions is the inclusion of expected salary increases in the projected amount.)

OPEB Expense

The net postretirement benefit expense[22] that a company recognizes includes the following components:

1. *Service Cost.* The service cost **is the actuarial present value of the expected postretirement benefit obligation attributed to services of the employees during the current period.** Typically, a company provides OPEB benefits on an all-ornothing basis. That is, benefits are generally not defined in terms of years of service. Therefore, an equal amount of the expected benefits is attributed to each year of

---

22. The FASB prefers this term to the more commonly used term, OPEB, because other benefits such as layoff benefits may be paid after employment but before retirement.

the attribution period (discussed later). The discount (interest) rate used to calculate the service cost is the rate of return on high-quality fixed-income investments currently available.

2. *Interest Cost.* **The interest cost is the increase in the accumulated postretirement benefit obligation due to the passage of time.** Since the OPEB is a deferred compensation plan in which future payments are discounted to their present values, interest accrues because of the passage of time. Thus, the interest cost is the accumulated postretirement benefit obligation at the beginning of the period multiplied by the discount rate. The interest rate used to calculate the accumulated postretirement benefit obligation is the same rate as that used for the service cost. The interest cost is added to the computation of the postretirement benefit expense.

3. *Expected Return on Plan Assets.* **The expected return on plan assets is the expected increase in the plan assets due to investing activities.** Plan assets are held by the funding agency and include investments in securities such as stocks and bonds, as well as other investments. The expected return is calculated by multiplying the fair value of the plan assets at the beginning of the period by the expected long-term rate of return on plan assets. The rate of return reflects the average rate of earnings expected on the assets invested to provide for the benefits included in the projected benefit obligation. Since OPEBs usually are *not* funded, we do not discuss this component further.

4. *Amortization of Unrecognized Prior Service Cost.* The prior service cost is the increase (decrease) in the accumulated postretirement benefit obligation that results from plan amendments (and at the initiation of the plan) and that is not recognized in total in the period granted. **The unrecognized prior service cost is amortized by assigning an equal amount to each remaining year of service until full eligibility for benefits is reached for each plan participant active at the date of amendment.** If all or almost all of a plan's participants are fully eligible for benefits, the prior service cost is amortized instead, based on the remaining life expectancy of the plan participants. Straight-line amortization over the average remaining years of service to full eligibility is also allowed for simplicity. The amortization amount is added (subtracted) in the computation of the postretirement benefit expense if the benefits are increased (decreased).

5. *Gain or Loss.* **Gains and losses are changes in the amount of either the accumulated postretirement benefit obligation resulting from experience different from that assumed, or from changes in assumptions.** Gains and losses may be recognized in the periods in which they occur, or recognition may be delayed. If the company chooses to delay recognition, it includes the amortization of any unrecognized net gain or loss in the postretirement benefit expense of a given year if, at the beginning of the year, the unrecognized net gain or loss exceeds 10% of the greater of the accumulated postretirement benefit obligation or the fair value of the plan assets. If amortization is required, the minimum amortization is the excess divided by the average remaining service period of active plan participants (or if most of the plan participants are retired, over their average remaining life expectancy). The total amount of any gain (loss) recognized is deducted (added) in the computation of the postretirement benefit expense.

Components of OPEB Expense

In summary, the OPEB expense a company reports on its income statement generally includes the following components:

	Service cost
+	Interest cost
−	Expected return on plan assets
+	Amortization of unrecognized prior service cost
±	Gain or loss
=	OPEB Expense

OPEB Liability or Asset

The *Statement* also addresses the calculation of the OPEB liability or asset because the amount of a company's net postretirement benefit expense to date may be different than the amount it has funded to date. Since a company usually does not fund the plan, it increases a liability, **accrued postretirement benefit cost**, each period by an amount equal to the expense. The company decreases this account by payments made to retired employees. However, in contrast to accounting for pensions, there is *no* provision for recognizing an **additional liability**.

Differences from Accounting for Pensions

You can see from the preceding discussion that the *Statement* requires accounting principles that closely parallel the accounting for pensions. The major differences are:

1. Although the attribution period is defined in the same way, the effect is different because the benefit formulas for most pension plans link benefits to years of service and salary levels. The result is that, for pension plans, the expected retirement date and date of full eligibility are the *same*. For many OPEBs, however, the benefit formula causes the two dates to be *different*. The attribution period for OPEBs generally begins with the date of hire (or the date on which credited service begins) and ends on the date the employee attains eligibility for full benefits. For example, for a plan that provides OPEBs to employees who render 15 years of service after age 35, the attribution (recognition) period is from 35 to 50 and, therefore, ceases prior to the retirement dates of the employees.
2. There is no provision for recognizing a minimum liability and the related intangible asset or component of accumulated other comprehensive income for OPEBs.
3. The interest component of the net postretirement benefit expense is based on the accumulated postretirement benefit obligation. However, the interest component of the pension expense is based on the projected benefit obligation.

FASB Statement No. 132R requires disclosures for OPEBs that are similar to those we discussed earlier for pension plans. In addition, the *Statement* requires disclosures not required for pensions:

1. The assumed healthcare cost trend rates,
2. The effect of a 1% increase and a 1% decrease in the assumed healthcare cost trend rates on the aggregate of the service cost and the interest cost, as well as on the accumulated post-retirement benefit obligation for healthcare benefits,
3. A description of the direction and pattern of change in the assumed healthcare cost trend rates, together with the ultimate trend rate(s) and when that rate is expected to be achieved,
4. If applicable, the amounts and types of securities included in the plan assets and the approximate amount of future benefits covered by insurance contracts,
5. If applicable, the cost of providing special or contractual termination benefits provided during the period and a description of the event, and
6. An explanation of any significant change in the benefit obligation or plan assets not otherwise apparent from the other disclosures.

The *Statement* also establishes some required disclosures in quarterly financial statements that are beyond the scope of the book.

EXAMPLE: ACCOUNTING FOR OPEBS

We show the basic accounting for OPEBs, using the following simplified example. Assume that the Livingston Company adopts a healthcare plan for retired employees on January 1, 2007. At that time the company has two employees and one retired employee,

9 Account for OPEBs.

as we show in Example 20-8. To determine eligibility for benefits, the company retro-actively gives credit to the date of hire for each employee. Based on the information in the exhibit, the company makes the following two journal entries to record the OPEB items at December 31, 2007:

Postretirement Benefit Expense	31,100	
Accrued Postretirement Benefit Cost		31,100

EXAMPLE 20-8   Accrual of Postretirement Healthcare Benefits

Basic Information

- The plan is started on January 1, 2007, and is not funded.
- The discount rate is 10%.
- All employees were hired at age 25.
- All employees become eligible for full benefits at age 55.
- Employee C was paid $1,500 postretirement healthcare benefits in 2007.
- The company elects to use straight-line amortization for any unrecognized prior service cost.

Additional information on January 1, 2007:

Employee	Status	Age	Expected Retirement Age	Accumulated Postretirement Benefit Obligation[a]
A	Employee	40	65	$ 15,000
B	Employee	60	65	60,000
C	Retired	70	—	25,000
				$100,000[b]

a. Actuarially determined at January 1, 2007.
b. This amount is the unrecognized prior service cost.

Computation of Postretirement Benefit Expense for 2007

1.	Service cost	$ 1,100[a]
2.	Interest cost	10,000[b]
3.	Expected return on plan assets	0
4.	Amortization of unrecognized prior service cost	20,000[c]
5.	Gain or loss	0
6.	Amortization of transition obligation	0
		$31,100

a. Actuarially determined based on expected postretirement benefit obligation. Note that there is no service cost for B and C because they have passed the date for full eligibility.
b. Accumulated postretirement benefit obligation at January 1, 2007 × Discount rate, or $100,000 × 10%.
c. $100,000 ÷ 5, or $20,000. Employees A, B, and C have 15, 0, and 0 years of remaining service to the full eligibility date (age 55), respectively. Therefore, the average remaining service period is 15 ÷ 3 = 5 years.

Note: If the company were changing from the cash to the accrual method, the accumulated postretirement benefit obligation of $100,000 would be the transition amount. The company could choose to recognize the amount immediately, or amortize it over 20 years.

The first entry records the expense for the year and, since the plan is not funded, the accompanying liability.

Accrued Postretirement Benefit Cost	1,500	
Cash		1,500

The second entry records the payment of retirement benefits.

CONCEPTUAL EVALUATION OF ACCOUNTING FOR OPEBS

Since *FASB Statement No. 106* is based on accrual accounting, you might expect that it would not be controversial. Instead, several aspects have been questioned by critics.

Relevance and Reliability

It is easy to argue that accrual accounting is more *relevant* than cash basis accounting because costs are matched as expenses against revenues in the period in which the benefits are earned. For OPEBs, the benefits are earned while the employee is working, not when he or she is retired. Therefore, the *relevance* of a company's income statement is enhanced by inclusion of the OPEB expense. There is relatively little disagreement about the nature of the obligation because of the similarity between the provisions of the *Statement* and the accounting for pensions.

> **10** Explain the conceptual issues regarding OPEBs.

Opposition did arise from companies that implemented the requirements of the *Statement*. In particular, the measurement problems created considerable controversy. The biggest argument is that OPEB costs cannot be measured with sufficient *reliability* to offset the increased relevance because of the numerous assumptions about future events that are required. The measurement of the various amounts used in accounting for OPEBs is even more difficult than for pensions. For example, healthcare plans agree to pay for some or all of a service, the amount and cost of which are unknown. However, pension payments are tied to more predictable variables of length of service and pay levels. Also, healthcare plans require an estimate of such items as the medical-cost trend rate and marital and dependency status during retirement. Furthermore, because of the totally new information that is required, companies were concerned that the costs of implementation would be fairly high and might well exceed the benefits obtained. As a result of these concerns, the FASB included in the *Statement*, for the first time, an extensive discussion of the costs and benefits.

Those who favored the current principles in *FASB Statement No. 106* argue that knowledge of these costs is essential for rational decision making by management and that accounting includes many estimates. Also, they argued that this OPEB cost information is useful for lending and investment decisions and that such decisions are never based on certainty. Therefore, they argued that it is better for a company to record the information based on the best estimates and provide disclosures of the subjectivity of the amounts rather than to report only cash payments.

Differences in Funding

As we discussed, there are few differences between pension and OPEB accounting. However, there are some differences in the practical impacts because the OPEB plans generally are not funded. Suppose, for example, that one company has an *unfunded* OPEB plan that is expected to provide exactly the same cash payments to retired employees as a *funded* pension plan of another company. The expense for the OPEB will be higher because the actual return on plan assets is not subtracted. This difference is appropriate because the company with the unfunded OPEB will have to pay more assets in the future. However, the company with the pension plan has already paid the assets into a fund which is earning a return on those assets.

Attribution Period

Attribution is the process of assigning the cost of postretirement benefits to periods of employee service. The attribution period begins with the date of hire or the date that credit for service begins, and ends on the date that the employee is eligible for full benefits, as we show in Exhibit 20-4. Thus, the expected postretirement benefit obligation is attributed to

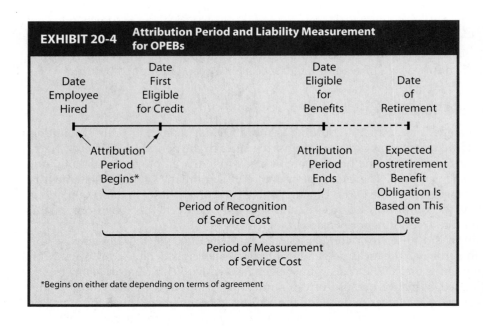

EXHIBIT 20-4 **Attribution Period and Liability Measurement for OPEBs**

the periods of employee service until the full eligibility date. However, the measurement of the accumulated postretirement benefit obligation at the full eligibility date is based on the benefits an employee is expected to receive and the expected retirement date. Thus, the attribution (recognition) period and the measurement period are different. Specifically, the period over which a company recognizes the service cost is based only on the period to full eligibility. However, measurement of the service cost is based on the period beyond that date to the expected retirement date.

The decision that the attribution period ends on the date the employee attains full eligibility was adopted by the FASB because it more closely follows the implicit contract between the company and the employee. Since employee service after the date of eligibility does not earn additional OPEB benefits, the FASB reasoned that a company should have recognized the expenses in full by then. However, it can be argued that this alternative follows legal form rather than economic substance, because employers expect employees to render services up to the date of expected retirement rather than only up to the date of full eligibility for the benefits.

Others argue that the attribution period should end at the expected retirement date because the company should recognize the OPEB cost over the entire employment period instead of recognizing only the interest cost after the date of eligibility. This argument is consistent with the basic exchange of retirement benefits for employee service. It follows that the use of this period is more consistent with the measurement of the expected postretirement benefit obligation, which is based on the expected retirement date. This alternative would also lower the annual expense and liability that a company accrues, thereby reducing the impact on its financial statements.

Some accountants suggest that a company should also amortize the prior service costs over the period to the expected retirement date.

Interaction with Deferred Income Taxes

As we discuss in Chapter 19, when a company recognizes a postretirement benefit expense for financial reporting without a related deduction for income tax reporting it creates a temporary deductible difference. OPEBs are one of the primary causes of companies reporting deferred tax assets.

Minimum Liability

As we discussed earlier, in contrast to accounting for pensions, there is no requirement for a company to recognize a minimum liability for OPEBs. The FASB decided that a minimum liability is not required because users can obtain enough information from disclosures in the notes to its financial statements. Also, it may be argued that the only liability of the company is the difference between the expense and the funding if it has no legal obligation to pay postretirement benefits. Therefore, recognition of the minimum liability would be inappropriate. Also, the corresponding intangible asset is conceptually questionable and may not be understood by users. However, it may also be argued that the difference between accounting for pensions and OPEBs is undesirable because the same concept is accounted for in a company's financial statements for pensions and by disclosure in the notes to its financial statements for OPEBs.

The requirement that a company recognize the minimum liability for pensions was based on the belief that most pension plans were adequately funded. The purpose of the minimum liability provision is to identify those relatively rare situations in which the plan is significantly underfunded. In contrast, virtually all OPEB plans are significantly underfunded, and recognition of a minimum liability by companies would not serve to identify exceptions. Instead, a company provides information about the funded status in the notes to its financial statements.

Impacts of the Adoption of FASB Statement No. 106

Adoption of the *Statement* has had two basic effects. One is on the financial statements of companies, and the second *may* be on the retirement benefits offered by companies. As an indication of the effect on the financial statements of companies, **IBM** adopted the new principles in 1991 and reported a cost of $2.26 billion on its income statement and balance sheet. The loss reduced earnings per share by about $4 per share, and IBM recorded its first-ever quarterly loss. Note that there was no impact on its cash flows. The company's cash flow statement included only the cash payments to retired employees (unless funding of the plan occurs). The General Accounting Office has estimated that the total liabilities of all companies to their current and retired employees for retiree health benefits is more than $400 billion.

Although the accounting issues and their impacts on the financial statements of companies are important, the effects of the *Statement* on benefit plans raise some difficult social issues. These effects are more difficult to evaluate because they involve management decisions that, in turn, may be affected by the financial reporting. Many companies have cut back on their coverages of retiree healthcare benefits. For some companies, the *Statement* made them aware of the costs of the benefits they had promised. Others have cut back because of the rising costs of providing health care benefits.

You may think that it is undesirable for companies to reduce benefits. However, you must remember that the *Statement* does not change the benefits promised to the retirees or the cost of the healthcare involved. Most people would argue that it is desirable to force companies to realistically face the costs of their promises and to acknowledge how much they can afford. Then, if necessary, companies should reduce the benefits now rather than face financial difficulty in the future because of their inability to pay costs they have not recognized. However, any cost reductions by companies will raise the costs incurred by other entities, whether it is the individual retirees or the public through state and federal taxation.

Most companies would prefer that the funding of OPEB plans be tax-deductible, but there do not appear to be any plans to lobby Congress for this. Some people may also argue that the principles place U.S. companies at a competitive disadvantage with foreign companies.

A qualitative characteristic of accounting information is *neutrality*. Accounting information is not intended to either encourage or discourage particular decisions, such as the offering of OPEBs, their funding, their tax-deductibility, or their impact on foreign trade.

Instead, its purpose is to provide useful information for those types of decisions. Accrual accounting does not change the nature, extent, or cost of the OPEB promise. However, it does require companies to report the effects of their commitments on their financial statements. This disclosure helps users understand the nature of the OPEB commitments and the ability of companies to fulfill their obligations.

There is a cost attached to implementing the accounting principles for OPEBs. Whether the benefits exceed the costs will, of course, never be known with certainty. However, the FASB, many accountants, many users of financial statements, and many company executives believe that they do.

SECURE YOUR KNOWLEDGE 20-3

- Postretirement benefits, or OPEBs, include all forms of benefits paid to former employees after their retirement, other than pensions. The cost of OPEBs is accrued during the periods that the employees earn the benefits by providing service.
- While the accounting for OPEBs is similar to that of pensions, two concepts should be understood:
  - The expected postretirement benefit obligation (EPBO) is the actuarial present value of the benefits a company expects to pay.
  - The accumulated postretirement benefit obligation (APBO) is the actuarial present value of the benefits attributed to employee service rendered to a specific date.
- Similar to pensions, the net postretirement benefit expense consists of service cost, interest cost (discount rate multiplied by the APBO at the beginning of the period), expected return (often zero because many OPEBs are not funded), amortization of prior service cost, and amortization of gain or loss.
- An OPEB liability or asset will be recorded if the amount of the postretirement benefit expense is different than the amount funded; however, in contrast to accounting for pensions, there is no provision for recognizing an additional liability.
- The cost of OPEBs is recognized over the attribution period (generally beginning with the date of hire and ending on the date the employee is eligible for full benefits). However, the APBO at the full eligibility date is measured from the date of hire to the expected retirement date.

APPENDIX: EXAMPLE OF PRESENT VALUE CALCULATIONS FOR DEFINED BENEFIT PENSION PLANS

11 Understand present value calculations for pensions.

In this chapter we show various situations related to defined benefit pension plans in examples using assumed amounts. This Appendix explains *how* a company computes the amounts of several key elements. The example involves applying *FASB Statement No. 87* for the Lonetree Company, which adopted a defined benefit pension plan on January 1, 2007. The following are the relevant facts:

1. Number of employees	100
2. Years to retirement at December 31, 2007	30
3. Years of life expectancy after retirement	18
4. Discount rate	10%
5. Benefit formula	Average of last five years' salary × Number of years of service × 0.02
6. Average of last five years' salary (based on expected salary levels)	$90,000 per employee
7. Annual pension benefit earned each year of service by each employee	$90,000 × 0.02 = $1,800

8. Expected long-term (and actual) rate of
   return on plan assets   8%
9. Amount funded each year   Equal to the annual service cost
10. Date of computation of pension expense
    and pension funding   December 31 each year

Note that for simplicity we assume all employees are the same age, retire at the same time, and have the same life expectancy after retirement, and that there are no gains or losses. The expected return on plan assets of 8% is less than the discount rate of 10% to create a liability at the time the company records the pension expense and makes the contribution. Example 20-9 shows the computations of the components of pension expense for the Lonetree Company (there is no gain or loss component). We discuss each component of the expense in the following sections.

EXAMPLE 20-9   **Computation of Pension Expense**

Date	Service Cost[a]	Projected Benefit Obligation[b]	Interest Cost[c]	Cash Payment[d]	Plan Assets[e]	Expected (and Actual) Return on Plan Assets[f]	Amortization of Prior Service Cost[g]	Pension Expense[h]
12/31/07	$ 84,603	$ 84,603		$ 84,603	$ 84,603			$ 84,603
12/31/08	93,062	186,123	$ 8,460	93,062	184,433	$ 6,768		94,754
12/31/09	102,368	307,104	18,612	102,368	301,556	14,755		106,225
12/31/10	118,236	472,944	32,246	118,236	443,916	24,124	$548	126,906
12/31/11	130,058	650,292	47,294	130,058	609,487	35,513	548	142,387

a. For current year. Annual benefits earned × present value of annuity for period of retirement × present value of $1 for remaining period of employment. In 2007, $180,000 × present value of annuity for 18 years at 10% × present value of $1 for 30 years at 10%. In each subsequent year the present value of $1 factor is reduced by 1 year. In 2010 the annual benefits earned are increased to $189,000.
b. At end of year. Total benefits earned to date × present value of annuity for period of retirement × present value of $1 for remaining period of employment. In 2007, $180,000 × present value of annuity for 18 years at 10% × present value of $1 for 30 years at 10%. In each subsequent year the benefits are increased by the service cost for that year and the present value of $1 factor is reduced by 1 year. In 2007 the benefits earned to date are increased by the prior service cost.
c. Projected benefit obligation at end of previous year × discount rate, or 10%. In 2007 beginning projected benefit obligation is $307,104 + $15, 355 adjustment due to amendment providing increased benefits to date.
d. Assumed equal to the service cost.
e. Balance at end of previous year + actual return on plan assets + contributions − payments ($0 in this example).
f. Plan assets at the end of previous year × expected long-term rate of return (8%), rounded.
g. Prior service cost ÷ average remaining service life of employees; $15,355 ÷ 28 years, rounded.
h. Service cost + interest cost − return on plan assets + amortization of prior service cost.

SERVICE COST

The service cost per employee each year is the present value of the future pension benefits earned *that* year by each employee. Under *FASB Statement No. 87*, a company computes this cost using the benefit/years-of-service method. We diagram the computation of the service cost for the current year as follows:

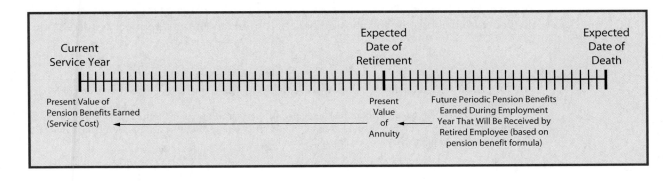

This diagram reads from right to left. Initially, the present value of the future periodic pension benefits earned during the current year is computed as of the expected date of retirement, based on the pension benefit formula, the discount rate, and the retirement period (from the expected date of retirement to the expected date of death).[23] Then, this present value as of the expected retirement date, is discounted back to the current year (based on the discount rate and the remaining years to the date of retirement) to determine the present value of the future pension benefits earned that year. This amount is the service cost for the current year. The equation for calculating the service cost is as follows:

$$\text{Service Cost} = \frac{\text{Present Value of Future Pension Benefits}}{\text{Earned by Employees in the Current Period}}$$

$$= \begin{array}{c} \text{Annual} \\ \text{Benefits} \\ \text{Earned} \end{array} \times \begin{array}{c} \text{Present Value of} \\ \text{Annuity for Period} \\ \text{of Retirement} \end{array} \times \begin{array}{c} \text{Present Value of \$1} \\ \text{for Remaining Period} \\ \text{of Employment} \end{array}$$

In our example the future pension benefits earned for each year of service by each employee of the Lonetree Company under the benefit formula is $1,800 ($90,000 × 0.02), as we calculated earlier. These benefits are earned by each of the 100 employees and therefore the company's service cost is based on the $180,000 ($1,800 × 100) of future pension benefits earned each year by the employees. The company expects each employee to receive these amounts each year during the 18 years of retirement.

At the end of 2007 we assume the remaining period of employment to be 30 years. Therefore, the Lonetree Company calculates the service cost in 2007, based on the 10% discount rate, as follows:

$$\text{2007 Service Cost} = \begin{array}{c} \text{Annual} \\ \text{Benefits} \\ \text{Earned} \end{array} \times \begin{array}{c} \text{Present Value of} \\ \text{Annuity for} \\ \text{18 Years at 10\%} \end{array} \times \begin{array}{c} \text{Present Value of \$1} \\ \text{for 30 Years at 10\%} \end{array}$$

$$= \$180,000 \times 8.201412 \times 0.057309$$

$$= \$84,603 \text{ (rounded)}$$

Each year the company makes a similar calculation, but the remaining period of employment decreases. In 2008 the present value of $1 factor for 29 years is used, and in 2009, for 28 years, and so on.[24] The second column of Example 20-9 summarizes the amount of the service cost for each year resulting from this calculation process. Note that the reason for the increase in amounts is that we have assumed, for simplicity, that there is no turnover of employees at the Lonetree Company. A typical company would have employees retiring each year and would be hiring new, younger employees. Thus, the service cost might increase or decrease depending on the characteristics of the particular employees. Note that if the Lonetree Company had selected a discount rate of 8%, the service cost in 2007 would be $167,643 ($180,000 × 9.371887 × 0.099377).

INTEREST ON PROJECTED BENEFIT OBLIGATION

The projected benefit obligation is the actuarial present value, at a specified date, of all the benefits attributed by the pension benefit formula to employee service rendered prior

---

23. The present value calculations in this Appendix use factors from the tables in the Time Value of Money Module.
24. As we discuss later, however, note that a change in the pension benefit formula in 2010 increases the annual benefits earned from $180,000 to $189,000. This change causes a corresponding increase (on a present value basis) in the service cost for 2010 and 2011.

to that date. We diagram the computation of the projected benefit obligation (PBO) at a particular date as follows:

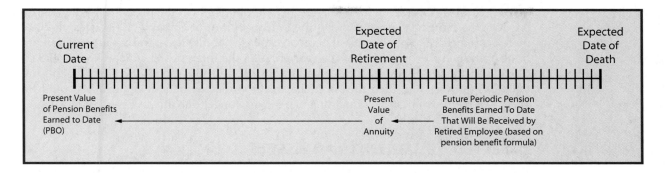

This diagram also reads from right to left. The present value of the future periodic pension benefits earned to date is computed as of the expected date of the retirement, based on the pension benefit formula, the discount rate, and the retirement period. Then, this present value as of the expected retirement date, is discounted back to the current date (based on the discount rate and the remaining years to the date of retirement) to determine the present value of the future pension benefits earned to date. This amount is the projected benefit obligation on the current date. Note that this diagram is similar to the one we showed for the service cost, except that it focuses on the projected pension benefits earned *to date*, while the service cost focuses on the future pension benefits earned *in a particular year*. There is a logical relationship between the two amounts, however. This is because the projected benefit obligation is the sum of the service costs to date (considering interest due to the passage of time and assuming there are no prior service costs and no employees have retired). The equation for the calculation of the projected benefit obligation is as follows:

$$\begin{array}{l} \text{Projected Benefit} \\ \text{Obligation} \end{array} = \begin{array}{l} \text{Present Value of Future Pension Benefits Earned by} \\ \text{Employees to Date (based on expected salary levels)} \end{array}$$

$$= \begin{array}{c} \text{Total} \\ \text{Benefits} \\ \text{Earned} \end{array} \times \begin{array}{c} \text{Present Value of} \\ \text{Annuity for Period} \\ \text{of Retirement} \end{array} \times \begin{array}{c} \text{Present Value of \$1} \\ \text{for Remaining Period} \\ \text{of Employment} \end{array}$$

In our example, at December 31, 2007, the employees have earned pension benefits for *one* year ($90,000 × 1 × 0.02 × 100 employees, or $180,000), and therefore the company calculates the projected benefit obligation as follows:

$$\begin{array}{l} \text{Projected Benefit} \\ \text{Obligation, 12/31/07} \end{array} = \begin{array}{c} \text{Total} \\ \text{Benefits} \\ \text{Earned} \end{array} \times \begin{array}{c} \text{Present Value of} \\ \text{Annuity for} \\ \text{18 Years at 10\%} \end{array} \times \begin{array}{c} \text{Present Value of \$1} \\ \text{for 30 Years at 10\%} \end{array}$$

$$= \$180,000 \times 8.201412 \times 0.057309$$

$$= \$84,603 \text{ (rounded)}$$

At December 31, 2008 the employees have earned pension benefits for *two* years ($90,000 × 2 × 0.02 × 100 employees, or $360,000), and therefore the projected benefit obligation is:

$$\begin{array}{l} \text{Projected Benefit} \\ \text{Obligation, 12/31/08} \end{array} = \$360,000 \times \begin{array}{c} \text{Present Value of} \\ \text{Annuity for 18} \\ \text{Years at 10\%} \end{array} \times \begin{array}{c} \text{Present Value of \$1} \\ \text{for 29 Years at 10\%} \end{array}$$

$$= \$360,000 \times 8.201412 \times 0.063039$$

$$= \$186,123 \text{ (rounded)}$$

The third column of Example 20-9 shows the amount of the projected benefit obligation at the end of each year. To determine its pension expense for each year, the Lonetree Company includes the interest cost on the projected benefit obligation. It computes this interest cost by multiplying the projected benefit obligation at the *beginning* of the year by the 10% discount rate, as we show in the fourth column of Example 20-9. Thus, in 2007 there is no interest cost included in pension expense because there was no projected benefit obligation at the beginning of the year. In 2008 the interest cost is $8,460 ($84,603 × 0.10), and the company includes this amount in pension expense.[25] Note that if any retired employees had died during the year, the projected benefit obligation would be decreased by the total of the remaining benefits no longer due the deceased employees.

EXPECTED RETURN ON PLAN ASSETS

The funding of a pension plan must be within the guidelines of ERISA. Since those rules are beyond the scope of the book, in this example we assume that the company funds an amount each year that is equal to the service cost. We also assume that the company makes its annual contribution on December 31 of each year. Therefore, the company makes its first payment of $84,603 to the plan on December 31, 2007, and the funding agency invests this amount in plan assets, such as bonds, stocks, and real estate. The fifth column of Example 20-9 shows the annual contribution (cash payment).

To determine its pension expense for each year, the Lonetree Company subtracts the expected return on its plan assets for that year. In 2007 no return was earned on the plan assets because the company did not make the contribution until the end of the year. In 2008 the company earns an expected return based on the plan assets available at the beginning of the year and held during the year. Thus, if we assume that the plan assets are expected to earn earn 8% per year, the expected return in 2008 is $6,768 ($84,603 × 0.08, rounded). This amount *decreases* the 2008 pension expense. On December 31, 2008 (before the contribution for 2008), the total assets are $91,371 ($84,603 + the actual return of $6,768). The contribution of $93,062 on that date increases the plan assets to $184,433. During 2009 the expected return on the assets is $14,755 ($184,433 × 0.08), which is deducted from the 2009 pension expense. As a result, the total plan assets on December 31, 2009, after the contribution for 2009, are $301,556 ($184,433 + the actual return of $14,755 + the contribution for 2009 of $102,368). The sixth and seventh columns of Example 20-9 show the plan assets and the expected and actual return on plan assets for each year, respectively. Note that if any employees had retired, the plan assets would be reduced each year by the payments made to the retired employees.

AMORTIZATION OF UNRECOGNIZED PRIOR SERVICE COST

Prior service cost is the cost of retroactive additional benefits granted by a company in a plan amendment or at the initial adoption of the plan. The cost causes an increase in the company's projected benefit obligation, and the company amortizes the unrecognized prior service cost as a component of its pension expense in later years. For example, assume that on January 1, 2010, the Lonetree Company changes the factor in the benefit formula from 0.02 to 0.021, retroactive to the adoption of the plan. This action creates additional pension benefits for each employee that the company calculates as follows:

$$\text{Additional Benefits per Employee} = \text{Average of Last 5 Years' Salary} \times \text{Number of Years of Service to Date} \times \text{Change in Formula}$$

$$= \$90,000 \times 3 \times 0.001$$

$$= \$270$$

---

25. As we discuss later, however, note that an amendment to the pension benefit formula in 2010 causes an increase in the projected benefit obligation. This change causes a corresponding increase in interest cost.

Since the Lonetree Company has 100 employees, the total additional benefits assigned to the employees is $27,000 ($270 × 100 employees). It calculates the prior service cost, which is the present value of those additional benefits, as follows:

$$\text{Prior Service Cost} = \frac{\text{Present Value of Additional Pension}}{\text{Benefits Granted by Plan Amendment}}$$

$$= \begin{array}{c} \text{Additional} \\ \text{Benefits} \end{array} \times \begin{array}{c} \text{Present Value of} \\ \text{Annuity for Period} \\ \text{of Retirement} \end{array} \times \begin{array}{c} \text{Present Value of \$1} \\ \text{for Remaining Period} \\ \text{of Employment} \end{array}$$

Recall that we assumed the life expectancy during retirement to be 18 years and, at the *beginning* of 2010, the remaining period of employment is 28 years. Therefore, the Lonetree Company calculates the prior service cost as follows:

$$\text{Prior Service Cost} = \begin{array}{c} \text{Additional} \\ \text{Benefits} \end{array} \times \begin{array}{c} \text{Present Value of} \\ \text{Annuity for} \\ \text{18 Years at 10\%} \end{array} \times \begin{array}{c} \text{Present Value of \$1} \\ \text{for 28 Years at 10\%} \end{array}$$

$$= \$27,000 \times 8.201412 \times 0.069343$$

$$= \$15,355 \text{ (rounded)}$$

The company amortizes the $15,355 unrecognized prior service cost as an element of pension expense in the current and future years. It amortizes its unrecognized prior service cost over the average remaining service life of its employees. Thus, the amortization in each year is $548 ($15,355 ÷ 28, rounded). The eighth column of Example 20-9 shows this amount for each year.

Adjustments of Service Cost and Projected Benefit Obligation

The amendment of the pension benefit formula at the beginning of 2010 causes not only an unrecognized prior service cost, but also an increase in the projected benefit obligation and the service cost for the current and future years. The increase in the service cost causes an increase in pension expense. The increase in the projected benefit obligation also causes an increase in pension expense because of the additional interest cost. Since the company continues to fund an amount equal to the annual service cost, there is no change in the plan assets at the beginning of 2010.

The service cost in 2010 and 2011 that we show in Example 20-9 is based on annual benefits earned of $189,000 ($90,000 × 0.021 × 100 employees), instead of $180,000. Thus, the company computes the 2010 service cost as follows:

$$\text{2010 Service Cost} = \begin{array}{c} \text{Annual} \\ \text{Benefits} \\ \text{Earned} \end{array} \times \begin{array}{c} \text{Present Value of} \\ \text{Annuity for} \\ \text{18 Years at 10\%} \end{array} \times \begin{array}{c} \text{Present Value of \$1} \\ \text{for 27 Years at 10\%} \end{array}$$

$$= \$189,000 \times 8.201412 \times 0.076278$$

$$= \$118,236 \text{ (rounded)}$$

The company makes a similar calculation in 2011 to determine the $130,058 service cost.

The company must include the present value of the additional benefits granted in the projected benefit obligation. Since the amendment occurred on January 1, 2010, the $307,104 projected benefit obligation on December 31, 2009 in Example 20-9 is not adjusted because it is based on the benefit formula at that time. The 2010 interest cost calculation, however, is based on the adjusted January 1, 2010 projected benefit obligation, which amounts to $322,459 ($307,104 + $15,355 prior service cost). Thus, the 2010 interest cost is $32,246 ($322,459 × 0.10).

The December 31, 2010 projected benefit obligation is based on the total benefits earned to date (after the amendment) and the company calculates it as follows:

$$\begin{array}{l} \text{Total} \\ \text{Benefits} \\ \text{Earned} \end{array} = \$90,000 \times \frac{\text{Number of Years}}{\text{of Service}} \times 0.021 \times 100 \text{ Employees}$$

$$= \$90,000 \times 4 \times 0.021 \times 100$$

$$= \$756,000$$

$$\begin{array}{l} \text{Projected} \\ \text{Benefit} \\ \text{Obligation} \end{array} = \begin{array}{l} \text{Total} \\ \text{Benefits} \\ \text{Earned} \end{array} \times \begin{array}{l} \text{Present Value of} \\ \text{Annuity for Period} \\ \text{of Retirement} \end{array} \times \begin{array}{l} \text{Present Value of \$1} \\ \text{for Remaining Period} \\ \text{of Employment} \end{array}$$

$$= \$756,000 \times \begin{array}{l} \text{Present Value of Annuity} \\ \text{for 18 Years at 10\%} \end{array} \times \begin{array}{l} \text{Present Value of \$1} \\ \text{for 27 Years at 10\%} \end{array}$$

$$= \$756,000 \times 8.201412 \times 0.076278$$

$$= \$472,944 \text{ (rounded)}$$

The company makes a similar calculation the next year to determine the projected benefit obligation on December 31, 2011 of $650,292.

PENSION EXPENSE AND LIABILITY

The pension expense each year for the Lonetree Company is the service cost, plus the interest on the projected benefit obligation, minus the expected return on plan assets, plus the amortization of the unrecognized prior service cost. (The gain or loss component does not arise in this example.) The company records any difference between the amount of the pension expense and the amount funded as a prepaid/accrued pension cost liability or asset. The ninth and fifth columns of Example 20-9 show the pension expense and amounts funded for the Lonetree Company, respectively. The journal entry to record the pension expense on December 31, 2007 is as follows:

Pension Expense	84,603	
Cash		84,603

The journal entry to record the pension expense on December 31, 2008 is as follows:

Pension Expense	94,754	
Cash		93,062
Prepaid/Accrued Pension Cost		1,692

The company makes a similar journal entry at the end of each succeeding year, and each year the debit to Pension Expense is greater than the credit to Cash. As a result, the company's pension liability account balance at the end of each year increases as follows:

Prepaid/Accrued Pension Cost (Liability)	
12/31/07	$ 0, or ($84,603 − $84,603)
12/31/08	1,692, or ($0 + $94,754 − $93,062)
12/31/09	5,549, or ($1,692 + $106,225 − $102,368)
12/31/10	14,219, or ($5,549 + $126,906 − $118,236)
12/31/11	26,548, or ($14,219 + $142,387 − $130,058)

In addition to the Prepaid/Accrued Pension Cost, the Lonetree Company must determine whether it needs to record an additional liability at the end of each year. Generally, a company recognizes an additional liability only in situations where it has a large, unrecognized prior service cost or has experienced substantial losses in the investment of its plan assets.

SUMMARY

At the beginning of the chapter, we identified several objectives you would accomplish after reading the chapter. The objectives are listed below, each followed by a brief summary of the key points in the chapter discussion.

1. **Understand the characteristics of pension plans.** A pension plan requires that a company provide income to its retired employees in return for services they provided during their employment. A defined benefit plan states the benefits to be received by employees after retirement or the method of determining such benefits. A defined contribution plan states the employer's contribution, and the future benefits are limited to the amount that can be provided by the contributions and the returns earned on the investment of those contributions.

2. **Explain the historical perspective of accounting for pension plans.** The first authoritative statement on pensions was *Accounting Research Bulletin No. 45* that recommended that companies recognize pension cost on the accrual basis. These principles were superceded by *APB Opinion No. 8* that required the use of the accrual method. These principles were then superceded by *FASB Statement No. 87*, which contains the current measurement and recognition requirements for the pension plans of employers. Accounting and reporting by the funding agency administering the pension plan is defined by *FASB Statement No. 35*. Disclosure requirements for employers' pension plans were established by *FASB Statement No. 87*, but were replaced by *FASB Statement No. 132* and *FASB Statement No.132* (revised 2003).

3. **Explain the accounting principles for defined benefit plans, including computing pension expense and recognizing pension liabilities and assets.** Pension expense includes the service cost, plus the interest cost, minus the expected return on plan assets, plus the amortization of the unrecognized prior service cost, minus or plus the gain or loss, which includes the effects of differences between actuarial assumptions and actual experience. The cumulative difference between the pension expense and funding is recognized as an asset or liability. The minimum total pension liability that a company must recognize is the unfunded accumulated benefit obligation. A company recognizing an additional pension liability may also recognize an intangible asset up to the amount of any unrecognized prior service cost. Any additional amount is recognized as a component of other comprehensive income.

4. **Account for pensions.** Compute the pension expense given the information about the components (e.g., service cost, interest cost). Record the pension expense and funding, and record any difference as an adjustment to prepaid/accrued pension cost. Compute and record any additional pension liability at an amount equal to the unfunded accumulated benefit obligation minus the accrued pension cost (or plus the prepaid pension cost).

5. **Understand disclosures of pensions.** The primary items a company must disclose about its pension plan(s) are listed on p.1005.

6. **Explain the conceptual issues regarding pensions.** The conceptual issues include the proper amount to recognize as pension expense (and when to record it), the identification and measurement of pension liabilities, and the balance sheet presentation of pension plan assets by the company with the pension plan and by the funding agency.

7. **Understand several additional issues related to pensions.** Additional recording and reporting issues include transition requirements when *FASB Statement No. 87* was adopted, vested benefits, defined contribution plans, disclosures by funding agencies, the Employee Retirement Security Act of 1974, pension plan settlements and curtailments, termination benefits paid to employees, multi-employer plans, and international accounting differences.

8. **Explain other postemployment benefits (OPEBs).** Postemployment benefits are paid to employees after employment but before retirement. Postretirement benefits are benefits paid to employees after their retirement, other than pensions. The most important of the OPEBs is healthcare benefits.

9. **Account for OPEBs.** Compute the postretirement benefit expense given information about the components (e.g., service cost and interest cost). Record the postretirement benefit expense and the increase in the accrued postretirement benefit cost (liability) assuming no funding. Record the payment of retirement benefits by decreasing the accrued postretirement benefit cost.

10. **Explain the conceptual issues regarding OPEBs.** The conceptual issues involve the relevance and reliability of the information, differences in funding between pensions and OPEBs, the attribution period, the interaction with deferred income taxes, the lack of a minimum liability recognition, and the impacts on companies of the adoption of *FASB Statement No. 106*.

11. **Understand present value calculations for pensions (Appendix).** Compute the components of the pension expense based on information about the employee (e.g., expected pension benefits and years of retirement) and the funding assumptions (e.g., discount rate). Use present value of annuity and present value of $1 calculations to determine the present values of the pension expense components.

ANSWERS TO REAL REPORT QUESTIONS

Real Report 20-1 Answers

1. YUM! Brands has noncontributory defined benefit pension plans. These plans are funded by YUM! Brands with no contributions by the employees (noncontributory) and the retirees receive fixed benefits based on a predefined formula.

2. YUM! Brand's pension expense for 2004 was $53 million (the net periodic benefit cost).

3. The actual return on plan assets of $53 million was greater than the expected return of $40 million.

4. At the end of 2004, the accumulated benefit obligation was $629 million and the projected benefit obligation was $700 million. The difference in these amounts is due to the fact that the projected benefit obligation includes projected salary increases while the accumulated benefit obligation is based on current employee salaries.

5. YUM! Brands is in a net liability position. An accrued liability of $111 million exists at the end of 2004. This amount is equal to the unfunded accumulated benefit obligation (accumulated benefit obligation of $629 million minus the fair value of the plan assets of $518 million). Furthermore, at the end of 2004, the projected benefit obligation (the present value of the benefits the company expects to pay) exceeds the fair value of plan assets by $182 million ($700 million − $518 million).

6. The use of a lower discount rate during 2004 would increase the ending balance in the projected benefit obligation, increase the ending balance in the accumulated benefit obligation, increase service cost, decrease the actuarial loss, and decrease interest cost for 2004. However, interest cost in 2005 would be higher (because of the increase in the projected benefit obligation at the end of 2004) relative to the amount that would have been reported if the discount rate were not changed.

7. YUM! Brands has a passive investment strategy with a targeted asset allocation of 70% equity securities and 30% debt securities which consists primarily of investments in mutual funds.

QUESTIONS

Q20-1 What is a pension plan? Explain how yearly income of retired employees is determined under a defined benefit pension plan.

Q20-2 Distinguish between a defined benefit pension plan and a defined contribution pension plan.

Q20-3 Distinguish between funded and unfunded pension plans; between contributory and noncontributory pension plans.

Q20-4 What is service cost? How does this differ from prior service cost?

Q20-5 Define *projected benefit obligation*. How does this differ from an accumulated benefit obligation?

Q20-6 In regard to pension plans, define *assumptions*. What is the relationship between a gain or loss and an assumption?

Q20-7 List and briefly define the five components of pension expense according to *FASB Statement No. 87*.

Q20-8 What is a company's accrued pension cost liability and when does it arise? What is a company's prepaid pension cost asset and when does it arise?

Q20-9 When does a company record an additional pension liability for a pension plan?

Q20-10 List the disclosures a company must make for its defined benefit pension plan in accordance with *FASB Statement No. 132* and *132R*.

Q20-11 List the conceptual issues of importance in regard to pension expense.

Q20-12 List the conceptual issues of importance in regard to pension liabilities and pension assets.

Q20-13 List and define the potential components of pension expense.

Q20-14 Conceptually, what are the four possible alternative methods for accounting for the prior service cost that arises from pension plan modifications?

Q20-15 What are the five possible alternative methods of determining the extent of a company's pension plan liability?

Q20-16 What is a defined contribution pension plan and what are the related accounting principles?

Q20-17 What must be included in the annual financial statements issued by a funding agency?

Q20-18 Does *FASB Statement No. 87* specify the minimum amount that a company must pay into its pension fund each year? If not, how is the amount determined?

Q20-19 What is a pension plan settlement? Curtailment? How should the net gain or loss from a settlement or curtailment be accounted for by a company according to *FASB Statement No. 88*?

Q20-20 What are other postemployment benefits? How are they distinguished from postretirement benefits?

Q20-21 List and briefly define the five components of OPEB expense according to *FASB Statement No. 106*.

Q20-22 How does accounting for other postemployment benefits differ from accounting for defined benefit pension plans?

MULTIPLE CHOICE (AICPA Adapted)

Select the best answer for each of the following.

M20-1 The actuarial present value of all the benefits attributed by the pension benefit formula to employee service rendered before a specified date based on expected future compensation levels is the
a. Projected benefit obligation
b. Prior service cost
c. Service cost
d. Accumulated benefit obligation

Items 2, 3, and 4 are based on the following information:

Spath Company adopted a noncontributory defined benefit pension plan on January 1, 2007. Spath Company uses the benefit/years-of-service method, which results in the following information:

	2007	2008
Service cost	$300,000	$450,000
Amount funded	240,000	390,000
Discount rate	10%	10%
Expected rate of return	10%	10%

The fair value of the plan assets at the end of each year exceeded the accumulated benefit obligation.

M20-2 What is the balance of the accrued pension cost as of December 31?

	2007	2008
a.	$ 0	$ 60,000
b.	$60,000	$ 60,000
c.	$60,000	$ 66,000
d.	$60,000	$126,000

M20-3 What is the pension expense for the year ended December 31, 2008?
a. $390,000   c. $456,000
b. $426,000   d. $480,000

M20-4 As of December 31, 2008, what is the balance in the pension plan asset fund?
a. $456,000   c. $654,000
b. $630,000   d. $840,000

M20-5 Which of the following is not a component of pension expense?
a. Amount funded
b. Service cost
c. Expected return on plan assets
d. Interest cost

M20-6 Davison Company has a noncontributory defined benefit pension plan for its employees. During 2007 the pension plan has a discount rate of 8%, service cost of $98,000, plan assets as of 1/1/07 of $432,000, and an expected return on plan assets of $34,560. On December 31, 2007 the company contributed $90,000 to the pension plan, resulting in a credit to Prepaid/Accrued Pension Cost of $6,300. What is the amount of the projected benefit obligation on January 1, 2007?
a. $332,000   c. $410,750
b. $345,600   d. $432,000

M20-7 On January 1, 2007 the Soloman Company changes the factor in the benefit formula from 0.02 to 0.022, retroactive to the adoption of the plan. The amendment will result in a(an)
a. Decrease in projected benefit obligation
b. Increase in service cost
c. Decrease in pension expense
d. Increase in plan assets

M20-8 The McCollum Company amended its noncontributory defined benefit pension plan at the beginning of 2004. The unrecognized prior service cost related to this amendment amounts to $240,000. Information regarding the four participating employees is as follows:

Employee	Expected to Retire After
A	Year 1
B	Year 2
C	Year 4
D	Year 5

Using the straight-line method, what is the amount of unrecognized prior service cost to be amortized in 2007?
a. $0   c. $60,000
b. $40,000   d. $80,000

M20-9 *FASB Statement No. 88* requires that a company record a loss and a liability for termination benefits paid to employees when
a. The employee accepts the offer
b. The amount can be reasonably estimated
c. The employee accepts the offer or the amount can be reasonably estimated
d. The employee accepts the offer and the amount can be reasonably estimated

M20-10 *FASB Statement No. 132R* requires a company with a defined benefit pension plan to make all of the following disclosures except
a. The amount of the pension expense, showing each of the components separately
b. The estimates of contributions for the next five years
c. The funded status of the plan
d. The discount rate

EXERCISES

E20-1 *Pension Expense* The Bailey Company has had a defined benefit pension plan for several years. At the end of 2007 the company's actuary provided the following information for 2007 regarding the pension plan: (1) service cost, $115,000; (2) expected return on plan assets, $14,000; (3) amortization of unrecognized net loss, $2,000; (4) interest cost on projected benefit obligation, $16,000; and (5) amortization of unrecognized prior service cost, $4,000. The company decides to fund an amount at the end of 2007 equal to its pension expense.

Required
Compute the amount of Bailey Company's pension expense for 2007 and prepare the related journal entry.

E20-2 *Pension Expense* On December 31, 2007 the Robey Company accumulated the following information for 2007 in regard to its defined benefit pension plan:

Service cost	$105,000
Interest cost on projected benefit obligation	12,000
Expected return on plan assets	11,000
Amortization of unrecognized prior service cost	3,000
Amortization of unrecognized net gain	1,000

On its December 31, 2006 balance sheet, the company had reported a prepaid/accrued pension cost liability of $14,000.

Required
1. Compute the amount of Robey Company's pension expense for 2007.
2. Prepare the journal entry to record Robey's 2007 pension expense if it funds the pension plan in the amount of: (a) $108,000, (b) $100,000, and (c) $112,000.

E20-3 *Interest Cost and Return on Assets* On December 31, 2007 the Palmer Company determined that the 2007 service cost on its defined benefit pension plan was $120,000. At the beginning of 2007 Palmer Company had pension plan assets of $520,000 and a projected benefit obligation of $600,000. Its discount rate (and expected long-term rate of return on plan assets) for 2007 was 10%. There are no other components of Palmer Company's pension expense; the company had a prepaid/accrued pension cost liability at the end of 2006.

Required
1. Compute the amount of Palmer Company's pension expense for 2007.
2. Prepare the journal entry to record Palmer's 2007 pension expense if it funds the pension plan in the amount of: (a) $128,000, and (b) $120,000.

E20-4 *Pension Expense Different Than Funding: One Year* The Verna Company has had a defined benefit pension plan for several years. At the end of 2007 the company accumulated the following information: (1) service cost for 2007, $127,000; (2) projected benefit obligation, 1/1/2007, $634,000; (3) discount rate, 9%; (4) plan assets, 1/1/2007, $589,000; and (5) expected long-term rate of return on plan assets, 9%. There are no other components of Verna Company's pension expense; the company had a prepaid/accrued pension cost liability at the end of 2006. The company contributed $128,000 to the pension plan at the end of 2007.

Required
Compute the amount of Verna Company's pension expense for 2007 and prepare the related journal entry.

E20-5 *Pension Expense Different Than Funding: Multiple Years* Baron Company adopted a defined benefit pension plan on January 1, 2006. The following information pertains to the pension plan for 2007 and 2008:

	2007	2008
Service cost	$160,000	$172,000
Projected benefit obligation (1/1)	120,000	289,600
Plan assets (1/1)	120,000	279,600
Company contribution (funded 12/31)	150,000	160,000
Discount rate	8%	8%
Expected long-term (and actual) rate of return on plan assets	8%	8%

There are no other components of Baron Company's pension expense.

Required
1. Compute the amount of Baron Company's pension expense for 2007 and 2008.
2. Prepare the journal entries to record the pension expense for 2007 and 2008.

E20-6 *Determination of Projected Benefit Obligation* Several years ago the Lewad Company established a defined benefit pension plan for its employees. The following information is available for 2007 in regard to its pension plan: (1) discount rate, 10%; (2) service cost, $142,000; (3) plan assets (1/1), $659,000; and (4) expected return on plan assets, $65,900. There is no amortization of unrecognized prior service cost and there is no gain or loss. On December 31, 2007, the company contributed $140,000 to the pension plan, resulting in a credit to Prepaid/Accrued Pension Cost of $8,200.

Required
Compute the amount of Lewad Company's projected benefit obligation on January 1, 2007.

E20-7 *Pension Expense Different Than Funding: Multiple Years* Carli Company adopted a defined benefit pension plan on January 1, 2006, and funded the entire amount of its 2006 pension expense. The following information pertains to the pension plan for 2007 and 2008:

	2007	2008
Service cost	$200,000	$215,000
Projected benefit obligation (1/1)	180,000	396,200
Plan assets (1/1)	180,000	406,400
Company contribution (funded 12/31)	212,000	220,000
Discount rate	9%	9%
Expected long-term (and actual) rate of return on plan assets	8%	8%

There are no other components of Carli Company's pension expense.

Required
1. Compute the amount of Carli Company's pension expense for 2007 and 2008.
2. Prepare the journal entries to record the pension expense for 2007 and 2008

E20-8 *Unrecognized Prior Service Cost* On January 1, 2007 the Smith Company adopted a defined benefit pension plan. At that time the company awarded retroactive benefits to its employees, resulting in an unrecognized prior service cost that created a projected benefit obligation of $1,250,000 on that date. The company decided to amortize the unrecognized prior service cost by the straight-line method over the 20-year average remaining service life of its active participating employees. The company's actuary has also provided the following additional information for 2007 and 2008: (1) Service cost: 2007, $147,000; 2008, $153,000; (2) expected return on plan assets: 2008, $34,000; and (3) projected benefit obligation: 1/1/2008, $1,522,000. The discount rate was 10% in both 2007 and 2008. The company contributed $340,000 and $350,000 to the pension fund at the end of 2007 and 2008, respectively. There are no other components of Smith Company's pension expense; ignore any additional pension liability.

Required
1. Compute the amount of Smith Company's pension expense for 2007 and 2008.
2. Prepare the journal entries to record the pension expense for 2007 and 2008.

E20-9 *Straight-Line Amortization* At the beginning of 2007 the Brent Company amended its defined benefit pension plan. The amendment entitled five active participating employees to receive increased future benefits based on their prior service.

The company's actuary determined that the unrecognized prior service cost for this amendment amounts to $330,000. Employee A is expected to retire after one year, employee B after two, employee C after three, employee D after four, and employee E after five years.

Required

Using the straight-line method, (1) compute the average remaining service life, and (2) prepare a schedule to amortize the unrecognized prior service cost.

E20-10 *Years-of-Future-Service Amortization* Refer to the information provided in E20-9.

Required

Using the years-of-future-service method, prepare a set of schedules to determine (1) the amortization fraction for each year, and (2) the amortization of the unrecognized prior service cost.

E20-11 *Methods to Amortize Unrecognized Prior Service Cost* Wolz Company, a small business, has had a defined benefit pension plan for its employees for several years. At the beginning of 2007 the company amended the pension plan; this amendment provides for increased benefits based on services rendered by certain employees in prior periods. The company's actuary has determined that the related unrecognized prior service cost amounts to $140,000. The company has four participating employees who are expected to receive the increased benefits. The following is a schedule identifying the employees and their expected years of future service:

Employee Numbers	Expected Years of Future Service
1	2
2	3
3	4
4	5

Required

1. Using the straight-line method, (a) compute the average remaining service life, and (b) prepare a schedule to amortize the unrecognized prior service cost.
2. Using the years-of-future-service method instead, prepare a set of schedules to determine (a) the amortization fraction for each year, and (b) the amortization of the unrecognized prior service cost.

E20-12 *Net Gain or Loss* Lee Company has a defined benefit pension plan. During 2006, for the first time, the company experienced a difference between its expected and actual projected benefit obligation. At the beginning of 2007 the company's actuary accumulated the following information:

Unrecognized net loss (1/1/2007)	$ 44,000
Actual projected benefit obligation (1/1/2007)	228,000
Fair value of plan assets (1/1/2007)	260,000

On December 31, 2007, the company is in the process of computing the net gain or loss to include in its pension expense for 2007. The company has determined that the average remaining service life of its employees is nine years. There was no difference between the company's expected and actual return on plan assets in 2007.

Required

Compute the amount of the net gain or loss to include in the pension expense for 2007. Indicate whether it is an addition to or a subtraction from pension expense.

E20-13 *Net Gain or Loss* The actuary of the Hudson Company has provided the following information concerning the company's defined benefit pension plan at the end of 2007:

Fair value of plan assets (1/1/2007)	$350,000
Actual projected benefit obligation (1/1/2007)	360,000
Expected projected benefit obligation (1/1/2007)	424,000
Average remaining service life of employees	10 years

The difference between the actual and expected projected benefit obligation first occurred in 2006.

Required

1. Compute the amount of the unrecognized gain or loss for the Hudson Company's pension plan at the beginning of 2007.
2. Compute the amount of the net gain or loss to include in the Hudson Company's pension expense for 2007. Indicate whether it is an addition to or a subtraction from pension expense.

E20-14 *Additional Pension Liability* Derosa Company has a defined benefit pension plan for its employees. Prior to 2007 the company has not had an additional pension liability. At the end of 2007 the company's actuary developed the following information regarding its pension plan:

Projected benefit obligation	$1,429,000
Accumulated benefit obligation	987,000
Plan assets (fair value)	852,000
Unrecognized prior service cost	200,000

Required

1. Calculate the additional pension liability required at the end of 2007 and prepare the appropriate journal entry, assuming that the company had a prepaid/accrued pension cost (liability) of $73,000 before considering the preceding information.
2. Repeat Requirement 1 assuming, instead, that the company had a prepaid/accrued pension cost (asset) of $46,000.
3. Indicate how the liability and asset in Requirement 2 would be disclosed on the 2007 ending balance sheet.

E20-15 *Accounting for an OPEB Plan* On January 1, 2007 Flash and Dash Company adopted a healthcare plan for its retired employees. To determine eligibility for benefits, the company retroactively gives credit to the date of hire for each employee. The following information is available about the plan:

Service cost	$ 30,000
Accumulated postretirement benefit obligation (1/1/07)	100,000
Accumulated postretirement benefit obligation for employees fully eligible	
to receive benefits (12/31/07)	40,000
Expected return on plan assets	0
Unrecognized prior service cost	12,000
Payments to retired employees during 2007	5,000
Interest rate	10%
Average remaining service period of active plan participants (1/1/07)	12 years

Required

1. Compute the OPEB expense for 2007 if the company uses the average remaining service life to amortize the unrecognized prior service cost.
2. Prepare all the required journal entries for 2007 if the plan is not funded.

E20-16 *Pension Plan Present Value Calculations (Appendix)* The Ark Company adopted a defined benefit pension plan for its employees on January 1, 2007. All its employees are the same age, retire at the same time, and have the same life expectancy after retirement. The company decided to compute its pension expense on December 31 of each year; it also decided to fund an amount on that date equal to the year's service cost. The following is a listing of other relevant facts:

Annual pension benefits earned by all employees for each year of service*	$100,000
Years to retirement (at end of 2007)	20
Years of life expectancy after date of retirement	15
Discount rate	9%
Expected long-term (and actual) rate of return on plan assets	8%

*Paid at end of each year

For the years 2007 through 2009 the company experienced no net gain or loss and did not have an additional pension liability in regard to the pension plan.

Required

1. Prepare a schedule to compute the Ark Company's pension expense for 2007 through 2009. Round to the nearest dollar.
2. Prepare the year-end journal entries to record the company's pension expense for 2007 through 2009.

PROBLEMS

P20-1   Components of Pension Expense The Nelson Company has a defined benefit pension plan for its employees. At the end of 2007 and 2008 the following information is available in regard to this pension plan:

	2007	2008
Expected return on plan assets	$ 27,000	$ 28,000
Amortization of unrecognized net gain	3,000	—
Amortization of unrecognized net loss	—	4,000
Amortization of unrecognized prior service cost	7,000	6,000
Company contribution (funded 12/31)	200,000	240,000
Interest cost on projected benefit obligation	32,000	35,000
Service cost	211,000	217,000

There are no other components of Nelson Company's pension expense in either year; ignore any additional pension liability.

Required
1. Compute the amount of Nelson Company's pension expense in 2007 and 2008.
2. Prepare the December 31 journal entry to record the pension expense in 2007 and 2008.
3. What is the total prepaid/accrued pension cost at the end of 2007, assuming no prepaid/accrued pension cost existed prior to 2007? Is it an asset or a liability?

P20-2   Pension Expense Different Than Funding On January 1, 2007 the Parkway Company adopted a defined benefit pension plan. At that time, the company awarded retroactive benefits to its employees, resulting in an unrecognized prior service cost of $2,180,000 on that date. The company decided to amortize these costs by the straight-line method over the 16-year average remaining service life of its active participating employees. The company's actuary and funding agency have also provided the following additional information for 2007 and 2008:

	2007	2008
Service cost	$ 340,000	$ 348,000
Projected benefit obligation (1/1)	2,180,000*	$2,738,000
Plan assets (1/1)	-0-	670,000
Discount rate	10%	10%
Expected long-term (and actual) rate of return on plan assets	—	9%

*Due to the unrecognized prior service cost

The company contributed $670,000 and $700,000 to the pension fund at the end of 2007 and 2008, respectively. There are no other components of Parkway Company's pension expense; ignore any additional pension liability.

Required
1. Compute the amount of Parkway Company's pension expense for 2007 and 2008.
2. Prepare the December 31 journal entry to record the pension expense for 2007 and 2008.
3. What is the total prepaid/accrued pension cost at the end of 2008? Is it an asset or a liability?

P20-3   Pension Expense Different Than Funding When Turner Company adopted its defined benefit pension plan on January 1, 2007, it awarded retroactive benefits to its employees. These retroactive benefits resulted in an unrecognized prior service cost of $980,000 that created a projected benefit obligation of the same amount on that date. The company decided to amortize the unrecognized prior service cost using the years-of-future-service method. The company's actuary and funding agency have provided the following additional information for 2007 and 2008: (1) service cost: 2007, $187,000; 2008, $189,000; (2) plan assets: 1/1/2007, $0; 1/1/2008, $342,000; (3) expected long-term (and actual) rate of return on plan assets: 2008, 9%; (4) discount rate for both 2007 and 2008: 8%; and (5) amortization fraction for unrecognized prior service cost: 2007, 80/980; 2008, 79/980. The company contributed $342,000 and $336,000 to the pension fund at the end of 2007 and 2008, respectively. No retirement benefits were paid in either year. There are no other components of Turner Company's pension expense; ignore any additional pension liability. The company rounds its calculations to the nearest dollar.

Required ☒
Prepare a pension plan worksheet that includes the calculation of the Turner Company's pension expense for 2007 and 2008, the reconciliation of the beginning and ending projected benefit obligation for 2007 and 2008, the reconciliation of the beginning and ending plan assets for 2007 and 2008, and the journal entry to record the pension expense at the end of 2007 and 2008, indicating whether each component is a debit or credit.

P20-4 *Pension Expense Different Than Funding* The Lane Company was incorporated in 1998. Because it had become successful, the company established a defined benefit pension plan for its employees on January 1, 2007. Due to the loyalty of its employees, the company granted retroactive benefits to them. These retroactive benefits resulted in $1,240,000 of unrecognized prior service cost on that date. The company decided to amortize these costs using the years-of-future-service method. The company's actuary and funding agency have provided the following additional information for 2007 and 2008:

	2007	2008
Expected long-term (and actual) rate of return on plan assets	—	9%
Amortization fraction for unrecognized prior service cost	48/620	46/620
Discount rate	9%	9%
Plan assets (1/1)	$ -0-	$ 690,000
Projected benefit obligation (1/1)	1,240,000*	1,814,600
Service cost	463,000	475,000

*Due to the unrecognized prior service cost

The company contributed $690,000 and $650,000 to the pension fund at the end of 2007 and 2008, respectively. No retirement benefits were paid in 2007. There are no other components of Lane Company's pension expense; ignore any additional pension liability. The company rounds its calculations to the nearest dollar.

Required
1. Compute the amount of Lane Company's pension expense for 2007 and 2008.
2. Prepare the December 31 journal entry to record the pension expense for 2007 and 2008.
3. What is the total prepaid/accrued pension cost at the end of 2008? Is it an asset or a liability?
4. Prepare a schedule that reconciles the beginning and ending amounts of the projected benefit obligation for 2007.

P20-5 *Pension Expense Different Than Funding* The Carpenter Company adopted a defined benefit pension plan for its employees on January 1, 2007. At the time of adoption the pension contract provided for retroactive benefits for the company's active participating employees. These retroactive benefits resulted in an unrecognized prior service cost of $1,860,000 that created a projected benefit obligation of the same amount on that date. The company decided to amortize the unrecognized prior service cost by the straight-line method over the 20-year average remaining service life of the employees. The following additional information is also available for 2007 and 2008: (1) discount rate for both 2007 and 2008: 8%; (2) company contribution (funded 12/31): 2007, $550,000; 2008, $510,000; (3) expected long-term rate of return on plan assets: 9%; (4) actual rate of return on plan assets, 10%; (5) service cost: 2007, $257,000; 2008, $264,000; and (6) plan assets: 1/1/2007, $0. The company paid pension benefits of $30,000 each year. There are no other components of Carpenter Company's pension expense; ignore any additional pension liability.

Required
Prepare a pension plan worksheet that includes the calculaion of the Carpenter Company's pension expense for 2007 and 2008, the reconciliation of the beginning and ending projected benefit obligation for 2007 and 2008, the reconciliation of the beginning and ending plan assets for 2007 and 2008, and the journal entry to record the pension expense at the end of 2007 and 2008, indicating whether each component is a debit or credit.

P20-6 *Amortization of Unrecognized Prior Service Cost* On January 1, 2007 the Baznik Company adopted a defined benefit pension plan. At that time the company awarded retroactive benefits to certain employees. These retroactive benefits resulted in an unrecognized prior service cost of $1,200,000 on that date. The company has six participating employees who are expected to receive the retroactive benefits. Following is a schedule that identifies the participating employees and their expected years of future service as of January 1, 2007:

Employee	Expected Years of Future Service
A	1
B	3
C	4
D	5
E	5
F	6

The company decided to amortize the unrecognized prior service cost to pension expense using the years-of-future-service method. The following are the amounts of the components of Baznik Company's pension expense, in addition to the amortization of the unrecognized prior service cost for 2007 and 2008:

	2007	2008
Service cost	$469,000	$507,000
Interest cost on projected benefit obligation	108,000	159,930
Expected return on plan assets	—	85,000

The company contributed $850,000 and $830,000 to the pension fund at the end of 2007 and 2008, respectively. Ignore any additional pension liability.

Required
1. Prepare a set of schedules for the Baznik Company to determine (a) the amortization fraction for each year, and (b) the amortization of the unrecognized prior service cost.
2. Prepare the journal entries to record the pension expense for 2007 and 2008.

P20-7 *Net Gain or Loss* For several years, Kent Company has had a defined benefit contribution plan for its employees. During those years the company experienced differences between its expected and actual projected benefit obligation. These differences resulted in a cumulative net gain or loss at the beginning of each subsequent year. The following schedule summarizes the amounts related to the preceding information for the years 2007 through 2009:

Year	Cumulative Unrecognized Net Loss (Gain)[a]
2007	$25,000
2008	26,000
2009	36,500

a. At beginning of year

The company's actuary and funding agency have also provided the following information about the company's actual projected benefit obligation and fair value of plan assets at the beginning of each year:

Year	Projected Benefit Obligation	Plan Assets
2007	$220,000	$200,000
2008	275,000	270,000
2009	320,000	325,000

The company amortizes any excess unrecognized gain or loss by the straight-line method over the average remaining service life of its active participating employees. Because of a consistent pattern of employee hirings and retirements, this average service life has remained at 20 years for 2007 through 2009.

Required
Prepare a schedule to compute the amount of the net gain or loss to include in the Kent Company's pension expense for 2007 through 2009. Indicate whether the gain or loss is added to or subtracted from the pension expense.

P20-8 *Additional Pension Liability* In the Fisk Company's negotiations with its employees' union on January 1, 2007, the company agreed to an amendment which substantially increased the employee benefits based on services rendered in prior periods. This resulted in an $80,000 unrecognized prior service cost that increased both the projected benefit obligation and the accumulated benefit obligation of the company. Due to financial constraints the company decided not to fund the total increase in its pension obligation at that time.

Prior to 2007 it had been the company's policy to fund enough of its pension expense each year so that the fair value of the plan assets at the end of the year was greater than the year-end accumulated benefit obligation. As a result the company reported a prepaid/accrued pension cost liability of $40,000 on its December 31, 2006 balance sheet.

The company appropriately amortized the unrecognized prior service cost as a component of pension expense in 2007 and 2008. The resulting pension and other information for 2007 and 2008 are as follows:

Year	Pension Expense	Company Contribution[a]	Accumulated Benefit Obligation[b]	Fair Value of Plan Assets[b]
2007	$137,000	$125,000	$562,000	$500,000
2008	145,000	160,000	682,000	637,000

a. Funded December 31
b. At year-end

Required
1. Prepare the December 31, 2007 journal entries related to the Fisk Company's pension plan.
2. List the amounts of any assets and liabilities to be reported on the company's December 31, 2007 balance sheet.
3. Prepare the December 31, 2008 journal entries related to the Fisk Company's pension plan.
4. List the amounts of any assets and liabilities to be reported on the company's December 31, 2008 balance sheet.

P20-9 *Determination of Pension Plan Amounts* Various pension plan information of the Kerem Company for 2007 and 2008 is as follows:

	2007	2008
Service cost	$100,000	(j)
Interest cost on projected benefit obligation	54,000	(g)
Accumulated benefit obligation, 12/31	(f)	(l)
Discount rate	9%	9%
Amortization of unrecognized prior service cost	4,000	4,000
Plan assets (fair value), 1/1*	500,000	615,000
Projected benefit obligation, 1/1	(a)	720,000
Deferred pension cost, 12/31	3,000	(k)
Expected long-term rate of return on plan assets	(b)	11%
Amortization of unrecognized net loss	(d)	700
Additional pension liability, 12/31	3,000	5,000
Accrued pension cost (liability), 12/31	17,000	26,000
Average service life of employees	10 years	10 years
Pension expense	(e)	110,850
Cumulative unrecognized net loss, 1/1	68,000	(i)
Expected return on plan assets	50,000	(h)
Corridor	(c)	72,000

* 1/1/2009: $740,000

Required
Fill in the blanks lettered (a) through (l). All the necessary information is listed. It is not necessary to calculate your answers in alphabetical order.

P20-10 *Comprehensive* The Jay Company has had a defined benefit pension plan for several years. At the beginning of 2007 the company amended the plan; this amendment provided for increased benefits to employees based on services rendered in prior periods. The unrecognized prior service cost related to this amendment totaled $88,000; as a result, both the projected and accumulated benefit obligation increased.

The company decided not to fund the increased obligation at the time of the amendment, but rather to increase its periodic year-end contributions to the pension plan. In the past the company has never had an additional pension liability at year-end.

The following information for 2007 has been provided by the company's actuary and funding agency, and obtained from a review of its accounting records:

Accumulated benefit obligation (12/31)	$740,000
Service cost	183,000
Discount rate	9%
Cumulative unrecognized net loss (1/1)	64,500
Company contribution to pension plan (12/31)	200,000
Projected benefit obligation (1/1)*	513,000
Plan assets, fair value (12/31)	728,000
Prepaid pension cost (asset) (1/1)	31,500
Expected (and actual) return on plan assets	48,000
Plan assets, fair value (1/1)	480,000

*Before the increase of $88,000 due to the unrecognized prior service cost from the amendment

The company decided to amortize the unrecognized prior service cost and any excess cumulative unrecognized net loss by the straight-line method over the average remaining service life of the participating employees. It has developed the following schedule concerning these 50 employees:

Employee Numbers	Expected Years of Future Service*	Employee Numbers	Expected Years of Future Service*
1–5	2	26–30	12
6–10	4	31–35	14
11–15	6	36–40	16
16–20	8	41–45	18
21–25	10	46–50	20

*Per employee

Required

1. Compute the average remaining service life and prepare a schedule to determine the amortization of the unrecognized prior service cost of the Jay Company for 2007.
2. Prepare a schedule to compute the net gain or loss component of pension expense for 2007.
3. Prepare a schedule to compute the pension expense for 2007.
4. Prepare a schedule to determine the additional pension liability (if any) at the end of 2007.
5. Prepare all the December 31, 2007 journal entries related to the pension plan.

P20-11 *Comprehensive* The TAN Company has a defined benefit pension plan for its employees. The plan has been in existence for several years. During 2006, for the first time, the company experienced a difference between its expected and actual projected benefit obligation. This resulted in a cumulative unrecognized loss of $29,000 at the beginning of 2007, which did not change during 2007. The company amortizes any excess unrecognized loss by the straight-line method over the average remaining service life of its active participating employees. It has developed the following schedule concerning these 40 employees:

Employee Numbers	Expected Years of Future Service*	Employee Numbers	Expected Years of Future Service*
1–5	3	21–25	15
6–10	6	26–30	18
11–15	9	31–35	21
16–20	12	36–40	24

*Per employee

The company makes its contribution to the pension plan at the end of each year. However, it has not always funded the entire pension expense in a given year. As a result, it had an accrued pension cost liability of $36,000 on December 31, 2006. Furthermore, the company's accumulated benefit obligation exceeded the fair value of the plan assets at the end of 2006, so that the company also had an additional pension liability (and excess of additional pension liability over unrecognized prior service cost) of $2,300 on December 31, 2006.

In addition to the preceding information, the following set of facts for 2007 and 2008 has been assembled, based on information provided by the company's actuary and funding agency, and obtained from its accounting records:

	2007	2008
Plan assets, fair value (12/31)	$620,500	$859,550
Cumulative unrecognized net loss (1/1)	29,000	29,000
Expected (and actual) return on plan assets	40,500	62,050
Company contribution to pension plan (12/31)	175,000	177,000
Projected benefit obligation (1/1)	470,000	686,000
Discount rate	10%	10%
Accumulated benefit obligation (12/31)	660,000	903,000
Service cost	169,000	175,000
Plan assets, fair value (1/1)	405,000	620,500

Required

1. Calculate the average remaining service life of the TAN Company's employees. Compute to one decimal place.
2. Prepare a schedule to compute the net gain or loss component of pension expense for 2007 and 2008. For simplicity, assume the average remaining life calculated in Requirement 1 is applicable to both years.

3. Prepare a schedule to compute the pension expense for 2007 and 2008.
4. Prepare a schedule to determine the adjustment (if any) to additional pension liability required at the end of 2007 and 2008.
5. Prepare all the December 31, 2007 and December 31, 2008 journal entries related to the pension plan.

P20-12 *Accounting for an OPEB Plan* On January 1, 2007 the Vasby Software Company adopted a healthcare plan for its retired employees. To determine eligibility for benefits, the company retroactively gives credit to the date of hire for each employee. The service cost for 2007 is $8,000. The plan is not funded, and the discount rate is 10%. All employees were hired at age 28 and become eligible for full benefits at age 58. Employee C was paid $7,000 for postretirement healthcare benefits in 2007. On December 31, 2007 the accumulated postretirement benefit obligation for Employees B and C were $77,000 and $41,500, respectively. Additional information on January 1, 2007 is as follows:

Employee Status	Age	Expected Retirement Age	Accumulated Postretirement Benefit Obligation
A Employee	31	65	$ 14,000
B Employee	55	65	70,000
C Retired	67	—	45,000
			$129,000

Required
1. Compute the OPEB expense for 2007 if the company uses the average remaining service life to amortize the unrecognized prior service cost.
2. Prepare all the required journal entries for 2007 if the plan is not funded.

P20-13 *Pension Plan Present Value Computations (Appendix)* On January 1, 2007 the Cromwell Company adopted a defined benefit plan for its employees. All the employees are the same age, retire at the same time, and have the same life expectancy after retirement. The following are the relevant facts concerning the pension plan factors and the employee characteristics:

Pension Plan Factors

Benefit formula	Average of last four years' salary $\times$ Number of years of service $\times$ 0.025
Expected average of last four years' salary	$80,000 per employee
Annual pension benefit earned each year of service by each employee	$80,000 $\times$ 0.025 = $2,000*
Date of computation of pension expense and pension funding	December 31
Amount funded each year	Equal to annual service cost
Discount rate	10%
Expected long-term (and actual) rate of return on plan assets	9%

*Paid at end of each year

Employee Characteristics

Number of employees	60
Age of employees	35
Years to retirement (at end of 2007)	25
Years of life expectancy after date of retirement	14

For the years 2007 through 2011 the company experienced no net gain or loss in regard to the pension plan. On January 1, 2010, however, the company agreed to an amendment of the pension plan. This amendment changed the factor in the pension benefit formula from 0.025 to 0.03. This amendment was made retroactive to the adoption of the plan. At the end of years 2007 through 2011 the company did not have an additional pension liability.

Required
1. Prepare a schedule to compute the Cromwell Company's pension expense for 2007 through 2011. Round to the nearest dollar.
2. Prepare the year-end journal entries to record the company's pension expense for 2007 through 2011.
3. Determine the balance in the Prepaid/Accrued Pension Cost account on December 31, 2011. Indicate whether it is an asset or liability.

CASES

COMMUNICATION

C20-1 Financial Reporting for a Defined Benefit Pension Plan

The Fink Company is considering establishing a defined benefit pension plan for its employees. The president of Fink Company is slightly familiar with *FASB Statement No. 87* and understands that accounting for a defined benefit pension plan may result in certain items being included in the financial statements of the sponsoring company. The president has come to you for help in better understanding these items.

Required

List each item, summarize how it is calculated, and briefly explain its meaning.

C20-2 Pension Cost Components

AICPA Adapted Carson Company sponsors a single-employer defined benefit pension plan. The plan provides that pension benefits are determined by age, years of service, and compensation. Among the components that should be included in the net pension cost recognized for a period are service cost, interest cost, and expected return on plan assets.

Required

1. What two accounting issues result from the nature of the defined benefit pension plan? Why do these issues arise?
2. Explain how Carson should determine the service cost component of the net pension cost.
3. Explain how Carson should determine the interest cost component of the net pension cost.
4. Explain how Carson should determine the expected return on plan assets component of the net pension cost.

C20-3 Pension and Future Vacation Costs

AICPA Adapted Essex Company has a single-employer defined benefit pension plan, and a compensation plan for future vacations for its employees.

Required

1. Define the interest cost component of net pension cost for a period. Explain how Essex should determine the interest cost component of its net pension cost for a period.
2. Define prior service cost. Explain how Essex should account for prior service cost.
3. What conditions must be met for Essex to accrue compensation for future vacations? Explain the theoretical rationale for accruing compensation for future vacations.

C20-4 Conceptual Issues

In the chapter the conceptual issues related to pension expense, pension liabilities, and pension plan assets are discussed.

Required

Explain how *FASB Statement No. 87* resolves each of these three conceptual issues.

C20-5 Other Postemployment Benefits

Companies often provide their employees with postemployment benefits other than pensions. These benefits may include health insurance, life insurance, and disability benefits.

Required

Explain how the accounting for these other postemployment benefits is similar or dissimilar to accounting for pensions.

CREATIVE AND CRITICAL THINKING

C20-6 Additional Pension Liability

The development of *FASB Statement No. 87* took many years and included compromises among competing arguments. One of the areas of compromise was the additional pension liability.

Required

Explain how the additional pension liability is calculated and describe any aspects that might be considered to be the result of compromises.

C20-7 Income Smoothing

Generally, accounting principles do not support the concept of income smoothing (the avoidance of year-to-year fluctuations in the amount of income). A friend of yours, however, after studying *FASB Statement No. 87*, claims, "Pension accounting includes income smoothing."

Required

Describe the methods by which *FASB Statement No. 87* avoids year-to-year fluctuations in the amount of pension expense.

C20-8 Pension Issues

The MacAdams Company had engaged in large amounts of R&D to develop a new product that would put the company ahead of its Japanese competition. As a result, the company's profits were severely reduced and the president was concerned about the possibility of a takeover by a European competitor. The president was discussing the situation with the controller and said, "Your accounting principles make me so mad. Here we are working hard to develop a product to beat the rest of the world and you won't let me treat any of those costs as an asset."

The controller replied, "I understand your frustration. And please remember they are not 'my' principles."

"I know," responded the president. "Do you have any suggestions?"

"Well," the controller replied, "we can't adjust R&D expense, but we can reduce our pension expense. One easy way to increase our profits would be for the board of directors to vote to increase the discount rate used for computing the present values and to increase the expected rate of return on plan assets. Both of those would have the effect of reducing the pension expense."

"Great idea. I will have to remember that when it is time for the year-end bonuses."

Required

Write a short report evaluating the controller's suggestion.

C20-9 OPEB Issues

"Will it cost your company your company? Ready for one of the most difficult challenges ever to confront corporate America? One that is estimated to cost up to $400 billion. New FASB regulations will force companies to measure and post as a debit their health expense obligation to current and *future* retirees. . . . We'll help you minimize the financial impact of these regulations and still enable you to remain responsive to the benefit needs of employees." (Excerpts from an advertisement by CIGNA, a large insurance company.)

"Forget about retiring with all-expenses-paid health care from your employer. About 65% of U.S. companies have reduced benefits. Some have asked retirees to pay more of the costs, while others have eliminated the plans altogether. Blame soaring medical expenses and a new accounting rule that requires companies to post long-term retiree medical benefits as liabilities on their balance sheets." (Adapted from *Business Week*, August 24, 1992, p. 39.)

Required

1. Critically evaluate the content of the advertisement.
2. Explain why companies may have reduced benefits when they adopted *FASB Statement No. 106*.

C20-10 OPEBs and Deferred Income Taxes

The following information is for the Dermer Company's OPEB plan, which it adopted on January 1, 2007:

Service cost, 2007	$100,000
Interest cost, 2007	20,000
Unrecognized prior service cost, 1/1/07	300,000
Benefits paid to employees, 2007	18,000
Pretax accounting income and taxable income for 2007 before any deductions for OPEB costs	500,000
Average remaining service period	15 years
Enacted tax rate for 2007	30%
Enacted tax rate for 2008 and beyond	35%
Any deferred tax assets are more likely than not to be realized	

Required

1. a. Prepare the journal entries to record the OPEB expense and payments for 2007.
   b. Prepare the income tax journal entry for 2007.
2. a. Assume instead that Dermer had an existing OPEB plan on January 1, 1996, and that the $300,000 was the accumulated postretirement benefit obligation at the date of adoption of *FASB Statement No. 106*,

instead of the unrecognized prior service cost. Prepare the journal entries to record the OPEB expense and payments for 2007 if the company uses the maximum period for the amortization of the transition liability and adopted the *Statement* on January 1, 1996.
   b. Prepare the income tax journal entry for 2007.
   c. What is the balance of the deferred tax asset at December 31, 2007, if it is assumed that in each year since 1996 pretax accounting income and taxable income before any deductions for OPEB costs have been $500,000? Also assume that each year, the OPEB expense and payments were the same as in 2007.
3. a. Assume instead that the $300,000 accumulated postretirement benefit obligation was recognized as a cumulative effect. Prepare the journal entries to record the activities related to the OPEB for 2007 if the *Statement* was adopted on January 1, 1996.
   b. Prepare the income tax journal entry for 2007.
   c. What is the balance of the deferred tax asset at December 31, 2007, if it is assumed that in each year since 1996 pretax accounting income and taxable income before any deductions for OPEB costs have been $500,000? Also assume that each year the OPEB expense (before including the cumulative effect adjustment) and payments were the same as in 2007.

C20-11 Analyzing Coca-Cola's Postemployment Benefit Disclosures

Refer to the financial statements and related notes of The Coca-Cola Company in Appendix A of this book. Answer each of the questions for (a) the company's pension benefits and (b) the company's other benefits.

Required

1. How much is the company's expense in 2004?
2. How much are the company's actual and expected return on plan assets?
3. How much is the benefit obligation at December 31, 2004?
4. Is the company in a net asset or liability position at December 31, 2004? Is this net amount greater or less than the net asset or liability reported on the balance sheet?
5. Conceptually, what were the effects of the decrease in the discount rate in 2004 on the amounts disclosed by the company (no calculations are required)?

C20-12 Ethics and Pensions

You are an accountant for the Lanthier Company. The president of the company calls you into the office and says, "We have to find a way to reduce our pension costs. They are too high and they are making us uncompetitive against our foreign competitors whose employees have state-funded pensions. I think we might have to abandon our defined benefit plan, but I know the employees would not be happy about that. I was also thinking that perhaps we could raise the discount rate we use up to the high end of the acceptable range. I also think we need a trustee who will pursue a more aggressive investment strategy for the pension funds; that way we can raise our expected rate of return."

Required

From financial reporting and ethical perspectives, discuss the issues raised by this situation.

Accounting for Leases

OBJECTIVES

After reading this chapter, you will be able to:

1   Explain the advantages of leasing.

2   Understand key terms related to leasing.

3   Explain how to classify leases of personal property.

4   Account for a lessee's operating and capital leases.

5   Understand disclosures by the lessee.

6   Account for a lessor's operating, direct financing, and sales-type leases.

7   Understand disclosures by the lessor.

8   Explain the conceptual issues regarding leases.

9   Understand lease issues related to real estate, sale-leaseback issues, leveraged leases, and changes in lease provisions. (Appendix).

Leasing—An Important Driver of the Economy

Leasing is an increasingly popular form of capital investment. Businesses lease many different assets including office equipment, medical equipment, and manufacturing machinery. Without the ability to lease, companies would find it more difficult to acquire the necessary capital and equipment which, in turn, would adversely affect business and economic growth. Attempting to capture the impact of equipment leasing on the U.S. economy, a 2004 study prepared for the Equipment Leasing Association estimates that equipment leasing contributed between $100 billion and $300 billion in real gross domestic product (GDP) annually. Furthermore, the study estimates that the equipment leasing industry is responsible for between 3 million and 5 million jobs. Clearly, the impact of leasing on our economy is significant.

One industry in which leasing has historically been used to make major capital investments is the airline industry. For example, **Southwest Airlines** leases approximately 21% of its aircraft through operating leases and paid over $400 million in rental expense in 2004. Why would a company choose to enter into an operating lease? First, the leased asset and the related obligation do not appear on the balance sheet. For Southwest, this unrecorded liability related to operating leases was over $2.6 billion. By not recording the leased property and the related obligation, Southwest was

Credit: Sandy Huffaker/Bloomberg News /Landov

able to show a more favorable debt ratio than it otherwise would have shown. Second, even though Southwest had to record rental expense related to the leased airplanes, in general, companies with operating leases report less interest, higher income, and more favorable returns on equity than companies with capital leases. These financial reporting advantages are considered critical to many companies.

However, airlines are not the only industry in which leasing is popular. As many companies make large investments in information technology, they are faced with a decision to lease or buy. To avoid expensive, long-term commitments in an industry for which rapid obsolescence is a problem, many companies are taking a conservative approach to information technology expenditures and turning to leasing. According to the Equipment Leasing Association, the market for leased information technology equipment will grow to $28 billion by 2005.

FOR FURTHER INVESTIGATION

For a discussion of leases, consult the Business & Company Resource Center (BCRC):

- New SEC Lease Accounting Rule Roils Books Again: 2nd Wave of Adjustments Snares Big Players, Poses Stock Delisting Threats for Some. Susan Spielberg, *Nation's Restaurant News*, 0028-0518, April 18, 2005.
- Crackdown on accounting for leases hits earnings. *Miami Daily Business Review*, 1070-6437, March 29, 2005.

Many companies choose to lease an asset rather than to purchase it. **FASB Statement No. 13 as Amended,** defines a lease as **"an agreement conveying the right to use property, plant, or equipment (land or depreciable assets or both) usually for a stated period of time."**[1] A lease involves a lessee and a lessor. **A lessee acquires the right to use the property, plant, and equipment; a lessor gives up the right.**

There are many kinds of leases: short-term, long-term, personal property, real property, cancelable, noncancelable, two-party, three-party, and others. Since it is a contractual agreement, the parties can include in the lease contract any provision that they desire. Many kinds of assets are leased. Among the most popular are cars, photocopiers, computers, airplanes, railroad boxcars, and buildings.

This chapter focuses on long-term noncancelable leases involving depreciable personal property such as equipment, machinery, and trucks. We discuss the lease of real property (land, buildings, and other items attached to the land) and certain other specialized lease issues in the Appendix to this chapter.

ADVANTAGES OF LEASING

1 Explain the advantages of leasing.

The primary disadvantage of leasing is that it is usually more expensive in the long run to lease than to buy. However, for many companies the advantages of leasing outweigh the disadvantages.

Advantages of Leasing from Lessee's Viewpoint

From the lessee's point of view, the advantages may include:

1. *Financing benefits*
   a. The lease provides 100% financing, so that the lessee acquires the asset without having to make a down payment.
   b. The lease contract contains fewer restrictive provisions and is more flexible than other debt agreements.
   c. The leasing arrangement creates a claim that is against only the leased equipment and not against all assets.
2. *Risk benefit.* The lease may reduce the risk of obsolescence, so that the risk is borne by the lessor.
3. *Tax benefit.* By deducting lease payments, the lessee can write off the full cost of the asset, including the part that relates to land. Also, the tax deduction may be accelerated, because it is often spread over the period of the lease rather than the actual economic life of the property.
4. *Financial reporting benefit.* For operating leases the lease does not add a liability or asset to the lessee's balance sheet. Therefore, it does not affect certain financial ratios, such as ratios using debt, and the rate of return. As a result, these ratios tend to be "better" because the leased asset and liability are omitted from the balance sheet. In particular, omitting the liability from the balance sheet may add to the perceived borrowing capacity of the lessee.
5. *Billing benefit.* For certain contract-type work, leasing may permit the contractor to charge more because the interest element contained in the rental payments is allowed as a contract charge, whereas interest on borrowed money to purchase assets usually is not.

Advantage number 4 is critical to some companies. Some leases (called "capital leases") enable lessees to acquire substantially all the risks and benefits associated with asset ownership. If a company can, in substance, acquire an asset without recording it or the

---

1. "Accounting for Leases," *FASB Statement No. 13 as Amended and Interpreted through January 1990* (Norwalk, Conn.: FASB, 1990), sec. L10.101.

liability in its accounts (an "operating" lease), it can greatly improve certain key ratios. The company would be using "off-balance-sheet financing."

Example: Purchasing versus Leasing Assume that in 2007, two identical companies, A and B, have the following financial data prior to any new acquisitions:

Current assets	$2,100,000
Noncurrent assets	2,900,000
Current liabilities	1,000,000
Noncurrent liabilities	1,600,000
Stockholders' equity	2,400,000

On December 31, 2007 Company A purchases equipment with a 10-year life, at a cost of $2,825,112. The company signs a 10-year, 12% note requiring $500,000 to be paid at the end of each year, starting on December 31, 2008. The payments include interest at 12% on the beginning-of-year principal balance. The remainder of each annual payment reduces the principal. Since this transaction is a purchase by the issuance of debt, Company A records the asset purchased and the note payable (part of which is a current liability). Company A's financial data show these changes:

- noncurrent assets increase to $5,725,112 ($2,900,000 + $2,825,112);
- current liabilities increase to $1,446,429 ($1,000,000 + the present value of $500,000 discounted for one year at 12%); and
- noncurrent liabilities increase to $3,978,683 ($1,600,000 + $2,825,112 − current amount of $446,429).

The remaining items do not change. Considering these changes, note the effect on two balance sheet ratios of Company A:

	Before Acquisition	After Acquisition
Current ratio (ratio of current assets to current liabilities)	2.10	1.45[a]
Ratio of debt to stockholders' equity	1.08	2.26[b]

a. Current assets of $2,100,000 divided by current liabilities of $1,446,429 ($1,000,000 + $446,429)
b. Debt of $5,425,112 ($1,446,429 + $3,978,683) divided by stockholders' equity of $2,400,000

The current ratio falls significantly, thus perhaps affecting the willingness of a bank to make a short-term loan. The ratio of debt to stockholders' equity more than doubles. This may affect the perceptions of long-term creditors or stockholders as to the risk of the company. These adverse changes, coupled with the impact that the purchase has on the rate of return on investment in 2008, might impair Company A's borrowing capacity or its ability to sell stock.

Next assume that at the end of 2007, Company B leases identical equipment, agreeing to pay $500,000 rent each year for the next 10 years. If the interest rate is 12%, then the present value of 10 payments of $500,000 discounted at 12% is $2,825,112 ($500,000 × 5.650223).[2] If Company B classifies the lease as a capital lease, it records an asset and a liability and the effects on its balance sheet are the same as the effects of the purchase on Company A's balance sheet. However, if the lease is classified as an operating lease, Company B does not record an asset or a liability. The current ratio after the lease remains at 2.10-to-1 and the ratio of debt to stockholders' equity remains at 1.08-to-1. Also, the rate of return on investment in 2008 (assuming that plant expansion was profitable) is significantly higher than for Company A, even though Company B acquires equipment identical to that acquired by Company A.

In summary, two virtually identical economic events are reported very differently in the financial statements of the two companies. Today, many companies lease certain

---

2. The present value calculations in this chapter use factors from the tables in the Time Value of Money module.

assets, but some prefer to structure the lease agreement to avoid capitalizing the lease payments (where required by *FASB Statement No. 13 as Amended*) because of the impact that reporting the asset and liability on the balance sheet has on key ratios. ♦

The preceding discussion is based on the lessee's point of view. The opposite effect occurs in regard to the lessor. Thus, for an operating lease, the asset remains on the lessor's balance sheet. The lessor also recognizes rent revenue periodically, usually at an amount equal to the amount of the rent receipts. For a capital lease, the lessor treats the asset as "sold" and records the related receivable. These alternatives affect significant ratios of the lessor.

Advantages of Leasing from Lessor's Viewpoint

From the lessor's point of view, the chief advantages are that leasing provides (1) a way of indirectly making a sale, and (2) an alternative means of obtaining a profit opportunity in a transaction that enables the lessor company to transfer an asset by the lease agreement. This transfer also permits the lessor to earn a rate of return in the form of interest on the selling price of the leased asset.

KEY TERMS RELATED TO LEASING

2 Understand key terms related to leasing.

FASB Statement No. 13 as Amended defines a number of terms that are used in leasing arrangements. We list these terms in Exhibit 21-1 because they are necessary for an understanding of accounting for leases.[3] You should study the terms now and carefully review each one as we introduce it in the chapter.

CLASSIFICATION OF PERSONAL PROPERTY LEASES

3 Explain how to classify leases of personal property.

We discuss the classification and accounting for leasing of personal property (mostly for equipment) here. We summarize the variations involving real property (land, buildings, and other property attached to the land) in the Appendix to this chapter.

The basic concept of *FASB Statement No. 13 as Amended* is that **a lease that transfers substantially all the risks and benefits of ownership is in substance a purchase by the lessee and a sale by the lessor and is a** *capital* **lease.** A lease that does *not* transfer substantially all the risks and benefits of ownership is an **operating lease.** Using the concept of economic substance over legal form (as we discussed in Chapters 5 and 18), a transaction that transfers substantially all the risks and benefits of ownership is an asset acquisition and a liability incurrence by the lessee. For the lessor, it is either a sale of an asset and the creation of a financing instrument (a sales-type lease) or just the creation of a financing instrument (a direct financing lease). The *Statement* provides criteria for determining the classification of leases by both the lessee and the lessor, as we show in Exhibit 21-2. We list the criteria that relate to the transfer of the risks and benefits of ownership in Column A. We list the criteria that relate to revenue recognition in Column B.

By using the criteria we show in Exhibit 21-2, a **lessee** classifies a lease as one of two types: (1) capital lease, or (2) operating lease. A lease that meets any *one* of the four criteria listed in Column A of Exhibit 21-2 is a *capital lease* for the lessee. Since the transfer of substantially all the risks and benefits of ownership is considered to have occurred, the lessee treats the lease as, in substance, a purchase of an asset and the creation of an accompanying liability. If the lease meets *none* of the four criteria, a transfer of the risks and benefits is considered *not* to have occurred, making the lease an *operating lease*. In this case, the lessee does *not* recognize an asset or a liability.

By using the criteria listed in Exhibit 21-2, a **lessor** classifies a lease as one of three types: (1) sales-type lease, (2) direct financing lease, or (3) operating lease. A lease that meets any *one* of the four criteria listed in Column A and *both* criteria in Column B of Exhibit 21-2 is either a sales-type or a direct financing lease for the lessor. The lease is a

---

3.   Adapted from *FASB Statement No. 13 as Amended and Interpreted through January 1990, op. cit.,* sec. L10.401–.424.

EXHIBIT 21-1	**Key Terms Related to Leasing**

Bargain purchase option. A provision allowing the lessee to purchase the leased property at the end of the life of the lease at a price so favorable that the exercise of the option appears, at the inception of the lease, to be reasonably assured.

Bargain renewal option. A provision allowing the lessee to renew the lease for a rental that is so favorable that the exercise of the option by the lessee appears, at the inception of the lease, to be reasonably assured.

Estimated economic life of leased property. Regardless of the lease term, the estimated remaining period during which the property is expected to be usable for the purpose that was intended at the inception of the lease, with normal repairs and maintenance.

Estimated residual value of leased property. The estimated fair value of the leased property at the end of the lease term. (Note that this value is a different concept from the estimated residual value at the end of the *economic* life of the property.)

Executory costs. Ownership-type costs, such as insurance, maintenance, and property taxes. These costs may be paid either by the lessor or the lessee. Normally, it is expected that the cost should be borne by the party to the contract who controls the asset essentially in the manner of an owner.

Fair value of leased property. The price for which the property could be sold in an arm's length transaction between unrelated parties. If the lessor is a manufacturer or dealer, the fair value of the property at the inception of the lease is normally the selling price. If the lessor is not a manufacturer or dealer, the fair value is usually the cost of the asset to the lessor.

Guaranteed residual value. The portion of the estimated residual value of the leased property that is guaranteed by the lessee or by a third party unrelated to the lessor.

Inception of the lease. The date of the lease agreement; or, if the leased property is being constructed, the date that title passes to the lessor.

Initial direct costs. Costs incurred by the lessor to originate a lease that (1) result directly from acquiring that lease, and (2) would not have been incurred had that leasing transaction not occurred. These costs also include costs directly related to specified activities performed by the lessor for that lease, such as evaluating the lessee's financial condition, negotiating lease terms, preparing and processing lease documents, and closing the transaction.

Interest rate implicit in the lease. The interest (discount) rate that, when applied on a present value basis to the sum of the minimum lease payments and any unguaranteed residual value accruing to the lessor, causes the resulting total present value to be equal to the fair value of the leased property to the lessor.

Lease receivable. The sum of the undiscounted (1) *minimum lease payments* plus (2) any unguaranteed residual value accruing to the benefit of the lessor at the end of the lease. Sometimes called *gross investment in the lease*.

Lease term. The fixed, noncancelable term of the lease plus (1) any periods covered by bargain renewal options, (2) any periods for which failure to renew the lease imposes a significant penalty on the lessee, (3) any periods covered by ordinary renewal options preceding the exercise date of a bargain purchase option, and (4) any periods during which the lessor has the option to renew or to extend the lease. The lease term, however, in no case extends beyond the date a bargain purchase option becomes exercisable.

Lessee's incremental borrowing rate. The rate that, at the inception of the lease, the lessee would have incurred to borrow, over a similar term, the cash necessary to purchase the leased property.

Manufacturer's or dealer's profit or loss. This profit or loss is the difference between the following two items: (1) the fair value of the property at the inception of the lease, and (2) the cost or carrying amount of the leased asset.

Minimum lease payments. These are the payments that are required to be paid by the lessee to the lessor over the life of the lease. Specifically, for a lease that contains a *bargain purchase option*, the minimum lease payments include (1) the minimum periodic payments required by the lease over the lease term, and (2) the payment required by the bargain purchase option. Otherwise, the minimum lease payments include (1) the minimum periodic payments plus (2) any guaranteed residual value, and (3) any payments on failure to renew or extend the lease. Executory costs are *not* included in minimum lease payments.

Unguaranteed residual value. The portion of the estimated residual value of the leased property that is not guaranteed by the lessee or by a third party unrelated to the lessor.

Unreimbursable cost. These costs may include commitments by the lessor to guarantee performance of the leased property that is more extensive than the typical product warranty, or to effectively protect the lessee from obsolescence of the leased property. However, estimating executory costs such as insurance, maintenance, and taxes to be paid by the lessor does not by itself constitute an important uncertainty.

sales-type lease if it results in a manufacturer's or dealer's profit (or loss). Otherwise, it is a *direct financing lease*. Since the transfer of the risks and benefits of ownership has occurred and the revenue recognition criteria are met, the lessor treats the lease as a sale of an asset and the creation of an accompanying receivable. The lease is an *operating lease* only if the lease meets *none* of the four criteria *or* fails *one* of the revenue recognition criteria. In this case, the lessor does *not* recognize a sale or a receivable, and the leased asset remains on its balance sheet along with the related depreciation on its income statement. We summarize the criteria and alternative classifications in Exhibit 21-3 using a flow chart. Exhibit 21-7 includes a summary of the accounting principles used by the lessee and lessor.

EXHIBIT 21-2   Classification of Leases Involving Personal Property

I. General criteria for classifying leases

Column A **Criteria Applicable to Both Lessee and Lessor**	**Column B** **Criteria Applicable to Lessor Only**
A. The lease transfers ownership of the property to the lessee by the end of the lease term.	A. The collectibility of the minimum lease payments is reasonably assured (i.e., predictable).
B. The lease contains a bargain purchase option.	B. No important uncertainties surround the amount of unreimbursable costs yet to be incurred by the lessor under the the lease.
C. The lease term is equal to 75% or more of estimated economic life of the leased property.[a]	
D. The present value of the minimum lease payments is equal to 90% or more of the fair value of the leased property to the lessor.[a]	

II. Classification by the lessee
   A. *Capital lease.* Lease that meets *one or more* of the criteria in Column A (Part I).
   B. *Operating lease.* Lease that does *not* meet any of the criteria in Column A (Part I). In other words, all leases other than capital leases are operating leases.

III. Classification by the lessor[b]
   A. *Sales-type lease.* Lease that meets these three criteria:
       1. *One or more* of the four criteria listed in Column A (Part I), *and*
       2. *Both* of the criteria listed in Column B (Part I), *and*
       3. It must result in a manufacturer's or dealer's profit (or loss) to the lessor. A profit (loss) exists when the fair value of the leased property at the inception of the lease is greater (less) than its cost or carrying value.
   B. *Direct financing lease.* Lease that meets these three criteria:
       1. *One or more* of the four criteria listed in Column A (Part I), *and*
       2. *Both* of the criteria listed in Column B (Part I), *and*
       3. It must *not* result in a manufacturer's or dealer's profit (or loss) to the lessor.
   C. *Operating lease.* Lease that meets none of the criteria in Column A (Part I) or that does *not* meet both of the criteria in Column B. In other words, all leases other than sales-type or direct financing leases are operating leases.

a. Items C and D do not apply if the beginning of the lease term falls within the last 25% of the total estimated economic life. This qualification was added by the FASB to prevent the possible manipulation of the kinds of leases that may result from renewal options. For example, without this qualification, for a tank car having an estimated useful life of 25 years and placed under five successive 5-year leases, the first four leases would be classified as operating leases and the last lease would be classified as a capital lease.
b. A fourth type of lease, from the lessor's viewpoint, is the leveraged lease. This type of lease is a special three-party lease which we discuss in the Appendix to this chapter.

SECURE YOUR KNOWLEDGE 21-1

• Compared to buying, leasing is usually more expensive in the long run; however, many companies choose to lease because of benefits related to less costly financing, reduced risk, lower taxes, off-balance-sheet financing, or higher billing rates.

(continued)

- From the lessor's viewpoint, the benefits of leasing may be the ability to indirectly make a sale and earn additional profit (interest) on the leased asset.
- The underlying concept used in classifying leases is based on substance over form:
  - A lease that transfers substantially all the risks and benefits of ownership is a capital lease and is accounted for as a purchase by the lessee and as a sale by the lessor.
  - A lease that does not transfer substantially all of the risks and benefits of ownership is an operating lease and is accounted for as a rental agreement.
- If a lease meets one of the four criteria in column A of Exhibit 21-2, the lessee classifies the lease as a capital lease and records an asset and a related liability; otherwise the lessee classifies the lease as an operating lease.
- If the lease meets one of the four criteria in column A of Exhibit 21-2 and both criteria in column B of Exhibit 21-2, the lessor classifies the lease as a:
  - Sales-type lease if the fair value of the leased property at the inception of the lease differs from its cost or carrying value (profit or loss exists), or a
  - Direct financing lease if there is no manufacturer's or dealer's profit or loss at the inception of the lease.

  Otherwise, the lessor classifies the lease as an operating lease.

LINK TO ETHICAL DILEMMA

Save-A-Lot, Inc. is a national retailer that specializes in selling a variety of household products at low cost. As a former auditor assigned to the Save-A-Lot audit, you were recently approached to become the controller for the company. After accepting the position, you began a review of several areas of operating risk faced by the company. During this review you noted that the company made extensive use of operating leases for its 3,000 retail stores as well as the majority of its property, plant, and equipment. During a meeting with the CFO to discuss this issue, the CFO stated that the company, like many retailers, has chosen to lease many of its assets due to the advantages of leasing. In particular, the CFO stated that the financial reporting benefits are particularly attractive. If the company were forced to record an asset and liability for the assets currently under operating leases, its debt ratio would be so adversely affected that the company would face considerable difficulty in attempting to obtain debt financing, putting the future of the company in considerable doubt. While you understand these benefits, you are particularly concerned that many of Save-A-Lot's operating leases for its more profitable stores will soon expire. Based on your knowledge of the real estate markets in these areas, you question whether the company will be successful in renewing the leases. The CFO stated that the renewals will not be a problem because she has personally executed side agreements for all of the company's operating leases that will require Save-A-Lot to renew the leases indefinitely. If these side agreements were included in the original lease agreements, the company would be forced to classify the leases as capital leases. However, by having the renewal option contained in a separate contract, the company is able to classify the leases as operating leases.

You are shocked by this admission. When you audited Save-A-Lot, you personally reviewed the lease documents and were never made aware of the side agreements. If you had been aware of their existence, you certainly would have insisted that the two contracts were, in substance, one contract and demanded that the company reclassify the leases as capital leases. To insist at this point that the company reclassify the leases would most certainly cost you your current job with Save-A-Lot, and the fact that you never discovered these side agreements may lead others to perceive you as an incompetent auditor which would make finding another job extremely difficult. What course of action do you take?

EXHIBIT 21-3 **Lease Criteria and Classifications**

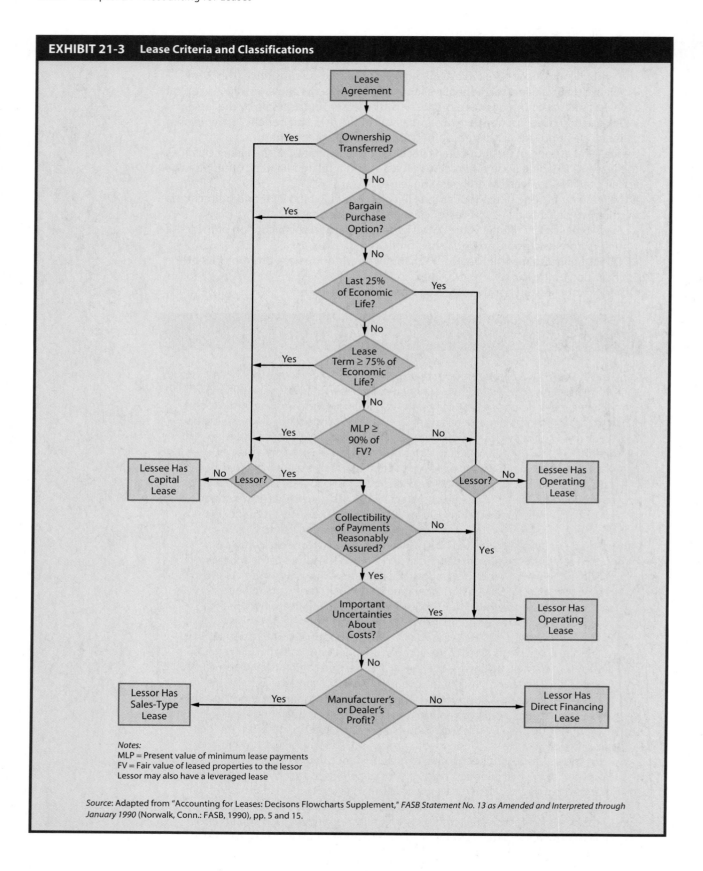

Notes:
MLP = Present value of minimum lease payments
FV = Fair value of leased properties to the lessor
Lessor may also have a leveraged lease

Source: Adapted from "Accounting for Leases: Decisons Flowcharts Supplement," *FASB Statement No. 13 as Amended and Interpreted through January 1990* (Norwalk, Conn.: FASB, 1990), pp. 5 and 15.

ACCOUNTING AND REPORTING BY A LESSEE

We include examples of accounting for leases by the lessee in this section. We will discuss accounting for leases by the lessor later in the chapter.

4 Account for a lessee's operating and capital leases.

Example: Operating Lease (Lessee)

Assume that a lease agreement signed between the User Company and the Owner Company contains the terms and provisions we list in Example 21-1. The lease does not transfer ownership or provide a bargain purchase option, and the lease term is 50% of the economic life. In addition, the present value of the minimum lease payments is $201,867, as we show in Example 21-1, which is only 67% of the fair value of the property. Therefore, this lease is an operating lease for the lessee because it does not meet any of the four criteria from Exhibit 21-2 (column A) (i.e., the risks and benefits are not transferred to the lessee), as we summarize in Example 21-2.

EXAMPLE 21-1   **Terms and Provisions of Lease Agreement Between Owner Company (Lessor) and User Company (Lessee) Dated January 1, 2007**

1. The lease term is five years. The lease is noncancelable and requires equal payments of $50,000 at the beginning of each year.
2. The cost, and also fair value, of the equipment to the Owner Company at the inception of the lease is $300,000. The equipment has an estimated economic life of 10 years and has a zero estimated residual value at the end of this time.
3. There is no guarantee of the residual value by the User Company.
4. The Owner Company agrees to pay all executory costs.
5. The equipment reverts to the Owner Company at the end of the five years. That is, the lease contains no bargain purchase option and no agreement to transfer ownership at the end of the lease.
6. The User Company's incremental borrowing rate is 12.5% per year.
7. For the Owner Company, the interest rate implicit in the lease is 12%.
8. The present value of an annuity due (in advance) of five payments of $50,000 each at 12% is $201,867 (4.037349 × $50,000 = $201,867.45).

EXAMPLE 21-2   **Application of Lease Classification Criteria by User (Lessee)**

Classification Criteria	Criteria Met?	Remarks
1. Transfer of ownership at end of lease	No	
2. Bargain purchase option	No	
3. Lease term is 75% or more of economic life	No	It is 50% (5 years ÷ 10 years)
4. Present value of minimum lease payments is 90% or more of fair value	No	The present value is $201,867.45, or 67% of the $300,000 fair value

Decision: A capital lease must meet one or more of the classification criteria; otherwise the lease is an operating lease.
Conclusion: The lease is an operating lease. It does no meet any of the criteria.

The only journal entry recorded by the User Company is the following, which it makes each year on January 1, 2007 through 2011.

Rent Expense	50,000	
Cash		50,000

If the company prepares monthly or quarterly interim statements, it reports the unexpired portion of the expense as an asset, Prepaid Rent. A lessee does not report the rented equipment in its balance sheet; however, it discloses the future minimum rental payments and other information in the notes to its financial statements, as we discuss at the end of this section. ♦

Capital Lease (Lessee)

When equipment is leased under a capital lease (i.e., the risks and benefits are transferred to the lessee), **the lessee records an asset and a liability equal to the sum of the present value, at the beginning of the lease term, of the minimum lease payments during the lease term.**[4] In accounting for the asset and liability, the lessee must consider the executory costs, the discount rate, amortization of the leased asset, and reduction of the lease obligation.

Executory Costs

Ownership-type costs such as insurance, maintenance, and property taxes are called **executory costs.** Executory costs may be *paid* by either the lessee or the lessor, depending on how the lease contract is written. However, since the risks and benefits of ownership have been transferred in a capital lease, the *lessee* usually *incurs* these costs. Many capital leases provide for the *lessee* to pay the executory costs directly. In these cases, the lessee expenses the executory costs as incurred. The lessee computes the values of the asset and liability by discounting the minimum lease payments without including the executory costs. Each lease payment includes the interest cost and the reduction of the lease liability.

Alternatively, the lessor may pay the executory costs and add the amount to determine the periodic lease amounts. Then the lessee *excludes* that portion of each lease payment that covers these executory costs from the minimum lease payments, and therefore from any present value calculations. That is, **the minimum lease payment is the lease payment minus the executory costs paid by the lessor.** The reason is that part of the lease payment is a reimbursement by the lessee of the executory costs paid by the lessor. The remainder of the payment is the interest cost and the reduction of the lease liability. If the executory costs are not specifically stated in the lease contract, the lessee estimates the amount of the executory costs included in each lease payment in order to determine the amount to subtract from each lease payment before computing the present value. The lessee expenses the portion of the total lease payment that is for the executory costs.

Discount Rate

The lessee computes the present value of the minimum lease payments by using the *lower* of:

1. *The lessee's incremental borrowing rate,* or
2. *The lessor's interest rate implicit in the lease,* if known by the lessee (or if it is practicable for the lessee to learn).[5]

Since the lessee is acquiring an asset, the rate it uses to borrow money to acquire an asset (the incremental borrowing rate) is appropriate. Alternatively, if it knows the rate in the contract (the implicit rate) and this rate is lower than the incremental borrowing rate, it is

---

4. *Ibid.*, sec. L10.106. Note also that the lessee must not record the asset at an amount that exceeds its fair value.
5. *Ibid.*, sec. L10.103.

a more relevant rate to use. The lessor may disclose its implicit rate. If it does not, the lessee can compute the implicit rate if there is a guaranteed residual value, a bargain purchase option, or if it knows the lessor's estimate of the unguaranteed residual value. If the lessee does not know any of these amounts, it does not have enough information to compute the implicit rate. If the lessor does not disclose the implicit rate and the lessee cannot compute it, the lessee would use its incremental borrowing rate.

Amortization (Depreciation) of Leased Asset

Since the lessee records an asset, it must compute amortization. The FASB uses the term *amortization* rather than *depreciation*, because the leased asset technically is an intangible asset. However, the lessee often includes the leased asset in the property, plant, and equipment section of its balance sheet. Either term can be used to name the expense. If the asset is written off over the estimated economic life of the property, the term that is usually used is *depreciation*. If the asset is written off over a shorter period of time (the term of the lease), the process is more often referred to as *amortization*. For simplicity, we use *depreciation* in this chaper.

Regardless of which term is used, if the capital lease agreement (1) transfers ownership of the asset to the lessee, or (2) contains a bargain purchase option, the lessee depreciates the asset over its estimated *economic* life to its estimated residual value. The lessee uses the estimated economic life because it expects to acquire ownership of the asset.

If the capital lease does not transfer ownership of the asset to the lessee or if it does not contain a bargain purchase option, the lessee depreciates the leased asset over the lease life because its rights to the use of the asset cease at the end of the lease. It depreciates the leased asset down to its guaranteed residual value at the end of the lease term.[6] The lessee uses a depreciation method that is consistent with its normal policy for similar, owned assets. We summarize the depreciation of leased property by the lessee (or the lessor if there is an operating lease) in Exhibit 21-4 on page 1076, using a flow chart.

Reduction of the Lease Obligation

Since the lessee records a liability, it computes interest expense and the reduction of the principal for each lease payment using the effective interest method (also called the interest method). This method produces a constant rate of interest on the outstanding balance of the lease obligation at the beginning of each period.

Examples of Lessee's Capital Lease Method

We provide several examples of capital lease transactions of the lessee in the following sections.

Example: Equipment Is Leased Without a Transfer of Ownership or Bargain Purchase Option

Assume that the Martin Company (the lessee) and the Gardner Leasing Company (the lessor) sign a lease agreement dated January 1, 2007 in which the Martin Company leases a piece of equipment from the Gardner Leasing Company beginning January 1, 2007. The lease contains the terms and provisions we show in Example 21-3 on page 1077.

First, Martin Company (the lessee) determines that the lease is a capital lease, as we show in Example 21-4 on page 1077. Since it is a capital lease, the lessee records the leased asset at the present value of the minimum lease payments (the lessee pays the executory costs). This amount does not exceed the fair value. The discount rate is 12%, the interest rate implicit in the lease. We assume that the lessee knows this rate and the rate is lower than its incremental borrowing rate of 12.5%.

---

6. *Ibid.*, sec. L10.107.

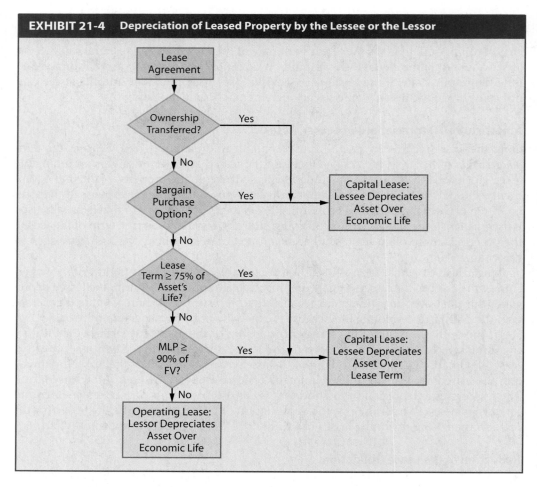

EXHIBIT 21-4   Depreciation of Leased Property by the Lessee or the Lessor

The Martin Company (the lessee) records the acquisition of the leased asset, the depreciation, and the minimum lease payments for two years as follows:

1. *Initial Recording of Capital Lease on January 1, 2007*

Leased Equipment	100,000.00	
Capital Lease Obligation		100,000.00

   The accounting methods we use in this chapter are those recommended by *FASB Statement No. 13 as Amended*. The *Statement* uses the $100,000 "net" present value for both the asset and the liability rather than the "gross" value of $131,693.80 (4 × $32,923.45). It is acceptable, however, for the lessee to record the liability at the gross amount with an accompanying debit to a contra-liability account, Discount on Capital Lease Obligation, for $31,693.80. This alternative procedure may be useful when the lessee prepares the required disclosures that we discuss later.

2. *First Annual Payment and Recognition of Interest Expense on Capital Lease on December 31, 2007*

Interest Expense	12,000.00	
Capital Lease Obligation	20,923.45	
Cash		32,923.45

   The annual payment is $32,923.45. This amount is

   - a payment of interest of $12,000 (12% × $100,000), and
   - a reduction of the lease obligation liability of $20,923.45 ($32,923.45 − $12,000).

   Note that this lease requires the payment to be made at the end of the year. Thus, the annuity is an ordinary annuity. If the lease requires the payments to be made at

EXAMPLE 21-3 | Terms and Provisions of Lease Agreement Between Gardner Leasing Company (Lessor) and Martin Company (Lessee) Dated January 1, 2007

1. The lease term is four years. The lease is noncancelable and requires equal payments of $32,923.45 at the end of each year.
2. The cost, and also fair value, of the equipment to the Gardner Leasing Company at the inception of the lease is $100,000. The equipment has an estimated economic life of four years and has a zero estimated residual value at the end of this time.
3. There is no guarantee of the residual value by the Martin Company.
4. The Martin Company agrees to pay all executory costs.
5. The equipment reverts to the Gardner Leasing Company at the end of the four years; that is, the lease contains no transfer of ownership or bargain purchase option.
6. The Martin Company's incremental borrowing rate is 12.5% per year.
7. The Martin Company uses the straight-line method to record depreciation on similar equipment.
8. For the Gardner Leasing Company, the interest rate implicit in the lease is 12%. The Martin Company knows this rate.
9. The present value of an ordinary annuity of four payments of $32,923.45 each at 12% is $100,000 (3.037349 × $32,923.45 = $100,000). (This is the only present value calculation necessary, since there is no guaranteed residual value or bargain purchase option.)

EXAMPLE 21-4 Application of Lease Classification Criteria by Martin Company (Lessee)

Classification Criteria	Criteria Met?	Remarks
1. Transfer of ownership at end of lease	No	Title reverts to lessor
2. Bargain purchase option	No	
3. Lease term is 75% or more of economic life	Yes	100% of estimated life
4. Present value of minimum lease payments is 90% or more of fair value	Yes	The present value is $100,000, or 100% of fair value

Decision: A capital lease must meet one or more of the classification criteria; otherwise, the lease is an operating lease.
Conclusion: The lease is a capital lease. It meets two of the four criteria.

the beginning of the year, the annuity is an annuity due (which we show later in this chapter).

3. *Recognition of Annual Depreciation of Leased Equipment on December 31, 2007*

Depreciation Expense: Leased Equipment	25,000.00	
Accumulated Depreciation:		
Leased Equipment		25,000.00

The lessee depreciates the asset over the lease term because the lease does not include a transfer of ownership or a bargain purchase option. The lessee uses the straight-line method, and the annual depreciation is $25,000 ($100,000 ÷ 4). The lessee credits an Accumulated Depreciation account.

On the balance sheet of Martin Company (the lessee) for December 31, 2007, it includes the Leased Equipment less the Accumulated Depreciation in the property, plant, and equipment section of its assets. It divides the Capital Lease Obligation between current liabilities and long-term liabilities, as we discuss in the next section.

4. *Second Annual Payment and Recognition of Interest Expense on December 31, 2008*

Interest Expense	9,489.19	
Capital Lease Obligation	23,434.26	
Cash		32,923.45

The amount of the second payment is the same as that for 2007, but the payment for interest is the effective rate of 12% multiplied by the balance of the lease obligation at the beginning of 2008.

- The interest is 12% × $79,076.55 ($100,000 − $20,923.45), or $9,489.19.
- The remainder of the annual payment is the reduction of the principal of $23,434.26 ($32,923.45 − $9,489.19).

Example 21-5 shows the interest expense and the reduction of the capital lease obligation over the life of the lease.

EXAMPLE 21-5   Summary of Lease Payments in Arrears and Interest Expense of Martin Company (Lessee)

(1) Date	(2) Annual Lease Payment	(3) Interest at 12% on Unpaid Obligation[a]	(4) Reduction of Capital Lease Obligation[b]	(5) Balance of Capital Lease Obligation[c]
January 1, 2007	—	—	—	$100,000.00
December 31, 2007	$32,923.45	$12,000.00	$20,923.45	79,076.55
December 31, 2008	32,923.45	9,489.19	23,434.26	55,642.29
December 31, 2009	32,923.45	6,677.07	26,246.38	29,395.91
December 31, 2010	32,923.45	3,527.54[d]	29,395.91	—

a. Column 5 at beginning of year × 12%
b. Column 2 − Column 3
c. Column 5 at beginning of year − Column 4
d. Adjusted for rounding error of $0.03

5. *Recognition of Annual Depreciation on December 31, 2008*

Depreciation Expense: Leased Equipment	25,000.00	
Accumulated Depreciation:		
Leased Equipment		25,000.00

Under the straight-line method, the depreciation entry for 2008 is the same as that for 2007.

The journal entries through 2010 follow a pattern similar to those presented for 2007 and 2008. For simplicity, we did not include the journal entries to record the payment of executory costs such as insurance, maintenance, and property taxes. A lessee records these types of costs in regular operating expense accounts. For example, if the Martin Company pays $3,000 for repairs on the leased equipment during 2007, it would record the payment as a debit to Repair Expense. ♦

Classification of Capital Lease Obligation

When a lessee classifies its capital lease obligation on its balance sheet, it considers the usual criteria for classifying the lease as current or noncurrent.[7] Since the FASB provided no guidelines to measure the respective amounts, a lessee may use two approaches to measure the amount of the current liability: (1) the present value of next year's payments, and (2) the change in the present value.[8]

Present Value of Next Year's Payments

Under the present value of next year's payments approach, the amount of the lessee's current liability is the payment(s) the lessee will make in the next year discounted to the

7. *Ibid.*, sec. L10.112.
8. R. J. Swieringa, "When Current Is Noncurrent and Vice Versa!", *The Accounting Review* (January 1984), pp. 123–130.

balance sheet date. For the Martin Company, the current liability each year is $29,395.93 (0.892857 × $32,923.45). The remaining portion of the obligation is classified as a noncurrent liability. This approach reports the same current liability each year for a given lease. It is conceptually sound and consistent with the theoretical measurement of liabilities in general. In this chapter we use the present value of next year's payments to determine the current liability portion of the lease obligation.

Change in the Present Value

The change in present value approach may be used by a lessee to measure the amount of its current liability. In this approach, the current liability is the amount by which the total balance of the lease liability will decrease in the next year. For the Martin Company the current portion of the liability on December 31, 2007 is $23,434.26 ($79,076.55 − $55,642.29); on December 31, 2008 it is $26,246.38 ($55,642.29 − $29,395.91). Note that the current liability on December 31, 2009 (the balance sheet preceding the final year's lease payment) is the same for each approach (with minor differences for rounding).

Example: Lease Payments Are Made at the Beginning of the Year

Assume that all the lease provisions described in Example 21-3 are the same *except* that the Martin Company (the lessee) is required to make the lease payments in advance, on January 1 of each year, and that the *cost* (and also fair value) of the equipment is $112,000. The annuity calculation is now the present value of an *annuity due* rather than that of an ordinary annuity. The value of the asset and the liability is different, as we show in the following calculation:

> **Present Value of Four Payments**
> **of $32,923.45 in Advance at 12% = $32,923.45 × 3.401831**
> **= $112,000 (rounded)**

Example 21-6 shows the information for the interest expense and the reduction of the capital lease obligation for each period. The journal entries through January 1, 2008 are as follows:

1. *Initial Recording of Capital Lease on January 1, 2007*

Leased Equipment	112,000.00	
Capital Lease Obligation		112,000.00

Martin records both the asset and the obligation at the present value.

EXAMPLE 21-6	**Summary of Lease Payments in Advance and Interest Expense of Martin Company (Lessee)**		
(1)	(2)	(3)	(4)
		Interest at 12%	
	Annual Lease	on Unpaid	Balance of Capital Lease
Date	Payment	Obligation[a]	Obligation[b]
January 1, 2007	Before the initial lease payment		$112,000.00
January 1, 2007	$32,923.45		79,076.55
December 31, 2007		$9,489.19	88,565.74[d]
January 1, 2008	32,923.45[c]		55,642.29
December 31, 2008		6,677.07	62,319.36[d]
January 1, 2009	32,923.45		29,395.91
December 31, 2009		3,527.54[e]	32,923.45[d]
January 1, 2010	32,923.45		0

a. Column 4 at beginning of year × 12%.
b. Column 4 at beginning of year − Column 2 + Column 3.
c. Each lease payment, after the initial payment, includes the accrued interest for the previous year.
d. $32,923.45 of this amount is a current liability; it will be paid January 1 of the next year. The remaining amount is a noncurrent liability.
e. Adjusted for $0.03 rounding error.

2. *First Annual Payment in Advance on January 1, 2007*

Capital Lease Obligation	32,923.45	
Cash		32,923.45

The first payment is entirely a reduction of principal, since no interest has accrued. (The preceding two journal entries could be made as one compound entry.)

3. *Recognition of Annual Depreciation of Leased Equipment on December 31, 2007*

Depreciation Expense: Leased Equipment	28,000.00	
Accumulated Depreciation: Leased Equipment		28,000.00

The straight-line depreciation is $112,000 \div 4$ years, or $28,000.

4. *Recognition of Interest Expense on Capital Lease on December 31, 2007*

Interest Expense	9,489.19	
Accrued Interest on Capital Lease Obligation[9]		9,489.19

Even though Martin (the lessee) will not make the next payment until January 1, 2008, the accrual concept requires that the lessee recognize interest expense in the year that it is incurred. In 2007 the amount is $9,489.19, or 12% of $79,076.55 ($112,000 − $32,923.45), as we show in Example 21-6. The lessee separates the Capital Lease Obligation into its current and noncurrent portions in its year-end balance sheet. In the December 31, 2007 balance sheet, it reports $32,923.45 as a current liability and the remaining part, $55,642.29, as a long-term liability.

5. *Second Annual Payment in Advance on January 1, 2008*

Accrued Interest on Capital Lease Obligation	9,489.19	
Capital Lease Obligation	23,434.26	
Cash		32,923.45

The interest applicable to 2008 is $9,489.19, as we show in Example 21-6. The remaining entries follow the pattern of those for 2008. ◆

Other Lessee Capitalization Issues

A lessee may also sign a lease agreement that includes: (1) a bargain purchase option, or (2) a guaranteed residual value.

Impact of Bargain Purchase Option

To show the impact of a bargain purchase option, assume that Redd Company leases equipment for four years and agrees to pay $40,000 at the end of each year. The lease also includes an option to pay $2,000 at the end of the fourth year to purchase the asset. This amount is so much lower than the expected fair value at the end of the fourth year that Redd (the lessee) is reasonably assured of exercising the option. Therefore, it is a bargain purchase option. Redd's incremental borrowing rate is 11%, and the lessor's implicit interest rate is 10%. The cost and fair value of the equipment is $128,160.63. This lease qualifies as a capital lease because there is a bargain purchase option. The lessee records the leased equipment at the present value of the

---

9. If not material, the lessee may credit this amount to the liability account, Capital Lease Obligation.

minimum lease payments (which includes the bargain purchase option) based on the lower 10% rate, calculated as follows:

Present value of the annual payments discounted at 10% ($40,000 × 3.169865)	$126,794.60
Add: Present value of the single sum of $2,000 (the bargain purchase option) discounted at 10% ($2,000 × 0.683013)	1,366.03
Present value of the minimum lease payments	$128,160.63

The lessee records the leased asset as follows:

Leased Equipment	128,160.63	
Capital Lease Obligation		128,160.63

The accounting by the lessee follows the same principles as in the previous capital lease examples, except that the lessee depreciates the Leased Equipment asset amount of $128,160.63 over its estimated *economic life* (not over the term of the lease) to its estimated residual value (*not* the bargain purchase option of $2,000). The lessee reduces the liability account, Capital Lease Obligation, by the effective interest method, as we previously illustrated. However, at the end of the fourth year, it has a balance of $2,000. When the lessee exercises the bargain purchase option, it debits Capital Lease Obligation and credits Cash for $2,000.

Impact of Guaranteed Residual Value

The lessee may agree to guarantee part or all of the residual value. That is, it guarantees that the value of the leased asset at the end of the lease term will be at least the stated amount of the guarantee. If the asset is not worth this guaranteed value, the lessee must pay the lessor any difference between this smaller value and the guaranteed value. A lessor would generally prefer a guaranteed residual value because it transfers the risk associated with the future value of the asset to the lessee. The guaranteed residual value is included in the minimum lease payments. Therefore, the lessee capitalizes the present value of the amount guaranteed.

Example: Guaranteed Residual Value Assume that Karpas Company leases equipment for four years that cost the lessor $147,284.99 (its fair value) and agrees to pay $40,000 at the end of each year. The equipment has an estimated residual value of $30,000 at the end of the fourth year. The Karpas Company agrees to guarantee the entire amount of this residual value (and there is no transfer of ownership or bargain purchase option). Assume an appropriate interest rate of 10%. This lease is a capital lease because the present value of the minimum lease payments ($147,284.99), as we show in the following calculation, is equal to 90% or more of the fair value of the leased property ($147,284.99).

Present value of the annual lease payments discounted at 10% ($40,000 × 3.169865)	$126,794.60
Add: Present value of the single sum of $30,000 (the guaranteed residual value) discounted at 10% ($30,000 × 0.683013)	20,490.39
Present value of minimum lease payments	$147,284.99

The lessee records the leased equipment at the present value of the minimum lease payments (which includes the guaranteed residual value) as follows:

Leased Equipment	147,284.99	
Capital Lease Obligation		147,284.99

The accounting for the lease follows the same principles as in the previous capital lease examples. The lessee depreciates the asset by an appropriate method over the *lease term* down to the guaranteed residual value. It reduces the liability using the effective interest method, so that at the end of the fourth year the liability has a balance of $30,000. The elimination of this balance depends on the condition of the leased asset at the end of the lease term and the terms of the lease agreement. ♦

Example: Disposal Where Lease Has a Guaranteed Residual Value

Based on the previous information, at the beginning of the fifth year the Karpas Company has the following accounts and balances:

Account	Balance
Leased Equipment	$147,284.99 (debit)
Accumulated Depreciation: Leased Equipment	117,284.99 (credit)
Capital Lease Obligation	30,000.00 (credit)

If the fair value of the leased asset is less than $30,000, the lessee may pay part of the liability by returning the asset to the lessor. It then pays the remaining part in cash and recognizes a loss on disposal of the asset. For example, assume that the Karpas Company returns the leased equipment to the lessor. Both the Karpas Company and the lessor agree that the equipment is worth only $20,000. The Karpas Company pays the lessor $10,000 in cash, and records the disposal as follows:

Accumulated Depreciation: Leased Equipment	117,284.99	
Capital Lease Obligation	30,000.00	
Loss on Disposal of Leased Equipment	10,000.00	
Leased Equipment		147,284.99
Cash		10,000.00

If the fair value is more than $30,000, the lessee may pay the liability in full by returning the asset to the lessor. In this case, the lessee does not recognize a gain or loss. Note that the lessee ignores any *unguaranteed* residual value.

Leases may be written with various provisions. For example, the lessee may be required to pay the lessor the full guaranteed residual value (in this case, $30,000) in cash. The lessee then may choose to sell the asset or keep it to use in its operating activities. ♦

Disclosure Requirements of the Lessee

FASB Statement No. 13 as Amended requires certain disclosures by the lessee for both operating and capital leases. We summarize the basic disclosures in Exhibit 21-5. The lessee discloses this information in its balance sheet or in the notes to its financial statements.[10] **Wal-Mart Stores** discloses its lease information in Note 9 of its 2005 financial statements, as we show in Real Report 21-1 on page 1084.

SECURE YOUR KNOWLEDGE 21-2

- A lessee accounts for an operating lease as a rental agreement. The lessee records rent expense each period and does not report the leased equipment nor any related obligation for future payments on the balance sheet.
- For a capital lease, the lessee records the leased asset and a liability equal to the present value of the minimum lease payments at the beginning of the lease term.
  - Executory costs (ownership costs such as insurance, maintenance, and property taxes) are not considered part of the minimum lease payment and are excluded from any present value calculations.
  - The lessee uses the lower of the lessee's incremental borrowing rate or the lessor's interest rate implicit in the lease (if it is known by the lessee) in any present value calculations.

(continued)

---

10. *FASB Statement No. 13 as Amended and Interpreted through January 1990, op. cit.,* sec. L10.112.

- The lessee depreciates the leased asset over its estimated economic life if it expects to acquire the asset at the end of the lease term (e.g., the lease agreement transfers ownership to the lessee or contains a bargain purchase option), or the lease term if the lessor is expected to retain ownership of the leased asset at the end of the lease term.
- Each lease payment consists of interest expense and a reduction of the principal of the recorded liability, computed using the effective interest method.
- The lease obligation is classified as current or noncurrent on the balance sheet using either the (1) present value of next year's payments approach or the (2) change in present value approach.
- If a lease contains a bargain purchase option, the bargain purchase option is viewed as an additional lease payment and is included in the computation of the present value of the minimum lease payments.
- If the lessee guarantees the residual value of the leased asset, it views the guaranteed residual value as an additional payment and includes this amount in the calculation of the present value of the minimum lease payments.

EXHIBIT 21-5 **Disclosure Requirements for Lessee: Operating and Capital Leases**

A. For operating leases having lease terms in excess of one year:
  1. Future minimum rental payments required as of the date of the latest balance sheet presented, for each of the five succeeding fiscal years and in total.
  2. The total of minimum rentals to be received in the future under noncancelable subleases.
B. For all operating leases, rental expense for each period.
C. For capital leases:
  1. The gross amount of assets recorded under capital leases by major classes according to nature or function.
  2. Future minimum lease payments for each of the five succeeding fiscal years and in total with separate deductions from the total (1) for the amount of executory costs included in the minimum lease payments, and (2) for the amount of the imputed interest required to reduce the net minimum lease payments to present value.
  3. The total of minimum sublease rentals to be received in the future under noncancelable subleases.
  4. Assets, accumulated depreciation, depreciation expense, and liabilities.
D. For all leases, a general description of the lessee's leasing arrangements including the following:
  1. The existence and term of renewal or purchase options and escalation clauses.
  2. Restrictions imposed by lease agreements, such as those concerning dividends, additional debt, and further leasing.

ACCOUNTING AND REPORTING BY A LESSOR

Recall that a lessor classifies a lease as follows:

1. *Operating Lease.* A lease that does not meet any of the criteria in Column A or does not meet both of the criteria in Column B of Exhibit 21-2.
2. *Sales-type Lease.* A sales-type lease results in a manufacturer's or dealer's profit (or loss) and meets one or more of the criteria in Column A and both the criteria in Column B of Exhibit 21-2.
3. *Direct Financing Lease.* A direct financing lease does not result in a manufacturer's or dealer's profit (or loss) and meets one or more of the criteria in Column A and both the criteria in Column B of Exhibit 21-2.
4. *Leveraged Lease.* A leveraged lease is a special three-party lease that is always considered to be a direct financing lease. We discuss these leases briefly in the Appendix to this chapter.

6 Account for a lessor's operating, direct financing, and sales-type leases.

We discuss the accounting method for each of the first three leases in the sections following Real Report 21-1.

Real Report 21-1 Wal-Mart Stores: Long-Term Lease Obligations

NOTE 9 (in part)

The Company and certain of its subsidiaries have long-term leases for stores and equipment. Rentals (including, for certain leases, amounts applicable to taxes, insurance, maintenance, other operating expenses, and contingent rentals) under all operating leases were $1.2 billion, $1.1 billion, and $1.1 billion in 2005, 2004, and 2003, respectively. Aggregate minimum annual rentals at January 31, 2005, under noncancelable leases are as follows (in millions):

Fiscal Year	Operating Leases	Capital Leases
2006	$ 730	$ 521
2007	700	514
2008	626	505
2009	578	490
2010	530	468
Thereafter	5,908	3,222
Total minimum rentals	$9,072	5,720
Less estimated executory costs		42
Net minimum lease payments		5,678
Less imputed interest at rates ranging from 4.2% to 14.0%		1,886
Present value of minimum lease payments		$3,792

Certain of the company's leases provide for the payment of contingent rentals based on percentage of sales. Such contingent rentals amounted to $42 million, $46 million, and $51 million in 2005, 2004, and 2003, respectively. Substantially all of the company's store leases have renewal options, some of which may trigger an escalation in rentals.

The company has entered into lease commitments for land and buildings for 46 future locations. These lease commitments with real estate developers provide for minimum rentals ranging from 5–30 years, which if consummated based on current cost estimates, will approximate $30 million annually over the lease terms.

Questions:

1. Why do you think Wal-Mart has chosen to use long-term operating leases instead of buying the assets?
2. What is the present value of the minimum lease payments? Where would this be found on Wal-Mart's balance sheet?
3. If Wal-Mart's operating leases were classified as capital leases, what would the effect be on Wal-Mart's debt ratio? For simplicity, assume that lease payments are made as a single annual payment at the beginning of each year. (On 1/31/05, Wal-Mart's total liabilities were $70,827 million and its total assets were $120,223 million.)

Operating Lease (Lessor)

Under an operating lease, a lessor company leasing an asset to a lessee retains substantially all the risks and benefits of ownership. The lessor includes the leased asset, say equipment, on its balance sheet in a subsection of property, plant, and equipment entitled Plant and Equipment Leased to Others.[11] It also records depreciation on the leased asset and includes it on its income statement. The lessor usually pays executory costs and records the rental receipts as revenue when they become receivable.

---

11. *Ibid.*, sec. L10.111.

Example: Operating Lease (Lessor)   Assume that the Owner Company leases a piece of equipment to User Company for five years under the terms described in Example 21-1 on page 1073. User Company agrees to pay $50,000 at the beginning of each year. In addition, the Owner Company purchased the equipment at a cost of $300,000. The equipment has an estimated life of 10 years and Owner Company uses the straight-line method of depreciation. On January 10, 2007 Owner pays the annual insurance premium of $2,000, and on December 15, 2007 it pays for repairs of $1,500. Assume that there are no initial direct costs involved in this lease. Owner records the preceding information as follows:

1. *Purchase of Equipment to Be Leased on January 1, 2007*

Equipment Leased to Others	300,000	
Cash (or Accounts Payable)		300,000

    We show the purchase of the equipment to reinforce your understanding of its classification. If the company already owned the equipment, in the preceding entry it would credit the Equipment account, and also would reclassify the related Accumulated Depreciation.

2. *Collection of Annual Payment on Operating Lease on January 1, 2007*

Cash	50,000	
Rental Revenue		50,000

    Owner Company collects the annual rental payments at the beginning of each year and records them as revenue. If the amount is receivable at this date but not yet collected, Owner debits a Rent Receivable account. If Owner prepares monthly or quarterly interim statements, it reports the unearned portion of the preceding revenue as a liability, Unearned Rent.

3. *Payment of Annual Insurance Premium on January 10, 2007*

Insurance Expense	2,000	
Cash		2,000

    Under operating leases, the lessor usually pays executory costs such as insurance. It records these costs as operating expenses and matches them against the gross rental revenue.

4. *Payment of Repairs on December 15, 2007*

Repair Expense	1,500	
Cash		1,500

    The repair expense is another example of an executory cost paid by the lessor.

5. *Recognition of Annual Depreciation Expense on December 31, 2007*

Depreciation Expense: Equipment Leased to Others	30,000	
Accumulated Depreciation: Equipment Leased to Others		30,000

    The lessor records depreciation on the leased equipment over its 10-year economic life. It reports the leased equipment and the accompanying accumulated depreciation on its balance sheet. ♦

Initial Direct Costs Involved in an Operating Lease

In the preceding lease example, we assumed that there were no initial direct costs. **Initial direct costs are costs that a lessor incurs directly from originating a lease that it would not have incurred if it had not entered into the lease contract.** For an operating lease, the lessor records these costs as an asset and allocates them as an operating expense in proportion to the rental receipts over the term of the operating lease. This procedure results in an appropriate matching of the initial direct costs as an expense against the rental revenue.

Direct Financing Leases (Lessor)

Under a direct financing lease, the lessor is usually a financial institution (or a financial subsidiary of a company). The lessor "sells" the asset at a fair value equal to its cost or carrying value and records an accompanying receivable. Since there is no manufacturer's or dealer's profit (or loss) in a direct financing lease, **the net amount at which the lessor records the receivable must be equal to the cost or carrying value of the property.** The *net* receivable is equal to the present value of the future lease payments to be received. There are, however, two components of the net receivable (net investment). These are the *gross receivable* (the total undiscounted cash flows) and the *unearned interest* (the interest to be earned over the life of the lease). The gross receivable of the lessor includes the sum of[12]

1. The *undiscounted* minimum lease payments to be received by the lessor, plus
2. Any unguaranteed residual value accruing to the benefit of the lessor.

Note that the gross receivable excludes any executory costs paid by the lessor. However, it includes the residual value, whether guaranteed or unguaranteed. If the residual value is guaranteed, it is included in the minimum lease payments. If it is unguaranteed, it is explicitly included as the second item. The lessor records the difference between the gross receivable (the Lease Receivable[13] account) and the cost or carrying value of the leased property as unearned revenue, with a title such as Unearned Interest: Leases. This account is a contra account and the lessor deducts this account from the Lease Receivable account to determine its net investment in the direct financing lease. The lessor reports this net investment on its balance sheet and divides the amount between the current and noncurrent asset sections. The current asset portion is determined by using the present value of next year's payments approach or by using the change in present value approach, as we explained earlier for the lessee's accounting.

Note that the lessor's accounting according to *FASB Statement No. 13 as Amended* follows the "gross" method whereas, as we discussed earlier, the lessee's follows the "net" method. It is acceptable, however, for the lessor to record the asset at the "net" amount, provided it makes the appropriate disclosures, as we show later. However, the main advantage of recording the receivable at the gross (undiscounted) amounts is that this accounting provides the information for the required disclosures, as we discuss later.

The lessor determines its interest revenue each period using the effective interest method to produce a constant periodic rate of return on the net investment in the lease. At the beginning of the lease, the net investment is equal to the original cost of the asset, if it is new, or the carrying value, if it has been owned in previous periods. **The interest rate implicit in the lease is the rate that, when applied to the gross receivable, will discount that amount to a present value that is equal to the net receivable.** Thus, there are three variables: the present value (the net receivable), the implicit rate, and the future cash flows (the gross receivable). If the lessor knows two of these three variables, it can calculate the third. We show three examples of accounting for a direct financing lease in the following sections.

---

12. *Ibid.*, sec. L10.114.
13. The title "Minimum Lease Payments Receivable" is appropriate when there is a *guaranteed* residual value. The title "Gross Investment in the Lease" is most appropriate if there is an *unguaranteed* residual value, because then the lessor has not "sold" the residual value. For simplicity, we use the title "Lease Receivable."

Example: Direct Financing Lease with No Unguaranteed Residual Value and Payments Made at End of Year

For the first example, we show the accounting by the Gardner Leasing Company (a financial institution) that leases equipment to the Martin Company as shown earlier in Example 21-3 on page 1077. In addition to the items in Example 21-3, assume that:

1. The collectibility of the lease payments is reasonably assured, and there are no uncertainties involved in the lease.
2. There are no initial direct costs of negotiating and closing the lease transaction.

The cost, and fair value, of the equipment is $100,000. The interest rate implicit in the lease is 12% on the net investment. Though given in the data for the lessee, the lessor calculates the annual rental payments it charges the lessee as follows:

$$\text{Annual Payments} = \frac{\text{Present Value Equal to the Cost of Equipment}}{\text{Present Value of an Annuity for 4 Periods at 12\%}}$$

$$= \frac{\$100,000}{3.037349}$$

$$= \$32,923.45$$

As we show in Example 21-7, based on the criteria from Exhibit 21-2 (columns A and B) the lease is a direct financing rather than a sales-type lease because the fair (present) value of the property is equal to its cost.

EXAMPLE 21-7	Application of Lease Classification Criteria by Gardner Leasing Company (Lessor)		
Classification Criteria		**Criteria Met?**	**Remarks**
Column A			
1. Transfer of ownership		No	
2. Bargain purchase option		No	
3. Lease term is 75% or more of economic life		Yes	100% of economic life
4. Present value of minimum lease payments is 90% or more of fair value		Yes	The present value is $100,000, or100% of fair value
Column B			
1. Collectibility reasonably assured		Yes	
2. No uncertainties		Yes	

Decision: If the lease meets one or more of the Column A criteria and both of Column B criteria, and there is no manufacturer's or dealer's profit or loss, it is a direct financing lease.
Conclusion: The lease is a direct financing lease, since appropriate criteria are met and there is no manufacturer's or dealer's profit or loss. The present (fair) value of the lease payments equals the

The lessor records the Lease Receivable at the sum of the undiscounted annual payments to be collected from the lessee plus the undiscounted unguaranteed residual value. Since there are no executory costs or unguaranteed residual value, the Gardner Leasing Company records this asset at $131,693.80 {[4 × ($32,923.45 − $0)] + $0}. The beginning balance of the account, Unearned Interest: Leases, is the difference between the Lease Receivable account and the cost or carrying value of the leased asset.

For the Gardner Leasing Company, this difference is \$31,693.80 (\$131,693.80 − \$100,000). Gardner records the following for 2007 and 2008:

1. *Initial Recording of the Lease on January 1, 2007*

Lease Receivable	131,693.80	
Equipment		100,000.00
Unearned Interest: Leases		31,693.80

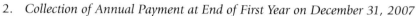

The effect of this transaction is to replace the equipment asset with a monetary asset of an equal amount. Again, note that Gardner records the receivable at the amount of the gross (undiscounted) rentals plus the estimated unguaranteed residual value of the leased asset (zero in this case). It credits the Equipment account for the cost of the item, because from an *economic-substance-over-legal-form* point of view it is the disposal of an asset, even though legal transfer of ownership has not occurred. Gardner records the Unearned Interest: Leases account as the difference between the cost of the equipment and the receivable; it is a contra account to the Lease Receivable account.

2. *Collection of Annual Payment at End of First Year on December 31, 2007*

Cash	32,923.45	
Lease Receivable		32,923.45

Gardner collects and records the payment of \$32,923.45.

3. *Recognition of Interest Revenue for First Year on December 31, 2007*

Unearned Interest: Leases	12,000.00	
Interest Revenue: Leases		12,000.00

Gardner amortizes the Unearned Interest account using the effective interest method. That is, it recognizes the interest revenue as 12% of the net investment at the beginning of the period (the January 1, 2007 balance of the Lease Receivable less the January 1, 2007 balance of the Unearned Interest: Leases) or \$12,000.00 (12% × \$100,000; that is, \$131,693.80 − \$31,693.80).

Gardner (the lessor) separates the receivable into its current and noncurrent portions for reporting the lease on its balance sheet. It calculates the current and noncurrent amounts of the Net Investment that it reports on its December 31, 2007 balance sheet as follows:

	Current	Noncurrent
Lease receivable	\$32,923.45	\$65,846.90[a]
Unearned interest: leases	(3,527.52)	(16,166.27)[b]
Net investment	\$29,395.93	\$49,680.63

a. 2 × \$32,923.45
b. [\$32,923.45 − (\$32,923.45 × 0.797194)] + [\$32,923.45 − (\$32,923.45 × 0.711780)]

Note that the \$29,395.93 current portion plus the \$49,680.63 noncurrent portion sum to the \$79,076.55 (with a \$0.01 rounding error) total Net Investment on December 31, 2007 shown in Example 21-8.

4. *Collection of Annual Payment for Second Year on December 31, 2008*

Cash	32,923.45	
Lease Receivable		32,923.45

Gardner records the receipt of the payment for the second period in the same way as during the first period.

5. *Recognition of Interest Revenue for Second Year on December 31, 2008*

Unearned Interest: Leases	9,489.19	
Interest Revenue: Leases		9,489.19

EXAMPLE 21-8	Summary of Lease Payments Received in Arrears and Interest Revenue Earned by Gardner Leasing Company (Lessor)						
(1) Date	(2) Annual Lease Payment Received	(3) Interest Revenue at 12% on Net Investment[a]	(4) Amount of Net Investment Recovered[b]	(5) Lease Receivable[c]	(6) Unearned Interest Leases[d]	(7) Net Investment[e]
January 1, 2007				$131,693.80	$31,693.80	$100,000.00
December 31, 2007	$32,923.45	$12,000.00	$20,923.45	98,770.35	19,693.80	79,076.55
December 31, 2008	32,923.45	9,489.19	23,434.26	65,846.90	10,204.61	55,642.29
December 31, 2009	32,923.45	6,677.07	26,246.38	32,923.45	3,527.54	29,395.91
December 31, 2010	32,923.45	3,527.54[f]	29,395.91	0	0	0

a. Column 7 at beginning of year × 12%
b. Column 2 − Column 3
c. Annual lease payment × Number of years remaining on lease, or Previous balance − Column 2
d. Previous balance − Column 3
e. Column 5 − Column 6
f. Adjusted for $0.03 rounding error

The calculation of the 2008 interest revenue by the effective interest method follows the same procedure as that for 2007. The only difference is that the net investment as of January 1, 2008 is less than that of January 1, 2007. The calculation for 2008 is 12% of the January 1, 2008 balance in the Lease Receivable account less the January 1, 2008 balance of the Unearned Interest: Leases. For 2008 the interest revenue is $9,489.19 (12% × $79,076.55; that is, $100,000 − $20,923.45).

Example 21-8 shows the interest revenue and the reductions in the receivable and the unearned interest over the life of the lease. The Gardner Leasing Company would use the information we show in Example 21-8 to record the journal entries for the remaining years of the lease. At the end of 2008 its net investment is zero. ♦

Example: Direct Financing Lease with No Unguaranteed Residual Value and Payments Received in Advance

To show a direct financing lease with a different timing of the payments, assume that on January 1, 2007 the Watkins Finance Company leases equipment to the Hutton Company, with the terms and provisions of the lease we show in Example 21-9. This lease is a direct financing lease because the provisions of the lease agreement we show in Example 21-9 meet one or more of the Column A and both of the Column B classification criteria from Exhibit 21-2, do not include any manufacturer's or dealer's profit, and the fair (present) value of the property is equal to its cost.

The Watkins Finance Company records the information for this lease in 2007 using the amounts from Example 21-10.

1. *Initial Recording of Lease on January 1, 2007*

Lease Receivable	500,000.00	
Equipment		391,371.20
Unearned Interest: Leases		108,628.80

Watkins (the lessor) records the Lease Receivable at the undiscounted five annual rental payments totaling $500,000 (5 × $100,000) plus the unguaranteed residual value ($0 in this case). It records the Unearned Interest at $108,628.80. Thus, the net receivable is the cost of the equipment of $391,371.20. Because the transaction is considered a disposal of an asset, Watkins also credits Equipment.

EXAMPLE 21-9 | Terms and Provisions of Lease Agreement Between Watkins Finance Company (Lessor) and Hutton Company (Lessee) Dated January 1, 2007

1. The cost, and fair value, of the equipment is $391,371.20.
2. The initial direct costs incurred by Watkins Finance Company are not material.
3. The term of the lease is five years, with annual payments of $100,000 received in advance at the beginning of each year.
4. The economic useful life of the equipment is five years and the estimated residual value to the lessor is zero.
5. The lease receipts are determined at an amount that will yield to the Watkins Finance Company a 14% annual rate of return on net investment.
6. The Hutton Company pays all the executory costs.
7. The equipment reverts to the Watkins Finance Company at the end of the fifth year; the lease contains no bargain purchase option.
8. The present value of the minimum lease payments receivable for the lessor is $391,371.20, calculated as follows:

Present value of 5 amounts of $100,000 in advance at 14% $= 3.913712 \times \$100,000$

$= \underline{\$391,371.20}$

9. The collectibility of the payments is reasonably assured, and there are no uncertainties involved in the lease.

EXAMPLE 21-10 | Summary of Lease Payments Received in Advance and Interest Revenue Earned by Watkins Finance Company (Lessor)

(1) Date	(2) Annual Lease Payment Received	(3) Interest Revenue at 14% on Net Investment[a]	(4) Lease Receivable[b]	(5) Unearned Interest: Leases[c]	(6) Net Investment[d]
January 1, 2007			$500,000	$108,628.80	$391,371.20
January 1, 2007	$100,000		400,000		291,371.20
December 31, 2007		$40,791.97		67,836.83	332,163.17[e]
January 1, 2008	100,000		300,000		232,163.17
December 31, 2008		32,502.84		35,333.99	264,666.01[e]
January 1, 2009	100,000		200,000		164,666.01
December 31, 2009		23,053.24		12,280.75	187,719.25[e]
January 1, 2010	100,000		100,000		87,719.25
December 31, 2010		12,280.75[f]		0	100,000.00[e]
January 1, 2011	100,000		0		0

a. Column 6 at beginning of year × 14%
b. Annual lease payment × Number of years remaining on lease, or Previous balance − Column 2
c. Previous balance − Column 3
d. Column 4 − Column 5
e. $100,000 of this amount is a current asset; it will be received on January 1 of the next year. The remaining amount is a noncurrent asset.
f. Adjusted for $0.05 rounding error

---

2. *Collection of Annual Payment for First Year on January 1, 2007*

Cash	100,000.00	
Lease Receivable		100,000.00

The payments are collected in advance. The first payment collected consists entirely of principal since no interest has accrued. (The two preceding journal entries could be made as one compound entry.)

3. *Recognition of Interest Revenue for First Year on December 31, 2007*

Unearned Interest: Leases	40,791.97	
Interest Revenue: Leases		40,791.97

As we show in Example 21-10, the interest earned in 2007 is $40,791.97 (14% × $291,371.20). Watkins would use the information we show in Example 21-10 to record the journal entries for the remaining years of the lease. At the end of the lease term, there will be a zero balance in both the Lease Receivable and Unearned Interest: Leases accounts. ♦

Example: Direct Financing Lease with an Unguaranteed Residual Value at the End of the Lease and Payments Made in Advance

To show a direct financing lease with additional issues, assume that on January 1, 2007 the Carlson Bank leases equipment to the Johnson Company, with the terms and provisions of the lease we show in Example 21-11.

EXAMPLE 21-11 **Terms and Provisions of Lease Agreement Between Carlson Bank (Lessor) and Johnson Company (Lessee) Dated January 1, 2007**

1. The cost, and fair value, of the equipment is $11,149.06.
2. The initial direct costs incurred by Carlson Bank are not material.
3. The term of the lease is four years, with annual payments of $3,000 received at the beginning of each year.
4. The estimated economic life of the equipment is five years, the lease is for only four years and there is an estimated residual value of $2,000 at the end of the lease. The Johnson Company does not guarantee any of the estimated residual value.
5. The lease payments are determined at an amount that will yield to the Carlson Bank a 14% annual rate of return on its net investment.
6. The Johnson Company pays all the executory costs.
7. The equipment reverts to the Carlson Bank at the end of the fourth year. The lease contains no renewal or bargain purchase options.
8. The present value of the minimum lease payments receivable for the lessor, plus the unguaranteed residual value, is $11,149.06, calculated as follows:

Present value of 4 amounts of $3,000 in advance at 14% (3.321632 × $3,000)	= $ 9,964.90
Add: Present value of a single sum of $2,000 (the unguaranteed residual value) = at 14% for 4 periods (0.592080 × $2,000)	1,184.16
Total present value	= $11,149.06

9. The collectibility of the payments is reasonably assured, and there are no uncertainties involved in the lease.

Since the provisions of the lease agreement in Example 21-11 meet one or more of the Column A and both of the Column B lease classification criteria from Exhibit 21-2, and do not include any manufacturer's or dealer's profit, this lease is a direct financing lease. The Carlson Bank records the information relevant to this lease for the year 2007 using the amounts from Example 21-12.

1. *Initial Recording of Lease on January 1, 2007*

Lease Receivable	14,000.00	
Equipment		11,149.06
Unearned Interest: Leases		2,850.94

Carlson (the lessor) records the Lease Receivable at $14,000 (the undiscounted four annual rental payments totaling $12,000, plus the $2,000 unguaranteed residual value). Note that the discounted amount of the $2,000 unguaranteed residual value included in the receivable to determine the net investment must earn a return (14% in this case), as well as the remaining part of the net investment. Carlson records the Unearned Interest at $2,850.94; thus, the net receivable is the cost of the equipment of $11,149.06. Because the transaction is considered a disposal of an asset, Carlson also credits the Equipment account.

2. *Collection of Annual Payment for First Year on January 1, 2007*

Cash	3,000.00	
Lease Receivable		3,000.00

The payments are collected in advance. This journal entry reduces the net investment that will earn interest.

3. *Recognition of Interest Revenue for First Year on December 31, 2007*

Unearned Interest: Leases	1,140.87	
Interest Revenue: Leases		1,140.87

As we show in Example 21-12, the interest earned during 2007 is $1,140.87.

The Carlson Bank would use the information we show in Example 21-12 to record the entries for the remaining years. At the end of the lease, there will be $2,000 left in the Lease Receivable account. When Carlson receives the asset, it records it at the lowest of the cost, carrying value, or fair value. Carlson records a loss if the asset value is less than $2,000. ◆

EXAMPLE 21-12	**Summary of Lease Payments Received in Advance and Interest Revenue Earned by Carlson Bank (Lessor)**				
(1)	**(2)**	**(3)**	**(4)**	**(5)**	**(6)**
Date	**Annual Lease Payment Received**	**Interest Revenue at 14% on Net Investment[a]**	**Lease Receivable[b]**	**Unearned Interest: Leases[c]**	**Net Investment[d]**
January 1, 2007			$14,000	$2,850.94	$11,149.06
January 1, 2007	$3,000		11,000		8,149.06[e]
December 31, 2007		$1,140.87		1,710.07	9,289.93
January 1, 2008	3,000		8,000		6,289.93
December 31, 2008		880.59		829.48	7,170.52[e]
January 1, 2009	3,000		5,000		4,170.52
December 31, 2009		583.87		245.61	4,754.39[e]
January 1, 2010	3,000		2,000[f]		1,754.39
December 31, 2010		245.61		0	2,000.00[f]

a. Column 6 at beginning of year × 14%
b. Annual lease payment × Number of years remaining on lease + $2,000 residual value, or Previous balance − Column 2
c. Previous balance − Column 3
d. Column 4 − Column 5
e. $3,000 of each of these December 31 balances is a current asset; the remaining amount is a noncurrent asset
f. The estimated unguaranteed residual value

Initial Direct Costs Involved in a Direct Financing Lease

The accounting for initial direct costs incurred by the lessor is different for each of the main types of leases. Recall that for an operating lease, the lessor records these initial direct costs as an asset, allocates them as an operating expense over the term of the operating lease, and matches them against the rental revenue. For a direct financing lease, **FASB Statement No. 91** states that the *initial direct costs* of a completed lease transaction include incremental direct costs and certain other direct costs. *Incremental direct costs* include those costs that result directly from and are essential to the leasing transaction and would not have been incurred by the lessor if the transaction had not occurred. The *other direct costs* that may be included are those costs of the lessor related to evaluating the lessee's financial condition, negotiating terms, preparing and processing lease documents, and closing the transaction.[14]

Since the lessor does not recognize any revenue at the time it signs a direct financing lease, it does *not* expense the initial direct costs at that time. Therefore, there is no effect on net income at the time it records the direct financing lease. Instead, it defers the initial direct costs. This accounting procedure requires that the lessor determine a *new* (lower) implicit rate that will discount the remaining future minimum lease payments to the net investment at the inception of the lease.[15] It expenses all other lease-related costs, such as the costs of advertising, servicing existing leases, unsuccessful lease originations, supervision, and administration, as incurred.

For example, if a lessor incurs initial direct costs of $5,000 on a direct financing lease, it records the costs as follows:

Unearned Interest: Leases	5,000	
Cash, etc.		5,000

This entry results in appropriate matching because the initial direct costs are deferred and recognized over the lease term. The reduction in the Unearned Interest: Leases account increases the net investment, but the future cash flows remain unchanged, thereby lowering the implicit rate. The lower rate results in less interest revenue being recognized each period. This achieves the goal of deferring the initial direct costs and including them as a reduction of income over the life of the lease.

The calculation of the new implicit rate requires the use of compound interest techniques, as we discuss in the Time Value of Money module. Since we do not show the calculation, we assume a new implicit rate and list it in the related problems at the end of the chapter.

Sales-Type Leases (Lessor)

In a sales-type lease, like a direct financing lease, the lessor "sells" the asset and records a receivable.[16] In contrast, however, in a sales-type lease the fair value of the asset that is "sold" is greater (or less) than its cost or carrying value. Thus, **the differences between a sales-type lease and a direct financing lease are the manufacturer's or dealer's (gross) profit or loss in a sales-type lease and the accounting for initial direct costs.** The manufacturer's or dealer's profit or loss is the difference between the following two items: (1) the present value of the minimum lease payments computed at the interest rate implicit in the lease (i.e., the sales price), and (2) the cost or carrying value of the asset plus any initial direct costs less the present value of the unguaranteed residual value accruing to the benefit of the lessor.[17]

Example: Sales-Type Lease   Assume that on January 1, 2007 the York Company leases specialty equipment to the Lake Company with the terms and provisions of the lease we show in Example 21-13. The test in Example 21-14 shows that this lease qualifies as a sales-type lease.

---

14. "Accounting for Nonrefundable Fees and Costs Associated with Originating or Acquiring Loans and Initial Direct Costs of Leases," *FASB Statement No. 91* (Stamford, Conn.: FASB, 1987), par. 5–7. This *Statement* was clarified by *FASB Statement No. 98.*
15. *FASB Statement No. 13 as Amended and Interpreted through January 1990, op. cit.,* sec. L10.114.
16. A lessor may not classify a lease involving real estate as a sales-type lease unless the lease agreement provides for the transfer of title to the lessee at or shortly after the end of the lease term.
17. *FASB Statement No. 13 as Amended and Interpreted through January 1990, op. cit.,* sec. L10.113.

EXAMPLE 21-13 **Terms and Provisions of Lease Agreement Between York Company (Lessor) and Lake Company (Lessee) Dated January 1, 2007**

1. The cost of the equipment is $120,000. The fair value is $190,008.49.
2. No initial direct costs are incurred by the York Company.
3. The term of the lease is 10 years, with annual payments of $30,000 received at the beginning of each year. The estimated economic life of the equipment is also 10 years.
4. The Lake Company agrees to pay all executory costs.
5. The Lake Company is given an option to buy the equipment for $500 at the end of the lease term, December 31, 2016. This is a bargain purchase option.
6. The interest rate implicit in the lease is 12%.
7. The present value of 10 payments of $30,000 at 12% on an annuity-due basis, plus the present value of the bargain purchase option is $190,008.49, calculated as follows:

Present value of 10 amounts in advance at 12% (6.328250 × $30,000)	=	$189,847.50
Plus: Present value of $500 discounted at 12% (0.321973 × $500)	=	160.99
Total present value	=	$190,008.49

8. The collectibility of the payments is reasonably assured, and there are no uncertainties involved in the lease.

Assuming that the York Company is a manufacturer or dealer in the specialty equipment being leased, it records the information relevant to the lease for 2007 as follows:

1. *Initial Recording of the Sales-Type Lease on January 1, 2007*

Lease Receivable	300,500.00	
Sales Revenue		190,008.49
Unearned Interest: Leases		110,491.51
Cost of Goods Sold	120,000.00	
Merchandise Inventory (or Equipment Held for Lease)		120,000.00

EXAMPLE 21-14 **Application of Lease Classification Criteria by York Company (Lessor)**

Classification Criteria	Criteria Met?	Remarks
Column A		
1. Transfer of ownership	No	
2. Bargain purchase option	Yes	
3. Lease term is 75% or more of economic life	Yes	100% of life
4. Present value of minimum lease payments is 90% or more of fair value	Yes	The present value is $190,008.49, or 100% of estimated fair value
Column B		
1. Collectibility reasonably assured	Yes	
2. No uncertainties	Yes	

Decision: If the lease meets one or more of the Column A criteria and both of Column B criteria and there is a manufacturer's or dealer's profit or loss, it is a sales-type lease.
Conclusion: The lease is a sales-type lease, since appropriate criteria are met and there is a manufacturer's or dealer's profit because the amount used as the selling price ($190,008.49) exceeds the cost ($120,000). That is, the present (fair) value of the lease payments is greater than the cost of the property.

The first journal entry records the "sale." Because this lease contains a bargain purchase option, York (the lessor) records the lease receivable at the sum of the undiscounted annual rental payments ($300,000) plus the undiscounted amount of the bargain purchase option ($500). It records the $190,008.49 sales revenue at the present value of the minimum lease payments, which is the present value of the annual payments ($189,847.50), plus the present value of the bargain purchase option ($160.99). The accounting for the bargain purchase option is the same as that for a guaranteed residual value since each is included in the minimum lease payments. Thus, the present value of the bargain purchase option (or a guaranteed residual value) is included as a part of the sales price of the equipment. The Unearned Interest: Leases amount of $110,491.51 is the difference between the receivable of $300,500 (the gross investment) and the sales revenue of $190,008.49. In general, however, the Unearned Interest: Leases amount is the difference between the gross investment in the lease and the sum of the present value of the two components of the gross investment. That is, the present value of the minimum lease payments and the present value of the unguaranteed residual value accruing to the lessor (none in this example because of the bargain purchase option).

The second journal entry records the cost of goods sold at the assigned inventory cost ($120,000) because there is no unguaranteed residual value. Thus the York Company reports a gross profit of $70,008.49 ($190,008.49 sales revenue − $120,000 cost of goods sold) on this sales-type lease at the time of the transfer of the property.

2. *Collection of Annual Payment for First Year on January 1, 2007*

Cash	30,000.00	
Lease Receivable		30,000.00

The lease provisions require that payments are collected in advance at the beginning of each year. Also, remember that this collection reduces the net investment (the amount on which interest revenue is calculated) by $30,000.

3. *Recognition of Interest Revenue for First Year on December 31, 2007*

Unearned Interest: Leases	19,201.02	
Interest Revenue: Leases		19,201.02

York amortizes the Unearned Interest: Leases account using the effective interest method. It recognizes interest as 12% of the net investment *after* the collection of the first rent, or $19,201.02, calculated as follows:

$$12\% \times [(\$300,500 - \$30,000) - \$110,491.51] = \$19,201.02$$

As we discussed for a direct financing lease, York may prepare a schedule of the periodic interest revenue, similar to the one we show in Example 21-12.

York's journal entries for the following nine years will show a pattern similar to the preceding ones. After it records the entries for the tenth year, its net investment on December 31, 2016 will be $500, the amount of the bargain purchase option. Also, as with a direct financing lease, since a sale is considered to have taken place, a lessor does not record any depreciation on the leased asset. The lessee typically would pay and record the executory costs. ♦

Initial Direct Costs Involved in a Sales-Type Lease

As we indicated previously, the accounting for the lessor's initial direct costs is different for each of the three main types of leases. In the preceding example of a sales-type lease, we assumed that there are no initial direct costs. If a lessor does incur initial direct costs on a sales-type lease, it expenses them in the same period.[18] The lessor could include them in cost of goods sold, but since the initial direct costs primarily relate to a selling activity it may report them as a selling expense entitled Initial Direct Sales-Type Lease

---

18. *Ibid.*

Expense. Either procedure results in an appropriate matching of the costs against the revenue recognized.

Unguaranteed and Guaranteed Residual Values

As we discussed in the introduction to sales-type leases, the lessor deducts the present value of any *unguaranteed* residual value from the cost or carrying value of the asset when it recognizes the expenses associated with the signing of the lease. Note that the unguaranteed residual value is *not* included in sales revenue because it represents an item that is *not* sold.

The present value of any *guaranteed* residual value, on the other hand, is *not* subtracted from the expenses (e.g., cost of goods sold) and is included in sales. Since both the expense and the revenue items contain the present value of the guaranteed residual value, the gross profit is the same as for an unguaranteed residual value of the same amount. The sales revenue and expenses for a sales-type lease with an unguaranteed residual value are both reduced by the present value of the unguaranteed residual value. This method of accounting for the guaranteed residual value in a sales-type lease indicates that there has been a transfer of the risks and benefits to the lessee usually associated with ownership of an asset. Since the unguaranteed residual value accrues to the lessor, there has been a transfer of fewer ownership risks and benefits. Note, however, as we indicated earlier, this distinction does not prohibit a lease containing an unguaranteed residual value from qualifying as a sales-type lease.

Disclosure Requirements for the Lessor

7 Understand disclosures by the lessor.

FASB Statement No. 13 as Amended requires the lessor to make certain disclosures in its financial statements or the related notes. Exhibit 21-6 shows the basic disclosures for operating, direct financing, and sales-type leases for a lessor whose leasing activities are a significant part of its business activities.[19]

EXHIBIT 21-6   Disclosure Requirements for Lessor: Operating, Direct Financing, and Sales-Type Leases

A. For operating leases:
1. The cost and carrying amount, if different, of property on lease or held for leasing by major classes of property, and the amount of the total accumulated depreciation.
2. Minimum future rentals on noncancelable leases for each of the five succeeding fiscal years and in total.
3. Total contingent rentals included in income for each period.
B. For direct financing and sales-type leases:
1. The components of the net investment in direct financing and sales-type leases including:
   a. The future minimum lease payments to be received, including any profit thereon.
   b. The unguaranteed residual values accruing to the benefit of the lessor.
   c. For direct financing leases only, initial direct costs.
   d. Unearned income.
2. Future minimum lease payments to be received for each of the five succeeding fiscal years and in total.
3. Total contingent rentals included in revenue for each period.
C. A general description of the lessor's leasing arrangements.

SUMMARY OF ACCOUNTING BY LESSEE AND LESSOR

The accounting issues involved in the various types of leases are numerous and sometimes complex. To assist in identifying the key issues involved, we include a summary of the accounting by the lessee and lessor in Exhibit 21-7.

---

19. *Ibid.*, sec. L10.119.

> **EXHIBIT 21-7   Summary of Accounting for Leases by the Lessee and the Lessor**
>
> ### LESSEE
>
> *Operating Lease*
>
> - Rent expense is recognized each period.
>
> *Capital Lease*
>
> - Leased property is recorded at the present value of the minimum lease payments.
> - Lease obligation is recorded at the present value of the minimum lease payments.
>   The minimum lease payments are discounted at the lessee's incremental borrowing
>   rate unless the lessor's implicit rate is both known and lower.
>   The leased property cannot be recorded at an amount that exceeds its fair value.
> - Depreciation of the leased property
>   Over the economic life if the lease is capitalized under either of the following criteria:
>   - the lease transfers ownership of the property to the lessee by the end of the lease term
>   - the lease contains a bargain purchase option
>   Over the lease life if the lease is capitalized but does not meet either of the preceding criteria
>   Use the normal depreciation policy
> - Interest expense is recognized by use of the effective interest method.
>
> ### LESSOR
>
> *Operating Lease*
>
> - Rent revenue is recognized each period.
> - Property leased to others is depreciated using the normal depreciation policy.
>
> *Direct Financing Lease*
>
> - Lease receivable is recorded at the sum of the minimum lease payments plus the unguaranteed
>   residual value (not discounted).
> - Unearned interest is recorded at an amount equal to the gross investment in the lease minus
>   the cost or carrying value of the leased property.
> - Initial direct costs are deferred and amortized over the life of the lease.
> - Interest revenue is recognized by use of the effective interest method.
>
> *Sales-Type Lease*
>
> - Lease receivable is recorded at the sum of the minimum lease payments plus the unguaranteed
>   residual value (not discounted).
> - Unearned interest is recorded at an amount equal to the gross investment in the lease minus
>   the sum of the present value of the two components of the gross investment.
> - Sales revenue is recorded at the present value of the minimum lease payments.
> - Expenses that are recognized include the cost or carrying amount of the leased property, plus
>   the initial direct costs, minus the present value of the unguaranteed residual value.
> - Interest revenue is recognized by use of the effective interest method.

ADDITIONAL LEASE ISSUES

This section discusses how to report lease transactions on the statement of cash flows. It also discusses several conceptual issues regarding accounting for leases, as well as international differences.

Statement of Cash Flows Disclosures

If a lessee records a lease as an operating lease, it classifies each lease payment as a cash outflow in the operating activities section of its statement of cash flows. If a lessee records a lease as a capital lease, it reports a noncash investing and financing activity at the signing of the lease agreement. For each lease payment, it classifies the interest portion as a cash outflow in the operating activities section, and the reduction of the lease obligation as a cash outflow in the financing activities section.

If a lessor records a lease as an operating lease, it classifies each lease receipt as a cash inflow in the operating activities section of its statement of cash flows. If a lessor records a lease as a direct financing lease, it classifies any cash paid to purchase the asset as a cash outflow in the investing activities section. Then, for each lease receipt, it classifies the interest portion as a cash inflow in the operating activities section, and the reduction of the lease receivable as a cash inflow in the investing activities section. If a lessor records a lease as a sales-type lease, it classifies any cash paid to purchase the asset as a cash outflow in the operating activities section. Then, for each lease receipt, it classifies the receipt as a cash inflow in the operating activities section.

Conceptual Evaluation of Accounting for Leases

8 Explain the conceptual issues regarding leases.

The four criteria used to determine if there is a capital lease are reasonable measures of whether the risks and benefits of ownership are transferred. Either of the first two criteria would be written into a lease agreement if both parties clearly wanted ownership of the leased property to transfer to the lessee. There is more controversy about the third and fourth criteria because they are fairly easy to avoid. For example, for the third criterion the economic life of the property may be "estimated" so that the lease life is less than 75% of that period. Note that for the fourth criterion, the inclusion of a guaranteed residual value in the lease agreement will typically result in a present value of the minimum lease payments that is equal to the fair value of the property. Therefore, companies will often try to find a way to effectively protect the lessor's risk related to the residual value of the property without meeting the definition of a guaranteed residual value. This would make the present value of the minimum lease payments equal to less than 90% of the fair value of the property. For example, third-party guarantees of the residual value have been fairly widely used to ensure that the present value of the minimum lease payments is less than 90% of the fair value, while providing the lessor with an effective guarantee of the residual value.

These examples raise the issue of why the lessee and lessor may want to avoid a capital lease. The motivation usually comes from the lessee who wants to avoid reporting the liability on its balance sheet. The lessee apparently believes that a "stronger" balance sheet allows it either to borrow more money or to borrow money at a lower interest rate. However, the lessee is required to disclose in the notes to its financial statements of the future cash flows each year for the next five years and all years thereafter. This allows the user to perform a present value calculation that determines the approximate amount of the balance sheet liability (and asset) that the lessee has avoided. Therefore, it appears that the lessee must assume that users do not read (or understand) the notes.

Many users believe that both the relevance and reliability of lease accounting would be enhanced by having a simple rule that requires capitalization of all leases with, say, a life of more than one year. However, companies lobbied not to have such a rule included in *FASB Statement No. 13*. Instead, the FASB opted for the four capitalization criteria. However, the *Statement* also has been criticized for being very "mechanical." That is, the criteria used for capitalization are "absolutes" and are either met or not, thereby leaving no room for professional judgment.

SECURE YOUR KNOWLEDGE 21-3

- A lessor accounts for an operating lease as a rental agreement.
  - The lessor records rental revenue each period and includes the leased equipment on its balance sheet as part of property, plant, and equipment.

(continued)

- The lessor depreciates the leased equipment over its estimated economic life.
- Executory costs paid by the lessor are recorded as operating expenses and matched against rental revenue.
- Any initial direct costs (costs incurred from directly originating the lease) are recorded as an asset and amortized over the lease term.
- For a direct financing lease, the lessor removes the carrying value of the leased equipment and records a gross receivable equal to the undiscounted minimum lease payments plus any unguaranteed residual value. The difference between the gross receivable and the carrying value of the leased property is recorded as unearned interest revenue (a contra-account to the lease receivable).
  - The gross receivable includes the residual value, whether it is guaranteed or unguaranteed.
  - Executory costs are not included in the gross receivable or the present value calculations.
  - The lessor's net investment in the lease (the lease receivable less unearned revenue) is reported as current or noncurrent using the present value of next year's payments approach or the change in present value approach.
  - Interest revenue is recorded each period and is computed using the effective interest method based on the interest rate implicit in the lease.
  - Any initial direct costs are deferred and recognized over the lease term by reducing unearned interest revenue based on a newly computed implicit interest rate.
- For a sales-type lease, the lessor recognizes a manufacturer's or dealer's profit or loss at the inception of the lease in addition to interest revenue over the lease term (like in a direct financing lease).
  - The manufacturer's or dealer's profit is measured as the difference between (1) the present value of the minimum lease payments (sales revenue) and (2) the cost of the asset less the present value of the unguaranteed residual value (cost of goods sold).
  - If the residual value is guaranteed by the lessee, the present value of this amount is not subtracted from the cost of the asset and is included in sales revenue.
  - Any initial direct costs are expensed at the inception of the lease.

LINK TO INTERNATIONAL DIFFERENCES

International accounting standards for leases are generally similar to U.S. standards. However, international standards focus more on the *substance* of the agreement rather than the *form* as defined by the four criteria in the U.S. standards. For this reason, international standards are generally less detailed and are considered more principles-based, while U.S. standards have more extensive form-driven requirements and are generally considered rules-based. Terminology differences exist. For example, under international standards, a lease is classified as either a finance lease or an operating lease. Under a finance lease, capitalization is required when substantially all of the risks and rewards of ownership are transferred, as demonstrated by several examples or indicators. While the first two indicators are very similar to U.S. standards, the third indicator is less precise because it states that "the lease term is for a major part of the asset's useful life," as compared to the 75% used in the United States. The fourth indicator also differs from the U.S. criterion in that it states that "the present value of the lease payments is equal to or greater than the fair value of the asset," as compared to the 90% used in the United States. Finally, international standards contain other indicators that are not specified under U.S. standards. U.S. standards also contain more detailed disclosures related to lease maturities.

APPENDIX: SPECIALIZED LEASE ISSUES AND CHANGES IN LEASE PROVISIONS

9 Understand lease issues related to real estate, sale-leaseback issues, leveraged leases, and changes in lease provisions.

Some companies engage in specialized leases. We discuss three specialized lease issues briefly in this Appendix: (1) real estate leases, (2) sales-leaseback transactions, and (3) leveraged leases. Other companies may be involved in lease agreements whose provisions are modified. We also briefly discuss changes in lease provisions.

LEASE ISSUES RELATED TO REAL ESTATE

In the main portion of this chapter we considered only the leasing of personal property (the example we used was equipment). Special issues are involved in the classification of leases that include land, either alone or in combination with buildings or equipment.[20] We show the differences in the classification of leases involving real estate in Exhibit 21-8.

Lease of Land Only

If land is the only item of property leased, the lessee accounts for the lease as a capital lease only if the lease transfers ownership at the end of the lease, or includes a bargain purchase option. Otherwise, the lessee accounts for the lease as an operating lease. (The criteria dealing with the 75% of the estimated economic life and the 90% of the fair value of the leased property do *not* apply because the asset would have to be depreciated over the lease life. Such a situation would be inappropriate for land.) The lessee does *not* depreciate the asset, Leased Land Under Capital Leases, because title to the land is expected to be transferred, and land is not subject to depreciation. The lessor accounts for the lease of land as a sales-type lease if (1) the lease transfers ownership or contains a bargain purchase option, (2) the lease meets both the collectibility and uncertainty criteria, and (3) there is a dealer's profit or loss. If the criteria for a sales-type lease are met with the exception that there is no dealer's profit or loss, then the lease qualifies as a direct financing one. Otherwise, it is an operating lease.

Lease of Both Land and Buildings That Transfers Title or Contains a Bargain Purchase Option

When both land and buildings are leased, a new issue arises as to the classification of the lease because one portion involves a depreciable asset with an estimated economic life and the other involves a nondepreciable asset. This lease is accounted for either as: (1) a lease of both land and buildings that meets criteria 1 and 2 of Column A (Part I) of Exhibit 21-8, or (2) a lease of both land and buildings that does *not* meet either criterion 1 or 2.

Lessee's Accounting

For a capital lease of land and buildings that transfers ownership or that contains a bargain purchase option, the lessee allocates the present value of the minimum lease payments between the two leased assets in proportion to their fair values at the inception of the lease (Exhibit 21-8, IIIA). It depreciates the amount assigned to Leased Buildings over the estimated economic life of the buildings. It does *not* depreciate the amount assigned to Leased Land.

Lessor's Accounting

The lessor accounts for the lease as a single unit, either as a direct financing, a sales-type, or an operating lease. The term **single unit** means that for a sales-type or direct financing

---

20. *FASB Statement No. 13 as Amended and Interpreted through January 1990, op. cit.*, sec. L10.120–.124.

EXHIBIT 21-8   Classification of Leases Involving Real Property

I. General Criteria for Classifying Leases
(Brief titles are given in this exhibit; see Exhibit 21-2 for fuller titles)

Column A **Criteria Applicable to Both Lessees and Lessors**	**Column B** **Criteria Applicable to Lessors Only**
1. Transfer of ownership 2. Contains bargain purchase option 3. Lease term is 75% or more of economic life 4. Present value of minimum lease payments is 90% or more of fair value	1. Collectibility reasonably assured 2. No uncertainties

II. Lease of Land Only

A. Lessee	B. Lessor

1. **Capital lease. Lease must meet either criterion 1 or 2 in**
    Column A (Part I). (Criteria 3 and 4 are _not_ applicable.)
 	
2. **Operating lease. Lease must not meet either criterion**
    1 or 2 in Column A (Part I).
	1. **Sales-type lease. Lease must**
	    a. **Meet either criterion 1 or 2 in Column A**
	        (Part I), _and_
	    b. **Meet both criteria in Column B (Part I), _and_**
	    c. **Results in a dealer's profit or loss.**
	2. **Direct financing lease. Lease must meet**
	    a. **Either criterion 1 or 2 in Column A(Part I), _and_**
	    b. **Both criteria in Column B (Part I).**
	3. **Operating lease. Lease that does _not_ qualify as a**
	    sales-type or direct financing lease.

III. Lease of Both Land and Buildings
A. Lease of both land and buildings that transfers ownership or contains a bargain purchase option

1. Lessee	2. Lessor

a. **Capital lease. The lease is a capital lease since**
    one or more of the criteria of Column A (Part I)
    are met. Land and buildings are separately capitalized.
	a. **Sales-type lease. The two assets,**
	    land and buildings, are considered as
	    a single unit and the lease must
	    (1) Meet either criterion 1 or 2 in Column A (Part I), _and_
	    (2) Meet both criteria in Column B (Part I), _and_
	    (3) Results in a dealer's profit or loss.
	b. **Direct financing lease. The lease of the two assets**
	    combined must meet
	    (1) Either criterion 1 or 2 in Column A(Part I), _and_
	    (2) Both criteria in Column B (Part I).

B. If lease meets neither criterion 1 nor criterion 2 in Column A (Part I), and if fair value of land is less than 25% of fair value of both land and buildings. (The land portion is ignored and the classification is determined using the characteristics of building.)

1. Lessee	2. Lessor

a. **Capital lease. Lease must meet either criterion 3 or 4**
    in Column A (Part I).
b. **Operating lease. Lease meets none of the criteria**
    in Column A (Part I).
	a. **Sales-type lease. Lease must**
	    (1) Meet either criterion 3 or 4 in Column A (Part I), _and_
	    (2) Meet both criteria in Column B (Part I), _and_
	    (3) Results in a dealer's profit or loss.
	b. **Direct financing lease. Lease must meet**
	    (1) Either criterion 3 or 4 in Column A (Part I), _and_
	    (2) Both criteria in Column B (Part I).
	c. **Operating Lease. Lease that does _not_ qualify as a**
	    sales-type or direct financing lease.

C. If lease meets neither criterion 1 nor criterion 2 in Column A (Part I), and if fair value of land is more than 25% of fair value of both land and buildings. (The lease is separated into land and building portions.)

1. Lessee	2. Lessor

a. **Land portion. Always an operating lease.**
b. **Building portion. Classified by remaining criteria**
    of Column A (Part I).
	a. **Land portion. Always an operating lease.**
	b. **Building portion. Classified by remaining criteria of**
	    Columns A and B (Part I).

lease, the lessor uses one Lease Receivable account to record the appropriate values for the lease of both land and buildings. In the original lease entry, however, the lessor credits both the land and the buildings accounts.

Credit: ©Tony Freeman/Photo Edit

Lease of Land and Buildings That Does Not Transfer Title or Contain a Bargain Purchase Option

Value of Land Is Less Than 25%

If a lease of land and buildings does not transfer ownership or contain a bargain purchase option, it is a capital lease if it meets one of the other two criteria. If the fair value of the land is less than 25% of the total fair value of the leased property at the inception of the lease, the land is considered to be immaterial. Therefore, *both* the lessee and the lessor treat the land and buildings as a single unit. Note that the estimated economic life of the building is used as the economic life of the unit.

1. *Lessee's Accounting.* If either criterion 3 or 4 of Column A (Part I) of Exhibit 21-8 is met, the lessee classifies the lease as a capital lease and recognizes the leased land and buildings as a single asset. It depreciates the total amount over the term of the lease, even though it is implicitly depreciating the land portion of the asset. If the lease does not meet any of the criteria in Column A (Part I), it is an operating lease.

2. *Lessor's Accounting.* If the lease meets either criterion 3 or 4 of Column A (Part I) of Exhibit 21-8 and both of the criteria of Column B (Part I), the lessor accounts for the lease as a single unit, as either a direct financing or a sales-type lease as appropriate. Otherwise, the lease is an operating lease.

Value of Land Is More Than 25%

On the other hand, if at the inception of the lease, the land represents 25% or more of the fair value of the leased property, the amount of the land is considered to be a material amount. Then, both the lessee and the lessor must treat the land and the buildings separately for purposes of applying the criteria listed in Exhibit 21-8. In this case, the lessee and lessor separate the minimum lease payments into amounts applicable to land and to buildings. Since the lease of the land results in an operating lease, the best way to make the preceding calculation is to determine the fair value of land, and then use the appropriate interest rate to determine the periodic minimum lease payments applicable to the land portion, as follows:

$$\text{Incremental Borrowing Rate} \times \text{Fair Value of Land} = \text{Periodic Minimum Lease Payment Applicable to Land}$$

The periodic minimum lease payments applicable to both land and buildings, less the amount calculated, is the amount attributed to the buildings.

1. *Lessee's Accounting.* Once the amount assigned to the buildings is determined, if the building portion of the lease meets either criterion 3 or 4 of Column A (Part I) of Exhibit 21-8, the lessee accounts for it as a capital lease. The lessee depreciates the present value amount assigned to the asset, Leased Buildings, over the life of the lease. It accounts for the land portion of the lease separately as an operating lease. Therefore, if the buildings portion of the lease meets neither criterion 3 nor 4 of Column A (Part I) of Exhibit 21-8, the lessee accounts for both the buildings and the land as a single operating lease.

2. *Lessor's Accounting.* If the buildings portion of the lease meets either criterion 3 or 4 of Column A (Part I) and both criteria of Column B of Exhibit 21-8, the lessee accounts for the lease as a direct financing or sales-type lease, depending on whether there is a manufacturer's or dealer's profit or loss. It accounts for the land portion of the lease separately as an operating lease. If the buildings portion of the lease does not meet the relevant criteria, the lessor accounts for both the buildings and land as a single operating lease.

Lease Involving Equipment as Well as Real Estate

If a lease involves both equipment and real estate, the portion of the minimum lease payments for the equipment portion of the lease is estimated. The equipment then is treated separately when applying the criteria we list in Exhibit 21-8. It is accounted for separately according to its classification by both the lessee and lessor. The accounting for the remaining real estate portion follows the accounting standards described in the preceding section.

SALE-LEASEBACK ISSUES

If a company has limited cash or decides it does not want to be responsible for owning the property, it may sell an asset (often land and buildings, but not real property exclusively) and then immediately lease it back from the buyer. This kind of transaction may be advantageous to both the lessee and lessor: The lessee receives cash from the sale that is needed for its activities, and may derive a tax advantage. The lessor acquires an asset.

The sale of the asset and the leaseback are considered to be a single transaction that is like a secured loan, with the creditor obtaining legal title to the asset. The sales price of the asset, any profit earned, and the minimum lease payments must be considered together. If the lease meets one of the criteria for treatment as a capital lease (see Exhibit 21-2), the seller-lessee accounts for the lease as a capital lease[21]. Otherwise, it accounts for the lease as an operating lease. It defers any profit on the sale. If the lease is a capital lease, the lessee amortizes the profit in proportion to the depreciation of the leased asset. If the lease is an operating lease, the lessee amortizes the profit in proportion to the payments over the period of time it expects the asset to be used. However, when the fair value of the property

---

21. A sale-leaseback transaction involving real estate must qualify as a sale under the provisions of *FASB Statement No. 66*, "Accounting for Sales of Real Estate."

at the time of the transaction is less than its undepreciated cost, it *recognizes a loss immediately* up to the amount of the difference between the undepreciated cost and fair value.[22]

Lessor's Accounting Issues

The purchaser-lessor follows the principles we discussed in the preceding sections to account for the purchase of the asset and the immediate lease of it back to the seller. From the lessor's point of view, no new issues are involved, so we do not show its accounting here.

Lessee's Accounting Issues

If the lease meets at least one of the four criteria in Column A of Exhibit 21-2, the seller-lessee accounts for the lease as a capital lease. If none of the criteria are met, the seller-lessee accounts for the lease as an operating lease. The accounting for the main provisions of the lease follows the procedures we already illustrated. The primary new issue from the lessee's viewpoint is the accounting for the profit or loss on the sale of the property by the seller-lessee.

Example: Sale-Leaseback (Lessee Accounting) Assume that on January 1, 2007 the High Point Railroad built ten boxcars costing $400,000. Because of a cash flow problem resulting from this new acquisition, High Point decided to sell these boxcars immediately to Landlord Company for $600,000, and then lease them back under the conditions we show in Example 21-15.

EXAMPLE 21-15	Terms and Provisions of Lease Agreement Between Landlord Company and High Point Railroad Dated January 1, 2007

1. The cost of the boxcars to High Point Railroad (the seller-lessee) is $400,000. The selling price to Landlord Company (the purchaser-lessor) is $600,000; thus, this amount becomes the new cost of the equipment to the seller-lessee.
2. The term of the lease is 15 years, with annual payments of $92,771.13 in advance at the beginning of each year. The estimated economic life of the equipment is 20 years, with no expected residual value at the end of this time. (The residual value at the end of 15 years is not considered because title passes at that time.)
3. The High Point Railroad agrees to pay all executory costs.
4. Title to the boxcars will be transferred to the seller-lessee at the end of lease term.
5. The interest rate implicit on the lease is 16%. High Point Railroad knows this rate, and the rate equals its incremental borrowing rate.
6. The present value of 15 payments of $92,771.13 at 16% on an annuity-due basis is $600,000, calculated as follows:

    Present value of 15 amounts in advance at 16% = 6.467529 × $92,771.13
    = $600,000 (rounded)

7. The lease qualifies as a capital lease to High Point Railroad, since it meets the criteria stated in Exhibit 21-2.

Typical journal entries to record the information related to the preceding sale-leaseback for High Point Railroad (the seller-lessee) for 2007 are as follows:

1. *Sale of the Boxcars to Landlord Company on January 1, 2007*

Cash	600,000.00	
Boxcars		400,000.00
Unearned Profit on Sale-Leaseback		200,000.00

---

22. *FASB Statement No. 13 as Amended and Interpreted through January 1990, op. cit.*, sec. L10.129.

2. *Initial Recording of the Leaseback as a Capital Lease on January 1, 2007*

Leased Boxcars	600,000.00	
Capital Lease Obligation		600,000.00

3. *Annual Payment on January 1, 2007*

Capital Lease Obligation	92,771.13	
Cash		92,771.13

4. *Payment of Executory Costs on Various Dates in 2007 (amounts assumed)*

Insurance Expense	2,600.00	
Repairs and Maintenance Expense	2,300.00	
Property Tax Expense	9,700.00	
Cash		14,600.00

5. *Recording Depreciation of Boxcars on December 31, 2007*

Depreciation Expense: Leased Boxcars	30,000.00	
Accumulated Depreciation: Leased Boxcars		30,000.00

High Point uses the straight-line method and a life of 20 years because owner-ship is transferred at the end of the lease. Depreciation for 2007 is $30,000 ($600,000 ÷ 20).

6. *Amortization of Unearned Profit on Sale-Leaseback on December 31, 2007*

Unearned Profit on Sale-Leaseback	10,000.00	
Profit on Sale-Leaseback (or Depreciation		
Expense: Leased Boxcars)		10,000.00

The amortization is $10,000 ($200,000 ÷ 20). Note that High Point amortizes the Unearned Profit on Sale-Leaseback and recognizes the profit over a 20-year period. For a capital lease, *FASB Statement No. 13 as Amended* requires that a seller-lessee recognize any profit using the same rate that it used to depreciate the Leased Boxcars. For an operating lease, the seller-lessee defers such profit (or loss) and amortizes the amount in proportion to the lease payments over the period it expects to use the leased assets. A loss would be recorded by the seller-lessee if the book value or carrying amount were larger than the fair value of the asset. The seller-lessee recognizes the entire amount of this loss in the year of the sale-leaseback.

7. *Recognition of Interest Expense on December 31, 2007*

Interest Expense	81,156.62	
Capital Lease Obligation		81,156.62

This year-end adjusting entry is the same as that made for any capital lease for which the payment is made in advance. High Point calculates the amount as $81,156.62 [16% × ($600,000 − $92,771.13)]. ◆

Leveraged Leases

A leveraged lease is a special arrangement involving three different participants to the agreement: (1) the equity participant (the owner-lessor); (2) the asset user (the lessee); and (3) the debt participant (the long-term creditor who provides nonrecourse financing for the leasing transaction between the lessee and lessor). Exhibit 21-9 shows the inter-related activities of the three parties to a leveraged lease. If the owner-lessor buys the equipment from a manufacturer, a fourth party to the transaction would be involved.

The SEC estimates that public companies have approximately $1.3 trillion of cash flow commitments for leases. Many of these leases are leveraged leases. Leveraged leasing arrangements began in the late 1960s and have grown rapidly since then. The lease is

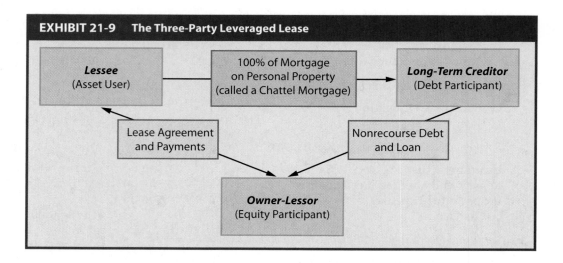

designed to provide income tax benefits to the three parties involved in the transaction. The lessor may be able to retain various tax credits, and also can immediately recognize all the cost of the asset as an income tax deduction. The lessee receives the right to income tax deductions for the rent of land, buildings, and other personal property. The creditor receives the tax protection provided for the leveraged lease contract.

From the standpoint of the lessee, no new accounting issues arise. It classifies a leveraged lease and accounts for it in the same way as a nonleveraged lease. *FASB Statement No. 13 as Amended* requires that the lessor classify a leveraged lease as a direct financing lease, since no manufacturer's or dealer's profit can arise from the transaction and therefore it cannot be classified as a sales-type lease.[23]

The lessor records its investment in a leveraged lease net of the nonrecourse debt, which usually consists of the (1) rental receivables, net of that portion applicable to the nonrecourse debt; (2) amount of any tax credits to be realized on the transaction; (3) estimated residual value of the leased asset; and (4) reduction for the unearned revenue items. Since leveraged leases are complex financial arrangements that vary in structure, the lessor's accounting for them is also complex and is beyond the scope of the book.[24]

CHANGES IN LEASE PROVISIONS

As we discussed earlier, lease contracts are written with many provisions, including renewal, extension, or purchase options, and penalties. Lessees and lessors may opt to change certain provisions that, in effect, change the classification of the lease. If at any time the lessee and lessor change a lease (other than by renewing or extending its term) so that the lease would have been classified differently *had the changed terms been in effect at the beginning of the lease term*, the revised agreement is considered a new agreement. The new agreement is reclassified as operating, direct financing, or sales-type, according to the criteria in Exhibit 21-2.

FASB Statement No. 13 as Amended also addresses the issue of renewals and extensions. A change in an operating lease to a direct financing or sales-type lease presents the fewest issues, since the accounting for the new lease would be similar to that described earlier in the chapter. The most complex issue involves a change in either a sales-type or direct financing lease. We briefly discuss some of the possible lease provision changes in the following sections.

---

23.   *Ibid.*, sec. L10.144.
24.   See Appendix E of *FASB Statement No. 13 as Amended and Interpreted through January 1990*, sec. L10.161, for an illustration of the accounting and financial statement presentation of leveraged leases.

Review of Estimated Unguaranteed Residual Value

A lessor reviews the estimated unguaranteed residual value annually. It *ignores* any upward adjustments in the estimated value, but must record any downward adjustment as a reduction in its net investment and a loss in the period. This recognition involves the calculation of a new implicit interest rate.

Impact of Renewal of Lease on Guarantee of Residual Value

Suppose, for example, a lessee records a lease as a capital lease while the lessor records it as a direct financing lease, and the lease contains a guarantee of the residual value of the leased property. If at the end of the lease term the lessee elects to renew the lease, this election would cancel the guarantee of residual value. The renewal, however, is *not* treated as a new agreement, because there is no change in the lease classification. The lessee adjusts the remaining balances of the asset and obligation from the original lease. The amount of the adjustment is equal to the difference between the present value of the future minimum lease payments under the new renewal agreement and the existing present balance of the obligation.

Changes to Sales-Type or Direct Financing Lease Prior to Lease Term Expiration That Change the Lease to an Operating Lease

If changes are made in either sales-type or direct financing lease provisions before the expiration of the lease, and if these changes would have caused the original agreement to be classified as an operating lease, the lessor removes the remaining net investment from its accounts. It replaces the Lease Receivable with an asset at its original cost, fair value, or carrying amount, whichever is lowest, and reports any net adjustment as an operating loss in the period of change. It then accounts for the new lease as any other operating lease.

An exception occurs when a guarantee or penalty becomes inoperative. In this case, if the renewal or extension results in an operating lease, the lessor continues to account for the existing lease as either a sales-type or direct financing lease (depending on the original classification) to the end of its original term. It then accounts for the renewal or extension as any other operating lease. The accounting by the lessee follows a similar pattern.

Renewal of Sales-Type or Direct Financing Lease Resulting in a New Lease That Qualifies as a Sales-Type Lease

The accounting for a renewal of sales-type and direct financing leases that results in a lease that qualifies again as a sales-type lease has been debated by the FASB since it originally issued *FASB Statement No. 13*. The original *FASB Statement No. 13* clearly indicated that when an existing sales-type or direct financing lease is renewed, the lessor could *not* classify the renewal lease as a sales-type lease even though it meets the necessary criteria. This renewal lease had to be treated as a direct financing lease. *FASB Statement No. 13 as Amended* qualifies the prior position. If the renewal takes place *during the term* of the lease, the position of the original *FASB Statement No. 13* will be followed. If the renewal takes place *at the end* of the lease (or during the last few months of the existing lease), the lease change can qualify as a sales-type lease. We discuss these two renewal situations briefly.

Renewal Occurring During Lease Term

The FASB concluded that if a lessor treated a renewal of a sales-type or direct financing lease as a sales-type lease at the time of an interim renewal, a "second sale" would result in recognition of revenue before its realization. For this reason, *FASB Statement No. 13 as Amended* requires that a lessor classify a renewal of an existing sales-type or direct financing lease that *otherwise qualifies as a sales-type lease* as a direct financing lease if the lease change occurs *during the term* of the lease.

Renewal Occurring at End of Lease Term

The FASB then altered its position regarding this type of lease change. It concluded that if the renewal occurred at the end of the lease term, and if the new agreement qualified as a sales-type lease (according to criteria stated in Exhibit 21-2), the lessor accounts for the renewal as a sales-type lease at the end of the original term of the existing lease.

Many other changes may be made in lease terms. These often involve complex changes in accounting and, thus, require careful consideration. The preceding discussion indicates the scope of the issues. An accountant faced with new changes should study carefully all current standards before taking action on a particular change.

SUMMARY

At the beginning of the chapter, we identified several objectives you would accomplish after reading the chapter. The objectives are listed below, each followed by a brief summary of the key points in the chapter discussion.

1. **Explain the advantages of leasing.** For the lessee, a lease may involve financing benefits, a risk benefit, a tax benefit, a financial reporting benefit, and a billing benefit. For the lessor, a lease may involve the benefits of indirectly making a sale, and an alternative means of obtaining a profit opportunity.
2. **Understand key terms related to leasing.** The key terms related to leasing are included in Exhibit 21-1.
3. **Explain how to classify leases of personal property.** A lessee classifies a lease as a capital lease if it meets any one of the four capitalization criteria (listed in Exhibit 21-2), and as an operating lease if it meets none of the four criteria. A lessor classifies a lease as a sales-type lease if it meets any one of the four capitalization criteria, both of the additional criteria, and involves a manufacturer's or dealer's profit or loss. A lessor classifies a lease as a direct financing lease if it meets any one of the four capitalization criteria, both of the additional criteria, and does not result in a manufacturer's or dealer's profit or loss. A lessor classifies a lease as an operating lease if it meets none of the four criteria.
4. **Account for a lessee's operating and capital leases.** A lessee accounts for an operating lease by expensing the periodic lease payments. For a capital lease, the lessee records an asset and a liability equal to the present value, at the beginning of the lease term, of the minimum lease payments during the lease term. The discount rate is the lower of the lessee's incremental borrowing rate or the lessor's implicit rate if known and lower. The lessee depreciates the asset over its economic life if the lease contained a transfer of ownership or a bargain purchase option. Otherwise, the lessee uses the lease life. The lessee computes interest expense using the effective interest rate, and reduces the lease obligation for the difference between the cash paid and the interest expense.
5. **Understand disclosures by lessees.** The disclosure requirements of the lessee are summarized in Exhibit 21-5. Among the most important are the future minimum lease payments for each of the succeeding five years and in total, separately reported for its operating and capital leases.
6. **Account for a lessor's operating, direct financing, and sales-type leases.** A lessor accounts for an operating lease by recording the amounts of the periodic lease receipts as revenue. It also reports the asset on its balance sheet and records depreciation on the asset. For a direct financing lease, the lessor records a receivable at the undiscounted minimum lease payments plus any unguaranteed residual value. The difference between the receivable and the carrying value of the leased property is recorded as a contra-account to the receivable. The lessor computes interest revenue on a direct financing lease using its implicit interest rate. For a sales-type lease, the lessor records a receivable at the undiscounted minimum lease payments plus any unguaranteed residual value. It records a contra-account to the receivable as the difference between the gross receivable and the present value of the components of the receivable. The lessor also expenses the cost or carrying value of the property, plus any initial direct costs, minus the present value of any unguaranteed residual value. The lessor computes interest revenue on a sales-type lease using its implicit interest rate.
7. **Understand disclosures by lessors.** The disclosure requirements of the lessor are summarized in Exhibit 21-6. Among the most important are the future minimum lease payments for each of the succeeding five years and in total, separately for operating and capital leases.
8. **Explain the conceptual issues regarding leases.** The primary conceptual issue is whether the four capitalization criteria appropriately measure the transfer of the risks and benefits of ownership. A related issue is whether it is too easy for a lessee to avoid meeting any of the criteria and therefore not reporting the lease liability (and asset) on its balance sheet.

9. **Understand lease issues related to real estate, sales-leaseback issues, leveraged leases, and changes in lease provisions (Appendix).** Leases of real estate follow special rules that are summarized in Exhibit 21-8. The primary issue in a sales-leaseback is that the seller-lessee recognizes a loss in the period of the transaction, but defers any gain and amortizes it over the remaining life of the lease. Leveraged leases involve three parties: the lessor, the lessee, and a long-term creditor who provides nonrecourse financing for the leasing transaction. When the lease provisions are changed in such a way that the lease would have been classified differently had the changed terms been in effect at the beginning of the lease term, the revised agreement is considered a new agreement.

ANSWERS TO REAL REPORT QUESTIONS

Real Report 21-1 Answers

1. Operating leases provide many benefits to the lessee. The use of long-term operating leases for stores and equipment may provide Wal-Mart considerable flexibility. For example, the renewal options allow Wal-Mart to continue to operate profitable locations, and for less profitable locations, the company may have lower expenses due to contingent rentals while relocating these stores can be accomplished relatively easily by choosing not to exercise renewal options. Such flexibility can be a significant reduction in the company's risk. In addition, the use of operating leases provides a financial reporting benefit in that the lease does not add an asset or liability to Wal-Mart's balance sheet which generally results in "better" debt and return ratios.

2. The present value of the minimum lease payments for Wal-Mart's capital leases is $3,792 million. This amount is included in the liability section of Wal-Mart's balance sheet with a portion classified as a current liability and a portion classified as a noncurrent liability (based on either the present value of next year's payments approach or the change in present value approach). In addition, the present value of the minimum lease payments at the inception of the lease

less accumulated depreciation is included in the property, plant, and equipment section of the balance sheet.

3. The classification of Wal-Mart's operating leases as capital leases would result in a deterioration of Wal-Mart's debt ratio. The current debt ratio is 58.9% ($70,827 million ÷ $120,223 million). Assuming a rate of interest of 10%, annual lease payments in advance, and a lease term of 15 years, assets and liabilities would be increased by the present value of the lease payments of approximately $5,160 million (see calculations in the following table). This would result in an increase in Wal-Mart's debt ratio to 60.6% ($75,987 million ÷ $125,383 million).

Payment Schedule (in millions)		
Year	Payment	Present Value
2006	$730	$ 730.00
2007	700	636.36
2008	626	517.36
2009	578	434.26
2010	530	362.00
Thereafter	591*	2,480.32
		$5,160.30

* ($5,908 ÷ 10 years)

QUESTIONS

Q21-1 What does *FASB Statement No. 13 as Amended* provide in reference to the measuring and reporting of leases?

Q21-2 List seven advantages to the lessee of leasing, as compared with purchasing, an asset.

Q21-3 Assume that a lessee leases equipment and insists on terms that qualify it as an operating lease, barely escaping the qualification as a capital lease. Discuss the impact that such an operating lease has on financial statements and related financial information as compared to the effect that a capital lease would have.

Q21-4 Define the following terms: (a) *lease*, (b) *sales-type lease*, (c) *direct financing lease*, (d) *sale-leaseback transaction*, (e) *operating lease*, (f) *leveraged lease*.

Q21-5 Define the following terms used in *FASB Statement No. 13 as Amended*: (a) *inception of lease*, (b) *bargain purchase option*, (c) *unguaranteed residual value*, (d) *implicit interest rate*, (e) *initial direct costs*.

Q21-6 What components make up the minimum lease payments of a typical capital lease?

Q21-7 List the four criteria used to determine if a lease is classified as a capital lease by the lessee.

Q21-8 Describe briefly the accounting procedures followed by the lessor and by the lessee for an operating lease.

Q21-9 Describe briefly the procedures followed by the lessee to account for a capital lease.

Q21-10 From the standpoint of the lessor, a sales-type lease must meet one or more of the criteria of a capital lease as well as two additional criteria. Name these two additional criteria.

Q21-11 What is the basic difference between the accounting procedures used by a lessor for a sales-type lease and those used for a direct financing lease?

Q21-12 Why are compound interest concepts appropriate and applicable in accounting for a direct financing lease?

Q21-13 The Owens Company leased equipment for four years at $50,000 a month, with an option to renew the lease for six years at $2,000 per month or to purchase the equipment for $25,000 (a price considerably less than the expected fair value) after the initial lease term of four years. How does Owens Company record this transaction?

Q21-14 McFarland Corporation leased equipment under a lease calling for the payment of $50,000 a year in rent. At the end of the current year, when the capital lease had a remaining term of 20 years, McFarland Company subleased the asset for a rental of $75,000 a year for 20 years. The new lease is acceptable to the lessor, who agrees that McFarland Company has completed its primary obligation. When will McFarland Company report the gain from this transaction? Explain.

Q21-15 (a) What disclosures are lessees required to make? (b) What disclosures are lessors required to make for various types of leases?

Q21-16 (Appendix) From the point of view of the seller-lessee, what is the primary accounting issue involved in accounting for a sale-leaseback transaction as compared to other lessee transactions? Discuss.

Q21-17 (Appendix) What distinguishes a leveraged lease from other leases? What, if any, is the major difference in the accounting of the lessee for a leveraged lease?

MULTIPLE CHOICE (AICPA Adapted)

Select the best answer for each of the following.

M21-1 The present value of the minimum lease payments should be used by the lessee in the determination of a(an)

	Capital Lease Liability	Operating Lease Liability
a.	Yes	No
b.	Yes	Yes
c.	No	Yes
d.	No	No

M21-2 East Company leased a new machine from North Company on May 1, 2007 under a lease with the following information:

Lease term	10 years
Annual rental payable at beginning of each lease year	$40,000
Useful life of machine	12 years
Implicit interest rate	14%
Present value factor for an annuity of 1 in advance for 10 periods at 14%	5.95
Present value factor for 1 for 10 periods at 14%	0.27

East has the option to purchase the machine on May 1, 2017 by paying $50,000, which approximates the expected fair value of the machine on the option exercise date. On May 1, 2007 East should record a capitalized lease asset of
a. $251,500
b. $238,000
c. $224,500
d. $198,000

M21-3 For a lease that transfers ownership of the property to the lessee by the end of the lease term, the lessee should

a. Record the minimum lease payment as an expense
b. Amortize the capitalizable cost of the property using the interest method
c. Depreciate the capitalizable cost of the property in a manner consistent with the lessee's normal depreciation policy for owned assets, except that the period of depreciation should be the lease term
d. Depreciate the capitalizable cost of the property in a manner consistent with the lessee's normal depreciation policy for owned assets

Items 4 and 5 are based on the following information:

Fox Company, a dealer in machinery and equipment, leased equipment to Tiger, Inc. on July 1, 2007. The lease is appropriately accounted for as a sale by Fox and as a purchase by Tiger. The lease is for a 10-year period (the useful life of the asset) expiring June 30, 2017. The first of 10 equal annual payments of $500,000 was made on July 1, 2007. Fox had purchased the equipment for $2,675,000 on January 1, 2007 and established a list selling price of $3,375,000 on the equipment. Assume that the present value at July 1, 2007 of the rent payments over the lease term, discounted at 12% (the appropriate interest rate), was $3,165,000.

M21-4 What is the amount of profit on the sale and the amount of interest income that Fox should record for the year ended December 31, 2007?
a. $0 and $159,900
b. $490,000 and $159,900
c. $490,000 and $189,900
d. $700,000 and $189,900

M21-5 Assuming that Tiger uses straight-line depreciation, what is the amount of depreciation and interest expense that Tiger should record for the year ended December 31, 2007?

a. $158,250 and $159,900
b. $158,250 and $189,900
c. $168,750 and $159,900
d. $168,750 and $189,900

	Interest Expense	Depreciation Expense
a.	$ 0	$ 0
b.	$7,717	$6,145
c.	$9,217	$6,145
d.	$9,217	$9,217

M21-6 Rent received in advance by the lessor for an operating lease should be recognized as revenue

a. When received
b. At the lease's inception
c. In the period specified by the lease
d. At the lease's expiration

M21-7 For a six-year capital lease, the portion of the minimum lease payment applicable in the third year to the reduction of the obligation should be

a. Less than in the second year
b. More than in the second year
c. The same as in the fourth year
d. More than in the fourth year

M21-8 On January 2, 2007, Lafayette Machine Shops, Inc. signed a 10-year noncancelable lease for a heavy-duty drill press, stipulating annual payments of $15,000 starting at the end of the first year, with title passing to Lafayette at the expiration of the lease. Lafayette treated this transaction as a capital lease. The drill press has an estimated useful life of 15 years, with no salvage value. Lafayette uses straight-line depreciation for all of its fixed assets. Aggregate lease payments were determined to have a present value of $92,170, based on implicit interest of 10%. For 2007 Lafayette should record

M21-9 On August 1, 2007 Kern Company leased a machine to Day Company for a six-year period requiring payments of $10,000 at the beginning of each year. The machine cost $48,000, which is the fair value at the lease date, and has a useful life of eight years with no residual value. Kern's implicit interest rate is 10% and present value factors are as follows:

Present value for an annuity due of $1
at 10% for six periods   4.791
Present value for an annuity due of $1
at 10% for eight periods   5.868

Kern appropriately recorded the lease as a direct financing lease. At the inception of the lease, the gross lease receivables account balance should be

a. $60,000   c. $48,000
b. $58,680   d. $47,910

M21-10 At its inception, the lease term of Lease G is 65% of the estimated remaining economic life of the leased property. This lease contains a bargain purchase option. The lessee should record Lease G as

a. Neither an asset nor a liability
b. An asset but not a liability
c. An expense
d. An asset and a liability

EXERCISES

E21-1 *Determining Type of Lease and Subsequent Accounting* On January 1, 2007 the Caswell Company signs a 10-year cancelable (at the option of either party) agreement to lease a storage building from the Wake Company. The following information pertains to this lease agreement:

1. The agreement requires rental payments of $100,000 at the end of each year.
2. The cost and fair value of the building on January 1, 2007 is $2 million.
3. The building has an estimated economic life of 50 years, with no residual value. The Caswell Company depreciates similar buildings according to the straight-line method.
4. The lease does not contain a renewable option clause. At the termination of the lease, the building reverts to the lessor.
5. Caswell's incremental borrowing rate is 14% per year. The Wake Company set the annual rental to ensure a 16% rate of return (the loss in service value anticipated for the term of the lease).
6. Executory costs of $7,000 annually, related to taxes on the property, are paid by Wake Company.

Required

1. Determine what type of lease this is for the lessee.
2. Prepare appropriate journal entries on the lessee's books to reflect the signing of the lease agreement and to record the payments and expenses related to this lease for the years 2007 and 2008.

E21-2 *Lessee Accounting Issues* The Sax Company signs a lease agreement dated January 1, 2007 that provides for it to lease computers from the Appleton Company beginning January 1, 2007. The lease terms, provisions, and related events are as follows:

1. The lease term is five years. The lease is noncancelable and requires equal rental payments to be made at the end of each year.
2. The computers have an estimated life of five years, a fair value of $300,000, and a zero estimated residual value.

3. Sax Company agrees to pay all executory costs.
4. The lease contains no renewal or bargain purchase option.
5. The annual rental is set by Appleton at $83,222.92 to earn a rate of return of 12% on its net investment. The Sax Company is aware of this rate, which is equal to its borrowing rate.
6. Sax Company uses the straight-line method to record depreciation on similar equipment.

Required
1. Determine what type of lease this is for Sax Company.
2. Calculate the amount of the asset and liability of the Sax Company at the inception of the lease (round to the nearest dollar).
3. Prepare a table summarizing the lease payments and interest expense.
4. Prepare journal entries for Sax Company for the years 2007 and 2008.

E21-3   *Lessee Accounting with Payments Made at Beginning of Year* The Adden Company signs a lease agreement dated January 1, 2007 that provides for it to lease heavy equipment from the Scott Rental Company beginning January 1, 2007. The lease terms, provisions, and related events are as follows:
1. The lease term is four years. The lease is noncancelable and requires annual rental payments of $20,000 each to be paid in advance at the beginning of each year.
2. The cost, and also fair value, of the heavy equipment to Scott at the inception of the lease is $68,036.62. The equipment has an estimated life of four years and has a zero estimated residual value at the end of this time.
3. Adden Company agrees to pay all executory costs.
4. The lease contains no renewal or bargain purchase option.
5. Scott's interest rate implicit in the lease is 12%. Adden Company is aware of this rate, which is equal to its borrowing rate.
6. Adden Company uses the straight-line method to record depreciation on similar equipment.
7. Executory costs paid at the end of the year by Adden Company are:

2007	2008
Insurance, $1,500	Insurance, $1,300
Property taxes, $6,000	Property taxes, $5,500

Required
1. Determine what type of lease this is for Adden Company.
2. Prepare a table summarizing the lease payments and interest expense for Adden Company.
3. Prepare journal entries for Adden Company for the years 2007 and 2008.

E21-4   *Lessor Accounting Issues* The Rexon Company leases equipment to Ten-Care Company beginning January 1, 2007. The lease terms, provisions, and related events are as follows:
1. The lease term is eight years. The lease is noncancelable and requires equal rental payments to be made at the end of each year.
2. The cost, and also fair value, of the equipment is $500,000. The equipment has an estimated life of eight years and has a zero estimated value at the end of that time.
3. Ten-Care Company agrees to pay all executory costs.
4. The lease contains no renewal or bargain purchase option.
5. The interest rate implicit in the lease is 14%.
6. The initial direct costs are insignificant and assumed to be zero.
7. The collectibility of the rentals is reasonably assured, and there are no important uncertainties surrounding the amount of unreimbursable costs yet to be incurred by the lessor.

Required
1. Assuming that the lease is a direct financing lease from Rexon's point of view, calculate the amount of the equal rental receipts.
2. Prepare a table summarizing the lease receipts and interest revenue earned by Rexon.
3. Prepare journal entries for Rexon for the years 2007 and 2008.

E21-5   *Lessor Accounting Issues* Ramallah Company leases heavy equipment to Terrell, Inc. on January 2, 2007 on the following terms:
1. Forty-eight lease rentals of $1,600 at the end of each month are to be paid by Terrell, Inc., and the lease is noncancelable.
2. The cost of the heavy equipment to Ramallah Company was $60,758.
3. Ramallah Company will account for this lease using the direct financing method. The difference between total rental receipts ($1,600 × 48 = $76,800) and the cost of the equipment ($60,758) was computed to yield a return of 1% per month over the lease term.

Required
Prepare journal entries for Ramallah Company (the lessor) to record the lease contract and the receipt of the first lease rental on January 31, 2007. Record the part of the $16,042 Unearned Interest that was earned during the first month and carry calculations to the nearest dollar.

E21-6   *Lessee and Lessor Accounting Issues* Lessor Leasing Company agrees to provide Lessee Company with equipment under a noncancelable lease for five years. The equipment has a five-year life, cost Lessor Company $30,000, and will have no residual value when the lease term ends. Lessee Company agrees to pay all executory costs ($500 per year) throughout the lease period. On January 1, 2007 the equipment is delivered. Lessor expects a 14% return. The five equal annual rents are payable in advance starting January 1, 2007.

Required
1. Assuming this is a direct financing lease for the lessor and a capital lease for the lessee, prepare a table summarizing the lease and interest payments suitable for use by either party.
2. On the assumption that both companies adjust and close books each December 31, prepare journal entries relating to the lease for both companies through December 31, 2007 based on data derived in the table. Assume that Lessee Company depreciates similar equipment by the straight-line method.

E21-7   *Lessor Accounting with Receipts at End of Year* The Berne Company, the lessor, enters into a lease with Fox Company to lease equipment to Fox beginning January 1, 2007. The lease terms, provisions, and related events are as follows:
1. The lease term is four years. The lease is noncancelable and requires annual rental payments of $50,000 to be made at the end of each year.
2. The cost of the equipment is $130,000. The equipment has an estimated life of four years and an estimated residual value at the end of the lease term of zero.
3. Fox agrees to pay all executory costs.
4. The interest rate implicit in the lease is 12%.
5. The initial direct costs are insignificant and assumed to be zero.
6. The collectibility of the rentals is reasonably assured, and there are no important uncertainties surrounding the amount of unreimbursable costs yet to be incurred by the lessor.

Required
1. Assuming that the lease is a sales-type lease from Berne's point of view, calculate the selling price and assume that this is also the fair value.
2. Prepare a table summarizing the lease receipts and interest revenue earned by the lessor.
3. Prepare journal entries for Berne Company, the lessor, for the years 2007 and 2008.

E21-8   *Lessor Accounting with Receipts at Beginning of Year* The Edom Company, the lessor, enters into a lease with Jebusite Company to lease equipment to Jebusite beginning January 1, 2007. The lease terms, provisions, and related events are as follows:
1. The lease term is five years. The lease is noncancelable and requires annual rental receipts of $100,000 to be made in advance at the beginning of each year.
2. The cost of the equipment is $313,000. The equipment has an estimated life of six years and, at the end of the lease term, has an unguaranteed residual value of $20,000 accruing to the benefit of Edom.
3. Jebusite agrees to pay all executory costs.
4. The interest rate implicit in the lease is 14%.
5. The initial direct costs are insignificant and assumed to be zero.
6. The collectibility of the rentals is reasonably assured, and there are no important uncertainties surrounding the amount of unreimbursable costs yet to be incurred by the lessor.

Required
1. Assuming that the lease is a sales-type lease from Edom's point of view, calculate the selling price and assume that this is also the fair value.
2. Prepare a table summarizing the lease receipts and interest revenue earned by the lessor.
3. Prepare journal entries for Edom Company, the lessor, for the years 2007 and 2008.

E21-9   *Lessee and Lessor Accounting Issues* The following information is available for a noncancelable lease of equipment that is classified as a sales-type lease by the lessor and as a capital lease by the lessee. Assume that the lease payments are made at the beginning of each month, interest and straight-line depreciation are recognized at the end of each month, and the residual value of the leased asset is zero at the end of a three-year life.

Cost of equipment to lessor (Anson Company)	$50,000
Initial payment by lessee (Bullard Company) at inception of lease	2,000
Present value of remaining 35 payments of $2,000 each discounted at 1% per month	58,817

Required
1. Record the lease (including the initial receipt of $2,000) and the receipt of the second and third installments of $2,000 in the accounts of the Anson Company. Carry computations to the nearest dollar.
2. Record the lease (including the initial payment of $2,000), the payment of the second and third installments of $2,000, and monthly depreciation in the accounts of the Bullard Company. The lessee records the lease obligation at net present value. Carry computations to the nearest dollar.

E21-10 *Comparisons of Operating and Sales-Type Leases* On January 1, 2007 Nelson Company leases certain property to Queens Company at an annual rental of $60,000 payable in advance at the beginning of each year for eight years. The first payment is received immediately. The leased property, which is new, cost $275,000 and has an estimated economic life of eight years and no residual value. The interest rate implicit in the lease is 12% and the lease is noncancelable. Nelson Company had no other costs associated with this lease. It should have accounted for this lease as a sales-type lease but mistakenly treated it as an operating lease.

Required

Compute the effect on income before income taxes during the first year of the lease as a result of Nelson Company's classification of this lease as an operating rather than a sales-type lease.

E21-11 *Lease Income and Expense* Reuben Company retires a machine from active use on January 2, 2007 for the express purpose of leasing it. The machine had a carrying value of $900,000 after 12 years of use and is expected to have 10 more years of economic life. The machine is depreciated on a straight-line basis. On March 2, 2007 Reuben Company leases the machine to Owens Company for $180,000 a year for a five-year period ending February 28, 2012. Under the provisions of the lease, Reuben Company incurs total maintenance and other related costs of $20,000 for the year ended December 31, 2007. Owens Company pays $180,000 to Reuben Company on March 2, 2007. The lease was properly classified as an operating lease.

Required

1. Compute the income before income taxes derived by Reuben Company from this lease for the calendar year ended December 31, 2007.
2. Compute the amount of rent expense incurred by Owens Company from this lease for the calendar year ended December 31, 2007.

E21-12 *Determining Type of Lease and Subsequent Accounting* The Ravis Rent-A-Car Company leases a car to Ira Reem, an employee, on January 1, 2007. The term of the noncancelable lease is four years. The following information about the lease is provided:
1. Title to the car passes to Ira Reem on the termination of the lease with no additional payment required by the lessee.
2. The cost and fair value of the car to the Ravis Rent-A-Car Company is $8,400. The car has an economic life of five years.
3. The lease payments are determined at an amount that will yield Ravis Rent-A-Car Company a rate of return of 10% on its net investment.
4. Collectibility of the lease payments is reasonably assured.
5. There are no important uncertainties surrounding the amount of unreimbursable costs yet to be incurred by the lessor.
6. Equal annual lease payments are due at the end of each year.

Required

1. What type of lease is this to Ravis Rent-A-Car Company? Why?
2. Prepare a table summarizing the lease receipts and interest revenue earned by the Ravis Rent-A-Car Company for the four-year lease term.
3. Prepare the journal entries for 2007 and 2008 to record the lease agreement, the lease receipts, and the recognition of income on the books of Ravis Rent-A-Car Company.

E21-13 *Sale-Leaseback (Appendix)* On January 1, 2007 the Stimpson Company sells land to Barker Company for $2.5 million, then immediately leases it back. The relevant information is as follows:
1. The land was carried on Stimpson's books at a value of $2 million.
2. The term of the noncancelable lease is 25 years.
3. The lease agreement requires equal rental payments of $357,007 at the end of each year.
4. The incremental borrowing rate of Stimpson Company is 15%. Stimpson is aware that Barker Company set the annual rental to ensure a rate of return of 14%.
5. The land has a fair value of $2.5 million on January 1, 2007.
6. Stimpson Company has the option of purchasing the land for $150 at the end of 25 years.
7. Stimpson Company pays all executory costs. These costs consist of insurance and property taxes amounting to $12,000 per year.
8. There are no important uncertainties surrounding the amount of unreimbursable costs yet to be incurred by the lessor, and the collectibility of the rentals is reasonably assured.

Required

1. Prepare the journal entries for the seller-lessee, Stimpson, for 2007 to reflect the sale and leaseback agreement. In calculating the present value of the lease payments, ignore the $150 bargain purchase option as immaterial.
2. Describe briefly the accounting treatment of the gain by the seller-lessee.

PROBLEMS

P21-1 *Determining Type of Lease and Subsequent Accounting* On January 1, 2007 the Alice Company leases electronic equipment for five years, agreeing to pay $70,000 annually at the beginning of each year under the noncancelable lease. Superior Electronics Company, the lessor, agrees to pay all executory costs, estimated to be $3,450 per year. The cost and also fair value of the equipment is $500,000. Its estimated life is 10 years. The estimated residual value at the end of five years is $200,000; at the end of 10 years, it is $5,000. There is no bargain purchase option in the lease nor any agreement to transfer ownership at the end of the lease to the lessee. The lessee's incremental borrowing rate is 12%. During 2007 Superior Electronics pays property taxes of $650, maintenance costs of $1,600, and insurance of $1,200. There are no important uncertainties surrounding the amount of unreimbursable costs yet to be incurred by the lessor. Straight-line depreciation is considered the appropriate method by both companies.

Required
1. Identify the type of lease involved for Alice Company and Superior Electronics Company and give reasons for your classifications.
2. Prepare appropriate journal entries for 2007 for the lessee and lessor.

P21-2 *Determining Type of Lease and Subsequent Accounting* On January 1, 2007 the Ballieu Company leases specialty equipment with an economic life of eight years to the Anderson Company. The lease contains the following terms and provisions:

The lease is noncancelable and has a term of eight years. The annual rentals are $35,000, payable at the beginning of each year. The interest rate implicit in the lease is 14%. The Anderson Company agrees to pay all executory costs and is given an option to buy the equipment for $1 at the end of the lease term, December 31, 2014.

The cost of the equipment to the lessor is $150,000 and the fair retail value is approximately $185,100. The lessor incurs no material initial direct costs. The collectibility of the rentals is reasonably assured, and there are no important uncertainties surrounding the amount of unreimbursable costs yet to be incurred by the lessor. The lessor estimates that the fair value is expected to be significantly greater than $1 at the end of the lease term.

The lessor calculates that the present value on January 1, 2007 of eight annual payments in advance of $35,000 discounted at 14% is $185,090.68 (the $1 purchase option is ignored as immaterial).

Required
1. Identify the classification of the lease transaction from the point of view of Ballieu Company. Give the reasons for your classification.
2. Prepare all the journal entries for Ballieu Company for the years 2007 and 2008.
3. Discuss the disclosure requirements for the lease transaction in the notes to the financial statements of the Ballieu Company.

P21-3 *Lessee Accounting Issues* The Timmer Company signs a lease agreement dated January 1, 2007 that provides for it to lease equipment from Landau Company beginning January 1, 2007. The lease terms, provisions, and related events are as follows:

The lease is noncancelable and has a term of five years. The annual rentals are $83,222.92, payable at the end of each year, and provide Landau with a 12% annual rate of return on its net investment. The Timmer Company agrees to pay all executory costs at the end of each year. In 2007 these were: insurance $3,760; property taxes, $5,440. In 2008: insurance, $3,100; property taxes, $5,330. There is no renewal or bargain purchase option.

Timmer estimates that the equipment has an economic life of five years and a zero residual value. Timmer's incremental borrowing rate is 16%, it knows the rate implicit in the lease, and it uses the straight-line method to record depreciation on similar equipment.

Required
1. Calculate the amount of the asset and liability of the Timmer Company at the inception of the lease. (Round to the nearest dollar.)
2. Prepare a table summarizing the lease payments and interest expense.
3. Prepare journal entries on the books of Timmer for 2007 and 2008.
4. Prepare a partial balance sheet in regard to the lease for Timmer for December 31, 2007.

P21-4 *Direct Financing Lease* Calder Company, the lessor, enters into a lease with Darwin Company, the lessee, to provide heavy equipment beginning January 1, 2007. The lease terms, provisions, and related events are as follows:

The lease is noncancelable, has a term of eight years, and has no renewal or bargain purchase option. The annual rentals are $65,000, payable at the end of each year. The interest rate implicit in the lease is 15%. The Darwin Company agrees to pay all executory costs.

The cost and fair value of the equipment to the lessor is $308,021.03. The lessor incurs no material initial direct costs. The collectibility of the rentals is reasonably assured, and there are no important uncertainties surrounding the amount of unreimbursable costs yet to be incurred by the lessor. The lessor estimates that the fair value at the end of the lease term will be $50,000 and that the economic life of the equipment is nine years.

The following present value factors are relevant:

$$PV_{n=8,i=15\%} = 4.487322; \quad PV_{n=8,i=15\%} = 0.326902; \quad PV_{n=1,i=15\%} = 0.869565$$

Required
1. Prepare a table summarizing the lease receipts and interest revenue earned by the lessor for this direct financing lease.
2. State why the lease is a direct financing lease.
3. Prepare journal entries for Calder Company for the years 2007, 2008, and 2009.
4. Prepare partial balance sheets for December 31, 2007 and December 31, 2008 showing how the accounts should be reported.

P21-5 *Comprehensive* Landlord Company and Tenant Company enter into a noncancelable, direct financing lease on January 1, 2007 for new heavy equipment that cost the Landlord Company $300,000 (useful life is six years with no residual value). The fair value is also $300,000. Landlord Company expects a 14% return over the six-year period of the lease. Lease provisions require six equal annual amounts payable each January 1, beginning with January 1, 2007. The Tenant Company pays all executory costs. The heavy equipment reverts to the lessor at the termination of the lease. Assume that there are no initial direct costs. The collectibility of the rentals is reasonably assured and there are no important uncertainties surrounding the amount of unreimbursable costs yet to be incurred by the lessor.

Required
1. (a) Show how the Landlord Company should compute the annual rental amounts. (b) Discuss how the Tenant Company should compute the present value of the lease rights. What additional information would be required to make this computation?
2. Prepare a table summarizing the lease and interest receipts that would be suitable for the Landlord Company. Under what conditions would this table be suitable for the Tenant Company?
3. Assuming that the table prepared in Requirement 2 is suitable for both the lessee and the lessor, prepare the journal entries for both firms for the years 2007 and 2008. Use the straight-line depreciation method for the leased equipment. The executory costs paid by the lessee in 2007 are: insurance, $700 and property taxes, $800; in 2008: insurance, $600 and property taxes, $750.
4. Show the items and amounts that would be reported on the comparative 2007 and 2008 income statements and ending balance sheets for both the lessor and the lessee. Include appropriate notes to the financial statements.

P21-6 *Direct Financing Lease with Unguaranteed Residual Value* Lessor Company and Lessee Company enter into a five-year, noncancelable, direct financing lease on January 1, 2007 for a new computer that cost the Lessor Company $400,000 (useful life is five years). The fair value is also $400,000. Lessor Company expects a 12% return over the five-year period of the lease. The computer will have an estimated unguaranteed residual value of $20,000 at the end of the fifth year of the lease. The lease provisions require five equal annual amounts, payable each January 1, beginning with January 1, 2007. The Lessee Company pays all executory costs. The computer reverts to the lessor at the termination of the lease. Assume there are no initial direct costs, no important uncertainties surrounding the amount of unreimbursable costs yet to be incurred by the lessor, and that the collectibility of rentals is reasonably assured.

Required
1. Show how the Lessor Company should compute the annual rental amounts.
2. Prepare a table summarizing the lease and interest receipts that would be suitable for the Lessor Company.
3. Prepare the journal entries for Lessor Company for the years 2007, 2008, and 2009.

P21-7 *Sales-Type Lease with Receipts at End of Year* The Lamplighter Company, the lessor, agrees to lease equipment to Tilson Company, the lessee, beginning January 1, 2007. The lease terms, provisions, and related events are as follows:

The lease is noncancelable and has a term of eight years. The annual rentals are $32,000, payable at the end of each year. The Tilson Company agrees to pay all executory costs. The interest rate implicit in the lease is 14%.

The cost of the equipment to the lessor is $110,000. The lessor incurs no material initial direct costs. The collectibility of the rentals is reasonably assured, and there are no important uncertainties surrounding the amount of unreimbursable costs yet to be incurred by the lessor. The lessor estimates that the fair value at the end of the lease term will be $20,000 and that the economic life of the equipment is nine years.

Required
1. Calculate the selling price implied by the lease and prepare a table summarizing the lease receipts and interest revenue earned by the lessor for this sales-type lease.
2. State why this is a sales-type lease.

3. Prepare journal entries for Lamplighter Company for the years 2007, 2008, and 2010.
4. Prepare partial balance sheets for Lamplighter Company for December 31, 2007 and December 31, 2008, showing how the accounts should be disclosed.

P21-8 *Various Lease Issues for Lessor and Lessee* Lessee Company leases heavy equipment on January 1, 2007 under a capital lease from Lessor Company with the following lease provisions:

The lease is noncancelable and has a term of 10 years. The lease does not contain a renewal or bargain purchase option. The annual rentals are $27,653.77, payable at the beginning of each year. The Lessee Company agrees to pay all executory costs. The interest rate implicit in the lease is 12%, which is known by Lessee Company. The residual value of the property at the end of 10 years is estimated to be zero.

The cost and fair value of the equipment to the lessor is $175,000. The lessor incurs no material initial direct costs. The collectibility of the rentals is reasonably assured, and there are no important uncertainties surrounding the amount of unreimbursable costs yet to be incurred by the lessor.

Lessee's incremental borrowing rate is 15% and it uses the straight-line method to record depreciation on similar equipment. In 2007 the lessee pays insurance of $1,900, property taxes of $1,300, and maintenance of $600; and in 2008 the lessee pays insurance of $1,800, property taxes of $1,200, and maintenance of $500.

Required
1. Identify the type of lease involved for the lessee and the lessor, and give reasons for your classifications.
2. Prepare all the journal entries for both the lessee and the lessor for 2007 and 2008.

P21-9 *Various Lease Issues for Lessor and Lessee* Benjamin Company has rented new equipment to Murrell Builders that cost $50,000. This equipment has a life of 4 years and no residual value at the end of that time. The lease is noncancelable and is signed on January 1, 2007. Murrell Builders assumes all normal risks and executory costs of ownership. The title to the property is transferred to Murrell Builders at the end of the four years. The Benjamin Company computes the rents on the basis of a 14% return. The lessee's incremental borrowing rate is also 14%. The collectibility of rentals is reasonably assured and there are no important uncertainties surrounding the amount of unreimbursable costs yet to be incurred by the lessor.

Required
1. Assuming the annual rentals are payable at the end of each year, complete the following:
   a. Lessor computation of periodic rental receipts.
   b. Lessee computation of the present value of the special property rights under the lease.
   c. A table summarizing lease and interest payments that would be suitable for both lessor and lessee.
2. Assuming the annual rentals are payable at the start of each year, compute the same three items listed in Requirement 1.
3. Prepare the journal entries for the lessor and lessee for Requirement 2 throughout 2007. Use the straight-line depreciation method.
4. Indicate the asset and liability amounts that the lessor and lessee would report on their balance sheets at December 31, 2007 under Requirement 2.

P21-10 *Initial Direct Costs and Related Issues* On January 1, 2007 the Amity Company leases a crane to Baltimore Company. The lease contains the following terms and provisions:

The lease is noncancelable and has a term of 10 years. The lease does not contain a renewal or bargain purchase option. The annual rentals are $4,000, payable at the beginning of each year. The Baltimore Company agrees to pay all executory costs.

The cost and fair value of the equipment to the lessor is $24,913.94. The lessor incurs initial direct costs of $1,364.98. The interest rate implicit in the lease is 12.5%. After including the initial direct costs, the implicit rate is 12%. The collectibility of the rentals is reasonably assured, and there are no important uncertainties surrounding the amount of unreimbursable costs yet to be incurred by the lessor. The lessor estimates that the fair value at the end of the lease term will be $3,000 and that the economic life of the crane is 12 years.

Required
1. What are initial direct costs? Discuss the accounting treatment of these costs. Are they treated in the same manner for (a) an operating lease, (b) a sales-type lease, and (c) a direct financing lease?
2. From the lessor's viewpoint, is the preceding lease a sales-type or direct financing lease? Give reasons to support your conclusion.
3. Prepare the journal entries for Amity Company for 2007.

P21-11 *Various Lease Issues* Farrington Company leases a computer from the Wilson Company. The lease includes the following provisions:

The lease is noncancelable and has a term of eight years. The annual rentals are $60,000, payable at the end of each year. The Farrington Company agrees to pay all executory costs and has an option to purchase the computer for $1,000 at the end of the life of the lease. The interest rate implicit in the lease is 12%, which is known to Farrington.

Farrington estimates that the computer has an economic life of 12 years and a value of $70,000 at the end of eight years. Farrington's incremental borrowing rate is 16% and it uses the straight-line method to record depreciation on similar equipment.

The computer cost Wilson $200,000 to manufacture. The lessor incurs initial direct costs of $10,000. The collectibility of the rentals is reasonably assured, and there are no important uncertainties surrounding the amount of unreimbursable costs yet to be incurred by the lessor.

Required

1. What is the correct classification of the lease for the lessee and lessor? Explain whether the lease meets *each* of the required criteria.
2. Assuming that the lease is signed on January 1, 2007, prepare all journal entries for 2007 for the lessor.
3. After six years, because of changes in the technology, the lessee and lessor independently conclude that the expected residual value of the computer at the end of the life of the lease is only $10,000. Discuss how the lessor should account for the change.

P21-12 *Accounting for Leases by Lessee and Lessor* Scuppermong Farms, the lessee, and Tyrrell Equipment, the lessor, sign a lease agreement on January 1, 2007 that provides for Scuppermong Farms to lease a cultivator from Tyrrell Equipment. The lease terms, provisions, and other related events are as follows: The lease is noncancelable and has a term of six years. The annual rentals are $56,100, payable at the beginning of each year. Tyrrell Equipment agrees to pay all executory costs, which are expected to be $1,100 annually, including property taxes of $500, insurance of $350, and maintenance of $250. Scuppermong Farms guarantees a residual value of $60,000 at the end of six years. The interest rate implicit in the lease is 14%, which is known by Scuppermong.

Scuppermong Farms' incremental borrowing rate is 15% and it uses the sum-of-the-years'-digits method to record depreciation on similar equipment.

The cost and fair value of the cultivator to Tyrrell Equipment is $271,154.68. The lessor incurs no material initial direct costs. The collectibility of the rentals is reasonably assured, and there are no important uncertainties surrounding the amount of unreimbursable costs yet to be incurred by the lessor.

Required

1. Identify the type of lease involved for both Scuppermong Farms and Tyrrell Equipment, and give reasons for your classifications.
2. Prepare the journal entries for both Scuppermong Farms and Tyrrell Equipment for 2007. (*Hint*: Scuppermong Farms should expense executory costs when annual payments are made to Tyrrell.)

P21-13 AICPA Adapted *Lessor's Income Statement* The Dahlia Company has two divisions, the Astor Division which started operating in 2005, and the Tulip Division which started operating in 2006. The Astor Division leases medical equipment to hospitals. All of its leases are appropriately recorded as operating leases for accounting purposes, except for a major lease entered into on January 1, 2007, which is appropriately recorded as a sale-type lease for accounting purposes.

Under long-term contracts, Tulip constructs wastewater treatment plants for small communities throughout the United States. All of its long-term contracts are appropriately recorded for accounting purposes under the percentage-of-completion method, except for two contracts which are appropriately recorded for accounting purposes under the completed-contract method because of a lack of dependable estimates at the time of entering into these contracts.

For the year ended December 31, 2007 the following information is available:

Astor Division:

Operating Leases. Revenues from operating leases were $800,000. The cost of the related leased equipment is $3,700,000, which is being depreciated on a straight-line basis over a five-year period. The estimated residual value of the leased equipment at the end of the five-year period is $200,000. No leased equipment was acquired or constructed in 2007. Maintenance and other related costs and the costs of any other services rendered under the provisions of the leases were $70,000 in 2007.

Lease Recorded as a Sale. The January 1, 2007 lease recorded as a sale is for a six-year period expiring December 31, 2012. The cost of this leased equipment is $3,500,000. This leased equipment is estimated to have no residual value at the end of the lease. Maintenance and other related costs, and the costs of any other services rendered under the provisions of this lease, all of which were paid by the lessee, were $120,000 in 2007. Equal annual payments under the lease are $750,000 and are due on January 1. The first payment was made on January 1, 2007. The present value for an annuity of $1 in advance at 10% is as follows:

Number of Periods	Present Value
5	4.170
6	4.791
7	5.355

Tulip Division:

Long-Term Contracts: Percentage-of-Completion Method. Long-term contracts recorded under the percentage-of-completion method aggregate $6,000,000. Costs incurred on these contracts were $1,500,000 in 2006 and $3,000,000 in 2007. Estimated additional costs of $1,000,000 are required to complete these contracts. Revenues of $1,740,000 were recognized in 2006 and a total of $4,800,000 has been billed, of which $4,600,000 has been collected. No long-term contracts recorded under the percentage-of-completion method were completed in 2007.

Long-Term Contracts: Completed-Contract Method. The two long-term contracts recorded under the completed-contract method were started in 2006. One is a $5,000,000 contract. Costs incurred were $1,400,000 in 2006 and $1,600,000 in 2007. A total of $3,100,000 has been billed and $2,800,000 collected. Although it is difficult to estimate the additional costs required to complete this contract, indications are that this contract will prove to be profitable.

The second contract is for $4,000,000. Costs incurred were $1,200,000 in 2006 and $2,600,000 in 2007. A total of $3,300,000 has been billed and $2,900,000 collected. Although it is difficult to estimate the additional costs required to complete this contract, indications are that there will be a loss of approximately $550,000.

Dahlia Company:

Selling, general, and administrative expenses exclusive of amounts specified earlier were $600,000 in 2007. Other income exclusive of amounts specified earlier was $50,000 in 2007.

Required

Prepare an income statement of the Dahlia Company for the year ended December 31, 2007, stopping at income (loss) before income taxes. Show supporting schedules and computations in good form. *Ignore income tax and deferred tax considerations.* Notes are *not* required.

P21-14 *Determining Types of Leases (Appendix)* Rigdon Company leases 50 acres of land to Christmas Tree International on January 1, 2007. The provisions of the lease are as follows:

The lease is noncancelable and has a term of 25 years. The annual rentals are $10,000, payable at the end of each year. The lease contains no bargain purchase option and the land reverts to Rigdon at the end of the lease. The incremental borrowing rate of Christmas Tree International is 12%.

The cost of the land to Rigdon Company is $60,000. The fair value is $78,431.39. The lessor incurs no material initial direct costs. The collectibility of the rentals is reasonably assured, and there are no important uncertainties surrounding the amount of unreimbursable costs yet to be incurred by the lessor.

Required
1. Determine the classification of this lease for both the lessor and the lessee.
2. Why are the final two criteria (lease term 75% of economic life and present value of lease payments 90% of fair value) not applicable when classifying a lease of land?

P21-15 *Sale-Leaseback (Appendix)* On January 1, 2007 the Orr Company sells heavy equipment to Foible Company for $3 million, then immediately leases it back. The relevant information is as follows:

The lease is noncancelable and has a term of eight years. The annual rentals are $603,908.50, payable at the end of each year. The seller-lessee agrees to pay all executory costs. The interest rate implicit in the lease is 12%.

The cost of the heavy equipment to Orr Company is $2,100,000. The purchaser-lessor incurs no material initial direct costs. The collectibility of the rentals is reasonably assured, and there are no important uncertainties surrounding the amount of unreimbursable costs yet to be incurred by the lessor.

Orr's incremental borrowing rate is 12% and the company estimates that the economic life of the equipment is eight years. The present value on January 1, 2007 of eight payments of $603,908.50, discounted at 12%, is $3 million ($603,908.50 × 4.967640). The executory costs for 2007 are:

Repairs and maintenance	$10,200
Property taxes	20,500
Insurance	18,000

Required
1. What type of lease is this to the seller-lessee? Discuss.
2. Prepare the journal entries for both the seller-lessee and the purchaser-lessor for 2007 to reflect the sale and leaseback agreement. Assume that the company uses the straight-line depreciation method.

CASES

C21-1 Initial Direct Costs

The Efland Company leases equipment to Orange Company. Efland pays $3,000 initial direct costs in negotiating the lease.

Required

1. Explain what initial direct costs are.
2. Indicate precisely how Efland should account for initial direct costs if this lease is (a) an operating lease, (b) a sales-type lease, (c) a direct financing lease.
3. For a sales-type lease, *FASB Statement No. 13 as Amended* requires that: "The cost or carrying amount, if different, of the leased property, plus any initial direct costs . . . , less the present value of the unguaranteed residual value accruing to the benefit of the lessor, computed at the interest rate implicit in the lease, shall be charged against income in the same period." Does this provision require that initial direct costs for sales-type leases be charged to cost of goods sold? Discuss the reasons for or against this accounting treatment.

C21-2 Sales-Type Lease Issues

Jordan Industries manufactures and leases to its customers five-ton construction dump trucks. The lease arrangements are usually as follows:

1. Payments on the lease are due for five years after its inception, but the present value is not greater than 90% of the fair value of the trucks at the time of sale.
2. The trucks revert to Jordan at the end of the lease. Estimated economic life of the trucks is 10 years.
3. No substantial uncertainties exist as to future payments Jordan must make, and potential customers are thoroughly checked for creditworthiness before the trucks are leased to them.
4. Jordan's accountant has informed the company that there are advantages from a reporting standpoint in treating the leases as sales-type instead of operating leases.

Required

1. Discuss the reasons why Jordan would want to treat the leases as sales-type instead of operating leases.
2. Explain what Jordan should do, under the requirements of *FASB Statement No. 13 as Amended*, to treat the leases properly as sales-type leases.

C21-3 Classification of Leases

AICPA Adapted *Part a.* Capital leases and operating leases are the two classifications of leases for the lessee.

Required

1. Explain how a capital lease is accounted for by the lessee, both at the inception of the lease and during the first year of the lease, assuming the lease transfers ownership of the property to the lessee by the end of the lease.
2. Explain how an operating lease is accounted for by the lessee, both at the inception of the lease and during the first year of the lease, assuming equal monthly payments are made by the lessee at the beginning of each month of the lease. Describe the change in accounting, if any, when rental payments are not made on a straight-line basis.

Do not discuss the criteria for distinguishing between capital leases and operating leases.

Part b. Sales-type leases and direct financing leases are two of the classifications of leases for the lessor.

Required

Write a short report that compares and contrasts a sales-type lease with a direct financing lease as follows:

1. Gross investment in the lease.
2. Amortization of unearned interest income.
3. Manufacturer's or dealer's profit.

Do not discuss the criteria for distinguishing between the leases described above and operating leases.

C21-4 Miscellaneous Lease Issues

AICPA Adapted On January 1, 2007 Von Company entered into two noncancelable leases for new machines to be used in its manufacturing operations. The first lease does not contain a bargain purchase option. The lease term is equal to 80% of the estimated economic life of the machine. The second lease contains a bargain purchase option. The lease term is equal to 50% of the estimated economic life of the machine.

Required

1. Explain the theoretical basis for requiring lessees to capitalize certain long-term leases. Do **not** discuss the specific criteria for classifying a lease as a capital lease.
2. Explain how a lessee should account for a capital lease at its inception.
3. Explain how a lessee should record each minimum lease payment for a capital lease.
4. Explain how Von should classify each of the two leases.

C21-5 Sale-Leaseback

AICPA Adapted On January 1, 2007 Metcalf Company sold equipment for cash and leased it back. As seller-lessee, Metcalf retained the right to substantially all of the remaining use of the equipment.

The term of the lease is eight years. There is a gain on the sale portion of the transaction. The lease portion of the transaction is classified appropriately as a capital lease.

Required

1. Explain the theoretical basis for requiring lessees to capitalize certain long-term leases. Do **not** discuss the specific criteria for classifying a lease as a capital lease.
2. a. Explain how Metcalf should account for the sale portion of the sale-leaseback transaction at January 1, 2007.

b. Explain how Metcalf should account for the lease-back portion of the sale-leaseback transaction at January 1, 2007.
3. Explain how Metcalf should account for the gain on the sale portion of the sale-leaseback transaction during the first year of the lease.

CREATIVE AND CRITICAL THINKING

C21-6 Capitalized and Operating Leases

AICPA Adapted On January 1 Borman Company, a lessee, entered into three noncancelable leases for brand-new equipment, Lease J, Lease K, and Lease L. None of the three leases transfer ownership of the equipment to Borman at the end of the lease term. For each of the three leases, the present value of the minimum lease payments at the beginning of the lease term, excluding that portion of the payments representing executory costs such as insurance, maintenance, and taxes to be paid by the lessor, including any profit thereon, is 75% of the fair value of the equipment to the lessor at the inception of the lease.

The following information is peculiar to each lease:

(a) Lease J does not contain a bargain purchase option. The lease term is equal to 80% of the estimated economic life of the equipment.

(b) Lease K contains a bargain purchase option. The lease term is equal to 50% of the estimated economic life of the equipment.

(c) Lease L does not contain a bargain purchase option. The lease term is equal to 50% of the estimated economic life of the equipment.

Required

1. Explain how Borman Company should classify each of the preceding three leases. Discuss the rationale for your answer.
2. What amount, if any, should Borman record as a liability at the inception of the lease for each of the preceding three leases?
3. Assuming that the minimum lease payments are made on a straight-line basis, how should Borman record the minimum lease payment for each of the preceding three leases?

C21-7 Disclosure of Leases and Related Issues

United Manufacturing Company manufactures and leases computers to its customers. During 2007 the following lease transactions take place:

1. On January 1 a computer is leased to Superior Microelectronics Industries and is guaranteed by United against obsolescence. The present value of the lease payments is greater than 90% of the fair value of the computer to both United and Superior.
2. Also on January 1 a computer is leased to Pitt Steel Company. Because of Pitt's unstable financial condition, its incremental borrowing rate is substantially greater than United's rate implicit in the lease (which Pitt did not know and could not estimate).

Required

1. For the first transaction, explain on whose financial statements the leased computer is shown.
2. Explain under what conditions in the second transaction the computer could fail to be shown on either United's or Pitt Steel's balance sheets at December 31, 2007.

C21-8 Types of Leases and Related Issues

AICPA Adapted Circuit Village Company entered into a lease arrangement with Thomas Leasing Company for a certain machine. Thomas's primary business is leasing, and it is not a manufacturer or dealer. Circuit Village will lease the machine for a period of four years, which is 50% of the machine's economic life. Thomas will take possession of the machine at the end of the initial four-year lease and lease it to another smaller company that does not need the most current version of the machine. Circuit Village does not guarantee any residual value for the machine and will not purchase the machine at the end of the lease term. Circuit Village's incremental borrowing rate is 16% and the implicit rate on the lease is 14%. Circuit Village has no way of knowing or estimating the implicit rate used by Thomas. Using either rate, the present value of the minimum lease payments is between 90% and 100% of the fair value of the machine at the time of the lease agreement. Circuit Village has agreed to pay all executory costs directly, and no allowance for these costs is included in the lease payments. Thomas is reasonably certain that Circuit Village will pay all lease payments, and because it has agreed to pay all executory costs, there are no important uncertainties regarding costs to be incurred by Thomas.

Required

1. With respect to Circuit Village (the lessee), answer the following:
   a. What type of lease has been entered into? Explain the reason for your answer.
   b. How should Circuit Village compute the appropriate amount to record for the lease or asset acquired?
   c. What accounts will be created or affected by this transaction, and how will the lease or asset or other cost be matched with earnings?
2. With respect to Thomas (the lessor), answer the following:
   a. What type of leasing arrangement has been entered into? Explain the reason for your answer.
   b. How should this lease be recorded by Thomas, and how are the appropriate amounts determined?
   c. How should Thomas determine the appropriate amount of earnings to be recognized from each lease payment?

C21-9 Capital Lease Issues

AICPA Adapted On January 1, 2007 Lani Company entered into a noncancelable lease for a machine to be used in its manufacturing operations. The lease transfers ownership of the machine to Lani by the end of the lease term. The term of the lease is eight years. The minimum lease payment made by Lani on January 1, 2007 was one of eight equal annual payments. At the inception of the lease, the criteria established for classification as a capital lease by the lessee were met.

Required

1. Explain the theoretical basis for the accounting standard that requires certain long-term leases to be capitalized by the lessee. Do not discuss the specific lease as a capital lease.
2. Explain how Lani should account for this lease at its inception and determine the amount to be recorded.
3. Explain what expenses related to this lease Lani will incur during the first year of the lease, and how they will be determined.
4. Explain how Lani should report the lease transaction on its December 31, 2007 balance sheet.

C21-10 Sale-Leaseback (Appendix)

AICPA Adapted On December 31, 2006 Port Co. sold six-month-old equipment at fair value and leased it back. There was a loss on the sale. Port pays all insurance, maintenance, and taxes on the equipment. The lease provides for eight equal annual payments, beginning December 31, 2007, with a present value equal to 85% of the equipment's fair value and sales price. The lease's term is equal to 80% of the equipment's useful life. There is no provision for Port to reacquire ownership of the equipment at the end of the lease term.

Required

1. a. Explain why it is important to compare an equipment's fair value to its lease payments' present value, and its useful life to the lease term.
   b. Evaluate Port's leaseback of the equipment in terms of each of the four criteria for determination of a capital lease.
2. Explain how Port should account for the sale portion of the sale-leaseback transaction at December 31, 2006.
3. Explain how Port should report the leaseback portion of the sale-leaseback transaction on its December 31, 2007 balance sheet.

C21-11 Ethics and Leasing

You are an accountant for the ABC Mining Company, and the CFO gives you a copy of a recent lease agreement to record. As you read the agreement you discover the company has leased 12 trucks from the XYZ Finance Co. The fair value of the trucks is $2.4 million. ABC has agreed to pay $250,000 semiannually, in advance. The lease term is five years, and the lessor's implicit rate is 8%. There is no option or requirement to purchase the trucks. This all seems straightforward, especially when you remember that the company recently borrowed from a bank and agreed to a 10% interest rate. Also, you recall that the company owns some similar trucks and depreciates them over eight years. You are about to leave the office early to meet some friends when you notice that there is a contingent rental of $97,592, payable by ABC Mining and starting with the seventh semiannual payment if the Consumer Price Index prevailing at the beginning of the lease increases in any one of the first three years of the lease.

Required

From financial reporting and ethical perspectives, discuss the issues raised by this situation.

RESEARCH SIMULATIONS

R21-1 Capital Lease Issues

Situation

The Cliborn Retail Company negotiated a lease for a retail store in a new shopping center that included 30 stores. The accountant for Cliborn, Gail Naugle, was given the lease agreement to analyze. She looked into whether the lease was a capital lease. The lease did not include a transfer of ownership or an option to purchase. The lease term was for 20 years and the present value of the minimum lease payments was $100,000. Unsure of the fair market value of the property or its life, she called the lessor's controller.

"That is easy," he replied. "There is no fair value because we would never sell a single store in a shopping center. And, let's see, 20 years divided by 75% is about 27 years, so the life of the property must be at least that much. Or do you want a capital lease?"

Directions

Assuming that you are Gail Naugle, research the generally accepted accounting principles and prepare a short memo to the controller of Cliborn that summarizes how to classify the lease. Cite your reference and applicable paragraph numbers.

R21-2 Capital Lease Issues

Situation

The Stirbis Company was negotiating a lease for a new building that would be used as a warehouse. Stirbis' accountant, Shannon Fenimore, had been invited to join Jim Stirbis (the president) in a meeting where the lease agreement was settled. The president of the company that owned the building said, "I assume you want an operating lease."

"That is correct," replied Jim Stirbis.

The president responded, "So we will not include a transfer of ownership or an option to purchase. Anyway, I am sure you do not want to get into the real estate business."

"No, of course not."

"And we agree that the lease term is 30 years."

"Yes, but that seems to present some problems. We would have to argue that the life of the building is more than 40 years."

"You should not have any trouble persuading your auditors to agree to that."

"Maybe not. But the present value of the $53,040 annual lease payment is $500,000, which is the fair value of the building."

"That is a problem. But I think I have a solution. We will adjust the annual payment to $45,000, so that the present value is only 85% of the fair value. Then we will add a clause that you also pay 1% of your total sales, up to a maximum of $8,040 each year."

Directions

Assuming that you are Shannon Fenimore, research the generally accepted accounting principles and prepare a short memo to the controller of Stirbis that summarizes how to classify the lease. Cite your reference and applicable paragraph numbers.

22

OBJECTIVES

After reading this chapter, you will be able to:

1 Define operating, investing, and financing activities.

2 Know the categories of inflows and outflows of cash.

3 Classify cash flows as operating, investing, or financing.

4 Explain the direct and indirect methods for reporting operating cash flows.

5 Prepare a simple statement of cash flows.

6 Use a worksheet (spreadsheet) for a statement of cash flows.

7 Compute and disclose interest paid and income taxes paid.

8 Identify the operating cash inflows and outflows under the direct method (Appendix).

9 Compute the operating cash flows under the direct method (Appendix).

The Statement of Cash Flows

Cash is King

Cash is the lifeblood of any company and is critical to its success. Cash flow information is used by both managers and analysts to understand a company's operations, assess its liquidity, gain insight into its ability to invest in new assets, and evaluate its financing decisions. While accrual accounting provides a company with a range of accounting choices as it records transactions, this same flexibility allows a company to manage its earnings. The statement of cash flows, much like a corporate bank statement, tracks the cash receipts and cash payments for a company and can be useful in exposing many of these manipulations. In light of recent earnings restatements, cash flow analysis has taken on an added importance as many users begin to question the faith they can put in a company's reported income numbers. With an increased emphasis on the analysis of cash flows when measuring a company's performance, a financial statement user should be aware of three red flags that may signal a company is not as healthy as its income statement makes it appear[1]:

- Negative operating cash flows—If a company is paying out more cash than it is generating from operations, the company will be forced to rely on issuing debt or stock or selling its assets to fund operations. This may often force a company into unfavorable financing options and possibly bankruptcy.

- High income but low operating cash flow—An examination of the ratio of income to operating cash flow can help identify high quality, sustainable earnings. If income is significantly

---

1. Adapted from "Watch for These 4 Cash-Flow Red Flags" by Harry Domash, http://moneycentral.msn.com.

Credit: Stone/George Chan

higher than operating cash flow, this may signal that the company is hemorrhaging cash (inventories and receivables are typical culprits) and the source of this cash drain should be investigated.

- Negative free cash flow—If a company must make continual investments in property, plant, and equipment to remain competitive, free cash flow (operating cash flow less capital expenditures) may be a more useful measure of cash flow than operating cash flow. While negative free cash flow may be a sign that a company is making large capital investments that may generate large future payoffs, it could also be a warning sign that the company is speculating as to the future payoff of these investments or that its investments are underperforming (not leading to cash generation).

Interpreting the statement of cash flows is not a straightforward, easy process. However, with a little time, patience, and diligent study, the use of cash flow information, along with information contained in the balance sheet and income statement, can help you identify many good investments and avoid many bad ones.

FOR FURTHER INVESTIGATION:

For a discussion of cash flows and its use in financial analysis, consult the Business & Company Resource Center (BCRC):

- Mind the Gap. Ronald Fink, *CFO, The Magazine for Senior Financial Executives*, 8756-7113, Dec 2003, v19, i16, p50(5).
- True Confessions: One Banker's Inner Struggle with Cash Flow. (Credit Fundamentals). Thomas P. Olson, *The RMA Journal*, 1531-0558, June 2003, v85, i9, p68(4).

Users of financial statements are interested in the operating, investing, and financing activities of companies. For a particular company they ask questions such as (1) What is the relationship between net income and cash provided by operations? (2) Why are dividends not larger, in light of rising income? (3) What expansion activities took place and how were they financed? (4) Why did cash decrease even though net income was reported? (5) What happened to the proceeds received from issuing capital stock? Each of these questions relates to the cash flows of the company. The FASB recognized the importance of providing answers to these questions by stating that financial reporting should provide information about how a company obtains and spends cash, about its borrowing and repayment of borrowing, about its capital transactions, including cash dividends and other distributions of resources to owners, and about other factors that may affect its liquidity or solvency.[2]

To satisfy these objectives, the FASB issued **FASB Statement No. 95** which requires a company to present a *statement of cash flows* for the accounting period along with its income statement and balance sheet.[3] The statement of cash flows is an integral part of a company's financial statements and the subject of this chapter.

CONCEPTUAL OVERVIEW AND REPORTING GUIDELINES

In Chapter 2 we noted that one of the specific objectives of financial reporting is to provide information about a company's cash flows. The FASB is concerned that a company's financial statements include information useful to external users about its cash inflows and outflows, borrowings and repayments, and capital transactions (including dividends). A company's receivables, payables, and inventory (i.e., items of working capital) are the links between its operations and its cash inflows and outflows. Information about these relationships is useful in understanding the operations of the company.

Information about a company's liquidity, financial flexibility, operating capability, and risk is related to these objectives as well. *Liquidity* is an indication of the company's ability to pay its bills as they come due. *Financial flexibility* is a measure of the company's ability to take effective actions to change the amounts and timings of its cash flows to adapt to change. Financial flexibility arises primarily from a company's ability to modify operations so as to increase net operating cash inflows. It also comes from the company's ability to raise cash from issuing new debt or equity securities or to obtain cash by disposing of assets. *Operating capability* is the company's ability to maintain a given physical level of operations, measured in terms of either the quantity of goods (inventory) produced and sold or the physical capacity of the company's property, plant, and equipment. *Risk* is the uncertainty or unpredictability of the future results of a company. The wider the range within which future results are likely to fall, the greater the risk associated with an investment in or extension of credit to the company.

The primary purpose of a company's statement of cash flows is to provide relevant information about its cash receipts and cash payments during an accounting period that is useful in evaluating the preceding items. The FASB states that the information in a statement of cash flows, if used with information in the other financial statements, helps external users assess (1) a company's ability to generate positive future net cash flows, (2) a company's ability to meet its obligations and pay dividends, (3) a company's need for external financing, (4) the reasons for differences between a company's net income and related cash receipts and payments, and (5) both the cash and noncash aspects of a company's financing and investing transactions during the accounting period.[4]

---

2. "Objectives of Financial Reporting by Business Enterprises," *FASB Statement of Financial Accounting Concepts No. 1* (Stamford, Conn.: FASB, 1978), par. 49.
3. "Statement of Cash Flows," *FASB Statement of Financial Accounting Standards No. 95* (Stamford, Conn.: FASB, 1987), par. 3.
4. *Ibid.*, par. 5.

Reporting Guidelines and Practices

To understand how to use and to prepare a statement of cash flows, it is important to have a definition of the statement and guidelines for preparing the statement. **A statement of cash flows is a financial statement of a company that shows the cash inflows, cash outflows, and net change in cash from its operating, investing, and financing activities during an accounting period, in a manner that reconciles the beginning and ending cash balances.**

1 Define operating, investing, and financing activities.

Operating Activities

A company's operating activities include all its transactions and other events that are not investing and financing activities. These include transactions involving acquiring (purchasing or manufacturing), selling, and delivering goods for sale, as well as providing services. Cash inflows from operating activities include *cash receipts from*:

- the sale of goods or services,
- collection of accounts receivable,
- collection of interest on loans, and
- receipts of dividends on investments in equity securities.

Cash outflows for operating activities include *cash payments to*:

- suppliers for inventory (or raw materials),
- employees,
- the government for taxes,
- lenders for interest (unless capitalized), and
- other suppliers for various expenses.

Investing Activities

A company's investing activities include its transactions involving acquiring and selling property, plant, and equipment, acquiring and selling investments (both current and noncurrent), and lending money and collecting on the loans. Cash outflows for investing activities include *cash payments for*:

- acquiring property, plant, and equipment,
- purchasing investments in other companies (e.g., stocks and bonds), and
- making loans to borrowers.

Cash inflows from investing activities include *cash receipts from*:

- sales of property, plant, and equipment,
- sales of investments in other companies, and
- principal repayments of loans by borrowers (e.g., collections of notes receivable).

How a company classifies certain items depends on its operations. For instance, if a company regularly factors its accounts receivable, then it treats the cash receipts as cash inflows from operating activities. Similarly, if a company requires its customers to sign notes for credit sales, then it treats the cash receipts from collections of these notes receivable as cash inflows from operating activities.

Financing Activities

A company's financing activities include its transactions involving obtaining resources from owners and providing them with a return on, and of, their investment, as well as obtaining money and other resources from creditors and repaying the amounts borrowed. Cash inflows from financing activities include *cash receipts (proceeds) from*:

- issuing equity securities (i.e., common stock and preferred stock),
- issuing bonds,

- issuing mortgages,
- issuing notes, and
- other short- or long-term borrowings.

Cash outflows for financing activities include *cash payments for*:
- dividends,
- repurchase of the company's equity securities, and
- repayments of amounts borrowed.

Most borrowings and repayments of borrowings are financing activities. However, as we noted, the settlement of liabilities such as accounts payable incurred to acquire inventory and salaries payable are operating activities.

Format

From a conceptual standpoint, **to predict the amounts, timing, and uncertainty of future cash flows, external users need financial information that is presented in homogeneous groups.**[5] To implement these guidelines and for consistent reporting, a company's statement of cash flows for the accounting period must clearly show (1) the cash provided by or used in its operating activities, (2) the cash provided by or used in its investing activities, (3) the cash provided by or used in its financing activities, (4) the company's net increase or decrease in cash, and (5) a reconciliation of the company's beginning cash balance to the ending cash balance reported on its year-end balance sheet.

As we will see, most financing and investing activities of a company affect its cash; however, some transactions (such as buying land by issuing common stock) are "simultaneous" investing and financing activities that do not affect its cash. These transactions are important in providing an overall picture of a company's investing and financing activities. The company is required to report these items either in a separate schedule or narrative explanation (in this chapter we will always use a schedule) that accompanies the statement of cash flows. Also, if a company uses the indirect method (which we discuss later) of reporting operating cash flows, it must also disclose the amounts of interest paid and income taxes paid during the accounting period. (We discuss this disclosure later in this chapter.)

Cash and Cash Equivalents

As we discussed in Chapter 7, as part of its cash management procedures, a company may invest its cash in short-term, highly liquid investments, such as treasury bills, commercial paper, and money market funds. These investments are called *cash equivalents*. Then, instead of reporting "Cash" as a current asset on its balance sheet, the company reports "Cash and Cash Equivalents." In this case, the company's statement of cash flows explains the change during the accounting period in its *cash and cash equivalents*. In this chapter, for simplicity, we focus only on changes in *cash*.

Example: Typical Statement of Cash Flows

Example 22-1 shows a typical statement of cash flows for the Ryan Corporation.

Content

Note that the statement of cash flows is divided into three sections, entitled (1) Net Cash Flow From Operating Activities, (2) Cash Flows From Investing Activities, and (3) Cash Flows From Financing Activities. These are the titles a company generally

---

5. "Recognition and Measurement in Financial Statements of Business Enterprises," *FASB Statement of Financial Accounting Concepts No. 5* (Stamford, Conn.: FASB, 1984), par. 20.

EXAMPLE 22-1   Typical Statement of Cash Flows

RYAN CORPORATION

Statement of Cash Flows
For Year Ended December 31, 2007

Net Cash Flow From Operating Activities		
Net income	$ 14,000	
Adjustments for differences between income flows		
and cash flows from operating activities:		
Add: Depreciation expense	8,000	
Decrease in accounts receivable	2,600	
Increase in salaries payable	800	
Less: Increase in inventory	(2,000)	
Decrease in accounts payable	(7,000)	
Net cash provided by operating activities		$16,400
Cash Flows From Investing Activities		
Payment for purchase of building	$(28,000)	
Payment for purchase of equipment	(4,000)	
Proceeds from sale of land, at cost	10,000	
Net cash used for investing activities		(22,000)
Cash Flows From Financing Activities		
Proceeds from issuance of common stock	$ 18,000	
Proceeds from issuance of bonds	12,000	
Payment of dividends	(9,000)	
Payment of note payable	(13,000)	
Net cash provided by financing activities		8,000
Net Increase in Cash (see Schedule 1)		$ 2,400
Cash, January 1, 2007		10,900
Cash, December 31, 2007		$13,300
Schedule 1: Investing and Financing Activities Not Affecting Cash		
Investing Activities		
Acquisition of land by issuance of common stock		$ (6,000)
Financing Activities		
Issuance of common stock for land		6,000

uses in its statement of cash flows. Note also the schedule of investing and financing activities not affecting cash.

Operating Cash Flows   A company reports the net cash provided by or used in its operating activities in the first section of its statement of cash flows. Over the long run, a company will be successful only if it is able to obtain positive cash flows from its operations. This situation occurs when the cash received from selling goods or services exceeds the cash paid to provide the goods or services. Generating cash from operations generally is the most important cash flow activity of a company. The Ryan Corporation provided a net cash inflow of $16,400 from its operating activities during 2007, as we show in Example 22-1. The company determined this $16,400 amount by adjusting the $14,000 net income for several differences between the income flows and cash flows from operating activities. This procedure is called the "indirect method" and we explain this method later in the chapter. External users can compare the company's net cash flow from operating activities with the same information from previous years to detect favorable or unfavorable *trends* in the company's liquidity, financial flexibility, operating capability, and risk. They can compare this information with the same information from other companies for the same purposes.

Investing Cash Flows A company reports the cash inflows and outflows from its investing activities in the second section of the statement of cash flows. It lists each investing cash inflow and outflow and subtotals the amounts to determine the net cash used for (or provided by) investing activities. During 2007 the Ryan Corporation paid cash of $28,000 to purchase a building and paid cash of $4,000 to purchase equipment. It received cash of $10,000 from the sale of land, at cost. The net result was that the company used $22,000 cash for its investing activities.

Financing Cash Flows A company reports the cash inflows and outflows from its financing activities in the third section of the statement of cash flows. It lists each financing cash inflow and outflow and subtotals the amounts to determine the net cash provided by (or used for) financing activities. During 2007 the Ryan Corporation had cash receipts of $18,000 and $12,000 from issuing common stock and bonds, respectively. It had a cash payment of $9,000 for dividends, and a $13,000 cash payment for a note. The net result was that $8,000 cash was provided by its financing activities.

Net Change in Cash and Reconciliation A company determines the net increase or decrease in cash by adding the amounts of the net cash flow from operating activities, the net cash flow from investing activities, and the net cash flow from financing activities. The $16,400 net cash provided by operating activities, combined with the $22,000 net cash used for investing activities, and the $8,000 net cash provided by financing activities resulted in a $2,400 net increase in cash for the Ryan Corporation in 2007. This $2,400 net increase in cash reconciles the $10,900 beginning cash balance to the $13,300 ending cash balance.

Non-Cash Items A company reports its investing and financing activities not affecting cash in a separate schedule accompanying the statement of cash flows. It lists each investing and/or financing activity and offsets the related amounts against each other. During 2007 the Ryan Corporation engaged in a simultaneous investing and financing transaction. It acquired land costing $6,000 by issuing common stock. The investing portion of the transaction was the acquisition of the land, while the financing portion was the issuance of common stock. Schedule 1 shows the investing activity as a $6,000 "outflow" which is offset by the $6,000 "inflow" from the financing activity. Although no cash was exchanged, both items are listed to show all of the Ryan Corporation's investing and financing activities during 2007. ♦

Usefulness

By reviewing the three sections of a company's statement of cash flows, external users can see how it obtained and used its cash. From the accompanying schedule, they can determine the types of investing and financing activities of the company that did not affect cash. They can examine the items in each section to see if important changes have occurred. For instance, the investing activities involving the acquisition of the building and equipment by the Ryan Corporation in 2007 may indicate an increase in its operating capability. In addition, the financing activities involving the issuance of both bonds and common stock by the Ryan Corporation in 2007 reveal a change in its capital structure and may indicate a change in its financial flexibility and risk.

A comparison with other companies can also show, for instance, whether the company is obtaining or using a greater proportion of its cash from financing or investing activities rather than operations. This may be important in assessing the relative risk of investing in the company. External users can evaluate the likelihood of future cash dividends, as well as the need for additional cash to finance existing operations or the expansion of operations. They also can evaluate the ability of the company to pay current obligations, make periodic interest payments, and pay off long-term debt when the debt reaches its maturity date. Thus, a company's statement of cash flows provides external users with information about its liquidity, financial flexibility, operating capability, and risk. In so doing, the statement enhances the predictive value and feedback value and, therefore, the *decision usefulness*, of a company's financial statements to help fulfill the objectives of financial reporting.

CASH INFLOWS AND OUTFLOWS

To understand a company's cash flows, the relationships between the *changes* in balance sheet accounts and the company's cash flows must be analyzed. A company's *inflows* of cash are caused by *decreases* in its assets (other than cash) and by *increases* in liabilities and in stockholders' equity during an accounting period. A company's *outflows* of cash are caused by *increases* in its assets (other than cash) and by *decreases* in liabilities and in stockholders' equity during the accounting period. The difference between the inflows and outflows is the change in cash during the accounting period. We show this relationship by the equations in Exhibit 22-1, starting with the basic accounting equation. Each equation is a modification of the previous equation, to eventually show the increases and decreases in cash. With this background in mind, we can refine the relationships we show in the last two equations of Exhibit 22-1.

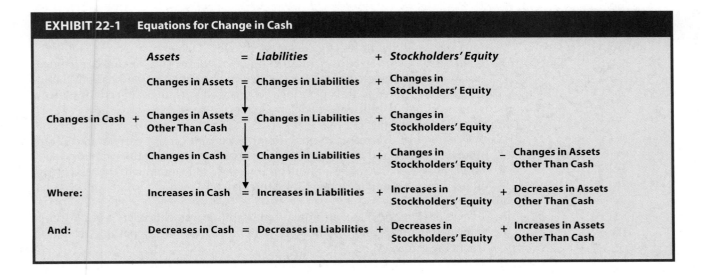

EXHIBIT 22-1   Equations for Change in Cash

Inflows of Cash

There are three categories of a company's inflows (increases) of cash:

1. *Decreases in Assets Other Than Cash.* The sale or other disposal of assets (other than cash) causes an increase in cash because cash is received in exchange for the assets.
2. *Increases in Liabilities.* The issuance or other incurrence of liabilities causes an increase in cash because cash is received in exchange for the liabilities.[6]
3. *Increases in Stockholders' Equity.* Stockholders' equity increases mainly because of net income and additional investments by owners. Additional investments cause an increase in cash because cash is received in exchange for the stock issued. Net income is slightly more complicated because the inflows and outflows of cash for operations are different than the revenues and expenses included in net income (we discuss this topic later).

2 Know the categories of inflows and outflows of cash.

---

6.   Alternatively, as we discuss later, the increase in a liability such as accounts payable results, in effect, in a "savings" (i.e., increase) in cash because of a smaller cash payment.

Outflows of Cash

There are also three categories of a company's outflows (decreases) of cash:

1. *Increases in Assets Other Than Cash.* The acquisition of assets (other than cash) causes a decrease in cash because cash is paid in exchange for the assets.[7]
2. *Decreases in Liabilities.* The payment of liabilities causes a decrease in cash because cash is paid to satisfy the liabilities.
3. *Decreases in Stockholders' Equity.* Stockholders' equity may decrease as a result of several transactions. Two common transactions are the payment of dividends and the acquisition of treasury stock. In each case, a decrease in stockholders' equity is accompanied by a decrease in cash.

Classifications of Cash Flows

We can further classify the cash inflows and outflows we just discussed into operating, investing, and financing cash flows.

3 Classify cash flows as operating, investing, or financing.

1. **Operating Cash Flows**
   A. *Inflows of Cash.* Increases in stockholders' equity (i.e., retained earnings) because of revenues, adjusted for changes in current assets and current liabilities that are related to the operating cycle, as well as changes in certain noncurrent assets and liabilities (e.g., deferred taxes).
   B. *Outflows of Cash.* Decreases in stockholders' equity (i.e., retained earnings) because of expenses, adjusted for changes in current assets and current liabilities that are related to the operating cycle, as well as changes in certain noncurrent assets and liabilities (e.g., deferred taxes).
2. **Investing Cash Flows**
   A. *Inflows of Cash.* Decreases in noncurrent assets and certain current assets (e.g., notes receivable and temporary investments related to investing activities).
   B. *Outflows of Cash.* Increases in noncurrent assets and certain current assets (e.g., notes receivable and temporary investments).
3. **Financing Cash Flows**
   A. *Inflows of Cash.* Increases in noncurrent liabilities, stockholders' equity (other than net income), and certain current liabilities (e.g., notes payable related to financing activities).
   B. *Outflows of Cash.* Decreases in noncurrent liabilities, stockholders' equity (other than a net loss), and certain current liabilities (e.g., notes payable and dividends payable).

Changes in assets (other than cash), liabilities, and stockholders' equity may be the result of investing and financing activities *not* affecting cash. Examples of these transactions include

- acquisitions of assets by issuing equity securities (noncash investing and financing activities),
- acquisitions of assets by assuming liabilities such as capital lease obligations (noncash investing and financing activities),
- exchanges of debt securities for equity securities such as the conversion of bonds to common stock (noncash financing activities),
- exchanges of assets for assets (noncash investing activities),
- exchanges of liabilities for liabilities (noncash financing activities), and
- exchanges of equity securities such as the conversion of preferred stock to common stock (noncash financing activities).

---

7. Alternatively, as we discuss later, the increase in an asset such as accounts receivable results, in effect, in a decrease in cash because of a smaller cash receipt.

Although these transactions are relatively rare, they do involve "simultaneous" investing activities and/or financing activities not affecting cash. They generally have a significant effect on the prospective cash flows of a company, so that the company reports them in a schedule (or narrative explanation) that accompanies its statement of cash flows, as we discussed earlier.

The operating cash flows involve several adjustments for items relating to the operating cycle. We further explain the net cash flow from operating activities in the next section.

SECURE YOUR KNOWLEDGE 22-1

- The statement of cash flows provides relevant information about a company's cash receipts and cash payments that is useful for assessing its liquidity, financial flexibility, operating capability, and risk.
- A company's cash flows are reported as:
    - Operating activities—cash receipts and cash payments relating to the earning activities of the company (generally resulting from transactions that enter into the determination of income).
    - Investing activities—cash receipts and cash payments relating to the acquisition and disposition of assets such as property, plant, and equipment, notes receivable, and investments in other companies.
    - Financing activities—cash receipts and cash payments relating to the external financing of a company such as the issuance and repurchase of common stock, issuance and repayment of bonds, and payment of dividends.
- A company's statement of cash flows must clearly show the three categories above as well as the net increase or decrease in cash and a reconciliation of the beginning and ending cash balance reported on the balance sheet. Furthermore, the disclosure of significant non-cash activities is required to be reported in either a separate schedule or narrative explanation that accompanies the statement of cash flows.
- A company's cash flow is related to the changes in its balance sheet accounts as follows:
    - Increases in cash are caused by decreases in assets (other than cash), increases in liabilities, and increases in stockholders' equity.
    - Decreases in cash are caused by increases in assets (other than cash), decreases in liabilities, and decreases in stockholders' equity.
- These cash flows can be further classified (consistent with the reporting guidelines above) as:
    - Operating activities—increases or decreases in stockholders' equity (e.g., retained earnings) because of certain revenues or expenses, adjusted for changes in the related current assets or current liabilities, and certain noncurrent assets and liabilities,
    - Investing activities—decreases or increases in noncurrent assets and certain current assets (e.g., notes receivable and marketable securities), or
    - Financing activities—increases or decreases in noncurrent liabilities, stockholders' equity and certain current liabilities (e.g., notes payable and dividends payable).

LINK TO ETHICAL DILEMMA

Polaris, Inc. manufactures and sells a variety of high-end electronic devices. Its most popular product, a portable satellite radio, has been a market leader for years and helped the company amass a large amount of cash. However, Polaris' financial performance has been somewhat disappointing over the last two years. Specifically, Polaris' return on assets has decreased by two percentage points, and its stock price has been stagnant. As the accountant for Polaris, the CEO has asked you to provide an analysis of the causes of these disappointing results and provide a recommendation that would increase the company's performance measures. Your examination of the company's financial results reveals that the company's large cash balance may be a factor in the company's disappointing performance. While the large cash balance increases the company's liquidity, the majority of these funds are invested in short-term financial instruments that yield approximately 2%. This low return is a significant cause of the company's declining return on assets measure and has many investors calling for an increased dividend which the CEO is adamantly against. Instead of paying a dividend, you suggest that Polaris use the excess cash to finance its customers' purchases of the company's products. The interest rate charged to provide this financial assistance will be much higher than the rate earned by the company's current investment strategy, and this increased return is expected to add at least one percentage point to the company's return on assets.

The CEO is very excited about this proposal but he is concerned about how the increased receivables created by the loans to the customers will affect the company's cash flow from operating activities. You state that while this is not specifically addressed by *FASB Statement No. 95*, you feel that since customer loans relate to the sale of the company's products, the associated cash outflow should be classified as an operating activity. The CEO disagrees and decides that the cash outflow associated with the lending transaction is an investing activity. He reasons that because generally accepted accounting principles do not address this issue, he has an obligation to the shareholders to make the company's financial statements look as good as possible. If the company classifies the lending transaction as an operating activity, it would report declining cash flow from operations and send an incorrect signal to the market as to the company's future. Furthermore, the CEO states that because the matter is simply a classification issue which does not change the company's total cash flow, no one would be hurt by classifying the transaction as an investing activity. How do you respond to the CEO's statements?

NET CASH FLOW FROM OPERATING ACTIVITIES

The calculation of a company's net cash flow from operating activities is usually the most detailed part of its statement of cash flows. To prepare this section, it is helpful to understand the relationship between sales revenues, expenses, and cash flows in a company's operating cycle.

Recall from Chapter 4 that a retail company's operating cycle is the average time it takes to spend cash for inventory, sell the inventory, collect the accounts receivable, and convert them back into cash. To begin a company's operating cycle, the company purchases inventory for cash or on credit. To make cash or credit sales, it incurs cost of goods sold and selling expenses and reduces inventory, and either pays cash, incurs current liabilities, or reduces prepaid items. In its operations, the company incurs general and administrative expenses and either pays cash, incurs current liabilities, or reduces prepaid items. Finally, the company collects its accounts receivable and converts them back into cash. This step completes the operating cycle.

As you can see from the previous discussion, the impact of each phase of the operating cycle is not the same on both the company's net income and its net cash flow from operating activities because of differences in when the company records revenues and expenses and when it receives and pays cash. A company "adjusts" for these differences to help calculate its net cash flow from operating activities.

There are also "non-cash" changes in certain noncurrent asset (and liability) accounts that affect a company's net income but do not result in a cash inflow or outflow for operating activities. For instance, when a company records depreciation, the journal entry involves a debit to Depreciation Expense (a reduction of net income) and a credit to Accumulated Depreciation (a reduction of noncurrent assets). Although depreciation expense reduces net income (and noncurrent assets), there is no cash outflow for operating activities. The recording of amortization expense for intangible assets (such as a patent) and depletion expense for natural resource assets (such as a coal mine) have the same effect. That is, there is a reduction in net income (and noncurrent assets) but no operating cash outflow. A company analyzes each of the changes in these noncurrent asset accounts to help determine the effect on its net cash flow from operating activities.

Direct Method

FASB Statement No. 95 allows a company to choose one of two ways to calculate and report its net cash flow from operating activities on its statement of cash flows. The first is called the *direct* method. **Under the direct method, a company deducts its operating cash outflows from its operating cash inflows to determine its net cash flow from operating activities.** Using this method, the cash inflows from operating activities are computed and reported first. A company's operating cash inflows are:

- collections from customers,
- collections of interest and dividends, and
- other operating receipts.

For simplicity, in the following example we focus on collections from customers.

Then, the cash outflows for operating activities are computed and reported. A company's operating cash outflows are:

- payments to suppliers,
- payments to employees,
- other operating payments,
- payments for interest, and
- payments for income taxes.

For simplicity, in the following example we focus on payments to suppliers, payments to employees, and payments for income taxes.

Example: Direct Method   Assume the Ryan Corporation presents the following simplified income statement information for the year ended December 31, 2007:

Sales revenue (cash and accounts receivable)		$70,000
Less:		
Cost of goods sold (cash and accounts payable)	$(29,000)	
Salaries expense (cash and salaries payable)	(13,000)	
Depreciation expense	(8,000)	(50,000)
Income before income taxes		$20,000
Income tax expense (cash)		(6,000)
Net income		$14,000

4 Explain the direct and indirect methods for reporting operating cash flows.

Further analysis reveals the following changes in its current asset and current liability accounts for 2007:

- accounts receivable decreased by $2,600,
- inventory increased by $2,000,
- accounts payable decreased by $7,000, and
- salaries payable increased by $800.

Under the direct method, Ryan Corporation reports the cash flows from operating activities on its statement of cash flows as follows:

Cash Flows From Operating Activities
    Cash Inflows:

Cash collected from customers	$ 72,600	
Cash inflows from operating activities		$72,600
Cash Outflows:		
Cash paid to suppliers	$(38,000)	
Cash paid to employees	(12,200)	
Cash paid for income taxes	(6,000)	
Cash outflows for operating activities		(56,200)
Net cash provided by operating activities		$16,400

The $72,600 cash collected from customers is computed by adding the $2,600 decrease in accounts receivable to the $70,000 sales revenue. This adjustment is made because the company's cash collections exceeded its sales during the year. This is the only cash receipt, so that cash inflows from operating activities are $72,600.

The $38,000 cash paid to suppliers is computed by adding the $2,000 increase in inventory and the $7,000 decrease in accounts payable to the $29,000 cost of goods sold. These adjustments are made because the company's purchases exceeded its cost of goods sold but some of these purchases were on credit. The $12,200 cash paid to employees is computed by deducting the $800 increase in salaries payable from the $13,000 salaries expense. This adjustment is made because the cash paid for salaries was less than its salaries expense. The entire $6,000 of income tax expense was paid in cash. These cash outflows for operating activities total $56,200, so that the net cash provided by operating activities is $16,400. Note that the depreciation expense is *not* included in the net cash flows from operating activities because it did not result in an outflow of cash. ♦

The direct method has the advantage of reporting a company's operating cash inflows separately from its operating cash outflows, which may be useful in estimating future cash flows. However, the direct method is criticized because it does not "tie" the net income reported on a company's income statement to the net cash provided by operating activities reported on its statement of cash flows. Also, the direct method does not show how the changes in the elements (i.e., current assets and current liabilities) of a company's operating cycle affected its operating cash flows.

Indirect Method

Use of the *indirect* method to report a company's net cash flow from operating activities on its statement of cash flows resolves the two criticisms of the direct method. **Under the indirect method, a company's net income is adjusted (reconciled) to its net cash flow from operating activities** on the statement of cash flows. To do so, net income is listed first and then *adjustments* (additions or subtractions) are made to net income:

1. to eliminate certain amounts (such as depreciation expense) that are included in its net income but do not involve a cash receipt or cash payment for operating activities, and
2. to include any changes in the current assets (other than cash) and current liabilities involved in the company's operating cycle that affect its cash flows differently than they affect net income.

In other words, under the indirect method, a company's income flows are converted from an *accrual* basis to a *cash flow* basis. In this manner, the indirect method shows the "quality" of a company's income by providing information about lead and lag intervals between its income flows and operating cash flows.

Example: Indirect Method   Refer back to the Ryan Corporation's income statement and additional information we showed earlier. Under the indirect method, Ryan Corporation reports the net cash flow from operating activities on its statement of cash flows as follows:

Net Cash Flow From Operating Activities

Net income	$14,000	
Adjustments for differences between income flows and cash flows for operating activities:		
Add: Depreciation expense	8,000	
Decrease in accounts receivable	2,600	
Increase in salaries payable	800	
Less: Increase in inventory	(2,000)	
Decrease in accounts payable	(7,000)	
Net cash provided by operating activities		$16,400

It is important to understand how each adjustment is used to convert the net income to the net cash provided by operating activities. First, the $8,000 depreciation expense is *added* to the $14,000 net income because it had been deducted to determine net income even though it did not involve an outflow of cash. The $2,600 decrease in the current asset, accounts receivable, is added to net income because it resulted in an additional cash receipt from operations. The $800 increase in the current liability, salaries payable, resulted in an increase in expenses and a decrease in net income. It is added to net income because it did not involve a cash payment for operations. The $2,000 increase in the current asset, inventory, and the $7,000 decrease in the current liability, accounts payable, are both deducted from net income because they resulted in additional operating cash payments. Note that by using either the direct method or the indirect method, net cash provided by operating activities is the same amount ($16,400). The indirect method is the method used by the Ryan Corporation in Example 22-1 at the beginning of the chapter. The Coca-Cola Company uses the indirect method in its statement of cash flows, as shown in Appendix A. ♦

Prior to *FASB Statement No. 95*, nearly all companies reported the results of their operating activities using the indirect method on their statements of cash flows. *FASB Statement No. 95* recommends the direct method, but allows the use of either the direct method or the indirect method. However, if a company uses the direct method on its statement of cash flows, it must also include a separate schedule that reconciles its net income to its net cash flow provided by (or used in) operating activities (i.e., the indirect method). Most companies (over 98%) use the indirect method[8] because of its prior use and the extra schedule required under the direct method. However, companies that use the indirect method must report the interest paid and income taxes paid. We use the indirect method in the main part of the chapter, but discuss the direct method in the Appendix at the end of the chapter. (**You should use the** *indirect method* **for** *all homework,* **unless otherwise indicated.)** ♦

Major Adjustments

In the previous example of the indirect method we made only a few simple adjustments to convert the net income to the net cash flow from operating activities. In reality, a company may have many adjustments involving both increases and decreases in its current assets and current liabilities, as well as other noncurrent accounts. Exhibit 22-2 lists the major adjustments used to convert a company's net income to its net cash flow from operating activities. We explain these adjustments in the examples that follow.

---

8.   *Accounting Trends and Techniques* (New York: AICPA, 2004), p. 549.

EXHIBIT 22-2 Adjustments to Convert Net Income to Net Cash Flow From Operating Activities

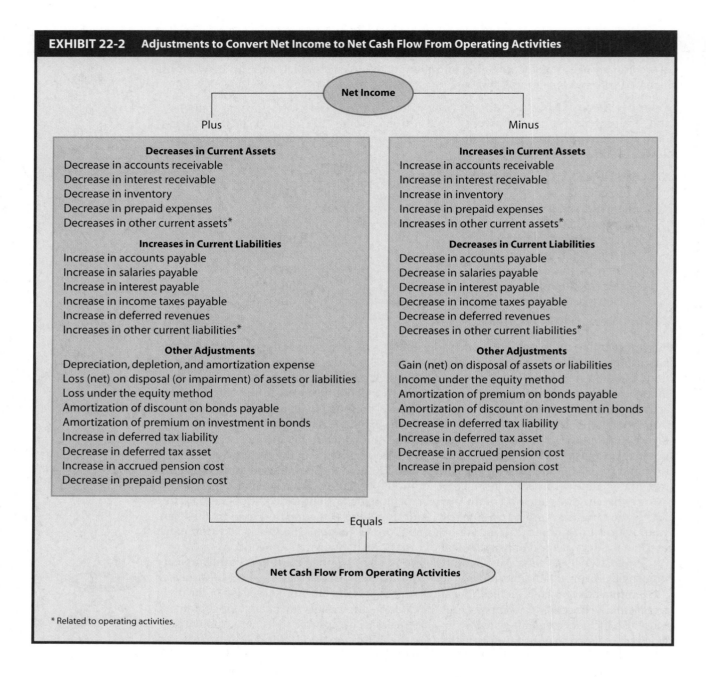

* Related to operating activities.

INFORMATION FOR PREPARATION OF STATEMENT

When a company prepares its statement of cash flows, it uses information for the accounting period from the following financial statements: (1) beginning and ending balance sheets, (2) income statement, and (3) retained earnings statement. In addition, it needs other information that explains the changes in its balance sheet accounts (other than cash). This additional information is obtained from its accounting records.

VISUAL INSPECTION METHOD OF ANALYSIS

There are two methods that you may use to prepare a company's statement of cash flows: the visual inspection method and the worksheet method.[9] Under the **visual inspection method**, you review the company's financial statements and prepare its statement of cash flows without using a worksheet. This method may be used when a company's financial statements are simple and when the relationships between changes in account balances can be easily analyzed. There are seven steps in the visual inspection method, as we show in Exhibit 22-3.

EXHIBIT 22-3   Steps in Visual Inspection Method

1. Prepare the heading for the statement of cash flows and list the three major sections: a) Net Cash Flow From Operating Activities, (b) Cash Flows From Investing Activities, and (c) Cash Flows From Financing Activities.
2. Calculate the net change in cash that occurred during the accounting period. This amount is a major subtotal, or "target figure," on the statement of cash flows.
3. List the company's net income as the first item in the net cash flow from operating activities section.
4. Calculate the increase or decrease that occurred during the accounting period in each balance sheet account (except cash).
5. Determine whether the increase or decrease in each balance sheet account (except cash) caused an inflow or outflow of cash and, if so, whether the cash flow was related to an operating, investing, or financing activity.
6. If no cash flow occurred in Step 5, determine whether the increase or decrease in each balance sheet account (except cash) was (a) the result of a noncash income statement item or (b) a simultaneous investing and/or financing transaction. If (a), then determine the adjustment (addition or subtraction) to help convert net income to the net cash flow from operating activities. If (b), then identify the components of the simultaneous investing and/or financing activity.
7. Complete the various sections of the statement of cash flows (based on the analysis in Steps 5 and 6), and check that the subtotals of the sections sum to the net change (increase or decrease) in cash (from Step 2). Also check that the sum of the net change in cash and the beginning cash balance is equal to the ending cash balance reported on the balance sheet.

Steps 5 and 6 do not have to be completed in sequential order. What is important is a complete analysis of the relevant information.[10] The visual inspection method is rarely used because there is no supporting documentation for the statement of cash flows.

---

9. Sometimes a third method involving T-accounts is used to analyze and develop the information for a company's statement of cash flows. The T-account method, however, results in cumbersome working papers when the analysis is complex. Because the worksheet method uses the same general technique as the T-account method, but in a more efficient format, we discuss only the worksheet method in this chapter.
10. If the company engaged in any investing and financing transactions not affecting cash, you must also prepare the heading for a schedule of Investing and Financing Activities Not Affecting Cash in Step 1 of Exhibit 22-3.

Simple Example (Visual Inspection Method)

5 Prepare a simple statement of cash flows.

Knowledge of the visual inspection method is helpful in understanding the more complex worksheet method. To explain the visual inspection method, Example 22-2 shows the condensed financial information of the Leyton Company (a small service company) for 2007. Example 22-3 shows the statement of cash flows prepared from that information. After preparing the heading and listing the three sections of the statement, the $2,600 net increase in cash is determined. This increase is computed by subtracting the $4,000 cash balance on the beginning balance sheet from the $6,600 cash balance on the ending balance sheet. Then, the $7,000 net income is obtained from the income statement and listed as the first item in the net cash flow from operating activities section. The following discussion explains the remaining steps in the visual inspection method by reviewing the items in each section of the statement.

EXAMPLE 22-2   Leyton Company: Condensed Financial Information

Income Statement Information for 2007

Service revenues		$31,800
Operating expenses		
Depreciation expense	$ 2,300	
Interest expense	1,400	
Other expenses	18,100	(21,800)
Income before income taxes		$10,000
Income tax expense		(3,000)
Net Income		$ 7,000

Retained Earnings Information for 2007

Beginning retained earnings	$11,300
Add: Net income	7,000
	$18,300
Less: Dividends	(3,500)
Ending retained earnings	$14,800

Balance Sheet Information

	Balances	
Accounts	**12/31/06**	**12/31/07**
Cash	$ 4,000	$ 6,600
Accounts receivable	6,300	9,000
Land	9,000	6,000
Buildings and equipment	48,000	60,000
Accumulated depreciation	(12,500)	(14,800)
Total Assets	$54,800	$66,800
Accounts payable	$ 7,500	$ 9,000
Notes payable, 10%	14,000	21,000
Common stock, $10 par	22,000	22,000
Retained earnings	11,300	14,800
Total Liabilities and		
Stockholders' Equity	$54,800	$66,800

Supplemental Information for 2007

(a) A building was purchased for cash during the year.
(b) Land was sold (at cost) for cash during the year.
(c) No buildings or equipment were sold during the year.
(d) A note payable was issued at the end of the year.

Net Cash Flow From Operating Activities

In this section there are three adjustments to convert the net income to the net cash flow from operating activities. The first adjustment involves the $2,300 depreciation expense. This amount is obtained from the income statement in Example 22-2. It is also the $2,300 increase (from $12,500 to $14,800) in the accumulated depreciation account on the balance sheets during the year.[11] Because depreciation is deducted in computing net income but does not cause a cash outflow, the $2,300 depreciation expense is added to net income. The second adjustment involves the $1,500 increase (from $7,500 to $9,000 in Example 22-2) in accounts payable. Accounts payable increased because other operating expenses recorded during the year exceeded the cash payments for these items. Therefore, the expenses deducted to compute net income are greater than the related cash payments. Consequently, the $1,500 increase in accounts payable is added to net income. The third adjustment involves the $2,700 increase (from $6,300 to $9,000) in accounts receivable. Accounts receivable increased during the year because service revenues on credit exceeded the cash collections on

---

11. No buildings or equipment were sold during the year. If they had been sold, the accumulated depreciation account would have decreased. The related cash flow analysis would have been more complicated. We discuss this situation later in the worksheet method.

account. Therefore, service revenues and net income are greater than the related cash receipts. Consequently, the $2,700 increase in accounts receivable is deducted from net income.

As a result of the preceding adjustments, the net cash flow from operating activities is $8,100 for the Leyton Company in 2007, as we show in Example 22-3. Note that, with the exception of depreciation, the adjustments to net income involve changes in current assets (except cash) and current liabilities.

EXAMPLE 22-3   Simple Statement of Cash Flows

LEYTON COMPANY

Statement of Cash Flows
For Year Ended December 31, 2007

Net Cash Flow From Operating Activities		
Net income	$ 7,000	
Adjustments for differences between income flows and cash flows from operating activities:		
Add: Depreciation expense	2,300	
Increase in accounts payable	1,500	
Less: Increase in accounts receivable	(2,700)	
Net cash provided by operating activities		$8,100
Cash Flows From Investing Activities		
Payment for purchase of building	$(12,000)	
Proceeds from sale of land, at cost	3,000	
Net cash used for investing activities		(9,000)
Cash Flows From Financing Activities		
Proceeds from issuance of note	$ 7,000	
Payment of dividends	(3,500)	
Net cash provided by financing activities		3,500
Net Increase in Cash		$2,600
Cash, January 1, 2007		4,000
Cash, December 31, 2007		$6,600

Cash Flows From Investing Activities

There are only two cash flows from investing activities: one cash payment and one cash receipt. During 2007 the Buildings and Equipment account increased by $12,000, from $48,000 to $60,000, as we show on the balance sheets in Example 22-2. This increase is the result of the purchase of a building, an investing activity, which required a cash payment of $12,000. This cash payment is listed as the first item in this section. During 2007 the Land account decreased by $3,000, from $9,000 to $6,000. This is the result of the sale of land, an investing activity. Because the land was sold at cost, there is no gain or loss.[12] The $3,000 cash receipt is listed as the second item in this section. As a result of these two cash flows, net cash of $9,000 is used for investing activities by the Leyton Company in 2007, as we show in Example 22-3.

Cash Flows From Financing Activities

There are also two cash flows from financing activities: one cash receipt and one cash payment. During 2007 the notes payable account increased by $7,000, from $14,000 to $21,000, as we show in Example 22-2. This increase is the result of issuing a note, a financing activity, which provided a cash receipt of $7,000 that is listed as the first item in this section. There was no change in the common stock account during the year, so there is no cash inflow or outflow related to common stock. During 2007 the company declared and paid dividends of $3,500. The amount of the dividends is obtained from

---

12.   We discuss the reporting of the sale of noncurrent assets at a gain or loss in a later example.

the retained earnings statement in Example 22-2. [Note also that the $7,000 net income, offset by the $3,500 dividends, accounts for the $3,500 increase (from $11,300 to $14,800) in the retained earnings account shown on the balance sheets.] The $3,500 cash payment of dividends, a financing activity, is listed as the second item in this section. As a result of these two cash flows, net cash of $3,500 is provided by the financing activities of the Leyton Company during 2007, as we show in Exhibit 22-3.

Summary

Note that in preparing the three sections of the cash flow statement in Exhibit 22-3, we account for all the changes in the assets (except cash), liabilities, and stockholders' equity accounts during 2007, as listed in Example 22-2. Note also that, with the exception of depreciation, the adjustments to net income in the net cash flow from operating activities section involve changes in current asset (except cash) and current liability accounts. On the other hand, all of the cash receipts and payments listed in the cash flows from investing activities section and the cash flows from financing activities section involve changes in noncurrent asset, noncurrent liability, and stockholders' equity accounts. The statement of cash flows in Example 22-3 is now complete. The $8,100 net cash provided by operating activities, less the $9,000 net cash used for investing activities, plus the $3,500 net cash provided by financing activities, equals the $2,600 net increase in cash. And, the $2,600 net increase in cash, added to the $4,000 beginning cash balance, is equal to the $6,600 ending cash balance (as reported on the company's December 31, 2007 balance sheet). With this background in mind, we now turn to the worksheet method of analysis. ♦

WORKSHEET (SPREADSHEET) METHOD OF ANALYSIS

Companies usually use the **worksheet method** to prepare their statements of cash flows. Under this method a company uses a worksheet to (1) record its cash receipts and payments according to the operating, investing, and financing sections of the statement of cash flows, (2) record the investing and financing activities *not* affecting cash, and (3) account for the *change* in each asset, liability, and stockholders' equity account. This method is most often used because it enables a company to analyze its complex transactions in a concise format. A common way of preparing an electronic worksheet is to use a software package such as Microsoft Excel. Because the worksheet method is used in more complex situations, it is helpful to follow a series of steps.

Steps in Preparation (Worksheet Method)

After gathering information from the financial statements and supplemental information from the accounting records, a company completes several steps to prepare the worksheet and its statement of cash flows. We list each step in Exhibit 22-4, followed by an explanation.

There are three issues related to the steps listed in Exhibit 22-4. First, other than usually starting with net income, there is no particular order in which the worksheet entries are reconstructed. You should develop a method to account for all the changes in the noncash accounts in an orderly way. Second, you may have to make *more than one* worksheet entry to reconcile the change in an account. For instance, the change in the Land account may be the result of both a sale and a purchase of land. In these cases, both the cash receipt and cash payment are accounted for, and reported, separately. Finally, remember that these worksheet entries are *not* posted to any accounts. They are recorded on the worksheet only to help prepare the statement of cash flows.

EXHIBIT 22-4   Steps in Worksheet Method

Step 1. Prepare the column headings on a worksheet (see Example 22-5). Then enter the account title Cash on the first line of the account titles column and list the beginning balance, ending balance, and change in cash in the respective columns.

Step 2. Enter the titles of all the remaining accounts from the balance sheets on the worksheet and list each beginning and ending account balance, and the change in the account balance directly below the cash information. (To simplify the worksheet, only the change in each account balance may be entered.) The accounts with debit balances are listed first, followed by the accounts with credit balances. Total the amount columns to verify that the debit totals equal the credit totals.

Step 3. Directly below these accounts, add the following headings:

A. Net Cash Flow From Operating Activities

B. Cash Flows From Investing Activities

C. Cash Flows From Financing Activities

D. Investing and Financing Activities Not Affecting Cash

Leave sufficient room below each heading so that each type of cash flow may be listed.

Step 4. Account for all the changes in the noncash accounts that occurred during the current period. *Reconstruct* the journal entries that caused the changes in the noncash accounts directly on the worksheet, making certain modifications to show the cash receipts and payments for operating, investing, and financing activities. Remember that you are preparing this worksheet at the *end* of the accounting period. The actual journal entries that caused the changes have already been made and posted to the accounts. In this step you are reconstructing the entries on the worksheet to prepare the statement of cash flows. Use the following *general rules*:

A. *Start with net income.* The net income is a summary of all the journal entries from operating activities that affect current assets or current liabilities (and some noncurrent) and retained earnings. The net income is adjusted on the worksheet to reconcile it to the net cash flow from operating activities. Therefore, the entry on the worksheet to list net income and to explain the impact on retained earnings is a debit to the caption Net Income under the heading Net Cash Flow From Operating Activities and a credit to Retained Earnings.[a]

B. *Account for the changes in the current asset (except cash) and current liability accounts.* Because nearly all the changes in the current assets and current liabilities relate to the company's *operating activities*, the impacts of these changes on cash are listed as *adjustments* (*additions or deductions*) to *net income* in the Net Cash Flow From Operating Activities section of the worksheet.[b] Review each current asset (except cash) and current liability account. Make an entry on the worksheet to record the change (debit or credit) in that account and the adjustment [credit (deduction) or debit (addition)] to net income.

C. *Account for the changes in the noncurrent accounts.* Review each noncurrent account and determine the journal entry responsible for its change. Identify whether the transaction involves an operating, investing, or financing activity. If the transaction involved an investing or financing activity, make the entry on the worksheet with the following changes:

1. If the entry affects cash, replace a debit to cash with either an investing or financing cash inflow caption, and list the item as a debit (receipt) under the proper heading. Replace a credit to cash with a proper cash outflow caption, and list the item as a credit (payment) under the proper heading.

2. If the entry involves an operating activity and affects a noncash income statement item (e.g., depreciation, gain, or loss), replace the debit or credit to this noncash item with an adjustment to net income under the Net Cash Flow From Operating Activities heading.

3. If the entry does not affect an operating activity or cash, it is a simultaneous financing and/or investing transaction. For this type of transaction, create expanded entries to record both the financing and/or investing activities.

Step 5. Make a final worksheet entry to record the net change in cash. The worksheet entries must account for all the changes in the noncash accounts recorded in Step 2. The difference between the total cash inflows and outflows must be equal to the change in the Cash account. The final worksheet entry to record a net increase in cash is a debit to Cash and a credit to Net Increase in Cash.[c] Total the debit and credit worksheet entries in the upper and lower portions to verify that the respective totals are equal.

Step 6. Prepare the statement of cash flows and accompanying schedule. Use the information developed in the lower part of the worksheet (and the beginning and ending cash balances). Under the major sections of the statement, list the various cash receipts and payments. Subtotal the items under each major section and add or subtract the subtotals to determine the net change in cash. Add the net change in cash to the beginning cash balance to determine the ending cash balance. In an accompanying schedule, list the various investing and financing activities not affecting cash.

a. The entry to show a net loss involves a debit to Retained Earnings and a credit to Net Loss. Any adjustments for noncash items included in net income, such as in Step 4C(2), are made as usual.

b. The major exceptions to this adjustment are changes in short-term notes receivable and notes payable, changes in temporary investments (i.e., marketable securities), and changes in dividends payable. These changes are the results of investing or financing activities and are handled like the changes in the noncurrent accounts discussed in Step 4(C), except that changes in temporary investments may require additional analysis as discussed in a later section.

c. For a net decrease in cash, an opposite entry (a debit to Net Decrease in Cash and a credit to Cash) is made.

Comprehensive Example (Worksheet Method)

To understand how to prepare a worksheet and statement of cash flows we discuss a comprehensive example. The example is not intended to be all-inclusive. However, it provides a basis from which to develop a logical approach to using a worksheet for analyzing similar operating, investing, and financing transactions. The example includes a discussion of each step in Exhibit 22-4. As you study this example, it will be helpful to reread these steps. Example 22-4 shows the condensed financial information of the Jones Company for 2007 that we use in the example. In Example 22-4 we include letters of the alphabet in parentheses beside amounts or items of information. These letters correspond to the letters we use to explain the worksheet entries in Example 22-5.

Steps 1, 2, and 3: Setting Up the Worksheet

Steps 1 and 2 involve setting up the worksheet, entering the account titles, their beginning and ending balances, and the changes in the account balances in the appropriate columns. The columns are totaled to check for accuracy. In Step 3 the major headings, Net Cash Flow From Operating Activities, Cash Flows From Investing Activities, Cash Flows From Financing Activities, and Investing and Financing Activities Not Affecting Cash, are then listed on the worksheet. Enough space is left under each heading so that the cash flows may be listed accordingly. Example 22-5 shows these accounts and their headings for the Jones Company.[13]

Step 4: Completion of the Worksheet

The worksheet entries to account for all the *changes* in the noncash accounts are entered directly on the worksheet in Step 4, as we show in Example 22-5. We explain each entry in the following discussion. Entries (a) through (j) generally affect current assets and current liabilities and relate to operating activities. Entries (k) through (w) generally affect noncurrent assets, noncurrent liabilities, and stockholders' equity items and relate to investing and financing activities. As you study each entry, it will be helpful to review the discussion under Step 4 of Exhibit 22-4, as well as the financial information in Exhibit 22-4.

Worksheet Entries for Operating Activities

Entry (a) records net income as the first item on the worksheet under the heading Net Cash Flow From Operating Activities. Adjustments are then made for noncash expenses and for changes in current assets and current liabilities.

Non-Cash Expenses   A review of the expenses on the income statement in Exhibit 22-4 shows three "noncash" expenses: depreciation expense on equipment, depreciation expense on buildings, and patent amortization expense. Each of these is added back to net income to help reconcile it to the net cash flow from operating activities, as we show in entries (b), (c), and (d). Note that entries (b) and (d) account for the changes in Accumulated Depreciation: Equipment and Patents (net), respectively. Entry (o), which we discuss later, is also recorded to account for the change in the Accumulated Depreciation: Buildings account.

Changes in Current Assets   A review of the changes in the current assets (except cash) reveals several additional adjustments that are made to help reconcile the net income to the net cash flow from operating activities. Accounts receivable increased by $2,000 during the year because the company collected less cash than the credit sales it made. To adjust net income for the lower operating cash inflow, entry (e) is made. Note that, for simplicity, we ignore bad debts here. If accounts receivable (net) are affected by a provision for bad debts, then both the change in accounts receivable because of recording bad

---

13.   Normally, in Step 3 the major headings are listed *below* the account titles. However, because Example 22-5 is so long, we show the lower portion of the worksheet on the facing page.

debts expense and the change because of cash collections in excess of (or less than) sales are treated as adjustments of net income.

EXAMPLE 22-4   Jones Company: Condensed Financial Information

Income Statement Information for 2007

Sales		$ 88,020
Less: Cost of goods sold	$ (52,200)	
Other operating expenses	(15,800)	
Depreciation expense: equipment	(2,820) (b)	
Depreciation expense: building	(5,100) (c)	
Patent amortization expense	(600) (d)	
Bond interest expense	(1,100)	
Income tax expense	(3,630)	
Plus: Gain on sale of land	1,700	(79,550)
Income before extraordinary items		$ 8,470
Extraordinary loss (net of income taxes)		(2,100)
Net Income		$ 6,370 (a)

Balance Sheet Information

	Balances	
Accounts	**12/31/06**	**12/31/07**
Cash	$ 3,200	$ 5,900 (w)
Accounts receivable	5,600	7,600 (e)
Inventories	7,300	7,000 (f)
Prepaid expenses	1,200	1,400 (g)
Land	10,000	18,200
Equipment	35,000	35,000
Accumulated depreciation: equipment	(12,000)	(14,820)
Buildings	144,000	149,000
Accumulated depreciation: buildings	(39,300)	(39,600)
Leased equipment	0	5,300
Patents (net)	5,000	4,400
Total Assets	$160,000	$179,380
Accounts payable	$ 8,600	$ 7,300 (h)
Income taxes payable	1,500	2,130 (i)
Interest payable	0	500 (j)
Note payable	0	2,600
Obligation under capital lease	0	5,300
Bonds payable, 10%	0	10,000
Discount on bonds payable	0	(900)
Deferred tax liability	1,920	2,100
Preferred stock, $100 par	6,000	0
Premium on preferred stock	1,000	0
Common stock, $10 par	34,000	37,400
Premium on common stock	67,000	73,700
Retained earnings	39,980	39,250
Total Liabilities and Stockholders' Equity	$160,000	$179,380

Retained Earnings Information for 2007

Beginning retained earnings		$39,980
Add: Net income		6,370
		$46,350
Less: Stock dividends	$ 3,100	
Cash dividends	4,000 (v)	(7,100)
Ending Retained Earnings		$39,250

Supplemental Information for 2007

(k) On December 31, 2007 the company borrowed $2,600 from a bank by issuing a 12%, 90-day note payable.

(l) During the year additional land was acquired at a cost of $10,400.

(m) During the year land that cost $2,200 was sold for $3,900, resulting in a $1,700 gain.

(n) During the year a new building was acquired at a cost of $15,000.

(o) During the year an earthquake completely destroyed a building that cost $10,000 and had a book value of $5,200. Settlement with the insurance company, combined with the tax credit, resulted in after-tax cash proceeds of $3,100 and an extraordinary loss (net of income taxes) of $2,100.

(p) On December 31, 2007 the company leased equipment under a long-term capital lease, recording the lease at $5,300.

(q) On January 1, 2007 the company issued $10,000 of long-term bonds at 90. The bonds pay interest semiannually on July 1 and January 1 at a 10% annual rate and mature in 10 years on January 1, 2017.

(r) The company uses straight-line amortization for the bond discount in (q); consequently, bond discount amortization was $100 for the year.

(s) On January 1, 2007 sixty shares of preferred stock with a total par value of $6,000 and book value of $7,000 were converted into 240 shares of common stock. The required book value method was used to record the conversion.

(t) Taxable income was less than pretax accounting income for the year, resulting in an increase in deferred taxes payable of $180.

(u) During the year, a small stock dividend was declared and issued. The stock dividend involved 100 shares of $10 par common stock. The market value of the stock on the declaration date was $31 per share.

EXAMPLE 22-5   Cash Flow Worksheet for 2007 (Jones Company)

	A	B	C	D	E		F	
1	Jones Company							
2	Cash Flow Worksheet							
3	For Year Ended Dec. 31, 2007							
4								
5		Balances		Change	Worksheet Entries			
6				Increase				
7	Account Titles	12/31/06	12/31/07	(Decrease)	Debit		Credit	
8	*Debits*							
9	Cash	3,200	5,900	2,700	(w)	2,700		
10	*Noncash Accounts:*							
11	Accounts receivable (net)	5,600	7,600	2,000	(e)	2,000		
12	Inventories	7,300	7,000	(300)			(f)	300
13	Prepaid expenses	1,200	1,400	200	(g)	200		
14	Land	10,000	18,200	8,200	(l)	10,400	(m)	2,200
15	Equipment	35,000	35,000	0				
16	Buildings	144,000	149,000	5,000	(n)	15,000	(o)	10,000
17	Leased equipment	0	5,300	5,300	(p-2)	5,300		
18	Patents (net)	5,000	4,400	(600)			(d)	600
19	Discount on bonds payable	0	900	900	(q)	1,000	(r)	100
20	Totals	211,300	234,700	23,400				
21								
22	*Credits*							
23	Accumulated depreciation:							
24	equipment	12,000	14,820	2,820			(b)	2,820
25	Accumulated depreciation:							
26	buildings	39,300	39,600	300	(o)	4,800	(c)	5,100
27	Accounts payable	8,600	7,300	(1,300)	(h)	1,300		
28	Income taxes payable	1,500	2,130	630			(i)	630
29	Interest payable	0	500	500			(j)	500
30	Note payable	0	2,600	2,600			(k)	2,600
31	Obligation under capital lease	0	5,300	5,300			(p-1)	5,300
32	Bonds payable, 10%	0	10,000	10,000			(q)	10,000
33	Deferred tax liability	1,920	2,100	180			(t)	180
34	Preferred stock, $100 par	6,000	0	(6,000)	(s-2)	6,000		
35	Premium on preferred stock	1,000	0	(1,000)	(s-2)	1,000		
36	Common stock, $10 par	34,000	37,400	3,400			(s-1)	2,400
37							(u)	1,000
38	Additional paid-in capital							
39	on common stock	67,000	73,700	6,700			(s-1)	4,600
40							(u)	2,100
41	Retained earnings	39,980	39,250	(730)	(u)	3,100	(a)	6,370
42					(v)	4,000		
43	Totals	211,300	234,700	23,400		56,800		56,800
44								

(Lower portion shown on facing page)

Inventories decreased by $300 during the year, indicating that the company purchased less inventory than it recorded as cost of goods sold. To adjust net income for the lower operating cash outflow, entry (f) is made. Prepaid expenses increased by $200 during the year, indicating that the company paid more cash for these items than the amount of expense it included in other operating expenses. To adjust net income for the higher operating cash outflow, entry (g) is made.

EXAMPLE 22-5   (Continued)

	A	B	C	D	E	F
45	Net Cash Flow From Operating Activities					
46	Net Income				(a) 6,370	
47	Add: Depreciation expense: equipment				(b) 2,820	
48	Depreciation expense: buildings				(c) 5,100	
49	Patent amortization expense				(d) 600	
50	Decrease in inventories				(f) 300	
51	Increase in income taxes payable				(i) 630	
52	Increase in interest payable				(j) 500	
53	Extraordinary loss				(o) 2,100	
54	Bond discount amortization				(r) 100	
55	Increase in deferred tax liability				(t) 180	
56	Less: Increase in accounts receivable					(e) 2,000
57	Increase in prepaid expenses					(g) 200
58	Decrease in accounts payable					(h) 1,300
59	Gain on sale of land					(m) 1,700
60	Cash Flows From Investing Activities					
61	Payment for purchase of land					(l) 10,400
62	Proceeds from sale of land				(m) 3,900	
63	Payment for purchase of building					(n) 15,000
64	Proceeds from building destroyed by earthquake				(o) 3,100	
65	Cash Flows From Financing Activities					
66	Proceeds from issuance of short-term note payable				(k) 2,600	
67	Proceeds from issuance of bonds				(q) 9,000	
68	Payment of dividends					(v) 4,000
69	Investing and Financing Activities Not Affecting Cash					
70	Incurrence of capital lease obligation for equipment				(p-1) 5,300	
71	Acquisition of equipment under capital lease					(p-2) 5,300
72	Issuance of common stock to convert preferred stock				(s-1) 7,000	
73	Conversion of preferred stock to common stock					(s-2) 7,000
74	Net Increase in Cash					(w) 2,700
75	Totals				49,600	49,600
76						

Changes in Current Liabilities   Accounts payable decreased by $1,300 during the year. This decrease indicates that the company's cash payments for operating activities exceeded expenses. To adjust net income for the higher cash outflow, entry (h) is made. Both income taxes payable and interest payable increased during the year, indicating that the company paid less cash than it reported as the respective expenses. To adjust net income for the lower cash outflows, entries (i) and (j) are made. A few entries which we record later also affect the net cash flow from operating activities.

Note that no adjustment is made to the net cash flow from *operating* activities for the $2,600 increase in the current liability, notes payable. This is because the increase was due to a *financing* activity, which we summarized in the supplemental information of Example 22-4. To record the cash receipt from this financing activity, entry (k) is made. At this point all the changes in the current assets (except cash) and current liabilities are accounted for.

Worksheet Entries for Investing and Financing Activities

Turning to the noncurrent assets and liabilities, a review of the supplemental information is needed to identify the various investing and financing activities.

Changes in Land During the year the company both purchased and sold land; both are investing activities. The acquisition of land resulted in a $10,400 cash payment, which is recorded in entry (l). Land that cost $2,200 was sold for $3,900, which resulted in a $1,700 gain (not extraordinary) that increased net income. Because the entire $3,900 is reported as a cash receipt from an investing activity, the gain is *subtracted* from net income to avoid double counting, and because there was no cash inflow from *operating* activities. Therefore, entry (m) is made.[14] Note that entries (l) and (m) account for the $8,200 increase in the Land account.

Changes in Buildings (and Extraordinary Loss) The acquisition of a new building during the year resulted in a $15,000 cash payment for an investing activity, which is recorded in entry (n). *FASB Statement No. 95* requires that a company report its cash flows from extraordinary items (as well as discontinued operations) as investing or financing activities and exclude them from its net cash flows from operating activities.[15] During the year, an earthquake (extraordinary event) occurred that destroyed a building owned by the company with a cost of $10,000 and a book value of $5,200. Because the company received after-tax cash proceeds of $3,100 from its insurance company, it incurred an extraordinary loss (net of taxes) of $2,100, which it included in (and reduced) net income. The proceeds are a cash receipt *from an investing activity*. To record the cash receipt, eliminate the book value, and *add back* the extraordinary loss to net income, entry (o) is made. Because worksheet entry (o) is complex, we show it below in journal entry form to help you in your analysis:

(o)	Cash Flows From Investing Activities:		
	Proceeds From Building Destroyed by Earthquake	3,100	
	Accumulated Depreciation: Building	4,800	
	Net Cash Flow From Operating Activities:		
	Extraordinary Loss	2,100	
	Buildings		10,000

Note that entries (n) and (o) account for the $5,000 increase in the Building account, and that entries (c) and (o) account for the $300 increase in the Accumulated Depreciation account. Note also that the Extraordinary Loss is shown on the worksheet as an addition to net income in the usual manner, along with the other added items.

Change in Leased Equipment At the end of the year the company leased equipment under a capital lease, recording the asset and liability at $5,300. Although not affecting cash, this is a simultaneous investing and financing transaction, and the company reports both activities in a schedule accompanying the statement of cash flows. Entries (p-1) and (p-2) record these events.

Changes in Bonds Payable (and Related Discount) On January 1 the company issued bonds payable with a face value of $10,000, at a discount, receiving proceeds of $9,000. This is a financing activity and the cash receipt is recorded in entry (q). Note that the $1,000 debit to Discount on Bonds Payable does not equal the net change ($900) in the account. This is because the company amortized part of the discount during the year. On the income statement in Example 22-4, note that the bond interest expense is $1,100; however, the cash paid or owed on the bonds is 10% of $10,000, or $1,000. The additional $100 of interest expense is due to the discount amortization. This amortization increased interest expense and reduced net income but did not involve a cash outflow. To

---

14. If the land was sold at a loss, the loss would decrease net income even though there was no outflow of cash for operating activities. In this case, the worksheet entry would be modified so that the caption Loss on Sale of Land is *debited* under the heading Net Cash Flow From Operating Activities to *add back* the loss to net income in a manner similar to depreciation expense.

15. *FASB Statement No. 95, op. cit.,* par. 28.

adjust for the lower operating cash outflow, entry (r) is made. The $900 increase in Discount on Bonds Payable is now accounted for. The adjustment for the amortization of a premium on bonds payable would be handled in a similar but opposite way. Bond premium amortization reduces interest expense to an amount *less* than the operating cash outflow. Therefore, the worksheet entry would involve a debit to Premium on Bonds Payable and a credit to Net Cash Flow From Operating Activities: Bond Premium Amortization for the amount of the premium amortization.

Change in Preferred Stock   During the year, sixty shares of convertible preferred stock with a total par value of $6,000 and a book value of $7,000 were converted to 240 shares of $10 par common stock; the company accounted for the transaction by the required book value method. Although not affecting cash, two simultaneous financing activities involving the exchange of equity securities occurred that the company reports in a schedule accompanying the statement of cash flows. Entries (s-1) and (s-2) record these events. Note that entry (s-1) did not account for all the changes in the Common Stock and Additional Paid-In Capital on Common Stock accounts. Entry (u) also affects these accounts, as we discuss below.

Change in Deferred Taxes   The deferred tax liability increased by $180 because the company's income tax expense was higher than the actual income taxes it paid or owes (because of a temporary difference between pretax financial income and taxable income). To adjust net income for the lower operating cash outflow, entry (t) is made.

Stock Dividend   The company declared and issued a small stock dividend during the year; it recorded the transaction at the market price of the stock. Recall that stock dividends affect only stockholders' equity accounts and do not involve the transfer of assets to stockholders or the exchange of equity securities. Consequently, the issuance of a stock dividend is *not* considered to be a financing activity and is *not* reported on a company's statement of cash flows. However, to account for the $3,100 effect on the company's stockholders' equity accounts, entry (u) is made in the *upper* part of the worksheet.

Cash Dividends   The $730 net decrease in retained earnings during the year has not yet been accounted for. Entry (a) increased retained earnings for the net income of $6,370, while entry (u) decreased it for the stock dividend of $3,100. The remaining decrease in retained earnings was due to the declaration and payment of $4,000 in cash dividends. This payment is a financing activity and is recorded in entry (v).

Step 5: Final Worksheet Entry

In Step 5 a check of the debit and credit entries in the upper portion of the worksheet shows that all the changes in the noncash accounts have been accounted for. A final worksheet entry is made to record the increase in cash and to bring the debit and credit column totals into balance. This is entry (w). The debit and credit totals in the upper portion of Example 22-5 are $56,800 and in the lower portion are $49,600. The worksheet for the Jones Company is now complete.

Step 6: Preparation of Statement

Example 22-6 shows the statement of cash flows and the accompanying schedule of investing and financing activities not affecting cash for the Jones Company. They were prepared from the *lower* part of the worksheet in Example 22-5, along with the beginning and ending cash balances. Note that in the Cash Flows From Investing Activities section, the company reports the payment for the purchase of land separately from the receipt from the sale of land. Similarly, it reports the payment for the purchase of the building separately from the receipt from the building destroyed by the earthquake. *FASB Statement No. 95* requires that a company report the cash inflows and cash outflows for related investing activities as well as for related financing activities *separately* and *not* "net" them against each other.[16] Note also that the reconciliation of the beginning and ending cash balances at the bottom of the statement of cash flows enables a user to trace the change in cash to related amounts on the company's balance sheets. Finally, note that the schedule of investing and financing activities not affecting cash discloses the $5,300 non-cash transaction that had both an investing and financing element, and the $7,000 other transaction that involved two financing elements.

EXAMPLE 22-6   Comprehensive Statement of Cash Flows

JONES COMPANY

Statement of Cash Flows
For Year Ended December 31, 2007

Net Cash Flow From Operating Activities		
Net income	$ 6,370	
Adjustments for differences between income flows and cash flows from operating activities:		
Add: Depreciation expense: equipment	2,820	
Depreciation expense: buildings	5,100	
Patent amortization expense	600	
Decrease in inventories	300	
Increase in income taxes payable	630	
Increase in interest payable	500	
Extraordinary loss (net) from earthquake	2,100	
Increase in deferred tax liability	180	
Bond discount amortization	100	
Less: Increase in accounts receivable	(2,000)	
Increase in prepaid expenses	(200)	
Decrease in accounts payable	(1,300)	
Gain on sale of land	(1,700)	
Net cash provided by operating activities		$13,500
Cash Flows From Investing Activities		
Payment for purchase of land	$(10,400)	
Proceeds from sale of land	3,900	
Payment for purchase of building	(15,000)	
Proceeds from building destroyed by earthquake	3,100	
Net cash used for investing activities		(18,400)
Cash Flows From Financing Activities		
Proceeds from issuance of short-term note payable	$ 2,600	
Proceeds from issuance of bonds	9,000	
Payment of dividends	(4,000)	
Net cash provided by financing activities		7,600
Net Increase in Cash (see Schedule 1)		$ 2,700
Cash, January 1, 2007		3,200
Cash, December 31, 2007		$ 5,900
Schedule 1: Investing and Financing Activities Not Affecting Cash		
Investing Activities		
Acquisition of equipment under capital lease		$ (5,300)
Financing Activities		
Issuance of capital lease obligation for equipment		5,300
Conversion of preferred stock to common stock		(7,000)
Issuance of common stock to convert preferred stock		7,000

---

16. *FASB Statement No. 95, op. cit.,* par. 31 and 75.

Secure Your Knowledge 22-2

- The calculation of a company's net cash flow from operating activities involves an adjustment of net income for differences in when the company records revenues and expenses and when it receives and pays cash, as well as for non-cash items (e.g., depreciation expense, amortization expense for intangible assets) that affect net income but do not result in a cash receipt or payment. These adjustments are made using either the direct or indirect methods.
- The direct method calculates and reports a company's net cash flow from operating activities by computing the company's cash inflows for each operating activity and then deducting its cash outflows for each operating activity.
  - The direct method requires that each income statement account be analyzed and adjusted for changes in current assets or liabilities, certain noncurrent assets or liabilities, and any non-cash items.
  - If the direct method is used, a company must include a reconciliation of net income to net cash flow from operating activities.
- The indirect method calculates a company's net cash flow from operating activities by converting its net income from an accrual basis to a cash flow basis.
  - The indirect method adjusts net income for changes in the appropriate current assets or liabilities, certain noncurrent assets or liabilities, and any non-cash items.
  - The indirect method is the most commonly used method for the preparation of net cash flow from operating activities.
- A company's net cash flows from investing and financing activities are identified through an analysis of the changes in the balance sheet accounts (generally noncurrent assets and liabilities) and a review of any supplemental information provided.
- The statement of cash flows may be prepared by using either the visual inspection method or the worksheet method. The steps for each method are outlined in Exhibit 22-3 and Exhibit 22-4, respectively.
  - Under either method, all of the changes in the assets (except cash), liabilities, and stockholders' equity accounts during the period are explained.

SPECIAL TOPICS

We designed the previous examples and discussion to show the common issues involved in using the worksheet to prepare the statement of cash flows. For simplicity, we omitted several topics. We briefly discuss these topics in the following sections.

Sale of Depreciable Asset

A company computes the gain or loss on the sale of a depreciable asset by comparing the current book value of the asset to the selling price. When the company records the transaction it increases cash, eliminates the book value (cost and accumulated depreciation), and recognizes a gain or loss that it reports on its income statement. At the end of the year, when preparing the worksheet for the statement of cash flows, this journal entry must be properly reconstructed on the worksheet to account for the changes in the various accounts.

Example: Sale of Depreciable Asset   Assume that during the year Brandt Company sold equipment with a cost of $2,200 and accumulated depreciation of $700 for $2,100. The company recorded an increase (debit) in Cash for $2,100, a decrease (debit) in Accumulated Depreciation for $700, and a decrease (credit) in Equipment for $2,200. Because the $2,100 selling price (proceeds) was more than the $1,500 ($2,200 − $700) book value, the company also recorded (credited) a Gain on the Sale of Equipment for $600.

The proceeds of $2,100 are a cash receipt from an *investing* activity. The gain increased net income but there was no cash inflow from *operating* activities. In preparing the worksheet entry for this transaction, two modifications are made: (1) instead of debiting cash, the caption Proceeds From Sale of Equipment under the heading Cash Flows From Investing Activities is debited for the $2,100, and (2) the caption Gain on Sale of Equipment is *credited* under the heading Net Cash Flow From Operating Activities to *subtract* the gain from net income to avoid double counting and to correctly show the cash provided by operating activities. The worksheet entry (in journal entry format) is as follows:

Cash Flows From Investing Activities:		
Proceeds From Sale of Equipment	2,100	
Accumulated Depreciation	700	
Equipment		2,200
Net Cash Flow From Operating Activities:		
Gain on Sale of Equipment		600

The sale of equipment (or other depreciable assets) at a loss is handled in a similar manner, except that the caption Loss on Sale of Equipment is *debited* under the heading Net Cash Flow From Operating Activities to *add back* the loss to net income because it did not involve an operating cash outflow. ♦

Retirement of Bonds

A company computes the gain or loss on the retirement of bonds by comparing the current book value of the bonds payable to the retirement price. When the company records the transaction, it decreases cash, eliminates the book value (face value and any related premium or discount), and recognizes a gain or loss that it reports on its income statement. At the end of the year, this journal entry must be properly reconstructed on the worksheet to account for the changes in the various accounts.

Example: Retirement of Bonds Assume that during the year, Rosen Company paid $8,900 to retire bonds with a face value of $10,000 and a book value of $9,700. The company recorded a decrease (debit) to Bonds Payable for $10,000, a decrease (credit) to Discount on Bonds Payable for $300, and a decrease (credit) to Cash for $8,900. Since the cash paid was less than the book value, the company also recorded (credited) an $800 ($9,700 − $8,900) Gain on Retirement of Bonds.

The cash paid of $8,900 is a cash payment for a *financing* activity. The gain increased net income but there was no cash inflow from *operating* activities. In preparing the worksheet entry for this transaction, two modifications are made: (1) instead of crediting cash, the caption Cash Flows From Financing Activities: Payment to Retire Bonds is credited for $8,900, and (2) instead of crediting gain, the caption Net Cash Flow From Operating Activities: Gain on Retirement of Bonds is credited for $800 to *subtract* the gain from net income to correctly show the cash provided by operating activities. The retirement of bonds payable at a loss is handled in a similar manner, except that the caption Net Cash Flow From Operating Activities: Loss on Retirement of Bonds is debited to *add back* the loss to net income because it did not involve an operating cash outflow. ♦

Interest Paid and Income Taxes Paid

7 Compute and disclose interest paid and income taxes paid.

FASB Statement No. 95 requires a company using the indirect method of reporting its operating cash flows to also disclose its interest *paid* and income taxes *paid*. This disclosure may be made in a separate schedule, narrative description, or the notes to the financial statements. Interest *expense* is affected by the cash paid, accruals, and any premium or discount amortizations on bonds (or notes) payable. Income tax *expense* is affected by the cash paid, accruals, and changes in deferred income taxes. To convert interest expense to interest paid, and to convert income tax expense to income taxes paid, the following adjustments[17] are necessary:

Interest	Income Taxes
Interest *expense*	Income tax *expense*
+ Decrease in interest payable	+ Decrease in income taxes payable
or	*or*
− Increase in interest payable	− Increase in income taxes payable
+ Amortization of premium on bonds payable	+ Decrease in deferred tax liability
or	*or*
− Amortization of discount on bonds payable	− Increase in deferred tax liability
= Interest *paid*	+ Increase in deferred tax asset
	or
	− Decrease in deferred tax asset
	= Income taxes *paid*

Example: Interest and Income Taxes   Refer back to the Jones Company information shown in Example 22-4 and 22-5. To determine its interest paid and income taxes paid for 2007, the Jones Company prepares the following schedules:

Bond interest expense	$1,100	Income tax expense	$3,630
− Increase in interest payable	(500)	− Increase in income taxes payable	(630)
− Bond discount amortization	(100)	− Increase in deferred tax liability	(180)
Interest paid	$ 500	Income taxes paid	$2,820

Based on these computations, Jones Company reports interest paid of $500 and income taxes paid of $2,820 with its 2007 statement of cash flows shown in Example 22-6. **Unless directed otherwise, you are *not* required to make these disclosures in the chapter homework.** ♦

Flexibility in Reporting

FASB Statement No. 95 permits flexibility in reporting a company's net cash flow from operating activities under the indirect method. That is, the company may show the reconciliation of net income to the net cash provided by (or used in) operating activities in a separate schedule accompanying its statement of cash flows. Thus, for instance, if the Jones Company used this approach, the first section of Example 22-6 would appear as follows:

Net Cash Flow From Operating Activities
Net cash provided by operating activities (Schedule 1) $13,500

Then the company would report the reconciliation of the $6,370 net income to the $13,500 net cash provided by operating activities in Schedule 1. The rest of the statement of cash flows would remain the same. (The schedule to report the investing and financing activities not affecting cash would be numbered as Schedule 2.) The advantage of reporting the reconciliation in a separate schedule is that it reduces the amount of detail that a

---

17. A company may have a valuation allowance related to its deferred tax asset. Since the valuation allowance is a contra account, it handles any changes in the account in the opposite way to that of the deferred tax asset.

company shows on its statement of cash flows. The disadvantage is that it removes from the statement a key factor in assessing the quality of the company's net income and its relationship to cash flows. By relegating the reconciliation to a separate schedule, this analysis may be overlooked by external users. For this reason, we advocate that a company include the reconciliation directly on its statement of cash flows, which most companies do.

Partial Cash Investing and Financing Activities

In the previous examples and discussion, we assumed that no cash was exchanged in any "noncash" transactions involving investing and financing activities. In some transactions, however, a company may exchange a small amount of cash even though most of the transaction involves a noncash exchange. In other transactions, it may exchange a large amount of cash even though some of the transaction is a noncash exchange. In these cases, there are alternative ways the company may use to disclose simultaneous investing and financing activities involving some cash.

Example: Small Amount of Cash Assume Hembrey Company acquired land for $10,000 by paying $1,000 down and signing a $9,000 note payable. One method it may use to disclose the effects of this transaction is to report the cash payment on its statement of cash flows and the noncash element on the accompanying schedule of investing and financing activities not affecting cash as follows:

Statement of Cash Flows
    Cash Flows From Investing Activities
        Payment for purchase of land $(1,000)
Schedule: Investing and Financing Activities Not Affecting Cash
    Investing Activities
        Purchase of land for $10,000 by issuance of note $(9,000)
    Financing Activities
        Issuance of note to acquire land   9,000

The advantage of this approach is that it keeps the significant noncash elements of the transaction separate from the cash elements. The disadvantage is that the external user cannot identify the relationships between the items. ♦

Example: Large Amount of Cash When the amount of cash is large in such an exchange, it may be more appropriate to report the items in the statement of cash flows. Several alternative disclosure formats are acceptable. For instance, if Lakewood Company acquired land for $18,000 by paying $15,000 down and signing a $3,000 note payable, it might report the effects on its statement of cash flows as follows:

Cash Flows From Investing Activities
    Purchase of land by issuance of note and cash $(18,000)
    Less: Issuance of note   3,000
    Cash payment for purchase of land $(15,000)

The advantage of this approach is that the related items are shown in close proximity. The disadvantage is that a financing element (issuance of note) is disclosed in an investing section. Each of the alternative disclosures has its advantages and disadvantages. You must use good judgment to determine the most informative disclosure for the given circumstances. ♦

Temporary and Long-Term Investments

As we discussed in Chapter 15, a company reports its investments (whether temporary or long-term) in "available-for-sale" debt and equity securities as assets at their fair value (by using an allowance account) on its year-end balance sheet. It also includes any resulting

unrealized increase or decrease in value as a component of its accumulated other comprehensive income[18] in its stockholders' equity. When the company sells this temporary or long-term investment, it eliminates the fair value (cost and allowance accounts) of the security, as well as any related cumulative unrealized increase or decrease in value, from its accounting records. It also records a realized gain or loss on the sale. It computes the realized gain or loss by comparing the proceeds to the *cost* of the security.

Because the company used an allowance account and an unrealized increase or decrease account to value the investment in available-for-sale securities, it must carefully analyze any changes in these accounts to determine the impact (if any) on its statement of cash flows. The company reports an increase in the investment account due to the *purchase* of the securities on its statement of cash flows as a cash payment for an investing activity. The entry on the worksheet to prepare the statement is also made in the usual manner. The company does *not* report any changes in the allowance and the unrealized increase or decrease accounts resulting from a *revaluation to fair value at year-end* on its statement of cash flows. However, it must account for the changes on the worksheet. The company reports a decrease in the investment account because of the *sale* of the securities on its statement of cash flows as a cash receipt from an investing activity in the usual manner. However, the worksheet entry must reconcile the changes in the investment, allowance, unrealized increase/decrease, and realized gain (or loss) accounts.

Example: Purchase and Sale of Investment Assume that on November 28, 2007, the Dougherty Company purchased 1,000 shares of Bear Company common stock for $40,000 as a temporary investment in available-for-sale securities. On December 31, 2007 the fair value of the stock has risen to $42 per share, so that the company reported the temporary investment as a current asset of $42,000 ($40,000 cost + $2,000 allowance). It also reported a $2,000 unrealized increase in value of available-for-sale securities as a component of its accumulated other comprehensive income in its stockholders' equity on the December 31, 2007 balance sheet. For its cash flow analysis, Dougherty Company would make the following worksheet entries at the end of 2007 to reconcile the $42,000 change in the carrying value of the temporary investment:

Temporary Investment in Available-for-Sale Securities	40,000	
Cash Flows From Investing Activities:		
Payment for Purchase of Temporary Investments		40,000
Allowance for Change in Value of Investment	2,000	
Unrealized Increase in Value of Available-for-Sale		
Securities		2,000

The debit portion of the first entry is listed in the upper part of the worksheet. This helps to reconcile the change in the temporary investment account. The credit portion of the

---

18. The company would first include the periodic *change* in the unrealized increase or decrease in value in its other comprehensive income for the period, as we discussed in Chapter 5.

first entry is listed in the lower part of the worksheet and accounts for the cash payment for the purchase of the temporary investment. The company reports this $40,000 cash payment in its 2007 statement of cash flows. Both the debit and credit portions of the second entry are listed in the upper portion of the worksheet and complete the reconciliation of the changes in the allowance and unrealized increase accounts. The company does *not* include this portion of the increase in the carrying value of the temporary investment on its 2007 statement of cash flows because there was no cash outflow.

Now suppose that the Dougherty Company sold its investment in Bear Company stock for $45,000 on January 16, 2008. Dougherty Company would make the following worksheet entries at the end of 2008 to reconcile the changes in the various accounts:

Cash Flows From Investing Activities: Receipt from Sale of Temporary Investment	45,000	
Temporary Investment in Available-for-Sale Securities		40,000
Net Cash Flow From Operating Activities: Gain on Sale of Temporary Investment		5,000
Unrealized Increase in Value of Available-for-Sale Securities	2,000	
Allowance for Change in Value of Investment		2,000

These two journal entries (1) record the $45,000 investing cash inflow from the sale of the securities, (2) treat the $5,000 gain on the sale as a subtraction from net income to reconcile it to the net cash flow from operating activities, and (3) reconcile the changes in the temporary investment, allowance, and unrealized increase accounts. The company reports the first two items on its 2008 statement of cash flows in the usual manner. ♦

A company may also make a long-term investment in debt securities (e.g., bonds) that it expects to hold to maturity. It amortizes any premium or discount each year as an adjustment to interest revenue, and reports the investment at its book value on the year-end balance sheet. For cash flow reporting purposes, it reports the purchase as a cash payment for investing activities. The company also adds any premium amortization on this type of investment to net income in the operating activities section of the statement of cash flows because the amortization reduced interest revenue to an amount lower than the cash received. The company subtracts any discount amortization from net income because the amortization increased interest revenue to an amount higher than the cash received. Each of these adjustments helps reconcile the net income to the net cash flow from operating activities. Although rare, if a company sells such an investment before maturity, it computes any gain or loss by comparing the proceeds to the unamortized cost. It reports the proceeds as a cash receipt from investing activities and deducts the gain from net income (or adds the loss to net income) in the usual manner on its statement of cash flows.

A company may also make short-term investments in trading securities. It reports the cash flows from purchases, sales, and maturities of trading securities as cash flows from operating activities. Also, as we discussed in Chapter 15, *FASB Statement No. 115* requires companies to report investments in trading securities at their fair value and report any resulting unrealized holding gain or loss in net income. Consequently, for reporting its operating cash flows under the indirect method, a company adds (deducts) an unrealized holding loss (gain) on trading securities to net income to help adjust net income from an accrual has is to a cash basis.

Financial Institutions

When the FASB was discussing the requirements of *FASB Statement No. 95*, one controversial issue was the proper reporting of interest collected and interest paid, and collections and payments of notes receivable and notes payable. Most companies do not deal with notes receivable and notes payable as a primary part of their operations. On the other hand, notes are a major aspect of the business of banks (and other financial institutions). Banks also frequently buy and sell notes, mortgages, and similar securities. The question arose as to whether companies should be required to report the related cash inflows and outflows (i.e., interest and principal) as operating activities or as investing and financing activities. As we discussed earlier in the chapter, the FASB concluded that companies must report interest collected and interest paid as cash flows relating to operating activities. The Board concluded that this would provide consistency with the reporting of the related interest revenue and interest expense on the income statement. However, the Board decided that companies must report the collections and payments of the principal of notes receivable and notes payable as cash flows relating to their investing and financing activities, respectively.

In *FASB Statement No. 102* the FASB reversed parts of its original requirements. For banks, brokers and dealers in securities, and other similar companies that hold loans for resale on a short-term basis or carry securities in a "trading account," other requirements now apply. (A trading account includes accounts that are acquired specifically for resale and are turned over very quickly.) The Board concluded that financial institutions must report the cash flows from the purchases or sales of these trading accounts in the operating activities section of the statement of cash flows.[19] In coming to this conclusion, the FASB reasoned that these types of assets for financial institutions are similar to inventory for other businesses and, as such, are part of the operating activities.

As we discussed earlier in the chapter, in most situations *FASB Statement No. 95* does *not* allow a company to "net" its cash outflows against cash inflows for reporting the results of related investing or financing activities. An exception is made for certain activities of banks and other financial institutions. These institutions are allowed to report the net cash flows for (1) deposits and withdrawals with other financial institutions, (2) time deposits accepted and repaid, and (3) loans made to customers and principal collections of these loans.[20] This exception is allowed because showing these items on a "gross" basis provides information that is costly for a company to accumulate and is of limited value to external users.

Cash Dividends Declared

In the previous examples, whenever we discussed cash dividends, we assumed that the dividends were declared *and* paid in the current year. The declaration and payment of cash dividends causes a decrease in both retained earnings and cash. A company reports this as a cash payment for financing activities.

In some instances a company will declare a cash dividend in the *current* year and pay the cash dividend in the *next* year. In this case the cash dividend is handled differently in preparing the worksheet for the statement of cash flows. The declaration of the cash dividend is recorded on the worksheet as a decrease (debit) in Retained Earnings and an increase (credit) in Dividends Payable. Because no cash outflow occurs in the current year, the company does not report dividends paid on its statement of cash flows. In the next year, the company records the payment of the cash dividends on the worksheet as a

19. "Statement of Cash Flows—Exemption of Certain Enterprises and Classification of Cash Flows from Certain Securities Acquired for Resale," *FASB Statement of Financial Accounting Standards No. 102* (Norwalk, Conn.: FASB, 1989), par. 8 and 9.
20. "Statement of Cash Flows—Net Reporting of Certain Cash Receipts and Cash Payments and Classification of Cash Flows from Hedging Transactions," *FASB Statement of Financial Accounting Standards No. 104* (Norwalk, Conn.: FASB, 1989), par. 7.

decrease (debit) in Dividends Payable and a decrease (credit) in Cash. The company then reports the dividends paid as a cash payment in the cash flows from financing activities section of its statement of cash flows.

When a company follows a policy of declaring a dividend in one year and paying the dividend in the next year, its Dividends Payable account balance will change during each year. A comparison of the change in the account balance to the dividends reported on the retained earnings statement will determine the worksheet entry necessary to account for the cash dividends.

Cash Flows for Compensatory Share Option Plans

In Chapter 16, we showed how a corporation records its estimated compensation expense for a compensatory share option plan. In Chapter 19, we explained how recording this compensation expense for financial reporting purposes but not recording any compensation expense for income tax purposes results in a deferred tax asset for the future deductible amount. Although both of these journal entries affect net income, neither results in a cash flow. Therefore, on the corporation's statement of cash flows, under the indirect method the increase in compensation expense must be *added* back to net income and the increase in the deferred tax asset must be *subtracted* from net income to help determine the net cash flow from operating activities.

When employees exercise the share options, the cash flow treatment is more complicated and we only provide a brief overview here. In Chapter 19, we explained that in the year an employee exercises the share options, the corporation is allowed to take a tax deduction (for compensation expense) equal to the difference between the market price of the shares on the exercise date and the exercise price. However, for financial reporting purposes, the corporation has already recorded all of the compensation expense during the service period. So, when the share options are exercised, the corporation has higher pretax financial income than taxable income because the previous future deductible difference has "reversed." Therefore, it eliminates the deferred tax asset (that it had previously recorded during the service period) and increases income tax expense. For cash flow purposes, this decrease in the deferred tax asset is *added* back to net income under the indirect method to help determine the net cash flow from operating activities.

If the actual market price used to record the compensation expense for income tax purposes is the same as the estimated market price (based on the option pricing model) used to record the compensation expense for financial reporting purposes, then there are no more cash flow issues. However, this is not likely because of the use of estimates, and a "permanent" difference will exist that provides a tax benefit by reducing the corporation's income tax expense and income taxes payable. Therefore, *FASB Statement No. 95* (as amended by *FASB Statement No. 123R*) requires that the corporation compute the excess realized tax benefit related to the difference between the compensation expense reported for income tax purposes and the compensation expense recorded for financial reporting purposes. The corporation is then required to report the excess realized tax benefit as a cash inflow from financing activities because it relates to the issuance of stock, which is a financing activity. The corporation is also required to *subtract* the excess realized tax benefit from net income to help determine its net cash flow from operating activities on its statement of cash flows.[21] The amount is subtracted because it reduced income tax expense but did not involve an operating cash savings.

---

21.   *FASB Statement No. 95*, op.cit., par. 19 and 23, as amended by *FASB Statement No. 123* (revised 2004) (Norwalk, Conn.: FASB, 2004), par. 68 and A96.

For example, suppose that Petricka Corporation reported net income of $500,000 and had a tax deduction of $800,000 in the current year for compensation expense because employees exercised share options. In previous years, for financial reporting purposes, the corporation had recorded compensation expense of $700,000 for this compensatory share option plan. If the corporation is subject to a 30% tax rate and uses the indirect method to report its cash flows from operating activities, then it would report the $30,000 [($800,000 − $700,000) × 0.30] excess realized tax benefit on its statement of cash flows for the current year as follows:

Cash flows from operating activities
Net income	$500,000
Less: Excess tax benefits from compensatory stock option plan	(30,000)
Cash flows from financing activities	
Excess tax benefits from compensatory stock option plan	$ 30,000

For more details, see Illustration 4 in Appendix A of *FASB Statement No. 123R.*

Effects of Exchange Rates

Many companies have operations in foreign countries. When a company with foreign operations prepares its statement of cash flows, the statement must disclose the "reporting currency equivalent" of the "foreign currency" cash flows using the exchange rates in effect at the time of the cash flows. It may use a weighted average exchange rate for the period if this yields similar results. On the statement, then, a company reports the effect of exchange rate changes on cash balances held in foreign currencies as a separate part of the reconciliation of the change in cash during the period.[22]

Cash Flow Per Share

A company must report its earnings per share on the face of its income statement, as we discussed in Chapter 17. Although the cash flow information presented in a company's statement of cash flows is useful in evaluating the performance of the company, the FASB believes that cash flow (or any component) is not an alternative to income as an indicator of a company's performance. Consequently, a company is *not* allowed to report a cash flow per share amount in its financial statements.[23] Users often compute other cash flow ratios, however, as we discussed in Chapter 6.

Disclosure

Real Report 22-1 shows the statement of cash flows for **Kellogg Company**. Note that Kellogg uses the indirect method to report net cash flow from operating activities and discloses the changes in current assets and current liabilities in the notes to its financial statements. Additionally, the effect of the exchange rate on cash is disclosed separately after net cash flow from financing activities.

---

22. *FASB Statement No. 95, op. cit.,* par. 25.
23. *Ibid.,* par. 33.

Real Report 22-1 Kellogg Company - Statement of Cash Flows

(millions)	2004	2003	2002
Operating activities			
Net earnings	$ 890.6	$ 787.1	720.9
Adjustments to reconcile net			
earnings to operating cash flows:			
Depreciation and amortization	410.0	372.8	349.9
Deferred income taxes	57.7	74.8	111.2
Other	104.5	76.1	67.0
Pension and other postretirement			
benefit plan contributions	(204.0)	(184.2)	(446.6)
Changes in operating assets and liabilities	(29.8)	44.4	197.5
Net cash provided from operating activities	$1,229.0	$1,171.0	$999.9
Investing activities			
Additions to properties	($ 278.6)	($ 247.2)	($253.5)
Acquisitions of businesses	—	—	(2.2)
Dispositions of businesses	—	14.0	60.9
Property disposals	7.9	13.8	6.0
Other	.3	.4	—
Net cash used in investing activities	($ 270.4)	($ 219.0)	($188.8)
Financing activities			
Net increase (reduction) of notes payable,			
with maturities less than or equal to 90 days	$ 388.3	$ 208.5	($226.2)
Issuances of notes payable, with maturities			
greater than 90 days	142.3	67.0	354.9
Reductions of notes payable, with maturities			
greater than 90 days	(141.7)	(375.6)	(221.1)
Issuances of long-term debt	7.0	498.1	—
Reductions of long-term debt	(682.2)	(956.0)	(439.3)
Net issuances of common stock	291.8	121.6	100.9
Common stock repurchases	(297.5)	(90.0)	(101.0)
Cash dividends	(417.6)	(412.4)	(412.6)
Other	(6.7)	(.6)	—
Net cash used in financing activities	($ 716.3)	($ 939.4)	($944.4)
Effect of exchange rate changes on cash	33.9	28.0	2.1
Increase (decrease) in cash and cash equivalents	$ 276.2	$ 40.6	($ 131.2)
Cash and cash equivalents at beginning of year	141.2	100.6	231.8
Cash and cash equivalents at end of year	$ 417.4	$ 141.2	$ 100.6

NOTE 15 SUPPLEMENTAL FINANCIAL STATEMENT DATA

Consolidated Statement of Cash Flows	2004	2003	2002
Trade receivables	$ 13.8	($ 36.7)	$ 14.6
Other receivables	(39.5)	18.8	13.5
Inventories	(31.2)	(48.2)	(26.4)
Other current assets	(17.8)	.4	70.7
Accounts payable	63.4	84.8	41.3
Other current liabilities	(18.5)	25.3	83.8
Changes in operating assets and liabilities	($ 29.8)	$ 44.4	$197.5

Questions:

1. How did Kellogg's net cash flow from operating activities differ from its net income for 2004? Explain this difference.
2. What type of activities did Kellogg invest in for 2004?
3. What kind of financing activities did Kellogg's engage in for 2004?

LINK TO INTERNATIONAL DIFFERENCES

International accounting standards require a company to include a cash flow statement as one of its basic financial statements. These standards define operating, investing, and financing activities in a manner similar to U.S. standards. A company may present its operating cash flows under either the indirect or direct method. However, contrary to U.S. standards, international standards do not require a company using the direct method to reconcile its net income to its operating cash flows. There are also a few differences in the way a company presents certain items under international standards as compared to U.S. standards. For instance, under international standards a company is (1) allowed to report dividends paid as either an operating cash outflow or a financing cash outflow, (2) allowed to report payments of income taxes identified with financing and investing transactions as financing and investing activities, (3) allowed to report cash flow per share, and (4) allowed more freedom in netting cash receipts and payments. Finally, contrary to U.S. standards, international accounting standards encourage a company to disclose any undrawn borrowing facilities that may be available for future operating activities, the cash flows that represent increases in its operating capacity separately from the cash flows that are needed to maintain its operating capacity, and the operating, investing, and financing activities of each of its reported industry and geographic segments.

SECURE YOUR KNOWLEDGE 22-3

- The sale of a depreciable asset generally involves an increase in cash (classified as an investing activity), the elimination of the book value of the asset, and the recognition of a non-cash gain or loss (the difference between the book value and the proceeds from the sale) which requires an adjustment to net income in the operating activities section of the statement of cash flows prepared under the indirect method.
- The retirement of bonds generally involves a decrease in cash (classified as a financing activity), the elimination of the book value of the bonds, and the recognition of a non-cash gain or loss (the difference between the book value of the bonds and cash paid to retire the bonds) which requires an adjustment to net income in the operating activities section of the statement of cash flows prepared under the indirect method.
- A company using the indirect method must disclose the interest paid and the income taxes paid in a separate schedule, narrative description, or the notes to the financial statements.
- The reconciliation of net income to the net cash flow from operating activities may be provided in a separate schedule.
- For simultaneous investing and financing activities that involve some cash, a company may choose to report the cash portion on its statement of cash flows and the non-cash portion in the accompanying schedule of non-cash activities, or it may choose to report both the cash and non-cash items on its statement of cash flows.
- Cash receipts or payments relating to the sale or purchase of investments in available-for-sale securities are classified as a cash inflow or outflow from investing activities.

(continued)

However, the unrealized change in the market value of these securities is not included on the statement of cash flows.

- The sale or purchase of debt securities classified as held-to-maturity is recorded as a cash inflow or outflow from investing activities. The amortization of any premium or discount related to this long-term investment is a non-cash item requiring an adjustment to net income in the operating activities section of the statement of cash flows prepared under the indirect method.
- Cash dividends declared in the current year and paid in the next year are recorded as a cash payment for financing activities in the year paid.
- The recognition of compensation expense (a non-cash item) related to compensatory share option plans results in an increase in a deferred tax asset. On a statement of cash flows prepared under the indirect method, a corporation must add the increase in compensation expense and subtract the increase in the deferred tax asset in determining net cash flow from operating activities. When the share options are exercised, the decrease in the deferred tax asset is added back to net income in the operating activities section of the statement of cash flows.

APPENDIX: DIRECT METHOD FOR REPORTING OPERATING CASH FLOWS

In the main part of this chapter, we used the *indirect* method to report the net cash flow from operating activities on the statement of cash flows. Most companies (over 98%) use this method. *FASB Statement No. 95* allows a company to use either the indirect method or the direct method to report the cash flows from operating activities on its statement of cash flows, but encourages the use of the *direct method*. As we briefly discussed earlier in the chapter, **under the direct method a company deducts its operating cash outflows from its operating cash inflows to determine its net cash provided by (or used in) operating activities.** This approach has the advantage of separating the company's operating cash receipts from operating cash payments, and of directly showing the cash it paid for interest and income taxes. Each of these disclosures may be useful in estimating its future cash flows. Because of the FASB's support for the direct method, use of this method is likely to increase. Therefore, we explain the direct method in this Appendix.

The direct method is an alternative to the indirect method for a company to report its net cash flow from *operating* activities. However, the company reports its cash flows from *investing* activities and cash flows from *financing* activities on the statement of cash flows in exactly the same manner as we discussed earlier. Therefore, in this Appendix we primarily focus on determining and reporting the cash flows from *operating* activities. However, because there are some slight differences in *preparing* information concerning investing and financing activities, we discuss these differences as well.

OPERATING CASH FLOWS

According to *FASB Statement No. 95*, under the direct method a company reports its operating cash inflows separately from its operating cash outflows. We discuss each of these classifications in the following sections.

Operating Cash Inflows

8 Identify the operating cash inflows and outflows under the direct method.

Under the direct method a company reports its cash inflows from operating activities in three categories: (1) collections from customers, (2) interest and dividends collected, and (3) other operating receipts, if any. Generally, these cash inflows from operating activities are calculated by an analysis of income statement and balance sheet items as follows:

1. *Collections from Customers.* Sales revenue, plus decrease in accounts receivable or minus increase in accounts receivable, and plus increase in deferred revenues or minus decrease in deferred revenues.

2. *Interest and Dividends Collected.* Interest revenue and dividend revenue, plus decrease in interest/dividends receivable or minus increase in interest/dividends receivable, and plus amortization of premium on investment in bonds or minus amortization of discount on investment in bonds.

3. *Other Operating Receipts.* Other operating revenues, minus gains on disposals of assets and liabilities, and minus investment income recognized under the equity method.

Operating Cash Outflows

A company reports its cash outflows from operating activities in five categories: (1) payments to suppliers,[24] (2) payments to employees, (3) other operating payments, (4) payments of interest, and (5) payments of income taxes. Generally, these cash outflows for operating activities are calculated by an analysis of income statement and balance sheet items as follows:

1. *Payments to Suppliers.* Cost of goods sold, plus increase in inventory or minus decrease in inventory, plus decrease in accounts payable or minus increase in accounts payable.

2. *Payments to Employees.* Salaries (wages) expense, plus decrease in salaries payable or minus increase in salaries payable.

3. *Other Operating Payments.* Other operating expenses, plus increase in prepaid items or minus decrease in prepaid items; minus depreciation, depletion, and amortization expense; minus losses on disposals of assets and liabilities; minus investment loss recognized under the equity method.

4. *Payments of Interest.* Interest expense, plus decrease in interest payable or minus increase in interest payable, plus amortization of premium on bonds payable or minus amortization of discount on bonds payable.

5. *Payments of Income Taxes.* Income tax expense, plus decrease in income taxes payable or minus increase in income taxes payable, plus decrease in deferred tax liability or minus increase in deferred tax liability.[25]

Under the direct method, the company's net cash provided by (or used in) operating activities is the difference between the cash inflows from operating activities and the cash outflows for operating activities.

Diagram of Operating Cash Flows

Under the *direct* method a company computes the cash inflows from operating activities for its statement of cash flows by adjusting the various revenue accounts for changes in certain asset accounts (primarily current assets involved in the operating cycle) and deferred revenues, and to eliminate certain "noncash" revenues (gains). The company computes the cash outflows for operating activities by adjusting the various expense accounts for changes in certain liability (and asset) accounts (primarily current liabilities and current assets in the operating cycle) and deferred revenues, and to eliminate certain "noncash" expenses (losses).

Exhibit 22-5 shows these adjustments. The adjustments may have to be modified depending on the way that the company reports and classifies the related items in its financial statements. For instance, an increase in deferred revenue of an airline would be due to selling tickets in advance. In this case the adjustment would be to sales revenue.

24. *FASB Statement No. 95* (par. 27) combines payments to suppliers and payments to employees into one category. However, it encourages companies to provide further breakdowns of operating cash receipts and operating cash payments, when useful. The authors believe that separating payments to suppliers from payments to employees may be useful to different external users, and do so throughout this Appendix. In a manufacturing company, a separation of payments to suppliers and payments to employees may not be practical. This is because the company may record various manufacturing costs, including direct and indirect materials as well as direct and indirect labor, directly in the work in process inventory and not show them as separate expenses. In this case it would be difficult to separate the related cash flows, so that reporting the combined payments to suppliers and employees may be the only practical disclosure.

25. For a company that has a deferred tax asset, it adds an increase in the deferred tax asset to income tax expense or subtracts a decrease. It handles a change in a related valuation allowance (contra account) in the opposite way.

EXHIBIT 22-5   Major Adjustments to Convert Income Statement Amounts to Operating Cash Flows

Income Statement Amounts	Adjustments	Operating Cash Receipts and Payments	Net Operating Cash Flows
Sales revenue	+ Decrease in accounts receivable or − Increase in accounts receivable + Increase in deferred revenues or − Decrease in deferred revenues	= Collections from customers	Cash Inflows From Operating Activities
Interest revenue and dividend revenue	+ Decrease in interest receivable or − Increase in interest receivable + Amortization of premium on investment in bonds or − Amortization of discount on investment in bonds	= Interest and dividends collected	
Other revenues	− Gains on disposals of assets and liabilities[a] − Investment income (equity method)[a]	= Other operating receipts	
Cost of goods sold	+ Increase in inventory or − Decrease in inventory + Decrease in accounts payable or − Increase in accounts payable	= Payments to suppliers	Cash Outflows For Operating Activities
Salaries expense	+ Decrease in salaries payable or − Increase in salaries payable	= Payments to employees	
Other expenses	+ Increase in prepaid items or − Decrease in prepaid items − Depreciation, depletion, and amortization expense[a] − Losses on disposals of assets and liabilities[a] − Investment loss (equity method)[a]	= Other operating payments	
Interest expense	+ Decrease in interest payable or − Increase in interest payable + Amortization of premium on bonds payable or − Amortization of discount on bonds payable	= Payments of interest	
Income tax expense	+ Decrease in income taxes payable or − Increase in income taxes payable + Decrease in deferred tax liability[b] or − Increase in deferred tax liability	= Payments of income taxes	

a.   Unless listed as separate items on income statement
b.   A change in a deferred tax asset is handled in an opposite manner.

On the other hand, an increase in deferred revenue of a retail company may be due to a collection of rent (for a sub-lease) in advance. In this case the adjustment is to other revenue instead of sales revenues.

Example: Adjustments for Operating Cash Flows

We now show the calculations for some of the adjustments in Exhibit 22-5. Assume for simplicity that the Smith Company made cash sales of $30,000 and credit sales of $42,000 during its *first* year of operations. So, its Sales Revenue account has a credit balance of $72,000 at the end of the year. It also collected $37,000 of the $42,000 accounts receivable during the year, so that its Accounts Receivable account has a debit balance of $5,000 at the end of the year. That is, the Accounts Receivable balance increased from $0 to $5,000 from the beginning to the end of the year. As we show in the top part of Example 22-7, by subtracting the $5,000 *increase* in Accounts Receivable from the $72,000 Sales Revenue, the company determines that it collected $67,000 from customers during the year. (You can verify the $67,000 cash collections by adding the $30,000 cash sales to the $37,000 cash collected from accounts receivable.) The company would include the $67,000 cash collected from customers in its cash inflows from operating activities.

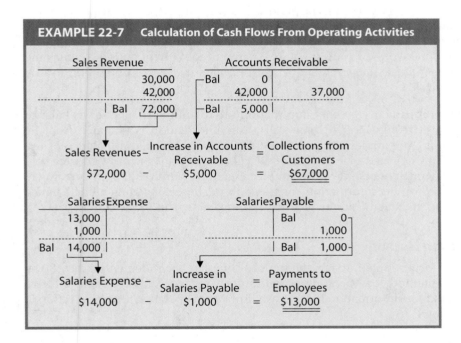

EXAMPLE 22-7   Calculation of Cash Flows From Operating Activities

Now assume that the Smith Company paid salaries of $13,000 during the year and that it accrued salaries of $1,000 at the end of the year. So, its Salaries Expense account has a debit balance of $14,000 at the end of the year. Its Salaries Payable account has a credit balance of $1,000 at the end of the year. That is, the Salaries Payable account increased from $0 to $1,000 from the beginning to the end of the year. As we show in the bottom part of Example 22-7, by subtracting the $1,000 *increase* in Salaries Payable from the $14,000 Salaries Expense, the company determines that it paid $13,000 to employees during the year. The company would add the $13,000 cash paid to employees in its cash outflows for operating activities. ♦

If a company uses the direct method of reporting its operating cash flows, *FASB Statement No. 95* requires the company to reconcile its net income to the net cash provided by (or used) in operating activities in a separate schedule accompanying its statement of cash flows. This reconciliation is, in effect, prepared under the *indirect* method.

Because we fully discussed the indirect method of reconciling net income to operating cash flows in the main part of the chapter, we do not repeat the discussion here.

PROCEDURES FOR STATEMENT PREPARATION

When a company uses the direct method to prepare the information for its statement of cash flows, it may use either the visual inspection method or the worksheet method. This depends on the complexity of its accounting information. The information is obtained, however, in a slightly different manner. Normally, under the direct method, a company obtains the information for its statement of cash flows from the following working papers:

1. **Post-closing trial balance (or balance sheet) from *previous* period.** Recall from Chapter 3 that a post-closing trial balance contains the debit and credit balances of all the *permanent* accounts in a company's general ledger. In other words, a post-closing trial balance of the previous period contains the same information as the *ending balance sheet* of the previous period.
2. **Adjusted trial balance of *current* period.** Recall from Chapter 3 that an adjusted trial balance contains the debit and credit balances (after adjustments but before closing) of all the temporary and permanent accounts in a company's general ledger. In other words, an adjusted trial balance of the current period contains the *balance sheet, income statement,* and *retained earnings statement* information for the current period.

In addition, the company needs other information to explain the changes in its balance sheet (permanent) accounts (other than cash). This information is obtained from its accounting records. In complex situations, use of the post-closing trial balance of the prior period and the adjusted trial balance of the current period is the most efficient way to prepare the statement of cash flows. In simpler situations, however, the statement may be developed based on the information contained in the beginning and ending balance sheets, the income statement, and the retained earnings statement of the current year.

Visual Inspection Method

9 Compute the operating cash flows under the direct method.

Under the visual inspection approach, the steps to complete the statement of cash flows using the direct method for operating activities are similar to those for the indirect method, except that the information for the cash flows from operating activities section is computed as follows:

- Make adjustments to the applicable revenues for the period (e.g., to sales revenue for change in accounts receivable and deferred revenues) to determine the amounts of collections from customers, interest and dividends collected, and other operating receipts.
- Make adjustments to the applicable expenses for the period (e.g., to cost of goods sold for changes in inventory and accounts payable) to determine the amounts of payments to suppliers, payments to employees, other operating payments, payments of interest, and payments of income taxes.

Exhibit 22-5 is helpful for making these adjustments. Once the operating activities section is completed, the investing activities section and the financing activities section are completed by analyzing the changes in the other balance sheet accounts in the same way as we discussed for the indirect method.

Example: Visual Inspection Method

Assume that the following income statement items were taken from the adjusted trial balance of the Betha Company at the end of 2007:

	Debit	Credit
Sales revenue		$94,000
Interest revenue		5,400
Cost of goods sold	$43,000	
Salaries expense	18,500	
Depreciation expense	11,000	
Other expenses	4,700	
Interest expense	9,200	
Income tax expense	3,900	

Also assume that a comparison of the post-closing trial balance for 2006 with the adjusted trial balance for 2007 shows the following *changes* in selected balance sheet accounts:

Accounts receivable	$ 8,200 credit (decrease)
Interest receivable	1,200 debit (increase)
Inventory	6,300 debit (increase)
Prepaid expenses	600 debit (increase)
Accumulated depreciation	11,000 credit (increase)
Accounts payable	4,800 credit (increase)
Salaries payable	500 debit (decrease)
Discount on bonds payable	200 credit (decrease)
Income taxes payable	300 credit (increase)
Deferred tax liability	400 credit (increase)

Based on the preceding information, Betha Company prepares Example 22-8 to determine each of the operating cash inflows and outflows.

EXAMPLE 22-8   Schedule to Compute Cash Flows

Income Statement Amounts		Adjustments			Operating Cash Flows
Sales revenue	$ 94,000	+ Decrease in accounts receivable of	$8,200 =	$ 102,200	Collections from customers
Interest revenue	5,400	− Increase in interest receivable of	1,200 =	4,200	Interest collected
				$ 106,400	Operating cash inflows
Cost of goods sold	$ (43,000) {	+ Increase in inventory of	6,300 } =	$ (44,500)	Payments to suppliers
		− Increase in accounts payable of	4,800		
Salaries expense	(18,500)	+ Decrease in salaries payable of	500 =	(19,000)	Payments to employees
Other expenses	(4,700)	+ Increase in prepaid expenses of	600 =	(5,300)	Other operating payments
Interest expense	(9,200)	− Decrease in discount on bonds payable (amortization) of	200 =	(9,000)	Payments of interest
Income tax expense	(3,900) {	− Increase in income taxes payable of	300 } =	(3,200)	Payments of income taxes
		− Increase in deferred tax liability of	400	$ (81,000)	Operating cash outflows
				$ 25,400	Net cash provided by operating activities

Operating Cash Inflows The $94,000 of sales revenue is increased by the $8,200 decrease in accounts receivable to determine the $102,200 collections from customers. This is because the company's cash collections exceeded its sales during the year. The

$5,400 interest revenue is decreased by the $1,200 increase in interest receivable to determine the $4,200 interest collected because the company received less cash than it recorded as interest revenue. The total operating cash inflows were $106,400 in 2007.

Operating Cash Outflows The $43,000 cost of goods sold is adjusted for two items. It is increased for the $6,300 increase in inventory because the company's purchases exceeded its cost of goods sold. It is decreased by the $4,800 increase in accounts payable because the company's cash payments were less than its purchases. Thus, payments to suppliers totaled $44,500 in 2007. The $18,500 of salaries expense is increased by the $500 decrease in salaries payable to determine the $19,000 paid to employees, because salaries paid exceeded salaries expense. The $4,700 of other expenses are increased by the $600 increase in prepaid expenses to determine the $5,300 other operating payments, because the company's cash payments for prepaid items exceeded its expenses. Note that the $11,000 depreciation expense is the same as the $11,000 credit to accumulated depreciation. Because this is a "noncash" income statement item and is listed separately from other operating expenses, no adjustment is made for operating cash flows.

The decrease in the discount on bonds payable resulted from the amortization of the discount. Recall that the amortization of the discount on bonds payable increases interest expense to an amount greater than the cash the company paid for interest. Therefore, the $200 decrease in the discount on bonds payable is subtracted from the $9,200 interest expense to determine the $9,000 interest paid. The $3,900 income tax expense is decreased by the $300 increase in income taxes payable and the $400 increase in the deferred tax liability to determine the $3,200 payments of income taxes, because the company paid less taxes currently than it recorded as an expense. The total operating cash outflows were $81,000 in 2007, so that $25,400 net cash was provided by operating activities during 2007 as we show at the bottom of Example 22-8.

Example 22-9 shows the cash flows from operating activities section of the Betha Company's statement of cash flows, under the direct method. The company includes cash flows from investing activities and the cash flows from financing activities in the usual manner to complete the statement of cash flows.

EXAMPLE 22-9 **Operating Cash Flows (Direct Method)**

BETHA COMPANY

Statement of Cash Flows (Partial)
For Year Ended December 31, 2007

Cash Flows From Operating Activities		
Cash Inflows:		
Collections from customers	$102,200	
Interest collected	4,200	
Cash inflows from operating activities		$106,400
Cash Outflows:		
Payments to suppliers	$(44,500)	
Payments to employees	(19,000)	
Other operating payments	(5,300)	
Payments of interest	(9,000)	
Payments of income taxes	(3,200)	
Cash outflows for operating activities		(81,000)
Net cash provided by operating activities		$ 25,400

Worksheet Method

Under the worksheet approach, the steps completed using the direct method are very similar to those of the indirect method. There are enough slight differences, however, that we list all of the steps using the direct method in Exhibit 22-6, after which we present an example.

EXAMPLE: WORKSHEET (SPREADSHEET) AND DIRECT METHOD

To learn how to use a worksheet under the direct method, look at Example 22-10. Assume that the post-closing trial balance and adjusted trial balance were obtained from the Copeland Company's accounting records. In addition, the following information was included in its accounting records for 2007:

1. Land costing $2,000 was sold for $2,800.
2. Equipment was purchased at a cost of $24,700.
3. Common stock was issued for $10,000.
4. Dividends of $3,500 were declared and paid.

After entering the accounts and amounts of the trial balances, the changes in the accounts are entered in the appropriate change column of the worksheet (spreadsheet). Then, based on the preceding information, entries (a) through (r) are entered on the worksheet to complete it. We briefly explain each of the worksheet entries next.

Operating Cash Flows

Entries (a) and (b) account for the sales revenue and interest revenue and record the "unadjusted" collections from customers and receipts of interest. (There are no other operating receipts.) Entries (c), (d), (e), (f), and (g) account for the cost of goods sold, salaries expense, other expenses, interest expense, and income tax expense, and record the "unadjusted" payments to suppliers, payments to employees, payments of interest, other operating payments, and payments of income taxes. Entry (h) accounts for the depreciation expense and increase in accumulated depreciation. Note that it is made in the normal manner in the upper part of the worksheet and, therefore, has no effect on the operating cash flows. The entry is necessary, however, to help account for the changes in all the income statement and balance sheet accounts.

Entries (i) through (m) account for the effect of the changes in the current assets and current liabilities on the "unadjusted" operating cash flows recorded earlier. Entry (i) reduces (adjusts) the collections from customers because of the increase in accounts receivable. Entries (j) and (k) reduce (adjust) the payments to suppliers because of the decrease in inventory and the increase in accounts payable. Entry (l) increases (adjusts) the payments to employees because of the decrease in salaries payable. Finally, entry (m) reduces (adjusts) the interest payments because of the increase in interest payable. There are no adjustments to the other operating payments or to the payments of income taxes in this example.

Investing and Financing Cash Flows

Entries (n) through (q) record the investing and financing cash flows. Entry (n) records the $2,800 investing cash receipt (proceeds) from the sale of land costing $2,000. Note that the $800 gain is recorded in the usual way. Entry (o) records the investing cash payment for the purchase of equipment. Entry (p) records the financing cash receipt (proceeds) from the sale of common stock. Entry (q) records the financing cash payment of dividends.

EXHIBIT 22-6   Steps in Worksheet Approach for Direct Method

Step 1. Prepare the column headings on a worksheet (see Example 22-10). Then enter the account titles and the debit and credit amounts of the post-closing trial balance from the previous year and the adjusted trial balance for the current year in the respective columns. Total the amount columns to check the equality.

Step 2. Compare each account balance in the post-closing trial balance and adjusted trial balance, and record the debit or credit difference in the Change column. Note that each revenue and expense account listed on the adjusted trial balance will not have a beginning balance; in that case the ending balance is the change amount. (To simplify the worksheet, sometimes the debit and credit amounts of the accounts in the trial balances are omitted, and only the changes in the accounts are listed.) Total the amount columns to check the equality.

Step 3. Directly below the account titles, add the following headings:

A.   Cash Flows From Operating Activities

B.   Cash Flows From Investing Activities

C.   Cash Flows From Financing Activities

D.   Investing and Financing Activities Not Affecting Cash

Under the heading Cash Flows From Operating Activities, list the eight possible inflow and outflow captions (e.g., collections from customers). Leave sufficient room below each of the subheadings so that each cash flow can be listed where appropriate.

Step 4. Account for all the changes in the noncash accounts that occurred during the current period. *Reconstruct* the journal entries that caused the changes in the noncash accounts directly on the worksheet, making the necessary modifications to show the cash receipts and payments related to operating, investing, and financing activities. Use the following general rules for the worksheet entries:

A.   *Start with the usual revenue and expense accounts.* The changes in these accounts during the year represent potential operating cash receipts or payments. Therefore, the entry on the worksheet is to debit or credit the related operating cash inflow or outflow caption and to credit or debit the revenue or expense account. Observe that these changes represent potential cash flows. They may have to be adjusted later for changes in certain current assets (e.g., accounts receivable) and current liabilities (e.g., accounts payable), as well as other accounts, to show the actual cash flows.

Note that there are two exceptions to the previous procedures. First, the worksheet entries for any noncash revenues and expenses (e.g., depreciation expense) are made in the usual manner, without any modifications.

Second, worksheet entries are *not* prepared at this time to account for gains or losses (either ordinary or extraordinary). The changes in these accounts will be accounted for later when dealing with the investing or financing transactions to which they relate (e.g., retirement of bonds at a gain).

B.   *Account for the changes in the current asset (except cash) and current liability accounts.* Because most of the changes in the current assets and current liabilities relate to the *operating activities,* the impacts of these changes on cash are listed as adjustments to the related operating cash inflow or outflow. There are several exceptions to this procedure. These exceptions involve changes in short-term notes receivable and notes payable, changes in temporary investments (i.e., marketable securities), and changes in dividends payable. These changes are the results of investing or financing activities and are handled like the changes in the noncurrent accounts discussed in Step 4(C).

C.   *Account for the changes in the remaining current assets (except cash) and current liabilities, as well as the changes in noncurrent accounts.* Review each account and determine the journal entry responsible for its change. Identify whether the transaction involves an operating,[a] investing, or financing activity. If the transaction involves an investing or financing activity, make the entry on the worksheet with the following changes:

1. If the entry affects cash, replace a debit to cash with either an investing or financing cash inflow caption, and list the item as a debit (receipt) under the proper heading of the worksheet. Replace a credit to cash with a proper cash outflow caption, and list the item as a credit (payment) under the proper heading of the worksheet. In the case of a transaction involving a gain or loss, record the gain or loss portion of the worksheet entry in the usual manner.

(continued)

EXHIBIT 22-6   (Continued)

2. If the entry does not affect an operating activity or cash, it is a "simultaneous" financing and/or investing transaction. For this type of transaction, create "expanded" entries on the worksheet to record both the financing and/or investing activities. The first entry shows the financing aspect of the exchange, while the second entry shows the investing aspect. These types of transactions are disclosed on a schedule accompanying the statement of cash flows.

Step 5. Make a final worksheet entry to record the net change in cash. The worksheet entries must account for all the changes in the noncash accounts recorded in Step 2. The difference between the total cash inflows and outflows must be equal to the change in the Cash account. Total the debit and credit worksheet entries in the upper and lower portions of the worksheet to verify that the respective totals are equal.

Step 6. Prepare the statement of cash flows and accompanying schedules[b]. Use the information developed in the *lower* portion of the worksheet, along with the beginning and ending cash balances.

a.   The primary examples of changes in noncurrent accounts that affect operating activities are the amortization of premiums or discounts on bonds payable or investments in bonds, changes in deferred taxes, and changes in prepaid/accrued pension costs. In these cases, the related income statement item (interest expense or interest revenue, income tax expense, and pension expense) has already been treated as an adjustment to an operating cash flow (payment of interest or receipt of interest, payment of income taxes, and payment of pensions) in Step 4A. Therefore, the worksheet entry involves a direct adjustment to the operating cash flow. For instance, a change (credit) in the discount on bonds payable due to amortization is accounted for as a debit to Cash Flows From Operating Activities: Payments of Interest and as a credit to Discount on Bonds Payable to adjust for the lesser cash outflow.

b.   The separate schedules include a schedule of the investing and financing activities not affecting cash and a schedule reconciling the net income to the net cash provided by operating activities.

Completion of Worksheet and Statement

Entry (r) is the final entry and records the increase in cash. The debit and credit columns in the upper and lower parts are totaled to check for equality and the worksheet is complete. Example 22-11 shows the statement of cash flows of the Copeland Company, prepared from the worksheet in Example 22-10. Note that the only difference between this statement, prepared under the direct method, and a statement of cash flows prepared under the indirect method is in the presentation of the cash flows from operating activities.

EXAMPLE 22-10   Cash Flow Worksheet for 2007 (Copeland Company)

	A	B	C	D	E	F	G	H		I	
1	Copeland Company										
2	Cash Flow Worksheet										
3	For Year Ended Dec. 31, 2007										
4											
5		12/31/2006 Post-Closing Trial Balance		12/31/2007 Adjusted Trial Balance		Change		Worksheet Entries			
6											
7											
8	Accounts	Debit	Credit	Debit	Credit	Debit	Credit	Debit		Credit	
9	Cash	5,300		9,800		4,500		(r)	4,500		
10	Accounts receivable	9,600		10,900		1,300		(i)	1,300		
11	Inventory	12,500		11,000			1,500			(j)	1,500
12	Land	22,000		20,000			2,000			(n)	2,000
13	Buildings and equipment	82,600		107,300		24,700		(o)	24,700		
14	Accumulated depreciation		32,800		41,900		9,100			(h)	9,100
15	Accounts payable		10,300		12,100		1,800			(k)	1,800
16	Salaries payable		1,100		800	300		(l)	300		
17	Interest payable		300		500		200			(m)	200
18	Notes payable		34,000		34,000		0				
19	Common stock, no par		30,000		40,000		10,000			(p)	10,000
20	Retained earnings		23,500		20,000	3,500		(q)	3,500		
21	Sales revenue				98,700		98,700			(a)	98,700
22	Interest revenue				2,500		2,500			(b)	2,500
23	Gain on sale of land				800		800			(n)	800
24	Cost of goods sold			51,000		51,000		(c)	51,000		
25	Salaries expense			23,000		23,000		(d)	23,000		
26	Depreciation expense			9,100		9,100		(h)	9,100		
27	Other expenses			1,900		1,900		(e)	1,900		
28	Interest expense			4,000		4,000		(f)	4,000		
29	Income tax expense			3,300		3,300		(g)	3,300		
30	Totals	132,000	132,000	251,300	251,300	126,600	126,600		126,600		126,600
31	Cash Flows From Operating Activities										
32	Collections from customers							(a)	98,700	(i)	1,300
33	Interest and dividends collected							(b)	2,500		
34	Other operating receipts										
35	Payments to suppliers							(j)	1,500	(c)	51,000
36								(k)	1,800		
37	Payments to employees									(d)	23,000
38										(l)	300
39	Other operating payments									(e)	1,900
40	Payments of interest							(m)	200	(f)	4,000
41	Payments of income taxes									(g)	3,300
42	Cash Flows From Investing Activities										
43	Proceeds from sale of land							(n)	2,800		
44	Payment for purchase of equipment									(o)	24,700
45	Cash Flows From Financing Activities										
46	Proceeds from issuance of common stock							(p)	10,000		
47	Payment of dividends									(q)	3,500
48	Net Increase in Cash									(r)	4,500
49	Totals								117,500		117,500
50											

EXAMPLE 22-11   Statement of Cash Flows (Direct Method)

COPELAND COMPANY

Statement of Cash Flows
For Year Ended December 31, 2007

Cash Flows From Operating Activities		
Cash Inflows:		
Collections from customers	$ 97,400	
Interest and dividends collected	2,500	
Cash inflows from operating activities		$99,900
Cash Outflows:		
Payments to suppliers	$(47,700)	
Payments to employees	(23,300)	
Other operating payments	(1,900)	
Payments of interest	(3,800)	
Payments of income taxes	(3,300)	
Cash outflows for operating activities		(80,000)
Net cash provided by operating activities		$19,900
Cash Flows From Investing Activities		
Proceeds from sale of land	$ 2,800	
Payment for purchase of equipment	(24,700)	
Net cash used for investing activities		(21,900)
Cash Flows From Financing Activities		
Proceeds from issuance of common stock	$ 10,000	
Payment of dividends	(3,500)	
Net cash provided by financing activities		6,500
Net Increase in Cash		$ 4,500
Cash, January 1, 2007		5,300
Cash, December 31, 2007		$ 9,800

SUMMARY

At the beginning of the chapter, we identified several objectives you would accomplish after reading the chapter. The objectives are listed below, followed by a brief summary of the key points in the chapter discussion.

1. **Define operating, investing, and financing activities.** A company's operating activities include all its transactions involving acquiring, selling, and delivering goods for sale, as well as providing services. Its investing activities include its transactions involving acquiring and selling property, plant, and equipment, acquiring and selling investments, and lending money and collecting on loans. Its financing activities include its transactions involving obtaining resources from owners and providing them with a return on, and of, their investment, as well as obtaining money and other resources from creditors and repaying the amounts borrowed.

2. **Know the categories of inflows and outflows of cash.** A company's inflows of cash come from decreases in assets other than cash, increases in liabilities, and increases in stockholders' equity. Its outflows of cash come from increases in assets other than cash, decreases in liabilities, and decreases in stockholders' equity.

3. **Classify cash flows as operating, investing, or financing.** Operating cash inflows (outflows) come from increases (decreases) in stockholders' equity because of revenues (expenses), adjusted for changes in certain current assets and current liabilities. Investing cash inflows (outflows) come from decreases (increases) in noncurrent assets and certain current assets. Financing cash inflows (outflows) come from increases (decreases) in noncurrent liabilities, stockholders' equity, and certain current liabilities.

4. **Explain the direct and indirect methods for reporting operating cash flows.** Under the direct method, a company deducts its operating cash outflows from its operating cash inflows to determine its net cash flow from operating activities. Under the indirect method, a company adjusts (reconciles) its net income for differences between income flows and cash flows for operating activities to determine its net cash flow from operating activities.

5. **Prepare a simple statement of cash flows.** To complete a simple statement of cash flows, use the visual inspection method. Prepare the heading and major sections, and list the net change in cash at the bottom. Next, list net income under the operating activities section. Then list the increase or decrease in each balance sheet account as a cash receipt or payment (or adjustment) in the appropriate operating, investing, or financing section. Subtotal each section, add them together to calculate the net change in cash, then add the net change in cash to the beginning cash balance to determine the ending cash balance. Verify that this amount is the same as the ending cash balance reported on the balance sheet.

6. **Use a worksheet (spreadsheet) for a statement of cash flows.** Set up a worksheet that shows the change in the balance of each balance sheet account at the top and the sections of the statement of cash flows (and a section for noncash investing and financing activities) at the bottom. Make worksheet entries to account for the changes in all the noncash balance sheet accounts, making certain modifications to show the cash receipts and payments for operating, investing, and financing activities. Make a final worksheet entry to record the net change in cash. Total the debit and credit worksheet entries in the upper and lower portions to verify that the respective totals are equal.

7. **Compute and disclose interest paid and income taxes paid.** To compute interest paid, start with interest expense and adjust this amount for any increase (decrease) in interest payable and any bond premium (discount) amortization. To compute income taxes paid, start with income tax expense and adjust this amount for any increase (decrease) in income taxes payable, deferred tax liability, and deferred tax asset. Disclose interest paid and income taxes paid in a separate schedule, narrative description, or notes to the company's financial statements.

8. **Identify the operating cash inflows and outflows under the direct method (Appendix).** The operating cash inflows are: (1) collections from customers, (2) interest and dividends collected, and (3) other operating receipts. The outflows are: (1) payments to suppliers, (2) payments to employees, (3) other operating payments, (4) payments of interest, and (5) payments of income taxes.

9. **Compute the operating cash flows under the direct method (Appendix).** To determine the operating cash inflows, make adjustments to the applicable revenues for changes in related balance sheet accounts to determine the collections from customers, interest and dividends collected, and other operating receipts. To determine the operating cash outflows, make adjustments to the applicable expenses for changes in related balance sheet accounts to determine the payments to suppliers, to employees, of interest, for other operating items, and for income taxes. Subtract the total operating cash outflows from the total operating cash inflows to determine the net cash flow from operating activities.

ANSWERS TO REAL REPORT QUESTIONS

Real Report 22-1 Answers

1. Net cash flow from operating activities is $338.4 million higher than net income ($1,229 million less $890.6 million). This difference is mainly due to non-cash charges for depreciation and amortization of $410 million. Kellogg's income tax expense was greater than its income tax payable, resulting in cash flow from operating activities being $57.7 million higher than net income. Finally, Kellogg contributed cash to its pension and postretirement benefit plans in excess of its expenses by $204 million.

2. While Kellogg disposed of businesses in 2003 and 2004, these dispositions were completed by 2005 and its most recent investments were for property, plant, and equipment.

3. A review of Kellogg's cash flows from financing activities reveals that the issuances and repurchases of common stock were approximately the same. Additionally, Kellogg experienced a net cash outflow related to debt of $286.3 million ($388.3 + $142.3 + $7.0 − $141.7 − $682.2). In addition, Kellogg was able to pay $417.6 million (almost one-half of its income) to shareholders in the form of dividends. The combination of a steady balance in its common stock account and a decreasing balance in its debt accounts indicates that Kellogg used its cash flow provided by operating activities to make capital investments and reduce its debt level.

QUESTIONS

Q22-1 What is a *statement of cash flows*?

Q22-2 Briefly describe the three types of activities of a company reported in its statement of cash flows.

Q22-3 What does the information in a statement of cash flows help external users to assess?

Q22-4 Name the five items a company's statement of cash flows must clearly show. What items are reported in a separate schedule accompanying the statement?

Q22-5 What are "cash equivalents"? How does a company's reporting on its cash and cash equivalents affect the statement of cash flows?

Q22-6 What are the three categories of a company's inflows of cash? What are the three categories of a company's outflows of cash?

Q22-7 Starting with the basic accounting equation, derive a set of equations that show the relationship between increases (decreases) in cash and increases (decreases) in assets other than cash, liabilities, and stockholders' equity.

Q22-8 Briefly describe a retail company's operating cycle and the relationship of its various stages to cash inflows and outflows.

Q22-9 What are the two ways to calculate and report a company's net cash flow from operating activities? Briefly describe each method.

Q22-10 Briefly describe the *indirect method* for reporting a company's net cash flow from operating activities. List several adjustments to net income and indicate whether they are additions or subtractions.

Q22-11 Give two examples of a company's (a) cash inflows from investing activities, and (b) cash outflows for investing activities.

Q22-12 Give two examples of a company's (a) cash inflows from financing activities, and (b) cash outflows for financing activities.

Q22-13 Give two examples of a company's investing and financing activities not affecting cash.

Q22-14 What is the *visual inspection method*? List the steps in this method.

Q22-15 Briefly describe the *worksheet method* of analyzing the information for a company's statement of cash flows. (Do *not* list the steps in preparation.)

Q22-16 Indicate how a company computes the amount of interest and income taxes that it paid during the year.

Q22-17 What two alternatives are allowed for *where* a company may disclose the net cash flow from operating activities prepared under the indirect method in regard to its statement of cash flows?

Q22-18 A company purchases equipment costing $12,500 by paying $5,000 down and signing a $7,500 note payable. Show two ways of disclosing the effects of this transaction in regard to the statement of cash flows.

Q22-19 (Appendix) Define the *direct* method of reporting the cash flows from operating activities of a company.

Q22-20 (Appendix) List the three operating cash inflows that a company reports under the direct method.

Q22-21 (Appendix) List the five operating cash outflows that a company reports under the direct method.

Q22-22 (Appendix) Briefly describe how to determine each of the operating cash inflows and operating cash outflows under the direct method.

MULTIPLE CHOICE

Select the best answer for each of the following.

M22-1 If a company issues a balance sheet and an income statement with comparative figures from last year, a statement of cash flows
a. Is no longer necessary, but may be issued at the company's option
b. Should not be issued
c. Should be issued for each period for which an income statement is presented
d. Should be issued for the current year only

M22-2 Selected information from Brook Corporation's accounting records and financial statements for 2007 is as follows:

Net cash provided by operating activities	$1,500,000
Mortgage payable issued to acquire	
land and building	1,800,000
Common stock issued to retire	
preferred stock	500,000
Proceeds from sale of equipment	400,000
Cost of office equipment purchased	200,000

On the statement of cash flows for the year ended December 31, 2007, Brook should disclose a net increase in cash in the amount of
a. $1,700,000
b. $2,400,000
c. $3,700,000
d. $4,200,000

M22-3 In a statement of cash flows (indirect method), the amortization of patents of a company with substantial operating profits should be presented as a (an)
a. Cash flow from investing activities
b. Cash flow from financing activities
c. Deduction from net income
d. Addition to net income

M22-4 The net cash provided by operating activities in Seat's statement of cash flows for 2007 was $8,000,000. For 2007, depreciation on fixed assets was $3,800,000, amortization of patents was $100,000, and dividends on common stock were $2,000,000. Based on the preceding information, Seat's net income for 2007 was
a. $2,100,000
b. $4,100,000
c. $8,000,000
d. $11,900,000

M22-5 The retirement of long-term debt by the issuance of common stock should be presented in a statement of cash flows as a

	Cash Flow From Financing Activities	Cash Flow From Investing Activities
a.	No	No
b.	No	Yes
c.	Yes	No
d.	Yes	Yes

M22-6 The net income for Mountain Corporation was $4,000,000 for the year ended December 31, 2007. Additional information is as follows:

Depreciation on fixed assets	$2,000,000
Proceeds from sale of land	200,000
Increase in accounts payable	300,000
Dividends on preferred stock	400,000

The net cash provided by operating activities in the statement of cash flows for the year ended December 31, 2007 should be

a. $6,000,000
b. $6,100,000
c. $6,300,000
d. $6,500,000

M22-7 Which of the following need not be disclosed in a schedule accompanying the statement of cash flows as an investing and financing activity not affecting cash?
a. Acquisition of fixed assets in exchange for capital stock
b. Dividend paid in capital stock of the company (stock dividend)
c. Retirement of a bond issue through the issuance of another bond issue
d. Conversion of convertible debt to capital stock

M22-8 The following information on selected transactions for 2007 has been provided by the Smith Company:

Net income	$20,000,000
Proceeds from short-term borrowings	1,200,000
Proceeds from long-term borrowings	4,000,000
Purchases of fixed assets	3,200,000
Decrease in inventories	8,000,000
Proceeds from sale of Smith's common stock	2,000,000
Depreciation expense	500,000

What is the net increase in cash for the year ended December 31, 2007 as a result of the preceding information?
a. $32,500,000
b. $25,700,000
c. $16,500,000
d. $12,500,000

M22-9 The following information was taken from the accounting records of Oregon Corporation for 2007:

Proceeds from issuance of preferred stock	$4,000,000
Dividends paid on preferred stock	400,000
Bonds payable converted to common stock	2,000,000
Payment for purchase of machinery	500,000
Proceeds from sale of plant building	1,200,000
2% stock dividend on common stock	300,000
Gain on sale of plant building	200,000

Oregon's statement of cash flows for the year ended December 31, 2007 should show the following amounts for investing and financing activities, based on the preceding information:

	Net Cash Flows From Investing Activities	Net Cash Flows From Financing Activities
a.	$700,000	$3,600,000
b.	$700,000	$3,900,000
c.	$900,000	$3,900,000
d.	$900,000	$5,600,000

M22-10 (Appendix) A company reports sales of $200,000 and interest revenue of $17,000 for the current year. During the year accounts receivable increased by $21,000 and interest receivable decreased by $3,000. Under the direct method, the company would report cash inflows from operating activities of
a. $235,000
b. $193,000
c. $241,000
d. $199,000

EXERCISES

E22-1 *Classification of Cash Flows* The following are several transactions and events that might be disclosed on a company's statement of cash flows:

1. Issuance of common stock
2. Purchase of building
3. Net income
4. Increase in accounts receivable
5. Depreciation expense
6. Sale of land at cost
7. Conversion of bonds to common stock
8. Increase in accounts payable
9. Payment of cash dividends
10. Issuance of a stock dividend

Required
Identify in which section (if any) of the statement of cash flows each of the preceding items would appear and indicate whether it would be an inflow (addition) or outflow (subtraction).

E22-2 *Net Cash Flow From Operating Activities* The following is accounting information taken from the Hyde Company's records for 2007:

1. Amortization of premium on bonds payable, $600
2. Purchase of equipment, $6,000
3. Depreciation expense, $7,400
4. Decrease in accounts receivable, $800
5. Decrease in accounts payable, $2,800
6. Issuance of long-term note for cash, $4,200
7. Increase in inventories, $7,500

8. Gain on sale of land, $8,000
9. Increase in prepaid assets, $500
10. Declaration and payment of cash dividends, $1,800
11. Increase in wages payable, $300
12. Patent amortization expense, $1,000
13. Net income, $10,800

Required
Prepare the net cash flow from operating activities section of the 2007 statement of cash flows for the Hyde Company.

E22-3 *Statement of Cash Flows* The following is a list of the items for the 2007 statement of cash flows of the Lombardo Company:

1. Depreciation expense, $4,200
2. Proceeds from sale of land, $5,600
3. Payment of dividends, $5,000
4. Net income, $7,900
5. Conversion of bonds to common stock, $7,000
6. Increase in accounts payable, $3,100

7. Proceeds from issuance of note, $6,200
8. Gain on sale of land, $1,800
9. Payment for purchase of building, $13,000
10. Increase in accounts receivable, $2,700
11. Ending cash balance, $13,900

Required
Prepare the statement of cash flows.

E22-4 *Statement of Cash Flows* The following is a list of items for the 2007 statement of cash flows of the Witts Company:

1. Receipt from sale of equipment, $2,700
2. Increase in inventory, $3,900
3. Net income, $13,500
4. Payment for purchase of building, $29,000
5. Depreciation expense, $8,700
6. Receipt from issuance of bonds, $8,000
7. Increase in prepaid expenses, $800

8. Loss on sale of equipment, $2,200
9. Payment of dividends, $5,200
10. Decrease in accounts receivable, $1,700
11. Issuance of common stock for land, $6,900
12. Decrease in accounts payable, $1,500
13. Beginning cash balance, $10,200

Required
Prepare the statement of cash flows.

E22-5 *Direct and Indirect Methods* The Dauve Company reported the following condensed income statement for 2007:

Sales		$100,000
Cost of goods sold		(58,000)
Gross profit		$ 42,000
Operating expenses		
Depreciation expense	$ 8,000	
Salaries expense	12,000	(20,000)
Income before income taxes		$ 22,000
Income tax expense		(6,600)
Net income		$ 15,400

During 2007, the following changes occurred in the company's current assets and current liabilities:

	Increase (Decrease)
Cash	$3,700
Accounts receivable	(5,500)
Inventories	8,900
Accounts payable (purchases)	(4,600)
Salaries payable	2,800

Required

1. By visual inspection, prepare the net cash flow from operating activities section of the Dauve Company's 2007 statement of cash flows using the indirect method.
2. By visual inspection, prepare the net cash flow from operating activities section of the Dauve Company's 2007 statement of cash flows using the direct method.

E22-6 *Fixed Asset Transactions* The following is an Equipment account and its associated Accumulated Depreciation account:

Equipment					Accumulated Depreciation				
Beginning		Machine A	8,100		Related to		Beginning		
balance	$49,000				Machine A	6,300	balance	$29,000	
Machine C	25,000	Machine B	5,200		Related to		Depreciation		
Ending					Machine B	4,600	expense	12,000	
balance	$60,700						Ending		
							balance	$30,100	

Additional data:

1. Machine A was sold at a gain of $900
2. Machine B was sold for its scrap value of $200
3. Machine C was acquired during the year

Required

Analyze the two accounts and show, in journal entry form, the entries that would be made in preparation of the statement of cash flows to reflect all of the changes listed in the accounts.

E22-7 *Visual Inspection* The following changes in account balances and other information for 2007 were taken from the accounting records of the Gordon Company:

	Net Changes for 2007	
	Debit	**Credit**
Cash	$ 1,000	
Accounts receivable		$ 1,100
Inventory	2,000	
Buildings and equipment	8,800	
Accumulated depreciation		2,900
Accounts payable	900	
Common stock, no par		5,500
Retained earnings		3,200
	$12,700	$12,700

Other information: Net income totaled $5,800. Dividends were declared and paid. Equipment was purchased for $8,800. No buildings and equipment were sold during the year. One hundred shares of common stock were sold for $55 per share. The ending cash balance was $4,200.

Required

Using visual inspection, prepare a 2007 statement of cash flows for the Gordon Company.

E22-8 *Visual Inspection* The following changes in account balances and other information for 2007 were taken from the accounting records of the Noble Company:

	Net Changes for 2007	
	Debit	**Credit**
Cash		$ 2,000
Accounts receivable	$ 1,900	
Inventory		2,400
Land		1,700
Buildings and equipment	23,000	
Accumulated depreciation		4,500
Accounts payable		1,600
Salaries payable	600	
Bonds payable		5,000
Common stock, no par		3,000
Retained earnings		5,300
	$25,500	$25,500

Other information: Net income was $9,900. Dividends were declared and paid. Land was sold for $1,700; a building was purchased for $23,000. No land was purchased and no buildings and equipment were sold. Bonds payable were issued at the end of the year. Two hundred shares of stock were issued for $15 per share. The beginning cash balance was $4,800.

Required

Using visual inspection, prepare a 2007 statement of cash flows for the Noble Company.

E22-9 *Balance Sheet* The following beginning balance sheet and statement of cash flows for 2007 are available for Fazzi Company:

Balance Sheet
January 1, 2007

Cash		$ 900	Accounts payable	$ 1,600
Accounts receivable		2,300	Notes payable	3,900
Land		4,900	Common stock, $5 par	4,500
Equipment	$20,000		Additional paid-in capital	1,800
Less: Accumulated depreciation	(9,100)	10,900	Retained earnings	7,200
Total Assets		$19,000	Total Liabilities and Stockholders' Equity	$19,000

Statement of Cash Flows
For Year Ended December 31, 2007

Net Cash Flow From Operating Activities		
Net income		$3,900
Adjustments for differences between income flows		
and cash flows from operating activities:		
Add: Depreciation expense		900
Increase in accounts payable		100
Less: Increase in accounts receivable		(700)
Gain on sale of land		(200)
Net cash provided by operating activities		$4,000
Cash Flows From Investing Activities		
Payment for purchase of equipment	$(5,000)	
Proceeds from sale of land	1,200	
Net cash used for investing activities		(3,800)
Cash Flows From Financing Activities		
Proceeds from issuance of common stock (200 shares)	$ 2,600	
Payment of long-term note	(900)	
Payment of dividends	(1,300)	
Net cash provided by financing activities		400
Net Increase in Cash		$ 600
Cash, January 1, 2007		900
Cash, December 31, 2007		$1,500

Required

On the basis of this information, prepare a balance sheet for the Fazzi Company as of December 31, 2007.

E22-10 *Erroneous Statement of Cash Flows* The 2007 statement of cash flows for the Andell Company, as developed by its bookkeeper, is shown here:

Cash Flows Statement
December 31, 2007

Inflows of Cash	
Operating Activities	
Net income	$10,600
Add: Proceeds from sale of equipment	4,400
Proceeds from issuance of stock	4,300
Less: Payment for investment in bonds	(6,000)
Payment of long-term note	(5,000)
Net cash inflows from operations	$ 8,300

Other Inflows

Decrease in accounts receivable	$ 2,100	
Depreciation expense	4,800	
Total other inflows of cash		6,900
Total inflows of cash		$15,200
Outflows of Cash		
Payment for purchase of land	$(5,200)	
Decrease in accounts payable	(2,800)	
Payment of dividends	(3,000)	
Gain on sale of equipment	(700)	
Total outflows of cash		(11,700)
Net Increase in Cash		$ 3,500
Cash, December 31, 2007		11,700
Cash, January 1, 2007		$ 8,200

You determine that the *amounts* of the items listed on the statement are correct, but in certain circumstances, incorrectly classified.

Required
Prepare a corrected 2007 statement of cash flows for the Andell Company.

E22-11 *Partially Completed Worksheet (Spreadsheet)* The Hanks Company has prepared the following changes in account balances for the worksheet to support its 2007 statement of cash flows:

	A	B	C	D
1				
2		**Increase**	**Worksheet Entries**	
3	**Account Title**	**(Decrease)**	**Debit**	**Credit**
4	*Debits*			
5	Cash	$ 830		
6	*Noncash Accounts*			
7	Accounts receivable	(290)		
8	Inventory	1,280		
9	Investments	1,550		
10	Land	(700)		
11	Equipment	2,300		
12	Patents (net)	(100)		
13	Total	$4,870		
14				
15	*Credits*			
16	Accumulated depreciation	$ 350		
17	Accounts payable	120		
18	Bonds payable	2,000		
19	Premium on bonds payable	300		
20	Common stock, $2 par	480		
21	Premium on common stock	1,120		
22	Retained earnings	500		
23	Total	$4,870		
24				

Additional information: The net income was $1,300. Depreciation expense was $350 and patent amortization expense was $100. At the end of 2007, long-term investments were purchased at a cost of $1,550. Land that cost $700 was sold for $900. On December 31, 2007, bonds payable with a face value of $2,000 were issued for equipment valued at $2,300. Two hundred shares of common stock were issued at $7 per share. Forty shares of common stock were issued as a "small" stock dividend, the relevant market price being $5 per share. Cash dividends declared and paid totaled $600.

Required
On the basis of the preceding information, complete the worksheet (spreadsheet).

E22-12 *Worksheet (Spreadsheet)* The following 2007 information is available for the Payne Company:

	Comparative Balance Sheets	
	January 1, 2007	**December 31, 2007**
Cash	$ 400	$ 600
Accounts receivable	220	200
Inventory	370	610
Land	250	410
Equipment	2,070	2,200
Less: Accumulated depreciation	(310)	(400)
Total Assets	$3,000	$3,620
Accounts payable	$ 800	$ 500
Notes payable (long-term)	900	720
Common stock, no par	600	1,000
Retained earnings	700	1,400
Total Liabilities and Stockholders' Equity	$3,000	$3,620

Partial additional information: The net income for 2007 totaled $1,600. During 2007 the company sold for $390, equipment that cost $390 and had a book value of $300. The company sold land for $200, resulting in a loss of $40. The remaining change in the Land account resulted from the purchase of land through the issuance of common stock.

Required
Making whatever additional assumptions that are necessary, prepare a worksheet (spreadsheet) to support the 2007 statement of cash flows for the Payne Company.

E22-13 *Worksheet (Spreadsheet) and Statement* The following 2007 information is available for the Stewart Company:

Condensed Income Statement for 2007	
Sales	$9,000
Cost of goods sold	(6,000)
Other expenses	(2,000)
Loss on sale of equipment	(260)
Gain on sale of land	400
Net income	$1,140

	Comparative Balance Sheets	
	December 31, 2006	**December 31, 2007**
Cash	$ 700	$1,130
Accounts receivable	450	310
Inventory	350	400
Land	300	500
Equipment	1,600	1,800
Less: Accumulated depreciation	(200)	(150)
Total Assets	$3,200	$3,990
Accounts payable	$ 600	$ 750
Bonds payable (due 1/1/2012)	1,000	1,000
Common stock, $10 par	900	1,400
Retained earnings	700	840
Total Liabilities and Stockholders' Equity	$3,200	$3,990

Partial additional information:
1. The equipment that was sold for cash had cost $400 and had a book value of $300.
2. Land that was sold brought a cash price of $530.
3. Fifty shares of stock were issued at par.

Required

Making whatever additional assumptions that are necessary,

1. Prepare a worksheet (spreadsheet) to support a statement of cash flows for the Stewart Company for 2007.
2. Prepare the statement of cash flows.

E22-14 *Retirement of Debt* Moore Company is preparing its statement of cash flows for the current year. During the year, the company retired two issuances of debt and properly recorded the transactions. These transactions were as follows:

1. Paid cash of $18,000 to retire bonds payable with a face value of $20,000 and a book value of $18,300.
2. Paid cash of $38,000 to retire bonds payable with a face value of $35,000 and a book value of $37,000.

Required

Record, in journal entry form, the entries that Moore Company would make for the preceding transactions on its worksheet to prepare its statement of cash flows.

E22-15 *Interest and Income Taxes* The Staggs Company has prepared its 2007 statement of cash flows. In conjunction with this statement, it plans to disclose the interest and income taxes it paid during 2007. The following information is available from its 2007 income statement and beginning and ending balance sheet:

Income Statement	
Interest expense	$12,000
Income tax expense	35,000

	Balance Sheet	
	Cr. Bal. 01/01/07	Cr. Bal. 12/31/07
Interest payable	$ 600	$ 2,300
Income taxes payable	5,000	3,000
Bonds payable	80,000	80,000
Premium on bonds payable	9,000	8,100
Deferred taxes payable	3,300	4,400

Required

Compute the amounts of interest paid and income taxes paid by the Staggs Company for 2007.

E22-16 *Investments* On October 4, 2007, Collins Company purchased 100 shares of Steph Company common stock for $64 per share as a temporary investment in securities available for sale. On December 31, 2007, the stock had a fair value of $63 per share, and on February 8, 2008, Collins sold the stock for $67 per share.

Required

In journal entry form, prepare the worksheet entries to record these transactions for the Collins Company's 2007 and 2008 statement of cash flows.

E22-17 *Operating Cash Flows (Appendix)* Use the information in E22-13.

Required

Based only on the information presented and using the direct method, prepare the cash flows from operating activities section of the 2007 statement of cash flows for the Stewart Company.

E22-18 *Operating Cash Flows (Appendix)* The following is accounting information taken from the adjusted trial balance of the Woodrail Company for 2007:

	Debit	Credit
Sales		$75,000
Interest revenue		4,300
Cost of goods sold	$43,600	
Salaries expense	13,600	
Interest expense	5,400	
Income tax expense	3,000	

In addition, the following changes occurred in selected accounts during 2007:

Accounts receivable	$5,700 credit
Inventory	9,800 debit
Accounts payable	7,000 credit
Salaries payable	900 debit
Interest payable	300 credit

Required

Using the direct method, prepare the cash flows from operating activities section of the 2007 statement of cash flows for the Woodrail Company.

E22-19 *Statement of Cash Flows (Appendix)* The following is a list of items to be included in the 2007 statement of cash flows of the Estes Company:

1. Payments to suppliers, $31,500
2. Other operating receipts, $1,200
3. Payments of dividends, $4,000
4. Payments of income taxes, $5,000
5. Collections from customers, $68,400
6. Payment for purchase of equipment, $18,500
7. Payments to employees, $19,300
8. Interest and dividends collected, $7,100
9. Other operating payments, $900
10. Proceeds from issuance of bonds, $11,300
11. Payments of interest, $8,400
12. Proceeds from sale of investments, $6,000
13. Beginning cash balance, $28,400

Required

Prepare the statement of cash flows using the direct method for operating cash flows.

E22-20 *Visual Inspection (Appendix)* The following changes in account balances were taken from the adjusted trial balance of the Walson Company at the end of 2007:

	Net Changes for 2007	
	Debit	Credit
Cash	$ 2,100	
Accounts receivable	8,700	
Inventory		$ 2,500
Land		1,900
Buildings and equipment	10,400	
Accumulated depreciation		6,800
Accounts payable	4,500	
Salaries payable		800
Income taxes payable		1,000
Common stock, no par		9,000
Retained earnings	4,000	
Sales		69,000
Cost of goods sold	34,000	
Salaries expense	17,200	
Depreciation expense	6,800	
Income tax expense	3,300	
Totals	$91,000	$91,000

In addition, the following information was obtained from the company's records:

1. Land was sold, at cost, for $1,900
2. Dividends of $4,000 were declared and paid
3. Equipment was purchased for $10,400
4. Common stock was issued for $9,000
5. Beginning cash balance was $17,000

Required

Using visual inspection and the direct method, prepare a 2007 statement of cash flows for the Walson Company. (A separate schedule reconciling net income to cash provided by operating activities is not necessary.)

PROBLEMS

P22-1 *Classifications of Cash Flows* A company's statement of cash flows and the accompanying schedule of investing and financing activities not affecting cash may contain the following major sections:

A. Net Cash Flow From Operating Activities
B. Cash Flows From Investing Activities
C. Cash Flows From Financing Activities
D. Investing and Financing Activities Not Affecting Cash

The following is a list of items that might appear on a company's statement of cash flows or in the accompanying schedule.

_____ 1. Decrease in accounts payable
_____ 2. Payment of dividends
_____ 3. Increase in income taxes payable
_____ 4. Proceeds from issuance of note
_____ 5. Payment for purchase of available-for-sale temporary investments

_____ 6. Amortization of premium on investment in bonds
_____ 7. Increase in prepaid expenses
_____ 8. Payment of note
_____ 9. Gain on sale of equipment
_____ 10. Proceeds from sale of land
_____ 11. Net income
_____ 12. Payment for acquisition of building
_____ 13. Depreciation expense
_____ 14. Issuance of common stock for land
_____ 15. Proceeds (principal) from collection of note

_____ 16. Amortization of discount on bonds payable
_____ 17. Decrease in deferred taxes payable
_____ 18. Proceeds from issuance of bonds
_____ 19. Issuance of stock dividend
_____ 20. Payment for purchase of treasury stock
_____ 21. Depletion expense
_____ 22. Increase in inventory
_____ 23. Conversion of preferred stock to common stock
_____ 24. Proceeds from issuance of stock
_____ 25. Lease of equipment under capital lease
_____ 26. Proceeds from sale of patent

Required

In the space provided and using the letters A through D, indicate in which section of the statement of cash flows (or the accompanying schedule) the preceding items would most likely be classified. After each letter indicate with a plus (+) or a minus (−) whether the items would be reported as an increase (inflow) or decrease (outflow). If an item would not be reported in the statement (or the accompanying schedule), put an X in the space provided.

P22-2 *Net Cash Flow From Operating Activities* The following is accounting information taken from the Verna Company's records for 2007:

1. Decrease in accounts payable, $4,600
2. Loss on sale of land, $1,900
3. Increase in inventory, $7,800
4. Increase in income taxes payable, $2,700
5. Net income, $68,400
6. Patent amortization expense, $1,600
7. Extraordinary loss (net), $6,200
8. Decrease in deferred taxes payable, $2,500
9. Amortization of discount on bonds payable, $1,300
10. Payment of cash dividends, $24,000

11. Depletion expense, $5,000
12. Decrease in salaries payable, $1,400
13. Decrease in accounts receivable, $3,500
14. Gain on sale of equipment, $6,100
15. Proceeds from issuance of stock, $57,000
16. Extraordinary gain (net), $3,700
17. Depreciation expense, $10,000
18. Amortization of discount on investment in bonds, $1,500

Required

Prepare the net cash flow from operating activities section of the 2007 statement of cash flows for the Verna Company.

P22-3 *Statement of Cash Flows* The following is a list of the items to be included in the preparation of the 2007 statement of cash flows for the Warrick Company:

1. Net income, $59,200
2. Payment for purchase of building, $98,000
3. Increase in accounts receivable, $7,400
4. Proceeds from issuance of common stock, $37,100
5. Increase in accounts payable, $4,500
6. Proceeds from sale of land, $7,000
7. Depreciation expense, $12,600
8. Payment of dividends, $36,000
9. Gain on sale of land, $5,300

10. Decrease in inventory, $3,700
11. Payment for purchase of long-term investments, $9,600
12. Amortization of discount on bonds payable, $1,900
13. Proceeds from issuance of note, $18,000
14. Increase in deferred taxes payable, $5,000
15. Equipment acquired by capital lease, $19,500
16. Decrease in salaries payable, $2,300
17. Beginning cash balance, $20,300

Required

1. Prepare the statement of cash flows.
2. Assume the company's preferred stock has been selling for $120 per share during 2007. How many shares would the company have had to issue to avoid having a decrease in cash during the year? Where would this issuance have been reported in the statement of cash flows?

P22-4 *Statement of Cash Flows* The following is a list of the items to be included in the preparation of the 2007 statement of cash flows for the Trone Company:

1. Extraordinary gain (net), $9,200
2. Proceeds from issuance of note, $25,000
3. Decrease in accounts receivable, $5,000
4. Payment for purchase of patent, $19,800
5. Increase in inventory, $6,700
6. Payment of dividends, $30,000

7. Decrease in accounts payable, $4,000
8. Proceeds from sale of investments, $8,500
9. Amortization of premium on bonds payable, $2,100
10. Net income, $49,200
11. Common stock exchanged for land, $14,000
12. Payment for purchase of equipment, $39,400

13. Loss on sale of investments, $4,800
14. Decrease in deferred taxes payable, $3,600
15. Proceeds from issuance of preferred stock, $52,800

16. Payment to retire bonds, $37,800
17. Depreciation expense, $10,700
18. Ending cash balance, $22,100

Required
1. Prepare the statement of cash flows.
2. What would have happened if the company had not issued the note during 2007? How did the issuance of the note affect the company's debt ratio (discussed in Chapter 6) at the end of 2007?

P22-5 *Infrequent Transactions* The following transactions were recorded on the books of the Baxter Company during the current year. The company:

1. Issued a "small" common stock dividend of 400 shares. The par value is $10 per share and the relevant market price was $20 per share.
2. Exchanged equipment with a cost of $10,000 and a book value of $3,800 for land valued at $12,000, paying an additional $8,500 in cash.
3. Converted preferred stock ($100 par) with a total par value of $20,000 and a book value of $22,800 to 1,500 shares of its $10 par common stock. The book value method was used to account for the conversion.
4. Recorded a loss of $4,200 as a result of retiring bonds payable with a face value of $30,000 and a related premium of $5,000 by paying $39,200.
5. Recorded an extraordinary gain (net of income taxes) of $6,000 as a result of a tornado that destroyed a building costing $100,000 and having an associated book value of $70,000. The insurance proceeds (net of income taxes) totaled $76,000.
6. Acquired equipment by entering into a capital lease. The lease required payments of $5,000 in advance; the present value of the lease payments (before the initial payment) was $34,000.

Required
For each of the preceding items, discuss *if* and illustrate *how* the transaction would be recorded on the worksheet to support the statement of cash flows. Use a journal entry format for your illustrations.

P22-6 *Partially Completed Worksheet (Spreadsheet)* The following partially completed worksheet has been prepared for the 2007 statement of cash flows of the Perrin Company:

	A	B	C	D	E	F
1						
2		**Balances**		**Change**	**Worksheet Entries**	
3	Account Titles	12/31/06	12/31/07	Increase (Decrease)	Debit	Credit
4	*Debits*					
5	Cash	$ 800	$ 1,540			
6	*Noncash Accounts:*					
7	Accounts receivable	1,500	2,180			
8	Inventory	3,100	6,055			
9	Investments in stock	—	2,800			
10	Land	6,000	9,200			
11	Buildings	20,000	20,000			
12	Office equipment	4,000	6,100			
13	Delivery equipment	3,000	5,900			
14	Treasury stock	—	2,000			
15	Totals	$38,400	$55,775	$?		
16						
17	*Credits*					
18	Accumulated depreciation	$ 7,000	$ 8,500			
19	Accounts payable	3,300	3,695			
20	Wages payable	600	500			
21	Bonds payable	—	5,000			
22	Premium on bonds payable	—	240			
23	Common stock, $10 par	6,000	8,200			
24	Additional paid-in capital	9,000	13,640			
25	Retained earnings	?	?	$3,500		
26	Totals	$38,400	$55,775	$?		
27						

Other relevant information:

(a) Beginning retained earnings $12,500

     Plus: Net income   8,000

                                              $20,500

     Less: Stock dividends $ 840

              Cash dividends   3,660   (4,500)

     Ending retained earnings $16,000

(b) Accumulated depreciation is a contra account for all the depreciable assets. Depreciation on these assets totaled $2,200 for the year.

(c) On January 1, 2007 the company issued 10% bonds with a face value of $5,000 at 106. Interest was paid semiannually on June 30 and December 31. The bonds mature on January 1, 2009. Straight-line amortization is used for bond discount or premium. Bond interest expense was $440.

(d) Land was purchased for $3,200 during the year.

(e) Two hundred shares of common stock were issued for delivery equipment valued at $2,900 and office equipment valued at $3,100.

(f) Twenty shares of stock were issued as a stock dividend. The market price per share was $42.

(g) Office equipment with a cost of $1,000 and a book value of $300 was sold for $50.

(h) Fifty shares of its own common stock were reacquired by the company as treasury stock. The company purchased the shares for $40 per share.

(i) One hundred shares of Doe Company stock were purchased for $28 per share at year-end.

Required ▨

Complete the worksheet (spreadsheet).

P22-7 *Worksheet (Spreadsheet) and Statement of Cash Flows* The following information was taken from the accounting records of the Lamberson Company:

	Account Balances	
	January 1, 2007	December 31, 2007
Debits		
Cash	$ 1,400	$ 2,400
Accounts receivable (net)	2,800	2,690
Marketable securities (at cost)	1,700	3,000
Allowance for change in value	500	800
Inventories	8,100	7,910
Prepaid items	1,300	1,710
Investments (long-term)	7,000	5,400
Land	15,000	15,000
Buildings and equipment	32,000	46,200
Discount on bonds payable	—	290
	$69,800	$85,400
Credits		
Accumulated depreciation	$16,000	$16,400
Accounts payable	3,800	4,150
Income taxes payable	2,400	2,504
Wages payable	1,100	650
Interest payable	—	400
Note payable (long-term)	3,500	—
12% bonds payable	—	10,000
Deferred taxes payable	800	1,196
Convertible preferred stock, $100 par	9,000	—
Common stock, $10 par	14,000	21,500
Additional paid-in capital	8,700	13,700
Unrealized increase in value of marketable securities	500	800
Retained earnings	10,000	14,100
	$69,800	$85,400

Additional information for the year:

(a)	Sales	$ 39,930
	Cost of goods sold	(19,890)
	Depreciation expense	(2,100)
	Wages expense	(11,000)
	Other operating expenses	(1,000)
	Bond interest expense	(410)
	Dividend revenue	820
	Gain on sale of investments	700
	Loss on sale of equipment	(200)
	Income tax expense	(2,050)
	Net income	$ 4,800

(b) Dividends declared and paid totaled $700.

(c) On January 1, 2007, convertible preferred stock that had originally been issued at par value were converted into 500 shares of common stock. The book value method was used to account for the conversion.

(d) Long-term nonmarketable investments that cost $1,600 were sold for $2,300.

(e) The long-term note payable was paid by issuing 250 shares of common stock at the beginning of the year.

(f) Equipment with a cost of $2,000 and a book value of $300 was sold for $100. The company uses one Accumulated Depreciation account for all depreciable assets.

(g) Equipment was purchased at a cost of $16,200.

(h) The 12% bonds payable were issued on August 31, 2007 at 97. They mature on August 31, 2017. The company uses the straight-line method to amortize the discount.

(i) Taxable income was less than pretax accounting income, resulting in a $396 increase in deferred taxes payable.

(j) Short-term marketable securities were purchased at a cost of $1,300. The portfolio was increased by $300 to a $3,800 fair value at year-end by adjusting the related allowance account.

Required

1. Prepare a worksheet (spreadsheet) to support the Lamberson Company's statement of cash flows for 2007.
2. Prepare the statement of cash flows.
3. Compute the cash flow from operations to sales ratio and the profit margin ratio for 2007. What is the primary reason for the difference in the results of the ratios?

P22-8 *Worksheet (Spreadsheet) and Statement of Cash Flows* The following information is available for the Bott Company:

	Account Balances	
	December 31, 2006	December 31, 2007
Debits		
Cash	$ 1,800	$ 2,000
Accounts receivable	4,600	4,720
Notes receivable (short-term)	0	1,000
Inventories	12,000	9,700
Prepaid items	1,700	1,380
Land	11,000	17,100
Buildings and equipment	78,000	110,000
Patent	4,400	4,000
Treasury stock (common, at cost, $25 per share)	2,500	1,000
Totals	$116,000	$150,900
Credits		
Accumulated depreciation	$ 24,000	$ 31,800
Accounts payable	6,000	8,210
Salaries payable	2,600	3,500
Miscellaneous current payables	1,400	1,200
Interest payable	0	140
12% bonds payable	0	7,000
Premium on bonds payable	0	650
Convertible preferred stock, $50 par	9,000	6,500

Premium on preferred stock	3,000	2,500
Common stock, $10 par	18,000	23,500
Premium on common stock	28,800	41,150
Retained earnings	23,200	24,750
Totals	$116,000	$150,900

Additional information for the year:

(a)

Beginning retained earnings, unadjusted		$23,200
Less: Prior period adjustment—correction of understatement of depreciation (net of income taxes)		(1,300)
Adjusted beginning retained earnings		$21,900
Add: Net income		11,500
		$33,400
Less: Cash dividends	$(4,000)	
Stock dividends (150 shares at $31 per share)	(4,650)	(8,650)
Ending retained earnings		$24,750

(b) Last year depreciation expense was inadvertently understated in the amount of $1,800. The correction was made this year to Accumulated Depreciation and to Retained Earnings as a prior period adjustment. The company also received a related income tax refund of $500.

(c) Sixty shares of treasury stock (common) were reissued at $30 per share.

(d) Bonds payable with a face amount of $7,000 were issued for $7,750 on April 30, 2007. The bonds mature on April 30, 2012, and pay interest semiannually. The straight-line method is used to amortize the bond premium. Interest expense totaled $460 for 2007.

(e) Fifty shares of preferred stock (originally issued at $60 per share) were converted into 100 shares of common stock.

(f) Land costing $2,900 was sold for $3,800.

(g) Three hundred shares of common stock were sold for $33 per share.

(h) Equipment costing $32,000 was purchased during the year.

(i) Land was acquired at a cost of $9,000 during the year.

(j) Depreciation expense was $6,000.

(k) Patent amortization was $400.

(l) The company loaned money to one of its executives and received a $1,000 short-term note receivable on December 31, 2007. The note matures 90 days from the date of issuance.

Required ◪

1. Prepare a worksheet (spreadsheet) to support a statement of cash flows for 2007.
2. Prepare the 2007 statement of cash flows for the Bott Company. Show the reconciliation of the net income to the net cash provided by operating activities in a separate schedule accompanying the statement.

P22-9 *Worksheet (Spreadsheet) from Trial Balance* The post-closing trial balance as of December 31, 2006 and the adjusted trial balance as of December 31, 2007 are shown here for the Heinz Company:

	December 31, 2006 Post-closing Trial Balance		December 31, 2007 Adjusted Trial Balance	
Cash	$ 2,700		$ 3,520	
Accounts receivable	5,900		6,215	
Inventories	15,300		15,530	
Prepaid items	1,400		1,000	
Investments in bonds (long-term)	8,300		7,300	
Land	16,300		19,000	
Buildings	68,700		60,700	
Accumulated depreciation: buildings		$ 35,000		$ 34,500
Equipment	29,600		25,600	
Accumulated depreciation: equipment		14,200		14,700
Patents (net)	8,700		9,185	
Accounts payable		8,900		9,195
Interest payable		630		300
Wages payable		2,500		2,600

Bonds payable		23,000	17,000
Discount on bonds payable	0	715	
Common stock, $10 par		22,000	22,650
Additional paid-in capital		15,320	15,970
Retained earnings		35,350	35,350
	$156,900	$156,900	
Sales (net)			49,550
Cost of goods sold		23,800	
Wages expense		16,510	
Other operating expenses		1,100	
Depreciation expense: buildings		2,700	
Depreciation expense: equipment		3,100	
Patent amortization		815	
Interest expense		1,715	
Loss (ordinary) on sale of investments		200	
Interest revenue			790
Gain (ordinary) on exchange of assets			1,300
Income tax expense		500	
Extraordinary loss (net of income taxes)		2,600	
Dividends declared		2,100	
Totals		$203,905	$203,905

A review of the accounting records reveals the following additional information:
(a) Bonds payable with a face value, book value, and market value of $14,000 were retired on June 30, 2007.
(b) Bonds payable with a face value of $8,000 were issued at 90.25 on August 1, 2007. They mature on August 1, 2012. The company uses the straight-line method to amortize bond discount.
(c) A tornado completely destroyed a small building that had an original cost of $8,000 and a book value of $4,800. Settlement with the insurance company resulted in after-tax proceeds of $2,200 and an extraordinary loss (net of income taxes) of $2,600.
(d) Equipment with a cost of $4,000 and a book value of $1,400 was exchanged for an acre of land valued at $2,700. No cash was exchanged.
(e) Long-term investments in bonds being held to maturity with a cost of $1,000 were sold for $800.
(f) Sixty-five shares of common stock were exchanged for a patent. The common stock was selling for $20 per share at the time of the exchange.

Required
Prepare a worksheet (spreadsheet) to support a statement of cash flows for 2007.

P22-10 *Prepare Ending Balance Sheet* On December 31, 2007 a fire destroyed a significant portion of the Richey Company accounting records. Only the January 1, 2007 balance sheet, the statement of cash flows for 2007, and several additional documents were saved as follows:

Balance Sheet
January 1, 2007

Assets			
Current assets:			
Cash			$ 1,900
Accounts receivable			5,100
Inventories			13,900
Prepaid items			1,300
Total current assets			$22,200
Property, plant, and equipment:			
Land			$12,000
Buildings	$60,000		
Equipment	20,000	$ 80,000	
Less: Accumulated depreciation		(29,000)	51,000
Total fixed assets			$63,000

Patents (net)		7,100
Total assets		$92,300

Liabilities

Current liabilities:

Accounts payable		$ 5,500
Income taxes payable		4,100
Miscellaneous payables		1,200
Total current liabilities		$ 10,800

Long-term liabilities:

10% bonds payable (due 12/31/2016)	$15,000	
Less: Discount on bonds payable	(1,000)	14,000
Total liabilities		$24,800

Stockholders' Equity

Preferred stock, $100 par	$17,000	
Premium on preferred stock	1,500	$18,500
Common stock, $10 par	$14,000	
Premium on common stock	11,200	25,200
Retained earnings		23,800
Total stockholders' equity		$67,500
Total liabilities and stockholders' equity		$92,300

Statement of Cash Flows
For Year Ended December 31, 2007

Net Cash Flow From Operating Activities		
Net income	$ 10,000	
Adjustments for differences between income flows and cash flows from operating activities:		
Add: Depreciation expense	5,100	
Patent amortization expense	600	
Loss on sale of land	400	
Decrease in accounts receivable (net)	1,100	
Decrease in inventories	3,010	
Increase in income taxes payable	190	
Increase in miscellaneous payables	200	
Bond discount amortization	100	
Less: Gain on sale of equipment	(180)	
Gain on sale of patent	(1,100)	
Increase in prepaid items	(120)	
Decrease in accounts payable	(400)	
Net cash provided by operating activities		$ 18,900
Cash Flows From Investing Activities		
Purchase of building by issuance of mortgage and cash	$(43,000)	
Less: Issuance of mortgage	20,000	
Payment for purchase of building	$(23,000)	
Proceeds from sale of land	2,800	
Proceeds from sale of equipment	500	
Proceeds from sale of patent	2,100	
Net cash used for investing activities		(17,600)
Cash Flows From Financing Activities		
Proceeds from issuance of common stock (150 shares)	$ 3,000	
Payment of dividends	(5,000)	
Net cash used for financing activities		(2,000)
Net Decrease in Cash (see Schedule 1)		$ (700)
Cash, January 1, 2007		1,900
Cash, December 31, 2007		$ 1,200

Schedule 1: Investing and Financing Activities Not Affecting Cash

Investing Activities

    Acquisition of land by issuance of preferred stock (40 shares) $(4,800)

Financing Activities

    Issuance of preferred stock to acquire land   4,800

The remaining financial documents reveal the following additional data:

1. The new building was acquired on December 31, 2007. The related mortgage requires equal annual repayments of the principal over a five-year period beginning December 31, 2009.
2. The company issued a stock dividend of 200 shares of common stock on December 14, 2007. On the date of declaration, the stock was selling for $18 per share.
3. The equipment that was sold had an original cost of $1,900.

Required

Prepare a December 31, 2007 balance sheet for Richey Company. Include supporting calculations.

P22-11 *Erroneous Statement of Cash Flows* The bookkeeper of the Ryan Company prepared the following 2007 statement of cash flows:

Flows of Cash Statement
December 31, 2007

Sources (Inflows) of Cash		
Net Source from Operations		
Net income	$ 47,800	
Add: Cash receipt from sale of land	6,500	
Inflow from issuing 10% bonds payable	25,000	
Depreciation expense	13,200	
Reduction in inventory	1,900	
Less: Outflow to buy equipment	(16,400)	
Increase in prepaid expenses	(700)	
Cash (principal) paid on long-term note	(9,500)	
Extraordinary gain (net)	(2,000)	
Total source from operations		$ 65,800
Other Sources (Inflows) of Cash		
Loss on sale of land	$ 2,300	
Increase in accounts payable	1,000	
Cash from issuing preferred stock	38,700	
Patent amortization expense	2,100	
Total other sources of cash		44,100
Sources (Financing) Not Affecting Cash		
Issuance of common stock for patent		11,000
Total inflows of cash		$120,900
Uses (Outflows) of Cash		
To purchase building	$(62,000)	
Increase in accounts receivable	(7,800)	
For acquiring marketable securities	(7,100)	
Decrease in income taxes payable	(1,400)	
Total uses of cash		(78,300)
Uses (Investing) Not Affecting Cash		
Acquisition of patent by issuing common stock		(11,000)
Net inflow before dividends		$ 31,600
Less: Cash dividends		(24,000)
Net Increase in Cash		$ 7,600
Cash, January 1, 2007		15,300
Cash, December 31, 2007		$ 22,900

After a thorough investigation, you have determined that the *amounts* of the items listed on the statement are correct. However, you notice several items that are incorrectly classified and reported.

Required

Prepare a corrected 2007 statement of cash flows for the Ryan Company.

P22-12 AICPA Adapted *Comprehensive* Angel Company has prepared its financial statements for the year ended December 31, 2007 and for the three months ended March 31, 2008. You have been asked to prepare a statement of cash flows for the three months ended March 31, 2008. The company's balance sheet data at December 31, 2007 and March 31, 2008, and its income statement data for the three months ended March 31, 2008, follow. You have previously satisfied yourself as to the correctness of the amounts presented.

	Balance Sheet Data	
	December 31, 2007	March 31, 2008
Cash	$ 25,300	$ 79,400
Marketable investments (at cost)	17,500	8,300
Allowance for decrease in value	(1,000)	(900)
Accounts receivable	24,320	49,320
Inventory	31,090	48,590
Total current assets	$ 97,210	$ 184,710
Land	40,000	18,700
Building	250,000	250,000
Equipment	—	81,500
Accumulated depreciation	(15,000)	(16,250)
Investment in 30% owned company	61,220	67,100
Other assets	15,100	15,100
Total	$448,530	$600,860
Accounts payable	$ 21,220	$ 38,417
Income taxes payable	—	13,529
Total current liabilities	$ 21,220	$ 51,946
Other liabilities	187,000	187,000
Bonds payable	50,000	115,000
Discount on bonds payable	(2,300)	(2,150)
Deferred taxes payable	510	846
Preferred stock	30,000	—
Common stock	80,000	110,000
Unrealized decrease in value of marketable investments	(1,000)	(900)
Dividends declared	—	(8,000)
Retained earnings	83,100	147,118
Total	$448,530	$600,860

	Income Statement Data For the Three Months Ended March 31, 2008
Sales	$242,807
Gain on sale of marketable investments	2,400
Equity in earnings of 30% owned company	5,880
Extraordinary gain on condemnation of land (net of tax)	8,560
Total revenues	$259,647
Cost of sales	$157,354
General and administrative expenses	22,010
Depreciation	1,250
Interest expense	1,150
Income taxes	13,865
Total expenses	$195,629
Net income	$ 64,018

Your discussion with the company's controller and a review of the financial records have revealed the following information:

(a) On January 7, 2008 the company sold marketable securities for cash. These securities had cost $9,200, and had a fair value of $8,600 at December 31, 2007. The remaining marketable securities were adjusted to their $7,400 fair value on March 31, 2008 by adjustment of the related allowance account. The dividend and interest revenue on these marketable securities is not material.

(b) The company's preferred stock was converted into common stock at a rate of one share of preferred for two shares of common. The preferred stock and common stock have par values of $2 and $1, respectively.

(c) On January 16, 2008, three acres of land were condemned. An award of $32,000 in cash was received on March 24, 2008. Purchase of additional land as a replacement is not contemplated by the company.

(d) On March 25, 2008 the company purchased equipment for cash.

(e) On March 26, 2008 bonds payable were issued by the company at par for cash.

(f) The investment in 30% owned company included an amount of $9,600 attributable to an increase in the recorded value of depreciable assets at December 31, 2007. This increase is being depreciated at a quarterly rate of $480.

Required

1. Prepare a worksheet (spreadsheet) to support the statement of cash flows for Angel Company for the three months ended March 31, 2008.
2. Prepare the statement of cash flows.

P22-13 **AICPA Adapted** *Comprehensive* The following are the balance sheets of Farrell Corporation as of December 31, 2007 and 2006, and the statement of income and retained earnings for the year ended December 31, 2007:

Balance Sheets

	December 31		Increase
	2007	2006	(Decrease)
Assets			
Cash	$ 225,000	$ 180,000	$ 45,000
Accounts receivable, net	295,000	305,000	(10,000)
Inventories	549,000	431,000	118,000
Investment in Hall, Inc., at equity	73,000	60,000	13,000
Land	350,000	200,000	150,000
Plant and equipment	624,000	606,000	18,000
Less: Accumulated depreciation	(139,000)	(107,000)	(32,000)
Patent	16,000	20,000	(4,000)
Total assets	$1,993,000	$1,695,000	$298,000
Liabilities and Stockholders' Equity			
Accounts payable and accrued expenses	$ 604,000	$ 563,000	$ 41,000
Note payable, long-term	150,000	—	150,000
Bonds payable	160,000	210,000	(50,000)
Deferred taxes payable	41,000	30,000	11,000
Common stock, $10 par	410,000	400,000	10,000
Additional paid-in capital	196,000	175,000	21,000
Retained earnings	432,000	334,000	98,000
Treasury stock, at cost	—	(17,000)	17,000
Total liabilities and stockholders' equity	$1,993,000	$1,695,000	$298,000

Statement of Income and Retained Earnings
For the Year Ended December 31, 2007

Net sales	$1,950,000
Operating expenses:	
Cost of sales	1,150,000
Selling and administrative expenses	505,000
Depreciation	53,000
	1,708,000
Operating income	242,000

Other (income) expense:

Interest expense	15,000
Equity in net income of Hall, Inc.	(13,000)
Loss on sale of equipment	5,000
Amortization of patent	4,000
	11,000
Income before income taxes	231,000
Income taxes:	
Current	79,000
Deferred	11,000
Provision for income taxes	90,000
Net income	$ 141,000
Retained earnings, January 1, 2007	334,000
	475,000
Cash dividends, paid August 13, 2007	43,000
Retained earnings, December 31, 2007	$ 432,000

Additional information:
1. On January 2, 2007 Farrell sold equipment costing $45,000, with a book value of $24,000, for $19,000 cash.
2. On April 2, 2007 Farrell issued 1,000 shares of common stock for $23,000 cash.
3. On May 14, 2007 Farrell sold all of its treasury stock for $25,000 cash.
4. On June 1, 2007 Farrell paid $50,000 to retire bonds with a face value (and book value) of $50,000.
5. On July 2, 2007 Farrell purchased equipment for $63,000 cash.
6. On December 31, 2007 land with a fair market value of $150,000 was purchased through the issuance of a long-term note in the amount of $150,000. The note bears interest at the rate of 15% and is due on December 31, 2012.
7. Deferred taxes payable represent temporary differences relating to the use of accelerated depreciation methods for income tax reporting and the straight-line method for financial statement reporting.

Required
1. Prepare a worksheet (spreadsheet) to support a statement of cash flows for the Farrell Corporation for the year ended December 31, 2007, based on the preceding information.
2. Prepare the statement of cash flows.

P22-14 *Operating Cash Flows (Appendix)* Use the information presented in P22-7.

Required
1. Using the direct method, prepare the cash flows from operating activities section of the 2007 statement of cash flows for the Lamberson Company.
2. *(Optional)*. If you completed P22-7 earlier, prepare the remaining portion of the statement of cash flows. (A separate schedule reconciling net income to cash provided by operating activities is not necessary.)

P22-15 *Statement of Cash Flows (Appendix)* The following is a list of the items to be included in the preparation of the 2007 statement of cash flows for the Yellow Company:

1. Proceeds from sale of land, $2,100
2. Payments of interest, $5,000
3. Equipment acquired by capital lease, $7,200
4. Proceeds from issuance of preferred stock, $11,000
5. Other operating payments, $1,300
6. Interest and dividends collected, $4,700
7. Payments to employees, $20,300
8. Payment for purchase of investments, $12,100
9. Collections from customers, $54,500
10. Payments of income taxes, $2,900
11. Payment of dividends, $5,200
12. Other operating receipts, $1,600
13. Payments to suppliers, $29,500
14. Beginning cash balance, $29,700

Required
Prepare the statement of cash flows using the direct method for operating cash flows.

P22-16 *Worksheet and Statement (Appendix)* Use the information presented in P22-13 for the Farrell Corporation.

Required
1. Using the direct method for operating cash flows, prepare a worksheet (spreadsheet) to support a 2007 statement of cash flows. (*Hint*: Combine the income statement and December 31, 2007 balance sheet items for the adjusted trial balance. Use a retained earnings balance of $291,000 in this adjusted trial balance.)
2. Prepare the statement of cash flows. (A separate schedule reconciling net income to cash provided by operating activities is not necessary.)

P22-17 *Comprehensive (Appendix)* The following are the December 31, 2006 post-closing trial balance and the December 31, 2007 adjusted trial balance of the Adair Company:

Accounts	12/31/06 Post-Closing Trial Balance Debit	Credit	12/31/07 Adjusted Trial Balance Debit	Credit
Cash	2,700		3,300	
Accounts receivable	7,300		6,200	
Inventory	8,100		9,900	
Investments in bonds	10,000		18,600	
Property and equipment	105,300		133,300	
Accumulated depreciation		42,400		49,200
Accounts payable		8,100		8,500
Salaries payable		1,300		700
Interest payable		0		300
Notes payable		0		9,000
Common stock, no par		43,600		58,100
Retained earnings		38,000		31,500
Sales				89,000
Cost of goods sold			48,800	
Depreciation expense			6,800	
Salaries expense			12,000	
Other operating expenses			1,700	
Interest revenue				1,200
Interest expense			900	
Income tax expense			6,000	
Totals	133,400	133,400	247,500	247,500

A review of the accounting records reveals the following additional information for 2007:
(a) Investments in bonds to be held to maturity were purchased at year-end for $8,600.
(b) A building was purchased for $28,000.
(c) A note payable was issued for $9,000.
(d) Common stock was issued for $14,500.
(e) Dividends of $6,500 were declared and paid.

Required
1. Using the direct method for operating cash flows, prepare a worksheet (spreadsheet) to support the 2007 statement of cash flows for the Adair Company.
2. Prepare the statement of cash flows. (A separate schedule reconciling net income to cash provided by operating activities is not necessary.)

P22-18 *Complex Worksheet (Appendix)* Use the information presented in P22-9 for the Heinz Company.

Required
Using the direct method for operating cash flows, prepare a worksheet (spreadsheet) to support a 2007 statement of cash flows.

CASES

COMMUNICATION

C22-1 Financial Statement Interrelationships
Prepare an outline of the general format of the statement of cash flows (indirect method). Include examples of cash inflows and outflows that would be reported under each major section. Finally, discuss the information that is disclosed on the income statement, balance sheet, and statement of cash flows, respectively, that is not disclosed on the other statements.

C22-2 Statement of Cash Flows

A friend of yours is taking an elementary accounting course. He says, "I understand the income statement and balance sheet, but I am confused by the statement of cash flows (and accompanying schedule). What is this statement, what is it useful for, what are its major sections, and what items are reported in each section and the accompanying schedule? I need to understand this statement better so I can do well in my class."

Required

Prepare a written response to your friend's questions.

C22-3 Cash Flow Activities

A company's statement of cash flows shows its cash inflows, cash outflows, and net change in cash from the operating, investing, and financing activities during an accounting period.

Required

Prepare a short memo that defines a company's operating, investing, and financing activities, and identifies the cash inflows and cash outflows related to each activity.

C22-4 Worksheet Method

The worksheet method is commonly used to analyze the information for preparing a company's statement of cash flows. This method involves the completion of several steps.

Required

Explain the worksheet method and list and briefly discuss the steps in this method.

C22-5 Operating Cash Flows

There are two methods to calculate and report a company's net cash provided by (or used in) operating activities.

Required

Prepare a short memo that identifies the two methods and explains the calculations necessary for each method.

CREATIVE AND CRITICAL THINKING

C22-6 Financing and Investing Activities Not Involving Cash

AICPA Adapted The statement of cash flows is normally a required basic financial statement for each period for which an earnings statement is presented. The statement should include a separate schedule listing the financing and investing activities not involving cash.

Required

1. What are financing and investing activities not involving cash?
2. What are two types of financing and investing activities not involving cash?
3. Explain what effect, if any, each of the following seven items would have on the statement of cash flows.
   a. Accounts receivable
   b. Inventory
   c. Depreciation
   d. Deferred tax liability
   e. Issuance of long-term debt in payment for a building
   f. Payoff of current portion of debt
   g. Sale of a fixed asset resulting in a loss

C22-7 Inflows and Outflows

AICPA Adapted Alfred Engineering Company is a young and growing producer of electronic measuring instruments and technical equipment. You have been retained by Alfred to advise it in the preparation of a statement of cash flows. For the fiscal year ended October 31, 2007, you have obtained the following information concerning certain events and transactions of Alfred:

1. The amount of reported earnings for the fiscal year was $800,000.
2. Depreciation expense of $240,000 was included in the earnings statement.

3. Uncollectible accounts receivable of $30,000 were written off against the allowance for uncollectible accounts. Also, $37,000 of bad debts expense was included in determining earnings for the fiscal year, and the same amount was added to the allowance for uncollectible accounts.
4. A gain of $4,700 was realized on the sale of a machine; it originally cost $75,000, of which $25,000 was undepreciated on the date of sale.
5. On July 2, 2007, a building and land were purchased for $600,000; Alfred gave in payment $100,000 cash, $200,000 market value of its unissued common stock, and a $300,000 mortgage.
6. On August 3, 2007, $700,000 of Alfred's convertible preferred stock was converted into $140,000 par value of its common stock. The preferred stock was originally issued at par.
7. The board of directors declared a $320,000 cash dividend on October 19, 2007, payable on November 16, 2007 to stockholders of record on November 5, 2007.

Required

For each of the seven items, explain whether each is an inflow or outflow of cash and explain how it should be disclosed in Alfred's statement of cash flows (indirect method) for the fiscal year ended October 31, 2007. If any item is neither an inflow nor outflow of cash, explain why it is not and indicate the disclosure, if any, that should be made of the item in Alfred's statement of cash flows for the fiscal year ended October 31, 2007.

C22-8 Analyzing Coca-Cola's Cash Flow Disclosures

Refer to the financial statements and related notes of The Coca-Cola Company in Appendix A of this book.

Required

1. What was the net cash provided by operating activities for 2004? What method was used to determine this amount? What was the largest positive adjustment to net income?
2. What was the net cash used in investing activities for 2004? What was the largest investing cash outflow? Investing cash inflow?
3. What was the net cash used in financing activities for 2004? What was the largest financing cash inflow? Financing cash outflow?
4. What was the interest paid in 2004? Income taxes paid?
5. Compute the "cash flow from operations to sales" ratio for 2004. How does this result compare to 2003? Why?
6. Compute the profit margin for 2004. How does this result compare to the cash flow from operations to sales ratio for 2004? Why?

C22-9 Ethics and Cash Flows

You are the accountant for Nello Company, which manufactures specialty equipment. Nello has been in financial difficulty, so its suppliers require purchases to be paid in cash. Furthermore, Nello has long-term debt with a debt covenant that requires it to maintain a 1:1 acid-test (quick) ratio. Nello's employees work a five-day week, Monday through Friday.

On Wednesday morning during the last week of the current year, Sam (the production supervisor) comes to you and says,

"I don't understand it. We have this large special order from a customer that must be delivered at the end of the first week in January. Once we get the raw materials, it is going to take five solid days of work without overtime to produce the order. If Bob (the president) would let me order the raw materials this morning, we could have them by late today. This would give us two days this week and the four days after New Years Day (Monday) of next week to complete the order without incurring overtime costs. But Bob says we must wait until next Tuesday to order the materials. This means we will have to work doubletime that Wednesday through Friday to finish the order. That overtime cost is going to really increase next year's factory salary expense, so our profit and operating cash flows from that order will be very low. Please talk to him."

When you approach Bob about buying the raw materials this morning, he says, "If we purchase those materials today, we will have to write a check. And that means our cash flow from operating activities for this year will be much lower, which our stockholders won't like. Furthermore, our quick ratio will go down from 1.01:1 to .90:1, so our creditors may be upset. I know our profit and operating cash flows for next year will be lower if we delay the purchase, but that seems to be the best decision. Don't you agree?"

Required

From financial reporting and ethical perspectives, how would you respond to Bob?

RESEARCH SIMULATION

R22-1   Researching GAAP

Situation

You are the new accountant for 12th National Bank and are preparing its 2007 statement of cash flows. The bank reports net income of $75,800 on its 2007 income statement. Included in this net income are the following items: $6,700 gain on sale of trading securities, $1,200 unrealized holding gain on trading securities, and $5,100 loss on sale of securities available for sale. Among its 2007 transactions, the bank sold trading securities with a carrying value of $22,900 for $29,600, and purchased trading securities for $65,200. The bank sold securities available for sale with a cost (and carrying value) of $58,700 for $53,600, and purchased securities available for sale for $39,400. It also made routine 90-day loans of $47,500 to customers and collected $20,000 principal on these customer loans. As a result of the preceding information, the bank's trading securities account increased by $43,500, the securities available for sale account decreased by $19,300, and the loans receivable account increased by $27,500. The bank uses the indirect approach to report operating cash flows on its statement of cash flows.

Directions

Research the applicable generally accepted accounting principles and prepare a written memo to the 12th National Bank's auditors that explains how you plan to report the preceding items on the bank's 2007 statement of cash flows. Cite your reference and applicable paragraph numbers.

23

Accounting Changes and Errors

Eating Up the Profits

According to a recent study released by Huron Consulting Group, the number of financial restatements climbed to record levels in 2004. After leveling off in 2003, the number of quarterly and annual restatements rose to the highest level since the group began its annual study.

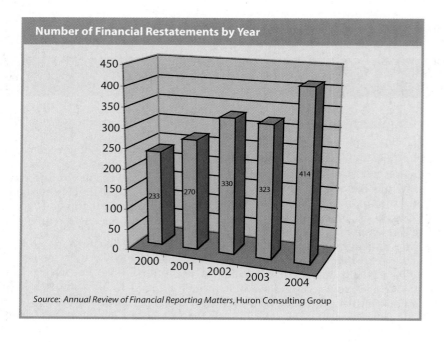

Number of Financial Restatements by Year

Source: *Annual Review of Financial Reporting Matters*, Huron Consulting Group

Improper revenue recognition was cited as the leading cause of financial restatements. This was closely followed by errors involving share (stock) option accounting, earnings per share, and accounting for other equity instruments. Other significant causes of restatements were errors in accounts receivable and inventory reserves, restructuring reserves, accruals, and loss contingencies.

Credit: Newswire RED LOBSTER

Although large misstatements, such as **WorldCom's** $74.4 billion restatement in 2004 and **American International Group's** (**AIG**) $3.9 billion restatement in 2005, have received considerable attention from the financial press, many restatements are much smaller in size and result from simple misapplication of accounting principles. For example, many restaurant chains have recently restated their earnings after taking a closer look at the way they account for leases. **Darden Restaurants**, which operates Red Lobster and Olive Garden, announced an estimated restatement of $74 million. Other restaurant chains issuing restatements include **CKE Restaurants** (Hardee's, Carl's Jr.), **Brinker International** (Chili's, Macaroni Grill), and **Ruby Tuesday**. Whether the restatements were caused by fraud, aggressive accounting, or simple mistakes, one thing is clear: the restatements certainly took a bite out of profits!

One of the qualitative characteristics of accounting is consistency (which we discussed in Chapter 2)—the conformity of accounting principles, policies, and procedures from period to period. However, in some instances a company may improve its reporting by changing its accounting to adopt a preferable or newly mandated generally accepted accounting principle, or to reflect changing economic conditions. When a company changes an accounting principle, the consistency of its financial statements is impaired. Therefore, it is important to report the effects of the change in its financial statements. Accounting for the effects of a change in an accounting principle is the primary topic of this chapter. We also discuss the related issue of accounting for a change in an estimate. Finally, we discuss accounting for errors.

Types of Accounting Changes

1 Identify the types of accounting changes.

The generally accepted accounting principles a company uses when it makes an accounting change are specified by **FASB Statement No. 154**, which defines three types of changes[1] as follows:

1. *Change in an Accounting Principle.* This type of change occurs when a company adopts a generally accepted accounting principle different from the one used previously for reporting purposes. For instance, changing from the LIFO to the FIFO inventory cost flow assumption is a change in accounting principle.
2. *Change in an Accounting Estimate.* This type of change is inherent in the periodic presentation of financial statements. Preparing financial statements requires the use of estimates to determine many revenues and expenses. These estimates sometimes must be changed as new events occur, as more experience is acquired, or as additional information is obtained. For example, a company may change the estimated life of a depreciable asset to reflect newly available information.
3. *Change in a Reporting Entity.* This type of change is caused by a change in the entity being reported. For example, a change in the subsidiaries that are included in a company's consolidated financial statements is a change in a reporting entity.

In addition to the preceding changes, *FASB Statement No. 154* specifies the accounting principles to be used when a company discovers an error in its published financial statements. *Errors* are not considered to be accounting changes, but are the results of mathematical mistakes or mistakes in the application of accounting principles.

Methods of Reporting an Accounting Change

2 Explain the methods of disclosing an accounting change.

There are two possible methods for a company to disclose an accounting change in its financial statements: (1) the **retrospective application of a new accounting principle** (restate its financial statements of prior periods, sometimes referred to as a **retrospective adjustment** or **restatement**), or (2) adjust for the change **prospectively**.

According to the provisions of *FASB Statement No. 154*:

- *A change in an accounting principle* is accounted for by the *retrospective application of the new accounting principle.*[2]
- *A change in an accounting estimate* is accounted for *prospectively.*
- *A change in a reporting entity* is accounted for by the *retrospective application of the new accounting principle.*

---

1. "Accounting Changes and Error Corrections," *FASB Statement of Financial Accounting Standards No. 154* (Norwalk, Conn.: FASB, 2005), par. 2.
2. If it is not practical to determine the cumulative effect of applying a change in any accounting period, the new principle is applied as if the change was made prospectively at the earliest date practical, as we discuss later in the chapter.

We discuss each of these methods and rules in greater detail in the following sections of the chapter. We provide a summary in Exhibit 23-1 at the end of the chapter. Note that a company reports an accounting change in its financial statements only if the amount is material.

ACCOUNTING FOR A CHANGE IN ACCOUNTING PRINCIPLE

FASB Statement No. 154 states that a change in accounting principle includes:

- A change from one generally accepted accounting principle to another generally accepted accounting principle when there are two or more generally accepted accounting principles.
- A change in accounting principle because the accounting principle formerly used is no longer generally accepted.
- A change in the method of applying an accounting principle.

Thus, a change in accounting principle can be a *voluntary* change from one generally accepted principle to another, or a *mandatory* change because the FASB has adopted a new principle. However, a change in an accounting principle does *not* include the initial adoption of a generally accepted accounting principle because of events or transactions occurring for the first time. It also does *not* include the adoption or modification of an accounting principle for transactions or events that are clearly different in substance from those previously occurring. Also, a change to a generally accepted accounting principle from one that is *not* generally accepted is a correction of an error and *not* a change in accounting principle.

Retrospective Adjustment Method

A company accounts for a change in accounting principle by the retrospective application of the new accounting principle to all prior periods as follows:

> **3** Account for a change in accounting principle using the retrospective adjustment method.

1. The company computes the cumulative effect of the change to the new accounting principle as of the beginning of the first period presented. That is, it computes the amounts that would have been in the financial statements if it had always used the new principle.
2. The company adjusts the carrying values of those assets and liabilities (including income taxes) that are affected by the change. The company makes an offsetting adjustment to the beginning balance of retained earnings to report the cumulative effect of the change (net of taxes) for each period presented.
3. The company adjusts the financial statements of each prior period to reflect the specific effects of applying the new accounting principle. That is, each item in each financial statement that is affected by the change is restated to the appropriate amount under the new accounting principle. The company uses the new accounting principle in its current financial statements.
4. The company's disclosures include (a) the nature and reason for the change in accounting principle, including an explanation of why the new principle is preferable, (b) a description of the prior-period information that has been retrospectively adjusted, (c) the effect of the change on income, earnings per share, and any other financial statement line item for the current period and the prior periods retrospectively adjusted, and (d) the cumulative effect of the change on retained earnings (or other appropriate component of equity) at the beginning of the earliest period presented.

Example: Retrospective Adjustment A retrospective adjustment requires that a company change the prior financial statements to what they would have been had it used the new method in previous periods. Examples 23-1, 23-2, 23-3, 23-4, and 23-5 illustrate a retrospective adjustment. In this example the Werner Company changes *from* the LIFO *to* the FIFO inventory method at the beginning of 2008. Example 23-1 shows the basic information for Werner Company.

EXAMPLE 23-1   Retrospective Adjustment for a Change in Accounting for Inventory

1. Werner Company starts operations on January 1, 2006.
2. The Werner Company changes from the LIFO method to the FIFO method on January 1, 2008.
3. The company reports the previous year's financial statements for comparative purposes. Therefore, the beginning of the first period presented is January 1, 2007.
4. Retained earnings on December 31, 2006 is $231,000. The company paid no dividends in 2006, 2007, and 2008.
5. The company's tax rate is 30% and there are no temporary or permanent differences.
6. The company pays its income taxes in a single payment in the following year.
7. The company must repay the taxes saved by using LIFO according to IRS rules but has *not* yet made any payments.
8. The company has 100,000 shares outstanding (for simplicity we only compute basic earnings per share).
9. The company calculated its inventory and cost of goods sold amounts under LIFO and FIFO as follows:

	Inventory Determined by		Cost of Goods Sold Determined by	
	LIFO Method	*FIFO Method*	*LIFO Method*	*FIFO Method*
12/31/2006	$ 70,000	$120,000	$720,000	$670,000
12/31/2007	90,000	160,000	780,000	760,000
12/31/2008	130,000	210,000	860,000	850,000

Example 23-2 shows the Werner Company's comparative income statements for 2007 and 2006. For those years, the company was using the *LIFO* method.

EXAMPLE 23-2   Comparative Income Statements under the LIFO Method

Werner Company
Income Statement
For Years Ended 12/31/2007 and 12/31/2006

	2007	*2006*
Sales	$1,700,000	$1,500,000
Cost of goods sold	(780,000)	(720,000)
Operating expenses	(500,000)	(450,000)
Income before income taxes	$ 420,000	$ 330,000
Income tax expense	(126,000)	(99,000)
Net income	$ 294,000	$ 231,000
Earnings per share	$ 2.94	$ 2.31

Since the Werner Company changed from the LIFO method to the FIFO method on January 1, 2008 and presents the previous year's (2007) financial statements for comparative purposes, it must report its comparative income statements for 2008 and 2007 using the *FIFO* method. Example 23-3 shows these statements. The income statement for 2007 shows the retrospective application of the change from the LIFO method to the FIFO method. Note that the 2007 income statement presented in 2008 is different than when it was originally presented in 2007. The cost of goods sold under FIFO is $760,000, whereas it was $780,000 under LIFO (see Example 23-2). This $20,000 difference also increased the 2007 income before income taxes, increased income tax expense by $6,000 ($20,000 × 0.30), and increased net income by $14,000 [$20,000 × (1 − 0.30)]. Although we don't show the balance sheet and statement of cash flows, Werner would also have reported these financial statements using the FIFO method for both 2008 and 2007.

EXAMPLE 23-3   **Comparative Income Statements under the FIFO Method**

Werner Company
Income Statement
For Years Ended 12/31/2008 and 12/31/2007

	2008	2007 As adjusted
Sales	$2,000,000	$ 1,700,000
Cost of goods sold	(850,000)	(760,000)
Operating expenses	(550,000)	(500,000)
Income before income taxes	$ 600,000	$ 440,000
Income tax expense	(180,000)	(132,000)
Net income	$ 420,000	$ 308,000
Earnings per share	$ 4.20	$ 3.08

Werner Company must also adjust its beginning retained earnings for the cumulative effect of the change from LIFO to FIFO (net of taxes) for 2007 and 2008. Example 23-4 shows Werner Company's retained earnings statements for these years.

EXAMPLE 23-4   **Comparative Retained Earnings Statements**

Werner Company
Retained Earnings Statement
For Years Ended 12/31/2008 and 12/31/2007

	2008	2007
Beginning unadjusted retained earnings	$525,000	$231,000
Plus: Adjustment for the cumulative effect on prior years' of retrospectively applying the FIFO inventory method (net of income taxes of $21,000 in 2008 and $15,000 in 2007)	49,000	35,000
Adjusted beginning retained earnings	$574,000	$266,000
Net income	420,000	308,000
Ending retained earnings	$994,000	$574,000

The $231,000 unadjusted beginning retained earnings for 2007 is the net income for 2006 under LIFO because Werner Company paid no dividends in 2006 (remember that we also assumed that the company started operations on January 1, 2006). The $35,000 retrospective adjustment to the beginning retained earnings for 2007 is the cumulative effect of the change from LIFO to FIFO for 2006. It is the difference between the $231,000 net income reported under the LIFO inventory method for 2006 and the $266,000 net income ($1,500,000 sales − $670,000 cost of goods sold − $450,000 operating expenses = $380,000 income before income taxes − $114,000 income taxes) that would have been reported under the FIFO method for 2006. The $266,000 adjusted beginning retained earnings is the retained earnings balance that Werner would have reported at the beginning of 2007 if it had been using FIFO during 2006. The $308,000 net income that Werner would have reported for 2007 if it had been using FIFO is then added to the $266,000 adjusted beginning retained earnings to determine the $574,000 ending adjusted retained earnings for 2007.

The $525,000 unadjusted beginning retained earnings for 2008 consists of the $231,000 unadjusted retained earnings balance at the end of 2006, plus the $294,000 net income for 2007 under LIFO because the company paid no dividends. The $49,000 retrospective adjustment to the beginning retained earnings for 2008 is the cumulative effect of the change from LIFO to FIFO for all previous years, which in this example is 2006 and 2007. It is the difference between the $525,000 cumulative net income ($231,000 for 2006 and $294,000 for 2007) under LIFO and the $574,000 cumulative net income ($266,000 for 2006 and $308,000 for 2007) under FIFO. The $574,000 adjusted beginning retained earnings is the balance that Werner would have reported at the beginning of 2008 if it had been using FIFO for 2006 and 2007. The $420,000 net income for 2008 (under FIFO) is then added to the $574,000 adjusted beginning retained earnings balance for 2008 to determine the $994,000 ending adjusted retained earnings for 2008.

At the beginning of 2008, Werner Company records the retrospective adjustment as follows:

Inventory	70,000	
Income Taxes Payable		21,000
Retained Earnings		49,000

Werner Company adds the $70,000 increase (debit) in the Inventory account to the $90,000 balance (under LIFO, see Example 23-1) to increase the balance to $160,000 (the beginning balance for 2008; see Example 23-1). The $21,000 increase (credit) in Income Taxes Payable is the amount that Werner is obligated under the Internal Revenue Code to repay for the income taxes it saved in 2006 and 2007 when the company was using LIFO. The $49,000 increase (credit) in Retained Earnings is the cumulative effect of the change from LIFO to FIFO for 2006 and 2007, net of income taxes, that we explained earlier in Example 23-4.

Example 23-5 shows the Werner Company's disclosures for its retrospective adjustment, as required by *FASB Statement No. 154*. Section 1 of Example 23-5 shows Werner's discussion of the nature and reason for the change from LIFO to FIFO, an explanation of why the new principle is preferable, and a description of the prior-period information that has been retrospectively adjusted. In Section 2 of Example 23-5, Werner discloses the effects of the change from the LIFO method to the FIFO method by reporting the effects on the entire income statement, but only on the line items affected for the balance sheet and statement of cash flows. (Under *FASB Statement No. 154*, a company may disclose the entire statements or just the line items affected.)

The first part of Section 2 shows the effects of the change from LIFO to FIFO on the line items of Werner Company's income statement for 2007 under both the old (LIFO) and the new principle (FIFO). Note that this shows how the new principle changed the income statement line items that were reported (and analyzed by users) under the old principle. It allows the user to understand how the income in 2007 under the new accounting principle (FIFO) is different from that reported under the old principle (LIFO).

EXAMPLE 23-5   Disclosure of the Effects of a Change in Accounting Principle

Section 1: Description of Accounting Change

On January 1, 2008, the company changed its method of valuing its inventory and cost of goods sold to the FIFO method from the LIFO method used in all previous years. The new method of accounting for inventory and cost of goods sold was adopted to recognize…(state justification for the change in accounting principle)…and financial statements of prior years have been retrospectively adjusted to apply the new method. The effect on retained earnings at January 1, 2007 was an increase of $35,000.

Section 2: Effects on Financial Statements

The following financial statement line items for 2008 and 2007 were affected by the change from the LIFO to the FIFO inventory method.

Werner Company
Income Statement Effects
For Year Ended 12/31/2007

	As Originally Reported under LIFO	As Adjusted to FIFO	Effect of Change
Sales	$1,700,000	$1,700,000	$ 0
Cost of goods sold	(780,000)	(760,000)	20,000
Operating expenses	(500,000)	(500,000)	0
Income before income taxes	$ 420,000	$ 440,000	$20,000
Income tax expense	(126,000)	(132,000)	(6,000)
Net income	$ 294,000	$ 308,000	$14,000
Earnings per share	$ 2.94	$ 3.08	$ 0.14

Werner Company
Income Statement Effects
For Year Ended 12/31/2008

	As Computed under LIFO	As Reported under FIFO	Effect of Change
Sales	$2,000,000	$2,000,000	$ 0
Cost of goods sold	(860,000)	(850,000)	10,000
Operating expenses	(550,000)	(550,000)	0
Income before income taxes	$ 590,000	$ 600,000	$10,000
Income tax expense	(177,000)	(180,000)	(3,000)
Net income	$ 413,000	$ 420,000	$ 7,000
Earnings per share	$ 4.13	$ 4.20	$ 0.07

Werner Company
Balance Sheet Effects
12/31/2007

	As Originally Reported under LIFO	As Adjusted under FIFO	Effect of Change
Inventory	$ 90,000	$160,000	$70,000
Income taxes payable	126,000	147,000[a]	21,000
Retained earnings	525,000[b]	574,000[c]	49,000

[a] ($50,000 × 0.3) + $132,000
[b] $231,000 + $294,000
[c] $231,000 + ($50,000 × 0.7) + $308,000

EXAMPLE 23-5   (Continued)

Werner Company
Balance Sheet Effects
12/31/2008

	As Computed under LIFO	As Reported under FIFO	Effect of Change
Inventory	$130,000	$210,000	$80,000
Income taxes payable	177,000	201,000[a]	24,000
Retained earnings	938,000[b]	994,000[c]	56,000

[a] $147,000 − $126,000 + $180,000
[b] $525,000 + $413,000
[c] $574,000 + $420,000

Werner Company
Statement of Cash Flows Effects
For Year Ended 12/31/2007

	As Originally Reported under LIFO	As Adjusted under FIFO	Effect of Change
Net income	$294,000	$308,000	$14,000
Adjustments to reconcile net income to net cash provided by operating activities:			
Increase in inventory	(20,000)	(40,000)	(20,000)
Increase in income taxes payable	27,000	33,000	6,000
Net cash provided by operating activities	$301,000	$301,000	0

Werner Company
Statement of Cash Flows Effects
For Year Ended 12/31/2008

	As Computed under LIFO	As Reported under FIFO	Effect of Change
Net income	$413,000	$420,000	$7,000
Adjustments to reconcile net income to net cash provided by operating activities:			
Increase in inventory	(40,000)	(50,000)	(10,000)
Increase in income taxes payable	51,000	54,000	3,000
Net cash provided by operating activities	$424,000	$424,000	0

The second part of Section 2 shows the effects of the change on the line items of the income statement for 2008 under both the old and the new principle. Note that Werner never reported the LIFO amounts in its 2008 income statement (because it switched to FIFO at the beginning of 2008) but these amounts are a required disclosure that helps users understand the effects of the change in accounting principle. When users were analyzing the company in 2007 and predicting the amount of income it would report in 2008, they would have expected the company to report using LIFO. This disclosure allows them to see the effects of the new principle on those predictions.

The remaining parts of Section 2 in Example 23-5 show the effects of the change in principle on the line items of Werner Company's balance sheet and statement of cash flows. The inventory amount in each balance sheet is taken from Example 23-1. The income taxes payable in each balance sheet as originally reported under LIFO is the amount of the income tax expense in that period's income statement (because we assumed Werner has no temporary or permanent differences and pays its income taxes in the following year.)

The income taxes payable in each balance sheet as adjusted under FIFO is more complex, because the company must repay the taxes it has saved under LIFO. The $147,000 balance on December 31, 2007 is the $132,000 income taxes from the 2007 income statement under FIFO plus the $15,000 ($50,000 change in income before income taxes for

2006 × 0.30) additional taxes that it owes for 2006 but has not yet paid. In 2008, the company pays the $126,000 of income taxes that were due from 2007 under LIFO and adds the $180,000 income taxes from the 2008 income statement under FIFO, which results in a balance of $201,000. The retained earnings balance in each balance sheet is the beginning balance for each year plus the appropriate income amount for that year. Note that the $574,000 adjusted retained earnings on December 31, 2007 includes the increase of $35,000 from the cumulative increase in net income (after taxes) that was measured on January 1, 2007, as we explained in Example 23-4. The adjusted retained earnings balance on December 31, 2008 includes the net income computed under FIFO over the three-year period (2006–2008).

The increase in inventory in each statement of cash flows is calculated as the difference in inventory amounts from year to year in Example 23-1. For instance, the $20,000 increase in inventory as originally reported under LIFO for 2007 is the difference between the $70,000 ending inventory for 2006 and the $90,000 ending inventory for 2007. The increase in the income taxes payable in each statement of cash flows is the change from one balance sheet to the next. For instance, the $27,000 increase in income taxes payable as originally reported under LIFO for 2007 is the difference between the $99,000 ending income taxes payable for 2006 and the $126,000 ending income taxes payable for 2007. ♦

ACCOUNTING FOR A CHANGE IN AN ESTIMATE

Generally accepted accounting principles frequently require a company to use estimates for items such as uncollectible accounts receivable, inventory obsolescence, service lives, residual values, recoverable mineral reserves, warranty costs, pension costs, and the periods that it expects to be benefited by a deferred cost. Since estimating future events is an inherently uncertain process, changes in estimates are inevitable as new events occur, as more experience is acquired, or as additional information is obtained.

FASB Statement No. 154 requires that **a company accounts for a change in an accounting estimate in the period of the change if the change affects that period only, or the period of the change and future periods if the change affects both.**[3] In other words, a change in an accounting estimate does *not* result in a retrospective adjustment, but is accounted for *prospectively*.

Example: Change in Estimated Service Life For example, if a company changes the estimated service life of an asset, it calculates a revised periodic depreciation expense based on the current book value, the estimated residual value, and the new estimated service life. Suppose that a company owns an asset with an original cost of $100,000, an estimated life of 20 years, an estimated residual value of zero, and the company is using straight-line depreciation. The company has recorded depreciation of $5,000 each year, so the asset's book value at the end of eight years is $60,000 [$100,000 − (8 × $5,000)]. Now suppose that at the beginning of the ninth year of the asset's life, the company changes the estimate of its life to a total of 23 years, so that 15 years now remain in the asset's life. The company depreciates the remaining book value over the remaining service life so that the depreciation expense of current and later years is $4,000 ($60,000 ÷ 15) per year.

In addition to including this new amount of depreciation in its financial statements, the company discloses the effect of the change on its income from continuing operations, net income, and the related earnings per share amounts of the current period in the notes to its financial statements. (This disclosure is not required for estimates made each period in the ordinary course of accounting for items such as uncollectible accounts or inventory obsolescence, unless the change is material.) To continue the preceding example, assume that the income tax rate is 30% and the company has 10,000 shares outstanding. The after-tax effect of such a change is an increase in income from continuing operations and

4 Account for a change in estimate.

3. *FASB Statement No. 154*, op. cit., par 19.

net income (because of lower depreciation expense) of $700 [($5,000 − $4,000) × 0.70], and the effect on earnings per share is an increase of $0.07 per share ($700 ÷ 10,000). The company discloses these amounts in the notes to its financial statements. We showed another example of a change in estimate in Chapter 11. ♦

SECURE YOUR KNOWLEDGE 23-1

- Consistent use of the same accounting principle enhances the usefulness of a company's financial statements. Generally accepted accounting principles define three types of accounting changes:
    - Change in an Accounting Principle—a change from one generally accepted principle to another generally accepted accounting principle.
    - Change in an Accounting Estimate—a change in an estimate due to new events occurring, more experience being acquired, or additional information being obtained.
    - Change in a Reporting Entity—a change in the entity being reported, which results in financial statements that are those of a different reporting entity.
- A change in accounting principle is accounted for by retrospectively applying the new accounting principle to all prior periods. Retrospective application requires:
    - The computation of the cumulative effect of the change as of the beginning of the first period presented,
    - An adjustment to the carrying value of the assets and liabilities (including income taxes) affected by the change,
    - An adjustment to the opening balance of retained earnings for the aggregate effect of the change on income (net of applicable income taxes),
    - A restatement of the financial statements of each prior period affected by the change, and
    - Appropriate disclosures.
- A change in an accounting estimate is accounted for prospectively in the period of the change, or the period of the change and future periods if the change affects both.

ADDITIONAL ISSUES

We discuss several additional issues related to accounting changes in the following sections.

Impracticability of Retrospective Adjustment

Sometimes, it may not be practicable to determine the effect of applying a change in accounting principle to any prior period. In this case, *FASB Statement No. 154* requires a company to apply the new accounting principle as if the change was made prospectively as of the earliest date practicable. For example, a change *to* LIFO would require the company to compute any appropriate cost indexes (as we discussed in Chapter 8) and to be able to monitor any LIFO liquidations that occurred in the past. This would often be impracticable. In this situation, the company would apply the new accounting principle in the year of the change without adjusting the financial statements of prior years. It would disclose information similar to what we showed in Section 1 of Example 23-5.

In other situations, a company might have sufficient information to retrospectively adjust to the new accounting principle for some, but not all, of the prior periods presented. In such a situation, the company applies the retrospective adjustment as of the earliest date practicable. That is, the company computes the cumulative effect of the change to the new accounting principle on the carrying amount of the assets and liabilities as of the beginning of the earliest period to which the new accounting principle can be applied. An offsetting adjustment (net of taxes) is made to the opening balance of retained earnings for that period. Effectively, we illustrated this situation with the Werner Company because we assumed the beginning of the first period presented was January 1, 2007. However, publicly-held companies must present three years of income statements. Therefore, if Werner Company were a publicly-held company, it would have used January 1, 2006 as the beginning of the first period presented. Note also that if a company provides a summary of its financial results for, say, 10 years, it must retrospectively adjust its disclosures for those periods, if practicable.

A Change in Principle Distinguished from a Change in an Estimate

Sometimes it is difficult for a company to distinguish between a change in an accounting principle and a change in an estimate. For example, a company may change from capitalizing and amortizing a cost to recording it as an expense when incurred because future benefits associated with the cost have become doubtful. The company adopted the new accounting method because of the change in estimated benefits and therefore the change in method is *inseparable* from the change in estimate. The company accounts for such a change as a *change in estimate.* That is, it accounts for the change prospectively.

   An additional complexity arises with respect to the depreciation (including amortization and depletion) of the cost of an asset over its useful life. It can be argued that a change in the method of depreciation is in fact a change in estimate. That is, the criteria that a company uses to select a method of depreciation are that it is systematic and rational, and results in an appropriate matching of costs and benefits. Therefore, if the estimate of the pattern of future benefits is changed, for example, from declining benefits to constant benefits, a change in the depreciation method is appropriate. Thus, a change in an accounting method (depreciation) results from a change in an estimate. Therefore, a change in the depreciation method is treated as a change in an estimate under the provisions of *FASB Statement No. 154.*[4] The *Statement* refers to this as *a change in accounting estimate effected by a change in accounting principle.*

Example: Change in Principle and Estimate   Assume that at the beginning of year 1, the Dowson Company purchased an asset for $20,000, which had an estimated life of four years and a zero residual value. The company was depreciating the asset using the sum-of-the-years'-digits method and decides to switch to the straight-line method at the beginning of year 3 because of a change in the estimated pattern of benefits the asset produces. Straight-line and sum-of-the-years'-digits methods produce the annual depreciation amounts we show in Example 23-6. In this example, we ignore the effects of income taxes.

EXAMPLE 23-6	**Alternative Depreciation Methods: Dowson Company**		
	Method		**Reduced Depreciation Amount Under**
Year	**Sum-of-the-Years'-Digits**	**Straight-Line**	**Straight-Line Method**
1	$ 8,000	$ 5,000	$ 3,000
2	6,000	5,000	1,000
3	4,000	5,000	(1,000)
4	2,000	5,000	(3,000)
	$20,000	$20,000	$ 0

---

4.   *Ibid.*, par 20.

The company writes off the unadjusted carrying value of the asset at the beginning of year 3 over the remaining life of the asset. In this case, under the sum-of-the-years'-digits method, the asset has a carrying value at the beginning of year 3 of $6,000 ($20,000 − $8,000 − $6,000). The company writes off this amount by the straight-line method through a depreciation expense of $3,000 per year over the remaining life of two years. Since the company accounts for the change prospectively, the only effect in the year of the change (year 3) is a depreciation expense of $3,000 instead of the $4,000 that the company would have reported under the sum-of-the-years'-digits method. No change is made in the financial statements for years 1 and 2. The company is also required to make the disclosures we discussed in a previous section. ♦

Preferability of the New Accounting Principle

After a company adopts an accounting principle, it should not change the principle unless a new principle is preferable. Therefore, when a company changes an accounting principle, management must justify the change on the grounds that the new principle is preferable to the old. For example, Nike justified its change to FIFO by stating that "this change was predicated on the fact that the LIFO method no longer matches the realities of how we do business." The SEC requires that when a company that files with it makes an accounting change, the auditor must submit a letter indicating whether the change is to an alternative principle that, in the auditor's judgment, is preferable under the circumstances. "Preferable" is defined to mean that the new method represents an improved method of measuring business operations in the particular circumstances. Some accountants object to the SEC's requirement because it relates only to a company making a change in an accounting principle. There is no requirement that the auditor make a statement about the preferability of the accounting principles the company is currently using.

The issuance of an FASB Statement is sufficient support for a change in accounting principle and does not require special justification. That is, the newly mandated principle is automatically considered to be preferable.

Direct and Indirect Effects

In the Werner Company example, we assumed that the change in the accounting principle used for inventory was the only item affecting the previous year's income. In more complex situations, a change in accounting principle might have an "interactive" effect on other items that affect prior years' income. For instance, a company might have bonus arrangements with management, profit sharing plans for employees, or royalty payments, all of which are based on the company's income. In these cases, a change in an accounting principle has both a "direct" and an "indirect" effect on the company's income of prior years. The direct effect is the amount by which its prior years' income is increased or decreased specifically as a result of the change in accounting principle. The indirect effect is the amount by which the company's income of prior years is affected by how the change in principle affects other elements of income. For instance, suppose the Werner Company also has a bonus arrangement with management based on net income. If the company had used FIFO instead of LIFO in prior years, the direct effect is an increase in income because of a lower cost of goods sold. However, this increase in income would have been partially offset by the indirect effect on the bonus arrangement. That is, because income was increased as a result of the lower cost of goods sold, the bonus expense also would have been higher, and this, in turn, would have offset some of the increase in income.

In situations in which a change in accounting principle has both a direct and indirect effect on prior years' income, *FASB Statement No. 154* states that **a company recognizes only the *direct effect* (net of applicable income taxes) in determining the amount of the retrospective adjustment.** Therefore, the indirect effects that would have been recognized if the newly adopted principle had been used in prior periods are *not* included in the retrospective application. For example, a bonus of a prior period that a company has paid to its employees would probably not be changed because of a change to an accounting principle that will be applied to the current and future periods. However, if indirect effects are actually incurred and recognized, they are reported in the year in which the accounting change is made.

Example: Indirect Effects The Werner Company's total pre-tax difference from the change to FIFO was $70,000 ($50,000 + $20,000) at January 1, 2008. Suppose the company pays a bonus of 10% of its income before income taxes and bonus to employees. If the company did *not* change the amount of the bonuses it paid in the past, then the amounts and disclosures we illustrated earlier would not change (except for the direct effect of the bonus on reported income in 2008). If the company *did* pay an additional bonus based on the change in income, then it would recognize an expense of $7,000 ($70,000 × 10%) in 2008, the year it adopted the new principle. ♦

Adoption of a New Accounting Principle for Future Events

If a company adopts a new accounting principle for use in the future but does not change the method currently used, it does not make a retrospective adjustment. For example, a company might use a new depreciation method for newly acquired assets, but continue to use the old method for currently owned assets. In this situation, the company should describe the nature of the change and its effect on net income of the period of the change, together with the earnings per share amounts, in the notes to its financial statements.

Initial Public Sale of Common Stock

If a company makes accounting changes when it makes an initial public distribution (the first sale of common stock made available to the general public), it retrospectively adjusts the financial statements for all prior periods presented. This procedure is available only once for changes made at the time a company first uses its financial statements to (1) obtain additional equity capital from investors, (2) effect a business combination, or (3) register securities. This approach is logical because the company's financial statements have never before been available to the public and therefore there is no need to explain the changes made to the statements.

Transition Methods Required by the FASB

As we discussed in a previous section, *FASB Statement No. 154* specifies the general rules to be applied for a change in an accounting principle. However, when issuing *Statements*, the FASB specifies transition rules, if appropriate. **Transition rules** define the accounting method a company uses when it changes an accounting principle to conform to a new principle required by the issuance of a *Statement*. In these situations, the accounting principle being used is no longer acceptable and a new principle is required. The transition rule usually requires a retrospective application of the new accounting principle. However, the change is sometimes accounted for prospectively, when obtaining the information for a retrospective application is costly or not practicable. You should carefully examine each *Statement* so that you follow the specific transition rules.

Accounting Changes in Interim Financial Statements

The principles to be followed when accounting changes are reported in interim financial statements are also established by *FASB Statement No. 154*. If a company makes a change in accounting principle in an interim period, it also reports the change by retrospective application. However, the impracticability exception we discussed earlier does not apply to earlier interim periods in the year in which the change is made. Therefore, the new principle is applied retrospectively to, at least, the beginning of the year in which the change is made. In summary, the effect is that **a company accounts for the change in principle at the beginning of the first interim period, regardless of the interim period in which the change occurs.**

Litigation Settlement

Another issue is whether a company should account for the results of a litigation settlement as a a retrospective adjustment or a prospective adjustment. It could be argued that such a settlement is a retrospective adjustment because it relates either to the period in which the event causing the litigation occurred or to the period in which the litigation was filed. Alternatively, it could be argued that the litigation settlement is an event of the period of settlement and should be included in the company's current period's income. This issue was resolved by **FASB Statement No. 16**, which specifies that a litigation settlement is not a retrospective adjustment.[5]

CONCEPTUAL EVALUATION OF ACCOUNTING FOR A CHANGE IN ACCOUNTING PRINCIPLE AND A CHANGE IN ESTIMATE

5 Explain the conceptual issues regarding a change in accounting principle and a change in estimate.

As we discussed in a previous section, there are two possible alternatives that a company uses to account for a change in an accounting principle or in an accounting estimate. These alternatives are retrospective application and prospective adjustment. We discuss the advantages and disadvantages of these alternatives, as well as selected additional issues, in the following sections.

Retrospective Application (Adjustment)

The major argument in favor of retrospective application is that all the financial statements that a company presents at a given date are prepared on the basis of consistent accounting principles. Thus, when a user of the financial statements evaluates the company's current financial results, it is possible to make a comparison with the previous year's financial statements without adjusting for a change in accounting principle. Retrospective application is the usual method required for a change in accounting principle mandated by the FASB because it does not penalize (or increase) a company's current year's earnings for an event that is beyond the control of the company's management.

On the other hand, the retrospective application method has several disadvantages. First, a company's financial statements issued in previous years are changed under this method. This creates the possibility that users may be confused by the change in the reported results, and that confidence in the information may be reduced because "the numbers changed." Second, the method is not consistent with the all-inclusive income concept, which is the basis of the generally accepted accounting principles as we discussed in Chapter 5. Third, there may be an impact on a company's contractual arrangements (such as bonus agreements, borrowing indentures, royalties, or profit sharing) when its previously reported income is changed. Fourth, the method lends itself to income manipulation by a company's management because items are excluded from its current year's income statement. When a company makes a retrospective application, it can decrease retained earnings without including the change as a reduction in its current year's income. Thus, the sum of the net incomes that it reports over the years would be more than the increase in its retained earnings (excluding consideration of dividends). Conversely, a retrospective application that increases the balance in a company's retained earnings does so without being added to its current year's net income.

---

5. "Prior Period Adjustments," *FASB Statement of Financial Accounting Standards No. 16* (Stamford, Conn.: FASB, 1977).

Prospective Adjustment

Accounting estimates used for periodic reporting inevitably change over time. A company also adopts new accounting principles from time to time. It may be argued that it is better for a company to account for such changes by considering their effects on the future and to make no attempt to change what has already been reported.

Since a company makes an estimate with the best information available at that time, and changes this estimate only to reflect new information, accounting for a change in an estimate with a prospective adjustment is especially appropriate. In addition, the alternative of reporting the effect of a change of estimate retrospectively might cause considerable confusion among users of financial statements because of the frequency of such changes.

In the case of a change in an accounting principle, the same arguments can be made about the desirability of a company not changing what it has already reported (that is, confusion and the all-inclusive income concept). Moreover, it may be argued that a change in an accounting principle, although it occurs in the current period, has little or no relation to the current period's economic events, or to the company's income generated from providing goods and services to its customers. Therefore, the change should be accounted for prospectively. Conversely, it can be argued that a change in an accounting principle is an event of the current period and a company should not account for it prospectively, but should report the cumulative effect in the income statement of the period of the change. Prior to 2006, this method was used for some changes in accounting principle.

ACCOUNTING FOR A CHANGE IN A REPORTING ENTITY

The third type of change defined by *FASB Statement No. 154* is a change in a reporting entity. As we noted earlier, **a company accounts for a change in reporting entity as a retrospective adjustment so that all the financial statements it presents are for the same entity.**[6] This procedure improves consistency.

6 Identify a change in reporting entity.

A change in an accounting entity occurs mainly when (1) a company presents consolidated or combined statements in place of the statements of individual companies, (2) there is a change in the specific subsidiaries that make up the group of companies for which a company presents consolidated financial statements, or (3) the companies included in combined financial statements change.

When a change in an accounting entity occurs, the company includes in the notes to its financial statements of the period in which it makes the change a description of the change as well as the reason for it, and the effect of the change on income before extraordinary items, net income, other comprehensive income, and related earnings per share amounts for all periods presented. However, financial statements of later periods need not repeat the disclosures. We do not discuss the accounting for a change in an entity here, but it is included in advanced accounting books.

SECURE YOUR KNOWLEDGE 23-2

- In situations for which it is impracticable to retrospectively adjust the financial statements for a change in accounting principle, a company may apply the new accounting principle as if the change was made prospectively as of the earliest date practicable.
- If a change in accounting estimate cannot be distinguished from a change in accounting principle (e.g., a change in depreciation, depletion, or amortization method), it is considered a change in estimate effected by a change in accounting principle and is accounted for prospectively.

---

6. *FASB Statement No. 154*, op. cit., par. 23.

- Any change in accounting principle must be justified on the grounds that the new principle is preferable to the old.
- When a change in accounting principle has both direct and indirect effects on the company's income, only the direct effect of the change in accounting principle is included in the retrospective adjustment. Any indirect effects are included in the year in which the accounting change is made.
- Any transition rule specified in a new accounting pronouncement is followed.
- A company accounts for a change in accounting principle at the beginning of the first interim period, regardless of the interim period in which the change occurs.
- A change in reporting entity is accounted for by retrospectively adjusting the financial statements of all prior periods presented.

ACCOUNTING FOR A CORRECTION OF AN ERROR

7 Account for a correction of an error.

A company may make a material error in the financial statements of a prior period that it does not discover until the current period. Examples of errors that a company might make include:

1. The use of an accounting principle that is not generally accepted;
2. The use of an estimate that was not made in good faith;
3. Mathematical miscalculations, such as the incorrect computation of its inventory; or logical errors, such as the omission of the residual value in the calculation of straight-line depreciation;
4. The omission of a deferral or accrual, such as the failure to accrue warranty costs.

The company must correct the error in the current period. The correction of an error made in a prior period is *not* an accounting change under the requirements of *FASB Statement No. 154.* **A company accounts for the correction of a material error of a past period that it discovers in the current period as a prior period restatement (adjustment).**

A prior period restatement (adjustment) requires the following:

1. The company computes the cumulative effect of the error correction on prior financial statements. That is, it computes the amounts that would have been in the financial statements if it had not made the error.
2. The company adjusts the carrying values of those assets and liabilities (including income taxes) that are affected by the error. The company makes an offsetting adjustment to the beginning balance of retained earnings to report the cumulative effect of the error correction (net of taxes) for each period presented.

3. The company adjusts the financial statements of each prior period to reflect the specific effects of correcting the error. That is, each item in each financial statement that is affected by the error is restated to the appropriate amount.
4. The company's disclosures include (a) that its previously issued financial statements have been restated, along with a description of the nature of the error, (b) the effect of the correction on each financial statement line item, and any per-share amounts affected for each prior period presented, and (c) the cumulative effect of the change on retained earnings (or other appropriate component of equity) at the beginning of the earliest period presented.

Therefore, the effect of a prior period restatement is very similar to a retrospective application of a new accounting principle, except for the reason that the company made the adjustments.

We do not illustrate the disclosures, but they would be similar to those we showed in Example 23-5. Real Report 23-1 provides an illustration of the disclosure of a correction of an error made in a prior period by **Darden Restaurants, Inc.** We discuss the journal entries required to correct errors in the next sections.

Real Report 23-1 Disclosure of the Correction of an Error Made in a Prior Period

DARDEN RESTAURANTS, INC.

NOTES TO CONSOLIDATED FINANCIAL STATEMENTS (in part)

NOTE 2 - RESTATEMENT OF FINANCIAL STATEMENTS (in part; amounts in thousands)

Following a December 2004 review of our lease accounting and leasehold depreciation policies, we determined that it was appropriate to adjust certain of our prior financial statements. As a result, we have restated our consolidated financial statements for the fiscal years 1996 through 2004. Historically, when accounting for leases with renewal options, we recorded rent expense on a straight-line basis over the initial non-cancelable lease term, with the term commencing when actual rent payments began. We depreciate our buildings, leasehold improvements and other long-lived assets on those properties over a period that includes both the initial non cancelable lease term and all option periods provided for in the lease (or the useful life of the assets, if shorter). We previously believed that these long-standing accounting treatments were appropriate under generally accepted accounting principles. We now have restated our financial statements to recognize rent expense on a straight-line basis over the expected lease term, including cancelable option periods where failure to exercise such options would result in an economic penalty. The lease term commences on the date when we become legally obligated for the rent payments.

The cumulative effect of the Restatement through fiscal 2004 is an increase in the deferred rent liability of $114,008 and a decrease in deferred income tax liability of $43,526. As a result, retained earnings at the end of fiscal 2004 decreased by $70,268. Rent expense for fiscal years ended 2004, 2003, and 2002 increased by $7,222, $10,145, and $7,874, respectively. The Restatement decreased reported diluted net earnings per share by $0.02, $0.04, and $0.03 for the fiscal years ended 2004, 2003 and 2002, respectively. The cumulative effect of the Restatement for all years prior to fiscal year 2002 was $54,364, which was recorded as an adjustment to opening stockholders' equity at May 27, 2001. The Restatement did not have any impact on our previously reported cash flows, sales or same-restaurant sales or on our compliance with any covenant under our credit facility or other debt instruments.

The following is a summary of the impact of the Restatement on (i) our consolidated balance sheets at May 30, 2004 and May 25, 2003 and (ii) our consolidated statements of earnings for the fiscal years ended May 30, 2004 and May 25, 2003. We have not presented a summary of the impact of the Restatement on our consolidated statements of cash flows for any of the above-referenced fiscal years because the net impact for each such fiscal year is zero.

Fiscal Year 2004	As Previously Reported	Adjustments	As Restated
Consolidated Balance Sheet			
Deferred income taxes	$ 176,216	$ (43,526)	$ 132,690
Deferred rent	—	122,879	122,879
Other liabilities	21,532	(8,871)	12,661
Total liabilities	1,534,578	70,482	1,605,060
Retained earnings	1,197,921	(70,268)	1,127,653
Accumulated other comprehensive income (loss)	(9,959)	(214)	(10,173)
Total stockholders' equity	1,245,770	(70,482)	1,175,288
Consolidated Statement of Earnings			
Restaurant expenses	$ 767,584	$ 7,222	$ 774,806
Total cost of sales	3,895,717	7,222	3,902,939
Total costs and expenses	4,663,357	7,222	4,670,579
Earnings before income taxes	339,998	(7,222)	332,776
Income taxes	108,536	(2,933)	105,603

Continued

Net earnings	231,462	(4,289)	227,173
Basic net earnings per share	1.42	(0.03)	1.39
Diluted net earnings per share	1.36	(0.02)	1.34

Fiscal Year 2003	As Previously Reported	Adjustments	As Restated
Consolidated Balance Sheet			
Deferred income taxes	$ 150,537	$(40,593)	$ 109,944
Deferred rent	—	115,296	115,296
Other liabilities	19,910	(8,567)	11,343
Total liabilities	1,468,442	66,136	1,534,578
Retained earnings	979,443	(65,979)	913,464
Accumulated other comprehensive income (loss)	(10,489)	(157)	(10,646)
Total stockholders' equity	1,196,191	(66,136)	1,130,055
Consolidated Statement of Earnings			
Restaurant expenses	$ 703,554	10,145	713,699
Total cost of sales	3,637,762	10,145	3,647,907
Total costs and expenses	4,307,223	10,145	4,317,368
Earnings before income taxes	347,748	(10,145)	337,603
Income taxes	115,488	(3,864)	111,624
Net earnings	232,260	(6,281)	225,979
Basic net earnings per share	1.36	(0.03)	1.33
Diluted net earnings per share	1.31	(0.04)	1.27

Questions:

1. What was the nature of the error that required Darden Restaurants to restate its financial statements?
2. What was the effect of the error on Darden Restaurants' 2004 income statement?

Error Analysis

Because errors, by their very nature, happen in unpredictable and often illogical ways, it is difficult to generalize about the kinds of errors that a company might make and the journal entries that may be required to correct them. Many errors are discovered automatically through proper use of the double-entry system. Others are found by the company's internal or external auditors before being included in its financial statements. In this section we are concerned about errors that escape detection until after they are included in a company's published financial statements. We categorize them according to the effect they have on the financial statements.

Errors Affecting Only the Balance Sheet

Some errors affect only balance sheet accounts. For example, a company may include a long-term note receivable as a current note receivable. Reclassification of the note only affects its balance sheet. Therefore, if the error occurred in a prior period, the company does not make a correcting journal entry. However, if it presents comparative financial statements in the current year, it corrects the financial statements of the prior period by reclassifying the item.

Errors Affecting Only the Income Statement

Errors that affect only income statement accounts usually result from the misclassification of items. For example, a company may include interest revenue with sales revenue.

Errors of this kind require reclassification but do not affect net income. Therefore, if the error occurred in a prior period, the company does not make a correcting journal entry. However, if it presents comparative financial statements in the current year, it corrects the financial statements of the prior period by reclassifying the item.

Errors Affecting Both the Income Statement and Balance Sheet

An error may affect both an income statement account and a balance sheet account, such as the failure to accrue a liability at the end of the period. For example, if a company fails to accrue interest, it understates interest expense on its current income statement and omits interest payable from its ending balance sheet.

Errors that affect both the income statement and the balance sheet can be classified as counterbalancing or noncounterbalancing. **Counterbalancing** errors are those that are automatically corrected in the next accounting period, even if they are not discovered. Consider the effect of unrecorded interest in the previous paragraph, and assume that the amount of the interest is $2,000 and the income tax rate 30%. The effects of the error on the company's financial statements of the period in which it made the error are as follows:

1. Interest expense is understated by $2,000.
2. Income before income taxes is overstated by $2,000.
3. Income tax expense is overstated by $600.
4. Net income is overstated by $1,400.
5. Retained earnings is overstated by $1,400.
6. Interest payable is understated by $2,000.
7. Income taxes payable is overstated by $600.

In the next period, when the company pays the interest and records the entire payment as an expense, the following additional errors occur:

1. Interest expense is overstated by $2,000.
2. Income before income taxes is understated by $2,000.
3. Income tax expense is understated by $600.
4. Net income is understated by $1,400.

Since the amount of the interest expense overstatement in the second period is equal to the understatement of the previous period, the net income understatement in the second period offsets the overstatement in the first period. Therefore, no balance sheet accounts are in error at the end of the second period. That is, the total liabilities are no longer understated, and the retained earnings balance is now correct. The errors have automatically counterbalanced. Note also that even though the errors counterbalance, the need for a correcting journal entry and for correction of the financial statements depends on *when* the error is discovered. If the company discovers the error *during* the second year, it must make a journal entry so that the interest expense and net income for the second year are reported correctly. If the company discovers the error *after* the second year, no correcting journal entry is needed. However, the financial statements for the two years are in error, so the company must correct (restate) the financial statements unless sufficient time has passed so that they are *not* being presented for comparative purposes.

Noncounterbalancing errors are those that are not offset in the next accounting period. For example, suppose that a company erroneously records the purchase of an asset costing $10,000 as supplies expense in the year of purchase. However, it should have capitalized and depreciated the asset by the straight-line method over 10 years with no residual value for both financial reporting and income tax purposes. Furthermore, the company records a full year's depreciation in the year of acquisition, the income tax rate is 30% and the MACRS depreciation is assumed to be $1,400. The effects of the error on the company's financial statements of the period in which it made the error are as follows:

1. Supplies expense is overstated by $10,000.
2. The asset is understated by $10,000.

3. Depreciation expense is understated by $1,000 ($10,000 ÷ 10).
4. Accumulated depreciation is understated by $1,000.
5. Income before income taxes is understated by $9,000 ($10,000 − $1,000).
6. Income tax expense is understated by $2,700 ($9,000 × 0.30).
7. Net income is understated by $6,300 ($9,000 − $2,700).
8. Retained earnings is understated by $6,300.
9. Deferred tax liability is understated by $120 [($1,400 − $1,000) × 30%]
10. Income taxes payable are understated by $2,580 ($2,700 − $120).

The understatement of the asset and the depreciation expense continues until the end of the asset's life. At this point the balance sheet accounts (asset, accumulated depreciation, income taxes payable, and retained earnings) are correct for the first time since the error was made. Consequently, if the company discovers the error before the end of the life of the asset, it must make a correcting journal entry.

LINK TO ETHICAL DILEMMA

As the controller for Coruscant Industries, you've just completed an extremely exhausting year with the issuance of Coruscant's annual report. After being surprised by the disappointing net income a year earlier, the Board of Directors charged you with improving the company's fortunes. Reviewing the previous year's financial results, you determined that the primary reason for Coruscant's disappointing results was higher than expected cost of goods sold. Seeking to improve the efficiency of operations and lower cost of goods sold, you had aggressively implemented several cost-containment measures to address this problem, which resulted in numerous complaints from the manufacturing supervisors. Despite these criticisms, the current annual report, which just met the analysts' projections of net income, should serve as validation that you successfully responded to the Board of Directors' challenges. As a reward for your efforts, you've decided to take a few days off to work on your golf game.

As you are preparing to leave the office, you receive an e-mail from a first-year staff accountant whom you had asked to double-check the accuracy of the current year inventory count. In the e-mail, the accountant informs you that while the current year inventory records appear in order, she had discovered an error in the beginning inventory records. It appeared that you had inadvertently transposed two numbers in the previous year's inventory balance, resulting in a material understatement of the previous year's ending inventory. The e-mail continues that since the current year inventory records are accurate, the error had "self-corrected" and there is no need to adjust the current year financial statements. Do you agree with the accountant's assessment? What ethical considerations does this situation present?

Error Correction

The approach to correcting an error is difficult to generalize because of the variety of errors that may occur. Each error must be examined carefully to determine how the transaction *was* recorded and how it *should have been* recorded. The correction can then be made by (1) recording a single comprehensive journal entry (which is the preferred method in practice), or (2) reversing the original incorrect journal entry and then recording the original transaction or event as it should have been recorded initially.

Example: Error Correction Approaches   Assume Larson Company recorded a building improvement costing $20,000 as Repair Expense when it should have capitalized the item. A single comprehensive journal entry to correct the error when it is discovered *in the next period* is:

Building	20,000	
Retained Earnings		20,000

Note that in this entry, we are ignoring income taxes and depreciation, which we will discuss later. Note also that the correction is not made by a credit to Repair Expense because the company discovered the error in the period following the one in which it was made. At this point the company's revenue and expense accounts for the previous period have been closed to retained earnings, so the correction of the previous year's income is made directly to the Retained Earnings account. The correction might also be made to an account, Correction of Prior Years' Income Due to Error in Recording Building Improvement, which is closed to Retained Earnings). If the company presents comparative financial statements, it corrects them as we discussed earlier.

If the second approach is used, two separate journal entries are required. First, the company reverses the original entry (but it again credits the Retained Earnings account because the Repair Expense account has been closed), and then the company makes the journal entry that it should have made, as follows:

Cash	20,000	
Retained Earnings		20,000
Building	20,000	
Cash		20,000

In this simple situation, the second approach may seem unnecessary, but it can prove useful in more complex circumstances.

In the previous example, Larson Company must also correct the recorded amount of depreciation. Since it discovered the error in the next period, it corrects Retained Earnings (for the previous period's depreciation expense understatement and income overstatement) and Accumulated Depreciation by the following journal entry (assuming a 10-year life, no residual value, straight-line depreciation, and that a full year's depreciation is recorded in the year of acquisition):

Retained Earnings	2,000	
Accumulated Depreciation		2,000

The company records depreciation expense for the second year in the normal way (because we assumed that it discovered the error during the second year). ♦

Steps in Error Correction

A logical sequence of steps for the analysis and correction of an error is indicated by the preceding discussion:

Step 1. Analyze the original erroneous journal entry and determine all the debits and credits that were recorded.

Step 2. Determine the correct journal entry and the appropriate debits and credits.

Step 3. Evaluate whether the error has caused additional errors in other accounts.

Step 4. Prepare the correcting entry (or entries), remember to record any corrections of the revenues and expenses for prior years as adjustments to retained earnings.

We show additional examples of some types of errors that can be expected to occur more frequently in the following sections for the Huggins Company, which uses a periodic inventory method. For simplicity, these corrections ignore the potential impact on taxable income, income tax expense, and deferred income taxes, although, in reality, correcting entries for these items may be required. Assume all errors are material.

Example: Omission of Unearned Revenue

In December 2007 the Huggins Company received $10,000 as a prepayment for renting a building to another company for all of 2008. The company recorded this transaction by a debit to Cash and a credit to Rent Revenue. The revenue should be reported in 2008, but the company erroneously included the revenue in its 2007 income. If the company discovers this error in 2008, it has overstated income for 2007 by including $10,000 rent revenue. Therefore, it has to decrease Retained Earnings by $10,000. Also, it has to record the rent revenue in 2008. Therefore, the company makes the following correcting entry:

Retained Earnings	10,000	
Rent Revenue		10,000

If the company does not discover the error until 2009, it does not make a correcting entry because the error has counterbalanced. However, if the company presents 2007 and 2008 financial statements for comparative purposes, the company corrects (restates) them as we discussed earlier. ♦

Example: Failure to Accrue Revenue

On December 31, 2007 the Huggins Company failed to accrue interest revenue of $500 that it had earned but not received on an outstanding note receivable. If the company discovered the error in 2008, it has understated income for 2007 by omitting interest revenue of $500. Therefore, it has to increase Retained Earnings by that amount. If we assume that the company credits any cash received in 2008 to Interest Revenue, it has overstated the revenue account by $500 in 2008, and so it makes the following correcting entry:

Interest Revenue	500	
Retained Earnings		500

If the company discovered the error in 2009, it does not make a correcting entry because the error has counterbalanced. However, if the company presents 2007 and 2008 financial statements for comparative purposes, it corrects them. ♦

Example: Omission of Prepaid Expense

In December 2007 the Huggins Company paid $1,000 for insurance coverage for the year 2008. It recorded the original entry as a debit to Insurance Expense and a credit to Cash, and did not record a year-end adjustment. If the company discovers this error at the end of 2008, it has understated its income for 2007 by the $1,000 overstatement of insurance expense. Therefore, it has to increase Retained Earnings by this amount. Since the company did not record prepaid insurance in 2007, it has understated Insurance Expense by $1,000 for 2008 and it makes the following correcting entry:

Insurance Expense	1,000	
Retained Earnings		1,000

Alternatively, if the payment of $1,000 in 2007 was for a two-year insurance policy, the correcting entry at the end of 2008 is:

Insurance Expense	500	
Prepaid Insurance	500	
Retained Earnings		1,000

If the company does not discover this error until 2009 and the payment in 2007 was for one year's insurance, it does not make a correcting entry because the error has counterbalanced. If the company discovered the error in 2009 and the payment was for two years' insurance, the correcting entry is:

Insurance Expense	500	
Retained Earnings		500

In this situation, $500 of the error has counterbalanced, leaving only $500 to be corrected. Once again, the company corrects the 2007 and 2008 financial statements if it presents them for comparative purposes. ♦

Example: Error in Ending Inventory

At December 31, 2007 the Huggins Company recorded its ending inventory at $50,000 based on a physical count. During 2008 it discovered that the correct inventory value should have been $55,000 because it made an error in the inventory count. Since it understated the ending inventory for 2007 by $5,000, it overstated cost of goods sold for 2007, and understated income. Therefore, it has to increase Retained Earnings by this amount. Since the company has understated its beginning inventory in 2008, it has to increase it by $5,000, and so it makes the following correcting entry:

Inventory	5,000	
Retained Earnings		5,000

If the company does not discover this error until 2009, it does not make a correcting entry because the error has counterbalanced, but it corrects the 2007 and 2008 financial statements because the error in the inventory affects cost of goods sold in both years. Many companies use a perpetual inventory system. Under this system they still take a physical inventory and may make similar errors. ♦

Example: Error in Purchases of Inventory

During December 2007 the Huggins Company made a purchase of inventory on credit that it had not paid at year's end. It recorded this transaction incorrectly at $17,000 although the invoice price of the inventory was $27,000. Since the company understated the purchases and accounts payable by $10,000, it understated cost of goods sold in 2007 (assuming it recorded the ending inventory correctly) and overstated income by $10,000. Therefore, it has to decrease Retained Earnings by this amount. The company understated Accounts Payable in 2008 by $10,000, and so it makes the following correcting entry:

Retained Earnings	10,000	
Accounts Payable		10,000

Because of the creditor's demand for payment, it is difficult to conceive of such an error remaining undetected until 2009, but if that did happen, the correcting entry is as shown. Since the ending inventory was correct, the error was not counterbalanced and the company has overstated its income for 2007 and retained earnings until it makes the correction. We illustrated more examples of the effects of errors in inventory and purchases in Chapter 9. ♦

Example: Failure to Accrue Estimated Bad Debts

The Huggins Company failed to accrue an allowance for doubtful accounts of $7,000 in its 2007 financial statements. The result of this error was the understatement of bad debt expense by $7,000. Therefore, the company has to decrease Retained Earnings by this amount. The discovery of the error in 2008 indicates that the company has overstated Accounts Receivable (net) by $7,000, and so it makes the following correcting entry:

Retained Earnings	7,000	
Allowance for Doubtful Accounts		7,000

Alternatively, if the company discovers the error after it makes the estimate of doubtful accounts and records it by the aging method at the end of 2008, it has overstated the bad debt expense because part of the charge relates to the 2007 error. Therefore, it makes the following correcting entry:

Retained Earnings	7,000	
Bad Debt Expense		7,000

It is obviously not possible to give examples of every possible error. In each situation the facts must be carefully examined, with particular consideration given to the time periods involved and the possibility of additional errors resulting from the initial error. For example, the effects of errors on the company's prior and current income tax expense and deferred income taxes must be assessed. Adjustments may have to be made to retained earnings if there were changes in income tax expense for prior periods. Also, if taxable income is incorrect for prior periods, amended tax returns may be necessary. ♦

Example 23-7 shows a schedule that summarizes the effects of the multiple errors of the Huggins Company on its income before income taxes for the years affected. The schedule includes each of the errors. Note that the omission of the prepaid expense assumes a two-year insurance policy (not a one-year insurance policy). The net effect of the errors is to reduce its pretax income for 2007 by $20,500, increase pretax income for 2008 by $4,000, and reduce assets by $6,500 and increase liabilities by $10,000 on its 2008 balance sheet. If the income tax rate is 30% and the correction of each of these errors affects taxable income, the 2007 errors enable the company to obtain a tax refund of $6,150 (30% × $20,500), and it also makes the following journal entry:

Income Tax Refund Receivable	6,150	
Retained Earnings		6,150

EXAMPLE 23-7   **Summary of Corrections of Errors Discovered in 2008**

Error	Effect of Correction on Income 2007	Effect of Correction on Income 2008	Increases on Balance Sheet December 31, 2008
Omission of unearned revenue	$(10,000)	$10,000	
Failure to accrue interest revenue	500	(500)	
Omission of prepaid expense (two-year insurance policy)	1,000	(500)	Prepaid insurance $500
Error in ending inventory	5,000	(5,000)	
Error in purchases	(10,000)		Accounts payable $10,000
Failure to accrue estimated bad debts	(7,000)		Allowance for doubtful accounts $7,000
Total pretax effect	$(20,500)	$ 4,000	
Less: Income tax effect	6,150		
After-tax effect	$(14,350)		

The 2008 corrections do not need a separate correction for income taxes in this example because we assume that the company has not closed its books for 2008.

SECURE YOUR KNOWLEDGE 23-3

- An error results from mathematical mistakes or mistakes in the application of generally accepted accounting principles.
- A material error of a past period that is discovered in the current period is accounted for as a prior period restatement (adjustment) which requires:
  - The computation of the cumulative effect of the error on prior period financial statements;
  - An adjustment of the carrying values of the assets and liabilities (including income taxes) affected by the error;
  - An adjustment to the opening balance of retained earnings for the aggregate effect of the error (net of applicable income taxes);
  - A restatement of the financial statements of each prior period affected by the error; and
  - Appropriate disclosures.
- Errors can be classified as:
  - Errors only affecting the balance sheet—reclassification of the balance sheet amounts affected is required.
  - Errors affecting only the income statement—reclassification of the income statement amounts affected is required.
  - Errors affecting both the income statement and the balance sheet—a correcting journal entry and correction of the financial statements may be required.
- If an error is a counterbalancing error (e.g., the error automatically corrects in the next accounting period), a correcting journal entry is needed if the error is discovered during the second year. If the error is discovered after the second year, no correcting journal entry is needed but the financial statements should be restated so that they are not misleading.
- If an error is a noncounterbalancing error (e.g., the error will not automatically correct in the next accounting period), a correcting journal entry is needed and any applicable financial statements must be restated.
- Every error should be carefully examined to determine how the transaction *was* recorded versus how it *should have been* recorded and then the appropriate journal entry to correct the error can be made.

LINK TO INTERNATIONAL DIFFERENCES

International accounting standards are similar to U.S. standards, but several differences exist. First, while both international and U.S. standards require errors to be corrected by restating previously issued financial statements, international standards allow an exception to this requirement. If restatement is impracticable for all prior periods, the error can be corrected by restating the financial statements for the earliest period practicable (which may be the current period). This exception could result in the correction of an error in a period other than that in which it initially occurred. Second, international standards do not address when the indirect effects of a change in accounting principle should be reported nor the disclosures required. Finally, the disclosure requirements of international standards for accounting changes and error corrections are considered less extensive than those required under U.S. standards.

SUMMARY OF EFFECTS ON FINANCIAL STATEMENTS

Exhibit 23-1 shows a summary of the effects of the retrospective adjustment, prior period restatement, and prospective adjustment methods on a company's financial statements.

EXHIBIT 23-1	Summary of Effects on Financial Statements of Methods Used for Accounting Changes and Errors

Retrospective Adjustment and Prior Period Restatement

Previous Years	Current Year
Income Statement	*Income Statement*
Change revenue and expense amounts to reflect new accounting principle, corrected information, or new accounting entity.	Compute revenue or expense amounts using new accounting principle, corrected information, or new accounting entity.
Balance Sheet	*Balance Sheet*
Change asset, liability, and stockholders' equity account balances to reflect amounts that would have been reported if the principle had always been used, the error had not been made, or the new entity had always existed.	No additional changes. Asset, liability, and stockholders' equity account balances are amounts that would have been computed if the new principle had always been used, the error had not been made, or the new entity had always existed.

Prospective Adjustment

Previous Years	Current Year
Income Statement	*Income Statement*
No change	Compute revenue and expense amounts using the new estimate or the newly adopted accounting principle for new events.
Balance Sheet	*Balance Sheet*
No change	Asset, liability, and stockholders' equity account balances include amounts based on the use of the old estimate or principle in past years and the new estimate or newly adopted principle for new events in the current (and future) year(s).

SUMMARY

At the beginning of the chapter, we identified several objectives you would accomplish after reading the chapter. The objectives are listed below, each followed by a brief summary of the key points in the chapter discussion.

1. **Identify the types of accounting changes.** The three types of accounting changes are a change in accounting principle, a change in accounting estimate, and a change in a reporting entity.
2. **Explain the methods of disclosing an accounting change.** There are two possible methods for a company to disclose an accounting change: the retrospective application of the new accounting principle, or adjust for the change prospectively.
3. **Account for a change in accounting principle using the retrospective adjustment method.** A company accounts for a change in accounting principle by the retrospective application of the new accounting principle to all prior periods as follows: (a) the company computes the cumulative effect of the change to the new accounting principle as of the beginning

of the first period presented, (b) it adjusts the carrying values of those assets and liabilities (including income taxes) that are affected by the change and makes an offsetting adjustment to the beginning balance of retained earnings to report the cumulative effect of the change (net of taxes) for each period presented, (c) it adjusts the financial statements of each prior period to reflect the specific effects of applying the new accounting principle, and (d) it makes related relevant disclosures in the notes to its financial statements.

4. **Account for a change in estimate**. A company accounts for a change in estimate in the period of the change if the change affects that period only, or the period of the change and future periods if the change affects both.

5. **Explain the conceptual issues regarding a change in accounting principle and a change in estimate**. The conceptual issues include the consistency of the information presented, the changing of previously reported information, the all-inclusive income concept, income manipulation, and any impact on contractual arrangements.

6. **Identify a change in a reporting entity**. A change in a reporting entity occurs mainly when a company presents consolidated or combined statements in place of statements of individual companies, there is a change in the specific subsidiaries that make up the group of companies for which the company presents consolidated statements, or the companies included in combined financial statements change.

7. **Account for a correction of an error**. A company accounts for a material error of a past period that it discovers in the current period as a prior period restatement (adjustment) as follows: (a) the company computes the cumulative effect of the error on periods prior to those presented, (b) it adjusts the carrying values of those assets and liabilities (including income taxes) that are affected by the error and makes an offsetting adjustment to the beginning balance of retained earnings to report the cumulative effect of the error correction (net of taxes) for each period presented, (c) it adjusts the financial statements of each prior period to reflect the specific effects of correcting the error, and (d) it makes related relevant disclosures in the notes to its financial statements.

8. **Summarize the methods for making accounting changes and correcting errors**. A summary of the methods for making accounting changes and correcting errors is included in Exhibit 23-1.

ANSWERS TO REAL REPORT QUESTIONS

Real Report 23-1 Answers

1. Darden Restaurants was not recognizing the expense related to its leases over the appropriate time period. Specifically, Darden recorded rent expense over the initial non-cancelable lease term. This initial lease term used in this calculation did not include any "rent holidays"—a period at the inception of the lease in which Darden had use of the leased asset but was not required to make payments—nor did it include any time periods associated with renewal options. Additionally, Darden depreciated its buildings (on leased land) and leasehold improvements (or other long-lived assets) over both the initial lease term plus any periods associated with renewal options. The correct procedure according to generally accepted accounting principles is to record rent expense over the initial lease term (which would include any "rent holidays") plus any periods where failure to renew the lease would result in an economic penalty, and to depreciate the assets over the shorter of the lease term plus any renewal periods or the expected life of the asset. The effect of these errors is described in the following answer.

2. The effect of these errors was to understate the total cost of the lease, which resulted in higher reported earnings. Because Darden did not include rent holidays in the initial non-cancelable lease term, rent expense was not recorded until actual payments were made. This delayed recognition of rent expense resulted in increased income. Furthermore, because a longer depreciation period was used, depreciation expense was understated, also leading to increased income. Darden corrected this error by restating its financial statements to reflect the proper recognition of expense over the initial non-cancelable lease term (which included any rent holidays) plus any renewal periods where failure to renew would result in an economic penalty. Furthermore, Darden corrected the period over which its buildings (on leased land) and leasehold improvements (or other long-lived assets) were depreciated. This restatement resulted in an increase in total liabilities in 2004 of $70,482 thousand. Furthermore, restaurant expenses for 2004 increased by $7,222 thousand and income taxes for 2004 decreased by $2,933 thousand. Together, this caused a decrease in 2004 earnings of $4,289 thousand.

QUESTIONS

Q23-1 Describe the three types of accounting changes.

Q23-2 Describe the two possible methods that a company could use to report the effect of accounting changes. Give one reason in favor of, and one against, each alternative.

Q23-3 Describe two situations in which a company could justify a change in an accounting principle.

Q23-4 What distinguishes a change in an accounting principle from a change in an estimate? How should a company account for each?

Q23-5 Give three examples of a change in an estimate. How does a company account for such changes?

Q23-6 In which situations may it be impracticable for a company to apply the retrospective adjustment method? What is the correct accounting in such cases?

Q23-7 How is a change in depreciation method accounted for? Why?

Q23-8 How does a company account for any indirect effects of a change in accounting principle?

Q23-9 How does a company account for the adoption of a new accounting principle for future events?

Q23-10 How does a company report a change in an accounting principle in its interim financial statements?

Q23-11 Describe a change in a reporting entity. How does a company account for such changes?

Q23-12 How does a company report an error of a prior period that it discovers in the current period?

Q23-13 Describe two errors that affect only a company's balance sheet.

Q23-14 Describe two errors that affect only a company's income statement.

Q23-15 Describe two errors that are counterbalanced in the following period.

Q23-16 Describe two errors that are not counterbalanced in the following period.

Q23-17 Why does a company correct errors even after they have counterbalanced?

MULTIPLE CHOICE (AICPA Adapted)

Select the best answer for each of the following.

M23-1 During 2007 White Company determined that machinery previously depreciated over a seven-year life had a total estimated useful life of only five years. An accounting change was made in 2007 to reflect the change in estimate. If the change had been made in 2006, accumulated depreciation at December 31, 2006 would have been $1,600,000 instead of $1,200,000. As a result of this change the 2007 depreciation expense was $100,000 greater. The income tax rate was 30% in both years. What should be reported in White's retained earnings statement for the year ended December 31, 2007 as the cumulative effect on prior years of changing the estimated useful life of the machinery?

a. $0
b. $280,000
c. $300,000
d. $400,000

Items 2 and 3 are based on the following information:

The Shannon Corporation began operations on January 1, 2007. Financial statements for the years ended December 31, 2007 and 2008 contained the following errors:

	December 31	
	2007	**2008**
Ending inventory	$16,000 understated	$15,000 overstated

Depreciation expense	$6,000 understated	—
Insurance expense	$10,000 overstated	$10,000 understated
Prepaid insurance	$10,000 understated	—

In addition, on December 31, 2008 fully depreciated machinery was sold for $10,800 cash, but the sale was not recorded until 2009. There were no other errors during 2007 or 2008 and no corrections have been made for any of the errors.

M23-2 Ignoring income taxes, what is the total effect of the errors on 2008 net income?

a. Net income understated by $1,800
b. Net income overstated by $5,800
c. Net income overstated by $11,000
d. Net income overstated by $30,200

M23-3 Ignoring income taxes, what is the total effect of the errors on the amount of working capital at December 31, 2008?

a. Working capital overstated by $4,200
b. Working capital understated by $5,800
c. Working capital understated by $6,000
d. Working capital understated by $9,800

M23-4 A change in the expected service life of an asset arising because additional information has been obtained is
a. An accounting change that should be reported by restating the financial statements of all prior periods represented
b. An accounting change that should be reported in the period of change and future periods if the change affects both
c. A correction of an error
d. Not an accounting change

M23-5 The cumulative effect of an accounting change on the amount of retained earnings at the beginning of the period in which the change is made should generally be included in the retained earnings statement for the period of the change for a

	Change in Accounting Principle	Change in Accounting Estimate
a.	Yes	Yes
b.	No	Yes
c.	Yes	No
d.	No	No

M23-6 On January 1, 2007 Belmont Company changed its inventory cost flow method to the FIFO cost method from the LIFO cost method. Belmont can justify the change, which was made for both financial statement and income tax reporting purposes. Belmont's inventories aggregated $4,000,000 on the LIFO basis at December 31, 2006. Supplementary records maintained by Belmont showed that the inventories would have totaled $4,800,000 at December 31, 2006 on the FIFO basis. Ignoring income taxes, the adjustment for the effect of changing to the FIFO method from the LIFO method should be reported by Belmont in the 2007
a. Income statement as an $800,000 debit
b. Retained earnings statement as an $800,000 debit adjustment to the beginning balance
c. Income statement as an $800,000 credit
d. Retained earnings statement as an $800,000 credit adjustment to the beginning balance

M23-7 When a cumulative effect-type change in accounting principle is made during the year, the cumulative effect on retained earnings is determined
a. During the year using the weighted average method
b. As of the date of the change
c. As of the beginning of the year in which the change is made
d. As of the end of the year in which the change is made

M23-8 Generally, how should a change in accounting principle that is affected by a change in accounting estimate be reported?

	Change in Accounting Estimate	Change in Accounting Principle
a.	No	No
b.	Yes	Yes
c.	No	Yes
d.	Yes	No

M23-9 On January 2, 2005 Garr Company acquired machinery at a cost of $320,000. This machinery was being depreciated by the double-declining-balance method over an estimated useful life of eight years, with no residual value. At the beginning of 2007 it was decided to change to the straight-line method of depreciation. Ignoring income tax considerations, the retrospective effect of this accounting change is
a. $0
b. $60,000
c. $65,000
d. $140,000

M23-10 A company has included in its consolidated financial statements this year a subsidiary acquired several years ago that was appropriately excluded from consolidation last year. This results in
a. An accounting change that should be reported prospectively
b. An accounting change that should be reported by retrospectively restating the financial statements of all prior periods presented
c. Neither an accounting change nor a correction of an error
d. A correction of an error

EXERCISES

E23-1 *Identification and Effects of Changes and Errors* The following are several independent events:
1. Change from the LIFO to the FIFO inventory cost flow assumption.
2. Reduction in remaining service life of machinery from 10 to 8 years.
3. A change from an accelerated method to the straight-line method of depreciating assets.
4. Write-down of inventories because of obsolescence.
5. Receipt of damages won in a court suit instigated five years ago.
6. Recording as an asset costs that were erroneously expensed in a previous period.
7. Write-down of property, plant, and equipment because of closure of inefficient plants.
8. A change from successful efforts to full cost accounting for oil exploration costs.

Required
Indicate how a company reports the preceding items (specify whether increases or decreases can generally be expected) in its financial statements of the current year.

E23-2 *Identification and Effects of Changes and Errors* The following are several independent events:
1. Change from the FIFO to the LIFO inventory cost flow assumption.
2. Write-off of patent due to the introduction of a competing product.
3. Payment to the Internal Revenue Service in settlement of a dispute over previous year's taxes.
4. Increase in allowance for uncollectible accounts from 2% to 4% of credit sales.
5. Change from straight-line to double-declining-balance method.
6. Write-down of an asset to reflect probable future losses.
7. A change from full cost to successful efforts accounting for oil exploration costs.

Required
Indicate how a company reports the preceding items (specify whether increases or decreases can generally be expected) in its financial statements of the current year.

E23-3 *Identification and Accounting for Changes and Errors* The following are several independent events:
1. A partnership is preparing to become a corporation and sell stock to the public. At this time, it is decided to switch from accelerated to straight-line depreciation.
2. A company has been debiting half its advertising costs to an intangible asset account and amortizing these costs over three years.
3. A company has been using accelerated depreciation. It now estimates that the pattern of benefits to be received in the future will be equal each period, so it decides to change to the straight-line depreciation method.
4. A company has been using straight-line depreciation in its property, plant, and equipment. It is now buying a new type of machine and elects to use accelerated depreciation on the new machines.
5. A company has been expensing all its manufacturing cost variances. It decides to allocate them between cost of goods sold and inventory in the future.

Required
Identify the correct accounting treatment for the changes (if any) related to the preceding events.

E23-4 *Change in Inventory Cost Flow Assumption* At the beginning of 2008 the Brett Company decided to change from the FIFO to the average cost inventory cost flow assumption for financial reporting purposes. The following data are available in regard to its pretax operating income and cost of goods sold:

Year	Reported Income Before Income Taxes	Excess of Average Cost of Goods Sold Over FIFO Cost of Goods Sold	Adjusted Income Before Income Taxes
Prior to 2007	$1,600,000	$130,000	$1,470,000
2007	600,000	50,000	550,000
2008	700,000		

The income tax rate is 30%, and the company received permission from the IRS to also make the change for income tax purposes. The company has a simple capital structure, with 100,000 shares of common stock outstanding. The company computed its reported income before income taxes in 2008 using the newly adopted inventory cost flow method. Brett's 2007 and 2008 revenues were $1,500,000 and $1,750,000, respectively. Its retained earnings balances at the beginning of 2007 and 2008 (unadjusted) were $1,120,000 and $1,540,000, respectively. The company paid no dividends in any year.

Required
1. Prepare the journal entry at the beginning of 2008 to reflect the change.
2. At the end of 2008 prepare comparative income statements for 2008 and 2007. Notes to the financial statements are not necessary.
3. At the end of 2008 prepare comparative retained earnings statements for 2008 and 2007.

E23-5 AICPA Adapted *Change in Inventory Cost Flow Assumption* The Berg Company began operations on January 1, 2007 and uses the FIFO method in costing its raw material inventory. During 2008 management is contemplating a change to the LIFO method and is interested in determining what effect such a change will have on net income. Accordingly, the following information has been developed:

	2007	2008
FIFO—Ending inventory	$240,000	$270,000
LIFO—Ending inventory	200,000	210,000
Income before income taxes (computed under the FIFO method)	120,000	170,000

Required
What is the effect on income before income taxes in 2008 of a change to the LIFO method?

E23-6 *Change in Inventory Method* The Fava Company began operations in 2006 and used the LIFO inventory method for both financial reporting and income taxes. At the beginning of 2007 the anticipated cost trends in the industry had changed, so that it adopted the FIFO method for both financial reporting and income taxes. The company reported revenues of $300,000 and $270,000 in 2007 and 2006, respectively. The company reported expenses (excluding income tax expense) of $125,000 and $120,000 in 2007 and 2006, which included cost of goods sold of $55,000 and $45,000, respectively. An analysis indicates that the FIFO cost of goods sold would have been lower by $8,000 in 2006. The tax rate is 30%. The company has a simple capital structure, with 15,000 shares of common stock outstanding during 2006 and 2007. It paid no dividends in either year.

Required

1. Prepare the journal entry to reflect the change.
2. At the end of 2007 prepare the comparative income statements for 2007 and 2006. Notes to the financial statements are not necessary.
3. At the end of 2007 prepare the comparative retained earnings statements for 2007 and 2006.

E23-7 *Change in Accounting for Construction Contracts* The Delta Company uses the completed-contract method of accounting for long-term construction contracts. The company started business in 2005 and prepared the following income statements:

	2005	2006
Construction revenue	$100,000	$300,000
Construction expense	(40,000)	(130,000)
Other expenses	(50,000)	(70,000)
Income before income taxes	$ 10,000	$100,000
Income tax expense (30%)	(3,000)	(30,000)
Net income	$ 7,000	$ 70,000
Earnings per share	$ 0.07	$ 0.70

The company changes to the percentage-of-completion method at the beginning of 2007. It determines the construction revenue and expense amounts under the percentage-of-completion method to be as follows:

	2005	2006	2007
Construction revenue	$200,000	$420,000	$900,000
Construction expense	80,000	182,000	420,000

The other expenses remain unchanged for 2005 and 2006, and are $80,000 in 2007. The company has not paid dividends on its 100,000 common shares outstanding. With the 2007 financial statements the company issues comparative statements for the previous two years. Under the completed-contract method, construction revenue and construction expense would be $600,000 and $280,000, respectively, in 2007. The company uses the percentage-of-completion method for income tax purposes.

Required

Prepare the income statements and the statements of retained earnings for 2007. Notes to the financial statements are not necessary.

E23-8 *Changes and Corrections of Depreciation* On January 1, 2002, the Klinefelter Company purchased a building for $520,000. The building had an estimated life of 20 years and an estimated residual value of $20,000. The company has been depreciating the building using straight-line depreciation. At the beginning of 2008, the following *independent* situations occur:

1. The company estimates that the building has a remaining life of 10 years (for a total of 16 years).
2. The company changes to the sum-of-the-years'-digits method. $n(n+1)/2$
3. The company discovers that it had ignored the estimated residual value in the computation of the annual depreciation each year.

Required

For each of the independent situations, prepare all of the journal entries related to the building for 2008. Ignore income taxes.

E23-9 *Journal Entries to Correct Errors* The following are several independent errors made by a company that uses the periodic inventory system:

1. Goods in transit, purchased on credit and shipped FOB destination, $10,000, were included in purchases but not in the ending inventory.
2. A purchase of a machine for $2,000 was expensed. The machine has a four-year life, no residual value, and straight-line depreciation is used.
3. Wages payable of $2,000 were not accrued.
4. Payment of next year's rent, $4,000, was recorded as rent expense.

5. Allowance for doubtful accounts of $5,000 was not recorded. The company normally uses the aging method.
6. Equipment with a book value of $70,000 and a fair value of $100,000 was sold at the beginning of the year. A two-year non-interest-bearing note for $129,960 was received and recorded at its face value. No interest revenue was recorded and 14% is a fair rate of interest.

Required

Prepare the correcting journal entry or entries for each of the preceding errors, assuming the company discovers the error in the year after it was made. (Ignore income taxes.)

E23-10 *Journal Entries to Correct Errors* Use the information in E23-9.

Required

Prepare the correcting journal entries if the company discovers each error two years after it is made and it has closed the books for the second year. (Ignore income taxes.)

E23-11 *Effects of Errors* The following are several independent errors made by a company:
1. Failure to record a purchase of inventory on credit.
2. Expensing the purchase of a machine.
3. Failure to accrue wages.
4. Failure to record an allowance for uncollectibles.
5. Including collections in advance as revenue.
6. Including payments in advance as expenses.
7. Failure to accrue warranty costs.
8. Discount on a note payable issued for purchase of a machine is ignored.
9. Failure to record depreciation expense on assets purchased during the year.

Required

Indicate the effect of each of the preceding errors on the company's (1) assets, (2) liabilities, (3) owners' equity, and (4) net income in the year in which the error occurs. State whether the error causes an overstatement ($+$), an understatement ($-$) (2), or no effect (NE).

E23-12 *Correcting Journal Entries for Errors* The following are several independent errors:
1. In January 2007 repair costs of $9,000 were debited to the Machinery account. At the beginning of 2007 the book value of the machinery was $100,000. No residual value is expected, the remaining estimated life is 10 years, and straight-line depreciation is used.
2. All purchases of materials for construction contracts still in progress have been immediately expensed. It is discovered that the use of these materials was $10,000 during 2006 and $12,000 during 2007.
3. Depreciation on manufacturing equipment has been excluded from manufacturing costs and treated as a period expense. During 2007, $40,000 of depreciation was accounted for in that manner. Production was 15,000 units during 2007, of which 3,000 remained in inventory at the end of the year. Assume there was no inventory at the beginning of 2007.

Required

Prepare journal entries for the preceding errors discovered during 2008. (Ignore income taxes.)

E23-13 *Omission of Accruals and Prepayments* The Dudley Company failed to recognize the following accruals. It also recorded the prepaid expenses and unearned revenues as expenses and revenues, respectively, in the year of payment or collection.

	2006	2007	2008
Prepaid expenses	$500	$ 900	$1,100
Accrued expenses	800	700	950
Revenue received in advance	300	400	1,300
Revenue earned but not received	600	1,000	1,200

The reported pretax income was $20,000 in 2006, $25,000 in 2007, and $23,000 in 2008.

Required
1. Compute the correct pretax income for 2006, 2007, and 2008.
2. Prepare the journal entries necessary in 2008 if the errors are discovered at the end of that year. Ignore income taxes.
3. Prepare the journal entries necessary in 2009 if the errors are discovered at the end of that year. Ignore income taxes.

PROBLEMS

P23-1 AICPA Adapted *Identification and Effects of Changes and Errors* On January 2, 2007, Quo, Inc. hired Reed as its controller. During the year, Reed, working closely with Quo's president and outside accountants, made changes in accounting policies, corrected several errors dating from 2006 and before, and instituted new accounting policies. Quo's 2007 financial statements will be presented in comparative form with its 2006 financial statements. Items 1 through 10 represent Quo's transactions.

1. Quo manufactures heavy equipment to customer specifications on a contract basis. On the basis that it is preferable, it switched accounting for these long-term contracts from the completed-contact method to the percentage-of-completion method.
2. As a result of a production breakthrough, Quo determined that manufacturing equipment previously depreciated over 15 years should be depreciated over 20 years.
3. The equipment that Quo manufactures is sold with a five-year warranty. Because of a production breakthrough, Quo reduced its computation of warranty costs from 3% of sales to 1% of sales.
4. Quo changed from LIFO to FIFO to account for its finished goods inventory.
5. Quo sells extended service contracts on its products. Because related services are performed over several years, in 2007 Quo changed from the cash method to the accrual method of recognizing income from these service contracts.
6. During 2007 Quo determined that an insurance premium paid and entirely expensed in 2006 was for the period January 1, 2006 through January 1, 2008.
7. Quo changed its method of depreciating office equipment from an accelerated method to the straight-line method to more closely reflect the pattern of benefits.
8. Quo instituted a pension plan for all employees in 2007 and adopted Statement of Financial Accounting Standards No. 87, *Employers' Accounting for Pensions*. Quo had not previously had a pension plan.
9. During 2007, Quo increased its investment in Worth, Inc. from a 10% interest, purchased in 2006, to 60%. As a result of its increased investment, Quo changed its method of accounting for investment in subsidiary from the fair value method to the consolidation method.

Required

1. Indicate whether Quo should classify each transaction as: (a) a change in accounting principle, (b) a change in accounting estimate, (c) a correction of an error in previously presented financial statements, or (d) neither an accounting change nor an accounting error.
2. Indicate the accounting treatment for each transaction as: (a) a retrospective adjusment approach, (b) a prior period restatement approach, or (c) a prospective approach.

P23-2 *Changes in Inventory Cost Flow Assumption* At the beginning of 2008 the Flynne Company decided to change from the LIFO to the FIFO inventory cost flow assumption. The following data are available:

Year	Reported Income Before Income Taxes	Excess of LIFO Cost of Goods Sold Over FIFO Cost of Goods Sold	Adjusted Income Before Income Taxes
Prior to 2007	$240,000	$42,000	$282,000
2007	80,000	18,000	98,000
2008	70,000	16,000	

The tax rate is 30%. The company has a simple capital structure and 10,000 shares of common stock outstanding. Assume that the balance in retained earnings is the sum of the company's reported income amounts (net of tax) and that the reported income before income taxes in 2008 uses the newly adopted method. Flynne's revenues for 2007 and 2008 were $225,000 and $230,000, respectively. Flynne's operating expenses (other than cost of goods sold) for 2007 and 2008 were $32,000 and $40,000, respectively.

Required

1. Prepare the journal entry at the beginning of 2008 to reflect the change.
2. At the end of 2008, prepare comparative income statements for 2008 and 2007.
3. At the end of 2008, prepare comparative retained earnings statements for 2008 and 2007.
4. Prepare a note to the comparative financial statements that discusses the nature and reason for the change from LIFO to FIFO and discloses the effects of the change on the company's income statements for 2007 and 2008. (Ignore the effects on the balance sheet and statement of cash flows because there is insufficient information to calculate these changes.)
5. Explain how your answer to Requirement 2 would change if the employees received a bonus of 10% of income before deducting the bonus and income taxes, and the company paid additional bonuses for prior years in 2008.

P23-3 *Change from FIFO to Average Cost* Koopman Company began operations on January 1, 2006 and uses the FIFO inventory method for financial reporting and the average-cost inventory method for income taxes. At the beginning of 2008 the company decided to switch to the average-cost inventory method for financial reporting. The company had previously reported the following financial statements for 2007:

Income Statement

	2007
Revenues	$100,000
Cost of goods sold	(60,000)
Gross profit	$ 40,000
Operating expenses	(25,000)
Income before income taxes	$ 15,000
Income tax expense	(4,500)
Net income	$ 10,500
Earnings per share	$ 1.05

Retained Earnings Statement

	2007
Beginning retained earnings	$15,000
Add: Net income	10,500
	$25,500
Less: Dividends	(6,000)
Ending retained earnings	$19,500

Balance Sheet (12/31/07)

Cash	$ 9,000	Accounts payable	$ 3,000
Inventory	38,000	Income taxes payable	1,800
Other assets	64,100	Deferred tax liability	4,800
		Common stock, no par	82,000
		Retained earnings	19,500
	$ 111,100		$111,100

An analysis of the accounting records discloses the following cost of goods sold under the FIFO and average-cost inventory methods:

	FIFO Cost of Goods Sold	Average Cost of Goods Sold
2006	$50,000	$57,000
2007	60,000	69,000
2008	70,000	80,000

There are no indirect effects of the change in inventory method. Revenues for 2008 total $130,000; operating expenses for 2008 total $30,000. The company is subject to a 30% income tax rate in all years; it pays the income taxes payable of a current year in the first quarter of the next year. The company had 10,000 shares of common stock outstanding during all years; it paid dividends of $1 per share in 2008. At the end of 2008 the company had cash of $10,000, inventory of $24,000, other assets of $70,800, and accounts payable of ?. The company desires to show financial statements for the current year and previous year in its 2008 annual report.

Required

1. Prepare the journal entry to reflect the change in methods at the beginning of 2008. Show supporting calculations.
2. Prepare the 2008 annual report. Notes to the financial statements are not necessary. Show supporting calculations.

P23-4 *Change from LIFO to Average Cost* Schmidt Company began operations on January 1, 2006 and used the LIFO inventory method for both financial reporting and income taxes. However, at the beginning of 2008 the company decided to switch to the average-cost inventory method for financial and income tax reporting. The company had previously reported the following financial statements for 2007:

Income Statement

	2007
Revenues	$128,000
Cost of goods sold	(78,000)
Gross profit	$ 50,000
Operating expenses	(25,000)
Income before income taxes	$ 25,000
Income tax expense	(7,500)
Net income	$ 17,500
Earnings per share	$ 1.75

Retained Earnings Statement

	2007
Beginning retained earnings	$27,000
Add: Net income	17,500
	$44,500
Less: Dividends	(6,000)
Ending retained earnings	$38,500

Balance Sheet (12/31/07)

Cash	$ 8,000	Accounts payable	$ 4,000
Inventory	42,000	Income taxes payable	7,500
Other assets	60,000	Common stock, no par	60,000
		Retained earnings	38,500
	$110,000		$110,000

An analysis of the accounting records discloses the following cost of goods sold under the LIFO and average-cost inventory methods:

	LIFO Cost of Goods Sold	Average Cost of Goods Sold		
2006	$62,000	$56,000	6k	6k
2007	78,000	69,000	9k	15k
2008	90,000	80,000	10k	25k more

There are no indirect effects of the change in inventory method. Revenues for 2008 total $130,000; operating expenses for 2008 total $30,000. The company is subject to a 30% income tax rate in all years; it pays all income taxes payable in the next quarter. The company had 10,000 shares of common stock outstanding during all years; it paid dividends of $1 per share in 2008. At the end of 2008 the company had cash of $12,000, inventory of $34,000, other assets of $76,000, income taxes payable of $6,000, and accounts payable of ?. The company desires to show financial statements for the current year and previous year in its 2008 annual report.

Required

1. Prepare the journal entry to reflect the change in method at the beginning of 2008. Show supporting calculations.
2. Prepare the 2008 annual report. Notes to the financial statements are not necessary. Show supporting calculations.

P23-5 *Change in Accounting for Construction Contracts* Since the Goode Construction Company was formed in 2006, it has used the completed-contract method for financial reporting, but at the beginning of 2008 it changes to the percentage-of-completion method. The company previously had reported the following pretax income:

	2006	2007	
Sales of completed contracts	$300,000	$800,000	820k
Less: Cost of completed contracts	(200,000)	(550,000)	350k
Gross profit	$100,000	$250,000	470k × 20%
			74k

Analysis of the accounting records discloses that the company earned the following gross profit on each of its projects based on the percentage-of-completion method:

	2006	2007	2008
Project A	$100,000	—	—
Project B	120,000	$125,000	—
Project C	—	75,000	$400,000
	220k	200k	400k

In 2008 the company would have reported sales and cost of completed contracts of $820,000 and $350,000, respectively, under the completed-contract method. The tax rate is 30%. The company has a simple capital structure, with 100,000 shares of common stock outstanding. It paid no dividends. Ignore other expenses (i.e., gross profit is income before income taxes). The company uses the percentage-of-completion method for income taxes.

Required

1. Prepare the journal entry to reflect the change in method at the beginning of 2008.
2. If the company also presents the 2006 and 2007 financial statements for comparative purposes, prepare the income statement disclosures (starting with income before income taxes) and retained earnings disclosures that are required in 2008.
3. What items (if any) would be restated on the financial statements?

P23-6 *Changes and Corrections of Depreciation* At the beginning of 2008, the controller of Holden Company asked you to prepare correcting entries for the following three situations:

1. Machine X was purchased for $100,000 on January 1, 2003. Straight-line depreciation has been recorded for five years, and the Accumulated Depreciation account has a balance of $45,000. The estimated residual value remains at $10,000, but the service life is now estimated to be one year longer than originally estimated.
2. Machine Y was purchased for $40,000 on January 1, 2006. It had an estimated residual value of $4,000 and an estimated service life of eight years. It has been depreciated under the sum-of-the-years'-digits method for two years. Now, the company has decided to change to the straight-line method.
3. Machine Z was purchased for $80,000 on January 1, 2007. Double-declining-balance depreciation has been recorded for one year. The estimated residual value is $8,000 and the estimated service life is five years. The computation of the depreciation erroneously included the estimated residual value.

Required

Prepare any necessary correcting journal entries for each situation. Also prepare the journal entry for each situation to record the depreciation for 2008. (Ignore income taxes.)

P23-7 **AICPA Adapted** *Change in Accounting for Inventory* The Kraft Manufacturing Company manufactures two products: Mult and Tran. At December 31, 2007 Kraft used the FIFO inventory method. Effective January 1, 2008, Kraft changed to the LIFO inventory method. The cumulative effect of this change is not determinable and, as a result, the ending inventory of 2007, for which the FIFO method was used, is also the beginning inventory for 2008 for the LIFO method. Any layers added during 2008 should be costed by reference to the first acquisitions of 2008, and any layers liquidated during 2008 should be considered a permanent liquidation.

The following information was available from Kraft's inventory records for the two most recent years:

	Mult		Tran	
	Units	**Unit Cost**	**Units**	**Unit Cost**
2007 purchases:				
January 7	5,000	$4.00	22,000	$2.00
April 17	12,000	4.50		
November 9	17,000	5.00	18,500	2.50
December 14	10,000	6.00		
2008 purchases:				
February 12	3,000	7.00	23,000	3.00
May 21	8,000	7.50		
October 15	20,000	8.00		
December 24			15,500	3.50
Units on hand:				
December 31, 2007	15,000		14,500	
December 31, 2008	16,000		13,000	

Required

Compute the effect on income before income taxes for the year ended December 31, 2008, resulting from the change from the FIFO to the LIFO inventory method.

P23-8 *First Issuance of Financial Statements* The Jackson Company has decided to issue common stock to the public in 2008. This will be the first public sale and therefore the company will issue its first publicly available financial statements since it was formed in 2005. The financial statements that it has prepared for its own use follow:

Income Statements

	For Years Ended December 31,		
	2005	**2006**	**2007**
Sales	$100,000	$130,000	$180,000
Cost of goods sold	(35,000)	(45,000)	(65,000)
Gross profit	$ 65,000	$ 85,000	$115,000
Other expenses	(62,500)	(75,000)	(83,200)
Income before income taxes	$ 2,500	$ 10,000	$ 31,800
Income tax expense	(750)	(3,000)	(9,540)
Net income	$ 1,750	$ 7,000	$ 22,260

Balance Sheets

	December 31		
	2005	**2006**	**2007**
Cash	$ 5,500	$ 12,500	$ 9,960
Accounts receivable	30,000	50,000	63,000
Inventory	40,000	60,000	65,000
Equipment	100,000	100,000	140,000
Less: Accumulated depreciation	(20,000)	(52,000)	(79,200)
	$155,500	$170,500	$198,760
Current liabilities	$ 19,250	$ 27,250	$ 33,250
Notes payable	50,000	50,000	50,000
Common stock	84,500	84,500	84,500
Retained earnings	1,750	8,750	31,010
	$155,500	$170,500	$198,760

These financial statements are audited for the first time at the beginning of 2008, and the following facts are discovered:

1. The company has not made any allowance for noncollection of accounts receivable. An allowance of 1% of total sales is considered appropriate. Uncollectible accounts of $630 should have been written off in 2007.
2. The notes payable are to officers of the company and have an interest rate of 12%. They were issued on January 1, 2005. No interest has been accrued or paid. (Assume simple interest and no compounding.)
3. The company has been using MACRS over a five-year life for both financial reporting and income tax purposes. It has been decided that the straight-line method should have been used for financial reporting, based on an economic life of 10 years and a zero residual value, with a full year's depreciation being recorded in the year of acquisition. No disposals of property, plant, and equipment have occurred.
4. After adjustments, with the exception of depreciation, expenses deducted for financial accounting purposes are the same as those deducted for income tax purposes.
5. The company is subject to a 30% income tax rate and pays its taxes at the end of each year.

Required

1. Prepare the financial statements for 2005, 2006, and 2007 that the company would issue at the beginning of 2008.
2. Describe what method the company would use to account for each item if the financial statements for all three years had been publicly issued previously.

P23-9 *Error Correction* At the end of 2008 while auditing the books of the Sandlin Company, *before* the books have been closed, you find the following items:

a. A building with a 30-year life (no residual value, straight-line depreciation) was purchased on January 1, 2008 by issuing a $90,000 non-interest-bearing, four-year note. The entry made to record the purchase was a debit to Building and a credit to Notes Payable for $90,000; 12% is a fair rate of interest on the note.
b. The inventory at the end of 2008 was found to be overstated by $15,000. At the same time it was discovered that the inventory at the end of 2007 had been overstated by $35,000. The company uses the perpetual inventory system.
c. For the last three years, the company has failed to accrue salaries and wages. The correct amounts at the end of each year were: 2006—$12,000; 2007—$18,000; 2008—$10,000.

Required

1. Prepare journal entries to correct the errors (ignore income taxes).
2. Assume, instead, that the company discovered the errors *after* it had closed the books. Prepare journal entries to correct the errors (ignore income taxes).

P23-10 *Error Correction* At the beginning of 2008 Tanham Company discovered the following errors made in the preceding two years:

	2006	2007
Overstatement of ending inventory	$5,000	$2,000
Omission of wages payable	700	800
Omission of allowance for doubtful accounts	1,300	1,700
Prepayment of insurance recorded as expense	500	200

Reported net income was $27,000 in 2006 and $35,000 in 2007. The allowance for doubtful accounts had a zero balance at the beginning of 2006. No accounts were written off during 2006 or 2007. Ignore income taxes.

Required

1. What is the correct net income for 2006 and 2007?
2. Prepare the adjusting journal entry in 2008 to correct the errors.

P23-11 *Error Correction* A review of the books of the Anderson Corporation indicates that the errors and omissions pertaining to the balance sheet accounts shown as follows had not been corrected during the applicable years.

The net income per the books is: 2005—$10,000; 2006—$12,000; 2007—$15,000; and 2008—$20,000. No dividends were declared during these years and no adjustments were made to retained earnings. The Retained Earnings balance on December 31, 2008, is $50,000.

December 31	Ending Inventory Overvalued	Ending Inventory Undervalued	Omissions			
			Prepaid Expense	Unearned Revenues	Accrued Expense	Accrued Revenues
2005	$ —	$4,000	$600	$ —	$300	$ —
2006	3,000	—	—	500	—	700
2007	2,000	—	400	—	100	—
2008	—	1,000	900	200	350	800

Required 🖾

Prepare a worksheet to determine the correct net income for the years 2005, 2006, 2007, and 2008, and the adjusted balance sheet accounts as of December 31, 2008. (Ignore possible income tax effects.)

P23-12 *Error Correction* The bookkeeper of the Cask Company, who has maintained its accounting records since the company's formation in January 2005, has prepared the unaudited financial statements. In your examination of these statements at the end of 2007, you discover the following items:

1. Sales taxes collected from customers have been included in the sales account. The Sales Tax Expense account is debited when the sales taxes are remitted to the state in the month following the sale. All sales are subject to a 6% sales tax. Total sales (excluding sales tax) for the three years 2005 through 2007 were $200,000, $300,000, and $500,000, respectively. The Sales Tax Expense account balance for the three years was $10,000, $15,000, and $26,000, respectively.
2. An account payable of $15,000 for merchandise purchased in December 2005 was recorded in January 2006. The merchandise was not included in inventory at December 31, 2005.
3. Merchandise with a cost of $4,000 was included twice in the December 31, 2006 inventory.
4. The company has used the direct write-off method of accounting for bad debts. Accounts written off in the three years 2005 through 2007 were $2,000, $4,500, and $6,500, respectively. The appropriate balances of Allowance for Doubtful Accounts at the end of 2005 through 2007 are $5,000, $6,000, and $8,200, respectively.
5. On January 1, 2006, 12%, 10-year bonds with a face value of $600,000 were issued at 102. The premium was credited to Additional Paid-in Capital. The bonds pay interest on June 30 and December 31, and use of the straight-line amortization method is appropriate.
6. Travel advances to the sales personnel of $18,000 were included as selling expenses for 2006. The travel occurred in 2007.
7. Salaries payable at the end of each year have not been accrued. Appropriate amounts at the end of 2005 through 2007 are $10,000, $11,000, and $7,000, respectively.
8. Installation, freight, and testing costs of $25,000 on a machine purchased in January 2005 were expensed at that time. The machine has a life of five years and a residual value of $10,000.

Required

Analyze the effects of the errors on income for 2005, 2006, and 2007, and the 2007 ending balance sheet (ignore income taxes), according to the following format:

Explanation	Income 2005		Income 2006		Income 2007		Balance Sheet December 31, 2007		
								Amount	
	Debit	Credit	Debit	Credit	Debit	Credit	Debit	Credit	Account

P23-13 **AICPA Adapted** *Comprehensive* The financial statements of the Gray Company showed income before income taxes of $4,030,000 for the year ended December 31, 2008, and $3,330,000 for the year ended December 31, 2007. Additional information is as follows:

1. Capital expenditures were $2,800,000 in 2008 and $4,000,000 in 2007. Included in the 2008 capital expenditures is equipment purchased for $1,000,000 on January 1, 2008, with no salvage value. Gray used straight-line depreciation based on a 10-year estimated life in its financial statements. As a result of additional information now available, it is estimated that this equipment should have only an eight-year life.
2. Gray made an error in its financial statements that should be regarded as material. A payment of $180,000 was made in January 2008 and charged to expense in 2008 for insurance premiums applicable to policies commencing and expiring in 2007. No liability had been recorded for this item at December 31, 2007.
3. The allowance for doubtful accounts reflected in Gray's financial statements was $7,000 at December 31, 2008, and $97,000 at December 31, 2007. During 2008, $90,000 of uncollectible receivables were written off against the allowance for doubtful accounts. In 2007, the provision for doubtful accounts was based on a percentage of net sales. The 2008 provision has not yet been recorded. Net sales were $58,500,000 for the year ended December 31, 2008, and $49,230,000 for the year ended December 31, 2007. Based on the latest available facts, the 2008 provision for doubtful accounts is estimated to be 0.2% of net sales.
4. A review of the estimated warranty liability at December 31, 2008, which is included in "other liabilities" in Gray's financial statements, has disclosed that this estimated liability should be increased $170,000.
5. Gray has two large blast furnaces that it uses in its manufacturing process. These furnaces must be periodically relined. Furnace A was relined in January 2002 at a cost of $230,000 and in January 2007 at a cost of $280,000. Furnace B was relined for the first time in January 2008 at a cost of $300,000. In Gray's financial statements, these costs were expensed as incurred.

Since a relining will last for five years, a more appropriate matching of revenues and costs would result if the cost of the relining were capitalized and depreciated over the productive life of the relining. Gray has decided to make a change in accounting principle from expensing relining costs as incurred to capitalizing them and depreciating them over their productive life on a straight-line basis with a full year's depreciation in the year of relining. This change meets the requirements for a change in accounting principle under *FASB Statement No. 154*, "Accounting Changes and Error Corrections."

Required

1. For the years ended December 31, 2008 and 2007, prepare a worksheet reconciling income before income taxes as given previously with income before income taxes, as adjusted for the preceding additional information. Show supporting computations in good form. Ignore income taxes and deferred tax considerations in your answer. The worksheet should have the following format:

	Year Ended December 31	
	2008	**2007**
Income before income taxes, before adjustments	$4,030,000	$3,330,000
Adjustments		
Net adjustments		
Income before income taxes, after adjustments	$	$

2. As of January 1, 2008, compute the retrospective adjustment of retained earnings for the cumulative effect of the change in accounting principle from expensing to capitalizing relining costs. Ignore income taxes and deferred tax considerations in your answer.

P23-14 **AICPA Adapted** *Comprehensive* The Ingalls Corporation is in the process of negotiating a loan for expansion purposes. The books and records have never been audited, and the bank has requested that an audit be performed. Ingalls has prepared the following comparative financial statements for the years ended December 31, 2008 and 2007:

Balance Sheet

	As of December 31,	
	2008	**2007**
Assets		
Current assets		
Cash	$163,000	$ 82,000
Accounts receivable	392,000	296,000
Allowance for uncollectible accounts	(37,000)	(18,000)
Available-for-sale securities	78,000	78,000
Merchandise inventory	207,000	202,000
Total current assets	803,000	640,000
Fixed assets		
Property, plant, and equipment	167,000	169,500
Accumulated depreciation	(121,600)	(106,400)
Total fixed assets	45,400	63,100
Total assets	$848,400	$703,100
Liabilities and Stockholders' Equity		
Liabilities		
Accounts payable	$121,400	$196,100
Stockholders' equity		
Common stock, par value $10, authorized 50,000 shares, issued and outstanding 20,000 shares	260,000	260,000
Retained earnings	467,000	247,000
Total stockholders' equity	727,000	507,000
Total liabilities and stockholders' equity	$848,400	$703,100

Statement of Income

	For the Years Ended December 31,	
	2008	2007
Sales	$1,000,000	$900,000
Cost of sales	(430,000)	(395,000)
Gross profit	570,000	505,000
Operating expenses	210,000	205,000
Administrative expenses	140,000	105,000
	(350,000)	(310,000)
Net income	$ 220,000	$195,000

During the course of the audit, the following additional facts were determined:

1. An analysis of collections and losses on accounts receivable during the past two years indicates a drop in anticipated losses because of bad debts. After consultation with management, it was agreed that the loss experience rate on sales should be reduced from the recorded 2% to 1%, beginning with the year ended December 31, 2008.
2. An analysis of the available-for-sale securities revealed that this portfolio consisted entirely of short-term investments in marketable equity securities that were acquired in 2007. The total market valuation for these investments as of the end of each year was as follows: December 31, 2007—$81,000; December 31, 2008—$62,000.
3. The merchandise inventory at December 31, 2007 was overstated by $4,000 and the merchandise inventory at December 31, 2008 was overstated by $6,100.
4. On January 2, 2007, equipment costing $12,000 (estimated useful life of 10 years and residual value of $1,000) was incorrectly charged to Operating Expenses. Ingalls records depreciation via the straight-line method. In 2008, fully depreciated equipment (with no residual value) that originally cost $17,500 was sold as scrap for $2,500. Noble credited the proceeds of $2,500 to Property and Equipment.
5. An analysis of 2007 operating expenses revealed that Ingalls charged to expense a three-year insurance premium of $2,700 on January 15, 2007.

Required

1. Prepare the journal entries to correct the books at December 31, 2008. The books for 2008 have not been closed. Ignore income taxes.
2. Prepare a schedule showing the computation of corrected net income for the years ended December 31, 2008 and 2007, assuming that any adjustments are to be reported on comparative statements for the two years. The first items on your schedule should be the net income for each year. Ignore income taxes. (Do not prepare financial statements.)

CASES

COMMUNICATION

C23-1 Accounting Changes

There are three types of accounting changes: changes in accounting principles, changes in accounting estimates, and changes in reporting entities.

Required

Explain the differences and similarities between each of these types of changes, and explain the correct accounting for each. Include a discussion of the advantages and disadvantages of the required accounting method.

C23-2 Accounting Changes

AICPA Adapted   The various types of accounting changes may significantly affect the presentation of a company's financial statements, and also affect the trends shown in its comparative financial statements and historical summaries.

Required

1. Explain a change in accounting principle and how a company reports it in the period of the change.
2. Explain a change in accounting estimate and how a company reports it in the period of the change.
3. Explain a change in reporting entity and how a company reports it. Give an appropriate example of a change in reporting entity.

C23-3 Accounting Changes

AICPA Adapted Berkeley Company, a manufacturer of many different products, changed its inventory method from FIFO to LIFO. The LIFO method was determined to be preferable.

In addition, Berkeley changed the residual values used in computing depreciation for its office equipment. It made this change on January 1, 2007 because it obtained additional information.

On December 31, 2007, Berkeley changed the specific subsidiaries comprising the group of companies for which consolidated financial statements are presented.

Required
1. What kind of accounting change is each of the preceding three situations? For each situation, indicate whether or not the company should show:
   a. The retrospective application of a new accounting principle.
   b. The effects on the financial statements of the current and future periods.
   c. Restatement of the financial statements of all prior periods.
2. Why does the company have to disclose a change in accounting principle?

CREATIVE AND CRITICAL THINKING

C23-4 Transition Methods for a Change in Accounting Principle

When the FASB issues a new *Statement*, it may require companies to apply the new principle prospectively, or to account for the change by the retrospective adjustment method.

Required

Why do you think that the FASB requires one of two different transition methods when a company adopts a newly required accounting principle? Do you agree with the use of two alternative methods?

C23-5 Accounting Changes

AICPA Adapted Sometimes a business entity may change its method of accounting for certain items. It may classify the change as a change in accounting principle, a change in accounting estimate, or a change in reporting entity.

The following are three independent, unrelated sets of facts relating to accounting changes.

Situation I A company determined that the depreciable lives of its fixed assets are presently too long to fairly match the cost of the fixed assets with the revenue produced. The company decided at the beginning of the current year to reduce the depreciable lives of all of its existing fixed assets by five years.

Situation II On December 31, 2009, Hyde Company owned 51% of Patten Company, at which time Hyde reported its investment using the cost method, owing to political uncertainties in the country in which Patten was located. On January 2, 2007, the management of Hyde Company was satisfied that the political uncertainties were resolved and the assets of the company were in no danger of nationalization. Accordingly, Hyde will prepare consolidated financial statements for Hyde and Patten for the year ended December 31, 2007.

Situation III A company decides in January 2007 to adopt the straight-line method of depreciation for plant equipment. The straight-line method will be used for new acquisitions, as well as for previously acquired plant equipment for which depreciation had been provided on an accelerated basis.

Required

For each of the preceding situations, provide the following information. Complete your discussion of each situation before going on to the next situation.
1. Type of accounting change.
2. Manner of reporting the change under current generally accepted accounting principles, including a discussion, where applicable, of how amounts are computed.
3. Effect of the change on the statement of financial position and earnings statement.
4. Note disclosures that would be necessary.

C23-6 Accounting Changes

AICPA Adapted It is important in accounting theory to be able to distinguish the types of accounting changes.

Required
1. If a public company desires to change from the sum-of-the-years'-digits depreciation method to the straight-line method for its fixed assets, what type of accounting change would this be? Discuss the permissibility of this change.
2. If a public company obtained additional information about the service lives of some of its fixed assets that showed that the service lives previously used should be shortened, what type of accounting change would this be? Include in your discussion how the change is reported in the year of the change, and what disclosures are made in the financial statements or notes.
3. If a company discovers halfway through a building's life that it ignored the residual value of the building in computing the straight-line depreciation, what type of accounting change would this be? Include in your discussion how the change is reported in the year of the change, and what disclosures are made in the financial statements or notes.
4. Changing specific subsidiaries comprising the group of companies for which consolidated financial statements are presented is an example of what type of accounting change? What effect does it have on the consolidated income statements?

C23-7 Ethics, Enron, Arthur Andersen, and Accounting Changes

In 2001, Enron Corporation filed financial statements in which it did not consolidate various Special Purpose Entities, thereby keeping large amounts of debt off its balance sheet. The company has since declared bankruptcy and admitted that it violated GAAP. Enron's auditor, Arthur Andersen LLP, issued an unqualified audit opinion stating that Enron had followed GAAP. Instead Enron should have changed its accounting principles to conform to GAAP, and Andersen should not have issued an unqualified opinion.

The U.S. Department of Justice began an investigation of Enron and Arthur Andersen. Some employees of Arthur Andersen shredded certain documents related to the audit. As a result the firm was found guilty of obstruction of justice and therefore was no longer able to perform audits. Only a few of the Arthur Andersen partners and employees were involved in the audit and even fewer in the shredding. However, thousands of Arthur Andersen employees lost their jobs.

Required

From an ethical perspective, discuss whether the actions of the Department of Justice were fair with regard to the employees of Arthur Andersen.

C23-8 Ethics and Accounting Changes and Errors

You are auditing the financial records of a company and reviewing the property, plant, and equipment records. Included in the assets are two buildings and numerous machines in each building. One of the buildings is used to manufacture components of toys; the other is used for assembly and packing, using the manufactured components as well as others purchased from suppliers. You see that the company has changed from the straight-line to the double-declining-balance depreciation method at the beginning of the year. You also discover that a $90,000 repair was added to the cost of the building in the previous year. You decide to ask the CFO about these calculations and she replies, "We decided to change the depreciation method because toys have such short lives and get obsolete so fast. You know how kids always want the latest fad. And that is partly why we are also going to recognize an asset impairment of $150,000 this year. And, as for that $90,000, those repairs should make the building last longer. But, anyway, the amount wasn't material to our depreciation calculations." As you walk back to your office, you recall from earlier in the audit that the company uses LIFO for its inventory and that income before income taxes has been around $1 million for each of the last several years.

Required

From financial reporting and ethical perspectives, discuss the issues raised by this situation.

The Coca-Cola Company 2004 Financial Statements and Supplementary Data

a

61   Consolidated Statements of Income

62   Consolidated Balance Sheets

64   Consolidated Statements of Cash Flows

65   Consolidated Statements of Shareowners' Equity

66   Notes to Consolidated Financial Statements

115   Report of Management on Internal Control Over Financial Reporting

116   Report of Independent Registered Public Accounting Firm

117   Report of Independent Registered Public Accounting Firm on Internal Control Over Financial Reporting

118   Quarterly Data (Unaudited)

ITEM 8. FINANCIAL STATEMENTS AND SUPPLEMENTARY DATA

TABLE OF CONTENTS

Page

Consolidated Statements of Income 61

Consolidated Balance Sheets 62

Consolidated Statements of Cash Flows 64

Consolidated Statements of Shareowners' Equity 65

Notes to Consolidated Financial Statements 66

Report of Management on Internal Control Over Financial Reporting 115

Report of Independent Registered Public Accounting Firm 116

Report of Independent Registered Public Accounting Firm on Internal Control Over
Financial Reporting 117

Quarterly Data (Unaudited) 118

CONSOLIDATED STATEMENTS OF INCOME

The Coca-Cola Company and Subsidiaries

Year Ended December 31,	2004	2003	2002
(In millions except per share data)			
NET OPERATING REVENUES	**$ 21,962**	$ 21,044	$ 19,564
Cost of goods sold	**7,638**	7,762	7,105
GROSS PROFIT	**14,324**	13,282	12,459
Selling, general and administrative expenses	**8,146**	7,488	7,001
Other operating charges	**480**	573	—
OPERATING INCOME	**5,698**	5,221	5,458
Interest income	**157**	176	209
Interest expense	**196**	178	199
Equity income — net	**621**	406	384
Other income (loss) — net	**(82)**	(138)	(353)
Gains on issuances of stock by equity investees	**24**	8	—
INCOME BEFORE INCOME TAXES AND CUMULATIVE EFFECT OF ACCOUNTING CHANGE	**6,222**	5,495	5,499
Income taxes	**1,375**	1,148	1,523
NET INCOME BEFORE CUMULATIVE EFFECT OF ACCOUNTING CHANGE	**4,847**	4,347	3,976
Cumulative effect of accounting change for SFAS No. 142, net of income taxes:			
Company operations	**—**	—	(367)
Equity investees	**—**	—	(559)
NET INCOME	**$ 4,847**	$ 4,347	$ 3,050
BASIC NET INCOME PER SHARE:			
Before accounting change	**$ 2.00**	$ 1.77	$ 1.60
Cumulative effect of accounting change	**—**	—	(0.37)
	$ 2.00	$ 1.77	$ 1.23
DILUTED NET INCOME PER SHARE:			
Before accounting change	**$ 2.00**	$ 1.77	$ 1.60
Cumulative effect of accounting change	**—**	—	(0.37)
	$ 2.00	$ 1.77	$ 1.23
AVERAGE SHARES OUTSTANDING	**2,426**	2,459	2,478
Effect of dilutive securities	**3**	3	5
AVERAGE SHARES OUTSTANDING ASSUMING DILUTION	**2,429**	2,462	2,483

Refer to Notes to Consolidated Financial Statements.

CONSOLIDATED BALANCE SHEETS

The Coca-Cola Company and Subsidiaries

December 31,	2004	2003
(In millions)		
ASSETS		
CURRENT		
Cash and cash equivalents	$ 6,707	$ 3,362
Marketable securities	61	120
	6,768	3,482
Trade accounts receivable, less allowances of $69 in 2004 and $61 in 2003	2,171	2,091
Inventories	1,420	1,252
Prepaid expenses and other assets	1,735	1,571
TOTAL CURRENT ASSETS	12,094	8,396
INVESTMENTS AND OTHER ASSETS		
Equity method investments:		
Coca-Cola Enterprises Inc.	1,569	1,260
Coca-Cola Hellenic Bottling Company S.A.	1,067	941
Coca-Cola FEMSA, S.A. de C.V.	792	674
Coca-Cola Amatil Limited	736	652
Other, principally bottling companies	1,733	1,697
Cost method investments, principally bottling companies	355	314
Other assets	3,054	3,322
	9,306	8,860
PROPERTY, PLANT AND EQUIPMENT		
Land	479	419
Buildings and improvements	2,853	2,615
Machinery and equipment	6,337	6,159
Containers	480	429
	10,149	9,622
Less allowances for depreciation	4,058	3,525
	6,091	6,097
TRADEMARKS WITH INDEFINITE LIVES	2,037	1,979
GOODWILL	1,097	1,029
OTHER INTANGIBLE ASSETS	702	981
TOTAL ASSETS	$ 31,327	$ 27,342

Refer to Notes to Consolidated Financial Statements.

The Coca-Cola Company and Subsidiaries

December 31,	2004	2003
(In millions except share data)		

LIABILITIES AND SHAREOWNERS' EQUITY

CURRENT

	2004	2003
Accounts payable and accrued expenses	$ 4,283	$ 4,058
Loans and notes payable	4,531	2,583
Current maturities of long-term debt	1,490	323
Accrued income taxes	667	922
TOTAL CURRENT LIABILITIES	**10,971**	7,886
LONG-TERM DEBT	**1,157**	2,517
OTHER LIABILITIES	**2,814**	2,512
DEFERRED INCOME TAXES	**450**	337

SHAREOWNERS' EQUITY

	2004	2003
Common stock, $0.25 par value		
Authorized: 5,600,000,000 shares;		
issued: 3,500,489,544 shares in 2004 and 3,494,799,258 shares in 2003	875	874
Capital surplus	4,928	4,395
Reinvested earnings	29,105	26,687
Accumulated other comprehensive income (loss)	(1,348)	(1,995)
	33,560	29,961
Less treasury stock, at cost (1,091,150,977 shares in 2004; 1,053,267,474 shares in 2003)	(17,625)	(15,871)
	15,935	14,090
TOTAL LIABILITIES AND SHAREOWNERS' EQUITY	$ 31,327	$ 27,342

Refer to Notes to Consolidated Financial Statements.

CONSOLIDATED STATEMENTS OF CASH FLOWS

The Coca-Cola Company and Subsidiaries

Year Ended December 31,	2004	2003	2002
(In millions)			
OPERATING ACTIVITIES			
Net income	$ **4,847**	$ 4,347	$ 3,050
Depreciation and amortization	**893**	850	806
Stock-based compensation expense	**345**	422	365
Deferred income taxes	**162**	(188)	40
Equity income (loss), net of dividends	**(476)**	(294)	(256)
Foreign currency adjustments	**(59)**	(79)	(76)
Gains on issuances of stock by equity investees	**(24)**	(8)	—
(Gains) losses on sales of assets, including bottling interests	**(20)**	(5)	3
Cumulative effect of accounting changes	**—**	—	926
Other operating charges	**480**	330	—
Other items	**437**	249	291
Net change in operating assets and liabilities	**(617)**	(168)	(407)
Net cash provided by operating activities	**5,968**	5,456	4,742
INVESTING ACTIVITIES			
Acquisitions and investments, principally trademarks and bottling companies	**(267)**	(359)	(544)
Purchases of investments and other assets	**(46)**	(177)	(141)
Proceeds from disposals of investments and other assets	**161**	147	243
Purchases of property, plant and equipment	**(755)**	(812)	(851)
Proceeds from disposals of property, plant and equipment	**341**	87	69
Other investing activities	**63**	178	159
Net cash used in investing activities	**(503)**	(936)	(1,065)
FINANCING ACTIVITIES			
Issuances of debt	**3,030**	1,026	1,622
Payments of debt	**(1,316)**	(1,119)	(2,378)
Issuances of stock	**193**	98	107
Purchases of stock for treasury	**(1,739)**	(1,440)	(691)
Dividends	**(2,429)**	(2,166)	(1,987)
Net cash used in financing activities	**(2,261)**	(3,601)	(3,327)
EFFECT OF EXCHANGE RATE CHANGES ON CASH AND CASH EQUIVALENTS	**141**	183	44
CASH AND CASH EQUIVALENTS			
Net increase during the year	**3,345**	1,102	394
Balance at beginning of year	**3,362**	2,260	1,866
Balance at end of year	$ **6,707**	$ 3,362	$ 2,260

Refer to Notes to Consolidated Financial Statements.

CONSOLIDATED STATEMENTS OF SHAREOWNERS' EQUITY

The Coca-Cola Company and Subsidiaries

Year Ended December 31,	2004	2003	2002
(In millions except per share data)			
NUMBER OF COMMON SHARES OUTSTANDING			
Balance at beginning of year	2,442	2,471	2,486
Stock issued to employees exercising stock options	5	4	3
Purchases of stock for treasury[1]	(38)	(33)	(14)
Adoption of SFAS No. 123	—	—	(4)
Balance at end of year	2,409	2,442	2,471
COMMON STOCK			
Balance at beginning of year	$ 874	$ 873	$ 873
Stock issued to employees exercising stock options	1	1	1
Adoption of SFAS No. 123	—	—	(1)
Balance at end of year	875	874	873
CAPITAL SURPLUS			
Balance at beginning of year	4,395	3,857	3,520
Stock issued to employees exercising stock options	175	105	111
Tax benefit from employees' stock option and restricted stock plans	13	11	11
Stock-based compensation	345	422	365
Adoption of SFAS No. 123	—	—	(150)
Balance at end of year	4,928	4,395	3,857
REINVESTED EARNINGS			
Balance at beginning of year	26,687	24,506	23,443
Net income	4,847	4,347	3,050
Dividends (per share—$1.00, $0.88 and $0.80 in 2004, 2003 and 2002, respectively)	(2,429)	(2,166)	(1,987)
Balance at end of year	29,105	26,687	24,506
OUTSTANDING RESTRICTED STOCK			
Balance at beginning of year	—	—	(150)
Adoption of SFAS No. 123	—	—	150
Balance at end of year	—	—	—
ACCUMULATED OTHER COMPREHENSIVE INCOME (LOSS)			
Balance at beginning of year	(1,995)	(3,047)	(2,638)
Net foreign currency translation adjustment	665	921	(95)
Net loss on derivatives	(3)	(33)	(186)
Net change in unrealized gain on available-for-sale securities	39	40	67
Net change in minimum pension liability	(54)	124	(195)
Net other comprehensive income adjustments	647	1,052	(409)
Balance at end of year	(1,348)	(1,995)	(3,047)
TREASURY STOCK			
Balance at beginning of year	(15,871)	(14,389)	(13,682)
Purchases of treasury stock	(1,754)	(1,482)	(707)
Balance at end of year	(17,625)	(15,871)	(14,389)
TOTAL SHAREOWNERS' EQUITY	$ 15,935	$ 14,090	$ 11,800
COMPREHENSIVE INCOME			
Net income	$ 4,847	$ 4,347	$ 3,050
Net other comprehensive income adjustments	647	1,052	(409)
TOTAL COMPREHENSIVE INCOME	$ 5,494	$ 5,399	$ 2,641

[1] Common stock purchased from employees exercising stock options numbered 0.4 million, 0.4 million and 0.2 million shares for the years ended December 31, 2004, 2003 and 2002, respectively.

Refer to Notes to Consolidated Financial Statements.

NOTES TO CONSOLIDATED FINANCIAL STATEMENTS
The Coca-Cola Company and Subsidiaries

NOTE 1: ORGANIZATION AND SUMMARY OF SIGNIFICANT ACCOUNTING POLICIES

Organization

The Coca-Cola Company is predominantly a manufacturer, distributor and marketer of nonalcoholic beverage concentrates and syrups. In these notes, the terms "Company," "we," "us" or "our" mean The Coca-Cola Company and all subsidiaries included in the consolidated financial statements. Operating in more than 200 countries worldwide, we primarily sell our concentrates and syrups, as well as some finished beverages, to bottling and canning operations, distributors, fountain wholesalers and fountain retailers. We also market and distribute juices and juice drinks, sports drinks, water products, teas, coffees and other beverage products. Additionally, we have ownership interests in numerous bottling and canning operations. Significant markets for our products exist in all the world's geographic regions.

Basis of Presentation and Consolidation

Our consolidated financial statements are prepared in accordance with accounting principles generally accepted in the United States. Our Company consolidates all entities that we control by ownership of a majority voting interest as well as variable interest entities for which our Company is the primary beneficiary. Refer to the heading "Variable Interest Entities" for a discussion of variable interest entities.

We use the equity method to account for our investments for which we have the ability to exercise significant influence over operating and financial policies. Consolidated net income includes our Company's share of the net earnings of these companies. The difference between consolidation and the equity method impacts certain financial ratios because of the presentation of the detailed line items reported in the financial statements.

We use the cost method to account for our investments in companies that we do not control and for which we do not have the ability to exercise significant influence over operating and financial policies. In accordance with the cost method, these investments are recorded at cost or fair value, as appropriate.

We eliminate from our financial results all significant intercompany transactions, including the intercompany transactions with variable interest entities and the intercompany portion of transactions with equity method investees.

Certain amounts in the prior years' consolidated financial statements have been reclassified to conform to the current-year presentation.

Variable Interest Entities

In December 2003, the Financial Accounting Standards Board ("FASB") issued FASB Interpretation No. 46 (revised December 2003), "Consolidation of Variable Interest Entities" ("Interpretation 46" or "FIN 46"). Application of this interpretation was required in our consolidated financial statements for the year ended December 31, 2003 for interests in variable interest entities that were considered to be special-purpose entities. Our Company determined that we did not have any arrangements or relationships with special-purpose entities. Application of Interpretation 46 for all other types of variable interest entities was required for our Company effective March 31, 2004.

Interpretation 46 addresses the consolidation of business enterprises to which the usual condition (ownership of a majority voting interest) of consolidation does not apply. This interpretation focuses on controlling financial interests that may be achieved through arrangements that do not involve voting interests. It concludes that in the absence of clear control through voting interests, a company's exposure (variable interest)

NOTES TO CONSOLIDATED FINANCIAL STATEMENTS
The Coca-Cola Company and Subsidiaries

NOTE 1: ORGANIZATION AND SUMMARY OF SIGNIFICANT ACCOUNTING POLICIES (Continued)

to the economic risks and potential rewards from the variable interest entity's assets and activities are the best evidence of control. If an enterprise holds a majority of the variable interests of an entity, it would be considered the primary beneficiary. Upon consolidation, the primary beneficiary is generally required to include assets, liabilities and noncontrolling interests at fair value and subsequently account for the variable interest as if it were consolidated based on majority voting interest.

In our financial statements as of December 31, 2003 and prior to December 31, 2003, we consolidated all entities that we controlled by ownership of a majority of voting interests. As a result of Interpretation 46, effective as of March 31, 2004, our consolidated balance sheet includes the assets and liabilities of:

- all entities in which the Company has ownership of a majority of voting interests; and additionally,
- all variable interest entities for which we are the primary beneficiary.

Our Company holds interests in certain entities, primarily bottlers, previously accounted for under the equity method of accounting that are considered variable interest entities. These variable interests relate to profit guarantees or subordinated financial support for these entities. Upon adoption of Interpretation 46 as of March 31, 2004, we consolidated assets of approximately $383 million and liabilities of approximately $383 million that were previously not recorded on our consolidated balance sheet. We did not record a cumulative effect of an accounting change, and prior periods were not restated. The results of operations of these variable interest entities were included in our consolidated results beginning April 1, 2004 and did not have a material impact for the year ended December 31, 2004. Our Company's investment, plus any loans and guarantees, related to these variable interest entities totaled approximately $313 million at December 31, 2004, representing our maximum exposure to loss. Any creditors of the variable interest entities do not have recourse against the general credit of the Company as a result of including these variable interest entities in our consolidated financial statements.

Use of Estimates and Assumptions

The preparation of our consolidated financial statements requires us to make estimates and assumptions that affect the reported amounts of assets, liabilities, revenues and expenses and the disclosure of contingent assets and liabilities in our consolidated financial statements and accompanying notes. Although these estimates are based on our knowledge of current events and actions we may undertake in the future, actual results may ultimately differ from estimates and assumptions.

Risks and Uncertainties

The Company's operations could be adversely affected by restrictions on imports and exports and sources of supply; prolonged labor strikes (including any at key manufacturing operations); adverse weather conditions; advertising effectiveness; changes in labeling requirements; duties or tariffs; changes in governmental regulations; the introduction of additional measures to control inflation; changes in the rate or method of taxation; the imposition of additional restrictions on currency conversion and remittances abroad; the expropriation of private enterprise; or product issues such as a product recall. In addition, policy concerns particular to the United States with respect to a country in which the Company has operations could adversely affect our operations. The foregoing list of risks and uncertainties is not exclusive.

Our Company monitors our operations with a view to minimizing the impact to our overall business that could arise as a result of the risks inherent in our business.

NOTES TO CONSOLIDATED FINANCIAL STATEMENTS

The Coca-Cola Company and Subsidiaries

NOTE 1: ORGANIZATION AND SUMMARY OF SIGNIFICANT ACCOUNTING POLICIES (Continued)

Revenue Recognition

Our Company recognizes revenue when title to our products is transferred to our bottling partners or our customers.

Advertising Costs

Our Company expenses production costs of print, radio, television and other advertisements as of the first date the advertisements take place. Advertising costs included in selling, general and administrative expenses were approximately $2.2 billion in 2004, approximately $1.8 billion in 2003 and approximately $1.7 billion in 2002. As of December 31, 2004 and 2003, advertising and production costs of approximately $194 million and $190 million, respectively, were recorded in prepaid expenses and other assets and in noncurrent other assets in our consolidated balance sheets.

Stock-Based Compensation

Our Company currently sponsors stock option plans and restricted stock award plans. Refer to Note 13. Effective January 1, 2002, our Company adopted the preferable fair value recognition provisions of Statement of Financial Accounting Standards ("SFAS") No. 123, "Accounting for Stock-Based Compensation." Our Company selected the modified prospective method of adoption described in SFAS No. 148, "Accounting for Stock-Based Compensation—Transition and Disclosure." The fair values of the stock awards are determined using a single estimated expected life. The compensation expense is recognized on a straight-line basis over the vesting period. The total stock-based compensation expense, net of related tax effects, was $254 million in 2004, $308 million in 2003 and $267 million in 2002. These amounts represent the same as that which would have been recognized had the fair value method of SFAS No. 123 been applied from its original effective date.

Issuances of Stock by Equity Investees

When one of our equity investees issues additional shares to third parties, our percentage ownership interest in the investee decreases. In the event the issuance price per share is more or less than our average carrying amount per share, we recognize a noncash gain or loss on the issuance. This noncash gain or loss, net of any deferred taxes, is generally recognized in our net income in the period the change of ownership interest occurs.

If gains have been previously recognized on issuances of an equity investee's stock and shares of the equity investee are subsequently repurchased by the equity investee, gain recognition does not occur on issuances subsequent to the date of a repurchase until shares have been issued in an amount equivalent to the number of repurchased shares. This type of transaction is reflected as an equity transaction, and the net effect is reflected in our consolidated balance sheets. Refer to Note 3.

Net Income Per Share

We compute basic net income per share by dividing net income by the weighted-average number of shares outstanding. Diluted net income per share includes the dilutive effect of stock-based compensation awards, if any.

Cash Equivalents

We classify marketable securities that are highly liquid and have maturities of three months or less at the date of purchase as cash equivalents.

NOTES TO CONSOLIDATED FINANCIAL STATEMENTS
The Coca-Cola Company and Subsidiaries

NOTE 1: ORGANIZATION AND SUMMARY OF SIGNIFICANT ACCOUNTING POLICIES (Continued)

Trade Accounts Receivable

We record trade accounts receivable at net realizable value. This value includes an appropriate allowance for estimated uncollectible accounts to reflect any loss anticipated on the trade accounts receivable balances and charged to the provision for doubtful accounts. We calculate this allowance based on our history of write-offs, level of past due accounts based on the contractual terms of the receivables and our relationships with and economic status of our bottling partners and customers.

Inventories

Inventories consist primarily of raw materials, supplies, concentrates and syrups and are valued at the lower of cost or market. We determine cost on the basis of average cost or first-in, first-out methods.

Recoverability of Equity Method and Cost Method Investments

Management periodically assesses the recoverability of our Company's equity method and cost method investments. For publicly traded investments, readily available quoted market prices are an indication of the fair value of our Company's investments. For nonpublicly traded investments, if an identified event or change in circumstances requires an impairment evaluation, management assesses fair value based on valuation methodologies as appropriate, including discounted cash flows, estimates of sales proceeds and external appraisals, as appropriate. If an investment is considered to be impaired and the decline in value is other than temporary, we record an appropriate write-down.

Other Assets

Our Company advances payments to certain customers for marketing to fund future activities intended to generate profitable volume, and we expense such payments over the applicable period. Advance payments are also made to certain customers for distribution rights. Additionally, our Company invests in infrastructure programs with our bottlers that are directed at strengthening our bottling system and increasing unit case volume. Management periodically evaluates the recoverability of these assets by preparing estimates of sales volume, the resulting gross profit, cash flows and considering other factors. Costs of these programs are recorded in prepaid expenses and other assets and noncurrent other assets and are subsequently amortized over the periods to be directly benefited. Amortization expense for infrastructure programs was approximately $136 million, $156 million and $176 million, respectively, for the years ended December 31, 2004, 2003 and 2002. Refer to Note 2.

Property, Plant and Equipment

We state property, plant and equipment at cost and depreciate such assets principally by the straight-line method over the estimated useful lives of the assets. Management assesses the recoverability of the carrying amount of property, plant and equipment if certain events or changes occur, such as a significant decrease in market value of the assets or a significant change in the business conditions in a particular market.

Goodwill, Trademarks and Other Intangible Assets

Effective January 1, 2002, our Company adopted SFAS No. 142, "Goodwill and Other Intangible Assets." The adoption of SFAS No. 142 required an initial impairment assessment involving a comparison of the fair value of goodwill, trademarks and other intangible assets to current carrying value. Upon adoption, we recorded

NOTES TO CONSOLIDATED FINANCIAL STATEMENTS
The Coca-Cola Company and Subsidiaries

NOTE 1: ORGANIZATION AND SUMMARY OF SIGNIFICANT ACCOUNTING POLICIES (Continued)

a loss for the cumulative effect of accounting change for SFAS No. 142, net of income taxes, of $367 million for Company operations and $559 million for the Company's proportionate share of impairment losses from its equity method investees. We did not restate prior periods for the adoption of SFAS No. 142.

Trademarks and other intangible assets determined to have indefinite useful lives are not amortized. We test such trademarks and other intangible assets with indefinite useful lives for impairment annually, or more frequently if events or circumstances indicate that an asset might be impaired. Trademarks and other intangible assets determined to have definite lives are amortized over their useful lives. We review such trademarks and other intangible assets with definite lives for impairment to ensure they are appropriately valued if conditions exist that may indicate the carrying value may not be recoverable. Such conditions may include an economic downturn in a geographic market or a change in the assessment of future operations.

All goodwill is assigned to reporting units, which are one level below our operating segments. Goodwill is assigned to the reporting unit that benefits from the synergies arising from each business combination. Goodwill is not amortized. We perform tests for impairment of goodwill annually, or more frequently if events or circumstances indicate it might be impaired. Such tests include comparing the fair value of a reporting unit with its carrying value, including goodwill. Impairment assessments are performed using a variety of methodologies, including cash flow analyses, estimates of sales proceeds and independent appraisals. Where applicable, an appropriate discount rate is used, based on the Company's cost of capital rate or location-specific economic factors. Refer to Note 4.

Derivative Financial Instruments

Our Company accounts for derivative financial instruments in accordance with SFAS No. 133, "Accounting for Derivative Instruments and Hedging Activities," as amended by SFAS No. 137, SFAS No. 138, and SFAS No. 149. Our Company recognizes all derivative instruments as either assets or liabilities at fair value in our consolidated balance sheets. Refer to Note 10.

Retirement Related Benefits

Using appropriate actuarial methods and assumptions, our Company accounts for defined benefit pension plans in accordance with SFAS No. 87, "Employers' Accounting for Pensions." We account for our nonpension postretirement benefits in accordance with SFAS No. 106, "Employers' Accounting for Postretirement Benefits Other Than Pensions." In 2003, we adopted SFAS No. 132 (revised 2003), "Employers' Disclosures about Pensions and Other Postretirement Benefits," ("SFAS 132(R)") for all U.S. plans. As permitted by this standard, in 2004 we adopted the disclosure provisions for all foreign plans for the year ended December 31, 2004. SFAS No. 132(R) requires additional disclosures about the assets, obligations, cash flows and net periodic benefit cost of defined benefit pension plans and other defined benefit postretirement plans. This statement did not change the measurement or recognition of those plans required by SFAS No. 87, SFAS No. 88, "Employers' Accounting for Settlements and Curtailments of Defined Benefit Pension Plans and for Termination Benefits," or SFAS No. 106. Refer to Note 14 for a description of how we determine our principal assumptions for pension and postretirement benefit accounting.

Contingencies

Our Company is involved in various legal proceedings and tax matters. Due to their nature, such legal proceedings and tax matters involve inherent uncertainties including, but not limited to, court rulings,

NOTES TO CONSOLIDATED FINANCIAL STATEMENTS
The Coca-Cola Company and Subsidiaries

NOTE 1: ORGANIZATION AND SUMMARY OF SIGNIFICANT ACCOUNTING POLICIES (Continued)

negotiations between affected parties and governmental actions. Management assesses the probability of loss for such contingencies and accrues a liability and/or discloses the relevant circumstances, as appropriate. Refer to Note 11.

Business Combinations

In accordance with SFAS No. 141, "Business Combinations," we account for all business combinations by the purchase method. Furthermore, we recognize intangible assets apart from goodwill if they arise from contractual or legal rights or if they are separable from goodwill.

New Accounting Standards

Effective January 1, 2003, the Company adopted SFAS No. 146, "Accounting for Costs Associated with Exit or Disposal Activities." SFAS No. 146 addresses financial accounting and reporting for costs associated with exit or disposal activities and nullifies Emerging Issues Task Force ("EITF") Issue No. 94-3, "Liability Recognition for Certain Employee Termination Benefits and Other Costs to Exit an Activity (including Certain Costs Incurred in a Restructuring)." SFAS No. 146 requires that a liability for a cost associated with an exit or disposal plan be recognized when the liability is incurred. Under SFAS No. 146, an exit or disposal plan exists when the following criteria are met:

- Management, having the authority to approve the action, commits to a plan of termination.

- The plan identifies the number of employees to be terminated, their job classifications or functions and their locations, and the expected completion date.

- The plan establishes the terms of the benefit arrangement, including the benefits that employees will receive upon termination (including but not limited to cash payments), in sufficient detail to enable employees to determine the type and amount of benefits they will receive if they are involuntarily terminated.

- Actions required to complete the plan indicate that it is unlikely that significant changes to the plan will be made or that the plan will be withdrawn.

SFAS No. 146 establishes that fair value is the objective for initial measurement of the liability. In cases where employees are required to render service beyond a minimum retention period until they are terminated in order to receive termination benefits, a liability for termination benefits is recognized ratably over the future service period. Under EITF Issue No. 94-3, a liability for the entire amount of the exit cost was recognized at the date that the entity met the four criteria described above. Refer to Note 17.

Effective January 1, 2003, our Company adopted the recognition and measurement provisions of FASB Interpretation No. 45, "Guarantor's Accounting and Disclosure Requirements for Guarantees, Including Indirect Guarantees of Indebtedness of Others" ("Interpretation 45"). This interpretation elaborates on the disclosures to be made by a guarantor in interim and annual financial statements about the obligations under certain guarantees. Interpretation 45 also clarifies that a guarantor is required to recognize, at the inception of a guarantee, a liability for the fair value of the obligation undertaken in issuing the guarantee. The initial recognition and initial measurement provisions of this interpretation are applicable on a prospective basis to guarantees issued or modified after December 31, 2002. We do not currently provide significant guarantees on a routine basis. As a result, this interpretation has not had a material impact on our consolidated financial statements.

NOTES TO CONSOLIDATED FINANCIAL STATEMENTS
The Coca-Cola Company and Subsidiaries

NOTE 1: ORGANIZATION AND SUMMARY OF SIGNIFICANT ACCOUNTING POLICIES (Continued)

During 2004, the FASB issued FASB Staff Position 106-2, "Accounting and Disclosure Requirements Related to the Medicare Prescription Drug, Improvement and Modernization Act of 2003" ("FSP 106-2"). FSP 106-2 relates to the Medicare Prescription Drug, Improvement and Modernization Act of 2003 (the "Act") signed into law in December 2003. The Act introduced a prescription drug benefit under Medicare known as "Medicare Part D." The Act also established a federal subsidy to sponsors of retiree health care plans that provide a benefit that is at least actuarially equivalent to Medicare Part D. During the second quarter of 2004, our Company adopted the provisions of FSP 106-2 retroactive to January 1, 2004. The adoption of FSP 106-2 did not have a material impact on our consolidated financial statements. Refer to Note 14.

In October 2004, the American Jobs Creation Act of 2004 (the "Jobs Creation Act") was signed into law. The Jobs Creation Act includes a temporary incentive for U.S. multinationals to repatriate foreign earnings at an effective 5.25 percent tax rate. Such repatriations must occur in either an enterprise's last tax year that began before the enactment date, or the first tax year that begins during the one-year period beginning on the date of enactment.

FASB Staff Position 109-2, "Accounting and Disclosure Guidance for the Foreign Earnings Repatriation Provision within the American Jobs Creation Act of 2004" ("FSP 109-2"), indicates that the lack of clarification of certain provisions within the Jobs Creation Act and the timing of the enactment necessitate a practical exception to the SFAS No. 109, "Accounting for Income Taxes," ("SFAS No. 109") requirement to reflect in the period of enactment the effect of a new tax law. Accordingly, an enterprise is allowed time beyond the financial reporting period of enactment to evaluate the effect of the Jobs Creation Act on its plan for reinvestment or repatriation of foreign earnings. FSP 109-2 requires that the provisions of SFAS No. 109 be applied as an enterprise decides on its plan for reinvestment or repatriation of its unremitted foreign earnings.

In 2004, our Company recorded an income tax benefit of approximately $50 million as a result of the realization of certain tax credits related to certain provisions of the Jobs Creation Act not related to repatriation provisions. Our Company is currently evaluating the details of the Jobs Creation Act and any impact it may have on our income tax expense in 2005. Refer to Note 15.

In November 2004, the FASB issued SFAS No. 151, "Inventory Costs, an amendment of Accounting Research Bulletin No. 43, Chapter 4." SFAS No. 151 requires that abnormal amounts of idle facility expense, freight, handling costs and wasted materials (spoilage) be recorded as current period charges and that the allocation of fixed production overheads to inventory be based on the normal capacity of the production facilities. SFAS No. 151 is effective for our Company on January 1, 2006. The Company does not believe that the adoption of SFAS No. 151 will have a material impact on our consolidated financial statements.

In December 2004, the FASB issued SFAS No. 123 (revised 2004), "Share Based Payment" ("SFAS No. 123(R)"). SFAS No. 123(R) supercedes APB Opinion No. 25, "Accounting for Stock Issued to Employees," and amends SFAS No. 95, "Statement of Cash Flows." Generally, the approach in SFAS No. 123(R) is similar to the approach described in SFAS No. 123. SFAS No. 123(R) must be adopted by our Company by the third quarter of 2005. Currently, our Company uses the Black-Scholes-Merton formula to estimate the value of stock options granted to employees and is evaluating option valuation models, including the Black-Scholes-Merton formula, to determine which model the Company will utilize upon adoption of SFAS No. 123(R). Our Company plans to adopt SFAS No. 123(R) using the modified-prospective method. We do not anticipate that adoption of SFAS No. 123(R) will have a material impact on our Company's stock-based compensation expense. However, our equity investees are also required to adopt SFAS No. 123(R) beginning no later than the third quarter of

NOTES TO CONSOLIDATED FINANCIAL STATEMENTS

The Coca-Cola Company and Subsidiaries

NOTE 1: ORGANIZATION AND SUMMARY OF SIGNIFICANT ACCOUNTING POLICIES (Continued)

2005. Our proportionate share of the stock-based compensation expense resulting from the adoption of SFAS No. 123(R) by our equity investees will be recognized as a reduction to equity income.

In December 2004, the FASB issued SFAS No. 153, "Exchanges of Nonmonetary Assets, an amendment of APB Opinion No. 29." SFAS No. 153 is based on the principle that exchanges of nonmonetary assets should be measured based on the fair value of the assets exchanged. APB Opinion No. 29, "Accounting for Nonmonetary Transactions," provided an exception to its basic measurement principle (fair value) for exchanges of similar productive assets. Under APB Opinion No. 29, an exchange of a productive asset for a similar productive asset was based on the recorded amount of the asset relinquished. SFAS No. 153 eliminates this exception and replaces it with an exception of exchanges of nonmonetary assets that do not have commercial substance. SFAS No. 153 is effective for our Company as of July 1, 2005. The Company will apply the requirements of SFAS No. 153 prospectively.

NOTE 2: BOTTLING INVESTMENTS

Coca-Cola Enterprises Inc.

Coca-Cola Enterprises Inc. ("CCE") is a marketer, producer and distributor of bottle and can nonalcoholic beverages, operating in eight countries. On December 31, 2004, our Company owned approximately 36 percent of the outstanding common stock of CCE. We account for our investment by the equity method of accounting and, therefore, our operating results include our proportionate share of income (loss) resulting from our investment in CCE. As of December 31, 2004, our proportionate share of the net assets of CCE exceeded our investment by approximately $366 million. This difference is not amortized.

NOTES TO CONSOLIDATED FINANCIAL STATEMENTS
The Coca-Cola Company and Subsidiaries

NOTE 2: BOTTLING INVESTMENTS (Continued)

A summary of financial information for CCE is as follows (in millions):

December 31,	2004	2003
Current assets	$ **3,264**	$ 3,000
Noncurrent assets	**23,090**	22,700
Total assets	$ **26,354**	$ 25,700
Current liabilities	$ **3,431**	$ 3,941
Noncurrent liabilities	**17,545**	17,394
Total liabilities	$ **20,976**	$ 21,335
Shareowners' equity	$ **5,378**	$ 4,365
Company equity investment	$ **1,569**	$ 1,260

Year Ended December 31,	2004	2003	2002
Net operating revenues	$ **18,158**	$ 17,330	$ 16,058[1]
Cost of goods sold	**10,771**	10,165	9,458[1]
Gross profit	$ **7,387**	$ 7,165	$ 6,600[1]
Operating income	$ **1,436**	$ 1,577	$ 1,364
Net income	$ **596**	$ 676	$ 494
Net income available to common shareowners	$ **596**	$ 674	$ 491

[1] These amounts reflect reclassifications related to the January 1, 2003 adoption of EITF Issue No. 02-16, "Accounting by a Customer (Including a Reseller) for Certain Consideration Received from a Vendor."

A summary of our significant transactions with CCE is as follows (in millions):

	2004	2003	2002
Concentrate, syrup and finished products sales to CCE	$ **5,203**	$ 5,084	$ 4,767
Syrup and finished product purchases from CCE	**428**	403	461
CCE purchases of sweeteners through our Company	**309**	311	325
Payments made by us directly to CCE	**646**	880	837
Payments made to third parties on behalf of CCE	**104**	115	204
Local media and marketing program reimbursements from CCE	**246**	221	264

Syrup and finished product purchases from CCE represent purchases of fountain syrup in certain territories that have been resold by our Company to major customers and purchases of bottle and can products. Payments made by us directly to CCE represent support of certain marketing activities and our participation with CCE in cooperative advertising and other marketing activities to promote the sale of Company trademark products within CCE territories. These programs are agreed to on an annual basis. Payments made to third parties on behalf of CCE represent support of certain marketing activities and programs to promote the sale of Company trademark products within CCE's territories in conjunction with certain of CCE's customers. Pursuant to cooperative advertising and trade agreements with CCE, we received funds from CCE for local media and marketing program expense reimbursements.

NOTES TO CONSOLIDATED FINANCIAL STATEMENTS
The Coca-Cola Company and Subsidiaries

NOTE 2: BOTTLING INVESTMENTS (Continued)

In the second quarter of 2004, our Company and CCE agreed to terminate the Sales Growth Initiative ("SGI") agreement and certain other marketing funding programs that were previously in place. Due to termination of these agreements, a significant portion of the cash payments to be made by us directly to CCE was eliminated prospectively. At the termination of these agreements, we agreed that the concentrate price that CCE pays us for sales made in the United States and Canada would be reduced. Total cash support paid by our Company under the SGI agreement prior to its termination was $58 million, $161 million and $150 million for 2004, 2003 and 2002, respectively. These amounts are included in the line item payments made by us directly to CCE in the table above.

In the second quarter of 2004, we and CCE agreed to establish a Global Marketing Fund, under which we expect to pay CCE $62 million annually through December 31, 2014 as support for certain marketing activities. The term of the agreement will automatically be extended for successive 10-year periods thereafter unless either party gives written notice of termination of this agreement. The marketing activities to be funded under this agreement will be agreed upon each year as part of the annual joint planning process and will be incorporated into the annual marketing plans of both companies. We paid CCE a pro rata amount of $42 million for 2004. This amount is included in the line item payments made by us directly to CCE in the table above.

Our Company previously entered into programs with CCE designed to help develop cold-drink infrastructure. Under these programs, our Company paid CCE for a portion of the cost of developing the infrastructure necessary to support accelerated placements of cold-drink equipment. These payments support a common objective of increased sales of Coca-Cola beverages from increased availability and consumption in the cold-drink channel. In connection with these programs, CCE agreed to:

(1) purchase and place specified numbers of Company approved cold-drink equipment each year through 2010;

(2) maintain the equipment in service, with certain exceptions, for a period of at least 12 years after placement;

(3) maintain and stock the equipment in accordance with specified standards; and

(4) annual reporting to our Company of minimum average annual unit case sales volume throughout the economic life of the equipment and other specified information.

CCE must achieve minimum average unit case sales volume for a 12-year period following the placement of equipment. These minimum average unit case sales volume levels ensure adequate gross profit from sales of concentrate to fully recover the capitalized costs plus a return on the Company's investment. Should CCE fail to purchase the specified numbers of cold-drink equipment for any calendar year through 2010, the parties agreed to mutually develop a reasonable solution. Should no mutually agreeable solution be developed, or in the event that CCE otherwise breaches any material obligation under the contracts and such breach is not remedied within a stated period, then CCE would be required to repay a portion of the support funding as determined by our Company. In the third quarter of 2004, our Company and CCE agreed to amend the contract to defer the placement of some equipment from 2004 and 2005, as previously agreed under the original contract, to 2009 and 2010. In connection with this amendment, CCE agreed to pay the Company approximately $2 million in 2004, $3 million annually in 2005 through 2008, and $1 million in 2009. Our Company paid or committed to pay $3 million in 2002 to CCE in connection with these infrastructure programs. These payments are recorded in prepaid expenses and other assets and in noncurrent other assets and amortized as deductions in net operating revenues over the 10-year period following the placement of the equipment. Our carrying values for these

NOTES TO CONSOLIDATED FINANCIAL STATEMENTS
The Coca-Cola Company and Subsidiaries

NOTE 2: BOTTLING INVESTMENTS (Continued)

infrastructure programs with CCE were approximately $759 million and $829 million as of December 31, 2004 and 2003, respectively. Effective in 2002 and thereafter, the Company had no further commitments under these programs.

In March 2004, the Company and CCE launched the Dasani water brand in Great Britain. The product was voluntarily recalled. During 2004, our Company reimbursed CCE $32 million for product recall costs incurred by CCE.

In March 2003, our Company acquired a 100 percent ownership interest in Truesdale Packaging Company LLC ("Truesdale") from CCE. Refer to Note 18.

If valued at the December 31, 2004 quoted closing price of CCE shares, the fair value of our investment in CCE would have exceeded our carrying value by approximately $2.0 billion.

NOTES TO CONSOLIDATED FINANCIAL STATEMENTS
The Coca-Cola Company and Subsidiaries

NOTE 2: BOTTLING INVESTMENTS (Continued)

Other Equity Investments

Operating results include our proportionate share of income (loss) from our equity investments. A summary of financial information for our equity investments in the aggregate, other than CCE, is as follows (in millions):

December 31,	2004	2003
Current assets	$ **6,723**	$ 6,416
Noncurrent assets	**19,107**	17,394
Total assets	$ **25,830**	$ 23,810
Current liabilities	$ **5,507**	$ 5,467
Noncurrent liabilities	**8,924**	9,011
Total liabilities	$ **14,431**	$ 14,478
Shareowners' equity	$ **11,399**	$ 9,332
Company equity investment	$ **4,328**	$ 3,964

Year Ended December 31,	2004	2003	2002
Net operating revenues	$ **21,202**	$ 19,797	$ 17,714[1]
Cost of goods sold	**12,132**	11,661	10,112[1]
Gross profit	$ **9,070**	$ 8,136	$ 7,602[1]
Operating income	$ **2,406**	$ 1,666	$ 1,744
Cumulative effect of accounting change[2]	$ **—**	$ —	$ (1,428)
Net income (loss)	$ **1,389**	$ 580	$ (630)
Net income (loss) available to common shareowners	$ **1,364**	$ 580	$ (630)

Equity investments include nonbottling investees.

[1] These amounts reflect reclassifications related to the January 1, 2003 adoption of EITF Issue No. 02-16, "Accounting by a Customer (Including a Reseller) for Certain Consideration Received from a Vendor."

[2] Accounting change is the adoption of SFAS No. 142.

Net sales to equity investees other than CCE, the majority of which are located outside the United States, were $5.2 billion in 2004, $4.0 billion in 2003 and $3.2 billion in 2002. Total support payments, primarily marketing, made to equity investees other than CCE were approximately $442 million, $511 million and $488 million for 2004, 2003 and 2002, respectively.

During the second quarter of 2004, the Company's equity income benefited by approximately $37 million for its share of a favorable tax settlement related to Coca-Cola FEMSA, S.A. de C.V. ("Coca-Cola FEMSA").

In December 2004, the Company sold certain of its production assets to an unrelated financial institution that were previously leased to the Japanese supply chain management company (refer to discussion below). The assets were sold for $271 million and the sale resulted in no gain or loss. The financial institution entered into a leasing arrangement with the Japanese supply chain management company. These assets were previously reported in our consolidated balance sheet caption property, plant and equipment and assigned to our Asia operating segment.

NOTES TO CONSOLIDATED FINANCIAL STATEMENTS
The Coca-Cola Company and Subsidiaries

NOTE 2: BOTTLING INVESTMENTS (Continued)

During 2004, our Company sold our bottling operations in Vietnam, Cambodia, Sri Lanka and Nepal to Coca-Cola Sabco (Pty) Ltd. ("Sabco") for a total consideration of $29 million. In addition, Sabco assumed certain debts of these bottling operations. The proceeds from the sale of these bottlers were approximately equal to the carrying value of the investment.

Effective May 6, 2003, one of our Company's equity method investees, Coca-Cola FEMSA consummated a merger with another of the Company's equity method investees, Panamerican Beverages, Inc. ("Panamco"). Our Company received new Coca-Cola FEMSA shares in exchange for all Panamco shares previously held by the Company. Our Company's ownership interest in Coca-Cola FEMSA increased from 30 percent to approximately 40 percent as a result of this merger. This exchange of shares was treated as a nonmonetary exchange of similar productive assets, and no gain was recorded by our Company as a result of this merger.

In connection with the merger, Coca-Cola FEMSA management initiated steps to streamline and integrate operations. This process included the closing of various distribution centers and manufacturing plants. Furthermore, due to the challenging economic conditions and an uncertain political situation in Venezuela, certain intangible assets were determined to be impaired and written down to their fair market value. During 2003, our Company recorded a noncash charge of $102 million primarily related to our proportionate share of these matters. This charge is included in the consolidated statement of income line item equity income—net.

In December 2003, the Company issued a stand-by line of credit to Coca-Cola FEMSA. Refer to Note 11.

The Company and the major shareowner of Coca-Cola FEMSA have an understanding that will permit this shareowner to purchase from our Company an amount of Coca-Cola FEMSA shares sufficient for this shareowner to regain a 51 percent ownership interest in Coca-Cola FEMSA. Pursuant to this understanding, which is in place until May 2006, this shareowner would pay the higher of the prevailing market price per share at the time of the sale or the sum of approximately $2.22 per share plus the Company's carrying costs. Both resulting amounts are in excess of our Company's carrying value.

In July 2003, we made a convertible loan of approximately $133 million to The Coca-Cola Bottling Company of Egypt ("TCCBCE"). The loan is convertible into preferred shares of TCCBCE upon receipt of governmental approvals. Additionally, upon certain defaults under either the loan agreement or the terms of the preferred shares, we have the ability to convert the loan or the preferred shares into common shares. At December 31, 2004, our Company owned approximately 42 percent of the common shares of TCCBCE. In 2004, we consolidated TCCBCE under the provisions of Interpretation 46.

Effective October 1, 2003, the Company and all of its bottling partners in Japan created a nationally integrated supply chain management company to centralize procurement, production and logistics operations for the entire Coca-Cola system in Japan. As a result of the creation of this supply chain management company in Japan, a portion of our Company's business has essentially been converted from a finished product business model to a concentrate business model, thus reducing our net operating revenues and cost of goods sold. The formation of this entity included the sale of Company inventory and leasing of certain Company assets to this new entity on October 1, 2003, as well as our recording of a liability for certain contractual obligations to Japanese bottlers. Such amounts were not material to the Company's results of operations.

In November 2003, Coca-Cola Hellenic Bottling Company S.A. ("Coca-Cola HBC") approved a share capital reduction totaling approximately 473 million euros and the return of 2 euros per share to all shareowners. In December 2003, our Company received our share capital return payment from Coca-Cola HBC equivalent to $136 million, and we recorded a reduction to our investment in Coca-Cola HBC.

NOTES TO CONSOLIDATED FINANCIAL STATEMENTS
The Coca-Cola Company and Subsidiaries

NOTE 2: BOTTLING INVESTMENTS (Continued)

Effective February 2002, our Company acquired control of Coca-Cola Erfrischungsgetraenke AG ("CCEAG"), the largest bottler of our Company's beverage products in Germany. Prior to acquiring control, our Company accounted for CCEAG under the equity method of accounting. Refer to Note 18.

In the first quarter of 2002, our Company sold our bottling operations in the Baltics to Coca-Cola HBC. The proceeds from the sale of the Baltic bottlers were approximately equal to the carrying value of the investment.

If valued at the December 31, 2004, quoted closing prices of shares actively traded on stock markets, the value of our equity investments in publicly traded bottlers other than CCE exceeded our carrying value by approximately $2.2 billion.

The total amount of receivables due from equity method investees, including CCE, was approximately $680 million as of December 31, 2004. This amount was primarily reported in our consolidated balance sheet caption trade accounts receivable.

NOTE 3: ISSUANCES OF STOCK BY EQUITY INVESTEES

In 2004, our Company recorded approximately $24 million of noncash pretax gains on issuances of stock by CCE. The issuances primarily related to the exercise of CCE stock options by CCE employees at amounts greater than the book value per share of our investment in CCE. We provided deferred taxes of approximately $9 million on these gains. These issuances of stock reduced our ownership interest in the total outstanding shares of CCE common stock by approximately 1 percent to approximately 36 percent.

In 2003, our Company recorded approximately $8 million of noncash pretax gains on issuances of stock by equity investees. These gains primarily related to the issuance by CCE of common stock valued at an amount greater than the book value per share of our investment in CCE. These transactions reduced our ownership interest in the total outstanding shares of CCE common stock by less than 1 percent. No gains or losses on issuances of stock by equity investees were recorded during 2002.

NOTE 4: GOODWILL, TRADEMARKS AND OTHER INTANGIBLE ASSETS

In accordance with SFAS No. 142, goodwill and indefinite-lived intangible assets are no longer amortized but are reviewed annually for impairment. Our Company is the owner of some of the world's most valuable trademarks. As a result, certain trademarks and franchise rights to bottle and distribute such trademarked products are expected to generate positive cash flows for as long as the Company owns such trademarks and franchise rights for a particular territory. Given the Company's more than 100-year history, certain trademarks and the franchise rights to bottle and distribute products under our trademarks have been assigned indefinite lives. Intangible assets that are deemed to have definite lives are amortized over their useful lives. The amortization provisions of SFAS No. 142 apply to goodwill and intangible assets acquired after June 30, 2001. With respect to goodwill and intangible assets acquired prior to July 1, 2001, the Company began applying the new accounting rules effective January 1, 2002.

The adoption of SFAS No. 142 required the Company to perform an initial impairment assessment of all goodwill and indefinite-lived intangible assets as of January 1, 2002. The Company compared the fair value of trademarks and other intangible assets to the current carrying value. Fair values were derived using discounted cash flow analyses. The assumptions used in these discounted cash flow analyses were consistent with our internal planning. Valuations were completed for intangible assets for both the Company and our equity method investees. For the Company's intangible assets, the cumulative effect of this change in accounting principle in 2002 was an after-tax decrease to net income of $367 million. For the Company's proportionate share of its

NOTES TO CONSOLIDATED FINANCIAL STATEMENTS
The Coca-Cola Company and Subsidiaries

NOTE 4: GOODWILL, TRADEMARKS AND OTHER INTANGIBLE ASSETS (Continued)

equity method investees, the cumulative effect of this change in accounting principle in 2002 was an after-tax decrease to net income of $559 million. The deferred income tax benefit related to the cumulative effect of this change for the Company's intangible assets in 2002 was approximately $94 million and for the Company's proportionate share of its equity method investees was approximately $123 million.

The impairment charges resulting in the after-tax decrease to net income for the cumulative effect of this change by applicable operating segment as of January 1, 2002 were as follows (in millions):

The Company:	
Asia	$ 108
Europe, Eurasia and Middle East	33
Latin America	226
	$ 367
The Company's proportionate share of its equity method investees:	
Africa	$ 63
Europe, Eurasia and Middle East	400
Latin America	96
	$ 559

Of the $108 million impairment recorded as of January 1, 2002 for the Company in Asia, $99 million related to bottlers' franchise rights in our consolidated bottlers in our Southeast and West Asia Division. Difficult economic conditions impacted our business in Singapore, Sri Lanka, Nepal and Vietnam. As a result, bottlers in these countries experienced lower than expected volume and operating margins.

Of the Company's $226 million impairment recorded as of January 1, 2002 for Latin America, approximately $113 million related to Company-owned Brazilian bottlers' franchise rights. The Brazilian macroeconomic conditions, the devaluation of the currency and lower pricing impacted the valuation of these bottlers' franchise rights. The remainder of the $226 million primarily related to a $109 million impairment for certain trademarks in Latin America. In early 1999, our Company formed a strategic partnership to market and distribute such trademarked products. The macroeconomic conditions and lower pricing depressed operating margins for these trademarks.

For Europe, Eurasia and Middle East equity method investees, a $400 million impairment was recorded as of January 1, 2002 for the Company's proportionate share related to bottlers' franchise rights. Of this amount, approximately $301 million related to CCEAG. This impairment was due to a prolonged difficult economic environment in Germany, resulting in continuing losses for CCEAG in eastern Germany. At that time, the market for nonalcoholic beverages was undergoing a transformation. A changing competitive landscape, continuing price pressure and growing demand for new products and packaging were elements impacting CCEAG. The $400 million impairment also included a $50 million charge for Middle East bottlers' franchise rights.

In our Africa operating segment, a $63 million charge was recorded for the Company's proportionate share of impairments related to equity method investee bottlers' franchise rights. These Middle East and Africa bottlers had challenges as a result of political instability and the resulting economic instability in their respective regions, which adversely impacted financial performance.

A $96 million impairment was recorded as of January 1, 2002 for the Company's proportionate share related to bottlers' franchise rights of Latin America equity method investees. In southern Latin America, the

NOTES TO CONSOLIDATED FINANCIAL STATEMENTS
The Coca-Cola Company and Subsidiaries

NOTE 4: GOODWILL, TRADEMARKS AND OTHER INTANGIBLE ASSETS (Continued)

macroeconomic conditions and devaluation of the Argentine peso significantly impacted the valuation of bottlers' franchise rights.

The following tables set forth the information for intangible assets subject to amortization and for intangible assets not subject to amortization (in millions):

December 31,	2004	2003
Amortized intangible assets (various, principally trademarks):		
Gross carrying amount	$ 292	$ 263
Accumulated amortization	$ 128	$ 98
Unamortized intangible assets:		
Trademarks	$ 2,037	$ 1,979
Goodwill[1]	1,097	1,029
Bottlers' franchise rights[2]	374	658
Other	164	158
	$ 3,672	$ 3,824

[1] During 2004, the increase in goodwill primarily resulted from translation adjustments.

[2] During 2004, the decrease in franchise rights primarily related to the impairment charge of $354 million related to CCEAG's franchise rights (see discussion below).

Year Ended December 31,	2004	2003
Aggregate amortization expense	$ 40	$ 23
Estimated amortization expense:		
For the year ending:		
December 31, 2005	$ 28	
December 31, 2006	$ 16	
December 31, 2007	$ 16	
December 31, 2008	$ 16	
December 31, 2009	$ 15	

The goodwill by applicable operating segment as of December 31, 2004 was as follows (in millions):

December 31,	2004	2003
North America	$ 140	$ 142
Asia	37	45
Europe, Eurasia and Middle East	828	742
Latin America	92	100
	$ 1,097	$ 1,029

In 2004, acquisition of intangible assets totaled approximately $89 million. This amount is primarily related to the Company's acquisition of trademarks with indefinite lives in the Latin America operating segment.

In 2004, our Company recorded impairment charges related to intangible assets of approximately $374 million. The decrease in franchise rights in 2004 was primarily due to this impairment charge, offset by an increase due to translation adjustment. These impairment charges primarily were in the Europe, Eurasia and

NOTES TO CONSOLIDATED FINANCIAL STATEMENTS
The Coca-Cola Company and Subsidiaries

NOTE 4: GOODWILL, TRADEMARKS AND OTHER INTANGIBLE ASSETS (Continued)

Middle East operating segment and were included in other operating charges in our consolidated statement of income. The charge was primarily related to franchise rights at CCEAG. The CCEAG impairment was the result of our revised outlook for the German market that has been unfavorably impacted by volume declines resulting from market shifts related to the deposit law on nonreturnable beverage packages and the corresponding lack of availability for our products in the discount retail channel. The deposit laws in Germany have led to discount chains creating proprietary packages that can only be returned to their own stores. These proprietary packages are continuing to gain market share and customer acceptance.

At the end of 2004, the German government passed an amendment to the mandatory deposit legislation that will require retailers, including discount chains, to accept returns of each type of non-refillable beverage containers which they sell, regardless of where the beverage container type was purchased. In addition, the mandatory deposit requirement was expanded to other beverage categories. The amendment allows for a transition period to enable manufacturers and retailers to establish a national take-back system for non-refillable containers. The transition period is expected to last at least until mid-2006.

We determined the amount of the 2004 impairment charges by comparing the fair value of the intangible assets to the current carrying value. Fair values were derived using discounted cash flow analyses with a number of scenarios that were weighted based on the probability of different outcomes. Because the fair value was less than the carrying value of the assets, we recorded an impairment charge to reduce the carrying value of the assets to fair value. These impairment charges were recorded in the line item other operating charges in the consolidated statement of income for 2004.

In 2003, acquisitions of intangible assets totaled approximately $142 million. Of this amount, approximately $88 million related to the Company's acquisition of certain intangible assets with indefinite lives, primarily trademarks and brands in various parts of the world. None of these trademarks and brands was considered individually significant. Additionally, the Company acquired certain brands and related contractual rights from Panamco valued at $54 million in the Latin America operating segment with an estimated useful life of 10 years.

NOTE 5: ACCOUNTS PAYABLE AND ACCRUED EXPENSES

Accounts payable and accrued expenses consist of the following (in millions):

December 31,	2004	2003
Trade accounts payable and other accrued expenses	$ 2,238	$ 2,014
Accrued marketing	1,194	1,046
Accrued compensation	389	311
Sales, payroll and other taxes	222	225
Container deposits	199	256
Accrued streamlining costs (refer to Note 17)	41	206
	$ 4,283	$ 4,058

NOTE 6: SHORT-TERM BORROWINGS AND CREDIT ARRANGEMENTS

Loans and notes payable consist primarily of commercial paper issued in the United States. At December 31, 2004 and 2003, we had approximately $4,235 million and $2,234 million, respectively, outstanding in commercial paper borrowings. Our weighted-average interest rates for commercial paper outstanding were approximately 2.2 percent and 1.1 percent per year at December 31, 2004 and 2003, respectively. In addition, we

NOTES TO CONSOLIDATED FINANCIAL STATEMENTS
The Coca-Cola Company and Subsidiaries

NOTE 6: SHORT-TERM BORROWINGS AND CREDIT ARRANGEMENTS (Continued)

had $1,614 million in lines of credit and other short-term credit facilities available as of December 31, 2004, of which approximately $296 million was outstanding. This entire amount related to our international operations. Included in the available credit facilities discussed above, the Company had $1,150 million in lines of credit for general corporate purposes, including commercial paper back-up. There were no borrowings under these lines of credit during 2004.

These credit facilities are subject to normal banking terms and conditions. Some of the financial arrangements require compensating balances, none of which is presently significant to our Company.

NOTE 7: LONG-TERM DEBT

Long-term debt consists of the following (in millions):

December 31,	2004	2003
Variable rate euro notes due 2004[1]	$ —	$ 296
5⅞% euro notes due 2005	663	591
4% U.S. dollar notes due 2005	750	749
5¾% U.S. dollar notes due 2009	399	399
5¾% U.S. dollar notes due 2011	499	498
7⅜% U.S. dollar notes due 2093	116	116
Other, due through 2013[2]	220	191
	$ 2,647	$ 2,840
Less current portion	1,490	323
	$ 1,157	$ 2,517

[1]   2.4 percent at December 31, 2003.

[2]   Includes $5 million and $27 million fair value adjustment related to interest rate swap agreements in 2004 and 2003, respectively. Refer to Note 10.

The above notes include various restrictions, none of which is presently significant to our Company.

After giving effect to interest rate management instruments, the principal amount of our long-term debt that had fixed and variable interest rates, respectively, was $1,895 million and $752 million on December 31, 2004, and $1,742 million and $1,098 million on December 31, 2003. The weighted-average interest rate on our Company's long-term debt was 4.4 percent and 3.9 percent per annum for the years ended December 31, 2004 and 2003, respectively. Total interest paid was approximately $188 million, $180 million and $197 million in 2004, 2003 and 2002, respectively. For a more detailed discussion of interest rate management, refer to Note 10.

Maturities of long-term debt for the five years succeeding December 31, 2004 are as follows (in millions):

2005	2006	2007	2008	2009
$ 1,490	$ 43	$ 21	$ 7	$ 406

NOTES TO CONSOLIDATED FINANCIAL STATEMENTS
The Coca-Cola Company and Subsidiaries

NOTE 8: COMPREHENSIVE INCOME

Accumulated other comprehensive income (loss), including our proportionate share of equity method investees' accumulated other comprehensive income (loss), consists of the following (in millions):

December 31,	2004	2003
Foreign currency translation adjustment	$ **(1,191)**	$ (1,856)
Accumulated derivative net losses	**(80)**	(77)
Unrealized gain on available-for-sale securities	**91**	52
Minimum pension liability	**(168)**	(114)
	$ **(1,348)**	$ (1,995)

A summary of the components of accumulated other comprehensive income (loss), including our proportionate share of equity method investees' other comprehensive income, for the years ended December 31, 2004, 2003 and 2002 is as follows (in millions):

	Before-Tax Amount	Income Tax	After-Tax Amount
2004			
Net foreign currency translation adjustment	$ **766**	$ **(101)**	$ **665**
Net loss on derivatives	**(4)**	**1**	**(3)**
Net change in unrealized gain on available-for-sale securities	**48**	**(9)**	**39**
Net change in minimum pension liability	**(81)**	**27**	**(54)**
Other comprehensive income (loss)	$ **729**	$ **(82)**	$ **647**

	Before-Tax Amount	Income Tax	After-Tax Amount
2003			
Net foreign currency translation adjustment	$ 913	$ 8	$ 921
Net loss on derivatives	(63)	30	(33)
Net change in unrealized gain on available-for-sale securities	65	(25)	40
Net change in minimum pension liability	181	(57)	124
Other comprehensive income (loss)	$ 1,096	$ (44)	$ 1,052

	Before-Tax Amount	Income Tax	After-Tax Amount
2002			
Net foreign currency translation adjustment	$ (51)	$ (44)	$ (95)
Net loss on derivatives	(284)	98	(186)
Net change in unrealized gain on available-for-sale securities	104	(37)	67
Net change in minimum pension liability	(299)	104	(195)
Other comprehensive income (loss)	$ (530)	$ 121	$ (409)

NOTES TO CONSOLIDATED FINANCIAL STATEMENTS
The Coca-Cola Company and Subsidiaries

NOTE 9: FINANCIAL INSTRUMENTS

Fair Value of Financial Instruments

The carrying amounts reflected in our consolidated balance sheets for cash and cash equivalents, non-marketable cost method investments, trade accounts receivable and loans and notes payable approximate their respective fair values. The carrying amount and the fair value of our long-term debt, including the current portion, as of December 31, 2004 was approximately $2,647 million and $2,736 million, respectively. As of December 31, 2003, the carrying amount and the fair value of our long-term debt, including the current portion, was approximately $2,840 million and $2,942 million, respectively. For additional details about our long-term debt, refer to Note 7.

Fair values are based primarily on quoted prices for those or similar instruments. Fair values for our derivative financial instruments are included in Note 10.

Credit Risk

With respect to our cash and cash equivalents balances, we manage our exposure to counterparty credit risk through specific minimum credit standards, diversification of counterparties and procedures to monitor concentration of credit risk. Based on these factors, we consider the risk of counterparty default to be minimal.

Certain Debt and Marketable Equity Securities

Investments in debt and marketable equity securities, other than investments accounted for by the equity method, are required to be categorized as either trading, available-for-sale or held-to-maturity. On December 31, 2004 and 2003, we had no trading securities. Securities categorized as available-for-sale are stated at fair value, with unrealized gains and losses, net of deferred income taxes, reported as a component of Accumulated Other Comprehensive Income (Loss) ("AOCI"). Debt securities, primarily time deposits, categorized as held-to-maturity are stated at amortized cost.

NOTES TO CONSOLIDATED FINANCIAL STATEMENTS
The Coca-Cola Company and Subsidiaries

NOTE 9: FINANCIAL INSTRUMENTS (Continued)

On December 31, 2004 and 2003, available-for-sale and held-to-maturity securities consisted of the following (in millions):

December 31,	Cost	Gross Unrealized Gains	Gross Unrealized Losses	Estimated Fair Value
2004				
Available-for-sale securities:				
Equity securities	$ 144	$ 146	$ (2)	$ 288
Other debt securities	5	—	(1)	4
	$ 149	$ 146	$ (3)	$ 292
Held-to-maturity securities:				
Bank and corporate debt	$ 4,479	$ —	$ —	$ 4,479
Other debt securities	107	—	—	107
	$ 4,586	$ —	$ —	$ 4,586

December 31,	Cost	Gross Unrealized Gains	Gross Unrealized Losses	Estimated Fair Value
2003				
Available-for-sale securities:				
Bank and corporate debt	$ 118	$ —	$ —	$ 118
Equity securities	147	97	(12)	232
Other debt securities	76	—	—	76
	$ 341	$ 97	$ (12)	$ 426
Held-to-maturity securities:				
Bank and corporate debt	$ 2,162	$ —	$ —	$ 2,162
Other debt securities	1	—	—	1
	$ 2,163	$ —	$ —	$ 2,163

NOTES TO CONSOLIDATED FINANCIAL STATEMENTS

The Coca-Cola Company and Subsidiaries

NOTE 9: FINANCIAL INSTRUMENTS (Continued)

On December 31, 2004 and 2003, these investments were included in the following captions (in millions):

December 31,	Available-for-Sale Securities	Held-to-Maturity Securities
2004		
Cash and cash equivalents	$ —	$ 4,586
Current marketable securities	61	—
Cost method investments, principally bottling companies	229	—
Other assets	2	—
	$ 292	$ 4,586

December 31,	Available-for-Sale Securities	Held-to-Maturity Securities
2003		
Cash and cash equivalents	$ 118	$ 2,162
Current marketable securities	120	—
Cost method investments, principally bottling companies	185	—
Other assets	3	1
	$ 426	$ 2,163

The contractual maturities of these investments as of December 31, 2004 were as follows (in millions):

	Available-for-Sale Securities		Held-to-Maturity Securities	
	Cost	Fair Value	Amortized Cost	Fair Value
2005	$ —	$ —	$ 4,586	$ 4,586
2006-2009	—	—	—	—
2010-2014	—	—	—	—
After 2014	5	4	—	—
Equity securities	144	288	—	—
	$ 149	$ 292	$ 4,586	$ 4,586

For the years ended December 31, 2004, 2003 and 2002, gross realized gains and losses on sales of available-for-sale securities were not material. The cost of securities sold is based on the specific identification method.

NOTE 10: HEDGING TRANSACTIONS AND DERIVATIVE FINANCIAL INSTRUMENTS

Our Company uses derivative financial instruments primarily to reduce our exposure to adverse fluctuations in interest rates and foreign exchange rates and, to a lesser extent, in commodity prices and other market risks. When entered into, the Company formally designates and documents the financial instrument as a hedge of a specific underlying exposure, as well as the risk management objectives and strategies for undertaking the hedge

NOTES TO CONSOLIDATED FINANCIAL STATEMENTS
The Coca-Cola Company and Subsidiaries

NOTE 10: HEDGING TRANSACTIONS AND DERIVATIVE FINANCIAL INSTRUMENTS (Continued)

transactions. The Company formally assesses, both at the inception and at least quarterly thereafter, whether the financial instruments that are used in hedging transactions are effective at offsetting changes in either the fair value or cash flows of the related underlying exposure. Because of the high degree of effectiveness between the hedging instrument and the underlying exposure being hedged, fluctuations in the value of the derivative instruments are generally offset by changes in the fair values or cash flows of the underlying exposures being hedged. Any ineffective portion of a financial instrument's change in fair value is immediately recognized in earnings. Virtually all of our derivatives are straightforward over-the-counter instruments with liquid markets. Our Company does not enter into derivative financial instruments for trading purposes.

The fair values of derivatives used to hedge or modify our risks fluctuate over time. We do not view these fair value amounts in isolation, but rather in relation to the fair values or cash flows of the underlying hedged transactions or other exposures. The notional amounts of the derivative financial instruments do not necessarily represent amounts exchanged by the parties and, therefore, are not a direct measure of our exposure to the financial risks described above. The amounts exchanged are calculated by reference to the notional amounts and by other terms of the derivatives, such as interest rates, exchange rates or other financial indices.

Our Company recognizes all derivative instruments as either assets or liabilities in our consolidated balance sheets at fair value. The accounting for changes in fair value of a derivative instrument depends on whether it has been designated and qualifies as part of a hedging relationship and, further, on the type of hedging relationship. At the inception of the hedging relationship, the Company must designate the instrument as a fair value hedge, a cash flow hedge, or a hedge of a net investment in a foreign operation. This designation is based upon the exposure being hedged.

We have established strict counterparty credit guidelines and enter into transactions only with financial institutions of investment grade or better. We monitor counterparty exposures daily and review any downgrade in credit rating immediately. If a downgrade in the credit rating of a counterparty were to occur, we have provisions requiring collateral in the form of U.S. government securities for substantially all of our transactions. To mitigate presettlement risk, minimum credit standards become more stringent as the duration of the derivative financial instrument increases. To minimize the concentration of credit risk, we enter into derivative transactions with a portfolio of financial institutions. The Company has master netting agreements with most of the financial institutions that are counterparties to the derivative instruments. These agreements allow for the net settlement of assets and liabilities arising from different transactions with the same counterparty. Based on these factors, we consider the risk of counterparty default to be minimal.

Interest Rate Management

Our Company monitors our mix of fixed rate and variable rate debt, as well as our mix of term debt versus non-term debt. This monitoring includes a review of business and other financial risks. We also enter into interest rate swap agreements to manage these risks. These contracts had maturities of less than one year on December 31, 2004. Interest rate swap agreements that meet certain conditions required under SFAS No. 133 for fair value hedges are accounted for as such, with the offset recorded to adjust the fair value of the underlying exposure being hedged. During 2004, 2003 and 2002, there has been no ineffectiveness related to fair value hedges. The fair values of our Company's interest rate swap agreements were approximately $6 million and $28 million at December 31, 2004 and 2003, respectively. The Company estimates the fair value of its interest rate management derivatives based on quoted market prices.

NOTES TO CONSOLIDATED FINANCIAL STATEMENTS
The Coca-Cola Company and Subsidiaries

NOTE 10: HEDGING TRANSACTIONS AND DERIVATIVE FINANCIAL INSTRUMENTS (Continued)

Foreign Currency Management

The purpose of our foreign currency hedging activities is to reduce the risk that our eventual U.S. dollar net cash inflows resulting from sales outside the United States will be adversely affected by changes in exchange rates.

We enter into forward exchange contracts and purchase currency options (principally euro and Japanese yen) and collars to hedge certain portions of forecasted cash flows denominated in foreign currencies. The effective portion of the changes in fair value for these contracts, which have been designated as cash flow hedges, are reported in AOCI and reclassified into earnings in the same financial statement line item and in the same period or periods during which the hedged transaction affects earnings. Any ineffective portion (which was not significant in 2004, 2003 or 2002) of the change in fair value of these instruments is immediately recognized in earnings. These contracts had maturities up to one year on December 31, 2004.

Additionally, the Company enters into forward exchange contracts that are not designated as hedging instruments under SFAS No. 133. These instruments are used to offset the earnings impact relating to the variability in exchange rates on certain monetary assets and liabilities denominated in nonfunctional currencies. Changes in the fair value of these instruments are immediately recognized in earnings in the line item other income (loss)—net of our consolidated statements of income to offset the effect of remeasurement of the monetary assets and liabilities.

The Company also enters into forward exchange contracts to hedge its net investment position in certain major currencies. Under SFAS No. 133, changes in the fair value of these instruments are recognized in foreign currency translation adjustment, a component of AOCI, to offset the change in the value of the net investment being hedged. For the years ended December 31, 2004, 2003 and 2002, approximately $8 million, $29 million and $26 million, respectively, of losses relating to derivative financial instruments were recorded in foreign currency translation adjustment.

For the years ended December 31, 2004, 2003 and 2002, we recorded an increase (decrease) to AOCI of approximately $6 million, $(31) million and $(151) million, respectively, net of both income taxes and reclassifications to earnings, primarily related to gains and losses on foreign currency cash flow hedges. These items will generally offset cash flow gains and losses relating to the underlying exposures being hedged in future periods. The Company estimates that it will reclassify into earnings during the next 12 months losses of approximately $35 million from the after-tax amount recorded in AOCI as of December 31, 2004 as the anticipated foreign currency cash flows occur.

The Company did not discontinue any cash flow hedge relationships during the years ended December 31, 2004, 2003 and 2002.

NOTES TO CONSOLIDATED FINANCIAL STATEMENTS
The Coca-Cola Company and Subsidiaries

NOTE 10: HEDGING TRANSACTIONS AND DERIVATIVE FINANCIAL INSTRUMENTS (Continued)

The following table summarizes activity in AOCI related to derivatives designated as cash flow hedges held by the Company during the applicable periods (in millions):

Year Ended December 31,	Before-Tax Amount	Income Tax	After-Tax Amount
2004			
Accumulated derivative net losses as of January 1, 2004	**$ (66)**	**$ 26**	**$ (40)**
Net changes in fair value of derivatives	**(76)**	**30**	**(46)**
Net losses reclassified from AOCI into earnings	**86**	**(34)**	**52**
Accumulated derivative net losses as of December 31, 2004	**$ (56)**	**$ 22**	**$ (34)**

Year Ended December 31,	Before-Tax Amount	Income Tax	After-Tax Amount
2003			
Accumulated derivative net losses as of January 1, 2003	$ (15)	$ 6	$ (9)
Net changes in fair value of derivatives	(165)	65	(100)
Net losses reclassified from AOCI into earnings	114	(45)	69
Accumulated derivative net losses as of December 31, 2003	$ (66)	$ 26	$ (40)

Year Ended December 31,	Before-Tax Amount	Income Tax	After-Tax Amount
2002			
Accumulated derivative net gains as of January 1, 2002	$ 234	$ (92)	$ 142
Net changes in fair value of derivatives	(129)	51	(78)
Net gains reclassified from AOCI into earnings	(120)	47	(73)
Accumulated derivative net losses as of December 31, 2002	$ (15)	$ 6	$ (9)

NOTES TO CONSOLIDATED FINANCIAL STATEMENTS

The Coca-Cola Company and Subsidiaries

NOTE 10: HEDGING TRANSACTIONS AND DERIVATIVE FINANCIAL INSTRUMENTS (Continued)

The following table presents the fair values, carrying values and maturities of the Company's foreign currency derivative instruments outstanding (in millions):

December 31,	Carrying Values Assets	Fair Values	Maturity
2004			
Forward contracts	**$ 27**	**$ 27**	**2005**
Options and collars	**12**	**12**	**2005**
	$ 39	**$ 39**	

December 31,	Carrying Values Assets (Liabilities)	Fair Values	Maturity
2003			
Forward contracts	$ (25)	$ (25)	2004
Options and collars	3	3	2004
	$ (22)	$ (22)	

The Company estimates the fair value of its foreign currency derivatives based on quoted market prices or pricing models using current market rates. This amount is primarily reflected in prepaid expenses and other assets in our consolidated balance sheets.

NOTE 11: COMMITMENTS AND CONTINGENCIES

On December 31, 2004 we were contingently liable for guarantees of indebtedness owed by third parties in the amount of $257 million. These guarantees are related to third-party customers, bottlers and vendors and have arisen through the normal course of business. These guarantees have various terms, and none of these guarantees is individually significant. The amount represents the maximum potential future payments that we could be required to make under the guarantees; however, we do not consider it probable that we will be required to satisfy these guarantees.

Additionally, in December 2003, we granted a $250 million standby line of credit to Coca-Cola FEMSA with normal market terms. As of December 31, 2004 and 2003, no amounts have been drawn against this line of credit. This standby letter of credit expires in December 2006.

We believe our exposure to concentrations of credit risk is limited due to the diverse geographic areas covered by our operations.

The Company is also involved in various legal proceedings. We establish reserves for specific legal proceedings when we determine that the likelihood of an unfavorable outcome is probable. Management has also identified certain other legal matters where we believe an unfavorable outcome is reasonably possible for which no estimate of possible losses can be made. Management believes that any liability to the Company that may arise as a result of currently pending legal proceedings, including those discussed below, will not have a material adverse effect on the financial condition of the Company taken as a whole.

NOTES TO CONSOLIDATED FINANCIAL STATEMENTS
The Coca-Cola Company and Subsidiaries

NOTE 11: COMMITMENTS AND CONTINGENCIES (Continued)

In 2003, the Securities and Exchange Commission ("SEC") began conducting an investigation into whether the Company or certain persons associated with the Company violated federal securities laws in connection with the conduct alleged by a former employee of the Company. Additionally, in 2003 the United States Attorney's Office for the Northern District of Georgia commenced a criminal investigation of the allegations raised by the same former employee. The Company is continuing to cooperate with the United States Attorney's office and the SEC.

During the period from 1970 to 1981, our Company owned Aqua-Chem, Inc. ("Aqua-Chem"). A division of Aqua-Chem manufactured certain boilers that contained gaskets that Aqua-Chem purchased from outside suppliers. Several years after our Company sold this entity, Aqua-Chem received its first lawsuit relating to asbestos, a component of some of the gaskets. In September 2002, Aqua-Chem notified our Company that it believes we are obligated to them for certain costs and expenses associated with the litigation. Aqua-Chem demanded that our Company reimburse it for approximately $10 million for out-of-pocket litigation-related expenses incurred over the last 18 years. Aqua-Chem has also demanded that the Company acknowledge a continuing obligation to Aqua-Chem for any future liabilities and expenses that are excluded from coverage under the applicable insurance or for which there is no insurance. Our Company disputes Aqua-Chem's claims, and we believe we have no obligation to Aqua-Chem for any of its past, present or future liabilities, costs or expenses. Furthermore, we believe we have substantial legal and factual defenses to Aqua-Chem's claims. The parties entered into litigation to resolve this dispute, which was stayed by agreement of the parties pending the outcome of litigation filed by certain insurers of Aqua-Chem. In that case, five plaintiff insurance companies filed a declaratory judgment action against Aqua-Chem, the Company and 16 defendant insurance companies seeking a determination of the parties' rights and liabilities under policies issued by the insurers. That litigation remains pending, and the Company believes it has substantial legal and factual defenses to the insurers' claims. Aqua-Chem and the Company have reached an agreement in principle to settle with five of the insurers in the Wisconsin insurance coverage litigation, and those insurers will pay funds into an escrow account for payment of costs arising from the asbestos claims against Aqua-Chem. Aqua-Chem and the Company will continue to litigate their claims for coverage against the 16 other insurers that are parties to the Wisconsin insurance coverage case. The Company also believes Aqua-Chem has substantial insurance coverage to pay Aqua-Chem's asbestos claimants. An estimate of possible losses, if any, cannot be made at this time.

Since 1999, the Competition Directorate of the European Commission (the "Commission") has been conducting an investigation of various commercial and market practices of the Company and its bottlers in Austria, Belgium, Denmark, Germany and Great Britain. On October 19, 2004, our Company and certain of our bottlers submitted a formal Undertaking to the Commission, and the Commission accepted the Undertaking. The Undertaking will potentially apply in 27 countries and in all channels of distribution where our carbonated soft drinks account for over 40 percent of national sales and twice the nearest competitor's share. It will take more than 12 months to fully implement the Undertaking and for the market to react to any resulting changes. The commitments we made in the Undertaking relate broadly to exclusivity, percentage-based purchasing commitments, transparency, target rebates, tying, assortment or range commitments, and agreements concerning products of other suppliers. The Undertaking will also apply to shelf space commitments in agreements with take-home customers and to financing and availability agreements in the on-premise channel. In addition, the Undertaking includes commitments that will be applicable to commercial arrangements concerning the installation and use of technical equipment (such as coolers, fountain equipment and vending machines). The commitments set forth in the Undertaking have been published for third-party comments. Following the comment period, the Commission presented to the Company certain comments it had received

NOTES TO CONSOLIDATED FINANCIAL STATEMENTS
The Coca-Cola Company and Subsidiaries

NOTE 11: COMMITMENTS AND CONTINGENCIES (Continued)

from third parties, as well as certain additional comments from the Commission's legal staff. The Company is in the process of addressing these comments with the Commission. The Company anticipates that the formal Undertaking will form the basis of a Commission decision pursuant to Article 9, paragraph 1 of Council Regulation 1/2003 to be issued in the second quarter of 2005, bringing an end to the investigation. The submission of the Undertaking does not imply any recognition on the Company's or the bottlers' part of any infringement of Commission competition rules. We believe that the Undertaking, while imposing restrictions, clarifies the application of competition rules to our practices in Europe and will allow our system to be able to compete vigorously while adhering to the Undertaking's provisions.

The Company is also discussing with the Commission issues relating to parallel trade within the European Union arising out of comments received by the Commission from third parties. The Company is fully cooperating with the Commission and is providing information on these issues and the measures taken and to be taken to address any issues raised. The Company is unable to predict at this time with any reasonable degree of certainty what action, if any, the Commission will take with respect to these issues.

The Spanish competition service made unannounced visits to our offices and those of certain bottlers in Spain in 2000. In December 2003, the Spanish competition service suspended its investigation until the Commission notifies the service of how the Commission will proceed in its aforementioned investigation.

The French Competition Directorate has also initiated an inquiry into commercial practices related to the soft drink sector in France. This inquiry has been conducted through visits to the offices of the Company; however, no conclusions have been communicated to the Company by the Directorate.

At the time of divesting our interest in a consolidated entity, we sometimes agree to indemnify the buyer for specific liabilities related to the period we owned the entity. Management believes that any liability to the Company that may arise as a result of any such indemnification agreements will not have a material adverse effect on the financial condition of the Company taken as a whole.

The Company is involved in various tax matters. We establish reserves at the time that we determine that it is probable that we will be liable to pay additional taxes related to certain matters. We adjust these reserves, including any impact on the related interest and penalties, in light of changing facts and circumstances, such as the progress of a tax audit.

A number of years may elapse before a particular matter, for which we may have established a reserve, is audited and finally resolved or when a tax assessment is raised. The number of years with open tax audits varies depending on the tax jurisdiction. While it is often difficult to predict the final outcome or the timing of resolution of any particular tax matter, we record a reserve when we determine the likelihood of loss is probable and the amount of loss is reasonably estimable. Such liabilities are recorded in the line item accrued income taxes in the Company's consolidated balance sheets. Favorable resolution of tax matters that had been previously reserved would be recognized as a reduction to our income tax expense, when known.

The Company is also involved in various tax matters where we have determined that the probability of an unfavorable outcome is reasonably possible. Management believes that any liability to the Company that may arise as a result of currently pending tax matters will not have a material adverse effect on the financial condition of the Company taken as a whole.

The Company is a party to various legal proceedings in which we are seeking to be reimbursed for costs that we have incurred in the past. Although none of these reimbursements has been realized at this time, the

NOTES TO CONSOLIDATED FINANCIAL STATEMENTS
The Coca-Cola Company and Subsidiaries

NOTE 11: COMMITMENTS AND CONTINGENCIES (Continued)

Company expects final resolution of certain matters in 2005. Management believes that any gains to the Company that may arise as a result of the final resolutions of these matters will not have a material effect on the financial condition of the Company taken as a whole.

NOTE 12: NET CHANGE IN OPERATING ASSETS AND LIABILITIES

Net cash provided by operating activities attributable to the net change in operating assets and liabilities is composed of the following (in millions):

	2004	2003	2002
Decrease (increase) in trade accounts receivable	$ (5)	$ 80	$ (83)
Decrease (increase) in inventories	(57)	111	(49)
Decrease (increase) in prepaid expenses and other assets	(397)	(276)	74
Increase (decrease) in accounts payable and accrued expenses	45	(164)	(442)
Increase (decrease) in accrued taxes	(194)	53	20
Increase (decrease) in other liabilities	(9)	28	73
	$ (617)	$ (168)	$ (407)

NOTE 13: RESTRICTED STOCK, STOCK OPTIONS AND OTHER STOCK PLANS

Prior to 2002, our Company accounted for our stock option plans and restricted stock plans under the recognition and measurement provisions of APB Opinion No. 25 and related interpretations. Effective January 1, 2002, our Company adopted the preferable fair value recognition provisions of SFAS No. 123. Our Company selected the modified prospective method of adoption described in SFAS No. 148. Compensation cost recognized in 2002 was the same as that which would have been recognized had the fair value method of SFAS No. 123 been applied from its original effective date. Refer to Note 1.

In accordance with the provisions of SFAS No. 123 and SFAS No. 148, $345 million, $422 million and $365 million were recorded for total stock-based compensation expense in 2004, 2003 and 2002, respectively. The $345 million and $365 million recorded in 2004 and 2002, respectively, were recorded in selling, general and administrative expenses. Of the $422 million recorded in 2003, $407 million was recorded in selling, general and administrative expenses and $15 million was recorded in other operating charges. Refer to Note 17.

Stock Option Plans

Under our 1991 Stock Option Plan (the "1991 Option Plan"), a maximum of 120 million shares of our common stock was approved to be issued or transferred to certain officers and employees pursuant to stock options granted under the 1991 Option Plan. Options to purchase common stock under the 1991 Option Plan have been granted to Company employees at fair market value at the date of grant.

The 1999 Stock Option Plan (the "1999 Option Plan") was approved by shareowners in April 1999. Following the approval of the 1999 Option Plan, no grants were made from the 1991 Option Plan, and shares available under the 1991 Option Plan were no longer available to be granted. Under the 1999 Option Plan, a maximum of 120 million shares of our common stock was approved to be issued or transferred to certain officers and employees pursuant to stock options granted under the 1999 Option Plan. Options to purchase common stock under the 1999 Option Plan have been granted to Company employees at fair market value at the date of grant.

NOTES TO CONSOLIDATED FINANCIAL STATEMENTS
The Coca-Cola Company and Subsidiaries

NOTE 13: RESTRICTED STOCK, STOCK OPTIONS AND OTHER STOCK PLANS (Continued)

The 2002 Stock Option Plan (the "2002 Option Plan") was approved by shareowners in April 2002. Under the 2002 Option Plan, a maximum of 120 million shares of our common stock was approved to be issued or transferred to certain officers and employees pursuant to stock options and stock appreciation rights granted under the 2002 Option Plan. The stock appreciation rights permit the holder, upon surrendering all or part of the related stock option, to receive common stock in an amount up to 100 percent of the difference between the market price and the option price. No stock appreciation rights have been issued under the 2002 Stock Option Plan as of December 31, 2004. Options to purchase common stock under the 2002 Option Plan have been granted to Company employees at fair market value at the date of grant.

Stock options granted in December 2003 and thereafter generally become exercisable over a four-year vesting period and expire 10 years from the date of grant. Stock option grants from 1999 through July 2003 generally become exercisable over a four-year vesting period and expire 15 years from the date of grant. Prior to 1999, stock options generally became exercisable over a three-year vesting period and expired 10 years from the date of grant.

The following table sets forth information about the fair value of each option grant on the date of grant using the Black-Scholes-Merton option-pricing model and the weighted-average assumptions used for such grants:

	2004	2003	2002
Weighted-average fair value of options granted	$ 8.84	$ 13.49	$ 13.10
Dividend yields	2.5%	1.9%	1.7%
Expected volatility	23.0%	28.1%	30.2%
Risk-free interest rates	3.8%	3.5%	3.4%
Expected lives	6 years	6 years	6 years

To ensure the best market-based assumptions were used to determine the estimated fair value of stock options granted in 2004, 2003 and 2002, we obtained two independent market quotes. Our Black-Scholes-Merton option-pricing model value was not materially different from the independent quotes.

A summary of stock option activity under all plans is as follows (shares in millions):

	2004		2003		2002	
	Shares	Weighted-Average Exercise Price	Shares	Weighted-Average Exercise Price	Shares	Weighted-Average Exercise Price
Outstanding on January 1	167	$ 50.56	159	$ 50.24	141	$ 51.16
Granted[1]	31	41.63	24	49.67	29	44.69
Exercised	(5)	35.54	(4)	26.96	(3)	31.09
Forfeited/expired[2]	(10)	51.64	(12)	51.45	(8)	54.21
Outstanding on December 31	183	$ 49.41	167	$ 50.56	159	$ 50.24
Exercisable on December 31	116	$ 52.02	102	$ 51.97	80	$ 51.72
Shares available on December 31 for options that may be granted	85		108		122	

[1] No grants were made from the 1991 Option Plan during 2004, 2003 or 2002.

[2] Shares forfeited/expired relate to the 1991, 1999 and 2002 Option Plans.

NOTES TO CONSOLIDATED FINANCIAL STATEMENTS
The Coca-Cola Company and Subsidiaries

NOTE 13: RESTRICTED STOCK, STOCK OPTIONS AND OTHER STOCK PLANS (Continued)

The following table summarizes information about stock options at December 31, 2004 (shares in millions):

Range of Exercise Prices	Outstanding Stock Options			Exercisable Stock Options	
	Shares	Weighted-Average Remaining Contractual Life	Weighted-Average Exercise Price	Shares	Weighted-Average Exercise Price
$ 30.00 to $ 40.00	6	0.8 years	$ 35.63	6	$ 35.63
$ 40.01 to $ 50.00	119	10.3 years	$ 46.03	53	$ 47.57
$ 50.01 to $ 60.00	48	9.1 years	$ 56.25	47	$ 56.30
$ 60.01 to $ 86.75	10	3.8 years	$ 65.85	10	$ 65.85
$ 30.00 to $ 86.75	183	9.3 years	$ 49.41	116	$ 52.02

Restricted Stock Award Plans

Under the amended 1989 Restricted Stock Award Plan and the amended 1983 Restricted Stock Award Plan (the "Restricted Stock Award Plans"), 40 million and 24 million shares of restricted common stock, respectively, were originally available to be granted to certain officers and key employees of our Company.

On December 31, 2004, 31 million shares remain available for grant under the Restricted Stock Award Plans. Participants are entitled to vote and receive dividends on the shares and, under the 1983 Restricted Stock Award Plan, participants are reimbursed by our Company for income taxes imposed on the award, but not for taxes generated by the reimbursement payment. The shares are subject to certain transfer restrictions and may be forfeited if a participant leaves our Company for reasons other than retirement, disability or death, absent a change in control of our Company.

The following awards were outstanding as of December 31, 2004:

- 513,700 shares of restricted stock in which the restrictions lapse upon the achievement of continued employment over a specified period of time (time-based restricted stock awards);

- 713,000 shares of performance-based restricted stock in which restrictions lapse upon the achievement of specific performance goals over a specified performance period. An additional 125,000 shares were promised, based upon achievement of relevant performance criteria, for employees based outside of the United States; and

- 1,583,447 performance share unit awards which could result in a future grant of restricted stock after the achievement of specific performance goals over a specified performance period. Such awards are subject to adjustment based on the final performance relative to the goals, resulting in a minimum grant of no shares and a maximum grant of 2,339,171 shares.

NOTES TO CONSOLIDATED FINANCIAL STATEMENTS

The Coca-Cola Company and Subsidiaries

NOTE 13: RESTRICTED STOCK, STOCK OPTIONS AND OTHER STOCK PLANS (Continued)

Time-Based Restricted Stock Awards

The following table summarizes information about time-based restricted stock awards:

	Number of Shares		
	2004	2003	2002
Outstanding on January 1,	**1,224,900**	1,506,485	1,492,985
Granted[1]	**140,000**	—	30,000
Released	**(296,800)**	(254,585)	(14,000)
Cancelled/Forfeited	**(554,400)**	(27,000)	(2,500)
Outstanding on December 31,	**513,700**	1,224,900	1,506,485

[1] In 2004 and 2002, the Company granted time-based restricted stock awards with average per share fair values of $48.97 and $50.99, respectively.

Performance-Based Restricted Stock Awards

In 2001, shareowners approved an amendment to the 1989 Restricted Stock Award Plan to allow for the grant of performance-based awards. These awards are released only upon the achievement of specific measurable performance criteria. These awards pay dividends during the performance period. The majority of awards had specific earnings per share targets for achievement. If the earnings per share target is not met, the awards will be cancelled.

The following table summarizes information about performance-based restricted stock awards:

	Number of Shares		
	2004	2003	2002
Outstanding on January 1,	**2,507,720**	2,655,000	2,605,000
Granted[1]	**—**	52,720	50,000
Released	**(110,000)**	—	—
Cancelled/Forfeited	**(1,684,720)**	(200,000)	—
Outstanding on December 31,	**713,000[2]**	2,507,720[2]	2,655,000[2]

[1] In 2003, 52,720 shares of three-year performance-based restricted stock were granted at an average fair value of $42.91 per share. In 2002, 50,000 shares of four-year performance-based restricted stock were granted at an average fair value of $46.88 per share.

[2] In 2002, the Company promised to grant an additional 50,000 shares at the end of three years and an additional 75,000 shares at the end of four years, at an average value of $46.88, if the Company achieved predefined performance targets over the respective measurement periods. These awards are similar to the performance-based restricted stock, including the payment of dividend equivalents, but were granted in this manner because the employees were situated outside of the United States. As of December 31, 2004, these grants were still outstanding.

The Company did not recognize compensation expense for the majority of these awards, as it is not probable the performance targets will be achieved.

NOTES TO CONSOLIDATED FINANCIAL STATEMENTS
The Coca-Cola Company and Subsidiaries

NOTE 13: RESTRICTED STOCK, STOCK OPTIONS AND OTHER STOCK PLANS (Continued)

Performance Share Unit Awards

In 2003, the Company modified its use of performance-based awards and established a program to grant performance share unit awards under the 1989 Restricted Stock Award Plan to executives. The number of performance share units earned shall be determined at the end of each performance period, generally three years, based on performance measurements determined by the Board of Directors and may result in an award of restricted stock for U.S. participants and certain international participants at that time. The restricted stock may be granted to other international participants shortly before the fifth anniversary of the original award. Restrictions on such stock lapse generally on the fifth anniversary of the original award date. Generally, performance share unit awards are subject to the performance criteria of compound annual growth in earnings per share over the performance period, as adjusted for certain items approved by the Compensation Committee of the Board of Directors ("adjusted EPS"). The purpose of these adjustments is to ensure a consistent year to year comparison of the specified performance measure.

Performance share unit Target Awards for the 2004-2006 and 2005-2007 performance periods require adjusted EPS growth in line with our Company's internal projections over the performance period. In the event adjusted EPS exceeds the target projection, additional shares up to the Maximum Award may be granted. In the event adjusted EPS falls below the target projection, a reduced number of shares as few as the Threshold Award may be granted. If adjusted EPS falls below the Threshold Award performance level, no shares will be granted. Of the outstanding granted performance share unit awards as of December 31, 2004, 741,985 and 769,462 awards are for the 2004-2006 and 2005-2007 performance periods, respectively. In addition, 72,000 performance share unit awards, with predefined qualitative performance measures other than adjusted EPS and other release criteria that differ from the program described above, are included in the performance share units granted in 2004.

The following table summarizes information about performance share unit awards:

	Number of Share Units	
	2004	2003
Outstanding on January 1,	**798,931**	—
Granted[1]	**953,196**	798,931
Cancelled/Forfeited	**(168,680)**	—
Outstanding on December 31,	**1,583,447**	798,931
Threshold Award	**950,837**	399,466
Target Award	**1,583,447**	798,931
Maximum Award	**2,339,171**	1,198,397

[1] In 2004 and 2003, the Company granted performance share unit awards with average fair values of $38.71 and $46.78, respectively.

The Company did not recognize any compensation expense in 2004 for awards from the 2004-2006 performance period, as it is not probable the Threshold Award performance level will be achieved.

NOTES TO CONSOLIDATED FINANCIAL STATEMENTS
The Coca-Cola Company and Subsidiaries

NOTE 14: PENSION AND OTHER POSTRETIREMENT BENEFIT PLANS

Our Company sponsors and/or contributes to pension and postretirement health care and life insurance benefit plans covering substantially all U.S. employees. We also sponsor nonqualified, unfunded defined benefit pension plans for certain members of management. In addition, our Company and its subsidiaries have various pension plans and other forms of postretirement arrangements outside the United States. We use a measurement date of December 31 for substantially all of our pension and postretirement benefit plans.

Obligations and Funded Status

The following table sets forth the change in benefit obligations for our benefit plans (in millions):

	Pension Benefits		Other Benefits	
December 31,	**2004**	2003	**2004**	2003
Benefit obligation at beginning of year[1]	**$ 2,495**	$ 2,182	**$ 761**	$ 651
Service cost	**85**	76	**27**	25
Interest cost	**147**	140	**44**	44
Foreign currency exchange rate changes	**71**	90	**1**	1
Amendments	**—**	(2)	**—**	(25)
Actuarial (gain) loss[2]	**124**	142	**(11)**	86
Benefits paid[3]	**(125)**	(122)	**(25)**	(22)
Curtailments	**3**	(23)	**—**	(6)
Special termination benefits	**—**	12	**—**	5
Other	**—**	—	**4**	2
Benefit obligation at end of year[1]	**$ 2,800**	$ 2,495	**$ 801**	$ 761

[1] For pension benefit plans, the benefit obligation is the projected benefit obligation. For other benefit plans, the benefit obligation is the accumulated postretirement benefit obligation.

[2] During 2004, our accumulated postretirement benefit obligation was reduced by $67 million due to the adoption of FSP 106-2. Refer to Note 1.

[3] Benefits paid from pension benefit plans during 2004 and 2003 included $25 million and $27 million, respectively, in payments related to unfunded pension plans that were paid from Company assets. All of the benefits paid from other benefit plans during 2004 and 2003 were paid from Company assets.

The accumulated benefit obligation for our pension plans was $2,440 million and $2,145 million at December 31, 2004 and 2003, respectively.

The total projected benefit obligation and fair value of plan assets for the pension plans with projected benefit obligations in excess of plan assets were $1,112 million and $388 million, respectively, as of December 31, 2004 and $941 million and $311 million, respectively, as of December 31, 2003. The total accumulated benefit obligation and fair value of plan assets for the pension plans with accumulated benefit obligations in excess of plan assets were $916 million and $341 million, respectively, as of December 31, 2004 and $770 million and $274 million, respectively, as of December 31, 2003.

NOTES TO CONSOLIDATED FINANCIAL STATEMENTS

The Coca-Cola Company and Subsidiaries

NOTE 14: PENSION AND OTHER POSTRETIREMENT BENEFIT PLANS (Continued)

The following table sets forth the change in the fair value of plan assets for our benefit plans (in millions):

	Pension Benefits		Other Benefits	
December 31,	**2004**	2003	**2004**	2003
Fair value of plan assets at beginning of year[1]	**$ 2,024**	$ 1,452	**$ —**	$ —
Actual return on plan assets	**243**	405	**1**	—
Employer contributions	**179**	208	**9**	—
Foreign currency exchange rate changes	**51**	54	**—**	—
Benefits paid	**(100)**	(95)	**—**	—
Fair value of plan assets at end of year[1]	**$ 2,397**	$ 2,024	**$ 10**	$ —

[1] Plan assets include 1.6 million shares of common stock of our Company with a fair value of $67 million and $82 million as of December 31, 2004 and 2003, respectively. Dividends received on common stock of our Company during 2004 and 2003 were $1.6 million and $1.4 million, respectively.

The pension and other benefit amounts recognized in our consolidated balance sheets are as follows (in millions):

	Pension Benefits		Other Benefits	
December 31,	**2004**	2003	**2004**	2003
Funded status—plan assets less than benefit obligations	**$ (403)**	$ (471)	**$ (791)**	$ (761)
Unrecognized net actuarial loss	**447**	429	**187**	203
Unrecognized prior service cost (benefit)	**47**	55	**(6)**	(7)
Net prepaid asset (liability) recognized	**$ 91**	$ 13	**$ (610)**	$ (565)
Prepaid benefit cost	**$ 527**	$ 407	**$ —**	$ —
Accrued benefit liability	**(595)**	(519)	**(610)**	(565)
Intangible asset	**15**	16	**—**	—
Accumulated other comprehensive income	**144**	109	**—**	—
Net prepaid asset (liability) recognized	**$ 91**	$ 13	**$ (610)**	$ (565)

NOTES TO CONSOLIDATED FINANCIAL STATEMENTS
The Coca-Cola Company and Subsidiaries

NOTE 14: PENSION AND OTHER POSTRETIREMENT BENEFIT PLANS (Continued)

Components of Net Periodic Benefit Cost

Net periodic benefit cost for our pension and other postretirement benefit plans consists of the following (in millions):

Year Ended December 31,	Pension Benefits			Other Benefits		
	2004	2003	2002	**2004**	2003	2002
Service cost	**$ 85**	$ 76	$ 63	**$ 27**	$ 25	$ 18
Interest cost	**147**	140	132	**44**	44	38
Expected return on plan assets	**(153)**	(130)	(137)	**—**	—	—
Amortization of prior service cost (benefit)	**8**	7	6	**(1)**	—	2
Recognized net actuarial loss	**35**	27	8	**3**	6	—
Net periodic benefit cost[1]	**$ 122**	$ 120	$ 72	**$ 73**	$ 75	$ 58

[1] During 2004, net periodic benefit cost for our other postretirement benefit plans was reduced by $12 million due to our adoption of FSP 106-2. Refer to Note 1.

In 2003, the Company recorded a charge of $23 million for special retirement benefits and curtailment costs as part of the streamlining costs discussed in Note 17.

Assumptions

The weighted-average assumptions used in computing the benefit obligations are as follows:

December 31,	Pension Benefits		Other Benefits	
	2004	2003	**2004**	2003
Discount rate	**5½%**	6%	**6%**	6¼%
Rate of increase in compensation levels	**4%**	4¼%	**4½%**	4½%

The weighted-average assumptions used in computing net periodic benefit cost are as follows:

Year Ended December 31,	Pension Benefits			Other Benefits		
	2004	2003	2002	**2004**	2003	2002
Discount rate[1]	**6%**	6%	6½%	**6¼%**	6½%	7¼%
Rate of increase in compensation levels	**4¼%**	4¼%	4¼%	**4½%**	4½%	4½%
Expected long-term rate of return on plan assets	**7¾%**	7¾%	8¼%	**8½%**	—	—

[1] On March 27, 2003, the primary qualified and nonqualified U.S. pension plans, as well as the U.S. postretirement health care plan, were remeasured to reflect the effect of the curtailment resulting from the Company's streamlining initiatives. Refer to Note 17. The discount rate assumption used to determine 2003 net periodic benefit cost for these U.S. plans was 6¾ percent prior to the remeasurement and 6½ percent subsequent to the remeasurement. This change in the discount rate is reflected in the 2003 weighted-average discount rate of 6 percent for all pension benefit plans and 6½ percent for other benefit plans.

NOTES TO CONSOLIDATED FINANCIAL STATEMENTS

The Coca-Cola Company and Subsidiaries

NOTE 14: PENSION AND OTHER POSTRETIREMENT BENEFIT PLANS (Continued)

The assumed health care cost trend rates are as follows:

December 31,	2004	2003
Health care cost trend rate assumed for next year	9½%	10%
Rate to which the cost trend rate is assumed to decline (the ultimate trend rate)	5¼%	5¼%
Year that the rate reaches the ultimate trend rate	2010	2009

Assumed health care cost trend rates have a significant effect on the amounts reported for the postretirement health care plans. A one percentage point change in the assumed health care cost trend rate would have the following effects (in millions):

	One Percentage Point Increase	One Percentage Point Decrease
Effect on accumulated postretirement benefit obligation as of December 31, 2004	$ 128	$ (111)
Effect on total of service cost and interest cost in 2004	$ 13	$ (11)

The discount rate assumptions used to account for pension and other postretirement benefit plans reflect the rates at which the benefit obligations could be effectively settled. These rates were determined using a cash flow matching technique whereby a hypothetical portfolio of high quality debt securities was constructed that mirrors the specific benefit obligations for each of our primary plans. The rate of compensation increase assumption is determined by the Company based upon annual reviews. We review external data and our own historical trends for health care costs to determine the health care cost trend rate assumptions.

Plan Assets

The following table sets forth the actual asset allocation and weighted-average target asset allocation for our U.S. and non-U.S. pension plan assets:

December 31,	2004	2003	Target Asset Allocation
Equity securities[1]	60%	60%	56%
Debt securities	31%	32%	35%
Real estate and other[2]	9%	8%	9%
Total	100%	100%	100%

[1] As of December 31, 2004 and 2003, 3 percent and 4 percent, respectively, of total pension plan assets were invested in common stock of our Company.

[2] As of December 31, 2004 and 2003, 4 percent of total pension plan assets were invested in real estate.

Investment objectives for the Company's U.S. pension plan assets, which comprise 72 percent of total pension plan assets as of December 31, 2004, are to:

(1) optimize the long-term return on plan assets at an acceptable level of risk;

(2) maintain a broad diversification across asset classes and among investment managers;

(3) maintain careful control of the risk level within each asset class; and

(4) focus on a long-term return objective.

NOTES TO CONSOLIDATED FINANCIAL STATEMENTS

The Coca-Cola Company and Subsidiaries

NOTE 14: PENSION AND OTHER POSTRETIREMENT BENEFIT PLANS (Continued)

Asset allocation targets promote optimal expected return and volatility characteristics given the long-term time horizon for fulfilling the obligations of the pension plans. Selection of the targeted asset allocation for U.S. plan assets was based upon a review of the expected return and risk characteristics of each asset class, as well as the correlation of returns among asset classes.

Investment guidelines are established with each investment manager. These guidelines provide the parameters within which the investment managers agree to operate, including criteria that determine eligible and ineligible securities, diversification requirements and credit quality standards, where applicable. Unless exceptions have been approved, investment managers are prohibited from buying or selling commodities, futures or option contracts, as well as from short selling of securities. Furthermore, investment managers agree to obtain written approval for deviations from stated investment style or guidelines.

As of December 31, 2004, no investment manager was responsible for more than 10 percent of total U.S. plan assets. In addition, diversification requirements for each investment manager prevent a single security or other investment from exceeding 10 percent, at historical cost, of the total U.S. plan assets.

The expected long-term rate of return assumption on U.S. plan assets is based upon the target asset allocation and is determined using forward-looking assumptions in the context of historical returns and volatilities for each asset class, as well as correlations among asset classes. We evaluate the rate of return assumption on an annual basis. The expected long-term rate of return assumption used in computing 2004 net periodic pension cost for the U.S. plans was 8.5 percent. As of December 2004, the 10 year annualized return on U.S. plan assets was 11.8 percent, the 15 year annualized return was 11.0 percent, and the annualized return since inception was 12.9 percent.

Plan assets for our pension plans outside the United States are insignificant on an individual plan basis.

Cash Flows

Information about the expected cash flow for our pension and other postretirement benefit plans is as follows:

	Pension Benefits	Other Benefits
Expected employer contributions:		
2005	$ 114	$ 9
Expected benefit payments[1]:		
2005	130	30
2006	121	32
2007	126	35
2008	128	37
2009	129	40
2010-2014	706	236

[1] The expected benefit payments for our other postretirement benefit plans do not reflect any estimated federal subsidies expected to be received under the Medicare Prescription Drug, Improvement and Modernization Act of 2003. Federal subsidies are estimated to range from $2.1 million in 2005 to $2.8 million in 2009 and are estimated to be $18.5 million for the period 2010-2014.

NOTES TO CONSOLIDATED FINANCIAL STATEMENTS
The Coca-Cola Company and Subsidiaries

NOTE 14: PENSION AND OTHER POSTRETIREMENT BENEFIT PLANS (Continued)

Defined Contribution Plans

Our Company sponsors a qualified defined contribution plan covering substantially all U.S. employees. Under this plan, we match 100 percent of participants' contributions up to a maximum of 3 percent of compensation. Company contributions to the U.S. plan were $18 million, $20 million and $20 million in 2004, 2003 and 2002, respectively. We also sponsor defined contribution plans in certain locations outside the United States. Company contributions to these plans were $8 million, $7 million and $6 million in 2004, 2003 and 2002, respectively.

NOTE 15: INCOME TAXES

Income before income taxes and cumulative effect of accounting change consists of the following (in millions):

Year Ended December 31,	2004	2003	2002
United States	$ 2,535	$ 2,029	$ 2,062
International	3,687	3,466	3,437
	$ 6,222	$ 5,495	$ 5,499

Income tax expense (benefit) consists of the following (in millions):

Year Ended December 31,	United States	State and Local	International	Total
2004				
Current	$ 350	$ 64	$ 799	$ 1,213
Deferred	209	29	(76)	162
2003				
Current	$ 426	$ 84	$ 826	$ 1,336
Deferred	(145)	(11)	(32)	(188)
2002				
Current	$ 455	$ 55	$ 973	$ 1,483
Deferred	2	23	15	40

We made income tax payments of approximately $1,500 million, $1,325 million and $1,508 million in 2004, 2003 and 2002, respectively.

NOTES TO CONSOLIDATED FINANCIAL STATEMENTS
The Coca-Cola Company and Subsidiaries

NOTE 15: INCOME TAXES (Continued)

A reconciliation of the statutory U.S. federal rate and effective rates is as follows:

Year Ended December 31,	2004	2003	2002
Statutory U.S. federal rate	**35.0 %**	35.0 %	35.0 %
State income taxes—net of federal benefit	**1.0**	0.9	0.9
Earnings in jurisdictions taxed at rates different from the statutory U.S. federal rate	**(9.4)**[1,2]	(10.6)[7]	(6.0)
Equity income or loss	**(3.1)**[3,4]	(2.4)[8]	(2.0)[10]
Other operating charges	**(0.9)**[5]	(1.1)[9]	—
Write-down/sale of certain bottling investments	**—**	—	0.7 [11]
Other—net	**(0.5)**[6]	(0.9)	(0.9)
Effective rates	**22.1 %**	20.9 %	27.7 %

[1] Includes approximately $92 million (or 1.4 percent) tax benefit related to the favorable resolution of various tax issues and settlements.

[2] Includes tax charge of approximately $75 million (or 1.2 percent) related to recording of valuation allowance on various deferred tax assets recorded in Germany.

[3] Includes approximately $50 million (or 0.8 percent) tax benefit related to the realization of certain foreign tax credits per provisions of the Jobs Creation Act.

[4] Includes approximately $13 million (or 0.1 percent) tax charge on our proportionate share of the favorable tax settlement related to Coca-Cola FEMSA.

[5] Primarily related to impairment of franchise rights at CCEAG and certain manufacturing investments. Refer to Note 16.

[6] Includes approximately $36 million (or 0.6 percent) tax benefit related to the favorable resolution of various tax issues and settlements.

[7] Includes approximately $50 million (or 0.8 percent) tax benefit for the release of tax reserves due primarily to the resolution of various tax matters.

[8] Includes the tax effect of the write-down of certain intangible assets held by bottling investments in Latin America. Refer to Note 2.

[9] Includes the tax effect of the charges for streamlining initiatives. Refer to Note 17.

[10] Includes the tax effect of the charges by equity investees in 2002. Refer to Note 16.

[11] Includes gains on the sale of Cervejarias Kaiser Brazil, Ltda and the write-down of certain bottling investments, primarily in Latin America. Refer to Note 16.

Our effective tax rate reflects the tax benefits from having significant operations outside the United States that are taxed at rates lower than the statutory U.S. rate of 35 percent. In 2003, our effective tax rate reflects further benefit from realization of tax benefits on charges related to streamlining initiatives recorded in locations with tax rates higher than our effective tax rate.

In 2003, management concluded that it was more likely than not that tax benefits would not be realized on Coca-Cola FEMSA's write-down of intangible assets in Latin America in connection with its merger with Panamco. Refer to Note 2. In 2002, management concluded that it was more likely than not that tax benefits would not be realized with respect to principally all of the items disclosed in Note 16. Accordingly, valuation

NOTES TO CONSOLIDATED FINANCIAL STATEMENTS
The Coca-Cola Company and Subsidiaries

NOTE 15: INCOME TAXES (Continued)

allowances were recorded to offset the future tax benefit of these items, resulting in an increase in our effective tax rate.

Undistributed earnings of the Company's foreign subsidiaries amounted to approximately $9.8 billion at December 31, 2004. Those earnings are considered to be indefinitely reinvested and, accordingly, no U.S. federal and state income taxes have been provided thereon. Upon distribution of those earnings in the form of dividends or otherwise, the Company would be subject to both U.S. income taxes (subject to an adjustment for foreign tax credits) and withholding taxes payable to the various foreign countries. Determination of the amount of unrecognized deferred U.S. income tax liability is not practical because of the complexities associated with its hypothetical calculation; however, unrecognized foreign tax credits would be available to reduce a portion of the U.S. liability.

As discussed in Note 1, the Jobs Creation Act was enacted in October 2004. One of the provisions provides a one time benefit related to foreign tax credits generated by equity investments in prior years. The Company recorded an income tax benefit of approximately $50 million as a result of this law change in 2004. The Jobs Creation Act also includes a temporary incentive for U.S. multinationals to repatriate foreign earnings at an effective 5.25 percent tax rate. As of December 31, 2004, management had not decided whether, and to what extent, we might repatriate foreign earnings under the Jobs Creation Act, and accordingly, the consolidated financial statements do not reflect any provision for taxes on the unremitted foreign earnings that might be remitted under the Jobs Creation Act. Based on our analysis to date, however, it is reasonably possible that we may repatriate some amount between $0 and $6.1 billion, with the respective tax liability ranging from $0 to $400 million. We expect to be in a position to finalize our assessment by December 31, 2005.

NOTES TO CONSOLIDATED FINANCIAL STATEMENTS

The Coca-Cola Company and Subsidiaries

NOTE 15: INCOME TAXES (Continued)

The tax effects of temporary differences and carryforwards that give rise to deferred tax assets and liabilities consist of the following (in millions):

December 31,	2004	2003
Deferred tax assets:		
Property, plant and equipment	$ **71**	$ 87
Trademarks and other intangible assets	**65**	68
Equity method investments (including translation adjustment)	**530**	485
Other liabilities	**149**	242
Benefit plans	**594**	669
Net operating/capital loss carryforwards	**856**	711
Other	**257**	195
Gross deferred tax assets	**2,522**	2,457
Valuation allowance	**(854)**	(630)
Total deferred tax assets[1]	$ **1,668**	$ 1,827
Deferred tax liabilities:		
Property, plant and equipment	$ **(684)**	$ (737)
Trademarks and other intangible assets	**(247)**	(247)
Equity method investments (including translation adjustment)	**(612)**	(468)
Other liabilities	**(71)**	(55)
Other	**(180)**	(211)
Total deferred tax liabilities	$ **(1,794)**	$ (1,718)
Net deferred tax assets (liabilities)	$ **(126)**	$ 109

[1] Deferred tax assets of $324 million and $446 million were included in the consolidated balance sheet line item other assets at December 31, 2004 and 2003, respectively.

On December 31, 2004 and 2003, we had approximately $194 million and $160 million, respectively, of net deferred tax assets located in countries outside the United States.

On December 31, 2004, we had $3,258 million of loss carryforwards available to reduce future taxable income. Loss carryforwards of $861 million must be utilized within the next five years; $550 million must be utilized within the next 10 years and the remainder can be utilized over a period greater than 10 years.

NOTE 16: SIGNIFICANT OPERATING AND NONOPERATING ITEMS

Operating income in 2004 reflected the impact of $480 million of expenses primarily related to impairment charges for franchise rights and certain manufacturing investments. These impairment charges were recorded in the consolidated statement of income line item other operating charges.

In the second quarter of 2004, we recorded impairment charges totaling approximately $88 million. These impairments primarily related to the write-downs of certain manufacturing investments and an intangible asset. As a result of operating losses, management prepared analyses of cash flows expected to result from the use of the assets and their eventual disposition. Because the sum of the undiscounted cash flows was less than the carrying value of such assets, we recorded an impairment charge to reduce the carrying value of the assets to fair value.

NOTES TO CONSOLIDATED FINANCIAL STATEMENTS
The Coca-Cola Company and Subsidiaries

NOTE 16: SIGNIFICANT OPERATING AND NONOPERATING ITEMS (Continued)

In the second quarter of 2004, our Company's equity income benefited by approximately $37 million for our proportionate share of a favorable tax settlement related to Coca-Cola FEMSA.

In the third quarter of 2004, we recorded impairment charges of approximately $392 million, which were primarily related to the impairment of franchise rights at CCEAG. The CCEAG impairment was the result of our revised outlook for the German market, which has been unfavorably impacted by volume declines resulting from market shifts related to the deposit law on nonreturnable beverage packages and the corresponding lack of availability of our products in the discount retail channel. Refer to Note 4.

In the fourth quarter of 2004, our Company received a $75 million insurance settlement related to the class-action lawsuit that was settled in 2000. Also in the fourth quarter of 2004, the Company donated $75 million to the Coca-Cola Foundation.

In the first quarter of 2003, the Company reached a settlement with certain defendants in a vitamin antitrust litigation matter. In that litigation, the Company alleged that certain vitamin manufacturers participated in a global conspiracy to fix the price of some vitamins, including vitamins used in the manufacture of some of the Company's products. During the first quarter of 2003, the Company received a settlement relating to this litigation of approximately $52 million on a pretax basis, or $0.01 per share on an after-tax basis. The amount was recorded as a reduction to cost of goods sold.

Refer to Note 2 for disclosure regarding the merger of Coca-Cola FEMSA and Panamco in 2003 and the recording of a $102 million noncash pretax charge to the consolidated statement of income line item equity income—net.

In the third quarter of 2002, our Company recorded a noncash pretax charge of approximately $33 million related to our share of impairment and restructuring charges taken by certain equity method investees in Latin America. This charge was recorded in the consolidated statement of income line item equity income—net.

Our Company had direct and indirect ownership interests totaling approximately 18 percent in Cervejarias Kaiser S.A. ("Kaiser S.A."). In March 2002, Kaiser S.A. sold its investment in Cervejarias Kaiser Brazil, Ltda to Molson Inc. ("Molson") for cash of approximately $485 million and shares of Molson valued at approximately $150 million. Our Company's pretax share of the gain related to this sale was approximately $43 million, of which approximately $21 million was recorded in the consolidated statement of income line item equity income—net, and approximately $22 million was recorded in the consolidated statement of income line item other income (loss)—net.

In the first quarter of 2002, our Company recorded a noncash pretax charge of approximately $157 million (recorded in the consolidated statement of income line item other income (loss)—net), primarily related to the write-down of certain investments in Latin America. This write-down reduced the carrying value of these investments in Latin America to fair value. The charge was primarily the result of the economic developments in Argentina during the first quarter of 2002, including the devaluation of the Argentine peso and the severity of the unfavorable economic outlook.

NOTE 17: STREAMLINING COSTS

During 2003, the Company took steps to streamline and simplify its operations, primarily in North America and Germany. In North America, the Company integrated the operations of three formerly separate North American business units—Coca-Cola North America, The Minute Maid Company and Coca-Cola Fountain. In Germany, CCEAG took steps to improve its efficiency in sales, distribution and manufacturing, and our German

NOTES TO CONSOLIDATED FINANCIAL STATEMENTS

The Coca-Cola Company and Subsidiaries

NOTE 17: STREAMLINING COSTS (Continued)

Division office also implemented streamlining initiatives. Selected other operations also took steps to streamline their operations to improve overall efficiency and effectiveness. As disclosed in Note 1, under SFAS No. 146, a liability is accrued only when certain criteria are met. All of the Company's streamlining initiatives met the criteria of SFAS No. 146 as of December 31, 2003, and all related costs have been incurred as of December 31, 2003.

Employees separated from the Company as a result of these streamlining initiatives were offered severance or early retirement packages, as appropriate, which included both financial and nonfinancial components. The expenses recorded during the year ended December 31, 2003 included costs associated with involuntary terminations and other direct costs associated with implementing these initiatives. As of December 31, 2003, approximately 3,700 associates had been separated pursuant to these streamlining initiatives. Other direct costs included the relocation of employees; contract termination costs; costs associated with the development, communication and administration of these initiatives; and asset write-offs. During 2003, the Company incurred total pretax expenses related to these streamlining initiatives of approximately $561 million, or $0.15 per share after-tax. These expenses were recorded in the line item other operating charges.

The table below summarizes the costs incurred to date, the balances of accrued streamlining expenses and the movement in those balances as of and for the years ended December 31, 2003 and 2004 (in millions):

Cost Summary	Costs Incurred in 2003	Payments	Noncash and Exchange	Accrued Balance December 31, 2003	Payments	Noncash and Exchange	Accrued Balance December 31, 2004
Severance pay and benefits	$ 248	$ (113)	$ 3	$ 138	$ (118)	$ (2)	$ 18
Retirement related benefits	43	—	(14)	29	—	(29)	—
Outside services— legal, outplacement, consulting	36	(25)	—	11	(10)	(1)	—
Other direct costs	133	(81)	(1)	51	(29)	1	23
Total[1]	$ 460	$ (219)	$ (12)	$ 229	$ (157)	$ (31)	$ 41
Asset impairments	$ 101						
Total costs incurred	$ 561						

[1] As of December 31, 2003 and 2004, $206 million and $41 million, respectively, was included in our consolidated balance sheet line item accounts payable and accrued expenses. As of December 31, 2003, approximately $23 million was included in our consolidated balance sheet line item other liabilities. As of December 31, 2004, this amount was reclassified to the pension and postretirement benefit accounts as such amounts will be paid out in accordance with the Company's defined benefit and postretirement benefit plans over a number of years.

NOTES TO CONSOLIDATED FINANCIAL STATEMENTS
The Coca-Cola Company and Subsidiaries

NOTE 17: STREAMLINING COSTS (Continued)

The total streamlining initiative costs incurred for the year ended December 31, 2003 by operating segment were as follows (in millions):

North America	$ 273
Africa	12
Asia	18
Europe, Eurasia and Middle East	183
Latin America	8
Corporate	67
Total	$ 561

NOTE 18: ACQUISITIONS AND INVESTMENTS

During 2004, our Company's acquisition and investment activity totaled approximately $267 million, primarily related to the purchase of trademarks, brands and related contractual rights in Latin America, none of which was individually significant.

During 2003, our Company's acquisition and investment activity totaled approximately $359 million. These acquisitions included purchases of trademarks, brands and related contractual rights of approximately $142 million, none of which was individually significant. Refer to Note 4. Other acquisition and investing activity totaled approximately $217 million, and with the exception of the acquisition of Truesdale, none was individually significant. In March 2003, our Company acquired a 100 percent ownership interest in Truesdale from CCE for cash consideration of approximately $58 million. Truesdale owns a noncarbonated beverage production facility. The purchase price was allocated primarily to property, plant and equipment acquired. No amount was allocated to intangible assets. Truesdale is included in our North America operating segment.

During 2002, our Company's acquisition and investment activity totaled approximately $1,144 million. Included in this $1,144 million, our Company paid $544 million in cash and recorded a note payable of approximately $600 million to finance the CCEAG acquisition described below.

In November 2001, we entered into the Control and Profit and Loss Transfer Agreement ("CPL") with CCEAG. Under the terms of the CPL, our Company acquired management control of CCEAG. In November 2001, we also entered into a Pooling Agreement with certain shareowners of CCEAG that provided our Company with voting control of CCEAG. Both agreements became effective in February 2002, when our Company acquired control of CCEAG for a term ending no later than December 31, 2006. CCEAG is included in our Europe, Eurasia and Middle East operating segment. As a result of acquiring control of CCEAG, our Company is working to help focus its sales and marketing programs and assist in developing the business. This transaction was accounted for as a business combination, and the results of CCEAG's operations have been included in the Company's consolidated financial statements since February 2002. Prior to February 2002, our Company accounted for CCEAG under the equity method of accounting. As of December 31, 2002, our Company had approximately a 41 percent ownership interest in the outstanding shares of CCEAG. In return for control of CCEAG, pursuant to the CPL we guaranteed annual payments, in lieu of dividends by CCEAG, to all other CCEAG shareowners. These guaranteed annual payments equal 0.76 euro for each CCEAG share outstanding. Additionally, all other CCEAG shareowners entered into either a put or a put/call option agreement with the Company, exercisable at any time up to the December 31, 2006 expiration date. In 2003, one of the other shareowners exercised its put option which represented approximately 29 percent of the outstanding

110

NOTES TO CONSOLIDATED FINANCIAL STATEMENTS

The Coca-Cola Company and Subsidiaries

NOTE 18: ACQUISITIONS AND INVESTMENTS (Continued)

shares of CCEAG. All payments related to the exercise of the put options will be made in 2006. Our Company entered into either put or put/call agreements for shares representing approximately a 59 percent interest in CCEAG. The spread in the strike prices of the put and call options is approximately 3 percent.

As of the date of the transaction, the Company concluded that the exercise of the put and/or call agreements was a virtual certainty based on the minimal differences in the strike prices. We concluded that either the holder of the put option would require the Company to purchase the shares at the agreed-upon put strike price, or the Company would exercise its call option and require the shareowner to tender its shares at the agreed-upon call strike price. If these puts or calls are exercised, the actual transfer of shares would not occur until the end of the term of the CPL. Coupled with the guaranteed payments in lieu of dividends for the term of the CPL, these instruments represented the financing vehicle for the transaction. As such, the Company determined that the economic substance of the transaction resulted in the acquisition of the remaining outstanding shares of CCEAG and required the Company to account for the transaction as a business combination. Furthermore, the terms of the CPL transferred control and all of the economic risks and rewards of CCEAG to the Company immediately.

The present value of the total amount likely to be paid by our Company to all other CCEAG shareowners, including the put or put/call payments and the guaranteed annual payments in lieu of dividends, was approximately $1,041 million at December 31, 2004. This amount increased from the initial liability of approximately $600 million due to the accretion of the discounted value to the ultimate maturity of the liability, as well as approximately $350 million of translation adjustment related to this liability. This liability is included in the line item other liabilities. The accretion of the discounted value to its ultimate maturity value is recorded in the line item other income (loss)—net, and this amount was approximately $58 million, $51 million and $38 million, respectively, for the years ended December 31, 2004, 2003 and 2002.

In July 2002, our Company and Danone Waters of North America, Inc. ("DWNA") formed a new limited liability company, CCDA Waters, L.L.C. ("CCDA"), for the production, marketing and distribution of DWNA's bottled spring and source water business in the United States. In forming CCDA, DWNA contributed assets of its retail bottled spring and source water business in the United States. These assets included five production facilities, a license for the use of the Dannon and Sparkletts brands, as well as ownership of several value brands. Our Company made a cash payment to acquire a controlling 51 percent equity interest in CCDA and is also providing marketing, distribution and management expertise. This transaction was accounted for as a business combination, and the consolidated results of CCDA's operations have been included in the Company's consolidated financial statements since July 2002. This business combination expanded our water brands to include a national offering in all sectors of the water category with purified, spring and source waters. CCDA is included in our North America operating segment.

In January 2002, our Company and Coca-Cola Bottlers Philippines, Inc. ("CCBPI") finalized the purchase of RFM Corp.'s ("RFM") approximate 83 percent interest in Cosmos Bottling Corporation ("CBC"), a publicly traded Philippine beverage company. CBC is an established carbonated soft-drink business in the Philippines and is included in our Asia operating segment. The original sale and purchase agreement with RFM was entered into in November 2001. As of the date of this sale and purchase agreement, the Company began supplying concentrate for this operation. The purchase of RFM's interest was finalized on January 3, 2002. In March 2002, a tender offer was completed with our Company and CCBPI acquiring all shares of the remaining minority shareowners except for shares representing a 1 percent interest in CBC. This transaction was accounted for as a business combination, and the results of CBC's operations were included in the Company's consolidated financial statements from January 2002 to March 2003.

NOTES TO CONSOLIDATED FINANCIAL STATEMENTS

The Coca-Cola Company and Subsidiaries

NOTE 18: ACQUISITIONS AND INVESTMENTS (Continued)

The Company and CCBPI agreed to restructure the ownership of the operations of CBC, and this transaction was completed in April 2003. This transaction resulted in the Company acquiring all the trademarks of CBC, and CCBPI owning approximately 99 percent of the outstanding shares of CBC. Accordingly, CBC was deconsolidated by the Company. No gain or loss was recorded by our Company upon completion of the transaction, as the fair value of the assets exchanged was approximately equal. Additionally, there was no impact on our cash flows related to this transaction.

Our Company acquired controlling interests in CCDA and CBC for a total combined consideration of approximately $328 million. As of December 31, 2003, the Company allocated approximately $56 million of the purchase price for these acquisitions to goodwill and $208 million to other indefinite-lived intangible assets, primarily trademarks, brands and licenses. This goodwill is all related to the CCDA acquisition and is allocated to our North America operating segment.

The combined 2002 net operating revenues of CCEAG, CBC and CCDA were approximately $1.3 billion.

The acquisitions and investments have been accounted for by the purchase method of accounting. Their results have been included in our consolidated financial statements from their respective dates of acquisition. Assuming the results of these businesses had been included in operations commencing with 2002, pro forma financial data would not be required due to immateriality.

NOTE 19: OPERATING SEGMENTS

Our Company's operating structure includes the following operating segments: North America; Africa; Asia; Europe, Eurasia and Middle East; Latin America; and Corporate. North America includes the United States, Canada and Puerto Rico. Prior-period amounts have been reclassified to conform to the current-period presentation.

Segment Products and Services

The business of our Company is nonalcoholic beverages. Our operating segments derive a majority of their revenues from the manufacture and sale of beverage concentrates and syrups and, in some cases, the sale of finished beverages. The following table summarizes the contribution to net operating revenues from Company operations (in millions):

Year Ended December 31,	2004	2003	2002
Company operations, excluding bottling operations	$ 18,871	$ 18,177	$ 17,123
Company-owned bottling operations	3,091	2,867	2,441
Consolidated net operating revenues	$ 21,962	$ 21,044	$ 19,564

Method of Determining Segment Profit or Loss

Management evaluates the performance of our operating segments separately to individually monitor the different factors affecting financial performance. Segment profit or loss includes substantially all the segment's costs of production, distribution and administration. Our Company typically manages and evaluates equity investments and related income on a segment level. However, we manage certain significant investments, such as our equity interests in CCE, within the Corporate operating segment. Our Company manages income taxes on a global basis. We manage financial costs, such as interest income and expense, on a global basis within the Corporate operating segment. Thus, we evaluate segment performance based on profit or loss before income taxes and cumulative effect of accounting change.

NOTES TO CONSOLIDATED FINANCIAL STATEMENTS
The Coca-Cola Company and Subsidiaries

NOTE 19: OPERATING SEGMENTS (Continued)

Information about our Company's operations by operating segment is as follows (in millions):

	North America	Africa	Asia	Europe, Eurasia and Middle East	Latin America	Corporate	Consolidated
2004							
Net operating revenues	$ 6,643	$ 1,067	$ 4,691[1]	$ 7,195	$ 2,123	$ 243	$ 21,962
Operating income (loss)[2]	1,606	340	1,758	1,898	1,069	(973)[3]	5,698
Interest income						157	157
Interest expense						196	196
Depreciation and amortization	345	28	133	245	42	100	893
Equity income (loss)—net	11	12	83	85	185 [4]	245	621
Income (loss) before income taxes and cumulative effect of accounting change[2]	1,629	337	1,841	1,916	1,270 [4]	(771)[3,5]	6,222
Identifiable operating assets	4,731	789	1,722	5,373 [6]	1,405	11,055 [7]	25,075
Investments[8]	116	162	1,401	1,323	1,580	1,670	6,252
Capital expenditures	247	28	92	233	38	117	755
2003							
Net operating revenues	$ 6,344	$ 827	$ 5,052[1]	$ 6,556	$ 2,042	$ 223	$ 21,044
Operating income (loss)[9]	1,282	249	1,690	1,908	970	(878)[10]	5,221
Interest income						176	176
Interest expense						178	178
Depreciation and amortization	305	27	124	230	52	112	850
Equity income (loss)—net	13	13	65	78	(5)[11]	242	406
Income (loss) before income taxes and cumulative effect of accounting change[9]	1,326	249	1,740	1,921	975 [11]	(716)[10]	5,495
Identifiable operating assets	4,953	721	1,923	5,222 [6]	1,440	7,545 [7]	21,804
Investments[8]	109	156	1,345	1,229	1,348	1,351	5,538
Capital expenditures	309	13	148	198	35	109	812
2002							
Net operating revenues	$ 6,264	$ 684	$ 5,054[1]	$ 5,262	$ 2,089	$ 211	$ 19,564
Operating income (loss)	1,531	224	1,820	1,612	1,033	(762)	5,458
Interest income						209	209
Interest expense						199	199
Depreciation and amortization	266	37	133	193	57	120	806
Equity income (loss)—net	15	(25)	60	(18)	131	221	384
Income (loss) before income taxes and cumulative effect of accounting change	1,552	187	1,848	1,540	1,081	(709)	5,499
Identifiable operating assets	4,999	565	2,370	4,481 [6]	1,205	5,795 [7]	19,415
Investments[8]	142	115	1,150	1,211	1,352	1,021	4,991
Capital expenditures	334	18	209	162	37	91	851

Intercompany transfers between operating segments are not material.

Certain prior-year amounts have been reclassified to conform to the current-year presentation.

[1] Net operating revenues in Japan represented approximately 61 percent of total Asia operating segment net operating revenues in 2004, 67 percent in 2003 and 69 percent in 2002.

[2] Operating income (loss) and income (loss) before income taxes and cumulative effect of accounting change were reduced by approximately $18 million for North America, $15 million for Asia, $377 million for Europe, Eurasia and Middle East, $6 million for Latin America and $64 million for Corporate as a result of other operating charges recorded for asset impairments. Refer to Note 16.

[3] Operating income (loss) and income (loss) before income taxes and cumulative effect of accounting change for Corporate were impacted as a result of the Company's receipt of a $75 million insurance settlement related to the class-action lawsuit settled in 2000. The Company subsequently donated $75 million to the Coca-Cola Foundation.

[4] Equity income (loss)—net and income (loss) before income taxes and cumulative effect of accounting change for Latin America were increased by approximately $37 million as a result of a favorable tax settlement related to Coca-Cola FEMSA, one of our equity method investees. Refer to Note 2.

[5] Income (loss) before income taxes and cumulative effect of accounting change was increased by approximately $24 million for Corporate due to noncash pre-tax gains that were recognized on the issuances of stock by CCE, one of our equity investees. Refer to Note 3.

[6] Identifiable operating assets in Germany represent approximately 46 percent of total Europe, Eurasia and Middle East identifiable operating assets in 2004 and 50 percent in 2003 and 2002.

[7] Principally cash and cash equivalents, marketable securities, finance subsidiary receivables, goodwill, trademarks and other intangible assets and property, plant and equipment.

[8] Principally equity investments in bottling companies.

[9] Operating income (loss) and income (loss) before income taxes and cumulative effect of accounting change were reduced by approximately $273 million for North America, $12 million for Africa, $18 million for Asia, $183 million for Europe, Eurasia and Middle East, $8 million for Latin America and $67 million for Corporate as a result of streamlining charges. Refer to Note 17.

[10] Operating income (loss) and income (loss) before income taxes and cumulative effect of accounting change were increased by approximately $52 million for Corporate as a result of the Company's receipt of a settlement related to a vitamin antitrust litigation matter. Refer to Note 16.

[11] Equity income (loss)—net and income (loss) before income taxes and cumulative effect of accounting change for Latin America were reduced by $102 million primarily for a charge related to one of our equity method investees. Refer to Note 2.

NOTES TO CONSOLIDATED FINANCIAL STATEMENTS
The Coca-Cola Company and Subsidiaries

NOTE 19: OPERATING SEGMENTS (Continued)

Compound Growth Rate Ended December 31, 2004	North America	Africa	Asia	Europe, Eurasia and Middle East	Latin America	Corporate	Consolidated
Net operating revenues							
5 years	4.2%	9.3%	0.5%	11.8%	3.2%	8.0%	5.5%
10 years	5.0%	6.5%	4.1%	4.1%	1.0%	19.2%	4.2%
Operating income							
5 years	2.1%	9.3%	8.0%	15.9%	5.2%	*	7.4%
10 years	5.7%	5.1%	4.2%	4.3%	3.4%	*	4.6%

* Calculation is not meaningful.

REPORT OF MANAGEMENT ON INTERNAL CONTROL OVER FINANCIAL REPORTING
The Coca-Cola Company and Subsidiaries

Management of the Company is responsible for the preparation and integrity of the Consolidated Financial Statements appearing in our Annual Report on Form 10-K. The financial statements were prepared in conformity with generally accepted accounting principles appropriate in the circumstances and, accordingly, include certain amounts based on our best judgments and estimates. Financial information in this Annual Report on Form 10-K is consistent with that in the financial statements.

Management of the Company is responsible for establishing and maintaining adequate internal control over financial reporting as such term is defined in Rules 13a-15(f) under the Securities Exchange Act of 1934 ("Exchange Act"). The Company's internal control over financial reporting is designed to provide reasonable assurance regarding the reliability of financial reporting and the preparation of the Consolidated Financial Statements. Our internal control over financial reporting is supported by a program of internal audits and appropriate reviews by management, written policies and guidelines, careful selection and training of qualified personnel and a written Code of Business Conduct adopted by our Company's Board of Directors, applicable to all Company Directors and all officers and employees of our Company and subsidiaries.

Because of its inherent limitations, internal control over financial reporting may not prevent or detect misstatements and even when determined to be effective, can only provide reasonable assurance with respect to financial statement preparation and presentation. Also, projections of any evaluation of effectiveness to future periods are subject to the risk that controls may become inadequate because of changes in conditions, or that the degree of compliance with the policies or procedures may deteriorate.

The Audit Committee of our Company's Board of Directors, composed solely of Directors who are independent in accordance with the requirements of the New York Stock Exchange listing standards, the Exchange Act and the Company's Corporate Governance Guidelines, meets with the independent auditors, management and internal auditors periodically to discuss internal control over financial reporting and auditing and financial reporting matters. The Committee reviews with the independent auditors the scope and results of the audit effort. The Committee also meets periodically with the independent auditors and the chief internal auditor without management present to ensure that the independent auditors and the chief internal auditor have free access to the Committee. Our Audit Committee's Report can be found in the Company's 2005 proxy statement.

Management assessed the effectiveness of the Company's internal control over financial reporting as of December 31, 2004. In making this assessment, management used the criteria set forth by the Committee of Sponsoring Organizations of the Treadway Commission (COSO) in *Internal Control—Integrated Framework*. Based on our assessment, management believes that the Company maintained effective internal control over financial reporting as of December 31, 2004.

The Company's independent auditors, Ernst & Young LLP, a registered public accounting firm, are appointed by the Audit Committee of the Company's Board of Directors, subject to ratification by our Company's shareowners. Ernst & Young LLP have audited and reported on the Consolidated Financial Statements of The Coca-Cola Company and subsidiaries, management's assessment of the effectiveness of the Company's internal control over financial reporting and the effectiveness of the Company's internal control over financial reporting. The reports of the independent auditors are contained in this Annual Report.

E. Neville Isdell
Chairman, Board of Directors,
and Chief Executive Officer

February 25, 2005

Connie D. McDaniel
Vice President
and Controller

February 25, 2005

Gary P. Fayard
Executive Vice President
and Chief Financial Officer

February 25, 2005

Report of Independent Registered Public Accounting Firm

Board of Directors and Shareowners
The Coca-Cola Company

We have audited the accompanying consolidated balance sheets of The Coca-Cola Company and subsidiaries as of December 31, 2004 and 2003, and the related consolidated statements of income, shareowners' equity, and cash flows for each of the three years in the period ended December 31, 2004. Our audits also included the financial statement schedule listed in the Index at Item 15(a). These financial statements and schedule are the responsibility of the Company's management. Our responsibility is to express an opinion on these financial statements and schedule based on our audits.

We conducted our audits in accordance with the standards of the Public Company Accounting Oversight Board (United States). Those standards require that we plan and perform the audit to obtain reasonable assurance about whether the financial statements are free of material misstatement. An audit includes examining, on a test basis, evidence supporting the amounts and disclosures in the financial statements. An audit also includes assessing the accounting principles used and significant estimates made by management, as well as evaluating the overall financial statement presentation. We believe that our audits provide a reasonable basis for our opinion.

In our opinion, the financial statements referred to above present fairly, in all material respects, the consolidated financial position of The Coca-Cola Company and subsidiaries at December 31, 2004 and 2003, and the consolidated results of their operations and their cash flows for each of the three years in the period ended December 31, 2004, in conformity with U.S. generally accepted accounting principles. Also, in our opinion, the related financial statement schedule, when considered in relation to the basic financial statements taken as a whole, presents fairly in all material respects the information set forth therein.

As discussed in Note 1 to the consolidated financial statements, in 2004 the Company adopted the provisions of FASB Interpretation No. 46 (revised December 2003) regarding the consolidation of variable interest entities. As discussed in Notes 1 and 4 to the consolidated financial statements, in 2002 the Company changed its method of accounting for goodwill and other intangible assets.

We also have audited, in accordance with the standards of the Public Company Accounting Oversight Board (United States), the effectiveness of The Coca-Cola Company and subsidiaries' internal control over financial reporting as of December 31, 2004, based on criteria established in *Internal Control—Integrated Framework* issued by the Committee of Sponsoring Organizations of the Treadway Commission and our report dated February 25, 2005, expressed an unqualified opinion thereon.

Ernst & Young LLP

Atlanta, Georgia
February 25, 2005

Report of Independent Registered Public Accounting Firm
on Internal Control Over Financial Reporting

Board of Directors and Shareowners
The Coca-Cola Company

We have audited management's assessment, included in the accompanying Report of Management on Internal Control Over Financial Reporting, that The Coca-Cola Company and subsidiaries maintained effective internal control over financial reporting as of December 31, 2004, based on criteria established in *Internal Control—Integrated Framework* issued by the Committee of Sponsoring Organizations of the Treadway Commission (the COSO criteria). The Coca-Cola Company's management is responsible for maintaining effective internal control over financial reporting and for its assessment of the effectiveness of internal control over financial reporting. Our responsibility is to express an opinion on management's assessment and an opinion on the effectiveness of the Company's internal control over financial reporting based on our audit.

We conducted our audit in accordance with the standards of the Public Company Accounting Oversight Board (United States). Those standards require that we plan and perform the audit to obtain reasonable assurance about whether effective internal control over financial reporting was maintained in all material respects. Our audit included obtaining an understanding of internal control over financial reporting, evaluating management's assessment, testing and evaluating the design and operating effectiveness of internal control, and performing such other procedures as we considered necessary in the circumstances. We believe that our audit provides a reasonable basis for our opinion.

A company's internal control over financial reporting is a process designed to provide reasonable assurance regarding the reliability of financial reporting and the preparation of financial statements for external purposes in accordance with generally accepted accounting principles. A company's internal control over financial reporting includes those policies and procedures that (1) pertain to the maintenance of records that, in reasonable detail, accurately and fairly reflect the transactions and dispositions of the assets of the company; (2) provide reasonable assurance that transactions are recorded as necessary to permit preparation of financial statements in accordance with generally accepted accounting principles, and that receipts and expenditures of the company are being made only in accordance with authorizations of management and directors of the company; and (3) provide reasonable assurance regarding prevention or timely detection of unauthorized acquisition, use, or disposition of the company's assets that could have a material effect on the financial statements.

Because of its inherent limitations, internal control over financial reporting may not prevent or detect misstatements. Also, projections of any evaluation of effectiveness to future periods are subject to the risk that controls may become inadequate because of changes in conditions, or that the degree of compliance with the policies or procedures may deteriorate.

In our opinion, management's assessment that The Coca-Cola Company and subsidiaries maintained effective internal control over financial reporting as of December 31, 2004, is fairly stated, in all material respects, based on the COSO criteria. Also, in our opinion, The Coca-Cola Company and subsidiaries maintained, in all material respects, effective internal control over financial reporting as of December 31, 2004, based on the COSO criteria.

We also have audited, in accordance with the standards of the Public Company Accounting Oversight Board (United States), the consolidated balance sheets of The Coca-Cola Company and subsidiaries as of December 31, 2004 and 2003, and the related consolidated statements of income, shareowners' equity, and cash flows for each of the three years in the period ended December 31, 2004, and our report dated February 25, 2005, expressed an unqualified opinion thereon.

Ernst + Young LLP

Atlanta, Georgia
February 25, 2005

Quarterly Data (Unaudited)

Year Ended December 31,	First Quarter	Second Quarter	Third Quarter	Fourth Quarter	Full Year
(In millions, except per share data)					
2004					
Net operating revenues	$ 5,078	$ 5,965	$ 5,662	$ 5,257	$ 21,962
Gross profit	3,325	3,935	3,610	3,454	14,324
Net income	1,127	1,584	935	1,201	4,847
Basic net income per share:	$ 0.46	$ 0.65	$ 0.39	$ 0.50	$ 2.00
Diluted net income per share:	$ 0.46	$ 0.65	$ 0.39	$ 0.50	$ 2.00
2003					
Net operating revenues	$ 4,502	$ 5,695	$ 5,671	$ 5,176	$ 21,044
Gross profit	2,885	3,568	3,503	3,326	13,282
Net income	835	1,362	1,223	927	4,347
Basic net income per share:	$ 0.34	$ 0.55	$ 0.50	$ 0.38	$ 1.77
Diluted net income per share:	$ 0.34	$ 0.55	$ 0.50	$ 0.38	$ 1.77

In the first quarter of 2004 as compared to the first quarter of 2003, the results were impacted by four additional shipping days. The increase in shipping days in the first quarter were largely offset in the fourth quarter of 2004.

In the second quarter of 2004, our Company's equity income benefited by approximately $37 million for our proportionate share of a favorable tax settlement related to Coca-Cola FEMSA. Refer to Note 2.

In the second quarter of 2004, our Company recorded impairment charges totaling approximately $88 million primarily related to write-downs of certain manufacturing investments and an intangible asset. Refer to Note 16.

In the second quarter of 2004, our Company recorded approximately $49 million of noncash pretax gains on issuances of stock by CCE. Refer to Note 3.

In the second quarter of 2004, our Company recorded an income tax benefit of approximately $41 million related to the reversal of previously accrued taxes resulting from a favorable agreement with authorities. Refer to Note 15.

In the third quarter of 2004, our Company recorded an income tax benefit of approximately $39 million related to the reversal of previously accrued taxes resulting from favorable resolution of tax matters. Refer to Note 15.

In the third quarter of 2004, our Company recorded an income tax expense of approximately $75 million related to the recognition of a valuation allowance on certain deferred taxes of CCEAG. Refer to Note 15.

In the third quarter of 2004, our Company recorded impairment charges totaling approximately $392 million primarily related to franchise rights at CCEAG. Refer to Note 16.

In the fourth quarter of 2004, our Company received a $75 million insurance settlement related to the class-action lawsuit that was settled in 2000. Also in the fourth quarter of 2004, the Company donated $75 million to the Coca-Cola Foundation. Refer to Note 16.

In the fourth quarter of 2004, our Company recorded an income tax benefit of approximately $48 million related to the reversal of previously accrued taxes resulting from favorable resolution of tax matters. Refer to Note 15.

In the fourth quarter of 2004, our Company recorded an income tax benefit of approximately $50 million related to the realization of certain foreign tax credits per provisions of the Jobs Creation Act. Refer to Note 15.

In the fourth quarter of 2004, our Company recorded approximately $25 million of noncash pretax losses to adjust the amount of the gain recognized in the second quarter of 2004 on issuances of stock by CCE. Refer to Note 3.

Certain amounts previously reported in our 2003 Quarterly Reports on Form 10-Q were reclassified to conform to our year-end 2003 presentation.

In the first quarter of 2003, the Company reached a settlement with certain defendants in a vitamin antitrust litigation matter. The Company received a settlement relating to this litigation of approximately $52 million on a pretax basis. Refer to Note 16.

In 2003, the Company took steps to streamline and simplify its operations, primarily in North America and Germany. Selected other operations also took steps to streamline their operations to improve overall efficiency and effectiveness. The pretax expense of these streamlining initiatives for the three months ended March 31, 2003, June 30, 2003, September 30, 2003 and December 31, 2003 was $159 million, $70 million, $43 million and $289 million, respectively. Refer to Note 17.

Effective May 6, 2003, Coca-Cola FEMSA consummated a merger with another of the Company's equity method investees, Panamerican Beverages, Inc. During the third quarter of 2003, our Company recorded a pretax noncash charge to equity income—net of $95 million primarily related to Coca-Cola FEMSA streamlining initiatives and impairment of certain intangible assets. During the fourth quarter of 2003, our Company recorded a pretax noncash charge of $7 million related solely to the streamlining and integration of these operations. Refer to Note 2.

In the fourth quarter of 2003, we favorably resolved various tax matters (approximately $50 million), partially offset by additional taxes primarily related to the repatriation of funds.

List of the Official Pronouncements of the AICPA and FASB

B2 Accounting Research Bulletins (ARBs), Committee on Accounting Procedure, AICPA

B2 Accounting Terminology Bulletins, Committee on Terminology, AICPA

B2 Accounting Principles Board (APB) Statements, AICPA

B2 Accounting Principles Board (APB) Opinions, AICPA

B3 FASB Statements of Financial Accounting Standards, Financial Accounting Standards Board

B8 FASB Statements of Financial Accounting Concepts, Financial Accounting Standards Board

B8 FASB Interpretations, Financial Accounting Standards Board

Listed below are the major official pronouncements of the AICPA and the FASB that have established generally accepted accounting principles or that have had a significant impact upon the establishment of these principles.

Number	Title	*Date of Issuance*

Accounting Research Bulletins (ARBs), Committee on Accounting Procedure, AICPA

43   Restatement and Revision of Accounting Research
Bulletin Nos. 1–42 . . . . .June 1953
Chapter
   1   Prior Opinions
   2   Form of Statements
   3   Working Capital
   4   Inventory Pricing
   5   Intangible Assets
   6   Contingency Reserves
   7   Capital Accounts
   8   Income and Earned Surplus
   9   Depreciation
  10   Taxes
  11   Government Contracts
  12   Foreign Operations and Foreign Exchange
  13   Compensation
  14   Disclosure of Long-Term Leases in Financial Statements of Leases
  15   Unamortized Discount, Issue Cost, and Redemption Premium on Bonds Refunded
44   Declining-Balance Depreciation (Revised July 1958) . . . . .October 1954
45   Long-Term Construction-Type Contracts . . . . .October 1955
46   Discontinuance of Dating Earned Surplus . . . . .February 1956
47   Accounting for Costs of Pension Plans . . . . .September 1956
48   Business Combinations . . . . .January 1957
49   Earnings per Share . . . . .April 1958
50   Contingencies . . . . .October 1958
51   Consolidated Financial Statements . . . . .August 1959

Accounting Terminology Bulletins, Committee on Terminology, AICPA

1   Review and Résumé (of eight original terminology bulletins) . . . . .August 1953
2   Proceeds, Revenue, Income, Profit, and Earnings . . . . .March 1955
3   Book Value . . . . .August 1956
4   Cost, Expense, and Loss . . . . .July 1957

Accounting Principles Board (APB) Statements, AICPA

1   Statement by the Accounting Principles Board . . . . .April 1962
2   Disclosure of Supplemental Financial Information by Diversified Companies . . . . .September 1967
3   Financial Statements Restated for General Price-Level Changes . . . . .June 1969
4   Basic Concepts and Accounting Principles Underlying Financial
    Statements of Business Enterprises . . . . .October 1970

Accounting Principles Board (APB) Opinions, AICPA

1   New Depreciation Guidelines and Rules . . . . .November 1962
2   Accounting for the "Investment Credit" . . . . .December 1962
3   The Statement of Source and Application of Funds . . . . .October 1963
4   Accounting for the "Investment Credit" (Amending No. 2) . . . . .March 1964
5   Reporting of Leases in Financial Statements of Lessee . . . . .September 1964

Number	*Title*	*Date of Issuance*

Accounting Principles Board (APB) Opinions, AICPA, Continued

6 Status of Accounting Research Bulletins . . . . .October 1965
7 Accounting for Leases in Financial Statements of Lessors . . . . .May 1966
8 Accounting for the Cost of Pension Plans . . . . .November 1966
9 Reporting the Results of Operations . . . . .December 1966
10 Omnibus Opinion—1966 . . . . .December 1966
11 Accounting for Income Taxes . . . . .December 1967
12 Omnibus Opinion—1967 . . . . .December 1967
13 Amending Paragraph 6 of the *APB Opinion No. 9*, Application to Commercial Banks . . .March 1969
14 Accounting for Convertible Debt and Debt Issued with Stock Purchase Warrants . . . . . .March 1969
15 Earnings per Share . . . . .May 1969
16 Business Combinations . . . . .August 1970
17 Intangible Assets . . . . .August 1970
18 The Equity Method of Accounting for Investments in Common Stock . . . . .March 1971
19 Reporting Changes in Financial Position . . . . .March 1971
20 Accounting Changes . . . . .July 1971
21 Interest on Receivables and Payables . . . . .August 1971
22 Disclosure of Accounting Policies . . . . .April 1972
23 Accounting for Income Taxes—Special Areas . . . . .April 1972
24 Accounting for Income Taxes—Investments in Common Stock Accounted
    for by the Equity Method . . . . .April 1972
25 Accounting for Stock Issued to Employees . . . . .October 1972
26 Early Extinguishment of Debt . . . . .October 1972
27 Accounting for Lease Transactions by Manufacturer or Dealer Lessors . . . . .November 1972
28 Interim Financial Reporting . . . . .May 1973
29 Accounting for Nonmonetary Transactions . . . . .May 1973
30 Reporting the Results of Operations—Reporting the Effects of Disposal of a Segment
    of a Business, and Extraordinary, Unusual and Infrequently Occurring Events and
    Transactions . . . . .June 1973
31 Disclosure of Lease Commitments by Lessees . . . . .June 1973

FASB Statements of Financial Accounting Standards, Financial Accounting Standards Board

1 Disclosure of Foreign Currency Translation Information . . . . .December 1973
2 Accounting for Research and Development Costs . . . . .October 1974
3 Reporting Accounting Changes in Interim Financial Statements
   (an amendment of *APB Opinion No. 28*) . . . . .December 1974
4 Reporting Gains and Losses from Extinguishment of Debt
   (an amendment of *APB Opinion No. 30*) . . . . .March 1975
5 Accounting for Contingencies . . . . .March 1975
6 Classification of Short-Term Obligations Expected to Be Refinanced
   (an amendment of *ARB No. 43*, Chapter 3A) . . . . .May 1975
7 Accounting and Reporting by Development Stage Enterprises . . . . .June 1975
8 Accounting for the Translation of Foreign Currency Transactions and Foreign
   Currency Financial Statements . . . . .October 1975
9 Accounting for Income Taxes—Oil and Gas Producing Companies
   (an amendment of *APB Opinion Nos. 11* and *23*) . . . . .October 1975
10 Extension of "Grandfather" Provisions for Business Combinations
    (an amendment of *APB Opinion No. 16*) . . . . .October 1975
11 Accounting for Contingencies—Transition Method (an amendment of *FASB
    Statement No. 5*) . . . . .December 1975
12 Accounting for Certain Marketable Securities . . . . .December 1975
13 Accounting for Leases . . . . .November 1976

Number	Title	Date of Issuance

FASB Statements of Financial Accounting Standards, Financial Accounting Standards Board, Continued

14 Financial Reporting for Segments of a Business Enterprise . . . . .December 1976

15 Accounting by Debtors and Creditors for Troubled Debt Restructurings . . . . .June 1977

16 Prior Period Adjustments . . . . .June 1977

17 Accounting for Leases—Initial Direct Costs (an amendment of *FASB
Statement No. 13*) . . . . .November 1977

18 Financial Reporting for Segments of a Business Enterprise Interim Financial
Statements (an amendment of *FASB Statement No. 14*) . . . . .November 1977

19 Financial Accounting and Reporting by Oil and Gas Producing Companies . . . . . . .December 1977

20 Accounting for Forward Exchange Contracts (an amendment of
FASB Statement No. 8) . . . . .December 1977

21 Suspension of the Reporting of Earnings per Share and Segment Information by
Nonpublic Enterprises (an amendment of *APB Opinion No. 15* and *FASB Statement
No. 14*) . . . . .April 1978

22 Accounting for Leases—Changes in the Provisions of Lease Agreements Resulting
from Refundings of Tax-Exempt Debt (an amendment of *FASB Statement No. 13*) . . . . . . .June 1978

23 Inception of the Lease (an amendment of *FASB Statement No. 13*) . . . . .August 1978

24 Reporting Segment Information in Financial Statements That Are Presented in
Another Enterprise's Financial Report (an amendment of
FASB Statement No. 14) . . . . .December 1978

25 Suspension of Certain Accounting Requirements for Oil and Gas Companies
(an amendment of *FASB Statement No. 19*) . . . . .February 1979

26 Profit Recognition on Sales-Type Leases of Real Estate
(an amendment of *FASB Statement No. 13*) . . . . .April 1979

27 Classification of Renewals or Extensions of Existing Sales-Type or Direct
Financing Leases (an amendment of *FASB Statement No. 13*) . . . . .May 1979

28 Accounting for Sales with Leasebacks (an amendment of *FASB Statement No. 13*) . . . . . . .May 1979

29 Determining Contingent Rentals (an amendment of *FASB Statement No. 13*) . . . . .June 1979

30 Disclosure of Information About Major Customers (an amendment of *FASB
Statement No. 14*) . . . . .August 1979

31 Accounting for Tax Benefits Related to U.K. Tax Legislation Concerning
Stock Relief . . . . .September 1979

32 Specialized Accounting and Reporting Principles and Practices in AICPA
Statements of Position and Guides on Accounting and Auditing Matters
(an amendment of *APB Opinion No. 20*) . . . . .September 1979

33 Financial Reporting and Changing Prices . . . . .September 1979

34 Capitalization of Interest Cost . . . . .October 1979

35 Accounting and Reporting by Defined Benefit Pension Plans . . . . .March 1980

36 Disclosure of Pension Information . . . . .May 1980

37 Balance Sheet Classification of Deferred Income Taxes (an amendment of *APB
Opinion No. 11*) . . . . .July 1980

38 Accounting for Preacquisition Contingencies of Purchased Enterprises
(an amendment of *APB Opinion No. 16*) . . . . .September 1980

39 Financial Reporting and Changing Prices: Specialized Assets—Mining and Oil
and Gas (a supplement to *FASB Statement No. 33*) . . . . .October 1980

40 Financial Reporting and Changing Prices: Specialized Assets—Timberlands and
Growing Timber (a supplement to *FASB Statement No. 33*) . . . . .November 1980

41 Financial Reporting and Changing Prices: Specialized Assets—Income-Producing
Real Estate (a supplement to *FASB Statement No. 33*) . . . . .November 1980

42 Determining Materiality for Capitalization of Interest Cost
(an amendment of *FASB Statement No. 34*) . . . . .November 1980

43 Accounting for Compensated Absences . . . . .November 1980

		Date of
Number	*Title*	*Issuance*

FASB Statements of Financial Accounting Standards, Financial Accounting Standards Board, Continued

44 Accounting for Intangible Assets of Motor Carriers (an amendment of Chapter 5 of *ARB No. 43* and an interpretation of *APB Opinion Nos. 17* and *30*) . . . . .December 1980

45 Accounting for Franchise Fee Revenue . . . . .March 1981

46 Financial Reporting and Changing Prices: Motion Picture Films . . . . .March 1981

47 Disclosure of Long-Term Obligations . . . . .March 1981

48 Revenue Recognition When Right of Return Exists . . . . .June 1981

49 Accounting for Product Financing Arrangements . . . . .June 1981

50 Financial Reporting in the Record and Music Industry . . . . .November 1981

51 Financial Reporting by Cable Television Companies . . . . .November 1981

52 Foreign Currency Translation . . . . .December 1981

53 Financial Reporting by Producers and Distributors of Motion Picture Films . . . . . . .December 1981

54 Financial Reporting and Changing Prices: Investment Companies (an amendment of *FASB Statement No. 33*) . . . . .January 1982

55 Determining Whether a Convertible Security Is a Common Stock Equivalent (an amendment of *APB Opinion No. 15*) . . . . .February 1982

56 Designation of AICPA Guide and Statement of Position (SOP) 81-1 on Contractor Accounting and SOP 81-2 Concerning Hospital-Related Organizations as Preferable for Purposes of Applying *APB Opinion 20* (an amendment of *FASB Statement No. 32*) . . .February 1982

57 Related Party Disclosures . . . . .March 1982

58 Capitalization of Interest Cost in Financial Statements That Include Investments Accounted for by the Equity Method . . . . .April 1982

59 Deferral of the Effective Date of Certain Accounting Requirements for Pension Plans of State and Local Governmental Units (an amendment of *FASB Statement No. 35*) . . . . .April 1982

60 Accounting and Reporting by Insurance Enterprises . . . . .June 1982

61 Accounting for Title Plant . . . . .June 1982

62 Capitalization of Interest Cost in Situations Involving Certain Tax-Exempt Borrowings and Certain Gifts and Grants . . . . .June 1982

63 Financial Reporting by Broadcasters . . . . .June 1982

64 Extinguishments of Debt Made to Satisfy Sinking-Fund Requirements (an amendment of *FASB Statement No. 4*) . . . . .September 1982

65 Accounting for Certain Mortgage Banking Activities . . . . .September 1982

66 Accounting for Sales of Real Estate . . . . .October 1982

67 Accounting for Costs and Initial Rental Operations of Real Estate Projects . . . . .October 1982

68 Research and Development Arrangements . . . . .October 1982

69 Disclosures about Oil- and Gas-Producing Activities . . . . .November 1982

70 Financial Reporting and Changing Prices: Foreign Currency Translation (an amendment of *FASB Statement No. 33*) . . . . .December 1982

71 Accounting for the Effects of Certain Types of Regulation . . . . .December 1982

72 Accounting for Certain Acquisitions of Banking or Thrift Institutions (an amendment of *APB Opinion No. 17*, an interpretation of *APB Opinion Nos. 16* and *17*, and an amendment of *FASB Statement No. 9*) .February 1983

73 Reporting a Change in Accounting for Railroad Track Structures (an amendment of *APB Opinion No. 20*) . . . . .August 1983

74 Accounting for Special Termination Benefits Paid to Employees . . . . .August 1983

75 Deferral of the Effective Date of Certain Accounting Requirements for Pension Plans of State and Local Governmental Units (an amendment of *FASB Statement No. 35*) . . . . .November 1983

76 Extinguishment of Debt (an amendment of *APB Opinion No. 26*) . . . . .November 1983

77 Reporting by Transferors for Transfers of Receivables with Recourse . . . . .December 1983

78 Classification of Obligations That Are Callable by the Creditor (an amendment of *ARB No. 43*, Chapter 3A) . . . . .December 1983

Number	Title	Date of Issuance

FASB Statements of Financial Accounting Standards, Financial Accounting Standards Board, Continued

79 Elimination of Certain Disclosures for Business Combinations by Nonpublic
Enterprises (an amendment of *APB Opinion No. 16*) . . . . .February 1984

80 Accounting for Futures Contracts . . . . .August 1984

81 Disclosure of Postretirement Health Care and Life Insurance Benefits . . . . .November 1984

82 Financial Reporting and Changing Prices: Elimination of Certain Disclosures
(an amendment of *FASB Statement No. 33*) . . . . .December 1984

83 Designation of AICPA Guides and Statement of Position on Accounting by Brokers
and Dealers in Securities, by Employee Benefit Plans, and by Banks as Preferable
for Purposes of Applying *APB Opinion No. 20* . . . . .March 1985

84 Induced Conversions of Convertible Debt (an amendment of *APB Opinion No. 26*) . . . .March 1985

85 Yield Test for Determining Whether a Convertible Security Is a Common Stock
Equivalent (an amendment of *APB Opinion No. 15*) . . . . .March 1985

86 Accounting for the Costs of Computer Software to Be Sold, Leased, or Otherwise
Marketed . . . . .August 1985

87 Employers' Accounting for Pensions . . . . .December 1985

88 Employers' Accounting for Settlements and Curtailments of Defined Benefit
Pension Plans and for Termination Benefits . . . . .December 1985

89 Financial Reporting and Changing Prices . . . . .December 1986

90 Regulated Enterprises—Accounting for Abandonments and Disallowances of
Plant Costs (an amendment of *FASB Statement No. 71*) . . . . .December 1986

91 Accounting for Nonrefundable Fees and Costs Associated with Originating or
Acquiring Loans and Initial Direct Costs of Leases . . . . .December 1986

92 Regulated Enterprises—Accounting for Phase-in Plans (an amendment of
FASB Statement No. 71) . . . . .August 1987

93 Recognition of Depreciation by Not-for-Profit Organizations . . . . .August 1987

94 Consolidation of All Majority-Owned Subsidiaries (an amendment of *ARB No. 51*,
with related amendments of *APB Opinion No. 18* and *ARB No. 43*, Chapter 12) . . . . .October 1987

95 Statement of Cash Flows . . . . .November 1987

96 Accounting for Income Taxes . . . . .December 1987

97 Accounting and Reporting by Insurance Enterprises for Certain Long-Duration
Contracts and for Realized Gains and Losses from the Sale of Investments . . . . .December 1987

98 Accounting for Leases: Sale-Leaseback Transactions Involving Real Estate,
Sales-Type Leases of Real Estate, Definition of the Lease Term, and Initial
Direct Costs of Direct Financing Leases (an amendment of *FASB Statement
Nos. 13, 66, and 91* and a rescission of *FASB Statement No. 26* and
Technical Bulletin No. 79-11) . . . . .May 1988

99 Deferral of the Effective Date of Recognition of Depreciation by Not-for-Profit
Organizations (an amendment of *FASB Statement No. 93*) . . . . .September 1988

100 Accounting for Income Taxes—Deferral of the Effective Date of
FASB Statement No. 96 (an amendment of *FASB Statement No. 96*) . . . . .December 1988

101 Regulated Enterprises—Accounting for the Discontinuation of Application of
FASB Statement No. 71 . . . . .December 1988

102 Statement of Cash Flows—Exemption of Certain Enterprises and Classification of
Cash Flows from Certain Securities Acquired for Resale (an amendment of
FASB Statement No. 95) . . . . .February 1989

103 Accounting for Income Taxes—Deferral of the Effective Date of
FASB Statement No. 96 (an amendment of *FASB Statement No. 96*) . . . . .December 1989

104 Statement of Cash Flows—Net Reporting of Certain Cash Receipts and Cash
Payments and Classification of Cash Flows from Hedging Transactions
(an amendment of *FASB Statement No. 95*) . . . . .December 1989

105 Disclosure of Information about Financial Instruments with Off-Balance-Sheet
Risk and Financial Instruments with Concentrations of Credit Risk . . . . .March 1990

Number	Title	Date of Issuance

FASB Statements of Financial Accounting Standards, Financial Accounting Standards Board, Continued

106 Employers' Accounting for Postretirement Benefits Other Than Pensions . . . . .December 1990

107 Disclosure about Fair Value of Financial Instruments . . . . .December 1991

108 Accounting for Income Taxes—Deferral of the Effective Date of *FASB Statement No. 96* (an amendment of *FASB Statement No. 96*) . . . . .December 1991

109 Accounting for Income Taxes . . . . .February 1992

110 Reporting by Defined Benefit Pension Plans of Investment Contracts (an amendment of *FASB Statement No. 35*) . . . . .August 1992

111 Rescission of *FASB Statement No. 32* and Technical Corrections . . . . .November 1992

112 Employers' Accounting for Postemployment Benefits (an amendment of *FASB Statement Nos. 5 and 43*) . . . . .November 1992

113 Accounting and Reporting for Reinsurance of Short-Term and Long-Term Contracts . . . . .December 1992

114 Accounting by Creditors for Impairment of a Loan (an amendment of *FASB Statement Nos. 5 and 15*) . . . . .May 1993

115 Accounting for Certain Investments in Debt and Equity Securities . . . . .May 1993

116 Accounting for Contributions Received and Contributions Made . . . . .June 1993

117 Financial Statements of Not-for-Profit Organizations . . . . .June 1993

118 Accounting by Creditors for Impairment of a Loan—Income Recognition and Disclosures (an amendment of *FASB Statement No. 114*) . . . . .October 1994

119 Disclosure about Derivative Financial Instruments and Fair Value of Financial Instruments . . . . .October 1994

120 Accounting and Reporting by Mutual Life Insurance Enterprises and by Insurance Enterprises for Certain Long-Duration Participating Contracts (an amendment of *FASB Statements No. 60, 97, and 113 and Interpretation No. 40*) . . . . .January 1995

121 Accounting for the Impairment of Long-Lived Assets and for Long-Lived Assets to Be Disposed Of . . . . .March 1995

122 Accounting for Mortgage Servicing Rights (an amendment of *FASB Statement No. 65*) . . . . .May 1995

123 Accounting for Stock-Based Compensation . . . . .October 1995

124 Accounting for Certain Investments Held by Not-for-Profit Organizations . . . . .November 1995

125 Accounting for Transfers and Servicing of Financial Assets and Extinguishments of Liabilities . . . . .June 1996

126 Exemption from Certain Required Disclosures about Financial Instruments for Certain Nonpublic Entities (an amendment of *FASB Statement No. 107*) . . . . .December 1996

127 Deferral of the Effective Date of Certain Provisions of *FASB Statement No. 125* (an amendment of *FASB Statement No. 125*) . . . . .December 1996

128 Earnings per Share . . . . .February 1997

129 Disclosure of Information about Capital Structure . . . . .February 1997

130 Reporting Comprehensive Income . . . . .June 1997

131 Disclosures about Segments of an Enterprise and Related Information . . . . .June 1997

132 Employers' Disclosures about Pensions and Other Postretirement Benefits (an amendment of *FASB Statements No. 87, 88, and 106*) . . . . .February 1998

133 Accounting for Derivative Instruments and Hedging Activities . . . . .June 1998

134 Accounting for Mortgage-Backed Securities Retained after the Securitization of Mortgage Loans Held for Sale by a Mortgage Banking Enterprise (an amendment of *FASB Statement No. 65*) . . . . .October 1998

135 Rescission of *FASB Statement No. 75* and Technical Corrections . . . . .February 1999

136 Transfers of Asset to a Not-for-Profit Organization or Charitable Trust That Raises or Holds Contributions for Others . . . . .June 1999

137 Accounting for Derivative Instruments and Hedging Activities–Deferral of the Effective Date of *FASB Statement No. 133* (an amendment of *FASB Statement No. 133*) . . . . .June 1999

Number	Title	Date of Issuance

FASB Statements of Financial Accounting Standards, Financial Accounting Standards Board, Continued

138 Accounting for Certain Derivative Instruments and Certain Hedging Activities (an amendment of *FASB Statement No. 133*) . . . . .June 2000

139 Rescission of *FASB Statement No. 53* and amendments to *FASB Statements No. 63, 89,* and *121* . . . . .June 2000

140 Accounting for Transfers and Servicing of Financial Assets and Extinguishments of Liabilities (a replacement of *FASB Statement No. 125*) . . . . .September 2000

141 Business Combinations . . . . .June 2001

142 Goodwill and Other Intangible Assets . . . . .June 2001

143 Accounting for Asset Retirement Obligations . . . . .June 2001

144 Accounting for the Impairment or Disposal of Long-Lived Assets . . . . .August 2001

145 Rescission of *FASB Statements No. 4, 44,* and *64,* Amendment of *FASB Statement No. 13,* and Technical Corrections . . . . .April 2002

146 Accounting for Costs Associated with Exit or Disposal Activities . . . . .July 2002

147 Acquisitions of Certain Financial Institutions . . . . .October 2002

148 Accounting for Stock-Based Compensation-Transition and Disclosure (an amendment of *FASB Statement No. 123*) . . . . .December 2002

149 Amendment of *Statement 133* on Derivative Instruments and Hedging Activities . . . . .April 2003

150 Accounting for Certain Financial Instruments with Characteristics of Both Liabilities and Equity . . . . .May 2003

132R Employers' Disclosures about Pensions and Other Postretirement Benefits (an amendment of *FASB Statements No. 87, 88,* and *106*) . . . . .December 2003

151 Inventory Costs (an amendment of *ARB No. 43,* Chapter 4) . . . . .November 2004

152 Accounting for Real Estate Time-Sharing Transactions (an amendment of *FASB Statements No. 66* and *67*) . . . . .December 2004

153 Exchanges of Nonmonetary Assets (an amendment of *APB Opinion No. 29*) . . . . . .December 2004

123R Share-Based Payment . . . . .December 2004

154 Accounting Changes and Error Corrections (a replacement of *APB Opinion No. 20* and *FASB Statement No. 3*) . . . . .May 2005

FASB Statements of Financial Accounting Concepts, Financial Accounting Standards Board

1 Objectives of Financial Reporting by Business Enterprises . . . . .November 1978

2 Qualitative Characteristics of Accounting Information . . . . .May 1980

3 Elements of Financial Statements of Business Enterprises . . . . .December 1980

4 Objectives of Financial Reporting by Nonbusiness Organizations . . . . .December 1980

5 Recognition and Measurement in Financial Statements of Business Enterprises . . .December 1984

6 Elements of Financial Statements (a replacement of *FASB Concepts Statement No. 3,* incorporating an amendment of *FASB Concepts Statement No. 2*) . . . . .December 1985

7 Using Cash Flow Information and Present Value in Accounting Measurements . . . .February 2000

FASB Interpretations, Financial Accounting Standards Board

1 Accounting Changes Related to the Cost of Inventory (an interpretation of *APB Opinion No. 20*) . . . . .June 1974

2 Imputing Interest on Debt Arrangements Made under the Federal Bankruptcy Act (an interpretation of *APB Opinion No. 21*) . . . . .June 1974

3 Accounting for the Cost of Pension Plans Subject to the Employee Retirement Income Security Act of 1974 (an interpretation of *APB Opinion No. 8*) . . . . .December 1974

4 Applicability of *FASB Statement No. 2* to Business Combinations Accounted for by the Purchase Method . . . . .February 1975

5 Applicability of *FASB Statement No. 2* to Development Stage Enterprises . . . . .February 1975

Number	Title	Date of Issuance

FASB Interpretations, Financial Accounting Standards Board, Continued

6 Applicability of *FASB Statement No. 2* to Computer Software .February 1975

7 Applying *FASB Statement No. 7* in Financial Statements of Established
Operating Enterprises . . . . .October 1975

8 Classification of a Short-Term Obligation Repaid Prior to Being Replaced by a
Long-Term Security (an interpretation of *FASB Statement No. 6*) . . . . .January 1976

9 Applying *APB Opinion Nos. 16* and *17* When a Savings and Loan Association
or a Similar Institution Is Acquired in a Business Combination Accounted for
by the Purchase Method . . . . .February 1976

10 Application of *FASB Statement No. 12* to Personal Financial Statements . . . . .September 1976

11 Changes in Market Value after the Balance Sheet Date (an interpretation of
FASB Statement No. 12) . . . . .September 1976

12 Accounting for Previously Established Allowance Accounts (an interpretation
of *FASB Statement No. 12*) . . . . .September 1976

13 Consolidation of a Parent and Its Subsidiaries Having Different Balance Sheets
Dates (an interpretation of *FASB Statement No. 12*) . . . . .September 1976

14 Reasonable Estimation of the Amount of a Loss (an interpretation of
FASB Statement No. 5) . . . . .September 1976

15 Translation of Unamortized Policy Acquisition Costs by a Stock Life Insurance
Company (an interpretation of *FASB Statement No. 8*) . . . . .September 1976

16 Clarification of Definitions and Accounting for Marketable Equity Securities
That Become Nonmarketable (an interpretation of *FASB Statement No. 12*) . . . . . . .February 1977

17 Applying the Lower of Cost or Market Rule in Translated Financial Statements
(an interpretation of *FASB Statement No. 8*) . . . . .February 1977

18 Accounting for Income Taxes in Interim Periods (an interpretation of
APB Opinion No. 28) . . . . .March 1977

19 Lessee Guarantee of the Residual Value of Leased Property (an interpretation of
FASB Statement No. 13) . . . . .October 1977

20 Reporting Accounting Changes under AICPA Statements of Position
(an interpretation of *APB Opinion No. 20*) . . . . .November 1977

21 Accounting for Leases in a Business Combination (an interpretation of
FASB Statement No. 13) . . . . .April 1978

22 Applicability of Indefinite Reversal Criteria to Timing Differences (an interpretation
of *APB Opinion Nos. 11* and *23*) . . . . .April 1978

23 Leases & Certain Property Owned by a Governmental Unit or Authority
(an interpretation of *FASB Statement No. 13*) . . . . .August 1978

24 Lease Involving Only Part of a Building (an interpretation of
FASB Statement No. 13) . . . . .September 1978

25 Accounting for an Unused Investment Tax Credit (an interpretation of
APB Opinion Nos. 2, 4, 11, and *16*) . . . . .September 1978

26 Accounting for Purchase of a Leased Asset by the Lessee during the Term
of the Lease (an interpretation of *FASB Statement No. 13*) . . . . .September 1978

27 Accounting for a Loss on a Sublease (an interpretation of
FASB Statement No. 13) . . . . .November 1978

28 Accounting for Stock Appreciation Rights and Other Variable Stock
Option or Award Plans (an interpretation of *APB Opinion Nos. 15* and *25*) . . . . . . .December 1978

29 Reporting Tax Benefits Realized on Disposition of Investments in Certain Subsidiaries
and Other Investees (an interpretation of *APB Opinion Nos. 23* and *24*) . . . . .February 1979

30 Accounting for Involuntary Conversions of Nonmonetary Assets to Monetary
Assets (an interpretation of *APB Opinion No. 29*) . . . . .September 1979

31 Treatment of Stock Compensation Plans in EPS Computations (an interpretation
of *APB Opinion No. 15* and a modification of *FASB Interpretation No. 28*) . . . . .February 1980

Number	Title	Date of Issuance

FASB Interpretations, Financial Accounting Standards Board, Continued

32 Application of Percentage Limitations in Recognizing Investment Tax Credit (an interpretation of *APB Opinion Nos. 2, 4,* and *11*) . . . . .March 1980

33 Applying *FASB Statement No. 34* to Oil and Gas Producing Operations Accounted for by the Full Cost Method (an interpretation of *FASB Statement No. 34*) . . . . .August 1980

34 Disclosure of Indirect Guarantees of Indebtedness of Others (an interpretation of *FASB Statement No. 5*) . . . . .March 1981

35 Criteria for Applying the Equity Method of Accounting for Investments in Common Stock (an interpretation of *APB Opinion No. 18*) . . . . .May 1981

36 Accounting for Exploratory Wells in Progress at the End of a Period (an interpretation of *FASB Statement No. 19*) . . . . .October 1981

37 Accounting for Translation Adjustments Upon Sale of Part of an Investment in a Foreign Entity (an interpretation of *FASB Statement No. 52*) . . . . .July 1983

38 Determining the Measurement Date for Stock Option, Purchase, and Award Plans Involving Junior Stock (an interpretation of *APB Opinion No. 25*) . . . . .August 1984

39 Offsetting of Amounts Related to Certain Contracts (an interpretation of *APB Opinion No. 10* and *FASB Statement No. 105*) . . . . .March 1992

40 Applicability of Generally Accepted Accounting Principles to Mutual Life Insurance and Other Enterprises (an interpretation of *FASB Statement Nos. 12, 60, 97,* and *113*) . . . . April 1993

41 Offsetting of Amounts Related to Certain Repurchase and Reverse Repurchase Agreements (an interpretation of *APB Opinion No. 10* and a modification of *FASB Interpretation No. 39*) . . . . December 1994

42 Accounting for Transfers of Assets in Which a Not-for-Profit Organization Is Granted Variance Power (an interpretation of *FASB Statement No. 116*) . . . . September 1996

43 Real Estate Sales (an interpretation of *FASB Statement No. 66*) . . . . .June 1999

44 Accounting for Certain Transactions involving Stock Compensation (an interpretation of *APB Opinion No. 25*). . . . . March 2000

45 Guarantor's Accounting and Disclosure Requirements for Guarantees, Including Indirect Guarantees of Indebtedness of Others . . . . November 2002

46R Consolidation of Variable Interest Entities (an interpretation of *ARB No. 51*) . . . . . . December 2003

47 Accounting for Conditional Asset Retirement Obligations (an interpretation of *FASB Statement No. 143*). . . . . March 2005

Note: The letter *n* following a page number indicates a footnote; the letter *f*, an exhibit; the letter *d*, a definition.

A

AAA (American Accounting Association), 11–12, 19

Accelerated depreciation method, 506

Account form, 148

Accounting, 4*d*; accrual, 50–51; cash basis, 50–51; changes and errors. *See* restatements; demand for, 3; estimates, change in, 200–202; financial, 6–7; managerial, 6–7; periods, 47, 47*f*; policies, 141–142; standards. *See* principles; standards; survey of trends, 3

Accounting cycle: accrued: expenses, 78–79; income taxes, 79, 79*n*; interest, 78–79; revenues, 79; salaries, 78; adjusted trial balance, 82, 82*d*, 82*f*; allowances, 86–87; bad debt expense, 80–81; control accounts, 93; deferred revenue, 77–78, 77*d*; depreciation expense, 80; discounts, 86–87; error detection, 74–76; estimated items, 80; general journal, 70*d*, 71; general ledger, 73*d*, 75*f*; journal entries, 71*d*; journalizing, 71*d*; major steps: adjusting entries, preparing, 76–81, 77*f*; closing entries, preparing, 84–86, 85*f*; financial statements, preparing, 81–84; general journal, recording in, 70–73; ledger, posting to, 73–76; net sales, 87; periodic inventory system, 71*n*, 87–88; perpetual inventory system, 71; posting, 73–74*d*; prepaid expenses, 76; purchases allowance, 87; purchases discount, 87; returns, 86–87, 87*n*; reversing entries, 90–91*d*, 91–92; sales allowances, 86–87; sales returns, 86–87; slide errors, 74–75; special journals, 71*d*, 93–94, 93*d*; subsidiary ledgers, 74*n*, 92–93, 93*d*, 93*f*; transactional analysis, 72–73*f*; transposition errors, 74–75; trial balances, 74–76, 74*d*; worksheets, 88–90, 89*f*

Accounting equation, 66–67, 68*f*

Accounting information. *See also* useful information: capital, obtaining, 4–5; capital markets, 4–5, 4*f*; external users, 5–6*d*, 6*n*; financial accounting, 6–7*d*, 7*f*; guiding principles. *See* generally accepted accounting principles (GAAP); principles; internal users, 5–6*d*; managerial accounting, 6–7*d*, 7*f*; primary markets, 4*f*, 5*d*; reporting, 6*n*. *See also* financial reporting; secondary markets, 4–5*d*, 4*f*; uses of, 4–5

Accounting Interpretations, 9*f*, 17–18

Accounting Principles Board (APB), 10

Accounting Research Bulletins (ARBs). *See* ARBs (Accounting Research Bulletins).

Accounting Research Study No. 10, 569–570

Accounting systems: accounts, 67*d*; balances, 69*d*; chart of, 67; contra, 69; credits, 68; debits, 68; double-entry system, 68, 68*f*; numbering, 67; permanent, 68–69; physical forms, 68; T-accounts, 68; temporary, 68–69; accrual-basis: converting from cash-basis, 95–97, 96*f*; principles, 50–51; transactional approach, 171–172; assets, 66*d*; cash-basis, 95–97; components of, 66–70; computer software for, 94–95; contributed capital, 67*d*; dividends, 67*d*; events, 67*d*; expenses, 67*d*; liabilities, 66*d*; major steps, 66–67; residual equity theory model, 66–67; retained earnings, 67*d*; revenues, 67*d*; source documents, 67*d*; stockholders' equity, 66*d*; transactions, 67*d*

Accounting Trends and Techniques, 9*f*, 18

Accounts, 67*d*; balances, 69; chart of, 67; contra, 69; credits, 68; debits, 68; double-entry system, 68, 68*f*; numbering, 67; payable, computer software for, 94; permanent, 68–69; physical forms, 68; receivable, 310*d*. *See also* receivables; asset valuation, 323; assigning, 325–326; cash (sales) discount, 313–314; computer software for, 94; credit policy, 312–313; disclosure of financing agreements, 328; factoring, 326–327; financing agreements, 323–328; generating cash from, 322–328; gross discount method, 313–314; as loan collateral, 324–328; net discount method, 313–314; net realizable value, 322–323; pledging, 324; selling, 326–327; T-accounts, 68; temporary, 68–69

Accounts receivable conversion (ARC), 304–305

Accrual of loss contingencies, 613–614

Accrual-basis accounting: converting from cash-basis, 95–97, 96*f*; principles, 50–51; transactional approach, 171–172

Accrued: expenses, 78–79; income taxes, 79, 79*n*; interest, 78–79; liabilities, current liabilities, 595–598; post retirement benefit cost, 1037; revenues, 79; salaries, 78

Accumulated: benefit obligation, 999*d*; other comprehensive income, 139–140; postretirement benefit obligation (APBO), 1035; rights, current liabilities, 596

Acid-test ratio, 271

Activity depreciation methods, 509–510

Activity ratios, 272–273

Actual return on plan assets, 999*d*

Actuarial funding method, 999*d*

Actuarial present value, 999*d*

Additional paid-in capital, 138, 770–771

Additions to property, plant, and equipment, 476

Adjusted trial balance, 82, 82d, 82f

Adjusting entries, preparing, 76–81, 77f

Administrative expenses, 184–185

Advances, current liabilities, 595

Advancing costs and expenses. *See* accrual-basis accounting.

Adverse opinions, 249

Advertising costs, current liabilities, 610–611

Aflac, 704–705

Aggregation, segment reports, 251

Aging accounts receivable, 318–320, 318d

AICPA (American Institute of Certified Public Accountants). *See* American Institute of Certified Public Accountants (AICPA).

AICPA Statement of Position: No. 81-1, 895; No. 97.2, 917; No. 98-1, 561; No. 98-5, 466, 562

AIG (American International Group's), 1199

Alcoa, 800

All-inclusive concept, 181–183

Allowance for doubtful accounts, 316

Allowance method, 316, 366n, 420

Allowances, 86–87

Alternative income captions, 189

Alternative minimum tax, 976–977

America Online (AOL), 611

American Accounting Association (AAA), 11–12, 19

American Institute of Certified Public Accountants (AICPA): history of, 17–18; history of GAAP, 8; publications, 17–18; survey of accounting trends, 3

American International Group (AIG), 1199

Amortization, 504d; bonds: acquired between interest dates, 718, 718n; discounts, 645–653, 715–717; effective interest, 648–651, 648n; premiums, 645–653, 715–717; straight-line, 645–647, 646n; debt securities, 714n; intangible assets, 552–553, 553n, 558f; loss, debt securities, 714n; unrecognized prior service costs, 1046–1047

Analysis. *See* financial analysis.

Anheuser-Busch, 514

Annual report (10-K form), 16, 145–146, 262d

Annual reports, 7, 69d

Annuities, M10d; future value: annuities due, M13–14; ordinary annuities, M10–13; present value: annuities, M14; annuities due, M18–21; deferred annuities due, M21–24; ordinary annuities, M14–18

APB (Accounting Principles Board), 10

APB Opinions, 10d. *See also* standards; *No. 4*, 32; *No. 8*, 998; *No. 9*, 195, 970; *No. 10*, 656, 909, 914; *No. 11*, 949; *No. 12*, 481, 513, 658, 855; *No. 14*, 656, 658, 795–796; *No. 16*, 181; *No. 18*, 729, 732n; *No. 19*, 210; *No. 21*, 312, 329, 645, 649, 651, 661–662, 664, 714–715; *No. 22*, 141; *No. 25*, 781; *No. 26*, 655; *No. 28*, 257, 387, 421; *No. 29*, 465–466, 844; *No. 30*, 181, 196, 655, 970; principles of accounting, 10; Securities and Exchange Commission (SEC), 17

APB Statement No. 4, 906

Apple Computer, Inc., 332

Appraisal systems, 518

ARBs (Accounting Research Bulletins): history of, 10; No. 43, 10, 424; No. 45, 895, 904; No. 47, 997–998

ARC (accounts receivable conversion), 304–305

Articles of incorporation, 767

Assets, 52d, 66d, 122d; in the accounting equation, 66; cost, depreciation, 504; current, 128–129, 128d; fixed, 133d; intangible, 134d; liquid, 132d; other, 134; retirement obligations, 479; return on total, 270; separable, 132d; valuation, 123–127, 124f; valuation, accounts receivable, 323

Assigning: accounts receivable, 325–326; notes receivable, 330–331

Assumptions, 46f. *See also* cost flow assumptions; principles; accounting period, 47, 47f; changes in value over time, 48; continuity, 46–47; economic entities, 45; fiscal year, 47; going concern, 46–47; monetary unit, 48; period of time, 47

Audit committee reports, 249–251

Auditing, 8, 308n

Auditor's reports, 248–249f; adverse opinions, 249; definition paragraph, 247; description, 246; disclaimer of opinion, 249; inherent limitations paragraph, 247; introductory paragraph, 246–247; opinion paragraph, 247–248; opinions expressed, 246; qualified opinions, 249; scope paragraph, 247

Authorized capital stock, 769

Available-for-sale securities, 707d; debt securities, 708–714, 709n, 724; equity securities, 708–714, 709n, 723

Average cost, 370–371, 370d, 378–379

Average cost flow assumption, 431

Average life expectancy, 996

B

Bad debts. *See also* impairments, loans; uncollectible accounts.: estimating, 316, 317. *See also* uncollectible accounts, valuation; expense, 80–81; failure to accrue, 1221–1222; short-term interest-bearing notes, 329

Baker Hughes, 615–617

Balance sheets, 52d, 69d, 84f, 130f. *See also* financial statements; reporting; reports; statements; assets, 52d, 122d; current, 128–129, 128d; fixed, 133d;

homogeneous classes, 136–137; intangible, 134*d*; liquid, 132*d*; other, 134; reporting, 136–137; separable, 132*d*; valuation, 123–127, 124*f*; capital, 120*d*; capital maintenance, 120–121, 120*d*; cash, 129; cash and cash equivalents section, 307; contributed capital, 137; current cost, 123*d*; current liabilities, 129–131; current market value, 123*d*–124; defined benefit pension plans, 1028–1029; elements, types of, 52–53, 121–123; fair value, 125*d*; financial capital, 121*d*; financial flexibility, 120; in financial reporting, 7; financial statements, 973–974, 973*n*; fixed assets, 133*d*; historical cost, 123*d*; income tax, 973–974, 973*n*; inventories, 129; liabilities, 52*d*, 122*d*; current, 129–131, 129*d*; homogeneous classes, 136–137; long-term, 134–135, 134*d*; other, 136; reporting, 136–137; valuation, 123–127, 124*f*; limitations, 126–127; liquid assets, 132*d*; liquidity, 120*d*; net realizable value, 124*d*; operating capability, 120*d*; operating cycle, 128*d*, 128*f*; pension plans, defined benefit, 1028–1029; physical capital, 121*d*; preparing, 84; present value, 125*d*; purpose of, 119–121; receivables, 129; recognition, 121; reporting classifications: accumulated other comprehensive income, 139–140; additional paid-in capital, 138; capital stock, 138; contributed capital, 137; current assets, 128–129, 128*d*; deferred charges, 134; intangible assets, 134*d*; long-term investments, 132–133, 132*d*; miscellaneous items, 140; other assets, 134; property, plant, and equipment (PP&E), 133–134, 133*d*; retained earnings, 139*d*; sample, 127–128; stockholders' equity, 137*d*; working capital, 131–132, 131*d*; restatements, 1216–1218; retained earnings, 139; separable assets, 132*d*; stockholders' equity, 123*d*, 803; temporary investments in marketable securities, 129; treasury stock, 803

Balances, 69*d*; adjusted trial balance, 82, 82*d*, 82*f*; trial balances, 74–76, 74*d*

Balancing bank accounts. *See* reconciling bank accounts.

Bank overdrafts, as cash, 306

Bankers Trust, 740

Bargain purchase option, 1069*d*, 1080–1081

Bargain renewal option, 1069*d*

Barings Bank, 740

Benefits *versus* costs, 43–44

Benefits/years-of-service approach, 1005

Betterments to property, plant, and equipment, 476–477

"Bill and hold" sales, 363–364

Black & Decker Corporation, 142

Boeing, 995

Bonds, 640*d*, 642*n*. *See also* notes; accruing interest, 652–653; acquired between interest dates, amortization, 718, 718*n*; amortization, 645–653; book value, 644; book value conversion, 659; carrying value, 644; characteristics of, 641, 642*f*; contract rate, 640; convertible, 657–660, 737–738; debt replacement, 654; debt retirement, 654; with detachable stock warrants, 656–657; discount, 135, 643; discounts and premiums, amortization, 715–717; effective interest amortization, 648–651, 648*n*; effective rate, 641–642; equity characteristics, 656–660; face rate, 640; face value, 640; induced conversions, 660; issue costs, 651–652; issued between interest payment dates, 644–645; less than face value, 135; market rate, 642; market value conversion, 659; maturity date, 640; more than face value, 135; nominal rate, 640; par value, 640; payable, 640–643; payable, cash flow, 1148–1149; premium, 135, 643; recalling the issue, 654; recording issuance of, 643–645; retiring, 654–656; sale before maturity, 719–720; selling prices, 641–643; serial: bonds outstanding method, 683–686; early redemption, 686; effective interest method, 683–686; interest expense, 683–686; issuance expense, 683–686; stated rate, 640; straight-line amortization, 645–647, 646*n*; yield, 641–642; zero-coupon, 653

Bonds outstanding method, 683–686

Bonus obligations, current liabilities, 602–605, 603*n*

Book value bond conversion, 659

Book value of bonds, 644

Book value per common share, 274–275

Brinker International, 1199

Bristol-Myers Squibb, 884

Buildings: acquisition, 462–463; changes and cash flow, 1148; leasing. *See* leasing, real estate.

Business reporting model, 54

Buy decisions, 5

C

Callable preferred stock, 797–798

Campbell Soup Company, 133

CAP (Committee on Accounting Procedure), 10

Capital, 120*d*; additional paid-in, 138; balance sheets, 120*d*; contributed, 137; financial, 121*d*; obtaining, 4–5; physical, 121*d*; primary markets, 4*f*, 5; private placements, 5; public offerings, 5; secondary markets, 4–5, 4*f*

Capital leases, 1068*d*; accounting and reporting, 1074–1075, 1075–1080, 1076*f*; examples, 1075–1080

Capital maintenance, 120*d*; in balance sheets, 120–121; and income, 170–171; income concept, 170–171

Capital markets, 4–5, 4*f*

Capital stock, 138, 769

Capital structure, 638, 768–771

Capitalized interest, revenue recognition, 904

Capitalizing *versus* expensing, 458–459. *See also* property, plant, and equipment (PP&E).

Carrybacks or carryforwards. *See* operating loss carrybacks or carryforwards.

Carrying value of bonds, 644

CASB (Cost Accounting Standards Board), 18

Cash, 306d. *See also* receivables; from accounts receivable, 322–328; auditing, 308n; balance sheets, 129; bank overdrafts, 306; bank reconciliation, 334–337; certificates of deposit (CDs), 306; coins and currency, 306; compensating balances, 309; current assets as, 306–307; discount, 313–314; dividends, 842–844; electronic funds transfer (EFT), 309; equivalent items, 307; excluded items, 306; funds on deposit, 306; included items, 306; internal controls, 333–337; managing, 307–308; negotiable checks, 306; petty cash, 333; planning systems, 308; postage stamps, 306; postdated checks, 306; receipts, assessing future, 35–36; travel advances, 306

Cash basis accounting, 50–51

Cash flows. *See* statement of cash flows.

Cash flow hedges, 745–746

Cash flow ratios, 275–276

Cash-basis accounting, 95–97

Ceiling, inventory.valuation, 414–415

CenterPoint Energy, Inc., 198

Certificates of deposit (CDs), 306

Certified Public Accountant (CPA), 42d

CFA Institute (CFAI), 11–12, 20

Check Clearing for the 21st Century Act, 305

Checks: as cash, 306; electronic, 304–305

Chief Accountant, 261

CISCO, 765

CKE Restaurants, 1199

Cliff vesting, 785–786

Closing entries, preparing, 84–86, 85f

Coca-Cola Company, 128, 142, 145, 148, 768

Code of Professional Conduct (CPC), 22f, 22n; description, 22–23; due care, 22f; integrity, 22f; objectivity and independence, 22f; public interest, 22f; responsibilities, 22f; scope and nature of services, 22f

"Codification of Financial Reporting Policies," 17n

Coins, as cash, 306

Colgate-Palmolive Company, 856–858

Combined accounts, 148

Committee on Accounting Procedure (CAP), 10

Common stocks, 138d; initial public sale, restatement, 1211; stockholders' equity, 772–779

Common-size statements, 265

Company profitability ratios, 269

Comparability, 43, 56, 256

Compensated absences, current liabilities, 595–598

Compensating balances, 309

Compensatory share option plans, 780d; cash flow, 1158–1159; cliff vesting, 785–786; conceptual evaluation, 792; disclosure, 790–791; exercise price, 780; fair value, 781, 783; fixed share option plan, 785–786; history of, 780–790; income tax issues, 975–976; intrinsic value method, 781; option price, 780; option pricing model, 783–784; overview, 780–790; performance-based share option plan, 786–787; political controversy, 782; recognition of compensation expense, 784–785; share appreciation rights (SARs), 788–790

Completed-contract method, 894d, 896–897, 898–901

Completion of production, revenue recognition, 892

Composite depreciation method, 516–518

Compound interest, M2–3

Compound-interest depreciation method, 515n

Comprehensive income, 139d, 172d, 207n. *See also* income; components of, 207; conceptual evaluation, 209; reporting alternatives, 207–209; reporting objectives, 36–37

Compromise, 14

Computer software costs, 559–560

ConAgra Foods, 391, 425

Conflict resolution, 14

Conservatism, 51

Consignment sales, revenue recognition, 923–924

Consignment transfers, 363

Consistency, 43

Consistency standards, 10

Consolidation reporting method, 707

Contingencies: gain: disclosure, 143–144, 615, 615–617; international differences, 617; loss: accrual of loss, 613–614; disclosure, 143–144, 614–615, 615–617; executory contracts, 615; international differences, 617; lawsuits, 614; loss, accounting for, 612–613; overview, 611–613; probable, 612; reasonably possible, 612; remote, 612

Continuing franchise fees, revenue recognition, 919, 921

Continuing operations. *See also* discontinued operations.: income from: administrative expenses, 184–185; alternative income captions, 189; classifying expenses, 184–185; cost of goods available for sale, 183–184; cost of goods sold, 183–184; general expenses, 184–185; gross margin on sales, 187–188; gross profit, 187–188; interperiod tax allocation, 186; intraperiod tax allocation, 186; multi-step formats, 187–188; operating expenses, 184–185; operating income, 187–188; other items, 185–186; sales revenue (net), 183; selling expenses, 184–185; single-step formats, 187–188; tax expenses, 186–187; variable expenses, 184–185

Continuity assumption, 46–47

Contra accounts, 69

Contract rate of bonds, 640

Contractual current liabilities: accrued liabilities, 595–598; advances, 595; compensated absences, 595–598; currently maturing long-term debt, 594; dividends payable, 594–595; holidays, 595–598; interest-bearing notes, 592–593, 592*n*; noninterest-bearing notes, 592–594; notes payable, 592–594, 593*n*; refundable deposits, 595; sick pay, 595–598; trade accounts payable, 591–592; vacations, 595–598

Contributed capital, 67*d. See also* stockholders' equity; stocks; on the balance sheet, 137; stockholders' equity, 771, 799–800

Contributory pension plans, 996*d*

Control accounts, 93

Convertible bonds, 657–660

Convertible preferred stock, 794–796

Convertible securities, earnings per share, 834–835

Copyrights, 559

Core earnings, 175–176

Corning, 524

Corporations, 137*d*; additional paid-in capital, 770–771; articles of incorporation, 767; authorized capital stock, 769; capital stock, 769; capital structure, 768–771; domestic, 767; foreign, 767; forming, 767–768; issued capital stock, 769; legal capital, 770; limits of liability, 767; no-par stock, 770; outstanding capital stock, 769; par value stock, 770; private, 767; public, 767; stock certificates, 768; stock transfer journal, 768; stockholders' ledger, 768; stockholders' rights, 769; subscribed capital stock, 769; treasury stock, 769; types of, 767

Cost Accounting Standards, 18

Cost Accounting Standards Board (CASB), 18

Cost depletion, 529

Cost flow, 361*f*

Cost flow assumptions, 367*d*, 367*f*; allowance method, 366*n*; alternatives: average cost, 378–379; earnings (income) management, 377–378; holding gain, 374–375; income measurement, 374–375; income tax effects, 375–376; inventory profit, 375; inventory valuation, 378; LIFO conformity rule, 375–376; LIFO liquidation profit, 376–377; liquidation of LIFO layers, 376–377; selecting, 379–380; average cost, 370*d*, 371; comparison of, 373–374; cost of beginning inventory, 367; cost of goods available for sale, 367; inventory valuation, 429–433; moving average cost, 371; physical flow, 367; specific identification, 367–369; weighted average cost, 370–371

Cost method, treasury stock, 801–803, 802*n*

Cost-recovery method, 177

Costs, 364*d*; advancing. *See* accrual-basis accounting; asset, depreciation, 504; average, 370–371, 370*d*, 378–379; of beginning inventory, 367; *versus* benefits, 43–44; continuing operations, 183–184; current, balance sheets, 123*d*; deferring, 50; depletion, 529; depreciable, 506; determining: gross price method, 365–367; net price method, 365–367; period costs, 365; product costs, 50, 365; purchases discounts, 365–367; trade discounts, 367; financing, 175–176; fixed overhead, 474–475; goods available for sale, 183–184, 367; goods sold, 183–184; historical, 48*n*; balance sheets, 123*d*; description, 48–49; property, plant, and equipment (PP&E), 460–461; moving average, 371; period, 50, 365–366; product, 50, 365; recognition. *See* recognition, expenses; weighted average, 370–371

Coupon obligations, current liabilities, 609–611

CPA (Certified Public Accountant), 42*d*

CPC (Code of Professional Conduct). *See* Code of Professional Conduct (CPC).

Creative and critical thinking, 24*d*, 24*f*; description, 23–25; partially structured problems, 25; problem-solving process, 24; structured problems, 24; unstructured problems, 24–25

Credit balance, 710

Credit card sales, exclusive agreements, 327

Credit policy, 312–313

Credits, 68

Critical thinking. *See* creative and critical thinking.

Cumulative preferred stock, 793–794

Currency, as cash, 306

Current asset changes, cash flow, 1144–1147

Current assets, 128*d*; balance sheet, 128–129; as cash, 306–307; receivables, 310

Current cost, balance sheets, 123*d*

Current liabilities. *See* liabilities, current.

Current market value, balance sheets, 123*d*–124

Current ratio, 271

Current Text (General Standards and Industry Standards), 12

Currently maturing long-term debt, 594

Curtailments of pension plans, 1031–1032

D

Darden Restaurants, 1199, 1215–1216

Days in operating cycle, 273

Dealer's profit/loss on leases, 1069*d*

Debit balance, 710–711

Debits, 68

Debt: current liabilities, 617–618; long-term: currently maturing, 594; liability issues, 594; maturing, cash flow from operations (CFO), 276; replacement, 654; retirement, 654; short-term: ability to refinance, 618; financing agreements, 618; intent to refinance,

617–618; liability issues, 617–618; refinancing, 617–618; repayment and replacement, 618; uncollectible. *See* bad debts.

Debt securities, 707*d*. *See also* investments; amortized loss, 714*n*; available-for-sale, 708–714, 709*n*, 724; bond discounts and premiums, amortization, 715–717; bonds, sale before maturity, 719–720; bonds acquired between interest dates, amortization, 718, 718*n*; credit balance, 710; debit balance, 710–711; dividend revenue, recording, 709–710; held to maturity, 714–720, 714*n*, 724; initial cost, recording, 709; interest revenue, recording, 709–710; realized gains and losses on sales, 712–714, 713*n*; reclassification adjustment, 714; trading securities, 708, 723; unrealized holding gains and losses, 710–712, 710*n*, 711*n*, 712*n*

Debt/equity ratio, 145, 273–274, 274*n*

Decision making, 5*f*. *See also* ethics; buy decisions, 5; financial accounting, 6–7*d*; financial reporting and, 35; hold decisions, 5; managerial accounting, 6–7*d*; sell decisions, 5

Decision usefulness, 41

Declining balance depreciation method, 507–509

Declining charge depreciation method, 506

Deere and Company, 666

Deferred: charges, 134; costs and expenses, 50; payments, PP&E acquisition, 464; revenues, 77–78, 77*d*, 598; tax: assets, 946*d*, 951–952; benefit, 946*d*; consequences, 946*d*; expense, 946*d*; liability, 946*d*, 950–951

Defined benefit pension plans, 996*d*; balance sheet, 1028–1029; expected return on plan assets, 1046; expense, 1026–1027, 1048; interest on projected benefit obligation, 1044–1046; liability, 1048; pension liabilities, 1027–1028; present value calculations, 1042–1048; prior service costs: overview, 1027; unrecognized, amortizing, 1046–1047; projected benefit obligation, 1047–1048; service costs: adjustments, 1047–1048; example, 1043–1044, 1044*n*

Defined contribution pension plans, 996*d*, 1029–1030

Definition paragraph, 247

Delaying. *See* deferred.

Depletion, 504*d*, 528*d*. *See also* depreciation; cost depletion, 529; determining, 528; examples, 528–529; percentage depletion, 529; recording, 528; statutory depletion, 529

Depreciable cost, 506

Depreciation, 504*d*, 514*f*. *See also* depletion; activity methods, 509–510; asset cost, 504; base for, 506; changes and corrections, 528; cost allocation methods: accelerated, 506; appraisal systems, 518; composite depreciation, 516–518; compound-interest, 515*n*; declining balance, 507–509; declining charge, 506; depreciable cost, 506; depreciation base, 506; group

depreciation, 515–516; inventory systems, 518; rational, 505; sinking-fund, 515*n*; straight-line, 506–507, 506*d*; sum of the year's digits, 507; systematic, 505; time-based, 506–509, 506*d*; disclosure, 513–515, 521–522; effects of 9/11, 525*n*; ethical dilemma, 523; evaluation of methods, 511–513, 512*f*; factors involved in, 504–506; fixed-percentage-of-declining-balance method, 509*n*; impairment of noncurrent assets, 520–524, 520*n*; impairment test, 521, 522; inadequacy, 505; income taxes, 524–527; international differences, 515, 524; MACRS principles, 525–527; measurement of loss, 521, 522–523; obsolescence, 505; partial periods, 518–520; property, plant, and equipment (PP&E), 520–524; recording, 510–511; recording the loss, 521; residual value, 505; salvage value, 505; service life, 504–505

Depreciation expense, 80

Derivative financial instruments, 142

Derivatives, 739–740

Development stage companies, 475–476

Differences between income statements and tax returns, 944*f*; causes of, 944–945; permanent differences, 945*d*, 946–947, 947*f*; temporary differences, 945*d*, 947–948, 947*n*, 948*f*

Diluted earnings per share, 831–837, 833*n*, 835*n*

Direct financing leases, 1083*d*, 1086–1093, 1093*n*

Direct (periodic) recording method, 419

Direct reporting method: cash flow: diagram of, 1163–1166, 1164*f*; direct reporting method, 1162–1166; inflows, 1162–1163; major adjustments, 1164*f*; outflows, 1163; visual inspection, 1166–1168; worksheets, 1169–1173, 1170*f*–1171

Direct response advertising, current liabilities, 610–611

DirecTV, 502–503

Disaggregation, 252, 255–256

Disclaimer of opinion, 249

Disclosure: cash flow, 1159–1160; contingencies, 614–615, 615–617; current liabilities, 620–621; depreciation, 513–515, 521–522; earnings per share, 837–840; financing agreements, 328; held-to-maturity debt securities, 724; importance of, 245; income tax, 974–975, 978–980; intangible assets, 567; interim reports, 260–261, 260*n*; issues: common stock market prices and dividends, 146; comparative financial statements, 145; debt ratio, 145; derivative financial instruments, 142; fair value, 142; intangible assets, 567; loss/gain contingencies, 143–144; management discussion and analysis (MD&A), 146; related party transactions, 144–145; risk of financial instruments, 142; SEC integrated disclosures, 145–146; selected financial data, 146; subsequent events, 144; summary of accounting policies, 141–142; summary of disclosures, 214–215; of leases: lessee, 1082–1083, 1083*f*; lessor, 1096,

1096*f;* statement of cash flows, 1097–1098; long-term inventory obligations, 423–424; pension plans: accounting examples, 1018–1019; defined benefit plans, 1005–1006; by funding agencies, 1030–1031; statement of cash flows, 1029; property, plant, and equipment (PP&E), 481–483; receivables, 331–332; revenue recognition, 905–909; segment reports, requirements, 253–254, 254*n*, 255–256

Discontinued operations. *See also* continuing operations: interim reports, 259; results from, 189*n*; disclosures, 195; held-for-sale components, 194; income, 187–189, 193; losses, 189–191, 193–195; purpose of, 189–193; sales in later period, 194–195; sales in same period, 193–194; selling components, 189–193

Discount bonds, 135, 643

Discounted notes receivable, 330–331

Discounting, M2*d*

Discounts, 86–87

Discussion Memorandum, 13

Disposal of property, plant, and equipment, 478–479, 479*n*

Distributions to owners, 54*d*

Dividends, 67*d. See also* retained earnings; accounting systems, 67; cash, 842–844; cash flow, 1149; disclosure issues, 146; ethical dilemma, 847; fractional shares, 850; GAAP, 848–850; large, 848–850; liquidating, 850; net, retained earnings, 204; nonreciprocal, nonmonetary transfer to owners, 844–846; opportunity cost, 848; ordinary stock, 846; overview, 841–842; participating preferred stocks, 843–844; payable, current liabilities, 594–595; preferred dividends coverage ratio, 274; preferred stock preference, 793; property, 844–846; ratio analysis, 851; revenue, recording, 709–710; scrip, 846; small, 848–850; special stock, 846; and splits, 736–737; stock, 846–848; yield, 269, 274

Division of Corporation Finance, 261

Dollar-value LIFO, 382*f. See also* LIFO (last-in, last-out); cost index, 383*d*; cost index, determining, 383–385; description, 381–382; double-extension method, 385; example, 382–383; inventory, valuation, 437–439; inventory pools, 385–387; link-chain method, 385

Domestic stocks, 767

Donated treasury stock, 804

Double-entry system, 68, 68*f*

Double-extension method, 385

Doubtful accounts. *See* bad debts.

Due care, 22*f*

E

Earned revenues, 177–178

Earning process, 49–50, 177–178

Earnings. *See also* income; revenue.: management, 377–378; per share, 199–200, 259–260, 268

Earnings per share, 827*n*; calculating, 827–829, 828*n*; components, 829–830; contingent issuances, 837; conversion ratios, 837; convertible securities, 834–835; diluted, 831–837, 833*n*; 835*n*; disclosures, 837–840; international differences, 840; overview, 826–827; potential common shares, 831; price/earnings ratio, 826; share options, 834–835; stock warrants, 834–835; treasury stock method, 832–834, 833*n*

Economic control, 363–364

Economic entities assumption, 45

Economic resource information, 36

EDGAR (Electronic Data Gathering Analysis and Retrieval System), 17

Effective interest method, 683–686

Effective rate, bonds, 641–642

Efficient market hypothesis, 244–245

Efforts-expended method, 896

Electronic funds transfer (EFT), 309

Emerging Issues Task Force (EITF), 18

Emerson Radio Corp, 978–980

Employee Retirement Security Act of 1974 (ERISA), 1031

Englehard, 615–617

Enron, 64

Entities, 45

EPBO (expected postretirement benefit obligation), 1035

Equipment. *See* property, plant, and equipment (PP&E).

Equity, 52*d. See also* stockholders' equity.

Equity accounting method, 729–736, 730*n*

Equity characteristics of bonds, 656–660

Equity reporting method, 707

Equity securities, 707*d. See also* investments; available-for-sale, 708–714, 709*n*, 723; credit balance, 710; debit balance, 710–711; dividend revenue, recording, 709–710; initial cost, recording, 709; interest revenue, recording, 709–710; realized gains and losses on sales, 712–714, 713*n*; reclassification adjustment, 714; trading securities, 708; unrealized holding gains and losses, 710–712, 710*n*, 711*n*, 712*n*, 728

ERISA (Employee Retirement Security Act of 1974), 1031

Error correction: restatements: analysis, 1216–1218; balance sheet errors, 1216–1218; corrective measures, 1218–1222; ethical dilemma, 1218; failure to accrue bad debts, 1221–1222; failure to accrue revenue, 1220; income statement errors, 1216–1218; international differences, 1223; inventory errors, 1221; omission of prepaid expenses, 1220–1221; overview, 1214

Error detection: inventory valuation, 439–441; trial balances, 74–76

Errors in accounting, adjusting. *See* restatements.

Estimated current liabilities: advertising costs, 610–611; coupon obligations, 609–611; direct response advertising, 610–611; expense warranty accrual method, 606–607; modified cash basis method, 608–609; premium obligations, 609–611; property taxes, 605–606; sales warranty accrual method, 607–608; warranty obligations, 606–609

Estimated economic life of property, 1069*d*

Estimated items, 80

Estimates, restatements, 1200*d*, 1207–1208

Estimating value of goodwill, 568

Ethical dilemmas, 22*d*; accounting for property, plant, and equipment, 49; cash flow, 1134; current liabilities, 603; depreciation, 523; dividends, 847; intangible assets, 561; interperiod tax allocation, 959; inventory, valuation, 423; inventory manipulation, 379; investments, 728; leases, 1071; liabilities, current, 603; lower of cost or market rule, 423; notes (securities) payable, 667; pension plans, 1030; property, plant, and equipment acquisition, 469; restatements, 1218; revenue recognition, 901; revising estimates, 126; segment reports, 254; stockholders' equity, 775; valuation of uncollectible accounts, 317

Ethics, 22*f*, 22*n*, 23*n*. See also assumptions; decision making; generally accepted accounting principles (GAAP); principles; standards; Code of Professional Conduct (CPC), 22–23, 22*f*, 22*n*; development process, 23; due care, 22*f*; integrity, 22*f*; introduction, 21–22; justice model, 23; moral reasoning, 23; objectivity and independence, 22*f*; public interest, 22*f*; responsibilities, 22*f*; rights model, 23; scope and nature of services, 22*f*; stakeholders, 23; utilitarian model, 23

Events, 67*d*

Exchange gains, 392–393

Exchange losses, 392, 393–434

Exchange rates, cash flow, 1159

Executory contracts, contingencies, 615

Executory costs, leases, 1069*d*

Exercise price, 780

Expected cash flows, M25

Expected postretirement benefit obligation (EPBO), 1035

Expected return on plan assets, 999*d*, 1000, 1000*n*

Expense warranty accrual method, 606–607

Expenses, 53*d*, 67*d*; in the accounting equation, 67; accrued, 78–79; administrative, 184–185; administrative, continuing operations, 184–185; advancing. See accrual-basis accounting; bad debts, 80–81; classifying, 184–185; continuing operations: administrative, 184–185; classifying, 184–185; general, 184–185; operating, 184–185; selling, 184–185; tax, 186–187; variable, 184–185; corporate interest, 255; deferring, 50; delaying, 50; depreciation, 80; general,

184–185; income statements, 178–179, 178*d*; interim reports, 257–258; operating, 184–185; prepaid, 76; recognition. See recognition, expenses; selling, 184–185; tax, 186–187; variable, 184–185

Expensing *versus* capitalizing, 458–459. See also property, plant, and equipment (PP&E).

Exposure Draft, 13

EXtensible Business Reporting Language (XBRL), 242*d*, 262

External users, 5–6*d*, 6*n*

Extraordinary items: criteria, 196–197, 196*n*; interim reports, 259; reporting procedures, 197–199

Exxon, 375

F

Face rate of bonds, 640

Face value of bonds, 640

Factoring accounts receivable, 326–327

Factory supplies, 360

Fair value, 707*d*; acquisitions at less than, 734; balance sheets, 125*d*; disclosure issues, 142; hedges, 740–744; investments, 727; liabilities, 727–728; property, leases, 1069*d*; share option plans, 781, 783–784

Fairness standards, 10

FARS (FASB Financial Accounting Research System), 8

FASAC (Financial Accounting Standards Advisory Board), 11–12

FASB (Financial Accounting Standards Board). See Financial Accounting Standards Board (FASB).

FASB Exposure Draft No. 213-B, 618, 675

FASB Financial Accounting Research System (FARS), 8

FASB *Interpretations*: No. 8, 618; No. 18, 257; No. 45, 675

FASB *Statements of Concepts*, 12*d*, 12*n*; conceptual framework, 32–33; No. 1, 33, 37, 37*n*; No. 2, 33, 40, 40*n*; No. 5, 33, 37*n*, 118; No. 6, 33, 140, 176, 774, 950; No. 7, 33, M25

FASB *Statements of Standards*, 12*d*, 12*n*; No. 2, 551, 556, 560; No. 4, 14; No. 5, 315, 612, 615, 855, 1033; No. 6, 421–422, 617–618; No. 7, 476; No. 13, 1066, 1068, 1082, 1096, 1106, 1107*n*; No. 14, 255; No. 15, 676, 680, 683; No. 16, 1212; No. 19, 17, 484; No. 34, 365, 462, 470–471, 472, 473; No. 35, 998, 1030; No. 43, 595–596, 598*n*, 1033; No. 45, 919; No. 47, 598; No. 48, 311; No. 49, 424, 598; No. 57, 144–145; No. 66, 921; No. 67, 462; No. 69, 484; No. 78, 619; No. 84, 660; No. 86, 560; No. 87, 998–1000, 1003, 1013*n*; No. 88, 998, 1031–1032; No. 91, 1092–1093; No. 95, 13–14, 210, 212, 973, 1126, 1135–1136, 1152–1153, 1162, 1163*n*, 1165–1166; No. 96, 949; No. 102, 1157; No. 106, 1034, 1041–1042; No. 107, 142, 331; No. 109, 945, 948*n*, 949–950, 963, 964, 973–974; No. 112, 1033; No. 114, 672*n*, 674*n*, 680, 683; No. 115,

17, 672n, 706, 710, 723, 726–729, 736–737, 845, 1156–1157; *No. 116*, 804; *No. 118*, 672n; *No. 121*, 520n, 523; *No. 123*, 781–782, 785n, 786n; *No. 123R*, 779, 782, 784–785, 788, 792; *No. 128*, 826; *No. 130*, 209, 970; *No. 131*, 252, 255, 257; *No. 132*, 998, 1005; *No. 132R*, 1005, 1037; *No. 133*, 142, 331, 740–741, 745; *No. 140*, 323, 330, 654; *No. 141*, 196, 564, 566; *No. 142*, 551; *No. 143*, 479; *No. 144*, 189, 191, 194, 195, 478, 520, 521, 523, 553; *No. 145*, 14; *No. 146*, 191; *No. 151*, 365; *No. 153*, 468; *No. 154*, 205, 321–322, 528, 970, 1200–1201, 1204, 1207–1208, 1209–1210, 1210–1211, 1214

FASB Technical Bulletin 85-6, 803

Feedback value, 42

FEI (Financial Executives International), 11–12, 20

FICA: current liabilities, 600–602, 601f; history, 996

FIFO (first-in, first-out), 369d; description, 369–370; income measurement, 374–375; inventory valuation, 378, 430–431, 431n; *versus* LIFO, 373–374; selecting, 379–380; valuation adjustment, 387–388

Financial accounting, 6–7d, 7f

Financial Accounting Foundation, 11, 11n

Financial Accounting Standards Advisory Board (FASAC), 11–12

Financial Accounting Standards Board (FASB): American Accounting Association (AAA), 11–12; American Institute of Certified Public Accountants (AICPA), 11–12; CFA Institute, 11–12; compromise, 14; conceptual framework, 32–34, 32n, 33f, 33n, 34f, 34n; conflict resolution, 14; *Current Text (General Standards and Industry Standards)*, 12; Discussion Memorandum, 13; Emerging Issues Task Force (EITF), 18; Exposure Draft, 13; Financial Accounting Foundation, 11, 11n; Financial Accounting Standards Advisory Board (FASAC), 11–12; Financial Executives International, 11–12; "Financial Performance Reporting..." project, 169, 176; Government Finance Officers Association, 11–12; *Guide for Implementation*, 12; history of GAAP, 8; Institute of Management Accountants, 11–12; *versus* International Accounting Standards Committee (IASC), 19–20; *Interpretations*, 12; Invitation to Comment, 13; National Association of State Auditors, 11–12; objectives-oriented standards, 16, 16n; online resources, 12; operating procedures, 13–14, 13f; operations, 12n; *Original Pronouncements*, 12; parent organization, 11; position papers, 13; principles-based standards, 31; pronouncements, 12; related organizations, 11–12; rules-based standards, 16; SEC forms, 16–17; and the Securities and Exchange Commission (SEC), 16–17; Securities Industry Association, 11–12; sociopolitical environment, 14–16, 15n, 16n; *Staff Positions*, 12; *Statements of Financial Accounting Concepts*, 12d, 12n; *Statements of Financial Accounting Standards*, 12d, 12n; structure, 11f; *Technical Bulletins*, 12; time to develop procedures, 13; web site, 12

Financial analysis: acid-test ratio, 271; activity ratios, 272–273; book value per common share, 274–275; cash flow from operations (CFO) to, 276d; maturing debt, 276; net income, 275; sales, 275; cash flow ratios, 275–276; common-size statements, 265; company profitability ratios, 269; comparisons between companies, 264–265; comparisons over time, 264–265; current company condition, 264; current ratio, 271; days in operating cycle, 273; debt ratio, 273–274; debt/equity ratio, 274n; dividend yield, 269; earnings per share ratio, 268; horizontal analysis, 265, 266f; intercompany comparisons, 264; interest coverage ratio, 274; intracompany comparisons, 264; inventory turnover ratio, 272; liquidity ratios, 270–271; payables turnover ratio, 273; percentage analysis, 264–265; preferred dividends coverage ratio, 274; price/earnings ratio, 268–269; profit margin, 269–270; quick assets, 271; quick ratio, 271; ratio analysis, 265–268; receivables turnover ratio, 272–273; return on stockholders' equity, 270; return on total assets, 270; stability ratios, 273–275; stockholder profitability ratios, 268–269; times interest earned ratio, 274; vertical analysis, 265, 267f; working capital ratio, 271

The Financial Analysts Journal, 20

Financial capital, balance sheets, 121d

Financial estimates: restatements: *versus* change in accounting principle, 1209–1210; prospective adjustment, 1213; retrospective adjustment method, 1212

Financial Executives International (FEI), 11–12, 20

Financial flexibility, 39d; balance sheets, 120; cash flow, 1126; liabilities, 590d; reporting guidelines, 176

Financial institutions, cash flow, 1156–1157

Financial instruments, 142, 739–740

Financial reporting. *See also* financial statements; reporting; reports; statements.: annual reports, 7; auditing, 8; business reporting model, 54; financial statements, types of, 7–8; liabilities, 136–137; major activities, 57f; notes, 8; objectives of, 34n, 35f; assessing future cash receipts, 35–36; cash flow information, 36, 37; comprehensive income information, 36–37; decision making, 35; economic resource information, 36; stewardship information, 37; understanding financial information, 37–38; public availability, 6n; reporting classifications: accumulated other comprehensive income, 139–140; additional paid-in capital, 138; capital stock, 138; contributed capital, 137; current assets, 128–129, 128d; deferred charges, 134; intangible assets, 134d; long-term investments, 132–133, 132d; miscellaneous items, 140; other assets, 134; property, plant, and equipment (PP&E), 133–134, 133d; retained earnings, 139d; sample, 127–128; stockholders' equity, 137d; working capital, 131–132, 131d; statement of comprehensive income, 7n; techniques: account form, 148; combined accounts, 148; notes, 149; parenthetical notations, 149; report form, 148; right of offset, 148, 148*n*; rounding, 148; statement format (balance sheets), 148; supporting schedules, 149; useful information characteristics: benefits *versus* costs, 43–44; comparability, 43; consistency, 43; decision usefulness, 41; feedback value, 42; hierarchical constraints, 43–45; hierarchy of, 40, 41*f*; materiality, 44–45, 44*n*; neutrality, 43; objectivity, 42; predictive value, 42; relevance, 41–43; reliability, 42; representational faithfulness, 42–43; timeliness, 42; understandability, 40; verifiability, 42; useful information types, 38*f*; financial flexibility, 39*d*; liquidity, 39; operating capability, 39–40, 39*n*; return on investment, 38; risk, 38; users of: assessing future cash receipts, 35–36; cash flow information, 36, 37; comprehensive income information, 36–37; decision making, 35; economic resource information, 36; objectives, 34; stewardship information, 37; understanding financial information, 37–38

Financial Reporting Releases, 17

Financial restatements. *See* restatements.

Financial statements, 51*n*, 52*f*, 118*n*. *See also* financial reporting; reports; *specific statements*; accounting period, 69*d*; annual report, 69*d*; assets, 52*d*; characteristics of, 56; comparability, 56; comparative, disclosure issues, 145; current liabilities, 620–621; disclosure issues: common stock market prices and dividends, 146; comparative financial statements, 145; debt ratio, 145; derivative financial instruments, 142; fair value, 142; loss/gain contingencies, 143–144; management discussion and analysis (MD&A), 146; related party transactions, 144–145; risk of financial instruments, 142; SEC integrated disclosures, 145–146; selected financial data, 146; subsequent events, 144; summary of accounting policies, 141–142; disclosures, 974–975; distributions to owners, 54*d*; effects of restatements, 1224; equity, 52*d*; error correction. *See* restatements; expenses, 53*d*; financing cash flows, 53*d*; gains, 53*d*; IASB framework, 56; income statement, 53*d*; interrelationships, 118–119, 119*f*; investing cash flows, 53*d*; investments by owners, 54*d*; losses, 53*d*; materiality, 56; objectives of, 56; operating cash flows, 53*d*; preparing, 81–84; recommended content, 118; relevance, 56; reliability, 56; revenues, 53*d*; statement of cash flows, 53*d*, 974; statement of changes in stockholders' equity, 54*d*; types of, 7–8; understandability, 56

Financing activities, cash flow: cash flow statement, 1141–1142; overview, 1127–1128; partial, 1154–1156; worksheet entries, 1147

Financing agreements, accounts receivable, 323–328

Financing cash flows, 53*d*, 1130, 1132–1133

Financing costs, 175–176

Finished goods inventory, 361

First-in, first-out (FIFO). *See* FIFO (first-in, first-out).

Fiscal year, 47

Fixed assets, 133

Fixed manufacturing overhead, 360

Fixed overhead costs, 474–475

Fixed share option, 785–786, 786*n*

Fixed-percentage-of-declining-balance depreciation method, 509*n*

Floor, inventory valuation, 414–415

FOB (free-on-board) shipping, 363–364

Ford Motor Credit Company, 323

Foreign currency transactions, 392–394

Foreign exchange rates, 392*f*

Foreign stocks, 767

Form 8-K (significant events report), 16

Form 10-K (annual report), 16, 145–146, 262*d*

Form 10-Q (quarterly operations report), 16, 262*d*

Forms, SEC. *See* Securities and Exchange Commission (SEC), forms.

Fractional shares, 850

Franchises, 559, 919–921

Full-cost method, 483–484

Funded pension plans, 996*d*

Funds, investments, 738–739

FUTA., current liabilities, 600–602, 601*f*

Future deductible amount, 946*d*

Future taxable amount, 946*d*

Future value: annuities due, M13–14; converting to present, M2; ordinary annuities, M10–13; single sum, compound interest, M3–7, M7*n*

G

GAAP (generally accepted accounting principles). *See* generally accepted accounting principles (GAAP).

Gains, 53*d*; contingencies, disclosure issues, 143–144; Income statements, 179–180, 179*d*

Gas and oil properties, 483–484

GASB (Government Accounting Standards Board), 20

General Electric, 375

General Electric Capital Services (GECS), 323

General expenses, 184–185

General journal, 70–73, 70*d*

General ledger, 73*d*, 75*f*. *See also* journal; ledgers; computer software for, 95; posting to, 73–76

General Mills, 358–359, 389–391, 620–621

General Motors, 139–140, 209, 375, 639

General Motors Acceptance Corporation (GMAC), 323

Generally accepted accounting principles (GAAP), 8*d*. *See also* assumptions; ethics; principles; standards; authoritative sources, 8–9, 9*f*; complexity, 30–32; development timeline, 10*f*; hierarchy of source categories, 8–9, 8*n*, 9*f*; history of, 8–9; policy-making bodies, 8–9; and the Securities and Exchange Commission (SEC), 8

GMAC (General Motors Acceptance Corporation), 323

Going concern assumption, 46–47

Goodwill, 563–566

Goodwill, investments, 732n

Government Accounting Standards Board (GASB), 20

Government Finance Officers Association, 11–12

Gross discount method, 313–314

Gross margin on sales, 187–188

Gross price method, 365–367

Gross profit, 187–188

Gross profit method of inventory valuation, 426–427

Group depreciation method, 515–516

Guaranteed residual value, 1069d; accounting and reporting by lessor, 1096; capitalization issues, 1081–1082; and renewal, 1107

Guide for Implementation, 12

H

HealthSouth, 64

Hedges, 740d; cash flow, 745–746; fair value, 740–744

Held-to-maturity debt securities, 707d, 707n; disclosure, 724; investments, 714–720, 714n

Hershey Foods Corp., 942

Hewlett Packard, 168–169, 390–391

Hierarchical constraints, 43–45

Hierarchy of useful information, 40, 41f

Historical cost, 48n; balance sheets, 123d; description, 48–49; property, plant, and equipment (PP&E), 460–461

Hold decisions, 5

Holding gain, 374–375

Holidays, current liabilities, 595–598

Honeywell, 138

Horizontal analysis, 265, 266f

I

IASB (International Accounting Standards Board), 19–20

IASB *International Financial Reporting Standards*, 9

IASC (International Accounting Standards Committee). *See* International Accounting Standards Committee (IASC).

IBM Company, 668–669, 839, 1041

Identifiable intangible assets, 557

IMA (Institute of Management Accountants), 11–12, 20

Impairment test, 521, 522

Impairments: goodwill, 564–565; investments, 722–723, 735; loans: accounting by creditor, 680–682; accounting by debtor, 676–680; conceptual evaluation, 683; equity or asset exchange, 679–680, 682; modification of terms, 677–679, 679–680, 681–682; notes receivable, 671–674, 672n, 673n; troubled debt restructuring, 676; property, plant, and equipment, 520–524, 520n

Implicit interest rate, 1069d

Improvements to property, plant, and equipment, 476–477

Inadequacy, 505

Inception of the lease, 1069d

Income. *See also* earnings; revenue.: accumulated other comprehensive income, 139–140; capital maintenance, 170–171; comprehensive, 139d, 172d, 207n; components of, 207; conceptual evaluation, 209; reporting alternatives, 207–209; reporting objectives, 36–37; from continuing operations: administrative expenses, 184–185; alternative income captions, 189; classifying expenses, 184–185; cost of goods available for sale, 183–184; cost of goods sold, 183–184; general expenses, 184–185; gross margin on sales, 187–188; gross profit, 187–188; interperiod tax allocation, 186; intraperiod tax allocation, 186; multi-step formats, 187–188; operating expenses, 184–185; operating income, 187–188; other items, 185–186; sales revenue (net), 183; selling expenses, 184–185; single-step formats, 187–188; tax expenses, 186–187; variable expenses, 184–185; core earnings, 175–176; earning process, 177–178; financing costs, 175–176; measuring, 171–172, 374–375; net, cash flow from operations (CFO), 275; noncash resources, converting to cash. *See* realization; non-core earnings, 175–176; nonrecurring items, 175, 181; reporting guidelines: financial flexibility, 176; general, 174; operating capability, 176d; return on investment, 175d; risk, 175d; specific, 174–175; user groups, 175–176; rights, converting to cash. *See* realization; on self-construction, 475; transactional approach, 171–172. *See also* accrual-basis accounting.

Income statement, 53d, 83f. *See also* financial statements; change in accounting estimate, 200–202; content: all-inclusive concept, 181–183; condensed statements, 183; current operating performance concept, 181–183; major components, 181; earnings per share, 199–200; elements of: expenses, 178–179, 178d; gains, 179–180, 179d; losses, 179–180, 179d; revenues, 176–178, 176d, 176n; extraordinary items: criteria, 196–197, 196n; reporting procedures, 197–199; in financial reporting, 7; income from continuing operations: administrative expenses, 184–185; alternative income captions, 189; classifying expenses, 184–185; cost of goods available for sale, 183–184; cost of goods sold, 183–184; general expenses, 184–185; gross margin on sales, 187–188; gross profit, 187–188; interperiod tax allocation, 186; intraperiod tax allocation, 186; multi-step formats, 187–188; operating expenses, 184–185; operating income, 187–188; other items, 185–186; sales revenue (net), 183; selling expenses, 184–185; single-step formats, 187–188; tax expenses, 186–187; variable expenses, 184–185; international differences, 203; limitations, 202; multiple-step, 182*f*; preparing, 82–83; purpose of, 69, 175; realization of revenue, 177–178; recognition of revenue, 176–178; recording and reporting items. *See* recognition; results from discontinued operations, 189*n*; disclosures, 195; held-for-sale components, 194; income, 187–189, 193; losses, 189–191, 193–195; purpose of, 189–193; sales in later period, 194–195; sales in same period, 193–194; selling components, 189–193; summary of financial information, 202

Income statement errors, restatements, 1216–1218

Income taxes: accrued, 79, 79*n*; alternative minimum tax, 976–977; benefits, 946*d*; compensatory share option plans, 975–976; continuing operations expenses, 186–187; deferred tax assets, 946*d*, 951–952; deferred tax benefit, 946*d*; deferred tax consequences, 946*d*; deferred tax expense, 946*d*; deferred tax liability, 946*d*, 950–951; depreciation, 524–527; differences between income statements and tax returns, 944*f*; causes of, 944–945; permanent differences, 945*d*, 946–947, 947*f*; temporary differences, 945*d*, 947–948, 947*n*, 948*f*; disclosures, 974–975, 978–980; effects of inventory cost flow assumptions, 375–376; expenses, 946*d*; financial statements: balance sheets, 973–974, 973*n*; disclosures, 974–975; statement of cash flows, 974; future deductible amount, 946*d*; future taxable amount, 946*d*; income tax benefit, 946*d*; income tax expense, 946*d*; income tax obligation, 946*d*; income tax refund, 946*d*; interim reports, 258–259; Internal Revenue Service (IRS), 18–19; international differences, 977; interperiod tax allocation, 186*d*, 949*f*; accounting principles, 949–950, 949*n*; current, recording and reporting, 953–961, 955*n*; deferred, recording and reporting, 953–961, 955*n*; ethical dilemma, 959; permanent differences, 945*d*, 946–947, 947*f*, 959–961; temporary differences, 945*d*, 947–948, 947*n*, 948*f*, 959–961, 967–970; intraperiod tax allocation, 186*d*, 945*d*, 970–973, 970*n*, 972*n*; obligations, 946*d*; operating loss carrybacks or carryforwards, 945*d*, 962–967, 962*n*, 967–970; paid, cash flow, 1152–1153, 1153*n*; payable, current liabilities, 602; rate changes, 975; refund, 946*d*; tax credits, 945*d*, 976–977; tax law changes, 975; taxable income, 946*d*; valuation allowance, 946*d*

Independence principle, 10

Indirect materials, 360

Indirect (periodic) recording method, 420

Induced bond conversions, 660

Industry Accounting Guides, 9*f*, 17

Industry Audit Guides, 9*f*, 17

Inflows, 1131

Information. *See* accounting information; useful information.

Inherent limitations paragraph, 247

Initial direct costs of leases, 1069*d*

Initial franchise fees, revenue recognition, 919–921

Installment method of revenue recognition, 177

Institute of Management Accountants (IMA), 11–12, 20

Intangible assets, 134*d*; amortization, 552–553, 553*n*, 558*f*; classifying, 550–551, 551*f*; cost of, 550–553; development, 554*d*; disclosure, 567–568; ethical dilemma, 561; finite life, 552–553; identifiable, 550*d*; copyrights, 559; deferred charges, 562; franchises, 559; internally developed, 551, 557, 568–569; leasehold improvements, 562; leases, 562; organization costs, 562; patents, 557–558; purchased, 551, 568–569; software, internal use, 561–562; software costs, 559–560; trademarks and tradenames, 562; impairment, 553, 558*f*; inconsistencies, 568–570; indefinite life, 553, 569; no alternative future uses, 555; research, 554*d*; research and development costs, 554–557, 555*f*; unidentifiable, 550*d*; estimating value of goodwill, 566; human resources, 563*n*; impairment of goodwill, 564–565; internally developed, 552; internally developed goodwill, 563, 569; negative goodwill, 565–566; purchased, 551; purchased goodwill, 563–564, 569–570

Integrity, 22*f*. *See also* ethics.

Intel Corporation, 724–725

Intercompany comparisons, 264

Interest. *See also* time value of money.: accrued, 78–79; compound, M2–3; during construction, 470–473; coverage ratio, 274; paid, cash flow, 1152–1153, 1153*n*; simple, M2–3

Interest-bearing notes, current liabilities, 592–593, 592*n*

Interest-rate swaps, 740

Intergraph Corp., 549

Interim reports, 257*d*; description, 257; disclosure, 260–261, 260*n*; discontinued operations, 259; earnings per share, 259–260; expenses, 257–258; extraordinary items, 259; income taxes, 258–259; international differences, 263; inventory valuation, 421; preparing, 260–261; restatement, 1211–1212; revenues, 257

Internal Revenue Service (IRS), 18–19. *See also* income taxes.

Internal users, 5–6*d*

Internal-use software, 561

International Accounting Standards Board (IASB), 19–20

International Accounting Standards Committee (IASC), 19

International differences: accounting, 147; cash flow, 1161; contingencies, 617; depreciation, 515, 524; earnings per share, 840; gain/loss contingencies, 617; income statement, 203; income taxes, 977; interim reports, 263; inventory, valuation, 423; investments, 729, 735; leases, 1000; LIFO (last-in, last-out), 388; long-term liabilities, 674; lower of cost or market rule, 423; notes receivable, 674; pension plans, 1032; property, plant, and equipment (PP&E), 466, 474; restatements, 1223; segment reports, 263; self-construction, 474; stockholders' equity, 857

Interperiod tax allocation, 186d, 949f; accounting principles, 949–950, 949n; current, recording and reporting, 953–961, 955n; deferred, recording and reporting, 953–961, 955n; ethical dilemma, 959; permanent differences, 945d, 946–947, 947f, 959–961; temporary differences, 945d, 947–948, 947n, 948f, 959–961, 967–970

Interpretations of the FASB, 12

Interrelationships, 118–119, 119f

Intracompany comparisons, 264

Intraperiod tax allocation, 186d, 945d, 970–973, 970n, 972n

Intrinsic value, share option plans, 781

Introductory paragraph, 246–247

Inventory, 360d; alternative systems, 362–363; balance sheets, 129; "bill and hold" sales, 363–364; classifications of, 360–362; computer software for, 94–95; consignment transfers, 363; cost, 364d; cost flow, 361f; cost flow assumptions, 367d, 367f. *See also* FIFO (first-in, first-out); LIFO (last-in, last-out); allowance method, 366n; average cost, 370–371, 370d; comparison of, 373–374; cost of beginning inventory, 367; cost of goods available for sale, 367; moving average cost, 371; physical flow, 367; specific identification, 367–369; weighted average cost, 370–371; cost flow assumptions, alternatives: average cost, 378–379; earnings (income) management, 377–378; holding gain, 374–375; income measurement, 374–375; income tax effects, 375–376; inventory profit, 375; inventory valuation, 378; LIFO conformity rule, 375–376; LIFO liquidation profit, 376–377; liquidation of LIFO layers, 376–377; mixing LIFO and FIFO, 375–376; selecting, 379–380; costs, determining: gross price method, 365–367; net price method, 365–367; period costs, 365; product costs, 50, 365; purchases discounts, 365–367; trade discounts, 366–367; depreciation method, 518; disclosures, 389–391, 389f; economic control, 363–364; exchange gains, 392–393; exchange losses, 392, 393–434; factory supplies, 360; finished goods, 361; fixed manufacturing overhead, 360; FOB (free-on-board) shipping, 363–364; foreign currency transactions, 392–394; foreign exchange rates, 392f; importance of, 360; indirect materials, 360; legal

title, transferring, 363–364; manufacturing supplies, 360; merchandise, 360; parts, 360; periodic systems, 362d; description, 362–363; FIFO (first-in, first-out) method, 369–370; income measurement, 375; LIFO (last-in, last-out) method, 372–373; *versus* perpetual, 363; specific identification, 367–369; weighted average cost method, 370–371; perpetual systems, 362d; FIFO (first-in, first-out) method, 369–370; LIFO (last-in, last-out) method, 372–373; *versus* periodic, 363; specific identification, 367–369; weighted average cost method, 370–371; pools, 385–387; profit, 374–375; quantities, determining, 363–364; raw materials, 360; reporting in financial statements, 361; of service companies, 362; transfer from seller to buyer, 363–364, 364f; turnover ratio, 272; variable manufacturing overhead, 360; work in process, 360

Inventory, valuation, 378; disclosure of long-term obligations, 423–424; dollar-value LIFO method, 437–439; errors, effects of, 439–441; FIFO (first-in, first-out), 378; gross profit method, 426–427; LIFO (last-in, last-out), 378; lower of cost or market rule, 414d; allowance recording method, 420; applying, 414–416; ceiling, 414–415; criticism of, 416, 422; direct (periodic) recording method, 419; ethical dilemma, 423; examples, 416–417; floor, 414–415; implementing, 418; indirect (periodic) recording method, 420; interim financial statements, 421; international differences, 423; loss recognition, 421–423; lower constraint, 414–415; perpetual recording method, 420; recording reduction, 419–421; reporting, 420–421; revenue recognition, 422; upper constraint, 414–415; product financing arrangements, 423–424; purchase obligations, 423–424; retail inventory method, 428d; additional costs, 433–434; additional markup, 429d; applying, 429–433; average cost flow assumptions, 431; comparison of methods, 434; cost flow assumptions, 429–433; examples, 428, 435–436; FIFO cost flow assumptions, 430–431, 431n; LIFO cost flow assumptions, 431–432; lower of cost or market rule, 433; markdown, 429d; markdown cancellation, 429d; markup, 429d; markup cancellation, 429d; net markdown, 429d; net markup, 429d; retail adjustments, 433–434; underlying assumptions, 434–436; summary of issues, 442; valuation above cost, 424–425

Inventory errors, restatement, 1221

Investing activities, cash flow: cash flow statement, 1141; long-term, 1154–1156, 1155n; overview, 1127; temporary, 1154–1156, 1155n; worksheet entries, 1147

Investing cash flows, 53d, 1130, 1132–1133, 1154–1156

Investments, 708f; available-for-sale securities, 706; categories, 706–707; classification, 706–708, 706n, 729; conceptual evaluation, 726–729; consolidation reporting method, 707; convertible bonds, 737–738; debt securities, 707d; amortized loss, 714n; available-for-sale,

708–714, 709n, 724; bond discounts and premiums, amortization, 715–717; bonds, sale before maturity, 719–720; bonds acquired between interest dates, amortization, 718, 718n; credit balance, 710; debit balance, 710–711; dividend revenue, recording, 709–710; held to maturity, 714–720, 714n, 724; initial cost, recording, 709; interest revenue, recording, 709–710; realized gains and losses on sales, 712–714, 713n; reclassification adjustment, 714; trading securities, 708, 723; unrealized holding gains and losses, 710–712, 710n, 711n, 712n; derivatives, 739–740; disclosures, 723–726; equity accounting method, 729–736, 730n; equity reporting method, 707; equity securities, 707d; available-for-sale, 708–714, 709n, 723; credit balance, 710; debit balance, 710–711; dividend revenue, recording, 709–710; initial cost, recording, 709; interest revenue, recording, 709–710; realized gains and losses on sales, 712–714, 713n; reclassification adjustment, 714; trading securities, 708; unrealized holding gains and losses, 710–712, 710n, 711n, 712n, 728; ethical dilemma, 728; fair value, 707d; acquisitions at less than, 734; hedges, 740–744; investments, 727; liabilities, 727–728; financial instruments, 739–740; in funds, 738–739; goodwill, 732n; hedges, 740d; cash flow, 745–746; fair value, 740–744; held-to-maturity debt securities, 707, 707n; impairments, 722–723, 735; interest-rate swaps, 740; international differences, 729, 735; management intent, 729; nonmarketable securities, 736; notional amounts, 740; by owners, 54d; plant expansion funds, 738–739; sinking funds, 738–739; statement of cash flows, 739; stock dividends and splits, 736–737; stock redemption funds, 738–739; stock warrants, 737, 737n; surrender value of life insurance, 738; trading securities, 706d, 708; transfers, 720–722, 722n; valuation, 706–708, 706n

Invitation to Comment, 13

IRS (Internal Revenue Service), 18–19. *See also* income taxes.

Issue Papers, 9, 18

J

J.C. Penney Company, 826

Johnson & Johnson, 129, 132, 148, 481–482, 567–568

Johnson Controls, 905

Journal entries, 71d

Journalizing, 71d

Journals. *See also* ledgers.: general, 70–73, 70d, 71; special, 71d, 93–94, 93d

Justice model of ethics, 23

K

Kellogg Company, 1160–1161

Kimberly-Clark, 135–136

Kohl's Corporation, 826

L

Land: acquisition, 462; changes, cash flow, 1148, 1148n; leasing. *See* leasing, real estate.

Last-in, last-out (LIFO). *See* dollar-value LIFO; LIFO (last-in, last-out).

Lawsuits, contingencies, 614

Lease receivables, 1069d

Lease terms, 1069d

Leased equipment changes, cash flow, 1148

Leasehold improvements, 463

Leasing: change of lease type, 1107; changes in provisions, 1106–1108; guaranteed residual value, 1069d; accounting and reporting by lessor, 1096; capitalization issues, 1081–1082; and renewal, 1107; renewals, 1107–1108; unguaranteed residual value, 1069d; accounting and reporting by lessor, 1096; estimated, 1107

Leasing, personal property: accounting and reporting by lessee: capital leases, 1074–1075, 1075–1080, 1076f; conceptual evaluation, 1098; operating leases, 1073–1074; summary of, 1096–1097, 1097f; accounting and reporting by lessor: conceptual evaluation, 1098; direct financing leases, 1083d, 1086–1093, 1093n; guaranteed residual value, 1096; leveraged leases, 1083d; operating leases, 1083d, 1084–1085; sales-type leases, 1083d, 1093–1096; summary of, 1096–1097, 1097f; unguaranteed residual value, 1096; advantages of, 1066–1068; bargain purchase option, 1069d, 1080–1081; bargain renewal option, 1069d; capital leases, 1068d; accounting and reporting, 1074–1075, 1075–1080, 1076f; examples, 1075–1080; classification, 1068–1072, 1070f, 1072; dealer's profit/loss, 1069d; direct financing leases, 1083d; disclosure: lessee, 1082–1083, 1083f; lessor, 1096, 1096f; statement of cash flows, 1097–1098; estimated economic life of property, 1069d; ethical dilemma, 1071; executory costs, 1069d; fair value of property, 1069d; guaranteed residual value, 1069d, 1081–1082, 1096; implicit interest rate, 1069d; inception of the lease, 1069d; initial direct costs, 1069d; international differences, 1000; lease receivable, 1069d; lease term, 1069d; lessee's incremental borrowing rate, 1069d; leveraged leases, 1083d; manufacturer's profit/loss, 1069d; minimum lease payments, 1069d; operating leases, 1068d, 1073–1074; sales-type leases, 1083d; unguaranteed residual value, 1069d, 1096; unreimbursible cost, 1069d

Leasing, real estate, 1101f; land and buildings: bargain purchase option, 1100–1103; transfer of title, 1100–1103; land only, 1100; leveraged leases, 1105–1106; plus equipment, 1103; sale-leaseback issues, 1103–1108, 1103n

Ledgers. *See also* journals: general, 73d, 75f; computer software for, 95; posting to, 73–76; subsidiary, 74n, 92–93, 93d, 93f

Legal capital, 770

Legal liabilities, 588*d*

Leveraged leases, 1083*d*; accounting and reporting by lessor, 1083; real estate, 1105–1106

Liabilities, 52*d*, 66*d*, 122*d*; in the accounting equation, 66; callable by creditors, 619; characteristics of, 588; deferred revenues, 598; financial flexibility, 590*d*; financial reporting, 136–137; gain contingencies: disclosure, 615, 615–617; international differences, 617; legal, 588*d*; liquidity, 589*d*; long-term, 134–135, 134*d*; loss contingencies, 612*d*; accrual of loss, 613–614; disclosure, 614–615, 615–617; executory contracts, 615; international differences, 617; lawsuits, 614; loss, accounting for, 612–613; overview, 611–613; probable, 612; reasonably possible, 612; remote, 612; noncancelable obligations, 598; nonlegal, 588*d*; obligations, 588*d*; operating cycle/year, 1589; other, 136; overview, 588–589; probable, 588*d*; product financing, 598; unearned items, 598; valuation, 123–127, 124*f*

Liabilities, current, 129*d*, 589*d*; accumulated rights, 596; on balance sheets, 129–131; changes, and cash flow, 1147; classification, 590, 591*f*; contractual amounts: accrued liabilities, 595–598; advances, 595; compensated absences, 595–598; currently maturing long-term debt, 594; dividends payable, 594–595; holidays, 595–598; interest-bearing notes, 592–593, 592*n*; noninterest-bearing notes, 592–594; notes payable, 592–594, 593*n*; refundable deposits, 595; sick pay, 595–598; trade accounts payable, 591–592; vacations, 595–598; disclosure, 620–621; estimated mounts: advertising costs, 610–611; coupon obligations, 609–611; direct response advertising, 610–611; expense warranty accrual method, 606–607; modified cash basis method, 608–609; premium obligations, 609–611; property taxes, 605–606; sales warranty accrual method, 607–608; warranty obligations, 606–609; ethical dilemma, 603; in financial statements, 620–621; operations dependent: bonus obligations, 602–605, 603*n*; FICA, 600–602, 601*f*; FUTA, 600–602, 601*f*; income taxes payable, 602; payroll deductions, 600–602, 601*f*; payroll taxes, 600–602, 601*f*; sales tax, 599–600; social security taxes, 600–602, 601*f*; unemployment insurance taxes, 600–602, 601*f*; use tax, 599–600; short-term debt to be refinanced, 617–618; valuation, 591; vested rights, 596

Liabilities, long-term: bonds, 640*d*, 642*n*; accruing interest, 652–653; amortization, 645–653; book value, 644; book value conversion, 659; carrying value, 644; characteristics of, 641, 642*f*; contract rate, 640; convertible, 657–660; debt replacement, 654; debt retirement, 654; with detachable stock warrants, 656–657; discount, 643; effective interest amortization, 648–651, 648*n*; effective rate, 641–642; equity characteristics, 656–660; face rate, 640; face value, 640; induced conversions, 660; issue costs, 651–652; issued between interest payment dates, 644–645;

market rate, 642; market value conversion, 659; maturity date, 640; nominal rate, 640; par value, 640; payable, 640–643; premium, 643; recalling the issue, 654; recording issuance of, 643–645; retiring, 654–656; selling prices, 641–643; stated rate, 640; straight-line amortization, 645–647, 646*n*; yield, 641–642; zero-coupon, 653; bonds, serial: bonds outstanding method, 683–686; early redemption, 686; effective interest method, 683–686; interest expense, 683–686; issuance expense, 683–686; impairment of loan: accounting by creditor, 680–682; accounting by debtor, 676–680; conceptual evaluation, 683; equity or asset exchange, 679–680, 682; modification of terms, 677–679, 679–680, 681–682; notes receivable, 671–674, 672*n*, 673*n*; troubled debt restructuring, 676; notes payable, 661–666, 662*n*; notes receivable: bad debts, 671–674, 672*n*, 673*n*; disclosure, 667–670, 670*n*; future developments, 675–676; guarantees, 675; impairment of loan, 671–674, 672*n*, 673*n*; international differences, 674; loan fees, 671; multiple component instruments, 675; reasons for, 640

Life insurance, surrender value, 738

LIFO (last-in, last-out), 371*d. See also* dollar-value LIFO; changing to or from, 388; conformity rule, 375–376; description, 371–373; disadvantages of, 380; *versus* FIFO, 373–374; income measurement, 374–375; interim statements, 387; international differences, 388; inventory disclosures, 389–391, 389*f*; inventory valuation, 378, 431–432; layers, liquidating, 376–377; liquidation profit, 376–377; selecting, 379–380; valuation adjustment, 387–388

Limits of liability, 767

Link-chain method, 385

Liquid assets, 132*d*

Liquidating dividends, 850

Liquidation of LIFO layers, 376–377

Liquidity, 39*d*, 120*d*, 306*d*; cash flow, 1126; liabilities, 589*d*; problems, 590; ratio analysis, 590; ratios, 270–271

Litigation settlement, restatement, 1212

Long-term: construction contracts, revenue recognition: capitalized interest, 904; completed-contract method, 894*d*, 896–897, 898–901; disclosure, 905–909; efforts-expended method, 896; long-term service contracts, 906; losses, 901–904; offsetting amounts, 904; operating cycle, 904; overhead costs, 904; percentage-of-completion method, 894*d*, 895–896, 897–901, 898*n*; proportional performance method, 906–908, 907*n*; reporting, 905–909; investments, 132–133, 132*d*; liabilities, 134–135, 134*d*; service contracts, revenue recognition, 906

Losses, 53*d*; contingencies, disclosure issues, 143–144; depreciation, measurement of, 521; Income statements, 179–180, 179*d*; measurement of, 522–523; recognition, 421–423; revenue recognition, 901–904

Lower of cost or market rule, 414*d*; allowance recording method, 420; applying, 414–416; ceiling, 414–415; criticism of, 416, 422; direct (periodic) recording method, 419; ethical dilemma, 423; examples, 416–417; floor, 414–415; implementing, 418; indirect (periodic) recording method, 420; interim financial statements, 421; international differences, 423; loss recognition, 421–423; lower constraint, 414–415; perpetual recording method, 420; recording reduction, 419–421; reporting, 420–421; retail inventory method, 433; revenue recognition, 422; upper constraint, 414–415

Lowe's Companies, Inc., 201

Lump-sum purchase, 463–464

M

MACRS principles, 525–527

Major components, 181

Management approach, 253, 256

Management discussion and analysis (MD&A), 146

Management intent in investments, 729

Management's reports, 249–251

Managerial accounting, 6–7*d*, 7*f*

Managing cash, 307–308

Manufacturer's profit/loss, leases, 1069*d*

Manufacturing supplies, 360

Marathon Oil, 389–391

Mariah Carey, 615

Markdown, inventory valuation, 429*d*

Markdown cancellation, 429*d*

Market efficiency, 244–245

Market rate of bonds, 642

Market value bond conversion, 659

Markup, inventory valuation, 429*d*

Markup cancellation, 429*d*

Matching, 50–51, 50*n*

Materiality, 44–45, 44*n*, 56

Maturing debt, 276

Maturity date of bonds, 640

Maytag, 639

McDonald's, 559

MD&A (management discussion and analysis), 146

Measuring income, 171–172

Merchandise inventory, 360

Merck & Co., Inc., 548, 854

Microsoft, 483, 639, 824

Midas Muffler, 559

Modified cash basis method, 608–609

Monetary unit assumption, 48

Moral reasoning, 23. *See also* ethics.

Morals. *See* ethics.

Moving average cost, 371

Multi-employer pension plans, 1032

Multiple-step income statements, 182*f*

Multi-step formats, 187–188

N

NASA, 64

National Association of Colleges and Employers, 3

National Association of State Auditors, 11–12

Negative cash flow, 1124–1126

Negative goodwill, 196, 565

Negotiable checks, as cash, 306

Net: credit sales method, 316–317; discount method, 313–314; income, cash flow from operations (CFO), 275; markdown, 429*d*; markup, 429*d*; price method, 365–367; realizable value: accounts receivable, 322–323; balance sheets, 124*d*; sales, 87

Net change in cash and reconciliation, 1130

Neutrality, 43

9/11, effects on depreciation, 525*n*

Nominal accounts. *See* temporary accounts.

Nominal rate of bonds, 640

Noncancelable obligations, 598

Non-cash items, cash flow, 1130–1131, 1144

Noncontributory pension plans, 996*d*

Non-core earnings, 175–176

Noncurrent assets, 310

Noninterest-bearing notes, current liabilities, 592–594

Nonlegal liabilities, 588*d*

Nonmarketable securities, 736

Nonmonetary asset exchanges, 466–469

Nonmonetary exchange, 776–777

Nonreciprocal, nonmonetary transfer to owners, 844–846

Nonreciprocal transfers, 465

Nonrecurring items, 175, 181

Nontrade receivables, 310*d*

No-par stocks, 138, 770

Norfolk Southern, 481–482

Normal revenue recognition, 311

Nortel Networks Corp., 884

Notes (annotations), 8, 149

Notes (securities). *See also* bonds.: current liabilities, 592*n*; payable: current liabilities, 592–594, 593*n*; disclosure of liabilities, 665–666; ethical dilemma, 667; exchanged for cash, rights, privileges, 663–664; exchanged for property, goods, services, 664–665; issued for cash, 662–663, 662*n*; long-term liabilities, 661–666, 662*n*

Notes (securities), receivable, 310d, 328d; assigning, 330–331; discounted, 330–331; impairment of loan: accounting by creditor, 680–682; accounting by debtor, 676–680; conceptual evaluation, 683; equity or asset exchange, 679–680, 682; modification of terms, 677–679, 679–680, 681–682; notes receivable, 671–674, 672n, 673n; troubled debt restructuring, 676; long-term liabilities: bad debts, 671–674, 672n, 673n; disclosure, 667–670, 670n; future developments, 675–676; guarantees, 675; international differences, 674; loan fees, 671; multiple component instruments, 675; ratio analysis, 666; short-term interest-bearing, 328–329; short-term non-interest-bearing, 329

Notional amounts, 740

Numbering accounts, 67

O

Objectives-oriented standards, 16, 16n

Objectivity, 42

Objectivity and independence, 22f

Obsolescence, 505

Office of the Chief Accountant, 261

Offsetting amounts, 904

Oil and gas properties, 483–484

OPEB (other postemployment benefits). See other postemployment benefits (OPEB).

Operating activities, cash flow, 1127d; cash flow statement, 1140–1141, 1140n; conceptual overview, 1127; diagram of, 1163–1166, 1164f; direct reporting method, 1135–1136, 1162–1166; indirect reporting method, 1136–1137; inflows, 1162–1163; major adjustments, 1137–1138, 1138f, 1164f; outflows, 1163

Operating capability, 39n; balance sheets, 120d; description, 39–40; reporting guidelines, 176d

Operating cash flows, 53d, 1129, 1132–1133

Operating cycle, 128d, 128f, 904

Operating expenses, 184–185

Operating income, 187–188

Operating leases, 1068d; accounting and reporting by lessee, 1073–1074; accounting and reporting by lessor, 1083d, 1084–1085

Operating loss carrybacks or carryforwards, 945d, 962–967, 962n, 967–970

Operating segments, segment reports, 252–255, 253d, 253n

Operations-dependent current liabilities: bonus obligations, 602–605, 603n; FICA, 600–602, 601f; FUTA, 600–602, 601f; income taxes payable, 602; payroll deductions, 600–602, 601f; payroll taxes, 600–602, 601f; sales tax, 599–600; social security taxes, 600–602, 601f; unemployment insurance taxes, 600–602, 601f; use tax, 599–600

Opinion paragraph, 247–248

Opinions of auditor. See auditor's reports.

Opinions of the Accounting Principles Board, 10

Opportunity cost, 848

Option pricing model, 783–784

Orange County, California, 740

Ordinary stock dividends, 846

Organization costs, 562

Organizations, standard-setting. See standard-setting bodies.

Original Pronouncements, 12

Other postemployment benefits (OPEB). See also pension plans.: accounting for: attribution period, 1039–1040, 1040f; example, 1037–1038; funding differences, 1039; impact of FASB Statements of Standards No. 106, 1041–1042; interaction with deferred income taxes, 1040; minimum liability, 1041; principles of, 1035; relevance, 1039; reliability, 1039; accrued post retirement benefit cost, 1037; accumulated postretirement benefit obligation (APBO), 1035; assets, 1037; expected postretirement benefit obligation (EPBO), 1035; expenses, 1035–1036; liabilities, 1037; versus pensions, 1034–1035, 1037; post employment benefits, 1033; post retirement benefits, 1033–1034

Outflows, 1132

Overhead costs, revenue recognition, 904

P

Paid-in capital, 771

Par value: bonds, 640; method, 804–805; stocks, 138, 770

Parenthetical notations, 149

Partially structured problems, 25

Participating preferred stocks, 794, 843–844

Partnerships, 137d

Parts inventory, 360

Patents, 557–558

Payables turnover ratio, 273

Payroll, computer software for, 95

Payroll deductions, current liabilities, 600–602, 601f

Payroll taxes, current liabilities, 600–602, 601f

PCAOB (Public Company Accounting Oversight Board), 20

Pension benefit formula, 999d

Pension Benefit Guaranty Corporation (PBGC), 994, 1031

Pension plans. See also other postemployment benefits (OPEB): accounting examples: additional liability, 1016–1018; disclosures, 1018–1019; expense equal to funding, 1007–1008; expense greater than funding, 1008–1009; expense less than funding, 1009–1011;

gains or losses, 1014–1016; unrecognized prior service costs, 1011–1014, 1013n; worksheet, 1019–1024; accumulated benefit obligation, 999d; actual return on plan assets, 999d; actuarial funding method, 999d; actuarial present value, 999d; assets, 1003–1004; assumptions, 999d; average life expectancy, 996; benefits/years-of-service approach, 1005; characteristics of, 996–997; contributory, 996d; curtailments, 1031–1032; deferred cost, 1004; defined contribution, 996d, 1029–1030; disclosures: accounting examples, 1018–1019; defined benefit plans, 1005–1006; by funding agencies, 1030–1031; statement of cash flows, 1029; discount rate, 999d; Employee Retirement Security Act of 1974 (ERISA), 1031; ethical dilemma, 1030; expected return on plan assets, 999d, 1000, 1000n; funded, 996d; gain or loss, 999d, 1002, 1002n; history of, 997–998; interest cost, 1000; international differences, 1032; legislation, 996, 1031; liabilities, 1003–1004; measurement methods, 1005; multi-employer plans, 1032; non-contributory, 996d; pension benefit formula, 999d; Pension Benefit Guaranty Corporation (PBGC), 1031; pension expense, 999–1003, 999n, 1002n; *Pension Reform Act of 1974*, 1031; prepaid/accrued cost, 1003; prior service cost, 999d, 1001, 1011–1014; projected benefit obligation, 999d; service cost, 999d, 1000; settlements, 1031–1032; summary of issues, 1024–1026; termination, 1032; unfunded, 996d; unfunded accumulated benefit obligation, 1003–1004; vested benefit obligation, 999d; vested benefits, 1029

Pension plans, defined benefit, 996d; balance sheet, 1028–1029; expected return on plan assets, 1046; expense, 1026–1027, 1048; interest on projected benefit obligation, 1044–1046; liability, 1048; pension liabilities, 1027–1028; present value calculations, 1042–1048; prior service costs: overview, 1027; unrecognized, amortizing, 1046–1047; projected benefit obligation, 1047–1048; service costs, 1044n; adjustments, 1047–1048; example, 1043–1044

Pension Reform Act of 1974, 1031

Percentage analysis, 264–265

Percentage depletion, 529

Percentage of outstanding accounts receivable, 317–318

Percentage of sales method, 316–317

Percentage-of-completion method, 50d, 177d, 898n; *versus* completed-contract method, 897–901; determining percentage completed, 895–896; long-term construction contracts, 894d

Performance-based share option, 786–788

Period costs, 50, 365

Periodic inventory systems, 71n, 362d; description, 362–363; FIFO (first-in, first-out) method, 369–370; income measurement, 375; LIFO (last-in, last-out) method, 372–373; *versus* perpetual, 363; preparing

financial statements, 87–88; specific identification, 367–369; weighted average cost method, 370–371

Period-of-time assumption, 47

Permanent accounts, 68–69

Perpetual inventory system, 71

Perpetual inventory systems, 362d; FIFO (first-in, first-out) method, 369–370; LIFO (last-in, last-out) method, 372–373; *versus* periodic, 363; specific identification, 367–369; weighted average cost method, 370–371

Perpetual recording method, 420

Personal property, leasing. *See* leasing, personal property.

Petty cash, 333

Pfizer, Inc., 190–191

Physical capital, 121d

Physical flow, 367

Pinnacle Entertainment Inc., 143–144

Plant. *See* property, plant, and equipment (PP&E).

Plant expansion funds, 738–739

Pledging accounts receivable, 324

Position papers, 13

Post employment benefits, 1033

Post retirement benefits, 1033–1034

Postage stamps, as cash, 306

Postdated checks, as cash, 306

Postemployment benefits. *See* other postemployment benefits (OPEB); pension plans.

Posting, 73–74d

Potential common shares, 831

PP&E (property, plant, and equipment). *See* property, plant, and equipment (PP&E).

Practice Bulletins, 9f, 17

Predictive value, 42

Preferred dividends coverage ratio, 274

Preferred stock, 138d, 793d; callable, 797–798; changes, and cash flow, 1149; convertible, 794–796; cumulative, 793–794; participating, 794; preference as to dividends, 793; preference in liquidation, 798; recalling, 797–798; redeemable, 798; retiring, 797–798; rights, 796–797; with stock warrants, 796–797; voting rights, 799

Premium bonds, 135, 643

Premium obligations, current liabilities, 609–611

Prepaid assets. *See* prepaid expenses.

Prepaid expenses, 76, 1220–1221

Present value: annuities, M14; annuities due, M18–21; balance sheets, 125d; converting from future, M2; deferred annuities due, M21–24; ordinary annuities, M14–18; role in financial reporting, M24–25; single sum, M7–9

Price/earnings ratio, 268–269, 826

Primary markets, 4f, 5d

Principles, 46f. *See also* assumptions; Code of Professional Conduct (CPC); ethics; generally accepted accounting principles (GAAP); standards; accrual accounting, 50–51; APB Opinions, 10; cash basis accounting, 50–51; conservatism, 51; historical cost, 48n; balance sheets, 123d; description, 48–49; property, plant, and equipment (PP&E), 460–461; inconsistencies, 2-11; independence, 10; matching, 50–51, 50n; period costs, 50; products costs, 50; prudence, 51; recognition of costs and expenses, 49d, 50n; advancing (accruing), 50; deferring (delaying), 50; earning process, 49–50; percentage-of-completion method, 50; realization, 49; representation, 10; response time, 10; restatements, 1200d; *versus* change in estimate, 1209–1210; components, 1201; direct and indirect results, 1210–1211; for future events, 1211; initial public sale of common stock, 1211; interim financial statements, 1211–1212; litigation settlement, 1212; preferability of new principle, 1210; prospective adjustment, 1213; retrospective adjustment method, 1201–1207, 1212; transition methods, 1211

Prior service cost, pension plans, 999d, 1001, 1011–1014

Private corporations, 767

Probable contingencies, 612

Probable liabilities, 588d

Problem-solving process, 24. *See also* creative and critical thinking.

Procter & Gamble, 740

Product costs, 50, 365

Product financing, liabilities, 598

Product financing arrangements, 423–424

Professional associations, 20

Profit margin, 269–270

Projected benefit obligation, 999d

Pronouncements of the FASB, 12

Property, plant, and equipment (PP&E), 133d, 460d; acquisition: buildings, 462–463; costs after, 476–478; deferred payments, 464; determination of cost, 461–463; by donation, 465–466; ethical dilemma, 469; issuance of securities, 464–465; land, 462; leasehold improvements, 463; lump-sum purchase, 463–464; nonmonetary asset exchanges, 466–469; nonreciprocal transfers, 465; additions, 476; asset retirement obligations, 479; balance sheet, 133–134; betterments, 476–477; characteristics of, 460–461; depreciation, 520–524; disclosure, 481–482; disposal of, 478–479, 479n; gas properties. *See* oil and gas properties; historical cost, 460–461; improvements, 476–477; international differences, 466; oil and gas properties, 483–484; property taxes, capitalizing, 462; rearrangement, 476–477; renewals, 476–477; repairs and maintenance, 477–478; replacements, 476–477; return on assets, 483n; self-construction: development stage companies, 475–476; fixed overhead

costs, 474–475; income on, 475; interest during construction, 470–473; international differences, 474

Property dividends, 844–846

Property taxes: capitalizing, 462; current liabilities, 605–606

Proportional-performance method, 50, 177, 906–908, 907n

Proxy statements, 16

Prudence, 51

Public Company Accounting Oversight Board (PCAOB), 20

Public corporations, 767

Public interest, 22f

Publications: *See also* APB Opinions. *See also* ARBs. *See also* FASB Interpretations. *See also* FASB *Statements of Concepts. See also* FASB *Statements of Standards. See also* Statements of Financial Accounting Standards; AICPA: *Accounting Interpretations*, 9f, 17–18; *Accounting Trends and techniques*, 9f, 18; *Industry Accounting Guides*, 9f, 17; *Industry Audit Guides*, 9f, 17; *Issue Papers*, 9, 18; *Practice Bulletins*, 9f, 17; *Statements of Position*, 9f, 17; *Technical Practice Aids*, 9; *Cost Accounting Standards*, 18; *Current Text (General Standards and Industry Standards)*, 12; FASB *Proposal Statement of Concepts*, 33–34; FASB *Statements and Interpretations*, 17. *See also* FASB *Statements of Standards; The Financial Analysts Journal*, 20; *Guide for Implementation*, 12; IASB *International Financial Reporting Standards*, 9; *Interpretations*, 12; *Opinions of the Accounting Principles Board*, 10. *See also* APB Opinions; *Original Pronouncements*, 12; pronouncements of the FASB, 12; SEC: "Codification of Financial Reporting Policies," 17n; *Financial Reporting Releases*, 17; *Staff Accounting Bulletins*, 17; *Staff Positions*, 12; *Technical Bulletins*, 12

Purchases: allowance, 87; discounts, 87, 365–367; obligations, 423–424

Q

Qualified opinions, 249

Quarterly operations report (10-Q form), 16, 262d

Quarterly report. *See* Form 10-Q (quarterly operations report).

Quick assets, 271

Quick ratio, 271

R

Ratio analysis: acid-test ratio, 271; activity ratios, 272–273; book value per common share, 274–275; cash flow from operations (CFO) to, 276d; maturing debt, 276; net income, 275; sales, 275; cash flow ratios, 275–276; company profitability ratios, 269;

current ratio, 271; days in operating cycle, 273; debt ratio, 273–274; debt/equity ratio, 274n; dividend yield, 269; dividends, 851; earnings per share ratio, 268; interest coverage ratio, 274; inventory turnover ratio, 272; liquidity, 590; liquidity ratios, 270–271; long-term liabilities, 666; payables turnover ratio, 273; preferred dividends coverage ratio, 274; price/earnings ratio, 268–269; profit margin, 269–270; quick assets, 271; quick ratio, 271; receivables turnover ratio, 272–273; return on stockholders' equity, 270; return on total assets, 270; stability ratios, 273–275; stockholder profitability ratios, 268–269; stockholders' equity, 806; times interest earned ratio, 274; working capital ratio, 271

Raw materials inventory, 360

Real accounts. *See* permanent accounts.

Real estate, leasing. *See* leasing, real estate.

Real estate sales, revenue recognition, 921–922

Realization, 49

Realized revenues, 177–178

Rearrangement of property, plant, and equipment, 476–477

Reasonably possible contingencies, 612

Recalling a bond issue, 654

Recalling preferred stock, 797–798

Receivables, 310d. *See also* accounts receivable; cash; uncollectible accounts; balance sheets, 129; current assets, 310; disclosures, 331–332; noncurrent assets, 310; nontrade receivables, 310d; normal revenue recognition, 311; notes receivable, 310d, 328d; assigning, 330–331; discounted, 330–331; short-term interest-bearing, 328–329; short-term non-interest-bearing, 329; revenue from credit sales, 311; revenue recognition, 311; right of return, 311; sales allowances, 314–315; sales returns: defective goods, 314–315; right of return, 311; trade receivables, 310–312, 310d; turnover ratio, 272–273; valuation issues, 311–312

Recognition: balance sheets, 121; expenses, 49d, 50n; advancing (accruing), 50; cause and effect, 178–179; deferring (delaying), 50; earning process, 49–50; immediate recognition, 179; percentage-of-completion method, 50; principles of, 178–179; realization, 49; systematic and rational allocation, 179; loss, 421–423; normal revenue, 311

Reconciling bank accounts, 334–337

Redeemable preferred stock, 798

Refinancing short-term debt: ability to refinance, 618; financing agreements, 618; intent to refinance, 617–618; liability issues, 617–618; repayment and replacement, 618

Refundable deposits, current liabilities, 595

Registration statement (S-1), 16

Regulation S-X, 17

Related party transactions, 144–145

Relevance, 41–43, 56

Reliability, 42, 56

Remote contingencies, 612

Renewals: leases, 1107–1108; property, plant, and equipment, 476–477

Repairs and maintenance on property, plant, and equipment, 477–478

Replacements of property, plant, and equipment, 476–477

Report form, 148

Reportable segments, 253, 255

Reporting entity, restatements, 1200d, 1213–1214

Reports. *See also* financial reporting; financial statements; reporting; reports; statements.: annual, 7, 69d; audit committee, 249–251; auditor's, 248–249f; adverse opinions, 249; definition paragraph, 247; description, 246; disclaimer of opinion, 249; inherent limitations paragraph, 247; introductory paragraph, 246–247; opinion paragraph, 247–248; opinions expressed, 246; qualified opinions, 249; scope paragraph, 247; classifications. *See also* financial reporting; financial statements; accumulated other comprehensive income, 139–140; additional paid-in capital, 138; capital stock, 138; contributed capital, 137; current assets, 128–129, 128d; deferred charges, 134; intangible assets, 134d; long-term investments, 132–133, 132d; miscellaneous items, 140; other assets, 134; property, plant, and equipment (PP&E), 133–134, 133d; retained earnings, 139d; sample, 127–128; stockholders' equity, 137d; working capital, 131–132, 131d; financial information. *See* financial reporting; flexibility, cash flow, 1153–1154; format, cash flow, 1128; guidelines, cash flow, 1126–1131; income, guidelines for: financial flexibility, 176; general, 174; operating capability, 176d; return on investment, 175d; risk, 175d; specific, 174–175; user groups, 175–176; interim, 257d; description, 257d; disclosure, 260–261, 260n; discontinued operations, 259; earnings per share, 259–260; expenses, 257–258; extraordinary items, 259; income taxes, 258–259; international differences, 263; preparing, 260–261; revenues, 257; inventory valuation, 420–421; management's, 249–251; revenue recognition, 905–909; SEC: 10-K form (annual report), 16, 145–146, 262d; 10-Q form (quarterly operations report), 16, 262d; Chief Accountant, 261; description, 261; Division of Corporation Finance, 261; Office of the Chief Accountant, 261; XBRL supplemental information, 262; segment, 252n, 256f; aggregation, 251; comparability issues, 256; corporate interest expense, 255; corporate interest revenue, 255; disaggregation, 252, 255–256; disclosure requirements, 253–254, 254n,

255–256; ethical dilemma, 254; international differences, 263; management approach, 253, 256; operating segments, 252–255, 253d, 253n; reportable segments, 253, 255; transfer pricing, 256

Representation principle, 10

Representational faithfulness, 42–43

Research and development costs, 554

Residual equity theory model, 66–67

Residual value, 505

Response time principle, 10

Responsibilities, 22f

Restatements: corrective measures, 1218–1222; reporting methods, 1200–1201; stockholders' equity, 852

Restatements, types of changes: accounting estimate, 1200d, 1207–1208; accounting principle, 1200d; *versus* change in estimate, 1209–1210; components, 1201; direct and indirect results, 1210–1211; for future events, 1211; initial public sale of common stock, 1211; interim financial statements, 1211–1212; litigation settlement, 1212; preferability of new principle, 1210; prospective adjustment, 1213; retrospective adjustment method, 1201–1207, 1212; transition methods, 1211; effects on financial statements, 1224; error correction: analysis, 1216–1218; balance sheet errors, 1216–1218; corrective measures, 1218–1222; ethical dilemma, 1218; failure to accrue bad debts, 1221–1222; failure to accrue revenue, 1220; income statement errors, 1216–1218; international differences, 1223; inventory errors, 1221; omission of prepaid expenses, 1220–1221; overview, 1214; estimates: *versus* change in accounting principle, 1209–1210; prospective adjustment, 1213; retrospective adjustment method, 1212; reporting entity, 1200d, 1213–1214; retrospective adjustments, 1208–1209

Retail adjustments, 433–434

Retail inventory method, 428d; additional costs, 433–434; applying, 429–433; average cost flow assumptions, 431; comparison of methods, 434; cost flow assumptions, 429–433; examples, 428, 435–436; FIFO cost flow assumptions, 430–431, 431n; LIFO cost flow assumptions, 431–432; lower of cost or market rule, 433; markdown, 429d; markdown cancellation, 429d; markup, 429d; markup, additional, 429d; markup, cancellation, 429d; net markdown, 429d; net markup, 429d; retail adjustments, 433–434; underlying assumptions, 434–436

Retail land sales, revenue recognition, 922–923

Retained earnings, 67d, 139d. *See also* dividends; appropriations, 853; balance sheets, 139; content of, 841; restrictions, 853; statements, 853–855; stockholders' equity, 771, 841. *See also* dividends.

Retained earnings statements. *See* statements, retained earnings.

Retained fair values, 775–776

Retirement: bonds, 654–656, 1152; employee. *See* other postemployment benefits (OPEB); pension plans; preferred stock, 797–798; treasury stock, 804

Retrospective adjustments. *See* restatements.

Return on assets, 483n

Return on investment, 38, 175d

Return on stockholders' equity, 270

Return on total assets, 270

Returns of purchased goods. *See* sales, returns.

Revenue, 53d, 67d. *See also* earnings; income; in the accounting equation, 67; accrued, 79; from credit sales, 311; deferred, 77–78, 77d; earned, 177–178; failure to accrue, 1220; Income statements, 176–178, 176d, 176n; interim reports, 257; realized, 177–178

Revenue recognition, 176–177d, 178f; after the sale period: cost recovery method, 914–915; installment method, 909–914, 915; purpose of, 892; alternatives, summary of, 892–894, 918f; completion of production, 892; consignment sales, 923–924; continuing franchise fees, 919, 921; cost-recovery method, 177; delayed until future event: deposit method, 915–916; purpose of, 893; description, 176–178; earned revenues, 177–178; earning process, 177–178; ethical dilemma, 901; franchises, 919–921; initial franchise fees, 919–921; installment method, 177; inventory valuation, 422; other than time of sale, 177–178; percentage-of-completion method, 177; proportional-performance method, 50, 177; real estate sales, 921–922; realized revenues, 177–178; receivables, 311; retail land sales, 922–923; right of return, 311; in the sale period, 892; software revenue, 917–918; substantial performance, 919; at time of sale, 177; timing, 177–178, 891–892

Revenue recognition, prior to the sale period: long-term construction contracts: capitalized interest, 904; completed-contract method, 894d, 896–897, 898–901; disclosure, 905–909; efforts-expended method, 896; long-term service contracts, 906; losses, 901–904; offsetting amounts, 904; operating cycle, 904; overhead costs, 904; percentage-of-completion method, 894d, 895–896, 897–901, 898n; proportional performance method, 906–908, 907n; reporting, 905–909; purpose of, 892

Reversing entries, 90–91d, 91–92

Right of offset, 148, 148n

Right of return, 311

Rights model of ethics, 23

Risk, 38, 175d

Rounding, 148

Ruby Tuesday, 1199

Rules-based standards, 16

S

S-1 (registration statement), 16

Salaries, accrued, 78

Sale of depreciable assets, cash flow, 1151–1152

Sale-leaseback issues, 1103–1108, 1103*n*

Sales: allowances, 86–87, 314–315; cash flow from operations (CFO) to, 275; returns, 86–87, 87*n*; defective goods, 314–315; right of return, 311; revenue (net), 183

Sales tax, current liabilities, 599–600

Sales warranty accrual method, 607–608

Sales-type leases, 1083*d*, 1093–1096

Salvage value, 505

Sam's Club, 327

Sarbanes-Oxley Act, 64–65

SARs (share appreciation rights), 788–790

Scope and nature of services, 22*f*

Scope paragraph, 247

Scrip dividends, 846

Secondary markets, 4–5*d*, 4*f*

Securities. *See* investments; *specific securities.*

Securities and Exchange Commission (SEC): APB Opinions, 17; and the FASB, 16–17; FASB Statements, 17; forms: 8-K (significant events report), 16; 10-K (annual report), 16, 145–146, 262*d*; 10-Q (quarterly operations report), 16, 262*d*; Electronic Data Gathering Analysis and Retrieval System (EDGAR), 17; *Financial Reporting Releases*, 17; proxy statements, 16; Regulation S-X, 17; required reports, 16–17; S-1 (registration statement), 16; *Staff Accounting Bulletins*, 17; fraud detection, 17; history of GAAP, 8; integrated disclosures, 145–146; reports: 10-K form (annual report), 16, 145–146, 262*d*; 10-Q form (quarterly operations report), 16, 262*d*; Chief Accountant, 261; description, 261; Division of Corporation Finance, 261; Office of the Chief Accountant, 261; XBRL supplemental information, 262; *Statements and Interpretations*, 17

Securities Industry Association, 11–12

Segment reports, 252*n*, 256*f*; aggregation, 251; comparability issues, 256; corporate interest expense, 255; corporate interest revenue, 255; disaggregation, 252, 255–256; disclosure requirements, 253–254, 254*n*, 255–256; ethical dilemma, 254; international differences, 263; management approach, 253, 256; operating segments, 252–255, 253*d*, 253*n*; reportable segments, 253, 255; transfer pricing, 256

Selected financial data, 146

Self Accounting Bulletins, 17

Self-construction: development stage companies, 475–476; fixed overhead costs, 474–475; income on, 475; interest during construction, 470–473; international differences, 474

Sell decisions, 5

Selling: accounts receivable, 326–327; expenses, 184–185

Separable assets, 132*d*

Serial bonds: bonds outstanding method, 683–686; early redemption, 686; effective interest method, 683–686; interest expense, 683–686; issuance expense, 683–686

Service cost, pension plans, 999*d*, 1000

Service life, 504–505

Settlements, pension plans, 1031–1032

Share appreciation rights (SARs), 788–790

Share options, 779*d*, 782*n*; cliff vesting, 785–786; compensatory, 780–792; in diluted earnings per share, 831–837; disclosures, illustration, 790–791; earnings per share, 834–835; exercise price, 780; fair value, 781, 783–784; fixed share option, 785–786, 786*n*; history of, 780–782; intrinsic value, 781; option pricing model, 783–784; performance-based share option, 786–788; political controversy, 782; recognition of compensation expense, 784–790, 784*n*; SARs (share appreciation rights), 788–790

Share purchase plans, 779–780, 779*d*

Short-term interest-bearing notes receivable, 328–329

Short-term non-interest-bearing notes receivable, 329

Sick pay, current liabilities, 595–598

Significant events report (8-K form), 16

Simple interest, M2–3

Single-step formats, 187–188

Sinking funds, 738–739

Sinking-fund depreciation method, 515*n*

Slide errors, 74–75

Social security. *See* FICA.

Sociopolitical environment, 14–16, 15*n*, 16*n*

Software revenue recognition, 917–918

Sole proprietorships, 137*d*

Source documents, 67*d*

Southwest Airlines, 1064–1065

Special journals, 71*d*, 93–94, 93*d*

Special stock dividends, 846

Specific identification, 367–369

Spreadsheets. *See* worksheets.

Spreadsheets (worksheets), 88*d*, 89*f*; cash flow: example, 1146–1147; preparation, 1142–1151, 1143*f*, 1144*n*; overview, 88–90

Stability ratios, 273–275

Staff Accounting Bulletin No. 104, 917

Staff Positions, 12

Stakeholders, 23

Standards. *See also* APB Opinions; assumptions; ethics; FASB *Statements of Standards*; Financial Accounting Standards Board (FASB); generally accepted accounting principles (GAAP); principles.: consistency, 10; development timeline, 10*f*; fairness, 10

Standard-setting bodies, 21*f. See also* Financial Accounting Standards Board (FASB); Accounting Principles Board (APB), 10. *See also* APB Opinions; American Accounting Associations (AAA), 19; CFA Institute (CFAI), 20; Committee on Accounting Procedure (CAP), 10; Cost Accounting Standards Board (CASB), 18; Emerging Issues Task Force (EITF), 18; Financial Executives International (FEI), 20; Government Accounting Standards Board (GASB), 20; Institute of Management Accountants (IMA), 20; Internal Revenue Service (IRS), 18–19; International Accounting Standards Board (IASB), 19–20; International Accounting Standards Committee (IASC), 19; professional associations, 20; Public Company Accounting Oversight Board (PCAOB), 20; relationships between, 20–21; Wheat Committee, 10–11

Stated value of stocks, 138

Statement of cash flows, 53d, 70d. *See also* cash flows; bonds payable, changes, 1148–1149; buildings, changes, 1148; cash and equivalents, 1128; cash dividends, 1149; cash dividends declared, 1157–1159; cash flows from financing activities, 211–212; cash flows from investing activities, 211; classifications, 1132–1133; compensatory share option plans, 1158–1159; conceptual evaluation, 1126–1131; current asset changes, 1144–1147; current liabilities changes, 1147; decreases in liabilities, 1132; decreases in non-cash assets, 1131; decreases in stockholders' equity, 1132; direct method, 212–214; direct reporting method: diagram of, 1163–1166, 1164*f*; direct reporting method, 1162–1166; inflows, 1162–1163; major adjustments, 1164*f*; outflows, 1163; reporting guidelines, 212–214; visual inspection, 1166–1168; worksheets, 1169–1173, 1170*f*–1171; disclosure, 1159–1160; ethical dilemma, 1134; exchange rates, 1159; expected, M25; financial flexibility, 1126; financial institutions, 1156–1157; financial reporting, 7; in financial reporting, 7; financing, 1130, 1132–1133; financing activities, 210–212; cash flow statement, 1141–1142; overview, 1127–1128; partial, 1154–1156; reporting guidelines, 210–212; worksheet entries, 1147; income tax, 974; income tax paid, 1153*n*; income taxes paid, 1152–1153; increases in liabilities, 1131; increases in non-cash assets, 1132; increases in stockholders' equity, 1131; inflows, 1131; information, 36–37; interest paid, 1152–1153, 1153*n*; international differences, 1161; investing, 1130, 1132–1133, 1154–1156; investing activities, 210–212; cash flow statement, 1141; long-term, 1154–1156, 1155*n*; overview, 1127; reporting guidelines, 210–212; temporary, 1154–1156, 1155*n*; worksheet entries, 1147; land changes, 1148, 1148*n*; leased equipment, changes, 1148; liquidity, 1126; major

sections, 211; negative, 1124–1126; net cash flows from operating activities, 211; net change in cash and reconciliation, 1130; non-cash items, 1130–1131, 1144; operating, 1129, 1132–1133; operating activities, 210–212, 1127d; cash flow statement, 1140–1141, 1140*n*; conceptual overview, 1127; diagram of, 1163–1166, 1164*f*; direct reporting method, 1135–1136, 1162–1166; indirect reporting method, 1136–1137; inflows, 1162–1163; major adjustments, 1137–1138, 1138*f*, 1164*f*; outflows, 1163; reporting guidelines, 210–212; from operations (CFO) to, 276d; maturing debt, 276; net income, 275; sales, 275; outflows, 1132; per share of stock, 1159; preferred stock changes, 1149; deferred tax changes, 1149; preparation: bonds payable, changes, 1148–1149; buildings, changes, 1148; cash dividends, 1149; cash flows from financing activities, 1141–1142; cash flows from investing activities, 1141; cash flows from operating activities, 1140–1141, 1140*n*; current asset changes, 1144–1147; current liabilities changes, 1147; financing activities, 1147; investing activities, 1147; land changes, 1148, 1148*n*; leased equipment, changes, 1148; non-cash expenses, 1144; preferred stock changes, 1149; deferred tax changes, 1149; statement example, 1145, 1150; stock dividends, 1149; visual inspection method, 1139–1142, 1139*n*, 1140*n*; worksheet example, 1146–1147; worksheet (spreadsheet) method, 1142–1151, 1143*f*, 1144*n*; purpose of, 210, 1126; ratios, 275–276; red flags, 1124–1126; reporting flexibility, 1153–1154; reporting format, 1128; reporting guidelines, 210–212, 1126–1131. *See also* statements, cash flow; retirement of bonds, 1152; sale of depreciable assets, 1151–1152; statements. *See* statements, cash flow; stock dividends, 1149

Statements. *See also* financial reporting; financial statements; reporting; reports.: changes in equity, 54d; distributions to owners, 140d; in financial reporting, 7; in financial statements, 54; investments by owners, 140d; comprehensive income, 7*n*; earnings. *See* income statement; financial position. *See* balance sheets; income. *See* income statement; operations. *See* income statement; retained earnings, 69d, 204d; adjustments, 204–206; change in accounting principle, 205; combined statements, 206; error correction, 205–206; net dividends, 204; net income, 204; preparing, 83, 83*f*

Statements and Interpretations, 17

Statements of Financial Accounting Concepts, 12d, 12n. *See also* FASB *Statements of Concepts.*

Statements of Financial Accounting Standards, 12d, 12n. *See also* FASB *Statements of Standards.*

Statements of Position, 9*f*, 17

Statutory depletion, 529

Stewardship information, 37

Stock option plans. *See* compensatory share option plans.

Stock transfer journal, 768

Stockholder profitability ratios, 268–269

Stockholders' equity, 66*d*, 137*d*, 771*d*. *See also* dividends; stocks; in the accounting equation, 66; balance sheets, 123*d*, 137*d*; capital stock reacquisition. *See* treasury stock; cash flow statements, 805; combined sales of stock, 775–776; common stock, 772–779; components, 771; contributed capital, 771, 799–800; disproportionate stock splits, 778; distributions to owners, 140*d*; earnings per share, 827*n*; calculating, 827–829, 828*n*; components, 829–830; contingent issuances, 837; conversion ratios, 837; convertible securities, 834–835; diluted, 831–837, 833*n*, 835*n*; disclosures, 837–840; international differences, 840; overview, 826–827; potential common shares, 831; price/earnings ratio, 826; share options, 834–835; stock warrants, 834–835; treasury stock method, 832–834, 833*n*; ethical dilemma, 775; international differences, 857; investments by owners, 140*d*; issuance of capital stock, 772–779; miscellaneous changes, 855; nonmonetary exchange, 776–777; paid-in capital, 771; preferred stock, 793*d*; callable, 797–798; convertible, 794–796; cumulative, 793–794; participating, 794; preference as to dividends, 793; preference in liquidation, 798; recalling, 797–798; redeemable, 798; retiring, 797–798; rights, 796–797; with stock warrants, 796–797; voting rights, 799; proportionate stock splits, 777–778; ratio analysis, 806; restatements, 852; retained earnings. *See also* dividends; appropriations, 853; content of, 841; restrictions, 853; statements, 853–855; retained fair values, 775–776; return on, 270; reverse stock splits, 778; rights to current stockholders, 779; share option plans, 779*d*, 782*n*; cliff vesting, 785–786; compensatory, 780–792; disclosures, illustration, 790–791; exercise price, 780; fair value, 781, 783–784; fixed share option, 785–786, 786*n*; history of, 780–782; intrinsic value, 781; option pricing model, 783–784; performance-based share option, 786–788; political controversy, 782; recognition of compensation expense, 784–790, 784*n*; SARs (share appreciation rights), 788–790; share purchase plans, 779–780, 779*d*; statement of changes, 7, 54, 54*d*, 855–859. *See also* financial statements; stock splits, 777–778; stock subscriptions, 773–775; stock warrants, 779; treasury stock: acquisition at greater than market value, 803; balance sheets, 803; cost method, 801–803, 802*n*; donated, 804; overview, 800–801; par value method, 804–805; reasons for, 800–801; retirement, 804

Stockholders' ledger, 768

Stockholders' rights, 769

Stocks, 138*n*, 146. *See also* stockholders' equity; additional paid-in capital, 138–139; capital, 138–139; certificates, 768; compensatory share option plans, cash flow, 1158–1159; dividend revenue, recording, 709–710; dividends. *See* dividends; preferred stock changes, cash flow, 1149; redemption funds, 738–739; splits, 736–737, 777–778; subscriptions, 773–775; warrants: detachable, 656–657; earnings per share, 834–835; investment issues, 737, 737*n*; preferred stock, 796–797; rights of current stockholders, 779

Straight-line depreciation method, 506–507, 506*d*

Structured problems, 24

Subscribed capital stock, 769

Subsequent events, 144

Subsidiary ledgers, 74*n*, 92–93, 93*d*, 93*f*. *See also* ledgers.

Substantial performance, 919

Successful-efforts method, 483–484

Summary of accounting policies, 141–142

Summary of financial information, 202

Sum-of-the-year's-digits depreciation method, 507

Supporting schedules, 149

T

T-accounts, 68

Target Corp., 790–791

Taxable income, 946*d*

Taxes, income. *See* income taxes.

Technical Bulletins, 12

Technical Practice Aids, 9

Temporary accounts, 68–69

Temporary investments in marketable securities, 129

10-K form (annual report), 16, 145–146, 262*d*

10-Q form (quarterly operations report), 16, 262*d*

Termination of pension plans, 1032

Thomson Analytics, 391

Time of sale, 177

Time value of money, M2*d*. *See also* interest; annuities, M10*d*; converting future values to present, M2; discounting, M2*d*; expected cash flows, M25; future value: annuities due, M13–14; converting to present, M2; ordinary annuities, M10–13; single sum, compound interest, M3–7, M7*n*; interest: compound, M2–3; simple, M2–3; present value: annuities, M14; annuities due, M18–21; converting from future, M2; deferred annuities due, M21–24; ordinary annuities, M14–18; role in financial reporting, M24–25; single sum, M7–9

Time-based depreciation method, 506–509, 506*d*

Timeliness, 42

Times interest earned ratio, 274

Timing, recognition of revenue, 177–178

Title, transferring, 363–364

Trade accounts payable, current liabilities, 591–592

Trade discounts, 366–367

Trade receivables, 310–312, 310d

Trademarks, 562

Tradenames, 562

Trading securities, 706d, 708, 723

Transactional analysis, 72–73f

Transactional approach, 171–172

Transactions, 67d

Transfer pricing, 256

Transfers of securities, 720–722, 722n

Transposition errors, 74–75

Travel advances, as cash, 306

Treasury Stock, 138–139

Treasury stock, 769d; acquisition at greater than market value, 803; balance sheets, 803; cost method, 801–803, 802n; donated, 804; overview, 800–801; par value method, 804–805; reasons for, 800–801; retirement, 804

Treasury stock method, 832–834, 833n

Trial balances, 74–76, 74d

Troubled debt restructuring, 676. *See also* bad debts; impairments, loans; uncollectible accounts.

U

UAL Corp., 994

Uncollectible accounts. *See also* bad debts; impairments, loans; receivables.: collecting after writeoff, 321–322; direct write-off method, 322; valuation, 316n; aging accounts receivable, 318–320, 318d; allowance for doubtful accounts, 316; allowance method, 316; estimate of bad debt expense, 316, 317; ethical dilemma, 317; net credit sales method, 316–317; percentage of outstanding accounts receivable, 317–318; percentage of sales method, 316–317; writing off, 320–321

Understandability, 40, 56

Unearned items, liabilities, 598

Unearned revenue. *See* deferred, revenues.

Unemployment insurance taxes, current liabilities, 600–602, 601f

Unfunded accumulated benefit obligation, 1003–1004

Unfunded pension plans, 996d

Unguaranteed residual value, 1069d; accounting and reporting by lessor, 1096; estimated, 1107

Unidentifiable intangibles, 550d; estimating value of goodwill, 566; human resources, 563n; impairment of goodwill, 564–565; internally developed, 552; internally developed goodwill, 563, 569; negative goodwill, 565–566; purchased, 551; purchased goodwill, 563–564, 569–570

UNIFI, 328

Union Carbide Corporation, 614

Universal, 615

Unreimbursible cost, 1069d

Unstructured problems, 24–25

U.S. Airways, 994

Use tax, current liabilities, 599–600

Useful information: characteristics: benefits *versus* costs, 43–44; comparability, 43; consistency, 43; decision usefulness, 41; feedback value, 42; hierarchical constraints, 43–45; hierarchy of, 40, 41f; materiality, 44–45, 44n; neutrality, 43; objectivity, 42; predictive value, 42; relevance, 41–43; reliability, 42; representational faithfulness, 42–43; timeliness, 42; understandability, 40; verifiability, 42; types, 38f; financial flexibility, 39d; liquidity, 39; operating capability, 39–40, 39n; return on investment, 38; risk, 38

User groups, reporting guidelines, 175–176

Utilitarian model of ethics, 23

V

Vacations, current liabilities, 595–598

Valuation: adjustment: FIFO (first-in, first-out), 387–388; LIFO (last-in, last-out), 387–388; assets, 123–127, 124f; inventory. *See* inventory, valuation; liabilities, 123–127, 124f; receivables, 311–312; securities, 706–708, 706n; uncollectible accounts, 316n; aging accounts receivable, 318–320, 318d; allowance for doubtful accounts, 316; allowance method, 316; estimate of bad debt expense, 316, 317; ethical dilemma, 317; net credit sales method, 316–317; percentage of outstanding accounts receivable, 317–318; percentage of sales method, 316–317

Valuation allowance, 946d

Value, changes over time, 48

Variable expenses, 184–185

Variable manufacturing overhead, 360

Verifiability, 42

Vertical analysis, 265, 267f

Vested benefit obligation, 999d

Vested benefits, 1029

Vested rights, current liabilities, 596

Visual inspection method, 1139–1142, 1139n, 1140n

Voting rights, preferred stock, 799

W

Wachovia Corporation, 250–251
Wal-Mart, 45, 47, 358, 436, 1084
Walt Disney Company, 116–117, 320
Warranty obligations, current liabilities, 606–609
Weighted average cost, 370–371
Wheat Committee, 10–11
Whirlpool, 615–617
Williams-Sonoma, Inc., 587
Work in process inventory, 360
Working capital, 131–132, 131d
Working capital ratio, 271
Worksheets (spreadsheets), 88d, 89f; cash flow: example, 1146–1147; preparation, 1142–1151, 1143f, 1144n; overview, 88–90
WorldCom, 64, 458, 1199

X

XBRL (eXtensible Business Reporting Language), 242d, 262

Y

Yum! Brands, 1021–1024

(Continued from inside front cover)

VII. FINANCIAL STATEMENTS

A. **Balance Sheet:**
   1. **Definition:** Summarizes a company's economic resources, economic obligations, and equity and their relationships on a particular date.
   2. **Assets:** Probable future economic benefits obtained or controlled as a result of past transactions or events.
   3. **Liabilities:** Probable future sacrifices of economic benefits arising from present obligations to transfer assets or provide services in the future as a result of past transactions or events.
   4. **Equity:** Residual interest of owners in assets after deducting liabilities.
   5. **Measurement Methods:** Alternative valuation methods of assets (and liabilities) include: (a) *Historical Cost*: Amount of cash (or equivalent) paid to acquire asset, (b) *Current Cost*: Amount of cash (or equivalent) that would be paid currently to acquire same asset, (c) *Current Market Value*: Amount of cash (or equivalent) that could be obtained currently by selling asset in orderly liquidation, (d) *Net Realizable Value*: Amount of cash (or equivalent) into which asset is expected to be converted in ordinary course of business, less direct conversion costs, and (e) *Present Value*: Present value of future net cash flows expected from conversion of asset in ordinary course of business.

B. **Income Statement:**
   1. **Definition:** Summarizes the results of a company's income-producing operations for an accounting period.
   2. **Revenues:** Inflows of assets or settlement of liabilities during a period from delivering or producing goods, rendering services, or other activities involving ongoing major operations.
   3. **Expenses:** Outflows of assets or incurrences of liabilities during a period from delivering or producing goods, rendering services, or other activities involving ongoing major operations.
   4. **Gains (Losses):** Increases (decreases) in equity from peripheral or incidental transactions and from all other events and circumstances during a period except those resulting from revenues (expenses) or investments by (distributions to) owners.

C. **Statement of Cash Flows:**
   1. **Definition:** Summarizes a company's cash inflows, cash outflows, and net change in cash from its operating, investing, and financing activities during an accounting period, in a manner that reconciles the beginning and ending cash balances.
   2. **Operating Cash Flows:** Inflows and outflows of cash from acquiring, producing, selling, and delivering goods for sale, as well as providing services. Reported under either *indirect* or *direct method*.
   3. **Investing Cash Flows:** Inflows and outflows of cash from acquiring and selling investments, property, plant, and equipment, and intangibles, as well as from lending money and collecting on loans.
   4. **Financing Cash Flows:** Inflows and outflows of cash from obtaining resources from owners and creditors, and providing a return on (and of) their investment, as well as repaying amounts borrowed on long-term credit.

D. **Supporting Statements, Schedules, and Notes:** Supplement the primary financial statements. May include: (1) statement of retained earnings, which primarily reconciles retained earnings for the net income and the dividends of the accounting period, (2) statement of changes in stockholders' equity, which primarily itemizes the changes in the various components due to investments by and distributions to stockholders, (3) schedule of investing and financing activities not affecting cash, which summarizes the results of noncash investing and/or financing activities, and (4) notes describing a company's required disclosures.

E. **Elements:** Items comprising a financial statement.